Brill's New Pauly

ANTIQUITY
VOLUME 4

Cyr-Epy

Brill's New Pauly

Brill's

Encyclopaedia of the Ancient World

New Pauly

Edited by
Hubert Cancik and
Helmuth Schneider

English Edition
Managing Editor *Christine F. Salazar*

Assistant Editors *Tina Chronopoulos, Susanne Hakenbeck, Ingrid Rosa Kitzberger, Sebastiaan R. van der Mije, Astrid Möller, Antonia Ruppel, Reinhard Selinger* and *David A. Warburton*

ANTIQUITY
VOLUME 4

CYR-EPY

BRILL
LEIDEN - BOSTON
2004

Originally published in German as DER NEUE PAULY. Enzyklopädie der Antike. Herausgegeben von Hubert Cancik und Helmuth Schneider. Copyright © J.B. Metzlersche Verlagsbuchhandlung und Carl Ernst Poeschel Verlag GmbH 1996ff./1999ff. Stuttgart/Weimar

Cover design: TopicA (Antoinette Hanekuyk)
Front: Delphi, temple area
Spine: Tabula Peutingeriana

Translation by protext TRANSLATIONS B.V.

Data structuring and typesetting:
pagina GmbH, Tübingen, Germany

The publication of this work was supported by a grant from the GOETHE-INSTITUT INTER NATIONES.

ISBN (volume) 90 04 12267 2
ISBN (set) 90 04 12259 1

This book is printed on acid-free paper.

PRINTED IN THE NETHERLANDS

Table of Contents

Notes to the User VII
List of Transliterations IX
List of Illustrations and Maps XI
List of Authors XV
Entries 1
Addenda 1173

Notes to the User

Arrangement of Entries

The entries are arranged alphabetically and, if applicable, placed in chronological order. In the case of alternative forms or sub-entries, cross-references will lead to the respective main entry. Composite entries can be found in more than one place (e.g. *a commentariis* refers to *commentariis, a*).
Identical entries are differentiated by numbering. Identical Greek and Oriental names are arranged chronologically without consideration of people's nicknames. Roman names are ordered alphabetically, first according to the *gentilicium* or *nomen* (family name), then the *cognomen* (literally 'additional name' or nickname) and finally the *praenomen* or 'fore-name' (e.g. *M. Aemilius Scaurus* is found under *Aemilius*, not *Scaurus*).
However, well-known classical authors are lemmatized according to their conventional names in English; this group of persons is not found under the family name, but under their *cognomen* (e.g. Cicero, not Tullius). In large entries the Republic and the Imperial period are treated separately.

Spelling of Entries

Greek words and names are as a rule latinized, following the predominant practice of reference works in the English language, with the notable exception of technical terms. Institutions and places (cities, rivers, islands, countries etc.) often have their conventional English names (e.g. *Rome* not *Roma*). The latinized versions of Greek names and words are generally followed by the Greek and the literal transliteration in brackets, e.g. *Aeschylus* (Αἰσχύλος; *Aischýlos*).
Oriental proper names are usually spelled according to the 'Tübinger Atlas des Vorderen Orients' (TAVO), but again conventional names in English are also used. In the maps, the names of cities, rivers, islands, countries etc. follow ancient spelling and are transliterated fully to allow for differences in time, e.g. both Καππαδόκια and *Cappadocia* can be found. The transliteration of non-Latin scripts can be found in the 'List of Transliterations'.
Latin and transliterated Greek words are italicized in the article text. However, where Greek transliterations do not follow immediately upon a word written in Greek, they will generally appear in italics, but without accents or makra.

Abbreviations

All abbreviations can be found in the 'List of Abbreviations' in the first volume. Collections of inscriptions, coins and papyri are listed under their *sigla*.

Bibliographies

Most entries have bibliographies, consisting of numbered and/or alphabetically organized references. References within the text to the numbered bibliographic items are in square brackets (e.g. [1.5 n.23] refers to the first title of the bibliography, page 5, note 23). The abbreviations within the bibliographies follow the rules of the 'List of Abbreviations'.

Maps

Texts and maps are closely linked and complementary, but some maps also treat problems outside the text. The authors of the maps are listed in the 'List of Maps'.

Cross-references

Articles are linked through a system of cross-references with an arrow → before the entry that is being referred to.
Cross-references to related entries are given at the end of an article, generally before the bibliographic notes. If reference is made to a homonymous entry, the respective number is also added.
Cross-references to entries in the *Classical Tradition* volumes are added in small capitals.
It can occur that in a cross-reference a name is spelled differently from the surrounding text: e.g., a cross-reference to Mark Antony has to be to Marcus → Antonius, as his name will be found in a list of other names containing the component 'Antonius'.

List of Transliterations

Transliteration of ancient Greek

α	a	alpha
αι	ai	
αυ	au	
β	b	beta
γ	g	gamma; γ before γ, κ, ξ, χ: n
δ	d	delta
ε	e	epsilon
ει	ei	
ευ	eu	
ζ	z	z(d)eta
η	ē	eta
ηυ	ēu	
θ	th	theta
ι	i	iota
κ	k	kappa
λ	l	la(m)bda
μ	m	mu
ν	n	nu
ξ	x	xi
ο	o	omicron
οι	oi	
ου	ou	
π	p	pi
ϱ	r	rho
σ, ς	s	sigma
τ	t	tau
υ	y	upsilon
φ	ph	phi
χ	ch	chi
ψ	ps	psi
ω	ō	omega
῾	h	spiritus asper
ᾳ	ai	iota subscriptum (similarly ῃ, ῳ)

In transliterated Greek the accents are retained (acute ´, grave `, and circumflex ˆ). Long vowels with the circumflex accent have no separate indication of vowel length (makron).

Transliteration of Hebrew

א	a	alef
ב	b	bet
ג	g	gimel
ד	d	dalet
ה	h	he
ו	w	vav
ז	z	zayin
ח	ḥ	khet
ט	ṭ	tet
י	y	yod
כ	k	kaf
ל	l	lamed
מ	m	mem
נ	n	nun
ס	s	samek
ע	ʿ	ayin
פ	p/f	pe
צ	ṣ	tsade
ק	q	qof
ר	r	resh
שׂ	ś	sin
שׁ	š	shin
ת	t	tav

Pronunciation of Turkish

Turkish uses Latin script since 1928. Pronunciation and spelling generally follow the same rules as European languages. Phonology according to G. Lewis, Turkish Grammar, 2000.

A	a	French a in *avoir*
B	b	b
C	c	j in *jam*
Ç	ç	ch in *church*
D	d	d
E	e	French ê in *être*
F	f	f
G	g	g in *gate* or in *angular*
Ğ	ğ	lengthens preceding vowel
H	h	h in *have*
I	ı	i in *cousin*
İ	i	French i in *si*
J	j	French j
K	k	c in *cat* or in *cure*
L	l	l in *list* or in *wool*
M	m	m

N	n	n
O	o	French o in *note*
Ö	ö	German ö
P	p	p
R	r	r
S	s	s in *sit*
Ş	ş	sh in *shape*
T	t	t
U	u	u in *put*
Ü	ü	German ü
V	v	v
Y	y	y in *yet*
Z	z	z

Transliteration of Arabic, Persian, and Ottoman Turkish

ا, ء	ʾ, ā	ʾ	ʾ	hamza, alif
ب	b	b	b	bāʾ
پ	–	p	p	pe
ت	t	t	t	tāʾ
ث	ṯ	s̱	s̱	ṯāʾ
ج	ǧ	ǧ	ǧ	ǧīm
چ	–	č	č	čim
ح	ḥ	ḥ	ḥ	ḥāʾ
خ	ḫ	ḫ	ḫ	ḫāʾ
د	d	d	d	dāl
ذ	ḏ	ẕ	ẕ	ḏāl
ر	r	r	r	rāʾ
ز	z	z	z	zāy
ژ	–	ž	ž	že
س	s	s	s	sīn
ش	š	š	š	šīn
ص	ṣ	ṣ	ṣ	ṣād
ض	ḍ	ḍ	ḍ	ḍād
ط	ṭ	ṭ	ṭ	ṭāʾ
ظ	ẓ	ẓ	ẓ	ẓāʾ
ع	ʿ	ʿ	ʿ	ʿain
غ	ġ	ġ	ġ	ġain
ف	f	f	f	fāʾ
ق	q	q	q, k	qāf
ك	k	k	k, g, ñ	kāf
گ	–	g	g, ñ	gāf
ل	l	l	l	lām
م	m	m	m	mīm
ن	n	n	n	nūn
ه	h	h	h	hāʾ
و	w, ū	v	v	wāw
ی	y, ī	y	y	yāʾ

Transliteration of other languages

Akkadian (Assyrian-Babylonian), Hittite and Sumerian are transliterated according to the rules of RLA and TAVO. For Egyptian the rules of the Lexikon der Ägyptologie are used. The transliteration of Indo-European follows Rix, HGG. The transliteration of Old Indian is after M. Mayrhofer, Etymologisches Wörterbuch des Altindoarischen, 1992ff. Avestian is done according to K. Hoffmann, B. Forssman, Avestische Laut- und Flexionslehre, 1996. Old Persian follows R.G. Kent, Old Persian, ^{2}1953 (additions from K. Hoffmann, Aufsätze zur Indoiranistik vol. 2, 1976, 622ff.); other Iranian languages are after R. Schmitt, Compendium linguarum Iranicarum, 1989, and after D.N. MacKenzie, A Concise Pahlavi Dictionary, ^{3}1990. For Armenian the rules of R. Schmitt, Grammatik des Klassisch-Armenischen, 1981, and of the Revue des études arméniennes, apply. The languages of Asia Minor are transliterated according to HbdOr. For Mycenean, Cyprian see Heubeck and Masson; for Italic scripts and Etruscan see Vetter and ET.

List of Illustrations and Maps

Illustrations are found in the corresponding entries. ND means redrawing following the instructions of the author or after the listed materials.
RP means reproduction with minor changes.

Some of the maps serve to visualize the subject matter and to complement the articles. In such cases, there will be a reference to the corresponding entry. Only literature that was used exclusively for the maps is listed.

Lemma Title AUTHORS Bibliography

Cyrene
Cyrene: (7th/6th cents. BC – c. 6th cent. AD)
ND: EDITORIAL TEAM TÜBINGEN/E. OLSHAUSEN/H. G. NIEMEYER

Daci(a)
The province of Dacia (AD 106–271)
ND: E. OLSHAUSEN
TIR L 35, 1969; N. GUDEA, Der Limes Dakiens und die Verteidigung der obermoesischen Donaulinie von Trajan bis Aurelian, in: ANRW II 6, 1977, 849–887; D. PROTASE, Der Forschungsstand zur Kontinuität der bodenständigen Bevölkerung im röm. Dazien (2.–3. Jh.), in: ANRW II 6, 1977, 990–1015; E. CHRYSOS, Von der Räumung der Dacia Traiana zur Entstehung der Gothia, BJ 192, 1992, 175–194; D. KNOPP, Die röm. Inschr. Dakiens, 1993 (diss.).

Damascus
Dimašqa/Damascus
ND: T. LEISTEN
J. SAUVAGET, Le plan antique de Damas, in: Syria 26, 1949, 314–358; K.A.C. CRESWELL, Early Muslim Architecture I, [2]1979; D. SACK, Damaskus, 1989.

Dark Ages
Greece and the Aegaean during the Dark Ages (12th – 9th cents. BC)
ND: S. DEGER-JALKOTZY/EDITORIAL TEAM TÜBINGEN ; V. R. D'A. DESBOROUGH, The Greek Dark Ages, 1972; F. SCHACHERMEYR, Die ägäische Frühzeit, vol. III, 1979; IV, 1980; G. KOPKE, Handel, ArchHom, Kap. M, 1990, esp. 78; J. VANSCHOONWINKEL, L 'Egée et la Mediterranée orientale à la fin du deuxième millénaire, 1991.

Daunian vases
Daunian vases
ND after: E. M. DE JULIIS, La ceramica geometrica della Daunia, 1977, plates 59, 65, 69, 87.

Dead Sea
Textual finds by the Dead Sea and in the Judaean desert
ND: A. LANGE

Defixio
Curse tablet from Hadrumetum (Tunisia)
RP after: U. E. PAOLI, Das Leben im alten Rom, 1948, 331 fig. 39.

Deinomenids
The Deinomenids and the Emmenids
ND: K. MEISTER

Deinostratus
Construction of the *quadratrix* according to Deinostratus
ND after: F. KUDLIEN, s.v. Hippias [6], KlP 2,1158; I. BULMER THOMAS, s.v. Dinostratos, Dictionary of Scientific Biography 4, 1971, 103–105.

Delian League
Delian League (478–404 BC)
W. EDER / EDITORIAL TEAM TÜBINGEN
Bibliography: B.D. MERITT, H.T. WADE-GERY, M.F. MCGREGOR, The Athenian Tribute Lists I-IV, 1939–1953
W. SCHULLER, Die Herrschaft der Athener im Ersten Attischen Seebund, 1974
R. MEIGGS, The Athenian Empire, 1975 (revised editon)
C.J. TUPLIN, The Athenian Empire, in: R.J.A. Talbert (ed.), Atlas of Classical History, 1985 (repr. 1994) 44
K.-E. PETZOLD, Die Gründung des Delisch-Attischen Seebundes, in: Historia 42, 1993, 418–443; 43, 1994, 1–31.

Delphi
[1] Delphi I, Layout plan
[2] Delphi II, Sanctuary of Apollo (detailed plan)
ND after plans of D. LAROCHE, in: M. MAASS (ed.), Delphi, Orakel am Nabel der Welt, 1996, 48 fig. 52, 49 fig. 53.

Deus ex machina
Deus ex machina: hypothetical reconstruction
ND: M. Haase

Diadochi and Epigoni
Kingdoms of the Diadochi (c. 303 BC)
ND: Editorial team Tübingen (based on: TAVO B V 2, author: W. Orth,
© Dr. Ludwig Reichert Verlag, Wiesbaden)
W. Orth, Die Diadochenreiche (um 303 v. Chr.), TAVO B V 2, 1992.

Didyma
[1] Cult precinct beside the Sacred Road from Miletus to Didyma (perspectival aerial view from SW)
ND after: K. Tuchelt (ed.), Didyma III 1,1996, 50 fig. 32 (reconstruction: Peter Schneider).
[2] Didyma, site-map of the excavations (as of 1995)
ND after: P. Schneider, Topographischer Übersichtsplan, 1995.

Diocletianus
[1] Dioeceses and provinces in the early 4th century
ND: B. Bleckmann
K. L. Noethlichs, Zur Entstehung der Diözesen als Mittelinstanz des spätröm. Verwaltungssystems, in: Historia 31, 1982, 70–81 B. Jones, D. Mattingly, An Atlas of Roman Britain, 1990, 149 T. D. Barnes, Emperors, Panegyrics, Prefects, Provinces and Palaces (284–317), in: Journal of Roman Archaeology 9, 1996, 532–552.
[2] Administration of the Empire after Diocletian and Constantine
ND: B. Bleckmann

Dipteros
Ephesus: Newer Artemision (schematic groundplan)
ND after: W. Schaber, Die archaische Tempel der Artemis von Ephesos, 1982, table 4.

Discus of Phaestus
Discus of Phaestus
ND after: J. P. Olivier, Le Disque de Phaistos, in: BCH 99, 1975, 32f.

Divination
Communication model according to Cicero, De divinatione
ND: M. Haase

Dodona
Sanctuary of Zeus (site map)
RP: L. Schneider, Ch. Höcker, Griech. Festland, 1996, 258.

Dome
Domes with circular and square bases
ND after: W. Müller, G. Vogel, dtv-Atlas zur Baukunst I, 1974, 48.

Duenos inscription
Duenos inscription; schematic view
ND after: CIL I2, 4; Transcription: R. Wachter, Altlateinische Inschr., 1987, 70.

Doric/Northwest Greek
Doric/Northwest Greek (in the Greek mother country)
ND: J. L. García-Ramón
Bechtel, Dial. II; J. Méndez Dosuna, Los dialectos dorios del Noroeste, 1985; M. Bile, Le dialecte crétois ancien, 1988; Id. et al., Bulletin de dialectologie greque, in: REG 101, 1988, 74–112.

Doric Migration
The Doric Migration
ND: B. Eder
E. Kirsten, Gebirgshirtentum und Seßhaftigkeit – die Bedeutung der Dark Ages für die griech. Staatenwelt: Doris und Sparta, in: S. Deger-Jalkotzy (ed.), Griechenland, die Ägäis und die Levante während der Dark Ages vom 12. bis zum 9. Jh. v. Chr, 1983, 356–443.

Duplication of the cube
Duplication of the cube: the mechanical solution by means of an angle bar, attributed to Plato
ND according to a design by M. Folkerts

Dura-Europus
Dura-Europus
ND: T. Leisten
A. Perkins, The Art of D.-E., 1973; P. Leriche, Doura-Europos: études, 1986.

Echinus
Different forms of echinus on Doric capitals
ND after: G. Rodenwaldt (ed.), Korkyra I. Der Artemistempel, 1940, Table 23; F. Kraus, Die Säulen des Zeustempels in Olympia, in: FS R. Boehringer, 1957, 384; A. K. Orlandos, Ἀρχιτεκτονική τοῦ Παρθενῶνος, 1977, 183; Th. Wiegand, H. Schrader, Priene, 1904, 190; J. T. Clarke, F. H. Bacon, R. Koldewey, Investigations at Assos, 1902, 153; R. Delbrueck, Hellenistische Bauten in Latium II, 1907, Table 18.

Education
Educational establishments in the Hellenistic period (330–133 BC)
Editorial team Tübingen / ND after TAVO (Author: H. Waldmann, © Dr. Ludwig Reichert Verlag, Wiesbaden).
Bibliography: H. Waldmann, Die hellenistische Staatenwelt im 2. Jh. v. Chr., TAVO B V 4, 1985; Id., Östlicher Mittelmeerraum und Mesopotamien. Wirtschaft, Kulte, Bildung im Hellenismus (330–133 v. Chr.), TAVO B V 5, 1987; H. Blanck, Das Buch in der Antike, 1992.

Egg-and-dart moulding
Miletus: Egg-and-dart moulding in relief
ND after: G. KLEINER, Die Ruinen von Milet, 1968, 41 figure 22a.

Egypt
[1] Egypt: economy (4th–2nd cents. BC)
EDITORIAL TEAM TÜBINGEN, according to TAVO B V 5 (Author: H. Waldmann, © Dr. Ludwig Reichert Verlag, Wiesbaden);
Bibliography: H. WALDMANN, Wirtschaft, Kulte und Bildung im Hellenismus (330–133 v. Chr.), TAVO B V 5, 1987

[2] Egypt in Roman times; administration (1st cent. BC–3rd cent. AD / –6th cent. AD)
EDITORIAL TEAM TÜBINGEN
Bibliography: H. HEINEN, W. SCHLÖMER, Ägypten in hell.-röm. Zeit, TAVO B V 21, 1989; P. HÖGEMANN, Nordostafrika und Arabische Halbinsel. Staaten und Kulturen (4.–1. Jh. v. Chr.), TAVO B V 22, 1987; E. KETTENHOFEN, Östl. Mittelmeerraum und Mesopotamien: Die Neuordnung des Orients in diokletianisch-konstantinischer Zeit (284–337 n. Chr.), TAVO B VI 1, 1984; Id., Östl. Mittelmeerraum und Mesopotamien: Spätrömische Zeit (337–527 n. Chr.), TAVO B VI 4, 1984; S. TIMM, Ägypten. Das Christentum bis zur Araberzeit (bis zum 7. Jh.), TAVO B VI 15, 1983

Ekphrasis
Garden architecture in the house of Loreius Tiburtinus (Pompeii)
ND after: E. Salza Prina Ricotti, The Importance of Water in Roman Garden Triclinia, in: Ancient Roman Villa Gardens, Dumbarton Oaks Colloquium on the History of Landscape 10, 1987, figure 8.

Eleusis
Sanctuary of Demeter (layout map)
ND after: H. R. Goette, Athen, Attika, Megaris, 1993, 228.

Ensigns:
[1] Ensigns of the Roman army
[2] Ensigns of the Roman army during the Principate
ND after an original by Y. LE BOHEC

Entasis
Contours of ancient columns
ND after: A. K. Orlandos, Ἀρχιτεκτονικὴ τοῦ Παρθενῶνος, 1977, 164 fig. 106; D. Mertens, in: Bathron. FS H. Drerup, 1988, 311 fig. 4; J. Leoni, The Ten Books on Architecture of Leone Battista Alberti, 1755, 148 (repr. 1955).

Ephesus
Ephesus: archaeological site-map
ND: P. SCHERRER / EDITORIAL TEAM TÜBINGEN
F. HUBER, Ephesos. Gebaute Geschichte, 1997.

Epic
The ancient epic: an inventory
ND: J. Latacz

Epidaurus
Sanctuaries of Asclepius and of Apollo Maleatas (layout plan)
ND after: D. Musti, M. Torelli (Ed.), Pausania, Guida della Grecia II, 1994, LXXVI.

Epinetron
Production of the roving with the help of the epinetron
ND after: A. PEKRIDOU-GORECKI, Mode im antiken Griechenland, 1988, 19 fig. 6.

Epistemology
Schematic representation of Stoic epistemology and theory of action
ND: M. HAASE

Epistylion
[1] Paestum, older Temple of Hera I (monolithic epistylion)

[2] Athens, Parthenon (drawing depicting the structure of an epistylion in three sections)
ND after: M. SCHEDE, Die Ruinen von Priene, 1964, 31 fig. 34; A. K. ORLANDOS, Ἀρχιτεκτονικὴ τοῦ Παρθενῶνος, 1977, 200 fig. 125.

[3] Priene, Temple of Athena (view of one of the long sides)
RP after: D. MERTENS, Der alte Heratempel in Paestum und die archaische Baukunst in Unteritalien, 1993, appendix 17.

Addenda

Constellations
[1] Zodiac
ND according to an original by W. HÜBNER

[2] Constellations north of the Zodiac
ND according to an original by W. HÜBNER

[3] Constellations south of the Zodiac
ND according to an original by W. HÜBNER

List of Authors

Albiani, Maria Grazia, Bologna	M.G.A.
Allam, Schafik, Tübingen	S.A.
Alonso-Núñez, José Miguel, Madrid	J.M.A.-N.
Ameling, Walter, Jena	W.A.
Apathy, Peter, Linz	P.A.
Auffarth, Christoph, Tübingen	C.A.
Bäbler, Balbina, Göttingen	B.BÄ.
Badian, Ernst, Cambridge, MA	E.B.
Bakır-Akbaşoğlu, Tomris, Izmir	T.B.-A.
Baltes, Matthias, Münster	M.BA.
Barceló, Pedro, Potsdam	P.B.
Bartels, Jens, Bonn	J.BA.
Baudy, Dorothea, Konstanz	D.B.
Baudy, Gerhard, Konstanz	G.B.
Baumhauer, Otto A., Bremen	O.B.
Belke, Klaus, Vienna	K.BE.
Bendlin, Andreas, Erfurt	A.BEN.
Bieberstein, Klaus, Fribourg	K.B.
Binder, Gerhard, Bochum	G.BI.
Binder, Vera, Gießen	V.BI.
Birley, A.R., Düsseldorf	A.B.
Blanc, Nicole, Paris	NI.BL.
Blänsdorf, Jürgen, Mainz	JÜ.BL.
Blech, Michael, Madrid	M.BL.
Bleckmann, Bruno, Bern	B.BL.
Bloch, René, Princeton, NJ	R.B.
Bloedhorn, Hanswulf, Jerusalem	H.BL.
Blume, Horst-Dieter, Münster	H.-D.B.
Böck, Barbara, Berlin	BA.BÖ.
Bodnár, István, Budapest	I.B.
Bollack, Jean, Paris	JE.BO.
Bowie, Ewen, Oxford	E.BO.
von Bredow, Iris, Stuttgart	I.v.B.
Bremmer, Jan N., Groningen	J.B.
Brennecke, Hanns, Erlangen	H.BR.
Brentjes, Burchard, Berlin	B.B.
Bringmann, Klaus, Frankfurt/Main	K.BR.
Briquel, Dominique, Paris	D.BR.
Brisson, Luc, Paris	L.BR.
Brock, Sebastian P., Oxford	S.BR.
Brodersen, Kai, Newcastle and Mannheim	K.BRO.
Burckhardt, Leonhard, Basle	LE.BU.
Burford Cooper, Alison, Ann Arbor	A.B.-C.
Burian, Jan, Prague	J.BU.
Caduff, Gian Andrea, Zizers	G.A.C.
Calboli, Gualtiero, Bologna	G.C.
Calboli Montefusco, Lucia, Bologna	L.C.M.
Calmeyer †, Peter, Berlin	PE.C.
Campbell, J. Brian, Belfast	J.CA.
Cartledge, Paul A., Cambridge	P.C.
Cassin, Barbara, Paris	B.C.
Chaniotis, Angelos, Heidelberg	A.C.
Chase, Michael, Victoria, BC	MI.CH.
Christes, Johannes, Berlin	J.C.
Christiansen, Birgit, Berlin	B.CH.
Clinton, Kevin, Ithaca N.Y.	K.C.
Colpe, Carsten, Berlin	C.C.
Courtney, Edward, Charlottesville, VA	ED.C.
Crawford, Michael Hewson, London	M.C.
Dammer, Raphael, Bochum	R.DA.
Daverio Rocchi, Giovanna, Milan	G.D.R.
de Libero, Loretana, Hamburg	L.d.L.
de Vido, Stefania, Venice	S.d.V.
Decker, Wolfgang, Cologne	W.D.
Degani, Enzo, Bologna	E.D.
Deger-Jalkotzy, Sigrid, Salzburg	S.D.-J.
Detel, Wolfgang, Frankfurt/Main	W.DE.
Di Marco, Massimo, Fondi (Latina)	M.D.MA.
Dietz, Karlheinz, Würzburg	K.DI.
Dingel, Joachim, Hamburg	J.D.
Docter, Roald Frithjof, Gent	R.D.
Domhardt, Yvonne, Zürich	Y.D.
Donohue, Alice A., Bryn Mawr	A.A.D.
Dorandi, Tiziano, Paris	T.D.
Döring, Klaus, Bamberg	K.D.
Drew-Bear, Thomas, Lyon	T.D.-B.
Dubourdieu, Annie, Paris	A.DU.
Duchesne-Guillemin, Jacques, Lüttich	J.D.-G.
Duridanov, Ludmil, Freiburg	L.D.
Dürkop, Martina, Potsdam	MA.D.
Eck, Werner, Cologne	W.E.
Eder, Birgitta, Vienna	BI.ED.
Eder, Walter, Bochum	W.ED.
Ego, Beate, Osnabrück	B.E.
Eigler, Ulrich, Trier	U.E.
Eleuteri, Paolo, Venice	P.E.
Elvers, Karl-Ludwig, Bochum	K.-L.E.
Engels, Johannes, Cologne	J.E.
Englhofer, Claudia, Graz	CL.E.
Erler, Michael, Würzburg	M.ER.
Errington, Robert Malcolm, Marburg/Lahn	MA.ER.
Euskirchen, Marion, Bonn	M.E.
Faist, Betina, Berlin	B.FA.
Falco, Giulia, Athens	GI.F.
Fantuzzi, Marco, Florence	M.FA.
Fell, Martin, Münster	M.FE.
Fey-Wickert, Beate, Hagen	B.F.-W.
Folkerts, Menso, Munich	M.F.
Fornaro, Sotera, Sassari	S.FO.
Forssman, Bernhard, Erlangen	B.F.
Förtsch, Reinhard, Cologne	R.F.
Frahm, Eckart, Heidelberg	E.FRA.

Frank, Karl Suso, Freiburg	K.-S. F.	Hünemörder, Christian, Hamburg	C. HÜ.
Frateantonio, Christa, Gießen-Erfurt	C. F.	Hunger, Hermann, Vienna	H. HU.
Frede, Michael, Oxford	M. FR.	Hurschmann, Rolf, Hamburg	R. H.
Frey, Alexandra, Basle	AL. FR.	Huß, Werner, Munich	W. HU.
Freyburger, Gérard, Mulhouse	G. F.	Ihm, Sibylle, Hamburg	S. I.
Freydank, Helmut, Potsdam	H. FR.	Inwood, Brad, Toronto, ON	B. I.
Frioli, Donatella, Rimini	D. F.	Jansen-Winkeln, Karl, Berlin	K. J.-W.
Funke, Peter, Münster	P. F.	Jastrzębowska, Elisabeth, Warsaw	E. JA.
Furley, William D., Heidelberg	W. D. F.	Johnston, Sarah Iles, Columbus	S. I. J.
Fusillo, Massimo, L'Aquila	M. FU.	Jori, Alberto, Tübingen	AL. J.
Gamauf, Richard, Vienna	R. GA.	Kalcyk, Hansjörg, Petershausen	H. KAL.
García-Ramón, José Luis, Cologne	J. G.-R.	Käppel, Lutz, Kiel	L. K.
Gärtner, Hans Armin, Heidelberg	H. A. G.	Karttunen, Klaus, Helsinki	K. K.
Gatti, Paolo, Triento	P. G.	Kearns, Emily, Oxford	E. K.
Gehrke, Hans-Joachim, Freiburg	H.-J. G.	Kienast, Dietmar, Neu-Esting	D. K.
Gerber, Jörg, Bochum	JÖ. GE.	Kierdorf, Wilhelm, Cologne	W. K.
Gerber, Simon, Berlin	S. GE.	Kinzl, Konrad, Peterborough	K. KI.
Giaro, Tomasz, Frankfurt/Main	T. G.	Klengel, Horst, Berlin	H. KL.
Gippert, Jost, Frankfurt/Main	J. G.	Knell, Heiner, Darmstadt	H. KN.
Gizewski, Christian, Berlin	C. G.	Koch, Heidemarie, Marburg/Lahn	H. KO.
Glei, Reinhold F., Bochum	R. GL.	Köckert, Matthias, Berlin	M. K.
Glock, Anne, Potsdam	A. GL.	Krafft, Fritz, Marburg/Lahn	F. KR.
Gordon, Richard L., Ilmmünster	R. GOR.	Kramer, Johannes, Trier	J. KR.
Görgemanns, Herwig, Heidelberg	H. GÖ.	Kramolisch, Herwig, Eppelheim	HE. KR.
Gottschalk, Hans, Leeds	H. G.	Krause, Jens-Uwe, Munich	J. K.
Goulet-Cazé, Marie-Odile, Antony	M. G.-C.	Krebernik, Manfred, Munich	M. KR.
Graf, Fritz, Princeton, NJ	F. G.	Kruschwitz, Peter, Berlin	P. KR.
Graßl, Herbert, Salzburg	H. GR.	Kuhrt, Amélie, London	A. KU.
Grieshammer, Reinhard, Heidelberg	R. GR.	Kunz, Heike, Tübingen	HE. K.
Gröschler, Peter, Mainz	P. GR.	Lafond, Yves, Bochum	Y. L.
Gruber, Joachim, Erlangen	J. GR.	Lakmann, Marie-Luise, Münster	M.-L. L.
Gschnitzer, Fritz, Heidelberg	F. GSCH.	Lambropoulou, Anna, Athens	A. LAM.
Günther, Linda-Marie, Bochum	L.-M. G.	Latacz, Joachim, Basle	J. L.
Gutsfeld, Andreas, Münster	A. G.	Lausberg, Marion, Augsburg	MA. L.
Haas, Volkert, Berlin	V. H.	Le Bohec, Yann, Lyon	Y. L. B.
Haase, Mareile, Erfurt	M. HAA.	Lehmann, Gunnar, Jerusalem	G. LE.
Habermehl, Peter, Berlin	PE. HA.	Leisten, Thomas, Princeton, NJ	T. L.
Hadot, Ilsetraut, Limours	I. H.	Leppin, Hartmut, Frankfurt/Main	H. L.
Harder, Ruth Elisabeth, Zürich	R. HA.	Ley, Anne, Xanten	A. L.
Harmon, Roger, Basle	RO. HA.	Lezzi-Hafter, Adrienne, Kilchberg	A. L.-H.
Harrauer, Christine, Vienna	C. HA.	Liebermann, Wolf-Lüder, Bielefeld	W.-L. L.
Hausleiter, Arnulf, Berlin	AR. HA.	Lienau, Cay, Münster	C. L.
Heimgartner, Martin, Basle	M. HE.	von Lieven, Alexandra, Berlin	A. v. L.
Heinz, Marlies, Freiburg	M. H.	Link, Stefan, Paderborn	S. L.
Hengstl, Joachim, Marburg/Lahn	JO. HE.	Linke, Bernhard, Dresden	B. LI.
Heyworth, Stephen, Oxford	S. H.	Liwak, Rüdiger, Berlin	R. L.
Hidber, Thomas, Göttingen	T. HI.	Lohmann, Hans, Bochum	H. LO.
Hiesel, Gerhard, Freiburg	G. H.	Lundström, Steven, Berlin	S. LU.
Hild, Friedrich, Vienna	F. H.	Maaß, Michael, Karlsruhe	MI. MA.
Hiltbrunner, Otto, Munich	O. HI.	Macuch, Maria, Berlin	M. MA.
Hitzl, Konrad, Tübingen	K. H.	Mahé, J. P., Paris	J. P. M.
Höcker, Christoph, Kissing	C. HÖ.	Makris, Georgios, Bochum	G. MA.
Hoesch, Nicola, Munich	N. H.	Manganaro, Giacomo, Sant' Agata li Battiati	GI. MA.
Högemann, Peter, Tübingen	PE. HÖ.	Mann, Wolfgang, New York	WO. M.
Hölkeskamp, Karl-Joachim, Cologne	K.-J. H.	Manthe, Ulrich, Passau	U. M.
Hossenfelder, Malte, Graz	M. HO.	Marek, Christian, Zürich	C. MA.
Hübner, Wolfgang, Münster	W. H.	Markschies, Christoph, Heidelberg	C. M.
Hülser, Karl-Heinz, Konstanz	K.-H. H.	Marzolff, Peter, Heidelberg	P. MA.

Maul, Stefan, Heidelberg	S. M.
Mehl, Andreas, Halle/Saale	A. ME.
Meier, Mischa, Bielefeld	M. MEI.
Meissel, Franz-Stefan, Vienna	F. ME.
Meister, Klaus, Berlin	K. MEI.
Menci, Giovanna, Florence	G. M.
Mennella, Giovanni, Genova	G. ME.
Meyer †, Ernst, Zürich	E. MEY.
Meyer-Schwelling, Stefan, Tübingen	S. M.-S.
Michel, Simone, Hamburg	S. MI.
Mlasowsky, Alexander, Hannover	A. M.
Mommsen, Heide, Stuttgart	H. M.
Montanari, Franco, Pisa	F. M.
Muckensturm-Poulle, Claire, Besançon	C. M.-P.
Müller-Kessler, Christa, Emskirchen	C. K.
Nercessian, Anne, Paris	A. N.
Nesselrath, Heinz-Günther, Göttingen	H.-G. NE.
Neudecker, Richard, Rome	R. N.
Neumann, Günter, Münster	G. N.
Neumann, Hans, Berlin	H. N.
Niehoff, Johannes, Freiburg	J. N.
Niehr, Herbert, Tübingen	H. NI.
Niemeyer, Hans Georg, Hamburg	H. G. N.
Nissen, Hans Jörg, Berlin	H. J. N.
Noethlichs, Karl Leo, Aachen	K. L. N.
Nünlist, René, Providence, RI	RE. N.
Nutton, Vivian, London	V. N.
Oakley, John H., Williamsburg, VA	J. O.
Oelsner, Joachim, Leipzig	J. OE.
Olshausen, Eckart, Stuttgart	E. O.
Osing, Jürgen, Berlin	J. OS.
Padgett, J. Michael, Princeton	M. P.
Pahlitzsch, Johannes, Berlin	J. P.
Parker, Robert, Oxford	R. PA.
Paulsen, Thomas, Bochum	TH. P.
Paulus, Christoph Georg, Berlin	C. PA.
Pekridou-Gorecki, Anastasia, Frankfurt/Main	A. P.-G.
Peter, Ulrike, Berlin	U. P.
Pingel, Volker, Bochum	V. P.
Plath, Robert, Erlangen	R. P.
Plontke-Lüning, Annegret, Jena	A. P.-L.
Podella, Thomas, Lübeck	TH. PO.
Pollmann, Karla, St. Andrews	K. P.
Pongratz-Leisten, Beate, Bryn Mawr	B. P.-L.
Portmann, Werner, Berlin	W. P.
Prayon, Friedhelm, Tübingen	F. PR.
Pressler, Frank, Freiburg	F. P.
Primavesi, Oliver, Munich	O. P.
Raepsaet, Georges, Brussels	G. R.
Rathbone, Dominic, London	D. R.
von Reden, Sitta, Bristol	S. v. R.
Reitz, Christiane, Rostock	CH. R.
Renger, Johannes, Berlin	J. RE.
Rhodes, Peter J., Durham	P. J. R.
Richmond, John A., Blackrock, VA	J. A. R.
Riedweg, Christoph, Zürich	C. RI.
Rist, Josef, Würzburg	J. RI.
Robbins, Emmet, Toronto, ON	E. R.
Roberts, Michael, Middletown	M. RO.
Rosen, Klaus, Bonn	K. R.
Runia, David T., Parkville (AU)	D. T. R.
Rüpke, Jörg, Erfurt	J. R.
Sallmann, Klaus, Mainz	KL. SA.
Salomone Gaggero, Eleonora, Genova	E. S. G.
Sancisi-Weerdenburg †, Helen, Utrecht	H. S.-W.
Sartori, Antonio, Milan	A. SA.
Šašel Kos, Marjeta, Ljubljana	M. Š. K.
Sauer, Vera, Stuttgart	V. S.
Sauer, Werner, Graz	W. SA.
Savvidis, Kyriakos, Bochum	K. SA.
Sayar, Mustafa H., Cologne	M. H. S.
Schachter, Albert, Montreal	A. S.
Schade, Gerson, Berlin	GE. SCH.
Schäfer, Alfred, Cologne	AL. SCH.
Schaffner, Brigitte, Basle	B. SCH.
Schanbacher, Dietmar, Dresden	D. SCH.
Schaus, Gerald P., Waterloo, Ontario	G. P. S.
Scheer, Tanja, Rome	T. S.
Scheibler, Ingeborg, Krefeld	I. S.
Scheid, John, Paris	J. S.
Scherrer, Peter, Vienna	P. SCH.
Schiemann, Gottfried, Tübingen	G. S.
Schirren, Thomas, Tübingen	TH. SCH.
Schlesier, Renate, Paderborn	RE. S.
Schmidt, Peter Lebrecht, Konstanz	P. L. S.
Schmitz, Winfried, Bielefeld	W. S.
Schmitzer, Ulrich, Erlangen	U. SCH.
Schneider, Helmuth, Kassel	H. SCHN.
Schön, Franz, Regensburg	F. SCH.
Schottky, Martin, Pretzfeld	M. SCH.
Schuler, Christoph, Tübingen	C. SCH.
Schulzki, Heinz-Joachim, Freudenstadt	H.-J. S.
Schürmann, Astrid, Mannheim	AS. S.
Schütrumpf, Eckart E., Boulder, CO	E. E. S.
Schwemer, Anna Maria, Tübingen	A. M. S.
Schwerteck, Hans, Tübingen	HA. SCH.
Sehlmeyer, Markus, Rostock	M. SE.
Seidlmayer, Stephan Johannes, Berlin	S. S.
Selzer, Christoph, Frankfurt/Main	C. S.
Senff, Reinhard, Bochum	R. SE.
Sharples, Robert, London	R. S.
Simon, Walter, Tübingen	W. SI.
Smolak, Kurt, Vienna	K. SM.
Sonnabend, Holger, Stuttgart	H. SO.
Sourvinou Inwood, Christine, Oxford	C. S. I.
Speck, Paul, Berlin	P. SP.
Speyer, Wolfgang, Salzburg	WO. SP.
Spickermann, Wolfgang, Bochum	W. SP.
Spoth, Friedrich, Munich	F. SP.
Stanzel, Karl-Heinz, Tübingen	K.-H. S.
Stein-Hölkeskamp, Elke, Cologne	E. S.-H.
Steinhart, Matthias, Freiburg	M. ST.
Stenger, Jan, Kiel	J. STE.
Stol, Marten, Leiden	MA. S.
Strauch, Daniel, Berlin	D. S.
Strobel, Karl, Klagenfurt	K. ST.

Strothmann, Jürgen, Bochum JÜ.STR.
Strothmann, Meret, Bochum ME.STR.
Suerbaum, Werner, Munich W.SU.
Szlezák, Thomas A., Tübingen T.A.S.
Thür, Gerhard, Graz G.T.
Tinnefeld, Franz, Munich F.T.
Todd, Malcolm, Exeter M.TO.
Tosi, Renzo, Bologna R.T.
Touwaide, Alain, Madrid A.TO.
Treggiari, Susan, Stanford SU.T.
Treidler, Hans, Berlin H.T.
Tuchelt, K., Berlin KA.TU.
Uggeri, Giovanni, Florence G.U.
von Ungern-Sternberg, Jürgen, Basle J.v.U. S.
Untermann, Jürgen, Pulheim J.U.
Uthemann, Karl-Heinz, Amsterdam K.U.
Vassis, Ioannis, Athens I.V.
Versnel, Hendrik S., Warmond H.V.
Voß, Wulf Eckart, Osnabrück W.E.V.
Wagner, Jörg, Tübingen J.WA.
Walde, Christine, Basle C.W.
Walser †, Gerold, Basle G.W.
Wartke, Ralf-B., Berlin R.W.
Weeber, Karl-Wilhelm, Witten K.-W.WEE.
Weiler, Gabriele, Cologne GA.W.
Weiß, Peter, Kiel P.W.
Weißenberger, Michael, Greifswald M.W.
Welwei, Karl-Wilhelm, Bochum K.-W.WEL.
Wiegels, Rainer, Osnabrück RA.WI.
Wiesehöfer, Josef, Kiel J.W.
Will, Wolfgang, Bonn W.W.
Willvonseder, Reinhard, Vienna R.WI.
Wilson, Nigel, Oxford N.W.
Wirbelauer, Eckhard, Freiburg E.W.
Wittke, Anne-Maria, Tübingen A.W.
Zahrnt, Michael, Kiel M.Z.
Zaminer, Frieder, Berlin F.Z.
Zauzich, Karl-Theodor, Sommershausen K.-T.Z.
Zelzer, Michaela, Vienna M.ZE.
Zimmermann, Bernhard, Freiburg B.Z.

C CONTINUATION

Cyranides (Κυρανίδες; *Kyranídes*). This treatise in four books of unknown authorship is preserved in Greek and in a Latin translation from 1169. It deals with the healing properties of stones, plants and animals (in alphabetic order) and is allegedly the work of Harpocration [3] of Alexandria and a certain Cyranus. Some scholars (e.g., M. WELLMANN [7]) prefer the form 'Coeranides', but in agreement with textual tradition, the spelling 'Cyranides' should be preferred [1]. The meaning of the name is unknown and so far attempts to explain the word and its cultural context have been unsatisfactory. The actual title of the work is: Βίβλος φυσικῶν δυνάμεων συμπαθειῶν καὶ ἀντιπαθειῶν συνταχθεῖσα ἐκ δύο βίβλων ... τῶν Κυρανίδων ..., 'The book of physical agencies, attractions and repulsions, compiled from two books ... of the Cyranides ...' (new edition: [3]).

The preserved text clearly has a long history of genesis. According to its own rather vague statements, it is a revised version of an 'archaic' text of similar content that is occasionally mentioned elsewhere. Both the revision and the 'original' are supposedly copied from steles. This treatise of an anonymous author pretends to be a translation from foreign languages (a familiar motif in occult literature): for Cyranus it is Syriac and for Harpocration Persian. But nothing indicates that the work is indeed a translation. Rather, many elements of language and content indicate a Greek original that was probably created in the 1st or 2nd cent. AD in Alexandria [1].

The first book — unlike the next three – constitutes an independent self-contained unit. Without a doubt it is the only one that is in true sense 'authentic', the other books are only later expansions of the concepts contained in the first book. In a dedicatory letter to his daughter, which prefaces the first book but is only preserved in strongly abbreviated form, Harpocration tells how he found the stele travelling to Babylon and Seleucia [1]. Then the actual text follows: at the beginning of each letter the lemmata discussed are listed — in each case a plant, a bird, a fish and a stone (usually in this order) and for the most part items with the same name or similar sounding adjectives are combined (e.g., *kinaídios botánē*, *kinaídios ichthýs*, *kinaídios líthos*, *kinaídios ptḗnos*). A short description of the individual item follows and then their magical and medical applications are explained. Usually, the end of each chapter provides instructions for making a talisman in the form of a cameo or intaglio, or an amulet (→ Magic, → *phylaktḗrion*), which mostly involves a combination of the four named objects [4].

The numerous allusions to pre-Christian circumstances — usually the deity to which the particular bird or stone is dedicated is named — clearly indicate that the author was not a Christian. For most part, the work of Cyranus in the first book overlaps with that of Harpocration but differs from it essentially through the addition of the other three books: in alphabetic order the second book discusses quadrupeds (τετράποδες/ *tetrápodes*), the third birds and the fourth fish. There is interesting agreement of these books with the → *Physiologus* (cf. [5; 8]) and especially the esoteric tradition of Hermes Trismegistus [6].

The four books provide valuable materials for the history of natural sciences and medicine but also for the history of religion and magic in antiquity. However, an influence of the 'Cyranides' on other literary works is not recognizable despite their fame in antiquity. The *Thesaurus Pauperum* of Peter Hispanus (written about 1270) is the first work to extensively refer to its wisdom; through its mediation some of its prescriptions became part of European folk medicine.

→ Medicinal plants; → Hermetic writings; → Lithica; → Magic

1 R. GANSZYNIEC, W. KROLL, s. v. Kyraniden, RE 12, 127–134 2 F. DE MELY, CH.-É. RUELLE (ed.), Les Lapidaires de l'antiquité et du moyen âge, vol. 2, 1898 3 D. KAIMAKIS, Die Kyraniden (Beitr. zur Klass. Philol., H. 76), 1976 4 M. WAEGEMANN, Amulet and Alphabet: Magical Amulets in the First Book of Cyranides, 1987 5 O. SCHÖNBERGER (ed.), Physiologus, 2001 (with German translation) 6 J. SCARBOROUGH, Hermetic and Related Texts, in: I. MERKEL, A. G. DEBUS (ed.), Hermeticism and the Renaissance, 1988, 19–44 7 M. WELLMANN, Marcellus von Side als Arzt und die Koiraniden des Hermes Trismegistos (Philologus Suppl. 27.2), 1935 8 K. ALPERS, Unt. zum griech. Philologus und den Kyraniden, 1984.

AL. J.

Cyrenaica (Κυρεναία; *Kyrenaía*, Lat. *Cyrenae*). Northeast African coastal region of the Cyrenaea (mod. Cyrenaica) with western border at → Arae [2] Philaenorum/ Φιλαίνων Βωμοί (mod. Ras el-Aáli) [1. 73f., 469] and its eastern one near → Catabathmus megas (mod. Solum); cf. Str. 17,3,22 [2. 509f.]. The region took its name from the Theraean → *apoikía* Cyrene. → Cyrene was part of the Libyan → pentapolis, together with Barca (mod. Barka), later outstripped by Ptolemaïs (mod. Tolemaide), also Euhesperides, later Berenice (mod. Benghazi), Tauchira, later Arsinoe (mod. Tokra), and Apollonia, later Sozusa (mod. Susa). However, the term itself is first documented only in Plin. HN 5,31 [3. 17, 23[16], 481[30]]. Little wonder, as these cities by no means always pulled together. Generally, however, it was Cyrene which determined what happened in the region.

In the wake of the intervention by the Spartan freebooter Thibron, the C. came under Ptolemaic control [4. 25–37]. The region was organized as a 'province' (321 BC?) and put under the administration of the *stratēgós* Ophellas. In the following period, the C. was at times linked with Egypt, at others governed by independent rulers. In a politically precarious situation (156/5 BC), Ptolemy VII Euergetes II took surprising and drastic action to ensure the support of the Roman Senate in his struggle against his brother Ptolemy VI Philometor: in his will, he named the people of Rome — albeit with certain conditions — as heirs to his 'kingdom' (βασιλεία) ([5. 204f.], SEG IX 7). However, a new turn of events prevented the implementation of this plan, but a similar testament by Ptolemy Apion (96 BC) was later put into practice: The C. became the Roman province of *Cyrenaica provincia* (74 BC) and was put under the administration of a *quaestor pro praetore* (Sall. Hist. fr. incerta 2,2; App. B Civ. 1,111,517). Between 40 and 34 BC (?), the provinces of Creta and Cyrenae were united (→ *Creta et Cyrenae*). From 27 BC, the double province was administered as a senatorial province by a praetorian proconsul (Cass. Dio 53,12,4).

Under Diocletian (end of 3rd/beginning of 4th cent. AD), the province (by then without *Creta*) was known as *Libya superior* — in contrast with the province of *Libya inferior*, whose territories adjoined to the east (Provinciarum Laterculus Veronensis 1,3f.). This rule still applied in AD 430 (Not. Dign. Or. 2,25f.). In 448/9, Polemius Silvius renamed the two provinces *Libya pentapolis* and *Libya sicca* (Pol. Silv. 1 p. 542,10). At the time of Justinian (1st half of the 6th cent. AD), the two Libyan provinces (*Libya superior* or respectively *inferior*) still existed (Λιβύη ἡ ἄνω and Λιβύη ἡ κάτω, Hierocles, Synekdemos 732,8; 733,4). Under Diocletian, these two provinces belonged to the diocese of *Oriens*, but around 430, in 448/9 and under Justinian to that of *Aegyptus*. Inscriptions: [6], also on that [7; 8; 9. 3–54; 10. 219–375]; AE 1969–1970, 601; AE 1972, 575; 616; AE 1973, 560.
→ Libyes

1 Huss 2 H. Kees, s.v. Pentapolis (3), RE 19, 509f. 3 A. Laronde, Cyrène et la Libye hellénistique, 1987 4 R.S. Bagnall, The Administration of the Ptolemaic Possessions outside Egypt, 1976 5 W. Huss, Die röm.-ptolem. Beziehungen in der Zeit von 180 bis 116 v.Chr., in: Roma e l'Egitto nell'antichità classica, 1992 6 G. Oliverio, Documenti antichi dell'Africa Italiana, 2 vols., 1932–1936 7 J.M. Reynolds, Twenty Years of Inscriptions, in: Society for Libyan Studies. Annual Reports 20, 1989, 117–121 8 S.M. Marengo, Lessico delle iscrizioni greche della Cirenaica, 1991 9 Quaderni di archeologia della Libia 4, 1961 10 ASAA 39/40, 1961/2.

G. Barker, J. Lloyd, J. Reynolds (ed.), Cyrenaica in Antiquity, 1985; F. Chamoux, La Cyrénaïque, des origines à 321 a.C., d'après les fouilles et les travaux récents, in: Society for Libyan Studies. Annual Reports 20, 1989, 63–70; A. Laronde, Cyrène et la Libye hellénistique, 1987; Id., La Cyrénaïque romaine, des origines à la fin des Sévères, in: ANRW II 10.1, 1006–1064 and pl. I–X; P. Romanelli, La Cirenaica romana, 1943. W.HU.

Cyrenaics (Κυρηναϊκοί; *Kyrēnaïkoí*).
A. History B. Doctrine

A. History

The term Cyrenaics — derived from the home town Cyrene of Socrates' pupil → Aristippus [3] — is used to describe those philosophers who subscribed to the tradition founded by the latter. A list of C. can be found in Diog. Laert. 2,86. Whenever ancient texts refer globally to Aristippus and the C., the topic is almost invariably that they considered → pleasure (*hēdonḗ*) the supreme good (*summum bonum*) and highest aim (*télos*). In the development of this view (and of the philosophy of the C. in general), two phases can be distinguished: the first, in which it was originally developed, and the second, in which → Anniceris, → Hegesias [1], and → Theodoros Atheos, by implementing different modifications, attempted its defence in the dispute with Epicurus at the end of the 4th and beginning of the 3rd cent. BC. Because of these modifications, some ancient philosophical historians separated the later C. from the earlier ones, and referred to them as Annicerians, Hegesians, and Theodorians (Diog. Laert. 1,19; 2,85; 93; 96; 97).

Extant sources attribute the formulation of the C.' philosophy of hedonism to Aristippus [3] the Elder and his grandson Aristippus [4] the Younger. However, the attribution of individual aspects to either of them is uncertain. Eusebius (Pr. Ev. 14,18,31–32) observed that although Aristippus the Elder conveyed the impression by his way of life and his statements that he believed in human happiness being solely based on pleasure, he never formulated an explicit hedonistic philosophy; that was only done by his grandson of the same name. The truth of this statement and its potential wider application beyond hedonism is disputed. As extant sources do not allow a reliable clarification of this question, early C.' philosophy is in the following presented as a homogenous doctrine, to which both Socrates' pupil Aristippus [3] and his grandson of the same name (Aristippus [4]) contributed, but these contributions are no longer individually discernible.

B. Doctrine

Sextus Empiricus (Adv. math. 7,191) reports the bases upon which the C. built their philosophy: 'The C. claim that the only criterion for truth are emotions (πάθη) and that only they were recognized and infallible; however, none of the objects that had caused these emotions were themselves recognizable or infallible. We can state infallibly and irrefutably that with our senses we perceive something as "white" and "sweet"; however, there is no way of proving that the cause of this particular sensation or emotion is in itself white or sweet'. This is a fact generally ignored — thus the C. continue with their argument —, mainly because we have all learned to describe the sensation, which objects create within us, with certain commonly used words. However, it does not follow that the emotions referred to with these same words are the same in themselves, as every person can only be certain of his or her own perceptions. On the contrary, it has to be expected that the sensory perceptions of individuals differ markedly as a consequence of the different constitution of their sensory organs (e.g. the colour of their iris). Thus we are only able to make reliable statements about our own sensory perceptions, but not about the nature of the objects themselves (S. Emp. Adv. math. 7,192–198).

In common with customary contemporary views, the C. explained the materialization of sensory perception as a physiological-psychological process: within a person's body, the influence of external objects causes certain motions or rather alterations (κινήσεις/ *kinḗseis*), which the sensory organs then transfer into the soul, where they are registered as a certain emotion.

This is the point on which the explanation of C. → ethics is based: if an individual can only ever be sure of his or her own emotions, it follows that a definition of good or bad must be restricted to within that selfsame sector. However, as 'good' in conjunction with emotions is synonymous with pleasant or pleasurable (ἡδύ/*hēdý*) and 'bad' with unpleasant or painful (ἀηδές/ *aēdés*; ἀλγεινόν/*algeinón*), it follows that good exists in pleasurable emotions and bad in painful ones. For that reason, the C. viewed → pleasure (*hēdonḗ*) as the supreme good and thus the ultimate aim of all human activity, and conversely pain as the greatest of all evils. Because they assumed that gentle motions were perceived as pleasurable and rough ones as painful, they defined pleasure as a 'gentle motion' (λεία κίνησις) and pain as a 'rough motion' (τραχεῖα κίνησις). In addition, they also recognized a third in-between state, in which neither of the two motions, i.e. neither pleasure nor pain, is perceived (S. Emp. Adv. math. 7,199; Diog. Laert. 2,85; 86; Euseb. Praep. evang. 14,18,32).

As each motion has to come to an end sooner or later, feelings of pleasure can be of varying intensity and length, but by necessity must always be of limited duration. For that reason, a C. will strive for the momentary sensory pleasure transmitted by his body; it is the ultimate aim of all of his actions (Ath. 12,544ab; Diog. Laert. 2,87–88). Everything else is only ever of relative value — if of value at all —, dependent on how much it contributes towards achieving a sensation of pleasure. It is a matter of reason (φρόνησις/*phrónēsis*) to judge from case to case and to determine through careful calculations how maximum pleasure is to be gained at each moment, while at the same time avoiding pain. One of the most important lessons thus learned is that all → affects, which are connected with the feeling of pain and which prevent the feeling of pleasure, are to be avoided as far as possible. In the case of some of these affects, namely those which like e.g. envy are rooted in delusion (κενὴ δόξα; in the case of envy the delusion that to achieve happiness one has to own something that someone else owns, but oneself does not), this is entirely achievable, but not in the case of those affects caused by nature, such as elemental terror (Diog. Laert. 2,91). Mental and physical training are required in order to fortify oneself against the latter (Cic. Tusc. 3,28–31; Diog. Laert. 2,91). With that, one might hope to learn the art which Aristippus himself allegedly demonstrated so masterfully: the art of not submitting oneself to *externalia* but of submitting these to oneself, as Horace, an admirer of Aristippus, put it (Hor. Epist. 1,1,19).

It is disputed whether even the early C. also recognized a purely mental form of pleasure alongside the sensual one. Diogenes Laertius (2,89; 90) claims that they did and quotes as examples of that particular kind of pleasure the 'delight in the simple welfare of the fatherland' ('simple' is used to exclude any reference to the physical welfare of the individual himself) and the enjoyment of art (cf. Plut. Symp. 5,1,674ab). However, there are a number of indicators that Diogenes Laertius wrongly attributes certain views to the early C. which were only voiced later by → Anniceris.

The modifications of the C. doctrine by Anniceris, Hegesias, and Theodoros Atheos in order to keep it competitive in the dispute with Epicurus were, however, unsuccessful. Epicurean hedonism completely supplanted the C.'s version.

EDITIONS: G. GIANNANTONI, I Cirenaici, 1958; E. MANNEBACH, Aristippi et Cyrenaicorum fragmenta, 1961; SSR IV A-H.

BIBLIOGRAPHY: K. DÖRING, Der Sokratesschüler Aristipp und die K., 1988; Id., Aristipp aus Kyrene und die K., GGPh² 2,1, 1998, § 19; G. GIANNANTONI, Il concetto di αἴσθησις nella filosofia cirenaica, in: Id., M. NARCY (ed.), Lezioni Socratiche, 1997, 179–203; V. TSOUNA MCKIRAHAN, The Epistemology of the Cyrenaic School, 1998; Id., The Cyrenaic Theory of Knowledge, in: Oxford Studies in Ancient Philosophy 10, 1992, 161–192. K.D.

Cyrene (Κυρήνη; *Kyrḗnē*, Lat. *Cyrene*).

I. HISTORY II. ARCHAEOLOGY

I. HISTORY

C. was founded by the Dorian island city of Thera in the mod. Cyrenaica, mod. Shahhat. Documentary evidence: Hdt. 4,150–158; SEG IX 3 (with a true core); Str. 17,3,21 [1. 9–67]. Overpopulation and famine — not internal political struggles — forced the inhabitants of Thera into the foundation of this → *apoikía* (differently in Menecles of Barca, FGrH 270 F 6). Initially, the emigrants occupied the island of Platea (mod. Bomba) off the Libyan coast, then the beach of Aziris, and finally in *c.* 631 BC founded the city of C. near the Cyre spring which was dedicated to Apollo (Callim. H. 2,88f.; in the Hellenistic period, the eponymous nymph C. was named as the founder of the city). Their leader Aristoteles adopted the genuine Greek epithet of Battus [2. 269–283] as his name (→ Battus [1]). In the following, this name alternated regularly with the name of Arcesilaus (→ Battiads). → Battus [2] II, who was in conflict with the indigenous → Libyes, enlisted new settlers from various Greek cities and brought them into the country. In 570 BC, he went to battle in the Irasa

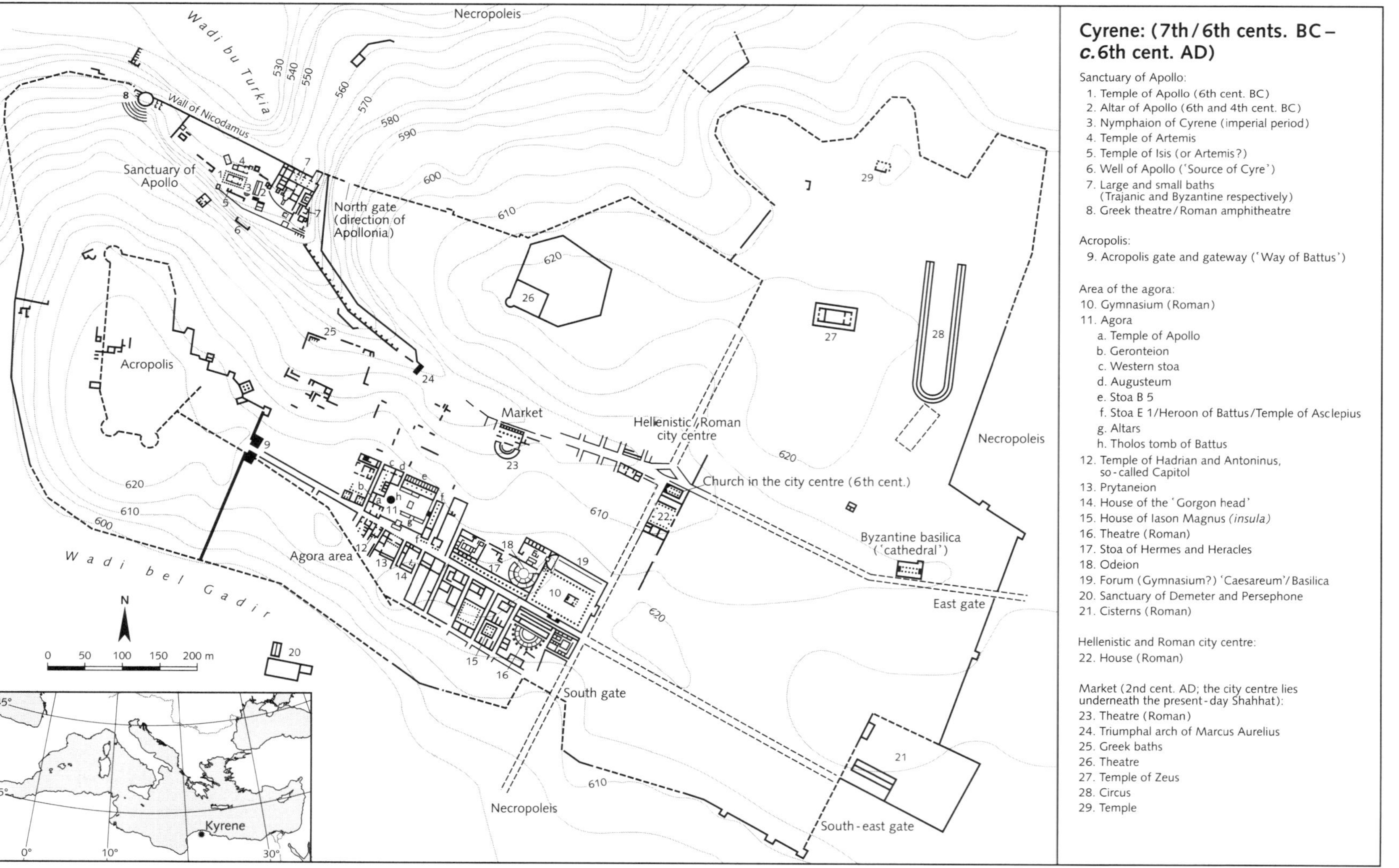
Cyrene: (7th/6th cents. BC – c.6th cent. AD)
Sanctuary of Apollo:
1. Temple of Apollo (6th cent. BC)
2. Altar of Apollo (6th and 4th cent. BC)
3. Nymphaion of Cyrene (imperial period)
4. Temple of Artemis
5. Temple of Isis (or Artemis?)
6. Well of Apollo ('Source of Cyre')
7. Large and small baths (Trajanic and Byzantine respectively)
8. Greek theatre/Roman amphitheatre
Acropolis:
9. Acropolis gate and gateway ('Way of Battus')
Area of the agora:
10. Gymnasium (Roman)
11. Agora
a. Temple of Apollo
b. Geronteion
c. Western stoa
d. Augusteum
e. Stoa B 5
f. Stoa E 1/Heroon of Battus/Temple of Asclepius
g. Altars
h. Tholos tomb of Battus
12. Temple of Hadrian and Antoninus, so-called Capitol
13. Prytaneion
14. House of the 'Gorgon head'
15. House of Iason Magnus (*insula*)
16. Theatre (Roman)
17. Stoa of Hermes and Heracles
18. Odeion
19. Forum (Gymnasium?) 'Caesareum'/Basilica
20. Sanctuary of Demeter and Persephone
21. Cisterns (Roman)
Hellenistic and Roman city centre:
22. House (Roman)
Market (2nd cent. AD; the city centre lies underneath the present-day Shahhat):
23. Theatre (Roman)
24. Triumphal arch of Marcus Aurelius
25. Greek baths
26. Theatre
27. Temple of Zeus
28. Circus
29. Temple
Necropoleis
Wadi bu Turkia
Wadi bel Gadir
Wall of Nicodamus
Sanctuary of Apollo
Acropolis
North gate (direction of Apollonia)
Agora area
Market
Hellenistic/Roman city centre
Church in the city centre (6th cent.)
Byzantine basilica ('cathedral')
East gate
South-east gate
South gate
0 50 100 150 200 m
Kyrene

region against the pharaoh Apries, whose help the Libyans had requested and was victorious (Hdt. 4,159). Under Battus [3] II, → Demonax [1] of Mantinea organized the citizenry in three phyles: those from Thera together with the *perioikoi*, the Peloponnesians together with the Cretans, and Greeks from other islands; furthermore, he restricted the powers of the king (Hdt. 4,161f.; Diod. Sic. 8,30,2). In 525, Arcesilaus III — as did the inhabitants of Barca and the Libyans — recognized the supremacy of the Persian king Cambyses, the conqueror of Egypt. With Arcesilaus IV, whose victories in Delphian chariot races are celebrated by Pindar (Pyth. 4; 5), the rule of the kings came to an end in *c.* 440 BC.

In the post-Alexandrian period, serious civil strife broke out in the city. One of the Cyrenean oligarchs, who had fled the city, asked Ptolemy, the new satrap of Egypt, for assistance in returning. In reply, Ptolemy sent heavily armed contingents under the leadership of the Macedonian → Ophellas into the → Cyrenaea (322). Ophellas succeeded in restoring peace and order (Diod. Sic. 18,19–21; Arr. Succ. fr. 1,16–19). Ptolemy reorganized the administration of the city in a *diagramma* (SEG IX 1; dating from 321?). Ophellas remained in the Cyrenaica as its provincial governor. In 308 BC, he died beneath the walls of Carthage [3. 193f.]. Later, the Cyrenaica was at times a province of the Ptolemaic kingdom, at times an independent kingdom (Magas, Demetrius the Fair, Ptolemy VII Euergetes II, and Ptolemy Apion). In 96 BC, Ptolemy Apion bequeathed to the Romans the *chṓra basilikḗ* ('royal land'), and in 74 BC, Rome granted provincial status to the Cyrenaica. In 34 BC, M. Antony appointed his daughter → Cleopatra [II 13] Selene queen regent of the Cyrenaica. In two edicts of 7/6 BC and 4 BC, Augustus reorganized C.'s judicial system (SEG IX 8). The Jewish revolt of AD 114 affected C. badly; the emperors Trajan and Hadrian supported its construction (SEG XVII 584).

The wealth of the city was based on grain and oil, but particularly in → silphium, which only grew in the Cyrenaica. In addition, there were profits from the trade with animals (sheep, cattle, and horses) and animal products (ostrich feathers). The city's most important sanctuary was the Apollo temple, linked with a sacred spring. C. was the birthplace of a number of important men: the mathematician → Theodorus, the philosopher → Aristippus [3] (→ Cyrenaics), the philosopher → Theodorus 'the Atheist', the poet → Callimachus, the universal scholar → Eratosthenes [2], the scholar → Carneades, and the bishop → Synesius.

Further documentation: Str. 17,3,22. Inscriptions: [4]; ASAA 39/40, 1961/2, 221 (no. 1)–268 (no. 94); 273 (no. 103)–329 (no. 200bis); 340 (no. 212)–357 (no. 294); AE 1972, 616; 1973, 561; 1974, 671; 672; 1995, 1630–1632.

1 J. Seibert, Metropolis und Apoikie, 1963
2 O. Masson, Le nom de Battos ..., in: Id., Onomastica Graeca selecta 1, 1990 3 Huss 4 Quaderni di archeologia della Libia 4, 1961, 5–39.

H. Ch. Broholm, s.v. Kyrene (2), RE 12, 156–169; F. Chamoux, Cyrène sous la monarchie des Battiades, 1953; R. G. Goodchild, Kyrene and Apollonia, 1971; R. Horn, Kyrene, in: Antike 19, 1943, 163–213; A. Laronde, Cyrène et la Libye hellénistique, 1987; S. Stucchi, Architettura cirenaica, 1975; A. A. I. Waisglass, An Historical Study of Cyrene from the Fall of the Battiad Monarchy to the Close of the Fourth Century B.C., 1954.

W.HU.

II. Archaeology

Excavations began early in the 19th cent. and have since revealed C. as one of the most important Greek cities of the ancient world. Of central importance was the richly adorned Apollo sanctuary, closely linked with the foundation myth (Apollo temple of the 6th cent. BC, repeatedly renewed, even as late as after the Jewish revolt of the 2nd cent. AD); it housed several altars, nymphaea, and votive offerings as well as temples for Artemis, Hades, Hecate *et al.*; in AD 98, Trajan endowed the baths later renewed by Hadrian. To the west, this was adjoined by a theatre, which in the Imperial period was altered into an amphitheatre. The cult image in the monumental Zeus temple, which had been rebuilt once under Augustus and then again under Marcus Aurelius in an archaic-Doric style, was a replica of the statue of the god which → Phidias had created in Olympia. *Extra muros* [1] was an important sanctuary of Demeter and Persephone; outside the town walls were also particularly extensive necropoleis (*i.a.* tombs hewn into the rock face).

1 D. White, The Extramural Sanctuary of Demeter and Persephone at Cyrene, Libya. Final Reports, 5. The Site's Architecture, its First Six Hundred Years of Development, 1993.

G. Barker (ed.), Cyrenaika in Antiquity, 1985; A. Laronde, La Cyrénaique romaine, des origines à la fin des Sévères, in: ANRW II 31.1, 1006–1064; Scritti di antichità in memoria di S. Stucchi, 1996.; regular reports in: Libyan Stud., Libya antiqua, Quaderni di archeologia della Libia.

H.G.N.

Maps: EAA s.v. Cirene, 658; A. Laronde, La Cyrénaïque romaine, des origines à la fin des Sévères (96 av. J.-C. — 235 ap. J.-C.), in: ANRW II 10.1, 1006–1064, esp. 1039; Id., Cyrène et la Libye hellénistique, 1987, 73 (according to R. G. Goodchild, K.); S. Raven, Rome in Africa, ³1993; D. White, The Extramural Sanctuary of Demeter and Persephone at Cyrene, Libya. Final Reports 1, 1984 (including map opposite of p. 1).

Cyrillonas (Diminutive form of *Cyrillus*). Name of an otherwise unknown author of six poems in the Syrian language; one of them is about a Hun attack on northern Mesopotamia (thus *c.* AD 396); the other five concern themselves with NT themes.

D. Cerbelaud, Cyrillonas, l'agneau véritable, 1984; S. Landersdorfer, Ausgewählte Schriften der syr. Dichter, 1913, 1–54; I. Vona, I Carmi di Cirillona, 1963.

S.BR.

Cyrillus (Κύριλλος; *Kýrillos*)

[1] **C. of Jerusalem.** Born *c.* AD 313, he was a member of the Jerusalem clergy (Jer. Chron. 2365 [GCS Eus. 7,236,7f. HELM/TREU]), and from 348 to 386 served as bishop of Jerusalem; he came to this office rather as a follower of the Homoeans (cf. Jer. loc. cit., Socr. 2,38,2 and Sozom. Hist. eccl. 4,20,1) than as a Nicaean (cf. Theod. Hist. eccl. 2,26,6). In 358 he was relieved of his office by → Acacius [2] of Caesarea and banished to Tarsus, rehabilitated in 359 and banished again in the following year. In 362 he returned briefly to Jerusalem and attempted to prevent the reconstruction of the Temple under the emperor → Iulianus [11] (Socr. 2,42,6; 45,17 and 3,20,7f.). Banished again under → Valens, he returned to his bishopric at the latest under → Gratianus [2] (Socr. 5,3,1). At the imperial council in Constantinople in 381 his anti-Arian (= anti-Homoean; → Arianism) position was emphasized (Socr. 5,8,3; Sozom. Hist. eccl. 7,7,3 and Theod. Hist. eccl. 5,9,17).

In addition to a letter to emperor → Constantius [2] concerning an apparition of the Cross (ed. see [1]), catecheses for candidates for baptism have survived; these expound *i.a.* the Jerusalem Creed, and are an important source for the liturgical changes laying emphasis on the commemorative character of the holy places of the life and death of Jesus. The five mystagogic catecheses on the other hand are probably not by C. but by his follower John of Jerusalem.

1 E. BIHAIN, in: Byzantion 43, 1973, 264–296.

EDITIONS: CPG 2, 3585–3618; E. BIHAIN, La tradition manuscrite grècque des œuvres de saint Cyrille de Jérusalem (phil. diss. Louvain), 1966; E.J. YARNOLD, s.v. Cyrillus von Jerusalem, TRE 8, 261–266. C.M.

[2] **C. (Cyril) of Alexandria**

A. LIFE B. WORK C. THEOLOGY

A. LIFE

Born in Alexandria [1], C. received a solid education from his uncle, bishop Theophilus. After attending the so-called Synod of the Oak together with him in 403, he succeeded him as bishop of Alexandria from AD 412 to 444. He immediately took severe measures against Novatians (→ Novatianus) and Jews, and turned against the *praefectus Augustalis* → Orestes. In connection with this, the Neoplatonic philosopher → Hypatia was murdered by Christians in 415 (partly the fault of C. according to [10. 500]). C. played a central role in the conflict over bishop → Nestorius of Constantinople, denouncing the latter's reserves against designating → Mary *theotókos* (θεοτόκος, 'mother of God') as a denial of the unity of God and humanity in Christ (important texts translated in [8. 244–399]). Pope Celestine I took C.'s part in the escalating conflict, and his position was confirmed at the Council of Ephesus (condemnation of Nestorius) in 431. In 433 C. reached an agreement with the remaining followers of Nestorius.

B. WORK

The writings of C. can be split into three phases, separated by the Nestorian controversy. The first (412–428) consisted of works of exegesis. C. directed his attention towards the OT (i.a. *Glaphyra in Pentateuchum*, CPG 5201), and produced the important commentary on John (CPG 5208) as well as the collection of sermons making up the commentary on Luke [1]. Early writings of his are also directed against the Arians (→ Arianism; *i.a. De sancta trinitate dialogi VII* [3]). Apart from letters [4; 7] and defensive writings, five volumes *Contra Nestorium* (CPG 5217) fall into the period of the dispute about Nestorius (428–433). The mature christological dialogue *Quod unus sit Christus* [2. 302–515] is seen as belonging to the third phase. The emperor → Iulianus [11] is opposed in *Contra Iulianum imperatorem*, which survives incomplete [5]. C. wrote annual 'Easter letters' [6].

C. THEOLOGY

Orientated as he was towards the Alexandrian ideological tradition (→ Athanasius), the oneness of Christ the divine Saviour is central for C. He understands the incarnation primarily as a divine realization, entailing an existential union of the deity and humanity (ἕνωσις φυσική/*hénōsis physikḗ* or καθ' ὑπόστασιν/*kath' hypóstasin*), in which the characteristics of each distinct nature nevertheless persist. Mary is accordingly God's mother. Conceptual weaknesses become apparent when C. speaks of the 'one nature of the *logos* become flesh' (μία φύσις τοῦ θεοῦ λόγου σεσαρκωμένη), and in so doing unintentionally employs a formula of → Apollinarius [3] of Laodicea. C. exercised a vital influence on the development of the christology of the ancient Church; he was at the same time the subject of greatly differing opinions.

EDITIONS: 1 CPG 5200–5438 2 CPG Suppl. 5201–5397 3 PG 68–77 (complete edition) 4 P.E. PUSEY (ed.), 7 vols., 1868–1877 (single texts) 5 J.-B. CHABOT, R.M. TONNEAU (ed.), CSCO 70, 1912; 140, 1953 (newer edition) 6 G.M. DURAND et al. (ed.), SChr 97, 1964 7 Id. (ed.), SChr 231, 237, 246, 1976–1978 8 L.R. WICKHAM (ed.), Select Letters, 1983 9 P. BURGUIÈRE, P. EVIEUX (ed.), SChr 322, 1985 10 P. ÉVIEUX et al. (ed.), SChr 372, 392, 434, 1991–1998 11 Acta Conciliorum Oecumenicorum IV 3/1, 1974, 161–199 (index).

BIBLIOGRAPHY: 12 J.A. MCGUCKIN, St. Cyril of Alexandria. The Christological Controversy, 1994 (bibliogr. 403–415) 13 B. MEUNIER, Le Christ de Cyrille d'Alexandrie, 1997 14 J. ROUGÉ, La politique de Cyrille d'Alexandrie et le meurtre d'Hypatie, in: Cristianesimo nella storia 11, 1990, 485–504 15 Theologische Quartalschrift 178, 1998, 257–326 (issue devoted to C.). J.RI.

[3] **C. of Scythopolis.** Born *c.* AD 524 as the son of a lawyer working for the metropolitan of Palaestina Secunda in Scythopolis (→ Beisan). In 542 he became a monk (→ Monasticism), and after some years lived as a hermit in various monasteries in the Judaean desert, from 556 in the great → Laura, whose founder Sabas

had profoundly impressed him in his youth (Vita Sabae p. 180f. SCHWARTZ). From 543 he wrote down the accounts of his fellow monks regarding the founding fathers of monasticism in the desert; these were handed down in collections of monks' lives and in menologies [1. 317–340]. The lives of seven monks in the Judaean desert have survived: Euthymius († 473), Sabas († 532), John Hesychastes († 557), Cyriacus († 556), Theodosius († 528), Theognius († 522) and Abraamius († 542/3). These texts, regardless of their hagiographic stylizations, are a major source for the history of monasticism in Palaestine, the controversies concerning the Council of Chalcedon (AD 451) and the teaching of → Origenes in this region after the Council of Constantinople in AD 553.

E. SCHWARTZ (ed.), K. von Skythopolis (texts and research 49/2), 1939; R. M. PRICE, Lives of the Monks of Palestine by Cyril of Skythopolis, 1991 (translation); CPG 3, 7535–7543; J. BINNS, Ascetics and Ambassadors of Christ. The Monasteries of Palestine 314–631 (Oxford Early Christian Stud.), 1994, 23–40; B. FLUSIN, Miracle et histoire dans l'œuvre de Cyrille de Scythopolis (Ét. Augustiniennes), 1983. C.M.

[4] **C. the Elder.** Teacher of law in Berytus in the 1st half of the 5th cent. AD [1]; whether he wrote a *Commentarius definitionum* [2] is doubtful [3].

1 PLRE II, 335 (Cyrillus 2) 2 SCHULZ, 388f. 3 P. E. PIELER, in: HUNGER, Literatur 2, 391.

[5] **C. the Younger.** Lawyer; under Justinian I wrote a Greek paraphrase (index) of the → *Digesta*, parts of which entered the Basilika scholia.

PLRE III, 372 (Cyrillus 3); ODB 1, 573. T.G.

[6] An encyclopaedia or lexicon, probably first written down in the 5th cent. AD, survives under the name of C. It contains biblical glosses, glosses from the Church Fathers, the Atticists and glosses derived from the tradition of 'classical' exegesis (esp. from the so-called Didymus scholia on Homer and a paraphrase of Euripides). It has survived in numerous manuscripts, which can be arranged into three or four families from different editions. Another indication of its extraordinary influence in the Byzantine period are interpolations in the lexicon of → Hesychius and the fact that a related collection, the source of one of the most fertile lexicographical traditions, reappears e.g. in the encyclopaedia of Photius and in the Suda.

3 R. REITZENSTEIN, Die Überarbeitung des Lexicons des Hesychios, in: RhM 43, 1888, 443–60; A. B. DRACHMANN, Die Überlieferung des Cyrillglossars (Danske Vidensk. Selskab. Hist.-filol. Meddedelser 21,5, 1936; K. LATTE (ed.), Hesychii Alexandrini Lexicon 1, 1953, XLIV–LI; S. LUCA, Il lessico dello Ps.-Cirillo (redazione VI): da Rossano a Messina, in: Rivista di Studi Byzantini Neoellenici 31, 1994, 45–80. R.T.

[7] Otherwise unknown author of a distich that, in prescribing the single distich as the measure for the perfect epigram, recommends brevity as a precept: more than two lines, and you have an epic (Anth. Pal. 9,369). This is an innovation, as the poets of Meleager preferred two distichs, those of the 'Garland' of Philip three. Evidence for the name C. is almost entirely absent prior to the 2nd cent. AD (FGE 115: the epigram is, however, not correctly understood there, cf. [1]).

1 M. LAUSBERG, Das Einzeldistichon. Studien zum ant. Epigramm, 1982, 43–44. M.G.A.

[8] The 'Apostle of the Slavs'. Constantinus, who shortly before his death adopted the monastic name Cyrillus (Vita Constantini 18,5), under which from the 14th cent. AD he and his brother Methodius have been venerated by the Slavs every 14 February as *Kiril i Metodi.* He came from → Thessalonica, where 'everyone speaks pure Slavonic' (Vita Methodii 5,4–8). He studied in → Constantinople (AD 843) in the Magnaura school (Vita Const. 4,1), at a time when the veneration of images had already taken up its undisputed place in Byzantine orthodoxy. As deacon (Vita Const. 4,15) and later librarian (ἄρχων τῶν κοντακίων rather than χαρτοφύλαξ) of the → Hagia Sophia he had the opportunity to become closely acquainted with the cathedral office. After a brief career as an official, Methodius became a Studite monk in the → Olympus monastery in Bithynia in AD 840. On the grounds of his powers of persuasion he was assigned to work among the heathen Saracens and → Chazars (Vita Const. 6,10).

The two Slav apostles were commissioned to make the entire liturgy (τάξις/*táxis*) (*vьsь činъ*) accessible to their Slavonic audience by translating it into the Slavonic language (2. Slav. Vita Naumi). This Slavonic liturgy (*činъ*) contained (Vita Methodii 15) morning (*utrьnnici*) and evening office (*večerьni i pavečerьnici*), the offices of the 'small hours' (*časovomъ*) and the *officium sacramentorum* (*tajnaja služba*). Before their journey to Moravia they had already written some sermons on the evangelists (*besědu evangelьsku*), and translated the Psalter (*psaltyrь*) with an Aprakos Gospel and the Praxapostolos (*evangelije sъ apostolomъ*) along with selected offices of the monthly cycle (parts of the Euchologion, the Lenten offices of the Triodion and the Oktoechos); in addition they put together a compilation that later became known as *Zakonъ sudnyj ljudjem* (*lex iudicialis de laicis*); the books of the Church Fathers (*otьčьkъye knigy*) and pericopic readings from the Old and New Testaments (*paremejnik*) are also extant.

→ Church Slavonic

M. ARRANZ, La tradition liturgique de Constantinople au IXe siècle et l'Euchologe Slave de Sinaï (manuscript), 1985; Id., La liturgie de l'Euchologe Slave de Sinaï, in: Orientalia Christiana Analecta 231, 1988, 15–74; M. EGGERS, Das Erzbistum von Method. Lage, Wirkung und Nachleben der kyrillomethodianischen Mission, 1996; I. GOŠEV, Starobălgarskata liturgija, in: Godišnik na sofijskija universitet. Bogoslovski fak. 6, 1932, 1–80; F. GRIVEC, F. TOMŠIČ, Radovi staroslavenskog instituta 4, 1960. L.D.

Cyrrhestice (Κυρρηστική; *Kyrrhēstikḗ*). Region in northern Syria south of → Commagene, between the Euphrates and the → Amanus; named after its capital Cyrrhus [2]. The name is used for the first time, but perhaps anachronistically, in connection with events of the year 286 BC (Plut. Demetrius 48,6). Attested with certainty is a revolt of 6,000 Cyrrhesticans against Antiochus [5] the Great in 221 (Pol. 5,50; 57). At the time Seleucid rule was ending, local dynasts appear to also have had their say in the political affairs in C: the Cyrrhestican and (apparently disloyal) Roman *socius* Channaeus/Pharnaeus, for example, is mentioned in connection with the battle of Gindarus in 38 BC, in which the Parthian crown prince → Pacorus perished (Cass. Dio 49,19,2; Frontin. Str. 1,1,6). During the Roman Imperial period C. was part of the province of Syria, then — after the separation of Phoenicia — of Syria Coele. When the province of Augusta Euphratensis was formed, probably under Constantius [2] II, the greater part of C. was included in it. The fertile areas around and to the north of Beroea remained with Syria Coele, later with its subsidiary province Syria Prima.
→ Syria

E. Frézouls, Cyrrhus et la Cyrrhestique jusqu'à la fin du Haut-Empire, in: ANRW II 8, 164–197; E. Honigmann, s.v. Kyrrhestike, RE 12, 191–198; E. Kettenhofen, Östl. Mittelmeerraum und Mesopotamien (TAVO B V 12), 1983; W. Orth, Die Diadochenzeit im Spiegel der histor. Geographie, 1993, 89.
M.SCH.

Cyrrhus (Κύρρος; *Kýrrhos*).
[1] Macedonian city near the modern Aravissos between Pella and Edessa, existed already in the 5th cent. BC (Thuc. 2,100,1); was to be the site of one of the gigantic temples supposedly planned by Alexander the Great (Diod. Sic. 18,4,5); half-finished partial structures in an ancient quarry near C. could be connected with this intended construction project [1]. An unpublished inscription (cf. [2]) attests to a municipal authority concerned with the building of roads and other structures. Mentioned in Plin. HN 4,34 as one of the Macedonian provincial cities, C. was taken by Ostrogoths in the 5th cent. AD; Theodemir, father of Theoderic the Great, died there (Jord. Get. 287f.). Justinian had the town fortified (Procop. Aed. 4,4).

1 G. Bakalakis, Archaia Makedonia 1, 1970, 172–183
2 A.K. Vavritsas, Archaia Makedonia 2, 1977, 7–9.

F. Papazoglou, Les villes de Macédoine, 1988, 152–154.
MA.ER.

[2] City in northern Syria, *c.* 90 km north-east of Antakya/Antioch. To judge by its name probably a Macedonian settlement existing already in the age of the Diadochi (→ Diadochi and Epigoni). Under the Seleucids, it was capital of → Cyrrhestice, the territory named after it, one of the four administrative districts of the satrapy of Seleukis. The strategic importance of C. was a result of its position on the main route from Antioch via Seleucia/Zeugma to northern Mesopotamia. After the difficulties of the 1st cent. BC it flourished during the Roman Imperial period, with extensive coinage. In the early 1st cent. AD C. was the garrison city of the *legio X Fretensis*, during the Parthian wars of the 2nd cent. an important staging post; it also was the home city of Avidius [1] Cassius, the military commander and later pretender to the throne in opposition to Marcus Aurelius. In AD 256, C. was taken by the Sassanids. The city subsequently declined in importance, even though Justinian constructed defences for it as late as the 6th cent. AD. In the 5th cent. AD, C. played a significant religious role under its bishop → Theodoretus. In 637 C. was captured by the Arabs, and thereafter affected by the frontier struggles with Byzantium. C. is mentioned as late as the 12th cent. AD. Archaeology: extensive ruins with a well-preserved walled circle, theatre and colonnaded street. Systematic archaeological investigation since 1952.

E. Frézouls, Recherches historiques et archéologiques sur la ville de Cyrrhus, in: Annales archéologiques arabes syriennes 4/5, 1954/5, 89–128; Id., L'exploration archéologique de Cyrrhus, in: J. Balty (ed.), Apamée de Syrie, 1969, 81–92; Id., Cyrrhus et la Cyrrhestique jusqu'à la fin du Haut-Empire, in: ANRW II 8, 164–197; J.D. Grainger, The Cities of Seleukid Syria, 1990.
J.G.

Cyrtii (Κύρτιοι; *Kýrtioi*, Lat. *Cyrtii*). Mentioned at Str. 11,523; 727 as nomads in northern Media and Persia. Pol. 5,52,5 mentions the C. as reserve troops of the Median governor Molon in the struggle against Antiochus III. Liv. 37,40,9 mentions them as opponents of the Romans in the battle of Magnesia (190 BC); at Liv. 42,58,13 they appear as Roman mercenaries with Callinicus (171 BC). On the basis of their name, they are seen as the ancestors of the Kurds.
B.B.

Cyrtones (Κύρτωνες; *Kýrtōnes*). Small Boeotian city (πόλισμα) on the border with eastern Locris, north-west of Hyettus on a pass to Korseia leading across the Chlomon mountains; probably to be identified with the sparse ancient remains near modern Kolaka. The old name was Cyrtone (Κυρτώνη; *Kyrtṓnē*, Paus. 9,24,4). In the Roman period there was a temple and grove of Apollo and Artemis in C., as well as a spring sacred to the nymphs. References: Paus. 9,24,4; cf. also Hdn. De prosodia catholica 3,1,293; 337; Hdn. De paronymis 3,2,861; Steph. Byz. s.v. Kyrtones.

J.M. Fossey, The End of the Bronze Age in the South West Copaic, in: id., Papers in Boiotian Topography and History, 1990, 53–57; W.A. Oldfather, Stud. in the History and Topography of Locris II, in: AJA 20, 1916, 157–168; N.D. Papachatzis, Παυσανίου Ἑλλάδος Περιήγησις 5, 21981, 166.
P.F.

Cyrus (Κῦρος; *Kŷros*, Lat. Cyrus).
[1] **C. I. (the Elder)** Grandfather of → Cyrus [2] (the Great), known from the cylinder inscription of his grandson (TUAT I 409,21). Here he is given the title 'great king, king of Anšān' (*šarru rabû šar Anšān*;

→ Anshan) and called 'descendant' (*liblibbu*) of → Teispes. The genealogical link C. (I.) — Cambyses (I.) — C. (II.) is also mentioned in Hdt. 1,111. C. the Elder may accordingly be interpreted as a petty king of Persian descent, ruling over (a part of (?) the formerly Elamite) Fārs in the 7th/6th cents. BC. Two fragments of an inscription of → Assurbanipal name a 'Kuraš, king of Parsumaš', who sent his eldest son Arukku to Niniveh 'with his contribution, to pay homage to me (A.)' [1. 191f., ii' 7'–13'; 280f., l. 115–118]; given the prevalence of the name C. and the fact that the attribution of Parsumaš to Fārs is by no means certain it remains a matter of dispute as to whether this refers to C.; the seal (PFS 93) with the Elamite legend 'Cyrus the Anšānite, son of Teispes' [2. fig. 2a/b] that was found on the five 'Persepolis Fortification Tablets' ([3], PFT 692–695,2033) however may be a reference to him.

1 R. Borger, Beitr. zum Inschriftenwerk Assurbanipals, 1996 2 M.B. Garrison, M.C. Root, Persepolis Seal Studies, 1998 3 R.T. Hallock, Persepolis Fortification Tablets, 1969 4 P. de Miroschedji, La fin du royaume d'Anšan et de Suse, in: ZA 75, 1985, 265–306 5 R. Rollinger, Zur Lokalisation von Parsu(m)a(š) in der Fārs, in: ZA 89, 1999. J.W.

[2] C. (II.?) Founder of the Persian empire (ruled 559?–Aug. 530 BC).

A. Descent and Genealogy B. The Medes and the Lydian empire C. Cyrus and the Neo-Babylonian empire D. Death and influence

A. Descent and Genealogy

From his cylinder inscription (TUAT I 409,21) we derive the information that he was descended from the lineage of Teispes, began his career as 'King of Anšān' and was 'son of Cambyses, the Great King, the King of Anšān, grandson of Cyrus, the Great King, the King of Anšān'. The father-son relationship between Cambyses (I.) and C. is also confirmed by an inscription from Ur (see below). The description of C. as 'Achaemenid' in the inscriptions from Pasargadae (CMa-c [4. 116]) was made retrospectively by → Darius [1] I (cf. DB I 27–29 [4. 117]); his purpose was probably to underpin the legitimacy of his own claims by constructing a relationship with the founder of the empire. In Herodotus (Hdt. 1,107f.; cf. Xen. Cyr. 1,2,1) C. was born from a marriage between Cambyses and → Mandane, the daughter of a Median king. Just as this tradition is an ideological expression of Persian claims to Media (and via Mandane's mother Aryenis to Lydia; cf. for Egypt Hdt. 3,2,1f.), so the legend of the miraculous rescue of the child C. (Hdt. 1,107–121; other versions of childhood and youth in Just. 1,4,10; Nicolaus of Damascus FGrH 90 F 66 and Ctesias FGrH 688 F 9; myths of → Exposure) with its Mesopotamian parallels (→ Sargon of Akkad) and its Iranian echoes is a token of the subsequent esteem in which the charismatic founder was held. According to Hdt. 1,214 C. ruled for 29 years. Of his sons, → Cambyses (II.) and → Bardiya [1] (Smerdis) are known by name; of his daughters, → Atossa and → Artystone (Hdt. 3, 88).

B. The Medes and the Lydian empire

Upon ascending the throne (559?) C.'s first achievement was probably to gain control of the region around Susa, the ancient centre of the Elamites, and thus strengthened to emerge victorious from the struggle against the onslaught of Astyages (Akkadian Ištumegu): the Median units rebelled against their commander-in-chief and delivered him to C., who subsequently seized Ecbatana, the Median royal capital, from which he had rich booty transported back to Anšān [3. no. 7, ii 1–4]. Grossly underestimating the Persians, and just as mistakenly overestimating his own military resources, the Lydian king → Croesus believed that he could redraw the political map of eastern Anatolia in the aftermath of C.'s victory (Hdt. 1,53–55; 73). When his invasion of Cappadocia (in the 540s; Hdt. 1,71) and the subsequent inconclusive battle of Pteria did not yield the desired success (Hdt. 1,76), he withdrew into his winter quarters in Lydia, meaning to prepare for a new campaign with the help of his allies in Babylonia, Egypt and Sparta (Hdt. 1,77). Determined to foil these plans, C. rather than dismissing his army had them pursue the Lydians (Hdt. 1,79), at the same time calling upon the Greek subjects of Croesus to abandon their commander (Hdt. 1,76). Even though the Greeks remained loyal to Croesus, after a further battle he soon found himself confined in his capital Sardis (Hdt. 1,80f.). After a two-week siege (Hdt. 1,84) — yet to be confirmed by archaeological finds — the city fell into the hands of the Persians; Croesus was probably killed during the fighting ([3. no. 7 ii 15–17] — but this reading is disputed; Eusebius, Chronikoi kanones [Armen.] p. 33,8f. Kaerst); he lived on only in one part of Greek tradition, which put a mythological (Bacchyl. 3,23ff.) or rationalizing (Hdt. 1,86ff.) 'gloss' on the catastrophe, at the same time establishing the tradition of C. as the 'generous victor' (Hdt.).

How little this image corresponds with reality is demonstrated by the reaction of the Persian king to the revolt of the Lydian Paktyes, whom he had appointed his treasurer, and who had won most of the Greek coastal cities to his side. C.'s commanders Mazares and → Harpagus [1] not only saw to the prompt punishment of the insurgent, but also took their revenge on his Greek allies: Mazares conquered Priene, enslaved its political elite and plundered the city and environs of Magnesia; Harpagus subsequently seized Smyrna, Phocaea and other cities, and secured the entire coastal strip of western Asia Minor as far as Lycia for C. (Hdt. 1,154–176). Only Miletus, which in Lydian times had been independent, and had supported C. against Croesus and not joined the revolt, retained its more favourable political status (Hdt. 1,169).

C. Cyrus and the Neo-Babylonian empire

Babylon under King → Nabonid cannot have remained unaffected by the collapse of its neighbour Media and its ally Lydia, or by the Persian rule over Susa. Owing to lack of surviving evidence, we are unable to determine what events preceded Babylon's own fateful confrontation with C. It is certain, however, that increasing tensions were exacerbated by C., in that he offered himself as a political alternative to those parts of the Babylonian population who were dissatisfied with Nabonid (such as the priesthood of Marduk). After his victory at Opis, the subsequent massacre of soldiers and the capture of Sippar, C. could afford to send his commander Ugbaru ahead to Babylon to take the city, which opened its gates to the representative without resistance, and to make Nabonid a prisoner ([3. no. 7, iii 12–18]; cf. Hdt. 1,191). C.'s own ceremonial entry into the city at the end of October 539 BC ([3. no. 7, iii 18–20]; Berossos FGrH 680 F 9) was designed to accord with the Babylonian model, as were his first official acts; Ugbaru and C.'s wife however, died immediately after the entry into the city [3. no. 7, iii 22f.]. The 'C. cylinder' (TUAT I 407–410), an architectural inscription similarly conceived under expert Babylonian tutelage, presents the Persian king as the legitimate king of Babylon, cherished and supported by → Marduk, complying for the welfare of his country with his obligations towards God and the people in respect of buildings, culture and social policy, and thus distinguishing himself from his predecessor (other eulogies: 'stanzaic poem': ANET 312–315; inscriptions from Ur [2. no. 194, 307]). By his behaviour, C. created the conditions needed for the elite of the country to be prepared to co-operate with their foreign master.

With the downfall of Nabonid, the former Neo-Babylonian territories from Palestine in the south-west to the Zagrus in the east also had a new ruler. It cannot be established to what extent C. integrated them into the empire following the Babylonian pattern, or to what extent he was able to set new political parameters there during the nine years of his rule. Although the role assigned to him in Jewish tradition (C. in the OT: 2 Chr. 36,22f.; Ezra 1,1–8; 3,7; 4,3–5; 5,13–17; 6,13f.; Is. 44,24–28; 45,1–9; Dan. 1,21; 6,29; 10,1) with regard to the repatriation of the Judaeans deported by Nebuchadnezzar and the rebuilding of the Temple in Jerusalem is probably to be understood as a process in which measures not authorized until later were (theologically) projected backwards onto the long-awaited liberator, C. may have had a particular interest in Syro-Palestinian affairs. Decisive events in this area, however, had to wait for his successors.

The importance C. placed on the task of integrating into the new empire the immense territory and unparalleled populations of the Neo-Babylonian empire is witnessed not only by the aforementioned ideological pains he was prepared to take, but also by concrete measures: the confirmation of high functionaries of Nabonid in their offices (e.g. the governor (*šakin māti*) Nabû-aḫḫē-bulliṭ) and the establishment of crown prince Cambyses as viceroy (538/7; cf. e.g. [7. 108]); although for reasons unknown to us the latter ceased to be 'king of Babylon' after just one year, making place for → Gobryas [2] as new governor (*bēl pīḫāti*) of the province of 'Babylon and *Ebir nāri* (Transeuphratene)' (evidence in: [6. 56 n. 1]). The fact that our sources — unlike those for Lydia — know nothing of revolts in Babylonia speaks for the success of early Persian policies in this region. This is also confirmed by the fact that in the 530s C. could evidently venture to bring large parts of eastern Iran under his control (cf. DB I 12–17 [4. 117] as a list of peoples for the year 522/1; no eastern campaigns are known for Cambyses II), although in this case both the strategy and the course of his campaigns, as well as the nature of his policies for securing the north-eastern and eastern frontiers, remain unclear owing to the lack of surviving records.

D. Death and influence

Greek sources speak of C.'s falling in the campaign against the steppe peoples (Hdt. 1,205–214; Ctesias FGrH 688 F 9), of his body being brought to Persis (Ctesias FGrH 688 F 13) and interred in his newly built capital at → Pasargadae (Aristob. FGrH 139 F 51b; cf. Arr. Anab. 6,29,4–11). Even today the remains of this structure set in artificially irrigated gardens bear witness to the orientation of the royal architect towards artistic models from the entire Near East, and to the creativity of the craftsmen engaged specifically for the project, in particular the Ionian stonemasons.

The traditional image of C. that we have even today errs on the positive side, due not least to the endeavours of the king himself, and draws a veil over the dark side of his person and politics; there is however no doubt that in C. we see an individual of extraordinary ability: in less than 30 years, by his strokes of military and strategic genius and his carrot and stick politics, he created an empire unparalleled in extent and in historic importance. It is no wonder that countless stories, to some extent following well-known patterns and models, soon began to circulate in Iran (cf. Xen. Cyr. 1,2,1), but also elsewhere, in praise of this extraordinary ruler.

1 Briant, passim 2 C.J. Gadd, Ur Excavation Texts 1, 1928 3 A.K. Grayson, Assyrian and Babylonian Chronicles, 1975 4 R. Kent, Old Persian, 1953 5 A. Kuhrt, Babylonia, in: CAH² 4, 1988, 112–138 6 M. San Nicolò, Beitr. zu einer Prosopographie der neubabylon. Beamten der Zivil- und Tempelverwaltung, 1941 7 A. Ungnad, Vorderasiatische Schriftdenkmäler 6, 1908 8 J. Wiesehöfer, Das ant. Persien, 1994, Index s.v.

J.W.

[3] **C. the Younger.** (*c.* 423–401 BC); son of Darius II and → Parysatis (Plut. Artaxerxes 1,2) and younger brother of → Artaxerxes [2] II. Born to the purple and favoured by his mother (Plut. Artaxerxes 2,4), C. became satrap of Lydia, Greater Phrygia and Cappadocia (Xen. An. 1,9,7), as well as supreme military commander (κάρανος: Xen. Hell. 1,4,3; cf. Xen. An. 1,1,2; 1,9,7)

in Asia Minor (408 or 407). His policy there was one of friendship with Sparta (cf. Thuc. 2,65,12), in close coordination with → Lysander.

After (alleged [?]), plans to mount a coup (reported by his opponent → Tissaphernes) on the occasion of his brother's coronation in 405/4 (Plut. Artaxerxes 3,3–5; cf. Xen. An. 1,1; Ctesias FGrH 688 F 16), C. was granted amnesty thanks to the intervention of his mother; he returned to his power base and there with the help of Sparta, the Ionian Greeks and enlisted Greek mercenaries (οἱ Κύρειοι, Xen. Hell. 3,2,7) prepared a military operation against Artaxerxes (Xen. An. 1,4,2; Xen. Hell. 3,1,1; Diod. Sic. 14,19,4). The expedition, exhaustively described in the *Anábasis* of → Xenophon, who participated in the campaign, collapsed in the autumn of 401 at → Cunaxa because C. fell in the decisive battle (Xen. An. 1,8,26f.; Diod. Sic. 14,23,6f.; Deinon FGrH 690 F 17; Plut. Artaxerxes 11,1–5). It is no surprise that Xenophon dedicated an encomium to C. (Xen. An. 1,9; cf. Xen. Oec. 4,6–25), nor that the Achaemenid royal inscriptions on the other hand do not mention him.

R. SCHMITT, s.v. Cyrus IV, EncIr. 6, 1993, 524–526; BRIANT, passim. J.W.

[4] **C. from Panopolis** (ὁ Πανοπολίτης; *ho Panoplítēs*). Poet and politician, *c.* AD 400–470. As *praef. urbis* he had Constantinople rebuilt after the earthquake of 437. He was the first to publish his decrees in Greek rather than Latin; 439–441 he also was *praef. praetorio Orientis*. As a follower of → Monophysitism he had a church built to the Mother of God. When at the end of 441 he fell into disfavour (he had become a consul only shortly before), he retired to Cotyaeum (Phrygia) and there took on the office of bishop. Of his many and diverse works only a short but impressive *Homilia in Nativitatem* ('Christmas Homily'; [1]), written in Greek, and three epigrams survive: Anth. Pal. 1,99 (an inscription on the pillar of Daniel Stylites in Anaplus); 9,136 (six hexameters declaimed by C. when he left Constantinople); and 15,9 (short panegyric poem to Theodosius II, in Homericising hexameters). Poems 7,557 (epitaph to a virtuous woman) and 9,623 (to a bath), as well as 808f. (to a luxurious villa and a statue of Pindar) and 813 (in praise of the empress Sophia, wife of Justin II), from the 'Kyklos' of Agathias, however probably belong to another C., living about a century later and perhaps to be identified as the father of → Paulus Silentiarius.

EDITION: 1 T.E. GREGORY, The Remarkable Christmas Homily of K. Panopolites, in: GRBS 16, 1975, 317–24.
BIBLIOGRAPHY: 2 D.J. CONSTANTELOS, K. Panopolites, Rebuilder of Constantinople, in: GRBS 12, 1971, 451–64 3 A. CAMERON, The Empress and the Poet: Paganism and Politics at the Court of Theodosius II, in: YClS 27, 1982, 217–89. M.G.A.

[5] Κῦρος; *Kŷros*, Str. 11,1,5; 2,17; 4,2; 7,3; 8,9; 14,4; Κύρος; *Kýros*, Ptol. 5,11,1; 3; Κύρνος; *Kýrnos*, Plut. Pompeius 34f.; Κύρτος; *Kýrtos*, App. Mith. 103; *Cyrus*, Plin. HN 1,6; 10; 6,25f.; 29; 39; 45; 52; the modern *Kura* (Russian, Turkish) or *Mtkvari* (Georgian). Greatest river of the southern Caucasus, rising in the uplands of modern Ardahan, and flowing in a NE-SE arc into the Caspian Sea. In antiquity it formed the frontier between Greater → Armenia, → Iberia [1] and → Albania [1] (Str. 11,3,2, Plin. HN 6,39). Mentioned at Str. 11,2,17; 7,3 as part of the inland waterway from India to Pontus via the Caspian Sea, with four-day land transport across the Ponia Pass (the modern Surami/Georgia) to the → Phasis.

F. WEISSBACH, s.v. Kyros (2), RE 12, 184ff. A.P.-L.

[6] River in Persis, according to Str. 15,3,6 in the vicinity of Pasargadae, the modern Pulvār. The modern Kur however is to be identified with the → Araxes [3].

J. SEIBERT, Die Eroberung des Perserreiches durch Alexander d.Gr., 1985, esp. 105f. J.W.

Cytaea (Κυταιίς; *Kytaiís*, Apoll. Rhod. 2,1267; Κύταια; *Kýtaia*, schol. ad Lycoph. Alexandra 1312; Κόταϊς; *Kótaïs* (τὸ φρούριον), Procop. Goth. 4,14,49; 4,14,51 Agathias 2,19,1). City in → Colchis, on the headwaters of the modern Kutaisi on the middle Rioni (→ Phasis) in Georgia. Archaeological finds indicate the existence of a settlement with acropolis from the 7th cent. BC; fragments of Greek pottery indicate contacts between inland Colchis and the Mediterranean region from the 7th/6th cents. BC. In the 5th/4th cents. BC the settlement was greatly extended (wattle-and-daub structures); constantly settled since.
→ Aea

O. LORDKIPANIDZE, Zur ersten Erwähnung Kutaisis in den schriftlichen Quellen, in: Id., T. MIKELADZE (ed.), Local Ethno-Political Entities of the Black Sea Area 7th–5th Cent. BC, 1988, 150–174. A.P.-L.

Cytenium (Κυτίνιον, Κύτινον, Κυτένιον; *Kytínion*, *Kýtinon*, *Kyténion*). Along with Boium, Erineus and Acyphas/Pindus one of the cities of central Greek Doris supposedly founded by → Dorus (Scyl. 62; Scymn. 592ff.; Diod. Sic. 4,67,1; Str. 9,4,10; 10,4,6; Conon, FGrH 26 F 1,27; Plin. HN 4,28; Ptol. 3,14,14; Aristid. 12,40; Steph. Byz. s.v. Κύτινα; schol. Pind. Pyth. 1,121; 126). Aeschin. Leg. 116 with schol. emphasizes the special status of C. among the Dorian cities; for Hsch. s.v. Λιμοδωριεῖς ('hungry Dorians') see → Doris [II 1].

C. is to be located on the southern slopes of the Kallidromon, near the modern Paliochori (traces of ancient settlement, inscriptions) on the junction of the most important ancient routes of central Greece. On account of its strategically favourable position C. was subject to repeated attacks: 458/7 BC a Phocian raid (Thuc. 1,107,2 with schol.; Diod. Sic. 11,79,4f.); 426 Athenian plans to attack (Thuc. 1,95,1; 102,1); 338 invasion of Philip II (Philochorus FGrH 328 F 56a; b); in 228 Antigonus Doson destroyed the city after it had been weakened by earthquakes; in 206/5 C. asked Lycian Xanthus for help in rebuilding (SEG 38, 1476).

E. W. KASE et al. (ed.), The Great Isthmus Corridor Route, 1991; D. ROUSSET, Les Doriens de la Métropole, in: BCH 113, 1989, 199–239; 114, 1990, 445–472; 118, 1994, 361–374; F. W. WALBANK, Antigonus Doson's Attack on Cytinium, in: ZPE 76, 1989, 184–192. P.F.

Cythera (Κύθηρα; *Kýthēra*, Lat. *Cythera*, the modern Kithira).
A. GEOGRAPHY OF THE ISLAND B. ECONOMY AND COMMERCE C. LOCATION OF THE CITY D. HISTORY

A. GEOGRAPHY OF THE ISLAND

Off the south-eastern tip of the Peloponnese, 30 km long and 18 km wide, C. covers an area of around 262 km², and is surrounded by several small, uninhabited islands. The coast consists mostly of steep cliffs, indented with small bays from which narrow, steep valleys lead into the interior. In antiquity, C. was regarded as favourable for seafarers (εὐλίμενος, 'with good harbours', cf. Str. 8,5,1). C. consists of limestone and slate; its interior comprises a high plateau at 300 to 380 m above sea-level, descending in the south to about 200 m and in the south-west rising to the summit of Mirmingari at 510 m. Remains of settlements are Early Helladic and particularly also Late Helladic [1. 11; 2; 3. 148ff.].

B. ECONOMY AND COMMERCE

The particular significance of the island lay in commerce, which evidently extended into the eastern Mediterranean and the Near East (various finds from the 3rd and 2nd millennium BC respectively). In an Egyptian itinerary (from the time of Amenophis III, 1402–1363 BC) the island is called *Kutira*. Bronze Age finds are concentrated in the region from Kastri in the south to the bay of Avlemona. Most frequently mentioned products of the island are: figs, cheese, wine and honey (Heraclid. FHG 2 fr. 24). Fishery for purple sea urchins was important (cf. description of the island as πορφύρουσα, Dionys. Per. 498; Steph. Byz. s.v. Kythera). This may also have brought Phoenicians to C.; a harbour location *Phoinikoûs* is attested for 303 BC (Xen. Hell. 4,8,7). The cult of Aphrodite Urania (→ Aphrodite B.2) may also be of Phoenician origin (Hdt. 1,105; Paus. 1,14,7; 3,23,1; Aphrodite Kythereia, Hes. Theog. 198).

C. LOCATION OF THE CITY

Phoenicus was possibly located in the bay of modern Avlemona. The ancient city of C. with its harbour Scandea was also here (Hom. Il. 10,268; Paus. 1,27,5; Thuc. 4,53,1); it was inhabited into the 6th/7th cents. AD. On steep chalk cliffs above Scandia was the acropolis, modern Paleokastro, with a sanctuary of Aphrodite. Parts of a former temple have been used in the chapels there. The northern cape was called Platanistus (Paus. 2,34,6).

D. HISTORY

Mentioned repeatedly in Homer (Il. 15,432; Od. 9,81), in historical times C. probably belonged to Argos into the 6th cent. BC (Hdt. 1,82), then to Sparta (Thuc. 4,53,2). C. was Perioeci territory and was administered by a *kythērodíkēs* (κυθηροδίκης, 'judge on C.', Thuc. 4,53,3). The value of C. to Sparta is emphasized in Hdt. 7,235 and Thuc. 4,53,3. in consequence, C. was frequently occupied by Athens (456, 426–410 and 393–387/6 BC: Paus. 1,27,5; Thuc. 4,53,1ff.; 57,4; 5,14,3; 18,7; 7,26,2; 57,6; Xen. Hell. 4,8,7; Isoc. Or. 4,119), where the favourable situation of the island for trade with Libya and Egypt had been recognized. After 195 BC, C. appears to have become independent of Sparta. It at any rate minted its own coins at this time. In the Augustan period C. again belonged to Sparta, being in the possession of C. Iulius Eurycles from Sparta, who as a participant in the battle of → Actium had been awarded Roman citizenship (Cass. Dio 54,7,2). Inscriptions: IG V 1,935–947; SEG XI 895–897; coins: HN 436 (3rd/2nd cent. BC); JNG 8, 1957, 81 no. 100; 102f.

In the 4th cent. AD Christianity was brought to C. from the Peloponnese.

1 D. FIMMEN, Die kret.-myk. Kultur, 1924, 11
2 V. STAIS, Ἀνασκαφαὶ ἐν Κυθήροις, in: AD 1, 1915, 191ff.
3 H. WATERHOUSE, R. HOPE SIMPSON, Prehistoric Laconia 3, in: ABSA 56, 1961, 114–175
4 G. DOUX, Chronique des fouilles 1964, s.v. Cythère, in: BCH 89, 1965, 879–881.

L. BÜRCHNER, O. MAULL, s.v. Kythera, RE 12, 207–215; W. HELCK, Die Beziehungen Ägyptens und Vorderasiens zur Ägäis bis ins 7. Jh.v.Chr., 1979, 15, 31, 130, 160, 162; G. L. HUXLEY, J. N. COLDSTREAM, Kythera, 1973; G. E. INCE et al., Paliochora, in: ABSA 82, 1987, 95–106; G. E. INCE, TH. KUKULIS, Paliochora, Kythera, in: ABSA 84, 1989, 407–416; H. KALETSCH, S. GRUNAUER V. HOERSCHELMANN, s.v. Kythera, in: LAUFFER, Griechenland, 362f.; H. LEONHARD, Die Insel Kythera, in: Petermanns Mitteilungen, supplement 128, 1899 with map; PHILIPPSON/KIRSTEN 3, 509ff.; J. A. SAKELLARAKIS, Minoan Religious Influence in the Aegean, in: ABSA 91, 1996, 81–99; R. WEIL, Kythera, in: MDAI(A) 5, 1880, 224ff., 293f. H.KAL. and E.MEY.

Cytheris Descriptive artist's name ('belonging to Aphrodite') of a Roman mime actress (*mima*) of the 1st cent. BC; bought out of slavery by Volumnius Eutrapelus, her official name was Volumnia (Cic. Phil. 2,58). Nothing is known about her stage performances, but all the more about her erotic qualities. She attained notoriety as mistress of Antonius [I 9]: before his marriage to Fulvia in 47 she accompanied him on his public appearances in an open litter (Cic. Att. 10,10,5; Plut. Antonius 9,7). Cicero avoids mentioning her name in his chronicle of scandals associated with Antony (Cic. Phil. 2). The poet Cornelius [II 18] Gallus too appears to have fallen for her charms; according to Serv. Ecl. 10,1 his love elegies to Lycoris were in fact addressed to C. [1].

1 R.D. ANDERSON, P.J. PARSONS, R.G.M. NISBET, Elegiacs by Gallus from Qaṣr Ibrîm, in: JRS 69, 1979, 148–155.

H. GUNDEL, s.v. Volumnius (17), RE 9, 883; W. KROLL, s.v. Kytheris, RE 12, 218–219; H. LEPPIN, Histrionen, 1992, 228f. H.-D.B.

Cytherus (Κύθηρος; *Kýthēros*). Attic *paralia*(?) deme of the Pandionis phyle, from 307/6 to 201 BC of the Antigonis; supplied two *bouleutaí*. According to Str. 9,1,20, one of the locations belonging to the Attic dodecapolis. Its localisation near Poussi Kalojerou by TRAILL [3] is methodologically unsustainable; Dem. Or. 42 suggests a site near a city, in a wooded area. In IG II² 2496 three houses belonging to the deme of C. in Piraeus are leased by otherwise unattested *Meritai* [4. 383 no. 72]. A cult association between Trikomoi, Erchia and C. can scarcely be deduced from IG II² 1213 (differently [1; 4. 185⁴⁶]). In Or. 42, Demosthenes negotiates an antidosis trial concerning a large estate in C. [2].
→ Phaenippus of Cytherus

1 P.J. BICKNELL, Clisthène et Kytherros, in: REG 89, 1976, 599–603 2 G.E.M. DE STE. CROIX, The Estate of Phainippos (Ps.-Dem., XLII), in: Ancient Society and Institutions. Studies Presented to V. Ehrenberg, 1966, 109–114 3 J.S. TRAILL, Demos and Trittys, 1986, 47ff., 130 4 WHITEHEAD, Index s.v. Kytheros

TRAILL, Attica, 8, 17, 43, 68, 111 no. 81, tables 3, 11. H.LO.

Cythnus (Κύθνος; *Kýthnos*, Lat. *Cythnus*, the modern Thermia). Island in the western → Cyclades (86 km²): 21 km long, 11 km wide; a monotonous, undulating plain (height 200 to 350 m.), predominantly slate. Its rugged coastline offers no good harbours. Two hot springs, already active in Roman times, are situated near Lutra on the north coast. C. is little fertile, short of water and virtually without trees. In antiquity C. was known for its fine cheese (Poll. 6,63; Eust. in Dionys. Per. 525; Plin. HN 13,134; Steph. Byz. s.v. Kythnos).

Finds in a Mesolithic-Neolithic cemetery suggest that C. played an intermediary role in the obsidian trade with Melos. A hoard of metal tools found there stems from the 3rd millennium BC. The ancient capital C. was on the west coast between two bays, the modern Briokastro. There survive remnants of city walls, foundations of temples, houses and conduits. The extent of the ancient city suggests a population of around 10,000.

C. participated in the Persian War, and is thus mentioned on votive offerings (Hdt. 8,46,4; Paus. 5,23,2; Syll.³ 31,31). C. was also a member of the → Delian League [1]; its relatively high contribution can probably be put down to ore-mining activities, which appear, however, to have been productive for only a short period. Demosthenes (Or. 13,34) gives C. as an example of a shabby city besieged by Attalus I (Liv. 31,45,9) in 199 BC; revolt of a false Nero in AD 69 (Tac. Hist. 2,8f.; Scyl. 58; Str. 10,5,3; Ptol. 3,14,24; Stadiasmus maris magni 273; 284; Ov. Met. 7,464).

1 ATL 1, 322f.; 3, 197f.

K. BRANIGAN, Early Aegean Hoards of Metalwork, in: ABSA 64, 1969, 1–12; L. BÜRCHNER, s.v. Kythnos (1), RE 12, 219ff.; N.H. GALE, Z.A. STOS-GALE, Cycladic Lead and Silver Metallurgy, in: ABSA 76, 1981, 169–224; G. GEROLA, Fermenia (Kythnos-Thermja), in: ASAA 6/7, 1923/4, 43ff.; A. GUNARIS, Ἡ Κύθνος, 1938; H. KALETSCH, s.v. Kythnos, in: LAUFFER, Griechenland 363–365; PHILIPPSON/KIRSTEN 4, 71ff. H.KAL.

Cytissorus (Κυτί(σ)σωρος; *Kytí(s)sōros*). C.'s parents are → Phrixus and Chalciope [2], a daughter of → Aeetes; grandson of → Athamas, king of the Minyae (Apoll. Rhod. 2,1148ff.; schol. Apoll. Rhod. 2,388; Apollod. 1,83), whom he rescues from being sacrificed when he returns from Aeetes to his homeland, Thessalian Achaea. Athamas was to have been sacrificed to → Zeus Laphystios as an act of atonement. C. having rescued his grandfather, the curse remains on his descendants (Hdt. 7,197). In Sophocles (schol. Aristoph. Nub. 257) it is Heracles who rescues Athamas. AL.FR.

Cytorus (Κύτωρος; *Kýtōros*). Port (*empórion*) in a sheltered bay east of → Amastris [4] on the Black Sea coast of Paphlagonia; the modern Gideruz. The bay with its heavily wooded (boxwood) cliffs is overlooked by the mountain of the same name. A foundation of → Sinope, C. was taken into the *synoikismós* of Amastris in 300 BC.

CH. MAREK, Stadt, Ära und Territorium in Pontus-Bithynia und Nord-Galatia, 1993, 17f.; L. ROBERT, À travers l'Asie Mineure, 1980, 147–150. C.MA.

Cyttarinii (Κυτταρῖνοι; *Kytattarĩnoi*). Community in the interior of Sicily; not located. Along with the Petrini and the Scherini the *koinón* of the C. paid a tax in wheat and barley to the *synoikismós* of → Entella [1. 264f. no. 208: 5th decree, l. 20]. In 254 BC the C. joined the Roman side in the 1st Punic War (Ἠνατταρῖνοι, Diod. Sic. 23,18,5). Ruined by Verres (*Cetarini*, Cic. Verr. 2,3,103). Cf. [2].

1 L. DUBOIS, Inscriptions grecques dialectales de Sicile, 1989 2 G. BEJOR, Città di Sicilia nei decreti di Entella, in: ASNP 12,3, 1982, 831–833. GI.MA.

Cyzicus (Κύζικος; *Kýzikos*). City in Mysia on the south coast of the → Propontis on the isthmus of the Arktonnesos (Kapıdağ) peninsula; the modern Balkız, to the east of Erdek. C. owed its prosperity to its double harbour and large territory (cf. the description with the city's location at Str. 12,8,11). From the beginning of coinage down to Philip II and Alexander the Great, the elektron coins of C. played an important role in international commerce (→ Cyzicene). Its eponymous founder C. was supposedly killed by the Argonauts (Apoll. Rhod. 1,949ff.). Founded towards the middle of the 7th cent. from Miletus (→ Colonisation), C. also had institutions adopted from there (calendar, phyles); influenced by Athens, C. later had a *hípparchos* as eponymous official. Ruled by tyrants under Persian sovereignty, C. then became a member of the → Delian League (Thuc. 8,107) and the 2nd → Athenian League. Repeatedly besieged and fought over, C. often succeeded in asserting its independence against the Persian empire. C. was incorporated into the Seleucid empire, and then befriended by the Attalids (Apollonis, wife of Attalus [4] I, came from C., Pol. 22,20,1).

Declared a free city in 188 BC by Manlius Vulso in the treaty of Apamea, in 154 BC C. gave naval support to Attalus [5] II in his war against Prusias II (Pol. 33,13,1), and opposed Aristonicus (IGR IV 134). Although blackmailed by Fimbria (Diod. Sic. 38,8,3), C. remained the ally of Lucullus and in 73 BC withstood the great siege of → Mithridates VI (Plut. Lucullus 9f.). In 67 BC the city was allied with Pompey against Mithridates, then with Caesar (IGR IV 135) and finally with Brutus (Plut. Brutus 28) against Sex. Pompeius (App. B Civ. 5,137). After C. had temporarily lost its freedom under Augustus (Cass. Dio 54,7; 23), Tiberius finally incorporated the city into the province of → Asia [2] (Tac. Ann. 4,36; Cass. Dio 57,24,6). In the aftermath of an earthquake, the emperor Hadrian helped C. build the great Temple of Zeus (Aristid. 27), held to be one of the Seven → Wonders of the World (Cyriacus of Ancona was still able to draw 33 pillars of this temple in 1433, but in the 18th cent. the temple was used as a quarry for buildings in Istanbul). Further earthquakes occurred under Antoninus Pius and Justinian. Under Diocletian, C. was the capital of the province of Hellespontus (Hierocles, Synekdemos 661,15; Not. Episc. *passim*). C. had a mint and a linen factory (Sozom. Hist. eccl. 5,15). Excavations have yet to be undertaken.

F. W. HASLUCK, Cyzicus, 1910; N. EHRHARDT, Milet und seine Kolonien, 1983; E. AKURGAL, s.v. Kyzikos, PE, 473f.

T.D.-B.

Cyzistra (Κύζιστρα; *Kýzistra*). Town and Byzantine fortress in the Cappadocian *strategia* of Cilicia (Ptol. 5,6,15), the modern Zengibar Kalesı, 56 km south-south-west of → Caesarea.

HILD/RESTLE, 219f.

K.ST.

D

D is used in Lat. as an abbreviation of the Roman praenomen → Decimus. As a numeral the letter D stands for the value 500. Like the numeral → C (= 100) it is derived from a letter of the western Greek alphabet not used in the Latin alphabet: Φ (phi), which stands for the value 1,000; the letter form D, indicating half the value of 1,000, was derived by bisection of the Greek symbol (right half).

W.ED.

D (linguistics) The fourth letter of the Greek and Latin → alphabet denoted a voiced plosive (as in New High German *Ding*, Modern English *dove*); its partial development into a fricative (Mod. Greek δέκα with ð as in Engl. *there*) did not take place until fairly late. The similarity in → pronunciation between Greek and Latin is shown by → loan-words: *diadēma*, κουστωδία (*koustōdía*).

In Greek and Latin inherited words, *d* frequently represents Proto-Indo-European *d*: δέκα; *déka*, *decem* < **dekm̥*; ἰδ-εῖν; *ideîn*, *uid-ēre* < **u̯id-*; δεξιτερός; *dexiterós*, *dexter* etc. On the other hand, e.g. Lat. *medius* and *uidua* go back to **medhi̯o-* or **u̯idheu̯ā* with *dh*; in Greek, *d* may also have derived from the labio-velar g^{w}: δελφ-ύς < **g^{w}elbh-*; see → Gutturals.

Geminate *dd* is relatively rare: Lat. *ad-dīcere*; Dor. Boeot. δικαδδω = Att. δικάζω [1; 2]; Homer. ἔδδεισα < **e-du̯ei̯sa* (a special case) and καδ-δῦσαι = Attic κατα-δῦσαι. For κάδδιξ (→ *kadískoi*) and the corresponding derivation καταδίχιον see [3].

In Lat. final *-d* disappeared, but only after long vowels: *mēd* > *mē*, but *aliŭd*.

→ Italy, alphabetical scripts

1 SCHWYZER, Gramm., 331 2 C. BRIXHE, Rev.: R. Arena, Note linguistiche a proposito delle tavole di Eraclea (1971), in: Kratylos 20, 1975, 60 3 J. WACKERNAGEL, KS II, 1955, 1042.

B.F.

Dachinabades Region of India to the south of → Barygaza, with the cities of Paithana and Tagara. Mentioned only in Peripl. m.r. 50f., where δάχανος has also been correctly explained as the Indian word for south, Old Indian dakṣiṇa. Probably following Middle Indian Dakkhiṇābadha (Old Indian dakṣiṇāpathad) as a term for the Indian peninsula.

K.K.

Daci, Dacia (Roman province of *Dacia*).

A. ORIGINS B. UP TO THE ESTABLISHMENT OF THE ROMAN PROVINCE C. THE ROMAN PROVINCE D. CULTURE AND ECONOMY IN THE ROMAN PERIOD E. DACIA IN LATE ANTIQUITY

A. ORIGINS

The Dacian group of tribes originally settled an extensive territory north of the lower Danube; in the west it reached to the Pathisus (Theiss), in the east possibly to the Hierasus (Sireth) or the Pyretus (Pruth); it was bordered to the north by the crescent of the Carpathians. The D. were a Thracian people. The location of their settlements enabled them to enter into various kinds of relations with neighbouring peoples, e.g. the Scythians and Gepidae, with whom they are often confused in ancient sources, and from the end of the 3rd cent BC *i.a.* with the (Germanic?) Bastarnae. The D. were stockbreeders and farmers, but to some extent also mined the ores that occurred in Transylvania. From the end of the 3rd cent. BC they became subject to Greek influence. At the same time, contacts developed with Italian merchants and Celtic tribes.

B. UP TO THE ESTABLISHMENT OF THE ROMAN PROVINCE

In the 1st cent. BC the D. were united under the leadership of king Burebista. The kingdom represented a considerable power, and directed attacks against Greek colonies on the Pontus coast and in the west against the Celtic Boii, who were then settling in *Pannonia superior* (Str. 5,1,6; 7,3,11). Caesar wanted to meet the threat posed from D. (Suet. Caes. 44,3), but his death intervened before he could act on his intentions. At about the same time Burebista too was murdered; his kingdom, which did not have a solid basis, collapsed. A new Dacian confederacy did not arise again until the 2nd half of the 1st cent. AD under king Decebalus. Armed confrontations occurred under Domitian, in the course of which the D. attacked Moesia in AD 85/86. After initial successes they were defeated at Tapae, with Decebalus having to recognize Roman rule. Existing tensions were however not removed by the peace settlement, and fighting broke out again under Trajan. In 101/2 the Romans defeated Decebalus and conquered the major part of his kingdom (Banat and Oltenia). But Decebalus did not give up, and war broke out again in 105 and 106, leading to his defeat and suicide (Cass. Dio 67,6f.; 68,6–14). This Roman victory brought the region of what then became the *provincia Dacia* (Romanian Transylvania, Oltenia and Banat) under Roman control. Excellent sources for the battles fought under Trajan in D. and the nature of the Roman victory are Trajan's Column in Rome and the Tropaeum Traiani in Adamklissi. A part of the Dacian tribes ('free Dacians') continued to live outside the Roman provincial system.

C. THE ROMAN PROVINCE

The Roman power establishing itself in D. had to overcome the resistance of neighbouring peoples (incursions of the Jazyges and Roxolani). In 118/9 this led to the appointment of a close friend of the emperor Hadrian, Q. Marcius Turbo, as head of the administration in Pannonia and D. (cf. CIL III 1462 or ILS 1324). During this period the province was divided into *D. inferior* (Oltenia with the eastern part of Banat) and *D. superior* (probably Transylvania and the region northwest of the Aluta). Probably in 124 *D. superior*, also known as *D. Apulensis*, was further divided, its northern section being separated from it under the name of *D. Porolissensis*. From 168 *D. inferior* was also called *D. Maluensis* (after Romula Malua, its capital). The autonomy of *Maluensis* and *Porolissensis* was restricted, however, as its administrators (*procuratores vice praesidis*) were subordinate to the imperial *legatus pro praetore*, who administrated *D. superior*. The wars against the Marcomanni also threatened D.; it probably was in this connection that the administration of the country was entrusted to a *consularis III Daciarum* in 168.

D. CULTURE AND ECONOMY IN THE ROMAN PERIOD

Under Roman rule rapid and varied development is to be noted in D.: the rise of urban life, development of a relatively dense road network, intensification of internal and external commerce; this last entailing the establishment of several customs posts. Gold mines played a significant role in economic life (*Alburnus maior* along with *vicus Pirustarum*, *Ampelum*). Silver, lead and iron were also mined. There were salt mines in the vicinity of Cluj (Ocna Mures). Commercial activities were restricted to local wood-, iron- and stone-working and the manufacture of ceramics. Romanization proceeded rapidly and to lasting effect. The existence *i.a.* of a common provincial parliament and cult in D. is attested from the time of Marcus Aurelius onwards. Sizeable cities were the primary foci of Romanization; of these Sarmizegethusa should be singled out as the main centre of Roman influence. The garrison in D. originally consisted of the *legio XIII Gemina*, stationed in Apulum; this was reinforced in 166/7 by the *legio V Macedonica* in Potaessa. The Roman military presence was particularly directed towards the external dangers threatening D. Accordingly, already under Hadrian a network of strongpoints was built in the east along the Aluta (*limes Alutanus*), and in the time of Severus was strengthened by a system of forward posts still further to the east (*limes Transalutanus*). Although strong auxiliary forces were stationed alongside the legions in D., the task of defence became ever more difficult, particularly against the tribes encroaching from the north-east.

TIR L 34 Budapest, 1968 (bibl.); TIR L 35 Bucarest, 1969 (bibl.); TIR K 34 Sofia, 1976 (bibl.); A. STEIN, Die Reichsbeamten von Dazien, 1944; C. DAICOVICIU, D. PROTASE, in: JRS 51, 1961, 63ff.; Id., Siebenbürgen im Altertum, 1943; Id., Dakia, 1969; D. TUDOR, Oltenia romana, 1959; A. KERÉNYI, Die PN von Dazien, 1944; V. CHRISTESCU, Istoria militară a Daciei romane, 1937; I. ROSSI, Trajan's column and the Dacian wars, 1971; A. ALFÖLDY, Stud. zur Gesch. der Weltkrise des 3. Jh. n. Chr., 1967; V. I. VELKOV, Die thrak. und dak. Stadt in der Spätant. (Bulgarian with Germ. summary), 1959; Dacia. Revue d'archéologie et d'histoire ancienne, Inst. d'Arch. V. Pîrvab de l'Acad. Roumaine (various articles). J.BU.

MAPS: TIR L 35, 1969; N. GUDEA, Der Limes Dakiens und die Verteidigung der obermoesischen Donaulinie von

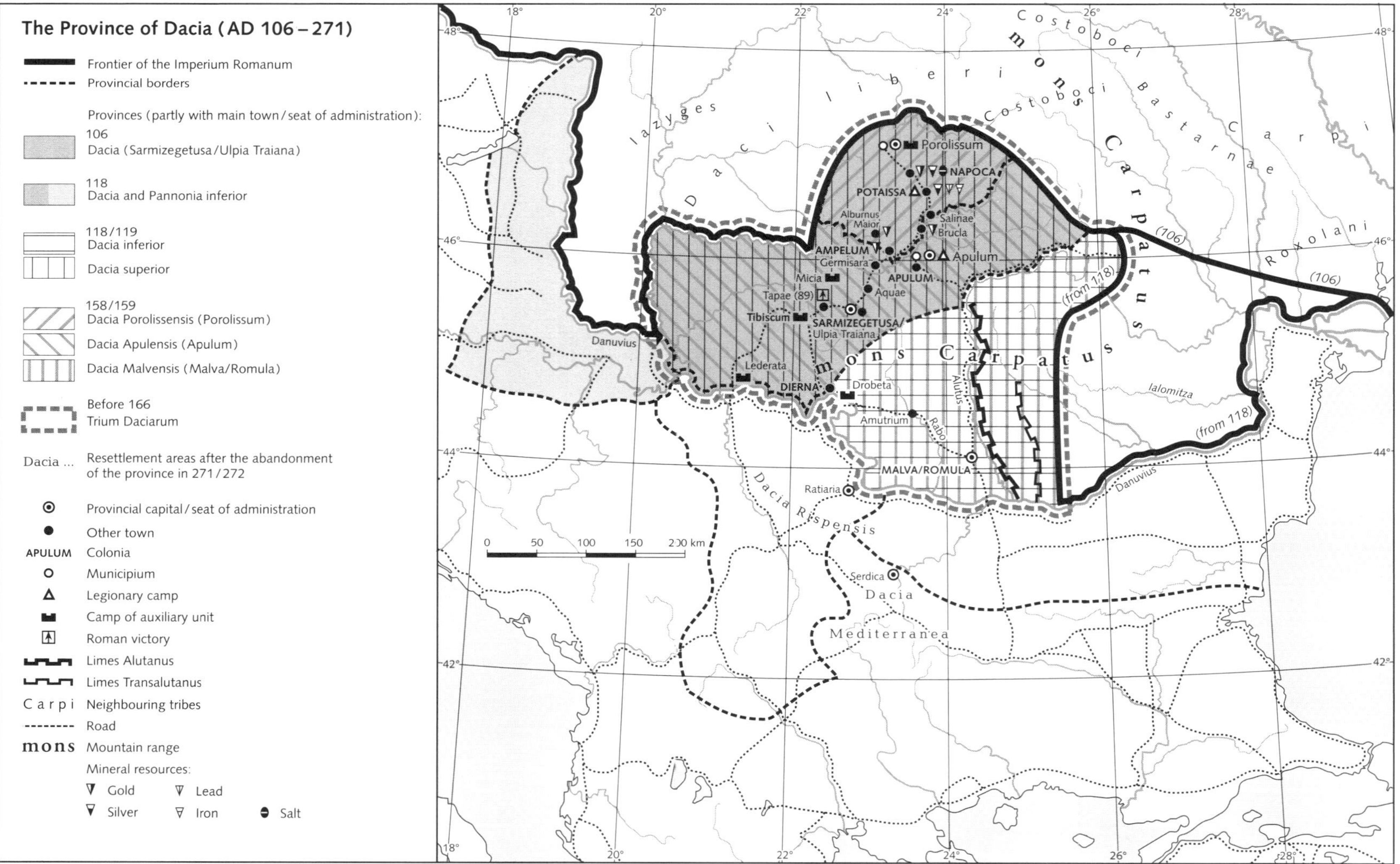

The Province of Dacia (AD 106 – 271)
Frontier of the Imperium Romanum
Provincial borders
Provinces (partly with main town / seat of administration):
106
Dacia (Sarmizegetusa / Ulpia Traiana)
118
Dacia and Pannonia inferior
118/119
Dacia inferior
Dacia superior
158/159
Dacia Porolissensis (Porolissum)
Dacia Apulensis (Apulum)
Dacia Malvensis (Malva/Romula)
Before 166
Trium Daciarum
Dacia ...
Resettlement areas after the abandonment of the province in 271/272
Provincial capital / seat of administration
Other town
APULUM
Colonia
Municipium
Legionary camp
Camp of auxiliary unit
Roman victory
Limes Alutanus
Limes Transalutanus
Carpi
Neighbouring tribes
Road
mons
Mountain range
Mineral resources:
Gold
Lead
Silver
Iron
Salt
Costoboci
mons
Daci liberi
Iazyges
Bastarnae
Carpi
Roxolani
Carpatus
(106)
Porolissum
NAPOCA
POTAISSA
Alburnus Maior
Salinae
Brucla
AMPELUM
Apulum
Germisara
APULUM
Micia
Tapae (89)
Aquae
Tibiscum
SARMIZEGETUSA/ Ulpia Traiana
Danuvius
mons Carpatus
(from 118)
Lederata
DIERNA
Drobeta
Alutus
Ialomitza
Amutrium
Rabo
MALVA/ROMULA
Ratiaria
Dacia Ripensis
Serdica
Dacia Mediterranea
0 50 100 150 200 km

Trajan bis Aurelian, ANRW II 6, 1977, 849–887; D. PROTASE, Der Forschungsstand zur Kontinuität der bodenständigen Bevölkerung im röm. Dazien (2.–3. Jh.), in: ANRW II 6, 1977, 990–1015; E. CHRYSOS, Von der Räumung der Dacia Traiana zur Entstehung der Gothia, BJ 192, 1992, 175–194; D. KNOPP, Die röm. Inschr. Dakiens, 1993 (diss.).

E. DACIA IN LATE ANTIQUITY

In the course of his efforts to re-establish imperial unity by overthrowing the Gaulish and Palmyran usurpations, Aurelian found himself obliged to stabilise the situation on the lower Danube by relinquishing the exposed province of D. in AD 271. Some accounts speak only of the withdrawal of the army and transfer of the name *Dacia* to territories south of the Danube (Jord. De summa temporum ... Romanorum 217: *Aurelianus imperator euocatis exinde legionibus in Mysia conlocauit ibique aliquam partem Daciam mediterraneam Daciamque ripensem constituit*), but most ancient authors speak of a complete evacuation of the Roman population and its resettlement on the south bank of the Danube (Eutr. 9,15,1: *prouinciam Daciam, quam Traianus ultra Danubium fecerat, intermisit uastato omni Illyrico et Moesia desperans eam posse retineri abductosque Romanos ex urbibus et agris Daciae in media Moesia collocauit*). It is quite possible that certain remnants of a Latin-speaking population remained north of the Danube, but a continuation of organised Roman life (with educational, cult and municipal structures) is scarcely conceivable; all of that migrated to the south bank of the Danube. In most cases, when D. is spoken of in late antiquity what is meant is the provinces of *Dacia ripensis* and *Dacia mediterranea,* thus named for propaganda purposes (e.g. Paul. Nol. carm. 17); occasional military expeditions to areas north of the Danube (e.g. in 332) do not alter the fact that the region remained abandoned to the West Goths and later the → Gepidae and → Slavs, while it was only in the course of the 6th cent. that the Danube had to be given up as the northern frontier of the Eastern Roman Empire. The majority of the Latin-speaking ancestors of the later Romanians came from south of the Danube into the Carpathian region not earlier than the early Middle Ages, in connection with the population movements caused by the Slav settlements.

DIGEST OF SOURCES: Fontes historiae Dacoromanae 1–2, 1970 (original with Roman. translation and comm.). BIBLIOGRAPHY: Römer in Rumänien, 1969; DACOROMANIA 1, 1973; G. SCHRAMM, Frühe Schicksale der Rumänen, in: Zschr. für Balkanologie 21, 1985, 223–241; 22, 1986, 104–125; 23, 1987, 78–94. J.KR.

Dacian see → Balkans, languages

Dacicus The victor's name D. was not assumed by Domitian, contrary to the report at Mart. 8 pr. Trajan was officially called D. only after 102; in 236 Maximinus assumed the name D. Maximus for himself and his son Maximus. In the case of later emperors the title was probably unofficial: Decius (D. maximus from 250, but only on Spanish milestones), Gallienus (D. max. only in ILS 552, from 257), Aurelian [3] (ILS 581, from 275). Constantine [1] I named himself D. Maximus in 336 (AE 1934, 158), probably on the basis of his short-lived conquests north of the Danube (Julianus, De Caesaribus 329C, cf. Fest. Brev. 26). A.B.

Dadastana (Δαδάστανα; *Dadástana*, also *Dabastana*). Town in Galatia on the border with Bithynia, *c.* 20 km west of Nallıhan on the road from Nicaea to Ancyra [2. 31, 106f.]; belonged to Bithynia from the time of Augustus, from that of Diocletian to the *prov. Galatia I* (Amm. Marc. 25,10,12) [1. 160]. The emperor Jovian died here on 17 February, AD 364, on his way home from the Persian war. Here, a corps belonging to the usurper Procopius went over to Valens in 365 (Amm. Marc. 25,10,12; 26,8,5).

1 MITCHELL 2 2 D. FRENCH, The Pilgrim's Road, 1981.

BELKE 154f.; K. STROBEL, Galatien und seine Grenzregionen, in: Forsch. in Galatien. Asia Minor Stud. 12 (1994), 29–40. K.ST.

Dadouchos see → Mysteria

Daedala (Δαίδαλα; *Daídala*).

[1] Fortified settlement north-west of Telmessus in the border region between Lycia and Caria, the eastern part of the Rhodian Peraea [2. 54–57, 97f.]. References: Str. 14,2,2; 3,1; Liv. 37,22,3; Steph. Byz. s.v. D.; Plin. HN 5,103. D. is identified with the ruins of Inlice Asarı [1. 32f.]; for location cf. Ptol. 5,3; Stadiasmos maris magni 256f.; inscriptions are lacking (origin of TAM II 163 from D. uncertain). D. possessed two offshore islands (Plin. HN 5,131). To the east of D. a mountain of the same name (Str. 14,3,2; 4), probably the modern Kızıl Dağ.

1 G.E. BEAN, Lykien, 1980 2 P.M. FRASER, G.E. BEAN, The Rhodian Peraea and Islands, 1954. C.SCH.

[2] City on Crete, mentioned only in Steph. Byz. s.v. D.; not locatable.

P. FAURE, La Crète aux cent villes, in: Kretika Chronika 13, 1959, 195. H.SO.

[3] Regions named in the context of the campaigns of Alexander the Great, at Curt. 8,10,19 as *Daedala regio* and at Just. 12,7 as *montes Daedali;* both on the lower reaches of the → Choaspes (the modern Kunaṛ), not far from the river Κωφήν; *Kōphēn* (the modern Kabul). H.T. and B.B.

[4] Mentioned only at Ptol. 7,1,49 N., situated in the country of the Κασπειραῖοι (*Kaspeiraîoi*) in the region of the modern (New) Delhi, perhaps to be identified with the modern Dudhāl. H.T.

[5] see → Hera

Daedalidae (Δαιδαλίδαι; *Daidalídai*). Attic *asty* deme of the Cecropis phyle, from 307/6 to 201/0 BC of the Demetrias phyle, from AD 126/7 of the Hadrianis. One → *bouleutes*. With the Daedalion, mentioned only in the *poletai* inscription [1] and probably the sanctuary of the eponymous hero of D., it bordered to the south with the Alopece deme.

1 J. YOUNG, Greek Inscriptions, in: Hesperia 10, 1941, 14ff., esp. 20f. no. 1, l. 10f.

TRAILL, Attica 10f., 50, 70, 109 no. 30, table 7, 12, 15; J. S. TRAILL, Demos and Trittys, 1986, 14, 135. H.LO.

Daedalion (Δαιδαλίων; *Daidalíōn*). Son of Heosphoros (Lucifer); brother of Ceyx; father of → Chione [2]. In his grief for the death of his only daughter, who scorned the beauty of Diana and was killed by her, he throws himself from the peak of Parnassus. Apollo, however, transforms him into a hawk (Ov. Met. 11,291–345; Hyg. Fab. 200). In Paus. 8,4,6 D. is the father of → Autolycus [1].

F. BÖMER, Kommentar zu Ov. Met. B. X–XI, 1980, 313. R.B.

Daedalus (Δαίδαλος; *Daídalos*).

[1] Mythical craftsman, sculptor and inventor, his very name belonging to a semantic field indicating objects created by astuteness and skill. In stories he is associated with Athens, Crete and Sicily. Judging from the development of artistic techniques, it is not impossible that the origins of the tradition lie at least partly in Crete, although whether D.'s name can be attested in the Linear B texts is a matter of dispute [1]. The first literary reference to D. (Hom. Il. 18,592) associates him with Crete; all sources mentioning his descent, however, agree that he is Athenian by birth. The names of his parents vary, but most of them reflect D.'s intelligence and manual skill: Metion, Eupalamus, Palamaon; Iphinoe, Metadousa, Phrasimedes and — less clearly — Merope. All genealogies agree in tracing D.'s descent back to → Erechtheus. Nevertheless, few of D.'s achievements are set in Athens; the folding-chair dedicated by him in the Erechtheium (Paus. 1,27,1) can scarcely be compared with his reported feats in Crete and Sicily. In fact the only story dealing with his time in Athens rather puts D. in an unfavourable light. Having brought up → Talus, Calus or Perdix, his daughter's son, he kills the boy out of jealousy for his greater gift of invention. Having been found guilty of the homicide in one of the early trials before the Areopagus (Hellanicus FGrH 323a F 22), he flees to Crete or is banished there, and becomes friends with king → Minos. In Crete he constructs *i.a.* the artificial cow in which → Pasiphae satisfies her passion for the bull, and later on the → Labyrinth, where the → Minotaurus that is the issue of this union is held captive. D. is once again forced to flee when Minos learns of his role in this affair, and in the popular version of the story escapes with his son → Icarus on artificial wings (rationalizing alternative in Diod. Sic. 4,77). Icarus' fall and death by drowning are well known; in the theme of the fall from a great height and transformation into the form of a bird parallels have been seen to the story of → Talus. D., who is more successful at steering the proper course, is supposed to have landed in Sicily, where he finds refuge with king Cocalus in Camicus (Hdt. 7,170; Soph.: Camicoe). A multitude of technical devices all over Sicily are attributed to his inventive talent; these frequently have to do with water, but among them we also find the transformation of Camicus into an impregnable fortress. When Minos sails to Sicily and demands the surrender of D., he is killed by Cocalus or his daughters, who channel boiling water into his bath — a reflection of D.'s hydraulic inventions.

D. undoubtedly stood out amongst the *technîtai* (τεχνῖται) of Greek mythology; it is said of other 'inventors' that they were his pupils (cf. Paus. 1,26,4; 2,15,1). To his métier belonged technical as well as artistic achievements, the two categories being basically ascribed to the same order of things: it is accordingly no surprise that the origins of various tools and techniques were ascribed to him, and that it was also believed that he had created many of the most ancient wooden statues (ξόανα) in all of Greece (Paus. 9,40,3 lists those he regards as genuine). In sculpture too D. is supposed to have introduced innovations: Diodorus (4,76) says he was the first to produce statues with open eyes and in walking pose. In this role he is to be regarded as a Panhellenic figure; but by his intelligence and gifts he also fits the Athenian self-image, and, just as all the stories make him an Athenian, so it is in Attica that we find the only hero worship of D. (Alopece, near the → Daedalidae deme, cf. [2]).

1 M. GÉRARD-ROUSSEAU, Les mentions religieuses dans les tablettes mycéniennes, 1968, 51 2 M. CROSBY, Greek Inscriptions, in: Hesperia 10, 1941, no. 1 11–12 (367/6 BC).

G. BECATTI, La leggenda di Dedalo, in: MDAI(R) 60/1, 1953/4, 22–36; M. DELCOURT, Héphaistos ou la légende du magicien, 1957, 157–162; F. FRONTISI-DUCROUX, Dédale, 1975. E.K.

From the mythical figure of D. is created the legendary father of all sculptors, craftsmen and architects. His synthetic biography with its various stages in Crete, Athens and Sicily mirrors the locations where Greek large-scale sculpture had its origins (→ Sculpture). Later genealogies of artists from → Dipoenus and Scyllis to → Endius are not historical, any more than are later attributions of anonymous wooden sculptures from antiquity, but the ancient characterization of his works as the first *kouroi* coincides approximately with the earliest stage of artistic style. Thus in classical archaeology early archaic sculpture from the 7th cent. BC is classed as 'Daedalian'. D. is depicted in all the figurative artistic media: in popular art as a craftsman; in reliefs and painting in the process of making his artificial wings, and in the fatal flight. Some have thought to identify three-dimensional images of him in a statue from Amman and in the 'Mozia Youth'.

FUCHS/FLOREN, 120–121, 236–237; S.P. MORRIS, Daidalos and the Origins of Greek Art, 1992; J.E. NYENHUIS, LIMC 3, 313–321 s.v. Daidalos nos. 1–11; OVERBECK, nos. 67, 68, 70–142, 261, 332, 340, 345, 348, 349, 428 (sources). R.N.

[2] Bronze sculptor from Sicyon. As son and pupil of → Patrocles he is assigned to the later Polyclitus school. He created statues of Olympic victors in 396/5 and 388/7 BC. He participated in the Elean victory monument at Olympia (399 BC) and the Arcadian at Delphi (369 BC). Bases with traces of statues survive in Halicarnassus and Ephesus. Attributions on this basis remain as uncertain as the suggestion that the bronze statue of the scraper from Ephesus should be identified as belonging to his *pueri destringentes se* mentioned by Pliny.

D. ARNOLD, Die Polykletnachfolge, in: 25th suppl. JDAI, 1969, 168–183; LOEWY, no. 88, 89, 103; J. MARCADÉ, Recueil des signatures de sculpteurs grecs, 1, 1953, no. 22–24.; OVERBECK, no. 987–994 (sources); L. TODISCO, Scultura greca del IV secolo, 1993, 54–55. R.N.

Daemon see → Demons

Daesitiates One of the most important peoples in the interior of the *prov. Dalmatia* (→ Dalmatae, Dalmatia), originally possibly in the loose confederation of the → Autariatae. They inhabited the valley of the upper Bathinus (Bosna) of the valley from the upper Urbanus (Vrbas) in the west to Rogatica in the east; their position has been confirmed through the discovery of an inscription (ILJug 1582 [1]) of a *Valens Varron(is) f(ilius), princeps Desitiati(um)* in Breza (22 km north-west of Sarajevo). The D. were perhaps attacked by the future Augustus in 35 BC (see SCHWEIGHÄUSER'S emendation of App. Ill. 17 where the manuscripts have *Daísioí te kaì Paiónes*). Under Bato as their leader they are listed by Cass. Dio 55,29,2 as one of the leading rebellious peoples in the great Pannonian uprising. Under Roman rule they were also significant: Pliny (HN 3,143) notes that in the early Augustan period they made up 103 *decuriae* in the *conventus* of Narona. Strabo (7,5,3) regarded them as a Pannonian people, a theory which is however neither confirmed by archaeology nor by onomastic material. Of their settlements we know a spa complex of sulphur thermal springs, the *res publica Aquarum S(——)* near modern Ilidža close to Sarajevo, the *municipium* → *Bistua Nova* in Bugojno, a *col. Ris*... in Rogatica; there also is archaeological evidence of a settlement in Breza (possibly Hedum). During the early Principate, a Roman road was built from Salona to Hedum, the *castellum* of the D. (CIL III 3201 = 10159). It is possible that its *praefectus* is named on a fragmentary inscription from *Bovianum Undecimanorum* in Samnium: a Marcellus, *centurio* of the *legio XI* (CIL IX 2564: [...*pr]aef. civitatis Maeze[ior(um) et civitat(um) Daesit]iatium*). At the end of the 1st cent. AD the soldiers who have left the army can still be identified by their ethnonyms (*Temans Platoris, Daesitias*, CIL III 9739; *Nerva Laidi f. Desidias*, CIL XVI 11, 18) while Roman citizens are documented no earlier than under Trajan, most of these being Aurelii.

1 A. ŠAŠEL, J. ŠAŠEL (ed.), Inscriptiones Latinae Jugoslaviae, 1986.

I. BOJANOVSKI, Bosna i Hercegovina u antičko doba (Bosnia and Herzegovina in antiquity), Akademija nauka i umjetnosti Bosne i Herzegovine, Djela 66, Centar za balkanološka ispitvanja 6 (Monographies, Acad. des sciences et des arts de Bosnie-Herzegovine 66, Centre d'études balk. 6), 1988, 144–154. M.Š.K.

Dagalaifus Was appointed *comes domesticorum* by Julian in AD 361 (Amm. Marc. 21,8,1) and *magister equitum* by Jovian; in 364 he was influential in the elections of Jovian and Valentinian I (Amm. Marc. 25,5,2; Philostorgius 8,8). In 364–366 as *magister peditum(equitum?)* he fought against the Alemanni (Amm. Marc. 26,5,9), in 366 he was *consul*. PLRE 1, 239. W.P.

Dagan (Akkadian *Dagān*, Hebrew *dāgōn*, Greek *Dagṓn* [1]). The etymology of the word is unknown. Descriptions equating him with the Hurrite god Kumarbi, who is called *halki* 'grain', however also suggest an agrarian nature [2]; this is taken up again in Philo of Byblus who lists D. as the third of the four sons of Uranus and describes him as 'Dagan who is wheat' (Euseb. Praep. evang. 1,10,36b [3]). Attested in western Semitic mythology as the son of → El and father of → Baal, D. is one of the central deities of the western Semitic pantheon. D. is first mentioned in texts from → Mari and → Ebla (24th cent. BC) [4] and during the time of Akkad appears in the Babylonian onomastikon. The kings Sargon and Narām-Sîn of Akkad trace their conquest of north-western Mesopotamia back to him. In the Ur III period, cult and onomastikon indicate worship of D. primarily amongst the middle and upper classes [5]. In the old Babylonian period, D. is one of the most important gods of the Amorite dynasty, as was also the case in the kingdom of Mari with centres of cult worship in Terqa and Tuttul, and in the dynasty of Isin in Assyria and Babylonia [3]. There D. is also mentioned in connection to Šala, otherwise attested as the wife of the weather god. One of the two main temples in → Ugarit was for D. In the town of → Assur 'the house of Dagan' in the 1st millennium BC was a type of slaughterhouse [6]. Among the Philistines D. was probably worshipped as a god of war and as the main god of their pantheon around 1100 BC (Judg. 16,23ff.; 1 Sam. 5; 31,10; 1 Chr. 10,10). There is evidence of a temple to D. in Ašdod as late as the time of the Maccabee Jonathan, who burnt this temple down (1 Macc. 10,83ff.; 11,4) [7].

1 W. Röllig, Syrien, WbMyth 1, 1965, 276f. 2 P. Mander, J.-M. Durand, Mitología y Religión del Oriente Antiguo II/1, 1995, 149 3 N. Wyatt, The Relationship of the Deities Dagan and Hadad, Ugarit Forsch. 12, 1980, 377 4 G. Pettinato, H. Waetzold, Dagan, in: Orientalia 54, 1985, 234–256 5 M. Hilgert, *erubbatum* im Tempel des Dagan, in: JCS 46, 1994, 29–39 6 K. Deller, Köche und Küche des Aššur-Tempels, in: BaM 16, 1985, 362ff. 7 J.F. Healey, Dagon, in: K. van der Toorn et al. (ed.), Dictionary of Deities and Demons, 1995. B.P.-L.

Dagisthaeus (Δαγισθαῖος; *Dagisthaîos*). As a young Roman commander D., who probably was of Gothic origin, unsuccessfully besieged Persian-occupied Petra in the area of the Lazi in AD 548/9 (Procop. Pers. 2,29 especially 33–43). On account of this he was later taken to court under Justinian on the charge of pro-Persian sentiments and arrested by the emperor (Procop. Goth. 4,9,1–4). For the Narses campaign to Italy he was released from custody and took part in the decisive battle against Totila at Busta Gallorum in AD 552 (Procop. Goth. 4,31,3–4). He also played a significant part in the subsequent conquest of Rome, that was hardly being defended by the Goths anymore (Procop. Goth. 4,33,24). M.MEI. and ME.STR.

Dagon see → Dagan

Dahae (Δάαι; *Dáai*, Δάοι; *Dáoi*; Latin: *Dahae*) The D. were a nomadic tribe in Persis; according to Strabo, they were originally one of the Scythian tribes in the region by the Caspian Sea (Str. 11,8,2; 11,9,2f.). Like the Mardi, Dropici and Sagartii, the D. are mentioned by Herodotus in connection with the revolt of Cyrus II against Astyages in 550 BC (Hdt. 1,125,4); in the Persepolis Inscription they are called *Daha*. The D. fought under Darius — and, after his death, under Spitamenes — against → Alexander [4] the Great (Arr. An. 3,11,3; 3,28,10; Curt. 4,12,6; 7,4,6). Eventually, Alexander incorporated them into his army (Curt. 8,3,16), using them as mounted archers in his campaign against the Indian king Porus (Arr. An. 5,12,2; cf. Curt. 8,14,5; 9,2,24). In the 3rd cent. BC, the D. supported Arsaces I, the founder of the Parthian kingdom (Str. 11,9,2), but they also formed part of the army of Antiochus III, fighting in 217 BC as lightly armed troops in the battle of Raphia, against → Ptolemaeus [7] IV (Pol. 5,79), and in 190 BC as *equites sagittarii* in the battle of Magnesia against the Romans (Liv. 37,40,8; cf. 37,38,3 and App. Syr. 32). They were still a noticeable presence in the internal conflicts dividing the Parthian kingdom in the 1st cent. AD (Tac. Ann. 11,8,4; cf. 2,3,1).

Literature:
J. Junge, Saka-Studien, 1939; P.L. Kohl, Central Asia. Palaeolithic Beginnings to the Iron Age, 1984 I.v.B., B.B. and E.O.

Dahistan Landscape on the lower → Atrek, western Turkmenia, named after the → Dahae. In the late Bronze and early Iron Age between 1500 and 600 BC, a well-developed irrigation culture with more than 30 attested settlements.

P.L. Kohl, Central Asia, Palaeolithic Beginnings to the Iron Age, 1984, 200–208. B.B.

Daimachus (Δαίμαχος; *Daímachos*).

[1] from Plataeae, Greek historian in the 4th cent. BC. He was the author of a contemporary history and was regarded by Jacoby, who can hardly have been correct in this regard, as the author of the Hellenica of Oxyrhynchus. FGrH 65 (with comm.).

F. Jacoby, The Autorship of the Hellenica of Oxyrhynchus, in: CQ 44, 1950, 1–11; S. Hornblower, in: Proc. of the Second Internat. Congr. of Boiotian Studies (1995; defends Jacoby); K. Meister, Die griech. Geschichtsschreibung, 1990, 65f.

[2] D. from Plataeae, Greek historiographer in the 3rd cent. BC. He was envoy of Antiochus [2] Soter at the Indian royal court in Palimbothra (FGrH 716 T 1). D. wrote *Indiká* with polemical criticism of his predecessor Megasthenes (FGrH 715), but was himself, according to Eratosthenes (at Str. 2,1,9 and 19) extremely unreliable. FGrH 716.

O. Lendle, Einführung in die griech. Geschichtsschreibung, 1992, 273; K. Meister, Die griech. Geschichtsschreibung, 1990, 142. K.MEI.

Daiphantus (Δαίφαντος; *Daíphantos*). Son of Bathyllios from Hyampolis. D. was one of the commanders of the Phocians in the clashes with the Thessalians shortly before the Persian Wars (Hdt. 8,27–31). The brilliant victory won by the Phocian army in these battles was still being commemorated in the home town of D. at the annual festival of the Elaphebolia in the time of Plutarch (Plut. Mor. 244B-C).
→ Elaphebolos; → Hyampolis E.S.-H.

Daitondas Bronze sculptor from Sicyon. He created victors' and portrait statues in Olympia and Thebes in the later 4th cent. BC, as well as one of Aphrodite in Delphi.

Lippold, 299; J. Marcadé, Recueil des signatures de sculpteurs grecs, 1, 1953, no.25; Overbeck, no. 1582 (sources). R.N.

Daktyloi Idaioi (Δάκτυλοι Ἰδαῖοι; *Dáktyloi Idaîoi*). The inventors of the blacksmith's craft described as *góēs* ('magicians') in the *Phoronis* (3) (PEG fr. 2; cf.Diod. Sic. 17,7,5; Str. 10,3,22) [1. 1054–5] (guild of mythical blacksmiths: [2. 269]). The same is attested not for the Troad (=Phrygia) but for Crete by Hes. fr. 282 M-W, Marmor Parium FGrH 239 A11 (Ephorus?)

and Diod. Sic. 5,64,3;5 who describes them as the original people of Crete. Their name ('fingers') was traced back by Soph. fr. 366 TrGF, who assumed ten Daktyloi Idaioi (DI), to the number of fingers, and by Hellanicus FGrH 4 F 89 to finger contact with the goddess Rhea. In spite of this, it is likely that the DI were originally goblins ('finger manikins'; Paus. 8,31,3: 'one cubit tall' against the *Phoronis*); the small stature of goldsmiths is shown on pictorial representations in Egypt [3. 79, 83–4]. The epithet is not derived directly from *ídē* (ἴδη, 'forest') but from the once densely wooded Ida massif in Asia Minor or Crete. The localisation of the DI runs parallel to the evidence for the cult of Cybele. The *Phoronis* calls the DI 'servants of the Adrestaea of the mountain', i.e. of Cybele worshipped there as 'mother of the mountain' (Eur. Hel. 1301f.) or 'Ida' (Eur. Or. 1453), who at Diod. Sic. 17,7,5 is their mentor and who on Crete continued Minoan traditions as the mountain goddess Rhea (Eur. fr. 472 TGF, schol. Apoll. Rhod. 1,1126) [4. 353]. According to Diod. Sic. 5,65,1 the Curetes were possibly sons of the DI; Paus. 5,7,6 however, equated the DI with the Curetes, the helpers of Rhea in the cave of the Cretan Ida. The DI were also connected with Olympia (via the Idaean Hercules: Paus. ibid.) and Cyprus (Clem. Al. Stromateis 1,16,75,4), all of which were places with rich archaeological evidence for metal import from the orient in the 8th–7th cents. BC [5. 15–9]. As possessors of special knowledge that made metal produce sound, they are said to have invented music (Plut. Mor. 1132F), to have had magic abilities (Pherecydes FGrH 3 F 47) and to have carried out the induction into mysteries (Porph. Vita Plotini 17); as teachers of Orpheus on Samothrace they assumed, according to myth, the role of the Cabiri (Ephor. FGrH 70 F 104) [6. 39–41]. Other identifications: Telchines (Eust. 771,44f.); Faunus, Picus (Plut. Numa 15,4 p. 70c); Lares (Arnob. 3,41).

1 A.S. Pease (ed.), M.T. Ciceronis de natura deorum, 1955–58 2 Burkert 3 R.J. Forbes, in: Stud. in Ancient Technology 8, 1964 4 M.P. Nilsson, MMR 5 W. Burkert, Orientalizing Revolution, 1992 6 Id., ΓΟΗΣ, in: RhM 105, 1962, 32–55. G.A.C.

Daktylos (δάκτυλος; *dáktylos*).

[1] The *daktylos*, Latin *digitus*, as a measure, is the term for the fingers' width, with four *dáktyloi* constituting a palm (παλαιστή; *palaistḗ*, Latin *palmus*), 16 *daktyloi* a foot (πούς; *poús*, Latin *pes*) and only in Greece 12 *daktyloi* making a span (σπιθαμή; *spithamḗ*). In Rome however the *daktylos* can also, according to the duodecimal system, be equated with the *uncia* and be counted up to the *as* (= *pes*). The guide for the *daktylos* is the foot that measures between 29.4 and 35.4 cm. It therefore fluctuates between 1.84 and 2.21 cm. Smaller distances are measured in fractions of the *daktylos*. Square and cubic *daktylos* were not in use.

→ Measures; → Palaiste; → Palmus; → Pes; → Pous; → Spithame

F. Hultsch, Griech. und röm. Metrologie, ²1882, 28f., 74f.; O. A. W. Dilke, Digit measures on a slab in the British Museum, in: The Antiquaries Journal 68, 1988, 290–294. A.M.

[2] see → Metrics

Dalheim Roman *vicus* in the Grand Duchy of Luxembourg, possibly identical with Ricciacus (Tab. Peut.); Indications of a late La Tène period settlement (*c.* 1st cent. BC). It was refounded as a road-station (*mansio*) during the construction of the Metz-Trier road in the Augustan period [1]. After the uprising of the Treveri in AD 69/70 the town developed into the economic and particularly religious centre of the region (CIL 13,1,2 p. 635–638) [2; 3]; in the 2nd half of the 3rd cent. it was devastated by invasions of Germanic tribes (in 260, around 268/270, around 275/6). Reconstructed as a smaller road-station it was destroyed again in 353/355 and finally declined at the beginning of the 5th cent.

1 J. Krier, Zu den Anf. der röm. Besiedlung auf dem Pëtzel bei D., in: Publications de la Section Historique de l'Inst. Grand-Ducal de Luxembourg 94, 1980, 141–194 2 Espérandieu, Rec. 5, 330–374 3 J. Krier, Neue Zeugnisse der Götterverehrung aus dem röm. vicus D., in: Hémecht 44, 1992, 55–82. F.SCH.

Dalisandus (Δαλισανδός; *Dalisandós*). Name of several towns that lay in Cilicia Tracheia, presumably near Sinabıç [1], near Belören in Lycaonia [2] or in eastern Pamphylia [3].

1 Hild/Hellenkemper, s.v. Dalisandos 2 D.H. French, The site of Dalisandus, in: EA 4, 1984, 85–98 3 J. Darrouzès, Notitiae episcopatuum Ecclesiae Constantinopolitanae, 1981. F.H.

Dalmatae, Dalmatia (Delmatae, Delmatia).
I. General II. Historical development

I. General

Important people of later Illyricum (degree of Celtization uncertain) in the hinterland of Salona between Tit(i)us (Krka) and Nestus/Hippius (Cetina) on the Glamočko, Livanjsko, Duvanjsko and Imotsko polje. Gave its name to the Roman *prov. Dalmatia*. Administratively separated from Illyricum at the beginning of the Flavian period. These areas were under the control of the Illyrian kingdom, notorious for its piracy (under the dynasty of the Ardiaeans, Agron and Teuta), which was fought by the Romans in 229 BC (1st Illyrian War against Teuta and Pinnes, 2nd Illyrian War in 219 BC, mainly against Demetrius of Pharus) and conquered in 168 BC (capture of Genthius).

II. Historical development
A. Greek and Roman Republican period
B. Roman province C. Geography D. Administration E. Society F. Late antiquity
G. Byzantine period

A. Greek and Roman Republican period

Roman intervention in the eastern Adriatic area superseded Greek settlement and influence to a large extent in D.; at the time of Pliny the Elder many Greek towns that once flourished were abandoned. The Greeks had colonized the southern Adriatic area in the late 7th cent. BC when they founded Epidamnus and Apollonia. According to Hdt., the Phocaeans were the first to explore the Adriatic area; the Greek colonists came into contact with the following peoples (Hecat. FGrH 1): Caulici, Liburni, Mentores, Syopii (otherwise unknown) and Hythmites (otherwise unknown). The first coherent report on the peoples in the Adriatic area is the description of the eastern Adriatic coast in Ps.-Scylax (4th cent. BC), where (from north to south) the Liburni, Hierastamnes (otherwise unknown), Hylli, Bulinii, Nesti, Manii, Autariati, Illyrii, Encheleis and the Taulantii are mentioned. The Liburnian thalassocracy was ended by the Greek expansion: in the 8th cent. BC they were driven out of Corcyra by the Corinthian colonists. The Cnidian colony on Corcyra Melaina (Korčula) in the 6th cent. BC was succeeded by colonization under Dionysius I in the 4th cent. BC : Pharus (Hvar), partially a Parian colony, and Issa (Vis) which for their part colonized Corcyra Melaina and the mainland: Tragurium (Trogir) and → Epetium (Stobreč).

After the decline of the Illyrian kingdom and the formation of the Roman protectorate in southern Illyricum, with Aous (Vjose) in the south (later the southern region up to Drilon became part of Macedonia) and with the river Naro (Neretva) forming the northern border, the D. with their centre at → Delminium became the major enemies of the Roman state. Because of their attacks on the colonies of Tragurium and Epetium — whose metropolis Issa was allied with Rome — and also on the → Daorsi who were under Roman protection, the Roman army under P. Cornelius Scipio Nasica marched into D. in 156–155 BC (the sources regarding these campaigns in [1]), and its capital city of Delminium (on Duvanjsko polje) was destroyed. The *consul* Ser. Fulvius Flaccus fought against the Ardiaei (=Vardaei) in 135 BC; in 129 the *consul* C. Sempronius Tuditanus fought against the Iapodes, Carni and Taurisci, and possibly also against the Liburni, in 119/8 L. Caecilius Metellus against the D. In 78–76 BC, C. Cosconius again waged war on the D., conquered Salona and freed the city from the D. Illyricum was set up as an independent province at the latest under Caesar in 59 BC. As *proconsul* (from 58 onwards) he kept a legion in Illyricum. In 56 BC a legation was sent from Issa to Caesar in Aquileia who probably confirmed the status of Issa as a free ally. After an uprising of the Pirustae in 54 BC Caesar visited the province for the second time. The Liburnian town of Promona was conquered by the D. in 50 BC. Centres of romanization at that time were Issa, where Caesar's legate Q. Numerius Rufus was active (ILLRP 389), as well as Caesar's *praesidium* → Epidaurum and *conventus civium Romanorum* in Salona, Narona and Lissus. With the exception of Issa, these took the side of Caesar after the outbreak of the conflict with Pompey. The D. joined Pompey and were victorious against Caesar's legate A. Gabinius at Synodium. Overall, Caesar's party (P. Cornelius Dolabella, Q. Cornificius and P. Vatinius, who was partly successful against the D.) fared worse in D. than the supporters of Pompey (M. Octavius, L. Scribonius Libo, M. Calpurnius Bibulus). In 43 Vatinius had to hand over his three legions to Brutus. There were further battles against the D.(recapture of Salona) and the Parthini under Cn. Asinius Pollio in 40–39 BC.

B. Roman province

The later Augustus conquered the entire coastal region during his Illyrian campaigns in 35–33 BC; his supposed successes in the hinterland however are disputed. In the course of his military campaigns a line of defence in the hinterland of the Dalmatian coast was set up in order to protect the already partly romanized coastal towns from attacks from the interior of D., a kind of Dalmatian *limes*. This perhaps connected Burnum with Siscia and went via Promona, Kadijina Glavica, Magnum, Andetrium, Tilurium to Bigeste in the region of Narona. The battles waged by Tiberius probably were more decisive than those of the later Augustus (11–9 BC; first uprising of the D. in 16 BC, in the course of which Agrippa was sent to fight against them in 12 BC, while peace finally came after the great Pannonian uprising in AD 6–9; among the leaders of the uprising were the → Daesitiates (*Bellum Delmaticum* in ILS 3320). After the final defeat Illyricum was possibly divided up into the *superior* and *inferior* regions (cf. ILS 938, unfortunately only a manuscript copy in which *civitates superiori provinciae Hillyrici* are mentioned; C. Vibius Postumus as *praepositus Delmatiae*, Vell. Pat.2,116,2, but probably only in the geographical sense). However, until Vespasian only one *legatus Augusti pro praetore* was securely attested for the whole of Illyricum as in no case is there documentation of two at the same time in later Pannonia and Dalmatia.

C. Geography

D. is a Dinaric karst region, sharply divided into coastal strips with several thousand islands and a Mediterranean climate, and a mountainous, wild hinterland that is only connected to the coastal area by a few narrow river valleys. As a result the north-eastern regions of D. were closely connected with Pannonia both geographically and ethnically; the border between the provinces stretched south of the river Savus (Sava). Both areas were linked by roads, most of which were built during the rule of Tiberius under P. Cornelius Dolabella.

Liburnia, the northern coastal area of D., a romanized and urbanized part of the province, on many occasions in history almost an independent unit, stretched from Arsia (Raša) in Histria via the Alpes Delmaticae/Albius Mons (Velebit) to the Zrmanja; the population was in contact with the Venetian-Etruscan peoples. Its centre was the colony of Caesar, or of the later Augustus, of Iader (Zadar), other important towns were Alvona, Flanona and Tarsatica in the Liburnian part of Histria; towns on the northern D. islands: Crexi, Absorus, Fulfinium, Curicum, Arba and Cissa, also Senia, Lopsica, Vegium, Aenona, Corinium, Nedinum, Asseria, Varvaria and Scardona on the mainland. The less romanized Iapodes settled east of it, with only a few urban settlements (Metulum, Terponus, Monetium, Avendo, Arupium); both the Liburni and the Iapodes belonged to the *conventus* of Scardona. The Iapodes became especially powerful in the course of the 3rd cent. and at times conquered part of the Liburnian coast below the Velebit. The earlier D. area with the towns of Aequum (a Claudian colony, the only veteran colony in D. although veterans were settled in all the large colonies and important coastal towns, also in Andetrium, Bigeste, Novae, Rider, Siculi and Tragurium), Delminium, Salvium, Rider and Magnum belonged to the *conventus* of Salona, while the towns in southern D. were assigned to the *conventus* of Narona; the most important urban centres were the colonies of Epidaurum and Scodra, the *municipia* Diluntum, Risinium, Acruvium, Butua, Olcinium and Lissus. The interior of the provinces was settled by the Maezaei, D., Daesitates, Dindari, Pirustae and a number of less significant peoples such as the Ditiones, Deuri, Siculotae, Glinditiones and Melcumani. The urbanization of these areas, rich in natural resources, advanced slowly with only a few relatively large urban settlements such as Raetinium, Salvium, Pelva, → Baloea, → Bistua Nova and Vetus, → Domavia and Maluesa; most of them are known as metallurgical centres or settlements along important roads; for many there is no evidence of pre-Roman settlements. Mining was one of the most important activities; miners from D. were so experienced that they were sent to mining areas in the *prov. Dacia*. While Roman citizenship was granted to the inhabitants of coastal towns mainly under Augustus, the giving of citizenship in the interior did not begin until the time of the Flavian emperors; it ended with the *constitutio Antoniana* under Caracalla. The coastal towns flourished thanks to their good harbours.

D. Administration

D. was a consular province governed by *legati Augusti pro praetore* who resided in Salona. In AD 42, L. Arruntius Camillus Scribonianus revolted against Claudius; after his defeat the legions *XI* (in Burnum — it remained in the province in AD 68/9) and *VII* (in Tilurium — it left D. under Claudius or Nero) were given the title *Claudia pia fidelis*. After the withdrawal of *III* or *IV Flavia* from Burnum to Moesia in *c.* AD 86, D. no

longer had a permanent garrison of legions. The *legio VIII Augusta* was occasionally stationed in the province along with a relatively small number of auxiliary troops, of whom the cohorts *III Alpinorum*, *Aquitanorum*, *I Belgarum*, *I Campana*, *I* and *II Milliaria Delmatarum* and *VIII Voluntariorum* should be mentioned. In the 1st cent. AD the *ala Claudia nova* was likewise stationed in the province for a long time. An important military outpost was set up in Bigeste (Humac) in the hinterland of Narona (probably under the later Augustus); it was a constant garrison of auxiliary troops and an important veteran settlement (Pagus Scunasticus).

Unlike Pannonia, D. was not affected by the Marcomannic Wars as the province was protected by its high mountains (modern Bosnia and Hercegovina); nevertheless there is evidence of contingents of the *legio II* and *III Italica* in Salona for this period. From the time of the reforms of Gallienus onwards, the province was administered by equestrian *praesides*. Under Diocletian the southern part was separated from the province, and an independent *Praevalitana* or *Praevalis* with the capital city of Scodra was created. While D. remained in the *dioecesis Pannoniarum*, the new province belonged to the *dioecesis Moesiarum*.

E. Society

Salona soon developed into a flourishing administrative, trade, religious and cultural centre and was one of the biggest towns in the Roman empire (with exceptionally rich epigraphic material), as well as a lively centre for early Christianity. The social structure of the D. population was complex, comparable with Italian society. The first senator of D. appears to have been Tarius Rufus, a supporter of Augustus, the second one being the well-known lawyer Iavolenus Priscus (end of the 1st/beginning of the 2nd cent. AD); the emperor Diocletian who withdrew to the new, magnificent palace of Spalatum (modern Split) should also be mentioned here. His residence influenced and shaped the urban basis of modern Split decisively; the palace still partly exists in its original form. St. Jerome was born in Stridon (exact location uncertain, in the border region of Pannonia) in northern D.

F. Late antiquity

After the defeat of Theodosius I the province of D. remained in the western part, while Praevalitana as a part of the Dacian diocese belonged to the eastern part. The administrative status of D. changed; under the *magister militum* Marcellinus in the mid 5th cent. it was even independent. His successor was the last Roman emperor in the West, Iulius Nepos, murdered in Spalatum in AD 480.

1 Broughton, MRR.

M. Zaninović, Ilirsko pleme Delmati I (The Illyrian Tribe of the D.), in: Godišnjak 4 (Centar za balkanološka ispitivanja 2), 1966, 27–92; II, in: ibid. 5/3, 1967, 5–101; G. Alföldy, Bevölkerung und Gesellschaft der röm.

Prov. Dalmatien (with a contribution by A. Mócsy), 1965; J.J. Wilkes, D., 1969; M. Suić, Antički grad na istočnom Jadranu, 1976; M. Zaninović, The Economy of Roman D., in: ANRW II.6, 1977, 767–809; I. Bojanovski, Bosna i Hercegovina u antičko doba (Bosnia and Herzegovina in antiquity) Akademija nauka i umjetnosti Bosne i Herzegovine, Djela 66, Centar za balkanoška ispitivanja 6), 1988; D. Rendić-Miočević, Illiri i antički svijet, 1989; E. Marin (ed.), Salona christiana (Starokršćanski Solin), 1994; S. Čače, *Civitates* Dalmatiae u 'Kozmografiji' Anonima Ravenjanina (The 'civitates' Dalmatiae in the 'Cosmographia' of the Anonymous Geographer of Ravenna), in: Diadora 15, 1993, 347–440. M.Š.K.

G. Byzantine period

The war against the Ostrogoths [1. 21ff.] brought D. back under the rule of eastern Rome. Detailed reports, not just about church life at the end of the 6th cent., are to be found in the letters of → Gregorius. The decisive turning point that was to leave its mark on D.until deep into the Middle Ages was the immigration of → Slavs [1. 24ff.] from the inland in the wake of the Avar destruction: in582 → Sirmium was destroyed by the Avars, and at the beginning of the 7th cent. the metropolis of → Salona must have met the same fate. The Byzantines were only able to retain several coastal areas and the islands to which the Christian romanized population fled, as e.g. from Salona to the old Greek colony of Ἀσπάλαθος/Spalatum, modern Split, to which the bishop's seat was also moved. After the Peace of Aachen (812) Charlemagne again had to yield possession of D. to Byzantium. Only in the later sixties of the 9th cent. did Basilius [5] I set up a → theme Δελματία (metropolis: Zadar; cf. the discussion in [2]) there; the local magnates (ἄρχοντες) appear however to a large extent to have exercised their rule unchallenged [2; 3]. Very soon D. that was by and large left to its own devices, got caught up in the tensions between Venice, Croatia, Hungary and Byzantium. Its ethno-political structure remained the same over the centuries (essentially right through into the 19th cent.): in towns such as Διάδωρα/Jadera/Zadar/Zara the romanized populace was able to hold out until the late Middle Ages; the various Slavic tribes lived (Croats, Serbs etc.) inland. In this way the romanized Byzantine culture was able to exert a significant influence on the kingdoms that were arising in the hinterland.

1 K. Jireček, Die Romanen in den Städten Dalmatiens während des MA, 2 vols., 1902 and 1904 2 J. Ferluga, L'amministrazione bizantina in Dalmazia (esp. administration history) 3 L. Steindorff, Die dalmatinischen Städte im 12. Jh., 1984 4 B. Krekič, s.v. Dalmatia, ODB, 578f. J.N.

Dalmatica Long-sleeved → tunica reaching down to the knees, named after its country of origin Dalmatia; mentioned in literature for the first time at the turn of the 2nd cent. AD. According to evidence from written sources and statues, the *dalmatica* was white with a purple → *clavus* that went vertically from the shoulders to the hem; the materials from which it was made were wool, silk, a half-silk and linen. The *dalmatica* was worn by men (with a *cingulum militiae* when on duty) and women. As early as the 3rd cent. AD it was adopted as liturgical church dress and became the typical attire of the deacons; as the (MHG) *korerock* or *lessrock* however it underwent great changes in the Middle Ages.

J.P. Wild, Clothing in the North-West Provinces of the Roman Empire, in: BJ 168, 1968, 222–223. R.H.

Dalmatius

[1] Fl. D. Son of → Constantius [1] and Theodora, half-brother of Constantine I. Nothing is known of his role in the initial period of Constantine's rule, although presumably he was given Toulouse as his abode during the tensions with Licinius in *c.* AD 320–324 (Auson. Prof. 16,11–12). Consul in 333, he was sent to Antioch at around the same time with the archaizing title of *censor* (Athan. c. Ar. 65,1ff.). There he was concerned with murder accusations against Athanasius. In Tarsus he had → Calocaerus burnt to death. In 337 he was killed together with other members of the younger line of the house of Constantine.

[2] Fl. D. Son of Dalmatius. [1]. After his education in Narbonne with the orator Exsuperius (Auson. Commemoratio professorum Burdigalensium 17,8–11) he was installed as fourth emperor on September 18, AD 335 after the three sons of Constantine (Consularia Constantinopolitana a. 335 in Chron. min. 1). He was entrusted with the defence of the lower Danube (*ripa Gothica*) against the Goths (Anonymus Valesianus 35), initially for the duration of the Persian campaign planned by Constantine. After Constantine's death, he was presumably still supposed to preside over the administration of Thrace, Macedonia and Achaea (Aur. Vict. Epitome de Caesaribus 41,20), but was, like his father, killed immediately after the death of Constantine, presumably with the knowledge or even at the order of his cousin Constantius. B.BL.

[3] Former guards officer, then a student of the ascetic Isaac. At the Council of Ephesus he sided with Cyril of Alexandria against his bishop Nestorius and persuaded the monks of Constantinople to join his side. From that time onwards he was the uncontested leading monk of the capital city (publication of his writings in Clavis Patrum Graecorum 3, 5776–8). PLRE 2,341.

G. Dagron, Les moines et la ville. Le monachisme à Constantinople jusqu'au concile de Chalcédoine (451), in: Travaux et mémoires du Centre de recherches ... byzantines 4, 1970, 229–276; Id., La romanité chrétienne en Orient, 1984, no. 8, 266ff. H.L.

Damage, Indemnity Damage is the loss suffered to property, or to a non-material item (e.g. honour) protected by law; indemnity is compensation for that loss. They are to be distinguished from forfeit, which has to do not with compensation for the damage but with punishment of the person who caused the damage and with appeasing the victim/plaintiff [1. 498–502; 6. 223–228]. Bound up in the concept of damage are the questions as to whether any additional expenses incurred and foregone profit are to be added to direct compensation, and whether compensation is to take the form of repayment in kind or replacement value. In each case, it is the legal system in force that determines the consequences of damage and the criteria to be applied.

Ancient legal systems other than Roman do not differentiate between damage and forfeit (cf. in that context 'composition'/'composition system' in the law of late antiquity and in medieval law [3. 120–129, 304–320]; and also [2; 5; 7]). Accordingly, modern literature on ancient law does not discuss the difference in any detail. Words denoting 'damage' (cf. e.g. Akkadian *bitiqtum* 'damage', 'loss'; *ḫabālum* 'commit violence against someone'; Old Egyptian *mn* 'loss'; *ngꜣw* 'loss', 'lack' and even Greek βλάβη/*blábē* 'damaging action, damage') have no technical legal sense; that first appears in Attic court speeches (→ *blábēs dikḗ*; [4]). The determining factor is not the objectively presented damage but the violation — where applicable acknowledged in an agreement ('contract') — of some area of the law. Abstract injury is the principal basis for assessing the (usually multiple) composition (also in the case of → talio). This had been agreed to right at the start in penalties for breach of → contract, which originally averted unconstrained revenge and later averted any legal enforcement. The damage was not calculated objectively; on the contrary, a cow is taken for a cow, just as in 'a tooth for a tooth'. For Roman law see → *damnum*; → *interesse*.

1 KASER, RPR 1 2 E. KAUFMANN, s. v. Buße, in: A. ERLER (ed.), HWB zur dt. Rechtsgesch., vol. 1, 1971, 575–577 3 E. LEVY, Weström. Vulgarrecht. Das Obligationenrecht, 1956 4 H. MUMMENTHEY, Die *dike blabes*, thesis Freiburg 1971 5 W. OGRIS, s. v. Schaden(s)ersatz, in: A. ERLER (ed.), HWB zur dt. Rechtsgesch., vol. 4, 1990, 1335–1340 6 HONSELL/MAYER-MALY/SELB 7 Z. O. SCHERNER, s. v. Kompositionssystem 2, in: A. ERLER (ed.), HWB der dt. Rechtsgesch., vol. 2, 1978, 995–997.

JO. HE.

Damagetus (Δαμάγητος; *Damágētos*). Mediocre epigrammatic poet of the 'Garland' of Meleager (Anth. Pal. 4,1,21), probably to be classified as part of the Peloponnesian School; he lived at the time of the war between the Achaean and the Aetolian Leagues (220–217 BC). Almost all of his 12 epigrams can be traced back directly (7,438; 541) or indirectly (praise of Sparta and its allies: 7,432; 540f., and in doricizing language 7,231; 16,1) to this event (perhaps also 6,277 to Arsinoe, the daughter of Ptolemy Euergetes), in view of the good relationships between Egypt and Sparta that developed in those years.

GA I,1,76–79; 2,223–230.

E.D.

Damania (name on Iberian coins [1. no. 86]: *dmaniu*) was an *oppidum stipendiarium* of the *conventus* of Caesaraugusta (Plin. HN 3,24) and part of the tribe of the Sedetani or Edetani (Ptol. 2,6,62); HÜBNER [2] presumes here that there were two different tribes while SCHULTEN sees both as one (cf. [3. 229]). In spite of inscriptions (CIL II 2960; 3990; 4249) its position cannot be ascertained more exactly. Spanish local researchers have identified it as modern Mediana (province of Zaragoza), others as Domeño (province of Valencia) [4. 859].

1 E. HÜBNER, Monumenta Linguae Ibericae 1, 1893 2 Id., s.v. D., RE 4, 2029 3 A. SCHULTEN, Fontes Hispaniae Antiquae 8, 1959 4 Enciclopedia Universal Ilustrada 17.

TOVAR, 3, 1989, 410.

P.B.

Damaratus (Δαμάρατος, Δημάρητος; *Damáratos*, *Dēmárētos*). Spartan king, Eurypontid, son and successor (around 510 BC) of King Ariston. The turning-point in his life was brought about by the enmity with Cleomenes I, whose intention to establish a Spartan satellite regime in Athens, with the help of an army campaign in 506 he thwarted at Eleusis (Hdt. 5,74f.). We do not know whether Athenian investigations became known to the Persian satrap in Sardeis [3. 273–276]. In 491 D. plotted against Cleomenes who, in view of a possible attack by the Persians, wanted to isolate the Aeginetes as possible collaborators (Hdt. 6,50f.). In a countermove Cleomenes succeeded in having D. no longer recognized as the rightful son of Ariston and consequently having him deposed by influencing the ephors and bribing the Pythia in Delphi (Hdt. 6,61–66). D. was not returned to favour when the conspiracy was revealed shortly after and he fled, offended also by his successor Leotychidas, to Darius I, who gave him vast lands in Mysia (Hdt. 6,70; 7,3). D. also accompanied Xerxes on the campaign against Greece in 480 (Hdt. 7,101–104; 209; 234f.; 239; 8,65; Plut. Mor. 864 E-F; Diog. Laert. 1,72); although his role as adviser has been embellished in legend [2. 156f., 166], Herodotus will have based his opinion on the so-called D. source (an oral tradition that goes back to D.) [1. 404, 476].

1 F. JACOBY, s.v. Herodotus, RE Suppl. 2, 205–520 2 J.F. LAZENBY, The Defence of Greece 490–479 B.C., 1993 3 M. ZAHRNT, Der Mardonioszug des Jahres 492 v.Chr. und seine histor. Einordnung, in: Chiron 22, 1992, 237–279.

K.-W.WEL.

Damarete (Δαμαρέτη; *Damarétē*).

[1] Daughter of Theron of Acragas and wife of Gelon of Syracuse, after his death wife of Polyzalus. Diod. Sic. (11,26,3) and the schol. 15 (29) to Pindar (Ol. 2) report that after the battle of Himera in 480 BC, D. spoke out in favour of making peace with the Carthaginians and treating them humanely. From the proceeds of the golden wreath weighing 100 talents which she received from them for her actions, she had so-called *damareteia*

minted—commemorative coins—that each had a value of 10 Attic drachmas or 50 *litrai* (17 specimens extant). For numismatic reasons, a later dating of the coins and hence also another reason for the minting is predominantly assumed today, with the dates fluctuating between the early seventies and 461. [1] suggests 465 = fall of the tyrants in Syracuse and Leontini. Overview of research [1. 1, n. 1].

1 H.B. MATTINGLY, The Damareteion Controversy, in: Chiron 22, 1992, 1–12

[2] Daughter of Hieron II of Syracuse, wife of Adranodorus, one of the guardians of Hieronymus; after the latter's death in 215 BC she was murdered in the course of the internal turmoil in Syracuse (Liv. 24,22–25). K.MEI.

Damas (Δάμας; *Dámas*).
[1] Hero from Aulis who travelled to Troy with Arcesilaus and was killed there by Aeneas (Q. Smyrn. 8,303–305: Dymas? [1]).

1 P. VIAN, Q. Smyrn., 1966.

[2] (Δαμᾶς; *Damâs*). Eponymous founder of → Damascus in Syria. He accompanied Dionysus to Asia where he established a shrine to him in Syria in the form of a hut (σκηνή), called Δαμᾶ σκηνή (*Damâ skēnḗ*, 'hut of Damas'), hence Damascus (Etym. m. s.v. Δαμσκός 247 GAISFORD). R.B.

[3] Wealthy citizen of Syracuse and patron of Agathocles [2]. Elected *strategos* in a war against Acragas, he appointed Agathocles as chiliarch and gave him the opportunity to distinguish himself for the first time. After the death of D., Agathocles married his widow and in this way became one of the richest men in Syracuse (Diod. Sic. 19,3,1–2; Iust. 22,1,12f.).

K. MEISTER, in: CAH 7,1, ²1984, 385. K.MEI.

[4] *Declamator* from the Augustan period with the surname ὁ σκόμβρος ('mackerel'), mentioned in Seneca (Controv. 2,6,12; 10,4,21. 10,5,21; Suas. 2,14); presumably identical with the Damasus of Tralles mentioned in Strabo (14,1,42). As the few remarks passed down to us by Seneca reveal, D. was an Asianist (→ Asianism).

H. BORNECQUE, Les déclamations et les déclamateurs d'après Sénèque le père, 1902 (repr. 1967), 164f. M.W.

Damascius (Δαμάσκιος; *Damáskios*)
A. LIFE B. WORKS 1. INDIRECTLY PRESERVED WRITINGS 2. 'TREATISE ON FIRST PRINCIPLES' 3. COMMENTARY ON THE PARMENIDES C. ACKNOWLEDGEMENT

A. LIFE
Neoplatonist, last head of the → Academy in Athens, born around AD 462 in Damascus, studied rhetoric around 479/80 with a certain Theon in Alexandria and there also was a member of the Platonist circle. Around 482/3 he went to Athens to teach rhetoric. Around 491/2 he gave up this career and initially studied propaedeutic sciences under → Marinus, who had succeeded Proclus in 485, then philosophy under → Zenodotus. Around 515 Damascius returned to Athens to succeed Zenodotus. As a result of the Justinianic decrees (closure of the Academy and prohibition of the teaching of philosophy), D., accompanied by other Neoplatonists, went to King Chosroes in Persia in 529. Disappointed by him, the philosophers did however ask for permission to return home and received this at the end of 532. Chosroes demanded of Justinian a guarantee of protection for them, and also their right to spend the rest of their days in complete freedom of thought—but without teaching. It is not known when or where D. died.

B. WORKS
1. INDIRECTLY PRESERVED WRITINGS
The works of D. can be divided into three groups: a) those that are only known from references or allusions made by D. himself in his other writings; b) those that are known from other authors: the most important work of this group is the 'Life of Isidore' (Βίος Ἰσιδώρου, *Vita Isidori*), known through notes made by Photius (*Bibliotheke*, cod. 181; cod. 242) and extracts in the Suda; it was written after 517 and before 526 and is dedicated to Theodora, a female student of D. and Isidore; in reality it presents a history of the Neoplatonist School in Athens from the end of the 4th cent.; c) the third group comprises works that are almost completely known either in the version edited by several students or in that by D. himself:

(a) The commentary on the *Phaedo* is made up of two sets of lecture notes. Olympiodorus edited his own *Phaedo* commentary by consulting a third version of the commentary of D. different from the first two.

(b) The commentary on the *Philebus* is a collection of notes which we owe to the student who wrote down the second version of the *Phaedo* commentary.

(c) The 'Treatise on First Principles' and the commentary on the *Parmenides* are the two most important works of D. Because of their presentation of the material and content, the question arises as to whether these two works are actually to be seen as separate.

2. 'TREATISE ON FIRST PRINCIPLES'
(Περὶ τῶν πρώτων ἀρχῶν, *De principiis* = princ.) It fills the gap in a commentary regarding the first hypothesis in the commentary on the *Parmenides*. Its goal is the search for the causes of every occurrence: it discusses the possibility of naming these causes and in this way identifying the cause of all causes. This endeavour is carried out top-down: 1. It begins with the question of the highest principles, the Ineffable, ἀπόρρητον, and the One, ἕν (princ. § 1 42); 2. Then the discussion leads to an investigation of the principles that change the One: the limiting One, the unlimited Many, the Unified, ἡνωμένον; § 43 — 89); 3. The treatise then dedicates

itself to the problems of the emergence of the Unified, which is identified with that which is intelligible, and the question of the relationships between philosophy and the various theologies (princ. § 90—125) in order to conclude with a discussion of participation (§ 126).

3. Commentary on the Parmenides (= In Parm.) This continues the discussion of participation (In Parm. § 127–138). The second hypothesis consequently begins with the first intelligible triad that according to Proclus is composed of the One, Power and Being and that according to D. corresponds to the triad of the Unified: Whole-One, One-Many, Unified. It then descends to the intelligible souls of which these higher beings, such as demons, angels and heroes consist (§ 139 — 196). According to D. the object of the third hypothesis is the human soul (§ 397–415). The fourth hypothesis describes the material forms that the soul can project into Becoming. The material forms that are not yet mixed with matter — by means of which they can be told apart from the perceptible forms — wait to be received into it (§ 416–423). The object of the fifth hypothesis is matter as a principle that withdraws from every form and every description (§ 424–431). The sixth hypothesis deals with the non-existent One in relation to the phenomenon that is composed of matter and the material forms (§ 432–440). The object of the seventh hypothesis is the principle of the Impossibility of the One, the purely imaginary nature of its absolute revocation (§ 441–447). The eighth hypothesis concerns the 'Others' of the non-existent One, the phenomena (§ 448–454). The object of the ninth hypothesis is finally the principle of the Impossibility of the 'Others' of the One, the purely imaginary nature of their absolute revocation (§ 455–60).

C. Acknowledgement

Essentially D. adopted the metaphysical system that had been formulated by → Syranus and perfected by Proclus. His hypercritical mind that multiplied difficulties in order to be able to better overcome them made him consider a number of Proclus' opinions. D. essentially demonstrated his originality when he allocated in a certain manner a principle to the One, the Ineffable, which lies completely buried in an abyss of silence. D. furthermore is the only Neoplatonist who lengthens the emergence through the negative hypotheses of the *Parmenides*: they represent the structure of the perceptible.

Editions and translations: Vitae Isidori reliquiae, ed. C. Zintzen, 1967; R. Asmus, Das Leben des Philosophen Isidoros von Damaskios aus Damaskos, 1911; The Greek commentaries on Plato's Phaedo. Vol. II: Damascius, ed., transl. L. G. Westerink, 1977; Lectures on the Philebus, wrongly attributed to Olympiodorus, ed., transl. L. G. Westerink, 21983; Damascii successoris Dubitationes et Solutiones de primis principiis, In Platonis Parmenidem, ed. C. A. Ruelle, Paris 1889; Damascius le Diadoque, Problèmes et Solutions touchant les Premiers Principes (...), transl. A. Ed. Chaignet, 1898, repr. 1964.; Traité des Premiers principes, ed. L. G. Westerink, transl. J. Combès, vol. I 1986, vol. II 1989, vol. III 1991. L.BR.

Damascus

A. Ancient Orient B. Persian period and Hellenism C. Roman period and early Islam

A. Ancient Orient

Oasis situated on the eastern edge of Antilebanon, watered by the undrained Barada, first mentioned in lists of Syrian towns of the pharaohs Thutmosis III and Amenophis III (*tmsq*, *Tamasqu*) and then in the → Amarna letters (*Di/Dumašqu*). In the 13th cent. BC too, D. was under Egyptian control. At the turn of the 2nd to the 1st millennium BC, D. became a city under Aramaic control. For the period of David and Salomo, the OT tradition mentions a strong Aramaic state of Aram-Zoba to which D. also belonged and which clashed with David over the issue of the control of important trading routes. For a certain period after David's victory D. became part of his kingdom. D. then appears as an independent political unit for the first time under a prince Rezon who was able to make use of the death of David and the dissolution of the power of Israel-Judah. Economically, D. profited particularly from the trade conducted by the camel caravans that linked Mesopotamia with the Phoenician coast and for which D. was an important station. In Assyrian tradition the first king of D. is Hadadezer who together with the king of Hamath (Epiphaneia [2]) headed an alliance that successfully fought Salmanassar III at the battle of Qarqar on the Orontes (853 BC). The alliance dissolved after 845. In 841 when D. was attacked again by the Assyrians, it was itself not captured, but the gardens of the oasis of D. were ravaged. In the period that followed D. had to pay tribute to Assyria but kept its independence until Tiglatpilesar III captured D. in 732 and made it the capital city of an Assyrian province. Later D. belonged to the New Babylonian Empire of Nebuchadnezzar II (604–562) and the Achaemenid Empire (→ Achaemenids [2]) until Parmenion, a general of Alexander the Great, conquered D.

W. T. Pitard, Ancient Damascus, 1987. H.KL.

B. Persian period and Hellenism

Because of its position as a trading junction, D. quickly recovered from the Assyrian destruction. As early as Ez 27,18, D. is again regarded as an important trading city, characterized by Str. 16,2,20 as the most important and splendid city in the entire Persian empire. Here, → Darius [3] III left his family and treasures before his campaign against Alexander the Great. As a result of Alexander's conquest of the Levant after 333 BC, D. became a Macedonian colony (Eus. Chronicon 1,260 Schoene). The Greek settlement must have predominantly been in the north and east of the Aramaic city, whose focus was in the south. Extended and fortified under the Ptolemies, the Seleucid → Antiochus [11] IX Cyzicenus elevated it to the status of capital city of Coele Syria and Phoenicia in 111 BC. With the exception of a hippodrome in the east of the city, no remains

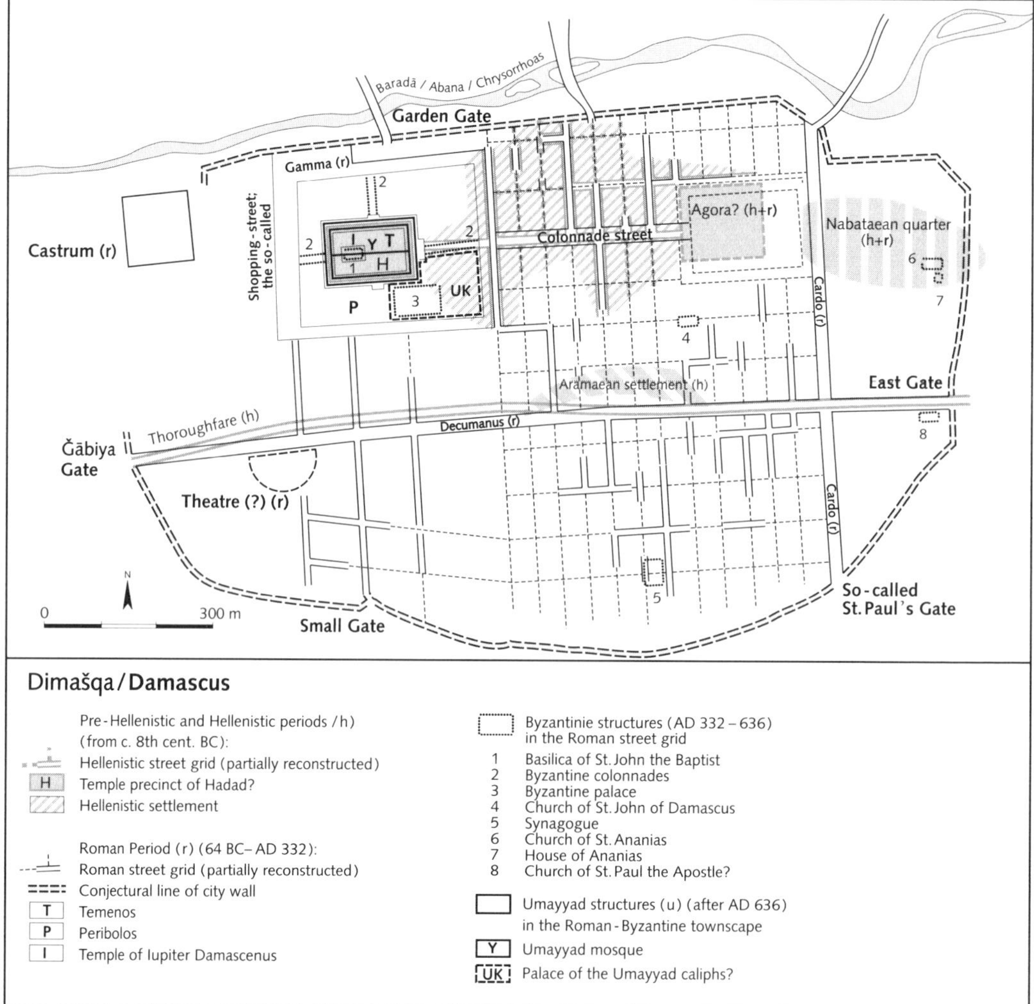

worthy of mention have been found of the Hellenistic settlement. Sections of the road network of today's old part of the city east of the Umayyad Mosque however are based on a Hippodamic system. → Aretas (al-Ḥāriṯ) [3] III Philhellenus of Petra introduced the first phase of Nabataean control over D. (85–66 BC). At that time a third district emerged in the north-east of D. that in the Middle Ages came to be the Christian quarter.

C. Roman period and early Islam

After D. was conquered by the Romans in 66 BC, it was incorporated into the Roman empire by Pompey at the same time as Syria (Jos. Ant. Iud. 14,27ff.; 33; Jos. Bell. Iud. 1,127; 131). According to Pliny (HN 5,47) and Ptolemy (Geogr. 5,14–22), D., as a free city, belonged to the → Decapolis, but was given to Cleopatra by Antony together with Coele Syria (38 BC). With the tacit permission of Rome, D. again fell to the Nabataeans (AD 37–54). The period shortly before this (15/6 and 37/8) was marked, as is inscriptionally attested, by the construction of the temple of Jupiter Damascenus, in all probability on the site of the sanctuary of the Aramaic city deity Hadad/Ramman. The temple was surrounded by a peribolos (380 m × 310 m) that was lined by colonnades and that in the 2nd cent. was widened in the west and north by shopping streets in the shape of the Greek letter gamma. Inside, a concentrically laid out temenos (156 m × 97 m) enclosed the shrine. Its eastern gate with its well-preserved propylon and the western gate today form the entrances to the Umayyad Mosque. The peribolos did not, as was customary, surround a market facility but represented the outer limit of the temple district. The agora of D. was located east of it to the north of the Zufle Tellet hill and probably related to the temple axis. Because of its increasing importance, D. was accorded the status of a metropolis by Hadrian; however, in the course of the reorganization of the Syrian provincial government in the 2nd cent., it had to cede this status to → Emesa/Ḥimṣ. After AD 222, Severus Alexander gave D. the status of a *colonia*. The erection of a *castrum* west of the temple and the building of armouries and magazines under Diocletian underlines the strategic importance of D. in securing the Euphrates line against the Sassanids at the end of the 3rd cent. AD. Changes made in the Byzantine period mostly concern the district of the temple of Jupiter, and the foundation of a church above the relics of John the Baptist by Theodosius (379–395). It is uncertain whether the temple was destroyed in the process or only altered. In AD 636, after only weak resistance, D. fell to the Muslims; under → Muʿāwiya I it became the capital city of the Umayyad empire in 656. The caliph al-Walīd (705–715) removed all the buildings from the interior of the temenos and used it as the frame for the new building of the first monumental Islamic mosque, for the completion of which numerous ancient reused stones (pillars, capitals), construction and decorative elements (saddleback roof, mosaics, marble strips) were taken over. Through the violent end of the Umayyads (750) and the shift of the centre of power under the → ʿAbbasids to ʿIraq, D. lost its importance and also to a large extent its patronage by the new rulers.

K. A. C. Creswell, Early Muslim Achitecture I, [2]1979,; Encyclopaedia of Islam II, 277ff.; K. Freyberger, Unters. zur Baugesch. des Jupiter-Heiligtums in Damaskus, in: Damaszener Mitteilungen 4, 1989, 61–86; D. Sack, Damaskus, 1989; J. Sauvaget, Le plan antique de Damas, in: Syria 26, 1949, 314–358; C. Watzinger, K. Wulzinger, Damaskus. Die ant. Stadt, 1921.
Maps: J. Sauvaget, Le plan antique de Damas, in: Syria 26, 1949, 314–358; K. A. C. Creswell, Early Muslim Architecture I, [2]1979; D. Sack, Damaskus, 1989. T.L.

Damasia Capital of the → Licates, a 'polis rising up like a fortress' (Str. 4,6,8). Tentatively identified with the early Imperial, fortified mountain settlement on the Auerberg (1055 m) near Bernbeuren (in modern Bavaria; finds of metal workshops and potters' ovens) that was settled by Rome in the 2nd decade AD and abandoned as early as *c.* AD 40.

G. Ulbert, Auerberg, in: W. Czsyz, K. Dietz, Th. Fischer, H.-J. Kellner (ed.), Die Römer in Bayern, 1995, 417–419. K.DI.

Damasias (Δαμασίας; *Damasías*). Athenian archon in 582/1 BC. He succeeded in remaining in office for longer than the usual term of a year. Only after a further 14 months could he be driven out of office by violent means. For the remainder of his period in office in 580/79 it is said that a working party of ten archons ruled, five of whom are said to have belonged to the *eupatrídai*, three to the *agroikoí* and two to the *dēmiourgoí* (Aristot. Ath. Pol. 13,2). It is disputed whether the assumption of this 'archontate compromise' is historically correct. Traill, PAA 300925.
→ Archontate

Develin, 40; Rhodes, 180ff. E.S.-H.

Damasichthon (Δαμασίχθων; *Damasíchthōn*).
[1] One of the sons of → Niobe (Apollod. 3,45) who like his brothers is killed by Apollo (Ov. Met. 6,254–260).

F. Bömer, Kommentar zu Ov. met. 6–7,1976, 78.

[2] Son of the Athenian Codrus. Together with his brother Promethus, who later murdered him, he was the leader of the Ionian colony in Colophon (Paus. 7,3,3). R.B.

Damasistratus (Δαμασίστρατος; *Damasístratos*). King of Plataeae who buried → Laius after he had been killed by Oedipus (Paus. 10,5,4; Apollod. 3,52). R.B.

Damasithymus (Δαμασίθυμος; *Damasíthymos*). Dynast of Calynda in Caria. His father, Candaules, bore a name attested for Lydia. In 480 BC as taxiarch of a Carian fleet contingent, D. took part in Xerxes' campaign against Greece (Hdt. 7,98). He died in the sea battle of Salamis when Artemisia [1] of Halicarnassus sank his ship in order to avoid being pursued by an Athenian ship (Hdt. 8,87; Polyaenus, Strat. 8,53,2).

J. Melber, in: Jahrbuch für Philologische Studien 14, 1885, 480–484. PE.HÖ.

Damastes (Δαμάστης; *Damástēs*). Son of Dioxippus from Sigeum, Greek geographer and historian of the 5th cent. BC, probably a student of → Hellanicus (Agathemerus 1,1). With the exception of a few fragments, his works do not survive.

FGrH 5. K.BRO.

Damasus Bishop of Rome (pope), * 305, † AD 384, son of a priest of the Roman parish; his mother Laurentina was ordained as a widow after the death of her spouse [1. 10], a sister Irene lived as a virgin dedicated to God [1. 11]. Deacon from 355 onwards, he was chosen as bishop of Rome in 366 against stiff opposition (opposing bishop Ursinus). Violent fights arose between the two parties, in the course of which D. managed to assert his position over that of his opponents.

During his term in office he single-mindedly advanced the pre-eminent position of the Roman bishop, the consequence of which was the momentous foundation of a Roman 'Petrinology' (Roman synod of 382, preserved in the so-called → *decretum Gelasianum*). D. promoted the representation of Christianity in Rome (construction of churches, decoration of the tombs of the martyrs); he entrusted to Jerome the revision of Old Latin biblical texts (→ Vulgate).
→ Epigrammata Damasiana

1 A. Ferrua, Epigrammata Damasiana, 1942.

J. Deckers, C. Carletti, D. und die röm. Märtyrer, 1956; Ch. Pietri, Roma Christiana 1, 1971, 407–884. K.-S.F.

Dameas

[1] (also: Demeas). Sculptor from Croton. In 532 BC he created the victor's statue of Milon in Olympia that is described by Pausanias; there is a base with fragmentary inscriptions that is seen as going together with it.

FUCHS/FLOREN, 428; LOEWY, no. 414; OVERBECK, no. 484 (sources).

[2] Bronze sculptor from Cleitor, student of Polycletus. In Delphi he created, for the victory statue of the Spartans who went to Aigospotamoi (405 BC), the statues of Artemis, Poseidon and Lysander, whose base is preserved and whom Cicero extols (Div. 1,75).

D. ARNOLD, Die Polykletnachfolge, 25. Ergh. JDAI, 1969, 6–7, 13, 33; OVERBECK, no. 978, 979 (sources); C. VATIN, Monuments votifs de Delphes, 1991, 103–138. R.N.

Damghan (Dāmġān). Town in Iran on the southern foothills of the Alborz, 342 km east of Teheran on the road to Nīšāpūr. The name possibly arose from the contraction of Deh-e Moġān (village of the Magi). The prehistoric antecedent of D. is Tepe Ḥeṣār with layers between the 5th millennium and the early 2nd millennium BC. After a hiatus of 1,500 years D. became the main settlement of the Parthian and Sassanid province of Qūmes, site of one of the holy state fires (ātaxš-ī xwarišnīh, 'unfed fire', hence Zoroastrians in D. right through to the 9th cent.). Nonetheless the traditional identification with Hecatompylus (Šahr-e-Qūmes) is not justified [1]. The Sassanid palace continued to be used in the Umayyad period. Important Islamic mosque and funeral architecture dates from the 1st half of the 11th cent.

1 J. HANSMANN, The problems of Qūmis, in: Journal of the Royal Asiatic Society 1968, 111–139 2 C. ADLE, A. S. MELIKIAN CHIRVANI, Les monuments du XIe siècle du Dâmġân, in: Studia Iranica 1/2, 1972, 229–297 3 E. F. SCHMIDT, Tepe Hissar Excavations, 1937. T.L.

Damia see → Charites; → Demeter

Damianus (Δαμιανός; *Damianós*).

T. Flavius Damianus. Sophist from Ephesus, where he financed public and private buildings, among them a dining-hall and *stoaí* the length of one *stadion* (Philostr. VS 2,23). In three discussions before his death at the age of 70 (*c.* AD 210?) he gave his student Philostratus the material for the biography of his teachers Aelius Aristides and Hadrianus of Tyre. As γραμματεύς (*grammateús*) he housed Roman troops returning from the Parthian Wars in 166/7 (IK 17.1,3080) and in 170/1 honoured the *proconsul Asiae* Nonius Macrinus with a statue (ibid., 3029). He married into the family of the Vedii Antonini; three sons became *consules suffecti*, two daughters married consuls (ibid., p. 90).
→ Philostratus, Second Sophistic

G. W. BOWERSOCK, Greek Sophists in the Roman Empire, 1969, 27f.; PIR F 253. E.BO.

Damippus (Δάμιππος; *Dámippos*). Spartan in the service of Hieronymus of Syracuse to whom he gave the advice of adherence to the alliance with Rome in 215 BC (Pol. 7,5,3). Later he also served Epicydes; in 212 he was sent as envoy to Philip V of Macedonia, and in the process fell into the hands of the Romans. The negotiations for his release, in the course of which M. Claudius [I 11] Marcellus noticed a tower that was only poorly guarded by the Syracusans, ultimately led to the successful Roman attack on Epipolae (Liv. 25,23,8ff.; Plut. Marcellus 18; Polyaenus, Strat. 8,11). M.MEI.

Damnameneus (Δαμναμενεύς; *Damnameneús*). One of the → Daktyloi Idaioi who invented the technique of forging iron (Phoronis fr. 2,3 EpGF = fr. 2,3 PEG I; Str. 10,3,22). R.B.

Damnatio in crucem Latin → *crux* or *damnatio in crucem* ('sentencing to crucifixion'), Greek during the Hellenistic period ἀνασταύρωσις/*anastaúrōsis* (which, however, in Hdt. 3,125 and probably also in Xenophon [10] of Ephesos 4,2 means 'impaling') was only one of several ways of exacting the → death penalty (II) in the Roman empire. It probably originated as deterrence against slaves in the context of the → *coercitio* ('power of coercion') by the → *tresviri* [1] *capitales. Damnatio in crucem* was perhaps based on Oriental and Punic precedents. At the time of the crucifixion of → Jesus it was a typical measure taken by provincial authorities against 'rebels'.
→ Punishment III

P. EGGER, Crucifixus sub Pontio Pilato. Das 'Crimen' Jesu von Nazareth im Spannungsfeld röm. und jüd. Verwaltungsund Rechtsstrukturen, 1997; H.-W. KUHN, Die Kreuzesstrafe während der frühen Kaiserzeit. Ihre Wirklichkeit und Wertung in der Umwelt des Urchristentums, in: ANRW II 25.1, 1982, 648–793. G.S.

Damnatio memoriae

I. HISTORICAL II. ARCHAEOLOGICAL/COINS

I. HISTORICAL

Damnatio memoriae (DM) was the process of erasing from the (public) memory of a person (usually a Roman emperor) whose name and images are removed from public inscriptions and buildings. Underlying this measure was the religious assumption, widespread in the Roman-Hellenistic world, that meritorious rulers, like heroes, had come from the realm of the gods and returned there after their death (Cic. Rep., *somnium Scipionis*; Verg. Aen. 6,734ff.). If divine origin was not sufficiently evident in the successes, good deeds and virtues of a politician or ruler, it could be called into public doubt. In Rome it was the Senate, and sometimes also the successor of the emperor, that passed judgement regarding the divine nature of the deceased emperor (Suet. Claud. 11; Cass. Dio 60,4). Given the concept of the divine genius of the emperor and of the divine quality that he assumes again after death, this could lead not only to *consecratio*, the cultic worship of the 'divinized one' (*divus Augustus*), but also to official condemnation through legal proceedings on charge of high treason or with the purpose of diminishing the emperor's honour, as was also possible against common Roman officials (*hostis iudicatio*: Dig. 48,19,8,1). The crimes and vices established in this process then provided the reason for the DM. Legal decrees, court rulings, and benefits granted by the condemned person could be revoked in whole or in part (*rescissio actorum*), which however rarely occurred. A DM was imposed on the emperors Domitian (AD 96), Commodus (192), Didius Iulianus (194), Maximinus Thrax (238), Maximianus Herculius (310) and Maximinus Daia (313); it was discussed with regard to others (e.g. Caligula: Suet. Calig. 60), while still others were subject to *hostis iudicatio* (e.g. Nero: Suet. Nero 49). Political conflicts and antagonism lay at the basis of each case (cf. Seneca's invective *Apocolocyntosis* against Claudius); hence a DM does not necessarily make a statement about the actual accomplishments and merits of an emperor.

CHRIST 426, 213ff., 239ff., 282ff., 348, 653ff., 734, 742; LATTE 313ff.; E. MEYER, Röm. Staat und Staatsgedanke, [4]1975, 407; MOMMSEN, Staatsrecht 2, 755, 1129ff.; 3, 1189ff. C.G.

II. ARCHAEOLOGICAL/COINS

The DM affected not just inscriptions and images but also coins. Aside from the melting down of coins, they could also be intentionally altered. On mintings of the emperors who suffered DM, such as Caligula, Nero and Elagabalus, marks are observable on the face in the area of the temples, cheeks and mouth; the inscription is also partly erased. The coin finds of Kalkriese near Osnabrück prove intentional destruction also of coins of Augustus. Adaptation of images on coins is also occasionally attested, such as e.g. the cuts made to a Nero *dupondius* to make it resemble Galba [1. 20ff.]. Some of the countermarks as well as the reminting of e.g. Claudius or even an early Tiberian Divus Augustus [2] over Caligula may fulfil the same intention; in this case, as well as in some others, however, they served mainly to restore the full value of the mintings of Caligula devalued when the coins were melted down by the Senate in AD 43 (Cass. Dio 60,22,3).

→ Countermarks

1 V. ZEDELIUS, Nero calvus? Ant. Veränderungen an Bronzemünzen des Kaisers Nero, in: Das Rheinische Landesmuseum Bonn 2, 1979, 20–22 2 C. M. KRAAY, Die Münzfunde von Vindonissa, 1962, 34 with n. 2.

F. VITTINGHOFF, Der Staatsfeind in der röm. Kaiserzeit. Untersuchungen zur 'damnatio memoriae', 1936; A. KINDLER, The Damnatio Memoriae of Elagabal on City-coins of the Near East, in: SM 30, 1980, 3–7; H. JUCKER, Die Bildnisstrafen gegen den toten Caligula, in: Praestant Interna. FS U. Hausmann, 1982, 110–118. A.M.

Damnum

A. MEANING B. REASONS FOR COMPENSATION C. CONTENT OF THE COMPENSATION FOR DAMAGES

A. MEANING

Originally 'expenditure', 'loss of assets'; in legal usage 'damage'. According to Roman law, only material loss can be counted as a replaceable *damnum*. Unlawful interference with other legal rights, e.g. insult or physical injury of a free Roman, are, to the Roman view, not assessable in monetary terms (*liberum corpus non recipit aestimationem*, Gaius Dig. 9,1,3). In these cases the victim may possibly be allowed an *actio iniuriarum* which is not meant to provide compensation for damages but to make amends through the payment of a fine (→ *iniuria*).

B. REASONS FOR COMPENSATION

The main reasons why a person might be obligated to pay compensation for damages were crime and infringement of a contract. According to Roman law, crimes necessitated fines (their function being one of punishment) paid to the injured party. The delinquent could therefore be fined as well as be involved in law suits to settle the claim for compensation for damages. In the case of the offence *damnum iniuria datum* of the *lex Aquilia* (*c.* 286 BC), the aspect of punishment already is of lesser importance than the settlement of damages: although the *actio legis Aquiliae* was still understood as a criminal legal suit (cf. Gai. inst. 4,9), it fundamentally concerned the reduction in value of the damaged good and hence essentially only resulted in compensation for damages. Crime-related claims for compensation for damages have as their prerequisite not only the fact of the damage but also the fault of the perpetrator. For some crimes (e.g. *damnum iniuria datum*) → *culpa* sufficed while for others → *dolus* was necessary (e.g. *furtum*). Liability irrespective of fault applied on the basis of the so-called quasi-crimes (Inst. Iust. 4,5) .

Contract-based claims for compensation also always required the presence of fault. Normally, the guilty party was liable for intent (*dolus*) and negligence (*culpa*), sometimes however already in the case of neglected supervisory obligation (→ *custodia*; e.g. in the case of a loan, *commodatum*). Sometimes they were only liable for *dolus* (e.g. in the case of safekeeping, *depositum*). In special cases compensation also had to be paid for damages incurred by chance (e.g. in the case of → *mora*, delay).

C. CONTENT OF THE COMPENSATION FOR DAMAGES

The extent of contractual compensation depended on the type of suit. In the case of strict legal suits aimed at *certum* (a certain amount of money) this was primarily the value of the object for which compensation was due; however there was a tendency to include in the calculation of the damages further disadvantages suffered by the creditor. The latitude of the *bonae fidei iudicia* allowed the Roman lawyer a particular degree of differential treatment depending on the circumstances of the individual case and led to the consideration of the concrete → interest in respect of the payment contractually owed (*id quod interest*). The compensation could cover reduced existing assets (*damnum emergens*), consequential damages of a defective service (e.g. Ulp. Dig. 19,1,13 pr.) or further indirect disadvantages, and could also include lost profits (*lucrum cessans*). If a service was provided late, damage caused by the delay had to be compensated for. The typical disadvantages of late payment of debts were compensated for by means of interest on arrears (cf. Dig. 18,6,20).

Many lawyers obligated a vendor at the signing of a contract, who had knowledge of a circumstance that caused the invalidity of the contract (Dig. 18,1,62,1; 18,1,70) to pay compensation for damage to someone's reputation (negative interest).

A contractual claim to compensation for damages was reduced if the injured party had the opportunity to limit the damage. If the injured party was also at fault, this did not lead to a sharing of the damage but could totally exclude a claim to compensation for damages (e.g. Dig. 50,17,203). Sometimes the person who caused the damage could subtract from a claim for compensation the profits gained in this legal relationship (so-called *compensatio lucri cum damno*; Dig. 3,5,10). For damage caused by those subject to the power of others or by particular animals, it was the person in power or the owner who was responsible. He did however have the choice between paying the compensation for damages and handing over the animal or the person who had caused the damage (*noxae deditio*).

Because of the principle of a monetary sentence in Roman civil law, the person who caused the damage could not be sentenced to restitution in kind but only to provide compensation for damages by way of a monetary payment. Intangible disadvantages generally had no effect on the amount of compensation (Dig. 9,2,33 pr.).

→ Delictum; → Iniuria; → Noxa; → Pauperies

KASER, RPR I, 498–502; H. HONSELL, TH. MAYER-MALY, W. SELB, Röm. Recht, 41987, 223–228; I. REICHARD, Die Frage des Drittschadensersatzes im klass. röm. Recht, 1993; R. ZIMMERMANN, The Law of Obligations, 1990, 824–833. R.GA.

Damocharis (Δαμοχάρις; *Damocháris*). Epigrammatic poet of the Justinianic period, *grammatikós*, friend and student of Agathias (according to the lemma of Anth. Pal. 7,206, a tomb epigram on the partridge loved by the master, cf. Agathias 7,204f.). Born on Cos, as can be seen from the epitaph of Paulus Silentiarius (7,588), he was proconsul and governor of Asia and was especially venerated both in Smyrna (cf. the anonymous poem 16,43) and in Ephesus (cf. SEG 18,474). Four epigrams of average standard from the 'Cycle' of Agathias are extant.

Av. und A. CAMERON, The Cycle of Agathias, in: JHS 86, 1966, 11. E.D.

Damocles (Δαμοκλῆς; *Damoklês*). Courtier and sycophant of the tyrant → Dionysius [1] I (according to Timaeus FGrH 566 F 32 of Dionysius II). The anecdote of the 'sword of Damocles' became famous through Cicero (Tusc. 5,61f.): as D. considered the powerful and rich tyrant to be the happiest person in the world, the latter had a sumptuous meal prepared for him but above his head had a sword suspended on a horse hair in order to demonstrate to him the true 'happiness' of a tyrant. K.MEI.

Damocrates (Δαμοκράτης; *Damokrátēs*).
(M.?) Servilius D. Freedman of M. Servilius (*cos. ord.* AD 3) whose daughter he cured (Plin. HN 24,7,28). Under Nero and Vespasian he wrote prescriptions in iambic trimeters in the didactic tradition of → Apollodorus [7]; some of these are extant in → Galen.

EDITION: F. CATS BUSSEMAKER, Poetae bucolici et didactici, 1862. E.BO.

Damocritus (Δαμόκριτος/*Damókritos*; also: Democritus [Δημόκριτος/*Dēmókritos*]). Sculptor from Sicyon, active during the first half of the 4th cent. BC. Pausanias saw a victor's statue of his in Olympia. Pliny chose the Attic form of the name, for a Democritus, who made statues of philosophers. In Rome his name was found on the statue of Lysis from Miletus in a lost collection of copies of 4th cent. works.

OVERBECK, no. 463, 466–468 (sources); LOEWY, no. 484; LIPPOLD, 247–248. R.N.

Damon (Δάμων; *Dámōn*)
[1] Prince of the → Telchines. Father-in-law of Minos and ancestor of Miletus. When the Telchines were struck dead by lightning by Jupiter because they poisoned crops, D. and his family were spared in gratitude for hospitality provided. Only his daughter Macelo and her husband were among the victims (Nic. in the schol. Ov. Ib. 475). R.B.
[2] A Pythagorean from Syracuse, friend of Phintias, for whom he stood surety with his life. According to Aristoxenus (fr. 31 WEHRLI = Iamblichus de vita Pythagorica 233–237; cf. Porph. Vita Plotini 59–61), who claimed to have heard the story directly from Dionysius II in exile in Corinth, Syracusian courtiers doubted the moral integrity and loyalty of the Pythagoreans and used a fictitious charge of conspiracy to put them to the test. Phintias was condemned to death (according to Diod. Sic. 10,4,3 he actually had planned a tyrannicide) and asked for a stay of execution so that he might put his domestic affairs in order and he arranged for D. to be his guarantor; against expectation, Phintias returned on time. Dionysius, was deeply impressed by this and tried in vain to become friends with this pair. For the

relationship between Aristoxenus' and Diodorus' versions and other sources (i.a. Polyaenus, Strat. 5,2,22; Cic. Off. 3,45. Tusc. 5,63. Fin. 2,79; Val. Max. 4,7,1; in Hyg. Fab. 257, the model for SCHILLER'S *Bürgschaft* (The Hostage), the friends are called Moerus and Selinuntius) see [1], esp. [2].
→ Pythagorean School

1 W. BURKERT, Lore and Science in Ancient Pythagoreanism, 1972, 104 n. 36 2 E. GEGENSCHATZ, Die 'pythagoreische Bürgschaft' — zur Gesch. eines Motivs von Aristoxenos bis Schiller, in: P. NEUKAM (ed.), Begegnungen mit Neuem und Altem, 1981, 90–154. C.RI.

[3] D. (Δάμων; *Dámōn*, with a short α: Plut. Pericles 4,153) of Athens, important sophist (→ Sophistic) and theoretician of music of the 5th/4th cents. BC. In antiquity insights about music and — in conjunction with it (Pl. Prt. 316e) — political advisory work for → Pericles [1] were attributed to him. Inseparable from D. in the research of the 19th and 20th cents. is Damonides (Δαμωνίδης; *Damōnídēs*: Plut. Pericles 9,307) of the Attic deme Oe, whether he be his father (the ΔΑΜΟΝ ΔΑΜΟΝΙΔΟ of the ostracon findings suggests this) or identical with D. (the vocal qualities are against this). Along with statements by or about D., there is a wide variety of modern hypotheses about his teachings, his writings and his ostracism (overview: [4]).

Depending on the way in which the question of identity is answered, widely divergent dating approaches within the 5th/4th cents. BC are possible. As a student of the Pythagorean Pythocleides in the 3rd generation (schol. Pl. Alc. 1, 118c), D. was frequently considered in antiquity to be a Pythagorean and connected with the Sophists (Isoc. Or. 15,235), esp. with → Prodicus (Pl. La. 197d). There are references to D.'s own school (Porph. Comm. in Ptol. Harmonika 3,5). Statements attributed to D. or to his school concern the character, effect and linguistic record of rhythms and tones. Plato has the pupil of D., Socrates [2] (Diog. Laert. 5,2,19), report with regard to D.'s view of rhythms (Pl. Resp. 3,400b) and has him quote him: 'Styles of music are never disrupted without <the disrupting of the > greatest political customs' (ibid. 3,424c, cf. 424d–425a) — a reference to the ethical power of music. According to the D. school, 'songs and dances arise when the soul is moved: frank, beautiful songs mould the soul accordingly, whereas the opposite kind of songs have the opposite effect' (Ath. 14,628c). The pedagogical function of music is consequently recognized and described for the first time. The D. school showed that 'sounds shape character (→ *ēthos*) in young and old' (Arist. Quint. 2,14). D. himself said that a 'singing, kithara-playing child ... should reveal bravery, level-headedness and justness' (Philod. De musica 7 and 55 KEMKE).

It has been assumed that D. wrote a dialogue and a list of keys [4. 39 f., 43 f.]. According to Philodemus (De musica 104 f. KEMKE), D. held a speech about the ethical power of music, possibly to the Areopagites. Questions regarding the content and influence of this speech led to the endeavour to reconstruct it with the help of the D. fragments and their textual surrounds [2].

According to Aristotle [6], Damonides (Damon?) was behind most of the measures of Pericles, with whom D. was related by marriage (And. 1,16), and was ostracized because of the introduction of judicial pay (Aristot. Ath. Pol. 27,4). Plutarch calls D. a megalomaniac with a tendency towards tyranny and sees in him the political trainer and rabble-rouser of Pericles disguised as a music teacher and mocked in the Old → Comedy (Plut. Pericles 4,153–154). In this way D. was regarded in the 19th cent. as the driving force in the Periclean period [1. 177–186]. However, in the 20th cent. Aristotle's and Plutarch's sources were questioned as biased [3. 34 f.].

Every attempt to make the testimonials about D. agree with each other is based on ignoring at least one source, the acceptance of the errors of an author or erroneous passing down of information etc. and can at best demonstrate a certain plausibility. The guardedness of scholars is increasing: whilst D. was mentioned four times in CAH[1] (vol. 5, 1927) and LESKY[2] (1963) dedicated a ch. to him (336–337), he is absent in CAH[2] (1992) and his ch. is missing in LESKY[3] (1971).
→ Music IV. E.; → Sophists

1 M. DUNCKER, Die Geschichte des Altertums, vol. 9, 1886 2 F. LASSERRE (ed.), Plutarque, De la musique, 1954, 53–87 (with French trans. and comm.)
3 K. MEISTER, D., der polit. Berater des Perikles, in: Riv. Storica dell' Antichità 3, 1973, 29–45 4 R. WALLACE, Damone di Oa, in: Quaderni Urbinati 5, 1991, 30–53 (for the fragment editions: 32). RO. HA.

Damophilus (Δαμόφιλος; *Damóphilos*).
[1] Coroplast and painter, probably from Magna Graecia. Together with Gorgasos he decorated the Temple of Ceres in Rome (493 BC) with murals and terracotta pediment figures and added artist's epigrams. Later renovations preserved both of these.

FUCHS/FLOREN, 427, 440; OVERBECK, no. 616, 1647 (sources); I. SCHEIBLER, Griech. Malerei der Ant., 1994. R.N.

[2] Rich property owner from Enna, who treated the slaves in an extremely inhumane fashion, as did his wife Megallis, thereby triggering the first Sicilian slave war in *c.* 136 BC. Following the occupation of Enna by the insurgents, he was murdered there in the theatre and his wife was thrown from the cliffs (Posid. FGrH 87 F 7 near Athens. 12,542b; Diod. Sic. 34,2,10ff., from Posid.).

K.R. BRADLEY, Slavery and Rebellion in the Roman World 140 B.C.–70 B.C., 1989, 48ff., 58, 62, 81, 105; W.Z. RUBINSOHN, Die großen Sklavenaufstände der Ant., 1993, 50; J. VOGT, Sklaverei und Humanität, [2]1972, 26. K.MEI.

Damophon (Δαμοφῶν; *Damophôn*) Sculptor from Messene. Based on prosopographic and historic evidence, it would seem that he was active from the end of the 3rd cent. BC until 168 BC; most of his divine statues known from written records must have been produced in Arcadia prior to the earthquake in 183 BC. He worked on colossal acroliths and was entrusted with the repair of Phidias' Zeus in → Olympia. Of a group of gods in the Asclepius shrine in Messene, the head and foot of the statues of Apollo and Hercules have survived. The most significant of his works is his group of colossal cult statues in → Lycosura with Despoina, Demeter, Artemis and Anytus. Three heads and a relief fragment of a cloak are still in existence. The reconstruction is based on an image on a coin from the imperial period.

P. MORENO, Scultura ellenistica, 1994, 502–519 (fig.); OVERBECK, no. 745,2, 1557–1564 (sources); R.R.R. SMITH, Hellenistic sculpture, 1991, 240–241 (fig.); STEWART 94–96, 303–304; P. THEMELIS, Damophon von Messene, in: AK 36, 1993, 24–40; Id., D. of Messene, in: K.A. SHEEDY (ed.), Archaeology in the Peloponnese, 1994, 1–37. R.N.

Damostratus (Δαμόστρατος; *Damóstratos*). Author of an epigram on Meleager's 'Garland' (Anth. Pal. 9,328): a 'Damostratus, son of Antilas' (v. 3) dedicates wooden statues and boar skins to the Naiads. The attribution seems questionable as does the very existence of the otherwise unknown author (D. of Apamea, author of *Halieutiká* (Ἁλιευτικά), dates from a time post-Meleager, i.e. after the first half of the first cent. BC).

GA I,1,80; 2,230f. E.D.

Damoxenus (Δαμόξενος; *Damóxenos*). Attic comedic author of the 3rd cent. BC, known to have been victorious at the Dionysia once [1. Testimonia 2]. There is evidence for two plays. His Σύντροφοι contains the longest speech by a cook preserved in a comedy (fr. 2: 68 verses); the speaker presents himself as a disciple of Democritus and more especially of Epicurus and is scornful of everyone who is not, even the Stoics.

1 PCG V, 1986, 1–7. H.-G.NE.

Dan (Hebr. *Dān*, Greek Δάν; *Dán*, in Ios. Δάνα, Δάνος; *Dána, Dános*).

[1] Son of Jacob and eponym of an Israelite tribe (Gen. 30,1–6), which eventually settled near the city of Laish/Leshem, which was then renamed after the tribe (Judg. 18,2–9; Jos. 19,40–48).

[2] City at the foot of Mt Hermon, 20 km north of Lake Hule, identified with Tall al-Qāḍī at the central source of the Jordan on the basis of a Greek-Aramaic bilingual inscription (3rd/2nd cents. BC) and the continuity of the name and particulars (Eus. On. 76,6–8; Jos. Ant. 5,178; 8,226). As the northernmost town in Israel, it features in stereotyped descriptions of the national boundaries (1 Sam. 3,20; 1 Kgs 5,5 and passim; → Bersabe). Under its pre-Israelite name of Laish/Leshem, it appears in Egyptian apotropaic texts (18th cent. BC) and in a list of towns made in the time of Thutmosis III (15th cent. BC). Excavations have provided evidence of intermittent settlement since Early Bronze II. A podium (18.5m × 18.5m) made of rusticated ashlars with a large stair dating from Iron II would seem to be either the substructure of a palace [5] or an open-air sanctuary or temple connected with the cult introduced by Jeroboam I (1 Kgs 12,26–33) [1; 4]. It is disputed as to whether the pre-deuteronomistic core of 1 Kgs 12 (v. 29a; 30b?) allows historical conclusions to be drawn regarding an 'imperial sanctuary' in D., as in the biblical texts only Bethel is mentioned in this respect (Am 7,13; cf. Hos. 10,5). The negative (!) aetiology of the sanctuary in Judg. 17–18 criticizes the local cult centring on D. (from the perspective of Bethel?), the existence of which has also now been proved via a Greek-Aramaic bilingual inscription dating from the 3rd/2nd cents. BC: 'Zoilus has taken a vow to the god in D. ...' (cf. Am 8,14). A fragment of an Aramaic stele [2] sheds some light on the complicated situation of the Northern Kingdom of Israel during the Aramaean Wars of the 9th cent. (1 Kgs 20; 22). D. was probably incorporated into the province of Megiddo in 733/32 by Tiglatpileser III (2 Kgs 15,29; Judg. 18,30).
→ Daphne [3]; → Judah and Israel

1 A. BIRAN, Die Wiederentdeckung der alten Stadt Dan, in: Antike Welt 15, 1984, 27–38 2 Id., An Aramaic Stele Fragment from Tel Dan, in: IEJ 43, 1993, 81–98 3 H.M. NIEMANN, Die Daniten, 1985 4 W.I. TOEWS, Monarchy and Religious Institution in Israel under Jerobeam 1, 1993 5 H. WEIPPERT, Palästina in vorhell. Zeit, 1988, 540 Ongoing reports on excavations can be found in: IEJ. M.K.

Danacia

D. Quartilla Aureliana. Wife of the senator Aiacius (AE 1968, 518, 523). W.E.

Danae (Δανάη; *Danáē*). Mythical daughter of → Acrisius, the king of Argus, and Euridice or Aganippe (Hom. Il. 14,319f.; Hes. fr. 129; 135MW; Hyg. Fab. 63). She was imprisoned by her father to keep her from any contact with the outside world following a pronouncement by the oracle that he would be killed by his grandson. Zeus approached D. in the form of a shower of gold and she became pregnant with → Perseus (Pind. Pyth. 10,44f.; 12,9ff.; Soph. Ant. 944ff.; Isocr. 10,59; Ov. Met. 4,610f.). When Acrisius discovered this he put her and the child into a chest and threw them in the sea (Simon. fr. 543 PMG). They were washed ashore in Seriphus and taken in by Dictys, the brother of King Polydectes. Supported by Perseus, D. refused to marry Polydectes. The king then sent Perseus on a mission to kill Medusa and tried to overcome D.'s resistance but she escaped to a sanctuary. On his return, Perseus turned Polydectes to stone using the head of the Gorgon and made Dictys the king. D. then returned to Argus with her son (Pherec. FGrH 3F10ff.; Apollod. 2,26; 34ff.). According to Verg. Aen. 7,410ff., D. ended up in → Latium, where she settled and became the progenitrix of → Turnus. The D. myth was a popular subject in Attic and Roman drama (Aeschyl., Soph., Eur., Cratin., Liv. Andron., Naev.).

J. Escher, s.v. D., RE 4, 2084–2086; J.-J. Maffre, s.v. D., LIMC 3.1., 325–337. R.HA.

Danai (Δαναοί; *Danaoí*). Middle Helladic ethnic group [1] of uncertain etymology; mentioned in Egypt in the 14th cent. BC on the base of the monument to Amenophis III in Karnak as *Danaia* (*tniw*) in connection with the Argolid/Peloponnese [2], possibly also connected with the *Danuna* belonging to the sea peoples, who were conquered by Ramses III in 1190 BC [3]. Used in the Homeric epics as a metric variant, as are 'Argeioi' and → 'Achaean', to describe the Greek population as a whole (e.g. Il. 9,34ff.; 9,370f.) [4]. Following the same tradition, it is used by Pindar as a collective term for Argives, Mycenaeans and Spartans (P. 4,48). The connection with Danaos [5], the mythical founder of Argus, after whom the Pelasgians were renamed as D., seems to have been made at a later stage (Hdt. 7,94; Eur. Archelaus, fr. 228 TGF; Str. 5,221; Steph. Byz. s.v. Ἄργος). Pausanias (7,1,7) mentions the D. as a special name for the Argives. The gifts of the D., which brought misfortune, — a reference to the wooden horse — became proverbial. (Verg. Aen. 2,49).

→ Sea Peoples, migration of

1 F. Schachermeyer, Griech. Frühgesch., 1984, 51 2 E. Edel, Ortsnamenlisten aus dem Totentempel Amenophis III., 1966 3 G.A. Lehmann, Umbrüche und Zäsuren im östl. Mittelmeeraum und Vorderasien z.Z. der 'Seevölker'-Invasionen um und nach 1200 v.Chr., in: HZ 262, 1996, 14, n. 18 4 G. Steiner, s.v. Δαναοί, Lex. des frühgriech. Epos, 1982, 217ff. 5 F. Schachermeyr, Die griech. Rückerinnerung im Lichte neuer Forsch., 1983, 105.

G. A. Lehmann, Die polit.-histor. Beziehungen der Ägäis-Welt des 15.–13. Jh. v. Chr. zu Ägypt. und Vorderasien, in: J. Latacz (ed.), Zweihundert Jahre Homerforsch., 1991, 105–126. B.SCH.

Danais (Δαναΐς; *Danaís*) or Danaídes (Δαναΐδες; *Danaides*). The title of a 6,500 hexameter epic dealing with the fate of the → Danaids and their flight from the sons of Aigyptos to Argus.

EpGF 141.

Danake (δανάκη; *danákē*). In ancient written sources (Hsch. 219; Poll. 9,82 i.a.) the *danake* is a silver Persian coin — the name derives from *danak* — which weighed slightly more than an Attic *obolós* (*c.* 0.9g). Together with the silver half-*danake* (ἡμιδανάκιον; *hēmidanákion*), the *danake* should probably be linked to coins from Sidon (1/16 shekel) and Aradus, as a provincial coinage, since the coins are mainly found in the Levant. The *danake* was occasionally used as an obolos for the dead.

→ Charon's fare; → Obolos; → Siqlu

F. Hultsch, Griech. und röm. Metrologie, ²1882, 592f.; BMC, Gr., Arabia cxxiv; Schrötter, s.v.D., 119. A.M.

Danaus, Danaids (Δαναός, Δαναΐδες; *Danaós, Danaídes*). Having quarrelled with his twin brother Aigyptos, according to the myth D. flees Egypt with his 50 daughters (the Danaids) for the Argolis and is given asylum there (Aesch. Supp. 1; Danaids TrGF 3 fr. 43–46; T 70 [1; 2]). However, the 50 sons of Aigyptos pursued the girls to Argos and wanted to force marriage on them. D. persuaded his daughters to pretend to go through with this, but then to decapitate the bridegrooms on the wedding night. Only one, Hypermestra, did not carry out the plan, but instead rescued her Lynceus (Pind. Nem. 10,6). A variety of resolutions of the murderous deed are recorded: a) the D. buried their husbands and were released from their blood guilt by Athene and Hermes on the orders of Zeus (Apollod. 2,22 according to Aesch. Suppl). b) D. became king of Argos, as successor to Pelasgus. Then he put Hypermestra on trial, at the Kriterion in Argus; but she was acquitted (Paus. 2,19,6). The other daughters, for whom no husbands could be found, were put forward as trophies in competitions (with varying degrees of success: Pind. Pyth. 9,111–116, or Paus. 3,12,2) [3]. Their unions resulted in the beginning of the Danai, who then superseded the Pelasgians. c) Lynceus killed his brothers' murderers; they prepared their bridal bath in the Underworld by continuously pouring water into a tub that had holes in the bottom. This was later seen as a 'fitting punishment' (Ov. Met. 4, 462 i.a.) [4], which went back to a tradition of Lower Italy, in which the D. were presented as examples of those not initiated into the Mysteries [5]; one of the first depictions of this is contained in the pictures of the Underworld by Polygnotus on Delphi (Paus. 10,31,9). By contrast, in the Argolis the D. were seen as the image of springs and beneficent in the dry area of the Argolis, as in the case of the Amymone spring, who married Poseidon [6; 7].

In genealogical terms, the origins in Belus (Baal) and Anchineo, the daughter of Neilus, emphasize the ancient nature of the culture of the → Argolis as does the primacy of cultural technologies such as the *pentekonteros* or irrigation techniques (Str. 1,23) and the → Thesmophoria, which the D. supposedly brought with them from Egypt (Hdt. 2,171). On the other hand, the foreign nature of the D. was used in polemics against the autochthony of Athens (in the early epic *Danais* PEG fr. 2; Isocr. 10,68; Plat. Menex. 245 D). In Aesch. Supp. the D. are, however, able (with black skin: v. 71) to explain their origins in Argos: when Io was fleeing from Hera, she bore Zeus' son Epaphus in Egypt, whose daughter Libye was Belus' mother

(Aesch. Supp. 291–325). The historicizing interpretation that the D. migrated from Egypt during the Bronze Age is put forward by Hdt.; the connection between Argos and Rhodos is integrated as a 'stop on the journey' (Hdt. 2,181 cf. [8. 151]). The evidence of an Egyptian inscription that there was a kingdom of the Danai in Greece did not lead to the myth [8; 9; 10].

Interpretations of the myth: a) narrative motif, the precursor to which was a Hittite myth in which 30 youths look for their 30 sisters [11; 12]. b) numerous metamythical associations which were locally linked with the springs bearing the names of the D. (→ Amymone), as well as with the festival of lights at Lyrceia, the place they landed (Paus. 2,38,4) or also Danaus' heroon. (Paus. 2,20,6–9) [13]. In the Roman era the → gerousia also derived from D. (IG IV 579). c) Social institution of young women (groups of 50, referred to polemically by Hecataeus FGrH 1 F 19) of an age entitled to start a family [14].

1 A.F. Garvie, Aeschylus, Supplices, 1969 2 H.F. Johansen, E.W. Whittle, Aeschylus, Supplices, 1980 3 L.R. Farnell, Pindar 2, 1932 4 F. Bömer, Ovids Met. 4, 1976, up to v. 462 5 Parker, Miasma, 1983, 212f., 381 6 A.B. Cook, Zeus 3, 1940, 355–370 7 M. Piérart, Argos assoiffée, in: Id. (ed.), Polydipsion Argos, BCH-Suppl. 22, 1992, 119–156 8 E. Meyer, Forsch. zur Alten Gesch. 1, 74 9 F. Schachermeyr, Die griech. Rückerinnerung, in: SAWW 404, 1983, 91–121 10 G.A. Lehmann, in: J. Latacz (ed.), 200 Jahre Homer-Forsch., 1991, 105–126; 11 W. Burkert, Typen griech. Mythen auf dem Hintergrund myk. und oriental. Tradition, in: D. Musti et al. (ed.), La transizione dal Miceneo all' alto arcaismo, 1991, 527–536, here 534 12 H. Otten, Eine althethit. Erzählung um die Stadt Zalpa, 1973 13 W.K. Pritchett, Topography 6, 1989, 98 14 K. Dowden, Death and the Maiden, 1989, 153–165; 224–229.

G. Steiner, s.v. Danaos, Lex. des frühgriech. Epos 2, 217–219; M. Bernal, Black Athena 1, 1987; M.L. West, The Hesiodic Catalogue of Women, 1985, 154; O. Waser, s.v. Danaiden, RE 4, 2087–2091; P. Friedländer, Argolica, diss. 1905, 5–30; G.A. Megas, Die Sage von Danaos, in: Hermes 68, 1933, 415–428; F. Graf, Eleusis und die orphische Dichtung, in: RGVV 33, 1974, 107–119; E. Keuls, The Water Carriers in Hades, 1974; Id., s.v. Danaides, LIMC 3.1, 337–341; 3.2, 249–253.

C.A.

Dance

I. Egypt and Ancient Orient II. Classical Antiquity

I. Egypt and Ancient Orient

As in all ancient culture, dance played an important role in the Ancient Orient as well as in Egypt; the documentary evidence for the latter, however, is incomparably better, both in pictures and in texts — there was hardly a part of life not involving dance: dances accompanied 'rites of passage' were magic-apotropaic, ecstatic, worshipful, amusing-entertaining, and even eroticizing. Children, women, and men danced together in separate groups; alongside, there were professional male and female dancers, who had been specifically trained in order to dance before deities, the king, or high-ranking dignitaries. Pictures and texts from Egypt make it possible to distinguish between various kinds of dance, without, however, enabling a detailed reconstruction. Dances could consist of sequences of measured steps, but could also involve jumping and stamping, they could be acrobatic and even wild; the latter applies in particular to Nubian and Libyan dances. Generally, dances were accompanied by rhythmic clapping, but also by rhythmic or melodic instruments or song.

In the Ancient Orient, dance scenes have been identified from the Ceramic Neolithic period onwards (*c.* 7th millennium BC). In academic research, dance is predominantly linked (particularly by means of textual sources) with regulated religious events as well as those of a magic and courtly-festive, sometimes also erotic nature. Alongside, there was the spontaneous dance of everyday life, outside of the official environment. In the Near East, men, women, and unclassifiable individuals are depicted dancing alone or in groups, amongst themselves or in front of deities. Dancers were dressed or naked, and musical accompaniment was not necessarily present. Several different kinds of dance can be distinguished by means of different postures of body and limbs.

→ Feasts I.–II.; → Music I.–II.

E. Brunner-Traut, s. v. Tanz, LÄ 6, 1986, 215–231 (literature); Y. Garfinkel, Dancing and the Beginnung of Art Scenes, in: Cambridge Archaeological Journ. 8, 1998, 207–237; S. De Martino, La danza nella cultura ittita, 1989; P. Calmeyer, Federkränze und Musik, in: A. Finet (ed.), Compte rendu de la XVIIe Rencontre Assyriologique Internationale (1969), 1970, 184–195.

AR. HA., H. J. N. and J. RE.

II. Classical Antiquity

A. Term and Sources B. History C. Later Reception

A. Term and Sources

Greek and Lat. terms for dance (χορός/*chorós*) derive from the following roots: 1) *chor-*: *chorós*, 'dancing ground' (Hom. Il. 18,590, Hom. Od. 8,260), 'round dance' [4. 119–120] (cf. Eng. '*choir*' [10. 37–38], also *carol* [21]); 2) *orch-*: Greek *orcheîsthai*, 'to move about' (Ath. 1,21a), 'to dance'; Greek *orchḗstra*, 'the lowered semi-circle in a → theatre, where the choruses sang and danced' (Phot. Lex. s. v. *orchḗstra*); 3) *mim-*: Greek *mimeîsthai*, 'to mimic', originally 'to express in a dance' ([13. 119], but cf. [7]); Greek *pantómimos*, 'who expresses everything through dance' (cf. Lucian De saltatione 67), Engl. 'pantomime'; 4) *pai-*: Greek *paízein*, 'to play, to dance' (Hom. Od. 8,251; H. Hom. 3,200 f., 206); 5) *ball-*: Greek *ballízein*, 'to dance' (Ath. 8,362b; cf. It. *ballo*, Engl. 'ballet'); 6) *sal-*: Lat. *saltare*, 'to dance' (contracted from *salitare*, iterative of *salire*, 'to jump').

These terms are all connected to central aspects of Greek intellectual life. Alongside sacrifices, ritual dances by the chorus were central to the → hero cult and the veneration of the gods, and even the great Athenian → festivals: e.g. the → *dithýrambos*., which was danced around an → altar (*thymélē*), or the *kýklios chorós* ('round dance'; [14. 175–176]), thus named in contrast with the → chorus of the Attic drama, which was traditionally arranged in a square (Poll. 4,108–109), both in honour of → Dionysus. Dance was mimetic (Pl. Leg. 655d, Aristot. Poet. 1,6, 1447a, Plut. Mor. 747e): The cultic dance evoked the deity ([20. 69–70, 117; 19. 76]), the serpentine chain dance of the *géranos* retraced the → labyrinth of → Cnossus (Plut. Thes. 21; [17]), the Pyrrhic dance (war-dance; → *pyrrhíchē*) represented fighting, etc. Chorus dances were ritualized play (*paízein*). They were instrumental and fundamental to human socialization (Pol. 4,21,3–4); they educated young people (*paideúein*: Pl. Leg. 654ab, cf. 672e) and trained them [14. 185]; they allowed adults once again to be a child (*paîs*) (cf. Pl. Leg. 7,803e; Mt 18,3) [20. 1, 33]. Dance, in combination with its accompanying song and instrumentals, constituted → *mousikḗ*, the unity of those arts in word, sound, and motion, which the → Muses themselves cherished (Hes. Theog. 2–10; Pl. Alc. 1,108cd).

There are literary and archaeological sources for the dance in antiquity: On the one hand, there are philosophical treatises (Pl. Leg. 2 and 7, Plut. Mor. 747a–748d, Lucian De saltatione, Lib. Or. 64), antiquarian-lexical compilations of excerpts (Ath. 1 and 14, Poll. 4,95–110), scattered references in various literary genres and — inasmuch as their rhythm allows to draw conclusions as to the dance steps — hexametric poetry [9. 117–118; 27. 65–66] as well as choral lyrics [10. 39–40; 28]; on the other hand, there are pictorial representations (ceramics, reliefs, clay figures, etc.) as well as inscriptions. These sources do not permit a reconstruction of actual motions, but transmit a notion of the function and meaning of dance.

Greek dance encompassed various kinds of rhythmic movement, e.g. acrobatics (Xen. Symp. 2,11; [30. 65–68]), ball games (Hom. Od. 8,370–380), and procession (*prosódion*; [16. 74]). With the exception of the → satyrs, who danced with the → maenads, and Apollo as → *chorēgós* ('leader of the chorus') of the → Muses, mixed-sex groups (*anamíx*: Eust. in Hom. Il. 1166) were rare (Hom. Il. 18,593–594; Hom. Od. 23,147; Lucian De saltatione 12, [30. 60–64; 27. 55]). On geometric vases, groups of dancing girls prevail [30. 55; 27. 54–55], and they were also a favourite with choral lyricists (Plut. Mor. 1136f). Thus, Greek lyric and dance genres overlap, as they did in the original Cretan → *hypórchēma* ('dance subordinate' to song: Ath. 14,628d). Performance practice seems to have been characterized by the pre-eminence of → *mímēsis*: apart from the holding on to wrists (Hom. Il. 18,594) or hips and the linking of arms in early Greek round dances [27. 56–58], physical contact between dancers is rare, presumably because it would restrict gestures (*cheironomía*: Ath. 14,629b) .

B. History

The earliest evidence of dance in the Aegean dates from the Minoan and Mycenaean period, e.g. clay figurine groups representing round dances [19. 34, fig. 7, 53, fig. 16]. Crete was seen as the cradle of dance (Ath. 5,181b, 14,630b, [18]); Homer (Hom. Il. 16,617–618, 18,590–592) as well as the fragment of an Aeolian poem (294,16 Lobel/Page) link dance with the island, which was also the home of the → Curetes, who were said to have received dance as a gift from → Rhea (Lucian De saltatione 8). Homer's description of the shield wrought by Hephaestus (Hom. Il. 18,490-496 and 593–602) contains the earliest dance scenes: circular and chain dances (as on 8th-cent. geometric vases [27]) at wedding celebrations or grape harvest festivals. From roughly the same period as these vases dates the 'Dipylon Krater' (Athens, NM 92), with the oldest alphabetic inscription: 'Whoever dances (*paízei*) the best of all dancers (*orchēstôn*), shall receive me' (LSAG 68) — early evidence for the competitive nature of Greek dance.

The earliest information about dance in → Sparta dates back to the 7th cent. BC. In Sparta, the → agora was called *chorós* (Paus. 3,11,9), and foreign artists such as → Terpander or the Cretan → Thaletas were entrusted with the composition (*katástasis*) of round dances and the teaching of their music; they then introduced the *Gymnopaidíai* festival with round dances performed in Apollo's honour (Plut. Mor. 1134bc). This was the beginning of Greek choral lyrics on the Peloponnese; its textual tradition begins with → Alcman's → *parthéneia* ('maiden songs'). According to Aristotle (Poet. 4,14,1449a), the *dithýrambos* in turn was the root of → tragedy. This statement is controversial [22. 89–97], but not the role of dance in Attic drama [23. 246–257; 24. 497]. *Emméleia*, → *kórdax*, and *síkinnis* were the names of the choral dances in tragedy, comedy or satyr play respectively (Ath. 1,20e), whose poets were called 'dancers' (*orchēstaí*: Ath. 1, 22a); Aeschylus is said to have invented numerous *schḗmata orchēstiká* ('dance positions': Plut. Mor. 747c, cf. Poll. 105, Ath. 629f) (Ath. 1,21de).

The increase in literary as well as archaeological Greek sources in the 5th/4th cents. BC allows a wider view on dance. Alongside the already mentioned round dances, the ecstatic dance of the → maenads (cf. Eur. Bacch. 862–866 with [16. figs. 12a–22]) stands out, as do Pyrrhic dances and sympotic dance performances, the latter often by professional female dancers (Xen. Symp. 2 and 9, [26. 223–233]). The most important source on dance in the → polis is → Plato's *Nómoi (Laws)*: on the road (Pl. Leg. 625a) between Cnossus, where Daedalus [1] set out the dancing-floor for Ariadne (Hom. Il. 18,590–592), and the cave, where the → Curetes with their dance protected the infant Zeus from his father → Kronos (Str. 10,3,11 and 13), travellers from Crete, Sparta, and Athens talk about the divine origin of dance (Pl. Leg. 653c–654a), the importance of dance in education (654b-e, 672e, 795e–796d), its mimetic quality (655d) and ethical power (656ab, 669b, 790e–791b), about choric institutions to advance and regulate dance (656d–672e, 798e–803b), as well as various kinds of dance (814e–816d).

In the Hellenistic period (3rd–1st cents. BC), choric dance lost its key position through the development of instrumental virtuosity and the fragmentation of *mousikḗ* — still described as intact by Plato — as well as the increasing professionalization of theatres and festivals (→ *technítai*). By the time of Diogenes [15] (2nd cent. BC), dramatic chorus dances had ceased to exist (cf. Philod. De musica 4,7,1–8). The → *pantómimos* took over the subjects of tragedy, which was turning into mere reading-matter (Lucian De saltatione 37 ff., 61), but he no longer possessed the religious-ethical power of its former dance, which had once prompted Plato to see the gods as 'fellow dancers' (Pl. Leg. 2,653e).

Thus it was that the Roman society of the Imperial age appeared ambivalent towards dance, prompting Seneca [1] maior for example to refer to dance as a — or more specifically *his* — 'disease' (*morbus*) (Sen. Controv. 3,10; cf. Sall. Catil. 25,2, Plin. Ep. 7,24,4–5, Macrob. Sat. 3,14,4–7), an attitude which in the Church Fathers, e.g. Augustine, turned into a generally negative view of dance (PL 36,254,11 and 277,1). Opponents of dance in the Imperial age as well as its Greek-speaking proponents (Plutarchus [2], Lucianus [1], Libanius) mainly referred to the *pantómimos*; references to other kinds of dance or even to ethical-religious aspects of dance are rare (Serv. Ecl. 5,73; Sen. Dial. 9,17,4; Acta Iohannis 94–96 [1. 198–207; 15. 59–67]; → Salii [2]). Overview of Roman dances: [29. 147–173; 31. 175–202].

C. Later Reception

Humanists such as J. C. Scaliger (*Poetices* 1,18, 1561) and J. Meursius (*Orchestra*, 1618) wrote scientific treatises on Greek dance, whereas popularizers like Th. Arbeau claimed it as the model for contemporary dance in an attempt to legitimize and ennoble the latter (*Orchésographie*, 1588, [2. fol. 2^v–6^v]) — two basic views which continued into the 19th cent. [25. 76]. Around the turn to the 20th cent., French scholars concluded from cinematographic insights that ancient depictions of several dancers 'analyzed' but one individual movement sequence, and that it was possible to 'reanimate' such sequences [8; 26; 24]; cf. in opposition to that German and English views from a historical-philological perspective [16; 29; 19; 28; 20]. As an alternative to the academic French ballet, perceived as soulless and mechanical [5. 75], some female dancers referred back to Greek dances [3. 58–97] (e.g. Isadora Duncan [6. 26]); this led to the development of 'free' or 'modern dance' [3. 33–39]. Jaques-Dalcroze, too, was inspired by Greek dance [12. 158; 26. 245–271]. Almost a century later, [11] declared the 'matriarchal' unity of *mousikḗ* with its ritual-maenadic dance the feminist alternative to the patriarchal models of art, science, and society.

→ Chorus; → Feasts (III. 6.); → Gestures; → Comedy; → Lyric poetry; → Metre; → Music; → Rhythm; → Tragedy; → Dance

1 E. Junod (ed.), Acta Johannis, in: Corpus Christianorum Series Apocryphorum 1, 1983 2 Th. Arbeau, Orchésographie, 1588 (repr. 1989) 3 G. Brandstetter, T.-Lektüren, 1995, 58–117, 182–206 4 A. Brinkmann, Altgriech. Mädchenreigen, in: BJ 130, 1925, 118–146 5 I. Duncan, My Life, 1927 6 Id., Écrits sur la Danse, 1927 7 G. Else, 'Imitation' in the Fifth Century, in: CPh 53, 1958, 73–90 8 M. Emmanuel, La danse grecque antique, 1896 (repr. 1987, etc.) 9 T. Georgiades, Der griech. Rhythmus, 1949 10 Id., Musik und Rhythmus bei den Griechen, 1958 11 H. Göttner-Abendroth, Die tanzende Göttin, 1991 12 E. Jaques-Dalcroze, Le rhythme, la musique et l'éducation, 1920 13 H. Koller, Die Mimesis in der Ant., 1954 14 Id., Ἐγκύκλιος Παιδεία, in: Glotta 34, 1955, 174–189 15 J. Kroll, Die christl. Hymnodik bis zu Klemens von Alexandreia, 1921 16 L. Lawler, The Maenads, in: Memoirs of the American Acad. in Rome 6, 1927, 69–112 17 Id., The Geranos Dance, in: TAPhA 77, 1946, 112–130 18 Id., The Dance in Ancient Crete, in: G. Mylonas (ed.), Stud. Presented to D. Robinson, 1951, 23–51 19 Id., The Dance in Ancient Greece, 1964 20 S. Lonsdale, Dance and Ritual Play in Greek Rel., 1993 21 Oxford English Dictionary², vol. 2, s. v. Carol, 907 22 Pickard-Cambridge/Webster 23 Pickard-Cambridge/Gould/Lewis 24 G. Prudhommeau, La danse grecque antique, 1965 25 S. Schroedter, T.-Lit. als Quelle zum T., in: S. Dahms (ed.), Der T. — ein Leben, FS F. Derra de Moroda, 1997, 161–179 26 L. Séchan, La danse grecque antique, 1930 27 R. Tölle, Frühgriech. Reigentänze, 1964 28 T. B. L. Webster, The Greek Chorus, 1970 29 F. Weege, Der T. in der Ant., 1926 30 M. Wegner, Musik und T. (ArchHom 4), 1968, 40–69 31 G. Wille, Musica Romana, 1967.

RO. HA.

Dandamis An Indian sage, who is supposed to have come into contact with Greeks at the beginning of 326 BC, when Alexander's army was encamped in Taxila. The Greeks with whom he had contact were either anonymous scouts (according to Megasthenes in Str. 15,1,68 and Arr. Anab. 7,2,2–4, according to Onesicritus in Str. 15,1,64–65, the name Mandanis is mentioned here; Plut. Alexander 65,1–3), or Onesicritus and Alexander himself (as per PGenev. 271 [1; 2], the basis is the 2nd section of the Palladius letter about the Brahmins [3]). D. was both master and scholar. He appears in almost all reports as the antagonist of the Indian sage → Calanus. The latter makes fun (as detailed by Strabo) of Onesicritus; D. in comparison is polite and open-minded: he asks him questions about the wisdom of the Greeks. Calanus accepts Alexander's suggestion to follow him to his country. D. on the other hand, stays in India and thereby demonstrates that as a sage he knows how to safeguard his freedom in relation to the ruler. In later texts D. appears as 'the wisest of all men', who is distinguished by his godliness, goodness of heart, selflessness and restraint.

No works by D. have been preserved, apart from two apocryphal Latin letters dating from the early 4th cent. AD, forming part of a fictitious exchange of letters between Alexander and D., here known as Dindimus, see [4].

1 V. Martin, Un recueil de diatribes cyniques; PGenev. inv. 271, in: MH 16, 1959, 77–115 2 W.H. Willis, K. Maresch, The Encounter of Alexander with the Brahmans, in: ZPE 74, 1988, 59–83 3 W. Berghoff, in: Beitr. zur klass. Philol. 24, 1967, 1–55 4 B. Kübler (ed.), Alexandri Magni regis Macedonum et Dindimi regis Bragmanorum de philosophia per litteras facta collatio, 1888.

J. André, Echos poétiques d'un brahmane, in: REL 60, 1983, 43–49; B. Berg, D. An Early Christian Portrait of Indian Asceticism, in: CeM 31, 1970, 269–305; B. Berg, The letter of Palladius on India, in: Byzantion 44, 1974, 5–16; G. Ch. Hansen, Alexander und die Brahmanen, in: Klio 45, 1965, 351–380; U. Wilcken, Alexander der Große und die ind. Gymnosophisten, in: SBAW 1923, 150–183. C.M.-P.

Daneion (δάνειον; *dáneion*). The → loan, limited assignment of fungible goods (in kind or money) was an everyday way of doing business throughout the regions inhabited by the Greeks. It took place between private individuals as well as in public life. The lenders were often banks or temples and the borrowers often states, which often also owed debts to private individuals (e.g. IG VII 3172: Orchomenus is indebted to Nicareta). This practise was generally known as *daneion*, but sometimes → *chrēsis* was used; the → *eranos* loan is a special type. The *daneion* was set up with a fixed repayment term, and the usual rate of interest was between 1 and 2 drachmae per mina per month (= 12–24 % p.a.). In the case of loans in kind, 50% interest (*hēmiólion*) had to be paid at the time of the next harvest. In terms of the financing of maritime trade, the *daneion* was used in the guise of a 'fenus nauticum' (only permissible in Athens for the import of grain), which entailed a higher rate of interest as a risk premium. However, the capital and interest only had to be repaid once the ship arrived intact at the destination for which the *daneion* had been arranged. The ship, and sometimes also the cargo, stood guarantee for the repayment of this *daneion*. In the case of defaulting on repayment of the *daneion* in Athens, → *blabes dike* was permissible against the borrower, with the charge that he was 'robbing' the lender. There are numerous instances of 'fictitious loans' to be found in the papyri, where a debtor knowingly falsely confirms the receipt of a certain sum as a *daneion*, when in fact, for example, he owes the amount as a purchase price.

H.-A. Rupprecht, Unt. zum Darlehen im Recht der graeco-ägypt. Papyri, 1967, 6ff.; Id., Einführung in die Papyruskunde, 1994, 118f.; G. Thür, Hypothekenurkunde eines Seedarlehens, in: Tyche 2, 1987, 229ff. G.T.

Dantheletae (Δανθηλῆται/*Danthēlêtai*; also *Dentheleti*). Thracian tribe inhabiting the area around the upper reaches of the → Strymon and the area to the west reaching as far as Axius. Earliest mention was by Theopompus (FGrH 115 F 221) for 340/339 BC. Philip V twice laid waste to their territory on his Thracian campaigns (184 and 181 BC: Liv. 39,53,12; 40,22,9; Pol. 23,8,4). In 88 BC, the D. acted as allies of Rome in the quelling of a Macedonian revolt. They attacked this province in 86/5 together with the Maedi, Dardani and Scordisci. In 57 and 56, the *proconsul* of Macedonia, L. Calpurnius Piso, caused the D. to rise up against Rome (Cic. Pis. 84; Prov. cons. 4; Sest. 94). In 29 and 28 BC, the → Bastarnae twice invaded their territory; at the request of their king, Sitas the *proconsul* of Macedonia, M. → Licinius Crassus, (Cass. Dio 51,23,4; 25,3) came to their aid each time. It is unknown whether they belonged to the Thracian vassal state prior to AD 45. The final occasion that they are mentioned as a tribe is by Cass. Dio 54,20 in 16 BC, when they invaded Macedonia together with the Scordisci. In the first cent. AD, many D. were forced into the *auxilia* of both Germaniae. During the Roman era in Thrace a strategia Δανθηλητική (*Danthēlētikḗ*) existed, which was divided on a temporary basis (ὀρεινή and πεδιασία, IGR 1,677).

B. Gerov, Proučvanija vărhu zapadnotrakijskite zemi prez rimsko vreme, in: Annales de l'université de Sofia 54,3 (1959/60), 1961, 74ff.; Id., Zum Problem der Strategien im röm. Thrakien, in: Klio 52, 1970, 130f.; Ch. Danov, Die Thraker auf dem Ostbalkan von der hell. Zeit bis zur Gründung Konstantinopels, in: ANRW VII.1, 1979, 90, 117, 124. I.v.B.

Danuvius (Danube) see → Ister [2]

Daochus (Δάοχος; *Dáochos*).

[1] **D.I.** from Pharsalus, son of Agias, was the → *tagos* of the Thessalian *koinon* for 27 years (*c.* 431–404 BC?); his *tageia* was reputedly a time of peace and prosperity (Syll.³ 273) [1. 110f.].

[2] **D. II.** high-ranking Thessalian, grandson of D. [1]. In 338 BC, Philip II sent him together with others to the Thebans to procure support against Athens (Pol. 18,4,4; Dem. Or. 18,211; Plut. Demosth. 18,1; Theopomp. FGrH 115 F 209 [2. 191]). After 336 he was a representative for the Thessalian *koinon* in the Delphic Amphictyony and played an important role in the establishment of the new staff of *tamiai* (FdD 3,5, 47 I 2, index s.v. D.).

1 M. Sordi, La lega tessala, 1958 2 J. R. Ellis, Philipp II and Macedonian Imperialism, 1976. M.MEI. and ME.STR.

Daorsi An 'Illyrian' *civitas* with only 17 *decuriae* in the *conventus* of Narona (prov. of *Dalmatia*, today in Bosnia Herzegovina and partly in Croatia), one of the most Hellenized peoples on the coast of Dalmatia. The D. settled on the left bank of the Naro (Neretva) from Bijelo polje as far as Trebinjska Šuma, i.e. in the hinterland between Narona and → Epidaurum, with access to the sea and a central settlement in Gradina near Ošanići in the region of Stolac (Herzegovina), built according to megalithic technique with cyclopean walls, some of which were up to 6m high; excavations have uncovered large quantities of imported Greek goods, mainly from the Hellenistic era. Stolac became the later *municipium Diluntum* (disregarding several other suggestions regarding the location), which continued as the main settlement of the D. in Ošanići (located here by Evans, Truhelka and Bojanovski, the epigraphic evidence of a *beneficiarii consularis* inscription confirms this). It is not known when D. was promoted to the category of *municipium*; in view of Imperial era gentilicia under possibly the Flavian emperors or Hadrian. In the 2nd cent. BC, the D. minted their own coins bearing the legend *Daorson* and with a ship on the reverse. Hecataeus (FGrH 1 F 175) considered them to be a Thracian people, which is not confirmed either by archaeological finds (e.g. burials) or by toponomastic or onomastic material (southern Illyrian names such as *Epicadus*, *Gentius*, Pinnes, Monunius, *Plassus*, *Bato*). The name appears in various forms on coins and in literary sources: *Dáorsoi* (Pol. 32,9,2); *Daorsei* (Liv. 45,26,14); *Daórizoi* (Str. 7,5,5); *Dársioi* (App. Ill. 2); *Daoúrsioi* (Ptol. 2,16,8); *Daursi* in Roman sources, both literary and epigraphical; *Duersi/Daversi* (Plin. HN 3,143); *Daverzus* (CIL XIII 7507); *Daversus* (CIL XVI 38, ex. tab. I, v. 26, from Salona). Dependent on the Illyrian kingdom, the D. joined the Romans' side even before the fall of Genthius in 168 BC and were rewarded with immunity; they must, however, have lost this in the course of the 2nd or 1st cent. BC. Their chief enemies were the → Dalmatae, who destroyed their fortress in Ošanići. The D. were probably conquered in 34–33 BC by the future Augustus. During the Imperial era they were one of the insignificant *civitates*, as indicated by the sparse epigraphical material on the region of the D.

I. Bojanovski, Bosna i Hercegovina u antičko doba [Bosnia and Herzegovina in antiquity], Akademija nauka i umjetnosti Bosne i Herzegovine, Djela 66, Centar zu balkanološka isptivanja 6 [Monographies, Academie des sciences et des arts de Bosnie-Herzegovine 66, Centre d'études des balk. 6], 1988, 88–102; Z. Marić, Die hell. Stadt oberhalb Ošanići bei Stolac (Ostherzegowina), Ber. der Röm.-German. Kommission 76, 1995, 31–72 (pl. 1–24).
M.Š.K.

Daphitas (Δαφίτας; *Daphítas*, also Δαφίδας; *Daphídas*). Greek grammarian ('sophist' according to Val. Max. 1,8), probably from the 2nd cent. BC, if it is accepted that he lived at the same time as Attalus III (see below). The Suda (δ 99 s.v. Δαφίδας) says that he came from Telmessus in Caria and made claims in a work about Homer that the poet was not telling the truth because the Athenians did not take part in the expedition to Troy. Strabo (14,647) tells that D. was crucified on Mt Thorax near Magnesia on the Maeander, because he had written an epigram insulting the Attalids (SH 70–371): this event seems to fit with the picture of the hostility towards the ruling house of Pergamum at the time of Attalus III. D.'s fate was recounted in the ancient world in an anecdotal fashion (other than Strabo ibid., cf. Suda and Val. Max. ibid.). He is also portrayed as someone who insulted the gods, whose punishment is linked amongst other things to the misinterpretation of an orade.

→ Philology

D.C. Braund, Three Hellenistic Personages: Amynander, Prusias II, Daphidas, in: CQ 32, 1982, 350–57; O. Crusius, s.v. Daphitas, RE 4, 2134–35; J. Fontenrose, The cruciphied Daphidas, in: TAPhA 91, 1960, 83–99; SH 370–371; B. Virgilio, Epigrafia e storiografia, 1988, 105–108; Id., Gli Attalidi di Pergamo, 1993, 14–15; U. v. Wilamowitz, Commentariolum grammaticum III, 1889, 11–12 = KS IV, 631–32.
F.M.

Daphnae Egyptian city on the edge of the East Delta, today known as Tall Dafana (Egyptian Ṯbn?). According to Hdt. 2,30, it was a border fortress of → Psametichus I; archaeological discoveries dating from the New Kingdom, the 26th Dynasty and later, including fortifications, weapons and Greek ceramics. It is possible that it could also have been one of the *stratópeda* of Greek and Carian mercenaries mentioned in Hdt. 2,154. It is disputed as to whether it is the same as the OT Thachpanches.

A.B. Lloyd, Herodotus, Book II, Commentary 99–182, 1988, 137; St. Timm, Das christl.-kopt. Ägypten in arab. Zeit, 1984–92, 551–555 (cf. 2510–2514).
K.J.-W.

Daphnaeus (Δαφναῖος; *Daphnaîos*).

[1] *Strategos* in Syracuse, was supposed to relieve Acragas in 406 BC when it was besieged by the Carthaginians, but this went wrong, apparently because of his corruption (Diod. Sic. 13,86,4ff.). This failure led to the removal from office of the group of commanders, the appointment of → Dionysius [1] as an authorized *strategos* and thereby to the latter's tyrannis. Dionysius killed D. in 405 (Diod. Sic. 13,96,3). K.MEI.

[2] Epiclesis of Apollo (Anth. Pal. 9,477; Nonnus, Dion. 13,82). There is an important Apollo sanctuary in Daphne, the suburb of Antioch [1].

Burkert 227; O. Jessen, s.v. Daphaios (1), RE 4, 2135f.
R.B.

Daphne

[1] (δάφνη; *dáphnē*). Used in antiquity as a name for the plant sacred to Apollo and Artemis — the → laurel *Laurus nobilis L.* of the *Lauraceae* family, not the *Thymelaeacea genus* of the daphne with which we are familiar today (→ Cneorum). C.HÜ.

[2] (Δάφνη; *Dáphnē*). The chaste nymph D. devoted to → Artemis and who loved to hunt, was a daughter of the river god Ladon (or Peneius) and → Gaia. She fled from Apollo, who tried to force his affections on her, and turned into the laurel tree, the branches of which

Apollo used for his crown (Palaephatus 50, Mythographi Graeci p. 309 WESTERMANN). The myth explains the function of the laurel in the Apollonian cults; it interprets the supplicants' branch as a wedding symbol. The initiatory character of the metamorphosis that ends the girl's life is clearer in the extended version of the myth: at first it is → Leucippus who desires the huntress (now portrayed as the daughter of the Spartan king Amyclas); he disguises himself as a girl in order to get close to her. Apollo's jealousy leads to his unmasking (Parthenius, Erotika pathemata 15, according to Diodorus of Elaea and Phylarchus, FGrH 81 F 32; Paus. 8, 20, 1–4); this is then followed by the famous pursuit. A similar fate to D. befalls → Manto and → Sibylle (Plut. Agis 9 p. 799; Diod. Sic. 4, 66, 5–6), both identified with D. The myth was also transferred to Antioch (Philostr. VA 1, 16; Lib. Or. 11 R 302). However, Ovid's version had the most lasting effect (Met. 1, 452–467). → Daphnephoria; → Laurel; → Nymphae

K. DOWDEN, Death and the Maiden, 1989, 174–179; J. FONTENROSE, Orion, 1981, 48–86; Y. GIRAUD, La fable de D. Essai sur un type de métamorphose végétale dans la littérature et dans les arts jusqu' à la fin du XVIIe siècle, 1968; O. PALAGIA, s.v. Daphe, LIMC 3.1, 344–348 with fig. in LIMC 3.2, 255–260; W. STECHOW, Apollo und D., [2]1965; J. WULFF, Die ovidische D. und ihre Rezeption in der engl. Lit. des 16. und 17. Jh., 1987. D.B.

[3] Town on the Nahr Laddan, the largest source river for the → Jordan, 3 km southwest of → Dan, today known as Ḫirbat Dafna (Jos. Bell. Iud. 4,3; Jer. Comm. in Ez 47,18). Archaeological investigations have uncovered two settlement mounds and burial complexes dating from the Roman era.

TIR/IP 108.

[4] Suburb of → Antioch [1] with a famous sanctuary dedicated to → Apollo Daphneios and Artemis, founded by → Seleucus Nicator (Str. 16,749f.). K.B.

Daphnephoria (Δαφνηφορία; *Daphnēphoría*). A ritual carried out everywhere Apollo bore the epithet *daphnēphóros* ('branch wearer') (e.g. IG IX 2, 1027). Only the Theban ritual has been verified; the sources are Pindar, Proclus and Pausanias, who each deal with a different stage in the process. The most detailed description is by Proclus, who explains the daphnephoric ode sung by a girls' chorus (Photius 321a–321b). The ritual is supposed to have been held on an enneaeteric basis (every ninth year). A *paîs amphithalḗs* ('child flourishing on both sides') led the procession; behind him his closest male relative carried a log from an olive tree (κωπώ) dressed in women's garments, and after him came the actual Daphnephoros, who held the laurel. He wore his hair loose, and wore a robe that reached to the ground and special shoes; he was followed by the girls' chorus. The procession led to the sanctuaries of Apollo Ismenios and Galaxios. This version probably has its origins in the 4th cent. BC. Pindar (1; fr. 94b) describes a boy whose father leads the procession and whose sister leads the chorus. The sister carries the laurel in this version (l. 8). Pausanias simply mentions that every year a boy from a good family and of excellent appearance was ordained as a priest of Apollo Ismenios and appointed Daphnephoros (9,10,4). Some or even all of the Daphnephoroi dedicated tripods to Apollo Ismenios (see IG XIV 1293b = FGrH 40F1).

There are at least four distinct stages in the development of this ritual: 1. the linking of one procession, bringing the laurel to Apollo, the divine patron of the Theban polis, with a second procession carrying a decorated piece of wood, perhaps a cult image, to the sanctuary. This ritual, which also occurs during the festival of the Daedala (→ Hera), could have reached Thebes around the time the polis was formed. 2. The ritual, as described by Pindar. 3. A reorganization in the 4th cent. (when Thebes was the driving force in the Delphic → Amphiktyonia), which introduced elements of the Delphic → Septerion [2; 3]. 4. A further reorganization in the Roman imperial period [4; 5].

1 L. LEHNUS, Pindar, in: BICS 31, 1984, 61–92 2 J. DEFRADAS, Les thèmes de la propagande delphique, 1972, 97–101 3 G. ROUX, Delphes, 1976, 166–168 4 I. LOUCAS, in: Kernos 3, 1990, 213 5 SCHACHTER 83–85. A.S.

Daphnephorikon (δαφνηφορικόν; *daphnēphorikón*). A song sung by maidens at the → Daphnephoria, a festival for Apollo Ismenios in Thebes (Paus. 9,10,4). Proclus (Phot. 321a34) reports *daphnephoriká* as part of Pindar's Partheneia; the Suda s.v. Πίνδαρος counts *daphnēphoriká* amongst the 17 books (in addition to the Partheneia). POxy. 4,659 (1904) = Pind. fr. 94b SNELL-MAEHLER provides us with a substantial fragment of a *daphnēphorikón*. The poem was written in honour of Agasicles, the grandson of an Aeoladas (l. 9), to whom fr. 94a is obviously addressed. Pagondas, the son of Aeoladas and father of Agasicles, known from Thuc. 4,91–93, is also mentioned (10). The *daphnēphóros* must be a παῖς ἀμφιθαλής, i.e. is not allowed to be an orphan (Phot. 321b23f.) — Agasicles's mother is probably Andaesistrota (71). The girls' chorus is lead by Damaina, the boy's sister (66). Fr. 94c seems to have been written for Pindar's own son Daiphantus, 'for whom he also wrote a *daphnephorikon* song' (Vita Ambrosiana 3,3–5 DRACHMANN). The fragment comes from a Pindar *vita* (POxy. 2438,24ff.), which also seems to indicate that Pindar's daughters Protomache and Eumetis were in the chorus of maidens. Fr. 104b is a quote from Plut. De Pythiae oraculis 29, supposedly addressed to Apollo Galaxios; scholars of Pindar tend to attribute this to Pindar on account of the statement by Proclus (Phot. 321b30–32) that the Daphnephoria was also celebrated in honour of Apollo Chalazíou; another point of view is represented in the adespoton PMG 997.

L. LEHNUS, Pindaro: Il Dafneforico per Agasicle, in: BICS 31, 1984, 61–92. E.R.

Daphnis (Δάφνις; *Dáphnis*).

[1] Mythical cowherd of Sicilian tradition, son of → Hermes (Stesich. fr. 102 PMG = Ael. VH 10.18; Timaeus, FGrH 566 F 83; Diod. Sic. 4,84,2). He died still a youth because of an unfortunate love affair with a → nymph and was honoured with ritual mourning songs typical of those for Adonis (Theoc. 1,64ff.; 7,73ff.). In bucolic poetry he served as the ideal for the adolescent shepherd and was seen as the originator of the shepherd's song (e.g. Diod. 4,84,3). Despite the Greek name (from → *dáphnē*: 'laurel'), the figure of D. did not originate in Greek mainland tradition, but was probably brought to Sicily by Phoenician colonists as a local variant of a god type similar to Adonis/ Tammuz [1. 27ff.; 2. 285]. In sociological terms, D. represents male initiands, who symbolically 'died' when they ceased to be one of the young shepherds before officially gaining the status of an adult farmer [2. 299ff.]. In typical fashion, in a satyr play by → Sositheus, the young D. just escapes death at harvest time, then marries and inherits the estate of the Phrygian farmer → Lityerses (TrGF I 99 F 1–3SNELL). The traditional tale has an analogously positive resolution in → Longus' novel 'Daphnis and Chloe'. The apotheosis of D. is interpretable as the mythical superelevation of the change in social status between youth and adulthood, as in this apotheosis nature withers at his death but then revives (Verg. Ecl. 5,56ff.). To commemorate his transport to heaven sacrifices were made to D. annually in Sicily at a spring named after him (Serv. Ecl. 5,20). In Virgil's 5th Ecloge the D. myth appears to be used as a typological model for a political soteriology related to Caesar/Octavian [2. 311ff.].

→ Adonis; → Bucolics

1 I. TRENCSÉNYI-WALDAPFEL, Werden und Wesen der bukolischen Poesie, in: Acta antiqua Academiae Hungaricae 14, 1966, 1–31 2 G. BAUDY, Hirtenmythos und Hirtenlied, in: Poetica 25, 1993, 282–318.

W. BERG, D. and Prometheus, in: TAPhA 96, 1965, 11–23; G. CIPOLLA, Folk Elements in the Pastoral of Theocritus and Vergil, in: Journal of the University of Durban-Westville 3, 1979, 113–21; D. M. HALPERIN, The Forebears of D., in: TAPhA 113, 1983, 183–200; R. MERKELBACH, Die Hirten des Dionysos, 1988; CH. SEGAL, Poetry and Myth in Ancient Pastoral, 1981, 25–65; F. G. WELCKER, D. (in Stesichorus), in: Id., KS zur griech. Literaturgesch. I, 1844, 188–202; U. v. WILAMOWITZ-MOELLENDORFF, D., in: Id., Reden und Vorträge 1, 1925, 259–91; G. WOJACZEK, Daphnis Unt. zur griech. Bukolik, in: Beitr. zur klass. Philol. 34, 1969. G.B.

[2] Architect from Miletus; mentioned by Vitruvius (7 praef. 16) together with → Paeonius from Ephesus as the architects of a Milesian temple of Apollo, probably the → dipteros in the sanctuary of Apollo at → Didyma. As Paeonius, according to Vitruvius, was previously involved in the late classical construction of the temple of Artemis at Ephesus, the otherwise unknown D. was probably linked to the building of the Didymeion begun in *c.* 300 BC, but not with its archaic predecessor. Any observations regarding D.'s actual activities or the how the work was divided between D. and Paeonius remain purely speculative.

H. SVENSON-EVERS, Die griech. Architekten archaischer und klass. Zeit, 1996, 74, 100; W. VOIGTLÄNDER, Der jüngste Apollontempel von Didyma, 14. Beih. MDAI(I), 1975, 10, 20. C.HÖ.

Daphnoides (δαφνοειδές or χαμαιδάφνη; *daphnoeidés* or *chamaidáphnē*). The name used for two types of daphne in the texts of Dioscorides (4,146 [1. 288 = 2. 444] and 4,147 [1. 289f.= 2. 444]), for *Daphne laureola L.* or *alpina L.* from the *Thymelaecea genus* with evergreen leaves similar to laurel. When drunk, an infusion of these leaves was said to have emetic, expectorant and diuretic properties and also to promote menstruation. They were also distinguished from the varieties with leaves similar to the olive tree such as *camelaiva* (Dioscorides 4,171 [1. 320] = 4,169 [2. 464]), the mountain daphne *D. oleoides L.*, and *Thymelea*, and the southern daphne (*D. gnidium L.*, → Cneorum [3. 119]) and also from the early-flowering, lime-loving common daphne *D. mezereum L.*

1 WELLMANN 2, 2 BERENDES 3 H. BAUMANN, Die griech. Pflanzenwelt in Mythos, Kunst und Lit., 1982. C.HÜ.

Daphnus (Δαφνοῦς; *Daphnoûs*). Port of the Locri Epicnemidii (Str. 9,3,17; Plin. HN. 4,27), today known as Agios Konstantinos, situated on the coastal plain of Longus on the Euboean Gulf. From the time of the first Sacred War (*c.* 590 BC) the entire coastal strip belonged to the Phocians (Scyl. 61; Str. 9,3,1), who secured an access to the Aegean Sea via D. After the third Sacred War D. was returned to Locris in 346 BC. It was destroyed by an earthquake in 426 BC (Str. 1,3,20).

J. M. FOSSEY, The Ancient Topography of Opountian Lokris, 1990, 7, 11, 84; PRITCHETT, 4, 1982, 149–151; F. SCHOBER, Phokis, 1924, 26f. G.D.R.

Dara

[1] City in the mountain region of Apavortene in Parthia. According to Pompeius Trogus (Iust. 41,5,2–4), this place was distinguished by its strategic and geographical merits (Plin. HN 6,46) and was founded by the Parthian king → Arsaces [1] I. As the region is mentioned elsewhere (as *Apauarktikene*, Isid. by Charax, 1,13, and *Partautikene/Artakana* Ptol. 6,5), but not the city, it is assumed that the settlement diminished in importance later [1. 199–201]. Its exact location is still unknown today.

1 M. L. CHAUMONT, Études d'histoire parthe II., in: Syria 50, 1973, 197–222. J.W.

[2] City in northern Mesopotamia (Δαραί; *Daraí* in Steph. Byz.) between Nisibis (modern Nusaybin) and Mardin, on the border between the Byzantine and Neo-

Persian empires. According to tradition, the city was founded in AD 507 by the Byzantine emperor Anastasius I (and was therefore also known as → Anastasioupolis). Iustinian extended the fortifications (Iustiniana Nea). D. (frequently mentioned in Syrian texts) was repeatedly attacked and captured in the wars between Byzantium and the Sassanid empire, e.g. in AD 573 under Justinian, and was finally taken over by the Arabs [2].

1 MILLER, 741 with outline 240 2 S. FRAENKEL, s.v. Dara 2), RE 4, 2150. J.OE.

Daras

[1] River which rises in the Upper Atlas (Δύρις; *Dýris*), flows through the region to the south of the Anti-Atlas mountains and into the Atlantic Ocean, today known as Oued Dra. Other forms of the name: *Dyris*, Vitr. De arch. 8,2,6; *Darat*, Plin. HN 5,9; Δάραδος or Δάρας; *Dárados* or *Dáras*, Ptol. 4,6,6; 9; 14; *Dara*, Oros. 1,2,31. It is possible that the D. can be identified with the Λίξος (*Líxos*) mentioned by Hanno, Periplus 6 (GGM 1,5) and the Χιῶν *Chiôn* mentioned by [Scyl.] 112 (GGM 1,93).

C. T. FISCHER, s.v. D. (1), RE 4, 2152. W.HU.

[2] A river flowing into the Persian Gulf and mentioned by Ptolemy (6,8,4 N.) and Marcianus of Heraclea (Periplus maris exteri, GGM I p. 531) (modern Daryāb and also Dargabind); mentioned by Marcianus in the course of a description of the coast moving from West to East; Ptolemy saw the D. as being part of the landscape of Carmania.

C. MÜLLER, GGM I, Tabulae, T. XXVIII; ANDRÉES, Allg. Handatlas 1924/5, 154f. H.T.

Dardae (Δάρδαι; *Dárdai*). A people in north-west India, *Darada* in Old Indo-Aryan, today known as the Dards and resident in the region known as Dardistan on the upper reaches of the Indus. Hdt. 3, 102ff. places them in the region below the sources of the Indus where the Δαράδραι (*Darádrai*) mentioned by Ptol. 7,1,4 are also to be found. Also mentioned by Plin. HN 6,67 and 11,111 (*Dardae*, probably following Megasthenes), Dionys. Per. 1138, Steph. Byz. i.a. According to Megasthenes (F 23b bei Str. 15,1,44), the Δέρδαι (*Dérdai*) live on a high plateau in the east and steal gold from the gold-digging ants.

P. H. L. EGGERMONT, Orientalia Lovanensia Periodica 15, 1984. K.K.

Dardanees

[1] A people living by the river → Gyndes (modern Diyālā), whose territory was traversed by → Cyrus II on his expedition to Babylon (Hdt. 1,189). J.OE.

[2] Another form of the name for the → Dardae (Δάρδαι; *Dárdai*) of northern India. H.T.

Dardani (Δάρδανοι; *Dárdanoi*).

[1] Another term for Trojans (→ Dardanidae), used as a synonym in Hom. Il. 3,456; 7,348 and *passim*; Hom. Il. 2,819f. specifically describes → Aeneas' retinue as D.

[2] Inhabitants of the probably mythical town of Dardania on Mt Ida, supposedly founded by → Dardanus as the precursor to Troy (Hom. Il. 20,216) and ruled by the family of Aeneas. Even Strabo found no trace of it (13,1,24).

[3] Inhabitants of the area known as Dardania or the city of Dardanus on the Hellespont between Zelia and Scepsis (Apoll. Rhod. 1,931; Diod. Sic. 13,45; Str. 13,1,50f.; Apollod. 3,139).

[4] A tribe identified with the Dardani in Moesia superior, which supposedly consisted of immigrant Trojans (Solin. 2,51). T.S.

[5] Powerful Illyrian tribal group in the south-western part of Moesia superior, strongly influenced by Thrace, particularly in the east of the region. The region was within the sphere of influence of the Macedonians, who gained control over Dardania in *c.* 335 BC. However, the D. continued to strive for a certain degree of independence. In 284 BC they were united under the rule of one king and waged prolonged wars against the Macedonians. In 229 the D. defeated Demetrius II, who died soon after his defeat. Rome asserted itself in Dardania during the 1st cent. BC (Sulla, Appius Claudius Pulcher, C. Scribonius Curio). The country was finally annexed in 29/8 by M. Licinius Crassus (*cos.* 30 BC).

The D. were known as a warlike people and there is evidence of their deployment in various auxiliary units during the Roman Imperial period. Their country was famous for its wealth of ore deposits (iron, lead, silver). The Dardanian ore mines were managed independently and constituted an important part of the imperial estate. From the time of Diocletian, Dardania was administrated as a separate province with its centre in Scupi (Plin. HN 3,149; Ptol. 3,9,2).

S. DUŠANIČ, s.v. D., Dardania TIR K 34 Sofia, 1976, 39 (with sources and literature). J.BU.

Dardanidae (Δαρδανίδαι; *Dardanídai*). Descendants of the Trojan progenitor → Dardanus, who produced the Trojan ruling dynasty. The genealogy of the D., save their heroines, is recounted by Aeneas in the Illiad (Hom. Il. 20,215ff.):

The son of Dardanus, the king of Dardania on Ida, is Erichthonius, whose son is Tros. Tros's three sons are Ilus, Assaracus and → Ganymede. The last is abducted by Zeus's eagle to serve the gods as a cup-bearer (Hom. Il. 5,265f.). Ilus founds Ilium (Conon narr. 12; Str. 13,1,25), his tomb is supposed to have lain before the gates to the city (Hom. Il. 11,166). Assaracus apparently continued to live in Dardania. The D. become divided in the fourth generation. The older branch produces the kings of Troy, → Laomedon, under whom Troy is destroyed for the first time by Hercules, and his son → Priamus, whom the Illiad frequently describes as a

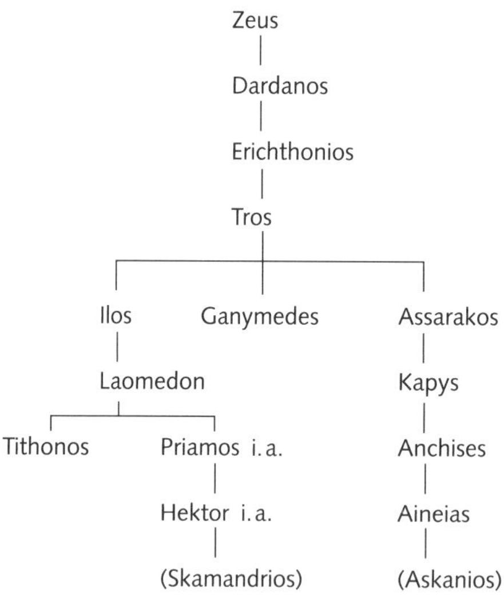

Dardanid (Hom. Il. 3,303 and *passim*); however, this line disappears together with Troy. Through Capys, Anchises and → Aeneas are descended from the younger branch of the D.; Poseidon prophesies that he will come to reign over Troy (Hom. Il. 20,302ff. with schol.; Hom. h. Ven. 5,196f.). Aeneas's son Ascanius appears as the ruler on Ida in Conon narr. 41. Scepsis was the long-term residence of the Aeneads and the descendants of Hector (Str. 13,1,52; Hellanic. FGrH 4 F 31). The legend of the Italian origins of Dardanus strengthened Roman self-perception as D., viewing the emigrant Aeneas as their ancestor (Verg. Aen. 3,94ff.; 7,195).

P. Grimal, Le retour des Dardanides, une legitimité pour Rome, in: Journal des Savants 1982, 267–282; T.J. Wiseman, Legendary Genealogies in Late Republican Rome, in: Greece and Rome 21, 1974, 153–164. T.S.

Dardanus (Δάρδανος; *Dárdanos*).

[1] Son of Zeus, who of all his mortal sons loved this one the most (Hom. Il. 20,215; 304), and either a mortal mother or the Atlantid Electra/Elektryone (Hes. fr. 177/80 MW; Hellanic. FGrH 4 F 23). Eponymous hero of the → Dardani, who lived on Mt Ida, and in Homer are linked with the Trojans and frequently synonymous with them. D. is the progenitor of the Trojan ruling dynasty. Possibly mentioned in the *Ilioupersis*, he originates from Arcadia, where he is supposed to have been born in a cave (Ilioupersis fr. 1 PEG I; Str. 8,3,19; Varro in Serv. Aen. 3,167) and is married to Pallas's daughter Chryse. She bore D. two sons, Deimas and Idaeus; Chryse also brought him as dowry two Palladia from Zeus and the sanctuaries later known as the 'Samothracian sanctuaries'. Zeus is also supposed to have given D. the statue of Dionysus Aisymnetes created by Hephaistus (Paus. 7,19,6). A great flood forced D. to flee and then settle in Samothrace, which some other sources (Hellanic. FGrH 4 F 23; Diod. Sic. 5,48) refer to as his place of birth.

After founding the Samothracian Mysteries, D. emigrates to Asia — also because of a flood according to some sources (Str. 7 fr. 50 and 13,1,25; Tzetz. Lycoph. 73), from which he saved himself by sewing himself in a skin. When he founded Dardania he erected the → Palladion on Mt Ida, an oracle proclaimed the significance of this as a protective pledge for the ruling dynasty. Dardania is not in the same location as the city later known as Troy, as this place is full of evil portents (Hellanicus FGrH 4 F 25; Lycoph. 29; especially Dion. Hal. Ant. Rom. 1,68,3f.; Apollod. 3,143). In Asia, D. married either the Cretan Arisbe (Cephalon FGrH 45 F 4; Lycoph. 1308) or Batea, the daughter of the local king, Teucer, whom D. then succeeded; he had a son by Batea, Erichthonius (Hellanicus FGrH 4 F 24; Diod. Sic. 4,75,1; Apollod. 3,140; Steph. Byz. s.v. Dardanus). Other children are Zacynthus (Dion. Hal. Ant. Rom. 1,50,3; Paus. 8,24,3; Steph. Byz. s.v. Zacynthus), Idaea (Apollod. 3,200) and Idaeus (Dion. Hal. Ant. Rom. 1,61). Together with his nephew Corybras, he is supposed to have introduced the cult of the Mother of the Gods into Phrygria (Diod. Sic. 5,49,2). At a later stage, D.'s great-grandson Ilus brought the Palladion to the Scamander Plain (or even received it first from Zeus: Apollod. 3,145) and founded Ilium, where the tomb of his ancestor D. was also shown in later times (Lycoph. 72 with schol.). This ancestor was the founder of the historical town of D. on the Hellespont (Hdt. 5,117; 7,43; Thuc. 8,104; Diod. Sic. 4,75; Str. 13,1,28).

The Italian version of the legend, either first created or merely specifically publicized during the Augustan period, said that D. was born in Tyrrhenian Corythus (possibly Cortona or Cora: Plin. HN 3,5,63) and gave him a brother named Corythus. Whilst his brother is supposed to have emigrated to Samothrace, D. took his Italian Penates with him to Phrygia (Verg. Aen. 7,205ff.). The commentator for Lycoph. (1129 Tzetz.) even mentions a town called D. in Italy. The Italian version of the legend facilitated the 'return' of the Trojan → Aeneas with Palladion and Penates to the land of his earliest forefathers, thereby legitimizing Rome as the supreme power in Italy. Probably because of the link with the Mysteries, D. was also seen as the author of a love spell, the 'Sword of D.' (see D. [2]), in which an image of Eros and Psyche played an important role (PGM IV 1716–1870).

→ Dardanidae; → Dardani

V. Buchheit, Vergil über die Sendung Roms, 1963, 151ff.; G.A. Caduff, Ant. Sintflutsagen, 1986, 142ff. and *passim*; L. Kahil, s.v. Dardanos, LIMC 3.1, 352–353; L. v. Sybel, s.v. Dardanos, Roscher 1.1, 962. T.S.

[2] Seen as identical with D. [1]. As founder of the Samothracian Mysteries and an authority on magic, he probably cannot be differentiated from *Hekate Dardanía* (PGM 4,2612; PGM 7,695; D. was an ancient name for Samothrace according to Steph. Byz.). The philosopher Democritus is supposed to have discovered writings by D. in his tomb and to have explained them

(Plin. HN. 30,9). Apul. Apol. 90,5 and Tert. Anim. 57,1 count him amongst the famous *magi* with Ostanes and Damigeron i.a. Fulgentius also mentions *volumina* by D., which had demonological content (cf. Fulgentius, Expositio Virgilianea continentiae 86,2 HELM). The 'Sword of D.' follows this tradition (Δαρδάνου ξίφος; *Dardánou xíphos*)—this is the title of a love spell in the 'Great Magic Papyrus of Paris' (4th cent. AD, cf. PGM 4,1716–1870). His hymn to Eros wields 'incomparable' power via a specially engraved magnetic stone 'imbued with fresh courage', which should explain the strange title, *Xíphos*. The 'triumphant-erotic' strength of the *mágnēs* combined with the 'sword' of Eros, the symbol of the association of Aphrodite and Ares (cf. the *Magnes* poem by Claudian), is supposed to have rendered the spell irresistible (different view [1]).
→ Hecate; → Ostanes; → Magic

1 K. PREISENDANZ, s.v. Xiphos, Roscher 6, 526f. C.HA.

[3] **from Athens.** Stoic philosopher; together with → Mnesarchus, a leading Stoic in the period *c.* mid 90's BC (Cic. Acad. 2,69), teacher of Apollonius of Ptolemais [1. col. 58]. He studied together with → Antipater of Tarsus and possibly with → Diogenes of Babylon [1. col. 51, 53].

1 T. DORANDI (ed.), Filodemo, Storia dei filosofi: La stoà da Zenone a Panezio, 1994. B.I.

[4] The city on the Asiatic bank of the Hellespontus, located 70 stadia south of → Abydus on the Sehitlik Batarya, was presumed to have been founded by the Aeolians in the 7th cent. BC. The settlement started → elektron coinage at an early stage. During the course of the Ionian Rebellion, D. was conquered by the Persians (Hdt. 5,117). In 411 BC, the Spartans suffered a devastating defeat in the waters near D., a member of the → Delian League (Thuc. 8,104). In the Hellenistic era, D. joined the *koinón* around Athena Ilias. Later D. was occupied for a short time by Abydus (Str. 13,1,28). During the war against → Antiochus [5] III, D. was on the side of the Romans, who used the coast near D. as their landing place. On account of this, D. was declared a *civitas libera* in the Peace of Apamea (Liv. 38,39,11). In 84 BC, Sulla met Mithridates I here, in order to end the (First Mithridatic) War. D. survived into the Byzantine era. In the Middle Ages the buildings were destroyed and the stones used elsewhere, and in modern times there have only been a few archaeological finds of ceramics and coins. However, in 1959 a burial mound containing lavish burial gifts was discovered 1 km to the southwest of the site of the city [1. 59f.]; [2].

1 J.M. COOK, The Troad, 1973 2 W. LEAF, Strabo on the Troad, 1923. HA.SCH.

[5] **Claudius Postumus D.** *consularis Viennensis, mag. libellorum, quaestor sacri palatii, praef. praet. Galliarum, patricius.* As a praetorian prefect in AD 412/3, he caused → Athaulf to fight on the side of → Honorius against → Iovinus; he murdered the captive usurper. The dating of his second prefecture is disputed (AD 401/04 or 406/07 in the PLRE, end of AD 415 according to [1]). D. was a Christian, and a correspondent of → Jerome and → Augustine. He withdrew to a settlement known as *Theopolis* ('City of God'), possibly due to Augustine's influence. PLRE 2, 346f.

1 DELMAIRE, 185f. H.L.

Dareikos (δαρεικός, δαρικός, δαριχός, *dareikós, darikós, darichós*). Greek name, deriving from Darius I, (Hdt. 4,166; 7,28f.; Thuc. 8,28) for the generally bean-shaped gold coins (στατήρ, *statḗr*) of the Great King of Persia. The occasionally used terms *dareikoi Philippeioi* and *argypoi dareikoi* are incorrect. The first coins, minted in *c.* 515 BC and the same weight as the *kroiseios* (*c.* 8.05g), which did not replace the latter until 30 years after the fall of the Lydian Empire, show a symbolic representation of the Persian king on the obverse — kneeling and shooting a bow. On later common coins this figure carries a lance in the right hand and towards the end of the 5th cent. BC, he is depicted with a dagger (the name τοξότης; *toxótēs* derives from this). The reverse side has an oblong depression, generally not subdivided. Soon after introduction, the weight was increased to *c.* 8.35g (= 1 shekel = $^1/_{60}$ mina), thereby putting them in a 1:13 $^1/_3$ weight ratio with the silver coins (*siglos*), with 20 *sigloi* to a *dareikos*. The fineness was 98. Lesser denominations of the *dareikos* are the gold *obolos* ($^1/_{12}$ *dareikoi*) and an uncertain nominal of $^1/_{54}$ *dareikoi* (= $^1/_{60}$ *dareikoi*?). The double *dareikos* was probably not minted until the time of Alexander the Great (in Babylon?). The *dareikos* remains the predominant gold coin in the Mediterranean until the minting of the *Philippeios* during the reign on the Macedonian Philip II in *c.* 345 BC.
→ Kroiseios; → Mina; → Obolos; → Philippeios; → Siglos; → Siqlu

E. BABELON, Les Perses Achéménides, les satrapes et les dynastes tributaires de leur empire Cypre et Phénicie, 1893; SCHRÖTTER, 120–121; J.H. JONGKEES, Kroiseios en Dareikos, Jaarbericht van het vooraziatisch-egypt. Gezelschap 'Ex Oriente Lux' 9, 1944, 163–168; E.S.G. ROBINSON, The Beginnings of Achaemenid Coinage, in: NC 6.18, 1958, 187–193; Id., A Hoard of Archaic Greek Coins from Anatolia, in: NC 7.1, 1961, 107–117, esp. 115ff. A.M.

Dares (Δάρης; *Dárēs*).
[1] Trojan priest of Hephaistus, whose sons Phegeus and Idaeus start the battle against → Diomedes. Whilst the former is killed by Diomedes, Idaeus is rescued by Hephaistus (Hom. Il. 5,9–26).

G.S. KIRK, The Iliad: A Commentary, vol. 2, 1990, 54; P. WATHELET, Dictionnaire des Troyens de l'Iliade, vol. 1, 1988, 408f.

[2] One of Aeneas' companions, excellent pugilist. However, at the funeral games in honour of → Anchi-

ses, he is unexpectedly beaten by Entellus (Verg. Aen. 5,362–484; Hyg. Fab. 273,17). Virgil's version is a free adaptation of the fist-fight between Epius and Euryalus (Hom. Il. 23,665ff.) [1].

1 R. Heinze, Virgils ep. Technik, ³1915, 154f.

L. Polverini, s.v. Darete, EV 1, 1000. R.B.

[3] The 'Phrygian D.' is the fictitious author of a supposedly contemporary account of the Trojan War (*Historia de excidio Troiae*). The anonymous Latin author (5th cent. AD?) poses as Cornelius → Nepos. He says that he discovered the report written by D. and translated and published it in order to correct the inaccuracies in Homer's narrative. The author presumably had a Greek version. The short chronicle (which, in all probability, is not an → epitome) was very highly valued in the Middle Ages and put into a poetic arrangement.

Edition: F. Meister, 1873 (repr. 1991).; A. Beschorner, Unt. zu D. Phrygius, 1992. J.D.

Dargamanes A river in → Bactria, which rises in the Paraponisus and supposedly joins the → Ochus to the west of the Zariaspes (Balhāb), and then flows together with the Ochus into the Oxus (→ Araxes [2]). In fact there were two different rivers called Ochus, confused by Ptolemy: the Zariaspes (Balḫāb) and the Harērud. The former must be the one referred to here, which joins the Oxus, as the D. or Qunduz river (Arabic Nahr al-Ḍarġm̄) flows into the latter. Ptolemy (or his predecessor Marinus) made a further mistake in confusing this D. with a canal of the same name near Maracanda (Samarkand).

J. Markwart, Wehrot und Arang, 1938. J.D.-G. and B.B.

Dargoidus River in → Bactria, which rises in the Parapanisus and flows northwards to join the Oxus (→ Araxes [2]) east of the Zariaspes, and which used to supply the region of Choana (today known as Qunduz) with water.

W. Henning, Surkh Kotal, in: BSO(A)S, 1956, 366f.; Id., The Bactrian inscription, in: BSO(A)S, 1960, 47–55. J.D.-G. and B.B.

Darioritum Principal city of the Veneti in the Gallia Lugdunensis, today known as Vannes, on the Gulf of Morbihan. Documentary evidence: Ptol. 2,8,6; Tab. Peut. (*Dartoritum*); Not. Galliarum 3,8 (*civitas Venetum*). A prosperous city during the Roman imperial period, D. was protected by a city wall during the troubled times of the 3rd cent., a wall which, as indicated by the remains, only enclosed part of D. Inscription.: CIL 13, 3140f.

L. Pape, La Bretagne romaine, 1995. Y.L.

Darius (Ancient Persian *Dārayava(h)uš*, 'Guardian of Good', Greek Δαρεῖος < Δαρειαῖος; *Dareîos* < *Dareiaîos*). The name of various Persian kings and princes [3]. D., the Mede (Dan. 9) cannot be identified historically.

[1] **D. I.** Son of → Hystaspes, grandson of → Arsames [1], from the Achaemenid family (→ Achaemenids), became king (522 BC) [1], after banding together with six accomplices from the country's most influential families and overthrowing the usurper → Gaumata. During the first year of his reign, D. had to quell numerous revolts, reported in his inscription of → Bīsutūn (TUAT 1, 421–441). In the second and third year, he fought against Skuncha, a prince of the northern Scythians [TUAT 1, 442]. This campaign is not the same as the unsuccessful campaign against the Scythians in Southern Russia (513 BC), recorded by Hdt. 4,83–143. Via marriages with → Artystone and → Atossa, daughters of → Cyrus, and with Parmys, daughter of → Bardiya, D. tried to legitimize an obvious link with the family of Cyrus, the founder of the kingdom, and thereby also to legitimize his own rulership [3. 63].

The → Ionian Revolt which broke out in 499 BC was quelled by D. in 493. Athenian help for the Ionians led to the (unsuccessful) Persian campaign against Athens (→ Marathon, in 490). After his death in 486, D. was interred in a rock-cut tomb in → Naqš-i Rustam. The inscriptions on the tomb provide important documentation of the ideology behind Persian rulership. D. boasts of having 'invented' → ancient Persian cuneiform [3. 333]. This was probably only used exclusively for ostentatious purposes (Naqš-i Rustam). He began the construction of the palace stairs at → Persepolis and the palaces there. D. was responsible for the administrative structures of the Persian Empire (→ Satrap), which endured until the end of the empire and were adopted by the Hellenistic states in the orient. Among others, these included the reorganization of the army, regular annual taxes, the introduction of the → dareikos, the construction of a communication system within the empire (→ Royal roads) and the use of the language known as → Aramaic as the 'official language'. In Egypt, he ordered a collection of Egyptian laws, but this cannot be seen as a general codification for the whole empire [4].

→ Bardiya; → Oroetes

1 Briant, 119–176, 982 2 R. Schmitt, The Name of Darius, in: Acta Iranica 30, 1990, 194–199 3 J. Wiesehöfer, Das ant. Persien, 1993 4 Id., 'Reichsgesetz' or 'Einzelfallgerechtigkeit'?, in: Zschr. für altoriental. und biblische Rechtsgesch. 1, 1995, 38–41.

[2] **D. II.** Throne name of Ochus, 6th king of the → Achaemenids (423–405 BC), son of → Artaxerxes [1] I and a Babylonian woman, hence referred to by later Greek authors as *nóthos*, 'bastard'; married his half-sister → Parysatis [4. 64]. The dating of Babylonian documents show his period of government as starting directly after then end of his father's reign. Greek

authors mention two half-brothers as interim kings [1. 605; 3. 114–124]. The Babylonian Murašû archive reflects the trouble surrounding the issue of the succession to the throne [3. 32–34]. Information about rebellions connected with the names Arsites, → Pissuthnes and Terituchmes is only found in Greek sources. Ctesias' sensational style presented a distorted picture of events.

The disputes between Sparta and Athens (→ Peloponnesian War) are exploited by the satraps → Tissaphernes and → Pharnabazus which results in military successes in the western part of Asia Minor. Influenced by Alcibiades, Sparta comes down on the side of Tissaphernes. The Persians continued to maintain their alliance with Sparta and in 408 sent Cyrus the Younger, the favourite son of Parysatis, to support Sparta, and in so doing won the upper hand over Athens.

Only a few ancient Persian inscriptions by D. have been preserved, all of which document his construction activities in Susa. He was the last Achaemenid to be buried in → Naqš-e Rustam.

1 Briant, 605–629 2 H. Sancisi-Weerdenburg, Darius II., in: EncIr 7, 1994, 50f. 3 M. Stolper, Entrepreneurs and Empire, 1985 4 J. Wiesehöfer, Das ant. Persien, 1993.

[3] **D. III.** Throne name of Artašata, last king of the Achaemenids (336–330 BC). The epithet *Kodomannus* (only in Iust. 10,3,3ff.) remains problematic. D. III was not part of the direct → Achaemenid line of descent (for line of descent see [1. 792]), and only came to power following the murder of both of his predecessors (→ Artaxerxes [3] III and IV), allegedly by the eunuch → Bagoas. He was defeated by → Alexander [4] the Great in two battles (Issus and Gaugamela). D. himself was murdered by two of his generals while fleeing to Bactria. The murder enabled Alexander to present himself as D.'s avenger and therefore as legitimate king of the Persians.

1 Briant.

E. Badian, Darius III., in: AchHist (in print); Briant, 837–891; C. Nylander, Darius III. the Coward King, in Alexander the Great: Reality and Myth, 1993, 145–159.

[4] Oldest son of → Xerxes I; murdered with his father in August 465 BC (Diod. Sic. 11,69).
[5] Oldest son of → Artaxerxes [2] II, executed by his father (Plut. Artaxerxes 26–29). A.KU. and H.S.-W.

Darius Crater Apulian voluted crater from → Canosa (found in 1851) in Naples (NM, Inv. 81947 [H 3,253], H 130cm, [1]), known as the eponymous work of the → Darius Painter named after it. The main face has the crown council of Darius in the centre [1] I., with paymasters and tribute bearers below and Athena with Hellas before Zeus and Apate before Asia above. Archaeological study interprets this as a representation of the victories of → Alexander' [4] the Great in Persia or an echo of contemporary theatre performances. The reverse shows a scene of the battle between → Bellerophon and the → Chimaera in the presence of gods and battling Middle Easterners.

1 Trendall/Cambitoglou 495, no. 38, pl. 176,1.

R. A. Tybout, Ziffern auf einem Zahltisch. Zum Problem des Originals der Perserdarstellung auf dem Dareioskrater, in: BABesch 52/3, 1977/78, 264–265; A. Geyer, Gesch. als Mythos, in: MDAI(A) 108, 1993, 443–455; Ch. Aellen, A la recherche de l'ordre cosmique, 1994, 115f., 139f. R.H.

Darius Painter Apulian vase painter working *c.* 340/320 BC, named after the main figure on the → Darius Crater. On the vessels he painted (including voluted craters, lutrophoroi, amphorae), some of which are monumental, he generally depicted scenes from classical tragedies (Euripides) and themes from Greek myth; some of these are only documented through his work. Other vases show scenes depicting weddings, women and Eros, as well as Dionysian motifs and rare sepulchral representations (→ Naiskos vases). His tendency to name people and representations in inscriptions (*Persai, Patroklou Taphos, Creusa*) is of particular interest. For images containing several figures, he used the entire surface of the body of the vase and set the compositions in two or three areas, some of which he separated from one another using opulent ornamental friezes. Some of his images refer to contemporary history.

Trendall/Cambitoglou, 482–522; Id., Second Supplement to the Red-figured Vases of Apulia, 1992, 145–154; Ch. Aellen, J. Chamay, A. Cambitoglou, Le peintre de Darius et son milieu, exposition cat. Geneva 1986; A. Geyer, Gesch. als Mythos, in: JDAI 108, 1993, 443–455. R.H.

Dark Ages

[1] (1200–800 BC)
A. Definition B. 12th century C. 11th century D. 10th century E. 9th century

A. Definition

Since the end of the 19th cent., the term Dark Ages (DA), coined by English speaking scholars, characterizes the time from the decline of the Mycenaean palaces *c.* 1200 to the beginning of the 'Homeric Period', i.e. the early archaic period of Greece in the 8th cent. BC. Archaeologically, the DA comprise the following periods: Late Helladic (LH) III C = Mycenaean III C (12th and early 11th cent.), sub-Mycenaean (early to middle 11th cent.), Protogeometric (PG; from the middle of the 11th cent. to *c.* 900), Early and Middle Geometric (EG, MG; 9th and early 8th cent.). LH III C and sub-Mycenaean were the last phase as well as the end of the Mycenaean culture, while PG, EG and MG are also regarded as the 'Early Iron Age' of Greece. The ideas associated with the term DA — cultural insignificance, impoverishment, lack of social differentiation, and the breaking-off of external relations — can no longer be supported. While it is true that, after the collapse of the Mycenaean palace states and palace culture (→ Aegean Koine B.4), Greek culture in almost all sectors sank to a level that does not compare well with either the highly advanced Mycenaean culture or the culture beginning around 750 BC, more recent research has revealed clearly creative and forward-looking achievements by the Greeks even during the DA. Already in the 11th cent., technological innovations were beginning to appear, referred to as 'the transition from the Bronze to the Iron Age', which made it possible, for example, to produce large vessels with a design consisting of concentric circles and semicircles drawn with a compass and a multiple brush, and thus to assign the art-historical term 'style' to the PG vase art of Athens and Euboea. In addition, it was during the DA that the Greek dialects developed; with epic '→ Oral Poetry', the basis for the large Homeric epics emerged. The formation of social strata and governmental institutions as well as shipping activity and intra-Aegean relations can be detected; even long-distance contacts were established time and again, albeit on a reduced scale.

Nevertheless, the term DA as the designation for an epoch is justified particularly because of the loss of writing and thus the lack of any written tradition (the Linear B script disappears around 1200, the Greek alphabet emerges around 800). Also lost were representational architecture, fortress and bridge building as well as art genres (the cult statuettes of Tiryns from the 12th cent. and the centaur of Lefkandi-Toumba from the 10th cent. are exceptions) while the skills of the palace workshops survived only in the crafts of pottery and weapons' manufacture. In the area of politics, the complex Mycenaean state structure, organised along centralist-bureaucratic lines, and the theocratic monarchy disappeared completely. There were no supraregional forms of rule, only the organisational forms of small states and municipalities were discernible, based on oikos, kinship and other personal associations. Change in the social and economic areas, can also be seen in the fact that the relevant Mycenaean Linear B terms mostly did not transfer into the alphabet-based Greek vocabulary.

B. 12TH CENTURY

The beginning of the LH III C was characterized by destruction and population movements ('Aegean Migration', 'Migration of the Sea Peoples'); settlements were shifted to safer places, but despite innovations (leaf blade swords, brooches for gowns, 'barbarian' ceramics) the culture remained Mycenaean and, in the late 12th cent. ('Middle' Late Helladic III C), it even demonstrated a final flowering in settlements (e.g. Mycenae, Tiryns, Lefkandi-Xeropolis, Paros-Koukounaries, Knossos, Kavousi), chamber graves (*i.a.* of Pera, Monemvasia, Elatea, Naxos, Kos, Rhodes, Mouliana) and sanctuaries (Kalapodi, Phylakopi, Keos-Hagia Irini, Kato Syme, Ida grotto). In contrast to the Mycenaean palace period, however, each region developed its own style, which is particularly evident in vase painting. In the centres of small domains, a warrior elite practised a courtly life style and portrayed its ideals on splendid vases and in elaborate warrior funerals. A lively trade and cultural exchange existed between the mainland, Crete and the islands. Long-distance contacts reached as far as Cyprus and Italy. In some places, peace and prosperity continued into the late LH III C period and then ended in new catastrophes.

C. 11TH CENTURY

The 11th cent. has not yet been researched sufficiently, but it appears that the Mycenaean culture ended quite differently in different regions. While destruction, the abandonment of settlements and a decline in population in the Mycenaean core lands (Peloponnese, Cyclades, and Dodecanese) lead to people turning away from Mycenaean culture and making a fresh start, the Mycenaean heritage was still maintained in the so-called periphery (Central Greece, Macedonia, Thessaly, and the Ionian islands) during the sub-Mycenaean and PG period. On Crete, the wealthy upper class of the urban settlement in Knossos maintained contacts to places as far away as Cyprus; the east of Crete remained Minoan into the PG period (Karphi, Praesus, Vrokastro, Kastri); and in Kalapodi, Kato Syme and in the Ida grotto, there is evidence of cultural continuity. Cyprus was Hellenized through immigration from Greece; large parts of coastal Asia Minor became Greek once and for all. While ancient tradition associates the demographic changes with migrations of Greek tribes (→ Dorian migration, → Ionian migration), new cultural elements (such as iron weapons and objects, pairs of long costume pins, individual graves, cremation, and hand painted old ceramics) cannot be associated with specific ethnic groups. In the 11th cent., the creation of the PG vase style in Athens proved to be very influential.

D. 10TH CENTURY

In the 10th cent., regional PG cultures emerged, among which Attica and Euboea played a leading role. More recent excavations provide evidence of remarkably different forms of political organization and economic activity: Nichoria, a village community of animal breeders, had a simple culture. A large house with apses probably served as the chieftain's residence and simultaneously as a meeting place for the nobility. In Lefkandi, the cemeteries present quite a different picture: numerous burial objects found in the Toumba cemetery are proof of the luxury and vigour of an enterprising aristocracy which had objects from Cyprus, Phoenicia and Egypt come to Euboea. Ceramic art was of no lesser quality than that of Athens and was influential for the styles of central Greece and the Cyclades. The monumental grave of a warrior lord (?) is reminiscent of a monarchic structure and Homeric death rites. In Athens and Knossos, which were urban centres already in the PG period, leading noble families maintained far-reaching international relations. On Crete,

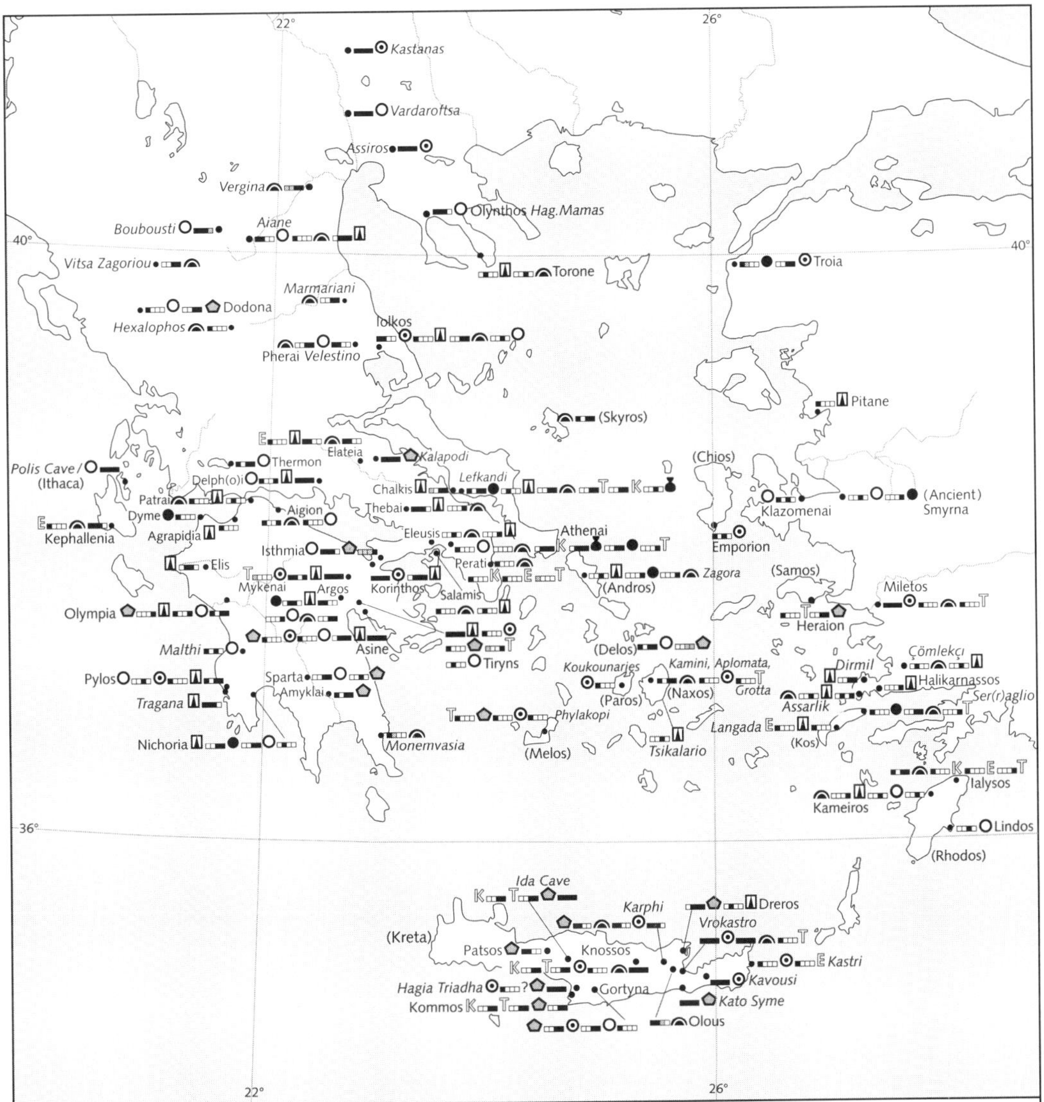

Greece and the Aegean during the Dark Ages (12th – 9th cents. BC); the most important sites

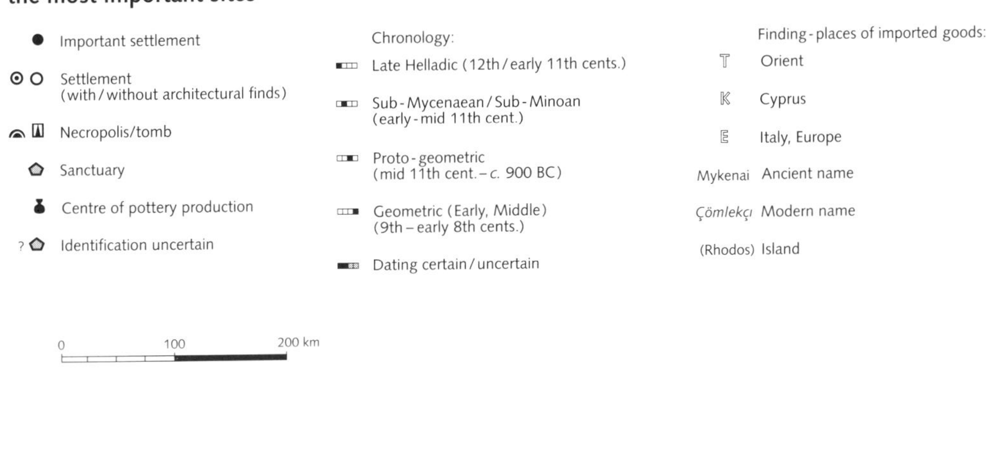

finds in Knossos and the early Iron Age temple of Kommos prove the presence of Phoenicians as of the 10th cent.

E. 9TH CENTURY

In the 9th cent., Athens, Euboea and Knossos also remain the leaders in matters of culture and trade. The urban structure is reinforced in settlements like Zagora (Andros), Emporion (Chios) or old Smyrna and initiated the later separation of polis and 'tribal state'. Alongside simple residential houses of oval, apsidal and rectangular shape, fortified structures occurred, only rarely also sacred architecture. In Crete (Knossos North Cemetery), phenomena could already be observed in the 9th cent. which occurred elsewhere only in the 8th cent.: 'nostalgic' turning towards a Bronze Age past, oriental influences in art due to more regular contacts with Cyprus and the Levant as well as a rapid rise in population numbers.

GENERAL WORKS: W.D. E. COULSON, The Greek Dark Ages, 1990; V.R. D'A.DESBOROUGH, The Greek Dark Ages, 1972; F.SCHACHERMEYR, Die ägäische Frühzeit, vols. 3 and 4, 1979/1980; A.SNODGRASS, The Dark Age of Greece, 1971; C.-G.STYRENIUS, Submycenaean Studies, 1967; J.VANSCHOONWINKEL, L'Egée et la Mediterranée orientale à la fin du deuxième millénaire, 1991.

CONGRESSES, REGIONAL STUDIES, INDIVIDUAL ASPECTS: P.A. CARTLEDGE, Sparta and Lakonia, 1972; Id., Early Lakedaimon, in: J.M. SANDERS (ed.), Philolakon. FS H. Catling, 1992, 49–55; R.W. V. CATLING, I.S. LEMOS (ed.), Lefkandi II/1, 1990; J.N. COLDSTREAM, H.W. CATLING (ed.), Knossos North Cemetery Early Greek Tombs, 1996; W.D. E. COULSON, The Dark Age Pottery of Sparta, in: ABSA 80, 1985, 29–84; Id., The Protogeometric from Polis Reconsidered, in: ABSA 86, 1991, 43–64; F.DAKORONIA, Spercheios Valley and the Adjacent Area in Late Bronze Age and Early Iron Age, in: La Thessalie, 1994; S.DEGER-JALKOTZY (ed.), Griechenland, die Ägäis und die Levante während der 'Dark Ages' vom 12. bis zum 9. Jh.v.Chr., 1983; Id., Elateia (Phokis) und die frühe Gesch. der Griechen, in: Anzeiger der Österreichischen Akad. der Wiss. 127 (1990) 1991, 77–86; B.EDER, Argolis, Lakonien, Messenien vom Ende der myk. Palastzeit bis zur Einwanderung der Dorier, 1998; K.FAGERSTRÖM, Greek Iron Age Architecture, 1988; R.HÄGG, Die Gräber der Argolis in submyk., protogeom. und geom. Zeit, 1974; R.HÄGG, N.MARINATOS (ed.), Sanctuaries and Cults in the Aegean Bronze Age, 1981; R.HÄGG, N.MARINATOS, G.C. NORDQUIST (ed.), Early Greek Cult Practice, 1988; V.KARAGEORGHIS (ed.), Proceedings of the International Symposium 'Cyprus in the 11th century B.C.', 1994; G.KOPCKE, Handel, in: ArchHom, M, 1990; J.LATACZ (ed.), Zweihundert Jahre Homer-Forsch., Colloquium Rauricum vol. 2, 1991; A.MAZARAKIS-AINIAN, Late Bronze Age Apsidal and Oval Buildings in Greece and Adjacent Areas, in: ABSA 84, 1989, 269–288; W.A. McDONALD, W.D.E. COULSON, Excavations at Nichoria in Southwest Greece III, 1983; D.MUSTI et al. (ed.), La transizione dal Miceneo all'alto arcaismo, 1991; M.R. POPHAM et al. (ed.), Lefkandi II/2, 1993; L.H. SACKETT, P.G. THEMELIS (ed.), Lefkandi I. The Iron Age, 1979/1980; M.L. WEST, The Rise of the Greek Epic, in: JHS 108, 1988, 151–172.

MAPS: V.R. D'A.DESBOROUGH, The Greek Dark Ages, 1972; F.SCHACHERMEYR, Die ägäische Frühzeit, vol. III, 1979; IV, 1980; G.KOPKE, Handel, ArchHom, Kap. M, 1990, esp. 78; J.VANSCHOONWINKEL, L'Egée et la Mediterranée orientale à la fin du deuxième millénaire, 1991.

S.D.-J.

[2] (AD 500–800) see → Textual history

Dascusa (Δασκοῦσα; *Daskoûsa*). City and fortress on the Euphrates limes in Cappadocia (strategia Melitene) on the border to *Armenia minor* (Plin. HN 5,84; 6,27; Oros. 1,2,23; Ptol. 5,6,19; 21 erroneously distinguishes D. and Dagusa), later counted as part of *Armenia II*, on the Satala-Melitene road (It. Ant. 209,3), located near Ağın, Elazığ. In the 4th cent., the *Ala Auriana* is stationed there (Not. Dign. Or. 38,22). Fortified settlement hill and late-antique fortress (Pağnık Öreni) [1; 2; 3]. The military camp was established in AD 80/82 [4].

1 R.P. HARPER, Ü.SERDAROĞLU, in: Keban Project 1968–1972 (1970–1976) 2 AS 21, 1971, 48f. 3 AS 23, 1973, 14f. 4 T.B. MITFORD, Some inscriptions from the Cappadocian Limes, in: JRS 64, 1974, 172f. (Troops incorrectly added).

W.RUGE, s.v. Daskusa, RE 4, 2219; R.P. HARPER, s.v. Daskusa, PE 258f.; HILD/RESTLE, 169f.

K.ST.

Dascylium (Δασκύλειον, Δασκύλιον; *Daskýleion*, *Daskýlion*).

[1] City in Bithynia, member of the → Delian League, whose name is thought to be contained in the place name Eşkel Liman (today Esence) on the coast of the Propontis west of Apamea Myrleia (Plin. HN 5,143; Steph. Byz. s.v. *Brýllion*).

[2] A more important settlement by the name of D. on the SE shore of Lake Daskylitis (today Manyas or Kuşgölü) near Hisartepe close to the village of Ergili was discovered in 1952 by K. BITTEL and E. AKURGAL (excavations initiated by AKURGAL in 1954–1960, since 1988 continued by T. BAKIR-AKBAŞOĞLU). As archaeological finds show, this settlement already existed during the 2nd millennium BC and had been settled by Aeolian colonists after the Trojan war (Str. 13,1,3). Excavations have uncovered city walls and polished, grey ceramics from this time, with parallels existing in Thrace and Macedonia. The remains of city walls, foundation walls of a temple to Cybele including a *bóthros* filled with cult objects, marble votive inscriptions in the Phrygian language and graffiti on clay shards show that this place was already settled from the 8th cent. BC onwards by a Phrygian population, following literary sources (Hom. Il. 24,545; Hdt. 3,90; Hell. Oxy. 22,3), the same can be said for the surrounding area. It is possible that the Phrygian population was reinforced by immigrants from the northern part of Phrygia Megale in central Asia Minor. The city came under Lydian rule (Nicolaus of Damascus, FGrH 90 F 63) and was named after Dascylus, the father of the Lydian king Gyges (Hdt. 1,8; Paus. 4,21); at this time,

Attic vases were imported into D., such as the kraters of Lydus and of the Gorgo painter.

D. is most famous as the residence of the Persian satrap of the Phrygian Hellespont (Hdt. 3,120; 126; 6,33; Thuc. 1,129,1); in 395 BC it served as winter quarters for the Spartan king → Agesilaus [2] during his campaign against Pharnabazus. A lively description can be found at Xen. Hell. 4,1,15: numerous wealthy settlements, *parádeisoi* ('hunting enclosures'), a river rich in fish, and birds in abundance; today, there is an important nature reserve nearby (Kuşcenneti). An Ionian votive capital as well as other architectural remains date from early Achaemenid times; there is also a Graeco-Persian stele with a relief depicting a ceremonial scene. Attic vases of the Amasis painter, of Euphronius and others, found there, are evidence of the prosperity and culture surrounding the satraps. An Aramaic inscription on a 'door lintel' from the 6th cent. BC identifies it as the gravestone of a Jew by the name of Pedejah who held a religious office in his community. A shrine to Zarathustra, enclosed by a *témenos* wall, and reliefs depicting *mágoi* with sacrificial animals date from middle Achaemenid times. After the battle at the Granicus, the Persian palace of Parmenion was taken over without a fight (Arr. Anab. 1,17,2); in contrast to the report in Arrian, the excavations show that D. was defended against the Macedonians. Under Roman rule, the area around D. was probably subject to Cyzicus for a certain period of time (Str. 12,8,11). In Byzantine times, it was a suffragan diocese of Nicomedia.

T. Bakir-Akbaşoğlu, Phryger in D., in: M. Salvini (ed.), Atti del Convegno internazionale 'Frigi e Frigio' (16–17 ottobre 1995), 1997; W. Ruge, s.v. Daskyleion (5), RE 4, 220. T.D.-B. and T.B.-A.

Dascylus (Δάσκυλος; *Dáskylos*).

[1] Son of Tantalus and Anthemoisia, father of Lycus, king of the Mariandyni in Bithynia (schol. Apoll. Rhod. 2,724; 752). D. or his son Lycus amiably received → Heracles as a guest during his travels when he was searching for Hippolyte's belt. In return, Hercules helped them to subjugate the neighbouring peoples (Apoll. Rhod. 2,775–791; Apollod. 2,100).

[2] Son of Lycus, grandson of D. [1]. His father offered him to the → Argonauts as a travel guide. On the return journey, he was dropped off again (Apoll. Rhod. 2,802–805; 4,298); → Dascylium.

[3] Father of → Gyges (Hdt. 1,8; Paus. 4,21,5; Anth. Pal. 7,709, there called Dascyles). R.B.

Dasius Messapic name in Lat. form (Schulze, 39, 44; ThlL Onom. s.v. D.). Respected bearers of that name in Apulia (in particular from Arpi and Sala) were still anti-Roman during the Second Punic War. ME.STR.

[1] D. from Brundisium, in 218 BC commander of the allied occupation forces of → Clastidium with large Roman stores which he betrayed to Hannibal after the victory at the Ticinus for 400 pieces of gold (Pol. 3,69; Liv. 21,48).

[2] Leader of the pro-Carthaginian party in Salapia; in 210 he was persuaded by his pro-Roman rival Blattius to betray the city to Claudius [I 11] Marcellus, as a result of which the Carthaginians lost 500 Numidian horsemen (Liv. 26,38).

[3] **D. Altinius.** respected aristocrat from Arpi. In 216 BC, he betrayed his city to Hannibal and in 213 offered its recapture to the Romans who jailed him in → Cales while his family was killed by the Punic occupation forces in Arpi (Liv. 24,45). L.-M.G.

Dassaretia Region in southern Illyricum near the western border of Macedonia (Liv. 42,36,9; cf. Plin. HN 3,145; 4,3; Mela 2,55; Str. 7,5,7; 5,12; Steph. Byz. s.v. D.) between the kingdoms of the Illyrians and the Macedonians, from the *Lychnidus lacus* (today Lake Ohrid; Ptol. 3,13,32; Liv. 43,9,7) to Antipatrea (today Berati, Albania) along the upper (H)apsus (Semani, Albania). Scerdilaedas and Philip V fought in 217 BC for the cities of Antipatrea, Chrysondyon and Gertus (Polyb. 5,108); otherwise, only *vici* and *castella* are mentioned. D. was conquered by Philip. In 200–199 BC, the *consul* Sulpicius and his legate L. Apustius crossed D. during the 2. Macedonian war (Liv. 31,33). In 167 BC, the Romans declared D. free; as part of the Roman protectorate in southern Illyricum D. remained outside the borders of Macedonia. As of the middle of the 2nd cent. BC, D. belonged to the *prov. Macedonia*. There is evidence of a *koinon* of Dassaretae. Inscriptions from Roman times indicate that D. was an administrative unit with its own magistrates; its centre was Lychidnus.

G. Zippel, Die röm. Herrschaft in Illyrien bis auf Augustus, 1877, 60ff.; F. Papazoglou, Les villes de Macédoine à l'époque romaine, BCH Suppl. 16, 1988. M.Š.K.

Dasumia

[1] Possibly wife of Calvisius [4].

Syme, RP 5, 526f.

[2] D. Polla. Mentioned in CIL VI 10229 and AE 1976, 77 [= 1] (cf. AE 1978, 16). Probably wife of Domitius [II 25] and possibly of Tullius Varro.

1 W. Eck, in: ZPE 30, 1978, 277ff. 2 Syme, RP 5, 521ff.

Dasumius

[1] Reputedly testator in the will handed down by CIL VI 10229; a new fragment (AE 1976, 77 = AE 1978, 16) shows that this is not the case [1]. Cf. Domitius [II 25].

1 W. Eck, Zum neuen Fragment des sogenannten *Testamentum Dasumii*, in: ZPE 30, 1978, 277ff.

[2] **(L.D.) Hadrianus.** Probably from Cordoba; *cos. suff* in 93, *proconsul Asiae c.* 106/107 [1; 2; 3]. Presumably related to Dasumia [2].

1 Vidman FO², 44, 85 2 W. Eck, in: Chiron 12, 1982, 43 3 Syme, RP 5, 521ff.

[3] **P. D. Rusticus.** Probably adopted by D. [2], biological son of P. Tullius Varro from Tarquinii; his son is D. [4]. *Cos. ord.* in 119 with Hadrian; originator of the *senatus consultum Dasumianum*. PIR [2] D 15.

SYME, RP 5, 521ff.

[4] **L. D. Tullius Tuscus.** Son of D. [3]. His long career is recorded in CIL XI 3365 = ILS 1081. Quaestor of Antoninus Pius; after only one Praetorian office as *praef. aerarii Saturni*, he became *cos. suff.* in 152, legate of Germania superior *c.* 155–158 and of Pannonia superior at the beginning of Marcus Aurelius' reign. PIR[2] D 16.

ECK, Statthalter 63f. W.E.

Datames (Hypocoristic of Old Persian **Datamithra-*). Son of the Carian Kamisares, satrap of southern Cappadocia, and a Paphlagonian princess, served at the court of → Artaxerxes [2] II and took part in the Cadusian war. After his father's death, D. became satrap of southern Cappadocia. His power grew until he finally administered the whole of Cappadocia for the Persians. He distinguished himself during the subjugation of Paphlagonia and Cataonia and was named as the commander of the army assembled against Egypt. Despite (or because of) these considerable merits, suspicions against him arose at court; around 370 BC, he complained about the king and in 362 BC, he was murdered. His life is well known because of the biography dedicated to him by Cornelius Nepos.

BRIANT, Index s.v. D.; N. SEKUNDA, Some Notes on the Life of Datames, in: Iran 26, 1988, 35–53.

Dataphernes (Old Persian **Datafarnah-*). Sogdian who, together with → Spitamenes, handed → Bessus over to Alexander the Great (329 BC); took part in the uprising against Alexander until the → Dahae handed him over to Alexander as a prisoner (328/7 BC). Sources: Arr. Anab. 4,1,5; 4,17,7; Curt. 7,5,21; 8,3,1–16.

F. HOLT, Alexander the Great and Bactria, 1989, 52, 65; M. MAYRHOFER, Onomastica Persepolitana, 1973, 149, no. 8.367. A.KU. and H.S.-W.

Dates see → Horticulture

Datetae (Δατηταί; *Datētaí*). 'Dividers', i.e. private arbiters in Athens, chosen by the parties, who presided over disputes amongst joint heirs. The procedure was initiated by private litigation for a division into shares, δίκη εἰς δατητῶν αἵρεσιν (Aristot. Ath.Pol. 56,6), against a joint heir who objected to a compromise. Usually, the archon was responsible for accepting the litigation while the Polemarch was responsible in exceptional cases if the litigation was directed against a metic (→ Archontes [I]). A court (→ Dikasterion) decided whether to proceed with or reject the division into shares. Later, this type of litigation was probably also applied to the division of co-ownership that was not based on an inheritance (Harpocr. s.v. δατεῖσθαι).

A.R. W. HARRISON, The Law of Athens I, 1968, 243
P.J. RHODES, A Commentary on the Aristot. Ath. Pol., 1981, 631. G.T.

Datianus Friend of Libanius (Lib. Ep. 409; 441 and *passim*). Initially, he was *notarius* (Lib. Or. 42,24f.), served under Constantine [1] the Great, was later an adviser of Constantius II (Lib. Ep. 114; 490). He became *patricius* and in AD 358 *consul*. As *comes*, in 346, he attempted to persuade Athanasius to return to Alexandria (Athan. Hist. Ar. 22). In 351, he was on the committee which had to decide on Photinus' heresy (Epiphany, adv. haer. 71). In 364, he was part of emperor Jovian's entourage (Philostorgius Hist. eccl. 8,8). He resided in Antioch for a long time and adorned the city with splendid buildings (Lib. Ep. 114; 1033). D. was a Christian (Epist. 81). PLRE 1, 243f. D. (1).
→ Libanius W.P.

Dating see → Manuscripts; → Papyri; → Writing, styles of

Dating systems see → Chronology

Datis (Δάτις; *Dátis*). Tragedian from Thoricus, son of Carcinus (Aristoph. Pax 289ff. with schol. R V; see also TrGF 21); D. is perhaps a nickname for Xenocles (TrGF 33), see also [1. 283–285].

1 DAVIES 2 TrGF 34. F.P.

Daton (Δάτον, Δάτος; *Dáton, Dátos*). Thracian region north-east of the Pangaeum mountains; here we find the Thasian mining colony of Crenides which was conquered *c.* 356 BC by Philip II and was absorbed into the newly founded Philippi. MA.ER.

Daulis, Daulia (Δαυλίς, Δαυλία; *Daulís, Daulía*). City in eastern Phocis, *c.* 1 km south of modern Davleia. Its location on one of the foothills of the Parnassus made access to it naturally difficult and gave it strategic importance because both the narrow pass between the lower and upper Cephissus valley as well as the road from → Chaeronea to → Delphi could be controlled by it (Hell. Oxy. 13,5; Liv. 32,18,7). Etymologically, its name is derived from the name of the nymph Daulia (Paus. 10,4,7) or from a geographical designation (δαυλός, 'ground thickly covered with dense vegetation', Str. 9,3,13). Initially the seat of a Thracian *dynasteía* (Thuc. 2,29,3), it appears in the Homeric catalogue of Phocian cities (Hom. Il. 2,520). In 480 BC the Persians set fire to it; in 346 BC it was destroyed by Philip II. D. is still mentioned as a *polis* by Hierocles (Synekdemos 643,10) as well as in Byzantine times (Steph. Byz. s.v. D.; Const. Porphyr. de them. 89). From the 9th cent. onwards, it was an important bishop's seat (Not. Episc. 533). On the acropolis, there are still remains of the circular city wall which also enclose the ruins of the church of St. Theodoros.

J. M. Fossey, The Ancient Topography of Eastern Phokis, 1986, 46–49; Müller, 461; N. D. Papachatzis, Παυσανίου Ἑλλάδος Περιήγησις [Pausaníou Helládos Periḗgēsis], 5, [2]1981, 461; F. Schober, Phokis, 1924, 27f.; TIB I, 142f.; L. B. Tillard, The Fortifications of Phokis, in: ABSA 17, 1910/1, 54–75. G.D.R.

Daunia (Δαυνία; *Daunía*). The region of D. roughly coincides with the northern part of today's Apulia; eventually incorporated into the *regio II* (Plin. HN 3,103), its extent however cannot be defined easily. In view of the importance of rivers for ancient geography, it can be assumed that the border in the north was the Fortore (Fertor in Ptol. 3,1,14), and the Ofanto (*Aufidus* at Plin. HN 3,103–105) in the south (Hor. Sat. 2,1,34f.: at *Venusia* as a border city; cf. also Mela 2,66; Str. 6,3,8; Pol. 3,88). In contrast to the historically unimportant coastal ranges of the *mons Garganus*, archaeological excavations allow the conclusion that, in the interior, Daunia extended as far as Lavello, Melfi and Banzi. Although true cities started to form in D. with its Romanization (the first Roman-Apulian alliance is dated to 326 BC by Liv. 8,25,3), cities such as Aecae, Arpi, Vibinum, Herdonia, Salapia, Canusium, Teanum Apulum and Ausculum were only founded during the Second Punic War; the same holds for two colonies (Luceria and Venusia became Roman in 291 BC) and rural *vici* such as Cannae and Gereonium. The road network was based on the *via Litoranea*, the *via Traiana* (where a pre-Roman road existed; Liv. 9,2,6–8) and the *via Appia* which crossed the interior parallel to the coast.

G. Angelini, G. Carlone, Atlante storico della Puglia 1. La Provincia di Foggia, 1986; A. Bottini, P. G. Guzzo, Greci e indigeni nel sud della penisola dall' VIII secolo a.C. alla conquista romana, in: Popoli e civiltà dell'Italia antica 8, 1986, 9–390; E. M. De Juliis, L'origine delle genti iapigie e la civiltà dei Dauni, in: G. Pugliese Carratelli (ed.), Italia omnium terrarum alumna, 1988, 591–650; A. Grilli, I geografi antichi sulla D., in: Atti del XIII Convegno di Studi Etruschi e Italici 'La civiltà daunia nel quadro del mondo italico, Manfredonia 1980', 1984, 83–92; M. Marin, Topografia storica della D. ant., 1970; G. Volpe, La D. nell'età della romanizzazione, 1990. S.D.V.

Daunian vases Pottery type found among the Italic peoples who inhabited the area of modern provinces around Bari and Foggia, with local production sites particularly in Ordona and Canosa.

From their early phase (around 700 BC), the vessels display a geometric ornamentation independent of the Greek range of subjects, which is applied in red and brown to black earthen colours onto the manually formed vessels. Among these are diamond and triangu-

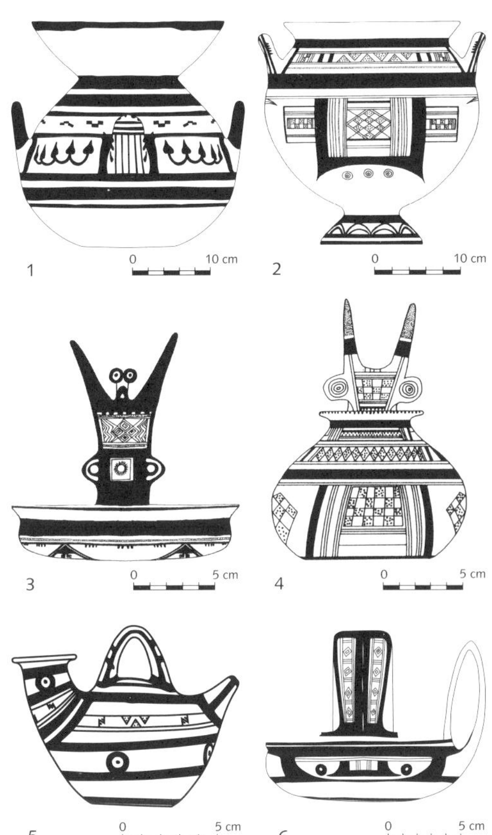

Daunian vases:
1. Funnel krater 2. Footed krater
3. Cup with anthropomorphic handle
4. Pitcher with anthropomorphic handle
5. Askos 6. Cup with high strap handle

lar patterns as well as band ornaments, wavy lines, circle, cross, square, arc, swastika and others (→ Ornaments). The initial development in vessel shape also took independently from Greek models. The typical Daunian vessels, divided into two groups (north and south Daunian pottery), are the foot crater, askos, funnel vessel and the bowl without a base featuring a looped handle; striking are the hand, animal and anthropomorphic protomes on the walls and handles or their drawn representations on the vessels. In the 5th cent. BC, the → potter's wheel is adopted and, in the course of the 4th cent. BC, Greek forms of decoration as well. As of 330 BC, bell and colonette craters, cantharus and kalathos become more frequent. In the early Canosine stage (*c.* 350 – 250 BC), the traditional forms of decor gave way to ivy and palmette friezes, the 'running dog', depictions of human figures and others. At that time only a few forms of vessel were dominant: double vessel, colonette crater, amphora, askos, thymiaterion.

D. Yntema, The Matt-Painted Pottery of Southern Italy, [2]1990. R.H.

Daunus (Δαῦνος; *Daûnos*).

[1] Hero who gave his name to the Daunians (→ Daunia); son of → Lycaon. Of Illyrian origin (Fest. p. 69), he immigrated to Italy together with his brothers Iapyx and Peuketios. There they expelled the native Ausonians and founded three kingdoms: Messapia, Peuketia and Daunia, which together are called → Iapygia (Nik. fr. 47 = Anton. lib. 31). When → Diomedes comes to Italy, D. receives him kindly and is supported by him against the Messapians. For this, Diomedes receives part of the land and D.'s daughter as his wife (Anton. Lib. 37). According to Tzetz. Lycophron 603f., D. killed Diomedes after a quarrel.

J. Bérard, La colonisation grecque de l'Italie méridionale et de la Sicile dans l'antiquité, 1957, 368–372.

[2] In Vergil, D. is the father of → Turnus and Iuturna (Verg. Aen. 10,616; 688 and passim). According to him, the Rutulians were also called *gens Daunia* (ibid. 8,146).

A. Russi, s.v. D., EV 2, 1002–1005. R.B.

Daversi see → Daorsi

David

[1] **King David.** In the biblical tradition, the figure of D. appears as a singer and musician (1 Sam 16,23), as a talented fighter (1 Sam 17; 30; cf. also his life as an irregular soldier in 1 Sam 22,1–5; 23) and finally as king of Judah, Israel, and Jerusalem (2 Sam 2,–5,10), who also subjugates the neighbouring states of Aram, Moab and → Edom [1] as well as Ammon (cf. 2 Sam. 8; 10; 12,26–31). His dynasty is promised eternal royal rule by god (cf. the so-called Nathan's prophecy 2 Sam. 7,12). After the fall of Judah and the end of the kingdom caused by the Babylonian Nebuchadnezzar (586 BC), D. becomes an idealized figure with whom both messianic hopes for a redemption of the people as well as spiritual dimensions of piety and prayer were associated. Thus, already during the time of exile and directly thereafter, the hope of a restitution of D.'s dynasty and the rule of a king of peace were expressed in prophecy (Ez 34,23f; 37,24f; Am 9,11ff; Mi 5,1–4; Hag 2,23; cf. 4 Q Flor 1,12). This eschatological dimension of the figure of D. also appears very clearly in the NT where Jesus is born in → Bethlehem, the city of D. (cf. the incorporation of Mi 5,1 in Mt 2,6; Lc 2,4; 2,11), and where he is also traced back to D. genealogically (Mt 1,1–16; Lc 3,23–38); furthermore, he carries the title 'son of D.' (Mt 9,27; 12,23; Mk 10,47; Joh 7,42; Romans 1,3 and passim; but cf. also the criticism of this title Mt 22,41ff. and parallels).

Through the association of numerous psalms with D.'s life (see the headlines of Ps 3; 7; 18; 34; 52; 54; 56; 57; 59; 60; 63)—nearly half of all psalms are attributed to D.—he becomes the ideal singer and prayer. Finally, he is regarded as the author of the entire book of psalms (cf. the non-canonical Ps 151 as well as 11QPsa DavComp).

These various developments find their form in the rabbinical tradition which emerged in the centuries after the destruction of the temple; the 'singer' D. as the author of the book of psalms becomes the ideal prayer (bBB 14a; bPes 117a; MTeh 1,6; cf. also the representation of D. in the synagogue mosaic of Gaza, where he is depicted in imperial Byzantine robes as the harp-playing Orpheus) in whose relationship to God the entire nation can participate (MTeh 24,3; bPes 117a; bBer 3; MTeh 4,1; 35,2 and passim). Simultaneously, he appears as a model for study of the Torah (bMak 10a). D.'s involvement in guilt (cf. the episode with Bathsheba, wife of the Hittite Uriah in 2 Sam 11, his census in 2 Sam 24 and parallels), for which he was punished, demonstrates God's just world order; at the same time, D.'s remorse and God's forgiveness serve as an encouraging example. D. can even appear as an intercessor to whose prayers Israel owes its existence (bSot 49a). Despite the rabbinical reluctance concerning messianic tendencies and eschatological speculations, here too D. is the archetype of the eschatological messiah (bMeg 17b; BerR 88,7; MTeh 5,4 and passim) for whose speedy appearance the 15th supplication of the eighteen-supplication prayer asks. Both the family of the patriarch in Palestine (*Nāśī*) and that of the → exilarch in Babylonia claimed, as their legitimization, their genealogical descent from the house of D.

A. Rosner, D.s Leben und Charakter nach Talmud und Midrasch, 1907; C. Thoma, s.v. D. II. Judentum, TRE 8, 384–387 (bibliography); L.A. Sinclair, s.v. D. I. Old Testament/ D. III. New Testament, TRE 8, 378–384, 387f. (bibliography). B.E.

[2] **David of Armenia.** Commentator on Aristotelian logic; it appears that he studied in Alexandria with → Olympiodorus, the pupil of → Ammonius [12], in the 2nd half of the 6th cent. AD. His works were translated into Armenian between the end of the 6th and the middle of the 7th cent. According to an Armenian tradition, which can be traced back to the 10th cent., he came from the otherwise unknown village of Nergin in Tarawn; the holy translators of the 5th cent. reportedly sent their pupil David abroad for study purposes where he earned himself the epithet 'the invincible' (Dawit' Anyalt') when, in the presence of the emperor Marcianus, he won a dialectic disputation against the Council of Chalcedon. After his return to his home country he reputedly translated into Armenian the *Organon* and the commentaries, which he had initially written in Greek, as well as many other works.

In addition to these, a panegyric of the holy cross and scholia on the grammar of Dionysius Thrax are attributed to him, two works which however were written by other authors of the same name; of the Armenian translations of the dialectic works attributed to D., the translation of the commentary on the categories was probably produced by another translator.

The Greek MSS attribute three titles to D.: (1) Prolegomena to Philosophy (Armenian), 'Definitions and categories of philosophy against four objections by Pyrrhon', a kind of protreptic writing that discusses traditional definitions of philosophy; (2) scholia on the *Isagoge* of Porphyrius, also translated into Armenian; (3) explanation of the ten categories; as it happens, the attribution of this work to D. is not directly confirmed in Armenian as the beginning of the text is damaged; (4) a fourth work, on the other hand, a commentary on the *Analytica*, has survived in Armenian only.

A. Busse, the editor of the Greek versions of these texts, wants to attribute (3) to → Elijah, another pupil of Olympiodorus, because, as he says, this text contradicts certain positions of (2); his arguments however are by no means conclusive. Text (4) on the other hand, surviving in Armenian only, has numerous parallels to (3). Therefore, there is no reason to doubt the tradition based on the MSS, which attributes this text to D. The coherence of the work also becomes evident when it is compared with that of Ammonius who also discusses, before the *Isagoge*, the six definitions of philosophy in the form of a preface on the various commentaries on logic.

Although the Armenian version often reflects an older tradition than the Greek MSS, it has never been evaluated systematically for the purpose of textual criticism.

A. Busse, ed., CAG 18.2, 1904; B. Kendall, R.W. Thomson, Definitions and Divisions of Philosophy by D. the Invincible Philosopher, 1983; J.P. Mahé, David l'Invincible dans la tradition arménienne, in: I. Hadot, Simplicius, Commentaire sur les Catégories I (Philosophia Antiqua, vol. 50), 189–207 (205–207: list of editions and secondary literature). J.P.M.

Day-labourers were among the wage-earners (μισθωτοί/*misthōtoí*; Lat. *mercenarii*, *operarii*) and supplemented the regular workforce when there was a need for additional, usually heavy, labour. In Athens they gathered at the Κολωνὸς μίσθιος/*Kolōnòs místhios*. They received → wages (μισθός/*misthós*: Hom. Il. 21,445; Lat. *merces*) or sometimes grain (σῖτος/*sîtos*, Lat. *frumentum*; → Ration).

Although there are not very many references to day-labourers in the agricultural sector, their work was of considerable importance, particularly at harvest time (Hom. Il. 18,550 ff.; Aristoph. Vesp. 712; Dem. Or. 18,51; Xen. Hier. 6,10; cf. also on women and slaves Dem. Or. 57,45; 53,20–22). Cato recommends recruiting workers basically for one day only (Cato Agr. 5,4), Varro allocates them the hardest jobs (Varro Rust. 1,17,2–3).

The public work records from Attica provide important source material. The accounts for the Erechtheum of 408/7 BC testify to μισθὸς καθ' ἡμέραν/*misthòs kath' hēméran* (day wages) for skilled craftsmen (IG I[3] 475,54; 475,65; 476,81; 476,87; 476,121) and for untrained labourers (IG I[3] 476,54–74; 476,141). On the building site at Eleusis around 330 BC day-labourers included brick-makers, porters, carpenters, trained building workers and drivers (IG II[2] 1672,28; 32; 45; 60; 110 f.; 126; 158; 160; 177; 240; 294; 1673,64 ff.). Day-labourers also played an important part in the Roman economy, although they are seldom attested.

The social status of day-labourers was low; in Athenian building accounts, unlike the skilled craftsmen, they are not mentioned by name. Their social position depended on whether they were continuously employed. The labourers on the Erechtheum received one drachma a day, while in Eleusis the daily wage was 1 $^1/_2$ drachmas, often more for craftsmen (IG II[2] 1672,28; 32; 45; 60; on Rome cf. Cato Agr. 22,3). The daily wage was normally sufficient for one day's sustenance. Day-labourers were held in little regard morally; the general opinion was that a day-labourer sold only his labouring ability, not his skill (Pl. Resp. 371d-e; Cic. Off. 1,150: *inliberales autem et sordidi quaestus mercennariorum omnium, quorum operae, non quorum artes emuntur*).

→ Crafts; → Wages; → Paid labour

1 A. Burford, Land and Labor in the Greek World, 1993
2 J. A. Crook, Law and Life of Rome, 1967, 195–197
3 A. Fuks, Kolonos misthios: Labour Exchange in Classical Athens, in: Eranos 49, 1951, 171–173 4 F. M. de Robertis, Lavoro e lavoratori nel mondo romano, 1963
5 S. M. Treggiari, Urban Labour in Rome: *mercennarii* and *tabernarii*, in: P. Garnsey (ed.), Non-Slave Labour in the Graeco-Roman World, 1980, 48–64. A. B.-C.

Dea Augusta Vocontiorum City of the Vocontii in Gallia Narbonensis, one of the two religious centres with *lucus Augusti* (Luc-en-Diois), today called Die. Ruins: Water pipes/channels, necropoleis (NE and NW), baths, bridges, *villae* inside and outside the walls. Inscriptions (CIL 12, 1556–1560; 1563) attest to the existence of temples (Jupiter, Cybele and Attis, Dea Augusta Andarta). Inscr.: CIL 12, 1554–1696.

Grenier, 1, 1931, 557–560; 4, 1960, 106–111; M. Leglay, s.v. D.A.V., PE, 259f. Y.L.

Dead, cult of the

I. Mesopotamia II. Egypt III. Etruria IV. Greece V. Rome VI. Christianity

I. Mesopotamia

The cult of the dead in Mesopotamia is documented in written as well as archaeological sources. In the written sources, the term *kispum* is used for the act of supplying the dead with food and drink (monthly or bimonthly). An important part of the ritual was the 'calling of the name' [3. 163] — *kispum* thus served to ensure not only the existence but also the identity of the dead in the → Underworld. In the absence of the cult of the dead, the Underworld changed into a dark, inhospitable place. The living also had an interest in performing the cult of the dead, since neglected spirits of the dead had the power to afflict the living with diseases and other punishment [2].

There is archaeological evidence of devices for the purpose of guiding libations into the earth or into the grave [3]. The ritual was usually performed in the building above the grave (a residence if within the city, a funeral chapel if outside of the city), where images (statues) of the dead could be placed. Finds from certain graves seem to indicate that the memory of the dead was not kept alive for very long (for example, old graves were disturbed by new installations, older remains were removed) [1; 2].
→ Burial B.; → Funerary architecture II.; → Death I.

1 G. Jonker, Topography of Remembrance, 1995, 187–212 2 S. Lundström, *kimaḫḫu* und *qabru*, in: Altoriental. Forsch. 27, 2000, 6 20 3 A. Tsukimoto, Unt. zur Totenpflege (*kispum*) im Alten Mesopot., 1985. S. LU.

II. Egypt

According to Egyptian beliefs, the continued existence of the dead in the afterlife required that they be provided with food. In addition to burial gifts and decorations, the supply of food was primarily ensured through sacrificial offerings that were presented at the grave by relatives of the deceased, ideally by the son. As a consequence, childlessness could have severe ramifications [4. 191–201]. We therefore find 'calls to the living' on burial steles or similar places in an attempt to entice strangers to at least say a sacrificial prayer [5; 4. 155–190]. Prayers not only served to replace material sacrifices, but also resulted in a 'calling of the name', another requirement for existence in the afterlife. Furthermore, one hoped to take part in the → sacrifices (II. B.) for the gods. During the so-called sacrificial circuit, sacrifices were first offered to the gods, then to the statues of the dead in the temple, then finally to the priests. For the same purposes, pilgrims erected steles at sacred sites such as Abydus. In Dair al-Madīnā, we furthermore have evidence of sacrifices made to ancestral busts in residential houses.

The royal cult of the dead was performed in the so-called mortuary temples, although they were not limited to this function [2]. Private citizens received cult chapels separate from their graves only in exceptional cases. The cult of the dead usually ended after a few generations, but in special cases it could blend into the beginning of → deification. Cults of the dead were occasionally also applied in connection with the vision of dying gods [3].
→ Burial B.; → Funerary architecture II.; → Pyramids; → Death I.

1 R. J. Demaree, The ꜣh ikr n Rꜥ-Stelae. On Ancestor Worship in Ancient Egypt, thesis Amsterdam 1983 2 G. Haeny, New Kingdom 'Mortuary Temples' and 'Mansions of Millions of Years', in: B. H. Shafer (ed.), Temples of Ancient Egypt, 1997, 86–126 3 F.-R. Herbin, Une liturgie des rites décadaires de Djême, in: Rev. d'Égyptologie 35, 1984, 105–126 4 M. Lichtheim, Maat in Egyptian Autobiographies and Related Studies, 1992 5 J. Sainte Fare Garnot, L'appel aux vivants, 1938. A. v. L.

III. Etruria

Since the rules of rituals of the *Etrusca disciplina* (→ Divination VII.) have not been preserved and are largely missing on inscriptions [4. 30–54; 10], the most important sources of the Etruscan cult of the dead are found in the form and in the furnishings of the burial complex. The wealthier graves of the → Villanova Culture already draw distinctions between burials of the body and cremation in the personal attributes used (fibulas, weapons etc.) as well as in the plates and cups for the 'funerary banquet' of the deceased [1. 30–33, fig.; 9. 11–14]. The ash container ('Villanova Urn') sometimes assumed anthropomorphous traits and can be regarded as the precursor of the burial sculpture, which became customary in Etruria from the 7th cent. BC and which represented the deceased either alone (canope in Clusium/Chiusi; statues in Clusium/Chiusi, Vetulonia, Volci/Vulci) or united with his ancestors (Caere/Cerveteri: [9. 81–115]). The latter motif also appeared on grave paintings in the 4th cent. BC: the deceased is welcomed by his ancestors to a meal with the gods of the Underworld (Volsinii: [11. 287, fig. 43; 44]).

One must differentiate, on the one hand, between cult acts during the burial phase, which can be identified through gifts such as drinking-cups and food on benches and tables or through altars for libations and through broken cups as relics of drink offerings, all presented at the entrance to the grave, and, on the other hand, cult acts that took place outside of the grave (which was closed after each burial process). These memorial celebrations were aided by ramps and stairs to the top of the burial complex, where the altar or cippus (as symbols of the deceased; → *cippus*) was located [9. 81–85]. Platforms at the foot of the → tumulus (Quintofiorentino, Cortona) possibly served for laying out the body (on representations of prothesis in the Etruscan visual arts, cf. [5. 368–373; 12. 131–132]). Necropoleis sanctuaries with temples, water basins, votive depositories, and inscriptions addressed to chthonic deities are documented for Volsinii and Capua [2]. A cult complex in the shape of a theatre with a monumental circular altar near Viterbo (6th cent. BC) suggests that animal sacrifices played a part in the cult of the dead and were performed in front of a large audience [9. 82–84; 3]. Funeral games with athletic and artistic competitions, including the bloody 'Game of Phersu' [6] which can be regarded as a precursor of gladiatorial games, are characteristic visual motifs of early Etruscan sepulchral art, esp. in Tarquinii and Clusium/Chiusi [12; 14]. Beginning in the 4th cent. BC, in the course of a change in visual themes, we find, among other things, processions of the dead in which the deceased actively participates accompanied by magistrates, surviving dependants, and demons of death [7].
→ Cippus; → Funerary architecture III. C.; → Procession; → Death II.; → Tumulus IV.; → Villanova Culture

1 G. Bartoloni, La cultura villanoviana, 1989
2 G. Colonna (ed.), Santuari d'Etruria, 1985, 116–126
3 Id., Strutture teatriformi in Etruria, in: [13], 321–347

4 J.-R. JANNOT, Devins, dieux et démons, 1998 5 Id., Les reliefs archaïques de Chiusi, 1988 6 Id., Phersu, Phersuna, Persona, in: [13], 281–320 7 R. LAMBRECHTS, Essai sur les magistratures des républiques étrusques, 1959 8 F. PRAYON, Die Anf. großformatiger Plastik in Etrurien, in: P. SCHAUER (ed.), Arch. Unt. zu den Beziehungen zw. Altitalien und der Zone nordwärts der Alpen, 1998, 191–207 9 Id., Frühetr. Grab- und Hausarchitektur, 1975 10 F. RONCALLI, Scrivere Etrusco, 1985, 65–73 (clay bricks from Capua) 11 S. STEINGRÄBER, Etr. Wandmalerei, 1985 12 J.-P. THUILLIER, Les jeux athlétiques dans la civilisation étrusque, 1985 13 Id. (ed.), Spectacles sportifs et scéniques dans le monde étrusco-italique, 1993 14 M. TORELLI, Il rango, il rito e l'immagine, 1997, 122–151.
F. PR.

IV. Greece

The duty of performing proper burial rites fell to the relatives, above all to the children of the deceased. If they were not performed, the dead were not regarded as dead 'to the full extent' and their souls were condemned to wander between earth and the Underworld [1. esp. 9 f.]. The enactment of the rites also confirmed the kinship of the surviving relatives with the deceased and therefore their right of inheritance [2nd ch. 7 and 11]. The details of the 'proper rites' varied. The absolute minimum was a respectable → burial of the body through burial in the ground or through cremation so that it would not become food for birds, dogs, or insects. If the body was not available, the rites could also be performed *in absentia,* and a→ *kenotáphion* was constructed (Hom. Od. 1,290–292; 4,583 f.; 9,65 f. with Eust. *ad loc.*; Eur. Hel. 1050–1068; 1239–1278; [1. 152, 155]).

In the ideal case, female relatives washed the body as soon as possible after death, dressed it and laid it out (→ *próthesis*). A day of lamentation followed; the informal lamentation of the relatives could be complemented by hired female mourners (→ Mourning; → *thrênos*). The body was carried out of the house (→ *ekphorá*) on the third day (also counting the day of death) and was buried or burned (on the varying proportion between inhumation and cremation depending on time and place, see [2. 96]). The deceased received gifts: among them were always → libations of honey, milk, wine, water and/or oil, which were repeated regularly, usually at least for the duration of one year (Aesch. Cho. 84–164; Soph. El. 894 f.). Even some smaller items of daily use that were owned by the deceased (mirror and make-up case for women, weapons and sports equipment for men, toys for children [3rd ch. 7 and 11]) and a meal were included (*deípnon*; Aesch. Cho. 483; Aristoph. Lys. 599–601; Plut. Aristides 21; [3. 76–79, 125 f.; 1. 41; 5]). The surviving relatives sometimes cut their hair and placed it on the grave; whoever was absent during the burial could dedicate his hair to the deceased at a later time (Hom. Il. 23,135; Aesch. Cho. 7–9; Soph. El. 52, 449). A monument (*sêma*; *stélē*) was erected and sometimes decorated with ribbons and boughs of myrtle [3. 84–90, 121–141, 218–246]. Additional rituals could also be performed depending on the wishes of the deceased and his family. For instance, we may assume that the → Orphicae Lamellae were placed on the bodies by the bereaved. The *póleis* repeatedly tried to limit the size and the extent of monuments, lamentations, and burials [3. 200–203; 4. 74–190] (→ Burial C.).

It was assumed that the souls of the people who did not receive the proper rites or who died early or unhappy would return in order to take revenge against those responsible, or in order to cause suffering to those whom they envied. Such cases required special rituals, additional libations and more, and the creation of statues of the dead. The statues were provided with food and/or left in uninhabited areas [1. 46–63; 5]. When a soul was restless, whole groups of people could be harmed and forced into the enactment of the necessary rituals. The Delphic Oracle, for instance, told cities that suffered from difficulties that they could find relief through performing burials or other honours for the dead (Hdt. 1,67,2; 1,167,2). A few cities performed rituals to appease the spirits of girls who had died unmarried in order to prevent them from enticing virgins to commit suicide [1st ch. 6]. At the → Anthesteria, the spirits were called back to earth and were honoured for three days in the hope that they would, having been satisfied on this occasion, remain in → Hades for the rest of the year. Even then, precautions were taken such as wearing apotropaic wreaths made of thorny *rhámnos*, so that the spirits would not take too many liberties (Phot. s. v. [pl.: vv.] ῥάμνος; cf. s. v. μιαρὰ ἡμέρα). A special libation and a ritual pronouncement at the end of the Anthesteria sent the spirits back to Hades [1. 63–66]. The festival of → Genesia, which honoured dead relatives, was also celebrated in many parts of Greece (Hdt. 4,26; [6. 100 f.; 7]).

The → hero cult can be regarded as a special form of the cult of the dead. Also, itinerant priests offered rites which were supposed to improve the lot of the dead in the Underworld (Pl. Resp. 354b 5–365a 3); a publicly performed ritual in Selinus [4] in the 5th cent. BC had a similar purpose [1. 49–58; 5].

→ Burial; → Funerary architecture; → Afterlife, concepts of; → Sacrifices III.; → Death; → Mourning; → Underworld

1 S. I. JOHNSTON, Restless Dead, 1999 2 C. SOURVINOU-INWOOD, 'Reading' Greek Death, 1995 3 D. C. KURTZ, J. BOARDMAN, Greek Burial Customs, 1971 4 R. SEAFORD, Reciprocity and Ritual, 1994 5 M. H. JAMESON *et. al.*, A 'Lex Sacra' from Selinous, 1993 6 S. C. HUMPHREYS, Family Tombs and Tomb Cult in Ancient Athens: Tradition or Traditionalism?, in: JHS 100, 1980, 96–126 7 F. JACOBY, GENESIA, in: CQ 38, 1944, 65–75.
S. I. J.

V. Rome

For the Romans, the world of the dead seemed dark and dangerous and was therefore carefully separated from the world of the living spatially (→ Necropoleis

VIII.) were located outside of the city walls along the highways) as well as by → ritual. Death was regarded as having a polluting effect on the entire family: the *flamen Dialis* (→ *flamines*) was not to touch a dead body, nor participate in a cremation (Gell. NA 10,15,24). The → priests were in charge of the legal governance of burials (Liv. 1,20,7), although burial and the cult of the dead were essentially private rituals arranged by the → *pater familias*.

Upon the arrival of the funeral procession at the burial site, the body was interred or cremated (→ Burial D.). According to Cicero (Leg. 2,56), burial was not complete in the case of cremation until the moment when the earth covered the ashes of the deceased; the grave (*sepulcrum*), however, was not considered as constructed and did not become on object of religious law until further ceremonies were performed: findings from the necropoleis indicate that perfume, wine and oil were burned. According to Cic. Leg. 2,57, a pig was sacrificed and the deceased was nourished by the smell of the animal, suggesting that he had already made the transition into the category of the Di → Manes. Since the living were not allowed to share food with the dead, they ate no part of the animal, only perhaps a second pig that was offered to the → Penates. After eight days had passed (*dies denicales*), another sacrifice took place on the domestic altar, where a 'ram for Lar' was slaughtered (Cic. Leg. 2,55). The family of the deceased was now released from the pollution of death.

The Romans also celebrated two ceremonies for the dead: the Feralia (Ov. Fast. 2,533–570) took place on 21 February, at the end of a month filled with various purification rites in preparation for the new year in ancient Rome. This was the final and closing day of a period of nine days (13–21 February), the *dies parentales* (→ Parentalia), which were dedicated to the dead (Varro, Ling. 6,13). According to Ovid (loc. cit.), families visited the graves and brought gifts, often modest ones, to the Di Manes: on a brick decorated with garlands — serving as an altar — grains of wheat and salt, flat loafs of wheat, and violets were spread out while ritual prayers were spoken. It was, however, not forbidden to make more lavish offerings. This ceremony, which allowed the living to fulfil their duties towards the dead, confirmed the place of both: the dead in the graves, and the living in the houses where the surviving family joined together on the following day (22 February), after a sacrifice to the Lar.

The second celebration for the dead, the Lemuria, took place on the 9th, 11th and 13th days of May (Ov. Fast. 5,419–661; → *lemures*). Ovid connects the name of the month (*Maius*) etymologically with the *maiores* ('ancestors'). The Lemuria were dedicated to the *lemures*, the souls of the dead, also regarded as nocturnal ghosts who supposedly visited their former homes (Non. 197 L). In the course of these days, gifts (*inferiae*) were brought to the graves. In the night, the *pater familias* conjured up the *lemures* in his house. This ritual, as described by Ovid, entailed magical elements (finger gestures of conjuration; words repeated nine times; the *pater familias* addresses the ghosts with his back turned in order to avoid any visual contact) and apotropaic aspects: the *lemures* leave after being fed beans, which is the price for the *pater familias* and his family to 'buy out'; the noise of beating metal with the hands then scares the ghosts away. There is, however, a connection to more traditional → sacrifices (IV): the ghosts were presented with black beans, similar to the black sacrificial animals offered to the → 'chthonic deities'. The introductory washing of the hands by the person performing the ritual is a typical act of purification before a sacrifice; the second washing, however, which is done to conclude the ceremony, aims at cleansing the performing person of the pollution that he incurred through his contact with the dead, and emphasizes the separation between the dead and the living.

Further finds in the excavations of Roman necropoleis, epigraphic documents, and analyses of the remnants of offerings, esp. of the animals sacrificed at the graves will offer more concrete knowledge about the relationships between the living and the dead.

→ Burial; → Funerary architecture III C.; → Necropoleis VIII.; → Sacrifices; → Ritual; → Death II.; → Underworld

F. Boemer, Ahnenkult und Ahnenglaube im alten Rom, 1944; F. Cumont, Lux perpetua, 1949; F. Hinard (ed.), La mort au quotidien dans le monde romain, 1995; I. Morris, Death-Ritual and Social Structure in Classical Antiquity, 1992; J. Scheid, Contraria facere: renversements et déplacements dans les rites funéraires, in: AION 6, 1984, 117–139.

A. DU.

VI. Christianity

In the beginning, the Christian worship of the dead adopted almost all of the traditional forms of the older Greek and Roman cults of the dead. [2. 46–53]. For instance, there were celebrations on the 3rd, 7th, 30th and 40th days after death (Ambr. Obit. Theod. 3), or the Novemdialia (→ *novendiale sacrum*) and → Parentalia (Aug. Quaestiones in Heptateuchum 1,172; Aug. Conf. 6,2), but most importantly on the 'birthday' (*dies natalis*), which Christians understood to be the day of death, esp. in the case of → martyrs [11. 230–239; 2. 54–67; 12. 219 f.]. However, the days of the deaths of martyrs and bishops do not appear in the written sources until the second half of the 4th cent. (→ Chronographer of 354). Beginning with bishop → Damasus of Rome (366–384), the first installations to suggest a martyr cult at the graves [9. 275–302] appeared in Roman → catacombs. Earlier and contemporaneous traces of the Christian cult of the dead are similar to the forms of the pagan cult in Salona, Tipasa, Sabratha, Cornus, Tarragona.

In the 3rd and 4th cents., the most popular form of the cult of the dead was the funerary banquet, which in Rome was not necessarily held at the grave, but, depending on space, in the → *schola* [4] *collegii* or in the private residence. The graves had special places for

→ libations and for lamps and flowers [3. 31–37; 4. 211–243; 7. 179–193]. Particularly in Northern Africa, the traditional meal was held in the context of the private cult of the dead, and also during the feast days of martyrs. Both practices are evidenced by the half-circular masonry berths (*stibadia*) at the necropoleis of Tipasa and Sabratha [3. 29 f.; 12. 315 f.]. The custom of having meals at the graves was judged negatively by the Church Fathers [10. 50 f., 100–102, 133–140; 12. 224–234]. This custom is documented in the catacombs in Rome on representations of funerary banquets, which also show the symbolic significance of → *agápē* and of peace during the meal [3. 31–35]. Here, we also find other traces of the traditional cult of the dead: seats hewn into the tuff (*cathedrae*) [8. 98–115; 7. 148–153], glasses for libations and other objects at the graves [4. 261–263], tables (*mensae*) for sacrifices [1]. In the course of the 4th cent., the old literal meaning of the *refrigerium* ('refreshment') at the grave changed into a more symbolic one: the wish and the hope for salvation and eternal life in paradise [5. 164–171].

The early 4th cent. witnessed the construction of the first exedra basilicas in Rome [7. 153–164], followed by other cemetery basilicas in the Christian necropoleis of various cities in the entire Imperium (esp. in Northern Africa) [10. 173–197]. These basilicas were the place for funerals as well as for burial and Eucharist celebrations. The celebration of the Eucharist in the context of the Christian cult of the dead can be found in written sources (already in Tert. De Corona 3,3 and Cypr. Epist. 1,2,1), [10. 69–73, 102–104; 12. 222–224, 234 f.]. Archaeologically, celebrations of the Eucharist are documented in the cemetary basilicas of the 4th cent. This close connection between → altar and grave is documented in the sources for as early as the mid 4th cent. Archaeologically, the oldest evidence to suggest this connection stems from the 5th cent. in Rome and was found in the Basilica of St. Alexander on the *via Nomentana* [9. 284 f.],.

→ Basilica (B.); → Saints; → Catacombs; → Martyrs; → Paradise; → Pilgrimage (II); → Death

1 E. Chalkia, Le mense paleocristiane, 1991 2 F. W. Deichmann, Einführung in die christl. Arch., 1983 3 P.-A. Février, À propos du repas funéraire: culte et sociabilité, in: Cahiers Archéologiques 26, 1977, 29–45 4 Id., Le culte des morts dans les communautés chrétiennes durant le IIIe siècle, in: Atti del IX congresso internazionale di archeologia cristiana, vol. 1, 1978, 211–273 5 Id., La tombe chrétienne et l'au-delà, in: J.-M. Leroux (ed.), Le temps chrétien de la fin de l'Antiquité au Moyen Age, 1984, 163–183 6 E. Jastrzebowska, Les scènes de banquet en peinture et en sculpture chrétienne du IIIe et du IVe s., in: Recherches Augustiniennes 14, 1979, 3–90 7 Id., Unt. zum christl. Totenmahl aufgrund der Monumente des 3. und 4 Jh. unter der Basilika des Hl. Sebastian in Rom, 1981 8 T. Klauser, Die Cathedra im Totenkult der heidnischen und christl. Ant., 1971 9 L. Reekmans, Les cryptes des martyrs romains, in: Atti, see [4], 275–302 10 V. Saxer, Morts, martyrs, reliques en Afrique chrétienne aux premiers siècles, 1980 11 A. Stuiber, s. v. Geburtstag, RAC 9, 217–243 12 W. Schmidt, Spätant. Gräberfelder in den Nordprov. des röm. Reiches und das Aufkommen christl. Bestattungsbrauchtums, Saalburg Jb. 50, 2000, 213–441. E. JA.

Dea Dia An otherwise unknown female deity to whom the → *Arvales fratres* devoted the sacrifice of the month of May; nothing is known about the connection of the Dea Dia (DD) with a Dia from Amiternum (CIL I² 2, 1546) and the Greek Dia. Her name derives from the adjective *dius* and is connected with the space of heaven, probably the 'good light of heaven'. The thesis that DD is an indigitation (→ Indigitamenta) of Tellus or of Ceres cannot be maintained.

R. Schilling, Rites, cultes, dieux de Rome, 1979, 366–370. J.S.

Dead Sea (textual finds) What is referred to as the textual finds of the Dead Sea (DS, → Asphaltitis limne) is the library of MSS that were found at locations on the DS, including Ketef Jericho, → Qumrān (= Q), Ḫirbat al-Mird, Wādī n-Nār, Wādī l-Ġuwair, Wādī l-Murabbaʿa (= WM), Wādī Sudair, Naḥal Ḥever (= NḤ), Naḥal Mišmār, Naḥal Ṣeʾelim and the Masada (= M), as well as in the Wādī d-Dāliya (= WD) located between Samaria and Jericho. A complete list of all the texts can be found in [3, vol. 39].

I. Wādī d-Dāliya II. Qumrān III. Masada IV. Naḥal Ḥever, Wādī l-Murabbaʿa and Ketef Jericho V. Smaller sites VI. Ḫirbat al-Mird

I. Wādī d-Dāliya

With the exception of WDSP 38 (Greek), the *Wadi ed-Daliyeh Samaritan Papyri* (= WDSP) were written in Aramaic and were found, badly damaged, in 1962–1964 in a cave of the WD. The documents (from the 4th cent. BC) had been in the possession of parts of the Samaritan upper class who had fled from Alexander's [4] armies. A large part of the documents deals with the buying and selling of slaves. More important than the documents themselves are the glyptics on the seal impressions. They suggest that a Hellenistic influence on Samaritan culture and religion existed already in the 4th cent. BC [vol. 3, 24; 51].

II. Qumrān

In 1947–1956, Bedouins and archaeologists found about 1,000 MSS in 11 caves near Ḫirbat Q (→ Qumran) in Hebrew, Aramaic, Greek and Nabataean, most of them badly damaged, which were dated palaeographically into the period from the 3rd cent. BC to the 1st cent. AD. Aside from biblical texts, they document apocryphs that were known already prior to 1947 (→ Apocryphal literature A.) and → pseudepigraphic literature as well as a large number of Essene (→ Essenes) and non-Essene texts that were unknown prior to 1947. A few texts from the last group (e.g. the Damascus Docu-

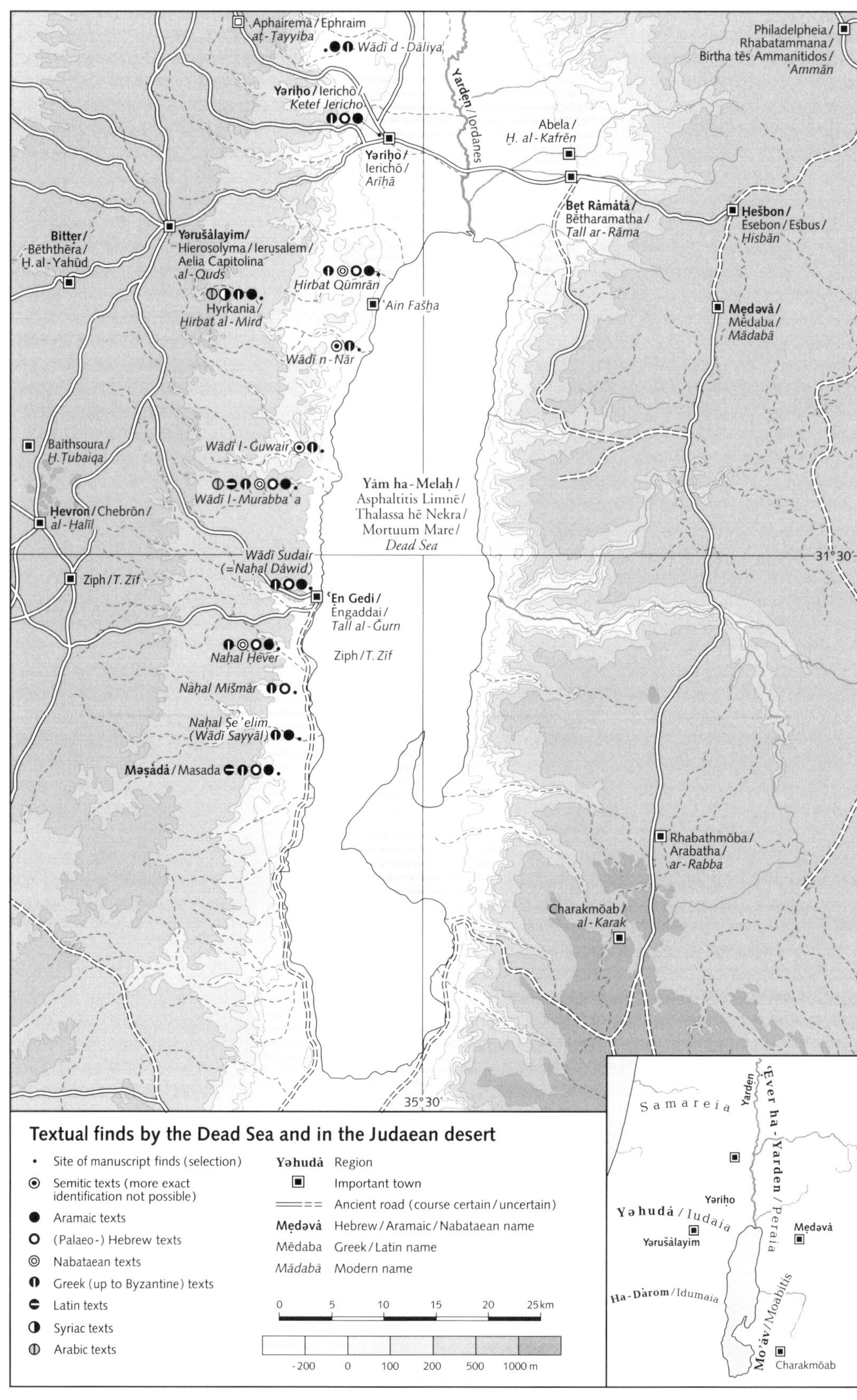
Aphairema / Ephraim
aṭ-Ṭayyiba
Wādī d-Dāliya
Yərīḥo / Ierichō /
Ketef Jericho
Yarden / Iordanes
Philadelpheia / Rhabatammana / Birtha tēs Ammanitidos / ʿAmmān
Abela / Ḫ. al-Kafrēn
Yərīḥo / Ierichō / Arīḥā
Bet Rāmātā / Bētharamatha / Tall ar-Rāma
Ḥešbon / Esebon / Esbus / Ḥisbān
Bitter / Bēththēra / Ḫ. al-Yahūd
Yərušālayim / Hierosolyma / Ierusalem / Aelia Capitolina / al-Quds
Ḫirbat Qumrān
Hyrkania / Ḫirbat al-Mird
ʿAin Fašḫa
Mədəvā / Mēdaba / Mādabā
Wādī n-Nār
Baithsoura / Ḫ. Ṭubaiqa
Wādī l-Ġuwair
Wādī l-Murabbaʿa
Yām ha-Melaḥ / Asphaltitis Limnē / Thalassa hē Nekra / Mortuum Mare / Dead Sea
Ḥevron / Chebrōn / al-Ḫalīl
Wādī Sudair (=Naḥal Dāwid)
31°30'
Ziph / T. Zīf
ʿEn Gedi / Engaddai / Tall al-Ġurn
Naḥal Ḥever
Ziph / T. Zīf
Naḥal Mišmār
Naḥal Ṣeʾelim (Wādī Sayyāl)
Məṣādā / Masada
Rhabathmōba / Arabatha / ar-Rabba
Charakmōab / al-Karak
35°30'
Textual finds by the Dead Sea and in the Judaean desert
Site of manuscript finds (selection)
Semitic texts (more exact identification not possible)
Aramaic texts
(Palaeo-) Hebrew texts
Nabataean texts
Greek (up to Byzantine) texts
Latin texts
Syriac texts
Arabic texts
Yəhudā Region
Important town
Ancient road (course certain / uncertain)
Mədəvā Hebrew / Aramaic / Nabataean name
Mēdaba Greek / Latin name
Mādabā Modern name
0 5 10 15 20 25 km
-200 0 100 200 500 1000 m
Samareia
Yarden
ʿEver ha-Yarden / Peraia
Yərīḥo
Yəhudā / Iudaia
Yərušālayim
Mədəvā
Ha-Dārom / Idumaia
Moʾav / Moabitis
Charakmōab

ment and the *Aramaic Levi Document*) are also known from the → Geniza. The library of Q therefore provides a non-representative cross-section of the literature of ancient → Judaism in the Hellenistic-Roman period. The texts authored by the Essene residents of Q can be identified according to the following criteria: the treatment or the quotation of an Essene text, the use of typical terminology (e.g. *anšy hyḥd*, that is 'men of the community'), radical observation of the Torah, cosmic-ethical dualism wherein everything non-Essene is rejected as sinful, critical distance to the Temple of Jerusalem, use of a 364–day solar calendar, and the mention of central figures from the history of the Essene community. In contrast, the free use of the tetragram, the 354–day lunar calendar, and the compilation of a text in a language other than Hebrew suggest the non-Essene origin of a text.

A. History of the canon and biblical manuscripts B. Para-Biblical Literature C. Exegetic Literature D. Literature dealing with religious law E. Calendarial Literature F. Poetic-liturgical Literature G. Wisdom literature (as a genre) H. Historical texts and narratives J. Apocalyptic and eschatological Literature K. Magical-divinatory Literature L. Other texts

A. History of the canon and biblical manuscripts

The library of Q indicates that ancient Judaism in the Hellenistic period observed authoritative texts and had developed an understanding of the Scriptures from the time of the Hellenistic religious reforms in 175–164 BC. We can, however, not assume a complete canon for this time. Altogether, *c.* 200 MSS of books of the later Hebrew Bible were found in Q: The oldest (4QSam[b]; 4QJer[a]) stem from the mid 3rd cent. BC. *C.* 35 % of the OT MSS from Q document the same inventory of consonants as the later Masoretic text; 5 % document a form of the Pentateuch, which was later adopted and altered by the Samaritans; 5 % document the Hebrew models of various books of the → Septuagint; *c.* 20 % use a full orthography common to Q; *c.* 35 % show types of texts that cannot be classified under any of the known versions. Especially the textual evidence of the last group allows insights into the editorial evolution of the OT books and shed doubt, at least for a part of the Hebrew Bible, on the postulate of an original text. MSS in Aramaic and Greek indicate that the translation process into Greek and Aramaic reaches far back into the past (→ Bible translations). To the extent that it is possible to date them, the non-Biblical texts from Q stem from the period between the 4th and the 1st cents. BC. These texts can be divided into various groups:

B. Para-Biblical Literature

Para-biblical texts are literary works which are closely connected to texts, topics, or persons of the later Hebrew Bible. Para-biblical literature is characterized by the endeavour to gain insights about the revelation that had occurred through interpretation of authoritative texts (such as the Torah) and to newly articulate it in new texts. These *relecture* processes represent the attempt to find answers to contemporary questions and to ground them in the revelation from the past. The Para-biblical literature from Q deals with texts and persons from the time of Creation to the time of exile. Aside from texts from the realm of the *rewritten Bible* (e.g. the books of Noah and Jubilees, Moses apocryphs), we also find narratives (Book of Giants), testaments, and apocalypses (see below).

C. Exegetic Literature

The library of Q is the primary source of exegetic literature in ancient Judaism from the time of the Hellenistic religious reforms (175–164 BC). The fact that exegetic literature appeared at that time suggests a change in the treatment of authoritative texts. Judaism did not develop an understanding of Scriptures until this period. The most widely used genre of exegetic literature are the *Pesharim* that originated in Essene circles. They share the common feature of introducing the interpretation of a cited lemma with an interpretative formula that can vary in its precise wording but always contains the word *pešer* ('interpretation'). There are thematic and continuous *Pesharim*. The word *pešer* and the interpretative techniques used by the *Pesharim* are reminiscent of ancient interpretations of dreams and omens (→ Omen; → Dreams, Interpretation of dreams). The interpretation of the Pesharists was regarded as a second act of revelation subordinate to the text of the prophet, which revealed to the interpreter the meaning of the text hidden to the prophet.

D. Literature dealing with religious law

The fact that the Essenes regarded this type of literature as largely exegetic is indicated by the designation of *midrāšîm* for two community rules. Community rules and a large part of the → Halakha are of Essene origin. Their exegetic character may be related to the Essene community's claim to have a special knowledge of the interpretation and the significance of the laws. Generally, we can observe the tendency towards a particularly strict interpretation of religious laws in the Essene Halakha. The reason for this may be found in the priestly origin of this community. Aside from issues of purity, the laws about the Sabbath and calendar issues are of particular interest. Community rules such as Serekh ha-Yaḥad or the Damascus Document govern the conduct of life in the Essene community and are reminiscent in their regulations of the structure of Hellenistic religious guilds. The fact that issues of religious law were not only relevant for the period in question is demonstrated by the so-called Rule of War and the community rule referring to the eschaton.

E. Calendarial Literature

The large number of calendarial MSS indicates that the Essenes regarded calendar issues as highly significant. The texts establish the times of service for the different ranks of priests and list the dates for the Sabbath and cult festivals. Mixed forms were not unusual. With the exception of 4QZodiology and Brontology (360-day solar calendar), all texts are committed to a 364-day solar calendar, similar to the one in astrHen and Jub, also the same one that governed the cult practices before 150 BC at least of the Jerusalem → Temple. In this calendar, months, weeks, and days do not have names, but are simply counted. It was used by the Essene movement even after 152 BC, while the temple at that time used the 354-day lunar calendar with Babylonian names, the same that is still being used by modern Judaism.

F. Poetic-liturgical Literature

The fact that poetic-liturgical literature forms one of the largest groups of texts in the library of Q has to do with the significance that the praise of God has for the → Essenes. Due to their distancing from the Jerusalem Temple, they regarded their community as a spiritual temple (*mqdš adm*, 'Temple of humans'), in which the praise of God took on the function of the sacrifice (see 4QMidrEschat[a] III). In general, one can ascertain that the poetic genres of the Hebrew Bible melt together in the texts of the Q library. Also, one finds more and more anthological poetry (see, for instance, the Hodayot). The liturgical poetry comprises collections of so-called daily prayers, songs for the sacrifice of Sabbath, texts dealing with a covenant renewal liturgy, purification rituals, and exorcism (see below K.). Aside from psalm collections in the style of the psalter and laments, the non-liturgical poetry consists essentially of Hodayot (songs of praise) and Hodayot-like poems.

G. Wisdom literature (as a genre)

The library of Q contained a surprisingly large number of wisdom texts, all of non-Essene origin with the exception of a didactic speech (4Q298). Their large number indicates that wisdom literature was much more prevalent in ancient Judaism than previously assumed. The dominant genre in this type of literature is constituted by a 'teaching' (*mūšar*). Such teachings are a combination of collections of sayings and of passages in the style of treatises, hymns, and parenesis. We also find a collection of what seem to be old sayings and two other didactic speeches. On the content level, most of the texts can be subsumed under the wisdom of the Torah, but it is also not unusual to find dualistic-eschatological ideas and an interest in cult.

H. Historical texts and narratives

Narrative texts other than those belonging to the para-biblical category are very rare in the library of Q. Aside from Tob, which was probably written in Hebrew originally (4Q196–200), we only find two Aramaic court narratives (Prayer of Nabonid: 4Q242; Proto-Esther: 4Q550–550e).

J. Apocalyptic and eschatological Literature

None of the apocalypses in the library of Q indicate Essene authors Many of the apocalypses are of para-biblical nature and proclaim to be revelations. Until recently, symbolic codification was regarded as a characteristic feature of apocalyptic revelation, and indeed, several of these symbolic apocalypses can be found in the library of Q (Book of Dreams: 1 Hen 83–90; 4Q204 4 etc.). However, some texts of revelation were found with ideas similar to those in symbolic apocalypses, but they did not use symbolic codification (e.g. Historical Text A: 4Q248) and should be categorized as non-symbolic apocalypses. Aside from pure texts of revelation, we also find works that take the visionary author into the world of transcendence, on what one would call *otherworldly journeys* (ascent to heaven; New Jerusalem: 1Q32 etc.). Furthermore, the library of Q contains a large number of other eschatological texts (e.g. Rule of War or community rule). Of these, at least a younger form of the Rule of War, the eschatological community rule, and possibly blessings derived from the Aaronitic blessing (Num 6,24–26) appear to be of Essene origin.

K. Magical-divinatory Literature

Only sparse amounts of magical-divinatory literature were found in Q and none of it appears to be of Essene origin. Aside from a physiognomical-astrological list of omens (4Q186, 4Q561), we find a brontologion attached to zodiacal astrology (4Q318). The surviving magical texts are largely exorcist in nature (→ Exorcism).

L. Other texts

In addition, the library of Q contained a small number of legal and religious documents, which clearly connect the library found in 1Q–11Q with the settlement of Q (→ Essenes; → Qumran). Furthermore, two letters (4Q342, Aramaic; 4Q343, Nabataean), four exercises by scribes as well as a list of treasures engraved in copper (3Q15) have survived.

III. Masada

The badly damaged MSS of the M (on the archaeology and the history of finds: → Masada) stem primarily from its Zelotic inhabitants during the first → Jewish War. Only the biblical MSS MasDtn and MasEzek could possibly stem from the period of Herod [1] I the Great. As far as it is still ascertainable, the seven biblical texts document a proto-Masoretic text [vol. 7, 6]. MasSir (Ma 1h) shows a textual form which deviates from the LXX and the Geniza MSS. Aside from biblical and deutero-canonical MSS, the following texts were found on the M: a Jub or psJub MS (Ma 1j), two MSS of texts that are also documented for Q, an apocryphon of Genesis or Joseph, a paleo-Hebrew MS (Ma 10 r), in which *hrgrzym* ('Mount Garizim') is written as a proper name in one word and which could be of Samaritan origin [vol.7, 6, 142–147], an Aramaic fragment, and several ostraka. The fact that Ma 1k-l is also documented in Q does not necessarily prove an Essene presence on M during the first Jewish War. In the remains of the Roman siegeworks, documents and letters were found that provide insights into the life of the legions at the end of the first cent. AD. One particular part of a text from Verg. Aen. (Ma 721 r) is remarkable in that it constitutes one of the oldest pieces of evidence for this work.

IV. Naḥal Ḥever, Wādī l-Murabbaʿa and Ketef Jericho

The altogether badly damaged MSS of the three locations are in Hebrew, Aramaic, Greek, and Nabataean, and were uncovered either by Bedouins or in systematic excavations. The Bedouins indicated that the places of origin for the MSS they found in NḤ were Wādī Sayyāl and Q, and only the study of the MSS themselves led to solid conclusions about their origin [3, vol. 27, 1–6; 3, vol. 39]. Literary texts, documents and letters from the 1st and 2nd cents. AD were found in refuge caves in NḤ and WM. The oldest known non-inscriptional Hebrew text, a paleo-Hebrew → palimpsest from the 7th cent. BC (the overwritten text consists of a list of names, the secondary text is a letter), was found in WM. In Ketef Jericho, two additional paleo-Hebrew MSS from the 4th cent. BC were found (Jer 1; Jer 6,5). Also in WM, Byzantine and Arabic MSS were found. Biblical MSS are known only from NḤ and WM. To the extent that they are legible, they document a proto-Masoretic text.

Particularly important for the textual history of the OT is 8ḤevXII gr. This scroll consists of an edition of the Greek translation of the Book of 12 Prophets in light of the proto-Masoretic text, a perspective also represented by → Theodotion or the LXX Lamentations. Due to its typical use of καίγε, this edition is called *Kaige* today. The paleographic dating of 8ḤevXII gr into the late 1st cent. BC [3, vol. 8, 19–26] evidences that the reworking of the LXX began much earlier than previously assumed and invalidates the idea that the Christian use of the LXX triggered the reworking process. The yield of non-biblical texts from the three locations is meagre. Aside from a few MSS from the time of the first Jewish War (these documents belonged to a group that fled from M to WM in AD 71 or later) and a few MSS that stem from the Roman occupation of WM following the second Jewish War, the *c.*160 MSS are documents from WM, NḤ, and Ketef Jericho and were in the possession of refugees from the last phase of the second Jewish War. The documents were written in Hebrew, Aramaic, Greek, and Nabataean and offer insights into the system of law, and the social and economic history of the period. Most of these documents belong to the following types: bills of sale or leases, lists of goods, promissory notes, marriage contracts, and letters of divorce. Generally, the laws that existed prior to the second Jewish War can also be found after AD 132. A new development, however, is the use of Hebrew in legal documents. Furthermore, the documents from before AD 132 suggest that the Jewish population around the DS participated in the system of law of their non-Jewish environment in this time period [12. 215]. The archives of documents of two women (Babatha: 5/6Ḥev 1–35; Salome Komaise: XḤev/Se 12, XḤev/Se 60–65) allow us to understand in detail the legal history of two Jewish families.

NḤ and WM provided us with a large number of letters, which became essential sources for the history of the second Jewish War. Many of these letters were written by → Bar Kochba himself and reveal, for instance, his true name (Shimʿon ben Kosiba); other letters stem from his administration. The fact that only two of these letters are written in Greek, the rest in Hebrew or Aramaic, suggests an effort towards revitalizing the Hebrew language.

V. Smaller sites

Smaller finds of MSS were made in Wādī n-Nār, Wādī l-Ġuwair, Wādī Sudair, Naḥal Mišmār, and Naḥal Ṣeʾelim. All of these MSS are badly damaged. In Wādī n-Nār, two Greek, one Semitic, and two linguistically unidentifiable fragments were found. Their speculative origin is Ḫirbat al-Mird. The complex at Wādī l-Ġuwair is possibly an Essene settlement. This complex is attributed with the finds of a Greek papyrus fragment and a Semitic paper fragment. According to information from Bedouins, four MSS from the period of the second Jewish War were found in Wādī Sudair (= Naḥal David) in 1952. These MSS consist of a proto-Masoretic Gen.-MS, an Aramaic promissory note, and two unidentified Greek documents. In Naḥal Mišmār, remnants of two Hebrew and one Greek document were found, so were parts of four Hebrew and of one Greek ostrakon from the period of the second Jewish War. The few MSS that are certain to stem from Naḥal Ṣeʾelim were discovered during an excavation campaign in 1960 in cave 34. They consist of a phylacterium, a Neh-MS, an Aramaic contract, a Greek census-list, and a Greek list of wheat.

VI. Ḫirbat al-Mird

The name refers to the Byzantine monastery of Kastellion, which was constructed in AD 492 near the DS, not far from Ḫirbat Q on the ruins of the ancient Hyrcania. Since 1873, surveys and partial excavations have been carried out there. The Arabic, Greek, and Syrian or Christian-Aramaic papyri of Ḫirbat al-Mird are badly damaged. Found in 1952 by Bedouins and in 1953 in excavations, they stem from the Byzantine and Arabic period. The 100 Arabic papyri can be divided into protocols, legal documents, letters, economic texts, literary texts, varia, and a drawing. Of the Syrian and Christian-Aramaic papyri, a letter, a magical amulet, and a MS of the Acts have so far been published.

Furthermore, reports exist of Jos-, Mt-, Lk-, and Col-MSS. Of the Greek papyri, Mt-, Mk-, Jn-, and Acts-MSS have been published as well as a monastic letter.

EDITIONS: 1 N. AVIGAD, Y. YADIN, A Genesis Apocryphon, 1956 2 J. H. CHARLESWORTH (ed.), The Princeton Theological Seminary Dead Sea Scrolls Project, 1991 ff. 3 Discoveries in the Judaean Desert (of Jordan), vol. 1 ff., 1955 ff. 4 F. GARCÍA MARTÍNEZ, E. J. C. TIGCHELAAR (ed.), The Dead Sea Scrolls Study Edition, vol. 1–2, 1997–1998 5 J. MAIER et al., Die Qumran-Essener: Die Texte vom Toten Meer, 3 vols., 1995–1996 6 N. LEWIS, Y. YADIN, J. C. GREENFIELD (ed.), The Documents from the Bar Kokhba Period in the Cave of Letters (Judaean Desert Studies), 1989 7 Masada. The Yigael Yadin Excavations 1963–1965, Final Reports, vol. 1–6, 1989–1999 8 Y. YADIN (ed.), The Temple Scroll, vol. 1–3, Jerusalem 1977–1983 9 A. YARDENI, Textbook of Aramaic, Hebrew and Nabataean Documentary Texts from the Judaean Desert and Related Material, vol. A-B, 2000.

BIBLIOGRAPHY: 10 D. BARTHÉLEMY, Les devanciers d'Aquila (VT, Suppl. 10), 1963 11 J. M. BAUMGARTEN, Studies in Qumran Law (Studies in Judaism in Late Antiquity 24), 1977 12 L. H. SCHIFFMAN et al. (ed.), Encyclopedia of the Dead Sea Scrolls, vol. 1–2, 2000 13 T. HERBERT, E. TOV (ed.), The Text of the Hebrew Bible in Light of the Discoveries of the Judaean Desert, 2001.

THE MAP IS BASED ON: D. JERICKE, G. SCHMITT, Palästina. Siedlungen in griech.-röm. Zeit (ca. 300 v. Chr.–300 n. Chr.; Nord- und Südteil), TAVO B V 18, 1992 L. H. SCHIFFMAN, Reclaiming the Dead Sea Scrolls, 1984 J. WAGNER, Die röm. Prov. Palaestina und Arabia (70–305 n. Chr.), TAVO B V 17.2, 1988.

Dea Roma see → Roma IV.

Dea Syria see → Syria Dea

Death

I. ANCIENT EAST AND EGYPT II. CLASSICAL ANTIQUITY

I. ANCIENT EAST AND EGYPT

A range of archaeological and textual sources from varied walks of life bear eloquent testimony to the intensity of the attempts of coming to term with death in ancient eastern cultures (→ Burial and mourning rituals and the related cult of the → dead), as displayed in forms of → funerary architecture, burial objects and the extensive → funerary literature. As is evident from textual sources, this struggle occupied a large part of everyday human existence [5]. On the one hand, belief in a continued human existence after death is a feature of the Egyptian, Mesopotamian and Hittite traditions. Body and soul — joined together in this life — are physically separated from each other after death. The mortal remains are placed in a grave, the dead person's soul travels to the → Underworld. The dependence of the dead person's soul on a/his/her body is evident in ritual burial (e.g. Egyptian mummification, Hittite anointment of the remains). Even the cult of the → dead takes this corporeality into account with the provision of food and drink. As well, there are other forms of communication between the living and the dead, such as the evocation of the spirits of the dead (cf. → Gilgamesh Epic, tablet 12).

On the other hand, death in ancient eastern cultures was a social event affecting not just the deceased and his or her family but the whole social milieu [4]. Death outside one's own surroundings, one's own culture, was something to be feared, as is shown for example in the Egyptian novel of → Sinuhe or the Sumerian Epic of Lugalbanda [4]. The death of a → ruler could endanger the social or cosmic order in its entirety: the beginning of the Hittite royal death ritual runs: 'If a great disturbance takes place in Ḫattusa as a king or queen becomes a deity' [3.56]. The variety mentioned above typifies the range of measures for coping with death. Thus, to the Mesopotamian mind, the journey to the → Underworld could take different forms (crossing the Underworld river, making the journey on foot). Varying regional, social or cultural traditions are mirrored in the literary texts, the literature on death and the archaeological evidence. The detailed description of the hereafter, especially typical of Egypt and Mesopotamia, articulates the attempt to acquaint the reader with an aspect of life inaccessible to humans and thus to remove the fear of the unknown (cf. the Egyptian guides to the hereafter, indicating the distances of individual sections). Common to all those belief systems is the concept that the deceased has to make a journey to reach the destination. Egyptian and Mesopotamian concepts view the deceased as an active agent; the Hittite perspective, on the other hand, sees him as essentially passive, dependent on propitiatory sacrifices to the sun-goddess of the Underworld (→ Sun-goddess III.), who is to be induced to let him pass (burial ritual: [6. 42]).

There are also texts that do not share the belief in a (good) life after death: Egyptian harp songs and the Gilgamesh Epic exhort people to enjoy life [1. 195–204], as only despair and oblivion await them thereafter — death as the end to a self-determined existence and the beginning of a shadowy existence that cannot be overcome with lavish funerary architecture and burial gifts: 'Gilgameš, where are you running to? You will not find the life that you are seeking! When the gods created mankind, they bestowed mortality ... Make of each day a festival of pleasure, dance and play by day and night! ... Such is the nature of human activity!' (Gilgamesh Epic, tablet 10). Even though the contrast between the two concepts could not have been greater, in view of the great (material) effort deployed for life after death (particularly in Egypt), they both nevertheless fix on the same objective — survival, by deeds and in literature, in posterity's memory: 'Man passes away, his body crumbles to dust. But a book conveys his memory in the mouth of the person reading aloud ...' (list of Old Egyptian writers); 'They have gone, their names would have been forgotten — but it is the book

that keeps their memory alive!' [2. 225–226].
→ Burial; → Funerary architecture; → Funerary literature; → Dead, cult of the; → Underworld

1 J. Assmann, Tod und Jenseits im Alten Äg., 2001 2 H. Brunner, Die Weisheitsbücher der Ägypter, ²1991 3 V. Haas, Hethit. Bestattungsbräuche, in: Altoriental. Forsch. 27, 2000, 52–67 4 S. Lundström, Zur Aussagekraft schriftlicher Quellen hinsichtlich der Vorstellungen vom Leben nach dem Tod in Mesopotamien, in: Altoriental. Forsch. 30, 2003, 30–50 5 G. J. Selz, Was bleibt?, in: see [4] (in print) 6 T. P. J. van den Hout, Death as a Privilege. The Hittite Royal Funerary Ritual: in J. M. Bremer et al. (ed.), Hidden Futures. Death and Immortality in Ancient Egypt, Anatolia, the Classical, Biblical and Arabic Islamic World, 1994, 37–75.

S. LU. and B. CH.

II. Classical Antiquity

(Greek θάνατος/*thánatos*; Lat. *mors*, *letum*).

A. Preliminary remark B. General overview C. Criteria of death D. Homicide and suicide E. Philosophy F. Religion and Mythology G. Literature H. Death of a ruler

A. Preliminary remark

Like → birth and → sexuality, death is one of the constants in the *condicio humana* [1]. Research into it, cutting across cultural boundaries, leads to compelling knowledge about cultural values in societies. In classical studies, too, the range of relevant ancient sources in the fields of literature, medicine, philosophy, epigraphy, iconography, legislation, legal wills etc. makes death an area of cultural studies *par excellence*.

B. General overview

As an entirely inexorable element in the framework of human existence, death was considered a sign that even the most powerful human being would never completely master destiny in this world [10. 13–27; 28]. The γνῶθι σαυτόν/*gnôthi sautón* ('Know thyself') of Delphic → Apollo calls for an acknowledgement of one's own mortality and consequent powerlessness. Of similar meaning is the *memento te hominem esse* ('Remember that you are a human being') that a slave used to whisper during a triumphal procession to the Roman being honoured with the → triumph. As a law of Nature, death was seen as analogous to the phenomena of animate and inanimate Nature (Arist. Spir. 17,478b 22 ff.), e.g. to the changing seasons of the year and to the destruction of cities by human violence (→ Consolatio). Transported to the personal level, even the death of favourite → domestic animals was mourned [15]. Death in antiquity was generally thought of as a transition and change into another form of existence, rather than as absolute finality (Cic. Tusc. 1,12) [14]. Popular metaphors for death are therefore change, journey, taking one's leave, sleep [3; 18]. As a causal link was accepted between life and post-mortal existence, the view of death as an event to be welcomed, or feared, or accepted with indifference, was also expressed in corresponding approaches to life.

That death, like sexuality, was subject to a strong taboo [1. 774 ff.], is shown by the high level of cultural activity that governed contact with the corpse and emotions accompanying death (cf. as well → Burial; → Mourning; → Dead, cult of the; → *laudatio funebris*; → *nenia* A.; → *thrēnos*; → *ekphorá*) in Greek, Etruscan and Roman cultures. In a relatively homogenous concept of the essence and character of death, a rich culture of death developed in the Mediterranean. For Greece, complex burial rites were crucial from the earliest items of evidence [4; 25]. With the Etruscans, death-culture was for example displayed in a rich funerary culture (→ Etruscans II. C. and III. C.; → Grave paintings; → Sarcophagus) that, in its artistic emphasis, is both a memorial to the dead and an expression of a pronounced zest for life and an expectancy of an afterlife. Distinctively Roman is a further institutionalization of burial rites and a culturally very advanced form of remembering the dead (cf. → *laudatio funebris*, → Manes, → *imagines maiorum*, → Lemures, → Parentalia) that finds almost unbroken continuity in Christianity in an *interpretatio christiana* [26; 27]. Even if death was undoubtedly more strongly visible in public consciousness — in contrast to contemporary European culture where it is virtually 'deprived of status' [1] — there were still distinct taboos (e. g. display of an 'ugly' death from illness).

C. Criteria of death

Already in antiquity there was a lively controversy, especially in medicine and philosophy, as to the criteria by which a human could be considered dead or by which death could be reliably determined (σημεῖα θανάτου/*sēmeîa thanátou*; Lat. *signa mortis*) [17]. Those same doctors who attributed a fundamental role to the brain in bodily functions (→ Hippocrates [6], → Galenus et al.) sided with Aristotle [6] (Part. an. 3,4 667a-b) in believing death to be caused by cardiac arrest, even if that could be brought about by other organs. Though as they were very familiar with conditions such as → hysteria, asphyxia and coma, in which respiration and cardiac activity could cease [17], they conceded that determining death by these criteria could be difficult (cf. Plin. HN 7,37,124; 26,8,15; unlike the situation today, determining death did not come under the area of competence of doctors but was part of the burial ritual cf. → *conclamatio*).

In philosophy there were several views as to what death meant (synopsis of views in Cic. Tusc. 1,8). Death was generally seen as a separation of body and soul, and that produced several possibilities (→ Soul, doctrine of the): if the soul is denied an existence independent of the body, the whole person dies (→ Epicurus, → Epicurean School); if a bodiless soul is considered possible (and there are varying estimates for the duration: for eternity, in Plato's view, cf. his *Phaídōn*, and that of → Pythagoras [2] and the → Pythagorean School; of limited duration, for → Stoicism), death is limited to the body, which is thought of as if it were a metonymy for man himself. The corpse, however, was essentially regarded as sacrosanct and its violation or dissection was therefore forbidden (as also its *maschalismós*, 'mutilation'). Greek and Roman legislation (→ Wills) shows that the deceased was thought of as a person with legal rights and with the corresponding social status.

D. Homicide and suicide

Even if the deliberate slaying of another human being was punished (with the exception of: → exposure of children and infanticide), the evaluation of → capital punishment (cf. → *munus* III.) and → suicide was dependent on the importance attributed to death as such. Other than, e.g., in Christianity, life was not essentially regarded as worthy of preservation. Cf. also → Homicide; → Killing, crimes involving.

E. Philosophy

→ Epicharmus' witticism: 'I would not like to die but I'm not worried about being dead' (Cic. Tusc. 1,8) gets to the heart of the philosophical discussion that sought rational elucidation. This looked at the question as to whether death was a bad thing, in order to reduce the fear of death as the greatest enemy to a good life in the fullest sense of the phrase. After → Plato [1] and in → Stoicism in particular, the individual's death was trivialized (and the Middle Ages adopted this thinking with gusto) and an *ars moriendi* ('art of dying') became the key to a genuine human existence: living well means dying well. → Consolatio as literary topic of various kinds also belongs to the context it this discussion. Important ancient philosophical reference texts on death are: Pl. Phd., Cic. Tusc. 1, Lucr. 3 and 4; Sen. Dial. 10, Sen. Ep.; on aspects of the soul see above II. C.; cf. general [2; 5; 16; 18].

F. Religion and Mythology

Concepts of an → afterlife derive from a reluctance to accept man's uncanny extinction by death. Death's sting is then removed in the concept of → deification (see H. below) or metempsychosis (→ Soul, migration of the). In Christianity the day of one's death is precisely 'the day of one's birth' into eternity (ἡμέρα γενέθλιος/ *hēméra genéthlios*, Martyrium Polycarpi 18,2; Lat. usually *dies natalis*; cf. → Dead, cult of the VI.). Religious rituals, which frequently form a counter-balance to the rituals at birth [12; 14], generally reflect the view of death as a changed state and a transition to another existence and should also prevent the mingling of forms of existence. If the deceased is not buried with all due care (e.g. Prop. 4,7), this causes an eery afterlife as a ghost or an undead [19] (→ Dead, cult of the). In the initiation rites of the cults of the mysteries (→ Mysteries) death is experienced symbolically [14. 218 ff.].

In Greece and Rome, the mythological figures representing death tend to depict the cruel moment of death (→ Ker): the handsome youth → Thanatos may not be the reaper but he is just as pitiless (Hes. Theog. 756–766; [14. 208 f.]). By contrast, Etruscan culture has a large number of demons of death [20].

G. Literature

The irrevocability of life, death on the battlefield (*Illiad*) and inglorious death far from home (*Odyssey*) become literary themes as early as the Homeric epics (→ Homer) ([1]). In → epic, heroic death, as an apparently more meaningful death — because suffered on behalf of one's community — remains a hotly discussed issue, the significance of which is finally taken *ad absurdum* in → Lucan's [1] almost macabre dance of death during the naval battle of Massilia (Luc. 3,567–751). Death resulting from bodily dismemberment exercises a special fascination for writers (e. g. → Hippolytus [1] in Sen. Phaedr. 1085–1114) [22]. Although → disease, only barely alleviated by medicine, was mankind's constant companion in antiquity, death through disease or the normal process of ageing was hardly ever described in ancient poetry and only rarely in prose (Plin. Ep. 1,22; 5,16 and passim [11]; Fronto p. 232 Naber). The death of the aged 'Oedipus at Colonus' in → Sophocles' [1] tragedy represents a notable exception.

The changing attitude towards heroic death in battle becomes sharper in the minor literary genres, as shown for example in a comparison of → Tyrtaeus (fr. 6 Diehl, middle of the 7th cent. BC) and → Horatius [7] (Hor. Carm. 3,2; 1st cent. BC) [8; 23]. Death is given *ex negativo* thematic treatment in the oft-repeated exhortation to make the most of one's transitory existence (collection of materials: [7]). An individual variation on heroic death, especially in the Roman elegist → Propertius [1], is the lovers' pact to die together as the culmination of a great love [24]. Gravestone poetry, in particular the *Carmina Latina Epigraphica* (CLE), offers a fascinating cross-section of the themes of lamentation, of concepts of afterlife and of unrestrained affirmation of life [21].

→ Burial; → Charon's fare; → Epitaphios; → Eschatology; → Funus imaginarium; → Funus publicum; → Funerary architecture; → Funerary inscriptions; → Afterlife, concepts of; → Martyrs; → Mors; → Necropoleis; → Rogus; → Soul, doctrine of the; → Soul, weighing of; → Mortality; → Suicide; → Testament; → Thanatos; → Capital punishment; → Dead, cult of the; → Mourning; → Underworld; → Deification

1 Ph. Ariès, L'homme devant la mort, 1978 (Engl. tr. by H. Weaver, The Hour of Our Death, 1981) 2 M. Baltes, Die Todesproblematik in der griech. Philos., in: Gymnasium 95, 1988, 97–128 3 C. von Barloewen (ed.), Der Tod in den Weltkulturen und Weltrel., 1996 4 G. Baudy, Exkommunikation und Reintegration. Zur Genese und Kulturfunktion frühgriech. Einstellungen zum T., 1980 5 E. Benz, Das Todesproblem in der stoischen Philos., 1929 6 G. Binder, B. Effe (ed.), T. und Jenseits im Alt., 1991 7 G. Binder, Pallida Mors, in: [6], 203–247 8 Id., Kriegsdienst und Friedensdienst, in: Acta Antiqua Academiae Scientiarum Hungaricae 39, 1999, 53–72 9 J. Bowker, Die menschliche Vorstellung vom T., in: [3], 406–431 10 J. Choron, Der T. im abendländischen Denken, 1967 11 M. Ducos, La vie et la mort dans la correspondance de Pline le Jeune, in: [27], 93–108 12 E. P. Fischer (ed.), Geburt und T., 1999 13 G. Gno-

LI, J.-P. VERNANT (ed.), La mort, les morts dans les soc. anciennes, 1982 14 F. GRAF, 'Allen Lebewesen gemeinsam': Geburt und T. in der Ant., in: [12], 205–238 15 G. HERRLINGER, Totenklage um Tiere in der ant. Dichtung, 1930 16 A. HÜGLI, Zur Gesch. der Todesdeutung, in: Studia Philosophica 32, 1972, 1–28 17 Id., s. v. Todeskriterien, HWdPh 10, 1245–1249 18 Id., s. v. T., HWdPh 10, 1237–1242 19 S. I. JOHNSTON, Restless Dead. Encounters between the Living and the Dead in Ancient Greece, 1999 20 I. KRAUSKOPF, Todesdämonen und Totengötter im vorhell. Etrurien, 1987 21 R. LATTIMORE, Themes in Greek and Latin Epitaphs, 1942 22 G. MOST, Disiecti membra poetae: The Rhetoric of Dismemberment in Neronian Poetry, in: R. HEXTER, D. SELDEN (ed.), Innovations in Antiquity, 1992, 391–419 23 C. W. MÜLLER, Der schöne T. des Polisbürgers oder 'Ehrenvoll ist es für das Vaterland zu sterben', in: Gymnasium 96, 1989, 317–340 24 T. D. PAPANGHELIS, Propertius. A Hellenistic Poet on Death and Love, 1987 25 C. SOURVINOU-INWOOD, 'Reading' Greek Death, 1996 26 J. M. C. TOYNBEE, Death and Burial in the Roman World, 1971 27 La vie et la mort dans l'Antiquité (Actes du colloque; Association G. Budé), 1990 28 H. WANKEL, Alle Menschen müssen sterben, in: Hermes 11, 1983, 129–154.

C. W.

H. DEATH OF A RULER

1. GREECE 2. ROME 3. BYZANTIUM 4. INDIVIDUAL ASPECTS

1. GREECE

From the Mycenaean period with its 'city-state palace culture' (heyday 14th/13th cents. BC) we know little of the rulers (*wanakes*, → *wanax*) and next to nothing about their deaths [1] (→ Burial C.; rich furnishings in the → funerary architecture III. B.); The same applies to the → Dark Ages (*c.* 1200–800 BC). In the Homeric epics we find impressive descriptions of the violent deaths of rulers (e.g. → Agamemnon, Hom. Od. 1,29–43; 3,248–312; 4,519–537); → Hector's death and the ensuing ceremonies are comprehensively depicted (Hom. Il. 22–24). Details of the ceremony for preparing the corpse and of the mourning rituals could reflect historical conditions of early kingship [2]. Hdt. 6,58 records the burial customs of the Spartan double kingship (9th–6th cents.): proclamation of the ruler's death, mourning lament, participation in the burial, period of mourning. On the deaths of some of the early tyrants we do have some information, e.g. on the natural death of → Cypselus [2] of Corinth, of his son → Periander or of → Peisistratus [4] of Athens [3]. Herodotus reports the murder (→ Tyrannicide) and crucifixion of → Polycrates [1] of Samos by the Persian Oroetes with the comment that his end was 'worthy neither of the ruler himself nor of his noble character' (3,120–125) [4. 120–125; 5. 36–42]. Cases are also known to us of violent death among the → tyrants of the classical period (*c.* 500–336 BC): → Evagoras [1] I and → Nicocles [1] of Cyprus or → Iason [2] of Pherae in Thessaly, whose murderers were fêted (Xen. Hell. 6,4,31 f.; Diod. Sic. 15,60,5). The Macedonian king Philip [4] II, father of Alexander [4] the Great, was the victim of assassination in 336 (Diod. Sic. 16,93 f.; [6]).

With Alexander [4], veneration of the → ruler enters a new stage: the ruler's death is closely connected with → hero cult, ruler cult and → deification. Even before his death (323), Alexander was occasionally worshipped as a god; thereafter, he was regarded as a protective deity for his successors, who also enjoyed cultic veneration already during their lifetimes ([7. 1054–1058] with bibliography). An outstanding example of a ruler's death is the double suicide of the Egyptian → Cleopatra [II 12] VII and the Roman M. → Antonius [I 9] in 30 BC during Octavian's advance on Alexandria [1] [8. 151–173; 9. 184–203].

2. ROME

The earliest literary depiction of a ruler's death is to be found as a fragment in the epic *Annales* of → Ennius [1] (1st third of the 2nd cent. BC); it treats the death and apotheosis of the legendary founder of the city, → Romulus [1], from a Hellenistic model (Enn. Ann. fr. 105–110 SKUTSCH) and was taken up by Cicero (especially Cic. Rep. 1,64: Romulus as protector of the people, father, patriarch; yearning and lament of the orphaned people; cf. Liv. 1,16); it can be seen as a model for ruler's death and deification (see also → *consecratio*, which later became part of the burial rite) after Caesar's death. The latter's was in effect the first ruler's death in Roman history and was described in detail, including the ensuing ceremonial proceedings, in historical and biographical literature (cf. especially Plut. Caesar 64–69; Suet. Iul. 81–85 with a compilation of the prodigies and dreams foretelling his death, as well as details of the funeral; also [4. 108–110] with sources). For the natural death of → Augustus cf. Suet. Aug. 97,1 f. (omens of death and apotheosis) and 99 f., for the funeral, in the most detailed account, Cass. Dio 56,34–42, [10. 69–72]; interment of the funerary urn occurred in the → *Mausoleum Augusti*, where two panels were installed with his *Res gestae*. In a similar fashion successive emperors had family tombs and monuments erected that were also intended to ensure their fame for posterity [11].

Impressive accounts of ruler's deaths can be found in the works of Tacitus, e.g. Tac. Ann. 12,66–69; 13,1–3: → Claudius [III 1] (whose death, funeral rite and consecration Seneca exaggerates satirically in the *Apocolocyntosis* [12]); Tac. Hist. 3,84,4–85: → Vitellius ([13. 227–229, 219–231]: other literary death scenes); the death of Agricola (Tac. Agr. 43) is undoubtedly stylized as a ruler's death, Tacitus makes his father-in-law 'immortal' in sharp contrast to the Emperor Domitian [14; 15]. In epic literature Virgil's tragedy of → Dido (Verg. Aen. 4; [16]) and the depiction, bridging two books, of the murder, apotheosis and veneration after death of → Pompeius [I 3] in Lucan (8,611–9,217; [17]) deserve mention.

3. BYZANTIUM

From 629 (→ Heraclius [7]) the Byzantine emperor also officially bore the title of → *basileús* (II.) that had been customary in everyday speech and in literature since Constantine [1] I and was crowned by his predecessor in a solemn ceremony in the presence of the patriarch and before representatives of the Senate, the people and the army ([18. 10–30] with sources). The transfer of power often took place on the death-bed, with the successor then participating in the burial ceremonies and his own public acclamation, thus registering the continuity between the deceased and the successor ([19. 1158 f.] with supporting evidence, including on Constantine's funeral rite, a Christian adaptation of the emperor-cult version).

4. Individual aspects

Historical and biographical literature frequently mentions the omens presaging the imminent death of the ruler (see above. H.2. on Caesar and Augustus). Quotation of the dying person's → *ultima verba* is also popular, as a means of recording the character and leadership qualities. Not infrequently various versions are transmitted; the contradictory accounts of Caesar's last words, for example, are well known ([4. 108–110]; for the *ultimae voces* cf. also [13. 220, 227–229]).

→ Ruler; → Ruler, birth of the; → Ruler cult; → Deification

1 R. Hägg, G. C. Nordquist (ed.), Celebrations of Death and Divinity in the Bronze Age Argolid, 1990 2 M. Andronikos, Totenkult (ArchHom vol. 3 ch. W), 1968 3 H. Berve, Die Tyrannis bei den Griechen, 1967 4 W. H. Friedrich, Der T. des Tyrannen, in: A&A 18, 1973, 97–129 5 A. Abramenko, Polykrates' Außenpolitik und Ende, in: Klio 77, 1995, 35–54 6 E. Badian, The Death of Philipp II, in: Phoenix 17, 1963, 244–250 7 J. R. Fears, s. v. Herrscherkult, RAC 14, 1047–1093 8 I. Becher, Das Bild der Kleopatra in der griech. und lat. Lit., 1966 9 H. Volkmann, Kleopatra. Politik und Propaganda, 1953 10 H. Chantraine, Der tote Herrscher in der röm. Kaiserzeit, in: Gesch. in Wissenschaft und Unterricht 39, 1988, 67–80 11 P. J. E. Davies, Death and the Emperor, 2000 12 G. Binder (ed.), L. Annaeus Seneca. Apokolokyntosis, 1999 (with German transl.) 13 Id., Pallida Mors, in: Id., B. Effe (ed.), T. und Jenseits im Alt., 1991, 203–247 14 K. Büchner, Die Darstellung des T. des Agricola durch Tacitus, in: Studii Clasice 13, 1971, 127–137 15 P. Schunk, Stud. zur Darstellung des Endes von Galba, Otho und Vitellius in den Historien des Tacitus, in: Symbolae Osloenses 39, 1964, 38–82 16 G. Binder (ed.), Vergils Dido-Drama und Aspekte seiner Rezeption, 2000 17 W. Rutz, Lucans Pompeius, in: Der altsprachliche Unterricht, R.11, H.1, 1968, 5–22 18 R.-J. Lilie, Byzanz. Kaiser und Reich, 1994 19 M. Whitby, s. v. Kaiserzeremoniell, RAC 19, 1135–1177.

E. Baltrusch, Sparta, 1998; P. Barceló, Basileia, Monarchia, Tyrannis, 1993; H.-J. Gehrke, H. Schneider (ed.), Gesch. der Ant., 2000; Ch. Habicht, Gottmenschentum und griech. Städte, [2]1970; M. Herford-Koch, T., Totenfürsorge und Jenseitsvorstellungen in der griech. Ant. Eine Bibliographie, 1992; F. Hinard (ed.), La mort, les morts et l' au-delà dans le monde romain, 1987; L. De Libero, Die archa. Tyrannis, 1996; G. Ostrogorsky, Gesch. des byz. Staates, [3]1963; A. Ronconi, s. v. Exitus illustrium virorum, RAC 6, 1258–1268; J. M. C. Toynbee, Death and Burial in the Roman World, 1971. CL. E.

Death, angel of (Hebrew *Malakh ha-mawet*). Figure of Rabbinical angelology, can be identified with → Sammael or → Satan (e.g. bBB 16a). The angel of death, given by God the power over life and death, stands at the side of someone who is dying. If that person opens his or her mouth in fright, the angel casts a drop of gall from his sword into the open mouth, whereupon death occurs (bAZ 20b). Up until the sin of the golden calf (Ex 32,1–24), the angel was intended only for the peoples of the world, because acceptance through the Torah meant freedom from death. → Rabbinical literature describes in detail how → Moses succeeds in opposing the power of the angel of death (SiphDt § 305, p. 326 f.; similar ideas appear also in pseudepigraphic literature, cf. SyrBar 21,23). Michael [1], Gabriel [1], Uriel, Rafael and other angels 'are assigned over the end' and attempt 'to bring forth' Esra's soul (Apc.Esr. 6,1 ff.). In connection with human death angels also appear as guides for the soul (cf. *i.a.* TestAsser 6,4 ff.) and may be present at the final judgement (TestAbr 12–12.; 1 Hen 55,3; 62,11; 2 Hen 10,2).

J. Michl, s. v. Engel (jüd.), RAC 5, 1962, 60–97, esp. 76 f.; P. Schäfer, Rivalität zw. Engeln und Menschen. Unt. zur rabbinischen Engelvorstellung, 1975, Index s. v. Todesengel; H. L. Strack, P. Billerbeck, Komm. zum NT aus Talmud und Midrasch, vol. 1, [9]1986, 145–149. B. E.

Death penalty

I. Ancient Orient
II. Classical Antiquity

I. Ancient Orient

The death penalty as a sanction for capital offences is attested in the ancient Near East from the latter part of the 3rd millennium BC as a penalty in varying frequency in the respective statute books and (less often) as a sentence in → documents of → procedural law. Capital offences were, in particular, homicide/killing (→ Killing, crimes involving), → robbery, abduction, adultery, various cases of sodomy and incest and other statutory definitions of offences, principally those threatening the political or social order. Moreover, the death penalty was sometimes threatened as a substitute (in cases of theft and embezzlement, for instance) if the perpetrator proved unable to pay the fine. It is also found as a threatened penalty in contracts. In certain cases it is likely that the death penalty (acting as a deterrent) was replaced by monetary and other (compensatory/penalty) payments. The investigation of capital offences (and therefore imposing the death penalty) was usually subject to royal jurisdiction or was delegated to other institutions by the → ruler. In what context the (public or private) death penalty was specifically enforced is unclear and controversial. The main methods of enforcement attested in Mesopotamia and Egypt are impaling, burning, drowning and beheading.

→ Punishment

W. Boochs, s.v. Strafen, LÄ 6, 68–72; S. Lafont, Femmes, droit et justice dans l'antiquité orientale, 1999; G. Ries, s.v. Kapitaldelikte, RLA 5, 391–399; C. Wilcke, Diebe, Räuber und Mörder, in: Xenia 32, 1992, 53–78.

H. N.

II Graeco-Roman

The death penalty was not recorded as a general term in either Greece or Rome. Instead, individual methods of enforcing it were mentioned (see below). In an early stage of development the death penalty was in each case an expression of private → revenge, which was not, or barely, legally channelled (cf. also → blood feud). In Rome the head of the family (→ *pater familias*) and the slave-holder (→ *dominus*) had long ago mitigated the right to impose and enforce the death penalty in respect of wife, children and slaves (probably since the 5th cent. BC), by the requirement of letting a domestic court, over which he presided, adjudicate. In the case of → slave revolts or where slaves had taken part in civil war, the slaves (→ Slavery IV.B.) were either returned to their *domini* for punishment or were immediately nailed to the cross by the victorious party (→ *crux*; in Greece *anaskolópisis* and *anastaúrōsis*). This method of the death penalty, principally of slaves, had probably been enforced in Rome from *c.* 200 BC. In Athens not only premeditated killing (→ *phónos*) and sedition and high treason (→ *katálysis toû dḗmou*, → *prodosía*) resulted in the death penalty, but also religious offences such as desecration of the temple (→ *hierosylía*) and (cf. in particular the case against → Socrates [2], 399 BC) publicly taught godlessness (→ *asébeia*). In a similar way, in Rome there was provision for the state death penalty for sedition and high treason (→ *perduellio*) by beheading (→ *decollatio*, in Greece *apokephalízein*) with an axe, later a sword. In the Roman Imperial period this was the typical death penalty for → *honestiores*, but now sometimes also for → homicide. A further method of enforcement was death by fire (→ *crematio*), at first perhaps the 'private' penalty for arson according to the Twelve Tables (→ *tabulae duodecim*; table 8,10, *c.* 450 BC), but in the Imperial period next to crucifixion and beheading one of the three most severe penalties (*summa supplicia*) for publicly prosecuted crimes.

In both Athens and Rome it was possible to escape blood feud, and then usually the public death penalty, by exile (→ *phygḗ*; → *exilium*), from which developed the alternative penalty of → banishment (for a fixed period or lifelong). For 'ordinary' criminals being used as → *gladiators* had a similar significance (→ *munus* III.).

→ Capitale; → Punishment; → Supplicium; → Killing, crimes involving; → Criminal law

E. Cantarella, I supplizi capitali in Grecia e a Roma, 1991; G. Thür, Die T. im Blutprozess Athens, in: Journal of Juristic Papyrology 20, 1990, 143–156.

G. S.

Debitor The *debitor* had an obligation to pay what he owed to the → *creditor*. For the origin of such an obligation arising from a contract (→ *contractus*) or a prohibited act (→ *delictum*) see → *obligatio*. The creditor could make his claims against a tardy debtor (→ *mora*) by litigation at court (→ Procedural law). If the creditor won or the debitor accepted his obligations, the 'personal liability' of the creditor came into effect (→ *nexum*). This, according to Gellius (20,1, especially 45ff.), might still have been taken literally in the law of the XII Tablets (5th cent. BC) (tab. 3,1–6). If the debt had not been paid within 30 days after the verdict or the debtor's acceptance, the creditor was allowed to seize the debtor (→ *addictus*, → *manus iniectio*). On three market days, the creditor had to present the debtor for redemption. If the *debitor* was not redeemed and if nobody came forward to resume the dispute in favour of the debtor (→ *vindex*), the creditor was allowed to sell the debtor *trans Tiberim* into slavery, or to kill him. Several creditors were allowed to divide the corpse of the debtor amongst themselves. In contrast to this legendary custom, the bondage of debtors is a recorded practice. Whether it was abolished in 326 BC by the *lex Poetelia Papiria* (cf. Varro, Ling. 7,105; Cic. Rep. 2,59) or still applied in the Imperial period (cf. Quint. Decl. 311) remains unclear. The typical form of enforcement in the jurisprudence during the time of the Principate were bankruptcy proceedings against the debtor's assets (*bonorum venditio*, Gai. Inst. 3,78ff.). The enforcement of a division into individual assets developed out of a recognition of the need to protect certain debtors, such as those who had promised an actionable financial contribution (→ *donatio*, → *stipulatio*) free of charge, or persons of senatorial rank.

H. Honsell, Th. Maier-Maly, W. Selb, Röm. Recht, [4]1987, 213–216, 519–523, 550.

R.WI.

Debt, Debt redemption

I. Ancient Orient II. Greece and Rome

I. Ancient Orient

Debt incurred by the population which lived on agriculture is a general phenomenon in agrarian societies. It ultimately led to debt bondage, thus threatening the social equilibrium. Debt redemption by sovereign decree was a common means of reducing or eliminating the consequences of debt, i.e. of restoring 'justice in the land'. Instances of debt redemption are well attested in Mesopotamia from the 3rd millennium BC, but more especially between the 20th and 17th cents. [4; 9]. Under the rulers of the 1st dynasty of Babylon (19th to 17th cents.) they usually took place at the beginning of the ruler's reign. They were especially necessary once the majority of the population (liable for compulsory service) were no longer supplied by regular → rations (as under the terms of the → *oikos* economy), but by allocation of fields to provide sustenance or leasehold land. The debt-engendering mechanism typical of agricultural societies—created by natural and military disasters and the resulting failed harvests — made such measures necessary. From the middle of the 2nd millennium the debt incurred by the population living on subsistence production led to increasing consolidation of land in the hands of a class of large landowners or institutional households (→ *oíkos*) consisting of members of the élite of urban officials. In the Neo-Assyrian period (9th to 7th cents. BC) the term *andurāru* designated on the one hand exemption from charges for privileged cities, with future effect, but on the other hand retrospective relief from debt obligations. The latter — in contrast to the ancient Babylonian period — could in this case be circumvented by appropriate contractual clauses. The existence of debt redemption (*andurāru*) is also attested for Assyria (20th/19th cents.), Mari (18th cent.), North Syria (Ebla [5] Alalaḫ, 18th cent.), Elam (18th cent.) and Nuzi (15th/14th cents.) [1. 116]. Instances of Hittite debt redemption are related to border or conquered territories [1. 116].

Texts from Egypt hardly ever mention debt redemption. [2; 10]. For the Ptolemaic period see instances of *philanthrōpía* decrees by Ptolemaic rulers [3].

According to Deut. 15,1–18, a form of debt redemption (*šᵉmiṭṭā*) which has its origins not in the authority of the king but in that of → Yahweh becomes effective every seven years. This presumably extends not only to consumer, but also to commercial loans. The *šᵉmiṭṭā* reflects the consequences of radical social changes in Judah at the beginning of the 7th cent. BC as resulting from the threat from the Neo-Assyrian kingdom. The *šᵉmiṭṭā* can be historically traced for the first time to 164/3 or 163/2 BC (1 Macc 6,49; Jos. Ant. Iud. 12,378). → Slavery

1 Chicago Assyrian Dictionary A/2, 1968, s. v. andurāru, 115–117 2 I. GRUMACH, Unt. zur Lebenslehre des Amenope, 1973 3 W. HUSS, Äg. in hell. Zeit, 2001 4 F. R. KRAUS, Königliche Verfügungen in altbabylonischer Zeit, 1984 5 Id., Ein mittelbabylonischer Rechtsterminus, in: J. A. ANKUM (ed.), Symbolae M. David, vol. 2, 1968, 9–40 6 E. NEU, Das hurritische Epos der Freilassung, 1996 7 H. NIEHR, The Constitutive Principles for Establishing Justice and Order in Northwest Semitic Societies with Special Reference to Ancient Israel and Judah, in: Zschr. für Altorientalische und Biblische Rechtsgesch. 3, 1997, 112–130 8 E. OTTO, Programme sozialer Gerechtigkeit: ibid., 26–63 (with bibliography) 9 J. RENGER, Royal Edicts of the Old Babylonian Period, in: M. HUDSON, M. VAN DE MIEROOP (ed.), The International Scholars Conference on Ancient Near Eastern Economics 3 (in print; with bibliography) 10 H. S. SMITH, A Note on Amnesty, in: JEA 54, 1968, 209–214. J. RE.

II. Greece and Rome

A. The general problem of debt B. Debt bondage C. Granting loans in Greece D. Social Problems E. Rome and the provinces F. The Roman Republic G. Principate

A. The general problem of debt

Debts and owing money were very common in antiquity and often caused by the fact that wealthy landowners lent implements, draught animals, food or seed grain to poor farmers. Once the → money economy had gained acceptance in various regions of the ancient world, it was no longer possible to separate the problem of debt from that of shortage of money and ability to pay. The social problem of the enslavement of debtors was associated with debt in ancient Greek and Roman history; debt bondage was eliminated by legislation (→ Slavery). In Greek *poleis* in the 4th cent. BC and in the Hellenistic period there were frequent requests for debt redemption. In classical Athens the granting of → fenus nauticum to fund grain imports was common. In general, in Greek cities members of the political élite lent large sums of money and in Rome in the last cent. of the Republic money-lending within the wealthy upper class and debt incurred from wealthy Romans even by kings and cities took on appreciable dimensions.

B. Debt bondage

According to Hesiod small farmers relied on borrowing from relations, friends and neighbours; however, Hesiod warns about becoming dependent on a creditor owing to a debt (Hes. Op. 349–354; 394–404). The tradition on → Solon [1] assumes that he put through a form of debt relief (→ *seisáchtheia*), freed debt slaves and abolished debt bondage altogether (Plut. Sol. 15). In Rome debt bondage is attested in the Twelve Tables; its abolition was attributed to a *lex Poetelia* of 326 or 313 BC (Varro Ling. 7,105; Cic. Rep. 2,59; Liv. 8,28,1–9). Menander [4] (around 300 BC.) on the other hand mentions two children in the Attic deme of Ptelea, who were in reality working as slaves because of their father's debts (Men. Her. 28–39; cf. Isoc. Or. 14,48). Similar testimony also exists for Rome: legislation probably did not abolish the → *nexum*, but did not allow people to be bound on the grounds of a *nexum*. In Athens it appears not to have been possible to file a suit in court for contracts which committed the debtor to work; this assumption is supported by Aristoteles, who mentions that in some cities there were no courts for certain kinds of loan contracts (Aristot. Eth. Nic. 1162b).

As well as in Athens, by 504 BC debt redemption had apparently been instigated in three other cities, in Megara, Croton and Cyme [2]; by 408 BC no further cases of this kind are known. It should not be concluded from this that, owing to the rise of the *polis*, debt no longer represented an acute social problem; it is rather to be assumed that in this period the wars against the Persians and Carthage and after that the growing tensions between Athens and Sparta were at the heart of politics and tended to supersede the internal conflicts.

C. Granting loans in Greece

The structure of granting loans and of debt is better attested for Athens than for other Greek cities, and this is especially true of → fenus nauticum which served to fund the purchase and transport of grain to Athens. There is a clear connection between the institution of the *fenus nauticum* and the money economy. Between 520 and 450 BC, Athenian silver coins were exported in vast quantities to Egypt and Asia Minor, but there are very few finds of Athenian coins in the Black Sea area, from which Athens imported large amounts of grain in the 2nd half of the 5th cent. and in the 4th cent. BC. The normal currency of the Black Sea area in the classical period was the elektron stater of Cyzicus, which was mainly used to pay for the grain. Accordingly, the money was not paid in Athens, but the debtor was allowed to pick up staters from Cyzicus on the way to the Black Sea, presupposing close co-operation between the provider of the loan in Athens and the money-lender in Cyzicus.

Academic discussion has primarily concentrated on two questions, (1) whether the → loan served for consumption or for funding production, and (2) in what social context granting of the loan took place. According to [3], Attic court speeches clearly show that it was customary to fund economic activities by means of loans. Some of these loans were granted by → banks, which were thus by no means any longer simply institutions for depositing money; the money resources of the → temple were also lent out, at least in part. For the social background of granting loans [10] has proved that an ideology of → reciprocity characterized all money transactions connected with loans. It should be emphasized in this context that these behavioural standards existed only between citizens of approximately equal status and that debt incurred by the poor could result in social dependence.

The boundary stones (ὅροι/→ *hóroi*) indicating that a plot of land had been pledged as security are further source material for loans in classical Athens. They also appear in the court speeches: for instance, it is reported that the estate of Phaenippus was unencumbered (Dem. Or. 42,5; cf. on the mortgaging of a house also 53,4–13). Mortgaging was probably designated as ὑποθήκη/ → *hypothḗkē*, sometimes also as πρᾶσις ἐπὶ λύσει/→ *prâsis epì lýsei* (purchase with the possibility of repurchasing; these terms frequently appear on the *hóroi* and probably refer to the same institution. In the 4th cent. BC and in the Hellenistic epoch cities also increasingly went over to raising loans, especially for funding warfare, including the building of city walls, and for → grain supply in times of shortage.

D. Social Problems

Granting loans and both public and private debt had been structural features of ancient history since the 4th

cent. BC and were not necessarily associated with social problems. However, many testimonies show that debt did indeed pose a serious social and consequently political problem. As early as in 427 BC debtors killed their creditors during the *stásis* (→ Social conflicts) in Cercyra (Thuc. 3,81,4), and Aeneas Tacticus feared that in the event of a siege indebted citizens might betray their city to free themselves of their burden of debt (Aen. Tact. 14,1). Many measures for debt redemption originate from the period between 408 and 324/3 BC [2. nos. 5–18], and only a few more can be dated to the period between 316/15 and 86/5 BC [2. nos. 19–40]. The measures for land distribution follow the same chronological pattern. According to Plato, debt relief was often promised by politicians who wanted to establish a → *tyrannis* (Pl. Resp. 566a; 566e; cf. Pl. Leg. 684d-e; 736c). The reason there was no *stásis* in Athens until the period of Roman supremacy is probably because the citizens received money from the *polis* for taking part in the people's assembly (→ *ekklēsía*) or for taking on offices and functions.

E. Rome and the provinces

In the 1st cent. BC public and private debt had reached a critical point in the Greek East; the situation in the western Mediterranean was probably similar, but there is less evidence for this. In 89 BC Nicomedes [6] IV of Bithynia attacked the territory of → Mithridates [6] VI in the hope of booty, with the aid of which he hoped to pay his debts to Roman officials and other Romans (App. Mith. 11). The contributions demanded by Cornelius [I 90] Sulla after the the province of Asia had been re-conquered had resulted at the time of the proconsulate of L. Licinius [I 26] Lucullus in 73 BC in the population of the province (Plut. Lucullus 20) ending up hopelessly in debt. The indebtedness of the provinces in the east in the post-Sullan period is attested by an almost casual remark by Suetonius on the recovery of debts in Bithynia by Caesar and further by Cicero's comments on the debts owed by the city of Sicyon to Pomponius [I 5] Atticus (Suet. Iul. 2; Cic. Att. 1,19,9; 1,20,4). In 66 BC a speedy victory over Mithridates [6] VI was in the interests of many Romans, as they had lent large sums in the province of Asia (Cic. Leg. Man. 18). Typical of circumstances in the western Mediterranean was the debt of the Allobrogians, who in the autumn of 63 BC were almost prepared to support → Catilina in the hope of debt relief (Cic. Cat. 3,4–13; Sall. Catil. 40 f.).

Neither the *lex Iulia de repetundis* (→ *repetundarum crimen*) of 59 BC nor the legislation of Clodius [I 4] in 58 BC or the provincial administration of Calpurnius [I 19] Piso and Gabinius [I 2], unjustly criticized by Cicero, contributed to an improvement in the situation. To avoid obligations, such as billeting, Roman magistrates in the provinces were bribed and so the circle of bribery and consequent debt continued to exist. Ptolemaeus [18] Auletes of Egypt, Brogitarus of Galatia and Ariobarzanes [5] III of Cappadocia were deeply in debt owing to these structures. As proconsul in Cilicia, Cicero was confronted with the fact that Iunius [I 10] Brutus recovered his debts in these provinces with great severity (Cic. Att. 5,21,10–13; 6,1,5–8; 6,2,7–9; 6,3,5–7). One of the main creditors of the provinces was Pompey [I 3] (cf. Cic. Att. 6,1,3); in one of his last letters to Atticus, Cicero mentions that the city of Buthrotum had debts with Caesar, which can probably be traced back to the attempt to persuade Caesar to withdraw a legion from the city in 48 BC (Cic. Att. 16,16A; Caes. B Civ. 3,16,1–2).

F. The Roman Republic

In the late Republic the Roman upper class was in debt to a quite spectacular degree. The reason for this was without doubt the increasing expenses of a political career (→ *cursus honorum*), which also included bribing voters or judges. The debt incurred by the *plebs* resulted primarily from the efforts of the wealthy upper class to obtain the highest possible levies from dependants, leaseholders and tenants. Populist politicians thought it necessary to alleviate the *plebs*' burden of debt; → Catilina, among whose followers were many who were in debt, promised debt redemption (*tabulae novae*; Sall. Catil. 21,2; Cic. Cat. 2,18 f.; Cic. Off. 2,84). Catiline's conspiracy can essentially be interpreted as a crisis of debt which was made even more acute by shortage of money. Caesar's measures after 49 BC represented a culmination of populist attempts to regulate the question of debt. All these measures were criticized by Cicero, who, towards the end of his life, regarded them as an attack on the *fundamenta rei publicae* (Cic. Off. 2,78–85).

G. Principate

The emergence of the Principate did not bring any fundamental improvement in the political behaviour of the provincial governors, though the end of the civil wars did bring economic recovery in the provinces. As the revolt of heavily indebted Gallic tribes in AD 21 shows, the problem of debt in the provinces had in no way been solved (Tac. Ann. 3,40–47). Later still wealthy Romans like → Seneca [2] lent money in the provinces in great style (Tac. Ann. 13,42,4). It was a characteristic of the early Principate that the *principes* and the upper classes of the provinces had a common interest in keeping the social circumstances unchanged. Therefore Dio [I 3] Chrysostomus decisively rejected debt relief and also land distribution (31,66–71). In Greece money-lending and debt served primarily to fund the luxury consumerism of the upper classes, as can be seen from a work by Plutarch directed against the incurring of debt (Plut. De vitando aere alieno, Mor. 827d–832).

In Italy there was a financial crisis in AD 33 when complaints about the high interest rates (→ Interest) had caused money-lenders to cancel the loans; the extent of this crisis makes clear that the upper class was still greatly in debt, even though the costs of a political career had dropped sharply. These events also clarify the connection between the money economy, shortage of money, ability to pay and debt; it cannot, however, be assumed that there was a structural problem of ability to pay: once Tiberius had intervened to mollify the effects of the crisis, there were no longer any difficulties of this kind on the money market. Pliny's complaints about the chronic indebtedness of his tenants and their inability to pay for the → leasehold give a good insight into agriculture (Plin. Ep. 3,18,6; 7,30,3; 9,30,3).

During the Principate, arrears in → taxes were often exempted; such measures were probably of particular benefit to the wealthy upper class. Granting loans and accepting credit within the Roman upper class continued to exist in late antiquity, as the Codex Iustinianus (5,37) and the polemic of Ambrose against money-lending (Ambr. De Tobia) show.

→ Poverty; → Banks; → Daneion; → Loans; → Money, Money economy; → Publicani; → Wealth; → Fenus nauticum; → Seisachtheia; → Slavery

1 J. Andreau, Banking and Business in the Roman World, 1999 2 D. Asheri, Leggi greche sul problema dei debiti (Studi classici e orientali 18), 1969, 5–122 3 E. E. Cohen, Commercial Lending by Athenian Banks: Cliometric Fallacies and Forensic Methodology, in: CPh 85, 1990, 177–190 4 J. A. Crook, Law and Life of Rome, 1967 5 M. I. Finley, Land Debt and the Man of Property in Classical Athens, in: Finley, Economy, 62–76 6 Id., Studies in Land and Credit in Ancient Athens, 500–200 B. C., 1952 ([2]1985) 7 M. W. Frederiksen, Cicero, Caesar and the Problem of Debt, in: JRS 56, 1966, 128–141 8 E. M. Harris, When Is a Sale Not a Sale? The Riddle of Athenian Terminology for Real Security Revisited, in: CQ 38, 1988, 351–381 9 L. Migeotte, L'emprunt public dans les cités grecques, 1984 10 P. Millett, Lending and Borrowing in Ancient Athens, 1991 11 G. E. M. de Ste. Croix, The Class Struggle in the Ancient Greek World, 1981 12 K. Shipton, Leasing and Lending in Fourth-Century B. C. Athens, 2000 13 B. Tenger, Die V. im röm. Äg. (1.–2. Jh. n. Chr.), 1993.

M. C.

Debt redemption see → Debt, Debt redemption

Decanus A soldier who commanded a → *contubernium*; he was appointed when the size of this unit was increased from eight to ten men (according to Ps.Hyg.). The inscription IGR I 1046 mentions δεκανοί (*dekanoí*) who were either persons of this rank or else commanders of a squadron of ten ships, a fact which can no longer be determined in detail. The decanus is still attested for the 4th cent. AD, sometimes carrying the title *caput contubernii* (Veg. Mil. 2,8; 2,13). In other documents, this term refers to persons belonging to the lowest level of the palace guard (Cod. Theod. 6,33; Cod. Iust. 12,26,1; 12,59).

→ Contubernium

1 O. Fiebiger, s.v. D., RE 4, 2245f. 2 D. Kienast, Kriegsflotten, 1966 3 M. Reddé, Mare nostrum, 1986, 542.

Y.L.B.

Decas (δεκάς; *dekás*). From Homeric into Hellenistic times, the basic unit in Greek and Macedonian infantry and cavalry armies (Hom. Il. 2,126; Hdt. 3,25,6; Xen. Hell. 7,2,6; Hipp. 4,9; Arr. Anab. 7,23,3; Anaximenes FGrH 72 F4; P. Cairo Zen. 1,7–11; 2,22–24; Frontin. Str. 4,1,6), which was commanded by a decadarch (Xen. Hipp. 2,2–6). Normally, the unit comprised ten men with a possible further division into groups of five; deviations from this practice occurred.

1 Kromayer/Veith 90f. 2 M. Launey, Recherches sur les armées hellénistiques, 1949, 560. LE.BU.

Decate (δεκάτη; *dekátē*), 'the tenth (part)', primarily refers to various forms of tithe:

1. Crop yield taxation, e.g. in Athens under → Peisistratus (Aristot. Ath. Pol. 16,4; but perhaps it is a 'twentieth', *eikostḗ*, in Thuc. 6,54,5, and *decate* is a generic term in the Ath. Pol.), in Crannon (Polyaenus, Strat. 2,34), in Delos (IG XI 2, 161, 27) and in Pergamum (IPergamon 158, 17–18; a twentieth on wine and a tenth on other field crops). The *lex Hieronica* for Sicily, too, includes a *decate* (Cic. Verr. 2,3,20).

2. Building taxation, e.g. in Delos (IG XI 2, 161, 26) and Egypt (P Tebt. 2,281).

3. Trade taxation, e.g. the transit toll at the Bosporus, which was charged by Athens in 410 BC under Alcibiades and in 390 by Thrasyboulos (Xen. Hell. 1,1,22; 4,8,27).

4. Votive offerings to the gods, especially weapons taken from defeated enemies (e.g. Xen. An. 5,3,4). The threat by the Greeks in 480 BC to dedicate a tenth of the property of cities collaborating with the Persians (Hdt. 7,132,2), presumed the destruction of these 'medizing' cities [1].

5. In Athens, the celebration on the tenth day after the birth of a child, the day it received its name, was called *decate* (e.g. Aristoph. Av. 494; Isaeus or. 3,30; Dem. Or. 39,20).

1 W.K. Pritchett, The Greek State at War, 1. vol., 1971, 93–100. P.J.R.

Decebalus (Δεκέβαλος; *Dekébalos*). D. was the last Dacian king, reigning from *c.* AD 87–106. In addition to modern-day western and central Transylvania, his kingdom included the Banat and the Walachian plains. According to Cass. Dio (67,6,1–2) he was a match for Rome thanks to his excellent military skills, uniting the Dacian tribes and even persuading Sarmatian and German groups to join him against Rome. After he had conquered parts of Iazygian territory and invaded Moesia in 85/86, a war against Domitian arose who, however, had to withdraw after unrest broke out along the middle part of the Danube. Thus, Tettius Iulianus' victory over D. near Tapae was not taken advantage of, and after the peace treaty D.'s kingdom was incorporated as a client state. But D. prepared for further attacks on Rome, which led to Trajan's two large Dacian campaigns in 101/102 and 105/106, in which both Dacia and Rome sustained heavy losses, and which led to the establishment of the province of Dacia. The main successes of the Romans in the much better documented first war were the securing of a line along the Danube, the conquest of the capital Sarmizegetusa and the reinforcement of the front line north of the Danube. D. had to fulfil the following conditions: 1. relinquishment of all weapons, 2. handing over of all Romans whom he had recruited in large numbers for military and civilian purposes, 3. razing of all fortresses (Cass. Dio 68,9,4–6). In the second war, Dacia was completely subjugated, and D. committed suicide (Cass. Dio 68,14,3; depictions 142–145 of Trajan's column in Rome). Despite well concealed hiding places, Trajan found his treasures (Cass. Dio 68,14,4–5).

W. Schuller (ed.), Siebenbürgen zur Zeit der Römer und der Völkerwanderung, 1994; K. Strobel, Untersuchungen zu den Dakerkriegen Trajans, 1984. ME.STR.

Decelea (Δεκέλεια; *Dekéleia*). Attic *Mesogeia* deme of the Hippothonti phyles; four → bouleutai. Part of the Attic Dodecapolis (Str. 9,1,20). In the former royal palace gardens of Tatoï (Thuc. 7,19,2) 120 stadiums north of Athens and south of the pass which, to the south-east of the Katsimidi, leads to Oropus and Tanagra (Thuc. 7,28,1; Hdt. 9,15). In 413 BC, the Spartans fortified D. (Thuc. 7,19,2; [1. 15 fig. 7; 3. 56f.; 4. 141f.]; hence the name of the 'Decelean War'); they occupied D. until 404 BC (Xen. Hell. 2,3,3) as well as the pass at the Katsimidi [2; 3. 57f.; 4. 142ff.]. At this time, the grain trade route from Oropus via D. to Athens (Thuc. 7,28) did not run across this pass but further to the east. The inscription of the Phratry of the Demotionidai from D. (IG II^2 1237; Syll.^{3} III 921) provides evidence of an altar to Zeus Phratrios, an assembly house of the Deceleians and a sanctuary of Leto; a hero named Decelus is mentioned at Hdt. 9,73,2. Wine from D. is derided as vinegar by Alexis (fr. 286 PCG).

1 Th.A. Arvanitopoulou, Dekeleia, 1958 2 E. Curtius, Sieben Karten zur Top. von Athen, 1868, 62 pl. 7 3 J.R. McCredie, Fortified Military Camps in Attica, 1966 4 J. Ober, Fortress Attica, 1985, 115, 141ff., 184, 196, 213.

Th.A. Arvanitopoulou, Ὄστρακα ἐκ Δεκελείας [*Óstraka ek Dekeleías*], 1959; Traill, Attica 21, 52, 59, 68, 110 no. 32 table 8; J.S. Traill, Demos and Trittys, 1986, 137; Whitehead, Index s.v. Decelea; F. Willemsen, Vom Grabbezirk des Nikodemos in Dekeleia, in: MDAI(A) 89, 1974, 173–191. H.LO.

Decempeda A measuring bar ten Roman feet (2.96 m) in length (*pertica*), derived from Lat. *decem* (ten) and *pes* (foot), which was used in architecture and especially in land surveying. There were 12 decempeda in one *actus*. As a square measure, the *decempeda quadrata* known as *scripulum iugeri* formed the smallest unit to be used in surveying = $^1/_{288}$ of the *iugerum* (8.76 m^2).

Measuring bars of more than ten foot have been recorded which were not referred to as decempeda.
→ Actus; → Iugerum; → Measures; → Pes; → Scripulum

F. Hultsch, Griech. und röm. Metrologie, ²1882; Schulten, s.v. D., RE 4, 2253–2254. A.M.

Decemprimi The term referred to the 'first ten' in a row (Greek δεκάπρωτοι, *dekáprōtoi*).
[1] *Decemprimi* was the name for the ten highest-ranking *decuriones* in the *curia* of a city with a constitution based on Roman or peregrine law. They handled various tasks; in particular, they were prominent in legations (Liv. 29,15,5; Cic. Verr. 2,2,162). In the Roman Imperial period, the *decemprimi* gradually become responsible for the legal duty of monitoring the municipal financial administration and, in case of improper economic utilization of the city's assets or outstanding taxes, are liable as debtors-in-common with their personal assets, being regarded as the representatives of the corporation that was their city. Depending on the municipal constitution, this liability could also extend to 20 or the entire *curia* (Cod. Theod. 16,2,39; Dig. 50,4,18,26; Cod. Iust. 10,30,14), which, in late antiquity, made unpopular both the rank as well as the originally honourable office of a → *decurio* (cf. Cod. Theod. 9,35,2; Cod. Iust. 10,38,1).
[2] Also called *decemprimi* were those who, with the *magister officiorum* in charge, commanded the *scholae domesticorum*, the military troupe protecting the court (Cod. Iust. 12,17,2; Not. Dign., Or. 11,3ff., Occ. 9,3ff.).
→ Curialis; → Decemviri

Jones, LRE 731, 734ff.; Liebenam, 267; Mommsen, Staatsrecht 3, 842. C.G.

Decemviri ('Ten Man (Committee)') occur in the following, historically recorded forms:
[1] According to tradition, the *decemviri legibus scribundis* were the committees selected in 451 and 450 BC to record the entire common and statute law valid in Rome (→ Tabulae duodecim), against which a → *provocatio* was not permissible. A first committee, consisting of patricians only, is said to have produced 10 tables while a second one, consisting of patricians and plebeians, a further two tables (including i.a. a prohibition of marriage between patricians and plebeians) (Liv. 3,33–57; Cic. Rep. 2,36f.; Dion. Hal. Ant. Rom. 10,1–6). In a factual sense, this most likely represented experimentation with state governing committees during the so-called class struggle of the early Republic because following the decemvirate up to the *leges Licinia Sextiae* (367/6 BC), e.g. in a 4–6 member consular tribunate, the development of the leading offices did not yet fully attain the dual principle of the consulate. Individual details as to the operation of the *decemviri* (daily rotation of the *summum imperium*, overthrow of the second committee, ratification of the laws by the people) are just as disputed as the historicity of the second *decemviri*.
[2] **Decemviri (st)litibus iudicandis,** according to tradition (Liv. 3,55,6f.), formed a sacrosanct judicial committee formed at the time of the *lex Valeria Horatia de tribunicia potestate* (449 BC), which was probably the responsible authority for disputes with the *plebs*. It is doubtful whether the later decemviral court, which made decisions in disputes over the status of liberty (*causae liberales*), developed from this. These *decemviri* were *magistratus minores* and, together with further committees (among others the *tresviri capitales* and *tresviri aere flando feriundo*), belonged to the XXVI-virate (Cic. Leg. 3,3,6) which was reduced to the XXvirate from the time of Augustus and became the first career station in the → *cursus honorum*. It seems likely that in this process the *causae liberales* were transferred from the *decemviri* to the consuls who now chaired the individual departments (*hastae*) of the centumviral court (cf. Cass. Dio 54,26; Suet. Aug. 36).
[3] **Decemviri agris (dandis) assignandis** were committees empowered to grant state-owned land to Roman citizens. Such committees could have between three and 20 members (Cic. Leg. agr. 1,17; 2,16; Liv. 31,4,2; Dion. Hal. Ant. Rom. 8,76).
[4] **Decemviri sacris faciundis** formed the committee of priests responsible for the interpretation of the Sibylline Books. Originally, it only had two members, but from the time of Sulla it was comprised of 15 (Gell. NA 1,19,11).
[5] **Decemviri** can also be the name given to members of a senatorial legation (Liv. 33,24,7) or a different senatorial commission (*decuria*) (Cod. Theod. 3,17,3; Cod. Iust. 5,33,1 pr.: for matters of guardianship, foster-care and trusteeship).
→ Lex agraria; → Sibyl; → Tribuni

Kaser, RZ 40f.; W. Kunkel, Staatsordnung und Staatspraxis der röm. Republik, 1995, vol. 2, 41, 326, 499, 533ff., 536, 559, 647, 654, 677; Latte, 160; Liebenam, 267; Mommsen, Staatsrecht 2, 592ff., 624ff., 702ff.; 3, 842. C.G.

Decennalia Feast days celebrating the tenth anniversary of an emperor's rule. *Decennalia* were probably first celebrated under Augustus (Cass. Dio 53,16,3), certainly under Tiberius in AD 24 and 34 (Cass. Dio 57,24,1; 58,24,1) and far beyond that: Cassius Dio still recorded them particularly for his own time (early 3rd cent.: 53,16,3), the *acta* of the Arval Brethren for the emperors Elagabalus and Gordian [1]. Further records point to still later times. The *decennalia* represented the fulfilment of vows made ten years earlier 'for the emperor's well-being and freedom from injury' [1]. On the coins of the adoptive emperors, these vows were symbolized by a shield (*clipeus*) surrounded with an oak wreath. An oak crown is also visible on a relief in the Villa Medici from the time of → Antoninus Pius where one can see a female figure write these vows on a shield: this figure probably represents Venus, who embodies

the eternal good fortune of the emperor. In addition, the *decennalia* were connected with the *victoria* and *providentia deorum*. The celebrations which marked the fulfilment of such vows, were accompanied by games (SHA Gall. 7,4).
→ Circus (II Games); → Votum

1 W. HENZEN, Acta fratrum Arvalium, 1874, 106.

J.-P. MARTIN, Providentia deorum, 1982; R. SCHILLING, L'évolution du culte de Vénus sous l'Empire romain, in: Dans le sillage de Rome, 1988, 162; P. VEYNE, Vénus, l'univers et les voeux décennaux sur les reliefs Médicis, in: REL 38, 1960, 306–322; G. WISSOWA, s.v. D., RE 4, 2265–2267. G.F.

Decennovium Straight, 19 mile (cf. the name) long section of the *via Appia* from the Forum Appii to Tarracina, continued through the *paludes Pontinae* by means of a viaduct, and possibly built under P. Claudius [I 29] Pulcher (*aedilis curulis* 255–253 BC). The decennovium was paved under Trajan in AD 110 (CIL X 6833–6835; 6839). The *mutatio* located at the halfway mark was called *Ad Medias*, the modern-day Mesa. There was a canal for tow boats parallel to the decennovium, which drained the swamps; Horace travelled on it (cf. the description at Hor. Sat. 1,5,3–26; Str. 5,3,6). Under Theoderic, after the canal had been drained by *patricius* Caecina Mavortius Basilius Decius in AD 507–511 (CIL X 6850–6852; Cassiod. Var. 2,32ff.), the name decennovium referred to the road section Tripontium – Tarracina. Cf. also Procop. Goth. 1,11.

M. CANCELLIERI, Le vie d'acqua dell'area pontina, in: Il Tevere (Quaderni Archeologici Etrusco-Italici 12), 1986, 143–156; Id., Il territorio pontino e la via Appia, in: S. QUILICI GIGLI (ed.), La via Appia, 1990, 61–72; G. UGGERI, in: ibid., 21–28; A. MOSCA, in: ibid., 102–105; F. BURGARELLA, Decio Cecina Mavorzio Basilio, in: Dizionario Biografico degli Italiani 33, 1987, 551–553. G.U.

Decentius

[1] Magnus D. *Caesar* during AD 350–353. A relative (possibly brother) of the usurper Magnus Magnentius ([Aur. Vict.] Epit. Caes. 42,2; Zon. 13,8,2) who made him *Caesar* in Milan at the end of 350 when the German tribes, encouraged by Constantius [2] II, had invaded Gaul. Commanding an insufficient force, he suffered a defeat against the Alamannic king Chnodomar (Julian Or. 1,35A; Amm. Marc. 16,12,4f.). When he heard of Magnentius' death, he committed suicide in Sens on 18 August 353 (Eutr. 10,12,2; Aur. Vict. Caes. 42,10; Chron. min. 1,238). PLRE 1, 244f. Decentius (3).

[2] *Tribunus et notarius* at the court of Constantius [2] II. In AD 361, he was meant to demand troops from the *Caesar* Julian (Amm. Marc. 20,4,2; 4,4; 4,11). Under Valens, he had an influential position, possibly as *magister officiorum* (cf. Lib. Ep. 1310; 1317). He was a non-Christian (ibid. 839). Many of Libanius' letters were addressed to him (Ep. 1463; 1476 et al.). PLRE 1, 244 Decentius (1). W.P.

Decetia City of the Haedui (Caes. B Gall. 7,33) in Gallia Lugdunensis, road junction (It. Ant. 367: *Decetia*; 460: *Deccidae*; Tab. Peut.: *Degetia*; Geogr. Rav. 4,26: *Dizezeia*); today's Decize (Nièvre). CIL 13, 2814–2816. Y.L.

Decianus Friend of Martial who came from Emerita in the province of Lusitania, but acted as a lawyer (*causidicus*) in Rome (Mart. 1,61,10; 2,5). He was a friend of literature to whom Martial dedicated his second book of epigrams. Follower of Stoic philosophy. In Martial, he only appears in book 1 and 2. PIR[2] D 20. W.E.

Deciates Ligurian people at the south-eastern coast of Gallia Narbonensis near → Antipolis (Mela 2,76; Plin. HN 3,35; Ptol. 2,10,8). The exact location of the *oppidum Deciatum* or *Dekieton* is unknown. In 154 BC, when the D. together with the neighbouring Oxybii besieged Nicaea and Antipolis, Rome sent the *consul* Q. Opimius upon the request of the city of Massalia and after a Roman legate had been injured. He defeated the D. and the Oxybii, disarmed them and granted the conquered territory to Massalia (Pol. 33,8–10; Liv. per. 47).

Fontes Ligurum et Liguriae antiquae, 1976, s.v. D.; J.-E. DUGAND, De l'Aegitna de Polybe au Trophée de la Brague, 1970; Y. ROMAN, L'intervention romaine de 154 avant J.-C. en Gaule Transalpine, in: Rev. archéologique de Narbonaise 24, 1991, 35–38. E.S.G.

Decidius Italic personal name, historically attested since the 1st cent. BC (ThlL, Onom. 3,70).

[1] Decidius Saxa, L. born in Spain (according to Cic. Phil. 11,5,12), but probably of Italic descent, he fought against the Pompeians in Spain in 49 BC (Caes. B Civ. 1,66,3) and in 45 probably against Pompeius' sons. Designated people's tribune by Caesar for 44, he joined M. Antonius [I 9] after Caesar's death and became a member of a commission for the distribution of land to veterans (MRR 2,324, 332f.). In 42, together with C. Norbanus, he commanded the advance guard of the army of the triumvirs. In 41, he became governor for Antonius in Syria (probably as *legatus pro praetore*, MRR 2,376), but in 40, he was defeated and killed by the Parthians under the leadership of Q. → Labienus (MRR 2,376, 384).

SYME, RP 1, 31–41. K.-L.E.

[2] T. Decidius Domitianus. *Procurator Caesaris Augusti* (AE 1935, 5), presumably in Lusitania, probably under Nero; related to Domitius Decidianus (DEMOUGIN, 468f. no. 563). W.E.

Decimatio In the Roman army, the *decimatio* was a rarely applied form of punishment for a whole unit (Pol. 6,38; Frontin. Str. 4,1,34; 4,1,37; Quint. Decl. 348). The tribunes selected every tenth man by drawing lots; the punishment could also be reduced by selecting just one man in a hundred (SHA Opil. 12,2). The victims decided on in this manner were not executed with an axe but clubbed to death (Tac. Ann. 3,21,1). This punishment, considered to be very severe, was applied in case of serious misdemeanours of the entire unit such as disobedience (Suet. Galba 12,2 SHA Opil. 12,2) or backing away from the enemy (Suet. Aug. 24,2; Tac. Ann. 3,21,1). The decision for the *decimatio* was made either by the commander of the legion, such as, for example, the *proconsul* of Africa (Tac. l.c.) or the *princeps*. The *decimatio* is documented for the Republican period; it was also practised in the period of the Principate, albeit rarely, and was perceived as a relic of an epoch long ago (Suet. Calig. 48,1. Galba 12,2. Tac. Ann. 3,21,1; Hist. 1,37,3; 1,51,5). This punishment is last mentioned in a text of AD 515, which however relates to the period of Diocletian's reign (Alcimus Avitus, hom. 25).

1 O. Fiebiger, s.v. D., RE 4, 2272. Y.L.B.

Decimius Roman family name, whose older and inscriptional form is Decumus (Schulze, 159), derived from → Decimus. Historic bearers of the name are documented since the 2nd half of the 2nd cent. BC.

[1] **D., C.** Legate in Crete in 171 BC, *praetor peregrinus* in 169, legate in Egypt in 168.

[2] **D., Num.** from Bovianum in Samnium; in 217, he brought timely help with a contingent of allies to the *magister equitum* Q. Minucius who was under heavy pressure from Hannibal near Gereonium (Liv. 22,24,11–14; Zon. 8,26).

[3] **Decimius Flavus, C.** *praetor urbanus* in 184 BC (Liv. 39,32,14). K.-L.E.

[4] **P. Decimius Eros Merula.** Doctor in Assisi (CIL XI, 5399–5400 = ILS 7812, 5369) who lived in the late 1st and early 2nd cent. AD. The former slave earned thousands of sesterces as *clinicus* (doctor at the sickbed), *chirurgus* (surgeon) and *ocularius* (eye specialist), which he used to buy his freedom, to enable him to become a priest (*seviratus*) and to donate at communal level. On his tombstone, his sources of income are listed in the same boasting manner as his various specialist fields. V.N.

Decimus Roman first name (ThlL, Onom. 3,73–76), probably did not indicate the place in a sequence ('the tenth') of births but the month of the birth; abbreviated D., in the Imperial period also Dec.; Greek Δέκμος, later Δέκιμος. The name was not used by patrician families and is otherwise rare as well (more frequent among the Iunii (→ Iunius) Bruti and the Laelii (→ Laelius)); in the Imperial period, it is also documented as a *cognomen* (for example with Aurelius, Flavius, Pacarius) and as a *nomen*.

Kajanto, Cognomina, 172; Salomies, 27f., 113f., 170. K.-L.E.

Decius Plebeian *nomen gentile*, documented in the literary tradition since the 5th cent.; the most important family were the Decii Mures (D. [I 1–3]), possibly from Campania [1], whose self-sacrifice (partly unhistorical) in battle made them much quoted examples in the tradition.

1 F. Càssola, I gruppi politici romani nell III secolo a.C., 1962, 152–154.

I. Republican period II. Imperial period

I. Republican period

[I 1] **D. Mus, P.** (Origin of the cognomen not known), in 352 BC, committee member dealing with a debt crisis in Rome (Liv. 7,21,6); as war tribune in 343, he is said to have saved the army of the consul A. Cornelius [I 22] Cossus Arvina from destruction by the Samnites (Liv. 7,34–36; usually regarded as a counterpart to the feat of M. Calpurnius [I 6] Flamma 258). As consul in 340, he fought against the Latini near Veseris in Campania and is said to have ensured the Roman victory in that he 'consecrated' (→ *devotio*) himself and his enemies to the gods of the Underworld and met a sacrificial death in battle (Liv. 8,6; 9–11). This is often regarded as a back-projection onto the father of a similar sacrifice by his son [I 2].

[I 2] **D. Mus, P.** Son of D. [I 1], one of the most influential Roman politicians around 300 BC and, due to a war on several fronts against Celts, Etruscans and Samnites, he was a consul four times (I 312, II 308, III 297, IV 295). In 308, he fought against the Etruscans; as censor in 304 with Q. → Fabius Maximus Rullianus, his colleague in the last three consulates, he limited the admission of citizens without property to the four urban tribus (Ap. → Claudius [I 2] Caecus); in 300, he supported the *lex Ogulnia* and thus is said to have belonged to the first plebeian pontifices (Liv. 10,7; 9,2). In 297, he defeated the Apulians near Malventum and in 296 remained in Samnium with an extended command (Liv. 10,15–17). In 295, he decided the battle near Sentinum in Umbria against the Celts by self-sacrifice (Duris FGrH 76 F 56; Liv. 10,26–30 and *passim*; cf. Pol. 2,19,5f.; 6,54,4, without giving the name). → Accius used the material in a play (*Aeneadae sive D.*, TRF[3] 326–328 [329–342 D.]).

Hölkeskamp; CAH 7^2, 2 (Index).

[I 3] **D. Mus, P.** Son of D. [I 2], consul in 279 BC, was defeated by Pyrrhus together with his colleague P. → Sulpicius Saverrio near Ausculum in Apulia (Plut. Pyrrh. 21). The tradition that, like his father and grandfather, he sacrificed himself in battle (Cic. Fin. 2,61; Tusc. 1,89), is unfounded. Late tradition makes him a *cos. suff.* in 265 (Vir. ill. 36,2).

CAH 7^2, 2 (Index).

[I 4] **Decius Subulo, P.** Follower of the Gracchi and a competent orator; as a people's tribune in 120 BC, he accused L. → Opimius (*cos.* 121) without success of suppressing C. Gracchus by force (Cic. De or. 2,132–136; Cic. Brut. 128). In 119 (?), a trial for reclaiming monies (?) against him failed because of his popularity [1]. As praetor in 115, he was severely humiliated by consul M. Aemilius [I 37] Scaurus (Vir. ill. 72,11).

1 ALEXANDER, 16f.

E. BADIAN, P. Decius P.f. Subulo, in: JRS 46, 1956, 91–96.

K.-L.E.

II. IMPERIAL PERIOD

[II 1] C. Messius Quintus Traianus Decius. Roman Emperor 249–251, * around 190 (Chron. pasch. 1 p. 505; different in [Aur. Vict.] Epit. Caes. 29,4) in Budalia, a *vicus* of the Pannonian Colonia Sirmium (Eutr. 9,4; Eus.; Hieron. Chron. pasch. 218 H; Aur. Vict. Epit. Caes. 29,1). Prior to the beginning of his reign, his name was C.M.Q. D. Valerinus (Valerianus, AE 1951, 9; 1978, 440; probably a spelling mistake [1; 2]), but frequently, he just called himself Q.D., an archaism for the 3. cent. AD that was probably intentional (SALOMIES, 350ff.; Q.L.D. unexplained on CIL II 6222; AE 1966, 217). Prior to his first consulate (*c.* 230), he was *candidatus Aug.* (AE 1985, 752) in an office not defined in any further detail, where the deletion of the name D. confirms that the senator is identical with the future emperor [2]. He was consular governor of the province of Moesia inferior (in 234, probably as of 232, THOMASSON 1, 142), Germania inferior (AE 1985, 752) and Hispania citerior (in 238, probably as of 235, THOMASSON 1, 18). In Spain, he remained faithful to Maximinus to the end [3] (AE 1978, 440). Only under Philip did D. emerge again as city prefect (Ioh. Ant. fr. 148, FHG 4, 597ff.). In 248, he was sent to the Danube with a special unit, but was proclaimed emperor by the troops in the early summer of 249 (Zos. 1,21,22; Zon. 12,19). D. tried in vain to remain faithful to Philip, then defeated him in a battle near Beroea (Ioh. Ant.), due to a scribal error referred to as Verona in Latin sources [4; 5]. Soon, D. took on the programmatic name of Traianus. He elevated his sons Herennius Etruscus and Hostilianus to Caesares while his wife Herennia Cupressenia Etruscilla became Augusta. According to evidence from coins, he wanted to head a peaceful regime and sought to maintain law and order particularly in the Danube provinces. Probably in order to restore the *pax deorum* and the unity of the empire (cf. AE 1973, 235, Cosa, where he was celebrated as *restitutor sacrorum*), D. proclaimed a general order to make sacrifices to the gods (*supplicatio*) in 249: all citizens of the empire had to make sacrifices to the official gods and had to obtain certificates (*libelli*) for this from local authorities (examples from Egypt in [6]). In this way D. triggered the great persecution of Christians, since many Christians refused to make these sacrifices (Euseb. Hist. eccl. 6,41,9f.; Lactant. De mort. pers. 4,2). The order to make sacrifices remained in force until D.'s death; among others, pope Fabian and Pionios of Smyrna died [7]. Little is reported on D.'s other activities in Rome; he built baths (Eutr. 9,4); the later emperor Valerianus was an important advisor (Zon. 12,20). *Cos. II* in 250, D. soon had to go back to the Balkans because of an invasion by the Goths. In the war against the Goths under Kniva in 250, he was at first successful near Nicopolis in Lower Moesia (Dacicus max., CIL II 4949, Germanicus max., AE 1942/43, 55, both probably unofficial), then suffered a severe defeat near Beroea in Thrace, but saved himself and reorganized the army [8]. The governor of Thrace, T. Iulius Priscus, joined forces with the enemy and attempted to make himself emperor (Dexippus, FGrH 100, F 26; Iord. Get. 18,103; AE 1932, 28; in Rome, a second pretender rose up, Iulius Valens Licinianus: Aur. Vict. Caes. 29,3; Epit. Caes. 29,5). Both were removed, but in the summer of 251, D. and Herennius (Augustus by now), who in that year shared the consulate (D. III, Herennius I), were annihilated by the Goths near Abrittus (between Marcianopolis and Sexaginta Prista, not in the Dobruja (IGBulg. 2 p. 153)) and lost their lives (Aur. Vict. Caes. 29,2–5; Zos. 1,23; Iord. Get. 18,101–103; Zon. 12,20). In the Christian sources, D. is called the 'great dragon' or the *metator antichristi* (Cypr. Epist. 22,1; cf. Apc. 16,13) while the pagan authors regarded him rather favourably (Aur. Vict. Epist. Caes. 29,2; Zos. 1,21,1ff; 22,1; 23,3). In SHA Aur. 42,6, D. and Herennius are put on the same level as the old Decians (*Vita et mors veteribus comparanda*).

1 BIRLEY 2 X. LORIOT, in: Empereurs illyriens: actes du colloque de Strasbourg, 1998 3 G. ALFÖLDY, Eine Inschr. auf dem Montgó bei Dianium an der span. Ostküste, in: Epigraphica 40, 1978, 59–90 4 S. DUSANIČ, The End of the Philippi, in: Chiron 6, 1976, 427–439 5 R. ZIEGLER, Festschr. Opelt, 1988, 385ff. 6 J. R. KNIPFING, The Libellis of the Decian Persecution, in: Harvard Theological Review 1923, 345–390 7 L. ROBERT, Le martyre de Pionios prêtre de Smyrne, 1994 8 B. GEROV, Beitr. z. Gesch. der röm. Prov. Moesien und Thrakien, 1980, 93ff., 361ff.

RIC 4/3, 107–150; KIENAST, ²1996, 204f.; K. WITTIG, s.v. Messius, RE 15, 1244–1284; R. SELINGER, The Mid-Third Century Persecutions of Decius and Valerian, 2002.

A.B.

[II 2] C. Messius Quintus D. Valerinus. identical with the (later) emperor D. [II 1]. A.B.

[II 3] D. Mundus. seduced Paulina, the wife of Sentius Saturninus, with the assistance of the Isis priests (on the literary topos of seduction [1. 144]) in AD 19. Thereupon, Tiberius had the priests killed, but D. only sent into exile (Jos. Ant. Iud. 18,66–80).

1 C. PHARR, The Testimony of Josephus to Christianity, in: AJPh 48, 1927.

ME.STR.

[II 4] Aelius D. Tricianus. From a soldier in the Pannonian army, he rose to prefect of the *leg. II Parthica* and accompanied Caracalla to the East. D. had knowledge of plans to murder Caracalla (8 April 217). Appointed by Macrinus as *leg. Aug. pro praet. Pannoniae inf.* with the rank of a consul (Cass. Dio 79,13,4; inscription in THOMASSON, 116), killed by Elagabalus in 219 (Cass. Dio 80,4,3). A.B.

Declamatio in Catilinam This imaginary trial speech, probably a rhetorical exercise from late antiquity, was ascribed in MSS to → Cicero but also to → Sallust and M. → Porcius Latro [4]. The assumption that it was a Renaissance forgery [2; 3] has been refuted by more recent MSS discoveries (earliest instance 1439) [1]. Other indications against this assumption are intrinsic criteria such as a quotation from the Twelve Tablets (8,26) and from a *lex Gabinia*, and an allusion to a Saturnalia on the Aventine Hill, not attested elsewhere. Of no value as a historical source for L. Sergius → Catilina, but not without relevance as regards the influence of Cicero.

1 H. KRISTOFERSON, D. in L. Sergium Catalinam, diss. 1928 2 A. KURFESS, Zur D. in L. Sergium C., in: PhW 57, 1937, 141–143 3 SCHANZ/HOSIUS 3, 154 4 R. HELM, s.v. Porcius 49, in: RE 22, 235. W.SI.

Declamationes Practice speeches, representing the ultimate stage of education in rhetoric. They treated (mostly fictitious) model cases (Suet. Gram. 25,9) with the aim of preparing pupils for the *pugna forensis* (Quint. Inst. 5,12,17), and were practised in schools of rhetoric modelled after the Greek pattern; the name is of later date (Cic. Tusc. 1,7; Sen. Controv. 1, pr. 12). Despite criticisms of excesses, Quintilian gives a more positive assessment of their pedagogical utility than, say, Messalla (Tac. Dial. 35), who takes the Republican educational ideal as his starting point. Historical themes or an established repertory of more or less fabulous events (poisonings, piracy, disinheritance etc.) were used as the basis for → *suasoriae* (analogous to the *genus deliberativum*) and → *controversiae* (analogous to the *genus iudiciale*). *Declamationes* remained a definitive element of higher education into late antiquity; the genre moreover provoked the artistic ambitions of teachers of rhetoric in the context of restrictions on political activity during the imperial period. *Declamationes* accordingly entered the public sphere alongside recitations of literary works. → Seneca the Elder provides a picture of this virtuoso pursuit in his anthology. Surviving examples from the educational sphere are two pseudo-Quintilian collections (*declamationes maiores/minores*), as well as excerpts of *declamationes* by one → Calpurnius Flaccus [III 2]. The practice model was then taken up again in the Renaissance.

→ Quintilianus; → Rhetoric

H. BORNECQUE, Les Declamationes, 1902; W. HOFRICHTER, Stud. zur Entwicklungsgesch. der Declamationes, 1935; S.F. BONNER, Roman Declamationes, 1949; Id., Education in Ancient Rome, 1977, 277ff.; 309ff.; D.L. CLARK, Rhetoric in Greco-Roman Education, 1957, 213ff.; F.H. TURNER, The Theory and Practice of Rhet. Declamationes from Homeric Greece through the Renaissance, 1972; P.L. SCHMIDT, Die Anfänge der institutionellen Rhet. in Rom, in: Monumentum Chilonense. FS E. Burck, 1975, 183–216; M. WINTERBOTTOM, Roman Declamationes, 1980 (extracts); D.A. RUSSELL, Greek Declamationes, 1983; M.G.M. VAN DER POEL, De Declamationes bij de Humanisten, 1987. P.L.S.

Declination see → Inflection

Decollatio In Roman law the 'simple' death penalty by decapitation (whence also: *capitis amputatio*), as opposed to being burned alive (→ *crematio*) and crucifixion (→ *crux*). All three methods of execution appear in Paulus, Sent. 5,17,2 as *summa supplicia* (most severe punishments). Certainly from the time of Caligula capital punishment by *damnatio ad bestias* (animal combat in the arena) was also current practice. *Decollatio* was typically reserved for higher-status freemen (→ *honestiores*), while *crematio* and *crux* were carried out on ordinary freemen (→ *humiliores*) and slaves. *Decollatio* may early on have been the punishment used in the few public (as opposed to private) executions, especially for high treason and treason (→ *perduellio*). In the late Republic it was largely replaced by banishment (→ *deportatio*), but remained in practice in the military, coming back into general use under Augustus. It was thereafter also the punishment for murder and many other offences, e.g. in late antiquity even for adultery (→ *adulterium*). In early times *decollatio* was carried out with the axe, from the time of Augustus with the sword.

1 E. CANTARELLA, I supplizi capitali in Grecia e a Roma, 1991, 154ff. 2 MOMMSEN, Strafrecht, 916ff. G.S.

Decor(um) see → Art, theory of

Decorations, military Decorations were used to reward soldiers' bravery and acts of courage in the Roman army as in all other armies, their advantage being that their cost to the common purse was slight, while at the same time they reinforced general awareness of military honour (Pol. 6,39). A pronounced feeling for hierarchical structures also had its influence on such decorations, as they were awarded according to the rank of the receiver (→ *dona militaria*). As A. BÜTTNER has shown, the origins of Roman decorations may be found not only in Italy, but also in the Celtic and Greek worlds as well as the Orient. They can be divided into various categories:

1. *Hasta pura*: this reward in the form of a weapon represents a problem for historians. According to Varro (Serv. Aen. 6,760), it was manufactured 'without iron'; it was accordingly assumed that this was a plain, blunt thrusting spear made of wood. But several funerary reliefs depict a *hasta pura* with a point. V. MAXFIELD therefore thinks that the lack of iron had a ritual basis, and that the *hasta pura* was never used as a weapon.

2. *Vexillum* was a cavalry decoration, and took the form of a piece of material hanging down from the *hasta*. The earliest mention of such decorations goes back to 107 BC, and is associated with Marius (Sall. Iug. 85,29).

3. *Corona* (crown): there was a great variety of *coronae* (Gell. NA 5,6), their origins lying far in the past. In the 5th cent. BC, L. Siccius Dentatus is supposed to have received, in addition to other decorations, 26 wreaths (Gell. NA 2,11). a) The grass crown (*graminea*) was the simplest but most prestigious decoration of this kind. It rewarded soldiers who had rescued an army in peril (Plin. HN 22,6f.). b) The citizens' crown (*civica*) was made from the leaves of the holm oak (*aesculus*), and was awarded to a Roman citizen who had saved the life of another Roman citizen (Gell. NA 5,6,11–14). c) The wall crown (*muralis, vallaris* or *castrensis*) was given the soldier who had been first to surmount the enemy's fortifications or defensive wall. The golden mural crown represented a crenellated wall (Pol. 6,39,5; Gell. NA 5,6,16). d) The siege crown (*obsidionalis*) belonged to the general who had forced the lifting of a siege (Plin. HN 22,7). e) The ship crown (*navalis, classica* or *rostrata*) resembled the bow of a ship, and was worn by soldiers who had been first to set foot on an enemy ship. f) Finally, the golden crown (*aurea*) was the reward for any deed of heroism not covered by one of the other listed crowns. Thus in 361 BC T. Manlius received a golden crown for having defeated a Gaul in single combat (Liv. 7,10,14).

4. The *dona minora*, a second-class decoration, was awarded to soldiers and centurions. There were four different kinds: a) the usually silver, in exceptional cases, gold bracelet (*armilla*) could be variously fashioned, with one or several spirals. The individual honoured wore the bracelet on one or both wrists. b) The *torques* (a circular piece of metal occasionally resembling a twisted cord) is generally ascribed a Celtic origin, although it is known that Persians and Scythians too possessed this kind of decoration. The *torques* was open, and could take quite different forms (twisted or not, with or without a clasp). In the Republican period gold was exclusively for the *socii*, silver for Roman soldiers. c) Equestrian decorations (*phalerae*) were also common. The helmet was originally adorned with small decorative rivets. Later these were simple or decorated small circular plates. During the Republic the decoration was given to riders who had killed an enemy. These decorations were often awarded during the Principate. M. Caelius, a centurion who fell at the defeat of Varus in AD 9, is depicted on his tombstone with several *phalerae*. d) The little sacrificial plate (*patella*), also called *phiálē* (φιάλη), was a simple emblem similar to *phalerae*. Prior to the Principate it was awarded to foot soldiers.

5. Soldiers and officers could be awarded with various items in recognition of particular deeds. We may cite here as examples the decorative brooch (*fibula*) and the shield of honour (*clipeus*). It is known that the Senate awarded Augustus the *corona civica* and the *clipeus* for his services (R. Gest. div. Aug. 34,2). These were in recognition of Augustus's political qualities (*virtus, clementia, iustitia* and *pietas*) as well as his military achievements. *Cornicula* should not, however, be regarded as military decorations in the traditional sense, for they did not represent awards for particular actions, but were badges of rank. Seen as a whole, the awarding of honours varied not only according to the rank of the recipient, but also displays specific characteristics at different periods. The development of honours in the first two centuries AD is well known to us from inscriptions, in spite of some obscure aspects. The questions raised by the differences in rank of the recipients reflect the social structures of the Imperium Romanum.
→ Corniculum; → Dona militaria

1 A. Büttner, Unt. über Ursprung und Entwicklung von A. im röm. Heer, in: BJ 157, 1957, 127–180
2 V. Maxfield, The Military Decorations of the Roman Army, 1981 3 P. Steiner, Die *dona militaria*, 1905.

Y.L.B.

Decretalia A text containing a *decretum* was called *decretale* (Sid. Apoll. Epist. 7,9,6) in later Latin. The term *decretum* (from *decernere* 'to decide') was used for judgements in individual cases as well as general rulings. In the individual case it denote the judicial verdict or decision of a magistrate or other judicial official or authority (also decisions of committees), by which a judicial decision was pronounced after examination of the evidence (*causae cognitio;* Dig. 37,1,3,8); to be contrasted to the → *rescriptum*, which comprised the evidence presented in unexamined form. General decrees were handed down by state authorities, also by the Senate or an *ordo decurionum* (→ *decurio*) in matters within their competence (Dig. 4,4,3 pr.; 11,7,8 pr.; 14,6,9,2; 50,9,5).

There are collections of guideline *decreta* from prominent authorities; these collections may contain other official acts besides *decreta* (such as *rescripta, edicta, orationes*), and are often called *decretales (libri)* (Siricius Epist. 1,15,20: *ad servandos canones et tenanda decretalia constituta*; Sid. Apoll. Epist. 1,7,4). The most prominent examples are the codes of imperial constitutions from late antiquity (codes of Theod. and Just.; Dig. 1,4,1,1) and other, more personal collections such as the *Variae* of → Cassiodorus. From late antiquity when bishops were able to promulgate decisions with legally binding effect in the ecclesiastical realm (Cod. Iust. 1, 4, *tit. de episcopali audientia*), their *decreta* and *rescripta* were also collected, in so far as they were of general significance. Already in antiquity, alongside the digests of *canones* of the Church councils in the western Empire particular prominence was accorded to *decretalia* in the historically literal sense of the word, that is to say the collection of papal *decreta*. Under Pope Gelasius at the beginning of the 6th cent. the monk Dionysius Exiguus was first to undertake an edited comprehensive collection of the *decretalia*; during subsequent centuries his work was continually expanded, culminating in 1170 in a comprehensive new edition, the so-called *Decretum Gratiani*. This formed the basis for the canonical branch of jurisprudence *utriusque iuris*, which came into being alongside the reception of Roman law from the 12th cent. An editorially remodelled version of the *decretum Gratiani* eventually found its way into the *Corpus Iuris Canonici* of the Catholic Church, published in 1917.

KASER, RZ 138, 352; W. KUNKEL, Staatsordnung und Staatspraxis der röm. Republik, 1995, vol. 2, 184f.; R. PUZA, Katholisches Kirchenrecht, 1991, 39ff.; WENGER, 427, 463ff. C.G.

Decretum Ruling, decision, decree of an official authority (from *decernere*). Legal texts, in their own peculiar language which does not fully conform with modern conceptions, use *decretum* primarily in relation to the following organs of authority: 1. praetors and provincial governors; 2. emperors; 3. the Senate; 4. decurions; 5. priestly colleges; 6. the councils (in the Christian period).

1. Gai. Inst. 4,140 divided judicial decrees of the praetor into *decreta* and → *interdicta*, depending on whether the praetor positively ordered something, such as the production of an object, or forbids something, such as the use of force against an innocent property-owner. *Decreta* were to be issued from the office of the praetor (*pro tribunali*: Dig. 37,1,3,8). Examples of enactments of a praetor (or of the provincial governor in the provinces) referred to as *decreta* are: those undertaken for the protection of dependents and minors, such as the appointment of a tutor or guardian or rescindment of such an appointment; approval for the sale of a ward's property; determination of the maintenance of the ward, → *restitutio in integrum* for a minor who has been cheated; decrees of the praetor in matters of inheritance, such as the establishment of an heir's right to an estate (granting of *bonorum possessio*); an order to an heir to take possession of an estate that is to be relinquished into trusteeship; the securing of an estate for an unborn heir; also the installation of creditors in a heavily indebted estate. By means of a *decretum* the praetor awarded a slave with freedom when earned, perhaps by uncovering a crime. The praetor proceeded by *decretum* against a property owner who was not prepared to secure the safety of a neighbour potentially affected by a danger proceeding from his property (→ *cautio damni infecti*). The first *decretum* provided the neighbour requiring protection with ownership of the property whence the potential danger proceeds (*missio in possessionem*); the second gives him (executive) property rights. As we know, e.g., from Cic. Quinct. 63, the people's tribunes (→ *tribunus plebis*) could intercede against the *decreta* of the praetors [1. 210], voiding them, just as they could against other measures taken by magistrates.

2. Any binding order given by an emperor is generally called a *decretum*, but the term is typically used to denote the emperor's decision in a case presided over by him in the capacity of judge. The emperor was able to intercede in a case in two ways: either by resolving a question of law, his decision being binding on the judge (*rescriptum*, usually at the request of one of the parties), in which case the determination of the facts and the verdict remained with the judge; or he might decide a case himself, either by personally taking control of the case or by allowing an *appellatio* against the verdict of the court. Imperial *decreta* soon take on a significance beyond the original case, in that they become precedents incapable of being set aside by judges in similar cases. These *decreta* could probably be accessed in the imperial archive, although only small numbers of texts by jurists on imperial *decreta* have survived [2. 181]. According to Gai. Inst. 1,2 and 1,5, the *decreta* formed a component part of Roman statute law; Papinian (Dig. 1,1,7 pr.) places them alongside the *leges* (→ *lex*) within *ius civile*; for Ulpian (Dig. 1,4,1,1) they are themselves *leges*, like any other formula of the → *constitutiones*.

3. The appointment of a provincial governor was an example of a *decretum* of the Senate. But other resolutions of the Senate were also termed *decreta*. It is reported by Festus (454,20 L.) that Aelius Gallus inquired what was the difference between a → *senatus consultum* and a *decretum senatus* [1. 185]. In juridical texts, *decretum senatus* appears merely as a variant of *senatus consultum* (e.g. Ulp. Dig. 14,6,9,2).

4. Decisions of the leading → *decuriones* of a community were called *decreta* in the Dig., as they are in the *lex Irnitana*, which required a quorum of two thirds of the membership for decisions (as in Ulp. Dig. 50,9,3), and only a qualified majority [3].

5. Priestly colleges were asked for their advice in cases with potential religious implications; they then gave their opinion either in advance (provisory) [2. 18ff.] or with regard to circumstances already pertaining (authoritative); the latter were binding on other organs of the state (e.g. Senate or consuls). Cic. Att. 4,2,3 gives an account of the *decretum* of the *pontifices* regarding the efficacy of the consecration of his house by his enemies [2. 21]. In the Christian era the Dig. still contained the somewhat anachronistic provision that human bones may be removed from a site only by *decretum* of the *pontifices* or imperial authorization (Ulp. Dig. 11,7,8 pr.).

6. In referring to council resolutions as *decreta*, legal texts of the Christian period followed the tradition of the Church Fathers, e.g. Augustine.

Unlike the *decretum* of a praetor or emperor, the judgements given by the *iudex* employed by the praetor to decide a case were not called *decreta*. The *iudex* pronounced a → *condemnatio* when he decided in favour of the plaintiff, or an → *absolutio* when he decided in favour of the defendant. The technical term for his verdict was *sententia* [1. 185]. The term *decretum* was likewise not used for decisions of the people's assembly [1. 184].

1 W. KUNKEL, R. WITTMANN, Staatsordnung und Staatspraxis der röm. Republik, 1995 2 SCHULZ 3 J. GONZÁLEZ, The lex Irnitana, in: JRS 76, 1985, 147–243.

R.WI.

Decrius

[1] Defender of a fort on the river Pagyda in Africa, captured in AD 20 by Tacfarinas; D. perished courageously in the action (Tac. Ann. 3,20,1f.).

DEMOUGIN, no. 233.

[2] **L.D.** Husband of Paconia Agrippina, honoured by the Rhodians (IGR 3,1126).

[3] **D. Calpurnianus.** *praef. vigilum*, killed in AD 48 as a consequence of his relationship with Messalina (Tac. Ann. 11,35,3).

DEMOUGIN, no. 461. D.K.

Decuma (= *decima sc. pars*). The law of Papia Poppaea (AD 9) limited to one-tenth of the inheritance (with additional allowances for children) the capacity (*capacitas*) of spouses in *manus*-free marriage to inherit from the testament of another. A wife in *manus*- marriage was, however, *sua heres* entitled to inherit the entire estate [2].The limit was abolished in AD 410 (Cod. Iust. 8,57,2). Apart from inheritance law, the tithe occurs as subject of a vow (Varro, Ling. 6,54; Dig. 50,12,2,2) and as the tax on crops from provincial land [1].

→ Caducum

1 KASER, Die Typen der röm. Bodenrechte in der späten Republik, in: ZRG 62, 1942, 61f. 2 H.L.W. NELSON, U. MANTHE, Gai Institutiones III 1–87, 1992, 223. U.M.

Decumanus is a technical term from Roman surveying (→ Limitatio), and denotes the perpendicular lines (*limites*) in a rectangular surveying system; originally it was a term from cosmology, for the east-west axis as sighting line for the apparent movement of the heavens [1. 199]: counterpart of the → *cardo*, which as north-south axis divides the world into the hemisphere of the sunrise and that of the sunset, or diurnal and nocturnal hemispheres [2. 147]. In the practise of land-surveying the *decumanus maximus* was established as an axis of orientation on the basis of topographical features, existing orientations of roads or the longest axis of the site to be surveyed, regardless of the cardinal directions. By means of a surveying instrument (→ *groma*), a system of coordinates was established within the site to be divided up, the main vertical axis (y axis) being called the *decumanus maximus* (*DM*), the main horizontal axis (x axis) the *cardo maximus* (*CM*), the two axes meeting at right angles at the centre of the area surveyed. As the widest and greatest *limes* of the survey, at 40 feet (*c.* 12 m) the *DM* always extended twice the width of the *CM*. In the language of surveying the *decumani* were always referred to as *prorsi* ('facing the enemy'), as opposed to the *cardines* (*transversi*).

1 O. BEHRENDS, Bodenhoheit und privates Bodeneigentum im Grenzwesen Roms. Feldmeßkunst, 1992
2 W. HÜBNER, Himmel- und Erdvermessung. Feldmeßkunst, 1992.
O. BEHRENDS, L. CAPOGROSSI COLOGNESI (ed.), Die röm. Feldmeßkunst — Interdiziplinäre Beiträge zu ihrer Bed. für die Zivilisationsgesch. Roms, 1992; O. DILKE, Archaeological and Epigraphic Evidence of Roman Land Survey, ANRW II.1, 564–592; E. FABRICIUS, s.v. Limitatio, RE 13, 672–701; U. HEIMBERG, Röm. Landvermessung, 1977; A. SCHULTEN, s.v. D., RE 4, 2314–2316. H.-J.S.

Decumates agri Problematic expression, attested only in Tac. Germ. 29,3: Tacitus does not count those peoples settled beyond the Rhine and Danube as belonging to the Germanic peoples, saying *eos qui decumates agros exercent: levissimus quisque Gallorum et inopia audax dubiae possessionis solum occupavere; mox limite acto promotisque praesidiis sinus imperii et pars provinciae habentur*. The partly fanciful discussion of this quotation, difficult as it is on linguistic and factual grounds, is as wide-ranging as it is fruitless. If *decumates* is generally viewed as an adjective modifying *agros* (acc. pl.), substantival nom. pl. is also possible (preferred by [1], cf. [13. 272, 274f.]). Conjectures involving *decumanos* and *decumatos* have failed, and the most recent [12] involving *desertos* (in the sense of ⟨*de*⟩*relictos* 'deserted') is scarcely plausible. The association with the concept of 'tenth' is certain, but a link with *decem pagi* does not hold up [2]. The remaining complex difficulties are expounded by TIMPE; see a summary of related research in LUND [12].

According to Tacitus, the settlements in question were adjacent to the → Chatti and thus in no-man's-land (*limite acto*, [3. 108f.]); modern scholarship expects the *decumates agri* to be in the narrower sense in the middle Neckar region with its domains [4], in the broader sense in the entire region between Rhine and Danube, including the Wetterau. *Levissimus quisque Gallorum* and *sinus imperii* are to be understood in the context of Domitian's triumphs over the Germanic tribes [5. 78ff.; 13. 275f.]. These represented the initial completion of the extension of the *decumates agri* with a road network protected by military posts, after the military occupation of the → *Abnoba mons* as far as → Arae [1] Flaviae by Pinarius Clemens in AD 73/74 had exploited territorial claims that, having been made under Augustus, had since been neglected (*dubia possessio* [3. 102, 102⁷]). The region flourished, with substantial suburban settlements (→ Aquae [III 6], Lopodunum, Sumelocenna, Arae [1] Flaviae) [7]. After the war between Gallienus and Postumus [8] the withdrawal of the army was followed by the collapse of the basic economic structure and progressive retreat of the population ([9], cf. [6]). The Roman claim was maintained into the 4th cent.; from the time of Julian the purpose of the Romans was to control the Germanic tribes that had settled in the meantime, esp. the → Alamanni and → Burgundiones (Amm. Marc. 18,2,15), as well as to retain the possibility of free passage (Pan. Lat. 8[5]2,1; Amm. Marc. 21,5,3; [10]). Continuity of Roman provincial settlement can be attested until the beginning of the 5th cent. [11].

1 G. Perl, Tacitus, Germania, 1990, 210f. 2 J. G. F. Hind, What ever happened to the Agri Decumates?, in: Britannia 15, 1984, 187–192 3 K. Dietz, Die Blütezeit des röm. Bayern, in: W. Czsyz, K. Dietz, Th. Fischer, H.-J. Kellner (ed.), Die Römer in Bayern, 1995, 100–176 4 R. Wiegels, Solum Caesaris, in: Chiron 19, 1989, 61–102 5 R. Wolters, Eine Anspielung auf Agricola im Eingangskap. der Germania?, in: RhM 137, 1994, 77–95 6 P. Kos, Sub principe Gallieno ... amissa Raetia?, in: Germania 73, 1995, 131–144 7 J. C. Wilmanns, Die Doppelurkunde von Rottweil und ihr Beitr. zum Städtewesen in Obergermanien, in: Epigraphische Stud. 12, 1981, 1–182 8 E. Schallmayer (ed.), Niederbieber, Postumus und der Limesfall, 1996 9 K. Strobel, Das Imperium Romanum im '3. Jh.', 1993, 292f. 10 I. Benedetti-Martig, I Romani ed il territorio degli agri decumati nella tarda antichità, in: Historia 42, 1993, 352–361 11 H. Castritius, Das E. der Ant. in den Grenzgebieten am Oberrhein und an der oberen Donau, in: Archiv für hessische Gesch. und Altertumskunde, N.F. 37, 1979, 9–32 12 A. A. Lund, Kritischer Forschungsber. zur 'Germania' des Tacitus, ANRW II.33,3, 1991, 1989–2222, esp. 2109–2124 13 G. Neumann, D. Timpe, H. U. Nuber, s.v. D.a., RGA 5, 271–286.

M. Clauss, s.v. D.a., LMA 3, 625f.

K.DI.

Decuria see → Decurio [4]

Decuriales (from *decuria* = a quantity made up of 10 parts, or the tenth part of a quantity) are members of a group of ten or the tenth part of a group (Varro, Ling. 9,86; Vitr. De arch. 7,1,).

[1] The members of an equestrian *decuria* under the orders of a → *decurio* (Varro Ling. 5,91), and in late antiquity the members of a *decuria* of foot-soldiers under the orders of a *decanus* (Veg. Mil. 2,8), are called *decuriales*.

[2] In the Republican period *decuriales* were members of particular groups within the civil service, e.g. the *scribae, lictores* or *viatores* (CIL II 3596; VI 1877; XIV 373).

[3] In late antiquity chancellery officials serving the Senate of Rome in various *decuriae* were also called *decuriales* (Cod. Iust. 11,14).

[4] *Decuriales* were members of departments (*decuriae*) created from time to time in the Roman Senate, and, in those cities with a constitution based on Roman Law, members of occasional committees of the city council (*decuriones*), to whom particular tasks could be delegated (Isid. Orig. 9,4,23; Vat. fr. 142,235; Dig. 29,2,25,1).

[5] *Decuriales* were members of the judicial departments created subsequent to the *lex Livia iudiciaria* (91 BC) in order to defuse partisan strife over membership of the jury courts (*quaestiones perpetuae*), and especially to ensure numerically equal participation by the groups (*decuriae*) of the senators and the knights (Liv. Per. 70, 71; Vell. Pat. 2,13,2; Suet. Aug. 32; Tac. Ann. 3,30).

[6] Members of particular sections within associations and organisations were also called *decuriales* (CIL VI 2192; 6719).

→ Curia; → Curialis; → Decemprimi

Kaser, RPR 2, 307ff.; W. Kunkel, Staatsorganisation und Staatspraxis der röm. Republik, 1995, Vol. 2, 112ff., 117; Mommsen, Staatsrecht, vol. 1, 341ff., 368ff.; vol. 3, 529ff.; 851.

C.G.

Decurio, decuriones *Decurio* (cf. *decuria*; → Decurio [4] via *decus(s)is* f. *dec-* and *as*) in general usage refers to a member or representative of a group of ten or tenth-part group (cf. Dig. 50,16,239,5); there is no shared etymology with *curialis*, a word of partly similar meaning derived from *co-viria*. In its specialized sense *decurio* denotes various functionaries:

[1] A member of a → *curia*, in those *municipia* and *coloniae* bound by Roman Law, was called *decurio*. Appointment of the usually 100 *decuriones* (occasionally smaller numbers) was regulated in various ways in accordance with *leges municipales* (cf. Tabula Heracleensis 85,126ff./ FIRA 1, 147ff.; Dig. 50,4,1), without a popular vote: by selection (*lectio, conscriptio*) from the circle of respected citizens (*honestiores*) by the city → *duoviri* acting in their censorial function as *quinquennales*; as a consequence of belonging to the *ordo decurionum* by virtue of holding office as city → *duovir* or → *aedilis*; or by co-option by the city council. The *duumviri* and *aediles* of the city and city legations (→ *decemprimi*) were drawn from the *decuriones*. The prerequisites for appointment to the *curia* were that the candidate was a citizen of the city, not disqualified by previous convictions or ill repute or by being a slave, freedman or eunuch or debtor to the city (Dig. 50,4,11), and at least of minimum age and minimum financial means. The normal minimum age was 25 years (Dig. 50,4,8). The minimum financial means varied according to the particular locality, standing at around the level of the equestrian census; but in small cities could be far less, in large cities far more than the average amount of 100,000 sesterces (Dig. 50,2,5–7; 12; 4,15). During the Republic and early Imperial period the decurionate as an honorary office (*honor*), was particularly desired, despite the lack of a salary and the considerable expenses entailed (Dig. 50,4,14,1). Membership of the highly regarded city council (honorifics: *splendidissimus ordo, senatores*) brought fame far beyond the confines of the city, underscored by places of honour at public gatherings and in the theatre (Tabula Heracleensis 135/FIRA 1,150), privileges under criminal law (no forced labour, no condemnation *ad bestias*: Cod. Iust. 9,47,3 and 12), immunity from *munera sordida* (Dig. 50,1,17,7). The decurionate nevertheless also involved burdens and obligations (*munera*). These derived in part from traditions associated with pre-Roman → *leiturgía* for city notables and the wealthy. These comprised in particular the obligation to undertake municipal office at reasonable intervals in alternation with other notables (Cod. Iust. 10,41 tit.; 10,42,1),

and to a certain extent personally provide funds for the poorer population or bear the costs of building works and the staging of official games (Dig. 50,4,10f.). One considerable legal obligation incumbent upon *decuriones* from time immemorial is that within the framework provided by city statute they were liable with their personal means not only for their own administrative obligations but also for the entire city's fiscal and financial conduct (Cod. Iust. 11,36 and 38; → *decemprimi*, → *curiales*). One of their duties was also to advise the city magistrates and, in consultation with the governor, decide on matters relating to municipal legislation and the distribution of offices (Tabula Heracleensis 126/FIRA 1,150; Cod. Iust. 10,32,2).

From the 3rd cent. AD, at the time of the soldier emperors, the of city finances were frequently overburdened through the costs of war, emergency disbursements and state-imposed burdens frequently led to excessive demands on the system of honorary office based on the decurionate. This made the decurionate so unattractive that efforts were increasingly made to escape the obligations of honorary office. Of course such tendencies also occurred earlier (Dig. 50,1,38: rescripts of emperors Marcus Aurelius and Verus; 50,2,1 and 50,4,9: Ulpian). Statutory measures directed against these tendencies led in late antiquity to the comprehensive statutory regularization of honorary duties as corporate obligations of rank incumbent on the *curiales* of a city. Among the consequences of this process are the statutory hereditary linkage of curial obligations with inheritable curial wealth (Cod. Theod. 12,1,53), the reduction of the minimum age for a *decurio* to 18 years, i.e. below the age of majority (25 years) (Cod. Theod. 12,1,7 and 19; probably only temporary), the punishment of unwilling or simply unworthy holders of the rank of *decurio* by compelling them to take on only its burdens (Cod. Theod. 12,1,66; Cod. Iust. 10,59), and to the strict legal ending of the right to voluntarily relinquish the *condicio* of a curial; this right was evidently often sought, on the basis of simple removal or assumption of imperial service or other corporate obligations, but also when an individual entered into a socially inferior or monastic way of life, or an agricultural existence remote from the city (Cod. Theod. 12,1,29; 33 and 53; Dig. 50,2,1; Cod. Iust. 1,3,52; 10,38,1; 12,33,2). Fundamentally, however, urban self-government organized on the basis of honorary office continues to function even in late antiquity, and for later periods of history retained the character of a model to be followed.

[2] *Decurio* could designate the chairman of a *decuria* in a public legal corporation (Cod. Iust. 11,14).

[3] The heads of the ceremonial service at the imperial court were called *decuriones*. In late antiquity three *decuriones* preside over 30 *silentiarii* (Suet. Dom. 17,2; Cod. Iust. 12,16).

Jones, LRE 737ff.; Liebenam, 226ff., 489ff.; Mommsen, Staatsrecht 3, 800ff., 814. C.G.

[4] **Decurio, decuria.** A *decurio* was an officer of the Roman army, commanding a group of ten riders (*decuria*). During the Republic 30 *decuriones* commanded the 300 mounted troops of a legion. These were subdivided into ten *turmae* (Pol. 6,25,1); each *turma* comprised three *decuriae*. During the Principate, the mounted troops of a legion were commanded by *centuriones*, while *decuriones* functioned as commanders of the *turmae* in the mounted auxiliary troops (*auxilia*). There were probably sixteen *turmae* in the *alae quingenariae* and twenty-four in the *alae milliariae*. The precise strength of such a *turma* is unknown, but it is apparent that it no longer, as originally, represented a unit of thirty riders. The oldest *decurio* was named *decurio princeps*; a *cohors equitata quingenaria* probably had four *decuriones*, a *milliaria* eight. *Decuriones* are also attested for the *equites singulares* and the *equites singulares Augusti*. Normally, riders were promoted to *decurio* of their own unit; riders of the legions or in some cases members of the *equites singulares Augusti* were also promoted *decurio*. The *decuriones* of the *alae* were the most important of the lower-ranking officers of the *auxilia*; they could even progress to becoming *centurio* of a legion. The German bodyguard set up by Augustus for the protection of the family of the *princeps* was also divided into *decuriae* (CIL VI 8802 = ILS 1729).

→ Ala; → Auxilia; → Equites militares; → Turma

1 S. Bellino, G. Mancini, s.v. Decuria, Decurio, in: Ruggiero, II.2, 1504–1552 2 K.R. Dixon, P. Southern, The Roman Cavalry, 1992, 20–31 3 J.F. Gilliam, The Appointment of Auxiliary Centurions, in: TAPhA 88, 1957, 155–168 4 P.A. Holder, Studies in the Auxilia of the Roman Army from Augustus to Trajan, 1980, 88–90. J.C.

Decursio see → Manoeuvres

Decussis (Decus). The *decussis* stands in general for the figure 10 (symbol: X), and the term is derived from the corresponding amount or value in asses. On the basis of the libral standard weight (1 Roman pound = 1 as = 327.45 g), the *decussis* weighs ten times one as, and as a value represents $^5/_8$ of a denarius of 16 asses. Numismatically speaking, the *decussis* is significant only as a bronze 10–as piece in the semilibral standard, cast during the years 215–212 BC (→ *aes grave*). The 'Roma in Phrygian helmet/prora' coin exists contemporaneously with the silver 10–as denarius, which was issued for the first time at this period [1. 151]. The weights of the three surviving examples vary between 1,106 and 652 g [2. 37].

→ As; → Denarius; → Small coinage, calculation of; → Libra

1 RRC, [2]1987 2 B.K. Thurlow, I.G. Vecchi, Italian cast coinage, Italian aes grave, Italian aes rude, signatum and the aes grave of Sicily, 1979.

Hultsch, s.v. D., RE 4, 2354–2356. A.M.

Dedicatio (from *dedicare*, 'dedicate/consecrate'). In Latin texts (inscriptions and literature) the most frequent expression for the transfer of objects and property (plots of land, temples, altars, votive offerings) to a divinity. The term was used in connection with private as well as official → dedications (private i.a. Suet. Vit. 7,10,3 and Dig. 24,1,5,12; official i.a. Suet. Tib. 3,40,1 and Dig. 1,8,6,3). The distinction between private and official *dedicatio* resided in the fact that in the case of official dedication the object or item of property acquired the status of a *res sacra* (*publica*), and concomitant privileged statutory standing (e.g. it could not be sold: Dig. 18,1,62,1), while a privately dedicated object remained legally speaking 'profane' [1. 385f.]. Especially in Cic. Dom. 45ff. and 53ff., but also in other texts where both terms are mentioned together (e.g. Festus p. 424), *dedicatio* is used synonymously and alternately with → *consecratio*.

1 G. Wissowa, Religion und Kultus der Römer, [2]1912.

W. J. Tatum, The Lex Papiria de dedicationibus, in: CPh 88, 1993, 319–328. C.F.

Dedication
I. Greek II. Latin

I. Greek
A. Definition B. Form C. Relationship to the Recipient D. Forerunners

A. Definition
The dedication of a literary work is the naming of a person from the author's surroundings with the intent of expressing an honour or gratitude to this person by association with the publication. (Occasionally the recipient was promised immortality [1. 25 f.]). Works which discuss the named person as a subject do not fall under this definition (e.g., → *enkṓmion*). It is apparent in works such as the 'Epinician Odes' of → Pindar that the author is aware of his role as a mediator of fame. A special case is the Homeric hymn to Apollo (Hom. H. 3) where the address to the Delian girls' chorus takes on aspects of a dedication. The first unambiguous example of a Greek dedication is considered to be the address to a certain Theodorus in an elegiac fragment by → Dionysius [30] Chalcus (fr. 1 IEG II 59, mid 5th cent. BC): the poem is handed to the friend like a cup of wine at the προπίνειν (*propínein*, 'toasting') and the link to the address form of lyrical poetry is evident (see below D.). → Isocrates (*Ad Nicoclem*) then transferred the custom to prose writing (example: Aristotle's [6]: *Protreptikós* to Themison). The act is often described as offering a present [1. 5–10] and is later also sacralized as a 'dedication offering' [2. 10]. A dedication copy is presented or sent. Since the book was published simultaneously (or after) (ἔκδοσις/*ékdosis*; → Publication), this is in a sense a public ritual. The situation is similar to letters intended for publication (→ Epistolography). The didactic letter may especially be considered as a type of dedication. How dedication and publication relate to each other cannot be stated with certainty. Sometimes publication is made dependent on the recipient's approval [1. 47–54]. This obviously relates to a common practice: an author circulates his work among friends and requests criticism before publication.

B. Form
The basic form of the Greek dedication is an address at the opening of the text. Its character as an address resulted in the term προσφώνησις/*prosphṓnēsis*: βιβλίον προσφωνεῖν τινι (*biblíon prosphōneîn tini*), which means 'to direct a book as an address to somebody', e.g., in Hypsicles (in Euc. 14, Praef.) and more often in Cicero when speaking of his literary plans in his letters to Atticus. Naming in other forms (e.g. in → Nicander and Meleager, Anth. Pal. 4,1,3–4) is only of secondary importance. The address may be expanded to a preface that explains origin and intention or in a collection of poems it may be a poem itself (Meleager [8]). A preceding dedicatory letter is even more detached (first documented in Archimedes [1], cf. → Epistolography D.). In dialogues a person may be honoured by being assigned a role (frequently found in Cicero and Plutarch [2]) though this is not a dedication in the strict sense [2. 33–40].

C. Relationship to the Recipient
(1) The recipient was an esteemed friend or colleague, as was already the case with Dionysius [30] Chalcus (see above I. A.: Theodorus also wrote poetry). Archimedes [1] sent his writings from Syracuse to the astronomer → Dositheus [3] in Alexandria. It is evident from statements in → Cicero's (II. C.) letters that reciprocal dedications were an important means of group contact in literary circles (→ Circles, literary). (2) The recipient is instructed, as is common in paraenetic and scientific treatises or in didactic poetry. The Romans liked to address didactic texts 'to a son' (*ad filium;* → Wisdom literature (as a genre) III). (3) A common motif in the Roman period, e.g., in Cicero, → Galenus, Christian authors (→ Origenes [2], → Hieronymus, → Augustinus), who all like to emphasize that the urgency of the request [1. 10–17] is due to the recipient posing a question or providing an inspiration: pressure overcomes the author's modesty. (4) Often the recipient is a protector or patron of the author (→ Literary activity I. B.1.–2.; → II). For example, Arcesilaus [5] addressed his dedication to king Eumenes [2] I because of his donations (Diog. Laert. 4,38) and Archimedes [1] the 'Sand-reckoner' to Gelon [2] of Syracuse. → Plutarch [2] dedicated many treatises to his Roman friends, undoubtedly to maintain contacts. An author also gained prestige through dedication to high-ranking individuals. A shift from (1) to (4): → Apollonius [13] of Perge dedicated books 1–3 of his Κωνικά (*Kōniká*, 'Conic Sections ') to his friend Eudemus in Pergamum, but after his death the remaining books to king Attalus [4] I, who had shown interest in Pergamum. (5) A spe-

cial case is the consolatory discourse, which sprang from the consolatory letter (→ Consolatio).

D. Forerunners

The custom of dedication originated from literary addresses that were rooted in oral culture and initially did not have the functions of honouring and thanking [2]. They are particularly common in archaic paraenesis: → Hesiodus to Perses, → Theognis to Cyrnus; in → Didactic poetry (II): → Empedocles [1] to his beloved boy Pausanias. The address forms of archaic → lyric poetry (I) may also be included. Symposium poetry (Dionysius [30] Chalcus; → Symposium literature) may have been a bridge between the paraenetic address and literary dedication. This would explain why dedications are first found in paraenetic and didactic works from which they eventually migrate to other genres. In the Roman period the custom of dedication strongly expanded in Greek and Latin literature until it virtually became the rule.

→ Epistolography; → Didactic poetry; → Literary activity

1 R. Graefenhain, De more libros dedicandi apud scriptores Graecos et Romanos obvio, thesis Marburg 1892 2 J. Ruppert, Quaestiones ad historiam dedicationis librorum pertinentes, thesis Leipzig 1911 3 R. J. Starr, The Circulation of Literary Texts in the Roman World, in: CQ 37, 1987, 213–233 4 F. Stephan, Quomodo poetae Graecorum Romanorumque carmina dedicaverint, thesis Berlin 1910. H. GÖ.

II. Latin

Modern practice considers the dedication as part of the paratext (along with title, book covers, prefaces) [1], but Greek and Latin dedications preserved from antiquity are part of the actual work, especially when they are part of a continuous volume of poetry (e.g., epic, didactic poem) as in Lucretius [III 1], Virgil [4] (Georgics 1) or in Catull. 1, where the dedicatory poem introduces the body of the poetry book. However, Latin dedications may also introduce prose writing (e.g., in the lost but reconstructable *praefatio* of Velleius [4] Paterculus) [2; 3].

The frequent use of dedications in Hellenistic and Roman poetry [4] is related to the inclusion of literature in the court system of Hellenistic monarchies and the Roman client system (→ *cliens*, → *patronus*) as well as the significance of literary → circles for the origin and distribution of works (→ Authors) [5; 6]. The recipients of a dedication may be rulers (Ov. Fast. 2,11–18) or members of the ruling house (Ov. Fast. 1,3–26), politically powerful persons, esp. patrons of poetry (Verg. G. 1,1–5: Maecenas [2]; Tib. 2,1,35: Valerius [II 16] Messala), often more highly ranked literary friends (Stat. Silv. 1 praef.: [II 12] Stella) and other close persons (Verg. Ecl. 6,6–12: Alfenus [4] Varus). Dedicating the first poem of a book extends the effect to the entire book (Prop. 2,1: Maecenas). A special case is a phenomenon occurring particularly in the → didactic poem: the dedication's recipient and actual addressee are not identical [7], e.g., Maecenas and Augustus in Verg. G. 1.

Regarding the specific form of the dedication (comparison to a gift, as means of instruction, to achieve material gain, dedicatory formulae etc.) see [8].

→ Literary activity II.; → Authors

1 G. Genette, Palimpseste. Die Lit. auf zweiter Stufe, 1993, 11 f. 2 T. Janson, Latin Prose Prefaces, 1964 3 E. Herkommer, Die Topoi in den Proömien der röm. Gesch.-Werke, 1968 4 M. S. Silk, M. Citroni, s. v. Dedications, OCD³, 438–439 5 B. K. Gold, Literary and Artistic Patronage in Ancient Rome, 1982 6 P. White, Promised Verse, 1993 7 E. Pöhlmann, Charakteristika des röm. Lehrgedichts, in: ANRW I 3, 1977, 813–907 8 R. Graefenhain, De more libros dedicandi apud scriptores Graecos et Romanos obvio, thesis Marburg 1892. U. SCH.

Dediticii Members of a community that, having been vanquished in war by Rome, has surrendered unconditionally to the hegemony of the Roman people (→ *deditio*), and may by a decree of Rome have forfeited its existence as a state. Thus *dediticii* were all provincial inhabitants (*provinciales*) whose community had been dissolved by Rome (Gai. Inst. 1,14): insofar as they had not already acquired Roman or Latin citizenship and been able to retain it, or were now granted it, or autonomous status had not been restored to their community. Dissolution of previous organizational structures and political subjection without Roman citizenship (even in restricted form), after sporadic use in Italy, became the regular means of establishing Roman rule outside Italy (App. Mith. 114,558). In this respect, Roman provincial government was a kind of perpetuated occupation regime, the subject people (*subiecti*) having in principle no rights of citizenship, and esp. in respect of their property depending on the whim of their Roman occupiers; Roman colonies are sometimes founded on the annexed former territories of *dediticii*, just as over all the territories of the *dediticii* a kind of supreme Roman ownership regime prevails. Indigenous forms of urban administration, taxation or legal custom (*consuetudines*) may be continued by the Roman administration, but they were always moulded to fit the Roman pattern, and liable to alteration by peremptory decree of the governor (*edictum provinciale*). How low the status of *dediticius* was becomes clear when one considers that in the early Imperial period freed slaves, if they had become slaves on dishonourable grounds, could not acquire Roman citizenship in the normal way, but had to remain in a *condicio dediticia* (Gai. Inst. 1,13–15). It was only when, from AD 212 with the *constitutio Antoniniana*, most members of the Roman Empire are granted Roman citizenship, that they could regard themselves as 'citizens of the Empire'; even the *condicio dediticia* of dishonourable *liberti* later disappears from legal practice (Cod. Iust. 7,5). But the original provincial form of subjection persisted in late antiquity, in the relatively strict rights of intervention, incompatible with the traditions of Roman citizenship, enjoyed by the state over its citizens (as in relation to → *coloni* or → *decuriones* [1]), and as a model for later forms of totalitarian state.

→ Provincia; → Imperium Romanum

CHRIST, 462, 622; W. DAHLHEIM, Gewalt und Herrschaft, 1977, 277ff.; JONES, LRE 737ff., 795ff.; MOMMSEN, Staatsrecht 3, 55f., 139ff., 655ff., 716ff. C.G.

Deditio *Deditio in potestatem* or — with a similar meaning — deditio *in fidem* (Pol. 20,9,10–12),was an autonomous state's, nominally, always voluntary surrender of sovereignty to Rome. It was the precondition for the peaceful end of war, and in peace for securing the protection of Rome. After formal acceptance of *deditio* by the Senate or an appropriately authorized (pro-)magistrate with *imperium* the surrendered community ceased to exist. Its citizens, gods and possessions became the property of Rome, and Rome could deal with them as it thought fit. Although prior promises became invalid by virtue of *deditio*, these were for the most part kept, especially as their breach could be legally pursued in Rome, probably as a breach of *fides*. The consequences of *deditio* ranged from the (rare) destruction or enslavement of the community to the return of freedom and property and re-establishment of the community (usual, but in war associated with conditions), possibly followed by a treaty.

The late Republican notion of the original procedure is made clear in Liv. 1,38,1–2; but at the time it must have looked very different. A bronze tablet found near Alcántara (Spain) contains the protocol of a *deditio* of 104 BC. Here it appears that the decision of the army commander had to be ratified in Rome, and restoration of property was uncertain ('so long as the people and Senate of Rome desire it'). Nothing of the kind is mentioned in the literary sources. Whether such a condition was the case only in the Spanish wars (cf. approx. App. Ib. 44,183), or whether it was assumed as self-evident, is at present unknown.

→ Fides; → Imperium

W. DAHLHEIM, Struktur und Entwicklung des röm. Völkerrechts, 1968, 1–109 (with older bibl.); J. S. RICHARDSON, Hispaniae, 1986, 199–201 (text of the tablet). E.B.

Deductio

[1] There are many different senses of *deductio* in specialized legal language: in civil case-law the expression *in iudicium deducere* usually indicates the transition of the dispute to the judgement stage, and so approximately corresponds to the modern concept of pendency. *Deductio in domum* is the ceremonial introduction of a wife into her husband's house (Dig. 23,2,5). A further frequent use of *deductio* is to denote the 'deduction' of specific components of a debt owed to a provider of services: for example the deduction of costs (Dig. 31,41,1); the deduction of certain counterclaims from the claim sued for by the *bonorum emptor* (enforcing creditor) (Gai. Inst. 4,65ff.; here the distinction between the *deductio* and the adjustment, *compensatio*, is explained by the dissimilarity between the underlying functions). Finally, *deductio* often denotes division, such as division of an estate (Dig. 37,4,13,3).

→ Comperendinatio

H. ANKUM, Deux problèmes relatifs à l'exceptio rei iudicatae vel in iudicium deductae ..., in: FS Petropoulos I, 1984, 173–195; G. JAHR, Litis contestatio, 1960, 126–133; G. THÜR: Vindicatio und Deductio im frühröm. Grundstücksstreit, in: ZRG 94, 1977, 293–305. C.PA.

[2] *Coloniam* or *colonos deducere* in the actual sense ordered in a military fashion, ('leading out a colony or colonists (*sc.* from Rome)') describes in Lat. technical terminology the departure of colonists under the leadership of an official collegium responsible (as a rule the → *tresviri* [2] *coloniae deducendae*) as part of the legal act of the foundation of a Roman colony (→ *coloniae*), in the further sense generally the process of founding the colony (for instance [1]; Cic. Leg. agr. 1,16–18; further evidence in [2]).

[3] *D. in forum* ('leading down to the Forum') is the term for the official presentation of a young Roman aristocrat in municipal Roman society at the beginning of his political education (Suet. Aug. 26,2; Suet. Nero 7,1; → *tirocinium fori*).

1 M. H. CRAWFORD (ed.), Roman Statutes, 1996, no. 2, l. 22–24; 61 2 ThlL 5.1, 273. K.-L. E.

Deer, red (Cervus, dama) For the most part, the names ἔλαφος/*élaphos* (from Hom. Il. 11,475 and passim) or *cervus* (= horned animal, from Plaut. Poen. 530) and νεβρός/*nebrós* (deer-calf, Hom. Il. 8,248; Od. 19,228: ἑλλός/*hellós*) or *inuleus* (Hor. Carm. 1,23,1; Prop. 3,13,35) refer to the red deer, *Cervus elaphus L.* The smaller fallow deer (or the roe?), *Dama dama (L.)* (Hom. Od. 17,295: πρόξ/*próx*), Lat. *dama* (confused with the → gazelle!), with its palmate antlers was introduced into Greece and to some extent Italy from Asia (reference: Arr. Anab. 7,20,4: herds on the estuary of the Euphrates; Ael. NA 5,56: Syrian deer from Lebanon and Carmel swam to Cyprus).

Many instances bear witness to knowledge of deer in Greece (on the Taygetus: Hom. Od. 6,104; in Elis: Xen. An. 5,3,10) and in Italy (Verg. G. 3,412f.) and Spain (Mart. 1,49,26). Aristotle provides a precise description with many anatomical details (i.a.: that the deer is a ruminant, Hist. an. 8(9),50,632b 4; that it has a large heart, Part. an. 3,4,667a 19f.; Plin. HN 11,183; incomplete clotting of the blood, Aristot. Hist. an. 3,6,515b 34–516a 4; lacks a gall bladder, 2,15,506a 22 and 31f.); in the ἀχαίνης/*achaínēs*, however, he locates this bladder in the tail (506a 23f.). Aristotle gives the gestation period of the hind prior to giving birth to 1–2 young in

May/June in the vicinity of trails (Hist. an. 8(9),5,611a 15–17) as about 8 months (Hist. an. 6,29, 578b 12–14). In the 2nd year the male calf ('brocket') grows straight horns (κέρατα εὐθέα, καθάπερ πασσάλους), in the third year ('two-pointer') forked antlers, and up to the 6th year compact antlers increasing by one point for every year. After shedding their old antlers in May/June the stags remain hidden until the growth of new ones, which they 'fray' against trees (Hist. an. 8(9),5,611a 25–b 17). Their well-known longevity was exaggerated in Plin. HN 8,119 (100 years). Characteristic of deer is swiftness, ability at jumping, and timidity or shyness (from Hom. Il. 1,225: κραδίην ἐλάφοιο; Aristot. Hist. an. 1,1,488b 15: φρόνιμος καὶ δειλός), esp. in the calf (νεβρός: Hom. Il. 4,243). The deer plays a considerable role in ancient similes [1. 494].

The Romans (e.g. Q. Hortensius) kept deer in preserves on their estates (Varro, Rust. 3,13,3), and to some extent as a household pet (Verg. Aen. 7,483–502, as the pet of Silvia, daughter of Tyrrhus; related allusion in Mart. 13,96). A tame deer (together with a bull and a horse) served as a guard at night for king Mithridates VI of Pontus. The zoo of the Roman emperor Gordianus [1] I was populated by 200 head each, of fallow and red deer (SHA Gordiani tres 3,7). The lean meat won by hunting from horseback with dogs was favoured by distinguished Roman ladies as a supposed prophylactic against fever (Plin. HN 8,119; 28,228). Galen (De facultatibus naturalibus 3,1,8 [2]) on the other hand condemns it as tough, difficult to digest and productive of noxious bile. The bones of deer were used for the mouthpieces of musical instruments, the skin for blankets (Hom. Od. 13,436) and the antlers apotropaically, as well as burnt in order to drive away snakes that were supposedly sensitive to odours (Plin. HN 8,118 and 115). Medical uses too are very specialized: e.g. the rennet from a calf killed in the womb against snakebites (Plin. HN 8,118), or the ashes from the antlers against toothache (Plin. HN 28,178) as well as against (tape)worms (ibid. 28,211).

In the cult of Artemis or Diana the deer is her companion as well as her mount (silver plate from the 4th cent. in Berlin [3. 131 and fig. 67]) and hunting prey (cf. her cognomen *elaphoktónos*, 'killer of deer': Eur. IT 1113). Deer sometimes also drew a priestess of Artemis seated on a carriage, as in a procession in Patras (Paus. 7,18,12; deer tamed for this purpose are mentioned in Ael. NA 7,46 and Plin. HN 8,117). There are also associations with Apollo (e.g. Paus. 10,13,5 on a statue at Delphi), and also with Eros and Nemesis (Paus. 1,33,3: statue of Phidias at Rhamnus). In the myth of → Cyparissus the latter unintentionally shoots his pet deer (cf. mosaic [3. 130 and fig. 70]). A deer or a hind may have been sacrificed in the Roman cult (cf. Fest. 57 M.: *cervaria ovis quae pro cerva immolabantur* [4. 380]). The hind figures as a sign (*omen*) in Liv. 10,27,8f. Images of deer as the prey of dogs, lions (e.g. on ancient coins [5]), panthers and griffins are known [6. 1948,34ff.]; mosaics from the 4th cent. AD survive in Sicily [3. 131 and colour illustrations 176] and England [3. 131 and fig. 72]. On a mosaic from the Byzantine imperial palace in Istanbul a deer fights a snake [3. 132 and fig. 71].

1 V. Pöschl, Bibliogr. zur ant. Bildersprache, 1964 2 G. Helmreich (ed.), Galenos, de facultatibus naturalibus, 1923 (CMG 5,4,2) 3 Toynbee, Tierwelt 4 Latte 5 F. Imhoof-Blumer, O. Keller, Tier- und Pflanzenbilder auf Mz. und Gemmen des klass. Alt., 1889, repr. 1972 6 F. Orth, s.v. H., RE 8, 1936ff. C.HÜ.

Defensor

I. In civil law II. In constitutional law

I. In civil law

Defensor is not a technical legal term for the defence counsel (but probably nevertheless thus in Quint. Inst. 5,3,13), but rather had various meanings, especially as the sponsor of the defendant primarily in a civil case, and here particularly of the absent defendant (*indefensus*). To take on such a defence was the duty of a friend (Dig. 4,6,22 pr.). Termed *defensor civitatis*, he is also the judicial representative of corporations (*universitates*, Dig. 3,4,1,3), above all of statutory public bodies (e.g. communities, provinces; cf. CIL X,1201 and *passim*).

→ Advocatus

R. M. Frakes: Some Hidden Defensores Civitatum in the Res Gestae of Ammianus Marcellinus, in: ZRG 109, 1992, 526–532; Kaser, RZ, 164, 437; D. Spengler, Studien zur Interrogatio in Iure, 1994, 42. C.PA.

II. In constitutional law

The typical duties of a *defensor* with regard to private individuals and corporations (Greek σύνδικος; *sýndikos*), in protecting their interests and defending them in court, could, as with the → *advocatus*, also give rise to the function of representing the interests of patrons in the public realm, and representing them at law (Dig. 50,4,18,13). Presumably arising from this function, during late antiquity various kinds of official position developed bearing the title *defensor*, among them the *defensor civitatis* as a representative of the state, acting in the interests of a *civitas*, but not counted as a member of the city administration (Cod. Theod. 1,29,1; Cod. Iust. 1,55 tit. *de defensoribus civitatum*; Nov. 15). His function was to protect the rural and urban population in an appropriate manner from 'unjustified tax assessments', 'insolence of administrative officials' (*officiales*) and 'dereliction of duty on the part of higher judges' (*iudices*) (Cod. Iust. 1,55,4). To this end, in the Justinianic period these *defensores* were nominally appointed for a term of five years by the responsible *praefectus praetorio*, on the basis of nominations from the *civitas*, from those qualified persons who were neither *decuriones* nor from the governor's office (Cod. Iust. 1,55,2 and 8). As lower-level judges they were competent in public and private cases including voluntary jurisdiction involving sums of less than 50 *solidi* (*tenuiores ac minusculariae res*), but not in criminal cases

(Cod. Iust. 1,55,1). With reports, hearing of statements and the referral of suspects to the appropriate court they had to assist in ensuring that offences against public order (*disciplina publica*), such as robbery, extortion, deception with weights and measures or encouragement of criminal activities (*patrocinia scelerum*), were rigourously prosecuted (Cod. Iust. 1,55,6; 7; 9). The office is not to be confused with that of the → *curator rei publicae* from the earlier Imperial period.

JONES, LRE 479f., 600, 726f.; KASER, RPR 2, 226, 288.
C.G.

Definitiones medicae The use of *definitiones* ('discussions') was extensive in medical teaching in the Greek as well as the Roman world (Gal. 1,306 K.; 19,346–7 K.). The most substantial surviving work of this genre is the *Definitiones medicae* ascribed to Galen (19,346–462 K.), the authenticity of which was doubted even in late antiquity (schol. in Orib. Syn, CMG 6,2,1, 250,29). WELLMANN [1. 66] was of the opinion that their author lived towards the end of the 1st cent. AD, and was a member of the Pneumatic school. Although the work contains Pneumatic teachings, the theoretical standpoint of its author cannot be explained by membership of an individual school. A date of origin previous to AD 200 suggests itself, as Agathinus of Sparta, who lived in the 1st cent. AD, is the most recent of the authors named in the *Definitiones medicae* (19, 353), and there is no reference to Galen. The author begins his text by defining the basic general concepts of medicine, and then proceeds to discuss parts of the body, bodily processes and finally illnesses. Although other introductory medical texts were formal question-and-answer dialogues, e.g. in the Greek Pap. Milan. Vogliano I,15 (1st cent. AD) or later in Lat. the *Quaestiones medicinales* of Ps.-Soranus or the *lectiones Heliodori* (5th cent.), they contain the same material as the *definitiones medicae* and have a similar layout.

→ Medicine

1 M. WELLMANN, Die Pneumatische Schule, 1895.
V.N.

Defixio (Greek κατάδεσμος; *katádesmos*, 'binding spell'). The most common form of black magic, in which curses written on thin lead tablets were supposed to have a negative influence on the affairs or well-being of people (or animals). Lead was preferred although potsherds, limestone, papyrus and wax tablets were also used: it was easily obtained and worked, was already used early on for correspondence (some of the earliest binding spells are termed *epistolḗ*, letter), was durable, and, what was more, associated with cold and darkness, to which the curses also referred. In the majority of curses the motive is not explicitly mentioned, and in the rest the grounds are envy [1] and emotions of rivalry, esp. sport, the (amphi)theatre, legal disputes, love and trade and business [2]. The texts are virtually without exception anonymous, without any justification, as e.g. by indicating the deserved punishment of the person(s) cursed. Where gods are called upon, they belong to the sphere of death, the underworld and sorcery (Demeter, Persephone, Gaia, Hermes, the Erinyes and → Hecate). In later periods the magical names of exotic → demons and divinities predominate. The spirits of the dead might also be called upon, for the tablets were often buried in the graves of those who died young (→ Ahoroi) or in chthonic sanctuaries and springs. The tablets were rolled up and pierced with a needle, and sometimes accompanied by magic dolls. More than 1,500 *defixio* texts are known to us at present. They appear for the first time in the late 6th cent. BC in Sicily and Olbia, and somewhat later also in Attica, especially in Athens. These early examples are at the same time the simplest, as they frequently contain only the name of the person cursed, occasionally adding 'I bind' and the name of the divinity they 'call upon'. The later curses, especially in the Imperial period, develop into complex texts, occasionally with extensive sequences of *voces magicae* and names of demons and divinities, which are often Egyptian or Semitic.

Curse tablet from Hadrumetum (Tunisia).

Although the verb *defigere* occurs frequently in literature and in magical texts with the meaning 'to bind', 'to curse' (ThlL 5.1, 342[E]31–41), the word *defixio* seems not to be attested before the 6th cent. AD (ThlL 5.1, 356 82). The act of binding magically is, however, already familiar in the Homeric epics, where gods, and also → Moira and Ate, perform acts of binding and deception (*deîn*, *pedân*). Here, *defixio* almost always occurs through the power of divine will, without the medium of a curse, but it is also performed by gods in response to human conjuration (Hom. Il. 9,454–7; 568–72). Occasional mentions of magical binding are to be found in widely differing literary genres; esp. in the field of poetry, entire works treat the theme (a celebrated example: Theocritus' 2nd Idyll) [3].

Throughout all periods, curses display a strongly formulaic bias (often clearly copying the manner of contemporary public inscriptions), suggesting the existence of models and books of formulae, as are in fact known in great numbers from the magical papyri of late antiquity [4]. Many formulae prescribed in these books are in fact found in surviving *defixiones*. Professional scribes and specialists are, however, also mentioned in the literature. Plato knows of seers and soothsayers who bewitch other people by *katadéseis* (sorcery) and magic dolls (Pl. Leg. 933a-e; rep. 364c). The existence of specialists is also to be surmised from a series of identical *defixiones* (apart from the names) found together and written by the same hand; inspired variations might indicate individual creativity. The formulaic elements of the binding spells display three main styles [2]: 1. the direct binding formula, a performative utterance designed to exert a direct manipulative effect on the victim; 2. an incantation to a divinity, in the form of a wish or a command to become active; and 3. a so-called *similia similibus* formula, an act to conjure an analogy in which the victim is to take on the nature of a powerless or tortured entity (e.g. the dead, a bound or tortured animal, the lead). Worthy of attention is the preference for particular regions of the body to be affected: the reasoning power and intellect of the orator, the voice of the actor, hands and feet of the athlete etc. [5].

Also to be found in the known collections of *defixiones*, but forming a distinct genus, are the prayers for justice or 'prayers of revenge' [6]. These too are often written on lead tablets, but differ from *defixiones* as such in that the name of the author is mentioned, the act is justified by indicating some wrong committed by the person cursed (theft, calumny), and particularly in that the gods are humbly called upon to punish the guilty party and set the injustice to rights. This form did not achieve popularity until the Hellenistic and Roman periods, and was widespread throughout the entire Imperium Romanum, especially in Britain. Collections are found i.a. in Cnidus [7. no. 1–13] and Bath [7]. In these imprecations, the lists of blighted bodily parts are expanded into comprehensive anatomical catalogues, in that they are directed not just at the particular body parts in question, but lay the entire body open to torture and punishment.

1 H.S. Versnel, Punish those who rejoice in our Misery: On Curse Texts and Schadenfreude, in: D.R. Jordan, H. Montgomery, E. Thomassen (ed.), Magic in the Ancient World (1998) 2 C.A. Faraone, The Agonistic Context of Early Greek Binding Spells, in: id., D. Obbink (ed.), Magika Hiera: Ancient Greek Magic and Religion, 1991, 3–32 3 L. Watson, Arae: The Curse Poetry of Antiquity, 1991 4 PGM 5 H.S. Versnel, And Any Other Part of the Entire Body there may be: An Essay on Anatomical Curses, in: F. Graf (ed.) Ansichten griech. Rituale. FS W. Burkert 1998 6 H.S. Versnel, Beyond Cursing: The Appeal to Justice in Judicial Prayers, in: as no. 2, 60–106 7 A. Autodollent, Defixionum Tabellae, 1904 8 R.S.O. Tomlin, The Curse Tablets, in: B. Cunliffe, The Temple of Sulis Minerva at Bath II, The Finds from the Sacred Spring, OUCA Monograph 16, 1988, 59–265.

R. Wünsch, Defixionum Tabellae Atticae, IG III.3, Appendix, 1897; W. Speyer, Fluch, RAC 7, 1969, 1160–1288; D.R. Jordan, A Survey of Greek Defixiones not Included in the Special Corpora, in: GRBS 26, 1985, 151–97; J. G. Gager, Curse Tablets and Binding Spells from the Ancient World, 1992; F. Graf, Gottesnähe und Schadenzauber, Die Magie in der griech.-röm. Ant., 1996, 108–154. H.V.

Deianira (Δηιάνειρα; *Dēiáneira*). Mythical daughter of king Oeneus of Calydon (Soph. Trach. 6f.) or of Dionysus (Apollod. 1,64; Hyg. Fab. 129) and → Althaea. After the death of her brother → Meleager, D., unlike her sisters, retained her human form (Ov. Met. 8,542ff.; Ant. Lib. 2 after Nicander; Hyg. Fab. 174). The river god Achelous wooed her; then → Heracles, who had heard Meleager singing D.'s praises, also arrived on the scene as a suitor (Pind. Fr. 249aSM; Bacchyl. 5,165ff. SM). Heracles defeated Achelous, after the latter had metamorphosed through many different forms (Archil. fr. 286ff. W; Soph. Trach. 9ff.; Diod. Sic. 4,35,3f.; Ov. Met. 9,8ff; Epist. 9,139f.; Sen. Herc. Oet. 495ff.; Apollod. 2,148; Hyg. Fab. 31). Of the couple's children, Hyllus and Macaria are the best-known. After the wedding the couple moved to Heracles's homeland of Trachis. Reaching a river, Heracles entrusted D. to the centaur Nessus to be carried across. When Nessus tried to violate her, Heracles killed him with a poisoned arrow. As he was dying, Nessus advised the bride to preserve his blood as a love potion (Soph. Trach. 555f.; Ov. Met. 9,101ff.; Epist. 9,141f.; 161ff.; Sen. Herc. Oet. 500ff.; Hyg. Fab. 34; somewhat differently in Archil. fr. 286ff. W; Diod. Sic. 4,36,2ff.). The couple proceeded to Trachis (Soph. Trach. 38ff.), whence Heracles defeated the Dryopes, with D. fighting at his side (Apollod. 1,64; 2,153). Later he conquered Oechalia and fell in love with the captured king's daughter → Iole, whom he brought back to Trachis. D. feared losing Heracles to Iole, and smeared the sacrificial robe intended for Heracles with the blood of Nessus. When Heracles put it on, the poison slowly ate away at him, and he decided to set fire to himself. D. thereupon committed suicide (Hes. fr. 25,14ff. MW; Bacchyl. 16,23ff. SM; Diod. Sic. 4,36; 38; Apollod. 2,157ff.; Hyg. Fab. 35f.). Her grave was pointed out in Heraclea on the Oete and in Argos (Paus. 2,23,5).

J. Boardman, s.v. Herakles, LIMC 4.1, 834–835; F. Díez de Velasco. s.v. Nessos, LIMC 6.1, 838–847; J. Escher, s.v. Deianeira 1), RE 4, 2378–2382; F. Jouan, Déjanire, Héraclès et le centaure Nessos. Le cheminement d'un mythe, in: H. Limet, J. Ries (ed.), Le mythe. Actes du Colloque Lièges, 1983, 225–243; J.R. March, The Creative Poet. Studies on the treatment of myths in Greek poetry, BICS Suppl. 49, 1987, 47–77. R.HA.

Deidamia (Δηιδάμεια; *Dēidámeia*).

[1] Daughter of king Lycomedes on the island of Scyros; wife of → Achilles and mother of Neoptolemus (Pyrrhus). According to an older tradition, Achilles conquered Scyros, married D. and fathered Neoptolemus. A later version has Thetis bringing her son Achilles disguised as a girl to Lycomedes on Scyros in order to prevent Achilles' death before Troy, which has been foretold to her. Achilles falls in love with D. and marries her (schol. Il. 9,668; Cypr. Arg. PEG I; Apollod. 3,174). After the fall of Troy, Neoptolemus gives D. in marriage to Helenus (Apollod. epit. 6,13). D. plays a central role in the lost tragedies *Skyrioi* of Sophocles and Euripides

(TrGF 4,551–561; PSI 12,1286; [1]). For iconographic representations cf. [2].

1 A. Lesky, Die tragische Dichtung der Hellenen, ³1972, 261, 329 2 A. Kossatz-Deissmann, s.v. Achilleus, LIMC 1.1, nos. 96–176.

[2] Daughter of → Bellerophon; mother by Evander (or by Zeus) of → Sarpedon (Diod. Sic. 5,79,3). In Hom. Il. 6,197 she is called Laodamia. R.B.

Deification

I. Ancient Orient II. Greece and Rome

I. Ancient Orient

In the Ancient Orient the deification of → rulers always occurred in the context of the legitimization and exercise of → rulership. Deified rulers and proper gods were always differentiated on principle.

A. Mesopotamia B. Egypt C. Iran

A. Mesopotamia

References to the deification of living rulers are geographically restricted to Babylonia and temporally to the late 3rd and early 2nd millennium BC: a) individual rulers claimed divine descent for themselves as a means of legitimizing their rule; b) rulers of the third dynasty of → Ur (21st cent.) and several rulers of the succeeding dynasty of Isin (20th cent.) were deified because of their participation in the ritual of sacred marriage as spouses of → Inanna (→ *hieròs gámos*); c) rulers of the Old Akkadian dynasty (24th/23rd cents.) had themselves deified during their lifetime because they assumed the dominium over the state's arable land for themselves, which originally was the prerogative of → city deities [1. 61 f.]. Because of his military success, divine honours were obtained from the major deities for → Naramsin 'as the deity of his city' and, consequently, a temple was built for him.

Deification was visibly expressed by prefixing the name of the deified person with the written symbol for 'god' and portraying him with divine insignia. Special ritual acts that resulted in deification are not known. Private persons were not deified. Assyrian royal ideology always considered the ruler to be merely a surrogate of the realm's deity, → Assur [2].
→ Divine kingship; → Rulers I

1 H. J. Nissen, Gesch. Alt-Vorderasiens, 1999
2 G. Selz, The Holy Drum, the Spear, and the Harp, in: I. J. Finkel, M. J. Geller, (ed.), Sumerian Gods and Their Representations, 1997, esp. 181 f. J. RE.

B. Egypt

The veneration of human beings as divinities is documented in all periods of Egyptian history. This special deification must be clearly differentiated from the aspect of the king's divinity derived from his office and descent. It affects the kings and their family members but also private persons. The reasons are not always clear but often these persons were the authors of wise sayings (→ Wisdom literature). Several degrees of divinity can be distinguished, though almost always a certain distance from the 'real' gods is maintained. The most noticeable exception is the rise of Imhotep (→ Imuthes [2]) to the status of a full divinity in the late period [5]. The cult could be locally restricted or spread through the entire country depending on the person. This was not only a phenomenon of popular religion: important cults also received royal patronage. Usually a person's deification only began after death. Only in special cases can a self-deification of a king during his lifetime be observed [2]. It should be noted that these were generally of short duration while some posthumous cults endured and even intensified over centuries [3].
→ Divine kingship; → Rulers II; → Pharaoh

1 J. Cerny, Le culte d'Amenophis Iᵉʳ chez les ouvriers de la nécropole thébaine, in: BIAO 27, 1927, 159–203
2 L. Habachi, Features of the Deification of Ramesses II (ADAIK 5), 1969 3 A. von Lieven, Kleine Beitr. zur V. Amenophis I., in: ZÄS 128, 2001, 41–64
4 D. Wildung, Die Rolle äg. Könige im Bewußtsein ihrer Nachwelt, 1969 5 Id., Imhotep und Amenhotep, 1977.
A. v. L.

C. Iran

Achaemenid rulers neither invoked their divine origin nor did they enjoy divine veneration [1. 55]. The Sassanid Šāpūr (→ Sapor [1]) described himself as being of divine ancestry and a deity (Middle Persian *bay*, Greek θεός/*theós*) venerating Mazda (→ Ahura Mazdā). Consequently, he faced his subjects as a ruler with divine attributes but a terminological differentiation between the divine ruler and the god Ahura Mazdā (*yazd*) [1. 220–222] was maintained.
→ Divine kingship; → Rulers III

1 J. Wiesehöfer, Das ant. Persien, 1993. J. RE.

II. Greece and Rome

As a meta-linguistic term deification describes the process of (spontaneous or institutionalized) interpretation and veneration of an object, an abstract term (→ Personification), a natural phenomenon or a human being — whether during their lifetime or after death — as divine. The 'apotheosis' (from Greek ἀποθέωσις/*apothéōsis*), i.e., the deification ritual for deceased emperors (Lat. → *consecratio*) from Augustus until its reinterpretation by Constantine [1] I in the context of his own funeral [1], is a particular case of this more general phenomenon. The ritual means of deification were derived from the cult of the gods and elevated the recipient of deification to their level: invocation (→ Epiklesis), → prayer and → *hýmnos*; religious → rituals such as → libation sacrifice) and veneration of a statue (Cic. Off. 3,80); also the establishment of a permanent cult with altar, sanctuary, priests and feast.

The sophist → Prodicus allegedly first postulated that early people had worshipped beneficial natural phenomena such as the → sun and the → moon, followed by human inventors (→ *prôtos heuretḗs*) (84 B 5 DK). The Stoic → Persaeus [2] of Citium elaborated this model with the idea that the gods were human beings deified for their good deeds (Philod. De pietate 9; Cic. Nat. D. 1,38). A very similar Prodicean model may have been formulated earlier by → Hecataeus [4] of Abdera (FGrH 264 F 25 = Diod. Sic. 1,11,1–13,1; [2. 9f.]), but the attribution is disputed [3. 283–287]. In the Hellenistic and Roman periods → Dionysus, → Hercules and the → Dioscuri (Cic. Leg. 2,19; Hor. Carm. 3,3) were considered paradigms of persons deified for benefactions, cultural achievements or conquests. → Euhemerus of Messene finally formulated that apart from good deeds and cultural achievements a → ruler's power was a fundamental condition for deification [3]. These Hellenistic deification discourses were also productively adapted in Rome, e.g., in → Ennius' Euhemerus translation and the debates over the deification of specific individuals from the 1st cent. BC. (Cic. Resp. 6,13; [2]; Cass. Dio 51,20,8). They converged in the Hellenistic and Roman periods in the actual deification of living and dead → rulers (cf. → Emperor cult); the relationship between the literary discourses and contemporary strategies of justification for the deification is evident in the Hellenistic ruler epithets of 'Benefactor ' (→ *Euergétēs*) and 'Saviour' (→ *Sōtḗr*).

To early Christian apologists and the early modern period, deification was an indicator of the absurdity of the 'pagan' concept of divinity and proof of the superiority of Judeo-Christian → monotheism. For a long time even modern research considered the Roman emperor cult to be no more than a purely politically motivated 'religion of loyalty' without deeper religious content (cf. [4. 11–16]). Only recent research has attempted to redefine its religious character and, thus, also the problem of deification: it positions the ruler between humans and gods though not as the equal of the latter [4. 233; 5] or interprets the emperor *as* a god [6. 17–38].

Decisive — and advancing the scientific debate — was the insight that the categorical dichotomy between humans and (apostasized) deity characteristic of Judeo-Christian dogma, as formulated by early Christian literature (cf. Acts 14,8–18), is not applicable in this form to the Graeco-Roman concept of god. The early Christian Trinitarian debates in the early Church already debated this dichotomy (→ Trinity III). Therefore, a model is required that can describe the entire range of the ancient reaction to deification from the affirmation of the deified person as a god to ambivalence regarding his status: in a religious world with largely anthropomorphic concepts of gods (cf. → Anthropomorphism) in which patterns of human social behaviour were projected according to sociomorphic categories on the gods, the term 'god' was debated (cf. → Pantheon [1] III ; → Polytheism I). Gods are differentiated from humans by their immortality and power, but the latter difference can be overcome, whereby the path to venerating individuals as divine together with the traditional deities became accessible: converging spheres of action are assigned to humans and gods, so that the process of deification becomes the religious expression of a feeling of gratitude for salvation, well-being and safety that is specific to a situation or institutionalized (Suet. Aug. 98,2). Philosophical discourse reacted to this modification of the image of humans, caused by the practice of deification, with ambivalence and a critique guided by a 'human' ideal of rulership (Cass. Dio 52,35,3–6; cf. Suet. Vesp. 23,4) as well as the damnation of individual 'unworthy ' cases (Seneca [2], *apocolocyntosis*).

→ Euergetes; → Rulers IV; → Emperor cult; → Trinity; → Dead, cult of the; → Katasterismos

1 S. Rebenich, Vom dreizehnten Gott zum dreizehnten Apostel?, in: Zschr. für ant. Christentum 4, 2000, 300–324 2 B. Bosworth, Augustus, the *Res Gestae* and Hellenistic Theories of Apotheosis, in: JRS 89, 1999, 1–18 3 R. J. Müller, Überlegungen zur Ἱερὰ Ἀναγραφή des Euhemeros von Messene, in: Hermes 121, 1993, 276–300 4 S. R. F. Price, Rituals and Power, 1984 5 D. Fishwick, The Imperial Cult in the Latin West, 1987–1992 6 M. Clauss, Kaiser und Gott, 1999. A. BEN.

Deikeliktai (Δεικηλίκται; *Deikēlíktai*). According to Ath. 14,621d-f a Laconic term for players in the simple street theatre, who acted out farcical scenes such as 'Fruit Thief' or 'The Foreign Doctor' (= μίμοι, μιμολόγοι). Despite variable spellings (δικηλισταί, δεικελισταί, δεικηλικταί), the Suda as well as MSS derive the word *deikeliktai* from δίκηλον, δείκελον (*díkēlon*, *deíkelon*) 'imitation', 'presentation' [cf. 1]. The anecdote in Plutarch (*Apophthegmata Laconica* 212ef; cf. *Agesilaus* 21) demonstrates the inferior status of *deikeliktai* as against actors of tragedy

1 I. Casaubonus, Animadversiones in Athenaei Deipnosophistas, 1805, vol. 7, 379f. W.D.F.

Deileon (Δηιλέων; *Dēiléōn*). Son of Deimachus of Tricca. With his brothers → Autolycus [2] and Phlogius he took part in the Amazon expedition of Heracles. They remained in Sinope and later returned with the Argonauts to Thessaly (Apoll. Rhod. 2,955–960; Val. Fl. 5,113–115). Other sources name him Demoleon (Plut. Lucullus 23,5; Hyg. Fab. 14,30). R.B.

Deilias graphe (δειλίας γραφή; *deilías graphḗ*). In Attic criminal law the indictment for cowardice. Although the existence of *deilias graphe* alongside other military offences (λιποταξίου γραφή, ἀστρατείας γραφή, γραφή τοῦ ἀποβληκέναι τὴν ἀσπίδα) is indicated in various places (And. 1,74; Lys. 14,5–7; Aeschin. 3,175f.; Aristoph. Ach. 1129; Equ. 368), it was disputed by older authorities [2; 5]. However, no concrete case of a *deilias graphe* is known. Distinction of the generalized *deilias graphe* from the more precisely defined offences given above is of course problematic; its prosecution was in any case formalized in only one statute (Lys. 14,5). The court of jurisdiction for all crimes in military service was composed of participants in the campaign in question, chaired by the responsible *strategos*; the guilty party was punished by → *atimía*.

1 G. BUSOLT/SWOBODA, 1127[2] 2 J.H. LIPSIUS, Das att. Recht und Rechtsverfahren 2, 1908, ND 1966, 453[6] 3 D. MACDOWELL, Andokides. On the Mysteries, 1989[2], 111f. 4 Id., The Law in Classical Athens, 1978, 160 5 TH. THALHEIM, RE 4, 2384. LE.BU.

Deima (Δεῖμα; *Deîma*). Like → Deimos and → Phobos a personification of fear. Pausanias describes an image of D. as a terrifying woman, which could be seen in his time in Corinth by the tomb of → Medea's sons. It was erected by the Corinthians in atonement for the murder of the children (Paus. 2,3,7).

S.I. JOHNSTON, Medea and the Cult of Hera Akraia, in: J.J. CLAUSS, S.I. JOHNSTON (ed.), Essays on Medea in Myth, Literature, Philosophy, and Art, 1997, 55–61; TH. KYRIAKOU, s.v. D., LIMC 3.1, 361f.; E. WILL, Korinthiaka, Recherches sur l'histoire et la civilisation de Corinthe des origines aux Guerres Médiques, 1955, 92–94.

Deimos (Δεῖμος; *Deîmos*). Personification of fear; usually associated with → Phobos. Together with → Eris the pair urge warriors into battle (Hom. Il. 4,440), and harness the horses to → Ares's chariot (Il. 15,119f.). → Antimachus [3] misinterpreted them as the horses of Ares, descended from Thyella ('storm') [1]; similarly, in Val. Fl. 3,89 Terror and Pavor are the horses of Mars. According to Hes. Theog. 934, D. and Phobos are the sons of Ares and Cythereia (Aphrodite). In Semus, FGrH 396 F 22, D. is the father of Scylla. D. and Phobos are depicted next to Gorgo on Agamemnon's shield (Hom. Il. 11,36f.); on the shield of Heracles the two of them stand next to Ares (Hes. Sc. 195f.; 463f.). No iconographic representation of D. can be established with certainty [2; 3]. Cf. for the Romans Pallor and Pavor (Liv. 1,27) or Metus and Terror (Apul. Met. 10,31).

1 V.J. MATTHEWS, Antimachos of Colophon, 1996, 150f. 2 J. BOARDMAN, s.v. Phobos, LIMC 7.1, 393f. 3 H.A. SHAPIRO, Personifications in Greek Art, 1993, 208–215. R.B.

Deinias (Δεινίας; *Deinías*). From Argos, lived in the 3rd cent. BC; he was the author of *Argoliká* in at least nine books. They ranged in scope from extensive treatment of the mythical period to the battle of Cleonae (*c.* 235), at which → Aratus [2] defeated the tyrant Aristippus of Argos (FGrH 306 F 5). His identity with the D. who murdered the tyrant Abantidas of Sicyon in 251/50 (T 1), is not established. FGrH 306 (with comm.). K.MEI.

Deinocrates (Δεινοκράτης; *Deinokrátēs*).

[1] Of Syracuse. Spared as a friend of → Agathocles [2] at the latter's seizure of power in 316 BC (Diod. Sic. 19,8,6), he soon became the leader of the exiles and of all opponents of Agathocles, took many towns in Sicily and fought with the Carthaginians against the tyrant (19,103f.). In 309 he marched with Hamilcar against Syracuse (20,29,5), and after the death of Hamilcar he was elected *strategos* by the exiles and the rest of the Greeks (20,31,2); when the Acragantines had to abandon their plans of establishing hegemony in their campaign against Agathocles's commanders, D. achieved the apogee of his career as the third power in Sicily alongside Agathocles and Carthage. D. then named himself 'leader of the common liberty', and his supporters increased so much (20,57,1) that Agathocles after the collapse of his African campaign offered to give up the tyranny and allow the exiles back (20,77,2f.). D., whose aim was to achieve sole power for himself, declined, and called upon Agathocles to leave Sicily (20,79,1–4). After Agathocles had made peace with Carthage in 306/5 (20,79,5) and won a victory over D. at Torgion, the latter surrendered and delivered up the occupied towns. Agathocles pardoned D., named him *strategos* and manifested confidence in him to the last (20,89f.).

K. MEISTER, in: CAH 7,1, [2]1984, 392f., 401ff.; J. SEIBERT, Die polit. Flüchtlinge und Verbannten in der griech. Gesch., 1979 (text 258ff., notes and index 569ff.). K.MEI.

[2] A Messenian, in 183 BC he hoped in vain for the help of his friend Quinctius Flamininus (Pol. 23,5) in winning independence for Messenia from Achaea [1. 220, 494]. When in 182, during the Achaeans' campaign against the renegades, D.'s old antagonist → Philopoemen was taken prisoner at Corone, D. quickly had him executed (Liv. 39,49,12; 50,7; Plut. Phil. 18; 20) [2. 189–194], but took his own life after Lycortas' victory shortly thereafter (Pol. 23,16,3.13; Liv. 39,50,9; Plut. Phil. 21,2). Polybius characterizes D. as a frivolous individual, whose exuberant lifestyle antagonized Flamininus i.a. (Pol. 23,5,4–5: Plut. Tit. 17,6).

1 GRUEN, Rome 2 R.M. ERRINGTON, Philopoemen, 1969. L.-M.G.

[3] Architect and urban planner of the early Hellenistic period; more precise dates for his life are not known. Owing to unclear spellings in MSS and confusion or conflation of names already in antiquity, his name has not come down to us with any clarity [1]. According to → Vitruvius (2 praef. 2), he came from Macedonia, according to Pseudo-Callisthenes 1,31,6 from Rhodes. Realistic plans as well as somewhat fantastical-seeming projects are associated with his name. He is supposed to have been commissioned by Alexander [4] the Great for the planning of → Alexandria (Vitr. De arch. 2 praef. 4; Plin. HN 5,62,7; 125). With its orthogonal network of streets, the city plan corresponded to ideas current at that time [2]. More unusual are D.'s draft plans for a platform for the cremation of → Hephaestion in Babylon, in the form of a six-stage, 60m-high stepped tower

(Diod. Sic. 17,114–115; Plut. Alex. 71). The rebuilding of the temple of Artemis at → Ephesus was mistakenly attributed to D. (Solinus 40,5). According to Vitr. De arch. 2 praef. 1–3, D. dressed as Heracles is supposed to have suggested to Alexander the Great that Mount Athos should be transformed into a colossal statue of the king [3]. The tale has the flavour of hyperbole, and may owe its origins to widespread aggrandizement of Alexander; the motif was the subject of imaginative illustrations in the Renaissance and Baroque periods (e.g. J.B. Fischer von Erlach, 1721).

1 G.A. Mansuelli, Contributo a Deinokrates, Alessandria e il mondo ellenistico-romano, in: Studi in onore di Achille Adriani 1, 1983, 78–90 2 B.R. Brown, Deinokrates and Alexandria, in: The Bulletin of the American Society of Papyrologists, 15, 1978, 39–42 3 H. Meyer, Der Berg Athos als Alexander. Zu den realen Grundlagen der Vision des Deinokrates, in: RA 10, 1986, 22–30.

J.E.M. Edlund, D. A Disappointed Greek Client, in: Talanta 8–9, 1977, 52–57; E. Fabricius, s.v. D. (6), RE 4, 2392f.; W. Müller, Architekten in der Welt der Ant., 1989, 153f. H.KN.

Deinolochus (Δεινολόχος; *Deinolóchos*). Writer of Doric Comedy, in our sources dated to the 73rd Olympiad (488–485 BC) and attested as the son or pupil [1. Test. 1], but also the rival [1. Test. 2], of → Epicharmus. He is supposed to have written 14 plays; thanks to a papyrus [2. no. 78] the sum of known titles by him has now grown to 12, of which ten suggest a mythical theme. Scarcely anything more can be said about the content and structure of these plays (except that they were probably comparable with those of Epicharmus). A single fragment of verse survives.

1 CGF I 1, ²1958, 149–151 2 C. Austin (ed.), Comicorum Graecorum Fragmenta in Papyris Reperta, 1973, 50f. H.-G.NE.

Deinomache (Δεινομάχη; *Deinomáchē*). Daughter (Plut. Alc. 1,1) of Megacles (son of Hippocrates from Alopece); great-niece of Cleisthenes; wife (Plat. Alc. 105d; Ath. 5,219c) of the Cleinias killed in 447/46 BC; mother of Alcibiades [3] (Plat., Ath. ibid.; Prt. 320a). Traill, PAA 302530; Davies 600, 9688, Table 1. K.KI.

Deinomachus (Δεινόμαχος; *Deinómachos*). Philosopher whose dates and school cannot be precisely determined; little can be deduced doxographically. He is mentioned only in association with Calliphon, who is scarcely more easily placed: both represent a position recorded in a discourse on the *divisio Carneadea* (→ Carneades) in Cic. Fin. 5,21, seeing virtue (*honestas*) allied with pleasure (ἡδονή) as the goal of human action (Clem. Al. Strom. 2,21,127; also critically commented upon in Cic. Off. 3,119; Tusc. 5,85). K.-H.S.

Deinomenes (Δεινομένης; *Deinoménēs*).

[1] D. from Gela, founder of the Deinomenid dynasty; father of the tyrants Gelon, Hieron, Polyzalus and Thrasybulus (cf. Simonides, fr. 141 Bergk = PLG 3,1166; Pind. Pyth. 1,79; 2,18; Hdt. 7,145; Timaeus FGrH 566 F 97; Diod. Sic. 11,67,2; Paus. 6,12,1ff.; 8,42,8).

[2] Son of Hieron by his first marriage with the daughter of the Syracusan Nicocles (Timaeus FGrH 566 F 97); as a boy he was installed under the guardianship of Hieron's brothers-in-law Chromius and Aristonus as king of the mercenary colony of Aetna, founded in 476 BC (cf. Diod. Sic. 11,76,3) (Pind. Pyth. 1,58ff. with schol.). At the death of his father in 467 he made votive offerings at Olympia in commemoration of the latter's victories (Paus. 6,12,1; 8,42,8). Murdered *c.* 451 (Diod. Sic. 11,91,1).

[3] Syracusan. In 214 BC played a leading role in the assassination of Hieron II the successor of Hieronymus, and was elected *strategos* by the Syracusans. Attempting to expel from Syracuse Hippocrates the enemy of Rome, he was killed by the people at Hippocrates' behest (Liv. 24,7,4ff.; 23,3; 30,6; 31,10; Paus. 6,12,4). K.MEI.

[4] Sculptor in bronze, whose acme is allocated by Pliny the Elder to 400–396 BC. Of his recorded works, statues of the athlete Pythodemus and of Protesilaus, the latter is frequently identified with a generic statue in New York, but this can hardly be dated after 430 BC, and is accordingly as frequently referred to as the *vulneratus deficiens* of → Cresilas. Pausanias saw statues of Io and Callisto by D. on the Acropolis; owing to the subject, these are usually ascribed to a 2nd–1st cent. BC sculptor of the same name, known from a signature on a statue base. Identifications with various classical generic statues have been suggested, but none of these suggestions has been established. The report by Tatian of a statue by D. of Queen Besantis may be ascribed to erroneous designation or imagination.

D. Arnold, Die Polykletnachfolge, 25. Ergb. JDAI, 1969, 7; J. Dörig, Deinoménès, in: AK 37, 1994, 67–80; Lippold, 203; Loewy, no. 233; Overbeck, no. 922–926, 983 (sources). R.N.

Deinomenids Ruling dynasty at first in Gela, later in Syracuse. Founded by → Deinomenes [1] of Gela and continued by his four sons Gelon, Hieron, Thrasybulus and Polyzalus. The marriage of Theron's daughter → Damarete to Gelon resulted in close relations of kinship between the Deinomenids and the Emmenids of Acragas (cf. fig.). K.MEI.

Deinostratus (Δεινόστρατος; *Deinóstratos*) D. is mentioned in Eudemus' list of mathematicians as the brother of Menachmus, who was a pupil of Eudoxus (Procl. in primum Euclidis elementorum librum comm., p. 67,11 Friedlein). He therefore lived in the middle of the 4th cent. BC

The Deinomenids and the Emmenids

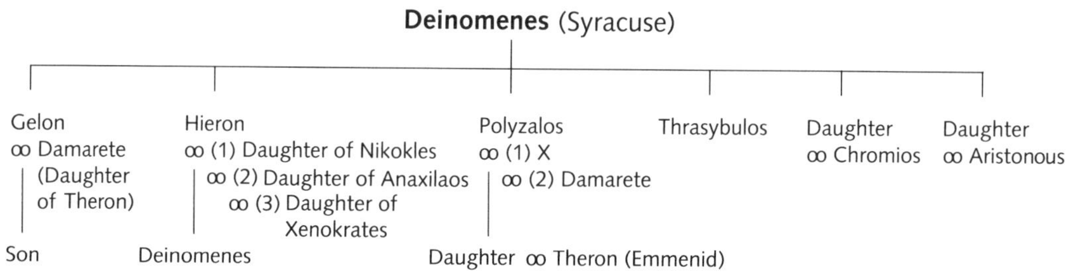

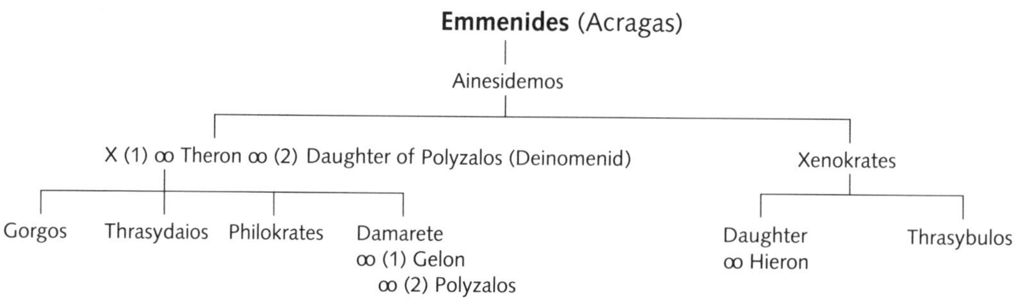

→ Pappus of Alexandria reports (4,30, p. 250,33–252,3 Hultsch) that to square the circle D. used a curve that was accordingly called the quadratrix (τετραγωνίζουσα). This curve, said to have already been used by Hippias of Elis for the trisection of an angle, is derived by displacing side BC of a square at a constant rate parallel to itself, until it coincides with the opposite side AD. At the same time, side AB is rotated around A until it coincides with AD. The points of intersection of the two line segments produce the quadratrix BFG. Using an indirect proof, Pappus shows that the arc BED

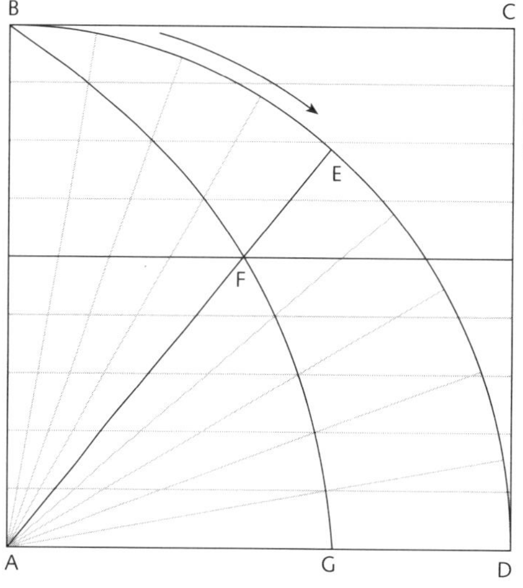

Construction of the *quadratrix* according to Deinostratus.

relates to AB as AB relates to AG. Thus the length of the quadrant (and therefore the circumference of the circle and hence its area) may be established by means of the end-point G of the quadratrix. If the proof given by Pappus derives from D., this would be one of the first indirect proofs in Greek mathematics.

Sporus (3rd cent.) raises two objections to the definition of the quadratrix: 1) coordination of the rates of displacement and rotation to create the quadratrix already assumes rectification of the circle (construction of a line segment the length of the circumference of a given circle); 2) the end-point G cannot be regarded as the point of intersection of the line segments rotated and displaced in parallel, because at the conclusion of the transposition both coincide. Both objections are today for the most part held to be unfounded, as by successive halving of the side of the square and the arc of the circle any number of points on the curve can be obtained, and the end-point of the quadratrix defined within as narrow limits as desired.

→ Mathematics

1 O. Becker, Das mathematische Denken der Ant., 1957, 95–97 2 I. Bulmer-Thomas, s.v. Dinostratus, Dictionary of Scientific Biography 4, 1971, 103–105 (104 with fig.) 3 Th. L. Heath, A History of Greek Mathematics, I, 1921, 225–230 4 G. Loria, Le scienze esatte nell'antica Grecia, [2]1914, 160–164 5 B. L. van der Waerden, Erwachende Wiss., [2]1966, 314–317.

M.F.

Deioces (Δηιόκης; *Dēiókēs*). According to Hdt. 1, the first ruler of the → Medes, said to have ruled for 53 years; elected by the Medes as their ruler, he is said to have had a fortress built (→ Ecbatana), surrounded himself with a bodyguard and introduced a court ceremonial designed to accustom his subjects to regard their ruler as a higher being. Herodotus' account combines contemporary elements of Achaemenid court protocol with Greek ideas on the ways of a tyrant (Hdt. 1, 96–101; [2]). The Greek personal name D. corresponds to the name *Daiakku* mentioned in Neo-Assyrian sources. But there is no identity as to persons. Daiukku is a Mannaean prince from the north-western Zagros, of whom Sargon II of Assyria reports in an inscription that he deported him to Ḫamat (715 BC).

1 S. Brown, Media and Secondary State Formation in the Neo-Assyrian Zagros, in: JCS 38, 1986, 107–119 2 P. Helm, Herodotus' Medikos Logos and Median History, in: Iran 19, 1981, 85–90 3 H. Sancisi-Weerdenburg, Herodotos' Medikos logos, in AchHist 8, 39–55.

A.KU. and H.S.-W.

Deion(eus) (Δηιών, Δηιονεύς; *Dēiṓn, Dēioneús*).
[1] Son of Aeolus [1] and Enarete the daughter of Deimachus. He was king of Phocis, and married Diomede the daughter of → Xuthus. From this marriage issued Asterodia, Ainetus, → Actor [2], → Phylacus and → Cephalus (Apollod. 1,51; 86; Hyg. Fab. 189,1; Callim. H. 3,209; Str. 10,2,14). The two last names show connections with Attica, as does the name Xuthus.

F. Graf, Greek Mythology, 1993, 127.

[2] A frequent erroneous spelling of → Eioneus, father of → Dia [2]. See also → Ixion R.B.

De Iona (105 hexameters) belongs to a group of pseudonymous biblical poems, presumably from the 5th cent. (the MSS attribute them to → Tertullianus). It comes from the same pen as → *De Sodoma* the content of which its opening part extends by a comparison of the fate of Sodom and Gomorrah with that of Niniveh. The poem follows the narration in Jon 1,1–2,1 with a poetically perfect description of a storm at sea. The last verses describe Jonah in the belly of the sea monster, which is interpreted as a symbol for Christ's death and resurrection. The poem is probably incomplete as there is no report on the events in Niniveh which, given the introduction, the reader might expect.
→ Biblical poetry; → De Sodoma

Edition: R. Peiper, CSEL 23,221–226. M.RO.

Deiopea (Δηιόπεια; *Dēiópeia*). A nymph in the vicinity of Cyrene, distinguished by her extraordinary beauty; she lives in the depths of the Peneius (Verg. G. 4,343). Juno promises her to Aeolus in marriage (Verg. Aen. 1,71–73).

R.A.B. Mynors, Virgil. Georgics (comm.), 1990, 303; M. Scarsi, s.v. D., EV 2,17. R.B.

Deiopites (Δηιοπίτης; *Dēiopítēs*). Trojan, son of → Priamus (Apollod. 3,153; Hyg. Fab. 90,6). Wounded by Odysseus (Hom. Il. 11,420); according to Dictys 3,7 killed by Agamemnon.

P. Wathelet, Dictionnaire des Troyens de l'Iliade, 1988, vol. 1, 414f. R.B.

Deiotarus (Δηιόταρος; *Dēiótaros*). Φιλορώμαιος (regarding Celtic composite name cf. [4. 190; 5. 155]). Born at the end of the 2nd cent. BC the son of Sinorix (IG III^2 3429); husband of Berenice; tetrarch of the Tolistobogii, king of the Galatians; died *c.* 40 BC. D. was a semi-Hellenized client prince of the Romans, and practised an energetic and unscrupulous form of power politics. He was one of the three Galatian tetrarchs who in 86 BC escaped the assassination attempts of Mithridates of Pontus. From then on he fought as an ally of the Romans, and in 73 BC succeeded in driving the Pontic general Eumachus out of Phrygia (App. Mith. 75; Liv. Epit. 94). In 63/62 BC Pompey rewarded him by recognizing him as sole king of the Tolistobogii, and granted him substantial parts of the kingdom of Pontus as well as Lesser Armenia. Caesar as consul in 59 BC had these awards confirmed by the Senate (Str. 12,3,13).

In 58–56 BC, D. drove Brogitarus out of Pessinus and in 52 BC also annexed his territory (Cic. Har. resp. 29; Sest. 56). With his considerable force of *c.* 12,000 foot soldiers and 2,000 horse troops, organized on the Roman pattern and later to become the *legio XXII Deiotariana*, he was able i.a. to support his friend Cicero against the Parthians in Cilicia in 51 BC (Cic. Fam. 15,1,6–2,2; 4,5–7; Att. 5,18,2; 6,1,14; Phil. 11,33–34).

During the Civil War in 49 BC, D. personally led 600 mounted troops for Pompey in the battle of Pharsalus, and accompanied him on his flight (Caes. B Civ. 3,4,3; App. B Civ. 2,71). Shortly afterwards he took over the territory of Domnilaus. In subsequent disputes with the Bosphoran king Pharnaces II (48 BC) he lost half of his troops while fighting at the side of Domitius Calvinus. At Nicaea after his victory at Zela (47 BC) Caesar took Lesser Armenia away from his former host, in spite of the intervention of Brutus. The tetrarchy of the Trocmi went to Mithridates of Pergamum (Bell. Alex. 34–41; 67,1; Cic. Brut. 5,21; Cass. Dio 41,62,5–63,1).

D. continued to sympathize with Republican circles, while his relationship to Caesar remained distant (Cic. Deiot. 8; Phil. 2,93–96). In early 45 BC he sent a petition to Caesar in Tarraco, requesting the return of the territory of the Trocmi now that Mithridates was dead (Cic. Deiot. 38). A Galatian delegation in Rome under the leadership of D.'s grandson Castor II thereupon accused him of an assassination attempt against Caesar. The hearing that took place at the end of November at Caesar's house was an example of 'cabinet justice', lacking any legal basis [2. 72–88]. Cicero's speech survives in which he skilfully defends his friend *in absentia* while at the same time denouncing the monarchical tendencies of Caesar's dictatorship (Cic. Deiot.) [1. 320–

344; 3. 109–123]. He succeeded in exposing the accusation as a fabrication, but no verdict was pronounced (Cic. Phil. 2,95).

After Caesar's murder D. removed his own son-in-law Castor Saocondarus, subsequently making himself king of all Galatia (Str. 12,5,1–3). Antonius [I 9] confirmed this conquest, falsifying Caesar's final dispensations in return for money (Cic. Phil. 2,94–96; Att. 14,12,1; 14,19,2). After the first battle at Philippi (42 BC) D.'s commander Amyntas [9] changed sides from Brutus to Antony (Cass. Dio 47,24,3; 47,48,2). D. Philopator, D.'s son, who since 51 BC had reigned alongside him, may already have been dead at the time of the second battle (Cic. Deiot. 36; funeral inscription from Blucion (Karalar): J. COUPRY, RA 6, 1935, 142). After D.'s death Antony appointed his grandson and accuser Castor II as his successor (Cass. Dio 48,33).

→ Amyntas [9]; → Antonius [I 9]; → Brogitarus; → Domnilaus; → Galatians; → Mithridates of Pergamum; → Mithridates of Pontus; → Pessinus; → Pharnaces II; → Sinorix; → Saocondaros; → Tarraco; → Tolistobogii

1 H. BOTERMANN, Die Generalabrechnung mit dem Tyrannen, in: Gymnasium 99, 1992, 320–344 2 K. BRINGMANN, Der Diktator Caesar als Richter? in: Hermes, 114, 1986 3 E. OLSHAUSEN, Die Zielsetzung der Deiotariana, in: FS. E. Burck, 1975 4 SCHMIDT 5 L. WEISGERBER, Galatische Sprachreste, in: Natalicium. FS J. Geffken 1931.

W. HOBEN, Unt. zur Stellung kleinasiatischer Dynasten in den Machtkämpfen der ausgehenden Republik, diss. 1969; HN 746.

W.SP.

Deiphobus (Δηίφοβος; *Dēíphobos*). Trojan prince and leader (Hom. Il. 12,94; 13,402–539), son of Priam and Hecuba (Apollod. 3,151). The tragedians have D. participating in the recognition of his once abandoned brother → Paris. D. threatens Paris, who flees to the altar and is there recognized by → Cassandra (Hyg. Fab. 91). D. is Hector's favourite brother, and Athena takes on his appearance when she entices Hector to his fatal single combat with Achilles (Hom. Il. 22,226ff.; 294ff.). With Paris he sets the ambush to which Achilles falls victim because of → Polyxena (Dictys 4,11; Hyg. Fab. 110). As the second most valiant hero of the Trojans, after Paris' death he wins Helen, who has been promised by Priam to the bravest in battle (Il. Parv. p. 74 PEG I; Dictys 4,22; Tzetz. Lycoph. 168), and who already loved D. while Paris lived (Hom. Od. 4,276). His defeated rival → Helenus thereupon leaves the city and is taken prisoner by the Greeks (Apollod. Epit. 5,9; Q. Smyrn. 10,345ff.). With Helen, D. attempts to outwit the Greeks in the Trojan Horse (Hom. Od. 4,276). In Dares (28) he is killed in battle; in Virgil (Aen. 6,494ff.) Helen betrays him to → Menelaus and Odysseus during the taking of the city. They kill him while he is unarmed, and his body is mutilated and remains unburied (Hom. Od. 8,517; Apollod. Epit. 5,22). His body is transformed into the plant *akephalon*. → Aeneas has a mound raised to D. at Rhoeteum (Aen. 6,505). D.'s mutilated body meets Aeneas in the Underworld.

→ Hector; → Helena

C. FUQUA, Hector, Sychaeus and D. Three mutilated figures in Aeneid 1–6, in: CPh 77, 1982, 235–240; L. KAHIL, s.v. D., LIMC 3.1, 362–367; L. v. SYBEL, s.v. D., ROSCHER 1.1, 981; R. WAGNER, RE 4, 2402–2405.

T.S.

Deiphontes (Δηιφόντης; *Dēiphóntēs*). Great-great grandson of Heracles (Heracles-Ctessipus-Thrasyanor-Antimachus-D.). He married → Hyrnetho, daughter of the Heraclid → Temenus. The latter had been awarded Argos in the land lottery after the conquest of the Peloponnese. Temenus' sons, who felt neglected compared with D. and Hyrnetho, had their father killed. As he was dying, Temenus handed over rule to D. and Hyrnetho. But the Temenids did not relinquish their claims to power. For this reason D. moved to Epidaurus, whose king Pityreus, a descendant of Ion, surrendered the country to him without a struggle. The Temenids attempted to abduct Hyrnetho to Argos. When it came to a battle, the pregnant Hyrnetho was murdered by her brother → Phalces. Her tomb was shown at Epidaurus and in Argos (Nicolaus of Damascus FGrH 90 F 30; Apollod. 2,179; Paus. 2,19,1; 2,23,3; 26,1f; 28,3–7; Diod. Sic. 7,13,1; Str. 8,8,5). Euripides wrote a *Temenos* and a *Temenidai* (TGF 728–751; POxy. 2455 fr.8; 10f.).

M. SCHMIDT, s.v. Herakleidai, LIMC 4.1, 723–725; H. W. STOLL, s.v. D., ROSCHER 1, 981–983.

R.B.

Deipnon (δεῖπνον; *deîpnon*). In the early Greek period a term applying to every daytime meal. But during the 5th cent. BC in Athens, probably as a consequence of urbanization, the meaning of *deîpnon* had become restricted to the main meal, which began at sunset.

There was a set order to the *deîpnon*. This comprised the actual meal, with the possibility of several courses, and the dessert, which might lead on to the drinking session (*sympósion*); not until the second part of the *deîpnon* was any amount of wine drunk. As the Greeks saw the *deîpnon* as the expression of a link with the gods, they began and ended every *deîpnon* with an invocation to the gods. The circle of participants in a private *deîpnon* depended on the particular occasion: ordinarily and on family occasions the family ate together, the women and children seated, while, from the 5th cent. BC onwards, the men usually lay in twos on dining couches after the oriental manner. When the head of the household invited guests from outside the family circle, marriageable women were excluded from the company. The degree of extravagance of the *deîpnon* differed from place to place. While Greek Lower Italy (esp. Sybaris) was marked by a high gastronomic culture even in the archaic period, in Athens into the 4th cent. BC even the elite ate relatively simply. In the Hellenistic age there was in general a growth in lavish eating habits at the upper stratum of society.

As well as private *deîpna* by invitation of a host there were also *deîpna* at which men met and shared the cost of a meal (so-called *éranoi*), besides official *deîpna* given by civic institutions such as the phyles. That the *deîpnon* gave expression to a shared Greek culture is shown by a regular *deîpnon* literature, knowledge of which we essentially owe to Athenaeus. The *deîpnon* was the model for the *cena* of the Romans, without its formality and strict etiquette. Depictions of the *deîpnon* are offered by Hom. Il. 2,399–432 and Ath. 4,128–131; 146f.
→ Cena

C. Morel, E. Saglio, s.v. Cena, DS 1, 1269–1276; J. Martin, s.v. D.-lit., RAC 3, 658–663; F. Orth, s.v. Kochkunst, RE 21, 944–957. A.G.

Deipyle (Δηιπύλη; *Dēipýlē*). Daughter of → Adrastus [1] and Amphithea; sister of → Argea [2], in whose company she is often portrayed [1]. Adrastus gave D. in marriage to → Tydeus, to whom she bore → Diomedes (Apollod. 1,103; 3,59; Hyg. Fab. 69A; 97,4).

1 G. Berger-Doer, s.v. Argeia, LIMC 2.1, 587–590. R.B.

Deipylus (Δηίπυλος; *Dēípylos*). Son of the Thracian king → Polymestor and of → Ilione, the eldest daughter of Priam. She exchanged him with her youngest brother → Polydorus, whose upbringing had been entrusted her by their father Priam. Her intention was to prevent the death of her brother should the outcome of the war be unfavourable. After the fall of Troy Polymestor allowed himself to be persuaded by Agamemnon to kill the last of the sons of Priam. Thus he unwittingly became the murderer of his own son. When later the real Polydorus learned the truth he killed Polymestor on the advice of his sister (Hyg. Fab. 109). R.B.

Deiradiotae (Δειραδιῶται; *Deiradiôtai*). Attic *paralia* deme of the Leontis phyle, from 307/6 to 201/0 BC of the Antigonis (→ Potamos Deiradiotae). Two → *bouleutai*. Finds of a gravestone and a mortgage marker stone (IG II^2, 2650, 5965) at Daskalio locate D. on the south-east coast of Attica east of Keratea.

Traill, Attica 44, 65, 68, 110 no. 31, tables 4, 11; Id., Demos and Trittys, 1986, 131. H.LO.

Deisidaimonia (δεισιδαιμονία; *deisidaimonía*). Although the term originally had a positive meaning ('conscientiousness in religious matters' in Xen.; Aristot.), it was primarily used in a derogatory sense, signifying a generally exaggerated zeal in religious practice, sanctimonious piety. Theophrastus (Char. 16) [1] was the first to characterize *deisidaimonia* as 'cowardice in the face of the divine', describing it as follows: agonizing fear of the gods; a bigoted inclination for worship and cult practise; superstitious fear of evil portents, in everyday life and in dreams; at the same time, the desire to ward off or prevent any negative effects by magical or ritual actions, especially continual cleansing. Plut. in *De superstitione* conveys more or less the same conception, attributing *deisidaimonia* to an erroneous or inadequate understanding of the gods. Roman observers such as Lucr., Cic. and Sen., employing in its place the Lat. word *superstitio*, to which Enn. and Plaut. had already given negative connotations such as private soothsaying, magic and more generally *prava religio* ('a distortion of religion'), were of the same opinion [2]. This last sense especially prevents us from simply translating *deisidaimonia* and → *superstitio* as 'superstition'. *Superstitio*, to a greater extent than *deisidaimonia*, developed into a term to describe the neglect of 'orthodox' religion in favour of other, mainly foreign and exotic, religions (e.g. Juv. 6,314ff; 511f. regarding foreign, esp. Egyptian, and 14,96ff. Jewish rites). Intellectual and spiritual positions were given clear social expression by such references to 'distortions of religion'. Christians appropriated both terms and used them in an inverse sense, esp. when condemning adherents of 'pagan' belief systems or the use in magic of Christian myth and rituals.
→ Superstition

1 H. Bolkenstein, Theophrastos' Charakter der Deisidaimonia, 1929. 2 S. Calderone, Superstitio, ANRW I 2, 377–396.

P. J. Koets, D.: A Contribution to the Knowledge of the Religious Terminology in Greek, 1929. H.V.

Deka (οἱ δέκα; *hoi déka*) 'the Ten'; a committee of ten men, elected after the overthrow of the Thirty in 403 BC to rule the oligarchy of Athens. According to Lysias (12,58) and some other sources, they were to work towards a peace settlement (accepted by [2]), but there is no hint of this in Xenophon (Hell. 2,4,23f.) and it is probably not so (cf. [1]), although the democrats around → Thrasybulus may have hoped that the change of regime in Athens would be followed by a change in direction. It is certain that the Ten made no efforts towards peace, but asked the Spartans for further help against the democrats. According to the author of the *Athenaion Politeia* (38,3) the Ten were replaced by a second group of ten who began to negotiate, but other sources offer no support for this: it is probably a question of confusion with the ten men from the city in the provisional government of twenty, appointed subsequently (And. 1,81; [3]). One of the Ten, however, Rhinon, after the restoration of democracy successfully submitted to an examination of his behaviour (→ Euthynai) and was elected *stratēgós* ([Aristot.] Ath. Pol. 38,4).

Under the regime of the Thirty, a committee of ten men had particular responsibility for the Piraeus; they were regarded as so thoroughly implicated in the oligarchy that, like the Thirty, they had to submit themselves to an examination of their behaviour if they wished to remain in Athens under the restored democracy ([Aristot.] Ath. Pol. 35,1; 39,6).
→ Athens

1 P. Cloché, La Restauration démocratique à Athènes, 1915 2 A. Fuks, Notes on the Rule of the Ten at Athens in 403 B.C., in: Mnemosyne[4] 6, 1953, 198–207 3 Rhodes. P.J.R.

Dekadarchia (δεκαδαρχία; *dekadarchía*).

[1] 'Rule by ten'; commissions of ten men, used in 405/04 BC by the oligarchically inclined Spartan Lysander, especially in the former Athenian sphere of influence; according to Diodorus (14,13,1), besides *dekadarchia* he also set up oligarchies, but according to Xenophon (Hell. 3,5,13; 6,3,8), Plutarch (Lys. 13) and Nepos (Lys. 1,4–2,1) *dekadarchia* persisted 'everywhere'. This is improbable, as Sparta had proclaimed freedom and autonomy as its goal in the war against Athens, and in Greek constitutional conceptions *dekadarchiai* resembled tyrannies, whereas oligarchies were seen as systems that were at least formally established on constitutional principles. The number of *dekadarchiai* cannot be determined. They are also attested in Greek cities of Asia Minor. As these did not immediately come under Spartan rule after the Peloponnesian War, and Spartan garrisons were therefore absent, troops of the younger Cyrus probably took on the protection of the *dekadarchiai* there.

The first *dekadarchiai* were presumably established after the battle of Aegospotami in 405. Despite the absence of contemporary testimony, it can perhaps be surmised that existing constitutional institutions survived in formal terms, but that the *dekadarchiai*, like the 'Thirty' (→ Triakonta) in Athens, used annual office-bearers, council members and other functionaries as they thought fit. As *dekadarchiai* are not comparable with ordinary oligarchies, their existence cannot be explained by a supposed specifically Spartan predilection for oligarchies. The indication in Plutarch (Lys. 13), that Lysander's use of *dekadarchia* was based on old connections and on friendship, shows that the system was entirely tailored to his person, and was designed by him to strengthen his position in Sparta; for Lysander's credibility amongst the Greeks was in its turn based on the greatness of Sparta. To this extent, *dekadarchiai* were at the same time instruments of Spartan state politics. When in 403 Lysander lost his influence on Spartan politics, the ephors in dissolving the *dekadarchiai* (Xen. Hell. 3,4,2) evidently sought to prevent him from regaining it. Lysander's attempt in 396 to restore the *dekadarchiai* in Asia Minor (Xen. Hell. 3,4,7–10) was foiled by the resistance of Agesilaus II.

J.-F. Bommelaer, Lysandre de Sparte, 1981, 209–211, 125–127, 165; D. Lotze, Lysander und der Peloponnesische Krieg, 1964, 68f. K.-W.WEL.

[2] According to Demosthenes, in 344 BC Philip II established a *dekadarchia* in Thessaly (Or. 6,22); but other sources attest only to his restructuring of Thessaly into tetrarchies. It is improbable that the *dekadarchia* consisted of a *koinon* of the 10 most important Thessalian cities (cf. [1. 99f.]). Possibly only one *dekadarchia* was established, in Pherae [2. 763f.]. Probably it is merely that our text of Demosthenes is corrupt, and he was originally referring to the structure involving tetrarchies [3. 275ff.].

1 F.R. Wüst, Philipp II. von Makedonien und Griechenland, 1938 2 J.R. Ellis, in: CAH 6, [2]1994 3 M. Sordi, La lega tessala, 1958. M.MEI.

Dekadrachmon (δεκάδραχμον; *dekádrachmon*). A silver coin to the value of 10 drachmas, occasionally minted to the Attic standard of 43.7 g to mark special events; thus in Athens after the battles of Salamis and Plataea, and in Syracuse after the Greek victory at Himera (480/79 BC), here as the *demaratium*. The splendid *dekadrachma* minted in Syracuse after 413 BC bear the signatures of the artists Evaenetus and Cimon. In the Hellenistic period the *dekadrachmon* is a more common denomination. Under Ptolemy III Euergetes *dekadrachma* are also minted in gold for Berenice II. The early 3rd cent. BC Punic *dekadrachma* in Sicily are lighter, weighing from 36 to 39 g.

→ Demaratium; → Drachme; → Evaenetus

Schrötter, 124; C.T. Seltman, The Engravers of the Akragantine Decadrachms, in: NC 6.8, 1948, 1–10; M.N. Tod, Epigraphical Notes on Greek Coinage, in: NC 6.20, 1960, 1–24; W.B. Kaiser, Ein Meister der Glyptik aus dem Umkreis Alexanders des Großen, in: JDAI 77, 1962, 227–239; G.K. Jenkins, Coins of Punic Sicily, SNR 57, 1978, 5–68, esp. 36ff.; O. Mørkholm, Early Hellenistic coinage, 1991, esp. 106.

Dekalitron (δεκάλιτρον; *dekálitron*) Exceptionally in Sicily, the Corinthian stater is associated not with the Euboean stater, later equated with the Attic *didrachmon* and divided accordingly, but with the *litron* system specific to the island, ten silver *litra* being equal to one stater (= 8.73 g according to the Attic standard). The *dekalitron*, also minted in silver, corresponds to the value of ten pounds of copper (109.15 g weight), and to a proportion of 1:250.

→ Didrachmon; → Stater

F. Hultsch, Griech. und röm. Metrologie, 1882, 541. 660f.; Id., s.v. Δεκάλιτρος στατήρ, RE 4, 2413f. A.M.

Dekanoummion (δεκανουμμίον; *dekanoummíon*). According to sources from late antiquity and Byzantium, the *dekanoummion* is a copper coin bearing a varying relationship to the denar unit. Despite this lack of certainty, it seems to be established that the *dekanoummion* was introduced in the reform of Anastasius in AD 498 as a 10–nummus piece with the denomination I (or X) and a weight of *c.* 2.25 g. In later coinage reforms the weight increased to 6.24 g, to sink again under Constantine IV to some 4.5 g and then towards the end of the 7th cent. AD to *c.* 2.1 g. Shortly thereafter the denomination fell into disuse.

→ Denarius; → Coinage reforms; → Nummus

PH. GRIERSON, Catalogue of the Byzantine coins in the Dumbarton Oaks Coll. and in the Whittemore Coll. 1, 1968, esp. 22ff.; W. HAHN, Moneta Imperii Byzantini 1, 1973, esp. 22ff.; M.F. HENDY, Studies in the Byzantine monetary economy c. 300–1450, 1985, esp. 476f. A.M.

Dekapolis (ἡ Δεκάπολις; *hē Dekápolis*). Term for a territory comprising a varying number of cities and with a predominantly Greek population, concentrated in northern Trans-Jordan, southern Syria and northern Palestine. Although some towns later to belong to the *Dekapolis* had already been in existence in pre-Hellenistic times, most of them claimed to have been founded by → Alexander [4] the Great. Archaeological investigations, however, have shown that the development of many towns into urban centres began only under Seleucid and Ptolemaic administration. After encroachments and occasional rule by Hasmoneans and Nabataeans in the 2nd and 1st cents. BC, the *Dekapolis* probably did not come into being until after Syria had come under Roman control in 64/63 BC (adoption of a new era on coins of the *Dekapolis*). There are, however, no indications pointing to the foundation of the *Dekapolis* as a political, military or economic league of cities. The member cities also had no unified administration in common. Inscriptions on the other hand show a Roman *praefectus* of the *Dekapolis*, which makes it an administrative area linked to the *provincia Syria,* with the individual cities and their territories within it enjoying local, i.e. municipal autonomy. The earliest literary mentions of the *Dekapolis* are in the gospels of Mark (Mk 5,20; 7,31) and Matthew (Mt 4,25). Pliny (HN 5,74) describes the *Dekapolis* as bordering on the Roman *provincia Iudaea*, and is the first to give a list of member-cities. According to him, these were: → Damascus, Canatha (al-Qanawāt, north-east of → Bostra), → Gadara (Umm Qais), → Gerasa (Ǧaraš), → Hippus (Qalʿat al-Ḥiṣn), → Pella (Tabaqat Faḥl on the eastern side of the Jordan valley), Abila (Quwailibī), Capitolias (Bait Raʾs), → Philadelphia (ʿAmmān), Raphana (perhaps ar-Raʾfa in southern Syria), Scythopolis (Beṯ-Šəʾān/→ Beisan, southern Galilee), and Dion/Dium (variously identified with towns in northern Jordan and southern Syria). A list in Ptolemy (Geogr. 5,14–22) gives the *Dekapolis* 18 cities. During the Jewish Revolt individual cities of the *Dekapolis* (e.g. Scythopolis) served as bases for Roman military operations. In AD 106 under Trajan the territory of the *Dekapolis* was divided between the provinces of Syria, Palastine, and the newly founded province of Nabataea.

H. BIETENHARD, Die syr. Dekapolis von Pompeius bis Trajan, in: ANRW II.8, 220–226; B. ISAAC, The Decapolis in Syria: A Neglected Inscription, in: ZPE 44, 1981, 67–84; C.H. KRAELING (ed.), Gerasa. City of the Decapolis, 1938; S. TH. PARKER, The Decapolis Reviewed, in: Journal of Biblical Literature 94, 1975, 437–441; A. SPIJKERMAN, The Coins of the Decapolis and the Provincia Arabia, 1978. T.L.

Dekaprotoi (δεκάπρωτοι; *dekáprōtoi*). College of the 10 highest ranked *decuriones* (→ Decurio), attested from the middle of the 1st cent. AD for communities in the east of the Roman empire. The obligations of the *dekaprotoi*, the western equivalent of which were the → Decemprimi, varied according to region and in the course of time. As a rule they represented their communities before the Roman magistrates, received the sworn public accounts of departing municipal officials and administered the community treasury. From the 2nd cent. onwards they were increasingly responsible for the collection of taxes, and in the 3rd cent. this became their main duty. As this involved personal liability, membership of the *dekaprotoi* gradually developed into a great burden, which was scarcely decreased even by privileges such as the status of *clarissimus* (→ Vir clarissimus, cf. CIL VIII 2403; ILS 1273) or the reduction of the period of duty from what was at first probably lifelong to 10, 15 or fewer years. Other functions of the *dekaprotoi* could include oversight of the price of corn, the control of pagan religious rites (from the 4th cent.) and similar supervisory duties. From the 3rd cent. they kept the lists of *decuriones* (*album decurionale*) and oversaw the administration of the *munera* (→ *munus*) for *decuriones*. They are not attested in Egypt until AD 202. The institution of the *dekaprotoi* is in principle already attested in the Republican period (Liv. 29,15,5; Cic. Rosc. Am. 25). The number of members could sometimes vary between 5, 10, 11 and 20. Admission to membership of the *dekaprotoi* was probably through election by the *ordo* (Cod. Theod. 12,1,171), perhaps also by → *cooptatio*.

JONES, LRE 730f.; W. LANGHAMMER, Die rechtliche und soziale Stellung der Magistratus Municipales und der Decuriones, 1973, 253ff.; O. SEECK, Decemprimat und Dekaprotie, in: Klio 1, 1901, 147–187. M.MEI.

Dekasmou graphe (δεκασμοῦ γραφή; *dekasmoû graphḗ*). In Athens the charge of active corruption of judges (Dem. Or. 46,26; see also Poll. 8,42; Harpocr. s.v. Δ. γ.). It concerned the offering of inducements to the chairman of a court, a member of a jury committee, the council or the people's assembly in the context of a legal case before them, to manipulate or decide the case to the advantage or disadvantage of a participant. The offence of *dekasmou graphe* was more precise than that of passive corruption (→ *dṓrōn graphḗ*), to which bearers of office were exposed irrespective of their judicial practise. The → *thesmothetai* were responsible for trying the charge, and the accuser presumably had to submit a bond (*parástasis*). Upon a guilty verdict and by request of the accuser (→ Antitimesis) the court could impose the death penalty.

BUSOLT/SWOBODA, 1098; A.R.W. HARRISON, The Law of Athens I, 1971, 15, 82. G.T.

Delatio nominis 'To indicate the name (of a suspect)' is originally only the very first step in initiating a public prosecution in Rome. Plaut. Aul. 416 uses the expression in this way regarding the campaign conducted by the → *tresviri capitales* against underclass criminality. In proceedings before these magistrates, a kind of police-court justice, the meaning of *delatio nominis* — entirely in the sense of a modern complaint to the police — is evidently confined to the sole process of reporting a criminal act [1. 60, 78].

In the 3rd and above all the 2nd cents. BC, alongside the older judgements based on private accusations and the unwieldy proceedings before committees (→ *comitia*), envisaged primarily for crimes against the state, state prosecutions had gravitated more and more to *quaestiones extraordinariae* (extraordinary proceedings for investigation and punishment, → *quaestio*), and victims of 'private' crime and their relatives also increasingly sought state prosecution of their cases in a *iudicium publicum*. Inevitably, this reduced the role of the former private accuser to that of providing the *delatio nominis*. Among the advantages of the new procedures were the public summoning and obligation of witnesses and the administration of punishment by the state [1. 92].

For the *iudicium publicum* of the 1st cent. BC, known to us primarily from the forensic practice of Cicero, the role of the *delatio nominis* has to some extent returned closer to the private accusation of former times: through the formal admission of the *delatio nominis* on the part of the magistrate (the → *receptio nominis*), the → *delator* acquired the status of an accuser (→ *accusatio*). We find the *delatio nominis* in such a form in the *lex Acilia* for *repetundae* proceedings (123/2 BC, text in [2]). This did not however change the situation that henceforth the *quaestio* opened by a *delatio nominis* remained an official procedure into the Imperial period. At first the *delatio nominis* in its new function is, like the complaint itself, presented orally. From the late classical period (3rd cent. AD) Paulus (Dig. 3,2,3 pr.) gives us a legal form for the *delatio nominis*, which is now to be presented in writing. Already in the Republican period the formal registration (*inscriptio*) of the accused had established a written form for the accusation admitted by the court (cf. e.g. Cic. Clu. 31,86).

1 W. KUNKEL, Unt. zur Entwicklung des röm. Kriminalverfahrens in vorsullanischer Zeit, 1962 2 C. G. BRUNS (ed. O. Gradenwitz), Fontes iuris Romani antiqui I, 1909, no. 10. G.S.

Delator The person who 'reports' something to a Roman authority, but in its narrower sense, esp. with regard to the → *delatio nominis*, the accuser. Considerable advantages were in prospect for the successful *delator*: as a rule, in the event of a guilty verdict he received a monetary reward in the form of a proportion of the accused man's property ([1]; with additional information in [2]). This naturally resulted in all kinds of abuse (cf. Cic. Rosc. Am. 55: Roscius was probably accused of political corruption in order to get hold of his wealth). If the accusation proved to be malicious, the *delator* himself was liable to prosecution for → *calumnia* (slander/libel). Even dropping his accusation during the trial could be risky for the *delator*: if the accused person demanded that the case be continued and was acquitted, he in his turn could demand the punishment of the *delator* (→ *tergiversatio*).

1 MOMMSEN, Strafrecht, 509ff. 2 W. KUNKEL, Unt. zur Entwicklung des röm. Kriminalverfahrens in vorsullanischer Zeit, 1962, 95[243]. G.S.

Delcus (Δέλκος; *Délkos*, Byzantine Δέρκος; *Dérkos*). Lake to the north of → Byzantium, today Derkoz Gölü/Turkey. According to Ath. 3,118b, the *delkanós* (δελκανός) was caught there, a fish that originated in the *Délkōn* (Δέλκων), which flowed into the D. In the Roman period an *oppidum* of the same name. I.v.B.

Delegatio In Roman private law, the *delegatio* is a three-person relationship by which the instructing party (delegant) authorizes the instructed party (delegate) to make a payment to or enter into an obligation with a third party, the recipient of the instruction (delegatee), in his own name but at the expense of the party instructing him. The basis of the *delegatio* is a unilateral informal declaration (→ *iussum*) accepting liability for the action of another person. It represents one of the most important transactions in Roman credit law, and has been thoroughly discussed by jurists.

In the case of a payment instruction (*delegatio solvendi*) the delegate is instructed to pay the delegatee. When the delegate proceeds to pay the delegatee, then in the covering relationship between delegant and delegate this is seen as a payment by the delegate to the delegant, so that by paying the third party the delegate liquidates his debt to the delegant. In the exchange relationship between delegant and delegatee on the other hand, the payment actually made by the delegate has the effect of a payment by the delegant to the delegatee. It is a matter of dispute whether Roman jurists here recognized a 'notional second' between payment from the delegate to the delegant and payment from the delegant to the delegatee (referred to as Celsus' transition theory, cf. Ulp. Dig. 24,1,3,12). Besides the payment of debts, in both the covering relationship and the exchange relationship a whole variety of purposes is to be considered (e.g. gifts, the payment of *dos*, lending). In the case of mistaken payment of a sum not owed and other deficiencies related to the purpose of the payment the compensatory settlement occurs either in the covering relationship or the exchange relationship. The payment in the covering relationship is therefore not affected by a deficiency in the exchange relationship, and vice-versa.

In the case of the instruction regarding a liability (*delegatio obligandi*), the delegate is instructed to enter into an obligation to the delegatee, in the form of a → *stipulatio*. If this obligation is to replace an existing liability of the delegant to the delegatee, then there ensues a → *novatio* with exchange of debtors (*delegatio debiti*). If on the other hand the *delegatio* is to replace an existing debt on the part of the delegate to the delegant, a *novatio* with exchange of creditors occurs (*delegatio nominis*), effected by a transfer of claim (→ *cessio*) from delegant to delegatee.

In public law the *delegatio* occurs as the transfer of an official authority (e.g. *iurisdictionem delegare*, cf. Dig. 39,2,1, Cod. Iust. 3,1,5). In a specialized sense in taxation law from the 4th cent. AD onwards *delegatio* is understood as the document in which the emperor establishes the annual level of taxation, and the instruction to collect it (e.g. Cod. Iust. 10,23,4). From this is derived the term *delegator* for the tax official.

R. Endemann, Der Begriff der Delegatio im Klass. Röm. Recht, 1959; G. Sacconi, Ricerche sulla delegazione in diritto romano, 1971; H. Honsell, Th. Mayer-Maly, W. Selb, Röm. Recht, [4]1987, 270–272; S. Weyand, Der Durchgangserwerb in der juristischen Sekunde, 1989.

F.ME.

Deliades, Deliastai see → Delius

Delian League (5th cent. BC). The Persian offensive on Greece was repelled in 480–79 BC, but nobody could know at the end of 479 that the Persians would never return. In 478 the Greeks continued the war under the leadership of Sparta, but the Spartan commander → Pausanias soon made himself so unpopular that Athens, either of its own record (Aristot., Ath. Pol. 23,4) or at the urging of its allies, decided to take over leadership (Thuc. 1,94–5). At this point, Athens established a standing alliance (nominally with the Ionians, but actually not limited to the Ionic Greeks) to continue the fight against the Persians in order to exact revenge and get booty (Thuc. 1,96,1), and surely (as Thuc. reports in another place), to free the eastern Greeks from Persian rulership and to protect them from any further offensive. Sparta and the other states of the Peloponnese did not join the alliance.

Originally, the alliance was a federation of free members who made themselves available to the leader Athens. The allies either provided ships for the war or paid monetary contributions (*phoros*). The alliance's treasury was kept in the sanctuary of Apollo in Delos, where the alliance assembly also met. But Athens assumed that a standing alliance also meant constant battles. By insisting upon the obligations of the allies and encouraging or forcing them to pay tribute rather than to provide their own ships, Athens strengthened its own position and weakened those of its allies, so that the naval league, which began as an alliance under the leadership of Athens, later became increasingly an empire under the control of Athens (Thuc. 1,96–7; 99).

Already in the earliest stages of the history of the league, Athens found ways to advance its own causes (Thuc. 1,98–101). The peaceful coexistence of Sparta's hegemony on the Greek mainland and the hegemony of Athens in the Aegean ended around 461 with the exclusion of the pro-Spartan → Cimon from politics. After this, the Athenians conducted the war against Persia in Egypt and began at the same time in the so-called first Peloponnesian War to expand their power over middle Greece (Thuc. 1,104–11). The war in Egypt ended in 454 with a disaster which probably provided the pretence for transferring the League treasury from Delos to Athens. Since 453, 1/60 of the tribute paid by the allies was dedicated to Athena and recorded every year in the 'Athenian tribute lists'.

The earliest lists show that Athens' control was in no way complete. After Cimon's death around 450 on a campaign in Cyprus, the regular war against Persia came to an end. It is possible but not certain that this was the consequence of a treaty, the so-called Peace of Callias. After a phase of uncertainty, Athens decided to continue the alliance and the collection of tribute: directly or indirectly, the tribute put the Athenians in the position to finance the Parthenon and other buildings in the 440s and 430s. Athens introduced, not systematically, but always if provoked, democratic constitutions for the allies; it established cleruchies (→ Klerouchoi) for Athenian citizens in their territory and held their trials before Athenian courts, which were likely to decide in favour of the supporters of Athens. In the prime of the League, when Athens still left its members nominal freedom and independence, it exercised power in a way previously unknown over a large number of Greek cities.

The territorial gains of the 450s on the Greek mainland were lost again in 447/6 as a consequence of rebellions, and in 446/5 Athens tried, with the conclusion of a 30-year peace to restore an equilibrium of power between Sparta and Athens (Thuc. 1,113–15). In the following years, it became clear, however, that Athens would expand its territorial power wherever it could, even if that meant violating Sparta's sphere of influence. As a result, Sparta began the Peloponnesian War in 431 with the declared goal of freeing the Greeks (Thuc. 2,8,4). In order to win the war, Sparta had to secure the support of Persia with the promise to forego the Greeks in Asia Minor. Sparta's victory in 404 led to the dissolution of the League and finally, after a phase of uncertainty, to the surrender of the Asiatic Greeks in the King's Peace of 386.

J. Bleicken, Die athenische Demokratie, [2]1994, especially 66–71; 396–97; R. Meiggs, The Athenian Empire, 1972; B. D. Meritt et al., The Athenian Tribute Lists, 1939–53; K.-E. Petzold, Die Gründung des Delisch-Att. Seebundes: Element einer 'imperialistischen' Politik Athens?, Parts 1 and 2, in: Historia 42, 1993, 418–443; 43, 1994, 1–31; P. J. Rhodes, The Athenian Empire, 1985, revised ed. [2]1993; Id., D. M. Lewis, The Thirty Years Peace, CAH 5[2], 34–61, 121–46; W. Schmitz, Wirtschaftliche Prosperität, soziale Integration und die Seebundpolitik Athens, 1988; W. Schuller, Die Herrschaft der Athener im Ersten Att. Seebund, 1974.

P.J.R.

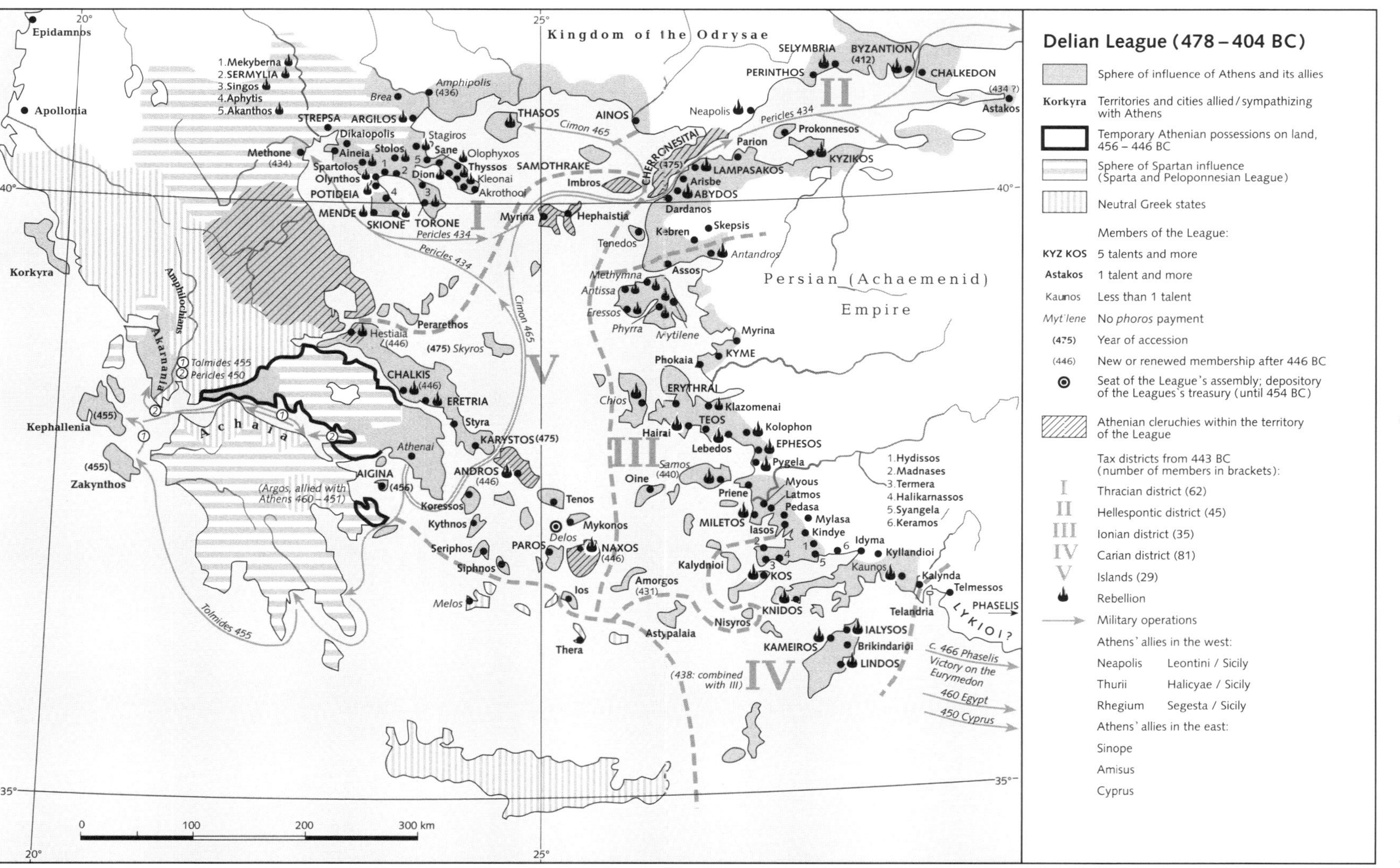
Delian League (478 – 404 BC)
Sphere of influence of Athens and its allies
Korkyra Territories and cities allied / sympathizing with Athens
Temporary Athenian possessions on land, 456 – 446 BC
Sphere of Spartan influence (Sparta and Peloponnesian League)
Neutral Greek states
Members of the League:
KYZ KOS 5 talents and more
Astakos 1 talent and more
Kaunos Less than 1 talent
Myt'lene No phoros payment
(475) Year of accession
(446) New or renewed membership after 446 BC
Seat of the League's assembly; depository of the Leagues's treasury (until 454 BC)
Athenian cleruchies within the territory of the League
Tax districts from 443 BC (number of members in brackets):
I Thracian district (62)
II Hellespontic district (45)
III Ionian district (35)
IV Carian district (81)
V Islands (29)
Rebellion
Military operations
Athens' allies in the west:
Neapolis Leontini / Sicily
Thurii Halicyae / Sicily
Rhegium Segesta / Sicily
Athens' allies in the east:
Sinope
Amisus
Cyprus
Kingdom of the Odrysae
Persian (Achaemenid) Empire
1. Mekyberna
2. SERMYLIA
3. Singos
4. Aphytis
5. Akanthos
1. Hydissos
2. Madnases
3. Termera
4. Halikarnassos
5. Syangela
6. Keramos
Epidamnos
Apollonia
Korkyra
Kephallenia
(455)
Zakynthos
Amphilochians
Akarnania
Achaia
① Tolmides 455
② Pericles 450
Tolmides 455
(Argos, allied with Athens 460 – 451)
AIGINA (456)
Athenai
Methone (434)
STREPSA
ARGILOS
Brea
Amphipolis (436)
Dikaiopolis
Aineia
Spartolos
Olynthos
POTIDEIA
MENDE
SKIONE
TORONE
Stolos
Stagiros
Sane
Olophyxos
Thyssos
Dion
Kleonai
Akrothooi
Pericles 434
THASOS
SAMOTHRAKE
Cimon 465
AINOS
Imbros
Myrina
Hephaistia
Hestiaia (446)
Perarethos
(475) Skyros
CHALKIS (446)
ERETRIA
Styra
KARYSTOS (475)
ANDROS (446)
Koressos
Kythnos
Seriphos
Siphnos
Melos
Tenos
Mykonos
Delos
PAROS
NAXOS (446)
Ios
Thera
Amorgos (431)
Astypalaia
CHERRONESITAI (475)
Neapolis
PERINTHOS
SELYMBRIA
BYZANTION (412)
CHALKEDON
(434 ?) Astakos
Prokonnesos
Parion
KYZIKOS
LAMPASAKOS
Arisbe
ABYDOS
Dardanos
Kebren
Skepsis
Tenedos
Antandros
Assos
Methymna
Antissa
Eressos
Phyrra
Mytilene
Myrina
KYME
Phokaia
ERYTHRAI
Chios
Klazomenai
Hairai
TEOS
Kolophon
Lebedos
EPHESOS
Samos (440)
Oine
Pygela
Priene
Myous
Latmos
Pedasa
MILETOS
Iasos
Mylasa
Kindye
Idyma
Kyllandioi
Kalydnioi
KOS
Kaunos
Kalynda
Telmessos
PHASELIS
LYKIOI?
Telandria
Nisyros
KNIDOS
IALYSOS
Brikindarioi
LINDOS
KAMEIROS
(438: combined with III)
c. 466 Phaselis
Victory on the Eurymedon
460 Egypt
450 Cyprus
20°
25°
35°
40°
0 100 200 300 km

MAPS: B.D. MERITT, H.T. WADE-GERY, M.F. MCGREGOR, The Athenian Tribute Lists IIV, 1939–1953; W. SCHULLER, Die Herrschaft der Athener im Ersten Att. Seebund, 1974; R. MEIGGS, The Athenian Empire, 1975 (corr. repr.); C.J. TUPLIN, in: R.J.A. TALBERT (ed.), Atlas of Classical History, 1985 (repr. 1994), 44; K.-E. PETZOLD, Die Gründung des Delisch-Att. Seebundes, Historia 42, 1993, 418–443; 43, 1994, 131.

Delicacies Mussels, fish, game and poultry were decided delicacies to the Greeks: for all of them → Archestratus [2] can provide the best source (Ath. 2,62c, 3,92d-e) and a good method of preparation (Ath. 9,384b). Hellenistic gastronomy reached Rome in the context of Roman conquests in the east, bringing with it not only new products (such as spices), but also food-related habits that were from then on inseparable from the sophisticated lifestyle of the upper classes: e.g. the use of *garum*, a sauce obtained by rendering fish intestines and small fish in salt (Gp. 20,46). The *lex Fannia* (161 BC) was the first in a whole series of laws seeking to restrict 'excess' at table, limiting the amount to be spent per meal and even forbidding certain foods (Gell. NA 2,24). These foods, spurned by moralists and ridiculed by satirists (who in this way inform us about the sequence of dishes; cf. Hor. Sat. 2,2,8), are meticulously described in Pliny's 'natural history' (see below), and their production portrayed by the specialist writers on agronomy. They featured in still-lifes or *xenia* that were the frequent subject of paintings and mosaics.

Rome's position and significance as political centre of the Empire allowed the city privileged access to all the products of the Mediterranean and beyond. Spices were imported — pepper from India; silphium from Cyrenaica, replaced during the 1st cent. AD by Parthian laser (*Asa foetida*) — or certain exotic fruits, like dates from North Africa; but also foods that, although produced in other places too, were better received when imported from their country of origin: plums from Damascus (*damascena*: Mart. 13,29), '*garum sociorum*' from Cartagena (Plin. HN 31,94; Mart. 13,102), caraway from Spain and Ethiopia (Plin. HN 19,161), conserved fish from Pontus (Ath. 6,275a). Some regions specialised in a particular product, in which they established a reputation: snails from Africa and Illyria (Varro, Rust. 3,14; Plin. HN 9,173–174), salted products from the Sequani (Str. 4,3,2), salted fish from Antibes (Plin. HN 31,94). In Italy itself there was oil from Liburnia, which attracted imitations (Apicius 1,5); olives from Picenum (Mart. 13,36), asparagus from Ravenna (Plin. HN 19,54,6f.), as well as smoked cheese from the Velabrum district of Rome (Mart. 13,32).

From the 2nd cent. BC the Romans sought to habituate fruits (peaches, apricots) and animal species (peacocks; the bird from Phasis: pheasant; poultry from Numidia: Guinea fowl) to Italy, even releasing exotic species of fish such as the parrot fish off the coasts (Plin. HN 9,62). To a great extent they developed those things that nature gave them only sparingly or at particular times of year, and in this way altered the economic structure of the *villa rustica*, which opened itself to luxury products to supply the owner's table as well as (with the surplus) the nearby city market. They favoured vegetable products such as asparagus (Cato Agr. 161) and table grapes (Columella 3,2,1), sold fattened dormice in cages (*gliraria*; Varro, Rust. 3,15), traded animals slaughtered young — kid, lamb, piglet — and especially parts of the sow such as the udder (*sumen*) and the uterus (*vulva*). The poultry yard and nest box were enriched by countless species (Varro, Rust. 3,4–11), with the fieldfare among those holding pride of place (Mart. 13,92); chickens and ducks were fattened, but also pigeons, quail and peacocks (Columella 8,1–15), not to forget geese for their livers (Plin. HN 10,52; Pall. Agric. 1,30). The *leporaria* ('game enclosures': Varro, Rust. 3,12–13) corrected the hazard of the hunt by supplying not only hares but also wild boar, the two kinds of game prized even above roe deer and red deer (Mart. 13,92). Coastal *villae* acquired fish ponds, which catered to pleasure as well as profit (Plin. HN 9,168–172). Morays, sole, bream and turbot were bred there (Columella 8,16–17); the most sought-after fish, however, the mullet (*mullus*), did not acclimatize: thus were explained the immoderate prices commanded by these items (Plin. HN 9,67; Juv. 4,15f.). Sergius Orata (Plin. HN 9,168) is accredited with the invention of the oyster bed, of which the most celebrated were those of the Lucrinus Lacus near Baiae, of Circei and Brundisium; ancient sources attesting enthusiasm for this mollusc, eaten fresh or salted, are found right up as far as the *limes*. But some foods, like the flycatcher (*ficedula*), remained subject to the hazard of the hunt, or, like mushrooms, the most sought-after of which was the cep, to the luck of the collector (Suet. Tib. 42). Almost all these delicacies still featured in Diocletian's 'maximum tarif' (AD 301), which proves that their success had not flagged, even if some, such as dormice, snails or even several different qualities of garum, seemed to have become more everyday fare (Edicta Diocletiani 3,6f.).

→ Fish dishes; → Spices

J. ANDRÉ, L'alimentation et la cuisine à Rome, [2]1981; N. BLANC, A. NERCESSIAN, La cuisine romaine antique, [2]1994; A. MICHA-LAMPAKIS, Η Διατροφη των αρχαιων κωμωδιογραφων, 1984; Recherches franco-tunisiennes sur la mosaïque de l'Afrique antique, 1, Xenia (Ecole Française de Rome), 1990; E. SALZA PRINA RICOTTI, L'arte del convito nella Roma antica, 1983. NI.BL. and A.N.

Deliciae (Also *delicia*, esp. on inscriptions [2]; but cf. [1. 2437]; see also Plut. Anton. 59,4, *delicium*, *delicati*). Children, mostly of unfree origin, who lived in rich households for the entertainment of their owners, particularly during the Imperial period. They were brought up in the *paedagogium*. The *pupulus* in Catull. 56,5 might be understood as an early example. They were esp. valued for their *garrulitas*, their impertinent loquacity (Suet. Aug. 83; Sen. De constantia sapientis

11,3; Stat. Silv. 2,1,45). Beautiful, beardless, long-haired boys (Sen. Ep. 47,7, 119,14; Mart. 3,58,30f.; a contr. picture in Petron. 28) from Egypt (Suet. Aug. 83; Stat. 2,1,73, 5,5,66f.) were preferred. They were often magnificently dressed (Sen. De vita beata 17,2; De tr. an. 1,8; Amm. Marc. 26,6,15). The majority of *deliciae* were purchased slaves [4. 308ff.]; many of them served at table and as catamites (Sen. Ep. 47,7, 95,24; Suet. Nero 28,1; on the consequences of sexual abuse [4. 310f.]). Dwarves and deformed persons could also be seen as *deliciae* (Quint. Decl. 298, cf. [1. 2438; 2. 1600]); there were more specialized terms for them such as *nani*, *pumili*, *pumiliones* (dwarves, often deformed), *fatui*, *fatuae*, *moriones* (fools), *scurrae* (clowns). The future fates of the children could vary greatly. Fictional texts are revealing in this respect, despite their presumed exaggerations: Horace (Epist. 1,20,6–18) jokingly prophesies for his latest book the fate of a catamite so long as it is fresh and youthful, and then the life of a teacher in the suburbs; Petronius' Trimalchio rises to the status of *dispensator* (29,3–5) and chief inheritor (76,1–2). The fate of → Antinous [2] in Hadrian's circle is entirely untypical. Sen. Ep. 12,3 depicts the decline of a *delicia* within the slave community. The presence of *deliciae* perhaps contributed to the predilection for portraying Cupids as children ([3. 135]: with caution). That less value was attributed to feelings for *deliciae* than to emotional ties to family members is shown in Stat. Silv. 5,5,66–87 (adopted son) and Dig. 7,7,6,2. On inscriptions the term is used in a non-technical sense for esp. loved individuals, above all children [2. 1596].
→ Family; → Sexuality; → Slavery

1 F. Mau, s.v. D., RE 4, 2435–2438 2 S. Auriyemma, s.v. Delicium, Dizionario Epigrafico 2, 1594–1603 3 W. J. Slater, Pueri, Turba minuta, BICS 21, 1974, 137–146 4 E. Herrmann-Otto, Ex ancilla natus (Forsch. zur ant. Sklaverei 24), 1994. H.L.

Delictum (*privatum*) is a forbidden act whose punishment is not, as for a → *crimen* (e.g. high treason, murder) pursued by a state body, but is left to the injured party himself, vengeance being gradually resolved in a claim for monetary compensation (→ *poena*). The latter usually amounts to a multiple of the damage sustained. There is *delictum* in *ius civile* (e.g. *iniuria*, *damnum iniuria datum*, *furtum*) as well as praetorian *delictum* (e.g. *dolus*, *metus*, *rapina*). Obligations on the defendant's part arising from *delictum* are non-heritable; many culprits accept cumulative liability. Responsibility for a *delictum* by a person subject to the power of another lies with the holder of power (→ *noxa*). During the imperial period, *delicta* are also punished judicially.
→ Actio; → Lex Aquilia; → Noxalis actio

Kaser, RPR I, 609–614; II, 425–433; H. Honsell, Th. Mayer-Maly, W. Selb, Röm. Recht, [4]1987, 223–226, 257–259; R. Zimmermann, The Law of Obligations, 1990, 913–921. R.GA.

Delium (Δήλιον; *Dēlion*). The name of several sanctuaries of Delian Apollo.
[1] Sanctuary to Apollo with a small settlement (πολίχνιον) and harbour on the Boeotian east coast, south-east of the modern Dilesi; a Theban, later Tanagran possession. The town was settled from the Mycenaean to the Byzantine period; few traces survive. Shared cult with Artemis and Leto. Frequently mentioned by sources, in particular owing to the severe defeat suffered there by the Athenians at the hands of the Boeotians in 424 BC, in which i.a. Socrates and Alcibiades participated. Sources: Hdt. 6,118,2f.; Thuc. 4,76,4f.; 89–101,2; Str. 9,2,7; Paus. 9,20,1; Liv. 35,51,1; Pl. Symp. 220e–221b.

Fossey, 62–66; Pritchett, II, 24–34, III, 295ff.; P. W. Wallace, Strabo's Description of Boiotia, 1979, 27ff.; N. D. Papachatzis, Παυσανίου Ἑλλάδος περιήγησις [*Pausaníou Helládos periḗgēsis*] V, [2]1981, 132f.; Schachter, I, 44–47. M.FE.

[2] Sanctuary of Apollo in Laconia on the east coast of the Parnon peninsula south of Monemvasia; precise location uncertain (Str. 8,6,1; Paus. 3,23,2–4: *Epidḗlion*).

A. J. B. Wace, F. W. Hasluck, South-Eastern Laconia, in: ABSA 14, 1907/08, 175f. Y.L.

Delius (Δήλιος; *Dḗlios*). Epithet of → Apollo, indicating his association with the island of → Delos: he was born there, and along with → Leto and → Artemis had a central cult site there. D. is as frequent an epiclesis for Apollo as → Pythius, which indicates his association with → Delphi. Whereas there are many cases where the cult of a divinity named Pythius was established (i.e. sanctioned) by the Delphic oracle, there is no comparable institution on Delos: the epiclesis D. is more the expression of the local Delian cult by a cult site. As well as D. Apollo, his sister Artemis is occasionally referred to as Delia (Δήλια) on the same grounds; Delia is also the name of a (fictitious) lover of the elegist → Tibullus.

It is also from Delos, more precisely from its central mountain, the Cynthus, that the epicleses Cynthios and Cynthia derive, attached esp. to Apollo and Artemis (and the name Cynthia given by the elegist Propertius to his lover in his poems).

Ph. Bruneau, Recherches sur les cultes de Délos à l'époque hellénistique et à l'époque impériale, 1970; C. Calame, Thésée et l'imaginaire athénien, 1990, 116–121. F.G.

Dellius (handwritten also Deillius, Deillios).
Q.D. (Name in Cass. Dio 49,39,2), referred to by Messalla Corvinus as *desultor bellorum civium*, as in 43 BC he defected from P. Cornelius [I 29] Dolabella to C. Cassius [I 10], the next year to Mark Antony and finally, shortly before the battle of Actium, to the camp of Octavian, with important information about Antony's troops (Sen. Suas. 1,7). Octavian held him in high

regard (Sen. Clem. 1,10,1; Horace dedicated Carm. 2,3 to him). Between 41 and 31 he undertook diplomatic missions in the east for Antony (MRR 2,559). In 40 BC Antony sent D. to Herod the Great in Judaea, to support him against the heir apparent Antigonus [5] (Ios. Ant. Iud. 14,394, Bell. Iud. 1,290). At the beginning of the Parthian War in 36 BC D. visited Cleopatra with the request for her to travel to Antony's headquarters. After defeat at the hands of the Parthians in 34, D. was supposed to persuade the Armenian king Artavasdes [2] to marry his daughter to Alexander Helios, Antonius' son (Cass. Dio 49,39,2). D., himself one of Antony's commanders in the Parthian War, wrote a history of the campaign (fragments HRR 2,53; Plut. Ant. 59; Str. 14,13,3).

SCHANZ/HOSIUS, 2, 327f. ME.STR.

Delmaticus Victor's name of L. Caecilius [I 24] Metellus D. (*cos.* 119 BC). K.-L.E.

Delminium (Delminenses, Delminum). Main town of the Dalmatae: Ptol. 2,16,11; App. Ill. 11; Florus 2,25; CIL III 3202; the name D. is possibly derived from the Albanian word *delme*, 'sheep'. Strabo (*Délmion*, 7,5,5) describes D. as a large city from which the people derived its name. In 156 BC, D. was besieged by C. Marcius Figulus. In 155 BC it was defeated and destroyed by P. Cornelius Scipio Nasica (cf. Strabo's *pedíon mēlóboton*; triumph over the Delmatae; ancient sources in [1. 448]). Up to now the ruins of D. were located in Lib, above Borčani, south-east of Županjac (= Duvno, the modern Tomislavgrad); according to ZANINOVIĆ it could also be identified with Gradina, near Gaj, above Tomislavgrad. D. still survives in the name Duvanjsko polje, the wider environs of Tomislavgrad. The Roman D., which became a *municipium* under Hadrian, has not yet been located with certainty; it must be sought on the plain within Duvanjsko polje. ZANINOVIĆ locates it at Tomislavgrad, BOJANOVSKI [2. 216ff., 230] in Borčani, in the immediate vicinity of prehistoric Delminium, locating Bistua Vetus at Tomislavgrad; this location better fits the data in the Tab. Peut. The town of D. was also placed at Prisoje in Buško blato (the wider environs of Tomislavgrad), because of the gravestone of a *IIvir* of the *municipium Delminensium*.

1 BROUGHTON, MRR, 448 2 I. BOJANOVSKI, Bosna i Hercegovina u antičko doba [Bosnia and Herzegovina in antiquity], Akademija nauka i umjetnosti Bosne i Hercegovine, Djela 66, Centar zu balkanološka isptivanja 6, [Monographies, Academie des sciences et des arts de Bosnie-Herzegovine 66, Centre d'études balk. 6], 1988 3 M. ZANINOVIĆ, Livanjsko polje u antici kao primjer delmatske zajednice (Livanjsko polje in antiquity as an example of a Dalmatian community), in: H. GJURAŠIN (ed.), Livanjski kraj u povijesti, 1994, 45–50. M.Š.K.

Delos (Δῆλος; *Dêlos*), also Lesser D. (ἡ μικρὰ Δῆλος; *hē mikrà Dêlos*).
I. GEOGRAPHY II. HISTORY III. ARCHAEOLOGY

I. GEOGRAPHY

Island at the centre of the Cyclades, separated from Rheneia or Greater Delos (17 km²) by a channel 1 km wide. The small, now uninhabited island is some 6 km long and 1.2 km wide; it covers an area of 3.5 km². D. is an elongated rocky ridge jutting from the sea, consisting mainly of gneiss, granite and granite gneiss. The west coast is accessed by three small bays: the bay of Skardana, the little harbour (in antiquity the 'sacred harbour') and the bay of Phourne. On the north-east coast lies the anchorage of Gourna. The interior of the island is mountainous. With the bare, conical Mount Cynthus it reaches a height of 113 m. In the south-west lies the arid gorge of the Inopus.

II. HISTORY

A. EARLY HISTORY B. CLASSICAL PERIOD C. HELLENISTIC PERIOD D. LATE REPUBLIC AND IMPERIAL PERIOD E. EARLY CHRISTIAN PERIOD

A. EARLY HISTORY

There was a settlement on Mount Cynthus in the Early Cycladic period (3rd millennium BC), and sanctuaries of Zeus and Athena in historical times. Ceramics from the Middle Helladic were found on the plain to the south of the precinct of Apollo next to the Delian Agora. Late Helladic wares were discovered at Treasury V. A Late Mycenaean settlement could be detected at the centre of the later sacred precinct; it probably owed its existence to the cult of a precursor of the Greek Artemis. At the Artemisium there is a semicircular platform cut from the rock, probably a Late Helladic cult site. Here was perhaps the *sema*, the tomb of the two Hyperborean maidens Hyperoche and Laodice, who according to legend made the first sacrifice to Apollo. The *theke* (Hdt. 4,33ff.), possibly the circular → *ábaton* (a Mycenaean ossuary near the stoa of Antigonus), is another witness to the early period; Arge and Opis, likewise two Hyperborean maidens, are supposed by legend to be buried there. Here sacrificial rites were performed, with origins reaching back to the Mycenaean or pre-Mycenaean period. These legends and cults may reflect the appropriation of the island by Apollo. At the period of the settlement of the Ionian Greeks in *c.* 1000 BC, the older female divinity, absorbed by Artemis, was joined by Leto as well as Apollo in the Delian triad of divinities, in which Apollo soon took pride of place. In the Greek legend the wandering Leto bore Apollo under a palm-tree, in another version on the peak of Cynthus. It was only then that Poseidon anchored the previously freely floating island.

Theseus is supposed to have established the great annual feast-day of the Ionian Greeks with its athletic and artistic *agones* and dances, esp. the primeval *geranos* ('Crane-dance') at the *keraton* ('goathorn altar'). It certainly goes back to the pre-Greek, at the latest early Greek period. The Homeric Hymn to Apollo sees D. as the centre of an amphictiony of the Ionian islands. The feast of Apollo, the Delia, was celebrated annually with choral and boxing contests. In the area of the earlier Mycenaean structures near to the precinct of Artemis there were similar contests for Leto and Apollo. The temple of Artemis, the Artemisium, was built *c.* 179 BC on the site of an archaic predecessor, itself successor to a Mycenaean temple. Leto acquired her temple north of the main sanctuary near the lion terrace by the mid 6th cent. BC at the latest. In the oldest temple of Apollo, the *pṓrinos naós* ('limestone temple'), probably established by Peisistratus from Athens, also stood the colossal 8.5 m-high bronze cult statue, created by → Tectaeus and → Angelion. Swans of Apollo and geese of Leto were kept on the lake. Apollo's guardians were the seated lions, made of marble from Naxos and today nine in number, on a 50m-long terrace; they were created towards the end of the 7th cent. BC, by craftsmen from Naxos. In the 7th and 6th cents. BC the rapidly growing precinct acquired an 'Ionian Island aspect' [1. 148], with the island of Naxos fulfilling the major role in constructing and equipping the site; this may esp. be seen in the Naxian *oíkos*, a simple 'house' in the form of an elongated rectangle, constructed from granite blocks and dating from the beginning of the 6th cent. BC, when the temple of Apollo did not yet exist. The enclosed *oíkos*, as built on D., is already known from → Delphi and Olympia as having functioned as a treasury. However in the Early Archaic period it also frequently occurs as a temple. An older, chapel-like building (probably 2nd millennium BC) was found before the east front of the *oíkos*. Before its east front stood the approx. 9 m-high marble statue of Apollo (*c.* 600 BC). In the middle of the 6th cent. BC, Athens took over control of the island from Naxos and Paros, the latter's influence having lain particularly in the *kouros* and *kore* statues.

B. Classical period

Peisistratus purified the island at the behest of the Delphian oracle, clearing away all the burials within sight of the temple, with the exception of those that were already the subject of cult veneration (Hdt. 1,64; Thuc. 3,104,1). Polycrates' gift of Rheneia is to be seen in this context. From then on D. remained under Attic control and administration. In 477 BC D. became the focus of the new Delian League. In the same year, work started on the construction of the 'Great' Temple of Apollo. In 454 BC the treasury of the League, at first still kept in the old temple, was transferred to Athens. Construction of the temple came to a halt, and was not completed until the 3rd cent. BC. In 426/5 BC Athens undertook a 2nd 'purification' of the island, removing the remainder of the burials; at the same time a ban on further burials was issued (only on Rheneia were burials still permitted). The same applied to births. This was followed by the establishment of the penteteric (five-yearly) Delia. In 422 the inhabitants were expelled from D., but only one year later brought back (Thuc. 5,1; 32,1).

C. Hellenistic period

In 314 BC the old regime came to an end. D. became the independent centre of the 'League of Islanders', and subsequently experienced a period of prosperity. Rich offerings flowed to the sanctuary. Decrees in honour of foreign benefactors attest to the significance of the sanctuary and the extent of its political and economic connections. Inscriptions give us a precise insight into the Delian temple administration and economy. The democratic *pólis* of D. came under an *árchon*, a council and a popular assembly. Care of the sanctuary fell to four annually elected *hieropoioí*. In around 250 BC the first Romans moved to D.; they soon predominated over other immigrants. At their urging and to counterbalance Rhodes as a commercial centre, in 166 BC Rome declared D. a free port, giving it back to the Athenians. The indigenous inhabitants were expelled a second time, to be replaced by an Attic *epimelētḗs* with cleruchs. D. experienced another upturn in prosperity; many foreign groups settled and erected magnificent club houses. Aegean and Syrian divinities were worshipped, and D. expanded to the extent still evident today from its ruins (cf. esp. Str. 10,5,2; 4; 14,5,2). On some days more than 10,000 slaves were traded on the Delian slave-market, the biggest in Greece.

D. Late Republic and Imperial period

In 88 BC D. was sacked by naval forces belonging to Mithridates VI; 20,000 people, mostly Italians, lost their lives (App. Mith. 28; Paus. 3,23,3ff.; for an estimate of the population [2]). In the following year D. was regained by Sulla. After a measure of rebuilding, in 69 BC pirates allied to Mithridates devastated D. once more (Phlegon, FGrH 257 fr. 12,13). D. never again recovered from this, even though C. Valerius Triarius built a wall around city and sanctuary [3]. D. declined in importance owing to changes in political relations in the Aegean and in trade routes, and was eventually abandoned by its inhabitants. Pausanias (8,33,2) reports D. as uninhabited apart from the custodians of the sanctuaries. Various attempts by Athens to sell the island came to nothing.

E. Early Christian period

So far as can be judged from the presence of several small churches, there was some degree of revival in the early Christian period. Traces of settlement become scarcer again from the 7th cent., and from the 14th cent. onwards it would seem that D. was entirely deserted.

III. Archaeology
A. The sanctuary B. Secular structures

A. The sanctuary

Excavations by the French School began in 1874 and continue to this day. The centre of the excavations, the Sanctuary of Apollo, lies in the west of the island by the harbour, which is open but protected by a 150 m-long breakwater of granite blocks (from the archaic period), still readily visible under the water. Designations for the many excavated structures, for the most part in a very ruinous state, are often uncertain, especially as there is no ancient description of D. The main entrance to the sanctuary lay to the south, right and left of the sacred way, and was flanked by two halls of columns. The westernmost of these was established by Philip V, who ruled over the Cyclades until his defeat at Cynoscephalae in 197 BC. The oldest part of the site is in the south-west, cut off to the south and west by the Stoa of the Naxians. Here may have stood the celebrated altar made of goats' horns, later protected by a building. The related building was probably the large Parian marble structure to the north of the paved square. North of the stoa was the Stoa of the Naxians, an assembly building with vestibule and inner row of columns, and bearing the base of the approx. 8.5 m-high Naxian statue of Apollo. The god was depicted in the characteristic archaic manner as a *kouros*, hands along his thighs and with a metal belt; its base is still visible today. Three small temples set side by side were dedicated to Apollo. The older *poros* temple with the cult image was probably an ante-structure; nearby to the south stood a peripteral temple, which, however, had scarcely progressed as far as the terrace stage when the Athenians moved the League's treasury in 454 BC. A long interval followed before it was completed as a temple of the Doric order by the Delian citizenry after 303 BC. Like the *poros* temple, this too was orientated to the west on the old cult site. In 425/417 BC the Athenians finally built the third temple, of Pentelian marble. Many aspects of the structure indicate the work of → Callicrates, who also built the Temple of Nike on the Acropolis. To the north and east was a wide arc of five buildings, termed 'treasuries' by analogy with similar buildings at Olympia and Delphi. The continuation to the north was formed by an elongated building interpreted as a → bouleuterion. The Sanctuary of Apollo is adjoined to the north-west by the Hellenistic Artemisium, a separate precinct within the sanctuary as a whole, enclosed by columned halls. Its focus was the small temple with Ionic columned frontage from the 2nd half of the 2nd cent. BC. In contrast to the temple of Apollo, it, like its predecessor structure, was orientated to the south-east. In the Hellenistic period the sacred precinct was appreciably extended to the east and north. Here in around 300 BC was built the so-called 'Sanctuary of the Bulls', a long building in which a trireme was probably installed. The hall was therefore a foundation of the Macedonian king Demetrius; but it was completed by his son → Antigonus [2] Gonatas, who also dedicated the ship to Apollo in thanks for his victory over Ptolemy's fleet. This Ship Hall or the cella in its rearmost section was lit by an Ionic-order lantern in its roof. The precinct was bounded to the north by Antigonus [2] Gonatas' 120 m-long stoa, built *c.* 253/250 BC.

B. Secular structures

The market and complexes serving the commercial life and administration of the *pólis* always lay outside the sacred precinct. Thus in 126/5 BC the Attic *epimelētēs* Theophrastes set up a new market outside the western edge of the sanctuary and north of the quayside. Already *c.* 208 BC the citizens of D. had built a great stoa further to the north. This area had been inhabited since time immemorial, even if no closed residential town had developed here. East of the great stoa and north of the Sanctuary of Apollo lay the Agora of the Italians. The rectangular, 70 × 100 m courtyard was surrounded by a two-storey hall of columns. A gate gave access to it from the direction of the harbour. Next to this gate were the foundations of the temple of Leto. Before this market was built, the entire area probably belonged to the goddess, including the sacred lake, on whose shore in the Delian version of the legend Leto supported by a palm-tree gave birth to Apollo and Artemis. The temple, which was orientated to the south, dated from the middle of the 6th cent. BC. The foundation of the marble seated statue of the goddess still survives. A processional way led to the lake, with a 50 m-long terrace on which stood nine (nowadays severely weathered) lions of Naxian marble (probably in the 7th cent. BC). Owing to the chronic danger of epidemic, at the beginning of the 20th cent. the lake was filled in; its original extent is today marked by a low, modern wall. In antiquity the lake probably received its water via a tributary stream of the Inopus. In this area stood the houses of the foreign merchant groups, such as that of the Poseidoniasts from → Berytus, several private houses, palaces, a *hippodromos*, a gymnasium, and after 88 BC a synagogue. Until the end of the 3rd cent. BC there was only one market on D., that of the Delian citizens. The buildings of the community administration were also adjacent to it. To the south and south-east the residential town with its narrow streets and rich Hellenistic houses, mostly of two storeys with peristyle, cisterns and often mosaic floors, hugged the slopes of Mount Cynthus. The theatre had room for an audience of 4,000–5,000. On various terraces on either bank of the Inopus were the sanctuaries of oriental gods. Also worthy of mention here is an ante temple of Hera from the 6th cent. BC, erected over an earlier structure. Inscr.: IG XI 2; 4, 1912/14 (no more have appeared); IDélos.

1 G. Gruben, Die Tempel der Griechen, 1966 ([4]1986), 146ff. 2 P. Roussel, La population de Délos à la fin du IIe siècle avant J.-C., in: BCH 55, 1931, 438–449 3 J. Delorme, Chronique des fouilles, s.v. Délos, in: BCH 74, 1950, 364ff.

D. VAN BERCHEM, Commerce et écriture, in: MH 48, 1991, 129ff.; E. BETHE, Das archa. D., in: Die Ant. 14, 1938, 81ff.; P. BRUNEAU, Recherches sur les cultes des Délos à l'époque hell. et à l'epoque impériale, 1970; P. BRUNEAU, Exploration arch. de D., 1972; Id., J. DUCAT, Guide des Délos, 31983; P. BRUNEAU, Deliaca VIII, in: BCH 114, 1990, 553ff.; Id., La céramique pergaménienne à reliefs appliqués de Délos, in: BCH 115, 1991, 597ff.; Id., Deliaca IX, in: BCH 115, 1991, 377ff.; A. CHAMDOR, D., l'île d'Apollon, 1960; F. COARELLI, D. MUSTI, H. SOLIN (ed.), Delo e l'Italia (Opuscula Instituti Romani Finlandiae II), 1982; P.L. COUCHOUD, J. SVORONOS, Les monuments des 'taureaux' à D., in: BCH 45, 1921, 270ff.; P. COURBIN, D., Fasc. XXXIII. L'Oikos des Naxiens (1980), 1982; F. COURBY, Notes topopographiques et chronologiques sur le sanctuaire d'Apollon délien, in: BCH 45, 1921, 174ff.; Délos. Études Déliennes publiées à l'occasion du centième anniversaire du début des fouilles de l'Ecole francaise d'Athèneà Délos, 1974; W. DÉOMA, La vie privée des Déliens, 1948; Exploration archéologique de D, 1902–1985 (35 vols.); H. GALLET DE SANTERRE, Délos primitive et archaique, 1958; Id., La terrasse des lions, le Létoon et le monument de granit à D., 1959; C. HABICHT, Zu den Epimeleten von D.167–88, in: Hermes 119, 1991, 194ff.; A.E. KALPAXIS, Die Pfostenlöcher unter dem Naxieroikos auf Delos, in: F. KRINZINGER, B. OTTO, E. WALDE-PSENNER (ed.), FS Bernhard Neutsch (Innsbrucker Beitr. zur Kulturwiss. 21), 1980, 237ff.; KIRSTEN/KRAIKER, 489ff.; LAUFFER, 181ff.; D. MERTENS, Der Tempel von Segesta, 1984, 220–227; A.C. ORLANDOS, D. chrétienne, in: BCH 60, 1936, 68ff.; J. PARIS, Les établissements maritimes de D., in: BCH 40, 1916, 5ff.; H.W. PARKE, Polycrates and D., in: CQ 46, 1946, 105ff., C. PICARD, J. REPLAT, Recherches sur la topographie du hiéron délien, in: BCH 48, 1924, 217ff.; A. PLASSART, Les sanctuaires et les cultes du mont Cynthe, 1929; N.K. RAUH, Was the Agora of the Italians an 'établissement du sport'?, in: BCH 116, 1992, 293ff.; PHILIPPSON/KIRSTEN, 4, 110ff; G. REGER, Private property and private loans on independent D. (314–167 B.C.), in: Phoenix 46, 1992, 322ff.; Id., The Public Purchase of Grain on Independent D., in: Classical Antiquity 12, 1993, H. 2. 300ff.; J. TRÉHEUX, L'administration financière des 'epi ta hiera a Delos', in: BCH 115, 1991, 349ff.; Id., L'unité de pesée et l'unité de compte des hiéropes à D. Economics of cult in the ancient Greek World. Proceedings of the Uppsala symposium, 1990; T. LINDERS, B. ALROTH (ed.), Uppsala: Acta universitatis Uppsaliensis. Boreas. Uppsala studies in ancient mediterranean and Near Eastern civiliations, 21, 1992, 21ff.; R. VALLOIS, Topographie délienne I, in: BCH 48, 1924, 411ff.; II, 53, 1929, 185ff.; R. VALLOIS, L'architecture hellénique et hellénistique à D. jusqu' à l'éviction des Déliens (166 av. J.-C.). I. Les monuments, 1944; II. Les constructions antiques de Délos, 1953; C. VIAL, D. indépendante (314–167 av. J.-C.), 1957; Id., Les sources de revenus des Déliens à l'époque hellenistique. L'origine des richesses dépensées dans la ville antique, in: PH. LEVEAU (ed.), Actes du colloque organisé à Aix-en-Provence par l'U.E.R. d'histoire, les 11 et 12 mai 1984 (Aix-en-Provence Cedex: Université de Provence), 1985, 47ff.; F. DURRBACH, Choix d'inscriptions de Délos I, Textes historiques, 1921/23; H. PHILIPPART, Bibl., in: Rev. belge de Philologie 1, 1912, 784ff.

H.KAL.

Delphi (Δελφοί; *Delphoí*), Delphi.

I. TOPOGRAPHY AND ARCHAEOLOGY II. ORGANIZATION AND HISTORY III. ORACLE

I. TOPOGRAPHY AND ARCHAEOLOGY

A. SITE B. SANCTUARY OF APOLLO C. ATHENA SANCTUARY IN MARMARIA D. SETTLEMENT E. QUARRIES F. NECROPOLEIS G. DISCOVERY AND EXCAVATION H. LITERARY ECHO

A. SITE

Delphi, with its sanctuary of Apollo, lies at an altitude of 533 to 600 m. on the south slope of Mt. Parnassus (main summit 2,457 m.), by the cleft of the Castalia Gorge. The Phaedriads (around 1,200 m.) overlook its rocky location resembling an amphitheatre (πετρώδες χωρίον, θεατροειδές; Str. 9,3,3) that looks out over the Pleistos Gorge at the Kirphis Mountains on the other side. The landscape has been shaped by powerful geological faults and fractures. The terrace consists of conglomerate and flysch over a base of limestone. Aquiferous strata make the ground unstable, and in repeated landslips rubble and rocks have come down on the site. The 'Rock of the Sibyl' is a typical earlier example (cf. detailed map, no. 23), but major landslides have also occurred in historical times: *c.* 373 BC on the NW of the sanctuary, in 1870 on the Castalia spring, 1905 on Marmaria and 1935 through the eastern part of the Apollo sanctuary.

B. SANCTUARY OF APOLLO

The approximately rectangular (*c.* 135 m. by 190 m.) sanctuary is surrounded by a late 6th-cent. wall (with 4th-cent. renovations), which negotiated the incline on the east and west sides in large gradations; simple openings served as gates. The crest of the wall was decorated with statues — hence the sanctuary's epithet χαλκοστέφανον, 'crowned with bronze' (Diod. Sic. 11,14,4 and Anth. Pal. App. 242; CID II 182). The main entrance is in the SE, from the Roman or early Byzantine marketplace (cf. detailed map, to which all the following numbers refer).

The cult of Apollo is attested by votive offerings from the early 8th cent. BC onwards and by buildings from the late 7th cent. BC. Written tradition describes a sequence of six temples; the scattered remains of a Doric building (early 6th cent. BC) belong to the fourth of these. The Doric style was retained for all subsequent buildings. The older wall of the sanctuary (*c.* 570 BC) runs 13.30 m. to the inside of the later wall on the east and west sides. Among the remains originating from this first, monumental phase are the foundations of treasuries (nos 26–30, in particular in the area of the later temple terrace), the delicate structural elements of a tholos and a small, canopy-shaped (?) rectangular construction, decorated with unusual metopes, both used as building material for the treasury of the Sicyonians (no. 10), the magnificent marble sphinx column of the Naxians (no. 24), the colossal statues of Cleobis

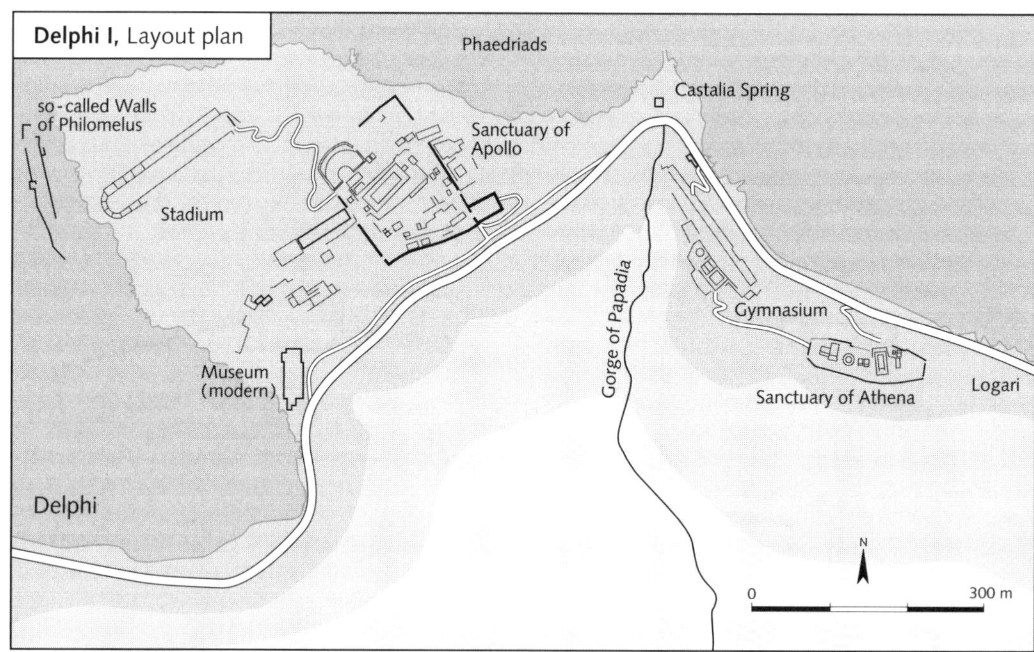

and Biton, as well as the golden and silver votive offerings dedicated by Croesus (Hdt. 1,50f., CID II 79, 81, cf. 102, 108). Votive offerings made of precious metals were melted down by the Phocians for the war of 356–346 BC, but although they are said to have dug for hidden treasures, the valuable items ritually buried in 400 BC in front of the Athenian portico (no. 22) were preserved, and unearthed in 1939.

The temple fire of 548/7 BC (Hdt. 2,180; Paus. 10,5,13) provided the opportunity for extending and renovating the sanctuary. This included the powerful 'curved polygonal' wall supporting the temple terraces (no. 25), which in the passage of time, like almost all suitable stone surfaces, has been covered with inscriptions. The new temple construction (no. 45) was completed around 500 BC by members of the Alcmaeonid family who had been exiled from Athens (Hdt. 5,62); artists from Athens collaborated in it. The treasury constructions of that time form two groups: the fine, mainland-Doric poros architecture and the incomparably well-preserved Cycladic marble architecture, lavishly decorated with figures and ornaments, foremost among them the Siphnian Treasury (no. 11). The treasury of the Athenians (no. 16) constitutes the programmatic synthesis of Doric architecture and insular marble art. Overall the votive offerings represent a monumental 'history' of the Greeks [1]. The forecourt of the temple with the large Altar of the Chians (no. 42) was bounded by the great Tripod of the Crotoniates (no. 39) and the victory monuments from the Persian and Carthaginian Wars: golden tripods (no. 50) on high columns (Bacchyl. 3,17: λάμπει δ᾽ ὑπὸ μαρμαρυγαῖς ὁ χρυσός, ὑψιδαιδάλτων τριπόδων σταθέντων πάροιθε ναοῦ, 'the gold of the high-built tripods in front of the temple glitters in the light'); of these the serpentine column of the Tripod of Plataea (no. 38) has been standing in the hippodrome of Constantinople since Emperor Constantine's time; the last monument from the Persian Wars was the statue of Athena on a palm marking the battle at the Eurymedon (no. 44); over all of these towered the colossal statue of Apollo for the victory at Salamis. Other monuments were added later: the 15 m-high statue of Apollo Sitalkas (no. 51) for the Amphictyonian victory over the Phocians in 346 BC, the Rhodian pillar with sun chariot (no. 37) and the commemorative pillars of Prusias (no. 52) and of Perseus (no. 49), the latter being appropriated by Aemilius Paullus after his victory at Pydna (168 BC).

The devastation from the rock-slide of 373 BC required the complete rebuilding of the north-west section including the temple. The *ischégaon* (no. 54) shored up the accumulated mound of rock debris and rubble. The famous 'Charioteer' of the bronze chariot, which Polyzalus probably erected for his brother Hieron, lay hidden here. All the votive offerings were new, as also the theatre (no. 55) above them and the temple (no. 45). The latter stands on the reinforced south-western base of its predecessor and after repeated damage and subsequent, increasingly insufficient, renovation survived until the end of antiquity. The inscriptions that document construction expenses mention entrepreneurs, artists, technicians and supplies of materials from the surrounding region, from the Peloponnese, from Attica and Macedonia. The building ruins provide only vague and oblique references to the conduct of oracles, and a more accurate analysis is still awaited in connection with the question posed by an opening in the roof over the cella (cf. Just. 24,8,4: *per aperta fasti-*

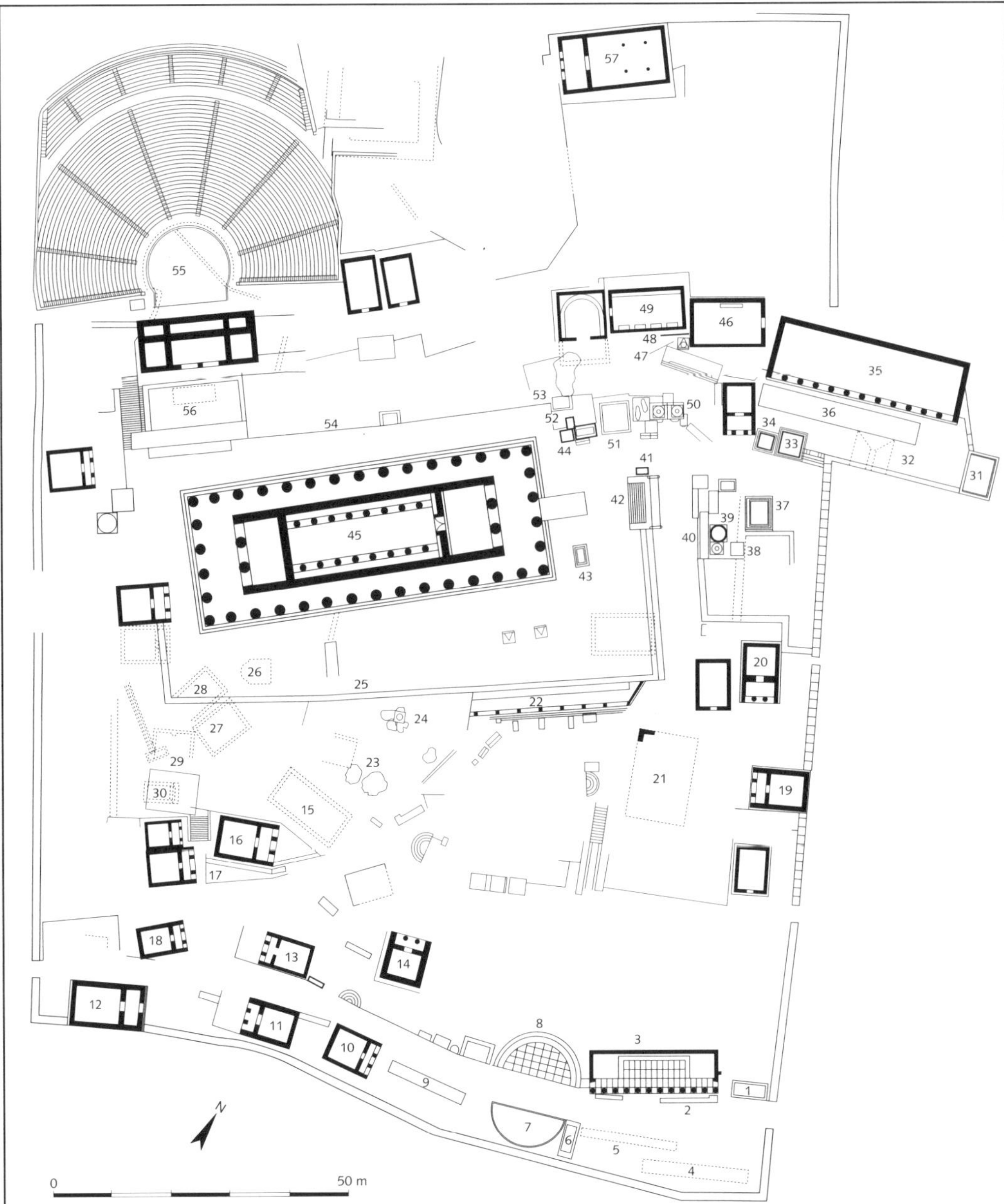

Delphi II, Sanctuary of Apollo (Detailed plan)

1 Lower votive offering of the Corcyreans: Bull
2 Votive offering of the Arcadians
3 Porticus
4 Votive offering of the Lacedaemonians: 'Nauarchoi'
5 Votive offering of the Athenians for Marathon: 'Eponymoi'
6, 7, 8 Votive offerings of the Argives
9 Lower votive offering of the Tarentinians
10 Treasury of the Sicyonians
11 Treasury of Siphnus
12 Treasury of the Thebans
13 Treasury of the Megarians
14 Treasury of Cnidus
15 Town Hall (?)
16 Treasury of the Athenians
17 Votive offering of the Athenians for Marathon
18 Treasury of the Boeotians
19 Treasury of Cyrene
20 Treasury of Acanthus
21 Treasury of Corinth
22 Porticus of the Athenians
23 Rock of the Sibyl
24 Sphinx votive offering of the Naxians
25 Polygonal wall supporting the temple terrace
26, 27, 28 buildings abandoned after 548/47
29 Well at the Asclepieion
30 So-called Etruscan Treasury
31, 32, 33, 34, 35, 36 Buildings and monuments on the Terrace of Attalus
37 Pillar of the Rhodians, with Sun chariot
38 Tripod from Plataeae (?)
39 Tripod of the Crotoniates
40 Upper votive offering of the Tarentinians
41 Pillar of the Aetolians for Eumenes II.
42 Altar of Apollo
43 Earlier so-called pillar of Paullus Aemilius
44 Votive offering of the Athenians: 'Palm of the Eurymedon'
45 Temple of Apollo
46 So-called district of Neoptolemus
47 Acanthus column
48 Archaic support wall
49 Votive offering of Daochus
50 Tripod votive offerings of Gelon and Hieron
51 Apollo Sitalces
52 Column of Prusias
53 Rock and Spring (so-called »Cassotis«)
54 Support wall ('Ischegaon')
55 Theatre
56 Votive offering of Craterus
57 Lesche of the Cnidians

gia). The Omphalos may well have been located in the opisthodome of the Temple [2].

The memorials of the Athenians (no. 5; 16; 17) ('Marathon-base'), Lacedaemonians (no. 4, 'Nauarch-Monument', for the victory of Aegos Potamos), Argives (*i.a.* the 'Doureios Hippos', the 'Trojan Horse', (no. 6; 7; 8) and Arcadians (no. 2) attest to the battles of the 5th and 4th cents. BC for dominance of Greece; they stand along the so-called Sacred Way. The nomenclature is modern; its course in the upper level is not ancient but Byzantine; the pavement contains inscriptions from the sanctuary. The Macedonians and their supporters had monuments above the temple: the monument of Craterus (no. 56) with the lion-hunt of Alexander and the votive offering of Daochus (no. 49). The 'female dancers'- or 'acanthus-column' with a tripod (no. 47) dates back to the Pythian pilgrimage from Athens in 336 BC, the unique sketches of hymns with musical notes on the Athenian Treasury (no. 16) to that of 128 BC.

The stoas were used, like the treasuries, for preserving the votive offerings but also for the comfort of pilgrims. The Stoa of the Athenians (no. 22) backed against the temple terrace. The West Stoa lies outside the sanctuary enclosure, the Attalus terrace, with the temple of Dionysus, monumental altar, pillar monuments and vestibule, protrudes into the sanctuary from the east (no. 31–36). The Lesche of the Cnidians (no. 57), a closed banquet construction in the north-east of the sanctuary, contained the famous paintings of Polygnotus. The stadium of the Pythian Games lies at the foot of the rock wall above the sanctuary. Its oldest visible components go back to the period of around 300 BC; Herodes Atticus (died AD 177) provided the last, though not quite completed, furnishings with stone seats, well structure and gate of honour. The location of the hippodrome is uncertain.

C. Athena Sanctuary in Marmaria

The sanctuary of Athena Pronaia (or *Pronoia*) stands on a stone terrace at the east of the site (cf. map). The oldest finds date from the Mycenaean period. The history of its construction runs roughly parallel to that of the main sanctuary: early archaic Doric temple around 600 BC, late archaic successors towards 500 BC, two treasuries with exquisite ornamentation. Representative of its construction heyday in the 4th cent. are the tholoi, an exemplary construction described in literature by its architect Theodorus (Vitr. De arch. 7, praef. 12), and a spaciously constructed prostylon temple with a delicate mixture of Doric exterior and Ionian interior architecture. Because of the scanty references in Pausanias, the significance of the construction is largely uncertain.

D. Settlement

In the Mycenaean period the Pleistos valley boasted a dense population. The significant locations are on the mountain spur at Chryso (Krisa) and the harbour area of Kirrha; the population decline in the 'Dark Ages' was less dramatic in D. than in the environs. The residential remains, especially in the north-east of the later sanctuary, date from the period of the 8th and 7th cents. BC.

The most important profane monumental constructions are wells, especially that of Castalia, and the gymnasium, a splendid early example of its kind (end of the 4th cent BC, restored by the Romans), with open and covered racetrack, swimming pool and rooms for instruction (bibliography: Syll.[3] 823). The constructions of the Roman and Byzantine periods, including thermal baths and the conversion of the Stoa of Attalus into a cistern, have left little of the earlier buildings. The city lacked any systematic fortification; only the hill in the west, probably in the 4th cent. BC, and the eastern approach, at a later undetermined period, were fortified.

Remains of churches, scattered building ornamentation and finds of small items, *i.a.* good-quality, locally produced lamps, date from the Christian period. The remains of a church with remarkable floor mosaics, found *extra muros* in the north of the modern site, were transferred to the forecourt of the museum.

E. Quarries

For the demanding constructions of the earlier period, large-scale supplies of stone material were obtained from the mainland or from the islands by the architects, whom we either know or suspect to have been from outside the area. From the 4th cent. BC very good local limestone was extracted from quarries that are amongst the area's attractions.

F. Necropoleis

The cemeteries extend west of the sanctuary and the city over the area of the protruding spine of rocks and east over the less steep slopes of the Pleistos valley; the burial sites held rich finds from the Mycenaean period onwards; Roman heroa, arcosolia and chamber graves are visible above ground, containing impressive sarcophagi. Of the imported ceramics, each typical of its period, the Apollo dish with its white background stands out; famous finds are the grave stele of an athlete and the Meleager Sarcophagus; the many exquisite terracottas have only been partly published [3].

G. Discovery and Excavation

The following is a brief outline: 1438 visit by Cyriacus of Ancona, further visits by Western travellers after 1676. Excavations by the Greek government in 1837/8, by the Berlin Academy with K. O. Müller in 1840, and in 1858 the location's change of name from Kastri to Delphi; first French excavation in 1860–62. In 1891 transfer of the location and start of the still ongoing excavation and investigation by the École Française in Athens. In 1903 dedication of the museum as a new construction. In 1906 restoration of the Athenian treasury; in 1935/6 extension of the museum; in 1938 restoration of the columns and entablature of the tholos, and of the columns at the eastern front of the temple in 1938–1941 [4].

H. Literary Echo

D. is the embodiment of a location where a dramatic sense of landscape, cult, myth, legend, poetry, science, art and history have come together as if by the divine inspiration of an oracle : 'Paysage inspiré! il est enthousiaste et lyrique' (Flaubert). The location's spiritual significance is reflected over and over in literature: H. Hom. ad Apollinem 282ff.; Pind. Pyth. 9,44–49; 8. Paean; Aesch. Eum. 1–33; Hdt. 1,46ff., 92 and passim; Eur. IT. 1234–1283; Eur. Ion; Pl. Resp. 4,427Bf., Pl. Leg. 5,738Bff., 6,759D, 8,828A; Plut. De E; Plut. De Pyth. or.; Paus. 10,5,5ff.; Heliodorus, Aithiopika 2,26ff.; 3,1; Angelos Sikelianos, Sibylla [5].

1 A. Jacquemin, Offrandes monumentales de Delphes, 1999 2 P. Amandry, Notes de top. et d'architecture delphique: IX. L'opisthodome du temple d'Apollon, in: BCH 117, 1993, 263–283 3 I. Konstantinou, in: AD 1964, 218–221 pl. 258–262 4 P. Amandry, Delphes oublié. Inst. de France, Académie des Inscr. et Belles-Lettres, Séance publique annuelle en commémoration du centenaire de la Grand Fouille de Delphes par l'École Française d'Athènes 1992, no. 16, 17–33 5 R. Jacquin, L'esprit de Delphes: Anghélos Sikélianos, 1988.

J.-F. Bommelaer, Guide de Delphes. Le site. Dessins de D. Laroche, 1991 (critical overview of earlier literature); M. Maass, Das ant. Delphi. Orakel, Schätze und Monumente, 1993; O. Picard (ed.), Guide de Delphes. Le musée, 1991.

MI.MA.

II. Organization and History

A. City, Territory and Sanctuary B. Civil administration and religious control C. History

A. City, Territory and Sanctuary

In antiquity the territory of D. (*Delphís*) extended from the wooded hills of Parnassus to the fertile coastal plains of Crisa, linked to Central Greece by the Lebadea road that ran over the hill of Arachova and joined the Chaeroneia-Panopeus-Daulis road (itinerary of the Athenian festival emissaries: Str. 9,3,12). Further to the south, a third road led through Ambryssus and Anticyra; from Thessaly, D. could be reached by a road leading across Parnassus to Amphissa. The harbour of Cirrha (today's Itea) offered easy access to travellers journeying from the Isthmus, the Peloponnese and the west.

The sanctuary of Apollo lay on a trapezoid-shaped stretch of ground, with main access to the south-east of the city and the Castalian spring, whence the Sacred Way (*hierà hodós*) led to the god's temple (cf. overview map). As well as the *témenos* with its sacred and profane buildings, the sanctuary of Apollo contained: the sacred soil (ἱερὰ χώρα, *hierà chṓra*), which encompassed the mountain area up to Parnassus, a plain that extended to Anticyra, a section of the Pleistus valley and, after the 1st Sacred War (see below), the dedicated area, the valley of Crisa. Movable goods (ἱερὰ χρήματα, *hierà chrḗmata*) increased through the contributions of the faithful (private citizens and states), through offerings and spoils of war and also through the *pélanos* (a tax imposed on the use of the oracle). The coexistence of the *hierà chṓra*, the dedicated territory and the *Delphís* with the *chṓrai* of neighbouring cities (Anticyra, Ambryssus, Phlygonium, Amphissa) was not easy; arbitration decisions and rulings by the amphictyonies sought, from the classical period to the Roman era, to bring some order to the contested territorial claims: FdD III 2,89,136,383; III 4, 276–283, 290–296; Sherk 37; [1].

Archaeological finds show that, in the middle of the 9th cent. BC, D. was a city that had commercial relationships with neighbouring territories, extended, in particular, northwards, in the 8th cent., and had a population increase in the 7th cent. The spread of the cult of Apollo proceeded more slowly. Imported ceramics (Achaean, Thessalian, Euboean, Boeotian, Attic) are to be found in the sanctuary only in the last quarter of the 8th cent., evidence of the cult's expansion beyond its own territory of origin, until it succeeded in establishing itself as a Panhellenic cult after 590 BC following the 1st Sacred War (see below).

B. Civil administration and religious control

The Panhellenic role of the sanctuary helped distance the city of D. from Phocian history (according to Paus. 4,74,11 the residents of D. denied their descent from the Phocians). Like all *póleis*, D. had political and administrative institutions: the popular assembly (*halía*), the council (*boulḗ*), magistrates, including the eponymous *árchōn*, the *gymnasíarchos* and two treasurers (*tamíai*), who were responsible for the administration of the public budget (CID II 31f.). The government had an aristocratic character. According to tradition, the sanctuary was erected on the spot in which Apollo, arriving from Delos (Hom. ad Apollinem 285–374), is said to have killed the snake (*Pythṓn*) — the origin of the epithet *Pýthios* for the god and of the name *Pythṓ* for Mycenaean D. —, a place that was already dedicated to divinities (principally Poseidon, Athena, Ge or Gaia, Themis) and seat of an oracle (possibly linked to local deities). This was also the home of the *omphalós*, the sacred stone that marked the centre of the earth. The authority of the oracle and the religious centre together had great significance for the political and legislative development of the Greek states. For, in his capacity as *archēgétēs*, Apollo directed the founding of colonies, as *nomothétēs* he intervened in the legislative process of the *póleis*, whether with his own proposals or by his acquiescence, and numerous decisions of the state authorities were subject to the response of the oracle, both on religious and profane matters [3]. Celebrations (*Pýthia*) were held in the sanctuary every four years with contests that had a predominantly musical and lyrical character; according to tradition, they were introduced for the first time in 586/5 BC and financed with the war booty acquired in the destruction of Crisa

(Paus. 10,7,2–8; cf. Str. 9,3,8–10). There was a list of the winners (from 582/1 onwards) compiled by Aristotle and Callisthenes (Plut. Solon 11,1; Syll.³ 275) [4]. The sanctuary and its property were administered by the council of the Amphictyons (*hieromnámones*) [5]. The city of D. appointed the clergy, who were selected from the local aristocracy, as well as the cult staff and the prophetess. In connection with the temple's reconstruction after 373 BC the college of *naopoioí* was created with the task of conducting the work and supervising expenses (CID II 1–36, 46–66) [6]. Every Greek had to be guaranteed free access to the sanctuary of Apollo (Thuc. 4,118,1; 5,18,1f.)

C. History

In the context of the development described above, the history of the sanctuary features phases of Thessalian supremacy (particularly in the 6th cent. BC), a short but dramatic controlling influence of Philip II (2nd half of the 4th cent BC), and a long period of Aetolian domination (3rd/2nd cents BC) until its liberation by M.' Acilius Glabrio in 191 BC. The 'Sacred Wars' represent an important chapter in D.'s archaic and classical history. The first (*c.* 600–590 BC), led by the Thessalian Eurilochus (Hyp.; Pind. Pyth. 2), punished the city of Crisa, whose citizens had attacked and robbed pilgrims travelling to the temple from the harbour of Cirrha (Str. 9,3,4). The city and the 'cursed' harbour were destroyed and the plain of Crisa was consecrated with a ban on cultivation imposed on it (Aesch. 3,108; Dem. Or. 45,149–155; cf. CID I 10). The city of D. had to defend its 'separate status' several times against the claims of the Phocians, who wanted to erect the traditional Phocian *prostasía* ('direction') over the sanctuary again (Diod. Sic. 16,25,5; 27,3). An unsuccessful Delphic attempt in the middle of the 5th cent. (2nd Sacred War) was followed by the occupation of the sanctuary and the plundering of treasure after the Phocians had refused to pay a penalty imposed on them for cultivating the Crisa plain, whereupon the council of the Delphic amphictyony had decided upon military involvement (3rd Sacred War, 356–346 BC). That war and the following one against the Locrians of Amphissa, who had also been guilty of cultivating the consecrated territory and had also rebuilt Cirrha harbour, provided Philip II with the pretext for intervening in Greece. Mythical-historical tradition recalls an attack on the temple by the Phlegyae from Orchomenus (Paus. 10,4,1f.; cf. 9,36,3). Tradition also recounts the unsuccessful attempt by the Persians to conquer the place in 480 (Hdt. 8,35–39; Diod. Sic. 11,14,3f.), and also the occupation by the Galatae (279 BC) that was ended by the intervention of the Aetolians, occasioning commemorative ceremonies (*Sōtḗria*) [7], and the pillaging by Sulla (87–83 BC). The temple was also damaged in natural disasters such as fire, earthquake and rockslides from the Phaedriads (Hdt. 8,35–39; according to Diod. Sic. 11,14,3f., thus thwarting the Persian attack; Callim. 44,172–185; according to Just. 24,6–8 during the attack by the Galatae).

Under Roman domination D. began its inexorable decline, notwithstanding short periods of prosperity due to the philhellenism of some Roman emperors (Nero, the Flavians, Nerva, Trajan and Hadrian, who declared D. a *hierà pólis*), and in spite of the interest on the part of cultured men like Plutarch (priests in D. between AD 105 and 126) and patrons like Herodes Atticus. A further short period of prosperity in the 4th cent. is attested by Amm. Marc. (22,12,8–13,4). D. is mentioned in the It. Ant. 325 as a stopover on the road between Nicopolis and Athens and is included in the cities list of Hierocles (643,13). An edict of Theodosius (391/2) led to the closure of all pagan cult sites, and Arcadius ordered the destruction of the temple. In the 5th cent. AD, D. housed a Christian community and was a bishopric (Not. Episc. 758). In the Byzantine period it was no more than a large village that was invaded by Slavic bands between the end of the 6th and beginning of the 7th cents. (Const. Porph. De them. 89). Inscriptions: FdD III 1–6; CID I-II.

→ Amphiktyonia; → Apollo; → Oracles; → Pythia; → Temple

1 G. Daverio Rocchi, La 'hiera chora' di Apollo, la piana di Cirra e i confini di Delfi, in: Mél. P. Lévêque 1, 1988, 117–125 Id., Frontiera e confini nella Grecia antica, 1988, 134–142 2 I. Malkin, Religion and Colonization in Ancient Greece, 1988 3 C. Morgan, Athletes and Oracles, 1989 4 J. Bousquet, Delphes et les 'Pythioniques' d'Aristote, in: REG 97, 1984, 374–380 W. Spoerri, Epigraphie et littérature: à propos de la liste des Pythioniques à Delphes, in: Comptes et inventaires dans la cité grecque, Actes Coll. Neuchâtel en l'honneur de J. Tréheux (1986), 1988, 111–140 5 G. Roux, L'Amphictyonie, Delphes et le temple d'Apollon au IVe siècle, 1979 6 M. Sordi, La fondation du collège des naopes et le renouveau politique de l'Amphictyonie au IVe siècle, in: BCH 81, 1957, 38–75 7 J. Flacelière, Les Aitoliens à Delphes, 1937 G. Nachtergael, Les Galates en Grèce et les Soteria de Delphes, 1977 8 TIB I, 143–144.

G. Daux, Delphes au IIe et au Ier siècles depuis l'abaissement de l'Etolie jusqu'à la paix romaine, 1936; J. Defradas, Etudes delphiques, in: BCH Suppl. 4, 1977; J. Fontenrose, The Delphic Oracle, 1978; H. W. Parke, D. E. W. Wormell, The Delphic Oracle, 1956. G.D.R.

III. Oracle

For the Delphic oracle see → Apollo; → Divination; → Pythia

Delphica The round decorative table on three legs (→ Household equipment; → Furniture) was called *delphica* by the Romans in imitation of the Delphic tripod (Procop. Vand. 1,21). The *delphicae* mentioned in literature (Mart. 12,66f.; Cic. Verr. 2,4,131) are probably to be identified with surviving tables from, in particular, the cities around Vesuvius.

G. M. A. Richter, The Furniture of the Greeks, Etruscans and Romans, 1966, 111–112. R.H.

Delphic Oracle see → Pythia

Delphic Paeans see → Athenaeus [NP 7]; → Limenius; → Music

Delphini In the Roman → Circus a pedestal erected on the → *spina*, visible at some distance, with seven revolving dolphin shapes or eggs, was used to indicate the number of circuits already elapsed or still remaining. According to Cass. Dio 49,43, the dolphins of the Circus Maximus in Rome were donated (or restored) by Agrippa in 33 BC; the dolphin symbolized the elegance and speed of the chariots and moreover highlighted the connection between the circus games and their 'patron' → Neptunus. In the hippodrome at Olympia there was at the starting-point a single dolphin shape in bronze as part of the complicated starting-mechanism described by Pausanias (6,20,10).

A. Balil, Ova, Delphini, Roman Circus, in: Latomus 25, 1966, 867–870; S. Cerutti, The seven eggs of the C. Maximus, in: Nikephoros 6, 1993, 167–176; W.K. Quinn-Schoffield, Ova and Delphini of the Roman Circus, in: Latomus 25, 1966, 99–100. C.HÖ.

Delphinium Member of the crowfoot plant family (Ranunculaceae) *delphínion* in Dioscorides 3,73 (only RV; [1. 84] = 3,77 [2. 310]). Because of the dolphin-like or pony-like nectaries on the larkspur, it is probably identical with *D. ajacis L.* (Modern Greek καπουτσῖνος) and consists of about 200 varieties, of which eight are to be found in Greece and Italy. That includes the common field weed *D. staphisagria L.* (στάφις ἀγρία in Dioscorides 4,152 [1. 84] = 4,153 [2. 451f.], Modern Greek ψειρόχορτο, ψειροβότανο, Lat. *astaphis agria* in Plin. HN 23,17, *herba pedicularis, passula mutula, granum capitis, rosa regis, pituitaria*, lousewort, naked-lady etc.). The multiplicity of names demonstrates that the black seeds resembling raisins (currants, στάφις) and poisonous because of their alkaloids, were, despite Pliny's warning (ibid.), not only applied as an emetic but also to combat lice, scabies, toothache and, in the form of crushed petals in wine, snakebite.

1 Wellmann 1 2 Berendes C.HÜ.

Delphinius (Δελφίνιος; *Delphínios*, in Crete also Delphidios). Epiclesis of Apollo, attested in both Ionic and Doric (Crete) territory and often linked in antiquity, after the Homeric hymn to Apollo, to Delphi and the → dolphin: he is said to have led his priests to Delphi as a dolphin. Many academics adopted this etymology, even though the cults could not confirm it; there the god is thoroughly bound up in the concerns of the young citizens of the polis. In Miletus (then in → Olbia) he is the god of the → Molpoi, a group of the city elite, in Cretan Dreros he is linked to a temple in the shape of a house for men's gatherings, in Athens with Theseus' being recognized by his father and a special form of sacrifice (Plut. Thes. 12,2–6; Paus. 1,19,1).

Ph. Bourboulis, Apollo D., 1949; A.S. Russjajeva, Religia i kultu antichnoi Olvii, 1992; F. Graf, Apollon D., in: MH 36, 1979, 2–22. F.G.

Delphus (Δελφός; *Delphós*). Hero who gave his name to → Delphi. He controlled the territory around Parnassus, when → Apollo, arriving from Delos, entered Delphi (Aesch. Eum. 16 with schol.). Apollo or Poseidon was mentioned as his father, and Melaena, Celaeno or Thyia as his mother (Paus. 10,6,3–5; schol. Eur. Or. 1094; Hyg. Fab. 161). In some accounts D. is said to have been the leader of the Cretans who came to Phocis and called themselves *Delphi* after him (Phylarchos FGrH 81 F 85). Delphi was also called Pytho after his son Pythes or his daughter Pythis (Paus. 10,6,5; schol. Apoll. Rhod. 4,1405). Iconographically D. cannot be firmly identified anywhere.

L. Lacroix, D. et les monnaies de Delphes, Études d'archéologie numismatique, 1974, 37–51; E. Simon, s.v. Delphos, LIMC 3.1, 369–371. R.B.

Delta

[1] Term for the area at the mouth of the Nile, deriving from its resemblance to the triangular shape of the Greek alphabetical letter *delta*. The delta is bounded in the west by the μέγας ποταμός (*mégas potamós*) with the Heracleotic Mouth at Alexandria, and in the east by the Bubastic arm of the Nile including the Pelusian Mouth.

[2] Site at the fork of the Nile below Memphis (Str. 17,788).

[3] Even in antiquity the term *delta* was applied to other river mouths (mouth of the Indus, Str. 15,1,33; Arr. Anab. 5,4,1).

K.W. Butzer, s.v. D., LÄ 1, 1975, 1043–1052. R.GR.

Deltion, Deltos see → Writing tablet

Delubrum One of the Latin terms for sanctuary. Modern and to some extent ancient thinking has the term deriving from the Latin *deluere* ('to wash off', 'to soak') (Serv. Aen. 2,225, cf. ThLL, 471 s.v.); the connecting link is to be found in the watering-points at sanctuaries or temple sites where ritual washing took place before performing the sacrifice. The oldest epigraphical evidence is CIL I 1291 (3rd cent. BC ?) from Amiternum, where *delubrum* refers to the sacred grove of Feronia. In the constitution of Urso from the 1st cent. BC (*magistri ad fana templa delubra* [1. 415], l. 6f.) *delubrum* probably meant 'sanctuary area with temple', since *fana* (grove) and *templa* (temple building) are mentioned separately. In the list of sacrifices of the → Argei quoted by Varro (Ling. 5,52) *delubrum* (in the sense of 'shrine'?) is distinguished from *aedes* (as temple of a divinity) (cf. Varro in Non. p. 494); elsewhere, *delubrum* is in literary usage synonymous with *aedes* in elevated style (since Plaut. Poen. 1175 and Acc. trag.

593). In Cicero (Leg. 2,19) *delubrum* appears as a deliberately chosen term to mean 'sanctuaries featuring temples and situated in cities', as distinct from rural groves and cults without temples. Unlike terms such as → *fanum*, → *sacellum* or → *templum*, *delubrum* was not adopted into post-antique terminology.

1 M. CRAWFORD (ed.), Roman Statutes (BICS Suppl. 64), 1996

Å. FRIDH, Sacellum, Sacrarium, Fanum and related Terms, in: S.-T. TEODORSSON (ed.), Greek and Latin Studies in Memory of Caius Fabricius, 1990, 173–187; A. MOMIGLIANO, The Theological Efforts of the Roman Upper Classes in the First Century B.C., in: CPh 79, 1984, 199–211. F.G. and C.F.

Deluge, legend of the

I. ANCIENT ORIENT II. CLASSICAL ANTIQUITY

I. ANCIENT ORIENT

In Mesopotamia, the legend of the deluge is preserved in a Sumerian as well as an Akkadian version; the Akkadian one is transmitted in 17th-cent. BC copies of the → Atraḫasīs myth[3. 612–645]. Extensive passages reappear verbatim on the 11th tablet of the recension of the Epic of → Gilgamesh from Niniveh [3. 728–738], and the myth is later also transmitted by → Berosus [1. 20 f.]. The gods perceive the noisy behaviour of the humans as hubris, causing them to eliminate mankind with the aid of a great flood, in which all but one righteous man perish (Atraḫasīs, 'the great sage', in the eponymous myth, Utanapištī, 'I have found my life', in the epic of Gilgamesh). This righteous man receives prior warning, builds an 'ark', and is rescued together with numerous animals. In the historical tradition (e.g. in the list of Sumerian kings), the great flood is seen as the dividing line between two primeval epochs [2. 42 f.]. Important elements of the biblical tale of the Flood in Gen 6–8 (presumably dating from the 6th cent. BC) have been copied from Mesopotamian models during the time of the Babylonian exile. In Gen 6–8, human depravity is seen as the cause for God's action. Both the Atraḫasīs myth and Gen 6–8 place the deluge within an aetiological context: the lifespan of humans, unlimited before the deluge, is limited afterwards [4. 98 f.]. One of the reasons for unrestricted human procreation is high rate of childhood mortality, for which the female demon Lamaštu (→ Demons) was blamed; for that reason, clay tablets with the text of the Atraḫasīs myth were worn as → amulets. Repeated attempts to prove the Flood archaeologically have so far remained unsuccessful, probably also because they fail to recognize the character of the underlying myth as aetiology.

1 S. M. BURSTEIN, The Babyloniaca of Berossos, 1978
2 J. RENGER, Vergangenes Geschehen in der Text-Überl. des alten Mesopot., in: H.-J. GEHRKE, A. MÖLLER (ed.), Vergangenheit und Lebenswelt, 1996, 9–60 3 TUAT, vol. 3 4 C. WILCKE, Weltuntergang als Anfang, in: A. JONES (ed.), Weltende, 1999, 63–112. J. RE.

II. CLASSICAL ANTIQUITY

In Graeco-Roman literature, the deluge is particularly linked with → Deucalion and → Pyrrha [1], who, warned by → Prometheus, escaped Zeus' great flood and founded the human race by casting stones (Epicharmus fr. 113–120 PCG; Pind. Ol. 9,41–56; Ov. Met. 1,253–415; Apollod. 1,46–48). Correspondence with oriental texts (→ Atrahasis; Epic of → Gilgamesh; Gen. 6–8; see above I.) point to the origin of the topos in that region; the first Greek epic to deal with this subject was presumably the → 'Titanomachy' [1]. The Greek myth exhibits the familiar features from the oriental sources [3. 489–493]: the highest god unleashes the flood in order to destroy mankind and thus to demonstrate his power. Depite this, there is one human who is warned by the gods and escapes. This hero of the flood builds a box-shaped boat (*lárnax*), in which both he and his wife survive the flood caused by a deluge of rain, until the receding waters let them strand on a high mountain. After their rescue, they make a sacrifice. The main difference between the biblical version (see above I.) and the Graeco-Roman myth is the fact that the flood was originally limited to a particular region (Locris, Thessaly), and that other humans survived apart from the hero and his wife (still evident in Apollod. loc. cit.; [2. 73–76]). Nonetheless, the flood marks the change to a new epoch, as the hero creates humankind afresh and acts as a founder of civilization. The end of the Brazen Race is at times also traced back to the great flood (Apollod. loc. cit.). The Graeco-Roman deluge is entirely anthropocentric and — in contrast with the OT — completely ignores the animal kingdom.

In philosophy, deluge myths are characterized by the periodical reappearance of such catastrophes, which because of the destruction in their wake become turning-points in human history (Anaximand. 12 A 27; Xenoph. 21 A 33 DK; Aristot. Mete. 1,14,352a-b; Pl. Ti. 22c-e). According to Plato [1], the first and greatest of these floods destroyed the state of Atlantis (Pl. Criti. 110d–112a; Pl. Ti. 25c-d; → Oceanus).

→ Origin myths; → Natural catastrophes

1 J. N. BREMMER, Near Eastern and Native Trad. in Apollodorus' Account of the Flood, in: F. GARCÍA MARTÍNEZ, G. P. LUTTIKHUIZEN (ed.), Interpretations of the Flood, 1999, 39–55 2 G. A. CADUFF, Ant. S., 1986
3 M. L. WEST, The East Face of Helicon, 1997. J. STE.

Dema (Modern Greek Δέμα). Incomplete (?) towerless, polygonal wall, 4.3 km in length with numerous sally gates and two watchtowers that, at Ano Liosia, sealed the northern access between Parnes and Aigaleos from Thriasia into the Pedion. Constructed either in 404 BC after the banishment of the Thirty [2] or in 378/375 BC in the Boeotian War [1].

1 M.H. MUNN, The Defense of Attica, 1993 2 A. SKIAS, Τὸ λεγόμενον Δέμα καὶ ἄλλα ἐρείπια [*Tò legómenon Déma kaì álla ereípia*], in: ArchE 1919, 35–36.

J.P. ADAM, L'architecture militaire grecque, 1982, 25f. fig. 27, 205 fig. 119, 243; TRAVLOS, Attika 81–84 fig. 92–94. H.LO.

Demades (Δημάδης; *Dēmádēs*). Orator from Athens, * around 380 BC, son of Demeas (deme of Paeania), † 319. Along with references by contemporary orators and epigraphical evidence (collected in [6]), we have information about him from an article in the Suda. Like his father, D. was initially a sailor and then, at a point in time that has not been authoritatively established, he turned to politics, initially and even later (cf. [4]) often in concert with Demosthenes. After 338 D. became one of the leaders of the pro-Macedonian party, achieved Alexander's lenient treatment of Athens after the destruction of Thebes (335), prevented support for Agis III, (330), proposed divine honours for Alexander (324/3) and negotiated peace with Antipater after the Lamian War (322), linked with the banning and death of Demosthenes. In 319, with his son Demeas, D. was himself killed by Cassander because of traitorous connections with Perdiccas.

It is uncertain whether his speeches were ever committed to writing but in any case none was available in the 1st cent. BC (Cic. Brut. 36), and there is uncertainty about even the titles that have survived. The extant speech carrying his name Ὑπὲρ τῆς δωδεκαετίας (*Hypèr tês dōdekaetías*) is generally regarded as not genuine. D.'s strength was (in contrast to Demosthenes) his art of improvisation, and he impressed with brilliant and witty phrasings that were soon collected and gained fame as Δημάδεια (*Dēmádeia*). Together with Demosthenes he was a popular subject of rhetorical → *declamationes*.

EDITIONS: F. BLASS, Dinarchi orationes, [2]1888 (repr. 1967) J.O. BURTT, Minor Attic Orators 2, 1954, 334–359 V. DE FALCO, [2]1954.
BIBLIOGRAPHY: 1 BLASS, [3]1962, 3,2, 266–278 2 M. DIECKHOFF, Zwei Friedensreden, in: Altertum 15, 1969, 74–82 3 M. GIGANTE, Fata D., in: Studi De Falco, 1971, 187–191 4 A. LINGUA, Demostene e D., in: Giornale italiano di filologia 30, 1978, 27–46 5 M. MARZI, D. politico e oratore, in: Atene e Roma 36, 1991, 70–83 6 A.N. OIKONOMIDES, Δημάδου τοῦ Παιανιέως ψηφίσματα καὶ ἐπιγραφικαί, περὶ τοῦ βίου πηγαί, in: Plato 8, 1956, 105–129 7 I. WORTHINGTON, The context of [D.] On the twelve years, in: CQ 41, 1991, 90–95.
M.W.

Demaenetus (Δημαίνετος; *Dēmaínetos*).
[1] Epithet of → Asclepius in Elis, from the name of the cult founder (Paus. 6,21,4).
[2] D. from Parrhasia, a town in Arcadia. He is said to have been transformed into a wolf after he ate the flesh of a boy whom the Arcadians had sacrificed to Jupiter Lycaeus. After 10 years he became human again and was victorious in boxing at Olympia (Scopas FGrH 413 F 1; Varro in Aug. Civ. 18,17). In Paus. 6,8,2 he is called Damarchos. R.B.
[3] Athenian, from the Buzyges clan. In the winter of 396/5 BC he sailed in an Athenian trireme to → Konon, thus risking another war with Sparta (so-called D. affair). On the advice of → Thrasybulus the Athenians informed Milon, the Spartan harmost on Aegina, who tried, in vain, to intercept him (Hell. Oxy. 9; 11 CHAMBERS; Aeschin. Or. 2,78). As *strategos* D., together with Chabrias, defeated the Spartan harmost Gorgopas at the end of 388, and D. was quartering in the Hellespont as *strategos* in the autumn of 387 (Xen. Hell. 5,1,10; 26). TRAILL, PAA 306140. W.S.
[4] Syracusan demagogue, who *c.* 340 BC harshly criticized → Timoleon's command in the field (Plut. Tim. 37,1–3). K.MEI.
[5] Citizen of Ptolemais/Akko. In 103 BC in the war with Alexander [16] Iannaeus, he prevented his homeland from surrendering to Ptolemy IX, who had been called upon to help (Jos. Ant. Iud. 13, 330). W.A.

Demagogue (δημαγωγός, *dēmagōgós*, 'leader of the people'). Aristophanes uses demagogue to mean a political leader in the mould of → Cleon (for example in Equ. 191–193; 213–222). The word was possibly coined in the 2nd half of the 5th cent. BC in Athens for the new style of populist politician whose position depended less on the clothing of office than the ability to speak persuasively at meetings of the popular assembly and at jury trials.

The older word for a political leader was *prostátēs*. Thucydides and Xenophon generally used *prostátēs*, but each of them twice used *dēmagōgós* to refer to democratic leaders (Thuc. 4,21,3; 8,65,2; Xen. Hell. 2,3,27; 5,2,7). Orators in the 4th cent. used the word occasionally, indeed as a neutral term for 'politician'; Isocrates used it for the great political leaders, Plato not at all. In Aristotle, however, it is used pejoratively for leaders of an extremely democratic bent (especially Pol. 4, 1292a4–37); in the author of the *Athēnaíōn Politeía* the word always has a democratic but not always hostile connotation.

1 W.R. CONNOR, The New Politicians of Fifth-Century Athens, 1971 2 M.I. FINLEY, Athenian Demagogues, in: Past & Present 21, 1962, 3–24 = Studies in Ancient Society, 1974, 1–25 3 R. ZOEPFFEL, Aristoteles und die Demagogen, in: Chiron 4, 1974, 69–90.
P.J.R.

Demarateion Famous silver coin from Syracuse with a weight of 10 Attic drachmas or 50 *litrai* (42.3 gm). After the victory of Gelon I over the Carthaginians at Himera in 480 BC, the latter donated to his wife Demarete, who had pleaded for lenient treatment on their behalf, a gold crown worth 100 talents in gratitude (Diod. Sic. 10,26,3). Shortly after 480/479 BC the coins were minted from the proceeds and 18 copies are known to us today. The obverse shows a chariot driver on a quadriga, the horses of which are crowned by a flying Nike; the reverse bears the image of Arethusa surrounded by four dolphins.
→ Dekadrachmon

E. BOEHRINGER, Die Münzen von Syrakus, 1929, 36ff.; SCHRÖTTER, 125; W. SCHWABACHER, Das D., 1958 (reviews: B. ANDREAE, in: Gymnasium 67, 1960, 270–272; P.A. CLEMENT, in: Gnomon 33, 1961, 823–826); H.A. CAHN (et al.), Griech. Münzen aus Großgriechenland und Sizilien. Basel, AM, und Slg. Ludwig, 1988, 125; H.A.

CAHN, Die bekränzte Arethusa. FS U. Westermark, 1992, 99–102; H.B. MATTINGLY, The D. controversy. A new approach, in: Chiron 22, 1992, 1–12; K. RUTTER, The Myth of the D., in: Chiron 23, 1993, 171–188. A.M.

Demaratus (Δημάρατος; *Dēmáratos*).

[1] Corinthian aristocrat, member of the → Bacchiadae family. D. made his fortune as a merchant around the middle of the 7th cent. BC, mainly through trade with Etruria. When he had to leave Corinth during the rule of → Cypselus he settled in Tarquinii with his followers and married an Etruscan aristocrat. According to ancient tradition the marriage produced two sons, one of whom became the first Etruscan king of Rome, → Tarquinius Priscus. While the Etruscan trade and D.'s emigration are probably historical, the traditional account of the sons should at least be treated with caution; it is possible that Greek authors attempted to construct an early connection between Etruscan and Greek aristocracies [1. 147f.] (cf. Pol. 6,11ᵃ,7; Dion. Hal. Ant. Rom. 3,46; Str. 5,2,2; 8,6,20; Cic. Rep. 2,19f.; Liv. 1,34,1ff.; 4,3,11; Plin. HN 35,16; 152).

D.'s story highlights the early contacts between Greece and Italy. His introducing the Greek alphabet into Italy is historiographic fiction.

1 A. BLAKEWAY, 'Demaratus', in: JRS 25, 1935, 129–149.

M. TORELLI, Die Etrusker, 1988, 144, 147ff.
M.MEI. and ME.STR.

[2] Athenian *stratēgós* who in 414/13 BC, with Pythodorus and Laispodias, brought assistance to Argus (Thuc. 6,105,2). TRAILL, PAA 306310; DEVELIN 153.
K.KI.

[3] (also Damaretus [1. 218]). From Heraea, in 520 BC (65th Olympiad) the first victor at Olympia in the newly instituted race in armour, with a second victory at the following Olympics (Paus. 6,10,4) [2. no. 132, 138]. Fragments of the easily misread inscription, mentioned by Paus. 6,10,5, on the victory statue for him and his son Theopompus (twice winner of the pentathlon [2. no. 189, 200]), have been preserved [3. 151f.]. Even his grandson Theopompus gained two victories at Olympia (wrestling) [4].

1 J. JÜTHNER, Philostratos, Über Gymnastik, 1909, repr. 1969 2 L. MORETTI, Olympionikai, 1957 3 CH. HABICHT, Pausanias und seine 'Beschreibung Griechenlands', 1985 4 H.-V. HERRMANN, Die Siegerstatuen von Olympia, in: Nikephoros 1, 1988, 119–183, no. 97–99.
W.D.

[4] Prominent pro-Macedonian Corinthian (Dem. Or. 18,295), known primarily through Plut. (Alex., Timol., Ages., mor.). He gave Alexander [4] the Great the famous → Bucephalus (Diod. Sic. 76,6). Unlikely to be identical to the *hetairos* featuring in the battle at the Granicus (Arr. Anab. 1,15,6).

BERVE no. 253; A.B. BOSWORTH, Comm. Arr. ad loc.
K.KI.

[5] Rhodian, released from prison in → Sardeis with his brother and two other Greeks at the request of → Phocion (Plut. Phoc. 18,6). In 321 BC, with a Rhodian fleet, he defeated a squadron formed by enemies of Antipater [1] (Arr. FGrH 156 F 11,1). E.B.

[6] Son of Theogenes, Athenian from Athmonon (IG II² 2322, 224) [1. 151, 70]. In 169 BC an emissary to the Ptolemaic court, later dispatched by the War Council to Antiochus [6] IV with other Greek emissaries for negotiations during the 6th Syrian War (Pol. 28,19,2.4; 20,3) [1. 151–152].

1 HABICHT. L.-M.G.

Demarchos (Δήμαρχος; *Dḗmarchos*). Holder of office with political and/or religious duties in Greek communities.

I. GREECE UNTIL LATE ANTIQUITY

(1) In Athens the *demarchos* was the highest officeholder in each of the 139 demes (→ Demos [2]), into which Cleisthenes had divided the polis ([Aristot.] Ath. Pol. 54,8). By no later than the 4th cent. BC the *demarchos* was elected by lot in each → *dḗmos* for one year; the *demarchos* for Piraeus on the other hand was appointed by the polis (Ath. Pol. 54,8). He convened and chaired the assembly of the deme. He could be called upon by the polis to maintain registers of confiscated property, to collect the *eisphorá* (before 387/86 BC) property tax from citizens who owned property in the *dḗmos*, to draw up a list of deme members available for rowing service (for 362: [Demosth.] Or. 50,6) and perform religious duties including the collection of votive offerings and disbursement of the *theōrikón*. He also had to ensure the burial of those who died in the *dḗmos*. On top of that, the *dḗmos* could confer various financial and religious duties upon its *demarchos;* if necessary, he had to represent the *dḗmos* in court. Some but not all demes used the *demarchoi* as a means of referring to dates (e.g. Rhamnus: IG I³ 248).

(2) In Chios in the 6th cent. BC the *demarchos* was an official who could be appointed along with the *basileús* and possibly had some judicial authority (ML 8).

(3) In Eretria the *demarchos* had religious obligations (IG XII 9, 90; 189).

(4) In the Italian Neapolis the *demarchos* was initially an important official (Str. 5,4,7); the title survived as a religious office that was held by the Emperors Titus (e.g. IG XIV 729) and Hadrian (for example SHA Hadrian 19,1) and is attested up until the 4th cent. AD.

(5) In Greek *demarchos* served as a term for the popular tribunes (e.g. Pol. 6,12,2).

→ Basileus; → Demos; → Eisphora; → Theorikon

WHITEHEAD, especially ch. 5. P.J.R.

II. BYZANTINE PERIOD

Dḗmarchoi cannot be defined by one function only in the Byzantine period. They were attested at various times: spokesmen for the *factiones* (→ Demos [2]), leaders of a city militia, responsible representatives, entrusted with a supervisory function, of a *geitonía* (citizenry of a city territory), but sometimes also as delegates of the state and holders of court titles.

K.-P. Matschke, in: Jb. für Gesch. des Feudalismus 1, 1977, 211–231; ODB 1, 602f. F.T.

Demarchus (Δήμαρχος; *Dḗmarchos*).

[1] Son of Taron, Lycian, rewarded with citizenship and privileges of honour for his services to the Samians (at the time of their banning) and to → Phila on Samos (Syll.³ 333). E.B.

[2] Syracusan *strategos*, who in 411 BC, as one of the followers of the exiled Hermocrates, commanded the Syracusan fleet in the Aegean (Thuc. 8,85,3; Xen. Hell. 1,1,29) and was removed in 405/4 by Dionysius I as a political rival (Diod. Sic. 13,96,3). K.MEI.

Deme judges see → *Dikastai kata demous*

Demeter (Ionian-Attic Δημήτηρ; *Dēmḗtēr*, Doric-Boeotian Δαμάτηρ; *Damátēr*, Aeolian Δωμάτηρ; *Dōmátēr*, Attic short form Δηώ; *Dēṓ*). Goddess of agriculture, especially grain cultivation, womanhood and the Mysteries.

A. Name B. Genealogy and Myth C. Functions D. Connection with Eleusis E. Cults F. Iconography

A. Name

The name is only partly comprehensible. In the second part of the word 'mother' is recognizable, for the first part ancient writers offer two interpretations, a connection with 'earth' (*gê/gâ*) or a word for grain (Cretan *dēaí*, 'barley'). The first has been in currency since the classical period (Derveni Papyrus, col. 18), the second is attested only in late antiquity (EM Gaisford s.v. Δηώ). Even if modern research has shifted its preference from one to the other, depending on a particular image of D., neither has prevailed; a derivation from *gê* is linguistically impossible, while *dēaí* is a secondary dialect form of the Greek *zeía* (**sdeía*).

B. Genealogy and Myth

D. is the daughter of → Kronos and → Rhea, and with → Hera and → Hestia sister of → Zeus, → Poseidon and → Hades (Hes. Theog. 454). Most closely connected with her is her daughter by Zeus, → Kore ('maiden'), who is also called → Persephone and embodies both maidenliness and mastery of the Underworld. Next is her lover → Iasion, whom Zeus kills (Hom. Od. 5,125–128, Eëtion Hes. fr. 177) and by whom she bears → Pluto ('wealth') (Hes. Theog. 969–971). The myth of the abduction of Kore-Persephone, first recounted in the Homeric D. Hymn, is central. According to it Hades-Pluto abducts D.'s daughter while she is picking flowers with her playmates and makes her mistress of the Underworld. D. searches for her daughter (together with → Hekate in the D. Hymn), learns of her being kidnapped and in response prevents the grain from growing any more. The subsequent famine for humans and gods forces Zeus to mediate. However, because Persephone has already eaten, unknowingly, a pomegranate seed and is consequently bound to the Underworld, she has to spend part of the year (a third in the hymn) in the Underworld, but may return to her mother in spring (Hom. H. 2, 401ff.). The Homeric D. Hymn links this to the aetiology for the Eleusinian → Mysteries and the sacrality of the corn on the field of Rharus at Eleusis where D. first allowed grain to re-grow; but this part of the tale is self-contained and is missing in other accounts (for example Ov. Met. 5,341–661 or the Sicilian version: Cic. Verr. 4,48,106f.). From the vase paintings of the later 6th cent. onwards, Athenian mythology attaches the tale that D. sent the Eleusinian → Triptolemus out into the whole world with grain [1]; and that was the basis of Athens' claim to be the home of grain cultivation and to be able to demand a grain-tithe from all members of the Delian League, if not from all Greeks (*aparche* decree of 423/22, LSCG 5; cf. Diod. Sic. 5,4,4).

C. Functions

1. Grain

Since Homer there has been no dispute about D.'s main sphere of influence being that of grain and its cultivation. Even in Homer 'bread' was metonymically described as *Dēmḗtros aktḗ* (Il. 13,322), and later as 'D.'s fruit' (Hdt. 1,193); D. is 'blonde' (*xanthḗ*) like ripe corn; the farmer attends to 'D.'s works' (Hes. Op. 393). A range of → epicleses refers to this subject-area: D. is *amallo-phóros* (Eust. 1162,27) or *karpophóros* (common in inscriptions), 'producer of sheaves or fruit', *anēsidṓra* (Paus. 1,31,4), 'sending up sheaves', *sitṓ* 'grain-woman' (Ath. Deipnosoph. 416 BC). Festivals such as the Attic Proerosia, Haloa and Kalamaia involved grain cultivation; ears of wheat are D.'s regular attribute in literature and the fine arts [2]; she helps in tilling the soil (Hes. Op. 465f.) and harvesting the grain (Hom. Il. 5,499–502), and from the cultural theory of the Sophists onwards she was regarded as the discoverer of grain cultivation (Prodicus, VS 84 B 5). Not by accident is Sicily, granary of the ancient world, 'wholly sacred to D.' (Diod. Sic. 5,2,3).

Myths confirm this. When D. punishes the sacrilegious → Erysichthon with hunger (Callim. H. 6,24–117), her power over the fundamentals of nutrition forms the background; the same applies to the myth of the abducted Kore. Ancient allegoresis reads this myth entirely as allegoresis of grain cultivation: Kore's time in the Underworld is an image for the seed of grain that has to be buried in the ground in order to sprout up again; modern interpretation went along with that for a long time. That is contradicted, however, by the fact that in Greece grain does not begin to sprout in late autumn shortly after being sown. Accordingly, NILSSON, in particular, has linked Kore's plight with that of grain in the underground silo, into which it is plunged after the harvest in early summer and from which it is brought out again before the autumn sowing [3]; that is more consistent but is at odds with the Greek interpretation. The epiclesis *Anēsidṓra* points to D. as goddess of agrarian fertility being close to the earth goddess → Gaia; Euripides identifies her in that way (Bacch. 275f.), but that is probably a secondary extension of her sphere of influence. As nurse of the underground hero → Trophonius, she is close to his sphere (Paus. 9,39,4f.). In Olympia she is venerated as *Chamýnē*, 'goddess of the earth' (Paus. 6,21,1), in Sparta (Paus. 3,14,5) and Hermione as *Chthonía* ('goddess of the earthly depths'; with the sacrifice of a pregnant cow that is killed by a group of elderly women 2,35,4–8). In some of her sanctuaries oaths of vengeance (Cnidus, Amorgus) and magical → *defixiones* are deposited (Lesbos, Cnidos, Corinth), as happens elsewhere only with Underworld gods.

2. GODDESS OF WOMEN

Next to grain, the life of married women in particular is subordinate to D. and, indeed, so specifically so that Athenian women invoke D. and her daughter as 'the two goddesses' (*tō theṓ*), whereas men turn to → Hercules. Men were excluded from some D. sanctuaries (Cic. Verr. 4,45,99; Paus. 2,35,7); when Miltiades broke into the D. sanctuary on Paros, he suffered an ultimately fatal injury (Hdt. 6,134). A large number of D. festivals are connected to women only; the festival of → Thesmophoria, is celebrated in practically every Greek city, and from it D. frequently bears the epiclesis *Thesmophóros* [4; 5]. The Thesmophoria are a festival for women lasting many days: in Athens, Sparta or Abdera it lasts three days, in Syracuse, ten. Rituals in which everyday routine is abolished predominate. In Syracuse women are said to have 'enacted a primeval lifestyle' (as in Diod. Sic. 5,4,7), in Eretria they burnt the sacrificial flesh in the sun without using any fire (as in Plut. Quaest. Graec. 298 BC). Fasting (Athens, see below), obscenities (*aischrología*) (Aristoph. Thesm. 539; Diod. Sic. 5,4,7; [7]) and an often radical rejection of the world of men were other features. The festival in Cyrene had 'women butchers', who were said to have emasculated King Battus when he tried to spy on them (Ael. frg. 47a D-F); Aristomenes of Messene was supposed to have been captured by women for the same reason (Paus. 4,17,1).

In Athens the festival took place on the 11th–13th → Pyanopsion. The first day was called *ánodos*, 'ascent': the women retreated to the Thesmophorion at the foot of the Acropolis (for the location [6]) and there built bowers in which they were to spend three days on beds of twigs (*stibádes*) (huts or tents, *skēnaí*, are also attested in Gela [8]). The second day was a fasting day, *Nēsteía*; in memory of D.'s fast after the Maiden's abduction, and accordingly a day of mourning when no garlands were worn. By contrast the third day offered up rich sacrifices in which *Kalligéneia*, the goddess of 'fine birth' was invoked: the object of the festival was to ensure the propagation of the citizenry.

The element that gave the festival its name is an unusual ritual: during the night (probably after the 1st day) 'images of snakes and male members', together with pine twigs and sacrificial piglets, were placed in underground pits (*mégara*), from which at the same time the remains of the pigs from the previous year were removed — they were *thesmoí*, 'that which is laid down'; crops were bound to flourish if they were mixed in (schol. Lucian Dial. meretr. 2,1 p. 275,23–276,28 RAVEN). Such pits are attested in varying forms in some D. sanctuaries (Priene, Cnidus, Agrigentum, Syracuse); they often contained pigs' bones and votive clay pigs. The ensuring of biological birth was accompanied by the parallel and inseparable agenda of agrarian fertility: both were indispensable for the continuity of the polis. The tendency in modern research since W. MANNHARDT to emphasize the agrarian aspect is just as unsatisfactory and unbalanced as the more recent preference for emphasizing the social function.

The goddess of women has two other special aspects. D. is occasionally considered a healer: offerings of limbs found in D. sanctuaries point to her curative function with illnesses of the breast or womb [10. 142f.], and for that reason she was also linked to → Asclepius [11]; other evidence points to her as a healer of eye afflictions, and this may have some link with the central role of sight in the mysteries. As well, she has a connection, especially in the Peloponnese, with the passage of young girls into adulthood, and as the deity for clan associations she has the epiclesis → *Patrṓia* (Thasos).

D. CONNECTION WITH ELEUSIS

The Homeric D. hymn links the myth of the abducted Kore with the creation of the Eleusinian Mysteries. They are the oldest Greek cult of mysteries, even if there is no evidence of continuity from the Mycenaean period [12]; building remains point to cult activity from the 8th cent. BC, and the Mysteries in the form that we know later were in any case largely shaped by the time of the Homeric D. Hymn (middle of the 7th cent.?). It is a characteristic feature that the cult was open to individuals on an entirely voluntary basis, without regard to distinctions of class or gender and without any ties to the polis; there was moreover a double promise of well-being in this life and of hopes for the afterlife (from Hom. H. 2,480–482); secret rites were central ('ineffable', *árrhēta* or 'forbidden', *apórrhēta*) during a night festival (→ Myesis, Epoptia), in which the individual is exposed to strong emotional impressions through the interplay of light and darkness (Aristot. fr. 15 ROSE). Historically, the Mysteries were originally derived from clan initiation cults, especially as D. *Eleusinía*, attested from the 5th cent. in Ionia (Ephesus) and also in the Doric Peloponnese (Sparta), is not linked to any other cult site with mysteries but is connected in the Peloponnese with rites of young women [13]. The model of the Eleusinian cult was adopted by other cults, by the Great Gods in → Samothrace as well as by some of the Peloponnesian cults of the Great Goddesses, who are to be interpreted as D. and Persephone (explicitly so in the Mysteries that were reformed in 92 BC in → Andania, LSCG 65; D. *Eleusinía* in Pheneus is also worth mentioning, Paus. 8,15,1). A cult subsidiary with Eleusinian involvement (→ Timotheus) was established in Alexandria at the end of the 4th cent. BC.

E. Cults

The name D. does not appear in the Linear B texts; an ivory fitting with the image of two goddesses and a young boy is not necessarily a representation of both goddesses and a divine child [14]. More evocative is a fresco found in Mycenae showing a goddess bearing sheaves [15]. Homer takes function and myth for granted as far as it is possible to do so, merely mentioning them in passing; that is in keeping with epic stylization. Throughout the whole of the pagan era D. remains a central divinity in the Greek Pantheon. Sanctuaries of D. are widely attested and indeed very often (as in Eleusis; cf. map of → Eleusis) halfway up a hill-slope [16] but in any case outside a residential area, often even actually outside the city (*prò póleōs*). Some ancient Arcadian cults of D. adopted a special position: for them the goddess was often linked to → Poseidon and her daughter was called *Déspoina* ('mistress') [17], like the daughter of D. *Erinýs* in Thelpusa (who after her rape by Poseidon in the shape of a horse bore her daughter and the horse Areion, Paus. 8,25,4–6), the cult of the 'black' D. (*Mélaina*) in Phigalia (child of D. and Poseidon, Paus. 8,42,1–3) or the cult of D. *Kidarís* in Pheneus (ritual masking of the priest, Paus. 8,15,3); in Lycosura D. was subordinate to the main divinity Despoina (Paus. 8,37,1–5). They may have involved vestigial reminiscences of Bronze Age cults. — after Hdt. D. was identified with the Egyptian → Isis: by way of the Alexandrian D. cult (cf. Callim. H. 6), this led to a range of the Greek D.'s characteristics being attributed to the Egyptian goddess, beginning with the Hellenistic aretalogies of Isis.

1 G. Schwarz, s.v. Triptolemos, LIMC 8.1, 56–68 2 L. Beschi, s.v. D., LIMC 4.1, 844–892 3 M. P. Nilsson, Die eleusinischen Gottheiten, in: ARW 22, 1935, 106–114 = Opuscula Selecta 2, 1952, 577–588 4 Nilsson, Feste, 313–325 5 Deubner, 50–60 6 K. Clinton, The Thesmophorion in Central Athens and the Celebration of the Thesmophoria in Attica, in: R. Hägg (ed.), The Role of Religion in the Early Greek Polis, 1996, 111–125 7 A. Brumfield, Aporreta. Verbal and Ritual Obscenity in the Cults of Ancient Women, in: R. Hägg (as n. 6), 67–74. 8 U. Kron, Frauenfeste in Demeterheiligtümern: das Thesmophorion von Bitalemi. Eine arch. Fallstudie, in: ArchAnz 1992, 611–650 9 G. Baudy, Ant. Religion in anthropologischer Deutung, in: E.-R. Schwinge (ed.), Die Wiss. vom Alt. am Ende des 2. Jt., 1995, 241–248 10 B. Forsén, Griech. Gliederweihungen, 1996. 11 Ch. Benedum, Asklepios und D. Zur Bed. weiblicher Gottheiten für den frühen Asklepioskult, in: JdI 101, 1986, 137–157 12 P. Darque, Les vestiges mycéniens découverts sous le télésterion d'Eleusis, in: BCH 105, 1981, 593–605 13 Graf, 274–277 14 E. Simon, Die Götter der Griechen, ³1985, fig. 90f. 15 St. Hiller, Spätbronzezeitliche Myth. Die Aussage der Linear B-Texte, in: Hellenische Myth./Vorgesch., 1996, 223–232 16 Y. Béquignon, Déméter, déesse acropolitaine, in: RA 1958/2, 149–177 17 R. Stieglitz, Die großen Göttinnen Arkadiens, 1967.

Farnell, Cults 3, 29–213; 311–376; H. Fluck, Skurrile Riten in griech. Kulten, 1931; Nilsson, GGR 456–481; N. J. Richardson (ed.), The Homeric hymn to D., 1974; Burkert, 247–251; P. Berger, The Goddess Obscured. Transformations of the Grain Protectress from Goddess to Saint, 1985; G. Sfameni Gasparro, Misteri e culti mistici di Demetra, 1986; S. G. Cole, D. in the Ancient Greek city and its countryside, in: S. E. Alcock, R. Osborne (ed.), Placing the Gods. Sanctuaries and Sacred Space in Ancient Greece, 1994, 199–216.
Cult centres: Eleusis: K. Clinton, The sanctuary of D. and Kore at Eleusis, in: N. Marinatos, R. Hägg (ed.), Greek Sanctuaries. New Approaches, 1993, 110–124; Attica: see above n. 6; A. C. Brumfield, The Attic Festivals of Demeter and Their Relation to the Agricultural Year, 1981; Boeotia: L. Breglia Pulci Doria, Aspetti del culto di Demetra in Beozia, in: G. Argoud, P. Roesch, La Béotie antique, 1985, 159–168; V. Suys, Les cultes de Déméter Achaia en Béotie. État actuel des connaissances, in: AntClass 63, 1994, 1–20; Eretria: P. Auberson, K. Schefold, Führer durch Eretria, 1972, 105; Greece: H. Petersmann, D. in Dodona und Thrakien. Ein Nachtrag, in: WS 100, 1987, 5–12; M. Lilibaki-Akamati, Ἱερὰ τῆς Πέλλας, in: Mneme Lazaridi, 1988, 195–203; Corinth: N. Bookidis, R. S. Stroud, D. and Persephone in Ancient Corinth, American Excavations in Old Corinth, 1987; Sparta: C. Stibbe, Das Eleusinion am Fuße des Taygetos in Lakonien, in: BABesch 68, 1993, 71–105; Arcadia: see above n. 17; Sicily: M.-Th. Le Dinahed, Sanctuaires chthoniens de la Sicile de l'époque archaïque à l'époque classique, in: G. Roux, (ed.), Temples et sanctuaires, 1984, 137–152; Gela: see above n. 8; Syracuse: L. Polacco, M. Trojani, A. C. Scolari, Il santuario di Cerere e Libera ad summam Neapolin de Siracusa, 1989; Paestum: A. Cipriani, A. M. Ardovino, Il culto di Demetra nella chora Pestana, in: G. Bartolini, G. Colonna, C. Grotanelli (ed.), Anathema. Regime delle offerte e vita dei santuari nel mediterraneo antico, Scienze dell'Antichità. Storia, archeologia, antropologia 3/4, 1989/1990, 339–351; Anatolia: M. U. Anabolu, Sanctuaries of D. and the chthonic deities in Western Asia Minor, in: Akten des 13. Internationalen Kongr. für Klass. Arch., 1990, 471; Priene: M. Schede, Priene, ²1964, 90–95; Libya: D. White, D. Libyssa. Her Cyrenaean cult in the light of recent excavations, in: QuadArchLibica, 12, 1987, 67–84.

F.G.

F. Iconography

Reliefs, vase paintings and numerous terracotta statuettes have transmitted the image of the goddess from the Archaic period onwards (assembly of the gods at the wedding of Thetis and Peleus: François Krater, Florence, Uffizi, about 570 BC). Her attributes, which make an identification possible, in particular on vase paintings without inscriptions, are polos (headdress), kalathos, veil, headbands, sheaves, torch, oinochoe or phiale; D. is generally dressed in a chiton or Doric peplos and himation. The D. Melaina of Onatas in Phigalia could not be identified beyond doubt (480/465 BC; Paus. 8,42,7). In the Classical period belong the original D. of Eleusis (often attributed to Agoracritus or his workshop, around 420/410 BC), D. Cherchel (Roman copy, original around 450/420 BC), the interpretation of the D. Capitolina is disputed (Rome, MC, Roman copy 1st cent. AD); in the Parthenon east frieze (442/38 BC) the mourning D. between Ares and Dionysus (cf. the unconfirmed interpretation of a two-figure group as D. and Kore in the Parthenon east gable, 438/432 BC); possibly contemporaneous, the representation on the 'great Eleusinian dedicatory relief' with the dispatch of Triptolemus (Athens, NM, around 440/430 BC); this was followed up by the Rheitos Bridge decree from Eleusis (421/420 BC: D. and Persephone with the *demos* of Eleusis and Athena) and the relief of the Nemesis base of Rhamnous (Munich, GL, around 425/420 BC: D. with Persephone). Representations dated to the 4th cent. BC are the enthroned D. of Cnidus (around 350/340 BC, London, BM), the prototype of the Roman D. Doria Pamphili, the wall-painting with the grieving figure in the 'Tomb of Persephone' in Vergina (2nd half of the 4th cent. BC) as well as a large number of votive reliefs, now with a distinct characterization of the older D., sitting on a cist, and the younger Persephone, standing. The colossal group of statues by Damophon from Lycosura/Arcadia has only been preserved in fragments (2nd half of the 2nd cent. BC; Paus. 8,37,3f.: D. and Persephone enthroned next to each other and flanked by Artemis and the Titan Anytus). On the large votive relief of Lacratides (Eleusis, around 100 BC) the figures are confirmed by inscriptions.

The Roman D./Ceres is often depicted on Republican and Imperial coins, gemstones and cameos (with Persephone: sardonyx, Paris, CM, Claudian). As agrarian goddess D./Ceres is often coupled with Annona, and becomes assimilated to Fides Publica (carnelian, Munich, SM, 2nd/3rd cents AD) and occasionally to Fortuna; from the early Imperial period goddess and cult are increasingly monopolized by the nobility and the imperial family, hence, *i.a.*, the portraiture of Livia in the likeness of Ceres on cameos in the 1st cent. BC (e.g. 'Grand Camée de France', Paris, CM) or various wives of emperors *i.a.*, Faustina Maior (statue: Paris, LV, AD 140/150); Messalina with Claudius as Ceres and Triptolemus (sardonyx, Paris, CM, Claudian). There are a large number of sarcophagi from the 2nd and 3rd cents. AD with the abduction of Persephone (with a stereotyped representation of D./Ceres, standing on a chariot with torch(es) in hand).

→ Agoracritus; → Ceres; → Damophon; → Onatas

St. de Angeli, s.v. D./Ceres, LIMC 4.1, 893–908; L.E. Baumer, Betrachtungen zur 'D. von Eleusis', in: AK 38, 1995, 11–25; L. Beschi, s.v. D., LIMC 4.1, 844–892 (with an older bibliography); T. Hayashi, Bed. und Wandel des Triptolemosbildes vom 6.–4. Jh.v.Chr., 1992; L.H. Martin, Greek goddesses and grain. The Sicilian connection, in: Helios 17, 1990, 251–261; M. Mertens-Horn, Bilder hl. Spiele, in: AW 28, 3/1997, 221–224, 227–230; G. Schwarz, Athen und Eleusis im Lichte der Vasenmalerei, in: Proceedings of the 3rd Symposium on ancient Greek and related pottery; conference in Copenhagen 1988, 575–584; B.S. Spaeth, The goddess Ceres in the Ara Pacis, AJA 98, 1994, 65–100. A.L.

Demetrias (Δημητριάς; *Dēmētriás*).

[1] Established around 290 BC, D. can be considered the most westerly of the large cities created in the Hellenistic period. The Macedonian founder, Demetrius I, gave the city his name. The choice of location in the annexed Thessalian border region of Magnesia, on the territory of Iolcus, was determined by the wish to create a base near the central → Aegean Sea for the European element of the three large Mediterranean kingdoms. D. did in fact serve the Antigonid dynasty 'for a long time as base for the fleet and as (second) residence' (Str. 9,5,1). At the same time, however, D. was a *pólis* in the Greek sense, with a complex constitution; while analysis of the city layout shows a distinctive interweaving of dynastic and civil elements, the everyday workings of this juxtaposition or integration is less clear. Initially populated by a *synoikismós*, in this case the melding of (almost) all the old communities of Magnesia, and then by an influx from all over the world that was promoted by trading privileges, D. was to become in Roman eyes, after scarcely 100 years, an *urbs valida et ad omnia opportuna* (Liv. 39,23,12). As such, D. was bound to get involved in the Roman-Macedonian conflict. After 168 BC, D. survived as the head of the later Magnesian League, i.e. as a regional centre of gradually increasing importance. In the restructuring of the late Roman Empire, D. was still the second city in Thessaly; at the same time D. split into several cores, with the centre of gravity shifting to Iolcus (now the old city of Volo). It was there that the bishopric was established, there that Justinian I constructed a fortress, there that D. sat out the Dark Ages to play a role at the height of the Middle Ages as a fairly well-known military and trading centre that was to change, but not end, under the Turks.

The area around D. had a particularly long tradition of settlement. The ancient city itself absorbed the harbour area of 'Pevkakia Maghoula' that had existed from Late Neolithic times. Shortly beforehand there had already been considerable town-planning going on on the nearby Ghoritsa mountain. The new development, however, far outstripped what it replaced; the fortification system, modified many times over, was one of the largest and strongest in the Greek world. The city centre was arranged in a largely orthogonal pattern; the residential area — itself much redesigned and architectonically innovative — was incorporated into this system. The putative grave-cult district of the founding king was only one of many features displaying an oriental influence. From an art-history perspective the find of well-preserved civilian grave-paintings is valuable. In the early Christian settlement complex there are, beyond the Kastro of Volo, some remarkable, very well furbished buildings, religious and profane, including the so-called Damokratia Basilica, interesting for its 'aniconic' painting cycle that drew on an unconventional biblical tradition.

A.S. Arbanitopulos, Γραπταὶ στῆλαι Δημητριάδος-Παγασῶν, 1928; P. Marzolff, D. und seine Halbinsel, D. III, 1980 (with maps); Id., Développement urbanistique de Démétrias, in: Actes du Coll. Int. 'La Thessalie'. Lyon 1990, II, 1994, 57–70 (with detailed bibliography); F. Stählin, E. Meyer, A. Heidner, Pagasai und D., 1934. P.MA.

[2] One of the post-Cleisthenian phyles of Attica, created in honour of → Demetrius [2] in 307/6 BC, together with Antigonis. Like the latter, it took over a total of 15 demes from seven Cleisthenian phyles [1. 28 table 11]. For more details see → Antigonis.

1 Traill, Attica, 25ff., 31ff. H.LO.

Demetrius (Δημήτριος; *Dēmétrios*).
I. Politically active personalities II. Christians III. Sophists, Philosophers IV. Poets, Historians V. Grammarians VI. Artists

Well-known personalities: the Macedonian King D. [2] Poliorketes; the politician and writer D. [4] of Phalerum; the Jewish-Hellenistic chronographer D. [29].

I. Politically active personalities

[1] Officer under Alexander [4], fought at Gaugamela as commander of a troop (*ile*) of → Hetairoi and in India he commanded a hipparchy.

Berve 2, no. 256. E.B.

[2] **D. Poliorketes.** Son of → Antigonus [1], born 337/6 BC (Diod. Sic. 19,96,1). In 320 he married → Phila, who bore him → Antigonus [2]. He took part in the war against → Eumenes [1]. As commander against → Ptolemaeus he was decisively beaten at Gaza. A campaign against the Nabataei was likewise unsuccessful. After the peace of 311, Antigonus sent him to defend the eastern satrapies against → Seleucus (Diod. Sic. 19,100, with an erroneous chronology). He occupied Babylon but when Ptolemy invaded Asia Minor he was recalled; Seleucus continued his conquests. Ptolemy was driven out of Asia Minor, but he gained Corinth and Sicyon. Thereupon Antigonus dispatched D. with a fleet and 5,000 talents to Europe, where he drove → Demetrius [4] of Phalerum out of Athens. Antigonus and D. were welcomed as gods: the first spontaneous deification by Greeks in Europe. Recalled once again by his father, he defeated Ptolemy in a decisive naval battle at → Salamis. As the death of → Alexander [5] had become known in the meantime, Antigonus and D. assumed the title of king in 306. Sent to Rhodes, D. was unable to get the island to defect from Ptolemy; a long and unsuccessful siege gained him the name *Poliorketes* ('the Besieger'). In 303 he reappeared in Greece, with the fleet, and renewed the Hellenic League under his and his father's leadership (StV 3, no. 446; see Philip). Close to victory, Antigonus missed his opportunity. His enemies united against him and D. had to rush to his aid. At → Ipsus D. allowed himself to be enticed away from the battlefield with the cavalry, and Antigonus lost the battle and his own life. D. retained control of the sea and the coasts, but lost almost all the Greek cities.

His enemies' alliance soon collapsed. In 299/8 Seleucus entered into an alliance with D. and married his daughter → Stratonice. This alliance did not last long, as D.did not cede the coast of Cilicia and Phoenicia to him. After → Cassander's death, though, D. began to plan an assault on Macedonia. In 295–4 he reconquered Athens. Summoned by Cassander's son Alexander in support against his brother → Antipater, he murdered Alexander, drove out Antipater and in 294 became king of Macedonia, but lost the coast of Asia Minor. On the gulf of → Pagasae he built the fortress city of → Demetrias [1].

An insurrection in Boeotia supported by → Pyrrhus evolved into a poorly documented war in which Ptolemy also had a hand. → Lanassa left Pyrrhus, married D. and handed over → Corcyra to him. In 288, however, Pyrrhus and → Lysimachus invaded Macedonia, and the war-weary army abandoned D. He retreated, handed over the Greek fortresses to Antigonus [2] and tried his luck with a mercenary army in Asia. Stalemated by a static war with → Agathocles [5], he surrendered in 286 to Seleucus, who interned him with royal honours until D. drank himself to death in 283. Antigonus buried his ashes after a ship-borne funeral procession to Demetrias. His fleet went over to Ptolemy who now dominated the seas. Main source: Plut. Demetrius.

R.A. Billows, Antigonus the One-Eyed, 1990; E. Will, in: CAH 7,1,²1984, 101–109.

[3] Son of → Antigonus [2], whom he succeeded, after a few years as co-regent, as king of Macedonia in 239 BC. The League of the → Aetoli, who had never warred with Antigonus, allied itself with the → Achaeans against D.: thus began the 'Demetrian War'. D. married Phthia, daughter of the recently deceased → Alexander [10] of Epirus, and helped Epirus in defending North Acarnania against the Aetolians. He supported Athens and Argus against the manoeuvrings of → Aratus [2] and got Boeotia and Locris Opuntia to defect from the Aetolians, but was unable to prevent → Megalopolis from joining the Achaean League. After the Epirote royal family had died out, the Aetolians won their capital → Ambracia (233 BC) and then attacked North Acarnania. Busy with the war in the north, D. invited the → Ardiaei to come to the aid of the Acarnanians. This led to Rome's deploying to the east (→ Teuta). D. died suddenly in 229. On behalf of his eight-year-old son → Philippus V, → Antigonus [3] took over government of a much-weakened kingdom.

Walbank in HM 3, 317–336. E.B.

[4] **D. of Phalerum.** (an Attic deme), son of Phanostratus, *c.* 360–280 BC pupil of → Theophrastus. In 322 (together with Phocion and Demades) a member of the Athenian delegation which, after the defeat at Crannon, negotiated terms for peace with the Macedonian victors → Antipater and → Craterus. When in 318 D., like → Phocion and his supporters, was condemned to death, he escaped execution. After → Cassander came to power, he installed his representative D. as governor of Athens (title possibly *epimelétēs* or *epistátēs*). In 309/8 D. was eponymous archon. The conquest of Piraeus in summer by → D. [2], the son of Antigonus I, put an end to D.'s rule over Athens. He found exile first in Thebes, and then, after Cassander's death (297), in Egypt, where he became an adviser to King → Ptolemy I. Accounts of his key role in founding the library at Alexandria are not credible [1]. A rift with → Ptolemy II Philadelphus (from 283 successor to Ptolemy I) is said to have led to D.'s enforced stay in the country, where he died from snakebite.

It was in D.'s regency in Athens that the seven 'guardians of the law' (*nomophýlakes*), elected for one year, were instituted (or had their duties expanded). D. was also responsible for laws restricting extravagance in burials and memorials, and at marriages and banquets (controlled by the newly appointed office of → *gynaikonómoi*). The Areopagus (→ Areios Pagos) council was assigned control of religious and moral behaviour. The → *choregia*, a liturgy imposed on the rich, was repealed, the relevant duties being funded from the city treasury and performed by an *agonothétēs*. The extent to which D.'s democratic reform (Str. 9,1,20), which favoured the propertied classes, was influenced by → Aristotle's political theory (in opposition [2]), is still a matter of debate.

D. was a productive writer (list of his writings in Diog. Laert. 5,80–81). His philosophical works were limited to ethics and the theory of the State and, like his research into constitutional history, rhetoric and poetry, point to the influence of Aristotle. On top of that are his historical works (e.g. the list of the archonts) and collections (e.g. the sayings of the Seven Sages, Aesop's Fables, but also of speeches).

D. was highly regarded by Cicero, as he excelled both in philosophical studies and in public administration (leg. 3,14). Quintilian regarded D. as the last Attic orator (inst. 10,1,80).

EDITIONS: WEHRLI, Schule W.W. FORTENBAUGH, E. SCHÜTRUMPF (ed.), Demetrius of Phalerum, Rutgers University Studies in Classical Humananities IX, 2000, 391–411 FGrH 228 (Collection of fragments of historical writings).
BIBLIOGRAPHY: 1 PFEIFFER, KP [1]1970, 128–133 2 H.-J. GEHRKE, Das Verhältnis von Politik und Philos. im Wirken des D. von Phaleron, in: Chiron 8, 1978, 149–199 3 CH. HABICHT, Athen. Die Gesch. der Stadt in hell. Zeit, 1995, 762–75 4 F. WEHRLI, D. von Phaleron, in: GGPh 3, 559–564.
E.E.S.

[4a] **D. of Pharus.** Illyrian prince of → Pharus [2] (modern: Hvar), in 230/29 BC governor of → Teuta on Cercyra. In the 1st → Illyrian War he went over to the side of the Romans to whom he owed his subsequent position of power (Pol. 2,10,8–2,11,17) [1. 43; 53 f.; 89]. As the husband of Triteuta he became the guardian of → Agron's [3] son Pinnes [1. 70; 2]. Together with → Scerdilaedas he repeatedly violated the shipping border at Lis(s)os and extended his robbery at sea (around 220) (→ Piracy) to the Cyclades; defeated by the Roman punitive expedition under L. → Aemilius [I 31] Paullus (in the 2nd Illyrian War), D. fled in 219 to the Macedonian king → Philippus [7] V (Pol. 3,16,2; 18–19,8) [1. 70–77], on whose side and in alliance with the Achaians he operated against the Aetolians and Scerdilaedas (Pol. 4,16,6–7; 4,19,7). On the Macedonian crown council D. worked towards an active Illyrian or Adriatic policy and energetically advocated the treaty with → Hannibal [4] which in 215 provided for the reinstatement of D. in the positions he had lost in 219 (Pol. 5,101,7; 5,108; 7,9,13 f.) [1. 145; 154]. Polybius [2] emphasizes the negative effect of D. on the young Macedonian king Philippus [7] V (5,12,5; 7,12,2; 7,13,4; 9,23,9). D. lost his life in the battles for → Messana [2] in 211 (?) [1. 78].

1 D. VOLLMER, Symploke, 1990.
L.-M. G.

[5] Son of → Philip V, from 197/6 to 191 BC a hostage in Rome (Pol. 18,39,5f.; 21,3,3); sent there in 184/3 with Apelles [2] and Philocles, and was courted by the Senate and → Quinctius Flamininus (Pol. 22,14; 23,1–2). As a candidate of the Macedonian friends of Rome for the succession to the throne, D. was suspected of highly treasonous dealings and executed in 180 (Pol. 23,7; 10; Liv. 40,7–16; 20; 23–24) [1. 67–76; 2. 190; 3. 471f.].

1 H.J. DELL, in: Ancient Macedonia 3, 1983
2 ERRINGTON 3 HM 3.
L.-M.G.

[6] **D. 'the Fair'** (ὁ καλός; *ho kalós*). Son of D. [2] Poliorketes and Ptolemais, half-brother of Antigonus [2] Gonatas, father of Antigonus [3] Doson (Plut. Demetr. 53,8). After the death of Magas (probably 250/249 BC), D. was summoned to Cyrene by the latter's widow → Apama to marry her daughter → Berenice [3], whom Magas had intended to marry to Ptolemy (III), and thereby prevent Ptolemaic domination of Cyrene. D.'s mission was certainly supported by Antigonus Gonatas, but after a short period of rule he was killed, because of his relationship with Apama, at the instigation of Berenice, who finally ended up marrying Ptolemy (Just. 26,3; allusion to D.'s murder in Catull. 66,27f.).

WILL, vol. 1, 243ff.
M.MEI. and ME.STR.

[7] **D. I Soter.** Son of Seleucus IV. On the death of his uncle Antiochus [6] IV in 164, D., who had been a hostage in Rome by virtue of the peace of Apamea (188 BC) — not recognized by the Senate as heir to the throne and, when king, acknowledged only belatedly and with ulterior motives — escaped to Syria in 162 with the help of the later historian Polybius, who was then interned in

Rome, and ordered the killing of his underage cousin, Antiochus [7] V, who had been recognized as king by Rome but was in political difficulties, as well as of his chancellor Lysias (Pol. 31,2; 11–15; 32,2; Jos. Ant. Iud. 12,389f.; App. Syr. 46f.; Just. 34,3,6–9). D. was successful ('Soter') against Timarchus, the governor-general of the Upper Satrapies, who had diplomatic support from Rome in his revolt, and, in 160, against the Jews who rose up under Judas Maccabaeus. In Judaea thereafter there prevailed a peace much appreciated even by pious Jews (1 Macc. 7ff.; 2 Macc. 14ff.; Diod. Sic. 31,27a; Jos. Ant. Iud. 12,391ff.; 13,1ff.). In the struggle for the Cappadocian throne (until 156 BC), D. took the side of the ultimately unsuccessful Orophernes against Ariarathes V, who was supported by Attalus II and had declined to marry D.'s sister Laodice, widow of Perseus of Macedonia (Pol. 32,10; Diod. Sic. 31,32; Just. 35,1–5). When in *c.* 158 Attalus II sent Alexander I (Balas) as the (putative) son of Antiochus IV into the struggle for the throne against D., a difficult man to get on with and soon unpopular in his own capital, Alexander quickly gained the support of Ariarathes V and Ptolemy VI, and finally also of the Maccabees (Jonathan) and was acknowledged by Rome. After defeats from 153 onwards D. died in the winter of 151/0 near Antioch (Pol. 33,19; Diod. Sic. 31,32a; Jos. Ant. Iud. 13,35ff.; 58ff.; Just. 35,1,6ff.).

[8] D. II Theos Nikator Philadelphos. Born shortly before 160, son of D. [7] I; from 147 was fighting in Syria against Alexander I (Balas) with the support of Ptolemy VI, and received as wife the latter's daughter, Cleopatra Thea, who had been married to Alexander, was installed as king by Ptolemy in Antioch and, together with his father-in-law, who died soon after from wounds received in the battle, defeated Alexander at Oinoparas in 145 (SEG 13,585; 1 Macc. 11,9ff.; Diod. Sic. 32,9c-d; Jos. Ant. Iud. 13,109; 116; Just. 35,2). In opposition to D., who was perceived in Antioch in particular as a despot, the *strategos* Diodotus Tryphon proclaimed the young son of Alexander Balas as Antiochus VI in 145 and soon afterwards proclaimed himself king. D. put an end to further Maccabean expansion only by acknowledging the high priest Simon, granting exemption from taxation and vacating Jerusalem (Diod. Sic. 33,4a; App. Syr. 68: divergent dating; Just. 36,1; 3,9). In combating the Parthian king Mithridates I, who had invaded Babylon after annexing Media, D. was captured in 140/139 after initial successes and later married to the Parthian princess Rhodogune (1 Macc. 14,1–3; Jos. Ant. Iud. 13,219; App. Syr. 67; Just. 38,9). In 129 D. was sent by the new king Phraates against his brother Antiochus [9] VII, who was harrying the Parthians, in the struggle for the Seleucid throne. After Antiochus' death in the Parthian War, D. had control over only North Syria and Cilicia. In support of his mother-in-law Cleopatra II he deployed to Egypt unsuccessfully against Ptolemy VIII. D. was defeated at Damascus in 126 by the rival king Alexander II (Zabinas), who had been installed by Ptolemy VIII, and after the defection of Syrian cities was killed at Tyre (Liv. per. 60; App. Syr. 68; Just. 39,1).

[9] D. III. Eukairos. Son of Antiochus [10] VIII, was installed as king in 95 in Damascus by Ptolemy IX, who at that time controlled only Cyprus, and shared the rule over the small kingdom with his brother Philip I. The pair were successful in the battle against their relative Antiochus X. D. helped the Jews against Alexander Iannaeus, fought in 88 against Philip, was handed over to the Parthian king Mithridates II in 87 and later died in his captivity. (Jos. Ant. Iud. 13,370; 376ff.; 384ff.). Other ruler epithets according to BMC, Sel. Kings 101: Theos Philopator Soter or Philometor Euergetes Kallinikos.

E. Bevan, The House of Seleucus, 1902; A. R. Bellinger, The End of the Seleucids, in: Transactions of the Connecticut Academy 38, 1949, 51–102; K. Bringmann, Hell. Reform und Religionsverfolgung in Judäa, 1983; A. Bouché-Leclercq, Histoire des Séleucides (323–64 avant J.-C.), 1913/14; Th. Fischer, Unt. zum Partherkrieg Antiochos' VII. im Rahmen der Seleukidengesch., 1970; Gruen, Rome; E. Grzybek, Zu einer babylon. Königsliste aus der hell. Zeit (Keilschrifttafel BM 35603), in: Historia 41, 1992, 190–204; G. Hölbl, Gesch. des Ptolemäerreiches, 1994; O. Mørkholm, Antiochus IV of Syria, 1964; W. Orth, Die frühen Seleukiden in der Forsch. der letzten Jahrzehnte, Gedenkschrift H. Bengtson, 1991, 61–74; A. J. Sachs, D. J. Wiseman, A Babylonian King List of the Hellenistic Period, in: Iraq 16, 1954, 202–211; H. H. Schmitt, Unt. zur Gesch. Antiochos' des Großen und seiner Zeit, 1964; S. Sherwin-White, A. Kuhrt, From Samarkand to Sardis, 1993; Will. A.ME.

[10] D. I. Son of the Bactrian king Euthydemus, around 206 BC led a delegation of his father's to Antiochus [5] III, who was seeking to recover the East, and became engaged to one of his daughters (Pol. 11,34,8). Probably around 184 D. forged over the Hindu Kush into the Punjab and beyond into India, extending the kingdom that he had inherited, becoming king also 'of the Indians'. With his sons Euthydemus III, Demetrius II [8], Pantaleon and Agathocles as subkings, he ruled over the mixed population of Greeks, Iranians and Indians. Coins were minted to the Attic standard with legends in Greek and Prakrit. D. met his death around 170 in battle against Eucratides, who had usurped Bactria (Str. 11,11,1; Just. 41,6,4).

The Cambridge History of Iran 3, 1984; A. N. Lahiri, Corpus of Indo-Greek Coins, 1965; A. K. Narain, The Indo-Greeks, 1957; W. W. Tarn, The Greeks in Bactria and India, ^{2}1951; Will; G. Woodcock, The Greeks in India, 1966. A.ME.

[11] came from Gadara (east of Lake Genezareth). As a freedman of Pompey he accompanied him on his campaigns in the East (Plut. Pomp. 2; 40). According to rumours in the capital he was richer than Pompey (Sen. De tranq. anim. 8,6) and with his money he financed the building of the Theatre of Pompey (Cass. Dio 39,38,6).

[12] (C. Iulius), freedman of Caesar, to whom M. → Antonius [I 9] in 39 BC handed over the administration of Cyprus (Cass. Dio 48,40,5f.; MRR 2, 390). W.W.

[13] Singing teacher for young girls, spoke ill of Horace (Hor. Sat. 1,10,79; 90).

[14] **D.**, who, perhaps in Capua, had forced commodity prices up under Nero, and was consequently impeached in Rome before the consuls (Plin. HN 33,164).

[15] Leading Alexandrian Jew, who married Mariamne, the daughter of King Agrippa I (Jos. Ant. Iud. 20,147).

[16] Commander of a *vexillatio* in Cappadocia under the governor Flavius Arrianus (Arr. ἐκτ. 1). PIR² D 42. W.E.

II. Christians

[17] **From Thessalonica.** Martyred saint, patron of the city of → Thessalonica. Two martyrs have been blended into the medieval hagiographical D. figure, a Greek *anthypatos* from Thessalonica under Maximianus (306) and a deacon from Sirmium. It can no longer be established whether the cult transfer that took place in late antiquity moved from Thessalonica to → Sirmium [1. II, 202] or vice versa [2. 348]. From the 5th cent. until now the centre of the cult [3] has been Thessalonica with its D. Basilica (used as a mosque 1493–1912) [4]. D. is venerated throughout the whole of Eastern and South-Eastern Europe, especially though among the Bulgarians and Greeks. No other saint in the Eastern Church can have had so many hagiographical and hymnographical works devoted to him [5; 6]. He is generally portrayed as a military saint, standing or enthroned in garments of peace, more rarely seated on a horse [7].

1 P. Lemerle, Les plus anciens recueils des miracles de Saint Démétrius, I-II, 1979/1981 2 M. Vickers, Sirmium or Thessaloniki? A Critical Examination of the St. Demetrius Legend, in: ByzZ 67, 1974, 337–350 3 A. Mentzos, Τὸ προσκύνημα τοῦ Ἁγίου Δημητρίου Θεσσαλονίκης στὰ βυζαντινὰ χρόνια [St. D's cult site of Thessalonica in the Byzantine period], 1994 (with a summary in English) 4 Ch. Mpakirtzes, Ἡ βασιλικὴ τοῦ Ἁγίου Δημητρίου Θεσσαλονίκης [The Basilica of St. D. in Thessalonica], 1986 5 F. Halkin, Bibliotheca hagiographica graeca, ³1957, 152–165 (no. 497–547z) 6 Id., Novum auctarium, 1984, 61–63 7 A. Xyngopulos, Ὁ εἰκονογραφικὸς κύκλος τῆς ζωῆς τοῦ Ἁγίου Δημητρίου [The iconographical cycle of the life of St. D.], 1970.

H. Delehaye, Les légendes grecques des saints militaires, 1909, 103–109; A. Kazhdan, N. Patterson-Ševčenko, s.v. D., ODB 1, 605–606. G.MA.

[18] Well known in connection with the biography of Origen, D. (AD 189–231/2) is the first historically verifiable bishop of → Alexandria [1]. By mutual agreement with Origen he transferred catechumenical instruction to him in 203 (Euseb. Hist. eccl. 6,3,8). D. later turned against his talented collaborator, reproached him for various offences (lay preaching and ordination in Palestine, self-mutilation) and forced him by means of a synod decision to give up teaching and to leave Egypt. As well as personal animosities (Euseb. Hist. eccl. 6,8,4: envy at Origenes' success) doctrinal differences may also have played a role. According to later (Alexandrian-Coptic) tradition, D. was the author of several non-extant letters on the question of the Easter festival. The creation of an Egyptian episcopal structure with Alexandria as its centre took place under D.

Bardenhewer, GAL II, 158–160; C. W. Griggs, s.v. D., in: Early Egyptian Christianity, 1990, 259; V. Grumel, s.v. D., patriarche d'Alexandrie, in: DHGE 14, 198f. J.RI.

[19] **of Tarsus.** Mentioned in Diog. Laert. 5,85 as a writer of satyr plays (σατυρογράφος; *satyrográphos*).

F. Susemihl, Gesch. der griech. Lit. in der Alexandrinerzeit I, 1891–1892. F.M.

III. Sophists, Philosophers

[20] Sophist in the middle of the 4th cent. AD (Lib. Ep. 33). He came from Tarsus (Ep. 1123), was *consularis Phoenices* (Ep. 234) and engaged in a lively exchange of correspondence with Libanius, who hailed him as the greatest orator of the time (Ep. 606; 621). He was a 'pagan' (Ep. 710). PLRE 1, 247 Demetrius (2). → Libanius

Schmid/Stählin II, 987; O. Seeck, Die Briefe des Libanius, repr. 1967, 117–119. W.P.

[21] **D. Lacon.** Epicurean, pupil of Protarchus of Bargylia and contemporary of Zeno of Sidon (*c.* 150–175 BC). It is quite out of the question that he was head of the Epicurean school after Apollodorus Cepotyrannus: he had a school for philosophers in Miletus, but probably also lived in Athens. Dedication of two of his writings to Roman personalities (Nero and Quintus) does not of itself constitute proof that he also stayed in Italy: D. could also have got to know them in Athens or Miletus. Remnants of his comprehensive work have survived through papyri from Herculaneum. D. dealt with physics, cosmology, theology (on divine anthropomorphism: PHerc. 1055), ethics (physiology is a means of combating confusion and passions: PHerc. 831), philology, which he applied to the texts of Epicurus (re-creating the correct way of reading the master's works is an essential condition for their use and enjoyment: PHerc. 1012), poetics (against Peripatetic rivals: PHerc. 188 and 1014), rhetoric (PHerc. 128) and geometry (against the Euclidean theorems, starting with the Epicurean theory of minima: PHerc. 1061). Such a breadth of interests and reappraisal, especially of the *enkýklia mathḗmata* (poetics, rhetoric, and mathematics), cannot however be taken as demonstrating D.'s intellectual deviation from Epicurean orthodoxy. Sextus Empiricus' anti-Epicurean polemic was aimed also at D.
→ Epicurean School; → Herculanean papyri

T. Dorandi, in: Goulet 2, 1994, 637–641; Erler, 256–265. T.D.

[22] **D. of Byzantium.** Peripatetic of the 1st cent. BC, mentioned by Diog. Laert. 5,83 and quoted in 2,20 as the source for an item of information on Socrates. His book on the art of poetry was quoted by Philodemus (Poem. 5,IX,34ff.), Athenaeus (452d, 548d, 633a) and an unknown writer in PHerc. 1012. He was perhaps the same D. who kept Cato the Younger company on the day before the latter's suicide in 46 BC (Plut. Cato Min. 65; 67ff.).

E. Martini, s.v. D. (87), RE 4, 2841f.; F. Wehrli, in: GGPh[2] 3, 1983, 594, 598. H.G.

[23] **D. Kythras.** Philosopher (non-Christian) from Alexandria; under Constantius II in AD 359 in Scythopolis accused of pagan sacrifice, tortured but acquitted (Amm. Marc. 19,12,12).

C. Vogler, Constance II, 1979, 190. ME.STR.

[24] Cynic philosopher of the 1st cent. AD, friend of Seneca, who saw him as a model of the Cynic-Stoic sage. He is known especially from Seneca's work, but Tacitus, Cassius Dio, Suetonius, Epictetus, Lucian and Philostratus also mention him. He belonged to the circle around the Stoic Thrasea Paetus; in the trial against P. → Egnatius Celer, one of the accusers of Barea Soranus, he took the side of the defendant. D. was confrontational in his attitude towards the rulers Caligula, Nero and Vespasian, the last of whom banished him to an island. His practically oriented Cynic philosophy was based on the principles of → Diogenes [14] of Sinope: an asceticism that aimed at suppressing one's needs, the desire of harmonizing deeds and words, and finally the reversal of values and openness of speech. Like the Stoics, he took the view that one should always be able to draw on (*in promptu et in usu*) maxims for living (*praecepta*) that, reflected upon daily, bring us inner peace and thus happiness. Various judgements were made of D., as is shown by Seneca's praise and by the reservations held by Tacitus and Cassius Dio. The picture painted by Philostratus in his 'Life of Apollonius of Tyana' derives more from novelistic structuring than historical accuracy.
→ Cynic school; → Seneca

M. Billerbeck, Der Kyniker Demetrius. Ein Beitrag zur Gesch. der frühkaiserzeitlichen Popularphilos., 1979; J. F. Kindstrand, Demetrius the Cynic, in: Philologus 124, 1980, 93–98. M.G.-C.

IV. Writers, Historians

[25] Writer of Old Comedy, two of whose play titles [1. test. 2] are known to us, as well as five fragments; the Σικελία (also quoted in one instance as Σικελικοί) is dated to after 404 BC (cf. fr. 2).

1 PCG V, 1986, 8–10. H.-G.NE.

[26] Author of a satyr play *Hesiónē* (?), end of the 5th cent. BC (Vas Neapol. 3240, see Beazley ARV[2] II 1336); possibly prizewinner in Athens around 400 BC; probably not identical with a writer of satyr plays of the same name from Tarsus (see Diog. Laert. 5,85).

TrGF 49 and 206. F.P.

[27] Writer of New Comedy, of whom we have four fragments (two uncertain) and a title of a play (Ἀρεοπαγίτης); the play is dated to after 294 BC (cf. fr. 1,8). In fr. 1 a cook boasts of having been chef to King Seleucus, to the Sicilian tyrant Agathocles and to the Athenian ruler Lachares.

1 PCG V, 11–13. H.-G.NE.

[28] **D. of Byzantium.** Greek writer of history, 1st half of the 3rd cent. BC. As a contemporary observer, he described in 13 bks the 'passage of the Galatians from Europe to Asia' (278/7) and in eight bks the history of Antiochus Soter (280–261) and Ptolemy Philadelphus (285/4–247) and the administration of Libya under those two rulers (FGrH 162 T 1). K.MEI.

[29] Jewish-Hellenistic chronographer (end 3rd cent. BC). The earliest Jewish author known to have written in Greek in → Alexandria [1]. In his treatise Περὶ τῶν ἐν τῇ Ἰουδαίᾳ βασιλέων ('On the kings in Judaea') he set out a Jewish chronology using the → Septuaginta and the dates it used. Unlike → Berossus and → Manetho, he is quite restrained in his calculations. D. explains away the contradictions in the OT tradition by the method of ἀπορίαι καὶ λύσεις (*aporíai kaì lýseis*) developed by Alexandrian philologists. → Alexander [23] Polyhistor's excerpts of his work have survived in Eusebius (Pr. Ev. 9,19,4; 9,21,1–19; 9,29,1–3.15.16c) and Clemens Alexandrinus (Stromateis 1,141,1–2 [F 6]). D.'s writing represented an outline of Jewish history from → Adam (F 2) up to the time of → Ptolemy IV Philopator (221–204 BC) (F 6) and was intended to illustrate the antiquity of the Jewish people and their writings (Eus. HE 6,13,7).
→ Chronicle

FGrH 3 C 722; N. Walter, Fragmente jüd.-hell. Historiker, in: JSHRZ III,2, [2]1980, 280–292; J. Hanson, Demetrius, in: J.H. Charlesworth (ed.), The Old Testament Pseudepigrapha 2, 1985, 843–854; Schürer 3,1, 1986, 521–525; G.F. Sterling, Historiography and Self-definition, 1992, 153–167 (Bibliography). A.M.S.

[30] **D. of Callatis.** Greek historian and geographer; at the end of the 3rd cent. BC he composed a work 'On Europe and Asia' in 20 bks (Diog. Laert. 5,83), a 'a general history (...) arranged geographically' [1. 2807]; its finishing-point is unknown, the death of Hieron II of Syracuse in 215 is mentioned in F 3 (5). He was used by, *inter alia*, → Agatharchides (FGrH 85 T 3) and perhaps influenced the latter's principle of representation (universal history according to geographical centres of influence). FGrH 85 with comm.

1 Ed. Schwartz, s.v. D. (77), RE 4, 2806f. K.MEI.

[31] Epic writer, mentioned by Diog. Laert. 5, 85 in a list of homonyms. Three hexameters are quoted there that address envious people.

SH 174. C.S.

[32] Undatable writer of epigrams, from Bithynia, author of a short but evocative poem, translated into Latin by → Ausonius (Epist. 30 PEIPER), about the cow of Myron (Anth. Pal. 9,730). Identification of this otherwise unknown writer with the philosopher D. of Bithynia (son of the Stoic Diphilus and pupil of Panaetius, cf. Diog. Laert. 5,84) or with the Hellenistic epic poet D. (SH 373) is purely conjectural.

FGE 37. E.D.

[33] Argive local historian, was quoted by Clement of Alexandria (Protreptikos 4,47,5 = I 36,13 STÄHLIN: ἐν δευτέρῳ τῶν Ἀργολικῶν); see especially JACOBY [1]. He has no connection with → D. of Troezen.

1 FGrH 304 2 FHG IV 383 3 E. SCHWARTZ, s.v. D. (82), RE 4, 2817. F.M.

V. GRAMMARIANS

[34] **D. Scepsius.** (ὁ Σκήψιος; *ho Skēpsios*). Scholar and antiquarian from Scepsis in the Troad. Born into a rich and noble family around 205 BC, he lived until roughly 130 BC, secluded in his own town (we know that he helped his fellow citizen Metrodorus of Scepsis: Diog. Laert. 5,84), where he devoted himself to composing his Τρωικὸς διάκοσμος. This was a huge commentary (30 bks) on the Catalogue of the Trojans in Hom. Il. 2,816–77, in which he supplied a large quantity of topographical and antiquarian information about his homeland (amongst other things he rejected identification of the Ilium of his day with the Homeric city); it was used by Apollodorus of Athens. The extant fragments appeared mainly in Strabo and Athenaeus. According to D., the tale of Aeneas' flight to the west was erroneous: he maintained instead that Aeneas had not survived the Trojan War and that a Trojan clan descended from Hector and Aeneas had controlled the area after the city's fall; and that was the basis of his debunking the Trojan origins of the city of Rome.

→ Apollodorus [1] of Athens; → Athenaeus [7] of Athens; → Strabo

EDITION: R. GAEDE, Demetrii Scepsii quae supersunt, diss. 1880.

BIBLIOGRAPHY: E. GABBA, Storiografia greca e imperialismo romano (III-I sec. a. C.), in: Rivista Storica Italiana 86, 1974, 630–633 = Aspetti culturali dell'imperialismo romano, 1993, 17–21; B. KREBBER, Ναυστολόγοι bei Strabon, ein neues Papyrusfragment, in: ZPE 9, 1972, 204–221 = B. KRÄMER, P.Köln I, 1976, 27–32 (no. 8); F. MONTANARI, Pergamo, in: Lo spazio letterario della Grecia antica, I 2, 1993, 651–52; F. MONTANARI, Demetrius of Phalerum on Literature, in: W.W. FORTENBAUGH, E. SCHÜTRUMPF (ed.), Demetrius of Phalerum, Rutgers University Studies in Classical Humananities IX, 2000, 391–411; PFEIFFER, KPI, 303–305, 312–314; E. SCHWARTZ, s.v. D. (78), RE 4, 2807–2813 = Griech. Geschichtschreiber, 1957, 106–114; R. STIEHLE, Der Τρωϊκὸς διάκοσμος des D. von Skepsis, in: Philologus 5, 1850, 528–546; F. SUSEMIHL, Gesch. der griech. Litt. in der Alexandrinerzeit, 1891–1892, I, 681–85.

[35] **D. Ixion.** (ὁ Ἰξίων; *ho Ixíōn*). From Adramyttium (Mysia), Greek grammarian from the Alexandrian period. The Suda (δ 430, s.v. Δημήτριος ὁ ἐπίκλην Ἰξίων) says that he was pupil of Aristarchus [4] of Samothrace, fell into conflict with the master and consequently went to Pergamum (probably to Crates). It is therefore difficult to date him to the Augustan period (Suda ibid.); it is more likely that he lived in the 2nd cent. BC, certainly before Tryphon of Alexandria (as the quotation in Apoll. Dyscolus, De Pronominibus 89,14 SCHNEIDER shows). He wrote various exegetical works on Homer, apparently attacking Aristarchus in part; attested title: Πρὸς τὰς ἐξηγήσεις, (or Πρὸς Ἀρίσταρχον), Πρὸς τοὺς ἠθετημένους (roughly thirty fragments from it are in the Homer scholia, transmitted by Didymus and Herodian). A commentary on Hesiod is mentioned only in the Suda (ibid.). A quotation in the Aristophanes scholia is genuine (Schol. Aristoph. Ran. 308 a), but the attribution to him of some other scholia in which just the name D. is mentioned is contentious. Of other works we have only a few fragments: Ἐτυμολογούμενα (or Ἐτυμολογία); Ἀττικαὶ λέξεις; Περὶ τῆς Ἀλεξανδρέων διαλέκτου; Περὶ ἀντωνυμιῶν; Περὶ τῶν εἰς μι ληγόντων ῥημάτων.

→ Aristarchus [4] of Samothrace; → Crates of Mallus

EDITION: T. STAESCHE, De Demetrio Ixione grammatico, diss. 1883.

BIBLIOGRAPHY: A. BLAU, De Aristarchi discipulis, 1883, 19–20; L. COHN, s.v. D. (101), RE 4, 2845–47; F. MONTANARI, Demetrius of Phalerum on Literature, in: W.W. FORTENBAUGH, E. SCHÜTRUMPF (ed.), Demetrius of Phalerum, Rutgers University Studies in Classical Humanities IX, 2000, 391–411; M. VAN DER VALK, Iliad III 35 and the Scholia, in: Mnemosyne 25, 1972, 80.

[36] **D. Chloros.** (Δημήτριος ὁ Χλωρός; *Dēmétrios ho Chlōrós*). Greek grammarian of uncertain dating, probably from the 1st cent. BC, exegetist of Nicander, mentioned several times in the scholia on the *Thēriaká* (158b; 377–378a; 382a; 541a; 585a; 622c; 748; 781b); he is probably the grammarian D., son of Menecles, quoted in the schol. Nic. Ther. 869a [cf. 3]. The fragment in Steph. Byz. 375,11, s.v. Κορόπη, must also be attributed to him; in it a hypomnema to Nicander was erroneously ascribed to D. of Phalerum, in confusion with this D. S. Emp. Adversus mathematicos 1,84, reproduces one of his definitions of grammar.

→ Nicander; → Stephanus of Byzantium

1 V. DI BENEDETTO, Demetrio Cloro e Aristone di Alessandria, in: ASNP 35, 1966, 321–324 2 C. GUHL, Die Fragmente des Alexandrinischen Grammatikers Theon, diss. 1969, 4 3 W. KROLL, s.v. Nikandros (11), RE 17, 262, 1ff. 4 W. KROLL, s.v. Demetrios (100a), RE Suppl. 7, 124 5 F. MONTANARI, Demetrius of Phaleron on Lit-

erature, in: Dicaearchus of Messene and Demetrius of Phaleron, Rutgers University Studies in Classical Humanities IX, 1997 6 F. SUSEMIHL, Gesch. der griech. Litt. in der Alexandrinerzeit, 1891–1892, II, 20.

[37] **D. of Magnesia.** (ὁ Μάγνης; *ho Mágnēs*). Grammarian and scholarly compiler from the 1st cent. BC; Dion. Hal. De Dinarcho 1, records his fame as *polyhístōr*. To his friend T. Pomponius Atticus he dedicated a treatise 'On Concord' (Περὶ ὁμονοίας), which Cicero mentioned at several points. His treatise 'On Homonymous Cities' (Περὶ ὁμωνύμων πόλεων) was used in some of the entries of Stephanus of Byzantium. His best-known work is the treatise 'On Homonymous Poets and Writers' (Περὶ ὁμωνύμων ποιητῶν τε καὶ συγγραφέων), from which Dion. Hal. ibid. polemically reproduces an excerpt on various people with the name Dinarchus and which is specifically quoted by Diog. Laert. 1,112. The work probably had the character of a compilation with a smattering of criticism: what is certain is that it was one of the sources of Diogenes Laertius, whose biographies of philosophers generally end with a list of homonymous people and a short characterization.

→ Diogenes Laertios; → Dionysius of Halicarnassus; → T. Pomponius Atticus; → Cicero; → Stephanus of Byzantium

EDITION: J. MEJER, Demetrius of Magnesia. On poets and authors of the same name, in: Hermes 109, 1981, 447–472.

BIBLIOGRAPHY: F. ARONADIO, Due fonti Laerziane: Sozione e Demetrio di Magnesia, in: Elenchos 11, 1990, 203–255; M. GIGANTE, Demetrio di Magnesia e Cicerone, in: Ciceroniana 5, 1984, 189–197; J. JANDA, D'Antisthène, auteur des Successions des philosophes, in: Listy Filologické 89, 1966, 341–364; F. LEO, Die griech.-röm. Biographie nach ihrer lit. Form, 1901, 39–45 (repr. 1990); J. MEJER, Diogenes Laertius and his Hellenistic Background, 1978, passim, especially 38–39; G. A. SCHEURLEER, De Demetrio Magnete, 1858; E. SCHWARTZ, s.v. D. (80), RE 4, 2814–17.

[38] **D. of Tarsus.** One of the people in Plutarch's treatise *De defectu oraculorum*, where he is termed 'the grammarian' (ὁ γραμματικός; *ho grammatikós*, 410a). For the suggested identification with a [S]crib(onius?) Demetrius, who dedicated two tablets with Greek inscriptions G XIV 2548) in British Eboracum (York), cf. [4]. By contrast, [2] would like to identify him with D. [41], the author of Περὶ ἑρμηνείας.

→ Plutarchus

1 L. COHN, s.v. D. (107), RE 4, 2847 2 W. RHYS ROBERTS, Demetrius. On Style, Loeb, ²1932, 270–281 3 SCHMID/STÄHLIN II, 425 and no. 4 4 A. STEIN, s.v. Scribonius (12), RE 2 A, 876.

[39] **D. Gonypesus.** (ὁ Γονύπεσος; *ho Gonýpesos*). Greek grammarian of uncertain dating but before the 2nd cent. AD, as Herodian quotes him (schol. Hom. Il. 8,233 b). He is also mentioned in schol. Hom. Il. 13,137 b; 15,683–4 (Eust. ad Hom. Il. 1037, 57).

→ Herodianus

L. COHN, s.v. D. (102), RE 4, 2847; F. MONTANARI, Demetrius of Phaleron on Literature, in: Dicaearchus of Messene and Demetrius of Phaleron, Rutgers University Studies in Classical Humanities IX, 1997.

[40] **D. Pyctes.** (ὁ Πύκτης; *ho Pýktēs*). Greek grammarian of uncertain dating but before the 1st cent. AD, as → Apollonius Sophistes (121,24f.) quotes his work Περὶ διαλέκτων. Another reference appears in EM 592,54.

L. COHN, s.v. D. (103), RE 4, 2847; M. SCHMIDT, Die Grammatiker Demetrius ὁ Πύκτης und Zenodotus Mallotes, in: RhM 20, 1865, 456. F.M.

[41] Author of the treatise 'On style' (Περὶ ἑρμηνείας), wrongly identified with D. of Phalerum in the most important MSS (including the oldest, the famous Parisinus graecus 1741, 10th cent. AD). Dating him has been contentious, with hypotheses ranging from the 3rd cent. BC to the 2nd, or early 1st cent. AD (cf. [3], who believes D. of Alexandria or Syria to be the author; Diog. Laert. 5.84; Cic. Brut. 315). After an introduction (§§ 1–35: Definition of phrase, clause, sentence, and line of reasoning (κῶλα, κόμμα, περίοδος, ἐνθύμημα) the work treats the four style types (§§ 36–304): elevated (μεγαλοπρεπής), elegant (γλαφυρός), simple (ἰσχνός), and the bitingly vehement (δεινός) and the variations in each case: frosty (ψυχρός), affected (κακόζηλος), dry (ξηρός), the repulsively charmless (ἄχαρις) under the three headings of content, style and composition (πράγματα, λέξις, σύνθεσις). D. is opposed to rigid schema (cf. § 37) and his complex analytical method does not at all resemble that of a textbook. The treatise has a decidedly Peripatetic flavour (Aristotle, Theophrastus) but also displays Stoic influences (e.g. the naturalistic theory of the origins of language). D. claims to be the first to treat elegant style (therefore apparently before Dion. Hal. Comp. 23). The excerpts on epistolary style §§ 223–235 were printed separately and translated in the 16th cent., by J. Sambucus (1567) and J. Lipsius (1591). Although D.'s treatise was already available in a Latin translation from the Middle Ages [11] and exercised a special influence in the 16th cent. (ed. princeps: Aldus Manutius 1508–09; comm. by Pier Vettori, 1562), it was more or less overshadowed later on by the treatise 'On the Sublime' (Περὶ ὕψους); the history of its rich later influence and aesthetic actuality has still to be written [8. 163–205].

EDITIONS: 1 L. Radermacher, 1901 2 W. RHYS ROBERTS, 1902 (repr. 1927 und 1953) 3 P. CHIRON, 1993 4 D. C. INNES, 1995.

BIBLIOGRAPHY: 5 H. GÄRTNER, Demetriana varia, in: Hermes 118, 1990, 213–236 6 G. M. A. GRUBE, A Greek Critic, 1961 7 G. A. KENNEDY, in: The Cambridge History of Literary Criticism, I, 1990, 196–198 8 G. MORPURGO-TAGLIABUE, D., dello stile, 1980 9 K. PAFFENROTH, A note on the dating of D.' On style, in:

CQ 44, 1994, 280–281 10 D. M. SCHENKEVELD, Studies in D.' On Style, 1964 11 B. V. WALL, A medieval Latin version of D.' De elocutione, 1937. S.FO.

[42] **D. from Troezen.** (ὁ Τροιζήνιος; *ho Troizénios*). Greek grammarian of uncertain dating but before the 3rd cent. AD: Diog. Laert. 8,74 quotes his work 'Against Sophists' (Κατὰ σοφιστῶν) on occasion of the death of Empedocles. He is quoted twice, without references to the title of the works, by Athenaeus: 1,29a on the title of the second 'Thesmophoriazusai' of Aristophanes; 4,139c on Didymus' [1] epithet βιβλιολάθας (this evidence is not given in SCHMIDT, Didymi Chalc. Fragmenta). He has nothing to do with the homonymous historian from Argos mentioned by Clement of Alexandria, Protreptikos 4,47,5 (I 36,13 STÄHLIN).
→ Demetrius [33]; → Diogenes Laertios

L. COHN, s.v. D. (106), RE 4, 2847; PFEIFFER, KPI, 332 n. 140; FHG IV 383 = DIELS, Poetarum Philosophorum Fragmenta, fr. 1. F.M.

[43] **D. Triclinius.** (*c.* AD 1280 to *c.* 1340; until 1316 the form of his name was: Triklines). Born in Thessalonica and worked there; teacher, copyist, editor and commentator of classical texts, the most important philologist and textual critic of the early Palaeologi period; follower (and pupil ?) of Thomas Magistros. For a short while he belonged to the circle of Maximus Planudes. As well as his work as copyist (MSS of → Aphthonius and → Hermogenes, → Theocritus, → Hesiod), he revised the oldest MS of → Babrius and compiled a complete edition of the Anthologia Planudea (→ Anthology [1]). He owes his reputation to his recensions of → Aristophanes [3] and the tragedians [1; 2], being the first to tackle works that were not read in schools. Like Planudes, he used several versions of a text as the basis for his annotated editions. As a rule he combined his own scholia with antique versions and those of Thomas Magistros and Manuel Moschopoulos. His strength, however, lay in his knowledge of ancient metrics, and that was his mainstay in making textual emendations. It is typical of D. Triclinius that he laboured over his editions, e.g. Aristophanes (cf. [3]) and Euripides (cf. [4]), for several years at a time. His treatise on the moon [5] attests to his interest in astronomy.

1 O. L. SMITH, Studies in the Scholia on Aeschylus. I: The Recensions of Demetrius Triclinius, 1975
2 R. AUBRETON, Démétrius Triclinius et les recensions médiévales de Sophocle, 1949 3 W. J. W. KOSTER, Autour d'un manuscrit d'Aristophane écrit par Démétrius Triclinius, in: Études paléographiques et critiques sur les éditions d'Aristophane de l'epoque byzantine tardive, 1957
4 G. ZUNTZ, An Inquiry into the Transmission of the Plays of Euripides, 1965 5 A. WASSERSTEIN, An unpublished treatise by Demetrius Triclinius on lunar theory ed. with introduction and notes, in: Jb. der Österr. Byzantinistik 16, 1967, 153 174.

HUNGER, Literatur, II, 73–77; N. G. WILSON, Scholars of Byzantium, 1983, 249–256; Prosopograph. Lexicon der Palaiologenzeit, 1976, 29317; A.-M. TALBOT, s.v. Triklinios, D., ODB 3, 2116. I.V.

VI. ARTISTS

[44] Son of Glaucon, epigraphically attested sculptor in Miletus around 100 BC. Identification with a priest who dedicated statues in Didyma is unconvincing.

E. THOMAS, Demetrios Glaukou Milesios, in: MDA I(Ist) 33, 1983, 124–133.

[45] Sculptor or workshop proprietor who signed the statue of a *dadophoros* in a Mithraeum in Emerita Augusta around AD 155. Other statues from that complex of finds were ascribed to him. In Sparta three Antoninian herms or bases of memorial statues are signed by a 'D., son of Demetrius'.

LOEWY, no. 347–349; G. LIPPOLD, s.v. D., RE Suppl. 3, 331 no. 127a. R.N.

[46] Greek painter from the 1st half of the 2nd cent. BC, at the Ptolemaic court in Alexandria, worked later on in Rome, where his stay in 164 BC was documented. In keeping with his epithet ὁ τοπογράφος ('the topographer') he painted landscapes in which the geographical characteristics of a region, in his case Egypt, were illustrated in a textbook fashion, like literary topographies. An example of this style of painting is preserved at Praeneste in a Nile landscape, populated with people, flora and fauna, on a mosaic copy. Influences of this Hellenistic-Alexandrian genre also in religious-idyllic landscape portraits of Roman-Campanian mural paintings with numerous Aegyptiaca.

L. GUERRINI, s.v. Demetrios 6, EAA 3, 70; H. MEYER, Kunst und Gesch., 1983, 116–118; OVERBECK, no. 2141–2142 (Sources); J. J. POLLITT, The Ancient View of Greek Art, 1974, 333; I. SCHEIBLER, Griech. Malerei der Ant., 1994, 179f. N.H.

[47] Son of D., sculptor from Rhodes. Together with Theon of Antioch, he signed a bronze statue in Lindos and a marble horse in Alexandria. The not uncommon name has made his classification difficult in an epigraphically based genealogy, and it was recently shifted from the 1st cent. into the 1st half of the 2nd cent. BC. In the absence of any other clues, none of the Hellenistic masterpieces (Laocoon, Scylla-Group) can be attributed to him.

V. GOODLETT, Rhodian sculpture workshops, in: AJA 95, 1991, 669–681; P. MORENO, Scultura ellenistica, 1994, 605, 638, 682; O. ROSSBACH, s.v. D. (124), RE 4, 2851; G. LIPPOLD, s.v. D. (124), RE Suppl. 3, 330.

[48] Bronze sculptor from the Attic deme Alopece, famous as *anthropōpoiós* ('creator of men') for the realistic detail of his portraiture. There is literary evidence for a statue of Athena with realistic snakes on the aegis and portraitures of Simon (hipparch 424/423 BC), Pelichus (fleet commander in Corinth in 434 BC) and the priestess Lysimache in old age. Her portrait is usually seen to be represented by a copy of an old woman's head in London (BM). A base from the Acropolis, which bore the likeness of Syeris (Lysimache's servant)

cannot be associated with D.'s work. Likewise other, generally restored signatures on bases from the early 4th cent. BC cannot be authoritatively ascribed.

LIPPOLD, 226; LOEWY, no. 62–64; OVERBECK, no. 897–903 (Sources); A.E. RAUBITSCHEK, Dedications from the Athenian Akropolis, 1949, 488, no.143; L.TODISCO, Scultura greca del IV secolo, 1993, 61–62. R.N.

Demeusis (Δήμευσις; *Dḗmeusis*). Confiscation of assets by the state.

1. *Demeusis* is encountered in Greek criminal law together with capital punishment, lifelong exile or penalties for severe crimes but the term *demeusis* is not always used. Occasionally, *demeusis* occurred in Athens on its own (cf. Dem. Or. 47,44). Plato (Leg. 855a) radically rejected confiscation, apparently because of the injustice to innocent heirs [1]. The property was always confiscated for the benefit of the community even though the sum wholly or partially went to a temple [2]. A precursor of later confiscation is evident in SIG³ 527,124 [3]. Normally the whole property was taken over, only in rare cases this was restricted to some assets.

2. In Athens' enforcement procedure *demeusis* was the last measure against defaulting debtors for collecting the debt to the state, which doubled after failing to meet the deadline. The sum was recovered from the sales value of the assets [4].

→ Demioprata

1 T.J. SAUNDERS, Plato's Penal Code, 1991, 290 2 G. THÜR, H. TAEUBER, Prozeßrechtliche Inschriften Arkadiens, 1994, no. 8 3 K. LATTE, Beiträge zum griech. Strafrecht, in: Hermes 66, 1931, 143 (= KS, 1968, 280) 4 A.R.W. HARRISON, The Law of Athens II, 1971, 178f. and 186. G.T.

Demigod see → Hero cult; → Hercules

Deminutio capitis

A. ANTIQUITY B. MIDDLE AGES AND MODERN PERIOD

A. ANTIQUITY

Deminutio capitis (DC) is a diminished legal position and a change in *status* (Gai. inst. 1,159: *prioris status permutatio*; Inst. Iust. 1,16 pr.). The differentiation of legal capacity in Roman law according to *status libertatis, status civitatis* and *status familiae* resulted in three *genera* of DC (Dig. 4,5,11). The Roman jurists distinguished between a *deminutio capitis maxima* (loss of freedom), *minor sive media* (loss of citizenship) and *minima* (change in family affiliation; Gai. Inst. 1,159ff.; Inst. Iust. 1,16).

The loss of freedom and with that the loss of legal capacity applied to prisoners of war (*captivitas*), in the Imperial period it was also a penalty, e.g., with sentencing to forced labour, *ad metalla*. Loss of citizenship and family affiliation were associated. Inversely, manumission of a slave was not considered as a DC (Inst. Iust. 1,16,4). Citizenship was also lost through emigration by transferring residence and by → *aqua et igni interdictio* (Gai. Inst. 1,161). All legal transactions that terminate *patria potestas* and agnatic kinship result in a *deminutio capitis minima*, i.e.→ *emancipatio, adoptio, conventio in manum, remancipatio*, giving a houseborn child into *mancipium* as well as acts by which a legally capable person (*persona sui iuris*) becomes a legally incapable person (*persona alieni iuris*) (*adrogatio*, establishment of *manus*). The effects of DC were equated with death (Gai.Inst. 3,153: dissolution of a *societas*) so that previous legal relationships were extinguished according to the *ius civile*. However, the praetor protected creditors after *adrogatio* (adoption) or *conventio in manum* (transfer into marital power) by reinstating the previous status (*in integrum restitutio*).

B. MIDDLE AGES AND MODERN PERIOD

Roman thought on *status* was adopted by the Middle Ages as well as in early common law and expanded by the terms *status naturalis* and *civilis*. However, the *status familiae* no longer had the same meaning as in Roman law because of children's ability to own property. However, the *patria potestas* did not generally end with the age of majority except in special local regulations but rather because of marriage, foundation of an independent household or entry into a monastery and declaration to the authorities. This was not considered as a DC. *Status naturalis* covers natural properties of humans, such as age and gender. By contrast, *status civilis* rests entirely on legal regulations such as distinctions regarding natives and foreigners or rank. Thus, the teachings on status helped integrate status differences in private law. Under the influence of natural law, the teaching of *status* was replaced by the recognition of birthrights (§ 16 ABGB) and a uniform legal capability.

COING I, 1985, §§ 35f.; F. DESSERTEAUX, Études sur la formation historique de la capitis deminutio, 3 vols., 1909–1928; M. KASER, Zur Gesch. der capitis deminutio, IURA 3, 1952, 48–89; KASER, RPR I, 1971, 271f. P.A.

Deminutivum see → Word formation

Demioprata (δημιόπρατα; *dēmióprata*).

[1] The public auction of goods for the benefit of the Athenian state treasury. They were initially submitted for confiscation in the course of the → *dḗmeusis* mostly by the plaintiffs in the main proceeding. After the index (the → *apographḗ*) of the goods to be confiscated had been read to the public assembly, 'to notify everyone of the dispossessed property' (Aristot. Ath. Pol. 43,4), it was forwarded to the Eleven, under whose chairmanship a court decided on the claims of third parties (→ *enepískēpsis*) with respect to claims and material rights (Poll. 8,61; Dem. Or. 49,45). Only then was it possible for the *poletai* to auction the goods to the highest bidder in the presence of the council (Aristot. Ath. Pol. 47,3). The archonts confirm the full rights that were based on the publication of the auction, the lapse

of the former title that was not enforced in due time and direct acquisition from the state.

[2] Indices of publicly auctioned goods compiled by the *poletai* (Poll. 10,96). Examples of such indices: IG II[2] 1582; Hesperia 5, 1936, 393; 10, 1941, 14 and 19; 1950, 244.

F. Pringsheim, Der griech. Versteigerungskauf, in: Gesammelte Abhandlungen, 1961, 305f. A. Kränzlein, Eigentum und Besitz im griech. Recht, 1963, 117f. G.T.

Demiourgos

[1] Epigram poet of an unknown period (with a peculiar, otherwise undocumented name), author of an insignificant distich on Hesiod (Anth. Pal. 7,52).

FGE 38. E.D.

[2] *Dēmiourgoí* (δημιουργοί, 'public workers') were occupied with public matters at various levels, depending on time and place. 1. In the Linear B tablets from Pylos *dḗmos* is found but not *demiourgoi*; it has been suggested [2] but not universally accepted that in the Mycenaean world *demiourgoi* were the workers of *dḗmos*-land as opposed to other kinds of land. 2. In Homer *demiourgoi* are independent craftsmen such as metal workers, potters and masons; also seers, doctors, bards and heralds (cf. e.g., Od. 17,382–385). 3. In the later Greek world the word is used sometimes in the Homeric sense (e.g. regularly by Plato and Xenophon), sometimes as the title of major officials in a state (cf. Aristot. Pol. 5, 1310b22). *Demiourgoi* in this second sense are found in Elis (e.g., [6. 61]) and many states of mainland Greece (e.g. Cleitor [6. 16] and Oeanthea [6. 58]), in Crete (e.g. Olus, ICret I 22,4) and several Aegean islands; and in the Roman period in Asia Minor. The federal Arcadia of the 360s had fifty *damiorgoí* (Tod 132). In the Achaean League as revived in the third cent. there was a board of ten *damiorgoí*, who with the *stratēgós* presided at meetings (Liv. 32,22,2). At Delphi the word at first referred to officials in general, but by the time of the Roman principate the *demiourgoi* were the citizens with full rights, eligible to hold office. 4. In Athens there are references to a division of the citizen body into *eupatrídai*, farmers and *demiourgoi*, and to the involvement of those classes in the appointment of the archonts after 580 BC (Aristot. Ath. Pol. fr. 2–3; 13,2), but the farmers and the *demiourgoi* are probably the result of 4th-cent. speculation.

Mycenaean period: 1 K. Murakawa, Demiurgos, in: Historia 6, 1957, 385–415 2 L.R. Palmer, Mycenaean Greek Texts from Pylos, in: TPhS 1954, 18–53b
Crete: 3 M. Guarducci, Demiurgi in Creta, in: RFIC 58 = [2]8, 1930, 54–70
Delphi: 4 C. Vatin, Damiurges et Épidamiurges à Delphes, in: BCH 85, 1961, 236–55
Athens: 5 Rhodes, 71–2, 182–4 6 C. D. Buck, Greek Dialects, [3]1955. P.J.R.

[3] In Plato's age δημιουργός (*dēmiourgós*) simply meant craftsmen. In a critical consideration of his predecessors' theories of causes, Plato emphasized in his cosmology and cosmogony the supremacy of the mind over matter or a nature creating without reason (Pl. Phd. 96a ff.; Leg. 886b ff.) and illustrates this with the introduction of a God who, like a versatile artist or craftsman [4. 35ff., 53f.], creates his work from available materials according to a predetermined plan (Pl. Resp. 507c; 530 a; 597b ff.; Pl. Soph. 265c ff.; Pl. Plt. 269c ff.; 272e ff.; Pl. Ti.). Instead of the *dēmiourgós,* Plato also speaks of ὁ ποιητὴς καὶ πατήρ (*ho poiētḕs kaì patḗr*), ὁ τεκταινόμενος (*ho tektainómenos*), ὁ συνιστάς (*ho synistás*), ὁ ποιῶν (*ho poiôn*), ὁ συνδήσας (*ho syndḗsas*), ὁ συνθείς (*ho syntheís*), ὁ γεννήσας (*ho gennḗsas*), ὁ κηροπλάστης (*ho kēroplástēs*). Later the synonyms τεχνίτης (*technítēs*), χειροτέχνης (*cheirotéchnēs*), χειρῶναξ (*cheirônax*), (ἀρχι)τέκτων (*árchitéktōn*), ἀριστοτέχνης (*aristotéchnēs*) are also used. In Latin the terms *aedificator, architecton, artifex, conditor, (con)formator, effector, fabricator, factor* are equivalents.

The demiurgic creations of the gods are just as pre-Platonic as the use of the term *dēmiourgós* for the creating god [17. 695ff.]. What is new in Plato is the absolute primacy of the mind in all natural creation because the work of the *demiourgos* is the work of reason (Pl. Ti. 36d8ff.; 39e7ff.; 47e3ff. [7. 425, 603ff.; 4. 76ff.]). Also new is that this *demiourgos* looks at an intelligible model in his creations (Pl. Ti. 28c f. etc.) and creates a world order obeying mathematical laws and a mathematically structured cosmos (*Timaeus*). The *demiourgos* not only produced the cosmos but also the World Soul (Pl. Ti. 34b10ff.) and the astral deities that are, in turn, demiurgical creators (Pl. Ti. 38c 3ff.).

In the period after Plato the idea of a world-creating god retreats [4. 55ff.], but both Aristotle as well as the Stoa and the Hellenistic physicians use the term δημιουργεῖν (*dēmiurgeîn)* to describe the purposeful creation of nature or the Logos (Bonitz, Index Aristotelicus 174 b 14ff.; SVF I 85,493 [17. 697f.]). By contrast, Epicurus rejected any notion of a reasoned and purposeful creation and maintenance of the world [2. 25, 30f.] and the scepticist Academy subjects them to doubt (Cic. Nat. D. 3,11,27f.; Lactant. Div. inst. 2,8,9ff.; 3,28,3f. [17. 698f.]).

In the Platonism of the Imperial period the thought of a world creation by the divine *demiourgos* is revitalized [4. 58ff.]; the *demiourgos* became an absolute mind (νοῦς/*noûs*) or as the soul (ψυχή/*psychḗ*) or mind of the divine soul; the ideal model is accordingly either ranked before, equal or after (Procl. In Tim. 1,322,20ff. Diehl [4. 66; 9. 238ff.; 16. 15ff.; 3. 39ff.; 6. 527Iff.; 12. 548ff.]). In Platonism before Plotinus, the *demiourgos* is usually equated to the idea of goodness [3. 40; 19. 135[427]], in Neoplatonism 'goodness itself' is ranked above it as 'the One'. As a metaphysical part of the tetradically structured model (Pl. Ti. 39e 7ff.), the *demiourgos* in Neoplatonism is called the *tetrás*

[13. 266ff.; 14. 242ff.], and because the *tetrás* potentially contains the *dekás*, it is also called the *dekás* [11. 98ff., 104]. Occasionally, the number of *demiourgoi* is increased to two [4. 61ff., 64f.; 1. 257ff.] or three [4. 65f., 68; 5. 831ff.; 8. 106ff., 111ff.]. The position of the *demiourgos* after the One continued to shift because of the continuous interposition of intermediary elements [4. 67ff.]. In Proclus the *demiourgos* takes the ninth and last position in the area of the mind [17. 703f.; 4. 68f.].

The concept of the demiurgic creating god also entered into medicine (Galen) [10. 334ff.], hermetics, the Chaldaean Oracles [17. 700ff.], Jewish [17. 704ff.; 15] and Christian philosophy as well as Gnosticism [17. 706ff.] — while strongly diminishing the *demiourgos*. On other consequences, see [18].

1 M. Baltes, Numenios von Apamea und der Platonische Timaios, in: Vigiliae Christianae 29, 1975, 241–270 2 H. Baltes, Die Weltentstehung des Platonischen Timaios nach den antiken Interpreten I, 1976 3 H. Baltes Zur Philosophie des Platonikers Attikos, in: Platonismus und Christentum, FS H. Dörrie, ed. by H.-D. Blume, F. Mann, 1983 (JbAC Supplement 10) 38–57
4 L. Brisson, Le même et l'autre dans la structure ontologique du Timée de Platon, 1974, 27–106 5 Id., Amélius: Sa vie, son oeuvre, sa doctrine, son style, in: ANRW II 36.2, 1987, 793–860 6 L. Brisson, M. Patillon, Longinus, in: ANRW II 36.7, 1994, 5214–5299 7 H. Cherniss, Aristotle's Criticism of Plato and the Academy, 1944 8 W. Deuse, Theodoros von Asine, 1973 9 W. Deuse, Der Demiourgos bei Porphyrios und Iamblich, in: C. Zintzen (ed.), Die Philosophie des Neuplatonismus, 1977, 238–278 10 P. Donini, Motivi filosofici in Galeno, in: PP 35,1980, 333–370 11 S. Gersh, From Iamblichus to Eriugena, 1978 12 S. Gersh, Middle Platonism and Neoplatonism I/II, 1986 13 I. Hadot, Ist die Lehre des Hierokles vom Demiourgos christl. beeinflußt? Kerygma und Logos, in: FS C. Andresen, ed. by A. M. Ritter, 1979, 258–271 14 I. Hadot, Le démiurge comme principe dérivé dans le système ontologique d'Hiéroclès, in: REG 103, 1990, 241–262 15 D. T. Runia, Philo of Alexandria and the *Timaeus* of Plato, 1986 16 W. Theiler, Die Vorbereitung des Neuplatonismus, 1930 17 W. Theiler, s.v. Demiourgos, RAC 3, 694–711 18 W. Ullmann, s.v. Demiourgos, HWdPh 2, 1972, 49–50 19 J. Whittaker, P. Louis (ed., transl.), Alcinoos, Enseignement des doctrines de Platon, 1990.

M.BA.

Demo (Δημώ; *Dēmṓ*). Shortened form of a compound (see D. [3], [4]).

[1] The daughter of → Celeus, king of Eleusis, and → Metaneira. Together with her sisters Callidice, Cleisidice and Callithoe, she has a friendly encounter with → Demeter who is wandering about in the shape of an old woman (Hom. H. 2,109).

[2] Name of the Cymaean → Sibyl, of whom, however, the Cymaeans did not know an oracle. They could only point to a water jug that contained the bones of the Sibyl (Hyperochus FGrH 576 2 = Paus. 10,12,8). D. is a short form for Demophile (Varro in Lactant. Div. inst. 1,6,10, where she is also called Amalthea or Herophile).

H. W. Parke, Sibyls and Sibylline Prophecy in Classical Antiquity, 1988, 71–94.

[3] Label on an Attic vase that shows → Amphiaraus with his family. Probably a shortened form for his daughter → Demonassa.

I. Krauskopf, s.v. Amphiaraos, no. 27, LIMC 1.1, 697

[4] Together with Deo a shortened form of Demeter (Suda s.v. D. 473 Adler; EM 264,8 Gaisford).

1 Schwyzer, Gramm. 636f. 2 E. Maass, Mythische Kurznamen, in: RH 23, 1888, 614.

R.B.

[5] Interpreter of Homer, probably of the 5th cent. AD; she is quoted in the scholia on Homer and Lucian, especially by Eustathius and Tzetzes. The fragments demonstrate that she offered interpretations of Homeric myths and deities from a rationalizing perspective on an astronomic and astrological basis in the context of the traditional allegorical exegesis of Homer.
→ Philology; → Eustathius

Editions: A. Ludwich, Die Homerdeuterin Demo, FS L. Friedländer, 1895, 296–321; A. Ludwich, in: Index lectionum in Regia Academia Albertina I e II, Regiomonti 1912/1913 and 1914)
Bibliography: L. Cohn, s.v. Demo (6), RE Suppl. 1, 345–46; K. Reinhardt, De Graecorum theologia, 1910, 47–49; W. Kroll, s.v. Demo. (2a), RE Suppl. 3, 331–333; H. Usener, KS III, 33–36.

F.M.

Democedes (Δημοκήδης; *Dēmokḗdēs*) of Croton. Greek physician, lived about 500 BC and according to Hdt. 3,125 was the best physician of his age. He was the son of Calliphon and practised in Croton before going to Aegina. After a year the town of Aegina employed him for one talent as the community's physician but a year later he moved to Athens for a higher salary and finally into the service of Polycrates of Samos who paid two talents. After Polycrates' assassination D. was taken as a slave to Susa, where he came to the notice of king Darius, who had seriously injured his ankle. D.'s treatment, which was gentler than that of the Egyptian court doctors, was successful and resulted in his release from prison. From then on he enjoyed wealth and influence at the court. Healing queen Atossa gave him the opportunity to escape to Italy where he again settled in Croton and married the daughter of the wrestler Milon. Although Herodotus' account (3,129–137) occasionally resembles an Oriental tale, it contains important information on the nascent institutionalization of medicine. In the Greek world D. was the first doctor employed by a community for whose services there was competition as Herodotus indicates. D. travelled in the Mediterranean world and in Aegina was able to transform himself within one year from a penniless immigrant to a respected healer. His success at the Persian court was at the expense of the Egyptian physicians who were considered the leading physicians, and brought him prosperity and influence.
→ Medicine

V.N.

Demochares (Δημοχάρης; *Dēmochárēs*).

[1] Mentioned by Seneca as an Athenian delegate to Philip II and compared to the Homeric → Thersites because of his open and bold style of speech (cf. Il. 2,212ff.) (Sen. De ira 3,23,2f.). Possibly identical with D. [3] PA 3716. M.MEI.

[2] The son of Demon of the Paeania deme, a relative of → Demosthenes, possibly as commander of the cavalry, he was Athenian delegate and witness of the oath of *symmachia* with Amyntas (IG II^2 102,19?) in 375/4 or 373/2 BC, syntrierarch (IG II^2 1612,313), sued as member of a *symmoria* for equipping the fleet, died before the summer of 356 (Dem. Or. 47,22–28; 32). DAVIES 144 see Demon 3737 (B); DEVELIN no. 744; PA 3718.

→ Athens J.E.

[3] The son of Laches, Athenian orator, historian and politician, nephew of Demosthenes, *c.* 350–271 BC. After the death of Demetrius of Phalerum in 307, D. achieved political significance (cf. the document in Ps.-Plut. Mor. 850F–51F). In the war against Cassander (307–303) he caused Athens to arm and fortify and concluded a treaty with the Boeotians. In 303 he was exiled for criticizing the cult of Demetrius [2] Poliorcetes (cf. FGrH 75 F 2); return during the archontate of Diocles (288/7?). He regained Eleusis from Macedonia and obtained financial support from Lysimachus, Antipater and Ptolemy I. In 280 he petitioned for a statue of Demosthenes and was given one himself after his death (Ps.-Plut. Mor. 847C-E = T 1).

Author of a contemporary history in 21 books rather more in the style of an orator than a historian (Cic. Brut. 286). The dates of his birth and death are uncertain, but since F 3 refers to the death of Demosthenes and F 5 to that of Agathocles, a period of 322–289/8 is conceivable. As a democrat by conviction his assessment of Demetrius of Phaleron is very negative (F 4). Only 5 fragments are attested. FGrH 75 (with commentary). PA 3716 D. TRAILL, PAA 321970.

R. A. BILLOWS, Antigonus the One-Eyed and the Creation of the Hellenistic State, 1990, 337ff.; O. LENDLE, Einführung in die griech. Geschichtsschreibung, 1992; K. MEISTER, Die griech. Geschichtsschreibung, 1990, 127; F. W. WALBANK, K.S. SACKS, s.v. Demochares, OCD, ^{3}1996, 451. K.MEI.

[4] **Papius** (?) **D.** Freedman of Sextus Pompeius, distinguished as a commander of the fleet at Cyme in 38 BC and operated successfully against Octavian (→ Augustus) and Lepidus, but at Mylai in 36, D. only escaped by chance. After the defeat of Naulochus he killed himself (App. B Civ. 5,83ff.; 105f.; Cass. Dio 49,2–10; Oros. 6,18,26, there Demochas).

M. HADAS, Sextus Pompey, 1966, 110ff., 130, 128^{29}. M.MEI.

Democles (Δημοκλῆς; *Dēmoklês*).

[1] At the baths the Athenian D. saved himself as an 'immature boy' (παῖς ἄνηβος; *paîs ánēbos*) from erotic pursuit by → Demetrius [2] Poliorcetes by jumping into a kettle of boiling water but was killed as a result (Plut. Demetrios 24,2–6). D. is not identical with the defender of the sons of Lycurgus against the suits of Moerocles and Menesaechmus (Ps.-Plut. Mor. 842E). → Athens J.E.

[2] Attic orator of the school of → Theophrastus; he defended the sons of Lycurgus (Ps.-Plut., Vitae decem oratorum, 842 E); perhaps he is identical to the Demokleides mentioned by Dionysius of Halicarnassus (De Dinarcho 11), according to Timaeus an opponent of → Demochares (Suda). M.W.

Democrates (Δημοκράτης; *Dēmokrátēs*).

[1] Attic orator of the 4th cent. BC from Aphidna, probably an older contemporary of Demosthenes [2] (about 338 BC he is called γέρων (*gérōn*; old man), cf. Stob. Floril. 3,22,43). As the descendant of → Harmodius or → Aristogeiton, he had a claim to free provisions in the Prytaneion (Hyp. 4,3). He belonged to the Pro-Macedonian party (Hyp. 4,2). He is also mentioned in Aeschin. Leg. 2,17 and Isaeus 6,22.

BLASS, 3,2. M.W.

[2] of Sicyon. Tragedian, late 3rd cent. BC (CAT A 6,5). Perhaps identical to the poet mentioned in DID A 3b, 41 (see TrGF 68) who once won at the Lenaea (*c.* 373).

TrGF 124. F.P.

Democriteans A Democritean school as an institution of education and research similar to Plato's Academy or Aristotle's Lyceum did not exist. Diog. Laert. 9,58 (Vita Anaxarchi), Euseb. Praep. evang. 14,17,10 and Clem. Strom. 1,64 essentially provide the same series of succession: → Democritus — Nessas or Nessus of Chios (69 DK) and also → Protagoras (80 DK, who was probably rather an older contemporary of Democritus) → Metrodorus of Chios (70 DK) — → Diogenes [13] of Smyrna (71 DK) — → Anaxarchus of Abdera (72 DK). This series names philosophers from Abdera and other cities who expounded completely different teaching opinions. This sequence emphasizes that the Democritean criticism of the senses was related to relativism and could effortlessly lead to it (Protagoras and possibly Diogenes of Smyrna) but also to other development phases and orientations in Scepticism (Metrodorus, Pyrrho). That one's teachings could also be turned into their opposite is suggested by the information that Pyrrho's student Nausiphanes (75 DK) was the teacher of → Epicurus. Thus, there is no proof that the Democriteans closely attached themselves to specific teachings of the Atomists (→ Atomism).

H. STECKEL, s.v. Demokritos, RE Suppl. 12, 221–3. I.B.

Democritus (Δημόκριτος; *Dēmókritos*).
[1] of Abdera
A. LIFE AND WRITING B. ATOMISTIC THEORY
C. OTHER TEACHINGS

A. LIFE AND WRITING

D. was active in the 2nd half of the 5th cent. and one of the main representatives of ancient → Atomism, which he adopted from → Leucippus. Their respective contributions to the theory of the atom are difficult to differentiate. It is characteristic in this context that the 'Great World Order' (Μέγας διάκοσμος; *Mégas diákosmos*) listed in an index of D.'s writings (by Diog. Laert. 9,45 = 68A33 DK) was a treatise by Leucippus according to Theophrastus, while Epicurus questioned the existence of Leucippus altogether.

D. was renowned for his long life. If he spent time in Athens, this was not preserved by tradition (68A1 DK). The long journeys attributed to D. do not necessarily indicate more than the encyclopaedic breadth of his works (cf. 68B64 and B65 DK).

D.'s writings were ordered according to thematic criteria as a tetralogical canon by → Thrasyllus. Tetralogies 1–2 contained works on ethics, 3–6 on physics, but also on psychology and logic (the list by Diogenes Laertius also includes nine unattributed treatises on physics); 7–9 on mathematics including astronomy; 10–11 on poetics and music; and 12–13 treatises on various arts (*téchnai*), among them also medicine. Diogenes Laertius again mentions nine non-Thrasyllic works and claims that everything else taking the name of D. are either compilations of the cited works or spurious. None of these writings have been preserved.

B. ATOMISTIC THEORY

The early atomists took up a number of Eleatic challenges: Parmenides' theorem that the Being must be one because nothing but it exists while Another would divide it into categories (28B8.42–9 DK); Zeno's thesis that continuous division of objects would lead to paradoxical results (29B1, B2 and B3 DK); Melissus' claims that motion is impossible because it requires emptiness (30B7,7ff. DK) and that even if there was a plurality, their constitutive units like the Eleatic One must be unchangeable and eternal (30B8 DK). In reply to these theses the Atomists conceded that there was a void or non-being to separate those things that are. However, being things are eternal and indivisible in this void.

Our sources indicate various reasons for the indivisibility of atoms: (1) the homogeneity of atoms can be founded on an indifference argument (οὐδὲν μᾶλλον; *oudèn mâllon*). Thus, there is no reason why a body should be *more* divisible at one than another point. The possibility that it is divisible everywhere would mean that the body would be divided into infinitely small components from which they could not possibly arise. Therefore, atoms must be one and indivisible (thus Aristot. Gen. corr. 1,8). This may be the same argument if (2) it is said that atoms are sluggish and, therefore, are *a fortiori* also indivisible because of their firmness (στερρότης; *sterrótēs* 68A57 DK) or, because they are solid (ναστaί; *nastaí*) and without part in the void (67A14 DK). (3) In Phys. 925,10ff. (= 67A13 DK) Simplicius explains that atoms are indivisible because of their smallness and because they have no parts. However, the smallness of atoms is a very questionable argument for their indivisibility (and contradicts the assumption that D. — unlike Epicurus — assumed extremely large atoms, 68A43 and A47 DK, cf. Epicurus ad Herodotum 55f.). The assumption that atoms have no parts could explain indivisibility but it is ruled out because of the manner in which atoms interact: it requires that they possess parts like hooks that are differentiated but inseparable from them [1. II,50–8]. The question if the physical theory of atomism is supported by an atomistic mathematics is related to this: 68B155 and B155a DK and the titles Περὶ ψαύσιος κύκλου καὶ σφαίρης (*Perì psaúsios kýklou kaì sphaírēs*; 'On the contact of a circle and a sphere ') and Περὶ ἀλόγων γραμμῶν καὶ ναστῶν (*Perì alógōn grammôn kaì nastôn*; 'On irrational lines and solid bodies') suggest that D. thought about the problem but we do not know what solution he proposed.

Atoms possess weight because of their mass (contrary to the testimony of 68A47 DK, cf. [2]) and, therefore, fall — probably at varying speeds — through the void (68A60, A61 and A135 DK, cf. also Aristotle's *reductio ad absurdum*, which Epicurus later joined, that in the void everything must fall with the same speed). Also, atoms could collide and entangle with each other or bounce into all directions.

What directions atoms and atom complexes actually take depends on three characteristics of atoms: (1) atoms differ from one another because of the *rhysmós* (ῥυσμός) or shape (which probably includes size and by derivation weight, cf. Aristotle in 68A41 DK, where size and shape are the only criteria of differentiation); (2) the *tropḗ* (τροπή) or position explains how the same atom or two atoms with identical *rhysmós* take on two different positions and can unfold very different effects; and (3) the *diathigḗ* (διαθιγή) or arrangement is the structure of a group of atoms which allows that the same type of atoms can be assembled into different phenomena (67A6 and A9 DK).

Atoms are completely characterized by their immutable shape — together with the void they are what actually (ἐτεῇ; *eteêi*) is. Atom complexes possess their sensual properties 'because of convention' (νόμῳ; *nómōi*). Therefore, they can change and under circumstances even depend on perception. Furthermore, these 'secondary' qualities can be explained in very different ways in their causality: cf. Theophrastus' restatement and criticism of D.'s various representations of sensual properties (68A135 DK).

C. OTHER TEACHINGS

Apart from sensual perception, which is restricted to these properties alone and which only is 'hazy cognition' (σκοτίη γνώμη; *skotíē gnṓmē*), there is genuine (γνησίη; *gnēsíē*) cognition. That which is real is recognized by this true cognition, which is separated from the senses (68B11 DK) but cannot be completely independent from them (cf. 68B125 DK), with some degree of certainty (cf. 68B117 DK).

Similar to the preceding natural philosophers, D. presented in detail how innumerable and extremely different *kósmoi* arise from the basic components. D. went over these processes up to the rise of living creatures and added a description of the prehistoric development of humans. In their original phase humans led a lonesome, animal-like existence. Then the necessity of mutual help against the attacks of wild animals drove them together. Language arose from cohabitation while various skills and arts developed from experience (68B5 DK).

The physical teachings of D. have largely come down to us indirectly. The alleged quotes of D. are for most part ethical teachings; about 80 are preserved under the name of a certain Democrates. These sayings praise moderation that enhances satisfaction (εὐθυμίη; *euthymíē*) and condemn extreme behaviour that leads to destabilization of the soul (68B191 DK). Such admonitions were commonplace and, therefore, it is unproven that they derive from D. However, if that is the case, one could assume that the optimal state of the soul has an equivalent in the atomic configuration but the sources contain no clue of a systematic linkage of ethics and physics/psychology.

The epistemic position in ethical questions that is evident in these fragments is similar to D.'s general epistemology: it is only about the realization of what is pleasant (ἡδύ, *hēdý*); the Protagorean thesis that the field of truth and goodness is affected by it is rejected (68B69 DK, cf. 68A114 DK).

→ ATOMISM; → MATERIALISM; → PRE-SOCRATICS

1 J. BARNES, The Presocratic philosophers, 1979
2 D. O'BRIEN, Theories of weight in the ancient world, vol. 1: Democritus, weight and size, 1981.

FRAGMENTS: Diels/Kranz II (68) 81–230; S. LURIA. Demokrit, 1970.
BIBLIOGRAPHY: H. STECKEL, s.v. Demokritos, RE Suppl. 12, 191–223.; T. COLE, Democritus and the Sources of Greek Anthropology, 1967; C. KAHN, Democritus and the origins of moral psychology, in: AJPh 106, 1985, 1–31; S. LURIA, Zur Frage der materialistischen Begründung der Ethik bei Demokrit, 1964; G. VLASTOS, Ethics and physics in Democritus (1945–46), in: G. VLASTOS, Studies in Greek Philosophy, vol. I, 1995, 328–350. I.B.

[2] Platonic philosopher, contemporary of Longinus (3rd cent. AD). Explanations on passages in Plato's *Alcibiades*, *Phaedon* and *Timaeus* quoted by Olympiodorus [1. 40], Damascius [1. 38] and Proclus [1. 52] suggest that D. wrote commentaries on these works [1. 191, 194, 218]. He also seems to have discussed the *Philebus* in detail [1. 198]. Little is known of his teachings. Only a note in Stobaeus (1,370,1f. WACHSMUTH-HENSE) is preserved, according to which D. derived all abilities of the soul from its substance, and another in Syrianus (In Arist. Met. 105,36ff. KROLL) according to which his theory of ideas was the same as that of → Atticus and Plutarch.

1 DÖRRIE/BALTES III, 1993.

L. BRISSON, Notices sur les noms propres, in: Id. et al., Porphyre, La vie de Plotin I, 1982, 78–79; GOULET 2, 716–717. M.BA. and M.-L.L.

[3] Epigram poet, no later than the 1st half of the 1st cent. AD, called 'clear and rich in images' (σαφὴς καὶ ἀνθηρός; 9,49) by Diogenes Laertius. Only one of his poems — a charming one describing the famous Aphrodite Anadyomene by Apelles — is preserved (Anth. Plan. 180, cf. Leonidas of Tarentum, Anth. Pal. 16,182; Antipater of Sidon, Anth. Pal. 178). He should be dated relatively early, i.e. no later than the 'Garland' of Philippus.

FGE 38f. E.D.

Demodice (Δημοδίκη; *Dēmodíkē*). Second wife of the Boeotian king → Athamas and stepmother of Phrixus whom she pursues in unrequited love. Phrixus takes flight for this reason (Pind. fr. 49, Damodika; Schol. Pind. Pyth. 4,288a). Usually she is called → Ino (Apollod. 1,80–84). In another version she is the wife of Cretheus, brother of Athamas. She slanders Phrixus, who will not return her love, before Cretheus, whereupon he demands Phrixus' death from Athamas. However, Phrixus is removed by his mother → Nephele (Hyg. Poet. Astr. 2,20).

P. ANGELI BERNARDINI et al., Le Pittiche (commentary), 1995, 471f.; B.K. BRASWELL, A Commentary on the Fourth Pythian Ode of Pindar, 1988, 243. R.B.

Demodocus (Δημόδοκος; *Dēmódokos*).
[1] Singer at the royal court of the → Phaeaces; as an indirect self-portrait, his slightly idealized description (Hom. Od. 8), just as that of → Phemius, constitutes an important source for the self-perception, working style and social status of the Homeric → *aoidoi*. D. is highly regarded in society; his name ('whom the people receives') is very telling and specifically explained in 'etymological' terms in Od. 8,472. D. presents his songs accompanied by a four-string phorminx at feasts in the palace and open popular assemblies. The songs, which are presented in free improvisations either according to his choice or upon request, treat heroic-epic ('The Quarrel of Achilles and Odysseus'; 'The Wooden Horse') as well as humoristic materials ('The Adultery of Ares and Aphrodite'). The intent of the singer appears to be to 'cheer' the audience (τέρπειν; *térpein*). D. repeatedly interrupts his presentation whereupon the audience encourages him by shouting to continue singing. The blindness of D., which is shared by the 'Singer of Chios' (Hom. H. 3,172) and from which the legend of a blind Homer derives, is compensated for by the Muses with the gift of song. They are also the ones who

cause D. in the current situation to follow 'the path of singing (οἴμη; *oímē*)'. — According to Pausanias (3,18,11), D. was depicted on the throne of Apollo in Amyclae.

A. THORNTON, Homer's Iliad: Its Composition and the Motif of Supplication, 1984, 23–45. RE.N.

[2] Poet from Leros (6th/5th cents. BC?). Aristot. Eth. Nic. 1151a6–11 quotes a witty elegiac distichon (1 WEST) that mocks the Milesians, and Diog. Laert. 1,84 cites a tetrameter praising Bias (6 WEST). The authorship of three distichs and a six-line poem in Anth. Pal. 11,235–238 = 2–5 WEST was questioned by [1], which is unjustified for 2 WEST (it begins καὶ τόδε Δημοδόκου, Str. 487C erroneously gives it as Φωκυλίδου). 5 WEST (quoted by Lydus, *De magistratibus populi Romani* 3,57 and, together with 4 WEST, in Constantinus Porphyrogennetus *De thematibus* 21) probably attacks the prefect Iohannes Cappadox (5th/6th cents. AD); another view in [2].

1 D.A. CAMPBELL, Greek Lyric Poetry, 1967, 343
2 A. CAMERON, The Greek Anthology, 1993, 295, 331.

EDITIONS: GENTILI/PRATO 1, ²1988; IEG 2, 56–58. E.BO.

Demokratia (δημοκρατία; *dēmokratía*, 'people-power') the standard Greek term for a form of government in which power resides with the many rather than with the few (*oligarchía*) or with a single man (*monarchía*). That threefold classification is first found in Pindar's *Pythia* (2,86–88), perhaps of 468 BC; it is used by Herodotus, in his debate about constitutions, set at the 6th-cent. Persian court (3,80–84) and is a commonplace thereafter. Aeschylus mentions the *dḗmou kratoûsa cheîr*, 'powerful hand of the people', (Suppl. 604; perhaps of 463 BC) and the power of the people to make their own decisions is a prominent theme in that play. It is possible that the word *demokratia* was coined in Athens about that time, though some believe it was already used in the late 6th cent. (cf. [2] and [4]). The word could be used to characterize any kind of constitutional government as opposed to despotism, (e.g., Hdt. 4,137,2; 6,43,3), but it came to be used, in accordance with the threefold classification, of the kind of constitutional government in which power resides with the many. Plato's *Politeia* uses a fivefold classification, in which *demokratia* ranks below different kinds of rule by the few but above tyranny. Plato's *Politikós* and Aristotle's 'Politics' distinguish between good and bad versions of each of the three forms of constitution: Aristotle uses *demokratía* for the bad form of rule by the many and *politeía* for the good.

There were two principal differences between a democratic and an oligarchic constitution in Greece. (1) Under a democracy all men of native descent were full citizens, all were able to attend the assembly and to sit in jury-courts, and all or at any rate all except the very poorest were able to hold office. In Athens the poorest citizens were by law debarred from holding office, but in the 4th cent. the law was no longer enforced; and from the middle of the 5th cent. the payment of stipends made it easier for poorer citizens to devote their time to public affairs. (2) Under a democracy power resided with the assembly (→ Ekklesia) rather than a smaller body: the council (→ Boule) and other offices were comparatively weak, and were appointed in a way which prevented the formation of a distinct class of office-holders. In Athens the council had considerable business but little power to act without the assembly's approval; and there were large numbers of offices, most of which were appointed by lot and could be held only for one year in a man's life.

A moderate democracy would not differ greatly from a moderate oligarchy, and which label such a state chose to use might depend on external politics. By the middle of the 5th cent. the Athenians were conscious that they had a democratic constitution and that some other states had a non-democratic constitution, and they were prepared to encourage or enforce democratic constitutions among their allies (e.g., in Erythrae: IG I³ 14 = ML 40). Support for Athens tended to be associated with democracy, and support for Sparta with oligarchy. The Spartan Lysander was fond of extreme oligarchy, and set up oligarchic governments among the former allies of Athens after the Peloponnesian War; there was turmoil in the Peloponnese after Sparta was defeated at Leuctra in 371 BC and became unable to sustain pro-Spartan oligarchies.

The Athenians at first gave the credit for their democracy to Cleisthenes, but later looked back to Solon or even to the legendary Theseus. The pressures of the Peloponnesian War led to the setting-up of oligarchic governments in 411 and in 404, but these were so unpleasant that they did not last long; and they left the Athenians with a determination to adhere to democracy, though in some respects the 4th-cent. constitution departed in practice from democracy as it had been understood in the 5th cent. [1; 6]. Demosthenes tended to identify *dēmokratía*, the freedom of the people to take decisions for their own city, with the freedom of the people from constraint by Philip of Macedon or any other outside power, while his opponents tended to regard him as undemocratic: the law threatening the Areopagus with suspension if the democracy were overthrown (SEG 12, 87), and the emphasis of the cult of *demokratia* in the 330s (e.g. the statue set up by the council of 333/2 (IG II² 2791 and [5]; cf. [3]), are to be understood in this context. There was a painting of Demos and Demokratia in the Stoa of Zeus (Plin. HN 35,129; Paus. 1,3,3); above the law of 337/6 threatening the Areopagus was carved a relief of Demos crowned by Demokratia; the priests of Demokratia and of Demos and the Charites had seats in the theatre (IG II² 5029a).

In the Hellenistic period the term *demokratia* sometimes retained its strong sense, but not always. Polybius writes of good and bad versions of the three constitu-

tions in the same way as Plato and Aristotle (Pol. 6,3,5–4,6). Athens had some periods of non-democratic government in the late 4th and early 3rd cents., mostly as a result of outside intervention, but for most of the time remained democratic in formal structure, though in practice the rich were able to exercise more influence than earlier. Elsewhere some states draw attention to their freedom and their traditional laws (e.g., Ilium, OGIS 218; Smyrna, OGIS 229; Cos, StV 3, 545); others in similar contexts do not use the word *demokratia* (e.g., Priene, IPriene 11; Iasos, IK Iasos 3), but do not seem to be less democratic than those which do; and there are some texts which use the word to refer simply to constitutional government, not necessarily of a democratic kind (e.g., Delphi, SIG^3 613 A; Pergamum, IPerg 413). Many states, like Athens, were democratic in their formal structure in the Hellenistic period and even in the Roman; the general direction of development was away from democracy; newly founded and newly Hellenized states were not usually very democratic; but in mainland Greece, the Aegean islands and the west coast of Asia Minor a significant degree of democracy persisted for a long time [7].
→ Cleisthenes; → Lysander; → Personification; → DEMOKRATIA

1 EDER, Demokratie 2 M.H. HANSEN, in: Liverpool Classical Monthly 11, 1986, 35f. 3 MDAI(A) 66, 1941, 221–27 no. 3 4 C. MEIER, Die Entstehung des Politischen bei den Griechen, 1980, 281–284 5 A.E. RAUBITSCHEK, Hesperia 31, 1962, 242f. 6 P.J. RHODES, in: CJ 75, 1979/80, 305–323 7 P.J. RHODES, D.M. LEWIS, The Decrees of the Greek States, 1997. P.J.R.

Demon (Δήμων; *Dḗmōn*).
[1] Uncle of → Demosthenes, honoured for the way in which he conducted his office as priest in 386/5 BC (IG II^2 1140); possibly trierarch in 373/2 (IG II^2 1607, 26; again later IG II^2 1609,13; [1. 115] see Demosthenes 3597 II).
[2] Son of Demomeles of the Paeania deme, nephew of → Demosthenes, priest of the urban Asclepius cult (IG II^2 4969), probably identical with the rhetor whose extradition was demanded by → Alexander [4] the Great in 335 BC (Plut. Demosthenes 23,4), accused by Timocles of accepting bribes in the Harpalus scandal (Timocles F 4 PCG). D. petitioned in 323 that Demosthenes who was convicted in the Harpalus trials be recalled to Athens (Plut. Demosthenes 27,6; Plut. Mor. 846D; [1. 116–118] see Demosthenes 3597 IV; [2; 3]).
→ Athens

1 DAVIES 2 PA 3736 3 DEVELIN no. 768. J.E.

[3] **D. of Athens.** about 300 BC. His local history of Attica with a broad description of the monarchical period caused Philochorus to write his treatise 'Against the Atthis of Demon' and to direct his own *Atthis* against Demon (FGrH 327 T 1). Other works: 'On the Mysteries in Eleusis', 'On Sacrifices', 'On Proverbs'. They all exhibit an antiquarian rather than a historical interest. FGrH 327 (with commentary). PA 3733. TRAILL, PAA 322625.
→ Atthis

O. LENDLE, Einführung in die griech. Geschichtsschreibung, 1992147 K.MEI.

Demonassa (Δημώνασσα; *Dēmṓnassa*).
[1] Daughter of the Argive seer → Amphiaraus and → Eriphyle, wife of → Thersander, a son of Polyneices, mother of Tisamenus (Paus. 3,15,8, 9,5,15). On the Cypselus Chest described by Pausanias she is shown standing with her siblings Eurydice and Alcmaeon before the house of Amphiaraus who is mounting the chariot (Paus. 5,17,7) [1]. On a late Corinthian crater that also depicts the departure of Amphiaraus the inscription calls her Damovanasa [2] while she is called → Demo [3] on an Attic vase. On an Attic bowl she is extending her hand to Thersander [3].

1 I. KRAUSKOPF, s.v. Amphiaraos, LIMC 1.1, 695 no. 15 2 Id., s.v. Amphiaraos, LIMC 1.1, 694 no. 7 3 U. FINSTER-HOTZ, s.v. Epigonoi, LIMC 3.1, 805 no. 4.

[2] Wife of Poeas, mother of → Philoctetes (Hyg. Fab. 97,8; 102,1). R.B.

Demonax (Δημῶναξ; *Dēmônax* or Δαμῶναξ; *Damônax*).
[1] **D. of Mantinea.** Respected aristocrat who was appointed as 'arbitrator' (καταρτιστήρ; *katartistḗr*) in → Cyrene about 550 BC on the advice of the Delphic Oracle (Hdt. 4,161). To resolve the internal conflicts, D. reformed the three *phylai* in which he redistributed the different groups of colonists and immigrants, the Theraeans and Perioeci, Peloponnesians and Cretans, 'Nesiotai', i.e. people from the (Ionian?) islands [1]. D. restricted the royal power of the Battiads to the religious and cultic sphere and transferred the other privileges (which are not specified in detail) to the *demos*. D. was considered the inventor of gladiatorial combats, which were also practised in Cyrene (Ephoros FGrH 70 F 54).

The measures mentioned were no revolutionary recreation of the entire order but a pragmatic solution to the colony's particular internal conflicts. Later D. was ranked with Solon and Lycurgus as a *nomothetes* (Hermippus fr. 82 WEHRLI).
→ Battus III.

1 K.-J. HÖLKESKAMP, D. und die Neuordnung der Bürgerschaft von Kyrene, in: Hermes 121, 1993, 404–421.

F. CHAMOUX, Cyrène sous la monarchie des Battiades, 1953, 138–142; A.A.I. WAISGLASS, Demonax ΒΑΣΙΛΕΥΣ ΜΑΝΤΙΝΕΩΝ, in: AJPh 77, 1956, 167–176. K.-J.H.

[2] A satrap (*praefectus*) appointed by the Parthians after the Armenian king Mithridates was imprisoned by Caligula. After Caligula's murder, Mithridates who had been freed by Claudius [II 50] returned and defeated D. in battle (Tac. Ann. 11,9).

M. KARRAS-KLAPPROTH, Prosopographische Studien zur Gesch. des Partherreiches, 1988; J. SANDALGIAN, Histoire documentaire de l'Arménie, 1917, 510; M. SCHOTTKY, Parther, Meder und Hyrkanier, AMI 24, 1991, 106f.; A. STEIN, s.v. Demonax (3), RE V 1, 144. M.SCH.

[3] of Cyprus. Cynic philosopher (*c.* AD 70 — 170) who is mainly known from the 'Life of Demonax' by his student → Lucianus. He was born as the son of a wealthy family on Cyprus. After studying literature and poetry D. turned to philosophy and lived in Athens. His teachers were → Epictetus, Timocrates of Heraclea, Agathobulus and Demetrius (of Sunium?). The Athenians, who saw in him a 'divine appearance' and a 'good spirit' (Lucian, Demon. § 63), granted him a state funeral. He has left no writings but in Stobaeus and other later collections, apophthegmata and moral aphorisms are preserved. D. was a representative of a moderate *kynismos* (→ Cynicism) that permitted him to 'honour Socrates, admire Diogenes and love Aristippus' (ibid. § 62).

→ Cynicism; → Lucianus

K. FUNK, Unt. über die lucianische Vita Demonactis, Philologus Suppl. 10, 1907, 558–674. M.G.-C.

Demonicus (Δημόνικος; *Dēmónikos*). Writer of comedies of unknown date, perhaps the 4th cent. BC [1]. D. is only attested in Ath. 9,410c where four verses are quoted from the piece Ἀχελῶιος (*Achelôios*) that describe hospitality extended to a voracious Boeotian (perhaps Hercules) (fr. 1).

1 PCG V, 1986, 14. T.HI.

Demonology

A. DEFINITION B. PREPLATONIC C. PLATO AND PLATONISM C.1 XENOCRATES C.2 PHILO C.3 PLUTARCH C.4 APULEIUS D. CHALDAEAN ORACLES E. CHRISTIAN

A. DEFINITION

Demonology is the philosophical doctrine of the *daímones* (→ Demons) — intermediate beings between gods and men — that the Platonic Academy first systematically developed subsequent to the problem posed by the Socratic *daimónion* (δαιμόνιον). M.BA.

B. PREPLATONIC

It is not possible to reconstruct a systematic Pre-platonic demonology although later philosophers, e.g., Aetius (1,8,2), Aristoxenus (fr. 34), Aristotle (fr. 192 ROSE) and Plutarch (De Is. et Os. 360e), believed that certain concepts important in later demonological systems were first formulated by → Pythagoras: for example, the ranking of god-demon-hero-man or god-demon-man, the belief in the omnipresence of demons and their possible association with the moon (regarding arguments on the Pythagorean origin of individual concepts [2], cf. [1. 2094–98; 3. 65–66; 169–70]). Some Pythagorean teachings and popular belief attempted to maintain the proper relationship between demonic beings and mortals: a cautious Pythagorean would silently pass by hero sanctuaries (ἡρῷα; *hērôia*) to avoid disturbing the 'higher forces' (κρείττονες; *kreíttones*) (Epicharm. fr. 165 CGF; cf. Hsch. s.v. *kreíttones*). Pythagoreans believed that the founder of their school was a 'demon', i.e. a being of superhuman intelligence and purity. (Aristot. fr. 192 ROSE).

1 F. BRENK, In the Light of the Moon: Demonology in the Early Imperial Period, in: ANRW II 16.3, 2068–2145 2 M. DETIENNE, De la pensée religieuse à la pensée philosophique. La notion de daïmon dans le pythagorisme ancien, 1963 3 W. BURKERT, Weisheit und Wissenschaft: Studien zu Pythagoras, Philolaos und Platon, 1962. S.I.J.

C. PLATO AND PLATONISM

Plato defined the *daímōn* as halfway and intermediary between gods and humans and a being that linked both groups (Pl. Symp. 202d ff.; cf. Ti. 40d ff.; Leg. 717a f.). In the whole of reality the demons exercised subordinate functions, as creator deities (Pl. Ti. 42d ff.), rulers over parts of the cosmos, protective deities of peoples (Pl. Plt. 271d ff.; Pl. Plt. 272e f.; Pl. Plt. 274b; Pl. Ti. 24c f.; Pl. Ti. 42e; Pl. Crit. 109b f.; Pl. Leg. 713c ff.) or individual persons (Phd. 107d ff.; 113d; Resp. 617d f.; 620d f.; Leg. 877a). The gap between demons and humans is not unbridgeable because already in life the innermost of a human being is a *daímōn*, whose well-being constitutes the *eudaimonía* ('happiness, well-being') of humans (Pl. Ti. 90c). After death the souls of great humans are worshipped as *daímones* (Pl. Resp. 540b f.; Crat. 398bf.). M.BA.

The Platonic dialogues contain the most important elements of later philosophic demonology: 1. the role of demons as intermediaries between gods and humans, and 2. the assignment of an individual demon to each soul whose life he guides (Pl. Phd. 107d). The most famous variation of this thought (Pl. Ap. 40a) is the Socratic *daimónion* (δαιμόνιον): something 'demonic' always kept Socrates from doing things that he should not do (cf. Pl. Tht. 151a; Euthphr. 3b; Xen. Mem. 1,1,2). The nature, mode of action and intention of this force were defined in later philosophical speculation, especially by Plutarch (*De Genio Socratis*) and Apuleius (*De deo Socratis*). Both were inclined to see this force as a god or at least a demon of particularly high quality and high rank. The demonology of the pseudo-Platonic *Epinomis* (usually attributed to Plato's student Philip of Opus) developed the idea that different types of beings inhabit different parts of the Cosmos: demons particularly sojourned in the air. This influenced later Platonism (e.g., Apul. De Platone 9–12 p. 233–38; Phil. De gigantibus 6–12; on the Epinomis and its influence, cf. [1]).

1 L. TARÁN, Academia: Plato, Philip of Opus and the Pseudo-Platonic Epinomis, 1975. S.I.J.

Plato's approaches were developed into a systematic demonology in his school, the Stoa and Platonism [1. 640ff.]. Demons were equated with the gods of mythology (Xenocrates, fr. 225; 228 Isnardi Parente); greater and lesser ones were distinguished (Xenocrates, fr. 225 I. P.; Ps.-Pl. *Epinomis* 984e [1. 640]; cf. already Pl. Symp. 202d) as well as good and bad demons because, unlike the gods, they were exposed to passions (Xenocrates, fr. 225ff. I.P.; Ps.-Pl. Epin. 985a [1. 614, 642, 646f.]). They were assigned a place in the sequence 'gods- (angels — iynges –) demons- (demigods- heroes –) humans' (Ps.-Pl. Epin. 984d ff., cf. Pl. Leg. 717a f.; Plut. De defectu oraculorum 415b; [1. 642, 648, 655f., 660, 665]). Among the duties of demons was the supervision of cosmic regions [1. 642, 647, 650, 656, 658], relaying oracles and dreams, protection of sanctuaries, participation in sacrifices and mysteries [1. 641, 643f., 646], the punishment of evildoers [1. 646f., 653]. From a psychologizing perspective they are the innermost of human beings — their conscience [1. 643, 654f.].

The most important information on systematized demonology is to be found in preserved specialized Platonic writings [1. 644ff.; 2. 315ff.] and summaries ([Alcinous] Albinus, Didascalicus 15; Porph. De abstinentia 2,36ff.; Procl. In Platonis Alcibiadem 67,19ff.; Olympiodorus, In Alc. 15,5ff.; 17,10ff.). On its influence cf. [3].

1 C. Colpe et al., s.v. Geister (Dämonen), RAC 9, 546–797 2 Dörrie/Baltes III, 1993. 3 H. M. Nobis, s.v. Dämonologie, HWdPh 2, 5–9.

F. Andres, s.v. Daimon, RE Suppl. 3, 267–322; R. Heinze, Xenokrates, 1892, 78–123. M.BA.

C.1 Xenocrates

→ Xenocrates attempted to systematize the position of gods, demons and humans. He emphasized the intermediate position of demons with a geometric metaphor: gods resemble equilateral triangles, humans scalene ones and demons isosceles ones: they are less balanced than equilateral triangles, but more balanced than scalene ones. Therefore, Xenocrates attributed both godlike powers and interfering human emotions to demons (fr. 23 Heinze = Plut. De def. or. 416c-d). Their natural residence was at the centre of three cosmic areas. With this he probably meant the moon and the area surrounding it (fr. 56 Heinze = Plut. Mor. 943f). Another important development was his division of demons into the two categories of good and bad. The latter demanded the ritual mutilation, mourning and human sacrifice that foolish people attributed to the gods (fr. 25 Heinze = Plut. De Is. et Os. 361b; De def. or. 417c).

C.2 Philo

→ Philo attempted to combine elements of Jewish written beliefs with the Middle Platonic demonology. He placed importance on the intermediary function of demons between gods and humans by particularly

emphasizing their role as guardians over humanity. He used the terms *angeloi* and *daimones* more or less as synonyms and equated both with individual souls that had purified their physicality and were supplied with divine *logoi*. These *angeloi*/demons filled the air even though some eventually became 'corporeal' (De Gigantibus 6–16; De somniis 1,134–5; 141–2; Legum allegoriae 3, 177). He considered bad demons (De Gigantibus 17–18) as punishers of sins on divine orders (Quaestiones in Exodum 1,23). He assumed that each individual not only possessed one but two personal demons — a good one and a bad one — who fought for supremacy (Quaestiones in Exodum 1,23, perhaps according to Pl. Leg. 896e).

C.3 Plutarch

Plutarch emphasized in a similar manner the intermediary role of demons between heaven and earth as being essential to preserving the community between gods and men. He followed Xenocrates with the idea that demons resided on the moon and in the air between moon and earth (De def. or. 416d-f). Like most Platonists he assumed that demons were disembodied souls although he also used the word 'demons' for Pan, Osiris and Isis (De def. or. 419b-e; Is. 360e) whom he did not consider real gods but only as higher forms of demons. Regarding the question if there were bad demons he seems to have been undecided; like Philo he suggested that if they existed they acted on divine orders. Elsewhere he said that demons became 'evil' if they had been lured into a body by physical pleasures (De def. or. 417b; Mor. 944c-d; De Is. et Os. 361b; cf. [1. 223–24]). Plutarch attempted to harmonize the Platonic demonology with popular belief by interpreting events like plagues and harvest failures as the work of evil demons (De def. or. 417d-e).

C.4 Apuleius

Apuleius argued along approximately the same lines. He developed the idea of demons as intermediaries and protectors of souls in his works *De Platone* and *De Deo Socratis*. He postulated three different types of demons: 1. the human soul in the body, 2. the soul that has left the body, and 3. demons that never enter a body including beings like Hypnos and Eros that are normally called *theoi* ('gods') (Socr. 14–16 p. 150–56). He also attempted to combine Platonic demonology with the traditional Roman belief in the power of the dead (*larvae, lemures and manes*; Socr. 15 p. 152–54).

D. Chaldaean Oracles

The demonology of the Chaldaean oracles illustrates three tendencies that became important in both philosophy and popular belief of late Antiquity and the Byzantine period. First, 'demon' is almost exclusively used as a term for a creature with evil intentions. Beings that do good and are intermediate are called *iynges* or, as in Philo, *angeloi* [3. 68–85]. Second, demons can harm the physical and psychological health of an individual as well as detract from spiritual efforts benefiting the soul (Orac. Chald. fr. 135 and [4. 134–37]). Third, demons are more strongly linked to physical nature than to the mental and spiritual world (Orac. Chald. fr. 88, cf. [4. 139–40]). The Oracles link demons to demonic hounds that belong to → Hecate's entourage in popular belief [5. Ch. 9].

1 J. Dillon, The Middle Platonists, 1977 2 R. Wallis, Neoplatonism, 1972 3 F. Cremer, Die chaldäischen Orakel und Jamblich, De Mysteriis, 1969 4 J. Gager, Curse Tablets and Binding Spells from the Ancient World, 1992 5 S. I. Johnston, Hekate Soteira, 1990.

P. Habermehl, 'Quaedam divinae mediae potestates'. Demonology in Apuleius' 'De Deo Socratis', in: Groningen Colloquium on the Novel 7, 1996, 117–142; C. Zintzen, s.v. Geister (Dämonen), Hellenistische und kaiserzeitliche Philosophie, RAC 9, 640–668. S.I.J.

E. Christian

In their confrontation with pagan religions early Christian authors deliberately fall back on philosophical demonology but interpret it from a new perspective (e.g. Tert. Apol. 22–23; Orig. Contra Celsum; Aug. Civ. 8–10; De divinatione daemonum). They counter the old pluralism of spirit beings with a separation of spirits based on Gen. 6,1ff. and 'angelify' or 'demonize' them. The intermediary function between gods and humans has become the task of angels, the dark traits of the spirit world are ascribed to fallen adherents of Satan that also include the ancient gods. At the same time the negative character of demons is accentuated into a dualistic principle: since they have rebelled against divine salvation they are responsible for evil in the world.

The concept that demons attempting to falsify the Christian doctrine are behind 'heretics' and 'schismatics' had serious consequences in the internal disputes among Christians after Constantine's changes (early 4th cent. AD). Demons remain omnipresent in popular belief as tales of hermits and monks prove who have dedicated themselves to the struggle against Satan and his followers since the temptation of → Antonius [5].
→ Demonology

J. B. Russell, Satan. The Early Christian Tradition, 1981; B. Teyssèdre, Le diable et l'enfer au temps de Jésus, 1985; P. G. van der Nat et al., s.v. Geister (Dämonen), RAC 9, 1976, 626–640 and 668–797. PE.HA.

Demons

I. Mesopotamia II. Egypt III. Syria-Palestine IV. Pre-Islamic Iran V. Greece and Rome

I. Mesopotamia

Mesopotamia did not develop a generic term for demons. A large number of immortal beings was known that each had their own name and acted as servants of the gods and as enemies or helpers of humans. They did not have cults of their own. Since demons were only able to exercise their limited powers, which manifested themselves in physical and psychological illnesses, with the approval of the gods, they were part of the existing world order. Thus, in the Babylonian tale of the Great Flood (→ Atraḫasis myth, see TUAT 3, 644 vii 3) the gods — after a promise to never again unleash a flood destroying all — installed the demoness Lamaštu, who was made responsible for childbirth fever and infant mortality, to prevent excessive multiplication of humans in the future. Other demons became 'watchmen' and worked on divine orders to the benefit or harm of humans. Some ancient Near Eastern myths relate that the demon-like creatures of the Primal Chaos were defeated by the hero gods that created the ordered world and then made guardians of sanctuaries. Many evil demons were personifications of diseases, epidemics or winds that were considered bearers of disease. Unlike the gods, who were always imagined as being anthropomorphic, demons were depicted as fear-inspiring → monsters. For example, the lion's head and paws, bird's wings and talons of bloodsucking Lamaštu [2] symbolized her dangerousness and fast attack. The residences of evil demons were the arid lands hostile to cultivation and the Underworld. Evil demons were often not clearly differentiated by their mode of action from vengeful spirits of the dead returning to earth. Often they were named together. Unlike the other demons, Lamaštu was considered a daughter of the highest god Anu that had been cast out of Heaven. In cuneiform texts exorcistic rituals played an important role. In them the renewed benevolence of the gods was effected, the demon was rendered harmless and banished to the Underworld, often being supplied with provisions for the journey. → Amulets provided protection against a renewed attack. The Babylonian belief in demons continues to this day in the Near East.

1 J. Black, A. Green, Gods, Demons and Symbols of Ancient Mesopotamia, 1992 2 W. Farber, s.v. Lamaštu, RLA 6, 1980–1983, 439–446. S.M.

II. Egypt

In Egypt demons existed both in this world and the next. They were mostly named according to their function but had no generic term. Underworld demons (and demons in general) played no special role in the official cult of the gods and the dead but they do in the Books of the Dead, especially as guardians at gates and other transitional areas. They were only dangerous to those dead who lack the requirements for entering the Underworld. Demons of this world are known especially from magical texts. Often they were messengers of the gods or illness demons. They differed in their properties (e.g., blind, dumb or deaf) and lifestyle (often in marginal areas such as the desert, foreign countries, darkness, swamps, watering holes) from humans and gods and did not belong to the 'orderly' world. They could be useful to humans but usually were a danger that people attempted to ward off in many ways. Demons were depicted as humans, animals or → monsters, often armed with knives, fire or snakes. The spirits of the dead could also have the (useful or threatening) functions of demons.

H. Te Velde, s.v. Dämonen, LÄ 1, 980–984; L. Kakosy, Zauberei im alten Ägypten, 1989, 66–84. K.J.-W.

III. Syria-Palestine

In the 14th/13th cents. BC, demons of illness and spirits of the dead can be identified in incantations from → Ugarit (KTU 82, 169 [1]). Incantations pleading that the gods Anat and → Baal drive them away were helpful in warding them off. Phoenician demons are named on amulets from → Arslantaş (1st millennium BC) but their authenticity is in doubt. In Judah and Israel the demons → Rešep and Deber ('plague'), Qeṭeb ('destruction'), Liliṯ, Šed, Ašmundai, Azāzel and Behemōṯ are documented (Deut. 32,17; 33,24; Hab. 3,5; Is. 28,2; 34,14; Ps. 91,3; 6; Hos. 13,14; Tob. 3,8; Lev. 16,8; 10; 26; Job 40,15 and *passim*). Partially they are personifications of illness or need. There are also evil spirits (1 Sam. 16,14), lying spirits (1 Kg 22,21–23), desert demons (Is. 13,21; 34,12; and *passim*), satyrs (Lev. 17,7 and *passim*), despoilers (Ex. 12,23) and destroying angels (2 Sam. 24,14–16 and *passim*). The motif of 'fallen angels' (Gen. 6,1–4; 1 Hen; Test XII Patr) can only be noted in passing. Exorcism is attested in 1 Sam. 16 and Tob. 8,2f. Aramaic amulets and magic bowls of the 4th–7th cents. AD for expelling demons are based on divine action in the OT. In this context the Mandaean magical texts, which express Mesopotamian ideas, must be mentioned. The NT in which the demons are subject to Satan is also based on divine action in the OT (1 Cor. 10,20; Lk. 10,19). In the NT the topic of human possession by demons as causative agents of disease is rather prominent. The importance of exorcism is closely related. The demonization of foreign gods is attested in both the OT and the NT (Ps. 95,5 LXX; Deut. 32,17 LXX; 1 Cor. 10,20f.).

1 M. Dietrich, O. Loretz, J. Sanmartin, Die keilalphabetischen Texte aus Ugarit einschließlich der keilalphabetischen Texte außerhalb Ugarits I (AOAT 24/1), 1976.

A. Caquot, Sur quelques démons de l'AT, in: Semitica 6, 1956, 53–68; C. Colpe, J. Maier, s.v. Geister (Dämonen), RAC 9, 562–585; W. Culican, Phoenician Demons, in: JNES 35, 1976, 21–24; W. Fauth, Lilits und Astarten in aramäischen, mandäischen und syrischen Zaubertexten, in: WO 17, 1986, 66–94; M. Görg, W. Kirchschläger, s.v. Dämonen, Neues Bibel-Lexikon I, 375–378; B. Janowski, Repräsentationen der gegenmenschlichen Welt, in: D. Trobitsch (ed.), FS Theißen, 1993, 154–163; J. C. de Moor, K. Spronk, More on Demons in Ugarit, in: Ugarit-Forschungen 16, 1984, 237–250; C. Müller-Kessler, The Story of Bugzan-Lilit, in: Journal of the American Oriental Society 116, 1996, 185–195 (with bibliography); J. Naveh, S. Shaked, Amulets and Magic Bowls, 1985; K. van der Toorn, B. Becking, P. W. van der Horst (ed.), Dictionary of Deities and Demons in the Bible, 1995; D. Trunk, Der messianische Heiler, 1994. H.NI.

IV. Pre-Islamic Iran

The key term for demon in the Iranian religious tradition, Old Persian *daiva-* (Avestic *daēuua-*, Middle Persian *dēw*, New Persian *dīw*), is etymologically equivalent to Old Indian *devá-* 'god'. In the Iranian language area it was thoroughly recoined in a sequence from 'god' > 'false god', 'idol' > 'demon' to 'devil' but because of scant references in the literature it is difficult to determine both in terms of chronology and religious history. In the Gathas of the Avesta, which are dated by consensus to about 1000 BC, the *daēuuas* are not yet demons but a separate category of gods that must be rejected. In the opinion of most researchers the demonization of the *daēuuas* is due to → Zoroaster's reform. He wanted to break their power, which was based on arbitrariness and strength. The re-evaluation process may have begun among the East Iranian tribes amongst whom he was active and he may have only accelerated it. In the texts of the Younger Avesta, which are more recent by several centuries, *daēuua-* is used for creatures that belong to the army of the 'Evil Spirit' in the context of Zoroastrian dualism. They appear as disease- and death-spreading demon hordes that pollute the world, that even attempted to destroy Zoroaster and must be kept at bay, for example, by the recitation of sacred prayer formulas and adherence to purification rules. In the Pahlavi literature of the 9th to 11th cents., which reflects religious ideas of the Sassanid period (3rd –7th cents.), one of the main duties of faithful Zoroastrians is fighting demons, who as counter-creations of the 'Evil Spirit', → Ahriman, personify almost every conceivable evil. Innumerable demons penetrate the sound creation of Ohrmazd (→ Ahura Mazda) at all levels whereby the world enters a state of 'heterogeneity' from which it will be liberated at the end of times by a separation of the forces of good and evil. Demons are sometimes described as creatures with faces, hair, claws and feet, sometimes as personifications of abstract concepts such as heresy or the embodiment of climatic evils (e.g., drought). Demons, which can also enter the body as diseases, maladies, impurities etc., must be warded off with good deeds and by adhering to purification rules. They are also scared off by fire and incestuous marriages, which are considered the most effective means of destroying demons.

E. Benveniste, Que signifie *vidēvdāt*?, in: Henning Memorial Vol., 1970, 37–42; A. Christensen, Essai sur la démonologie iranienne, 1941; L. H. Gray, The Foundations of the Iranian Rel., in: Journ. of the Cama Oriental Institute 15, 1929, 1–228; S. Shaked, Bagdāna, King of the Demons, and other Iranian Terms in Babylon. Aramaic Magic, in: Acta Iranica 25, 1985, 511–525. M.MA.

V. Greece and Rome

A. Definition B. Development of word meaning C. Popular belief

A. Definition

The word 'demon' (δαίμων; *daímōn*) is often derived from δαίω (*daíō*) 'divide, distribute' because of the role it often plays in allotting destiny, but this etymology is rather uncertain [1. 1, 247; 2. 1, 369]. It is often equally uncertain which kind of being the term demon means. Often it describes a being that is called θεός (*theós*, god) by others (Hom. Il. 1,222; Eur. Bacch. 42, cf. 84 *passim*). Already in Hesiod (Op. 121–126) the word demon was also used for the soul of a deceased. In philosophical texts since Plato (Symp. 202d-e), demon may refer to a being that is with regard to power between gods and humans and intermediates between them. Later authors sometimes linked Platonic and Hesiodic concepts by equating intermediating demons with souls (Phil. De gigantibus 16; Plut. De def. or. 415f; 419a). In Greek and Roman antiquity, demons could be beings with good or bad intentions but already in Homer, especially in the *Odyssey*, demons were more commonly associated with disagreeable events (cf. [4. 2073–79] on earlier discussions).

1 Chantraine 1, 247 2 Wilamowitz 1, 369
3 F. Andres, s.v. Daimon, RE Suppl. 3, 267–322
4 F. Brenk, In the Light of the Moon: Demonology in the Early Period, in: ANRW II 16.3, 2068–2145. S.I.J.

B. Development of word meaning

A summary of Homeric word usage is found in [1. 2071–82]. Two points are particularly important: first, demons were cited when the speaker did not know which god had caused a certain event. Homer himself rarely uses it since, as the omniscient narrator, he can always name the acting deity. This is probably the reason why the physical appearance of demons is never described. Therefore, demons indicate divine forces that cannot be identified with certainty by mortals. Second, demons are often held responsible for psychological phenomena like delusion and insanity (Hom. Od. 14,488; 12,295) but rarely for physical actions (exceptions: Hom. Il. 15,468; Hom. Od. 12,169 and perhaps Od. 5,396).

Hesiod adds two important ideas: demons help in punishing evil-doers and they are the souls of the dead (Op. 122–26). Classical sources, especially tragedies, offer numerous examples of the former idea (Aesch. Pers. 601; Eur. Alc. 1003; Eur. Rhes. 971; Pl. Resp. 469b; 540c; cf. Emp. fr. 31 B 115, 5 and 13 DK). The idea of demons as avengers of wrongs appears to have developed in classical texts into the → Alastor (Aesch. Pers. 354; Aesch. Ag. 1501) and the → Erinyes (Aesch. Cho. 1048–62; Eur. Med. 1389). Like demons both had contact with the souls of the dead. However, the enraged dead can also avenge themselves (Pl. Leg. 865d-e). In the classical period the actions of demons were linked to misfortune and even death (Aesch. Ag. 1175; Aesch. Sept. 812; Soph. OC 76; Antiph. 3,3,4), even though demons in the broader sense could still represent any change in fortune (Lys. 13,63; Hdt. 5,87; cf. Pind. Pyth. 5,123).

The related concept of a 'personal' demon that positively or negatively influences or guides the life of each individual is already encountered in archaic sources (e.g., Thgn. 1, 161–4; Heracl. 22 B 119 DK) but only clearly emerged in the classical period (Pind. Ol. 13,28; 105; Soph. Trach. 910f.; Eur. Med. 1347; Pl. Phd. 107d). Although *olbiodaímōn* (ὀλβιοδαίμων) and *eudaimoníē* (εὐδαιμονίη) each occur once in Homer (Il. 3,182; h. 11,5), the greater frequency of *eudaimoníē* and its derivations as well as the opposites *dysdaímōn* (δυσδαίμων) and *kakodaímōn* (κακοδαίμων) in the classical period indicate an increasing interest in the concept of a personal demon. As well, the tendency of seeing demons as a category of beings separate from the gods gained strength in the classical period (Aristoph. Plut. 81). At the same time the philosophical concept of demons as intermediaries between goods and mortals arose (see below).

The popular meaning of demon persisted to the end of Graeco-Roman Antiquity. Only under the influence of Christianity and some forms of Neoplatonic philosophy did it become exclusively associated with harmful beings, which resulted in the modern meaning of the term 'demon'.

C. Popular belief

In addition to beings that were explicitly called demons, there was a large number of immortal or long-lived beings that were neither described as demons or gods but to whom superhuman powers were clearly attributed. In scholarship they are frequently discussed as a part of Greek → demonology [2]. Sometimes these beings are called → *eídola* (εἴδολα) or *phásmata* (φάσματα), terms that are also used for dreams and illusions. This apparently reflects their fleeting and often illusory appearance in the human world. However, ancient authors often use no definite term.

Most of these beings are treacherous and cause problems that extend from child death (Gello, Lamia, Mormo), nightmares (Ephialtes) and breaking of pots in kilns (Ps.-Hdt. Vit. Hom. 32 = Hom. Epigr. 14) to defeat in athletic competitions or court [3. ch. 1 and 3]. In particular, they were made responsible for misfortune whether unexpected or otherwise difficult to explain. The 'Mid-Day Demon' [2. 121] and Empusa belong here although their functions are not quite clear [4]. Many such beings were considered the souls of the dead that returned because of envy, rage or restlessness (→ Ahoroi). Some were called heroes (Paus. 6,6,7; Aristoph. fr. 322), whereby the heroic dead could bring fortune or misfortune [5. 192–201].

That many of these beings have adjectival names that describe the nature and activity of the demon (Lamia from λαιμός (*laimós*), 'throat'; Mormo from μόρμω (*mórmō*), 'to be scared'; Ephialtes from ἐφάλλομαι (*ephállomai*), 'spring upon'), and many of these terms appear in plural shows that the beings individualized by myths and genealogies are only representations of 'spirits' imagined to be threatening. → Hecate is sometimes portrayed as their leader (Adespota fr. 375 TGF; PGM 4, 2708–84) [6], which fits with her being able to protect an individual against them [7]. Protection was also provided by an inscription above the door naming Heracles Kallinikos as the house occupant [8], as well as amulets worn on the body or hung up in the house [9]. The awareness that invisible, potentially destructive forces were omnipresent is evident both in Plato's statement that *kêres* (κῆρες) hang above all things in life (Pl. Leg. 937d) and the personification of ills and illnesses since Hesiod (Op. 100–104; cf. Eur. Phoen. 950 and Soph. Phil. 42, where the *kêres* bring blindness and disease). In late antiquity this evil is imagined as a physical shape: the 'pestilence demon' in Ephesus manifested himself as a disgusting beggar, then as a great fear-inspiring hound (Philostr. VA 4,10). Many such demonic beings are well attested in the Byzantine period and even today in rural areas [10].

In magic demonic beings — especially disembodied souls — could be called upon for various tasks (*áhoroi*, → Nekydaimon). The souls of the dead, including dead heroes, were considered prophetic (Plut. De def. or. 431e–432e; → Trophonius).

Iconographically many of these demonic beings are linked to demons in other cultures: they are ugly, of terrifying countenance and often half human, half animal. Sometimes it was believed that they could change their shape (→ Mormo, → Empusa) [11. 429f.; 4].

The beings depicted on bronze seals are often called demons or '*genii*'. Sometimes they are represented as half human, half animal (especially with dog- or serpent-like traits). Occasionally, they appear to provide service in another, completely anthropomorphic shape that is interpreted as a deity. Attempts to link these beings, for example, with the → Erinyes are interesting but in the end cannot be proven [12; 13. 196–200].

The only demon to be honoured in a traditional cult was the *agathòs daímōn*, who received the first libation of wine (Aristoph. Equ. 85; Vesp. 525; Plut. Symp. 655e; LSCG 134). In ancient art it was depicted as a snake [14. 213–218].

→ DEMONOLOGY

1 F. BRENK, In the Light of the Moon: Demonology in the Early Imperial Period, in: ANRW II 16.3 2068, –2145 2 H. HERTER, Rheinisches Jb. Volkskunde 1, 1950, 112–43 3 J. GAGER, Curse Tablets and Binding Spells from the Ancient World, 1992 4 S. I. JOHNSTON, Defining the Dreadful: Remarks on the Greek Child-Killing Demon, in: P. MIRECKI, M. MEYER (ed.), Ancient Magic and Ritual Power, 1995, 361–87 5 A. HENRICHS, Namenslosigkeit u. Euphemismus. Zur Ambivalenz der chthonischen Mächte im attischen Drama, in: H. HOFMANN, A. HARDER (ed.), Fragmenta Dramatica, 1991, 161–201 6 S. I. JOHNSTON, Hekate Soteira, 1990. 7 Id., Crossroads, in: ZPE 88, 1991, 217–24 8 O. WEINREICH, De dis ignotis quaestiones selectae, in: ARW 18, 1915, 8–15 9 R. KOTANSKY, Incantations and Prayers for Salvation on Inscribed Greek Amulets, in: C. FARAONE, D. OBBINK (ed.), Magika Hiera, 1991, 107–137 10 C. STEWART, Demons and the Devil, 1991 11 J. Z. SMITH, Towards Interpreting Demonic Power in Hellenistic and Roman Antiquity, in: ANRW II 16.1, 425–39 12 D. SANSONE, The Survival of the Bronze age demon, in: Illinois Classical Studies 13, 1988, 11–17 13 N. MARINATOS, Minoan Religion, 1993, 196–200 14 NILSSON, GGR, vol. 2.

H. NOWAK, Zur Entwicklungsgesch. des Begriffes Daimon, Eine Unt. epigraphischer Zeugnisse vom 5.Jh. v.Chr. bis zum 5. Jh. n.Chr., diss. 1960; J. TER VRUGT-LENZ, s.v. Geister (Dämonen), Vorhell. Griechenland, RAC 9, 598–615. S.I.J.

Demonstratio In general civil law the specific designation of a thing or person (Dig. 6,1,6). This term lies at the origin of the interpretative formula *falsa demonstratio non nocet* ('a wrong expression does not affect the matter's validity'), which was used by the Romans mainly when interpreting a will (Inst. Ius. 2,20,30) and which is still current today. In the context of civil proceedings *demonstratio*, set out at the beginning of a large number of legal arguments, refers to the concise exposition of the circumstances of the disputed issue (Gai. Inst. 4,39; 40; 44; 58; 136). If the part of the legal address known as → *intentio* did not adequately characterize the disputed issue and the underlying legal issues to be settled by the judge, a *demonstratio* would precede it; especially in cases brought against an *incertum* ('someone/something unidentified'). While a wrongly chosen *demonstratio* could result in the loss of a case, it did not prevent a new suit, as the substance of a case was not legally binding.

→ Formula

KASER, RZ, 240; W. SELB, Formeln mit unbestimmter intentio iuris, 1974. C.PA.

Demophile see → Sibyl

Demophilus (Δημόφιλος; *Dēmóphilos*).

[1] Athenian orator who, in 346/45 BC, proposed the scrutiny of citizen lists which resulted in loss of citizenship for many (Aeschin. In Tim. 77,86; Androtion FGrH 324 F 52 = Philochorus FGrH 328 F 52; Sch. Aeschin. In Tim. 77) [1; 2].

[2] Athenian, accused → Aristotle in 323 BC (Diog. Laert. 5,5; Ath. 696a) of *asébeia*,impiety, because of the hymn and epigram to Hermias of Atarneus (cf. [3]). D. was successful in the charge he brought against Phocion in 319 but fled from Athens after the latter's rehabilitation (Plut. Phocion 38,2).

→ Athens; → Demokratia

1 PA 3664 2 DEVELIN no. 775 3 I. DÜRING, Aristotle in the Ancient Biographical Tradition, 1957, 343f. J.E.

[3] Writer of comedies, generally classified with New Comedy even though his period of writing is unknown

[1]. D. is attested to only in Plaut. Asin. 10f (Prologue): ... *huic nomen Graece Onagost fabulae; | Demophilus scripsit, Maccus vortit barbare;|* ... As the *Asinaria* does not elucidate what role an 'ass driver' (ὀναγός; *onagós*) might have had in the Greek play and as a dotal slave — something seemingly inconsistent with Athenian law [2. 21ff.] — plays a key part in Plautus, any inferences about D.'s comedy are questionable [2. 34].

1 PCG V, 1986, 15 2 G. VOGT-SPIRA, 'Asinaria' oder 'Maccus vortit Attice', in: E. LEFÈVRE, E. STÄRK, G. VOGT-SPIRA, Plautus barbarus, 1991, 11–69. T.HI.

Demophon (Δημοφῶν; *Dēmophôn*).

[1] Youngest son of the Eleusinian prince Celeus and Metaneira. According to myth D. was nurtured by the goddess → Demeter, who had been hired as a wet-nurse; she anointed him with ambrosia and hardened him at night in the fire so as to burn away his mortality (cf. Thetis: Achilles), until his mother noticed and cried out. Demeter then placed D. on the ground and threatened the Eleusinians with civil wars (Hom. Il. 2,233–255); in another version of the myth she killed the child (Apollod. 1,31; Orph. Fr. 49). This 'nurturing episode', possibly a motif of the Thesmophoriae, was not carried over into the mysteries [1]. In Ov. Fast. 4,539–560, where Celeus is a poor farmer, D. is replaced by his brother → Triptolemus (cf. schol. Nic. Ther. 484; Hyg. Fab. 147).

→ Thesmophoria

1 K. CLINTON, Myth and Cult: the Iconography of the Eleusinian Mysteries, 1992, 30–34, 87, 97f., 100–102.

F. GRAF, Eleusis und die orphische Dichtung Athens in vorhell. Zeit, 1974, 157, 159f., 167f.; N. J. RICHARDSON, The Homeric Hymn to Demeter, 1974, 231–236. K.C.

[2] King of Athens, son of → Theseus and Phaedra, and brother of → Acamas, with whom he is frequently confused (Diod. Sic.4,62; Hygin. Fab.48). The mother's name is not uniformly preserved. When their grandmother → Aethra was abducted by the Dioscuri, the two grandsons fled (Apollod. epit. 1,23), but returned to free her after the destruction of Troy (Ilias Parva fr. 20 PEG I; Iliup. arg. PEG I); her release is depicted in Polygnotus' painting *Ilioupersis* (Paus. 10,25,7), on several Attic vases and the Tabula Iliaca [1]. Both brothers took part in the Trojan War and are even said to have been part of the forces inside the Trojan Horse (Paus. 1,23,8; Homer does not mention them) [2]. The Athenians owed possession of the → Palladion to D. According to one version, D. had sent it to Athens after Diomedes had entrusted it to his safekeeping (Polyaenus, Strat. 1,5); according to another version, D. unintentionally killed an Athenian while taking possession of the Palladion (Paus.1,28,9). In Eur. Heracl., D. pledged Hercules the protection of Athens when Hercules was fleeing from Eurystheus. The unhappy relationship with the Thracian woman → Phyllis was ascribed to Acamas as well as to D. Both brothers had altars in the harbour of Phalerum (Paus. 1,1,4).

1 U. KRON, s.v. Aithra 1, LIMC 1.1, 426–28 no. 59–78 2 PRELLER/ROBERT, 1238f.

U. KRON, s.v. Akamas et D., LIMC 1.1, 435–446; STOLL, in: ROSCHER 1, s.v. D., 988–991. R.B.

[3] Athenian *strategos* in the war of 379/378 BC against Agesilaus II of Sparta; one of the leaders of the Athenian forces at Thebes in 378 (Diod. Sic. 15,26,2f.) [1; 2].

[4] Son of Demon; cousin, brother-in-law and from 376/5 BC guardian of → Demosthenes; successfully prosecuted by the latter, after 366, for embezzling from the estate and for illegal use of his sister's substantial dowry (Dem. Or. 27–29; Plut. Mor. 844D) [3].

→ Athens; → Strategoi

1 PA 3693 2 DEVELIN, no. 786 3 DAVIES, 116 (under Demosthenes 3597 III). J.E.

Demos (δῆμος; *dêmos*).

[1] *Demos*, meaning 'people', could refer to either the entire citizenry of a community or only the 'common people' as distinct from its more privileged members. As an extension of the first meaning it also served to designate the popular assembly, so that political decisions in many states were seen as being 'issued by the council and the people' (ἔδοξεν τῇ βουλῇ καὶ τῷ δήμῳ). Adjectives such as *dēmotikós* and the description of a democratic leader as προστάτης τοῦ δήμου ('champion of the people'; e.g. in Thuc. 3,82,1) are derived from the second meaning. The ambiguity of meaning enabled advocates of democracy to present it as power-sharing among all the citizens, and its opponents to present it as rule by the masses. This caused Aristotle to slip from treating democracy as rule by the masses to treating it as rule by the poor (Pol. 3,1279a–1280a).

The *demos* of the first meaning is personified in Aristophanes' 'Knights' as an old man, good-natured but easily manipulated. In Athens *Demos* was depicted in paintings, for example together with *Demokratia* in the Zeus-Stoa (Plin. HN 35,129; Paus. 1,3,3), and in reliefs: above the text of the Law of 337/6, which threatened the dissolution of the Areopagus (SEG 12, 87), *Demos* is shown being crowned by Democracy. In Hellenistic and Roman Athens there was a sanctuary of the *demos* and the Charites, with its own priesthood (e.g. IG II^2 844, 41; 4676; 5029a). P.J.R.

[2] *Demos, dêmoi* (δῆμοι), small and topographically defined communities (demes), subdivisions of a polis.

A. ATHENS B. OTHER GREEK CITIES C. BYZANTINE PERIOD

A. ATHENS

In Athens *dêmoi* with this special meaning existed even before → Cleisthenes (see perhaps Plut. Solon 12,4), but it was only through his reform of the phyles in 508/7 that the word gained its institutional sense, meaning components of the Athenian polis (Hdt. 5,69,2: [Aristot.] Ath. Pol. 21,4–5). Strabo (9,1,16) names 170 or 174 *dêmoi* but examination of the inscriptions reveals that there were in fact only 133, of which six *dêmoi* were divided into 'larger' and 'smaller' units. Each of the ten new Cleisthenian *phylaí* ('tribes') consisted of three *trittýes* ('thirds'), each of which was situated in, or was designated as being in one of the three regions: *ásty* (city), *paralía* (coast) or *mesógeios* (inland). Each *trittýs* contained one or more *dêmoi*, not necessarily related to one another. The phyles had approximately the same surface area; currently under discussion ([4] and [7] against [5] and [6]) is the question of whether the *trittýes* were of equal size or were situated together in one region, as the two propositions cannot both be correct. The *dêmoi* were of varying size (the largest was Acharnae); for the location of the *dêmoi* and their relationship to the *trittýes* and *phylaí* see [6] and [7].

Even before Cleisthenes there were in fact many *dēmoi* designated as such, as e.g. Marathon. Some *dêmoi* were named after local landmarks, plants or professions practised there (Potamos = River; Phegous = Oak; Kerameis = Potters), others after Athenian families (e.g. Butadae; for the possible meaning of this see [2]). The *dêmoi* had their own political institutions, a deme assembly and a leading official, the → *dḗmarchos*; instituting local administration may have of itself created Cleisthenes' popularity [1]. The *dêmoi* were represented in the Council of the 500, in proportion to their size.

In 508/7 citizens were registered in the *dêmoi* in which they lived or owned land, but later on membership was made hereditary; foreigners who received Athenian citizenship could choose their own *dêmos*. A man's full name consisted of his own name, that of his father and that of his *dêmos* (thus: Pericles, son of Xanthippus, from [the deme] Cholargus); in fact, membership of a *dêmos*, and the *trittýs* and *phylḗ* to which the *dḗmos* belonged, defined a man's status as Athenian citizen. Citizens could also be recognized as owners of property (*enkektēménoi*) outside their own *dêmos*; metics were accepted as 'residents' in a *dêmos*.

The *dêmoi* also conducted the *dokimasía* of 18-year-old males whose membership was to be recognized (Aristot. Ath. Pol. 42,1–2), and maintained the register of their acknowledged members in the *lexiarchikón grammateîon*. On occasion the *dêmoi* could be called upon to carry out a special scrutiny (*diapsēphismós* or *diapsḗphisis*) of the qualifications of all current members.

Dêmoi had their own religious festivals and disposed of property that belonged more to the *dêmos* as a whole than to its individual members and which was allocated to leaseholders. As in modern states and their regional entities, people who had a prominent place in the life of the polis generally did not also play a significant role in the life of their *dêmos*.

1 D. Kienast, Die innenpolit. Entwicklung Athens im 6. Jh. und die Reformen, in: HZ 200, 1965, 265–83 2 D.M. Lewis, Cleisthenes and Attica, in: Historia 12, 1963, 22–40 3 R. Osborne, Demos: The Discovery of Classical Attica, 1985 4 P. Siewert, Die Trittyen Attikas und die Heeresreform des Kleisthenes, 1982 5 G.R. Stanton, The Trittyes of Kleisthenes, in: Chiron 24, 1994, 161–207 6 Traill, Attica 7 J.S. Traill, Demos and Trittys, 1986 8 Whitehead.

B. Other Greek cities

In various other states local structures are spoken of that are occasionally but not always known as *dêmoi*. Official terminology can only be determined from inscriptions, as the same administrative units are described in literary texts in a variety of terms. Diodorus (11,54,1) reports that the *pólis* of Elis had been established from several small *póleis*; Strabo (8,3,2), however, says of Elis at one point that people had settled there in *kṓmai* ('villages'), but at another he maintains that the *pólis* consisted of *dêmoi* after the Persian wars. Furthermore, Strabo (8,3,2) speaks of several *póleis* in Arcadia and Achaea consisting of *dêmoi*, but reports of the dissolution of the *pólis* Mantinea in 385 BC mentioning *kṓmai* (Xen. Hell. 5,2,7); when Helisson was integrated into Mantinea in the early 4th cent. BC it officially became a 'village' (*kṓmē*) of Mantinea (SEG 37, 340).

Dêmoi are mentioned for the cities on Euboea (in Eretria *dêmoi* were subdivisions of *chóroi*; the latter, on the other hand, may have been parts of phyles), as also in Aegina, in Aegiale on Amorgos (but not in the other cities of the island), in Macedonian Thessalonica (according to Stephanus of Byzantium; not attested epigraphically), in Ionian Miletus, Stratoniceia in Caria and Ptolemais in Egypt. Aulon was a *dêmos* of Naxos (IG XII 5, 36 = Syll.[3] 520). Rhodes was divided into three phyles, each of which derived from the former cities of Camirus, Ialysus and Lindus. On Rhodes, as in its dependent territories, there were *dêmoi* subordinate to one or the other of those phyles. An extended dependent community could consist of more than one *dêmos*, a small one could (as a *koinón*) form part of a *dêmos*. Cos and Calymna were also divided into *dḗmoi*, the latter maintaining its *dêmoi* after its own integration into the polis of Cos at the end of the 3rd cent. BC, while itself becoming a *dêmos* of Cos.

N. F. Jones, Public Organization in Ancient Greece, 1987.

P.J.R.

C. Byzantine period

Greek *dêmoi* (δῆμοι) at times synonymous with the singular *dêmos*, other times specifically the people who had political representation, *inter alia*, it could also mean the supporters of sport clubs designated by colours (in Byzantium, mainly green and blue) in Rome and Byzantium (*factiones*, so-called circus factions). The concept of the regional, social, political and religious categorization of Greens and Blues in Constantinople was refuted by A. Cameron [1].

1 A. Cameron, Circus Factions, 1976, especially 44, 103.

LMA 3, 686; ODB 1, 608f.

F.T.

Demosioi (δημόσιοι; *dēmósioi*, amplified with ὑπηρέται; *hypērétai*, 'servants'). Public slaves who were used by Greek states for a variety of lowly administrative tasks. In Athens they looked after the official records (Aristot. Ath. Pol. 47,5; 48,1), helping the *astynómoi* in keeping the city clean (Ath. Pol. 50,2) and the *hodopoioí* in road maintenance (Ath. Pol. 54,1), as well as working in the courts (Ath. Pol. 63–65; 69,1). In the 4th cent. they were used to check coins in silver mints (Hesperia 43, 1974, 157–88); in the 2nd cent., and undoubtedly even earlier, they are said to have been supervisors of official weights and measures (IG II[2] 1013). The Scythian archers ('Scythae') who kept order in the public assembly formed a special category of *demosioi*. (cf. schol. Aristoph. Ach. 54).

O. Jacob, Les esclaves publics à Athènes, 1928. P.J.R.

Demosthenes (Δημοσθένης; *Dēmosthénēs*).

[1] Prominent Athenian commander during the Peloponnesian War. Appointed *strategos* for the first time in 427/6 BC, he entered Aetolia with Western Greek allies so as to be able to attack Boeotia from the west. Through tactical errors D. suffered a severe defeat and fear prevented him from returning to Athens (Thuc. 3,94–98). However, in the Aetolian and Spartan assault on the Athenian stronghold of Naupactus in 426, D., with 1,000 Acarnanian hoplites, was able to prevent its capture and with the Acarnanian troops secured two victories over the Peloponnesians and Ambracians (Thuc. 3,100–102; 105–114). Thus rehabilitated, he deployed in 425 on the Messenian cape of Pylos, where he was surrounded by Spartans. The Athenian fleet sent as a reinforcement succeeded in blockading the Spartan garrison on the offshore island of Sphacteria. The Spartans felt obliged to make a peace offer to the Athenians. With his unacceptable demands, the Athenian demagogue → Cleon forced a breakdown in the negotiations. As a quick victory was no longer in the offing, Cleon had to go himself to Pylos as *strategos*. Together with D., who was already planning an assault on Sphacteria, Cleon succeeded in capturing some 120 Spartans (Thuc. 4,2–23; 26–41). In 424 D.'s surprise attack on Megara, facilitated by local traitors, failed because of the unexpected intervention of → Brasidas (Thuc. 4,66–74). Likewise, an assault that D. led against Boeotia from Naupactus with Acarnanian support also failed (Thuc. 4,76f.; 89–101). D. was not reappointed *strategos* until 418/7 and 414/3. Early in 413 D. was dispatched with a large contingent to Syracuse in support of Nicias. A night raid on Epipolae resulted in defeat. The subsequent withdrawal from Sicily proposed by D. was unduly delayed by Nicias. After the catastrophe that befell the Athenian fleet in Syracuse harbour, the Athenian army withdrew into the interior, was surrounded and forced to surrender. Nicias and D. were executed in Syracuse (Thuc. 7,86). Traill, PAA 318425.

J. Roisman, The General Demosthenes and his Use of Military Surprise, 1993. W.S.

[2] **Attic Orator and Politician** b. 384/3 BC in Athens, son of Demosthenes (deme of Paiania, phyle Pandionis) and Cleobule, d. 322 on Calauria.

A. Life B. Work C. Later influence

A. Life

The most informative biographical sources are his own speeches and those of his contemporaries (Aeschines, Dinarchus, Hypereides), as well as the *Vita* by Plutarch and that by Ps.-Plutarch, two treatises by Dionysius of Halicarnassus (De Dem., Ep. 1 ad Am.), together with notes in the scholia on Didymus and later writers (Libanius, Zosimus, Suda, Photius). D.'s father, owner of a weapons factory, died in 377, the guardians (Aphobus, Onetor, Therippides) entrusted his upbringing to his mother but misappropriated a portion of the legacy. On reaching maturity D. prepared himself through his training with Isaeus for a legal contest with his guardians. Although successful with a conviction against Aphobus, and most likely a settlement with the other two, he recovered only a portion of the estate (364/3). In the ensuing years he completed his study of oratory, somewhat credibly believed to have included an intensive study of Thucydides and with Isocrates, as well as thorough training in gesture, mime and voice modulation; schooling with Plato, on the other hand, was a later invention. M.W.

D. was regarded as one of the most influential rhetors of Athens in the second half of the 4th cent. BC. He worked initially as a logographer, perhaps also a teacher of oratory, and gained a high reputation as orator in the Athenian courts. In the course of his political career from 355 to 322 D. acquired substantial financial assets to add to his inherited wealth. Large sums of money, from the Persian king in particular, were paid to him to influence politics in Athens. On the other hand, a large number of public offices and extravagant financial grants for Athens from D. are attested to between 363 and 324.

His political career began with charges against Androtion and Leptines in 355 and Timocrates in 353. The speech against Leptines was the first prosecutorial speech D. delivered in public himself. As Aristophon defended Leptines, people suspected that he was really D.'s opponent. In the *symmoria* speech (→ Symmoria), his first foreign policy speech before the public assembly and the one that really launched his career as orator, he warned Athens in 354/3 against entanglement in a war with the Persian Empire. Although the *symmoria* speech marked D.'s entry into foreign policy, it was the relationship between Athens, Philip II and Alexander the Great that decisively formed his political activity until his death.

In the speech on → *syntaxeis* in 353/2 D. directed his criticism at the accumulation of surpluses of public money in the → *theorikon* fund, and thus at → Eubulus of Probalinthus. That marked the start of the second phase of his political life in which D. established an independent profile. His proposals, in the speech for the

Megalopolitans in 352, for an active Athenian policy in the Peloponnese were not, however, adopted. In the speech against Aristocrates, the Thracian Cersobleptes was still described as Athens' main opponent in northern Greece, even though the Macedonian → Philip II was already at war with the Athenians at that time; however Philip's attack on Cersobleptes towards the end of 352, brought about a strategic turn. From 351 (First Philippic) D. considered the dynamically expanding Macedonia as Athens' main adversary. Attacked by Philip II, Olynthus sought Athenian assistance in 349. In the Olynthiac speeches D. argued firmly for immediate and comprehensive support, but too little came too late to prevent the destruction of Olynthus in 348. Although D. was in 347/6, together with Aeschines, one of the negotiators of the → Peace of Philocrates of 346, he soon began to oppose it publicly. In 344/3, negotiations aimed at expanding it into a general and enduring peace (*koinē eirḗnē*, → Peace, concept of) and settling contentious issues, broke down. In 343 D. brought a suit against Aeschines for his part in the negotiation of the Peace of Philocrates (Dem. Or. 19). Aeschines was however acquitted with the support of Phocion and Eubulus.

The third phase of D.'s political life, in which he determined the foreign policy of the polis until 338, began in 343. He pressed to have negotiations for a renewal of the Peace of Philocrates broken off, to have soundings taken for an alliance with the Persian king, to have a new Hellenic League formed against Macedonia and to have open war declared against Philip II. In the Third and Fourth *Philippika* D. sharpened his attacks on Philip in 341 and in 339 he achieved a reform of the *theorikon* system and an increase in Athens' maritime defences. In the autumn of 340 Philip opened hostilities with the seizure of an Athenian grain-ship in the Hellespont. Shortly before the decisive battle D. was still able to create an alliance between Athens and Thebes, which did not, however, prevent the defeat of the Hellenic League at Chaeronea in 338. After that, with supportive orators and *strategoi*, he introduced defensive measures in Athens, looked after the grain supply and the repair of the walls in particular and, notwithstanding the defeat, was able to deliver the memorial address (*epitaphios*) for those who had fallen in that year of war.

Even in the fourth phase of his political life, from 338 to 330, D. remained one of the leading orators. He argued that Athens exploit the crises after the assassination of Philip II in 336 and during the Theban revolt of 335 to secure a military reversal of the situation of 338/7. During the war against Darius III he advocated only the obligatory support for → Alexander [4] the Great, denounced breaches of the guarantees of 338/7, and until Gaugamela, hoped for Alexander's defeat in Asia. Initially D. appears to have even recommended Athens' support for Agis III but Athens did not openly take up arms against Alexander or Antipater between 336 and 330. With his famous speech 'On the Crown' in 330 (Dem. Or. 18) D. gained a triumphant victory in court over his rival Aeschines, who as early as 336, had brought an action against Ctesiphon's nomination of D. for a garland as a reward for his services to the state. The outcome of the affair also led to a plebiscite on Athens' recent past and to a confirmation of D.'s policy.

In 324, discontent with the status of Athens in Alexander's universal empire after 330, → Harpalus' flight to Athens, the decree on mercenaries, the decree on exiles, and the debate about divine honours for Alexander in the Greek states, all combined to create a crisis in the course of which D., in the final phase of his political biography, together with Leosthenes and Hypereides, fixed the broad features of policy in Athens. As the principal ceremonial delegate (*architheṓros*) of Athens at the Olympic Games of 324, D. negotiated with Nicanor on the decree on exiles, the implementation of which would mean the loss of Athens' cleruchy on Samos. The actual extent of D.'s involvement in the Harpalus scandal can no longer be established. His conviction in 323 as the principal accused in the Harpalus proceedings was a consequence of the judges' dissatisfaction with the limited success of his diplomacy from summer 324 to early 323. After his arrest D. escaped into exile. Thence, and after his quick return to Athens, he supported Hypereides and Leosthenes, who after Alexander's death led Athens at the head of a new Hellenic League against Macedonia in the 'Lamian War'. After the defeat at Crannon, D. was condemned to death *in absentia* in Athens following a motion by Demades. He committed suicide in 322 when tracked down to the Poseidon sanctuary on Calauria. His political biography is typical of an Athenian rhetor in the 4th cent. The military failure of his foreign policy against Philip II and Alexander the Great should not be interpreted as evidence of a mistaken conceptual basis.

PA; Davies 3597; P. Carlier, Démosthène, 1990; G.L. Cawkwell, D.'s Policy after the Peace of Philocrates I, in: CQ 57, 1963, 120–138 and II, ibid. 200–213; G.L. Cawkwell, The Crowning of D., in: CQ 19, 1969, 163–180; M.M. Markle, D.'sSecond Philippic: A Valid Policy for the Athenians against Philip, in: Antichthon 15, 1981, 62–85; H. Montgomery, The Way to Chaeronea, 1983; A.W. Pickard-Cambridge, D. and the Last Days of Greek Freedom 384–322 B.C., 1914 (repr. 1978); Schäfer passim; R. Sealey, D. and his time, 1993; H. Wankel, D. Rede für Ktesiphon über den Kranz, 2 vols., 1976.

J.E.

B. Work

The extant *Corpus Demosthenicum* contains 63 titles: 60 speeches, a letter of Philipp's ([12]), a collection of 56 proems and a collection of six letters. While it is probably only a small part of the speeches that D. composed and actually delivered, almost everything that was still available at the time of his death has survived (schol. Aeschin. Leg. 18 mentions 71 speeches of D., Ps.-Plut. speaks of 65; we also know the titles of nine lost speeches). The Corpus probably derives from a collection that was assembled uncritically by Callimachus in Alexandria around 240 BC; the means used by Dionysius of Halicarnassus and Caecilius to separate authentic from non-authentic works are known to us in only a few cases. The arrangement of the speeches varies in transmission but certain groups have always been kept together (e.g. the Philippics or the Olynthian speeches). The sequence followed in two of the most important MSS was adopted in the *editio princeps* (Venice 1504) and in modern complete editions. The speeches can be divided into four groups: (1) courtroom addresses in private cases (27–59), (2) courtroom addresses in political trials (18–26), (3) public addresses in the public assembly (1–17), (4) epideictic speeches (60; 61). A few of them are certainly not authentic (7; 11; 17; 25; 26; 58; 61), those held by Apollodorus, son of Pasion [10], may well have been his own (46; 49; 50; 52; 53; 59), others are of arguable authenticity (10; 33–35; 43; 44; 48; 56 as well as the letters and proems).

The style in the speeches from D.'s early period (364–359) still displayed a certain dependence on models like Isaeus and Isocrates, only reaching its own unique character and highest development in the public addresses of the middle period (355–341) and, in particular, in the speech 'On the Crown' (330 BC). When compared with other Attic orators, D. is characterized by a greater freedom in the choice of words, including vocabulary from common everyday speech as well as from poetic diction, a tendency towards abstract expression and substantivization (in this respect similar to Thuc.), rich use of sustained graphic metaphors, as well as a certain predilection for accumulating synonyms. Word order is very free and inclines towards hyperbata; it is moreover marked by an avoidance of hiatus (initially like Isocrates, less severely so later on), striving for rhythmic responsion at the beginning and end of cola and the 'tribrachys law' (a combination of three or more short syllables is avoided as far as possible), discovered by Blass and confirmed by later research [16; 18]. In sentence construction there is a regular alternation between longer periods and shorter clauses; the use of word and thought images is similarly rich and variable. In the general handling of all forms of linguistic and oratorical techniques and their apposite use to suit the subject matter, D.'s art surpasses that of all other Attic orators.

C. Later influence

D.'s oratorical ability received the highest acclaim from his contemporaries, even from his political adversaries (e.g. Aeschines); the only negative judgement was from Demetrius of Phalerum; opinions are divided, however, on the question of his political achievement, a dichotomy that was to mark D.'s reception into the 20th cent. In his honour the Athenians erected a bronze statue by Polyeuctus in 280 BC that was commissioned by D.'s nephew Demochares and served as the model for the extant marble portrait from the Roman period. Polybius (18,14) criticizes D.'s politics but Cicero admires his exemplary resistance against 'tyranny' and entitled his own speeches against Antonius *Philippicae* (43 BC); for him, who had translated the speech 'On the Crown' into Latin, D. was already what he was to become from the Augustan period onwards, namely the unchallenged top orator (*facile princeps*) of the Greeks (in contrast to the Roman 'Atticists' like Brutus, who favoured Lysias [21. 107ff.]. With the victory of Atticism (from Dion. Hal. onwards) D. became the model orator *par excellence*, the object of diligent study, of commentaries and glorification, who acquired the same status in his field as Homer in poetry (ὁ ποιητής, ὁ ῥήτωρ; *ho poiētḗs, ho rhḗtōr*; 'The poet', 'The orator') in papyrus manuscripts only Homer is better represented. Of the many writers from the Imperial period who studied his life and work, we only mention the author of the treatise *Perì hýpsous*, Quintilian, Plutarch, Hermogenes, Lucian, and Libanius. Even during the Byzantine period, D. scholarship seems never to have dropped off altogether and, in contrast to many others, his work survived the age of iconoclasm almost unscathed. With the end of the Byzantine Empire, D. came to be known again in Western Europe and used for political purposes: Cardinal Bessarion translated the first Olynthian speech into Latin to foment war against the Turks; under the influence of D.'s works Elizabeth I of England compared Philip II of Macedonia with Philip II of Spain [3. 287]. From then on, D. was assiduously translated into Latin but less so, and only much later, into modern languages. In the 17th and 18th cents. the assessment of D. was coloured by attitudes towards monarchy during the age of absolutism (e.g. Rollin, Mitford) and into the middle of the 19th cent. by predominantly favourable voices (Niebuhr, Grote, Schäfer) [3. 288–93]. The Hegelian-based criticism of the short-sighted, local patriot who stood against the spirit of his age without any prospect of success (Droysen) reached its apogee in Kahrstedt and Drerup (D. as a perfidious pettifogger and agent of the Persian king) [3. 293–5]. During both World Wars the orator was used by the Allies as a model of resistance against military aggression (Clemenceau, Adam) [3. 296–300]. Since the end of the last war interest has turned more to D. the orator while academic appraisal of D. as a politician continues to be controversial.

Editions: S.H. Butcher, W. Rennie, 3 vols., 1903–31 (repr.); M. Croiset, O. Navarre, P. Orsini, J. Humbert, L. Gernet, G. Nathieu, R. Clavaud, 13 vols., 1924–87.

Individual editions, Translations, Commentaries: A. Sakellariou, 1988 (or. 1–3) P. Collin, 1965 (or. 4) N.D. Vasilopoulos, 1969 (or. 4) L. Canfora, 1992 (or. 9) L.J. Bliquez, 1968 (or. 11; 12) L. Canfora, 1974 (or. 16) G. Ballaira, 1971 (or. 18) S. Usher, 1993 (or. 18) H. Wankel, 1976 (or. 18) W. Zuercher, 1983 (or. 18) D.M. MacDowell, 1990 (or. 21) G. Xanthakis Karamanos, 1989 (or. 21) L. Volpis, 1936 (or. 23) L. Pearson, 1972 (or. 27; 28; 30; 31; 32; 34) M. Kertsch, 1971 (or. 30) F.A. Paley, J.E. Sandys, 1896–8 (repr. 1979) (34–37; 39; 40; 45; 46; 53–56) U. Albini, S. Aprosio, 1957 (or. 35) C. Ca-

REY, R.A. REID, 1985 (or. 37; 39; 54; 56) T.N. BALLIN, 1978 (or. 50) E. AVEZZÙ, 1986 (or. 59) C. CAREY, 1992 (or. 59) A.J. PATTESON, 1978 (or. 59) J.A. GOLDSTEIN, 1968 (Letters) B. HAUSMANN, 1978/1981 (papyrus fr.).
SCHOLIA: M.R. DILTS, 2 vols., 1983–86 Didymus, In D. Commenta, edd. L. PEARSON, S. STEPHENS, 1983.
INDEX: S. PREUSS, 1892.
LITERARY AND RESEARCH PAPERS: D.F. JACKSON, G.O. ROWE, in: Lustrum 14, 1969 (*bis* 1966) U. SCHINDEL (ed.), D., 1987, 431–449 (*bis* 1983).
GENERAL: 1 BLASS, 3,1, [2]1893 (repr. 1962) 2 L. CANFORA, Per la cronologia di D., 1968 3 P. CARLIER, Démosthène, 1990 4 P. CLOCHÉ, D. et la fin de la démocratie athénienne, [2]1957 5 E. DRERUP, Aus einer alten Advokatenrepublik, 1916 6 W. JAEGER, D. Der Staatsmann und sein Werden, [2]1963 7 J. LUCCIONI, D. et le Panhellénisme, 1961 8 U. SCHINDEL, D., 1987 9 P. TREVES, D. e la libertà greca, 1933 10 J. TREVETT, Apollodorus, the Son of Pasion, 1992.
TRANSMISSION: 11 L. CANFORA, Inventario dei manoscritti greci di D., 1968 12 Id., Per la storia del testo di D., 1968 13 D. IRMER, Beobachtungen zur D. Überlieferung, in: Philologus 122, 1968, 43–62 14 Id., Zur Genealogie der jüngeren D.-MSS, 1972.
LANGUAGE, STYLE: 15 G. BARTHOLD, Studien zum Vokabular der polit. Propaganda bei D., diss. 1962 16 W. BARTSCHELET-MASSINI, Neue Versuche zum demosthenischen Prosarhythmus, in: H.U. CAHN, E. SIMON (ed.), Tainia, FS R. Hampe, 1980, 503–28 17 R. CHEVALLIER, L'art oratoire de D. dans le discours sur la couronne, in: BAGB 1960, 200–16 18 D.F. McCABE, The Prose-Rhythm of D., 1981 19 L. PEARSON, The Art of D., 1976 20 G. RONNET, Études sur le style de D. dans les discours politiques, 1951.
INFLUENCE BEYOND HIS LIFETIME: 21 D. ADAMS, D. and his Influence, 1927 (repr. 1963) 22 A.A. ANASTASSIOU, Zur ant. Wertschätzung der Beredsamkeit des D., diss. 1965 23 J. BOMPAIRE, L'apothéose de D., de sa mort jusqu'à l'époque de la IIe sophistique, in: BAGB 1984, 14–26 24 E. DRERUP, D. im Urteil des Alt., 1923 (repr. 1968) 25 M. LOSSAU, Unt. zur ant. D.-Exegese, 1964 26 A. MICHAELIS, Die Bildnisse des D., in: K. FITTSCHEN (ed.), Griech. Porträts, 1988, 78–100 27 U. SCHINDEL, D. im 18. Jh., 1963. M.W.

[3] from Bithynia. (presumably from 3rd/2nd cent. BC; possibly belonging to the Imperial period). He composed a work in prose or verse with legends of foundings, *Ktíseis*, as well as an epic, *Bithyniaká*, in at least ten books.

FGrH 3C, 1, 552–554; CollAlex 25–27; K. ZIEGLER, Das Hell. Epos, 1966, 15–22. C.S.

[4] D. Philalethes. Physician, author of ophthalmological writings, from the first half of the 1st cent. AD. He took the name Philalethes after his teacher, Alexander Philalethes of Men Karou (Asia Minor), who followed the Herophilean tradition, and whose views on the pulse he largely echoed in his three-volume work 'On Pulses' (Gal. 8,726–7). His greatest contribution was, however, in the field of ophthalmology. His *Ophthalmikós* became the basis for many later works on the subject: from Rufus of Ephesus in the late 1st cent. AD (Aetius 7,53) to an anonymous Byzantine tract from around AD 900 [1] as well as texts in Latin by the writers Simon of Genoa and Matthaeus Silvaticus from the early 14th cent., who were familiar with a mutilated manuscript from the Bobbio monastery, a Latin version of D.'s treatise.

The *Ophthalmikós* opened with chapters on the anatomy and physiology of the eye, drawing heavily on Herophilus, followed by sections on pathology, symptomatology and therapy. It contained descriptions of over 40 eye disorders, including short-sightedness, glaucoma, and staphyloma, as well as a series of treatments such as fomentations, various eye-salves and phlebotomy. D.'s description of an operation for cataract (Silvaticus, Liber Pandectarum, s.v. Paracentesis, Venice 1480) is the oldest extant by a Greek author and may well be even older than that of Celsus (De med. 7,7,14). Identification with Demosthenes of Massilia (Gal. 13,855) or the author of a green plaster (Gal. 12,843) could not be confirmed.

→ Ophthalmology; → Laodicea; → Medicine

1 T. PUSCHMANN (ed.), Nachträge zu Alexander Trallianos, 1886, 134–179.

M. WELLMANN, RE 9, 189–190 s.v. Demosthenes [11]; Id., Demosthenes' ΠΕΡΙ ΟΦΘΑΛΜΩΝ, in: Hermes 38, 1903, 546–566; VON STADEN, 570–578. V.N.

Demostratus (Δημόστρατος; *Dēmóstratos*).

[1] Athenian, deme uncertain, from the clan of the → Buzygae (Aristoph. Lys. 397 with schol.; Aristid. 3,51). 'Demagogue' (Plut. Nic. 12,6) who in 415 BC proposed that the *strategoi* of the Sicilian expedition be given full powers as → *autokrátores* (Plut. Alc. 18,3; Aristoph. Lys. 391; unnamed in Thuc. 6,25,1) and also that Zacynthian hoplites be recruited (Aristoph. Lys. 393 with schol.).

TRAILL, PAA 319245; DEVELIN, 149; DAVIES, 3276(B)(4). K.KI.

[2] D.P...anus. Fronto, Marcus Aurelius' teacher, delivered a speech in his defence and sent it to Marcus Aurelius and Verus (Fronto p. 102,11f.; 113,8 VAN DEN HOUT); may well be identical to the Athenian archon Ti. Claudius D. [1].

1 E. CHAMPLIN, Fronto and Antonine Rome, 1980, 63f., 160[14]. W.E.

Demotic Term coined by Hdt. (2,36) for an Egyptian cursive script attested from the 7th cent. BC; initially used exclusively for recording everyday texts (documents, letters, receipts, lists and the like) and thus distinct as a 'common' script from 'holy' script (→ Hieroglyphs, → Hieratic). From the 4th cent. BC other texts were written in demotic script: narrative and instructional literature, scholarly, religious, mythological, funereal and magic texts, monumental inscriptions (→ Bilingual inscriptions) decrees (→ Rosetta Stone), graffiti etc. The language of most of the texts written in demotic script is likewise termed demotic (link between Late Egyptian and → Coptic). Some texts written in demotic were, however, partly or completely composed in an earlier language (Middle Egyptian; → Egyptian). In the first cents. AD demotic was replaced by Greek as an archival script and language but it survived in other textual forms—especially in literary and magic papyri, labels on mummies and graffiti—until at least the 3rd cent. AD. Individual instances are still found in the 4th and 5th cents.; the latest dated inscription comes from → Philae: 11 December AD 452 [2].

→ Demotic law

1 F. DE CENIVAL, L'écriture démotique, in: Bibliothèque d'Étude, Inst. Français d'Archéologie, 64/1, 37–44 2 D. DEVAUCHELLE, 24 Août 394 — 24 Août 1994. 1600 ans, in: Bull. de la Soc. Française d'Égyptologie, 131, Oct. 1994, 17f. 3 E. LÜDDECKENS, s.v. Demotisch, LÄ 1, 1975, 1052–1056 4 Id., s.v. Papyri, Demotisch, LÄ 4, 1982, 750–898 5 H.-J. THISSEN, H. FELBER, Demotist. Lit.-Übersicht, in: Enchoria 1, 1971ff.

K.-T.Z.

Demotic law → Demotic (the later stage of Egyptian language/script) was used in everyday life in Egypt from the middle of the 7th cent. BC and continued even during Hellenistic and Roman foreign domination. Therefore the law found in demotic documents will have probably been exposed to foreign influence, but this cannot be assumed. Thus, for example, the Romans were not the first to introduce a form of property law into Egypt. Rather, it has its roots in the Pharaonic period, as demonstrated by a long inscription from the 10th cent. BC [1].

The situation that emerges from texts of the Pharaonic period points initially to an empirically acquired law based on well-established facts. In time, however, the Egyptians learned to observe issues in isolation and developed an abstract elaboration of rules, as several demotic writings indicate. In them, legal propositions, even if casuistical, are coherent and developed in a logical sequence; the legal issue is not only methodically treated but a certain depth of content is also discernible. The authors of such works were thus capable of writing legal books, they were perhaps professional jurists [2; 3]. They represent the first steps towards real jurisprudence.

The increasing stock of formulae also points in this direction, in so far as they provided the law with a higher degree of practicability and flexibility. This can be seen, for example, in the institution of marriage. From the 9th cent. BC we come across documents of dealing with matrimonial property and matters of inheritance that use strongly contrasting turns of phrase. These differences are to be explained not only in terms of the geographical origins of the married couple and the lawyers but probably also in terms of chronological progress in developing a legal lexicon. On the whole, these documents do indeed reflect an advanced level of judicial thinking [4].

Even the institution of guarantee/surety is encountered in demotic documents from the Ptolemaic period. The main basic principles are essentially similar in demotic and contemporary Greek documents in Egypt. Through the entire material stretching in unbroken sequence into the Byzantine period it can be established that this form of commerce was also known to lawmakers of the → *corpus iuris* from the practice of their time. There was unmistakable interaction between Egyptian and Greek law in the area of guarantee/surety [5]. Similarly, the marriage documents mentioned earlier exercised some influence on the formation of matrimonial property law in Greek papyri [6]. Other examples also demonstrate that foreign legal systems affected demotic documents and that the latter made a positive contribution to development of those laws.

→ Egyptian law

1 S. ALLAM, Publizität und Schutz im Rechtsverkehr, in: Id. (ed.), Grund und Boden in Altägypten, 1994, 35–43 2 E. SEIDL, Eine demot. Juristenarbeit, in: ZRG 96, 1979, 17 3 S. ALLAM, Réflexions sur le 'Code légal' d'Hermopolis dans l'Égypte ancienne, in: Chronique d'Égypte 61, 1986, 50–76 4 s.v. Ehe, Eheurkunden, in: LÄ I, 1162–1183 5 J. PARTSCH, in: K. SETHE, Demot. Urkunden zum ägypt. Bürgschaftsrechte vorzüglich der Ptolemäerzeit, 1920, 518f. 6 G. HÄGE, Ehegüterrechtliche Verhältnisse in den griech. Papyri Ägyptens bis Diokletian, 1968, 17.

S.A.

Demotikon Modern word formation to describe a name component of a full Greek citizen: apart from the person's name (e.g., Δημοσθένης/*Dēmosthénēs*) and the father's name (genitive, e.g., Δημοσθένους/*Dēmosthénous*), the *demotikon* indicates origin from a → *dḗmos* [2], a local unit of a → *pólis* (e.g., *Paianieús*, 'from the deme Paeania') and was primarily used in epigraphic contexts, i.e. in texts directed at the public. In Attica the *demotikon* became customary after the political elevation of the *dḗmoi* by → Cleisthenes [2] and obligatory after the reorganization of democracy in 403 BC (cf. Aristot. Ath. Pol. 21,4) [1. 69–78; 223 f.; 2. 171 f.; 176 f.]. The *demotikon* differentiates the citizen with full rights (*polítēs*) from the *métoikos*, who had no appendage to his name, and the foreign non-citizen, who had an → *ethnikon* instead of a *demotikon*. Among the Rhodians, for example, the *demotikon* identified citizens of incorporated communities in the state's far-flung territories from inhabitants of subjugated communities ([3. 53,2]; cf. [4]).

1 D. WHITEHEAD, The Demes of Attica 508/7 — ca. 250 B. C., 1986 2 M. H. HANSEN, City-Ethnics as Evidence for Polis Identity, in: Id., K. RAAFLAUB (ed.), More Studies in the Ancient Greek Polis, 1996, 169–196 3 P. M. FRASER, G. E. BEAN, The Rhodian Peraea and Islands, 1954 4 I. C. PAPACHRISTODOULOU, Archaioi Rhodiakoi Demoi, 1989.

L.-M. G.

Demotionidae see → Phratry

Denarius Standard Roman silver coin, worth 10 *asses* — hence the ancient term 'tenner' —, later 16 *asses*. Named δηνάριον (*dēnárion*) in Greek. After the breakdown of the gold system during the Second Punic War, the *denarius* was introduced between 214 and 211 BC, together with the fractional pieces *quinarius* ($^1/_2$ *denarius*) and *sestertius* ($^1/_4$ *denarius*), as the new prime monetary unit (with a value marking of X or ⳩) to replace the *quadrigatus*. With a weight of 4 *scrupula* (*c.* 4.55 gm = $^1/_{72}$ of a Roman pound of 327.45 gm) the *denarius* corresponded to 10 sextantal *asses* and departed from the old currency of didrachms at 6 *scrupula*, probably so as to prevent an outflow of Roman gold into enemy territory [1. 8ff.; 360ff.]. The ratio of silver to bronze was 1:120 [2. 626]. The fineness of over 95% was maintained up to the end of the Republic [2. 569ff.]. Even before 200 BC the weight was reduced to roughly 3.8 gm ($^1/_{84}$ of a Roman pound) [2. 594f.]. Around 141 BC the value marking of XVI, which appeared only briefly, attests to a ratio of 16 to the *as*, which had dropped to the uncial standard, while the value markings of X or ⳩ continued to be used (Table of Values, → Aureus) [2. 613; 624f.]. After the *aureus* became the real principal monetary unit in the early Imperial period, the *denarius* began to drop in value. In AD 64 Nero devalued the *denarius* to $^1/_{96}$ of a pound, i.e. to three *scrupula* or roughly 3.4 gm with a fineness of *c.* 93 % [3. 76; 4. I 25, III 110ff.]. In the course of the 2nd cent. AD it sank to around 3 gm with 73–72 % silver [4. II 60, III 121ff.] and under Septimius Severus and Caracalla, to *c.* 50 % silver [4. III 49]. With the currency reform of Caracalla around AD 215 the *antoninianus* became the principal monetary unit, as double *denarius* (→ Medallion, for other multiples of the *denarius*) [4. III 64ff.]. Following the end of the Severan dynasty (AD 235) the *denarius* was minted only sporadically and in small quantities as a copper coin with an ultrathin silver overlay [5. 49]. The diameter was reduced from 23 to 18 mm. After the collapse of silver coinage in the 3rd cent. AD, the *denarius* survived as a unit of computation from the Diocletian currency reform (AD 301) [6. 328]. In Diocletian's revaluation edict the value of the gold pound was set at 72,000 *denarii*. [7. 450]; in the 4th cent. AD at 6,000 *denarii*, and later in the 6th cent. up to 7,200 *denarii* made up the *solidus* [8. 15f.]. Towards the end of the 7th cent. AD a silver coin emerged under the Merovingians that was termed *denarius*, later *denier* [9. 102].

As a unit of weight the *denarius* was set at $^1/_{84}$ of a pound and, especially from Nero onwards, at $^1/_{96}$ of a pound and, also under the name *drachma*, was equivalent to the new Attic drachma of three *scrupula* (3.41 gm) [10. 210].

→ Antoninianus; → As; → Aureus; → Didrachmon; → Drachma; → Medallion; → Counterfeiting of coins; → Coinage reforms; → Coinage systems; → Quadrigatus; → Quinarius; → Sestertius; → Solidus

1 J. Seibert, Forsch. zu Hannibal, 1993 2 RRC, [2]1987 3 A.N. Zograph, Ancient coinage I, 1977 4 D.R. Walker, The metrology of the Roman silver coinage I, Brit. Archeol. Rep. Suppl. Ser. 5, 1976; II, Ser. 22, 1977; III, Ser. 40, 1978 5 A. Burnett, Coinage in the Roman world, 1987 6 S. Bolin, State and currency in the Roman Empire to A.D. 300, 1958 7 M.F. Hendy, Studies in the Byzantine monetary economy, c. 300–1450, 1985 8 P. Grierson, Byzantine coins, 1982 9 Id., M. Blackburn, Medieval european coinage I, 1986 10 Hultsch, s.v. D., RE 5, 202–215, here 210.

D. Sperber, Denarii and Aureii in the Time of Diocletian, in: JRS 56, 1966, 190–195; M.H. Crawford, Coinage and money under the Roman Republic, 1985. A.M.

Dendara (Egyptian *Jwnt*[*–tꜣ-nṯrt*], Greek Τεντυρα; *Tentura*), city in Upper Egypt, located on the west bank of the Nile opposite today's Qena, capital of the 6th Upper Egyptian *nome*. From earliest times, D. was an important centre, and especially significant from the Old Kingdom to the early Middle Kingdom. Details of a large number of the *nome*'s *strategoi* from the Ptolemaic and Roman periods have been preserved on their monuments. The most important deity was the goddess of love, Hathor. Her sanctuary, dating from the Old Kingdom, was extended and rebuilt several times. The structure extant today dates from the late Ptolemaic and early Roman period and is one of the best-preserved temples in Egypt.

F. Daumas, LÄ 1, 1060–1063. K.J.-W.

Dendrophoroi (δενδροφόροι; *dendrophóroi*). *Collegium*, probably founded by the Emperor Claudius in connection with the reorganization of the cult of → Mater Magna. The first epigraphical evidence, dating from AD 79, is CIL X 7 (Regium Iulium). The founding date (*natalicium*) was 1 August. The association's ritual function involved felling, decorating and carrying the sacred pine in the mourning procession on 22 March in memory of Attis (Lydus, Mens. 4,59; cf. the bas-relief in the Musée d'Aquitanie, Bordeaux [1]). The association's Greek name suggests that a formalization of earlier practices may have taken place [2].

In the Roman world the *dendrophoroi* were doubtless linked, albeit nebulously, with woodworking associations, especially the *collegia fabrum tignariorum*. In the 2nd cent. such associations were quite widespread, with the usual patrons and office-bearers, especially in the western part of the empire and often in connection with the Imperial cult. The sharing of *sportulae* ('donations') amongst the members (men and women) is attested many times (e.g. AE 1987, 198) [3]. From the 3rd cent. the *dendrophoroi* were also active as 'fire-fighters' (cf. Cod. Theod. 14,8,1); in 415 the *Collegium* of *dendrophoroi* was banned by Emperor Theodosius in the course of the prohibition of pagan cults (Cod. Theod. 16,10,20 [6]).

→ Attis; → Cannophori; → Collegium; → Mater Magna; → Sportula

1 M.J. Vermaseren, Cybele and Attis, 1977, pl. 73 2 W. Burkert, Stucture and History in Greek Myth, 1979, 119, 137 3 Y. de Kisch, in: Ktema 4, 1979, 265f.

R.GOR.

Dengizich (Dintzic, Greek Δεγγιζίχ, Δινζίριχος; *Dengizích*, *Dinzírichos*). Son of Attila, king of the Huns; after the latter's death D. assembled an army from the elements of the Hun empire that were still under his control, to fight the Goths. He was, however, defeated at Bassianae (Pannonia) by the Goths (probably after AD 456/57, Iord. Get. 272f.). He later conducted several wars against the Romans but was killed in 469 by the *mag. mil. per Thracias* Anagestes (Prisc. fr. 36 [FHG 4,107f.]; Chron. pasch. 323d Dindorf). PLRE 354f.

M.MEI. and ME.STR.

Dentatus Cognomen ('born with teeth') of M'. Curius [4] D.

Kajanto, Cognomina 224.

Denter Cognomen (cf. Dentatus) of the Caecilii [I 25] and M. → Livius D. (cos. 302 BC).

Kajanto, Cognomina 224.

K.-L.E.

Denthalii (Δενθάλιοι; *Denthálioi*). Laconian border region near Messenia on the western slope of the northern Taygetus around the source of the Nedon, with a sanctuary of Artemis Limnatis, contested by Sparta and Messenia and finally granted to Messenia by Tiberius (Steph. Byz. s.v. D.; Tac. Ann. 4,43; Paus. 4,4,2; 31,3). Inscription: IG V 1 p. 260f. no. 1371–1378.

L. Ross, Reisen im Peloponnes, 1841, 1ff.; F. Bölte, s.v. D., RE 3A, 1312, 67ff.; N. Valmin, Études topographiques sur la Messénie ancienne, 1930, 189ff.; Philippson/Kirsten, 3, 423; Nilsson, GGR 1, 493.

C.L. and E.O.

Dentistry

I. Ancient Orient II. Classical Antiquity

I. Ancient Orient

A. I. Sources B. Dental diseases and treatment

A. I. Sources

The main source for Mesopotamian dentistry consists in two chapters from the medical manual 'When the top of a person's head is feverishly hot' (1st millennium BC; cf. → Medicine I) and there are also isolated texts of prescriptions. The oldest textual evidence is a cuneiform tablet from the ancient Babylonian period (*c.* 18th to 16th cents. BC). The majority of the texts is accessible only in cuneiform autographs; for partial translations cf. [1].

B. Dental diseases and treatment

Various periodontal illnesses, caries and grinding of the teeth [2] were known. Wobbly teeth and bleeding gums were regarded as concomitants of diseases formerly interpreted as diphtheria and lichen.

The following types of treatment are attested. 1. Medical-therapeutic: application of powders or cataplasms; in serious cases also extraction of teeth. A wild herb was used for cleaning teeth. 2. Magic-medical: amulets in the form of stone necklaces or leather bags; recitation of incantations [2]. Unique as an example of sympathetic magic is an instruction for producing a model of the jaw in which the painful tooth is indicated by a black barley-corn and the model is then treated [3].

Treatment was usually by plant substances (on the problem of identification cf. → Pharmacology I.); alkali and alum were used for cleaning the mouth.

1 Chicago Assyrian Dictionary, vol. Š/3, 1992, 48b, s.v. *šinnu* A 2 B. Böck, Babylon. Divination und Magie als Ausdruck der Denkstrukturen des altmesopot. Menschen, in: J. Renger (ed.), 2. Internationales Colloquium der Deutschen Orient-Ges., 1999, 409–425 3 F. Köcher, Babylon.-assyr. Medizin in Texten und Unt. vol. 6, 1980, xix.

R. D. Biggs, s. v. Medizin, RLA 7, 627, § 3.6 (short survey of the texts); R. C. Thompson, Assyrian Medical Texts II, in: Proceedings of the Royal Society of Medicine 19/3, 1926, 58–69 (obsolete partial translation).

BA. BÖ.

II. Classical Antiquity

Dental specialists are attested in Egypt from 2600 BC — though seldom designated by the character for doctor. In antiquity dentistry was frequently part of surgery. Palaeopathological finds show considerable tooth decay and also wear of teeth, which can be attributed to the consumption of bread baked with very coarse flour. Tooth caries was also widespread. Furthermore, Egyptian, Babylonian and Greek texts speak of the torments of teething. Rubbing the gums with ointments based on myrrh or with warm oil were used as remedies.

The holes in carious teeth, which in Babylon and Greece were often regarded as the work of → worms, were cleaned with a metal scraper before being filled with a powder made of → terebinth and malachite. Unbearably painful teeth could be removed manually or with special forceps (cf. → Surgical instruments, fig. no. 4), as Cornelius → Celsus [7] explains in *De medicina* 7,12. In particularly difficult cases trepanation with the aid of a drill was also recommended. The Hippocratic treatise *De articulis* and the illustrations in the corresponding commentary by → Apollonius [16] show that around 400 BC the principles of repositioning a dislocated temporo-maxillary joint were quite well known.

Teeth which had fallen out could be replaced by false teeth made of bone or even gold and fixed by caps which were placed round the false tooth and fastened to adjacent, more stable teeth. Well-preserved examples of this kind of tooth replacement come from Palestine, Etruria and Greece, possibly also from Egypt, though no mummies have yet been discovered with dentures of this kind.

In numerous prescriptions from the field of dentistry it seems to have been more a matter of eliminating bad breath than of preserving the teeth or gums. Toothpastes, which often contained cleaning agents like soot, were likewise recommended to keep the teeth white: Messalina [2] used an agent of this kind which had been blended using burnt stag horn, gum mastic from Chios and salts of ammonia (Scribonius Largus, Compositiones 60) as a basis.

W. HOFFMANN-AXTELT, Die Gesch. der Zahnheilkunde, [2]1985; H. E. LÄSSIG, R. A. MÜLLER, Die Z. in Kunst- und Kulturgesch., 1985; C. PROSKAUER, F. H. WITT, Bildgesch. der Z., 1962. V. N.

Denuntiatio can in a legal context be any communication made to another person, orally or in writing, in pursuit of a legal objective. The person making the declaration and the person receiving it do not have to be private individuals but can also be office-holders or even the curule aediles' edict (Dig. 21,1,37). If such a communication is addressed to someone who is absent, it is termed *detestatio* (Dig. 50,39,2). The *denuntiatio* can have an informative or communicative character, as for example the requisite (in late antiquity, threefold) notification of a proposed sale of property pledged as security (Dig. 13,7,4) or have a restraining character, as for example with a *denuntiatio operis novi nuntiatio* (objection to a new construction project; Dig. 39,1,5,10) or finally have a challenging character as in an injunction (Dig. 22,1,32,1), notice of legal proceedings or notification of dispute in the → *litis denuntiatio*. Given the term's ambiguity, it is not possible to set out all the legal features held in common, particularly in respect of the requisite form and substance. Among the more noteworthy features are (1) the *comperendinatio* that is termed *denuntiatio* in Gai. Inst. 4,15 (see also Ps.-Ascon. Verr. 164); (2) *denuntiatio domum* is the *denuntiatio* to be delivered at the home of the addressee (Dig. 39,1,4,5); (3) *denuntiatio ex auctoritate magistratus facta* is a *denuntiatio* issued on the instructions of a magistrate (Dig. 16,3,5,2); (4) in a procedural context the *denuntiatio* is often the summons of a witness (Valerius Probus 5,9) or a summons issued by a magistrate against the defendant. See also → *denuntiator*.

H. ANKUM: Der Verkäufer als cognitor und als procurator in rem suam im röm. Eviktionsprozeß ..., in: D. NÖRR, S. NISHIMURA (ed.), Mandatum und Verwandtes, 1993, 285–306. C.PA.

Denuntiator Someone who has something to announce or proclaim. In a narrower sense the term is applied to those who, whether as a private individual or on behalf of an office, report a criminal offence. *Denuntiator* is then very often synonymous with → *delator*. The excesses of the latter had a lasting effect on the public opinion on denunciation. *Denuntiatores* crop up in Rome even as junior officials in the role of heralds. For similar functions in Greek law → *menysis*, → *sykophantes*. G.S.

De orthographia see → Flavius Caper

Depas (δέπας; *dépas*). Wine bowl, mentioned several times in Homer and probably also attested in Hittite, for drinking, libations, mixing and ladling, made from precious metal and decorated ('Nestor's cup', Hom. Il. 11,632ff.). As synonyms Homer uses ἄλεισον (*áleison*), ἀμφικύπελλον (*amphikýpellon*), κύπελλον (*kýpellon*); from which the *depas* has been understood to be a two-handled cup, similar to the cantharus (→ Pottery, shape and types of). Archaeological finds and interpretation of Linear-B tablets from Pylos and Knossos (where it appears as *di-pa*) seem to have brought some clarity to the question of its shape, a long-standing subject of controversy among scholars [1]. On that basis it is an amphoroid krater with two, three or four handles on its rim or without any handle at all. On the tablets the diameter of the vessel's opening varied widely, and thus the narrow opening shown on clay tablet Ta 641 from Pylos [4] makes any wine-mixing, as Homer described in the case of Nestor's cup, virtually impossible. The Homeric *depas amphikýpellon* (e.g. Il. 9,656; 13,219f; Od. 8,89) was probably a double cup linked by an eyelet [3].

1 G. BRUNS, Küchenwesen in myk. Zeit, ArchHom Q, 1970, 25–27, 42–44, 52 2 F. CANCIANI, Bildkunst II, ArchHom N, 1984, 40 3 G. DAUX, in: BCH 94, 1965, 738–740 fig. 12–14, 89 4 S. HILLER, Der Becher des Nestors, in: AW 7/1, 1976, 22–31. R.H.

Deportatio Banishment to an island or a desert oasis was a capital punishment in Roman law; in the Principate (at the latest from Trajan's time, soon after AD 100), it replaced the → *aqua et igni interdictio*, which had replaced the death penalty for upper-class citizens towards the end of the Republic. The *aqua et igni interdictio* and *deportatio* involved lifelong loss of citizenship rights and property. As the offender had not escaped penalty by voluntary flight into exile, banishment — generally to a quite specific location (Dig. 48,22,6,1) — became part of the verdict. As the literal meaning of *deportatio* implies, this usually meant that the person found guilty was forcibly transported to the place of banishment. Commutation of the sentence was possible with imperial clemency. In that event citizenship rights and the right to own property could be restored (→ *postliminium*). A milder form of *deportatio*, intentionally of more limited duration, was the → *relegatio*. The *deportatio* was imposed for the most varied range of offences: from 'political offences' such as *lèse majesté* (→ *maiestas*) and various forms of abuse of office (e.g. → *repetundae* and → *peculatus*) to murder, kidnapping or sexual crimes. Even adultery (→ *adulterium*) was sometimes punished by *deportatio*.

E. L. GRASMÜCK, Exilium, 1978. G.S.

Deportation

I. Ancient Orient and Egypt II. Classical Antiquity II. Christian

I. Ancient Orient and Egypt

Forcible deportations of combatants and civilians during wars were common practice (though on varying scales) in many periods of the history of the Ancient Orient and Egypt. Deportations had a dual purpose: they made possible the creation of an unfree and, therefore, easily exploited labour force, and they were a convenient means of lastingly weakening the military and economic potential of defeated tribes, cities and states.

In Mesopotamia deportations appear to have been a source of unfree labour as early as the late 4th millennium (symbol 'woman + foreign country ' = 'female slave', 'man + foreign country ' = 'male slave') [1. 244]. Deportations on a large scale were first performed by the kings of the territorial states of Akkad (2334–2154 BC) and Ur (2112–2004). The deported — almost all members of foreign ethnicities, including women and children separated from their husbands and fathers — were used as labour in the palace and temple sector — the men as mercenaries and (often blinded) as rural labourers, the women e.g. in the textile industry. The Sumerian terms LÚ+KÁR 'bound person', sag/arad 'slave' and érin/guruš '(semi-free) labourer' mark the progress in stages of the integration of deportees [2].

While there is limited evidence of deportation in the Old Bablylonian period (1st half of the 2nd millennium; e.g., Codex Ḫammurapi, § 32, 133 135), Middle Assyrian [3. 2[5]] and Hittite royal inscriptions [4] record tens of thousands of deportees, with Hittite sources distinguishing between captured warriors ([LÚ]ŠU.DAB/*appant-*) and civilians ([LÚ]NAM.RA/*arnuwala-*). An abundance of iconographic and textual sources provide information on deportation under the Neo-Assyrian empire. Especially in the 8th and 7th cents. entire peoples were deported from conquered territories and settled in the opposite corner of the Assyrian sphere (e.g., in 722/720 the Israelites were deported from → Samaria to Media) or employed in public works in the major Assyrian cities. To undermine the religious identity of opponents, divine images were also deported. The legal status of deportees (described as *šallatu* like the material booty) seems to have varied from case to case; for example, political hostages had a special status [3].

Deportations as a means of conducting war are also attested in the 1st millennium for → Urarṭu, → Elam [1. 246] and the Syro-Palestinian region [3. 48 n47, 49 n50]. While it was the rule that deported peoples integrated into their new surroundings albeit often not until the second or third generation, the Jews who were deported by Nebuchadnezzar [2] II into the Babylonian captivity in 597 and 587 appear to have found their specific identity there [5. 109–114] (→ Juda and Israel; → Judaism). The Achaemenids permitted the Jews to return to their homeland (Ezra 1), but otherwise continued the Ancient Oriental practice of deportation and resettled, for example, Greeks [6].

Likewise, the Egyptians deported prisoners of war (*sqr-ʿnḫ*, see [7. 786]). In the Old and Middle Kingdoms, especially Nubians [8] were brought to Egypt; in the New Kingdom predominantly Asians and members of the Sea Peoples (→ Sea peoples, migrations of) were taken and — some branded — used as workers and soldiers. Syrian girls were deported because of their erotic charm [9]. In Egypt the practice of deporting criminals to marginal areas as forced labour was widespread [10. 69]; banishment of this type is also attested in Israel and for the Hittites but only rarely in Mesopotamia [3. 41–43].

→ Diaspora; → Prisoners of war; → Slavery

1 H. Klengel, s. v. Krieg, Kriegsgefangene, RLA 6, 243–246 2 I. J. Gelb, Prisoners of War in Early Mesopotamia, in: JNES 32, 1973, 70–98 3 B. Oded, Mass Deportations and Deportees in the Neo-Assyrian Empire, 1979 4 S. Alp, Die soziale Klasse der NAM.RA-Leute und ihre hethit. Bezeichnung, in: Jb. für kleinasiatische Forsch. 1, 1950/51, 113–135 5 W. Röllig, Deportation und Integration, in: CollRau 4, 1996, 100–114
6 E. Olshausen, Griechenland im Orient, in: Stuttgarter Beitr. zur Histor. Migrationsforsch. 2, 1995, 24–40
7 W. Helck, s. v. Kriegsgefangene, LÄ 3, 786–788
8 R. Gundlach, Die Zwangsumsiedlung auswärtiger Bevölkerung als Mittel äg. Politik bis zum Ende des MR, 1994 9 W. Helck, Die Beziehungen Vorderasiens zu Äg. im 3. und 2. Jt. v. Chr., 1962, 359–390
10 W. Boochs, s. v. Strafen, LÄ 6, 68–72. E. FRA.

II. Classical Antiquity

Deportation of individuals and larger population groups was also common in the Graeco-Roman world. Usually, it was related to military confrontations, with the victims being soldiers as well as civilians (cf. → War, consequences of). In contrast to expulsion — such as the → *xenēlasía* (Plut. Lycurgus 27; Thuc. 1,144) practiced in Sparta and the periodical expulsions of foreigners from Rome, e.g., the Jews (Val. Max. 1,3,3; cf. → Tolerance) — a constituent element of deportation (apart from forced removal from the home or adopted home) is the assignment of a defined new home. According to this criterion, the notorious Athenian action against the inhabitants of → Aegina (431 BC) was not a deporta- tion because it was not the Athenians but the Spartans who assigned them a new location (Thyrea; cf. → Cynu- ria [2]) (Thuc. 2,27). Deportation differs from → exile (→ *exilium*) in being instigated not by one's own country's political powers but by foreign powers and usually without a legal basis.

In the Classical period the typical deportation was perpetrated with the dual motivation of punishment while gaining new settlements. The case of Samos [3] is exemplary: in 365 BC the Athenian Timotheus [4] retaliated against the disloyalty of its inhabitants by deporting them to Iasos [4] and settling 2,000 Athenian → *klēroúchoi* on the island (Nep. Timotheus 1,1; Isocr. Or. 15,111; Diod. Sic. 18,8,7). Deportation was also a customary political method of Hellenistic rulers. (The depiction in Pol. 23,10,4–6 of the deportation of coastal inhabitants by Philip [7] V and their replacement by Thracians considered loyal is particularly relevant) In 223 BC Antigonus [3] Doson was particularly harsh against the city of → Mantinea (III. B.) whose population was for most part deported to Macedonia (Plut. Aratus 45,4).

The Romans repeatedly resorted to deportation during their expansion; in 241 BC the insurgent population of the town of Falerii [1] (Val. Max. 6,5,1; Eutr. 2,18) met this fate. In 167 BC, 1,000 members of the Achaean elite (among them Polybius [2]) were deported to Italy (Pol. 30,13,6 f.; Paus. 7,10,7–12). 17 years later, 300 of them were able to return to Greece. The Romans, too, became victims of deportation, e.g., when Roman legionaries were deported by the Parthians after the battle of Carrhae (53 BC; → Ḥarran) to the → Margiana region (Plin. HN 6,47). Agrippa [1] settled the Germanic → Ubii in 38 (or 19) BC from the east to the west bank of the Rhine (App. B Civ. 5,386; Str. 4,3,4).

Particularly in the Roman Imperial period deportees were responsible for certain public duties. Under Tiberius [1], numerous adherents of the Isis cult and the Jewish faith were deported to Sardinia to combat banditry there (Tac. Ann. 2,85,4). Forced labour was used in AD 67 during Nero's [1] attempt to cut through the → Isthmus of Corinth (Cass. Dio 63,16,2), among them 6,000 Jewish captives from the First → Jewish War (AD 66–74; Jos. BI 3,10; → Prisoners of war).

The deportation of individuals as an instrument in criminal law (*poena legis*) had existed in Rome since the early Imperial period in the form of the → *relegatio* and the → *deportatio*.

→ Deportatio; → Exilium; → War, consequences of; → Prisoners of war; → Mobility (B.); → Relegatio; → Piracy; → Slave trade; → Slavery; → Tolerance; → Exile

P. Ducrey, Le traitement des prisonniers de guerre dans la Grèce antique, 1968; J. Seibert, Die polit. Flüchtlinge und Verbannten in der griech. Gesch., 2 vols., 1979; H. Sonnabend, Deportation im ant. Rom, in: A. Gestrich et al. (ed.), Ausweisung und Deportation (Stuttgarter Beitr. zur Histor. Migrationsforsch. 2), 1995, 13–22; H. Volkmann, G. Horsmann, Die Massenversklavungen der Einwohner eroberter Städte in der hell.-röm. Zeit, [2]1990.

H. SO.

Depositio see → Feriale

Depositum The Roman safekeeping agreement materialized as a real contract when the depositor entrusted an object to the custodian (bailee) for cost-free safekeeping. Paid safekeeping comes under → *locatio conductio*.

The bailee became neither the owner nor possessor of the object but merely its *detentor* (→ *posessio*): he was not permitted to use the object, use of the object qualified as → *furtum*. At the depositor's request the custodian was expected to return the object intact.

In cases of intentional unauthorized appropriation, even the XII Tables provided for a penalty of double value (*duplum*) against the custodian (Paulus coll. 10,7,11). Even later the *duplum* could be sought if the deposit took place in an emergency such as an *incendium* (fire) or *naufragium* (shipwreck) (Dig. 16,3,1,1, non-Roman *depositum miserabile*). In addition there was in the early Republic a praetorian *actio in factum concepta* (analogous complaint) of the depositor against the bailee; its provisions compensated for bad faith (→ *dolus*), as well as (somewhat later) an *actio* according to *ius civile*, with which the obligations were established in trust and confidence (*bona fides*) (Gai. Inst. 4,47).

In general the bailee is liable only for *dolus*; many classicists equate gross negligence (*culpa lata*) and a breach of the *diligentia quam in suis rebus* (care as with one's own affairs) with *dolus* (cf. Nerva und Celsus in Dig. 16,3,32). The limited liability of the bailee is explained in a practical sense by the fact that he gains no advantage or financial reward for his efforts (cf. Coll. 10,2,1). Within the framework of *depositum* he can seek, in the *actio depositi contraria*, compensation from the depositor for expenses and for damages (Coll. 10,2,5).

A later so-called *depositum irregulare* arises if money is deposited on the understanding that it may be used by the guarantor and simply repaid in the same amount. Here the guarantor has possession of the money and as such bears the risk (as in a loan agreement, → *mutuum*) of accidental mishap (cf. Coll. 10,7,9). With the *depositum irregulare* interest can also be agreed upon and pursued with the *actio depositi* (Dig. 16,3,24).

With the *depositum sequestre* an object is entrusted by several people to the *sequester* on the understanding that he is to hold it in safekeeping and return it under specified conditions (Paul. Dig. 16,3,6). The most frequent case in point is safekeeping during a dispute (cf. Dig. 50,16,110), in which the *sequester* has to hand over the object to the person who eventually prevails in the dispute. Unlike the usual bailee the *sequester* enjoys the protection of ownership.

→ Culpa; → Custodia

Kaser, RPR I, 534–536, II, 371–373; H. Honsell, Th. Mayer-Maly, W. Selb, Röm. Recht, [4]1987, 301– 04; R. Zimmermann, The Law of Obligations, 1990, 205–220.

F.ME.

Derbe (Δέρβη; *Dérbē*). City in the south of Lycaonia, now Devri Şehri, north-east of → Laranda. Known first as the residence of Antipater of D. (Cic. Fam. 13,73; Str. 12,1,4; 6,3). The Apostle Paul visited the city on his first and second missionary journeys (Acts 14,6; 16,1). Assigned by Ptolemy to the 'Cappadocian' *stratēgía Antiochiánē* (Ptol. 5,6,16); from the middle of the 2nd cent. AD member of the *koinòn Lykaonías* which was limited to south Lycaonia [1. 38–40, 67]. A Lycaonian diocese from no later than 381 (suffragan of Iconium). In the 8th/9th cent. the city was abandoned, probably as a result of Arab incursions [2. 53,88,157]. The existence of a second D. in Isauria (Steph. Byz. s.v. D.) is unlikely.

1 H.v. Aulock, Mz. und Städte Lykaoniens, 1976 2 Belke. K.BE.

Dercylidas (Δερκυλίδας; *Derkylídas*). Spartan; regarded as a talented and cunning military commander. He won Abydus and Lampsacus in 411 BC without a battle (Thuc. 8,61f.), was harmost in Abydus in 407/6 (Xen. Hell. 3,1,9) and in 399 in Sparta's war against the Persian satrap Tissaphernes in Asia Minor he relieved the unpopular Thibron, who was unable to keep discipline in the army, including the former mercenaries (including Xenophon) of Cyrus the Younger (Xen. Hell. 3,1,8–10). In 399 in a 'lightning campaign' D. snatched the Troad from the satrap Pharnabazus, fought the Thracians in Bithynia during a truce, wintered there and in 398 secured the Chersonese against Thracian invasion (Xen. Hell. 3,1,16–2,11; Isoc. Or. 4,144; Diod. Sic. 14,38,2–7) and besieged Atarneus, which surrendered in the spring of 397 after an eight-month siege. When, on instruction from the ephors, he advanced on Caria to compel Tissaphernes to sue for peace, the latter and Pharnabazus united their forces and forced D. to withdraw. In view of the Persian superiority in numbers, D. accepted the truce offered at Magnesia (Maeander) in the early summer of 397, the terms of which provided for the withdrawal of the Spartans and the autonomy of the Greek cities in Asia Minor (Xen. Hell. 3,2,12–20; Diod. Sic. 14,39,5f.; StV 2, 219) — a delusive treaty because the Persian Great King continued to impose claims on those cities. As the preparations of the Persian fleet gave rise to fears of an invasion of Greece [1. 29], D. was relieved by Agesilaus II in 396. After the battle of Cnidus in 394 D. defended Abydus, where he remained harmost until 389 (Xen. Hell. 4,8,32). D. demonstrated political and strategic vision but had to conduct war in Asia Minor with inadequate means.

1 Ch.D. Hamilton, Agesilaus and the Failure of Spartan Hegemony, 1991. K.-W.WEL.

Dercylides (Δερκυλίδης; *Derkylídēs*) Philosopher from the 1st cent. BC [3. 180] or AD [4. 64]. Although nowhere described as a Platonist, he seems to have studied Plato's philosophy intensively, especially the mathematical and astronomical sections of his dialogues. Significant was his work of at least eleven volumes 'On Plato's philosophy', which was still being quoted by Porphyrius [1. 82ff., 296; 3. 60, 236]. The treatise 'On the spindle and the whorl, treated in Plato's *Politeia*', is perhaps part of that work [3. 44, 202f., 236]. Proclus transmits two commentaries on Pl. Resp. 545d ff. (In rep. 2,24,6ff.; 25,15ff. Kroll [1. 110ff., 342]) and reports elsewhere that D. had identified the unknown fourth participant in Plato's *Timaeus* as Plato himself (In Tim. 1,20,9ff. Diehl [3. 212]). According to Albinus [2. 98], D. — like Thrasyllus — divided Plato's dialogues into tetralogies.

1 Dörrie/Baltes I, 1987 2 Dörrie/Baltes II, 1990 3 Dörrie/Baltes III, 1993 4 J. Mansfeld, Prolegomena, 1994.

J. Glucker, Antiochus and the Late Academy, 1978,123; H. Tarrant, Thrasyllan Platonism, 1993, 11–13; 72–84. M.BA. and M.-L.L.

Dercylus (Δερκύλος; *Derkýlos*). Son of Autocles of Hagnous, Athenian emissary to → Philippus II for the Peace of Philocrates in 346 BC (Aeschin. Leg. 47; 140; Dem. Or. 19,60,125. 175). D. was guarantor for Athenian ships in 341/40 (IG II² 1623, 179–180) and was *strategos* in 319/8 (Plut. Phocion 32,5; Nep. Phocion 2,4; IG II² 1187: honour conferred by the *demos* of the Eleusinians). (PA and APF 3249).
→ Athens J.E.

Derdas (Δέρδας; *Dérdas*). A common name in the royal family of Elimea.
[1] Son of → Arrhidaeus [1] and a princess of → Elimea, who in alliance with Philippus, son of → Alexander [2], and with Athenian support, attacked Athens' confederate → Perdiccas (Thuc. 1,57). In a later Athenian treaty with Perdiccas (IG I³ no. 89), he, along with other Macedonian princes, swore the oath (l. 69).

E. Badian, From Plataea to Potidaea, 1993, 172–4; S. Hornblower, Greek Historiography, 1994, 127–30; HM 2, 18, 122f. E.B.

[2] A D., probably the grandson of D. [1], murdered Amyntas 'the Short' of Macedonia (cf. → Amyntas [2]) (Aristot. Pol. 5,1311b3). He later supported Sparta in the war against Olynthus (Xen. Hell. 5,2).
[3] Probably the son of D. [2], brother-in-law of → Philippus II and commander in his Olynthian war (349 BC). In Philippus' absence D. was defeated by → Charidemus and taken prisoner (Theopomp. FGrH 115 F 143). E.B.

Derieis (Δεριεῖς; *Derieîs*). Tribe and district in the east of Acarnania, destination of the Peloponnesian ceremonial emissaries (IG IV² 96, l. 61ff.; SEG 36,331, l. 41ff.). In 314 BC *synoikismós* in → Agrinium (Diod. Sic. 19,67,4). Capital not located.

Pritchett, vol. 8, 81–85. D.S.

Derivation see → Word formation

Dermatikon see → Sacrifices

Derris (Δέρρις; *Dérris*). Cape at the southern end of Sithonia opposite Cape Canastraeum on Pallene.

M. Zahrnt, Olynth und die Chalkidier, 1971, 180. M.Z.

Dertona *Oppidum* of the Ligurian Dectunini or Irienses, now Tortona. Founded as a *colonia* between 211 and 118 BC, possibly re-established before 27 BC, *tribus Pomptina* (Vell. Pat. 1,15,5), *regio IX*, intersection of the *via Fulvia* (from 159 BC), the *via Postumia* (from 148 BC and the *via Aemilia Scauri* (from 109 BC; Str. 5,1,11; Ptol. 3,1,35; Plin. HN 3,49; Tab. Peut. 3,5). In the late Imperial period centre of the *annona* (Cassiod. Var. 10,27,2), bishopric (Agatho Papa, Ep. 3, 1239) and probably *praesidium* of the military (Not. Dign. Occ. 42). Maiorianus was defeated by Ricimer at D. in AD 461. Archaeological Remains: necropolis, city walls.

Fontes Ligurum et Liguriae antiquae, 1976, s.v. D.; G. BINAZZI (ed.), Inscriptiones Christiana Italiae 7, 1990, 3–118; P. FRACCARO, Opuscula 3, 1957, 124–150.

G.ME.

Dertosa In the 6th cent. BC the rich trading city of Tyrichae lay on the mouth of the Ebro (Avien. Ora maritima 498–503). A 'very rich' city is again mentioned there for 215 BC: *Hibera* (Liv. 23,28,10). It is doubtless identical with the later *Hibera Iulia Ilercavonia* (for the tribe Ilercavones see [4. 1092]) D. (according to [1. 1269], Iberian, according to [2. 63; 3. 4, 233f.], Ligurian). According to Livy, Hibera lay on the southern bank and this is consistent with the favourable strategic position and the extant remains [3. 3, 79]. Strangely enough, it is termed a *colonia* on inscriptions (CIL II Suppl. p. 1144) and on Augustan coins but a *municipium* on Tiberian coins [5]. Thus, two locations must have been quite close to each other, possibly on different banks, as suggested by the fact that today's Tortosa is situated on the northern bank (on this problem [6]; cf. also Mela 2,90; Plin. HN 3,23; Str. 3,4,6.9, according to which a ford and not a bridge provided a crossing over the Ebro here; Geogr. Rav. 4,42; 5,3).

In AD 506, D. was besieged by Alaric II (Chron. Caesaraug., in: Chronica minora 2,222 MOMMSEN). In the 6th and 7th cents D. is often mentioned as a diocese: [3. 9, 446]. King Reccared I (586–601) had coins minted here: [9]. For the later history of the locations see [8].

1 HOLDER, I 2 A. SCHULTEN, Numantia 1, 1914 3 Id., Fontes Hispaniae Antiquae, 1952ff. 4 Id., s.v. Ilurcavones, RE 9, 1092f. 5 A. VIVES, La Moneda Hispánica 2, 1924, 1, LXXXIX 4,17 6 E. HÜLSEN, s.v. D., RE 5, 246f. 7 A. HEISS, Monnaies des rois wisigoths d'Espagne, 1872, 90, Pl. 2 8 Enciclopedia Universal Ilustrada 62, 1545, s.v. Tortosa.

TOVAR, 3, 1989, 433f.

P.B.

Descriptio see → Ekphrasis

Desert (ἡ ἔρημος/*érēmos*, ἡ ἐρημία/*erēmía*, τὰ ἔρημα/*érēma*; Lat. *deserta*, *regio deserta*). In geographical terms the arid desert zones were part of the marginal areas of the Ancient World (North Africa, the Middle East with Syria, Palestine, Arabia). Politically and to a greater extent economically they, had close relationships to the Graeco-Roman cultural sphere. A large part of the east-west trade devolved over long-distance routes across the Arabian deserts. Desert towns such as Ḥatra [1], Palmyra and Petra [1] achieved considerable, politically significant prosperity as a result. In North Africa the Trans-Sahara trade was significant (Plin. HN 5,34; 5,38). The → oases of Egypt supplied → salt, → grain and → wine, but like the Siva oasis, which became famous as a result of Alexander [4] the Great's visit, they also had cultic functions (→ Ammoneum). In Late Antiquity the hermit Anthony [5] made the desert the starting point of Christian → asceticism and → monasticism.

→ Camel; → Caravan trade; → Oasis; → Steppe; → Incense route

H. J. W. DRIJVERS, Hatra, Palmyra und Edessa. Die Städte der syr.-mesopot. W. in polit., kulturgesch. und rel.-gesch. Bed., in: ANRW II 8, 1977, 799–906; L. HEMPEL, Die Mittelmeerländer — Grenzen in einem geoökologischen Spannungsfeld zw. Waldland und W., in: E. OLSHAUSEN, H. SONNABEND (ed.), Stuttgarter Koll. zur Histor. Geogr. des Alt. 4, 1990 (Geographica Historica 7), 1994, 309–333.

H. SO.

Deserti agri Reclamation of wasteland was a concern of imperial lawmaking as early as the height of the Imperial period. On the imperial estates in North Africa leaseholders who had cultivated fallow land enjoyed particularly favourable lease conditions under the *lex Manciana* (CIL VIII 25943). Jurists from the Classical period commented on a case in which agricultural land that had been neglected by its owner was cultivated by a third party (Gaius, Inst. 2, 51). Pertinax is supposed to have tried to allocate uncultivated land in AD 193 with a tax exemption for 10 years (Herodian. 2, 4,6).

Emperors of late antiquity intensified their efforts to cultivate fallow land. Aurelianus made the *curiae* liable for abandoned land and at the same time granted a three-year tax exemption. Constantine repeated this; if the *curiales* of a community had not been able to meet the taxes due on fallow land, the burden had to be shared among all property owners in the community (Cod. Iust. 11,59,1). Even from the beginning of the 4th cent. AD abandoned *ager publicus* was granted with full title to a developer (cf. Cod. Iust. 11, 63, 1, AD 319). Anyone who cultivated privately owned wasteland was in any case assured of the produce from it (Cod. Theod. 7,20,11). Theodosius decided that the previous owner still had two years in which he could reclaim the abandoned property but thereafter he would forfeit it (Cod. Theod. 5,11,12). In 386 a takeover of unowned wasteland enjoyed immunity for two years (Cod. Iust. 11,59,7,1). *Deserti agri* are attested in widespread areas of the empire: *inter alia* in Gaul, Italy, Syria, North Africa.

Earlier research espoused the view that the *deserti agri* had increased in surface area in late antiquity; the causes seen responsible for this were a putative decline in agriculture, a reduction in population and not least an excessive tax burden that had led to a rural exodus (cf. e.g. Lib. Or. 2, 32; Theod. Epist. Sirmond. 42). Recently, a more cautious appraisal of the problem is preferred [2; 3]: around AD 400 no more than *c.* 10% of agricultural land lay fallow (Cod. Theod. 11,28,2). In AD 422 in *Africa Proconsularis* and *Byzacena* some 5,700 or 7,615 *centuriae* of the land were not cultivated (compared to 9,002 or 7,460 *centuriae* of cultivated land; Cod. Theod. 11,28,13); those values however correspond to the natural realities of North Africa: even at present only *c.* $^5/_9$ of the land surface there are agriculturally productive [2]. Legislation in late antiquity on the *deserti agri* applied principally to marginal lands which were cultivated or left fallow according to the state of the economy and the level of taxation.

1 Jones, LRE 812–823 2 C. Lepelley, Déclin ou stabilité de l'agriculture africaine au Bas-Empire?, in: AntAfr 1, 1967, 133–144 3 C.R. Whittaker, Agri deserti, in: M.I. Finley (ed.), Studies in Roman Property, 1976, 137–165; 193–200. J.K.

Desertion see → Deilias graphe; → Desertor

Desertor The Roman army regarded as a *desertor* anyone who did not appear at roll-call (Liv. 3,69,7) or who during a battle was beyond the range of the trumpet or who left his unit in time of peace without permission, without *commeatus* (Suet. Oth. 11,1; SHA Sept. Sev. 51,5; Dig. 49,16,14) ('distanced himself from the *signa*'). The punishments were merciless: depending on the case a person was at risk of slavery (Frontin. 4,1,20), mutilation (SHA Avid. Cass. 4, 5) or death (the condemned person was beaten with canes and then thrown down from the *Tarpeium saxum* or crucified). The *decimatio* was a punishment for the desertion of a whole unit. During the Principate, desertion became rarer which was the result of the strictness of individual *principes*: in peace-times a prison sentence was the most common form of punishment (Tac. Ann. 1,21,3), although capital punishment was not abolished (Suet. Aug. 24; Jos. Bell. Iud. 3,103). Despite the often expressed view that penalties were increased in late antiquity, this is uncertain. Deserters were still at risk of mutilation (Amm. Marc. 29,5,22; 29,5,31; 29,5,49) and capital punishment (Amm. Marc. 21,12,20; 29,5,22) but there was also the option of deporting them or transferring them to another unit. Moreover the law recommended leniency for recruits (Dig. 49,16,3,9). On the other hand, the law also regarded as *desertores* those who had left their superiors in the lurch (Dig. 49,16,3,9) and sold their weapons (Dig. 49,16,3,17). The laws of late antiquity attempted above all to stop landowners from taking in *desertores* on their estates and hiding them there (Cod. Theod. 7,18).
→ Commeatus; → Decimatio; → Deilias graphe

1 O. Fiebiger, RE 5, 249–250. Y.L.B.

Design see → Building trade

Desire (ἐπιθυμία; *epithymía*).
A. Definition B. Plato and Aristotle
C. The Stoa and Epicureanism

A. Definition

In Homer ἔρος (*éros*) is used as a very general expression for desire; later the word also had, above and beyond its sexual core meaning, a usage that was so wide that it was often merely a synonym for ἐπιθυμία (*epithymía*) (B.) [1]. Prodicus differentiated between desire in general and ἔρως (*érōs*) by means of a difference in intensity as he defined *érōs* as double desire (84 B 7 DK; similar to Xen. Mem. 3,9,7); from the point of view of the object, the intention was that ἔρως be distinguished from desire in general, separating it as desire for sexual intercourse (Pl. Symp. 192e–193a; Aristot. Top. 146a9). Nevertheless the boundaries of language usage remained fluid so that Aristotle was still to refer to the cosmological Eros of Hesiod as ἔρωτα ἢ ἐπιθυμίαν (Mete. 1,984b24).

B. Plato and Aristotle

In his *Politeia*, Plato formulates a large-scale theory of desire. Initially the *epithymíai* are the stirrings of the lowest part of the soul (ἐπιθυμητικόν, *epithymētikón*) with which the soul feels hunger and thirst, desires sexually (ἐρᾷ) and the like (Resp. 439d). He does not regard a general definition of this part of the soul to be possible because of its lack of uniformity and its diversity (Resp. 580d-e). But he does mention a criterion that clearly separates that which belongs to the *epithymētikón* from the part of the soul that gives 'courage and spirit' (θυμοειδές, *thymoeidés*): whilst a desire as such is independent of the values held by the person with the desire and can conflict with them, a phenomenon like anger cannot possibly be directed against the values held by the angry person (Resp. 440a-d).

But desire is not limited to the *epithymētikón*. The *thymoeidés* and the rational part of the soul (λογιστικόν, *logistikón*) have their own desire, that which strives for honour and insight so that desire like the soul itself is tripartite (Resp. 580d-e). This involves the concept of 'channelling' of the whole of one's desire from one part of the soul to the other (Resp. 485d) so that desire ultimately appears as a single psychic energy distributed among the three parts of the soul in a variable manner. In his description of the effectiveness of this energy in the *logistikón* or for the philosopher, Plato uses erotic terminology as well as explicitly erotic imagery (especially Resp. 490b) so that *érōs* becomes part of the model not just in the lowest but also in the highest part of the soul. In this way desire in the *Politeia* comes to resemble *érōs* in the Diotima speech of the *Symposium*, in which the tendency to understand sexual desire alone as *érōs* in the actual sense is also rejected (Symp. 205a-d) [2; 3].

Aristotle conceptually limits desires to the 'primitive' strivings, just as Plato had classified them as belonging to the *epithymētikón*. His general term for the conative aspect of the soul is striving (ὄρεξις, *órexis*), and desire as the striving for that which is full of pleasure (ἡδύ, *hēdý*) constitutes together with *thymós* (*thymós*) the irrational part of the ὀρεκτικόν, *orektikón* (An. 414b 2–6; 432b 3–6). In theology however it remained linked with Plato's view and language, for the Prime Mover moves ὡς ἐρώμενον (Mete. 12,1072b 3). In the case of desire itself, Plato's inheritance can be seen particularly from the fact that it is different from θυμός because from the point of view of values it is deeper and has similar demarcations (Eth. Nic. 1149a 24–b 3); and although it is different from reason it is capable of 'obeying' reason (κατήκοον, *katēkoon*, Eth. Nic. 1102b 31) so that it is not just subject to it but can also be positively in harmony with it (συμφωνεῖν, Eth. Nic. 1119b 15; συμφωνία, Resp. 442c 10) — because this is the nature of prudence.

C. The Stoa and Epicureanism

→ Stoa and → Epicurus then intellectualized desire in a way that was foreign to the two classical authors in connection with their concept of philosophy as 'psychotherapy'. The Stoa dealt with desire in the theory of the → affects (πάθη, *páthē*). An affect is an excessive impulse (πλεονάζουσα ὁρμή) which as such goes against 'proper and natural reason' (SVF III 378; 389). Of the four types of affect (desire, fear, pain, pleasure), desire is the one that strives for that which appears to be good (τὸ φαινόμενον ἀγαθόν) (SVF III 378; 386). From this it becomes evident that the *thymós* phenomena belong to desire (SVF III 394–397). On the other hand, desire is already limited by definition to that desire which the classical authors viewed as irrational. The most significant innovation is that for the (older) Stoa, explicitly in any case for → Chrysippus, the affect and hence desire does not originate from a capacity of the soul that is foreign to reason, but, like error, is irrational only in the normative sense because it goes against proper reason: the affects are none other than types of opinions (δόξαι, *dóxai*) or judgements (κρίσεις, *kríseis*) (SVF III 378, 456, 459), which should explain the great extent to which the affects — and hence also the goal of ἀπάθεια, *apátheia* — *in nostra sint potestate* (Cic. Tusc. 4,14).

Epicurus viewed desire in terms of goal of the realization of happiness through passion. Pleasure has a 'size limit' that lies in freedom from physical and mental displeasure (pain, fear) (Ad Menoeceum 128,131; RS 3,18). Epicurus thus divides desire into natural and 'empty' (κεναὶ ἐπιθυμίαι) forms, and the natural forms further into merely natural and necessary ones that are again necessary for happiness, for the health of the body or for life itself (Epic. ad Menoeceum 127; cf. RS 29; Cic. Fin. 2,26. Anticipations: Pl. Resp. 558d–559c; Aristot. Eth. Nic. 1118b 8–15). Necessary desires that bring with them pain if unfulfilled are desires for food, drink and clothing (Us. 456; SV 33; Schol. re RS 29; desire that is particularly necessary for happiness is the desire for freedom from psychological displeasure [4]). Merely natural is desire that does not lead to pain when unfulfilled (RS 26,30), and empty desires are ultimately those that are only natural arising through 'empty opinions' (παρὰ κενὴν δόξαν γίνονται) and demonstrate intensive urges (σπουδὴ σύντονος) (RS 30; in the extant material the classification of individual desires as belonging to either of these two classes is ambiguous: cf. Us. 456 with Schol. re RS 29). The essential contrast is the one between necessary and empty desire. The latter has a maximum limit with regard to its fulfilment because of the limits to pleasure and is easily satisfied (Ad Menoeceum 130; RS 15,18,21; Us. 469). Empty desire on the other hand is unlimited (ἀόριστος καὶ κενὴ ἐπιθυμία, Us. 485), hence hard to satisfy and a source of displeasure (ad Menandrum 130; RS 15). The remedy for empty desire is the elimination of its cause, the kenodoxy, through right thinking (Ad Menoeceum 132–133; Us. 221,457; cf. Cic. Fin. 1,42–46).

1 K.J. Dover, Greek Homosexuality, 1979, 42–48
2 F.M. Cornford, The Unwritten Philosophy and Other Essays, 1950, 68–80
3 G. Santas, Plato and Freud, 1988, 26–34, 75–79
4 R. Müller, Die Epikureische Ethik, 1991, 82.

J. Annas, The Morality of Happiness, 1993; M.C. Nussbaum, The Therapy of Desire, 1994.

W.SA.

Desmoterion (δεσμωτήριον; *desmōtērion*). In Athens at the market (on location [1]) there was a prison (Dem. Or. 24,208f.) that owed its name to the fetters, δεσμά (*desmá*) that were put on the prisoners usually in the form of chains and shackles. The places of detention were not safe from breakouts in other cities either. The supervisory authority, in Athens the Eleven, decided the nature of custody (in chains, permission for visits). Prisoners were always held with others and imprisonment was not imposed as punishment but to secure the accused, condemned and state debtors. The *desmoterion* was encountered in numerous Greek states and in the Hellenistic period also in Egypt (cf. P.Tebt. 567: δεσμευτήριον, *desmeutērion*). Other terms for it are οἴκημα (*oíkēma*, cell or cage), ἀναγκαῖον (*anankaíon*, house of forced detention), κέραμος (*kéramos*, pot) and — only in Plato's state utopia — σωφρονιστήριον (*sophronistērion*, 'house of reflection'). In the field of prisons, Plato was an innovator insofar as he (Leg. 908a ff.) classified prisons using three special grades that also differed externally according to their position and description: the detention prison, the penitentiary and the reformatory [2]. Plato suggested imprisonment as physical punishment (in the same way that Dem. Or. 24,146 already had) and in Hellenistic Egypt it was also gradually put into practise [3. 74]. In individual cases prisoners in Athens were chained (in stocks or neck irons) to increase their punishment (Dem. Or. 24,103 and 114), in other cases this occurred as a substitute punishment for state and private debtors unable to pay their debts [4. 243f.]. In most cases imprisonment served to secure the prisoner so that the state debtor could not escape his obligation (Aristot. Ath. Pol. 63,6) or the criminal could not escape punishment [5. 107]. Capital punishment was also carried out in prison (Dem. Or. 25,52). Before the trial it was, however, strictly forbidden to arrest a citizen — even if he was accused of a serious crime — if he could provide three bailsmen. The exceptions, according to the council oath (Dem. Or. 24,144), were state tenants unable to pay and those accused of high treason. In Ptolemaic Egypt the police authorities often ordered, against a royal decree to protect personal freedom (PTebt. 5,255–264), that a person be arrested for civil offences (ἴδια ἀδικήματα) [3. 58f.].

→ Capital punishment

1 A. L. Boegehold, The Lawcourts at Athens. Site, Buildings, Equipment (Ath. Agora, vol. 28), 1995, 85 u. 95f. 2 T.J. Saunders, Plato's Penal Code, 1991, 309ff. 3 R. Taubenschlag, Das Strafrecht im Rechte der Papyri, 1916 4 A. R. W. Harrison, The Law of Athens II, 1971 5 U. E. Paoli, Zum att. Strafrecht und Strafprozeßrecht, in: ZRG 76, 1959, 107f. G.T.

De Sodoma (167 hexameters, attributed to → Tertullianus or → Cyprianus [2] in the MSS) belongs to a group of pseudonymous biblical poems normally dated to the 5th cent. The poem comes from the same pen as → *De Iona*, the content of which it extends; it tells the story of Lot and Sodom's destruction following Gen. 19,1–29. The poet uses mythological and geographical motifs (particularly a comparison with the Phaeton myth and curiosities about the Dead Sea).

→ Biblical poetry; → De Iona

Edition: R. Peiper, CSEL 23, 212–220.
Bibliography: R. Hexter, The Metamorphosis of Sodom, in: Traditio 44, 1988, 1–35. M.RO.

Despeñaperros Ravine in the Sierra Morena, linking New Castilia (Oretania) with Andalusia (Baetica). On the ancient road above the gorge in the Collado de los Jardines there is a grotto sanctuary above which is a fortified Iberian settlement. Stratigraphically the shrine goes back to the 4th cent. BC, and the earliest types of statuettes even to the 6th cent. BC. A total of 3,000 bronze figurines were found in front of it, *c.* a quarter of all Iberian statuettes (among these anatomical *ex votos*).

G. Nicolini, Les bronzes figurés des sanctuaires ibériques, 1964, 37–43.; S. Ramallo Asensio, La monumentalización de los santuarios ibéricos en época tardo-republicana, in: Ostraka 2, 1993, 117–144.; L. Prados Torreira, Los santuarios ibéricos, in: Trabajos de Prehistoria 51, 1994, 127–140. M.BL.

Despoina see → Artemis; → Demeter; → Persephone

Despoteia (Δεσποτεία; *Despoteía*). In Greek 'rule' (from δεσπότης, *despótēs*, lord) did not initially have a specific legal meaning. The expression referred to the relationship in which the lord ruled over his slaves based on tradition (Aristot. Pol. 1253b) or in the political sense to despotism (Pl. Leg. 698a). *Despoteia* first appeared in Ptolemaic papyrus documents as the power of disposal possessed by the owner (BGU 1187,32, 1st cent. BC), together with the term *kyrieía* already used in the Greek city states. It was only in Roman Egypt that *despoteia* became a permanent component of the powers of the owner enumerated in the documents. The expression entered into the Greek legal literature of the Roman east in late antiquity as a translation of *dominium* or *proprietas* (ownership in the technical sense) (Nov. Iust. 2,2 pr.). The political meaning of *despoteia* underwent a positive change and came to describe the rule of the emperor.

→ Dominium

A. Kränzlein, Eigentum und Besitz im griech. Recht, 1963. G.T.

Despotes (δεσπότης; *despótēs*, Classical: 'lord, master'). Byzantine term initially for God, Christ, the emperor and high clerics and nobles, *despotes* was from the 12th cent. onwards the highest title bestowed by the emperor in the Byzantine ranking system. In the late Byzantine period *despótai* — the sons-in-law, afterwards also the brothers and younger sons of the emperors — who did not have a right to the imperial title. Often they administered semi-autonomous parts of the empire (e.g. the Peloponnese or Morea); their insignia, clothing and self-description in the documents were close to those of the emperor. In the Greek vernacular, the word has been used as a salutation for bishops since late antiquity.

A. Failler, Les insignes et la signature du despote, in: REByz 40, 1982, 171; L. Ferjančić, s.v. D., LMA 3, 1986, 733f.; R. Guilland, Le despote, in: REByz 17, 1959, 52–89; G. Ostrogorsky, Urum — Despotes. Die Anfänge der Despotenwürde in Byzanz, in: ByzZ 44, 1951, 448–460. G.MA.

Destinatio (from reconstr. *de-stanare*, 'determine') generally means the determination of a purpose or a decision, legally also a legally-binding unilateral declaration of will (Cod. Iust. 6,30,6; Dig. 50,17,76). In political life *destinatio* means the delegation of a subordinate or the installation in an office of a person envisaged for the task by a person authorized to do so. The imperial recommendation of a → *candidatus* to the Senate was also called *destinatio* as was the direct appointment of an office bearer by the emperor (Dig. 4,4,18,4; Cod. Iust. 11,74,2; 12,12,2). In the imperial period the occasional (and in late antiquity the more frequent) appointment of a co-emperor or the entrusting of a person viewed as a successor with an important office by the emperor was described as *destinatio* (CIL VI 932). For this and for the appointment to a normal office, *designatio* (in the case of appointment at a future point in time: Tac. Hist. 1,12,21; 26; 2,1) or → *creatio* was also used.

→ Magistratus

CHRIST, 97; JONES, LRE 322ff.; KASER, RPR 2, 242ff., 718; W. KUNKEL, Staatsorganisation und Staatspraxis der röm. Republik, 1995, vol. 2, 89f.; MOMMSEN, Staatsrecht 1, 578ff.; 2,2, 1157, 1169. C.G.

Detestatio sacrorum We are not well informed about the *detestatio sacrorum* (DS) (Gell. NA 15,27,3: cf. also *alienatio sacrorum*: Cic. Or. 144; Leg. 3,48), which had to precede the adoption of a *persona sui iuris* in the place of the son (→ Adoption) through a legal decision of the *comitia curiata* or the establishment of a *testamentum calatis comitiis*. Nothing is preserved of the work *De sacris detestandis* (Gell. NA 7,12,1) written by Servius Sulpicius Rufus.

The DS is a solemn declaration (Dig. 50,16,40, pr.; *ibid.* 238,1) with which the man who is to assume a right frees himself in front of the assembled committees from his previous family shrines (*sacra familiaria*) and his *gens*. This is preceded by an investigation by the *pontifices* to ensure that the previous *sacra* are not left unattended. The DS disappeared with the *adrogatio per populum* in the post-classical period.

KASER, RPR I, 66, 106; B. KÜBLER, s.v. D. s., RE IA, 1682–1684. P.A.

Deucalion (Δευκαλίων; *Deukalíōn*). Attested as a proper name since the discovery of the Linear B Tables (PY An 654,12: *de- u-ka-ri-jo*), for Hes. fr. 234 M-W and for Deinolochus (Comicorum Graecorum Fragmenta in Papyris 78 fr. 1) also in the form *Leukaríōn* (Λευκαρίων). This either involves differently dissimilated derivations of *leukós* (λευκός, 'white') (cf. Ov. Epist. 15,165ff.) [1], or D. represents a pre-Greek word [2. 96–7]. In the post-Mycenaean period the name referred, apart from some epigraphical evidence (CIL III 2211; VI 6396) to mythical persons: the father of Cretan Idomeneus (Hom. Il. 13,451; Od. 19,180f.), a Trojan (Hom. Il. 20,478), an Argonaut from Achaea (Val. Fl. 1,366), the son of Abas (schol. Apoll. Rhod. 3,1087), the father of the founder of Candyba (cf. [3. 385]).

D. was described, from the time of Epicharmus (CGFP 85 fr. 1), Pind. Ol. 9,41ff. and probably as early as by Hes., as the hero of the Flood. Linked with him and Pyrrha is an etymology-related legend of human creation that in Hes. and Pind. was limited to eastern Locris and that later (Ov. Met. 1,381ff.) became universal and in Acusilaus (FGrH 2 F 35) for the first time took the form of the stone-throwing legend. Correspondingly, older sources (Apollod. 1,47; Pl. Ti. 22a) in contrast to the Vulgate of the Imperial period (Ov. Met. 1,291f.) refer only to a local flood. Commemorative rituals in which D. was named expressly are known from Athens (Paus. 1,18,7) and Hierapolis/Bambyce (Lucian. Syr. D. 13; 28) [2. 239–58].

D. was considered from the time of Hes. fr. 2; 4 to be the son of Prometheus; a number of mothers are named. The paternal link is more stable because Prometheus as the one providing warning of the Flood took on the function of the Oriental Ea/Enki [4. 130–5]. Oriental influence can also be seen from the evacuation to → Parnassus (Apollod. 1,48) or the Othrys (Hellanic. FGrH 4 F 117) by means of a *larnax* ('ark') [2. 129–30]. D. was a cultural hero like Prometheus because he taught humans not just to roast the sacrificial meat on the fire but also to boil it in a cauldron (Aristot. Pr. 3,43b [2. 229–30]). In the works of historians this myth is mirrored in D. or the flood driving out the original people, the Pelasgians, cf. Dion. Hal. Ant. Rom. 1,17,3 (Hellanicus?) and Diod. Sic. 5,81,2f. From the time of Hdt. 1,56,3 and Hellanicus FGrH 4 F 6a the sources have released D. from the tie with Locris and placed him in Thessaly. There is evidence of additional secondary adoption in Dodona (Aristot. Mete. 352a 35), Athens (Marm. Par. FGrH 239 A4) and Argus (Arr. FGrH 156 F 16). The Vulgate (Apollod. 1,49; cf. Hes. fr.9) made Deucalion's son → Hellen the father of Dorus, Xuthus (father of Ion) and Aeolus, the eponyms, of the three dialect groups. This development was the result of the emergence of a common Greek sense of belonging together [2. 84–7].

D.'s classification in the synopses of the historians after the prehistory of Argus and Arcadia, to whom a flood tradition was unknown, and the restriction of the flood to Thessaly connected with this [2. 153–6] became, from the time of Theophilus of Antioch onwards (ad Autolycum 3,18f.), the main argument of Christian polemics against the identification with Noah justified by Philo (De praem. 23). In spite of the proverbial nature of D. (Anth. Pal. 11,19; 67; 71) pictorial representations are rare [3. 384–5].

→ Prometheus

1 FRISK 2 G.A. CADUFF, Sintflutsagen, 1986 3 P. LINANT DE BELLEFONDS, C. AUGÉ, s.v. D., LIMC 3.1 4 S. WEST, Prometheus Orientalized, in: MH 51, 1994, 129–149. G.A.C.

Deultum (Δεβελτός; *Debeltós*). Settlement *c.* 25 km west of → Burgas, modern Debelt/Bulgaria. Traces from the late Bronze Age, and afterwards Thracian Hallstatt settlement that later flourished because of its trade with the Greek colonies of the Black Sea. D. was connected with the sea via Lake Mandra which in antiquity stretched further south than it does today. Attic goods of the 1st half of the 4th cent. BC, Hellenistic ceramics, coins and amphora stamps etc. from Heraclea Pontica, Thasos and Chios. No pre-Roman literature or epigraphical evidence but Pliny's reference (HN 4,45) leads us to assume that there was an older Greek precursor settlement. D. was probably founded by Vespasian in AD 70 as the sole veteran colony in Thrace (veterans of the *legio VIII Augusta*, CIL VI 31692 of AD 82:

colonia Flavia Pacis Deultensium) in order to secure the bay of Burgas and the road from Moesia to Propontis. Because of the archaeological research that to date has only been inadequate, the size and type of the colony are still unknown (the Silenus on coins from D. in any case indicates the status of a *colonia libera*). The wall remains that can be seen today date to the Middle Ages. Coin minting under Trajan and from Caracalla to Philippus Arabs. In the 4th cent. D. probably declined, as Ammianus (31,8,9) only describes D. as *oppidum Dibaltum*. According to the treaty between the Bulgarian Khan Tervel and Theodosius III of 716, D. became a Byzantine border town and the starting-point for the defensive trenches of the Erkesia (Theophanes 1,497).

B. Gerov, Zemevladenie v rimska Trakija i Mizija, 1983, 41–49; Zlatarski, Istorija na bălgarskata dăržava prez srednite vekove, 1,1, 1918, 177ff. I.v.B.

Deunx In the Roman system of measures and weights, *deunx* refers to $^{11}/_{12}$ of the whole (as) and the term is derived from *deesse* and *uncia*, i.e. 1 as (12 *unciae*) less 1 *uncia*. *Deunx* is used in the measurement of length (*pes*), the measurement of area (*iugerum*) and the measurement of capacity (*cyathus*, *sextarius*) as well as in the calculation of interest (*fenus*) and in the law of succession. Based on the Roman pound (*libra*: 327,45 g), the *deunx* weighs 300.16 g. Coins of this weight were not minted.

→ As; → Cyathus; → Iugerum; → Libra; → Pes; → Sextarius; → Uncia

Hultsch, RE 5, s.v. D., 276–277. A.M.

Deus ex machina (Θεὸς ἀπὸ μηχανῆς; *theòs apò mēchanês*). Crane-like stage machinery (μηχανή, γέρανος, κράδη; *mēchanḗ*, *géranos*, *krádē*) that became proverbial as early as the 4th cent. BC, by which a deity could suddenly appear hovering and traversing the air, and imbue the plot with fresh momentum or bring it to an end (cf. Pl. Cleit. 407a; Crat. 425d; Antiphanes 189,13–16 PCG; Alexis 131,9 PCG; Men. Theophorumene fr. 5 Sandbach = 227 Körte; Cic. Nat. D. 1,53). Its use in the parodies of Aristophanes (Pax 174ff.; Nub. 218ff.; Av. 1184ff.; Fr. 192 PCG, perhaps Thesm. 1098ff.) confirms it for 5th cent. tragedy: Aesch. PV 284ff. (Oceanus); Eur. Med. 1317ff. (Medea), Andr. 1226ff. (Thetis), El. 1233ff. (Dioscuri), Herc. 815ff. (Lyssa and Iris), Or. 1625ff. (Apollo) are definite examples; it was probably used in Eur. Hipp. 1283ff. (Artemis), Suppl. 1183ff. (Athena), Ion 1549ff. (Athena), IT. 1435ff. (Athena), Hel. 1642ff. (Dioscuri), before the lacuna at Bacch. 1330ff. (Dionysus); rather unlikely in Soph. Phil. 1409ff. (Hercules).

The *deus ex machina* scenes in Euripides often include a critical interpretation of the myth (Herc., El., Ion) or an interpretation of the occurrence (Bacch., Hipp.) and are also partly used as criticism of contemporary events: through the epiphany of Apollo in the

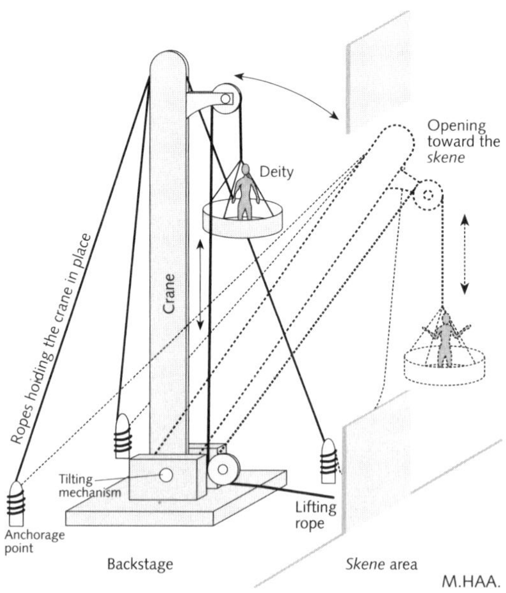

Deus ex machina; hypthetical reconstruction.
The crane (according to Hero) conveys the deity from backstage to the stage.

Orestes that has the effect of being superimposed and through which the plot is forcibly returned to the path prescribed by the myth, it becomes clear that a good outcome of the events is only possible on the stage but not in real life. A special variety is presented in the exodus of *Medea*: as Medea, like a deity, saves herself from Jason with the help of the *mēchanḗ*, her superhuman traits are dramatically portrayed. Aristot. Poet. 1454a 37–b 2 (cf. Hor. Ars P. 191f.) criticizes this use of the *mēchanḗ*, as the solution (λύσις; *lýsis*) does not develop from coherence within the plot itself but is imposed from outside.

→ Aeschylus [1]; → Euripides [1]; → Sophocles; → Mechane

W.S. Barrett, Euripides. Hippolytos, 1964, 395f.; N. Hourmouziades, Production and imagination in Euripides, 1965, 146–169; H.-J. Newiger, Drama und Theater, 1996, 97–102; W. Schmitt, Der d.e.m. bei Euripides, 1967; A. Spira, Unt. zum d.e.m. bei Sophokles und Euripides, 1960; O. Taplin, The Stagecraft of Aeschylus, 1977, 443–447. B.Z.

Fig.-Lit.: H. Bulle, H. Wirsing, Szenenbilder zum griech. Theater des 5. Jh. v.Chr., 1950; M. Bieber, A History of the Greek and Roman Theater, ²1961, 74–78; S. Melchinger, Das Theater der Tragödie, 1974, 191–200; A. Schürmann, Griech. Mechanik und ant. Gesellschaft, 1991, 146f., 155f. M.HAA.

Deuteragonistes (δευτεραγωνιστής; *deuteragōnistḗs*). 'Second actor', introduced by Aeschylus, but the designation *deuteragonistes* is more recent. Whilst the 'first actor' (*prōtagōnistḗs*) traditionally took on the main role (*Átossa*, *Oidípous*, *Mḗdeia*) and could identify with this, the *deuteragonistes* — or even the 'third actor' (*tritagōnistḗs*)—had to cope with a large number of different roles. The amount of text that had to be mastered by the *deuteragonistes* was considerable and rapid mask changes required great declamatory skill but brought less fame than the role of the first actor. He did not take part in the agon of the tragic actors (in Athens from the middle of the 5th cent. onwards). In this way the second actor was regarded as second-class, as the metaphorical usage of *deuteragonistes* proves.

→ Hypokrites; → Protagonistes; → Skenikoi agones; → Tritagonistes

A.W. Pickard-Cambridge, The Dramatic Festivals of Athens, [2] 1968, 132–135; K. Schneider, s.v. ὑποκριτής, RE Suppl. 8, 190. H.BL.

Deva Modern Chester. Legionary camp, originally set up for the *legio II Adiutrix* in *c.* AD 75 [1] as a wooden/earthen fort, with baths (stone); water pipes of lead date the completion to AD 79. The *legio XX Valeria Victrix* took over the camp in *c.* AD 86/7. The rebuilding in stone began in *c.* AD 102. A large amphitheatre situated outside the walls was constructed in the 2nd cent. [2]. West of the camp on the bank of the Dee is a mooring place. The fortress wall was renovated in the 3rd cent. using reused stones, among these inscriptions and sculptures [3]. The garrison was reduced in size after AD 300; before 400 the camp was abandoned.

1 V.E. Nash-Williams, The Roman Frontier in Wales, [2]1969, 33 2 F.H. Thompson, Excavation of the Roman amphitheatre at Chester, in: Archaeologia 105, 1975, 127–239 3 R.P. Wright, I.A. Richmond, The Roman Inscribed and Sculptured Stones in the Grosvenor Museum, 1955, 4f. M.TO.

Devaluation of money Ancient monetary systems were in principle based on the value of their substance: the value of coins related to the metal quota of the material from which they were made — gold, silver or bronze — and this was determined by weight and fineness. Based on these prerequisites the devaluation of money in antiquity could primarily be traced back to manipulations in the weight or fineness of the coins. As the quantity of money issued essentially depended on the level of public expenses, which could seldom be reduced arbitrarily, the devaluation of money can usually be explained in terms of → public finances and an inadequate supply of precious metals. In this way the devaluation of money in antiquity is fundamentally different from the phenomenon of inflation in the 20th cent. AD that has as its prerequisite an excessive growth in the quantities of money: the imbalance between the supply of money and the actual demand for money leads to price increases; modern inflation should therefore be regarded as closely correlated with government monetary policy and the amount of money.

Greek currencies were generally stable, and the silver level in the coins was only rarely reduced. The minting of bronze coins instead of silver coins occurred occasionally as an emergency measure. The report about the Athenian general Timotheus, who in a campaign against Olynthus issued a fiduciary bronze currency so that he could pay his troops (Ps.- Aristot. Oec. 1350a), is not necessarily historically correct, nonetheless it indicates options in Greek monetary policy.

Manipulations in the weight standard of silver coins are known for the mintings of the Ptolemies and the Attalids. Ptolemy I Soter gradually reduced the weight of the Egyptian silver tetradrachma to 14.2 g in view of the lack of silver deposits in Egypt, which fell below — by about 3 g — the Attic standard upon which the international Alexander currency was based. The Attalids had → tetradrachmas called *kistophóroi* struck, for instance from 170 BC onwards, that only weighed *c.* 12 g and therefore actually corresponded to 3 Attic → drachmas. Manipulations in the fineness are also well known from Carthaginian and Celtic mintings. The fineness of the Carthaginian minting declined in the 1st Punic War to 33% and in the 2nd Punic War was reduced to 18%. In consequence of the Gallic War the fineness of the indigenous mintings declined dramatically in Gaul and Britain.

Already in the early Principate period the weight and metal content of important denominations was reduced; the *principes* attempted in this way to finance the rising expenditure of the army. Under Nero 45 *aurei* instead of the previous 40 were struck from 1 Roman pound of gold and 96 *denarii* instead of the previous 84 were minted from 1 pound of silver. In this way the → *aureus* weighed *c.* 7.4 g, and the → *denarius* 3.41 g. By the time of Commodus the weight of both coins was further reduced to 7.22 g (*aureus*) and 2.93 g (*denarius*), with the silver content of the *denarius* sinking to *c.* 85 %. The → *antoninianus* struck under Caracalla with a value of 2 *denarii* weighed only 5.11 g. Prior to the coin reform of Diocletian the silver coins had a fineness of only *c.* 4 %.

The relationship between the devaluation of money and price increases in the Roman Empire during the 3rd and 4th cents. AD has not been fully explained to date. Before the Aurelian coin reform (AD 274/5) the devaluation of the Egyptian silver drachma from 32% to 3% silver content did not influence the price level, whilst in the 4th cent. AD any deterioration in the coins in Egypt immediately had an effect on the price level. Although it is clear that in antiquity coins were generally valued according to their level of precious metal and deteriorations in coins resulted in price increases, the Egyptian example is proof of the spread and recognition of fiduciary money. Certainly the precondition for this was confidence that all market players acted in the same way; as P Oxy. 1411 (AD 260) shows, coins were not accepted if for political reasons this confidence no longer existed. Consequently factors that had previously not been taken into account and that were very complex influenced the question of whether coins whose fineness and weight had been reduced were treated according to their nominal or their real value.

1 R. BAGNALL, Currency and Inflation in 4th Century Egypt, Bull. of the American Soc. of Papyrologists Suppl. 5, 1985 2 F. BEYER, Geldpolitik in der röm. Kaiserzeit, 1995 3 R.A.G. CARSON, Coins of the Roman Empire, 1990 4 R. DUNCAN-JONES, Money and Government in the Roman Empire, 1984 5 K. HASLER, Studien zu Wesen und Wert des Geldes in der röm. Kaiserzeit von Augustus bis Severus Alexander, 1980 6 C. HOWGEGO, Ancient History from Coins, 1995 7 A.H.M. JONES, Inflation under the Roman Empire, in: JONES, Economy, 187–227 8 K. MARESCH, Brz. und Silber. Papyrologische Beiträge zur Gesch. der Währung im ptolemäischen und röm. Ägypten bis zum 2. Jh. n.Chr., 1996 9 K. STROBEL, Das Imperium Romanum im 3. Jh., 1993, 270–279.

S.v.R.

Devehöyük Iron Age cemeteries south-west of → Karkemish, Syria. Most of the graves which are mainly urn graves (phase I) date to the 8th cent. BC. Worth stressing in particular are imported Cypriot, eastern and island Greek, Phrygian (?), Egyptian-Phoenician and locally imitated wares, also pottery decorated with figures as well as terracotta figurines and plaques. Phase II (to the 4th cent. BC) with inhumations, partly in constructed tombs, yielded not just metal objects and small sculptures but also imported Greek pottery.

P.R.S. MOOREY, Cemeteries of the First Millenium B.C. at Deve Hüyük, 1980.

A.W.

Development see → Progress, idea of

De verbis dubiis see → Flavius Caper

De viris illustribus Latin collection of → biographies of important authors with the exclusion of statesmen and commanders (exception: Aurelius → Victor), initially as an introduction to a work. Its origins can be found in the peripatetic and Alexandrian literature business (e.g. → Neanthes; important: → Callimachus' *Pínakes*). It is this tradition that influenced the biographical collections of → Varro, of → Hyginus, and especially of → Suetonius' *De viris illustribus*. The genre experiences a new zenith with Jerome (→ Hieronymus), who in AD 392/3, following Suetonius (but also Cicero's *Brutus*), compiled 135 short *vitae* of Greek and Lat. Christian authors in chronological sequence. A Greek translation has erroneously been attributed to the patriarch Sophronius († AD 638). The tradition was continued by → Gennadius of Marseilles (477/8), → Isidore of Seville (615/618) and finally Ildefons of Toledo (*c.* 605–667).
→ Literature, historiography of; → PETRARCH

S. PRICOCO, Storia letteraria e storia ecclesiastica dal D.v.i. di Girolamo a Gennadio, 1979; R.A. KASTER, C. Suetonius Tranquillus, De Grammaticis et Rhetoribus, 1995.

U.E.

Devotio Ritual in which a person dedicates either the enemy, himself or both to the gods of the Underworld and to death [1]. Macr. (Sat. 3,9,9ff.) reports that in earlier times enemy towns were, according to the *evocatio* (the 'calling out') of the gods, dedicated to the gods of the Underworld (Dis pater, Veiovis, Manes) (*devoveri*). The prayer (*carmen devotionis*) that Macr. cites on the occasion of the *devotio* of Carthage, calls the enemies a 'substitute' (*vicarios*) for the Roman commander and his army who in this way could remain alive. A known variation of this genuine *votum* ('vow') is the *devotio*, evidence of which is only provided for P. Decius Mus (340 BC battle at Vesuvius, Liv. 8,9–10) and less uniformly for his son (295 BC Sentinum, Liv. 10,28) and his grandson (279 BC Ausculum, Cic. Fin. 2,61; Tusc. 1,89). In this case the Roman army commander laid down his life binding this act of self-*consecratio* to a *devotio* of the enemies as described above ([1], cf. [3. 32]). Liv. (8,9,14ff.) reproduces the prayer (not in the original wording) with which Decius dedicated the enemy army and himself to the → Di Manes and Tellus (*legiones auxiliaque hostium mecum Deis Manibus Tellurique devoveo*). The *pontifex maximus* recited the words whilst the commander in the *toga praetexta*, with a covered head and resting on a spear laid his hand under the toga on his chin. After that the commander girded in the *cinctus Gabinus* committed suicide by dashing on horseback into the enemy lines. If the gods did not accept this self-*consecratio*, the commander remained incapable of sacred acts during his lifetime. If a legionary was devoted in his place, an image of the commander at least seven feet tall had to be buried. The place was then a *locus religiosus*. In the case of the loss of the commander's spear, a suovetaurilia sacrifice had to be conducted.

Despite these ritual provisions [2; 3], it is doubtful whether the nature of the *devotio* described was one of the firmly established Roman rituals. In the Imperial period, the concept of *devotio* became an expression for various types of 'self-sacrifice' 'for the well-being of the emperor' (*pro salute principis*) [4]. Legions were given the honourable title *devoti numini maiestatique (Augusti/Augustorum)* [5] as a sign of their devotion unto death; there is also plenty of evidence for the invocation *de nostris annis tibi augeat Iuppiter annos* ('of our years may Jupiter increase your years') (Tert. Apol. 35; [6. 197; 207]). If the ruler was ill, people made public vows to lay down their lives for the recovery of the emperor's health. Here the influence of the *devotio Iberica* can be seen [6]. Caligula forced P. Afranius Potitus to actually honour the *devotio* (Cass. Dio 59,8,3; Suet. Cal. 27,2). In the later period *devotio* also simply meant the cursing of a person, especially in → *defixiones* ('bewitching').
→ Consecratio; → Evocatio

1 H.S. VERSNEL, Two Types of Roman D., in: Mnemosyne 29, 1976, 365–410 2 L. DEUBNER, Die Devotion der Decier, ARW 8, 1905, Bh. 66ff. 3 H. WAGENVOORT, Roman Dynamism, 1947, 31–34 4 H.S. VERSNEL, Destruction, D. and Despair in a Situation of Anomy, in: G. PICCALUGA (ed.), Perennitas. Studi in onore di Angelo Brelich, 1980, 541–618 5 H.G. GUNDEL, Devotus numini maiestatique, in: Epigraphica 15, 1953, 128–150

6 G. HENZEN, Acta Fratrum Arvalium, 1874 7 R. ÉTIENNE, Le culte impérial dans la Péninsule Ibérique d'Auguste à Dioclétien, 1958, 357–362.

WISSOWA, Rel. und Kultus der Römer, ²1912, 384f.; K. WINKLER, RAC III, 849–58. H.V.

Dexamenus (Δεξαμενός; *Dexamenós*).
[1] Mythical king of → Olenus in Achaea, host of → Hercules; his name indicates that hospitality is his main function in the narrative. Hercules repaid his hospitality by saving D.'s daughter who was being pursued by the centaur Eurytion. There are various versions of the story: either D. was forced to betroth his daughter Mnesimache to Eurytion who was, however, killed by Hercules (Apollod. 2,91); or Eurytion tried to rape D.'s daughter Hippolyte at her wedding feast and was killed by Hercules (Diod. Sic. 4,33); or Hercules abducted D.'s daughter → Deianira, promised to marry her, then killed her suitor Eurytion and fulfilled his promise (Hyg. Fab. 31; 33). It is not only the last of these versions that reminds us of Hercules' rescue of Oeneus' daughter Deianira from the centaur Nessus. Tales and names are also mixed up on a vase (Beazley ARV² 1050) on which Hercules is shown killing a centaur called D. whilst Oeneus and Deianira stand beside it. D. himself appears in literary sources as a centaur; in the schol. Callim. H. 4,102 he is the centaur who owns herds of cattle in Bura in Achaea (cf. Etym. s.v. *Búra*).

D. GONDICAS, s.v. D., LIMC 3.1, 385–6; R. VOLLKOMMER, s.v. Deianeira II, LIMC 3.1, 359–61. E.K.

[2] **of Chios.** the most important gem cutter of the period around 400 BC, workshop probably in Athens [1. 130, 134]. Initialled four scarabaeoids: heron flying (chalcedony, St. Petersburg, ER) [1. 130f.[29] pl. 31,1], heron standing (jasper, ibid.) [1. 132[31] pl. 31,2], portrait of a man (jasper, Boston, MFA) [1. 132[32] pl. 31,3] and the 'Mike cameo' (chalcedony, Cambridge, FM) [1. 134[33] pl. 31,4]. Countless works attributed [1. 131[28], 134ff.[35ff.], 147[115], 157[162], 159 pl. 31,5–10 and pl. 32,1–5].

1 ZAZOFF, AG.

J. BOARDMAN, Greek Gems and Fingerrings. Early Bronze Age to Late Classical, 1970, 194–199, 408f.; O. NEVEROV, D. von Chios und seine Werkstatt, 1973 (Russ.); M.L. VOLLENWEIDER, Le criquet de la collection Seyrig dans l' œuvre de Dexaménos, in: RN 6. Ser. 16, 1974, 142–148 pl. 15f; ZAZOFF, AG 127 (bibliography). S.MI.

Dexicrates (Δεξικράτης; *Dexikrátēs*). Comedy writer of the 3rd cent. BC and hence belonging to the New Comedy if his name is correctly supplied on the epigraphical list of Lenaean victors [1. test. *2]. Ath. 3,124b cites two verses from the play Ὑφ' ἑαυτῶν πλανώμενοι (fr. 1); the Suda article is based on this passage, and the addition that D. was an Athenian was probably a conclusion drawn from this [1. test. 1]. A brief mention is also to be found in the work of the grammarian Herodian (fr. 2).

1 PCG V, 1986, 16. T.HI.

Dexion see → Amynus; → Sophocles

Dexippus (Δέξιππος; *Déxippos*).
[1] Lacedaemonian, 406 BC mercenary leader of Acragas in the war against Carthage in which he played an obscure role. The Syracusans appointed him as the commander in Gela where he refused to support Dionysius I and was then sent back to his homeland (Diod. Sic. 13,85,3f.; 87,4f.; 88,7f.; 93; 96,1). D. is perhaps identical with a perioecus who drew attention to himself in the army of Cyrus the Younger through his wicked machinations and was finally executed by Nicander (Xen. An. 5,1,15; 6,1,32; 6,5ff.). M.MEI.
[2] **P. Herennius D.** * *c.* AD 200/205 [1. 19f.]. Historian from the Attic deme of Hermus, in 262 agonothete for the Panathenaea, then eponymous archon (PIR 4/2, 104). In 267 with 2,000 men he launched an attack on the Heruli who were invading Athens (D. FGrH 100 F 28; Sync p. 717,15; Zos. 1,39,1). According to Phot. Bibl. 82, p. 64 a 11–20, he wrote a historical work about primeval times up to 270 in 12 vols., continued by → Eunapius, a history of the Diadochi in 4 vols. that was an abridged extract from → Arrian in which the German Wars from 238 to 274 were described; Iordanes in the *Gothica* adopted from them the material relayed by Cassiodorus, probably also imparted by Eunapius and others for Zosimus. Quotations from D. are also in the SHA [2] (Fragments: FGrH 2 no. 100, p. 452–480 with the commentary by JACOBY p. 304–311). TRAILL, PAA 303780.

1 F. MILLAR, P. Herennius Dexippus, in: JRS 59, 1969, 12–29 2 F. PASCHOUD, L'Histoire Auguste et Dexippe, in: Hist. Aug. Coll., n.s. I, 1991, 217–269. A.B.

[3] **of Cos.** Physician, student of Hippocrates. He wrote a one-volume treatise on medicine and a prognostic in two volumes. His healing of the sons of the Carian king Hecatomnus prevented a war with Cos (Suda s.v. Dexippus). He was known for his starvation cure for fever which involved allowing his patient no food and only a small quantity of fluid. Treatment of such kind was scorned by Erasistratus (Gal. 1,144; 15,478, 703; CMG Suppl. orient. 2,106). D. believed that the epiglottis controlled the passage of fluid that it partly steered into the lungs and partly into the stomach (Plut. Mor. 669f.). Any change in the human body was the consequence of excess whilst disease, on the other hand, was the result of bile and mucus-producing food remnants. Bile and mucus could merge into serum and sweat or thicken into pus or throat and nasal mucus. By drying they formed solid components like fat and flesh. A mixture of phlegm and blood produced white phlegm or turned into black bile (Anon. Lond. 12,14–15).
→ Medicine V.N.

[4] Neoplatonic philosopher of the 4th cent. AD, student of → Iamblichus of Chalcis, writer of a three-volume commentary on Aristotle's 'Categories' in dialogue form [1]. He is certainly not the same person as the historian P. Herennius Dexippus [2]. Very little is known about his life although he is the person to whom the letter 'On Dialectics' from his teacher Iamblichus was addressed (Stobaeus 2,18 WACHSMUTH-HENSE). D.'s commentary, his sole extant work, was probably written in the mid 4th cent. AD. It is largely dependent on Iamblichus' and Porphyrius' lost commentary on Aristotle's 'Categories'[3]. The passages in which scholars used to suspect traces of the oral teaching of Plotinus also appear to be based on Porphyrius' lost *Categories* comm. *Ad Gedalium*, as D.'s Platonizing is a reaction to Plotinus' criticism of the 'Categories' [5; 6; 7].
→ Aristotle; → Philosophy

1 A. BUSSE (ed.), CAG 4.2., 1888, 1–71 2 Id., Der Historiker und der Philosoph Dexippus, in: Hermes 23, 1888, 402–409 3 P. HADOT, The Harmony of Plotinus and Aristotle according to Porphyry, in: R. SORABJI, Aristotle Transformed, 1990, 125–140 4 K. KALBFLEISCH (ed.), Simplicii in Aristotelis categorias commentarium (= CAG 8), 1907, 2, 25ff. 5 P. HENRY, Trois apories orales de Plotin sur les Catégories d'Aristote, in: Zetesis. FS E. de Strycker, 1973, 234–265 6 P. HENRY, The oral teaching of Plotinus, in: Dionysios 6, 1982, 2–12 7 P. HENRY, Apories orales sur les Catégories d'Aristote, in: J. WIESNER (ed.), FS P. Moraux, II, 1987, 120–156.

J. DILLON, Dexippus on Aristotle, Categories, 1990; W. KROLL, s.v. D. (6), RE 5, 293f. MI.CH.

Dexius C.D. Staberianus. *Cos. suff.* together with L. Venuleius Montanus in an unknown year (AE 1958, 262; [1. 111]; for possible identifications see [2. 338ff.]).

1 W. ECK, RE Suppl. 14 2 SCHEID, Collège. W.E.

Dextans In the Roman system of weights and measures, *dextans* describes $^{10}/_{12}$ of the whole and is derived from *deesse* and *sextans*, i.e. 1 *as* (12 *unciae*) less 1 *sextans*. The *dextans* was used in the measurement of length (*pes*), the measurement of area (*iugerum*), in the law of succession and in the calculation of hours. Based on the Roman pound (*libra*: 327.45 g), the *dextans* weighs 272.88 g [1. 296]. Bronze mintings of 10 *unciae* in the sextantal or somewhat lighter standard were issued in Luceria as a compensatory coin for the Roman as shortly after 211 BC for a few years and bear the value symbol S···· [2. 185ff.; 3. 65f.].
→ As; → Iugerum; → Libra; → Pes; → Uncia

1 HULTSCH, s.v. D., RE 5, 296 2 RRC, ²1987 3 M.H. CRAWFORD, Coinage and money under the Roman Republic, 1985 4 SCHRÖTTER, 137. A.M.

Dexter Widespread Roman *cognomen* in the families Afranius, Calpurnius, Cassius, Cestius, Claudius, Cornelius, Domitius, Egnatius, Nummius, Pomponius, Subrius, Turpilius. K.-L.E.

Dextrarum iunctio see → Wedding customs

Dia (Δῖα, Δία; *Dîa*, *Día*).
[1] The female equivalent of → Zeus, as *Diwiya* on the Linear B inscriptions from Pylos and Knossos, with her own sanctuary, just as → Poseidon also has his female counterpart in the Mycenaean pantheon [1]. In the post-Mycenaean period the three heroines who can be linked with the Mycenaean goddess by name, are all linked with Zeus, but the individual derivation is problematical.
[2] The heroine is most likely D. in the local cults of Phlius and Sicyon, a daughter of Zeus also called Ganymede or identified with → Hebe (Str. 8,6,24; Paus. 2,12,4; 13,3).

1 GÉRARD-ROUSSEAU, 67–70. F.G.

[3] Wife of → Ixion, daughter of → Eïoneus (Deïoneus). Ixion promised his father-in-law Eïoneus many gifts in exchange for his daughter. As the latter wanted to claim them, Ixion threw him into a ditch filled with hot coals where he came to a miserable end (Pherecydes of Soron in schol. Apoll. Rhod. 3,62). D.'s and Ixion's son was → Peirithous (Diod. 4,69,3; Apollod. 1,68), but Zeus is mostly regarded as his father (Hom. Il. 2,741; 14,317f.; Hyg. Fab. 155,4).
[4] Daughter of the Arcadian Lycaon, mother by Apollo of → Dryops (schol. Lycophr. 480; schol. Apoll. Rhod. 1,1213). R.B.
[5] Name given to several islands in the Aegean (schol. Theoc. 2,45b; Steph. Byz. s.v. D.), such as (1) the island on which Artemis killed Ariadne (Hom. Od. 11,325), and (2) the uninhabited island off the northern coast of Crete in front of Iraclion, today also Standia. Evidence found in the following passages: Str. 10,5,1; Stadiasmus maris magni 348 (GGM 1,514); Ptol. 3,15,8; Plin. HN 4,61; Apoll. Rhod. 4,424.

C. BURSIAN, Geogr. von Griechenland, 1862–1872, 560; M. GUARDUCCI, Inscr. Cret. I, 1935, 93f. H.KAL.

[6] (Δία; *Día*, also *Dióspolis*). Emporion in eastern Thynis (Bithynia, Steph. Byz. s.v. D. [229]; *Dióspolis* in Ptol. 5,1,2), modern Akçakoca (formerly Akşehir); probably the port for Cierus/Prusias ad Hypium, to which territorium D. belonged.

G. PERROT et al., Exploration archéologique de la Galatie et de la Bithynie, 1862, 20; G. MENDEL, Inscriptions de la Bithynie XX, in: BCH 25, 1901, 49–55; W. RUGE, s.v. D. 7), RE 5, 299; F.K. DÖRNER, W. HOEPFNER, Vorläufiger Bericht über eine Reise in Bithynien 1961, in: AA 1962, 564–594; F.K. DÖRNER, Vorbericht, in: AAWW 99, 1962, 31–33; T.S. McKAY, s.v. Akçakoca, PE, 23; C. MAREK, Stadt, Ära und Territorium in Pontus-Bithynia und Nord-Galatia, 1993, 16, 39; K. BELKE, Paphlagonien und Honorias, TIB 9, 1996, 189f. K.ST.

Diabateria see → Sacrifices

Diacira Mesopotamian town on the right bank of the Euphrates, not far from modern Hīt, exact location unknown. Amm. Marc. 24,2,3 and Zos. 3,15,2 (here variation Δάκιρα, *Dákira*) report on the destruction of the town situated in Sassanid territory and the rich booty in the battles of the Romans on the eastern border of the empire against the Sassanid empire under Julian (AD 363). According to Zosimus, the surrounding area had asphalt resources. The form of the name is Aramaic (analyzed as *dī/d* and *qīrā* '[place] of asphalt', ʾaqīrā would be expected).

TAVO B VI 4. J.OE.

Diacria (Διακρία; *Diakría*), also Hyperacria and Epacria. Term for the mountainous northeast of Attica [2], probably also the Attic east coast as far as Brauron, the ancestral home of the → Peisistratids (Pl. Hipparch. 228b; Plut. Solon 10,3; [4. 224]). Supported by a group of *Hyperakrioi* (Hdt. 1,59) or *Diakrioi* (Aristot. Ath. Pol. 13,4; [1; 2; 3. 184–188]), Peisistratus [4] established his tyrannis in Athens in 561 BC.

1 K. H. Kinzl, Regionalism in Classical Athens?, in: Ancient History Bull. 3, 1989, 5–9 2 R. J. Hopper, 'Plain', 'Shore' and 'Hill' in Early Athens, in: ABSA 56, 1961, 189–219 3 Rhodes 4 K.-W. Welwei, Athen, 1992.

H. LO.

Diacritical signs

I. Greek II. Latin

I. Greek

Texts by Greek authors were already supplied in antiquity with a whole range of symbols; aids to reading (→ Punctuation) such as punctuation marks and accenting, as well as critical and, finally, colometrical signs (→ Colometry) can be differentiated.

Although → Aristophanes [4] of Byzantium (*c.* 265 — *c.* 190 BC) is regarded as the inventor of punctuation [8. 222], he was by no means the first person to use it. Punctuation to separate metric units is already encountered in the *dikolon* on the cup from Ischia called, because of the inscription, the Nestor Cup (CEG 454; before 700 BC), in the form of a symbol in the shape of a bird in the Timotheus Papyrus (PBerolinensis 9875; 4th cent. BC); Isoc. Or. 15,59 and Aristot. Rh. 3,8,1409a 20f. with the word *paragraphḗ* also refer to punctuation. Aristophanes [4] is however the first grammarian whose markings with accents are mentioned (schol. Hom. Od. 7,317); we do not know which grammarians are responsible for the other aids to reading — such as spiritus, long and short symbols (these are considered to be the modern 'metrical signs'), apostrophe, diaeresis and the hyphen arch that (comprising several letters) marks a unity of words, e.g. in a compound. Frequently these aids to reading do not appear until the papyri of the Imperial period, and the early Ptolemaic Homeric papyri still lack punctuation marks and accents [12. 10], although we occasionally encounter prosodic aids to reading in papyri of the 1st cent. BC. The accenting system changed fundamentally from the 3rd/4th cents. AD: before every unstressed syllable could get a grave accent, it is then only still used on the final syllable of oxytones [6].

Aside from the aids to reading there were a number of → editorial signs like the → obelus are attributed partly to → Zenodotus and partly to Aristophanes [4] [8. 221]; however, the long tradition did not develop into a detailed system until the work of the grammarian → Nicanor in the 2nd cent. AD [2; 3; 7].

The arrangement of lyric poetry, which previously had been written like prose, into one-line *kola* (*kōlízein*) can be traced back to Aristophanes [4]; evidence for this can be found for Pindar and Simonides (Dion. Hal. comp. 22,26). The end of sections relating to one another was marked by Aristophanes [4] with a *paragraphos* (a short stroke between the lines) whilst the end of the last strophe or of the epode in a triadic composition strophe-antistrophe-epode was marked by a *koronis*, a type of embellished *paragraphos*. If a poem followed in a different metre, Aristophanes used the *asteriskos* (⁜, cf. in Heph. 73–76 Consbruch the section 'On the Signs'/Περὶ σημείων). It appears that Aristophanes [4] edited Alcaeus (Heph. 68 Consbruch) and Pindar (schol. Pind. Ol. 2,48) in this way. The Cod. Marcianus Graecus 483 that contains the metric scholia to Pindar with the manuscript corrections of Demetrius [43] Triclinius [4. 93–106; 5; 9] provides a fine example of the work of Byzantine philologists.

Finally, it is worth at least mentioning the musical symbols, evidence for which is also already to be found in inscriptions and in papyri [11. 277–326].

→ Colometry; → Punctuation

1 G. Cavallo, H. Maehler, Greek Bookhands of the Early Byzantine Period A.D. 300–800 (BICS Suppl. 47), 1987 2 B. A. van Groningen, Short Manual of Greek Palaeography, ³1963 3 A. Gudeman, s.v. Kritische Zeichen, RE 11, 1916–1927 4 J. Irigoin, Les scholies métriques de Pindare, 1958 5 M. Lamagna, Segni diacritici in Demetrio Triclinio, in: F. Conca (ed.), Byzantina Mediolanensia, 1996, 235–245 6 C. M. Mazzucchi, Sul sistema di accentazione dei testi greci in età romana e bizantina, in: Aegyptus 59, 1979, 145–167 7 K. McNamee, Sigla and Select Marginalia in Greek Literary Papyri, 1992 8 Pfeiffer, KPI 9 A. Tessier, Demetrio Triclinio revisore della colometria pindarica, in: SIFC 80, 1987, 67–76 10 E. G. Turner, P. J. Parsons, Greek Manuscripts of the Ancient World (BICS Suppl. 46), ²1987 11 M. L. West, Ancient Greek Music, 1992 12 S. West, The Ptolemaic Papyri of Homer, 1967.

GE.SCH.

II. Latin

In the ancient Latin texts extant in inscriptions, papyri or parchment codices, diacritical signs are to be found that provide either aids to reading — to mark syntactic (→ Punctuation) or metric *kola*, lengths and stresses — or additional information on the transmitted of the wording — to mark text-critical concerns [2. 131]. For the field of Roman music, diacritical signs (notes) have previously only been known from secondary sources [6. 489ff.].

Symbols to mark points of metre, presumably adopted from Greek tradition along with the genre, are already to be found in the oldest epigrams passed down in inscriptions from the 3rd/2nd cents. BC, the Scipionic inscriptions: aside from the conventional and natural practice of marking verse changes through line changes (CLE 6), relatively long horizontal strokes (CLE 7) or relatively large spatia (CLE 8, here also with line changes between verses 1 and 2) are used [5. 352f.]. These forms observable here — line changes, word separators and spacing — are used throughout the whole of Latin antiquity. In principle all symbols used for word division or as decorative elements such as dots, dashes or *hederae* (stylized ivy leaves) can also be employed to mark verse changes and emphasize *kola* within verses. The beginning of metric sections and changes in metre are marked from time to time by a *paragraphos* (a short stroke between the lines) [7. 140ff.].

To stress the lengths of vowels, various concepts were developed in the history of the Latin language which, however, tended to prove unsuccessful overall: in the inscriptions these are the so-called *geminatio Acciana* (i.e. the double writing of prosodically long vowels), apices and the so-called *i longae* [1. 34ff.] (jutting out over the top line); there are also forms of linguistically erroneous dipthongization (inverted spellings [3. 73]). In the papyri there are symbols similar to the apex (´) for noting the prosodic length of vowels, as well as — especially in papyri (used as school editions?) from more distant, predominantly Greek-speaking provinces — symbols to interpret word stress [2. 104, 107, 116, 131].

→ Inscriptions; → Punctuation; → Metre; → Music; → Papyri

1 E. Meyer, Einführung in die lat. Epigraphik, ³1991
2 R. Seider, Paläographie der lat. Papyri, vol. 2.1, T.2: plates. Lit. Papyri, 1. Halbband: Texte klass. Autoren, 1978
3 Sommer
4 P. Steenbakkers, Accent-Marks in Neo-Latin, in: Acta Conventus Neo-Latini Hafniensis, 1994, 925–934
5 B. Vine, Studies in Archaic Latin Inscriptions, 1993
6 G. Wille, Musica Romana. Die Bed. der Musik im Leben der Römer, 1967
7 E. O. Wingo, Latin Punctuation in the Classical Age, 1972. P.KR.

Diadema (διάδημα; *diádēma*). The term was originally used to describe all bands worn round the head; different from → wreath. The *diadema* decorates, consecrates and raises its wearer above others; in this way *diademata* are symbols of dignity, particularly in cult; to this belong the 'bust crowns' or the 'griffin *diadema*' of the priests and deities; of a religious nature are also the ribbon-, gable- and rhomboid-shaped '*diademata* of the dead' that from the Mycenaean period onwards (shaft tomb IV, Mycenae) in many cases adorn the forehead of the deceased and that in the Classical and Hellenistic periods are also furnished with not just decorative ornamentation but also with mythical images related to the hereafter (Hercules, Dionysian Thiasos).

As a symbol of royal dignity it was adopted from the Persian kings by → Alexander [4] the Great; since then the *diadema* was part of the royal vestments and regalia (exception: Sparta); on coins of Ptolemy IV the *diadema* is surrounded by a radial → wreath. In Rome it was likewise a symbol of kingship; the Republican rejection of this symbol of absolute power resulted in it initially remaining rare in the regalia of the early Imperial period. Not until the 4th cent. AD did the *diadema*, with the special form of the pearl *diadema*, become the common insignia of the Roman emperors in the east and west.

This should be distinguished from the item of jewellery also frequently called *diadema* that was originally made of metal, was ring-shaped and was worn in the hair, evidence for which can be found from the 5th cent. BC onwards among goddesses and heroines; in the Hellenistic period the queens adopted it, then the empresses (Livia); from the Flavian period onwards it was also worn by women who were not empresses as part of their private apotheosis.

A. Alföldi, Insignien und Tracht der röm. Kaiser, in: MDAI(R) 50, 1935, 145–150; H. Jucker, Röm. Herrscherbildnisse aus Ägypten, in: ANRW II 12.2, 1981, 667–725; U. Kron, Götterkronen und Priesterdiademe, in: Armagani. FS for J. Inan, 1989, 373–390; M. Pfrommer, Unt. zur Chronologie früh- und hochhell. Goldschmucks, IstForsch 37, 1990; H. Wrede, Consecratio in formam deorum, 1981, 75. R.H.

Diadematus Cognomen of L. Caecilius [I 26] Metellus D. (*cos.* 117 BC). K.-L.E.

Diadikasia (διαδικασία; *diadikasía*). In Athens a judicial procedure aimed at organizing the legal situation without plaintiffs and defendants. It was not introduced as part of the usual civil action (δίκη, *díkē*) and took place in two main groups of cases, namely in disputes in which two or more opponents asserted a better claim to a private or public right, or in those cases in which it was a matter of exemption from a duty under public law. In the first group the most common case involved a claim by several persons to a legacy in an inheritance dispute [1. 159ff.].

The object of the claim could, however, also be a usufructuary right (Dion. Hal. De Dinarcho 12), a reward offered by the state (And. 1,27), assets seized unlawfully by the state (Lys. 17) or the right to a guardianship (Aristot. Ath. Pol. 56,6) or a position as an official or priest (Xen. Ath. Pol. 3,4). The second group included disputes regarding the obligation to equip a chorus or a ship, or similar matters. The jurisdiction of the court differed according to the type of issue. In inheritance disputes the archon (→ Archontes) was responsible.

There is also evidence of the *diadikasia* outside Athens in proceedings between private individuals and the state regarding property (Syll.[3] 279,20) but the opinion that the *diadikasia* served in Greek law to determine ownership is probably unwarranted [1. 214ff.; 2; 4] [3].

1 A.R.W. Harrison, The Law of Athens I, 1968 2 A.Kränzlein, Eigentum und Besitz im griech. Recht, 1963, 142 3 G.Thür, Kannte das altgriech. Recht die Eigentumsdiadikasie?, in: J.Modrzejewski, D.Liebs (ed.), Symposion 1977, 1982, 55ff. 4 A.Maffi, in: G.Thür, J.Vélissaropoulos (ed.), Symposion 1997, 17ff.

G.T.

Diadochi, wars of the The term refers to the wars between the former companions and generals of king Alexander [4] (→ Diadochi and Epigoni) for his inheritance, lasting from his death in 323 BC to the formation of the Hellenistic state system. The period of the D. can be roughly divided into two periods: the wars leading up to the death of → Antigonos [1] Monophthalmos (301 BC), who championed most forcefully the unity of the empire, and the subsequent phase, beginning as early as *c.* 305, in which the Hellenistic successor states of Alexander's empire slowly took on the characteristics of sovereign states.

As Alexander left no descendants capable of taking over the government, and as the Macedonian monarchy had no strict system of succession, tensions between ambitious generals were to be expected. The earliest agreements drawn up in Babylon clearly show the attempt to combine preserving the unity of the empire with satisfying the interests of certain individuals; however, the appointment of Philip III → Arrhidaeus [4], Alexander's feeble-minded brother, together with Roxane's unborn child, later Alexander [5] IV, as dual but equal kings under the guardianship of the absent → Craterus and the simultaneous recognition of the → chiliarch → Perdiccas as regent could not be a solution, as particular interests immediately became apparent: thus → Ptolemaeus signalled his claim to direct succession by abducting Alexander's body to his own satrapy of Egypt. At the same time, Alexander's mother → Olympias tried to keep power in the family through the marriage of her daughter → Cleopatra to → Leonnatus; after the latter's death, she therefore turned to Perdiccas. Perdiccas' ambitions for the empire as a whole roused the resistance of → Antipater [1] (*strategos* of Europe), Craterus, Antigonus (satrap of Greater Phrygia), → Lysimachus (satrap of Thrace), and Ptolemy, resulting in the First War of the Diadochi. The compromise drawn up in 320 in Triparadeisus in Syria following the death of Craterus and the murder of Perdiccas (i.a. by → Seleucus), appointing Antipater as royal guardian and regent, failed only a year later with Antipater's death, because his designated successor → Polyperchon was not recognized by the other Diadochi nor by his son → Cassander.

In the course of the subsequent Second War of the Diadochi, the elimination of Olympias as well as of Philip III and his wife weakened the dynastic concept,

but Cassander then assumed the role of legitimate successor to the empire by arranging for their lavish funerals and by marrying the last surviving daughter of → Philippus II. Meanwhile, Antigonus pursued offensive power politics in the east—supposedly in the interest of the unity of the empire; in his proclamation of Tyre in 314, he demanded i.a. the release of Alexander IV, who had been interned by Cassander. He was also able to exploit the interests of the Greek cities for his own aims. In the Third War of the Diadochi, though, he was forced to sign a treaty (311), confirming the *status quo* until the king reached the age of majority. However, it was this which moved Cassander to eliminate the king and thus reopen the war for his succession. Antigonus was the first to seize the opportunity: following the spectacular success of his son → Demetrius [2] in Greece and in the Aegean region, he had himself proclaimed king by his army (306). In order to at least make an outward demonstration of their claims, the remaining Diadochi soon followed his example with proclamations of their own. The conflicts with Antigonus in the Fourth War of the Diadochi finally peaked in 301 with the battle of Ipsus (Phrygia), in which Antigonus was killed, and his son fled.

As the settlements after Ipsus worked to his disadvantage, Seleucus sought closer links with Demetrius in 299 and gave him his daughter → Stratonice in marriage, particularly, as at the same time, closer links were also forged between Lysimachus and Ptolemy with the latter marrying the former's daughter → Arsinoe [II 3]. These unions — even though they were undoubtedly directed at short-term tactical aims — demonstrate for the first time clearly the recognition of each partner as the autonomous ruler of his territories. However, after Demetrius had used Cassander's death in 298/7 to intervene in Greece and to have himself proclaimed king of the Macedonians in 294, his aggressive politics in Asia resulted in the other Diadochi entering into an alliance with the Molossian prince → Pyrrhus; in 285, Demetrius fell into Seleucus' captivity, where he died in 283. The death of further Diadochi calmed the situation: Lysimachus, whose kingdom extended as far as Thessaly after Pyrrhus' expulsion from Macedonia in 285, died in 281 near Curupedion while battling against Seleucus, who himself was killed the same year by → Ptolemaeus Ceraunos. In 282, → Ptolemaeus II was able to succeed his father directly to the throne, whereas Seleucus' son → Antiochus [2] I only succeeded with great difficulty (281–278). The anarchy following the death of Ptolemaeus Ceraunos in the fight against the Celts was ended in 278 by Demetrius' son → Antigonus [2] Gonatas with a military success over the Celtic forces. With the death of Pyrrhus in 272, Antigonus became the undisputed king of the Macedonians.

The period of the Diadochi is characterized by two main features: whereas the Diadochi in the early years still took their bearing from Alexander's official successors, later claims were increasingly legitimized by military success. Conversely, the concept of a unified empire gradually gave way to a more pluralistic thinking; after 301 at the latest, it had lost its practical political basis.

H.-J. GEHRKE, Gesch. des Hellenismus, 1990; P. GREEN, Alexander to Actium, 1990; J. SEIBERT, Das Zeitalter der Diadochen, 1983. M.MEI.

Diadochi and Epigoni *Diádochoi*, 'successors', is a literary collective term for the generals of Alexander who after his death in 323 BC made themselves heirs to his empire both co-operating and opposing each other. Their successors, the second generation after Alexander, were then grouped together as *epígonoi*, 'those born later'. The memory of the Epigoni of the legend, the sons of the Seven against Thebes, probably played a larger part in naming them than Alexander's Epigoni, the group of 30,000 young Oriental troops who were meant to supplement the Macedonian phalanx (Arr. Anab. 7,6,1).

Jerome of Cardia may have been the first to refer in a group-specific sense to Diadochi and Epigoni. However we would be going too far were we to conclude from remarks in Diodorus (18,42,1 = FGrH 154 T 3) and Josephus (c. Ap. 1,213 = FGrH 154 F 6) that because Jerome wrote 'the history of the Diadochi' that his work had a corresponding title [1. 76–80]. Diodorus and Josephus simply summarized the main epoch that Jerome had treated with terms that had since become familiar. Dionysius of Halicarnassus who remarked that Jerome had mentioned Rome 'in the history of the Epigoni', i.e. in the last part of his work (Dion. Hal. Ant. Rom. 1,5,4 = FGrH 154 F 13) proceeded in a similar manner. Probably, however, Jerome's younger contemporary Nymphis of Heraclea could have used as a heading the terms Diadochi and Epigoni that the predecessor had introduced, and in this way facilitated their spread. As he included Alexander in his historical work, he gave the 24 vols. 'On Alexander, the Diadochi and the Epigoni' (Suda s.v. Nymphis = FGrH 432 T 1) a plausible and catchy overall title which firmly distinguished him from the growing number of people writing solely about Alexander. Josephus who summarized the 'European History' and the 'Asian History' of Agatharchides of Cnidus as History of the 'Diadochi' proves how common the epoch terms Diadochi and Epigoni had become; the two works obviously proved influential right through to the 3rd. cent. (Jos. Ant. Iud. 12,5 = FGrH 86 F 20b). Correspondingly Strabo used the two concepts to divide the history of Persia into periods (15,3,24). It is not possible to tell from the fragments of Jerome, Nymphis and Agatharchides where the authors drew the boundary between Diadochi and Epigoni and what they viewed as the end of the time of the Epigoni.

J.G. DROYSEN, the 'discoverer of Hellenism' introduced the two terms to modern literature. To the two vols. following the 'History of Alexander the Great' — the 'History of Hellenism' — he had in the first edition of 1836/43 given the subtitle 'History of the Successors of Alexander' and 'History of the Development of the Hellenistic State System'. In the second edition of 1877/8, in which he collected all three vols. under the overall title of 'History of Hellenism', the second and the third vol. were given the subtitles 'History of the Diadochi' and 'History of the Epigoni'. He ended the second volume with the death of Ptolemy Ceraunus in the battle against the Celts in 279 and the transfer of Pyrrhus to Italy in the preceding year. The battle of Sellasia in 222 marked the end of the third volume. Later authors shifted the final point in the history of the Diadochi to the year 281 when Lysimachus, who was fighting against Seleucus, fell at Curupedion and the latter, the last survivor of Alexander's generals, was murdered shortly afterwards by Ptolemy Ceraunus.

The epoch name Diadochi became widespread in the literature that followed DROYSEN, not least because the history of the empire of Alexander (cf. the map in → Alexander [4]) after 323 was determined exclusively by men who already under Alexander had held positions of leadership in the conquest and administration of the empire. While the settlement at Babylon in 323 was based on the continued existence of the entire empire, three groups opposed each other in the subsequent period. The first group comprised those who strove for independent rule over a section of the empire. These included Ptolemy who in Babylon was made the *strategos* of Thrace, and Seleucus who in 321 became satrap of Babylonia. A second group wished to preserve the unity of the empire under rulers from the Macedonian royal house. Antipater, Craterus, Eumenes and Polyperchon were the champions of this solution. When Antipater died in 319 it had basically failed. Finally there were those Diadochi who wished to become successors of Alexander and rule the entire empire. The first was Perdiccas who, however, as early as 321 became the victim of an officers' conspiracy. In his footsteps trod Antigonus [1] Monophthalmos, supported by his son Demetrius [2] Poliorketes. But the first group — to which belonged after 319 Antipater's son Cassander in Macedonia — proved to be stronger in several so-called Wars of the Diadochi. In 315 an initial formally legal strike against the unity of the empire occurred when Ptolemy, Lysimachus and Cassander entered into a *symmachia*, i.e. an interstate alliance whilst the previous changing coalitions were informal amalgamations, which Diodorus, following its main source Jerome, calls *koinopragíai* ('common enterprises') [2]. In 306 Antigonus and Demetrius assumed the royal title to emphasize their claim to the entire empire. This was a fatal step. For in 305 Ptolemy, Lysimachus, Seleucus and Cassander also elevated themselves in their respective domains to the status of kings and in this way destroyed the lawful basis of the unity of the empire [3]. When Antigonus opposed them at the Battle of Ipsus in 301 he was defeated and fell. Then with the Battle of Curupedion in 281 the rule of Lysimachus also ended. From then on only three Diadochi

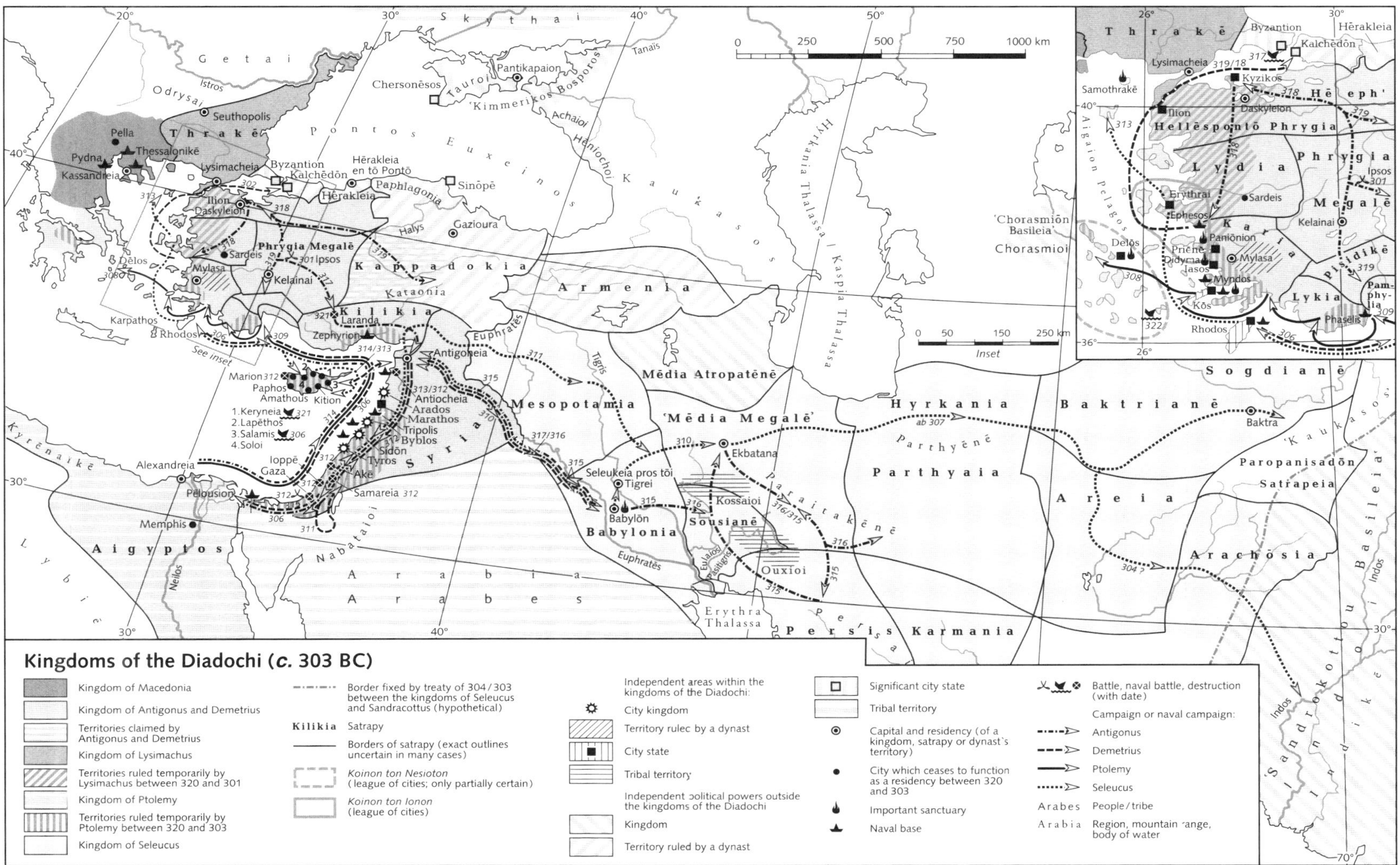

Kingdoms of the Diadochi (c. 303 BC)
Kingdom of Macedonia
Kingdom of Antigonus and Demetrius
Territories claimed by Antigonus and Demetrius
Kingdom of Lysimachus
Territories ruled temporarily by Lysimachus between 320 and 301
Kingdom of Ptolemy
Territories ruled temporarily by Ptolemy between 320 and 303
Kingdom of Seleucus
Border fixed by treaty of 304/303 between the kingdoms of Seleucus and Sandracottus (hypothetical)
Kilikia Satrapy
Borders of satrapy (exact outlines uncertain in many cases)
Koinon ton Nesioton (league of cities; only partially certain)
Koinon ton Ionon (league of cities)
Independent areas within the kingdoms of the Diadochi:
City kingdom
Territory ruled by a dynast
City state
Tribal territory
Independent political powers outside the kingdoms of the Diadochi
Kingdom
Territory ruled by a dynast
Significant city state
Tribal territory
Capital and residency (of a kingdom, satrapy or dynast's territory)
City which ceases to function as a residency between 320 and 303
Important sanctuary
Naval base
Battle, naval battle, destruction (with date)
Campaign or naval campaign:
Antigonus
Demetrius
Ptolemy
Seleucus
Arabes People / tribe
Arabia Region, mountain range, body of water
0 250 500 750 1000 km
0 50 150 250 km
Inset
See inset

monarchies still belonged to the 'Hellenistic system' — the Ptolemies, Seleucids and Antigonids.

For the following generations of rulers in the three dynasties the term Epigoni was not generally accepted. It was certainly very vague and did not describe a group with fixed dimensions like the Diadochi. The political trend was also significant: whilst the Diadochi derived their claims to rule from their personal relationship with Alexander despite their different goals, that no longer applied to the same extent to their sons and grandsons. The longer the Hellenistic monarchies lasted, the more they became independent entities.

J. HORNBLOWER, Hieronymos of Cardia, 1981 2 K. ROSEN, Die Bündnisformen der Diadochen und der Zerfall des Alexanderreiches, in: Acta Classica 11, 1968, 182–210 3 O. MÜLLER, Antigonos Monophtalmos und 'das Jahr der Könige', 1973. K.R.

MAPS: W. ORTH, Die Diadochenreiche (um 303 v.Chr.), TAVO B V 2, 1992.

Diadoumenos see → Polyclitus

Diaeta Room in a Roman → villa; however, it is not possible within the framework of Roman villa architecture to define a *diaeta* typologically or historically either on the basis of the villa letters of Pliny the Younger (Plin. Ep. 2,17; 5,6) or on other traditions. In both *Laurentinum* and *Tusci*, Pliny provides descriptions of seven *diaeta* each (Plin. Ep. 2,17,2; 2,17,13; 2,17,20; 5,6,20; 5,6,27). Their symmetry in numbers as well as in their aesthetic evaluation is a deliberate literary design, linking both letters compositionally, without implying that the descriptions are purely fictitious. Four of Pliny's *diaetae* are clearly identifiable as an ensemble of rooms, others could have been individual rooms. Conversely, Pliny refers to individual, isolated *cubicula* and also to an ensemble of *cubicula*, without using the term *diaeta*. Their only difference compared with *diaetae* 13 and 14 of the *Tusci* may have been that they comprised a total of three, respectively four *cubicula*. It is therefore possible that in his letters compositional criteria guided Pliny in distinguishing between *diaeta* and *cubiculum*.

The remaining literary references are so vague that they can not be compared with Pliny's descriptions (Plin. Ep. 6,16,14; 7,5,1; Plut. Poplicola 15). It is possible, however, that this somewhat blurred terminology is a true reflection of reality since there were no strict rules governing the arrangement of an ensemble of rooms, which rather evolved flexibly. For that reason, Pliny's use of the term *diaeta* may be linked with those ensembles of rooms in Roman villas, which display a certain autarchy, combined with a certain degree of seclusion: they may have been rooms or ensembles of rooms which were isolated without a direct link to the remainder of the villa, or rooms situated at the end of crypto-porticos or porticos, or finally ensembles of rooms which were integrated into the structure of the villa but whose seclusion was defined more by conventions governing their usage.

R. FÖRTSCH, Arch. Komm. zu den Villenbriefen des jüngeren Plinius, 1993, 48–53; A. MAU, s.v. D., RE 5, 1903, 307–309. R.F.

Diaeus (Δίαιος; *Díaios*) of Megalopolis; a radical opponent of Rome, *strategos* of the Achaeans in 150/49, 148/7, and 146 BC. In 146 BC, D., together with → Critolaus led the league into catastrophe (Pol. 38,10,8; 18,7–12) [1. 127, 228]. Following a dispute with Menalcidas of Sparta over bribery and capital jurisdiction, D. travelled to Rome in 149/8, where the former had fled; the Senate, however, did not come to any decision (Paus. 7,11–12) [1. 220–222]. After an Achaean-Spartan passage at arms, Menalcidas' suicide, and D.'s terror against supporters of Rome (Pol. 38,18,6; Paus. 7,13), Aurelius [I 14] Orestes demanded in 147 that Sparta together with other *poleis* should leave the league, strengthening the opponents of Rome around D., whose punishment was called for in vain by Sex. Iulius Caesar (Pol. 38,9–10; Paus. 7,14) [1. 223–227]. In the Achaean War, D. assumed the leadership in 146 following the defeat at Scarphea against Caecilius [I 27] Metellus, but was himself defeated on the Isthmus by Mummius (Pol. 38,15–18; Paus. 7,15–16) [1. 234–237]; together with his family, he chose to die [1. 238,33]. According to his own statements, D.'s critic Polybius rejected any personal gain from D.'s confiscated assets (Pol. 39,4).

→ Achaeans

1 J. DEININGER, Der polit. Widerstand gegen Rom in Griechenland, 1971. L.-M.G.

Diagoras (Διαγόρας; *Diagóras*).

[1] of Eretria. Towards the end of the 6th cent. BC (between 539 and 510?), D. overturned the 'oligarchy of the knights', allegedly for personal motives (Aristot. Pol. 5,5, 1306a 35–37) [1]. In posthumous tribute, a statue of D. was erected (Heraclides Lembus fr. 40 DILTS). Whether D. as *nomothetes* introduced a 'democratic constitution' [2], has to remain a moot point.

1 F. GEYER, Topographie und Gesch. der Insel Euboia 1, 1903, 66f. 2 H.-J. GEHRKE, Stasis, 1985, 63f. K.-J.H.

[2] of Melos, lyric poet. Eusebius' dating of his creative period to between 482/1 and 468/7 probably refers to dates of birth, because D. wrote in the late 5th cent.: Aristophanes (Av. 1072ff., with scholia) reports of a trial, in which D. was condemned to death because of his godlessness and desecration of the mysteries. He is supposed to have written dithyrambs and a paean [1. 8, 334–339]. His few surviving verses (PGM 738) are in contradiction with his reputation as an atheist, which later brought him fame. The attribution of an atheistic treatise to him has been rejected [2; 3].

1 D.A CAMPBELL, Greek Lyric 4, 1992 2 L. WOODBURY, The Date and Atheism of Diagoras of Melos, in: Phoenix 19, 1965, 178–211 3 M. WINIARCZYK, Diagoras von Melos: Wahrheit und Legende, in: Eos 67, 1979, 191–213; 68, 1980, 51–75. E.R.

[3] Progenitor of a very successful Rhodian family of athletes, descendants of the hero Aristomenes (Third Messenian War). At the 79th Olympiad (464 BC), he won the boxing contest (Pind. Ol. 7, praising his size) and was *periodonikes* [1. no. 252]. His sons Acusilaus (boxing) [1. no. 299] and Damagetus (*pankration*) [1. no. 287, 300] were both victorious on the same day of the 83rd Olympiad (448 BC), whereupon according to an unreliable ancient tradition D. died of joy (Gell. NA 3,15). His youngest son → Dorieus [2] was particularly successful: three times *periodonikes* in the *pankration* (Olympic victories in 432, 428, 424 BC = 87th–89th Olympiads) [1. no. 322, 326, 330]. His grandsons Peisirodus (son of his daughter Pherenice) [1. no. 356] and Eucles (son of his daughter Callipateira) [1. no. 354] gained Olympic victories in boxing — probably in 404 BC —, the former in the boys' class, the latter in the men's. It is said that the mothers of the victorious grandsons gained entry to the Olympic contest disguised as coaches (Paus. 6,7,2f.; 5,6,7–9); although married women were generally barred from admission, their particular transgression supposedly remained unpunished. Remains of the bases of the victors' statues of this family of athletes, with fragments of the inscriptions, have survived [2. no. 55, 63–66].

1 L. Moretti, Olympionikai, 1957 2 H.-V. Herrmann, Die Siegerstatuen von Olympia, in: Nikephoros 1, 1988, 119–183.

M. B. Poliakoff, Combat Sports in the Ancient World, 1987, 119–121; W. Decker, Sport in der griech. Ant., 1995, 136ff. W.D.

Diagraphein, diagraphe (διαγράφειν, διαγραφή; *diagráphein, diagraphḗ*).

(1) In Attic procedural law, *diagraphḗ* referred to the deletion of a suit from the court list after the prosecutor had either abandoned the case or failed to pay the court fees, or if the defendant objected to the admissibility of the action either by → *paragraphḗ* (παραγραφή) or by → *diamartyría* (διαμαρτυρία).

(2) The term *diagraphḗ* is also used for the registration of shares in mines leased from the polis, with their respective boundaries, in a register (Harpocr. s.v. διαγραφή).

(3) Additionally, it is a banking term, meaning 'to pay' and 'order payment', derived from that the technical term *diagraphḗ* referring both to the payment procedure itself as well as to the entry in the bank register and the bank's certificate confirming the transaction conducted, be it a cash payment of a transfer between accounts. *Diagraphaí* are known since the 3rd cent. BC; from the late 1st cent. AD, they are no longer just bank receipts confirming transactions — a kind of statement of account by the bank — but also serve as documents for the underlying business transaction. Their use ceased towards the end of the 3rd cent. AD.

→ Banks

1 R. S. Bagnall, K. A. Worp, SPP XX 74: The Last Preserved Bank-Diagraphe, in: Tyche 10, 1995, 1–7 2 R. Bogaert, Banques et banquiers dans les cités grecques, 1968, 50–54, 57–59 3 A. R. W. Harrison, The Law of Athens 2, 1971, 104f. 4 J. F. Healy, Mining and Metallurgy in the Greek and Roman World, 1978, 103–110 5 Wolff, 95–105. W.S.

Diaitetai (διαιτηταί; *diaitētaí*).

[1] In Greek law, *diaitetai* was the general term used for 'private' arbitrators, appointed with the agreement of both parties; empowered either to mediate or to settle the dispute in a binding and final decision (Dem. Or. 27,1; 59,47). Frequently, each party nominated an arbitrator assured of their confidence, and these then agreed on the appointment of a third, so that the arbitration was accomplished by a total of three *diaitetai*.

[2] In Athens, every citizen who had reached the age of 59 was obliged to serve for a year under the supervision of the 'official' *diaitetai*. These — instead of the *thesmothetai* — carried out the preliminary proceedings in cases of proprietary litigation in which the sum in dispute exceeded 10 drachmas (Aristot. Ath. Pol. 53, 2–6). A decision by one of these *diaitetai* could be accepted by both parties as binding, but each party was also entitled to insist on a decision by the → *dikastḗrion* (→ *éphesis*). In this case, the documentary evidence was sealed in two separate clay vessels, and only this evidence could be used by either party in the case. Perversions of justice by the *diaitetai* were punished with → *atimía*. After the completion of their year in office, the *diaitetai* were honoured by decree (e.g. list of the *diaitetai* of 325/4 BC, ordered according to phyles, IG II² 1926).

A. Steinwenter, Die Streitbeendigung durch Urteil, Schiedsspruch und Vergleich, ²1971 G. Thür, Beweisführung vor den Schwurgerichtshöfen Athens, 1977, 75ff. 316f. G. Aicher-Hadler, Das 'Urteil' des amtlichen Diaiteten, RIDA³ 36, 1989, 57ff. G.T.

Diakonos (διάκονος; *diákonos*, literally 'servant'). The word group διακονεῖν/*diakoneîn*, *diákonos*, διακονία/*diakonía* — 'to serve' (especially at table), 'servant', 'service' — emphasized service as a favour to someone while δουλεύειν/*douleúein* etc. emphasized the dependency relationship in service. Therefore, in the NT *diakonía* generally describes a 'service' modelled on the brotherly love of Jesus, whose work of salvation was understood as a 'service' to humanity (Mk 10,45). *Diakonos* as the term for a church office is only tentatively encountered in the NT (Phil 1,1; Rom 16,1; 1 Tim 3,8–13) and has parallels in Greek associations (see [1. 92]), where the *diákonoi* who are named after cooks in inscriptions probably served the meals, e.g., IG IV 774 (Troezen, 3rd cent. BC) and IG IX 1,486 (Acarnia, 2nd/1st cents. BC; cf. also CIG II 1800: τὸ κοινὸν τῶν διακόνων, 'Attendants' association', [1. 92]). The specific field of duties (which was probably regionally differentiated) only becomes tangible in the 2nd and 3rd cents.: the *diákonoi* were employees directly assigned to the bishop (→ *epískopos* [2]) with originally broad duties (announcements, independent baptismal celebrations, administration of assets) that became increasingly restricted (assistance during baptism, fetching and setting up the offerings during the Eucharist). Female deacons (originally *diacona*: Rom 16,1, latter διακονίσσα/*diakonissa*) were active in social care, pastoral care of women and the annointment of female baptized children.

In the course of the formation of a three-level hierarchy of offices — *diakonos*-priest-bishop — by the year 1000 the *diakonos* had declined to a minor degree of consecration on the career path to → priest (VI.); female deacons disappeared entirely in the East, while in the West 'diaconissa' became the name for monastic women.

→ Episkopos [2]; → Priest VI

1 H. W. Beyer, s. v. διακονέω etc., ThWB 2, 1935, 81–93 2 A. Weiser, s. v. διακονέω, in: H. Balz, G. Schneider (ed.), Exegetisches WB zum NT 1, ²1992, 726–732 3 C. Osiek et al., s. v. Diakon/Diakonisse/Diakonat, in: RGG⁴ 2, 1999, 783–792. M. HE.

Dialect Dialect (Greek διάλεκτος; *diálektos*) is defined as a geographical variation of a linguistic continuum whose spatial extent can be classified in a variety of ways. For example, the → Arcadian or → Thessalian dialects of Greek are themselves differentiated by a number of local variations. Isoglosses (common features, esp. phonological, morphological, and lexical ones) result in a dialect geography.

The earliest levels of a dialect structure of the Greek language, beginning in the 2nd millennium BC, and, linked with that, the homelands and movements of Greek tribes, can to a certain extent be derived from the isoglosses of the dialects of the 1st millennium (→ Greek dialects); e.g. the *-ti*(–) > *-si*(–) in the Ionian-Attic and Arcadian-Cypriot dialects points to an earlier continuum ('Eastern Greek') in Mycenaean Greece. In the classical period, almost every region had its own dialect, often with its own orthography, although supradialectic trends can be detected (→ Attic); these are the forerunners of later common languages.

In contrast with neighbouring → Oscan-Umbrian, Latin with its origins in an urban dialect of the Latium dialect region, did not develop its own dialects, despite its later wide geographical spread.

→ Greek dialects; → Italy: Languages; → Koine; → Latin

W. Besch et al. (ed.), Dialektologie, 1982f.; Knobloch, I, 590–603 (with bibliography); E. Risch, Histor.-vergleichende Sprachbetrachtung und Dialektgeographie, in: Kratylos 11, 1966, 142–155 (= KS 255–268). J.G.-R.

Dialecticians The term dialectician (διαλεκτικός; *dialektikós*), 'practised in discourse', was initially used to describe someone 'who knows how to ask questions and answer them' (Pl. Crat. 390c), i.e. a logician according to the contemporary appreciation of his most important ability. The understanding of the term then shifted, so that it either continued to comprise all logicians (as e.g. in Aristot. Top. 8,2,157a 19; Cic. Acad. 2,143; S. Emp. P.H. 2,166) or only referred to a certain group of logicians of the 4th and 3rd cents. BC. Its most famous representatives were → Diodorus [4] Cronus and his pupil Philo, but at the very least, Eubulides, Alexinus, and Dionysius of Chalcedon were also among its members. It remains uncertain firstly, whether the name means that these logicians 'presented their arguments in the form of questions and answers' (Diog. Laert. 2,106), and secondly, whether they were Megarians: earlier academic discussion had seen the → Megarian School as a school of several phases, the third of which was understood to be dialectic. The controversy between Döring, who sees the dialecticians as part of the Megarian School, which he subdivides into various circles [1], but does not understand as an institution in itself [3], and Sedley, who views the Megarians and dialecticians as two rivalling schools [2. 74–78], remains unsolved.

More of the logic of the dialecticians around → Diodorus Cronus seems to have been preserved than previously known. According to Ebert [4], → Sextus Empiricus' reports of the dialecticians refers to that very group, and his account of *Stoic* logic is predominantly pre-Chrysippan and to a large extent still identical with the logic of the dialecticians. Apart from their discussion of modality and the meaning of implication, we thus also know their views on signs as well as their classification of statements, their teachings on proof, their classification of paralogisms, and their theory of sophisms.

1 K. Döring, Die Megariker. Komm. Sammlung der Testimonien, 1972 2 D. Sedley, Diodorus Cronus and Hellenistic Philosophy, in: Proc. of the Cambridge Philological Society 203 N.S. 23, 1977, 74–120 3 K. Döring, Gab es eine Dialektische Schule?, in: Phronesis 34, 1989, 293–310 4 Th. Ebert, Dialektiker und frühe Stoiker bei Sextus Empiricus. Unt. zur Entstehung der Aussagenlogik, 1991. K.-H.H.

Dialectics (ἡ διαλεκτική; *hē dialektikḗ*) is an elliptic expression for ἡ διαλεκτικὴ τέχνη (*hē dialektikḕ téchnē*), 'the art of discourse'. In both versions, it is first found in Plato (Plt. 7,534e 3 or respectively Phdr. 276e5f.), where it is used to describe an ability which is characteristic of philosophers. This, then new, definition of dialectics was widely adopted, but also frequently modified even in antiquity.

For a better understanding, the descriptor 'art' (*téchnē*) is of importance. It clarifies from the very outset that dialectics comprise a practical knowledge, a knowledge of how to do something; only secondarily, can it through reflection also comprise a kind of theoretical knowledge and, depending on the definition of science, even become a scientific discipline in its own right. Plato had very specific discussions in mind, where expertise was to be developed: the *élenchoi*, a strictly regulated dialogue between two participants, the set-up of which has been variously described ([4; 5], → Refutation). In an *élenchos*, one participant assumes the role of questioner, the other that of respondent; according to clearly defined rules, both test any kind of thesis to examine its basis or refute it. The general purpose of this exercise is to find out something about the truth or falsehood of these theses. Expertise in respect of such dialogues means the ability to master both of these roles and thus to approach questions regarding truth with the necessary circumspection. Plato clearly had in mind these dialogues and their specific demands, which is i.a. evident in his definition of dialectician whom he saw throughout and directly as someone 'who knows how to ask questions and answer them' (Crat. 390c 10f.; see also Plt. 7,534d 3–10). Dialectics is thus the art of the question-and-answer discussion.

Because of their characteristics, these discourses are ideally suited for the testing of ethical standards. In the upheaval of the 5th and 4th cents. BC, this was a concern that was both urgent and difficult; in Plato's view, it was philosophy's central task. For that reason, the art of the question-and-answer discussion became in his view the crucial ability of a true philosopher. This understanding of Platonic dialectics corresponds to that of [5]. Others do not want to link Plato's dialectics so closely to the *élenchos*, thus endowing it with philosophy's central mission. However, once that link is loosened, there is hardly anything precise and reconstructible left to say about Plato's understanding of dialectics.

The statement that dialectics were the art of the question-and-answer discussion, became the standard explanation and was even frequently repeated after the beginning of our era. Nevertheless, this definition of dialectics soon became anachronistic, because *élenchoi* lost their status and eventually were no longer practised. Even Plato himself warned of the danger that the elenctic fervour was not employed for the examination of important questions, but degenerated to a mere joke, used only out of the delight of refutation, thus leading to scepticism (Plt. 7,537 e–539 d). When soon thereafter Aristotle set out his own understanding of dialectics in his 'Topics', he still took question-and-answer discussions and their regulations as given; yet regretted that there was a noticeable decrease in the ability to formulate appropriate yes/no-questions (Soph. el. 17,175b 10–14). It seems that this ability survived where it could be used for the deduction of sophisms (cf. e.g. Gell. NA 16,2,1). There are other later indicators, too, pointing to elements of dialogue, such as the strange definition originating from the early Stoa [1] that only those arguments were conclusive, 'in which, provided the premise is conceded to be correct, this concession also seems to lead to the acceptance of the consequences' (S. Emp. adv. math. 8,303 = [3. 1059]). But question-and-answer discussions were no longer used for the prudent examination of assertions. In order to preserve some continuity after the loss of the *élenchoi*, it was possible to refer back to the original purpose of these dialogue games and arrive at the statement that dialectics was the science of true and false; such formulae soon became as common as the standard explanation (cf. e.g. Diog. Laert. 7,42; 62; Cic. Acad. 1,28,91). Still, even then it became necessary to redefine the art of discourse and its place amongst the various forms of intellectual activity, as well as its relation to the central concerns of philosophy.

Aristotle himself still conceives dialectics in relation to *élenchoi*: on the one hand, *élenchoi* are not concerned with scientifically proven statements, but with statements that are as plausible as possible, and with the conclusions to which they lead. Because dialectics is thus concerned with presumptions, Aristotle makes a clear distinction between a dialectic conclusion — independently of its formal logical qualities — and a scientifically proven conclusion (Top. 1,1,100a 25–30); elsewhere, he compares dialectics with rhetoric, its counterpart (Rh. 1,1,1354a 1). On the other hand, in the 'Topics' it is Aristotle's intent, which he himself perceives as novel, to develop a method for elenctic debates which would make it possible successfully to assume both roles in the discussion of any and every topic (Top. 1,1,100a 18–21; 2,101a 25ff.; Soph. el. 34,183a 37–184b 8); furthermore, such a method would be suitable for the detection of errors. Dialectics can thus be described as a prudent and skilful application of this method. In addition, *élenchoi* provide a clarification of our assertions, especially, when methodically supported. In that way, dialectics enriches people's intellectual lives and is therefore given a high rank in Aristotle's opinion of the various intellectual pursuits. [2] However, it is probably for this same reason that he did not develop a particularly close link between dialectics and philosophical competencies and concerns.

However, because of the sparsity of the source material, it is uncertain how one should envisage dialectics in around 300 BC. Undoubtedly, sophisms played a major part; they were developed in the form of questions and answers, and their resolution studied. They were also quite entertaining. Nonetheless, dialectics must have comprised more. The statement of Ariston of Chios [3. 208–215] means that many of the negative effects of dialectical instruction, as feared by Plato, actually occurred; in addition, it implies that this must have been instruction in refutation. Furthermore, the dialecticians around Diodorus Cronus devoted a lot of time and thought to logical topics, and these topics would also have been part of dialectics; they later resurface in the dialectics of the Stoics. Thus the dialectics of this period is richer than initially assumed, but the little information available to date is insufficient to come to a comprehensive understanding of dialectics at that time. The period around 300 BC constitutes a definite gap in the reconstruction of the history of dialectics.

The early Stoa essentially continued with dialectics of Diodorus Cronus and his circle, but with their own motive: as dialectics helps to uncover falsehood, it is of great support to the overall programme of developing a single non-contradictory concept according to which one can live happily—philosophy's ultimate aim in the eyes of the Stoics. For that reason, Zeno of Citium and his successors placed great value on dialectics. Chrysippus reformed the Stoic dialectics and essentially gave it the form in which it is transmitted to us. To judge by its content, it now appears as a new discipline with the status of a more or less comprehensive reflective science, and which claims to be the first to combine and systematically discuss all topic areas concerned with language and argumentation, esp. the philosophy of language, formal logic, and grammar. The fact that this new discipline was called dialectics, harks back to older uses of this term without, however, explaining it sufficiently. Attempts at reconstructing the structure of this new discipline have also only been partially successful. However, as far as the importance of dialectics for philosophy as a whole is concerned, the claim of the Stoic dialectics matches the Platonic one.

The concept of such a comprehensive academic discipline was a new development in the history of science; with it, language became one of the main concerns of philosophy. It seems that the Stoics made very definite statements on this aspect of their dialectics. The report of the Stoics on their dialectics, as transmitted by Diogenes Laertius, ends with a reference to the central role of logic and dialectics in wisdom in general: According to the Stoics, 'all objects were investigated with the help of language-based — discursive or argumentative — theories, irrespective of whether they fell into the field of physics or ethics' (Diog. Laert. 7,83 = [3. 87]). The meaning of this statement seems to be that logic and dialectics are of such importance because the development of theories always takes place in the medium of language, nowhere more so than in philosophy. If this interpretation is correct, then language as a medium of all theories is the constituent factor which unifies this new discipline, and at the same time the reason for the close link between dialectics and wisdom; it ensures 'that the true dialectician is the sage'. The Stoics thus claim an importance for dialectics similar to Plato's, even if it is not quite clear which methods could be used to realize this claim.

→ DIALECTICS

1 TH. EBERT, Dialektiker und frühe Stoiker bei Sextus Empiricus. Untersuchungen zur Entstehung der Aussagenlogik, 1991, 241–245, 288–297 2 J.D.G. EVANS, Aristotle's Concept of Dialectic, 1977 3 K. HÜLSER, Die Fragmente zur D. der Stoiker, 4 vols., 1987 4 E. KAPP, Der Ursprung der Logik bei den Griechen, 1965 5 P. STEMMER, Platons Dialektik. Die frühen und mittleren Dialoge, 1992.

K.-H.H.

Dialogue

A. DEFINITION B. PRECURSORS AND STIMULI C. SOCRATES DIALOGUES D. POST-PLATONIC PERIOD; HELLENISM E. ROMAN PERIOD F. CHRISTIANITY G. SURVIVAL

A. DEFINITION

Dialogue is defined as a prose genre, in which a conversation between several participants is recorded in direct speech. In Greek and Latin literature, this form of representation is mostly used for theoretical debates, particularly philosophical ones. Somewhat lesser developed were the entertaining humorous scenes (see below for Lucian: E. Roman Period), which were close in genre to the → mimos. The most important author of dialogues is Plato; he has been seen throughout as the classic proponent of this genre. In reality, he was very close to its origin, because dialogue as a genre was a creation of the first generation of Socrates' pupils.

B. PRECURSORS AND STIMULI

Historians included dialogues as well as speeches in their narrative: Herodotus 3,80–83 ('constitutional debate') and *passim*, Thucydides 5,84–115 ('Melian Dialogue'). Presumably, conversations of the → Seven Sages were circulating in the 5th cent. BC [10. 197–201]. → Ion of Chios at times reported anecdotes about famous men in the form of conversations. It is uncertain whether the *Homilíai* (ὁμιλίαι) of → Critias were dialogues. The art of conducting oral debates along fixed rules was developed by the Sophists (eristics, main source: Plato, Euthydemus). For Plato, it is noticeable that he imitated the dialogue technique of the comedy, but most of all the mimetic prose of → Sophron.

C. SOCRATES DIALOGUES

According to Aristot. Poet. fr. 72 ROSE), these were first written by Alexamenus of Teos. This is an otherwise unknown author, and the significance of this reference is disputed (cf. POxy 45, no. 3219). Only fragments have survived of dialogues by Aeschines of Sphettus, Euclides of Megara, Phaedon of Elis, Antisthenes *et al.* [8]. Dialogues by → Plato and → Xenophon are extant. Undoubtedly, the main motivation for their creation was the visualization of Socrates' personality and his teachings as a holistic entity. However, the authors did not feel bound by documentary faithfulness, but felt free to include fiction within the framework of the historically possible. Plato endowed this form with a deeper philosophical meaning [5; 7; 11; 14; 20; 21]. It opposes the didactic lectures of the sophists, and demonstrates that knowledge is not merely transferred but acquired by each individual himself—under the encouragement and corrective direction of Socrates. Occasionally, considerable effort has gone into a vivid and vibrant description of the situation (*Symposium*; *Phaedon*; less so e.g. in the *Menon*). On a formal level, a distinction can be made between 'dramatic' and 'diegematic' dialogues (Diog. Laert. 3,50; Plut. Symp. 7,8,1

[17]). The latter have a narrative framework. This may be the original form, as in the *Theaetetus* (143c) this descriptive form is described as cumbersome and replaced with the dramatic one. Plato retained the form of the dialogue, although increasingly frequently interspersed with continuous lectures (an extreme example: *Nomoi*). For him the principle that perception required intersubjective examination may have been important. Later Socratic dialogues by unknown authors have become part of the *Corpus Platonicum* as spurious texts [15].

D. Post-Platonic Period; Hellenism

Of Plato's successors, only → Speusippus wrote dialogues in the definition as described above. However, Aristotle and the Peripatetics cultivated this form and developed it further, but none have survived. Aristotle [3. 294–301; 9. 248–253] wrote at least eight dialogues, the most important of which were *Eudemus* and *De philosophia*. Some of Plato's titles reappear (e.g. *Politikos*). These works were directed at the wider public, and (in contrast with the didactic works) their style was carefully and impressively crafted. Innovations: Aristotle himself appeared as the main speaker (Cic. Att. 13,19, ad Q. fr. 3,5). The individual books were prefaced by prooemia (Cic. Att. 4,16). → Dicaearchus (i.a. 'the descent into Trophonius' cave') and → Heraclides Ponticus (i.a. 'The woman who appeared to be dead') introduced dramatic, entertaining, and even sensational elements into the dialogues, Dicaearchus has critical remarks on the oracular cult, Heraclides scenes from the past centring around Empedocles and Pythagoras, associated with a reawakening from apparent death and subsequent disclosure of the experiences. Aristotle made an appearance in → Clearchus of Soli's 'On Sleep' (Περὶ ὕπνου). → Praxiphanes ('On Poets') had Plato and Isocrates engage in conversation during a visit to Plato's country villa; the intention was presumably to convey the atmosphere of dignified leisure, so beloved by Cicero subsequently. In 'On Old Age' (Περὶ γήρως), → Ariston [3] of Ceos went back into mythical times with an appearance of → Tithonus. → Eratosthenes dealt with mathematical problems in *Platonikos* (Πλατωνικός). → Satyrus wrote a biography of Euripides in dialogue form. These examples show that dialogue became a vehicle for didactic content (Xenophon's *Oikonomikos*).

Another related subject area is the *symposion*. Plato and Xenophon were the first to make conversations at a symposium the subject of a dialogue. Symposia with cultured conversations were namely cultivated in the Academy, and a distinctive → symposium literature in the form of dialogues developed, ranging from parodies such as → Petronius' *Cena Trimalchionis* to the literary-philosophical *Saturnalia* by → Macrobius. Dialogues are also found in the early Cynical authors (Antisthenes, Diogenes of Sinope, Philiscus); → diatribe (Bion) and → satire (Menippus) with strong elements of dialogue can be viewed as offshoots. Dialogues from other philosophical schools: → Hegesias (Cyrenaics), Ἀποκαρτερῶν; → Stilpon (Megarian School); → Timon of Phleius (Sceptics), *Python*, → Antiochus [21] of Ascalon, *Sosus*.

E. Roman Period

The first Latin dialogues were the three books *De iure civili* by M.→ Iunius Brutus: legal instructions of the author for his son in conversations at various country estates; as 'villa dialogues' (cf. Praxiphanes) probably inspiring Cicero. M. Terentius → Varro with his *Res rusticae* also set out a textbook in the form of dialogues. C.→ Scribonius Curio wrote an anti-Caesar dialogue (cf. Cic. Brut. 60,218) as a political pamphlet. It was → Cicero, who then led Latin dialogue literature to its zenith. With reference to Plato (from whom he took titles such as *De re publica* and *De legibus*), but formally rather following Aristotle and Heraclides (longer continuous expositions, prooemia to the books, Aristotelian: the author as lead speaker, Heraclidean: author absent, story often located in the past), he presented Greek philosophy to the Roman world [4. 1021–1023] and also his representation of rhetoric as an art form and a cultural tradition. The dialogue form suited Cicero's sceptical-eclectic attitude and his method of *disputatio in utramque partem*. The narrative framework is that of the circles of an idealized Roman aristocracy, the characters of the various speakers carefully portrayed.

→ Tacitus follows Cicero with his *Dialogus de oratoribus*. → Seneca's *Dialogi*, however, are wrongly designated as such, they are more like diatribes. → Plutarch's dialogues, splendid and vivid in form and content, convey an impression of the lost Peripatetic dialogue. A separate development is noticeable in → Dion [I 3] of Prusa: dialogues with anonymous participants or with mythical characters, some dialogues dealing with philosophy, others portraying only myths. This type of dialogue is thought to derive from rhetorical exercises. It is comparable with → Philostratus' *Heroikos*. → Lucianus could take this as his starting point, but he experimented with various forms of dialogue and created new ones by crossing typical comedy motifs (Prometheus 5–7) with those of the cynical satire of Menippus (Bis accusatus 33). Allegorical characters also make an appearance (e.g. in the *Bis accusatus*). This form of dialogue later became part of the mix of genres of → Boethius' *Consolatio philosophiae*. Didactic works with a dialogical framework are: (Lat.) Macrobius, *Saturnalia*; → Martianus Capella, *De nuptiis Philologiae et Mercurii*; → Fulgentius, *Mythologiae*; (Greek) Ps.-Orpheus, *Lithica*. → Athenaeus' *Deipnosophistai* are part of the → symposium literature.

F. Christianity

In Christian literature, dialogue played an important role, especially as a vehicle for theological debate [22]. G. Bardy [12] distinguishes five types:

1. Apologetic dialogue, initially in the conflict with the Jews: Ariston of Pella (*c.*140, lost); → Justin, *Dialogus cum Tryphone*; → Aeneas of Gaza, *Theophrastus sive de animarum immortalitate* (*c.* 500, against a Neoplatonist); → Minucius Felix, *Octavius* (against pagans, following Cicero).

2. Theological dialogue, in controversies among Christians. Records of a historical disputation: → Origenes, Διάλεκτος πρὸς Ἡρακλείδαν [19]. Origenes, *De resurrectione* [16. 251]; → Methodius of Olympus, *Symposium* (following Plato); → Adamantius, *De recta in deum fide* (anti-Gnostic).

3. Philosophical dialogue: → Bardesanes, 'On Fate' or 'Book of the Laws of the Countries' (Syrian); → Gregorius of Nyssa, *Contra fatum*; *Macrinia De anima et resurrectione* (imitating Plato's *Phaedon*); → Augustinus, several dialogues, esp. from the period of his conversion; the *Soliloquia* introduce a novelty: a conversation of *ratio* personified with Augustinus.

4. Biographical dialogue (from the pre-Christian period only known from Satyrus): → Sulpicius Severus, appendix to *Vita Martini*; → Palladius, *De vita S. Joannis Chrysostomi*; → Gregorius the Great, *De vita et miraculis patrum Italicorum* (4 bks.).

5. Biblical dialogue: according to Socr. 3,16, Apollinaris the Younger supposedly rendered the material of the NT in dialogue form (in reply to Julian's edict on teaching, as a substitute for Platonic dialogues).

G. Survival

During the Middle Ages, the dialogue forms of Christian literature were developed further, noticeably more so in the west than in Byzantium. The special form of dialogue with Jews is particularly firmly established (e.g. Abaelardus, *Dialogus inter philosophum Judaeum et Christianum*). The Renaissance [2] led to a new bloom, esp. in turning to Cicero (see below) and Lucian. During the Reformation, Ulrich von Hutten's dialogues (modelled on Lucian's examples) were very effective journalism. Dialogue was also used in the presentation of scientific problems to a wider audience (Galilei, 'Dialogo sopra i due massimi sistemi del mondo', 1632). The Enlightenment led to a further wave of dialogue literature [6]. After Hegel questioned the value of the dialogue form, it lost validity in the course of the 19th cent. Some recent scientists (e.g. W. Heisenberg, 'Der Teil und das Ganze', 1969) have rediscovered dialogue. 'Dialogical philosophy' (Martin Buber) develops the idea of dialogue to an anthropological category.

→ Dialogue; → Philosophical literature, genres of

1 K. Berger, Hell. Gattungen im NT, in: ANRW II 25.2, 1031–1432 (Dialogue: 1301–1316) 2 V. Cox, The Renaissance dialogue. Literary dialogue in its social and political contexts, Castiglione to Galileo, 1992 3 I. Düring, s.v. Aristoteles, RE Suppl. 11, 159–336 4 H. Flashar (ed.), Die Philos. der Ant., vol. 4, 1994 5 P. Friedländer, Platon, ³1964–1975, I, ch. 8 6 Th. Fries, Dialog der Aufklärung. Shaftesbury, Rousseau, Solger, 1993 7 K. Gaiser, Platone come scrittore filosofico, 1984 8 G. Giannantoni, Socratis et Socraticorum Reliquiae, 1990 9 O. Gigon (ed.), Aristotelis Opera III, 1987 10 Id., Sokrates. Sein Bild in Dichtung und Gesch., ³1994, ch. III 11 H. Gundert, Dialog und Dialektik, 1971 12 A. Hermann, G. Bardy, s.v. D., RAC 3, 928–955 13 R. Hirzel, Der Dialog, Ein lit.-histor. Versuch, 2 vols., 1895 14 J. Laborderie, Le dialogue platonicien de la maturité, 1978 15 C.W. Müller, Die Kurzdialoge der Appendix Platonica, 1975 16 P. Nautin, Origène, 1977 17 O. Nüsser, Albins Prolog und die D.-Theorie des Platonismus, 1991 (Beiträge zur Alt.-Wiss. 12) 18 M. Ruch, Le préambule dans les œuvres philosophiques de Cicéron, Essai sur la genèse et l'art du dialogue, 1958 19 J. Scherer, (ed.), Entretien d'Origène avec Héraclide, 1960 20 M. C. Stokes, Plato's Socratic Conversations. Drama and Dialectic in Three Dialogues, 1986 21 Th. A. Szlezák, Platon lesen, 1993 22 B.R. Voss, Der Dialog in der frühchristl. Lit., 1970 (Studia et Testimonia Antiqua 9) 23 G. Zoll, Cicero Platonis aemulus, 1962.

H.GÖ.

Dialysis (διάλυσις; *diálysis*).

[1] The procedural law of the Greek states was based on the principle of the reconciliation of both parties involved (διαλύειν, *dialýein*). Only after the failure of that step a formal verdict was to decide on the matter. *Dialysis* proceedings thus constituted the first procedural step in 'preliminary proceedings', irrespective of whether heard by a magistrate (→ *anákrisis*) or by public or private → *diaitētaí*, in international arbitration or in proceedings heard by 'foreign judges' called from one or more cities to decide on a case.

[2] In late antiquity, a special form of document evolved in Egypt in Greek as well as Coptic documents: following from the *dialysis* of the arbitration courts, an agreement was set out in the form of a settlement, with the intention of providing more assurance.

A. Steinwenter, Die Streitbeendigung durch Urteil, Schiedsspruch und Vergleich, ²1971 Id., Das byz. D.-Formular, in: Studi Albertoni 1, 1935, 73ff. G. Thür, Formen des Urteils, in: D. Simon (ed.), Akten des 26. Deutschen Rechtshistorikertags, 1987, 472f.

G.T.

Diamartyria (διαμαρτυρία; *diamartyría*). A 'testimonial decision', an archaic procedure different from normal witness evidence: based on the testimony of one or more witnesses, it was an act with formal determining powers, which in Athens was predominantly admissible in administrative proceedings in respect of inheritance. Such proceedings were initiated by someone with a claim to the estate who was not one of the direct heirs. He would apply for the assignment of the estate (→ *epidikasía*). A direct heir would then appear as respondent, and supply evidence for his assertion that the 'estate was not subject to *epidikasia*' (μὴ ἐπίδικον εἶναι τὸν κλῆρον) by means of a *diamartyria*. Exceptionally, it was admissible for an individual to give evidence on his own behalf here. The application of the claimant was then immediately annulled. There is no record of a positive *diamartyria* — i.e. one in favour of the applicant—in any such procedure. It was probably excluded in any case since the direct heir's right to inheritance without official approval (→ *embateúein*) had been violated by the application of the claimant from outside the family to whom the reduced onus of proof had been accorded. It was possible to contest a *diamartyria* with a charge of false or illegal testimony (→ *pseudomartyrías díkē*), but losing such a case had serious consequences (→ *epōbelía*). There is evidence of two cases in which *diamartyria* was employed outside of inheritance disputes (Isoc. Or. 18,15 and Lys. 23,13ff., with evidence of a positive *diamartyria*); in both cases, the *diamartyria* appear before the → *paragraphḗ*.

→ Succession, law of

E. Berneker, s.v. Ψευδομαρτυριῶν δίκη, RE 23, 1372ff.
H.J. Wolff, Die att. Paragraphe, 1966, 106ff. G.T.

Diamastigosis see → Artemis

Diamond see → Precious stones

Diana

A. Name B. Functions C. Cult and cult sites

A. Name

The name *Dĭāna* (in older documents sometimes scanned as *Dīāna*) is derived from *dĭus*, 'light as day, shining'; D. is the 'bright one'. Varro's derivation of the name from Diviana (Ling. 5,68) or Deviana (GRF 226, no. 103) is only of aetiological value.

B. Functions

Little is known about the original nature of the Italian D. As with all of the goddess' other characteristics, her name is laden with Hellenizing interpretations such that one can hardly approach the original form of Diana. D.'s close links with the spheres of the Greek → Artemis (see [1]) facilitated these interpretations. Both Artemis and D. were *phōsphóros* (φωσφόρος, 'Bringer of Light'). This function must be viewed as a general one and is in itself insufficient to classify D. as a moon goddess, but it explains why she could continue to be associated with the moon and also with the goddess → Hecate. Like Artemis, D. was closely linked to the dividing line between the wilderness of nature and the ordered world of the *civitas*; she was a 'goddess of the outside' (Wilamowitz) and offered protection in all situations that in reality or imagination were linked with this 'dividing line'.

Many sources indicate that her sanctuaries and sacred groves were more likely associated with the surrounding territory of towns than the town centres themselves. In Latium, for example, the groves and woodlands of D. were situated outside the towns: in Anagnia, at the crossing of the *via Latina* and the *via Labicana* (Liv. 27,4,12), in the *suburbano Tusculani agri, qui Corne appellatur* (Plin. HN 16,242), on Mons Algidus (Hor. Carm. 1,21,5; Carm. saec. 69), as well as near Tibur (*silva*, Mart. 7,28,1), and esp. near Aricia (*lucus Dianius in nemore Aricino*, Cato fr. 58 Peter; Str. 4,1,4f. et al.). In Rome itself, the documented, apparently ancient, *Diania* (Diana sanctuaries) were located on the Caeliculum (destroyed in 58 BC and rebuilt in 54 as a temple of D. Planciana), on the Esquiline, and in the *vicus patricius*, i.e. rather outside the → Pomerium; the important D. sanctuary on the Aventine was very clearly built outside of the city. Another example is the very ancient D. sanctuary on Mons Tifata to the north of → Capua [2]. The famous rites of the *rex Nemorensis* as well as the tradition concerning Virbius and the Taurian Artemis show that D. was also associated with wild savagery, as is also known of Artemis [3]. As goddess and protectress of the division between 'inside' and 'outside', D. was also venerated as huntress and mistress of animals (*nemorum comes, victrix ferarum*, CIL VIII 9831), and traditionally depicted as such [4]. For that reason, she was often connected with → Silvanus (CIL III 8483; XIII 382), and well into the Imperial period, D. was privately venerated in poetry and dedicatory inscriptions as the goddess of the hunt (e.g. CIL VI 124; II 5638; III 1937). This also explains why she (frequently in conjunction with Silvanus) was invoked by troops stationed at the 'frontier' (e.g. CIL II 2660; III 1000; 3365; VIII 9831).

She also protected girls and women in all exigencies of the female gender (e.g. the fact that in childbirth both mother and child were considered to be under threat from the 'outside' is evident in the rites protecting against persecution by Silvanus, Varr. = Aug. Civ. 6,9). D. thus became one of the important goddesses for women, alongside → Juno and → Venus. As birth goddess. D. often appeared alongside Apollo and Aesculapius (CIL III 986). Two other deities, also venerated in the Nemi grove, were interpreted in a similar way: the nymph → Egeria assisted in childbirth (Fest. p. 67), and Virbius also served his mistress D. on these occasion. Her connection with slaves (*dies natalis*, dedication day, of the Aventine temple was a *servorum dies*), who were outside the circle of the free, is therefore hardly a surprise either (see also CIL V 5668; III 1288; 5657).

C. Cult and cult sites

The cult of D. developed on two levels. On the one hand, she appears in private veneration as the goddess of women and hunters, on the other hand, she was from very early on endowed with a political function, as in Nemi and Rome; the latter was later extended through her relationship with Apollo and e.g. expressed in the celebrations of the *Ludi saeculares*.

Of the *Dianium* in the Roman quarter of *vicus patricius*, it is only known that men were not admitted (Plut. Mor. 264c). On the Ides of August, also the foundation day of the Aventine D. temple, women would carefully comb their hair and then carry torches in a procession to the grove at Nemi in order to keep their vows (Ov. Fast. 3,263; Prop. 2,32,9f.; Stat. 3,1,55f.). In the sanctuary itself, votive offerings (vulvae, phalli, mothers with babies, arms, legs, hands etc.) have been found, as well as inscriptions that hint at such vows (e.g. CIL I² 2,42; 45). Elsewhere, too, D. was often venerated by women (CIL V 2086; XI 6298; II 5387; VIII 8201), frequently together with their husbands and families (CIL VI 132; XI 1211; 3552; III 1154). In her role as a goddess for women, she was invoked as a protectress of the family (CIL VI 131; 135; XI 3552). Dedications by hunters, often *collegia venatorum* or *iuvenes*, are also more private in character (CIL V 3222; X 5671; XI 2720; 3210; 5262; II 2660; XIII 1495).

From the beginning of the Republic, D. was also venerated as a goddess of the state, as the mistress of the grove at Nemi, meeting-place of the Latin League [5], and in Rome in the temple on the Aventine. The grove at Nemi had been dedicated by a dictator of the Latin League in *c.* 500 BC [6]. The three-figured cultic statue points to Campanian influence [7]. Within the grove was a D. temple as well as other buildings, i.a. a chapel dedicated to Isis. In the Imperial period, a theatre and baths were built alongside the cultic terrace [8]. Nothing is known about the exact proceedings of these rites apart from a single reference regarding the *rex Nemorensis*, the priest of the grove (?), who had to kill his predecessor in office (Str. 5,3,12; Serv. Aen. 6,136 et al.). According to tradition (Liv. 1,45; Dion. Hal. Ant. Rom. 4,25,6ff.), the Aventine temple, founded by → Servius Tullius in *c.* 540 BC and modelled on the Artemisium in Ephesus ('community sanctuary'), originally had no connection with the grove near Aricia. According to Strabo (4,1,4f.) the cult statue resembled the *xóanon* ('cult image') of Artemis of Massilia, which once again points to Ephesus [9]. In the archaic period, the temple was not a Latin federal sanctuary, but an ancient Roman cult site, set up as an asylum sanctuary after the example of Massilia-Ephesus [10]. Later it was assigned its new role (e.g. Varro, Ling. 5,43). The statute of the temple is extant (*lex arae Dianae in Aventino*), to which other statutes refer (CIL IX 361; XII 433; III 1933).

In parallel with the development of the Apollo cult in Rome, as his mythical sister, D. also gained greater honour. At the *lectisternium* (cultic feast for the gods) of 399 BC, they formed one of the divine pairs. A further temple for D. was built in 179 BC near to the Circus Flaminius, and rebuilt by Octavian after his victory over Sextus Pompeius at Naulochus; on the same occasion, the legionary legate L. Cornificius restored the Aventine temple, which was henceforth called the temple of Diana Cornificiana. Under Augustus, D. was generally venerated in conjunction with Apollo. A cult statue of D. stood in the Apollo temple, together with Apollo D. was among the deities celebrated in the secular games, and together with him had several altars and temples both in Rome (CIL VI 33; 35) and the provinces (CIL II 964). As a goddess for hunters and women as well as Apollo's sister, she was venerated across the entire Roman empire. D. was also occasionally used for the *interpretatio* of foreign deities (e.g. Abnoba, Arduinna, Caelestis).

→ Apollo; → Artemis

1 GRAF 2 A. DE FRANCISCIS, Templum Dianae Tifatinae, 1965 3 F. GRAF, Das Götterbild aus dem Taurerland, in: Antike Welt 10, 1979, 33–41 4 E. SIMON, s.v. Artemis/ D., LIMC 2.1, 792–855 5 C. AMPOLO, Boschi sacri e culti federali: l'esempio del Lazio, in: Les bois sacrés (Collection du Centre Jean-Bérard, 10), 1993, 103–110 6 Id., Ricerche sulla lega Latina. II. La dedica di Egerius Baebius (Cato fr. 58 PETER), in: PdP 212, 1983, 321–326 7 F.-H. PAIRAULT, D. Nemorensis, déesse latine, déesse hellénisée, in: MEFRA 81, 1969, 425–471 (with bibliography) 8 F. COARELLI, I santuari del Lazio in età repubblicana, 1987, 165–185 9 C. AMPOLO, L'Artemide di Marsiglia e la D. dell'Aventino, in: PdP 25, 1970, 200–210 10 M. GRAS, Le temple de Diane sur l'Aventin, in: REA 89, 1987, 47–61.

TH. BLAGG, Mysteries of D. The Antiquities from Nemi in Nottingham Museums, 1983; Id., Le mobilier archaïque du sanctuaire de Diane nemorensis, in: Les bois sacrés, 1993, 103–110; G. RADKE, Zur Entwicklung der Gottesvorstellung und der Gottesverehrung in Rom, 1987, 160–172; R. SCHILLING, Rites, cultes, dieux de Rome, 1979, 371–388; G. WISSOWA, Religion und Kultus der Römer, ²1912, 247–252. J.S.

Diana Veteranorum Town in Numidia, north-northwest of Lambaesis, mod. Aïn Zana. Documentary evidence: It. Ant. 34,3 (*Diana*); 35,4 (*Diana Veteranorum*); Tab. Peut. 3,1 (*ad Dianam*). The town, which was probably only founded in Roman times, started out as a very simple settlement with a community council (CIL VIII 1, 4587, AD 141) and was only elevated to a *municipium* in AD 162 (CIL VIII 1, 4589; 4599). From the mid 3rd cent., a bishop resided in Diana Veteranorum (Cypr. epist. 34,1). Inscriptions: CIL VIII 1, 4575–4625; Suppl. 2, 18646–18653; AE 1956, 40–42 no. 124; [1].

1 Bull. Archéologique du Comité des Travaux Historiques 1930f., 49–55; 1932f., 432–440, 467–473.

AAAlg, sheet 27, no. 62. W.HU.

Dianium Small island in the *mare Tyrrhenum* opposite → Cosa in Etruria, named Artemisia by the Greeks because of its crescent shape (Plin. HN 3,81), mod. Giannutri (Prov. Grosseto). Roman *villa*.

R.C. BRONSON, G. UGGERI, in: Studii etruschi 36, 1970, 201–214; BTCGI 8, 108–114. G.U.

Diapsephismos, diapsephisis (διαψηφισμός, διαψήφισις; *diapsēphismós*, *diapsḗphisis*). Literally, a ballot using pebbles to select alternatives. Both terms were occasionally used to designate votes in legal proceedings (e.g. Xen. Hell. 1,7,14; cf. the verb *diapsēphízesthai* e.g. in Antiph. 5,8). In Athens, however, they refer specifically to ballots with the purpose of confirming or refuting the citizenship of people who at a certain time laid claim to that right. That happened in 510 BC, when the tyranny of the Peisistratids ([Aristot.] Ath. Pol. 13,5: *diapsēphismós*) was overthrown, again 445/4 in conjunction with grain distribution (schol. Aristoph. Vesp. 718 uses *diakrínein*), and also in 346/5 (Aeschin. 1,77; Dem. Or. 57,26: *diapsḗphisis*); on the occasion of this latest *diapsephisis*, both Demosthenes (Or. 57) and Isaeus (Or. 12) wrote speeches. In 346/5, and presumably also in 445/4, the ballot was held in the *dḗmoi*. The decrees of the Demotionidae (IG II[2] 1237) used *diadikasía* for a similar procedure in conjunction with a *phratria*.

→ Demes; → Psephos P.J.R.

Diaspora The term diaspora (Greek διασπορά; *diasporá*, 'scattering') refers to Israelite or rather Jewish settlements outside Palestine. The main reason for their formation was the → deportation of the population as a consequence of military conquest; but alongside that, flight for political reasons, emigration in response to economic hardships, as well as expansion of trade also played a part. Despite considerable cultural differences, the country of Israel and in particular the temple in Jerusalem were the central focus of all of these communities, concretely expressed in the payment of the temple tax.

Babylonia and Egypt were the most important Jewish centres of the ancient world, where Jews lived with various degrees of self-government and the right to practice their religion and observe its laws. Other important diasporan centres were Cyrenaica, North Africa, Cyprus, Syria, Asia Minor, the offshore island of Chios, Samos etc., and finally Greece and Rome.

The Egyptian diaspora, dating back to the immediate pre-exile or exile period (cf. 2 Kg. 25,26) and according to Philo (In Flaccum 43) comprising a million people, had its centre in → Alexandria [1]. A fertile interchange with Greek culture ensued, eventually (from about the 3rd cent. BC) bringing forth the Septuagint, the Greek translation of the Hebrew → Bible. Between AD 115 and 117, there were uprisings in North Africa, Cyrenaica, Egypt, Cyprus, and parts of Syria, the beginning of the decline of the Hellenistic Jewish diasporan culture.

The Babylonian diaspora, dating back to the time of the Bablylonian exile (cf. the events of 598/7, 587/6, with 2 Kg 24,12–16; 25,1–21), and of whose first centuries little is known, experienced a significant influx of refugees who had to leave Israel after the failed uprising of → Bar Kochba (AD 132–135). From the period of the → Amoraim to the high Middle Ages, numerous scholars, working particularly in the cities of Neharde'a, Sūra, and Pumbedita, made Babylonia the spiritual and religious centre of Judaism (cf. also the formation of the Babylonian Talmud, whose final form probably dates to the 6th cent.). Polemic disputes between the scholars of the diaspora and those of Israel itself are evidence of the rivalry which existed between these communities.

→ Exilarch

A. Kasher, s.v. D. I/2. Frühjüd. und rabbinische Zeit, TRE 8, 711–717; J. Maier, Zw. den Testamenten. Gesch. und Rel. in der Zeit des zweiten Tempels, Die Neue Echter Bibel, Ergänzungsband zum Alten Testament 3, 1990; E. Schürer, The History of the Jewish People in the Age of Jesus Christ III/1, 1986, 1–176 (all with extended bibliography). B.E.

Diatessaron (τὸ διὰ τεσσάρων [εὐαγγέλιον]; *tò dià tessárōn [euangélion]*). The Diatessaron is the earliest extant harmonization of the gospels, dating back to Tatian, who in the latter third of the 2nd cent. combined the four canonical gospels into one homogenous presentation by embedding the synoptic tradition within the chronological framework of the gospel of John. He also used some apocryphal material and furthermore showed his encratitic, anti-Jewish, and docetic (→ Docetics) leanings.

Whether the Diatessaron was originally written in Greek or Syriac, in Rome or in → Syria, remains as unclear as whether it was written before or after Tatian's break with the Roman Church. Despite its wide distribution and considerable effect and influence, not a single manuscript has survived. A fragmentary reconstruction is possible with the help of quotes from the Diatessaron in → Aphrahat and in → Ephraim's commentary on the Diatessaron. Extant Arabic and Persian translations are based on Syrian originals and show evidence of considerable revision. The very early Latin translation is also lost. In 1933, the first papyrus fragment dating from before AD 234 was discovered in → Dura Europus. The Diatessaron was used in the liturgy of the Syrian Church into the 5th cent. and directly influenced the Syrian text of the gospels. It is uncertain whether the Diatessaron was a model for the Western gospel text or merely a very early piece of evidence.

→ Apocryphal literature; → Tatianus

C. Peters, Das D. Tatians (Orientalia Christiana analecta 123), 1939; R. M. Grant, Tatian and the Bible (Texts and research on the history of Early Christian literature 63), 1967; J. Molitor, Tatians D. und sein Verhältnis zur altsyr. und altgeorg. Überlieferung, in: Oriens Christianus 53, 1969, 1–88; 54, 1970, 1–75; 55, 1971, 1–61. K.SA.

Diatheke (διαθήκη; *diathḗkē*).

A. Meaning and essence B. Age and history of origins C. Transmitted documents D. Power and freedom of testation E. Form of the testament F. Safekeeping G. Delineation from adoption H. Content of the Diatheke I. Reading of the will J. Alteration and revocation of the Diatheke

A. Meaning and essence

The *diatheke* represents Greek law's central instrument for testate succession. The word is derived from διατίθεσθαι (*diatíthesthai*): the 'putting aside' of items of personal possession by the testator for persons who did not belong to the family household (οἶκος, *oîkos*) and thus could not be legal heirs. *Diatheke*, somewhat fuzzily translated as 'testament', describes the act of disposal itself as well as the associated document. Its purpose was to order the proprietary and family affairs after the death of the testator, sometimes also in the form of testamentary contracts between the parties concerned [3. 189]. The meaning of 'covenant' in the biblical sense can be disregarded here.

B. Age and history of origins

The origins of the Greek testament are disputed. The existence of two roots is assumed: the testate disposition of individual components of a testator's assets (bequests) or the clarification of the entire position of the testator in respect of sacral and proprietary law in the absence of direct male descendants (testate succession). Such procedures were instituted in Magna Graecia even before the 6th cent. BC (Pl. Leg. 922e). In Athens, Solon specified testate succession in his laws on inheritance (Dem. Or. 46,14) [4. 151f.]. He, too, accepted the basic principle that testation was only admissible in the absence of legitimate sons. Sons were the natural heirs. New additions were probably the regulations barring adoptive sons from testation and stipulating that a *diatheke* must be set up of the testator's own free will. The freewill clause — temporarily removed from inheritance law by the Thirty (→ Triakonta) in order to ease the burden of public courts in dealing with private legal disputes (Aristot. Ath. Pol. 31) — became, with slight variations in the wording, a fixed component of testamentary formulae. In Sparta, *diatheke* was only introduced by a *rhetra* (law) of the ephor Epitadeus in *c.* 400 BC (Plut. Agis 5); it was unknown in the Gortyn law code, as this had not progressed beyond the archaic level of a substitute instrument, i.e. the *donatio mortis causa* (a gift in prospect of death). Both Doric states had long operated a system of inalienable grants of land, which precluded the power of testation [5. 128ff.]. Plato recognized a testament with certain restrictions.

C. Transmitted documents

A large number of Greek *diathēkai* are preserved verbatim in Diogenes Laertius (the philosophers' testaments), also in inscriptions and papyri (documentary evidence [6. 111f.]).

D. Power of testation and freedom of testation

Only a legally capable person could institute a *diatheke*, i.e. a slave could not, but a foreigner could. Power of testation was linked to the age of majority, which differed in individual Greek cities. Solon's law denied legal capacity to those impaired by insanity, old age, drugs, disease, under the influence of a woman, and also to a testator who found himself in a predicament, especially if he signed under the threat of personal execution by his creditors. Limited power of testation was granted in Alexandria to freedpersons of citizens, in Attica generally to women, who could only testate up to the value of one bushel of barley (Isaeus 10,10), for anything more she required the assistance of her guardian (→ Kyrios) [1. 307]. The right to set up a *diatheke* was temporarily suspended for those liable to account until their accounts were settled (Aeschin. In Ctes. 21). In Egypt, children of a marriage with a written contract also had only limited power of testation, inasmuch as they could not testate as long as their father was alive [7]. The testator's freedom of will with respect to his dispositions was only curtailed by the rights of his children to a statutory share in his estate [1. 197f.].

E. Forms of testament

There was no compulsory provision in Greece for a testament to be of a certain form. Originally, the last will and testament was given orally by the testator in person in the presence of witnesses (whose number was not subject to legal regulation, but it is likely that it became customary from early on, maybe even in the pre-Solonic period, to commit a testament to writing. In Egypt, too, there were no legal provisions for the testator to write the will in his own hand or to sign a copy. Recording a will in written form ensured the preservation of evidence and also made it easier to keep the contents secret, because the witnesses named in the document were generally not informed about the content of the *diatheke (*Isaeus 4,13); they only had to witness the fact that a testament had been written. The document was sealed by the testator and the witnesses in order to prevent tampering. In Egypt, a *diatheke* always had to be arranged before a notary, either through an oral declaration which was then officially recorded or by delivery of the actual document. The *diatheke* had thus evolved from a simple record of evidence to a dispositive document [1. 315].

F. Safekeeping

In Athens, the testator handed the sealed testament for safekeeping either to a trustee (Isaeus 9,5. 6,7) or to an official body, e.g. the city magistrates (*astynomoi*, Isaeus 1,15). In Egypt, Greek testaments were always lodged with an official body for safekeeping.

G. Delineation from adoption

A testator could arrange in his testament for the posthumous adoption of his chosen heir, and even in the absence of such clause, an heir could apply for admission to the *phratria* of the deceased testator, but in Athens at least, adoption and testation were clearly distinct legal transactions. For soldiers' wills of the Ptolemaic period, see [1. 12f, 407].

H. Content of the Diatheke

There were no specific rules governing the nomination of one or more heirs (κληρονόμοι, *klēronómoi*); in particular, there was no requirement for testate succession to be set out explicitly (exemplary in Diog. Laert. 10,16). It was also possible to appoint a substitute heir (POxy. 490,5) as well as providing for subrogation.

There was no strict distinction between the appointment of heirs and the making of bequests, because a legatee is also at times referred to as *klēronómos*. Individual objects or groups of assets as well as entitlements could be the subject of legacies, which the legatee could receive immediately from the testator. The distinction between a real *legatum per vindicationem* and a *legatum per damnationem,* which established a legal claim, was foreign to the Greek legal system. Sometimes certain conditions were included, but it is not clear for Athens how compliance was enforced [2. 980]; in Greek-Egyptian law, by contrast, non-compliance carried the threat of legal punishment [1. 372]. Finally, Greek testaments also contain manumissions as well as the nomination of guardians and executors. Testaments remain noticeably uniform from the period of the Attic orators through to the end of the Byzantine epoch.

I. Reading of the will

In Athens, a testator could remove his testament from safekeeping at any time, open it, and then reseal it. After his death, the keeper of the testament opened it on his own initiative or on that of one of the parties concerned. Witnesses who were still alive when the will was opened may have also been consulted or present. In Egypt, the testator had to submit a special application to the relevant authorities if he wanted to reopen his will. After the death of a testator, one of the concerned parties had to apply for the will to be read, which then took place in an official audience in the presence of all concerned parties and the majority of surviving witnesses (who had to verify their seals); an official copy was then made, the original resealed and deposited in the archives ([1. 399f.], BGU XII 2244).

J. Alteration and revocation of a Diatheke

A testator could, even without particular testamentary proviso, alter or revoke his *diatheke* at any time up to his death. By contrast, it was presumably not permitted unilaterally to revoke a joint testament, such as those evident in the papyri (cf. POxy. 75,15). A *diatheke* was altered or revoked by a later one which, however, had to refer explicitly to the revocation of the earlier one, otherwise they were assumed to be jointly valid. Furthermore, in Attic as well as Greek law, a *diatheke* could be revoked by removal from safekeeping. For the procedure for revocation according to the laws on papyri, see [1. 392f.].

→ Succession, law of; → Legatum; → Testament

1 H. Kreller, Erbrechtliche Untersuchungen auf Grund der graeco-ägypt. Papyrusurkunden, 1919 2 E.F. Bruck, Totenteil und Seelgerät im griech. Recht, [2]1970 3 B. Kübler, s.v. D., RE 5, 966–985 4 A.R.W. Harrison, The Law of Athens I, 1968, 149ff. 5 G. Thür, Armut. Gedanken zu Ehegüterrecht und Familienvermögen in der griech. Polis, in: D. Simon (ed.), Eherecht und Familiengut, 1992, 121ff. 6 H.-A. Rupprecht, Einführung in die Papyruskunde, 1994, 111f. 7 P.M. Meyer, Juristische Papyri, 1920. G.T.

Diatribe

A. Concept B. Older diatribes C. Christian diatribes

A. Concept

Diatribe is a modern concept which owes its existence to the fact that, based on Wilamowitz's [3] formal description of the Cynic → Teles' popular-philosophical 'sermons' (3rd cent.BC), Usener [1. LXIX] and Wendland [2] introduced for these 'diatribe' as a generic term. It has stood the test of time, as long as it is taken as a kind of ancient *dialexis* (first in [4]); originally as a synonym of *dialogos, dialexis* referred to any kind of conversation, but in the usage of philosophers and rhetors, it then came to mean a didactic, but also entertaining, lecture with specific formal elements such as questions and objections fabricated by the speaker and not arising from the audience itself in the actual delivery (*fictivus interlocutor*). Thus, a diatribe is a popular-philosophical *dialexis* and not an original literary genre, but a 'presentational style', which could also be referred to as *homilia* or *sermo*.

1 H. Usener, Epicurea, 1887 2 P. Wendland, Philo und die kynisch-stoische D., in: P. Wendland, O. Kern (ed.), Beitr. zur Gesch. der griech. Philos. und Religion, 1895, 3–75 3 U.v. Wilamowitz-Moellendorf, Antigonos von Karistos, 1881, 292–319 4 O. Halbauer, De diatribis Epicteti, 1911. K.U.

B. Older diatribes

There is documentary evidence that Διατριβαί (*Diatribaí*) was used as a title for the works of Bion of Borysthenes (Diog. Laert. 2,77) and those of Epictetus (subscriptiones of the MSS, but not in Arrian's letter of dedication). The term *diatribḗ* (διατριβή) is ambiguous. From 'pastime', one can derive 'occupation (of a non-vocational or non-political nature)', specifically 'philosophical activities within a circle of like-minded participants', and concretely 'philosophical exposition or presentation' (e.g. Pl. Ap. 37d; Plut. De facie 19,929b). Apart from Bion and Epictetus, writings with the title *diatribaí* were attributed to quite a number of philosophers after Aristippus [3] of Cyrene (Diog. Laert. 2,84) [5]. Certain, almost stereotypically applied, elements are considered typical. Form: short paratactic sentences; simple or even vulgar or coarse language; emphatic accentuation with the help of certain stylistic means (antithesis parallelisms, isokola); affected syntax (rhetorical questions, exclamations); dialogical elements (objections by an anonymous partner, often introduced by a subjectless 'said he' (φησίν, *inquit*); prosopopoeia of abstracts); polemic and ironic idioms; comparisons taken from nature and everyday life; citation of well-known (including mythical) persons; quotations, preferably in verse form, sometimes parodied; anecdotes and exemples. Content: ethical questions of everyday life such as wealth and poverty, gossiping, nosiness, marriage, friendship, misfortune, and death. The tendency is rather Cynical or Stoic: the natural is recommended as opposed to convention and luxury; opposing affects, a search for gratification and fear of death (list of topics in [6. 44–65 and 263–292]). Diatribes were restricted in duration; being true to life takes precedence over ethical theory. For the social context and the self-image of those popular philosophers, who from the 1st to 3rd cent. AD were the predominant users of the diatribe as a form of speech, see [11]; in the early Christian context, the evolution from itinerant preacher to resident teacher and preacher must be added. For Latin texts, the term diatribe — apart from its use in reference to satire [7; cf. 8] and Lucretius [10; cf. 8. 36–37] — is most appropriate for Seneca's letters [8. 69–75, passim; 11–12]. 2. No coherent texts of the earliest author of diatribes — → Bion of Borysthenes — are extant, but some from his successor → Teles are preserved. A papyrus of the 2nd cent. BC contains a dialogue and a letter, both in the manner of a diatribe (MH 16, 1959, 77–139). Particular developments are the iambs of → Phoenix of Colophon and → Cercidas as well as the peculiar writings by → Menippus of Gadara, characterized by a mixture of the serious and the comic (σπουδογέλοιον), of prose and verse, and an element of mimicry and dialogue. Menippus' influence (→ Varro) and that of the diatribe in general on Roman satire are much discussed [7]. 3. In Roman times, the diatribe was predominantly used by the Stoics, resulting in diatribes gaining in seriousness and weight. In a pure form, it can be found in → Musonius Rufus, more school-related in → Epictetus. Elements of diatribes in authors of other literary genres: → Seneca, → Dion of Prusa, → Plutarchus, → Maximus of Tyrus, → Lucianus.

5 H.D. Jocelyn, Diatribes and sermons, in: Liverpool Classical Monthly 7, 1982, 3–7 (cf. also H.B. Gottschalk ibid. 91–92) 6 A. Oltramare, Les origines de la d. romaine, 1926 7 E.G. Schmidt, D. und Satire, Wiss. Zschr. der Univ. Rostock 15, 1966, 507–515 8 St. K. Stowers, The D. and Paul's Letter to the Romans, 1981 9 J. Hahn, Der Philosoph und die Ges., 1989 10 B.P. Wallach, A History of the D. from its Origin up to the First Century B.C. and a Study of the Influence of the Genre upon Lucretius, 1974 11 W. Trillitzsch, Senecas Beweisführung, 1962, 18–23 12 H. Cancik, Unt. zu Senecas epistulae morales, 1976.

H.GÖ.

C. Christian diatribes

It is striking that the diatribe as a rhetorical form influenced Christian → sermons and theological tractates so deeply. Traces are already present in the NT (Paul's address to the Areopagus, Acts 17; parts of the genuine Pauline epistles [13; 14; 15]). Apart from rudimentary studies on Tertullian [17] and Augustinus [18; 19], there is as yet no comprehensive investigation of Latin texts. In individual cases (e.g. Augustine) it is very difficult to determine in which tradition a text is rooted. For example, the influence of Gorgian rhetorical figures of speech [19. 367–368] has to be taken into account, i.e. elementary rhetorical tools of which every late antique person of average education would have been aware. It is understandable that some essentially cynical topics are absent from Christian texts and that certain stylistic means such as irony are generally avoided, with the exception of → Tertullianus (esp. *De pallio*). As the Bible became the main source of maxims and comparisons (*synkriseis*), quotations from poets — even in the NT (1 Cor. 15,33: Menander; Tit 1,12: Epimenides; Acts 17,28: Arator) — become comparatively rare (e.g. Aug. Serm. 105,10: Verg. Aen. 1,278f.); The same applies to historical exemples. On the other hand, as in pagan texts, one finds plays on words and comparisons drawn from the life of farmers, fishermen, soldiers, sailors, athletes etc. Even in the pagan context, the rhetorical concept of the thesis [21] — because of its connection with the dialectical method [13. 31f.] — fails fully to embrace the phenomenon of the diatribe as the rhetorical form used by dogmatic popular philosophers; this applies even more to Christian sermons and tractates with their dogmatic roots, which also determined their protreptic and paraenetic imperatives.

→ Diatribe

13 St. K. Stowers, The D. and Paul's Letter to the Romans, 1981 14 Th. Schmeller, Paulus und die D., 1987 15 C.J. Classen, Paulus und die ant. Rhet., in: ZNTW 82, 1991, 1–33 (research report) 16 E.G. Schmidt, D. und Satire, in: Wiss. Zschr. Univ. Rostock 15, 1966, 507–515 17 J. Geffcken, Kynika und Verwandtes, 1909, 58–138 18 M.I. Barry, St. Augustine the Orator, 1924 19 Chr. Mohrmann, Études sur le latin des chrétiens 1, ²1961, 323–349; 351–370; 391–402 20 M. Bernhard, Der Stil des Apuleius von Madaura, 1927 (repr. 1965) 21 H. Throm, Die Thesis, 1932 22 K. Berger, Hell. Gattungen im NT, in: ANRW II 25.2, 1031–1432 (D.: 1124–1132) 23 R. Bultmann, Der Stil der paulinischen Predigt und die kynisch-stoische D., 1910 24 W. Capelle, H.I. Marrou, s.v. D., RAC 3, 990–1009 25 B.P. Wallach, Epimone and D.: Dwelling on the Point in Ps.-Hermogenes, in: RhM 123, 1980, 272–322 26 P. Wendland, Die hell.-röm. Kultur, ²³1912 (Hb. zum NT 1, 2/3), 75–96. 27 Norden, Kunstprosa.

K.U.

Diaulos (δίαυλος; *díaulos*) 'double flute' and by analogy 'double run'; Greek athletic event, run over two lengths of the stadium or about 385 m overall [1. 69f.]. To prevent the runners on the outermost track from being disadvantaged during the relatively short distance, each runner had a separate turning-post and the neighbouring track was kept free for the second lap [2. 106–110; 3]. In this way the number of actual starting places was half the number of those actually available. A central turn as at Dolichus would inevitably have caused scrimmages and fouls. At Olympia the *diaulos* seems to have been introduced for the 14th Olympiad in 724 BC (Africanus, Olympionicarum Fasti 7 Rutgers; Philostr. Gymn. 12). Good *stadion* runners were generally also successful *diaulos* runners [4. nos. 45, 50, 54], many recording double victories at Olympia [e.g. 1. 74]. The fifteen victories the sprinter (σταδιοδρόμος) Dandis of Argos achieved at the

Nemean Games can only be understood as including the *diaulos* [5. no. 15]. Pausanias (5,17,6) introduces a *diaulos* to account for the boustrophedon inscriptions on the Cypselus Chest.
→ Dolichus; → Cypselus Chest

1 W. Decker, Sport in der griech. Ant., 1995
2 R. Patrucco, Lo sport nella Grecia antica, 1972
3 P. Aupert, Athletica I: Epigraphie archaïque et morphologie des stades anciens, in: BCH 104, 1980, 309–315
4 L. Moretti, Iscrizioni agonistiche greche, 1953
5 J. Ebert, Epigramme auf Sieger an gymnischen und hippischen Agonen, 1972.

J. Jüthner, F. Brein, Die athletischen Leibesübungen der Griechen II 1, 1968, 102–105; I. Weiler, Der Sport bei den Völkern der Alten Welt, ²1988, 151f. W.D.

Diazoma see → Theatre

Dibon The village of Dhiban, 4 km north of the Arnon, has retained the name of the nearby Dibon of antiquity, one claimed by two of the Israelite tribes: Gad (Num. 32,34) and Ruben (Josh. 13,17). A stele, the Moabite Stone, with an inscription of Mesha' king of Moab (TUAT 1, 646–650; cf. 2 Kg. 3,4), was found here in 1868, confirming it as Moabite from the 9th cent. BC (Num. 21,30; Isa. 15,2; Jer. 48,18; 22). Apart from some remains of the Early Bronze Age, excavations revealed an Iron Age settlement, most of which has been obliterated by later Nabataean, Roman and Byzantine building on the site.
→ Judah and Israel; → Royal inscriptions; → Moab; → Moabite

A. D. Tushingham et al., Excavations at Dibon (Dhiban), AASO 36/37, 1964; AASO 40, 1972. R.L.

Dicaea (Δίκαια; *Díkaia*). This colony of → Eretria was probably founded in the middle of the 6th cent. BC with the help of Peisistratus; it lay east of Aineia in the interior, probably near Trilofo. As late as the early years of the Peloponnesian War it was a member of the → Delian League. It was able to keep its autonomy into the first half of the 4th cent., becoming Macedonian no later than 349/8. Its later history is unknown.

F. Papazoglou, Les villes de Macédoine à l'époque romaine, 1988, 202; D. Viviers, Pisistratus' Settlement on the Thermaic Gulf: a Connection with the Eretrian Colonization, in: JHS 107, 1987, 193–195; M. Zahrnt, Olynth und die Chalkidier, 1971, 181f. M.Z.

Dicaearchus (Δικαίαρχος; *Dikaíarchos*) from Messene (in Sicily [1. 43]), student of → Aristotle.
A. Life B. Works C. Theory of the soul
D. Social-political theory

A. Life
D. (born *c.* 375 BC?) spent a part of his life in the Peloponnese (Cic. Att. 6,2,3; fragments and testimonials in [1]; list of writings in [2]). As with other early

Peripatetics, the breadth of D.'s interests is remarkable; Varro (Rust. 1,2,6) and Pliny (HN 2,162) describe him as 'highly learned', Cicero (Att. 6,2,3) as 'very well instructed' (ἱστορικώτατος).

B. Works
A work on the history of culture entitled 'The life of Greece' (Βίος Ἑλλάδος, *Bíos Helládos*) began with a Golden Age, which was followed by a pastoral age. It included mythological materials from Greece but also from Babylonia and Egypt. D. wrote biographies of Pythagoras and Plato as well as works on Homer and Alcaeus. His introductory comments ('hypotheses') on the dramas of Sophocles and Euripides seem to have mainly treated the details of staging. The relationship to later information about the content of Euripidean drama is disputed (see [3] and the notes there). His works on drama and music competitions were an important source for later scholars. D. also significantly contributed to the development of mathematical geography; he divided the inhabited world with a straight line running from the Pillars of Hercules to the Himalayas (Agathemerus, Geogr. inform. Proem. 5 = fr. 110 Wehrli). The treatise on the height of mountains in the Peloponnese (the Suda s.v. Dikaiarchos = Fr. 1 Wehrli) probably was a part of the general geographical treatise rather than an independent work ([1. 75], but cf. [4. 538]). The texts that are attributed to D. in GGM 1,97–110 and 1,238–243 are false [1. 80; 5. 562f.].

C. Theory of the soul
According to reports from antiquity (fr. 5–12 Wehrli), D. either denied the existence of the soul or claimed that it should be defined as 1) a 'harmony' of the four elements, 2) nothing more than the body in a particular state, 3) a force located in such a body. The latter two definitions, from Cic. Tusc. 1,10,21 (which quotes a dialogue by D. set in Corinth) and S. Emp. 1–7,349, are probably the closest approximation to D.'s theories [6]. However, the significance of 'harmony' was probably conferred upon D. in the doxographic tradition since Aristoxenus, while the view of a harmony of the four elements or primary qualities (Nemesius, De natura hominum 2,17,10 Morani) derives from a theory discussed by Plato (Phd. 86a-d, 92a–94e). The relationship of D.'s thesis in terms of chronology and content to that of Aristotle, who rejected the theory of harmony (An. 1,4), is disputed [6; 7; 8]. Atticus (fr. 7,10 des Places) and Nemesius (De natura hominum 2,17,10 Morani) link D. to Aristotle himself since both deny the substantiality of the soul. However, this criticism is based on a Platonic bias, and D.'s perspective is perhaps not far removed from a functionalist interpretation of Aristotle's position (see also → Alexander [26] of Aphrodisias). D. certainly denied any immortality of the soul (Cic. Tusc. 1,31,77 quoted his 'Lesbian Dialogue' on this point).

Reports (Diels, DG p. 416,1; 639,27) that D., like Aristotle, explained soothsaying in dreams and prophetic inspiration with the soul's share in the divine can be derived from the concept of nature as a whole being divine (e.g., Aristot. Somn. 463 b 14ff.). Assumptions in Cic. (Div. 1,50,113; 2,48,100) that the soul separates from the body during sleep perhaps reflect a transfer of Cratippus' opinion on D. ([1. 46], but cf. [9]). D.'s writings also included a work on the oracle of Trophonius.

D. Social-political theory

In the *Tripolitikos*, D. developed a theory of a mixed constitution that Plato () and Aristotle (Pol. 2,6,1265b 33) had already applied to Sparta: it unites elements of monarchy, aristocracy and democracy and therefore is superior to each of them. This theory was applied to Rome by Polybius (6,11,11) and Cicero (Rep. 1,69–70; 2,65), but whether D. was the source is uncertain (cf. [1. 65f.], also [10; 11]). The *Tripolitikos* is perhaps identical with a work on the Spartan constitution [1. 64]; the existence of works on the constitutions of Corinth, Athens and Pellene is doubtful [1. 64f.]. The work 'On the Sacrifice at Troy' was perhaps a criticism of Alexander the Great [2. 761].

Cicero portrays D. as a representative of the active life (Att. 2,16,3) even though D. defends the contemplative life against Theophrastus. The debate already reflects passages preserved in Aristot. Eth. Nic. 10,7–8. A work 'On the Destruction of Humans' contained the assumption (Cic. Off. 2,5,16) that humans are more threatened by other humans than by anything else.

→ Alexander [26]; → Aristotle; → Aristoxenus; → Cratippus; → Theophrastus

1 Wehrli, Schule 1, ²1967 2 J.-P. Schneider, Dicéarque de Messène, in: Goulet 2, 760–764 3 P. Carrara, Dicaearco e l'hypothesis del Reso, in: ZPE 90, 1992, 35–44 4 F. Wehrli, D. von Messene, in: GGPh² 3, 535–539 5 E. Martini, s.v. D. (3), in: RE 5, 546–563 6 H.B. Gottschalk, Soul as harmonia, in: Phronesis 16, 1971, 179–198 7 G. Movia, Anima e intelletto: ricerche sulla psicologia peripatetica da Teofrasto a Cratippo, 1968, 71–93 8 J.E. Annas, Hellenistic Philosophy of Mind, 1992, 30f. 9 Moraux I, 1973, 243–247 10 F.W. Walbank, A Historical Commentary on Polybius, I, 1957, 639–641 11 I.G. Taifacos, Il De republica di Cicerone e il modello Dicaearcheo della costituzione mista, in: ΠΛΑΤΩΝ 31, 1979, 128–134.

G.J.D. Aalders, Die Theorie der gemischten Verfassung im Alt., 1968, 72–81; W.W. Fortenbaugh, E. Schütrumpf (ed.), Dicaearchus of Messana: text, translation, and discussion, 2001. R.S.

Dicaeogenes (Δικαιογένης; *Dikaiogénēs*).

[1] Athenian from a wealthy and respected family (Davies, 145–149 pl. II). When trierarch of the state trireme Paralos he fell at Cnidus in 412/11 BC. An action was brought in 389 concerning the testamentary disposal of his wealth (Isaeus, Or. 5). Traill, PAA 324245. W.S.

[2] **of Athens.** (?), tragedian and dithyrambic poet. In the 4th cent. BC victor at the rural Dionysia in the deme of Acharnae in the tragic or dithyramb class (DID B 6). Surviving titles are *Mḗdeia* and *Kýprioi*, for which Aristot. Poet. 1554b 37ff. records an *anagnorisis* διὰ μνήμης.

TrGF 52. F.P.

Dice (game) (κυβεία/*kybeía*; Lat. *alea*). Allegedly invented by the Lydians (Hdt. 1,94,3), → Palamedes [1] before Troy (Paus. 2,20,3; 10,31,1) or the Egyptian god Thot (Pl. Phdr. 274c-d). Dice are occasionally mentioned in mythology (Hdt. 2,122,1), e.g., Eros plays with Ganymede (Apoll. Rhod. 3,114–126), Hercules with a temple guard (Plut. Romulus 5,1 f.) and Patroclus with Clysonymus (Hom. Il. 23,87 f.). Either four-sided knuckle bones (→ astragalos [2], Lat. also *talus*) that had inscribed on them the values one and six as well as three and four, or six-sided dice (κύβοι/*kýboi*; Lat. → *tesserae*; knuckle bones and dice were also called *aleae* by the Romans) similar to the ones employed today and made of ivory, clay, bronze or other materials, were used for dice games. The value of each side was marked by dots, strokes or words. As with the knuckle bones, the numbers of two opposite sides always added up to seven (cf. Anth. Pal. 14,8).

Usually the game was played with three and sometimes four dice that were thrown from the back of the hand, the palm or a cup (→ *fritillus*) to ensure a correct throw (Mart. 14,16) on a → *tabula* or *alveus* (cf. → board games) with elevated rim. The sum of points won the game (this type of game was called πλειστοβολίνδα/*pleistobolínda*: 'highest toss game', Poll. 9,95), with the highest possible number of points being triple sixes and the lowest triple ones (cf. Aesch. Ag. 32 f.). The combination of different dice scores received specific names (Plaut. Curc. 357 f.; Poll. 7,203–206), e.g., the triple six was called *Venus*, 'the Aphrodite/Venus throw', and the lowest value *canis*, 'the dog throw', (both terms in Suet. Aug. 71,2; Prop. 4,8,45 f.; *canis* also Ov. Ars am. 2,206). Detailed description: Ov. Ars am. 3,353–366; Ov. Tr. 2,473–482.

Games were played for objects (in Plaut. Curc. 354–356 a coat and a ring), but especially for money, with the sums played often being huge and driving the looser to ruin (Alci. 3,6; Hor. Epist. 1,18,21–23, cf. Suet. Aug. 71,2 f.). As a result, the authorities attempted to ban dice playing (e.g., Plaut. Mil. 164; Hor. Carm. 3,24,58; indirectly Suet. Aug. 71,1). These prohibitions were only waived at the → Saturnalia. Members of all classes, from the emperor to the simplest soldier, were devotees of the dice. Like → Augustus, Claudius [III 1] was also known to be a passionate gambler who even had his travel wagon remodeled for this purpose and wrote a book on dice games (Suet. Claud. 33,2). By contrast, Caligula was feared as a cheat (Suet. Cal. 41,2). Dice games were particularly popular in inns and hostels.

Representations of dice games in art can be found in numerous scenes of Greek vase painting, murals in Pompeiian taverns, mosaics, book illustrations from late antiquity etc. The number of preserved dice is very

large, among them are loaded specimens that had been hollowed out and weighted on one inner side with lead, etc. Dice cups are also preserved. Regarding dice in other games cf. → board games.
→ Fritillus; → Gambling; → Betting

J. VÄTERLEIN, Roma ludens. Kinder und Erwachsene beim Spiel im ant. Rom (Heuremata 5), 1976, esp. 7–13; 54; M. FITTA, Spiele und Spielzeug in der Ant., 1998, 110–122. R.H.

Dichalkon (δίχαλκον; *díchalkon*). A Greek measure of weight and bronze coin worth twice as much as a *chalkous*. It corresponded to $^1/_4$ (Athens), $^1/_6$ (Delphi, Epidaurus) or $^1/_8$ (Priene) of an obolos [1]. Variants of the mark of the value were e.g. B X (stamp of Antiochus IV, Seleucea on the Tigris at about 9.6 g) [2. 271f.] or ΔΙΧΑΛΚ(on) (stamp of Apollonia Pontica at 2.1 g) [3].
→ Chalkous; → Obolos

1 M.N. TOD, Epigraphical Notes on Greek Coinage, in: NC 6.6, 1946, 47–62 2 E.T. NEWELL, The coinage of the Eastern Seleucid mints from Seleucus I to Antiochus III, 1978 3 SNG London, British Mus. 1, 1993, 7, 178ff.

RPC I, 370ff. A.M.

Dicta Catonis Versified handbook of popular ethics from the 3rd cent. (cf. Carm. epigr. 1988, 51; [1. LXXIII]); widely known by the end of the 4th cent. at the latest. The text, of which the Dutch philologist M. BOAS made a lifelong study [1. LXXXff.], exists in version Y (or V) with 306 vv. and in a more extensive version F, with 331 vv. but altered by interpolations and recasting, aside from the Barberini recension [1. XXXVIff.]. The title of Y runs *Marci Catonis ad filium libri*, where F (Codex Verona cap. 163) has *Dicta M. Catonis ad filium suum* [1. LXVff.; 2. 30ff.], since ERASMUS (ed. Löwen [2]1517) *Catonis Disticha. Dionysius Cato*, an invention of S. BOSIUS, was accepted from the edition of J. SCALIGER (Leiden 1598) until well into the 19th cent. [2. 40f.].

Content: a) an introductory epistle in prose; b) 57 interpolated *breves sententiae* in prose; c) four books of ethical advice, each comprising two hexameters; a clear structure cannot be recognized. Political advice takes second place to private counsel: people are admonished to keep a sense of proportion (2,6), not to despair in adversity (2,25), to enjoy the pleasures of the moment, etc. 1,26 & 2,18 are among the most overtly opportunist. There is thus no need to inquire about the author's philosophical position. Many thoughts stem from Seneca, succinct formulations also from Horace [cf. 1. app.].

As a handbook *Dicta Catonis* enjoyed its greatest influence in the Middle Ages [cf. 6], with quotations [1. LXXIIff., app.], commentaries like that by Remigius of Auxerre, renderings, sequels and translations into virtually every major European language all testifying to the general validity of certain minimal requirements.

The anonymous *Monosticha* (FPR 3,236–240) boasts 77 hexameters in two recensions [cf. 4. 614 and for the title 3. 44ff.; 4. 608, n. 2] with even pithier advice on life. Alcuin represents a *terminus ante quem* for this text, and a late classical origin is also likely; the transmission follows that of the *Dicta Catonis* but is always separate [1. LXIII].

EDITION: 1 M. BOAS, 1952.
LITERATURE: 2 Id., Die Epistola C., 1934 3 Id., Alcuin und Cato, 1937 4 Id., Die Lorscher Hs. der sog. Monosticha C., in: RhM 72, 1917/8, 594–615 5 P. ROOS, Sentenza e proverbio nell antichità e i Distici di Catone, 1984 6 SCHANZ-HOSIUS, 3, 37ff. P.L.S.

Dictamnus An uncommon subshrub growing in Crete, properly called Dittany in English (δίκταμνος; *díktamnos* or δίκταμνον; *díktamnon* in Aristot. Hist. an. 8(9),6,612a 3–5 and Mir. ausc. 4,830b 20–22, Theophr. Hist. pl. 9,16,1, Dioscorides 3,32 [1. 41f.] = 3,34 [2. 284ff.] and *dictamnus* in Verg. Aen. 12,412 and Pliny HN 25,92). It is considered to be not our native Rutacea the aromatic Burning Bush, *Dictamnus albus* L., the *diptam* or *diptamnus* of the Middle Ages, whose leaves have a lemon-like fragrance when rubbed, but rather the Mediterranean labiate *Amaracus* (Amarakos) *dictamnus Benth.* (= *Origanum dict. L.*). A decoction of the rounded, grey, downy leaves was supposed to ease birth pains or to expel a foetus that had miscarried (Dioscorides), reputedly even hunting-arrows could be expelled by goats (Aristot. and Theophr. loc. cit.: 3. 119ff.), who liked to graze on the plant when wounded (Pliny HN 25,92). Shifted to → deer on the authority of Pliny HN 8,97 & 25,92, Isid. Orig. 12,1,18 and Serv. on Aen. 4,73, the story was retold in one form or another in many a medieval bestiary such as that by Thomas of Cantimpré (12,11 [4. 345]).

1 M. WELLMANN, vol. 2 2 J. BERENDES 3 H. BAUMANN, Die griech. Pflanzenwelt in Mythos, Kunst und Literatur, 1982 H. BOESE (ed.), Thomas Cantimpratensis, Liber de natura rerum, 1973. C.HÜ.

Dictation see → Copy

Dictator (from *dictare*, 'to dictate', 'to have recorded in writing', 'to arrange'; other etymologies in Cic. Rep. 1,63: *quia dicitur*). The holder of an exceptional, emergency, comprehensive — yet temporary — appointment under the Roman Republic. An empowered civil servant, i.e. a consul or if necessary even a praetor, could name a dictator (*dictatorem dicere*), theoretically on his own initiative, but in practice after consultation with the Senate and other officials. The dictator would then hold an → *imperium* limited to six months, free from collegial intercession or appeals to the populace (*provocatio*). This was actually a way to transfer absolute military power, not subject to law, into the civil sector of public life (Cic. Leg. 3,9; Liv. 4,17,8; 4,26,8; Dig. 1,2,2,18).

The early development of the office of *magister populi*, as it came to be known, is shrouded in mystery (Cic. Leg. 3,3,9; 4,10; Varro, Ling. 5,82; Festus 216,11ff.; differing in Isid. Orig. 9,3,11). Initially a *magister equitum* should have been named as representative. That it was closely connected with the official power (→ *magistratus*) and the devolution of royal power is indicated by the existence of similarly constituted and perhaps original offices in formerly independent Latin areas. The power of the dictator comes close to kingship (Cic. Rep. 2,59: *novumque id genus imperii visum est et proximum similitudini regiae*; cf. the Greek equivalents: στρατηγὸς αὐτοκράτωρ or μόναρχος; Plut. Cam. 18,6).

At first used only under a military state of emergency, for the last time in 202 BC (Liv. 30,39), from the 4th cent. BC the office, now held by a 'prodictator', was increasingly used for internal purposes (Liv. 7,3,4; 8,16,12), e.g. for the policing of a public assembly (*comitiorum habendorum causa*). In the Second Punic War there was an attempt in 217 BC to impose the office legally through collegiate control (*lex Metilia de aequando magistri equitum et dictatoris iure*: Liv. 22,25f). In the following cent. the post fell into disuse, only to be revived by L. Cornelius Sulla in 82 BC to give his extraordinary official power as *dictator legibus scribundis et constituendae rei publicae* a constitutional context (App. B Civ. 1,99; MRR 2,66f.) and again invoked, retroactively as it were, by Caesar as *dictator perpetuus* in 45 BC (MRR 2,305). With the beginning of the Principate the necessity of the post disappeared.

W. Kunkel, Staatsordnung und Staatspraxis der röm. Republik II, 1995, 665ff.; Mommsen, Staatsrecht 2, 141ff. C.G.

Dicte (Δίκτη; *Díktē*). Mountain in Crete, not identifiable with certainty. In particular Str. 10,4,12 indicates that in antiquity, D. was not in the Lassithi Hills as today, but rather designated the Modi ridge (539 m) on the eastern tip of Crete and that this was the birthplace of Zeus (cf. Dion. Hal. Ant. Rom. 2,61; Diod. Sic. 5,70,6; Ath. 9,375f.). At the Minoan town of Palaikastro there was a sanctuary of Zeus Diktaios.

P. Faure, Nouvelles recherches de spéléologie et de topographie crétoises, in: BCH 84, 1960, 189–220; E. Meyer, s.v. D., RE suppl. 10, 137f.; R.F. Willets, Cretan cults and festivals, 1962. H.SO.

Dictinius Bishop of Astorga (Asturica); son of Symphosius, who was likewise bishop there. The most eminent Priscillianist writer after → Priscillianus himself; he declared his disaffection with the doctrine at the first Council of Toletanum (Toledo) in AD 400 and repudiated his own writings, whereupon he was again acknowledged. Later Innocent I defended him (Epist. 3,1ff. = PL 20,485ff.) against rigourist bishops in Baetica and Africa, protesting against the indulgence shown him by the Synod of Toledo. The Priscillianist tracts he wrote exercised a persistent influence; Pope Leo the Great regretted that they were still being read with respect (Epist. 15,16 = PL 54,688), and the Council of Bracarense (563) forbid even reading them. In his *Libra* ('Scales') of which we can gain some knowledge from Augustine (CSEL 41, C. mendacium 5–35), D. justifies white lies in religious matters and Priscillianist utilitarian morals (*iura, periura, secretum prodere noli*).

Bardenhewer, GAL 3,413; V. Burrus, The Making of a Heretic. Gender, Authority, and the Priscillianist Controversy, 1995; C.-M. Molas, s.v. D., DHGE (bibliography); Ch. & L. Piétri (ed.), Die Gesch. des Christentums, vol. 2, 1996, 496–500. R.B.

Dictio dotis Under Roman law a unilateral promise to provide a dowry (→ *Dos*). Proculus (Dig. 50,16,125) gives the form of words used to make the promise: *dotis filiae meae tibi erunt aurei centum* ('as dowry for my daughter you will have 100 gold pieces'). The words were said by the father or another male ancestor of the bride, or by herself, or by someone in her debt designated by her (such as a previous husband forced to return the dowry he himself had once received, following an *actio rei uxoriae*, a divorce). Despite its one-sided declaration the *dictio dotis* was considered a settlement. It is true that it was a pact rather than a full contract requiring a *promissio*, a bilateral binding oath in the form of a → *stipulatio*. A claim for *dos* could be made on the basis of a legacy in the donor's will. As there was a strong moral pressure for *dos* to be given, the lack of actionability will not have been of decisive import. An imperial ruling of AD 428 (Cod. Theod. 3,13,4) made it clear that a general right to dowry existed regardless of how it was expressed rendering the *dictio dotis* obsolete.

1 H. Honsell, Th. Mayer-Maly, W. Selb, Röm. Recht, [4]1987, 405f. 2 M. Kaser, RPR I, 335f. G.S.

Dictum see → Gnome

Dictynna (Δίκτυννα; *Díktynna*). Goddess of fishing, and of the hunt, in Crete. Samians established her sanctuary in about 519 BC on the steep slope of the Tityrus (Rhodopou) peninsula of western Crete [1; 2], according to Hdt. 3,59. Her cult became widespread (Plut. Mor. 984a) as did that of the equivalent figure of Britomartis (Callim. H. 3, 189–205), aside from western Crete, at Aegina and Aphaea (Paus. 2, 30,3), in Gythium, Sparta and Laconia, Athens, Phocis, Massalia and Commagene [3; 4]. Callimachus related the myth of how, in an attempt to escape Minos, pursuing her with lustful intent for nine months, she jumped from the precipice to be rescued in the net (*díktys*, δίκτυς) of some fishermen (popular etymology found as early as Aristoph. Vesp. 368). The relationship of D. to Artemis is a) by association as epiclesis (Aristoph. Ran. 1359; Eur. Hipp. 145; IT 127; portrayed there as the epiclesis of Isis and the nurse of Zeus, see [5]); b) as a nymph of Artemis (Callim. H. 3, 197–200); c) as a goddess along with Artemis in the oath of Dreros (ICreticae 1. 1 A29; Delos IG XI 2, 145) [6]. The iconography is identical. NILSSON holds that D. and Artemis alike are mere distinctions derived from the Minoan mother goddess [7]. It is uncertain whether the etymological link to the Dicte Mountains is based on the geographical ignorance of later writers, or was present from the beginning, as HEUBECK [8] suggests.

1 G. WELTER, U. JANTZEN, in: F. MATZ, Forsch. auf Kreta, 1951, 106–117 2 E. KIRSTEN, in: Proceedings of 4th Cretol. Congr., A 1, 1980, 261–270 3 D. JESSEN, RE 5, 584–588 4 A. RAPP, RML 1, 1884/86, 821–828 5 M. GUARDUCCI, ICreticae 2, 1939, 128–140 6 J. WAGNER, G. PETZL, in: ZPE 20, 1976, 201–223, l. 6f. 7 NILSSON, MMR, 510–513 8 A. HEUBECK, Praegraeca, 1961, 52f.

J. B. HARROD, The Tempering Goddess. The Britomartis-D.-Artemis Mythologem, 1980; R. F. WILLETTS, Cretan Cults, 1962, 179–193; C. BOULOTIS, LIMC 3.1, 391–394; H. VAN EFFENTERRE, LIMC 3.1, 169–170. C.A.

Dictys (Δίκτυς; *Díktys*).

[1] Son of Magnes and a Naiad, brother or half-brother to → Polydectes (Apollod. 1,88), the king of the island of Seriphos. Other sources stress his descent from Poseidon direct or in the fourth degree (Tzetz. Lycoph. 838; Pherecydes FGrH 3 F 10f.). As a fisherman (D. = 'netsman') he lodges → Danae and her infant son → Perseus, who are swept onto the shore at Seriphos in a box. The story has been frequently staged [1]. In Aeschylus' satyr-play *Diktyulkoi* (TrGF 3 F 46–47) satyrs help D. and another fisherman to land the heavy and mysterious catch [2; 3]. Perseus used the Medusa's head to turn Polydectes to stone, after the latter had fallen in love with Danae and despatched Perseus to fetch the → Gorgoneion as a trophy. D. was then made king of Seriphos by Perseus (schol. Ap. Rhod. 4,1515; Hyg. Fab. 63; Apollod. 2,36; 45; Strabo 10,5,10). In Athens D. and the Nereid Clymene were worshipped as the saviours of Perseus (Paus. 2,18,1). Euripides wrote a tragedy entitled *Dictys* (TGF 331–348).

1 J.-J. MAFFRE, s.v. Danae, LIMC 3.1, 332f., nos. 54–67 2 A. LESKY, Von neuen Funden zum griech. Drama, in: Gymnasium 61, 1954, 296f. 3 R. PFEIFFER, Die Netzfischer des Aischylos (1938), in: B. SEIDENSTICKER, Satyrspiel, 1989, 58–77.

J. H. OAKLEY, Danae and Perseus on Seriphos, in: AJA 86, 1982, 111–115.

[2] One of the Tyrrhenian sailors turned into dolphins by Bacchus (Ovid Met. 3,615; Hyg. Fab. 134,4).

[3] Centaur, killed by Peirithous for disturbing his wedding feast (Ov. Met. 12,334–340).

[4] Son of Neptune and Agamede, the daughter of Augias (Hyg. Fab. 157,2).

[5] Foster child of Isis (Plut. Is. 8 p. 353 F). R.B.

Dictys Cretensis 'Dictys of Crete' is the fictitious author of an alleged, laboriously corroborated authentic eyewitness account of the Trojan War (*Ephemeris toû Troikoû polémou*). It not only includes a prelude that omits the judgement of Paris, but also relates the fate of the returning heroes. Only a few fragments remain of a possibly 2nd-cent. AD (?) Greek original, though we have a rendering in Latin by one L. Septimius some two cents. later. His 6 vols. are made to resemble the *Commentaries* of → Caesar, with echoes of the style of Sallust. The work is strongly anti-Trojan, while at the same time critical of the Greeks. Its influence in the Middle Ages was less than that of the similar → Dares, but extends as far as Goethe's 'Achilleis'.

EDITION: W. EISENHUT, [2]1973.
BIBLIOGRAPHY: S. MERKLE, Die Ephemeris belli Troiani des D. von Kreta, 1989. J.D.

Didache (διδαχή; *didachḗ*, 'teaching' *sc.* 'of the Twelve Apostles'). The earliest Church regulations, usually attributed to the → Apostolic Fathers. Highly prized in antiquity, frequently used in other works, the *Didache* has been known since 1873. The most important textual witness to this influential document of early Christian communality is the 11th-cent. Codex Hierosolymitanus 54. Greek and Coptic fragments, Ethiopic and Georgian translations, as well as considerable indirect transmission, including the Apostolic Constitutions 7,1–32, all complement the basic text. It is generally agreed to date to the early 2nd cent., but this, like its origin — in Syria/Palestine, possibly Egypt — is contested.

The 16 mostly short chapters of the *Didache* fall into five logical divisions. At the beginning in the shape of a doctrine of the two paths, (the Path of Life and the Path of Death), is some expository ethical teaching (ch. 1–6), complemented by a short gospel insert (1,3b–2,1). This tract, like the Epistle of → Barnabas (18–20), must be from a Jewish source, reworked into Christian form before reaching the author [6. 15]. Further chapters lean heavily on contemporary Jewish practice as they cover the liturgy (7–10): regulations concerning baptism (7), the weekly fast (8,1) and the repetition of the paternoster thrice a day (8,2f.) are found here as well as the Eucharistic prayers (9,1–10), interpretation of which is controversial. A third section concerns itinerant teachers and members of other churches who are travelling (11–13): as far as possible they should be guaranteed support. In the rules for communal life (14–15) aside from the imperatives of confession of sins and forgiveness (14), the selection of experienced 'bishops and deacons' to lead the faithful is stressed (15,1f.), as is the imposition of fraternal discipline (*correctio fraterna*) as communal corrective (15,3). The *Didache* concludes with an eschatologically justified exhortation to vigilance suffused with apocalyptic themes (16). A prominent place in the book is allotted to the charismatic offices (role of apostles, prophets and teachers).

The question of sources for the *Didache*, its background, and of course the establishment of a fair text that adequately conveys the different strains that have come down to us, whether selected text or synoptic *editio maior*, is an important field of research.

Editions, translations: 1 K. Niederwimmer, Die D., [2]1993 2 W. Rordorf, A. Tuilier, La doctrine des douze apôtres, 1978. (SChr 248) 3 G. Schöllgen, D., [2]1992 (Fontes Christiani 1) 4 K. Wengst, D. (Apostellehre), [2]1984.

Bibliography: 5 J. A. Draper (ed.), The D. in modern Research, 1996 (1–42 on research history)
6 K. Niederwimmer, Der Didachist und seine Quellen, in: C. N. Jefford (ed.), The D. in Context, 1995, 15–36 (368–382 for other literature) 7 F. E. Vokes, Life and Order in an Early Church: the D., in: ANRW II/27.1, 1993, 209–233. J.RI.

Didactic poetry

I. Ancient Orient II. Greek & Latin

I. Ancient Orient

see → Wisdom literature

II. Greek & Latin

A. Definition and characteristics
B. Intention and typology C. History
1. Greek 2. Latin

A. Definition and characteristics

The relation of form to content is typical of the problems of didactic literature, as even a definition is difficult: formal poetics treats didactic poetry [DP] as a subdivision of epic while a classification derived from content denies it any poetic quality. As both attempts stem from non-consensual normative premises, only a phenomenological approach can have meaning here. The main formal feature is a reliance on metrics, language and style of the → epic, its style lying between the elevated and middle levels depending on the subject. Stock epic elements are: the invocation of the muse, similes and narrative excursus; also hymns to the gods are stock elements in most DP, later assuming a panegyric function. Unlike the narrative-dramatic heroic epic, DP forms a coherent exposition addressed to someone who is either not present in the work at all or only as a source of pretended questions and objections. DP may be composed on any subject, but mostly concerns some practical discipline or science. From Hellenistic times it was usually based on a prose work. Accordingly both didactic and poetic claims of the genre must be considered.

B. Intention and typology

Ever since antiquity literary criticism denied either the poetic or the didactic aspects of the genre: Aristotle's verdict that Empedocles was not a poet, but rather a natural scientist (Poet. 1447b 17–20), was influential, but acted as a stimulus for → Hellenistic poetry, as versification of a most 'unpoetical' subject was seen as a challenge. It is matched by Cicero's verdict that → Aratus [4] understood nothing of astronomy but captured it marvellously in verse (De or. 1,69). The perspective of the reader determined whether DP was criticized as unpoetic or unscientific. The dilemma was resolved by replacing the alternative — *aut prodesse aut delectare* ('either to be useful or to please') — by a synthesis (Hor. Ars P. 333f.).; at one paradoxical stroke DP was transformed from the most unpoetic of genres to the most poetic, insofar as it realized in exemplary fashion both the didactic and the aesthetic purpose of poetry.

For interpreting individual works and the history of the genre as a whole the typology evolved by B. Effe with its distinction between the formal and the factual type is helpful. In the formal type the virtuosity of the poetic treatment is paramount, while the subject matter is indifferent — indeed, the more contrived and 'unpoetic', the better. The factual type, on the contrary, should be scientifically correct and factually accurate, the form serving merely as a vehicle for the content. Between the two stands the transparent type of DP, in which the merely selective poetic treatment of the subject-matter makes the latter appear secondary (not, however, random or 'superficial' in the sense of allegory or mystification), while its obvious philosophical and moral seriousness points to a more important object in the background. It is in a certain sense the ideal, 'synthetic' form of DP, as it tends neither to the purely artistic, turning the object of the lesson into an object of curiosity, nor to the ideologic or missionary, degrading the form into a vehicle for indoctrination and propaganda (Brecht's 'cunning in writing the truth'), but seeks instead to enhance the dignity of the object by the sublimity of the epic form.

C. History

1. Greek

The three phases to be outlined here correspond to the three types defined above: DP of the archaic period (→ Hesiodus) is transparent; that of classical times (→ Presocratics) factual; that of Hellenistic times (→ Aratus [4], → Nicander) formal. Hesiod in his 'Works and Days' (Ἔργα καὶ ἡμέραι) covers agriculture, not of course as a practical handbook would, despite some technical sections, but as a moral guide for the reader he is addressing, his greedy and unscrupulous brother Perses. Hesiod seeks to confront him with the ideal of 'honest work' in his paraenetic poem. The transparency of Hesiodic DP is not a sophisticated and elaborate construction, but more an expression of its time: practical instruction in animal husbandry against a background of theological and philosophical reflections aimed at the moral education of society — all this could only be accomplished through the medium of epic DP. The other poetic achievements of the archaic period with more or less didactic content or at any rate of didactic intent (→ Epic: Inventory, II B.), are not considered here except for philosophical DP, as they are not strictly didactic works from a phenomenological viewpoint.

The rhapsode → Xenophanes of Colophon (*c.*540–470 BC) began the tradition of fact-driven philosophical DP with his 'On Nature' (Περὶ φύσεως/*Perì phýseōs*) and with it the second phase in the history of didactics. While in his *silloi* and 'Parodies' he makes a satirical attack on the anthropomorphic gods of Homer and Hesiod, in his DP he seems to postulate a transcendent God and a rational explanation of natural phenomena. That he does not avail himself of the medium of scientific prose which originated at the same time, but deliberately chooses to retain the epic form is because of his avowed polemic intent to replace the 'unscientific' poetry of Homer and Hesiod using their own means of expression.

→ Parmenides of Elea (6th to 5th cent. BC) continued the esoteric tendencies of his (alleged) teacher. Against the false ideas (*dóxai*) of mankind he sets the 'well-rounded truth' (*alētheíē eukyklḗs*), ontologically 'annulling' all becoming and leaving only the one immutable Being. He goes so far in his extreme ontology (28 B 3 DK), maintaining Non-being as inconceivable, that he utterly denies the epistemological value of perceptions. The last step is to make Being itself communicable only in poetic metaphor. This is the first instance of DP acquiring the function of metaphorically intimating matters beyond the sphere of everyday discourse.

On the other hand the DP of → Empedocles [1] (5th cent. BC) embodies the factual type *par excellence*. The poem addressed to one Pausanias argues a rational cosmology with the aid of numerous didactic strategies. In it, the addressee becomes a mere representative for the general reader, always being lectured and exhorted to pay attention; important lessons are usually repeated and illustrated with comparisons and examples from everyday experience. The argument, including the exposition of myth, is rationalist and intended to convince.

After Empedocles the tradition of DP was abandoned for nearly 200 years. The *Hedypatheia* of → Archestratus [2] of Gela (in 330 BC), given a Latin form by → Ennius [1], was scarcely DP in the strict sense, but more like a culinary tour of the ancient world. A revival of DP takes place in early Hellenistic times with the *Phainomena* of → Aratus [4] of Soli. This work did not take up the philosophical DP of the → Presocratics but directly from Hesiod, bringing its author literary recognition (Callim. Epigr. 27). This confirms that the quality of the *Phainomena* lies primarily in the formal mastery of difficult material, in part from Eudoxus [1] of Cnidus. The themes (astronomy and weather) supplement and refine the peasants' wisdom of the 'Works and Days' but totally lacks the moral didactic pretensions of Hesiod. Even the Stoical colouring one might expect such a poem remains at best superficial — it does not seek to expound Stoic cosmology or astrology but to give practical knowledge about the skies and the weather. Aratus' work is accordingly not of the transparent but of the formal type: the subject-matter was not intended to further any particular philosophical doctrine, but is the result of striving to renew an obsolete genre within the framework of the poetology of → Callimachus [3].

There is no doubt about the formal nature of the DP of → Nicander of Colophon (*c.* 2nd cent. BC). The *Theriaka* (on poisonous animals and cures) as well as the *Alexipharmaka* (on poisons and antidotes of all kinds) even more explicitly than the *Phainomena* display a *recherché* learning and ambitious virtuosity in versifying disparate material. Other Hellenistic writings are mostly known only from titles: Nicander's *Georgika* must have been as didactically formal as → Numenius' and → Pancrates' poems 'On fishing' (*Halieutika*); the *Ornithogonia* by a poetess → Boeo (or maybe Boeus?) was probably not truly didactic in intent, containing only stories of metamorphosis. Others emulated Aratus' 'On the Heavenly Phaenomena' and in Rome too Aratus' legacy was immense (see below).

In the Empire a return to factual, practically relevant matter is noticeable: the most influential work is the *Oikouménēs Perihḗgēsis* or 'Description of the World' by → Dionysius [27] of Alexandria writing under Hadrian, a geography of the whole of the known world in barely 1,200 lines of verse, whose language and metre recall Callimachus [3] and Apollonius [2]. This work came to be the most popular and widely read geography of antiquity and later ages, the author as the single most authoritative geographer being called 'the Periegete'. Also of considerable poetic worth, admittedly rather on the formal side, are *Halieutika* ('On Fishing') by → Oppian (written under Caracalla, or by different criteria under Marcus Aurelius); in 5 books the species, life cycle and catching of fish are described. However, another book credited to Oppian, the *Cynegetika* (under Caracalla) reveals a lesser command of language and metre: the author takes 4 bks. to deal with equipment, animals and the technique of the hunt. Finally, included in the pseudo-Orphic corpus (→ Orphica) of the 4th cent. AD are the → *Lithika* in just 800 lines of verse, the sole poetic work on gems to have come down to us, a type common in antiquity, at first almost entirely of mineralogical interest but later acquiring overtones of magic. The author invokes Hermes to explain to his public the secret powers of gems and professes Neoplatonic beliefs coloured by popular superstition.

2. LATIN

In 1st-cent. BC Rome there was a productive reception of the three types of Greek DP in reverse chronological order. It began with → Cicero's version of Aratus (*Aratea*), an early work that was deliberately composed as an *exercice de style* and so was of the formal type. The *Aratea* aims at formal refinement, but also fits facts and the addressee into a Latin background: more exhaustive information and explanation is provided for the reader, so that its scope will have surpassed that of the original and not insignificantly.

After the reception of the formal Hellenistic type with Cicero there follows a reversion to the Presocratic factual type exemplified by Empedocles in → Lucretius' long philosophical didactic poem *De rerum natura*. Its poetic form is a means for the author to sugar the bitter pill of Epicurean doctrine the reader has to swallow (4,11–25). The method is intended to trick, not deceive, cf. 4,16. Other didactical devices are employed — repetitions, admonitions, demonstrations and proofs — yet the argument always remains rational, intersubjectively consistent, and it would be wrong to speak of fanaticism or quasi-religious zeal. The formal structure of *De rerum natura* is extremely elaborate, despite (or perhaps precisely because) of its functional role, as has been pointed out by the poet himself (1,136–145) and certain critical readers (Cic. Ad Q. Fr. 2,9,3; Ov. Am. 1,15,23f.).

In → Virgil's 'agricultural' poem (*Georgica*) Latin reception of Greek DP is at its best. By his choice of theme and the transparent nature of the work Virgil puts himself consciously in the tradition of Hesiod (cf. *Ascraeum carmen* 2,176), and like Hesiod he uses agriculture as a moral paradigm. The poetic form is for Virgil neither an indulgence nor merely a didactic vehicle but a necessary component of the transparent conception. Where Hesiod has a natural unity, Virgil has a deliberate innovation, a classical synthesis of form and content that the many writers of DP of later ages were unable to achieve.

After the *Georgica* → Ovidius' *Ars amatoria* fundamentally transformed the genre. In this work Ovid opens up the form and content of the genre, using instead of the traditional hexameters the elegiac distich and offering a study of love, a subject which cannot be taught. Ovid diagnoses and demonstrates in this way the impossibility of a further innovative creative extension of the genre; for that reason alone it seems quite unlikely that he should have composed *Halieutica* in exile (Pliny HN 32,11) — and certainly not the poor hack work that has come down to us under his name.

However, the DP tradition did not die away; the successors of Virgil and Ovid respectively resist typological and thematic organization. Among thoroughly original works we find epigons of Virgil as well as more or less successful attempts to give poetic treatment to subjects as yet untried (which were thus sometimes remote). The DP of the Augustan poet Grattius (a contemporary of Ovid: Ov. Pont. 4,16,34) on hunting (*Cynegetica*) for example seeks to follow the culture theory of Lucretius and Virgil and to elevate hunting to a cultural accomplishment of Herculean proportions. The pretence of transparency turns out to be merely a predictable attempt at exaggerating material that is essentially trivial. Germanicus' [2] Aratus translation blends formal skill with panegyric aspiration: as Jove reigns above so does the Emperor Tiberius reign on earth, and the earthly *Pax Augusta* is a reflection of the divine order. The intended transparency is admittedly only for the sake of appearances, the result of polite courtly convention, not inner need. Even in Aratus [4] Stoic Zeus-theology was an ornament rather than serious philosophical background, but in Germanicus it fades to adulatory gesture.

The case of → Manilius' *Astronomica* (probably dating to Tiberius) is different. It is the first independent poem about stars in Latin (only the first book owes anything to Aratus) and takes a decidedly Stoic and at times anti-Lucretian stance. Manilius gives what is by ancient standards a scientific account of astrology based on Posidonius' doctrine of *sympatheia*; as with Lucretius, the poetic form has a didactic and persuasive intent. Naïve Virgil worship is, however, to the fore in the technical writer → Columella. The tenth bk. of his textbook *Res Rusticae* (under Nero) on horticulture were composed because Virgil explicitly left the theme to a successor (Verg. G. 4,147f.) — a formal amusement done out of reverence for his great predecessor with no deep ambition. To Nero's time belongs another pseudo-Virgilian work → *Aetna*, a didactic poem on vulcanism which maintains a scientific approach throughout.

A few original examples of the factual type have come down to us from the late Empire: the three 'linguistic' poems of → Terentianus Maurus (3rd cent.), *De litteris*, *De syllabis* and *De metris*, are a virtuoso treatment in different metres of those subjects, an approach adopted primarily for mnemonic ends. Similarly the *Liber medicinalis* of → Serenus (4th cent.?), the only didactic poem of antiquity on medicine, seeks to reach a wider public for its scientific matter (mainly drawn from Pliny the Elder) by its verse, as it offers a catchy 'collection of cures' for some 80 familiar complaints (from headaches to piles down to podagra). A true epigone on the other hand appears to be the *Cynegetica* of → Nemesianus (3rd or 4th cent.), who seems not to have read Grattius. Similarities between the two can be explained by the nature of the subject and their imitation of Virgil.

A final peak is attained with the reworking of Greek DP by → Avienus in the 4th cent. After the less important earlier Aratus renderings by Cicero and Germanicus the *Phaenomena* of Avienus is an imposing improvement on Aratus, both by its syncretic 'Jupiter-theology' with an admixture of Stoic, Orphic, Hermetic and Neoplatonic elements and by its masterly use of material from the Aratus commentaries and additions thereto. From Avienus, too, comes a Latin version of the *Perihegesis* of Dionysius (*Descriptio orbis terrae*) and a fragmentary → Periplus (*De ora maritima*; 'On the sea coast') from an unknown Greek source. In this way the unity of Greek and Latin DP was once again forcefully demonstrated at the end of antiquity.

This is not the place to attempt to sketch the intensive and still largely unexplored survival in particular of Latin DP in medieval and modern times, since the range of themes extends to virtually all practical, technical, scientific and philosophical areas.

→ DIDACTIC POETRY

L. L. Albertsen, Das Lehrgedicht — eine Gesch. der antikisierenden Sachepik, 1967; B. Effe, Dichtung und Lehre, 1977; B. Fabian, Das L. als Problem der Poetik, in: H. R. Jauss (ed.), Die nicht mehr schönen Künste, 1968, 67–89; T. Haye, Das lat. L. im MA, 1997; W. Ludwig, Neulat. L. und Vergils Georgica, in: Id., Litterae Neolatinae, 1989, 100–127; C. Meier, Pascua, rura, duces, in: FMS 28, 1994, 1–50; F. Oudin, Poemata didascalica (3 vols.), 1749, 1813; E. Pöhlmann, Charakteristika des röm. L., in: ANRW I 3, 813–901; G. Roellenbleck, Das ep. L. Italiens, 1975. R.GL.

Didaskaliai (αἱ διδασκαλίαι; *hai didaskalíai*).
I. Greek II. Roman

I. Greek

Derived from the verb διδάσκειν, the singular *didaskalía* has the general meaning of 'teaching', 'instruction' (Pind. Pyth. 4,102; Xen. Cyr. 8,7,24) and in a special sense of 'choral training' (Pl. Grg. 501e); in the plural it is a technical term for lists of dramatic and choral productions with associated details: year of performance (archon), poet, title, festival, *choregos*, actors. The entries were made in the archive of the authority responsible for the production, such at least was the case in Athens. Aristotle collected this material and published it in his Διδασκαλίαι (*Didaskalíai*) and Νῖκαι Διονυσιακαὶ ἀστικαὶ καὶ Ληναικαί.

Peripatetic research is based on Aristotle (→ Dicaearchus) and the fragmentary inscriptions preserved, epigraphical notices that partly continue his work, so particularly the following lists from Athens: 1) IG 2²,2318 + fr. nov. (ed. [1]), made soon after 346 BC, in 13 columns (but cols. VI and X missing, as are two or three at the start), collectively known as *Fasti*, comprising, from 473/2 BC until 329/8 BC, in stereotyped succession the following information: name of the presiding archon; winning phyle in the dithyramb class for boys with *choregos*; winning phyle in the dithyramb class for men with *choregos*; winning *choregos* and poet in the comedy contest; winning *choregos* and poet in the tragedy contest; from 450/49 the name of the winning actor in the tragedy contest is added. As nothing remains of Aristotle's 'Victories' (Νῖκαι) except the title, no definite link between the inscription and Aristotle's work can be determined. 2) IG II², 2319–2323, made soon after 288 BC and called *Didaskalíai* contains in the same ordered sequence the tragedies and comedies entered in the Great Dionysia together with those performed at the Lenaea with the following headings: archon, names of poets and their plays with the respective characters in order of merit. 3) IG II², 2325. List of winning writers, tragedy and comedy, and actors at the Great Dionysia and Lenaea and the sum total of their victories at the respective festival. 4) Other inscriptions about Athens can be deciphered on the monument of Xenocles (IG 2²,3073) with reference to the Lenaea of 307/6, and fragmentary lists found in Rome for Athenian comedy contests (IG XIV, 1097+1098). In addition are the remains of the list found in the Athenian Agora for 255/4 with the three leading players for the contest for old tragedy and comedy and for old satyr plays. The information provided in the *didaskaliai* made its way from the monumental lists into the → hypotheseis for the separate plays, into the → scholia, the → Marmor Parium and the → Suda.

About the remaining performances we are much less well informed. Notices of dramatic performances at the rural Dionysia in Attica are found for the demes of Myrrhinous (IG II²,1183,36, second half of the 4th cent. BC) and Piraeus (IG II²,1496 for 334–330 BC). For Eleusis there is evidence of dithyramb and tragedy performances from mid 4th cent. (IG II²,1186), and of a comedy contest (IG II²,3100). For Icarion IG II²,1178 records *choregoi* and IG II²,3099 tragedies. Whether the IG II²,3091 inscription found at Aexone refers to the rural Dionysia is arguable.

→ Dionysia; → Lenaea

Edition: 1 E. Capps, Greek inscriptions: a new fragment of the List of Victors at the City Dionysia, in: Hesperia 12, 1943, 1–11
Bibliography: 2 Mette 3 Pickard-Cambridge/Gould/Lewis 4 TrGF I 3–52.

II. Roman

In Latin literature two comedies by Plautus (Codex Ambrosianus: Stichus, 200 BC; Pseudolus, 191 BC), and all six by Terence can be dated from *didaskaliai*. The Hellenistic Aristotelian-Peripatetic *didaskalia* literature found its way into Latin literature via → Accius' *Pragmatica* and *Didascalica* which related the beginnings of dramatic literature in Rome — incorrectly — and questioned the authenticity of Plautus' comedies. → Varro deals with the question of *didaskaliai* (deciding against Accius, cf. Cic. Brut. 72), probably particularly in *De scaenicis originibus* and *De actionibus scaenicis*.

G. E. Duckworth, The Nature of Roman Comedy, 1952, 52–61; H. Juhnke, Terenz, in: E. Lefèvre (ed.), Das röm. Drama, 1978, 231f.; Leo, 386–391; P. L. Schmidt, Postquam ludus in artem paulatim verterat. Varro und die Frühgesch. des röm. Theaters, in: G. Vogt-Spira (ed.), Stud. zur vorlit. Periode im frühen Rom, 1989, 77–135. B.Z.

Didia Clara Daughter of Didius [II 6] and wife to Cornelius [II 47] Repentinus. Coins bearing her name and the title Augusta were minted in April and May of AD 193.

Raepsaet-Charlier, no. 312. W.E.

Didius Roman plebeian gentile name (also spelled Deidius on coins and inscriptions, Schulze, 438). The name is attested from the 2nd cent. BC.

E. Badian, The Consuls, 179–49 BC, in: Chiron 20, 1990, 404f.

I Republic

[I 1] **D., T.(?)** Probably instituted as people's tribune in 143 BC (MRR 1,472) a law to regulate expenditure on banquets, so extending the *lex sumptuaria* of C. → Fannius Strabo (Macrob. Sat. 3,17,6).

E. Baltrusch, Regimen morum, 1989, 85f.

[I 2] **D., C.** In 46/5 BC fleet commander for Caesar (Flor. 2,13,75), in 46 beat the Pompeians at Carteia; after another victory at Munda in 45 BC he destroyed Pompey's fleet and indeed Pompey himself; the same year saw him killed by the Lusitanians (Bell. Hisp. 37; 40; Plut. Caesar 56 and elsewhere; MRR 2,300; 311).

[I 3] **D., Q.** was sent by Octavian to Syria as governor immediately after the battle of Actium (his title his not recorded). Once there, he promptly eliminated the remnants of Mark Antony's army (Marcus Antonius [I 9]) and particularly the Red Sea fleet (Cass. Dio 51,7; MRR 2, 421).

[I 4] **D., T.** The most distinguished bearer of this name in the Republic, *homo novus*, mint master in 113 or 112 BC (RRC 294). When people's tribune in 103 he tried in vain to prevent his fellow tribune C. → Norbanus from prosecuting Q. → Servilius Caepio (Cic. De or. 2,197; MRR 1,563f.). As praetor in 101 in Macedonia he defeated the Caeni in eastern Thrace (Roman Statutes 1, no. 12, Cnid. col. IV, l. 8f.; [1. 213]) and celebrated his first triumph in 100 or 99 (MRR 3,81). As consul with Q. Caecilius [I 28] Metellus Nepos in 98, he introduced the *lex Caecilia Didia*, imposing delays (*trinundinum*) to be observed between successive legislative procedures and preventing extraneous clauses from being introduced (*lex satura*). In the same year he went to Spain, staying there as proconsul until 93 and thanks to a grim campaign against the Celtiberians being awarded a second triumph (Cic. Planc. 61; Inscr. Ital. 13,1,85); one of his military tribunes was Q. → Sertorius. In the → Civil War he fought in 90 and 89 as legate in the southern field of action, taking Herculaneum in 89 (Vell. Pat. 2,16,2), and fell on 11 June 89 (Ovid Fast. 6,567f.). On the coins of P. → Fonteius Capito in 55 BC (RRC 429) he appears as rebuilder of the → *villa publica*, the censors' office.

1 M. Hassall et al., Rome and the Eastern Provinces at the End of the Second Century B.C., in: JRS 64, 1974.

K.-L.E.

II Empire

[II 1] **D. Balbinus.** *Epistrategos* of Heptanomia, recorded in AD 229 (BGU II 659; POxy. 3348/9) [1].

1 D. Thomas, The Roman Epistrategos, 1982, 191, 204.

[II 2] **A. D. Gallus.** Part of his career can be traced in CIL III 7247 = ILS 970 (cf. Vogel-Weidemann 348ff.). Quaestor in AD 19 (EOS I 515ff.; so he could scarcely have been the *quaestor imp.* named in ILS 970, *proconsul Siciliae, cos. suff.* in 39 (AE 1973, 138) and then or immediately afterwards *curator aquarum* until 49 (Frontin. Aq. 102). Legate and *comes* with Claudius in Britain in 43, and afterwards legate in Moesia, where he was awarded triumphal insignia for making Cotys ruler of the Bosporus kingdom; between about 49 and 52 proconsul of Asia, from 52–57 governor of Britain, where nothing of note disturbed his period in office. He may well have come from Histonium, perhaps the son of A. D. Postumus, *procos. Cypri* (AE 1934, 86). His own adoptive son was perhaps D. [II 3] below. PIR² D 70.

M. Torelli, in: EOS II, 183; Devijver, 1540; Birley, 44ff.

[II 3] **A. D. Gallus Fabricius Veiento.** → Fabricius

[II 4] **L. D. Marinus.** An *eques* from Syria whose long career as procurator raised him at least to the office of *a cognitionibus* with the rank of *vir perfectissimus* under Caracalla; later he may have become a member of the Senate. CIL III 6753 = ILS 1396; PIR² D 71.

Devijver, D 8; V, 2088; R. Haensch, in: ZPE 95, 1993, 177f.

[II 5] **D. Secundus.** Figures in a rescript of Trajan; held equestrian or senatorial office. PIR² D 76.

W. Eck, in: Chiron 13, 1983, 205.

[II 6] **M. D. Severus Iulianus.** Emperor in 193. Son of one Q. Petronius Didius Severus and Aemilia Clara (PIR² P 279; A 414), he was probably a native of Mediolanum (Milan) and possibly related to the senator and lawyer Salvius Iulianus. Born on 30 Jan. 133 (Cassius Dio 73,17,5; though SHA Did. Iul. 9,3 gives 2 Feb. 137). Brought up by Domitia [II 8] Lucilla, the mother of Marcus Aurelius; she is said to have furthered his career. A relatively slow rise carried him to the command of the legio XXII Primigenia in Mainz, and then to praetorian governorship of Belgium. *Cos. suff.* in 175. Consular legate in Dalmatia between 176 and 180; then held a similar position in Germany until 184/5, where under his tenure the Cologne praetorium was rebuilt [1]; afterwards legate in the province of Pontus and Bithynia and *c.* 189/190 proconsul of Africa. The town of Bisica honoured him with a large monument in Rome (CIL VI 1401 = 41122). After the death of Pertinax he succeeded in getting the praetorians to acclaim him *imperator*; eventually being recognized by the Senate. He ruled 66 days from 28 Mar 193 (Cass. Dio 73,17,5). His wife, Manlia Scantilla, received the title of Augusta, as did their daughter. In the provinces both Septimius Severus and Pescennius Niger pronounced themselves against him. As Septimius Severus invaded Italy and soon stood before Rome, the Senate deposed Iulianus on 1 June; the following day he was murdered in the imperial palace. He failed to evolve any distinctive policy as emperor. PIR² D 77.

1 W. Eck, in: BJ 184, 1984, 97ff.

Eck, Statthalter 184ff.; V. Zedelius, Unt. zur Münzprägung von Pertinax bis Clodius Albinus, diss. 1976; A. M. Woodward, The Coinage of Didius Iulianus and his

Family, in: NC 121, 1961, 71ff.; Fittschen & Zanker I, 93 (portrait). W.E.

Dido Mythical founder of → Carthage; called *Elissa* by Phoenicians, *Theiosso* by Greeks, and *Deido* by Africans because of her wanderings (so Timaeus in *FGrH* 566 F 82; but see Serv. auct. Verg. Aen. 1,340). The myth to be lastingly established by Virgil (Aen. 1 and 4) is in its outlines present already in Timaeus; a far more detailed pre-Virgilian version is to be found in Pompeius Trogus (Just. Epit. 18,4–6), but as in Timaeus without mention of → Aeneas. Her father, king of Tyre, was variously called Mutto (Tim.), Methres (Serv. on Verg. Aen. 1,343) or Belus (Verg. Aen. 1,621). Fleeing her brother → Pygmalion, who had killed her husband Acherbas (Just.) or Sychaeus (Verg.) out of greed, she came to Libya and founded Carthage. For that she acquired as much land as she could enclose in an ox-hide (Verg.; vaguer in Just.), hence the name Byrsa for the Carthaginian citadel [1]. To escape marriage to the Libyan prince Hiarbas (Just.; Iarbas: Verg.) and to save her city, she burned herself to death on a pyre. Only in Virgil (Aen. 4) is her unhappy love for Aeneas specific reason for her death on the pyre [2] and cause of the enmity between Carthage and Rome. Whether Virgil adapted this from Naevius' *Bellum Poenicum* or made it up himself is a matter of dissension among scholars; but that the portrayal is Virgil's alone is indisputable [2; 3]. Recent criticism confirms Virgil's originality. The story is omitted by Dionysius of Halicarnassus, while Varro makes not Dido but her sister → Anna burn herself for love of Aeneas (Serv. auct. Verg. Aen. 4,682; Serv. Verg. Aen. 5,4).

Since Virgil (cf. too Aen. 6,450–476) the tragic tale of Dido and Aeneas has become one of the great love stories of literature. Augustine (Conf. 1,13) testifies to its influence in late antiquity.

1 J. Scheid, J. Svenbro, Byrsa. La ruse d'Elissa et la fondation de Carthage, in: Annales (ESC) 40, 1985, 328–342 2 R. Heinze, Virgils ep. Technik, 1915, 115–119 3 A.-M. Tupet, Didon magicienne, in: REL 49, 1970, 229–258.

E. Griset, La leggenda di Anna, Didone ed Enea, in: RSC 9, 1961, 302–307; R. Martin (ed.), Enée et Didon. Naissance, fonctionnement et survie d'un mythe, 1991; M. Sala, s.v. Didone, EV 2, 48–63; E. Simon, s.v. D., LIMC 8.1, 559–562. F.G.

Didrachmon (δίδραχμον; *dídrachmon*). A unit of weight and a silver coin worth two drachmas, the *didrachmon* was the largest value in circulation, mostly struck in Asia Minor, southern Italy, Rome and part of Sicily, as well as Corinth, Elis and on Aegina, seldom in Athens, and rated variously at 12.48 g in Aegina, at 8.73 g in Attica or at the south Italian standard of 7.9 g, later 6.6 g. As a unit it represented a stater, so esp. for gold coinage. Rhodian 1st-cent. bronze coins and Neronian coins from Antioch on the Orontes bear the legend ΔΙΔΡΑΧΜΟΝ; *DIDRACHMON* [1; 2].
→ Drachma; → Stater

1 A. Kromann, The Greek imperial coinage from Cos and Rhodos, in: S. Dietz, I. Papachristodoulou, Archaeology in the Dodecanese, 1988, 213–217 2 RPCI, 606ff., 616, 4178.

Schrötter, 159–161; H. Küthmann, Zur röm.- campanischen Didrachmenprägung, in: JNG 9, 1958, 87–97; M. N. Tod, Epigraphical Notes on Greek Coinage, in: NC 6.20, 1960, 1–24; H. A. Cahn, Knidos. Die Münzen des sechsten und fünften Jh.v.Chr., AMuGS 6, 1970, esp. 178–192; M. H. Crawford, Coinage and money under the Roman Republic, 1985, esp. 32f. A.M.

Didyma (Δίδυμα; *Dídyma*).
A. General B. Pre-greek times to classical period C. Hellenistic times D. Roman Empire E. Christian Era F. Apollo Sanctuary G. Artemis Sanctuary H. Sacred Way I. Hellenistic and Roman remains J. Byzantine settlement

A. General

D., formerly Branchidae, on a limestone plateau by the gulf of Iasus, regional sanctuary between Caria and Ionia (Strabo 14,1,2), famed as the source oracle of Apollo (Hdt. 1,92; 2,159; Paus. 7,2,6) and for the size of its temple of Apollo (Strabo 14,1,5), is reckoned one of the best-preserved monuments of antiquity. Investigations in 18th and 19th cents. by English and French archaeologists, the clearing of the temple site by the Berlin museums from 1906 to 1925; the excavations of the German Archaeological Institute since 1962 — all produced archaeological evidence going back to about 700 BC. Neolithic obsidian finds nearby. It is the richest site in Asia Minor for statuary of the archaic period.

B. Pre-greek times to classical period

The presence of fresh water lies at the root of the cult; Apollo's cult spring lay in a depression in the landscape, that of Artemis lay on a rock outcropping. In pre-Greek times (Hdt. 1,157; Paus. 7,2,6) one can probably assume worship of a female nature-god (union of Zeus and Leto, Syll.[3] 590). Prophets, priests and cult founders in pre-Hellenistic times were the local aristocratic family of the Branchidae. Herodotus mentions foundations of Necho (2,159) and Croesus (1,92) there. Darius is said to have approved asylum protection at the sanctuary (Tac. Ann. 3,63). Its destruction by fire by the Persians cannot be confirmed archaeologically, the dating to 494 (Hdt. 6,19) or 479 BC (Paus. 8,46,3) 'during the second secession of Ionia' (Hdt. 9,104) is disputed. The reported surrender of the sanctuary to the Persians by the Branchidae can be traced to later Milesian invention (Callisthenes, FGrH 124 F 14; Str. 17,1,43). From 479 BC the processions from Miletus were resumed.

C. Hellenistic times

The last third of the 4th cent. BC brought fundamental changes in the organization and oracular activity:

Cult precinct beside the Sacred Road from Miletus to Didyma (perspectival aerial view from SW).

Miletus commissioned the construction of a new temple for Apollo, and appointed an official as προφήτης (*prophḗtēs*) and sacrificial priests for Apollo on an annual basis. The Seleucids supported the sanctuary, and the polis *anathema* (the Canachus Apollo), appropriated by the Persians, to Miletus (Paus. 1,16,3; 8,46,3). From *c.* 200 BC, the *Didýmeia* were celebrated as a penteteric festival. D. was plundered during an attack by Galatians in 277/6 BC and in 67 BC by pirates.

D. Roman Empire

In Roman times there was an extension of the sanctuary by Caesar (44 BC), and under Trajan the ceremonial avenue was widened and the interior of the sanctuary paved (AD 100/1). The reported intention of Caligula to rededicate the temple to himself (Cass. Dio 59,28,1), is questionable. From 177 the imperial cult was celebrated there as the Κομμόδεια (*Kommódeia*, or 'Feast of Commodus').

E. Christian Era

The first indication of Christian reaction to the Greek cults dates to the 4th cent. In the 5th and 6th cents. and between the 10th and 12th cents. D. was a diocese, although no Christian monuments seem to have been built. Earthquakes devastated the site in the 7th and at the end of the 15th cent.; it has been resettled since the late 18th cent.

F. Apollo Sanctuary

The foundations of the brick wall of a court yard in which the central cult spring lay date from *c.* 700 BC. In the 6th cent. a proper → temple was built with a dipteral peristasis of limestone and marble (→ Dipteros) and a spring house or naïskos to protect the sanctuary and site of the oracle (μαντεῖον, *manteîon*). Halls were built to the south-west and east as well as a rotunda. Towards the middle of the 4th cent. the older buildings were demolished and a start made on a larger dipteros on a seven-stepped platform covering almost two and a half times the area of what had stood there before. Inscriptions and builders' marks on the temple walls document the construction process. The building material consists of marble quarried at Heraclea by Latmus.

By 170 BC a main building with sanctuary and prodomos (portico with twelve columns and two-columned hall) had been built. The forecourt and roof of the adytum were not completed. A grove of trees (ἄλσος, *álsos*, Str. 14,1,5) was planted in the sanctuary. After AD 250 the eastern intercolumnar space was walled up. In the 5th/6th cents. a basilica with galleries was erected in the forecourt and in the 7th the temple was fortified. A 10th-cent. fire, earthquakes and plundering of stones in the 19th cent. completed the destruction of the temple.

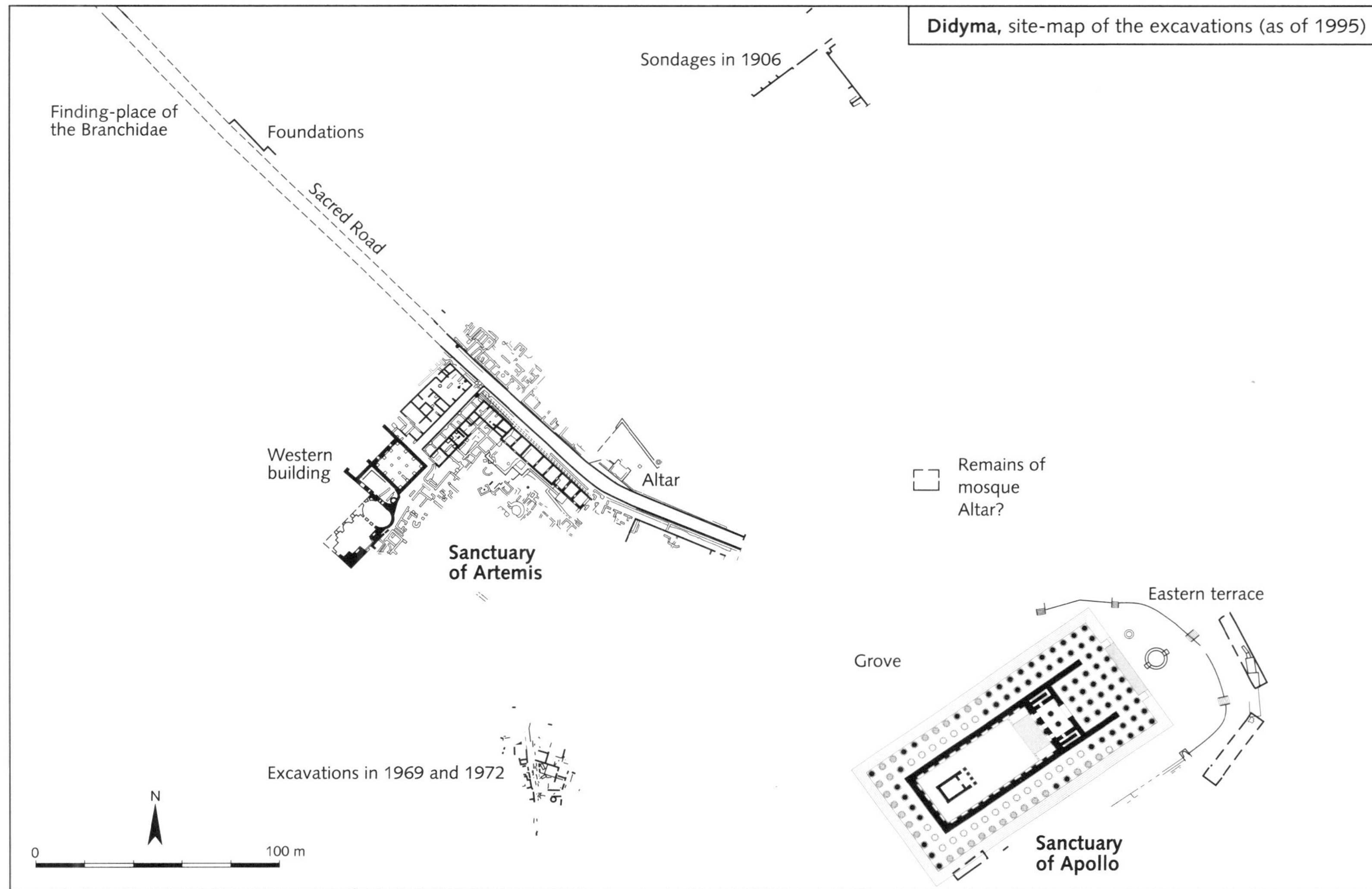

Didyma, site-map of the excavations (as of 1995)
Sondages in 1906
Finding-place of the Branchidae
Foundations
Sacred Road
Western building
Altar
Remains of mosque
Altar?
Sanctuary of Artemis
Eastern terrace
Grove
Excavations in 1969 and 1972
N
0
100 m
Sanctuary of Apollo

G. Artemis Sanctuary

The structures on a rock outcrop dating to *c.* 700 BC have been identified as the source precinct with the cult of Artemis (ὑδροφορία, *hydrophoría*). It was extended since the 6th cent. BC; from the 3rd–1st cents. BC the dried-up spring was replaced with a well. A wall, to which were added colonnades (limestone columns and wooden beams), separated the group of separate buildings from the Sacred Way. In the 2nd cent. AD the sanctuary was restructured, only to be abandoned in the 4th cent.

H. Sacred Way

In the 6th cent. BC a raised road some 5 to 6 metres wide and more than 20 kilometres long was built linking Miletus to D. for processions, with stations dedicated to local deities along the way (a nymph sanctuary has been identified). On the highest point is a sanctuary with a group of seated statues and sphinx sculptures also from the 6th cent. BC. The last section of the road should be assumed to run to the west and south of the Apollo temple ('stadium').

I. Hellenistic and Roman remains

Outside the sanctuaries are cemeteries; other inscriptions suggest hitherto unidentified cult sites and buildings.

J. Byzantine settlement

After the destruction of older buildings, the Sacred Way was rebuilt with arcade halls and church buildings in the 5th and 6th cents.; from the 8th cent. rural settlements and erection of new churches.

L. Büchner, s.v. D., RE 5, 437–441 (older literature); J. Fontenrose, D. Apollo's oracle, cult and companions, 1988; G. Gruben, Das archa. Didymaion, in: JDAI 78, 1963, 78–182; W. Günther, Das Orakel von D. in hell. Zeit, Istanbuler Mitt. Beih. 4, 1971; W. Hahland, D. im 5. Jh.v.Chr., in: JDAI 79, 1964, 142–240; L. Haselberger, Ber. über die Arbeit am Jüngeren Apollontempel von D., in: Istanbuler Mitt. 33, 1983, 90–123; H.W. Parke, The massacre of the Branchidae, in: JHS 105, 1985, 59–68; P. Schneider, Zur Top. der Hl. Strasse von Milet nach Didyma, in: AA 1987, 101–129; K. Tuchelt, Die archa. Skulpturen von D., in: IstForsch 27, 1970; Id., Vorarbeiten zu einer Top. von D., Istanbuler Mitt. Beih. 9, 1973; Id., Einige Überlegungen zum Kanachos-Apollon von D., in: JDAI 101, 1986, 75–84; Id., Die Perserzerstörung von D., in: AA 1988, 427–438; Id., Branchidai-D. (Zaberns Bildbände zur Arch. 3), 1992 (with bibliography); Id., P. Schneider, T.G. Schattner, H.R. Baldus, Didyma III 1: Ein Kultbezirk an der Hl. Straße von Milet nach D. (with a bibliography of the D.-excavations, 1962–1995), 1996; W. Voigtländer, Der jüngste Apollontempel von D., Istanbuler Mitt. Beih. 14, 1975; T. Wiegand, A. Rehm, D. 2: Die Inschr., 1958; T. Wiegand, H. Knackfuss, D. 1: Die Baubeschreibung, 1941. KA.TU.

Didymarchus (Διδύμαρχος; *Didýmarchos*). Author of 'Metamorphoses' in at least three books, which seem to have included the → Battus myth. Rather than a heavenly origin for Pan he prefers the version with Pan as the son of → Gaia (Theoc. schol. 1, 3–4).

SH 20 & 175; U. v. Wilamowitz-Moellendorff, Antigonos von Karystos, 1881, 172, n. 5. C.S.

Didyme (Διδύμη; *Didýmē*). Egyptian (Ethiopian) mistress of Ptolemy II; see in Anth. Pal. 5,210?

A. Cameron, Two Mistresses of Ptolemy Philadelphus, in: GRBS 31, 1990, 287; F.M. Snowden Jr., Asclepiades' D., in: GRBS 32, 1991, 239–259. W.A.

Didymus (Δίδυμος; *Dídymos*).

[1] of Alexandria

A. Philological activity B. Musical theory

A. Philological activity

The most important Greek grammarian of the latter half of the 1st cent. BC. The biographical entry in the Suda (δ 872) tells us that he was still alive in the reign of Augustus, and mentions a nickname 'Chalkenteros' (Χαλκέντερος, 'Brazen-guts', cf. the Suda ι 399, χ 29). To his strong constitution he attributed an untiring assiduity that extended to different branches of philology. The Alexandrine tradition of exegesis and scholarship had persisted through several generations of Aristarchan scholars. It culminated in D., who worked in Alexandria and was already renowned in antiquity for having written between 3,500 and 4,000 books — more than he could himself remember and earning him another ironic title, that of 'Bibliolathas' (Βιβλιολάθας, 'book-forgetter', cf. Ath. 4,139 c).

Much of what we know of D. has to do with Homeric philology. An unknown grammarian of late antiquity compiled a commentary using his works and those of Aristonicus, Nicanor and Herodian. Excerpts from this Four-Men Commentary found their way into various learned collections, above all into the rich scholia of the Codex Venetus A of the *Iliad*, in which this note appears at the end of nearly every single book: 'the notes of Aristonicus presented, together with the writings of D. on Aristarchus' edition, also some from Herodian's *Iliad* prosody and from Nicanor's writing on the → *stigme*.' So we know that D. was at pains to present Aristarchus' definitive Homer text and its sources; in this way he became the person responsible for handing down a large amount of exegetic material stemming from the master. D.'s commentaries on the *Iliad* and the *Odyssey* are to be distinguished from work on the Aristarchan *diórthōsis* (διόρθωσις). Influential too is the complex of his detailed and learned *hypomnḗmata* on the works of a large number of important epic, lyric, tragic and comic poets of classical times. We have testimony of varying quality to his commentaries on Hesiod, on Bacchylides and Pindar (some 80 fragments in the scholia), on Sophocles, Euripides and perhaps Aeschylus as well, on Ion of Chios, on Aristophanes (over 60 mentions in the scholia), Phrynichus, Menander and perhaps also on Eupolis and Cratinus. Among writers of prose he concerned himself with Thucydides and in particular with the orators Demosthenes, Aeschines, Hypereides, Isaeus and perhaps others too. A 2nd-cent. papyrus with the general title of 'On Demosthenes' (Περὶ Δημοσθένους) gives part of the commentary on the *Philippics* in the form of an epitome.

The copious lexicographical work of D. is definitely related to the exegesis of authors. In this field two works stand out: *Léxis tragikḗ* (Λέξις τραγική) and the *Léxis kōmikḗ* (Λέξις κωμική), on tragic and comic idiom, dedicated to the linguistic peculiarities of tragedians and comedians. We know, too, of a work on the language of Hippocrates, and of another, quoted by Harpocration s.v. δερμηστής, in at least seven books with the title *Aporouménē léxis* (Ἀπορουμένη λέξις; 'Disputed usage'; the fragment MILLER published about the *lexis Platonica* is a pseudepigraph). Over and above these are the numerous monographs on various themes from literary history and antiquity including 'On Lyric Poets' (Περὶ λυρικῶν ποιητῶν), perhaps part of a larger work 'On Poets' (Περὶ ποιητῶν); *Symmiktá* (Συμμικτά) and/or *Symposiaká* (Συμποσιακά); a collection of abstruse and unusual tales (Ξένη ἱστορία); and paroemiography (Περὶ παροιμιῶν). In the field of grammar Περὶ παθῶν (on linguistic 'Pathology': explaining problematic words on the basis of adopted modifications to obviously related words), 'On Orthography' (Περὶ ὀρθογραφίας) and a monograph on the Latin language.

D.'s work is like a pool collecting the results of previous centuries. He collected, compiled and passed his material on to different scholia, corpora and countless learned miscellanies, perhaps, as has often been said, with no great originality, yet certainly with much learned care. He was probably aware that the work of the great Alexandrine philologists was doomed to disappear, so he devoted himself to arranging, selecting and compiling the essentials, salvaging from them much of what we know today. His work built a platform for later generations, and his influence in the fields of scholastics, lexicography, grammar and paroemiography is beyond estimation.

→ Aristarchus [4]; → Aristonicus [5]; → Grammarians; → Herodianus; → Nicanor; → Philology; → Scholia; → Four-Men Commentary

EDITIONS: M. SCHMIDT, Didymi Chalcenteri fragmenta, 1854; L. PEARSON, S. STEPHENS, Didymi in Demosthenem commenta, 1983; A. LUDWICH, Aristarchs Homerische Textkritik nach den Fragmenten des D., 1884/5; FGrH 340.

BIBLIOGRAPHY: E. MILLER, Didyme d'Alexandrie. Περὶ τῶν ἀπορουμένων παρὰ Πλάτωνι λέξεων, in: Mélanges de Littérature Grecque, 1868, 399–406 (= Lexica Graeca Minora, 1965, XIV-XV e 245–252 [Ps.-Didymos]; G. ARRIGHETTI, Poeti, eruditi e biografi, 1987, 194–204 and *passim*; P. BOUDREAUX, Le texte d'Aristophane et ses commentateurs, 1919, 91–137; L. COHN, s.v. D. (8), RE 5, 445–472; H. DIELS, W. SCHUBART, Berliner Klassikertexte I, 1904; E.M. HARRIS, More Chalcenteric Negligence, in: CPh 84, 1989, 36–44; J. IRIGOIN, Histoire du texte de Pindare, 1952, 67–76 and *passim*; K. LEHRS, De Aristarchi studiis Homericis, [3]1882, 16–29 and *passim*; F. LEO, D. Περὶ Δημοσθένους, Nachrichten der Ges. der Wiss. zu Göttingen 1904, 254–261 (= Ausgewählte kleine Schriften, ed. E. FRAENKEL, 1960, II 387–394); M.J. LOSSAU, Unt. zur ant. Demosthenesexegese, 1964; O. LUSCHNAT, Die Thukydidesscholien, in: Philologus 98, 1954, 14–58; F. MONTANA, L' "Athenaion Politeia" di Aristotele negli "Scholia Vetera" ad Aristofane, 1996, 29–31 and *passim*; F. MONTANARI, in: CPF I 1, 258–264; PFEIFFER, KPI, 228, 261–267, 271, 275, 284, 292, 331–337; A. RÖMER, Aristarchs Athetesen in der Homerkritik, 1912, 98ff.; L.E. ROSSI, I generi letterari e le loro leggi scritte e non scritte, in: BICS 18, 1971, 69–94; K. RUPPRECHT, s.v. Paroimiographoi, RE 18, 1747–1751; M. SCHMIDT, Die Erklärungen zum Weltbild Homers und zur Kultur der Heroenzeit in den bT-Scholien zur Ilias, 1976, 28–32; M. VAN DER VALK, Researches on the Text and Scholia of the Iliad, I, 1963–4, 536–553; C. WENDEL, Die Aristophanes-Scholien der Papyri, in: Byzantion 13, 1938, 631–690; Id., s.v. Mythographie, RE 16, 1358–1362; S. WEST, Chalcenteric Negligence, in: CQ 20, 1970, 288–296; U.v. WILAMOWITZ, Einleitung in die Griech. Tragödie, [2]1895, 158–167; G. ZUNTZ, An Inquiry into the Transmission of the Plays of Euripides, 1965, 253ff.

F.M.

B. MUSICAL THEORY

D. also made a contribution to musical theory. For the intervals of the three tonic genera (diatonic, chromatic, enharmonic; → Music) he developed his own theory of harmonic division. The excess of a major tone, ratio 9 : 8, over a minor, ratio 10 : 9, leaves a difference of 81 : 80, and is still termed a Didymic or syntonic comma [1. 70–73; 2. 85–88]. A lost work, his Περὶ τῆς διαφορᾶς τῶν Ἀριστοξενείων τε καὶ Πυθαγορείων [3. 5, 25; 2. 139, 144ff., 152ff.], was the source of Ptolemy's and Porphyry's information about Aristoxenian and Pythagorean teaching, and included references to the otherwise unknown → Ptolemais Cyrenaicae.

1 I. DÜRING, Harmonielehre des Klaudios Ptolemaios, 1930 2 Id., Ptolemaios und Porphyrios über die Musik, 1934 3 Id., Komm. des Porphyrios zur Harmonielehre des Klaudios Ptolemaios, 1932.

F.Z.

[2] **Minor.** (Δίδυμος ὁ νεώτερος; *Dídumos ho neṓteros, D. minor*). Greek grammarian from Alexandria, active in Rome (the Suda δ 873), distinguished from D. [1] Chalkenteros by being called ὁ νέος or ὁ νεώτερος, the Younger. We have no biographical details about him. Usually he is placed a little later than D. [1] Chalkenteros, in the 1st cent. AD. The Suda (loc. cit.) says he wrote Πιθανά (a subject Apollonius [11] Dyscolus also treated) and Περὶ ὀρθογραφίας καὶ ἄλλα πλεῖστα καὶ ἄριστα. Hypotheses have been made that he was to be identified with D. [3] Claudius, or with D. Chalkente-

ros or with other grammarians of the same name and his works attributed to these accordingly.
→ Didymus [1] Chalkenteros; → Didymus [3] Claudius; → Apollonius [11] Dyscolus.

H. v. ARNIM, s.v. D. (6), RE 5, 444f.; G. BERNHARDY, Suidae Lexicon, I, 1834–53, s.v. Δίδυμος νέος; L. COHN, s.v. D. (9), RE 5, 472f.; DIELS, DG, 86; M. SCHMIDT, Didymi Chalcenteri fragmenta, 1854, 3, 335–349; M. WELLMANN, s.v. D. (7), RE 5, 445. F.M.

[3] **Claudius.** (ὁ Κλαύδιος; *ho Klaúdios*). Greek grammarian, active in Rome at the beginning of the Empire; titles of his work in the Suda δ 874. In Περὶ τῆς παρὰ Ῥωμαίοις ἀναλογίας (some fragments found in Priscian) D. attempted to explain grammatic and syntactic aspects of Latin through a comparison with Greek (cf. Philoxenus). No trace remains of another work, Περὶ τῶν ἡμαρτημένων παρὰ τὴν ἀναλογίαν Θουκυδίδῃ, apparently about faulty analogies in Thucydides. Another title Ἐπιτομὴ τῶν Ἡρακλέωνος affords no clue to the contents. This D. may have composed a polemical work against Cicero's *De re publica*, which has come down as the work of D. [1] Chalkenteros (Amm. Marc. 22,16,16). The possibility that D. [4] and D. [2] were one and the same person can not be ruled out.
→ Cicero; → Philoxenus; → Priscianus; → Thucydides

L. COHN, s.v. D. (10), RE 5, 473; A. DAUB, Studien zu den Biographika des Suidas, 1882, 90f.; H. FUNAIOLI, Grammaticae Romanae Fragmenta, 1907, 447–450; M. SCHMIDT, Didymi Chalcenteri fragmenta, 1854, 3, 345–349; M. DUBUISSON, Le latin est-il une langue barbare?, in: Ktema 9, 1984, 55–68. F.M.

[4] **Son of Heraclides.** (ὁ τοῦ Ἡρακλείδου; *ho toû Hērakleídou*), Greek grammarian and musician, worked in 1st-cent. Rome at the time of Nero (the Suda δ 875). He is unlikely to have been son to the grammarian Heraclides Ponticus the Younger, who studied under Didymus [1] Chalkenteros in Alexandria. To equate him with his close contemporary Claudius D. (D. [3]) seems difficult; less so to make him the author of works on Pythagorean philosophy mentioned by Clement of Alexandria (in Strom. II 52,12 STÄHLIN) and by Porphyry.
→ Didymus [1] & [3]; → Heraclides Ponticus the Younger

L. COHN, s.v. D. 11, RE 5, 473f.; A. DAUB, Studien zu den Biographika des Suidas, 1882, 90f.; M. SCHMIDT, Didymi Chalcenteri fragmenta, 1854, 345f. F.M.

[5] **'the Blind'** Important theologian from → Alexandria [1] (313–398). Despite being blinded while very young, this lay ascetic became a famous teacher and, so Rufinus in Historia Ecclesiastica 11,7, was entrusted by Athanasius with the leadership of the catechete school in Alexandria. In the field of systematics (pre-existence of the soul) and exegesis he relied on Origen. In Rufinus, Palladius, Jerome and Ammonius he had influential students. He was posthumously condemned as an Origenist (Synod of Constantinople 543) and much of his work was destroyed. The papyrus find in Egypt at Tura in 1941 increases the textual basis considerably.

Of the numerous commentaries on practically the entire Bible that remain in predominantly fragmentary form in scholia, excerpts and linked works, the most significant are on Gen. [1], Pss. [2], Job [3], Zech. [4], Eccles. [5] as well as on the catholic letters. The exposition is handled in the usual Alexandrine manner. Of the dogmatic writings little remains; the same is true of a treatise *De spiritu sancto* [6]. D. defended the Nicene creed against the heresies of his time.

1 P. NAUTIN, L. DOUTRELEAU, 1976; 1978 (SChr 233; 244) 2 E. MÜHLENBERG, 1, 1975, 121–375; 2, 1977 (Patristic Texts and Studies 15f.) 3 A. HEINRICHS, U. and D. HAGEDORN, L. KOENEN, 1968; 1985 (Papyrologische Texte und Abhandlungen 1–4) 4 L. DOUTRELEAU, 1962 (SChr 83–85) 5 G. BINDER et al., 1969–1983 6 L. DOUTRELEAU, 1992 (SChr 386).

EDITION: CPG 2544–2573.
BIBLIOGRAPHY: B. KRAMER, s.v. D., TRE 8, 741–746; E. PRINZIVALLI, Didimo il Cieco e l'interpretazione dei Salmi, 1988. J.RI.

[6] Slave of emperor Tiberius, who kept Germanicus' son Drusus in captivity. PIR[2] D 83. W.E.

[7] Spaniard, related to → Theodosius I. Together with his brother Verinianus and supported by a private army, he rebelled against → Constantinus [3] III in AD 408, was defeated in 409, captured and put to death. PLRE 2, 358. H.L.

Dieburg Roman civilian settlement, main settlement of the *civitas Auderiensium* with good infrastructure (archaeological finds: e.g., a Mithraeum). Heyday about AD 300, but victim of Alamannic raids.

E. SCHALLMAYER, D., in: D. BAATZ, F.-R. HERRMANN (ed.), Die Römer in Hessen, [2]1989, 250–255. K.DI.

Diegylis (Διήγυλις; *Diḗgylis*, Val. Max. 9,2 ext. 4: Diogyris). King of the Thracian tribe of the Caeni and brother-in-law of the Bithynian king → Prusias II, whom he supported in the war against → Attalus [5] II of Pergamum (App. Mith. 6). He attacked Attalus' possessions on the Thracian Chersonesus and destroyed Lysimachea (Diod. Sic. 33,14,2–5) but was defeated by Attalus in 145–141 BC (Str. 13,4,2; Pomp. Trog. prol. 36; OGIS 330, 339 [1; 2]). Diodorus (33,14–15; 34,12) and Valerius Maximus (9,2 ext. 4) emphasize the cruelty of his reign and that of his son Zibelmius.

1 BENGTSON, 2, 227–229 2 J. KRAUSS (ed.), Die Inschr. von Sestos und der thrakischen Chersones, 1980, no. 1, 14–63.

CH. M. DANOV, Die Thraker auf dem Ostbalkan von der hell. Zeit bis zur Gründung Konstantinopels, in: ANRW II 7.1, 1979, 21–185, 102f.; J. HOPP, Unt. zur Gesch. der letzten Attaliden, 1977, 96–98. U.P.

Dierna (Δίερνα; *Díerna*). Originally a Dacian settlement, Romanized since Trajan, modern Orşova in Banat/Romania. Supposedly already a *colonia iuris Italici* in Trajan's time (Ulpianus in Dig. 50,15,1,8) and a *municipium* in the Severian period (CIL III 14468). D. was located on the Danube west of Drobeta and was the starting point of the rural road to Tibiscum and Sarmizegetusa. A ports, toll station and brick production were located nearby. The military garrison was supplied by the *cohors I Brittonum miliaria*, who established a camp there (CIL III 8074,10). In the 4th cent. the *legio XIII Gemina* and its *praefectus* are mentioned (Not. Dign. Or. 42,37). The settlement is documented up to the time of Justinian. Sources: Ptol. 3,8,10; Tab. Peut. (*Tierna*); Dig. 50,15,1,8 (*Zerna*); Not. Dign. Or. 42,37; Procop. Aed. 4,6,288 (Ζέρνης). The form *Dierna* (*Tsierna*) is attested in inscriptions.

TIR L 34 Budapest, 1967, 53 (bibliography). J.BU.

Dierum (Διερόν; *Dierón*). Fortification on Mt. Olympus, occupied by the troops of Q. Marcius Philippus during the invasion of Macedonia in 169 BC (Liv. 44,3). Located near the village Karia at *c.* 1,450 m altitude.

A. Rhizakis, Une forteresse macédonienne dans l'Olympe, in: BCH 110, 1986, 331–346; G. Lucas, La Tripolis de Perrhébie et ses confins, in: I. Blum (ed.), Topographie antique et géographie historique en pays grec, 1992, 114 n. 243. HE.KR.

Dies atri see → Hemerology

Dies fasti see → Fasti

Dies imperii The day of assuming power, usually also the official recognition of the ruler by the Senate or the army (→ Soldier emperors). The exception is → Vespasian: his *dies imperii* was 1 July 69 AD but the recognition by the Senate came on 21 December 69. The *dies imperii* is attested, for example, for Caligula in the Acta Arvalium (*quod Imperator appellatus est*, Acta Arvalium, CIL VI 32347, 9c 10, see [1]). As in the Hellenistic model, the annually repeated public celebration was the most important after the *dies natalis* (→ Birthday B.) of the → *princeps* [2. 1137–1145]. The *dies imperii* may frequently be determined indirectly from the date of dedications and donations in the ruler's honour [3. 11]. The *tribunicia potestas* of the ruler was renewed on the *dies imperii*; the tribunic New Year was reconciled with the *dies imperii* by dating the act granting *tribunicia potestas* to the *dies imperii*. Even under the Tetrarchy (→ *tetrárchēs* IV) the regnal years were counted according to the *tribunicia potestas* and the imperial acclamations, which changed annually on the *dies imperii*. → Constantinus [1] I counted his imperial acclamations from the *dies Augusti*, which was a change in terminology but not in substance.

1 J. Scheid (ed.), Commentarii Fratrum Arvalium, 1998, 29; 34 2 P. Herz, Kaiserfeste der Prinzipatszeit, in: ANRW II 16.2, 1978, 1135–1200 3 Kienast ([2]1996). ME. STR.

Diespiter see → Jupiter

Dietetics

I. Greece II. Rome

I. Greece

Greek medicine is fundamentally different from Egyptian and Babylonian medicine because it allots dietetics in the broader sense of a regime of eating, drinking, exercise and bathing, a key role within therapeutics [2. 395–402; 3]. Originally, dietetics referred to the administering of balanced foods in liquid, pasty or solid form, depending on the degree of illness (Hippocr. De medicina vetere 5 [4. 241–257]). However, about the mid 5th cent. BC it expanded well beyond a pure theory of nutrition. At times the Pythagoraeans have been credited with the invention of dietetics (Iambl. VP 163). However, Plato (Resp. 406 A-C, Prt. 316 D) associated it with Herodicus of Selymbria, who as a teacher of sports felt the need to incorporate both nutritional and exercise prescriptions in his catalogue of measures for maintaining and improving health. Plato probably rejected this 'new-fangled medicine that pampers disease' (Resp. 406A), but many others immediately joined the 'fashion' (Hippocr. De victu 1,1), among them Democritus (58 A 33 DK). Later authors such as Soranus (Vita Hippocr. 2) and Porphyrius (in Iliad. 11,514) believed that Hippocrates had further developed the ideas of Herodicus, since he was believed to have been his student. Without doubt, dietetics as the most reliable healing method, [11. 343–350] had a preferred place in the Hippocratic Corpus of texts such as *De victu*, *De alimento* and *De victu in morbis acutis*. The author of *De arte* even believed that the medical ability to affect healing by way of dietetics was the most conclusive proof that medicine was an art as the balancing of competing elements was a very demanding task.

The new dietetics also required an understanding of lifestyle in the wider context of thought about the structure of the world (Hippocr. De victu 1,2). By placing the preservation of health at the forefront of all activities, it was directed at the wealthy who did not have to worry about their subsistence. The new trend of dietetics was further expanded upon by Praxagoras, Chrysippus the Elder and Diocles in the late 4th cent. BC. The latter adapted dietetics more closely to the requirements of daily life (fr. 141 Wellmann). In his treatise 'On Health (for Pleistarchus)' he formulated an objection to those who believed that dietary instructions had to contain a justification of the nutritional value of the food recommended in each case (fr. 112 Wellmann; [10. 232–242]). For one part, these justifications could not always be supplied and for another, a different effect than the one desired could occasionally occur. Diocles was convinced he knew the properties of foods from experience (Gal. De exper. med. 13,4–5), even though his descriptions of these properties are less detailed than those of Mnesitheus (fr. 23 BERTIER), whose explanations, particularly on grain he quoted extensively [1. 30–56]. Other authors of important treatises on dietetics were Diphilus of Siphnus, who was active around 300 BC (extensively cited by Athenaeus of Naucratis; [8. 194–201]), and Herophilus, who was active around 280 BC and emphatically recommended gymnastics (fr. 227–229 STADEN 398).

II. ROME

The Greek dietetic tradition, in particular its link to bathing and physical exercise, were adopted by the Romans without reservations. In their therapeutic efforts in the 1st cent. AD, Celsus (Med., prooem. 1,1) and Scribonius Largus (praef. 6) put an undiminished trust in diet, and Asclepiades [6] of Bithynia also owed part of his success to prescribing a 'wine therapy' combined with mild exercise. It remains uncertain whether the incorporation of intellectual activities — listening to music or attending theatre performances —, as found in his dietary prescriptions and those of Athenaeus of Attaleia, were unusual in their age [3. 262–270]. Celsus (Med. 1,1f.) presumably picked up on a Hellenistic development with his offer of dietary consultation under consideration of status and profession. In the next cent. Rufus of Ephesus and Galen followed his path in this.

Galen wrote in great detail about dietetics, both in a therapeutic and a prophylactic sense, and aimed to combine theory and practice, by associating individual foods with the four primary qualities (wet-dry, hot-cold) or the four bodily humours [11. 358–370]. His short treatise *De subtiliante diaeta* stands alone insofar as it focuses on the question of weight reduction, which has become important in 20th-cent. dietetics [5. 2–4]. Galen's recommendations in this respect were taken up by the Greek encyclopaedists [11. 371–379] and Byzantine authors such as Simeon Seth. Latin transmission was secured by texts such as the letter of Anthimus in the 6th cent. AD.

The choice of foods was more strongly determined by medical considerations than judgements of taste or personal preferences. Many authors attempted to maintain an equilibrium among the humours with their advice. Occasional agreement with modern concepts of a balanced diet is purely accidental. They recommended foods rich in protein, especially fish, cheese and pulses —, also whole-grain bread, fatty foods — with a moderate share of animal fats — and some fresh or dried fruit. However, it must not be forgotten that some dietary prescriptions (e.g., Jewish ones), had a ritual rather than medical basis, even if they brought about a healthy lifestyle [6. 553–580], and, as Galen often emphasized, the personal circumstances of those seeking advice, e.g., poverty or urban life, could render the best advice ineffective. His own recommendations were based on the one hand on thorough observation of local grain types or excessive physical training for example, on the other hand possibly on pure prejudice, such as a dislike of fresh fruit, a preference for pork (because it was supposedly most similar to human flesh) and the belief that most types of white meat are beneficial to the chronically ill [11. 362–367]. Like his predecessors, he was concerned that his dietetics should be differentiated from mere culinary skill or teachings on physical fitness. However, the transitions were clearly fluid [11. 374–377]. Galen was well aware that excessive sports could be detrimental to ones health (Gal. 1,23–25). Holistic dietetics, which he claimed as his own, is similar to that of modern advocates of a healthy lifestyle and probably had a similar effect among those who had sufficient time and money for it. However, the basis of each dietetic recommendation differed significantly from modern ones, and the ancient classification of foods into those that promoted and those that were detrimental to health can hardly be reconciled with modern knowledge of vitamins, proteins, carbohydrates, etc.

→ Gymnastics; → Cooking; → Medicine; → DIETETICS

1 J. BERTIER, Mnésithée et Dieuchès, 1972, 30–86 2 E.M. CRAIK, Diet, *Diaeta*, and Dietetics, in: C.A. POWELL, The Greek World, 1995, 387–402 3 L. EDELSTEIN, Antike Diätetik, in: Die Antike, 1931, 255–270 4 I.M. LONIE, A structural Pattern in Greek Dietetics, in: Medical History, 1977, 235–269 5 N. MARINONE, Galeno. La Dieta dimagrante, 1973 6 J. PREUSS, Biblical and Talmudic Medicine, 1978 7 A. RATTRAY, Divine Hygiene, 1903 8 J. SCARBOROUGH, Diphilus of Siphnos and Hellenistic medical Dietetics, in: JHM 1970, 194–201 9 STADEN, 397–407 10 P. VAN DER EIJK, Diocles and the Method of Dietetics, in: R. WITTERN, Hippokratische Medizin und ant. Philos., 1996, 230–257 11 J. WILKINS, D. HARVEY, M. DOBSON, Food in Antiquity, 1995.

V.N.

Dieuches (Διεύχης; *Dieúchēs*).

[1] Physician and author of medical texts in the 4th and possibly even the early 3rd cent. BC. He viewed the human body from the perspective of the four elementary qualities (Gal. 10,452), approved of bloodletting (11,163) and was positively disposed towards anatomy (11,795). He became particularly respected for his methods of treatment (Gal. 10,28; 11,795), especially because of greater care in prescribing dangerous medication (Orib. CMG VI 1,1,245; 292f.). Pliny considered him an authority in his medical books (20–27) and cites him in five places (fr. 8–12 BERTIER). The only literally preserved passages are found in Oribasius (fr. 13–19 BERTIER), who quotes him in detail in connection with a series of foods, especially those containing different types of flour. If the title is not by Oribasius himself, then its source might be a work of D. ('On the preparation of foods').

In the case of seasickness, D. simply recommends omitting the administration of an anti-emetic drug because vomiting could well provide relief. For novices in maritime travel it was deemed to be more important to eat light foods after vomiting and to avoid looking at the waves until they had become accustomed to the sea. Also, one should always carry thyme or similarly fragrant substances to counteract the pervasive stench on ships (fr. 19 BERTIER).

D., the teacher of Numenius of Heraclia (Ath. 1,5 B), was regularly quoted by Galen as being one of the great Dogmatist physicians (→ Dogmatics) with whose views every experienced doctor should be familiar (Gal. 10,28,461; 11,163,795; CMG V 9,1,70; CMG Suppl. or. 4,69). With the exception of Gal. 11,795, D.'s name always follows that of → Diocles [6], which suggests a period of activity around 300 BC [2], though an earlier dating to about 340 BC cannot be ruled out. In later sources D. was often associated with Mnesitheus — whether as his teacher or as his student is uncertain. This supports the possibility of D. and Mnesitheus or their family members being the ones who are mentioned on a dated votive gift of *c.* 350 BC from the temple of → Asclepius in Athens (IG II² 1449 [1]). He is probably not identical with Dieuches of Cos, who was honoured in Delphi in the 3rd cent. BC (FdD 3,1,515).
→ Medicine

1 P. GIRARD, BCH 1878, 65–94 2 M. WELLMANN, s.v. D., RE 5, 480.

J. BERTIER, Mnésithée et Dieuchès, 1972, V.N.

[2] Author of the New Comedy, son of Mnasiteles. Only attested in inscriptions; as the victor of the Amphiaraea/Rhomaea of Oropus (early 1st cent. BC) [1].

1 PCG V, 1986, 17. T.HI.

Dieuchidas (Διευχίδας; *Dieuchídas*). Son of Praxion of Megara, 4th cent. BC. Author of the *Megariká* in at least five vols. with broad treatment of the early period. The terminal date is uncertain, as is the chronological relationship with → Ephorus. In accounts of the temple of Delphi, a D. appears in the college of the *naopoioí* ('temple builders') in 338–329 (Syll.³ 241 C 141; 250 I 21). He is usually identified with this D. contrary to [1. 13ff.]. Only 11 fragments preserved. FGrH 485 (with commentary).

1 L. PICCIRILLI, Megarika, 1975. K.MEI.

Diffarreatio The *actus contrarius* of a → *confarreatio*, which dissolved a marriage joined in this form and followed the same ceremony. At the same time it effected the termination of the (former) husband's spousal powers (→ *manus*).

1 W. KUNKEL, s.v. matrimonium, RE 14, 2277
2 TREGGIARI, 24. G.S.

Differentiarum scriptores In antiquity the interest in identifying more closely the specific meaning (*proprietas ac differentia*; Quint. Inst. 1 pr. 16) of synonyms that are related in their root or different in form but semantically very close (*polliceri/promittere, nullus/nemo, intus/intro,* [1. 47]) extends back to Greek philosophy of language (Plato and the Sophists, the Stoa, later Cicero, Nigidius Figulus). In Rome it finds its place in oratory (Cato), rhetoric (Quint. Inst. 9,3,45ff.), jurisprudence and especially among the grammarians of the Imperial period who attempted to identify correct linguistic use ('orthoepia'). Respective materials in → Varro, → Verrius Flaccus and → Pliny's *Dubius sermo* became part of independent, alphabetized compilations only in late antiquity, via compilations such as → Flavius Caper's *De Latinitate* (HLL § 438 W.2). These introduce the relevant pair of terms usually with *inter .... (hos interest)* and also to explain homonyms. → Charisius [3] (4th cent. AD), for example, refers via → Iulius Romanus (*qui de differentiis scribunt*, p. 266, 22f.) back at least to authors of the 3rd cent. His *Glosulae multifariae idem significantes* (B. 5, p. 408–412) are later (cf. HLL 5,126f.) supplemented by chains of synonyms without explanations, the so-called *Synonyma Ciceronis* (p. 412–449) and actual *Differentiae* (p. 387–403). Nonius followed in about 400, c. 5 (p. 681–718 L.). Famous names were often attached to the originally probably anonymous collections (Cicero, Remmius Palaemon, Probus, Fronto etc.).

EDITIONS: 1 M. L. UHLFELDER, De proprietate sermonum vel rerum, 1954 2 C. CODOÑER, Isidoro de Sevilla, Diferencias, 1992.
BIBLIOGRAPHY: 3 J. W. BECK, De D.S. Latinis, 1883
4 G. BRUGNOLI, Studi sulle Differentiae verborum, 1955
5 C. CODOÑER, Les plus anciennes compilations de 'Differentiae', in: RPh 59, 1985, 201–219. P.L.S.

Digamma Sixth letter of the Greek alphabet representing the sound value /u̯/at the beginning of a syllable (bilabial pronunciation as in *water*). The name digamma ('double gamma', i.e. 'one gamma above another ', cf. ὥσπερ γάμμα διτταῖς ἐπὶ μίαν ὀρθὴν ἐπιζευγνύμενον ταῖς πλαγίοις, Dion. Hal. Ant. Rom. 1,20,3) refers to the appearance of the letter Ϝ and unlike other letter names was coined by the Greeks themselves. The model for the digamma was the consonant wāw /u̯/ of Phoenician [3]. The digamma stands for a sound inherited from proto-Indo-Germanic that originally occurred in all Greek dialects and, therefore, was still noted in archaic inscriptions: e.g. ἔργον (Argive Ϝεργον) < proto-Indo-Germanic **u̯érgom*, cf. OHG *werc* > NHG *Werk* [1. 222–230]. This sound was first lost in Ionic-Attic and only later in other dialects. To the extent that it was still pronounced, Β or Γ were in part used as substitutes [4]. In the uniform East Ionic alphabet (→ Alphabet, → Attic), which gradually supplanted all local writing systems after *c.* 400 BC, the symbol is missing. However, as the cipher for '6', the digamma continued to live in the → stigma, which was later considered as the ligature of σ + τ [1. 149]. In the Homeric epics, the oldest literature in alphabetized Greek, certain prosodic characteristics in verse structure suggest that this sound must have still existed in a preliminary stage of epic poetry. This discovery was made by R. BENTLEY in the 18th cent. The clearest indicator is the hiatus, which in contrast to other poetry is fairly common in Homer: the use of the digamma, which is also confirmed by linguistic history, results in a non-glottal sound. Often the digamma has a position-forming (→ Metrics) effect: in Il. 1,108 ἐσθλὸν δ' οὐδέ τί πω εἶπες ἔπος it not only effects the length required by verse technique in the second syllable of εἶπες: (Ϝ)εἶπες (Ϝ)ἔπος, but also avoids a hiatus with πω (Ϝ)εἶπες. Occasionally the word-initiating aspirate, if arising from *su̯ (in part still noted in dialects as Ϝh- or Ϝ[1. 226]) can effect position length: φίλε ἑκυρέ (Il. 3,172) < proto-Indo-Germanic *su̯ekuro- (cf. Old Indian *śváśura-* < **svaś-*, Latin *socer*, OHG *swehur*) [2]. Therefore, the digamma must have been spoken in the pre-Homeric period when the phrases concerned were coined. In Homer's time the sound had already disappeared from Ionic. This affected the verse structure because the syntagmas were retained. The digamma effect therefore allows for a separation of old and new word pronunciation and, given the peculiarity of → Homeric language, even in the same verse: e.g., Il. 6,478 Ἰλίου ἶφι ἀνάσσειν (no digamma effect in ἶφι, because the hiatus shortening of –ου is metrically required; [Ϝ]ανάσσειν with digamma effect).

In the Latin alphabet the digamma was simplified from *FH* (*FHE:FHAKED* on the Fibula Praenestina) to reproduce a phenomenon that only arose in this language, the frictive/f/ [5]: cf., e.g., *frāter*.

→ Homeric language

1 SCHWYZER, Gramm., 149, 222–230 2 P. CHANTRAINE, Grammaire homérique, vol. 1, 1958, 116–164 3 LSAG 24/5 4 O. MASSON, Remarques sur la transcription du *w* par *bêta* et *gamma*, in: H. EICHNER, H. RIX (ed.), Sprachwiss. und Philologie, 1990, 202–212 5 LEUMANN, 3, 9.

R.P.

Digentia Stream in the *ager Sabinus*, received the *fons Bandusia*, passed by the villa of Horatius Flaccus (Hor. Epist. 1,18,104) and entered the Anio on the right side between Mandela and Varia; modern Licenza.

NISSEN 2, 616.

G.U.

Digesta

A. NAME AND GENERAL SIGNIFICANCE
B. EXTERNAL COURSE OF THE LEGISLATION AND REFORM OF STUDIES C. THE WORKING METHOD OF THE COMPILERS D. TRANSMISSION

A. NAME AND GENERAL SIGNIFICANCE

The *Digesta* (from *digerere*, 'to order') formed the core of emperor Justinian's legal reforms: after the collection of the Imperial constitutions (→ *Codex*) in AD 529, the *Institutiones* followed in 533 as an introductory legal text book with binding legal force, then in the same year came the collection of classical writings of jurists, the *Digests*, and, finally, in 534 the revision of the *Codex*. *Digesta* is originally a genre of legal literature for treating legal questions both in the *ius civile* and the *ius honorarium*. The naming invoked the significant works of this title (the *Digesta* of Alfenus Varus, Celsus, Iulianus and Marcellus) while collections already belonging to late antiquity such as the *Fragmenta Vaticana* and the → *Collatio legum Mosaicarum* as well as an occasionally postulated *Praedigestum* of the classicist legal school probably no longer had much significance.

B. EXTERNAL COURSE OF THE LEGISLATION AND REFORM OF STUDIES

On 15 December 530, a legal basis was provided with the constitution *Deo auctore* for the work of a commission whose mandate was to examine the works of authors that had been distinguished by the *ius respondendi* (§ 4). Lasting works were to be collected in the *Digesta sive Pandectae* (§ 12), arranged in 50 books and subdivided according to titles, with the *Codex* or the classification of the *edictum perpetuum* serving as models.

Tribonianus as the *quaestor sacri palatii* was to appoint the most capable jurists to the commission, according to his preference (Const. Deo auctore § 14). Towards the end of its activity (533), the commission consisted of Tribonianus (now *magister officiorum*) as its head, Constantinus (*comes sacrarum largitionum et magister scrinii libellorum sacrarumque cognitionum*) from the head of the imperial chancelleries, the professors Theophilus (*magister iurisque peritus*) and Cratinus (*comes sacrarum largitionum et optimus antecessor*) of the law school of Constantinople, the professors Dorotheus (*facundissimus quaestorius*) and Anatolius (*magister et iuris interpres* from an old family of jurists) of the law school of Berytus as well as the eleven advocates admitted at the court of the *praefectus praetori Orientis* (*viri prudentissimi, patroni causarum*). In three years almost 2,000 book rolls with a total of more than three million lines were read, excerpted, in part amended and arranged (Const. Tanta § 1). Even authors who had written before Augustus were considered. This anthology, which eventually comprised 150,000 lines, was published on 16 December 533 together with the introductory law *Tanta* (Greek: *Dédōken*) in Latin and Greek 533. According to the detailed but not entirely accurate information in the *Index Florentinus*, excerpts from 1,505 books by 38 authors were incorporated in the *Digesta*. According to one calculation it was 1,625 books, according to another 1,528 [1. 147, 286]. If the (unknown) number of books that the commission read but did not consider is included (Const. Deo auctore § 4), a certain harmonization of the inconsistencies can be achieved.

This work — together with the *Institutiones* and the *Codex* — was intended not only to standardize the application of the law, but also, as a reform law, to reform, standardize and improve the training of jurists at the law schools of Rome, Constantinople and Berytus. Simultaneously, education was to be focused on these three places; training locations such as those in Caesarea (Palestine) and Alexandria were closed due to a lack of quality (Const. Omnem § 7). A plan for a reformed course of study, probably still of 5 years' duration, was developed in 533 (ibid. § 1) and fleshed out in Const. *Tanta* (535). For purposes of education, the *Digesta* were divided into seven sections (Const. Tanta § 2–8): in the first year the *novi Iustiniani* had to study the institutions and the first section of the Digest (*Digesta* 1–4; Const. Omnem § 2). The *edictales* of the second year of study either had to deal with the seven books on court proceedings (*Digesta* 5–11: *secundus articulus*, Const. *Tanta* § 3) or the eight books on property law (*Digesta* 12–19: *tertia congregatio*, Const. Tanta § 4), and also with another book from each of four groups containing a sequence of fourteen books in total, i.e., the law of marital property (*Digesta* 23–25, part of the *quartus locus* or *umbilicus*, ranging from *Digesta* 20 to *Digesta* 27), the laws on guardian- and wardship (*Digesta* 26–27), the complete law of wills, bequests and trusts (*Digesta* 28–34) as well as further inheritance law material (*Digesta* 35–36), i.e., the fifth section (*Digesta* 28–36: *quintus articulus*, Const. *Tanta* §§ 6–6 b). The *Papinianistae* of the third year had to read the books not selected in the previous year as well as the books on the suits pertaining to movable and immovable collateral (*Digesta* 20), the Aediles' Edict and related materials (*Digesta* 21) and book 22 (Const. *Tanta* § 5) with accumulated opening fragments from Papinian's *Responsae* and *Quaestiones* (hence the name of this section of studies). The 'case-solvers' (*lytai*) of the fourth year of study had to take the books of the fourth and fifth section that had been omitted so far (*Digesta* 23–36). The remainder (*Digesta* 37–50, including the two *terribiles libri* (*Digesta* 47; 48) on offences and criminal procedure (Const. *Tanta* § 8a), were reserved for later independent study. The studies of the advanced 'case-solvers' (*prolytai*) were dedicated to the imperial constitutions of the Justinianic *Codex*.

C. The working method of the compilers

Regarding the method by which the commission was able to complete the *Digesta* in such a short time, 'Bluhme's theory of masses' remains unchallenged. In 1830, Fr. Bluhme assumed three sub-commissions that had to handle varying amounts of material: the *ius civile* ('Sabinus mass'), the *ius honorarium* ('Edicts mass') and the literature on *quaestiones* and *responsae* ('Papinian mass'). When another text group arose during the commission's work, the fragments were assigned to an 'appendix mass', which was distributed after the three commissions had combined their results.

D. Transmission

The most important manuscript of the *Digesta* is the Littera Florentina (905 folios in 2 vols.), which probably dates to the 6th cent. According to recent research it was kept in southern Italy before it was taken as booty from Amalfi to Pisa in 1135 and finally came to Florence in 1409, where it has been kept in the Biblioteca Medicea Laurenziana since 1783 (a somewhat shortened facsimile print with clipped margins was published in Florence in 1988). The Florentina (*F*) had already been corrected in antiquity with the aid of two control manuscripts (F^1 and F^2). Individual fragments of the Digest that should also be attributed to late antiquity but are independent of the Florentina are found in the Greek sources of the Byzantine law schools. Also, there are a few papyrus fragments that might be contemporary with *F*. All other medieval texts are probably derived from a lost Beneventan copy that also points to *F* via a lost *codex secundus* (*S*). However, since *S* corrects *F* in a few places, there must also be a subsidiary text independent of *F* and that was perhaps only an excerpt of the Digest. The Littera Bononiensis, i.e., the text used by Bolognese glossators, may have better readings than *F*.

The tripartite division of the *Digesta* into a *digestum vetus* (*Digesta* 1,1–24,2), *infortiatum* (*Digesta* 24,3–38) and a *digestum novum* (39,1–end) has been customary since the Littera Bononiensis (the text of the law school of Bologna) and was only given up in the humanistic editions. There are only speculative assumptions on the reason and origin of this tripartite division.

Modern texts (especially P. Krüger, Berlin 1872, and the two-volume paperback, Milano 1908, ed. by Bonfante, Fadda, Ferrini, Riccobono and Scialoja) are based on the *editio maior* produced by Th. Mommsen in 1870, with the Milanese edition taking the Florentina more strongly into account.

Regarding the significance and reliability of the *Digesta* as a historical source, including the issues of interpolation and text stages, see → Legal history (Romance Studies), also → Humanism, legal. Regarding the unique influence of the *Digesta* as the foundation of European legal studies since the school of Bologna and the reception of Roman law in the late Middle Ages see → Digests; → Glossators; → Ius Commune.

1 T. Honoré, Tribonian, 1978.

Th. Mommsen, Digesta Iustiniani Augusti, 2 vols., 1870; Wieacker, RRG, 122ff.; P. Jörs, s.v. D., RE 5, 484–543; Dulckeit/Schwarz/Waldstein, §§ 43, 44; L. Wenger, Die Quellen des röm. Rechts, 1053, 576–600, 853–877; L. Mitteis, E. Levi, E. Rabel (ed.), Index Interpolationum quae in Iustiniani Digestis inesse dicuntur I, 1929, II, 1931, III, 1935, Suppl. I, 1929; O. Behrends, R. Knütel, B. Kupisch, H. H. Seiler (ed.), Corpus Iuris Civilis, Text und Überlieferung, II Digesten 1–10, 1995. W.E.V.

Diglossia The term 'diglossia' (not to be confused with → bilingualism) was already used late in the 19th cent. to characterize the Greek language situation. However, it only became a central concept in sociolinguistics with Ch. Ferguson's essay [1] in which he developed the canonical definition using Swiss German, (Modern) Greek, Arabic and Haitian Creole as examples. It considers diglossia to be a language situation in which the spoken primary language (which FERGUSON labelled 'L' as in 'Low'; in the Greek language area this was the δημοτική, *dhimotikí*), whether regionally strongly differentiated or largely uniform, is subordinate to a genetically not necessarily related, codified language (labelled 'H' as in 'High', for example, the καθαρεύουσα, *katharévusa*) that strongly differs in sound, morphology and vocabulary. It usually is the language of an extensive literary corpus that is considered to be definitive. While the L-variety is acquired without direction 'in a natural manner' by all members of the language community and is responsible for routine communication needs, the prestigious H-variety that is considered mandatory in written and formal communication is learned during the education process; the relationship of the two is complementary and there is social consensus on their use. The H-variety is the sole object of language care and language expansion, which is why H can replace L in all functions but not the other way round. Therefore, the elimination of diglossia must be preceded by linguistic planning to equip L for all communication needs, which is often done by borrowing from H.

This modern concept is suited indeed to describing adequately the social relations of Ancient standard languages: the relationships between Middle Egyptian and New Egyptian, Akkadian and Aramaic, Hebrew and Aramaic, finally Attic and Koine as well as Latin and Vulgar Latin are comparable in principle. The ultimate causes are the conditions of communication in premodern states: written competence is only required and desirable for a small elite. Specifically in the cases of the two 'classical' languages the conditions, which originated in antiquity would persist into the 19th cent.; in Arabic, the youngest ancient written language, they still apply [2].

→ MODERN GREEK

C. FERGUSON, Diglossia, in: Word 15, 1959, 325–340, 336; J. NIEHOFF-PANAGIOTIDIS, Koine und D., 1995.

V.BI. and J.N.

Dikaspolos (δικάσπολος; *dikáspolos*). In the Homeric epics this term applied to a king or *geron* (member of the council of elders) in the role of judge or magistrate (Il. 1,238). Wielding a sceptre he would deliver the judgement (θέμιστες, *thémistes*) coming from Zeus. It depends on one's theory about the course of a lawsuit (→ *dikázein*) how this is to be imagined in practice.

M. SCHMIDT, LFE 2, 1991, 302.

G.T.

Dikastai kata demous (*dikastaì katà dḗmous*) are itinerant judges who in Athens visited the demes to resolve minor matters of litigation. Appointed first by Peisistratus ([Aristot.] Ath. Pol. 16,5) to counteract the power of the nobles in their places of residence, they were probably abolished after the fall of the tyrants. They were revived in 453/2 BC (Ath. Pol. 26,3) to relieve the increasingly overburdened jury courts of minor cases. Their number then totalled 30, perhaps one judge per *trittys*. In the last years of the Peloponnesian War they were probably unable to visit all demes any longer; the oligarchy of 404/3 had moreover allowed 'thirty' to become a less propitious number: after the war the number was increased to forty. They held office then in Athens. Each group of four was assigned to defendants from one phyle; they ruled on private suits involving an amount in dispute of up to ten drachmas and referred more serious private suits to the *diaitetai* (Ath. Pol. 53,1–2).

→ Demes; → Trittys

A.R. W. HARRISON, The Law of Athens, 2nd vol., 1971, 18–21.

P.J.R.

Dikasterion (δικαστήριον; *dikastḗrion*).
A. ATHENS B. OTHER PARTS OF GREECE

A. ATHENS
1. COURT SITE 2. DECISION-MAKING BODY
3. PROCEDURE

1. COURT SITE

There were two types of court sites, those at which homicidal crimes were judged (φονικά, *phoniká*) and those at which other public or private suits were negotiated. The former, of which there were five, were at the edge of the town for ritual reasons and had no roof to avoid being tarnished by the accused (Antiph. 5,11; Aristot. Ath. Pol. 57,4) while the latter were at the market or in its immediate vicinity. Except for the two largest ones, the *Hēliaía* (Ἡλιαία) and the site of the → *ekklēsía* (ἐκκλησία), they had a roof. The *phoniká* were named after sanctuaries, e.g., 'the council on the hill of Ares' (ἡ ἐν Ἀρείῳ πάγῳ βουλή; → Areopagus), 'the court site by the Palladion' (τὸ ἐπὶ Παλλαδίῳ) next to a temple dedicated to the goddess Pallas Athena, 'the one by the Delphinion' (τὸ ἐπὶ Δελφινίῳ), 'the one by the office of the Prytaneis' (τὸ ἐπὶ Πρυτανείῳ; → Prytaneion) and *tò en Phreattoî* (τὸ ἐν Φρεαττοῖ) after the holy compound of the hero Phreatto on the coast of the Piraeus peninsula.

In front of court sites that were reserved for jury court sessions in the → Agora a large space was fenced off from which all court sites could be entered. This is where the judges of the jury courts were chosen by lot. The → Heliaia was a particularly large court site attested from the 4th cent. BC. In the exceptional cases where it voted on freeing or condemning an accused [1] the popular assembly also held sessions in the Agora under a chair selected by lot from among the → prytaneis. Several other sites of popular courts are known, though their use as such is not obvious from their names; e.g., the → Odeum, the → Stoa poikile and the → Stoa basileios (Dem. Or. 25,23). At the entrance of each court site stood an effigy of *Hḗrōs Lýkos* (Ἥρως Λύκος), the defender of the accused, who was named for his wolf-like appearance. The jurors sat on wooden benches covered with reed mats, the presiding officials on a podium (βῆμα, *bêma*) and the parties with their advisers on another podium. A third podium was reserved for the parties' presentations and witness statements. A stone table for counting the votes stood near this speaker's podium (Aristoph. Vesp. 333). Two ballot jars (→ *kadískoi*) and a water clock (→ *klépsydra*) were also part of the furnishings. Spectators were barred from the court sites by barriers (*drýphaktoi*) and a paled gate (*kinklís*). On the rocky crest of the Ares Hill the speakers used two natural stones as podiums: that of the defendant was called 'Stone of Arrogance' (λίθος Ὕβρεως) and that of the plaintiff 'Stone of Irreconcilability' (λίθος Ἀναιδείας). This was also the location of the stele on which the blood laws were recorded (Lys. 1,30). An altar dedicated to Athena → Areia and a sanctuary of the Erinyes were located in the immediate vicinity.

2. DECISION-MAKING BODY

In Athens, *dikasterion* was also the name of the numerous collegial courts (a binding decision by a single judge in a proceeding was alien to the Athenians). The origin of the 51 → *ephetaí*, who have been attested since Dracon (before 600 BC), is uncertain. The uneven number prevented tied votes. The Areopagus consisted of former archontes (→ Archontes [I]), who belonged to the college for life. Here, there could be tied votes but they resulted in the acquittal of the accused (Ant. 5,51; Schol. Dem. Or. 24,9). The Areopagus decided on intentional and (direct) killing, while the *ephetai* were responsible for unintentional (or indirect) killing and other blood cases. Other trials were brought before the Heliaia, which was staffed with jurors (→ *dikastḗs*). It was attributed to Solon and experienced its flowering during the democracy of the 5th and 4th cents. In civil cases a *dikasterion* of 201 or (if the value of the dispute was over a thousand drachmas) 401 jurors was chosen by lot, in political trials 501 to 2,501 jurors are attested, and once even 6,000. Originally the *dikasteria* were selected annually but according to Aristot. Ath. Pol. 63,4, lots were drawn every day to prevent bribery. The council (→ *boulḗ*) and the popular assembly (→ *ekklēsía*) were not described as *dikasteria* when they acted as courts.

3. PROCEDURE

Athenian mass courts required tight organization. The 'court chair' (→ Attic law C.) had to accept the suit, conduct the preliminary proceeding (→ *anákrisis*), have a date allotted and preside over the proceeding on the appointed day (ἡγεμονία τοῦ δικαστηρίου). The chair had no influence on the decision, which was automatic with the count of the secret ballots cast in the *dikasterion*. The vote followed immediately after the speaking turns of the parties, which was precisely measured by means of the → *klepsýdra*.

B. OTHER PARTS OF GREECE

Dikasteria are frequently attested but the circumstances of Athenian democracy cannot simply be transferred. Syll.³ 953 (Calymna) and IPArk 3 appear most comparable, contrary to 5 (both Tegea), 8 (Mantinea) and 17 (Stymphalus). In Ptolemaic Egypt a *dikasterion* ('ten-man court') was set up for Greeks and other immigrants in the 1st half of the 3rd cent., among other courts..

1 BUSOLT/SWOBODA, 990.

A.R. W. HARRISON, The Law of Athens II, 1971, 43ff.; G. THÜR, The Jurisdiction of the Areopagos, in: M. GAGARIN (ed.), Symposion 1990, 1991, 53ff.; H.-A. RUPPRECHT, Einführung in die Papyruskunde, 1994, 143; A.L. BOEGEHOLD, The Lawcourts of Athens (Ath. Agora 28), 1995. G.T.

Dikastes (δικαστής; *dikastḗs*). In the Greek city states lay persons rather than professional judges were appointed to the → *dikastḗrion*. *Dikastes* is therefore best translated as 'juror'. Any male citizen of more than 30 years of age and of blameless reputation could register in Athens as a *dikastes*. As an 'identification' he was given a small tablet that bore his name and each year he had to swear the 'Heliastic oath' that he would vote according to the law (Dem. Or. 24, 149–151). The *dikastes* was paid for the day that he was in court (→ *dikastikòs misthós*). Whoever exercised the function of *dikastes* as a state debtor was punished with death (Aristot. Ath. Pol. 63,3). In Stymphalus the member of a small court was also called a *dikastes*. The minimum age there was 40 years. Originally, the official in Athens who initiated court procedure was also called a *dikastes* (Dem. Or. 23,28).

A. R. W. HARRISON, The Law of Athens II, 1971, 44–49
G. THÜR, H. TAEUBER, Prozeßrechtliche Inschr. Arkadiens, 1994, no. 17, l. 16 G.T.

Dikastikos misthos (δικαστικὸς μισθός; *dikastikòs misthós*). Daily payment for Athenian jurors from the mid 5th cent. BC (Aristot. Ath. Pol. 2,2). In early Athenian democracy the principle of democratic equality of all citizens applied. Increasing economic and social inequality resulted in only the economically independent citizens, i.e. the wealthy part of the population, being able to participate in courts while the less wealthy and poor citizens, especially the rural population, could not abandon the work that fed them to serve as jurors. The more established democracy under Pericles therefore introduced daily payments, which the Athenians described as *dikastikos misthos* (judge's salary). The amount was about equal to a daily wage and probably originally was one → obolos. Pericles was accused of self-serving motives because of this reform (Aristot. Ath. Pol. 27,3; Plut. Pericles 9). It was also believed that a deterioration of the courts was the immediate consequence of the introduction of daily payments (Aristot.

Ath. Pol. 27,4; Pl. Grg. 515e). Because of the dire need of the citizenry, the rate was increased to two oboles for each session during the Peloponnesian War (Schol. Aristoph. Vesp. 88) and in 425 by Cleon to a → triobolon. In 411 the reactionary oligarchy returned to the principle of paying no compensation for excercizing state functions (Thuc. 8,65,3; 67,3; Aristot. Ath. Pol. 29,5), a principle to which the subsequent democracy also adhered (Thuc. 8,97,1). After restoring the popular courts following the fall of the Thirty, daily payments of the old amount of three oboles were restored. This rate continued to the time of Aristotle in the 4th cent. BC (Ath. Pol. 62,2). However, by that time it was hardly sufficient for satisfying even the most basic needs (Isoc. Or. 7,54).

→ Dikasterion

A.R. W. HARRISON, The Law of Athens II, 1971, 48ff. J. BLEICKEN, Die athenische Demokratie, ²1994, 208.

G.T.

Dikazein (δικάζειν; *dikázein*). The word (approximately: 'to exercise a right') is associated with the ending of a dispute with a sentence. Whether the sentence was originally passed by an 'arbitrator' who was consensually appointed by both parties is highly questionable. Rather, *dikazein* in the early period was the activity of a council of elders or of an official (→ *dikastḗs*) that was at least rudimentarily provided with state authority. In what form this *dikazein* would occur is also uncertain: either an official decided in the matter on his own or a formal procedure of proof was initiated, the success or failure of which indirectly brought about the decision (e.g., a particular oath could be imposed on one of the parties to the dispute by means of the *dikazein*, Hom. Il. 23,574; 579). In later times *dikazein* simply meant 'making a judicial decision' as jurors (→ *dikastḗs*) in court (→ *dikastḗrion*) did by means of a secret ballot.

G. THÜR, Zum *dikazein* bei Homer, in: ZRG 87, 1970, 426ff.; M. SCHMIDT, s.v. D., LFE 2, 1991, 301f. (from 1982).

G.T.

Dike (Δίκη; *Díkē*).

[1] (Religion). Personification of human law made concrete in legal pronouncements (as opposed to → Themis, the divine order): the legal order breaks down if it is eroded by corrupt judges (Hes. Op. 220). She is a central figure of mythological and poetic reflection on the foundation of social existence in the archaic and classical period. The genealogies incorporate D. in a value system. She is the daughter of Zeus and Themis (Hes. Theog. 902) and, as one of the three → Horae, the sister of Eunomia and Eirene — the trinity of 'orderly government', peace and law — secures the community's well-being. Therefore, she may be called the mother of Hesychia, (domestic) tranquillity (Pind. Pyth. 8,1). She is closely associated with Zeus, the guarantor of order; she is his daughter, presents complaints to him and calls on him to inflict punishment (Hes. Op. 258–260). Aeschylus follows on from here: he persistently and explicitly calls her daughter of Zeus (especially Suppl. 145; Choeph. 949), beside whom she is enthroned (TrGF Fr. 281a) and whose messenger she is among humans while also recording their transgressions on Zeus' tablets. Whoever has trespassed against her will be haunted by Poine's ('Punishment') sword and the → Erinyes (Choeph. 639–651, cf. Eum. 511f.). Sophocles brings out this punishing role more strongly. Although she is still enthroned with Zeus (OC 1382), she is also a companion of the gods of the Underworld (Ant. 451) such as the punishing Erinyes (Aj. 1390). In Lower Italian vase imagery she is depicted with a sword among the punishing powers of the Underworld. She is even more active in an image of the → Cypselus Chest (Paus. 5,18,2) and an Attic red-figured amphora in Vienna, where she slays the homely Adikia ('Injustice') in the guise of a powerfully built woman. Aeschylus already speaks of the altar of D., which must be honoured with reverence (Eum. 539f.). However, the cult is only attested in the poleis after the mid 4th cent. BC.

Natural philosophical reflection emphasized D. as the preserver of extensive cosmic laws: D. and the Erinyes ('her enforcers') keep → Helios in his path (Heraclitus 22 B 94 DK). 'Much-punishing' D. has the keys to the gate of the paths of day and night (Parmenides 28 B 1,14 DK). D. also is the daughter of Time (Eur. TGF Fr. 223). In Aratus (Phaen. 96–136) and Roman poets she is the constellation Virgo or Astraea: she was the last of the gods to leave earth before the beginning of the 'Iron Age' (Verg. Ecl. 4,6; Georg. 2,473f.; Ov. Met. 1,149f.).

R. HIRZEL, Themis, D. und Verwandtes, 1907; H. LLOYD-JONES, The Justice of Zeus, 1971, 1983; H.A. SHAPIRO, Personifications in Greek Art. The Representation of Abstract Concepts 600–400 B.C., 1993, 38–44.

F.G.

[2] (Law). The basic meaning is 'enforcing action' (to be examined by court, → *dikastḗrion*); the meanings 'suit' and 'trial' are derived from this, likewise 'sentence' and 'punishment'. In Athens *dike* in the broader sense included both private and public suits. A private suit (*dike* in its narrow sense) was only open to the injured or damaged party. This also included the murder suit (δίκη φόνου, *díkē phónou*); the → *diadikasía* is also sometimes called *dike*. The public suit (technically → *graphḗ*) as a popular suit could be submitted by any reputable citizen of Athens. Depending on whether or not the plaintiff was allowed to submit a petition for an appraisal in his written suit (also called *dike* or → *én-klēma*), the sources speak of → *tímētos agṓn* or → *atímētos agṓn*. Outside Athens the terms *dike* and *graphḗ* merge. In the Egyptian papyri *dike* can sometimes be translated as 'claim' without abandoning the basic meaning. In the enforcement clause of the documents 'as if according to the sentence (of a → *dikastḗrion*)' (καθάπερ ἐκ δίκης) the Greeks took into account that

the dikasteria of their home towns did not exist in Ptolemaic Egypt.
→ Dikasterion; → Dikazein

H. J. Wolff, Beiträge zur Rechtsgesch. Altgriechenlands, 1961, 248f.; H.-A. Rupprecht, Einführung in die Papyruskunde, 1994, 103143147f. G.T.

Dikolon see → Punctuation

Dill (OHG *tilli*, related to NHG Dolde [umbel], Lat. *anetum*). Probably identical with the umbellifera (*Anethum graveolens L.*, ἄ[ν[ν]ηθον; *á[n[n]ēthon*, Aeolic ἄνητον; *ánēton*, Alc. in Ath. 15,674d), which was introduced from Asia Minor in antiquity. This popular kitchen herb (sown according to Palladius, Opus agriculturae 3,24,5 and 4,9,5 or 10,13,3 and 11,11,4, in February/March and September/October) with bare seeds (Theophr. Hist. pl. 7,3,2 = Plin. HN 19,119) is mentioned in Theophr. Hist. pl. 1,11,2 and Plin. HN 19,167; also as medicinal, for example, in Dioscorides 3,58 ([1. 70f.] = 3,60 [2. 303]) and Plin. HN 20,196 and *passim*. Dill differs, mainly in size, from fennel (*Foeniculum vulgare Mill.= officinale All.*) [3. 78f.]), which is closely related and used similarly.

1 Wellmann 2 2 Berendes 3 J. Billerbeck, Flora classica, 1824, reprint 1972. C.HÜ.

Dillius

[1] C.D. Aponianus. Senator, originally from Cordoba, entered the Senate under Nero. As legate of the *legio III Gallica* he joined Vespasian and fought for him at Cremona. Of his career only a *cura alvei Tiberis* is certain (AE 1932, 78 = CIL II[2] 7, 275); related to D. [2]. PIR[2] D 89.

[2] C.D. Vocula. Related to D. [1]. Also from Cordoba, probably also accepted, like D. [1], into the Senate under Nero. As a praetorian he commanded the *legio XXII Primigenia* in Germania superior in 69/70. Hordeonius Flaccus gave him the command against Iulius Civilis, who was besieging Vetera. At the instigation of Iulius Classicus he was murdered in 70 by a Roman deserter. CIL VI 1402 = ILS 983 was erected for him posthumously by his wife Helvia Procula (cf. [1]; PIR[2] D 90).

1 Caballos, 1, 122f. W.E.

Dilmun D., which was first mentioned in the early 3rd millennium BC in Mesopotamian economic texts, was once exclusively identified with the island of → Baḥrain. However, archaeological evidence from the eastern province of Saudi Arabia, Failaka Island and Qaṭar demonstrates that D. varied in size over time. According to written and archaeological records, D. was a crossroads of trade in the Persian Gulf during the 3rd and early 2nd millennium BC. In the mid 2nd millennium, D. became a colony of the Kassites who ruled Mesopotamia and in the 13th cent. BC it became a tributary of the Assyrians. Under lose Assyrian suzerainty in the 8th/7th cents. BC, D. once again became an important centre of the Omani copper trade. Texts from Failaka attest to D.'s economic ties to the Neo-Babylonian and later Achaemenid empires. After the 4th cent. BC, *Tylos*, the Greek version of Akkadian *Tilmun*, only described the main island of Baḥrain. Hellenistic remains are especially present in the fortified city V of Qalʾat al-Baḥrain, the chamber burials of Janussan in northern Baḥrain and the coin hoard of Raʾs al-Qalaʾat of the late 3rd cent. BC. However at this time the town of → Gerrha had assumed the function of the port of trade. The identification of Tylos with Baḥrain is based on Androsthenes of Thasos, an admiral of Alexander the Great. The identity of the name of Tylos with Tylos on the Phoenician coast has led to the question of whether the Phoenicians had come from the Gulf coast to the Mediterranean [1]. Palmyrene texts from the 2nd cent. AD indicate that *Thiloua*, the Aramaic form of Tylos and also the name of Baḥrain in the 2nd cent. AD, was a satrapy of the southern Mesopotamian kingdom of → Characene. During the Sassanid period the main island of Bahrain is known as *Talūn* from texts of the Nestorian Church.
→ Baḥrain; → Gerrha

1 G. W. Bowersock, Tylos and Tyre: Bahrain in the Graeco-Roman World; in: Sh. H. A. Al-Khalifa, M. Rice (ed.), Bahrain through the Ages — the Archaeology, 1986, 399–406 2 R. Englund, D. in the Archaic Uruk Corpus, in: D. Potts (ed.), D. Berliner Beiträge zum Vorderen Orient 2, 1983, 35–37 3 H. I. McAdam, D. revisited, Arabian Archaeology and Epigraphy 1, 1990, 49–87 3 D. Potts, The Arabian Gulf in Antiquity, 1990 4 M. Rice, The Archaeology of the Arabian Gulf, 1994. M.H.

Diluntum see → Daorsi

Dimachaerus see → Munera

Dimensuratio provinciarum and Divisio orbis terrarum Two anonymous lists of lands and islands of the Roman *oikoumene* with their length and width in Roman miles, probably created in the 5th cent. AD [1; 2]. Like similar information in Plin. HN 3–6, they can also be traced back to → Agrippa [1] [3].

1 Editions: GLM 9–20 2 K. Brodersen, C. Plinius Secundus: Naturkunde VI, 1996, 329–336 3 A. Klotz, Die geogr. commentarii des Agrippa, in: Klio 24, 1931, 38–58, 386–466.

J. J. Tierney, Dicuili Liber de mensura orbis terrae, 1967, 22–26. K.BRO.

Dimini Neolithic hilltop settlement about 5 km to the east of Volos/→ Iolcus (Thessaly), half way to → Sesklo, whose key ranking in this region it assumed in the late Neolithic (1st half of the 5th millennium BC).

The excavation by V. STAIS in 1901 conformed to the expectations of the time: a fortification surrounded by several walls with a → megaron in the centre. The publication of the excavation by Ch. TSOUNTAS [4] created a paradigm that placed fortifications and megara chronologically before → Troy — with appropriate consequences in the secondary literature. In the 1970s D. was reexamined by G. Ch. CHOURMOUZIADIS [1]. He recognized four sectors around the central court that were separated by radial roads and circuit walls. All units were equally furnished with a court, hearths, work and storage rooms. Since the finds only diverged a little (polychrome and unpainted pottery with incised and notched decoration), he concluded that a territorial delimitation of social groups was present but was unable to define them more closely.

It is certain that the six circuit walls found so far are not stable enough to be defensive. The so-called megaron is a reconstruction from the final, Chalcolithic phase of the settlement. The site was only resettled in the late Mycenaean period (about 12th –11th cents. BC). The remains of a large corridor house on the more level northern side and a domed tomb among the Neolithic house ruins indicate an elevated rank of the location. The Neolithic culture of Thessaly that chronologically follows the Sesklo culture is named after D.

1 G. CH. CHOURMOUZIADIS, Το νεολιθικό Διμήνι, 1979 2 K. KOTSAKIS, in: G. A. PAPATHANASSOPOULOS, Neolithic Culture in Greece, 1996 3 D. THEOCHARIS, Neolithic Greece, 1973 4 CH. TSOUNTAS, Αἱ προιστορικαῖ ἀκροπόλεις Διμηνίου καὶ Σέσκλου, 1908 (see review by E. PFUHL, in: GGA 1910, 827–854). G. H.

Dimum *Statio* on the Danube in Moesia inferior, modern Belene, apparently in the tribal territory of the Getic Dimenses. The identification with Δίακον (Ptol. 3,10,10) is questionable. In the 4th cent. a *cuneus equitum Solensium* was stationed there (Not. Dign. Or. 40,12). Attestations: Itin. Ant. 221; Tab. Peut.; CIL III 12399; Not. Dign. Or. 40,6; 12; Procop. Aed. 307,19 (Διμώ).

V.I. VELKOV, Die thrak. und dak. Stadt in der Spätant., 1959, 60, 67, 88, 163. J.BU.

Dinarchus (Δείναρχος; *Deínarchos*).
A. LIFE B. WORKS

A. LIFE

Attic orator, born about 361 BC in Corinth, son of Sostratus, died after 292.

The source of information on his life is the (incompletely transmitted) treatise *De Dinarcho* of Dionysius of Halicarnassus, who relied in particular on a lost speech by D. ('Against Proxenus'); the other lives (Ps.-Plut., Photius, Suda) depend on Dionysius. D. relocated in his younger years (*c.* 340/38) to Athens, lived there as a metic and had links to the Peripatetic school. After about 336/5 he was active as a → logographer. M.W.

Despite his successful activity as a logographer and friendship with Theophrastus, Demetrius of Phalerum and Cassander, D. did not become a successful politician. This exemplifies that a metic in Athens could not play an independent political role without citizenship despite outstanding rhetorical talent and considerable wealth. As a logographer D. only became prominent when he composed three accusatory speeches against the democratic rhetors Demosthenes, Aristogeiton and Philocles during the → Harpalus trials. The note in the Suda (Suda s.v. D.) that Antipater made a D. the *epimelētḗs* for the Peloponnese does not relate to D. The Vita of D. explains the great success of D. in Athens after 323 with his friendship to Cassander (Plut. Mor. 850C). This tradition may have arisen from the known friendship of D. with Demetrius of Phalerum. In any case, no political actions by D. in the interest of Cassander can be demonstrated. D. must not be seen simplistically as an enemy of Athenian democracy because of his speeches against the democratic rhetors. After all, he had made his home in the democratic Athens of *c.* 340/338 to 322 BC and in 338 had fought as a metic for Athens at Chaeronea (Din. 48 F 2 CONOMIS). However, after the overthrow of Demetrius in 307, D. escaped the accusations of his opponents because of collaboration with Antipater and Cassander and went into exile in Chalcis. After returning to Athens in 292, he pursued a proceeding against his host Proxenus before the court of the polemarch (Plut. Mor. 850D/E with Aristot. Ath. Pol. 58,2–3) that had no recognizable political background. Nothing is known of his final years and death. J.E.

B. WORKS

Of the 160 speeches available in antiquity (cf. Dion. Hal.), which were mostly spurious, the three cited ones, 'Against Demosthenes' (Or.1), 'Against Aristogeiton' (Or. 2) and 'Against Philocles' (Or. 3) are preserved; Or. 2 and 3 are damaged towards the end. D. wrote them for unknown speakers at the Harpalus trials (324/23). Four other speeches attributed by ancient critics to D. are contained in the *Corpus Demosthenicum* (Or. 39; 40; 47; 58).

D. has been considered a second-rate orator since antiquity. His style is characterized by abundant borrowing from his predecessors, esp. Demosthenes, seemingly exaggerated excitement and overextended ellipses (e.g., Or. 1,18–21), and a lack of clear logic and structure (contrary position in the commentary of WORTHINGTON).

→ Rhetors

COMPLETE EDITIONS: N.C. CONOMIS, Dinarchus, Orationes cum fragmentis, 1975; M. NOUHAUD, L. DORS-MÉARY, Dinarque. Discours, 1990.
INDIVIDUAL EDITIONS: Or. 2 and 3: L. GIOVANNUCCI, 1971, 1973.
COMMENTARY: I. WORTHINGTON, A Historical Commentary on Dinarchus, 1992.
INDEX: L. L. FORMAN, 1897 (reprint 1962)
BIBLIOGRAPHY: BLASS, 3,2, 289ff.; G. SHOEMAKER, Din-

archus, 1968; D. WHITEHEAD, The Ideology of the Athenian Metic, 1977. M.W.

Dindymene see → Cybele

Dindymum (Δίνδυμον; *Díndymon*). Mountain on the border between Galatia and Phrygia (modern Arayit or Günüzü Dağı), 1,820 m high, near the spring of the Sangarius (Claud. in Eutropium 2,262f., cf. Str. 12,3,7). Some ancient authors derived the mountain's name from its 'double' or 'forked' appearance (Nonnus, Dion. 48,855). D. was famous for the cult of Cybele, whose temple was located in the nearby town of Pessinus and who also bore the name *Dindyménē* (Str. 12,5,3), here and elsewhere. Attis was buried there (Paus. 1,4,5, who calls this mountain *Ágdistis*). A base of Alexius' I during his campaign against the Turks in 1116. Remains of a Byzantine fortress located on one of the peaks.

BELKE, 158f. T.D.-B.

Dinogetia (Δινογέτεια; *Dinogéteia*). Roman fortification in Moesia inferior (Scythia minor) on the right bank of the lower Danube in a strategically important location north of Troesmis near the delta, modern Garvăn, Tulcea in Romania. A pre-Roman Geto-Dacian settlement is attested. In the Roman period the town (πόλις in Ptol. 3,8,2; 10,1) represented a significant starting-point for travel along the Pyretus into the Scythian hinterland. In the course of the 3rd and 4th cents., especially under Diocletian, systematic fortifications were carried out. Archaeological, epigraphic and numismatic finds demonstrate relative prosperity (agricultural tools, domestic implements, pottery, bricks; remains of buildings, e.g., thermal baths; Christian basilica). The *cohors I Cilicum*, the *legio I Iovia Scythica* and in the 4th cent. the *milites Scythici* constituted the garrison of D. Under Anastasius I and Justinian the town was restored and fortified. Attestations: Ptol. 3,8,4; 10,1; 10,11 (Δινογέτεια); It. Anton. 225,5 (*Diniguttia*); Geogr. Rav. 4,4,4 (*Dinogessia*); Not. Dign. Or. 39,24 (*Dirigothia*).

TIR L 35 Bucarest, 1969, 38 (bibliography). J.BU.

Dinon (Δίνων; *Dínōn*) of Colophon, the 4th cent. BC, father of Cleitarchus, a historian of Alexander (FGrH 690 T 2), and the author of the *Persiká* in at least three parts (*syntáxeis*) with several books each (F 3) from Semiramis (at least) to the reconquest of Egypt by Artaxerxes [3] III (343/2). The often novel-like and sensationalist representation (cf. F 10; 17; 22) was influenced by Ctesias and was used, e.g., by Pompeius Trogus and Plutarch (Artaxerxes). FGrH 690.

O. LENDLE, Einführung in die griech. Geschichtsschreibung, 1992, 271; H. SANCISI-WEERDENBURG, A. KUHRT (ed.), Achaemenid History 2, 1987, 27ff. K.MEI.

Dinos Wrong term for a cauldron (→ Pottery, shapes and types of; → Lebes). I.S.

Dinos Painter Attic red-figured vase painter, active *c.* 425–410 BC. He is considered a student of the → Cleophon Painter, whose style he continued in 'a less exalted and delightful manner' (BEAZLEY). He only painted large vessels (→ Pottery, shapes and types of), especially bell craters, calyx craters and stamnoi, but also volute craters, an amphora and a loutrophoros as well as four dinoi, one of which is the eponymous Berlin piece (Berlin, SM). Some of his vases show complex compositions, e.g., Dionysus seated amongst satyrs and maenads; and he decorated a calyx crater with a double series of images. He preferred Dionysian themes, e.g., on one of the latest Lenaea stamnoi, maenads dance around an image of Dionysus. Further themes include komos, symposion and the 'Warrior's Farewell', often with standardized cloaked figures on the reverse. Other mythological themes, such as Apollo and Marsyas, the death of Actaeon, and the heroic deeds of Theseus are rare. His figures are full-bodied, with full curly hair and eyes with heavy lids. The rich fall of folds and languid posture as well as considerable application of additional opaque white introduce the more richly ornamented style of the next generation where his influence is noticeable in the works of the → Pronomus Painter.

BEAZLEY, ARV², 1151–1158, 1685; M. MENDONCA, The Dinos Painter, 1990; M. ROBERTSON, The Art of Vase-Painting, 1992, 242–245. M.P.

Diobelia (διωβελία; *diōbelía*). A payment of two → *oboloí* in Athens. According to the author of the Aristotelian *Athenaion Politeia* (28,3), the *diobelia* was introduced by Cleophon whereupon a certain Callicrates promised to increase the sum but in fact abolished the *diobelia*. The *diobelia* is attested from 410 to 406/5 BC from inscriptions (in 406 temporarily reduced to an obolos) and in 405/4 was probably replaced by a distribution of grain. The basis for the payment is uncertain but it was probably granted during the Decelean War as a subsistence subsidy for needy citizens who did not receive other payments from the state.

J.J. BUCHANAN, Theorika, 1962, 35–48; RHODES, 355–357. P.J.R.

Diobolon (διώβολον; *diṓbolon*). Silver coin worth two → *oboloí* (= $^{1}/_{3}$ drachma, e.g., according to the Attic coinage standard of 1.4 g. The *diobolon* occasionally has a value marker (ΔΙΩ, ΔΙΟ, Δ). The Attic *diṓbola* bear a head of Athena on the obv. and an owl with two bodies on the rev. In Athens during the classical period the *diobolon* was the amount that had to be paid for visiting the theatre (θεωρικόν) or was paid to a participant in the popular assembly (ἐκκλησιαστικόν).
→ Drachma; → Coinage, standards of; → Theorikon

SCHRÖTTER, 143f.; M.N. TOD, Epigraphical Notes on Greek Coinage, in: NC 6.7, 1947, 1–27, especially 9–12; J.N. SVORONOS, B. PICK, Corpus of the Ancient coins of Athens, 1975, pl. 17, 34–36. A.M.

Diocaesarea (Διοκαισάρεια; *Diokaisáreia*).

[1] Temple settlement around the Zeus sanctuary of Olba in Cilicia Tracheia, which became an independent town under Tiberius and later a diocese (suffragan of Seleucia on the Calycadnus). Archaeological finds: generous extension of the settlement with city walls, colonnade street, aqueduct, theatre, temple of Tyche; during the early Byzantine period the temple of Zeus was converted into a three-aisled colonnaded basilica.

HILD/HELLENKEMPER, s.v. D. F.H.

[2] Town in Cappadocia, 38 km east of Nazianzus, modern Tilköy (formerly Kaisar Köy), founded in the 1st cent. AD, in the 6th cent. a Monophysite diocese.

W. RUGE, s.v. Nazianzos, RE 16, 2099–2101; HILD/RESTLE, 171. K.ST.

Diocese see → Dioikesis

Diocleides see → Megarian School

Diocles (Διοκλῆς; *Dioklês*).

[1] Hero in Megara. He supposedly died in battle, bravely covering a youth with his shield. At his grave boys competed for who could give the sweetest kiss. This agon, which took place every spring, was called Dioclea (Schol. Pind. Ol. 7,157; 13,156a; Theoc. 12,27–33 with Schol.: Aition). Perhaps the kisses represented farewell kisses repeated in the cult of the hero ([1]; to the contrary [2]). According to Schol. Aristoph. Ach.774 the agon was founded by → Alcathous [1], the son of Pelops. In Hom. H. 2,153; 474, D. is a prince of Eleusis, in Plut. Thes. 10 a Megarian commander in Eleusis.

1 NILSSON, Feste 459 2 A.S. F. GOW, Theocritus (comm.), 1950, 227.

[2] Prince in Messenian Pherae, whom → Telemachus visits on his journey from Pylos to Sparta and back (Hom. Od. 3,488; 15,186; 21,15f.; Paus. 4,1,4; 30,2). His sons Crethon and Orsilochus were killed by Aeneas outside Troy (Hom. Il. 5,541f.). R.B.

[3] Lawmaker and popular leader and lawmaker in Syracuse. In 413 BC he effected severe punishment of the Athenian prisoners of war (Diod. Sic. 13,19,4; 13,33). In 412 he transformed the constitution (Diod. Sic. 13,34,6) from a moderate polity into a radical democracy (Aristot. Pol. 1304a27ff.) by means of laws, among them the appointment to public offices by lot, and (involuntarily) prepared the ground for the tyranny of → Dionysius [1]. In 409/8 he commanded Syracusan relief troops against the Carthaginians in Himera, but abandoned the town to them on the basis of mere rumours (Diod. Sic. 13,60–62) and was therefore banned in 408/7 at the instigation of Hermocrates.

The comprehensive legislation ascribed to D. by Diodorus (13,34f.) is probably due to confusion with a nomothete of the Archaic period (thus, first [1. 78, 417], most recently [2. 24ff.] and [3. 125ff.]).

1 A. HOLM, Gesch. Siziliens, vol. 2, 1874 2 B. CAVEN, Dionysius I., 1990 3 D.M. LEWIS, in: CAH 6, ²1994.

[4] Apart from Peisarchus the foremost leader of the oligarchy of the 600, which assumed power in Syracuse soon after the death of Timoleon in 337 BC. When Agathocles seized power in 316, the 600 were overthrown and D. and the other leaders were murdered (Diod. Sic. 19,6; Polyaenus, Strat. 5,3,8).

K. MEISTER, in: CAH 7,1, ²1984, 389. K.MEI.

[5] Comedy writer during the transition form the Old to the Middle Comedy, contemporary of the comedians Sannyrium and Philyllius (late 5th/early 4th cents. BC), from Athens or Phleius [1. test. 1]. Six titles of plays are known: Βάκχαι, Θυέστης Β', Κύκλωπες (apparently all with mythological content), Θάλαττα (name of a hetaera [1. 20]) as well as Μέλιτται and Ὄνειροι. The few remaining small fragments are insignificant.

1 PCG V, 1986, 18–24. T.HI.

[6] of Carystus

A. LIFE B. TEACHINGS C. WRITINGS D. CATEGORIZATION

A. LIFE

The son of Archidamus, Greek doctor and author of medical treatises, who was highly esteemed by the Athenians as a 'second Hippocrates' (fr. 5 WELLMANN). His biographical dates are disputed. According to WELLMANN [10. 802] he lived in the first third of the 4th cent. BC, that is before Aristotle, because Galen (fr. 23) attributed to him the very first anatomy book. However, JAEGER [2. 70–113; 3. 15–17] considered him a Peripatetic who lived from 340 to 260 BC because a dietetic letter allegedly written by D. about 305 BC and transmitted by Paul of Aegina (CMG 9,1,68) was supposedly authentic. Also, a reference to Antioch [1] in fr. 125 of his treatise on health appears to suggest that he lived at least until the foundation of that city on the Orontes in 300 BC. The reference to Galatia in the same passage apparently even permits a later date of his death so that some statements may be interpreted as polemics against Herophilus in the 260s. However, the alleged reference to Galatia is very uncertain and a dispute with Herophilus more than improbable [1. 146–148]. Even if the letter was authentic (with regards to justified doubts, cf. [8. 257–263]) and if the reference to Antioch were certain, it would merely prove that D. lived to the end of the 4th cent. Therefore, most researchers have come to consider him a contemporary of Aristotle even if their relationship remains speculative. If the mineralogist Diocles (Theophrastus De lapid. 5,28 = Diocles Fr. 166) is our D., which is more than uncertain ([9. 253f.] contrary to [8. 251–4]), he probably knew Theophrastus, but his role in the Lyceum would remain obscure.

B. Teachings

As a 'younger Hippocrates' (fr. 2), D. followed the theory of the four elements (earth, air, fire and water) and the four primary qualities (wet, dry, hot, cold). Their excess or deficiency represents the main cause of diseases (fr. 30) but there were also external causes of diseases (fr. 31). He paid particular attention to *pneûma*, which was distributed throughout the body by the vascular system. The arteries represent the channels of voluntary movement (fr. 57); epilepsy and apoplexy result from a blockage of the flow of *pneuma* when the aorta is clogged by *phlégma* (mucus) (fr. 51,55) — an opinion he shared with → Praxagoras. If the flow of *pneuma* through the pores was blocked because of corruption of the blood caused by gall or because of mucus in the veins (fr. 40; 43; 51; 59; 63), this could lead to various fevers, due to the absence of the cooling properties of *pneuma*. D. took on the idea of sympathetic relationships and believed that every season and phase of life was characterized by its characteristic mixture of elementary qualities (fr. 84,141).

In his embryology D. assumed the necessary existence of both male and female seed (fr. 172), which is affected by the mixture of bodily fluids (fr. 173). The male seed originates in the brain and spinal cord and excessive sex can therefore be harmful (fr. 172,170). The development of the embryo takes 40 days with male embryos developing faster in the uterus than female ones (fr. 175f.). D. attempted to confirm some of his theories by means of animal dissections (fr. 29). However, his conclusions on the existence of nipples in the human uterus (fr. 27) rested upon a false analogy. It is uncertain whether D.'s explanations on the uterus and heart corrected Aristotle or *vice versa*.

In his discussion of various fevers (fr. 104f.), D. emphasized the significance of prognosis and of critical days that determine the further course of the illness — he wrote a *Prognostikon* – and paid particular attention to each seventh day of the course of an illness (fr. 106–110). His views on a multitude of acute and chronic diseases such as, e.g., tetanus, are transmitted in the Anonymus Parisinus (1st cent. AD).

C. Writings

D. wrote treatises on topics as varied as digestion, fever and nutrition. In his *Archidamos* (Gal. 11,471), he developed his father's opinions on the advantages of oil in massaging and anointing the body. His most important therapeutic work was his treatise on health 'To Pleistarchus'. Like many other authors of Hippocratic treatises, D. focused his attention on nutrition and physical movement — Galen (5,879; 898) considered him particularly knowledgeable on gymnastics. In a long passage that is preserved verbatim in Galen, D. expressed the opinion that effects caused by foods could not always be reliably predicted from their properties and that inversely a causal explanation of effects was not always possible. Overall, he considers it more advisable to be guided by experience than by theory, with the fewest errors arising if one looks at the overall effects of foods. As much as these discussions may be philosophically sophisticated, they neither laid the foundations for a new scientific method, as claimed by Jaeger [2. 25–43], nor did they make D. the predecessor of the Empiricist or Sceptical schools, as Kudlien thought [5. 6].

D.'s medical interests were broad. A medical device for removing arrowheads is attributed to him [3. 101]. Among his treatises we know the titles 'On Bandages' and 'On Surgery'. He wrote on poisons and the herbal *Rhizotomikon*, a treatise on roots with medicinal effects (cf. the medication contained in the P. Antin. 123).

D. Categorization

Even though he was considered one of the great figures of the 'Dogmatic' tradition and though his theories entered the doxographies of this school (cf. Gal. CMG Suppl. Or. 4,69,115), D.'s relationship to his immediate predecessors and successors remains obscure. Neither Aristotle nor Theophrastus' biological treatises mention him by name. Despite his familiarity with thoughts that also occur in Hippocratic treatises, there is no evidence of D.'s direct familiarity with any work in the *Corpus Hippocraticum* [7. 181–189; 8. 233; 9. 243–249]. In many respects D. picks up on ideas already present in the fields of medicine, pharmacology and natural history and develops them with other objectives and interests than Aristotle and his students, which may explain the paucity of overlap.

→ Dietetics, Medicine

1 Edelstein, Ancient medicine, 145–151 2 W. Jaeger, D. von Karystos, 1938 3 W. Jaeger, Vergessene Fragmente des Peripatetikers D. von Karystos, in: ABAW 1938, 3, 1–46 4 A. Krug, Heilkunst und Heilkult: Medizin in der Ant., ²1993 5 F. Kudlien, Probleme um D. von Karystos, in: AGM 1963, 456–464 6 F. Kudlien, s.v. D., Kl.P. 2, 52–53 7 W. D. Smith, Hippocratic Tradition, 1979 8 H. v. Staden, Jaeger's 'Skandalon der histor. Vernunft': Diocles, Aristotle, and Theophrastus, in: W. M. Calder, Werner Jaeger reconsidered, 1992, 227–265 9 P. van der Eijk, Diocles on the Method of Dietetics, in: R. Wittern, Hippokratische Medizin und ant. Philos., 1996, 229–258 10 M. Wellmann, s.v. D., RE 5, 802–811.

M. Wellmann (ed.), Die Fragmente der sikelischen Ärzte, 1901; P. J. van der Eijk, Diocles of Carystus: A Collection of the Fragments with Translation and Commentary, 2000.

V.N.

[7] of Peparethus, probably the first author of a *Rhṓmēs ktísis* ('The Founding of Rome'; Plut. Rom. 8), probably in the 3rd cent. BC. According to Plutarch (Romulus 3 and 8), Fabius Pictor (late 3rd cent.) used D.'s tragically embellished tale, which is strongly reminis-

cent of Sophocles' *Tyro*. [1. 61–63], while Dionysius of Halicarnassus (Ant. 1,79 and 83) cited Fabius for the same version of the founding of Rome. Therefore, NIEBUHR [3] dated Fabius to before D. and found many successors (e.g., [2]). According to SCHWARTZ, Plutarch did not use D. directly but via an 'antiquarian of the Augustan period' [2]. However, direct use by Plutarch and an earlier date of D. than Fabius are almost certain. FGrH 820.

1 D. FLACH, Einführung in die röm. Geschichtsschreibung, [2]1992 2 ED. SCHWARTZ, s.v. D. (47), RE 5, 797f. 3 B.G. NIEBUHR, Röm. Gesch. 1, 113.

ALBRECHT, vol. 1, 300; A. MOMIGLIANO, in: CAH 7,2 [2]1989, 89; D. TIMPE, Fabius Pictor und die Anfänge der röm. Historiographie, ANRW I 2, 941f. K.MEI.

[8] Mathematician around 190–180 BC. He wrote a book Περὶ πυρ(ε)ίων (*Perì pyr(e)íōn*) that is only preserved in an Arabic translation [1]. It discusses parabolic and spherical burning mirrors, a problem in the division of spheres in → Archimedes' *De sphaera et cylindro* and the → duplication of the cube (using conic sections and the cissoid, which D. probably invented). Apart from → Eutocius [2. 66–70, 160–176] this work is not mentioned in the preserved Greek literature.

1 G.J. TOOMER (ed.), Diocles. On Burning Mirrors. The Arabic Translation of the Lost Greek Original Edited, with English Translation and Commentary, 1976 2 J.L. HEIBERG (ed.), Archimedis opera omnia, 3, [2]1915 3 TH.L. HEATH, A History of Greek Mathematics, 1921, I, 264–266; II, 47–49, 200–203 4 J.P. HOGENDIJK, Diocles and the geometry of curved surfaces, in: Centaurus 28, 1985, 169–184 5 J. SESIANO, Les miroirs ardents de Dioclès, in: MH 45, 1988, 193–202. M.F.

[9] **of Magnesia.** Hellenistic author of biographies and summaries of the teachings of philosophers, who is only known from 19 occurrences in → Diogenes Laertius. It is not known from which Magnesia he was. Two works are quoted: 'Survey of the Philosophers' (Ἐπιδρομὴ τῶν φιλοσόφων; Diog. Laert. 7,48; 10,11) and 'Lives of the Philosophers' (Βίοι τῶν φιλοσόφων; Diog. Laert. 2,54; 82). Since NIETZSCHE many scholars have identified the two works with each other, but the first work is better considered as essentially doxographic (7,48 Diogenes begins to cite a passus on Stoic logic; the quote probably closes with § 53 [1. 351–373] but some scholars extend it to § 82) while the other is biographical. The earliest mentioned is Xenophon, the latest Chrysippus; Cynics and Stoics are the main focus.

The identification of D. with the addressee in the dedication of the Garland of → Meleager [2], which was accepted for a considerable time, is based on a doubtful interpretation of Diog. Laert. 6,99 [3]. If it is rejected there is no reliable indication for dating (possibly 2nd or 1st cent. BC). NIETZSCHE considered D. the main source of the entire work of Diogenes Laertius [4. 201; 5] but that is a crass exaggeration. However, it is proven that Diogenes had direct access to the work of D. and what is owed to him is perhaps greater than can be reliably determined today.

1 J. MANSFELD, Diogenes Laertius on Stoic Philosophy, in: Elenchos 7, 1986, 297–382 2 E. MAASS, De biographis Graecis quaestiones selectae, 1880, 8–23 3 GOULET 2, 1994, 775–777 4 F. NIETZSCHE, De Laertii Diogenis fontibus, in: RhM 24, 1869, 187–228 5 J. BARNES, Nietzsche and Diogenes Laertius, in: Nietzsche-Studien 15, 1986, 16–40.

V. CELLUPRICA, Diocle di Magnesia fonte delle dossografia stoica in Diogene Laerzio, in: Orpheus 10, 1989, 58–79; E. MARTINI, RE 5, 798–801; J. MEJER, Diogenes Laërtius and his Hellenistic Background, 1978, 42–45. D.T.R.

[10] **Iulius D.** Poet of epigrams from Carystus, author of four poems in the 'Garland' of Philip: three are no more than repetitions of commonplaces (Anth. Pal. 6,186; 7,393; 12,35), the fourth — about a shield that saved its owner from the treachery of the sea by serving as a boat (9,109) — appears to have an original theme (cf. Zos. 9,40; Theon 9,41; Leonidas of Alexandria, Anth. Pal. 9,42). Identification with the orator D. of the Augustan period, who was repeatedly praised by Seneca [12] (Sen. Controv. 1,8,15f.; 7,26 etc.), is possible.

GA II,1,230–233; 2,260–263. E.D.

[11] A definitely post-Aristarchic grammarian D. is quoted four times in the scholia on Homer (Schol. Il. 13,103 c; 22,208 b; Schol. Od. 14,132; 19,457). If this is the D. mentioned in POxy. 1241 II 19–20, he would have been a contemporary of Apollodorus and Dionysius [17] Thrax (with whom he is placed in Schol. Il. 13,103 c) or would have lived a generation later, but the testimony is very problematic. On the other hand, D. is the name of the grammarian from Phoenicia who was a student of Tyrannion the Elder in Rome, a student so eager that he earned the nickname Tyrannion the Younger (*T. minor*), which has caused some confusion in the sources (cf. HAAS). In that case the prime of D. = *Tyrannion minor* must be dated to the Augustan period (approximately at the same time as Didymus [1]: this is not contradicted by the possibility that the Schol. Od. 14,132 may actually be by Didymus), and the works that can be attributed to him with certainty (leaving aside the attribution problems resulting from the confusion with Tyrannion the Elder) would be the Ἐξήγησις τοῦ Τυραννίωνος μερισμοῦ and the Διόρθωσις Ὁμηρική. Despite the problems stemming from POxy. 1241, the two should probably be equated. Whether the grammarian D. who was quoted by Artemidorus (Oneirokritika 4,70) is the same person is almost impossible to prove.

→ Tyrannion

W. HAAS, Die Fragmente der Grammatiker Tyrannion und D., SGLG 3, 1977, 177–181; L. COHN, s.v. D. (54), RE 5, 812–813; E. MARTINI, s.v. D. (51), RE 5, 801; PFEIFFER, KP I, 309; J. TOLKIEHN, Der Grammatiker D., in: Wochenschrift für Klass. Philol. 35, 1915, 1143–46; C. WENDEL, RE 7 A, 1819–20. F.M.

[12] Declamator of the Augustan period, from Carystus. Repeatedly mentioned and esteemed by → Seneca the Elder, upon whom our entire knowledge depends (Controv. 1,3,12. 8,16; 2,3,23; 7,1,26; 10,5,26). He perhaps was a moderate Asianist and may be identical with the author of Anth. Pal. 7,393.

H. Bornecque, Les déclamations et les déclamateurs d'après Sénèque le père, 1902 (reprint 1967), 165. M.W.

[13] **C. Appuleius D.** → Circus.

Diocletianus

A. Origin and career
B. Organization of the rulership
C. Reform of the Empire

A. Origin and career

Roman emperor AD 284–305. Full name (first adopted after his elevation): C. Aurelius Valerius D. (CIL III 22), previously Diocles (Lactant. De mort. pers. 9,11; 19,5; 52,3; Lib. Or. 19,45f.; [Aur. Vict.] Epit. Caes. 39,1; POxy 3055). Born in 241 or 244 in Dalmatia (Malalas 311 Bonn; [Aur. Vict.] Epit. Caes. 39,1), presumably in Salona (Theoph. 10,13 de Boor). In a purely military career he advanced to the position of *dux Moesiae* (Zon. 12,31) and after that to commander of the bodyguard (*protectores domestici*) of Emperors Carus and Numerianus (Zon. 12,31; Aur. Vict. Caesares 39,7). The entry in Syncellus (725 Mosshammer) is a misunderstanding of a source also used by Eutropius 9,19,2 and does not prove any suffect consulship of the later emperor. After the death of Numerianus on 20 November 284, he was elevated to the rank of Emperor (Lactant. De mort. pers. 17,1; PBeatty Panopolis, 2, 162f., 260f.), probably in a place located in the vicinity of Nicomedia (Zos. 1,73,2; Jer. Chron. a. 2302), where later the elevation of Galerius to Caesar and the abdication occurred and which was probably decorated with a Jupiter column by D. (cf. Lactant. De mort. pers. 19,2; Jer. a. 2321). On 1 January he took up the consulship (Chron. pasch. p. 511) in Nicomedia and in the spring marched against Carinus who was ruling in the West. Although Carinus defeated D. in the vicinity of the mouth of the Morava, he fell victim to a conspiracy of his own officers (Aur. Vict. Caes. 39,11). In order to win over Carinus' supporters for himself, he left Aristobulus, the praetorian prefect of Carinus, in office and even accepted him as co-consul for 285 (Aur. Vict. Caes. 39,14f.; Amm. Marc. 23,1,1). In spite of demonstrative attestations of respect towards the Senate (SHA Car. 18,4), D. did not travel to Rome (incorrect Zon. 12,31), but proceeded from Upper Italy to the Danube to fight there against Teutons and Sarmatians. Since overcoming the Bagaudae rebellions demanded a large detachment, he sent officer Maximianus, whom he had previously appointed Caesar in December 285 (perhaps on 13 December, cf. [1. 28ff.]) to Gaul. From Danube D. returned to the East and stayed in Nicomedia, the beginning of 286 (Cod. Iust. 4,21,6). During the course of the year, perhaps in summer, Maximianus was elevated to Augustus. As D.'s 'brother' (Pan. Lat. 6,15,6) Maximianus also carried the names Aurelius Valerius.

B. Organization of the rulership

Soon after the elevation of Maximianus to Augustus both emperors seem to have adopted in parallel the epithets Iovius and Herculius. It is disputed whether D., who by reserving for himself the name derived from Jupiter, intended to maintain priority over his 'brother' Maximianus, who otherwise was on equal footing (→ Tetrarchy). From 286 to 288, D. appears to have been mainly concerned with the fortification of the eastern border that was threatened by the Sassanids, mainly by starting the extension of the *strata Diocletiana* from Sura on the Euphrates to the Arabian Desert [2. 136ff.]. In 287, it was presumably inner political difficulties that induced the Sassanid ruler Bahram II to conclude a truce with D., whereby the Euphrates border was respected (Pan. Lat. 10,7,5–6; 9,1–2; 10,6). Upon receiving news of usurpation of → Carausius', D. travelled west. After battles with Alemannians and Iuthungi in the Raetian region, he met with Maximianus in the vicinity of Augsburg (Pan. Lat. 2,9,1) to coordinate the battle against Carausius and measures to defend the border. Via the middle Danube, where he fought against the Sarmatians, D. returned to the eastern border, where he was able to gain victories against invading Saracen tribes (Pan. Lat. 11,5,4), who presumably were in alliance with the Sassanids. Whether therefore the Arsacid Trdat, who only a short time later conveyed his congratulations to the ruler Narseh on his coming to power, was in turn installed as ruler over part of Armenia, remains an open question. However, obviously Armenia was considered a Roman sphere of influence only a few years later (Amm. Marc. 23,5,11). Renewed battles against the Sarmatians, upheavals in Egypt and the still unresolved problem of the Carausius' usurpation finally prompted D. to implement a step that had perhaps been planned for a long time, namely the elevation of Constantius [1] and Galerius Maximianus to subordinate Caesars on 1 March 293 (Tetrarchy). Galerius was successful in suppressing the rebellions in Egypt [2. 62], while Constantius Chlorus and his praetorian prefect Allectus were able to defeat Carausius' successor. Probably in 297, the uprising of → Domitius [II 14] Domitianus compelled D. to travel to Egypt, while Galerius, from Syria, took action against Narseh, who attacked simultaneously, but was defeated in the Osrhoene between Kallinikon and Carrhae. For the controversial chronology cf. now [5; 9]. After eight months, D. put an end to the usurpation of Achilles by cutting off the water supply of besieged Alexandria (Aur. Vict. Caes. 39,33; 38; Eutr. 9,23; Malalas 308 Bonn) and he inspected the southern border of Egypt overrun by the Blemmyes, where he decided to give up

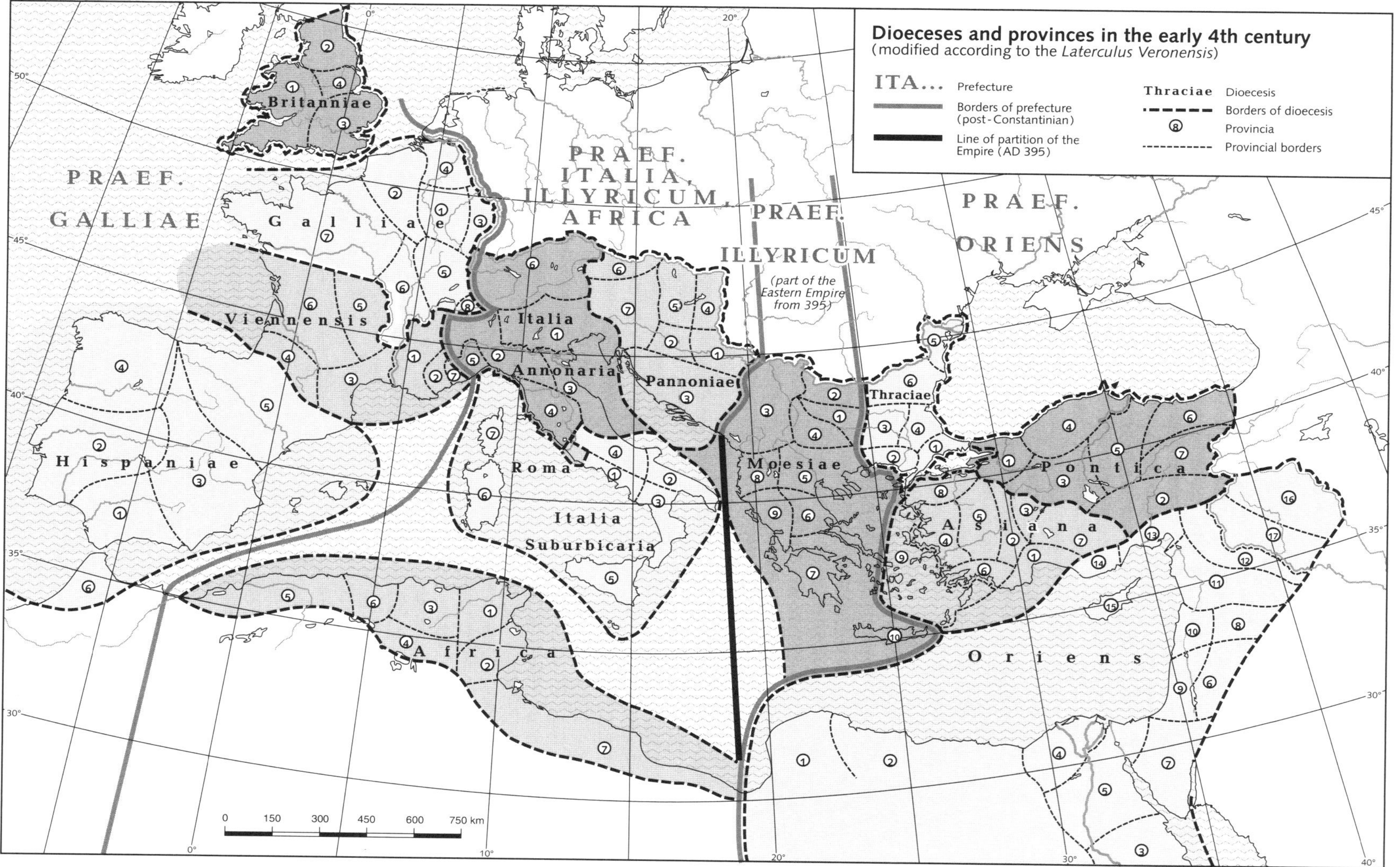
Dioeceses and provinces in the early 4th century
(modified according to the Laterculus Veronensis)
ITA... Prefecture
Borders of prefecture (post-Constantinian)
Line of partition of the Empire (AD 395)
Thraciae Dioecesis
Borders of dioecesis
Provincia
Provincial borders
PRAEF. GALLIAE
PRAEF. ITALIA, ILLYRICUM, AFRICA
PRAEF. ILLYRICUM
(part of the Eastern Empire from 395)
PRAEF. ORIENS
Britanniae
Galliae
Viennensis
Hispaniae
Italia
Annonaria
Pannoniae
Roma
Italia Suburbicaria
Africa
Moesiae
Thraciae
Asiana
Pontica
Oriens
0 150 300 450 600 750 km

Britanniae

1. Britannia Prima
2. Britannia Secunda
3. Maxima Caesariensis
4. Flavia Caesariensis

Galliae

1. Belgica Prima
2. Belgica Secunda
3. Germania Prima
4. Germania Secunda
5. Sequania
6. Lugdunensis Prima
7. Lugdunensis Secunda
8. Alpes Graiae et Poeninae

Viennensis

1. Viennensis
2. Narbonensis Prima
3. Narbonensis Secunda
4. Novem Populi
5. Aquitanica Prima
6. Aquitanica Secunda
7. Alpes Maritimae

Hispaniae

1. Baetica
2. Lusitania
3. Carthaginiensis
4. Gallaecia
5. Tarraconensis
6. Mauretania Tingitana

Italia Annonaria

1. Venetia et Histria
2. Aemilia et Liguria
3. Flaminia et Picenum
4. Tuscia et Umbria
5. Alpes Cottiae
6. Raetia

Italia Suburbicaria

1. Campania
2. Apulia et Calabria
3. Lucaniae et Brutii
4. Samnium
5. Sicilia
6. Sardinia
7. Corsica

Africa

1. Proconsularis
2. Byzacena
3. Numidia Cirtensis
4. Numidia Militiana
5. Mauretania Caesariensis
6. Mauretania Sitifiensis
7. Tripolitana

Pannoniae

1. Pannonia Inferior
2. Savensis (Savia)
3. Dalmatia
4. Valeria
5. Pannonia Superior
6. Noricum Ripense
7. Noricum Mediterraneum

Moesiae

1. Dacia (Mediterranea)
2. Dacia Ripensis
3. Moesia Superior vel Margensis
4. Dardania
5. Macedonia
6. Thessalia
7. Achaea
8. Epirus Nova
9. Epirus Vetus
10. Creta

Thraciae

1. Europa
2. Rhodope
3. Thracia
4. Haemimontus
5. Scythia
6. Moesia Inferior

Asiana

1. Lycia et Pamphylia
2. Phrygia Prima
3. Phrygia Secunda
4. Asia
5. Lydia
6. Caria
7. Pisidia
8. Hellespontus
9. Insulae

Pontica

1. Bithynia
2. Cappadocia
3. Galatia
4. Paphlagonia
5. Diospontus
6. Pontus Polemoniacus
7. Armenia Minor

Oriens

1. Libya Superior
2. Libya Inferior
3. Thebais
4. Aegyptus Iovia
5. Aegyptus Herculia
6. Arabia
7. Arabia Nova
8. Augusta Libanensis
9. Palaestina
10. Phoenice
11. Syria Coele
12. Augusta Euphratensis
13. Cilicia
14. Isauria
15. Cyprus
16. Mesopotamia
17. Osrhoene

Administration of the Empire after Diocletian and Constantine

(at the time of Valentinian I and Valens: AD 364 – 375)

Augustus (emperor)

EMPEROR'S IMMEDIATE ENTOURAGE

Staff
comes domesticorum
- protectores et domestici
candidati (bodyguards, recruited from the scholae palatinae)
tribuni scholarum
- scholae palatinae (palace guards)
tribunus et cura palatii
tribunus stabuli
- stratores

sacrum cubiculum (Palace)
praepositus sacri cubiculi (chamberlain)
primicerius sacri cubiculi (vice-chamberlain)
- cubiculari (eunuchs)
- silentiarii
castrensis (palace administration)
- castrensiani

sacrum consistorium (Council)
comites consistoriani
- quaestor sacri palatii
- magister officiorum
- comes sacrarum largitionum
- comes rei privatae
- magistri militum } if employed at court
- praefecti praetorio }
comites primi ordinis inter consistorium (extraord. members)
Secretariat of the sacrum consistorium: primicerius notarioum
- (tribuni et) notarii

CENTRAL IMPERIAL ADMINISTRATION AND COURT

Military
2 magistri militum
(magister militum)
magister militum praesentialis
magister equitum praesentialis

Central administration
Apparatus for the implication of imperial decisions

Disciplinary authority; no military command

magister officiorum
officia palatina
- magister dispositionum
(secretary for travels and appointments)
scrinium dispositionum
- magister admissionum
(master of audiences)
admissionales
- interpretes (interpreters)
- mensores (quartermasters)
- decani (door-keepers)
- cursores (couriers)

agentes in rebus ('secret police')
cursus publicus (postal service)
fabricae (from 388; workshops producing weapons)

quaestor sacri palatii
sacra scrinia
- magister memoriae
memoriales
- magister epistolarum
epistulares
- magister libellorum
libellenses

Finances

Taxes (without annona) Mint, donatives, etc.
comes sacrarum largitionum
- officium largitionum
(largitionales)
procuratores sacrae monetae

Imperial private property; Domains
comes rei privatae
- officium (privatiani)

Jurisdiction Administration (in the capitals)
praefectus urbis Romae
vicarius urbis
(responsible also for Italia Suburbicaria)
- praefectus annonae
- praefectus vigilum
- curatores
praefectus urbis
Constantinopolitanae

EMPIRE

Military
magister militum per Orientem
magister militum per Thracias
magister militum per Illyricum
magister militum per Gallias
→ comites rei militaris → comitatenses
→ duces → limitanei

Finances
comites sacrarum largitionum
= comites thesaurorum

rationales
= magistri rei privatae

procuratores

Jurisdiction; general administration; Taxes (annona) in the provinces

3 prefectures
Praefecti praetorio
Galliarum
Italiae, Illyrici, Africae
per Orientem
- officium
(praefectiani)

12-14 dioceses
vicarii
- officium

c. 110 provinces
Governors
proconsules
Africae
Achaiae
Asiae
- officium

consulares
praesides
correctores
- officium
(cohortales)

TOWNS

the Dodekaschoinos (Procop. Pers. 1,19, 29–37). In Antioch he met up with Galerius, who had been defeated. The tale that he humiliated his Caesar by forcing him to walk on foot in front of his chariot (Eutr. 9,24; Fest. 25; Amm. Marc. 14,11,10) is a tendentious misunderstanding of a conventional gesture of demonstrating respect [3. 25f.]. In the second campaign, Galerius invaded Armenia, where he was able to capture the Persian camp. While Galerius penetrated far into Persian territory, D. occupied former Roman Mesopotamia with a second army. Working from reconquered Nisibis, D. (via Sicorius Probus, who was sent to Narseh) pursued peace negotiations with the Sassanid ruler. He, in turn, ceded Nisibis and Mesopotamia in exchange for the return of his imprisoned relatives and acknowledged Roman sovereignty over Armenia and Iberia (on Petrus Patricius fr. 14 = FHG 4,189; [4. 133]).

C. Reform of the Empire

The long-lived government, secured by foreign policy successes, enabled D. to carry out many administrative and military reforms (cf. fig.). However, it can no longer be determined how much of this can actually be attributed to D. With regard to fiscal issues, in addition to supporting measures of coin reform and the Price Edict, the tax system of the → *capitatio-iugatio* was to guarantee continuity of public revenue. Italy was subjected to taxation for the first time and divided into numerous (over 100) new provinces like the rest of the empire. Generally, it is presumed that D. created a new middle authority between province and *praef. praet.* at the same time as the dioceses (different to [6]). The extension of large residences — in D.'s part of the empire Antioch and above all Nicomedia — provided the appropriate architectonic framework for the new ceremony that corresponded to the monarchical superelevation decisively expedited under D. The reform was rounded off by religious policy. Immediately following the successful war against the Sassanids, Christian soldiers and palace staff were to face repressive measures (Lactant. De mort. pers. 10,4). In 297 or 302, following the inquiry of the governor of Africa D. issued a rescript with sharp regulations against the Manichaeans. On 23 February 303, persecution of Christians began (Lactant. De mort. pers. 12,2) with the church in Nicomedia being destroyed. One day later, a (most likely the only) general persecution edict against the Christians was made public [7]. The motive for the persecution of Christians remains in the dark, but it seems probable that, in addition to the program of a conservative renewal, there was a connection with D.'s long-planned retreat from rulership and with the planned perpetuation of the tetrarchic order, which had to be guaranteed by the favour of the gods. After the Vicennalia (20 November 303), combined with a triumph that D. celebrated together with Maximianus in Rome, he resigned simultaneously with Maximianus on 1 May 305 and travelled as *senior Augustus* from Nicomedia to Salona, where the construction of a palace had already begun in 300. In November 308 he met with Galerius and Maximianus in Carnuntum to re-organize the tetrarchy that was in the process of breaking up, and he elevated Licinius to Augustus [8] and his daughter, the wife of Galerius, to Augusta on 11 November 308. Presumably in the summer of 313, D. committed suicide after he had to fear the worst for himself with the end of Maximinus Daia and the successful alliance between Constantinus [1] and Licinius ([Aur. Vict.] Epit. Caes. 39, 7; Socr. 1,2,10). He was divinized and interred in Salona (Eutr. 9,28; Sid. Apoll. Carm. 23,497).
→ Dominatus

1 F. Kolb, Diocletian und die Erste Tetrarchie, 1987 2 T.D. Barnes, The New Empire of Diocletian and Constantine, 1982 3 W. Seston, Dioclétien et la Tetrarchie, vol. 1, 1946 4 M.H. Dodgeon, S.C. Lieu (ed.), The Roman Eastern Frontier and the Persian Wars, AD. 226–363, 1987 5 F. Kolb, Chronologie und Ideologie der Tetrarchie, in: Antiquité tardive 3, 1995, 21–31 6 K.L. Noethlichs, Zur Entstehung der Diözesen als Mittelinstanz des spätröm. Verwaltungssystems, in: Historia 31, 1982, 70–81 7 K.H. Schwarte, Diokletians Christengesetz, in: R. Günther, S. Rebenich (ed.), E fontibus haurire, 1994, 203–240 8 H. Chantraine, Die Erhebung des Licinius zum Augustus, in: Hermes 110, 1982, 477–487 9 T.D. Barnes, Emperors, Panegyrics, Prefects, Provinces and Palaces (284–317), in: Journal of Roman Archaeology 9, 1996, 532–552.

Maps: K.L. Noethlichs, Zur Entstehung der Diözesen als Mittelinstanz des spätröm. Verwaltungssystems, in: Historia 31, 1982, 70–81; B. Jones, D. Mattingly, An Atlas of Roman Britain, 1990, 149; T.D. Barnes, Emperors, Panegyrics, Prefects, Provinces and Palaces (284–317), in: Journal of Roman Archaeology 9, 1996, 532–552. B.BL.

Diodorus (Διόδωρος, Διόδορος; *Diódōros, Diódoros*). Well-known representatives of the name: the philosopher D. [4] Kronos, the mathematician D. [8] of Alexandria, the universal historian D. [18] Siculus, the early Christian theologian D. [20] of Tarsus.

[1] Athenian, fleet commander with Mantitheus at the end of 408–407 BC at the Hellespont with a sufficient number of ships, so that Alcibiades [3] was able to sail to Samos and Thrasyllus and Theramenes to Athens (Diod. Sic. 13,68,2). (Traill, PAA 329550; Develin 171).

[2] Athenian from Erchia, son of Xenophon, after 399 BC with his brother Gryllus in Sparta, fled with both of them to Lepreum and Corinth. Fought without fame (Gryllus fell) as an Athenian at Mantinea in 362 (Diog. Laert. 2,52–54). Traill, PAA 330570.

W. Kirchner, s.v. D., RE 5, 459 K.KI.

[3] **of Aspendus.** Pythagorean of the 4th cent. BC included by the then head Aresas supposedly only 'due to a lack' of members (Iambl. VP 266; his Pythagoreanism is unjustly disputed by Timaeus FGrH 566 F 16 = Ath. 163e), after his return to Greece supposed to have 'circulated the Pythagorean sayings (likely *Akoúsmata*)'

(Iambl. VP 266); stood out due to his strict vegetarianism (Archestratus fr. 154,19f. SH = Ath. 163d) and attire, novel for Pythagoreans: robe of animal skin (Stratonicus fr. 737 SH = Iambl. VP 266) or *tríbōn* (worn coat), satchel and staff, long beard, long hair, barefoot, dirty (Hermippus fr. 24 WEHRLI = Ath. 163e; Sosicrates fr. 19f. FHG IV p. 503 = fr. 15f. GIANNATTASIO ANDRIA = Diog. Laert. 6,13 and Ath. 163f); he was a precursor of the Cynics.

→ Pythagorean School

W. BURKERT, Lore and Science in Ancient Pythagoreanism, 1972, 202–204; WEHRLI, Schule, Suppl. I: Hermippos der Kallimacheer, 1974, 59–60. C.RI.

[4] Son of Aminias, from Iasos in Caria, with the epithet 'Kronos' ('old fool'), which is supposed to have skipped over to him from his teacher Apollonius from Cyrene, a student of → Eubulides. D. taught in Athens toward the end of the 4th cent. BC. No later than the 80s of the 3rd cent., he made his way to Alexandria; whether this was for a limited period of time or for the rest of his life is unclear. He had five daughters who all studied dialectics. Students of D. were → Philo of the 'Megarian School' and → Zeno of Citium.

D. was one of the most influential philosophers in the period around 300 BC. The following theories are documented as his:

1. No word is ambiguous. Whatever a person says always means only that which the speaker meant to convey. If something said is not comprehended in the sense in which the speaker means it, then the reason for this is not that what was said is ambiguous, but rather that the speaker has expressed himself vaguely (Gell. NA 11,12,2–3). It appears to have been a radical application of this view when D. named his slaves after conjunctions such as Ἀλλὰ μήν ('But now') (Ammonius in De interpretatione 38,17–20).

2. In reference to motion, D. set up the paradoxical thesis: 'Not a single object moves, however it did move' (κινεῖται μὲν οὐδὲ ἕν, κεκίνηται δέ, Sext. Emp. 10,85). Of the arguments with which he tried to prove this thesis, the one quoted here as an example is the one that was probably the most important to him. Presupposing undivided bodies (ἀμερῆ σώματα) and undivided places (ἀμερεῖς τόποι), he argued this way: 'The undivided body must be located in an undivided place, and therefore it neither moves there — because after all it fills it; something that is supposed to move must have a place that is bigger than itself — nor in a place where it is not — because it is not yet there to move there. Therefore, it does not move at all' (Sext. Emp. 10,86). It is disputed whether D.'s thesis should be understood as a physical theory, or whether he was solely concerned with the paradox as such.

Two further theories that are documented as D.'s approach to modal logic: 3. According to D., a conditional statement is true when it neither was nor is possible that the protasis is true and the apodosis is false (Sext. Emp. 8,112–117). 4. According to D., possible is what is either true or will be true (Cic. Fat. 13; 17). D. tried to prove that this concept of possibility was the only correct one with his 'master conclusion' (κυριεύων sc. λόγος) that is described in the following manner in the only documentation that contains more exact information about him (Epict. Dissertationes 2,19,1): D. is to have recognized that the following three statements are incompatible with one another: a) Everything that is bygone is necessarily true. b) Something impossible does not derive from something possible. c) Something possible exists that is neither true nor will be true. Since D. is to have considered the first two statements as being self-evident, he is to have concluded that the third is false, and consequently its negation is true: Nothing is possible that is neither true nor will be true. This argument was fiercely debated in antiquity, especially because D.'s concept of possibility proven with this argument appeared to request that all events be seen as determined (cf. esp. Cic. Fat. 12–13; 17).

→ Dialecticians; → Logic; → Megarian School

EDITIONS: 1 K. DÖRING, Die Megariker, 1972, III 2 2 SSR II F.

BIBLIOGRAPHY: 1 S. BOBZIEN, Chrysippus' modal logic and its relation to Philo and Diodorus, in: K. DÖRING, TH. EBERT (ed.), Dialektiker und Stoiker, 1993, 63–84 2 N. DENYER, The atomism of Diodorus Cronus, in: Prudentia 13, 1981, 33–45 3 K. DÖRING, Die sog. kleinen Sokratiker und ihre Schulen bei Sextus Empiricus, in: Elenchos 13, 1992, 81–118, here 94–118 for D. 4 Id., D. Kronos, Philon und Panthoides, in: vol. 3: Die Philosophie der Antike, 1983, vol. 4: Die hellenistische Philosophie, 1994 2.1, § 17 G (with bibliography) 5 D. SEDLEY, Diodorus Cronus and Hellenistic philosophy, in: Proc. of the Cambridge Philological Soc. 203, 1977, 74–120 6 H. WEIDEMANN, Zeit und Wahrheit bei Diodor, in: K. DÖRING, TH. EBERT (ed.), Dialektiker und Stoiker, 1993, 314–324. K.D.

[5] Mercenary leader under → Demetrius [I A 2]. After the battle of Ipsus (301 BC) appointed by Demetrius to commanding officer in Ephesus, he intended to hand over the city to → Lysimachus, but Demetrius was able to take him prisoner through a trick (Polyaenus, Strat. 4,7,3–4). Identified with the tyrant murderer D. (Polyaenus, Strat. 6,49) by DROYSEN [1].

G. DROYSEN, Gesch. des Hellenismus, vol. 2, ²1952, 355. E.B.

[5a] **D. Pasparos.** of Pergamum (politically active: 1st half of the 1st cent. BC). In a series of inscriptions found in the Great Gymnasium in → Pergamum (with site maps), D. emerges as the perfect example of the late Hellenistic → *euergétēs* (e.g. IPerg 256; IGR 4, 292–294). In Pergamum he was the *archiereús* (municipal high priest) and → priest of Zeus Megistos. After 85, D. achieved in Rome for Pergamum relief from L. Cornelius [I 90] Sulla's punishments and protection from interference by the → *publicani*. In 69 or a little later as gymnasiarch (→ Gymnasiarchy) he financed renovation work, etc. in the Great Gymnasium and the cel-

ebration of several festivals. His fellow citizens showed their gratitude to him by, among other things, setting up a cult for D. in its own → *témenos* (the heroon of the city excavation?) and in an → *exédra* in the Great Gymnasium (room B on the top terrace).

C. P. Jones, D. Pasparos Revisited, in: Chiron 30, 2000, 1–14; W. Radt, Pergamon, 1999. J. BA.

[6] Son of Timarchides, respected member of the council of Syracuse; in 70 BC spokesman for the complaint about Verres before Cicero (Cic. Verr. 2,4,138).

[7] Famous cithara player, defeated by Nero in AD 67 in a competition (Cass. Dio 63,8,4); supposedly presented with 200,000 sesterces by Vespasian at the official opening of the reconstructed Marcellus theatre (Suet. Vesp. 19,1). M.MEI.

[8] Mathematician in Alexandria from the first cent. BC (Edwards [1. 153–157] considers possible that there were three bearers of this name). D. wrote a commentary to → Aratus [4] that was directed against the critique of the Stoics and of Hipparchus [4. 16, 48f., 97, 183f., 203f.]. Fragments from D.'s writings are especially preserved in → Achilles Tatius [2] and Macrobius (Somn.) that deal with the difference between astronomy and physics, the meaning of the terms 'cosmos' and 'star' as well as the nature of the stars and the Milky Way (printed in [1. 168–171]).

D. is among the early authors who dealt with the → analemma, which enabled the representation of points and circles on the celestial sphere with the aid of orthogonal projection in a plane. An important application was the possibility to indicate the position of the sun at any point in time. In his treatise Ἀνάλημμα (*Analēmma*), documented by → Pappus (4,246,1) and → Proclus (Hypotyposis, p. 112), D. certainly also treated the projection of the apparent daily course of the sun and in so doing provided rules for the production of sundials. D.'s method of determining the local meridian from three shadow lengths is known through al-Bīrūnī, Hyginus Gromaticus and aḍ-Ḍarīr [5. 841–843]. Pappus wrote a commentary to D.'s Analemma. The knowledge of the Analemma among the Arabs is due predominantly to D.'s writings.

D. also dealt with the parallel postulate (Anaritius [an-Nairīzī], in dec. lib. prior. elem. Eucl., p. 35,1. 65,23 Curtze) and with the mathematical meaning of the term τεταγμένον (*tetagménon*, 'given'; Marinus, comm. to Euclid's *Data*, p. 234,17 Menge).

→ Analemma; → Gnomon

1 D. R. Edwards, Ptolemy's 'Peri analemmatos' — an annotated transcription of Moerbeke's Latin translation and of the surviving Greek fragments with an Engl. version and comm., 1984, 152–182 (thesis Brown Univ.)
2 Th. L. Heath, A History of Greek Mathematics, II, 1921, 286–292
3 F. Hultsch, RE 5, 710–712
4 J. Martin (ed.), Scholia in Aratum vetera, 1974
5 O. Neugebauer, A History of Ancient Mathematical Astronomy, 1975, 840–843, 1376–1378 M.F.

[9] from Sardeis. Poet of the 'Garland' of Philippus (Anth. Pal. 4,2,12), friend of Strabo, who calls him author of historical writings (ἱστορικὰ συγγράμματα, μέλη καὶ ἄλλα ποιήματα (13,4,9 = SH 384). In spite of a few uncertainties, 11 carefully composed epigrams can be ascribed to him, mainly epitaphs (actual inscriptions were perhaps 7.627; 700f. = GVI 1472; 1819; 664) and epideictic epigrams (eulogies for Tiberius and Drusus, 9,219 and 405). He is to be distinguished from D. of Tarsus, with the epithet Grammatikos, author of five epitymbia on personalities of the past, including Themistocles (7,74; 235), Aeschylus (7;40), Aristophanes (7,38) and Menander (7,370).

GA II,1,232–243; 2,263–276 E.D.

[10] of Sinope. New Comedy poet, son of Dion and brother of comedian Diphilus. Coming from Sinope, D. later received Athenian citizenship [1. test. 2], to which perhaps the inscription IG II² 648 refers [1. Testimonia 2]. At the Lenaea of the year 284 BC, D. came in second and third [1. Testimonia 4], another time he appears to have been victorious [1. Testimonia *3]. Five work titles are recorded as well as three fragments, including a longer one (42 vv.) about the divine origin of the art of the parasite (fr. 2). One can only speculate about the identity of D. with an actor from Athens or Sinope with the same name [1. Testimonia *5].

1 PCG V, 1986, 25–30 T.HI.

[11] According to mention in Plutarch (Theseus 36,5; Cimon 16,1), Athenaeus (13, 591 B; FGrH 372 F 36) and Harpocration (FGrH 372 F 1; 7; 10; 14), a periegetic writer. Origin unknown, active around 300 BC. He is described by Harpocration (FGrH 372 F 1; 15; 16; 25; 32) as the author of a work about the Attic demes (Περὶ τῶν δήμων). Plutarch mentions his writing Περὶ (τῶν) μνημάτων in at least three books (Themistocles 32,5); apparently it was a description of Attic gravestones. The questionable work title Περὶ Μιλήτου could also refer to this writing. A.A.D.

[12] of Elaia. (ὁ Ἐλαΐτης). Alexandrian poet of elegies, who treated, among others, the unhappy love that Leucippus harboured for Daphne (Parthenius, Erotica 15 = SH 380). Very likely he is to be equated with the homonymous author from *Korinthiaká* (Κορινθιακά), who is quoted in schol. Theoc. 2,120a (= SH 381) as witness for a version of the myth in which the golden apples that Hippomenes used at the competition with Atalanta actually belonged to the wreath of Dionysus (cf. Philetas fr. 18 Powell). M.D.MA.

[13] Greek grammarian and lexicographer, author of a collection of Ἰταλικαὶ γλῶσσαι, quoted by Ath. 11,479a. A total of five references by Athenaeus are traced back to him (11,478b; 479a; 487c; 501d; 14,642e), one by Erotianus (51,16 s.v. καμμάρῳ) and one in schol. Dion. Thrax 183,29 (in reference to a work Περὶ τῶν στοιχείων). The fact that he is quoted twice by Athenaeus (11,501d; 14,642e) and again in schol. Dion. Thrax together with → Apion, allows us to infer that he was their contemporary and therefore younger than D. [14] of Tarsus; however, the recon-

struction is certainly not beyond all criticism.
→ Apion; → Diodorus [14] of Tarsus

L. Cohn, s.v. D. (52), RE 5, 709f.

[14] of Tarsus. Greek grammarian of the Alexandrian period, quoted by Strabo 14,5,15 and by Steph. Byz. 23,24 s.v. Ἀγχιάλη. He was also a poet of epigrams: Anth. Pal. 7,235 is certain, 7,700 and 701 are likely; however, it is impossible to distinguish between the different authors of the same name in Anth. Pal. when no further details are given. Since Strabo (ibid.) mentions two grammarians from Tarsus together, D. and Artemidorus, who elsewhere is called ὁ Ἀριστοφάνειος, one tends to equate this D. of Tarsus with D. ὁ Ἀριστοφάνειος, who is quoted by Ath. 5,180e (regarding a problem of Homeric philology) and in schol. Pind. Isthm. 2,54; however, this hypothesis can claim no certainty. The schol. Il. 2,865 tracing back to Didymus is allocated to the same author. Hsch. s.v. Διαγόρας = schol. Aristoph. Ran. 320 is problematical. As in many other cases, here there are also problems with homonymy: cf. Cohn and D. [13] for other uncertain places.
→ Anthology; → Artemidorus [4] of Tarsus; → Diodorus

H.L. Ahrens, Bucolicorum Graecorum reliquiae, 1855–1859, vol. II, p. XL; L. Cohn, s.v. D. 52), RE 5, 708f.; A. Ludwich, Aristarchs Homer. Textkritik, I, 1884–85, 228, 535; Pfeiffer, KPI, 258; Ch. Schäublin, Diodor von Tarsos gegen Porphyrios?, in: MH 27, 1970, 58–63
F.M.

[15] Originator of a definition of rhetoric as 'the ability to find the possible means of persuasion for each speech and to express them elegantly' (δύναμις εὑρετικὴ καὶ ἑρμηνευτικὴ μετὰ κόσμου τῶν ἐνδεχομένων πιθανῶν ἐν παντὶ λόγῳ, Nicolaus Progymnasmata, p. 451.7 column 3, schol. in Aphthon. p. 7 Walz 2). Almost the same definition is ascribed by Quint. Inst. 2,15 and 16 to an Eudorus (varia lectio: Theodorus) and explained as an expansion of the Aristotelian (Aristot. Rh. 1356a 25) definition. Whether this D. is identical with → Diodorus [16] of Tyre is questionable; a less positive evaluation of rhetoric would have been expected from the pupil of Critolaus.

[16] of Tyrus. Peripatetic, pupil and follower of Critolaus (mid 2nd cent. BC). He is known due to his definition of the goal of life (*télos*; fr. 3–5 Wehrli), according to which the highest good is the union of virtue and freedom from pain, but virtue far outweighs all other goods — a merging of the doctrines of Critolaus and of Hieronymus of Rhodus.
→ Aristotelianism

F. Wehrli, Schule 10, ²1969, 87ff.; Id., in: GGPh 3, 590f.
H.G.

[17] Zonas. Epigram poet from the 'Garland' of Philippus (Anth. Pal. 4,2,11) from Sardeis. He was also a speaker and as such had managed to attain some fame in Rome at the time of the Mithridatic Wars (89–67 BC) (cf. Str. 13,4,9). At least nine anathematic, sepulchral and epideictic epigrams (Anth. Pal. 11,43 is sympotical) can be allocated to him; due to confusions with D. [9] of Sardeis and D. [14] of Tarsus, however, a few uncertainties remain. These poems allow an ingenious imitator of Leonidas to be identified, who is superior to his model in virtuosity and linguistic creative power (the *hapax legomena* are relatively numerous, cf. 6,22; 6,98; 9,226; 9,556, etc.).

GA II,1,380–387; 2,263f., 413–418.
E.D.

[18] D. Siculus. from Agyrium (modern Agira) in Sicily, Greek universal historian of the first cent. BC, who intended with his *Bibliothḗkē* (title according to Plin. praef. at B. 25) to replace an entire (historical) library. Details of his *vita* are to be found especially in the prooemium: The earliest date is a stay in Egypt in the 180th Olympiad, i.e. 60–57 BC (1,44,1; 46,7; 83,9), the latest date (16,7,1) is the founding of the colony of Tauromenium by Octavian/Augustus (likely already 36, not 21 BC). D. laboured for 30 years on his work (1,4,1), lived in Rome for a longer period and also used Latin authors (1,4,4).

His model was Ephorus of Cyme (4,1,2–3; 5,1,4), however, D. also took into detailed consideration the mythical period and Roman history. The 'library' consists of 40 bks., covering the beginnings of the world to the beginning of Caesar's Gaulish War 60–59 BC (1,4,6; 5,1) or to the conquest of Britain in the year 54 (3,38,2; 5,21,2; 22,1) and according to 1,4,6f. it structured roughly into the period before the Trojan War with geography, ethnography, theology and mythography of the *oikoumene* (bks. 1–6: bks. 1–3 barbarians, bks. 4–6 Greeks), the history from the fall of Troy up to the death of Alexander the Great in 323 BC (bks. 7–17), and the period from 323 to 60/59 or 54 BC.

Bks. 1–5 and bks. 11–20 have been transmitted completely, otherwise only fragments and excerpts (Constantinian excerpts, Excerpta Hoescheliana for bks. 21–26 and Photius starting with bk. 31). The reports about Egypt (1,10–98, main source Hecataeus of Abdera), India (2,35–42, Megasthenes), the people on the Arabian gulf (3,12–48, Agatharchidas) and the rationalistic interpretation of myths (6,1–5, Euhemerus) are of special ethnographic and historiographic significance. Historically precious are bks. 11–20 with the only continuous account of the years 480–302 BC. Focus in the universal historical concept is on the Greek, Sicilian, and starting in bk. 23 (1st Punic War) Roman history, with the central parts: Greek history of the classical period (11–15, main source Ephorus), history of Sicily from 480 to 289/88 (11–21, Timaeus), history of Philip II (16, model unknown), Alexander the Great (17, Cleitarchus), history of his successors (18–20, Hieronymus of Cardia), early Roman history (7–12, unknown but reliable annalist), Roman history 171–146 (28–32, Polybius), and Roman history 146–88 (33–38, Posidonius). D. organizes annalistically according to Olympiads, Athenian archonts and Roman consuls with the aid of an (unknown) chronographic source (with dates on rulers, philosophers, poets and historians; overview at [1. 666–669]), however he does not always manage synchronous alignment.

The assessment of D. has been extremely negative since NIEBUHR (1828) in the 19th cent. (NISSEN, 1869; MOMMSEN, 1859) and at the beginning of the 20th cent. [1. 663–704], to some extent until most recent times [2; 3; 4]: D. is regarded primarily as a shallow 'compiler', who mechanically copies models, uses only one model for long stretches (so-called one-source theory), excerpts superficially, falls into errors and contradictions, does not recognize duplicates, and is chronologically confused and historically too uncritical. He is also lacking autopsy and political and military experience. Only for the last decades a more positive assessment has emphasized the unified and easily comprehensible style [5. 63ff., 110–139], the consistent use of standard authors, the flexible working method (always a main source as well as one or more secondary sources: [6]), the magnificent representation of the history of Sicily of Philip II, the successors of Alexander the Great, and of early Rome. Furthermore, references to the unified view of history and philosophy of life [7; 8] as well as the convincing overall concept [6] result in partial rehabilitation.

1 ED. SCHWARTZ, s.v. D. (38), RE 5, 663–704 2 J. HORNBLOWER, Hieronymus of Kardia, 1981 3 J. MALITZ, Die Historien des Poseidonios, 1983 (Zetemata 79) 4 L. PEARSON, The Greek Historians of the West, 1987 5 J. PALM, Über Sprache und Stil des D. von Sizilien, 1955 6 K. MEISTER, Die sizilische Gesch. bei Diodor, 1967 7 M. PAVAN, La teoresi storica di Diodoro Siculo, in: RAL 16, 1961, 19–52, 117–151 8 K. S. SACKS, Diodorus Siculus and the First Century, 1990.

EDITIONS: E. VOGEL, K. FISCHER, 1888–1906; C. H. OLDFATHER et al., 1933–1967 (12 vols. with Engl. trans.); E. CHAMOUX et al., 1972ff. (with French trans.); O. VEH, U. WILL, 1992–93 (up to now bks. 1–10, German trans.); J. F. MCDOUGALL, 2 vols., 1983 (lexicon).
LITERATURE: F. CASSOLA, Diodoro e la storia romana, in: ANRW II 30.1, 1982, 724–733; E. GALVAGNO, C. MOLÈ VENTURA, Diodoro e la storiografia classica, 1991; O. LENDLE, Einführung in die griech. Geschichtschreibung, 1992, 242ff.; K. MEISTER, Die griech. Geschichtsschreibung, 1990, 171ff.; M. PAVAN, Osservazioni su Diodoro, Polibio e la storiografia ellenistica, in: Aevum 61, 1987, 20–28. K.MEI.

[19] Metrologist (doctor?) of the 4th–5th cents. AD. He drew up an overview on weights and measures of capacity. In the scholia to the *Iliad* (5,576) a fr. from the work Περὶ σταθμῶν ('On Weights') is preserved, in which parts of the talent are quoted.
→ Weights; → Measures of capacity; → Talent

1 F. HULTSCH, s.v. D. (54), RE 5, 712 2 Id., Metrologicorum scriptorum reliquiae, vol. 1, 1864, 156f., 299f. 3 Id., Griech. und röm. Metrologie, ²1882, 8, 339f. M.F.

[20] of Tarsus. Famous early Christian theologian († before AD 394). After a thorough education, D. first worked in → Antioch [1] as a lay catechist. Later he was ordained as a priest under Meletius and took over the leadership of the ἀσκητήριον (*askētḗrion*), monastery-like. Thereby, the Antiochene exegetical school (→ Antiochene School) was founded as an institution (students: → Iohannes Chrysostomos, → Theodoros of Mopsuestia). From 378 D. was bishop of Tarsus. As a defender of the faith against paganism and heresy, D. belongs among the pioneers of the Nicaenum and plays an important role at the Council of Constantinople in 381. Branded posthumously as a precursor of Nestorius, his writings were condemned in 449 (Synod of Constantinople). Therefore, only fragments are preserved from a varied work. Among them are numerous commentaries on the OT and NT that give preference to an interpretation according to the literal sense, among them a Ps.-comm. [1. 3–320], as well as dogmatic and apologetic-polemic writings.

1 J.-M. OLIVIER, 1980 (Corpus Christianorum Series Graeca 6) 2 CH. SCHÄUBLIN, s.v. D., TRE 8, 763–767 (bibliography).

EDITION: CPG 3815–3822. J.RI.

[21] see → Socratics

Diodotus (Διόδοτος; *Diódotos*).

[1] In 428/27 BC author of the *psḗphisma* ('people's resolution') about the fate of the Mytileneans. D. gave a speech against Cleon (Thuc. 3,41–49,1). TRAILL, PAA 328540.

B. MANUWALD, Der Trug des D., in: Hermes 107, 1979, 407–422; C. ORWIN, in: American Political Science Review 78, 1984, 485–494; W. C. WEST III, (bibliogr.), in: P. A. STADTER (ed.), Speeches in Thuc., 1973, 156f. K.KI.

[2] Also recorded as Theodotus, satrap of Bactria and Sogdiana, made himself independent around the time of Antiochus' II death (246 BC). A few years later, at about the same time as the establishment of the Arsacid rulership in Parthyene or during the fratricidal war between Seleucus II and Antiochus Hierax, D. made himself king and adopted the ruler epithet Soter (dating varies in [1] and [2]). In 234 he left the so-called Graeco-Bactrian kingdom that since then had been independent of the Seleucids to his son of the same name (Str. 11,9,515; Iust. 41,4,5; 8f.).

1 K. BRODERSEN, The Date of the Secession of Parthia from the Seleukid Kingdom, in: Historia 35, 1986, 378–381 2 D. MUSTI, CAH 7² 1, 219f.

The Cambridge History of Iran 3, 1984; A.N. LAHIRI, Corpus of Indo-Greek Coins, 1965; A.K. NARAIN, The Indo-Greeks, 1957; E.T. NEWELL, The Coinage of the Eastern Seleucid Mints, ²1978, 245ff.; W.W. TARN, The Greeks in Bactria and India, ²1951; WILL; G. WOODCOCK, The Greeks in India, 1966. A.ME.

[3] D. Tryphon. see → Tryphon

Diogeiton (Διογείτων; *Diogeítōn*). In 401/400 BC, D. was on trial because of abuse of the custody of his brother Diodotus' children and the embezzlement of his fortune. The prosecutor was one of the children of Diodotus, who had died in 409/408; he was also D.'s grandchild, since Diodotus had married the daughter of D. (Lys. or. 32, contra D.). TRAILL, PAA 325580.

J.M. MOORE, D.'s Dioikesis, in: GRBS 23, 1982, 351–355. ME.STR.

Diogenes (Διογένης; *Diogénēs*). Known personalities: the Cynic D. [14] of Sinope, the philosophical historian D. [17] Laertius.

I. POLITICALLY ACTIVE PERSONALITIES II. PHILOSOPHERS III. POETS, SCULPTORS

I. POLITICALLY ACTIVE PERSONALITIES

[1] Athenian (?) [1. 341,1], Macedonian troop commander in Attica since 233 BC, who is supposed to have demanded Corinth from the Achaeans (Plut. Arat. 34,1–4) [2. 168,63] at the rumour of the death of → Aratus [2]; after the death of → Demetrius [3] II in 229, he facilitated the liberation of Athens from Macedonian rule by the abandonment of Piraeus and other garrisons for 150 talents (Plut. Arat. 34,6) [1. 340f.; 2. 176] and was therefore honoured as *euergétēs* (IG II² 5080) [2. 182].

1 HM 3 2 HABICHT. L.-M.G.

[2] In 221 BC, as *strategos* of Susiane, D. defended the castle of Susa for Antiochus III against the rebellious Molon, became *strategos* of Media, and in 209 accompanied Antiochus III on his eastern campaign (Pol. 5,46,7; 48,14; 54,12; 10,29,5; 30,6). A.ME.

[3] Envoy of → Orophernes of Cappadocia, in 157 BC in Rome together with Timotheus for the renewal of *amicitia* and for defence against the deposed Ariarathes V (Pol. 32,10,4–8; Diod. Sic. 31,32b). L.-M.G.

[4] Friend of the Jewish king Alexander [16] Iannaeus. The Pharisees gave him a share of the blame for the death of 800 of their party supporters whom the king had had crucified; coming to power under Alexandra Salome, they killed D. (Jos. BI 1,113; Ant. Iud. 13,410). K.BR.

[5] Commander of Mithridates VI Eupator. D. was the stepson of Archelaus [4] (Plut. Sulla 21,6) and not his son ([1. 98] contrary to App. Mith. 49; Eutr. 5,6,3; Oros. 6,2,6). He fell in the battle against Sulla's troops at Orchomenus in 86 BC.

1 A. KEAVENEY, Sulla, 1982. ME.STR.

[6] Son of Numenius, *syngenḗs* of Cleopatra VII and Caesarion, documented in 38 BC as the last Ptolemaic *strategos* of Cyprus and Cilicia.

E. VAN'T DACK, Ptolemaica Selecta, 1988, 177, 179, 182 W.A.

[7] Notary under Constantius II, sent to Alexandria in 355 to implement the deposition of Athanasius (Athan. ad Const. 22; Hist. Ar. 48,1; PLRE 1, 255, D. 2).

[8] Former governor in Bithynia, executed under Valens in connection with the trial against → Theodorus (Amm. Marc. 29,1,43). B.BL.

[9] Officer in the private guard of Belisarius, fought against the Vandals in Africa (in AD 533/34), against the Goths in Italy (starting in 536), against the Persians (in 542) and in 549 again in Italy, where on behalf of Belisarius he took over the defence of Rome against the siege of the Gothic king Totila. After the fall of the city in January 550 due to betrayal, he fled to the fortress of Centumcellae (Civitavecchia). He is last mentioned as its defender (Procop. Goth. 3,37; 39). PLRE 3A, 400f. no. 2. F.T.

[10] Bishop of Amisus (at Pontus Euxinus) in the 6th cent. AD, author of an *epitaphios* (perhaps actually an inscription, [cf. [1]) to his brother's son (Anth. Pal. 7,613). Its origin from the 'Kyklos' of Agathias is not certain.

1 P. WALTZ, Acropole 6, 1931, 17 E.D.

II. PHILOSOPHERS

[11] **of Ptolemais.** Stoic philosopher, life dates unknown. According to Diog. Laert. 7,141, he began philosophical instruction with ethics (instead of logic or physics). B.I.

[12] Natural philosopher, active around 440–430 BC. In 423, when Aristophanes' 'Clouds' was performed, D.'s doctrines must have been so well-known that they could falsely be attributed to Socrates (64 C 1 DK). Demetrius [4] of Phalerum records that D. was also in danger in Athens due to the hate (probably directed at philosophers) (Diog. Laert. 9, 57 = 64 A 1 DK). D.'s hometown Apollonia can be located on Crete (according to Steph. Byz. 64 A 3 DK) or at the Pontus (a Phrygian D. appears in Aelianus' list of *átheoi*, also 64 A 3 DK).

D.'s treatise 'On Nature' (Περὶ φύσεως) refers, according to Simplicius, who still was in possession of a copy, to the following further works of its author: 'Against the Sophists' (Πρὸς σοφιστάς — as D. called other natural philosophers), 'Meteorologia' (Μετεωρολογία, again philosophical discussions of a general nature), and 'On the Nature of Man' (Περὶ ἀνθρώπου φύσεως; 64 A 4 DK). All extant quotes of D. go back to Περὶ φύσεως, the doxographical reports, however, likely go back to Theophrastus' script 'Collection of D.' Opinions' (Τῶν Διογένου συναγωγή), a compilation of several works of D. [1. 249].

Different to most of the post-Parmenidean philosophers, D. represented a monistic position: Everything originates through change from the same thing and is the same thing, otherwise the things in the world could not interact (64 B 2 DK). This common nature is air (64 B 4–5 DK), which is eternal, immortal and strong and knows much (64 B 7–8 DK). The divine air directs and permeates everything, reaches everywhere and is present in everything. Since it is so changeable and diversified in form, everything shares in it in a different manner (64 B 5 DK). Outstanding examples of participation in the air are breath and soul (for these doctrines, cf. the theses of the → Milesian School). Since blood is a carrier of air in the organism, D. offered a detailed discussion of the blood-vessel system (64 B 6 DK, cited in Aristot. Hist. an. 3,2,511b31– 513b11).

Theophrastus calls D. the 'almost youngest natural philosopher' (Democritus perhaps lived later) and pointed out that D. combined (incompatible) doctrines of Anaxagoras and Leucippus (recorded by Simplicius, 64 A 5 DK; cf. [1. 93] on the meaning of Theophrastus' claim). Whether he was an eclecticist or not, D. appropriated Anaxagorean doctrines in an original way. He rejected the countless particles of being mixing with each other, he removed the dualism foisted on them and the self-sufficient spirit, and decided in favour of an all-permeating monism. Most likely, Leucippus' contribution to D.'s concept was not the void (64 A 6 and A 31 DK, however, the void need not necessarily be the Atomist's absolute void, but rather the spontaneous origin of infinite worlds (64 A 6 DK).

A thought that can be termed teleological can be found in the fragment 64 B 3 DK: The optimum order of the world documents the existence of an organizing intelligence. However, this does not result in the teleological explanation of each and every natural phenomenon. The intelligence of the air and the measures that it contains can guarantee that causal chains emerging from the principle generate optimum orders without intended interactions.

When the Sophists came up in the middle of the 5th cent. BC, D.'s project had already acquired an old-fashioned appearance. However, his influence on the Stoic concept of *pneûma* has perhaps been substantial.

1 A. Laks, Diogène d'Apollonie, 1983.

Fragments: Diels/Kranz, II 51–69; R. Hanslik, s.v. D. (42), RE Suppl. 12, 233–236.

[13] of Smyrna. (*c.* 380–320 BC) appears in the line of succession of the → Democriteans. The assertion that he represented the same doctrines as → Protagoras (71 A 2 DK) is unproductive. He is perhaps the D., who is reported to have held the opinion, together with Leucippus and Democritus, that perceptions result from convention (νόμῳ) and not by nature [1. 397 b 9–11].

1 Diels, DG.

Diels/Kranz II 235.

I.B.

[14] of Sinope The founder of the → Cynic School, 412/403 — 324/321 BC, is mainly known to us through Diog. Laert. 6,20–81, as well as from the numerous *apophthegmata* and *chreiai*. Truth and legend are mixed throughout his biography.

A. Life B. Doctrine

A. Life

D. was born in Sinope on the Black Sea as the son of one Hicesias, who managed the public bank and one day committed counterfeiting. D. is supposed to have participated in this, which forced him to go into exile in Athens (Diog. Laert. 6,20–21). Based on this episode, D.'s Cynic doctrine adopted 'counterfeiting' in the sense of reversing the generally acknowledged values (νόμος) as its motto. The chronology does not allow any positive statement about whether D. could have been in contact with → Antisthenes in Athens, as it is maintained in the so-called 'Successions' (→ Doxography; cf. Diog. Laert. 21–23), but it is certain that he was under the influence of this student of Socrates at least indirectly. In Athens he presented himself for the first time in the attire of the Cynic, with a beggar's purse, staff and *tríbōn* (worn-out cloak) and began to lead a life of extreme frugality; this earned him the nickname 'the Dog' (κύων, *kýōn*), which he not only readily accepted, but later on even claimed it for himself because of the openness, shamelessness and simplicity in the dog's behaviour. On a journey to Aegina he was taken prisoner by pirates, brought to Crete and sold as a slave (Diog. Laert. 6,29–30; 75). A rich citizen of Corinth, Xeniades, bought him and made him the teacher of his children; it is not known whether at that time he lived with Xeniades or in a tub on the Kraneion. According to tradition, he is said to have met Alexander the Great one day while he was lying on this hill in the sun and is said to have told him, 'Don't block the sun!' (*nunc quidem paululum, inquit, a sole*; Cic. Tusc. 5,92).

There are several versions of his death and burial. D. had numerous students: → Crates of Thebes, Monimus of Syracuse, Onesicritus of Aegina or Astypalaea who participated in Alexander's campaign in Egypt, another Onesicritus of Aegina with his two sons Androsthenes and Philiscus, the well-known politician Phocion 'the Good' and the Megarian philosopher Stilpon.

B. Doctrine

The authenticity of D.'s works has been questioned since antiquity. Diog. Laert. 6,80 presents two lists of his writings, in which only four titles are identical; the first list is anonymous, while the second is attributed to → Sotion and likely of Stoic origin and therefore suppresses the philosopher's most daring writings, among them in particular the famous 'State' and the tragedies.

As moral art (τέχνη), D. proposes a 'short path' to achieve happiness, namely the way of physical asceticism with a moral goal that prefers the power of action to the hair-splitting remarks of discussion and gives special emphasis to the experience of life of the sage. Asceticism requires that one frees oneself of all material goods, is content with only the bare necessities of life, and practises taking on voluntary privations (πόνοι) daily: one should take in only minimal food, drink only water, sleep on the hard ground or roll in the hot sand in summer, in order to be in the position of bearing all vicissitudes in good spirits when fortune and fate strike one day.

D. pursues his 'counterfeiting' in all areas of human action. In politics, he refuses to belong to any particular city and declares himself a *kosmopolítēs*, a citizen of the world (κοσμοπολίτης; → Cosmopolitanism); in his 'State' he repudiates all prohibitions that are an expression of the social will, and expresses scandalous views with regard to family and sexuality; he even recommends anthropophagy, i.e. cannibalism, and incest, the shared possession of women and children, the nudity of women at sports activities, and total sexual permissiveness. In morals, he breaks with Socratic intellectualism, emphasizes the power of the will according to the example of Antisthenes, and exhorts people to profess autarky (αὐτάρκεια), apathy and freedom as prerequisites of happiness. In religion, he professes a form of agnosticism and opposes all types of religious practice of his day, since he believed religion to be an expression of origin and presents a barrier on the path toward apathy due to the inhibition it arouses. In philosophy, he relies on poverty as an 'instinctive aid to philosophy'; the 'short path' of the Cynic School, therefore, abstains from any type of *paideía* and requires no special knowledge. D. strongly influenced the early Stoics such as → Zeno, and the latter wrote a 'State' that is inspired by that of D.; others, such as the contemporaries of Panaetius, however, were shocked by D.'s excessive statements.

→ Antisthenes; → Cosmopolitanism; → Crates of Thebes; → Cynic School; → CYNICISM

SSR Vol. II, Section V B, vol. IV, 413–559; M.-O. GOULET-CAZÉ, L'ascèse cynique. Un commentaire de Diogène Laerce VI 70–71, 1986; L. PAQUET, Les Cyniques grecs. Fragments et témoignages, [2]1988, 49–100; H. NIEHUES-PRÖBSTING, Der Kynismus des D. und der Begriff des Zynismus, 1988. M.G.-C.

[15] of Babylon. Most significant head of Stoic school after Chrysippus, *c.* 240–150 BC. He studied with → Chrysippus and his successor → Zeno of Tarsus, and was teacher of → Antipater [I 10] of Tarsus, → of Panaetius of Rhodus and of less significant Stoics. He is known for his debates with the Academician → Carneades and his participation in the Athenian delegation of philosophers to Rome (156–55 BC), where he also presented philosophical lectures — the first formal introduction of Stoic concept in Rome. He wrote on numerous topics: logic, physics and theology, ethics and politics, but especially on rhetoric and music. The fragments of Philodemus' writing 'On Music' contain an important representation of D.'s thought, especially with regard to politics. D. participated intensively in the discussion on the nature of *télos* (life goal), on the balance of ethical principles and pragmatic action (cf. Cic. Off. 3,50–56; 91), and on the nature of the gods.

1 SVF III, pp. 210–243 2 C. GUERARD, in: GOULET vol. 2, 807–810 (bibliogr. n. by J.-P. DUMONT, D. DELATTRE, with notice of a planned publication of fragments and testimonia) 3 M. POHLENZ, Die Stoa, vol. 1, 1948, 180–190 4 G. STRIKER, Antipater, or the art of living, in: Essays of Hellenistic Epistemology and Ethics, 1996, 298–315 5 J. ANNAS, Cicero on Stoic Moral Philosophy and Private Property, in: J. BARNES, M. GRIFFIN (ed.), Philosophia Togata, 1989, 151–173 6 M.C. NUSSBAUM, Poetry and the Passions: Two Stoic Views, in: J. BRUNSCHWIG, M. NUSSBAUM (ed.), Passions and Perceptions, 1993, 115–121 7 D. OBBINK, P. VANDER WAERDT, Diogenes of Babylon. The Stoic Sage in the City of Fools, in: GRBS 32, 1991, 355–396 8 J. BRUNSCHWIG, Did Diogenes of Babylon invent the Ontological Argument?, in: Id., Papers in Hellenistic Philosophy, 1994, ch. 8. B.I.

[16] of Tarsus. Epicurean of uncertain date. He wrote 'Selected School Lectures' (Ἐπίλεκτοι σχολαί) contained in almost 20 books (Diog. Laert. 10,26; 97; 120; 138) and an 'Outline of the ethical doctrines of Epicurus' (Ἐπιτομὴ τῶν Ἐπικούρου ἠθικῶν δογμάτων; Diog. Laert. 10,118). If he is identical with the author of the same name D. [20] of 'Poetical Inquiries' (Ποιητικὰ ζητήματα; Diog. Laert. 6,81) and of tragedies (Str. 14,5,15), he should be dated in the 2nd half of the 2nd cent. BC. The orthodoxy of D. within the school is disputed (Diog. Laert. 10,26).

T. DORANDI, in: GOULET 2, 1994, 823f. T.D.

[17] Laertius Author of the only extant work from antiquity that offers a comprehensive representation of the history of Greek philosophy to the beginning of the Christian Era.

A. PERSONAL DETAILS B. THE LIVES OF THE PHILOSOPHERS

A. PERSONAL DETAILS

Our knowledge of the author is based only on what can be derived from his name and his work. The epithet Laertius probably does not indicate that he came from Laerte in Caria or Cilicia, but is to be understood as a 'nickname' that goes back to Homer's name for Odysseus, διογενὲς Λαερτιάδη (*diogenès Laertiádē*), to differentiate him from his namesakes. The words παρ' ἡμῶν (9,109) can be interpreted in terms of Nicaea in Bithynia (not far from Byzantion) being his hometown; but this remains uncertain. The assumption that D. came from such a provincial town has its appeal in the fact that it would explain his somewhat old-fashioned erudition. D. scarcely mentions philosophers from the Roman period, apart from a list of Sceptics in 9,116 (but cf. the catalogue, *pínax*, Stoic philosophers below). The one named last in this list is a student of Sextus Empiricus. A dating in the middle of the 3rd cent. is therefore likely. But D. does not mention representatives of Middle Platonism and of Neoplatonism, nor does he know any philosophers who are in contact with Neo-Pythagoreanism and the reawakening of Aristotelianism. This is surprising since a passage of the text at 3,47 suggests that his book was dedicated to a lady with sympathies for Platonic philosophy (although it is unlikely, but certainly not impossible, that this passage was transferred from another source).

B. The Lives of the philosophers
1. Title 2. Structure 3. Description

1. Title

Since Byzantine time the work of D. was known as Βίοι φιλοσόφων or *Vitae philosophorum* ('Lives of the Philosophers'). The MSS offer longer titles that likely do not go back to the author: Φιλοσόφων βίων καὶ δογμάτων συναγωγὴ τῶν εἰς δέκα ('Lives and Doctrines of the Philosophers in 10 Books') or Βίοι καὶ γνῶμαι τῶν ἐν φιλοσοφίᾳ εὐδοκιμησάντων καὶ τῶν ἑκάστῃ αἱρέσει ἀρεσάντων τῶν εἰς δέκα ('Lives and Maxims of Famous Philosophers and Doctrines of the Corresponding Schools in 10 Books'). The first title alludes to the mixture of biographical and doxographical material characteristic of this work; the second draws attention to the book's great treasure of anecdotal material and to its presentation according to leading philosophers and their schools (→ Hairesis).

2. Structure

The basis for the structure of the work is outlined in prologue 1,13–16. D. divides the history of Greek philosophy into two main lines according to the pattern of the succession literature (διαδοχαί, → Doxography). These determine the division of the *vitae* into ten books, as the following summary indicates:

Book 1: The Seven Sages, including Thales; Book 2: The Ionian Line, including Anaximander, Anaxagoras, Socrates and the Socratics; Book 3: Plato; Book 4: Plato's successors in the Academy to Cleitomachus; Book 5: Aristotle, Theophrastus and their successors in the Lykeion; Book 6: Antisthenes, Diogenes and the Cynics; Book 7: Zeno and the Stoics (according to a *pinax* in a later MS, about twenty *vitae*, ending with the Roman philosopher Cornutus have dropped out here); Book 8: The Italian stream, led by Pythagoras and Empedocles; Book 9: The 'scattered' philosophers, including Heraclitus, Parmenides, Democritus and Pyrrho; Book 10: Epicurus.

The work, as it is preserved, is for sure in an unrevised condition. Various chapters or *vitae* are of unequal length and contain material of remarkable variety, which results in the work's uneven and compilatory character. In most chapters, biographical material is presented under the following headings: (1) Patronymic and philosopher's origin, (2) his teachers, (3) his heyday, (4) anecdotes from his life, often of a sensational or scandalous nature, (5) maxims and *bon mots*, (6) a list of other known persons of the same name (homonyms). For the more significant philosophers, D. also offers extremely valuable lists of works that go back to Hellenistic library stocks, and other documents such as testaments and letters (the latter usually being fictitious). A special characteristic is the inclusion of 52 epigrams of rather poor quality, whose subject matter are mainly the circumstances of the death of the respective philosopher. In 1,39 and 1,63 D. mentions that these epigrams come from a collection of his poems entitled *Pámmetros* (Πάμμετρος), which were published in at least two books. As the title indicates, it contained poems in a variety of metres, a few of which cannot be found anywhere else. In Byzantine time a number of these poems were included in the *Anthologia Palatina*.

3. Description

The presentation of the philosophical doctrines is unevenly distributed in the *vitae*. Extensive descriptions are provided for the doctrines of the founders of the large schools. The long doxographies of the Stoa (7,39–160) and of Pyrrho (9,69–108, actually a summary of Neo-Pyrrhonian doctrine) are especially notable. The doxography of Plato is a relatively short and confusing description. It is supplemented by a version of the *Divisiones Aristotelicae*, which are regarded to be Platonic. In Book 10, D. deviates from his usual method and quotes word for word the text of three long letters in which Epicurus summarizes his doctrines on physics, meteorology and ethics, and also his collection of main maxims (Κύριαι δόξαι). The emphasized final position allotted to Epicurus, is allotted together with the enthusiastic comments in 10,8–10, has led some scholars to the conclusion that D. himself sympathized with Epicurean philosophy.

D.'s aim is not to write a history of philosophy. He combines biographical and doxographical material because like most ancient philosophical historians he was convinced that there was an inner relationship between the life (βίος) and the doctrine (λόγος) of every philosopher.

The value of the information provided by D. depends totally on the literary genre and the quality of his sources. The character and extent of the use of sources have long been a matter of heavy debates in research. The thesis of Nietzsche, based mainly on 7,49, that his main source was → Diocles [9] of Magnesia, is well known; however it is now generally agreed that it is wrong to search for a single main source behind the extremely varied types of information that D. offers. Further sources, no longer extant, referred to often are → Hippobotus, Hermippus of Smyrna, Sotion, Apollodorus of Athens, Heracleides Lembos, Alexander Polyhistor, Demetrius of Magnesia and Favorinus. Some of them are certainly quoted second- or third-hand.

In recent times, the search for sources has been disregarded in order to concentrate on understanding the methods of editing. D. excerpted and processed material from widely dispersed sources. Due to his antiquarian tendencies (and perhaps also because he was limited by insufficient access to recent works), he shows a clear preference for older and sought-after material from the Hellenistic period. Therefore, he hands down many fragments from philosophical-historical works that are no longer extant. Despite the intellectual mediocrity of D.'s achievement, his value for the history of ancient philosophy remains unsurpassed.

EDITIONS: H.S. LONG, 1964 (on tradition); T. DORANDI (crit. ed., Coll. Budé, expected for 2000); D. KNOEPFLER, La vie de Ménédème d'Érétrie de Diogène Laërce: contribution à l'histoire et à la critique du texte des Vies des Philosophes, 1991 (on LONG).
BIBLIOGRAPHY: E. SCHWARTZ, s.v. D. (40), RE 5, 737–763; J. MEJER, D. Laertius and his Hellenistic Background, 1978; Diogene Laerzio storico del pensiero antico, Elenchos 7, 1986 (contributions by M. GIGANTE, J. MANSFELD et al.); J. MEJER, D. Laertius and the transmission of Greek philosophy, in: ANRW II 36.4–5, 1990–1992, 3556–4307; J. MEJER, s.v. Diogène Laërce, in: GOULET 2, 824–833, 1011–1012 (with addendum by S. MATTON on the medieval tradition). D.T.R.

[18] **of Oenoanda.** Epicurean around the turn from the 2nd to the 3rd cent. AD (possibly 1st quarter of the 2nd cent. AD [1], according to the most recent literature even between the 1st cent. BC and the 1st cent. AD [3]). Author of a popular work about the philosophy of Epicurus that was made public as a wall inscription on a stoa at the agora of Oenoanda in Lycia. The limited secured knowledge about his life originates from this inscription. The stoa was presumably destroyed by an earthquake that shook Oenoanda in AD 140–01; the stone blocks were reused for the construction of the New Agora.

When D. set up the inscription, he was already old and sick; he had traveled to Rhodes to meet his friends Menneas, Carus and Dionysius. D. wanted to make the healing doctrine of Epicurus accessible to contemporary and future mankind, which was tormented by evils due to false views. D. was Epicurus' fervent supporter and interpreted his thinking correctly and in a balanced manner, but commensurate with the changed historical and overall conditions. The importance of the 'Epicurean Stoa' of D. lies not only in his contribution to the understanding of the Epicurean philosophy, but also in the underlying political message.

Only 212 fragments of uncertain arrangement and composition of contents are preserved. At least three treatises of D. together with a few texts of Epicurus were set up in seven lines on the wall of the stoa. Reading from the top to the bottom, the first three lines (VII-V) contain D.'s work *De Senectute* (fr. 137–179; defence of old age against the common complaints: inactivity, disease, loss of pleasures, imminent death); line IV presents a collection of writings of D. and of Epicurus (fr. 97–116); line III contains the letters of D. to his friends Antipater (fr. 62–67), Dionysius (fr. 68–74) as well as to Menneas and Carus. Line II comprises the treatise on physics (fr. 1–27; doctrine of nature, theory of atoms, parts of epistemology, doctrine of the gods, history of culture, astronomy). The contents of line I is ethics (fr. 28–61; blessings and virtue, virtue and pleasure, principles of *Tetraphármakos*, classification of desires, relationship soul-body). These lines are located above a base of 15 continuous lines with maxims of Epicurus (a few of which were unknown until then). The disposition addressed to friends and acquaintances (fr. 117–118) can be attributed either in line II or I. The arrangement of other fragments (fr. 75–96; 129–136) is uncertain. According to D.'s will, however, the texts should be read and understood in the following order according to the original regulations of the Epicurean tradition: first the text on physics (II), then on ethics (I), the letters (III), the tenets of Epicurus (basis), D.'s advice for his family members and his friends (II or V), the collection of D.'s and of Epicurus' writings (IV), and finally (V-VII) the treatise *De Senectute*.

EDITION: 1 M.F. SMITH, D. of Oinoanda. The Epicurean Inscription, 1993.
BIBLIOGRAPHY: 2 B. PUECH, R. GOULET, in: Goulet 2, 1994, 803–806 3 M.F. SMITH, L. CANFORA, Did D. of Oinoanda know Lucretius?, in: RFIC 121, 1993, 478–499. T.D.

[19] **from Athens.** Son of Diogenes, poet of satyr plays, honoured as Attic participant in the III Pythaïs of the *technitai* of Dionysus in Delphi in the year 106–05 (or 97 BC, cf. TrGF app. crit. 145–151) (FdD III 2, 48 36, Syll.³ 711 L).

METTE, 72; TrGF 148. F.P.

III. POETS, SCULPTORS

[20] **from Tarsus.** Philosopher, also author of tragic *Poiḗmata* (*c.* 150–100 BC; Str. 14,675). He is perhaps identical with the Epicurean of the same name (see [1]).

1 V. ARNIM, s.v. D. (46), RE 5, 776, 37ff. 2 TrGF 144.

[21] **from Thebes.** Tragedian, son of Theodotus. Victory in the 1st cent. BC at the Soteria in Acraephia (DID A 9[b]).

METTE, 62; TrGF 176.

[22] D. or Oenomaus (Οἰνόμαος), tragedian from Athens, first performance likely in 403 BC. The Suda δ 1142 mentions eight pieces; his name is still mentioned by Plutarch (*De recta ratione audiendi* 7,41C). The information of the Suda is probably contaminated with that of Diogenes [14] of Sinope (see also TrGF 88); Oenomaus probably refers to the Cynic from Gadara, who also wrote tragedies (see TrGF 188).

B. GAULY (ed.), Musa Tragica, 1991, 45; TrGF 45. F.P.

[23] Sculptor from Athens. His pediment figures and caryatids between the columns of the Pantheon of Agrippa (25 BC), probably copies of the Erechtheion *korai*, were highly praised (Plin. HN 36,38).

G. CRESSEDI, EAA 3, 106, s.v. D. 1; C. ROBERT, s.v. D. (53), RE 5, 777. R.N.

Diogenianus (Διογενιανός; *Diogenianós*).

[1] Epicurean, dating uncertain (perhaps 2nd cent. AD). Eusebius (Pr. Ev. 4,3; 6,8), who cites long excerpts from his script against the doctrine of Chrysippus 'On Fate'

(περὶ εἱμαρμένης), falsely labels him as a Peripatetic. D. accepted the truth and reliability of mantics. He taught the existence of fortune (τύχη) and of fate; but this does not exclude the freedom of the will.

T. Dorandi, in: Goulet 2, 833f.; J. Hammerstaedt, in: JbAC 36, 1993, 24–32. T.D.

[2] **from Heraclea.** (according to the Suda, not Heraclea Pontica). Greek grammarian of the 2nd cent. AD. He compiled a Παντοδαπὴ λέξις ('All Types of Sayings') in five bks., one of the first significant lexicographical works in alphabetical order: To a great extent it consisted of an epitome of the enormous collection of Pamphilus and of Zopyrion. With D.'s lexicon, the late antique and Byzantine lexicography had one of the most respected sources, in the original or as an epitome: The Περιεργοπένητες of D. were the main model for Hesychius (6th cent. AD), probably a compendium of the *Pantodapḕ léxis* (the thesis advocated by Reitzenstein, rejected by Latte, that the two works were identical, was long debated); are also two papyrus fragments are likely belonging to his compendia (Papiri della Società Italiana 892 and POxy. 3329). Material derived from D. can also be found in numerous scholiastic corpora (e.g. on Plato, Aeschines, Callimachus, Nicander).

The Suda entry on D. (δ 1140), originating from the *Onomatológos* of Hesychius Milesius also documents a geographical work 'On Rivers, Lakes, Springs, Mountains and Mountain Ranges' (Περὶ ποταμῶν λιμνῶν κρηνῶν ὀρῶν ἀκρωρειῶν), none of which, however, is extant. Remnants from one of his collections of satirical and sympotical songs in alphabetical order can be found in the *Anthologia Palatina* (mostly in bk. 11). It is not documented, however, whether D. wrote paroemiographic collections; nevertheless, a Byzantine collection of proverbs in eight codices has finally been transmitted under his name (in different versions: D1–D3 Bühler (cf. Corpus Paroemiographorum Graecorum = CParG I 177–180) and D. Vindobonensis (CParG II 1–52) need to be distinguished); it is uncertain whether he is the author of the short treatise Περὶ παροιμιῶν (CParG I 176–180).

H. Weber, Unt. über das Lexikon des Hesychios, in: Philologus Suppl. 3, 1878, 449ff.; R. Reitzenstein, Die Ueberarbeitung des Lexicons des Hesychios, in: RhM 43, 1888, 443–460; K. Latte, Hesychi Alexandrini Lexicon, 1, 1953, IXff., XLIIff.; W. Bühler, Zenobii Athoi Proverbia, 1 (Prolegomena), 1987, 188–275. R.T.

Diognetus (Διόγνητος; *Diógnētos*).

[1] Athenian, son of Niceratus, from Cyantidae; brother of Nicias and Eucrates [2], father of Diomnestus. Winner at the Dionysia in 415 BC (Pl. Grg. 472a), afterwards exiled; in Athens in 404–03. Intervened in 403 with Pausanias on behalf of Nicias' sons. Died *c.* 396 (Lys. 18,4; 9f.; 21; And. 1,47). Perhaps identical with the person named by Traill (PAA 327535, 327540).

Traill, PAA 327820; Davies 10808. K.KI.

[2] As nauarch of Antiochus III, led Antiochus' bride Laodice, daughter of Mithridates II of Pontus, to Seleucia near Zeugma in 222–21 BC. In 219, he took the then Ptolemaic Seleucia in Pieria by storm in the 4th Syrian War, and accompanied by fleet Antiochus' land attack on south Syria (Pol. 5,43,1; 59,1; 60,4; 62,3; 68,9; 69,7; 70,3). A.ME.

[3] Tragedian. His name appears on a *technitai* inscription in Ptolemais in the Thebais/Egypt (in 270–246 BC, time of Ptolemy Philadelphus; i.a. OGIS 51).

Mette, 71; TrGF 115. F.P.

[4] **D.-Letter.** Anonymous Christian apologia of a protreptic nature, written in Greek. In a short, literarily ambitious form, the writing answers three questions (ch. 1) of the otherwise unknown D.: questions about the God of the Christians (chs. 2–4), their way of life (chs. 5–6), as well as — after laying the foundations of the concept of God (chs. 7–8) — the late entrance of Christianity into history (ch. 9–10). The two following chapters 11–12 are mostly viewed as an appendix (contrary: [2. 174–181]). Perhaps written shortly before 200, good arguments are in favour of → Alexandria [1] as the location of writing.

1 R. Brändle, Die Ethik der 'Schrift an Diognet', 1975
2 M. Rizzi, La questione dell'unità dell' 'Ad Diognetum', 1989 (bibliography).

Edition: P. Marrou, [2]1965 (SChr 33bis).
Concordance: A. Urbán, Concordantia in Patres Apostolicos I, 1993. J.RI.

[5] Teacher of → Marcus Aurelius.

Dioikesis (διοίκησις; *dioíkēsis*, Lat. *dioecesis*).
I. Greece II. Rome

I. Greece

'Housekeeping' in the sense of administration, especially in the financial realm. *Dioikesis* is used for the administration of the state in general (for example, Pl. Prt. 319d; [Aristot.] Ath. Pol. 43,1), also for the financial administration (for example, Xen. Hell. 6,1,2; Dem. Or. 24,96f.), and, in an extended sense by the author of the Aristotelian *Athenaion Politeia*, for maintenance payments made by the state (24,3). In later 4th-cent. BC Athens, an office for the upper financial administration existed with the title of *epì tē̃i dioikḗsei* ('at the top of the administration'): this title may have been held by Lycurgus and his successors (cf. Hyp. fr. 118 Jensen = Kenyon, SEG 19, 119) and was definitely in use from 307/6 up into the 2nd cent. Earlier opinions held that this office was executed by a single person during the oligarchic regimes of the Hellenistic period and by a committee of ten during the democratic phases. Records available today, however, give rise to the assumption that a single official was in charge until the year 287 BC, then followed by a committee, although several texts mention only a single member instead of the whole committee. But it is also quite possible that even for the time before 287, references might be found that point to a committee rather than a single official.

P. J. RHODES, The Athenian Boule, 1972, 107–109; Id., in: Tria Lustrum ... FS J. Pinsent, 1993, 1–3. P.J.R.

II. ROME

The term is used in the sense of 'administrative district', in Cicero occasionally referring to the *conventus iuridici* in Asia or Cilicia which had grown out of the Attalid administration. During the Principate it is also used for parts of the western provinces and occasionally for the territory of a city [1. 1056ff.]. The term did not grow in significance until the administration of late antiquity. → Diocletianus' division of the imperial territory into more than 100 small provinces made it reasonable to combine several of these into medium-sized administrative districts for certain administrative purposes, first in the financial administration, where *rationales* had to contend with a business realm reaching across several small provinces [2. 181], later also in the judicial system and the general administration, where certain individuals could be entrusted with the authority over groups of provinces. Depending on the individual case, these individuals could be representatives of the praetorian prefects (*vices agentes*), vicars (*vicarii*, who apparently must be distinguished from the *vices agentes*), or individuals from the immediate surroundings of the emperor (*comites*, cf. the *comes Orientis* as a relic). It is still contested at what point in time these groups of provinces became fixed administrative units subordinate to the vicars, the period of Constantine certainly being a possibility [3]. The *Laterculus Veronensis* however, written towards the end of 314 [4. 548–550], already takes the existence of strictly divided *dioeceses* for granted, these being: 1. Oriens, 2. Pontica, 3. Asiana, 4. Thraciae, 5. Moesiae, 6. Pannoniae, 7. Italia, 8. Africa, 9. Galliae, 10. Viennensis (Septem Provinciae), 11. Britanniae, 12. Hispaniae (cf. map for → Diocletianus). This division was only slightly modified in the period following, in that, for instance, southern Italy was put under the control of the *vicarius urbis* as *Italia suburbicaria*, the *dioecesis* of *Moesia* was divided into *Macedonia* and *Dacia*, and Egypt was put under the control of the *praef. Augustalis* as a separate *dioecesis*. Even after the establishment of regions of the praetorian prefectures, the *dioeceses* never became true mid-level authorities; instead, the assignment of authorities remained open. The competition in the Western empire was tempered by the fact that each prefect assumed direct control over the *dioecesis* in which he resided [5]. In the East, the *dioecesis* quickly attained the significance of a hierarchical level superior to the church provinces and equal to the imperial administration, while in the West, the term was used for regions subordinate to the bishop, starting in the Carolingian period, first alongside παροικία (*paroikía*) and similar terms, later even as an exclusive designation.

1 A. SCHEUERMANN, s.v. Diözese, RAC 3, 1957, 1053–1062 2 R. DELMAIRE, Largesses sacrées et res privata, 1989 3 K. L. NOETHLICHS, Zur Entstehung der Diözese als Mittelinstanz des spätröm. Verwaltungssystems, in: Historia 31, 1982, 70–81 4 T. D. BARNES, Emperors, Panegyrics, Prefects, Provinces and Palaces (284–317), in: Journal of Roman Archaeology, 9, 1996, 532–552 5 J. MIGL, Die Ordnung der Ämter, 1994. B.BL.

Dioiketes (διοικητής; *dioikētḗs*). In Ptolemaic Egypt as well as in other parts of the Greek world, the word *dioíkēsis* was used to designate the administration in general and the financial administration in particular. The title of *dioiketes* was held by the official in charge of the king's financial administration (see, for instance, OGIS 59; Cic. Rab. Post. 28). Local financial officials may also have held this title (Pol. 27,13,2 with WALBANK, Commentary on Polybius, ad. loc.).
→ Dioikesis P.J.R.

Diolkos, Diholkos (Δίολκος; *Dí(h)olkos*). Paved trackway for transporting goods and ships between the Saronic Gulf (→ Saronikos Kolpos) and the Gulf of → Corinth across the → Isthmus of Corinth at its narrowest point. The *diolkos* describes a slight southerly curve between the moorings at its ends. It is *c.* 8 km long, the gradient is a max. 6 % and the track is 1.5 m wide. By connecting the harbours of Cenchreae [2] and → Lechaeum, it strengthened the infrastructure of Corinth, though ancient sources shed no light on its economical significance. Although Diog. Laert. 1,99 ascribed to Periander only an attempt to cut through the isthmus, the *diolkos* is usually dated to the archaic period, on the basis of stonemasons' symbols, though similar stonemasons' symbols were still used in the 5th cent. BC. Thuc. 3,15,1, who for 428 BC reports the setting up of *holkoí* (towpaths) by the Spartans for transporting the fleet across the isthmus, does not mention the term '*diolkos*', which first appears in Str. 8,2,1. The transport of a largish number of ships across the isthmus is attested for 220 and 217 BC (Pol. 4,19,7–9; 5,101,4). After the battle of → Actium, the future Augustus used the *diolkos en route* to Asia (Cass. Dio 51,5,2). The *diolkos* was in use well into the Byzantine period (Georgios Sphrantzes 1,33: [1]). Excavations have revealed important remains at the western end of the *diolkos*. — Sources: Thuc. 3,15,1; 8,7; 8,8,3; Aristoph. Thesm. 647f.; Pol. 4,19,7–9; 5,101,4; Str. 8,2,1; 8,6,22; 8,6,4; Plin. HN 4,10; 18,18; Cass. Dio 51,5,2; Hsch. s.v.. *diolkos*.

1 I. BEKKER (ed.), Corpus Scriptorum Historiae Byzantinae 31, 1838, 96.

J. W. DRIJVERS, Strabo VIII 2,1 (C 335). Porthmeia and the D., in: Mnemosyne 45, 1992, 75–78; K. FREITAG, Der Golf von Korinth, 1997, 195–202; B. R. MACDONALD, The D., in: JHS 106, 1986, 191–195; G. RAEPSAET, M. TOLLEY, Le D. de l'Isthme à Corinthe, in: BCH 117, 1993, 233–261; N. M. VERDELIS, Der D. am Isthmus von Korinth, in: MDAI(A) 71, 1956, 51–59; Id., Die Ausgrabung des D. während der J. 1957–1959, in: MDAI(A) 73,

1958, 140–145; W. Werner, Der D. Die Schiffsschleppbahn am Isthmus von Korinth, in: Nürnberger Blätter zur Arch. 10, 1993/4, 103–118; Id., The Largest Ship Trackway in Ancient Times, in: International Journ. of Nautical Archaeology 26, 1997, 98–117. H. LO.

Diomea (Διόμεια; *Diómeia*). Attic *paralia*(?) deme of the Aegeis phyle, from 307/6 until 201/0 BC of the Demetrias phyle. One → bouleutes. D. was located outside the walls of Athens and south of the Ilissus between Alopece to the South and Ancyle to the East [1], where, not far from the Diomeic Gate (Alci. 3,51,4; Hsch. s.v. Δημίαισι πύλαις; [2. 83, 112, 160 fig. 219 'X'), the Hercules sanctuary and gymnasium were situated in → Cynosarges (Diog. Laert. 6,13; [2. 340f.]).

1 W. Judeich, Top. von Athen, ²1932, 169f. fig. 14 2 Travlos, Athen.

Traill, Attica 7, 16, 39, 62, 69, 110 no. 33, table 2, 12; J. S. Traill, Demos and Trittys, 1986. H.LO.

Diomede (Διομήδη; *Diomḗdē*).
[1] → Deïon.
[2] Mistress of Achilles, daughter of Phorbas, one of the seven women of Lesbos whom Achilles took prisoner (Hom. Il. 9,128f.; 664f.). In the *Iliad*, she plays a secondary role to → Briseis and is rarely represented [1]. Together with Briseis and Iphis, she was depicted on a painting by Polygnotus in Delphi (Paus. 10,25,4). According to Zenod. in schol. Il 9,664a, D. was from Caria. Anth. Pal. 14,18 and 16,29 play with the double meaning of Διομήδης ἀνήρ; *Diomḗdēs anḗr* ('Diomedes the man'/'the husband of Diomede').

A. Kossatz-Deissmann, s.v. D., LIMC 3.1, 396 no. 2. R.B.

Diomedes (Διομήδης; *Diomḗdēs*).
[1] Hero of the city of Argos in the Trojan War, as opposed to Agamemnon of Mycenae, the lord of north-eastern Argolis (Hom. Il. 2,559–568; cf. Il. 23,471f. [1; 2]). Son of Tydeus and Deipyle, the daughter of Adrastus. In his *aristeia* before Troy (Il. 5 and 6), he killed Pandarus, wounded Aphrodite when she tried to save Aeneas (Il. 5, 290–351), and later also wounded Ares (Il. 5, 825–863). As a friend of the family, he exchanged weapons with Glaucus the Lycian (on the side of the Trojans), (Il. 6, 119–236). As a spy, he crept into the hostile city with Odysseus and killed Dolon and Rhesus (Il. 10). Paris wounded him so that he could no longer take part in the ongoing battle (Il. 11, 369–400); he could not replace Achilles after all. During the funeral games for Patroclus, he won the chariot race with Athena's help (Il. 23,388–390; 499–513) and fought a duel with Ajax (Il. 23,811–825). In the *Ilias parva*, he became essential for the seizure of Troy together with Odysseus by fetching Philoctetes from Lemnos (fr. 1; cf. Eur. Phil.; Soph. Phil. 570f; 592–594), stealing the → Palladion (cf. Conon FGrH 26 F 1,34: D. tricks Odysseus), and hiding in the wooden horse (Hyg. Fab. 108). He killed Cassandra's betrothed, Coroebus (PEG arg. 2). D. returned home effortlessly (Hom. Od. 3,167; 180–182; Nostoi PEG arg.), but found his wife Aegiale(ia) (who is also his aunt, Il. 5,412) unfaithful and continued on his way (Lycoph. 592–632; Dictys 6,2). In Italy, King Daunus supposedly offered him residence in Apulia and gave him his daughter Euippe as a wife. He founded cities and was worshipped as a god (Str. 5,9,1; 6,3,9), as it is said already in Ibycus (PMG fr. 294; Pind. Nem. 10,7–3), all the while staying on good terms with the Trojan fugitives (Verg. Aen. 11,243–295; Paus. 1,11,7). He shared the right to the Palladion with Aeneas in Italy [4] by means of one or more copies (Ilioupersis PEG fr. 1; Alcmaeonis fr. 9); D. brought it to Argos (Paus 2,23,5).

Genealogically, D. did not originally stem from Argos but from Aetolia on his father's side (Il. 23,471). He avenged his grandfather Adrastus and the 'Seven against Thebes' as a descendant of the Epigoni. He punished Agrius for the bad treatment of his grandfather Oeneus (Alcmaeonis PEG fr. 9). Regarding the mythological reason for the founding of the Amphilochian Argos, cf. Ephorus FGrH 70 F 123b.

Several cities worshipped D. with a cult: the fight in which D. supposedly died points to hero cults. Athena was said to have turned him into an immortal god (thus Pind. Nem. 10, 7). In Mothone, Messenia, he was connected to Athena (Paus. 4,35,8). In Argos, his shield was carried in a procession to the bath of Pallas (Callim. H. 5,355). However, he did not have his own heroon in Argos, but with the Epigoni (Paus. 2,20,5; cf. Il. 4,406f. [8]). D. is a newly created name [9], but his legendary character was already established before the *Iliad* [2]. A reference to Mycenaean tradition [11] is unlikely; it is more probable that the name had been introduced by Doric immigrants, at least with regard to the catalogue of ships (Il. 2–9).

1 G. S. Kirk, The Iliad 1, 1985, 180f. 2 W. Kullmann, Quellen der Ilias, 1960, 85–89; 380 3 Farnell, GHC, 289–293 4 N. Horsfall, in: CQ 29, 1979, 374f. 5 H. Kleinknecht, Λουτρὰ τῆς Παλλάδος, in: Hermes 74, 1939, 300–350 6 W. Bulloch, Callimachus: Fifth Hymn, 1985 7 J. R. Heath, The Blessings of Epiphany, in: Classical Antiquity 7, 1988, 72–90 8 A. Pariente, F. Bommelaer, in: M. Piérart (ed.), Polydipsion Argos, BCH-Suppl. 22, 1992, 195–230; 265–304 9 Kamptz, 31a2; 66 10 B. Mader, LFE 2, 1991, 309f. 11 T. B. L. Webster, From Mycenae to Homer, ²1964, 228 12 F. Schachermeyr, Griech. Rückerinnerung, SAWW 404, 1983 13 A. Giovannini, Les origines du catalogue des vaisseaux, 1969 14 W. Burkert, in: D. Musti et al. (ed.), La transizione dal miceneo al alto arcaismo 1991, 530f.

J. Boardman, C. E. Vafopoulou-Richardson, LIMC 3.1, 396–409; O. Andersen, Die D.-Gestalt in der Ilias, 1978. C.A.

[2] Poet of the New Comedy, son of Athenodorus, citizen of Pergamum [1. test. 1] and Athens [1. test. 2] (double citizenship as for → Diodorus of Sinope? [1. ad test. 1]). Inscriptions document a victory in Magnesia [1. test. 1] during the later 2nd cent. BC, honours in Epidaurus and Athens [1. test. 2, 3] as well as in Delphi for the year 97/96 [1. test. 4]. We can count D. among the winners of the Dionysia only if we accept an unconfirmed supplement to the list of winners (Δι̣[), [1. test. * 5]. No traces have survived of D.'s literary production.

1 PCG V, 1986, 31. T.HI.

[3] **D. Soter.** Indo-Greek king of the early 1st cent. BC. The only sources are coins (middle Indian *Diyumeta*).

BOPEARACHCHI 101f., 295–298. K.K.

[4] Latin grammarian of the late 4th cent. AD. D. is the author of an *Ars grammatica* which was probably published between 370 and 380 and which addresses an audience from the eastern part of the Roman empire. The three books represent the didactic programme: parts of speech — fundamentals of grammar — style and metrics. As a whole, the work is undeniably influenced by → Charisius [3] and → Donatus, more specifically, by → Terentius Scaurus in bks. 1–2, and by → Flavius Caper in bk. 1. With regard to bk. 3 on metrics, → Terentianus Maurus and → Caesius [II 8] Bassus come to mind. Less certain indeed is the influence of → Suetonius on the other parts. The entire *Ars* was used by → Rufinus and → Priscianus. A shortened version, which circulated under the name of → Valerius Probus, was used by → Consentius, Pompeius, and by a scholiast of Virgil. This shortened version was also adapted in the Anglo-Saxon area (Anon. ad Cuimnanum, Ars Ambrosiana, Malsacanus, Aldhelm), but has only survived in excerpts. It also seems to have been available in its entirety to Boniface, Tatuinus, Murethach, and others. The archetype of the *Ars* (already a partially shortened version, kept in the palace library in Aachen) appears in a large number of copies, which means that it was used by the grammarians of the Carolingian period, for example Rabanus Maurus. A new edition does not exist.

EDITION: GL 1,299–529.
BIBLIOGRAPHY: P.L. SCHMIDT, HLL § 524. P.G.

Diomedon (Διομέδων; *Diomédōn*).

[1] As the commander of Seleucia on the Tigris under Antiochus III, he fled from Molon, the advancing rebel satrap of Media (Pol. 5,48,12). A.ME.

[2] Athenian commander during the Peloponnesian War. As *strategos*, he brought reinforcements to the Athenian troops in Asia Minor in 412–11 BC, regained control over seceding Lesbos together with Leon, and was victorious against the Rhodians (Thuc. 8,19,2; 23f.; 55,1). Although he was in favour of the democratic countermovement against the 400, he was removed from office (8,73,4; 76,2). In 407, D. was once more elected *strategos* and came to the aid of Conon. Following the victory at Arginusae, he recommended that the shipwrecked be rescued, but to no avail. In spite of this, he was condemned to death and executed with the other *strategoi* for failing to undertake the rescue (Xen. Hell. 1,6,22f.za; 7,1–34; Diod. Sic. 13,100–102). TRAILL, PAA 334600.

D. KAGAN, The Fall of the Athenian Empire, 1987, 51–60; 94; 168–171; 354–375; W.K. PRITCHETT, The Greek State at War IV, 1985, 204–206. W.S.

Diomosia (Διωμοσία; *Diōmosía*). At least from the time of Dracon (before 600 BC) Athenians of both parties and their helpers (witnesses) were obliged to swear a solemn oath, the *diomosia*, to the archon basileus during the official preliminary hearings (*prodikasíai*) for murder trials. The prosecutor swore (while calling upon the goddesses of revenge and other deities) to his right of prosecution at the risk of his own person, lineage, and house, and to the fact that the defendant really had committed the crime (Antiph. 6,16; Dem. Or. 23,67). Following this, the defendant was immediately handed over to the prosecutor for him to privately execute his revenge, unless the defendant denied the deed with an equally solemn counteroath (Lys. 10,11). In case of an oath on both sides, which was the usual case, the decision of which was the better oath was reached through a process involving legal formalism, that is, the secret vote of 51 → *ephetaí* (IG I[3] 104,12/13). This kind of formalism can be compared to a divine judgement. The double oath by the two parties was later recognized as meaningless (Dem. Or. 23,67f.; Pl. Leg. 948d), but still remained part of preliminary hearings. Over time, the term also came to represent the statements sworn by the parties and witnesses in other trials. In the 4th cent. BC, when the act of swearing in came after the charge and the plea (→ Antomosia), the meaning of the term extended to even the case files. Records of *diomosia* exist also outside of Athens (IG IX 1, 334).

BUSOLT/SWOBODA, 548f., 1184 D.M. MACDOWELL, Athenian Homicide Law, 1963, 90ff. G.THÜR, in: L.FOXHALL, A.D.E. LEWIS, Greek Law, 1996, 62ff. G.T.

Diomus (Δίομος; *Díomos*). Son of Colyttus, eponymous hero of the Attic deme → Diomea. D. is understood to be connected to the aetiology of the first 'ox murder' (→ Bouphonia), although the name of the bull killer (βουτύπος; *boutýpos*) varies. D., priest of Zeus Polieus, was the first to kill an ox at the Dipolieia after the latter had eaten from the sacrificial grain (Porph. De abstinentia 2,10). The bull killer is also called Thaulon (Androtion FGrH 324 F 16) or Sopater (Porph. ibid. 2,29). D. also plays a central role in the aetiology of → Cynosarges: when D. sacrificed to the deified Hercules, a white dog snatched the sacrificial meat away from him. Following this, D. erected a sanctuary on the spot where the dog dropped the sacrificial parts. The festival that was celebrated there for Hercules was called Diomeia (Steph. Byz. s.v. Κυνόσαργες 393f. MEINEKE; Etym.m. s.v. Δίομος 277 GAISFORD; Aristph. Ran. 651; schol. Aristoph. Ach. 603c).

W. BURKERT, Homo necans, 1972, 156; DEUBNER, 162; PARKE, 166. R.B.

Dion

I. PERSONS II. CITIES

I. PERSONS

(Δίων; *Díōn*)

[I 1] Son of Hipparinus, brother-in-law and son-in-law of Dionysius I of Syracuse, b. 409 BC, close friend of Plato and defender of his philosophy since Plato's first visit to Syracuse in 388. He gained prestige and wealth as Dionysius' I' trusted friend and advisor and also remained an influential person under Dionysius II. In 366, he arbitrated the peace with Carthage and called Plato to Syracuse in order to transform the despotic rule of Dionysius II according to the Platonic ideal state. This effort was a complete failure because Dionysius proved to be ill-suited personally, and because his friends and advisors opposed it, particularly Philistus. Accused of high treason, D. was banished to Greece; the immediate cause was found in D.'s letter to his Carthaginian friends not to conclude peace without his arbitration (Pl. Ep. 7,329; Plut. Dion 14f.; Mor. 53E). During his nine years of exile, D. lived as a princely gentleman in Athens, maintained a close relationship with the Academy, received Spartan citizenship, and visited Corinth amongst other places. After learning in 360 from Plato in Olympia that Dionysius II was unwilling to end his exile despite Plato's intercession, D. landed near Minoa in the Carthaginian part of Sicily in 357 with a few ships and 600 mercenaries. On his way to Syracuse he drew a lot of support from Acragas, Gela, Camarina, and the Sicilian communities, while the population in Syracuse rose up against Dionysius. D.'s triumphal entry was followed by unsuccessful negotiations and battles of varying success with the tyrant who was locked in on Ortygia. D. and his brother Megacles were elected as plenipotentiary *strategoi*, but his high-handed demeanour caused the distrust of the democrats, led by his former brother-in-arms Heraclides. Accused of striving towards → tyrannis and deposed, D. withdrew to Leontini, but was soon called back into battle against Nypsius, the general of Dionysius II. D. now worked rigourously towards the realization of Plato's ideal state. He dissolved the fleet as a breeding-ground for democracy, forced Dionysius to go to Locri in 355, and assumed an authoritative and quasi-tyrannical position. D. called a constituent assembly of Syracusians and Corinthians and ordered the execution of his adversary Heraclides. Several kings, among them D., and 35 guardians of the law, were supposed to take the top positions of the state, while council and public assembly were largely deprived of their authority. In 354, the general disapproval of this reorganization led to the murder of D., who was regarded increasingly as a tyrant, on the order of Callippus, himself a close associate of the Academy. D.'s attempt at 'liberating' Sicily only resulted in a period of anarchy that lasted a good ten years.

While Plato idealized D., modern research regards him soberly and at times very negatively as a man lacking both in statesmanlike skill and character, who started on the road to tyranny (cf. [1. 290]).

Main sources: Plato, 7th and 8th letters (their authenticity is recognized today; only FINLEY differs); Plutarch, Dion. (primarily from Timaeus); Diodorus (15,74,5 — 16,36,5).

1 B. BENGTSON, Griech. Gesch., [5]1977.

H. BERVE, D., 1957; Id., D., in: HZ 184, 1957, 1–18; Id., Die griech. Tyrannis 1967, vol. 1, 260ff., vol. 2, 657ff.; H. BREITENBACH, Platon und D., 1960 (in reference to this, H. BERVE, in: Gnomon 35, 1963, 375–77).; B. CAVEN, Dionysios I., 1990, 213ff.; M.I. FINLEY, Das ant. Sizilien, 1979, 117ff.; K. VON FRITZ, Platon in Sizilien und das Problem der Tyrannenherrschaft, 1968; G.A. LEHMANN, Dion und Herakleides, in: Historia 19, 1970, 401–413; J. SPRUTE, D.s syrakusanische Politik und die polit. Ideale Platons, in: Hermes 100, 1972, 294–313; M. SORDI, in: E. GABBA, G. VALLET (ed.), La Sicilia antica, vol. 2,1, 1980, 225ff.; Id., La Sicilia dal 368/7 al 337/6, 1983, 1ff.; H.D. WESTLAKE, in: CAH 6, [2]1994, 693ff. K.MEI.

[I 2] Belonged 87–86 BC in Alexandria to the circle surrounding → Antiochus [20] of Ascalon, but later, in Athens, he attended lectures by Antiochus' brother Aristus, then finally went over to the Peripatos (Cic. Luc. 12; Philod. Academia 35,8 p. 171 DORANDI); author of table talk (Plut. Mor. 612E; Ath. 1,34b). A famous proverb probably refers to him (τὸ τοῦ Δίωνος γρῦ: Stob. 3,19; Zenob. 5,54; Ps. Plut. Prov. Alex. 29). In 56, D. went to Rome as the leader of an Alexandrian legation with the purpose of preventing Ptolemy XII's return. After eluding a poison attack in the house of Lucceius, he was murdered as one of the last of the legation before his appearance in front of the Senate. PP 6,16749.

J. GLUCKER, Antiochus and the Late Academy, 1978, 94ff. W.A.

[I 3] **D. Cocceianus of Prusa.** (also called Chrysostomus since Menander, the rhetor). Orator and philosopher, b. *c.* AD 40 in Prusa (Bithynia), son of Pasicrates, died after 112. He came from a rich and distinguished family and was active first as a sophist and enemy of philosophy, but then became a student of the Stoic → Musonius. In the 70s, under Vespasian and Titus, D. lived primarily in Rome but was expelled from Italy and Bithynia by Domitian because of his open criticism of the emperor (AD 82). Until 96, D. led the life of a wanderer, oriented towards the ideal of the Cynic sage, in the north-east part of the empire and with the Getae. His exile was revoked by Nerva, from whom D. obtained privileges for his hometown. As the leader of a legation, he thanked Nerva's successor Trajan for these privileges and became his friend. Eager to act in accordance with Trajan's wishes, D. devoted his efforts to Prusa, and promoted the city through endowments and public buildings. A conflict erupted with the citizenry which escalated into a trial (111/2), the background of which is known to us through Plin. Ep. 10,81f. Nothing further is known about D.'s life.

Of D.'s writings, a collection of 80 speeches and lectures is extant (37 and 64 were written by D.'s student → Favorinus) which, apparently, were published posthumously (some of them obviously lack a final revision). D.'s work distinguishes itself through a great variety of topics: 'moral lectures' from the realm of moral philosophy appear alongside with speeches with political admonitions and statements about the issues of the time, and essays of literary criticism appear alongside sophist declamations and theological and cosmological discussions; the *Euboikos* [7] even contains a kind of novel in shortened form. But all of D.'s writings reveal a fundamental attitude marked by a philosophical syncretism, in which Socratic-Platonic influences mix with the ideas of the → Stoa and of → Cynicism, as well as his sentimental and nostalgic enthusiasm for the culture of old Hellas. He writes in a moderately Atticizing language oriented towards the ideal of *aphéleia* (simplicity) and without strictly avoiding *coine* influences, which made him the stylistic model for later writers (Philostratus, Eunapius, Maximus of Tyre, Synesius i.a.). D.'s writings are a precious source for the cultural history of the Greek East around AD 100. Numerous other works which were still extant in antiquity (historical writings, e.g. *Getica*, cf. FGrH 707; playful pieces in small format, e.g. an → *encomium* of the parrot and one of the gnat, an → ekphrasis of the Tempe valley; philosophical writings, e.g. 'On the Question whether the Cosmos is Transitory', as well as a defence of Homer against Plato) have been lost. The six letters transmitted under D.'s name are probably spurious.

EDITIONS: H. VON ARNIM, 1893–6 (repr. 1962) G. DE BUDÉ, 1916–1919 J.W. COHOON, H. LAMAR CROSBY, 1932–51 D.A. RUSSELL, 1992, (orr. 7. 12. 36).
TRANSLATION: W. ELLIGER, 1967.
INDEX: R. KOOLMEISTER, TH. TALLMEISTER, edited by J.F. KINDSTRAND, 1981.
RESEARCH REPORT: B.F. HARRIS, D. of Prusa, in: ANRW II.33,5, 1991, 3853–3881.
BIBLIOGRAPHY: 1 H. VON ARNIM, Leben und Werke des D. von Prusa, 1898 2 W.D. BARRY, Aristocrats, orators, and the 'mob', in: Historia 42, 1993, 82–103 3 A. BRANCACCI, Struttura compositiva e fonti della terza orazione 'Sulla regalità' di D.C., in: ANRW II.36,5, 3308–3334 4 P. DESIDERI, D. di Prusa, 1978 5 Id., D. di Prusa fra ellenismo e romanità, in: ANRW II.33,5, 3882–3902 6 M. HILLGRUBER, D.C. 36 (53), 4–5 und die Homerauslegung Zenons, in: MH 46, 1989, 15–24 7 C.P. JONES, The Roman World of D.C., 1978 8 J. MOLES, The kingship orations of D.C., in: F. CAIRNS, M. HEATH (ed.), Papers of the Leeds International Latin Seminar 6, 1990, 297–375 9 J. MOLING, D. von Prusa und die klass. Dichter, PhD thesis 1959 10 M. MORTENTHALER, Der Olympikos des D. v. Prusa als lit.histor. und geistesgesch. Dokument, PhD thesis 1979 11 A.M. RITTER, Zwischen 'Gottesherrschaft' und 'einfachem Leben', in: JbAC 31, 1988, 127–43 12 W. SCHMID, Attizismus vol. 1, 1887, 72–191 13 G.A. SEECK, D.C. als Homerkritiker (or. 11), in: RhM 133, 1990, 97–107 14 H. SIDEBOTTOM, The date of D. of Prusa's Rhodian and Alexandrian orations, in: Historia 41, 1992, 407–419.

M.W.

II. CITIES
(Δῖον; *Dîon*)

[II 1] City on the peninsula of Lithada near Cape Cenaeum on the north-eastern tip of → Euboea (Hom. Il. 2,538: αἰπὺ πτολίεθρον, 'the city at high elevation'). Only few traces have survived in a medieval tower near Lithada (formerly Lichas) built from ancient workpieces. Near D., remnants were found of a sanctuary for Zeus Kenaios, which, as legend holds, was consecrated by Hercules. Just like the neighbouring city of Athenae Diades, D. was long able to maintain its political independence before becoming a member of the 1st → Delian League with a tribute of 1,000 drachmae, and after 450/49 with a tribute of 2,000 drachmae (Διῆς or Διῆς ἀπὸ Κηναίου). D. was also a member of the 2nd → Athenian League (Syll.[3] 1, 147,88). Str. 10,1,5; Plin. HN 4,64; Ptol. Geog. 3,14,22; Steph. Byz. s.v. D.; Nonnus, Dion. 13,161.

C. BURSIAN, Geogr. von Griechenland, 1868, 409f.; F. GEYER, Top. und Gesch. der Insel Euboia I, 1903, 99ff.; PHILIPPSON/KIRSTEN, 570; ATL 1, 1939, 264f., 482.

H.KAL.

[II 2] City surrounding the national sanctuary of the Macedons below Olympus on the → Baphyras in Pieria, near modern Malathria. Temple and (since Archelaus [1]) festival for Zeus Olympius. Under the rule of the Macedonian kings, D. and the sanctuary were endowed with buildings and statues (Liv. 44,7,3), among them Lysippus' bronze statues of the 25 *hetaíroi* of Alexander the Great who fell 334 BC on the Granicus (Arr. Anab. 1,16,4), statues that were taken to Rome by Q. Caecilius Metellus (Plin. HN 34,64) after the war against Aristonicus in 148 BC. Even prior to this (in 219), D. had been plundered by the Aetolians (Pol. 4,62). D. was given a Roman *colonia*, possibly soon after Caesar's death or, at the latest, under Augustus, who gave D. the title *colonia Iulia Augusta Diensis*. At the same time, the territory of D. apparently was expanded to all the other cities of Pieria. In the Roman imperial period, D. once again achieved prosperity, as evidenced by preliminary excavations. D. became a bishop's seat before 343 (council of Serdica) at the latest, and still existed in the 6th cent. (Hierocles Synekdemos 638,5) despite looting by the Goths *c.* AD 472 (Iord. Get. 287). So far, there is no evidence for a medieval settlement.

19–cent. efforts at uncovering the site and the systematic excavations carried out by the university of Thessalonica since 1963 have laid bare parts of the walled Hellenistic and Roman residential city: *insulae* with houses and workshops from the 2nd and 3rd cents. AD along the main street that runs through the city — uncovered in its entire length — in a north-easterly direction, parts of the Hellenistic water supply (→ Cistern), public buildings (walls, gates, odeum, latrines), remnants of an early Christian basilica. Various buildings were found outside of the walled-in area: sanctuaries (probably for Asclepius, Isis, and Demeter), additional remnants of early Christian buildings as well as a Hellenistic and a Roman theatre (3rd cent. BC; 2nd cent. AD). The findings are kept in the museum of Dio.

F. Papazoglou, Les villes de Macédoine, 1988, 108f.; D. Pandermalis, D., n.d. MA.ER. and C.HÖ.

[II 3] The city of D., of unknown origin, was located on the north-eastern coast of the Athos peninsula near the Isthmus. In the 5th cent. BC, it was a member of the → Delian League, breaking away from Athens as late as 417. In the 4th cent., D. belonged to the 2nd → Athenian League and was able to maintain its independence until it was seized by Philip II. The city's later history is unknown.

M. Zahrnt, Olynth und die Chalkidier, 1971, 182–185. M.Z.

[II 4] City located in Achaea Phthiotis. In 302 BC, Cassander wanted to combine it through *synoikismos* with Thebae in Phthiotis, but this was prevented by Demetrius Poliorcetes (Diod. Sic. 20,110). D. is presumed to be one of the cities in ruins on the northern slope of the Othrys mountains.

R. Reinders, New Halos, 1988, 157; F. Stählin, Das hell. Thessalien, 1924, 173, 185. HE.KR.

Dione (Διώνη; *Diṓnē*, cf. Ζεύς, Διός; *Zeús, Diós*). Perhaps Zeus' original wife [1], though she was already replaced by → Hera in Mycenaean times (cf. PY Tn 316). A coin from Epirus [2] shows an enthroned D., with Zeus on the verso; in the Zeus sanctuary at → Dodona, she was worshipped alongside Zeus [3]. → Aphrodite was also regarded as the daughter of the two (Hom. Il. 5,370; Eur. Hel. 1098; [4]; Theoc. Id. 15,106; 17,36; cf. Pl. Symp. 180d). In Cic. Nat. D. 3,23, D. is the mother of the third Venus, though usually she is identified in Latin literature with → Venus (Ov. Fast. 2,461; 5,309; [5]). Pherecydes (FGrH 3 F 90) counts her among the Dodonic nymphs who raised → Dionysus, and in Euripides (TGF 177) D. is even his mother. Several Attic vases from the 5th cent. BC show her in Dionysus' circle, which indicates an Athenian interest in Dodona [6].

1 G.E. Dunkel, Vater Himmels Gattin, in: Die Sprache 34, 1988–1990, esp. 16–18 2 E. Simon, s.v. D., LIMC 3.1, 412, no.4 3 H.W. Parke, The Oracles of Zeus, 1967, 259–273 4 R. Kannicht, Eur. Hel. vol. 2 (comm.), 1969, 274f. 5 F. Bömer, P. Ovidius Naso, Die Fasten, vol. 2 (comm.), 1958, 310 6 E. Simon, s.v. D., LIMC 3.1, 413, no. 10–12.
J.N. Bremmer, Götter, Mythen und Heiligtümer im ant. Griechenland, 1996, 19; E. Simon, s.v. D., LIMC 3.1, 411–413. R.B.

Dionysia (Διονύσια; *Dionýsia*). Term for the festival of → Dionysus, characteristic for the cult of Dionysus in many Greek poleis; the Dionysia often took place in the winter months.

(1) In Athens, the Dionysia were a part of a cycle of festivals extending over four winter months, which started with the rural Dionysia (τὰ κατ' ἀγροὺς Δ., in the month of Poseideon), was followed by the Lenaea (month of Gamelion) and the Anthesteria (month of Anthesterion), and culminated in the urban or Great Dionysia (τά ἐν ἄστει Δ., month of Elaphebolion) [1]. The rural Dionysia had usually adopted numerous elements of the urban Dionysia — particularly the performances of tragedies, comedies, and dithyrambs — as well as the ritual presence of male sexuality. Aristophanes presents their main ritual, a phallic procession, in his comedy the 'Acharnians': the song of the chorus to Phales (263–279), the deified phallus, shows that the ritual could be connected to male fantasies of sexual pleasure, even fantasies of violence. The urban Dionysia in honour of Dionysus Eleuthereus, on the other hand, were the creation of a later period. Although they are usually attributed to Pisistratus, it is also conceivable to date them into the period of Cleisthenes [2]. The god was supposedly taken to Athens from his cult centre Eleutherae on the Attic-Boeotian border. The local myth of Dionysus Melanaigis of Eleutherae is not related to the urban Dionysia but is connected with the → Ephebeia instead [3]. Central features were the performances of tragedies and dithyrambs in the theatre at the foot of the Acropolis as well as an impressive procession which enacted the entrance of the god with his entourage of satyrs and maenads into the city [4].

(2) Processions and dramatic performances following the Athenian model also characterized the Dionysia of Hellenistic cities. The significance of the celebration for the polis is evident in the fact that honours given to important citizens or foreigners were a part of the celebration, usually prior to the performances. The particularly splendid procession of the Dionysia in Alexandria under Ptolemy II was recorded in an → *ekphrasis* by Callixenus of Rhodes (FGrH 627 F 1) [5]. The degree to which the Dionysia were regarded as constitutive of Greek cultural identity in Hellenistic times is indicated, for instance, by the fact that Antiochus IV Epiphanes forced the Jews of Jerusalem to carry out Dionysia complete with processions in the framework of his comprehensive agenda of Hellenization (2 Macc. 6,168 BC).

1 A.W. Pickard-Cambridge, The Dramatic Festivals of Athens, ... [2]1968 2 W.R. Connor, City D. and Athenian democracy, in: Classica et Mediaevalia 40, 1989, 7–32 3 P. Vidal-Naquet, Le chasseur noir et l'origine de l'éphébie athénienne, in: Annales. Economies, Sociétés, Civilisations 23, 1968, 947–964 4 F. Graf, Pompai in Greece, in: R. Hägg (ed.), The Role of Religion in the Early Greek Polis (1996) 55–65 5 E.E. Rice, The Grand Procession of Ptolemy Philadelphus, 1983. F.G.

Dionysiades (Διονυσιάδης; *Dionysiádēs*). Son of Phylarchides, tragedian from Mallus (Suda δ 1169), according to Str. 14,6,759, from Tarsus, counted among the *Pleias*. Possibly identical with the poet named among the winners of the Dionysia (TrGF 110, see also DID A 3a, 67).

METTE, 163; TrGF 105. F.P.

Dionysius (Διονύσιος; *Dionýsios*). Famous personalities: D. [1], the tyrant of Syracuse; the historian D. [18] of Halicarnassus. Dionysios (month), → Months, names of the. The chronicle of Ps.-D. by Tell Maḥre see D. [23].

I. POLITICALLY ACTIVE PERSONALITIES II. PHILOSOPHERS III. GRAMMARIANS, HISTORIANS IV. SCIENTISTS, GEOGRAPHERS, DOCTORS V. POETS VI. ARTISTS VII. BISHOPS

I. POLITICALLY ACTIVE PERSONALITIES

[1] D. I. of Syracuse, son of Hermocritus, born in *c.* 430 BC, died in 367 BC. Founder of the 'greatest and longest tyrannical rule in history' (Diod. Sic. 13,96,4; appearance: Timaeus FGrH 566 F 29).

Possessing a sophist education (Cic. Tusc. 5,63), D. had enormous ambitions and a will to power (Isoc. Or. 5,65). He supported the (unsuccessful) *coup d'état* by Hermocrates in 408/7 and, in 406/5, as a secretary of the assembly of *strategoi*, he accused the commanders who failed to stop Carthage from capturing Acragas of treason in front of the assembly. The resulting fine that was imposed on the 'troublemaker' was paid by the future historian Philistus, so that D. could continue to agitate against the 'rich and powerful' and work towards the dismissal and subsequent new election of the assembly (Diod. Sic. 13,91–96). Now himself a member of the assembly in spite of his youth, D. accused his own colleagues of corruption, achieved his election to the position of plenipotentiary *strategos* (spring 405) and remained in the realm of legality with this office, which was intended by the constitution for times of crisis. Only after obtaining a bodyguard, an act that was approved following a bogus assassination attempt, he completed the step to → tyrannis (summer 405). He attempted to relieve Gela, which was occupied by Carthage, by turning away from phalanx tactics in a revolutionary way and by fighting a battle dispersed into various encounters. However, the attempt was a complete failure due to lack of co-ordination in troop movements, so that Gela and Camarina also fell to the Carthaginians, whose army advanced to the gates of Syracuse. He was able to suppress an uprising of the Syracusian oligarchs in the aftermath of the defeat through his quick return, but it brought about the death of his wife, the daughter of Hermocrates. At the end of 405, an epidemic in the Carthaginian army in front of Syracuse led Himilco to a peace agreement, which acknowledged D.'s rulership over Syracuse but also entailed the loss of the Syracusian hegemony, and which intended the recognition of Carthaginian rulership over western Sicily, including the Elymi and Sicani. Himera, Selinus, Acragas, Gela, and Camarina were to pay tribute to Carthage, while Leontini, Messana and the Sicils received autonomy (Diod. Sic. 13,114,1; cf. StV 2, no. 210).

In this situation, D. attempted to strengthen the power of Syracuse again, but primarily for the purpose of solidifying his own position: he developed Ortygia into an enormous fortress, expanded the citizenry by freeing slaves, confiscated the possessions of the oligarchs, redistributed the land to former slaves, poor free men and others, created a large army of mercenaries, and conferred offices and positions on friends and relatives, all of which gained him a huge following. As a result, the citizens' troops rose up in 404 in Syracuse, joined also by the poleis of eastern Sicily: D. was locked into his citadel (Diod. Sic. 14,8,4ff.) and could not be freed until months later by Campanian mercenaries (Diod. Sic. 14,10,2ff.).

After the revolt, D. subjugated the Chalcidian cities of eastern Sicily and moved their inhabitants mostly to Syracuse, which thereby became the largest city of the Greek world as well as the most colossal fortress in the world at the time due to a wall surrounding the Epipolai (the 'plateau') and the building of fort Euryalus on a strategically important spot. Above all, D. was now arming for the imminent war against Carthage (Diod. Sic. 14,18ff.; 41ff.): His orders included the recruitment of a large number of mercenaries, the manufacture of modern weapons, the building of a huge fleet of the new type of ship called *penteres* (= with five benches for oarsmen on each side), and the construction of siege equipment including the newly invented catapult. Last but not least, he formed marriage alliances with Syracuse (Andromache) and Locri (Doris). In the year 398, armament was complete: with the slogan 'the liberation of Sicily' (Diod. Sic. 14,45,4), D. and his army of (allegedly) over 80,000 men and 300 warships marched against the unprepared Carthaginians and advanced unstoppably to the extreme west of Sicily, where he captured the island city of Motya, the main Carthaginian base, thanks to an ingenious siege technology. Only one year later, the Carthaginians launched a counter attack under Himilco with supposedly even greater force. 100,000 men on foot and 400 warships moved along the northern coast, caused several cities to break away and, after a victory against D.'s fleet near Catana, occupied Syracuse, while D. freed large numbers of slaves and was determined to resist to the very end with the help of Sparta. Yet again, an epidemic decimated the enemy army camped on the Anopus, and it was almost completely destroyed by a successful attack. When the Carthaginian fleet suffered the same fate (summer 396, cf. Diod. Sic. 14,71,1ff.), an uprising among the African dependants of Carthage made it possible for D. to win back eastern Sicily and stop a Carthaginian offensive (Diod. Sic. 14,95ff.). The peace of 392 limited Carthage's rulership to the west, that is, the old Punic strategic bases of Motya, Panormus, and Solus as well as the region of the Elymi and Sicani, while almost the entire rest of Sicily came under D.'s rule (Diod. Sic. 14,96,3; cf. StV 2, no. 233).

D.'s intervention in Italy was aimed primarily at freeing the rear in the face of Carthage. Allied to Locri since 399, D. inflicted a devastating defeat on the Italiot League led by Croton in 388 at the Elleporus and, after a long siege in 387/6, captured and cruelly punished Rhegium. From this point on, D. controlled the Straits of Messina. Mostly for economic reasons, D. founded the colonies of Lissus and Issa in 385–384 on the Dalmatian coast as well as Ancona and Adria (at the mouth of the river Po) on Italian soil. He befriended the Illyrians, made contact with the Celts and weakened the Etruscans by conquering Pyrgi, the harbour of Caere. In *c.* 382, he began the third war against Carthage, which had formed widespread alliances with the Greek poleis in Lower Italy. D. recognized the danger, captured Croton first (379), then defeated the Carthaginians in *c.* 375 near Cabala on Sicily (location unknown!), but later, after the rejection of his demand that Sicily be cleared, he suffered a serious defeat at Cronion (near Palermo). The peace treaty of 374 established for the first time the border from Halycus (modern Platani) in the south to the Himeras (modern Imera Settentrionale) in the north. This border essentially separated Greek Sicily from the Carthaginian epicracy until Roman intervention.

After a short peace, D. began the fourth Carthaginian war in 368 and advanced to Lilybaeum (modern Marsala), the new Carthaginian base, which he besieged unsuccessfully. D. died in the spring of 367 in the midst of war (Diod. Sic. 15,73,5).

With his restless foreign policy which had made the war against Carthage his life's work, D. created one of the first territorial states of the Greek world comprising the larger part of Sicily, the south of Lower Italy, and regions along the Adria. As a result, he stepped out of the framework of the polis, but could only do so successfully by employing means that contradicted its nature. D. operated within the framework of the constitution as a plenipotentiary *strategos* only in the beginning; later he apparently used the title of '*archon* (ruler) of Sicily' and was, *de facto*, a tyrant. Technically, he did not infringe upon the institutions of the polis such as council and public assembly, but he only allowed them a shadowy existence. He based his power mostly on foreign mercenaries and filled all key positions with his relatives and 'friends'. Nevertheless, his connections to the Greek homeland were intensive, especially towards the end of his rule: in 369 he saved Sparta from collapse with a corps of mercenaries, a year later he was given the freedom of the city of Athens, and in 367, D. and Athens formed a defensive alliance (cf. StV 2, no. 280).

Doubtless D. was a skilled politician, organizer, and commander, yet he also owed his successes to his cruelty, his scrupulous actions against those opposed to him, and the work of his secret police. Those who see D. as the greatest military genius after the Macedonian kings, (thus e.g. [1]; cautiously [2. 256f.]) do not take into account the fact that he was saved repeatedly due to epidemics in the enemy army and that his life's work, the expulsion of the Carthaginians from Sicily, was not completed. In fact, the antagonism between Greeks and Carthaginians that D. promoted for reasons of legitimizing his own rulership was to bring much suffering to the island.

Sources: the most important among the no longer extant sources is the panegyrical representation by Philistus, D.'s long-term advisor and officer (cf. FGrH 556, T 1–13, F 57f.). It formed the basis for Ephorus (in bks. 16 and 28 of his universal history, cf. FGrH 70 F 68; 89–91; 201–04; 218), Theopompus (in the Sicilian excursus of the *Philippica*, cf. FGrH 115 F 184), and Timaeus, who portrays D. extremely negatively (cf. FGrH 566 F 25–29; 105–112) and calls him the 'evil spirit of Sicily and Italy' (F 29). Since these sources are lost as well, the surviving parts of Diodorus' 'Library' have taken on great importance. His representation in bks. 13–15 falls into two unequal parts: while 13,91–14,109 presents a detailed description of the first half of D.'s rule (from 406/5 to 387/6), largely following Timaeus (thus [3. 70ff.]; incorrectly [4]: Philistus), the second half (from 386/5 until 368/7), 15,13–74, is described only in summary form, mainly following Ephorus. The remaining sources (esp. Cic. Tusc. 5,57–63 and elsewhere) are of mostly anecdotal character with stories about the cruel tyrant.

1 B. Caven, Dionysius I., 1990 2 H. Berve, Die Tyrannis bei den Griechen, 1967 3 K. Meister, Die sizilische Gesch. bei Diodor, 1967 4 L.J. Sanders, Dionysius I of Syracuse and Greek Tyranny, 1987.

H. Berve, Die Tyrannis bei den Griechen, 1967, vol. 1, 222ff., vol. 2, 637ff.; B. Caven, s.v. D. (1), in: OCD [3]1996, 476f.; M.I. Finley, Ancient Sicily, 1979, 101ff.; D.M. Lewis, in: CAH 6, [2]1994, 120ff.; M. Sordi, in: E. Gabba, G. Vallet (ed.), La Sicilia antica, vol. 2,1, 1980, 207ff.; K.F. Stroheker, Dionysios I., 1958.

K.MEI.

[2] **D. II.** Tyrant of Syracuse, oldest son of D. I and his wife Doris of Locri, b. in *c.* 396 BC. His father kept him away from government matters, but after his father's death in 367, D. was recognized by the military as the successor in the interest of an orderly transition of rulership, and was confirmed by the people. He made peace with Carthage in 366, helped Sparta in 365, led a short-term war against the Lucanians, fought pirates in 359/8 in the Adria, and rebuilt Rhegium, which had been destroyed by his father, under the name of Phoebia. However, his interest in women and keeping a luxurious court far outweighed his interest in politics and diplomacy. At his court, two factions fought each other from the beginning: one was led by his brother-in-law → Dion, who wanted to change D.'s lifestyle and realize the ideal state as conceived by Plato, whom he

brought to the court in 367 for this purpose. The other was led by Philistus and the old monarchical guard who categorically rejected any change of the status quo and who succeeded in removing Dion to Greece in 366. Plato, who also left Syracuse, was unable to change D.'s attitude during another visit to Syracuse in 361 and also failed to achieve Dion's recall, even though D., who dabbled in literature and philosophy, was strongly interested in Plato's friendship and outwardly seemed open towards his ideas. Dion's violent return home forced D. to Locri in Lower Italy in 357–55. The murder of Dion by Callippus in 354 was followed by anarchy, in which first Callippus became tyrant, then two of Dion's half brothers, Hipparinus in 353 and Nysaeus in 351, and finally again D. in 347. D. was able to maintain his rule for three years until Sicily was liberated from his tyrannis in 344 by Timoleon. He then went into exile in Corinth where he lived as a private citizen. His weakness of character and political incompetence did serious harm to the position and significance of western Greece. Sources: Plato, 7th and 8th letters; Diodorus Siculus 15,74,5–16,36,5; 65–70; Plutarch, Dion and Timoleon.

H. Berve, Die Tyrannis bei den Griechen, 1967, vol. 1, 260ff.; B. Caven, D. I., 1990, 213ff.; M. I. Finley, Das ant. Sizilien, 1979, 117ff.; H. D. Westlake, in: CAH 6, ²1994, 693ff. K.MEI.

[3] **D. Soter.** One of the last Indo-Greek kings in the 1st cent. BC. The only evidence for him are his coins (middle-Indian *Diyanisiya*).

Bopearachchi 137f., 361f. K.K.

[4] Son of Cephalas, lived in Acoris in the late 2nd cent. BC; priest of an Egyptian cult, king's farmer, soldier. D. gave out loans of grain which were recorded in an extant archive.

N. Lewis, Greeks in Ptolemaic Egypt, 1986, 124ff.; H. Heinen, in: Gnomon 60, 1988, 128–131 (review). W.A.

[5] Son of the tyrant Clearchus of Heraclea and himself a tyrant 337–36 BC. After the death of Alexander [4] the Great, he joined the enemies of → Perdiccas and later served under → Antigonus [1]. He fought for the latter on Cyprus and expanded his own power under his protection. He died in 306/05. E.B.

[6] D. Petosarapis (Διονύσιος Πετοσάραπις; *Dionýsios Petosárapis*). Egyptian? Influential *phílos*, who, in *c.* 168–64 BC, tried to use the tensions between Ptolemy VI and VIII as an opportunity for a palace revolt. He was defeated by the kings at Eleusis, retreated to the *chora* where he apparently found followers among the residents. It is not known when the revolt ended (Diod. Sic. 31,15a; 17b).

L. Mooren, The Aulic Titulature in Ptolemaic Egypt, 1976, 70f. no. 026. W.A.

[7] Cicero's slave and reader (Fam. 5,9,2), who stole several books of his. He fled to Illyria in 45 BC where he made himself out to be a freedman and where Cicero searched for him through the governors. K.-L.E.

II. Philosophers

[8] **D. of Heraclea.** Philosopher and student of the Stoic → Zeno of Citium [1. col. 10, 30–32]. He was born in the late 4th cent. BC and reached the age of 80 years. Diogenes Laertius reports that he had first studied with Heraclides Ponticus, Alexinus, and Menedemus before coming to Zeno (7,37,166–7: an incomplete list of his numerous works known for their elegant style). His interest in poetry led him to → Aratus, and from there to the teachings of the Stoa. His nickname was 'the Apostate' (ὁ μεταθέμενος; *ho metathémenos*) because he renounced Stoicism and went over to hedonism: suffering due to disease caused him to doubt the Stoic notion that pain does not matter in regard to happiness (different versions of the story can be found in Cic. Tusc. 2,60; Fin. 5.94; Ath. 281de; Lucian Bis accusatus 21).

1 T. Dorandi (ed.), Filodemo, Storia dei filosofi: La stoà da Zenone a Panezio, 1994. B.I.

[9] **D. from Chalcedon.** lived in the decades before and after 350 BC. D. presumably was the first person to use the term → 'dialecticians' for the members of the Megarian school (Diog. Laert. 2,106). O. Primavesi [1] has presented plausible arguments for the assumption that the same D., whose definition of 'life' is shown by Aristotle to be insufficient in his *Topica* (148a26–31), is D. of Chalcedon.
→ Megarian School

1 O. Primavesi, D. der Dialektiker und Aristoteles über die Definition des Lebens, in: RhM 135, 1992, 246–261.

Edition: SSR II P.
Bibliography: K. Döring, D. aus Chalkedon, in: GGPh 2.1, § 17F. K.D.

[10] **D. from Cyrene.** Stoic philosopher and mathematician of the mid 2nd cent. BC, perhaps student of → Diogenes of Babylon. His writings were aimed against a certain Demetrius, presumably a rhetor [1. col. 52].

1 T. Dorandi (ed.), Filodemo Storia dei filosofi: La stoà da Zenone a Panezio, 1994. 2 Id., s.v. D., Goulet 2, 865f. B.I.

[11] **D. of Lamptrae.** Epicurean, third leader of the Epicurean school according to Polystratus (220/19–201/0 BC). Few extant notes can be found in Diog. Laert. 10,25 and in the fragments of PHercul. 1780 (Philodemus).

T. Dorandi, s.v. D., Goulet 2, 866. T.D.

[12] Stoic philosopher who was active in Athens during the 1st cent. BC. In his lectures, he is claimed to have often quoted verses in an uncritical way, without paying attention to metre (Cic. Tusc. 2,26). B.I.

III. Grammarians, historians

[13] **D. Scytobrachion.** (Σκυτοβραχίων; *Skytobrachíōn*). In the scholia on Apoll. Rhod., he is called 'Milesian' in places, 'Mytilenean' in others, probably due to a copying mistake ([1,71–76], following F.G. Welker), not because D. himself invented the existence of a second 'D. of Miletus' as a source (as claimed by C. Müller through to F. Jacoby). The Suda (s.v. Δ. Μυτιληναῖος, δ 1175 Adler) gives the unexplained epithet *Skytobrachíōn* ('leather arm'; also in Suet. Gram. 7; Ath. 12,515d-e; schol. Hom. Il. 3,40) or *Skyteús*. He was the author of 'Libyan Stories', which contained narratives about the Amazons, the Atlanteans, and the Libyan Dionysius, *Argonautiká* (according to the Suda in 6 bks., according to the scholia on Apoll. Rhod. and [1] in 2 bks.), and 'Trojan Stories'. He treated the myths in a rationalistic and aetiological manner. The main source for D. is Diodorus Siculus, as well as the fragments of PHibeh 2186, POxy. 2812, PMich. inv. 1316ᵛ. Based on the first fragment, D. can be dated to the mid 3rd cent. BC (in temporal proximity to → Euhemerus).

Edition: 1 J.S. Rusten, D. Scytobrachion, 1982 (includes testimonia, fr., and a detailed bibliography).
Bibliography: 2 A. Corcella, Dionisio S., i 'Phoinikeia' e l' alfabeto pelasgico, in: Atti della Accademia delle Scienze di Torino 120, 1986, 41–82. S.FO.

[14] **D. from Phaselis.** in Lycia, at times simply called ὁ Φασηλίτης; *Phasēlítēs*. Greek Grammarian of the Alexandrian period, but prior to Didymus [1] (schol. Pind. Nem. 11 inscr. a; cf. schol. Pind. Pyth. 2 inscr.; perhaps schol. Pind. Ol. 9,55b). In the *vita* by Nicander (p. 61 Westermann = p. 33 Crugnola, schol. Nic. Ther.), he is mentioned as the author of a text entitled 'On the Poets' (Περὶ ποιητῶν) and of another, entitled 'On the Poetry of Antimachus' (Περὶ τῆς Ἀντιμάχου ποιήσεως). Regarding other, uncertain passages, see [2]: as in many other cases, homonyms present problems for the attribution of quotations which mention a D. without any further information.
→ Pindarus; → Didymus [1]; → Nicander

1 A. Boeckh, Pindari Opera, II 1, 1821, ad schol. O. 9, 55b 2 L. Cohn, s.v. D. (136), RE 5,984 3 FHG III, 27.

[15] **D. Iambos.** (ὁ Ἴαμβος; *ho Íambos*). Alexandrian grammarian of the 3rd cent. BC, one of → Aristophanes [4] of Byzantium's teachers (Suda α 3933, s.v. Ἀριστοφάνης Βυζάντιος). The exact reason for the epithet is unknown. Athenaeus, 7,284b, refers to a work 'On Dialects' (Περὶ διαλέκτων; *Perì dialéktōn*). In Ps.-Plut., De musica 15 (1136 C), he is cited in connection with a report about the inventor of Lydian harmony, but there is no title. He was also a poet: Clem. Al. Strom. V 8 = II,358,2f. Stählin records a hexameter written by him.
→ Mnesarchus

A. Nauck, Aristophanis Byzantii Fragmenta, 1848, 2 n. 3; G. Knaack, s.v. D. (93), RE 5, 915; Pfeiffer, KPI, 213, 249; SH, 179 (nr. 389); F. Susemihl, Gesch. der griech. Lit. in der Alexandrinerzeit, 1891–1892, I, 346. F.M.

[16] **D. from Sidon.** (occasionally cited simply as ὁ Σιδώνιος; *ho Sidṓnios*). Greek grammarian from Aristarchus' school whose most productive period falls into the 2nd half of the 2nd cent. BC. His work as an exegete of Homer is documented (through Didymus, Aristonicus, and Herodianus) in the scholia to Homer and in Apollonius [12] Sophistes. The fragments deal with issues of textual criticism, prosody, and grammar, wherein he followed his teacher as a representative of analogy. We only have one certain quotation regarding Pindar in schol. Pind. Pyth. I 172 (the attribution of schol. Pind. Pyth. I 109 to D. is questionable, since it only cites a grammarian D. without any further information).
→ Aristarchus [4]; → Apollonius [12] Sophistes; → Didymus [1]; → Aristonicus [5]; → Herodianus; → Homer; → Pindarus.

A. Blau, De Aristarchi discipulis, 1883, 45–48; L. Cohn, s.v. D. (135), RE 5, 983–984; A. Ludwich, Aristarchs Homer. Textkritik, 1884–85, I, 50, 75 n., 97 passim; F. Susemihl, Gesch. der griech. Lit. in der Alexandrinerzeit, 1891–1892, II, 716; M. van der Valk, Iliad III 35 and the Scholia, in: Mnemosyne 25, 1972, 80. F.M.

[17] **D. Thrax.** (ὁ Θρᾷξ; *ho Thrâix*). Greek philologist and grammarian who lived from *c.* 180/170 to *c.* 90 BC. The reason for the epithet is unknown (possibly connected to the typically Thracian name of his father Teres): Alexandria is generally assumed to be the city of his origin, but the designation 'Alexandrian' in the Suda δ 1172 could also refer to the place of his education and work. Apollodorus [7] of Athens and D. were the most important direct students of Aristarchus [4] of Samothrace. Both were involved in the political crisis of 145/144 surrounding Ptolemy VIII's ascension to the throne. Following his escape from Alexandria, perhaps in 144, D. taught in Rhodes (he also wrote a work Περὶ Ῥόδου (*Perì Rhódou*) 'On Rhodes': fr. 56 = FGrH 512), where Tyrannion was his student. As far as we know, he devoted himself primarily to the philology of Homer and wrote *hypomnḗmata* and *syngrámmata* (one of them polemical against Crates) according to the example set by his teacher. He also worked on Hesiod and possibly Alcman. Several fragments with grammatical content are still extant. In this area, D. is known for his Τέχνη γραμματική; *Téchnē grammatiké* (*Ars Grammatica*), a small treatise on normative grammar, which would be the first work by an Alexandrian philologist to have survived almost completely if the attribution were not uncertain.

The question of the *Téchnē*'s authenticity is important for the history of Hellenistic grammar as well as for the question of whether a normative system of grammatical rules emerged as early as the 2nd cent. BC or later, and at what time the discipline was recognized as scientifically autonomous. Some researchers regard the observation of linguistic phenomena undertaken by Aristophanes of Byzantium and Aristarchus of Samothrace as the stage of identifying morphological rules, which, however, does not yet achieve the abstraction of a normative system. Others view Aristophanes and Aristarchus as the founders of the study of inflection, which was subsequently defined and specified by the generation of Aristarchus' students in the 2nd half of the 2nd cent. BC. In the context of this development, the status of the *Téchnē* is important. If we regard it as a compilation from the 4th cent. AD at the earliest, we must move the beginning of grammar as an autonomous science to at least the 1st cent. BC, the generation of Tyrannion, Philoxenus, and Tryphon. The arguments against its authenticity can be summed up in three points: (1) according to the scholia (124,7ff.; 161,2ff. HILGARD), several ancient grammarians argued that it was false by pointing to contradictions between D. and the *Téchnē*. (2) It contains Stoic elements that go beyond the degree to be expected from a direct student of Aristarchus. (3) There is no indication that ancient authors knew the treatise until the early Byzantine era, and the few grammatical fragments extant on papyrus from the time between the 1st and the 3rd/4th cents. AD seem to differ from the *Téchnē* in a substantial way (a papyrus from as late as the 5th cent. contains the beginning). The defenders of authenticity view the first argument as invalid; the second as not conclusive because stoic influences on grammar began relatively early; the third one as merely an argument *ex silentio*, arguing that the question of the text's authorship must be differentiated from the question of its influence on successive studies. Furthermore, it is likely that the text has changed during its transmission (most recent survey in [16]).

A correct approach to solving the problem [17; 24] must proceed from the assumption that §§ 1–4 are authentic: this never has been questioned, because it is attested in S. Emp. math. 1,57 and 250 (Dionysius Thrax, ἐν τοῖς παραγγέλμασι). It is therefore certain that D. wrote a grammatical treatise (*parangélmata*) whose beginning reveals the conception of a systematic educational text. The definition of *grammatikḗ* as 'experience of what is said by poets and prose writers' (ἐμπειρία τῶν παρὰ ποιηταῖς τε καὶ συγγραφεῦσιν λεγομένων) is entirely in line with the philological work of the Alexandrians. These facts thus confirm the role and influence of D. within the history of grammar in the 2nd cent. BC, regardless of whether or not the larger part of the *Téchnē* is authentic (§§ 6–20; § 5 is certainly interpolated). This latter presents a coherent and technical treatment of the foundations of grammar as influenced by Stoicism.

→ Aristophanes [4] of Byzantium; → Aristarchus [4] of Samothrace; → Apollodorus [7] of Athens; → Tyrannion

EDITIONS: 1 K. LINKE, Die Fragmente des Grammatikers D. Thrax, SGLG 3, 1977 2 FGrH 512.
ARS GRAMMATICA: 3 G. UHLIG, Dionysii Thracis Ars Grammatica, 1883 4 J. LALLOT, La grammaire de Denys le Thrace, 1989 5 A. HILGARD, Scholia in Dionysii Thracis artem grammaticam, in: Grammatici Graeci I 3, 1901.
BIBLIOGRAPHY: 6 W. AX, Aristarch und die 'Gramm.', in: Glotta 60, 1982, 96ff. 7 L. COHN, s.v. D. (134), RE 5, 977–983 8 V. DI BENEDETTO, Dionisio il Trace e la Techne a lui attribuita, in: ASNP II 27, 1958, 169–210; II 28, 1959, 87–118 9 ID., La Techne spuria, ASNP s. III 3, 1973, 797–814 10 ID., At the origins of Greek grammar, Glotta 68 (1990), 19–39 11 F.W. HOUSEHOLDER, Word-classes in ancient greek, in: Lingua 17, 1967, 103–128 12 H. ERBSE, Zur normativen Gramm. der Alexandriner, in: Glotta 58, 1980, 236–258
13 M. FUHRMANN, Das systematische Lehrbuch, 1960, 29ff., 145ff. 14 A. KEMP, The 'Tekhne Grammatike' of D. Thrax, in: D.J. TAYLOR (ed.), The History of Linguistics in the Classical Period, 1987, 169–189 15 ID., The Emergence of Autonomous Greek Grammar, in: P. SCHMITTER (ed.), Gesch. der Sprachtheorie II, 1991, 302–333 16 V. LAW, I. SLUITER (ed.), Dionysius Thrax and the 'Techne grammatike', 1995 17 F. MONTANARI, L'erudizione, la filologia, la grammatica, in: Lo spazio letterario della Grecia antica, I 2, 1993, 255–56, 277
18 R. NICOLAI, La storiografia nell'educazione antica, 1992, 186ff. 19 M. PATILLON, Contribution à la lecture de la Technê de Denyse le Thrace, in: REG 103, 1990, 693–98 20 PFEIFFER, KPI, 279, 307, 321–329
21 J. PINBORG, in: Current Trends in Linguistics, 13, 1975, 69ff. 22 R.H. ROBINS, Dionysius Thrax and the Western grammatical tradition, TAPhA 1957, 67–106 23 ID., The Techne grammatike of Dionysius Thrax in its historical perspective, in: P. SWIGGERS, W. VAN HOECKE, Mot et parties du discours, La pensée linguistique 1, 1986, 9–37 — 24 D.M. SCHENKEVELD, Scholarship and grammar, in: Entretiens XL, 1994, 263–301 25 M. SCHMIDT, Dionys der Thraker, in: Philologus 8, 1853, 231–253, 510–520 26 E. SIEBENBORN, Die Lehre von der Sprachrichtigkeit und ihren Kriterien..., 1976 27 D.J. TAYLOR, Rethinking the History of Language Science in Classical Antiquity, in: D.J. TAYLOR, The History of Linguistics in the Classical Period, 1987, 1–16 28 A. TRAGLIA, La sistemazione grammaticale di Dionisio Trace, in: Studi Classica e Orientali 5, 1956, 38–78 29 H. WOLANIN, Derivation in the Techne grammatike by Dionysios Thrax, in: Eos 77, 1989, 237–249 30 A. WOUTERS, The grammatical papyri from Graeco-Roman Egypt, 1979 31 ID., Dionysius Thrax on the correptio Attica, in: Orbis 36, 1991–93, 221–228.

F.M.

[18] D. of Halicarnassus. Historian.

A. BIOGRAPHY B. WORKS 1. HISTORICAL WRITINGS 2. RHETORICAL WORKS C. AESTHETIC VIEWS D. RECEPTION AND HISTORY OF RESEARCH

A. BIOGRAPHY

Born in Halicarnassus *c.* 60 BC. In Rome from *c.* 30/29 BC, at least until the first book of the 'Roman History' was published in 8/7 BC (1,7,2; on the publication in two parts cf. 7,70,2). His writings, including those that were unpublished, were popular with a circle of Greek intellectuals (Epist. ad Pompeium Geminum

1,1; 3,1). He had Roman patrons, for example Q. Aelius Tubero (De Thucydide 1,1) and was a teacher of rhetoric (comp. 20, 23).

B. Works

1. Historical writings

a) The 'Roman History' (Ῥωμαικὴ ἀρχαιολογία, *Antiquitates Romanae*). The following have survived of the 20 bks.: 1–10, 11 incomplete; 11–20 in excerpts. The work deals with the period from the mythical beginnings to the 1st Punic War (1,8,1–2), i.e. up to the beginning of Polybius' history. The basic premise is that the Romans are Greeks and that their superiority is based on Greek virtues (1,5,1 [16]), which, however, have been perfected (Rome as the ideal polis: [19]). b) 'About Time' (Περὶ χρόνων, not extant (FGrH 251).

2. Rhetorical writings

The chronology is contested [8; 11; 25 incl. bibliography]). a) 'Against the Critics of Political Philosophy' (Ὑπὲρ τῆς πολιτικῆς φιλοσοφίας πρὸς τοὺς κατατρέχοντας αὐτῆς ἀδίκως): De Thucydide 2,3: this lost piece was probably aimed against the Epicureans.

b) 'On the Old Orators' (Περὶ τῶν ἀρχαίων ῥητόρων, *De oratoribus veteribus*): a history of eloquence and, at the same time, a textbook for future writers and orators. The first part (*Lysías, Isokrátēs, Isaíos*) and *Dēmosthénēs*, with a garbled beginning, have survived [32]. Despite praef. 4,5, it is uncertain whether D. had completed the works on Hypereides and Aeschines. The treatises contain primarily a short biographical sketch of each orator, which amounts to an analysis of the quality of their respective styles and the structure (οἰκονομία, *oikonomía*) of their works, and finally a series of good as well as bad examples from these same works. In the *praefatio*, D. expresses his admiration for the Roman government which wants to promote a renaissance of rhetoric, philosophy, and culture in general.

c) 'On Dinarchus' (Περὶ Δεινάρχου, *De Dinarcho*): deals with questions of authenticity.

d) 'On Imitation' (Περὶ μιμήσεως, *De imitatione*): a textbook in three bks. Extant are an epitome from the period following the 5th cent. AD and the self-quotation in Epist. ad Pomp. 3–6 on historians [15].

e) D. had intended to write a treatise on historians (De Thucydide, praef. 4,4), but only 'De Thucydide' (Περὶ Θουκυδίδου) is complete [25; 26]. The latter was followed by a supplement entitled 'Second Letter to Ammaeus on the Figures of Speech by Thucydides' (Περὶ τῶν Θουκυδίδου ἰδωμάτων πρὸς Ἀμμαῖον).

f) A study of stylistics (Περὶ συνθέσεως ὀνομάτων, *De compositione verborum*): in this 'phono-stylistics', D. regards poetry and prose as 'an art of imitation created for the sense of hearing' [17].

g) The 'First Letter to Ammaeus' (Πρὸς Ἀμμαίον ἐπιστολή) discusses the relative chronology of Aristotle's rhetoric in relation to Demosthenes with the purpose of proving that Demosthenes was not influenced by Aristotle.

h) The 'Letter to Cn. Pompeius Geminus' (Πρὸς Πομπήϊον Γεμῖνον ἐπιστολή, *Epist. ad Cn. Pompeium Geminum*) 1–3: D. repeats the criticism of Plato's style found in *De Demosthene* with a verbatim quotation of chapters 5–7. He adds yet another quotation from *De imitatione*, wherein he discusses Herodotus and Thucydides, thus establishing a canon of historians that are exemplary in style.

j) The 'Rhetoric' (Τέχνη ῥητορική, *Ars rhetorica*) is not authentic.

C. Aesthetic views

D.'s cultural ideal is a 'philosophical rhetoric' in the tradition of Isocrates and Cicero, which can be acquired through reading the classics (that is, the authors of the 5th–4th cents. [20]). In addition to a focus on style, orators are also supposed to pay attention to the philosophical content. Furthermore, the orator's goal should lie in being useful to many people; therefore ideal rhetoric is by nature also 'political', as we can witness in the example of Isocrates' 'philosophical rhetoric' (De Isocrate 4,4). In following these 'rules' of the skill combined with an intuitive sense for 'the beautiful' (De imitatione, fr. 2 A [13; 14; 28]), he does not hesitate 'to rewrite' Plato and Thucydides in order to juxtapose the originality of his own method with a banal adherence to textbooks (Epist. ad Ammaeum 2,1,2–2,1; comp. 22,7–8). He thereby proposes an eclectic imitation [20], that is, he follows the principle of distilling specific stylistic qualities from each author. The goal is a 'mixed' style which is clear and abstains from the vagueness inherent in excessive formality (the 'Gorgianisms' and the 'Dithyrambic' of Platonic and Thucydidian prose). D. is also eclectic in his use of different movements in literary criticism such as the Peripatetic (e.g., in the study of *genera loquendi*, cf. [31]), the Stoic (e.g., in the theory about the origin of language, cf. [11]), the Platonic (irrationality of judgement, cf. [18]), or the Alexandrian (generally, in the type of commentary made by historians; cf. [30] and [15]).

In the rhetorical writings and in the *Antiquitates*, D. follows the same guiding principles: 1. the necessity of comparison in judging the models; 2. the achievement of truth (ἀλήθεια; *alḗtheia*) as the highest goal of historical research as well as literary criticism (Epist. ad Ammaeum 1,2,3). The stylistic models and the historical examples contribute in the effort 'to improve life and the speeches' (Epist. ad Pompeium 1,2). Thus, 'philosophical rhetoric' finds its 'most useful' and absolutely 'true' realization [15] in historiography.

D. Reception and history of research

As a theorist of historiography and after his *Thoukydídēs* was translated into Latin by A. Dudith (1560), D. shared and competed with Lucian's *De historia conscribenda* in exerting a strong influence on the *artes historicae* of the Renaissance [15]. Held up as a model by J. Bodin (*Methodus ad facile historiarum cognitionem*, 1566) and I.Vossius (*Ars historica*, 2nd edition

1653), used by J. Scaliger for the chronology and by Montesquieu as a source [21], D.'s poetic conception of historiography resonates in the 18th cent. in the works of Abbot Geinoz (1749), F. Schlegel (the only German translator of the *Isokrátēs*, 1796), and F. Creuzer [12]. However, beginning with L. de Beaufort (1738), D.'s reconstruction of archaic Roman history is regarded as unreliable and D. himself is viewed as a *graeculus* (E. SCHWARTZ [27]), 'an uncritical and unhistorical mind' (SCHMID/STÄHLIN II, 473). On the debate between J. Perizonius (1651–1715) and B.G. Niebuhr (1811) i.a. over using D. as a source for the origins of Rome, cf. [10; 24], also regarding the 'Etruscan issue' by K.O. Müller (1828) through G. De Sanctis (1907) until today [9. 1–35]. What still remains to be written is a history of the reception of D. the rhetor (despised by E. NORDEN and U. v. WILAMOWITZ), and especially of the *De compositione*, for example in the *Prose della volgar lingua* by P. Bembo (1525 [14]), up to and including the influential translation by Ch. Batteux (1788).

EDITION: 1 F. SYLBURG 1586 (ed. princeps, complete edition).
ANT.: 2 C. JACOBY 1885–1925 3 E. CARY, 1937–50.
OPUSCULA: 4 USENER, RADERMACHER, 1899–1929 (repr. 1997) 5 S. USHER, 1974–85 6 G. AUJAC, 1978–92
BIBLIOGRAPHY: 7 D. BATTISTI, De imitatione, 1997 8 S.F. BONNER, The Literary Treatises of Dionysius of Halicarnassus, 1939 9 D. BRIQUEL, Les Tyrrhènes, 1993 10 L. CANFORA, Roma 'città greca', in: Quaderni di Storia 39, 1994, 5–41 11 P. COSTIL, L'esthétique littéraire de Denys d'Hal., 1949 12 F. CREUZER, Herodot und Thucydides (1794), Italian tr. with introduction and notes by S. FORNARO, 1994 13 C. DAMON, Aesthetic response and technical analysis in the rhetoric writing of Dionysius of Halicarnassus, in: MH 48, 1991, 33–58 14 F. DONADI, Il 'bello' e il 'piacere' ..., in: SIFC 89, 1986, 42–63 15 S. FORNARO, Epistola a Pompeo Gemino, 1997 16 E. GABBA, Dionysius and the History of Archaic Rome, 1991 (Italian ed. ²1996) 17 B. GENTILI, Il 'de comp. verb.' di Dionigi di Alicarnasso, in: QUCC 36, 1990, 7–21 18 K. GOUDRIAAN, Over classicisme, 1989 19 F. HARTOG, Rome et la Grèce: les choix de Denys d'Halicarnasse, in: S. SAID (ed.), Hellenismos, 1991, 149–67 20 TH. HIDBER, Das klassizistische Manifest des D. von Halikarnassos, 1996 21 A. HURST, Un critique grec dans la Rome d'Auguste: Denys d' Halicarnasse, in: ANRW II 30.1, 839–65 22 G. MARENGHI, Dionisio di Alicarnasso, Dinarco, 1970 23 P.M. MARTIN, Denys d'Halicarnasse source de Montesquieu, in: R. CHEVALLIER (ed.), Caesarodunum XXII bis, 1987, 301–336 24 A. MOMIGLIANO, Perizonius, Niebuhr and the Character of Early Roman Tradition (1957), in: Id., Secondo Contributo, 1960, 69–88 25 G. PAVANO, Saggio su Tucidide, 1958 26 W.K. PRITCHETT, On Thucydides, 1975 27 L. RADERMACHER, E. SCHWARTZ, s.v. D., RE 5, 934–71 28 D.M. SCHENKEVELD, Theory of evaluation in the rhetorical treatises of Dionysius of Halicarnassus, in: Museum Philologum Londiniense 1, 1975, 93–107 29 C. SCHULTZE, Dionysius of Halicarnassus and his audience, in: Past perspectives, 1986, 121–41 30 H. USENER, Epilogus, in: Dionysii Halicarnassensis Libri de imitatione reliquiae Epistulaeque criticae duae, 1889, 110–43 31 C. WOOTEN, The Peripatetic Tradition in the Literary Essays of Dionysius of Halicarnassus, in: W.W. FORTENBAUGH, D.C. MIRHADY (ed.), Peripatetical Rhetoric after Aristotle, 1994, 121–30 32 J. WYK CRONJÈ, Dionysius of Halicarnassus: De Demosthene (Spudasmata 30), 1986.

S.FO.

[19] D. Tryphonus. (ὁ Τρύφωνος; *ho Trýphōnos*). Greek grammarian of the 1st cent. AD, probably the son (or the student?) of the grammarian Tryphon of Alexandria (Augustan period). Harpocration and Athenaeus used his treatise Περὶ ὀνομάτων which comprised at least 10 bks. Several fragments are also quoted by Stephanus of Byzantium. This work was probably connected with Tryphon's onomastic writings.

→ Tryphon of Alexandria; → Harpocration; → Athenaeus; → Stephanus of Byzantium.

L. COHN, s.v. D. (137), RE 5, 985; E. ROHDE, De Iulii Pollucis in apparatu scaenico enarrando fontibus, 1870, 66.

[20] D. Musicus. (ὁ Μουσικός; *ho Mousikós*), of Halicarnassus. Greek grammarian of the Hadrianic period (1st half of the 2nd cent. AD). He owes his epithet to his voluminous works about musicology and the history of music (only few fragments have survived in various scholarly sources). Three titles can be found in the Suda δ 1171 (where he is also referred to as *sophistḗs*): 'Treatises on Rhythmics' (Ῥυθμικὰ ὑπομνήματα; *Rhythmikà hypomnḗmata*) in 24 bks.; 'History of Music' (Μουσικὴ ἱστορία; *Mousikḕ historía*) in 36 bks., which contained information about aulos players, cithara players, and poets of the various genres; 'Musical Education' (Μουσικὴ παιδεία; *Mousikḕ paideía*) in 22 bks. Porphyry (comm. on Ptolemy, *Harmoniká*, 37,15f. DÜRING) cites a Περὶ ὁμοιοτήτων. The D. cited in the Suda ο 656 (s.v. Ὀρφεὺς Ὀδρύσης) is most likely the same person. It is still questionable whether he can be identified with the contemporary Aelius D. [21] Atticista.

→ Dionysius [21]; → Dionysius [22]

L. COHN, s.v. D. (142), RE 5, 986–991; A. DAUB, De Suidae biographicorum origine et fide, in: Jbb. für. Philol. Suppl. 11, 1880, 410ff.; A. GRIFFIN, A new fragment of D. of Halikarnassos ὁ μουσικός, in: Historia 28, 1979, 241–246; C. SCHERER, De Aelio Dionysio musico qui vocatur, thesis 1886; SCHMID/STÄHLIN II, 870–871; R. WESTPHAL, Die Fragmente und die Lehrsätze der griech. Rhythmiker, 1861, 46 and *passim*; Id., Die Musik des griech. Alterthumes, 1883, 248–250.

[21] Aelius D. of Halicarnassus. Grammarian from the period of Hadrian (Suda δ 1174), founder of Atticist lexicography together with Pausanias. He is known to us as the author of the 'Attic Terms' (Ἀττικὰ ὀνόματα; *Attikà onómata*) in five bks., a collection of Attic expressions in alphabetical order. The purpose of this work (which appeared in a second edition enlarged mostly by quotations from writers) was to offer lexical and grammatical explanations and to indicate the linguistically and stylistically correct use of Attic. Numerous fragments can be retrieved from various scholarly

sources, primarily works of lexicography and scholiography. The lexica by D. and Pausanias were known to Photius (Bibliography 99b–100a, codd. 152 and 153) and were still used by Eustathius in the 12th cent. It is still questionable today whether the Atticist lexicographer can be identified with the contemporary D. [20].
→ Pausanias; → Dionysius [20] Musicus

EDITIONS: E. SCHWABE, Aelii Dionysii et Pausaniae atticistarum fragmenta, 1890; H. ERBSE, Unt. zu den attizistischen Lexika, 1950.
BIBLIOGRAPHY: L. COHN, s.v. D. (142), RE 5, 987–991; ERBSE, see above; SCHMID/STÄHLIN II, 873–874; M. VAN DER VALK, A few observations on the Atticistic lexica, in: Mnemosyne s. IV, 8, 1955, 207–218; G. WENTZEL, Zu den atticistischen Glossen in dem Lex. des Photios, in: Hermes 30, 1895, 367–384.

[22] Greek grammarian of unknown date, author of commentaries on Euripides which are cited as one of the major sources in the *subscriptio* to the scholia on *Orestes* and on *Medea*. He is perhaps the same person as the grammarian D. who is cited as a source by Tzetzes and also in the treatises 'On Comedy' (Περὶ κωμῳδίας; *Perì kōmōidías*). The suggestion that he is identical with D. [28] is unfounded.
→ Euripides (scholia); → Dionysius [28]

L. COHN, s.v. D. (141), RE 5, 985–986. F.M.

[23] **The chronicle by [Ps.]-D. of Tell-Maḥrē.** Syrian chronicle of the world from creation to the year AD 775/6. It originated in the monastery Zuqnīn (near Amīda) and was erroneously attributed to D. of Tell-Maḥrē (died in 845) by the first publisher. A short preface is followed by a) the time from creation to the year 313, using Eusebius as a reference and a few other sources as well, b) the years 313–485, partially based on → Socrates [9], c) the years 497–506/7, an independent work from Edessa which is also known as the Chronicle of → Iossua Stylites, d) the years 489–578, based in large parts on the lost second part of the church history by → Iohannes of Ephesus, and e) the years 587–775 (of particular importance for northern Mesopotamia of the early Abbasid period). The first sections contain a detailed narrative about the Magi and a variation on the legend about the Seven Sleepers of Ephesus.

EDITION: J.B. CHABOT, CSCO Scr. Syri 43 [a)-c)], 53 [d)-e)].
TRANSLATIONS: Scr. Syri 66 [a)-c), Lat.]; Scr. Syri 213 [d)-e), French]; P. MARTIN, 1876 [c), French] W. WRIGHT, 1882 [c), Engl.]; J. WATT [c), Engl., 2000]; W. WITAKOWSKI, 1996 [d), Engl.]; A. HARRAK [d)-e), Engl., 1999].
BIBLIOGRAPHY: W. WITAKOWSKI, The Syriac Chronicle of Pseudo-Dionysius of Tel-Maḥre, 1987; Id., Sources of Pseudo-Dionysius of Tel-Maḥre for the Second Part of His Chronicle, in: Leimon. Studies presented to L. Ryden, 1996, 181–210 [on the sources of b)]; Id., in: Orientalia Suecana 40, 1991, 252–275 [on the sources of d)]; U. MONNERET DE VILLARD, Le leggende orientali sui Magi evangelici (Studi e Testi 163), 1952; M. WHITBY, The era of Philip and the Chronicle of Zuqnin, in: Classica et Medievalia 43, 1992, 179–185; S.P. BROCK, Studies in Syriac Christianity, 1992, 10–13; A. PALMER, The Seventh Century in the West-Syrian Chronicles, 1993. S.BR.

IV. DOCTORS, SCIENTISTS, GEOGRAPHERS

[24] Physician from the late 4th cent. BC, who advocated the bandaging of limbs to stop a patient's bleeding (Caelius Aurelianus, Chronicae passiones 2,186). He may be identical to the D. who gave the name of *epanthismos* to a vessel similar to a vein (Rufus, Nom. part. 205), whereby he expressed his interest in anatomy, as well as to the D. mentioned by Pliny (HN 20,19,113) who is cited in connection with remedies along with Diocles and Chrysippus.
→ Medicine V.N.

[25] Astronomer, active in the years 275–241 BC, probably in Alexandria. In 285, the year Ptolemy II Philadelphus ascended the throne, he reformed the Egyptian calendar (twelve times 30 days, with five leap days a year and six leap days every three years) by naming the months after the signs of the zodiac: Καρκινών (*Karkinṓn*, 'Cancer'), Λεοντών (*Leontṓn*, 'Leo'), Παρθενών (*Parthenṓn*, 'Virgo') etc. Summer solstice and the new year was the 1st *Karkinṓn* = 27th Pharmuti, corresponding to June 26. The yearly markers seem to indicate that he accounted for anomalies in the sun's motion. He wrote about the fact that the length of a person's shadow can be used to calculate the time of day, similar to Sextos ὁ ὡροκράτωρ (*ho hōrakrátōr*; 'the Lord of the Hours'). His observations about Mercury, Mars, and Jupiter are as a reference used by Ptolemy (Synt. 9,7; 9,10; 10,9; 11,3). He may be identical to the D. mentioned by Pliny (HN 6,58) who was sent on a mission to India by Ptolemy Philadelphus [2].

EDITION: 1 J. HEEG, CCAG, 5,3, 76–78 (although attributed in part to a Theodorus).

Bibliography: 2 H. BERGER, s.v. D. (117), RE 5, 972f. 3 A. BÖCKH, Über die vierjährigen Sonnenkreise der Alten, 1863, 286–340 4 W. GUNDEL, H.G. GUNDEL, Astrologumena, 1966, 253 5 K. MANITIUS (ed.), Ptolemäus, Hdb. der Astronomie 2, 1912 (repr. 1963), 406–408. W.H.

[26] Son of Calliphon (according to the acrostic in his *Descriptio Graeciae* v. 1–23), Greek geographer of the Sullan period, author of a description of Greece in iambic trimeters (Ἀναγραφὴ τῆς Ἑλλάδος; *Anagraphêtês Helládos*) in the form of a → *períplous*. Two fragments have survived: following the prologue, 1–109b deal with Hellas, Ambracia, Amphilochia, Acarnania, Aetolia, Ozolian Locris, Phocis, Boeotia, Megaris, and Corinthia, 110–150 deal with Crete as well as the Cyclades and Sporades.

GGM 1, 238–243; D. MARCOTTE, Le poème géographique de D. fils de Calliphon, 1990.

[27] **D. Periegetes.** From Alexandria (cf. the acrostic in his *Orbis descriptio* vv. 112–134). Under Hadrian he wrote (according to the acrostic vv. 513–532) a didactic poem in hexameters with a poetic description of the

world (Οἰκουμένης περιήγησις; *Oikouménēs periḗgēsis*): after an introduction (1–26), it deals with the ocean (27–169), the continents of Africa (170–269) and Europe (270–446), the islands (447–619), and Asia (620–1165). The work was much read in antiquity, the Middle Ages, and into the 19th cent. It was loosely translated into Latin by → Avienus and → Priscianus, and was commented thoroughly by → Eustathius i.a.

GGM 2, 103–176; C. JACOB, La description de la terre habitée de Denys, 1990; I. O. TSAVARI, Histoire du texte de la description de la terre de Denys le Périégète, 1990; K. BRODERSEN, D. von Alexandria: Das Lied von der Welt, 1994. K.BRO.

[28] **D. of Byzantium.** Greek geographer of the 2nd cent. AD. His detailed and stylized description of the Thracian → Bosporus (Ἀνάπλους Βοσπόρου; *Anáplous Bospórou*) has only survived in copies of Cod. Palatinus gr. 398. The missing passages must be supplemented from a 16th-cent. Latin paraphrase. According to the Suda δ 1176 ADLER (SH 386) ἐποποιός (*epopoiós;* 'poet of epics'), he can be identified with the author of θρῆνοι (*thrênoi*; 'poems of lamentation') and with the geographer, but this is highly doubtful.

1 GGM 2, 1–101 2 R. GÜNGERICH, D. Byzantii Anaplus Bospori, 1927, XLIIIf. K.BRO. and M.D.MA.

[29] Author of *Ornithiaká*, who probably used Alexander of Myndus as the main source for his didactic poem. The *Ornithiaká* are attributed in part to D. [27] Periegetes, in part to D. of Philadelphia (Vita Chisiana 81, 15). In addition, a Byzantine paraphrase (1. land fowl, 2. waterfowl, 3. bird catching) of the didactic poem is extant as well. The three parts of the paraphrase probably follow the three bks. of the original.

M. WELLMANN, Alexander von Myndos, in: Hermes 26, 1891, 506–520. C.S.

V. POETS

[30] **D. Chalcus.** (Χαλκοῦς; *Chalkoús*). Athenian elegist and rhetor. He received his nickname (listed in the library catalogue of Callimachus) after his suggestion to introduce bronze coins into Athens (Ath. 669d). Plut. Nicias 5,3 refers to him (or to his son?) as the founder of Thurii in 444/3 BC. Colourful metaphors (one of them criticized in Aristot. Rh. 1405a31–35), often used metasympotically [1], characterize the citations from his innovative [2] elegies (all of them in Athenaeus, who supposedly said [602b-c] that one of them began with a pentameter).

1 K. BORTHWICK, The Gymnasium of Bromius, in: JHS 84, 1964, 49–53 2 A. GARZYA, Dionisio Calco, in: RFIC 30, 1952, 193–207 C. MIRALLES, La renovación de la elegía en la época clásica, in: Boletín del Inst. de Estudios helénicos 5.2, 1971, 13ff.

EDITION: GENTILI/PRATO, Poetarum elegiacorum testimonia et fragmenta 2, 1985, 74–78; IEG 2, 58–60. E.BO.

[31] Author of comedies, from Sinope [1. test. 1], victor in the Lenaea (2nd half of the 4th cent. BC) [1st test. 2]. The titles of four plays (Ἀκοντιζόμενος, Θεσμοφόρος, Ὁμώνυμοι, Σῴζουσα or Σώτειρα) and 10 fragments have survived, the longer two of which both contain a lecture by a cook: fr. 2, describing the correct way in which the cooking profession should be practised, and fr. 3 (addressed to a 'student'), describing how to help oneself inconspicuously while cooking. This is the first text for either one of these themes to be presented in detail [2. 305f.].

1 PCG V, 1986, 32–40 2 H.-G. NESSELRATH, Die att. Mittlere Komödie, 1990. T.HI.

[32] Author of the *Bassariká* and the *Gigantiás*, which are extant only in fragments (in Steph. Byz. and in a papyrus from the 3rd/4th cents. AD). In the at least 18 bks. (perhaps altogether 24) of the *Bassariká*, D. describes the campaign of the god Dionysus against the Indian king Deriades. Bks. 3 and 4 contained a catalogue of warriors. The *Gigantiás* focuses on the → gigantomachy on Pallene and on episodes from its prehistory (Hercules' return from Troy to Cos; the robbery of Helios' cattle instigated by Alcyoneus). The style of the epics is Homeric. Furthermore, they are clearly influenced by Hellenistic poetry on a linguistic as well as thematic level (Callimachus, Apollonius Rhodius, Nicander). → Nonnus made extensive use of both epics.

E. HEITSCH (ed.), Die griech. Dichterfragmente der röm. Kaiserzeit 1, 1961, 60–77; A. S. HOLLIS (ed.), Ovid, Metamorphoses Book 8, 1970, app. 2 (151–153); E. LIVREA (ed.), Dionysii Bassaricon et Gigantiadis Fragmenta, 1973. C.S.

[33] **D. of Rhodes.** Author of a funeral epigram from the 'Garland' of Meleager, dedicated to the poet Phaenocritus (the name is otherwise unknown) of Ialysus (Anth. Pal. 7,716). This D. (the name is too common to allow definite identifications) could also be the author of the 'Meleagrian' poems 6,3; 7,462; 12,108, simply entitled Διονυσίου; *Dionysíou* (the title in 6,3 seems suspicious, since the dedicator's name is also Διονύσιος; it is remarkable that the last verse can also be read in P.Berol. 9812 from the 3rd cent. BC, followed by remnants of two further epigrams, probably by the same author).

GA I,1, 80f.; 2, 231–235; FGE 40–44.

[34] **D. of Cyzicus.** Author of an epitaph for Eratosthenes (Anth. Pal. 7,78) from the 'Garland' of Meleager which, if not composed for the grave (as the τόδε in v. 6 might suggest), was written a short time after the death of the scholar (*c.* 194 BC). This D. (whose name is too common to allow definite identifications) could also be the author of the 'Meleagrian' poems 7,462 and 12,108, which are signed with the simple mention of Διονυσίου.

GA 1,1, 80f.; 2, 231–235. E.D.

[35] Writer of the New Comedy, documented only on the inscription list of Lenaea winners, which indicates that he was active in the 2nd cent. BC [1].

1 PCG V, 1986, 41. T.HI.

[36] **D. from Cyprus.** Tragedian, his name appears in an inscription in Paphos (SEG 13,586, between 144 and 131 BC).

TrGF 138.

[37] **D. from Athens.** Son of Cephisodorus, writer of satyr plays, honoured in an inscription on the south wall of the Athenian treasury (FdD III 2, 48 36, SIG^3 711 L) as an Attic participant in the 3rd Pythaïs of the *technitai* of Dionysus in Delphi in the year 106/05 BC (or 97, cf. TrGF app. crit. 145–151). He apparently belonged to the Pythaists in the year 128/27 as well (FdD III 2 no. 15 col. 2, 18).

METTE, 72; TrGF 149.

[38] **D. from Anaphlystus.** Son of Demetrius. According to an inscription on Delos (DID B 13, *c.* 112 BC), he was the winner in an agon of tragedy and satyr-play writers.

TrGF 141. F.P.

[39] **D. from Thebes.** He worked in the tradition of the old μουσική (*mousikḗ*) and was mentioned along with Pindar, Lamprus, and Pratinas (Aristox. fr. 76 Wehrli), teacher of Epaminondas (Nep. Epam. 2). F.Z.

[40] **D. from Miletus.** Ti. Claudius Flavianus D., sophist from Miletus, student of Isaeus. Philostr. VS 1,22,521f. praises his declamations (μελέτη; *melétē*) for their natural style, structure and discipline. D. taught primarily in Ephesus; his students were Alexander of Seleucia and Antiochus (VS 2,5,576; 4,568). The emperor Hadrian made him a knight (*eques equo publico*), nominated him twice as *procurator* οὐκ ἀφανῶν ἐθνῶν (Philostr. VS 1,22,524; cf. IK 17.1,3047), and granted him board (σίτησις; *sítēsis*) in the Mouseion of Alexandria. D.'s sarcophagus was found near the Library of Celsus in Ephesus (IK 12,426; cf. Philostr. VS 2,22,526).
→ Philostratus, Second Sophistic

G.W. BOWERSOCK, Greek Sophists in the Roman Empire, 1969, 51–53; PIR D 105. E.BO.

[41] **D. from Scymnus.** (Σκιωναῖος; *Skiōnaîos* in Tzetzes). Dramatist; it is uncertain, whether he was a tragedian or a writer of comedies. A fragment in connection with his name is extant in the schol. Lycoph. 1247, 357 SCHEER. The name D. also appears in an inscription in the Dionysus theatre in Athens (2nd cent. AD).

TrGF 208.

[42] **D. from Heraclea.** Called ὁ Μεταθέμενος; *ho Metathémenos* (see also → D. [8]). According to Diog. Laert. 5,92f., he authored a *Parthenopaeus* under Sophocles' name, which is claimed to have been remarkably authentic.

TrGF 113. F.P.

[43] **D. of Corinth.** (ὁ Κορίνθιος; *ho Korínthios*). An epic poet according to the Suda δ 1177 ADLER (= SH 387), author of Ὑποθῆκαι, Αἴτια, Μετεωρολογούμενα and of a commentary on Hesiod written in prose. An Οἰκουμένης περιήγησις δι' ἐπῶν was also attributed to him, but he was obviously mistaken for D. [27] Periegetes, as was already surmised in the Suda (ibid.), at least for the latter work. Only one quotation from the *Aítia* (Plut. Mor. 761b = SH 388) has survived. M.D.MA.

[44] **D. of Andros.** Author of a short epigram, which originates either from the 'Garland' of Meleager or from that of Philippus. It deals with the popular topic of the fateful connection between Zeus and Bromios, that is, the connection between rain and wine (Anth. Pal. 7,533; cf. Theoc. 7,660; Antipater of Thessalonica, Anth. Pal. 7,398, etc.). Nothing is known about the author; the common name does not allow any identification.

FGE 44. E.D.

[45] **D. Sophistes.** Author of two charming love epigrams—one is addressed to a girl who sells roses (Anth. Pal. 5,81), the other, whose attribution is not clear, is addressed to a bath attendant (5,82); their origin can no longer be clearly determined. The very common name of the otherwise unknown poet sheds doubt on any identifications (including the one with the musician and grammarian from the period of Hadrian, D. of Halicarnassus the Younger).

FGE 44f. E.D.

[46] **D. of Antioch.** Christian sophist from *c.* AD 500. He was the recipient of testimonial 17 by Aeneas [3] of Gaza, in which he praises the suburb of Daphne, where D. lived, as a place of inspiration. D.'s 85 letters, although poor in content (paraphrases: [1. 64–71]), were used as stylistic models in Byzantine schools of rhetoric, along with → Synesius and → Procopius of Gaza [2].

EDITION: R. HERCHER, Epistolographi graeci, 1873, 260–274

BIBLIOGRAPHY: 1 M. MINNITI COLONNA, Le epistole di D., in: Vichiana 4, 1975, 60–80 2 A. PIGNANI, Un' inedita raccolta metabizantina di temi epistolari, in: AFLN 13, 1970–71, 91–105. O.HI.

VI. ARTISTS

[47] Bronze sculptor from Argus. In Olympia, he created the votive group of Micythus (after 476 BC), consisting of 12 statues of gods and poets. The bases, with traces of the statues, are extant. Attempts at identifying the Orpheus statue with the Munich-St. Petersburg head type as well as the Homer statue in the so-called blind style have been unsuccessful. D.'s votive-statue, dedicated by Phormis for winning a chariot race in

Olympia, was famous due to the lifelike representation of the horse.

W. DITTENBERGER, Die Inschr. von Olympia, 1896, no. 267–269; F. ECKSTEIN, Αναθηματα, 1969, 33–43; LIPPOLD, 103–104; LOEWY, no. 31; OVERBECK, no. 401–402 (sources).

[48] Son of Timarchidus, from the Athenian sculptor family of Polycles. After 149 BC, he and his brother → Polycles created the statues of Jupiter Stator and of Juno Regina in Rome. In Delos, *c.* 130 BC, D. created together with → Timarchides Polycles the portrait statue of the slave trader Ofellius Ferus, larger than life and in the heroic → nudity of the Hermes Richelieu type.

J. MARCADÉ, Recueil des signatures de sculpteurs grecs, 2, 1957, no. 41–42 fig.; OVERBECK, no. 2207 (sources); F. QUEYREL, C. Ofellius Ferus, in: BCH 115, 1991, 389–464; A. STEWART, Attika, 1979, 42–46.

[49] Son of Apollonius, sculptor from Athens. He created the extant statue of Agrippina minor from the Heraeum in Olympia.

K. HITZL, Die kaiserzeitliche Statuenausstattung des Metroon, 1991, 43–46, 83–84; LOEWY, no. 331. R.N.

[50] Roman portrait painter of the 1st cent. BC. Pliny's mention of the same artist (HN 35,113; 148) refers to him with the epithet *anthrōpográphos*. He was apparently highly respected and was specialized in painting likenesses. His numerous paintings, which may have resembled contemporary Republican portrait sculptures in style, appear to have been in great demand with private clients.

M. NOWICKA, Le Portrait dans la peinture antique, 1993, *passim*. N.H.

VII. Bishops

[51] Bishop of Corinth (*c.* AD 170). Eusebius, as the main source for D., refers to eight 'catholic letters' (HE 4,23,1) written by D. Seven of them are replies to requests from various Christian communities in Greece (Athens, Cnossus, i.a.), Asia Minor (Nicomedia, i.a.), and Rome. The eighth is a private devotional letter to the Christian woman Chrysophora. It centres around a defence against heretics (Marcionites) and rigorist tendencies. In the letter to the Roman community, D. reports the use of the 1st letter of Clement in the liturgy (Euseb. Hist. eccl. 4,23,11). The corpus of letters that were available to Eusebius also included a reply from bishop Pinytus of Cnossus addressed to D.

BARDENHEWER, GAL I 439–442; W. KÜHNERT, D. von Korinth — eine Bischofsgestalt des 2. Jh., in: SCHMITT-LAUBERT et al. (ed.), Theologia scientia eminens practica. FS F. Zerbst, 1979, 273–289.

[52] Bishop of Alexandria (247/8–264/5). D. was educated in rhetoric and philosophy, and in 231/2, according to Eusebius (HE 6,29,4), he took over the education of the catechumens from Heraclas, then succeeded him as bishop. His name is connected to the conflict surrounding Novatianus, the baptism of heretics, Trinitarian problems (conflict surrounding his alleged tritheism with → D. [53] of Rome), as well as the fight against chiliastic tendencies in Egypt. Only few fragments of his numerous writings have survived (in Eusebius and Athanasius, i.a.). The tradition of ceremonial Easter letters probably goes back to D. His relationship to Origen and his theology (pre-existence of the soul) is controversial.

EDITION: CPG 1550–1612.
BIBLIOGRAPHY: W. A. BIENERT, D. Zur Frage des Origenismus im 3. Jh., 1978; Id., s.v. D., TRE 8, 767–771; J. DE CHURUCCA, Das polit. Denken des Bischofs D. von Alexandrien, in: A. A. ALBERT et al. (ed.), Mélanges F. Wubbe, 1993, 115–140.

[53] Bishop of Rome (22 July AD 259/260 – 26 December 267/8). Probably from Greece, D. becomes bishop of Rome after the seat had been vacant for a long time. He reorganizes the community, which had been weakened by the Valerian persecution, on the basis of a presbyteral constitution. Following the request by Libyan presbyters, D. holds a synod, which condemned Sabellianism and a tritheistically influenced theory of the trinity as it was supported by bishop → D. [52] of Alexandria. The reply from the Alexandrian D. gave rise to the 'argument between the two Dionysii'. D., who was buried in the papal crypt of the Calixtus catacombs, is one of the most important Roman bishops of the 3rd cent.

J. N. D. KELLY, Reclams Lexikon der Päpste, 1986, 34f. J.RI.

[54] **(Ps.)-D. Areopagites.** Pseudonym of an author who claimed to be the 'bishop of Athens' and probably lived around the turn of the 5th to the 6th cent. He may have been of Syrian origin, and it is possible that he belonged to the circle from which emerged Damascius and Marinus, among others. At the Academy of Athens, he probably attended the lectures of Proclus (died in 485) and of Damascius, both of whose influence on D. is evident. The older layer of his writings definitely seems to date from the period after 482 (*Henotikón*) and prior to 532 (first reference by the Severians in Constantinople) and probably spread first through Antiochan circles.

Four theological works with a Neoplatonist (Plotinic) orientation have come down to us, while seven other works that are quoted by the author seem to have been lost. *Perì tês ouranías hierarchías* ('On the Heavenly Hierarchy'; 15 ch.) organizes the world of the angels (who are regarded as symbols) into a hierarchy of decreasing perfection, which the spirit has to ascend in order to elevate itself onto the level of the immaterial and the intelligible. *Perì tês ekklēsiastikês hierarchías* ('On the Hierarchy in the Church'; 7 ch.) describes and interprets the rites of the Church in allegorical fashion and analyses their structure, which is understood as the image of the heavenly structure. The light of God which shines on the angels and which is handed down by them from level to level corresponds to the light of the Church which the bishop spreads over the ranks subordinate to him, while the source of the light is Christ, whom the bishop represents symbolically. Heaven and earth are divided into three levels which in turn have the same number of functions (purification, enlightenment, and becoming one), those who initiate others (bishops, priests, servants) and the initiated (the purified, the enlightened, those who have achieved perfection), whereby each rank possesses the qualities and functions of the next subordinate rank. *Perì theíōn onomátōn* ('On Divine Names'; 13 ch.) analyses the designations which the Bible assigns to the deity: it is transcendent, unnameable, and nameless (*anónymon*), even if it possesses the designations of all its creations (*polyónymon*). All of the forms of address (being, life, wisdom, truth, greatness, etc.) which are studied in this treatise are understood as emanations. In *Perì mystikês theologías* ('On Mystical Theology'; 8 ch.), D. equates the following three notions: becoming one with God, being ignorant of God, and the darkness characterized by the absence of words and thoughts. The ten letters confirm this theology (1; 5); they clarify issues such as the priority of the first principle over the deity (2) and the nature of Jesus (3; 4), they encourage steadfastness (6), they emphasize the power of the proof of truth (7), they encourage meekness and respect for the hierarchical structure of the Church (8), they deal with the symbolism of the Holy Scriptures (9), and they announce the return of St. John the Evangelist to Asia Minor (10).

Prior to 550, scholia were added by John, the bishop of Scythopolis, and up until Maximus Confessor (early 7th cent.), who was attributed with all of them. The corpus was translated by Sergius of Rēšʿainā (died in 536) into Syrian and reached the Occident in the 9th cent. where it exerted an enormous influence in the form of a Greek MS without any scholia (Par. gr. 437), given to Louis the Pious by Michael II in 827. This MS was given to the Abbey of Saint-Denys in Paris (due to the assumed identity of the author with its founder) and its text was translated into Latin in the 9th cent. under abbot Hilduin, then also by John Scotus Eriugena and Anastasius, the librarian, who used MSS that were annotated with scholia. The translation revised by John the Saracen between 1150 and 1167 received official status at the University of Paris and was confirmed by the translation of Robert Grosseteste (*c.* 1168–1263) in Oxford. Ambrogio Traversari (died in 1439) authored the first Renaissance translation (ed. princeps: Bruges 1480). The authenticity of the corpus has been questioned since Lorenzo Valla, followed by Erasmus.

→ Damascius; → Henotikom; → Iohannes of Scythopolis; → Marinus; → Michael II; → Maximus Confessor; → Neoplatonism; → Proclus; → Sergius of Rēšʿainā

P. Chevalier, Dionysiaca, 4 vols., 1937 (repr. 1989); G. Heil, A.M. Ritter, Corpus Dionysicum, 2nd vol., 1991/1; S. Lilla, Introduzione allo studio dello Ps. Dionigi l'Areopagita, in: Augustinianum 22, 1982, 533–577; M. Nasta, CETEDOC, Thesaurus Pseudo-Dionysii Areopagitae, 1993; R. Roques, L'univers dionysien, 1983; P. Rorem, Biblical and Liturgical Symbols within the Pseudo-Dionysian Synthesis, 1984. A.TO.

[55] **Exiguus.** ('the insignificant one', 'the small one'), important canonist, computist, and translator (*c.* 470–prior to 556). A monk from Scythia minor and close friend of → Cassiodorus (Cassiod. Inst. 1,23) who came to Rome *c.* 500. Equipped with an excellent knowledge of languages, he translated numerous works of Greek Christian literature into Latin. Among them are hagiographic texts (*Vita Pachomii i.a.*), Gregory of Nyssa's Περὶ κατασκευῆς ἀνθρώπου (*Perì kataskeuês anthrṓpou*) as well as diverse dogmatic writings from the 5th cent. (letters from Cyril of Alexandria to Nestorius, i.a.). The canonistic writings are very significant. On the request of bishop Stephan of Salona he put together a comprehensive collection and translation of Latin and Greek council canons (*Codex canonum ecclesiasticorum*). The revised Codex was later combined with the collection of decretals completed under Pope Symmachus (papal letters from Siricius, AD 384–399, up to Anastasius II, AD 496–498) into the *Collectio Dionysiana*. In his writings on the Easter calculations that had been suggested to him in 525 by Pope John I, he continued the Easter chart by Cyril of Alexandria. His use of the birth of Christ as the chronological fixed point (25 December 753 *ab urbe condita*) makes him the founder of Christian time-reckoning.

Edition: PL 67, 9–520; 73, 223–282; PL Suppl. 4, 17–22.
Bibliography: H. Mordek, s.v. D. (3), LMA 3, 1088–1092 (bibliography); Ch. Munier, L'œuvre canonique de Denys le Petit d'après les travaux du R.P. Wilhelm Peitz S.J., in: Sacris Erudiri 14, 1963, 236–250; G. Teres, Time computations and D. Exiguus, in: Journal for the History of Astronomy 15, 1984, 177–188. J.RI.

[56] **Dionysius.** *Procurator Asiae* in the year 211 (AE 1993, 1505), perhaps identical with Claudius D. (s.v. Claudius [II 22]). W.E.

Dionysodorus (Διονυσόδωρος; *Dionysódōros*).

[1] Taxiarch to Theramenes, betrayed to the Thirty by Agoratus (Lys. or. 13,30; 39–42). The latter was taken to court in 399/98 BC by D.'s brother and brother-in-law, Dionysius, the speaker of the 13th oration written by Lysias. ME.STR.

[2] Theban and Olympic winner. Sent as an ambassador to → Darius [3] and taken prisoner together with other Greek ambassadors by Parmenion in Damascus after the battle of Issus, then released unharmed by Alexander [4] the Great (Arr. Anab. 2,15,2f.). E.B.

[3] From Caunus (?), lived in the 2nd half of the 3rd cent. BC (for possible identification with other bearers of this name see [1. 108]). He solved the cubic equation arising from division of a sphere in a specified volu-

metric ratio dealt with by → Archimedes via the bisection of a parabola with a hyperbola (Eutocius, 152,27–160,2 HEIBERG). It is presumed that the same D. wrote a treatise entitled Περὶ τῆς σπείρας (*Perì tês speíras*, cf. Heron Alexandrinus, 3,128,3f. [5]), in which he defined the content of a → torus.

1 I. BULMER-THOMAS, s.v. Dionysodorus, Dictionary of Scientific Biography 4, 1971, 108–110 2 TH. L. HEATH, A History of Greek Mathematics, 2, 1921, 46, 218f., 334f. 3 J. L. HEIBERG (ed.), Archimedis opera omnia, 3, ²1915 4 W. SCHMIDT, Über den griech. Mathematiker Dionysodorus, in: Bibliotheca Mathematica, 3. Ser., 4, 1903, 321–325 5 H. SCHÖNE (ed.), Heronis Alexandrini opera quae supersunt omnia, 3, 1903. M.F.

[4] In 169/8 BC, D. was sent as an ambassador of Ptolemy VI and Ptolemy VIII to ask the Achaean League for help against Antiochus [6] IV.

E. OLSHAUSEN, Prosopographie 1, 1974, 71 no. 48. W.A.

[5] Sophist, see → Euthydemus

[6] **D. of Troezen.** Greek grammarian of the Alexandrine era (probably active in the 2nd half of the 2nd cent. BC), pupil of Aristarchus [4] of Samothrace. there is evidence that he had a very broad range of interests. The only Homeric fragment is to be found in schol. Hom. Il. 2,111 b, where Didymus [1] quotes him together with Ammonius in connection with a version of Aristarchus. Plutarch mentions him in connection with paroemiology (Vita Arati 1) as does Hesych (γ 616). He is quoted in relation to the grammatical question of pronouns by Apollonius Dyscolus (Grammatici Graeci II 1, De Pronomibus 3,16). The two treatises 'On rivers' (Περὶ ποταμῶν, schol. Eur. Hipp. 123) and 'Errors of the tragicians' (Τὰ παρὰ τοῖς τραγικοῖς ἡμαρτημένα, schol. Eur. Rhes. 508) are attributed to him in Euripides' scholia. Lucian (Pro lapsu inter salutandum 10) mentions him as the collector of the letters of Ptolemy Lagus. There is, however, a difficulty about attributing schol. Apoll. Rhod. 1,917 to this D. or the Boeotian historian of the same name from the 4th cent. BC [cf. 3].
→ Aristarchus [4]; → Didymus; → Ammonius [3] of Alexandria

1 A. BLAU, De Aristarchi discipulis, Jenae 1883, 43–44 2 L. COHN, s.v. D. (18), RE 5, 1005 3 F. JACOBY, FGrH 68 e Comm. 4 F. MONTANARI, SGLG 7, 1988, 89, 99 5 F. G. SCHNEIDEWIN, Paroemiographi Graeci I, praef. VII. F.M.

Dionysodotus From Sparta, presumably 6th cent. BC. Author of → paeans, which were performed at the Gymnopaedia together with the songs of → Thaletas and → Alcman (Sosibius FGrHist 595 F 5). L.K.

Dionysopolis (Διονυσόπολις; *Dionysópolis*). Settlement on the western coast of the Black Sea, today Balčik/ Bulgaria. There is evidence of settlement dating from Neolithic times. Nothing is known about the founding of the ancient city. On the basis of Ionic elements in inscriptions and the six indirectly identified Miletian phyles (IGBulg 1,15 ter), it is assumed that D. was probably founded by the Miletians in the 7th cent. BC. According to Ps.-Scymn. 75ff., D. was previously known as *Krounoí*; but according to Mela 2,22 *Krounoí* was the port for D. The first evidence of prosperity is found in the 3rd–2nd cents. BC: valuable marble statues, many imported goods and the autonomous minting of coins. D. was conquered in 71 BC by Lucullus, but 30 years later was in the hands of → Burebista, who spared the city following the intervention of a citizen by the name of Acornion (IGBulg 1,13). In 28 BC D. was re-conquered by M. Licinius Crassus, the proconsul of Macedonia, and incorporated into the province of Moesia under Tiberius. Member of the West Pontic *koinón* (IGBulg 1,14). Coin minting from the time of Commodus until that of Gordianus. Has yielded many valuable archaeological finds, including surgical instruments from a Roman grave. D. was destroyed in the 6th cent. by a flood; the city was supposedly a bishop's seat in 787, however there is no archaeological evidence of this except the 11th cent. Inscriptional evidence: IGBulg 1, p. 49ff.

B. GEROV, Zemevladenieto v rimska Trakija i Mizija, 1983, 17, 94ff.; N. EHRHARDT, Milet und seine Kolonien, 1983, 65f. I.v.B.

Dionysus (Διόνυσος; *Diónysos*)
I. RELIGION II. ICONOGRAPHY

I. RELIGION
A. SPECIAL FEATURES AND GENEALOGY
B. TRADITION C. AREAS OF INFLUENCE D. CULTS
E. MYTHS F. LATER RECEPTION

A. SPECIAL FEATURES AND GENEALOGY

D. is amongst the oldest of the Greek gods. Of all the Greek gods, his cult is the most widespread and his image is depicted most frequently; today, he is still the most fascinating and the most attractive from a modern point of view [1]. At the same time he is mythically one of the most untypical of the Greek gods. Amongst the untypical factors are: his double birth; the fact that he was regarded from birth as a deity, despite his mortal mother; his second, divine, mother; his death, and the opportunity for those initiated into his Mysteries to become divine beings or to be reincarnated.

According to Homer (Il. 14,325), D. is the last of Zeus' sons mentioned by name, by Semele, a mortal (cf. Hes. Theog. 940f.). Records of Persephone as D.'s mother are part of the knowledge of the Mysteries and therefore only appear at a later date (e.g. Diod. Sic. 5,75,4, according to Cretan tradition); veiled references to this can possibly already be found in the works of Pindar and Euripides [2. 318f.].

B. Tradition

1. Written records 2. Imagery and attributes

1. Written records

The earliest reference to the name of D. (*di-wo-nu-so*) is found in the Bronze Age, on three fragmentary Linear B tablets from Pylos and Chania on Crete (*c.*1250 BC). One of the Pylos tablets possibly refers to him in association with wine, as on the reverse the tablet lists women from a town named after wine (*wo-no-wa-ti-si*). The tablet from Chania provides evidence of a joint cult of Zeus and D. with honey libations [3. 76–79]. D. worship in an even older Cycladic cult shrine in Ayia Irini on Ceos [4. 39–42] remains unproven, as does the interpretation of the name *di-wi-jeu* on other Pylos tablets as 'son of Zeus' (= D.). Further to the linguistic explanation of the name D. as *nýsos* (in the sense of son) of Zeus, it has been suggested that the name derives from → Nysa, a location (mountain or plain) connected with D. since the time of Homer (Il. 6,133). There are references to D. in every type of literature ranging from Homer to Nonnus' *Dionysiaka*, with Attic drama containing the most references. D.'s marginal role in the Homeric epics (only mentioned on two occasions in both the *Iliad* and the *Odyssey*) corresponds to that of Demeter and has become even more puzzling following the discovery of Minoan-Mycenean D. worship. Written records of the cult (constantly being added to through new finds) document lively worship of D. over a period of 2,000 years, but only seldom provide generalizations or insights into specific ritual details.

2. Imagery and attributes

The earliest images, supported by addition of the name, are found in Attic black-figured vase painting dating from the 6th cent. BC and show D. as the god of wine (demonstrated by the attributes of a grape-bearing branch or an amphora). It is possible that he is depicted on a Cycladic ceremonial vessel dating from the 7th cent., together with a woman in bridal apparel [5. 55–58, fig. 10], possibly also evidenced by the depiction of an attribute later used as a specific reference to D., a → kantharos, a drinking vessel mainly used in cults worshipping heroes and the dead seen already in geometric Mycenean-influenced art [6. 45]. From the time of the first appearance of the god in pictorial art, D., his attributes (such as wine vessels, creeping ivy and later also vine foliage) and figures associated with him were widely represented into the period of Late Antiquity on all varieties of items bearing images, although initially the images appeared primarily on ceramics used by aristocratic citizens at → symposia or during cult worship of the dead. The images also appeared in increasing numbers on sarcophagi. The most important of the figures associated with him are the half-beast and often ithyphallic silenes and satyrs, with donkey, horse or ram attributes, and women (either grouped together with them or shown separately), who (dating in particular from the era of red-figured vase painting) are depicted as Maenads, shown by the use of specific clothing (animal skins), hair worn loose and ecstatic dance movements, snakes are also pictured with them and also the deer they have ripped to pieces. Beasts of prey (lions, leopards and panthers) are prominent amongst the animals depicted with D. and his associates. The → thyrsos, a stem of narthex or giant fennel with a pine cone on the end, is also often used as an attribute linking D. with his retinue. In general it can be stated that in (ceramic) pictorial art there is no area connected with myths, cults or 'everyday' issues that cannot be associated with D. and his sphere of influence. Even the 'ornamental' use of ivy leaves can denote that a picture has connections with Dionysian omens.

C. Areas of influence

1. Ritual ecstasy 2. Women 3. Wine 4. Eroticism 5. Music and dance 6. Theatre 7. Masks 8. Initiations and hopes for the afterlife 9. Polis society

1. Ritual ecstasy

The first mention of D. in literature (Hom. Il. 6,132) identifies him using the epithet *mainómenos* as the 'ecstatic' god. However, D. does not appear here or anywhere else in Homer as the god of wine. In respect of one special trait of his divinity — the transfer of his specific attributes to his worshippers — it is characteristic that ritual ecstasy, 'divine madness' (*theía manía*), plays a central role in his worship, both in terms of myth and the cult. Although other gods can also induce *ekstasis* (coming out of oneself; → Ecstasy) and *enthousiasmos* (inspiration — possession of a human by a god), ecstasy does not count as one of their identifying characteristics as it does in the case of D. In addition, the term (not verified in inscriptions before the advent of the Hellenistic age) *mainás*, literally 'frenzied woman', first appears in Homer (Il. 22,460), whilst women's ritual ecstasy seems to be an implicit prerequisite of D. worship. The cult's technical term for this is *bákchē*. Ritual ecstasy, *bakcheúein*, is often accentuated with (literary and cult-related) epithets and epicleses common to D., such as *Bakchios*, *Bakcheios* and *Bakcheus*. Analogous with the deity, a male worshipper may also be called *bákchos* (particularly in initiations into the Mysteries).

2. Women

The pre-eminence of women in D.'s circle is shown to advantage in the first Homeric reference to the god. There, the frenzied god is (Il. 6,132–134) in Nysa, surrounded by his wet-nurses, bearing *thýsthla* (thyrsi?). Like D., other Greek gods could also be worshipped by both sexes, however in cults it was often the case that women had a preference for female deities and men opted for male deities. But D. was predominantly worshipped by women. This would later seem to account for the physical effeminization of D. (of which there is literary and pictorial evidence dating from the Classical era and more thereafter). During ritual ecstasy (a state never stimulated by wine-drinking), married women apparently had access to more cult privileges (higher levels of initiation?) than young girls, and closer communion with the deity (cf. Diod. Sic. 4,3,3).

3. WINE

In Hesiod, D. is explicitly associated with wine production as a masculine sphere of influence (Op. 614). In addition, D.'s characterization as a 'joy to mortals' (according to Hom. Il. 14,325), has its origins, according to Hesiod, in the gift of wine. This gift is seen, however, as a 'mixed blessing', linked with toil or trials (Hes. Sc. 400; fr. 239, 1MW). Wine has appeared in lyric poetry as a source of poetic inspiration since the time of Archilochus (fr. 120 WEST). The danger of (undiluted) wine as a madness-inducing drug, or *phármakon*, was well known; it was therefore generally diluted with water. Viewing wine as a manifestation of D. (and therefore usable as a metonym) is known from the time of Eur. Bacch. 284 (cf. Eur. El. 497) onwards. The gift of wine is D.'s crucial cultural deed, reducing suffering; it makes life bearable and is a welcome complement to Demeter's gift of bread (cf. Eur. Bacch. 274–283). Images on vases generally show the god holding a drinking vessel (ancient drinking horn type: rhyton or cantharus). There are no images of a drunken D. before the Hellenistic Era. The images in Attic vase painting show wine production as a preserve of male beings, particularly satyrs, whilst the ladling and pouring of the wine is predominantly carried out by women in connection with D. worship. Except for aulos players and hetaera, women were excluded from the symposium — the principle point of which was the consumption of wine (from drinking vessels with Dionysian connotations). There are no pictures of women drinking wine (with the exception of drunken old women) and they are derided in Attic comedy (cf. Sappho fr. 2,16 PAGE on women's wine consumption on Lesbos in connection with the worship of Aphrodite). Drunkenness in men was also frowned upon, except on the occasion of specific organized feasts from which women were excluded.

4. EROTICISM

It was not a given in Greek tradition that eroticism and wine were linked together. The realization that excessive wine consumption has a deleterious effect on male potency is not a modern discovery. The Greeks primarily attributed the ecstasy associated with eroticism to the area of influence governed by Aphrodite and Eros. In black-figured vase painting, however, promiscuous sexuality and even erotic violence are more often associated with D.'s sphere of influence, although never with the actual figure of the deity and only infrequently with wine-drinking. According to the Homeric Hymn of Aphrodite (Hom. h. 5,263), the sileni enjoyed romantic trysts with nymphs in dark corners of caves. D. himself could be worshipped using the epithet χοιροψάλας (from χοῖρος, 'piglet', 'female genitals'; *choîros*: as a name for Maenads it has also been found on vase paintings [7. 176f.]) (in Sicyon [8. 208 No. 172]). In Euripides' 'Bacchae', the Theban king Pentheus wrongfully accuses the women of his city acting as Maenads of engaging in wild sexual union with men (Bacch. 217–225), however the Lydian Bacchae in the chorus know that during their ceremonies D. will lead them to places inhabited by Aphrodite, the Charites and Pothos, the god of yearning (Bacch. 402–416). It is impossible to judge whether the emphasis of Dionysian legitimized sexual promiscuity outside the limits of both the city and of marriage is male wishful thinking dating from antiquity, or whether its rejection touches on the undoubtedly greater repression on the part of modern male scholars [9]. It is assumed both by Euripides and other authors writing in antiquity that the bacchic women (and men?) were connected by a visionary erotic dynamic in their close contact with D. during ecstatic dances. This can also be inferred from the images seen in art. The important role of eroticism in D. worship is reflected in the pictorial, cultural and literary association of the god with Aphrodite and in the Phallophoria specific to his cult.

5. MUSIC AND DANCE

Dancing and music formed an integral part of the festive worship of all Greek deities. Chorus dancing, *choreúein*, was even regarded as synonymous with religious practice [10]. However, the most widely known dances were performed as the preparation to and part of dramatic performances connected to D. as god of the theatre. Drama is supposed to have evolved from the cult song specific to D., the → dithyrambus [11] (Aristot. Poet. 1449a10–12). The connection between this cult song and the initiation into the Dionysian Mysteries could possibly be traced back to Archil. fr. 120 WEST [12]. The predominance of wind and percussion instruments (*aulós*, *týmpanon*, *kýmbala*, *krótala*) in performances and worship associated with Dionysus is evidenced in particular by vase paintings. The use of string instruments was also permitted. The particular affinity of *aulós* music (both on stage and in cult settings) with cathartic orgies and Dionysian initiation ceremonies or *bakcheía*, was emphasized by Aristotle (Pol. 1341a21–25, 1341b32–1342b18), who therefore regarded this type of music as unsuitable for young boys.

6. THEATRE

D. reigned supreme in this area. This is particularly well documented in the case of Athens, the home of the great Attic tragedians and comic writers of the Classical era. Of the five most important Attic festivals dedicated to D., three (the rural Dionysia, the Lenaea, the Great Dionysia; → Dionysia) were heavily influenced by the theatre. In antiquity, the theatre buildings themselves often belonged to D. sanctuaries (e.g. in Athens). All stage productions were assigned to D. in the festival calendars of the Greek motherland, Asia Minor and the Italian and Pontic colonies. The festival preparations included sacrifices, processions and musical performances in his honour. As a statue he was present as a spectator at the performances. Of the three types of drama, D.'s links with the satyr plays are the most obvious (on account of the chorus of satyrs). In Attic comedy the divine patron of the theatre was, however, often used in a variety of ways for the communication of comic and politically critical intentions. The notion that plots of Attic tragedies had 'nothing to do with D.' has been abandoned as recent scholarship has increasingly highlighted the fact that the plays were actually determined by D. and Dionysian themes, his cult characteristics, areas of influence and functions [13; 14; 15].

7. Masks

There is also evidence of the use of masks in the cult worship of other (particularly female) deities (Artemis, Demeter), however in the case of D. the mask represents a manifestation of the god himself. Only he is 'the Mask God'. The Lenaea vases document the worship of the god in the form of his mask (or double mask) hung on a tree, a pillar or a column. The worshippers are women 'serving wine' or circle dancing (also dancing with satyrs) [16. 212–214; 17]. In a wide variety of ways, vase painting conveyed to the symposiasts the simultaneous presence and absence of D. through frontality, not least in, black-figured eye cups. Art and drama exploited the ecstatically effective qualities (simultaneous distance and proximity, deathly rigidity and suggestive liveliness) of the frontal aspect of the mask under the sign of D. Masks were inextricably linked to theatrical performances in antiquity (initially only to distinguish the age and genders of the players and not to identify their roles [18. 85–98]). The mask enabled the 'transforming union' and 'unifying transformation', which is characteristic of acting in antiquity (performed by male players only) and which qualifies the mask, also in a cult context, as an 'instrument of mystery' [19].

8. Initiations and hopes for the afterlife

Together with Demeter, D. must be regarded as the most important Greek deity of the Mysteries. Plato (Phdr. 265b4) even identifies D.'s characteristic *manía* as *telestikḗ* ('integral to the initiations'). However, the verb *bakcheúein,* which has its origins in cult language, covers the entire spectrum of ecstatic Dionysian rituals and is not used solely for the Mysteries. In contrast to those of Demeter, D. Mysteries were not limited in terms of location and were organized by private cult associations (in private houses?). They were clearly outside the areas governed by the polis societies. There is no definite evidence in the case of Attica. Cult documents were uncovered by burial site finds of small gold tablets in the 19th cent. (from Greek Southern Italy, Thessaly and Crete) but only more recent discoveries have enabled the interpretation of the former as evidence of Bacchic Mysteries [20]. The documents (e.g. Hdt. 4,79) show that it is probable that the cult was practiced (by men and women) at least since the 5th cent. BC [21. 27f.]; it is even possible that details in archaic lyric poetry dating from the 7th cent. could be interpreted in this sense [12; 22]. Dionysian initiation cults were practiced into Late Antiquity [23]. The Bacchic Mysteries did not only convey the hope of a blissful afterlife, but promised rebirth, even deification. Death by lightening, animal metamorphosis and wine can be determined as central elements of the experience of the Mysteries. These obviously also included all the specific qualities that Aristotle (without reference to the Mysteries) listed in the characterization of Attic tragedy (*páthos*, *éleos* and *phóbos*, *hedonḗ*, *peripéteia*, *anagnṓrisis*, *metabolḗ*, *mímēsis*, *kátharsis*). Shared qualities of and differences between D. Mysteries and tragedy lead to many as yet unanswered questions [24]. This is also true of the supposed connection between Orphicism and the D. epiclesis → *Zagreus* (as yet unproven in cult documentation).

9. Polis society

D. was one of the most important deities for the Greek city-states. Like Artemis, he was a god 'outside' as well as 'inside' the polis, even (as in Athens) at its centre [25]. More than all other deities, he accentuates all the ways in which boundaries may be crossed, including the boundaries between the city and the countryside or wilderness. During the reign of the Peisistratids in Athens, or at the latest during the reforms introduced by Cleisthenes, he became the most important city god after Athena. The main festival in his honour, the City (or Great) Dionysia, which in the Classical era also included the staging of the most important drama agones (contests), specifically integrates the whole polis regardless of phratria membership, including metics and any guests, particularly those from the colonies. The power (by no means limited to Athens) of D. worship to politically integrate encompassed men, women and children of all strata in society, with the result that D. was far from being just a 'rustic' or 'aristocratic' deity.

D. Cults

1. Sacrifices 2. Epicleses 3. Festivals and cult sites 4. Joint cults 5. Cult colleges 6. Ruler cult

1. Sacrifices

As was the case with other polis deities, D. was worshipped with sacrifices and food offerings. The 'classic' sacrifices of cattle were (as was always the case) reserved for special festive occasions, whilst sacrifices of pigs, sheep and goats were more usual occurrences [26]. He was also brought non-meat sacrifices and gifts such as cakes. In addition, his presence in the wine libations which accompanied the sacrificial proceedings as a matter of course, were a constitutive element of the worship of almost all other deities.

2. Epicleses

In the case of D., as with all other Greek deities, the cults and cult epicleses were strongly differentiated in terms of topography and heortology. In Etruria from the 5th, perhaps even from as early as the 7th cent. BC, he was identified with → Fufluns [27], in Rome he was worshipped as Liber pater and known in literature by the epiclesis → *Bacchus*, which had its origins in the cult. The image of the deity in the cult is influenced mainly by material determined by Athens, which is only applicable to a limited extent for other regions. D. had a number of cults outside Attica under a variety of epicleses (the most obvious: D. *Mystes*, in Arcadian Tegea). Amongst the most important epicleses, with evidence found at several sites (aside from the more generally widespread epicleses, those emphasizing the *bakcheúein* and those often connected with ecstatic cults) are *Lysios* (Corinth, Sicyon) or *Lyaios* (Mantinea), the 'liberator', and *Phleus* (only in Ionia: Chios, Ephesus, Erythrae), 'he who swells'. In addition, numerous other epithets emphasize the god's close relationship to flourishing nature, both animal and botanical, to wine, to certain landscapes and also to the organization of the polis (e.g. D. *Polites*: Heraea in Arcadia). The D. who 'feeds on raw flesh' *Omestes* (Lesbos) and *Omadios* (Chios) were seen of particular importance in the history of the religion by means of their assumed links to the ecstatic shredding of flesh and Dionysian *ōmophageín* — brought to particular mythic prominence by Euripides' 'Bacchae' — (cf. LSAM 48); there is, however, no historical evidence of human sacrifices. A more likely assumption is that (as at the → Agrionia festival in Boeotia) antagonism between the sexes was acted out in ritual form in the cult [28].

3. Festivals and cult sites

In additional to the festivals celebrated annually, D. worship also included a rule (there is also evidence that this was sometimes also the case for other gods such as Athena, Zeus and Poseidon) that certain festivals could only be celebrated after an interval of two years, i.e. every third year. In the case of D., there is evidence of this triennial festival system for example in Delphi, Thebes, Camirus, Rhodus, Miletus and Pergamon (cf. also his epiclesis *Trieterikos* on Melos). In principle, D. is distinguished in particular by his temporary absence. However, this does not mean that D. was the 'foreign' god, the 'coming' god, on account of his historically late adoption from non-Greek regions, as per the influential claims made by Rohde and Dodds. Rather, the welcome 'coming' of the god reflected to a great extent his striking powers of liberation, which could also be politically effective (in Eretria: LSCG, Suppl. 46 [29]). He is welcomed as a guest, *xénos*, in the polis, fed and entertained, and this to a particularly impressive extent during the City or Great → Dionysia in Athens (in the month of Elaphebolion). In addition to this main festival and the two other festivals mainly dedicated to drama, there are two other significant festivals for D. in Athens: the → Anthesteria (preceding the Great Dionysia in the festival calendar), the 'oldest Dionysia' (Thuc. 2,15,4), predating the Ionic Migration, and the → Oschophoria after the conclusion of the grape harvest in Pyanopsion, the month following the Eleusinian Mysteries. In regions other than Attica, the significance of the god in the festival calendar is emphasized by references to D. contained in the names of the months, such as *Bakchiō̃n* (Mykonos and Ceos). Despite the presence of D. Lenaios in Athens and his festival the → Lenaea (derived from *lênai*, 'frenzied women'), Bacchic frenzies were forbidden to women in Attica; they were only permitted to go to Delphi to attend joint Bacchic ceremonies and dances as *thyiádes* (meaning the same as *lḗnai* and *bákchai*) together with the Delphic women in Parnassus [30]. The propagation of the Bacchic women's cult from Delphi is documented by an oracle of the Hellenistic era, I. Magn. 215(a), according to which three Theban *mainádes* are dispatched to establish the Bacchic *órgia* (cult rituals) and *thíasoi* of D. Bacchus in Magnesia on the Maeander [31].

4. Joint cults

Some of the oldest cult comrades of D. are Zeus (in Bronze Age Crete), Hera (Lesbos; cf. Heraea in Aracadia) and Demeter and Core (Eleusis, Sicyon and Thelpusa). There is also evidence of joint cults with numerous other deities (in particular Aphrodite, Apollo, Artemis and Hermes), with Semele, his Theban mother, and also with Hercules.

5. Cult colleges

The spread of Dionysian associations was particularly pronounced during the Hellenistic and Roman eras (e.g. the → *Iobakchoi* in Athens in the 2nd cent. AD, with strictly regulated drinking practices). Amongst those cult colleges connected to the Bacchic D. (although specific D. worship is not always documented) are the *Bakchi(a)stai* (Cos and Thera) and the *Bakcheastai* (Dionysopolis). The relationship of the aristocratic family of the Bacchiadae, who ruled Corinth from the 8th to the 7th cent. BC, to D. is uncertain.

6. Ruler cult

In Hellenism, D. was awarded a central role in the ruler cult (e.g. Ptolemy IV as the 'New D.'). The autocratic D. of Euripides' 'Bacchae' is the precursor of these rulers and the corresponding Hellenistic deities [32. 204f.].

E. Myths

The few details about D. in the works of Homer already include key elements of the mythic image (and probably also of the cult variant) in poetic form. These include the ecstatic experience of the switch from one extreme to the other and, in particular, the pursuit of Dionysian women by a man. In Homer, it is → Lycurgus (Il. 6,130), who is identified as an Edonian king in the later tradition and whose hostile role is represented, for instance, in Thebes by King Pentheus, in Argus by Perseus, and in Thrace by → Orpheus. His punishment corresponds to the law of myth, as with any other *theomáchos*. Non-Homeric tradition also includes groups of women rebelling against the god: the daughters of Minyas from Orchomenus in Boeotia, the daughters of Proetus from Argus and, in particular, the Theban daughters of Cadmus, sisters of D.'s mother Semele (the best dramatic representation is in Euripides' Bacchae). The pinnacle of the women's punishment is when Dionysus uses the ritual ecstasy which distinguished his worship to drive the women to kill their own sons. In later versions, both women named by Homer as having an intimate connection with D., his mother Semele and his lover → Ariadne, remain examples to which his female followers aspire. Thebes becomes a Bacchic *mētrópolis* on account of Semele (Soph. Ant. 1122). Ariadne, daughter of Minos, who, according to Homer is the lover of D. and is killed by Artemis,(Od. 11,321–325) and is then, according to Hesiod, made immortal by D. (Theog. 947–949), serves as a model for later Dionysian women (other mortal lovers of D.: Althaea, Carya, Physcoa, perhaps also Erigone; sons: e.g. Oenopion). The identification of anonymous brides of D. in vase paintings as Ariadne (or Aphrodite) remains unverified, particularly in the case of early antiquity. The exemplary image of Dionysian women (as of D. himself), probably also a cult prerequisite, is also applied to his mother, Semele, whom according to later records he also made immortal (Iophon fr. 22 F 3 TGF). According to the myth, when she died following being struck by Zeus' thunderbolt, D. was born prematurely and then born a second time from Zeus' thigh. Even the mythical hints of D.'s particular proximity to the cult of the dead are already apparent in Homer, when the god gives Achilles' mother Thetis a golden vessel (also used for wine) (*amphiphoreús*, Od. 24,74) in which to gather the mortal remains of her dead son. The sea goddess Thetis (later analagous with Persephone), with whom D. finds a safe haven when he is pursued by Lycurgus (Hom. Il. 6,136), also has a fairly prominent position in early Dionysian art, as the god appears at her wedding with Peleus (even shown on the François Vase with an amphora as a gift). In D.'s arrival myths, the sea represents the origin of his epiphany and scene of his miracles (specifically: wine miracles, the god's metamorphosis into a lion and the metamorphosis of the hostile sailors into dolphins, Hom. h. 7,35–53). Miracles involving fluids also distinguish the power of the mythical D. in other areas (e.g. springs of water, wine, milk and honey, Eur. Bacch. 704–711; the maenads also suckle the young of wild animals, ibid. 699f.). D.'s own experience of a violent death, as demonstrated in the cult, probably particularly in the Mysteries (god's grave in Delphi: Callim. fr. 643), is reflected in the ways that both Semele and Ariadne die, as well as in the figures of his male antagonists, who are mythically aligned with him (cf. also the Titans in the myth of D. Zagreus). In the myths, the overcoming of death is demonstrated by the women closely associated with him. He masters death and can even be equated with Hades (Heracl. fr. 15 D.-K.). Mythically, D. actually appears as the 'most terrible and the most lenient' of all gods (*deinótatos, ēpiótatos*: Eur. Bacch. 861).

F. Later reception

Even after the end of pagan cult practice, D. continued to pose a challenge to artists and academics both in representation and significance (the first instances date from the Renaissance and the later mainly from the 19th cent.). The D. of antiquity cannot merely be reduced to the lighthearted 'wine, women and song', but must be regarded both culturally and mythically as a polyvalent god and a blend of divine and mortal, female and male, animal and human, pain and desire, sacrificial object and subject — this is all contained in the current interpretational consensus with its critical roots in NIETZSCHE'S *The Birth of Tragedy*. In recent times, efforts to understand the myths, in particular those concerning *sparagmós* and the omophagy practiced by maenads as an accurate reflection of common cult practice, have been abandoned. The complexity of the relationships between Dionysian myths and cults does, however, still encompass many problems to which a satisfactory solution has not yet been found. W.F. OTTO's view of D. as a deity revealed is now superseded by the concept of D. as the representation of complete 'Otherness' (VERNANT). Many of the god's polarities, empathetically defined by OTTO, found expression in the emphasis of either his embodiment of the 'indestructibility of life' (KERÉNYI) or his quality of being intoxicated by death (DETIENNE). Anthropological comparisons shed more light on 'the Dionysian'. However, the D. of antiquity remains 'different' and 'elusive' (HENRICHS).

1 A. HENRICHS, Loss of Self, Suffering, Violence: The Modern View of Dionysus from Nietzsche to Girard, in: HSPh 88, 1984, 205–240 2 W. BURKERT, Homo necans, 1972 3 E. HALLAGER, M. VLASAKIS, B.P. HALLAGER, New Linear B Tablets from Chania, in: Kadmos 31, 1992, 61–87 4 M. E. CASKEY, The Temple at Ayia Irini, Ceos 2, 1986 5 D. PAPASTAMOS, Melische Amphoren, 1970 6 C. ISLER-KERÉNYI, Dioniso con una sposa, in: Metis 5/1–2, 1990, 31–51 7 A. KOSSATZ-DEISSMANN, Satyr- und Mänadennamen auf Vasenbildern des Getty-Museums und der Sammlung Cahn, in: Greek Vases in the J.P.Getty Museum 5, 1991, 131–199 8 A. TRESP, Die Fragmente der griech. Kultschriftsteller, 1914 9 R. SCHLESIER, Mischungen von Bakche und Bakchos. Zur Erotik der Mänaden in der ant. griech. Tradition, in: H. A. GLASER (ed.), Annäherungsversuche. Zur Gesch. und Ästhetik des Erotischen in der Lit., 1993, 7–30 10 A. HENRICHS, 'Warum soll ich denn tanzen?' Dionysisches im Chor der griech. Tragödie, 1996 11 B. ZIMMERMANN, Dithyrambos. Gesch. einer Gattung, 1992 12 D. MENDELSOHN, ΣΥΓΚΕΡΑΥΝΩΘ: Dithyrambic Language and Dionysiac Cult, CJ 87, 1992, 105–124 13 R. SEAFORD, Dionysiac Drama and the Dionysiac Mysteries, in: CQ 31, 1981, 252–275 14 R. SCHLESIER, Die Bakchen des Hades. Dionysische Aspekte von Euripides' Hekabe, in: Metis 3, 1988, 111–135 15 A.F.H. BIERL, D. und die griech. Tragödie. Polit. und 'metatheatralische' Aspekte im Text, 1991 16 J.-P. VERNANT, Figures, idoles, masques, 1990 17 F. FRONTISI-DUCROUX, Le dieu-masque. Une figure du D. d'Athènes, 1991 18 C. CALAME, Le récit en Grèce ancienne. Énonciations et représentations de poètes, 1986 19 K. KERÉNYI, Mensch und Maske (1948), in: Id., Humanistische Seelenforschung, 1996, 265–277, 321–323 20 F. GRAF, Dionysian and Orphic Eschatology: New Texts and Old Questions, in: T.H. CARPENTER, C.A. FARAONE, 1993, 239–258 21 W. BURKERT, Ant. Mysterien. Funktionen und Gehalt, 1990 22 R. SCHLESIER, Das Löwenjunge in der Milch. Zu Alkman, Fragment 56 P. [= 125 CALAME], in: A.

Bierl, P.v. Möllendorff (ed.), Orchestra: Drama – Mythos – Bühne. FS H. Flashar, 1994, 19–29 23 R. Merkelbach, Die Hirten des D. Die D.-Mysterien der röm. Kaiserzeit und der bukolische Roman des Longus, 1988 24 R. Schlesier, Lust durch Leid: Aristoteles' Tragödientheorie und die Mysterien. Eine interpretationsgeschichtliche Studie, in: Eder, Demokratie, 389–415 25 C. Sourvinou-Inwood, Something to do with Athens: Tragedy and Ritual, in: R. Osborne, S. Hornblower (ed.), Ritual, Finance, Politics. Athenian Democratic Accounts Presented to David Lewis, 1994, 269–290 26 F.T. van Straten, Hierà kalá. Images of Animal Sacrifice in Archaic and Classical Greece, 1995 27 L. Bonfante, Fufluns Pacha: The Etruscan Dionysus, in: T.H. Carpenter, C.A. Faraone, 1993, 221–235 28 Graf, 74–80 29 A.-F. Jaccottet, Le lierre de la liberté, in: ZPE 80, 1990, 150–156 30 M.-C. Villanueva Puig, À propos des thyiades de Delphes, in: L'association dionysiaque dans les sociétés anciennes, 1986, 31–51 31 A. Henrichs, Greek Maenadism from Olympias to Messalina, in: HSPh 82, 1978, 121–160 32 H.S. Versnel, Ter Unus. Isis, D., Hermes. Three Studies in Henotheism, 1990.

Burkert, 251–260, 432–443; T.H. Carpenter, Dionysian Imagery in Archaic Greek Art. Its Development in Black Figure Vase Painting, 1986; Id., Dionysian Imagery in Fifth-Century Athens, 1997; T.H. Carpenter, C.A. Faraone (ed.), Masks of Dionysus, 1993; G. Casadio, Storia del culto di Dioniso in Argolide, 1994; S.G. Cole, Voices from beyond the Grave: D. and the Dead, in: T.H. Carpenter, C.A. Faraone, 1993, 276–295; M. Daraki, D., 1985; M. Detienne, D. mis à mort, 1977; Id., D. à ciel ouvert, 1986; E.R. Dodds, The Greeks and the Irrational, 1951; A. Geyer, Das Problem des Realitätsbezuges in der dionysischen Bildkunst der Kaiserzeit, 1977; J.E. Harrison, Prolegomena to the Study of Greek Religion, 1903; G.M. Hedreen, Silens in Attic Black-figure Vase-painting. Myth and Performance, 1992; A. Henrichs, Changing Dionysiac Identities, in: B.F. Meyer, E.P. Sanders (ed.), Jewish and Christian Self-Definition, vol. 3: Self-Definition in the Graeco-Roman World, 1982, 137–160, 213–236; Id., Myth Visualized: D. and His Circle in Sixth-Century Attic Vase-Painting, in: Papers on the Amasis Painter and His World, 1987, 92–124; Id., Der rasende Gott: Zur Psychologie des D. und des Dionysischen in Mythos und Lit., in: A&A; 40, 1994, 31–58; H. Jeanmaire, D. Histoire du culte de Bacchus, 1951; M. Jost, Sanctuaires et cultes d'Arcadie, 1985; K. Kerényi, D. Urbild des unzerstörbaren Lebens, 1976; F. Lissarague, Un flot d'images. Une esthétique du banquet grec, 1987; M. Massenzio, Dioniso e il teatro di Atene. Interpretazioni e prospettive critiche, 1995; F. Matz, Die dionysischen Sarkophage, 4 vols., 1968–1975; G. Maurach, D. von Homer bis heute. Eine Skizze, in: Abh. der Braunschweig. Wiss. Ges. 44, 1993, 131–186; O. Murray, M. Tecusan (ed.), In Vino Veritas, 1995; R. Osborne, The Ecstasy and the Tragedy: Varieties of Religious Experience in Art, Drama, and Society, in: C. Pelling (ed.), Greek Tragedy and the Historian, 1997, 187–211, fig. 1–13; W.F. Otto, D. Mythos und Kultus, 1933; A. Pikkard-Cambridge, The Dramatic Festivals of Athens, 21968; G.A. Privitera, Dioniso in Omero e nella poesia greca arcaica, 1970; E. Rohde, Psyche. Seelencult und Unsterblichkeitsglaube der Griechen, 1890/1894; A. Schachter, Cults of Boeotia 1, 1981; A. Schöne, Der Thiasos. Eine ikonographische Unt. über das Gefolge des D. in der att. Vasenmalerei des 6. und 5. Jh. v.Chr., 1987; R. Seaford, Reciprocity and Ritual. Homer and Tragedy in the Developing City-State, 1994; Id. (ed.), Euripides. Bacchae, 1996; E. Simon, Festivals of Attica. An Archaeological Commentary, 1983; J.-P. Vernant et al., La cité des images. Religion et société en Grèce ancienne, 1984; J.J. Winkler, F.I. Zeitlin (ed.), Nothing to Do with D.? Athenian Drama in Its Social Context, 1990. RE.S.

II. Iconography

Early representations of D. on a Melian amphora dating from the 7th cent. BC (Athens; British School; in front of woman wearing chiton and himation), and in Attic vase painting from the early 6th cent. BC (Dinus of → Sophilus, London, BM, *c.* 580 BC: marriage of Peleus and Thetis; in the same scene and in the return of Hephaestus to Olympus on the François Vase, Florence, *c.* 570 BC; → Siana cups by the Heidelberg and Amasis Painters, 575/555 BC). Vase paintings of D. and his retinue, in particular from the 6th cent. BC. Frequently the scenes with Ariadne (in addition to Attic vase paintings, see also bronze craters from Derveni, Thessalonica, *c.* 330 BC). D. appears in the scene of the battle with the giants in the northern frieze of the Siphnian treasury at Delphi (*c.* 525 BC), on the Pergamon altar (western frieze, southern projection, 180/160 BC: see also D. Kathegemon as patron god of the Attalids). There are few depictions of D.'s sea journey, such as on an eye cup by Execias (Munich, SA, *c.* 530 BC) or on an amphora in Tarquinia (end of 6th cent. BC).

Large sculptural representations date from somewhat later: torso of a seated statue from Icaria (Athens, NM, *c.* 520 BC, identified via Cantharus); the cult image of D. 9,20,4 by → Calamis in Tanagra (475/450 BC) as recorded by Paus. 9,20,4 has not been preserved. The image of the bearded D. in a long robe, known as Sardanapal (Athens, NM, 360–330 BC; unverified attribution to → Cephisodotus the Elder and → Praxiteles) is taken from the D. Theatre in Athens. The column masks, common in the 6th–5th cents. BC, also showed a bearded image; these masks were the method by which D.'appeared' at cult festivities (marble mask from Icaria, Athens, NM, 2nd half of the 6th cent. BC). From the 5th cent. BC: D. is shown as a youthful god, clean-shaven and athletic (in the eastern frieze in the Parthenon, 442–438 BC; cf. lying figure of D. in the eastern pediment of the Parthenon, 438–432 BC).

D.'s attributes are ivy wreaths, vine branches, the thyrsus, the cantharus, the nebris and panther skin; D. often appears accompanied by wild animals; his retinue consists of maenads, satyrs and sileni. As is the case with very few other gods, D. is shown in the form of a child: statue groups with Hermes (Praxiteles, Olympia, *c.* 330 BC) and with Silenus (Munich, GL; Paris, LV, Roman copies of Early Hellenistic originals.).

There are numerous Roman images of D./Bacchus to be found in murals (D. and Ariadne: Villa dei Misteri, Pompeii, *c.* 60 BC), and also in mosaics: drunk D. leaning on a satyr (D. mosaic in Cologne, *c.* AD 225), the dispatch of Icarius (Nea Paphos/Cyprus, end of 3rd cent. AD), triumph of D. (Sousse/Tunisia, from Hadrumentum, beginning of the 3rd cent. AD.; Tunis, Bardo Museum, from Acholla, beginning of the 2nd cent. AD). There are also many images in relief: stucco relief from the Villa Farnesina (Rome, MN, *c.* 20 BC), stucco relief on the tomb of the Pancratii (Rome, AD 165/170) and the sarcophagi dating from the 2nd–3rd cents. AD. Amongst the statues which have been preserved are the D./Bacchus portrayed as a hunter in a belted chiton and boots, with thyrsus and panther (Copenhagen, NCG, 2nd cent. AD), the bronze D. from the Tiber (Rome, TM, beginning of the 1st cent. AD). There are also images of D. following the tradition of Apollo Lykeios with his arm bent over his head: the Bacchus of Versailles, with *nebris* (formerly Paris, LV, Hadrianic) and D./Bacchus in the Villa Albani in Rome, with the himation around his hips (Hadrianic).

F. BERTI (ed.), D. Mito e Mistero. Conference Commacchio 1989, 1991; S. BOUCHER, LIMC 4.1, s.v. D./Bacchus, 908–923 (with older bibliography); T.H. CARPENTER, Dionysian Imagery in Archaic Greek Art, 1986; F. FRONTISI-DUCROUX, Le dieu-masque, 1991; C. GASPARRI et al., LIMC 3.1, s.v. D., 414–540 (with older bibliography); Id., LIMC 3.1, s.v. D./Bacchus, 540–566 (with older bibliography); F.W. HAMDORF, D.-Bacchus. Kult und Wandlungen des Weingottes, 1986; C. ISLER-KERÉNYI, D. und Solon, in: AK 36, 1993, 3–10; E. POCHMARSKI, D.-Rundplastik der Klassik, 1974; S.F. SCHRÖDER, Röm. Bacchusbilder in der Tradition des Apollon Lykeios, 1989; D. WILLERS, Typus und Motiv. Aus der hell. Entwicklungsgesch. einer Zweifigurengruppe, in: AK 29, 1986, 137–150. A.L.

Diopeithes (Διοπείθης; *Diopeíthēs*).

[1] Author of Old Comedy, only known from inscriptions; probably won at the Dionysia for the first time in 451 BC [1. test.].

1 PCG V, 1986, 43. B.BÄ.

[2] Athenian oracle consultant and fanatical opponent of the enlightenment promoted by → Pericles. Following his petition it was decided in 437/6(?) BC to prosecute those who did not believe in the gods or who disseminated teachings on supernatural matters (→ *eisangelía*). The petition resulted in the *asebeia* case against → Anaxagoras [2], but was ultimately directed at Pericles (Plut. Pericles 32; Diod. Sic. 12,39,2). It is possible that he was the same D. who spread the word in Sparta of the oracle prophecies counselling against → Agesilaus [2] succeeding to the throne (Xen. hell. 3,3,3; Plut. Agesilaus 3; Lysander 22).

M. OSTWALD, From Popular Sovereignty to the Sovereignty of Law, 1986, 196–198 and 525–536; PH. A. STADTER, Plutarch's Pericles (comm.), 1989, 298–300. R.B.

[3] D., son of Diphilos from the deme of Sunium; follower of → Demosthenes and an Athenian *strategos* active in the northern Aegean region between 343/2 and 341/40 BC. With official orders to escort Athenian kleruchs to the Thracian area of the Chersonnes, D. intervened on his own authority — with Athen's silent support — in the battle between → Philippus II and Cardia, put together a company of mercenaries with which he went to war in Thrace — also without any official orders from Athens — thereby provoking Philip II. Demosthenes expressly approved this action and ensured that D.'s unauthorized action was not only forgiven, but that he received reinforcements in March 341. D.'s activities contributed significantly to the escalation of the tension between Athens and Philip. This D. was presumably the same prominent Athenian connected to Ephialtes' legation whose gift of money from the Persian king did not arrive until after his death. This would mean that D. died in 340/39 (cf. Aristot. Rh. 2,8,11 1386a14; Dem. Or. 8 passim with lib. hypothesis; Dem. Or. 9,15; 73; Ps.-Dem. Or. 12,3f.; 16; schol. Aeschin. In Ctes. 83; Dion. Hal. ad Amm. 10; Dion. Hal. De Deinarcho 13; Philochorus FGrH 328 F 158; Lucian Enc. Dem. 35; 37).

→ Athens; → Strategos

DAVIES 168; DEVELIN no. 910; PA 4327; SCHAEFER 2[2], 451–480. J.E.

Diophanes (Διοφάνης; *Diophánēs*).

[1] *Strategos* of the Arsinoites 224–18 BC; most of the P. Enteuxeis texts date to his time in office. PP 1,247.

N. LEWIS, Greeks in Ptolemaic Egypt, 1986, 56ff. W.A.

[2] 2nd-cent. BC Greek rhetor from Mytilene; exiled from his homeland for political reasons, he went to Rome and became the teacher and friend of Tib. → Gracchus. Together with C. → Blossius [2] from Cumae, he is supposed to have had a strong influence on Gracchus' politics. In 132 he was killed shortly after Tib. Gracchus (Cic. Brut. 104; Str. 13,2,3; Plut. Tib. Gracchus 8,5).

M. GELZER, KS 2, 1963, 77f. M.W.

[3] Epigrammatic poet from Myrina, author of a witty distichon of unknown origin (from the 'Garland' of Philippus?) about Eros (Anth. Pal. 5,309). E.D.

Diophantus (Διοφαντός; *Diophantós*).

[1] Author of comedies, dates unknown; one fragment and the title of one play (Μετοικιζόμενος) have been preserved.

1 PCG V, 42. H.-G.NE.

[2] From Sinope, son of Asclepiodotus, commander to Mithridates VI Eupator. In 110 BC he provided skilful military and diplomatic support to the inhabitants of the city of Chersonesus and thus enabled them to withstand the Scythians (Str. 7,3,17). In return for this he was rewarded with an inscription in his honour (SIG[3] 709; SEG 30, 963, see [1]). He conquered Theodosia and Panticapaeum and founded Eupatoria in the Western Crimea.

1 Z.W. RUBINSTEIN, Saumaktos: Ancient History, Modern Politics, in: Historia 29, 1980, 50–70.

CAH 9, [2]1994, 139; A. MEHDI BADI[C], D'Alexandre à Mithridate, vol. 5, 1991, 69–71, 78–83, 89.

[3] Son of Mithares, commander to Mithridates VI, who sent him to Cappadocia in 73 BC (Memnon c. 37, FHG 545). He and his army were completely vanquished there in 71 BC (Memnon c. 43, FHG 549). ME.STR.

[4] Greek mathematician

A. LIFE B. WORKS C. LATER RECEPTION

A. LIFE

D. worked in Alexandria. He must have lived after → Hypsicles and before → Theon of Alexandria; it is generally assumed that his *akmḗ* was *c.* AD 250. If the dates contained in an epigram in the *Anthologia Graeca* [1. vol. 2, 60f.] are correct, D. reached the age of 84.

B. WORKS

D.' sprincipal work is the 13 books of the Ἀριθμητικά (*Arithmētiká*), six books of which have been preserved in Greek (editions in [1]) and four books (presumed to be the original bks 4–7) have only been preserved in the Arabic translation (editions in [2] and [3]). The work itself is unusual for Greek mathematics and follows the Babylonian algebraic tradition. D. deals with determinate and, more especially, indeterminate (i.e. problems where there are more unknowns than equations) linear and quadratic equations using symbols in a very abbreviated algebraic form. The problems are formulated in straightforward arithmetic. They are ordered only partially in a systematic fashion; there is wide variation in the methods — these are tailored to the individual problems and surprising tricks are often used. The problems dealt with in the surviving Greek and Arabic books are listed in modern form in [2. 461–483].

In the introduction D. explains how to multiply and divide the powers of unknowns, how to multiply polynomials and how to combine terms to the same power. The method is to reduce all identical terms until one equation remains with only one term on each side.

Book 1 is concerned with linear and quadratic equations which only have a positive solution. These problems are similar to phrased algebraic problems, which had been very popular since the time of → Archimedes; they do not reveal any new content.

The remaining books are more interesting. Here indeterminate linear and quadratic equations are dealt with in expert fashion. D. only allows positive rational numbers as solutions and is generally satisfied with one solution from amongst a usually infinite number of solutions. Equation systems are reduced to equations with only one unknown. D. knew the general solution of the equation $x^2 + y^2 = z^2$ (which the Babylonians and the Pythagoreans could already solve), special methods of solving indeterminate solutions in the form $Ax^2 + Bx + C = y^2$, when A or C are squares, and a method of solving the equation system $ax^2 + bx + c = y^2$, $dx^2 + ex + f = z^2$. D. was also aware that certain numbers could not be written as the sum of three squares.

D. already used symbols for the unknowns, their powers, the reciprocal powers and the absolute term; they are usually the initial letters of the corresponding words: M^o = μονάς (*monás*) = unit; ς = ἀριθμός (*arithmós*) = unknown x; Δ^Y = δύναμις (*dýnamis*) = x^2; K^Y = κύβος (*kýbos*) = x^3; $\Delta^Y\Delta$ = δυναμοδύναμις (*dynamodýnamis*) = x^4; ΔK^Y = δυναμόκυβος (*dynamókubos*) = x^5; K^YK = κυβόκυβος (*kybókybos*) = x^6. In terms of the calculations, he only knew the sign for subtraction (⋔), which is either an inverted Ψ or a combination of the initial letters Λ and I of the stem of λείπειν (*leípein*). Terms to be added together are simply written next to each other. Other elements of calculation (e.g. multiplication and equals signs) are expressed in words.

Fragments also survive of a (not very significant) treatise on polygonal numbers (Περὶ πολυγώνων ἀριθμῶν, *Perì polygṓnōn arithmôn* [1. vol. 1, 450–481]). Other works that have been lost are *Porísmata*, which D. refers to in the *Arithmētiká*, and *Moriastiká* (calculating with fractions). The presumably not genuine manuscripts are edited in [1. vol. 2, 3–31].

C. LATER RECEPTION

The Greek MSS of the *Arithmētiká* (see [8]) go back to an archetype (now lost) dating to the 8th or 9th cent. This work was known to Arab mathematicians; there was a comm., and in the 9th cent. Qusṭā ibn Lūqā translated (at least) four books into Arabic. In Byzantium Maximus → Planudes wrote a comm. on books 1 and 2. In 1463 Regiomontanus discovered a Greek D. manuscript. BOMBELLI dealt with some of D.'s work in his 'Algebra' (1572). In the Early Baroque era P. DE FERMAT in particular was active in developing the modern theory of numbers via the continuation of D.'s trains of thought. The Greek first edition was produced by BACHET DE MÉZIRIAC (1621); the 2nd edition (1670) contains FERMAT's comments.

→ Mathematics

EDITIONS AND TRANS.: 1 P. TANNERY (ed.), Diophanti Alexandrini opera omnia cum Graecis commentariis, 2 vols., 1893–1895 2 J. SESIANO, Books IV to VII of Diophantus' *Arithmetica* in the Arabic Translation Attributed to Qusṭā ibn Lūqā, 1982 3 R. RASHED (ed.), Diophante. Les arithmétiques. Tome III, livre IV. Tome IV, livres V, VI, VII. Texte établi et traduit, 2 vols., 1984 4 P. VER EECKE (ed.), Diophante d'Alexandrie. Les six livres arithmétiques et le livre des nombres polygones. Oeuvres traduites pour la première fois du grec en français. Avec une introduction et notes, 1926 (repr. 1959) 5 G. WERTHEIM, Die Arithmetik und die Schrift über Polygonalzahlen des Diophantus von Alexandria, 1890 6 A. CZWALINA, Arithmetik des D. aus Alexandria, 1952 7 TH. L. HEATH, Diophantus of Alexandria. A Study in the History of Greek Algebra, [2]1910.

LITERATURE: 8 A. ALLARD, La tradition du texte grec des *Arithmétiques* de Diophante d'Alexandrie, Rev. Hist.

Textes 12/3, 1982/3, 57–137 9 I.G. Bašmakova, Diophant und diophantische Gleichungen, 1974 10 J. Christianidis, *Arithmetike stoicheiosis*: Un traité perdu de Diophante d'Alexandrie?, in: Hist. Math. 18, 1991, 239–246 11 Th. L. Heath, A History of Greek Mathematics, II, 1921, 448–517 12 E. Lucas, Recherches sur l'analyse indéterminée et l'arithmétique de Diophante, 1961 13 J.S. Morse, The reception of Diophantus' *Arithmetic* in the Renaissance, 1981 (diss. Princeton Univ.) 14 K. Vogel, s.v. Diophantus of Alexandria, Dictionary of Scientific Biography 4, 1971, 110–119 15 J. Sesiano, s.v. Diophantus of Alexandria, ibid., 15, 1978, 118–122 (supplements K. Vogel) 16 B.L. van der Waerden, Erwachende Wiss., [2]1966, 457–470.

M.F.

Diophilus, Diophila Preserved on the POxy. 20, 2258C fr. 1 in addition to the fragments of the *Plokamós Bereníkēs* by Callimachus are nine hexameters of an astrological poem which have thematic and linguistic links to Aratus and Callimachus. An exact identification of the author's name (Diophilos/Diophila) is not possible. The verses were quoted on the papyrus as they also concern the 'Lock of Berenice'.

R. Pfeiffer, Callimachus 1, 1949, 118–120; SH 179–181

C.S.

Dioptra (ἡ διόπτρα; *hē dióptra*). Surveyor's instrument for measuring angles and distances or the lateral width of distant objects (e.g. the apparent distance of stars from one another and the height of walls and mountains). The applications included the construction of aqueducts, house-building or fire-telegraphy (cf. Pol. 8,37,2; 9,19,8f.). At the beginning of his work entitled *D.*, which covers the theory and practice of surveying and mapping (πραγματεία διοπτρική), Hero of Alexandria (1st cent. AD?) documented in detail the construction and operation of this measuring instrument. Following his description, the *dioptra* can be pictured in its simplest form as a 1.85m long, 7.7cm wide ruler equipped with a builder's level (ὁ πλάγιος κανών) and a metal tile with a viewing hole attached to one end ('eye piece'). Another metal tile could be moved by the observer up and down a groove in the ruler. Focussing on the object to be measured through the viewing hole, the movable metal tile is pushed to the point where it obscures the observer's view of the object. After reading the measurement from the ruler and noting the measurement from the movable metal tile it was then possible to determine the angle or the apparent distance using Hipparchus' chord tables (cf. also Vitr. De arch. 8,5,1; Suda s.v. D.; and the outline in [1]).

Sources on D.: Eucl. Phaen. 1; Pappus, In alm. Ptolem. p. 87–108 Rome; Geminus, Introductio in astron. 1,4–6 (astronomical uses); Pol. 8,37,2; 9,19 (military uses); 10,45,6ff. (invention of a double tube system by Cleoxenus and Democleitus for the observation of light signals); Theon of Smyrna, p. 124f. Hiller (measurement of mountain heights by Dicaearchus and Eratosthenes)

→ Surveyors

1 S. Sambursky, s.v. D., LAW, 1965, 758.

A.G. Drachmann, D., in C. Singer (ed.), A History of Technology 3, 1957, 609ff.; Id., s.v. D., RE Suppl. 6, 1287–1290 (with fig. 1–3); P. Delsedime, Uno strumento astronomico descritto nel corpus Archimedo: La d. di Archimede, in: Physis 12, 1970, 173–196; F. Hultsch, s.v. D., RE 5, 1073–1079; Id., Winkelmessung durch die Hipparchische D. (Abh. zur Gesch. der Mathematik 9), 1899, 191–209; A. Lejeune, La dioptre d'Archimède, in: Annales de la société scientifique de Bruxelles (1)61, 1947, 27–47; O. Neugebauer, A History of Ancient Mathematical Astronomy 2, 1975, 845–848.

E.O. and V.S.

Diores (Διώρης; *Diṓrēs*).

[1] Son of → Amarynceus [1]. One of the four leaders of the Epeians from Elis who went to Troy. He was killed by the Thracian Peirous (Hom. Il. 2,622; 4,517; Paus. 5,3,4).

W. Kullmann, Die Quellen der Ilias, Hermes ES 14, 1960, 98 and 162; E. Visser, Homers Katalog der Schiffe, 1997, 569–573.

[2] Father of → Automedon, chariot driver to Achilles and Patroclus (Hom. Il. 17,429).

[3] Son of Priamus, companion of → Aeneas. At the funeral games for Anchises he participated in the race (Verg. Aen. 5,297; Hyg. Fab. 273,16). He was later killed by → Turnus (Verg. Aen. 12,509).

L. Polverini, s.v. D., EV 2,87f.

R.B.

Diorthotes see → Copy

Dioscorides (Διοσκουρίδης; *Dioskourídēs*).

[1] Son of Polemaeus, nephew of → Antigonus [1] Monophthalmus. Led the fleet to a few victories as naval commander in 314–13 BC. Nothing further is known about his life.

R.A. Billows, Antigonus the One-Eyed, 1990, 381f.

E.B.

[2] Polyhistor of the 4th and 3rd cents. BC, pupil of Isocrates (Ath. 1,18,11 A). Of his works, the following titles are known (cf. FGrH 3 B 594): 1. *Apomnēmoneúmata* ('Memorabilia'), a manuscript of which the contents are unknown, with which Hegesander (*c.* 150 BC) was familiar; 2. *Lakṓnōn politeía* ('The Spartan State'; Plut. Lyc. 11,9); 3. *Nómima* ('Customs'); 4. *Perí tōn hērṓōn kat' Hómēron bíou* ('Lives of heroes according to Homer'). The individual attributions are uncertain, not least because one or several of the works could have been written by D. of Tarsus, mentioned in an inscription (Inscr. Cret. Cnossus 12, p. 66 Guarducci = Syll.[3] 721), a grammarian who lived around AD 100.

E. Schwartz, s.v. D. (7), RE 5, 1125–29.

M.W.

[3] Writer of epigrams of the 'Garland' of Meleager (cf. Anth. Pal. 4,1,24, where the wording Διοσκουρ- is favoured over the more widely used Διοσκορ-) who

came from an otherwise unspecified Nicopolis (according to the lemma of 7,178). He lived in the 2nd half of the 3rd cent. BC, as suggested in the *epitaphios* for the comic actor Machon (7,708, cf. Ath. 6,241f.), in Egypt, mostly in Alexandria (cf. Anth. Pal. 11,363 and 6,290; 7,76; 7,166; 9,568). 40 of his epigrams have been preserved; these are mainly funerary or erotic (9,734 may perhaps be added here): of his funerary epigrams, those dealing with authors of the past (Sappho, Anacreon and Thespis, Aeschylus, Sophocles, Sositheus) are particularly informative — they demonstrate a strong interest in historical literary forms (cf. in particular. 7,37; 410f.); the erotic epigrams, however, do in places show a particular dependence on Callimachus and more especially Asclepiades [1], but are also distinguished by an equally lively and prejudice-free realism. It is particularly noticeable that he has a certain preference for exotic rituals and customs (cf. 6,220 on the cult of the Cybele; 5,53 about Adonis; 7,162 regarding Pers. beliefs) and for antiquarian questions (cf. 9,340 on the invention of the *aulós*); and thus should one understand the attempts to rehabilitate the reputation of Philaenis (7,450) and the unfortunate daughters of Lycambes (7,351), against Archilochus. As in the case of other contemporary writers of epigrams (Damagetus, Alcaeus of Messene etc.) his works contain characteristic praise of Spartan ideals (7,229; 430; 434). From the time of Antipater of Sidon onwards, D. is often emulated by the later epigram writers. It is possible that he is the same person as the epic poet D. mentioned in the schol. Apoll. Rhod. 1,740 (cf. Anth. Pal. 11,195).

GA I,1, 81–94; 2, 235–270. E.D.

[4] Author of New Comedy, only known from inscriptions; victorious at the Lenaea in the 3rd cent. BC [1. test.].

1 PCG V, 1986, 43. B.BÄ.

[5] Known as Phacas on account of his facial warts, lived in Alexandria and was a Herophilean physician and influential adviser to Ptolemy Auletes and Ptolemy XIII. On the orders of the latter, he undertook an ambassadorial mission to Achillas in 48 BC during which he was killed or at least seriously wounded (Caes. B. Civ. 3,109). He wrote 24 medical books, which 'were all very well-known' (Suda s.v. D.), and a polemic about hippocratic lexicography in seven vols. (Erotianus [1] 91), quoted by Galen 19,105 and Paulus of Aegina (CMG 9,1,345) in connection with the treatment of swellings. It is possible that this is the same D. who together with Poseidonius wrote about an epidemic of bubonic plague in Libya (Orib., CMG 9,1,345), this has, however, not been verified.
→ Medicine

1 E. Nachmanson, Erotianos, 1918. V.N.

[6] Courtier of Ptolemy XII and his envoy to Rome; D. accompanied Serapion in BC 48 as an envoy for Ptolemy XIII (i.e. for Caesar) to → Achillas, where he or his co-envoy were murdered. If D. survived, it is possible that he was identical with D. the physician [5], Phacas. (PP 6,14601; 16594). W.A.

[7] Mosaicist from Samos; used the signature ΔΙΟΣΚΟΥΡΙΔΗΣ ΣΑΜΙΟΣ ΕΠΟΙΗΣΕ for two *emblemata* (→ Mosaic) from the 'Villa of Cicero' at Pompeii (Naples, MN) showing scenes from New Comedy, probably copies of originals from the 3rd cent. BC. The type of script used in the signatures dates the mosaics to the 1st cent. BC.

R. Bianchi Bandinelli, EAA 3, 132f., s.v. D. (fig., bibliography). C.HÖ.

[8] Most famous gem cutter of the Augustan era, probably from Aegeae (Cilicia), as implied by the signature of his son, → Eutyches [2. 541ff.]. D. was the *praepositus* ('manager') of the imperial workshop in Rome, where apart from his sons Eutyches, → Herophilus and → Hyllus he also employed the apprentices Agathopus, Saturnius and Epitynchanus [1. 317f.]. Around 28–17 BC according to Plin. HN 37,8 and Suet. Aug. 50, he is reputed to have cut the (lost) seal bearing the portrait of → Augustus [1. 315f.[54], 317[62]; 2. 542f.]. Seven intaglii bearing his signature demonstrate that his works generally consisted of portraits and reproductions of mythical scenes and statues: bust of → Io (cornelian, Florence, AM), bust of → Demosthenes (amethyst, private collection), theft of the Palladion (cornelian, Devonshire Collection), → Bellerophon tames → Pegasus (cornelian fragment, Boston, MFA), → Hermes with the head of a ram (cornelian, London, BM), → Hermes, frontal view (cornelian, Cambridge, FM) — in the same vein as the 'Phocion' in the Vatican —, and also similar to the standing → Achilleus (cornelian Naples, MN) [1. 317[63–69] pl. 91,5–9, pl. 92,1.2]. The sardonyx with → Hercules and → Cerberus (Berlin, SM) also provides evidence that in addition to his mastery of intaglio cutting, he was also an accomplished cameo craftsman [1. 316[61] pl. 91,4; 2. 542f. fig. 1, 2]. Several unsigned works are attributed to him and his workshop on the basis of the style: the 'Gemma Augustea' and the 'Great French Cameo' [1. 318f.[82]] and Winckelmann's 'Drunken Bacchus' being among these [1. 338[253ff.]; 2. 543 fig. 3]. Gems bearing D.'s forged signature are common. [3. 400f. fig. 50]. The numerous copies bear witness to the influence of his works [1. 338f.[258f.]].
→ Gem and cameo cutters; → Gem cutting

1 Zazoff, AG 2 E. Zwierlein-Diehl, Griech. Gemmenschneider und augusteische Glyptik, in: AA 1990, 539–557 3 Id., Antikisierende Gemmen des 16.–18. Jh., in: Pact. Revue du Groupe européen d'études pour les techniques physiques, chimiques et mathématiques appliquées à l'archéologie 23, 1989, 373–403 4 U. Pannuti, Cataloghi dei Musei e gallerie d'Italia. Mus. Arch. Naz. di Napoli. La collezione glittica II, 1994, 216f. no. 183.

T. Gesztelyi, Die Probleme der Meister, der Werkstatt und der Koine in der Steinschneidekunst, in: Der Stilbegriff in den Altertumswiss. conf. Rostock 1993, 19–21. S.MI.

[9] D. the Younger, known as ὁ νεώτερος or ὁ γλωττογράφος. Grammarian in the early 2nd cent. AD. His edition of Hippocrates was as highly regarded as that of his relation and contemporary, Artemidorus, and was used by Galen together with other editions as the basis for his commentary on works by Hippocrates. D. used highly scientific methods (Gal. CMG V,10,2,2,66; 319) and was completely prepared to emend the Hippocratic texts, including numerous older and more complex versions. He used the punctuation marks and diacritics typical for Alexandrian editors of literary texts; made corrections where necessary and removed sections he deemed not to be authentic (CMG V,10,2,2,415; V,9,1,58). His notes on the authenticity of individual sections of *De natura hominis*, *De morbis* and *Epidemiae VI* must have been used in an introductory hypothesis on or brief biography of Hippocrates. D. compiled a glossary of Hippocratic terms, which filled several books, (Gal. 19,63,68), and in which he was forced to leave out three quarters of the lexis because of a lack of space, although he claimed to have explained every single word used in the writings of Hippocrates. Galen, however, complained that D. included many entries that needed no explanation or were immediately understandable. Although his glossary did not form part of his edition of Hippocrates, it was closely linked to the text selected by D. and demonstrated his excellent knowledge of the Hippocratic corpus as well as his familiarity with etymological issues. Galen made consistent reference to D.'s edition and to that of Artemidorus. Some of his notes as to which version he preferred have been preserved in medieval manuscripts of Hippocratic texts.

→ Medicine; → Philology

J. Ilberg, Die Hippokratesausgaben des Artemidoros Kapiton und D., in: RhM 45, 1890, 111–137; D. Manetti, A. Roselli, Galeno commentatore di Ippocrate, in: ANRW II 37.2, 1617–1633; W. D. Smith, The Hippocratic Tradition, 1979, 235–240; M. Wellmann, s.v. D. (11), RE 5, 1130–1131. V.N.

[10] **Pedanius D.** see → Pedanius

Dioscorus (Διόσκορος; *Dióskoros*).

[1] Patriarch of Alexandria (444–451). In terms of ecclesiastical politics, he aimed to achieve the highest standing for his patriarchy and in terms of theology he promoted the teaching of the pre-eminence of the divine nature of Christ (moderate → Monophysitism). When the radical Monophysite → Eutyches was sentenced in 448, D. took his side and, with the help of the Emperor Theodosius II, asserted his will at the 'Robber Synod' of Ephesus (451) and deposed Flavianus, the patriach of Constantinople. However, he was soon himself removed from office by the Emperor Marcianus after the Council of Chalcedon in 451, although only on the charge of misuse of authority. He died in exile on 4th Sept. 454. The Monophysites regarded him as a saint, as evidenced by his Syriac *vita* [1].

1 F. Nau (ed.), Histoire de Dioscore, patriarche d'Alexandrie, écrite par son disciple Théopiste, in: Journal Asiatique 1, 1903, 5–108, 241–310 (Syriac with French trans.).

W. H. C. Frend, The Rise of the Monophysite Movement, 1972, 25–48; A. Grillmeier, H. Bacht, Das Konzil von Chalkedon, I-III, [5]1979; F. Haase, Patriarch Dioskur I. von Alexandrien nach monophysitischen Quellen, Kirchengesch. Abhandlungen 6, 1908, 141–236. G.MA.

[2] Coptic advocate and poet from Aphrodito in Upper Egypt (*c.* AD 520 — 585). He visited Constantinople around AD 550. The preserved papyrus fragments include petitions, contracts and an essay on weights and measures. D. compiled a Greek-Coptic glossary. In addition Greek occasional poems have also been preserved: encomia in hexameters and iambs, epithalamia, panegyric poetry — all with a variety of mythical content. D. had no feel for the quantities in verse; it is possible that his language was influenced by Coptic phonology and syntax.

E. Heitsch (ed.), Die griech. Dichterfragmente der röm. Kaiserzeit 1, 1961, 127–152; A. H. M. Jones, The Later Roman Empire 1, 1964, 407–408; L. S. B. Mac Coull (ed.), Dioscorus of Aphrodito, 1988. C.S.

Dioscuri (Διόσκουροι, Διοσκόρω; *Dióskouroi, Dioskórō*).

I. Religion II. Iconography

I. Religion

Divine twins, regarded as sons of Zeus; they appear repeatedly in Greek mythology. The most important (alongside the Theban D. → Amphion and → Zethus) were the Spartan ones, whose most ancient name probably was *Tindarídai*. In Attica, they were often invoked as Ἄνακτες (*Ánaktes*: 'masters'). Their individual names — Castor (Κάστωρ) and Polydeuces (Πολυδεύκης) — as well as their characters in general are presumed to be of Indo-Germanic origin, and academic studies frequently link them with the Indo-Germanic twin riders '*Aśvin*'. In Rome, they were called Castores.

Whereas the D. in the great Homeric epics were sons of the Spartan king → Tyndareus (Hom. Od. 11,298ff.), the Cypriots considered Castor, the tamer of horses, to be mortal, his siblings — Polydeuces, the boxer, and → Helena by contrast were immortal children of Zeus and → Leda (Cypria fr. 8 PEG I; Apollod. 3,126; Hyg. Fab. 77).

The spread of the D. cult beyond Laconia probably led to the emphasis of the descent of both (Hom. h. Diosc.17,2; 33,1; Pind. Pyth. 11,62). They were frequently opposed by other heroic pairs: They defended their sister Helena against the Hippocoontids and also rescued her from Attica, where she was kept after being abducted by → Theseus and Peirithous. Attica, and, according to some, Athens itself were laid waste (Alcm. fr. 21 PMGF; Hellanicus FGrH 4 F 168). The fortress of Aphidna, where Helena was hidden, fell after the betrayal by Academus or respectively Deceleus, whose town traced its historic friendship with Sparta back to this deed (Hdt. 9,73; Plut. Thes. 32 p. 15d-f). Theseus' mother Aethra had to accompany Helena as her handmaid, and the D. installed → Menestheus as king in Athens (Ael. VH 4,5; Apollod. epit. 1,23). The D. were not involved in Helena's return from Troy; the explanation being that they had already found their end by then (Hom. Il. 3,236–244). Their most important dispute was with the Apharetidae → Idas and → Lynceus. In what is probably the original version, they quarrelled over cattle which they had rustled together: Idas, being greedy, had divided the animals up unfairly and driven them to Messenia (Cypria fr. 15 PEG I; Pind. Nem. 10,60ff.; Apollod. 3,135f.). An ambush by the D. (Castor lying in hiding in a hollow tree) was discovered by the eagle-eyed Lynceus, who then stabbed the mortal brother. Polydeuces revenged his brother's death by killing Lynceus; Zeus struck Idas with lightning; both Apharetidae were incinerated. According to the version which was more common later on, the D. abducted the brides of the Apharetidae, Hilaeira and Phoebe, daughters of Leucippus (Theoc. 22.137ff.; Ov. Fast. 5.699; Hyg. Fab. 80). In the fight for the girls, both Apharetidae were killed, but in most of the records, the mortal Castor also died. However, Polydeuces was permitted to share his immortality with his fallen brother, so that the twins spent alternate days in Hades and in the upper world or rather Olympus (Hom. Od. 11,301ff.; Pind. Nem. 10,55ff.).

The D. were seen as participating in most of the mythical group adventures, such as the Argonautic expedition, when Polydeuces won victory over Amycus, king of the Bebryces (Theoc. 22,27), and the Calydonian boar hunt (Apollod. 1,67); they were at the funeral games for Pelias (Stesich. fr. 178 PMGF) and appeared as victors in Heracles' Olympic Games (Paus. 5,8,4). Reputedly, they founded the city of Dioscurias on the Pontus, and they bore an image of Ares out of Colchis (Paus. 3,19,7). The → Leucippids bore them their sons Anaxis and Mnasinos (Paus. 2,22,5, in Apollod. 3,134: Anogon and Mnesileos). They were initiated into the mysteries of Eleusis (Xen. Hell. 6,3,6) and Samothrace (Diod. Sic. 5,49); from the Hellenistic period onwards, they seem at times to merge with the Samothracian → Cabiri (Paus. 10,38,7). Like the latter, the D. were called upon particularly in distress at sea, when their epiphany as a stellar constellation, possibly also by way of St. Elmo's fire, brought help (Hom. H. Diosc. 33,10f; Alc. fr. 34 Poet. Lesb. Fr. LOBEL PAGE; Hdt. 2,43; Eur. Hel. 1495ff.; Lucian Nav. 9). Later, they were identified with the constellation of Gemini (Ps.-Eratosth. Katast.10). They appear as helpers in distress, σωτῆρες (*sōtêres*) generally (Str. 5,3,5; Ael. VH 1,30), and in battle. In Sparta, where they had reputedly invented the armed war-dance and the Spartan attack formation was named after Castor (Plut. Mor. 1140C), they were closely linked with the royal house: If a king stayed at home during an armed conflict, it was believed that one of the D. also stayed behind (Hdt. 5,75). As riders on white mounts, they allegedly came to the help of the Italian Locrians in the battle at the Sagra river (Iust. 20,2–3). They were frequently worshipped with a *theoxenia*, a banquet shared with divine guests (Pind. Ol. 3 with schol.; Nem. 10,49f.), however, they also had their own temples (Argos: Paus. 2,22,5) and occasionally strangely shaped cult images (Pephnus: Paus. 3,26,3).

Their cult was particularly widespread in the Peloponnese: Sparta, Therapne, and Argos all claimed to posses graves of the D., where they were assumed to live underground (Alcm. fr. 7 PMGF; Pind. Nem. 10,56ff.). Furthermore, in Sparta their house was known (Paus. 3,16,2); families in both Argos and Sparta claimed to be descendants of the D. The *Anaktes* enjoyed their own cult all over Greece, as well as in Attica and also Cyrene and Sicily. The D. were also worshipped separately.

The veneration of the D. probably reached Rome via Italian cities such as Lavinium, Ardea, or possibly also Tusculum (Cic. Div. 1,43,98), which in turn had adopted it from the *poleis* of Magna Graecia — without Etruscan intermediaries. A D. cult was instituted in Rome at the latest after their epiphany in the battle at Lake Regillus 499–6 BC (Cic. Nat. 2,2,6; 3,4,11; Liv. 2,20,12; Dion. Hal. Ant. Rom. 6,13,1–3); in 484, their temple on the Forum Romanum was dedicated (Liv. 2,42,5), with Castor, the equestrian hero, becoming the more eminent: In Rome, the D. were referred to as *Castores* and were closely linked with the water nymph → Iuturna from Ardea. It was at her spring on the forum that they watered their horses after the battle of Lake Regillus. The large-scale → *transvectio equitum* was dedicated to them (Dion. Hal. Ant. Rom. 6,13,4). The brothers were also frequently invoked in oaths.

E. BETHE, s.v. D., RE 5, 1087–1123; F. CASTAGNOLI, L'introduzione del culto dei Dioscuri nel Lazio, in: Studi Romani 31, 1983, 3–12; P. FAURE, Les Dioscoures à Delphes, in: AC 54, 1985, 56–65; A. FURTWÄNGLER, s.v. D., Roscher 1.1, 1154–1177; M. GUARDUCCI, Le insegne dei Dioscuri, in: ArchCl 36, 1984, 133–154; F. GURY, s.v. D./Castores, LIMC 3.1, 608–635; A. HERMARY, s.v. D., LIMC 3.1, 567–593; W. KRAUS, s.v. D., RAC 3, 1122–1138; TH. LORENZ, Die Epiphanie der D., in: Kotinos, FS E. Simon, 1992, 114–122; B. POULSEN, The Dioscuri and ruler ideology, in: Symbolae Osloenses 66, 1991, 119–146; Il senso del culto dei Dioscuri. Atti del Convegno svoltosi a Taranto nell'aprile 1979, Taranto 1980. T.S.

II. ICONOGRAPHY

In Sparta, where the D. were known as Tyndarids, they were depicted with their Laconian cultic attributes, the *dokana* (marble stele, Sparta, 1st half of the 6th cent. BC), two amphoras and two snakes (marble stele, Sparta, early 5th cent. BC?); comparable are also the D. on Tarentine votive tablets or the 4th/3rd cents. BC (Taranto, National Museum). An Attic kylix by Oltus provides early evidence of the Etruscan Dioscuri cult, the Tinas Cliniar (Tarquinia, National Museum, late 6th cent. BC). The oldest and most characteristic attribute of the D. is the horse (skyphos fragment from Perachora, Athens, NM, 590–580 BC, with inscriptions); other attributes: lance and sword, *piloi* (sometimes encrusted with stars), stars (without *piloi*: cf. cameo in Vienna, Kunsthistor. Mus., 3rd cent. BC). In pictorial representations, they also mostly appear as twins, often identical, facing each other. As protectors and saviours of their sister Helena, they appeared, according to Paus. 3,18,14f. on the throne of Apollo in Amyclae (2nd half of the 6th cent. BC). On a painting by Polygnotus in the Anakeion on the Athenian Agora, they were depicted together with the Leucippids (2nd half of the 5th cent. BC: Paus. 1,18,1), the abduction of the Leucippids also features on the south frieze of the Siphnian treasury in Delphi (*c.* 525 BC), on the north frieze of the Heroon of Gölbaşı-Trysa (Vienna, KM, *c.* 370 BC) as well as on vase paintings particularly of the 5th cent. BC (column krater in Ferrara, 440/30 BC). They are depicted as participants in the Calydonian boar hunt (François Crater, Florence, UF, *c.* 570 BC; from the Roman period on the Meleager sarcophagi) and in the voyage of the Argonauts — for the latter particularly the duel between the D. Polydeuces and Amycus, king of the Bebryces (see also image of the Argonauts on a metope of the tuff-built Sicyonian Treasury in Delphi, *c.* 560 BC; a second metope shows the Dioscuri's cattle raid) — or in a theoxenia, their cultic banquet. The 'Boxer at Rest' (Rome, TM) is possibly also depicted as one of the D. (probably a portrait of Attalus II of Pergamum, *c.* 170 BC).

In Italy, numerous representations of the D./Castores (temple on the Forum Romanum, early 5th cent. BC) are extant: of Roman sculpture, one can mention the group from Lacus Iuturnae adjacent to their temple, with horse protome (Rome, Ant. Forense, late 2nd cent. BC), as well as the colossal group on the Capitolium in Rome (*c.* AD 120) and also the 'Horse Tamers of Monte Cavallo' (Rome, Quirinal, presumably AD 150/180), the latter two both with fully sculpted horses. In Venice, there is also a statue of one of the D. as a horse-tamer (Arch. Mus., AD 175–195); this type of representation also appears frequently on coins and reliefs (altars, tomb steles); cf. also the group of statues from San Ildefonso in Madrid (Prado, early 1st cent. AD, interpretation uncertain).

→ Dioscuri of Monte Cavallo

P.J. Connor, Twin Riders, in: AA 1988, 27–39; S. Geppert, Castor und Pollux, 1996; N. Kunisch, Zwillingsreiter. Studien zur Mythologie. FS K. Schauenburg 1986, 29–33; L. Nista (ed.), Castores. L'immagine dei Dioscuri a Roma, 1994; R.D. de Puma, LIMC 3.1, s.v. Dioskouroi/Tinas Cliniar, 597–608; R. Stupperich, Das Dioskurenrelief in Dortmund, in: Boreas 8, 1985, 205–210.

A.L.

Dioscurias (Διοσκουρίας; *Dioskourías*). Greek *pólis* and port (Ps.-Scyl. 81) on the eastern shore of the Black Sea, mod. Suḫumi/Abhazia, according to Eratosthenes (Str. 1,3,2; 2,5,25) the easternmost coastal town of the Pontus Euxinus. No exact dates of foundation; the pottery suggests that it was founded by Milesians in the 6th cent. BC (Arr. Peripl. p. eux. 10,4; Anon. Per. p. E. 7B). Important commercial centre for trade with the tribes of the Caucasus. 70 tribes gathered there to trade in wood, honey, flax, wax, pitch, and salt (Str. 11,2,16; 5,6). Mithridates VI retreated to D. after his defeat by Pompey in 66 BC (App. Mith. 101). After that the town presumably fell into ruin and was flooded. Under Augustus, Sebastopolis was founded nearby. The only autonomous coinage dates to the period of Mithridates VI. There is hardly any archaeological evidence, as the site of the ancient D. is partly submerged, partly beneath the mod. city of Suḫumi.

V.A. Kuftin, Materialy k arheologii Kolhidy, 1, 1949; N. Ehrhardt, Milet und seine Kolonien, 1983, 84f. (with bibliography).

I.v.B.

Diospolis

[1] **D. Magna.** (μεγάλη Διόσπολις; *megálē Dióspolis*) in the Graeco-Roman era the name of the ancient *wꜣst* in Upper Egypt, thus named because of the identification of → Zeus and → Amun, whose greatest temple was located there. In the name *Djeme* (*Ḏꜣmt*/*Ṯꜣmt*), a southern district of the city on the west bank of the Nile, the Greeks recognized their *Thēbai* (→ Thebes) [2. 465–473].

[2] **D. Parva.** (μικρά or respectively ἄνω Δ; *mikrá* or *anō D.*), in the Graeco-Roman era the name of the ancient *ḥwt sḫm*, indicating a local Amun cult, mod. Hu, capital of the 7th nome of Upper Egypt on the west bank of the Nile [3. 64].

[3] **D. Inferior.** (κάτω Δ; *kátō D.*), in the Graeco-Roman era the name of the ancient (*pꜣ*) *jw-n-jmn*, 'Island of Amun', mod. Tall al-Balāmūn, south-west of Damiette. In the New Kingdom capital of the 17th Nome of Lower Egypt [1. 319–321].

1 J. Malek, s.v. Tell el-Belamun, LÄ 6
2 R. Stadelmann, s.v. Theben, LÄ 6 3 K. Zibelius, s.v. Hu, LÄ 3, 64–68.

R.GR.

[4] see → Cabyle

[5] see → Dia [5]

Diotima (Διοτίμα; *Diotíma*). In the introduction of his discourse on Eros in Plato's *Symposium* (201d), Socrates claims that he would only pass on what he had learned from D., a wise priestess from Mantinea, who allegedly obtained for Athens a ten-year moratorium of the plague from the gods. The dialogue of the *Symposium* is thus interrupted. The D.-interlude consists of two parts: the first explains the nature of Eros, the second his power. In his epilogue, Socrates indicates his conviction that these teachings are correct. It is impossible to conclude whether or not D. was a historical person. Hölderlin adopted the character of D. as a result of his studies of Plato [1].

1 P. Wapnewski, Der umarmende Buchstabe. Zu Hölderlins Gedichtentwurf D., in: D.H. Green et al. (eds.), From

Wolfram and Petrarch to Goethe and Grass, 1982, 563–568.

D.M. HALPERIN, Why is D. a woman? Eros and the Figuration of Gender in: Id. et al. (eds.), Before Sexuality, 1990, 257–308; K. SIER, Die Rede der D., 1997. R.B.

Diotimus (Διότιμος; *Diótimos*).

[1] Athenian, son of Strombichides, from Euonymon (his family is known into the 3rd cent.). *Strategos* in Corcyra in 433/32 BC (Thuc. 1,45,2; IG I³ 364,9); 439–32 *nauarchos* at Neapolis (Timaeus FGrH 566 F 98); he may have led a legation to Susa (Str. 1,3,1). Perhaps identical with D. in Ath. 10,436e.

FRASER/MATTHEWS (1); DAVIES, 4386. K.KI.

[2] Athenian *strategos*. Commander of the Athenian mercenary force near Corinth in 390/89 BC. In 388/7 and 387/6 he operated off Abydos. He was able to refute a charge of unlawful enrichment by giving a full account of his activities. In 376, he was commander of the Athenian garrison on Syros. DAVIES 162f.

[3] Great grandson of → D. [1], from a noble and wealthy family. He is epigraphically documented from *c.* 350 BC as a landowner in Laurion, lessee of mines, and owner of ore processing plants. He served repeatedly as *triarchos*, and in 338/7 as well as 335/4 as *strategos* and naval commander. For his donation of shields, he was honoured with a garland, and Lycurgus proposed a further tribute to him. It is uncertain whether Alexander demanded his extradition in 335. Between 332 and 325, he was as *strategos* responsible for the security of grain transport to Athens. He died before 325/4. DAVIES, 163f.

H. WANKEL, D. Rede für Ktesiphon über den Kranz 1, 1976, 623–625. W.S.

[4] **of Athens.** Epigrammatic poet of the 'Garland' of Meleager (Anth. Pal. 4,1,27), author of at least seven poems (in addition, 7,173 is disputed, and 9,391 as well as 16,158 are not certain, as they could also belong to D. [5] of Miletus). These are votive epigrams (6,267; 358) and epigrammatic epitaphs (7,227; 261; 420; 475; 733), traditional in their choice of subject, but well executed. Not too much credence should be given to the lemma Διοτίμου Ἀθηναίου τοῦ Διοπείθους ('by the Athenian Diotimus, son of Diopeithes'), found in poem 7,420 *in rasura* (presumably this refers to the famous *triarchos*, a contemporary of Demosthenes); more likely is a confusion with D. [7] of Adramyttium, grammarian and poet, who lived in the first half of the 3rd cent. (cf. Aratus 11,437) and wrote epic poems on Hercules (SH 393f.).

GA I,1, 94–96; 2, 270–280. E.D.

[5] **of Miletus.** Epigrammatic poet, undoubtedly the author of a delightful love poem from the 'Garland' of Philip (Anth. Pal. 5,106); however, the author of the ecphrastic poems 9,391 and 16,158 cannot be named with any degree of certainty; under the simple header of Διοτίμου ('by Diotmos'), they could also have been written by the Meleagrian poet D. [4].

GA II,1, b 244f.; 2, 276f. (cf. GA I,1, 96; 2, 278f.). E.D.

[6] Author of mythological epics about the deeds of Hercules; Ath. 13,603d reports that the hero of the *Herakleía* did his deeds out of his love for Eurystheus. The fragment of the *Hērakléus ā̓thla*, consisting of three hexameters, refers to the Cercopes (the Suda s.v. Εὐρύβατος 3718 EAGLE). C.S.

[7] **of Adramyttium.** Meleager mentions an epigrammatic poet D. (Anth. Pal. 4,1,27); a total of eleven epigrams are attributed to a D. in the *Anthologia Palatina* and the *Anthologia Planudea*. Both the attribution of individual epigrams and the identity of D. are disputed. He is presumably identical with the grammarian and epic poet from Adramyttium, derided by Aratus (Anth. Pal. 11, 437).

SH 181–182; GA 2, 270–280. C.S.

Diotogenes Name uncertain, missing in Iamblichus' Pythagorean catalogue (v. P. 267), also in Photius' catalogue of Stobaeus' philosophical sources (Bibl. c. 167,114a-b). Author of pseudo-Pythagorean treatises on kingship and piety, fragments of which can be found in Stobaeus. The date of their composition is a matter of dispute. There is no indication in the treatise on kingship which would indicate a reference to the Principate; nor is there an attempt to legitimize monarchy as part of the world order. It explains how a king legitimizes his role by preserving an existing order, by meeting all of his obligations, by copying Zeus, and is thus divine.

H. THESLEFF, The Pythagorean Texts, 1965, 71ff. M.FR.

Dioxippus (Διώξιππος; *Diṓxippos*). Poet of the Middle Comedy; titles of five plays have survived [1. test. 1]: *Antipornoboskós* [2], *Diadikazómenoi*, *Thēsaurós*, *Historiográphos* (possibly mocking the oligarchic, pro-Macedonian politician Callimedon, fr. 3), and *Philárgyros*. He was probably involved in the Lenaea of 349 BC as *didaskalos* for a play by Anaxandrides [1. test. 2].

1 PCG V, 1986, 44–46 2 H.-G. NESSELRATH, Die att. Mittlere Komödie, 1990, 324. B.BÄ.

Diphilus (Δίφιλος; *Díphilos*).

[1] Athenian operator of a silver mine. In 330 BC, he was charged by Lycurgus with illegally mining the *mesokrineís* (pillars), which served both as markers to separate the various leases within the mine but also as safety props, and sentenced to death. His assets of 160 talents were confiscated and distributed amongst the citizens (Ps.-Plut. Mor. 843D).

→ Mining

J. ENGELS, Studien zur polit. Biographie des Hypereides, ²1993, 224–237; M.H. HANSEN, Demography and Democracy, 1986, 45–47. W.S.

[2] Appointed by → Antigonus [1] Monophthalmos in 315 BC commandant of the citadel of Babylon, D. gathered around him those officers who remained loyal to Antigonus in his conflict with → Seleucus. The citadel was captured by Seleucus in 312 BC (Diod. Sic. 19,91,3f.). Nothing is known of his later fate. E.B.

[3] Author of an epic *Thēsēïs* and of choliambs [1. 1152; 2. 541], or of a *Thēsēïs* in choliambs [3. 61]. This dispute stems from alternative interpretations of the only relevant testimonium, schol. Pind. Ol. 10,83b Σῆμον ... νενικηκέναι, ὥς φησι Δίφιλος ὁ τὴν Θησηΐδα ποιήσας ἔν τινι ἰαμβ(εί)ῳ οὕτω, followed by the quotation of two choliambs (fr. 1 West = Theseïs T 2 Bernabé). It is uncertain whether he is identical with the author of a ὁλόκληρον ποίημα against the philosopher Boïdas (schol. Aristoph. Nub. 96 = DK no. 34), who wrote in the 5th [1. 1153; 2. 541f.] or perhaps the 3rd cent. BC [4. 213ff.].

1 O. Crusius, s.v. D. (11), RE 5, 1,1903 2 W. Schmid, Gesch. der griech. Lit. I/2, München 1934 3 West, IEG II, ²1992 4 G.A. Gerhard, Phoinix von Kolophon, 1909. M.D.MA.

[4] see → Histrio

[5] **D. of Sinope** Comic poet, alongside → Menander and → Philemon the most important representative of the Attic New → Comedy [1. test. 1. 13–16].

A. Life B. Works

A. Life

In the epigraphical list of comic poets who gained most victories at the Lenaea, D. appears almost immediately after Menander and Philemon [1. test. 4], an indication that he might have begun producing plays at the same time they did, or shortly thereafter. Of his life, little is known: Some anecdotes were in circulation regarding his amorous affair with the well-known Athenian hetaera Gnathaena [1. test. 7. 8]. It is not clear how long into the 3rd cent. BC he survived; however, as early as 262 or 258 BC, one of his plays was restaged again as an example of 'Old Comedy' [1. test. 5]. D. died in Smyrna [1. test. 1], but was buried in Athens; his tombstone, which also lists his brother, the comic poet → Diodorus [10] (who apparently in contrast with D. had adopted Athenian citizenship), is extant.

B. Works

D. was three times victorious in the comedy contest of the Lenaea [1. test. 4]; there is no knowledge of other successes during his lifetime. Of a total of 100 documented plays [1. test. 1], 61 titles are extant, in some cases revisions (διασκευαί) of works that had already been performed (cf. fr. 5. 75). Three of D.'s plays are only known from Roman adaptations: → Plautus adapted the Κληρούμενοι (*Klēroúmenoi*) for his *Casina* [1. test. 10]; a scene from Συναποθνήσκοντες (*Synapothnḗskontes*) was used by → Terence in his *Adelphoe*, after Plautus had earlier used the same play as a model for his *Commorientes* [1. test. 12]; Plautus' *Rudens* is also based on one of D.'s plays, the title of which, however, is not transmitted [1. test. 11]. D.'s Σχέδια (*Schédia*), only known as a single fragment (79), was probably the basis of Plautus' *Vidularia* [2].

The fragments themselves are sufficient to make it clear that in his choice of subjects and characters, D. still took his lead from plays produced by Attic comedians in the period preceding Menander: In the *Hairēsiteíchēs* (Αἱρησιτείχης), which D. later staged again in a new adaptation under the title of 'The Eunuch or the Soldier' (Εὐνοῦχος ἢ Στρατιώτης), the character of the swaggering soldier takes centre stage, in the *Apoleípousa* (Ἀπολείπουσα), a cook thirsty for knowledge appears, in the *Zōgráphos* (Ζωγράφος), another cook holds forth about the right kind of customer one has to try and select, only to make it clear at the end of his long speech that he is on his way to a celebration in a brothel (fr. 42). Hetaeras, too, take a quite prominent roles in D.'s plays: In his *Synōrís* (Συνωρίς, named after a well-known Athenian demimondaine), the eponymous heroine appears in a dice game with a literarily educated parasite (fr. 74); it is likely that the three Samian women, whose guessing game in fr. 49 ends with an obscenity, unimaginable in Menander, also were hetaeras. D. also frequently used parasites as protagonists in his comedies: in the already mentioned *Synōrís*, the parasite is not only shown playing dice, but also getting angry (fr. 75) and defending his professional honour (fr. 76); he is also given centre stage in *Telesías* (Τελεσίας), described in Ath. 6,258e almost as showpiece of parasite representation, and not least in *Parásitos* (Παράσιτος) itself. In fr. 87 (the title of the play is unknown), a brothel keeper complains about the hardships of his profession, in fr. 125 (equally without title), a charlatan utters mysterious-sounding hexameters. In *Boiṓtios* (Βοιώτιος), there is mockery of the Boeotians (fr. 22), similar to that of earlier authors of the Middle Comedy; equally, D.'s relatively — in comparison with Menander and Philemon — high number of titles on mythological subjects (altogether at least five, if not nine) harks back to the comedies of the preceding age. The same applies to *Sapphṓ* (Σαπφώ), where Archilochus and Hipponax apparently appeared as rival admirers of the poetess (fr. 71); plays with this title are otherwise only known from earlier comic poets.

The later Plautus was far more comfortable with the more robust and probably also more traditional comic fare which D. presented to his audience than with Menander, and which apparently brought him success (even though there is documentary evidence of only three victories for D., see above); the liveliness of his dialogues is evident in some of the fragments (e.g. 74; 76) as well as in Plautus' adaptations. Later, as an author whose plays were read rather than performed, he could not compete with Menander: Our knowledge of him has thus far hardly profited from the papyri (although some information may still be hidden among the adespota), and in the transmission of quotes (especially the gnomic-sentencious), he lags far behind Menander and also Philemon.

1 PCG V, 1986, 47–123 2 R. CALDERON, Plautus, Vidularia: introd., testo crit. e comm., 1982, 90–113. H.-G.NE.

[6] **of Siphnos.** Greek physician of the early 3rd cent. BC (Ath. 2,51). His book 'On Diets for the Sick and Healthy' took into account a wide range of everyday food, such as nuts, damsons, cherries, and mushrooms, and contained advice for their preparation. In his treatise 'On Seafish', possibly a part of the aforementioned larger work, he advised against the consumption of oysters, mussels, and sea fish because of their low nutritional values. D. was one of the main sources for the dietary notions of Athenaeus [3] of Naucratis, but is not quoted by any of the transmitted medical authors.

→ Dietetics; → Medicine V.N.

Diphros Four-legged stool, generally with turned legs. A seat for gods and heroes (west frieze of the Siphnian treasury in Delphi; east frieze of the → Parthenon), as well as for common people in scenes from everyday life (geometric amphora Athens, NM Inv. no. 804: workshop scenes). They were made of simple wood or valuable ebony, the inventory lists of the Parthenon even record silver-footed *diphroi*. A special form is the folding stool (δίφρος ὀκλαδίας; *díphros okladías*), whose legs end in claw-shaped feet.

→ Furniture; → Sella curulis

G. M. A. RICHTER, The Furniture of the Greeks, Etruscans and Romans, 1966, 38–46; TH. SCHÄFER, Diphroi und Peplos auf dem Ostfries des Parthenon, in: MDAI(A) 102, 1987, 188–212. R.H.

Diple (διπλῆ; *diplê*). Editorial mark of the Alexandrian philologists, used in textual criticism, simple (generally >, but also <) or accompanied by two dots (⸖). Documentary evidence relates it predominantly with Homeric philology: The simple *diple* (ἀπερίστικτος or καθαρά; *aperístiktos* or *kathará*) was used by Aristarchus of Samothrace, to refer to various critical-exegetic observations on the interpretation of a text, on its language, the realia etc., and the *diplê periestigménē* (διπλῆ περιεστιγμένη) by contrast, to mark those passages in which he polemicized against Zenodotus' views. With reference to Plato's text, Diog. Laert. states in 3,65–6 that the simple *diple* draws the reader's attention to Plato's characteristic teachings and opinions, whereas the dotted *diple* marks the 'text-critical interventions by some editors' (ἐνίων διορθώσεις). Hephaestion (Περὶ σημείων; *Peri semeíon* 4 and 11, pp. 74 and 76 CONSBRUCH) provides some information about the various uses of *diplai* in dramatic and lyric texts.

→ Aristarchus of Samothrace; → Homer; → Critical signs; → Plato; → Zenodotus

A. GUDEMAN, s.v. Kritische Zeichen (1–2), RE 11, 1918–1920; PFEIFFER, KPI, 233 n. 118, 267, 279. F.M.

Diploma (plur. *diplomata*; from the Greek διπλόω; *diplóō* = to double, fold over; Lat. *duplico*) generally refers to a duplicate object, which is folded or in two parts, but in particular to a document on parchment, papyrus or also in the form of a → diptych which has been folded and sealed in order to safeguard the written content. Important private and public records were set down in the form of *diplomata*, which thus became almost synonymous with document: private letters (Cic. Att. 10,17,4) and legal transactions (testaments, witnessed treaties and contracts, declarations, copies), official letters of safe conduct, passports, permits for the state postal service (Tac. Hist. 2,54,1; 65,1; Sen. Clem. 1,10,3), documents for the award of Roman citizenship (Suet. Nero 12,1) and other legal awards and orders by the emperors (Sen. Ben. 7,10,3; Suet. Calig. 38,1). In order to safeguard the contents, a decree of the Senate of the 1st cent. AD (Suet. Nero 17) ordered that all documents regarding private or public contracts had to be closed and sealed in a particular manner (Paulus, Sent. 5,25,6/FIRA 2, 411; ...*adhibitis textibus ita signari, ut in summa marginis ad medium partem perforatae triplici lini constringantur atque impositae supra linum cerae signa imprimantur*...). However, legally accepted forms of documents changed and varied widely. At times, the imperial court included a dedicated office *a diplomatibus* (CIL VI 8622; X 1727) along with those of *a libellis* and *ab epistulis* (Suet. Aug. 50).

→ Tabula

KASER, RPR 1, 233ff.; WENGER, 72 (n. 57), 83, 146. C.G.

Diplomacy (from the Greek-Lat. → *diploma*, Latin *diplomaticus*, late Latin *diplomatus*) etymologically derives from the similar late antique word for the holder of a passport, who on imperial business was permitted to use the state postal service for the transfer of documents and to cross the borders into foreign lands (*evectio* — Cod. Iust. 12,50). In all international relations governed by *ius gentium* throughout antiquity, such activities were always linked with a national system of rules governing the dispatch and reception of messengers and plenipotentiaries (*nuntii, missi, legati*; ἄγγελοι, ἀπόστολοι, πρέσβεις), the drafting, documentation, and execution of treaties, i.e. rules governing diplomacy in an ancient sense of the word, as it appears in numerous ancient sources [1]. A wide range of obligations, some anchored in religious beliefs (such as the protection of envoys, the adherence to sworn peace treaties, a declaration of war and of the cessation of war), were recognized in most ancient communities (e.g.: Hdt. 7,133; Xen. Hell. 5,1,31; Liv. 30,36–45). In ancient communities foreign relations was the responsibility of central decision-making bodies (in Rome, for example, the Senate, or authorized magistrates, or the citizens' assembly: cf. Pol. 6,12 and Liv. ibid.), or particular officials, often with special authority, with set procedures for the reception of, and attendance to, the representatives of foreign powers (e.g. the late antique *magister officiorum*: Not. Dign. Or. 19; Lydus, Mag. 2,2), as well as technical regulations regarding the organization of transport (e.g. the Roman *cursus publicus*: Cod. Iust. 12,50).

Compared with modern international relations, ancient forms of diplomacy lacked a strictly defined national sovereignty of the various communal entities that were represented, as well as permanent diplomatic representations of one state at another [2. 26ff., 33ff.]. On the other hand, there are ancient rudiments of both, such as in the Greek sphere the emphasis on autonomy as a criterion for a community, sovereign in its foreign relations (Thuc. 5,18), also the institution of the → *proxenoi*, in the Roman sphere the system of envoys (within the empire: Dig. 50,7; Cod. Iust. 10,65), as well as the norms of an international law which permanently governed relations with foreign states (→ *ius gentium*: Dig. 1,1,5).

1 StV 2 W.G. Grewe, Epochen der Völkerrechtsgeschichte, 1984.

J. Bleicken, Athenische Demokratie, [2]1994, 161f.; Ch. Gizewski, Hugo Grotius und das ant. Völkerrecht, in: Der Staat, 1993, 325ff.; Jones, LRE 366ff., 575ff.; Mommsen, Staatsrecht 3, 1147ff. C.G.

Dipoenus Sculptor from Crete. Like his brother Scyllis, assumed to be a pupil or son of the legendary → Daedalus and one of the original exponents of the art of marble sculpture. Tales of his flight from Cyrus and his first commissions in Sicyon reflect the fact that the 'Daedalic' marble-sculpture of the Greek islands preceded that of the mainland and date its arrival on the mainland to the earlier half of the 6th cent. BC. Even in ancient literature, some archaic works were attributed to D. Through the sculpture of a group of gods with the Dioscuri in Argos, D. was also linked with the chryselephantine technique.

Fuchs/Floren, 121; Overbeck, no. 321–327, 329–332, 334 (sources); Stewart 242–243. R.N.

Dipolieia (τὰ Διπολίεια sc. ἱερά; *tà Dipolíea hierá*, also Dipolia/Διπόλια), an Attic festival for → Zeus Polieus, central to which was the sacrifice of a bull (flight ritual of the → Bouphonia). The Greeks derived the aetiological explanation for this from the myth of → Diomus, a priest of Zeus. The *dipolieia* were celebrated in high summer on the 14th of the month of Skirophorion; they were no longer customary in the Hellenistic period.
→ Poplifugia; → Regifugium

W. Burkert, Homo necans (Engl. edition), 1983, 136–143; Deubner, 158–174; H. W. Parke, Festivals of the Athenians, [3]1994, 162–167; R. Parker, Athenian Rel., 1996, 270. M.SE.

Dipteros (Greek δίπτερος; *dípteros*: two-winged; building equipped with double *pterón* = gallery or perambulatory). Technical term for a Greek → temple with a frontage of at least eight columns, whose → cella is enclosed on all sides by at least two, on the ends even three rows of columns; the term is only known from Vitruvius (3,1,10; 3,2,1; 3,2,7; 3,3,8; 7 praef. 15), but not elsewhere in Greek architectural terminology. In comparison with a → peripteros with its simple set of columns, the dipteros — an expensive building concept with far greater requirements in labour, transport, and material (a dipteros of 8 × 17 columns required at least 92 columns, but a peripteros of similar outline only 48) — was developed in the mid 6th cent. BC in Ionian Asia Minor in the course of a veritable explosion in scale of the previously comparatively small-scaled sacral architecture of the Ionic order. In Greek temple architecture, only very few dipteroi were actually built. Apart from the archaic dipteroi of → Samos (→ Rhoeicus, → Polycrates), and those preserved in the form of later constructions at → Ephesus (→ Chersiphron, → Metagenes, → Wonders of the World) and → Didyma (→ Daphnis), the only other building with a definite dipteral ground plan is the unfinished Peisistratid Olympieion in Athens, which was designed in the Doric order. It is uncertain whether the — probably hypaethral — Doric temple G in → Selinus can be reconstructed as a dipteros; Vitruvius mentions a further Doric dipteros (the lost, possibly legendary temple of Quirinus in Rome, Vitr. De arch. 3,2,7). An example of a → pseudodipteros is the Hellenistic peripteral temple at → Baalbek. The frequently voiced assumption that a hypaethral *sekos* (→ Roofing) with a separate sanctuary, almost independent of the peripteros — as in the temple of Apollo in Didyma — was part of the basic concept of a dipteros, remains problematic; both the temple of Rhoeicus on Samos and the archaic temple of Artemis in Ephesus (cf. Str. 14,22 p. 640 C) seem to have been roofed buildings. In further contrast with Didyma, both buildings also boasted large altar terraces adjoining the main building, richly endowed with the tradition of their respective cults (→ Altar).

The splendidly varied ornamentation (→ Ornaments) of these giant archaic Ionian temples is striking. Alongside the customary Ionic order decor of the entablature, bases as well as necks of columns were decorated with anathematic reliefs (*columnae caelatae*, → Column), a sculptured frieze and marble as building material are found in Ephesus, and there were deliberate variations in the profiles of column bases (Samos, dipteros of Polycrates; the different base profiles were produced on a large-scale lathe; → construction technique). This 'uniqueness' of individual columns, produced at great expense, together with extant or literary transmitted votive inscriptions, documenting the donation of individual columns and with it their anathematic functionality (e.g. votive offerings to Croesus in Ephesus, cf. Hdt. 1, 92), lead to the assumption that these archaic Ionic dipteroi were monuments, in which indi-

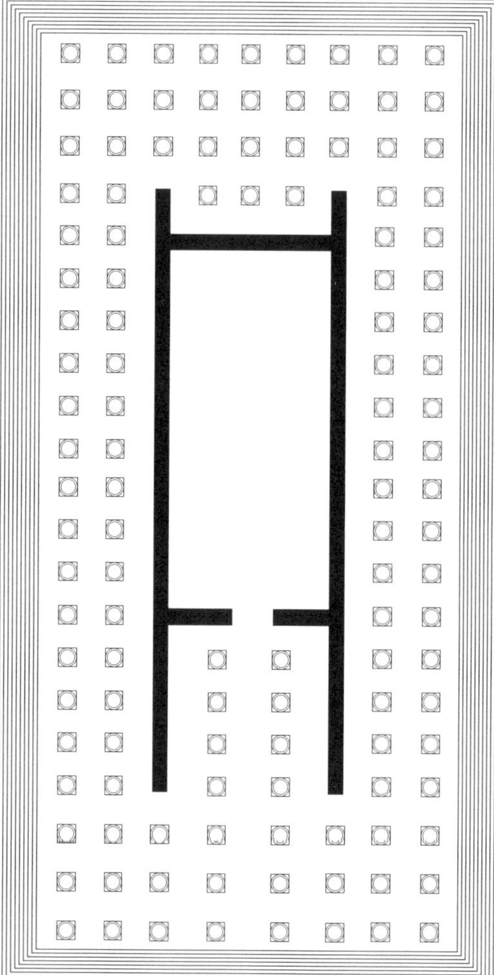

Ephesus: Newer Artemision (schematic ground-plan).

vidual votive offerings to these Ionic sanctuaries of supraregional importance were brought together in a deliberate move to create a greater whole, a veritable 'forest of columns': a levelling factor within a design deliberately intended to explode anything that had been done before, and appeared on the background of an Ionic-Greek identity which in those times had to be redefined at the interface of the Greek sphere and Achaemenid-Oriental civilization, striving to harmonize aristocratic-oligarchic group ideals with autocratic components; for a more detailed analysis of these aspects, cf. → temple.

A. Bammer, U. Muss, Das Artemision von Ephesos, 1996, 45–79; B. Fehr, Zur Gesch. des Apollonheiligtums von Didyma, in: MarbWPr 1971/72, 14–59; Id., Zur Gesch. des Apollontempels von Didyma: Nachtrag, in: Hephaistos 9, 1988, 163–166; W. Müller-Wiener, Griech. Bauwesen in der Ant., 1988, 142–145; O. Reuther, Der Heratempel von Samos, 1957; W. Schaber, Die archa. Tempel der Artemis von Ephesos, 1982; H. v. Steuben, Seleukidische Kolossaltempel, in: Antike Welt 3/1981, 3–12; R. Tölle-Kastenbein, Zur Genesis und Entwicklung des D., in: JDAI 109, 1994, 41–76; Id., Das Olympieion in Athen, 1994; W. Voigtländer, Der jüngste Apollontempel von Didyma, 14. Beih. MDAI(I), 1975.

C.HÖ.

Diptychon (from the Greek δίς; *dís* = two times and πτύσσω; *ptýssō* = fold) can refer to anything folded or appearing as a double, such as mussel shells or twins (Eur. Orest. 633 or respectively Ambr. Hex. 6,8,25), but in particular refers to a folded piece of writing on paper or parchment, or two foldable linked writing tablets — or a writing tablet with lid — and a writing surface made from wax, gypsum or other, mostly light-coloured, material (λεύκωμα; *leúkōma*), which would be written on with a stylus, a reed, or a brush. As *diptycha* protected texts against damage or forgery, it became customary to use them in the production and safekeeping of documents or valuable texts (Hdt. 7,239,3; Symmachus, Ep. 2,80); a number of examples are extant (FIRA 1, 221ff. — military certificates; 3, 129ff. — testaments, 3, 283ff.; — sales contracts). Some *diptycha* take transitional forms leading to the → *codex* (Dig. 32,52, pr.: *in codicibus membraneis, chartaceis, eborei vel alterius materiae vel in ceratis codicillis*).

In late antiquity, an ornamental form of the *diptychon*, made with valuable materials (Cod. Theod. 15,9,1, pr.) and often with pictorial illustrations ('consular *diptycha*', several examples extant), developed in conjunction with the appointment of high-ranking officials Even earlier, the diptych was used in the liturgy of the Christian church (Aug. Epist. 78,4), and contributed towards the further development of an ecclesiastical art of writing and pictures (codices, triptychs, polyptychs, reliquaries).

→ Diploma; → Writing tablet; → Tabula

F. Gehrke, Spätant. und frühes Christentum, 1967, 180ff.; H. Hunger et al., Textüberlieferung der ant. Lit. und der Bibel, 1975, 27ff., 54ff.; Wenger, 72ff., 74ff.

C.G.

Dipylon Painter Attic vase painter of the geometric period (Late Geometric I, mid 8th cent. BC; → Geometric vase painting), named after the cemetery at the Dipylon Gate in Athens, where most of his works were found. The Dipylon Painter (DP) and the other painters of his workshop created about 20 monumental vases (kraters; amphorae), which were placed on tombs as receptacles for offerings (→ Burial); of these, the amphora Athens, NM 804, with a height of 155 cm (the stand has been replaced and thus the vase may have been even higher originally) is the best-known work of the DP. His artistic repertoire included representations of prothesis and ekphora, rows of human figures in mourning, kneeling, or sitting on → *diphroi*, chariots in motion, and images of warriors. The vessels are clearly structured by the horizontal dividers, separating the ornamental bands or figure friezes; of great importance are the meanders, which appear in a number of variations, diamond shapes, vertical waves; in addition, there are several other decorative embellishments, such as stars, rosettas, zigzag bands, rows of dots and many others, which were used to fill empty spaces (horror vacui; → ornaments). His animal friezes are innovative, depicting grazing deer or resting goats, and birds; narrative elements are evident in the fragment in Paris, which originated from his workshop (LV Inv. A 519 [2. 50, fig. 19]), showing in a number of scenes the battle between two differently armed groups, as well as an image of the Molione/→ Actorione (in reference to Hom. Il. 11, 709–711?).

1 J.N. Coldstream, Greek Geometric Pottery, 1968, 29–41 2 Id. The Geometric Style: Birth of a Picture, in: T. Rasmussen, N. Spivey (ed.), Looking at Greek Vases, 1993, 47–51 3 Th. Rombos, The Iconography of Attic Late Geometric II Pottery, 1988 4 K. Schefold, Das Frühwerk des Dipylonmeisters, in: AK 4, 1961, 76–78.

R.H.

Dirae Bucolic poem of the early Imperial period, in which the poet puts a curse on his expropriated land. The link with Verg. Ecl. 1 and 9 resulted even before the Vergil biographies of Donatus (based on Suetonius) (§ 17) to its attribution to → Vergilius (but cf.[3]). Maintaining the topic, v. 104 begins a new poem without a topical break (cf. v. 41. 89. 95 with 107), known as *Lydia*, but without ancient evidence regarding that title, probably written by the same author (cf. [5]). It is an elegiac lament of a lover separated from his Lydia. Both pieces have been transmitted together in two strands in the → Appendix Vergiliana (M and SFL).

→ Curse

Editions: C.v.d. Graaf, 1945 W.V. Clausen et al., App. Verg., 1966, 3–14 (E.J. Kenney) E. Fraenkel, in: JRS 56, 1966, 142–155 (only D.), opposed by F.R.D. Goodyear, in: PCPhS 1971, 30–43.

Bibliography: 1 K. Büchner, P. Vergilius Maro, 1955, 109–116 2 B. Luiselli, Studi sulla poesia bucolica, 1967, 117–144 3 E. Van den abeele, Remarques sur les 'D.', in: RhM 112, 1969, 145–154 4 H. Zaboulis, App. Verg.: D., in: Philologus 122, 1978, 207–223 5 J. Richmond, D., in: ANRW II 31.2, 1122–1125 6 F. della Corte, s.v. D., in: EV 2, 91–94 7 A. Salvatore, Da un 'dramma' politico a un dramma esistenziale, in: Storia, poesia e pensiero nel Mondo Antico. FS M. Gigante, 1994, 549–564.

P.L.S.

Dirce (Δίρκη; *Dírkē*).

[1] Daughter of Ismenus (Callim. H. 4,75ff.), wife of king → Lycus. Both are hostile to Lycus' niece → Antiope [2]; after Antiope had failed in her attempt to escape, D. and Lycus handed her over to her twin sons → Amphion and Zethus, whom she had abandoned at birth, to have her dragged to death by a bull. However, the sons recognize their mother just in time and then proceed to make D. suffer that very punishment (Eur. in Hyg. Fab. 7f.; Plaut. Pseud. 199f.; Apollod. 3,43f.; Petron. Sat. 45,8); they throw D.'s body into a river, which thenceforth bears her name (Pind. I.6,74; Aesch. Sept. 273). Dionysus was bathed in this river, before Zeus sewed him into his thigh (Eur. Bacch. 519ff.). A nocturnal rite was performed on D.'s tomb (Plut. Mor. 578b).

E. Bethe, s.v. Dirke, RE 5, 1169–1170; F. Heger, s.v. Dirke, LIMC 3.1, 635–644.

R.HA.

[2] Small river, rising immediately south-west of Thebes, mod. name also Plakiotissas (Str. 8,7,5; 9,2,24; Paus. 9,25,3; Plin. HN 4,25). In mythology and literature closely linked with Thebes (cf. Pind. I.6,73–76; 8,20f.; Eur. HF 784); for that reason, the adjective Διρκαῖος/*Dircaeus* is often used synonymously with Θηβαῖος/*Thebanus* (e.g. Verg. Ecl. 2,24; Hor. Carm. 4,2,25).

E. Bethe, s.v. Dirke, RE 5, 1169f.

P.F.

Diribitores *Diribitores*(from *diribere* = *dis-habere*) are 'distributors' or 'regulators', also 'stewards', or 'preparers' (e.g. of food: Apul. Met. 2,19). In the Roman Republic, *diribitores* were the publicly appointed and sworn officials of the *tabulae/suffragia* responsible for the counting of votes in courts of law or in the citizens' assembly (CGIL 5,62,6; *lex Malacitensis* 55/FIRA 1, 211).

→ Comitia; → Suffragium

Mommsen, Staatsrecht 3, 406ff.

C.G.

Disability In Greece and Rome disability in the sense of permanent functional damage of a physical or mental nature (acquired by congenital defect, disease, accident, old age or in war) was thought of as a deviation from the customary norm. The term disability is outlined vaguely in the sources (e.g. Greek ἀσθένεια/*asthéneia*, Lat. *debilitas*, literally 'weakness'). People with disabilities are sometimes called ἀδύνατοι/*adýnatoi* ('powerless') or Lat. *debiles* ('weak'; [8]; cf.. Cic. Leg. 1,55; Sen. Controv. exc. 3,1; Plin. HN 7,104 f.). The afflictions are specifically named in each case (e.g. Lys. 24; Plaut. Merc. 630; AE 1971, 88, col. II, l. 6 f.). Deformities or malformations are designated i.a. as ἀμορφία/*amorphía* or πηρός/*pērós* or Lat. *deformitas*, *deformis* or *mancus* ([8]; e.g. Cic. Leg. 3,8,19; Lucil. 332 f.). The mentally ill are called μαινόμενος/*mainómenos* or Lat. *furiosus* [6].

The prevailing ideal of beauty and the capabilities required by ancient society determined acceptance by the community. Reactions to people who did not conform to these standards or did so only to a limited extent were many and varied in both Greece and Rome. They ranged from mockery and disgust via fear and sympathy to respect and awe. Disability could be seen as punishment by the gods and the physical manifestation judged to be the reflection of a bad character (e.g. → Thersites; see [4]). The social position of the disabled, the influence of their families and the type and extent of their disability decided the degree of exclusion or integration of those concerned. Even among aristocrats equality of status did not prevent discrimination [10; 13]. The physically disabled attempted to compensate for their deficiencies by particular capabilities and skills, in the field of music and the arts, for instance. They attempted to deny or conceal their disability, tried to fit in with the expectations of society, even to prove their capability in the military sector or to overcome social exclusion by self-mockery [4; 10; 13]. Ancient sources also, however, cite resignation, withdrawal from social life and → suicide in cases of disability acquired later in life—such as blindness, for instance (e.g. [10]).

People with disabilities relied on the material support of their → families. State care for the disabled, which originally applied only to war invalids, existed only in classical Athens in a recognizable form (cf. → war, consequences of). Mentally handicapped people were excluded from this, however (Lys. 24; Aristot. Ath. Pol. 49,4; Plut. Solon 31). Some disabled new-born babies were subject to the → exposure of children, while others were brought up [15]. Without social support or education the disabled eked out their existence as → beggars or acted as clowns on festive occasions, displaying their physical anomalies (cf. → Entertainers). The entertainment value of the physically deformed is also reflected in art [16]. Τέρατα/*térata* or Lat. *monstra* (literally 'monsters') were regarded as divine signs. In Republican Rome they were killed in the context of measures of atonement (→ *prodigium*). In the Roman Imperial period, on the other hand, they seem to have been shown at markets and were used to amuse Roman emperors [1; 3; 14].

The possibility of a professional life was not barred to people with a physical disability. Records show lame craftsmen and soldiers, blind poets (e.g. Homer [1]) and legal scholars, dumb painters, magistrates with amputated arms or with speech disabilities, deformed kings and emperors. People with disabilities could sometimes become priests, even though this met with religious scruples [5; 8; 10; 13]. Women with disabilities are seldom mentioned in ancient testimonies. Interest in them was primarily directed at their ability to bear children (→ Labda) [8]. While there was nothing to stop physically disabled people taking part in political and social life, the mentally ill were as far as possible locked away by their families. They were accorded hardly any rights and were more likely to be exposed to attacks on the street than the physically disabled [6]. Sticks, prostheses, carts, sedan chairs, litters, horses or mules were used as mobility aids by people with disabilities. Guide-dogs and wheelchairs were unknown in antiquity [8; 10].

→ Marginal groups

1 R. GARLAND, The Eye of the Beholder, 1995 2 N. VLAHOGIANNIS, Disabling Bodies, in: D. MONSERRAT (ed.), Changing Bodies, Changing Meanings, 1998, 13–36 3 I. WEILER, Körperbehinderte aus der Sicht des Althistorikers, in: G. FETKA-EINSIEDLER, G. FÖRSTER (ed.), Diskriminiert?, 1994, 7–23 4 H. GRASSL, Behinderte in der Ant., in: Tyche 1, 1986, 118–126 5 Id., Behinderung und Arbeit, in: Eirene 26, 1989, 49–57 6 Id., Zur sozialen Position geistig Behinderter im Altertum, in: I. WEILER (ed.), Soziale Randgruppen und Außenseiter im Alt., 1988, 107–116 7 A. ESSER, Das Antlitz der Blindheit in der Ant., ²1961 8 M. L. EDWARDS, Physical Disability in the Ancient Greek World, 1995 9 A. MEHL, Behinderte in der ant. griech. Ges., in: M. LIEDTKE (ed.), B. als pädagogische und polit. Herausforderung, 1996, 119–135 10 L. DE LIBERO, Dem Schicksal trotzen. Behinderte Aristokraten in Rom, in: The Ancient History Bulletin 16, 2002 11 A. RÖSGER, Der Umgang mit Behinderten im röm. Reich, in: (see [9]), 137–150 12 A. KÜSTER, Blinde und Taubstumme im röm. Recht, 1991 13 L. DE LIBERO, Mit eiserner Hand ins Amt?, in: J. SPIELVOGEL (ed.), Res publica reperta. FS J. Bleicken, 2002, 172–191 14 I. WEILER, Hic audax subit ordo pumilorum, in: Grazer Beitr. 21, 1995, 121–145 15 M. SCHMIDT, Hephaistos lebt, in: Hephaistos 5/6, 1983/84, 133–161 16 L. GIULIANI, Die seligen Krüppel, in: AA 1987, 701–721.

L. d. L.

Discens In a military context, this term denotes a soldier who has received special training for a certain special tasks or roles. There is epigraphical evidence that among soldiers serving in a legion were some who had received special training to prepare them for service as cavalry (CIL VIII 2882 = ILS 2331), medical orderlies, architects, or to act as standard or eagle bearers (*discens aquiliferu(m) leg(ionis) III Aug(ustae)*, CIL VIII 2988 = ILS 2344). It is not clear whether the *discentes* were of the same rank and standing as the *immunes*, i.e. soldiers who had special responsibilities and were exempt from the *munera*, ordinary heavy duties. There were also *discentes* among the Praetorians.

1 Dizionario epigrafico, 1910–1911, (II.3), s.v. Discens.

J.CA.

Discessio General 'dispersal', in assemblies also 'closure' (Gell. NA 1,4,8; Ter. Andr. 5,68; Cic. Sest. 77). In legal terms, *discessio* describes the loss of a right or withdrawal from a contract (Dig. 18,2,17,18; Dig. 6,1,35 pr.).

Politically, *discessio* was used as a general term for the formation of parties, splits and internal conflicts, such as between patricians and plebeians (Greek ἀπόστασις; *apóstasis*; Gell. NA 2,12; Sall. Hist. fr. 1,11). In the Roman Senate, *discessio* refers to the voting procedure in which voters go and assemble on different sides of the voting chamber (Plin. Ep. 8,14,19; *lex de imperio Vespasiani* 4, FIRA 1, 154–156; Tac. Ann. 14,49,1). In Christian usage, *discessio* (in correspondence with Greek ἀπόστασις) describes the fall from true faith (Vulg. act. ap. 21,21).

→ Senatus; → Senatus consultum

MOMMSEN, Staatsrecht 3, 983f.

C.G.

Disciplina arcani (arcane discipline) *Disciplina arcani* (DA) refers to a religiously motivated obligation to secrecy to be observed by members of religious communities, not to divulge their religious teachings and practices to strangers and those who are not yet full members. Despite documentary evidence of various forms of religious secrecy in ancient religions, predominantly in some of the → Mysteries, the term DA refers specifically to the ancient Christian obligation to maintain secrecy. However, this theory of a Christian DA is a historical construct based on post-Reformation denominational controversies, used by each side for their own legitimization [3]. No such obligation to secrecy is known from early Christianity itself; in the confrontation with → Gnosticism, the very openness of Christian teachings itself became a criterion for orthodoxy. The explanation for occasional references to the exclusive nature of Christian mysteries for those not baptized and the resulting prohibition from participation in certain aspects of the cult (sacrament) or the unauthorized divulgence of ritual formulae, known particularly from the late 3rd and 4th cents. AD in conjunction with preparation for baptism, cannot be explained by a theory of DA, but only through religious epistemology.

1 H. Clasen, Die Arkandisziplin in der Alten Kirche, 1956 2 C. Jacob, »Arkandisziplin«, Allegorese, Mystagogie, 1990 3 R. Rothe, de d.a. origine, 1841.

H.BR.

Disciplina etrusca see → Divination

Disciplina militaris The Latin term *disciplina* designates a) a field of knowledge or an academic discipline and b) obedience. According to Livy (Liv. 9,17,10), in Rome *disciplina militaris* had evolved into an *ars*. In conjunction with the Roman military, *disciplina* generally appears in its second meaning; Frontinus calls the knowledge of military matters *rei militaris scientia* (Frontin. Str. 1 praef. 1). The phrase is used by Valerius Maximus as well as Pliny and is furthermore epigraphically documented (Val.Max. 2,7; Plin. Ep. 10,29; S.c. de Cn. Pisone patre, 52; ILS 3809; cf. *disciplina militiae*: Liv. 28.24.9). Tacitus used the phrase *militia disciplinaque nostra* to refer to the Roman military service (Tac. Ann. 3,42,1; cf. *veteris disciplinae decus*: Ann. 1,35,1), and Vegetius cites *disciplina* as a reason for Roman military success (Veg. Mil. 1,1: *Nulla enim alia re videmus populum Romanum orbem subegisse terrarum nisi armorum exercitio, disciplina castrorum usuque militiae*. Cf. Veg. Mil. 2, praef.: *de usu ac disciplina ... bellorum*). According to Flavius Josephus, Rome's military strength was essentially based on obedience and constant practice in the use of weapons (Joseph BJ 2,577, cf. 3,70–75). It is significant that, for foreigners in particular, absolute obedience was seen as the characteristic of the Roman army; thus a centurion is quoted in the gospel: 'I am a man with soldiers under my command. I tell this one »Go«, and he goes; and that one »Come«, and he comes.' (Mt 8,9). In Republican times, military discipline was largely dependent on the behaviour of the magistrates and promagistrates in command of the legions; its implementation was predominantly the task of the officers. During the Principate, the *princeps* also exercised increasing influence on the discipline of his soldiers. Frontinus, who devotes lengthy expositions to the topic *disciplina*, documents in a great number of examples, how consuls were able to restore discipline in a legion with the help of hard drill and strict punishments (Frontin. Str. 4,1). In the 1st cent. AD, Ser. Sulpicius Galba and Cn. Domitius Corbulo in particular had the reputation of being very able, but also exceedingly strict military leaders (Suet. Galba 6; Tac. Ann. 11,18). Especially during the Civil Wars of AD 69, it became very obvious that soldiers modelled themselves on the example of their commanders (Tac. Hist. 2,76,5); in such situation, the better discipline of one's own troops was a decisive argument in guiding the choice of military intervention (Tac. Hist. 2,77,2–3). Augustus tried to impose strict discipline in the Roman army (S.c. de Cn. Pisone patre, 52: *militarem disciplinam a divo Aug institutam*; Suet. Aug. 24,1: *disciplinam severissime rexit*); Cn. Piso, *cos.* 7 BC, was accused in the trial of AD 20 of having considerably compromised *disciplina militaris* (DM) by accepting gifts. Pliny praises Trajan for re-establishing the *displina castrorum* (Plin. Paneg. 6,2), later authors (Cassius Dio, SHA) passed judgement on the *principes* based on whether they had increased the discipline in the legions, as Hadrian did (SHA Hadr. 10,2–3; cf. the coin BMCRE III Hadrian 1484; ill. in Birley, 118, pl. 10), or rather corrupted the soldiers.

The maintenance of discipline was the responsibility of the centurions, who had the right to beat a Roman soldier with a vine staff. For that reason, they were hated by the legionaries; in mutinies, the soldiers' anger was directed first at the centurions, resulting in some instances in brutal murder (Tac. Ann. 1,17,4; 1,18,1; 1,23,3f.; 1,32,1). Even in the Republican era, a graduated system of rewards and punishments was in place (Pol. 6,37–39): a brave soldier could receive distinctions and be promoted. But it was also possible to punish entire units, e.g. by dissolving a legion, with the soldiers being dishonourably discharged from military service; units which had retreated in the face of the enemy or refused obedience, could be subjected to → *decimatio* (Suet. Aug. 24; Tac. Ann. 3,21,1). In some instances, cohorts were forced to camp outside of the ramparts (Frontin. Str. 4,1,18; 4,1,21). Individual soldiers faced a number of different punishments dependent on the severity of their offence; officers who had failed were publicly shamed by having to stand in camp during daylight, dressed in ragged and torn clothes (Suet. Aug. 24,2; Frontin. Str. 4,1,26; 4,1,28), soldiers had their pay confiscated or were incarcerated (Tac. Ann. 1,21,3). Executions also took place, justified with the observation that no soldier was worth having discipline corrupted on his behalf (Frontin. Str. 4,1,41: *negavit tanti esse quemquam, ut propter illum disciplina corrumperetur*).

DM was also steeped in religion: Recruits had to swear an oath (*sacramentum militiae*), which included the acceptance of DM (Pol. 6,21; Gell. NA 16,4). For the duration of his military service, a soldier had to do what the gods or his superiors ordered him to do (*fas disciplinae*). The term *disciplina* in its double meaning of 'knowledge' and 'obedience' occupied such an important position in military thinking that *disciplina* finally became personified as a goddess, to whom altars were dedicated (e.g. ILS 3810). In late antiquity, DM remained one of the fundamental values, as shown in Vegetius' description of the training of recruits: oriented on the *antiqua consuetudo* (Veg. Mil. 1, praef.).
→ Decorations, military; → Centurio; → Decimatio; → Dona militaria

1 G. BRIZZI, I 'manliana imperia' e la riforma manipolare. L'esercito romano tra 'ferocia' e 'disciplina', in: Sileno 16, 1990, 185–206 2 W. ECK, A. CABALLOS, F. FERNÁNDEZ, Das senatus consultum de Cn. Pisone patre, 1996 3 C. GIUFFRIDA, Disciplina Romanorum, in: Le trasformazioni delle cultura, 1985, 837–860 4 Y. LE BOHEC, ²1990 5 J. VENDRAND-VOYER, Normes civiques et métier militaire à Rome sous le Principat, 1983 6 M. ZIÓLKOWSKI, Il culto della Disciplina nella religione degli eserciti romani, in: Riv. Stor. Ant. 20, 1990, 97–107 A. R. BIRLEY, Hadrian. The Restless Emperor, 1997, 113–120. Y.L.B.

Discobolus see → Victor statues

Discoduratera (Δισκοδουρατέραι; *Diskodouratérai*). A considerable emporium between the modern villages of Gostilitsa and Slaveikovo on the left bank of the Yantra (ancient *Iatrus*), 12 km west of Drianovo, 32 km south-west of Nicopolis ad Istrum, founded by Augusta Traiana probably during the reign of Marcus Aurelius. Enjoyed considerable prosperity under the Severan emperors, when it was fortified; under Aurelian incorporated into the territory of Nicopolis ad Istrum. Numerous inscriptions ([1. 21ff.], IGBulg II, 137–145) and important ruins.

1 SULTOV, in: Mitt. des Bezirkmuseums von Tirnowo 1, 1962.

I. WELKOW, in: Jb. des arch. Nat. Mus. Sofia 1922–1925, 1926, 127–137. J.BU.

Discordia The Latin equivalent of the Greek → Eris. In contrast with → Concordia, D. was never more than a literary personification, and not a cult goddess. Ennius (Ann. 225f.) has D. break down the gates of war (cf. Hor. Sat. 1,460f.). According to Hyg. Fab. praef. 1, D. is a daughter of the 'night' (→ Nox) and of → Erebos. In Virgil (Aen. 6,280), she stands guard at the entrance to the Orcus; in Aen. 8,702 she appears — in a torn cloak — on Aeneas' shield amidst the tumult of the battle of Actium (cf. also Val. Fl. 2,204, and also the warmongering D. in Petron. Sat. 124, v. 271–295). In Mart. Cap. 1,47, D., alongside Seditio, is a deity of the third celestial region.

A. GRILLI, s.v. D., EV 2,97f.; E. NORDEN, Ennius und Vergil, 1915, 15–18; O. SKUTSCH, The Annals of Q. Ennius, 1985, 403–405. R.B.

Discourse, standards of Standards of discourse is not a term used in ancient → rhetoric nor → dialectics. They are the requirements met in a speech or conversation, by an orator or a participant in a dialogue, which achieves the desired effects. These standards are the subject of empirical, practice-related theories (τέχνη; *téchnē*, *ars*) of public as well as private 'discourse', including within the conversational setting long or short monologues as well as questions and longer or shorter answer (Pl. Grg. 449b9–c8, Prt. 334d6–335c2) — thus the topic of rhetoric, eristics, and dialectics.

The standards of discourse are first and foremost based on the general purpose of a speech or a conversation. As these purposes are subject to debate, so are the standards of discourse: those who expected a speech or oration to lead to the perception of truth and knowledge (→ Plato/→ Socrates), must reject standards of discourse that apply only to convictions and opinions (→ Sophistic). Those who conduct conversation with the aim of testing the probability of statements (Aristotelian dialectics), must reject the standards of discourse of the sophistic eristics, whose main purpose was to appear in the eyes of the audience as the winner of a competitive dialogue. Protagoras (Pl. Tht. 167b2–7) thought that speeches should create a communal consensus in the polis as to the justness of the useful and the practical, attaining concord about the meanings of the words 'just', 'legal', 'honourable' and 'useful'; speeches must therefore be adapted to the situation (καιρός, *kairós*), and thus the orator must adjust to his audience. For → Georgias of Leontini (Helena 13), speeches produced conviction by guiding the soul (ψυχαγωγία, *psychagōgía*: Pl. Phd. 271c10) so that they had to be both correctly crafted (*téchnē*) and also delight the audience; this had nothing to do with the transmission of knowledge or truth, but rather the correct use of rhetorical technique (*téchnē;* Pl. Grg. 457b1–5). For → Aristotle (Aristot. Rh. 1355b10–11) a speech must persuade (πείθειν, *peíthein*) through plausibility (πιθανόν, *pithanón*), relying on convincing elements: the character of the orator, the mood which he evokes among listeners, i.e. proofs and apparent proofs (Aristot. Rh. 1356a1–4; → *probationes*). The characteristic of discourse norms remained the object of convincing the audience/judges of the speaker's partial point of view (ἀρετή; *aretḗ*, *virtus*: Quint. Inst. 2,15,1–38; → *virtutes dicendi*).

Furthermore, standards of discourse are functions of the purpose of the various genres, kinds, parts, and elements of speech in respect of the specific role of the listener as judge or spectator (Aristot. Rh. 1358b2–13). A didactic dialogue (e.g. Pl. Prm. 137a6–166c5) has to be conducted in such a way that the student acquires knowledge and understanding of a scientific tenet or discipline, based on its principles or axioms. The main aim of a sophistic argument is to win, i.e. to change the audience's agreement to the opponent's notions with the help of a quick and lively presentation (Grg. Helena 13). In examining proofs by dialogue, as by Zeno of Elea and Socrates, one takes the opponent's opinion as a starting point and then draws conclusions from that which show that they are untenable. The purpose of a dialectic dialogue is to ascertain whether one can assent to a statement or reject it (Aristot. Soph. el. 165b1–8). Standards of discourse stipulate that the teacher, examiner, attacker assume the role of the questioner. Plato's demand (Grg. 448d5–449c5, Prt. 334d6–335c2) that sophists should restrict themselves to short and precise replies, is in essence a dispute about standards of discourse. Only to pose one question, and only to refute by further questions (Pl. Grg. 466c7–8, 467c1–2), are standards of discourse, as are Protagoras' call not to deceive by questions (Pl. Tht. 167e1–168a2), and Aristotle's instructions on questions and answers in his *Topica* and *Sophistici elenchi*.

O.A. Baumhauer, Die sophistische Rhet., 1986; Lausberg. O.B.

Discus of Phaestus The discus of Phaestus is a round disc of fired clay (*c.* 16 cm in diameter, 2 cm thick); it was found in the palace of → Phaestus and stratigraphically dated to the 16th cent. BC. Both sides display a linear spiral of stamped signs (242 in total). 45 different letters can be distinguished, several of them bearing images from the Minoan cultural sphere. Side A has 31 groups of signs, separated by lines, side B 30. Undoubtedly, this is some kind of script. It was probably read from the outside in, from right to left — as was the stamping sequence. The number of signs points to a syllabic script, the groups indicate words, oblique strokes at the end of words probably indicate syntagmata. As the discus of Phaestus is the only evidence of this script and as the text is too short for any certain statistical analysis, neither its language nor its content can be discovered.

→ Greece: Writing systems; → Pre-Greek languages

L. Pernier, Il disco di Phaestos con caratteri pittografici, in: Ausonia 3, 1908, 255–302; J.-P. Olivier, Le disque de Phaistos, 1975; Y. Duhoux, Le disque de Phaestos, 1977; L. Godart, Il disco di Festo, 1994. G.N.

Discus of Phaestus. Heraklion, Archaeological Museum.

Discussor A *discussor* (Greek *logothétēs*, etym. from *discutere* in the meaning of 'to check, investigate') was an official of the late antique Roman state, to whom article 10,30 of the Cod. Iust. was dedicated. The main tasks of the *discussores* lay in tax administration. In that context, they apparently carried out external audits of the tax bases set by the → *census* through self-assessment (*professio*). They also appear as auditors for customs, public building projects, and state regulated prices. Administrative acts issued by the *discussores* were called → *sententiae* (Cod. Iust. 7,62,26). Several Imperial constitutions dealt with attempted bribery, a particular hazard for *discussores*.

Similar or the same tasks were carried out by the *inspectores* and *peraequatores* (Cod. Iust. tit. 11,58); it is no longer possible to reconstruct the division of responsibilities or their place within the hierarchy. It seems that the *peraequatores* had higher rank (cf. Cod. Theod. 13,11,11). G.S.

Discus throwing The discus (δίσκος, *dískos*) was originally a product of copper smelting, a solidified puddle. In origin a desirable Bronze Age commodity, it developed into a piece of sports equipment. In the *Iliad* (23,826–849), where it appears as σόλος (*sólos*) (23,826, 839, 844; this poetic term also in Quint.

Smyrn. 4,436), this link is still tangible, because in the discus throwing contest, the discus is both projectile and prize, however, anachronistically made of iron [2]. As a throwing disc made of metal (occasionally stone), between 17 and 32 cm in diameter and *c.* 4–5 kg in weight [3; 4. 236–246], it was hurled as far as possible. Described in the epics as a single discipline (see above and also Hom. Od. 8,129, 186–190), discus throwing (DT) was later only performed as part of the pentathlon, probably as the first of the five competitions [5. 18–20]. In Philostratus' view (Gymn. 3), it was one of the more demanding exercises.

In Olympia, pentathletes could choose between three discs, which were stored in the Syconian treasure house (Paus. 6,19,4). There is hardly any record of distances thrown [4. 260–261]. There is no consensus regarding the technicalities of ancient DT [6]; it is debated whether the throw was preceded by a turn (as in the modern discipline) [4. 256–258]. Judging by Myron's famous Diskobolos statue [7], it seems likely that the throwing action was a pendular swing [8]. DT is frequently depicted on vase paintings [4. pl. 56–57, 60–61, 63–64, 66–67]. The distance thrown is marked by a wooden stick stuck in the ground [4. fig. 65a]. DT was also known in the Etruscan sports culture [9. 295–306]. For an illustration, see → Sports.

1 W. Decker, Zum Ursprung des Diskuswerfens, in: Stadion 2, 1976, 196–212 2 S. Laser, ArchHom T, 58–62 3 J. Jüthner, Über ant. Turngeräthe, 1896, 18–36 4 Id., F. Brein, Die athletischen Leibesübungen der Griechen II 1, 1896, 225–303 5 J. Ebert, Zum Pentathlon der Ant., 1960 6 M.K. Langdon, Throwing the Discus in Antiquity: The Literary Evidence, in: Nikephoros 3, 1990, 177–187 7 B. Schröder, Zum Diskobol des Myron, 1913 8 W. Anschütz, M.-L. Huster, Im Olympiajahr 1984: Der 'Diskobol' zwischen Leistungssport und Regelzwang, in: Hephaistos 5/6, 1983/84, 71–89 9 J.-P. Thuillier, Les jeux athlétiques dans la civilisation étrusque, 1985.

M. Lavrencic, G. Doblhofer, P. Mauritsch, Diskos, 1991; R. Patrucco, Lo sport nella Grecia antica, 1972, 133–170; I. Weiler, Der Sport bei den Völkern der Alten Welt, ²1988, 161–166.

W.D.

Disease

A. Terminology B. Mesopotamia and Egypt C. Sources from Antiquity and Late Antiquity D. Pathocenosis and epidemiology E. The Diseases according to Dioscorides 1. Skin diseases 2. Gastrointestinal tract 3. Toxicology 4. Gynaecology and midwifery 5. Urinary tract, liver, spleen 6. Respiratory system and tract 7. Sensory organs and perception 8. Bones, joints, fractures 9. Fevers, inflammations and infections

A. Terminology

Νόσος/*nósos* (Ionic νοῦσος/*noûsos*, 'D'.; etym.: 'being weakened') describes disease in an imagery of aggression, which remained in use for a long time [17], as a result of external (divine) or internal origin, which 'ruled over people and struck them down' (e.g.: ἱερὰ νόσος; *hierà nósos*, 'the sacred disease', epilepsy). From about the 5th cent. BC, the term was increasingly rivalled by the derivation *nósēma* [30], perhaps an expression coined by the Sophists; in any case, it rapidly spread through the medical world. It does not have the religious connotation of *nósos*, even less so, as it was used within nosology, which was being developed at the time. The Latin terms *morbus* and *infirmitas* (both at least partially equivalent to *nósos*), and *aegritudo*. In Byzantine Greek, the meaning of the term ἀρρωστία; *arrōstía*, which hailed from the classical period, was narrowed down to being synonymous with *nósēma*..

B. Mesopotamia and Egypt

Since the early Mesopotamian cultures, disease was seen as a consequence of an attack by animated beings (spirits and deities), unless it was the result of behaviour seen as morally deviant, or of magic [2]. The activity of the → physician was mainly restricted to the identification of the cause [1]. Although these conditions made a diagnosis particularly difficult [29; 34], doctors were confident of being able to identify diseases such as dysentery, tuberculosis, meningitis, epilepsy, gangrene, and osteitis [18].

Egyptian medicine was also based on an animistic system, which was, however, widened by speculations about physiopathological processes [3. 60–138; 24. 42–63]. The difficulties which such a system poses for interpretation are more than made up for by the wealth of mummified material, allowing a fairly accurate diagnosis of several diseases [24. 64–95]: parasitoses (esp. bilharziasis), malaria, tuberculosis, leprosy (not earlier than the 6th cent. BC), tetanus, as well as infections with abscesses. It is also conceivable that cardiovascular, gastrointestinal, and urinal afflictions as well as paralyses can be identified from the written sources. Strangely enough, skin diseases are only rarely in evidence, although it can be assumed that they were fairly frequent.

C. Sources from Antiquity and Late Antiquity

The majority of Graeco-Roman sources are texts, both literary and technical. The latter first appeared from the mid 5th cent. BC onwards with the nosographic treatises from the time of → Hippocrates [6] (4th cent. BC), and finally culminate in → Galen's *De locis affectis* (2nd cent. AD), the last great treatise of antiquity, a synthesis of the entire subject matter (even more so, as Galen wrote it towards the end of his medical career). In these works, pathological phenomena are topically ranked in accordance with the method of *a capite ad calcem* ('from head to heel'), i.e. in each case, the afflicted organs are listed from the head down.

Within the period mentioned above and even beyond, specialist works (literary as well as technical)

were written on a variety of topics such as toxicology (Nicander and both the treatises attributed to Pedanius Dioscorides), gynaecology (Soranus), kidneys and the urinary tract, melancholia, gout (Rufus), helminthology (worm diseases), and ophthalmology (Alexander [29] of Tralles); furthermore, in late antiquity, general and specialized treatises from the classical period were translated into Latin, e.g. the works of Soranus by Caelius [II 11] Aurelianus.

In Byzantine times, the body of ancient texts underwent a renewal through the inclusion of data resulting from the change in pathocenosis (see below), and also the inclusion of contributions by Arabian nosography (e.g. the description of smallpox in the treatise by Rhāzes/ar-Rāzī, translated perhaps in the 11th cent. by Symeon Seth).

For the earliest period, the lack of written accounts can be made up for by osteopathological data [38; 15]. Although they could also supplement the accounts in later treatises, the indicative value of this source is limited by its very nature.

Pictorial documents are rare: plastic representations of malformations, whose interpretation is particularly difficult, and illustrations in Byzantine mosaics and MSS, restricted, however, to scenes of Christ miraculously curing diseases and afflictions.

The identification of nosological symptoms with the help of retrospective diagnosis is particularly problematic because of the different systems of terminological (physiological or respectively pathological) reference in ancient and modern medicine.

D. Pathocenosis and epidemiology

Although the number of nosological phenomena increased with the number of treatises, the appearance of new diseases is less frequent than a broadening of the range of those diseases already described [5]. Some diseases, however, first appeared in classical and early Byzantine times, such as → leprosy (*elephantíasis*), which possibly first emerged after 300 BC and was endemic by the beginning of the common era, or the plague (Yersinia pestis), which had been endemic in the Near East for ages [7. 60–71], but was not found in Byzantium prior to Justinian's reign (6th cent. AD).

The pathocenosis (overall picture of common diseases) of the classical period [4] seems to have been characterized by infectious and parasitic diseases including → fever (esp. malaria), by typhoid (probably providing at least a partial explanation of the 'Plague of Athens' of 430 BC, Thuc. 2,51), by exceedingly frequent diseases of the respiratory and gastrointestinal systems (in the latter case predominantly caused by parasitoses), by forms of rheumatism, arthritis, and sciatica, by possibly widespread poliomyelitis with a variety of paralyses, by diseases of the nervous system which are insufficiently differentiated and difficult to identify, and finally by numerous eye infections, i.e. in total by a comparatively homogenous nosological complex, which is significantly different from that of other

regions such as Egypt. To this background must be added a number of great → epidemics; however, they were generally limited in space and time and frequently linked to wars or famines.

This pathocenosis underwent at least three changes through the 6th cent. AD: the first in the Hellenistic and Roman (Republican) periods with the large-scale movement of armies and the introduction of leprosy to Greece and Italy as well as that of smallpox to Italy (even though neither disease became endemic). Furthermore, the early Imperial period seems to have been marked by an increase in civilizational diseases[23], particularly gout.

The second change took place after the 1st cent. AD and the unification of the Roman Empire; it manifested itself in the appearance of large pandemics, often linked to the movement of people or armies: *leichḗn* ('lichen') in AD 46, the 'Antonine Plague' of AD 167 (smallpox?), measles (?) in 189 and other insufficiently identified contagious diseases in 232, 238, 252, 302, 312, 359, 376, 408–410. The third change occurred in the middle of the 6th cent. with the arrival of leprosy, smallpox becoming endemic (from 541), and the arrival of bubonic plague in Constantinople 542, called 'Justinianic Plague' and its quick spread across all of Europe (543: Italy, Provence, Rhone valley) [7. 40–49].

The lack of reliable data or respectively representative clinical descriptions of the afflicted population makes it very difficult to judge the spread and severity of individual diseases. Although the diseases described in the *Corpus Hippocraticum* and mentioned on votive offerings found in Epidaurus have been studied, these data can not be considered representative: the former represent actual cases treated by Hippocratic physicians, paying more attention to the individual sufferer than the disease in general, the second group cases where medicine failed [43] and the sufferer's final hope lay in divine miracles. The therapeutic indications of the medical substances in the various treatises seem to be of greater significance: In accordance with the basic assumption that there is necessarily a balance in the medical culture of pre-industrial societies between the therapeutic demands generated by pathocenosis and the reaction to it through medication, the frequency with which a particular therapy is mentioned can be taken as an indicator for the relative importance of an individual disease. The data in the following tables have been compiled based on the accounts in → Pedanius Dioscorides' treatise Περὶ ὕλης ἰατρικῆς (*Perì hýlēs iatrikês*, *De materia medica*) [44].

E. The Diseases according to Dioscorides

Despite the fundamental difficulties faced by this kind on investigation, it is possible to identify individual symptoms of ancient diseases through analysis of osteopathological data and though retrospective diagnostics — if necessary, through a combination of both techniques. In this framework, the following nosological facts pertaining to antiquity have been identified, presented in the following in groups and then tables ranked according to their frequency (not all of the ancient diseases are included here; cf. also the summary and overview at the end of this article).

1. Skin diseases

Their frequency is perhaps caused by the fact that they are fairly obvious. Their causes differ widely: facial erysipelas, probably a streptococcal dermatitis; λέπρα/*lépra*: not leprosy, but a skin disease attributed to a dyscrasia of the black gall, same as λειχήν/*leichḗn*; ἀλφός/*alphós*, characterized by depigmentation; ἕρπης/*hérpēs* or scabies, ψώρα/*psṓra*. Other skin problems are of an aesthetic nature (e.g. ἔφηλις/*éphēlis*) or traumatological, benign, or serious (e.g. scars).

	Number of cases	Percentage
Total	626	100.00
Erisypelas	49	7.82
lépra	47	7.66
leichḗn	33	5.27
alphós	33	5.27
hérpēs	30	4.79
psóra	26	4.15
éphēlis	28	4.47

2. Gastrointestinal tract

The gastrointestinal tract was particularly badly afflicted, not only by mainly unspecified stomach and abdominal pains, but also by diarrhoea, dysentery, colic, and bloating. The digestive organs themselves were also afflicted, i.a. by problems of the anus (prolapse and fissures, fistulas, and haemorrhoids) or ruptured intestines, or even by parasites [16; 7. 326–331]. Additionally there were a number of lesser afflictions, from anorexia to bradypepsia, dyspepsia, nausea and constipation.

	Number of cases	Percentage
Total	596	100.00
Stomach pain	105	17.61
Diarrhoea	99	16.61
Bellyache	97	16.27
Dysentery	74	12.41
Colic	54	9.06
Flatulence	36	6.04
Prolapse or fissures of the anus	36	6.04
hélmis and *askarís*	36	6.04
Fistulas and Haemorrhoids	23	3.85
Hernias	14	2.34

3. Toxicology

Poisonings with animal poisons constituted two thirds of the documented toxicological illnesses: alongside undefined cases, these are predominantly scorpion stings as well as snake and spider bites. Rabies, recognized by one of its symptoms (hydrophobia) and thought to be a kind of poisoning, was already quite common. Poisonings with plant poisons (a third) are mostly caused by fungi and also include the absorption of leeches, accidentally swallowed with water (for toxicology in general: [39]).

	Number of cases	Percentage
Total	481	100.00
Poisoning (animal venom)	322	67.00
Poisoning (plant poison)	159	33.00
Poisoning (animal venom)	322	100.00
Uncertain	153	49.90
Scorpion	39	11.90
Rabies	34	10.42
Snakebite	25	7.66
Spider bite	24	7.36
Poisoning (plant poison)	159	100.00
General	48	30.01
Mushrooms	15	10.56
Aconite	8	5.63

4. Gynaecology and midwifery

Undoubtedly, the importance of this area must have been greater than suggested by Dioscorides' records, even more so, as the recorded problems mostly deal with amenorrhea (absence of menstrual flow), general disorders of the uterus (esp. induration and occlusion), and miscarriages; in line with ancient aetiology, 'hysterical choking fits' (→ Hysteria) were also included, whereas there is no notable mention of sterility, problems in childbirth or miscarriages.

	Number of cases	Percentage
Total	377	100.00
Amenorrhoea	136	36.07
Hardening and Occlusion of the womb	130	34.48
Miscarriages	47	12.46
'Hysterical suffocation'	27	7.17
Gynaecology / Obstetrics	7	1.85

5. Urinary tract, liver, spleen

Problems when passing urine, unspecified as well as δυσουρία/*dysouría* or στραγγουρία/*strangouría* seem to have been quite common; in addition, there were illnesses of bladder or kidneys, particularly lithiasis. The male urinary tract is rarely mentioned, but with a variety of afflictions: ὑδροκήλη/*hydrokḗlē*, discharge of semen, and a single mention of a φίμωσις/*phímōsis*. Both liver and spleen seem to have been badly afflicted, without these afflictions necessarily being linked with specific problems of the urinary tract, even though such a link was frequently assumed because of their swelling as a consequence of malaria. Hydropsy and oedema are well represented, as well as gout.

	Number of cases	Percentage
Total	504	100.00
Difficulties in urinating	195	38.69
Bladder diseases	50	10.00
Kidney diseases	50	10.00
Dropsy	49	9.72
Gout	48	9.52
Oedema	47	9.32
Lithiasis	37	7.34
Diseases of the male urinary tract	28	5.55

6. Respiratory system and tract

Most prevalent were undefined affections of the πλευρά/*pleurá* and the thorax; amongst the identifiable illnesses, coughs feature prominently, as do breathing problems (*orthópnoia*, *ásthma*, *dýspnoia*); colds are mentioned in a variety of forms (*katárrhous*, *kóryza*, and *bránchos*) is a bit more common than *phthísis*, which is equated with tuberculosis. The 'cough of Perinthus' (Hippoc. Epid. 6,7,1), dated to *c.* 400 BC and perhaps observed by Hippocrates himself, undoubtedly comprises several nosological cases, amongst them whooping cough. It is possible that angina, which was mainly seen as a difficulty in breathing, also included diphtheria.

	Number of cases	Percentage
Total	327	100.00
Coughs	79	24.15
Diseases of the *pleurá*	41	12.53
Diseases of the thorax	39	11.92
orthópnoia	29	8.86
ásthma	26	7.95
katárrhous, *kóryza* and *bránchos*	18	5.50
phthísis	17	5.19
dýspnoia	10	3.05

7. Sensory organs and perception

Eyes and vision as well as ears and hearing were particularly afflicted by illnesses. Almost half of the documented afflictions concerning eyes and vision were unspecified, the remaining cases concerned the following (in decreasing order of frequency): cataracts (*tá episkotoúnta taîs kórais*), weak sight (*amblyōpía*), pterygium (*pterýgion*), inflammation of the tear sac (*aigílōps*), scarring of the cornea (*leúkōma*), white speck cataracts (*árgemos*), as well as inflammations of the eye lids and conjunctivitis (*psōrophthalmía*), to which comes the peculiar feature of night blindness (*nyktalōpía*). It must be emphasized that the afflictions of eyes and vision were not necessarily caused by greater light intensity, but possibly also by nutritional deficiencies and bacteria (in the latter case an infectious disease [7. 378–385]).

Ears and hearing were very frequently afflicted by otalgia (earaches), suppurations, inflammations, as well as other injuries; undoubtedly, frequently mentioned hearing problems such as tinnitus and deafness were symptoms.

	Number of cases	Percentage
Total	436	100.00
Eyes and eyesight	316	72.47
Ears and hearing	120	27.53
Eyes and eyesight	316	100.00
Uncertain	135	42.72
Clouding of the pupil(s)	28	8.86
amblyōpía	24	7.59
árgemos, *psōrophthalmía*, *nyktalōpía*	16	5.06
pterýgion	15	4.74
aigílōps	12	3.79
leúkōma	11	3.48
Ears and hearing	120	100.00
Otalgia	44	36.66
Pain; various conditions	32	26.66
Suppuration	16	13.33
Impaired hearing; tinnitus; Deafness	16	13.33

8. Bones, joints, fractures

Apart from fractures, luxations, and severe traumatic injuries, which make up more than half of the recorded afflictions of the skeletal system, the most important afflictions were pains in the hip joints, equivalent to modern sciatica (neuralgia of the sciatic nerve); for the remainder, painful joints dominate, whose causes are difficult to specify and which are also difficult to distinguish from the pain caused by gout.

	Number of cases	Percentage
Total	231	100.00
Fractures, luxations and serious traumatic lesions	126	54.54
ischiás	67	29.00
Joint pains	32	9.96

9. Fevers, inflammations and infections

The various forms of → fever were not clearly defined; where referred to as *tritaîos* or *tetartaîos* ('occurring on the third or fourth day') [32], they can be linked with malaria which was widespread at the time [14; 7. 230–247]. The 'Plague of Athens' of 430 BC can without doubt be identified as typhoid fever [7. 24–39]. Inflammations were common, general as well as local; they could affect all of the internal and external organs, in the case of the latter frequently in conjunction with all kinds of phlegmons and abscesses. Infections mostly occurred as a consequence of injuries or wounds; if they became worse, sepsis could develop.

10. Iatrogenic complications

They were distinguished from poisonings and clearly presented as consequences of the abuse of medical drugs or as side effects of drugs; they appear in many variations, with a total of 38 illnesses listed (the most important of which are included in the table below).

	Number of cases	Percentage
Total	120	100.00
Stomach problems and abdominal pain	35	29.16
Haematuria; bladder and kidney problems	18	15.06
Headaches	14	11.66
Stupefaction or mania	11	9.16
Ulceration	7	5.83
Various conditions	7	5.83
Exitus	4	3.33

11. Neuropsychological disorders

These were not or only very rarely recognized; in antiquity, they were linked with humoral physiological phenomena (melancholia) or organic disorders (hysteria or phrenitis) [36; 11; 25; 26; 27; 10. 17–37].

Furthermore come disorders of limited geographical range, such as bean allergy, and others which were wide-spread, but not clearly identified, such as the various forms of anaemia (thalassemia) [7. 348–355]. Particularly remarkable is that epidemics of sexually transmitted diseases (→ Venereal diseases), recognized and described as such, are missing (even though framboesia is presumed to be an ancient disease [7. 104–109]), as is the recognition of the special medical features of disorders in childhood or old age.

12. Synopsis

Synoptic table of medical topics in Pedanius Dioscorides' treatise *De materia medica* (*Perí hýlēs iatrikḗs*) with their frequency (in absolute figures and percentages):

Skin, nails, mucous membranes	626	11.64
Digestive apparatus	596	11.08
Toxicology	481	8.94
Gynaecology and obstetrics	377	7.01
Urinary apparatus	348	6.47
Respiratory tract	327	6.08
Eyes; eyesight	316	5.87
Bones; joints; fractures	231	4.29
Wounds and ulcers	223	4.14
Bodily fluids	140	2.60
Inflammation	138	2.56
Mouth; gums; throat; voice	130	2.42
Ears; hearing	120	2.23
Iatrogenic conditions	120	2.23
Nervous system; spasms and tremors	110	2.04
Blood; veins	107	1.99
Flatulence; dropsy	96	1.78
Hepatic system	92	1.71
Slight injuries	90	1.67
Nutrition; digestion	82	1.52
Spleen	76	1.41
Head	69	1.28
Fever	65	1.20
Teeth	54	1.00
Nerves; muscles; paralysis	51	0.94
Gout	48	0.89
Hair	36	0.66
Tuberculosis	33	0.61
Male genitalia	28	0.52
Discharge	27	0.50
Ganglion system	27	0.50
External parasites	24	0.44
Pain	21	0.39
Asthenia	20	0.37
Psychology	13	–
Tetanus	10	–
Vertigo	9	–
Leprosy	6	–
Excessive food intake	5	–
Sleep	4	–
Contagious diseases	2	–
TOTAL	5,375	98.98

→ Alexander [29] of Tralles; → Caelius [II 11] Aurelianus; → Pedanius Dioscorides; → Empiricists; → Erasistratus; → Galen; → Hippocrates [6]; → Medicine; → Methodists; → Rufus [6] of Samaria; → Soranus; → Medicine; → History of Medicine

1 H.I. Avalos, Illness and Health Care in the Ancient Near East, 1995 2 Id., Medicine, in: Oxford Encyclopedia of Archaeology in the Near East, vol. 3, 1997, 452–459 3 T. Bardinet, Les papyrus médicaux de l'Egypte pharaonique, 1995 4 J.-N. Biraben, Le malattie in Europa: equilibri e rotture della patocenosi, in: Storia del pensiero medico occidentale 1, 1993, 439–484 5 S. Byl, Néologismes et premières attestations de noms de maladies, symptômes et syndromes dans le Corpus Hippocraticum, in: D. Gourevitch (ed.), Maladie et maladies, Mélanges Grmek, 1992, 77–94 6 J.-N. Corvisier, Santé et société en Grèce ancienne, 1985 7 F.E.G. Cox (ed.), Illustrated History of Tropical Diseases, 1996
8 K. Deichgräber, Die griech. Empirikerschule, repr. 1965 9 J. Desautels, L'image du monde selon Hippocrate, 1982 10 M.W. Dols, Majnûn: the Madman in Medieval Islamic Society, 1992 11 L. Garcia Ballester, Soul and Body, Disease of the Soul and Disease of the Body in Galen's Medical Thought, in: P. Manuli (ed.), Le opere psicologiche di Galeno, 1988, 117–152
12 I. Garofalo, Erasistrati fragmenta, 1988 13 M.D. Grmek, Il concetto di malattia, in: Id., Storia del pensiero medico occidentale 1, 1993, 323–347 (English: Western Medical Thought from Antiquity to the Middle Ages. Cambridge, MA: Harvard University Press, 1999)
14 Id., Bibliographie chronologique des études originales sur la malaria dans la Méditerranée orientale préhistorique et antique, in: Lettre Jean Palerne 24, 1994, 1–7
15 M.D. Grmek, D. Gourevitch, Spicilège d'études

paléopathologiques concernant la partie européenne du territoire de l'Empire Romain, in: Lettre Jean Palerne 27, 1996, 2–25 16 D. GROVE, A History of Human Helminthology, 1990 17 J. JOUANNA, La maladie comme agression dans la collection hippocratique et la tragédie grecque, in: P. POTTER et.al. (eds.), La maladie et les maladies dans la collection hippocratique, 1990, 39–60 18 J. V. KINNIER WILSON, Diseases in Babylon: An Examination of Selected Texts, in: Journal of the Royal Medical School 89, 1996, 135–140 19 J. C. LARCHET, Théologie de la maladie, 1991 20 C. LICCIARDI, Les causes des maladies dans les sept livres des Epidémies, in: P. POTTER et al. (eds.), La maladie et les maladies dans la Collection Hippocratique, 1990, 323–337 21 J. LÓPEZ-FÉREZ, La strangurie dans le corpus Hippocraticum, in: P. POTTER et al. (ed.), La maladie et les maladies dans la Collection Hippocratique, 1990, 221–226 22 G. LORENZ, Ant. Krankenbehandlung in histor.-vergleichender Sicht, 1990 23 P. MIGLIORINI, Scienza e terminologia medica nella letteratura latina di età neroniana, 1997 24 J. F. NUNN, Ancient Egyptian Medicine, 1996 25 J. PIGEAUD, Folie et cures de la folie chez les médecins de l'Antiquité gréco-romaine, 1987 26 Id., La psychopathologie de Galien, in: P. MANULI (ed.), Le opere psicologiche di Galeno, 1988, 153–183 27 Id., La maladie de l'âme, 1989 28 Id., Il medico e la malattia, in: S. SETTIS (ed.), I Greci 1, 1996, 771–814 29 M. POWELL, Drugs and Pharmaceuticals in Ancient Mesopotamia, in: The Healing Past, 1993, 47–67 30 G. PREISER, Allg. Krankheits-Bezeichnungen im Corpus Hippocraticum, 1976
31 E. SCHÖNER, Das Viererschema in der ant. Humoralpathologie, 1964 32 F. SKODA, Les noms grecs de fièvres, in: Centre de recherches comparatives sur les langues de la Méditerranée ancienne, Documents 10, 1989, 226–238 33 W. D. SMITH, Pleuritis in the Hippocratic Corpus, and after, in: P. POTTER et.al. (eds.), La maladie et les maladies dans la Collection Hippocratique, 1990, 189–207 34 M. STOL, Diagnosis and Therapy in Babylonian Medicine, in: Jaarbericht van het Voorasiatische-Egyptische Genootschap Ex Oriente Lux 32, 1990–1992, 42–65 35 O. TEMKIN, Hippocrates in a World of Pagans and Christians, 1991 36 Id., The Falling Sickness. A History of Epilepsy from the Greeks to the Beginnings of Modern Neurobiology, 21971 37 J. THÉODORIDÈS, Histoire de la rage, 1986 38 P. THILLAUD, Paléopathologie humaine, 1995 39 A. TOUWAIDE, Galien et la toxicologie, in: ANRW II 37.2, 1994, 1887–1986 40 A. TOUWAIDE et al., Medicinal Plants for the Treatment of Urogenital Tract Pathologies according to Dioscorides' De Materia Medica, in: American Journal of Nephrology 17, 1997, 241–247 41 J. T VALANCE, The Lost Theory of Asclepiades of Bithynia, 1990 42 Id., The Medical System of Asclepiades of Bithynia, in: ANRW II 37.1, 1993, 693–727 43 H. VON STADEN, Incurability and Hopelessness: the Hippocratic Corpus, in: P. POTTER et al. (eds.), La maladie et les maladies dans la Collection hippocratique, 1990, 61–112 44 M. WELLMANN, Pedanii Dioscuridis de materia medica libri quinque, 3 vols., 1906–1914 (repr. 1958).

B. ARENSBOURG, M.S. GOLDSTEIN, A Review of Paleopathology in the Middle East, in: H. WASERMAN (ed.), Health and Disease in the Holy Land, 1996, 19–36; P.F. BURKE, Malaria in the Greco-Roman World. A Historical and Epidemiological Survey, in: ANRW II 37.3, 1996, 2252–2281; G. COOTJANS, La stomatologie dans le Corpus aristotélicien, 1991; M.W. DOLS, The Black Death in the Middle East, 1977; A.C. EFTYCHIADES, *Eisagōgē eis tēn Byzantinēn therapeutikēn*, 1983; G.B. FERNGREN, D.W. AMUNDSEN, Medicine and Christianity in the Roman Empire: Compatibilities and Tensions, in: ANRW II 37.3, 1996, 2957–2980; D. GOUREVITCH, Le triangle hippocratique dans le monde gréco-romain, 1984; Id., Bibliogr. du vocabulaire de la pathologie en latin ancien, in: Lettre Centre Jean Palerne 23, 1993, 1–23; Id., La gynécologie et l'obstétrique, in: ANRW II 37.3, 1996, 2083–2146; M.D. GRMEK, Les maladies à l'aube de la civilisation occidentale, 1983; R. JACKSON, Eye Medicine in the Roman Empire, in: ANRW II 37.3, 1996, 2228–2252; M.H. MARGANNE, L'ophtalmologie dans l'Egypte gréco-romaine d'après les papyrus littéraires, 1994; F. MAWET, Recherches sur les oppositions fonctionnelles dans le vocabulaire homérique de la douleur (autour de pêma-algos), 1979; P. POTTER, G. MALONEY, J. DESAUTELS (eds.), La maladie et les maladies dans la collection hippocratique, 1990; F. SKODA, Médecine ancienne et métaphore. Le vocabulaire de l'anatomie et de la pathologie en grec ancien, 1988; J. STANNARD, Diseases of Western Antiquity, in: Cambridge World History of Human Diseases, 1993, 262–270; F. STOCK, Follia e malattie mentali nella medicina dell'età romana, in: ANRW II 37.3, 1996, 2282–2409; R. STRÖMBERG, Griech. Wortstud. Unt. zur Benennung von Tieren, Pflanzen, Körperteilen und Krankheiten, 1944. A.TO.

Dishes, Meals (Greek ἐδέσματα/*edésmata*; Lat. *cibi, esca*). A classification of dishes in antiquity is unknown to us and can be deduced only from antique → cookery books. They generally organize dishes according to their basic ingredients, thus according to such food groups as fish, meat (quadrupeds), poultry, vegetables, grains and legumes [1]. Ancient sources attest to a variety of dishes; apart from cookery books, comedies (Aristophanes; Plautus) are especially informative sources of information, as well as technical agricultural (Cato Agr.; Columella) and medical tracts (Hippoc. De alimento; Cels. De medicina; Pedanius Dioscorides; Gal. De alimentorum facultatibus; cf. also Plin. HN; Gellius; Macrob. Sat.). Surpassing all of them was the 'Banquet of the Learned' of Athenaeus [3] (end 2nd cent. AD), that mentions a large number of mainly Greek dishes by name and also includes the most important ingredients. Athenaeus also often records the place of a particular dish within a meal (appetizer, main course, dessert; 128c–130d) and within a classification of meals: everyday meals, (156c-d); festive meals (267e–269e); cult meals (364d-e). His work thus provides information on the social, religious and cultural dimension of meals in antiquity.

Cookery books are the main source of information for the composition and preparation of dishes. In this context the 4th-cent. AD work *De re coquinaria*, ascribed to → Caelius [II 10] Apicius, has to be singled out, the only cookery book from antiquity extant in its entirety. The book contains 478 recipes. While the foodstuffs and other ingredients are mentioned in each case, the quantities generally are not; also, the recipes only rarely give information on the manner and length of preparation, the method of cooking and temperature. As that information cannot be obtained from other sources, it is impossible to determine exactly the consistency, appearance and shape, but especially the seasoning and taste, of the dishes in Apicius' work. The instructions for assembling and preparing the individual dishes are nevertheless clear. They regularly consist of more than ten ingredients and their preparation calls for high technical skills and special kitchen equipment. The dishes were invariably thinly cut up or prepared in such a way as to ensure a soft consistency. The dishes were all intended to be served up with a rich helping of sauce, the real source of taste. The sauces were produced with a base of cooking or frying juices, supplemented with ready-made sauces (*garum*), sweet wine-based mixtures or → honey and a variety of → spices. The dishes had a strong aroma, a powerful flavour and frequently combined contrasting taste sensations. The underlying objective was to achieve a harmony of sweet, sour, bitter and salty [2. 191].

Apicius' cookery book's instructions for assembling and preparing dishes ought not to be extrapolated to antiquity in general. Apart from differences in place and time, it should also be especially borne in mind that dishes and eating habits, were dependent also on the social background of the consumer. Thus, if Apicius' cookery book, which targeted well-to-do gourmets of the Roman Imperial period, contained many recipes for meat and → fish dishes, this in no way reflects the eating habits of the wider population. In the Imperial period and in antiquity generally the population at large predominantly ate dishes with legumes (→ vetch), → grain and → vegetables. The use of spices and sauces also varied according to social standing. If the upper classes happened to prefer sauces that were based on choice ingredients and could only be produced at great expense (cf. καρύκη/*karýkē*, a sauce, invented in Lydia, from blood and spices; Ath. 516c), simple folk had to be content with mainly ready-made sauces like the various varieties of *garum*. Finally, eating habits were subject to the spirit of the age. Thus, classical Greek cuisine rarely used more than four spices for a dish, whereas ten or more were included in refined Roman cooking of the Imperial period (cf. especially Apicius 10). Gourmets from the classical Greek period may have preferred fish dishes [3. 25–57], but in the chapter addressed to the gourmet *par excellence*, as its title (*polyteles*, 'expensive') implies, Apicius lists only → meat dishes.

Overall, antiquity boasted a large number of dishes from which the sources have passed on only a small proportion. It is regrettable that we are so deeply ignorant of everyday dishes, as well as the dishes and eating habits, among the lower social levels. The same is true of the nature and role of dishes in a cultic context (→ Meal offerings).

→ Nutrition; → Table culture; → Fish dishes; → Meat dishes; → Vegetables; → Beverages; → Spices; → Cook; → Meals; → Food

1 F. Bilabel, s. v. Kochbücher, RE 11, 932–943 2 J. André, Essen und Trinken im alten Rom, 1998 (French [2]1981) 3 J. N. Davidson, Courtesans and Fishcakes: The Consuming Passions of Classical Athens, 1997.

A. Dalby, Siren Feasts: A History of Food and Gastronomy in Greece, 1996; F. Orth, s. v. Kochkunst, RE 11, 944–982. A. G.

Dishypatos (δισύπατος; *dis(h)ýpatos*). Middle-ranking administrator within the Byzantine bureaucracy, first recorded in 804 [1. 153*, 39]. The title of a *dishypatus* was given to judges and administrators. Of frequent occurrence from the 12th cent. on; after 1178 exclusively as a family name.

1 G. Fatouros, Theodori Studitae epistulae, I, 1992.

J. Bury, The Imperial Administrative System, 1911, 27; R. Guilland, Recherches sur les Institutions byzantines, II, 1967, 79–81; W. Seibt, Die byz. Bleisiegel in Österreich, I, 1978, 237–240. G.MA.

Dis Pater Roman equivalent of the Greek ruler of the Underworld, → Hades or respectively → Pluto. According to ancient tradition, the name *Dis* derives from *dives*, 'rich', in the same way as Pluto derives from *ploûtos*, 'wealth' (Cic. Nat. D. 2,66; Quint. Inst. 1,6,34). Dis Pater (DP) was only worshipped in cult within the context of the *ludi Tarentini*, a celebration of atonement introduced by the Sibylline oracles in 249 BC, and its associated secular festival; together with → Proserpina, he was venerated at → Tarentum with the sacrifice of black animals (Varro in Censor. 17,8; Val. Max. 2,4,5): this low-profile cultic presence in a context, which is Greek-dominated though the Sybillines and the link with Proserpina, provides support for the ancient explanation that the cult originated in the Greek world. Its origins probably lay in lower Italy, where Pluto and Persephone were frequently venerated together, as e.g. in Elea or in Locri. Furthermore, a hammer-bearing masked figure called DP was charged with removing bodies from the arena (Tert. Ad nat. 1,10,47; cf. Apol. 15). This is more than a mere literary-inspired spectacle, as is evident from the hammer, pointing to the Etruscan → Charon [1]. — In the image of the other world by Vibia, a follower of → Sabazius, the dead woman faces a bearded DP and a lady ruler of the dead, called Aeracura [2]; the same couple — with the graphic variations of Hera/Era and (H)erecura — is also found on dedications from the Gallic and Germanic provinces (ILS 3961–3968). This, too, is assumed to be a Greek development in the inner circle of mysteries; the goddess is perhaps to be seen as an underworldly Hera in a combination of → Hera and → Kore.

In contrast with the low-level cultic presence, the metrically unproblematic name DP is very common in literature as the Roman equivalent of Hades-Pluto.

1 F. Altheim, Griech. Götter im alten Rom, 1930, 90f. 2 E. Lane, Corpus Cultus Iovis Sabazii 2, 1985, 31 no. 65.

G. WISSOWA, Religion und Kultus der Römer ²1912, 309–313. F.G.

Dispensator (*ab aere pendendo*, Varro, Ling. 5,183). In earlier times the *dispensator* would presumably weigh unminted precious metals for his master or the state. The post developed into that of bookkeeper, cashier and steward, much like the Greek *oikonómos*. It is frequently encountered in Roman inscriptions. Many *dispensatores* were slaves or freedmen. In Gaius Inst. 1,122 they are distinguished as a special type of slaves: *servi, quibus permittitur administratio pecuniae, dispensatores appellati sunt* ('slaves entrusted with the management of money are called *dispensatores*'). Great influence was exercised by the *dispensator Caesaris* or *Augusti* as administrators of the private fortune of the emperor or a member of the imperial family. They worked not only in close proximity of the Emperor, but also on his estates and in other enterprises. In addition *dispensatores* were responsible for manning customs warehouses (→ *horrea*) and overseeing the grain supply. In late antiquity the function of *dispensator* was also included in church administration.

LIEBENAM, s.v. D., RE 5, 1189–1198. G.S.

Display scripts

A. DEFINITION B. GREEK C. LATIN

A. DEFINITION

Lettering designed to highlight certain parts of a manuscript such as the title, subtitle, opening, scholia, lemmata, subscription, contents and initials; single sentences such as Biblical quotations from the surrounding text; and book and chapter numberings (→ Scripts).

B. GREEK

For Greek scripts it is usual, apart from rare examples in majuscule codices, to talk of display scripts only after the → minuscule became established, and to distinguish three styles (there are also mixed types): 1. The Alexandrinian display majuscule, also called Coptic uncial [1], commonly used in conjunction with the Pearl script (10th–11th cents.), is characterized by alternating thick and thin letters, thicker extremities and distinctive forms for *alpha, my, ypsilon* and *omega*. 2. The Byzantine display majuscule, also known as pointed arch majuscule, with an alphabet stemming from the Biblical majuscule, was frequently employed in conjunction with older minuscules and Italo-Greek scripts. Typical are the pronounced shading and breaks in the curves. 3. The term 'epigraphic display majuscule' was minted because of its possible descent from inscriptions [2]. Typical of it are minuscule forms, juxtapositions and ligatures, as well as the superposition and enclosure of individual letters. We can distinguish a narrow and balanced variant and a square and broad one. Both these variants, which were sometimes used in combination, were in use from the end of the 10th cent.

→ Uncial; → Majuscule; → Minuscule

1 J. IRIGOIN, L'onciale grecque de type copte, in: Jb. der Österreichischen Byz. Ges. 8, 1959, 29–51 2 H. HUNGER, Epigraphische Auszeichnungsmajuskel, in: Jb. der Österreichischen Byz. Ges. 26, 1977, 193–210 3 H. HUNGER, Minuskel und Auszeichnungsschriften im 10.–12. Jh., in: La paléographie grecque et byzantine, 1977, 204–209. P.E.

C. LATIN

Display scripts are typical of the history of Latin script from the earliest documents. At first different patterns of writing were used: smaller hands for running titles and larger ones for the *explicit*. The initial letter on each page, even columns, may be enlarged irrespective of any break in the text. At the start of a textual unit not just single letters but whole words or sections could be graphically highlighted.

By the 5th cent. at the latest the principle had been adopted of using a script distinct from that of the text proper. By and large older scripts were preferred. In uncial codices, the headings, chapter titles, texts in miniatures, *incipit, explicit*, colophons and quotations would be written in capitals and sometimes, quotation marks in the margin and the use of indented or jutting-out lines were employed for emphasis. Both capitals and uncials were used as display scripts in half-uncial codices. Besides different inks, space between lines and decorative frames were used. The text could likewise be underlined and letters embellished. It went so far that in scriptoria like Luxeuil and Lindisfarne majuscule alphabets were developed solely for display.

In Carolingian times, a strict hierarchy of writing styles was codified. Square or, less frequently, rustic capitals of various sizes were most important, followed by uncials and half uncials, the latter confined to environments like the 'court schools' of Charlemagne and at Tours. Within the text *auctoritates* and *nomina sacra* were set off by a type of display script that mixed capitals and uncials. Uncials in particular were the basis for the heavier display script in the Gothic era, achieved by doubling and thickening the lines. Minuscules with enlarged letters, which were used in any case to distinguish between text and commentary remained in use and were now donned with doubled strokes, reinforced elements and distinguishing marks. *Textura* was used as a display script in both cursive and bastarda manuscripts. Humanists were later to rediscover the capitals of antiquity and were inspired partly by inscriptions — there is a constant relation between display scripts and contemporary inscriptions — and partly by examples from book scripts. Later a lightly rounded form of square capital predominated, illuminated with the help of coloured, sometimes golden inks and enclosed in an ornamental frame in the image of inscriptions, column breaks and suchlike.

→ Capitals; → Uncials

1 J. AUTENRIETH, 'Litterae Virgilianae'. Vom Fortleben einer Schrift, 1988, 5–35 (*passim*) 2 B. BISCHOFF, Paläographie des röm. Altertums und des abendländischen

Mittelalters, 1979, 77–79; 92; 100–102; 127; 134; 148; 162; 179; 244; 259 J.J. JOHN, s.v. A., LMA 1, 1259–1260 (with bibliography) E. KESSLER, Die A. in den Freisinger Codices von den Anfängen bis zur karolingischen Erneuerung, 1986 O. MAZAL, Buchkunst der Gotik, 1975, 30–31. D.F.

Dispositio The *dispositio* (τάξις, *táxis*) was considered in the text books of rhetoric an indispensable stage, serving to mould the results a speaker had reached in the → *inventio* into a speech (Rhet. Her. 3,16; cf. Cic. Inv. 1,9; Quint. Inst. pr. 1; 7,1,1 and *passim*). For this reason most authors discuss it immediately after the *inventio* (Quint. Inst. 7, pr. 2). Occasionally it is placed after *inventio* and → *elocutio* (Cic. De or. 1,187; 2,79; also Arist. Rh. 1403b6ff.), as the organizing criterion for the two essential parts of a speech: *res* and *verba*. Its primary object was *utilitas*; this distinguished it from the normal arrangement (*ordo*). Other relevant points were *decor* and *necessitas* (Cic. De or. 1,142; Iul. Vict. Rhet. 81,24ff.). Already in the Rhet. Her. 3,16 two types of *dispositio* are listed: one, *ab institutione artis*, concerns the logical order of the parts of a speech (*principium, narratio, divisio, confirmatio, refutatio, epilogus*) and of its arguments (*expositio, ratio, confirmatio rationis, exornatio, conclusio*); the other frees itself from the *ordo artificiosus* to follow the *iudicium* of the speaker on the respective case. Unlike *partitio*, which was simply a *species* of the *dispositio* (Quint. Inst. 3,9,2), the *dispositio* applied to all parts of the speech, not only regulating their sequence but determining their presence, their lack or their division. Of fundamental importance was the strategic ordering of the arguments within the → *argumentatio* part, which would vary according to the position of the parties to a case. For an accusal the 'Homeric' order, setting the weakest arguments in the middle, was particularly effective (Quint. Inst. 5,12,14), while the descending order from strongest to weakest was to be avoided (ibid.). Also, it was to the prosecutor's advantage to lump several feeble arguments together hoping they would support each other, while it was more convenient for the defence to refute each argument separately.

G. CALBOLI, Rhetorica ad C. Herrenium, 1969; L. CALBOLI MONTEFUSCO, Consulti Fortunatiani Ars Rhetorica, 1979; Id., s.v. Dispositio, HWdR, vol. 2, 1994, 831–839; P. HAMBERGER, Die rednerische Dispositio in der alten ΤΕΧΝΗ ΡΗΤΟΡΙΚΗ (Korax-Gorgias-Antiphon), thesis 1914. L.C.M.

Dissimilation see → Graßmann's law, see → Phonetics

Dissoi logoi (Δισσοὶ λόγοι; *dissoì lógoi*), i.e. 'double argument', a title taken from the opening words of an anonymous treatise appended to the manuscripts of Sextus Empiricus and written in the Dorian dialect probably at the beginning of the 4th cent. BC, in any case after the end of the Peloponnesian War in 404 BC. The basic structure is the systematic opposition of arguments for and against a number of apparent opposites: good and evil, beauty and ugliness, just and unjust, true and false. The source of this hard-to-classify work has been sought in Pythagorean [1] and in particular sophist sources, and more recently closely compared with the anti-logical method of sophistic thought in the 5th cent., as in the so-called 'overturning arguments' (Καταβάλλοντες; *Katabállontes*) ascribed to → Protagoras, but also apparent in the dialectics of Zeno and in the arguments of Gorgias' treatise 'On What is not'.

1 A. ROSTAGNI, Un nuovo capitolo nella storia della retorica e della sofistica, in: SIFC, 52, N.S. 2,1–2, 1922, 201–236.

EDITIONS AND TRANSLATIONS: DIELS & KRANZ II (90) 405–416; T.M. ROBINSON, Contrasting Arguments, an Edition of the D. L., 1979; A. LEVI, On Twofold Statements, in: AJPh 61, 1940, 292–306; M. UNTERSTEINER, I sofisti, 1949, 2

LITERATURE: C.J. CLASSEN, in: Elenchos, 6, 1985. B.C.

Dithyramb (ὁ διθύραμβος; *dithýrambos*). Choral song in honour of → Dionysus. The origin and meaning of this term has caused much speculation since ancient times. The word itself is certainly not a Greek, perhaps a Phrygian composition; most likely from a combination of *íambos* (ἴαμβος; two-step) and *thríambos* (θρίαμβος; three-step) [1]. In a contested passage of his *Poetics* () Aristotle makes the dithyramb the harbinger of tragedy — or, say others [2], of comedy.

Three phases can be distinguished in the history of the genre: the pre-literary dithyramb; the institutional phase of the 6th cent.; and the new dithyramb from the middle of the 5th cent. At first the dithyramb was a hymn of Dionysiac content, performed by a group of singers led by an exarch, as confirmed by the oldest testimony, Archil. fr. 120 WEST. The next phase arose from the cultural and religious policies of the tyrants and of the young Attic democracy: according to Herodotus 1,23 Arion was the first to compose (ποιήσαντα) a choral hymn in Corinth at the end of the 7th cent., to rehearse and perform it (διδάξαντα) and finally to bestow the existing name of dithyramb on the new art or, alternatively, give his song a title [3] (ὀνομάσαντα). In Athens the dithyramb is associated with the name of Lasus of Hermione, who organized the dithyrambic agons, probably in the early years of Attic democracy. Each of the ten Attic phyles would enter a male voice and a boys' choir of fifty singers apiece for the contest. Funding — settlements for the poet, the choir-leader, flautist and the outfitting of the choir — fell to the → choragos, who in the event of victory was entitled to place a tripod with a dedicatory inscription on the tripod way. The dithyrambic agon was a contest between phyles, not between poets, who were not even mentioned in the victory inscriptions. This underlined the political function of the dithyrambic agon; in the newly-established political order, the participation of the dithyrambic choir helped to build a tradition. *Dithýramboi* were performed during the following feasts in Athens: the Great → Dionysia and → Thargelia, the Lesser → Panathenaea, → Prometheia and Hephaesteia (cf. Lys. 21,1–4; ps.-Xen. Ath. pol. 3,4; Antiph. 6,11). The first victory at the Athenian Dionysia was carried off by an otherwise unknown Hypodicus of Chalcis (509/8 BC).

In the first half of the 5th cent. Simonides (56 victories in the agon), Pindar and Bacchylides dominated the field. The dithyrambs of Pindar (fr. 70–88 MAEHLER) reveal stereotyped elements: the occasion of its performance, the hosting polis, praise of the poet, the recounting of myths and especially Dionysian theology seem to belong to the standard repertoire of Pindaric dithyramb. Bacchylides' dithyrambs, however, with exception of the *Io* (c. 19) lack topical allusions. From this come the difficulties connected with their classification since Alexandrian times (cf. fr. 23 MAEHLER: the discussion between → Aristarchus of Samothrace and → Callimachus on how to classify the *Cassandra*).

Later in the cent. the genre was appropriated by the musical avant-garde of the time (the so-called new dithyramb) as → Pherecrates' musical innovations (fr. 155 PCG VII) and → Pratinas' reaction to them (fr. 708 PMG) make clear [4]. → Melanippides, → Cinesias, → Timotheus and → Philoxenus were prominent in this movement. Among their innovations were the astrophic form (ἀναβολή; *anabolḗ*; Melanippides, cf. Aristot. Rh. 3,9,1409b 30–33), instrumental and vocal solos, rhythmic variations (μεταβολαὶ κατὰ ῥυθμόν; *metabolaì katà rhytmón*), modulation of one tone into others (καμπή; *kampḗ*, cf. Aristoph. Nub. 333), the mixing of the original Phrygian harmony of the dithyramb with the Doric harmony of the → paean (Philoxenus in the Mysians, so Aristot. Pol. 8,7,1342b 8–15) and mimetic dances and music (cf. the parody of Philoxenus' dithyramb 'Cyclops or Galatea' in Aristoph. Plut. 290ff.).

The increasing separation of the dithyramb from its religious context and its resultant literary nature finds its expression in the compositions of Licymnius of Chios, which Aristotle Rh. 3,9,1413b,14–16 qualifies as fit for reading more than for choral performance. Reading the dithyrambs of → Telestes became so popular in the 4th cent. BC that Alexander the Great had them sent into his camp (Plut. Alex. 8,3). The same cent. saw a new art form emerge from the dithyramb, something like a lyric koine that also influenced other lyric genres. Plato uses *dithyrambôdes* (διθυραμβῶδες) and dithyrambs figuratively as a stylistic category to characterize swollen, overloaded diction (Plato Crat. 409b12–c3, Pl. Phdr. 241e2). Poems were composed with dithyrambic content and of dithyrambic style (Philoxenus, Deipnon, fr. 836 *PMG* Arion's Thanksgiving, fr. 939 *PMG*). The Middle Comedy contains long passages in dithyrambic style (e.g. Eubulus fr. 42 *PCG* V; Antiphanes fr. 55 *PCG* II) [4].

Dithyrambic music strongly influenced the religious poetry of the following cent.: both → Isyllus of Epidaurus and the Epidauric and Delphic hymns are shaped by the musical innovations of the new dithyramb. In the Hellenistic era dithyrambs were performed on Delos at the Delia and Apollonia festivals, and at the Great Dionysia in Athens until the 2nd cent. AD. The few fragments we have, make it hard to judge the poems of this period.

→ Dionysia; → DITHYRAMB

1 W. BRANDENSTEIN, Ἴαμβος, θρίαμβος, διθύραμβος, in: IF 54, 1936, 34–38 2 J. LEONHARDT, Phalloslied und Dithyrambos. Aristoteles über den Ursprung des griech. Dramas, AHAW 1991, 4 3 J. LATACZ, Einführung in die griech. Trag., 1993, 63 4 H.-G. NESSELRATH, Die att. Mittlere Komödie, 1990, 241–266.

O. CRUSIUS, s.v. Dithyrambos, RE 5, 1203–1230; H. FRONING, Dithyrambos und Vasenmalerei, 1971; A. PIKKARD-CAMBRIDGE, Dithyramb, Tragedy, and Comedy, [2]1966; G. A. PRIVITERA, Laso di Ermione nella cultura ateniese e nella tradizione storiografica, 1965; G. A. PRIVITERA, Il ditirambo fino al V secolo, in: R. BIANCHI BANDINELLI (ed.), Storia e civiltà dei Greci V, 1979, 311–325; H. SCHÖNEWOLF, Der jungatt. Dithyrambos. Wesen, Wirkung, Gegenwirkung, 1938; D. F. SUTTON, Dithyrambographi Graeci, 1989; B. ZIMMERMANN, Dithyrambos. Gesch. einer Gattung, 1992. B.Z.

Dius Fidius see → Sancus

Diverbium With few exceptions [2.220] all scenes in the manuscripts of Plautus' plays that are written in iambic senarii bear the direction *diverbium* (cf. Donat. II p. 5 W.), marking those sections of the play to be performed without musical accompaniment (cf. Plautus Stichus 758–768: the metre changes to the iambic senarius during a pause by the flautist). The oldest testimony (Liv. 7,2,10) confirms this. In late antiquity the grammarian Diomedes (1,491,22–24) was alone in taking *diverbium* in its literal Greek sense of 'dialogue' (and → canticum as 'monologue' [2. 220]).

1 G. E. DUCKWORTH, The Nature of Roman Comedy, 1952 ([2]1994), 362–364 2 W. BEARE, The Roman Stage, [3]1964, 219–232. H.-G.NE.

Divers It is doubtful whether representatives of the two orders of the grebes (*Podicipidae*) or the northern European loons (*Colymbidae*) were known to antiquity. In any case almost all grebes spent the winter at the Mediterranean. The οὐρία/*ouría* (Ath. 9,395e), which is about the size of a duck and dirty brown in colour, has been interpreted as a diver [1. 220], the κολυμβίς/*kolymbís* (Ath. 9,395d; cf. Aristot. Hist. an. 1,1,487a 23 and 7(8),3,593b 17) as a little grebe (*Podiceps ruficollis*) [1. 158] and the καταρράκτης/*katarrháktēs* (Aristot. ibid. 2,17,509a 4 and 8(9),12,615a 28–31) as a Slavonian grebe (*P. auritus*) [1. 132; 2. 73]

1 D'ARCY W. THOMPSON, A Glossary of Greek Birds, 1936 (repr. 1966) 2 LEITNER.

KELLER 2, 240–242. C. HÜ.

Dives Cognomen indicating wealth in the case of L. Baebius [I 7] D. and L. Canuleius [I 5] D. It became hereditary for the descendants of P. → Licinius Crassus D. (*pontifex maximus* in 212 BC; cf. Plin. HN 33,133). Wrongly attributed to the triumvir M. → Licinius Crassus (cos. 70, 55 BC). K.-L.E.

Diviciacus

[1] (also Divitiacus). Celtic name derived from *divic-* 'avenge' [2. 81–82; 3. 194]; for spelling see *CIL* XIII 2081. King of the Suessiones, the most powerful man in Gaul in 80 BC, whose rule extended even as far as Britain (Caes. B Gall. 2,4,6). Possibly evidenced by bronze coinage [1. 421].

1 B. Colbert de Beaulieu, Monnaie Gauloise au nom des chefs mentionnés dans les Commentaires de César, in: Hommages A. Grenier, 1962, 419–446 2 Evans 3 Schmidt.

[2] Pro-Roman ruler and druid of the Haedui, brother of Dumnorix. In 61 BC he unsuccessfully sought the help of the Roman Senate against the Sequani and Ariovistus (Caes. B Gall. 6,12,5). When his brother assumed tribal power he was forced to retire. Caesar restored his status in 58 and used his help against Ariovistus (Caes. B Gall. 1,16,5; 18,1–8; 19,2–3; 20,1–6; 31; 32,4; 41,4). D. remained Caesar's key instrument in dealings with the Haedui. In 57 BC he supported him against the Belgae and achieved mercy for the → Bellovaci (Caes. B Gall. 2,5,2; 10,5; 14,1–15,2). After that Caesar mentions him no more. In Rome Cicero was introduced by him to the Celtic art of divination (Cic. Div. 1,90).
→ Ariovistus; → Dumnorix; → Haedui

B. Kremer, Das Bild der Kelten bis in augusteische Zeit, 1994.

Divico Celtic name, see Diviciacus [1]. Commanded the → Helvetii when they defeated L. → Cassius [I 11] Longinus in 107 BC. In 58 BC he was spokesman for the embassy sent to Caesar to make terms for ending the war after the defeat on the Saône (Caes. B Gall. 1,13–14). W.SP.

Divinatio Roman term for the procedure of allowing one of several litigants in a private case (→ *delatio nominis*) to appear before a public criminal court (*iudicium publicum*); the origin of this term is unknown. What Gellius NA 2,4 has to say about the word expresses no confidence; it would therefore seem that its history was no longer known to Romans of the 2nd cent. AD. The employment of a religious term would indicate a very early origin. There is however no basis for a reconstruction. In [1] it is convincingly suggested to come from the old practice, at least in private prosecutions for murder by several male relatives of the victim, of choosing one agnate as plaintiff by *divinatio*.

The basic principle of *ne bis in idem* did not allow of two trials in the same case. If there were several plaintiffs they had so to arrange the accusal as to have a main plaintiff with the others ranked as joint plaintiffs (cf. → *subscriptio*). If the plaintiffs could not reach an agreement, the magistrate responsible for the case (→ *quaestio*) would decide, before the admission of the complaint (→ *receptio nominis*), who would be plaintiff. He would be advised in this by a *consilium*, though this was not yet the jury of the high court.

1 W. Kunkel, Quaestio, in: KS, 1974, 76f.
2 Mommsen, Strafrecht, 373 with n. 6. G.S.

Divination

I. Mesopotamia II. Egypt III. Hittites IV. Syria and Palestine V. Iran VI. Greek VII. Rome

I. Mesopotamia

While attention in old Egyptian culture was largely centred on existence after death, the concerns of Mesopotamia were almost exclusively with the present. A significant part of the cultural energy of ancient Mesopotamia was devoted to keeping human actions in harmony with the divine, so as to ward off such misfortunes as natural catastrophes, war, sickness and premature death. As such, heavy responsibility rested on the ruler as mediator between the world of gods and that of men.

In Mesopotamia everything which is and happens was seen as a manifestation of divine will. There was no such thing as 'chance'; any disaster was attributed to the gods turning away from mankind, provoked to divine anger by pollution or the breaking of taboos. A break in their relations with the gods would not be revealed to the people of Mesopotamia only by a catastrophe but by warning signals in their surroundings deviating from the rules established at creation. Thus signs when properly interpreted revealed information on public and private concerns. The causal relationship between the observed phenomenon and the prophesied future event was seldom empirical in the way weather lore is, although the prehistoric origins of the art of divination may well lie in the observing of natural portents. Rather, analogies springing from these peoples' world view and not always immediately transparent to us, were at the bottom of these causal connections; analogies having their justification in the assumption that all conceivable observed phenomena, whether their appearance is provoked or not, are inextricably linked and reflect a single divine purpose. In this sense, the causal relationship between protasis and apodosis as established in an → omen, reveals the cosmic order. Hence omens, laws and medical diagnostic texts all share the same outward form. For the same reason very different divinatory methods, applied in combination and complementing one another, would together convey a more precise insight into the future. Thus it was expressly stressed in a cuneiform handbook of divination [1] that the weighing of terrestrial signs can only lead to a reliable forecast when astral signs are taken into account and vice versa.

The interpretation attained in this way could then be verified by hepatoscopy. Also significant is the fact that trial by ordeal, i.e. divine judgement, was admitted as evidence in the highly developed Babylonian legal system.

Divine will became apparent not only in the immediate signs of nature: it could be asked through provoked signs. Accordingly oracular expertise during the course of Mesopotamian history gradually rose to primary importance among the different forms of divination, as with its help it was possible to determine forthwith whether the gods approved a certain course of action and what results it would have. Haruspicy in particular came to be an important instrument of → kingship, legitimizing its decisions. More, the divine will could be communicated in coded or immediate form in dreams (→ Dreams, Interpretation of dreams) [2], or through → ecstasy and → prophecies (TUAT 2, 84ff.; [3]).

Assyrian and Babylonian omens (protasis and apodosis) were recorded on clay tablets in the 2nd but mostly in the 1st millennium BC; there are few in Sumerian. There were collections of divinatory examples, organized according to divinatory technique, some with more than 10,000 items. These occasionally amounted to comprehensive treatises of over 100 tablets that were partly compiled for the first time at the command of → Assurbanipal, and served soothsayers as handbooks. The entries were arranged in a fixed order for each of the natural phenomena observed and graphically organized so that the required entry could easily be found. Despite a considerable oral tradition, the written records carried more authority in the 1st millennium BC — not least so that augurs could refute any accusation of having misled the king or not having researched properly. Especially the series of tablets recording terrestrial [4] and astral omens (→ Astrology) and those about entrails [5], the occurrence of deformed births, human or animal [6], the physiognomy and behaviour of men [7], reveal a surprisingly detailed and strangely modern system of recording the world surrounding man. The spirit that emerges from this is typical for Mesopotamian culture and has laid the foundations of modern science, showing not only amazing medical knowledge but also in Seleucid and Parthian times leading to calculations in → astronomy even though they were always subservient to the divinatory aim.

The most important divinatory way of sounding the will of the gods was by examining entrails, for which there is evidence from as early as the middle of 3rd millennium. It had the status of an art, that the sun-god Šamaš and the weather god → Hadad, the gods of divination from sacrifice, had revealed to Enmeduranki, an antedeluvial king of Sippar [8]. It was carried out by a professional 'seer' (*bārû*), who was required to be physically intact. The examination of entrails had a sacramental character and was part of a complex ritual [9; 10]. A lamb of perfect proportions would be sacrificed to the personal god of the supplicant. As well as its liver, the lungs, spleen and bowels would be inspected. The liver was seen as the 'slate of the gods', that Šamaš 'wrote upon', once the *bārû* had whispered the oracular query into the ear of the sacrificial animal. A sheep liver has an intricate topography that made it in a way a representation of the world. Its parts, given labels like 'Palace gate', 'Throne base' and 'Way', were vetted for form, colour, direction etc. and related to markings (growths, channels left by liver fluke etc.), called 'Weapon' as an example [11]. If the eyelid sign called the 'Look' that was normally found was lacking, it meant that Šamaš refused communication with the enquirer. The recorded apodoses of hepatoscopy and omens show them to have been of great significance in military campaigns. The royal archives of later Assyrian kings → Asarhaddon and Assurbanipal contain countless records detailing not only oracular queries but the findings, too, and sometimes their interpretation [12]. The queries deal with the appointment of priests and worthies, the loyalty of associates, the progress of political and historical enterprises and even the efficacy of medication. As a protection against deceit and manipulation, the kings would have important cases investigated by several teams of augurs working independently. In the interests of study not only were commentaries attached to the omen series, but also clay models of the liver were made that reproduced the findings of the entrails observed before an historically important event [13]. This is to be seen as part of a daring attempt to discern a purposeful pattern in historical facts, and to make use of it for one's own advantage. The divine will was further indicated in the flight of birds [14], the pouring of oil [15] and the smoke of incense.

Of help to the kings in their need to subject their relationship with the gods to an ongoing testing by divination were astrological calculations. Asarhaddon and Assurbanipal covered their entire territory with observatories. Watchers were charged with sending regular reports to the royal court. These would then be analysed and evaluated by specialists with the help of the relevant collection of omens [16]. Governors and civil servants were required to report unaccustomed happenings. Future disasters revealed by divination could be forestalled by means of precautionary rites [17].

Although we meet with texts that express the view that divination may be limited in its scope and even point out the option to ignore its suggested course of action, belief in the reliability of divination remained unbroken in Mesopotamia.

The influence of Mesopotamian omen texts can be traced in both Greek [18] and Indian civilizations [19].

1 A.L. Oppenheim, A Diviner's Manual, in: JNES 33, 1974, 197–220 2 Id., The Interpretation of Dreams in the Ancient Near East, 1956 3 M. Weippert, Assyr. Prophetien, in: M. Fales, Assyrian Royal Inscriptions, 1981, 71–115 4 S. Moren, The Omen Series *Šumma Alu*, PhD Pennsylvania 1978 5 U. Jeyes, Divination as Science in Ancient Mesopotamia, in: Jaarbericht. Ex Oriente Lux 32, 1991/92, 23–41 6 E. Leichty, The Omen Series *Šumma Izbu*, 1970 7 F.R. Kraus, Die physiognomischen Omina der Babylonier, 1935 8 W.G. Lambert,

Enmeduranki, in: JCS 21, 1967, 126–138 9 I. STARR, The Rituals of the Diviner, 1983 10 H. ZIMMERN, Beitr. zur Kenntnis der babylon. Rel., 1901, 96ff. 11 R. LEIDERER, Anatomie der Schafsleber, 1990 12 I. STARR, Queries to the Sungod, 1990 13 J.-W. MEYER, AOAT 39, 1987 14 J.-M. DURAND, La divination par les oiseaux, in: Mari: Annales de Recherches Interdisciplinaires 8, 1997, 273–282 15 G. PETTINATO, Die Ölwahrsagung bei den Babyloniern, 1966 16 H. HUNGER, Astrological Reports to Assyrian Kings, 1992 17 S. M. MAUL, Zukunftsbewältigung, 1994 18 C. BEZOLD, F. BOLL, Reflexe astrologischer Inschr. bei griech. Schriftstellern, 1911/17 19 D. PINGREE, Mesopotamian Astronomy and Astral Omens in other Civilizations, in: H. J. NISSEN, J. RENGER, (ed.), Mesopotamien und seine Nachbarn 1992, 375–379. S.M.

II. Egypt

Before well into the first millennium BC divination was of scant importance in Egypt. Eclipses of the sun and moon or other omens were seldom recorded; instances of interpretation of → dreams and auspicious days (hemerology) are recorded from the New Kingdom onwards, but the interpretation of stars, wind and bird flight only in isolated instances [1]. There was no systematic collecting of signs (Hdt. 2,82) to our knowledge. In general the extraordinary was thought less worthy of note than the regular, the cosmic process, which had to be maintained every day. Only later, under Iranian, Mesopotamian and Hellenistic influence did omens and → astrology win ground, so much so that Egyptian astrology was prominent in late antiquity.

Oracles were important from the New Kingdom onwards. If the cult image was carried around on a float at the festival, questions could be asked of it: the motion of the float indicated approval or not. Oracles were consulted less frequently to predict the future, their main purpose being to determine legal and administrative policy. In the 21st dynasty (*c.* 1070–945 BC) the upper Egyptian 'State of God' was officially ruled by the oracle of → Amun of Thebes. It lost that influence later, but Herodotus (2,83) still ranked it particularly high.

1 H. BRUNNER, Das hörende Herz, in: OBO 80, 1988, 224–229.

J. ASSMANN, Ägypten. Eine Sinngesch., 1996, 233f.; L. KÁKOSY, s.v. Orakel, LÄ 4, 600–606; A. B. LLOYD, Herodotus, Book II, Commentary 1–98, 1976, 345–349; s.v. Omen, RÄRG, 542f. K.J.-W.

III. Hittites

The Hittites were acquainted with various forms of divination: in dreams (incubation; → Dreams, Interpretation of dreams) man sought to decipher the will of god; in dreams the god revealed for example the succession of Ḫattušilis III. The examination of entrails, probably taken over from Babylon, was mainly performed during the sacrificial ceremonies at the great ritual festivals at which the 'message of the god' was made known. Occasionally, omens were observed in order to set the correct time to carry out ritual procedures. The most important divinatory practice of the Hittites were drawing lots and observing the flight of birds. In successive oracles, recorded there and then, the principle 'favourable-unfavourable' was employed to settle the route of march, or to ask for the consent of the gods to changes in the festive rituals. Oracles at which lots were drawn elicited the gods' will using lots that were either marked or had words like 'God', 'King', 'Enemy', 'Fire' etc. written on them. Bird oracles concentrated on the movement and special behaviour of particular birds at a site marked out in advance.

E. LAROCHE, Catalogue des textes hittites, 1971, 91–102; A. ARCHI, L'ornitomanzia ittiata, in: SMEA 16, 1975, 119–180; A. ÜNAL, Zum Status der Augures bei den Hethitern, in: RHA 31, 1973, 27–56; A. KAMMENHUBER, Orakelpraxis, Träume und Vorzeichenschau bei den Hethitern, 1976; A. ÜNAL, Ein Orakeltext über die Intrigen am hethitischen Hof, 1978; V. HAAS, Marginalien zu hethitischen Orakelprotokollen, Altorientalische Forschungen 23, 1996, 76–94. V.H.

IV. Syria and Palestine

In 14th–13th cents. BC in → Ugarit the practice of entrail observation, especially of the liver and lungs is attested. Then there are astrological omens and necromancy. The sacrificial augur in Emar enjoyed an important cultic position extending beyond augury. Hurrian divinatory texts from Emar are concerned with liver augury and medical prognosis. Two model livers were also found there; other sites in Syria and Palestine are Mumbaqa (Ekalte) on the → Euphrates, Hazor and Megiddo.

The Phoenicians and Arameans of the following millennium seem not to have read entrails. Perhaps the Phoenician inscribed arrowheads belong in a divinatory context; the same may be true of the prophets of Hamath (KAI 202). Exhaustive information on oracular gods and their rites are given in Hellenistic and Roman times. Divinatory practices in Israel and Judah are incubation, interpretation of → dreams, lots, priestly oracles and necromancy. Prophecy, too, (→ Prophets) mostly belongs to the field of divination.

F. H. CRYER, Divination in Ancient Israel, 1994; M. DIETRICH, O. LORETZ, Mantik in Ugarit, 1990; D. E. FLEMING, The Installation of Baal's High Priestess at Emar, 1992, 87–92; Y. HAJJAR, Divinités oraculaires et rites divinatoires en Syrie et en Phénicie à l'èpoque gréco-romaine, ANRW II 18.4, 2236–2320; A. JEFFERS, Magic and Divination in Ancient Palestine and Syria, 1996; A. LEMAIRE, s.v. Divination, DCPP, 131f.; J. W. MEYER, AOAT 39, 1987; S. RIBICHINI, L'aruspicina fenicio-punica e la divinazione a Pafo, in: UgaritForsch. 21, 1989, 307–317; J. TROPPER, Nekromantie, 1989. H.NI.

V. Iran

We know of divination in Iran from contemporary Greek accounts and from Arab and Persian writers of post-Sassanid times. In Hellenistic and even Roman literature, the Persian Zoroastrian tradition was sometimes seen—wrongly from a historical point of view—as the very cradle of divinatory learning and practice, and its religious and didactic 'experts', the magi, as adepts *in rebus magicis* (cf. e.g. Plin. HN 30). More reliable are Herodotus' observations on the magi as interpreters of dreams (1,107 and *passim*) and heavenly phenomena (7,37) and on the belief of the Achaemenid kings in omens; his account of hippomancy in 3,84–87 on the other hand can scarcely be grounded on historical fact. For the Sassanid epoch Agathias (2,25,1f.) records pyromantic practices of the 'magi'; the middle Persian story of Ardaxšīr and Ardavān has them regularly consult seers, interpreters of dreams, and astrologers. The Arab writer Ibn an-Nadīm knew of several Persian works of divination in the 10th cent.; his Persian contemporary Balʿamī quotes a 'Book of Omens', that allegedly contained all omens from the time of Persian rule.

M. Boyce, F. Grenet, A History of Zoroastrianism III, 1991, 491–565; M. Omidsalar, EncIr VII, 1996, 440–443. J.W.

VI. Greek

A. Definition B. Methods C. Seers D. Sanctuaries E. Politics F. Criticism

A. Definition

In the Greek-speaking world, divination consisted of an oracular pronouncement about the future or a solution in consort with supernatural powers. This fundamental element of Greek religion was usually practiced by interpreting the flight of birds, sacrifices, dreams and omens, as for instance a sneeze or chance saying at a decisive moment; less usual methods were coscinomancy (sieve-divination [1]) and, especially in late classical times, hydromancy, lecanomancy or catoptromancy [10; 21]. The intermediary between the suppliant and the supernatural was the seer. Divination preferably took place at a special site, which often developed into an influential sanctuary [27; 12].

B. Methods

The most important method in the early days was the interpretation of the flight of birds [29. 148f.], a near Eastern method already recorded in Homer. Admittedly only the more imposing birds, raptors like eagles, hawks and falcons, were important (Hom. Od. 2,182); those flying from the right were favourable, those from the left boded ill. Likewise the calls of birds and their plumage could be relevant. Homer mentioned bird augurs (Hom. Il. 1,69; 6,76), though non-professionals like → Helen (Hom. Od. 15,160–81) as well as the seven Persian conspirators against Smerdis (Hdt. 3,76) could likewise read the signs. Also from the near East came divination from sacrifice [7. 41–53], which is mentioned by Homer (Il. 24,221; Od. 21,145; 22,318–323), and which was later to be more fully described. Three important divisions were distinguished. 1. Hepatoscopy concerned the liver and is depicted on vases from 530 BC. In Plato's time it was more common than divination by bird signs (Phdr. 244c). The liver had to be healthy, its lobes normal (Aesch. Prom. 495). 2. Before a battle, the entrails of a sacrifice and the intensity of the fire that consumed them were inspected — only those that burned well meant victory (Eur. Phoen. 1255–8). 3. The examination of the burning tail and sacred bone of the sacrificial animal on a high altar (a recurrent motif on Athenian vases). It was important that the tail curled. Tail bones are missing from the finds made in the Heraion of Samos and in the Artemis sanctuary in Kalapodi. Other signs too were possible: the lack of flames, splashes of liquid and gall were bad omens (Soph. Ant. 1005–11). At the Zeus Altar in Olympia the flames on the altar were interpreted (empyromancy). The 'oldest oracle' (Plut. Sept. sap. 15), namely dreams, remained throughout the whole of antiquity an important way of deciphering the future. In the strongly hierarchical society the interpretation of dreams came to be the preferred method of the social and religious elite, as for the light task of interpreting one could do without a seer. The dreams of kings in particular (Hom. Il. 2,79–83; 11,45f. Artem. 1,2), but also of priests (Aeschin. 2,10) were significant. In the 5th cent. BC professional interpreters of dreams made their appearance (Aristoph. Vesp. 52f.; Theophr. Char. 16,11) and there were books on the subject, the first of which was perhaps by Antiphon, a contemporary of Socrates [11. 132f.]. Practically all the writings on dreams are lost, save Artemidorus' *Onirocritica*, which has an approach very different from dream interpretation today [22]. Chance omens, like sneezes (Xen. An. 3,2,9), random sayings at special times (Eustath. Il. 10,207; Hom. Od. 20,95ff.; Aristoph. Lys. 391ff.) are called *phḗmē* or *klēdṓn* in Homer [15. 203]. Chance encounters on the road (*sýmbola/sýmboloi*, Aesch. Ag. 144) or weather phenomena [20. 51] could also assume significance; in the uncertain world of Greek antiquity practically anything unaccustomed could have meaning read into it. For this reason among others, divination played an important role in Greek literature: the omens, seers, oracles and dreams in Homer, Herodotus [14] and in the tragedies [3; 4; 24] have a meaningful part to play in working upon the reader, spectator or listener and in particular the way in which expectations are worked into the development of literary works.

The oracles of → Clarus [26] and → Didyma peppered their utterances with philosophy, philosophical and theological ideas (stoic, 'monotheistic') and later turned against Christianity [6], whose rise and entry into civil activity in the 3rd cent. AD led to the end and the closing of the last oracle sites in the late 4th cent. [2].

C. Seers

The most important interpreter of signs was the *mántis*, from the root *ma* 'reveal, unveil') [9]. Interpretation was made possible through the special relationship to the gods that the seers claimed [8. 17ff.], one underlined by the terms *thésphata* (divine utterings) for oracles, *theiázein* for prophecy, *theoprópos, theomántis* for seers and personal names like Mantitheos (Andocides 1,44) or Theoklos (Paus. 4,16,1) [5. 105]. The truth so disclosed was not esoteric, though Xenophon claimed enough skill on his own account to prevent his *mántis* from tricking him (An. 5,6,29). Seers, like → oracles, made no direct predictions, but rather expressed opinions on the possibilities raised by the consultants or clarified the present by pointing to misconduct in the past (Soph. OT). To be successful a seer had to have experience and be able to adapt his differentiated insights to fit separate possibilities. Seers often belonged to particular families, like the Iamidai of Olympia, who remained until the 3rd cent. AD [23]. Early seers were nobles, sometimes kings, important above all in war [5. 99–101], presumably the main sphere of divination. Seers accompanied the great mythical expeditions (→ Amphiaraus, → Mopsus, → Calchas). There are several historical records of seers being killed in battle (Hdt. 7,228f.; SEG 29, 361). Seers would also wander [5. 108], particularly, it must be assumed, those whose influence became unwelcome to local notables (→ Melampus). The most influential gods in the field were → Apollo as divider of order from chaos, the known world from the unknown, wisdom from ignorance, in the past, present and future, and Zeus as patron of → Dodona, the oldest of Greek oracles.

The seers had some renowned female counterparts, but such priestesses were rarely noble and mostly sedentary (but see the epitaph on a 3rd-cent. *mántis*, Satyra of Larissa, SEG 35, 626); they spoke in trance mostly and not with any technical knowledge [5. 102f.]. That → Cassandra spoke in the first person is because she was 'possessed' by Apollo. The Delphic → Pythia, a priestess of Apollo, was reputed to have a sexual relation with the god — a typical way to account for 'possession' by a godhead [25]. The Pythia did indeed receive the revelation, but it was put into words by male *prophē̆tai*. Trance and → ecstasy were prominent in the prophesying of the → Sibyl (Heracl. B 92) and remained so in the 2nd cent. AD for the priestesses of Dodona, who were unable to recall their pronouncements on waking (Aristid. 45,11).

D. Sanctuaries

As well as submitting questions to *mánteis* supplicants could turn to one of over 20 oracles in the Greek world. Most lay in remote places on the margins of civilization, like the Zeus Ammon oracle in the oasis of Siwa in the western wastes of Egypt, or in Hainen, in Clarus, Didyma, Grynium [16]. In that way they could remain free from political pressure and partisanship. The absence of a familiar environment and the frequent need for a prolonged stay would allow the priests time to acquaint themselves with the anxieties and wishes of their 'clients', while simultaneously making the questioner more receptive to their often enigmatic pronouncements (Aesch. Ag. 1255), forcing him moreover to make his own interpretation and so freeing the oracle from responsibility in tricky matters. Divination at the well-known oracles of Apollo in Asia Minor and perhaps Delphi too was based on ecstatic states [29]; that of the medicinal sanctuaries (→ Amphiaraus, → Asclepius) on prophetic dreams (incubation). In many an oracle even the dead were consulted; renowned under that head was that of → Trophonios in Lebadea (Paus. 9,39,2–14; SEG 39, 434). In the realm of private concerns, the matter of the questions had mostly to do with pregnancy (Eur. Ion 540f.; 1547f.). In public life oracles functioned as agencies of arbitration, justification and renewal. While internal politics, legislation and jurisdiction as institutions of the state could not immediately be made to depend on oracle pronouncements — as little as it was allowed to seek advice on a possible war against other Greek states (Xen. Hell. 3,2,22) — they played an important part in cult concerns (Plat. Resp. 427bc). Occasionally religious questioning nevertheless assumed definite political colouring (Hdt. 5,67; IG III 78, 24–6). Apollo was frequently asked about the founding of colonies and the despatch of expeditions (e.g. Thuc. 3,92,5).

E. Politics

Little is known about political structures outside the larger *poleis*. In Sparta the Pythii were appointed by the king as official attendants of the Delphic oracle. The ephors for their part regularly consulted the incubation oracle at Thalamae near Sparta; in their official building there lay the grave of the Cretan oracle founder Epimenides. As the ephors were in possession of the legendary 'Skin of Epimenides', probably a parchment roll of oracular pronouncements, giving them access to the gods independently of the kings [5. 104; 31. 154–63]. In Athens the Peisistratids attempted to monopolize divination as an instrument of power and guarded an official collection of oracles on the Acropolis. In democratic Athens individual seers (→ Diopeithes, Lampon, who was the first to sign the peace treaty between Athens and Sparta in 421 BC) gained influence. Private seers were consulted (cf. Aesch. Ag. 409); unlike their archaic forerunners, these were not members of the → Eupatrides [5. 104ff.]. From the 6th cent. BC unofficial seers, the chresmologoi, began to appear who forecast from existing written prophecies: → Bacis in Athens [5. 104], → Musaeus (Hdt. 7,6,3) and the Sibyl [30; 5.103]. Later still, the *engastrimýthoi* (ventriloquists) appeared, who finally attained a certain status [5. 107] and are referred to by the apostle Paul alluding to Delphi as 'Python' [19].

F. Criticism

Even in antiquity the divine authority of seers and oracles was continually being questioned. Furthermore, already in Homer competition between seers and singers is evident (Il. 5,149–51; 2,830–4; Od. 22,328f.,

379f.). The 5th cent. brought with it a change in attitude. In Athens in particular oracles were consulted on internal policy less and less after the Persian wars. Questions on colonies stopped in the early 4th cent., and counsel on cults was seldom asked after 300 BC. The political processes available in a democracy made divination in certain matters apparently superfluous. The catastrophe of the Sicilian expedition in 413 BC, one all seers prophesied success for (Thuc. 8,1,1) marks the end of the public role of the seer. From now on neither seers nor oracles are paid any attention to Thucydides or Aristophanes, and divination is no longer mentioned in the numerous speeches of the 4th cent. [32]. There were still seers (SEG 41, 328; 30, 82), though stripped of their prestige; Plato rated them on a par with the contemptible mendicant priests of Cybele (Resp. 364b). Philosophical schools were divided, Epicureans (SEG 39, 1412) and Cynics [17] rejecting divination and Stoics continuing to accept it [28. 211–4].

Oracles and prophecies never completely disappeared. The battle of Chaeronea (Plut. Dem. 19f.) and the fall of Rome in AD 410 were accompanied by oracular activity; Philip II and Alexander [4] the Great employed seers for military ends (according to Aristander of Telmessus [23. 25–9]). In general however both seers and oracles lost their former central position as traditional public authorities, not least because of the rising intellectual self-awareness of the Greeks, the growth of a professional army and of a philosophical understanding of the behaviour of beasts and men. In the private sector divination still continued, even experiencing an upturn in the first cent. AD [29; 13. 168–261] and diversifying: using dice, letters [18] (SEG 37.1829) and alphabetic oracles (SEG 38, 1328; 1338; 39, 1377b).

1 G. Arnott, Coscinomancy in Theokr. and Kazantzakis, Mnemosyne 4.3, 1978, 27–32 2 P. Athanassiadi, The Fate of Oracles in Late Antiquity, in: Deltion Christianikes Archaiologikes Hetaireias 15, 1990, 271–8 3 S. Vogt, das Delphische Orakel in den Orestes-Dramen, in: A. Bierl, P. von Moellendorff (ed.), Orchestra, Drama, Mythos, Bühne, 1994, 97–104 4 E. Bächli, Die künstlerische Funktion von Orakelsprüchen, Weissagungen, Träumen usw. in der griech. Tragödie, 1954 5 J. Bremmer, The Status and Symbolic Capital of the Seer, in: R. Hägg (ed.), The Role of Religion in the Early Greek Polis, 1996, 99–109 6 R. van den Broek, Apollo in Asia, 1981 7 W. Burkert, The Orientalizing Revolution, 1992 8 Id., From Epiphany to Cult Statue, in: A. B. Lloyd, What is a God?, 1997, 15–34 9 M. Casewitz, Mantis: le vrai sens, in: REG 105, 1992, 1–18 10 A. Delatte, La Catoptromancie grecque et ses dérivés, 1932 11 E.R. Dodds, The Greeks and the Irrational, 1951 12 J.-P. Vernant, Mortals and Immortals, 1990, 303–317 13 R.L. Fox, Pagans and Christians, 1985 14 P. Frisch, Die Träume bei Herodot, 1968 15 Graf 16 F. Graf, Bois sacrées et oracles en Asie Mineure, in: Les Bois Sacrées, 1993, 23–9 17 J. Hammerstaedt, Die Orakelkritik des Kynikers Oenomaus, 1988 18 F. Heinevetter, Würfel- und Buchstabenorakel in Kleinasien und Griechenland, 1911 19 J.W. van Henten, s.v. Python, in: K. van der Toorn et al. (ed.), Dictionary of Deities and Demons in the Bible, 1995, 1263ff. 20 P. Stengel, Die griech. Kunstaltertümer, 1898 21 T. Hopfner, Mittel- und neugriech. Lekano-, Lychno-, Katoptro- und Onychomantien, in: FS F. L. Griffith, 1932, 218–32 22 S. Price, The Future of Dreams: From Freud to Artemidorus, in: Past & Present 113, 1985, 3–37 23 P. Ken, Prosopographie der hist. griech. Manteis bis auf die Zeit Alexanders des Grossen, 1966 24 R. Lennig, Traum und Sinnestäuschung bei Aischyl., Soph., Eur., 1969 25 I. Maurizio, Anthropology and Spirit Possession, in: JHS 115, 1995, 69–86 26 R. Merkelbach, J. Stauber, Die Orakel des Apoll von Klaros, in: Epigraphica Anatolica 27, 1996, 1–54 27 Nock, 534–550 28 D. Obbink, What all men believe—must be true, in: Oxford Studies in Ancient Philosophy 10, 1992, 193–231 29 H. W. Parke, The Oracles of Apollo in Asia Minor, 1987 30 Id., Sibyls and Sibylline Prophecy in Classical Antiquity, 1992² 31 R. Parker, Spartan Religion, in: A. Powell (ed.), Classical Sparta, 1989, 142–72 32 N.D. Smith, Diviners and D. in Aristophanic Comedy, in: CA 8, 1989, 140–158.

J.B.

VII. Rome

The term *divinatio* occurs i.a. in Cicero, who defines it as *praesensio et scientia rerum futurarum* (Div. 1,1), or the 'science of future events'. The word itself is derived from *divus* 'divine': knowledge of the future is therefore a significant divine attribute, and its possible transference to mankind an important aspect of religion (Orig. C. Cels. 4,88).

Divination in the strict sense was not part of official Roman cult. Nearest to official Roman divination was the office of augur. Cicero makes a clear distinction when he points out that Roman → augures were unable to pronounce on the future from their observance of birds or other signs (Cic. Div. 2,70). The opposing view although not a representative one for the collegium is advocated by App. Claudius Pulcher (Cic. Div. 1,105). The augurs as interpreters of Jupiter Optimus Maximus (*interpretes Iovis Optimi Maximi*, Cic. Leg. 2,8,20) merely tried to determine whether the gods approved the decisions made by men. The answer held future relevance insofar as the Roman state got an indication on whether the proposed action could be accomplished successfully with the consent of the gods or whether it should be given up so as not to rouse their ire, the *ira deorum*.

A fundamental rejection of both personal and official or state divination, which is seen especially in Christian late antiquity proved impracticable. Despite the banning of the *divinandi curiositas*, which Constantine II in AD 357 believed to have eliminated for ever (Cod. Theod. 9,16,4), the multiplicity and practice of various divinatory divisions showed no sign of diminishing, rather the opposite. A father of the church, → Arnobius of Sicca, took the list of divinatory practices made by Cicero (Div. 1,132 and Nat. D. 1,55) as relevant to his own times, adding to it various *fanatici* of his own time (Arnob. 1,24,2).

Already in the Republic need and necessity had arisen, particularly for prodigies and other signs regarded as

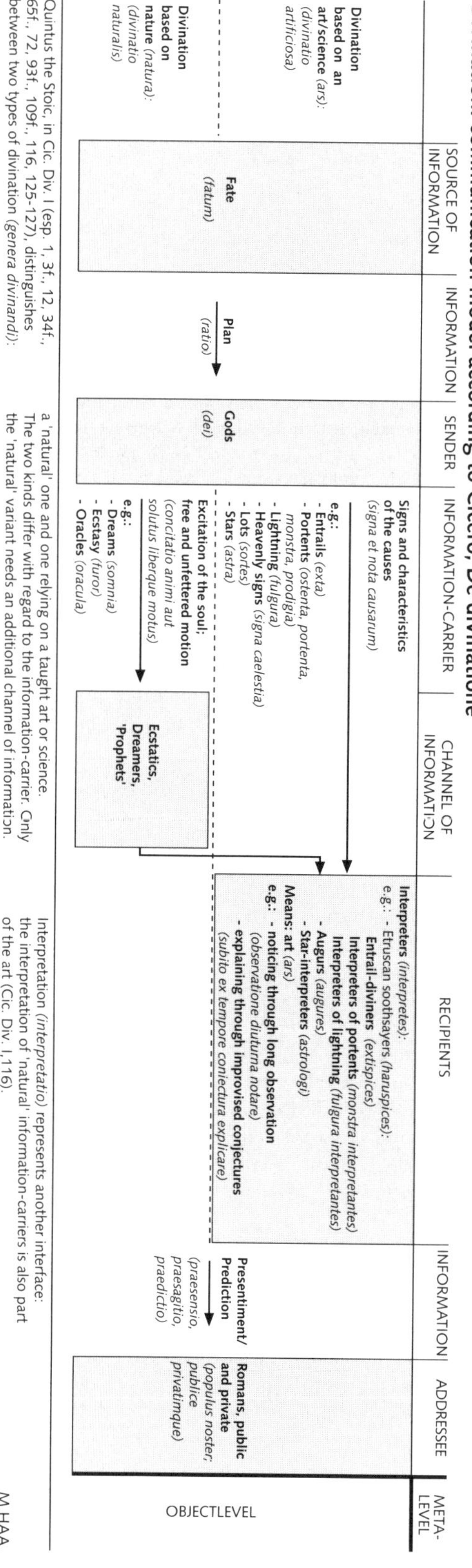

Quintus the Stoic, in Cic. Div. I (esp. 1, 3f., 12, 34f., 65f., 72, 93f., 109f., 116, 125-127), distinguishes between two types of divination (*genera divinandi*): a 'natural' one and one relying on a taught art or science. The two kinds differ with regard to the information-carrier. Only the 'natural' variant needs an additional channel of information. Interpretation (*interpretatio*) represents another interface: the interpretation of 'natural' information-carriers is also part of the art (Cic. Div. I,116).

M.HAA.

coming from the gods, to move beyond the powers of the augurs. In particular any danger to the 'peace of the gods' (*pax deorum*), which was indicated, in the opinion of the Romans, by such unprovoked signs, required an appropriate procedure (*procuratio*), in order to ward off possible damage to the state [1]. To that end the Senate availed itself of two different non-Roman procedures concurrently: consulting the *libri Sibyllini* (→ Sibyls) and carrying out the *Etrusca disciplina* with *haruspices* [2]. The *libri Sibyllini* were a collection of prophecies from the Sibyl of Cumae, reputedly sold by a mysterious old woman to king Tarquin (Priscus in Lactant. Div. inst. 1,6,18; Superbus in Dion. Hal. Ant. Rom. 4,62; Pliny HN 13,27,88; Solin. 2,17; Gell. NA 1,19; Zon. 7,11; Tzetz. ad Lycophronem 1279; unspecified in Serv. Aen. 6,72). Their contents points to the Greek society of southern Italy [4. 65–88] rather than to the Etruscans [3. 21–28]. Consulting the *libri Sibyllini* was the prerogative of a special college, originally the *Duumviri* (Livy 3,10,7; 5,13,6), later the *Decemviri* (from 369 BC: Livy 6,37,12; 6,42,2) and finally the *Quindecimviri sacris faciundis* (Serv. Aen. 6,73: after Sulla; Cic. Fam. 8,4,1: 51 BC), who were entrusted by the Senate with the task of finding amidst the collection what had caused the occurrence of prodigies (*prodigia*). This procedure led to various modifications to Roman religion and in some cases to the introduction of foreign practices, frequently borrowed from Greek usage (*lectisternia* since 399: Livy 5,13,6; alleged burial alive of a Gallic and a Greek couple on the Forum Boarium in 228 BC: Plut. Marcellus 3,4; Cass. Dio fr. 48; Zon. 8,19; or in 216 BC: Livy 22,57,6; later only Plut. Quaest. Rom. 83).

The *Etrusca disciplina* was a divinatory discipline in the narrow sense. It was undertaken by → *haruspices* at the behest of the Senate; the exercise of the *Etrusca disciplina* in Rome probably began when Tuscany was conquered [2] in the form of a collegium of sixty members, the *ordo LX haruspicum*. They were recruited from the sons of prominent families of the twelve Etruscan cities (Cic. Div. 1,92; Val. Max. 1,1,1); its seat was in Rome [5]. When a *prodigium* occurred the *haruspices* would analyze it and attempt to determine its meaning, so as to pinpoint the religiously 'correct atonement' (*procuratio*) or generally necessary course (cf. Cicero's Har. resp.). The 'scientific' basis for the technique of the *haruspices*, which was in outlines recorded in a written corpus, was largely divinatory: the Etruscan books were subdivided into sections on *haruspicini*, *fulgurales*, and *rituales* (Cic. Div.1,72; cf. 2,49), of which the first two concerned hepatoscopy, i.e. *haruspicium* proper, the analysis of the liver and other organs of sacrificial animals, and brontoscopy (the analysis of thunder and lightning), while the third besides its ritual aspect (Fest. 397) included the analysis of prodigies [6; 7. 3–115].

What distinguished the Etruscan method from the predictions of an augur was not so much the object observed as the inferences drawn from it: the *haruspex* was less concerned with divine approval than in extracting precise information about the future (see → Tanaquil's interpretation of the sign of the eagle that stole a felt cap (*pilleus*) from Tarquinius Priscus: Livy 1,34,8–9 [8. 1371–8] about the analysis of *exta*). The underlying concept of divination was of a god-ruled world, in which the gods used natural phenomena to give men signs (Sen. Nat. 2,32). In the case of hepatoscopy ('The Bronze Liver of Piacenza'), where the outer fringe of the heavens shows subdivisions into 16 fields, each under the patronage of a god (Cic. Div. 2,42; Plin. HN 2,55,143), there is a parallel system between microcosm (liver of a sacrificial animal) and macrocosm (the universe) [9. 53–88; 10], from which the *haruspices* through the divinatory discipline could arrive at the information sought.

Despite the *Etrusca disciplina* being incorporated into officially sanctioned Roman religious practice, its use in the private sector was met with scepticism (Tacitus [11]. For the renewal of the *ordo LX haruspicum* by Claudius, in order to combat *externae superstitiones*, see Tac. Ann. 11,15). The most disparate forms of divination, frequently of oriental origin, and astrology in particular [12], nevertheless gained an ever stronger foothold in the society of Imperial Rome [13], where its position was strengthened by → Celsus, → Apuleius of Madaurus or Neoplatonism in general, constituting a radical break with the sceptical attitude of Cicero and the Academy [14]. On the other hand, as power was being concentrated in the Emperor, such divination roused suspicion and its use was traced to politically motivated ambition and the desire to know the chances a new pretender to the throne. Under Augustus (Cass. Dio 56,25) and Tiberius (Suet. Tib. 63) laws were issued that regulated and restricted private divination until finally it was entirely prohibited by the Christian emperors (measures AD 357 under Constantius II; Theodosius' general ban of 391–392; Cod. Theod. 16,10,7 & 9; 16,10,10–12) [15].

→ Astrology; → Augures; → ; → Fate; → Haruspices; → Neoplatonism; → Omen; → Prodigium

1 R. Bloch, Les prodiges dans l'antiquité, 1963 2 B. MacBain, Prodigy and Expiation: a Study in Rel. and Politics in Republican Rome, 1982 3 R. Bloch, Origines étrusques des Livres sibyllins, in: Mélanges A. Ernout, 1940 4 D. Briquel, Les enterrés vivants de Brindes, in: Mélanges J. Heurgon, 1976 5 M. Torelli, Elogia Tarquiniensia, 1975 6 C. O. Thulin, Die etruskische Disziplin, 1905–9 7 A. Bouché-Leclercq, Histoire de la divination dans l'Antiquité IV, 1882 8 R. Shilling, A propos des exta, l'extispicine étrusque et la litatio romaine, in: Mélanges A. Grenier, 1962 9 A. Maggiani, Qualche osservazione sul fegato di Piacenza, SE 50, 1982 10 L. B. van der Meer, The Bronze Liver of Piacenza: Analysis of a Polytheistic Structure, 1987 11 P. Grimal, Tacite et les présages, in: Rev. des Etudes Latines 67, 1989, 170–178 12 F. Cumont, Astrology and Rel. among the Greeks and Romans, 1921 13 E. R. Dodds, Pagans and Christians in an Age of Anxiety, 1965 14 F. Guillaumont, Philosophe et augure, recherches sur la théorie cicéronienne de la divination, 1984 15 S. Moreno, Politica y adivinacion en el Bajo Imperio Romano, 1991.

D.BR.

Divine kingship Divine kingship in the sense of J. G. Frazer (1854–1941) and I. Engnell [1], i.e. connected with the New Year's festival and the death and rebirth of the god (→ Tammuz) is not encountered in the ancient Near East. H. Frankfort's distinction between 'divine kingship' and 'sacral kingship' [2], i.e. between the venerated king and the venerator king as priest, was a step towards but narrows the perspective to the area of cult. As already outlined by Labat [3], ancient Near Eastern texts and pictures indicate that rulers could be linked in more than one way (e.g. descent, legitimization or manumission) with the world of the gods (= sacralization of the ruler).

→ Ruler; → Pharaoh

1 I. Engnell, Stud. in Divine Kingship in the Ancient Near East, 1943 2 H. Frankfort, Kingship and the Gods, 1946 3 R. Labat, Le caractère religieux de la royauté Assyrio-Babylonienne, 1939.

B.P.-L.

Divio (Dibio). An important centre where trade routes crossed at the confluence of the Saône and the Ouche, on the boundary between the *civitates* of the Lingones and the Aedui, now Dijon. The *castrum Divionense* described by Gregory of Tours in his *History of the Franks* 3,19 was built in the 3rd cent. near the road from Lyons to the Rhine frontier.

E. Frézouls, Les villes antiques de la France II, 1, 1988, 179–274; C. Rolley, s.v. D., PE, 278.

Y.L.

Division of angles and circles

I. Ancient Orient
see → Mathematics I

II. Classical Antiquity
A. Division of circles B. Trisection of angles

A. Division of circles

The division of circles, i.e. the division of the circumference of a circle into any number of arcs of equal length, is directly correlated to the regular polygons: if a regular n-gon is inscribed in a circle, the circumference of the circle is divided into n sections and the angle at the centre belonging to the side of the n-gon has the value $360°/_n$. The Pythagoreans (→ Pythagoras [2]) were already interested in the regular polygons and their properties. They could inscribe the regular triangle, rectangle and hexagon in a circle, in the case of the hexagon making use of the fact that its side is equal to the radius of the circle. They also knew that the side s_5 of the regular pentagon divides the diagonal d_5 according to the 'golden ratio' ('division in extreme and mean ratio'; Euc. 6, def. 3: εὐθεῖα ἄκρον καὶ μέσον λόγον τετμῆσθαι λέγεται), i.e.: $d_5 : s_5 = s_5 : (d_5 - s_5)$ applies. Determining the partial lengths by division in extreme and mean ratio results, from an algebraic point of view, in a quadratic equation.

The Greeks could solve all types of quadratic equation — and therefore also the problem of division in extreme and mean ratio occurring in constructing a pentagon — geometrically with the aid of so-called planar geometry (see on this [5. 60–64]). This meant they were able to construct the regular pentagon inscribed in a circle and they presumably discovered while doing this that there are irrational dimensions (see [5. 71–73]). Pythagorean knowledge of the regular polygons is summarized in bk. 4 of Euclid's (→ Euclides) [3] 'Elements'; construction of the regular *n*-gons for *n* = 3, 4, 5, 6 and 15 is illustrated there. Another construction of the pentagon, which simultaneously directly provides the side of the decagon, was used by → Ptolemy [65] (Almagest 1,9.)

The construction of the side of a regular heptagon results in a cubic equation. An exact solution to this problem is handed down in an Arabic text that Ṯābit ibn Qurra (826–901) translated from the Greek; attribution of the Greek original to → Archimedes [1], as in the MS, is not entirely certain [6. 204–213]. In this treatise an interpolation (→ *neûsis*) is performed in such a way that two triangles thereby arising are equal in area [7. 429 f.]. From the Arabic-Islamic region there are numerous further constructions of the regular heptagon [6]. The Arabs also worked on the construction of the regular nonagon in a given circle. They found interpolation methods with the aid of which the side of the nonagon sought can be determined. The figure used for this can easily be extended in such a way that the side of any *n*-gon with an uneven number of corners can be ascertained [7. 434–436].

B. Trisection of angles

In the case of the regular nonagon an angle of 40° (or 20°) has to be constructed. This is not possible simply with compasses and ruler. This is a special case of trisection of the angle. The problem of trisection of the angle results in a cubic equation. This equation cannot in normal circumstances be solved geometrically simply with compasses and ruler, but only by using conic sections, higher curves or interpolation; in this respect trisection of the angle is related to → duplication of the cube. Trisection of the angle, duplication of the cube and → squaring the circle (now become proverbial) are designated as 'classical problems of mathematics'. Greek scholars made great efforts to solve these problems by geometric means. It is possible that the question of trisection of the angle became topical once it had become known how to construct the regular pentagon and there was a desire to continue the construction of regular polygons ([3. 235]; on the problem and ways of solving it in general: [4]).

→ Hippias [5] of Elis invented a special curve, the 'quadratrix' (τετραγωνίζουσα/*tetragōnízousa* sc. γραμμή/*grammḗ*); cf. → Deinostratus for trisection of the angle. This curve arises owing to the combination of two movements; it enables not only the division of an angle into any number of parts, but also the rectification of the arc of a circle (Pappus, collectio 4: [1. 252 f.]; cf. [5. 95–97]). A solution by interpolation is handed down by → Pappus (Collectio 4: [1. 272–276]; cf. [5. 86 f.; 3. 235–237]); he shows that a circle and a hyperbole can be used instead of intperpolation. The conchoid used by → Nicomedes [3] (with fig.) for → duplication of the cube is also suitable for carrying out trisection of the angle (Pappus, Collectio 4: [1. 242–244]; cf. [5. 87; 3. 238–240]). Another construction for trisection of any angle, which also uses an interpolation, is handed down in the *Liber assumptorum*, extant in Arabic, which goes back in content at least partially to → Archimedes [1] (bk. 11.) ([2. 518]; cf. [5. 88; 3. 240 f.]). This solution was known in the Arab world, e.g. in the *Liber trium fratrum* of the Banū Mūsā (the three sons of Mūsā ibn Šākir, 9th cent., Baghdad), and also reached the west through Lat. translations.

1 F. Hultsch (ed.), Pappi Alexandrini Collectionis quae supersunt, vol. 1, 1876 2 J. L. Heiberg (ed.), Archimedis opera omnia, vol. 2, ²1913 3 T. L. Heath, A History of Greek Mathematics, vol. 1, 1921, 235–244 4 W. Breidenbach, Die Dreiteilung des Winkels, ²1951 5 O. Becker, Das mathematische Denken der Ant., 1957 6 J. P. Hogendijk, Greek and Arabic Constructions of the Regular Heptagon, in: Archive for History of Exact Sciences 30, 1984, 197–330 7 J. Tropfke, Gesch. der Elementarmathematik, vol. 1, ⁴1980. M. F.

Divisor ('One who apportions endowments'). From the 2nd cent. BC or earlier war spoils of the Roman state were occasionally distributed among the people of Rome. In the absence of an official 'Body of Apportionment' it fell to private citizens, *divisores*, to assume that function. By the end of the Republic this had led to a system of canvassing that has been described in detail in Cicero Planc. 48ff. *Divisores* promised in single → *tribus* a 'reward' to a sufficient number of tribus members in the event of a particular candidate being elected. If the *tribus* was won over and the candidate elected, the money that had been deposited with a sequester would be distributed by the divisor. This particular type of → *ambitus* was probably made punishable by the *lex Calpurnia* in 67 and certainly by the *lex Tullia* in 63 BC.

W. Kunkel, Staatsordnung und Staatspraxis der röm. Republik II, 1995, 83. G.S.

Divitia The modern Cologne-Deutz. Starting as a bridgehead across the Rhine opposite → Colonia Agrippinensis [1] early in the 1st cent. AD and rebuilt with a bridge by Constantine the Great to harbour 1,000 men on the Rhine border that is above flood level (Paneg. 6 [7],11,3; 13,1–5); parts of the structure lasted until Frankish times (*Divitia civitas*: Greg. Tur. Franc. 4,16).

1 B. Päffgen, W. Zanier, Überlegungen zur Lokalisierung von Oppidum Ubiorum und Legionslager im frühkaiserzeitlichen Köln, in: W. Czysz, C. M. Hüssen et al. (eds.), Provinzialröm. Forschungen. Festschrift G. Ulbert, 1995, 111–130, esp. 127f.

M. CARROLL-SPILLECKE, Das röm. Militärlager D. in Köln-Deutz, in: Kölner Jbb. 16, 1993, 321–444. K.DI.

Divodurum The chief town of the Gallo-Roman *civitas* of the Mediomatrici, now Metz, on a long ridge between the Moselle and the Seille before their confluence (Ptol. 2,9,7). A Hallstatt *oppidum* destroyed in the 6th cent. BC was succeeded by a La Tène age camp taken in the war against Caesar. When the Augustan settlement fell victim to a conflagration under Tiberius, the new town was given a typical Roman 'grid pattern', whose main coordinates were formed by the roads between Lyons and Trier (→ *cardo*) and between Reims and Strasbourg (→ *decumanus*) crossed (It. Ant. 240; 363–365; 371). Divodurum is first named after the death of Nero in AD 68 (Tac. Hist. 1,63) when a massacre of the population took place. Traces of fire point to its destruction towards the end of the 1st cent.

From its prime, which lasted until the mid-3rd cent., the following remains are preserved i.a.: the 'Maison Quarrée' (temple or civil basilica), the basilica at the church of St.-Pierre-aux-Nonnains, the amphitheatre to the south, a small theatre on the bank of the Moselle, parts of an aqueduct and three baths constructions. Burnt layers dating to 240/250 can be traced back to barbarian attacks. As a result the town boundary was reduced and surrounded by a wall some 3,500 m long. Divodorum was then named after the *civitas Mediomatrici* or *Mettis* (Amm. Marc. 15,11,9; 17,1,2; Not. Galliarum 5,3; Not. Dign. Occ. 11,59; 12,27). There was further destruction during the attack by Vandals in 406 and on 7 Apr. 451 the ancient city of Metz finally succumbed in the fight against → Attila (Greg. Tur. Franc. 2,6).

E. FRÉZOULS, Les villes antiques de la France I, 1, 1982, 235–350 (with collected documents and inscriptions); B. VIGNERON, D. Mediomatricorum, 1986. F.SCH.

Divona Main town of the Celtic → Cadurci in Aquitania (now Cahors. dép. Lot); sources: Ptol. 2,7,9; *CIL* XIII 1541 [1].

A. AUDIN, J. GUEY, P. WUILLEUMIER, Inscriptions latines découvertes à Lyon dans le pont de la Guillotière, in: REA 56, 1954, 297–347. E.O.

Divorce The dissolution of → marriage through divorce appears to have been possible everywhere in antiquity from Mesopotamia to Rome, of course not always in the same way for men and women. Thus in Egypt in the 1st millennium BC it was possible for women as well as men to make a declaration of divorce; in ancient Jewish law, as probably also in Mesopotamia, on the other hand, the repudiation was only declared by the husband. In any case, Jewish law also linked the dissolution of the marriage in the later, Talmudic period (→ Halakha) with grounds for divorce (→ Marriage IV.). In antiquity there were also many divorce penalties. Testimonials for this are already known from the Ancient Orient in the form of a type of contractual penalty based on the marriage contract (→ Marriage I.). Fines for groundless divorce or divorce based on fault were also known in classical Greece; such sanctions were no obstacle to the effectiveness of a divorce. There was no Greek technical term for divorce. People spoke of 'repudiating' (*apopémpein*) or 'leaving' (*apoleípein*) and simply of 'separation' (*apallagḗ*). Consequently, divorce tended to be an actual rather than a legal or even legally structured process. The 'divorce documents' of the Hellenistic period from Egypt contain contracts regarding the consequences of divorce (return of the dowry, → *phernḗ*, permission to remarry); divorce itself was not a 'legal entity' even in the 3rd–1st cents. BC.

In Roman law only the → *diffarreatio* was a formal divorce for a long time. It was the counterpart of → *confarreatio*, which as the basis of a → *manus* marriage (with 'the authority of the husband') was probably no longer very widespread during the Principate period. Other *manus* marriages were like the *manus*-free marriage divorced informally by the spouses themselves. To dissolve the *manus* a → *remancipatio* was then required. The typical form of the simple Roman divorce (→ *divortium*) was the → *repudium* (declaration of divorce) that also became the basis of the letter of divorce (*libellus repudii*) necessary as a prerequisite for divorce in late antiquity. The Christian concept of marriage did not yet lead to divorce becoming inadmissible in late antiquity. However divorce became increasingly difficult until Justinian [1] in AD 542 finally stipulated in Nov. 117 the grounds for divorce (esp. in the case of crimes). However a divorce without such grounds was not ineffective but of course led to considerable penalties (esp. loss of the dowry/→ *dos*; ban on remarriage), following the official penalties that had already been applicable since about the time of the birth of Christ for → *adulterium* (adultery) that could even be punished with death in late antiquity.
→ Adulterium; → Marriage; → Adultery; → Marriage contracts; → Wife

E. LEVY, Der Hergang der röm. Ehescheidung, 1925; H. A. RUPPRECHT, Kleine Einführung in die Papyruskunde, 1994, 108; TH. THALHEIM, s. v. Ehescheidung, in: RE 5, 2011–2013; TREGGIARI, 435–482. G. S.

Divortium (from *divertere*, to turn away) is divorce in Roman law. Its basis is clearly set out in a rescript of Alexander Severus in AD 223 (Cod. Iust. 8,38,2): *libera matrimonia esse antiquitus placuit* (it was recognized of old that marriage is free). Whether this was true of marriages in the early times that were celebrated with special rites is doubtful. But even here extant sources mention that provision was made for a form of divorce (→ *diffarreatio*). The 'freedom' of marriage meant in particular that no grounds were required for its dissolution: neither the guilt of one of the parties nor even an established breakdown of marriage. Morally, however, only a divorce for which there were grounds will have been acceptable (and accepted by the censor). The authority for initiating a divorce was originally vested in the husband or his *paterfamilias*, since the wife, being subject to his domination (→ *manus*), had no legal status to do so. Under the influence of the free dissolution —by husband and wife alike — of a *manus*-free marriage, the adage quoted above was extended to include *manus* marriages no later than under the principate.

Neither moral disapproval nor even the punishments for guilty divorces that were introduced in Christian times had any influence on the effectiveness of the *divortium*. On the other hand, custom and the threat of punishment undoubtedly exercised considerable indirect pressure not to proceed with a divorce without relevant grounds. So too did the imposition of considerable financial disadvantages connected with groundless divorce (cf. → Marriage contracts). Mutually agreed divorce was however not only permissible throughout the period Roman law held sway, it was not penalised even in Christian times.

Other than in the case of *diffarreatio* no stipulations were made as to the form a divorce should take. It was effected by a simple declaration by the party wishing to divorce (see also → *repudium*). If the parties resumed their matrimonial state or omitted to abandon it despite the declaration of divorce, the actual state was legally decisive. It was usual to communicate the wish to divorce by messenger. This *nuntium remittere* apparent was so widespread it came to be the normal term for a divorce. In late classical times (from the 3rd cent.) a letter of divorce, *libellus repudii,* was usual.

If a *manus* marriage was dissolved, the divorce did not of itself end the dominion of the husband. For that a special form was required such as *diffarreatio* or → *remancipatio*, by which the father of the wife reassumed domestic power over her.

1 E. Levy, Der Hergang der röm. Ehescheidung, 1925, 55ff. 2 Treggiari, 435–482. G.S.

Diyllus (Δίυλλος; *Díyllos*) of Athens. Greek historian of the first half of the 3rd cent. BC, son of the atthidographer Phanodemus. Author of *Historíai* in 27 bks., a universal history in two parts (cf. FGrH 73 T 1 and 2), which continued → Ephorus and covered the period from the 3rd Sacred War (357/6) to the death of Cassander's son Philip. D. was continued in his turn by Psaon of Plataeae (FGrH 78 T 1).

According to Plutarch, D., who wrote entirely in the 'tragic' manner (Plut. Mor. 345E and F), was 'not insignificant in historiography' (Plut. Mor. 862B = T4). Whether Diodorus used D. for the history of Alexander in bk. 17 (thus [1]) or for the Diadochi period in bks. 18–20 (cf. [2. 19ff.]), is still debatable (cf. [3. 126f.]). FGrH 73 and 257 a F 3.

1 N. G. L. Hammond, Three Historians of Alexander the Great, 1983 2 J. Seibert, Das Zeitalter der Diadochen, 1983 3 K. Meister, Die griech. Geschichtsschreibung, 1990. K.MEI.

Djoser (Egypt. *Ḏsr*, only the Horus name *Nṯrj-ḫt* is attested in contemporary sources; in Manetho Τόσορθρος/*Tósorthros* or Σέσορθος/*Sésorthos*). First or second king of the 3rd Dynasty; according to the Turin Papyrus of Kings ruled for 19 years (*c.* 2650 BC); no political events from his period are known. Probably with the collaboration of Imhotep (→ Imuthes), D. erected a monumental funerary complex in Saqqara, in the centre of which was the first pyramid, a stepped building developed from a mastaba on an almost square base and surrounded by temples to the dead and palace façades. Later transmission saw it as the beginning of stone → architecture. Because of his grave construction, which was the inspirational source of other royal burial complexes in the Old Kingdom and was still frequently visited in the New Kingdom, D. was visibly the founder of the Old Kingdom tradition and enjoyed lasting veneration. Even a falsely, backdated document from the Ptolemaic era rests its claim on his authority.
→ Dodekaschoinos; → Pyramid(s)

J. von Beckerath, s.v. D., LÄ 1, 1975, 1111f. S.S.

Doberus (Δόβηρος; *Dóbēros*). City in Paeonia, probably in the valley of the Strymon. Place of assembly for Sitalces' assault on the Macedonian kingdom in 432 BC (Thuc. 2,98,2). Absorbed into Macedon (possibly under Philip II), D. became a *civitas* of the Roman province of Macedonia (Plin. HN 4,35). Pillaged by the Goths in AD 267 (Zos. 1,43); diocese (Council of Chalcedon).

F. Papazoglou, Les villes de Macédoine, 1988, 328f. MA.ER.

Docimus (Δόκιμος; *Dókimos*). Appointed satrap of Babylon by → Perdiccas in 323 BC (Arr. Succ. 24,3–5). Condemned after Perdiccas' death, he fled to Asia Minor and supported → Alcetas [4] and → Attalus [2] against → Eumenes. Defeated along with his allies by → Antigonus Monophthalmus and imprisoned in a fortress, he betrayed them in an escape attempt and went over to Antigonus (Diod. Sic. 19,16), who quickly promoted him. In Phrygia he founded a city Dokimeion. In 302 he allied himself with Lysimachus (Diod. Sic. 20,107,3). His later history is unknown.

R. A. Billows, Antigonus the One-Eyed, 1990, especially 382f. E.B.

Dockyards (νεώρια/*neōria*, neut. pl.; Lat. *navalia*, neut. pl.). There is no evidence of dockyards as permanent structural establishment for → shipbuilding in the early Greek period; shipbuilding took place as a specialized part of the → *materiatio* at places chosen on an *ad hoc* basis in each case close to coasts or harbours (Pylos [1]; cf. Hom. Od. 6,263–272). At the latest since the early 6th cent. BC, as a feature of the autonomy of the Greek → polis, dockyards were part of the infrastructure of the navy (→ navies) in the same way as boat sheds and storehouses for rigging (→ skeuotheke). To what extent these dockyards were of military character or served for the construction and maintenance of civilian ships is unclear; designating remains of structures as 'dockyards' (e.g. in → Oeniadae [1], → Gytheum, → Syracusae: see Addenda, → Thurii) is often uncertain. In the → Peloponnesian War dockyards were a prime target for naval attacks [3]. Destroying them caused great damage to an opponent; the timber store, which was an essential component of a dockyard, attracted particular attention in this respect.

It can be assumed that there were also extensive dockyards at the centres of the Roman fleet (in particular → Ravenna, → Brundisium, → Misenum, → Baiae, → Puteoli, → Ostia), though there are no archaeological finds showing exactly what they looked like or they cannot be specifically distinguished from the documented architectural remains of harbours (cf. Vitr. De arch. 5,12). Dockyards did not necessarily have to be in the immediate vicinity of the coast; there is evidence of land transport even of large ships and over long distances (resplendent ships from → Lacus Nemorensis/Lake Nemi, which had probably been built in Misenum). The literary tradition shows dockyards with slipways and ramps, slips for ship maintenance and in isolated instances even dry docks (→ Motya). Cf. → harbours/harbour complexes; → navigation; → shipbuilding (with bibliography in each case).

1 L. Cassons, Ships and Seamanship in the Ancient World, ³1986 2 P. A. Gianfrotta, A Roman Shipyard at Minturno, in: H. Tzalas (ed.), 2nd International Symposium on Ship Construction in Antiquity (Congress Delphi 1987), 1990, 195–205 3 O. Höckmann, Ant. Seefahrt, 1985, 153–156, 184 n. 37. C.HÖ.

Doclea Settlement of the Illyrian Docleates (Ptol. 2,16,12; App. Ill. 16,46; Ptol. 2,16,8; Plin. HN 3,143; *princeps civitatis Docleatium*, ILJug 1853 [1]) in the interior of Crna Gora (Montenegro), now Duklja, at the junction of the Zeta and Morača in the Podgorica (formerly Titograd) region; was later a Flavian *municipium Docleatium* in the *prov. Dalmatia* (→ Dalmatae, Dalmatia), confirmed in several inscriptions (collected by Sticotti [2]) as *res p(ublica) Docleatium*. Ruler cult attested. Excavations have brought to light numerous remains of Roman buildings: aqueduct, forum, early Christian basilica, necropoleis. Several bases with inscriptions in honour of emperors from *Divus* Titus onwards. Birthplace of Diocletian (Epitoma de Caesaribus 39,1). After Diocletian's reforms D. belonged to *Praevalitana*; it regained its prosperity after 536, when Justinian's authority was consolidated also in the *prov.* No coin finds after Honorius. A diocese in the 6th cent.

1 A. Šašel, J. Šašel (ed.), Inscriptiones Latinae Jugoslaviae, 1986 2 P. Sticotti, Die röm. Stadt D. in Montenegro (Schriften der Balkankommission, Ant. Abt. 6), 1913 3 J. J. Wilkes, Dalmatia, 1969 A. Cermanović-Kuzmanović, D. Srejović, O. Velimirović-Žižić, Antička Duklja nekropole (The Roman Cemetery at D.), 1975. M.Š.K.

Doctor
[1] see → Medicine
[2] see → Munus, Munera III E

Doctrina Addai This Syrian tale recounts Addai's legendary missionary activity in Edessa and the subsequent conversion of King Abgar 'the Black' (→ Abgar Legend). The beginning, which has its only parallel in the Greek version by Eusebius (HE 1,13), describes Abgar's exchange of correspondence with Jesus and Addai's arrival in → Edessa (in Eusebius: *Thaddaios*). The Doctrina Addai however, provides additional new information, in particular about a portrait of Jesus by Ḥannan, Abgar's emissary, the precursor of the Mandylion of later tradition, and continues the narrative up to Addai's successors Aggai and Palūṭ. As well, it records the discovery of the cross by Claudius' wife Protonice. The work was composed around 420 and stems from the same environment as the legend of the martyrdom of Šarbel and Barsamya.

Editions/Translations: G. Phillips, The Doctrine of Addai, 1876; G. Howard, The Teaching of Addai, 1981 (photographic ed. of 5th-cent. MS, in: E. N. Meščerskaya, Legenda ob Avgare, 1984); A. Desreaumaux, Histoire du Roi Abgar et de Jésus, 1993.
Bibliography: H. J. W. Drijvers, 'Abgarsage', in: W. Schneemelcher (ed.), Neutestamentliche Apokryphen, ⁵1987, 389–396; S. P. Brock, Eusebius and Syriac Christianity, in: H. W. Attridge, G. Hata, Eusebius, Christianity and Judaism, 1992, 212–234; S. Heid, Zur frühen Protonike- und Kyriakoslegende, in: Analecta Bollandiana 109, 1991, 73–108. S.BR.

Doctrina Iacobi The *Doctrina Iacobi nuper baptizati*, believed to date from the 7th cent., recounts how in his youth the Jew Jacob amused himself by beating up Christians. How, during a stay in → Carthage he was compulsorily baptized, like all Jews in the Empire, on the order of Emperor → Heraclius, and then, after a vision, he confessed to the baptism and acquired a comprehensive theological knowledge; and how, in long, secret debates, he convinced all compulsorily baptized Jews and a passing Jewish traveller, Iustus, of the validity of Christianity. While this story had previously been regarded as contemporary and even historically reliable, it was recently demonstrated to have been a medieval compilation of various writings, e.g. an apocalyptic dialogue, a picaresque novel, etc. These writings survived into the Middle Ages in a strongly corrupted form and, because of the identical names of the characters, were then thought to be remnants of one single text and were elaborated with long expositions designed to illustrate the correctness of the Christian interpretation of the Old Testament. That was the origin of the Doctrina Iacobi that we have today. All historical informations in the work, including the compulsory baptism by Heraclius, are unreliable. Fragments of the outstanding semi-vulgar literature from the 'dark ages' of Byzantium are, however, contained within it.

G. DAGRON, V. DÉROCHE, Juifs et Chrétiens dans l'Orient du VIIe siècle, Traveaux et Mémoires 11, 1991, especially 47–229 (ed. of *D.I.*: DÉROCHE), 230–273 (comm.: DAGRON and DÉROCHE).; P. SPECK, Die *Doctrina Iacobi nuper baptizati*, in: Varia VI. Beiträge zum Thema 'Byzantinische Feindseligkeit gegen die Juden' im frühen siebten Jahrhundert (ΠΟΙΚΙΛΑ ΒΥΖΑΝΤΙΝΑ 15), 1997, 263–436. P.SP.

Doctrina patrum de incarnatione verbi Dogmatic florilegium, dating from the end of the 7th into the 8th cent. AD, that was put together from already existing but now partially lost Christological collections (i.a. ch. 24 and 33) and wrongly ascribed to the apocrisiary → Anastasius [3] († 666) or the abbot → Anastasius Sinaites [5] (died shortly after 700).

EDITION: F. DIEKAMP, D., 1907.
BIBLIOGRAPHY: A. GRILLMEIER, Jesus der Christus im Glauben der Kirche 2/1, ²1991, 94–100. J.RI.

Document hand

I. GREEK II. LATIN

I. GREEK

The Greek → documents passed down on papyri (→ Papyrus) and ostraka (→ *óstrakon*) are mostly written in cursive script (→ Writing, styles of) or chancellery script. However, in the case of the earliest testimonials of the Greek script in Egypt (4th to the beginning of the 3rd cent. BC) when there was still no significant difference between an actual cursive script and the book hand in the → epigraphical style, the few documents passed down were written in book hands. In the following epoch people used cursive script for the majority of private documents, but for administrative documents they used chancellery script. However between the 1st and 3rd cent. AD, too, fluid, elegant and easily legible script types were used that are hard to assign to a strict classification even though they were described as 'semi-cursive book scripts' because of their mixed nature. Especially in the 2nd cent. AD, documents (even private ones) often have a clear, neat script with very few → ligatures and barely any distorted letters (cf. on the other hand the contemporary round majuscule; → Uncial I.) whose softer and more fluid ductus was well suited for documents.

G. MESSERI, R. PINTAUDI, Documenti e scritture, in: G. CAVALLO et al. (ed.), Scrivere libri e documenti nel mondo antico, 1998, 39–53. G. M.

II. LATIN

From the 1st cent. BC at the latest, the majuscule cursive script (also called capitalis cursive or older Roman cursive; → Majuscule) occurs, which in the subsequent cent. achieved a clearly stylized form: its letters are sharply vertical and unconnected, with *A, E, F, O, R* regularly formed cursively. This script was used particularly in graffiti, on wax tablets (→ Writing tablets) and documentary papyri (on which its cursive nature is especially effective), but seldom for literary works. The → minuscule as a book and everyday script was also used from the 3rd cent. AD for the documents and administrative writings of the Roman empire until ultimately the majuscule cursive (then called minuscule cursive or newer cursive) was superseded in the 5th cent.; in addition this script was also used for marginal notes in MSS and for main texts and formed the graphic basis for the new book hands of the high Middle Ages.

B. BISCHOFF, Paläographie des röm. Alt. und des abendländischen MA, ²1986, 85–91. P. E.

Documents

I. GENERAL II. ANCIENT ORIENT III. EGYPT IV. JEWISH LAW V. CLASSICAL GREECE AND HELLENISM VI. ROMAN LAW

I. GENERAL

A. TERM B. BUSINESS DOCUMENTS

A. TERM

In legal terms, a document is a written declaration regarding a legal transaction. In modern opinion it is a declaration of intent in a suitable written form that is intended to provide proof in legal transactions and that permits recognition of the issuing party (e.g., [2; 8]). In general, documents include all non-literary and partially literary texts (exceptions are, e.g., poetry and amulets), i.e., apart from business documents, trial and administrative documents, letters and accounts. Preferred media for documents were clay, → papyrus, ostraca (→ *óstrakon*), stone, wood and wax tablets, as well as metal.

B. BUSINESS DOCUMENTS

1. FORMAL ASPECTS 2. EFFECT 3. SAFEKEEPING, ISSUERS AND ARCHIVING

1. FORMAL ASPECTS

The appearance of documents (e.g., material and shape, language, text arrangement, necessary components, style, clauses, attachment of verification means such as → seals) was often the product of (local, period etc.) practice. Observing the formal characteristics contributes to an understanding of documents and may permit further conclusions (e.g., place and period of origin, administrative procedure). In contrast to medieval documents ('diplomatics'; see [1; 3]), only a limited theory of documents exists for antiquity.

2. EFFECT

Documents of proof and constitutive documents must be distinguished. The former prove a legal declaration made outside the document, the latter bring about a legal transaction. Legal historians often use the term 'dispositive document' rather than constitutive document, which actually means a document embodying law and is connected to asset papers. This terminological imprecision is harmless ([9. 489[5]]). The content must be differentiated according to dispositive and declarative clauses: the former only express legal practice whereas the latter modify it. Special authentication forms and an associated increased value as proof ('private/public documents') only emerged in the Hellenistic period (see V.). Despite the widespread written notation, there was no mandatory written form.

3. Safekeeping, issuers and archiving

Securing the document statement against change is an important concern with both the external form (multiple authentication, sealing, cf. → seal: by means of illustrations, autography, signature) and witnesses being used for this purpose. Literacy was not general in antiquity [4] (→ Writing). Private persons often used professional → scribes or could only write in a clumsy manner. For this reason private letters — which were in any case only written with the participants' knowledge in mind — are often unclear. Professional scribes usually expressed themselves professionally and followed conventions or models in writing and form. The level of experience of individual scribes varied but did not necessarily result in legal differences. Private documents were kept by the entitled party (legal documents) while letters, notes etc. were held by the recipient. The former were destroyed, invalidated or returned to the other party after completion. Associated documents formed 'archives' (that were preserved in association) or (modern compiled) 'dossiers' [5]. Administrative archives only contain administrative documents [7]. Deposition and registration of private business documents only occurred in the Hellenistic period.

→ Demotic law; → Fajum; → Papyrus; → Writing materials; → Contract; → Administration

1 H. Bresslau, Hdb. der Urkundenlehre für Deutschland und It., [4]1968 ff. 2 Th. Frenz, s. v. U. (rechtlich), in: Handwörterbuch der deutschen Rechtsgesch. 5, 1998, 574–576 3 Id., s. v. U.lehre, in: ibid., 584–591 4 W. V. Harris, Ancient Literacy, 1989 5 A. Jördens, Papyri und private Archive. Ein Diskussionsbeitrag zur papyrologischen Terminologie, in: E. Cantarella, G. Thür (ed.), Symposion 1997, 2001, 253–268 6 W. Kunkel, s. v. Συγγραφή, syngrapha, RE 4 A, 1376–1387 7 E. Posner, Archives in the Ancient World, 1972 8 H. Steinacker, Die ant. Grundlagen der frühma. Privatu., 1927 9 F. Wieacker, review of: H. Steinacker, 'Traditio cartae' und 'traditio per cartam', ein Kontinuitätsproblem (1959/60) in: ZRG Rom. Abt. 79, 1962, 488–493.

II. Ancient Orient

There is no current theory of documents covering the entire cuneiform region (but s. [18. 114–174]). However, information may be found in studies on individual periods (e.g., [3; 17. 19–78]), studies of groups of documents (e.g., [11. 13–25; 7. 46–52; 16; 10]) and scattered comments on document editions.

A. General B. Administrative documents C. Business documents

A. General

Administrative (initially especially economic administration), legal (business, court documents; → state treaties) and other documents (e.g., letters) existed in → cuneiform writing from the early Dynastic to the Hellenistic periods (→ Cuneiform, legal texts in). Clay tablets were an important document medium (Sumerian *dub*; Akkadian *ṭuppum* without specifying the business type; Aramaic epigraphy of the Achaemenid period reveals that document designations differentiated content, cf. [17. 52]). In the later period, the clay tablet became reserved only for certain business types [14. 108]. Stone (as well as clay) was used for official inscriptions, likewise also in the Early Dynastic (29th/28th cents. BC) and Middle to Neo-Babylonian periods, e.g., the Akkadian *kudurru* ('boundary stones'), which documented land distributions [4; 1]. The wax tablet (Sumerian ^{giš}DA; Akkadian *lēʾu*, Hittite ^{GIŠ}*lēʾu*, literally 'wooden tablet') is attested since the Middle Assyrian/Middle Babylonian/Hittite period. It was used in non-literary contexts, esp. in administration and accounting [6; 19], but rarely or never as a legal document (presumably because of the ease of alteration). Hittite DUB.SAR.GIŠ ('wooden tablet scribe') might indicate the use of wooden tablets, possibly for Luwian texts. → Parchment (Akkadian *kussu*) and → papyrus (*niāru*) have been attested in images and noted since the 1st millennium BC.

In size, form and arching of the surface as well as column numbers, clay tablets exhibit clear qualitative and use-related, chronological and geographical differences: e.g., writing exercises, short administrative texts (→ Ebla); accounts for small stock and harvests as well as large tablets with continuous documentation of revenues and expenditures (Ur III), as opposed to tabulated documents (Middle Babylonian); broad formats for business documents and elongated formats for receipts (Neo-/Late Babylonian) etc.

B. Administrative documents

The origin of → writing lies in economic administration, which requires documentation. The precursors of administrative documents written on clay tablets were clay bullas (clay envelopes) used for inventories: the number and type of goods were represented by clay symbols that were sealed into the envelope [13]. About 90% of cuneiform material consists of legal and administrative documents. The latter are by far in the majority and in some periods and areas even constitute the only preserved documents. (→ Administration).

C. Business documents

1. Formal aspects 2. Effect 3. Safekeeping, issuers and archiving

1. Formal aspects

The Sumerians first began putting legal matters into a written form and even used formularies before the Old Babylonian period [4]. It must be emphasized that a great variety of documentary elements with local and chronological significance exists, but these details has often been overlooked. These documents, which are very brief and almost exclusively objective in style, are witness protocols of business transactions. Essential elements of documents are the transaction record, information on the parties, supplementary clauses (e.g., non-contestability and punitive clauses), naming of the witnesses and (including or separately) the document's scribe, and possibly the date. The 'commitment record' played a significant role as a document. It essentially announces a payment in abstract terms but its purpose is only rarely stated. Other significant documents were the Sumerian *šu ba(n)ti* document [11. 17 f.], stylized promises of payment by the debtor [11. 14–17], the *ina-pāni c*redit contract (Akkadian) [16. 50 f.] and the 'dialogue document' (Neo-Babylonian/Hellenistic period [18. 152; 159 f.]). Qualified receipts, i.e. the contract details are given (e.g., in → Nuzi), take the place of contract documents. Formularies could be adapted to various legal transactions. On occasion formalities [12] and publicity forms (e.g., [18. 120 f.; 200 f.; 9. 67–81]) are recognizable apart from the authentication in legal acts and contracts, but neither a Roman-style formalism nor a public document of enhanced credibility are identifiable. This also applies to agreements recorded in court.

Sealing (by the author or a third party using a cylinder or imprinted seal [8], → seal; or even a seal substitute: fingernail or shell imprints, carvings [17. 35–40; 22]) was used instead of the modern signature. The parties to the document (both or only the party entering the commitment, including women and the unfree) as well as witnesses sealed; sealing essentially was a proof of authenticity but attaching seals to clay envelopes at times seemed to have also constituted sealing. Sealing was subject to local and chronological variations, e.g., in → Lagaš documents to be sealed were not made up as clay envelopes but regularly were in neighbouring Umma (during Ur III in both cases). Commitment records often were not sealed except in the Old Assyrian kingdom.

2. Effect

Business documents were primarily documents of proof, but a dispositive effect also developed [18. 137; 162–168]. Issued to an abstract person (Old Assyrian *tamkārum*, 'merchant'), the Old Assyrian/Babylonian commitment record could be used as a document of title to goods [2. 14 f.]. Documents could be used as collateral or inherited; they embodied the rights described in them (Middle/New Assyrian [17. 72 f.]).

3. Safekeeping, issuers and archiving

Clay tablets, which were only dried after having been inscribed, could be altered after rewetting — as is reflected by instructions. The envelope tablet was a precaution — regardless of the business at hand — against forgery (Ur III to Middle Babylonian/New Assyrian, late 3rd to mid-1st millennium BC). For this purpose the finished document was wrapped in a flat piece of clay, which was laterally compressed, inscribed and sealed; in cases of doubt regarding the correctness of the envelope text, the envelope was broken and the (unshortened) text of the inner tablet was checked. It is uncertain if the envelope tablet influenced the creation of duplicates elsewhere [18. 127–130]. Duplication was used for security (Neo-Babylonian); copies, collected documents and notices were used to create order (e.g., in → Kaneš, cf. [20]). For security a (promissory) → oath, a → curse, the non-contestability clause or (an on occasion bloody) contractual penalty might be used. The participation of persons entitled to object (in the document) effected the loss of this right. Writing was performed by professional scribes or literate private persons. There are indicators that the knowledge of writing was fairly widespread (→ Writing II; [5]). Formulae and clauses were practiced as part of the writing exercises (→ Scribes I). Documents were stored in (on occasion sealed) clay jars etc. as well as on shelves. A general archiving of legal documents was unknown but public and private → archives existed (e.g., [15; 21]). Commitment records were destroyed after fulfilment [17. 75 f.].

1 J. A. Brinkman, s. v. Kudurru A, RLA 6, 267–274 2 G. Eisser, E. Lewy, Die altassyrischen Rechtsu. vom Kültepe, vol. 1–2 (MVAG 33), 1930 3 G. Eisser, Zur U.lehre der altassyrischen Rechtsu. vom Kültepe, in: FS P. Koschaker, vol. 3, 1939, 94–126 4 I. J. Gelb et al., Earliest Land Tenure Systems in the Near East. Ancient Kudurrus, vol. 2, 1989 5 P. D. Gesche, Schulunterricht in Babylonien im ersten Jt. v. Chr., 2000 6 H. Hunger, s. v. Holztafel, RLA 4, 459 f. 7 B. Kienast, Die altbabylonischen Briefe und U. aus Kisurra, 1978 8 E. Klengel-Brandt (ed.), Mit Sieben Siegeln versehen. Das Siegel in Wirtschaft und Kunst des Alten Orients, 1997 9 P. Koschaker, Neue keilschriftliche Rechtsu. aus der El-Armarna-Zeit, 1928 10 U. Lewenton, Stud. zur keilschriftlichen Rechtspraxis Babyloniens in hell. Zeit, 1970 11 H. Lutzmann, Die neusumer. Schuldu., thesis Erlangen 1971, 1976 12 M. Malul, Studies in Mesopotamian Legal Symbolism, 1988 13 H. J. Nissen et al., Frühe Schrift und Techniken der Wirtschaftsverwaltung im alten Vorderen Orient, 1990 14 J. Oelsner, Recht im hell. Babylonien, in: M. J. Geller, H. Maehler (ed.), Legal Documents of the Hellenistic World, 1995, 106–148 15 Id., Siegelung und Archivierung von Dokumenten im hell. Babylonien, in: M.-F. Boussac, A. Invernizzi (ed.), Archives et sceaux du monde hellénistique, 1996, 101–112 16 H. Petschow, Neubabylonisches Pfandrecht, 1956 17 K. Radner, Die neuassyrischen Privatrechtsu. als Quelle für Mensch und Umwelt, 1997 18 M. San Nicolò, Beitr. zur Rechtsgesch. im Bereiche der keilschriftlichen Rechtsquellen, 1931 19 Id., Haben die Babylonier Wachstafeln als Schriftträger gekannt?, in:

Orientalia 17, 1948, 59–70 20 A. M. ULSHÖFER, Die altassyrischen Privatu., 1995 21 K. R. VEENHOF, Cuneiform Archives, in: Id. (ed.), 30e Rencontre Assyriologique Internationale 1983, 1986, 1–36 22 R. WALLENFELS, Private Seals and Sealing Practices at Hellenistic Uruk, in: M.-F. BOUSSAC, A. INVERNIZZI (ed.), Archives et sceaux du monde hellénistique, 1996, 113–129.

III. EGYPT

A. GENERAL B. HIERATIC AND CURSIVE HIERATIC DOCUMENTS C. DEMOTIC DOCUMENTS

A. GENERAL

The visual appearance of Egyptian documents was determined by the script (→ Hieroglyphs; → Hieratic; → Demotic) and the writing medium (stone inscription; papyrus; especially limestone ostraca, → *óstrakon*). Ostraca were used for notes and other short texts. Depending on the available space, they were inscribed using the usual phraseology but only for short texts (e.g., render receipts, formulas). In inscriptions → hieroglyphs were used in Egypt up to the Graeco-Roman period. The inscribed documents of public and private acts (→ contract) make this material important in many respects. The → hieratic and → demotic scripts mark (approximate) periods (i.e., before and after the 7th cent. BC). The term → archive (B.1.) denotes related phenomena: public and private, hieratic and demotic, later also Greek and, finally, Coptic document archives are recorded and attested up to the Arab conquest in AD 643 [11; 14. 248–261; 575–578]. The tradition of administrative records began in the 4th millennium BC with small wood or ivory tablets (e.g., [6]) and vessel inscriptions, which characterized the original content as render payments [10. 33 f.].

Cylinder seals, which belong to the same period (→ Seal), do not relate to the documentation system but were used for sealing the products after checking [9. 370 f.]. The artificially produced → writing material → papyrus is preserved since the 5th Dynasty (about 2575–2465 BC) in the (inscribed) original. The character of the material (roll/sheet size, grain, cf. [7]) permits the distinction of local, chronological and content-specific types, which are recognizable with sufficient representation in both chronologically older and younger inscriptions [7. 10–54; 142–145]. The content of documents captures the life of a developed court culture with the full range from royal decrees, administration, legal transactions to private letters [7; 20. 21–31].

B. HIERATIC AND CURSIVE HIERATIC DOCUMENTS

Formats, formulas, writing styles and phraseology have characteristics related to chronology, location and content with relatively few changes from the Old to the New Kingdom (*c.* 2700–1070 BC) [7] and beyond. The most important private legal document type was the house document (*jmt-pr*; → testament II. B.), which was used to transfer objects of importance. It begins with the date, followed by the document soma (the dispositive document part) and witnesses' names. The writer is not named, the document was sealed [20. 22–25].

Another noteworthy type of document is the cursive hieratic, scribe or witness document in a subjective style [19. 18 f.]. Also important in terms of legal actions are protocols of fictional trials that contain recognitions of commitments [20. 27–29].

C. DEMOTIC DOCUMENTS

A survey of the types of documented business transactions is provided by [5. 123–152; especially 139–148]. The documents follow a strict scheme that precludes retroactive changes. Their formulation is unilateral. Document types of the late Egyptian and Ptolemaic-Roman period are subjectively and objectively stylized scribe and witness documents, also the letter form. Double documents are not attested for the pre-Ptolemaic period [19. 19–24; 21. 49–61]. On the registration and archiving of demotic documents in Graeco-Roman Egypt cf. [15] and below (V. B.).

A striking peculiarity is the division of legal transactions into several documents: economic transactions are divided into the letter of payment and the compensation letter (*sẖꜣ ḏbꜣ ḥḏ/sẖꜣ n wꜣj*); in the process the receipt of the payment is confirmed and the seller declares that he no longer has any right to the sold item (document examples in [12]). A similar division is found in → marriage contracts [19. 72–79]. Legal documents function as proof; in acquisitions this is expressed in the issuing of a pre-acquisition document, but the document also embodies the acquired right (cf. [13. 328 f.]). Completion of the transaction can be suspended by temporarily not using the document [18; 19]. Witnesses appear with their names or their own statement pertaining to the documented event. The document text closes with the → scribe's name. Sealing is rare [2; 3]. Oaths and contractual penalties are used as affirmation and surety.

Only a small part of the extensive stock of extant demotic documents has been published so far (index of editions [4; 22]). The analysis of document production, formulas and design is still incomplete despite work such as [19; 21] (more in [1. 105–111]) because the bulk of the demotic material is still waiting for publication. In particular, the relationship between demotic and Greek documents created in the same environment in Ptolemaic Egypt (cf. below V. B.-C.) and their social background have only been in the focus of research in recent decades (e.g., [8]).

1 W. BOOCHS, Altäg. Zivilrecht, 1999 2 Id., Siegel und Siegeln im Alten Äg., 1982 3 E. BRESCIANI, Gli archivi demotici dai templi di Fayum, in: M.-F. BOUSSAC, A. INVERNIZZI (ed.), Archives et sceaux du monde hellénistique, 1996, 303–306 4 J. F. OATES et.al., Checklist of Editions of Greek, Latin, Demotic and Coptic Papyri, Ostraca and Tablets, 52001. 5 M. DEPAUW, A Companion to Demotic Studies, 1997 6 G. DREYER, Umm el-Qaab: Das Grab U-j, 1998 7 W. HELCK, Altäg. Aktenkunde des 3. und 2. Jt. v. Chr., 1974 8 J. H. JOHNSON (ed.),

Life in Multi-Cultural Society. Egypt from Cambyses to Constantine and Beyond, 1992 9 P. KAPLONY, Die Inschr. der äg. Frühzeit, vol. 1, 1963 10 Id., Die Inschr. der äg. Frühzeit, Suppl., 1964 11 E. LÜDDECKENS, s. v. U.archive, LÄ 6, 876–886 12 Id., Demotische U. aus Hawara, 1998 13 Id., Äg. Eheverträge, 1960 14 O. MONTEVECCHI, La Papirologia, ²1988 15 P. W. PESTMAN, Les papyrus démotiques de Tsenhor (P Tsenhor), 1994, vol. 1, 26–32 (with fig.) 16 Id., Registration of Demotic Contracts in Egypt, P. Par. 65, 2nd Cent. B. C., in: J. A. ANKUM et al. (ed.), FS R. Feenstra, 1985, 16–25 17 Id., Some Aspects of Egyptian Law in Graeco-Roman Egypt. Title Deeds and ὑπάλλαγμα, in: E. VAN'T DACK et al. (ed.), Egypt and the Hellenistic World, 1983, 281–302 18 Id., Ventes provisoires de biens pour sûreté de dettes. ὠναὶ ἐν πίστει à Pathyris et à Krokodilopolis, in: Id. (ed.), Textes et études de papyrologie grecque, démotique et copte (Papyrologica Lugduno-Batava 23), 1985, 45–59 19 E. SEIDL, Äg. Rechtsgesch. der Saiten- und Perserzeit, ²1968 20 Id., Einführung in die äg. Rechtsgesch. bis zum E. des NR, 1957 21 Id., Ptolem. Rechtsgesch., ²1962 22 S. P. VLEEMING, A. A. DEN BRINKER, Check-List of Demotic Text Editions and Re-editions, 1993 23 TH. ZAUZICH, Die äg. Schreibertradition in Aufbau, Sprache und Schrift der demotischen Kaufverträge aus ptolem. Zeit, 1968.

IV. Jewish law

Ancient documents that allow conclusions on a formally independent Jewish document system are lacking. Among the Old Hebrew ostraca and papyri (10th–6th cents. BC) only a few legal and economic documents may be found among letters, bills of delivery, lists etc. [11]. After the return from the Babylonian captivity → Hebrew, as the holy language, was no longer used in daily life and → Aramaic, Greek and also → Nabataean were used instead. Documents on ostraca, papyri and leather are available from Achaemenid and Nabataean-Roman Palestine (e.g., [3; 8]) as well as from Achaemenid to Roman Egypt (e.g., [10; 7; 1]). Reflections of ordinary life are found in the OT (e.g., sale of real estate: Gen 23,10–16, cf. [9]; divorce letter: Deut 24,1) and the Talmud [4]. Overall, it is clear that the document form was adapted to the respective cultural environment (cf. also [5; 6]).

1 V. A. TCHERIKOVER (ed.), Corpus Papyrorum Iudaicarum, vol. 1–3, 1957–1964 2 D. BARTHOLÉLEMY et al. (ed.), Discoveries in the Judean Desert of Jordan, 1955 ff. 3 I. EPH'AL, J. NAVEH, Aramaic Ostraca of the Fourth Century B. C. from Idumaea, 1996 4 A. GULAK, Das U.wesen im Talmud im Lichte der griech.-äg. Papyri und des griech. und röm. Rechts, 1935 5 E. KOFFMAN, Die Doppelu. aus der Wüste Juda, 1968 6 C. SIRAT et al., La Ketouba de Cologne. Un contrat de mariage juif à Antinoopolis, 1986 7 J. M. S. COWEY, K. MARESCH, Papyri aus den Slgg. von Heidelberg, Köln, München und Wien, 2001 8 N. LEWIS et al. (ed.), The Documents of the Bar Kokhba Period in the Cave of Letters, 1989 9 H. PETSCHOW, Die neubabylonische Zwiegesprächsu. und Genesis 23, in: JCS 19, 1965, 103–120 10 B. PORTEN et al. (ed.), The Elephantine Papyri in English: Three Millennia of Cross-Cultural Continuity and Change, 1996 11 J. RENZ, W. RÖLLIG, Hdb. der althebräischen Epigraphik, vol. 1–3, 1995.

JO. HE.

V. Classical Greece and Hellenism

A. Documents of the classical period B. The significance of Graeco-Egyptian documents C. Document types of the Hellenistic period D. Development in the Roman period E. Document security and special clauses

A. Documents of the classical period

The transmitted Greek documents especially of the 5th–4th cent. BC are all → epigraphical (II.). However, there must have been documents on other, unpreserved materials such as wood and → papyrus. Therefore, the significance of documents cannot be assessed from direct transmission but must be deducted from literary evidence, in particular the court speeches of → Demosthenes [2] (also → *syngraphaí*; → *syngraphḗ*).

Apart from an abundance of governmental documents (laws, → state treaties, lists of office holders and public expenses), there were documents that concerned legal transactions among private individuals (fundamental [1], cf. also [2; 3]). For example, numerous → *hóroi* ('boundary markers') are known especially from Attica (especially [4]). However, most documents pertain to sureties, according to their legal structure sales with a right of redemption and use (→ *prâsis epì lýsei*) for the 'seller'. Functionally, this is similar to a mortgage in modern law. In this way → loans and also the return, e.g., of dowry, was ensured (→ *proíx*). Another important type of classical document is the manumission document (→ manumission B.). It particularly occurs in temple inscriptions (especially in Delphi; cf. on this [5]). Apart from the 'transfer' of the slave to the deity, these documents often contain the payment of the → freed person, especially service obligations, to the former master (→ *paramonḗ*). Finally, documents regarding various contracts in the form of the → *syngraphḗ* ('written text') must have played a significant role.

The technical importance of documents in classical Greek law cannot be deduced with certainty from the available sources. However, it may be assumed that they had no stronger effect than documents in the Hellenistic period (see [6]). Therefore, today one may assume that the documents served as proof rather than being the actual means of making private transactions effective. Effectiveness resulted from other characteristics such as a downpayment (→ *arrabṓn*) or, more generally, from a → purpose-specific order (s. also → contract). In juristic terminology documents were pure documents of proof but not dispositive or constitutive documents.

B. The significance of Graeco-Egyptian documents

In terms of preservation, Greek documents from Ptolemaic and Roman Egypt are particularly important (*c.* 300 BC –*c.* AD 300). These testimonials are preserved in a particular abundance that, nevertheless, is not matched by a literary corpus similar to that of classical Greece and especially the *Corpus Iuris* of Roman law. As a result, the legal history of Egypt (or at least the Greek-speaking part of the population) must be reconstructed directly from documents (regarding the demotic documents of Egypt s. III. C.). Scientific work has focussed on the countless Graeco-Egyptian → papyrus documents (summary in [7]). Moreover, there is a substantial number of inscribed clay shards (→ *óstrakon*) though they usually only contain notices, short letters and internal calculations but not documents relating to legal transactions. The number of preserved parchment documents is rather insignificant. The documentary history of Egypt may therefore be limited to (legal) papyrology. The subject matter of the papyri is the entire sphere of public and legally relevant private life. They concern the state (in the Roman period after 30 BC the provincial) and local → administration, tax collection, office holders, the military, temples and churches as well as the burdens of public renders on private persons (→ *munus*; → Liturgy I.). Business documents, court protocols and documents regarding foreclosure are at the centre of legal historical interest.

C. Document types of the Hellenistic period

The oldest Greek document type, which is already known from the classical period, is the → *syngraphḗ* (see especially [6. 57–80]). Before the late 2nd cent. BC, it was a purely private document that was established with the participation of six witnesses. It 'objectively' reproduced the business transaction, i.e., without the business partners formulating their declarations as their own (cf. below VI. A.). In Egypt this type was initially designed as a double document with identical inner and outer inscriptions to better secure proof. The *kýria* ('attestation of truth') clause of the document also secured proof. [7. 139]. Finally, a private keeper of the document is often (*syngraphophýlax*) stated. The double document fell from use because of the rise of agoranomic documents (see [6. 81–105]): state notaries (→ *agoranómoi*) provided private documents with a 'title' (*anagraphḗ*) and officially registered it. The notaries also entered the private declaration into a protocol and only then permitted the parties to enter their 'signature' (*hypographḗ*) below. As a result, the notarial document replaced the private *syngraphḗ*. This transformation was already complete by the Roman period (after 30 BC).

The → *cheirógraphon* ('hand written text') was also common in the Ptolemaic period (see [6. 106–114]). It was available for all transaction types and contained the personal ('subjectively' stated) acknowledgement of having received or owing something. In these documents, too, the *kýria* clause was widely used. Unlike the six-witness *syngraphḗ*, the *cheirógraphon* continued into the Roman period and, as the *chirographum*, was accepted as a *testatio* into transactions among Romans like the notarial document (see VI; Cic. Fam. 7,18,1; Gai. Inst. 3,134). By submitting a copy or the original to an → archive, the document's value as proof was enhanced [6. 129–135].

D. Development in the Roman period

The Roman period *hypómnēma* ('confirmation of remembrance') was designed as a private, subjective contract offer — primarily as a rental/leaseholding/service or work contract (→ *místhōsis*; see [6. 114–122]). Despite its wording, it probably offered proof of the contract itself. Finally, in the Roman period the objectively formulated private document pertaining to a legal transaction without witnesses or notarial recording developed. In the secondary literature it is described as a 'private record' (see [6. 122–127]). Whether the *hypómnēma* or the private record were used appears to have depended on local customs among professional scribes. Objective legal requirements for the choice cannot be identified. This also largely applies to choice of public and private document types. [6. 113].

In the Roman period the public documents of Egypt included the → *synchṓrēsis*, which was used particularly in Alexandria [1] and took the shape of a (fictional) court settlement (with the same terminology; see [6. 91–95]). The → *katalogeîon* was a 'state authority with notarial functions' responsible for documents of this type [6. 28]. From the recording of business processes in banking, another 'public' document, the *diagraphḗ* (→ *diagráphein*; see [6. 95–105]) eventually developed in the Roman Imperial period. Initially, this was an entry into a bank register. Notification by the → banks of this fact was considered to be the same as documents with 'public credibility' or like public certifications. In the last phase of this development, there was a shift towards including not merely the payment process but also the → sale, → loan or any other transaction upon which the payment was based (in modern terms the causal transaction) in the bank document. Like all public documents, it was 'objectively' formulated. Towards the late 2nd cent. AD, the 'independent' *diagraphḗ*, which was divorced from the mere payment process, was generally used like the notarial document. However, it fell out of use towards the late 3rd cent. AD just as the notarial document and the *synchṓrēsis*.

E. Document security and special clauses

In Egypt registration and archiving (see [7. 139–141]) were used to secure the document and, consequently, to increase its value as proof. In the Ptolemaic period the means for this purpose was the *katagraphḗ* (registration, → land register). It was mandatory or at least customary for purchases of property, houses and slaves as well as manumissions. In the Roman period the *bibliothḗkē enktḗseōn* for properties and the *anákrisis* for slaves had an equivalent function. A particularly important component of many Greek documents since the classical period is the → *prâxis* [1] clause. It made possible an enforcement (*prâxis*) against the debtor's assets after an admonition procedure (see [7. 143 f.]).

The continuation and, in part, even the securing and reform of the documentation system in Roman Egypt demonstrates a vitality of Hellenistic documents even when faced with highly developed Roman law. However, increasing influence of Roman law becomes quite evident in the 3rd cent. AD through the adoption of the 'stipulation clause', which hints at the question and answer interplay of the Roman → *stipulatio* in a schematic manner but which has as little to do with the immediate documented legal transaction unlike with Greek and Hellenistic legal thinking in general [8]. This external formal approach was not able to secure the continuity of the Greek public document: towards the late 3rd cent. AD this document was replaced by the private document — *cheirógraphon* and *hypómnēma* — in Egypt and documents of the Roman → *tabelliones* (see VI.).

1 D. Behrend, Att. Pachturkunden, 1970 2 W. Schwahn, s. v. Syngraphai, RE 4 A, 1369–1376 3 G. Thür, Bemerkungen zum altgriech. Werkvertrag, in: Studi in onore di A. Biscardi, vol. 5, 1984, 471–514 4 M. I. Finley, Studies in Land and Credit in Ancient Athens, reprint (1951, ²1985) 5 K. D. Albrecht, Rechtsprobleme in den Freilassungen der Böotier, Phoker, Dorier, Ost- und Westlokrer, 1978 6 Wolff 7 H. A. Rupprecht, Kleine Einführung in die Papyruskunde, 1994 8 D. Simon, Studien zur Praxis der Stipulationsklausel, 1964.

G. S.

VI. Roman Law

A. Style B. External form C. Duplicates D. Effect E. Creation F. Transmission

A. Style

The *testatio* (witnessed document) and the *chirographum* ('hand-written statement', cf. → *cheirógraphon*) must be differentiated. The *testatio* takes an objective style, i.e. the documented process is reported in the third person (e.g., [1. 60,2,6]: *petiit et numeratos accepit*, 'he has requested and received the money'). By contrast, the issuer of a *chirographum* describes in the first person what has happened (e.g., [1. 53,2,3–4]: *scripsi me accepisse et debere*, 'I have written down that I have received and owe') — it is a document in the subjective style. Ideally, the *chirographum* is written by the issuer in his own hand, but in the case of illiterate persons it is expressly noted that it was written by a slave (*scripsi iussu domini mei coram ipso*, 'I have written this at the order of my master in his presence', cf. [1. 45,5,4–5]) or an agent (*scripsi rogatu et mandatu Titii*, 'I have written this at the request and by assignment from Titius'; *coram ipso*, 'in his presence', cf. [1. 78,3,4–6]).

Witnesses usually participated in both document types and sealed the document (→ Seal, with Fig.). The issuer also sealed the *chirographum*, normally at the beginning and end[1. 36 f.]. While witnesses confirmed the truth of the facts reported in the *testatio*, they merely authenticated the issuer's identity in the case of the *chirographum*, i.e., only the signature. The fact to be proven, i.e., the written declaration of the issuer, was embodied in the document itself in the case of the *chirographum*. In the mid-4th cent. AD documents in the objective style fell out of use [12. 744; 13. 78⁴¹].

B. External form

Writing material usually consisted of → tablets (*tabulae, tabellae*) made of wood that were depressed on the inner side and coated with a writing surface (→ *cera*; 'wax tablets', *tabulae ceratae*). The preferred substance was made of a secretion of *Laccifer lacca*, the lac insect ([14]; on other coating materials [15], [16]) into which the text was carved by means of a → stylus (*graphium, stilus*). In a heated state the compound was easily formed so that writing was easily cancelled using a hot spatula. The bare wooden surface of the outer side was inscribed with → ink (*atramentum*). Occasionally, a short table of contents (*index*), which provided quick information on the document's content, was found there or at the edges of the tablet. Usually two or three tablets were tied together to form a → diptych or triptych. Documents with more than three tablets were rare (polyptychs). In triptychs the second tablet had an outer groove (*sulcus, stria*) in which the cords ran and the witnesses' seals were placed in order that the third tablet would lie flat on the second. Beside the seal, the witnesses' names were written in the genitive form. The tablets combined into a document were described as a → *codex* (Sen. Dial. 10,13,4) or with a plural as → *codicilli* especially in the case of wills. The term → *pugillares* (Gai. Dig. 50,16,148, literally: 'fist-held') was also used.

With the arrival of → papyrus (*charta*) and → parchment (*membrana*), documents were also written on these writing materials [12. 78–89]. Ulpian (Dig. 37, 11,1 pr.) makes it clear that *tabulae testamenti* were not just made of wood but also of papyrus and parchment. Gaius [2] (Dig. 2,13,10,2) already describes a banker's records as *membranae*.

C. Duplicates

To protect documents against forgery and yet be able to access their content, a duplicate format [12. 72–82; 17. 2408–2430], in which the text to be documented was recorded twice, was often chosen. One version, the inner writing (*scriptura interior*), was tied up and sealed and, consequently, was secured against retroactive forgery. The seal was only broken when the document was needed as proof in case of a dispute. The outer writing (*scriptura exterior*) was freely accessible so that it continued to be possible to see the content of the document at any time.

In wax tablets the *scriptura interior* was located on the inner side of the first two tablets. The *scriptura exterior* was written in ink on the outside of the second tablet in the case of diptychs. Triptychs contained the *scriptura exterior* on the inside of the third tablet, which — like the inner side of the first two tablets — was coated with a writing layer. Occasionally, a third text version (*tertia scriptura*), which was recorded on the outer side of the first two tablets, was found in triptychs; the function of this third version has not yet been definitively determined [1. 31 f.[88]]. To render retroactive falsification even more difficult, the strings had to run through two additional holes on the edges of the tablets according to *SC Neronianum* (AD 61; Suet. Nero 17; Paulus, Sent. 5,25,6; [18]).

The concept of duplicate documents is also found for papyri [12. 80–82; 19; 20. 6–12]. The text was written on the papyrus sheet in two superimposed versions. The upper part of the document was rolled up, folded down and sewn with strings in several loops before being finally knotted up. The witnesses signed in their own hand on the document's reverse side next to the loops. Subsequently, the entire document was rolled up into an easily stored cylinder (→ roll).

→ Military diplomas, which consisted of two bronze tablets in which the inner writing was enclosed with wire and sealed, were also duplicate tablets.

D. Effect

Regarding the effectiveness of documents, Roman law differentiated between documents of proof and debt-creating (dispositive, constitutive) documents [21. 518 f.]. In a debt-creating document the creation of the document is both an essential and a sufficient precondition for the effectiveness of the documented legal transaction. The proof of the document's falsehood is precluded from the outset because the legal situation of the content was only created by the document. Only the proof of a forgery is conceivable. However, a document of proof could be rendered ineffective by demonstrating the actual facts when the legal transaction did not take place or at the least did not occur in the documented manner.

The entry of a transfer claim (*nomen transscripticium*) by the creditor in his house book (cf. → *litterarum obligatio*) had a debt-creating effect. Together with the debtor's authorization letter (*litterae*) the entry was a debt-creating document. [21. 499, 503–506, 519]. By contrast, booking a cash demand (*nomen arcarium*) based on an actual payment was not constitutive for the debtor's commitment. As a document of proof it merely provided proof of payment [22. 77–79].

Gaius (Gai. Inst. 3,134) also considered the Hellenistic *cheirógraphon* and the *syngraphai* (see above, V.C.) as dispositive documents, which he classified as contract types under peregrine law [21. 521–523; 22. 303–306[24]].

After the mid-2nd cent. AD, Roman documents of proof began to resemble debt-creating documents [21. 512 f., 520 f.]: in a rescript of Antoninus [1] Pius the proof that an act of emancipation had in fact not occurred was not admitted against a testament with seven seals (Gai. Inst. 2,120 f., 149a). Although the objection of non-payment of a loan (*exceptio non numeratae pecuniae*) was recognized, its temporal restriction resulted in the irrefutable consequence of the loan document after the term had expired (Cod. Iust. 4,30,8: AD 228). In the proceeding both the testament with seven seals and the loan document had the same effect as a debt-creating document. In Inst. Iust. 3,21 and Theophilus (on this point [7]) the commitment of a loan document is, therefore, described as a new form of the *litterarum obligatio*.

E. Creation

Apart from creating a document by one's own hand, the possibility of entrusting a person skilled in writing and the law with the writing of a document, e.g., of → wills (Cic. De or. 1,57,245; 2,6,24), already existed in the Republic. In the Imperial period private professional document scribes (→ *tabelliones*) began to offer their services. The *formula Baetica* (CIL II 5042 = FIRA III 92), a model contract of the 1st or 2nd cent. AD engraved on a copper plate, which includes various types of credit transactions, was probably the store sign of a professional document scribe [12. 757 f.; 21. 501 f.].

In a trial of late antiquity (→ Procedural law IV.), the documents of *tabelliones* as publicly created documents (*instrumenta publice confecta*, Cod. Iust. 4,29,23,1: AD 530) had an enhanced force as proof [13. 80]. *Instrumenta quasi publice confecta*, i.e., documents signed by at least three witnesses [23. 1039], were equivalent. Private legal acts could also be made the object of public documents (*instrumenta publica*) if the declarations were given to an authority with certification powers (*ius actorum conficiendorum*) for recording [12. 748–754; 13. 80–82; 24. 30–38]. These documents enjoyed a full and lasting force as proof (*perpetua firmitas*, Cod. Theod. 16,5,55: AD 414 = in part Cod. Iust. 7,52,6) [25. 601].

F. Transmission

The most important collection of Roman private documents (→ *tabulae privatae*) is the → Murecine archive of the bank of the Sulpicii (*Tabulae Pompeianae Sulpiciorum*, cf. [1]), which was discovered in 1959 in the environs of → Pompeii (see [26; 27]). Apart from the great number of well-preserved documents, this find is distinguished by the large range of documented subjects, which covers procedural and auction documents, business documents, → sales (III.), → rent (IV.), orders (→ *mandatum*), → loans , → surety (C.) and arranging of collateral (→ hypothecary law; → *pignus*), debt recognition, receipts and documents concerning the → bank's accounting. A permanent preservation of the documents proved unsuccessful, and photographs that were made shortly after the excavation are the current foundation of the text.

Another important though less rich find was made in the 1930s during excavations at → Herculaneum (*Tabulae Herculanenses*). The first edition of the Herculaneian tablets does not contain all documents and occasionally has erroneous readings ([2]–[4]). A new, complete edition is in progress ([5]–[9]). The archive of the Pompeian banker L. → Caecilius [III 4] Iucundus, which was discovered in 1875, contains an abundance of receipt documents [10]. Between 1786 and 1855 documents from the period AD 139 to 167, which provide insight into legal affairs in the province of Dacia [11], were found in a gold mine near → Alburnus maior (Romania).

The most important recent find pertaining to provincial law are the (PYadin) papyri found in 1960/61 in the so-called 'Cave of Letters' near the → Dead Sea [20], which includes the archive of Babatha. These documents are from the period between AD 93/94 and 132, i.e., before the uprising of → Bar Kochba. They include, e.g., the dispute over Babatha's guardianship, loans, leases, donations and marriage contracts.

EDITIONS: 1 G. CAMODECA, Tabulae Pompeianae Sulpiciorum, 2 vols., 1999 2 G. PUGLIESE CARRATELLI, Tabulae Herculanenses I-III, in: PdP 1, 1946, 379–385; 3, 1948, 165–184; 8, 1953, 455–463 3 V. ARANGIO-RUIZ, G. PUGLIESE CARRATELLI, Tabulae Herculanenses IV-VI, in: PdP 9, 1954, 54–74; 10, 1955, 448–477; 16, 1961, 66–73 4 M. DELLA CORTE, Tabelle cerate ercolanesi, in: PdP 6, 1951, 224–230 5 G. CAMODECA, Per una riedizione delle tabulae herculanenses, in: Cronache Ercolanesi 23, 1993, 109–119; 24, 1994, 137–146 6 Id., in: Ostraka 2.2, 1993, 197–209 7 Id., in: Cahiers Glotz 7, 1996, 167–178 8 Id., Nuovi dati dalla riedizione delle tabulae ceratae della Campania, in: Atti. XI congresso internazionale di epigrafia greca e latina (Rome 1997), vol. 1, 1999, 521–544 9 Id., Tabulae Herculanenses 59–62, in: U. MANTHE (ed.), Quaestiones Juris. FS J. G. Wolf, 2000, 53–76 10 K. ZANGEMEISTER, Tabulae ceratae Pompeis repertae annis MDCCCLXXV et MDCCCLXXXVII, in: CIL IV Suppl. 1, 1898, 273–454 11 TH. MOMMSEN, Instrumenta Dacica in tabulis ceratis conscripta aliaque similia, in: CIL III 2, 1873, 921–960.
BIBLIOGRAPHY: 12 L. WENGER, Die Quellen des röm. Rechts, 1953 (repr. 2000) 13 KASER, RPR, vol. 2 14 S. AUGUSTI, Sulla natura e composizione delle 'tavolette cerate', in: Rendiconti dell'Accademia di archeologia, lettere e belle arti di Napoli, N. S. 37, 1962, 127f. 15 R. BÜLL, Lit. und experimentelle technologische Studien über Wachsbeschreibstoffe, 1969 16 Id., E. MOSER, s. v. Wachs, RE Suppl. 13, 1366–1369 17 L. WENGER, s. v. Signum (duplicate documents), RE 2 A, 2378–2448 18 G. CAMODECA, Nuovi dati dagli archivi campani sulla datazione e applicazione del 'S. C. Neronianum', in: Index 21, 1993, 353–364 19 WOLFF, 78f. 20 N. LEWIS, The Documents from the Bar Kokhba Period in the Cave of Letters, Greek Papyri, 1989 21 H. L. W. NELSON, U. MANTHE (ed.), Gai institutiones III 88–181, 1999 (with commentary) 22 P. GRÖSCHLER, Die tabellae-U. aus den pompejanischen und herkulanensischen U.funden, 1997 23 M. KASER, s. v. Testimonium, RE 5 A, 1021–1061 24 A. STEINWENTER, Beitr. zum öffentlichen U.wesen der Römer, 1915 25 M. KASER, K. HACKL, Das röm. Zivilprozeßrecht, ²1996 26 J. G. WOLF, J. A. CROOK, Rechtsurkunden in Vulgärlatein (AHAW 1989.3), 1989 27 J. G. WOLF, Der neue pompejanische U.fund, in: ZRG 118, 2001, 73–132.
P. GR.

Dodekadrachmon (only adjective δωδεκάδραχμος; *dōdekádrachmos*). Silver twelve drachmas coin that was minted in northern Greece in the Attic standard and in Ptolemaic Egypt and in Carthaginian Sicily with a weight of 44,3–45,5 g.
→ Drachma; → Coinage, standards of

SCHRÖTTER, 150; M.N. TOD, Epigraphical Notes on Greek Coinage, in: NC 6.20, 1960, 1–24; G.K. JENKINS, Coins of Punic Sicily, in: SNR 57, 1978, 5–68, especially 36ff.; J.M. JONES, A dictionary of Ancient Greek coins, 1986, 81; O. MØRKHOLM, Early Hellenistic coinage, 1991, 106.
A.M.

Dodekapolis (Δωδεκάπολις; *Dōdekápolis*, 'Twelve Town'). Name of several, not always historically verifiable, Greek leagues of towns

1. Hdt. 1,145 mentions → Aegae [2], → Aegira, → Aegium, → Bura, → Dyme, → Helice [1], → Olenus, → Patrae, → Pharaea and → Tritaea [2] as members of the Achaean *dodekapolis*, which the Achaeans are said to have taken from the Iones when they drove them out.

2. On the Aeolian *dodekapolis* cf. Aeoles [2].

3. According to Hdt. 1,142, in the 6th cent. BC the Ionian *dodekapolis* consisted of → Chios, → Ephesus, → Erythrae, → Clazomenae, → Colophon, → Lebedus, → Miletus, → Myus, → Phocaea, → Priene, → Samos and → Teos, which as amphiktyonia practised the cult of Poseidon Heliconius in the → Panionium on Mt. Mycale [1; 3. 55–57, 70–74, 90–95]. Typical of the Ionian *dodekapolis* are collegia of → *molpoí*. The delegates of the member *poleis* were called *basileîs*.

4. The Attic *dodekapolis* of the original king → Cecrops (Philochorus FGrH 328 F 94) is largely a product of ancient historiographical speculation. The l.c. mentioned eleven towns of → Aphidna, → Brauron, → Decelea, → Eleusis, → Epacria, Cecropia, → Cephisia, → Cytherus, → Sphettus, → Tetrapolis and → Thoricus are supplemented either by → Phalerum, Tetracomi or → Athens itself as the twelfth.

1 G. RAGONE, La guerra meliaca e la struttura originaria della lega ionica in Vitruvio 4,1,3–6, in: RFIC 114, 1986, 173–205 2 A. D. RIZAKIS, La politeia dans les cités de la confédération achéenne, in: Tyche 5, 1990, 109–134 3 K. TAUSEND, Amphiktyonie und Symmachie, 1992.
H. LO.

Dodekaschoinos 'Twelve mile land', term in the Graeco-Roman period (Ptol. 4,5,74 and Hdt. 2,29) for the *c.* 135 km long northern sector of Nubia between → Syene and Takompso (*Tꜣqmps*)/Hierosycaminus (al-Maharraqa) [1] that was transferred by the rulers to the temple of → Isis at → Philae mainly for the levy of taxes on the transport of goods. In a stone stele at Seḥel claiming to date back to the Old Kingdom, but in fact probably from the time of Ptolemy V, the priesthood of the Chnum temple at → Elephantine claims older rights to this region [2].

1 A. BURKHARDT, Ägypter und Meroiten im D., 1985 2 P. BARGUET, La stèle de la famine, 1953.
S.S.

Dodona, Dodone (Δωδώνη; *Dōdṓnē*).
I. TOPOGRAPHY, HISTORICAL DEVELOPMENT
II. ARCHAEOLOGICAL FINDS III. ORACLE

I. TOPOGRAPHY, HISTORICAL DEVELOPMENT

Sanctuary and settlement in Epirus, 22 km southwest of today's Ioannina in the 640 m high plain of Hellopia beneath the Tomarus [1. 85–87, 92]. D. is the oldest oracle site in Greece attested in literature (myth of its founding in Hdt. 2,54f. [2. 51–54]), already known to the Homeric epics (Il. 16,233–235; Od. 19,296–301). The original cult venerated Dione Naia, who was joined in the 8th cent. BC by the oracle god Zeus Naios; in the Hellenistic period Dionysus, Demeter and Themis were added. Priestesses (→ *Peleiades*) gleaned the god's will from the rustling of the sacred oak and also from the flight of doves, later from the clanging of bronze cauldrons; the → Selli interpreted Zeus' counsel. Especially in the Archaic-Early Classical period, votive offerings and questions for the oracle were sent from Greece, Southern Italy and Asia Minor. Originally situated in the territory of the Thesprotians (Str. 7,7,11; FGrH 1 F 108), D. came under the influence of the Molossians in the 5th cent. D. became the cultural and political centre of Epirus, in which the decisions of the Molossians and of the *koinon* of the Epirotans were also displayed. In 219 BC D. was pillaged by the Aetolians; it was rebuilt by Philip V, and then destroyed by the Romans in 167 BC, but the cult continued until the 4th cent. AD. At the penteteric Naia Games [3], which are documented from the 3rd cent. BC to the 3rd cent. AD, gymnastic, tragic and equestrian contests took place. Inscriptions: [2. 55–60; 4. 259–273; 5. 534–592]; Coins: [6].

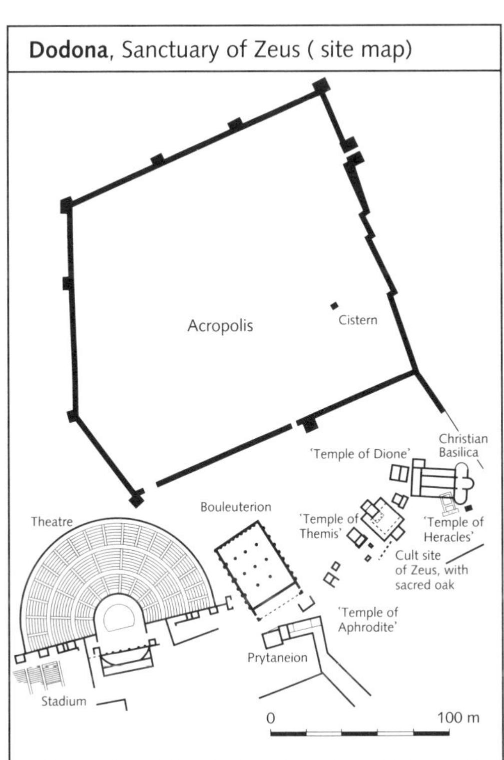

II. ARCHAEOLOGICAL FINDS

Since 1875 archaeological excavations have brought to light large parts of the sanctuary to the south of the fortified acropolis: various cult buildings in the vicinity of the Sacred Oak, buildings for the assemblies that took place there (the so-called bouleuterion and prytaneion; → assembly buildings), a theatre for almost 20,000 spectators that in the Roman period was converted into an arena (→ Amphitheatre) as well as a stadium in front of it. The monumental configuration of buildings began only around 400 BC; until then it was a cult site that was largely set in the open without any architectonic structure. For a short period in the 6th cent. AD, D. was a diocese before the locality was destroyed around AD 550 in the wake of Slavic migrations and abandoned; the basilica with a nave and two aisles in the east of the sanctuary dates from that period.

1 PHILIPPSON/KIRSTEN, 2, 1 2 P. CABANES (ed.), L' Illyrie méridionale et l'Épire dans l' Antiquité 2, 1993 3 P. CABANES, Les concours des Naia, in: Nikephoros 1, 1988, 49–84 4 H. W. PARKE, The oracles of Zeus, 1967 5 P. CABANES, L'Épire, 1967 6 P. R. FRANKE, Die antiken Münzen von Epirus, 1961, 27–39, 317–322.

S.I. DAKARIS, D., 1993; N.G. L. HAMMOND, Epirus, 1967. D.S. and C.HÖ.

III. ORACLE

No later than the 4th cent. BC, D. belonged to the lot-oracles, at which lots were drawn from a pot under the supervision of a priestess (Callisthenes FGrH 124 F 22 = Cic. Div. 1,76; 2,69). The fact that Herodotus compares the oracle with that of Amun-Re at Thebes demonstrates that even in his time the drawing of lots was the most widespread method of → divination (Hdt. 2,57). The numerous responses, written on narrow lead strips, to the questions put to Zeus Naios and Dione (from the 5th cent.; many still unpublished, cf. SEG 43, 1993, 318–341; [1; 2; 3]) should be seen in connection to those lots. The epigraphically attested practice at the lot-oracle of Apollo Koropaios in Demetrias (SIG[3] 1157, *c.* 100 BC) constitutes an even closer parallel than the numerous Italian lot-oracles [4] — though D. must actually have had close relations with Italy [5]. Our literary sources only partly concur with this. Hom. Il. 16,233–235 is familiar with the Selli, barefooted and living on the ground, as guardians of the oracle, Od. 19,296–299 with the (talking) oak as the source of knowledge about Zeus' will (similarly Hes. fr. 240,8; 319; Aesch. PV 832). The oak's ability to speak is presupposed in the myth of the talking beam made of Dodonian oak which was part of the ship Argo (Apollod. 1,110). Soph. Trach. 171f. indicates two doves on the Sacred Oak as the source of the oracle; likewise, the myths of the sanctuary's origins link the Sacred Oak with a (talking) dove (Proxenos FGrH 703 F 7; Philostr. Imag. 2,33; Schol. Il 16,234). Hdt. 2,54–57 on the other hand interprets the doves allegorically as priestesses, and in several later sources 'dove' (*peleiás*) is explained as a term for the priestesses of D.

If the early testimonies speak of oak and doves as the givers of signs, that tallies with the ancient view that D. gave oracles in signs and not in words (Str. 7 fr. 1 CHR.), but is not consistent with extant texts and other information on oracles in prose (Dem. Or. 21,53) or hexameters (Paus. 10,12,10). This suggests an originally very archaic and perhaps pre-Greek oracle (Zeus Pelasgikos: Hom. Il. 16,233; Pelasgians: Hdt. 2,54), that was cared for by a priesthood characterized by its particularly marginalized ritual and that expressed itself through natural signs (oak), later switched to priestesses (thus Str. 7,7,12) and provided answers in textual form, in keeping with Greek practice elsewhere. Harder to reconcile with newer findings and literary testimony is the information that priestesses of D. had given their oracles in ecstasy (Pl. Phdr. 244b; Paus. 10,12,10). The long resonating bronze cauldron that has been mentioned since Menander (fr. 66 CAF) and Polemon (Steph. Byz. s.v. Δωδώνη) as an astonishing votive offering (cf. Callim. Fr. 483) has nothing to do with divinatory practise.

1 C. CARAPANOS, Dodone et ses ruines, 1878, 70–83
2 H. POMTOW, Die Orakelinschr. von D., in: Jahrbücher für Philol. 29, 1883, 306–360 3 H.W. PARKE, The Oracles of Zeus, 1967, 126, n. 18, 259–273
4 J. CHAMPEAUX, Sors oraculi. Les oracles en Italie sous la République et l'Empire, in: MEFRA 102, 1990, 271–302
5 J. GAGÉ, Pyrrhus et l'influence religieuse de Dodone dans l'Italie primitive, in: RHR 145, 1954, 150–167; 146, 1955, 18–50. F.G.

Dodrans In the Roman system of weights and measures the *dodrans* denotes $^{3}/_{4}$ ($^{9}/_{12}$) of the whole unit (the whole *dempto quadrante*). The *dodrans* was used in measuring length (*pes*) and surface area (*iugerum*), in laws of inheritance and obligations and in calculating time. Based on the Roman pound (*libra*: 327,45 gm), it weighed 245,59 gm [1. 150]. The *dodrans* appeared as a coin under M. Metellus in 127 BC (bust of Vulcanus/Prora), as also a year later under C. Cassius, together with the *Bes*, minted in bronze with the value marking S:· [2. 288; 290].
→ Bes; → Iugerum; → Libra; → Pes

1 SCHRÖTTER, 150 2 RRC, ²1987.

Hultsch, s.v. D., RE 5, 1265–1266. A.M.

Dodwell Painter Middle Corinthian vase-painter from around 580/570 BC, who specialized in pyxides and oinochoai but also painted neck-amphoras and hydriai; generally with friezes of animals and riders. The pyxis in Munich (SA, so-called Dodwell Pyxis) with the Calydonian boar hunt and other mythical figures (the accompanying names are partly incorrect) is outstanding, as are also two careful friezes on the olpe in Rome (VG): revellers dancing around a krater, and Hercules fighting the Hydra. In other cases, the slickly churned-out paintings are not very precise. We have some 70 pieces by D. According to AMYX, ten painters can be regarded as associated with D. on stylistic grounds; they painted predominantly pyxides and oinochoai with animal friezes.

AMYX, CVP, 205–210, 320f., 346–348, 565 no.33; AMYX, Addenda 59. M.ST.

Doedalses

[1] Sculptor whose existence is contested. Pliny (HN 36,35) mentions a work in marble in Rome *Venerem lavantem †sesededalsa† stantem*, from which the Bithynian name D. is gleaned, an emendation which is largely accepted. This D. is then identified with Daedalus, who according to a Byzantine source created a Zeus Stratios for the Bithynian King Nicomedes. The statue type of that Zeus has not been established with any certainty. The statue of the standing Venus that Pliny referred to is generally taken to be of the 'crouching Aphrodite' type, but neither the connection with Nicomedes I and the dating deriving from it (264–247 BC) nor the existence of a D. has been credibly demonstrated.

D. BRINKERHOFF, Hypotheses on the History of the Crouching Aphrodite Type in Antiquity, in: The J.P. Getty Museum Journal, 6–7, 1978–79, 83–96; P. MORON, Scultura ellenistica, 1994, 218–225; OVERBECK, no. 2044 (Quellen); B.S. RIDGWAY, Hellenistic sculpture, 1, 1990, 230–232 fig. R.N.

[2] (Δοιδάλσης; *Doidálsēs*). The Bithynian dictator was at the head of a list of rulers by Memnon [5] of Heraclea. He lived at the time of the re-colonization of Astacus [1] by Athens in 435/4 BC (Memnon FGrH 434 F 12,3). The information in Strabo (12,4,2) that D. himself had later undertaken to re-establish the city is probably a misunderstanding. D.'s successor was Boteiras, who died in 377/6 at the age of 76 (Memnon FGrH 434 F 12,4). Whether D. was the father of Boteiras and therefore the grandfather of his son → Bas (see Addenda) is not known. M. SCH.

Dog

[1] (κύων/*kýōn*, κυνίδιον/*kynídion*, κυνίσκος/*kyniskos*, σκύλαξ/*skýlax*, σκυλάκιον/*skylákion*, *canis*, *canicula*, *catellus*).

A. BREEDS B. LITERATURE, RELIGION, MEDICINE

A. BREEDS

One of the oldest domestic animals, bred in various parts of the world, probably starting in the Mesolithic era, from varieties of wild dogs that have now died out. The theory of its descent from the golden jackal (*Canis *aureus*) [2] has now been abandoned. From bone remains and from graphic representations several early breeds can be identified as the ancestors of today's breeds: 1. *Canis familiaris Putjatini Studer*, similar to the dingo, broad and robust, represented in the 'boar hunt' of Tiryns (14th cent. BC) 2. *Canis familiaris matris optimae Jeitteles*, the 'bronze-dog', according to HAUCK the ancestor of the pariah- and greyhounds. 3. The brach (*bracci*), heavy hunting dogs with floppy ears, the result of crossing with another wild dog. 4. The large herding dog, developed from crossing with the *Canis inostranzewi Anutschin*, the lineage of the bulldog and mastiff. 5. *Canis familiaris palustris Rütimeyer*, the turf-dog or marshdog, the ancestor of the spitz and similar breeds.

From about 3000 BC some of these breeds can be recognized in illustrations from the Ancient Orient: mastiffs in Mesopotamia and Egypt, and greyhounds and terrier varieties in Egypt (3rd millennium BC). From Greek visual representations and ancient descriptions, PLACHT [1] discerns four groups, namely Melitans (Pomeranians), Laconians (i.e. καστόριαι/*kastóriai* and ἀλωπεκίδες/*alōpekídes*), Cretans (greyhounds) and Molossians (mastiffs and sheepdogs). HAUCK on the other hand speaks of six types (pariah- and sheepdogs, greyhounds, brachs, mastiffs and herding dogs) and cautions against taking the images too realistically. Homer (about 90 instances) and other ancient authors classify dogs only according to their functions, for example hunting (Hom. Il. 8,338–340; 10,360–362; 11,292f.; Hom. Od. 19,428ff. and *passim*), guarding and defending herds (Il. 5,476; 10,183f. and *passim*) or an estate (Od. 14,29–36; 20,13–15 and *passim*). Only from the 5th cent. are breeds distinguished: Laconians (Pind. Fr. 106 B. = 121 TU.; Soph. Aj. 8), Indians (Hdt. 1,192), Molossians (Aristoph. Thesm. 416). From zoological and hunting literature there emerge the following characteristics for recognized breeds:

1. Molossians (Epirotans): the largest, sharpest and strongest breed used as herding dogs and watch-dogs but also for hunting large game. They unarguably belong to the mastiff variety but there are grounds for thinking that they were crossed with Laconians. The watch-dog of Eumaeus (Hom. Od. 14,29–36) certainly belonged with them, as did the 'Indian' dogs. (Aristot. Gen. an. 2,7,746a 34f.; Xen. Cyn. 10,1).

2. Laconian (Spartan dogs): probably a cross of mastiffs and other types. They were as strong as bulldogs but smaller and faster and were used for hunting. Because of their careful breeding (cf. Xen. Cyn. 4) they were very expensive. Xenophon (Cyn. 3) differentiates between the main type, the Castorian (after the man Castor who is said to have first bred them) and the Alopekides ('vulpine') — after their fox-like heads as shown on many classical vase-paintings.

3. Cretan and Sicilian dogs were greyhounds. The Cretans in particular were often crossed with Laconians and were especially suited to accompanying hunters on horseback. Coins from the Sicilian towns Panormis, Segesta and Eryx show the breed flourishing there.

4. Melitans, named after Malta as their original place of breeding, were small, weak, long-haired spitz dogs with short legs, used as watchdogs but primarily as lapdogs (Str. 6,277; Ael. NA 7,40).

5. The cross-breed herding-dog was an inexpensive working animal and is discussed in specialist agricultural literature (Varro, Rust. 2,9; Columella 7,12; cf. Verg. G. 3,404f.; Columella 7,12,3).

From the earliest times in Greece dogs were bred for hunting but, in contrast to the East, not for martial combat, with rare exceptions (Hdt. 5,1; Plin. HN 8,143; Plut. De sollertia animalium 13 = Mor. 969; Ael. NA 7,38: battle at Marathon). Only the Britons had fighting dogs. (Claud. De Consulatu Stilicho 3,301). Apart from the common, ugly 'Segusian' dog, the Celts had (Arr. Cyn. 3,4) the swift and noble greyhound *vertragus* (Arr. Cyn. 3,6f.; Opp. Kyn. 1,373; Plin. HN 8,148; Grattius 156; Mart. 3,47). References to dogs that had run wild and were roaming around and living off carcasses and garbage are to be found in the East (Ps. 59,7 and 15; Jer. 15,3; Ex. 22,31; 1 Kgs 21,19ff.), Greece (Hom. Il. 8,379f.; 17,241; 18,271f.; 22,66; Hom. Od. 3,259; 14,133f.) and Italy (Liv. 41,21,7; Hor. Epod. 5,23). In the Archaic period dogs were not only given the corpses of enemies to eat but also their torn-out genitalia (Od. 18,86 and 22,476; cf. Il. 22,75).

B. LITERATURE, RELIGION, MEDICINE

A tame dog was considered the epitome of loyalty (Hom. Od. 17,291ff.; Plin. HN 8,143f.; Ael. NA 6,25; 7,40 and *passim*) and prudence (e.g. Xen. Oec. 13,8; Aristot. Hist. an. 8(9),1,608a 27; Theoc. 21,15; Plin. HN 8,147; Plut. Soll. an. 19 = Mor. 973e-f; Ael. NA 7,13). His master spoiled him (Od. 10,216f.; Arr. Cyn. 9,1; 18,1) and gave him a proper name (Xen. Cyn. 7 [3]; Plin. HN 8,143f.). Loyal and vigilant men could be described favourably as dogs (Aesch. Ag. 607; 896; Aristoph. Equ. 1023) and so could animals like the eagle, termed dog of Zeus (Aesch. PV 1021f.; Soph. fr. 884), or the griffin (Aesch. PV 803). In a negative sense the dog represents a lowly, impudent and servile person (of women: Hom. Il. 6,344; 356; 8,423; 21,481; Hom. Od. 18,338; Aristoph. Vesp. 1402; of men: Hom. Il. 8,299; 13,623; Od. 17,248). Aggressiveness, too, was characterized by comparison to dogs (Aesch. Supp. 758: κυνοθρασεῖς; Soph. fr. 885; Eur. fr. 555; Theoc. 15,53: κυνοθαρσής; referring to the Furies: Soph. El. 1388; Eur. fr. 383). That *kýōn* as an epithet of → Antisthenes [1], → Diogenes [14] and the Cynic philosophers was meant pejoratively (Aristot. Rh. 3,10,1411a 24; Anth. Pal. 7,65; 413; Plut. Mor. 717c) is obvious.

As man's favourite domestic animal (cf. Hom. Od. 17,309; Prop. 4,3,55; Phaedr. 3,7,22; Mart. 1,109) the dog gave rise to many proverbs [4] and is encountered in animal fables (Aesop. 41; 52; 64; 93; 94; 129; 134–139; 283 HAUSRATH; Phaedr. 1,4,17–19; 22; 3,7; Babr. 42; 48; 74; 79; 85; 87; 99; 104; 110). By contrast with East Asia the dog was not eaten anywhere any more in the historical period (cf. the misinterpretation in the

Roman cult [5. 68[1]]). Darius I's order to the Carthaginians to renounce human sacrifice and the consumption of dog-meat is to be explained by the religious protection of dogs in Iran as guardians against evil spirits (Just. 19,1,10). The dog was probably used as an animal sacrifice only in purification rites (Clearchus in Ael. NA 12,34; Ath. 3,99e; Plut. Quaest. Rom. 52,277b; Plin. HN 29,58 [6. 27f.; 40ff.].

In art the dog characterized—as their companion—the hunter and gods of the forest and of hunting (Apollo, Pan, Priapus, Silvanus and Diana) and of course Jupiter Custos on the Roman Capitoline. The dog was also linked to → Hecate. The dog of Hades was → Cerberus. In Roman superstition important functions were ascribed in particular to a barking, black and pregnant dog [7. 32ff.]. The abundant magic-organotherapeutic use of individual body parts and blood, fat, milk, urine, etc. recorded in Plin. HN 29,99–101 attest to the secret powers attributed to the dog (as in the case of the → vulture).

Zoological knowledge of the dog was on the other hand rather sketchy. Aristot. Hist. an. 3,7,516a 16f. even maintained that its skull consisted of only one bone. Aristotle (Hist. an. 2,2,501b 5–14) and Pliny (HN 11,160; cf. Cic. Nat. D. 2,134) discuss second dentition. Plin. HN 11,265 understands keeping the tail under the body not as a general gesture of humility and he attributes it only to inferior dogs. Rabies (*rabies canum*), which is transferable to humans, was accurately observed (Aristot. Hist. an. 7(8),22,604a 4–8; Plin. HN 2,207; 7,64; 8,152f. etc.) and—unsuccessfully—combated with many remedies (e.g. Plin. HN 24,95; 28,156; 29,99–101 etc.). Ancient literature provides rather good information on the upbringing and training of dogs (e.g. Varro, Rust. 2,9; Opp. Kyn. 1,376–538; Plin. HN 8,151; Columella 7,12,11–14; Sen. Clem. 1,16). Columella devotes a short chapter to canine illnesses (7,13).

1 W. Placht, Die Darstellung des Hundes auf griechischen Bildwerken, diss. Vienna 1933 (typescript) 2 K. Lorenz, So kam der Mensch auf den Hund, 1950, [28]1966 3 E. Baecker, Hunde-Namen des Altertums, diss. Königsberg 1884 4 Otto, Sprichwörter 5 Latte 6 H. Scholz, Der Hund in der griechischen-römischen Magie, diss. Berlin 1937 7 E.E. Burriss, The Place of the Dog in Superstition, in: CPh 30, 1935, 32ff.

Keller 1, 91–151; O. Antonius, Grundzüge einer Stammesgeschichte der Haustiere, 1922, 89–138; F.E. Zeuner, Geschichte der Haustiere, 1967, 69–98; Toynbee, Tierwelt, 94–109. C.HÜ.

[2] see → Constellations (Volume 4, Addenda)

Dogmatists

[1] **Philosophers.** Originally a sceptical expression to designate those who adopt as their own a view (*dógma*; cf. S. Emp. P.H. 1,13)—especially a philosophical or scientific view—which, in sceptical thinking, cannot be justified let alone proven (S. Emp. P.H. 1,3). Also applied by the Pyrrhonians in an extended sense to those Academicians who adopted views such as that nothing can be known (cf. the ἰδίως/*idíōs* in S. Emp., ibid.). Because of the close link between empiricism and Scepticism in medicine, the term 'Dogmatists' was often also applied by Empiricists to physicians otherwise known as Rationalists (Gal. de sect. 1, S. 2, 10 Helmreich). Because of its origin the expression readily came to connote an attitude that holds firm to a view despite all counter-arguments or that simply follows some authority. M.FR.

[2] **Schools of medicine.** In medical handbooks from the Roman and Byzantine periods medicine is often divided into three schools of thought, that of the → Empiricists, that of the → Methodists and that of the Dogmatists, and their exponents in each case. While the Empiricists and Methodists each had their own narrowly circumscribed tradition deriving from an identifiable founder, the multiplicity of names and doctrines in the Dogmatist camp suggests that this school was defined by later authors [1. 165–166] not so much by the teachings which the Dogmatists actually espoused as by the teachings from which they distanced themselves [3. 76–100]. In opposition to the Empiricists the Dogmatists were united in the view that the physician should discover the cause(s) of illnesses first and then remedy them. Unlike the Methodists the Dogmatists possessed differentiated conceptions of bodily structures and composition, their physiology and pathology, and probably regarded as a simplification the Methodists' teaching that the range of causes could be reduced to the three basic states of the body (*status strictus, medius, laxus*). In diagnosis and therapy the Dogmatists relied upon the application of rational observation, and for that reason they were also known as *rationales* or *logikoí*. However, the question of the exact form of rational observation and of how a cause could be identified not only separated the Dogmatists from non-Dogmatist physicians but also set up divisions amongst themselves (for Galen's attempt to make distinctions within the Dogmatist school's tradition, cf. Gal. 19,12).

Generally Hippocrates heads the lists of the most significant Dogmatists followed by, i.a., Diocles, Praxagoras, Mnesitheus, Herophilus and Erasistratus (cf. e.g. Gal. 19,683; Anon. Bambergensis, fol. 6[r] [4. 66] and a few late Alexandrian commentators [5. 188]). Galen's frequent references to this group of outstanding physicians and the school's representatives Pleistonicus, Phylotimus and Dieuches, who were active at the end of the 4th or the beginning of the 3rd cent. BC, suggest the doxography of the Dogmatists developed in Hellenistic Alexandria. The list was later extended with other names, in particular with those of Asclepiades, Pneumatists like Athenaeus and Agathinus and finally those of Antyllus, Philumenus and Galen (2nd cent. AD). That such an intellectual schema of classification is not unproblematic can be seen from the fact that the lists of the names of the School's members frequently vary, that notable differences exist among the physicians named and that a large number of Dogmatists engaged in polemic against rivals from their own camp. Nevertheless, the Dogmatist School's appeal to reason ensured it the highest reputation until well into the 17th cent. and allowed writers of medical history to talk of the Dogmatists as a homogeneous group until well into the 20th cent. [2. 59].

→ Medicine

1 G.E.R. Lloyd, Science, Folklore, and Ideology, 1983 2 Staden 3 Id., Hairesis and Heresy, in: B.F. Meyer, E.P. Sanders (ed.), Self-definition in the Graeco-Roman World, vol. 3, 1982, 76–100; 199–206 4 U. Stoll, Das 'Lorscher Arzneibuch', 1992 5 O. Temkin, The Double Face of Janus, 1977. V.N.

Doiptunus

Tib. Iulius D. (also Doiptounos or Douptounos; IPE 2,49). The name is not Greek and appears here for the first time. Probably appointed by Byzantium as administrator of the Bosporus after AD 620, since the inscription with Christian symbols also mentions a *comes*.

V.F. Gajdukevič, Das Bosporanische Reich, 1971, 517. I.v.B.

Dok

Dok (Δώκ; *Dṓk*, Δαγών; *Dagṓn*). Fortress from the Hasmonean period north-west of Jericho, in which Simon Maccabaeus was murdered, together with his two sons, by his son-in-law Ptolemy (1 Macc. 16,15f.; Jos. Ant. Iud. 13,230; Bell. Iud. 1,56). Chariton founded a *laura* here in AD 340. The name is preserved in the spring ʿAin Dūk.

C. Möller, G. Schmitt, Siedlungen Palästinas nach Flavius Josephus, TAVO B 14, 1976, 77f.; Y. Hirschfeld, List of Byzantine Monasteries in the Judean Desert, in: FS Virgilio Corbo, 1990, 29ff.; G. Schmitt, Siedlungen Palästinas in griech.-röm. Zeit, TAVO B 93, 1995, 135. A.M.S.

Doketai

Doketai (δοκηταί; *dokētaí*). With this generic term or τῶν ... δοκιτῶν αἵρεσις (*tôn ... dokitôn haíresis*, Theod. Epist. 82,1) ancient Christian theologians from the middle of the 5th cent., as also recent academic research, designated various points of view that (in the minds of their critics at any rate) call into question or even repudiate the real humanity of → Jesus Christ and postulate a 'pseudo-body'. Opponents of → Ignatius of Antioch maintained for example that Christ had only appeared to suffer (τὸ δοκεῖν, Epist. ad Smyrnaeos 2; 4,2). Docetism in that sense is not only ascribed to individual theologians classed by the Church mainstream as 'heretical' but is also to be found in embryonic form in so-called → apocryphal literature. While the term Docetism in this wide sense has been used since late antiquity for greatly varying phenomena, it originally had a more restricted meaning. Before it came to be used, particularly in the context of trinitarian theological and Christological debates of the 4th to 6th cents., as a label for one's opponent's position.

The term ἡ (αἵρεσις) τῶν δοκητῶν (the heresy of the *Doketai*) probably occurs first in Clem. Al. Strom. 7,108,2; he calls Iulius Cassianus ὁ τῆς δοκήσεως ἐξάρχον (the leader of the *Doketai*; Str. 3,91,1), without however quoting any relevant text from that author. Not much later, → Hippolytus outlines a doxography of the *Doketai* whose teachings can be regarded as variations of the Valentinianic Gnosticism (Haer. 8,2–11,2; 10,16,1–6). Apparently included amongst them was the view that a heavenly saviour had been 'clothed' in the body with which he was born from Mary but had then shed it at the crucifixion (8,10,7). It has been suggested [1. 305] that the term 'docetic' be reserved for that group and that 'docetistic' be used to describe those who question Christ's actual humanity altogether: in that case the Docetists would have held a docetistic Christology. The view expressed earlier that Gnosticism (→ Gnostics) was fundamentally docetist (i.e. docetistic; thus still [3]), is incorrect [5. 45–52]. It arose i.a. in the polemic of the Anti-Gnostic fathers but has now been refuted by finds of the originals.

1 N. Brox, 'Doketismus' — eine Problemanzeige, in: ZKG 95, 1984, 301–314 2 A. Hilgenfeld, Ketzergeschichte des Urchristentums, 1963, 546–550 (repr.; first 1884) 3 A. Jülicher, s.v. δοκηταί, RE 5, 1268 4 M. Slusser, Docetism: A Historical Definition. The Second Century 1, 1981, 163–172 5 K.W. Tröger, Doketistische Christologie in Nag-Hammadi-Texten, in: Kairos 19, 1977, 45–52. C.M.

Dokimasia

Dokimasia (Δοκιμασία; *Dokimasía*). In the Greek world it means the procedure of determining whether certain conditions have been met.

In Athens the following *dokimasíai* are attested: 1. The *dokimasía* of young men who at the end of their eighteenth year were presented to the father's *dḗmos* to be recognized as a member of the deme and a citizen. The *dḗmos*, a college of judges and the council took part in this procedure. 2. The *dokimasía* of the → *bouleutaí* (council members) in the council and before a college of judges, that of the archontes likewise in the council and before a college of judges and that of other officials before a college of judges ([Aristot.] Ath. Pol. 45,3; 55,2–5, with the questions that were put to the archontes at the *dokimasía*; 56,1; 59,4; 60,1). Lysias wrote his speeches 16, 26 and 31 for *dokimasíai* of this kind. The *dokimasía* of a herald also included the test of a good voice (Dem. Or. 19,338). 3. The *dokimasía* of the knights and their horses in the council ([Aristot.] Ath. Pol. 49,1–2). 4. The *dokimasía* of invalids seeking state support, in the council (ibid. 49,4); Lysias composed a speech (Or. 24) for one such occasion. 5. The *dokimasía* of speakers before the public assembly; on demand, the speaker had to undergo this check before a college of judges, if suspected of not having the requisite qualifications (Aeschin. In Ctes. 28–32). 6. The *dokimasía* in a jury court in connection with the grant of citizenship and other significant honours in Hellenistic Athens, under some regimes at least (see for example IG II² 496 with 507, citizenship; 682, commemorative statues) [1] and [3]. 7. *Dokimasía* of silver coins, the owners of which required confirmation of authenticity, by a *dēmósios* (Hesp. 43, 1974, 157–188, Law of 375/74 BC; cf. IG II[2] 1492 B, 102, 137 = SIG[3] 334, 10, 45). Cf. the reference to a *dokimastḗs* for weight and measures (Anecd. Bekk. 1, 238).

The conduct of *dokimasíai* is also attested outside Athens, as for example in Erythrae, in the context of a constitution fashioned by Athens in the 5th cent. (*dokimasía* of the *bouleutaí*, IG I[3] 14 = ML 40), in Coressus in the 3rd cent. (sacrifices, SIG[3] 958) and Ephesus in the 2nd cent. AD (*bouleutaí*, SIG[3] 838).

→ Boule; → Demosios

1 A.S. Henry, Honours and Privileges in Athenian Decrees, 1983 2 Rhodes 3 P.J. Rhodes, Tria Lustra ... J. Pinsent, 1993, 1–3. P.J.R.

Dokimasia Painter Attic red-figured vase painter, active around 485–465 BC. As a junior member of the Brygus-workshop (→ Brygus painter) the Dokimasia Painter (DP) represents the 'milder' side of this cup-tradition. He is named after a cup-painting (Berlin) that shows ephebes at the inspection (*dokimasía*) of their horses through the polis. Other paintings show contests of arms, school education, the pleasures of the symposium and the komos; mythical subjects include the deeds of Theseus and Odysseus. Late in his life the DP preferred the stamnos (Orpheus' death), perhaps also the calyx krater and the kalathos.

Beazley, ARV[2], 412–414; Id., Paralipomena 372–373; Id., Addenda[2], 233–234; D. Williams, CVA London 9, 69 (with older literature). A.L.-H.

Dokimastes see → Coin counterfeit, see Subaeratus

Dokimeion (Δοκίμειον; *Dokímeion*). Town in Phrygia maior (Steph. Byz. s.v. Δ.; Str. 12,8,14: Δοκιμία κώμη; Ptol. 5,2,24: Δοκίμαιον; Hierocles [8], Synecdemus 677: Δοκίμιον; → Asia Minor III E.) on the road from Apamea [2] to Amorion (modern Hisar Köyü) near modern İscehisar. On the broken marble at D. cf. → Syn(n)ada.

→ Marble (with map)

Belke/Mersich, 237f. E. O.

Dolabella Roman cognomen, became hereditary in the family of the Cornelii Dolabellae (→ Cornelius [I 23–29]). K.-L.E.

Dolates Members of a community in the *regio VI*, called *Sallentini* in the Augustan list (Plin. HN 3,113), because in 266 BC they were deported to Umbria from Soletum in Calabria (Liv. Ep. 15; Eutr. 2,17).

Nissen, 1, 543 n. 2. G.U.

Doliche

[1] (Δολίχη; *Dolíchē*). City of the Perrhaebic Tripolis (with Azorus and Pythium) in western Olympus on the border of Macedonian Elimiotis. D. is now identified not with today's village of Duklista but with the ruins at the village of Sarantaporo.

G. Lucas, La Tripolis de Perrhébie et ses confins, in: I. Blum (ed.), Topographie antique et géographie historique en pays grec, 1992, 93–137; F. Stählin, Das hellen. Thessalien, 1924, 21; Th. Tzaphalias, in: Thessaliko Himerologio 8, 1985, 140–144 (exploration). HE.KR.

[2] City in Commagene (modern Dülük), 10 km north of Gaziantep on Keber Tepe (1210 m. in height), the caves of which attest to prehistoric settlement. D. became known through the cult of Jupiter → Dolichenus, who began his triumphal march through the Roman empire from here. D. was destroyed in AD 253 by the Persian king Sapor [1] I.

The sanctuary of Jupiter Dolichenus was on Dülük Baba Tepesi, situated within view of Dülük to the south, already suspected to be there from [1. 173–302] and now attested by a priests' necropolis and an altar (AD 57/58) with the relief of a priest of Dolichenus. No cult image of the god standing on a bull with a lightning bolt and a double axe, otherwise typical of such cult sites, has yet been discovered there, though several reliefs of this kind are known from the immediate surrounding area.

In recent years D. has also gained significance for research into Mithras, since two interconnected caves, each with a Mithras relief, were discovered at the foot of Keber Tepe, rekindling discussion about Mithras' route out of Persia into the Roman empire.

1 F. Cumont, Études syriennes, 1917.

R. Ergeç, J. Wagner, D. und Iupiter Dolichenus, in: J. Wagner (ed.), Gottkönige am Euphrat, 2000, 85–91; A. Schütte-Maischatz, E. Winter, Kultstätten der Mithrasmysterien in D., in: ibid., 93–99. J. WA.

Dolichenus Jupiter Optimus Maximus D., highest divinity of Dolichē in → Commagene, now Dülük near Gaziantep. The original temple on the Dülük Baba Tepe has not been excavated. However, the god's pose on the bull, his thunderbolt and his double axe suggest his descent from the Hittite storm-god Teššub. In Rome he was venerated as *conservator totius mundi*, preserver of the universe (AE 1940, 76). The counterpart of Jupiter Optimus Maximus D. was named → Juno Sancta/Regina. Two other pairs occur, sun and moon, and the Dioscuri. There is no literary or archaeological evidence at all from the Achaemenid or Hellenistic periods. The cult first spread in the 2nd cent. AD, long after Dolichē had been integrated into the Roman province of → Syria. Most features of the cult in the West derive directly from Dolichē but the modest sanctuaries there do not show a common pattern. Those known to be members of the cult very often bear the names of first-

or second-generation immigrants; its organization is obscure. Outside Rome the cult spread mainly in the Rhine-Danube region and in Britain. In a sense it is a cult with an avowed loyalty to the Emperors, especially the Severians. Many sanctuaries were pillaged by Maximinus Thrax in AD 235–238 and never restored. The cult was clearly weakened by the destruction of Dolichē by → Šāpūr (Šābuhr) I (AD 252), although the Aventine temple was used until the 4th cent.

M. Hörig, E. Schwertheim, Corpus cultus Iovis Dolicheni, 1987; M. Hörig, in: ANRW II 17.4, 1984, 2136–79; M.P. Speidel, The Religion of Iuppiter D. in the Roman Army, 1978.

R.GOR.

Dolichos (δόλιχος; *dólichos*). Longest running race at Greek sporting events. At Olympia, where the *dolichos* reportedly came into the program in 720 BC (15th Olympiad) as third sport, it probably covered a stretch of 20 stades (*c.* 3,845 m) [1. 108f.]. Over that distance the disadvantage of turning around a central post (→ Diaulos), was reduced. Graphic [2] and archaeological (Nemea [3]) evidence to this effect should therefore be taken seriously. A good turning technique created distinct advantages. Successful *dolichos*-runners were, by way of example, the *periodonikai* (victors in all the great games) Dromeus of Stymphalus [4. no. 188, 199], Ergoteles of Knossos (or Himera) [4. no. 224, 251], Damatrius of Tegea [4. no. 593, 600] and T. Flavius Metrobius [4. no. 814; 5. no. 814]. Also well-known was the runner Ladas of Argus [3. no. 260], whose victor's statue, masterly fashioned by Myron, helped contribute to his fame [6. 29, 68, 70, 101–103]. The victor's statue of an unknown long-distance runner was recently recovered from the sea off Cyme (now in the museum of Izmir) [7]. The link between the *dolichos* and the work of couriers is obvious [8]; the achievement of Ageus, victor at Olympia [4. no. 464], who reported his success at Argus on the same day, is credible enough.

1 J. Jüthner, F. Brein, Die athletischen Leibesübungen der Griechen II 1, 1968 2 J. Neils, Goddess and Polis, 1992, Pl. 24 3 St. G. Miller, Turns and Lanes in the Ancient Stadium, in: AJA 84, 1980, 159–166
4 L. Moretti, Olympionikai, 1957 5 Id., Nuovo supplemento al catalogo degli olympionikai, in: MGR 12, 1987, 67–91 6 F. Rausa, L'immagine del vincitore, 1994 7 T. Uçankus, Die bronzene Siegerstatue eines Läufers aus dem Meer vor Kyme, in: Nikephoros 2, 1989, 135–155 8 Y. Kempen, Krieger, Boten und Athleten, 1992, 52–126.

W. Decker, Sport in der griechichen Antike, 1995, 70f.; R. Patrucco, Lo sport nella Grecia antica, 1972; I. Weiler, Der Sport bei den Völkern der Alten Welt, ²1988, 152f.

W.D.

Doliones (Δολίονες; *Dolíones*). Thracian tribe on the southern coast of the Propontis (Str. 12,4,4), first mentioned by Hecataeus (FGrH 1 F 219) [1. 1283]. According to legend they migrated from Thessaly and under their King Cyzicus gave hospitality to the → Argonauts; through a misunderstanding the king was killed by Jason (Apoll. Rhod. 1,947–1077). The area settled by the D., Dolionis, was bounded by the river → Aesepus, Lake Dascylitis and the river Rhyndacus. Milesian settlers founded the colony Cyzicus on the coast probably in 679 BC. The D. kept within their area of settlement but by no later than the Roman era the Dolionis was entirely within the territory of Cyzicus (Str. 12,8,10f.); [2].

1 L. Bürchner, s.v. D., RE 9, 1283 2 F.W. Hasluck, Cyzicus, 1910.

HA.SCH.

Dolium The largest clay vessel used by the Romans for storage and transport of provisions (like the Greek → pithos; cf. → Pottery, shapes of; → Pottery, production of II B). *Dolia* were primarily used for preserving provisions like wine, olive oil and grain. As part of the wine-production process wine underwent fermentation in the *dolium* in the *cella vinaria*. The *dolia* intended for wine had their interior treated with tar, like → transport amphorae. The *dolia* were often sunk into the floor. Because of their size their function as a transport vessel was secondary. Especially in the 1st cents. BC and AD, however, *dolia* were also used for bulk transport of *vin ordinaire*, as shipwrecks reveal, which were laden with 12 to 24 *dolia* that stood in rows and contained a volume amounting to 75 to 100 → amphorae. Choice wines were stored in sealed amphorae. Transport *dolia* had either a rounded, pot-bellied shape or a cylindrical shape, with a stable base and a large, wide opening. They were sometimes closed with ceramic lids. *Dolia* were shaped by hand on a slow potter's wheel. The process sought to achieve standard volumes like 1.5 *culeus* (= 30 *amphorae* = *c.* 786 litres: *dolia sesquicularia*, cf. Columella 12,18,7), and sometimes the volume was indicated with figures scratched on the vessel. *Dolia* are rarely mentioned as being made from other materials (wood: Plin. HN 8,16. lead: Dig. 33,7,26).

R. Hampe, A. Winter, Bei Töpfern und Töpferinnen in Kreta, Messenien und Zypern, 1962; A.J. Parker, Ancient Shipwrecks of the Mediterranean and the Roman Provinces, 1992.

R.D.

Dolius (Δόλιος; *Dólios*).

[1] 'The cunning', epithet of Hermes (Aristoph. Thesm. 1202; Soph. Phil. 133; Cornutus 16). On the road to Pellene there stood a statue of Hermes D. (Paus. 7,27,1).

[2] Old slave of → Penelope, who looked after her garden on Ithaca for her (Hom. Od. 4,735–741; 24,222). He put his sons at Odysseus' disposal for the battle with the relatives of the slain suitors (Hom. Od. 24,386–411; 492–501). According to Hom. Od. 17,212; 18,321f. D. was the father of the goatherd Melantheus and the maid Melantho.

G. Ramming, Die Dienerschaft in der Odyssee, diss. 1973.

R.B.

Dolls (κόρη/*kórē*, νύμφη/*nýmphē*; Lat. *pup[p]a*) were made in antiquity from wood, bone, wax, cloth, clay, precious metals and the like and have been preserved in very large quantities from the early Bronze Age until the end of antiquity. We know of dolls in human as well as animal shape (Gell. NA 10,12,9) and of toys like e.g. items of furniture (beds, tables, chairs) and household objects (crockery, combs, lamps, mirrors, thymiaterion etc.). Human dolls were fitted out with great care. The clothing was colourfully patterned, the — occasionally portrait-like — faces were given makeup, the hair coifed, lips painted red; the dolls were i.a. given jewellery (diadem, rings). There were two types of doll: those that were immobile, as their extremities were securely fastened, and the so-called jointed dolls, the extremities of which were linked by chains (Petron. Sat. 34,8f.) or threads in holes at the shoulders and waist and could thus be moved. Animal and human figures were also set on wheels or a platform and could be pulled along. In the visual arts dolls were mainly shown in the hands of young girls, especially on Attic grave reliefs ([1. no. 0.851, 0.853a, 0.869a, 0.915, 0.918, 1.311, 1.757]; other examples from the Greek and Roman world [2. 45, 54–65, 69–72, 83–86]). As children entered adulthood the dolls were offered up in sanctuaries (cf. e. g. Pers. 2,70; Anth. Pal. 6,280). Dolls were laid in the graves with dead children. They were not used as grave offerings with adults.

→ Children's games; → Puppet theatre; → Games

1 C.W. Clairmont, Classical Attic Tombstone, vol. 1, 1993 2 M. Fittà, Spiele und Spielzeug in der Ant., 1998 (fig.).

C. Bauchhenss, Zwei Terrakotten aus Kleinasien, in: AA 1973, 5–13; S. Laser, Sport und Spiel (ArchHom. 3), 1987, T 96–98.

R.H.

Dolon (Δόλων/*Dólōn*, cf. δόλος/*dólos*, 'guile'). Son of the Trojan herald Eumedes. During a night reconnaissance raid in the Greek camp, for which he had volunteered in order to gain Achilles' immortal horses, he fell into the hands of the Greek scouts Diomedes and Odysseus. In an (unsuccessful) bid to save his skin, he readily betrayed his own cause, which cost the life of the Trojan ally, the Thracian King Rhesus (Hom. Il. 10, so-called Doloneia, probably post-*Iliad* [1]; [Eur.] Rhes.). By contrast with this portrait of D. — for the Stoa he was the archetypical coward (Plut. Mor. 76a) — he is depicted more favourably in Virgil (Aen. 12,346ff.).

1 G. Danek, Studien zur Dolonie, 1988.

D. Williams, s.v. D., LIMC 2.1, 660–664.

RE.N.

Dolonci (Δόλογκοι; *Dólonkoi*). Thracian group of tribes that settled on the → Chersonesus [1] in the 6th/5th cents. BC. Harassed by the Apsinthii in the north, the D. on the advice of the Delphic Oracle in 561/560 BC brought in → Miltiades [1], who was considered the *oikistḗs*. He arrived in the Chersonesus with political opponents of Peisistratus and ruled over them as tyrant. His second successor, Miltiades [2], fled at the Scythian invasion of the Chersonesus (516/5), but was then recalled by the D. (Hdt. 6,34–40 [1. 79–82, 565–567]). Later reminiscences are to be found, generally with a wrong location, in Plin. HN 4,41 and Sol. 68,3.

1 H. Berve, Die Tyrannis bei den Griechen, 1967.

I.v.B.

Doloneia (Δολώνεια; *Dolṓneia*, 'poem about Dolon'), a probably old (cf. e.g. Διομήδεος ἀριστείη already in Hdt. 2,116,11; further examples in [1. 148] term for the 10th book of the *Iliad*, in which the Trojan → *Dólōn* (a name etymologically derived from δόλος: 'guile', so perhaps 'Foxy', 'Wily', 'Sneaky' [2. 186]) plays a major role. In the night after the unsuccessful embassy to Achilles both the Achaeans and the Trojans send scouts into their opponents' camp: Odysseus and Diomedes come upon Dolon, take him prisoner, interrogate him and kill him and the sleeping Thracian King → Rhesus, who had arrived the day before, with twelve of his men; they return safely to their camp with Rhesus' snow-white steeds, wagon and equipment. Behind this story lies an old Rhesus-legend which the *Doloneia*-poet used, as did the author of the pseudo-Euripidean *Rhesus* [3]. The *Doloneia*-poet adapted the legend (the character of *Dolon* probably being his own invention) to suit the narrative requirements of the *Iliad* (probably already available in written form) and inserted his version at its current place in the *Iliad*; as no other narrative threads from other parts of the *Iliad* point in any way to the *Doloneia*, it has the effect, as ancient scholars first observed (Homer schol. T on K 1), of being a pointless intrusion, alien to the rest of the *Iliad* ([4] with the history of the problem and relevant literature). Its author is probably to be found from among the circle of writers of the → epic cycle [3]: Rhesus is a copy of the 'late helpers in the time of extreme need' (like Penthesilea, Memnon, Eurypylus), but here situated within the *Iliad*, not after it.

1 R. Pfeiffer, KPI 2 B. Hainsworth, The Iliad: A Commentary, Vol. III, books 9–12, 1993 3 B. Fenik, 'Iliad X' and the 'Rhesus'. The Myth (Coll. Latomus, Vol. LXXIII), 1964 4 G. Danek, Studien zur Dolonie (WS, Beiheft 12), 1988.

J.L.

Dolopians (Δόλοπες; *Dólopes*). The D. were the south-western neighbours of the Thessalians, possibly split off from them during their immigration and driven out of the plains. Their area of settlement — without access to the coast — lay between Achaea Phthiotis in the east, Spercheus valley in the south, Epirus in the west and the central Pindus, a mountainous country, very sparsely settled then as now and, since the southern Pindus has a strong north-south folding, passable only in that direction. In Homer the D. are regarded as subjects of the King of Phthia, Peleus (Il. 9,484; sources: [1; 2]). They belonged to the 12 tribes of the Delphic amphictyony. In 480 BC they were allied to the Persians. In the classical period they were under the rule of tyrants from Pherae. After 346 BC they sided with the Macedonian king and lost one of their votes as *hieromnemones* in Delphi. From 278/7 they belonged to the Aetolian League, and from *c.* 207 to 167, not unchallenged, to Macedonia. In 198 → Aetolians engaged in a raid from the Spercheus valley northwards, in the course of which they conquered and pillaged i.a. the cities of Dolopia. In 174 Perseus put down an uprising of the D., and that provided the Romans with the pretext for the 3rd Macedonian War. After 167 the D. were considered a free tribe in terms of the Roman concept of peace for Greece. In 57/55 BC the proconsul L. Calpurnius Piso drove the Agraii and the D. from their place of residence (Cic. Pis. 91; 96; [3]). They appear for the last time in 48 as allies of Caesar. When Augustus re-established the Delphic amphictyony, the city of Nicopolis received the vote of the D., 'because the D. no longer existed as a people' (Paus. 10,8,3). Only a few locations of the D. are known from literature. Assigning those locations to ruin sites or to modern settlements is as speculative now as it ever was: → Angeae; Ellopia; → Ctimenae; → Menelais.

1 J. Miller, s.v. D., RE 5, 1903, 1289f. 2 F. Stählin, Das hellenische Thessalien, 1924, 145–150 3 Kirsten/Kraiker, 758, Index.

Y. Béquignon, La vallée du Spercheios, 1937, 324ff.; R. Flacelière, Les Aitoliens à Delphes, 1937 (Index); B. Helly, Incursions chez les D., in: I. Blum (ed.), Topographie antique et géographie historique en pays grec, 1992, 48–91. HE.KR.

Dolphin (δελφίς/*delphís* and δελφίν/*delphín*, Lat. *delphinus* and *delphin*).

[1] A frequent representative in the Mediterranean of the small viviparous → whale, with a spout (αὐλός; *aulós*), articulation of sounds, and pulmonary respiration (Aristot. Hist. an. 1,5,489a 35–b 5; 4,9,535b 32–536a 4; 8,2,589a 31–b 11 with a discussion of its role as an aquatic animal, ἔνυδρος; *énydros*), was admired chiefly by the Greeks as 'king of marine animals' (or of fishes; Ael. NA 15,17; Opp. Hal. 1,643 and 5,421 or 441). Its scant fear of man (Ps.-Aristot. Hist. an. 9,48,631a 8f.), its speed and acrobatics were all esteemed (631a 20–30), as also its intellectual qualities, which it employed to escape from a fishing net (Ael. NA 11,12) and also to save singers like → Arion from Methymna (in Hdt. 1,23f.; Plin. HN 9,28; Cic. Tusc. 2,67; Ov. Fast. 2,83; Prop. 2,26,17; Gell. NA 16,19; Paus. 3,25,7; Plut. Sol. anim. 36 = Mor. 984A—985B and others) or Coeranus from Miletus (Ath. 13,606e). Its pleasure in music was well known (e.g. Eur. El. 435; Aristoph. Ran. 1317; Ael. NA 2,6 and 11,12) and also its fondness for handsome youths (Ps.-Aristot. Hist. an. 9,48,631a 10f.; Gell. NA 6(7), 8), whom in some cases it followed to its own death (Ael. NA 6,15; Plin. HN 9,25; Gell. NA loc. cit.). Dolphins were said to collaborate willingly with fishermen for their share of the catch (Opp. Hal. 5,425–447; Ael. NA 2,8; Plin. HN 9,29–33). Because of their intelligence these animals that were sacred to the Greeks (Ath. 7,282e) were thought to be humans transformed by Dionysus (Opp. 1,648–651; H. Hom. 7,53). River dolphins were known in antiquity in the Ganges (Str. 15,719 following Artemidorus; Curt. 8,9,9) and the Nile (Sen. Q Nat. 4,2,13f.; Plin. HN 8,91; according to [1. 110] it was a case of sharks or siluroids); they could defeat crocodiles. On the Black Sea, Thracians, for example, hunted dolphins as food (Opp. Hal. 5,519–588; Xen. An. 5,4,27; Str. 12,549) and to use its (train-)oil. In mythology the dolphin is encountered in → Poseidon's entourage and brings → Amphitrite to him as a wife (Hom. Od. 12,96; Bacchyl. 17,97; Aristoph. Equ. 560; Ov. Fast. 2,81). It is however also linked to → Apollo (Str. 4,179,6), → Dionysus (see above; Hyg. Fab. 134), Aphrodite (Gell. NA 6 (7),8; Nonnus, Dion. 13,439) and other gods. The motif of the rider on the dolphin is widespread, e.g. with Arion. In art the dolphin is encountered on Crete, often on reliefs, gemstones, lamps etc., on mosaics as in Piazza Armerina in Sicily and on gravestones. In early Christian art many antique motifs survive. Occasionally the dolphin stands as a symbol for Christ [3. 1,503f.].

1 Leitner 2 W. Richter, in: RhM 104, 1961 3 LCI.

E. B. Stebbins, The Dolphin in the Literature and Art of Greece and Rome, 1929; M. Rabinovitch, Der Delphin in Sage und Mythos der Griechen, 1947; K. Czernohaus, Delphin-Darstellungen von der minoischen bis zur geometrischen Zeit, 1988. C.HÜ.

[2] see → Constellations (Volume 4, Addenda)

[3] see → **Delphini.**

Dolus means (in a narrow sense) malicious deception. Servius Sulpicius defines *dolus* in that sense as *machinationem quandam alterius decipiendi causa, cum aliud simulatur et aliud agitur* (a form of dealing to deceive others, in that something is feigned while something else is [actually] done, Ulp. Dig. 4,3,1,2). Along with that meaning *dolus* in Roman law encompasses a variety of other unacceptable forms of behaviour. In the early Republic *dolus* first appears as a form of culpability that constitutes an essential element in certain offences (e.g. → *furtum*) and *crimina* (e.g. killing *dolo sciens* in connection with *parricidium*).

In the area of *bonae fidei iudicia* (actions of good faith, e.g. → *emptio venditio*, → *locatio conductio*, → *mandatum* and → *societas*), *dolus* includes any deliberate breach of good faith by one of the parties. *Dolus* or *fraus* — appears here as the opposite of the (flexibly applied) concept of *bona* → *fides*. As a measure of liability the meaning of *dolus* changes when (as early as the late Republic) a liability for → *culpa* (negligence) is also acknowledged. From then on *dolus* is seen as a culpability, distinguished from *culpa* (negligence) by the subjective element of intent to cause damage or loss.

In the context of *iudicia stricti iuris* (actions involving strict [application of] law, e.g. → *rei vindicatio*) a plaintiff's *dolus* is taken into account if the defendant appeals, *in iure* (before the Praetor), to an → *exceptio doli*. In that case the → *iudex* has to investigate either previous, 'dolous' behaviour on the part of the plaintiff (*exceptio doli praeteriti ac specialis*) or a dolous institution of proceedings (*exceptio doli praesentis ac generalis*).

The *actio de dolo* is said to go back to Cicero's friend C. Aquilius Gallus (Cic. Nat. D. 3,30,74, cf. Cic. Off. 3,14,60). In this (subsidiary) action a person who had suffered through dolous behaviour was able to reclaim his → *interesse*. Even in the context of *actio de dolo*, the *dolus* is not only understood in the narrower sense of a private action against an offence of deception but also encompasses various instances of behaviour injurious to → *aequitas*.

→ Parricidium; → Exceptio

Kaser, RPR I, 504–512; M. Brutti, La problematica del dolo processuale nell'esperienza romana, I/II, 1973; A. Wacke, Zum dolus-Begriff der actio de dolo, in: RIDA 27, 1980, 349–386; R. Zimmermann, The Law of Obligations, 1990, 662–677; P. Mader, Dolus suus neminem relevat, in: FS Waldstein, 1993, 215–229. F.ME.

Domain The word domain (from the Lat. [*res*] *dominica* through Late Latin *domenica*, Old French 'domenie', 'domaine') describes in the Middle Ages and in early modern times, rather more narrowly than the Late Latin original, the 'feudal' or 'allodial real estate' of a 'landowner' ('noble') and may denote the property as a whole or a single segment of it. In Roman legal language the *res dominica* is roughly covered by *dominium* (Dig. 50,16,195,2; 1,5,20), with the property being taken as plots or other things but possibly also applying to the whole property complex. The term was not limited to real estate (Dig. 7,2,1,1; 14,3,13,2) but acquired more or less this meaning in describing particular large holdings of property (large estates, *fundi*; in late antiquity termed *res domenica* or *domus divina*) that were at the emperor's disposal or were used for the personal needs of members of the imperial household (Cod. Iust. 11,66; 67; 68). Despite attempts at drawing a distinction between that and other state property at the emperor's disposal into state property (*fiscus, rationes, largitiones*), crown property (*patrimonium, res privata*) and personal property of the emperor and his family (*domus augusta, domus divina*: Dig. 30,39,8–10) and the consequential distinction between taxable and leasable property (Cod. Iust. 11,65ff.), there was no boundary that was legally defined and institutionally durable, because the emperor, with his sovereign authority over everything, was able to make his own rulings (Dig. 43,8,2,4: *res fiscales ... quasi propriae et privatae principis sunt*). The way state and imperial large holdings were organized goes back to the Republican → *aerarium*, but partly also to various forms of personal-imperial wealth or special property in earlier phases of the Imperial period and, by way of tradition, maintained the corresponding names even though there was no functional justification for them (*rationes, fiscus, res privatae, patrimonium, largitiones Caesaris*; Cod. Iust. 3,26,2; 7). Real estate was the backbone of state and imperial property in all its forms. The proceeds from it, which for the most part went to swell the state coffers, the rights to tax-exemption for it and the forms of colonate and emphyteutic law (Cod. Iust. 11,62; 63; 75) in late antiquity are at the root of the later character of domains, which until modern times depended on special laws for the monarchy and nobility in the areas of property, taxation, fiefdoms and inheritance. This is also true for the distinction between personal property of the ruler-owner and his family and state property that was available only for politically-defined purposes. A fundamental separation occurred only in the context of the constitutional movements of the 18th/19th cents. (*vis-à-vis* Parliament's budgetary powers) and was completed in connection with the abolition of monarchies after the First World War.

E. Heilfron, Deutsche Rechtsgesch., [7]1908, 594ff.; Jones, LRE 411ff.; Kaser, RPR 2, 152f., 308; H. Mitteis, H. Lieberich, Deutsche Rechtsgesch., [13]1974, 287ff. C.G.

Domavia *Municipium* in the late 2nd cent. AD, possibly under Septimius Severus (CIL III 12732); after AD 230 *colonia m(etalli?) D(omaviani)* (CIL III 12728f.) in the *prov. Dalmatia*, now Gradina close to Sas (near Srebrenica, Bosnia-Herzegovina); from no later than Marcus Aurelius a centre of administration of both the Pannonian and the Dalmatian mines (*procurator metallorum Pannon*[*icorum*] *et Delmat*[*icorum*], CIL III 12721), that were developed in the area around Srebrenica; the mining district was called *Argentaria* (Tab. Peut. 6,1); large quantities of silver, lead, zinc; lead sarcophagi were discovered in D. and Sirmium. Several inscriptions of *procuratores* attest to the construction of public buildings (*macellum, balneum*), while D. had several inscriptions fashioned in honour of emperors (from Septimius Severus to Volusianus). Roman settlers and Greek-speaking colonists from the East are epigraphically attested but indigenous people are rarely documented. The last epigraphical evidence for construction activities: renovated baths in AD 274 under Aurelius Verecundus, the *procurator* of the silver mines (CIL III 12736), while coin finds attest to mining activity in the 4th cent.

I. Bojanovski, Bosna i Hercegovina u antičko doba [Bosnia and Herzegovina in antiquity], Akademija nauka i umjetnosti Bosne i Herzegovine, Djela 66, Centar zu balkanološka isptivanja 6, [Monographies, Academie des sciences et des arts de Bosnie-Herzegovine 66, Centre d'études des balk. 6], 1988, 193–203. M.Š.K.

Dome, Construction of domes 'Non-genuine' dome constructions from layered corbel stone vaults (→ Vaults and arches, construction of) are to be found throughout Mediterranean cultures from the 3rd millennium BC; they seem to have entered largely independently the architectural repertory of Minoan Crete (tholos graves at Mesara and Knossos), Mycenaean Greece ('Treasure-house' of Atreus in Mycenae; 'domed grave' at Orchomenus), Sardinia (*nuraghe*), Thrace and Scythia (so-called 'beehive'-domes on graves and also Etruria (domed grave at Populonia). This form is mostly used in → funerary architecture (→ Tholos).

Domes with circular and square bases

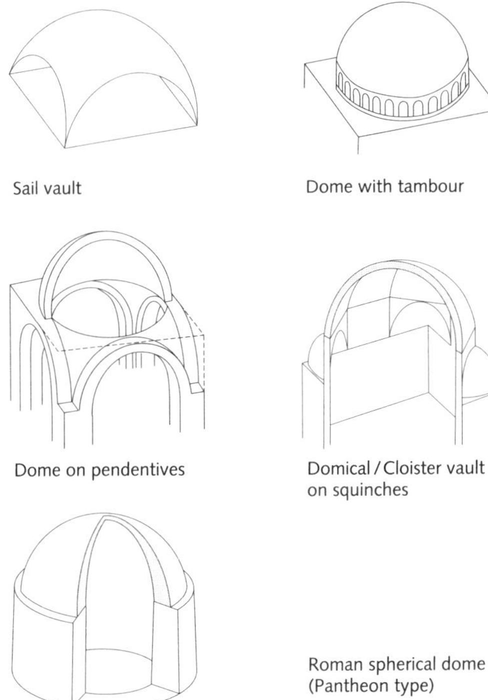

Only with the development of the Roman technique of pouring concrete in the 1st cent. BC (→ Construction technique; → *opus caementicium*) did the 'genuine', completely radially structured, self-centred hemispherical dome become an architectural feature, initially as a 'half-dome' linked to the → roofing, derived from vault construction, of an → apse or → exedra ('apsidal room' in Praeneste; Mercati Traiani in Rome, later in bath constructions of all kinds); from late Republican-Augustan times on, we also find as a 'complete dome' over a circular, square or multi-cornered (generally octagonal, or 12– or 16–cornered) frame. The earliest dome construction finished with poured concrete is thought to be the so-called 'temple of Mercury' in → Baiae, probably a dining hall in connection with baths (recreational or medical). With the domed roof over the Octagon in Nero's → Domus Aurea the feature moves beyond the construction of baths and enters into the architectural repertory of the → palace; in fact, it becomes a topos here, as later in temple construction (Rome, → Pantheon), church construction (→ Hagia Sophia; → Central-plan building) and, in late antiquity, in mausoleums (Galerius rotunda in Thessaloniki; 'Tempio della Tosse' in Tibur).

All along, the joining of a square frame to the three-dimensional, circular dome as its roofing constituted a crucial problem in dome construction. With the 'outer circle dome' the square is entirely encompassed by the outer dome circle, i.e. the dome transversely intersects the supporting square in the shape of a bow. The 'inner circle dome', by contrast, fits entirely within the interior of the square and thus needs pendentives (spherically cut triangles) or squinches (niches) to act as 'corner-resolvers'; in a formal sense, the earliest completed pendentive dome is held to be the first dome of the → Hagia Sophia, that collapsed shortly after the building's consecration in AD 558 (precursors to the squinches are to be found at several Sassanid palaces in Iran). Less technically demanding were domes over an octagon or polygon that were generally shaped in a 'cloister vault' in which the number of corners in the frame were, as a rule, precisely integrated. A circular frame was usually vaulted by an 'melon dome' like a curved octagon (the so-called 'Venus temple' in Baiae; Diocletian baths in Rome). The solution adopted with Hadrian's Pantheon in Rome, where the hemispherical dome over the cylindrical support rests on a complex system of struts and relieving arches in the area of the eight niches of the frame, remains the exception from a statistically-technical perspective.

Until the early modern times dome construction was approached by 'trial and error', a procedure of which—apart from the few written accounts like that of the collapse of the dome of the Hagia Sophia in Constantinople (see above) — only the 'positive' results, i.e. those remaining in existence for some time as monuments, have come to our knowledge; attempts to calculate or accurately estimate statics of dome constructions are not attested. Buildings with a diameter of over 40 m were capable of being domed (as in the Pantheon in Rome with *c.* 43 m.; *c.* 37 m diameter at the so-called 'Apollo temple', a thermal hall on the shore of Lake Avernus on the *Campi Flegrei*); but the building diameter was generally under 30 m. The dome was erected over centring and forms (→ Materiatio) from concrete poured in radial layers in which especially light material like pumice or volcanic soil was increasingly used in the upper layering. As also in vault construction, clay pipes, brick ribs, and even disused amphorae were added for a stable structuring of hollow spaces and thus reducing the weight in the overall composition ('Helena-Mausoleum' on the *via Labicana* in Rome). → Lighting in dome constructions was achieved by an → *opaeum* (Pantheon) or by a window loft (Baiae).

In all the cultural subsystems that followed Roman-pagan late antiquity (Western-Latin and Eastern Byzantine Christianity; Islam) the endomed space was conceived as a metaphor for the all-encompassing vault of heaven and in that sense as a topos of early medieval churches, as also for early mosque constructions.

J. Fink, Die Kuppel über dem Viereck, 1958; A. Müfid-Mansel, Trakya-Kirklareli Kibbeli Mezarları ve Sahte Kubbe ve Kemer Problemi, 1943; G. Pelliccioni, Le cupole romane: La stabilità, 1986; F. RAKOB, Römische Kuppelbauten in Baiae, in: MDAI(R) 95, 1988, 257–301; J. J. RASCH, Die Kuppel in der römischen Architektur: Entwicklung, Formgebung, Konstruktion, in: Architectura 15, 1985, 117–139; Id., Das Mausoleum der Kaiserin Helena an der Via Labicana in Rom, 1998; L. SCHNEIDER, CH. HÖCKER, P. ZAZOFF, Zur thrakischen Kunst im Frühhellenismus, in: AA 1985, 593–643; E.B. SMITH, The Dome, 1950; D. THODE, Untersuchungen zur Lastabtragung in spätantiken Kuppelbauten, 1975. C.HÖ.

Domestic animals

I. DEFINITION II. BIRDS, FISHES, INSECTS III. MAMMALS IV. FURTHER ASPECTS

I. DEFINITION

Domestic animals — in the sense of lap or favourite animals — are animals that are kept without any practical purpose, who share the home, and to whom people develop an emotional attachment. The latter also holds true for certain working animals, in particular for → horses (cf. Ael. NA 11,31; [8. 156–161]), → dogs [1] (see below), and → cats (see below). For Egypt, there is evidence — some of it going as far back as the 3rd millennium — that the dog, the cat, the → monkey, the → gazelle, and the Egyptian goose were favourite animals [2. 37]. In a man's grave in Israel from 10 000 BC, whelps were found as burial objects, proving his love of animals [1. 76]. Odysseus shows love to his dog Argus (Hom. Od. 17,291–327); in Hom. Od. 10,216 f., the master spoils his dog.

II. BIRDS, FISHES, INSECTS

Due to their ability to imitate the human voice, → thrushes, starlings (Plin. HN 10,120), → jays [cf. 3], → magpies (Petron. Sat. 28,9), → ravens (Macrob. Sat. 2,4,29), and, above all, → parrots (Ov. Am. 2,6,14–26) were kept as domestic animals. As songbirds, one kept → blackbirds (Plin. Ep. 4,2) and → nightingales (Plin. HN 10,120); ornamental birds were the → finch, *passer* (→ sparrow, blue rock thrush or bullfinch; famous was the one kept by Lesbia: Catull. 2; 3), → crane [5th vol. 2, fig. 57b], → dove / pigeon (Plin. HN 10,106; 110), less commonly the → owl (Ael. NA 1,29), → goose (Ael. NA 5,29 [6. 297]), → jackdaw, → duck, → quail (Plaut. Capt. 1002 f.), and → eagle (Ael. NA 6,29; Plin. HN 10,18). → Fishes were tamed and pampered (Cic. Att. 2,1,7; Ael. NA 8,4). Even → snakes were domestic animals (Sen. De ira 2,31,6). → Cicadas were children's pets (Theoc. 1,52 f. [5th vol. 2, 404]).

III. MAMMALS

Animals kept as domestic animals were the gazelle (Mart. 13,99), → hare [8. 190], → deer (Verg. Aen. 7,483–485), less commonly the → bear (see addenda; Sen. De ira 2,31,6), → ichneumon, *lagalopex* (perhaps a lynx: only in Mart. 7,87), → hedgehog (Aristot. Hist. an. 9,6, 612b 4–11), → lion (Sen. De ira 2,31,6), and → tiger (Ael. NA 6,2), the latter probably only in the surroundings of rulers. It was common to keep → monkeys (Plin. HN 8,215 f.; Plut. Pericles 1; Eubulus at Ath. 12,519). The → weasel was used as a mouser and was also regarded as a playmate for children [5. vol. 1, 164]. Written evidence indicates that domestic cats (→ Cat) were kept in Athens since the early 5th cent. BC and since the late 5th cent. in lower Italy; images on vases and coins depict people playing with cats [5th vol. 1, fig. 24; 25; pl. 2, 4]. In the Roman period, the cat became a popular pet in all of Italy, progressively so in the provinces of the empire as well [8. 75–79]. The → dog was highly valued as man's loyal companion (Hom. Od. 2,11; Plin. HN 8,142; Sen. Apocol. 13,3; Phaedr. 3,7,22). The documents bear witness to the emotional attachment of humans to animals. This impression is supported by images of dogs in burial art [7].

IV. FURTHER ASPECTS

In the Roman period, considerable sums were occasionally invested in purchasing and keeping domestic animals. Plin. Ep. 4,2 enumerates the following animals owned by a rich boy: ponies for driving and riding, smaller and larger dogs, nightingales, parrots and blackbirds. A famous source about the love of animals is Catull. 2 and 3. Martial 1,109 describes how the lap dog Issa was being spoiled. The exaggerated love of animals (Petron. 64,6) was used by Mart. 7,87 in a satirical comparison.

→ Domestication; → Household equipment; → Onomastics; → Stables, keeping of animals in; → Zoo, Animal reserve

1 N. BENECKE, Der Mensch und seine H., 1994
2 J. BOESSNECK, Die H. in Altägypten, 1953
3 H. GOSSEN, A. STEIER, s. v. Krähe, RE 11, 1556–1566
4 E. VON KEITZ, Ueber Tierliebhaberei im Altertume, 1883 5 KELLER 6 O. KELLER, Tiere des klass. Altertums, 1887 (repr. 2001) 7 F. ORTH, s. v. Hund, RE 8, 2540–2582 8 TOYNBEE, Tierwelt 9 K.-W. WEEBER, s. v. H., in: Id., Alltag im alten Rom, 1998, 172–174
10 J. WIESER, s. v. H., LAW, 1209–1217. S. I.

Domestication By this is meant the gradual and purposeful transformation of wild animal species into domesticated animals by human agency. Because of their biological characteristics, only a few of the wild mammals living during and immediately after the Ice Age were suitable for domestication. Only 5 of 19 orders of mammals provide domesticated species; these are the *Lagomorpha* (rabbits), *Rodentia* (guinea-pigs), *Carnivora* (dog, cat, ferret), *Perissodactyla* (horse, donkey) and the *Artiodactyla* (pig, sheep, goat, cattle, camel, llama). Domesticated animals however do not represent separate species: they can produce fertile offspring with their wild species of origin, and are sub-units of these. They are therefore to be systematically assigned to their species of origin, i.e. domesticated cattle to the (extinct) wild ox *Bos primigenius* as *B. p. forma taurus* or *Bos taurus*. As the various races of domestic animal vary in colour of coat rather than skeletal structure, little information can be gleaned from surviving skeletal remains. Apart from maintenance in captivity with a more plentiful and varied diet, a decisive role is played by selective breeding by human beings, so that particular desirable characteristics of physique (size and strength) and behaviour (passivity and tameness) eventually become inheritable. Such selective breeding is directed at working performance (e.g. endurance while drawing the plough or bearing a rider) or the optimization of milk-production for offspring, production of meat or fat, or the quality of the coat or wool. The stages of the domestication process can be reconstructed by means of archaeological finds, as for example in the litter from ancient farm buildings, from accompanying artefacts as well as by the use of archaeometric (scientific) methods. Finds have established that the → dog was the first animal to be domesticated, on multiple occasions in Eurasia and America as early as the transition from Pleistocene to Holocene (i.e. *c.* 10000–8000 BC), from the → wolf (and not the Golden or Asiatic Jackal, as K. LORENZ [1] believed) [2. 69–98].

The Greeks and Romans distinguished many races [3. 94–109]. The use of herd-dogs enabled → goats [2. 113–133; 3. 148–150] and → sheep [2. 133–173; 3. 146–148] to be domesticated. The domestication of → horses began during the 3rd millennium BC, probably from the Ukraine eastwards [2. 254–287; 3. 151–172]. The → donkey, originating in North Africa and evidently first domesticated in Egypt [2. 316–323; 3. 180–185], played a significant role in antiquity as a beast of burden. → Cattle were bred in Europe from the → aurochs before 4000 BC [2. 174–20; 3. 138–145]. From the 3rd millennium onwards several races of → pig, from time immemorial forbidden to Jews as unclean [2. 220–232; 3. 116–122], were bred from the wild pig by sedentary settlers. The two-humped → camel and the riding-camel or dromedary, probably already domesticated in Arabia during the 4th millennium BC [2. 288–311; 3. 123–126], were known to Greek colonists from the 5th/4th cents. BC (first attested in Hdt. 1,80). The → cat [2. 325–336; 3. 75–79] came to the Greeks from Egypt, where it had certainly been domesticated since about the 5th dynasty. The → ferret, as the domesticated form of the → polecat, or more precisely the East European steppe polecat [2. 336–338], is not known until very late, from the 4th cent. BC. In the 1st cent. AD Strabo (3,2,6) reports the use of the ferret (γαλῆ ἀγρία) on the Balearics for hunting rabbits (γεώρυχοι λαγιδεῖς; → Hare). This rodent spread to the west from the Iberian peninsula after the last Ice Age; it was raised in *leporaria* by the Romans, but not domesticated until the Middle Ages [2. 341–347].

1 K. LORENZ, So kam der Mensch auf den Hund, 1950 2 F. E. ZEUNER, Gesch. der Haustiere, 1967 3 TOYNBEE, Tierwelt.

N. BENECKE, Der Mensch und seine Haustiere, 1994; W. HERRE, W. RÖHRS, Haustiere — zoologisch gesehen, 1990; I. L. MASON, Evolution of Domesticated Animals, 1984.

C.HÜ.

Domesticus In the general sense, a slave in a house (*domus*), or a person bound to the family or to the head of the household (Dig. 48,19,11,1).

However, the word having originally signified the opposite of *publicius*, during the Republic it already entered the political sphere, to designate the entire *cohors* of a Roman provincial governor: free and unfree servants (*servi, ministri*), subordinate officials (*apparitores, officiales*), even subordinates assigned by statute (*adiutores, comites, consiliarii*) and the military escort. Although Cicero advised that there should be a distinction between domestic and official duties (Cic. ad Q. fr. 1,10ff.), already in his time the functions of the two spheres were similar (Cic. Phil. 12,1), and this situation later became the norm (Cod. Iust. 1,51). Military commanders and political legates outside Rome also had *domestici*, and, while these were not allowed to act independently or in a deputising role (Cod. Iust. 1,51,4; 5,2,1), their function in practice influenced the work of their employer.

Thus arose the intermingling of public and private functions as between the staff and household of the emperor (*familia, comitatus Caesaris*), and consequently at the imperial court (*palatium, domus Augusta*), where officials in the emperor's service executed functions at once of a political/public and a personal nature (Suet. Aug. 89,2; Cod. Iust. 11,66); terms originally relating to the personal sphere of the emperor, such as *domesticus* (as also *domus, patrimonium, res privata, ministri*) acquired an 'official' flavour.

In late antiquity *domestici* are a military escort at the imperial court, organized in five to seven *scholae* each of some 500 men under the supervision of the *magister officiorum*; in addition there was an imperial bodyguard (*protectores et domestici*), each troop under the command of a → *comes* (Not. Dign. Or. 15; 11,3ff. Cod. Iust. 3,24,3 pr.; 12,17,1–4). *Domestici* at court are called *domestici praesentales*, elsewhere *domestici deputati*. As the military character of their functions at court declines, from the 5th cent. *excubitores* appear as a guard detachment (Lydus, Mag. 1,16,3).

Those in receipt of an imperial subvention or of privileges associated with the honorary rank of *protector* are not in the stricter sense members of the *domestici* (Cod. Iust. 12,46,2).

JONES, LRE 593, 602f.; MOMMSEN, Staatsrecht 1, 320ff.; 2, 836ff.

C.G.

Domicilium Dwelling (Dig. 11,5,1,2), as for example the matrimonial dwelling (Dig. 23,2,5: *domicilium matrimonii*), but particularly a domicile. This is the place where one usually resides and where one intends to remain (Cod. Iust. 10,40,7,1: *ubi quis larem rerumque ac fortunarum suarum summam constituit*). It became recognized that someone might have two *domicilia* (Dig. 50,1,6,2). *Domicilium* is the basis for liability to tax and for legal jurisdiction. Someone who is a citizen (*civis*) of one community and has his *domicilium* in another, thus being *incola* there (Dig. 50,16,239,2), can be arraigned in either location at the choice of the plaintiff (Gai. Dig. 50,1,29). Since the late Middle Ages according to the common law theory of statutes, a person's legal relations (*ius ac conditio seu qualitas personalis*, personal statute) depend on his domicile. P.A.

Dominatus (Lat. *dominatus*) sometimes has the legal sense of *dominium* (cf. Nov. Theod. II. 22,2,16), meaning the position of a *dominus* as mandated authority, master or owner, esp. in family and property law (Dig. 12,6,64; 29,2,78). In the political realm, *dominatus* stands for 'foreign' or 'arbitrary' power (Greek *tyrannís*; Cic. Rep. 1,61). At the core of the concept is statutory power that is freely exercised and not susceptible of control, and thus is subject to abuse (Cic. Rep. 1,61).

The modern German loan-word *Dominat* is a 19th-cent. neologism, and according to [1. 749ff.] and [2. 347ff.] signifies a form of imperial rule arising with the reign of → Diocletianus (end of the 3rd cent. AD), following an 'oriental'-Hellenistic pattern, and by its openly monarchic concept of the state and the imperial office clearly distinguished from the earlier 'Principate' regime founded on a kind of co-dominion with the Senate. Thus during the *dominatus* of late antiquity the emperor stands as the categorical and pre-eminent fount of justice, and when necessary sovereign arbiter of the law (*lege solutus*). The structure of the high offices of state (→ *cursus honorum*), and the composition of the imperial aristocracy and its conception of itself in relation to the imperial court, differs significantly from early Imperial period structures. It is, however, hardly possible to make a strict separation of the epochs (Principate/*dominatus*): many traits of the *imperium* of late antiquity already appear in embryonic form during the earlier Imperial period (as e.g. 'emancipation from the law', the tendency of many emperors towards oriental-Hellenistic forms of self-portrayal, or their stance as possessors of power independent of the Senate, and primarily backed by the military), and on the other hand the *imperium* of late antiquity, with some exceptions, holds to the law, to state traditions and to the interests of the aristocracy who bear the burden of the state [3].
→ Autocrator; → Princeps; → Tyrannis

1 Mommsen, Staatsrecht 2,2 2 Th. Mommsen, Abriß des röm. Staatsrechts, ²1907 3 J. Bleicken, Prinzipat und Dominat, 1978.

A. Demandt, Die Spätantike, 1989, 211ff.; Ch. Gizewski, Zur Normativität und Struktur der Verfassungsverhältnisse in der späten röm. Kaiserzeit, 1988, 15ff.; Jones, LRE 321ff. C.G.

Dominium Originally signified the domestic power of the → *pater familias* (Ulp. Dig. 50,16,195,2: *in domo dominium*). From the beginning of the Imperial period *dominium* occurs in the sense of property (Labeo Dig. 18,1,80,3; Sen. Benef. 7,5,1; 7,6,3). In the early period, the Roman conception of property is uniform, being understood at first solely as *dominium ex iure Quiritium*: property rights accessible to Roman citizens and at the limit to *peregrini* with → *commercium*. Later on, in honorary law established by the → *praetor* (*in bonis habere*, → *bona*), allowed claims giving absolute priority over those of any other person, even the Quirite owner (Gai. 2,40–41). From this time onwards, two kinds of property right exist in Rome: *duplex dominium*. *Dominium* occurs in the general sense of ownership, where it is a question of *dominium usufructus* (Dig. 7,6,3) or *dominium proprietatis* (Dig. 7,4,17; cf. also Ulp. Dig. 7,1,15,6 *dominus proprietatis*). In 530/31 Justinian entirely eliminated *dominium ex iure Quiritium*, which had been superseded in law and become all the more confusing to law students, and with it *duplex dominium*, thus once again unifying the conception of property rights (Cod. Iust. 7,25,1).

1 H. Honsell, Th. Mayer-Maly, W. Selb, Röm. Recht, ⁴1987, 142–149 2 Kaser, RPR I, 400–404; II, 238–242, 246–251, 261f. D.SCH.

Dominus 'Master' (generally, e.g. Cic. Leg. 2,15; Plin. Ep. 4,11,6). *Domine/domina* is from time immemorial the form of address used by children to their parents (Suet. Aug. 53,1; CIL X 7457 *domine pater*); the form also occurs between husband and wife (as in Scaevola Dig. 32,41 pr. *domina uxor*, Paulus Dig. 24,1,57 *domine carissime*), between close relatives, friends, and in commercial intercourse as well (cf. Dig. 13,5,26: to a creditor). Peculiar is the use of the word in relation to one's own children (CIL VI 11511; VI 17865; VIII 2862) or a ward (Dig. 32,37,2). In legal terms *dominus* signifies a person to whom certain items or affairs are assigned: a house (Plaut. Most 686 *aedium domini*); slaves (Sen. Ep. 47,14, *pater familias* in the terms used by the *maiores*); an inheritance (Marcianus Dig. 28,5,49 pr., *hereditatis dominus*); property (*proprietas*: Ulp. Dig. 29,5,1,1); a business deal (*negotium*: Neratius Dig. 3,3,1 pr.); a legal case (*lis*: Neratius Dig. 2,11,14). *Dominus* can also mean a ruler (thus in Ov. Pont. 2,8,26 in relation to Augustus: *terrarum dominus*, Tert., Adv. Marcionem 5,5,3 in relation to God and Christ); in pejorative terms tyrant (Cic. Rep. 2,47). Augustus did not tolerate being addressed as *dominus*, not even by his children and grandchildren (Suet. Aug. 53,1). Tiberius too forbade it (Suet. Tib. 27; Cass. Dio 57,81). Antoninus Pius replied with subtle self-irony to a plaintiff at appeal who used the term, Κῦριε βασιλεῦ Ἀντωνῖνε, (Dig. 14,2,9). Other emperors were less modest. Caligula demanded to be addressed as *dominus* (Aur. Vict. 3,13). Domitian claimed the title *dominus et deus* (Suet. Dom. 13; Aur. Vict. 11,2), as did Diocletian (Aur. Vict. 39,4): thus begins the epoch called the → Dominatus, after this designation for the ruler. According to an anecdote in Bolognese learned tradition (12th cent.), Frederick Barbarossa is said to have been assured by the jurist Martinus that he was *dominus mundi* ('master of the world'); the jurist Bulgarus denied this *quantum ad proprietatem* (so far as property is concerned) [1].

→ Dominatus

1 F.K. v. Savigny, Gesch. des röm. Rechts im MA IV, 1850, 180–183 2 Friedländer, IV, 82–88 3 E. Meyer, Röm. Staat und Staatsgedanke, ⁴1975, 435–438 4 Mommsen, Staatsrecht II 1, 760–763. D.SCH.

Domitia

[1] Daughter of Domitius [II 2]; sister of D. [5]; Nero's aunt on his father's side. Possibly she was frequently married [1. 162f., 166], but her only husband known to us by name is C. Sallustius Passienus Crispus, *cos. II* 44, who left her probably in AD 41 to marry Agrippina the Younger, which was the cause of the deepest aversion between the two women. Thus in AD 55 she was involved in an intrigue against Agrippina. Shortly after Agrippina's death in AD 59, D. also died, supposedly poisoned by Nero, who appropriated her immense fortune [1. 159ff.; 2]. PIR² D 171.

1 Syme, AA 2 Raepsaet-Charlier no. 319.

[2] **D. Calvina.** Daughter of (Calpurnius) Bibulus, a follower of Mark Antony, and Domitia, daughter of Domitius Calvinus, whose name she took; married to M. Iunius Silanus, *cos.* 19 BC PIR² D 173.

Raepsaet-Charlier, no. 321.

[3] **D. Decidiana.** Probably the daughter of T. Domitius Decidianus, from Narbonensis; wife of Agricola from *c.* 62; two sons are known, who died young, and a daughter who married Tacitus; she accompanied Agricola to the provinces. She lived at least until AD 98, when Tacitus wrote his *Agricola* (Tac. Agr. 6; 29; 43,4; 44,4; 45f.). PIR² D 174.

Raepsaet-Charlier, no. 322.

[4] **D. Faustina.** Eldest daughter of Marcus Aurelius and Faustina; granddaughter of Antoninus Pius; b. AD 30.11.147 [1]. She took her gentile name from Domitia [8]. She died before 161. PIR² D 177.

1 Vidman, FO² 51.

[5] **D. Lepida.** Daughter of Domitius [II 2], sister of D. [1]; Nero's aunt on his father's side. Married to Valerius Mesalla Barbatus, then to Faustus Cornelius Sulla, *cos. suff.* 31, and finally to C. Appius Iunius Silanus, *cos. ord.* 28; this last marriage took place on the orders of the emperor Claudius, who had married Valeria Messalina, Lepida's daughter. But Silanus was executed in 42, probably as a consequence of Messalina's intrigues. When Claudius had Messalina executed in 48, Lepida was with her (Tac. Ann. 11,37,3). She was very close to her brother's son, later to become Nero; she looked after him when Agrippina was banished (40/41). Longstanding enmity with Agrippina; her influence on Nero was associated with this. In 54 she was prosecuted for having used magical practices against Agrippina; she was also supposed to have endangered the security of Italy with her hordes of slaves in Calabria; D. was accordingly executed (Tac. Ann. 12,65,1). She was portrayed as being rich, scheming and morally unscrupulous. PIR² D 180.

Raepsaet-Charlier no. 326; Syme, AA 164ff.; G. Camodeca, in: Le ravitaillement en blé de Rome, 1994, 108.

[6] **D. Longina.** Daughter of Domitius [II 11] and of one (Cassia?) Longina, thus from a leading family of Nero's time (cf. [1]). Married by 69 at the latest to L. Aelius Plautius Lamia Aelianus, *cos. suff.* 80; by AD 70 she was married to → Domitianus [1]. In 73 she bore him a son, and subsequently one or two more, of whom none survived. In 81 she received the epithet Augusta, which also appeared on coins. She was alleged to have had a close relationship with Domitian's brother Titus, but Domitian separated from her because of her adultery with the actor Paris. But he later took her back. In 96 she was instrumental in the conspiracy at court against Domitian. After his murder she lived on unmolested into Hadrian's reign. In 140 one of her freedmen erected a temple in her honour at Gabii (CIL XIV 2795 = ILS 272). She was extraordinarily rich; property is attested in Rome and Peltuinum. PIR² D 181.

1 Syme, AA 187.

Raepsaet-Charlier, no. 327; U. Hausmann, Herrscherbild II 1, 1966, 63ff. (portraits).

[7] **D. Lucilla.** Daughter of Cn. Domitius [II 18] Lucanus; adopted by her uncle Domitius [II 25] Tullus so that he might acquire her inheritance from her maternal grandfather Curtilius Mancia (Plin. Ep. 8,18). Married to P. Calvisius Tullus Ruso, *cos. ord.* 109. She is the main heiress in testament CIL VI 10229 [1; 2], referred to in Plin. Ep. 8,18; regarding her *horti* in Rome [3]. She was the mother of D. [8], and so grandmother of Marcus Aurelius. PIR² D 182.

1 W. Eck, J. Heinrichs, Sklaven und Freigelassene, 1993, 189, no. 285 2 Syme, RP 5, 521ff. 3 Liverani, s.v. D., LTUR 3, 58f.

Raepsaet-Charlier, no. 328.

[8] **D. Lucilla.** Daughter of D. [7] and P. Calvisius Tullus Ruso, *cos. ord.* 109. Married to M. Annius Verus before AD 121; her children were the later emperor → Marcus Aurelius (b. 121) and Annia Cornificia Faustina. She is frequently mentioned in Marcus Aurelius' 'Meditations' and in Fronto's letters. She was extraordinarily rich, primarily through her inheritance from her mother; many *figlinae* in the vicinity of Rome were in her possession; after her death (before 161) they went to Marcus Aurelius. PIR² D 183.

Raepsaet-Charlier, no. 329; Liverani, s.v. D., LTUR 3, 58f.

[9] **D. Paulina.** Mother of Hadrian; married to P. Aelius Hadrianus Afer. PIR² D 185.

A. Birley, Hadrian, 1997.

[10] **D. Paulina.** Daughter of D. [9] and sister of Hadrian; married to L. Iulius Ursus Servianus, *cos. suff.* 90, *cos. ord. II* 102, *III* 134. She lived at least until 125 (ICret. I 201.43). As Hadrian's sister honoured at Fundi, at Lyttus on Crete and at Attaleia. PIR[2] D 186.

RAEPSAET-CHARLIER, no. 12.

[11] **D. Regina.** Wife of the legionary legate L. Calpurnius Proculus (AE 1930, 27).

[12] **D. Vetilla.** Daughter of L. Domitius Apollinaris; married to L. Neratius Marcellus, *cos. suff.* 95.

W. ECK, in: ZPE 50, 1983, 197ff.; RAEPSAET-CHARLIER, no. 333; SYME, RP 7, 588ff.

[13] **D. Vetilla.** Daughter of Domitius Patruinus; married to L. Roscius Paculus, *cos. suff.* in the Hadrianic-Antonine period. PIR[2] D 189.

RAEPSAET-CHARLIER, no. 334; SYME, RP 7, 588ff. W.E.

Domitianus

[1] Roman emperor; original name T. Flavius Domitianus = Imperator Caesar Domitianus Augustus.

A. UP TO THE DEATH OF TITUS B. RELATIONSHIP WITH THE SENATE C. THE IMAGE OF DOMITIAN IN ROMAN LITERATURE AND EXTERNAL POLITICS
D. FINANCIAL POLICY AND BUILDING ACTIVITIES
E. POLICY TOWARDS RELIGION

A. UP TO THE DEATH OF TITUS

Born on 24 Oct. AD 51 in Rome; his parents were T. Flavius → Vespasianus and Flavia Domitilla. D. spent his childhood in Rome; he did not accompany his father Vespasian to Judaea. His life was first threatened in the 2nd half of 69 during the reign of Vitellius, when D.'s father had already been proclaimed emperor, and fighting broke out between Flavius Sabinus, Vespasian's brother and city prefect of Rome, and the Vitellians. He escaped from the burning Capitol disguised as a follower of Isis; consequently, in later years he particularly venerated Isis. After Rome was taken he was acclaimed Caesar by the troops, the name having already been given him in the east. For a short period D. was the highest representative of the imperial family in Rome, actual power being in the hands of → Licinius Mucianus (Tac. Hist. 4,39,2). D. received the praetorate for the year 70 with consular power, but quickly sought a command against the rebellious Germans, so as to compete with the military fame of his brother Titus. Although Mucianus did not prevent the command, the military undertaking came to a premature end before Lugdunum; Vespasian also later failed to transfer to D. the command he wanted against the Parthians. This public slight had an influence on D.'s later policies. Whereas Vespasian made his elder son Titus *collega imperii*, D. was kept remote from real power. Although he was named *princeps iuventutis* and was consul six times (in 71, 73, 75, 76, 77, 79), only once, in 73, as *cos. ord.* He was additionally a member of all the priestly colleges. He had married Domitia Longina, daughter of Domitius Corbulo, as early as AD 70: probably a stratagem to obtain support in senatorial circles. In spite of all his setbacks, D. was certainly part of Vespasian's dynastic project. Under Titus too, it became clear that D. was the 'natural' successor to the imperial throne.

B. RELATIONSHIP WITH THE SENATE

Thus, when Titus died on 13 September 81, D.'s succession to power was smooth; he had his brother deified. On the very day of his brother's death D. was acclaimed emperor by the praetorian guard, and on 14 September the Senate transferred to him the name of Augustus; *tribunicia potestas*, with effect from 14 September, was officially determined by the *comitia* on 30 September 81. Almost from the beginning of his reign, D.'s relations with sections of the Senate seem to have been strained. The situation was compounded by the fact that he wished to distinguish himself from his brother, who (supposedly) had lived in perfect harmony with the Senate. D. had also never himself been a senator, and so did not understand the Senate's mentality. He early on made no bones about his more or less autocratic standpoint, while on its part the majority of the Senate met halfway those of D.'s desires it was aware of, resolving upon numerous honours: i.a. the right always to be accompanied by 24 lictors; to bear the title of *censor perpetuus* (from 85); to be consul on an uninterrupted basis (in the event D. was *cos. ord.* ten times during his reign: 82–88, 90, 92, 95). The months of September and October were renamed Germanicus and Domitianus (86); numerous statues and triumphal arches were erected; the square of the *Forum Romanum* was dominated by a gigantic equestrian statue of D. Early on there were conspiracies against him, to which he reacted with executions. Thus his cousin T. Flavius Sabinus, *cos. ord.* 82, was executed probably soon after his consulship. A conspiracy was uncovered in 87 (CIL VI 2065 II 62ff.). Antonius Saturninus, legate of Upper Germany, rebelled against D. at the end of 88; the rebellion was put down. Not a few senators were executed during his reign: 14 are known by name. In particular, at the end of 93 senators influenced by the ideas of Stoicism were condemned to death or banishment, among them Herennius Senecio and Helvidius (Priscus). Flavius Clemens (likewise a cousin of D.), whose sons the emperor had adopted, was executed shortly after his consulship in 95 (Suet. Dom. 15,1). The grounds for his execution are not known; certainly not an inclination to Christianity, although there were measures against Christians under D. The fear thus aroused in the hearts of many was the cause of the final conspiracy, in which D.'s wife, a praetorian prefect and some of his freedmen took part; whether senators too were implicated, among them his successor Nerva, is uncertain. D. was murdered on 18 September 96, and his ashes deposited in secret in the *templum gentis Flaviae*. The Senate expunged his memory (→ *damnatio memoriae*), and many of his statues and many inscriptions mentioning him were accordingly destroyed, altered or rewritten to other emperors (cf. I. Eph. 232–242; 1498, 2048).

C. THE IMAGE OF DOMITIAN IN ROMAN LITERATURE AND EXTERNAL POLITICS

It is difficult to penetrate to the real character of his reign, as almost all literary sources apart from Martial and Statius (who wrote only in panegyric terms about D. in his lifetime) begin after his death: Tacitus' *Agricola* and *Historiae* (period of Domitian not extant), Pliny's *Epistulae* and *Panegyricus*. But these were conditioned by the transition to Nerva and Trajan, and by a compulsion for self-justification, and described D. as a *princeps* perverted. Although the account of Suetonius is less hostile, to a large extent he adopts the negative senatorial assessments. Cassius Dio is dependent on his sources, who are hostile to Domitian. Modern scholarship has attempted to correct the generally negative picture, but without arriving at a consistent view of its own (cf. in the last instance [1]). Correctives are especially possible in the area of his military undertakings on the frontiers. In the spring of 83 D. was personally present at the opening of a campaign against the Chatti (probably already planned in 82), thus continuing the slow advance begun under his father on the right bank of the Rhine. Territorial gains in Hesse up to the line of the later *limes* were evidently achieved without major battles, with the result that the triumph over the Chatti celebrated by D. probably as early as 83 was characterized as a farce (Plin. Pan. 16,3; 17,1f.). In 83 the Senate voted D. the victor's name Germanicus. After a renewed campaign against the Chatti in 85 D. officially founded the provinces of Germania superior and Germania inferior, thus declaring an end to the problem of the German tribes that had remained unresolved since Augustus (cf. [2]). In Britain D. allowed Iulius Agricola to pursue his conquests; it was only after Agricola had been governor for seven years in all and been victorious in the battle at Mons Graupius that D. recalled him, and then only because he realized that a stronger commitment was necessary on the Danube frontier against the Dacians and other tribes. Tacitus interprets the recall as being occasioned by D.'s envy of Agricola's military successes in contrast to his own allegedly unjustified triumph against the Chatti. But already in 85 in Lower Moesia the governor there, Oppius Sabinus, had been killed in battle during a Dacian raid under Diurpaneus. D. himself went to the Danube, command being taken by his *praef. praet.* Cornelius Fuscus. After initial successes D. celebrated a triumph over the Dacians, probably in 86; but shortly afterwards Fuscus was defeated by Diurpaneus. D. again went to the Danube, command in battle being at first taken over by Cornelius Nigrinus. In order to better defend the Danube frontier, and so that the transfer of further troops should not lead to an overlarge military force being concentrated in the hands of one legate, Moesia was divided into two provinces (Moesia inferior und Moesia superior) not later than 86. Campaigns were now directed against Decebalus, who suffered a severe defeat at Tapae (Cass. Dio 67,10,1ff.). The rebellion of Antonius Saturninus in Upper Germany prevented the victory from being exploited. While a peace was concluded with Decebalus (who was recognized as a client king, to whom subsidies had to be paid), further attacks were directed against the Iazyges and Sarmatae; these campaigns were not brought to a conclusion until 93. Trajan continued D.'s policy on the middle and lower Danube, which demonstrates the correctness of D.'s reorientation of his military dispositions.

D. FINANCIAL POLICY AND BUILDING ACTIVITIES

D.'s wars required considerable financial backing; yet, contrary to claims, no financial difficulties seem to have arisen thereby during his reign. At first he even increased the silver content of the *denarius*, although this did have to be decreased again owing to the increase in the wages of legionaries from 900 to 1,200 sesterces per year (probably in 85). Confiscation of the property of condemned senators was not, however, due to financial problems. In contrast with his father, D. granted unassigned land (*subseciva*) to cities in Italy without requiring compensatory payment (e.g. CIL IX 5420 = FIRA I² no. 75). In his policies towards provincial citizens too he appears to have had regard for their interests, as in relation to the financial burden caused by the *cursus publicus* (AE 1958, 236 = IGLS 5, 1998). He subjected governors to a strict regime: according to Suetonius (Dom. 8,2) there were never fairer public officials. This is confirmed by the fact that, contrary to the claims of Tacitus and Pliny, his awarding of official positions in Rome and the provinces was based not on politics but on 'practical ability', as was also the case under Trajan [3]. It is also true that he attempted to protect Italian agriculture against competitive pressure from the provinces. Towards the end of his reign he developed the road network in Italy. But it was in Rome that he carried out his greatest construction projects, with the reconstruction of the Capitol, the construction of the Forum Transitorium, the completion of the Colosseum; the most significant of his projects was the imperial palace on the Palatine Hill, used by all future rulers.

E. RELIGIOUS POLICY

D. appealed to *mos maiorum*; he made pointed use of his censorial power, i.a. in the maintenance of Roman religion and its precepts. He accordingly executed several Vestal Virgins who had broken their vows. The celebration of secular games in 88, goes back to the games under Augustus, and is a further indication of his traditionalism. In 86 he also established the *Agon Capitolinus* as a competition for orators, poets, singers and athletes [4]. In particular, however, he accepted the cult of his own person, although the claim that he demanded to be addressed as *dominus ac deus* was an erroneous generalisation of a habitual form of address, perhaps among the imperial household. Intensification of the veneration of the ruler is to be detected in the erection of the gigantic imperial temple at Ephesus, and the reflection of that event in John's Apocalypse. For Christians, D. was one of the greatest persecutors of the Church (Lactant. De mort. pers. 3). This factor and the dominance of senatorial sources have perpetuated into the 20th cent. the image of D. as a *tyrannus*.

1 B.W. JONES, M. GRIFFIN, The Flavians, CAH XI (in print) 2 K. STROBEL, in: Germania 65, 1987, 423ff. 3 ECK, Senatoren 48ff. 4 M.L. CALDELLI, L'agon Capitolinus, 1993.

W. ECK, Senatoren von Vespasian bis Hadrian, 1970, 48–76; S. GESELL, Essai sur la règne de l'empereur Domitien, 1894; B.W. JONES, The Emperor Domitian, 1992; A. MARTIN, La titulature épigraphique de Domitien, 1987; H. NESSELHAUF, Tacitus und Domitian, in: Hermes 80, 1952, 222ff.; J.-M. PAILLER, R. SABLAYROLLES (ed.), Les années Domitien, 1994; K. STROBEL, Die Donaukriege Domitians, 1992; R. SYME, Domitian: The Last Years, in: Chiron 13, 1983, 121ff. = RP 4, 252ff.; Id. Tacitus, 1958, I 19–29; CHR. URNER, Kaiser Domitian im Urteil ant. lit. Quellen und moderner Forsch., 1993.
COINS: BMC Emp. II 297ff.; RIC I 149ff.
PORTRAITURE: M. WEGNER, Das röm. Herrscherbild II 1, 1966, 30ff.; FITTSCHEN-ZANKER, I 35ff. no. 31–33. W.E.

[2] Usurper emperor proclaimed at the beginning of the reign of Aurelianus [3], and soon eliminated (Zos. 1,49,2). The only alleged coin of D. is a modern alteration of a coin of Tetricus [1]. Perhaps to be identified with D. the military commander who *c.* 261 under the command of Aureolus is said to have defeated Macrianus (SHA Gall. 2,6; Tyr. Trig. 12,13; 14 with fictitious derivation; 13,3), but whose existence is in any case dubious.

1 KIENAST [2]1996, 237. A.B.

[3] *Notarius* of Constantius II (Lib. Or. 42,24f.). He rose to *comes sacrarum largitionum* and in AD 353 to *praef. praet. Orientis* (Amm. Marc. 14,7,9). In Antioch he was to persuade the Caesar Gallus to travel to the court of Constantius II. During a commotion provoked by Gallus he was killed by soldiers (Amm. Marc. 14,7,9–16; Zon. 13,9). PLRE 1, 262 D. (3). W.P.

[4] This learned monk was one of the main figures in Palestinian Origenism, and at the urging of Leontius of Byzantium he was appointed bishop of → Ancyra by → Justinian *c.* 540. He was an Origenist with Monophysite tendencies, and was one of those who instigated the dispute of the Three Chapters, i.e. the dispute over works by the three theologians → Theodorus of Mopsuestia, → Theodoretus of Cyrrhus and → Ibas, which led to the verdicts of condemnation (κεφάλαια, *kephálaia*) at the 5th Ecumenical Council in → Constantinople.

Of D.'s works only a short fragment of his *libellus* to Vigilius of Rome is extant (CPG 3, 6990; in Facundius: CCL 110A, 126).

L. PERRONE, La Chiesa di Palestina e le controversie Cristologiche, 1980, 204–207. C.M.

Domitilla see → Flavia

Domitius Roman plebeian family name, attested from the 4th cent. BC onwards (ThlL, Onom. 3,217–227). The most important families into the 1st cent. AD are the Ahenobarbi [I 1–8] and the Calvini [I 9–12]. Identification of some members of the family in the 2nd cent. BC is uncertain.

MÜNZER, Index s.v. D.; SYME, RR, Index s.v. D.; SYME, AA, Index s.v. D.

I. REPUBLICAN PERIOD II. IMPERIAL PERIOD
III. ORATORS AND WRITERS

I. REPUBLICAN PERIOD

DOMITII AHENOBARBI

Family history in Suet. Ner. 1–5. Legend of the origin of the cognomen (ThlL, 1,135; in manuscript also Aenobarbus) 'Red-beard', 'Bronze-beard' in Suet. Ner. 1,1; Plut. Aem. 25. The family was probably accorded patrician status in 29 BC by Octavian (Suet. Ner. 1,2; [1. 72f.]). Related to the Julio-Claudian dynasty via L.D. [II 2] Ahenobarbus (*cos.* 16 BC); his grandson of the same name, later → Nero, was adopted by Claudius in AD 50. The family tomb of the D. was on the Pincio (Suet. Ner. 50). *Praenomina*: Cn. and L.

Genealogy: MÜNZER, s.v. Domitius, RE 5, 1315f. (Republic); PIR 3[2], 126 (Imperial period).

1 TH. MOMMSEN, Röm. Forsch. 1, 1864.

[I 1] D. Ahenobarbus, C. The first consul in the family. As plebeian *aedile* in 196 BC he prosecuted leaseholders of the *ager publicus*, and with the fines began building the Faunus Temple on the Tiber island, consecrating it as *praetor urbanus* in 194 (Liv. 33,42,10; 34,53,4). As consul in 192 and proconsul in 191 he fought against the Boii (Liv. 35,22,3f.; 40,2f.; 36,37,6; use in the campaign of auxiliary troops from Achaea: MORETTI, 60). In 190 he took part as a *legatus* in the war against Antiochus III, but in the battle of Magnesia did not play the decisive role accorded him by tradition (Plut. Mor. 197Df.; App. Syr. 159–189).
[I 2] D. Ahenobarbus, Cn. Son of D. [I 1]; 170 (?) *praetor* (MRR 1,420), 169 and 167 ambassador to Greece and Macedonia, 162 *cos. suff.* (InscrIt 13,1,462).
[I 3] D. Ahenobarbus, Cn. Son of D. [I 2] ?; *legatus pro praetore* under M'. Aquillius [I 3] 129–126 (?, MRR 1,505) in Asia (letter to D. from Bargylia: [1. 179–198]). On his return he represented the Samians in a *repetundae* action (IGR 4, 968; [2. 167–178]). After his praetorate in 125 at the latest, as consul in 122 he fought successfully in southern Gaul against the Allobroges, and in 121 with his successor Q. Fabius Maximus against the allied Allobroges and Arverni (→ Bituitus); both men erected victory monuments

(Flor. 1,37,6). He built a road to southern Gaul, the *via Domitia*, along with the station Forum Domiti and probably a Roman garrison in Narbo (milestone: ILLRP 460a), perhaps remaining in Gaul until 118; the year of his triumph in Rome falls between 120 and 117 (InscrIt 13,1,83; Vell. Pat. 2,10,2). In 115 he was censor together with L. Caecilius [I 24 or 26] Metellus (Delmaticus ?, MRR 1,531), expelling 32 individuals from the Senate and forbidding lavish theatrical productions. He was *pontifex* until his death (perhaps in 104).

1 M. Holleaux, Études d'epigraphie et d'histoire grecques 2, 1938 2 Cl. Eilers, Cn. Domitius and Samos: A New Extortion Trial (IGR 4, 968), in: ZPE 89, 1991.

[I 4] D. Ahenobarbus, Cn. Son of D. [I 3]. *IIvir* at the colonial foundation at Narbo in 118 BC (?, [1. 94–96] coinage: RRC 282); 116 or 115 perhaps master of the mint (RRC 285). As people's tribune in 104 or 103 he wanted to succeed his father as *pontifex*, but failed; he proceeded to have a law passed replacing the existing system of co-option into the four priestly colleges with a plebiscite of 17 tribes; he brought an unsuccessful action against his opponent M. Aemilius [I 37] Scaurus (MRR 1,559). In 103 he was elected *pontifex maximus* and filled this post until his death *c.* 89. In 100 he took part (as *praetor* ?) in the struggle against L. Ap(p)uleius [I 11] Saturninus (Cic. Rab. perd. 21f.). Consul in 96 with C. Cassius [I 8] Longinus; *censor* in 92 with the orator L. → Licinius Crassus: although at loggerheads, they enacted a famous edict against the teaching of rhetoric in Latin (text in Suet. Gram. 25; Gell. NA 15,11,2; cf. Cic. De or. 3,24,93; Quint. Inst. 2,4,42; Tac. Dial. 35).

1 G.V. Sumner, The Orators in Cicero's Brutus, 1972.

[I 5] D. Ahenobarbus, Cn. Son of D. [I 4]; son-in-law of L. Cornelius [I 18] Cinna; in 82 ostracized by Sulla, he assembled an army in Africa with the backing of king Hiarbas, but in 81 was comprehensively defeated by Pompey, dying in the action (Plut. Pomp. 12).

[I 6] D. Ahenobarbus, Cn. Son of D. [I 8]. In 49 BC captured with his father by Caesar at Corfinium, both being pardoned (Caes. B Civ. 1,23,2); D. is nevertheless supposed to have been one of the conspirators in 44 (Suet. Ner. 3,1). From 44–42 he was the fleet commander of the murderers of Caesar (precise title unknown); in the autumn of 42 he defeated Cn. D. [I 10] Calvinus, and from then on bore the title of *imperator* (gold coinage: RRC 519); after Philippi he received his own command and fought very successfully against the triumvirate (siege of Brundisium), until in 40 he reconciled himself with M. Antonius [I 9], → Asinius Pollio acting as mediator (Vell. Pat. 2,73,2; 76,2). Under Antony's protection and against the initial opposition of Octavian (→ Augustus), his former rights were restored (gold coinage for Antonius: RRC 521), and until 34 (?) he was governor in Bithynia, in 36 taking part in Antony's campaign against the Parthians and in 35 supporting the governor of Asia, C. Furnius, against

Sex. Pompeius. In 32 with C. Sosius, another follower of Mark Antony, he occupied the consulacy already promised him in the peace of Misenum. Both men soon left Rome, and in March met Antony at Ephesus. D. turned emphatically against the influence of Cleopatra VII; although he had supreme command of a part of the fleet, already a sick man he went over to Octavian shortly before the battle of Actium in 31, and died shortly afterwards. (Vell. Pat. 2,84,2; Tac. Ann. 4,44; Suet. Ner. 3. Plut. Ant. 63,4). He or his son D. [II 2] dedicated a temple to Neptune *in circo Flaminio* (Plin. HN 36,4,26). His life was the subject of a tragedy by Curiatius Maternus (Tac. Dial. 3; Schanz/Hosius 2,524f.).

Syme, RR, Index s.v. D.

[I 7] D. Ahenobarbus, L. Son of D. [I 3]; younger brother of D. [I 4]; 97 BC (?) *praetor* in Sicily and 94 consul with C. Coelius [I 4] Caldus (MRR 2,12). As a follower of Sulla, in 82 he was murdered on the threshold of the Curia Hostilia by the Marians under the leadership of *praetor* L. → Iunius Brutus Damasippus (Vell. Pat. 2,26,2; Oros. 5,20,4 i.a.).

[I 8] D. Ahenobarbus, L. Son of D. [I 4]; probably the younger brother of D. [I 5]; father of D. [I 6]; bitter opponent of Caesar. In 73 BC he appeared in the case against the Oropians as counsel for the leaseholders (Sherk 23, l. 7), was a witness in the Verres trial in 70 (Cic. Verr. 2,1,139f.), and in 61 as curule *aedile* gave magnificent games (Plin. HN 8,131); with his brother-in-law M. → Porcius Cato he opposed Pompey and later also the triumvirate, so that in 59 he was denounced for alleged conspiracy against Pompey in the Vettius affair (Cic. Att. 2,24,3; Vatin. 25). In 58 as *praetor* he tried in vain to rescind Caesar's measures as consul. He had to abandon a sure campaign for the consulate for 55 because of the opposition of Pompey and Crassus, who in consequence of the Luca agreements wished themselves to take on the office for that year; but with Ap. Claudius [I 24] Pulcher he received it for 54; both consuls promised the election to the next candidates to the office, Cn. D. [I 10] Calvinus and C. → Memmius, which led to a scandal (Cic. Att. 4,15,7; 17,2). At the beginning of 52 he was reconciled with Pompey and became presiding *quaesitor* in the trial of Milo (Cic. Mil. 22). At the beginning of January 49 he was named as successor to Caesar's governorship (Caes. B Civ. 1,6,5). In February he assembled troops and attempted to hold up Caesar at Corfinium in the territory of the Paeligni, but failed entirely because he ignored Pompey's order to withdraw. He was captured by Caesar, but along with his son generously pardoned (Caes. B Civ. 1,15–23). D. soon proceeded to Massalia, where he took a leading part under D. Brutus and C. Trebonius in the fighting against the besieging army, but fled shortly before the fall of the city (Caes. B Civ. 1,34,2; 36,1f.; 56–59; 2,3–7; 22,2–4). He went to Pompey in Thessaly, on 9 August 48 led the left wing at Pharsalus, and was cut down during the rout (Caes. B Civ. 3,99,4f.; Cic. Phil. 2,29,71; Luc.

7,599ff. i.a.). Character portrayal in Ps.-Sall. epist. 2,9,2.

Gelzer, Caesar, Index s.v. D.; Gruen, Last Gen., Index s.v. D.

Domitii Calvini

[I 9] D. Calvinus, Cn. Consul 332 BC, (Liv. 8, 17,5; for the cognomen 'bald-headed', from *calvus*, see Kajanto, Cognomina 235).

[I 10] D. Calvinus, Cn. Opponent, later a follower of Caesar. 62 BC *legatus* in Asia; in 59 as people's tribune he supported the *cos.* M. Calpurnius [I 5] Bibulus, was *praetor* in 56 (Cic. Sest. 53,113) and gave magnificent *ludi Apollinares* (Cic. Att. 4,16,6; 17,3). In 54 he sought to obtain election as consul by bribing the incumbent consuls. The elections did not take place, but after the interregnum at the beginning of 53 he did become consul for the 2nd half of that year (MRR 2,227f.). He then went over to Caesar, in 48 fought in Greece against Q. Caecilius [I 32] Metellus Pius and led the centre of Caesar's army at Pharsalus (Caes. B Civ. 3,89,3). He then went to Asia Minor, where he was defeated by Pharnaces at Nicopolis, but held out in the province of Asia (Bell. Alex. 34–40; MRR 2,277). After Caesar's victory at Zela in 47 D. forced Pharnaces to capitulate at Sinope (MRR 2,88f.). In 46 he supported Caesar in Africa (Bell. Afr. 86,3; 93,1). In 45 in Rome he appeared as a witness for the defence on behalf of Deiotarus and swore to a treaty between Rome and Cnidus (IKnidos 33). Perhaps in 45 he became *pontifex*, and it was probably in this function that he received Caesar and the *haruspex* Spurinna at his house on the morning of 15 March 44 (Val. Max. 8,11,2). In 42 he was to bring reinforcements to Mark Antony and Octavian from Brundisium, but was comprehensively defeated by L. Staius Murcus and Cn. D. [I 6] Ahenobarbus (App. B Civ. 479–487; MRR 2,363). In 40 he was *cos. II* with C. Asinius [I 4] Pollio. As governor in Spain 39–36 he fought against the Pyrenean tribes, was victorious at Osca and took on the title of *imperator* (coins: RRC 532), celebrating a triumph in 36 (InscrIt 13,1,87; inscr. evidence of a votive offering from the booty: ILS 42). From the booty he rebuilt the burnt-out Regia on the Forum (Cass. Dio 48,42,4–6). He is probably attested in 21 as a member of the prominent college of the *fratres Arvales*, and had perhaps previously been their *magister* (CIL VI 32338; cf. CIL I² p. 214f.; [2. 42f.]); he probably died soon after. PIR² D 139.

1 Syme, RR, Index, s.v. D. 2 Scheid, Recrutement, 42f. 3 Syme, AA, Index, s.v. D.

[I 11] D. Calvinus, M. *Praetor* 80 BC (?) and governor of Spain, where he was defeated and killed on the Anas by troops of Sertorius under the *quaestor* L. Hirtuleius (Sall. Hist. 1,111M; Liv. Per. 90; Plut. Sert. 12,3f. i.a.).

C.F. Konrad, Plutarch's Sertorius, 1994, 130f.

[I 12] D. Calvinus Maximus, Cn. Son of D. [I 9]. His office as curule *aedile* in 299 BC (Piso fr. 28 HRR in Liv. 10,9,12; Plin. HN 33,17) is disputed (MRR 1,173). As consul in 283 he fought successfully with his colleague P. Cornelius [I 27] Dolabella against the Celts. In 280 D. was the first plebeian *censor* (Liv. Per. 13), and probably at the same time *dictator* for the holding of elections, which is singular (InscrIt 13,1,41; MRR 1,191; [1. 515, n. 1]).

1 Mommsen, Staatsrecht, vol. 1. K.-L.E.

II. Imperial period

[II 1] Cn. D. Ahenobarbus. Son of D. [II 2] and Antonia the elder; related to Augustus through his grandmother Octavia. Born on 11 December, year unknown. Supposedly *comes* to Gaius Caesar in the east, but on grounds of age this is highly problematical (Suet. Nero 5,1; cf. [1]). He is attested as *frater Arvalis* in 27, 33, 38 and 39. In 28 Tiberius married him to Agrippina the younger; in 32 as consul he held the *fasces* for 12 months, which was unusual. In 36 he was a member of a commission for the evaluation of fire damage in Rome. In 37 at the instigation of the praetorian prefect Sertorius Macro he was accused of incest with his sister Lepida. Shortly after the death of Tiberius, Agrippina bore him Nero, the emperor to be. He probably died in the year 40. Nero had the *fratres Arvales* make an annual sacrifice in front of his father's house on the *via sacra*. Tradition has him a person of inferior character (Suet. Nero 5,1; Quint. 6,1,50). PIR² D 127.

1 Scheid, Frères 137ff.

[II 2] L.D. Ahenobarbus. Son of Cn. D. [I 6] Ahenobarbus; married to Antonia the elder, niece of Augustus. A patrician probably from 29 BC, in 16 BC he became consul; he staged his magnificent games with such cruelty that Augustus sent him a warning. He was proconsul of Africa in 12 BC [1]. As legate of Illyricum he advanced as far as the Elbe; subsequently he was probably commander of the army in Germania, where he tried in vain to return the Cherusci to their tribal homelands. Attested as *frater Arvalis*. Died in 25. His children are D. [II 1] and Domitia [1] and [5].

1 Thomasson, Fasti Africani, 1996, 21f.

PIR² D 128; Scheid, Frères, 74ff.; Syme, AA 141ff. and *passim*.

[II 3] L.D. Ahenobarbus. Son of D. [II 1] → Nero. W.E.

[II 4] D. Alexander. *vicarius Africae* under → Maxentius (Aur. Vict. Caes. 40,17; Zos. 2,12,2); seized imperial power in AD 308, presumably in connection with the rift between Maxentius and his father. D. was unable to ally himself with any of the opponents of Maxentius, even though he sought recognition by Constantine (ILS 8936). His power remained restricted to Africa; his possession of Sardinia can only have been for a short period (AE 1966, 169). In 309 or 310 D. was defeated by Maxentius' *praef. praet.* → Ceionius [8] Rufius Volusianus. B.BL.

[II 5] **D. Antigonus.** Equestrian from Macedonia; son of one Philippus. *Tribunus militum* and *procurator*; received into the praetorians by Caracalla. Legate of the *legio XXII Primigenia* (*c.* 220) and *V Macedonica*. *Cos. suff.* under Severus Alexander; consular legate of Moesia inferior 235/236 (AE 1966, 262; CIL III 14429; AE 1964, 180; PIR² A 736). Two texts from Rome perhaps relate to him [1].

1 A. Illuminati, in: Iscrizioni Greche e Latine del Foro Romano e del Palatino, ed. by S. Panciera, 1996, 208ff. no. 64. 2 Leunissen, 183.

[II 6] **L. D. Apollinaris.** Senator from Vercellae, to whom presumably IGR III 558 = TAM II 569 can be assigned (but cf. [1]). He was then legate of two legions, *praef. aerarii militaris* and between 93 and 96 legate of Lycia-Pamphylia. Suffect consul July-August 97 [2]. Married twice, latterly to Valeria Vetilla, daughter of Valerius Patruinus, *cos. suff.* 82. His sons were D. [II 20] and [II 23], his daughters Domitia [12] and one Valeria Polla. PIR² D 133.

1 M. A. Speidel, in: MH 47, 1990, 149ff. 2 Vidman, FO² 45.

Syme, RP 7, 588ff.

[II 7] **D. Balbus.** Senator of praetorian rank, attributed a counterfeit will by his relative Valerius Fabianus (Tac. Ann. 14,40,1).

[II 8] **D. Caecilianus.** An intimate friend of Clodius Thrasea, in AD 66 he brought him the Senate's death sentence (Tac. Ann. 16,34,1).

[II 9] **D. Celer.** *Comes* to the governor of Syria, Cn. Calpurnius Piso, to whom he lent vigorous support in his attempt to win back Syria in the autumn of AD 19 (Tac. Ann. 2,77–79). He was presumably already dead by the time of Piso's trial in December 20 [1].

1 W. Eck, A. Caballos, F. Fernández, Das s.c. de Cn. Pisone patre, 1996, 98.

[II 10] **Cn. D. Corbulo.** From Peltuinum; born perhaps between 30 and 25 BC [1. 810]. *Quaestor* in Asia under Augustus, later *praetor* (not in AD 17). In AD 21 in the Senate he attacked the *curatores viarum* and building contractors for mismanagement with regard to road maintenance; trials and sentences followed (Tac. Ann. 3,31). Dio Cassius 59,15,3 has a similar account for the year 39; apparently Caligula channelled the proceeds to his own account, and made Corbulo consul. The account of the consulacy at least is now generally related to the son, D. [II 12] [1. 809f.; 2]. Under Claudius he was compelled to pay back a part of the proceeds from the trials [3]. Married to Vistilia, Plin. HN 7,39; Caligula married her daughter Caesonia in 39. PIR² D 141.

1 Syme, RP 2 2 Vogel-Weidemann, 373ff. W. Eck, Die staatliche Organisation Italiens in der hohen Kaiserzeit, 1979, 71f. W.E.

[II 11] **Cn. D. Corbulo.** From Peltuinum; son of D. [II 10] and Vistilia (Plin. HN 7,39), thus half-brother of Milonia Caesonia, Caligula's wife (cf. in this regard, as well as for his wider, substantial circle of relations [1. 805ff.]). It is probably through her mediation that he received a suffect consulate in AD 39 (cf. in this regard D. [II 10]); there is no evidence of earlier offices held. Claudius appointed him legate to the army of Lower Germany, where he is attested for the year 47 [2. 117ff.]. There he proceeded successfully against the Chauci; he had their leader Gannascus murdered, which later became the cause of a new uprising. He resettled the Frisii and gave them a new political structure. But, as Corbulo was supposedly too successful, Claudius ordered the bases on the right bank of the Rhine to be relinquished; this was presumably to avoid more substantial military entanglements. Corbulo nevertheless received the *ornamenta triumphalia* for building a canal between the Maas and the Rhine. It was only after a long period out of office that he became proconsul of Asia, still under Claudius, perhaps 52/53 [3. 372ff.]. As early as 54 he was appointed by Nero to apply the new policy towards Armenia and Parthia. The official position he held is disputed. He may have been *legatus Augusti pro praetore*, thus governor of Armenia, or may have received a military command (regarding which [4. 201ff.]). After arriving in the east in 55 Corbulo proceeded militarily against Armenia, although no spectacular battles were fought. This was celebrated in Rome as a conclusive victory. A new client king, Tigranes, was installed in Armenia; Corbulo was made governor of Syria. When the Parthians reconquered Armenia and re-installed Tiridates as their client king, → Caesennius Paetus was entrusted with command in Armenia. It was only after his defeat, for which Corbulo's inaction was partly to blame, that conduct of the war was returned to Corbulo; he was granted extraordinary powers over all office-bearers in the east. C. himself was soon consular legate of Cappadocia-Galatia, if C. Iulius Proculus was at the same time financial procurator of Cappadocia and Cilicia (AE 1966, 472; 1914, 128), and Rutilius Gallicus deputy governor in Galatia (I. Eph. III 715). Eventually, following an offer by the Parthians, the old client king Tiridates was formally recognized by Nero in Rome, without Corbulo's having had to assert himself militarily (cf. [4. 86–135]). Corbulo is therefore in no way to be regarded as the splendidly successful soldier and far-sighted politician, prevented by his opponents from achieving complete success. But this view was promulgated in Corbulo's writings, and became established in historiography. Corbulo remained in the east until 66/67, until Nero called him to Greece, where he killed himself on the emperor's orders. It is presumed that the grounds were his involvement in the conspiracy against Nero by his son-in-law Annius Vinicianus [3. 385ff.]. One of his daughters, Domitia Longina, later became the wife of Domitian. PIR² D 142.

1 SYME, RP II 2 ECK, Statthalter 3 VOGEL-WEIDEMANN 4 M. HEIL, Die oriental. Außenpolitik des Kaisers Nero, 1997.

[II 12] T. D. Decidianus/Decidius. Regarding the form of the name see CIL VI 1403 and [1]. Senator from Narbonensis, who after serving his three years as *quaestor aerarii Saturni* rose to the praetorship under Claudius (CIL VI 1403 = ILS 966). Probably the father of Domitia Decidiana; father-in-law of Agricola (Tac. Agr. 6,1). The customs statute of 62 refers to his conditions for leasing the customs franchise in Asia ([1], it also gives the cognomen Decidianus, otherwise Decidius).

[II 13] C. D. Dexter. Suffect consul probably during the final years of Marcus Aurelius; consular governor of Syria, attested for 189. 193 city prefect, probably until 196, when he received a second consulate; he must therefore have been a close follower of Septimius Severus. PIR² D 144.

1 ENGELMANN-KNIBBE, in: Epigr. Anat. 14, 1989, 20, 38.

LEUNISSEN, 308. W.E.

[II 14] L. D. Domitianus. Egyptian usurper from the tetrarchic period, known only from papyri and coins; his uprising is to be dated to AD 296/297 or 297/298. Literary sources (Aur. Vict. Caes. 39,23 and 38; Eutr. 9,22,1 and 23; [Aur. Vict.] Epit. Caes. 39,3) mention only D.'s supporter, the equestrian *corrector* Aurelius Achilleus (P Cairo Isid. 62; P Michigan 220). Diocletian put down the revolt by conquering Alexandria (Eutr. 9,23). B.BL.

[II 15] L. D. Gallicanus Papinianus. Originating from Vina in Africa, consul probably in 238; thereafter governor in Dalmatia, Hispania citerior and Germania inferior; in what order is unknown. PIR² D 148.

ECK, Statthalter 216.

[II 16] M. Aurelius L. D. Honoratus. Procurator of Arabia between 212 and 217; honoured in Gerasa with his wife Aurelia Iulia Heraclia. 221/222 *praef. Aegypti*, thereafter praetorian prefect; he is listed in the Album of Canusium as *clarissimus vir* (AE 1993, 1641). PIR² D 151.

R. HAENSCH, in: ZPE 95, 1993, 163ff.

[II 17] D. Leo Procillianus. Governor of Syria Phoenice in 207; as he is called *hypatikós*, he may already have received a suffect consulate (AE 1969/70, 610; IGLS VII 4016 bis). Probably to be identified with the city prefect Leo under Elagabal (Cass. Dio 79,14,2).

W. ECK, s.v. D. 63), RE Suppl. 14, 114; LEUNISSEN, 311.

[II 18] Cn. D. Lucanus = Cn. D. Afer Titius Marcellus Curvius Lucanus. He and his brother D. [II 25] were adopted by the senator D. Afer, and in 59 inherited his fortune (Plin. Ep. 8,18,5ff.). D.'s career comes down to us in CIL XI 5210 = ILS 990 and IRT 527 (for an interpretation [1; 2]). Begins his career under Nero, takes part in the Batavian war as *praef. auxiliorum omnium adversus Germanos*, receiving the *dona militaria* under Vespasian; given patrician status; praetorian legate in Africa, suffect consul under Vespasian, proconsul of Africa under Domitian, then legate to his brother in the same province. An equestrian statue was erected to him in Lepcis Magna (IRT 527). His daughter Domitia Lucilla was adopted by his brother Tullus so that she could come into the inheritance of her grandfather Curtilius Mancia. PIR² D 152.

1 G. ALFÖLDY, Die Hilfstruppen, 1969, 131ff. 2 THOMASSON, Fasti Africani, 1996, 46ff.

[II 19] L. D. Paris. Slave, later a freedman of Domitia [1]. Pantomime artist. A friend of Nero. In 55 on the instructions of Domitia he prosecuted Agrippina of high treason. Although the case failed, he suffered no consequences. In 56 he brought a court case against his patroness (Dig. 12,4,3,5). In 67 he was executed by Nero, because he was supposedly unable to teach him to dance. PIR² D 156.

[II 19a] see → Paris [3] (see Addenda)

[II 20] D. Patruinus. Son of D. [II 6]. Father of Domitia [13] (CIL V 6657 = ILS 6741a)

SYME, RP 7, 588f.

[II 20a] D. Peregrinus. *Procurator ad Mercurium* in Alexandria [1] in AD 161 (POxy. 4060, 40–42), replaced by Manius Severus.

[II 21] D. Philippus. From Macedonia; father of D. [II 5], cf. [1].

1 A. ILLUMINATI, in: Iscrizioni Greche e Latine del Foro Romano e del Palatino, ed. by S. PANCIERA, 1996, 208ff. no. 64.

[II 22] Cn. D. Ponticus. Praetorian legate to the proconsul of Africa, Paccius Africanus, in 77/78 (IRT 342).

[II 23] D. Seneca. Son of D. [II 6]; cf. AE 1981, 826c. Military tribune to the *legio XVI Flavia* (IGR III 559 = TAM II 570). Married to Clodia Decmina (AE 1981, 826e). Father of D. [II 24].

[II 24] D. Seneca. Son of D [II 23]. Legate of Lycia-Pamphylia 135–138 (IGR III 738 c. 24).

W. ECK, in: Chiron 12, 1982, 174 n. 431; M. WÖRRLE, Stadt und Fest, 1988, 39, 43.

[II 24a] M. D. Tertius. Equestrian office-holder; after positions of military service, e.g. as *tribunus* and *praepositus*, he became *procurator* of Cyrenae (patrimonial procurator, not praesidial procurator), *procurator* of Moesia superior, *procurator et praefectus provinciae Sardiniae*, probably in AD 208/9. (CIL X 7517; 8025; ILSard. I 15; [1] = AE 1928, 117; 1971, 123 = 1974, 359).

1 A. TARAMELLI, in: Notizie degli Scavi 1927, 257–261.

R. ZUCCA, Un nuovo procurator provinciae Cyrenarum, in: E. CATANI, S. M. MARENGO (ed.), La Cirenaica in età antica, 1998, 623 ff. W. E.

[II 25] Cn. D. Tullus = Cn. D. Afer Titius Marcellus Curvius Tullus. Brother of D. [II 18]; like him adopted by D. Afer. His career comes down to us in CIL XI 5211 = ILS 991 and IRT 528 (Lepcis Magna). In the Senate from the time of Nero, took part as *praef. equitum* in the fighting against the Batavi. Even before his tenure of the praetorate he was sent as imperial legate to the army in the province of Africa; given patrician status; probably consul under Vespasian; proconsul of Africa under Domitian; a monumental equestrian statue was erected to him at the time in Lepcis Magna (IRT 528). He adopted his brother's daughter Domitia Lucilla, who also became his chief heiress (Plin. Ep. 8,18). The will CIL VI 10229 and AE 1976, 77 = [1], drawn up between May and August 108, is to be attributed to him; he died shortly afterwards.

1 W. Eck, in: ZPE 30, 1978, 277ff.

Syme, RP 5, 521ff.; di Vita-Evrard, in: Epigrafia juridica Romana, 1989, 159ff.

[II 26] M. D. Valerianus. Senator honoured in Prusias in Bithynia, AE 1957, 44 = SEG 20, 28: he went through the gamut of public offices up to *praetor*, then became legate to the *legio XII Fulminata* and the *legio VII Claudia; corrector civitatium Pamphyliae, proconsul Siciliae*, praetorian legate of Galatia, then of Cilicia, finally in 238/9 of Arabia, where he presumably became suffect consul *in absentia*. AE 1907, 67; PIR[2] D 168.

Dietz, 143ff.; W. Eck, s.v. D. 85), RE Suppl. 14, 114.

W.E.

III. Orators and writers

[III 1] Cn. D. Afer. Latin orator of the Claudian period, treated in Suetonius' *De oratoribus* (cf. Jer. Chron. a. Abr. 2060). Born in Nemausus (Nîmes) in modest circumstances; AD 25 *praetor*, subsequently becoming prominent as a prosecutor (Tac. Ann. 4,52 with general assessment; 4,66). In 39 his astuteness saved him from a dangerous situation, to the extent that he was even appointed suffect consul (Cass. Dio 59,19f.; with A. Didius Gallus, cf. [3]); from 49 he was *curator aquarum* (Frontin. Aq. 102, 8f.); particularly active under Claudius as a defense counsel; died in 59 of gluttony (Hier.; cf. Tac. Ann. 14,19). His brickworks (CIL XV 979–983) went to his adoptive sons (Plin. Ep. 8,18,5ff.). D. was regarded as the leading orator of his time (Tac. Dial. 13,3; Quint. Inst. 10,1,118 next to the *veteres*). Besides quick-witted epigrams, his pupil → Quintilianus (Inst. 10,1,86 and *passim*; Plin. Ep. 2,14,10) emphasizes his *maturitas* (12,10,11), the *grave et lentum* (Plin. Ep. 2,14,10ff.) of his style. His rejection of the practices of modern → Declamation shows him to be a proponent of *eloquentia incorrupta* (Tac. Dial. 15,3).

Works (only fragments extant): (1) Speeches: confirmed titles (cf. also Tac. Ann. 4,52,1; 4,66) *Pro Cloatilla* (Quint. Inst.), *Pro Voluseno Catulo* (10,1,24), *Pro Laelia* (9,4,31), *Pro Taurinis* (Charis. p. 184 B.). (2) Several bks. of *Urbane dicta* from the speeches (Quint. Inst. 6,3,42, and many quotations; Jer. Ep. 52,7, cf. [4]), published after 41. (3) Two bks. *De testibus* (Quint. Inst. 5,7,7).

Fragments: H. Meyer, ORF [2]1842, 563–570.
Bibliography: 1 PIR D[2] 126 2 Bardon 2,158f. 3 J.W. Humphrey, P.M. Swan, Cassius Dio on the Suffect Consuls of A.D. 39, in: Phoenix 37, 1983, 324–327 4 R.S. Rogers, Domitius Afer's Defence of Cloatilla, in: TAPhA 76, 1945, 264–270 5 W.C. McDermott, Saint Jerome and Domitius Afer, in: VChr 34, 1980, 19–22.

P.L.S.

[III 2] D. Marsus. Writer of epigrams; a contemporary of Ovid (Pont. 4,16,5), probably to be identified with the addressee of a letter from Apollodorus, teacher of rhetoric to Augustus (Quint. Inst. 3,1,18); according to Mart. 8,55(56), 21ff a protégé of Maecenas. → Martial's frequent naming of him (B. 1 praef. named i.a. as his model; regarding Catullus, D. and Albinovanus Pedo cf. also 5,5,6; Catullus and D. 2,71,3; 7,99,7; D. and Pedo 2,77,5f.) gives us an idea of D.'s significance for the art of the literary → epigram in Rome. The few extant fragments allow only an outline reconstruction of his work. From a *Cicuta* come four distichs (fr. 1): → Bavius (with Mevius, cf. Hor. Epod. 10,2 with fr. 5 — an *obtrectator Vergilii*) and his brother, the concord between them dissolved by a woman, are subjected to ridicule. Involvement in literary feuds of the period also shows the caustic side of the grammarians → Orbilius (Suet. Gram. 9,3 = fr. 4) and → Caecilius Epirota (16,3 = fr.3); from the *Cicuta* also frgg. incl. 40 folios (cf. [10])? The title 'Hemlock' indicates a book of scoptic, 'satirical' epigrams, whereas poems treating other themes were probably collected in other books: the *Fusca Melaenis* read by Maecenas (Mart. 7,29,7f.) indicates epigrams of erotic content; examples of → funerary epigrams are the oration to Tibullus (fr. 7), whose first lines are a variation on Tib. 1,3,57f., and the two distichs on Atia, mother of Augustus (fr. 8f., regarding which [7]). If Martial 4,29 apologizes for the *turba* of his *libelli*, regarding the *Amazonis* v. 7f. as opposed to the *liber* of Persius he also alludes to a number of books of epigrams (regarding substantial epigrams also 2,77,5f.), not to an epic. Finally, whether the 9 books of *Fabellae* (fr. 2) comprise a collected edition is uncertain. Regarding witty aphorisms from a rhetorical text *De urbanitate*, Quintilian has critical comments in *De risu* (inst. 6,3,102–109; already used previously, cf. [8; 9]), cf. also Plin. HN 34 ind. auct.; 34,48.

Fr.: D. Fogazza, 1981 FPL [3]278–283 (bibl. 278f.) Courtney, 300–305.
Research papers: 1 L. Lombardi, in: BSL 7, 1977, 343–358 2 L. Duret, ANRW II.30,3, 1480–1487.
Bibliography: 3 A. Traglia, Poeti latini dell'età giulio-claudia misconosciuti, in: C&S; 26 (101), 1987, 44–53 4 S. Mariotti, Intorno a Domitius Marsus, in: FS A. Rostagni, 1963, 588–614 5 E. Paratore, Ancora su Domitius Marsus, in: RCCM 6, 1964, 64–96 6 F. della Corte et al., Domitius Marsus, in: Maia 16, 1964, 377–388; 17, 1965, 248–270 7 M. Lausberg, Zu einem Epi-

gramm des Domitius Marsus auf die Mutter des Augustus, in: ΜΟΥΣΙΚΟΣ ΑΝΗΡ. FS M. Wegner, 1992, 259–268 8 E.S. Ramage, The De urbanitate of Domitius Marsus, in: CPh 54, 1959, 250–255 9 F. Kühnert, Quintilians Erörterung über den Witz, in: KS, 1994, 111–143 (first publ. 1962) 10 R. Reggiani, Un epigramma di Domitius Marsus in Quintiliano?, in: Prometheus 7, 1981, 43–49. P.L.S.

Domnacus see → Dumnacus

Domnilaus (Δομνέκλειος; *Domnékleios*). Celtic name; tetrarch of the Trocmi, the son and successor of Brogitarus [1. 1303; 2. 155]. D. was killed on Pompey's side at Pharsalus in 49 BC. After the death of Deiotarus his territory was awarded to his son Adiatorix by Antony but Augustus had him executed after the battle of Actium (Caes. B Civ. 3,4,5; Str. 12,3,6).
→ Antonius [I 9]; → Brogitarus; → Deiotarus; → Trocmi

1 Holder, vol. 1 2 L. Weisgerber, Galatische Sprachreste, in: Natalicium. FS J. Geffken 1931. W.SP.

Domus As the term for house, *domus* is etymologically derived from the Indo-European root **dem*, which conferred the idea of 'building' but also had a personal and a religious meaning. However, while in Greek the term *dómos* was restricted to the fabric of the building, the social connotations prevailed in Latin *domus*. This is, for example, evident in the rigidified locative *domi*, which in its terminological field of meaning unified both the idea of the social home and a state of peace and as such was the opposite of the state of war, *militiae*. The house and the community of cohabitation united in it were the critical locus of protection from an outside world that was considered hostile and from which Romans believed they were separated by the door posts (*ianua*). As a result, the domestic sphere took an important place in the religious ideas of the Romans (*di penates*).

It is telling that the cultic space of the early *rex* was called *domus regia,* which points to the role of the house as a metaphor for the social edifice. The cohabitation of several generations, the exercise of a joint ancestor cult and the focussing of material subsistence, which was transferred by laws of succession from one generation to the next, resulted in the *domus* increasingly acquiring the meaning of social origin, kinship and legal descent. However, the terminology remained imprecise because on the one hand both ancestors and descendants could be included, but on the other hand maternal and paternal relatives were not distinguished.

In the course of the terminological differentiation, *domus* with its concentration on true relatives was juxtaposed to the *familia*, which was primarily defined by the inclusion of slaves and other dependents. While originally, *familia* was the typical expression for the most influential aristocratic family associations, this meaning had been transferred to the *domus* in the late Republic. This emphasized the function of the houses of the *nobiles* as important centres for political decisions. It also levelled the ground for transferring the term to the imperial court (*domus Caesaris*). In the course of this development, *domus* acquired an ambivalence that is typical for court-related terminology: for one, it meant the concentration of important persons at the ruler's place of residence, for another, the representation of the claim to power in the exalted architectural design. In the course of the 2nd cent. AD the expression *domus Caesaris* was replaced by the Greek *aula*.
→ Familia; → Lares; → Penates

G. Buti, The Family and the Tribe, in: W. Meid (ed.), Studien zum indogermanischen Wortschatz, 1987, 9–20; R. Saller, Patriarchy, property and death in the Roman family, 1994; D. Wachsmuth, Aspekte des antiken mediterranen Hauskults, in: Numen 27, 1980, 34–75. B.LI.

Domus Augustana see → Mons Palatinus

Domus Aurea As the successor building of the → *domus transitoria*, which was destroyed in the fire of AD 64, the *domus aurea* (DA) was still uncompleted at the time of Otho (Suet., Otho 7). Its main aspects were the extensive expropriation and inclusion of public space and the mobilization of all technical and artistic means in shaping an artificial world. After Nero's death the main areas, apart from the Palatine, were systematically returned to public use by the Flavians and Hadrian.

The DA included the Palatine, the Oppius, the Caelius and the Velia. The city wall of the 4th cent. BC may have constituted its southern and eastern limits. In the north and east the area seems to have stretched from the outer limits of the *domus* in the Giardino Rivaldi to the still preserved remains under S. Pietro in Vincoli and the garden of the Palazzo Brancacci but exempted the Porticus Liviae. Preserved remains can be attributed with varying degrees of certainty. The Neronian understorey of the → *arcus Constantini* may be considered a possible monumental entrance. The *vestibulum* should, at least in general opinion, be identified with the *porticus triplices miliariae* mentioned by Suetonius and, therefore, would be a large square bordered on three sides by colonnades located in the area of the temple of Venus and Roma (SHA. Hadr. 19,12) that was to contain the *c.* 40 m tall bronze statue of Nero (Plin. HN 34,45; Suet. Nero 31; Mart. Epigr. 2); cf. → Colossus Neronis. Remains of porticoes can be seen along the *sacra via* near the *clivus Palatinus* and the *clivus ad Carinas*. Recent excavations have confirmed its dating to Nero's reign. However, the interpretation of older structures in the podium of the temple of Venus and Roma is hypothetical.

Facilities that belonged to the artificial lake in the valley between the Caelius, Esquiline and Palatine (Tac. Ann. 15,42; Suet. Nero 31; with location: Mart. 2,5) have been stratigraphically dated in excavations at the

Meta Sudans to the phase after the fire of AD 64 but before the construction of the → Colosseum (AD 70–80). These are substructures of areas bordering on an east-west street and possibly bore porticoes. In the area of the later Meta Sudans (after AD 80) the street entered a north-south route. These areas extended close to the lake and possibly were meant to provide a view. The lake was probably fed from the Caelius, perhaps by the Nympheum on the Caelius, which was a reshaping of the substructures of the Claudius temple.

The most important and largest preserved parts are located on the Oppius, the south-western extension of the Esquiline, now covered by the substructures of the Baths of Trajan. A series of important innovations can for the first time be observed here at a qualitatively high level, but they are not necessarily all new inventions. On the lower floor, which had been known for some time, the existence of a second polygonal inner court has been demonstrated so that the part known so far can be symmetrically completed and the octagonal hall was shown to be the central axis of the tract. The opening in its vault shows arrangements for mechanical systems and may be identified with the well-known rotating sky dome. The western part of the tract was possibly already under construction before the fire of AD 64. Rooms 123 and 125 beside the octagonal hall are among the oldest examples of cross vaults (→ Vaults and arches, construction of) in Roman architecture. Parts of the upper floor were uncovered above the octagon and the inner court adjoining to the east. No round shapes were used there. Instead, the transitions were evened out by using triangular compartments that served as *impluvia* or contained rectangular exedras. A separation of round and rectangular systems by floor is typical for the manner in which forms were handled in the DA. Plans similarly rich in variation and change are unknown from earlier villas.

The remains in the *domus Augustana* (→ Mons Palatinus) have been known since the excavations of Pirro Ligorio but remained unidentified. There the buildings of the DA remained in use to AD 80 and were then destroyed by another large fire (Tac. Ann. 15,52). In many areas the layout of Domitian's new residence made use of the ruins from Nero's reign. However, for the *cenatio Iovis* a round building with two concentric circular foundations within a rectangular water basin was taken down. It represented a kind of precursor to the Teatro marittimo in the *villa Hadriana* at Tivoli. For the western part of this complex, the underlying nymphaeum of the *domus transitoria* had already been destroyed in Nero's time. Likewise, the *aula regia* followed the design of two large precursor rooms. At the transition from the lower to the upper peristyle, two symmetrical groups of rooms of Neronian origin as well as the outer walls of the lower garden and the walls along the eastern outer suite were found.

The furnishings of the DA were already legendary among contemporaries; of these, the famous 'grotesques' of the murals were the first to receive attention

during the Renaissance. More recently, the sizeable remains of the stucco work, mosaic murals (→ Stucco; → Mosaic) and marble incrustations applied in masterful combinations have been recorded. The → murals of the Fourth Style, whose creation is now no longer attributed to the DA alone, but at least they achieved a grandiose appearance in this large project. Their playful, condensed joy in detail was a complement to the room structure.

The surrounding landscape was not only used as a view (Tac. Ann. 15,42 mentions the *arva et stagna et in modum solitudinum hinc silvae, inde aperta spatia et prospectus*) but was also the object of a demonstrative remodelling. New excavations have shown that the southern extensions of the Velia and the northern ones of the Palatine were removed for the sake of the *vestibulum*, and that the north-west slope of the Palatine, which was oriented towards the Forum Romanum, received a large substructure for establishing a terraced garden.

Tradition and innovation are the prerequisite for an overall understanding which has hitherto been barely possible. Already the → *domus transitoria*, its immediate predecessor, extended from the Palatine to the Esquiline. Before it and contemporaneously there were more, ever larger *domi* that occupied the areas adjoining the Palatine and the Forum Romanum. There, however, the true predecessors were the *horti* of the city of Rome and especially the residences of Hellenistic rulers with their incorporations of public space. However, there the public functions were retained unlike at the DA (→ Palace).

With the exclusion of all aspects relating to public policy and their transfer into a more comprehensive view of the world purely focussed on the emperor, traditions experienced a profound reinterpretation For one, the exquisitely artful forms of architecture were enhanced by furnishings of a degree of material luxury that overshadowed everything else — particular conspicuous were the technical 'simulations' of the notorious (Sen. Ep. 90) *magistri et machinatores* Severus and Celer (Tac. Ann. 15, 42), which ranged from showers of flowers and small-scale model towns on the shore of the *stagnum* to thermal baths with their own sea and fresh water aqueducts (to the Palatine and the Caelius) and culminated in a revolving 'sky dome' above the round dinner hall on the Oppius (Suet. Nero 31). But apart from this, the Colossus Neronis must have been accorded its semantic place in this system as well. Aspects of the world were concentrated here and made available to its 'user' Nero in a kind of permanent staging. This is also a tradition in Roman villa culture, though man and nature were usually juxtaposed in a general manner. In the DA not nature but the earthly world and the cosmos as a whole were meant to appear and to be related to a single person. This new orientation of traditional ways of thought, makes it comprehensible that Nero believed he would finally be able to live 'like a human being' (Suet. Nero 31): in rural solitude with a rare domestic and wild animal fauna, the 'latest technical achievements', a collection of art works and the famous paintings of Fabullus (Plin. HN 35,120). A similarly complex ensemble was not again achieved until the *villa Hadriana*.

How negatively the occupation of public urban space was viewed by contemporaries (Mart. Epigr. 2; Suet. Nero 39) is demonstrated in the treatment of the DA after Nero's death. The Colosseum was placed into the area of the *stagnum*. The *vestibulum* was opened as a thoroughfare to create a link between the Velia and the Colosseum valley and under Hadrian the temple of Venus and Roma took its place. The works of art placed into the DA were returned to the public by Vespasian, who had them put into the *templum pacis* (Plin. HN 34,84). On the Palatine Domitian began building the *domus Flavia* (→ Mons Palatinus) after the fire of AD 80 and eliminated the remains of the DA, though they continued to determine the layout. The Oppius, on which some of the most important buildings were located, was turned over to a new public use by the Baths of Titus and later the Baths of Trajan, which practically buried the building suite in its substructures.

M. Bergmann, Der Koloß Neros, die Domus Aurea und der Mentalitätswandel im Rom der frühen Kaiserzeit. Trierer Winckelmann-Programm 13, 1993; A. Cassatella et al., in: LTUR 3, 1995, 49–64; Richardson, 119–121 (bibliography). R.F.

Domus Laterani In the written sources an *aedes Lateranorum* by Plautius Lateranus, the designated consul of the year 65, is attested in Rome during the Neronian period (Juv. 10,15,18; more regarding location near the Lateran basilica later: Jer. Ep. 77,4). An *aedes Laterani* (Ps.-Aur. Vict. Epit. 20,6) was created when Septimius Severus donated the *aedes Parthorum* to his senior commander T. Sextius Lateranus (PIR[1] S 469). Three water pipelines (CIL XV 7536) bearing the names of Sextius Lateranus and his brother Sextius Torquatus (PIR[1] S 478) were found in 1595 near the Lateran Basilica, enabling an approximate localization. Whether it is the same building as the Neronian one is as uncertain as its identification with preserved building remains. Possible candidates are the remains of two (judging from the building technique) post-Neronian *domi* that lie below the *castra equitum singularium*, which were in its turn covered by the Lateran Basilica, and a house with trapezoid outline behind the apse of the Lateran basilica that is clearly later. However, the *aedes Parthorum* existed before this storehouse.

P. Liverani, in: LTUR 3, 1995, 127; Richardson, 129–130. R.F.

Domus Tiberiana see → Mons Palatinus

Domus transitoria In the period of his reign before the great fire of AD 64, which was followed by the building of the → *domus aurea*, Nero combined the *horti Maecenatis* on the Esquiline (→ Esquiliae) with the palatial buildings on the Palatine (→ Mons Palatinus) (Suet. Nero 31; Tac. Ann. 15,39). Preserved are a building section of the *domus Tiberiana*, walls at the sunken peristyle as well as under the *aula regia* and the *cenatio Iovis* of the later Flavian palace. The affinity of an elaborate vaulted hall in the terraces of the Hadrianic temple of Venus and Roma by the Velia is disputed. A qualitatively outstanding testimony for the quality of the furnishings are the 'Bagni di Livia', a possibly hypaethral complex that was already sunk in before overbuilding by the *cenatio Iovis* and which could only be reached by stairs. Virtually symmetrical resting rooms with small staggered back wall niches and a pair of small rooms along their sides opened into both its east and west side. On the south side a series of columns was set up on a paving of large stones. This has been interpreted as a pavilion over a *triclinium*. The north side of the court was occupied by a nymphaeum structure in the style of a *scenae frons*, which rises above a flat water basin. The porphyry and serpentine columns possessed Corinthian capitals made of gilded bronze. This was crowned by a spacious niche architecture with flat pilasters.

We cannot be sure whether the building complex was abandoned because of the fire of 64. This is suggested by the fact that one half of the building was destroyed for a circular building that is also dated as Neronian and, therefore, may have belonged to the *domus aurea* and, in turn, was destroyed by the *cenatio Iovis*. Later finds, such as a water pipe and a brick with Vespasian's stamp (CIL XV 664 c), merely provide *termini ante quem*. The insulation between the vaults of the resting rooms and the floor level of the building above resembles that of the garden in the early phase II of the → *domus Tiberiana* (→ Mons Palatinus), which also suggests attribution to the *domus aurea*. Remains of the paintings on the ceiling vault with depictions, e.g., of an amazonomachy and a Dionysian *thiasos*, which were removed after being found in 1721, are located in the stores of the National Museum in Naples; the columns from the court can no longer be found.

Richardson, 138–139; M. de Vos, in: LTUR 3, 1995, 199–202 (bibliography). R.F.

Dona militaria Particularly deserving soldiers and officers of the Roman army were granted marks of honour (→ Decorations, military), with the rank of the recipient playing an important role. The practice of presenting such marks of honour changed in the course of the Republican period and the Principate. The older tradition reported the granting of decorations in the early Republic (Plin. HN 22,6–13) but the first credible information is found in Polybius (6,39). Honorary distinctions are documented in the literature pertaining to the 4th cent. AD (cf. Amm. Marc. 24,4,24; 24,6,15) and to the Byzantine period; however, epigraphic evidence only extends from the end of the Republic to the beginning of the 3rd cent. AD. Under the Republic *dona militaria* (DM) were awarded by commanders in the name of the Roman Senate and people, but under the Principate in the name of the *princeps*. Apart from individual soldiers and officers, units such as *alae* (→ *ala* [2]) or → *cohortes* could be honoured; in inscriptions they were then called *torquatae* or *armillatae*. The distinction of individual soldiers or officers was noted in various ways, for example, with the formula *donis donatus*, abbreviated *don. don.* (ILS 2710), by naming the marks of honour awarded or by combining the quoted formula with a list of distinctions. On grave reliefs images of DM are often found. The decorations were worn at official occasions, which increased the impression the units made on the public (Tac. Hist. 2,89,2).

Which and how many decorations were awarded to a soldier or officer depended on the recipient's rank. Four possibilities must be clearly differentiated:

1. Simple soldiers (*milites*), soldiers freed of the *munera* (*immunes*) and soldiers who were paid a higher salary (*principales*) received at least *torques* and *armilla*, but normally the triad of *torques*, *armilla* and *phalerae* (*dona minora*); they could also aspire to be distinguished with the *corona civica* or the *corona aurea* (CIL XIV 3472 = ILS 2637, CIL V 4902). The *evocati* (soldiers who served beyond the ordinary period of service) received with few exceptions (such as CIL XIII 1041 = ILS 2531) four types of decorations — *torques*, *armilla* and *phalerae* like other soldiers and also the *corona aurea* (CIL XI 2112).

2. In the decoration of centurions, certain fluctuations can be detected up to the Flavian period. The Flavians created a new system that took the differences of rank among centurions into account: a centurion of the → *auxilia* could receive the usual triad of *torques*, *armilla* and *phalerae* but the sources are unclear as to whether other decorations could be added. A centurion who commanded the *cohortes* II-X of a legion was decorated like the centurion of the praetorians with the three *dona minora* and also a *corona* (CIL III 14387i = ILS 9198). The centurions of the first *cohors* or those of the first *cohortes* of the praetorians received a *corona* and a *hasta pura* (CIL XI 1602).

3. As numerous inscriptions show, officers of the *ordo equester* or *ordo senatorius* received *coronae*, *hastae purae* and *vexilla* as decorations; the finely graded system of rules for decorating officers was also introduced by the Flavians, though each *princeps* followed his own rules which were more generous or restrictive to varying degrees. The officers of the *ordo equester* as well as those of senatorial status were not distinguished for special deeds but only for their participation in a war — even if they did not see action. Nevertheless, there were two degrees in each rank so that two officers of the same service rank would not necessarily receive the same number of decorations; that way it was possible to reward special merit. As MAXFIELD [2] has shown, an officer of the *ordo equester* could expect to be decorated with a *corona*, a *hasta pura* and a *vexillum*.

4. The same rules applied to members of the *ordo senatorius*: the number of DM depended on the rank of the recipient and varied under the Principate with a reorganization under the Flavians. For the period between Vespasian and Commodus there is much epigraphic evidence for the *donae militariae* so that the rules for awarding decorations to senators can be reconstructed.

Dona militaria for officers from the *ordo senatorius* (c: *corona*; h: *hasta pura*; v: *vexillum*)

1. Julio-Claudian period (based on [2])		
Former tribune		2c – 2h – 2v
Former praetor		3c – 3h – 3v
Former consul		4c – 4v
2. Between Vespasian and Commodus		
Former tribune	minimum	2c – 1h – 1v
		2c – 2h – 1v
	maximum	2c – 2h – 2v
Former praetor	minimum	3c – 2h – 2v
		3c – 3h – 2v
	maximum	3c – 3h – 3v
Former consul	minimum	4c – 3h – 3v
		4c – 4h – 3v
	maximum	4c – 4h – 4v

After the beginning of the 3rd cent. AD the inscriptions no longer mention the DM. The almost matter of fact awarding of decorations caused the interest in them to dwindle; however, during the 3rd-cent. crisis the number of inscriptions also strongly declined.

1 J. FITZ, Auszeichnungen der Praefekten der *alae milliariae*, in: Klio 52, 1970, 99–106 2 V. MAXFIELD, The Military Decorations of the Roman Army, 1981 3 T. NAGY, Les dona militaria de M. Macrinius Avitus Catonius Vindex, in: Homm. M. Renard, Coll. Latomus 102, 2, 1969, 536–546 4 P. STEINER, Die d.m., 1905.

Y.L.B.

Donatio The assignment of a benefit in assets without any return (e.g., by transferring ownership of an object, relinquishing a claim or waiving a debt of the beneficiary). If an object is transferred to the recipient with the intent to give (*animus donandi*), the *donatio* constitutes a *iusta causa* of property acquisition by → *traditio* or occupancy (→ *usucapio*). A mere promise of donation is according to Roman law only binding in the form of a → *stipulatio*.

The *lex Cincia de donis et muneribus* (a → *plebiscitum* of 204 BC) prohibited acceptance of donations above a certain (unknown) value. Not included were donations among *personae exceptae* (especially close relatives). The purpose of this prohibition was probably the fight against luxury, presumably for the purpose of protecting weaker members of society against forced donations. A donation completed contrary to the *lex Cincia* was effective, but a suit for fulfilment of a promise violating the *lex* could be countered by the donor (but not by his heir) with an → *exceptio (legis Cinciae)*.

A *donatio inter virum et uxorem* (donation among spouses) probably was forbidden from the earliest times. In the Augustan period jurists derived this prohibition from the *mores maiorum*. As justification they stated that the mutual affection of spouses should not be affected by excessive gifts (cf. Dig. 24,1,1). The underlying objective probably was to preserve the assets in the family of the respective marriage partner. This *donatio* is utterly void according to the *ius civile*. Only in the Severian period an (unrevoked) donation becomes valid on the donor's death (Dig. 24,1,32 pr.).

Not included in the gift prohibition was a donation undertaken before the → marriage with a view towards it. According to classical law, such donations can be reclaimed by means of a → *condictio* if the marriage does not come about. In the course of the legal upgrading of engagement, Constantine made the reclamation dependent on the condition-imposing party not being at fault in breaking off the engagement (Cod. Theod. 3,5,2 = Cod. Iust. 5,3,15). In late antiquity the *donatio ante nuptias* developed into an independent institution of marital property. This was a gift by the man to the woman, which, like the → *dos* provided by the wife's side, was to provide support for the wife and legitimate children after the end of the marriage. Imperial law often required a certain value ratio of this *donatio* to the *dos*. Under Justinian it could also be granted during the marriage (*donatio propter nuptias*).

A *donatio mortis causa* is a *donatio* that will only become effective if the recipient survives the donor. The most important application is a *donatio* that the donor undertakes in the face of death. If the donor unexpectedly survives the recipient, the gift may be demanded back (Dig. 12,1,19 pr.). The *donatio mortis causa* is also a promise of a donation that is conditionally delayed by the death of the donor. The rules that limit a → *legatum* also apply to the *donatio mortis causa*.

→ Causa; → Condicio; → Condictio; → Matrimonium

Kaser, RPR I, 331f., 601–604, 763– 65, II, 394–400; R. Zimmermann, The Law of Obligations, 1990, 477–507; H. Schlei, Schenkungen unter Ehegatten, 1993, 4–85.

F.ME.

Donatists see → Donatus [1]

Donativum A *donativum* is a one-time special gift to soldiers by the Roman *principes* that was paid out in money. The practise of the *donativum* presupposes the power to dispose of the army and the public treasury as well as the institutionalized closeness of the commander and his troops. Therefore, it is a typical phenomenon of the Imperial period. It continues practices of the late Republic, under different conditions, in which the distribution of booty could be mixed with motives of rewarding for loyalty in the civil war, the provisioning of veterans and securing a following (Suet. Iul. 38). A *donativum* was usually not granted on the occasion of a victory or triumph but typically when securing the dynasty or the reign were at stake, e.g., in the testaments of the first two *principes* Augustus and Tiberius, at family events such as the attiring of the young Nero with the *toga virilis* under Claudius, the adoption of Aelius Caesar (Hadrian), the marriage of the younger Faustina (Antoninus Pius), as well as the suppression of real or imagined conspiracies such as the events surrounding Seianus (Tiberius), Lepidus (Caligula), Agrippina the Younger, Piso (Nero) and Geta (Caracalla), or at an accession.

The *donativa* constituted a decisive factor in the change of rulers from the early Principate. Particularly in precarious situations they offered an effective means for securing or gaining the favour of certain units, especially the praetorians but also other parts of the army (e.g., in AD 68/9). In an extreme case it lead to an auction of the imperial title (the succession from Pertinax to Didius Iulianus in 193; Cass. Dio 74,11). As the case of Galba demonstrates, a promised *donativum* that was not paid could be fateful (Suet. Galba 16,2). The *donativa* tended to increase and amounted to a multiple of the *stipendium* (annual soldier's pay). During the rapid turnover of emperors in the 3rd cent. the legions (but probably not the *auxilia*) enjoyed a *donativum* more often. Sometimes exorbitantly high *donativa* were paid in this period, which were in turn based on a repeatedly increased *stipendium*. Under Diocletian the *donativa* became regular payments on the occasion of the annual holidays celebrating the ruler and governmental jubilees (in addition to the *stipendium*). This practice continued in late antiquity and was taken over by some Germanic kingdoms. The amount of a share in a *donativum* apparently depended at all times on the service rank of the recipient.

→ Congiarium; → Largitio; → Liberalitas; → Praetoriae cohortes; → Soldier's pay

1 Jones, LRE, 623–624 2 Le Bohec 3 G.R. Watson, The Roman Soldier, 1969, 108–114.

P.W.

Donatus

[1] D. of Carthage, Donatists

A. Definition B. History C. Assessment

A. Definition

Donatism is a derogatory term for an ethically radical Christian movement that attached itself to traditional elements in the African Church in Roman North Africa in the 4th–7th cents. AD. It led to a schism in the African Church during disputes over the consequences of the Diocletian persecutions of Christians, i.e. the question of how to deal with lay persons and clerics who had given in to the governmental authorities and in some way had become *lapsi*, e.g. had surrendered Holy Scriptures (*traditores*). A separate Donatist Church formed that was considered schismatic by other churches and, therefore, was polemically labelled with the name of D. of Carthage, who for many years was its leading bishop.

B. History

The Diocletian persecution, which had only lasted a brief period in Africa (303–305), claimed many victims. Because of governmental coercion, even clerics handed over holy books (sometimes 'heretical' writings, which however was also considered a lapse from faith because it served to avoid martyrdom). Apparently, many false accusations also circulated. Already in 305 there were severe disputes in the Church over how to handle such *traditores*. Traditionally, the African Church was radical in questions of Church discipline: lapsed persons could no longer be members of the Church, leave alone of the clergy because the Church was the community of those free of sin. Bishop Mensurius of Carthage and his deacon Caecilianus were suspected of not having sufficiently supported arrested Christians (probably to avoid provoking the authorities). When after the death of Mensurius (309/311) Caecilianus was consecrated as his successor, opposition arose above all among Numidian bishops. The validity of his consecration was disputed because a *traditor* had participated in it. In 312 a synod of 70 bishops in Carthage called by the Numidian primate deposed Caecilianus and consecrated a certain Maiorinus († 313) in his place. The deposition of Caecilianus was not recognized outside of Africa and caused a schism in the Church in Africa. This is the situation that → Constantine [1] found in 312. The group around Maiorinus appealed against the emperor's matter-of-fact recognition of Caecilianus, whose clergy was freed from the *munera* and who was to receive the emperor's compensation payments for the damage resulting from the persecution, by claiming to be the sole Catholic Church in Africa and also demanded an investigation of its accusations against Caecilianus.

In the meantime Donatus had become bishop of Carthage as the successor of Maiorinus [5. 292–303]. Until his death in exile in 355 he was the dominating figure of Donatism. He viewed his office as bishop entirely in the tradition of Cyprian and was later venerated as a martyr. No writings are preserved but Jerome mentions a *Liber de spiritu sancto*.

Constantine commissioned Miltiades of Rome and three Gallic bishops with the investigation demanded by Donatus. The bishops sat as an imperial court in the traditional form of a synod. This marked the creation of the imperial synod called by the emperor as a new institution of state and Church [2]. In line with Roman/Occidental ecclesiastical tradition the consecration of Caecilianus was considered valid and Donatus was condemned. When Donatus' supporters did not accept the judgement and again appealed to the emperor, Constantine called a synod in 314 in Arles, which confirmed Rome's judgement. Constantine initially countered a renewed protest of the Donatists in 316/17 with governmental measures but in 321 gave in to the solid resistance. In contradiction to Constantine's ideology of unity, two churches existed side by side in Africa, with the Donatists probably being in the majority. Probably in 336 Donatus was able to hold a synod attended by 270 Donatist bishops in Carthage. The relationship of the → Circumcelliones, who appeared more frequently in this period, to the Donatists is uncertain.

After the death of Caecilianus (346), Donatus demanded that emperor Constans recognize the Donatists as the only Catholic Church in Africa. The latter reacted after 347 with severe persecutions, which Constantius continued and which claimed many victims while producing Donatist martyr cults and martyr literature. In 347 Donatus had to go into exile (died 355). Under emperor → Iulianus the banned persons returned in triumph. Under the episcopate of Donatus' successor → Parmenianus († 392/393), the Donatists experienced their true flowering; they were the Church in Africa (with uneven geographical distribution [1]) and there were also Donatist groups in Italy (Rome), Gaul and Spain, some even with bishops. Links to the Spanish Priscillians are unclear. A Donatist schism after the death of Parmenianus weakened their position and support for → Gildo's usurpation in 397/398 led to new state measures. After 403 the laws against heretics were also applied to the Donatists (Cod. Theod. 16,5,37–43; 6,3–5). Following the anti-Donatist work of Optatus of Mileve, the actual theological discussion with the Donatists (especially with Petilianus of Cirta) began with Aurelius of Carthage and → Augustinus. In 411 a great debate of more than 500 Donatist and Catholic bishops took place under state guidance in Carthage (on the Catholic side especially Aurelius and Augustine) at which the fate of Donatism had actually already been sealed. A pro-Catholic edict of unity by Honorius (Cod. Theod. 16,5,52) prohibited Donatism and resulted in mass conversions to Catholicism. Remnants of Donatism maintained themselves despite severe persecutions under Vandal and Byzantine rule until the Arab invasions.

C. Assessment

It is not easy to establish a theological profile. The Church had to be pure without sinners. From this it followed that the validity of the sacraments was also dependent on the purity of the person performing them. This was the justification of the Donatist practice of anabaptism, which was traditional in Africa but rejected elsewhere in the Church. This theology placed the Donatists in the tradition of → Cyprian. It is clear that African Donatists and Catholics basically shared the same concept of the Church, except that they weighted it differently in the specific case [7]. In both Churches the cults of martyrs and relics played an outstanding role (The Donatists even had suicide martyrs). The often emphasized radical rejection of the new alliance between Church and state [1] appears less fundamental and rather more a by-product of the emperor's siding with the Catholics. It is difficult to place the theology of Tyconius, the most important Donatist who also had an influence on Augustine, within the spectrum of Donatism. Because the theological differences appear to be unspecific in the explanation of the schism, English and American scholarship [1] in particular has interpreted Donatism as a primarily anti-Roman social movement with a view especially towards the Circumcelliones; but they cannot be the standard for interpretation. The clearly religious motivation of Donatism probably later allied itself with a social motivation in the face of the serious social problems of late antiquity.

1 W.H.C. Frend, The Donatist Church, ³1983 2 K.M. Girardet, Kaisergericht und Bischofsgericht, 1975 3 E.L. Grasmück, Coercitio. Staat und Kirche im Donatistenstreit, 1964 4 C. Lepelley, Les cités de l' Afrique romaine au Bas-Empire I/II, 1979/1981 5 A. Mandouze, Prosopographie chrétienne du Bas-Empire I, 1982 6 P. Monceaux, Histoire littéraire de l' Afrique chrétienne depuis les origines jusqu'à l'invasion arabe I-VII, 1901–1923 (1966) 7 A. Schindler, s.v. Afrika I, TRE 1, 640–700.

S. Lancel (ed.), Acta Concilii Carthaginensis, SChr 194/195/224/373, 1972–1991 Augustinus, Traités anti-donatistes I-V, BAug 28–32, 1963–1968 J.-L. Maier, Le dossier du donatisme I/II, TU 134/135, 1987/1989 Optat de Milève, Traité contre les donatistes I/II, SChr 412/413, 1995/1996. H.BR.

[2] Attested in AD 408 as *procos. Africae*. Augustine (Epist. 100) calls upon him for a determined but non-violent proceeding against the Donatists (→ D. [1]). Another letter by Augustine to D. is Epist. 112. PLRE 2, 375f.

Prosopographie de l'Afrique chrétienne (303–533) 1, 1982, 309f. H.L.

[3] **Aelius D.** Latin grammarian, perhaps born around 310 in Africa, teacher of → Hieronymus in Rome. He composed an *Ars grammatica* (edition: [1; 4]) and commented on Virgil and Terence. An introduction in dialogue format preceded the *Ars*, which was written according to the rules of the art. It is dedicated to the *partes orationis*, which are introduced in abbreviated form. The work was a synthesis of everything produced so far by grammarians and became one of the fundamental texts of grammatical teaching. It was soon commented upon by → Servius and was distributed throughout the Latin world. Between late antiquity and the Middle Ages a division occurred in manuscript transmission between the *Ars minor*, the introduction, which was used as an elementary grammar, and the *Ars maior*. The latter was very famous throughout the entire Middle Ages and was commented upon in its entirety by Ercambertus of Freising and Remigius of Auxerre. It was also continued, in part, by Murethach, Sedulius Scotus, Smaragdus, Paul the Deacon (→ Paulus [4]), Pietro da Pisa and others (comprehensively discussed in [4]).

The commentary on the works of Virgil, the original version of which is lost, is one of the most important exegetical works of late antiquity. However, it was frequently replaced by → Servius' more manageable commentary. Of D.'s original only the dedication letter, Virgil's *vita* (edition: [2. 1–11]) and two introductions [2. 11–19] are preserved. Remains of D.'s commentary are most likely found in the additions of → Servius auctus/Danielis. Apart from Servius, → Macrobius, → Isidorus and many glossaries refer to D.'s commentary. The commentary on Terence (edition: [3]) is preceded by a *vita* taken from → Suetonius and an introduction to the genre of comedy. However, the commentary on the *Heauton Timoroumenos* is lost. → Eugraphius and the → Scholia Bembina, as well as Priscianus and Isidore refer to D.'s text. They were almost certainly able to use a version that is more complete than the one available to us (abbreviations and interpolations). In the Middle Ages D. was known to Lupus of Ferrières and Hugo Primas. D. probably also wrote *De structuris*, a lost treatise on metric clausulae.

Editions: 1 GL 4,355–402 2 J. Brummer, 1912 (reprint 1969) 3 P. Wessner, 1902–5.
Bibliography: 4 L. Holtz, D. et la tradition de l'enseignement grammatical, 1981, 585–674 5 P.L. Schmidt, HLL § 527. P.G.

[4] **Ti. Claudius D.** wrote an extensive, almost completely preserved commentary on Virgil's *Aeneid*, the *Interpretationes Vergilianae*, probably around AD 400. He identified the *Aeneid* as a rhetorical showpiece of the [2. 91–102] *genus laudativum*, as a praise of Augustus (p. 2,7–25 G.), and interpreted the literal meaning without resorting to → allegoresis, which is why he had little influence in the Middle Ages. The commentary has just begun to be used as source for the literary standards of late antiquity regarding criticism and morality [2. 103–119; 3].

Editions: 1 H. Georgii, 2 vols., 1905/6.
Bibliography: 2 M. Squillante Saccone, Le Interpretationes Vergilianae di T.C.D., 1985 3 R.J. Starr, Explaining Dido to your son, in: CJ 87, 1991, 25–34. K.P.

Donkey Just as today, the donkey was in many regions of the Mediterranean one of the most often used domestic animals of antiquity. It was ridden, burdened with a packsaddle or hitched in front of a cart and was one of the most commonly used sources of living mechanical energy. As for many material possessions, the literary and archaeological sources for the use of donkeys are sparse and archaeozoology is only slowly beginning to offer interesting evidence.

A. Systematic zoology, origin and domestication B. The wild ass C. The domestic donkey D. Uses of the donkey E. The donkey in ancient culture F. Religious significance

A. Systematic zoology, origin and domestication

This genus of ungulates (*Equidae*) belongs to the family of Perissodactyla. The species *equus* is divided into four subspecies: zebras, wild asses, Asian wild asses and horses. The wild donkey of African origin is divided into two main groups: the Nubian wild ass (*Equus asinus africanus africanus*) and the Somalian wild ass (*Equus asinus africanus somaliensis*). The domestic donkey (*Equus asinus asinus*) appears to be descended from the Nubian wild ass rather than from the wilder and more shy Asian species. → Domestication may have originally occurred in the early 4th millennium in Egypt; after that it became widespread throughout the Middle East. However, a domestication in the Middle East that possibly used hybrids of African and Asian wild asses cannot be ruled out [1. 144–145]. In any case, in the 3rd millennium *Equus asinus asinus* was used from Mesopotamia to Egypt in agriculture and transportation [3. 217–225]. The presence of the domestic donkey in Greece is documented from Lerna in the Argolis around 2000 BC [1. 144–145] and from Macedonia around 1400 BC. In the territory on the Black Sea it appeared about the 9th cent. BC, in Italy at the sites of Tortoreto-Fortellezza (10th–6th cents. BC) and Spina as well as in Spain in the 8th and 7th cents. BC. Its spread throughout Mediterranean Europe seems to have gone hand in hand with the Phoenician expansion and Greek city foundation. In the late Hallstatt period donkeys were kept at the Heuneburg and in the La Tène period in Provence. Its spread through Gaul, the Rhineland and the Danube area at the beginning of the Principate is probably due to troop movements of the Roman army. So far the donkey has not been documented in northern Gaul. The question whether it was bred on a large scale in the regions north of the Alps or if there was dependence on imports is disputed.

B. The wild ass

Ancient authors do not seem to have clearly distinguished between the true wild asses (*Equus asinus*) and the Asiatic wild ass (*Equus hemionus hemionus*, *Hemionus kiang*, *Hemionus hemippus*, *Hemionus onager*). The terms ὄνος ἄγριος (*ónos ágrios*), ὄναγρος (*ónagros*, Lat. *onager, onagrus*) probably describe the wild ass or the Asiatic wild ass (onager); it is a robust, wild and untameable race with a graceful head and small ears that in the opinion of ancient authors was native to Asia Minor, Syria, Armenia, Mesopotamia, Persia and Arabia. Pliny (HN 8,174) considered the wild asses of Phrygia and Lycaonia exceptional. The African onager, a wild ass with fiery temperament, speed and long ears, is mentioned less frequently. The Indian wild ass ὄνος ἰνδικός (*ónos indikós*), described as having one horn in the centre of the forehead, might be the origin of the → unicorn legend. The wild ass was hunted with spears or lassos. Its meat is comparable to that of the stag and was prized in the Orient and Rome. The foals of the African wild ass, the *lalisiones*, were particularly famous (Plin. HN 8,170–174). Jacks were caught for breeding donkeys and mules (Varro, Rust. 2,6,3; Columella 6,37,4).

C. The domestic donkey

Ancient authors usually call *equus asinus asinus* ὄνος (*ónos*), *asinus*, sometimes *asellus* in poetry, κανθήλιος (*kanthḗlios*) or κάνθων (*kánthōn*, the donkey burdened with a packsaddle), μυχλός (*mychlós*) among the Phoenicians and later γαϊδάριον (*gaïdárion*). Coming from north-eastern Africa the domestic donkey reached Greece via the Middle East. It appears on Mycenaean clay tablets as *o-no* and its presence has been demonstrated from bones findings. Homer mentions it only once (Il. 11,558–562) and Hesiod does not mention it at all. After the 6th cent. BC the donkey is frequently depicted and described. The most detailed descriptions are found in Aristotle (Gen. an. 747b–748b; Hist. an. 577a–578b), Plautus (*Asinaria*), Varro (Rust. 2,6), Columella (6,36–7,1), Pliny (HN 8,167–175), Ps. Lucian (*Asinus*), Apuleius (Met. 7–11), Palladius (4,14) and the *Geoponica* (16–21). According to ancient perception the donkey belongs to the category of μώνυχα (*mṓnycha*) or *solidipedes*; its age can be determined from changes in its teeth, its skin is hard, its fur ash grey to black, dark stripes decorate its legs, neck or back. Its mane is not very thick, its ears are long and mobile, from a physiological point of view its blood was considered thick and black, its arteries are narrow and its heart is large. The females have two teats and can at most nourish two young. Donkeys are rarely ill and can live for more than 30 years. Its character and behaviour were considered to be slow. It is lazy, stubborn, undisciplined and hardened from beatings. It has a pronounced sexual desire and shies away from water. This negative assessment, which is also found with other opinions in the *Physiognomonica*, is clichéd and was not necessarily shared by those who knew donkeys well. Columella and Palladius considered donkeys as enduring, frugal and good workers.

The donkey had the reputation of being very frugal in feeding and of being satisfied with pasture grass, mediocre feed and hay, leaves, twigs and chopped straw. It would also eat thistles and nettles. The more valued donkeys appreciated hay, barley and bran but wheat was probably only rarely fed (Ps. Lucian. Asin. 37). The donkey drinks little and prefers pasture water to which it is accustomed (Plin. HN 8,169). Added to its legendary frugality are its great resistance to fatigue and illnesses and that it hardly ever is infested by fleas and ticks (Aristot. Hist. an. 557a). However, it may poison itself with yew and laurel leaves. It is prone to dysentery and cholera. A special disease μηλίς (*mēlís*), the symptom of which is excess production of nasal mucus, can become its doom (Aristot. Hist. an. 605a). Its worst enemy in the countryside is the wolf. Crows and birds defending their nests have supposedly attacked its eyes. In shared pastures horses give it a hard time. But its most frequent and severe health problems result from the harsh treatment meted out by humans. To heal it the *veterinarius* or the specialized *mulomedicus* was called.

The most prized breeds were those of Reate, Arcadia and Magnesia. The breeding jacks of Reate were fairly large and sold at prices of up to 60,000 and even 100,000 HS (Varro Rust. 2,1,14). The breeds of Illyria, Thrace and Epirus were smaller. The rules of breeding concerned the quality of the breeding jacks and mating in summer, which was followed twelve months later by the birth. The jenny awaited darkness for the birth; she bears one foal, rarely two, and produces milk after the tenth month of the gestation period. Donkey foals were weaned at the age of one year and the jenny can conceive again only seven days after the birth. Donkeys may mate at the age of thirty months but for the breeding jack it is better to wait to the age of three years. Training can be begun in the third year of life. The agronomists allot a special significance to the breeding of hybrids, → mules and hinnies [4. 200–201]. The technique of crossing a horse mare with a jack for mule breeding was well mastered in antiquity. Mules from Arcadia and of Reate owed their reputation in particular to the crossing with carefully selected jacks (*admissarii*). Apart from the *hemionus mulus* another cross, the hinny (horse stallion and jenny) was bred, which in antiquity was called γίννος (*gínnos*), Latin *hinnus*, *hinnulus* or *burdus*. For improving the breed, crossing with wild asses was recommended.

D. Uses of the donkey

In the economy and daily life the donkey is the animal that is used for all purposes (cf. also [2. 7–14]; → Land transport). In particular, it is used for transportation: carrying, drawing, pulling and transporting — in the country and in town — yoked alone or in pairs. For cultivating an olive orchard of 240 *iugera*, three donkeys were needed for transportation and one for the mill according to Cato (Agr. 10,1). For cultivating a vineyard of 100 *iugera*, Cato and Varro calculated two oxen and two donkeys and another donkey for the mill (Cato Agr. 11,1; Varro Rust. 1,19,3). Led by the halter (*capistrum*), equipped with various carrying devices, donkeys and hinnies could perform numerous transports of goods and persons. Covered by a blanket, they served as mounts for Dionysus and his followers; even persons of high rank relied on them in difficult terrain with narrow and stony paths. In late antiquity they were used in the → *cursus publicus* for transport along with horses and hinnies. Donkeys with a packsaddle were especially used as draught and pack animals in the transportation of goods. There were several devices for carrying burdens: baskets (κανθήλια, *kanthḗlia*; *clitellae*) or a frame (*sagma*). On occasion considerable weights were transported. In the price edict of Diocletian (→ Edictum Diocletiani) a load of 65.5 kg is mentioned (14,11) but often the load weighed more than the animal, as can be observed even today in certain regions of Asia and Africa. Donkey caravans were part of the *impedimenta* of ancient armies. According to one anecdote Philip II of Macedonia had to forego a militarily favourable location because of a lack of fodder. He bitterly complained that the needs of donkeys took precedence over his (Plut. Mor. 178A). Caravans of *aselli dossuari* took oil, wine and grain to the coast in southern Italy (Varro, Rust. 2,6,5).

The use of donkeys as draught animals is less frequently documented. However, the *asini plaustrarii* must have been as frequent in town as yoked oxen. Donkeys, like oxen, were part of the essential furnishings of rural estates. The efficiency of donkey gear cannot be doubted (→ Land transport). The *mola asinaria*, a rotating mill for grinding grain or crushing olives (*trapetum*) must have been among the cruellest labours. The description of the baker's mill in Apuleius is famous (Met. 9,10–13): with blindfolded eyes the donkey moves the upper millstone by means of a rope (*helcium*). Walking in circles, burdened as much by the heavy pulling as by the beating that continuously comes down on its back, the work is most exhausting. The iconography of the subject (Zimmer no. 18–25) shows horses, undoubtedly for aesthetic reasons. On light soil the donkey was 'a species that rendered great services with its work' (Plin. HN 8,167). In Campagnia, Andalusia, Baetica and Libya two donkeys were hitched to the plough, sometimes a donkey and an oxen and in the province of Byzacena even a donkey and a woman. The donkey pulled the threshing sledge (*tribulum*) or threshing cart (*plostellum punicum*, cf. fig. → Threshing); or it was used in threshing along with horses, mules and oxen to stomp out the grain (Anth. Gr. 9,301).

Other products were also generated by the donkey: donkey manure was used as fertilizer and its urine as an insect repellent on trees. Eating donkey meat was unusual but it was not shunned altogether. In Athens there was a market for donkey meat; in Rome it was the food of the poor but the meat of donkey foals was esteemed in the Augustan period. However, on the whole the question regarding the eating of donkey and horse meat is disputed. The meat was recommended as a cure against several diseases, for example as a soup against epilepsy or against a tendency towards dizziness. The fat was used as a wound-closing balm. Some bones were used to produce flutes (Plin. HN 11,215; 16,172). Milk and cheese from the jenny hardly ever appeared on the menu but the medicinal qualities of this particularly low-fat milk were recognized; in particular, whey was prepared. Hippocrates and Galen recommended it because of its mildly laxative effect for many digestive illnesses. It was also used in cases of arthritis and diarrhoea, as an antidote and to strengthen teeth. The cosmetic and dermatological qualities of donkey milk were particularly valued by Poppaea Sabina: her herd of 500 donkeys supplied her with the milk for her baths (Plin. HN 11,238). Other ladies of the upper classes satisfied themselves with washing their faces. Hoses, drum skins, parchment and narrow thongs for whips were produced from donkey skin and leather, and the mane was made into various kinds of ropes.

Except for the pure-bred jacks used for breeding mules, the commercial value of donkeys was generally very low. In Macedonia during the 2nd cent. AD 30 drachmae were paid for a donkey and for a donkey from Arsinoë (Egypt) 600 drachmae were paid in AD 219. The case of the Celtiberian jenny who earned her owner more than 400,000 HS for her foals must have been very rare indeed (Plin. HN 8,170).

E. The donkey in ancient culture

Since Graeco-Roman antiquity stereotypes of donkeys have developed more than for any other animal in western culture, making them symbols of misfortune, suffering and forbearance. The examples of contempt, mockery and negative connotations regarding donkeys are beyond count. The label 'donkey' was an insult and only rarely an expression of compassion. In many proverbs and fables the donkey symbolizes sluggishness and stupidity. This includes sayings such as 'the donkey who hears the lyre' (ὄνος λύρας ἀκούων) for someone who has a very poor ear for music, or 'to tell a donkey a story' (ὄνῳ μῦθον λέγειν), i.e. someone who understands nothing. Often humans are cruel to donkeys. The donkey's fate is truly not enviable: 'between the mill and the loads its life is endless torment' (Aesop. 16). Usually, an *asellus miserandae sortis* is described in the fables of Aesop and the novels of Ps.Lucian and Apuleius. The circumstances often fluctuate between realism and parody, between mockery and paradigm. In Hellenistic and Roman Egypt and in the Latin agronomists, however, a more positive attitude towards donkeys is often found.

F. Religious significance

In Egypt the donkey belonged to the god Typhon, a god of misfortune who was placated with sacrifices. In the Graeco-Roman world the donkey was essentially associated with the god Dionysus/Bacchus and his following: a donkey carried the child Dionysus through Boeotia to Euboea and helped the god put the giants to flight, it accompanied him from Lydia to India and it saw to it that Dionysus arrived at Dodona after travelling through the swamps. For this the gods rewarded it by assigning it a constellation. It climbed Mt. Olympus while carrying Hephaestus and his tools. In the Dionysian procession of Ptolemy II the satyrs and maenads rode on donkeys. Participation in orgiastic ceremonies, especially in honour of the → Bona Dea, was attributed to donkeys. They were the subject of superstitions: the ghost → Empusa, which was sent by Hecate (Aristoph. Ran. 288ff.), the donkey Nicon in Actium, the donkey call as an ill omen, the donkey with three hooves are all examples of this. → Epona protects them as she does with other equids. Donkeys are also encountered as sacrificial animals, in Italy for Vesta, in Lampsacus for Priapus and in Tarentum for favourable winds.

→ Donkey cult

1 N. Benecke, Archäologische Studien zur Entwicklung der Haustierhaltung in Mitteleuropa und Südskandinavien, 1994 2 L. Bodson, L'utilisation de l'âne dans l'antiquité gréco-romaine, in: L'âne. Actes de la journée d'études (21/11/1985), 1986 3 S. Bökönyi, The Earliest Occurrence of Domestic Asses in Italy, in: R.H. Meadow, H.-P. Uerpmann (ed.), Equids in the Ancient World, 1991 4 S. Georgoudi, Des chevaux et des boeufs dans le monde grec. Réalités et représentations animalières à partir des livres XVI et XVII des Géoponiques, 1990, 196–205 5 E. Lagarde, L'âne Grand Noir du Berry, 1995 6 G. Nachtergael, Le chameau, l'âne et le mulet en Egypte gréco-romaine, in: Chronique d'Égypte 64, 1989, 287–336 7 M. Ventris, J. Chadwick, Documents in Mycenaen Greek, [2]1973. 8 Ch. Willms, Der Hausesel nördlich der Alpen, in: Saalburg-Jahrb. 45, 1990, 78–82.

O. Antonius, Grundzüge einer Stammesgeschichte der Haustiere, 1922; J. Clutten-Brock, A Natural History of Domestical Animals, 1987; A. Dent, Donkey. The Story of the Ass from East to West, 1972; O. Keller, Die antike Tierwelt I, 1909; A. Leone, Gli animali da lavoro da allevamento e gli hippoi nell' Egitto greco-romano e bizantino, 1992; W. Olck, s.v. Esel, RE 6, 626–676; E. Zeuner, Gesch. der Haustiere, 1966. G.R.

Donkey cult With donkey cult is meant the worship of a donkey, a donkey's head or a donkey-shaped deity. The origins of this ancient custom are largely obscure despite its relatively wide distribution (e.g. in ancient Egypt and Babylon). Egyptians and Romans also claimed, usually from a hostile position, that Judaism worshipped donkeys. According to Flavius → Iosephus, → Apion was the initiator of this slander (c. Ap. 2,7), the content of which is the accusation that the Jews had set up a donkey's head that they hailed during the divine service. This idea of Jewish donkey worship was facilitated by the similarity in sound of the Jewish term for God, *Jahu*, and the Egyptian word for donkey.

E. Bickermann, Ritualmord und Eselskult, in: Monatsschrift für die Geschichte und Wissenschaft des Judentums 7/8, 1927; Judaica, FS für H. Cohen, 1912, 297; S. Schiffer, in: REA 1919, 242. Y.D.

Dontas Sculptor from Sparta, active as an alleged student of → Dipoenus and Scyllis about the middle of the 6th cent. BC. The treasury of the Megarians at Olympia contained a wooden relief set in gold by him depicting Hercules and figures of the gods. According to Pausanias it was clearly older than the late 6th cent. building. The treasury's sculpture therefore cannot be attributed to D.

Fuchs/Floren, 215; Overbeck, no. 330–331 (sources). R.N.

Door

I. Ancient Orient and Egypt
II. Graeco-Roman Antiquity

I. Ancient Orient and Egypt

Apart from their architectural function as the transition between inside and outside or between spatial units of a building, doors possessed a symbolic and magical meaning in the Ancient Orient and Egypt. For example, in the Neo-Assyrian period (9th -7th cents. BC), doors and passages of public buildings were flanked by apotropaic hybrid creatures.

In the Ancient Orient doors mostly consisted of wooden posts to which a panel of wood or reed was firmly attached. The post, which was anchored at the top, turned on a pivot stone, which was usually made of stone (but also, e.g., of metal) and in public buildings bore the name of the builder and/or the purpose of the building in an inscription. Fittings of a double temple door richly decorated with reliefs were found in → Balāwāt (9th cent. BC). (Lime) stone doors were occasionally used in tombs. According to iconographic representations, which mostly referred to temple doors, most doors had a flat lintel.

In Egyptian stone architecture the threshold, sides and lintel were also made of stone, often even in brick buildings. The door panel was made of wooden planks with carved-out cones, which turned in an upper anchoring and a lower (metal-fitted) pan. The edges or even the entire door panel of important buildings might have metal fittings. Wooden or bronze sliding bolts were used for locking.

→ Architecture

M. S. Damerji, Die T. nach Darstellungen in der altmesopot. Bildkunst von der ʿUbaid- bis zur Akkad-Zeit, in: BaM 22, 1991, 231–311; H. Brunner, s. v. Tür und Tor, LÄ 6, 778–787.

AR. HA.

II. Graeco-Roman Antiquity

(θύρα/*thýra*; Latin *fores; ianua; valvae*). Already in early Greek architecture (8th/7th cents. BC), doors were the most important building accessories along with the → windows. Their form and furnishings reliably indicated the rank of the building and the status of its owner. Doors are subdivided into the frame, which is firmly integrated into the architecture, the locking mechanism (metal cones, pans or closing edges and locks, thresholds; hinges were comparatively rare) and one or two inset door panels. The latter were usually made of wood and decorated more or less richly and beyond purely structural needs with metal, sometimes also with ivory, ebony and other precious materials. Door panels, like roofing tiles and window shutters, were generally part of the → household inventory in domestic architecture (and not in a strict sense part of the architecture).

In Greek representational architecture two door types emerged in which the type of frame but not the panel was characteristic: the Ionian door with a rich frame decoration and occasionally a bracket-like *hyperthyron* as the upper end of the frame, and the Doric door with rather simple frame ornamentation. A detailed description of the respective building proportions and their distinguishing characteristics is found in Vitr. De arch. 4,6 (on the nomenclature of details on Greek temple doors [1. 19–22]). A further type was the 'Attic door', a special form described in Vitruvius 4,6,1–6. These concepts of form were largely repeated in the Roman period, with the ostentation of the Ionian door clearly being preferred.

Wooden doors have only occasionally been preserved (usually in tombs), but numerous marble and decorated stone doors (e.g., on the mausoleum of Belevi, or Macedonian chamber tombs) imitate these doors with their fittings. Also, illustrations of doors in paintings permit conclusions on their original appearance. A good impression of the material and creative investment in doors is provided by the bronze doors of the → Pantheon [2] and those of the Temple of Romulus, both of which are preserved in the original, as well as the wooden door of Santa Sabina (all in Rome), which is entirely covered with carvings. On religious aspects cf. → Gate deities.

1 Ebert.

A. Büsing-Kolbe, Frühe griech. Türen, in: JDAI 93, 1978, 66–174; G. and D. Gruben, Die T. des Pantheon, in: MDAI(R) 104, 1997, 3–74; W. Hoepfner, E. L. Schwandner, Haus und Stadt im klass. Griechenland, [2]1994, 356 (s. v. T.); G. Jeremias, Die Holzt. der Basilika S. Sabina in Rom, 1980; H. Klenk, Die ant. T., 1924; Ch. Löhr, Griech. Häuser: Hof, Fenster, T., in: W. D. Heilmeyer (ed.), Licht und Architektur, 1990, 10–17; A. Oliver Jr., Ivory Temple Doors, in: J. L. Fitton (ed.), Ivory in Greece and the Eastern Mediterranean Period (conf. London 1990), 1992, 227–231; W. Müller-Wiener, Griech. Bauwesen in der Ant., 1988, 104–107.

C. HÖ.

Dora (Hebrew *dōʾr*). Port town identified with Ḫirbat al-Burǧ near the village aṭ-Ṭanṭūra 15 km north of Caesarea (Eus. Onom. 9,78; 16,136) and 21 km south of Haifa. Settlement since the Middle Bronze Age IIA was demonstrated in excavations from 1980–1991. D. was attested in the city lists of Ramses II (region of the *via maris* between Saron and Akko). In the travel report of Wen Amun (about 1100 BC), however, D. appeared in the possession of the *Tkl*, who were one of the Sea Peoples (→ Sea Peoples, migrations of). D. was assigned to the tribe of Manasse in Jos. 17,11, but initially was outside the settlement area of the Israelite tribes. Only Solomon appears to have incorporated it as the 4th district (1 Kgs 4,11; cf. Jos. 12,23). Tiglatpileser III made D. the centre of the province Dūʾrū in 732 BC. The Phoenician influence, which is archaeologically demonstrable since Iron Age I (pottery and small finds), is illuminated by a contract of Asarhaddon, in which Baʿlu of Tyrus was granted special rights in the port of Dor

(TUAT 1, 158f.), the inscription on the sarcophagus of Ešmunazar of Sidon (TUAT 2, 590ff.) from the Persian period, which includes Dor, Jaffa and the Saron plain as part of → Sidon, and the description of the coast by Scyl. (§ 104). Neither Antiochus [5] III (Pol. 5,66) nor Antiochus [9] VII (1 Macc. 15; Jos. Ant. Iud. 13,7,2) were able to conquer the strong fortress. Only Alexander Iannaeus was able to take it and placed the town, which had become Seleucid in 201 BC, under Hasmonaean rule. → Pompeius granted it autonomy and minting rights in 63 BC. By contrast, Pliny (AD 70) calls D. a 'mere memory' even though the town had a mint until AD 222 and remained an episcopal see until the 7th cent.

E. Stern, Dor, Ruler of the Seas, 1994. M.K.

Dorcatius Under this name (which is also found in CIL 5,2793) Isid. Etym. 18,69 quotes two hexameters about stuffing a ball with stag hair. [1] identifies the author with an anonymous poet to whom Ovid (Tr. 2,485) refers in a listing of humorous didactic poems.

1 M. Haupt, Coniectanea, in: Hermes 7, 1873, 11–12 Opuscula vol. 3, 1876, 571 2 Courtney, 341. ED.C.

Dorea (δωρεά, *dōreá*; 'gift, present'). As a technical term the word has so far been attested only from Ptolemaic Egypt (→ Ptolemies), though the underlying practice of giving away land is known from all Hellenistic monarchies (→ Hellenistic politics). In Egypt the *dōreaí* are well documented as an independent category of land holding. The institution can be traced to both Oriental and Macedonian roots. It concerns the transference of land holding and/or any income derived from it by the kings to individuals among their followers, high functionaries and family members. It could involve single plots of land, larger estates, whole villages or even towns (an example of the latter from the part of Lycia under Ptolemaic control in [1]). In most cases it seems to have been given subject to revocation, in other words it was insecure; permanent possession was accordingly dependent on the favour of the king. However, gifts of land intended as irrevocable are also attested, in particular for the Seleucid kingdom (→ Seleucids),.

1 M. Wörrle, Epigraphische Forsch. zur Gesch. Lykiens II, in: Chiron 8, 1978, 201–246.

R. A. Billows, Kings and Colonists. Aspects of Macedonian Imperialism, 1995, 111–145; H. Kreissig, Wirtschaft und Ges. im Seleukidenreich, 1978, 40–46; 96–109. JÖ. GE.

Doric/Northwest Greek

A. Spread B. Characteristics C. Classification and History up to the 4th–3rd cent. BC D. Samples E. Doric since the 4th cent. BC

A. Spread

The Doric dialects in the broader sense are well documented since the pre-classical period (see map): in central and northwest Greece (Phocis: 1, with Delphi, Western and Eastern Locris: 2 and 3), Peloponnese and Isthmus (only Elis: 15, Laconia: 13, Argolis: 11–12, Corinthia: 10, Megaris: 9), Crete (16) and the Doric Islands (Thera: 17c, Rhodos: 17a, etc.: 17), and since the classical period also in Cos (17b), Cyrene and in the Doric colonies of → Magna Graecia (above all → Heraclea, → Locri Epizephyrii) and → Sicilia. The remaining northwest Greek regions (4–7), Achaea (8) and Messenia (14) only offer relatively later and unproductive inscriptions. Whether a Northwest Greek dialect was spoken in Macedonia in the classical period remains unknown. Literary Doric is not very reliable (→ Greek literary languages).

B. Characteristics

Almost all Doric dialects have the following in common: a) a West Greek component, b) specific Dorisms and c) characteristics that are seen as Doric, but also appear in other dialects.

Ad a): preserved *-ti(–)*; $^{*}t^{(h)}$*i̯* (type τόσσος) as well as $^{*}t^{(h)}$*-i̯*, $^{*}k^{(h)}$*i̯* (in the present tense to –σσω); **tu̯*,**ts* > *ss* (in the Cretan still t^{s}); nom. pl. τοι, ται; athematic infinitive in –μεν; ὅκα; αἴ κα; δήλομαι/δείλομαι 'to intend' (**g^u̯el-*); πρᾶτος; ἱαρός; (Ϝ)ίκατι 'twenty', –κάτιοι (= -κόσιοι).

Ad b): 1. Pl. in –μες; 3. Pl. ἔθεν (= ἔθεσαν); τέτορες 'four'.

Ad c): *ā* + *ŏ* > *ā*, *ā* + *e* > *ē* (gen. singular -ᾱ, pl. -ᾶν, 3. singular ἐνίκη); 3. singular ἦς 'he was'; 'Doric' future tense in –σέω (**-séi̯o/e-*); aorist and future tense with –ξ- to present tense with **-di̯o/e-* (aorist ψᾱφιξα-, δικαξα-/δικασσα-; but Argolic –σσα-); furthermore, isoglosses with the Attic-Ionian (**r̥* > *ra*, thematic inflection of the vocalic verbs).

For each dialect, one should expect, in addition to a)-c), d) isoglosses (of varying chronology) with neighbouring dialects and e) individual dialectal peculiarities. Ad d) cf. ἐν /*ἐν-ς with accusative; *ē/ō* or *ẹ̄/ọ̄* from compensatory lengthenings and contractions (see below); *-s-* > *–^{h}-* (> –∅–) in Argolic, Laconian, later also in Elean. Ad e) cf. e.g. → psilosis in Elean and Cretan; *–nt*-participles in Heraclea having dat. pl. in –ασσιν; presents in –είω (= -εύω) in Elean; infinitive in –μειν in Rhodian; also some characteristics that are to be ascribed to the pre-Doric substratum (e.g. Laconian Ποhοιδᾶν, cf. Arcadian Ποσοι-; Cretan οἰ, αἰ, ἰν/ἰς, cf. Arcadian οἱ, αἱ, ἰν). In spite of d) and e), a) points clearly to a continuum that originally was close to 'West Greek' (→ Greek dialects) dating to the end of the 2nd millen-

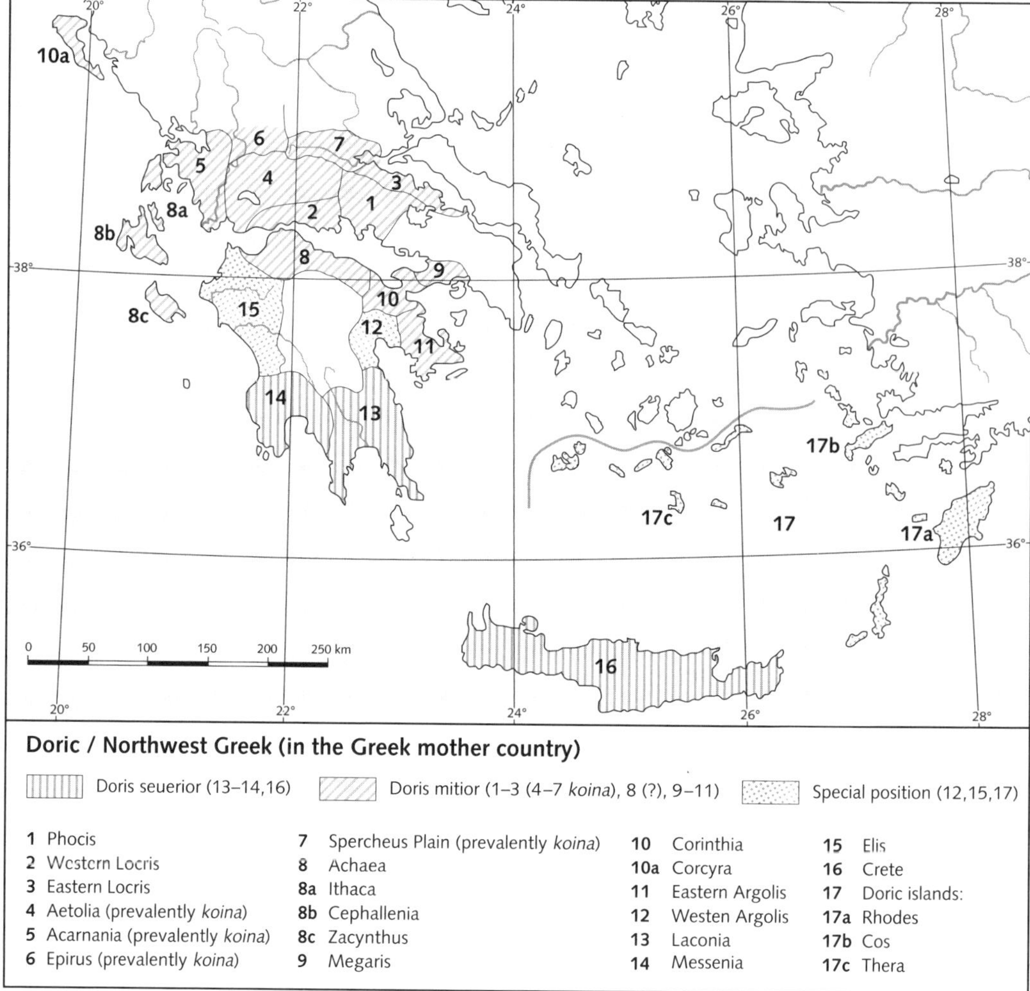

nium and first spreading into Greece in the course of the → 'Doric migration'; the assumption of a proto-Doric continuum is justified by b) and c).

C. Classification and History up to the 4th–3rd cent. BC

An initial, presumably post-Mycenaean classification of the Doric dialects is based on the isoglosses ἐν (Northwest Greek, Elean) / *ἐν-ς (Doric in the stricter sense) on the one hand and on the first compensatory lengthening and the contractions *e+e*, *o+o*, which result in *ē*/*ō* (ἠμί, βωλά; τρῆς, τῶ: also Arcadian) or *ẹ̄*/*ọ̄* (εἰμί, βουλά; τρεῖς, τοῦ: also Ionian-Attic) on the other (*Doris seuerior* and *Doris mitior* respectively in the terminology going back to H.L. Ahrens). As a result of further developments, differences between the individual dialects increased. Belonging to the *Doris seuerior* are Laconian (also Heraclean as well as the dialects of Magna Graecia) and Cretan (only in the Classical period [3. 92ff.]); Elean (*ā̈* from originally **ē*, e.g. δικασταμεν = δικασθῆναι), West Argolic, Island. Doric and Cyrenaean (*ē*, *ẹ̄* and *ō* [6. 31ff.]) all take a special position. Belonging to the *Doris mitior* are the dialects of the Saronic Gulf (East Argolic, Corinthian, Megarian [1. 113f.]) and the Northwest Greek dialects. The latter stand out by means of characteristics that they partially have in common with Elean (e.g. ΣΤ for *st^h*, opening of *e* before *r*, athematic dat. pl. in –εσσι and in –οις, later also thematic dat. singular in –οι), which however also appear sporadically in other dialects [10. 333ff.]. It is uncertain whether Elean originally belongs to the Northwest Greek dialects: its vowel system i.a. indicates the contrary (see above).

Att.	Lacon.	Cret.	Cyren.	Rhod.	Ele.	Delph.
εἰμί	ἠμί	ἠμί	ἠμί	ἠμί	ἠμί	εἰμί
τοῦ	τῶ	τῶ	τῶ	τοῦ	τῶ	τοῦ
Acc. pl.						
-ους	-ως	-ο(ν)ς	-ος	-ους	-ο(ι)ς	-ους
F. -ουσα	-ω$^{(h)}$α?	-ονσα	-οισα	-ουσα	-ωσα	-ουσα
ξένος	ξένος	ξῆνος	ξῆνος	ξεῖνος	ξένος	ξένος
Inf. -ειν	-ην	-εν	<-Εν>	-ειν	-ην	-εν

From the 4th cent. on, various forms of a 'Doric' *Koiná* partially shaped by common Doric characteristics (e.g. ᾱ, –(ν)τι; ἱαρός, αἴ κα) and based on the Attic officialese, were evident practically everywhere, including the Aetolian (with athematic dat. pl. in –οις, ἐν with acc.), especially in the north-west, as well as those of the Achaean Confederacy (→ Achaeans, Achaea), especially in the Peloponnese. The relationships between dialects and *Koinaí* differ according to each region.

D. Samples

Laconian (242 BC): δεξωμεσα ταν εκεχηριαν ταν τω Αιγλαπιω αη, ταν τοι Κωοι εφενεποντι. Corresponding Attic: δεξόμεθα τὴν ἐκεχειρίαν τὴν τοῦ Ἀσκληπιοῦ ἀεί, ἣν οἱ Κῷοι ἐπαγγέλλουσι.

Heraclea (4th cent.): κατεταμομες δε μεριδας τετορας. Corresponding Attic: κατετάμομεν δὲ μερίδας τέτταρας.

Cretan (Gortyn, 3rd cent.): νομισματι χρηтθαι τωι καυχωι ... · τοδ δ' οδελονς μη δεκετθαι τονς αργυριος. Corresponding Attic: νομίσματι χρᾶσθαι τῷ χαλκῷ ... · τοὺς δ' ὀβολοὺς μὴ δέχεσθαι τοὺς ἀργυρίους.

Cyrenaean (4th cent.): αυτα δε ουχ υπω[ροφος] ... τενται ουδε μιασει μεστα κα [ες] Αρταμιν ενθηι · ... αι δε κα μη εκοισα μιαι κα[θ]αρει το ιαρον. Corresponding Attic: αὕτη δὲ οὐκ ὑπωροφος ... ἔσται οὐδὲ μιανθήσεται ἕως ἂν εἰς Ἄρτεμιν ἔλθῃ · ... ἐὰν δὲ μὴ ἑκοῦσα μιανθῇ, καθαρεῖ τὸ ἱερόν.

Elean (4th cent.): ταιρ δε γενεαιρ μα φυγαδειημ μαδε κατ οποιον τροπον · ... εξηστω δε ... τοι δηλομενοι νοστιττην και ατταμιον ημεν · ... τοιρ δε επ' ασιστα μα αποδοσσαι ... τα χρηματα τοιρ φυγαδεσσι. Corresponding Attic: τὰς δὲ γενεὰς μὴ φυγαδεύειν μηδὲ καθ' ὁποῖον τρόπον · ... ἐξέστω δὲ ... τῷ βουλομένῳ νοστεῖν καὶ ἀζήμιον εἶναι ... τοὺς δὲ ἐπ' ἄγχιστα μὴ ἀποδόσθαι ... τὰ χρήματα τοῖς φυγάσι.

Delphian (5th cent.): τον Ϝοινον μὲ φαρεν ες του δρομου· αι δε κα φαρε̃ι, hιλαξαστο̃ τον θεον. Corresponding Attic: τὸν οἶνον μὴ φέρειν ἐκ τοῦ δρόμου · ἐὰν δὲ φέρῃ, ἱλασάσθω τὸν θεὸν. (About 400): ταγε[υ]σεω ... κ]ατα τουν νομους ... · των δε προστα τεθνακοτων εν τοις σαματεσσι μη θρηνειν μηδ' οτοτυζεν. Corresponding Attic: ταγεύσω κατὰ τοὺς νόμους ... · τῶν δὲ πρόσθεν τεθνηκότων ἐν τοῖς σήμασι μὴ θρηνεῖν μηδ' ὀτοτύζειν.

→ Doric migration (with map); → Greek dialects; → Greek literary languages; → Koine

Sources: 2–3, 6–12.

Bibliography: 1 A. Bartoněk, Classification of the West Greek Dialects at the time about 350 BC, 1972 2 Bechtel, Dial. II 3 M. Bile, Le dialecte crétois ancien [with: Recueil des inscriptions postérieures aux IC], 1988 4 M. Bile et al., Bulletin de dialectologie grecque, in: REG 101, 1988, 74–112 (research report) 5 C. Brixhe, Le déclin du dialecte crétois: essai de phénomenologie, in: E. Crespo et al. (ed.), Dialectologica Graeca Miraflores 1993, 37–71 6 C. Dobias-Lalou, Le dialecte des inscriptions grecques de Cyrène, 1998 7 L. Dubois, Inscriptions grecques dialectales de Sicile, 1989 8 Id., Une table de malédiction de Pella: s'agit-il du premier texte macédonien?, in: REG 108, 1995, 190–197 9 A. Landi, Dialetti e interazione sociale in Magna Grecia, 1979 (inscription 223–343) 10 J. Méndez Dosuna, Los dialectos dorios del Noroeste. Gramática y estudio dialectal, 1985 11 J. J. Moralejo Álvarez, Gramática de las inscripciones délficas (fonética y morfología) (siglos VI-III a.C.), 1973 12 Thumb/Kieckers.

Maps: Bechtel, Dial. II J. Méndez Dosuna, Los dialectos dorios del Noroeste, 1985 M. Bile, Le dialecte crétois ancien, 1988 Id. i.a., Bulletin de dialectologie grecque, in: REG 101, 1988, 74–112.

J.G.-R.

E. Doric since the 4th cent. BC

With the spread of the written Ionian-Attic *Koinḗ* (*K.*), which in some places supersedes a short-lived Doric-coloured *K.*, Doric as a written dialect disappears with varying speed according to the area. This does not affect all dialect characteristics at the same time; typically, beginning Koineization can be documented first in the colonies less committed to the mother country traditions, as on the Heraclea tables (4th cent. BC), there above all in numerals (e.g. Ϝικατι next to — rarer — εικοσι). Likewise in Panhellenic Delphi, influences of the *K.* appear quite early (2nd half of the 4th cent.), but the dialect is used on private inscriptions well into the early Imperial period. Forms such as νακορος and σατες are still preserved on papyri of the 3rd cent. BC. On Crete, hybrid forms such as ειμεν ('crossed' from ἦμεν and εἶναι) appear since the end of the 3rd — beginning of the 2nd cent.; in this the type of document also plays a role: the Doric dialect is to be found in its 'purest' form on inscriptions that are concerned with inner-Cretan matters, while a contract with → Antigonus [3] Doson is completely written in *K.* In Cyrenaica around the turn of the historical periods, *K.*-inscriptions take the upper hand, while dialect inscriptions do not completely disappear until the 2nd–3rd cent. AD; in particular, genitives in –α to stems in a and in –ω to stems in o are retained longer than the article forms τοί and ταί. In Laconian, *K.* inscriptions are in the majority starting in the 1st cent. AD (in Messenia even later). Rhodes appears as especially resistant to the *K.*, where prose inscriptions are written predominantly in dialect up into the 1st–2nd cent. AD.

To the extent the fragmentary knowledge of the vocabulary peculiar to Doric allows such statements, as a whole the contribution of Doric to the *K.* is to be described as minor, with the exception of a few words from the military and judicial area (e.g. λοχαγός, which however was already absorbed into Attic and presumably spread from there; or for instance μοιχᾶν for μοιχεύειν which Xen. Hell. 1,6,15 makes a Spartan say); agreements between phenomena documented in Doric and in the *K.* or in modern Greek, e.g. λαός for Attic λεώς, genitives in –α to nominatives in –ας or the thematization of athematic verbs (in Messenian ὀμνύω and ἀνοίγω have been documented quite early), are difficult to judge insofar that it could also be a matter of early Koineization (after all, archaic inscriptions from Doric dialect regions are rare; the sources often do not become more ample until the Hellenistic period) or of convergence phenomena. Knowledge of the development of Late and New Greek will also make the classification as specifically Doric-Northwest Greek characteristics of, for example, a dat. ἀγώνοις or of the change from/st^h/>/ st/ : <σθ> : <στ> appear problematic.

With the archaism of the Imperial period, for a short period Doric is used once again not only in literature but also in inscriptions; Late Laconian is of special mention here. The basic question raised by this as by related phenomena in Aeolic is to what extent learned traditions were at play here or whether one could still draw on living knowledge of the dialect; in particular, the assessment of hyperdialecticisms is controversial. In the case of the Late Laconian inscriptions, much speaks in favour of continuity: although obsolete spelling conventions are revived (e.g. <ϝ> again introduced, although the sound had been <β> already in the 3rd cent. BC), it demonstrates a few innovations in contrast to the older Doric, such as the → rhotacism, which is incompatible with the assumption of an artificial revival without a spoken language background.

Independent of the fate of Doric as a local writing variety, it is also worth asking about spoken Doric; evidence from Theocritus (Adoniazusai 15) points to Doric being spoken in the Hellenistic period in Alexandria, and various testimonies refer to Doric spoken in the motherland as late as the imperial period: Strabo (8,1,2: ἔτι καὶ νῦν κατὰ πόλεις ἄλλοι ἄλλως διαλέγονται, δοκοῦσι δὲ δωρίζειν ἅπαντες), of Suetonius (Tib. 66 about spoken Doric on Rhodes) and of Pausanias (4,27,11 about the population of Messenia); Dion Chrysostomos claims to have met an old woman speaker of the dialect in → Elis (1,54 δωρίζουσα τῇ φωνῇ). These testimonies are credible insofar as traces of the Doric have been preserved to modern times, recognizable above all in the retaining of the /ā/; apart from toponyms and loan-words in Lat. (*malum* < μᾶλον 'Apple', cf. however Italian *mela* < μῆλον), which prove nothing for the living on of the dialect after the Hellenistic period, southern-Italian dialect words (such as Sicilian *casentaru* < γᾶς ἔντερον 'earthworm') and Doric vocabulary in the Greek dialect of lower Italy spoken yet today (*nasída* < νᾶσος or *lanó* < λανός), are especially relevant and support ROHLFS' thesis of Greek being spoken continually in lower Italy since the archaic colonization, not only since the Byzantine period, as argued by PARLANGÈLI. Indeed there even exists a New Greek dialect that can almost be described as New Doric: Tsaconian with its highly archaic character such as, e.g., retention of /ā/(*fona* < φωνά), retention of the digamma sound (*vanne* < ϝαρνίον), retention of/u/(*psjuχa* < ψυχά) and the rhotacism first occurring in Late Laconian (*tar amer* for τᾶς ἁμέρας); the fact that dialect testimonies completely disappear from the 3rd cent. AD should therefore not lead to the conclusion that the spoken dialect died out at the same time or shortly afterwards.

M. BILE, C. BRIXHE, Le dialecte crétois, unité ou diversité?, in: C. BRIXHE (ed.), Sur la Crète antique: histoire, écritures, langues, 1991, 85–138; C. BRIXHE, La langue comme reflet de l'histoire ou les éléments non doriens du dialecte crétois, in: Id. (ed.), ibid., 43–77; Id., Le déclin du dialecte crétois: essai de phénoménologie, in: E. CRESPO, J. L. GARCÍA-RAMÓN (ed.), Dialectologica Graeca. Actas del II Coloquio Internacional de Dialectología Griega (Miraflores de la Sierra 19–21 de Juni de 1991, 1993, 37–71 (on the Koineization on Crete); V. BUBENÍK, Hellenistic and Roman Greece as a Sociolinguistic Area, 1989, 73–138 (on the proportion of dialect to Koine inscriptions in single Doric-language regions); S. CARATZAS, L'origine des dialectes néogrecs de l'Italie méridionale, 1958; A. DEBRUNNER, A. SCHERER, Gesch. der griech. Sprache II: Grundfragen und Grundzüge des nachklassischen Griech., 1969; C. DOBIAS-LALOU, Dialecte et Koinè dans les inscriptions de Cyrénaïque, in: Verbum 10, 1982, 29–50 (also in: Actes de la première rencontre internationale de dialectologie grecque, Nancy, 1–3 Juillet 1981) (on the retention of the dialect in the Cyrenaica); E. FRAENKEL, Griech. und Italisch, in: IF 60, 1952, 131–155 (135–137 on the dialectization of Koine forms); E. KIECKERS, Das Eindringen der Koine in Kreta, in: IF 27, 1910, 72–118; A. MORPURGO DAVIES, Geography, History and Dialect: The Case of Oropos, in: E. CRESPO, J. L. GARCÍA-RAMÓN (ed.), Dialectologica Graeca (see above), 261–279 (i.a. also on the Late Laconian); H. PERNOT, Introduction à l'étude du dialecte tsakonien, 1934; G. ROHLFS, L'antico Ellenismo nell'Italia di oggi, in: Id., Latinità ed Ellenismo nel Mezzogiorno d'Italia, 1985, 33–54; Id., Grammatica storica dei dialetti italogreci, [2]1977; A. THUMB, Die griech. Sprache im Zeitalter des Hellenismus, 1901 (28–101 on the dying out of the old dialects and their contribution to the origin of the Koine; 38f. on the relationship of the dialect to the Koine inscriptions on Rhodes); A. THUMB, E. KIECKERS, Hdb. der griech. Dialekte I, [2]1932.

V.BI.

Doric Migration The migration of Doric tribes from north-western and central Greece into their historical settlement areas in southern Greece was already considered in antiquity the divide between the Heroic Age and the historical period (Thuc. 1,12). In the 1st millennium BC Megaris, Corinthia, Argolis, Laconia and Messene constituted the Doric regions of the Peloponnese, especially on the evidence of their dialect. Furthermore, the islands of the southern Aegean, Crete and the coast of Asia Minor around Halicarnassus were part of Doric territory. The testimony of Linear B texts from the Mycenaean palaces of the Argolis and Messene confirms that towards the end of the 2nd millennium BC a Greek dialect was spoken in the Peloponnese that was not Doric. Therefore, it may be assumed that the arrival of Doric-speaking populations only occurred in the post-Mycenaean period, i.e. after 1200 BC. Nevertheless, Doric is part of the group of Greek dialects that formed after the immigration of Indo-Germanic tribes into Greece about 2000 BC and does not represent a post-Mycenaean development. Therefore, it must have been spoken during the Bronze Age in Greece. The close relationship of the Doric dialect with the north-western Greek dialects suggests the regions of central and north-western Greece as the home of the Dorians [1; 2].

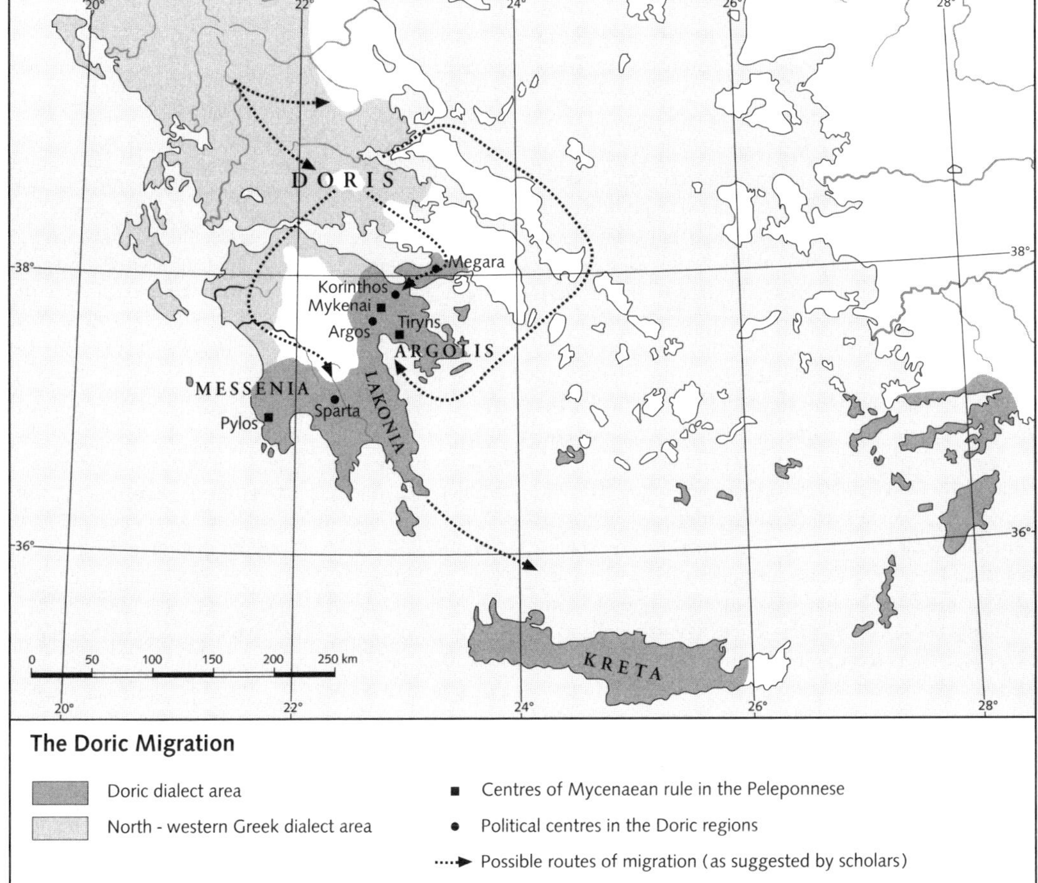

J. CHADWICK has challenged this assumption and argued that traces of the Doric dialect can already be detected in the Mycenaean Greek of the Peloponnese; as a result he has doubted the Doric migration (DM) altogether. In this view, the Doric tribes already resided in the 2nd millennium as a lower social layer within the boundaries of the Mycenaean kingdoms and only came to power in an uprising against Mycenaean rule [3; 4]. This view is not only contradicted by details of the linguistic situation (see above) but also by the historical tradition.

The DM was mythologically expressed in the legend of the return of the → Heraclidae. It told of the descendants of Hercules who sought refuge with → Aegimius [1], king of the Dorians, in central Greece after the death of the hero on the Oeta and three generations later conquered the Peloponnese with the Dorians. By lot → Temenus received Argolis, the twin sons of → Aristodemus [1] Laconia and → Cresphontes the region of Messene. According to this tradition the return of the Heraclids terminated the ruling families known from the epics. It is the origin of the view that the DM brought about the end of Mycenaean palace culture. Although the legend mainly served to justify the historical settlement and power situation in the Peloponnese and its origin cannot be dated before the 7th cent. BC, it presupposes the concept that the Dorians were migrants into the Peloponnese [5]. Homer's presentation, which deliberately archaizes and avoids reference to events more recent than the Trojan War, is also based on the assumption that the Doric immigration and settlement occurred later. Homer's epics show no knowledge of the legend of the return of the Heraclids and the Dorians were only mentioned in a single anachronistic passage (Hom. Od. 19,177) as a people on Crete.

The fact that the distribution of the three Doric *phylai* (→ Phyle) Hylleis, Dymanes and Pamphyloi, the festivals (Karneia, cf. Thuc. 5,54; Paus. 3,13,4) and the names of the months are the same in the entire Doric settlement area points to a common origin of the Doric tribes (→ Dorieis) before the DM. An origin in north and central Greece is suggested by their dialect and also several names of months which they shared with the tribes of northern and central Greece (e.g., Apellaios), the legend of the Doric king Aegimius, which is located in the area about the Gulf of Malis, their claim that the small region of → Doris in central Greece is their metropolis (Tyrt. Fr. 2 WEST; Hdt. 8,31; 8,43; Thuc. 1,107,2; 3,92,3) and the early contacts of the Spartan

Dorians with the Apollo sanctuary of Delphi. Traces of their life as semi-nomadic shepherds and pastoral warriors appear to be preserved in the archaic customs of Sparta. The model of a pastoral migration dominates the image of the DM in current research [6].

The DM is not tangible in archaeological terms: certain objects and customs which include, for example, the production of a handmade alien pottery, wearing of pairs of long clothes pins and the introduction of cist tombs, and that were new in the material culture of the → Dark Ages have in vain been linked to the Dorians and their immigration. Current research holds factors other than the DM responsible for the destruction of the Mycenaean palaces and the demise of the Mycenaean palace system *c.* 1200 BC (bibliography in [7; 8]). The lack of archaeological evidence for the DM has been the reason for doubting the credibility of the historical tradition [9. 166–180]. However, the end of the DM becomes tangible with the beginnings of their historical settlements: the foundation of → Sparta occurred with the building of the Artemis Orthia sanctuary about the middle of the 10th cent. BC [6. 370–376]. The Doric settlement of Argus probably began as early as the 11th cent. BC if the earliest post-Mycenaean settlement there is interpreted in this sense. The settlement of Dorians in Messene before the first Messenian War and the rule of Sparta remains uncertain. Essentially, one must assume that various Doric tribal groups migrated into the former core areas of Mycenaean culture in the Peloponnese and settled there at various times, but only *c.* 150–300 years after the destruction of the Mycenaean palaces [8]. Subsequently, Dorians also settled on Crete and the Doric islands of the Aegean.

→ Aegean Koine; → Greek dialects; → Linear B; → Mycenaean Culture

1 E. Risch, Die griech. Dialekte im 2. vorchristlichen Jt., in: SMEA 20, 1979, 91–110 2 Id., La posizione del dialetto dorico, in: D. Musti (ed.), Le origini dei Greci, 1985, 13–35 3 J. Chadwick, Who were the Dorians?, in: PP 31, 1976, 105–131 4 Id., Der Beitrag der Sprachwissenschaft zur Rekonstruktion der griech. Frühgesch., in: AAWW 113, 1976, 183–204 5 F. Prinz, Gründungsmythen und Sagenchronologie, 1979, 206–213 6 E. Kirsten, Gebirgshirtentum und Seßhaftigkeit — die Bedeutung der Dark Ages für die griech. Staatenwelt: Doris und Sparta, in: S. Deger-Jalkotzy (ed.), Griechenland, die Ägäis und die Levante während der 'Dark Ages' vom 12. bis zum 9. Jh.v.Chr., 1983, SAWW 418, 356–443 7 J. Vanschoonwinkel, L'Égée et la Méditerranée orientale à la fin du deuxième millénaire, 1991 8 B. Eder, Argolis, Lakonien, Messenien vom Ende der myk. Palastzeit bis zur Einwanderung der Dorier, 1998 9 J. T. Hooker, Mycenaean Greece, 1977.

Maps: E. Kirsten, Gebirgshirtentum und Seßhaftigkeit — die Bedeutung der Dark Ages für die Griech. Staatenwelt: Doris und Sparta, in: S. Deger-Jalkotzy (ed.), Griechenland, die Ägäis und die Levante während der 'Dark Ages' vom 12. bis zum 9.Jh. v.Chr., 1983, 356–443.

BI.ED.

Dorieis (Δωριεῖς; *Dōrieîs*, 'Dorians'). The name D., documented in the Mycenaean as yet only in the personal name *Dōrieús*, describes in the Classical period on the one hand the inhabitants of a small nation state in central Greece in the uppermost section of the Cephissus valley, and on the other hand the entirety of the inhabitants — who according to legend set off from there — of the eastern and southern Peloponnese (Argolis with Sicyon, Corinth, Megara and Aegina, Laconice and Messenia), of the islands of the southern Aegean (Crete, Melos, Thera, Anaphe, Astypalaea and the Dodecanesus) and the cities situated on the Carian coast, Halicarnassus and Cnidus, as well as of the overseas colonies settled by these Dorian regions. The D. in this second sense of the word did not form a political unit, but they were connected by closely related dialects, by many similar types of institutions, specifically in the political and cultic realms (e.g. Phyles, festivals, related calendars) and by the consciousness of a common descent. However, this did not find expression in concerted action because the largest Dorian cities of the motherland, Argus and Sparta, were enemies.

This geographical distribution indicates that the D. had advanced from the east and the south of the Peloponnese over the island chains of the southern Aegean up to the coast of Asia Minor. The existence of the central Greek D. also suggests that the Peloponnesian D. came from the Greek mainland. Further observations confirm this:

1) The Doric dialects are scarcely different in their old characteristics from the Northwest Greek dialects (from Epirus to Phocis, Elis and Achaea), yet markedly different from all other Greek dialects.

2) The close kinship of the Mycenaean, Arcadian and Cypriot dialects indicates that the Peloponnese and Crete were inhabited by speakers of this dialect group before the D. settled there.

3) According to the tradition of the D., they had not conquered their Peloponnesian places of residence until towards the end of the legendary period under the leadership of the Heraclidae (→ Doric Migration).

4) As foreign conquerors, they still ruled widely over servile farmers (→ Helots) in the archaic and classical period.

Therefore, it is best to accept the traditional view of the Peloponnesian and insular D. as a post-Mycenaean immigrant stratum of north-west Greek origin. An important clue to the time of their immigration — not securely tangible archaeologically — is the fact that although the later Arcadian-Cypriot dialects derive from Mycenaean, yet they exhibit a number of joint innovations, so that the bulk of the later Cypriot Greeks cannot have left the Peloponnese (under the pressure of the D.) until some considerable time after the destruction of the palaces around 1200 BC. Incidentally, the process of Dorianization of the Peloponnesian and south-Aegean regions is likely to have taken several generations, since the D. to all appearances first established themselves at just a few points and then from

there occupied more and more new regions through colonization campaigns; tradition also derives individual cities of the islands and of Caria from certain Peloponnesian mother cities. However, at the time when the coherent historical records begin for us (8th cent. BC), all of these movements had long been completed.
→ Doric/Northwest Greek; → Doric Migration

J. CHADWICK, Who were the Dorians?, in: PdP 31, 1976, 103–117; S. DEGER-JALKOTZY (ed.), Griechenland, die Ägäis und die Levante während der 'Dark Ages' (Symposion Zwettl 1980), 1983; A. MALKIN, Colonisation spartiate dans la Mer Égée, in: REA 95, 1993, 365–381; D. MUSTI (ed.), Le origini dei Greci, 1985; V. PARKER, Zur Datierung der Dorischen Wanderung, in: MH 52, 1995, 130–154. F.GSCH.

Dorieus (Δωριεύς; *Dorieús*).
[1] Spartan, Agiad, son of Anaxandridas II and his first wife, older brother of the kings Leonidas and Cleombrotus, younger half-brother of Cleomenes I, who was born before D., but to the second wife of Anaxandridas, whom he due to the initial infertility of his first wife had additionally married at the direction of the ephors and gerontes. After Cleomenes as the eldest son had succeeded to the throne (Hdt. 5,41f.; Paus. 3,3,9f.), D. organized—allegedly due to outrage over this ruling—a colonist campaign to Libya *c.* 515–14 BC and founded an → Apoikia in the oasis region at the river Cinyps (Oued Caam). The Carthaginians, who regarded it as a threat, destroyed it in league with the nomadic Macae *c.* 512. D. returned with his people to Sparta, but took off once again two years later and founded Heraclea at Eryx in Sicily. There, with the majority of his companions, he soon fell in battle against the allied Carthaginians and Segestans (Hdt. 5,46; Diod. Sic. 4,23,3; Paus. 3,16,4). His previous participation in the destruction of Sybaris in league with the Crotoniates (Hdt. 5,44f.) remains dubious. His campaigns exemplify the possibilities and limits of the actions of representatives of higher Greek nobility at the end of the archaic period. The later attempt by Gelon of Gela to exploit the memory of D. in *c.* 489 in order to gain Sparta's aid against Carthage remained unsuccessful (Hdt. 7,158).

D. ASHERI, Carthaginians and Greeks, in: CAH 4, 1982, 751f.; H. BERVE, Die Tyrannis bei den Griechen I, 1967, 178f.; HUSS, 60f.; G. MASTRUZZO, Osservazioni sulla spedizione di Dorieo, in: Sileno 3, 1977, 129–147. K.-W.WEL.

[2] Youngest son [1. no. 322] of → Diagoras [1. no. 252], who was the progenitor of a famous Rhodian athletic lineage [2. 136–138] of the 5th cent. BC. According to Delphian inscriptions [3. no. 23], he was one of the most successful athletes in antiquity as three-time *periodonikes* [4. no. 13] in the pankration. He had victories in Olympia in 432, 428, 424 BC [1. no. 322, 326, 330], where base fragments have been found with remains of victory inscriptions [5. no. 153]. After a sports career of *c.* 15 years, he took up political activities predominantly against Athens, which released him as a prisoner in consideration of his athletic fame; after the island Rhodes seceded from the Lacedaemonians in 395 BC, he was executed by the same (Paus. 6,7,4–6).

1 L. MORETTI, Olympionikai, 1957 2 W. DECKER, Sport in der griechischen Antike, 1995 3 L. MORETTI, Iscrizioni agonistiche greche, 1953 4 R. KNAB, Die Periodoniken, 1934, repr. 1980 5 W. DITTENBERGER, K. PURGOLD, Die Inschriften von Olympia, 1896.

H. SWOBODA, s.v. D., RE 5, 1560f.; M.B. POLIAKOFF, Combat Sports in the Ancient World, 1987, 119–121. W.D.

[3] Author of an epigram that is recorded in Ath. 10,412f, whose authority is an historian of the 3rd cent. BC, Phylarchos (FGrH 81 F 3): the amusing anecdote tells of the Herculean gourmet feasting achievement by the famous athlete Milon of Croton (Anth. Pal. append. 3,95 COUGNY = SH 396). The hypothesis that this D. is to be identified with the same-named gourmand that Leonidas of Tarent makes the subject of a satire (Anth. Pal. 6,305) is attractive.

FGE 45f. E.D.

Dorillus (Δόριλλος; *Dórillos*). Tragedian; mocked in the *Lémniai* of Aristophanes (PCG III 2,382, *c.* 413–05 BC) as *doríallon* ('female private parts' [1. 130ff., especially 146 and 148]); possibly the same as Dorilaus, a contemporary of Euripides (see DID C 18).

1 J. HENDERSON, The Maculate Muse, 1975.

TrGF 41. F.P.

Dorimachus (Δωρίμαχος; *Dōrímachos*). Aetolian from Trichonion, son of Nicostratus, was victorious as *stratēgós* of the Aetolian league in 221–20 BC with → Scopas against Messenia (Pol. 4,10–13). In 220–19 he plundered Epirus and set the temple of Zeus in Dodona on fire (Diod. Sic. 26,4,7; Pol. 4,67). He turned against Thessaly in order to withdraw Philipp V from the siege of Pale (Pol. 5,5,1), then heard of Philipp's invasion in Aetolia, from where on his arrival the Macedons had already withdrawn victoriously (Pol. 5,17,5–8). In 211, D., who as *princeps Aetolorum* (Liv. 26,24,7) had spoken for an alliance with Rome against Philipp V a year earlier, attempted with the aid of Roman troops to stop Philipp V from capturing Echinus, however without success (Pol. 9,42,1–4; for D.'s office as strategist in the same year cf. WALBANK). D. and Scopas (205–04?) were elected as *nomothêtai* in order to reduce the high debt of Aetolia. However, their proposals met with strong resistance (Pol. 13,1; 1a). Later, as an Aetolian envoy, D. contributed to the condemnation of Scopas in Alexandria (IG IX² 30; Pol. 18,54,4).

CAH 7,1 ²1984, 474–75; HM 3, 370, 372, 376; F.W. WALBANK, Philipp V. of Macedon, 1940, Index s.v. D. ME.STR.

Dorion see → Cookery books

Doris (Δωρίς; *Dōrís*).
I. Personal names II. Place names

I. Personal names
Feminine shortened version of the name *Eúdōros* and similar, likely often understood as 'the giver' (cf. *dōron*, 'Gift').
[I 1] One of the → Oceanids, the daughters of Oceanus and of Tethys (Hes. Theog. 350); cf. Polydore and Eudore in Hes. Theog. 354; 360 and the 'Dorids' in Goethe's 'Faust'. Wife of Nereus, mother of the 50 → Nereids (Hes. Theog. 241; Apollod. 1,11; Ov. Met. 2,11; 269).
[I 2] Daughter of Nereus and of D. [I 1], one of the → Nereids (Hom. Il. 18,45; Hes. Theog. 250; cf. Eudore, Dotho at Hes. Theog. 244; 248). D. can stand for 'sea' metonymically (Arat. 658; Verg. Ecl. 10,5 D. *amara*; Ov. Fast. 4,678).

A. Lesky, Thalatta, 1947, 115f.; R. Wachter, Nereiden und Neoanalyse: Ein Blick hinter die Ilias, in: WJA 1990, 19–31. R.B.

II. Place names
[II 1] A basin landscape in central Greece at the headwaters of the Cephissus surrounded on three sides by high mountain ranges (Parnassus and Corax — modern Giona — in the south and south-west, Oete and Kallidromon in the north and north-west); bordering on D. were Oitaia, Malis and the eastern Locris in the north, Phocis in the east, the western Locris in the south and Aetolia in the west [2; 3]. D. certainly had fertile soil for planting (re. the term Λιμοδωριεῖς, 'Hunger Dorians', at Scyl. 62, Hsch. s.v., cf. [2. 422; 3. 236f.]). Although, only c. 190 km² large, D. was strategically important due to the control of important north-south connections that led between Oete and Kallidromon into D. and from there through the Cephissus valley to the south-east or over a further pass between Corax and Parnassus directly to the south [1].

During their migration to the south, the → Dorieis are reported to have driven out the first inhabitants of the land, the Dryopes, and founded the cities Boeum, Erineus and Cytenium, which then by adding Acyphas/Pindus became the Doric tetrapolis. From the 7th cent. BC on, D. was regarded as the *mētrópolis* and homeland of the Dorieis (References: Tyrtaeus fr. 2 West; Hdt. 1,56; 8,43; Scymn. 592ff.; Diod. Sic. 4,67,1; Str. 8,6,13; 9,3,1; 4,10; 10,4,6; Conon, FGrH 26 F 1,27; Plin. HN 4,28; Ptol. 3,14,14; Aristid. 12,40; schol. Pind. Pyth. 1,121; schol. Aristoph. Plut. 385; schol. Lycoph. Alex. 980). D. was a member of the Delphian amphictyony. Constantly besieged in the Classical and Hellenistic period by neighbouring states, D. became a member of the Aetolian league in the 3rd cent. BC; from 166 BC on, D. existed as a federal state up into the Roman Imperial period (compilation of sources at [3. 238f.]).

1 E.W. Kase et al. (ed.), The Great Isthmus Corridor Route, 1991 2 Philippson/Kirsten, I,2, 419ff. 657ff. 3 D. Rousset, Les Doriens de la Métropole, in: BCH 113, 1989, 199–239.

D. Rousset, Les Doriens de la Métropole, in: BCH 114, 1990, 445–472; Id., Les Doriens de la Métropole, in: BCH 118, 1994, 361–374. P.F.

Doriscus (Δορίσκος; *Dorískos*, *Doriscum*). Settlement in the west of the Hebrus estuary (modern Evros) in the plain of the same name (Hdt. 7,59). In 512 BC it was laid out by Darius I as the starting point of his campaign against the Greeks and as a provisions storehouse, and it was also used in this way by Xerxes (Hdt. 7,25, 108; inspection of troops by Xerxes: 7,59f.; Plin. HN 4,43). The commander of the Persian garrison was Maskames (7,105f.). It was captured in 346 BC by Philippus II (Aeschin. In Ctes. 82; Liv. 31,16,4). It was newly founded by Trajan as Traianopolis [1. 137–140]

B.H. Isaac, The Greek Settlements in Thrace until the Macedonian Conquest, 1986. I.v.B.

Dormouse (Lat. *glis*). The biggest central and southern European species of the nocturnal rodent family of dormice with a body length of 13–20 cm and a tail length of 10–18 cm. From the 2nd cent. BC onwards the dormouse was fattened for gourmet consumption by the Romans in special breeding enclosures (*gliraria*, description in Varro, Rust. 3,15) with beech nuts, chestnuts and walnuts (example of the high return: Varro, Rust. 3,2,14; roasted and coated with honey and sprinkled with poppy: Petron. Sat. 31,10; Apicius 8,408). In 115 BC this was prohibited in vain by a luxury law (Plin. HN 8,233) and again in 78 BC by the *Lex Aemilia*. Dormice live in grass nests in the hollows of trees and in crevices in rocks, are sleepy during the day (*somniculosus*: Mart. 3,58,36) and hibernate in self-excavated holes in the ground, which are up to 1 m deep. Pictorial representations are to be found in [1].

1 Keller 1,191–193.

H. Gossen s. v. S., RE 2 A, 2240–2242. C. HÜ.

Doron graphe (Δώρων γραφή; *Dṓrōn graphḗ*). In Athens, the charge of corruptibility (Poll. 8,42), also including the corruptibility of a judge. Active bribery in connection with jurisdiction was prosecuted with → *dekasmoû graphḗ*. The offence consisted in presents given to, and accepted by, officials, among whom the lawyers in public and private trials were also counted (Dem. Or. 46,26), to the detriment of the state (Lys. 21,22: ἐπὶ τῆς πόλεως κακῷ; Dem. Or. 21,113: ἐπὶ βλάβῃ τοῦ δήμου). The charge was filed in lighter cases with the → *logistaí*, in graver cases with the → *thesmothêtai* (Aristot. Ath. Pol. 59,3). In grave cases the punishment was death, in lighter cases a sum of money ten times the value of the gift or bribery was required (Aristot. Ath. Pol. 54,2). In each case, it involved the complete loss of civil rights, which extended to the descendants.

BUSOLT/SWOBODA, 1077, 1098 J. BLEICKEN, Die athenische Demokratie, [2]1994, 358. G.T.

Dorotheus (Δωρόθεος; *Dōrótheos*).

[1] Sculptor of bronze from Argos. Known by two signatures from the middle of the 5th cent. BC on bases in Delphi and in Hermione (Crete), with traces of an inlet for a horse or rider statue.

J. MARCADÉ, Recueil des signatures des sculptures grecques, 1, 1953, no. 30–31; P. ORLANDINI, I donari firmati da Kresilas e Dorotheos a Hermione, in: ArchCl 3, 1951, 94–98. R.N.

[2] Painter from the middle of the 1st cent. AD. Commissioned by Nero to replace the damaged picture of Aphrodite by → Apelles [4] in the temple of Caesar with a copy (Plin. HN 35,91).

L. GUERRINI, s.v. D. 3, EAA 3, 177.; I. SCHEIBLER, Griech. Malerei der Antike, 1994, 23. N.H.

[3] Greek grammarian and lexicographer from Ascalon (Steph. Byz. 132.6, s.v. Ἀσκάλων), probably from the early Imperial period, author of a lexicographical work that is quoted as Λέξεων συναγωγή or as Ἀττικὴ λέξις/Ἀττικαὶ λέξεις and was still available, at least partially, to Phot. (Bibl. 100a 156). Since Athenaeus (who quotes the work several times) mentions the 108th book in VII 329 d, it must have been a rather substantial collection. In schol. Hom. Il. 10,252a, an opinion of D. in opposition to Aristonicus and Tryphon is reported (from bk. 31). Porphyrius (on Hom. Il. 9,90) says that D. wrote an entire book about the word κλίσιον (probably a section from the main work). From Ath. 14,662f we know that he occupied himself with Antiphanes (cf. PCG II, p. 313) and the poets of the New Comedy. Equating him with the D. mentioned by Clem.Al. strom. I 21 = II 82,21 STÄHLIN is very dubious. [1].
→ Antiphanes [1]; → Aristonicus; → Tryphon

1 L. COHN, s.v. D. (20), RE 5, 1571–72 2 H. ERBSE, Beiträge zur Überlieferung der Iliasscholien, 1960, 117–119 3 M. H. E. MEIER, Opuscula academica II, 1863, 42–43. F.M.

[4] from Chalcis. Son of Pythippus, listed in IG 7,543,5 (90–80 BC) as victor at the Sarapieia in Tanagra as tragedian (?). Perhaps brother of Gorgippus from Chalcis (TrGF 175).

TrGF 160. F.P.

[5] of Sidon. Author of an astrological didactic poem in five books (1st cent. AD) that was used by → Firmicus Maternus. Only a few hexameters and parts of a prose version are extant. An expanded Arabian translation points to an intensive use of this poem by Islamic astronomers.

D. PINGREE (ed.), Dorothei Sidonii Carmen Astrologicum, 1976. C.S.

[6] Antiochian presbyter (around AD 290). Eusebius is our source for this highly-educated eunuch who had a command of Hebrew and the classics (HE 7,32,2–4). According to him, Emperor Diocletian transferred supervision of the purple dye work of Tyrus to D. as a mark of favour. This contemporary of Lucianus of Antioch is not identical with a martyr and court official of the same name also mentioned by Eusebius (HE 8,1,4; 8,6,1; 5).

BARDENHEWER, GAL II 285f.; L. ABRAMOWSKI, s.v. D. 5), DHGE 14, 685f. J.RI.

[7] Bishop of Marcianopolis (Moesia inferior). Follower of → Nestorius and one of his most stubborn defenders at the oriental synod in Ephesus in AD 431, he allegedly publicly declared himself against the *theotókos* Maria. Later, D. was defrocked and banned; several letters by him (i.a. to the people of Constantinople, Iohannes of Antioch, Emperor Marcianus) and the fragment of an explanation of the Credo are preserved.

EDITIONS: CPG 5781–5786.
BIBLIOGRAPHY: A. VAN ROEY, s.v. D. 8), DHGE 14, 688. J.RI.

[8] Legendary bishop, who according to Theophanes (Chronographia 1, 24 DE BOOR) died as a martyr under Emperor Iulianus. A compilation drawn from different sources, probably created in the 8th–9th cents., as proof of the apostolic founding of Constantinople (disciple and apostle catalogues i.a.) was accredited to him.

EDITIONS: TH. SCHERMANN, Prophetarum vitae fabulosae, 1907, 131–160.
BIBLIOGRAPHY: TH. SCHERMANN, Propheten- und Apostellegenden, 1907, 144–153, 174–198; B. DE GAIFFIER, 'Sub Iuliano Apostata' dans le martyrologe romain, in: Analecta Bollandiana 74, 1956, 19f. J.RI.

[9] Monk in Alexandria (around AD 500). According to an isolated report by Theophanes (chronogr. 1,152f. DE BOOR), author of a lengthy work by the title of τραγῳδία ἤγουν προφητεία τῆς νῦν καταστάσεως ('Tragedy or prophecy of the current conditions') that defends the Council of Calchedon against Emperor Anastasius, who is compared with Iulianus. Anastasius had the author banned and the work burned.

A. JÜLICHER, s.v. D. 27), RE 5, 1574. J.RI.

[10] Professor of law in Berytus in the 1st half of the 6th cent. AD, member of Justinian's commissions for the compilation of the digests (*Tanta*, § 9), of the institutions (*Imperatoriam*, § 3) and of the second reworking of the Codex (*Cordi*, § 2), D. wrote a paraphrased translation to the digests.

F. BRANDSMA, Dorotheus and His Digest Translation, 1996. T.G.

[11] see → Visio Dorothei

Dorticum (Δορτικόν; *Dortikón*). Roman fort on the right bank of the Danube at the mouth of the Timacus (modern Timok), originally in Moesia Superior, in

Dacia Ripensis after 271, today Vrav, Vidin in Bulgaria. In the 4th cent., location of the *cuneus equitum Dalmatarum Divitensium*. Still known as a fortress under Justinian. On its localization cf. also [1. 60, 77,248]. References: Geogr. Rav. 4,7,8; Tab. Peut.; It. Ant. 219,1; Not. Dign. Or. 42,3,14; Ptol. 3,9,4 (Δορτικόν); Procop. Aed. 4,6,20.

1 V.I. Velkov, Die thrakische und dakische Stadt in der Spätantike, 1959 (Bulgarian with Ger. summary).

TIR L 34 Budapest, 1968, 55. J.BU.

Dorulatus Celtic name; prince of the Insubres. In 194 BC, D. led an army over the Po, but then endured a crushing defeat by the proconsul L. → Valerius Flaccus at Mediolanum (Liv. 34,46,1). W.SP.

Dorus (Δῶρος; *Dôros*). Mythological first ancestor of the Dorians, son of Hellen and of Orseis, grandson of Deucalion, brother of Xuthus and of Aeolus. His sons are Tectamus and → Aegimius (Hes. Cat. fr. 9,2; Apollod. 1,49–50; Diod. Sic. 4,58,6; 60,2). Starting from Phthia, D. led the people into the Thessalian Hestiaiotis (Diod. Sic. 5,80,2), into the central Greek landscape of Doris (Str.8,7,1) or to southern Aetolia (Apollod. 1,57).

F. Graf, Greek Mythology, 1993, 132–133; I. Malkin, Myth and Territory in the Spartan Mediterranean, 1994, 39–41. R.B.

Dorylaeum (Δορύλαιον, Δορύλλειον; *Dorýlaion, Dorýlleion*). Important city in the north of Phrygia (modern Eskişehir) between the river Tembris (Porsuk Çayı) and its tributary Bathys (called *Hermus* by Plin. HN 5,119; modern Sarısu). The ancient site is located on a hill (Şarhüyük, 'Hill of the city'), that was inhabited already in the Hittite and Phrygian period (currently Turkish excavations); founded anew as a Greek city by Dorylaus of Eretria (otherwise unknown); mythological founder is → Acamas, son of Theseus. The city, in Phrygia Epictetus in the *conventus* of Synnada, was famous for its warm springs (Ath. 2,17). D. was at all times an important traffic centre and therefore a military centre: support point of Lysimachus in the struggle against → Antigonus [1] Monophthalmus before the battle at Ipsus; seat of a *schola* in the 6th cent. Of the numerous inscriptions, mostly from the Imperial period, the civil documents derive to a large extent from the city walls that were erected in great haste against the barbarian invasions of the end of the 3rd cent.; an entire series of dedications (especially for Zeus Bronton) and epitaphs were found in the surrounding villages. The relatively few coin mintings come from the period from Vespasianus to Philippus II. D. was the first suffragan diocese of Synnada in the province Phrygia Salutaris.

MAMA 5, xi-xxv, 1–91; Belke/Mersich, 238–242. T.D.-B.

In the early and middle Byzantine period, D. remained an important traffic centre that controlled the routes from → Constantinople to south-east Anatolia. Up until the crusades the city served as troops assembly point for all Byzantine military expeditions in a south-east direction and took second position among the fortified army camps named *áplēkta* (ἄπληκτα, for Lat. *applicatum*) [1]. In 742–43, the city served as bastion for the → strategists of → Thema Opsikion and rival emperor Artabasdus during their attempt to usurp Emperor Constantine V. In the 8th–10th cents., D. was the target of numerous Arabian attacks, but it was never captured. Under Godfrey of Bouillon in 1097, a crusader victory at D. over the Seljuks and Turkmens opened the route through Asia Minor to Jerusalem for the 1st crusade; in the same region, however, the German unit of the 2nd crusade suffered a defeat in 1147 under Conrad III. The Seljuks conquered and destroyed D. in the year 1080. Emperor Manuel I rebuilt the fortress in 1175 again [2], but lost it once again to the Seljuks after the defeat of Myriokephalon (1176).

G. Huxley, A List of ἄπληκτα, in: GRBS 16, 1975, 87–93 2 P. Wirth, Kaiser Manuel Komnenos und die Ostgrenze. Rückeroberung und Wiederaufbau der Festung D., in: ByzZ 55, 1962, 21–29.

Belke/Mersich, 241–242; S. Vryonis Jr., The Decline in Medieval Hellenism in Asia Minor and the Process of Islamization from the Eleventh through the Fifteenth Century, 1971, passim. G.MA.

Dorylaus (Δορύλαος; *Dorýlaos*).

[1] From Amisus, great-great-grandfather of the geographer Strabo, recruited mercenaries in Thrace, Greece and Crete as *anḕr taktikós* and friend of Mithridates V of Pontus. In Knossos he was chosen as *stratēgós* and defeated the Gortynians. After the assassination of Mithridates in 120 BC he remained in Knossos (Str. 10,4,10).

[2] Son of Philetaerus, nephew of D. [1]. Raised as syntrophos of Mithridates VI in Sinope, D. later became ὁ ἐπὶ τοῦ ἐγχειριδίου ('secretary') of the king and priest of Comana (OGIS 372). In the 1st Mithridatic War D. went to Greece in 86 BC with allegedly 80,000 men, where he merged his army with the troops of → Archelaus [4], who had been beaten by Chaeronea; however both were defeated at Orchomenus by Sulla (Str. 10,4,10; App. Mith. 49; Plut. Sulla 20; Oros. 6,2,6; Eutr. 5,6,3). According to Memnon FGrH 434 F 23, he was to carry out the punishment of Chios. In the 3rd Mithridatic War D. was killed due to betrayal to the Romans (Str. 12,3,33; but cf. Plut. Lucullus 17, according to which D. died at Cabira).

Th. Reinach, Mithridate Eupator, 1890, 42–50 (on D. [1]), 52, 56, 122, 335, 459 (on D. [2]). M.MEI.

Doryphorus

[1] see → Polyclitus

[2] **D., Doryphoros.** Being a freedman of Claudius or Nero, his full name was Ti. Claudius D. He exercised the function of *a libellis* and had great influence on

Nero, who is to supposed to have even married him. Since D. opposed Nero's marriage with Poppaea, he was removed by him in the year 62 with poison. His possessions, even those in Egypt, fell back to the emperor. PIR[2] D 194.

BESSONE, GFF 2, 1979, 105ff. W.E.

Dos The *dos* was in Roman law the dowry. Marriage in and of itself had no influence on the property rights of the spouses. According to old custom, a dowry belonged to a marriage, although it was not prescribed by law. A wife who entered into the legal power (*manus)* of her husband merged her property, as well as future acquisitions, with the property of her husband or his *paterfamilias*. If a wife was under the legal power of a *paterfamilias*, he handed over a dowry to the husband; if the woman was legally independent (*sui iuris*), she transferred a dowry to her husband herself that could consist of money or landed property, slaves, animals etc. or any combination of these things. The dowry became the property of the husband; however, for dowry lands his right to disposal was limited by the required consent of the wife according to a *lex Iulia* of Augustus. Income that was drawn from the property handed over as a dowry was to be used, according to general opinion, for the appropriate maintenance of the wife during the marriage. In the event of a divorce, the earnings remained the property of the husband, however he was obliged to repay the dowry.

For women of the *ordo senatorius,* the usual value of a dowry amounted in the Principate to a million HS (the minimum fortune of a senator), a high sum that however could certainly be raised by a rich family. The *dos* could be handed over at the wedding, but often sums of money were paid in three annual instalments, beginning one year after the wedding. An agreement to postpone the payments, e.g. until the death of the person who was to pay the dowry, could also be concluded. From the 3rd cent. BC on, the Praetors developed rules for the just handling of the dowry. The property brought into the marriage by a woman *in manu* was equated with the dowry.

After the end of the marriage, the *dos* was viewed as *res uxoria* (wife's goods) and consequently, the woman or her heirs could start a *actio rei uxoriae* for the return of the *dos*. A marriage partner who caused a divorce due to an offence on his/her part, or arranged to be divorced from a respectable partner, could be disadvantaged; the woman on the basis of the *retentio propter mores*; if she committed a severe offence, her husband would retain a sixth or else an eighth of the dowry as well as a sixth for each child up to three children; the man by means of the *actio rei uxoriae*; if he committed a severe offence, he would have to repay the dowry immediately or else within six months. The husband could demand the reimbursement of expenses for possessions that were given as a dowry; further compensation payments could be necessary in individual cases. Goods such as land that could not be divided had to be transferred immediately; money could be paid back in three annual instalments.

If the wife died first, the dowry remained with her husband; if the dowry originally had been given by a male ancestor of the woman, he received the dowry back, if he was still alive, a fifth of the dowry being deducted for each of the children resulting from the marriage. If the husband died first, the widow was to claim her dowry from his heirs; in this case, no deductions could be made, not even for children.

The general rulings could be changed by an agreement (*pactum*) that was usually drawn up at the time of the wedding. This type of agreement could list the individual components of the dowry, take care of the children from the marriage and determine what measures were to be taken in the event of the death of one of the partners or of a divorce. Such *pacta dotalia* were observed in the decision about the *actio rei uxoriae*. Rulings concerning the *dos* were generally seen as important because the dowry of a widowed or divorced woman enabled her to remarry. If a family was too poor to give the woman a *dos*, her husband could provide it himself. Later the dowry was offset by a wedding present from the husband to his wife (*donatio ante nuptias*).
→ Adulterium; → Dictio dotis; → Divortium; → Marriage; → Marriage contracts

1 HONSELL 2 A. SÖLLNER, Zur Vorgeschichte und Funktion der actio rei uxoriae, 1969 3 TREGGIARI 4 R. P. SALLER, Patriarchy, Property and Death in the Roman Family, 1994. SU.T.

Dosiadas (Δωσιάδας; *Dosiádas*). Author handed down by Anth. Pal. 15,26, also in the Codex of the bucolic poets under the Τεχνοπαίγνια (*Technopaígnia*). The poem is a γρῖφος (*gríphos*) or riddle, in the way of the *Alexandra* of → Lycophron, with dark references and allusions to known mythological figures which are explained by the scholia in some MSS. Its subject is a literary dedication of an altar that Jason erected on Lemnos and at which → Philoctetes was injured. The language is a mixture of Doric and epic forms (e.g. Τεύκροιο βούτα = Paris) in iambic verses of varying lengths that form the shape of an altar (βωμός; *bōmós*) in accordance with the title of the poem. Anth. Pal. 15,25 is a second class imitation from the time of Hadrian.

A. S. F. GOW, Bucolici Graeci, 1952, 182f.; CollAlex 175. E.R.

Dosis The noun is derived from διδόναι (*didónai*) 'to give' and like the verb has no specific legal meaning. The legal institutions gift and endowment are quite inadequately covered by the term *dosis* : the Attic orators use διδόναι (*didónai*) and διατιθέναι (*diatithénai*; → Diatheke) alternately when they justify testamentary gifts of money from Solon's law. In the large law inscription of Gortyn, *didónai* means 'to bestow' (col. IX

15–30, with legal limitations). When setting up an endowment, 'giving' naturally plays an important role, but it depends on the contents of the endowment document. *Dosis* is used (as is χάρις, *cháris*) in the papyri of Egypt for 'gifting in the event of death' (sometimes with a revocation clause) and among the living (further synonym: δῶρον, *dōron*).
→ Doron graphe

R. Koerner, Inschriftliche Gesetzestexte der frühen griech. Polis, 1993, 544f. H.-A. Rupprecht, Einführung in die Papyruskunde, 1994, 111, 129. G.T.

Dositheus (Δωσίθεος; *Dositheos*).
[1] Son of Drimylos, Jewish apostate. He is supposed to have saved the life of Ptolemy IV Philopator before the battle at Raphia (217 BC)(3 Macc. 1,3). Around 240 BC he was one of the two leaders of the royal *secretariat* and accompanied Ptolemy III in 225–24 on a trip in Egypt; he held the highest priestly office in Hellenistic Egypt around 222 as the priest of Alexander [4] the Great and the deified Ptolemies. PP 1/8,8; 3/9,5100.

V. Tcherikover, A. Fuks, Corpus Papyrorum Judaicarum I, 1957, 230–236, no. 127; M. Hengel, Juden, Griechen und Barbaren, in: SBS 76, 1976, 55, 125.

[2] Officer, fought on the side of → Judas Maccabaeus. Together with Sosipater, he destroyed a Syrian garrison left in eastern Jordan by Timotheus (2 Macc. 12,19). Timotheus himself fell into the hands of D.'s people, but he was set free (2 Macc. 12,24f.); he is probably identical to the cavalry officer D., whose heroic feat is mentioned in 2 Macc. 12,35.
→ Timotheus

M. Hengel, Judentum und Hellenismus, [3]1988, 119, 502. A.M.S.

[3] Pupil of the astronomer → Conon in Alexandria. D. was a friend of → Archimedes [1], who dedicated the treatises *Tetragōnismòs parabolês*, *Perì sphaîras kaì kylíndrou*, *Perì helíkōn*, *Perì kōnoeidéōn kaì sphairoeidéōn* to him. He flourished around 230 BC.

Nothing is known about any mathematical scripts of his own. D.'s astronomical works had apparently mainly to do with the calendar. Observations are mentioned about the appearance of the fixed stars (in the appendix to Geminus' *Eisagōgḗ* [5. 210–233]) and over 30 weather predictions (in Ptol. Phaseis, see [2. 1–67] and [6]). He wrote about the eight-year calendar cycle of → Eudoxus (Περὶ τῆς Εὐδόξου ὀκταετηρίδος). He is perhaps identical with the D. of Pelusium who gave information about the life of → Aratus [4] [4. § 2].
→ Calendar

1 D. R. Dicks, s.v. Dositheus, Dictionary of Scientific Biography 4, 1971, 171f. 2 J. H. Heiberg (ed.), Claudii Ptolemaei opera astronomica minora, 1907 3 F. Hultsch, s.v. Dositheos (9), RE 5, 1607f. 4 E. Maass (ed.), Theonis Alexandrini vita Arati, 5 K. Manitius (ed.), Gemini elementa astronomiae, 1898 6 A. Rehm, Parapegmastudien, ABAW, N.S. 19, 1941. M.F.

[4] Jewish general of Ptolemy VI Philometor and of Cleopatra (Jos. Ap. 2,49). In the past, it was assumed that he had been the model for the 'legendary' D. [2] in 3 Macc. 1,3.

V. Tcherikover, A. Fuks, Corpus Papyrorum Judaicarum I, 1957, 20ff., 230; Schürer III, 135f., 539. A.M.S.

[5] Idumaean, changed parties from → Hyrcanus II to → Herodes I; he was caught up in the judicial murder of Hyrcanus (Ios. ant. Iud. 15,168–173) and was executed by Herod I in connection with the conspiracy of Costobarus (Jos. Ant. Iud. 15,252.260).

A. Kasher, Jews, Idumaeans, and Ancient Arabs, in: Texte und Stud. zum antiken Judentum 18, 1988, 217f. A.M.S.

[6] Son of Cleopatrides, Alexandrian Jew. He applied for the exemption of Jews of Asia Minor with Roman citizenship from Roman military service for religious reasons; the privilege was granted by a decree from L. → Lentulus Crus in 49 BC (Ios. ant. Iud. 14,236f.).

Schürer III, 120f.; P. R. Trebilco, Jewish Communities in Asia Minor, 1991, 17, 197. A.M.S.

[7] Founder of the Samaritan sect of Dositheans that probably came into existence in the 1st cent. AD. He claimed to be the prophet announced by Moses (Deut. 18,15) and expected by the Samaritans (Orig. contra Celsum 1,57). He is supposed to have rejected the prophetic writings which reportedly called the Sadducees into being (Ps.-Tert. adversus omn. haer. 1). Furthermore, he is supposed to have denied the existence of angels, the Resurrection and the Last Judgement (cf. Philastrius). According to Islamic sources, this sect had its own calendar and its own purity laws.

1 Caldwell, in: Kairos 4, 111 2 A. Loewenstamm, s.v. Dustan, in: Encyclopedia Iudaica 6, 1971, 313–316 3 H. G. Kippenberg, Garizim und Synagoge, Traditionsgeschichtliche Untersuchungen zur samaritanischen Rel. der aramäischen Periode (RGVV 30), 1971, 128–137. B.E.

[8] Christian writer (around AD 350). Only Macarius of Magnesia (Apocriticus ad Graecos 3, 43 [1]) reports that the Cilician-born D. had been a κορυφαῖος (*koryphaîos*) of the Encratites of Isauria and the surrounding area. From a work of his in eight books, in which he lays out the doctrine of his sect, Macarius quotes a sentence which emphasizes the double creation of the world by means of the *enkráteia*.

1 C. Blondel (ed.), 1867, 151.

A. Jülicher, s.v. Dositheos (11), RE 5, 1609; G. Gasparro, Enkrateia e antropologia, 1984, 234, 378f. J.RI.

[9] Latin grammarian, probably lived towards the end of the 4th cent., according to → Cominianus. His *Ars grammatica*, written in Latin and Greek, was intended for pupils of both languages. It is possible that the Greek text is the translation of the Latin original and

that D. is solely the translator. Already in ancient times, changes and additions were made to the Ars (Editions: [1. 424–436]). Without any grounds, D. is credited with the *Hermeneumata* [3], a bilingual manual with texts of varying but mostly elementary character. In Carolingian Europe these were widely distributed and are documented in at least 9 different versions [4; 5].

EDITIONS: 1 GL 7,376–436 2 J. TOLKIEHN, 1913 3 G. GOETZ, CGL 3.
BIBLIOGRAPHY: 4 A.C. DIONISOTTI, From Ausonius' Schooldays?, in: JRS 72, 1982, 83–125 5 Id., Greek Grammars and Dictionaries in Carolingian Europe, in: M.W. HERREN (ed.), The Sacred Nectar of the Greeks, 1988, 26–31 SCHANZ/HOSIUS 4,1,177–179. P.G.

Dossennus

[1] One of four standard roles of the *fabula* → *Atellana*, the type of the glutton (*Manducus*, Varro, Ling. 7, 95 MÜLLER; Paul Fest. 115 L; representation as god of death in Etruscan graves), obscene (in *Maccus Virgo*) and clever hunchback (derived from *dorsum*). According to Horace (Epist. 2,1,173), he appeared *edacibus in parasitis* (among gluttonous parasites). His supposed epitaph alludes to his shrewdness (Sen. Ep. 89,7). In the *Philosophia* of Pomponius, he played the avaricious fortune-teller (p. 49 FRASSINETTI = p. 241 RIBBECK). He also appears in Novius (*Duo Dossenni,* p. 75 FRASSINETTI = p. 257 RIBBECK), and as a role in *Campani* and *Maccus Virgo*. *Dorsennus* in Suet. Galba 13 rests on conjecture.
[2] Documented as a proper name by an Oscan-Greek coin from Posidonia (end of the 4th cent. BC) and in Rome by the mint master L. Rubrius D. (in 87–86 BC) [2]. Pliny (HN 1,14f.; 14,92) cites a poet Fabius D.; Porphyrio and Ps.-Acro misunderstand D. at Hor. Epist. 2,1,173 to refer to an Atellana poet.

1 P. FRASSINETTI (ed.), Atellanae Fabulae, 1967, p. VII 2 G. MANGANARO, La *Sophia* di D., in: RFIC 37, 1959, 395–402 3 F. MARX, s.v. Atellanae fabulae, in: RE 2, 1896, 1919 4 O. SKUTSCH, s.v. D., in: RE 5, 1905, 1609f. JÜ.BL.

Dothan

(Hebr. *Dotān*, *Dotayin*; Greek Δωθάειμ/ *Dōtháeim*; Arab. *Tall Dūṯān*). Town 15 km north-west of Samaria, not mentioned except in the Bible (finds of the name *t/dn* in Egyptian lists of the 18th dynasty refer to a town in Lebanon), named in the Joseph story as a station on the trading route from Gilead to Egypt (Gen. 37,17; 25), in the Elisha cycle surrounded by Arameans (2 Kgs 6,13), scene in the fictitious Judith novella from the Hellenistic period (Jud. 3,9; 4,6; 7,3; 18; 8,3). As excavations by S. FREE (1953ff.) have shown, the city was fortified in the 3rd millennium and 18th–16th cents. BC; tomb chambers date from the 14th–12th cents. BC; renewed prosperity in the 10th until the beginning of the 7th cent. BC; later settlement came in the Hellenistic period.

D. USSISHKIN, R.E. COOLEY, G.D. PRATICO, s.v. D., NEAEHL I, 1993, 372–374. K.B.

Dotium

(Δώτιον πεδίον; *Dôtion pedíon*). The northern part of the eastern Thessalian plain between river Peneius in the north, the Ossa and Pelion range in the east, Lake Boebe in the south and Lake Nessonis as well as Erimon mountain-range in the west was designated as Dotium. An old road to the → Tempe valley led through the initially densely forested, fertile alluvial land. D. was considered the birthplace of Asclepius (Hom. h. 16). Most of the places known from literature, i.a. a Demeter sanctuary, have not yet been indisputably located (Elatea, Gyrtum, Mopsium, Sycyrium and others).

PHILIPPSON/KIRSTEN, 1, 1950, 110; F. STÄHLIN, Das hellenische Thessalien, 1924, 57; I. BLUM (ed.), Topographie antique et géographie historique en pays grec, 1992, Index starting at 237. HE.KR.

Doto

(Δωτώ; *Dōtṓ*). Feminine short form, presumably understood as 'the giver' [1] (cf. δώτωρ, δωτήρ, δώτης etc.). One of the → Nereids (Hom. Il. 18,43; Hes. Theog. 248; Apollod. 1,11; Verg. Aen. 9,102; Hyg. Fab. praef. 8; IG XIV 2519). She occupied a sanctuary in the Syrian coastal town of Gabala (Paus. 2,1,8).

1 KAMPTZ, 126.

G. GARBUGINO, s.v. D., EV 2, 137. R.B.

Dove/Pigeon

I. SPECIES II. ZOOLOGY III. HUNTING AND OTHER USES IV. RELIGIOUS SIGNIFICANCE V. ETHNOLOGY VI. ILLUSTRATIONS

I. SPECIES

The pigeon and dove family, περιστεροειδῆ/*peristeroeidê* (Aristot. Hist. an. 5,13,544a 33–b 11 and also 6,4, 562b 3–563a 4), includes several species:

1) Wild pigeons: a) Πέλεια/*péleia* (derived from πολιός/*poliós* = 'dark, blueish grey'), the rock dove (*Columba livia L.*), the wild progenitor of the domestic pigeon. Homer only speaks of this species, which he labels 'fearful' because of its shyness towards people (τρήρων/*trḗrōn; e.g.*, Hom. Il. 5,778; Hom. Od. 12,62). Its enemies are birds of prey (Hom. Od. 15,525–527 and *passim*). Aristot. Hist. an. 5,13,544b 1–5 differentiates the *peleiás* from the domestic pigeon. It was apparently rare among the Romans. Varro, Rust. 3,7,1 calls it *columba saxatilis sive agrestis*. b) Φάσσα/*phássa* or φάττα/*phátta*, Latin *palumbes* (*-bus, -ba*), the wood-pigeon (*Columba palumbes L.*), identical with φάψ/ *pháps* (Aristot. ibid. 7(8),3,593a 15, not so in Ath. 9,393f; the name since Aeschyl. Philoctetes fr. 232 TGF). It is described as dark grey with an iridescent head (Alexander of Myndus in schol. Theoc. 5,96), and occurs in Greece as a migrant (Aristot. ibid. 7(8),12, 597b 3 f. and 16,600a 24 f.) as well as a year-round tree-nesting breeding bird (ibid. 7(8),3,593a 16 f.; Theoc. 5,96 f.; Verg. Ecl. 3,69). In Italy it only occurs as a migrant (Plin. HN 10,72 and 78; Serv. Ecl. 1,58). Its long lifespan (25–40 years: Aristot. ibid. 6,4,563a 1 f.;

Plin. HN 10,106) is a fable. c) Οἰνάς/*oinás*, the (cave-nesting) stock dove (*Columba oenas L.*), intermediate in size between wood- and rock pigeon (Aristot. ibid. 7(8),3,593a 18–20), was caught as a migrant in the autumn especially while drinking water (Aristot. ibid. 593a 20 f.; Ath. 9,394b). The Romans had no special name for it. d) Τρυγών/*trygṓn*, the ash grey (or rather brown) turtle dove (*Streptopelia turtur*) with its conspicuous cooing (t.t. τρύζειν/*trýzein*, Poll. 5,89; Latin *turtur*, cf. Isid. Orig. 12,7,60), the smallest dove, was likewise a migrant (Aristot. ibid. 7(8),12, 597b 4; Varro, Rust. 3,5,7). The alleged hibernation in Aristot. ibid. 7(8),3,593a 17 f. is a mistaken observation.

2) Tame pigeons: a) The domestic pigeon is descended from the rock dove (*Columba livia domestica L.*), Greek περιστερά/*peristerá* (sometimes –ός/ -*ós*), diminutive περιστέριον, -ίδιον, -ιδεύς, Latin *columba* and -*bus* (mostly the male, exception, e.g., Hor. Epist. 1,10,5; Columella 8,8,1; Plin. HN 10,25), diminutive *columbulus* (e.g., Plin. Epist. 9,25,3). From Sophocles on (fr. 781 TGF), many (e.g., Aristot. Hist. an. 1,1,488b 3 and 5,13,544b 2 f.) emphasized their tameness towards humans. Roman literature frequently mentioned them beginning with Plaut. Asin. 693 and Plaut. Cas. 138. White doves had been known in Greece since the Persian Wars (e.g., Ath. 9,394e). b) The green imperial pigeon (*Ducula aenea aenea*; [5. 247, cf. 231]) of India, according to Ael. NA 15,14 a popular gift for Indian princes, is perhaps already recorded as περιστεραὶ μηλίναι/*peristeraì mēlínai* ('quince-yellow pigeon') in → Daimachus [2] (in Ath. 9,394e) and in Aristot. Hist. an. 8(9),1,609a 18 f. (= Plin. HN 10,204) as πυραλλίς/*pyrallís* (Callim. Fr. 416 Pf., but cf. the beetle of same name in Plin. HN 11,119!).

II. Zoology

The frequent ancient observations, which usually refer to domestic pigeons, concern their crop (Aristot Hist. an. 2,17,508b 26–28), the peculiar closing of the eyes (Aristot. Part. an.2,13,657b 10 f.) and their sucking way of drinking (e.g., Plin. HN 10,105). Their peacefulness was attributed to the absence of gall (more precisely of the gall-bladder; Aristot. Hist. an. 2,15,506b 20 f.; cf. Plin. HN 11,194). The billing (t.t. κυνεῖν/*kyneîn*, Latin *osculari* = 'kissing') before mating as well as the early and significant fertility were well known and exploited by breeders (Columella 8,8; Pall. Agric. 1,24; cf. Varro, Rust. 3,7,5 ff.). A popular pigeon food is verbena (περιστερεών/*peristereṓn* or περιστέριον/*peristérion*; → verbenaca) and ἑλξίνη/*helxínē* (probably wall pellitory, *Parietaria officinalis L.*), which supposedly annually cleaned the pigeon's stomach. Timidity, tenderness, conjugal love and faithfulness after death — which Christians later claimed in particular of the turtle dove — were attributed to their character.

III. Hunting and other uses

Pigeons were shot with arrows (in Hom. Il. 23,850 ff. only as sport), caught using snares (Hom. Od. 22,468), nets, fowling rods and blinded stool pigeons (παλλεύτριαι/*palleútriai*, Latin *illices*) for food. In Rome captive wood-pigeons were fattened to make their dry meat (Cato Agr. 90; Varro, Rust. 3,7,9) juicier. Apicius 6,2,1 and 4,4 describes their culinary preparation. On the raising of domestic pigeons, see → Small domestic animals, breeding of II.

In medicine the meat, internal organs and blood had multiple uses in diet and therapy. Pigeon dung (*fimus columbarum*) was also commonly used. It was recommended (e.g., in Plin. HN 22,123 and 125; 30,80 and 117) for internal and external application against eczema, swelling, poisoning and especially to staunch bleeding and dissolve haematomas.

The homing instinct of carrier pigeons was already known in the Old Kingdom of Egypt and is noted in Ael. VH. 9,2 (cf. Paus. 6,9,3) in the context of carrying news of Taurosthenes' victory at the Olympic games from Olympia to Aegina (444 BC). During the Roman Civil War pigeons maintained communications with → Mutina, which was surrounded (Frontin. Str. 3,13,8; Plin. HN 10,110). In Anacr. Fr. 149 B.[4] a carrier pigeon was the messenger of love.

IV. Religious significance

Probably in the 4th cent. BC the Greeks adopted white doves as sacred animals from the cult of → Astarte into that of → Aphrodite (e.g., Ael. NA 4,2), and later the Romans into the cult of Venus. In all Aphrodite sanctuaries influenced by the Orient (e.g., in Amathus and → Paphus on Cyprus, on → Cythera, and on the → Eryx [1] in Sicily) pigeons were kept. The pigeon as the most important attribute of Aphrodite was transferred to → Dione, → Eros [1], → Adonis etc. In oracles it was particularly significant in the founding legends of Siwa by the god Ammon (→ Ammoneum) and of → Dodona (III) by Zeus. In Judaism doves were frequently sacrificed, while to Christians doves became a symbol of the Holy Spirit, Christ and the Church, the soul and some virtues [1].

V. Ethnology

In ancient proverbs pigeons stood for love, gentleness, timidity [2. 88 f.] and naive credulity (Hsch. s. v. ἡμέρα πελειάς; Plaut. Poen. 676: *palumbis*) because of their alleged character. The contrast of the peaceful pigeon and the warlike eagle (Hor. Carm. 4,4,31 f.; Mart. 10,65,12) or raven (Juv. 2,63) was used to characterize the range of human behaviour. Frequently, 'dove' was used as a pet name for female lovers (e.g., Plaut. Cas. 138). Pigeons did not have a specific meaning in fables (cf. Aesop Romance 129, 201 f., 235 and 238 Perry).

VI. Illustrations

Pigeons are often shown in ancient mosaics [3. 253]. They are also often found on coins [4. Taf. 5,28–37], esp. from cult locations of Aphrodite, and cameos [4 Pl. 21,22 and 24,41].

→ Small domestic animals, breeding of

1 J. Poeschke, s. v. T., LCI, vol. 4, 241–244 2 A. Otto, Die Sprichwörter und sprichwörtlichen Redensarten der Römer, 1890 (reprint 1988) 3 Toynbee, Tierwelt 4 F. Imhoof-Blumer, O. Keller, Tier- und Pflanzenbilder auf Mz. und Gemmen des klass. Alt., 1889 (reprint 1972) 5 D'Arcy W. Thompson, A Glossary of Greek Birds, 1936 (reprint 1966), 210 f., 225–231, 238–247, 290–292 und 300–302.

J. Kosswitz, Ph. Oppenheim, s. v. Columbarium, RAC 3, 1957, 245–247; D. Lorentz, Die T. im Alt., 1886; V. Hehn, Kulturpflanzen und Haustiere (ed. O. Schrader), [8]1911 (reprint 1963), 341–354; Keller 2, 122–131; F. Sühling, Die T. als rel. Symbol, 1930; A. Steier, s. v. T., RE 4 A, 2479–2500. C. HÜ.

Dowry

I. Ancient Orient and Egypt II. Classical Antiquity

I. Ancient Orient and Egypt

The dowry in old Mesopotamia was given with the bride generally by her father (more rarely also by the mother or other family members) into the marriage, that (together with the means of the husband) served to secure the economic position of the wife if the man died first or in the event of a divorce. As a widow or a divorced (by the man) wife, she was entitled to the dowry, which in the event of her death went to her children, if childless went back to the father of the bride. If the wife passed away first, the dowry remained with the widower until his own death, at which time the dowry fell in full to the children of the deceased wife.

In the late Babylonian period (6th–4th cents. BC), the husband had the right to use the dowry, but it remained the property of the wife (or of her parental home). Claims to a dowry had preference over other claims to assets by third parties. According to the regulations of the so-called 'Neo-Babylonian law fragment', the bride's father had the right in the event of financial collapse to reduce the level of the dowry contrary to prior agreements according to the principle of equitableness (*aequitas*), which had the protection of the parental home of the woman from economic ruin as its goal [2. 80, 90 with n. 161]. Delayed handing over of the dowry on the part of the bride's father until after the birth and survival of a child by the married couple is documented. Depending on the financial position of the bride's father, the components of the dowry were not only real property (fields, gardens and land for houses) and chattel (slaves, livestock), but also silver, gold, furniture, household goods and toiletries, textiles and jewellery [3].

In Egypt during the Ptolemy period, a part of the dowry over which the husband had the power of disposal served as alimentation capital (for the provision of the wife), which was to be returned by the husband — as were other parts of the dowry — in the event of a divorce.

→ Marriage; → Family; → Woman

1 E. Lüddeckens, s.v. Mitgift (demotic), LÄ 4, 152–155 2 H. Petschow, Das neubabylonische Gesetzesfragment, in: ZRG 76, 1959, 37–96 3 M.T. Roth, The Material Composition of the Neo-Babylonian Dowry, in: AfO 36/37, 1989/90, 1–55 4 R. Westbrook, s.v. Mitgift, RLA 8, 273–283. H.N.

II. Classical Antiquity

For the legal forms of the dowry in Greece and in the Hellenistic world, see → *pherne* and → *proix*, for that under Roman law see → *dos*.

Doxa see → Opinion

Doxography The term doxography denotes the method which is frequently used by ancient writers in the realm of philosophy of recording the views or opinions (δόξαι, *dóxai*) of philosophers. It can also refer to texts or passages that contain such accounts.

The term doxography is derived from the neologism *doxographus*, which the German scholar Hermann Diels (1848–1922) introduced and which literally means 'writer of opinions'. In his work *Doxographi Graeci* (1879), Diels collected various ancient documents that summarize the philosophical doctrines of the ancient philosophers (especially in the area of natural philosophy). He understood the term to be in contrast to *biographus*, 'recorder of lives'. In practice, however, it is difficult to differentiate clearly between these two types of writings, as an examination of the documents collected by Diels and others makes clear. Then it becomes clear that at least three different types of writings are connected with the broad term doxography.

In the narrowest sense of the word, doxography is to be understood as the so-called *placita* (ἀρέσκοντα; *aréskonta*) literature, works in which *dóxai* on certain topics are collected, each being allocated to a philosopher or a school, e.g. 'Plato declared that the cosmos is unique. Democritus and Epicurus maintained that there is an infinity of worlds...'. The organizing principle is in general systematic (although occasionally the principle of succession is used), with frequent application of antithesis and diaeresis in the presentation. The most famous example is Περὶ ἀρεσκόντων ξυναγωγή ('Collections about Opinions') of → Aetius [2] (1st cent. AD) which is summarized in the ps.-Plutarchean *Epitome* 'Opinions of the natural philosophers' and was extensively used by → Stobaeus in his *Eclogae*. This work treated topics of physics with special consideration of the pre-Socratic philosophers. There appear not to have been any works of this type in the areas of logic or ethics (otherwise [1]).

A second genre of doxography is the so-called 'About the Schools' (Περὶ αἱρέσεων; *Perí haireséōn*) literature, in which systematic summaries of the philosophers of a school (e.g. the Stoa) or of an important philosopher (e.g. its founder Zeno) are offered. These types of works concentrate on the post-Socratic period and cover the various areas of philosophy that usually are subdivided into physics, ethics and logic (or dialectics). Good examples of such doxographies are to be found in the preserved fragments of → Arius Didymus and in → Diogenes [17] Laertius (e.g. on the Stoa in Book 7,38–160). → Hippobotus and → Panaetius also wrote works with this title.

A third genre that is related to doxography is the so-called 'Successions' literature (Διαδοχαί; *Diadochaí*), in which generations of philosophers are linked to one another by a teacher-pupil-relationship, both before and during the development of the philosophical schools of the Hellenistic period (e.g. Anaximander was the pupil of Thales in the so-called Ionian succession etc.). Authors of such works were → Sotion and → Antisthenes. Philodemus' Σύνταξις τῶν φιλοσόφων ('Survey of the philosophers'), of which segments about the Academy and the Stoa were in found in Herculaneum, can be counted among this sort. It also constitutes the principle of organization of the *Vitae philosophorum* of → Diogenes Laërtius. These writings offer mostly institutional and anecdotal information, including bibliographical aspects. The basis of their organization, however, is ideological, and they mention philosophical teachings in order to differentiate between schools and their individual members. This type of writing is situated between biography and doxography.

Apart from these specific writings, doxographical passages are frequently to be found with other authors when they treat special philosophical topics (mainly in the areas of physics and ethics). A famous example is to be found in Cicero's *De natura deorum*: it begins with a long doxographic overview on theological views that is imbedded in an Epicurean invective (1,18–41). Such use of doxographic material reflects the origin of this practice, which, as J. Mansfeld has shown, is to be positioned in the dialectic method introduced by Aristotle. When Aristotle sets about examining a philosophical theme, he often first collects and examines the so-called ἔνδοξα (*éndoxa*, serious opinions) in order to use the results of his analysis as a springboard for the introduction of his own views. A clear example is to be found at the beginning of *De anima* (1,2,403b 20): 'For our study of the soul it is necessary, while formulating the problems of which in the course of our examination we are to find the solutions, to consider the views (δόξαι; *dóxai*) of our predecessors, in order that we may profit by whatever is sound in their suggestions and avoid their errors.'

Aristotle's practice was continued and expanded by his colleague and successor → Theophrastus. His extensive collection of Φυσικαὶ δόξαι ('Opinions about Physics') in 18 Books, in which the views of the philosophers up to Plato on natural philosophy were systematically introduced, appears to have been especially influential. It is assumed of this lost work that it has been the source for much material on the Pre-Socratics in later doxographic works and accounts, although it has proven difficult to determine the exact contours of its influence.

From its origins in the Peripatos on, the doxographic method developed further and found wide circulation in philosophical writings of antiquity. An important contribution came from the New Academy that used it to prove the incompatibility of the philosophical doctrines and the impossibility of attaining scientific cognition. Later it was frequently applied in patristic writings in order to give a quick overview of heathen thinking. A disadvantage of doxography is that in the course of time it tends to become rather schematic and to abandon arguments and analyses in order to concentrate mainly on the juxtaposition of views or on a thin skeleton of the doctrine. Due to this lack of argumentation, the doxographic tradition came into bad repute. Nevertheless, it should be recognized that it has distinctive methods (especially the use of disjunction and diaeresis), which give us important insights on how ancient philosophers handled their own past. And beyond this, it has preserved a considerable amount of invaluable information about the doctrines of the philosophers that otherwise would have been lost.

→ Aetius [2]; → Arius Didymus; → Aristotle; → Diogenes [17] Laertius; → Philodemus; → Theophrastus

1 M. Giusta, I dossografi di Etica, 1964–7.

Editions: H. Diels, DG; R. Giannattasio Andria, I frammenti delle Successioni dei filosofi, 1989

Bibliography: D.E. Hahm, The Ethical Doxography of Arius Didymus, ANRW II 36.4, 2935–3055; J. Mansfeld, Physikai doxai and Problemata physica from Aristotle to Aëtius (and Beyond), in: W.W. Fortenbaugh, D. Gutas (ed.), Theophrastus: His Psychological, Doxographical and Scientific Writings, 1992, 63–111; J. Mansfeld (ed.), Doxography and Dialectic. The Sitz im Leben of the 'Placita', ANRW II 36.4, 3057–3229; J. Mansfeld, D.T. Runia, Aëtiana: the Method and Intellectual Background of a Doxographer, 1996.

D.T.R.

Drabescus (Δράβησκος; *Drábēskos*). City of the Edones near Zdravik *c.* 12 km north of → Amphipolis, where the Athenians were defeated by the Thracians in *c.* 465 BC (Thuc. 1,100,4). Traces of settlement are existing up into the Roman Imperial period, when D. was a station on the *via Egnatia* (Tab. Peut.: *Daravescos*).

F. Papazoglou, Les villes de Macédoine, 1988, 391f.; TIR K 35,1, 25.

MA.ER.

Drachme (δραχμή; *drachmḗ*).

[1] Coin. According to finds from the Argive Heraeum and Sparta, six small iron spits each in the value of one obol, form a 'handful' *drachmaí* (derived from δράττεσθαι), both hands encompassing 12 pieces and resulting in one didrachme. The first silver drachmai are minted in the Aeginetic standard of coinage at 6.24 g. Other standards are the so-called Phoenician at 3.63 g, the Chian-Rhodian at 3.9 g (and less), the Corinthian at 2.8 g and the Attic standard, which became dominant since the late Classical period, at 4.37 g. In the Hellenistic era, the weight of the Attic drachme is reduced until the Romans set it at 4.31 g, corresponding to $^{3}/_{4}$ of the Neronian denar.

The drachme or its double (didrachme) are handled analogously to the Persian siglos and the stater as whole units. 100 drachmai correspond to a mina, 6,000 drachmai to one talent, while, in Corinth four oboli (instead of the usual six) go into one drachme. The multiple pieces are described with reference to the drachme (didrachme, decadrachme etc.). Drachmai in gold occur as half-pieces of the gold staters, while the copper drachmai are only minted in Ptolemaic Egypt in a value of 120 drachmai to 1 silver drachme. Δ and variations form the value symbol on coins.

→ Denar; → Didrachme; → Decadrachme; → Coinage, standards of; → Obolos; → Siglos; → Stater; → Talent

SCHRÖTTER, 159–161; H. CHANTRAINE, Literatur-Überblick Peleponnes, in: JNG 8, 1957, 70–76; K. KRAFT, Zur Übers. und Interpretation von Aristoteles, Athenaion politeia, ch. 10, in: JNG 10, 1959/60, 21–46; M. N. TOD, Epigraphical Notes on Greek Coinage, in: NC 6.20, 1960, 1–24; H. A. CAHN, Knidos. Die Münzen des sechsten und fünften Jh.v.Chr., 1970, 178–192; C. M. KRAAY, Archaic and Classical Greek Coinage, 1976. A.M.

[2] **Weight.** Every drachme → weight was dependent on the theoretical heaviness of a Greek drachme coin. Hence, a drachme weighed exactly as much as the silver drachme of the minting city concerned; the multiplications (multiples) and also the subordinate units, the → oboloi, worked accordingly. Modern calculations assuming heavier weight drachmai in contrast to coin drachmai in Athens are false. Weights on the drachme basis served predominantly to complete the → mina weights and its subdivisions, i.e. its weight lies mostly well under 100 g. There were drachme weights in lead, bronze and precious metals. Up to now only the Attic drachme weights as well as two specimens of the Aeginetic standard in Olympia have been reliably identified and published. Weights are known from Athens at 1, 2, 3, 4, 5, 6, 7(?), 8, 10, 12, 16, 20 and 25 drachmai; they consist mostly of lead, seldom of bronze. Identification features include the number signs on the top of the weight in addition to the heaviness that must approximately amount to one or multiple times the theoretical drachme weight of 4.366 g. These signs were either cast in relief or embossed upon pouring. Δ stands for DEKA = 10, Π for PENTE = 5 and the halved Eta ⊦ for one drachme. All common values could be combined with these three symbols. In Olympia a three-level stepped-off bronze weight (height 1.1 cm) of 12 g must be viewed as a two-drachmai-piece of the Aeginetic standard. A singular silver weight that likely originally weighed five Aeginetic drachmai (5 × 6.237 = 31,185 g) was secondarily reduced in its weight.

K. HITZL, Ant. Gewichte im Tübinger Arch. Institut, in: AA 1992, 243–257; K. HITZL, Die Gewichte griech. Zeit aus Olympia, Ol. Forsch. XXV, 1995, passim; M. LANG, M. CROSBY, Agora X, 1964, 26, 30f.; E. PERNICE, Griech. Gewichte, 1894, 45–47, 144–160. K.H.

Draco (Δράκων; *Drákōn*)

[1] see → Dragon slayers

[2] Athenian lawmaker said to have enacted in 621/20 BC the first 'statutes' (θεσμοί; *thesmoí*) set down in writing. We know as little about D. personally as we do about his activity as a lawmaker: he was perhaps one of the → Thesmothetai and/or given special authority [1. 31]. His laws were written down and publicly displayed on numbered blocks of wood (ἄξονες; *áxones*) that were hung up vertically and could be swivelled on their → axes [2].

A fragment of the blood-law — the law for the prosecution of 'unpremeditated' (μὴ ἐκ προνοίας) homicide — is epigraphically preserved (IG I³ 104 from 409/8 BC) [3; 4]. The procedure, which for the first time involved establishing the motivation of the offender and the circumstances of the offence, had several stages: specified relatives of the victim or fellow phratry members had first to publicly accuse the offender and call on him to avoid the agora and sanctuaries. The traditional demand for a blood feud proclaimed in this way was then restricted by the following procedure before the courts of the polis: the 'kings' (βασιλεῖς; *basileîs*) — probably the *árchōn basileús* (→ *Archontes* [I]) and the phyle kings — had to determine who perpetrated the offence and to pronounce judgement, which involved exile in the case of unpremeditated murder. Before that, the 51 → *Ephetai* (ἐφέται) had to identify the perpetrator's intentions. In exile the perpetrator enjoyed protection from revenge. He was even able to return if the victim's closest living relatives unanimously extended 'forgiveness' (αἴδεσις) — probably after payment of compensation.

Other specific provisions — for example, immunity for killing in self-defence — follow. The law on adultery, which provided immunity for the killing of the adulterer, possibly belongs here as well (Paus. 9,36,8; Ath. 13,569d, cf. Dem. Or. 23,53). D. probably also set out the prosecution of other crimes involving killing, in particular the punishment and procedure before the → Areopagus in cases of premeditated murder. Overall, these laws aimed at limiting blood feuds, which had possibly become an issue requiring regulation as a result of the reciprocal use of force in suppressing → Cylon's putsch.

D.'s other laws have gained prominence because of the proverbial severity of the punishments: according to Plutarch (Solon 17,1–4), the death penalty applied to 'idleness' and theft of field crops as well as to temple theft. Nothing is known of the actual substance of these measures, perhaps because → Solon is said to have rescinded them (with the exception of the blood law) (Aristot. Ath. Pol. 7,1; Plut. ibid.). Whether the pre-

Solonic law against tyrants and the procedure against usurpers (Aristot. Ath. Pol. 16,10; Plut. Solon 19,4) are to be ascribed to D. must remain a matter for conjecture [5]. Other laws — on education, oaths before a court, cults — are poorly attested and probably not authentic.

D.'s 'constitution' (πολιτεία; *politeía*), said to have provided, for example, for a council of 401 members and for restricting citizenship to hoplites (Aristot. Ath. pol. 4,2–5), is certainly a later invention, given that D., like → Theseus and Solon, became iconized as the founder of a 'constitution' [6; 7]. At the same time it cannot be denied that the few soundly attested laws represent an important stage in the process of institutional consolidation in the polis → Athens.

1 Develin 2 R.S. Stroud, The Axones and Kyrbeis of Drakon and Solon, 1979 3 R. Koerner, Inschr. Gesetzestexte der frühen griech. Polis, 1993, no. 11 (trans., comm. and bibliography) 4 H. van Effenterre, F. Ruzé, NOMIMA I, 1994, no. 02 5 M. Ostwald, The Athenian Legislation against Tyranny and Subversion, in: TAPhA 86, 1955, 105–121 6 Rhodes, 112–118 7 E. Ruschenbusch, ΠΑΤΡΙΟΣ ΠΟΛΙΤΕΙΑ, in: Historia 7, 1958, 398–424.

M. Gagarin, Drakon and Early Athenian Homicide Law, 1981; R.S. Stroud, Drakon's Law on Homicide, 1968; K.-W. Welwei, Athen, 1992, 138–146. K.-J.H.

[3] From Stratoniceia in Caria. Greek grammarian, of uncertain date but before the 2nd cent AD. → Apollonius [11] Dyskolos (Grammatici Graeci II 1, De Pronomibus 17,1) recounts that D. named possessive pronouns *diprósōpoi* (διπρόσωποι). As that term resurfaces in the *Téchnē grammatikḗ* (Τέχνη γραμματική) attributed to → Dionysius [17] Thrax, D. was thought to predate him and thus assigned to the 2nd cent. BC; but uncertainty about the attribution of the *Téchnē* makes that dating quite doubtful. According to the Suda (δ 1496, s.v. Δράκων), he wrote works about technical-grammatical, metrical and philological-critical questions, mainly in connection with lyric poetry. Other references are to be found in Herodian (Περὶ μονήρους λέξεως 34,17) and Photius (Lex. s.v. πάμπαν). It has been established that the extant treatise on prosody (Περὶ μέτρων ποιητικῶν) ascribed to D. is a 16th cent. AD forgery (other details and bibliography in [1]).

1 L. Cohn, s.v. Drakon (13), RE 5, 1662–1663 2 V. Di Benedetto, Dionisio il Trace e la Techne a lui attribuita, in: ASNP 28, 1959, 110 3 J. Lallot, La Grammaire de Denys le Thrace, 1989, 205. F.M.

[4] see → Ensigns/Standards

Draconarius see → Ensigns

Dracontides (Δρακοντίδης; *Drakontídēs*).

[1] Athenian, son of Leogoras from the deme Thorae; in 446/5 BC *epistátēs*, in 433/2 *stratēgós* and in that capacity one of the commanders of a relief fleet for Cercyra in the autumn of 433 (cf. Thuc. 1,51,4; on the corruption of the text at that point see [1. 95]). D. was a bitter opponent of Pericles and in 430 aided in his removal (Plut. Pericles 32,3) [2]. Davies 4551.

1 S. Hornblower, Commentary 1, 1991 2 F.J. Frost, Pericles and Dracontides, in: JHS 84, 1964, 69–72. W.W.

[2] Athenian politician. In the autumn of 404 BC he tabled the motion for transferring management of the state to thirty men (Aristot. Ath. Pol. 34,3; Lys. or. 12,73) and himself became one of the 'Thirty' (Xen. Hell. 2,3,2). After the oligarchy's fall, his property was confiscated and sold in 402/1 by the *pōlētaí* (SEG 32, 161 IV 14f.). W.S.

Dracontius

[1] *Praepositus monetae* in Alexandria. On 24 December AD 361 he was murdered as a Christian by the heathen mob because he had knocked over an altar (Amm. Marc. 22,11,9f.; Historia acephala 8). PLRE 1, 271 D. (1).

[2] **Antonius D.** Attested only epigraphically (ILS 758; 763 et al.) and as a recipient of laws (Cod. Theod. 11,7,9; 11,30,33), *vicarius Africae* from AD 364 to 367 PLRE 1, 271f. D (3). W.P.

[3] **Blossius Aemilius D.** Latin poet of senatorial origin (*vir clarissimus*) of the late 5th cent. AD, advocate in Carthage; in a secure position and already recognized as a poet through his recitals, he composed (in 484?) a (lost) poetical *Panegyricus* to a foreign ruler, probably the Byzantine Emperor → Zeno, whose efforts to help the Catholic Romans under the domination of the Arian vandals were well known. That poem earned D. and his family imprisonment for many years under King Guntamund (484–496) probably ending only under Thrasamund. A poem of thanks to that king, probably in connection with his release, is likewise lost. Nothing else about his life has survived. The *Romulea* (the title hints at Roman content and self-conscious Roman identity), a collection of 10 poems in hexameters, dates to the period before and after his imprisonment. It contains epithalamia (→ Hymenaeus), mythological → epyllia (e.g. *Medea, Helena, Hylas*: a favourite classroom topic, cf. Verg. G. 3,6), → *controversiae* and → *suasoriae*, as well as two dedications to the grammarian Felicianus, who was famous for having raised Latin literature in Carthage to new heights and for having taught Romans as well as Vandals. It is uncertain whether the extant monody in hexameters *Orestis tragoedia* originally belonged to the *Romulea*. It is not likely that D. was the composer of the → *Aegritudo Perdicae*. Two fairly short poems on classroom topics in the style of Ausonius have survived only in a printed edition by the Humanist Corio (*De mensibus* and *De rosis nascentibus*) and display points of — perhaps indirect — contact with contemporary Greek-Egyptian poetic schools.

D.'s main works, however, were written while in prison, beginning with *Satisfactio*, an 'expiatory poem' to King Guntamund in elegiac distichs (probably drawing on Ov. Tr. 2). In it, even the pardon of God is requested. D. continued this parallel theme of God and ruler more subtly in his *opus magnus*, the three books of hexameters *De laudibus Dei*: God's acts of kindness to mankind are portrayed with distinct features of the Biblical epic with the narrative element subordinate to the hymnal-lyrical aspects. Guntamund is thus challenged to the *imitatio Dei*. D.'s language and style display characteristic devices (asyndetic sequences, anaphora), his metres betray great licence. D. was just as familiar with the Classic poets (Virgil, Ovid, Statius, Juvenal) as with Christian authors, in particular Ambrosius (*Hexaemeron*) and Augustine (*Civitas Dei*). His works influenced not only Latin poetry in Africa (e.g. the solar-hymn, Anth. Lat. 389 = 385 ShB), but also persisted into the early Middle Ages (revision of *Satisfactio* and *De laudibus* B.1 by → Eugenius of Toledo).

→ Biblical poetry

EDITIONS: F. VOLLMER, MGH AA 14, 21–228 (first complete edition); J. M. DIAZ DE BUSTAMANTE, 1978; J. BOUQUET, 1995 *(carmina profana)*; C. MOUSSY, C. CAMUS, 1985–88 *(Laud.; Satisf.)*.

BIBLIOGRAPHY: F. VOLLMER, s.v. D. (49), RE 5, 1635–1644; P. LANGLOIS, s.v. D., RAC 4, 250–269; K. SMOLAK, Die Stellung der Hexamerondichtung des D. innerhalb der lat. Genesispoesie, in: Antidosis. FS Walther Kraus, 1972, 381–397; D. KARTSCHOKE, Bibeldichtung, 1975, 48–50; M. ROBERTS, Biblical Epic and Rhetorical Paraphrase in Late Antiquity, 1985; W. SCHETTER, Über Erfindung und Komposition des Orestes des D., in: FMS 19, 1985, 48–74; D. F. BRIGHT, The Miniature Epic in Vandal Africa, 1987.

K.SM.

Dragon slayers Dragons, from the Greek δράκων (*drákōn*) derived from δέρκομαι (*dérkomai*) 'to look at penetratingly' (Porph. De abstinentia 3,8,3), are mythical beings combining the superhuman qualities of various animals [1]. In mythology the world of humans was threatened by amphibious snakes (synonym: ὄφις; *óphis*, Hom. Il. 12,202/208), fish (κῆτος; *kētos*) or composite creatures. Only a hero could hold up against their power, gaze, odour and fiery breath, multiple heads and limbs. Victory over the dragon freed mankind from mortal peril, and the victor founded and ensured a stable order, as when Zeus tamed → Typhon (Hes. Theog. 820–880), Kronos Ophioneus, Cadmus the dragon in Thebes, Apollo the → Python of Delphi, Bellerophon the → Chimaera, Hercules, the → Hydra and the Hesperid dragon (linked with the liberation of a maiden in the Perseus-Andromeda myth and the Jason-Medea myth; cf. the hundred-eyed dragon → Argus).

The cosmic dimension of Typhon suggests an origin in the Ancient Near East (cf. Hecataeus FGrH 1 F 300 in Hdt. 2,144 [2]), first in the Hittite dragon Illuyankas and later in the (female!) → Tiamat of the Babylonian creation-myth *Enuma eliš*. The body of the vanquished dragon formed heaven and earth, and the space in between formed an area for mankind to live in [3; 4]. The zoomorphic imagery of flood and famine, foreign peoples and war, in the form of the dragon endowed the mythical primeval struggle with the menace of impending doom [5]. Victory in the creation games at New Year's celebrations confirmed the city god of Babel and its king as guarantors of order [6]. As the threat of downfall could also be directed at the king, the image of the dragon had an attraction even in non-monarchical societies, in Israel (e.g. the Leviathan [7; 8; 9]) and in Greece [5; 10]. There the slaying of the dragon lost its cosmic scope and is connected with the founding of a city (e.g. Pind. Pyth. 1,16 [11; 12]). An euhemeristic reduction of dragon myths is to be found in Ephoros (FGrH 70 F 31b = Str. 9,42f.) with the Python as thief (cf. Paus. 10,6,6), or Alexander the Great as dragon, fathered by the Egyptian king-magician Nectanebus, cf. [13].

Ancient tradition lived on to influence Christian tradition through a) the identification of the dragon with Satan (Apc. 12), b) the figure of Saint George as a dragon-slayer, and through Martha, who tamed Taras.

1 L. RÖHRICH, s.v. Drache, Drachenkampf, Drachentöter, Enzyklopädie der Märchen 3, 1981, 787–820 2 M. L. WEST, Hes. Theog. Commentary, 1966, on 820–80 3 W. STAUDACHER, Die Trennung von Himmel und Erde, diss. 1942 4 M. K. WAKEMAN, God's Battle with the Monster, 1973 5 C. AUFFARTH, Der drohende Untergang, 1991 6 B. PONGRATZ-LEISTEN, Ina šulmi irub, 1994 7 O. KAISER, Die mythische Bed. des Meeres, ZATW Beih. 78, [2]1962 8 J. DAY, God's Conflict with the Monster and the Sea, 1985 9 E. ZENGER, Gottes Bogen in den Wolken, [2]1987 10 W. BURKERT, Orientalisierende Epoche, AHAW 1984, 82–84 11 Id., Oriental and Greek Mythology, in: J. BREMMER (ed.): Interpretations of Greek Mythology, 1987 12 J. TRUMPF, Stadtgründung und Drachenkampf, in: Hermes 86, 1958, 129–157 13 O. WEINREICH, Der Trug des Nektanebos, 1911.

R. MERKELBACH, s.v. Drache, RAC 4, 226–250; C. DOUGHERTY, Poetics of Colonization, 1993.

C.A.

Drainage The meagre productivity of ancient agriculture rendered the effective use and cultivation of any suitable land imperative for growing grain, viticulture, and planting olive trees. Hills and mountain slopes in Greece were prepared for cultivation through terracing, and drainage measures were used to gain virgin land or to protect land from flooding after the winter rains. The requirements were different in Greece and Italy: in the Greek interior, there are fairly large plains in which lakes are formed by surface inflow; run-off is often subsurface (*katavothra*) and is sometimes insufficient to prevent the water table from rising and flooding inland regions. In Italy, on the other hand, it was the formation of marshes in the coastal plains that constituted a serious problem.

Even in the Mycenaean period the Greeks went to great lengths to use drainage measures to extend the areas for cultivation and protect them from flooding. At Lake Copais in Boeotia a ditch 25 km long and 40 m wide was excavated, through which the water flowing into the lake was diverted, with the result that the lake completely dried out in summer. Virgin land was reclaimed by building dikes in parts of the lake. In Alexander's time, Crates of Chalcis renewed efforts to drain the lake; these works, which had to be broken off because of internal political difficulties in Boeotia, were at least partly successful (Str. 9,2,18). Likewise, in Arcadia the Olbios was diverted at a very early stage so as to develop the eastern section of the plain of Pheneus; similar projects are attested for Thisbe in Boeotia and Caphyae in Arcadia (Paus. 8,14,3; 8,23,2; 9,32,3).

In Italy the Etruscans were the first to drain the valleys by using underground canals (*cuniculi*); these *cuniculi* all had vertical shafts every 30–40 metres to facilitate access. In the vicinity of Veii they are often almost 3 kilometres long. To divert water from the Po valley, the Etruscans built a canal near the coast (Plin. HN 3,120). Even the *cloaca maxima* in Rome should be understood as a drainage canal for the marshy plain between the Palatine, the Capitol and the Quirinal (Liv. 1,38,6). During the early Roman Republic an underground canal diverted water from Lake Albano (Liv. 5,15,2; 5,15,11; 5,16,9; 5,19,1), and an outlet for Lake Velinus was created by M. Curius Dentatus (Cic. Att. 4,15,5); the drying-out of the basin of Reate led to feuding between Reate and Interamna in Cicero's time. The two largest projects of this kind were the draining of the Pomptine marshes and Lacus Fucinus. The planning was said to go back to Caesar (Suet. Iul. 44,3; Plut. Caes. 58); Claudius then tried in vain to drain the lake with an underground canal to Liris (Suet. Claud. 20,2; 32; Tac. Ann. 12,56f.; Plin. HN 36,124), and the *Historia Augusta* wrongly claims that Hadrian achieved that goal (SHA Hadrianus 22,12). The first works for draining the Pomptine marshes are attested for 160 BC (Liv. per. 46), and in the Augustan period a canal existed along *via Appia*, perhaps also having a drainage function (Str. 5,3,6; Hor. Sat. 1,5,1–23). Whether the canal planned by the architects of Nero, Severus and Celer had some connection with this remains a matter of debate (Tac. Ann. 15,42,2). These ambitious plans were not to be realized with the technical means available to antiquity, and it was thus Prince Alessandro Torlonia who had the honour of transforming Lago Fucino into fertile agricultural land in 1854–1876.

1 K. GREWE, Planung und Trassierung röm. Wasserleitungen, [2]1992, 73f. 2 J. KNAUSS, Die Melioration des Kopaisbeckens durch die Minyer im 2. Jt.v. Chr., 1987 3 Id., Myk. Wasserwirtschaft und Landgewinnung in den geschlossenen Becken Griechenlands, in: Kolloquium Wasserbau in der Gesch., 1987, 25–63 4 J. KNAUSS, B. HEINRICH, H. KALCYK, Die Wasserbauten der Minyer in der Kopais, 1984 5 J.B. WARD PERKINS, Etruscan Engineering: Road-Building, Water-Supply and Drainage, in: Hommages à Albert Grenier III, 1962, 1636–1643.

H.SCHN.

Drama Derived from the verb δρᾶν (*drân*), predominantly attested in Attic, the noun δρᾶμα (*drâma*; 'action', 'deed' in a general sense) is the antonym of 'what is experienced' (πάθος/*páthos*) (Aesch. Ag. 533); it can also mean 'duty', 'task' (Pl. Tht. 150a, Resp. 451c). For the most part, though, drama is a technical term meaning 'theatrical play' (tragedy, comedy, satyr play) in the context of its performance (Aristoph. Ran. 920); it appears in the plural form in the title of Aristophanes' play Δράματα ἢ Νίοβος (*Drāmata ē Níobos*; fr. 289–298 PCG III[2]; fr. 299–304 PCG III[2]), in Telekleides fr. 41 PCG VII, and frequently in Aristotle's 'Poetics' (e.g. 3,1448a 34). This sense was also the origin of its metaphorical use as 'theatrical effect' (Pl. Pol. 35b) and 'dramatic event' (Polybius 23,10,12).

The observation transmitted through Johannes Diaconus (comm. on Hermogenes, Περὶ μεθόδου δεινότητος, ed. [4]) that Solon wrote in his elegies that → Arion composed the first drama or the first tragedy (τῆς δὲ τραγῳδίας πρῶτον δρᾶμα Ἀρίων ὁ Μηθυμναῖος εἰσήγαγεν) ought not be interpreted as meaning that drama was known as a literary technical term as early as Solon; it should instead be seen as a retrospective projection of the development of the → dithyramb into a 'miniature drama' onto its early phase, as indeed Hdt. 5,67 also does with the 'tragic choirs' (τραγικοὶ χοροί; *tragikoì choroí*) in honour of the hero Adrastus in Sicyon [2]. Whether this can be regarded as a mimetic-pantomimed representation of the hero's πάθη (*páthē*) [1], and in turn used in discussion of drama's origins and linked to cult 'activities' (δρώμενα; *drṓmena*), must remain a matter of speculation.

The documents on dramatic performances (→ Didaskaliai) used drama as a literary technical term right from the very start. Thence the term appeared both in literary texts and, in particular, the didascalic writings of Aristotle, who in turn influenced the Hellenistic peripatetic scholars and their successors (→ Hypotheseis, → Scholia, → Suda). In the language of the documents, stereotyped formulations, such as 'the drama was performed (sc. on ...)', 'the drama is set in ...', 'characters in the drama ...' (ἐδιδάχθη τὸ δρᾶμα, ἡ σκηνὴ τοῦ δράματος, τὰ τοῦ δράματος πρόσωπα), appear over and over again.

→ Arion; → Didaskaliai; → Tragedy; → DRAMA

1 B. ZIMMERMANN, Dithyrambos. Gesch. einer Gattung, 1992, 24f., 20f. 2 J. LATACZ, Einführung in die griech. Trag., 1993, 62f. 3 H. SCHRECKENBERG, Δρᾶμα. Vom Werden der griech. Trag. aus dem Tanz, 1960 4 H. RABE, Aus Rhetoren-Hss. no. 5, in: RhM 63, 1908, 149f.

A. LESKY, Die trag. Dichtung der Hellenen, [3]1972, 17–48; J. LEONHARDT, Phalloslied und Dithyrambos. Aristoteles über den Ursprung des griech. Dramas, AHAW 1991, 4; A. PICKARD-CAMBRIDGE, Dithyramb, Tragedy, and Comedy, [2]1962; Id., The Dramatic Festivals of Athens, [2]1968 (1988).

B.Z.

Drangae Eastern Iranian people (Σαράγγαι, *Sarángai*, in Hdt. 3,93) on the lower course of the → Etymander (the modern Hilmand/Helmand Rūd); the country itself was called → Drangiana, and that seems in any case to be the Medio-Persian form. Together with some tribes of the central desert and Carmania, the Sarangae appear in Herodotus as linked to a tax district, on the southern side of the Parthians and Hyrcanians. In the army of Xerxes the Sarangai bore Median weaponry (Hdt. 7,67,1). A legendary cycle is bound up with the hero-names Keršāsp and Rōstam.

R. GHIRSHMAN, Iran, Parthians and Sassanians, 1962.

J.D.-G. and B.B.

Drangiana (or Zarangiana), as the name of the region around the lower course of the → Etymander (the modern Hilmand/Helmand Rūd) in the Iranian province of Sīstān, goes back to the original Iranian name *Zranka*, which also described the inhabitants of the region and which has a disputed etymology. It appears in the inscription of → Bīsutūn of Darius I (1,16) and in Greek and Latin derivations; the 'Persian' variants have an initial *d*-. According to Strabo, D. (in the Parthian period) adjoined Areia in the north and west, Carmania in the west, Gedrosia in the south and Arachosia in the east; together with → Areia [1] it formed a 'tax district'. Along with the names of tribes and rivers, Ptol. 6,19 also mentions the cities Prophthasia (Phrada) and Ariaspe. Str. 15,2,9f. refers to tin deposits and to the Persian lifestyle of the inhabitants. In the late Achaemenid period D. formed a satrapy, together with Arachosia under Barsaentes, the ally of Bessus.

After Alexander's conquest (330/29 BC) D., together with Areia, was governed by Arsames, later by Stasanor and Stasander. As a Seleucid possession the region quickly fell to Euthydemus of Bactria, and then to the Parthians in the middle of the 2nd cent. Isidor of Charax describes Paraetacene or Sakastene, on the shores of the middle → Etymander, which the Sacae had seized around 128 BC. Also archaeologically attested with the (mainly Parthian) ruins at Kūh-ī Xwāğah, D. played an important role in the Avesta- und 'historical' tradition of Iran as well.

R. SCHMITT, EncIr VII 5, 1995, 535–537; P. DAFFINÀ, L'immigrazione dei Sakā nella Drangiana, 1967; G. GNOLI, Ricerche storiche sul Sīstān antico, 1967; A. HINTZE, Der Zamyād-Yašt, 1994, 40ff.

J.W.

Drappes (Draptes). Celtic or pre-Celtic name; leader of the Senones (EVANS, 445–446).

Together with the Cadurcian Lucterius, D. tried to invade the Gallic *provincia* in 51 BC. Pursued by Roman forces, the Gallic troops entrenched themselves at Uxellodunum. In an attempt to resupply the city, D. was blocked and captured by C. Caninius Rebilus. He thereupon committed suicide (Caes. B Gall. 8,30–36; 44,2; Oros. 6,11,20–22).

→ Senones; → Uxellodunum W.SP.

Drapsaca (Δράψακα; *Drápsaka*). City in → Bactria, first mentioned in connection with Alexander the Great's campaigns, also attested in the forms Δάραψα and Δρέψα (*Dárapsa* and *Drépsa*; Arr. Anab. 3,29,1; Str. 15,725; Ptol. 6,12,6; 8,23,13 N; Steph. Byz. p. 218). The form Δάραψα is preserved in the rural name of modern Andarāb north of Kābul (Hindu kush), while modern Qunduz should be regarded as the ancient D. [1]. Ptolemy includes D. in Sogdiana and also mentions the inhabitants (6,12,4: Δρεψιανοί; *Drepsianoí*). The Hyrcanian Ἄδραψα (*Ádrapsa*) mentioned by Ptol. 6,9,6 has nothing to do with D. but is etymological evidence for earlier links between Bactria and Hyrcania. Alexander passed through D. in 329 BC on the way to Ἄορνος (*Áornos*) and Βάκτρα (*Báktra*).

1 Atlas of the World II, Plate 31.

H.T. and B.B.

Dra(v)us A navigable river having its source in the Norian Alps (Plin. HN 3,147), flowing into the Danube at Mursa in Pannonia, modern Drava. Some cosmographers also have the Draus rise in the Danube (cosmographia 1,20; 24; Iulius Honorius, cosmographia B 24). The Draus was an important transportation route (Ven. Fort. Vita Martini 4,649) and enjoyed veneration in Pannonia as a river deity. H.GR.

Dreams; Interpretation of dreams

I. ANCIENT ORIENT II. CLASSICAL ANTIQUITY

I. ANCIENT ORIENT

Dreams and their interpretation were a popular topic in the written tradition of the Ancient Orient and Egypt since the 22nd cent. BC. Both spontaneously experienced dreams as well as dream incubation are attested. Preserved dreams relate divine messages (in the form of theophanies). Though usually contained in literary texts [3; 5. 746; 6], they also occur in letters [1]. Dreams also contained ethical maxims and wisdom for life reflecting personal experience and state of health. The 'Assyrian Book of Dreams' (7th cent. BC, with Old Babylonian precursors in the 18th cent. BC) compiles dream images considered typical, such as omina (→ Divination), and interprets them in an appended apodosis ('postscript', which interprets the omen). Psychoanalytic interpretation of these dream images has been unsuccessful so far. An Egyptian Book of Dreams is preserved from the Ramesside period (13th cent. BC) and appears to contain Babylonian influences [5. 747]. Dream visions, like → prayer, were a plot device in literary works for representing the thoughts, moods and fears of the protagonists.

Dream interpretation was the task of experts of whose 'training' nothing is known. The Akkadian term *šā'ilu*, 'questioner', hints at the practice of dream interpretation, which involves narrating the dream, questioning the dreamer and providing a 'solution', i.e., interpretation [4. 217 f.]. In dream interpretation symbols, assonance, paronomasia, word-play, association, etc. played a role. The evil consequences of a dream were countered with unbinding rituals. The dreams and their professional interpretation related in the correspondence of → Mari (18th cent. BC) exhibit considerable structural and typological proximity to the dream visions of OT → prophets.

→ Divination

1 S. Butler, Mesopotamian Conceptions of Dreams and Dream Rituals, 1998 2 A. Kammenhuber, Orakelpraxis. T.e und Vorzeichenschau bei den Hethitern, 1976 3 A. L. Oppenheim, The Interpretation of Dreams in the Ancient Near East, 1956 4 J. Renger, Unt. zum Priestertum in der altbabylon. Zeit II, in: ZA 59, 1969, 104–230 5 P. Vernus, s. v. Traum, LÄ 6, 745–749 6 A. Zgoll, T. und T.-Erleben im ant. Mesopot. — Beitr. zu einer Kulturgesch. des T., 2002.

J. RE.

II. Classical Antiquity

A. General points B. Theories of sleep and dream genesis C. Discourses on dream interpretation D. Technique of dream interpretation E. Mythology and poetry

A. General points

Encounters with dreams and dream interpretation are reflected in Graeco-Roman antiquity in the discourses of philosophy, medicine, religion, mantic, magic, popular awareness and poetry [20. 24] and provide insights into the mentality and self-image of dreamers and interpreters [5; 13; 20; 21]. Regarding the conceptual framework, s. II. C. and D.

Despite the empirically gained knowledge that all higher beings dream (Lucr. 4,985–1036; Plin. HN 10,209 ff.), dreaming was considered a specifically human trait in antiquity. It was noted with horror and astonishment when humans (supposedly) could not dream (Suet. Nero 46; Plin. HN 5,8,44 f.: the Atlantes). The difference between dreaming and being awake was considered the guarantee of human → rationality, which is also a theme in competing origin myths of dream interpretation: its mythical 'inventor' (→ *prṓtos heuretḗs*) was → Apollo (Eur. IT, especially 1234–1275) or → Prometheus (Aesch. PV 467 ff.). In both myths encryptation and the need for interpretation of dream images served to secure the gods their empowering knowledge. Against this background, dream interpretation by mortals becomes a subversive act of enlightenment.

B. Theories of sleep and dream genesis

By contrast, for example, to Freud's psychoanalytical dream theory, antiquity established a fundamental link between sleep and dream types [11; 14. 16–21]. In essence, experential knowledge may be recognized implicitly or explictly behind any form of using or interpreting a dream. (This also applies to magical practices that were supposed to manipulate people by generating dreams [6], and the rites accompanying incubation sleep (→ incubation)). Nevertheless, some physiological and materialistic theories were antagonistic to mantic dream interpretation because they did not assess dreams as messages sent to humans (by gods: Pl. Symp. 203a; by → demons: Pythagoreans, Diog. Laert. 8,32).

A functional biological and physiological explanation of dreams and sleep, to which ancient medicine also adhered, was first provided by Aristotle [6] (Aristot. Somn.; Aristot. An. 2; 3,1), even though he did not wish to rule out prophetic dreams on principle (but prefered to explain them as coincidence): the subject, which is perceived as a functioning organism, was suffering a privation of sensory perception in its sleep due to vapours arising from the stomach that, in turn, eliminated the soul's ability to be in community with other humans (cf. Heraclitus' concept of the *ídios kósmos*, the 'separate world' of the sleeper: Heracl. 22 B 89 DK). In other respects, the state of sleep has a positive connotation, e.g., because it allowed digestion and was seen as life-preserving recuperation and preservation for all living creatures. Therefore, dream images are remainders of the day and indicators of the psychophysical state. The link between dreaming and (abundant) food intake, mood, being in love, sexual desire [15] and mourning was empirical knowledge in antiquity (e.g., Ps.-Theocr. 21). Plato [1] (Resp. 571c–572b) and, centuries later, early Christian writers proposed a close link between one's moral stance and dream images (humans are what they dream) [22].

A monistic materialistic explanation was provided by → Atomism and the → Epicurean school (→ Epicurus; tangible in Lucr. 4,452–468; 757–826; 906–1036): the sensory organs are largely subject to the same bombardment of atoms in sleep as when they are awake, but the ability for rational thought is reduced, which is why the more or less senseless dream images that arise through the combination of atoms are withdrawn from a direct examination of their reality. Unenlightened persons misinterpreted them, therefore, as evidence of the existence of fabulous creatures and the Underworld or as a glimpse into the future. Consistent with their teaching, any form of dream interpretation for mantic purposes was rejected in the Epicurean program, which aimed at reducing the fear of the gods and of death. Summary: Tert. De anima 41,1–9; cf. → Soul, doctrine of the.

C. Discourses on dream interpretation

Ancient terms for dream interpretation: ὀνειροκρισία/*oneirokrisía*, Latin *coniectura*, *interpretatio*; for dream interpreter: ὀνειροκρίτης/*oneirokrítēs*, Latin *interpres*, *coniector*.

Two areas emerge as the objective of interpretation and frame of reference in ancient dream use and dream interpretation: (1) dreams and the body; (2) dreams and the future (mantic). Philosophical discourse, on the other hand, was primarily concerned with the theoretical foundations and possibilities of dream interpretation as well as the function of the dream in human thought [16]. In many phases of → Stoicism, a dream interpretation geared towards a recognition of the → *lógos* in connection with the concept of *sympátheia* played an important role (Cic. Div. 1,6; → Chrysippus [2], → Posidonius [3] D.). In → Neoplatonism, dream divination was made useful for theurgical operations (cf. → Divination; → Theurgy). In Christianity downgrading of dreams in favour of visions occurred, but dreams were to some extent seen as indicators of the depth of faith [10; 22].

Medical dream interpretation, which sought indicators of the function or dysfuntion of the body or soul in the dreamed experience, was already practiced as part of a wholistic diagnostics since → Hippocrates [6] (reference texts: Hippocr. regimen 4; Gal. De dignotione ex insomniis; cf. [18. 280–306]; cf. → Incubation), especially in association with the theory of the four humours.

Dream interpretation was essentially considered the most democratic form of mantic because every person dreams and dreams may be interpreted without aids or costs. The usurpation of dreams by various population and educational groups, which ranged from routine practice, which is difficult to access, and incubation to the secularized dream interpretation of → Artemidorus [6], cannot be reduced to a single formula of 'lay versus professional dream interpreters' because all groups (private individuals, semi-professionals, scientific interpreters [3]) considered dreams in a form suited to their needs. Even 'lay persons' arrived at respectable results by means of intuition and empiricism (cf. Artem. 1 proem).

A history of dream interpretation, which essentially appears as a Greek and Oriental art in antiquity, is not possible because of the state of the preserved tradition. Dream interpreters are already mentioned in the Homeric epics (presumably priests/oracle readers with special abilities; Hom. Il. 1,62), although dreams in the 'Iliad' and 'Odyssey' are not professionally interpreted. Even in the later period, the dream interpreter remained a marginal literary figure (exceptions: Ov. Am. 3,5; Lucian Somnus). Members of certain peoples (e.g., the Hyblaeans and Telmessians: Clem. Al. Strom. 1,16,74; Tert. De anima 46,39) were considered naturally gifted as dream interpreters.

The precondition of a systematic tradition of examining the relationship of the world of those who are awake to the dream experience in the form of cataloguing of dream images and their fulfilment that can be passed on, i.e., dream interpretation as a proper 'existential technique' (FOUCAULT), is → literacy. Beginning in the 5th cent. BC, several Greek treatises on methodological foundations and individual problems (images, dream types) are attested [20. 127–143]; but only the *Oneirokritiká* of Artemidorus [6] are preserved (2nd cent. AD).

The existence of a genuine Etruscan dream interpretation is disputed; the appearance of *coniectores* at the court of Tarquinius [12] Superbus in Accius' *Brutus* (2nd cent. BC) is more probably attributable to a genre characteristic of tragedy than an Etruscan touch [9]. In Rome, dream interpretation, which was considered a Greek → *téchnē*, was less important than other types of divination (cf. Cic. Div. 1,58; 1,132; [4]). Like all forms of mantic, dream interpretation was officially prohibited in the Roman empire in the mid 4th cent. AD but, as dream books with Christian shades show (e.g., *Somnium Danielis*), still enjoyed great inofficial popularity [2].

D. TECHNIQUE OF DREAM INTERPRETATION

The main characteristic of mantic dream interpretation was a differentiation of dream types with and without significance for seeing the future (→ Divination). Often an improvized five-tiered classification into three meaningful (ὄνειρος/*óneiros*, Latin *somnium*; ὅραμα/*hórama*, Latin *visio*; χρηματισμός/*chrēmatismós*, Latin *oraculum*) and two meaningless (ἐνύπνιον/ *enhýpnion*, lat. *insomnium*; φάντασμα/*phántasma*, Latin *visum*) dream types was used [12]. In this context Artemidorus [6], who is representative of professional dream interpretation, applied different schemes and typologies that (1) classify the manifest content of the dream and its discrepancy with the phenomena of awakeness and, depending on the degree of presumed encryptation, permit conclusions on the dream type; (2) determine the specific meaning of the image, by approximately identifying the dominant element of the image against the background of the dreamer's life (status, age, profession, family history, character etc.) and — on this basis — subject of the dream (often by means of analogies, Artem. 2,25) to an interpretation similar to textual interpretation and certain rhetorical practices. Inversely, → Macrobius [1] (*Commentarii in Somnium Scipionis*) attempts to render the criteria of dream interpretation useful to literary interpretation [19. 457–465].

It is noteworthy that unlike psychoanalytical dream interpretation, a mutual representation of objects is assumed in principle and sexual dreams, for example, were also interpreted as the expression of other matters. Because of the strong inclusion of the social position of the dreamer in the interpretative process and the assumption that the dreams of high-ranking persons had a great significance for the common good, ancient dream interpretation has a decidedly social dimension. Cf. in general on technique [20. 171–222].

E. MYTHOLOGY AND POETRY

While the routinely recurring phenomenon of sleep (Greek *hýpnos*, Latin *somnus*) was personified in religion and mythology as a deity (→ Somnus), there is no (constant) personified equivalent for dreams, but according to the nature of the dream only temporary messengers (e.g., Hom. Il. 2,1–49) or hordes of dreams (→ Morpheus).

The Homeric epics open a literary discourse [19] that cannot be reduced to non-literary interpretative discourses but through the manifold functions of the dream motif in literary art demonstrates deep psychological insight into the dream phenomenon (examples of especially densely written dream representation: Aesch. Cho. passim; Eur. IT 52 ff.; Prop. 1,26A; 4,7;

Verg. Aen. 1,353–360; 2,268–302 and passim; Luc. 3,1–40; 7,1–44); regarding other genres (shorter pieces, novels, historiography) cf. [7; 21].
→ Divination; → Incubation; → Somnus; → DREAM INTERPRETATION

1 G. BENEDETTI, T. WAGNER-SIMON (ed.), T. und Träumen. T.-Analysen in Wiss., Rel. und Kunst, 1984 2 K. BRACKERTZ, Die Volks-Traumbücher des byz. MA, 1993 3 D. DEL CORNO (ed.), Graecorum de re oneirocritica scriptorum reliquiae, 1969 4 H. CANCIK, Idolum and Imago, in: D. SHULMAN, G. STROUMSA (ed.), Dream Cultures, 1999, 169–178 5 P. COX MILLER, Dreams in Late Antiquity, 1994 6 S. EITREM, Dreams and Divination in Magical Ritual, in: C. A. FARAONE, D. OBBINK (ed.), Magica Hiera, 1991, 175–187 7 P. FRISCH, Die T. bei Herodot, 1968 8 G. GUIDORIZZI (ed.), Il sogno in Grecia, 1988 9 CH. GUITTARD, Le Songe de Tarquin ..., in: La divination dans le monde etrusco-italique (Caesarodunum Suppl. 54), 1986, 47–67 10 J. S. HANSON, Dreams and Visions in the Graeco-Roman World and Early Christianity, in: ANRW II 23.2, 1980, 1395–1427 11 H. HOMANN, s. v. Schlaf, HWdPh 8, 1296–1299 12 A. H. M. KESSELS, Ancient Systems of Dream Classifications, in: Mnemosyne 22, 1969, 389–425 13 A. KROVOZA, Nachwort, in: [20], 223–233 14 P. LAVIE, Die wundersame Welt des Schlafs, 1999 15 J. PIGEAUD, Il sogno erotico nell'antichità: l'oneirogmos, in: [8], 137–146 16 S. ROTONDARO, Il sogno in Platone, 1998 17 R. G. A. VAN LIESHOUT, Greeks on Dreams, 1980 18 O. VEDFELT, Dimensionen der T., 1999 19 C. WALDE, Die T.darstellungen in der griech.-röm. Dichtung, 2001 20 Id., Ant. TD und mod. T.forsch., 2001 21 G. WEBER, Kaiser, T. und Visionen in Prinzipat und Spätant., 2000 22 M. WEIDHORN, Dreams and Guilt, in: Harvard Theological Review 58, 1965, 69–90. C. W.

Drepanon (Δρέπανον; *Drépanon*). Name of several foothills; the external shape of the mountain may have given rise to the name D. ('sickle').
[1] On the north coast of western Crete (Ptol. 3,15,5), known in antiquity and today as D.

M. GUARDUCCI, Inscript. Cret. 2,10. C.L. and H.SO.

[2] Northernmost outcrop of the Peloponnese into the Corinthian Gulf, 7 km north-east of Rhion (with which it is identified in Str. 8,2,3 and Ptol. 3,14,29), the blunt end of the cone of a mountain stream; the (otherwise unknown) 'fortress of Athena' (Paus. 7,22,10; 23,4). was located there.

E. CURTIUS, Peloponnesos, 1, 447; A. PHILIPPSON, Der Peloponnes, 261; PHILIPPSON/KIRSTEN 3, 67, 189. C.L. and E.O.

[3] (Δρέπανον μικρόν; *Drépanon mikrón*). Even today the name of a cape on the western coast of Cyprus, wrongly located by Ptol. 5,14,1 on the southern coast. Archaeological finds: extensive field of ruins with necropolis; a theatre was also visible here in the 19th cent. At Hagios Georghios Peyias a large church complex with three basilicas has been partly excavated.

D. CHRISTOU, Chronique des fouilles à Chypre en 1992, in: BCH 117, 1993, 753; D. G. HOGARTH, Devia Cypria, 1889, 10–12; E. OBERHUMMER, Die Insel Cypern 1, 1903, 129f. R.SE.

[4] (also *Drépana, Drepánē*). Foothills and harbour town on the north-western tip of Sicily north of Lilybaeum at the foot of the → Eryx, modern Trapani. Settled since the Palaeolithic period, attested for the first time in literature as harbour of the → Elymi in Eryx (cf. Diod. Sic. 24,11) in the war of Dionysius I against Carthage in 367 BC (Diod. Sic. 15,73). Neither coins nor inscriptions are available from the Classical period. Developed as a military harbour by the Carthaginians at the start of the 1st Punic War, with part of the population of Eryx (Diod. Sic. 23,9) being resettled. In the summer of 249 BC P. Claudius Pulcher suffered a devastating defeat in an attempt to take D. from the sea (Pol. 1,49–51; Diod. Sic. 24,1), in 242 D. was unexpectedly occupied by C. Lutatius Catulus. Base for the decisive naval battle at the *insulae Aegates* in 241 BC that ended the war (Pol. 1,59f.; Diod. Sic. 24,8; 11), thereafter a harbour locality without city status (Cic. Verr. 2, 2,140; 4,37; Plin. HN 3,88; 90f.). Cf. CIL 10, p. 747. Archaeology: minor remains.
[5] Settlement in Bithynia on the southern coast of the Gulf of Astacus, birthplace of Helena, mother of Constantine the Great (AD* 250/257), and therefore elevated to city status as Helenopolis (Amm. Marc. 26,8,1; Procop. Aed. 5,2). Archaeology: a few remains on the cape of Hersek in the Gulf of Izmit. C.L. and E.O.

Drerus (Δρῆρος; *Drêros*). Town in north-east Crete in a mountainous position, with a double acropolis, from which there is a view of the Gulf of Mirabello, modern Hagios Antonios near Neapolis. Already populated in the Minoan period, D. reached its peak between the 8th and 6th cents. BC. The Temple of Apollo Delphinios from the mid 8th cent. BC, combining Minoan and Doric elements (with cult images of Apollo, Leto and Artemis) [1], testifies to archaic Cretan religiosity. The most important source for D. in the Hellenistic period is the epigraphically preserved oath of the 180 ephebes (2nd half of the 3rd cent. BC; Syll. I³ 527) with details about an alliance with → Knosos and opposition to Lyttus (→ Lyctus) [2]. D. seems later to have become a dependency of Lyttus. There are no further informative traces of settlement from the Roman period. Archaeologically notable, besides the Temple of Apollo, are the remains of the Hellenistic cistern on the agora.
→ Crete (with map)

1 I. BEYER, Die Tempel von D., 1976 2 A. CHANIOTIS, Die Verträge zw. kret. Poleis in der hell. Zeit, 1996, 195, no. 7.

H. BEISTER, s. v. D., in: LAUFFER, Griechenland, 202; H. VAN EFFENTERRE, s. v. D., in: J. W. MYERS et al., Aerial Atlas of Ancient Crete, 1992, 86–90; I. F. SANDERS, Roman Crete, 1982, 141. H. SO.

Dress regulations see → Clothing; → Costume, clerical

Drilae (Δρῖλαι; *Drîlai*). Tribe in the north Anatolian mountains south of → Trapezus; the Greeks with Xenophon were unable to capture their mountain refuge in 400 BC (Xen. An. 5,2,1–27; cf. Steph. Byz. s.v. D.), identified with the Sanni by Arr. Peripl. p. eux. 15. E.O.

Drilon (modern Drim, Albanian Drini). River formed in Albania near Kukësi from the union of the Beli Drim (Drini i Bardhë, which rises at the foot of the mountain Rusolije in Kosovo) and the Crni Drim (Drini i Zi), which emerges from *Lichnidus lacus*, modern Lake Ohrid, Macedonia/Albania. Ptol. 2,16,6 is almost correct in observing that the river flows from the *Scardus mons* (modern Šar planina in Macedonia) and another (unnamed) mountain through the interior of Moesia superior. Str. 7,5,7 describes its course as navigable eastwards to Dardania. The Romans termed it wrongly *Dirinus*, *Drinius* (Plin. HN 3,144: *amnis Drino* [or *Drilo*]; 3,150: *Illyrici ... longitudo a flumine Arsia ad flumen Drinium* [or *Dirinum*] *DXXX* ...) or *Drinus* (Dimensuratio provinciarum 18: *Illyricum* [*Pannonia*] *ab oriente flumine Drino, ab occidente desertis*), partly because the upper course of the → Drinus (modern Drina) with its tributary Lim almost reaches the Drilon's river valley. In the vicinity of the *Labeatis lacus* (Skadarsko jezero, Albanian Liqeni Shkodres), the rivers Clausal and Barbanna join and form an arm of the Drilon, which from here on is called *Oriundes flumen* (corresponding to the lower course of the Drilon) in Liv. 44,31,3–5 and flows south from Lissus into the Adriatic. Eratosthenes (in Steph. Byz.) mentions it in connection with → Dyrrhachium.

C. PATSCH, s.v. D., RE 5, 1707. M.Š.K.

Drinus Right-hand tributary of the Savus (Sava), modern Drina (length: 346 km); Ptol. 2,16,7 records that the D. flows west of Taurunum (Zemun) into the Savus. The D. is formed from the union of the Tara and Piva in the border region of Bosnia-Herzegovina and Montenegro; it forms the border between Bosnia-Herzegovina and Serbia. In some sources the name D. was erroneously applied to the river → Drilon, no doubt because both rivers flow close to each other in the extreme north of Albania. A road station *ad Drinum* (modern Brodac, north of Bijeljina) is mentioned in Tab. Peut. 5,3; the river is named *Drinius* in Geogr. Rav. 4,16.

C. PATSCH, s.v. D, RE 5, 1709. M.Š.K.

Drobeta Garrison and civilian settlement on the Danube east of the 'Iron Gate' in Dacia inferior or Dacia maluensis, modern Turnu Severin (Oltenia, Romania). Near it was Pontes, where Apollodorus of Damascus erected the famous Danube bridge for Trajan. In the 2nd Dacian War D. was used as a military base by the Romans. In Trajan's time the *cohors Cretum sagittariorum* built a large garrison here, in which various auxiliary troops were later stationed (*cohors III campestris*: CIL III 14216,8,10; *cohors I sagittariorum* in the 3rd cent.: CIL III 1583, 8074; *cuneus equitum Dalmatarum Divitensium* with *auxilium primorum Daciscorum* in the 4th cent.: Not. Dign. Or. 42,16,24). In the same period a *praefectus legionis XIII geminae* was appointed in Transdrobeta (Not. Dign. Or. 42,35). Under Hadrian D. became a *municipium*, and under Septimius Severus, a *colonia*. A toll station was located in D. Worthy of note are the thermal baths and a temple of Cybele. Under Constantine the Great the garrison had to be refurbished. The last work on the fortifications took place under Justinian. References: Ptol. 3,8,10 (Δρουφηγίς/Δρουφηγύς); Tab. Peut. (*Drubetis*); Not. Dign. Or. 42,6,16,24 (*Drobeta*).

TIR L 34 Budapest, 56 (Bibliography). J.BU.

Dromedarii Camel riders (καμηλῖται; *kamēlítai*) were put to military use in the East very early on; thus, during the campaign against Croesus (547/6 BC), Cyrus deployed camel riders in front of the foot soldiers, and in 480 BC Arab camel riders formed part of the army of Xerxes (Hdt. 1,80,2–5; 7,86,2; 7,184,4). Camel riders later fought in the armies of both the Seleucids and the Parthians against Roman legions (190 BC: Liv. 37,40,12; AD 217: Herodian. 4,14,3; 4,15,2–3). According to Vegetius, however, camels were useless in battle (Veg. Mil. 3,23). In the Roman army, camels were used for logistics (Tac. Ann. 15,12,1). *Dromedarii* were therefore camel drivers rather than soldiers deployed in combat situations; *dromedarii* are attested for the 2nd cent. AD in the Thebais (EEpigr. 7,458f.). They are depicted on the Arch of Galerius, on the Arch of Constantine in Rome and on the column of Theodosius in Constantinople. In late antiquity the *dromedarii* were classified after the *alae* (for the Thebais cf. Not. Dign. Or. 31,48; 31,54; 31,57). According to Procopius, Justinian's reduction in the number of camels contributed substantially to the weakening of the Roman army (Procop. Arc. 30,15f.).

→ Camel

1 G. BECATTI, Colonna coclide istoriata, 1960, pl. 77a 2 H.P. LAUBSCHER, Der Reliefschmuck des Galeriusbogens, 1975, 44 3 K. SCHAUENBURG, Die Cameliden, BJ 155/6, 1955/6, 83. S.L.

Dromedary see → Camel

Dromichaites (Δρομιχαίτης; *Dromichaítēs*; in Oros. 3,23,52 Dori or Doricetis). Ruler of the Getae at the end of the 4th/beginning of the 3rd cent. BC. Bitter political rival of → Lysimachus, who undertook two campaigns against D. probably in 297 and between 293–291 (chronology disputed); D. captured Lysimachus' son Agathocles [5] and then Lysimachus himself but released them both, in exchange for their withdrawal from conquered territories north of the Ister and for the pledge of marriage between D. and one of Lysimachus' daughters. One of D.'s fortresses was the so far unidentified Helis. Literary Sources: Diod. Sic. 21,11–12; Paus. 1,9,6; Pol. fr. 102; Str. 7,3,8; 14; Plut. Demetrius 39, 6; 52,6; Plut. Mor. 183D1; Polyaenus, Strat. 7,25; Iust. 16,1,19; Memnon, FGrH 434 F 5,1; [1]. The location, extent and character of D.'s empire are matters of scholarly debate.

1 W. Schubart, Griech. lit. Papyri, no. 39.

C. Franco, Il regno di Lisimaco, 1993; K. Jordanov, Getae against Lysimachos, in: Bulgarian Historical Review 1, 1990, 39–51; J. Lens Tuero, El encuentro entre Dromijaites y Lisimaco, in: J. Lens (ed.), Estudios sobre Diodoro de Sicilia, 1994, 201–207; H. S. Lund, Lysimachus, 1992, 45–50. U.P.

Dromocleides (Δρομοκλείδης; *Dromokleides*).
[1] Athenian archon 475/4 BC. (Diod. Sic. 11,50,1). E.S.-H.
[2] Influential and active Athenian demagogue, supporting → Demetrius [2] Poliorketes. In 295 BC he proposed that Piraeus and Munychia be handed over to Demetrius and, probably in 292/1, that the 'saviour' Demetrius be asked for an oracle (Plut. Demetrius 13,1–3; 34,1–7).
→ Athens; → Kolakes

Habicht, 94; 98–100; Id., Unt. zur polit. Geschichte Athens im 3. Jh.v.Chr., 1979, 34–44. J.E.

Dromon (Δρόμων; *Drómōn*). Poet of the 4th cent. BC; two fragments of his play *Psaltria* are extant [1].

1 PCG V, 1986, 124–125. B.BÄ.

Dromos see → Funerary architecture

Dromos (δρόμος; *drómos*). The Greek word *dromos* means 'course' (also course of the stars), hence running, race (e.g. of the Greek heroes in Hom. Il 23,758), but also racetrack and running track. In archaeological terminology *dromos* designates a corridor leading to a room, primarily in burial complexes. The term *dromos* was first used for the entrance paths to the burial complexes of the → Aegean Koine, which include in particular, apart from the Cretan → tholos tombs with their short *dromoi*, the Mycenaean domed and chamber tombs. The open *dromoi* of the domed tombs had often been cut into the neighbouring rock or hill and the side walls partially disguised by carved square stone blocks (so-called treasure-house of → Atreus at Mycenae). Both the entrance paths to → funerary architecture of other cultures and the avenue-like approaches to Egyptian temples are called *dromoi* today.
→ Tumulus

1 P. Bruneau, Le Dromos et le Temple C du Sarapieion C de Délos, in: BCH 104, 1980, 161–188 2 O. Pelon, Tholoi, tumuli et cercles funéraires (Bibliothèque des Écoles Françaises d'Athènes et de Rome 229), 1976, 277–297. K. H.

Droop cups see → Little-master cups

Dropides (Δρωπίδης; *Drōpídēs*). From an aristocratic Athenian family (an ancestor with the same name was an archon in 645/4 BC and related to → Solon); according to Curtius 3,13,15, he was one of the three Athenian emissaries to → Darius [3] captured by → Parmenion after the battle of → Issus (in 333). The account in Arrian An. 3,24,4, needs to be corrected in some details where it deviates from Curtius [1. 1, 233f.] but reports credibly that → Alexander [4] had him arrested. His fate is unknown.

1 Bosworth, Commentary. E.B.

Druentia Modern river Durance, rises in the → Alpes Cottiae and flows into the Rhône (Str. 4,1,3; 11; Ptol. 2,10,4). It was along this torrential river (Str. 4,6,5; Plin. HN 3,33; Auson. Mos. 479) that Hannibal marched with his army (Liv. 21,32,8; 32,6; Sil. Pun. 3,468; Amm. Marc. 15,10,11). *Nautae Druentici* are mentioned in inscriptions (CIL XII 731; 982). In late antiquity the region's security was maintained by fortresses (Cassiod. Var. 3,41,2). H.GR.

Drugs see → Poisons; → Pharmacology; → Salves

Druids (Druides, Druida). Latinization of the Celtic stem **drui(d)*, 'the very wise'; the ambiguity with the Greek δρῦς (*drys*) 'oak' was apparently intentional (cf. Plin. HN 16,249) [1. 1321f.; 2. 430]. They were first referred to by the Peripatetic Sotion 200/170 BC (Diog. Laert. 1,1,6f.), later references are based at least in part on the lost historical work by Posidonius. According to them, the *druidae* formed, together with the *bardi* and → *vates*, a hierarchically organized branch of the Celtic priestly caste, with an orally-transmitted secret teaching, of which little is known. Their origins lie in obscurity; they probably had Indo-European roots; according to Caesar (B Gall. 6,13), their teachings reached the continent from Britain. Archaeological evidence is rare, and generally inconclusive. In Gallic society, which Caesar divided into *druidae*, *equites* and *plebs*, the *druidae*, as priests, teachers and judges, held a pre-eminent position and were responsible for cult, public and private sacrifices, divination, soothsaying, and interpreting religious obligations, including the festival calendar. They also embodied knowledge of medicine, botany, as well as the history and culture of their peoples and were tutors to the young nobility. Once a year, at a secret location in the region of the → Carnutes, they met as a judicial court and, when necessary, elected their leader. They exercised an influence over the election and term of office of tribal princes and took decisions on war and peace (Diod. Sic. 5,31,2; Str. 4,4,4; Caes. B

Gall. 6,13; Dion. Chrys. 49,8,1). Their doctrine of the migration of the soul (Caes. Gall. 6,13,5) led to the story that they were adherents of the Pythagoreans, with the result that they were also described as philosophers (Diod. Sic. 5,28,6, from Alexander Polyhistor; Luc. 1,450–458; Mela 3,19; Hippolytus, Philosophumena 1,25; Orig. contra Celsum 1,16,17; Clem. Al. strom. 1,15). Whereas Caesar made some use of their assistance, shown by the example of the only *druida* known by name, → Diviciacus, the *druidae* were persecuted by emperors Tiberius and Claudius on the pretext of their involvement in human sacrifice (Plin. HN 30,13; Suet. Claud. 25). A ritually sacrificed nobleman was discovered in Lindow Moss, Cheshire in 1984 [3]. In AD 61 → Suetonius Paulinus destroyed the Druid centre on the island Mona (Isle of Man; Tac. Ann. 14,29–30). As late as 69/70 *druidae* interpreted the burning of the Capitol as the end of Roman control of the world (Tac. Hist. 4,54); thereafter, their influence seems to have declined dramatically on the continent; later references, which also include female *druidae*, refer only to simple soothsayers (SHA Alex. Sev. 60, Car. 14,15, Aurelian. 44). According to Christian accounts from the early Middle Ages, the *druidae* seem to have still had influence in Britain and especially in Ireland as → *magi* and *filid*. From the 18th cent. onwards the supposedly secret teachings of the *druidae* led to a wealth of speculation that in turn gave rise to the lodge-like male society of the order of Druids and numerous other occult groups [4].

→ Celts; → Druids

1 Holder 2 A. Ross, Ritual and the Druids, in: M. Green (ed.), The Celtic World, 1995, 423–444 3 Id., Der Tod des Druidenfürsten, 1990 4 E. Türk, s.v. Druidenorden, LThK³ 3, 381f.

1 D.O. Cróinín, s.v. Magi (Druids), LMA 6, 81f. 2 F. Le Roux, C.J. Guyonvarc'h, Les Druids, ³1986 3 G.-Ch. Picard, César et les Druides, in: Hommage J. Carcopino 1977, 227–233. W.SP.

Druna Modern Drôme, tributary of the Rhône (Auson. Mos. 479). H.GR.

Drusilla Daughter of the Jewish king Agrippa I, born AD 38. As a child she was engaged to Epiphanes, son of king Antiochus IV of Commagene. The marriage did not take place because Epiphanes did not get circumcised as promised. In 53 she married king Azizus of Emesa, who did get circumcised. The Procurator of Judaea → Antonius [II 6] Felix, who was smitten by her beauty, got her to marry him and thus break the law forbidding a Jewess to marry a non-Jew (Jos. ant. Iud. 18,132; 19,354f.; 20,139–143). K.BR.

Drusipara (Δρουσιπάρα; *Drousipára*). Important station on the Amphipolis — Hadrianopolis — Byzantium road in south-east Thrace, east of Büyük Karıştiran/Turkey (earliest reference Ptol. 3,11,7; also in It. Ant. 137,7; 323,3; It. Burd. 569; Theophanes, 1,234,2). I.v.B.

Drusus Initially cognomen in the *gens* → Livia (ThlL, Onom. 3,256–260). According to Suet. Tib. 3,2, an otherwise unknown Livius (in the 3rd cent. BC) assumed the epithet, after he had won a duel with the Celtic leader Drausus, and passed it on to his family. Through → Livia's first marriage, with Ti. Claudius [I 19] Nero, the cognomen passed into the Claudian branch of the *domus Augusta* through her son Nero Claudius [II 24] (D. Maior), brother of the second Princeps → Tiberius; D. appears in the name of the son of D. Maior, → Germanicus, of the latter's son D. [II 2], of the son of Tiberius (D. Minor [II 1]), in the birth-name of → Claudius and of his son Claudius [II 23], as well as that of → Nero after he was adopted by Claudius.

Salomies, 328. K.-L.E.

I. Republican period II. Imperial period

I. Republican period

[I 1–4] → Livius Drusus

[I 5] D. (Claudianus), M. (Livius) Cousin of Clodius [I 4], father of Livia, grandfather of Tiberius (for adoption from the family of the Claudii Pulchri into the Livii Drusi see [1]). His first (known) political appearance dates to 59 BC (Cic. Att. 2,7,3) and sees him associated with the then *consul* Caesar. In 50, D. was *praetor* or *iudex quaestionis* (MRR 2, 248); it is not known with which political party he sided during the Civil War that started in 49. In the *bellum Mutinense* of 43 he took the side of the Senate and was therefore placed on the proscription list by the Triumvirate (M. → Antonius [I 9]) in November (Cass. Dio 48,44,1). He fled to the east and fought at Philippi in 42 in the army of Cassius [I 10] and Brutus [I 9]. After the defeat he committed suicide (Vell. Pat. 2,71,3).

1 F. Münzer, s.v. D., RE 13, 881f. W.W.

II. Imperial period

[II 1] D. the Younger= Nero Claudius D. = D. Julius Caesar. Son of Tiberius and Vipsania Agrippina. Born on 7 October 15 or 14 BC, and thus only a little younger than Germanicus [1]. When his father went into exile on Rhodes, he remained in Rome. After his father's return in AD 2 he received the *toga virilis*. In AD 4, on his father's adoption by Augustus, he received the name D. Julius Caesar. Shortly thereafter he married Livia Julia, the sister of Germanicus and widow of Gaius Caesar. He participated in senate sessions as early as AD 9; in 11 quaestor; allowed to apply for the consulate without having been a praetor. After Augustus' death he read the testament to the Senate and delivered a funeral oration from the rostra. In September 14, on Tiberius' orders. he was sent to Illyricum with the Praetorian prefect Sejanus to bring the mutinying troops under control, which he did successfully. In 15 *consul*. That marked the start of conflict with Sejanus, whom he had struck in public. Many people tried to play Drusus off against Germanicus; but, according to Tacitus, neither allowed himself to be manipulated (Ann. 2,43,6). In 17 he was given, along with Germanicus, a proconsular command; he went to Illyricum to keep the Germans in check. In 18 an *ovatio* was approved for him, as also for Germanicus, to mark his successes. At the end of 19/early 20 he returned to Italy because of Germanicus' death and participated in the funeral ceremony. Contrary to the version in Tacitus (Ann. 3,19,3), he celebrated his *ovatio* on 28 May 20 [1], and not after the trial of Calpurnius Piso; the latter event took place late November/early December [2] and D. took part in it in the second half of 20 after he had returned to Illyricum. On the occasion of his *ovatio,* a triumphal arch was erected on the Forum Augusti (CIL VI 40352), which was not dedicated until 12 March 30 [2]. In 21 *cos. II* with Tiberius; in 22 he received the *tribunicia potestas*. He was thought to have been poisoned by Sejanus, who had an affair with D.'s wife, Livia. After D.'s death in 23 the Senate conferred honours upon him similar to those granted to Germanicus in 19/20 (cf. CIL VI 912 = 31200 = [3] = [5]). An *elogium* was affixed on the Mausoleum Augusti, where he was buried (CIL VI 40367). Numerous statues and altars were erected in his honour both in his lifetime and after his death.Of the three sons that Livia Julia bore him, only Ti. Iulius Caesar = Tiberius Gemellus survived him. PIR² J 219.

1 SUMMER, in: Latomus 26, 1967, 427ff. 2 VIDMAN, FO² 41 3 W. ECK, A. CABALLOS, F. FERNÁNDEZ, Das s.c. de Cn. Pisone patre, 1996, 109ff. 4 M.H. CRAWFORD (ed.), Roman Statutes I (BICS Suppl. 64), 1996, 510f., 544f. 5 LEBEK, in. ZPE 95, 1993, 81ff.

[II 2] D. = D. Julius Caesar. Son of Germanicus and Agrippina the Younger. Born AD 7 or 8. It is not certain whether he accompanied his father to the East. In 23 he received the *toga virilis* and the privilege of early assumption of office, at the same time; to mark the occasion, a *congiarium* was distributed to the populace. After the death of D. [II 1], he and his brother Nero were commended to the Senate's favour by Tiberius; both of them were thus designated as his future successors. About 23 he married Aemilia Lepida, who belonged to the Augustan family line. He assumed a number of priestly offices; in 25 he was also *praef. urbi* during the Latin Festival (?). D. became caught up in the conflict between his brother Nero, his mother Agrippina and Sejanus. His wife made accusations against him; at Sejanus' behest, Cassius Longinus accused him in the Senate. Condemned by the senate as *hostis,* he was imprisoned on the Palatine. In 33 he starved to death. He was rehabilitated only after Caligula came to power; his portraiture appeared on coins; his remains were interred in the Mausoleum Augusti; cf. CIL VI 40374. PIR² J 220.

J. PIGÓN, in: Antiquitas 18, 1993, 183ff. W.E.

Drusus maior (Drusus the Elder) see → Claudius [II 24]

Dryads see → Nymphai

Dryas (Δρύας; *Drýas*, 'man of oak'; ThlL, Onom. s.v.D.).

[1] Thessalian Lapith. He was a friend of Peirithous, at whose wedding he fought with the Centaurs (Hom. Il. 1,263; Hes. Sc. 179; Ov. Met. 12,290–315).

[2] Thracian, a son of Ares. He took part in the Calydonian Hunt (Ov. Met. 8,307). Unlikely to be identical to the D. who was murdered by his brother → Tereus, after an oracle's pronouncement that Tereus' son would be murdered by a relative (Apollod. 1,67; Hyg. Fab. 45,3; 159) [1].

1 F. BÖMER, P. Ovidius Naso Met. B. 8–9 (comm.), 1977, 113; B. 12–13 (comm.), 1982, 106.

[3] Father of the Thracian king → Lycurgus, who was opposed to Dionysus (Hom. Il. 6,130; Soph. Ant. 955). In a fit of madness Lycurgus thought his son, also called D., was a vine bough and killed him (Apollod. 3,34f.; Hyg. Fab. 132).

W. BURKERT, Homo necans, 1972, 198.

[4] A Thracian, who in a chariot contest for the hand of → Pallene was brought to ruin through a plot, and killed by his rival in love, Cleitus (Parthenius 6 = MythGr p. 13f.; Konon FGrH 26 F 1,10). R.B.

Drymus (Δρυμός; *Drymós*).

[1] (Δρυμαία; *Drymaía*). City situated at the foot of the Callidromon, in the northern foothills of the central Cephissus valley, *c.* 1.5 km south-east of Drymea (in antiquity *Nauboleís*, Paus. 10,33,12; cf. Hom. Il. 2,518); set ablaze by the Persians (480 BC, Hdt. 8,33), destroyed by Philip II (346 BC Paus. 10,3,2) and conquered by Philip V (207 BC, Liv. 28,7,13), still mentioned in late antiquity (Hierocles, Synekdemos 643; Not. Episc. 737–762). Well-preserved walls on the acropolis (4th cent. BC) and inscriptions (2nd cent. BC; Imperial period: IG IX 1, 226–231; BCH 26, 1902, 340 no. 51; SEG 14, 468).

MÜLLER, 485; N.D. PAPACHATZIS, Παυσανίου Ἑλλάδος Περιήγησις [Pausaníou Hellágos Periḗgēsis], 5, ²1981, 431–432; F. SCHOBER, Phokis, 1924, 28; TIB I, 150; L.B. TILLARD, The Fortifications of Phokis, in: ABSA 17, 1910/1, 54–75. G.D.R.

[2] Location in north-west? Attica, with limited arable land, on the border with Boeotia (Skurta plain?), toponymically forest or wasteland (δρυμός; *drymós*, 'thicket, copse'). A *pólis* according to Harpocrates (s.v. D.) and the Suda (s.v. D.). As part of the military district of → Eleusis [1] and → Panactum (IG II² 1672), probably also a fortress: χωρίον καὶ φρούριον (*chōríon kaì phroúrion*, 'site and fortress', Hsch. s.v. D., cf. Dem. Or. 19,326). Another D. in Boeotia is mentioned in Aristot. dikaiomata (fr. 612 ROSE).

C. EDMONSON, The Topography of Northwest Attica, 1986, 115ff.; J. OBER, Fortress Attica, 1985, 98, 116, 194,

223, 225; E. VANDERPOOL, Roads and Forts in Northwestern Attica, in: California Studies in Classical Antiquity 11, 1978, 227–245, especially 232f. H.LO.

Dryope (Δρυόπη; *Dryópē*).

[1] Name of a nymph. Two widely diverging accounts exist of D.'s metamorphosis. According to Nik. in Antonius Liberalis 32, D. was the daughter of → Dryops and wife of → Andraemon [2]. She took onto her lap Apollo, who had been transformed into a tortoise, and subsequently gave birth to → Amphissus. D. was abducted by the nymphs with whom she played as a girl and to whose world she originally belonged. In her place, a black poplar and a spring appeared, whereas she herself became a nymph. Thus, D. returned to her own kind, while Amphissus founded a nymphaeum (for which the story provides the aition). According to Ov. Met. 9,324–393, on the other hand, D. was the daughter of Eurytus and half-sister of Iole. When she plucked a lotus flower for her son Amphissus, it bled because the nymph → Lotis lived inside. D. was thereupon transformed into a tree. An old tree cult lies behind both versions.

F. BÖMER, P. Ovidius Naso Met. B. 8–9 (comm.), 1977, 375–376; NILSSON, Feste, 442,3.

[2] Nymph, mother of Rutulian Tarquitus by Faunus (Verg. Aen. 10,550f., probably an invention of Virgil's). R.B.

Dryops (Δρύοψ; *Drýops*, 'man of oak'). Gave his name to the Dryopians [1]; son of the river → Spercheus and the Danaid Polydora, or of Apollo and → Dia [3], daughter of the Arcadian Lycaon. D. himself was also thought to be an Arcadian (Str. 8,6,13; Pherecydes FGrH 3 F 8; Nik. in Ant. Lib. 32; Tzetz. Lycoph. 480). One of his daughters bore Pan to Hermes (Hom. h. 19,33–39). D. had a cult (temple with statue) in the Dryopian town of Asine in Messenia (Paus. 4,34,11), whence occasional coins showing D. [2].

1 I. MALKIN, Myth and Territory in the Spartan Mediterranean, 1994, 231 2 C. ARNOLD-BIUCCHI, s.v. D., LIMC 3.1, 670.

NILSSON, Feste, 422. R.B.

Dryton Born before 192 BC, died 126/123, from Crete, citizen of Ptolemais, active at various locations as a soldier and hipparch (Archive with documents from 174–99). On 4.3.150 he wed Apollonia, in his second marriage, and thus set an example, promoting Graeco-Egyptian society as the blend of the two cultures.

N. LEWIS, Greeks in Ptolemaic Egypt, 1986, 88ff.; R. SCHOLL, D.s Tod, in: CE 63, 1988, 141–144. W.A.

Dual Numerical category, which in contrast to the sg. (singular) and pl. (plural) denotes a (conjugate or accidental) duality. While the dual was used extensively in

the Indo-European parent language throughout the whole inflection system for nouns and verbs, in most individual Indo-European languages it survives only in a more rudimentary form. The most extensive dual-system is preserved in Indo-Iranian, whereas in Latin, for example, the only vestiges of dual inflection are to be found in *duo* < *duō* 'two' and *ambō* 'both' (dat.-abl. *duōbus*, *ambōbus*). Dual forms occur more frequently in Early Greek (e.g. Homeric nom./acc. dual. ὤμω compared with nom. singular ὦμος, nom. plural. ὦμοι; aorist indicative active 3rd dual ἐβήτην compared with 3rd singular ἔβη, 3rd plural ἔβαν). Nevertheless, they already display considerable modification vis-à-vis the pattern in the parent language (dual verbal endings replaced by plural forms in the 1st person, one ending [Homeric -οιϊν, Attic -οιν] for the dual genitive and dative in all declensions) and in the course of time are completely replaced by the corresponding plural forms. Today a dual is used in modern Indo-Germanic languages in (Baltic) Lithuanian and (Slavonic) Slovene; outside the Indo-Germanic language group, e.g. in Arabic.

→ Inflection

A. CUNY, La catégorie du duel dans les langues indo-européennes et chamito-sémitiques, 1930; SOMMER, 348 § 199 n.4, 464f. § 294; SCHWYZER, Gramm. 557, 666f. J.G.

Dubis River in Gallia, modern Doubs, rises in the French Jura, crosses the territory of the Sequani and flows into the → Arar at Verdun-sur-le-Doubs (Caes. B Gall. 1,38; Str. 4,1,11; 14; 4,3,2; Ptol. 2,10,3). F.SCH.

Dubrae Modern Dover, was of great importance during the period of Roman occupation of → Britannia, as a port and coastal fortress. The first-rate port may well have been used during the invasion of AD 43. A fort was built in the late 2nd cent. to accommodate a unit of the *classis Britannica* [1]. The fort was replaced in the late 3rd cent. by a coastal fortress as protection against the Saxons. Parts of the docks and the moles have been discovered in the port area of Dover. A well preserved Roman lighthouse on East Hill, octagonal in the exterior but rectangular internally, is extraordinary. Another lighthouse once stood to the west on the other side of the valley [2].

1 B. PHILP, The Excavation of the Roman Forts at Dover, 1981 2 R. E. M. WEELER, C. J. AMOS, The Roman Lighthouse at Dover, in: Archaeological Journal 86, 1929, 47–71. M.TO.

Ducarius Celtic compound name formed from *-caro-* 'dear'. Knight, in a unit of Insubres in Hannibal's army, who in the battle at Lake Trasimene in 217 BC killed the *consul* C. → Flaminius (Liv. 22,6,3–5; Sil. Pun. 5,644–658).

→ Hannibal W.SP.

Ducenarius (*duceni* = 'two hundred each') generally indicates a reference to the number 200, as for example in weights (*duceni pondo* = two *centenarii*/two 'hundredweight'). In the political sphere, after Sulla's judicial reform (82 BC) *ducenarius* denoted the 200 judges belonging to the equestrian class in the jury panels (→ *decuriae*) (Vell. Pat. 2,32,3; Liv. per. 89; Suet. Aug. 32 concerns the Augustan reform).

In the Principate the term *ducenarius* derives from the salary of 200,000 HSS for equestrian officials in the Emperor's service and generally refers to the highest rank used in the provinces, for example provincial procurators, in a hierarchical framework ranging from *sexagenarii* through *centenarii* to *tricenarii* (Suet. Aug. 32, Claud. 24,1; CIL V 7870).

In late antiquity *ducenarius* refers to an equestrian official holding the *officium* of a senior appointment or serving at the Imperial court (financial administration; → *agentes in rebus*), lower in rank than a *perfectissimus* but superior to *centenarii* and *sexagenarii* and non-equestrian ranks. The rank of *ducenarius* could also be conferred on an honorary basis on an official's retirement (Cod. Iust. 12,20,3; 12,23,7; 12,31 and 32; Cod. Theod. 8,4,3: *perfectissimatus vel ducenae vel centenae vel egregiatus dignitas*).

JONES, LRE 578, 599, 634; HIRSCHFELD, 432ff.; MOMMSEN, Staatsrecht 3, 531, 536, 564. C.G.

Ducenius

[1] **A.D. Geminus.** Originally from Patavium. *Cos. suff.* in 61 or 62. In 62 appointed, with two senators, *curator vectigalium publicorum* by Nero (Tac. Ann. 15,18,3); the issuing collection of regulations, the tax law of the Province of Asia, are now known through an inscription from Ephesus (H. ENGELMANN, D. KNIBBE, EA 14, 1989 = SEG 39, 1180 = AE 1989, 681). Subsequently legate of Dalmatia; appointed *praef. urbi* by Galba but quickly replaced by Flavius Sabinus. If ILS 963 refers to him, he became proconsul of Asia under Vespasian. PIR² D 201.

W. ECK, in: ZPE 43, 1981, 230; VOGEL-WEIDEMANN, 462ff.; SYME, RP 4, 362ff., 382ff.; A. BÉRENGER, in: MEFRA 105, 1993, 75ff.

[2] **C.D. Proculus.** *Cos. suff.* in 87. PIR² D 202.

SYME, RP 4, 383f.

[2a] **P. D. Verres.** Suffect consul in AD 124 (CIL VI 2081; [1]). son of Ducenius [3]. The cognomen Verres (instead of Verus, apparently his father's cognomen) is surprising.

1 W. ECK, P. WEISS, Hadrianische Suffektkonsuln: Neue Zeugnisse aus Militärdiplomen, in: Chiron 32, 2002, 449–489 W. E.

[3] **P.D. Verus.** *Cos. suff.* in 95 [1]; *pontifex*. PIR² D 200, 203.

1 DEGRASSI, FCIR, 28. W.E.

Ducetius One of the few Sicels known by name, mentioned only by Diodorus (11,76–12,30, drawing on Timaeus) in an overly dramatic account (see [1. 50ff.] and [2. 99ff.]). In 466–461 BC, supported by the Sicels, D. attempted to use the chaotic conditions after the fall of the tyrants to establish a power base in Sicily (cf. Diod. Sic. 11,72,3–73; 76,4–6; 86,2–87). In 461/0 he moved with Syracuse against → Aitne [2] and expelled the mercenaries of the tyrant Hieron. Two years later he founded Menainon (near Mineo), conquered Morgantina and in 453/2 completed the unification of the Sicels (with the exception of Hybla). With the founding of Palice (near Palagonia) at the sanctuary of the Palici, the Sicelian 'national deities' (cf. Diod. Sic. 11,88–89), he established a representative capital. In 451 he conquered Inessa, attacked the Acragantian city of Motyon and, also in 451, defeated the combined forces of the now alerted powers of Syracuse and Acragas but was defeated by the allies in 450. Pardoned by the Syracusans and banished to Corinth, he was able to return with their approval in 448/7. As Acragas felt snubbed, as indeed at the time of the pardon given to D., war broke out and Syracuse won. D. founded Kaleakte on the northern coast and died in 440 trying to unite the Sicels in the north. Their communities achieved unity under the rule of Syracuse; Palice (in Diod. Sic. 12,29: Trinakria) was destroyed (Diod. Sic. 11,90,1–2).

D.'s endeavour should be seen less as a Sicel national movement than an indigenous attempt to emulate Greek tyranny.

1 K. MEISTER, Die sizilische Geschichte bei Diodor, 1967
2 E. GALVAGNO, Ducezio 'eroe': storia e retorica in Diodoro, in: E. GALVAGNO, C. MOLÉ VENTURA (ed.), Diodoro siculo e la storiografia classica, 1991.

D. ADAMESTEANU, L'ellenizzazione della Sicilia ed il momento di Ducezio, in: Kokalos 8, 1962, 167ff.; D. ASHERI, in: CAH 5, ²1992, 161ff.; G. MADDOLI, in: E. GABBA, G. VALLET (ed.), La Sicilia antica, Vol. 2,1, 1980, 61ff.; F.P. RIZZO, La repubblica di Siracusa e il momento di Ducezio, 1970 (as well K. MEISTER, in: Gnomon 47, 1975, 772–777). K.MEI.

Duck Athenaeus (9,395D-E, drawing on Alexander from Myndus, Περὶ ὀρνίθων; *Perì ornithōn*, 'On birds') recorded that several varieties of the family of *Anatidae*, widely dispersed throughout the world, were found in the Mediterranean region. These were: 1) the very common stock duck (or wild duck, mallard) (*Anas platyrhynchos*), νῆττα; *nêtta*, lat. *anas* (diminutive form νηττάριον; *nēttárion*, lat. *aneticula*); 2) the smaller βοσκάς; *boskás*, perhaps the migratory garganey (or querquedule) (*Anas querquedula*), but according to GOSSEN [1. 418] the red-crested pochard (*Netta rufina*); 3) the green-winged (or common) teal (*Anas crecca*), φασκάς; *phaskás*; 4) the unidentifiable γλαύκιον; *glaúkion*, a small variety with bluish eyes, and it is this that GOSSEN [1. 418] relates to the corresponding feather-colouring of the garganey; 5) the 'fox-goose' or 'Egyptian (or Nile) goose ' χηναλώπηξ; *chēn-*

alṓpēx (description in Ael. NA 5,30; cf. Ael. NA 10,16; 11,38 on defending their young), in Central Europe, however, the sheldrake/shelduck (according to [1. 418], without explanation, the φλέξις; *phléxis*, *Tadorna tadorna*), which broods in rabbit- and fox-burrows and is identified by many with the '→ Diomedean birds' (Verg. Aen. 11,271–274; Ov. Met. 14,508f.; Plin. HN 10,126f.) with their serrated beaks; 6) the pin-tailed duck, depicted as somewhat larger than the stock duck but smaller than the Egyptian goose, ἄλλο γένος βοσκάδων (*állo génos boskádōn*; *Anas acuta*); 7) the πηνέλοψ (*penélops*), mentioned by some Greek lyricists, by Aristophanes (Av. 298, 1302) and Aristotle (Hist. an. 7(8),3,593b 23), perhaps the European widgeon (or whistling duck) (*Anas penelope*) or white-eyed duck (or pochard) (*Aythya nyroca*) [1. 418].

Although considerably less so than in Egypt and Mesopotamia, ducks were caught with traps and nets, by day and night, while migrating through Greece (on methods of capture see Dionysius, 3,23 [2]) and sold, for example at the market in Athens (Aristoph. Pax 1004, Ach. 875). Egyptians and Mesopotamians had very early on begun breeding ducks, something the Greeks did not take up until the Hellenistic period (Arat. 918, 970). The Romans operated profitable breeding stations (*nessotrophia*), described by Varro (rust. 3,5,11) and very extensively by Columella (8,15,1–7) until the late Imperial period. Incubation of their eggs by domestic hens is mentioned by Cicero (Nat. D. 2,124) and Pliny (HN 10,155), as well as Columella. Of the roast duck, noble Romans ate only the breast and backbone (Petron. Sat. 13,52; 93,2). In contrast to physicians, who pronounced the meat difficult to digest (beginning with Galen. fac. nat. 3,18,3, CMG 5,4,2), Cato (according to Plut. Marcus Cato 23,5 p. 350d) is said to have recommended it as food for the ill. According to Dioscorides (2,79,1 [6. 160] and 2,97 [7. 191] et al., duck's blood was added to antidotes (ἀντίδοτα; *antídota*).

From the late Minoan and Mycenaean periods ducks were a popular decorative motif in vase painting. There were also ointment vessels in duck-shape. Late Roman mosaics in North Africa, for example one from the 3rd cent. AD from El Djem, depict the bird very graphically, usually in the context of a villa [3. fig. 30]. Beautiful miniatures of stock-ducks are to be found in medieval book illustration, e.g. [4. pl. 22]. They are rarely depicted on coins [5. pl. 6,20].

→ Poultry farming

1 H. Gossen, Zoologisches bei Athenaios, Quellen und Studien zur Gesch. der Naturwiss. 7, 1940, 375–436 2 A. Garzya (ed.), Dionysii Ixeuticon libri, 1963 3 A. Driss, Die Schätze des Nationalmuseums in Bardo, 1962 4 B. Yapp, Birds in medieval manuscripts, 1981 5 F. Imhoof-Blumer, O. Keller, Tier- und Pflanzenbilder auf Münzen und Gemmen des klass. Altertums, 1889 (repr. 1972) 6 Wellmann 2 7 Berendes. C.HÜ.

Ductus In the palaeographic terminology of medieval MSS and papyri *ductus* is usually associated with the speed of execution of individual letterforms or ligatures. Sometimes (especially in French scholarship) the term refers to the number, sequence and direction of individual pen-strokes [1. 22]; that, however, is more a matter of the structure of the letters. Accordingly, the *ductus* can be described as 'slow' (calligraphic) or cursive, without excluding either calligraphic or cursive elements from some writing styles. In the first case, the writing, which is vertical or only slightly sloping, is painted, as it were, with the hand supported by the little finger, and thick and thin strokes are carefully differentiated in completing the letters. This calligraphic technique, which allows only a few ligatures, is normally used only in the canonical book hands such as the → Capital scripts, the half uncials, the Carolingian → Minuscule scripts, the → Beneventa script and the Gothic Textura, in Latin, and the → Majuscule scripts and the Pearl script in writing Greek. On the other hand, the cursive script, which was generally used as the everyday script, was written slanting, quickly and smoothly, without lifting the pen off the page, and with the use of a great many → ligatures (right and left). In the process the number of structural components in the letterforms was sharply reduced and the writing style was less bound to any prescribed model. That could result in combining or dividing of hand movements, leading in turn to changes in style and form. Striving for simplification led in particular to the abandonment of ornamental strokes and to a rounding of angles.

1 J. Mallon, Paléographie romaine, 1952, 22.

B. Bischoff, Paläographie des röm. Alt. und des abendländischen Mittelalter, [2]1986, 71–75; R. Kottje, s.v. Duktus, Lexikon des gesamten Buchwesens 2, [2]1989, 393; H. Hunger, Duktuswechsel und Duktusschwankungen ..., in: Bollettino della Badia greca di Grottaferrata 45, 1991, 69–71; F. Gasparri, Introduction à l' histoire de l' écriture, 1994, 51–56. P.E.

Duenos inscription An inscription in archaic Latin on the so-called 'Vasculum Dresselianum', a ceramic vessel discovered in Rome, south-east of the Quirinal, in 1880 by H. Dressel. The triangular object with rounded tips and concave sides (length of sides: 10,3–10,5 cm; max. height: 4,5 cm; cf. [1. 55]) has a round opening at each tip. The inscription is on the outer side, written in three lines to be read from right to left (see fig.; other fig. in [1; 2. 134f., 140]; a version of transcription in [3. 70]).

The dating of the text ranges from the 7th to the late 3rd cent. BC; archaeologically the vessel should date to around 600 but the text may have been added some time later (this view in [2. 134]; differing view in [1. 57]), and this is not precluded by epigraphical clues (e.g. the writing of the k-sounds, cf. [1. 56ff.; 4. 252]). The interpretations of the inscription differ in significant details, partly because the limits between the words are not clear. The phrase *duenos med feced* offers a sound basis for interpretation ('a »good man« has

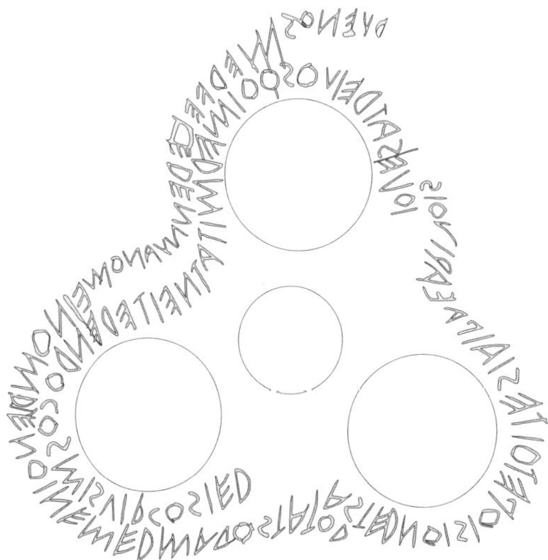

iouesatdeiuosqoimedmitatneitedendocosmisuircosied
astednoisiopetoitesiaipacariuois
duenosmedfecedenmanomeinomduenoinemedmalostatod

Duenos inscription; schematic view

made me/had me made', l. 1, starting from the outer right and moving left; *duenos* = class. *bonus* is unlikely to be a name). The many uncertainties have given rise to debate about the function of the text and the vessel. The inscription probably comes from private life (mention of a *cosmis uirco* = *comis virgo*, at the end of l. 1, starting at the inner top right moving left). Suggestions about the vessel's purpose range from its being a lamp, to a container for various utensils, through to possible magic or cult practices (love-charm, libation etc.); GJERSTAD's idea that it was a container for toiletry articles [2. 137] remains pure speculation.

For all of the many problems, the duenos inscription is, in a historical-linguistic sense, one of the most important examples of Old Latin and, along with the somewhat older Forum-inscription (CIL I² 1), represents the only document in Old Latin from the city of Rome (cf. [3. 72–75]). Inscription: CIL I² 4 = ILS 8743; Vessel: Antiquity Collection, Altes Mus. Berlin, inventory no. 30894,3.

1 A.E. GORDON, Notes on the Duenos-Vase Inscription, in: CSCA 8, 1975, 53–72 2 E. GJERSTAD, The Duenos-Vase, in: Septentrionalia et Orientalia. FS B. Karlgren, 1959, 133–143 3 R. WACHTER, Altlat. Inschr., 1987, 70–75 4 H. SOLIN, Zur Datierung ältester lat. Inschr., in: Glotta 47, 1969, 248–253.

G. COLONNA, Duenos, in: Studi Etruschi 47, 1979, 163–172; G. DUMÉZIL, Idées romaines, 1969; M. DURANTE, L'iscrizione di Dueno, in: Incontri linguistici 7, 1981, 31–35; E. GOLDMANN, Die Duenos-Inschrift, 1926; M. LEJEUNE, Notes de linguistique italique, in: REL 44, 1966, 141–181; A.L. PROSDOCIMI, Studi sul Latino arcaico, in: Studi Etruschi 47, 1979, 173–221, especially 173–183; B. VINE, Notes on the Duenos-Inscription, in: Atti del XI Congresso di Epigrafia Greca e Latina (Preatti, Roma), 1997, 133–139. M.MEI. and ME.STR.

Dürrnberg The D. near Hallein (Salzburg) was a centre of Celtic culture in Central Europe from the Hallstatt period (6th cent. BC). Early salt-mining brought the partly fortified settlement in the upper valley of the D. economic prosperity rendering it important well beyond the region. This is attested by rich burials, esp. from the early La Tène period (5th/4th cent. BC), with lavish grave-goods and many southern imports. D. lost importance in the late Celtic period (2nd/1st cent. BC), and the settlement shifted to the valley of the Salzach around Hallein.
→ Mining; → Princely burial, Princely seat; → Commerce; → Celtic archaeology; → Salt

E. PENNINGER et al., Der D. bei Hallein I-IV, 1972–1995; L. PAULI (ed.), Die Kelten in Mitteleuropa Ausstellungskatalog Hallein, 1980, esp. 150ff.; C. BRAND, Zur eisenzeitlichen Besiedlung des D. bei Hallein, 1995. V.P.

Duilius Name of a plebeian family that died out in the 3rd cent. BC; in inscriptions *Duilius*, in manuscripts *Duillius* (ThlL, Onom. 3, 266f.); mistaken etymology derived the name from *duellum-bellum*, in the form *Duellius*, *Bellius* (Cic. Or. 153; Quint. Inst. 1,4,15; cf. Pol. 1,22,1).

WALDE/HOFMANN 1,100.

[1] **D., C.** Consul 260 BC with Cn. Cornelius [I 74] Scipio Asina. After Scipio was captured at Lipara, D. also took over command of the fleet at Messana; he provided its ships with portable boarding bridges (*corvus*), and trained the fleet in their use. At Mylae on the north coast of Sicily he inflicted on the Carthaginians under Hannibal, son of Gescon, their first defeat at sea. In the land war he raised the siege of Segesta and took Macella. On his return to Rome he was the first Roman to celebrate a *triumphus navalis* (main source Pol. 1,21–24; MRR 1,205). The memory of his victory was maintained by a column decorated with the prows of enemy ships (the so-called *columna rostrata*) on the Forum Romanum; it was renovated in the Imperial period together with its inscription, and survives to this day (ILLRP 319; Plin. HN 34,20; Quint. Inst. 1,7,12 i.a.; Ill. in NASH 1, fig. 333). With the booty from his victory he built the Janus Temple on the Forum Holitorium (Tac. Ann. 2,49). 258 censor with L. Cornelius [I 65] Scipio (InscrIt 13,1,43). In old age in 231 he was again dictator for the holding of elections (InscrIt 13,1,45). Fragmentary elogium from the Augustan period: InscrIt 13,3, no. 13.

[2] **D., K.** First of the family to become consul, in 336 BC along with L. Papirius Crassus (Liv. 8,16,1; MRR 1,139); in 334 a member of the commission for the establishment of a colony at Cales (Liv. 8,16,14).

[3] **D., M.** According to annalistic tradition he belonged to the first college of people's tribunes, said to have been elected in 471 BC by the *comitia tributa* (Piso fr. 23

HRR in Liv. 2,58,1f.); in 470 he prosecuted Ap. Claudius Caecus (Dion. Hal. Ant. Roman 11,46). In 449 he is supposed to have instigated the *secessio plebis* (Liv. 3,52,1); after his return he is said to have again been elected tribune, and i.a. brought in a law ensuring the continued existence of the people's tribunate and the right of *provocatio* (Liv. 3,55,14; MRR 1,48). K.-L.E.

Dulgubnii According to Tac. Germ. 34,1 (a conjecture after Ptol. 2,11,9 = 'the war-ready') a German tribe, neighbours of the Chasuarii, Chamavi, Angrivarii and Langobardi, presumably situated east of the Weser on the middle Aller and middle Elbe and in the Südheide. Probably not politically autonomous [1].

1 G. Neumann et al., s.v. D., RGA 4, 431 2 Id., et al., s.v. D., RGA 6, 274–276. K.DI.

Dumnacus (Domnacus). Celtic name; leader of the Andes (Evans, 345). In 51 BC D. besieged Duratius at Lemonum with his army. When he failed to storm the camp of the legate C. Caninius Rebilus, who had hastened to the aid of Duratius, he attempted to flee across the Loire before the advancing forces of C. → Fabius. There he was overtaken, and cut down in the subsequent battle (Caes. B Gall. 8,26–29).
→ Duratius W.SP.

Dumnonii The D. lived in south-west Britannia. Their name may be derived from a pre-Roman divinity *Dumnonos*. During the Iron Age the D. were widely dispersed, without centres or *oppida*. After the Roman conquest (AD 50/65) the territory was secured by a legionary camp at Isca, later to become the capital of the tribe [1]. Settlements during the Roman period remained dispersed and un-Romanized, some small *villae* appearing in the vicinity of Isca. The economy was pastoral; ore was mined (e.g. tin in western Cornwall and Dartmoor, silver in eastern Cornwall [2]).

1 P.T. Bidwell, The Legionary Bathhouse and Forum and Basilica at Exeter, 1979 2 M. Todd, The South-West to AD 1000, 1987, 185–188.

A. Fox, South-West England, 1971. M.TO.

Dumnorix (Dubnoreix; Celtic composite name: 'world king' [1. 85–86]). Prince of the Haedui, brother of Diviciacus and son-in-law of Orgetorix, with whom he is supposed to have planned the conquest of the whole of Gaul (Caes. B Gall. 1,3). D. was the most powerful man in the tribe; he possessed his own mounted troop, and by means of gifts and matrimonial connections enjoyed great influence among foreign tribes, so that in 58 BC he was able to help the Helvetii to cross the territory of the Sequani (Caes. B Gall. 1,18,3–19,4). Caesar suspected him of conspiracy, but, to avoid endangering the alliance with the Haedui, limited himself to observing D. (Caes. B Gall. 1,18,10–20,6). D. evidently behaved himself in the following years, but, in 54 BC when he was to accompany Caesar as a hostage on his second British campaign, he used all his means to avoid the crossing and to encourage others to remain behind. Eventually he attempted to flee, and was pursued and killed by Roman troops (Caes. B Gall. 5,6–7). His importance prior to the arrival of Caesar is demonstrated by numerous silver coins bearing his name [2. 429–431].
→ Diviciacus; → Haedui; → Helvetii; → Orgetorix

1 Evans 2 B. Colbert de Beaulieu see Diviciacus [1].

B. Kremer, Das Bild der Kelten bis in augusteische Zeit, 1994, 219–239. W.SP.

Dumnovellaunus (Dubnovellaunus; Celtic composite name: 'he who sees the world'? [1. 196–197; 272–277]). King of some tribes in eastern Kent *c.* 15 BC — *c.* AD 15 [2. no. 275–291A]. Around the beginning of our era he conquered the territory of the Trinovantes north of the Thames and established himself in Camulodunum. In *c.* AD 10 he was driven out by Cunobellinus. It is probably this event that caused him to flee to Augustus, who mentions him in his *Res Gestae* (R. Gest. div. Aug. ch. 32).
→ Camulodunum; → Cunobellinus

1 Evans 2 R.P. Mack, The Coinage of Ancient Britain, 1964, 95, 103. W.SP.

Dunax (Δοῦναξ; *Doûnax*, *Dunuca*, *Dinax*). Mountain range in western Thrace, probably the Rila mountains in Bulgaria (Ptol. 34,10,15 = Str. 4,6,12; Liv. 40,58,2: battle of the Thracians with the Bastarnae, 179 BC). It is not really possible to link homonymous personal names with this name. I.v.B.

Dunius L.D.Severus. Proconsul of Pontus-Bithynia under Claudius.

PIR² D 207; W. Weiser, in: ZPE 123, 1998, 275–290. W.E.

Duodecim scripta Board game in which a player attempted to remove his own 15 counters by reaching the end of the other side of the board. Moves were determined by throwing two or three dice; if two or three of the opponent's counters occupied a line, the first player's own counter could not be placed on that line; if only one counter was there, it could be removed. According to Isid. Orig. 18,60, *duodecim scripta* was played with a dice shaker or 'tower', dice and counters. The board consisted of 36 squares decorated with geometrical figures such as circles or squares, letters or groups of letters, and sayings. Dice towers and boards (esp. scratched in paving stones) have survived, as well as artistic portrayals of the game being played.
→ Board games

H. Lamer, s.v. Lusoria Tabula, RE 13, 1979–1985; J. Väterlein, Roma Ludens, in: Heuremata 5, 1976, 55–57;

H. G. Horn, Si per me misit, nil nisi vota feret. Zu einem Spielturm aus Froitzheim, in: BJ 189, 1989, 149–154. R.H.

Duoviri, Duumviri ('[office filled by]' two men; singular '*duum vir*', hence also '*duumviri*') denotes various kinds of office known to have been occupied by pairs of men. Many of these occur solely or for the most part at particular periods during the Roman Republic.

Duumviri perduellionis were judges in matters of high treason in the early Republican period, and by the 1st cent. BC were hardly named any longer (Liv. 1,26,5f.; Cic. Rab. perd. 12f.).

Duumviri sacris faciundis are the officials to whom the task of consulting the Sybilline Books was transferred in the 4th cent. BC; they were later replaced by *Xviri* and then by *XVviri sacris faciundis* (Liv. 3,10,7; Cic. Fam. 8,4,1; Varro, Ling. 7,88).

Duumviri agris dandis assignandis (other numbers of members also possible) are officials of the Roman state entrusted with the distribution of land to Roman colonists (*lex agr.* 28 and 52ff./FIRA 1, 102ff., 109, 113).

Duumviri navales are officials occasionally employed in the 4th and 3rd cent. BC for the construction as well as the command of fleets (Liv. 9,30,4; 41,1,3).

Duumviri aedi dedicandae, faciundae, locandae were responsible for the construction, administration and use of temples (Liv. 7,28,5); known until the beginning of the Imperial period, their functions then being taken over by particular *procuratores* (Cass. Dio 55,10,6).

Other dual offices might be created for particular functions, as e.g. the *duumviri viis purgandis* for street cleaning (*tabula Heracleensis* 51/FIRA 1, 140 152) or the *duumviri aquae perducendae* for water supply (Frontin. Aq. 1,6; Cass. Dio 46,45,4).

The best-known form of the *duoviri* is the chief office in *municipia* and *coloniae* constituted under Roman law. When not headed by '*quattuorviri et aediles*' (lex municipii Tarentini 9,2, 1st half of the 1st cent. BC, FIRA 1, 167), a → *praefectus* (lex de Gallia cisalpina 20ff. (*c.* 50 BC, FIRA 1, 169–175) or a state commissioner (→ *curator rei publicae*), city government was always in the hands of *duoviri*. In some (Latin) cities the office existed even prior to subordination to Rome; in others, esp. the *coloniae*, it is to be explained as a copy of the consulate in the city of Rome. Like the historical development of city government in *coloniae* and *municipia* as a whole, the function of the *duoviri* in these places prior to the 1st cent. BC is known to us only in its general principles; besides *duoviri* there were probably also other forms of administration specific to particular localities. From the 1st cent. BC onwards we find more precise indications of the duties and rights of the *duoviri*, in some *leges datae* and in the *lex municipii Malacitani* (52 BC; FIRA 1, 202–219), the *lex coloniae Genetivae Ursonensis* (44 BC; FIRA 1, 177–199) and the *lex municipii Salpensani* (AD 82; FIRA 1, 202–208), as well as in juridical texts on the *officium* of the *proconsul*. As *duoviri iure dicundo* they are officers of record, and have *iurisdictio* at a lower level, without possessing the *imperium* of the Roman *consul* or *praetor*. In the provinces such *imperium* lay with the governor (Dig. 50,1,26), who decided all questions concerning the *lex municipalis* by edict. The *duoviri* convened the *ordo decurionum* and the popular assembly, conducted the election of other officials and functionaries (cf. lex municipii Malacitani 52; Dig. 50,4,14 and 18), and represented the city before the emperor, as well as representing it legally before the official authorities and also in other cities (Dig. 3,4,1 and 6; 44,7,35,1). The office continued with this level of jurisdiction into late antiquity. In this period too the *duumviri* were elected either by the population of the city (Cod. Theod. 12,5,1) or by the municipal *dekuriones* (Cod. Iust. 10,31,46) from among their own number (Dig. 50,2,7,2).

→ Collega; → Colonia; → Curiales; → Decurio; → Magistratus; → Municipium

Jones, LRE 737ff.; Liebenam, 256ff.; Mommsen, Staatsrecht 2,1, 579, 615, 618, 667. C.G.

Duplication of the Cube (κύβου διπλασιασμός/*kýbou diplasiasmós* according to Eratosthenes, in [1. 88,16]).

I. General II. Origin of the problem III. Solution attempts IV. Afterlife

I. General

The duplication of the cube — besides the → division of angles and circles and the → squaring of the circle — belongs to the three classic problems in Greek → mathematics. The challenge is such: to find — through the use of geometry — for a given cube with a side-length of a (and thus the volume of a^3) the side x of another cube whose volume is twice as big as that of the given cube. The problem is therefore to find the value of x, to which applies: $x^3 = 2a^3$ (that is: $x = a^3\sqrt{2}$). The problem thus amounts to a calculation or formation of the cubic root. In contrast to the Greeks, we now know that a general cubic equation (which also means the duplication of the cube) cannot be solved through the use of compass and ruler alone; geometrical solutions are, however, possible through the use of conical sections, higher curves, or interpolations (→ *neúsis*) or if one allows approximate solutions (on the problem of possible solutions in general: [5]).

II. Origin of the problem

Greek authors clothed the problem of duplicating the cube into various mythical forms that partially contradicted each other [2. 244–246; 3. 262–266]. According to one version, the problem is connected to a legend about → Minos. Another version that probably goes back to → Eratosthenes [2] holds that the Delians received an order from Apollo in the time of Plato [1],

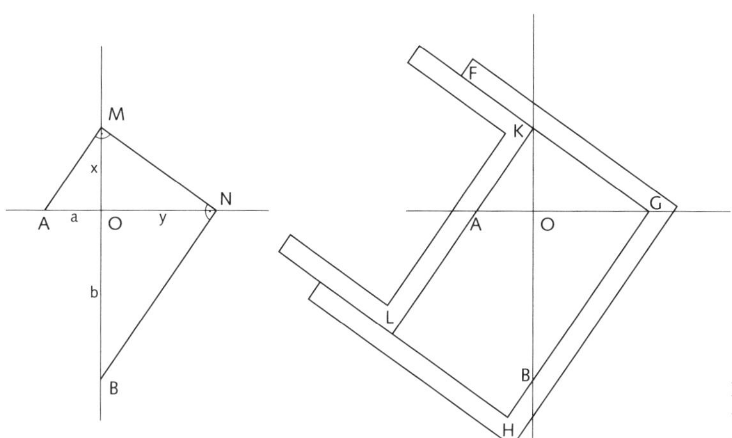

Duplication of the cube: the mechanical solution by means of an angle bar, attributed to Plato

when they suffered from a plague, to enlarge his cube-shaped altar in such a way that the form would remain the same while the content would be doubled; supposedly the Delian craftsmen, unable to solve the problem, turned to → Plato [1]. This historically less plausible version became widespread, i.a. by → Plutarch [2] and Iohannes → Philoponus, and was the reason why the problem of duplicating the cube is also called the 'Delian Problem'.

III. Solution attempts

Our main source for the history of the problem is → Eutocius, who hands down several ancient approaches to a solution in his commentary to → Archimedes' [1] (B. 4.) 'On the Sphere and the Cylinder' [1. 54–106]. → Hippocrates [5] of Chios (*c.* 450 BC) is the first mathematician known by name who worked on the problem. Eutocius [1. 88,17–23] and → Proclus [2] (Procl. in Euc. p. 213,7–9 Friedlein) document the fact that Hippocrates transformed this problem into another: between a and b, the two mean proportionals x and y should be found, so that $a / x = x / y = y / b$ [2. 183, 200 f.]. It is true that $ay = x^2$, $bx = y^2$, $xy = ab$ and therefore $x^3 = a^2b$. If one posits $b = 2a$, then x is a solution to the problem of duplicating the cube. In this way, the given cubic equation is replaced by two quadratic equations with two unknowns. Hippocrates' idea was very influential: all subsequent attempts to solve the duplication of the cube proceeded from the equivalent problem of finding two mean proportionals to the given values of a and $b = 2a$.

→ Archytas [1] (early 4th cent. BC) solved the duplication of the cube by means of a bold spatial construction involving sections of a circle, a cylinder, and a cone ([1. 84–88]; cf. [2. 246–249; 3. 249–252; 4. 76–78]). → Eudoxus [1] (*c.* 370 BC), whose solution has been lost, probably projected Archytas' spatial construction orthogonally onto a plane [2. 249–251; 4. 78 f.]. → Menaechmus [3] (*c.* 350 BC) used conical sections for the solution: he presented a construction which is regarded as the 'geometrical locus' of a parabola or hyperbola ([1. 78–84]; cf. [2. 251–255; 3. 266 f.; 4. 82–84]). In modern terms, he made the parabola $x^2 = ay$ intersect with the hyperbola $xy = ab$; their point of intersection offers a solution to the problem.

Mechanical attempts to solve the problem of duplicating the cube amount to the construction of interpolations (→ *neúsis*). Eutocius attributes Plato with a mechanical solution of that sort [1] ([1. 56–58]; cf. [2. 255–258; 3. 267–271]; cf. fig.): on two axes perpendicular to each other, one checks off the given values a (= AO) and b (= OB). When the angles AMN and MNB form right angles, then OM = x and ON = y are the desired mean proportions between a and b. In order to find M and N, one attaches an angle bar (with two right angles) to A and B, then turns the angle bar around A and B until the vertices of the right angles lie straight on the axes. The two resulting points of K and G are the desired positions of M and N on the axes. Since the solution requires mechanical aids, it surely does not stem from Plato; it is probable that Eratosthenes [2] put them into Plato's mouth in the Dialogue *Platōnikós*.

→ Eratosthenes [2] (*c.* 230 BC) also used a mechanical device: the → *mesolábion* ([1. 94–96]; cf. [2. 258–260; 3. 384 f.; 5. 18 f.]). There, three congruent right-angled triangles slide along two fixed tracks and are moved against each other until the intersections of the hypotenuses lie on a straight line with the verticals; thereby the desired mean proportionals are determined.

Solutions with the aid of higher curves stem from → Nicomedes [3] (probably shortly after Eratosthenes) and → Diocles [8] (*c.* 190–180 BC.). In this context, Nicomedes used the conchoid ([1. 98–100]; cf. [2. 260–262; 3. 390–395]), while Diocles used the cissoid ([1. 66–70]; cf. [2. 264–266]). Small variations of Diocles' solution, in which an interpolation (→ *neúsis*) is used instead of the cissoid, are documented in → Sporus [1. 76–78] and → Pappus (collectio 3, p. 64–68; 8, p. 1070–1072) [2. 266–268]. Three additional proposals of solutions are known which also make use of an interpolation and which are very similar to each other: by → Apollonius [13] ([1. 64–66]), → Hero [1. 58–60], and → Philo [7] ([1. 60–64]; also cf. [2. 262–264]). Pappus also presents the solution by approximation by an author whose name he does not mention (Pappus, Collectio 3, p. 30–48; cf. [2. 268–270]).

IV. Afterlife

With the knowledge of the ancient approaches, the problem of duplicating a cube was also dealt with in the Arab world and since the 12th cent. by western mathematicians. In modern times, the study of the problem has furthered the knowledge of higher curves and has led to interesting constructions of approximation. The list of authors who have worked on the problem includes M. Stifel, J. Buteo, J. Praetorius, R. Descartes, F. Sluse, and A. C. Clairaut.

→ Mathematics IV. A.

1 J. L. Heiberg (ed.), Archimedis opera omnia, vol. 3, [2]1915 2 T. L. Heath, A History of Greek Mathematics, vol. 1, 1921, 244–270 3 B. L. van der Waerden, Erwachende Wissenschaft, 1956, 230–232, 249–252, 262–271, 384 f., 393–395 4 O. Becker, Das mathematische Denken der Ant., 1957, 75–84 5 W. Breidenbach, Das Delische Problem (Die Verdoppelung des Würfels), [2]1952.

M. F.

Dupondius (*dupondium*). A doubling of the → As, in the Roman system of measurement, the *dupondius* represented twice the 'unit' of length (twice the *pes*) and in weight two Roman pounds (one *libra* = 327.45 g). *Dupondius* also signified simply the number two, and in Roman law the doubled whole. The earliest *dupondii* were cast in bronze with a dose of lead as two libral asses (hence also *dussis*) with the denomination II between 269 and 240 BC in the Roma/wheel series (→ Aes grave) [1. 23]. As a result of the debasement of the currency in the 2nd half of the 3rd cent. BC, the *dupondius* was issued again between 217 and 213 BC (Roma/prora series) in the semilibral standard (221.3–133.6 g) [1. 27]. *Dupondii* were also cast in Etruria under a different standard [1. 38]. Shortly after the introduction in Rome of the *denarius*, between 214 and 211 BC, the *dupondius* (Minerva/prora) was minted on the basis of an uncial *as* (*c.* 27 g), while at the same time the nominal *as* was coined under the sextantal standard (*c.* 54 g) [2. 159]. Thereafter, the *dupondius* was not minted again for some 160 years. Presumably during the years 38–37 BC, the fleet prefects of Mark Antony in the Gr. east minted bronze *dupondii* in a heavy series (17.64–11.99 g) and a light series (7.55 g). The twofold appearance of the reverse motif (a ship) as well as the denomination B signifies the doubling of the *as* and indicates circulation in the Gr. world [3. 284ff.].

After the Augustan reform of the coinage, from 18 BC the *dupondius* is coined in Rome at a weight of *c.* 12.5 g in brass without denomination, with 25 *dupondii* to one pound weight. Under Tiberius and Caligula, the weight increased to a maximum of 16 g, gradually falling from the time of Claudius [4. 3, 90, 102, 114]. The abbreviation SC on the reverse, which became the norm under Augustus, was dropped for a short time under Nero when the denomination II appeared in its place. From the time of Nero the *dupondius was* distinguished from the *as* by the emperor's likeness with radiate crown (instead of with laurel wreath) [4. 136ff.; 5. 58f., 78f.]. Down to the introduction of the *antoninianus* by Caracalla in AD 215, the *dupondius* was progressively reduced in weight to around 12 g, then in the course of the 3rd cent. AD, although infrequently minted, fell rapidly to 6 g, until under Carus at the latest it was no longer minted. During the imperial period the *dupondius* served imperial propaganda. On the obverse it bore the likeness of the emperor or his family, and on the reverse a personification or motifs of a political kind, related to the self-image of the emperor.

→ Aes Grave; → Antoninianus; → As; → Denarius; → Libra; → Coinage, standards of; → Coinage; → Pes; → Senatus Consultum

1 B.K. Thurlow, I.G. Vecchi, Italian cast coinage, Italian aes grave, Italian aes rude, signatum and the aes grave of Sicily, 1979 2 RRC, [2]1987 3 RPC I, 1992 4 RIC [2]I, 1984 5 D.W. MacDowall, The Western coinages of Nero, 1979.

H. Willers, Gesch. der röm. Kupferprägung, 1909; M.H. Crawford, Coinage and money under the Roman Republic, 1985.

A.M.

Dura-Europus City on the west bank of the middle Euphrates (Arab. aṣ-Ṣāliḥiya, south-eastern Syria). D.-E. was founded *c.* 300 BC by Macedonian colonists as one of the Seleucid fortresses for securing links to the Euphrates. After the Parthian conquest *c.* 141 BC it rose to become a military station and important staging post on the caravan route to Palmyra. Trajan's advances against Mesopotamia restored the status of D.-E. as a Roman garrison city on the Syrian *limes*. A shift in the course of the Euphrates and the stationing of various Roman detachments led to its decline. D.-E. fell before the assault of the Sassanid Šāpur I (*c.* AD 256), and soon afterwards ceased to exist [1. 10–31]. The history of D.-E. is characterized by the coexistence and mutual influence of Macedonians, Greeks, Iranians, Romans and Semitic-speaking inhabitants. The rectilinear street layout betrays its Hellenistic foundation, but the Parthian city took on an increasingly Semitic-Iranian character. Excavations of the well-preserved ruins (especially the first rows of houses behind the walls, filled in with earth shortly before 256) produced highly significant finds, among them a very early *domus ecclesiae* [2], a synagogue with extensive figurative frescos [3; 4] and a number of temples both syncretic Graeco-Semitic as well as purely oriental in character.

1 M. Rostovtzeff, D.-E. and its Art, 1938 2 L.M. White, Building God's House in the Roman World, 1990 3 H. Stähli, Ant. Synagogenkunst, 1988, 69–99 4 J. Gutmann, The D.-E. Synagogue, A Reevaluation, 1992, Introduction.

P. Leriche, Doura-Europos: études, 1986; A. Perkins, The Art of D.-E., 1973.

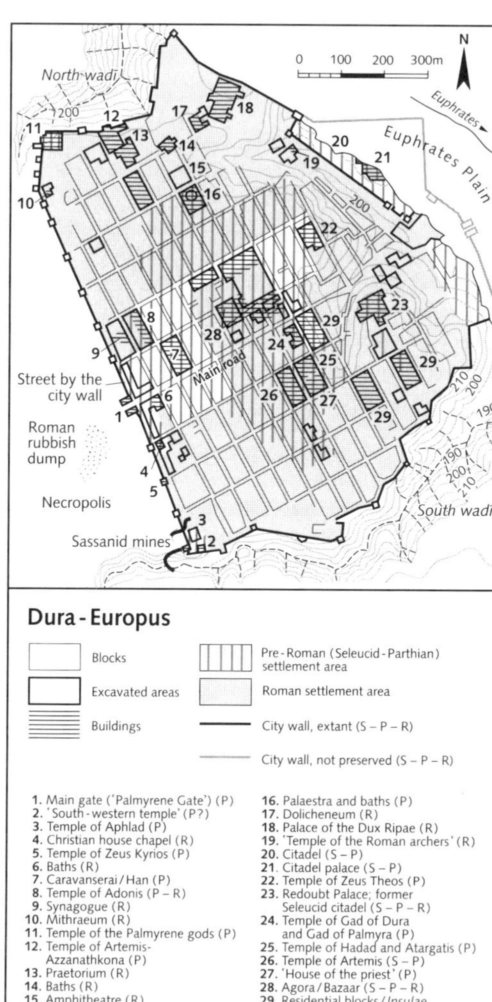

MAPS: A. PERKINS, The Art of D.-E., 1973; P. LERICHE, Doura-Europos: études, 1986. T.L.

Duranus River in Aquitania, modern-day Dordogne; rises at 1680 m. on the Puy de Sancy (Mont-Dore), and after a course of 490 km flows into the Atlantic with the Garumna to its left (Auson. Mos. 464; Geogr. Rav. 4,40). E.O.

Duratius Celtic composite name: 'the unfortunate' [1. 87]. Pro-Roman chieftain of the Pictones, besieged by Dumnacus in 51 BC. His name is attested to on silver coins [2. 431–432].
→ Dumnacus; → Pictones

1 EVANS 2 B. COLBERT DE BEAULIEU see Diviciacus [1]. W.SP.

Duria Name of two tributaries of the Po (Plin. HN 3,118). The shorter of the two, today called the Dora Riparia, flows along the Alpine pass at Mont Genèvre (Liv. 5,34,8); the longer, gold-bearing (Str. 4,6,7) Dora Baltea flows through the Aosta valley past Ivrea, and joins the Po near Industria (near modern Crescentino). H.GR.

Duris (Δοῦρις; *Doûris*)

[1] Epigrammatic poet from Elea (in Aeolis); author of a remarkable poem on the flood that destroyed Ephesus *c.* 300 BC (Anth. Pal. 9,424, cf. Steph. Byz. 289,3–16), in all probability from the 'Garland' of Meleager. The city was rebuilt shortly afterwards by Lysander, who renamed it Arsinoeia after his wife: this happened before 289/8 (cf. Syll.[3] 368, 24), after the epigram had been written.

GA I,1, 97; 2, 280f. E.D.

[2] One of the most productive and significant painters of Attic red-figure bowls of the late Archaic period (*c.* 505–465 BC); he occasionally decorated other vessels, among them some splendid white-ground *lekythoi*. D.'s vases were frequently labelled; he signed more than 50 vases as painter and two as potter.

His early work was experimental in effect, every figure painstakingly drawn and positioned; D. did not yet exploit the contrast between thinned and black slip. At this stage of his career he worked with several potters, → Euphronius among them, and favoured the *kalos* names (→ *Kalos* inscriptions) Chaerestratus and Panaetius.

In a subsequent transitionary phase D. experimented with two styles of painting. In the one, his images were economical (simple borders and an absence of handle palmettes); solitary figures, athletes and courtship scenes predominated in his motifs. Against this there were compositions of more expansive execution, the subjects often mythical, with many figures, opulent drapery and unusual decorative motifs with complex ornamental bands. The figures were more naturalistic and more compact than previously. At this time his enduring association with the potter Python began, during which, however, he also worked with Kleophrades.

His middle period was characterized by the consolidation of both styles; the harmony and elegance of his figures compensated for the occasional paucity of detail. Characteristic of this phase was the single maeander, always ending with an inward hook, and alternated with panels containing crosses (→ Ornamentation; so-called Duris maeander); genre images, especially symposium scenes, predominated. D. now signed less often; Hippodamas became his most frequent *kalos* name.

New → vessel forms occurred in his late period (*rhyta*, *pyxides* and *oinochoai*). *Kalos* inscriptions became increasingly rare; signatures were entirely absent. The ornamentation of the handles of his bowls was now more ornate. There were often two 'Duris maeanders' where there was previously only one, while the figures were less lively. Overall, however, accomplished figure-drawing was as characteristic of D. as his complex mythical scenes, although the latter were less numerous than the portrayals of everyday life.

BEAZLEY, ARV², 425–453, 1652–1654, 1701, 1706; D. BUITRON-OLIVER, Douris, 1995; M. ROBERTSON, The Art of Vase-Painting in Classical Athens, 1992, 84–93.

J.O.

[3] **D. of Samos.** *c.* 340–270 BC a pupil of → Theophrastus (Ath. 4,128a) and from *c.* 300 tyrant of his home island (FGrH 76 T 2). Versatile writer, author of the following (lost) works: 'Homeric Problems', 'On Tragedy', 'On Sophocles and Euripides', 'On Painting', 'On Reliefs', 'On Laws', 'On Competitions'. Historical works (fr. extant): 'Samian Annals' (Σαμίων ὧροι/ *Samíōn hôroi*, a local chronicle of Samos: F 22–26; 60–71); 'History of Agathocles' (τὰ περὶ Ἀγαθοκλέα/ *Tà perì Agathokléa* in 4 bks.: F 16–20; 56–71), used by Diodorus [18] (bk. 19–21), though not as his main source (as [1]), but only as a secondary one (as [2]). His main work was a 'Macedonian History' (Μακεδονικά/ *Makedoniká*) in at least 23 bks., covering the period from the death of → Amyntas [3] III. 370/69 to that of Lysimachus [2] in 281 BC (F 1–15; 35–55), with a general anti-Macedonian tendency.

In the prooemium (F 1), D. polemicized against → Ephorus and → Theopompus [3]: their only concern was γράφειν (*gráphein*, 'style'), and they had completely neglected μίμησις καὶ ἡδονή (*mímēsis kaì hēdonḗ*), i.e. a realistic and lifelike depiction with its ensuing pleasures (sc. to the reader). The classification and origin of this historiography, described by [3] as 'tragic' or respectively 'Peripatetic', are still controversial, but it seems advisable to refer to it as an example of 'mimetic' historiography [4]. On D.'s credibility, which has been overrated by many scholars (e.g. by[5], [6], [7], and [8]), cf. esp. [4] and [9]. For an excellent commentary on all fragments as well as a comprehensive account of the literature, see [10].

D.'s antipode was → Hieronymus [6] of Cardia with his history of the Diadochi, which was based on a sober investigation of facts and causes.

→ Historiography II. C.; → Samos

1 T. ORLANDI, Duride in Diodoro XIX-XXI, in: PdP 19, 1964, 216–226 2 K. MEISTER, Die sizilische Gesch. bei Diodor, thesis München 1967, 131–165 3 E. SCHWARTZ, s. v. D. (3), RE 5, 1853–1856 = Id., Griech. Geschichtsschreiber, 1957, 27–31 4 K. MEISTER, Die griech. Geschichtsschreibung, 1990, 96–101 5 H. STRASBURGER, Die Wesensbestimmung der Gesch. durch die griech. Geschichtsschreibung, ³1975, 78–85 6 R. B. KEBRIC, In the Shadow of Macedon. D. of Samos, 1977 7 P. PÉDECH, Trois historiens méconnus. Théopompe, D., Phylarque, 1989, 257–389 8 O. LENDLE, Einführung in die griech. Geschichtsschreibung, 1992, 181–189 9 K. MEISTER, Historische Kritik bei Polybios, 1975, 109–126 10 F. LANDUCCI GATTINONI, Duride di Samio, 1997.

EDITION: FGrH 76 with commentary (JACOBY). K. MEI.

Durius The modern river Duero (Span.; Portug. Douro). The pre-Celtic name is *D.* (Sil. Pun. 1,438; 5,323; [1. 1380]), possibly with variant *Duris* (CIL II 2370). All references (Str. 3,3,2; 4; 6; 3,4,12; 20; Mela 3,8; 10; Plin. HN 4,112f.; 115) indicate that its course was the same in antiquity as it is today. That it was navigable by large vessels for 800 stadia upstream (Str. 3,3,4) is still true today: from its mouth to Barca d'Alva; sailing even small boats on its upper course is today not possible, whereas in 133 BC it supported sailing vessels (App. Ib. 91). As a consequence of deforestation, the flow of all Spanish rivers is less regular and less in volume today. According to Sil. Pun. 1,234 the D. was gold-bearing. The most important town on the D. was Numantia.

1 HOLDER 1.

G. DELIBES, F. ROMERO, El ultimo milenio a.C. en la Cuenca del Duero, in: M. ALMAGRO-GORBEA, G. RUIZ ZAPATERO (ed.), Paleoetnologia de la Península Ibérica, 1992, 233–258; SCHULTEN, Landeskunde 1, 1955, 346ff.; TOVAR, 2, 1976, 187ff., 197ff., 201ff. P.B.

Durnomagus The modern Dormagen. Late Flavian *alae* fort (3.3 ha) between Cologne and Neuss. Second construction phase in the mid 2nd cent. AD, probably the *ala Noricorum* (CIL XIII 8523f.); burnt down *c.* 200, and in *c.* 275 very briefly occupied. In the north-eastern corner was a reoccupation fort from late antiquity.

M. GECHTER, Das röm. Kavallerielager Dormagen, in: Arch. im Rheinland 1994, 1995, 85–87. K.DI.

Durocortorum Capital of the Gallo-Roman *civitas* of the Remi; modern Reims, on the northern edge of Champagne (Ptol. 2,9,6; 8,5,6); whether it should be identified with the centre of the autonomous Remi (Caes. Gall. 6,44) remains an open question. After sporadic settlement since the end of the Hallstatt period it expanded during La Tène III. In the course of the 1st cent. BC an *oppidum* arose, *c.* 90 ha. in area, with a massive earth rampart and ditch and surrounded by a second concentric rampart of the same type (550 ha. in area). The importance of the location as a communications centre goes back to pre-Roman times (It. Ant. 356; 362–365; 379–381; Tab. Peut.). The beginnings of effective urbanization at the end of the rule of Augustus were oriented on existing communications routes. From the time of Tiberius, however, typical divisions on an orthogonal plan were attested; the SE/NW-orientated → *cardo* and the corresponding → *decumanus* are still recognizable in the modern street pattern (Caes. B Gall. 6,44). D. reached the zenith of its prosperity in the Severan period as the seat of the governor and the metropolis of the Provincia Belgica (Str. 4,3,5). In that period, at the latest, the inner rampart was levelled and the two main axes spanned with gates at each exit point from the central city zone; the northern one, the *Porte* *de Mars* (32.5 m wide), is extant. On the forum, parts of the cryptoporticus of a temple have been excavated and conserved. The other public buildings known to us — an amphitheatre on the northern periphery, baths near the present-day cathedral (CIL 13,3255), and presumably a theatre in the vicinity of the forum — were on the *cardo*. D. suffered during the invasions of AD 275, and probably also those of 252–254 and 259–260. As a consequence, the settlement was reduced in size, the 'symbolic' gates transformed into actual city gates and linked by a strong fortified wall. In Diocletian's Imperial reforms (→ Diocletianus, with map) the city, in sources of late antiquity called *Remi* after the name of the indigenous tribe (Amm. Marc. 15,11,10; 16,2,8; 11,1; 17,2,1; 25,10,6; 26,5,14; Jer. Ep. 123), became the metropolis of *Belgica II* (Not. Gall. 6,1). It was the location of several state production centres (Not. Dign. Occ. 9,36; 11,34; 56; 76), and, still extended over a sizeable area of 60 ha., retaining a portion of its former glory. Valentinian came to Remi in 365 in the course of the war against the Alemanni, and spent the next two years there (Amm. Marc. 26,5,14). Already Christianized by the mid 3rd cent., when the Vandals attacked in 407, Remi was the scene of the execution of bishop Nicasius. Here in 498 (?) bishop Remigius performed the baptism of the Frankish king Chlodwig (→ Chlodovechus; Greg. Tur. Franc. 2,31). While the bishopric developed behind the shelter of the Roman walls, a new Christian city arose *extra muros* in the south, on the site of the necropolis.

F. Berthelot, R. Neiss, Reims antique et médiéval, in: Archeologia 300, 1994, 50–57; R. Neiss, La structure urbaine de Reims antique et son évolution du Ier au IIIe siècle ap. J.-C., in: Actes du colloque: Les villes de la Gaule Belgique au Haut-Empire, Saint Riquier 1982, 1984, 171–191; Reims Fouilles Archéologiques, in: Bull. de la Société Archéologique Champenoise (regular arch. reports). F.SCH.

Duronia One of the first women of the nobility to patronize the cult of the Bacchanalia [1. 214f.], to which in 186 BC, at the instigation of her husband T. Sempronius Rufus, she introduced her son P. Aebutius [2] (Liv. 39,9,2–4); this event contributed to the exposure and suppression of the cult (Liv. 39,18,6).
→ Bacchanal(ia)

1 R.A. Bauman, Women and Law in Ancient Politics, 1992.

Duronius Plebeian family name, from *Durnius* (Schulze, 160; ThlL Onom. s.v. D.). ME.STR.

[1] **D., C.** Friend (*amicissimus*) of Annius [I 14] Milo, whom he helped during or after his trial for the murder of → Clodius [I 4]. Cic. Att. 5,8,2f. W.W.

[2] **D., L.** 181 BC *praetor* in Apulia. When Tarentum and Brundisium complained about piracy, he received the praetorship of Istria additionally, and thus probably the task of protecting the Adriatic coast against the plundering raids of → Genthius (Liv. 40,18,3; 42,1–5). D. led the inquiry into the → Bacchanalia in Italy.

Gruen, Rome, 421–422.

[3] **D., M.** As people's tribune he had wanted to repeal a *lex sumptuaria*, and in 97 BC [1. 434] was as a consequence struck off the senatorial roll (Val. Max. 2,9,5; cf. also [2. 272,77]). He later attempted to prosecute M. Antonius [I 7], one of the censors responsible (Cic. De or. 2,274).

1 J. Suolahti, The Roman Censors, 1963
2 W. Kunkel, Staatsordnung und Staatspraxis in der röm. Republik, HdbA 3.2.2, 1995. ME.STR.

Durostorum Settlement on the right bank of the lower Danube in Moesia inferior, the modern Silistra (northern Bulgaria). Customs post and important junction between the country road from Marcianopolis and the road along the bank of the Danube leading into the delta zone. The military importance of D. is demonstrated by the presence there of the *legio IX Claudia* (from AD 105/6). It was probably under Antoninus Pius that a civilian settlement (*canabae*) arose in D., elevated to the status of *municipium* under Marcus Aurelius. At the end of the 2nd cent. D. was threatened by the incursions of the Costoboci; in the 3rd cent. further opportunities for D. to develop were prevented by the attacks of the Carpi. Under Diocletian, D. became the capital of the province of Scythia. D. is mentioned in Not. Dign. Or. 40,26,33 (cf. 35) as the headquarters of the *milites quarti Constantiniani* and the *praefectus legionis XI Claudiae*.

Abundant archaeological finds (structures, statues, sarcophagi, ceramics, coins, wall-paintings from the closing years of the 4th cent.) attest to the prosperity of the city's inhabitants, esp. in late antiquity. D. was one of the centres of Christianity in Scythia Minor, the centre of activity of St. Dasius and the birthplace of Aëtius (*c.* 390). Attested until the beginning of the 7th cent. References: Ptol. 3,10,5 (Δουρόστορον; *Douróstoron*); Procop. Aed. 4,7 (Δορόστολος; *Doróstolos*); It. Ant. 223,4 (*Durostoro*); Tab. Peut. (*Durostero*); Amm. Marc. 27,4,12 (*Durostorus*); Geogr. Rav. 4,7,1 (*Durostolon*); Not. Dign. Or. 40,26,33 (*Durostoro*); Cod. Iust. 8,41,6; 9,22,20 (*Dorostolo*).

V.I. Velkov, Die thrak. und dak. Stadt in der Spätant., 1959; TIR L 35 Bucarest, 40 (sources and lit.). J.BU.

Durotriges The *civitas* of the D. comprised the region of Dorset, south Wiltshire and south Somerset. Its most important Roman centre was located at Durnovaria (Dorchester) with a further main centre at Lindinis (Ilchester). During the late Iron Age there were large hillforts here, among them Maiden Castle, Hod Hill, Ham Hill and Hambledon. Some of them were stormed by the Romans shortly after AD 43 [1]. Subsequently the *civitas* remained for the most part rural. Many *villae* were built in the late Roman period.

1 I. A. RICHMOND, Excavations at Hod Hill, 1968.

R. E. M. WHEELER, Maiden Castle, 1943.

Durovernum Modern Canterbury; arose in the form of an Iron Age *oppidum* on the Stour in the late 1st cent. BC. The Roman city developed shortly after AD 43, perhaps revealing the pre-Roman character of the tribes of Cantion (Kent). Public buildings were erected in the late 1st and early 2nd cents. A large theatre was added in the late 2nd cent. [1]; defensive works were built in the late 3rd cent. An *extra muros* Christian church, probably from the 4th cent., survived until *c.* AD 700 (Bede, Hist. Eccl. 1,26). After AD 400 the area within the walls was settled by Anglo-Saxon migrants.

1 S. S. FRERE, The Roman Theatre at Canterbury, in: Britannia 1, 1970, 83–113.

S. S. FRERE, S. STOW, Excavations on the Roman and Medieval Defences of Canterbury, 1982. M.TO.

Dusares At the head of the Nabataean pantheon was the god Dusares (e.g. in Tert. Apol. 24,8; Nabatean Dušarā/*dw-šr*ʾ; Δουσαρης in Greek inscriptions) (Répertoire d'Épigraphie Sémitique (=RES) 1401; CIS II 350,3–4). His name ('he from the Šarā[-mountains]') shows him as a local mountain or → weather god of the → Petra [1] region. The oldest evidence for the name of this deity dates from *c.* 96/95 BC, an inscription from the Triclinium of Aṣlaḥ in Petra (RES 1432).

More insight into the character of this god is provided by bilingual inscriptions, which mention his name, as well as by translations and assimilations: thus, D. appears as → Zeus, i.e. the highest god, as well as as Helios (→ Sol) and → Dionysus [3. 97–107]. Extant epithets of D. include: 'god of our lord' (sc. of the king; CIS II 201; 208; 209; 211; 350 and passim); 'god of Gaia', i.e. the Nabataean core settlement in the Wādī Mūsā [3. 89–91]; 'god of Madrasa' (CIS II 443), i.e. a sacrificial hill south of the entrance to the Sīq, and as 'master of the temple' (RES 1088; 1436). Originally, D. was venerated as Betyl (→ *baitýlia*); under the influence of Hellenistic-Roman depictions of gods, he was also represented anthropomorphically. Alongside, he was depicted theriomorphically as an eagle. The Qaṣr al-Bint is considered his main temple in Petra. Other places of worship to D. are evident from the Nabatene to Miletus and Delos and as far as Puteoli [1].
→ Nabataioi; → Petra [1]

1 H. J. W. DRIJVERS, s. v. D., LIMC 3.1, 670–672; 3.2, 532 2 M. GAWLIKOWSKI, Les dieux des Nabatéens, in: ANRW II 18.4, 2659–2677, esp. 2662–2665 3 J. HEALEY, The Religion of the Nabataeans, 2001, 80–106. H. NI.

Duty The concept of duty in the strict (Kantian) sense of absolute obligation is unknown in antiquity, when the way of thinking was thoroughly eudaemonistic: i.e. happiness was seen as the greatest good. It is, however, customary to equate the Stoic καθῆκον (*kathêkon*, lit. that which is 'befitting' or 'appropriate'), translated by Cicero into Lat. as *officium*, with the English 'duty'; but this is not to be recommended, owing to potentially erroneous associations. *Kathêkon* is a concept used in assessing and classifying human actions. For the Stoics these are complex phenomena, consisting of outward behaviour and inner state of mind. Arising from the idea that wrong behaviour cannot arise from a correct state of mind, there are initially three classes of action: 'perfect actions' (κατορθώματα/*katorthṓmata*: correct behaviour from a correct state of mind), 'qualified actions' (μέσαι/*mésai*: correct behaviour from a false state of mind) and 'wrong actions' (ἁμαρτήματα/*hamartḗmata*: wrong behaviour from a wrong state of mind; SVF 3,491ff.). Thus perfect and qualified actions are mutually differentiated not by outward behaviour but solely by inner state of mind. As this last is often not known, it cannot be decided whether any given action is a perfect or a qualified action. The Stoics accordingly need a further class of action that obviates this distinction while at least allowing correct behaviour in general to be clearly distinguished from wrong actions. Thus in addition to absolute and qualified actions they arrive at the generic concept of 'appropriate action', *kathêkon*, defining it as 'a consistency in life, so that any action arising from it allows of rational justification' (SVF 3, 494). All correct behaviour now falls under this concept — whether of the wise man or the fool, even that of animals and plants. It embraces quite simply all behaviour in keeping with nature, for only such behaviour (as a condition of happiness) can allow rational justification.

Neither should one impute to the Romans any conception of unconditional obligation. The word *officium*, whose meaning ranges from favour through recognition of a service owed to the idea of public office, never has this sense. → Cicero's *De officiis*, inspired by → Panaetius [4], nevertheless exerted considerable influence over Christian doctrine regarding duty, via the Church Father → Ambrosius of Milan, and it was in the tradition of that doctrine that the concept of an absolute obligation developed, insofar as it bases duty on the will of God, to whom is owed absolute obedience. Ambrosius adopted the distinction between absolute and qualified duty, but applied it to external behaviour (De officiis ministrorum 1,11,36f.). At a later time the new distinction was added between duty to God, to one's fellow human beings and to oneself.
→ Ethics; → Happiness; → Stoicism

M. HOSSENFELDER, Das 'Angemessene' in der stoischen Ethik, in: B. MERKER et al., Angemessenheit. Zur Rehabilitierung einer philos. Metapher, 1998, 83–99. M.HO.

Duumviri see → Duoviri

Duvius

L. D. Avitus. One of the earliest senators to come from Gaul (Vasio Vocontiorum). After his praetorship he became praetorian governor of Aquitania; *cos. suff.* with Thrasea Paetus in the last months of AD 56. In 57/8 he became commander of the army of Lower Germany, presumably through the influence of the praetorian prefect Afranius Burrus (likewise from Vasio Vocontiorum) (CIL XII 1354 = ILS 979; AE 1976, 391). He drove out the Frisians, who occupied the right bank of the Rhine. With the commander of the army of Upper Germany, Curtilius Mancia, he proceeded against the Ampsivarii, who had formed a coalition of German tribes.

PIR² D 210; Eck, Statthalter, 123f. W.E.

Dux

[1] The term *dux*, which had already appeared in the Republican period with the general meaning of 'a leader in a military action or of a troop of soldiers' (cf. e.g. Cic. Dom. 12: *seditionis duces*), was in the 2nd cent. AD occasionally used in a semi-official way as the title for the commander of a military unit established for a particular purpose and not necessarily subordinate to the governor of a province. Thus Ti. Claudius Candidus was *dux exercitus Illyrici* in the war waged by Septimius Severus against Pescennius Niger in AD 193–195 (CIL II 4114 = ILS 1140); *dux* was also used to describe lower-ranking officers with an unusual command, as for example a *centurio* who commanded a legion (CIL III 4855 = ILS 2772). A *dux ripae* is attested at → Dura-Europos in Mesopotamia in the mid 3rd cent. AD; he probably held a territorial command, although subordinate to the governor of Syria.

At the time of the Tetrarchy higher-ranking officers from the *ordo equester*, who evidently held supreme military command over a region, received the title *dux*. An inscription dated between AD 293 and 305 bears the name of Firminianus, *vir perfectissimus*, who was *dux* of the border territory (*limes*) of Scythia (CIL III 764 = ILS 4103); according to Eutropius, Carausius, who had tried to kindle a rebellion from Brittania, had been responsible for Belgica and Armorica. It would therefore appear that the command of a *dux* could extend over several provinces. In Egypt in AD 308/9 there was a *dux Aegypti Thebaidos utrarumque Libyarum* (AE 1934, 7–8). It is nevertheless improbable that the naming of *duces* was an intentional policy of Diocletian; at the time of the Tetrarchy such appointments were perhaps an immediate response to local emergencies, but there is no doubt that they contributed to the emergence of a professional officer corps. Codex Theodosianus uses *duces* as a general term for commanders of border regions (Cod. Theod. 7,22,5: *duces singulorum limitum*; cf. for the Rhine frontier Cod. Theod. 7,1,9).

The eventual outcome was the complete separation of the civil provincial administration under the *praesides*, from the military realm, which fell to the *dux*. But there were continual exceptions to this rule, thus in Isauria the offices of *dux* and *praeses* appear to have been linked. A *dux* frequently commanded the armies of two provinces, for example the troops of Armenia and Pontus as well as Syria Euphratensis were organizationally combined. The *dux* had command over all → *limitanei* within his area, and frequently units of the → *comitatenses* as well, thus he often commanded larger forces than the governors of earlier times. Yet he had little to do with the payment and supply of his troops, he also had no administrative or judicial duties in the cities and communities of his command. It was accordingly more difficult for him to instigate a rebellion.

The *dux* had the rank of *vir perfectissimus*; as a rule, tribunes who had commanded a unit of *comitatenses* or a cohort of *limitanei* were promoted *dux* after long years of military service. Owing to their purely military career, many *duces* were relatively uneducated. They were immediately subordinate to the *magister peditum*, each *dux* having his own administrative staff (*officium*). Valentinian I gave *duces* the rank of senator, so granting them the title of *vir clarissimus*.

→ Limitanei

1 R.E. Smith, Dux, Praepositus, in: ZPE 36, 1979, 263–278 2 D. Van Berchem, L'Armée de Dioclétien et la réforme constantinienne, 1952 3 S. Williams, Diocletian and the Roman Recovery, 1985. J.CA.

[2] Byzantine military rank, used since Anastasius [1] in AD 492 for the leader of the mobile army of the *comitatenses*, but from the later 6th cent. also for lower-ranking functions. With the emergence of the theme system in the 7th cent. the *dux* was at first subordinate to the governor (→ *stratēgós*, στρατηγός) of a military province (→ *théma*, θέμα). Not until about the middle of the 10th and early 11th cent. were frontier provinces in particular, but later increasingly former themes, frequently placed directly under a *dux*, also called *katepánō* (κατεπάνω); with the professional army under his command he was henceforth able to defend the territories more effectively than could the *stratēgós*, who had at his disposal only local theme forces that had often lapsed into decline.

H.-J. Kühn, Die byz. Armee im 10. und 11. Jh., 1991; ODB 1, 659. F.T.

Dwarf (Greek νᾶν[ν]ος/*nân[n]os*; Lat. *pumilio*, *pumilus*). Egyptian art has handed down a rich and varied image of the dwarf: in Egyptian popular belief dwarf gods such as Ptah-Pataikos (→ *pátaikoi*) and → Bes, the friend of children and women, (see Addenda; cf. → Monsters I) had been represented as helpful powers and omnipresent in the form of → amulets. In human daily life the dwarf took on the tasks of a craftsman and assisted in looking after children and in personal hygiene. Most illustrations show dwarves who, like cripples, served as entertainment for their masters.

The image in Greece is more one-sided and less positive. Mythical dwarves like the → pygmies and → cercopes are impious and malicious. In the human domain the dwarf was regarded as a luxury and prestige object. He acted as servant and → entertainer at drinking sessions. Dwarves were professional creators of fun in Roman cultural circles too. The new multiplicity of leisure architecture allowed performances at → theatres, amphitheatres (→ *amphitheatrum*) and the → thermal baths.

→ Disability (see Addenda); → Fringe groups

N. Himmelmann, review of V. Dasen, Dwarfs in Ancient Egypt and Greece (1993), in: Klio 77, 1995, 448 f.

AL. SCH.

Dwellings on flood resistant mounds These mound dwellings (German: *Wurte*) originated as individual farms in the marshes between Denmark and the Netherlands (where they are called *terpen*) in the Germanic settlement area along the southern North Sea coast in the 2nd/1st cents. BC during regression phases of the North Sea. In the course of subsequent cents., these locations were deliberately elevated into settlement mounds because of the rise in sea level and increasing numbers of storm floods. Mounds of several meters height that could consist of as many as 20 farms were created (e.g., Feddersen Wierde near Wesermünde, Germany). The farms consisted mostly of three-aisled stall and dwelling combinations, storage buildings and workshops. The arrangement and division of the farms was planned, at Feddersen Wierde first in rows and later a star pattern around an open square with a central farm. The largely self-sufficient economy was based on livestock husbandry and cultivation in neighbouring dry areas as well as various crafts. These mound dwellings are archaeologically particularly significant because the water-logged soil provides good conditions for preserving many objects of daily life in Germanic culture (wooden tools, textiles, building parts, animal dung, plant remains etc.). → Germanic archaeology; Agriculture

W. Haarnagel, Die Grabungen Feddersen Wierde, 1979; G. Kossack et al., Zehn Jahre Siedlungsforsch. in Archsum auf Sylt, in: BRGK 55, 1974, 261–427; Probleme der Küstenforsch. im südl. Nordseegebiet 1 ff., 1940 ff.; P. Schmid, s. v. Feddersen Wierde, RGA 8, 1994, 249–266; R. Uerkvitz, Norddeutsche Wurten-Siedlungen im arch. Befund, 1997.

V. P.

Dyas (δυάς; *dyás*). 'Indeterminate duality' (ἀόριστος δυάς, *aóristos dyás*): the non-reducible counter-principle essential for the 'creation' of phenomena in Plato's oral teaching on principles, according to the testimony of Aristotle (Metaph. A 987b 25ff.; M 1081a 14; N 1088a 15 and *passim*) and Theophrastus (Metaph. 11a 27ff.). Plato set it beside the 'One' or the 'Good' (ἕν or ἀγαθόν) as the definitive principle of reality. While Speusippos ascribed the introduction of *interminabilis dualitas* (= *aóristos dyás*) to the *antiqui*, thus probably the Pythagoreans (fr. 48 Tarán, cf. Theophr. ibid.), Aristotle viewed this an innovation by Plato (Metaph. A 987b 25–27). Other Platonic terms for indeterminate duality were τὸ ἄνισον (*tó ánison*, the unequal) and τὸ μέγα καὶ μικρόν (*tó méga kaì mikron*, 'the large and small'). To the 'One Good' belong concepts such as equality, similarity, rest etc.; to *dyas* belong evil, inequality, movement etc. (Aristot. Metaph. M 1084a 5). Reality is the product of the successive 'restriction' and determination of indeterminate duality by the form-giving principle of the One and its derivatives. Numbers are the first of these products (M 1081a 21ff.; N 1091a 23 and passim). Duality is thus contained in everything except in the One (Λ 1075 a35). The χώρα (*chṓra*) of the world of the senses (Pl. Ti. 49aff.) is to be understood as a regional form of *dyas* (cf. Aristot. Ph. 209b 11–16). *Dyas* as a concept of matter remains important later on in Numenius (fr. 11 des Places), in the Chaldaean Oracles (fr. 8 des Places), in Plotinus (Enneades 5,4,2,1–11: *aóristos dyás* as the intelligible substance of the *nous* hypostasis deriving from the One), in Iamblichus (Theologumena arithmethicae 7,3–13 de Falco, in Nicomachi arithmeticam introductionem 31,13 Pistelli and passim), Syrianus (in Aristot. Metaph. 9,16 and *passim* Kroll), and above all in Proclus (e.g. in Pl. Resp. 1,98,30; 2,173,23; in Pl. Prm. 661,29 Cousin) and Damascius (e.g. De principiis 1,86,20; 91,12ff. Ruelle).

L. Robin, La theórie platonicienne des idées et des nombres d'après Aristote, 1908, 276f., 533–553, 635–660; H. Happ, Hyle. Studien zum aristotelischen Materie-Begriff, 1971, 85–208; Th. A. Szlezák, Platon und Aristoteles in der Nuslehre Plotins, 1979, 54–79; J. Narbonne, Plotine, Les deux matières [Ennéade II,14 (12)], 1993, 110–124.

T.A.S.

Dyeing (Textiles). By dyeing (βάπτειν; *báptein*, *tinguere*) is meant the steeping of the material to be coloured in a vat of dye (βάμμα; *bámma*). The colour produced is the result of a chemical bond between the molecular structure of the textile and the dye.

The art of dyeing (βαφική; *baphikḗ*, *tinctura*) was highly developed in antiquity, as is demonstrated by extant remains of original textiles; these provoke continual amazement, with regard not only to the craftsmanship and artistry they display, but also the freshness and brilliance of their colours. The essential aspect of dyeing is to obtain a lasting and wash-resistant colour, and this necessitated a series of preparatory processes. In order for the smallest amounts of natural dyes to penetrate sufficiently deeply into the fibres to achieve a colour that was resistant both to washing and to light, the material to be dyed had to be carefully prepared. The fibres were first cleaned, soapwort for example being used for wool (στρούθιον, *stroúthion*). This rendered the wool soft and elastic, and free of grease and dirt. After that, the fibres were mordanted with acidic, soluble metallic, and mineral salts. In the alkaline baths the metal separated from the acid was then absorbed by the fibres, and finally in the dyeing process formed a firm bond with the dye. Decisive in determining the result of the process was the amount and quality of mordant used (besides alum also various plants such as the leaves or the roots of the pomegranate were used). The fibres might be dyed in spun form, as yarn, or already woven. The material was laid in the vat of dye, prepared according to particular formulae, and brought to a boil. Animal fibres such as wool were heated gently, to avoid felting. Silk was treated with great care as compared to cotton, linen or hemp. Once the fabric had taken on the desired colour, it was rinsed until the rinsing water contained no more dye residues.

Dyes were extracted from various organic materials of vegetable and animal origin. Most → pigments were obtained from plants. Pigment-bearing plant parts, such as leaves, shoots, blossoms, fruits or roots, were collected, dried, crushed, and used in this form as dye. Among the animal dyes was the expensive and much-prized → purple (πορφύρα; *porphýra*, *purpura*), a liquid excreted at death by a particular species of snail (Plin. HN 9,124–140; Str. 16,2,23). Also valued was the dye obtained from the various kinds of coccid (κόκκος, *coccus*), a parasite living on trees and plants (Plin. HN 9,141; 16,32; Paus. 10,36,1f.).

Antique authors give no information as to the actual work of dyers, so that dyeing techniques and working processes are largely unknown. Dyers themselves were not esteemed (Plut. Pericles 1). Because of the dyes used, and especially the process involved in producing purple dye, a very bad odour must have emanated from the workshops. Tyre may have become rich on account of its numerous purple-dye works, but it was also notorious for the accompanying noxious smells (Str. 16,2,23). In spite of this, archaeological discoveries (e.g. at Pompeii) demonstrate that dyers' workshops were not always excluded from cities. A Hellenistic dye-works was found at Isthmia near Corinth; numerous vessels were found that had been used for dyeing or for storing pigments, the discovery of loom-weights makes it probable that weaving was also carried out at this workshop.

1 E.J.W. Barber, Prehistoric Textiles. The Development of Cloth in the Neolithic and Bronze Ages with special Reference to the Aegean, 1991 2 Blümner, Techn. 1, 225–256 3 C. Kardara, Dyeing and Weaving Works at Isthmia, in: AJA 65, 1961, 261–266 4 C.P. Kardara, Βαφή, βαφεία και βαφαί κατά την αρχαιότητα, in: Hesperia 43, 1974, 447–453 5 W.O. Moeller, The Wool Trade of Ancient Pompei, 1976, 35–39 6 J.P. Wild, Textile Manufacture in the Northern Roman Provinces, 1970, 79–82.

A.P.-G.

Dymanes (Δυμᾶνες; *Dumânes*). On the one hand, this name is borne by one of the three old Dorian phyles (D., Hylleis and Pamphyli); on the other, it is that of a small community in western Locris, probably in the vicinity of Physcus [2]. Both may go back to a tribe of this name from north-western Greece, the larger part of which in prehistoric times joined the → Dorieis, while a splinter group went up into western Locris.

1 L. Lerat, Les Locriens de l'Ouest 1, 1952, 28f.

F.GSCH.

Dymas (Δύμας; *Dýmas*).

[1] Phrygian king on the Sangarius; father of Hecuba the wife of Priam, and of Asius (Hom. Il. 16,718; Apollod. 3,148; Hyg. Fab. 91,1; Ov. Met. 11,761).

[2] A Phaeacian, whose daughter was a friend of Nausicaa (Hom. Od. 6,22).

[3] A Trojan who joined Aeneas at the fall of Troy, and was killed (Verg. Aen. 2,340; 428).

T. Gargiulo, s.v. Dimante, EV 2, 75.

[4] **D.** or Dyman. Son of the Dorian king → Aegimius [1]; brother of Pamphylus. Like the latter, he perished during the migration of the Heraclidae into the Peloponnese, in the battle against Tisamenus, son of Orestes. It is from D., Pamphylus and their adoptive brother Hyllus that the three Dorian phyles are supposed to have received the names → Dymanes, Pamphyli and Hylleis. D. also gave its name to the city of → Dyme [1] in Achaea (Apollod. 2,176; Paus. 7,17,6; schol. Pind. Pyth. 5,92; Steph. Byz. s.v. Δυμᾶνες).

I. Malkin, Myth and Territory in the Spartan Mediterranean, 1994, 40.

R.B.

[5] From Iasus. Son of Antipater; tragic poet; in IG 12,8, p. 38 and Suppl. S. 149 B (*c.* beginning of the 2nd cent. BC) he is celebrated as the author of a Dardanus drama.

TrGF 130.

F.P.

Dyme (Δύμη; *Dýmē*).

[1] City on the west coast of Achaea near the modern Kato-Achaia, on a broad plateau on the left bank of the Peirus, protected on three sides by precipices. Protected by a fortress (Pol. 4,59,4), D. was able to exploit the natural riches of the land on Cape Araxus. One of the old 12 cities of Achaea (Hdt. 1,145), D. arose from the amalgamation of eight villages (δῆμοι; *dêmoi*) (Str. 8,3,2), among them Paleia and Stratos (Str. 8,7,5; Paus. 7,17,6f.; Steph. Byz. s.v. D.). Before 280 BC it incorporated the territory of the abandoned city of Olenus. D. was one of the four cities that founded the Achaean League after 280 BC (Pol. 2,41). In spite of many conflicts with → Elis and Aetolia, archaeological finds attest to the prosperity of D. in the Hellenistic period. In 66 BC Pompey settled pirates in D. (Str. 8,7,5; Plut. Pompeius 28,7; App. Mith. 96). Already planned by Caesar and Antony as a Roman *colonia*, D. was elevated to the status of *Colonia Augusta Dumaeorum* by Augustus, and after his death probably joined with Patrae (Paus. 7,17,5). D. went into decline during the Roman Imperial period. Extant ruins: city wall, necropoleis, remains of buildings, ancient streets and wells.

A.D. Rizakis (ed.), Paysages d'Achaïe I (Meletemata 15), 1992.

Y.L.

[2] Δύμη; *Dýmē*, *Dimae*. Fortified settlement in south-eastern Thrace (the modern Ardanion/Greece), *c.* 30 km from the estuary of the Hebrus (Ptol. 3,11,7). In the Roman period an important road station (It. Ant. 322,5; It. Burd. 602,6). I.v.B.

Dynamis (Δύναμις; *Dýnamis*). Daughter of Pharnaces; wife and successor of Asander. For a short time autonomous queen of the → Bosporan kingdom. Her second husband was the anti-Roman → Scribonius; he died during the attack of Agrippa [1] and Polemon, whom D. had to marry on Roman orders (in 14 BC, Cass. Dio 54,24,4–6). Shortly afterwards she retired with her son → Aspurgus (perhaps to the residence found 15 km from Novorosijsk). Augustus restored her to the throne after the death of Polemon. She ruled until AD 7/8. Many inscriptions testify to her friendship with Rome (IPE 2,354; 4,420 i.a.).

V.F. Gajdukevič, Das Bosporanische Reich, 1971, 326ff. I.v.B.

Dynasteia (δυναστεία; *dynasteía*, cf. also δυνάστης; *dynástēs*, 'Ruler'). Derived from δύνασθαι; *dýnasthai*, 'to be capable', 'to be able'; 'to have influence', 'to be wealthy' [1. 116]. *Dynasteia* was primarily the rule (→ rulership) of a small, influential group, within which high offices were inherited. Two basic levels of meaning are to be distinguished for *dynasteia*: in the first of them, its character as the term for a group of rulers or an individual ruler expresses more the original sense of the word; in the second the inheritance of leading positions as an impetus for continuity complements that sense in a defining way (cf. the dynasties of the kingdoms of ancient Egypt).

There was an early example of the second kind in Thessaly, whose *dynasteia* was characterized by established right and patriarchal power exercised over families living in dispersed localities, as well as by the lack of centralized institutions (e.g. an advisory assembly and laws) (Pl. Leg. 680b). Aristotle was later to distinguish the fourth form of oligarchy, corresponding to democracy in its lawlessness, as *dynasteia* (Aristot. Pol. 1293a 30–34). Whereas in the third form sons took up their fathers' place by law (Aristot. Pol. 1293a 26–30), in the fourth the process of inheritance was accompanied by the suspension of political institutions and laws: in their place, a few powerful individuals held sway, exercising great influence with their wealth, and passing on their positions of power to their sons. Its arbitrariness brought *dynasteia* close to → tyrannis (Aristot. Pol. 1292b 5–10. In Mytilene and Corinth *dynasteia* was an early form of *tyrannis*: Dem. Or. 40,37; Diod. Sic. 7,9,2–6). A precondition for the emergence of *dynasteia* was the enfeeblement of institutional order by the formation of a small group within the oligarchy, who shared and inherited offices among themselves (in Elis, this form of government brought rebellion and anarchy; cf. Aristot. Pol. 1306a 10–20). It is in this context that the Thebans are to be understood, when they attempt to justify their pro-Persian stance by asserting that a group of dynasts, intent solely on increasing their personal power, had taken over the government (Thuc. 3,62). In reaction to the coup in Athens in 411 BC, Andocides remarked that democracy had turned into *dynasteia* (And. 2,27). Discussing contemporary events, *dynasteia* was contrasted with → *demokratia* (→ *Isonomia* in Plato Polit. 291c-d), but with → *oligarchia* in texts orientated towards the past; in any case, it was never one of the canonic forms of constitution.

Cassius Dio uses the term *dynasteia* in the original sense of the word. Observing the concentration of power in Rome in the hands of particular private individuals who, owing to their wealth, did not feel themselves bound by laws, he describes the period between 133 and 127 BC as *dynasteia* (Cass. Dio 52,1); in Rome too, he claims, disruption of the aristocratic order paved the way for *dynasteia*. A striving for *dynasteia* was esp. imputed to Scipio Africanus, the Gracchi in their exceptional status as people's tribunes, and to other members of the elite up to and including Augustus. In the Roman Imperial period the selection of a successor occurred not only by the dynastic principle, but also—according to contemporary propaganda—by the criterium of *virtus*, which became the basis for the legitimation of rule, alongside inheritance.

→ Diadochi and Epigoni

1 Frisk.

P. Barceló, Basileia, Monarchia, Tyrannis, 1993; H. Berve, Die Tyrannis bei den Griechen, 1967, Index s.v. D.; J. Martin, D., in: R. Koselleck (ed.), Histor. Semantik der Begriffsgeschichte, 1978, 228–241; M. Stahl, Aristokraten und Tyrannen im archa. Athen, 1987; L. Whibley, Greek Oligarchs, 1967, 124–126.

M.MEI. and ME.STR.

Dyrrhachium (Δυρράχιον; *Dyrr[h]áchion*, *Dyrrhachium*).

I. Graeco-Roman period
II. Byzantine period

I. Graeco-Roman period

Harbour town on the Illyrian coast, the modern Durrës in Albania; founded on a peninsula by Corinth and Corcyra, probably in 626/625 BC, as the colony of Epidamnus (Eus. Chronicon 88f.; Thuc. 1,24–26; Scymn. 435–439). The name D. (coinage), which became established in the Roman period, was in use alongside Epidamnus from the 5th cent. BC onwards (so Thuc.; Hdt.; inscr.). Despite clashes with the Illyrians (Thuc. 1,24,4), D. flourished from commerce with its neighbours, and possessed a treasury at Olympia (Paus. 6,19,8). Interventions by Corcyra, Corinth and Athens in 433 BC, occasioned by internal conflicts, were a cause of the Peloponnesian War. Cassander captured the city in 314 (Polyaenus, Strat. 4,11,4). At the end of the 1st Illyrian War in 229 BC, D. came under the protection of Rome, and later became *civitas libera* (Cic. Fam. 14,1), and under Antonius or Augustus *colonia* under Italic law. As an important harbour for ships from Italy (Brundisium), and starting-point for the *via Egnatia* to Thessalonica, D. played an important role in the Roman civil wars (Pompey's base in 48 BC, unsuccessfully besieged by Caesar) and in the Imperial period. The inhabitants were held to be depraved and dissolute. Written sources: [1. 19–28]; inscriptions: [1]; coins: [2; 3; 4].

1 P. Cabanes, F. Drini, Corpus des inscr. grecques d' Illyrie méridionale et d' Épire 1, 1996 2 P. Cabanes (ed.), L'Illyrie méridionale et l'Épire dans l'Antiquité 1, 1987, 209–219 3 BMC, Gr (Thessaly), 65–78 4 HN, 315, 406.

P. Cabanes, L'Épire, 1976; N.G.L. Hammond, Epirus, 1967; J. Wilkes, The Illyrians, 1992. D.S.

II. Byzantine period

D. in the Byzantine period is mentioned *i.a.* in the *Itinerarium Antonii* (317, 5; 7; 337, 4; 339, 5; 497, 6; 520, 3), in the *Tabula Peutingeriana* (6,2 Weber), as well as in Hierocles (653,1; cf. also Konstantinos Porphyrogennetos, De administrando imperio 30, 96; 32,82 Moravcsik/Jenkins, De thematibus 93 Pertusi) and Anna Komnene ([2] *passim*). Efforts at reconstruction after earthquakes in 314 and 522, and partially successful sieges by Theoderic in 481, the Bulgars in the 10th and 11th cents., Normans 1081–1085, 1107/8, 1185, and by crusaders in 1203 confirm its continuing strategic importance in peace and in war, not fading until the late Middle Ages under the rule of Anjou, Venice and the Turks. D. was bishopric and metropolis of the province of Νέα Ἤπειρος (*Néa Épeiros*, *Epirus nova*), later a theme; bishops are attested from the 5th cent. [1. 1249ff.]. Until the 8th cent. D. belonged to Rome, from 1020 to Ochrid. Some archaeological remains survive (continuity of settlement), among them the aqueduct, Roman baths, the frequently renewed city walls, and the chapel in the amphitheatre with mosaic of the emperor Alexander (911–913).

→ Apollonia[1]

1 DHGE 14, 1960, 1248–1252 2 D.R. Reinsch, 1996 (tr. and comm.).

LMA 3, 1986, 1497–1500; ODB 1, 1991, 668; A. Philippson, s.v. D., RE 5, 1882–1887; for further lit. see Apollonia [1]. E.W.

Dysaules (Δυσαύλης; *Dysaúlēs*). Brother of Celeus in Eleusis; banished by → Ion, brought the Eleusinian Mysteries to Celeae near Phleius; according to local cult legend also buried there (Paus. 2,12,4; sceptical: 2,14,1–4). The name D. does not occur in the Homeric epic cycle. The 'Orphics' were the first to place him at Eleusis in a poem on Demeter's visit there [1]. In that poem he was a native of the place, married Baube, was father of Eubuleus and → Triptolemus, and welcomed → Demeter as a guest.

1 F. Graf, Eleusis und die orphische Dichtung Athens in vorhell. Zeit, 1974, 159f., 167f.

O. Kern, s.v. D., RE 5, 1888f. K.C.

E

E (linguistics) The fifth letter of the Greek → alphabet was at first called εἶ (pronounced *ẹ̄*; see below), later ἒ ψιλόν (*èpsilón*) [1. 140]. It could indicate various *e* vowels in local alphabets, e.g in Old Attic: 1) the Early Greek short *ĕ* (ΕΧΣΕΝΕΝΚΕΤΟ (*EXSENENKETO*); also in ΤΕΙΧΟΣ (*TEICHOS*) with 'true ει'), only the first value surviving (i.e. as short *ĕ*: ἐξενεγκέτω; *exenenkétō*; τεῖχος (*teîchos*) soon became *tẹ̄khos*); 2) an open, long *ę̄* from original Greek *ē* (ΑΝΕΡ; *ANER*, ΑΝΕΘΕΚΕ; *ANETHEKE*, later ἀνήρ; *anḗr*, ἀνέθηκε; *anéthēke*) or *ā* (ΜΝΕΜΑ, later μνῆμα; *mnêma*); 3) a closed, long *ẹ̄* [2. 232f.], which did not arise until the post-Mycenean period by contraction (ΙΔΕΝ, ΒΟΕΘΕ̣Ν; *IDEN*, *BOETHEN*), pseudo-lengthening (ΝΕ̣ΜΑΝΤΕΣ; *NEMANTES*) or metric lengthening (ΗΕ̣ΝΕΚΑ; *ĒENEKA* [3. 347]), and was later written down as 'false ει' (ἰδεῖν, βοηθεῖν; νείμαντες; εἵνεκα; *ideîn*, *boētheîn*; *neímantes*, *héneka*); as a result, the old *e̯i* (as in τεῖχος; *teîchos*) collapsed. The long vowels mentioned under 2) and 3) are represented differently in the various Gr. dialects. Thus already in the pre-Christian period *ẹ̄* became *ī*, and later *ę̄*; see → itacism The Lat. letter *E* stands for both the short *ĕ* (twice in *septem*) and for the long *ē* (twice in *hērēs*).

The Gr. and Lat. *ĕ* goes back to numerous original forms, the basic vowels of the proto-Indo-Germanic → ablaut: φέρω; *phérō*, *fero* < **bherō*; γένος *genus* < **genə₁os*; the Gr. *ĕ*, e.g. in θετός, θεός; *thetós*, *theós*, on the other hand maintains the proto-Indo-Germanic → laryngeal *ə₁* [4. 179f.; 5. 72]. The original Gr. and Lat. *ē* may represent the extended *ē* (ἡμι-; *hēmi*, *sēmi-* < **sēmi-*) or the full *ĕə₁* (εἴης; *eíēs*, Old Lat. *siēs* < **ə₁sieə₁s* 'that you be (Ger. »*du seist*«)'); as an exceptional case, we have the Gr. –γνητος (–*gnētos*, < **gn̥ə₁tos*; another form in Lat. *gnātus*). The Lat. *ĕ* and *ē* have various further origins, e.g. in *(sept)em* < **(sept)m̥*; *uester* < *uoster*; *certus* < **kritos*; *agellus* < **agr̥los* < **agrolos*; *ac-ceptus* < **ad-kaptos*; *trēs* < **trei̯es* (contraction); *aēnus* < **ai̯esnos* (pseudo-lengthening); *ēnsis* < **ensis* (lengthening by nasalisation).

e and *ē* in Lat. and Gr. reciprocal → loan-words [6] can be traced back for the most part to similar vowels: *ĕphēbus* from ἔφηβος (*éphēbos*); κεντηνάριος (*kentēnários*) from *centēnārius*. But e.g. in *talentum*, *camera* from τάλαντον (*tálanton*), καμάρα (*kamára*) the vowel has changed in Lat.

→ Pronunciation; → H (linguistics); → Itacism

1 Schwyzer, Gramm. 2 M. Lejeune, Phonétique historique du mycénien et du grec ancien, 1972 3 Chantraine 4 H. Rix, review of: R. S. P. Beekes, The development of the Proto-Indo-European laryngeals in Greek, in: Kratylos 14, 1969 5 Id., Histor. Gramm. des Griech., [2]1992 6 F. Biville, Les emprunts du latin au grec II, 1995.

B.F.

Eagle (ἀετός; *aetós*, *aquila*). Most distinguished bird of antiquity (Il. 8,247; 24,315; Aesch. Ag. 112; Pind. Pyth. 1,6 al.; Plin. HN 10,6). Description of the six types in Aristot. Hist. an. 8(9),32,618 b 18–619 b 12 and with alterations in Plin. HN 10,6–8. (1) πύγαργος, νεβροφόνος (*pýgargos*, *nebrophónos*; 'deer calf killer') (in Plin. no. 2), with white tailfeathers, living on plains, in forests, mountains and in towns, perhaps snake eagle [1. 208]. (2) πλάγγος, νηττοφόνος (*anataria*) or μορφνός, Homer. (= περκνός, Il. 24,316), in damp lowlands or by lakes, a large, strong bird (in Plin. no. 3), probably the lesser spotted eagle [1.18]. (3) μελανάετος or λαγωφόνος (*leporaria*, *valeria* cod., cf. [1. 31, 162], booted eagle (?), in mountainous areas and in forests, smallest, but strongest species (in Plin. no. 1). (4) περκόπτερος (according to Plin. no. 4), ὀρειπέλαργος 'mountain stork' (because of black and white markings) or ὑπάετος, large, but weak and inferior to the raven, scavenger and (in spite of [1. 195]) the Egyptian vulture. (5) ἁλιάετος (*haliáetos*), the fish or sea eagle, as the two were not distinguished (in Plin. no. 6), with a large, thick neck, curved wings and a broad tail [1. 133]. (6) γνήσιος (*gnḗsios*), the genuine, i.e. pure-race, medium-sized, with reddish colouration, but rare, perhaps the imperial eagle or (according to [1. 129]) the griffon-vulture (in Plin. no. 5). Plin. HN 10,11 recognizes another 7th species, *Aquila barbata* = *ossifraga* among the Etruscans, the bearded eagle [1. 31].

Apart from no. 4 all eagles hunt living prey (Aristot. 619 a 6–8: sea eagle = Plin. HN 10,8: fish eagle; Aristot. 619 a 31–b12 = Plin. HN 10,14 (general); Aristot. 620 a 6–12 = Plin. HN 10,9: sea eagle, but wrongly related to *anataria*! As birds with curved claws (γαμψώνυχα; *gampsṓnycha*) eagles do not drink (Aristot. Hist. an. 8(9),18,601 a 31–b3), by contrast with the there mentioned Hesiod, they fight with bulls, deer and snakes according to Aristotle, in Ael NA 2,39; Plin. HN 10,17. Reproduction: Aristot. Hist. an. 6,6,563 a 17–28; b4–9; Plin. HN 10,12–13 (with the aid of the → eagle-stone). Killing and repelling the young out of jealousy: Aristot. 619 a 27–31 (exception: no. 3) and 619 b 26–31; Plin. 10,6 and 13. Rearing of the ejected birds by the φήνη (*phḗnē*; bearded vulture?): Aristot. Hist. an. 7(8),3,592 b 5–6; 8(9),34,619 b 23–25 and 34 and Plin. HN 10,13. Much quoted in the Middle Ages was the claim by Aristotle (Hist. an. 8(9),34,620 a 1–5; Plin. HN 10,10) that the sea eagle (ἁλιάετος) reared only the young who could look at the sun without their eyes watering. Further peculiarities [2] are, for instance, the strengthening of sight by brain and gall (Plin. HN 29,118 and 123; Ael. NA 1,42; Dioscorides 2,78,2 = 2,96 [3. 190]; Gal. 10,1012a). Immune to being struck by lightening (Plin. HN 10,15), eagles protected against hail (Gp. 1,14,2) and other things (Gp. 13,8,8; Plin. HN 37,124: against drunkenness, though Pliny is sceptical). Eagles were used as hunting birds in India (Ctesias in Ael. NA 4,26). Byzantine illustration on ancient zoological texts are extant [4].

As the only divine (Aristot. 619 b 6; Anth. Pal. 9,222,2) and mantic bird (Hesiod in Aristot. 601 b 2; Sen. Nat. 2,32,5 and passim), it is the herald of victory, messenger and helper of Zeus (since the Iliad, cf. [5]; [6. 1,392] only interprets it as a symbol of lightening; on the two eagles on the Omphalos of Delphi see [5,178 ff.]) and linked to many Oriental kings, especially the Achaemenids (therefore on coins and coats of arms with Alexander the Great, the Diadochi, Augustus and other emperors [see 7. 2,1–6; 8. esp. pl. 4,28–40; 9. 12; 10. 228–231]. Zeus transforms himself into an eagle (Ov. Met. 6,108; Lucian. dialogi 4). Further transformations → Periphas, Merops, Nisus, Pandareus, Periclymenus. Eagle → constellations: Arat. 313 f., Hyg. Fab. 10 et al. As symbol of the ruler's apotheosis: [11. 309[1]]. Use as → ensigns (*aquila*)

1 Leitner 2 Oder, s. v. Adler, RE 1, 372 f. 3 J. Berendes, Des Pedanios Dioskurides Arzneimittellehre übers. und mit Einl. versehen, 1902, repr. 1970 4 Z. Kádár, Survivals of Greek zoological illuminations in Byzantine manuscripts, 1978, plate 129,1 = VIII,3; 239,2 = 187,2 5 Cook, Zeus 1.2 6 Nilsson, GGR 7 Keller 8 F. Imhoof-Blumer, O. Keller, Tier- und Pflanzenbilder auf Münzen und Gemmen des klass. Altertums, 1889, repr. 1972 9 D'Arcy W. Thompson, A glossary of Greek birds, 1936, repr. 1966, 2–16 10 Toynbee, pl. 120–121 11 Latte.

C.HÜ.

Eagle-stone (ἀετίτης; *aetítēs*). According to Plin. HN 36.149 (cf. Plin. HN 10.12) a so-called rattle stone found in both sexes in eagles nests, which like a pregnant woman contained a further stone inside it, of which Pliny according to Sotacus (3rd cent. BC) [1.468] distinguished a total of four kinds in Africa, Arabia, Cyprus and near Leucas. Without its presence the eagle would not produce any progeny. According to the stone book of Evax ch. 1 [2.234–236], the eagle brought it from the periphery of the earth to protect its eggs. Already from the time of Plin. HN 36.151 and Ael. NA

1.35 it was considered to be an antiabortifacient, fastened to the body of pregnant women, according to Evax though it also brought luck to its wearer and defended against bad luck. Via Isid. Orig. 16,4,22, Solin. 37,14 f. and the Latin lapidaries, the 'ethites' entered the highly mathematical, scientific encyclopaedias such as Thomas of Cantimpré 14,28 [3.361].

1 M. Wellmann, Die Stein- und Gemmenbücher der Ant., in: Quellen und Studien zur Gesch. der Naturwiss. und der Medizin 4, 1935, repr. 1973, 426–489 2 R. Halleux, J. Schamp (ed.), Les Lapidaires Grecs, 1985 3 H. Boese (ed.), Thomas Cantimpratensis, Liber de natura rerum, 1973.

C.HÜ.

Ear ornaments

I. Ancient Orient II. Classical Antiquity

I. Ancient Orient

see → Jewellery

II. Classical Antiquity

Ear ornaments (ἐνώτια/*enṓtia*, ἐνωτάρια/*enōtária*, ἐνωτίδιον/*enōtídion*, Lat. *inaures*) are seldom mentioned in Gr. myth (Hom. Il. 14,183; Hom. Od. 18,298; Hymn. Hom. ad Ven. 8), but numerous finds and representations attest that already in early times they formed part of the → jewellery of men (Hom. Od. 18,298) and women. In the classical period and later, the wearing of ear ornaments by men was regarded as denoting effeminacy or an Oriental origin (e.g. Hdt. 7,47; Xen. An. 3,1,31; Plaut. Poen. 981; Plin. HN 11,136). The materials used for the manufacture of such ornaments varied greatly: gold, elektron, jasper, cornelian, silver, emerald, pearl, glass paste, shell and much more. Information on the appearance of ear ornaments comes not only from pictorial representations on vases and in wall-paintings and sculptural representations, but can also be gleaned from numerous finds of treasure from the early period (Aegina hoard, 17th/16th cents. BC, now in London, BM) to the end of Antiquity. Ear ornaments show a rich variety of forms, of which only a few can be mentioned here.

Ornate jewellery was produced as early as the 2nd millennium BC; hardly any finds, however, are known from the Gr. mainland for the period from the 15th cent. BC to the 12th cent. BC: unlike Crete and Cyprus, where the stylised bull's head was popular as a pendant on an earring. The latter remained current into the Hellenistic period, as did the earring in the form of a boat, occurring on the Gr. mainland. Besides these, simple earrings of gold and silver wire are found. Forms worthy of mention from subsequent centuries are spiral earrings of thin, sometimes doubled gold wire; the spirals might be terminated by a gold disk or ball. There were also crescent-shaped ear ornaments with pendants fastened to short chains.

In the Gr. Archaic period (7th–6th cents. BC) the main form is the ball- or pyramid-shaped earring; there were also spirals or hoops with or without pendants, disks, and pendant earrings of gold wire in the form of a fishhook, ending in disks, protomes of animals or rosettes. From the early Archaic period come hoop earrings (hoard from the Artemisium of Ephesus), which seem to be absent in the 6th cent. but to come back into fashion in the 5th. Here the 'ear caps' worn by Cypriot women from the 6th to the 5th cent. BC may be mentioned; these were probably made from fabric and metal and lay on the earlobe, usually covering it completely.

In the Classical period (5th–4th cents. BC) the number of varieties of ear ornaments increased. One of the most important of these is the vase-shaped pendant (amphora, less frequently *loutrophoros*), which came into fashion at the beginning of the 5th cent. BC and was also worn by Etruscan women. Ear pendants with figurative representations below an ornamented gold disk now became popular. The richness of variety of these ear pendants increased with the Hellenistic period (3rd–1st cents. BC). Motifs now come from the plant and animal worlds as well as from mythology; of especial note are pendants in the shape of doves, swans, images of Eros and Aphrodite. The ear pendants were often linked together with an (amaranth) chain (see → Neck ornaments). The simple hoop earring with lion or antelope protome and the boat-shaped earring were also worn. From the 5th to the beginning of the 3rd cent. BC the spiral earring was also in fashion. The grave finds from Tarentum give an impression of the rich variety of the Hellenistic earring [5].

Italian and Etruscan ear ornaments are attested to by finds and by representations on clay votive statues [4. passim; 3]. The magnificent basket earring, a special Etruscan form of which almost 300 examples survive, is restricted to the Archaic period (7th–6th cent.) [7]. The Roman ear ornament from the Imperial period onwards also displays a great variety of form. The simplest was the gold wire earring, with the wire bent into a ring shape on which stones or pearls were either mounted or hung; the wire was closed with a hook and eye arrangement. Hook earrings, so called from the S-shaped hook by which they are attached in the ear, have a soldered disk; the pendant was then attached to the bend of the hook. The disk may also be replaced by a mounted stone, to whose mounting the pendant was then fixed directly. The so-called baretta earring (named after the crossbar, It. *baretta*) enjoyed great popularity from the early Imperial period onwards; the underside of the crossbar bears two or three eyelets to which pendants with precious stones or pearls were attached. Probably of southern Italian origin is the hemisphere earring, attached to the ear by means of an S-shaped hook soldered to the hemisphere; the fastening was covered by a second hemisphere or a disk. Pendant earrings comprising three pearls occurred in the Severan period (2nd–3rd cents. AD).

1 J. M. Hemelrijk, Some Ear Ornaments in Archaic Cypriot and Eastern Greek Art, in: BABesch 38, 1963, 28–51 2 B. Pfeiler, Röm. Goldschmuck des 1. und 2. Jh.n.Chr. nach datierten Funden, 1970 3 P. Sommella, in: Enea

nel Lazio, Ausstellung Rom, 1981, 221–269 4 M. CRISTOFANI, M. MARTELLI (ed.), L'oro degli Etruschi, 1983 5 T. SCHOJER, in: E. M. DE JULIIS et al., Gli ori di Taranto, 1984, 127–192 6 B. DEPPERT-LIPPITZ, Griech. Goldschmuck, 1985 7 CH. TRÜMPLER, Die etr. Körbchen-Ohrringe, in: H. HERES, M. KUNZE (ed.), Die Welt der Etrusker. Internat. seminar 24th–26th Oct. 1988 in Berlin, 1990, 291–297, pl. 57–61 8 D. WILLIAMS, J. OGDEN, Greek Gold. Jewellery of the Classical World, 1994 9 A. BÖHME-SCHÖNBERGER, Kleidung und Schmuck in Rom und den Prov. (Schriften des Limesmuseum Aalen 50), 1997 10 G. PLATZ-HORSTER, Röm. Schmuck bei Mumienporträts aus Ägypten, in: K. PARLASCA (ed.), Augenblicke. Mumienporträts und ägypt. Grabkunst aus röm. Zeit, exhibition at Frankfurt a.M., 1999, 89–91.

R.H.

Earthquake

I. MESOPOTAMIA II. GRAECO-ROMAN WORLD

I. MESOPOTAMIA

The push of the Arabian peninsula to the north-east against the Eurasian plate caused the uplift of the Zagros and Taurus mountains. Seismic release of tensions can lead to earthquakes in the whole of Mesopotamia, particularly in the north. Earthquakes were considered to be expressions of wrath by → Enlil, king of the gods, by various → chthonic gods and by Inanna/Ištar as the star of Venus. They were regarded as severe warnings to the king and as precursors of further disasters. Earthquake omens were recorded from the middle of the 2nd millennium BC on and are preserved in cuneiform script from as late as Hellenistic times. They were incorporated into Greek tradition with almost no changes [1]. From observation stations all over Mesopotamia, reports were made to the Neo-Assyrian kings → Asarhaddon and → Assurbanipal (7th cent. BC) not only about astrological omens, but also about earthquakes. Thanks to the preserved reports [3], several earthquakes of the 7th cent. can be dated accurately. In order to calm the wrath of the gods, the king had to carry out extensive expiatory rites. The oldest historical report about earthquake damage can be found in an Assyrian royal inscription of 13th cent. BC. Earthquake damage can also be detected with archaeological methods.

1 C. BEZOLD, F. BOLL, Reflexe astrologischer Inschr. bei griech. Schriftstellern, 1911, 50ff. 2 A. FADHIL, Erdbeben im Alten Orient, in: BaM 24, 1993, 271–278 3 H. HUNGER, Astrological Reports to Assyrian Kings, 1992.

S.M.

II. GRAECO-ROMAN WORLD

Due to its tectonic structure (in Magna Graecia also its volcanic structure), the entire Greek area of settlement was so susceptible to seaquakes and earthquakes [1] that this phenomenon not only played a role in myths (→ Poseidon) and popular belief, but also in every attempt to explain the world as a natural system (in this case also in order to remove the fear of earthquakes being seen as supernatural, arbitrary acts of the gods). Seneca's detailed book on the subject *De terrae motu* (Sen. Q. Nat. 6) also contains a doxographic overview, based on the Αἰτίαι φυσικαί (*Aitíai physikaí*) of Posidonius' pupil Asclepiodotus, without, however, always mentioning the originator of the theory; of the older doxography going back to Theophrastus, → Aetius [2] (placita 3, 15) offers only scanty remnants which are to be complemented by Aristot. Mete. 2,7: While → Thales in his comparison of the earth with a floating ship equated an earthquake with the rolling of the ship in a storm and → Anaximander and → Anaximenes [1] think of a collapse due to cracks caused by excessive dryness, which for → Empedocles [1] and Antiphon caused fire in the earth's interior, the following thinkers made materials in the earth's interior responsible, which have collected there under pressure and whose explosive expansion results in earthquakes: Anaxagoras [2] and Archelaus [8] thought of air that penetrated the terrestrial disc from below, Democritus [1] of water collected in underground caves, Aristotle of hot and dry *pneúma* (*spiritus*) created from vapours emerging from the earth or evaporation on the earth's surface which would penetrate the earth and be compressed by surface water draining into the earth's crevices (Aristot. Mete. 2,8; similarly in Theophrastus and Posidonius, Sen. Q. Nat. 6,21ff. and most of the subsequent authors). Volcanic activities were usually seen as peripheral phenomena while a theory mentioned in Sen. Q. Nat. 6,11 had the *pneúma* compressed from below by vapours created as a result of volcanism in the earth's interior; → Straton of Lampsacus, however, thought of an antiperistatic motion of cold and warm matter in the earth's interior. The zenith of ancient seismology is represented by the detailed theory of → Posidonius, which incorporated experiences from the entire oikoumene; this theory divides the earth geologically into regions at risk and 'immune' regions, assumes the place of origin to be at a great depth, includes numerous peripheral phenomena and furthermore classifies earthquakes, subsequent to Aristotle (Mete. 2,8), according to the direction of their thrust. Earthquakes were compiled by Demetrius of Callatis around 200 BC (Str. 1,3,20 with a longer excerpt) and Demetrius of Skepsis (Str. 1,3,17). A summary of the literary references to earthquakes in Greece and the eastern Mediterranean from 600 BC till AD 600 can be found in CAPELLE [1. 346–358].

Whether the fabled Atlantis in Plato's *Critias* perished as a result of an earthquake is being debated. Apart from Seneca, Pliny the Elder (HN 2,191ff.) proves to have a good knowledge about the theories on earthquakes (which he called *motus terrae*) adopted by Aristotle and Seneca, about indications of earthquakes, which were used by many scientists to make predictions about earthquakes, and about the many ways in which earthquakes manifest themselves, which could also lead to the emergence of land at other locations. He mentions (HN 2,199f.) an earthquake during the reigns of Tiberius (AD 17) and of Nero (AD 68). Pliny himself, as is reported by his nephew (Plin. Ep. 6,16), lost his life in August of AD 79 during the eruption of Vesuvius after days of earth tremors (Plin. Ep. 6,20).

1 W. Capelle, s.v. Erdbebenforschung, RE Suppl. 4, 344–374 2 O. Gilbert, Die meteorologischen Theorien des griech. Altertums, 1907, 293–324. F.KR.

Easter chronicle see → Chronicon paschale

Easter computation see → Calendar

East Greek pottery

A. Introduction B. Geometric Period (9th–8th Cent. BC) C. Archaic Period (7th–6th Cent. BC) 1. Orientalizing Phase and Wild Goat Style 2. Fikellura-Vases 3. Black-figured Vases 4. Special Groups 5. East Greek Pottery in Etruria

A. Introduction

The region of eastern Greece, i.e. the west coast of Asia Minor and the offshore islands, was settled by Greeks in part during the late Bronze Age and more comprehensively in the early Iron Age. Culturally and politically, the region was subdivided into the Aeolian north, the Ionic middle and the Doric south; artistically, the prosperous cities of Ionia (Miletus, Samos, Ephesus and Smyrna) were the leading ones in the region. Local pottery workshops influenced by the style developed in Athens at the time, can be distinguished from protogeometric times on.

B. Geometric Period (9th–8th Cent. BC)

Based on the evidence provided by the finds of Kos and Rhodes, the geometric style became established in East Greek Pottery from *c*. 850 BC again following Attic examples, but also developing local variants. Amongst the latter were: hatching in one direction, triangles filled with hatched lozenges, quadratic hooks and occasionally Cypriot forms and motives. In the late geometric period (*c*. 740–680 BC), the east Greek vase painters tended towards conservatism in their motifs and the arrangement of ornaments. Only water birds occurred more frequently as figurative representations, e.g. in the handle zone of bowls (kotylai). From these bird kotylai, the widely spread bird dishes of the 7th cent. were developed which were drinking vessels of nearly hemispherical shape. They were lower and wider than the kotylai and they bore a decor with cross-hatched water birds between lozenges in the handle zone. The bird was replaced in the late 7th and 6th cent. by a simple dotted rosette.

C. Archaic Period (7th–6th Cent. BC)

1. Orientalizing Phase and Wild Goat Style

Orientalizing attempts (cf. → Orientalizing Vase Painting) first emerged in the late 8th cent. in East

Greek Pottery and became more common from *c*. 675 BC onwards, but East Greek Pottery was slow to give up its subgeometric appearance. In Miletus and Chios, it remained until the middle of the 7th cent., when a pleasant style of little sophistication, which depicted animals, often called 'Wild Goat Style', gained acceptance: goats, red deer, dogs, lions, geese, hares and sphinxes occurred which in the early and middle phase were represented in reservation technique and as outline drawings, in the late phase after 600 BC in reservation and black-figured technique. The black-figured technique (→ Black-figured vases) had been adopted from Corinth and, on vases which employed both techniques, featured more prominently. Filler ornaments became dense and rich in variants. Superimposed red was used frequently, white was quite common after *c*. 600. Clay analyses have shown that, in the middle phase, most of the exported Wild Goat Style pottery came from southern Ionia, principally from → Miletus, but in the late phase came from northern Ionia. Oinochoai, plates and dishes were usual forms while, amongst the very fine, white-based vases from Chios, the chalices with high rims and the bowls (phialai) stand out in particular. On Chios in the 6th cent., experimentation occurred with polychrome figurative scenes ('Grand Style' — some of it is mythological) as well as with a black-figured technique ('sphinx and lion' group, 'Comast cups') carried out with little care. Other centres to be mentioned are Ephesus and Sardeis where variants of the 'Wild Goat Style' were produced. Aeolian cities preferred their 'Grey Ware', but there, too, a provincial Wild Goat Style was at home, especially from Larisa and Pitane. In the Doric south, the Wild Goat Style was particularly common on the flat dishes of the 'Nisyrus' group. The picture background was often divided into a lower segment, which was decorated with a radial tongue pattern, and a main field with animal or human figures.

2. Fikellura-Vases

While the late Wild Goat Style continued in northern Ionia in the 1st half of the 6th cent., the vase production in Miletus diminished dramatically, possibly caused by local political unrest. Shortly before the middle of the 6th cent., the 'Fikellura' pottery emerged which clearly followed the Wild Goat Style of the middle period. Its centre, again, was Miletus. Locally produced vessels from a Carian necropolis near Mylasa display a combination of Wild Goat and Fikellura motifs — possibly a reflection of the low production of vases in Miletus itself during the 1st half of the 6th cent. Fikellura pottery obtained its name from a town in the vicinity of ancient → Camirus on Rhodes where these vases were first found. Animals, plants and human beings were painted as outlines, leaving out details, with influences of the Attic black-figured style evident. The typical vessel shape was a squat amphora of medium size. The decoration often consisted of complex woven bands or meander patterns on the neck as well as rows of half moons and volutes on the vessel body. Figurative decoration could occur on the shoulder, the vessel body or on both. The Altenburg painter started with simple scenes of animal fights and with dog-hare-hunts and then, around 540 BC, introduced scenes with dancing revellers (comasts, see → Komos). In the last quarter of the century, the 'Painter of the Running Satyrs' added some mythological figures (centaurs, satyrs, winged 'demons'), and the 'Running Man Painter' made vigourous use of the decoration without placing a frame around the picture. The end of the Fikellura vases coincided with the → Ionian Revolt uprising of 499–493 BC.

3. Black-figured Vases

The Ionian → Little Master cups are few in number, but they are amongst the best works of East Greek Pottery. They imitate the structure, form and partly the decoration of Attic drinking cups with a high foot. For the representation of details, some preferred reservation techniques over the black-figured style of painting. The 'Vineyard bowl' (Paris, LV F 68) is the most well-known, some fragments in Samos with a lion and dog are similar to the Fikellura work of the Altenburg painter. They belong to the middle part of the 3rd quarter of the cent.

Some groups of black-figured vases were produced in the area of → Clazomenae in the 2nd half of the 6th cent. They used copiously applied superimposed red and white and zones with animal and human representations. The 'Tübingen' group is the oldest: It is characterized by a carefully detailed decoration that covers the entire surface of these large-sized vessels; the main field often displays a row of dancing women. In the 'Petrie' group, where all the vessels were probably produced by one painter, we also find several slim amphorae decorated with rows of dancing women. The 'Urla' group takes up once more the theme of dancing women, but also Komos scenes, riding youths and mythical images. Related to the Petrie painter is the Borelli painter, the inventor of figured painting on the Clazomenian (clay) sarcophagi. The sarcophagus rims were extended and a white coating (*slip*) was put on before the decoration in the Wild Goat Style with reservation technique (→ Orientalizing vase painting) was applied. Attic influence led to attempts to imitate the black-figure style of painting, especially with scenes of hoplite fights and horse races, but the representation of details with white paint was preferred over incision. The Albertinum painter in the early 5th cent. BC was the best of these artists, but his connection to older east Greek works was already tenuous.

4. Special Groups

Two groups of vases, which use incised drawings and applied purple as decoration, were probably manufactured on Rhodes. The 'Vroulia' group (named after the town in the south of Rhodes) is characterized most of all by high quality drinking cups on a low, conical foot. Bold plant ornaments decorated the main fields outside and inside. The group belongs in the late 7th and the 1st half of the 6th cent. The 'Situla' group was related in terms of the ornaments, but under the lip offers simple figured scenes. The characteristic form was the → situla, a high cylindrical vessel with a flat pouring lip, with small round handles directly under this lip and a low support ring as a base. Black and purple plant decoration often adorns the two lower fields. Mostly, they belonged in the last third of the 6th cent., but an example from Samos is decorated in the way of the middle Wild Goat Style.

5. East Greek Pottery in Etruria

East Greek Pottery has produced some unusual examples of good quality in Etruria, possibly produced by immigrants from northern Ionia where the Persian conquest after the middle of the cent. had a particularly strong impact. The 'Northampton' group consisted of four amphorae which come close in quality to the Attic works. The 'Campana' group, mostly dinoi, had similarly colourful black-figured works, but they have been executed with less care. The → Caeretan hydriae belong in the last third of the 6th cent. and were characterized by a few striking scenes from mythology.

→ Pottery, shapes and types of; → Orientalizing vase painting; → Ornaments

R.M. Cook, P. Dupont, East Greek Pottery, 1998 (with individual finds); R.M. Cook, Greek Painted Pottery, [3]1997, 109–134; R.M. Cook, Clazomenian Sarcophagi, 1981; J.M. Cook, A List of Clazomenian Pottery, in: ABSA 60, 1952, 123–152; A.A. Lemos, Archaic Pottery of Chios, 1991; G.P. Schaus, Two Fikellura Vase Painters, in: ABSA 81, 1986, 251–295; W. Schiering, Werkstätten orientalisierender Keramik auf Rhodos, 1957.

G.P.S.

Ebionaei (Greek Ἐβιωναῖοι; *Ebiōnaîoi*, from Hebr. אֶבְיוֹנִים < *æbyōnīm*, '[the] Poor'). Since → Irenaeus (Haer. 1,26,2); the usual collective term for selected, heterodox Jewish-Christian groups in antiquity. The name was wrongly interpreted as pejorative by Patristic authors (Euseb. Hist. eccl. 3,27; Orig. contra Celsum 2,1: 'poor of mind') or, since Tertullianus (De praescriptione haereticorum 10,8; also Hippolytus, refutatio omnium haeresium 7,35,1), ascribed to a homonymous namegiver Ebion, supposedly a pupil of → Cerinthus. In fact, this was an honorary title of pious Jews (Ebionaei: 'those poor before God', cf. Ps 25,9; 68,11; Romans 15,26; Gal 2,10) which is also documented in the NT. Apart from the notes of the Christian heresiologists, the so-called Ebionaei gospel, which can be reconstructed from quotations in → Epiphanius of Salamis (panarion 30, 13–22), deserves consideration as a source. The assessment of an interaction between the Ebionaei and the original community ('not likely', [3. 312]) as a result of missionary activities and Christian emigration into the land east of the Jordan; the same applies to the Ebionitic influence on the older strata of the Pseudo-Clementines.

Despite the various ways in which the Ebionaei manifested themselves, single characteristics can be identified (cf. [4. 951]): 1) the adherence to the law of

Moses (Sabbath, circumcision, Jewish feasts) combined with professing monotheism and the worship of Jacob, the Lord's brother, as an example of piously abiding by the law, 2) the (later) rejection of sacrifices in cult, 3) the recognition, made possible by the coming of Jesus as the one chosen by God, of 'forged' pericopes, 4) the rejection of parts of the OT (prophets) and of Paulus as a renegade in terms of the law, 5) a gnosticly influenced Christology which emphasized the human nature of Jesus. The presence of the Ebionaei can be demonstrated in Asia Minor, Egypt and Syria well into the 5th cent. They also influenced the Mandaeans and Islamic literature (→ Koran).

1 A.F. J. Klijn, G.J. Reinink, Patristic evidence for Jewish-Christian Sects, 1973 (Sources) 2 J.M. Magnin, Notes sur l'Ebionisme, in: Proche-Orient Chrétien 23, 1973, 233–265; 24, 1974, 225–250; 25, 1975, 245–273; 28, 1978, 220–248 3 G. Strecker, s.v. Judenchristentum, TRE 17, 310–325 4 H. Merkel, s.v. Ebjoniten. Evangelisches Kirchenlexikon³ 1, 949–951 5 D. Vigne, Christ en Jourdain. Le baptême de Jésus dans la tradition judéo-chrétienne, 1992, 32–36, 108–115, 147–152.

J.RI.

Ebla Town in North West Syria (today Tall Mardīḫ, *c.* 60 km southwest of Aleppo). Excavations since 1964 show proof of extensive building developments from the 3rd and 2nd millennia BC; since 1974, substantial archives with *c.* 17,000 clay tablets and fragments (24th/23rd cents. BC) have come to light. They are written in the → Cuneiform script adopted from Mesopotamia and composed in an archaic Semitic language on whose character there are differing opinions (→ Eblaite). So far, they represent the earliest written documents from North West Syria. These are principally administrative documents. Texts of significance in terms of the history of events are hardly represented (i.a. the letter of a ruler from → Mari to the one of E. as well as a trade contract with a city state on the Euphrates). Archaeological and written sources confirm the role of the state of E. as an important centre in North West Syria in the 24th/23rd cents. BC, but its territory cannot be delineated exactly. It is likely that, in the east, it reached as far as the Euphrates and, in the west, as far as the Orontes. It appears that, in the north, Ḥalab/Aleppo (already mentioned in the E. texts) was associated with E. and, in the south, possibly the region of Ḥama. In the palace, the 'House of the King', numerous servants were employed. Attached to the palace was an administrative centre where several thousand dependent workers as well as specialized craftsmen and messengers were employed. Agriculture, animal husbandry and commerce formed the economic base of the state of E. The most important agricultural area was the densely populated plain of → Aleppo controlled by E. and the undulating country adjoining in the west. E. maintained various commercial contacts, but in particular with Emar (today Maskana), an important entrepôt on the → Euphrates, as well as with Mari situated further down river. Thus, E. enjoyed a connection with trade links reaching far into the East. On the other hand, finds of Egyptian origin indicate connections to the eastern Mediterranean region as well. For the Mesopotamian rulers → Sargon and → Naramsin, E. was one of the targets of their military campaigns into northern Syria. Whether the massive destruction of buildings, which occurred during the 24th/23rd cents. BC, can be traced back to this event or a different one is not clear. During the time of the 3rd Ur dynasty (21st cent. BC), E. maintained commercial contacts with south Mesopotamia. For the 1st half of the 2nd millennium BC, a connection with the Middle Kingdom in Egypt has been demonstrated with the aid of archaeological finds. Parts of a literary text from → Ḫattuša [2. 189] refer to a destruction of E. in the 18th cent.; after that, E. lost its importance and was given up for good in the 2nd cent. BC [3. 182].

1 A. Archi, Fifteen Years of Studies in Ebla: A Summary, in: OLZ 88, 1993, 461– 471 2 V. Haas, I. Wegner, Stadtverfluchungen aus Boghazköy, in: U. Finkbeiner et al. (ed.), Beitr. zur Kulturgesch. Vorderasiens, 1996 3 P. Matthiae, s.v. E., The Oxford Encyclopedia of Archaeology in the Ancient Near East, 1997.

H.KL.

Eblaite The texts from palace G in → Ebla (24th cent. BC) are the oldest written records found in North West Syria so far. They reflect a complex linguistic situation: along with the cuneiform script, Sumerian and Akkadian texts from Mesopotamia were also imported, and the local material itself is not homogenous. The Semitic idiom (→ Semitic languages) used in local texts (of which the bilingual lexical lists are particularly important), which is closely related to → Akkadian, is called Eblaite. To be differentiated from that language is a linguistic layer that can be associated with the later → northwest Semitic languages, which is evident most of all in personal names. After all, numerous personal names and place names belong to a non-Semitic layer. Eblaite is to be classified rather as an Akkadian dialect than as an independent branch of 'east Semitic'. The phonetic level is more archaic than that of Old Akkadian. Apart from important morphological correspondences with Akkadian, phonological changes related to the substrate language can be observed. Apart from significant isoglosses with Akkadian, the vocabulary also shows many peculiarities.

L. Cagni (ed.), La Lingua di Ebla, 1981; P. Fronzaroli, Per una valutazione della morfologia eblaita, in: Studi Eblaiti 5, 1982, 93–120; Id. (ed.), Studies on the Language of Ebla, 1984; M. Krebernik, The Linguistic Classification of Eblaite, in: J.S. Cooper, G.M. Schwartz (ed.), The Study of the Ancient Near East in the 21st Century, 1996, 233–249.

M.KR.

Ebony As *ébenos* (ἔβενος) or *ebénē* (ἐβένη; since Hdt. 3,97: 200 logs of ebony as tribute of the Ethiopians to the Persian Great King) and *hebenus* (since Verg. G. 2,115f.), the precious and very long lasting (Plin. HN

16,213) heartwood imported from India (cf. Str. 15,1,37) and black Africa (cf. Str. 17,2,2) was famous in antiquity; it was derived from various deciduous trees of the genus *Diospyros* (*D. ebenum* in India, *hirsutum* and *haplostylis* in Africa) belonging to the family of the Ebenaceae. In his report on Indian trees, Pliny (HN 12,20), like his source Theophrastus (Hist. pl. 4,4,6), differentiated a treelike Ethiopian type from a less valuable one from India. The best description of the two types is given by Dioscorides (1,98 [1. 89] and 1,129 [2. 113f.]). Reportedly, the Artemis statue in the temple of → Ephesus was made of ebony (Plin. HN 16,213). Crushed with a grinding stone, it was supposed to help against eye ailments (Theophr. Hist. pl. 9,20,4, in Plin. HN 24, 89; similarly Dioscorides). Because of its high price, fakes already occurred in those times (thus Dioscorides; [3. 134]).

1 M. Wellmann 2 2 J. Berendes 3 K. Koch, Die Bäume und Sträucher des alten Griechenlands, [2]1884.

C.HÜ.

Ebora Whether the name E. is Iberian, Ligurian or Celtic, remains unclear [1. vol. 1, 1394; vol. 2, 205; 2. 68; 3. 150].

[1] Town of the Carpetani, today Montalba on the Tajo. The town *Aebura* referred to in Livy (40,30; 32f.) is probably identical with *Libora* (Ptol. 2,6,56; Geogr. Rav. 4,44, *Lebura*; but cf. CIL II p. 111 s. *Caesarobriga*).

[2] Today Évora in Portugal (Alentejo); its identity is confirmed by inscriptions and archaeological remains (fort, aqueduct, temple) (CIL II p. 13; no. 110; 114; 504; 339; Suppl. p. 805; no. 5187; 5199; 5450). Plin. HN 3,10: *Ebora, quae Ceriaralitas Iulia* ... . Both are probably identical, as well as with the place names mentioned in Str. 3,1,9 (*Eboûra*), Ptol. 2,4,9 (*Ebora*) and Ptol. 2,5,6 (*Ebura*). There are also suppositions about other towns with the same name [4. 1896; 5. 2753]. E. was no doubt important, even during the times of the Visigoths as the location of a mint and a diocese. [6. 446]: *Elbora, Elvora, Ebora*. Coins: [7. vol. 3, 105; vol. 4, 119].

1 Holder 2 A. Schulten, Numantia 1, 1914 3 Id., Fontes Hispaniae Antiquae 6 4 E. Hübner, s.v. E., RE 5, 1896–1898 5 Enciclopedia Universal Ilustrada 18, s.v. Ebura 6 A. Schulten, Fontes Hispaniae Antiquae 12, 1947 7 A. Vives, La moneda hispánica, 1926.

Tovar, 1, 1974, 52; Tovar, 2, 1976, 217f.; Tovar 3, 1989, 232f., 302, 420.

P.B.

Eboracum (Today York). With its strategically favourable location in the heart of the Vale of York, E. presented itself to the Romans as a base for their military control of northern Britannia. The earliest garrison was stationed in E. under Q. Petilius Cerealis in AD 71/74 [1]. The legionary camp (*legio IX Hispana*) was a wood-earth fort of the 70s; the reconstruction in stone took place in the early 2nd cent. The *legio VI Victrix* replaced the *legio IX Hispana* between 109 and 120. The fortifications were renovated in connection with the military campaigns of the Severi in the early 3rd cent.; a further building program under Constantius Chlorus was carried out after 296. He planned the reinstatement of the defences at the river, including the towers which were located outside; the western corner tower still exists. The military occupation forces were probably reduced in the 4th cent., but the fortress remained a centre for the defence of → Britannia up to the end of Roman rule. Civil settlements developed starting from the fortress and extending across the River Ouse and attained special importance in the 2nd cent. In the 3rd cent., possibly during Septimius Severus' stay, E. was elevated to a *colonia*. E. flourished and expanded, of which buildings and grave sites are testimony [2]. Apart from other crafts, the use of jet (bituminous lignite/brown coal) was continued. E. remained important up to the time of the kingdom of Northumbria.

1 B. Hartley, L. Fitts, The Brigantes, 1988, 19 2 Royal Commission on historical monuments, York 1: E., 1962.

M.TO.

Eborarii see → Ivory

Eburnus Cognomen ('ivory coloured'), derived from the skin or hair colour of Q. Fabius Maximus Eburnus, *cos.* 116 BC (Ps. Quint. Decl. mai. 3,17; with an obscene meaning in Arnob. 4,26).

Kajanto, Cognomina 227.

K.-L.E.

Eburodunum

[1] Main town of the Caturiges. On a rocky plinth towering above the Durance, the pre-Roman *oppidum* and the Roman town occupied the place of today's urban development (Embrun). Important station on the road from southern Gaul to northern Italy.

P.-A. Fevrier, Archéologie dans les Hautes-Alpes, 1991, 242–244.

Y.L.

[2] Gallo-Roman *vicus* with a pre-Roman sulphur spring still in use today, extended to a fort in late antiquity, today's Yverdon-les-Bains.

W. Drack, R. Fellmann, Die Römer in der Schweiz, 1988, 562–565.

G.W.

Eburones People in Gallia Belgica, the most important one amongst the Germani Cisrhenani (Caes. B Gall. 2,4); they were clients of the Treveri in the south; in between the two were the lands of the Germanic → Condrusi and Segni (Caes. B Gall. 4,6; 6,32). In the north, the E. shared a border with the coastal people of the Menapii (Caes. B Gall. 6,5). The core of their areas of settlement between Maas and Rhine (Caes. B Gall. 5,24) comprised the northern Ardennes, the Eiffel and the plains extending across the lower reaches of the rivers. With the → Aduatuci in the west, there was a possible partial congruence (Caes. B Gall. 5,27; 6,32; 38) [1]. Under their leaders → Ambiorix and Catavolcus, the E. in 54 BC inflicted on Caesar one of his worst defeats (Caes. B Gall. 5,24–52; Liv. Epit. 106f.; Cass. Dio 40,5–11). The revenge campaigns of the following years lead to the thorough destruction of the E. (Caes. B Gall. 6,5; 29–34; 8,24f.); but their complete annihilation is unlikely. The E. were partly absorbed by newly emerged tribes, the Tungri and the immigrated Ubii. It is possible that the Sunuci (Plin. HN 4,106; Tac. Hist. 4,66) are the remainders of the E. mentioned in Str. 4,3,5.

1 L. Rübekeil, Suebica, 1992, 174f.

H. Galsterer, Des Éburons aux Agrippiniens, in: Cahiers du Centre G. Glotz 3, 1992, 107–121; TIR M 79. F.SCH.

Ebusus (Ἔβουσος; *Ébousos*). According to archaeological finds, the larger one of the two → Pityussae ('Spruce islands'), Ibiza and Formentera, was settled around the middle of the 7th cent. BC, initially under the name of *'ybšm* by Phoenician colonists from the Straits of Gibraltar. The founding of a settlement by Carthage reported in Diod. Sic. 5,16,1–3, evidently refers to an expansion carried out by the north African metropolis some 100 years later. Thanks to its prominent position, the town of E. became an important Punic entrepôt with acropolis, port quarters (covered by buildings today), extensive necropoleis (Puig des Molins) and rural sanctuaries (e.g. for Tanit, cave of Es Cuieram); in the 5th cent. BC, it had approximately 5,000 inhabitants. Already *civitas foederata* (Plin. HN 3,76) in the 2nd cent. BC, E. became *municipium Flavium Ebusitanum* in AD 79.
→ Tinnit

M. E. Aubet, Tiro y las colonias fenicias de Occidente, [2]1994, 289–293; C. Gómez Bellard, Die Phönizier auf Ibiza, in: MDAI(M) 34, 1993, 83–107; J. H. Fernández, s.v. Ibiza, DCPP, 222–226. H.-G.N.

Ecbatana (ancient Persian *Hāgmātana*, Greek Ἐκβάτανα, Ἀκβάτανα; *Ekbátana, Akbátana*), today Hamadān. Median capital, summer residence of the → Achaemenids (Xen. An. 3,5,15; Xen. Cyr. 8,6,22; Ael. NA 3,13; 10,6; Ezra 6,2) and Arsacids (→ Arsaces; Curt. 5,8,1; Str. 11,524), Seleucid Ἐπιφάνεια/*Epipháneia* (Steph. Byz. s.v. Ἀκβάτανα), later overtaken by Rhages. Today, the ruins of E. are largely buried under the modern city and thus are not accessible for archaeological research. The best description of E. can be found in Pol. 10,27,4–13, according to which the citadel — not the city — was fortified. This concurs with the fact that, today, no rampart is visible [11], but a massive brick platform instead. The seven walls around the 'house' of → Deioces (Hdt. 1,98f.) are probably a legend, but here, too, the people lived on the outside. Of the numerous objects having ended up in museums via the trade in antiques, their claimed provenance being E./Hamadān is doubtful in some cases [3]. The temple of 'Aiñe,' referred to by Polybius, is probably the one of → Anahita in which Aspasia was consecrated (Plut. Artoxerxes 26,3; 27,3; Iust. 10,2); Arrianus (An. 7,14,5) also mentioned a 'seat' of Asclepius, which Alexander destroyed in anger over the death of → Hephaestion. The lion erected as a result of that incident, removed in the Islamic period [7], but a worshipped symbol today [10], was previously regarded as being Arsacid. In the surroundings of Hamadān, M. Azarnoush excavated a cemetery (1st cent. BC — 1st cent. AD) — the only published excavation [1; 2; 8]. The graves of 'Esther and Mordecai', first documented by Benjamin of Tudela, were traced back to a late, Jewish Sassanid queen [6]; but Jos. Ant. Iud. 10, 265 already recorded that, here, a Jew cared for the graves of the kings.

1 M. Azarnoush, Excavations at the Cemetery of Sang-e Šir area, in: Proc. of the 3rd Annual Symposium on Arch. Research in Iran (=ASARI), 1975, 51–72 2 Id., Second Season of Excavations at the Site of Sang-e Šir in Hamadan 1975, in: A. Abedi (ed.), Proc. of the 4th ASARI, 1976, 40–59 3 P. Calmeyer, s.v. Hamadan, RLA 4, 1972, 64–67 4 Id., Zu einigen vernachlässigten Aspekten medischer Kunst, in: Proc. of the 2nd ASARI, 1973, 112–127 5 I. M. Diakonoff, Media, Cambridge History of Iran II, 36–148 6 E. Herzfeld, Archaeological Hist. of Iran, 1935, 105f. 7 H. Luschey, Arch. Mitt. aus Iran, N.F. 1, 1968, 115–122 8 M. Mehryar, in: Proc. of the 3rd ASARI, 1975, 41–50 9 O. W. Muscarella, Annual Symposium, in: D. Schmandt-Besserat (ed.), Ancient Persia. The Art of an Empire, 1980, 23–42 10 S. Nadjmabadi, G. Gropp, in: Arch. Mitteilungen aus Iran, N.F. 1, 1968, 123–128 11 E. F. Schmidt, Flights over Ancient Iran, 1940, plate 91f. 12 L. Vanden Berghe, Archeologie de l'Iran ancien 1959, 108–110, 190f. plates 135–138. PE.C.

Ecclesiastical/Religious law

I. Old Testament II. Graeco-Roman Antiquity

I. Old Testament

A religious law in the sense of a legal system existing alongside profane law or even preceding it, cannot be reconstructed for the old Israel. At the centre of recent discussions is the question of the 'theologizing' or the 'Jahvism' of the law. This refers especially to the concept occurring in Exodus (Ex 20,1 ff.: Decalogue and book of the covenant) of a God → Jehova as a lawgiver who thus functionally occupies a domain which in the Old Orient was reserved for royalty. By way of this construction, the Israelite law is not only legitimized by the divine, but also promulgated. As a consequence, social and criminal regulations (e.g. 2nd Tablet of the Decalogue) appear alongside those that regulate practising the cult and the Jehovah worship (1st Tablet of the Decalogue; altar law in Ex 20,22 ff.; so-called 'cultic Decalogue' in Ex 34,10–26). Here, the juxtaposition of religious and profane articles of law accentuates the fact that social action always has a religious dimension as well, which also becomes evident in the prayer literature of the → psalms. The background to this new concept of law is the social and political experiences of crisis in the 8th cent. BC, which in the Book of Deuteronomy result in the factual ties of the king to the Torah and prophecy (→ Prophet) via the so-called 'office laws' (Deut. 17,14–20). The question whether this 'legal system' was ever practised in the sense of current law or — which is more probable — it has to be understood as a literary compilation of legal scholarship motivated by the loss of sovereignty in the 6th cent. BC, is not yet settled.

1 R. BACH, Gottesrecht und weltliches Recht in der Verkündigung des Propheten Amos, in: W. SCHNEEMELCHER (ed.), FS G. Dehn, 1957, 23–34 2 B. JANOWSKI, JHWH der Richter — ein rettender Gott. Psalm 7 und das Motiv des Gottesgerichts, in: JBTh 9, 1994, 53–85 3 H. NIEHR, Rechtsprechung in Israel. Unt. zur Gesch. der Gerichtsorganisation im Alten Testament, 1987 4 E. OTTO, Wandel der Rechtsbegründungen in der Gesellschaftsgesch. des antiken Israel, 1988 5 Id., Theologische Ethik des Alten Testaments, 1994. TH.PO.

II. GRAECO-ROMAN ANTIQUITY

For the history of ancient religion, the concept of 'religious law' is a common neologism since the end of the 19th cent., which particularly wants to emphasize the legalization process (set off against Greek → mythology) of Roman religion (fundamental treatment in [1]; see also [2. 380] with the Latinization *ius sacrum*). There is no ancient concept for this, and it cannot be there because there is no comprehensive concept of → religion.

The *ius divinum* refers to the property claims of the Gods; regarding other 'special rights', they are usually modern collective terms formed on an *ad hoc* basis (*ius pontificale*, pontifical law), which in antiquity were systematically regarded as part of public → law (*ius publicum*), not as areas of independent concepts of law.

The neologism 'religious law' is sometimes also used by scholars in connection with the so-called 'sacred laws' (*leges sacrae*) of Greek and Roman antiquity, but these texts are cultic and administrative temple statutes as well as 'stage directions' for ritual activities laid down in writing; they are not a genre of text that could be adequately described by the modern legal concept contained in the term 'religious law'.

1 E. PERNICE, Zum röm. Sakralrecht I, in: SB der königl. Preuss. Akademie der Wiss. zu Berlin 2, 1885, 1143–1169 2 G. WISSOWA, Rel. und Kultus der Römer, [2]1912 ([1]1902). J.R.

Ecdemus (Ἔκδημος; *Ékdēmos*) or Ecdelus (Ἔκδηλος; *Ékdēlos*, thus Plutarch, Polybius) from Megalopolis. Academic philosopher of the 3rd cent. BC, pupil of Arcesilaus who is mainly known because of his many and diverse political activities (Plut. Aratus 5: 'a philosopher and a man of action at the same time', ἀνὴρ φιλόσοφος καὶ πρακτικός cf. Id., Philopoemen 1); (Pol. 10,22; cf. Paus. 8,49,1): he was a teacher of Philopoemen; together with Demophanes, he liberated his home town of Aristodemus' tyranny and supported Aratus of Sicyon during the expulsion of the tyrant Nicocles; finally, he followed a call to Cyrene for the establishment of a new constitution.

→ Aratus; → Philopoemen K.-H.S.

Ecdicius (Ἐκδίκιος; *Ekdíkios*)

[1] Born in Ancyra, 'Heathen' (Lib. Ep. 267; 1419). In AD 360, he was governor (*consularis*?) in Galatia (Lib. Ep. 308). Ecdicius is the recipient of numerous letters from Libanius (Epist. 267; 1419 and others). But he is probably not identical with the *praef. Aegypti* of AD 362/3, Ecdicius Olympus (Cod. Theod. 15,1,8f.) who came from Cilicia and studied with Libanius in Athens (Lib. Ep. 147). PLRE 1, 276, 647f. W.P.

[2] Arvernian from a senator's family, son of the emperor → Avitus [1], brother-in-law of Sidonius Apollinaris, received an excellent education (in Clermont). Around AD 469, he was probably at the court of → Anthemius [2]; probably in 471 he organized the defence of Clermont against the Visigoths using his own means. During a famine in Burgundy in 473, he supplied the (suffering) population with food. In 474, Iulius Nepos awarded the *patricius* title to him for his achievements and probably made him a *magister utriusque militiae* (Sid. Apoll. Epist. 3,3; 5,16; Iord. Get. 240; Greg. Tur. Franc. 2,24). PLRE 2, 383f., no. 3. M.MEI.

Ecetra Main settlement of the Volsci; its exact location to the north of the Monti Lepini is not known (Liv. 4,61,5; 6,31,5). An ongoing obstacle for the Romans [1. 649; 2. 100] (Liv. 3,10,8; Dion. Hal. Ant. Rom. 8,4), E. even stood up to them (at the end of the 5th cent. BC) after the fall of → Antium [3. 434], which was allied to E. (Liv. 4,59,1; Diod. Sic. 14,16,5). The Ecetrani, *de facto* displaced by the Privernati, are still found in Liv. 6,31 for 378 BC; thereafter, their traces vanish. The name of the town, which particularly in its Greek form Ἐχέτρα (*Echétra*), similar to *Cimetra* (Liv. 10,15,6) or *Velitrae*, is possibly of Etruscan origin.

1 NISSEN 2 2 G. DE SANCTIS, Storia dei Romani 2, 1960 3 L. PARETI, Storia di Roma 1, 1952.

G. COLONNA, I Latini e gli altri popoli del Lazio, in: G. PUGLIESE CARRATELLI (ed.), Italia omnium terrarum alumna, 1987, 519–521; M. NAFISSI, s.v. Volsci, EV 5.1, 617–619. A.SA.

Echeclus (Ἔχεκλος; *Écheklos*).

[1] Son of the Trojan Agenor, killed by Achilles (Hom. Il. 20,474). Paus. 10,27,2 points to a parallel motive in the *Iliad parva* (18 PEG I) where the son of Achilles, Neoptolemus, kills the father of E.

W. KULLMANN, Die Quellen der Ilias, Hermes ES 14, 1960, 354; P. WATHELET, Dictionnaire des Troyens de l'Iliade, vol. 1, 1988, 555f.

[2] Trojan, killed by Patroclus (Hom. Il. 16,694).

P. WATHELET, Dictionnaire des Troyens de l'Iliade, vol. 1, 1988, 556.

[3] Centaur (Ov. Met. 12,450). R.B.

Echecrates (Ἐχεκράτης; *Echekrátēs*).
[1] Thessalian condottiere of Ptolemy IV, whose training of the army and especially the cavalry significantly contributed to the victory at Raphia in 217 BC. In that battle, he commanded the right wing of the cavalry. An anecdotally coloured representation of the battle is recorded in Diod. Sic. 16,26,6. PP 2, 2161. W.A.
[2] Pythagorean from Phleius, who together with Phanton, Polymnastos and Diocles, who also came from Phleius, as well as Xenophilus from Chalcidice, was one of the last representatives of the 'mathematical' branch of Pythagoreanism (Aristox. fr. 18f. WEHRLI = Iambl. VP 251 and Diog. Laert. 8,46; [1. 198]; cf. Diod. Sic. 15,76,4; Iambl. VP 267). Granting his wish, Phaedo reported in Plato's dialogue of the same title about Socrates' death. In Pl. Phd. 88d, E. expresses sympathy for the (Pythagorean?) idea that the soul is a *harmonía* (ἁρμονία) [2]. Cic. Fin. 5,87 and Val. Max. 8,7,3 make him into Plato's teacher; in the Pseudo-Platonic 9th letter, he is referred to as a 'youth' (νεανίσκος; *neanískos*) (358b). There is no consensus on his being identical with the E. who is the source of the historian Timaeus on the southern Italian Lokrians [1. 92 n. 40].
→ Pythagorean School

1 W. BURKERT, Lore and Science in Ancient Pythagoreanism, 1972 2 C. A. HUFFMAN, Philolaus of Croton, 1993, 324, 326f. C.RI.

Echedemus (Ἐχέδημος; *Echédēmos*). Prominent Athenian from Cydathenaeum [1. 189–193], tried in vain in 190 BC to mediate between the Aetolians and the Romans, i.a. with P. Cornelius Scipio (Pol. 21,4–5; Liv. 37,6; 7) [2. 277–288], and in 185/4 contributed decisively to the reorganization of the Delphian → amphictyony [3. 213].

1 C. HABICHT, Studien zur Gesch. Athens in hell. Zeit, 1982 2 P. PANTOS, E., the Second Attic Phoibos, in: Hesperia 58, 1989 3 HABICHT. L.-M.G.

Echeia (ἠχεῖα; *ēcheîa*). Instruments/objects producing or amplifying sound (echo). Vitruvius refers to *echia* as bronze vessels with a wide opening, which were used for resonance reinforcement in the theatre (Vitr. De arch. 1,1,9; 5,5). Tuned to various keys, they were supposedly installed under the rows of seats according to mathematical calculations. They did not exist in Rome, but L. Mummius is said to have brought pieces of loot of this type back from Corinth. However, nothing in the theatre of Corinth points to such an installation [1. 28]. Neither in Greek theatres, whose acoustics are excellent anyway [2. 58–60], nor in Italic ones are there any conclusive traces so far. It is possible that Vitruvius, following the teachings on harmony by → Aristoxenus, took speculation for reality [3. 270].

1 R. STILLWELL, Corinth 2: The Theatre, 1952 2 H.-D. BLUME, Einführung in das antike Theaterwesen, [3]1991 3 H. BULLE, Unt. an griech. Theatern, 1928.

E. GRAF, s.v. ἠχεῖα, RE 5, 1908f.; A. LESKY, Noh-Bühne und griech. Theater, in: Maia 15, 1963, 42–44; P. THIELSCHER, Schallgefäße, in: FS Dornseiff, 1953, 334–371. H.BL.

Echelidae (Ἐχελίδαι; *Echelídai*, from ἕλος; *hélos*, 'Swamp'?). Locality (*dḗmos* according to Steph. Byz. s.v. Ἐχελίδαι; EM s.v. Ἔχελος) in Attica in the plain near the mouth of the Kephisos close to the 'Long Wall' leading to Phalerum, slightly north of today's Neofaliron on the territory of the Demos Xypete [2; 3. 87]. JUDEICH and MILCHHÖFER [1; 2] suspect that the hippodromos of Athens was located there.

1 W. JUDEICH, Top. von Athen, [2]1931, 456 2 A. MILCHHÖFER, s.v. E., RE 5, 1911 3 TRAILL, Attica, 50, 86f., 114 no. 10. H.LO.

Echembrotus (Ἐχέμβροτος; *Echémbrotos*) Arcadian aulode and elegist. Paus. 10,7,5–6 reports about his victory in the aulode competition during the newly arranged Pythian Games in 586 BC and quotes his verse(?) epigram on a tripod in Thebes dedicated to Hercules. His description as a singer of μέλεα καὶ ἐλέγους is the earliest record of the term *élegoi*.

IEG 2, 62; M. L. WEST, Studies in Greek Elegy and Iambus, 1974. E.BO.

Echemmon (Ἐχέμμων; *Echémmōn*).
[1] A son of Priamus. He was killed at the same time as his brother Chromius of Diomedes (Hom. Il. 5,160; Apollod. 3,153).

P. WATHELET, Dictionnaire des Troyens de l'Iliade, vol. 1, 1988, 557f.

[2] A Nabataean who was killed by Perseus (Ov. Met. 5,163; 176). Ovid at this point adopts the Homeric motif from Hom. Il. 5,159–165 (cf. E. [1]).

F. BÖMER, P. Ovidius Naso, Met. B. 4–5 (comm.), 1976, 264. R.B.

Echemus (Ἔχεμος; *Échemos*).
[1] King of Tegea in Arcadia, son of Aeropos, married to Leda's daughter Timandra who left him (Hes. Cat. fr. 23a, 31–35; 176,3–4; Paus. 8,5,1; Apollod. 3,126). E. won in an Olympic wrestling match (Pind. Ol. 10,66). Due to his victory in single combat against Heracles' son Hyllus, E. is said to have checked the advance of the Heraclids into the Peloponnese by 50 (Diod. Sic. 4,58,3–5) or 100 years (Hdt. 9,26). A relief fragment

shows E. as an heroic fighter [1]. Paus. 8,53,10 describes the grave of E. in Tegea.

1 U. KRON, s.v. E., LIMC 3.1, 676 no. 1.

[2] Dicaearchus (fr. 66 WEHRLI) associates E. with the revenge campaign of the Dioscuri to Attica and equates him with the eponym of the academy (→ Academus). R.B.

Echephron (Ἐχέφρων; *Echéphrōn*).
[1] Son of Nestor (Hom. Od. 3,413; 439; Apollod. 1,94).
[2] Son of Hercules and Psophis, twin brother of → Promachos. R.B.

Echepolus (Ἐχέπωλος; *Echépōlos*, 'Horse owner').
[1] Pelopid, son of an Anchises from Sicyon. He gave Agamemnon the mare Aithe and thus bought his release from the journey to Troy (Hom. Il. 23,296 with schol.)

W. KULLMANN, Die Quellen der Ilias, Hermes ES 14, 1960, 261.

[2] A Trojan who was killed by Antilochus (Hom. Il. 4,458).

P. WATHELET, Dictionnaire des Troyens de l'Iliade, vol. 1, 1988, 558–560. R.B.

Echestratus (Ἐχέστρατος; *Echéstratos*). Legendary Spartan king, son of Agis I, father of Labotas and thus the third king from the house of the Agiads (Hdt. 7,204). According to Paus. 3,2,2, the Cynureans are said to have been expelled from the Argolis in the reign of E. M.MEI.

Echetla (Ἐχέτλα; *Echétla*). Town in the interior of Sicily, neighbouring Leontini, Syracusae and Camarina (Diod. Sic. 20,32), in the border region between the spheres of influence of Carthage and Hieron II (Pol. 1,15,10). Besieged by the Romans at the beginning of the 1st Punic War. Plin. HN 3,91 calls the citizens of E. *stipendiarii*. Judging from the similarity in name, E. was located on the hill Occhialà near Grammichele east of Caltagirone where Siculan-Greek remains and a Demeter sanctuary were found.

D. PALERMO, s.v. Grammichele, BTCGI 7, 164–169; R. M. ALBANESE PROCELLI, La necropoli di Madonna del Piano presso Grammichele: osservazioni sul rituale funerario, in: Kokalos 38, 1992, 33–68. GI.F.

Echetlus, Echetlaeus (Ἔχετλος, Ἐχετλαῖος; *Échetlos, Echetlaîos*). A man of peasant demeanour who in the battle of Marathon killed many Persians with his plough (*echétlē*, 'plough handle') and subsequently disappeared. Because of an oracle, the Athenians worshipped him as the Hero Echetlaeus. On the painting of the battle of Marathon in the Stoa Poikile, he was depicted with a plough in his hand (Paus. 1,15,3; 32,5)

M.H. JAMESON, The Hero Echetlaeus, in: TAPhA 82, 1951, 49–61; J.G. SZILÁGYI, s.v. Echetlos, LIMC 3.1, 677–678. R.B.

Echetus (Ἔχετος; *Échetos*, 'Holder'). Cruel king with whom the suitor Antinous threatened the beggar Irus and Odysseus (Hom. Od. 18,85; 116; 21,308; Suda s.v. E. 493 ADLER). He blinded his daughter Amphissa (or Metope) and had her crush ore in a chamber; he dismembered her lover Aechmodicus (Apoll. Rhod. 4,1093 with schol.). Schol. Hom. Od. 18,85 (= Marsyas FGrH 135–136 F 19) explains that he was a Sicilian tyrant who tortured strangers, but who was eventually stoned by his own subjects.

J. RUSSO et al., Homer's Odyssey, vol. 3 (comm.), 1992, 52f. R.B.

Echidna (Ἔχιδνα; *Échidna*). Primeval female creature in the shape of a snake, introduced into Greece due to the influence of Near East narrative art and iconography (Iluyanka for the Hittites, Tiamat in Mesopotamia). In Hesiod, E. is the daughter of the sea creatures Phorcys and Ceto (Theog. 295–303) and, together with → Typhon who also often occurs in the body of a snake, mother of a series of monsters — of Orthrus the dog of the triple-bodied → Geryoneus, of → Cerberus, of → Hydra, of → Chimaera, of the → Sphinx (Φίξ; *Phíx* in Hesiod) and of the lion of → Nemea. Later authors add → Scylla (Hyg. Fab. 151) as well as the snake of the Hesperids and the eagle of → Prometheus (Apollod. 2,113; 119). Her abode is either at the edge of the known world – amongst the Arimoi in Lydia (Hes. Theog. 304; cf. Hom. Il. 2,783) or amongst the Scythians as whose progenitress she was regarded by the Greeks (Hdt. 4,8f.) – or in the Underworld (Aristoph. Ran. 473). A local story makes her into a Peloponnesian highway robber who is killed by Argus (Apollod. 2,4). In the Greek reflection of the Scythian myth of origin, she is the mother by Hercules of three sons, i.a. of the eponymous Scythes (Diod. Sic. 2,43,3; cf. IG XIV 1293 A 96).

J. FONTENROSE, Python. A Study of Delphic Mythology, 1959, 94–97; R. HOSEK, s.v. E., LIMC 3.1, 678f.; F. MORA, Religione e religioni nelle storie di Erodoto, 1985. F.G.

Echinades (Ἐχινάδες, Ἐχῖναι; *Echinádes, Echînai*). Archipelago off the SW coast of Acarnania and the mouth of the Achelous; today, it belongs to the nomos Cephallenia. The islands were largely uninhabited, but they were exploited economically (Dion. Hal. Ant. Rom. 1,51). Already in antiquity it was observed that the islands became joined to the mainland due to the → Achelous [1] depositing debris into the area (Hdt. 2,10; Thuc. 2,102; Scyl. 34; Str. 1,3,18; 10,2,19 [1; 2]). This phenomenon was also incorporated into the myths. No later than the 2nd cent. AD (Paus. 8,24,11), the silting-up process was completed because the deposits now reached into the deep Cephallenia trench. Individual islands were sometimes regarded as being part of the E., sometimes they are mentioned separately: in the south the Oxeiai islands Artemita, Dolicha and the former island of Nasos near Oeniadae [3], in the north the Taphiai islands situated between Leukas and the mainland. Because of their prominent location, the E. were frequently mentioned in itineraries and portulans right up to the Middle Ages (Plin. HN 4,53f. with all names; It. Ant. 488; [4]).

1 Philippson/Kirsten 2, 2, 396, 406–409 2 W. M. Murray, The coastal sites of W-Akarnania, thesis 1982, 18–30 3 Id., The location of Nasos, in: Hesperia 54, 1985, 97–108 4 Soustal, Nikopolis, 96f.

E. Oberhummer, Akarnanien, 1887, 15, 20–23, 241f. D.S.

Echinoderms (Greek ὀστρακόδερμα/*ostrakóderma*) or crustaceans. They partly correspond with today's phylum of the *Echinodermata*, i.e. the marine feather stars, starfishes and brittle stars, the → sea urchins and sea cucumbers. Aristotle who gave them the name and lists in Hist. an. 1,6,490b10 the phylum as that of the → shells (*óstrea*), does however also include the → sponges (modern phylum *Porifera*), sea anemones (modern class *Anthozoa* of the phylum jellyfish, *Cnidaria*), sea squirts (*ascidia*, modern class of sea squirts, tunicates), and the marine and land snails (modern phylum molluscs, *Mollusca*). Despite this erroneous classification he had the best knowledge in antiquity of the echinoderm cf. Aristot. Hist. an. 4,4–7,527b35–531b17; 4,11,537b24 f. and 537b31–538a1; 5,12,544a15–24 and 5,15–16,546b15–549a13 as well as 7(8),2,590a18–b3; 7(8),13,599a10–20 and 7(8), 20, 603a12–28.

Keller 2, 571–574 (only echinoderms in the modern sense). C. HÜ.

Echinus (Ἐχῖνος; *Echînos*).

[1] Town on the northern shore of the Gulf of Malia near today's village of Achino. Originally part of the Achaea Phthiotis, Echinus was granted by Philippus II to the Malieis in 342 with whom E. belonged to the Aetolian league from *c.* 235. In 210, E. was conquered by Philippus V (Pol. 9,41; [1]) who refused to return it to the Aetolians; after 193, the Romans conquered it and assigned E. to Malis again in 189. In Roman times, E. was considered part of Achaea Phthiotis or Thessalia. New finds testify to a blossoming during the Imperial period. Under Justinian I, the fortifications were renovated. In 551, an earthquake with a tidal wave caused severe damage. From the 5th to the end of the 13th cent., there is evidence of E. being a bishop's seat while the town itself probably came to an end with the Slavic invasion of the 7th cent.

1 F. Stählin, Das hellenische Thessalien, 1924, 186f.

L. W. Daly, E. and Justinian's Fortifications in Greece, in: AJA 46, 1942, 500–508; M. P. Papakonstantinou, in: AD 90, 1985 II, 167f. (excavation report); id., Το νοτιό και το δυτικό τμήμα της Αχαΐας Φθιώτιδος απο τους κλασικούς μέχρι τους Ρωμαϊκούς χρόνους, in: R. Misdrache-Kapon, La Thessalie, quinze années de recherches archéologiques, 1975–1990: Act. du colloque international (Lyon 1990), 1994, 2, 229–238; TIB 1, 1976, 152. HE.KR.

[2] Town in Acarnania on the Gulf of Ambracia, its actual location being unknown. In the 4th cent. BC, ambassadors were sent to Athens (Stv 2, 305f.); several times target of the Peloponnesian *theōrodókoi*. Testimonies: Plin. HN 4,5; Steph. Byz. s.v. Ἐχῖνος

Pritchett 8, 93–101. D.S.

[3] from ἐχῖνος; *echînos*, 'Hedgehog; Sea urchin'. According to Vitruvius, it is the cushion-like support piece of the Doric (4,3,4) or the Tuscan (4,7,1) capital, which is located between the square abacus on top of it and the hypotrachelium, which merges into the shaft of the → column and was initially separated from the echinus with decorative ornamental bands and later with three or four rings (*anuli*); these three elements of the capital usually consisted of a single workpiece. What is called the echinus of the Ionian capital (without a basis in ancient usage) is the support pad between the volutes and the start of the shaft flutes which is often decorated with an → egg-and-dart moulding. The term echinus is not found in Greek architectural inscriptions; neither is any consistent terminology for the individual components of the capital; apparently the term ἐπίκρανον (*epíkranon*), alongside its local variants (for the capital overall), served as a collective term for all components of this workpiece. That the term echinus is based on the similarity of this building element with a sea urchin is etymological speculation.

Just as the → entasis, the echinus has an essential function for the visualising of load and tension conditions in Greek columned buildings which, particularly in the 6th cent. BC, is sometimes overemphasized by shaping the echinus with a broad and squashed flat appearance (1. Corfu, temple of Artemis; 2. Assus, temple of Athena). Furthermore, the continuous modifications of the echinus profiles from classically balanced round shapes (3. Olympia, temple of Zeus; 4. Athens, Parthenon) to the steeply rising funnel shape of the Hellenistic echinus (5. Priene, Agora) and to the button-like reduced mass of the Roman echinus (6. Cori, Hercules temple) provide an important dating aid for ancient architecture.

→ Column

Ebert, 25–27; K. Herrmann, Zum Dekor dorischer Kapitelle, in: Architectura 13, 1983, 1–12; D. Mertens, Der Tempel von Segesta und die dorische Tempelbaukunst des griech. Westens in klassischer Zeit, 1984, 134–138, suppl. 31, 32; Id., Der alte Heratempel in Paestum und die archaische Baukunst in Unteritalien, 1993, 18–27, 105–111; W. Müller-Wiener, Griech. Bauwesen in der Antike, 1988, 114f., 126; B. Wesenberg, Kapitelle und Basen, 32. Beih. BJ, 1971, 57–59. C.HÖ.

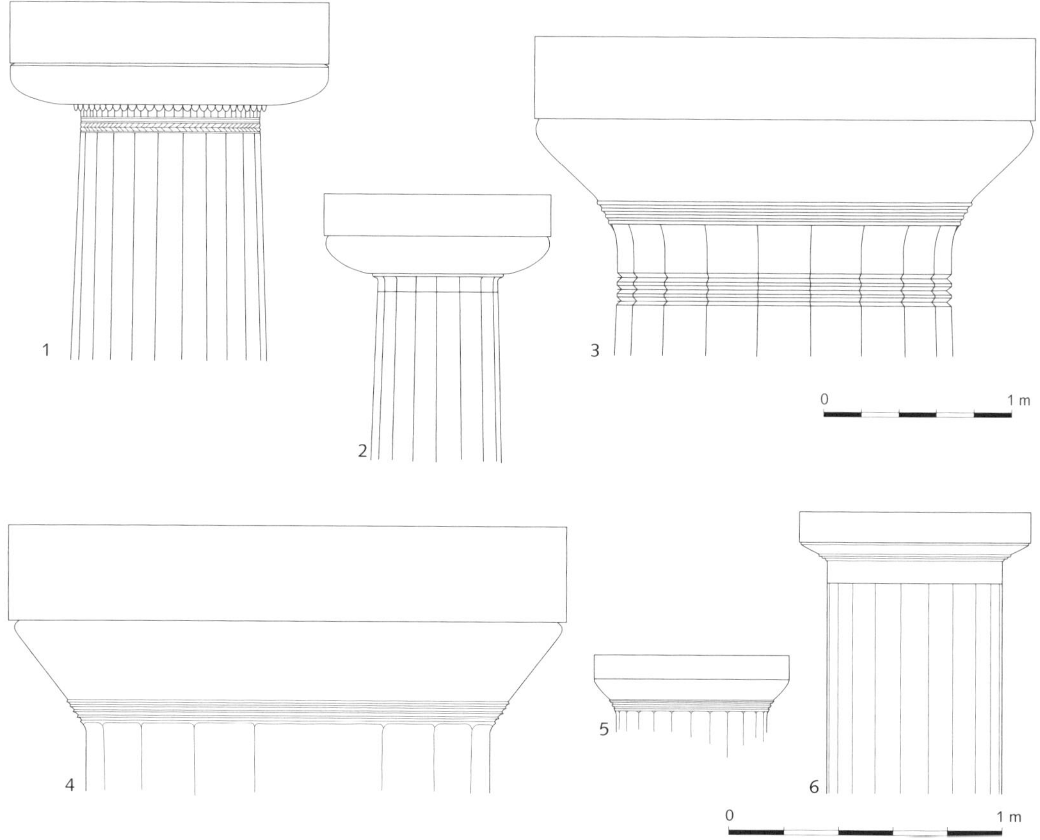

Different forms of echinus on Doric capitals
1. Corfu: Temple of Artemis (c. 580 BC)
2. Assos: Temple of Athena (6th cent. BC)
3. Olympia: Temple of Zeus (c. 472/1-457 BC)
4. Athens: Parthenon (447-438 BC)
5. Priene: Agora, southern stoa (Hellenistic)
6. Cori: Temple of Hercules (Roman)

Echion (Ἐχίων/*Echíōn*, 'Snake man', from ἡ ἔχις/*échis*, 'the Snake').

[1] One of the five 'Spartoi', the men who grew from the dragon teeth sown by → Cadmus into the Theban earth. He married Cadmus' daughter Agave and was the father of Pentheus (Paus. 9,5,3f.; Apollod. 3,26; 36; Hyg. Fab. 178,6; 184,1; Ov. Met. 3,126; cf. Hor. Carm. 4,4,64: *Thebae Echioniae*). Aeneas killed the Rutulian Onites, a son of E. and Peridia (Verg. Aen. 12,514f.).

R. Rocca, s.v. E., EV 2, 164f.

[2] Son of Hermes and Antianeira, his home being at the Pangaeum (Pind. Pyth. 4,178–180), in Thessaly (Apoll. Rhod. 1,52; Hyg. Fab. 14) or in Arcadia (Val. Fl. 7,543). Argonaut (Val. Fl. 4,734) and Calydonian hunter (Ov. Met. 8,311; 345). R.B.

Echnaton see → Amenophis [4] IV, see → Amarna

Echo (ἠχώ; *ēchṓ*).

[1] The origin and propagation of sound is explained as (contiguous) air moved by a blow (→ Acoustics); its reflection within a sound box (reverberation) or on a suitable, usually a smooth object, conceived of as reversal (resounding, echo), is also included in this explanation (Theophr. de sensu 9 [Empedocles], 53 [Democritus]; Aristot. An. 2,8, 419b 25ff., Probl. 11,6,899a 24–25 and 11,8,899b 25ff., probably after Aristoxenus; Lucr. 4,572–594). Echos were considered unfavourable for apiculture (Varro, Rust. 3,16,12; Verg. G. 4,50; Columella 9,5,6; Plin. HN 11,65); in buildings it was used i.a. in echo halls in Olympia (Plin. HN 26,100; Paus. 5,21,17) and Hermione (Paus. 2,35,10). F.KR.

[2] As a personification, it is documented since the 5th cent. BC (Pind. Ol. 14,20f.; Aristoph. Thesm. 1059ff. after Eur. fr. 118 TGF; Eubulus fr. 34 PCG). Its mythology is only fully developed in Hellenistic times. As a natural creature, she is almost always a → nymph (an Oread), rarely the daughter of a nymph and a mortal (Longus 3,23); as a mountain creature, she is associated most of all with → Pan. She regularly is his lover; if the love is consummated, she gives birth to the daughters Iambe (schol. Eur. Or. 964) and Iynx (Callim. Fr. 685) who are the embodiments of two powerful types of speech: the satirical poem and the enchanted love poem. Frequently, the outcome of this love is

unhappy (Mosch. 6 Gow; Dion. Chrys. orat. 6,20). In Longus' account (ibid.) Pan's revenge is the aition for the natural phenomenon. Another aition reports that because of her support for Zeus' love affairs, Juno robbed her of her independent voice so that she could only repeat words after someone. Ovid connected this story in an effective manner with the story of her unrequited love to → Narcissus, because of which she faded away to a disembodied voice (Ov. Met. 3,356–510). Pictorial representations are mentioned in the literature (Philostr. Imag. 2,33 and Anth. Plan. 4,153–156; with Pan: Callistratus, Ekphraseis 1 p. 421f. Kayser) and are found in archaeological objects (lamps, Pompeian wall paintings).

J. Bazant, E. Simon, s.v. E., LIMC 3.1, 680–683. F.G.

Eclecticism The eclecticists are a school of philosophers documented in one source only (Diog. Laert. 2,12). Their founder, Potamon of Alexandria, taught that the aim was to select the most plausible teachings of the various schools. In the same manner, Galenos refused to identify with any branch of philosophy or medicine (De libris propriis 1; De dignot. affect. 8). Modern research often refers to eclecticism, most of all in respect of the philosophy of the early Imperial period. This often proves to be misleading; it hides the fact that the phenomenon of eclecticism is nourished by quite different sources, but it is also prone to overlook that this eclecticism, as a rule, follows narrow tracks and does not blur the school identity of the philosophers. Amongst the sources and starting points could be listed (1) classicism, which afforded philosophers such as Plato and Aristotle an authority stretching beyond the boundaries of the schools, (2) the reinvigoration of Platonism and Aristotelianism which demanded that their philosophy be brought up to the contemporary level, (3) the endeavour to at least find a common philosophical language, but often also to reduce school differences to a few central points and to put them aside in certain contexts, (4) the widespread academic scepticism which allowed individuals to have philosophical opinions, but not the attachment to the authority of a school, and (5) the shear fact that, with the dissolution of the schools as institutions in the 1st cent. BC, the unity of the teachings was reduced to central theses. Eclecticism occurred on narrow tracks to the extent that Epicuraeans were excluded from it and that it was most of all the Platonists and Peripatetics who borrowed from the Stoics, and the Platonists who used Aristotle or later Peripatetics as a basis. Often, this was favoured by a view of history according to which, with certain exceptions, the difference between Plato, Aristotle and the Stoa is negligible. Often, as is the case with Plotin, eclecticism was unconscious (cf. Porph. VP 14). → Eclecticism

M. Albrecht, Eklektik. Eine Begriffsgesch., 1994. M.FR.

Eclecticist sculpture see → Sculpture

Eclectus (Ἔκλεκτος; *Éklektos*, also Electus, Eiectus). E. from Egypt, freedman of Verus, later lived in the palace of Marcus Aurelius (SHA Ver. 9,5f.) after whose death he became *cubicularius* of that emperor's nephew M. Ummidius Quadratus. When the latter was executed in AD 182, Commodus took on E. (Herodian. 1,16,5; Cass. Dio 72,4,6) with whom he appeared in gladiator games (SHA Comm. 15,2; Cass. Dio 72,19,4). In 193, together with the praetorian prefect Aemilius Laetus and Marcia, the *concubina* of Commodus, he instigated the murder of the Emperor (Hdn. 1,17,6; 2,1,3; Cass. Dio 72,22,1+4). He married Marcia and, together with Aem. Laetus, he carried out government business for Pertinax with whom he was killed in 193 (Cass. Dio 73,1,1f.; 10,1f.). PIR 3, 67 (Eclectus). M.MEI. and ME.STR.

Eclipses

A. In Superstition B. In Astrology C. In Astronomy

A. In Superstition

Eclipses disturbed the usual regularity of day and night and frightened people as long as they were unable to explain these phenomena. In early times, it was believed that the heavenly bodies suffered under the power of the → demons and attempts were made to end this suffering with banging or loud shouting. On the other hand, Thessalian witches are supposed to have forced the moon down to earth with their magical practices (Pl. Grg. 513a, Hor. Epod. 5,46; 17,77, Verg. Ecl. 8,69, Ov. Met. 7,207f.). Eclipses were also interpreted as signs of nature's mourning or horror (συμπάθεια, *sympátheia*; Diog. Laert. 4,64) because of human sacrilege or the fall or death of a hero right up to the death of Christ. The opposition of sun and moon was interpreted as a fight (Liv. 22, 1,9) and transferred to a warlike antagonism (Greeks and Persians in April 480 BC: Hdt. 7,37, conversely Lydius De ostentis 9). In Rome, the eclipses belonged to the *prodigia*, i.e. the indications of divine wrath which had to be appeased by *procuratio* (→ Expiatory rites). They were recorded in the annals and thus found their way into literary works. Poetry gained from the eerie mood of eclipses; apart from lyric poetry, it was epic poetry in particular that gained, after two passages in Homer (Il. 17,366; Od. 20,356) had already been interpreted — no later than in Plutarch — as referring to eclipses [3. 2331f.].

B. In Astrology

Eclipses announced the death of a ruler or hero, malformation, famine, pest, war, rebellion or the destruction of cities. In that context, the relevant signs of the zodiac indicated the countries affected according to the different systems of astrological geography [4. praef. XII-XVII] (Nechepso-Petosiris frg. 6 Riess in Heph. 1,21, cf. Lydius De ostentis 9, furthermore Manil. 4,818–865 about the *signa ecliptica*). Ptolemy takes the colours of the eclipses into account (Apotelesmatika 2,10). Since the 1st cent. AD, the pseudo-planets of the rising and falling lunar nodes (ἀναβιβάζων/*anabibázōn* and καταβιβάζων/*katabibázōn*; → Ecliptic) with an orbit time of *c.* 18.5 years in opposite directions, namely from east to west, as a draconitic body of the ninth sphere with head and tail were also included in the prognoses [5]; the oldest evidence comes from Dorotheus Sidonius 5,43 in Heph. 3,16,11–13 (388 PINGREE).

C. IN ASTRONOMY

In Mesopotamia, eclipses of the moon are recorded on clay tablets since the 2nd half of the 2nd millennium BC, the oldest message that can be safely dated relates to the eclipse of the sun on May 3rd 1375 BC [9]. This data was entered into the Babylonian moon calculations of the 'System A' invented around 500 BC. Since the 4th cent., the Saros period of 223 synodical months (= 18 years and 10 $^1/_3$ days, three times that period = ἐξελιγμός/*exeligmós*, 54 years and 31 days) was used for calculations. Records of predictions are available since the 7th cent. Hipparchus and Ptolemy used Babylonian records of 730 to 82 BC [7]; conversely, the late Babylonian astronomy is influenced by Greek science. Observations of the Egyptians are documented by Diod. Sic. 1,50,1–2; they are supposed to have collected 373 eclipses of the sun and 832 eclipses of the moon in 48,863 years (Diog. Laert. pr. 2), but these reports are uncertain.

Thales of Miletus is reputed to be the first who predicted to the Ionians the eclipse of the sun of August 24th 585 BC (Hdt. 1,74,3) [6. 52–54], whereas Anaximenes (A 16 DK) is said to have been the first to recognize that the moon receives its light from the sun. Others assume Pythagoras to be the discoverer. Thucydides knew that eclipses of the sun only take place during a new moon and he reports that, during a total eclipse of the sun, individual stars became visible (2,28). Hipparchus is said to have produced eclipse tables for 600 years in advance for different localities (Plin. HN 2,53). While the predictions for an eclipse of the moon were quite accurate, those for eclipses of the sun were sometimes less exact because they did not take the parallax of the moon into account. Ptolemy provides a valid summary of the method of calculation (Syntaxis, B. 6) with references to earlier methods which were probably compiled in the time around 200 BC already and also spread to India.

As phenomena associated with an eclipse, reference is made to earthquakes, winds, clouds and rain, shooting stars and aureoles as well as thunder. The eclipsed sun was observed in reflective surfaces (also water), *pelves* (pans or bowls) filled with oil or pitch (Sen. Q. Nat. 1,12,1), with a sieve, a broad tree leaf or with clasped hands. The observations also had the purpose of determining the size of heavenly bodies (Cleomedes 2,3,67–80: the earth has to be larger than the moon) and the distance between them, the parallax as well as the geographical length of observation points (Plin. HN 2,180; Ptol. geographia 1,4). Philippus of Opus wrote a work Περὶ ἐκλείψεως σελήνης ('About Lunar Eclipses'), further works by Orion, Apollinarius, and then also by Hipparchus and Ptolemy are documented by Achilles, introductio in Aratum 19 p. 47,14 MAASS. Usually, one differentiated between total (τέλειοι, *téleioi*) and partial eclipses (ἀπὸ μέρους, *apò mérous*: Cleomedes 2,6,152), unique is the division into three categories by Ps.-Eudoxus, ars 19,12–15 BLASS: μηνοειδεῖς; *mēnoeideîs* (= ἐλάσσους; *elássous*; moon-like, smaller ones) — ἁψιδοειδεῖς; *hapsioeideîs* (μείζους; *meízous*; loop-like, larger ones) — ᾠοειδεῖς; *ōioeideîs* (ἔτι μείζους; *éti meízous*; egg-shaped, even larger ones).

A useful list of the eclipses for the years 900 BC to AD 600 is offered by [2] and (with special consideration of the mostly inaccurate or incorrect ancient documents) [3. 2352–2364], corrections [8. 509–519].

1 A. BOUCHÉ-LECLERCQ, L'astrologie grecque, 1899 2 F.K. GINZEL, Spezieller Kanon der Sonnen- und Mond-Finsternisse für das Ländergebiet der klass. Altertumswiss., 1899 3 F. BOLL, s.v. F., RE 6, 2329–2364 4 A.E. HOUSMAN (ed.), M. Manilii astronomicon liber quartus, 1920, repr. 1972, [2]1937 5 W. HARTNER, The pseudoplanetary nodes of the moon's orbit in Hindu and Islamic iconographies, in: Ars Islamica 5, 1938, 113–154 6 O. GIGON, Der Ursprung der griech. Philos., 1945 7 B.L. VAN DER WAERDEN, Drei umstrittene Mond-Finsternisse bei Ptolemaios, in: MH 15, 1958, 106–109 8 A. DEMANDT, Verformungstendenzen in der Überlieferung antiker Sonnen- und Mondfinsternisse, 1970 9 F.R. STEPHENSON, The earliest known record of a Solar Eclipse, in: Nature 228, 1970, 651f. 10 O. NEUGEBAUER, A History of Ancient Mathematical Astronomy, 1975 11 W. RICHTER, Lunae labores, in: WS NF 11, 1977, 96.

W.H.

Ecliptic (ἐκλειπτική sc. γραμμή, cf. schol. Arat. 550, p. 323,8 MARTIN: τὴν μέσην γραμμὴν τοῦ ζῳδιακοῦ; and ThlL V,2, 48,56 *ecliptica linea*, but mostly ἐκλειπτικὸς sc. κύκλος). One of the five fixed celestial orbits (→ *kýkloi*), limited by the two tropics and intersecting the equator, i.e. an oblique orbit (λοξός, *loxós*) whose stars do not rise and set at the same point; it originally referred to the orbit of the sun during its year. The name is derived from the fact that the → eclipses take place on this orbit (Ach.Tat. Isagoga 23, p. 53,10 MAASS, dist. ζῳδιακός, cf. Anon. ibid. p. 130,25f.). Furthermore, in a more general sense, the word refers to the totality of all planes of the lunar and planetary orbits for which Manil. 1,682, Geminus 5,53 et al. give a width (πλάτος) of 12° (table in Ptol. Syntaxis 13,10). According to one incorrect theory, the sun also deviates from the centre line [2. 2212f.]. With a value of 12°, the moon deviates most. For Venus, however, Pliny (HN 2,66) indicates an additional deviation of 2°. The incline of the ecliptic was calculated by → Eratosthenes [2] almost correctly by arriving at 23° 51' 19", and this value was adopted by Hipparchus and Ptolemy (Syntaxis 1,12): Twice the value is greater than 47° 40' and smaller than 47° 45' (pl. the ecliptic degrees 0°–90° in relation to the meridian arcs 0°–23° 51' 20"). Mostly, however, the round value of 24° is used for calculations, i.e. the chord of a polygon with 15 corners (Geminus 5,46: = 4 sixtieth parts at 6° each).

The ecliptic is divided into 12 × 30 = 360°. According to Geminus (18,7), the average daily arc of the moon is 13° 10' 35", it passes through one twelfth of the ecliptic in 2.25 days (Geminus 1,30). The Babylonians worked with synodical months as is evident from the text mulApin going back to about the year 1000 BC and adapted around 500 BC by incorporating an additional month. But the Greeks neither followed this system nor the Indian system of the 28 moon stations, which only reached them in Byzantine times, but exclusively used the sun which only passes through about one degree per day. As a result of the two solstices and the two equinoxes, at which the ecliptic intersects the equator, the solar year is divided into four parts which, due to the eccentricity of the solar orbit and the resultant anomaly, have different lengths: The sun is slowest at its apogee (in the star sign of Gemini), and it is fastest at its perigee (sign of Sagittarius). Geminus (1,13–16) arrives at 94.5 days for spring, 92.5 days for summer, 88.125 days for autumn and 90.125 days for winter. The start of the year is arbitrary (Ptol. Apotelesmatika 2,11), but in terms of astronomy, one initially preferred the summer solstice (sign of Cancer), later the vernal equinox (sign of Aries). As a result of the precession, the four points of the year slowly move against the direction of the planets, namely from east to west, so that the twelve signs of the zodiac shift from their original ecliptic twelfths (δωδεκατημόρια; *dōdekatēmória*). This realization prevailed over the rarely documented hypothesis of a trepidation according to which the year points swing backwards and forwards with a speed of 1° in 80 years up to an amplitude of 8° (Attalus and Eudoxus fr. 63 Lasserre in Hipparchus 1,9,1–8). Hipparchus discovered the precession by observing the position of *spica* in comparison the one determined by Timocharis around 270 BC (Ptol. Syntaxis 7,2 p. 12,21); Ptolemy increased his data in a mechanical fashion by 2° 40'. While the two Greek scholars assumed too large a value of 36" per year or 1° in 100 years, i.e. one revolution in 36,000 years, the Islamic astronomy used too low a value of 1° in 66.6 years. The oldest ecliptic fixing of the year points determines 8° for the 'tropic' signs (Meton and Eudoxus, fr. 144f. Lasserre, in Columella 9,14,12). This value was sanctioned by the Julian calendar and plays a part in the astrological interpretation of the → Paranatellonta in Teucer, Manilius and Firmicus Maternus. Geminus (5,52), however, assumes the sign limits to be at 1° (or 0°), Manilius (3,680–682) mentions the variants 1°, 8° (which he otherwise follows) and 10°, the Babylonians assumed either 8° (System B) or, since they proceeded in blocks of five days, 10° (System A) as the basis for their calculation based on the moon. Apart from 8°, Achilles (Isagoga 23, p. 54,18f. Maass) also mentions the values 12° and 15°, i.e. the centre of the zodiac sign, which astrologically also plays a part.

On average, one ecliptic degree rises in four minutes and one ecliptic twelfth in two hours, but duration and speed of the rise are dependent on the geographical latitude: The sections either rise and set fast at a low gradient or slowly at a steep one [10. 52–62]. Rise and set times are complementary (Geminus 7,37): Degrees or degree ranges equidistant from the turning points (τροπαί, *tropaí*) have complementary rise and set times, i.e. the one rises for as long as the other sets and vice versa (ἰσοδυναμοῦντες, *isodynamoûntes*), the degrees equidistant from the equinoxes (ἰσημερίαι, *isēmeríai*) have the same rise and set times (ἰσαναφόροι, *isanaphóroi*, Geminus 7,32). While Hipparchus (3,3–4) records the rises of the true constellations for the third climate (Rhodes: 36°), → Hypsicles in his *Anaphorikós* (*c.* 170 BC) refers to the first climate (Alexandria), but the round values of the second climate (Babylon) were mostly preferred [3. 42]. The corresponding lengths of day and night vary in the same manner.

Close to the original meaning of the ecliptic comes the theory of a draconitic body with head and tail, which moves on a ninth sphere, as a symbol for the rising and falling lunar nodes, Ἀναβιβάζων; *Anabibázōn* and Καταβιβάζων; *Katabibázōn* [1.121–123; 4; 10. 294f.].

→ Dorotheus [5]; → Ecliptic

1 A. Bouché-Leclercq, L'astrologie grecque, 1899 2 A. Rehm, s.v. Ekliptik, RE 5, 2208–2213 3 E. Honigmann, Die sieben Klimata und die ΠΟΛΕΙΣ ΕΠΙΣΗΜΟΙ. Eine Unters. zur Gesch. der Geogr. und Astrologie im Altertum und MA, 1929 4 W. Hartner, The Pseudo-planetary Nodes of the Moon's Orbit in Hindu and Islamic Iconographies, Ars Islamica 5, 1938, 113–154 (in: Oriens — Occidens, 1968, 349–404) 5 B.L. van der Waerden, History of the Zodiac, Archiv für Orientforschung 16, 1952/3, 216–230 6 Id., Erwachende Wiss. II: Die Anfänge der Astronomie, 1966 7 R. Böker, H.G. Gundel, s.v. Zodiakos, RE 10 A, 462–709
8 O. Neugebauer, A History of Ancient Mathematical Astronomy, 1975 9 B.L. van der Waerden, Die Astronomie der Griechen, 1988 10 W. Hübner, Die Eigenschaften der Tierkreiszeichen in der Antike, 1982. W.H.

Ecloga (Ἐκλογή; *eklogḗ*, 'excerpt', 'selection').
[1] Varro (in Charisius, gramm. p. 154 B.) uses the foreign term in its literal meaning ('selection'). It is unclear how the meaning has developed into the usage we encounter from the end of the 1st cent. AD on: *Ecloga* may refer to individual lyrical poems (Stat. Silv. 3, pr. 23 = 3,5; 4, pr. 21 = 4,8, later in a similar way Auson. 8 Peiper) and in the plural form *Eclogae* to the entire collection (Plin. Ep. 4,14,9). The term is used in particular for → Horatius (Suet. Vita: Epist. 2,1; Sid. Apoll. Epist. 9,13,2, v.12: Carm., Auson. 16 Praef.: 3,19; in grammarians for Hor. Epod. and Sat. as well) and for the *bucolica* by → Virgil (initially Suet. Vit.), which guarantees the continued use of the title in the → Bucolics.

ThlL 5,2,48. P.L.S.

[2] Law book of the East Roman Empire issued in March of AD 741. The Ecloge was a compilation in 18

titles (chapters) of civil and criminal legal matter relevant for everyday life (for example, marriage, divorce, gifts) influenced to a moderate degree by Christianity and by the rights of habit, based on Justinian's overwrought and no longer practical jurisdiction. Although replaced by the → Epanagoge after 867, the Ecloge continued to be handed down. It helped shape the legislation of cultures under Byzantine influence, for example the Old Slavic law book *Zakon Sudnyj Ljudem* (9th/10th cents.) and was translated into various languages [1. 533f.], for instance into Arabic [2] and Armenian.

1 D. Gkines, s.v. Ἐκλογὴ τῶν Ἰσαύρων, Θρησκευτικὴ καὶ ἠθικὴ ἐγκυκλοπαιδεία 5, 1966 2 S. Leder, Die arab. Ecloga, 1985.

L. Burgmann (ed.), Ecloga. Das Gesetzbuch Leons III. und Konstantinos' V., 1983; E. H. Freshfield, A Manual of Roman Law: The Ecloga, 1926 (Engl. trans.); C. A. Spulber, L'Eclogue des Isauriens, 1929 (French trans.); P. E. Pieler, in: Hunger, Literatur, II, 458ff.; B. Sinogowitz, Studien zum Strafrecht der Ekloge, 1956.

G.MA.

Economical Ethics

I. Definition II. Greece III. Rome IV. Christianity

I. Definition

Economical ethics (EE) deal with those aspects of economical actions that can be judged according to ethical criteria. It is a modern theoretical discipline which analyzes primarily those normative ideas and attitudes that exert considerable influence on the economic activities of individuals or social groups as well as on the → economy at large. These ideas are not necessarily motivated by morals but often serve only to legitimize the economic actions of certain social groups. The subjects of EE include the evaluation of different professions, in particular physical → work, the control of → prices, the charging of → interest as well as the estimation of → wealth. In antiquity, systematic writings about EE did not exist, however, one can find isolated discussions esp. in philosophical texts.

II. Greece

Ancient → economy was embedded into the society at large and was originally characterized by the dominance of domestic economics which, to a large extent, shaped economical actions and thinking. First signs of an EE can already be found in the *Érga* by → Hesiodus, who demands respect for the law, praises agricultural work, and puts wealth as well as prestige down to work (Hes. Op. 213–281; 298–316). Furthermore, economical activities follow the postulates of maintaining good relationships to the → neighbours (Hes. Op. 342–358). Price fixing is the subject of the court speech by → Lysias [1] against the grain traders: Lysias polemicizes against the exploitation of a shortage for the purpose of attaining high → prices (Lys. 22,11–22).

The first systematic treatment of economic issues and EE can be found in → Plato [1] and → Aristotle [6], in the context of ethics and political theory. Plato, for example, demands that the political leadership (the φύλακες/*phýlakes*) of a just city should not have any personal property; Plato held that the pursuit of economical interests of such a leadership would necessarily lead to → social conflicts (Pl. Resp. 415d–417b). In the *Nómoi*, Plato discusses many different questions regarding economy and financial circumstances (→ Private property; → Wealth, distribution of). He strongly recommends that the financial assets of the citizens should be as equal as possible and criticizes the emergence of wealth (Pl. Leg. 735a–745a). The basis of all economic activity of the citizens is → agriculture, while → commerce and the → crafts lie in the hands of strangers (Pl. Leg. 846d–850c). A variety of rules concern the → market, sale and → purchase, and → prices; → loans and credit were rejected in general and → interest was only accepted in the case of delayed payments (Pl. Leg. 915d–921d).

In his 'Nicomachian Ethics', Aristotle raises the question of how to determine the equal value of traded goods and how to establish their value. → Money, in this context, appears as the means to measure value without which the fair exchange of different types of goods would not be possible (Aristot. Eth. Nic. 1133a–1133b). In political theory, the issue of establishing the appropriate goals of economic activities is treated thoroughly: Aristotle regards the → *oíkos* as the point of reference for economic activities, so that the issue comes down to the effort of obtaining food and other basic commodities for the *oíkos*. Appropriate activities are therefore those that aim at the appropriate provision of the people living in the *oíkos* (Aristot. Pol. 1253b–1256b). On the level of the → *pólis*, trade is necessary, since no single city has all necessary goods at its disposal on its own territory (Aristot. Pol. 1257a–1257b). This view implies a rejection of the acquisition of money that is not limited to the need of obtaining necessary goods but strives towards the unlimited accumulation of wealth. An unlimited accumulation of money (χρηματιστική/→ *chrēmatistikḗ*) draws a similar kind of criticism as interest — which is regarded as unnatural because it allows money to bring forth more money. Money-lending therefore does not correspond to the original function of money, that is, a means of exchange (Aristot. Pol. 1257b–1258b).

In his *Oikonomikós*, Xenophon [2] made an important contribution to EE, one that is typical of its time in many ways: he argues for a division of labour within the *oíkos* that is based on the natural constitution of man and woman and requires the man to procure goods from outside of the *oíkos* while the → woman is in charge of storing supplies (→ Storage economy). The accomplishment of a rich land owner (→ Large estates / Latifundia) lies primarily in his ability to drive his slaves to incessant and diligent work (Xen. Oec. 7,15–43). The writing about the public revenue of the city of

Athens (*Póroi*) contains hardly any remarks about EE, however, it is significant that Xenophon attempts to secure the existence of Athenian citizens by increasing esp. the income from silver mining in order to achieve their liberation from the need to work (Xen. Vect. 4,33; 4,52; → Mining; → Silver).

III. Rome

The *praefatio* of → Cato's [1] *De agricultura* ('On Agriculture') can be regarded as the classical Roman text on EE. This text makes clear that the choice of how to earn money is not solely dependent upon the expected income, but also on the social prestige connected with the activity. A further aspect in evaluating an economical activity is the risk it entails. On the basis of these considerations, lending money (→ Loan) and → commerce are either not socially respectable or are rejected as too risky, while → agriculture is praised as the activity least likely to cause envy (Cato Agr. praef.).

The evaluation of professions remained an important topic in the literature of the Roman Republic and the Principate. In his groundbreaking work on the social norms and values of the Roman senatorial class, → Cicero devoted a long passage to professions (Cic. Off. 1,150 f.). He evaluates the professions according to their social prestige, while their economical significance plays no role at all: first, he names the tax collectors and money-lenders who attract the people's hatred due to their activities, thus his disapproval. The job of → day-labourers is also not acceptable, since they are paid for their → work, not for their professional skills (*artes*). Retail merchants are accused of making a profit through lying. The craftsmen are judged all as one, since no workshop can offer any kind of freedom. In particular, Cicero criticizes the → crafts that serve immediate consumption—following Terence, Cicero lists fish vendors, butchers, cooks, poultry vendors and fishermen (*cetarii*; *lanii*; *coqui*; *fartores*; *piscatores*: Cic. Off. 1,150).

As a positive contrast, Cicero presents three professional groups: on the one hand, the *artes*, whose practice is based on intelligence, leading to greater benefit—the examples given by Cicero are → medicine and → architecture—, on the other hand, wholesale trading, and finally, → agriculture, of which he says that 'nothing is better, nothing more fruitful, nothing more pleasant, nothing more worthy of a human, a free citizen' (*nihil est agri cultura melius, nihil uberius, nihil dulcius, nihil homine, nihil libero dignius*: Cic. Off. 1,151). Also worth mentioning are Cicero's discussions of the late Republic's socio-political activities; he proceeds from the proposition that communities were formed so that each citizen could keep his property (Cic. Off. 2,73: *hanc enim ob causam maxime, ut sua tenerentur, res publicae civitatesque constitutae sunt*). He therefore rejects any type of activity aimed at redistribution (Cic. Off. 2,72–85). For Cicero as well as for Cato, agriculture is the most valued actvity for the members of the senatorial upper class. This opinion is based upon Platonic, Aristotelian, and Stoic thoughts that go back to Greek ideas, but also on the norms of the Roman aristocracy (→ *nobiles*).

In the period of the Principate, the discussion about professions was continued by Dio Chrysostomus (Dion. Chrys. 7,105–138). First, Dio states that people in the cities who have no possessions are economically pressured to work in order to be able to purchase all the goods necessary for living. This raises the question of which professions are acceptable. In this context, Dio especially criticizes → prostitution, because it forces previously free women into sexual intercourse purely for profit, not affection.

Price fixing is the subject of critical considerations in the *praefatio* of the Price Edict of Diocletian (→ *Edictum* [3] *Diocletian*). The reason for rising prices was explained not as a result of economical mechanisms nor of the decline in value of coins, but only as a result of the *avaritia* ('greed') of the merchants; economical developments were therefore explained on the basis of character flaws in the persons participating in the economical process (Edictum Diocletian praef. 6–19).

IV. Christianity

Christian ethics are characterized by a positive attitude towards → poverty and a simultaneous critical view of wealth. However, in the course of the rise of the Church, Christian ethics assign a function to wealth as well: as long as a rich person uses his fortune to give to charity, he is justified (Clem. Al. Quis dives salvetur?). In late antiquity, the ascetic movement led to an increasingly positive view of physical labour, which becomes a requirement in particular for monks set forth in the rules of the order (Aug. De opere monachorum; → Monasticism).

→ Economy; → Economy

1 P. A. Brunt, Aspects of the Social Thought of Dio Chrysostom and of the Stoics, in: Proceedings of the Cambridge Philological Society 199 (N. S. 19), 1973, 9–34 2 M. I. Finley, Aristotle and Economic Analysis, in: Id. (ed.), Studies in Ancient Society, 1974, 26–52 3 Finley, Ancient Economy 4 H. Grassl, Sozialökonomische Vorstellungen in der kaiserzeitlichen griech. Lit., 1.–3. Jh. n. Chr., 1982 5 H. Lenk (ed.) Wirtschaft und Ethik, 1998 6 S. Meikle, Aristotle's Economic Thought, 1995 7 B. Schefold, Die griech. Ant.: Eine andere wirtschaftliche Mentalität, in: Id., Wirtschaftsstile, vol. 1: Studien zum Verhältnis von Ökonomie und Kultur, 1994, 111–248 8 J. Wieland (ed.), Wirtschaftsethik und Theorie der Ges., 1993.

J. M. A.-N.

Economy see → Volume 5, Addenda

Ecphantides (Ἐκφαντίδης; *Ekphantídēs*). Early playwright of the Old Comedy [1. test. 4]. After 458 BC, he won four times in the Dionysia [1. test. 1]. Two titles of his plays are known: *Peírai* and *Sátyroi*. An unknown play is the origin of fr. 3, in which E. criticizes the Megarian Comedy.

1 PCG V, 1986, 126–129.

B.BÄ.

Ecphantus (Ἔκφαντος; *Ékphantos*).

[1] Greek painter from Corinth, active probably in the mid 7th cent. BC. According to Pliny (HN 35,16), he was the founder of the *secunda pictura*, a style of painting which completely covered all surfaces with paint; an example of this style are the wooden plates handed down from Pitsa. The *monochromata* mentioned by Pliny in this context may refer to the unbroken and precious mineral pigments that were used.

N.J. Koch, De picturae initiis, PhD thesis Bochum 1995, 23ff, 33ff, 47f.; G. Rembado, Il problema delle origini delle pittura corinzia, in: Sandalion 8/9, 1985/86, 109–119. N.H.

[2] Pythagorean of probably the 4th cent. BC from Syracuse, but according to Iambl. VP 267 from Croton. Testimonies can be found in Hippolytus (Refutatio 1,15), Stobaeus, Ps.-Plutarch, and Theodoretus. He presupposes knowledge of Democritus and apparently of Plato as well. E. assumes the existence of extensive yet indivisible Pythagorean monads which are distinguished by size, form, and a certain power. They are moved by this power, not by their weight or by an external power. This power, also called 'soul' or 'intellect', is the result of providence and works according to a certain order or idea, an idea which also posits that the world is spherical. It is Earth that spins around its own axis. However, we cannot obtain definitive knowledge from all this but must follow our own best judgement, the *nómos*. E.'s name was falsely attached to a treatise about kingship from probably the 2nd or 3rd cent. AD (fragments in Stobaeus). It is characterized by the attempt to justify the position of the emperor as part of the divine world order, which can also be found in Celsus and other 2nd-cent. sources. 'E.' differs from this in his emphasis on the divine quality of the emperor and in his recourse to ideas that show parallels to gnostic, hermetic, and Jewish thought (perhaps a reference to Gen. 1–2).

Editions: Diels/Kranz 51, vol. 1, S. 442; H. Thesleff, The Pythagorean Texts, 1965, 79ff. M.FR.

Ecstasy

I. Ancient Orient II. Greek and Roman Antiquity

I. Ancient Orient

In Mesopotamia, the ecstatic state is described as *maḫû*, 'to be outside of oneself, to be crazy, to rave'. It is possible that the verb *tebû*, 'to elevate oneself', used in the Mari-Letters already points to the special mental state of a → prophet. The term *maḫḫû*, 'ecstatic', is documented again and again since the 24th cent. BC [1]. Ecstasy occurs primarily in the context of delivering oracles at the temple and is therefore controllable. Ecstasy is a method of legitimizing divine communication (→ Divination). For the most part, ecstasy is documented in Syria and Israel, along the middle course of the Euphrates in the 18th cent. BC, in → Byblus in the 11th cent. (travel report by Wen-Amun [2]), as well as in the OT with the ecstatic *nabī* [3], and is still discernible in → Lucianus of Samosata's writing against → Alexander [27] of Abonutichus. In the period of → Asarhaddon and → Assurbanipal, the messages of ecstatics (*šipir maḫḫê*) play a central role in legitimizing the line of succession as well as military enterprises. Ecstasy was used as a tool for criticizing the king's decision only in exceptional cases [7]. Only few of the Mari-Letters contain indications that ecstasy was consciously evoked through intoxicating beverages [4]. In the annals of Asarhaddon, ecstasy is used in a figurative sense as the reason for the revolt of the brothers [5], in Late Babylonian hymns as the reason for chaotic circumstances in the country [6].

1 Chicago Assyrian Dictionary (CAD) M/1, s.v. *maḫḫû*
2 ANET, 25ff. 3 K. Koch, Die Profeten, 1978 4 J.-M. Durand, Archives Epistolaires de Mari I/1, 1988, 392, no. 207, no. 208, no. 212, no. 392 5 R. Borger, Asarhaddon, 1967, 42 6 CAD M/1, s.v. *maḫû*
7 S. Parpola, Letters from Assyrian Scholars to the Kings Esarhaddon and Assurbanipal, 1983. B.P.-L.

II. Greek and Roman Antiquity

A. Greece B. Rome C. Christianity

A. Greece

In the Greek world, ecstasy (Greek ἐνθουσιασμός; *enthousiasmós*, 'to hold god within oneself', μανία; *manía*, 'frenzy', late ἔκστασις; *ékstasis*, 'to be outside of oneself') is connected to a number of phenomena. Important for the period that followed are Plato's categories of different forms of *manía*, where he relates each form to a god: 1) prophetic (→ Apollo), 2) telestic (→ Dionysus), 3) poetic (→ Muses), and 4) erotic (→ Aphrodite, Eros; Phaedr. 265B). The first two categories are the most central ones [1. 64–101]. Mantic ('prophetic') ecstasy is connected, on the one hand, to the established oracle locations, esp. Delphi (where the Pythia prophetizes in ecstasy), Didyma and Clarus (where it is the priests), and on the other hand, with the unattached figures of the → Sibyl and → Bacis. Virgil (Aen. 6,77–80) explicitly regards this type of mantic ecstasy as the medium's act of divine possession. Telestic ('initiatory') ecstasy is a part of various cults that developed into mysteries from late archaic times. In this context, the cult of Dionysus was central. Here, the god himself is regarded as ecstatic (*mainómenos*, Hom. Il. 6,132), and his ritual and mythological admirers, the → Maenads, are named after their ecstatic state. They have been documented since the Homeric Epics (Hom. Il. 22,460; in a mythological reflection as Dionysus' wet-nurses: Il. 6,132).

Besides that, oriental cults in which the experience of ecstasy could be reached existed since late archaic times, such as that of → Sabazius or of → Cybele. The mysteries of → Eleusis are also attributed with ecstatic experiences, at least in later times (→ Iacchus; Synesius,

Dion 8,48A) [2]. In these cults, ecstasy is an experience sought by the individual for the attainment of momentary joy induced either by drinking wine or through frenetic dancing [3]. The meaning of *manía*, however, is ambivalent: it was sent down as a disease by the same gods who are worshipped in the ecstatic cults (Eur. Hipp. 141–144). Possessed individuals may be referred to in Greek/Latin as *pýthōnes*. Cathartic rites were performed in order to free individuals from possession (Pl. Resp. 364 BC; Hippoc. De morbo sacro 1,4). The fact that women appear to dominate in ritual ecstasy has to do with the social function of these cults [4]. In the Imperial period and under Platonic influence, ecstasy increasingly becomes a means to escape corporeality through ascent to the divine. As such, it is important in → theurgy and Neoplatonism [5; 6]. Poetic ecstasy as a poetological model of inspired writing had been formulated since Democritus (68 B 17; 18; 21 DK) and Plato (Ion 534B *i.a.*) and was developed into a final version valid for European tradition by Horace (Ars 295–298; cf. Cic. De or. 2,46,194) among others, but this version always had to compete with other poetological concepts.

B. Rome

Rome knew only few indigenous appearances of ecstasy; even the terminology (*furor*) is pejorative. While ancient ecstatic prophecy probably underlies the term → *vates*, this type of divination is already obsolete in historical times [7]. The practices of → *augures* and → *haruspices* are the dominant ones. Ritual ecstasy, on the other hand, which came to Rome with Dionysus (Bacchus) from lower Italy and Etruria, was tolerated only marginally in the Republican period (Bacchanalia scandal of 187 BC) [8].

C. Christianity

Similarly, Christian tradition also does not know ecstasy, at least outwardly. In the NT, ecstatics are regarded as possessed by → demons and healed (for example. Acts 16,16), and the same holds true in the legends of saints. The demonic interpretation of ecstasy prevents the acceptance of prophetic ecstasy, which survives only on the fringes [9].

1 E.R. Dodds, The Greeks and the Irrational, 1951 2 F. Graf, Eleusis und die orphische Dichtung Athens, 1974, 54–58 3 J. Bremmer, Greek maenadism reconsidered, in: ZPE 55, 1984, 267–286. 4 R.S. Kraemer, Ecstasy and possession. The attraction of women to the cult of Dionysos, Harvard Theological Review 72, 1979, 55–80 5 J.P. Culianu, Esperienze dell'estasi, 1969 6 Id., Psychanodia 1, 1983 7 J.K. Newman, The Concept of Vates in Augustan Poetry, 1967 8 J.-M. Pailler, Bacchanalia, 1988 9 D.E. Aune, Prophecy in Early Christianity and the Ancient Mediterranean World, 1983.

F.G.

Edessa (Ἔδεσσα; *Édessa*).

[1] City in central Macedonia at the eastern entrance to the Kara-Burun pass from Lower to Upper Macedonia, today known as Edessa, formerly as Vodena. In previous times, E. was wrongly regarded as the old Macedonian royal seat of → Aegae [1]. E. was first mentioned in 217 BC (Pol. 5,97) but must be significantly older. One traditional view holds that the neighbouring community of Euboea was founded by homecomers from the Trojan War (Str. 10,1,15), but more important is perhaps the fact that the name of E. was passed on to the early Seleucid settlement in Syria (modern Şanliurfa). In the 3rd cent., E. was a rest station on the travel route of Delphic *theōroí* [1]. Until 167 BC, E. was as important as Beroea [1] and Pella, with which E. was integrated into *Macedonia III*. The *via Egnatia* (Pol. 34,12,7) ran through E., a fact that guaranteed the town's importance within the Roman province: it became the site of a *conventus* of Roman business men — inscriptions show many Roman names — and it is the site of the earliest Christian inscriptions in Macedonia (2nd–3rd cents. AD) [2. 1–54]. MA.ER.

In the Byzantine period, E. is mentioned among others in the It. Ant. (319, 3; 330), in the It. Burd. (606,4), in the Tab. Peut. (7,1 Weber) as well as in Hierocles (638,8) and Constantinus Porphyrogennetus (De Thematibus 88 Pertusi) as belonging to the Ἐπαρχία Μακεδονίας πρώτης. Inscriptions show that a Christian community existed since the 3rd cent. [2. no. 1–54], bishops are recorded in a funeral inscription from the 5th/6th cents. [2. no. 2] and at the council in Constantinople of 692 ([3. 152 no. 64] cf. [3. 214, 222, 230]). In 479, E. was conquered by Theoderic. The immigration of Slavs began in the 6th cent. The fortress of Βοδινά/*Bodiná* (the name is derived from Slavic *voda*, described and first mentioned in Skylitzes 345,20–23 Thurn) is evidence of E.'s strategic significance from the 10th to the 14th cent. E.W.

1 A. Plassart, Liste delphique des théorodoques, in: BCH 45, 1921, 17,III,60 2 D. Feissel, Recueil des inscriptions chrétiennes de Macédoine du IIIe au VIe siècle, 1983 3 H. Ohme, Das Concilium Quinisextum und seine Bischofsliste, 1990.

DHGE 14, 1420f.; Lauffer, Griechenland, 205–207; LMA 3, 1565–1567; F. Papazoglou, Les villes de Macédoine, 1988, 127–131; A.B. Tataki, Macedonian E., in: Meletemata 18, 1994. MA.ER. and E.W.

[2] (Urfa). Northern Mesopotamian city on the headwaters of the river Nahr al-Baliḥ, in a region that now belongs to Turkey on the border to Syria, known today as (Şanlı) Urfa. The pre-Greek name of E., Urhai, graecized into Ὀρρόη (*Orrhóē*), became the designation for the region and the state as Orrhoëne or Osroëne in the Hellenistic period, but after the re-establishment of the city through → Alexander [4] the Great, (331 BC) or → Seleucus I (304 BC), it was named after the Macedonian city of E. [1]. From *c.* 132 BC on, E. was the capital of the Osroënic-Arabic kingdom of the Abgarids

which was able to maintain relative independence between the power centres of the Roman and the Parthian-Sassanid Empires until the 3rd cent. AD. E. was home to cults of Syrian-Mesopotamian deities (Atargatis, Nabu, Bel) until Christianity became the state religion following the conversion of → Abgar IX (179–214). E. quickly developed into a centre of Christian learning, with the language and the writing of E. significantly shaping both the literature and the liturgy of the Syrian Church. In the Byzantine period, E. became a bulwark against the western expansion of the Sassanids before it was taken by Muslims in AD 639.

E. MEYER, s.v. E., RE 5, 1933–1938. T.L.

[3] see → Bambyce

Edessa Chronicle Local Syrian chronicle, written in *c.* AD 540 based on Edessenic archives. The beginning as well as the end of the work consists of a description of local floods. The first one (November 201) includes informative details about the region's topography (→ Edessa [2]). Furthermore, there is mention of a Christian church. Only eight of the 104 preserved headwords that are mostly presented in concise form can be dated back to the period before the 4th cent. The dominant topic is the appointment of bishops; besides that, wars, taxes, construction projects, and natural catastrophes are dealt with as well. The latest date mentioned is the year 540. A few later Syrian chronicles use a lost version of the Edessa Chronicle. The designation of 'Edessa Chronicle' is occasionally mistaken for an anonymous chronicle of the years 497–506/7 which was inserted into the chronicle of → [Ps.]-Dionysius [23] of Tell-Maḥrē.

EDITION: I. GUIDI (CSCO III,4, 1903 (with Lat. trans.). BIBLIOGRAPHY: L. HALLIER, Unters. über die E.Ch. (Texte und Unters. IX,1, 1892; with Ger. trans.); I. ORTIZ DE URBINA, Patrologia Syriaca ²1965, 206; W. WITAKOWSKI, Chronicles of Edessa, in: Orientalia Suecana 33/35 1984/5, 487–498; S. P. BROCK, in: Studies in Syriac Christianity, 1992, 3f. S.BR.

Edetani Iberian tribe on the Spanish east coast. The main city was Liria, today still known as Liria on the Guadalaviar (CIL II p. 509), and the tribal area corresponded roughly to the hinterland of Valencia and Saguntum ([1. 111]). SCHULTEN [2. 326] refers to them as the inhabitants of the province of Teruel further to the north. The location can be deduced from that of the main city and from other sources (cf. also [3. 58]: *Edeta[nia]*). The E. are mentioned for the years of 209 and 141 BC: Pol. 10,34,2 (uncertain reading); App. Ib. 330f. (here, *Sedetania* should clearly be read as *Edetania*, a common mistake; cf. [4. 40]), also, in several inscriptions: CIL II 3786, 3793, 3874(?), 4251 (= ILS 2711), but rarely in the rest of literature (Str. 3,4,1; 12; 14; Plin. HN 3,20; Ptol. 2,6,15). The name is probably derived from the personal name of *Edeco*, *Edesco* [2. 235,4] and is most likely Iberian ([5] *Ed-ec-o*).

1 H. SIMON, Roms Kriege in Spanien, 1962
2 A. SCHULTEN, Numantia 1, 1914 3 Enciclopedia Universal Ilustrada 19 4 Fontes Hispaniae Antiquae 4, 1937, 40 5 HOLDER, 1.

J. UROZ SAEZ, La regio Edetania en la época ibérica, 1983; TOVAR, 3, 1989, 32–34. P.B.

Edfu (Egypt. *Ḏbꜣ*; Greek Ἀπολλωνόσπολις μεγάλη; *Apollōnóspolis megálē*). City on the western shore of the Nile in the south of Upper Egypt, at the end of important caravan routes to the red Sea and to the gold mines of the Eastern desert. Capital of the second Upper Egyptian district. The temple of Horus from the Ptolemaic period (built by Ptolemy III-XII) is excellently preserved, and its rich decorations with images and writing are an important source for the religion of late Egypt [1; 2].

1 Le temple d'Edfou I-XV, 1897–1985 2 D. KURTH, Treffpunkt der Götter, 1994 3 B. PORTER, R. MOSS, Topographical Bibliography V, 1937, 200–205. S.S.

Edictum

[1] *Edictum* (from *edicere*) is a binding public announcement by Roman office bearers (→ *magistratus*), which presented either concrete orders or a 'governmental agenda' [1. 58] for the coming term of office. The word suggests an originally oral announcement [2. 178], but the historically documented form is a recording on an → *album* ('white wooden plate') at the magistrate's office. Literary tradition refers to edicts by → *consules*, → *aediles*, → *praetores*, provincial governors, tribuni plebis (→ *tribunus*), → *censores*, but also by the emperors. It is not clear whether the authority to issue an *edictum* was anchored in a special *ius edicendi* as mentioned by Gaius (Inst 1,2; 6), or if it arose automatically from the respective area of responsibility [2. 180]. The *edictum* was no law in the formal sense (→ *lex*), although especially the *edictum* of the praetor became the basis for all legal practices. The legal advisors of office bearers helped shape the *edictum* and would interpret it in the *libri ad edictum* (→ *Edictum* [2] *perpetuum*). Since the *edictum* was largely adopted from the respective predecessor, it is very difficult to connect particular regulations with specific office bearers. One of the rare exceptions is the case described by Cic. Off. 3,58–60 which allegedly motivated C. Aquilius Gallus to introduce a *iudicium de dolo* (legal remedy due to malicious actions). No inscriptions of edicts by court magistrates have survived. Attempts to reconstruct them from the jurists' commentaries on edicts and from Cicero's writings date back to the 16th cent. Still of fundamental value is LENEL's reconstruction [3].

1 L. WENGER, Die Quellen des röm. Rechts, 1953
2 W. KUNKEL, R. WITTMANN, Staatsordnung und Staatspraxis der röm. Republik, 2, 1995 3 O. LENEL, Das edictum perpetuum, ³1927. R.WI.

[2] **Edictum perpetuum.** Among the various meanings of an *edictum perpetuum*, the so-called jurisdictionary edicts stand out in the procedural context. In these edicts, the magistrate who bore the authority of jurisdiction at the beginning of his term in office proposed those regulations according to which he planned to enforce and develop his jurisdiction for the duration of his office — thus *perpetuum* —, Dig. 1,2,2,10. According to Papinian, Dig. 1,1,7,1, its function was to complete, clarify, and correct the *ius civile*. Apparently due to the prior development of a bad state of affairs, a *lex Cornelia* from the year 67 BC tied the author of the edicts to his own propositions. This legal corps, the *ius honorarium*, was rendered unchangeable and fixed as *de iure* probably under Hadrian. It consists primarily of trial formulas, that is, promises of legal protection which spell out the factual requirements in making various legal charges. Other (material and) procedural regulations concerned, for example, the initiation of legal proceedings, *exceptiones*, *interdicta*, commitments of possessions, the granting of quasi-rights of succession (*bonorum possessio*), *in integrum restitutio*, legal aids, etc. The magistrate could offset a lack of precision not only through the granting of analogous charges (*actiones utiles* or *in factum*), but also through imposing the condition that certain cases required individual examination (*causae cognitio*).

→ Formula; → Cognitio

A. Guarino, Le ragioni del giurista ..., 1983, 265ff.; M. Kaser, Ius honorarium und ius civile, in: ZRG 101, 1984, 1–114; W. Selb, Das prätorische Edikt: Vom rechtspolit. Programm zur Norm, in: FS M. Kaser, 1986, 259–272; Id., La fonction originale de l'édit du préteur ..., in: IURA 36, 1985, 115–118. C.PA.

[3] **Edictum Diocletiani.** The price edict by Diocletian handed down on inscriptions, together with the reorganization of the tax system and two coin edicts, was part of a comprehensive administrative and financial reform whose primary goal was to secure provisions for the Roman army. The term 'edict' was derived, beginning with Mommsen, from the expression *dicunt* in the *praefatio* (praef. 4). In the text itself, we find the terms *lex* (praef. 15) or *statutum* (praef. 15; 18; 19; 20). The only literary mention of the *ED* is found in Lactant. (De mort. pers. 7,6f). The *c.* 150 fragments of the Latin text and of various Greek translations found so far all appear to originate from the east of the Imperium Romanum. However, this does not mean that the law was not valid in the empire as a whole (cf. praef. 16; 20). The *ED* was issued between 21 November and 31 December 301 (*trib. pot. XVIII* of Diocletian, counting from 20 November 284) in the name of the two *augusti* C. Aurelius Valerius Diocletianus and M. Aurelius Valerius Maximianus as well as the *caesares* Flavius Valerius Constantius and Galerius Valerius Maximianus. With this, we can create a direct temporal and thematic connection to the second coin edict, which came into force on 1 September 301 according to [11]. The ordered doubling of the nominal value of → *nummus* and → *argenteus* probably caused a general price increase which needed to be counteracted quickly.

The *ED* consists of a *praefatio* and a list of foods, goods, and services, indicating more than a thousand (so far) maximum prices in denars. The *praefatio* names the cause and the purpose of the *ED*: fixing maximum prices was a way to control the *avaritia* of merchants and tradespeople, who sometimes demanded eight times the usual amount on the market. Soldiers above all were affected by this, who often had to spend a significant share of their yearly pay for the purchase of few items of food and other goods. In cases of overcharging, or if buyers and sellers entered into illegal negotiations, or if goods were hoarded, the edict threatened capital punishment.

This is the most detailed list of goods and services up to this point (with up to three quality grades and a distinction between new and used objects) but it does not follow any kind of strict system. Foods appear first on the list, then the wages for agricultural workers, craftsmen, and teachers, as well as the prices for raw materials and the products of craftsmen (of which textiles take up a large part), and for transportation services. The prices in the *ED* can be assessed relative to the prices listed for gold (1 pound = 72,000 denars) and silver (1 pound = 6,000 denars). In this way, the price relation between gold and silver can be established as 12:1. According to Lactantius (De mort. pers. 7,7), goods soon disappeared from the market as a reaction to the *ED*; after a short time, the *ED* had to be annulled. More recent research seems to indicate, however, that Diocletian succeeded in slowing price increases.

The fixing of maximum prices was not a fundamental innovation. For instance, price controls for grain existed in Athens (Aristot. Ath. Pol. 51,3), and Roman magistrates had determined maximum prices for grain in different cities during times of grain shortages (edict by Antistius Rusticus, AE 1925, 126). After Diocletian, it was still attempted occasionally to counteract supply problems with price edicts on a short-term basis (cf. for Antioch in AD 362 for instance Julian. Mis. 368–369; Lib. Or. 1,126; Amm. Marc. 22,14,1).

→ Diocletianus; → Price; → Price control

Editions: 1 Th. Mommsen, H. Blümner, Der Maximaltarif des Diokletian, ²1958 2 S. Lauffer, Diokletians Preisedikt, 1971 3 M. Giacchero, Edictum Diocletiani et Collegarum de pretiis rerum venalium in integrum fere restitutum e Latinis Graecisque Fragmentis, 1974

New finds after 1974: 4 M.H. Crawford, J. Reynolds, The Publication of the Prices Edict: a New Inscription from Aezani, in: JRS 65, 1975, 160–163 5 M.H. Crawford, J. Reynolds et al., The Aeziani Copy of the Prices Edict, in: ZPE 26, 1977, 125–151 6 Id., in: ZPE 34, 1979, 163–210 7 J. Reynolds, Diocletian's Edict on Maximum Prices: The Chapter on Wool, in: ZPE 42, 1981, 283f. 8 A. Chaniotis, G. Preuss, Neue Fragmente des Preisedikts von Diokletian und weitere lat. Inschr. aus Kreta, in: ZPE 80, 1990, 189–193.

BIBLIOGRAPHY: 9 H. BLÜMNER, s.v. e.D., RE 5, 1948–1957 10 H. BÖHNKE, Ist Diokletians Geldpolitik gescheitert?, in: ZPE 100, 1994, 473–483 11 K.T. ERIM, J. REYNOLDS, M. CRAWFORD, Diocletian's Currency Reform. A New Inscription, in: JRS 61, 1971, 171–177 12 P. HERZ, Studien zur röm. Wirtschaftsgesetzgebung. Die Lebensmittelversorgung, 1988, 208–220 13 G. and W. LEINER, Kleinmünzen und ihre Werte nach dem Preisedikt Diokletians, in: Historia 29, 1980, 219–241 14 K.L. NOETHLICHS, Spätant. Wirtschaftspolitik und Adaeratio, in: Historia 34, 1985, 102–116. K.L.N.

[4] **Edictum Theodorici.** Law from the period of the Germanic empires on the territory of the West Roman Empire. Traditionally, the King of the Ostrogoths, Theoderic the Great, is named as the ruler under whom the *ET* was promulgated. The attempts at attributing the *ET* to other kings, especially to Theoderic II (453–466), King of the Visigoths [1], have clearly failed. The main reason why doubt is expressed again and again at locating the *ET*'s origin in the Empire of the Ostrogoths is the fact that Iustinian never mentions the *ET* (as a law to be annulled) in the *pragmatica sanctio* of 554 through which the *corpus iuris* came into force in Italy. The style of the prologue and epilogue especially speaks for its creation in the royal chancellery of Ravenna [2. 191].

The thematic foundation of the *ET* is Roman common law. The main sources are the *Codex Theodosianus* with the *Novellae* that belong to it up to Maiorianus, and less importantly, the *Pauli sententiae* with their *Interpretatio*. Furthermore, the pre-Theodosian collections of imperial law (→ *codex*) and the *Responsa* by → Paulus are used, but not the *Institutiones* by Gaius, which were otherwise common in late antiquity. Although the *ET*'s content lacks a meaningful structure, it is still useful in a practical sense due to its moderate volume (154 *capita* = individual regulations) and the preceding index. The *ET* contains regulations regarding (public and private) criminal law, procedural law, and — admittedly quite incomplete — civil law and property rights. The sparseness of these regulations reflects the 'personality principle' of the Ostrogothic Empire: each ethnic group followed its own traditional laws. According to LIEBS [2. 194], the *ET* represents the 'minimum of Roman legal culture prescribed to his Goths' by Theodoric the Great.

1 G. VISMARA, E. Theodorici, Ius Romanum Medii Aevi I 2 b aa, 1967 2 D. LIEBS, Die Jurisprudenz im spätant. Italien, 1987.

G. MELILLO, A. PALMA, C. PENNACCHIO, Lessico dell 'E. Theodorici Regis', 1990 (foreword by A. MAZZACANE); H.J. BECKER, E. Theodorici, in: A. ERLER, E. KAUFMANN (ed.), Handwörterbuch zur Dt. Rechtsgesch., vol. 1, 1971, 801–803. G.S.

Editio The term *editio* is derived from the verb *edere* ('to present, to show, to announce') and has several meanings within the legal realm:

(1) The *editio actionis* (Dig. 2,13) refers to the announcement required, in order for a trial to be sub judice in the formulary procedure, from the plaintiff towards the defendant, stating the type of charge(-formula) the plaintiff intends to initiate against the defendant. As long as the defendant accepts the formula (*accipere iudicium*), the → *litis contestatio* (attestation of conflict) is established. For a long time, modern research was dominated by the opinion that the *editio actionis* had to occur in two steps, that is, firstly out of court in a simple notice of one party to the other, and secondly, in front of the court magistrate (*in iure*) as a binding commitment to the desired litigation programme — an opinion for which there exists hardly any evidence in the sources. Today, a different understanding of the conflict development up to the trial in front of the magistrate (*in iure*) is forming. According to this new understanding, the magistrate (who is already very busy) participates to a much smaller degree than previously thought and, with that, the entire procedure is less formal. In this sense, the *editio* is the process as well as the result of informing the adversary about the charge initiated against him by the plaintiff.

Ulpianus refers to the necessity of such information as *aequissimum* (Dig. 2,13,1 pr.), so that the prospective defendant can direct his further actions or defence accordingly. The information was not tied to a certain form — it could be given in writing or orally (for instance by dictation or in the joint reading of the edict) (Dig. 2,13,1,1). The *editio* did not have to be repeated a second time in front of the magistrate, but the adversary was not coerced into silent acceptance of the information. Instead, as reported in an exemplary way by Cic. Part. or. 99f., he was allowed to hold out his own views towards the plaintiff, and, with that, corrections he deemed necessary (for example, a different type of charge) and supplements (for example → *exceptiones*). Similar to negotiating a contract, this private form of interaction allowed the parties to work out the *editio* which then determined the procedural programme. The Pompeian trial records show that psychological pressure certainly played a role in that the place of the negotiation was moved close to the seat of the magistrate, so that he could be reached quickly if negotiations should fail. If a unanimous *litis contestatio* was reached, the magistrate's contribution was essentially reduced to the appointment of a judge and his confirmation as well as authorizing him to rule.

In contested cases, on the other hand, the magistrate could play a larger role, and his ability to refuse the charge (*denegatio actionis*) gave him an effective means of exerting pressure. The *editio* spelled out not only the formula but also the *instrumenta*, that is, the evidence (documents, the questioning of witnesses) which the judge was to use in the trial (Dig. 2,13,1,3; formerly, these were understood as an independent category of the *editio*). The mutual communication between the prospective parties therefore went so far as to require the disclosure of the body of evidence. The evidence as well as the duty of determining the formula were sanctioned in that any other evidence or any alternative charges were precluded in the trial to follow. This rule is the reason why it was highly important — in difficult cases even unavoidable — to obtain legal assistance for the *editio*, while the part of the trial in front of the judge, on the other hand, could be handled by rhetors, because there the legal framework was rigidly predetermined. In cognitio procedures (→ *cognitio*), this *editio* was maintained for a long time further.

(2) In criminal trials, the plaintiff was occasionally allowed to determine the judges through a selection listed in the *editio*. In this case, the defendant was entitled to a limited right of rejection (*reiectio*).

→ Libellus

A. Bürge, Zum Edikt De edendo, in: ZRG 112, 1995, 1–50; G. Jahr, Litis Contestatio, 1960, 165–206; W. Kunkel, Quaestio, in: KS, 1974, 69–73; M. Wlassak, Die klass. Prozeßformel, 1924, 72; J. G. Wolf, Die Streitbeilegung zwischen L. Faenius Eumenes und C. Sulpicius Faustus, in: Stud. Sanfilippo VI, 1985, 771–788. C.PA.

Editions, second We can speak of a second edition (SE) of an ancient text if the author has revised a work after its release for publication or if an unauthorized version has entered into circulation. The difference between the circulation of the first draft and the publication of a work was never as big in Antiquity as it became after the introduction of book printing. Occasionally, the author stopped working on the text before showing or reading it to others, but more often, the publication was carried out in different steps. Authors performed plays, gave speeches, held recitations (Donat. vit. Verg. 31–4; Tac. Dial. 2–3), and showed drafts to friends in order to inform them (Apollonius of Perge, Conica 1 *init.*) or to hear their criticism (Hor. Ars P. 438–52; Ov. Pont. 2,4,13–8). The use of the term ὑπομνηματικόν (*hypomnēmatikón*), which is documented in PHerc. 1427, 1506, 1674 for the first three books of Philodemus' 'Rhetoric' [1; 2], suggests that a relatively formal first draft stage existed before the production of the fair copy (PHerc. 1426, 1672). Writers allowed the production of multiple copies (Ov. Tr. 1,7,23–6) and sent short presentation scrolls to friends and patrons which differed from those given out to the general public, as has been shown for Martial and Statius' *Silvae* [3]. Another complication results from the fact that the SE can be arranged by another party, as is the case in modern times. Euclid's 'Elements' has been handed down in two versions, one of them by Theon of Alexandria. Furthermore, the older version (only represented by the Codex Vatic. graec. 190) shows numerous → interpolations. Places covered by several lemmata overlap each other at times.

With the development of → book-trade, works could be published in a more formal manner. The author (or the editor/publisher for posthumous works such as the *Aeneid*) could thereby make it known that he agreed to the public distribution of the text. In a

small number of cases we have the appropriate evidence to show that the author himself revised his text once more in view of a second publication. The 'Clouds' are a good example of such a revision [4]. Aristophanes altered several passages in the text of the original which had only reached third place among the applicants in the urban Dionysia in the year of 424/3. In the Parabasis (518–62), he even described the unfavourable reaction of the audience and pleaded for their renewed favour. The surviving play is a partially revised version (which was probably never performed), but the original was preserved into Hellenistic times. In books 12–13 of Cicero's letters to Atticus, we gain insight into the author's thoughts while he reworked the two books originally dedicated to Catullus and Lucullus into the four books of the *Academica* dedicated to Varro (cf. [5]). As it is a discussion with the actual publisher, one could have expected not to find a single trace of the earlier versions, but the *Lucullus* of the so-called *Academica priora* and a part of the first book of the *Academica posteriora* have survived. Two later Latin authors introduced their works with the statement that they were improved editions. Solinus' second letter (p. 217 Mommsen) can only be found in one group of the MSS (cf. [6]), while Tertullian reports of his work *Adversus Marcionem* that the preserved version was the third edition (1,1,1–2): the first supposedly was too cursory and the second contained unauthorized excerpts, which had been spread by an apostate. In Columella's case, only the second book (*De arboribus*) of his initial work about agriculture (in three of four books) is preserved yet so are all of the 12 books *De re rustica* (cf. [7], still the most thorough treatment of the topic, and [8]). The idea that it does not belong where tradition has placed it is supported by the reference to the content of the *primum volumen* and by the fact that its content overlaps with books 3–5 of the longer work.

The Hellenistic period presents two cases in which the body of evidence is very different but the reason is the same. The scholia to certain verses of the first book of the *Argonautika* by Apollonius [2] Rhodius show alternative versions which are attributed to a προέκδοσις (*proékdosis*, 'previous edition'). Seeing that they are intelligible and stylistically accomplished, they may well be → author's variants stemming from an earlier distribution-phase of the text (cf. [9]). The third and fourth book of Callimachus' *Aetia* are framed by panegyric poems to Berenice, which were written after 246/5 BC and do not continue the conversation of the muses from the first two books. It is therefore conceivable that the four books were published in pairs. However, the famous prologue with its emphasis on the author's old age appears to have been written later for the edition of all four books (thus [10]). A. Cameron recently presented the thesis that books 1–2 did not undergo any changes when books 3–4 were added. According to his chronological scheme, the *Argonautika* were published after the *Aetia* 1–2 [11. 247–262], but he fails to adequately consider the probable assumption that these works circulated in draft form (therefore προέκδοσις) among the poet scholars of the Mouseion. And even CAMERON is of the opinion that Callimachus 'published' *Acontius and Cydippe* twice, first as a separate poem, then as part of *Aetia* 3.

CAMERON's view also represents an extreme in the case of Ovid [11. 115; 12]: he claims that we are dealing with a SE only in the case of the *Amores*, and that this SE was formed by merely deleting a few poems and rearranging the others. The introductory epigram which announces the abridgement from five to three books confirms that we are dealing with a revision; we can be quite certain that at least poem 2,18 was written for the SE (cf. [13]). In a series of articles (last in [14]), C.E. MURGIA presented the view that the *Ars amatoria* and the *Remedia amoris* were revised as well. Some of his arguments are indeed interesting; however, in construing dependencies between different places in the text, he fails to consider Ovid's tendency towards contamination.

Because the *Fasti* show only few changes, such as the dedication to Germanicus (1 passim, and 4,81–4), while the original form remained largely intact, it has been considered to be a posthumous publication [15]. It is, however, somewhat surprising that only six books have survived. Newer studies have clearly identified elements of closure at the end of book 6 [16; 17] and, in 6,725, a reference to Trist. 2,549, which describes the state of the work when Ovid was expelled: *sex ego Fastorum scripsi totidemque libellos*. These observations suggest a deliberately fragmentary revision of the earlier text. But the phrasing of the verse from the *Tristia* from a passage intended to prove Ovid's seriousness to Augustus opens up the possibility that a poem spanning the length of six books already existed.

Augustus' death was one of the reasons for the revision of the *Fasti*, after all, such changes in the political landscape led to other SEs as well, for example, in Martial's tenth book (cf. 10,2 and [18]), and the different versions of Eusebius' 'Ecclesiastical History' (cf. [19]). More famous — and more questionable — is the case of the *Georgica*: in his notes to Ecl. 10,1 and Georg. 4,1, Servius states that after his friend Cornelius Gallus was forced to commit suicide, Virgil removed the *laudes Galli* in an effort to satisfy Augustus, thereby shaping the text into the form we know today. Many scholars remain sceptical of the entire story (for example, [20]). On the one hand, one should not use chronological arguments against it: we do not know whether the *Georgica* were officially published before the death of Gallus (27 or 26 BC), but the revision of an unpublished text obviously does not constitute a SE. On the other hand, connections to the Gallus of the 'Ecloges' are still discernible (for example, Arethusa 4,351: cf. Ecl. 10,1; Orpheus 4,454ff.: cf. Ecl. 6,71; and notice Lycorias 4,339), and it is possible that a commentator who had no access to Gallus' poetry attempted to explain what could still be found by earlier readers (cf. [21]). But if we can agree to the assumption that a SE existed which was published three years after the first one and in which the new text replaced the old, plausible reconstructions can be made (for example, [22]).

It follows from this survey that the differences between different editions sometimes leave traces in the tradition, and these may be direct (Solinus) or indirect (Apollonius Rhodius, Virgil). Sometimes a version has completely disappeared (Aristophanes, *Clouds*; Ovid, *Amores*; Martial 10), in which case the later or authorized text usually replaced the earlier text completely, but not always (Cicero *Academica*). The assumption that SEs can be ruled out *e silentio* seems mistaken.

→ Copy

1 T. DORANDI, Per una ricomposizione dello scritto di Filodemo sulla Retorica, in: ZPE 82, 1990, 65–67 2 D. DELATTRE, En relisant les Subscriptiones des PHerc. 1065 et 1427, in: ZPE 109, 1995, 40–41 3 P. WHITE, The Presentation and Dedication of the 'Silvae' and the Epigrams, in: JRS 64, 1974, 40–61 4 K.J. DOVER, Aristophanes, Clouds, 1968, lxxx — xcviii 5 O. PLASBERG, Ciceronis Academicorum reliquiae cum Lucullo, 1922, iii xv 6 H. WALTER, Die 'Collectanea rerum memorabilium' des C. Iunius Solinus (Hermes Einzelschriften 22), 1969 7 H. EMONDS, Zweite A. im Alt., 1941, 108–35 8 R. GOUJARD, Le 'De arboribus' de Columelle: problèmes de l'authenticité, in: RPh 53, 1979, 7–28 9 M. FANTUZZI, Varianti d'autore nelle Argonautiche di Apollonio Rodio, in: A&A; 29, 1983, 146–61 10 P.J. PARSONS, Callimachus: Victoria Berenices, in: ZPE 25, 1977, 1–50 11 A. CAMERON, Callimachus and his critics, 1995 12 Id., The First Edition of Ovid's 'Amores', in: CQ 18, 1968, 320–33 13 A.S. HOLLIS, Ovid, Ars amatoria 1, 1977, 150–151 14 C.E. MURGIA, Influence of Ovid's 'Remedia amoris' on 'Ars amatoria' 3 and 'Amores' 3, in: CPh 81, 1986, 203–220 15 G. KNÖGEL, De retractatione fastorum ab Ovidio Tomis instituta, 1885 16 A. BARCHIESI, Il poeta e il principe, 1994, 264–277 17 C.E. NEWLANDS, Playing with Time, 1995, 209–236 18 L. FRIEDLÄNDER, Martialis epigrammaton libri, 1886 19 T.D. BARNES, The Edition of Eusebius' Ecclesiastical History, in: GRBS 21, 1980, 191–201 20 E. NORDEN, Orpheus and Eurydice. Ein nachträgliches Gedenkblatt für Vergil, in: KS zum klass. Alt., 1966, 468–532 21 R.G.M. NISBET, Pyrrha among Roses: Real Life and Poetic Imagination in Augustan Rome. Review and discussion of Jasper Griffin, Latin Poets and Roman Life, in: Collected Papers on Latin Literature, ed. by S.J. HARRISON, 1995, 223 22 M.L. DELVIGO, in: O. PECERE, M.D. REEVE (ed.), Formative Stages of Classical Traditions, 1995, 14–30.

S.H. and N.W.

Edobicus Franc, *mag. militum* of → Constantinus [3] III, whom he freed from Valencia in AD 407. E. tried to win the *Germani* as allies. During his attempt to relieve the usurper who was besieged in Arelate, he was defeated by → Constantius [6] III and Ulfila, and was killed while attempting to escape in 411. H.L.

Edom

A. Historical Development up to the 4th cent. B. Hellenistic Period C. Edom within Rabbinical Tradition

A. Historical Development up to the 4th cent.

'The Red One' primarily refers to the mountain region east of the Wādī al-ʿArabā, to its population only secondarily. Under Merenptah, a report emerged that the 'Schasu (*Šśw*) of E.' were received in Egypt (ANET 259). Their settlement began in the 12th/11th cents. BC from the north and reached its peak in the 8th–6th cents. BC. The Esau-Jacob cycle (Gen. 25*, 27*, 32–33) demonstrates a special relationship to E., at least from an israelitic perspective. David achieved a limited supremacy (2 Sam. 8,13f.). Salomon and Joshafat used the harbour of Ezjon-Geber (Ǧazīrat Faraʿūn) for commerce with Ofir (1 Kgs 9,26–28; 22,48–50). E. did not develop into an independent tribal principality until the mid 9th cent. under Joram (2 Kgs 8,20–22) and became a state in the 8th cent. BC with the capital of Boṣrā. Records indicate that Qausmalak, Ḥairām, and Qausgabar were tributaries of Tiglatpileser III, Sanherib, Asarhaddon, and Assurbanipal. While Juda suffered under Assyrian pressure, E. was the silent winner. The animosity towards E. in Juda's prophecy during and after his exile is grounded in its occupation of the Judaic south (Ez 35,10; 12) and is reflected in ostraca with PN carrying the theophoric element of the Edomite national god Qaus ('bow'), a form of the Syrian-Arabic → Weather god(s). In 552, Nabonid put an end to E.'s independence. In the early 5th cent. BC, immigrating Arabic Qedar and the Nabataeans that developed out of them seized power in the central area, and in the Negev the province Idumaea emerged in the early 4th cent.

→ Edomite; → Nabataeans

J.R. Bartlett, E. and the Edomites, 1989; P. Bienkowski (ed.), Early Edom and Moab, 1992; E.A. Knauf, Supplementa Ismaelitica, in: Biblische Notizen 45, 1988, 62–81; M. Weippert, s.v. E., TRE 9, 291–299. K.B.

B. Hellenistic Period

E. denotes the area of the Edomite tribe or, as was their name in the Hellenistic period, the Idumaeans. In Biblical times, the area originally reached east of the ʿĂrābā valley over the mountain range of Śəʿir. However, due to the expansion of the → Nabataeans, the Edomite settlement territory moved into the Negev up to Hebron, Bet-Ṣur and Mārešā in the late 4th cent. BC After the area was conquered by Iohannes Hyrcanus (135/4–104 BC), he imposed the conversion to Judaism on the residents by enforcing circumcision as well as Jewish law (Jos. Ant. Iud. 13,257f.; 15,254). During the 1st Jewish War, Idumaean troops fought on the side of the Zelots (Jos. BI 4,224ff.).

C. Edom within Rabbinical Tradition

After the historical E. fell as a result of the 1st Jewish War (66–70), the term E. becomes a code name for the Roman Empire in rabbinical tradition, a name which served as a projection of all the repression and humiliation which Judaism had to suffer from the Romans. The reason for this projection can be found not only in the phonetic as well as written similarities (cf. Hebr. Daleth and Reš) and the obviously negative Biblical statements about E. (see *i.a.* Is. 34; Jer 49,7–22; Ez 35; Mal 1,2–5), but apparently also in the fact that Herod, whose kingdom was entirely based on Roman power, was Idumaean. The identification of E. with Rome is already suggested in the pre-rabbinical records 4 Ezra 6,7–19, where Esau represents the passing eon and Jacob holding onto his heel (who already in Biblical tradition was regarded as the progenitor of the Edomites; cf. Gen. 36,1; 9) represents the time of salvation that follows immediately after. In rabbinical literature, we already find records of this image here and there in early Tannaitic texts (→ Tannaites). It becomes widespread from the end of the 2nd cent. on, in Amoraic texts as well (→ Amoraim). After the fall of Rome, the metaphor was transferred to the Christian occident.

→ Herodes

F. Avemarie, Esaus Hände, Jakobs Stimme, in: R. Feldmeier, U. Heckel, M. Hengel, Juden, Christen und das Problem des Fremden, WUNT 70, 1994, 177–210; H. Donner, Gesch. des Volkes Israel und seiner Nachbarn in Grundzugen, 2 vols., ATD Ergänzungsreihe 4/1.2, 1984, Index s.v. E.; A. Kasher, Jews, Idumaeans, and Ancient Arabs. Relations of the Jews in Eretz-Israel with the Nations of the Frontier and the Desert during the Hellenistic and Roman Era (332 BCE — 70 CE), Texte und Stud. zum Ant. Judentum 18, 1988 (lit). B.E.

Edomite Name of the language used by the residents of the country of → Edom (→ Idumaea) south-east of the Dead Sea. Linguistically, E. should be placed between → Phoenician and → Hebrew. It is recorded in only a few inscriptions on ostraca and seals (7th/6th cents. BC).

→ Bersabe; → Canaanite

W.R. Garr, Dialect Geography of Syria-Palestine, 1985; L. Herr, The Scripts of Ancient Northwestsemitic Seals, 1978. C.K.

Edones (Ἠδωνοί; *Ēdōnoí*, Ἠδῶνες; *Ēdônes*). Thracian tribe on the lower reaches of the Strymon and on the Pangaeum. Their region was rich in mines and forests and therefore much embattled. Records of the E. exist for the 6th to the 4th cent. BC. They were subjugated in Megabazus' first European campaign. The Milesian tyrant Histiaeus received the settlement of Myrcinus from Darius and had a city built in its place (Hdt. 5,11; 23; 124). His son-in-law Aristagoras [1] fell in the fight against the E. during the attempt to secure the surroundings of Myrcinus (Hdt. 5,126; Thuc. 4,102,2).

Xerxes marched through the land of the E. as well (Hdt. 7,110; 114). The coins of the Edonic King Geta, which are of great interest for numismatic history, date from the early 5th cent. BC. The first unsuccessful attempt by the Athenians to found Amphipolis in the area of the E. occurred in 475. The second attempt under Hagnon took place in 465/4 and ended with the Athenians' defeat at → Drabescus (Thuc. 1,100,3). It is possible that the information in Herodotus (9,75) about the Athenian commander Sophanes, who was killed by the E. at → Daton, belongs in this context. The founding of Amphipolis was not achieved until 437 BC. Alexander [2] annexed the western part of the Edonic area (Thuc. 2,99). Despite Attic colonization, the Edonic ruling house maintained control over the hinterland until the Peloponnesian War. Sparta tried to ally itself with Pittacus, the king of the E. who was sympathetic towards Athens, but he fell victim to a court intrigue (Thuc. 4,107). The last literary reference to the E. occurs in connection with → Brasidas' battle of 1,500 Thracian and Edonic mercenaries against Cleon at Amphipolis in 422 BC (Thuc. 5,6). In later sources, the E. are mentioned only in a mythological and archaistic context (Ov. Rem. am. 593; Men. 11,69). Still in use, however, is the name of the region Ἠδωνίς; *Ēdōnís* (Ptol. 3,12,28; Plin. HN 4,40).

A. Fol, Političeskata istorija na trakite, 1972, 89–93, 104–106; Y. Youroukova, Coins of the Ancient Thracians, 1976.

I.v.B.

Educa (Edula, Edusa, Edulia). Roman 'special deity' (→ Indigitamenta), which, according to Varro (antiquitates rerum divinarum 114 Cardauns) was named in Christian Polemic (Tert. Ad nat. 2,11,8: *Edula*; Aug. Civ. 4,34; 6,9) together with → Potina. According to Varro in Non. 151, E. (*Edusa*) supposedly watched over the food for the children. Sacrifices were made to her when children had their first meal. In Donat. Ter. Phorm. 1,1,15, her name is *Edulia*. According to [1], E. was originally a *gens* deity.

1 F. Altheim, Röm. Religionsgesch. 1, 1931, 78–79.

B. Cardauns, M. Terentius Varro. Antiquitates rerum divinarum (comm.), 1976, 206; G. Radke, Die Götter Altitaliens, 1965, 111.

R.B.

Education

A. Concept B. Greece C. Rome D. Late Antiquity and Christianity E. Later reception

A. Concept

Education is understood here as the act of imparting techniques and skills, also as the shaping of morals, character, and mental development — in short: 'the sum total of a society's reaction to development' [1. 13] — whereby the growing human being is 'raised' to take his/her place in the world of adults. The concept of education differs from the concept of 'socialization' in that 'the decisive criterion of education lies in the fact that the process is intentional' (E. = 'to render social', socialization = 'to become social') [1. 17]. While an individual can endeavour to gain knowledge and culture throughout life, education generally ends with the individual's integration into society [1. 21].

A person can become a 'productive' member of society without cultivation but not without education. At no time in antiquity could more than 20–30% of adult men and *c.* 10% of the population read and write [2; 3]. The following therefore only describes the education of a minority. The education of the largest part of the population, on the other hand, occurred in all historical epochs through the process of the older generation's modelling and the younger generation's emulation as well as through oral teaching. Ideas fixed in writing contributed to education by being read out loud, through lectures, recitations, scenic performances, or in the form of songs or inscriptions (conveyed to 'those eager to learn' by literate persons).

B. Greece

a) Educational conceptions of the Homeric period: *The Iliad* and *Odyssey* contain the educational goals and principles directed towards an aristocratic society. Education thus refers to the process of turning noblemen into individual warriors and leaders (Hom. Il. 9,443). Honour as the most precious good and fame as the highest goal elevate chivalrousness and the agonistic principle to the fundamentals of education (Hom. Il. 6,208, cf. 11,784). The most important educational method is emulation, the most important educational method is to serve as a model, the most important educator is the older generation: the father, and often an older constant companion as well (Hom. Il. 9,434–605: Phoenix). In addition, education included a component of the fine arts. In this primarily oral culture, the education in the fine arts was based on emulation as well: similar to the Rhapsodes, Achilles also sings of heroic deeds (Hom. Il. 9,185–189; [27. 33–50; 4; 5. 17–22]). → Homer provides 'self-assurance and support' [6. 63] not only to the aristocratic society of the 8th cent. BC, but also, according to ancient opinion (for example, Pl. Resp. 606e), functions as the educator for all of Greece [7. 1, 23–88; 27. 44–46].

b) The educational conception of the polis: the clearest picture of education within the framework of the polis can be found in Sparta and Athens. It was tied to the community but continued to be geared to the particular needs of the leading class: in Sparta, it was the class of the → Spartiatae, in Athens, that of the wealthy citizens. In the beginning, the educational goals and principles were identical: the educational ideal was the καλοκαγαθία (*kalokagathía*). It required the possession of personal aptitude, which noblemen at first claimed exclusively for themselves as a matter of course. But the individual warrior was replaced by the → Hoplitai; actions were no longer guided by the ambition to gain personal fame, but by the needs of the polis. This role was gradually accepted by the property-owning citizenry as well, who had the material resources to also provide their sons with an education that remained aristocratic in its core [27. 92–94]. This education included gymnastic and artistic components. In Sparta, education in gymnastics was aimed at military training while neglecting artistic pursuits. It also promoted the health of future mothers through 'girl sports' (Plut. Lycurgus 15). Education in the fine arts doubled as the ethical education of a polite, a fact that can be observed in the songs of → Alcaeus and → Alcman as well as in → Solon's elegies [27. 51–104; 5. 28–33].

c) Innovations of the → sophists: the sophists revolutionized ancient pedagogy in the 5th cent. BC primarily through the following basic ideas: the distinction between culture as a human construct and nature as given (*nómos-phýsis*-opposition), and the claim that all humans are fundamentally equal and that inter-human inequalities are products of cultural influences. In accordance with these ideas, education has the purpose of bringing out the aptitudes that are inherent in each individual. Since the sophists taught in exchange for a fee, their programme of enabling individuals to meet the demands of house and polis (Pl. Prt. 318cd) ultimately reached only the property-owning citizenry.

The sophistic conception of education went far beyond artistic and gymnastic education in its focus on the training of intellectual abilities. By relegating societal conventions, the laws of the state, and anthropomorphous notions of god to the humanly constructed realm of culture, sophistic education promoted independent thinking, but, according to its critics, it displayed a relativist attitude towards ethical norms and questioned traditional religion [8].

→ Socrates' dispute with the sophists resulted in the development of philosophical schools with their philosophically orientated educational forms. A much broader influence, however, was exerted by the sophistic ideas developed in the school of → Isocrates, where the educational conception of a rhetorical education based on → *enkýklios paideía* was further developed [7. 3,105–130; 27. 105–184; 5. 67–156].

d) Educational conception of Hellenism: the polis lost its normative power, and education gained the function of conveying to Greeks the → *paideía* (regarded as their highest good: Isocr. panegyricus 50; Men. monostichoi 275; Plut. de liberis educandis 8e) through which they defined themselves as 'Hellenes' wherever they settled. In this context, education was understood as the shaping of the immature child into a socially acceptable person. Characteristic is the dominance of the literary element in education. This focus on literature now absolutely required the ability to read and write (Aristot. Pol. 1338^{a} 15–17, 36–40). Studies were guided by the *grammatikós* (γραμματικός) and were aimed at intellectual as well as ethical education [27. 307–333] through the discussion of literary texts: Homer (esp. *The Iliad*), Euripides and Menander, but also Hesiodus, Apollonius Rhodius, the lyric poets, the dramatists Aeschylus and Sophocles, and among the prose writers primarily the historians (Herodotus, Xenophon, Hellanicus, esp. Thucydides), the Attic orators probably on occasion, although the intensive study of the latter remained in the domain of rhetoric teaching. These literary pursuits were supplemented — most likely only by those who were interested [27. 334–352] — with the mathematical sciences (arithmetic, geometry, astronomy, and music theory) and were completed through training in rhetoric with the σοφιστής (*sophistḗs*) or the ῥήτωρ (*rhḗtōr*). The initiates of the old philosophical schools crowned or replaced them — depending on their attitude towards rhetorical education — with philosophical education [27. 389–407]. Thus, ancient education had found its final character. In this form it was adopted by the Romans and survived until the end of Antiquity, in the east until the Byzantine period.

e) Patronage and course of education: (1) private: the demand by philosophers that education should be a public task (Pl. Resp. 7,520c–541b, Leg. 7,788a–824a; Aristot. Pol. 8,1337a–1342b) remained unanswered for a long time. As a private matter, education favoured the children of the rich (Pl. Prt. 326c). In the classical period, the domestic education by mother and wet nurse was followed, after age eight, by instruction in gymnastics (running, long jump, discus and javelin throwing, wrestling, boxing, pancratium) in the → *palaístra* taught by the → *paidotríbēs*, and by education in the fine arts (singing and instrumental music) taught by the citharist. Parallel to these, lessons in reading, writing, and arithmetic were taught by the *grammatistḗs*/*grammatodidáskalos*. On their way to school, children from good families were accompanied and protected by the → *paidagōgós* (among other things from paederasty [9. 199]). The elementary instruction by the grammatist laid the foundation for higher education [27. 227–306].

(2) State and municipal institutions of education: aside from the Cretes, only the Spartans had state education. In Sparta, this was a result of an exceptional socio-political situation (maintaining rulership over Helots and Messenians), in which the father-son relationship was replaced by the relationship between adolescents and the older generation [10. 90–94], a circumstance which also makes comprehensible the educational element of homosexual love [9. 163, 215; 27. 72–88]. State supervision intended education only for healthy and strong children. At the age of seven, the boys were grouped into formations in which they remained for 13 years under the supervision of the → *paidónomoi* and where they received an education geared towards military fitness and strength of character [7. 1, 113–139; 27. 51–71]. Even beyond the time of their education, they remained quartered in barracks until the age of 30. The highest goal was the creation of a military elite. Therefore, physical education and toughening up took precedence over intellectual education. A moral education aimed at unbending toughness was supposed to

produce Spartans who were ascetic and obedient towards the laws and institutions of the state.

(3) *Ephebeia* and → Gymnasium: except for Sparta, the Greek poleis left it at a supervisory function when it came to education [27. 201f.[8]]. This did not change until Athens institutionalized the military instruction of 18–20 year olds in the → *ephēbeía*, probably in 338 BC [11. 19; 27. 204]. Although initially founded as a military institution, it was apparently linked from the start to a minimal programme in literary education. After the discontinuation of its original function, the *ephebeia* could therefore transform itself into the *ephebeia*-gymnasium. It is not clear in what form the *ephebeia* was adopted by other poleis; in the Hellenistic period, it is documented for over 100 communities. It is the first state school. The reason for its emergence lies in the fact that the polis now marked the line of division between Greeks and non-Greeks. The *ephebeia*-gymnasium was often supplemented with sections for adolescents (Pergamum even had a gymnasium with three sections [11. 31f.]), which, however, were no longer financed by the communities but generally by wealthy citizens and sponsor organizations of former students, while state supervision only occurred at games and at festivals (in official examinations of school achievements in competitions) [12. 60–64; 27. 204–226].

(4) Other school institutions (for girls): in *c.* 600 BC, → Sappho directed a kind of boarding school for young girls on Lesbos (organized as → Thiasos). It clearly focused on fine arts, but a gymnastic component was also included. The closeness between the female teacher and students brought — just as in Spartan education — an erotic element into education. 'Boarding schools' such as Sappho's probably existed up until Roman-Hellenistic times [7. 1, 183–186; 27. 85–88]. In the Hellenistic period, girls apparently were sent to school or to the gymnasium as well ([27. 200], more sceptically [11. 60]). Public instruction for girls is documented for Teos (it is questionable whether education occurred together with boys [11. 47, 53]) and Pergamum (special supervisor for girls), perhaps also for Smyrna [27. 219].

(5) Philosopher schools: see → Philosophy, teaching of.

C. Rome

(a) Educational conceptions: (1) Ancient Rome: the educational goal of the Roman aristocracy was to prepare the adolescent for his duties as → *pater familias* and his role in political and military life. Education grew out of the → *mos maiorum* and was carried out directly within practical life, through it and for it. A strictly utilitarian attitude disallowed artistic elements altogether. Gymnastic components remained foreign to the Roman emphasis on sports solely aimed at military training (riding, swimming, fencing). Although elementary schools (introduced by the Etruscans) existed from as early as the 7th cent. BC on [27. 459f.], the theoretical part of ancient Roman education hardly went beyond the practical skills of reading, writing, and arithmetic. The primary purpose was similar to the educational ideal of the polis in that it aimed for the moral education of individuals willing to make personal sacrifices in the service to → *gens* and → *civitas*. However, the ancient Roman ideal of education is, as it were, reduced to an agathist ideal, namely the ideal of the *vir bonus*: it contains the virtues attributed to the citizen who practices agriculture, such as *labor, industria, parsimonia, temperantia, severitas,* as well as statesmanlike virtues such as *gravitas, constantia, magnitudo animi, probitas, fides* (Cic. Tusc. 1,2). The educational goal also included oratory skills, and here again, practical life offered the necessary training (Cato fr. 15 p. 80 J: *rem tene, verba sequentur*) [27. 425–444].

(2) Greek education in Rome: the steadily growing cultural influence of Greece in the 3rd and 2nd cents. BC finally opened up to noble young Romans an intellectual dimension of education that had been largely absent before. Greek education essentially means education through literary and rhetorical studies. It remains to be seen how much educational value the Romans granted the *paideía*: → Cato Censorius regarded the imported goods as an endangerment of ancient Roman educational principles (Plut. Cato maior 22,5). → Scipio Aemilianus, on the other hand, already believed that Greek education had contributed to his achievement (Pol. 32,9f.). → Cicero completely recognized Greek education as full compensation for the gentilistic requirements he lacked for playing a leading role in society. The Augustan period saw the completion of a unity between Hellenistic and Roman culture (Verg. Aen. 6,847–853, Hor. Epist. 2,1,156–160). With regard to the Roman educational experience, one could speak of a Roman humanism [13; 14].

(b) Patronage of education: (1) House and family: while Polybius criticizes the lack of state supervision in Rome from his Hellenistic point of view, Scipio regards the same as an advantage with regard to Cicero (Cic. Rep. 4,3). In contrast to the Spartans, the Romans found promise of political strength in supporting family structures (*patria potestas*) [9. 94–98]. An education loyal to the state was intended to ensure the individual's identification with the *res publica* [12. 66f.]. Even the adoption of the Greek paideia as an element of education remained the responsibility of the family. Education by private teachers in the homes of senatorial families — quite often by the head of household's slaves or freedmen [15] — continued as a custom until late antiquity. Aristocratic families also concerned themselves with the education of the slaves who belonged to the *familia urbana* (often organized in *paedagogia* [27. 491–493]). Likewise, it was up to the family to send their children to the schools of grammarians, rhetors, and philosophers.

An idealized picture of the course of education is painted by Messalla in the tacitaean *Dialogus* (28–35). This depiction also applies to the education of girls from noble families during their first 12–15 years, intended as a foundation for the active participation of the young married woman in the literary, artistic, and intellectual life [16. 296–302; 17. 221–223]. We must emphasize the influence of mothers on their children's education and culture. Examples of highly educated women are Cornelia (Plut. C. Gracchus 19) and Sempronia (Sall. Catil. 25,2). When it came to moral education, they were assisted by an older relative. Following elementary education, the bilingually raised child (Greek was taught primarily by the *paidagogos*) was taught by the *grammaticus Graecus* and the *grammaticus Latinus* as well as the rhetor (→ Rhetoric), who taught rhetoric first in Greek only, but from the 1st cent. BC on (→ Plotius Gallus) in Latin as well. The attitude of *dissimulatio* favoured by republican minded Romans loved to diminish the contribution of Greek rhetoric in the education of young Romans (Cic. De or. 2,75, 77–84, 162 and *passim*; Tac. Dial. 35) and to stress instead the importance of the 'political apprenticeship' (*tirocinium fori*, after the 16th year) (Cic. De or. 1,109; Tac. Dial. 34). The latter was supervised by an older friend of the family and could — as it did for Cicero (Cic. Lael. 1; Brut. 106; Leg. 1,13) — introduce the student to the practice of law. Relatives and friends of the family usually also supervised the military service of young noblemen [27. 432–435]. Education in philosophy only played a role for the intellectual elite; the most intensive philosophical studies were afforded by attending the philosopher schools in Athens.

(2) Public instruction: its organization was left up to the initiative of the teacher; its success depended on the teacher's reputation. → School.

(c) Developments in the Imperial period: cultural education retained its traditional function for the senator class and the local upper class. Again and again, it became an object of philosophical reflection [18. 512–515]: theoretical treatises on education are documented for the peripatetics → Theophrastus and → Aristoxenus as well as for the stoics → Zeno, Cleanthes and Chrysipp (basic ideas: self-education; the propaedeutic value of the sciences, character development as the main goal; educational optimism). A treatise handed down under Plutarch's name entitled *Perí paídōn agōgḗs* develops the triad of *phýsis/lógos/máthēsis*, and *ḗthos/áskēsis*, and argues that learning and practice can compensate for deficiencies in aptitude [4]. It rejects 'brutal pedagogy' [12. 16; 18] and advises the father to be lenient and to remember his own youth (12,18). We should also mention → Musonius, Seneca, Quintilian, Epictetus, and Marcus Aurelius in this context.

The need for leading officials in the imperial administration resulted in a professionally oriented education. It opened up new careers esp. for members of the equestrian class [12. 68f.; 19]. The organizational structures and educational institutions of the cities in the Hellenized East were transferred to the communities in the West as well [20. 1, 176–180]. In accordance with the pyramidal structure of the educational system, evidence of elementary schools can be found in even the smallest settlements, gymnasia were kept in small towns, instruction in rhetoric was offered generally only in bigger cities, the study of philosophy was best pursued in Athens, that of jurisprudence in Rome or Berytus, and that of medicine in Alexandria [12. 70; 21. 2737–2739]. Women also — at least of the upper class — participated in education and culture and were present in the economic and professional life as well as in self-administration and municipal politics [17. 211–223].

The educational interests of members of the upper class (*honestiores*) found expression in private initiative and voluntary work in the municipal realm (example: Pliny the Younger). As wealth began to decline, these tasks were increasingly forced on them by the state [20. 2, 23f.]. The state's interest in education and in the training of leading officials also resulted in state patronage. Depending on their particular interests, the emperors only paid attention to higher general studies and universal education. The ancient state never took care of elementary education: elementary teachers were always poorly paid and excluded from the privileges enjoyed by the teachers of the → *artes liberales*. By far the largest part of the population was left in a state of illiteracy. Here, the extent of deliberate moral education and the development of intellect and character beyond spontaneous socialisation depended on a person's social environment, just as the level of technical training depended on one's place in working life.

D. Late Antiquity and Christianity

(a) Christian education: Christian education is primarily religious education, dogmatics and morals are its main subjects [27. 573]. The guiding principle is the παιδεία Κυρίου (*paideía Kyríou*, Eph 6,4, → Clemens Alexandrinus and → Origenes interpreted it as surpassing the pagan *paideía*) [22. 196; 23. 150f.]. It establishes a kyriocentric educational thinking, in contrast to the Greek anthropocentric and the Jewish nomocentric educational conceptions [22]. Intellectual development was relegated to a serving role [18. 521]. Christian education was meant equally for boys and for girls, the social role of women was considered within the educational subjects. In general, education was not the privilege of only the few, but a common good [18. 523]. As opposed to education in the general sense, yet similar to the Hellenistic paideia with which it stood in competition, Christian education never ended (sermon, repentance) [24. 877f.], since the perfection that depends on divine grace could only be reached in the hereafter according to Christian thought [18. 523; 23. 154]. Christian virtues (humility, faith, hope, the love of God and compassion) dominated the educational subjects. Humility in particular (*tapeinótēs, humilitas*), which as a virtue was foreign to pagan antiquity, and the strict requirement of controlling physical desires which was regarded as absolute in contrast to the pagan, philosophical emphasis on self-control, combine to give Christian education a new character [23. 156f.].

(b) Christianity and ancient education: Christian education originally entailed the education of simple people and simple minds who found the promise of eternal bliss in living according to the *regula fidei*. In the end, however, it cannot get by without literary education: Christianity is based on written revelation and must administer a growing body of traditional rules and regulations regarding moral discipline, spiritual literature, apologetics, polemics against → heresy, and dogmatics [27. 576f.]. From the 2nd cent. on, more and more wealthy individuals accepted the new religion. They held on to their lifestyle and were not satisfied with simple answers concerning issues of faith. Their 'elitist class consciousness ... corresponded to a great openness towards ancient culture' [25. 53].

As a result, Christian schools modelled on Jewish rabbinical schools emerged only in the so-called 'barbaric' countries (Egypt, Syria, Mesopotamia), while the area of Greek and Latin education brought forth a 'cultural osmosis' [27. 582] between classical and religious education [27. 579–583]. This osmosis did not take place without internal Christian opposition [25. 54–62; 27. 583–587]. Still, the share of Christian teachers grew steadily on all levels: Origenes, for example, at first had worked only as grammarian, a priest with the name of Malchion had a rhetoric school in Antiochia in *c.* AD 268, → Anatolius was professor of Aristotelian philosophy in Alexandria in AD 264. The school law by Iulianus Apostata, which excluded Christians from the teaching profession, remained a non-representative episode (enacted on 17 June AD 362, repealed on 11 January AD 364, Cod. Theod. 13,3,5–6). But even a Christian majority among teachers and students did not result in the Christianization of ancient school instruction: its propaedeutic function (first recognized by → Clemens following the Jew → Philo[25. 71–74]) for Christian education remained unchallenged [18. 532–534; 27. 587–594].

(c) Patrons of Christian education: (1) Family: a primarily ethical education uses emulation above all. Therefore, the parents' role as models — in continuation of the Jewish tradition [18. 517f.] — is of great importance; they bear the main responsibility for the education of their children in the eyes of God and the community. Other household members — such as grandparents, siblings, servants — as well as godparents also shared in the educational responsibility [18. 525–531; 26; 27. 573f.].

(2) Church: the moral education by the parents was aided by the introduction into dogmatics by specially appointed teachers of religion, generally priests, whose schooling was examined and completed by bishops (baptismal catechumenate) [27. 574–576].

(3) Christian schools: because elementary and secondary general education took place in the schools of antiquity, no Christian schools developed for these levels. The demand for religion teachers and the striving of the → gnostics for a 'holy science', however, lead us to expect the emergence of theological universities. In fact, such schools emerged since the 2nd cent. AD, but they were not able to engender a tradition [18. 536f.; 27. 594–599], despite their great temporary importance (on Clemens [25. 68–81], on Origenes [25. 81–100]). 'Spirituality is not brought up in schools, but through the personal contact with the bishop and the older priests of the local clergy, who often accepted students as readers from early childhood on' [27. 598]. In the East, where the tradition of ancient education continued unbroken into the Byzantine period, a tradition of monastery instruction (limited in its influence) developed early on. In the West, the situation changed beginning in the 4th cent. AD: the decline (more or less rapid in the different parts of the empire) of the ancient educational system that resulted from Germanic invasions forced the church more and more to take charge of propaedeutics as well (monastery, bishop, and presbyterian schools) [27. 600–634].

E. Later reception

We can talk about a continued influence of ancient education, but hardly about its later reception (stronger emphasis on connections in [1. 39–71]). The breaks between Late Antiquity and the Middle Ages and between the Middle Ages and modernity are too far-reaching. The continued influence of ancient education during the Renaissance is a result more of overcoming than continuing the old education, because it brought forth the emancipation of the human being: education no longer is a private affair; illiteracy (which increased once again in the Middle Ages) is eliminated today due to universal compulsory school attendance; receiving an education no longer depends on belonging to 'better society' but on individual talent and performance motivation, which, of course, in turn is determined by the social environment; modern pedagogy tries to be child-centered. The moral and religious conceptions of education are visibly shaped by cultural diversity.

→ Life Stages; → Education; → Education; → Rhetoric; → School

1 H.-E. Tenorth, Gesch. der Erziehung, 1988 2 W.V. Harris, Ancient literacy, 1989 3 W.H. Pleket, in: Mnemosyne 45, 1992, 416–423 4 J. Latacz, Das Menschenbild Homers, in: Gymnasium 91, 1984, 15–39 5 W. Reichert, Erziehungskonzeptionen der griech. Ant., [2]1993 6 J. Latacz, Homer, [2]1989 7 W. Jaeger, Paideia, vol. 1 [5]1973, vol. 2 [4]1973, vol. 3 [4]1973 8 J.V. Muir, in: P.E. Easterling, J.V. Muir(ed.), Greek Rel. and Society, 1985, 191–218, 228–230 9 C. Reinsberg, Ehe, Hetärentum und Knabenliebe im ant. Griechenland, [2]1993 10 J. Martin, in: H. Süssmuth (ed.), Histor. Anthropologie, 1984, 84–109 11 M.P. Nilsson, Die hell. Schule, 1955 12 J. Christes, Gesellschaft, Staat und Schule in der griech.-röm. Antike, in: H. Kloft (ed.), Sozialmaßnahmen und Fürsorge, GB Suppl. 3, 1988, 55–74 13 K.-H. Abel, in: A&A; 17, 1971, 119–143 14 W. Schadewaldt, Romanitas Humana, in: ANRW I 4, 43–62 15 J. Christes, Sklaven und Freigelassene als Grammatiker und Philologen im ant. Rom, Forsch. zur ant. Sklaverei, vol. 10, 1979 16 Friedländer 17 K. Thraede, s.v. Frau, RAC 8, 197–269 18 P. Blo-

MENKAMP, s.v. E., RAC 6, 502–559 19 D. NELLEN, Viri litterati, [2]1981 20 J. BLEICKEN, Verfassungs- und Sozialgesch. des röm. Kaiserreichs, vol. 1 [4]1995, vol. 2 [3]1994 21 U. SCHINDEL, s.v. Schulen, LAW, 2735–2740 22 W. JENTSCH, Urchristl. Erziehungsdenken, 1951 23 B. SCHWENK, Hell. Paideia und christl. Erziehung, in: C. COLPE et al. (see below), 141–158 24 G. PRIESEMANN, M. RITTER, s.v. Erziehung, LAW, 874–878 25 R. KLEIN, Christl. Glaube und heidnische Bildung, in: Laverna 1, 1990, 50–100 26 M. GÄRTNER, Die Familienerziehung in der Alten Kirche, 1985 27 MARROU.

Bibliography: L. ALFONSI, Augustin und die ant. Schule, AU 17, 1975, 5–16; S.F. BONNER, Education in ancient Rome, 1977 · A.K. BOWMAN, G. WOOLF (ed.), Literacy and power in the ancient world, 1994; C. COLPE, L. HONNEFELDER, M. LUTZ-BACHMANN(ed.), Spätant. und Christentum, 1992; A. DIHLE, s.v. Demut, RAC 3, 735–778; C. A. FORBES, The education and training of slaves in antiquity, in: TAPhA 86, 1955, 321–360; H.-G. GADAMER, Platon und die Dichter, 1936; Id., Platos Staat der E., 1941, repr.: Platos dialektische Ethik, 1958, 205–220; L. GRASBERGER, Erziehung und Unterricht im klass. Alt. 1–3, 1864–1880, repr. 1971; A. GWYNN, Roman education. From Cicero to Quintilian, 1926; F.-P. HAGER, Zur Bed. der griech. Philos. für die christl. Wahrheit und Bildung bei Tertullian und bei Augustin, A&A; 24, 1978, 76–84; H.-TH. JOHANN (ed.), Erziehung und Bildung in der heidnischen und christl. Ant., 1976; M. LECHNER, Erziehung und Bildung in der griech.-röm. Ant., 1933; S.L. MOHLER, Slave education in the Roman empire, TAPhA 71, 1940, 262–280; K. WENGST, Demut, Solidarität des Gedemütigten, 1987. J.C.

Education / Culture

A. TERM B. HISTORY: GREECE 1. EDUCATIONAL IDEALS AND CONCEPTS 2. GENERAL AND SPECIFIC EDUCATION 3. DESIRE FOR EDUCATION AND SPECIALIST ERUDITION 4. BANAUSIA C. ROME 1. THE SITUATION IN EARLY ROME 2. GREEK EDUCATION IN ROME 3. DEVELOPMENT IN THE IMPERIAL PERIOD D. LATE ANTIQUITY AND CHRISTIANITY 1. CONTINUATION OF ANCIENT EDUCATIONAL CONCEPTS 2. CHRISTIANITY AND ANCIENT EDUCATION 3. THE CHRISTIAN IDEA OF EDUCATION E. TRADITION OF ANCIENT EDUCATION

A. TERM

On one hand, the Greek term → παιδεία (*paideía*), like παίδευσις (*paídeusis*; Aristoph. Nub. 986,1043), describes an → education that comprises both intellectual and ethical teaching as a process (Aristoph. Nub. 961; Thuc. 2,39,1), but on the other hand also education as an asset and as the result of the teaching process (Democr. 180; Pl. Prt. 327d; Grg. 470e; Resp. 378e; Aristot. Pol. 1338a30). Today, a distinction is usually made between education = teaching by means of theoretical insight and education = forming of character and behaviour by discipline and training. Ancient education always intended to include character training but there is agreement with the conventional modern differentiation to the extent that teaching without education existed in antiquity but education that did not address the intellect (through music and/or literary educational elements) was unimaginable. In addition, teaching concluded with the integration of the individual in society while education could be a process continuing throughout life. In various periods the content and ideal of education changed in tandem with the image of man.

B. HISTORY: GREECE

1. EDUCATIONAL IDEALS AND CONCEPTS

a) The educational ideal of the Homeric period: the heroes of the Iliad and the Odyssey reflect the educational ideal of their 8th-cent. audience [1]: at the centre of this aristocratic view of man held by a court culture was the ability to perform, which had to be demonstrated over and over again (ἀρετή, *aretḗ*). It enabled achieving the goals of 'wealth', 'honour' and 'glory'. It was as much part of the education of the Homeric hero to wield the lance as it was to speak knowledgeably in the council or assembly (Hom.Il. 9,442). Chivalric behaviour, sensitive discretion, polite but also worldly behaviour characterized his appearance [2. 37–40], musical skills (lyre play, Hom.Il. 9,186) were familiar to him.

b) The educational ideal of the polis period: in the course of the 7th cent. the individual knightly warrior gave way to the hoplite phalanx. The polis had become the new centre of life. This was particularly pronounced in Sparta, but essentially similar in all Greek aristocratic societies [2. 89]. The lyric poets were the propagandists of polis culture: they sang of subordination to the political community, obedience to the law, and dedication of life to the polis (Tyrtaeus Fr.6,1–3; 9,1–18; Callim. Fr.1,6–11; 18–19). Their educational ideal was the καλὸς κἀγαθός (*kalòs kagathós*), the good man with pleasing physique and perfect ethical and social behaviour. Among the virtues preserving the state, Aeschylus (Sept. 610; similar Aristoph. Ran. 727–729) lists the virtues of thoughtfulness, justice, capability and piety. Aristophanes [3. 36] still supported the ἀρχαία παιδεία (*archaía paideía*, Old Education) in the first half of the 5th cent. Thucydides described in the Periclean *Epitaphios* (2,39–40, cf. the speech of the Corinthians, which is characterized by a perceptive hatred 1,70) the new dynamic that grew from the fusion of democratic thought with aristocratic traditions of education.

c) The educational ideal of Hellenism: the image of man that developed with the end of the polis world in the course of the 4th cent. was characterized by free personal development. Musical education dropped in rank relative to a literary education, the educational route that included grammar, dialectics and rhetoric, in the context of the → *enkýklios paideía*. Already at the transition to this period, Democritus (*c.* 430–370 BC) conceived of *paideía* as the indestructible educational asset belonging to humans (68 B 180 DK). Everywhere where Greeks lived they cared for its transmission through communal educational institutions and de-

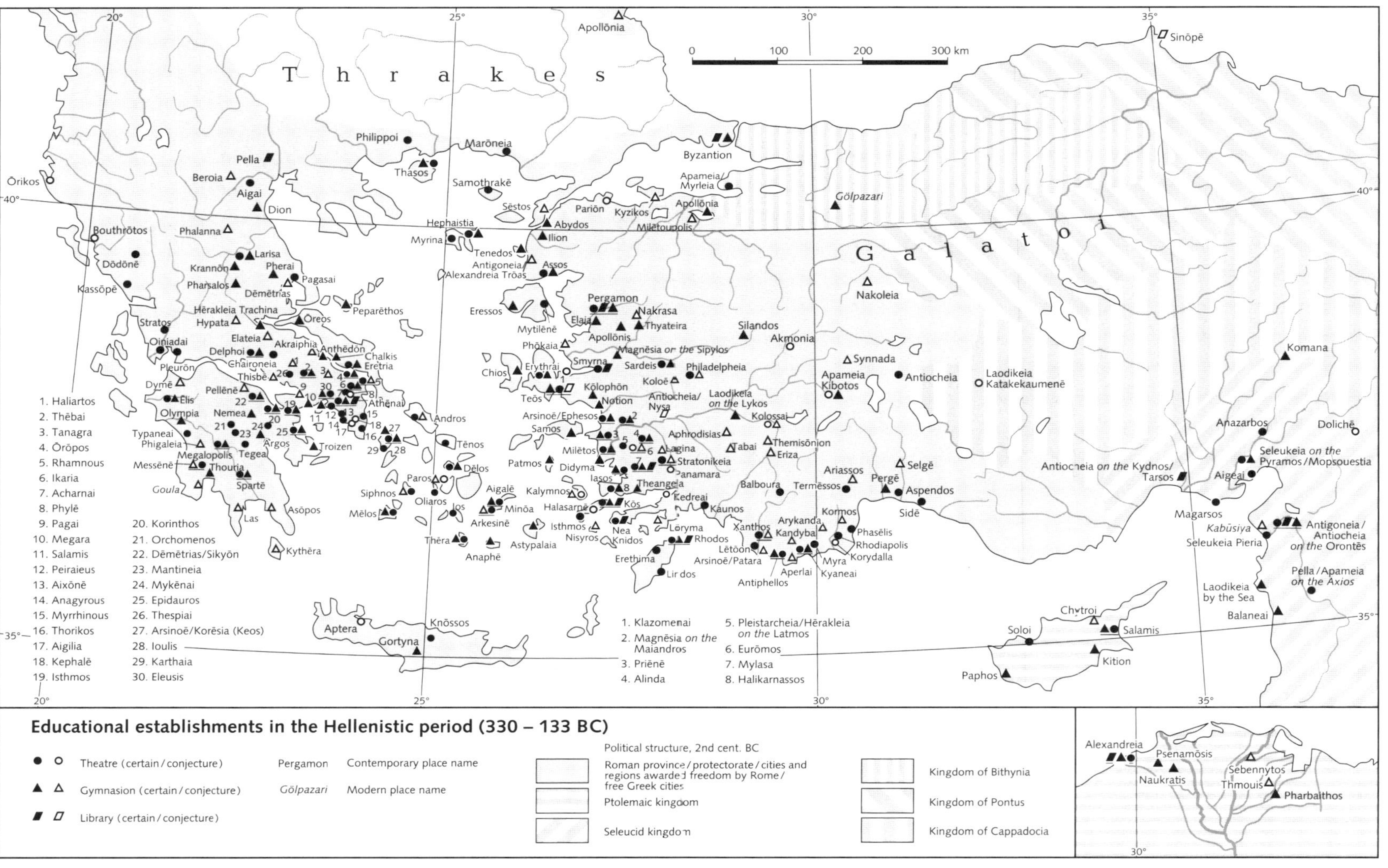

Educational establishments in the Hellenistic period (330 – 133 BC)

fined their identity by possessing this cultural asset.

d) Educational concepts: in the case of the → Seven Sages, the claim of self-acquired σοφία (*sophía*) is found (an ethical knowledge and superior cleverness in social and political questions, cf. Cic. De or. 3,137), which is why adherents of the theoretical-scientific and the practical-political ideal of life can equally claim it as their predecessor [6].

In the philosophy of → Pythagoras and his 'order', the theory of numbers was central. Therefore, arithmetic, geometry, music and astronomy were fixed components of the educational curriculum [4. 115f.].

The development of democracy in the course of the 5th cent. made the benefits of education in political activity apparent. This involved the → Sophists in the programme as professional mediators of education [4. 42–50]. The concept of encyclopaedic learning, the *polymathía* (→ Hippias of Elis, cf. Pl. Hp. mi. 368b-d) was criticized by → Heraclitus (Diels, 22 B 40 DK) and → Democritus (68 B 65 DK) as an overload of knowledge. A selection of material that seemed suited to the handling of duties in home and polis (Pl. Prt. 318c-d) appeared called for and led to the development of the subject canon of the *enkýklios paideía* [4. 42–50]. → Gorgias of Leontini believed that all that was needed was taught by teaching rhetorical technique (Pl. Grg. 449a-b; d-e). However, most sophists valued the transmission of knowledge; some also dealt with questions in theology, ethics and politics. The conviction that talent and intellect decide on the success of educational efforts [3. 36] essentially made education available to all — unlike the aristocratic ideal of the *kalokagathía*. Nevertheless, it remained a privilege of the aristocracy and the wealthy.

According to the critique of antiquity, the teachings of the sophists bore the seeds of a relativization of standards in its practical application — 'man is the measure of all things' (Protagoras, 80 B 1 DK), a formalization and technicalization of education that was guided by success (Gorgias) (cf. in Plato Thrasymachus, Resp. 327–354, and Callicles in *Gorgias*; on the decay of values accelerated by the Peloponnesian War, Thuc. 3,82–83). → Socrates attempted to counter this tendency. He turned to questions of the human soul and the proper conduct of life. He attempted to unmask the knowledge transmitted by the sophists as an illusion.

According to his own admission, his pupil → Plato (Pl. Ep. 7) repeatedly sought to enter politics. He blamed corrupt politics for his ideal of the philosopher king (Resp. 473c-e) not being accepted as the ideal of a new political elite. His *paideía* is inextricably linked to his design for a state and derived from his fundamental philosophical convictions, which were influenced by Pythagorean teachings [2. 129–159; 4. 112–117; 7. vol. 3,337–344] and had the objective of elevating the human soul to an aware perspective on goodness. This difficult route can only be travelled by philosophical spirits and led through the stages of a musical and gymnastic education — the heritage of the old aristocratic

education — and a general propaedeutics of mathematical sciences — the influence of Pythagorism on Platonic pedagogic (but cf. also Hippias of Elis) — to a crowning by dialectics, which trains the mind for an intellectual view of the idea of goodness. His ideal was the philosophically educated person, who knows how to shape earthly reality — and if he is permitted, also political reality — with knowledge of true being.

However, lasting success fell to → Isocrates [4. 118–121; 8] and not Plato. He recognized the formal educational value of the mathematical disciplines but also viewed the contribution of dialectics as restricted to it. A rhetorical education that he called φιλοσοφία (*philosophía*) (Isoc. Or. 15,261–271; 12,26–29) crowned the educational route that he proposed (on this use of the term philosophy, which was correct in his time [7. vol. 3. 108–109]). His educational concept comprised a 'broad knowledge of literature, a clarity of thought achieved by mathematical training, and skilled expression' [5. 347]. However, in the subsequent period the ideal and reality generally separated from each other and the mathematical disciplines were neglected in the educational practice. Recently, it was wrongly concluded as a result that there never was a concept of *enkýklios paideía* that included the mathematical disciplines and one that only in late antiquity included the → *artes liberales* [9]: the recognition of the formal educational value of the mathematical disciplines secured their place in the education concept of Isocratic character. However, since this educational value did not seem as obvious in a rhetorical education as in a philosophical education, it was in practice neglected.

As with Isocrates, the complete programme of the *enkýklios paideía* is also found in → Aristotle [4. 121–126]. He also considered the mathematical subjects and dialectics as subjects in the education of youth that aided the training of reason. He also affirmed the usefulness of grammar and rhetoric in practical life.

2. General and specific education

The canon of general educational disciplines required their learning as a precondition in a non-expert capacity but, nevertheless, emphasis on individual subjects as the crowning of the educational concept led to specialized study [4. 71–99, 112–128]. This applied to rhetoric in the Isocratic educational concept, to dialectics and philosophy in philosophical educational programmes, and also to the mathematical disciplines in the Platonic Academy. This is why the most important mathematicians were in contact with it or were members of it [4. 73]. The specialized studies of the Peripatetics resulted in the emancipation of literary and natural sciences, a development that was continued in the → Mouseion at Alexandria. From then on the distinction made by Aristotle (Part. an. 639a 1–13; Pol. 1282a 1–7; Eth. Nic. 1094b 23–27) between the educated person and the expert [4. 126–128] applied. At the same time the relationship of general and specialized education had to be defined [2. 408–422; 4. 74–99, 128–146]. The utility of a general education was seen in the training of the mind before any specialization and in the unfolding of personal inclination ('non-predetermined variety': [2. 419f.]), but also — a view that is alien to the basic concern of general education — in making available useful subject knowledge for a later profession. Understandably, the philosophers emphasized the formal aspect, while adherents of a rhetorical education and experts (e.g., the architect → Vitruvius, the geographer → Strabo and → Ps.-Soranus in medicine) more strongly emphasized the material aspect. However, rejection of a general education that was considered useless and, therefore, superfluous can also be found [4. 99–111].

3. DESIRE FOR EDUCATION AND SPECIALIST ERUDITION

Although originally only a non-expert involvement with the subjects of education was considered appropriate to status, Aristotle (Pol. 1337b 15–21) conceded that expert treatment could also be considered ἐλευθέριον (*eleuthérion*, worthy of a free man), providing it is not done to obtain a professional income [10. 42–44]. The practical/political ideal of life had lost its obligatory aspect and, consequently, a liberated intellectual potential turned towards the sciences and flowered. Figures like → Archimedes (Plut. Marcellus 14,17) and → Nicolaus of Damascus (FGrH 90 fr.132) are ideal-typical of the devotion to a science or a universal desire for education as the content of noble leisure [10. 110–116]. It was even possible to speak of a religion of education: the belief was widespread that use of educational assets purified the soul and founded the right to happiness, which is why it became popular to be portrayed on a grave stele or a sarcophagus as an intellectual (professor, musician, writer) [2. 195–197; 5. 348].

4. BANAUSIA

The τέχναι ἐλευθέριοι (*téchnai eleuthérioi*) were wrongly equated with the τ. λογικαί (*t. logikaí*), just as the τ. βάναυσοι (*t. bánausoi*) were with the τ. χειρωνακτικαί (*t. cheirōnaktikaí*) [10. 71–86]. *Eleuthérioi téchnai* (skills worthy of a free man) were warfare and agriculture (Xen. Oec. 4,2–11; Dion. Hal. Ant. Rom. 2,28), the one as unpaid service to the state, the other as the basis of material existence. Inversely, any intellectual activity, if it distracted from the true duties as perceived by the dominant ideal of life or was practised for gain, was considered unworthy of status and banausic ([10. 86–129, s. also 25–70]; on the etymology of *bánausos* [10. 79–81]). At the threshold of Hellenism, Aristotle (see above) recognized that a specialized education was appropriate to elevated status. Thus, the *enkýklios paideía* was joined by the ἐλευθέριοι ἐπιστῆμαι (*eleuthérioi epistēmai*) and only their professional exercise remained inappropriate to higher status. However, this viewpoint of the better members of society lost its general acceptance. The professional intelligentsia profited increasingly from the value placed on the educational assets related by them and developed its own professional ethos. Their distinction of *t. logikaí* and *t. cheironaktikaí* did not relate to status appropriateness but to the higher prestige of intellectual professions in the world of work.

C. ROME

1. THE SITUATION IN EARLY ROME

Initially one cannot speak of education in Rome; the intellectual element of the Greek polis with the educational medium of literature and a counterpart to musical education is largely missing. Instead, ethical educational postulates dominate; therefore, see → education (= teaching).

2. GREEK EDUCATION IN ROME

a) Development: the Hellenization of Rome began with the conquest of Southern Italy and Sicily in the 3rd cent. and reached its climax in the 2nd cent. Cato stands for a somewhat overwrought and in the end futile resistance while Scipio Aemilianus and his circle dealt with the foreign intellectual influences while preserving a Roman identity [2. 445–453; 5. 348; 10. 152–166]. Cicero and Varro combined active participation in public life with a literary activity through which they decisively propagated Greek cultural heritage [2. 464–465; 10. 166–189; 11; 12. 387–389].

b) The subjects of education: apart from occasional exuberance (Plut. Aem. Paulus 6,9), the selection of subjects soon focussed on the → *artes liberales*, i.e. the subjects of the Greek *enkýklios paideía*. As in Greek culture, arithmetic, geometry, astronomy and music played a minor role (Cic. Tusc. 1,5; Hor. Ars P. 323–332). However, the undeniable value of rhetoric opened the doors for a rhetorical education in the tradition of Isocrates. The origin of this education presupposed bilingualism for its acquisition, beginning with the teaching by the *grammaticus Graecus* and the *grammaticus Latinus*. Philosophy was ranked low in the education of the average Roman while rhetoric ranked high [2. 505–530].

c) Utilitarianism and desire for education: the Roman desire for education is characterized in the Republican period by the practical use for education, by *utilitas* and *usus* [10. 169–180; 13]. This does not just apply to the sketched rhetorical education. In the sciences only the practical uses of mechanics, architecture and surveying [2. 466] were of interest. The origin of legal studies is also explained by its relationship to practice [2. 530–533]. Typically enough, encyclopaedias are a specifically Roman literary genre [4. 50–70; 10. 171–173]. Cicero, too, essentially justified his educational ideal for the perfect speaker, for whom he required the study of history, law and philosophy, in utilitarian terms [11]. His never tiring desire for education and his receptiveness to philosophy enabled him to become the most important mediator of Greek cultural heritage in the Latin world.

3. DEVELOPMENT IN THE IMPERIAL PERIOD

The changing political and social framework also altered the role of education [10. 228–241]. Philosophy and rhetoric continued competing in the claim to education [2. 396–400]. On the one hand, a rhetorical education served the elegant leisure of the high society, on the other — with increased professionalization and specialization — also a career as, for example, → *causidicus* or in the Imperial service. At that time a specialized legal training opened attractive career perspectives. However, philosophy gained in importance for giving meaning to human life [13. 37]. Stoic philosophy equipped members of the senatorial class to retain their personal dignity even under undignified conditions (e.g., Thrasea Paetus, Helvidius Priscus, Annaeus Seneca in Tac. Ann. 14–16).

On the Greek side, the representatives of the → Second Sophistic maintained epideictic eloquence. Their Atticistic attitude was matched on the Roman side by the classicistic retrospective to Cicero of the first publicly appointed rhetoric teacher → Quintilian. The bilingualism of Hellenistic Roman education was exposed to an initially unnoticeable but steady erosion that became clearly recognizable during the 3rd cent. [14. 34–41; 2. 475–489] because a Roman literature of equal quality (e.g., Virgil and Cicero) and independent Roman rhetoric teaching had come into existence. In late antiquity 'there were two Mediterranean cultures, a Latin West and a Greek East' [2. 479].

D. Late Antiquity and Christianity

1. Continuation of ancient educational concepts

In late antiquity education was equivalent to the preservation of the much admired classical literature. On the country domains of the *clarissimi*, esp. in Gaul (→ Apollinaris Sidonius) and in Africa (→ Martianus Capella), a rich literary activity unfolded. But in Rome as well the classical education remained alive (→ Symmachus and his circle). It offered the dignitaries everywhere in the empire a framework of privileging behaviour in handling Imperial power [15]. Martianus Capella let philosophy, as the bride of Mercury and a mystic, rise to the Gods [9. 142–146] — it stood as the last dam against the rising flood of Christianity [2. 564–570; 5. 349–350].

2. Christianity and ancient education

Jesus and his disciples were removed from ancient education. The Bible's 'language of fishers' as well as the *rusticitas* and *simplicitas* of Christians — mostly simple people — was looked down upon for a long time. Only in the course of the 2nd cent. did persons with a higher education increasingly join Christianity. The first attempts of the Apologists to elevate its status were unable to impress anyone. The rigid opposition of → Tatian in the East and → Tertullian in the West threatened to lead to increasing isolation. However, in Alexandria wealthy and educated Greeks constituted a high proportion of the Christian communities. In response to their needs, → Clemens recognized the value of ancient philosophy and its compatibility with the Christian religion, which was in turn considered a philosophy. On the other hand, he also conceded to the common believer a faith solely based on the *regula fidei*. → Origenes finally succeeded in reducing the social tension: he shared Clemens' views of the value of ancient education but also emphasized the Christian idea of fraternity. Origenes also supposedly transferred the methods of Alexandrian philology to the text of the Bible. In the West → Hieronymus applied his classical education to the texts and exegesis of the Bible. However, his famous dream vision (Jer. Ep. 22,30) is symptomatic for the greater torment of the conscience of educated Christians in the West. The change of → Augustinus from enthusiastic admiration of ancient education to sceptical reserve and the rejection expressed by → Isidorus, who, however, in his *Etymologiae* — as did → Cassiodorus in his *Institutiones divinarum et saecularium litterarum* — made an inventory of what was worth knowing from a Christian perspective [9. 191–214; 5. 350–359;].

3. The Christian idea of education

The primacy of religious education even remained unaffected when the value of a literary and philosophical education was recognized. From a Christian perspective ancient education could only have an ancillary and propaedeutic function. In his catechism school, which he first set up in Alexandria (215–230), and then in Caesarea (230–250) in Palestine [2. 595–597; 16. 92–100], Origenes developed a coherent teaching programme of the materials that Clemens had practised in an open education: 'beginning with the *enkýklia mathēmata*, primarily the dialectics..., followed by physiology and mathematics, geometry and astronomy, and continued via the principles of ethical action to theology' [16. 92].

In the East the ancient school education was maintained without any discontinuity during the Byzantine period. But in the West the contribution of literary and philosophical education to the Christian education, which was almost exclusively understood as Biblical exegesis and theology, was continuously eroded [2. 597–616]. It is due to the monastic preservation of old texts (Cassiodorus; Benedictines) that the educational heritage survived in the Occident.

E. Tradition of ancient education

Ancient education repeatedly surfaced in humanistic endeavours: in the Carolingian and the Italian Renaissance as well as in Neo-Humanism (the Third Humanism see → Paideia). All humanistic movements share the ancient educational concept of a development of man's personal abilities. It continues to this day in the educational mission of modern schools (e.g., the German Gymnasium system) and its implementation of a curriculum of education subjects despite all debates on their selection and weighting.

→ Ephebeia; → Gymnasium; → School; → Artes liberales; → Education/Culture

1 J. Latacz, Das Menschenbild Homers, in: Gymnasium 91, 1984, 15–39 2 Marrou 3 D. Bremer, s.v. Paideia, HWdPh 7, 35–39 4 F. Kühnert, Allgemeinbil-

dung und Fachbildung in der Antike, 1961 5 H. FUCHS, s.v. Bildung, RAC 2, 346–362 6 W. JAEGER, Über Ursprung und Kreislauf des philosophischen Lebensideals. SB Berlin, 1928, 25 7 Id., Paideia 1 (1933) ⁵1973; 2 (1944) ⁴1973; 3 (1947) ⁴1973 8 F. KÜHNERT, Die Bildungskonzeption des Isokrates, in: Bildung und Redekunst in der Antike, KS ed. by V. RIEDEL, 1994, 42–56 9 I. HADOT, Arts libéraux et philosophie dans la pensée antique, 1984 10 J. CHRISTES, Bildung und Gesellschaft, 1975 11 R. MÜLLER, Die Wertung der Bildungsdisziplinen bei Cicero, in: Klio 43–45, 1965, 77–173 12 H. FUCHS, s.v. Enkyklios Paideia, RAC 5, 365–398 13 U. SCHOLZ, Von der Bildung eines röm. Politikers, in: Humanistische Bildung 16, 1992, 25–39 14 H.I. MARROU, Augustin und das Ende der antiken Bildung, (French 1938, ⁴1958) 1982 15 P. BROWN, Macht und Rhetorik in der Spätantike, 1995 16 R. KLEIN, Christlicher Glaube und heidnische Bildung, in: Laverna 1, 1990, 50–100.

M.L. CLARKE, Higher education in the ancient world, 1971; R. HARDER, Die Einbürgerung der Philosophie in Rom, in: Antike 5, 1929, 291–316 (= KS 330–353 = Das neue Cicerobild, Wege der Forschung 27, ed. by K. BÜCHNER, 1971, 10–37); H.-TH. JOHANN (ed.), Erziehung und Bildung in der heidnischen und christlichen Antike, 1976; M. LECHNER, Erziehung und Bildung in der griech.-röm. Antike, 1933; H.I. MARROU, Μουσικὸς ἀνήρ, 1938; W. STEIDLE, Redekunst und Bildung bei Isokrates, in: Hermes 80, 1952, 258–296; H. FUCHS, Die frühe christliche Kirche und die antike Bildung, in: Antike 5, 1929, 107–119 (= Das frühe Christentum im röm. Staat, Wege der Forschung 267, ed. by R. KLEIN, 1971, 33–46); F.-P. HAGER, Zur Bedeutung der griech. Philosophie für die christliche Wahrheit und Bildung bei Tertullian und bei Augustin, in: A&A; 24, 1978, 76–84; W. JAEGER, Das frühe Christentum und die griech. Bildung, 1963; F. KLINGNER, Vom Geistesleben im Rom des ausgehenden Altertums (1941), in: Id., Röm. Geisteswelt, ⁴1961, 514–564; A. WIFSTRAND, Die alte Kirche und die griech. Bildung, 1967; CURTIUS; E. HOFFMANN, Pädagogischer Humanismus, 1955; U. HÖLSCHER, Selbstgespräch über den Humanismus, in: Id., Die Chance des Unbehagens, 1965, 53–86; E. LEFÈVRE, Die Gesch. der humanistischen Bildung, in: Humanistische Bildung 2,1979, 97–154; H. OPPERMANN (ed.), Humanismus, 1970; H. RÜDIGER, Wesen und Wandlung des Humanismus, 1937. J.C.

MAPS: H. WALDMANN, Die hellenistische Staatenwelt im 2.Jh. v.Chr., TAVO B V 4, 1985; Id., Östlicher Mittelmeerraum und Mesopotamien. Wirtschaft, Kulte, Bildung im Hellenismus (330–133 v.Chr.), TAVO B V 5, 1987; H. BLANCK, Das Buch in der Antike, 1992.

Educational journeys see → Travels

Eduma (Ἐδουμά; *Edoumá*, modern Dūmā). According to the Onomasticon of Eusebius (255,74) a settlement in the region of Acrabattene in Transjordan southeast of Neapolis (Nablūs).

S. HERRMANN, Die Operationen Pharao Schoschenks I. im östlichen Ephraim, in: Zschr. des deutschen Palästina-Vereins 80, 1964, 61, 67ff. T.L.

Eel (ἔγχελυς; *éngchelus*, *anguilla*), hardly distinguished from the sea eel (γόγγρος; *góngros*, *conger/congrus*). In the *Iliad* (21,203; 353) contrasted with fish as an amphibian. Its way of life and behaviour were well known to Aristotle (Hist. an. 8,2,591 b 30–592 a 24; 1,5,489 b 26 f.; 2,13,504 b 30 f.; Part. an. 4,13,696 a 3 f.: only two fins). Theophr. fr. 171,4 explains the ability to live on land by its small gills and low requirement of water and believes (fr. 171.9), like Plin. HN 9.160, that it is of asexual procreation. Aristot. Hist. an. 6.16.570 A 3–24 maintains its generation from the earth's intestines (γῆς ἔντερα; *gês éntera*) in mud, and refutes an alleged sexual dimorphism (4,11,538 a 3–13). Plin. HN 9,74 f. mentions, i.a. a mass catch in the autumn on Lake Garda in 'receptacles' (*excipulae*), Aristot. Hist. an. 4,8,534 a 20–22 in clay vessels like fish traps in the sea, to which it wanders from the rivers (Hist. an. 6,14,569 a 8 f.). Highly valued among the Greeks (cf. criticism of the comedians on culinary luxury [1]), for the Romans it was a food of the people (cf. Juv. 5,103). Famous catching sites: Strymon, Lake Copais and the Sicilian Straits. Eel keepers (ἐγχελυστρόφοι; *enchelystróphoi*) were already known by Aristot. 8.2.592 A 2 f., but Gal. De diaet. succ. [2. 8], considered the soft flesh harmful for extenuating diets. The fish was sacred in Egypt (Hdt. 2.72) and elsewhere. The smoothness of the skin, serving among other things as cane, (Plin. HN 9.77) was legendary (Aristoph. Equ. 864; Nub. 559; Plaut. Pseud. 747). If it was killed in wine it was supposed to create an aversion to it (Plin. HN 32,138). The giant eels of the Ganges (Plin. 9.4) were known to the Middle Ages through Isid. Orig. 12.6.41.

→ Fishes

1 KELLER, 2,357–360 2 K. KALBFLEISCH (ed.), De diaet. succ., 1923 (CMG V,4,2). C.HÜ.

Eeriboea (Ἠερίβοια; *Ēeríboia*).

[1] Stepmother of the → Aloads, who kept Ares prisoner. However, E. told Hermes the location of the prison (Hom. Il. 5,389 f.).

[2] (also Eriboea/Periboea). The daughter of Alcathous, spouse of Telamon and mother of → Ajax [1] (Pind. Isthm. 6,45; Soph. Aj. 569; Paus. 1,42,2; Apollod. 3,162). R.B.

Eetion (Ἠετίων; *Ēetíon*, linguistically probably not of Greek origin [1]). Name, especially of foreign heroes.

[1] King of the Cilicians in Mysian Thebe (Hom. Il. 1,366). His daughter → Andromache told her husband Hector how Achilles killed her father E. and her seven brothers during the conquest of Thebe: Achilles set up a monument for the father. The wife of E. was ransomed but later killed by Artemis (Hom. Il. 6,394–428). Among the booty from the conquest of Thebe was the horse Pedasus (Hom. Il. 16,152–154), a phorminx (Hom. Il. 9,186–188) and a disc that Achilles used in the competition at the funerary games for Patroclus (Hom. Il. 23,826–829). The poet of the Iliad probably

had sources available for descriptions of the conquest of Thebe ([2]; cf. Cypria fr. 28 PEG I).

1 Kamptz, 135, 372 2 W. Kullmann, Die Quellen der Ilias, Hermes ES 14, 1960, 287–291.

P. Wathelet, Dictionnaire des Troyens de l'Iliade, vol. 1, 1988, 563–569.

[2] An Imbrian. He ransomed Lycaon, a son of Priamus captured by Achilles and sold to Lemnus, who then could return to Troy (Hom. Il. 21,33–43).
[3] Trojan, father of Podes, highly respected by Hector (Hom. Il. 17,575; 590).

P. Wathelet, Dictionnaire des Troyens de l'Iliade, vol. 1, 1988, 570f.

[4] → Iasion, son of Zeus and the Pleiades' Electra.

Ph. Williams Lehmann, s.v. Aëtion, LIMC 1.1, 249f.

[5] Eponymus of Attic → Eetioneia (Steph. Byz. s.v. Ἠετιώνεια).
[6] Corinthian, father of Cypselus (Hdt. 1,14; 5,92; Paus. 2,4,4). R.B.
[7] (also Aetion). Sculptor who created a cedar wood Asclepius statue for the physician Nicias in Miletus. It was praised in an epigram by Theocritus (Anth. Pal. 6,337). It is insufficient for identification with the painter → Aëtion that Pliny (HN 34,50) listed the latter among bronze artists.

Lippold, 322f.; Overbeck, No. 1067, 1083, 1728,2, 1754, 1937–1941, 2055 (sources). R.N.

Eetionia (Ἠετιώνεια; *Ēetiṓneia*, Ἠτιώνεια; *Ētiṓneia*). Narrow peninsula that borders the main harbour (*Kántharos*) of Piraeus on the northwest (Harpocr. s.v. E.). In 411 BC 'the 400' had the wall on the Eetionia made into a fort of the Piraius fortification (Munichia, → Athens [1]) (Aristot. Ath. Pol. 37; Thuc. 8,90–92). Its reconstruction after the razing in 404 is attested by construction documents of 395/4 or 394/3 BC on the base of the Hellenistic Eetionia wall (IG II² 1656, 1657; [1. 28; 3. 21ff. No. 1, 2]). Restored in 337/6 BC (in stone?) (IG II² 244; [3. 36ff. No. 10]). The Aphrodisium was located outside the Eetionia gate with its two round towers [1. 38ff., 145 Fig. 19, 20, 85] (IG II² 1035 l. 46, 1657; [1. 115f.; 2. 175ff.]). A Thiasos (→ Associations) ['Ε]τιονιδôν (*[E]tionidôn*) [4].

1 K.-V. von Eickstedt, Beitr. zur Top. des Piräus, 1991, 34ff. 2 P. Funke, Konons Rückkehr nach Athen im Spiegel epigraphischer Zeugnisse, in: ZPE 53, 1983, 149–189 3 F.G. Maier, Griech. Mauerbauinschr. I, 1959 4 A. Papagiannopoulos-Palaiou, Ἀττικαὶ ἐπιγραφαὶ 2. Ὁ ἀρχαιότατος ἐν Ἀττικῇ θίασος [Attikai epigraphaí 2. Ho archaiótatos en Attikêi thíasos], in: Polemon 1, 1929, 107f. H.LO.

Effatio, effatum *Effatum* is a specialist term in the augural language (*verbum augurale*, Serv. auct. 3,463), which appears in the definitions of the augur Messala (Gell. NA 13,14,1) and in Cic. Leg.2,21. In the *effatio* the augur limits the precinct of the auspices with a ritual formula (Varro, Ling. 6,53: *finem auspiciorum caelestum*; Serv. Aen. 6,197: *ubi captabantur auguria*); it effected the site's liberation from the (disturbing) presence of the unknown deities that occupied it (Serv. auct. 1,446: *ut* [...] *per augures locus liberaretur effareturque*. This *liberatio* is not the only example of a 'deconsecration' — reprofaning through rituals — of existing cult sites, that is an *exauguratio*, which cancels the preceding *inauguratio* [1. 42]). The *effatio* was used for three types of location (Cic. Leg. 2,21: *urbem* [...] *et agros et templa liberata et effata habento*): for a town, i.e. within the limits of the *pomerium* for the *auspicia urbana* (Serv. auct. 1,13: *effata urbe* a reference to Ostia), the *ager Romanus antiquus*, which had its own auspices (Varro, Ling. 6,53: thus the term *ager effatus*; Serv. Aen. 6,197), and for the *templa* (Varro, Ling. 6,53; Cic. Att. 13,42,3; Liv. 10,37,15, *aedes*; Serv. Aen. 1,446; Fest. p. 146) both in the meaning of cult sites and augural temples [2. 193–207]. The *effatio* and the *liberatio* [2. 209–228] were complemented by the → *consecratio* (Serv. Aen. 1,446: *locus* [...] *tum demum a pontificibus consecr*[*atur*]) in the case of cult sites and, for the *urbs* and *templa*, by the *auspicatio*, obtaining of auspices, which turned the locations into inaugurated districts (Serv. Aen. 3,463: *loca sacra, id est ab auguribus inaugurata, effata dic*[*untur*]).
→ Augures

1 Latte 2 A. Magdelain, Jus, imperium, auctoritas, 1990. D.BR.

Effractor In Roman law the thief who obtains his loot through break and entry. According to Dig. 47,18 he commits a criminal act that is prosecuted as a → *crimen* (*publicum*). In the Republic it was still a civil offence. An escapee was called an *effractor* (*carceris*) and was also prosecuted as the perpetrator of a *crimen* in a → *cognitio extra ordinem*. G.S.

Egelasta This Iberian [1. 58] settlement was located near the salines of Men Baca between → Castulo and Linares and Vilches (CIL II 5091, p. 710) and belonged to the *conventus* of → Carthago Nova (Plin. HN 3,25). The identification with Iniesta in [2. 175] is mistaken. Pliny praised the salt of Egelasta because of its unique medicinal effect (HN 31,80). Otherwise only rarely mentioned (Str. 3,4,9; Ptol. 2,6,56, *Egelésta*).

1 A. Schulten, Numantia 1, 1914 2 Enciclopedia Universal Ilustrada 19.

Tovar, 3, 1989, 155f., 234. P.B.

Egeria
[1] Deity ('Nymph') of the inlet of the same name into Lake Nemi near Aricia, related to the sanctuary of → Diana there (Str. 5,3,12; Verg. Aen. 7,761–777; Schol. Juv. 3,17). Wife or lover of the Roman king

→ Numa [1], whom she advised with respect to his cultic arrangements (Dion. Hal. Ant. Rom. 2,60; Ov. Fast. 3,273–299; Plut. Numa 4,2). Ennius already reports that she gave him the *ancilia* (Ann. 114). A rationalizing reading makes this myth an invention with which Numa legitimized his religious reforms (Dion. Hal.; Plut., already indicated in Cic. Leg. 1,4). A unique tale is Ovid's invention that the nymph E. retreated to Aricia after Numa's death and in tearful mourning transformed herself into the spring (Met. 15,478–551).

There was a cult of E. in Rome in the grove of the → Camenae (cf. Ov. Met. 15,482), where the original → *ancile* supposedly fell from the sky. She was considered a deity of birth (Fest. p. 67). This fits with the interpretation of E. and the Camenae as nymphs and their association with Diana. The prehistory is largely unclear. Normally, it is assumed that E. came with Diana from Aricia to Rome [2; 3] because of the local link. The link to Manius → Egerius, the founder of the grove of Aricia, as the male counterpart, is interesting but uncertain [4].

1 J. Gagé, Les femmes de Numa Pompilius, in: Mélanges Pierre Boyancé, 1974, 281–298 2 G. Wissowa, Religion und Kultus der Römer, ²1912, 160, 219, 248–250 3 Latte, 170f. 4 F. Altheim, Griech. Götter im alten Rom, 1930, 94.

G. Dumézil, La religion romaine archaïque, 1974, 397.

F.G.

[2] see → Peregrinatio ad loca sancta

Egerius

[1] Son of Arruns, grandson of Demaratus. E. was only born after the death of his father and grandfather, which is why the entire fortune went to Arruns' brother Lucumo. His nephew supposedly received the name E. because of his poverty (*egere*, 'to suffer want'). When Lucumo later became Roman king with the name L. Tarquinius Priscus, E. was granted rule over the Latin town of Collatia by him and took the epithet Collatinus. His son L. Tarquinius Collatinus was the husband of → Lucretia (Liv. 1,34,2f.; 57,6; Dion. Hal. 3,50,3; 4,64,3, critically referring to Fabius Pictor).
[2] According to Festus p. 128, a Manius E. dedicated the grove of Diana Nemorensis (→ Egeria).

T.F.C. Blagg, The Cult and Sanctuary of Diana Nemorensis, in: M. Henig, A. King (ed.), Pagan Gods and Shrines of the Roman Empire, 1986, 211–219.

R.B.

Egg (ᾠόν; *ōión*, *ovum*). In the ancient kitchen eggs of all domestic birds, such as ducks, pheasants, geese, chicken, peafowl, partridges and pigeons and occasionally even wild fowl, were used. In general usage the meaning of 'egg' was narrowed to chicken egg, which was known in Greece no later than the 6th cent. BC and was later much esteemed in the Roman world. The chicken egg was a quite affordable food (Edictum Diocletiani 6,43), which was popularly served as an appetizer at meals (Hor. Sat. 1,3,6f.: *ab ovo usque ad mala*). It also had a place in haute cuisine: → Apicius occasionally used eggs for preparing sauces, puddings and deserts (e.g. 4,2,13).
→ Chicken

J. André, L'alimentation et la cuisine à Rome, ²1981.

A.G.

Egg-and-dart moulding Distinct → ornamentation in the decorative canon of Ionic architecture, in modern architectural terminology also known as the 'Ionian → kymation': a profiled ledge with an arched cross section whose relief or painted ornamentation consisted of an alternation of oval leaves and lancet-shaped spandrel tips and which often concludes at the lower end with pearl staff (astragal) corresponding to the rhythm of the egg-and-dart moulding. Apart from decorating the → epistylion or the → frieze, egg-and-dart-moulding was particularly used to decorate the → echinus of the

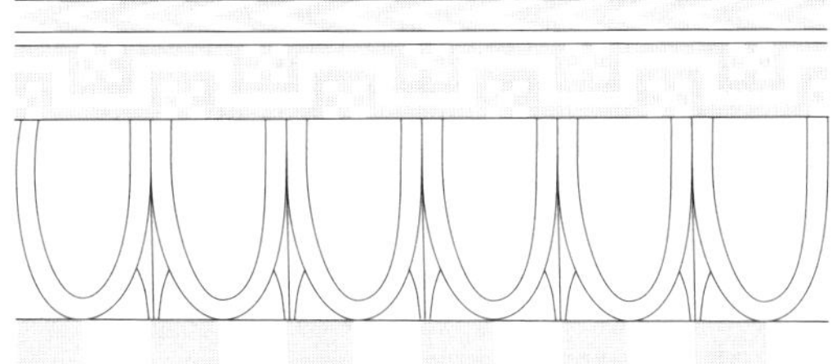

Miletus: Egg-and-dart moulding in relief
between painted ornamental bands,
from the temple on the Kalabak Tepe (6th cent. BC).

Ionian volute capital, later also on walls with doors and other visually emphasized building parts; the development of its form constitutes an important aid in dating ancient architecture. Egg-and-dart-moulding is initially restricted to Ionian architecture, but already in the 5th cent. BC it is found as a decorative element on Doric buildings (the → Parthenon at Athens) and — at the latest in the early 5th cent. BC — as an ornamental band in vase painting; in the Hellenistic period it became a universal motif in all decorated types of architecture, → painting, → mosaic, → toreutics, → terra sigillata and other forms of small arts and crafts.

W. Müller-Wiener, Griech. Bauwesen in der Antike, 1988, 120–121; W. Kirchoff, Die Entwicklung des ionischen Volutenkapitells im 6. und 5. Jh. und seine Entstehung, 1988, 158–161.

C.HÖ.

Eggius

[1] **L. Eggius.** *praef. castrorum* of Varus in Germania (Vell. Pat. 2,119,4).
[2] **C.E. Ambibulus.** Identical with [C. Eggius] Ambibulus Pom[ponius Lon]ginus Cassianus L. Maecius Pos[tumus] of CIL IX 1123. His career began as a sena-

tor's son under Trajan, who admitted him among the patricians, and in 126 he became an ordinary consul. Like all other senatorial Eggii, he was from Aeclanum.

G. CAMODECA, in: EOS 2, 132ff.; PIR² E 5, 6.

[3] **C.E. Marullus.** Senator of praetorian rank, who belonged in 41 and 42 to the *collegium* of the *curatores riparum et alvei Tiberis*. PIR² E 7.
[4] **L.E. Marullus.** *Cos. suff.* in 111. PIR² E 9.
[5] **L. Cossonius E. Marullus.** Grandson of E. [4]. Patrician. *Cos. ord.* in 184; proconsul of Africa 198/9. AE 1942/3, 111; 1958, 142; I. Eph. III 660; G. CAMODECA, EOS II 134; PIR² E 10. His son was Cossonius Scipio Orfitus. W.E.

Eghiše see → Elishe

Egnatia
[1] **(E.) Mariniana.** On coins from Viminacium she appears as Diva Mariniana. In all probability she was the wife of the later emperor Valerianus, whose accession she predeceased. Probably the sister of Egnatius [II 12] and [II 13].

PIR² E 39; M. CHRISTOL, Essai, 1996, 190ff.

[2] **E. Maximilla.** Wife of P. Glitius Gallus, whom she accompanied into exile on Andros under Nero. Later she obviously returned to Italy. PIR² E 40.
[3] **E. Taurina.** Named on a *fistula* from Velitrae (Suppl. It. II Velitrae No. 17). Probably of senatorial rank and related to Egnatius Taurinus. W.E.

Egnatius Roman family name, maybe originally Samnitic (cf. SCHULZE, 187f.), epigraphically also attested from central Italy. Name bearers in Rome are known from the 2nd cent. BC onwards. Egnat(i)us is uniquely also transmitted as a praenomen (Val. Max. 6,3,9. Plin. HN 14,89; [1]).

1 SALOMIES, 102.

I. REPUBLICAN PERIOD II. IMPERIAL PERIOD

I. REPUBLICAN PERIOD

[I 1] **E., Gellius.** Leader of the Samnites in the 3rd Samnite War, who brought about a coalition between the Samnites, Etruscans, Umbrians and Celts against Rome in 296. Their united army was defeated in 295 in the battle of Sentinum, E., the leader, was killed in the struggle for the Samnites' camp (Liv. 10,18–21; 29,16).
[I 2] **E., Cn.** Praetor and proconsul in Macedonia about the mid–140s BC; he built the → Via Egnatia (milestone: AE 1976, 643); also mentioned in the same period as a witness in the senatus consultum on Corcyra (SHERK 4). MRR 3,84f. (for dating).
[I 3] **E., Marius.** Probably a descendant of E. [I 2], one of 12 generals of the Italians in the → Social War (Vell. Pat. 2,16,1; App. B Civ. 1,181). In 90 he captured Venafrum in the southern theatre of war by treason and then

inflicted heavy losses on the consul L. → Iulius Caesar, probably near the Via Latina (App. B Civ. 1,183; 199). According to Livy he was killed in 89 in a battle against C. Cosconius [I 1] (Liv. per. 75). K.-L.E.
[I 4] Perhaps identical to the Spaniard attacked by Catullus (Carm. 37,17ff.; 39), author of a didactic poem *De rerum natura* in several books; two fragments from book 1 are preserved in Macrob. Sat. 6,5,2 (according to Accius) and 12, where E. is enumerated among the *veteres*, the predecessors of Virgil. The title suggests an imitation of → Lucretius.

FRAGMENTS: COURTNEY, 147f.; FPL³, 143f.
BIBLIOGRAPHY: N. MARINONE, I frammenti di E., in: Poesia latina in frammenti, 1974, 179–199. P.L.S.

II. IMPERIAL PERIOD

[II 1] **E. Capito.** Senator of consular rank and *frater Arvalis*; killed by Commodus in 182 or 183. PIR² E 17; LEUNISSEN, 196.
[II 2] **Q.E. Catus.** Legionary legate in Pannonia in 73; in 75/6 legate of the *legio III Augusta* in Africa.

PIR² E 18; B.E. THOMASSON, Fasti Africani, 1996, 135f.

[II 3] **P.E. Celer.** Friend of the senator and stoic Q. Marcius Barea Soranus. Nevertheless, he wrongfully accused him and his daughter in 66 before the senate for which he received an accuser's bounty. Musonius Rufus accused him late in 69 for this reason and he was sent into exile in 70 (regarding the reasons for the trial [1]). PIR² E 19.

1 J.K. EVANS, The Trial of P. Egnatius Celer, in: ClQ 29, 1979, 198ff.

[II 4] **C.E. Certus.** *Cos. suff.* in an unknown year in the 1st half of the 3rd cent. PIR² E 20.

G. CAMODECA, in: EOS 2, 138.

[II 5] **C.E. Certus Sattianus.** Senator, originating from Beneventum, honoured there in 254.

W. ECK, RE Suppl. 14, 115; G. CAMODECA, in: EOS 2, 137f.

[II 6] **M.E. Marcellinus.** Quaestor about 104; probably identical with the *cos. suff.* of 116, M. Egnatiu[s—]. PIR² E 14, 24.

VIDMAN, FO², 48.

[II 7] **M.E. Postumus.** *Cos. suff.* in 183. PIR² E 26.
[II 8] **A.E. Proculus.** Senator, who after a long praetorian career made it to the praefectura of the *aerarium Saturni* and the suffect consulate; buried in Rome. CIL VI 1406 = ILS 1167. PIR² E 30.

B. E. THOMASSON, Fasti Africani, 1996, 124f.

[II 9] **Q.E. Proculus.** Praetorian legate of Thracia between 198 and 209 (VELKOV, Cabyle 2, 1991, 18 No. 10). The *cos. suff.* of same name in CIL IX 6414b = ILS 1166 is probably identical with him. Cf. PIR² E 31.

[II 10] **M.E. Rufus.** Senator of the Augustan period. *Aedil* probably in 21 BC; won high praise by establishing a private fire fighters' squad; thus, he was able to achieve the praetorship immediately after his rank of aedile. When he wanted to gain an open position as *consul* in 19, the office-holding *consul* Sentius Saturninus prevented him. A conspiracy (for this reason?) resulted in his execution. PIR² E 32.

PH. BADOT, in: Latomus 32, 1973, 600ff.

[II 11] **E. Victor.** *Consul* under Septimius Severus, in 207 consular legate of Pannonia superior. PIR² E 35.

LEUNISSEN 163.

[II 12] **L.E. Victor Lollianus.** Praetorian legate of Galatia in 218; later *cos. suff.*; *corrector Achaiae*; *proconsul* of Asia for three years (THOMASSON, Laterculi I 236); on πολλάκις (*pollákis*) AE 1993, 10; *praef. urbi* 254. Famous orator in his age, son of E. [II 11]. PIR² E 36.

LEUNISSEN, 185; DIETZ, 149ff.; M. CHRISTOL, Essai sur l'évolution des carrières senatoriales, 1986, 190ff.; J. REYNOLDS, in: L'Afrique, la Gaule, la religion à l'époque romaine. Mélanges à la mémoire de Marcel Le Glay, 1994, 675ff.

[II 13] **E. Victor Marinianus.** Praetorian legate of Arabia, later *cos. suff.*; consular legate of Moesia superior; according to CHRISTOL [1] he was a brother of E. [II 12] and Egnatia [1] Mariniana and, therefore, the brother-in-law of emperor Valerianus. His offices most likely were held during the time of Severus Alexander.

1 M. CHRISTOL, Essai sur l'évolution des carrières senatoriales, 1986, 109, 190ff. W.E.

Egrilius

[1] **M. Acilius Priscus E. Plarianus.** An E. by birth but adopted by a M. Acilius Priscus. The family came from Ostia. Senator. He rose via the proconsulate in the Narbonensis, the command of the *legio VIII Augusta*, to the praefectura of the *aerarium militare* and then the *aerarium Saturni* 126 [1. 301]. It is unknown if he became consul. In Ostia *pontifex Volcani* after 105. PIR² E 48 [1. 285–308].
[2] **A.E. Plarianus.** *pater. Cos. suff.* in 128. VIDMAN, FOst 49 [1. 302].
[3] **A.E. Plarianus.** Probably the son of E. [2]. Senator. *Praef. aerarii militaris.* CIL XIV 4445 [1. 309].

1 F. ZEVI, in: MEFRA 82, 1970.

[4] **Q.E. Plarianus La[rcius—]** CIL VIII 800 and 1177 = AE 1942/3, 85 = Catalogue des inscriptions Latines païennes du Musée du Bardo, 1986, No. 211. *Cos. suff.* probably in 144; *proconsul Africae* in 159

B. E. THOMASSON, Fasti Africani, 1996, 63f.

[5] **Q.E. Plarianus.** Son of E. [4]; legate during the proconsulate of his father. PIR² E 49.

[6] **[E. Plarianus Larcius L]epidus Flavius [—]** Senator, belonging to the Ostian family of the Egrilii; his career path is uncertain; he was almost certainly legate of the *legio XXX Ulpia* and then probably legate of the Lugdunensis. AE 1969/70, 87.

W. ECK, RE Suppl. 14, 115f. W.E.

E Group Modern technical term for an Attic black-figure ceramics workshop *c.* 560–540 BC; named after → Exekias, who began his career as a potter in this group; two extant signatures from this time. Characteristic are conventional belly amphorae, decorated with just a few standard themes uniformly repeated. Alongside these, this group also includes some unusual works, and especially several pioneering innovations: the type A belly amphora; the new, broad-shouldered neck amphora with ornamented handles; the first → *kalos*-inscriptions (for Stesias); the first appearance of the motif of the turning team of horses.

BEAZLEY, ABV, 133–138; BEAZLEY, Paralipomena, 54–57; BEAZLEY, Addenda², 35–37; E. E. BELL, An Exekian Puzzle in Portland, in: W. G. MOON (ed.), Ancient Greek Art and Iconography, 1983, 75–86. H.M.

Egypt

A. INTRODUCTION B. PREHISTORY AND STATE FORMATION C. THE OLD KINGDOM AND THE FIRST INTERMEDIATE PERIOD D. THE MIDDLE KINGDOM AND THE SECOND INTERMEDIATE PERIOD E. THE NEW KINGDOM F. THE LATE PERIOD

A. INTRODUCTION

The country on the Nile from the 1st Cataract to the Mediterranean, Egyptian *km.t*, 'the Black (Land)', Greek Αἴγυπτος (*Aígyptos*). The division of Egyptian history into 'kingdoms', 'intermediate periods' (periods of unified and divided states) and 'dynasties' essentially derives via Manetho from Egyptian annalists. The absolute chronology, which is based on contemporary information on dates, lists of kings and astronomical calculations, is only (more or less) firm for the late period and the New Kingdom. In earlier periods uncertainties may accumulate to give a margin of error of as much as a century. Life in the river oase surrounded by deserts was determined by the rhythm of the → Nile. Before the introduction of efficient water-lifting devices in the Ptolemaic period, irrigation from retaining basins was the basis of food production for 1.5–2 million people. The dry climate of the present originated in the third quarter of the 3rd millennium BC; before that the adjoining deserts had a partially steppe-like character.

B. PREHISTORY AND STATE FORMATION

In the Nile valley epipalaeolithic cultures were able to maintain themselves for a relatively long period. Neolithic cultures emerged first in the 6th millennium in the Delta-Fajûm region, later in all of Egypt; they used the resources of the steppe and practised livestock husbandry and crop cultivation supported by natural holding basin irrigation. Irrigation buildings only began in Egypt during the Old Kingdom and never achieved more than local importance. Intensification of agricultural production, technological progress in crafts and the formation of superregional trade networks constituted in the 2nd half of the 4th millennium the background to social differentiation and the formation of 'proto-states' in Upper Egypt. Tradition named king → Menes (Thinites, 1st–2nd dynasty) as the unifier of the empire and founder of the 1st dynasty. The identity of this state rested on the institution of kingship, the central role of which was expressed in the doctrine of the king's divinity. In the context of state creation both the notation and symbolic forms of the hieroglyphic script were independently developed and, in turn, created the base for writing administrative documents and image captions. Though it initially integrated motifs of Middle Eastern origin, the art represented the self-awareness of the new elite in representations of hunting, warfare and rituals. With its capacity for extensive military action, Egypt gained a powerful position in the sphere of its neighbours.

In the Old Kingdom (3rd–6th dynasty, *c.* 2700–2190 BC) a complex administrative apparatus was developed surrounding king and court. To systematize organic settlement structures, the country was divided into administrative districts (later 22 Upper and 20 Lower Egyptian districts), the population was recorded and required to perform services. The foreign policy interests were oriented towards acquiring copper, ivory, precious woods, for example, by sending expeditions and establishing permanent outposts. Under Pharao → Djoser the → pyramid shape was invented as the form of the royal tomb. In monumental tombs of the residential elite the canonical style of art developed and a discourse on ethics and wisdom was created by biographical texts, which preconfigured form and content of the literature during the Middle Kingdom. Internal colonization brought a decentralization of state structure. With the establishment of permanent administrative centres in the district capitals the development of regional urbanization was promoted, which produced a provincial elite that became increasingly rooted in local social structures.

C. The Old Kingdom and the First Intermediate Period

(7th–11th dynasties, *c.* 2190–1990 BC.) The monarchy was not able to counter this development and after → Phiops II lost its role as the centre of the political and economic system. Rulers established themselves in the countryside who portrayed themselves as saviours of the individual and the community in periods of crisis and famines. No longer restrained by canonical norms, a flowering of regional and popular culture created images of new originality and texts of outstanding linguistic power. In the south of Upper Egypt military conflicts led to the unification of larger territories until Theban princes opposed the heirs of the Old Kingdom (9th — 10th dynasties, Heracleopolites) as the 11th dynasty and gained the victory.

The Middle Kingdom (11th–13th dynasties, *c.* 1990–1630 BC) deliberately attached itself to the conventions of the Old Kingdom but kings appeared as an omnipresent and active institution. Local dynasties were gradually pushed back, the administration was reorganized and the country divided into urban districts. The same striving for clear structures of power also characterized the Middle Kingdom's foreign policy. In the south Nubia was conquered to the 2nd cataract and secured with a series of massive fortifications. Fortifications and patrolling can also be documented at Egypt's other boundaries. After classicistic beginnings, artists acquired the ability of representing physiognomic individualism. Literature is attested for the first time. Wisdom teachings (in part ascribed to invented authors of the Old Kingdom) formulated the codex of norms for the elite of officials. Narratives, prophecies, complaints etc. make the kingdom's ideology their topic (the king as protector, often against the foil of a chaotic, kingless period) but also the tensions between the ideal and reality of the state, between individual fate and the norm. This literature and the language of the Middle Kingdom were later considered as classical.

D. The Middle Kingdom and the Second Intermediate Period

(14th–17th dynasties, *c.* 1630–1550 BC) During a period of dynastic discontinuity after the 12th dynasty, leaders of Canaanitic immigrants seized power in Egypt (→ Hyksos, 15th dynasty). Residing in Avaris in the eastern Delta (Tell el-Dabʿa), their rule extended in the north at least to southern Palestine. In the south their suzerainty extended at least to southern Upper Egypt, where successors of the native kings were able to maintain themselves (17th dynasty). The effect of this culturally alien rule must have been significant. The introduction of horse and chariot are tangible in the late Hyksos period. The effects on the structure of the Egyptian elite, monarchy and religion are still being debated. In the south of Egypt a state also formed, the kingdom of Kush south of the 3rd cataract. Thus, the native 17th dynasty found itself in a new situation surrounded and threatened by other powerful states. Using nationalist propaganda the kings of the 17th dynasty attempted a 'war of liberation'. According to tradition, Ahmose's victory over the Hyksos ushered in the 18th dynasty and the New Kingdom (18th–20th dynasty, *c.* 1550–1070 BC).

E. The New Kingdom

Concluding a series of earlier campaigns, Thutmose I succeeded in smashing the kingdom of Kush and conquering the Nile valley beyond the 4th cataract. → Nubia was organized into a stable colonial empire. In the North military advances reached northern Syria and the Euphrates, but during the collision with the Mittanni kingdom (peace treaty under Thutmose IV) and in

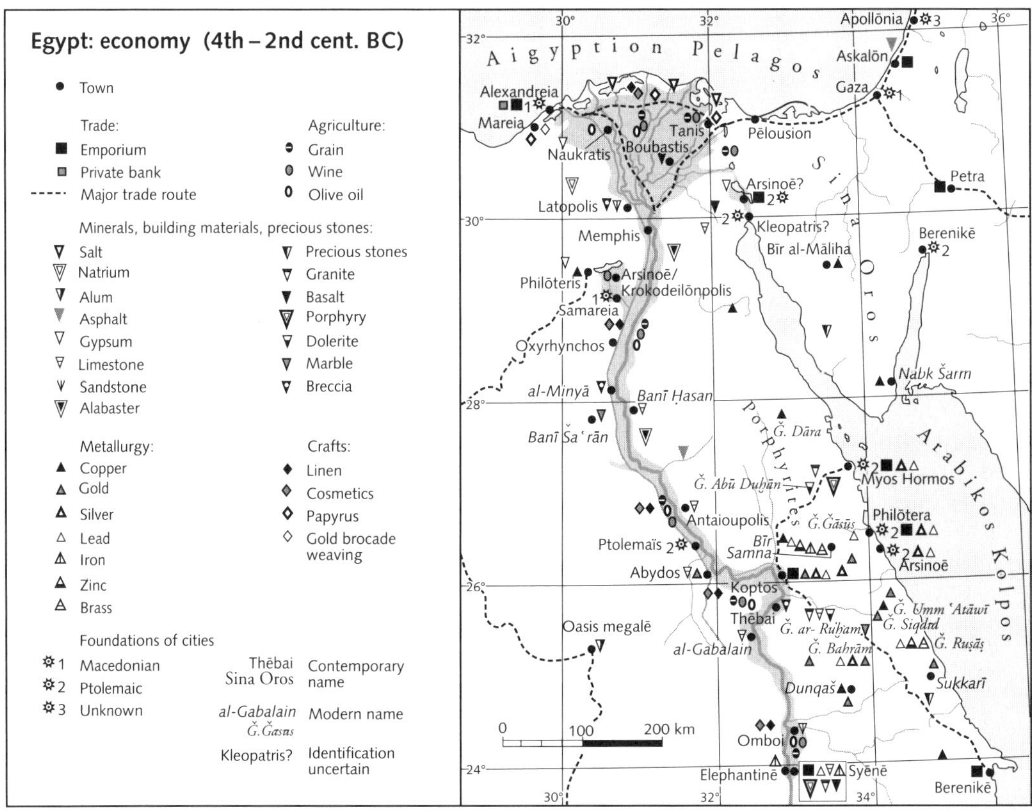

the struggles to subjugate the princes of the Palestinian towns a northern frontier of Egyptian rule formed at the upper Orontes. The end of the 18th dynasty was marked by the crisis of the Amarna period. In conflict with established elites, → Amenophis IV proclaimed a new religion that exclusively worshipped the 'living orb of the sun' (→ Aton). He even changed his name to 'Akhnaton', had the old temples closed and founded a new residence at → Amarna. This state contrary to all tradition was untenable after the death of its creator. A return to the old cults occurred under → Tutenchamun. The capital was relocated to Memphis while Thebes remained the ritual centre. The restoration of the state by → Haremhab laid the foundation for the Ramessid period (19th–20th dynasty, 1294–1070 BC). During the reconsolidation of the Egyptian claim to the Syro-Palestinian region, Egypt clashed with the Hittite kingdom. Despite the unfortunate outcome of the battle of → Qadesh, → Ramses II essentially managed to maintain the boundary of the Egyptian sphere of influence in this peace treaty with Hattushili III. The new threat from Libyan tribes, who were pushing towards the Nile valley from the west, was repeatedly defeated. However, the settlement of Libyan groups created a Libyan element in Egypt. The defeat of the migration of the → Sea Peoples demonstrates how Egypt came under pressure. Domestically the 20th dynasty was characterized by crises (economic problems, administrative failure, corruption) and under the successors of Ramses III the crown lost its power over the external territories and control over the domestic situation.

The necessity of self-defence strengthened the role of the military and being a soldier and general became a central attribute of kings. Their victories brought untold wealth into the country and the temples that received those for administration became powerful institutions. Wealth and refinement characterized the genesis of an urban life style and a tendency towards decorative art provided an opening for foreign influences. Far reaching intellectual changes attest to a theological discourse that experienced god in the Cosmos beyond all conventional mythical constructs and that sought to reconcile the unity of a creator god with polytheistic practice. In 'personal piety' god could be subjectively experienced; pious people put 'god into their heart', interpreted their lives in the categories of obedience and mercy, sin and punishment. Apart from maintaining classical works, the characteristic creations of literature are narratives (tales), and a lyric that articulated an atmosphere of privacy and sensibility that characterized the mentality of the New Kingdom.

J. Assmann, Ägypten, Theologie und Frömmigkeit einer frühen Hochkultur, 1984; W. Helck, Gesch. des Alten Ägypten, HdOr I.1.3, [2]1981; M. Lichtheim, Ancient Egyptian Literature I-III, 1973–1980; B. Trigger (et al.), Ancient Egypt, A Social History, 1983; C. Vandersleyen (ed.), Das Alte Ägypten, PropKg 15, 1975. S.S.

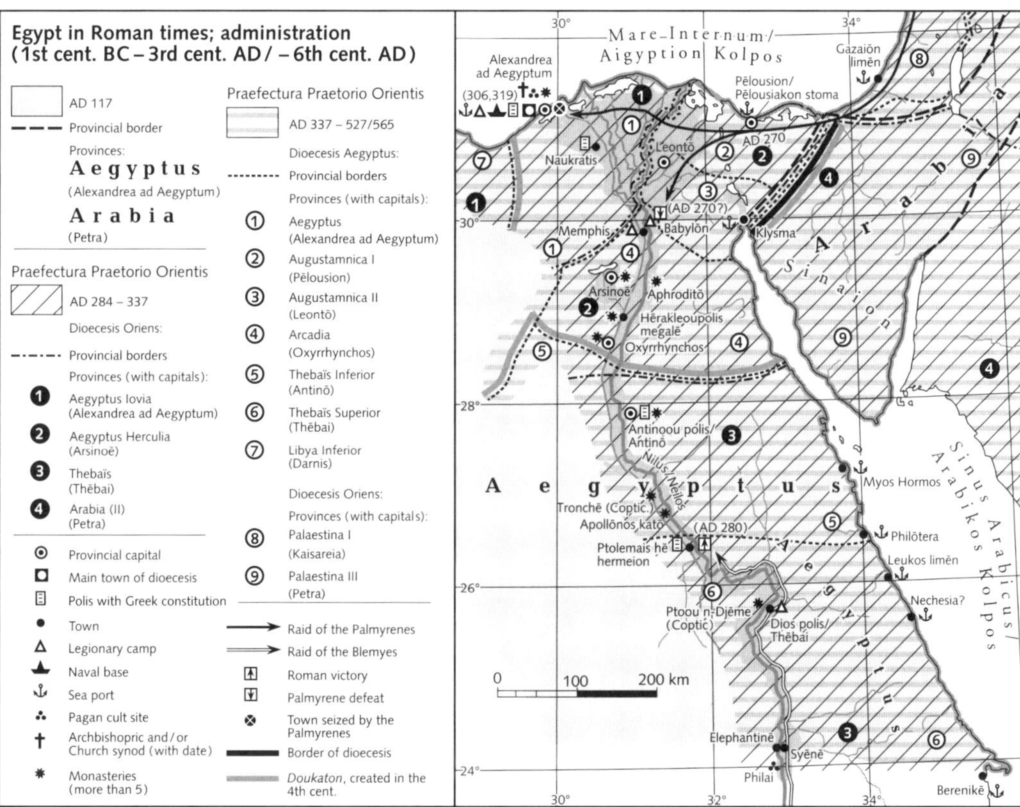

F. The Late Period

From the 21st dynasty until fairly recently Egypt was ruled by foreigners. The loss of independence is the great break in Egyptian history that is felt in all areas. After successful defensive battles against the 'Sea Peoples' and the Libyans, Egyptian resistance collapsed at the end of the 20th dynasty under unclear circumstances. The rulers of the new (21st) dynasty were Libyan tribal leaders under whom the country was divided into two: Upper Egypt (where hardly any Libyans settled) was secured by numerous fortifications and ruled by a military commander who was also the high priest of Amun in Thebes, while Lower Egypt (with a large Libyan population) was ruled by the king in Tanis. Beginning in the 22nd dynasty Egyptians were again progressively included in government but military functions were exclusively reserved for Libyans until the latest times. After 900 BC the feudal tendencies became stronger and Egypt split into petty principalities. In the later 8th cent. the influence of the Nubian kings on Upper Egypt grew, while in the Delta the power of the principality of Sais grew. About 730 BC the Nubian king Pianchi (Pije) conquered Egypt but was largely satisfied with suzerainty over the largely independent petty princes. Only his successor Shabaco completely subjugated the country to Nubian control. Between 674 and 664 BC the Nubians and Assyrians disputed the possession of Egypt. Of several Assyrian campaigns, three were successful, the last (664/3), in which Thebes was also conquered and plundered, permanently drove the Nubians out of Egypt.

There is only scant evidence from a few areas for the Third Intermediate Period (21st–25th dynasties). Texts of historical content as well as letters and documents are very sparse. Therefore, the chronology and the circumstances of government are still unclear. However, private sculpture is well documented since the 22nd dynasty. In particular portraits reach a climax during the 25th dynasty. After the 25th dynasty new graves of high dignitaries were again built in Thebes, in part on a grand scale. With the beginning of Nubian influence a strongly archaizing tendency set in: in many areas (architecture, sculpture, funerary decoration, writing style, language, titles, names etc.) models were sought from earlier periods.

The 26th dynasty was founded by a prince of Sais, → Psam(m)etich(us) I. Initially still under Assyrian supremacy, he managed to make himself lord of all Egypt within a decade and eliminated the fragmentation into petty principalities. After the subjection of the other Delta rulers Middle and Upper Egypt also submitted to the rule of Sais. In 656 BC the daughter of Psametich I was installed as the successor of the 'divine bride' in Thebes and, thus, the independence of the Upper Egyptian 'theocracy' was brought to an end. The almost 140-year rule of the 26th dynasty was domestically successful; the power of the Libyan military caste was countered by Greek and other mercenaries. In foreign policy

Egypt was able to react to changes in the Near East. It attempted to support the respectively weaker parties and to find allies. Military interventions in the Near East under → Necho II and → Apries brought little success. Necho II, who was particularly active in foreign policy, built a fleet and began to dig a canal to the Red Sea. On his orders Phoenician ships circumnavigated Africa in an East-West direction according to Hdt. 4,42. Although the kings of the 26th dynasty were of Libyan origin and dynastically probably continued the 24th dynasty, its government completely broke with the old feudal situation: petty principalities were eliminated and independent rulers were replaced by royal officials. For the first time since the New Kingdom a unified state was recreated, this time with its centre of gravity in Lower Egypt. Likewise the (Lower Egyptian) → 'demotic' script established itself for daily use in all of Egypt. Although at the beginning of the 26th dynasty high officials in Thebes were still able to build huge funerary palaces for themselves, Upper Egypt and Thebes were becoming increasingly provincial. For the first time Egypt developed close contacts with the Greek world, first through mercenaries who became an established part of the Saitic military system, but then also through Greek merchants in Egypt (→ Naucratis). These relationships are reflected in the sources: the most important source for the history of the 26th dynasty is Hdt. 2,147–182. The Egyptian sources only rarely contain concrete historical statements and texts of ordinary life are only preserved in small numbers. Culturally, a smooth transition from the 25th dynasty and a definite and increasing attachment to its 'archaizing' tendencies may be observed. Reliefs and inscriptions are often exact copies of old models. The individual districts of Egypt developed a kind of particularism and the bearers of religious tradition increasingly referred to the past and were hostile towards what was new and foreign. Shortly after the long and successful government of → Amasis, Egypt was conquered in 525 BC by → Cambyses and was from then on a Persian satrapy. The new masters were extremely unpopular and there were continuous uprisings of the Libyans in the Delta, in part with Greek (and especially Athenian) aid. in 404 BC Persian rule was shaken off and the last three native 'dynasties' (28th–30th) of Libyan delta lords ruled to 343 BC. Several Persian attempts at reconquest were warded off with the aid of Greek mercenaries until in 343/2 BC Artaxerxes III once more turned Egypt into a satrapy for a decade.

Persian rule did not fundamentally change the internal order of Egypt; under Darius I an effort was made to restore the old situation (codification of Egyptian law of the 26th dynasty) and even new temples were built. However, his predecessors and successors pursued a far more repressive policy. Apart from their own troops the Persians used foreign mercenaries to rule the country (Jewish colony in → Elephantine). The last 'native' dynasty (404–343 BC) once again developed a very extensive building activity. In sculpture and relief art a close link to the works of the 26th dynasty was sought.

In 332 BC the Macedons conquered Egypt and ruled it for three centuries. After Alexander's death Egypt went to his general Ptolemy, who made himself king in 304 BC following the example of the other diadochs. He and his successors ruled in the newly founded → Alexandria, which soon became the most important metropolis of the Hellenistic world. Ptolemy I-III succeeded in considerably enlarging their territory: their realm included the Cyrenaica, Cyprus and parts of Syria and Asia Minor. Decline set in with Ptolemy IV: Syria is retained in the 4th Syrian War (battle of Raphia in 217 BC) but the external power of the Ptolemies decayed. They were barely able to hold out against the other Diadochan states and became increasingly dependent on Rome. Domestically the situation also became unstable because of succession disputes, economic difficulties and uprisings of the Egyptian peoples (temporary independence of Upper Egypt in 206–186 BC). In the 1st cent. foreign policy became entirely dependent on Rome, to which the Cyrenaica and Cyprus were lost. The administration introduced by the Ptolemies was tight and centralized. Egypt consisted of 40 districts (νομοί; *nomoí*) that were subdivided into toparchies and villages (κῶμαι; *kômai*). The two Greek poleis Alexandria and → Ptolemais (in Upper Egypt) stood outside this system. This administration with its strict controls and exploitation of the native population made Egypt into the most wealthy state of that time. This wealth permitted influencing other Hellenistic countries and the expansion of Alexandria into the greatest metropolis and cultural centre of the Mediterranean world. Particularly successful was the pursuit of Graeco-Hellenistic natural science and philology. However, the wealth of Ptolemaic Egypt also benefited the native religious tradition through the new construction and the restoration of Egyptian temples. The cult of → Isis soon spread throughout the entire Hellenistic world. Already under Ptolemy I an Egyptian-Hellenistic deity was introduced and worshipped with → Serapis.

With the beginning of Roman rule (30 BC), Egypt as an Imperial province was directly ruled by the emperor, who was represented by a prefect and controlled the country with three legions. At first the economic and religious policies of the Ptolemies were continued. Priests and temples received considerably fewer funds, however, and the integration of Egyptians into the upper positions of society, which was increasingly encouraged by the Ptolemies since the 2nd cent. BC, was not continued. The native population had even less rights than in other provinces. The exploitation of the rural population increasingly led to tax evasion and the forced liturgies to impoverishment of the propertied classes. No later than the 2nd cent. AD, the pagan religion and literary traditions, which were only maintained in the temples (last remnants in the 4th and 5th cents.) decayed. The result was an increased influence of Christianity, which grew stronger despite persecutions. Egyptian (Coptic) Christianity developed a pronounced national character and the Egyptian church became officially independent after the council Chalcedon (AD 451). Anchoritism and monasticism were characteristic of Egypt and spread from there. In AD 642/3 Egypt was conquered by the Arabs.

→ Irrigation; → Coptic; → Ptolemaeus

G. HÖLBL, Gesch. des Ptolemäerreiches, 1994; F.K. KIENITZ, Die politische Gesch. Ägyptens vom 7. bis zum 4. Jh. vor der Zeitwende, 1953; K.A. KITCHEN, The Third Intermediate Period in Egypt, [2]1986. K.J-W.

MAPS: H. WALDMANN, Wirtschaft, Kulte und Bildung im Hellenismus (330–133 v. Chr.), TAVO B V 5, 1987; H. HEINEN, W. SCHLÖMER, Ägypten in hell.-röm. Zeit, TAVO B V 21, 1989; E. KETTENHOFEN, Östlicher Mittelmeerraum und Mesopotamien: Die Neuordnung des Orients in diokletianisch-konstantinischer Zeit (284–337 n. Chr., TAVO B VI 1, 1984; Id. Östlicher Mittelmeerraum und Mesopotamien: Spätröm. Zeit (337–527 n. Chr.), TAVO B VI 4, 1984; S. TIMM, Ägypten. Das Christentum bis zur Araberzeit (bis zum 7. Jh.), TAVO B VI 15, 1983.

Egyptian Language of Pharaonic Egypt, in contrast to modern Egyptian (= Arabic), also known as Ancient Egyptian in the context of Afro-Asian languages. In the course of its long tradition from the end of the 3rd millennium BC, it went through several stages: Old, Middle, and New Egyptian (in the Old Kingdom, Middle Kingdom, and from the → Amarna period), → Demotic (from the 7th cent. BC) up to → Coptic, the language of Christian Egypt that survived well into Arabic times. These transitions took place around the language's fixed core and led to significant changes, grammatically above all in the transition to New Egyptian, lexically above all in the radical break that occurred with the transition to Christian culture. Middle Egyptian, the language of the earliest literary works that later were handed down in the schools, received the status of a 'classical language', which it maintained until the end of Pharaonic culture. The Egyptian language shares many similarities with the Afro-Asian languages in its 'word roots' based on consonants, in its grammatical forms and constructions, and in its vocabulary, esp. in pronouns. But lexically and grammatically, it often stands on its own, so that it has been difficult to define so far the types of linguistic relationships it shares with other languages. In the New Kingdom, after the Egyptian expansion to the Near East, Egyptian adopted many Semitic foreign words and loan-words, and with the transition to Christian culture, many Greek words were added. From the period of → Ramesses II, we have indications that great differences existed within the Egyptian language between Assuan and the Delta. However, the differences in dialect in this period cannot be exactly determined. As was the case later in the Coptic language, these differences may have concerned vocalism, but since Egyptian writing had no vowels, they could not find written expression.

→ Egypt; → Hieratic; → Hieroglyphs

A.H. GARDINER, Egyptian Grammar, [3]1957; J. OSING, s.v. Dialekte, LÄ 1, 1074–75. J.OS.

Egyptian law Egypt was a centralized state at least from the middle of the 3rd millennium. Important factors that led to this development were, among others, the monumental construction of the pyramids, which required that all resources and workers had be accounted for, and the introduction of technologies for large-scale artificial irrigation ('hydraulic hypothesis': the emergence of high culture from the irrigation economy). Finally, Egypt experienced the rise of a thoroughly organized and far-reaching administration, a treasury with a special tax system, and a judiciary with established procedures.

Ancient Egyptian society was religiously oriented and saw the world in the hands of divine powers that watched and ruled over the social order. This gave rise to an ideology based on origin in which the order of life was experienced as divine and where human activity took place within the boundaries of that order. This ideology was imagined as a goddess named *Maat* (= order/correctness/truth). She ties all human actions to certain ethics and morals. The king has the obligation to achieve this, by, among other things, enacting laws. She served as a guideline and an embodiment of the right way to conduct official business for the organs of the state. At the same time, *Maat* is a moral imperative given to all human beings: in the afterlife, everyone must render account for how well they abided by the principle of rightful actions on earth.

An example for the step-by-step emergence of legal forms in Egyptian law can be found in endowments. Images and texts in tombs show that the Egyptians were always concerned about food in the afterlife. In the course of time, they increasingly took the initiative themselves to prepare for and to secure their continued maintenance. Therefore, for generations they took people into their service and put them in charge of sacrifices and ceremonies, in exchange for endowments of fields and other sources of income, on a heritable basis. Thereby, the service was guaranteed forever. The religious and moral commandment to take care of the dead, which had become weak, was thus replaced with a legal relationship. In an effort to lend even greater permanence to endowments of this sort, the Egyptians devised the establishment of the temple and its priests. Because of its 'immortality' the eternal institution of the temple, represented by its respective priests, had the function of a modern legal entity. Sometimes the pious endowment is even established for the king, while the priests are entrusted with the enactment of its dedication to the donor and his tomb. Thereby, the permanent existence of the endowment is guaranteed and placed under supervision of state and temple, as it were.

Thus, legal life began to take shape roughly in the time of the pyramids (mid 3rd millennium BC) and gradually became more independent, while the significance of religious and moral principles in governing everyday human relationships steadily declined. This is evident in the large variety of extant documents: royal decrees, administrative acts, land *registers* (predecessors of a real estate register), taxation lists, archives of temple administrations, (court) protocols, statutes of pious endowments, legal arrangements between private persons such as sales (without fixing the payment: service and payment were estimated and settled according to a standard), loans, leaseholds, agreements in family law, divisions of inheritances, publicly established testaments, etc. The effectiveness of law even found expression in the area of religion, e.g. in mythology where the gods Horus and Seth go to court in order to settle their conflict through a judgement. Furthermore, the last judgement, which occupied a large part in the Egyptian concepts of the afterlife should be mentioned.

To sum up, it is obvious that Egypt made an essential contribution to the development of legal culture in the Mediterranean. The clear recognition of this fact is impeded by the peculiarity of the sources, which were not yet formulated in a technically legal way and from which we must, therefore, reconstruct Ancient Egyptian law, an effort which is in full swing today.

→ Demotic law

1 E. Seidl, Altägypt. Recht, in: Oriental. Recht, Hdb. der Orientalistik, I. Abt.-Ergbd. III, 1964, 1–48
2 W. Helck, s. v. Recht, in: LÄ 5, 1984, 182–187 (lit.)

S.A.

Egyptizing Sculpture see → Sculpture

Eidolon (εἴδωλον; *eídōlon*, Lat. *idolum*, picture, image, delusion).

[1] Refers to a smaller-than-life portrait (cf. the votive gift of a female statue in Delphi, in Hdt. 1,51).

[2] In Greek mythology, esp. in Homer, *eidolon* refers to a delusion (Hom. Il. 5,449), but especially to the soul of the deceased in Hades (Hom. Od. 11,213; Il. 23,104; the *eidolon* is disembodied but still has the shape of the living person: Hom. Il. 23,107). In pictorial representations, it is often depicted with wings and in miniature form (cf. the scene of the 'weighing of fates' on a black-figured Dinus from Caere *c.* 540 BC [1]. Here, the Keres ('Fates') of the still living are usually represented as *eidola*). For the Orphics, the soul participates in the divine. As *eidolon aionos* ('image of life'; Pindar, fr. 116 Bowra), it exists not merely as a shadow after death, a notion which is different from Homer's.

[3] According to Plato (Tht. 191d 3–e 1), the *eidolon* is the imprint of the first perception in consciousness, which ensures later recognition. Through name, definition, and the *eidolon*, understanding of an object is accomplished (Pl. Ep. 7,342a 7ff.). Epicurus regarded *eidola* as atomic images that emanate from an object and enable its perception and understanding (cf. Cic. Fin. 1,21).

[4] In Jewish and Christian terminology (LXX and NT), *eidolon* means 'idol'.

→ Image; → Ker; → Psyche

1 A. Kossatz-Deissmann, s.v. Achilleus, LIMC 1.1, no. 799.

HE.K.

Eidyllion (εἰδύλλιον; *eidýllion*). Diminutive of εἶδος (schol. Aristoph. Ran. 942; Proleg. E, schol. Theoc. p. 5,10f. Wendel; cf. [1]). In the oldest known source, Plin. Ep. 4,14, *eidyllion* seems to have the general meaning of 'short poem' (cf. also Sozom. Hist. eccl. 6,25). The term is very rare outside the scholia on Theocritus. It is therefore used specifically for the short poems by Theocritus, including the epic and erotic poems, not only the bucolic poems, as one might assume according to the modern meaning ('rural-pastoral work') with its usual connotations of sentimental characters and peaceful surroundings. These specialized connotations result from the idealized Renaissance notion of bucolic poetry, which was based on Virgil and which certainly does not come from Theocritus himself (in his only reference to one of his poems, he calls it 'little song', μελύδριον: 7,51). Whether the more general meaning of 'short poem' was the original meaning and the more specialized one was secondary, cannot be determined because the meaning of the root (εἶδος) is uncertain (already for the scholiasts: cf. Proleg. E, Theoc. p. 5,7–19).

A common interpretation postulates that the term emerged in relation to the πολυείδεια (diversity) of literary genres which is characteristic for the Theocritan corpus. According to this interpretation, *eidyllion*, as the 'genre of little songs' (so already Proleg. E, p. 5, 14–19 = Anecdot. end S. 12, 26 — 13, 2 Wendel: εἰδύλλιον < εἴδη λόγου: diegetic, mimetic, mixed) becomes the designation for odes according to the meaning of *eídos* in the late metric scholia on Pindar, since these odes come in a variety of forms: p. 3, 8; 4, 6, etc. Tessier; Apollonius [9a], the editor of Pindar, received the nickname of *eidográphos*, because he classified his poems according to their musical *eídē* — Doric, Phrygian, etc. (cf. EM 295,52; Eustathius, Prooem. Pind. Comm. III, p. 303, 14ff. Drachm. and schol. Genev. Theoc. II, p. 7, 11f. Ahrens connect the term *eídē* to the epinicia by Pindarus and *eidyllion* to Theocritus). In Suda σ 871, *eídē* also seems to have the more general meaning of 'works of various genres'. However, according to an interpretation by Zucker (*eidyllion* = 'component', cf. i.e. Isoc. Antid. 74, who uses it as 'textual passage'), one should not assume any specific reference to Theocritus' corpus.

1 M. Leumann, Diminutiva auf –ύλλιον und Personennamen mit Kennvokal –υ im Griech., in: Glotta 32, 1953, 215.

E. Bickel, Genus, εἶδος und εἰδύλλιον, in: Glotta 29, 1942, 29–41; F. Zucker, ΕΙΔΟΣ und ΕΙΔΥΛΛΙΟΝ, in: Hermes 76, 1941, 382–392.

M.FA.

Eikoste (εἰκοστή; *eikostḗ*). Duty or tax at the rate of a twentieth (5%).

1. In Athens, the Peisistratidae presumably were the first to impose tax on agricultural yields in order to finance wars, magnificent buildings, and ceremonial sacrifices, according to Thuc. 6,54,5, at the rate of 5%. In Aristot. Ath. Pol. 16,4; 16,6, tax is called 'tithe' (δεκάτη), (cf. Hdt. 1,64,1).

2. In 413/2 BC, the Athenians imposed import and export tax at the rate of 5% on their *symmachoi* (allies) in the Delian-Athenian League instead of the → *phoroi* in order to cover the rising costs of the Peloponnesian War (Thuc. 7,28,4: τὴν εἰκοστὴν ... τῶν κατὰ θάλασσαν ἀντὶ τοῦ φόρου). The *phóroi* were probably reinstituted in or shortly before 410.

3. In Aristoph. Ran. 363 (405 BC), we find the name of εἰκοστολόγος (*eikostológos*), which probably refers to a taxed leaseholder who exacted an *eikoste*. Apparently this refers to income from customs duties, which were imposed in Attic cleruchies or in allied cities, and which served as a model for the *eikoste* in the Attic *symmachia*.

4. In going back to the forms of rulership of the Attic *symmachia*, the Athenian *strategos* Thrasybulus re-imposed an *eikoste* on the allies for the benefit of Athens in 390/389 (IG II² 28; = TOD 114; = IEry II 502 l. 7f.: ...τὴν ἐπὶ Θρασυβούλο εἰκοστήν; IG II² 24). This tax most likely came to an end with the Peace of Antalcidas.

5. Certain legal transactions, primarily land sales and the establishment of taxed leaseholds, were often subject to sales taxes (ἐπώνια, *epōnia*). In Delos, a tax of 5% was applied to leaseholds.

6. Following the recapture of the city of Sardeis and the execution of the usurper → Achaeus [5], → Antiochus [5] III imposed a sales tax of 5% on the residents of Sardeis payable to the king, a tax which was added to an already existing *eikoste*, whose yields went into the municipal treasury. At the request of Laodice, Antiochus freed the city from this tax in a letter preserved on an inscription from the year 213 BC (SEG 39,1083 l. 5f.).

7. In a letter preserved on an inscription by an Attalid king from the 2nd cent. BC, settlers who had received lots for land were obligated to pay taxes. A group of coloni had to pay a tax of ten percent (δεκάτη) on agricultural yields, and an *eikoste* on yields of wine (WELLES no. 51, lines 15–18).

8. In Anaea, the mainland property of Samos, a natural tax in grain was imposed at the rate of 5%. The tax went to the temple, probably that of Hera. The grain officials of the city of Samos bought up this grain at a minimal price with the interest income of a governmental bond and distributed it to the citizens (Syll.³ 976).

9. In Ptolemaic Egypt, there was a 5% tax on wool (εἰκοστὴ ἐρεῶν; PHibeh 115 Z. 20; O.Bodl. I 14.16.25f.; PRyl. 70 Z. 24) and a tax on income from leaseholds of οἰκόπεδα (residences).

10. In Roman Egypt, a tax of two *choínikes* (διχοινικία) or a twentieth of an *artaba* was imposed on each *ároura* in the district of Arsinoites. Additional taxes of 5% are also documented for the districts of Mendes and of Tentyra (ESAR II 508; 518f.; 559).

11. In the Roman period, *eikoste* is the Greek term for the → *vicesima*, a tax of 5% on being set free or on inheritances.

→ Taxes

1 BUSOLT/SWOBODA 2 P. FUNKE, Homónoia und Arché, 1980 3 D. J. GARGOLA, Grain distributions and the revenue of the temple of Hera on Samos, in: Phoenix 46, 1992, 12–28 4 PH. GAUTHIER, Nouvelles Inscriptions de Sardes 2, 1989, 13–45 5 I. KERTÉSZ, Zur Sozialpolitik der Attaliden, in: Tyche 7, 1992, 133–141 6 B. R. MACDONALD, The Phanosthenes Decree. Taxes and Timber in Late Fifth-Century Athens, in: Hesperia 50, 1981, 141–146 7 R. MEIGGS, The Athenian Empire, 1972 8 L. MIGEOTTE, Les souscriptions publiques dans les cités grecques, 1992 9 PRÉAUX, 112, 300f. 10 P. J. RHODES, A Commentary on the Aristotelian *Athenaion politeia*, 1981 11 B. SMARCZYK, Unt. zur Religionspolitik und polit. Propaganda Athens im Delisch-Attischen Seebund, 1990 12 S. L. WALLACE, Taxation in Egypt, 1938 13 K. W. WELWEI, Athen, 1992.

W.S.

Eileithyia (Εἰλειθυία; *Eileithyíai*, Doric Ἐλευθ(υ)ία; *Eleuth(y)ía*, Mycenaean in Knosos *e-reu-ti-ja*). Greek goddess, worshipped almost exclusively by women in the context of pregnancy and birth, also in the context of children's and women's diseases (Diod. Sic. 5,73,4; [1]). Already known by Homer in this function (μογοστόκος, 'concerned with the effort of giving birth', Hom. Il. 16,187). The name itself seems to be telling — it can be connected with *eleuth-*, 'to go, to come' [2]. She has almost no independent myths: she was born at her important cult centre of Amnisus (Paus. 1,18,5). Whenever she is regarded as the daughter of → Hera (since Hes. Theog. 291f.; cf. Hom. Il. 11,270f.) her cultic function is reflected. Parallel to this, a group of 'Eileithyiai' exists as reflecting practical assistance at birth (Hom. Il. 11,270; 19,119), similar to the functionally related Genetyllides (Aristoph. Thesm. 130) or → Moirai.

On Crete, her cult goes back to the Bronze Age, and her sanctuary in Amnisus on Crete, already mentioned by the Od. (19,187 'Grotto of E.'), is the continuation of a Minoan-Mycenaean cult centre [3; 4; 5]. She often has her own sanctuary (endowment by → Helena in Argus, Paus. 2,22,6; images consecrated by → Phaedra in Athens, Paus. 1,18,5) with a priestess (sacred law of Chios [6]; on other cult centres: Paus. 3,14,6; [7; 8]), or was connected to Artemis, Apollo, or Asclepius. Her cult is characterized by unusual rites and the votives of limbs [9. 97ff.]. At many cult centres, esp. in Northern Greece, but also on Delos (Hdt. 4,35), she is actually invoked as a form of → Artemis, whose functional realm includes birth as a central event within the stages of a woman's life (i.e. Boeotia [10], Gonnoi [11]).

1 C. VORSTER, Griech. Kinderstatuen, 1983, 72f. 2 W. SCHULZE, Quaestiones Epicae, 1892, 260–266 3 P. FAURE, Fonctions des cavernes crétoises, 1964, 82–90 4 R. F. WILLETTS, Cretan Eileithyia, in: CQ 52, 1958, 221–223 5 N. MARINATOS, Cult by the sea-shore. What happened at Amnisos?, in: R. HÄGG (ed.), The Role of Religion in the Early Greek Polis, 1996, 135–139 6 S. N. KOUMANOUDIS, A. P. MATTHEOU, Horos 3, 1985, 105 7 D. KNOEPFLER, in: AK 33, 1990, 115–128 8 D. BERRANGER, Recherches sur l'histoire et la prosopographie de Paros à l'époque archaïque, 1992, 82f. 9 B. FORSÉN,

Griech. Gliederweihungen, 1996, 135 10 J.M. Fossey, Epigraphica Boeotica 1, 1991, 152–155 11 B. Helly, Gonnoi, 1973, vol. 2 no. 175–196; cf. 168–172.

P.V. C. Baur, E., Philologus, Ergänzungs-Bd. 8, 1901, 453–512; N.D. Papachatzis, Μογοστόκοι Εἰλείθυιαι καὶ κουροτρόφοι θεότητες, in: AD 33, 1978, 1–23; Th. Hadzisteliou-Price, Kourotrophos. Cults and Representations of the Greek Nursing Deities, 1978; S. Pingiatoglu, E., 1981; R. Olmos, s.v. E., LIMC 3.2, 534–540. F.G.

Eileithyiaspolis (Εἰλειθυίας πόλις; *Eileithyías pólis*). City in Upper Egypt, 15 km north of → Edfu on the eastern shore of the Nile, Egyptian *Necheb* (*nḫb*), today al-Kāb. Very early traces of settlements. Important location in the pre-dynasty and early dynasty periods. Aside from the snake goddess Uto of Lower Egypt, the vulture goddess Nechbet is worshipped here and plays an important role as an Upper Egyptian crown goddess at the birth of kings, and, in the Graeco-Roman period, is identified with → Eilithyia. Archaeological findings: Remnants of the temples of Nechbet and Thot.

B. Porter, R. L. B. Moss, Topographical Bibliography of Ancient Egyptian Hieroglyphic Texts, Reliefs and Paintings V, 1937, 171–191. R.GR.

Eilesium (Εἰλέσιον, Εἱλέσιον, Εἰρεσίαι, Εἰρέσιον, Ἐρέσιον; *Eilésion*, *Heilésion*, *Eiresíai*, *Eirésion*, *Erésion*; on the names: [2. 106f.]). City mentioned already by Homer (Il. 2,499; H. in Apollinem 32) in the south-east of Boeotia near modern Asopia (formerly: Khlembotsari) [1. 127–130]; a description of the ancient remnants (with a different identification) also in [2. 91]. Sources: Str. 9,2,17; Plin. HN 4,26; Dionysius Kalliphontos 90; EM s.v. Εἰρέσιον; Suda s.v. Ἐρέσιον; Steph. Byz. s.v. Εἰλέσιον.

1 Fossey 2 P. W. Wallace, Strabo's Description of Boiotia, 1979. P.F.

Einsiedeln Eclogues Two → bucolic poems in the Codex Einsidlensis 266 from the Neronian period. In the first poem, Nero is identified with Jupiter and Apollo (22–34; differing: [3]), and his poetry — probably the *Troica* (38–41) — is regarded as superior to that of Homer and Virgil (43–49). The second poem (probably by the same author) is characterized by the tension between the worries of the shepherd Mystes (1. 11) and his description of a new golden age under Nero (15–38; following → Verg. Ecl. 4 but lacking its anticipatory quality).
→ Panegyrics; → Calpurnius Siculus

Editions: 1 C. Giarratano, [3]1943 (repr. 1973) 2 D. Korzeniewski, Hirtengedichte aus neronischer Zeit, [2]1987.
Bibliography: 3 S. Döpp, Hic vester Apollo est, in: Hermes 121, 1993, 252–254 4 H. Fuchs, Der Friede als Gefahr, in: HSPh 63, 1958, 363–385 5 B. Effe, G. Binder, Die ant. Bukolik, 1989, 130–140 6 D. Korzeniewski, Die "Panegyrische Tendenz" in den Carmina Einsidlensia, in: Hermes 94, 1966, 344–360. B.F.-W.

Eion (Ἠιών; *Ēiṓn*).
[1] (ἡ ἐπὶ Στρυμόνι). City on the left shore of the Strymon, harbour of Amphipolis (Thuc. 1,98; Dem. Or. 12,23; 23,199), archaeological traces near Ofrini (Greece). Phoenix is said to have been buried there by Neoptolemus (Lycoph. 417 with schol.). It became a military base under Darius I and was used as a supply camp under Xerxes, commanded by → Boges (Hdt. 7,24f.). Cimon conquered it in 476 BC, and Athens shaped it into an Attic colony. Starting-point for further Attic expansion along the Thracian coast (Hdt. 7,107; Thuc. 1,98), important Athenian base in the Peloponnesian War (Thuc. 4,50,1; 5,10,3–10). Conquered by the Spartans in 406 (Xen. Hell. 1,5,15). Destroyed by Athens around the mid 4th cent. BC (Theopomp. FGrH 115 F 51). I.v.B.
[2] Colony of → Mende which cannot be exactly localized; it was taken by Athens in 425, but lost again shortly thereafter. Its further history is unknown.

M. Zahrnt, Olynth und die Chalkidier, 1971, 187. M.Z.

Eioneus see → Dia

Eiras (Εἰράς; *Eirás*). Sometimes also called Náeira; lady-in-waiting of Cleopatra VII who in Octavian's propaganda was attributed decisive political influence. E. died together with the queen. PP 6,14720.

H. Heinen, Onomastisches zu E., Kammerzofe Kleopatras VII, in: ZPE 79, 1989, 243–247. W.A.

Eirenaeus, Irenaeus
[1] (Εἰρηναῖος; *Eirēnaîos*). Grammarian, student of Heliodorus the metrician, 1st cent. AD (*terminus ante quem* due to the quotation in the Hippocratic lexicon by Erotianus, 116,8 Nachmanson). He probably taught also in Rome under the Latin name of Minucius Pacatus (perhaps the *rhetor Pacatus* in Sen. Controv. 10, praef. 10). He was not a freedman [2]. The Suda mentions him in the praefatio and s.v. 'E.' (ει 190) as well as s.v. 'Pacatus' (π 29), and lists numerous titles of grammatical and lexicographical writings, one of which περὶ τῆς Ἀθηναίων προπομπίας (*De Atheniensium honoribus in pompis deducendi*, trans. by Bernhardy), may have had antiquarian aspects too. He was the first reported to have authored linguistic writings about Atticism (this is why the Etymologicum Gudianum 317,16 De Stefani supposedly called him 'the Atticist', ὁ Ἀττικιστής): 3 bks. 'Attic Names' (Ἀττικῶν ὀνομάτων) or Ἀττικῆς συνηθείας, if the entries in the Suda refer to the same work under different titles; 'On Atticism' (Περὶ ἀττικισμοῦ); the encyclopedia 'On the Attic origin of the Alexandrian dialect' (περὶ τῆς Ἀλεξανδρέων διαλέκτου, ὅτι ἔστιν ἐκ τῆς Ἀτθίδος); 'On Hellenism' (the pure, correct Greek — Περὶ Ἑλληνισμοῦ), supplemented by the 'rules of correct Greek' (Κανόνες Ἑλληνισμοῦ). It is difficult to say to what extent he had anticipated the rigourous Atticism of the 2nd cent. AD.

In the sparse extant fragments (21 in [1], to which has to be added [4. 2121] and [5]), E. appears as a representative of the thesis that the Alexandrian dialect should be elevated to standard Greek (κοινὴ διάλεκτος), and as an advocate of analogy and the application of etymology, as in the case of other Alexandrian grammarians (esp. Philoxenus). It is controversial, whether the grammarian is identical to the person of the same name who wrote commentaries on Apollonius Rhodius (textual constitution, identification of geographical points [6. 111]), Herodotus, and Euripides' *Medea* (opposing [3] and—incl. bibliography—[6]), whose sources are the object of polemics that can still be discerned in the collections of scholia.

EDITION: 1 M. HAUPT, Opuscula, II, 1876, 435–440.
BIBLIOGRAPHY: 2 J. CHRISTES, Sklaven und Freigelassene als Grammatiker und Philologen im ant. Rom, 1979, 104–105 3 SCHMID/STÄHLIN, II,2, 870, 873
4 L. COHN, s.v. E., RE 5, 2120–2124 5 R. REITZENSTEIN, Gesch. der griech. Etymologika, 1897, 382–387
6 C. WENDEL, Die Überlieferung der Scholien zu Apollonios von Rhodos, 1932, 106–107, 111, 115. S.FO.

[2] E. (Irenaeus) of Lyons
A. BIOGRAPHY B. WORKS C. THEOLOGY

A. BIOGRAPHY
E. was most likely born between AD 130 and 140 and, as a youth, lived in Smyrna, where he still heard the local bishop and apostle's student → Polycarpus before his martyrdom (156 or 167), (Euseb. Hist. eccl. 5,20,6). He later left Asia Minor for unknown reasons and moved to the west without breaking his ties to home. According to a (late?) report that is contested in its validity as a source, he was in Rome at the time of Polycarpus' martyrdom (epilogue of the Polycarpus martyrdom in the Moscow MS), but then moved to south Gallia. Even before he became bishop of Lyon as successor of the murdered Potheinus in AD 177, he approached Rome once in the name of this south Gallian community: he travelled (between 174 and 189, perhaps in 178/9) to the *urbs* in order to delineate the Gallic position in the conflict surrounding the prophetic movement of → Montanus (Euseb. Hist. eccl. 5,3,4–4,2; → Montanism). He was probably already bishop when he intervened in the conflict over the date of Easter and admonished the Roman bishop Victor to even things out with the communities of Asia Minor (Euseb. Hist. eccl. 5,24,12–17; additional letter-fr. CPG I, 1310). The traditional view claiming that he died as a martyr under → Septimius Severus is late and probably invalid. Jerome was the first to mention martyrdom (com. in Is. 17).

B. WORKS
Aside from the 4th-cent. Latin trans. of his main work in five volumes under the title Ἔλεγχος καὶ ἀνατροπὴ τῆς ψευδωνύμου γνώσεως ('Analysis and Refutation of the Incorrectly called Gnosis', Adversus haereses, CPG 1, 1306; larger fr. of the original Greek text in → Epiphanius and Hippolytus, *i.a.*), there exists an Armenian trans. of the work εἰς ἐπίδειξιν τοῦ ἀποστολικοῦ κηρύγματος ('Presentation of the Apostolic Kerygma', CPG 1, 1307). The main work, probably created between 180 and 189, aims primarily at refuting the gnostic movement (→ Gnostics), and for this purpose offers a genealogy of the contemporary 'heresies' and partly extensive contents descriptions of the gnostic schools, which have not decreased in significance even after the most recent findings of original Coptic texts. In addition, the books offer a detailed account of the theology of the Church majority. Fragments of two further writings and letters (CPG 1, 1308–1312) have survived. The authenticity of various catenae fragments is contested and improbable (CPG 1, 1315–1317). A modern *editio critica maior* of the entire work is lacking, the critical edition of the main work by A. ROUSSEAU/ L. DOUTRELEAU (SChr 100, 152f., 210f., 263f., 293f., 1965–1982) has been met with criticism (S. LUNDSTRÖM).

C. THEOLOGY
E. is clearly shaped by his background of Asia Minor. His thinking operates within the continuity of traditions and he aims at opposing a 'Church' *diadochḗ* (continuous tradition of teachings) to the (gnostic) 'heretics': For him, the unbroken link from Christ through the apostles to the contemporary presbyters of the Church, the *successio presbyterorum* (haer. 3,2,2), exists precisely in that it preserves the *traditio, quae est ab apostolis* in contrast to the *diadochḗ* of the philosophers and 'heretics'. This *traditio* can be summarized as a *regula veritatis* (κανὼν τῆς ἀληθείας, 'canon of truth') in short formulas (Adversus haereses 1,10,1). In E.'s historical-theological concept of the ἀνακεφαλαίωσις of all things in Christ's return, a (later) excerpt from the *Panarion* ('medicine chest') by Epiphany (according to Eph 6,12; cf., i.e. Haer. 1,10,1).

N. BROX, Offenbarung, Gnosis und gnostischer Mythos bei Irenäus von Lyon, 1966; S. LUNDSTRÖM, Studien zur lat. Irenäusübers., 1943; Id., Die Überlieferung der lat. Irenaeusübers., 1985; R. NOORMANN, Irenäus als Paulusinterpret, 1994. C.M.

Eirenarches see → Police

Eirene (Εἰρήνη; *Eirḗnē*). The word is perhaps pre-Greek [1; 2].
[1] Personification and deification of peace (Orph. H. 15,11). E. is one of the → Horae, daughter of Zeus and Themis, sister of Dike and Eunomia (Hes. Theog. 901–902; Pind. Ol. 13,6–8). She is often mentioned in Greek literature as a central figure for the prospering of the political community. Thus, E.'s gifts are praised, for instance, in Bacchyl. fr. 4,61 SNELL-MAEHLER and in Euripides (Bacch. 419–420; TGF 453) while usually being connected, as 'a giver of wealth', to *ploûtos* ('wealth'), (cf. already in Hom. Od. 24,486). In Phile-

mon fr. 71, she is called 'philanthropic' (*philánthrōpos*). In the 'Peace' by Aristophanes (421 BC; shortly prior to the Peace of Nicias), E. is released from a dark cave, into which she was thrown by war ('Polemos'), (Aristoph. Pax 223; 292–300). The fact that sacrifices were made to her and that she was addressed as *semnotátē basíleia theá* (parody of sacrifice: Aristoph. Pax 973–1016) [3] in this same comedy does not necessarily suggest that an official cult existed at this time [4], but underscores the significance of E. as a political catchword [5], and shows that here, as in all other personifications, a cult is an inherent potential from the beginning. E. received an official cult in Athens after the peace of 371 BC (Philochorus FGrH 328 F 151; Isocr. 15,109–110; Nep. Timotheus 2,2) [6]. This cult also had a statue of → Cephisodotus, which showed E. with the child Plutos in her arms and which stood on the Agora (Paus. 1,8,2; 9,16,2) [7]. E. appears on Attic vases, usually in the circle of other Horae, but also in the circle of Dionysus [8]. → Cimon consecrated an altar to her as early as 465 BC after his victory at Eurymedon (Plut. Cimon 13,5 487b). For the Hellenistic period, several Greek cults are documented in literature and on inscriptions (Syll.[3] 307–308).

1 FRISK 1,467 2 A. DEBRUNNER, RLV 4.2, 526 3 F.T. VAN STRATEN, Hiera Kala, 1995, 31–33 4 M.P. NILSSON, Kult. Personifikationen, in: Eranos 50, 1952, 37 n. 2 5 G. GROSSMANN, Polit. Schlagwörter aus der Zeit des peloponnesischen Krieges, 1950 6 DEUBNER, 37–38 7 E. SIMON, s.v. E., LIMC 3.1, 703 no. 8 8 Id., s.v. E., LIMC 3.1, 704 no. 11–12.

H.A. SHAPIRO, Personifications in Greek Art, 1993, 45–50; E. SIMON, E. und Pax. Friedensgöttinnen in der Ant., 1988. R.B.

[2] Daughter of Ptolemy I and Thais, married → Eunostus after 307 BC under unknown circumstances. PP 6,14507.

[3] Hetaera of Ptolemy 'the Son'. Killed in the defeat of Ptolemy's revolt in 259/8 BC in the Ephesian Artemisium. PP 6,14721.

[4] Daughter of Ptolemy Agesarchou, mother of Andromachus [3]. Priestess of → Arsinoe in 199–171/0 BC [II 4] III; was victorious at the Panathenaea in an unknown year.

C. HABICHT, Athen in hell. Zeit, 1994, 109f.

[5] Concubine of Ptolemy VIII from Cyrene. She supposedly induced him to kill Cyrenian legates upon his return to Alexandria in 145 BC (political cleansing at the time of the king's departure?). The traditional account in Jos. Ap. 2,53–55 is not historical. E. was perhaps the mother of Ptolemy Apion. PP 6,14722. W.A.

Eirenoupolis (Εἰρηνούπολις; *Eirēnoúpolis*). Today Çatalbadem (formerly İrnebol) in Cilicia Tracheia (in the region of Lacanitis, Ptol. 5,7,6). Founded by Antiochus IV of Commagene. From AD 355 to 359, the city was surrounded by a wall. From the early 4th cent., it belonged to the province of Isauria; diocese (suffragan of Seleucea on the Calycadnus).

G. BEAN, T.B. MITFORD, Journeys in Rough Cilicia 1964–1968, 1970, 205ff.; HILD/HELLENKEMPER, s.v. E. 1). F.H.

Eiresidae (Εἰρεσίδαι; *Eiresídai*). Attic *asty* deme of the phyle Acamantis. One (or two) → bouleut(ai). A plot of land owned by Plato in E. bordered on the river Cephissus to the west (Diog. Laert. 3,41), which probably formed the boundary of the demos. Therefore, E. was probably located west of the Colonus Hippios and north-west of the Platonic Academy (an epitaph from the 4th cent. BC of two *dēmótai* from E. was found in the north-west [1. 8 fig. 8]) between the Hodos Kephissou and the Leophoros Athenon.

1 P.D. STAVROPULLOS, Ἀνασκαφαὶ Ἀρχαίας Ἀκαδημείας [Anaskaphai Archaías Akadēmeías], in: Praktika 1963, 5–28.

TRAILL, Attica, 19, 47, 59, 70, 110 no. 34, table 5; J.S. TRAILL, Demos and Trittys, 1986, 132. H.LO.

Eiresione (Εἰρεσιώνη; *Eiresiṓnē*). Olive or laurel branch, entwined with wool, dressed with figs, ceremonial breads, and small containers of honey, oil, and wine (Pausanius Rhetor in Eust. in Il. 22,496, 1283, 7ff.; EM 303, 17ff.; Suda s.v. E.). Boys carried it from house to house while singing a song of supplication, which (just as the custom itself: Harpocr. p. 162,1ff.; Suda s.v. *diakónion*) was also called *eiresione* (Ps. Hdt. v. Hom. 33). After the procession, the *eiresione* was fastened to the door so that it could be seen (Aristoph. Vesp. 398f. as well as Equ. 729 and Plut. 1054 with schol.). The boys referred to Apollo in their song. In Athens, a *paîs amphithalḗs* (παῖς ἀμφιθαλής, 'child surrounded by flowers') brought the *eiresione* to the temple of Apollo during the festival of Pyanepsia. An aition for the custom was provided by the myth of Theseus: the *eiresione* was claimed to have been offered to give thanks for the happy return from Crete and as a sign for the end of infertility, as a counterpart to the branch of supplication that was set up before the departure (Plut. Thes. 22). An alternative aetiology, also rooted in the cult of Apollo, bases the custom on an oracle occasioned by a famine (Pausanius Rhetor ibid.). As far as the date of the festival is concerned, documents also indicate the Thargelia (schol. Aristoph. Equ. 729) and, as further recipients, Helios and the Horae (ibid.) or Athena (schol. Clem. Al. Protrepticus 10, 2). The *eiresione* can be related to customs of initiation that mediate between childhood and adulthood and which are linked to the seasonal breaks in the agricultural year.

→ Amphithaleis paides; → Daphnephoria; → Oschophoria; → Pyanopsia

D. Baudy, Heischegang und Segenszweig, in: Saeculum 37, 1986, 212–227; O. Schönberger, Griech. Heischelieder, Beitr. zur klass. Philol. 105, 1980. D.B.

Eisagogeus (εἰσαγωγεύς; *eisagōgeús*). Every office holder who was entitled to preside over a court in Athens (→ Archontes) was responsible for introducing (εἰσάγειν, *eiságein)* his subjudice cases into a law court (→ *dikastḗrion*) and, concerning this act, was also referred to as *eisagogeus*. In a narrower, technical sense, the *eisagogeus* was part of a five-member collegium which was entitled to preside over certain urgent legal affairs (Aristot. Ath. Pol. 52,2). In Ptolemaic Egypt, the *eisagogeus* was a permanent official of Greek nationality and nominated by the king, who acted as the chairman of the courts in the country and in the capital of Alexandria. Among the → *chrematistaí*, the verdict chambers were named after their *eisagogeus*.

A. R. W. Harrison, The Law of Athens II, 1971, 21ff.; H. J. Wolff, Das Justizwesen der Ptolemäer, ²1970. G.T.

Eisangelia (εἰσαγγελία; *eisangelía*). In Athens, *eisangelia*, in the technical sense, refers to a type of public complaint in criminal matters from Solon's times (Aristot. Ath. Pol. 8,4.). *Eisangelia* designates the statement of claim (Lycurg. 34,137) as well as the proceedings it institutes. The charges were submitted in writing and argued in detail. The proceedings went through a series of changes over the course of time. Originally, they were designed for criminal acts not covered by the laws. Later, the criminal acts were differentiated by individual laws, and, around the middle of the 4th cent. BC, summarized in a *nómos eisangeltikós* and subjected to a unified process. We can assume that in the beginning only the → Areios pagos was in charge of the execution of laws in the role of a supervisory office, while later there were several authorities; the following are documented: the public assembly when public welfare was seriously harmed, the council of five hundred for violations of official duties, the archon for the protection of orphans and inheriting daughters (the judgement was made by the → *dikastḗrion*), and the entirety of the → *diaitetaí* for duty violations by arbitrators.

M. H. Hansen, E., 1975; R. W. Wallace, The Areopagos Council to 307 B.C., 1995, 64ff.; O. DeBruyn, La compétence de l'Aréopage en matière de procès publics, 1995. G.T.

Eisphora (εἰσφορά; *eisphorá*). In Athens, the *eisphora* was an extra-budgetary, direct wealth-tax imposed on wealthy Athenians during financial crises, primarily during wars, by order of the public assembly. According to Aristot. Ath. Pol. 8,3, an *eisphora* supposedly existed already in the Solonic period. However, the wording of the law cited there mentions only a general collection of taxes through the → *naukraroi*. According to Thuc. 3,19,1, an *eisphora* was imposed in 428/7 BC for the first time (πρῶτον) in the amount of 200 talents due to the high costs of war. Since an *eisphora* is already documented (B Z. 17) in the so-called Callias decree (IG I³ 52) of 434/3 BC, the πρῶτον in Thuc. apparently must be referred to the stated amount of 200 talents (SEG 40,4). According to Pollux 8,129f., the *eisphora* was a progressive tax imposed in various rates on *pentakosiomedimnoi*, *hippeis*, and *zeugitai*. It is a matter of debate whether the frequent *eisphora* during the last years of the Peloponnesian War dampened the war enthusiasm of rich Athenians or whether this contributed to the oligarchic revolution. In 378/7, the system of *eisphora* was reformed (Philochorus FGrH 328 F 41): Following an estimation of wealth among the richest citizens of Athens (Pol. 2,62,7: 5750 talents; Philochorus F 46 and Dem. Or. 14,19: 6000 tal.), the 1,200 or more taxpayers (regarding this number: Isocr. 15,145; Dem. Or. 20,21–28) were divided into 100 tax groups (→ *symmoria*) of c. 15 persons (Cleidemus FGrH 323 F 8). It is contested whether these tax groups are identical to the *symmoriai* introduced in 358/7 for the → trierarchy. Within the *symmoria*, the individual paid the *eisphora* in an amount proportionate to his wealth. The liability to pay this tax began at a wealth of 3–4 talents (Davies, XXIIIf.). The metics were also liable to pay the *eisphora*. The 300 richest individuals, the *hēgemónes*, and the second as well as third richest in each *symmoria* (Dem. Or. 18,103; 18,312) were obligated to pay the entire tax amount in advance and then collected it from the other taxpayers in their *symmoria* (→ *proeisphorá*). It was possible to be exempt from this liability by way of → *antidosis* and → *diadikasia* proceedings. In the *symmoria*, *diagrapheís* kept registers of the members with their share of wealth (*diágramma*; Hyp. F 102. 152 Jensen). Between 347/6 and 323/2, a yearly *eisphora* of 10 talents was imposed.

1 J. Bleicken, Die athenische Demokratie, ⁴1995 2 P. Brun, Eisphora – Syntaxis – Stratiotika, 1983 3 M. R. Christ, Liturgy avoidance and *antidosis* in classical Athens, in: TAPhA 120, 1990, 147–169 4 V. Gabrielsen, The *antidosis* procedure in classical Athens, in: CeM 38, 1987, 7–38 5 J. G. Griffith, A note on the first *eisphora* at Athens, in: AJAH 2, 1977, 3–7 6 M. H. Hansen, The Athenian Democracy in the Age of Demosthenes, 1991 7 H. Leppin, Zur Entwicklung der Verwaltung öffentlicher Gelder im Athen des 4. Jh.v.Chr., in: Eder, Demokratie, 557–571 8 P. J. Rhodes, Problems in Athenian *eisphora* and liturgies, in: AJAH 7, 1982, 1–19 9 W. Schmitz, Reiche und Gleiche, in: Eder, Demokratie, 573–597 10 Id., Wirtschaftliche Prosperität, soziale Integration und die Seebundpolitik Athens, 1988 11 G. E. M. de Ste. Croix, Demosthenes' *timema* and the Athenian *eisphora* in the fourth century BC, in: CeM 14, 1953, 30–70 12 R. Thomsen, Eisphora, 1964 13 R. W. Wallace, The Athenian *proeispherontes*, in: Hesperia 58, 1989, 473–490. W.S.

Eispoiesis (εἰσποίησις; *eispoíēsis*). In Athens, *eispoiesis* referred to a legal institution comparable to modern adoption, similar to the *ánpasis* in Gortyn (Great Law,

col. X 33–XI 23). The *eispoiesis* was conceived from the perspective of the law of succession (→ *diatheke*). In Athens, as opposed to Gortyn, a man was only allowed to adopt if he had no marital son. The *eispoiesis* was also possible in the case of death, even 'posthumously', without the professed intention of the 'adoptive father'. In Athens, *eispoiesis* was enacted through registration in the list of the respective → phratria; in Gortyn, it was brought in front of the public assembly.
→ Adoption

A.R. W. Harrison, The Law of Athens I, 1968, 83ff.; L. Rubinstein, Adoption in IV. Century Athens, 1993; R. Koerner, Inschr. Gesetzestexte der frühen griech. Polis, 1993, 547ff.

Eispraxis (εἴσπραξις; *eíspraxis*). 'Collection' in the largest sense; in Athens, for instance, it was the collection of tribute payments for the naval alliance (IG II² 1273, 24), in Egypt that of all taxes, but also of private debts (→ Praxis). G.T.

Eisthesis see → Rubrication

Eitea (Εἰτέα; *Eitéa*).
[1] Attic *asty*(?) deme of the phyle Acamantis, from 307/6 to 201/0 BC of Antigonis, from AD 126/7 that of Hadrianis. Two *bouleutai*. The location is unknown (north-east Attica? [3. 140–142]). The fact that it belonged to the city trittys of Acamantis is deduced from the inscriptions [1] and IG II² 2363 ([2. 101]).

1 B.D. Meritt, J.S. Traill, in: Agora 15, 50ff. no. 42 2 J.S. Traill, Diakris, the Inland Trittys of Leontis, in: Hesperia 47, 1978, 89–109 3 Id., Demos and Trittys, 1986, 68, 132, 139–142.

Traill, Attica, 9, 48, 69, 110 no. 35, 124 no. 3, table 5, 11, 15; Whitehead, 25 n. 90, 371, 377, 426.

[2] Attic *asty*(?) deme of the phyle Antiochis, two (or one) → *bouleutai(es)*). The finding place of the deme decree [1; 4] combined with prosopographic evidence [3], speaks for a location near Grammatiko in north-eastern Attica. In favour of an attribution to the city trittys, s. [2. 104].

1 A. Kalogeropoulou, Ψήφισμα ἐξ Εἰτέας Ἀττικῆς [*Psēphisma ex Eitéas Attikês*], in: AD 25, 1970, A, 204–214 2 J.S. Traill, Diakris, the Inland Trittys of Leontis, in: Hesperia 47, 1978, 89–109 3 Id., Demos and Trittys, 1986, 139–142 4 E. Vanderpool, The Two Attic Demes of Eitea, in: AD 25, 1970, A, 215f.

Traill, Attica 22, 54, 69, 110 no. 36, 124; Whitehead, Index s.v. E. H.LO.

Eiwan see → Liwan

Ekdikos (ἔκδικος; *ékdikos*). Probably in the Hellenistic period, the basic meaning of 'avenger' developed into 'representative before the court' and 'person entitled to take legal action' in the private as well as the public area, esp. in the trans. of → *defensor civitatis*.

H.-A. Rupprecht, Einführung in die Papyruskunde, 1994, 64, 144.

Ekdosis (ἔκδοσις; *ékdosis*).
[1] In Greece, the second part of a wedding that started with → *engýēsis*, the 'handing over' of the bride to the groom by her → *kyrios*. In the papyri, the *ekdosis* is left as the only act in a wedding (aside from its written form), carried out by the father, the mother, or the bride herself.
→ Marriage

H.J. Wolff, Beiträge zur Rechtsgesch. Altgriechenlands, 1961, 155ff.; H.-A. Rupprecht, Einführung in die Papyruskunde, 1994, 108; St. Perentidis, in: G. Thür, J. Vélissaropoulos (ed.), Symposion 1995, 1997, 179ff.

[2] see → Publication

Ekecheiria (ἐκεχειρία; *ekecheiría*). Technical term for 'armistice', 'court rest', and the 'divine peace' as agreed upon by Iphitus of Elis and Lycurgus of Sparta for the games in Olympia (Plut. Lycurgus 1,2; Paus. 5,20,1), claimed by the other great festival locations as well.

StV II no. 185; III S. 414 (II A6) L. Robert, Études Anatoliennes 2, 1937, 177ff. G.T.

Ekklesia (ἐκκλησία; *ekklēsía*). Assembly of the adult male citizens, which was entitled to the ultimate decision-making authority in the Greek states. At times also called *(h)ēliaía* (with differences due to dialect) or *agorá*. The frequency of meetings, the areas of authority, the degree to which independent actions were restricted by the officials' and/or the council's realm of authority, and the number of members of the *ekklesia* varied depending on the type of the political organisation; thus, oligarchies can exclude the poor from the *ekklesia* by requiring a minimum of wealth.

In the Homeric world, the assemblies met occasionally in order to deal with the duties of the king or the nobleman who called them. Active participation was reserved to leading men and religious experts, the masses expressed agreement through cheering, disapproval through silence. In the *Iliad* (2,211–277), Thersites, a man from the people, gives a speech, but is reprimanded by Odysseus.

In Sparta, the Great Rhetra (Plut. Lycurgus 6) of the full citizens' assembly attributed to Lycurgus guaranteed regular meetings and the authority to make ultimate decisions. The question of co-operation between the council of elders and the public assembly is not quite clear (the presentation in [3] is based on late sources); in Thucydides and Xenophon, the assembly appears to be more powerful, the *gērousía*, in contrast, less powerful than in the Great Rhetra or in the *Politika* by Aristotle [2]. Common members were not allowed to speak nor to propose motions. Presumably, the assembly was most powerful when the *gērousía* was divided. The vote was taken through loud yelling (Thuc. 1,87,2).

In Athens, the poorest citizens were probably never excluded from the *ekklesia*, but they were not expected to play an active role at first. When Solon created a new council which was to prepare the work of the public assembly, he apparently intended regular meetings of the assembly. His *(h)ēliaía* seems to be identical with the public assembly, but with the function of making court decisions. In 462 BC, the *ekklesia* received additional areas of authority through the reform of the Areopagus instigated by Ephialtes, perhaps even including the right to carry out the proceedings of *eisangelía* in serious offences against the state. By no later than the 2nd half of the 5th cent. BC, all of the more important decisions and many of the less important ones were made by the *ekklesia*. Every citizen was allowed to speak and to propose motions as long as he was not expressly excluded. The role of the council in preparing the agenda was not regarded as a significant interference with the freedom of the public assembly.

In the 30s of the 4th cent., perhaps even earlier, four regular assemblies took place in each of the ten prytanies of the year, with specific tasks assigned to each of them ([Aristot.] Ath. Pol. 43,4–6). One of them was known as *kyría* ('principal assembly'). In other places, *kyría ekklesia* refers to a regular assembly. In Athens, the ten *kyríai* apparently were the only regular assemblies in earlier times. The *sýnklētoi* ('the summoned') *ekklesiai* presumably were extraordinary assemblies which were held in addition to the regular ones. In the beginning, the assemblies may have been chaired by the nine archonts, from Ephialtes up to the early 4th cent. by the fifty *prytaneís*, afterwards by a committee of nine *próhedroi* made up of council members from each of the ten phyles with the exclusion of the respective managing prytany. Certain decisions that concerned persons mentioned by name required a quorum of 6,000 and a vote on small ballot plates, which were used to check the quorum. Otherwise, the vote was taken by a raising of hands, probably without taking an exact count. Participation in the *ekklesia* was not paid for until after the Peloponnesian War.

There is no evidence that *ekklesiai* met just as frequently outside of Athens. In many states, a regular assembly took place each month, in some of them participation was paid (e.g. in Iasos: SEG 40, 959; [10]). In some communities, the right to propose motions was limited. Legislative bodies that comprised more than one city sometimes had a public assembly, but not always. The Boeotian League had no assembly before 386 BC, but apparently it did so after 378. In the Delphic amphiktyony, decisions were regularly made by a representative council, but public assemblies could be held as well. In the Achaean and Aitolian Leagues of the Hellenistic period, public assemblies as well as council meetings took place.

→ Amphiktyonia; → Eisangelia; → Gerousia

IN GENERAL: 1 BUSOLT/SWOBODA
SPARTA: 2 A. ANDREWES, in: Ancient Society and Institutions, FS V. Ehrenberg, 1966, 1–20 3 W. G. FORREST, in: Phoenix 21, 1967, 11–19
ATHENS: 4 R. M. ERRINGTON, ἐκκλησία κυρία in Athens, in: Chiron 24, 1994, 135–160 5 M. H. HANSEN, The Athenian Ecclesia, 1983 6 Id., The Athenian Assembly in the Age of Demosthenes, 1987 7 Id., The Athenian Ecclesia 2, 1989 8 P. J. RHODES, E. Kyria and the Schedule of Assemblies in Athens, in: Chiron 25, 1995, 187–198 9 R. K. SINCLAIR, Democracy and Participation in Athens, 1988, chs. 3–5
IASOS: 10 P. GAUTHIER, in: BCH 104, 1990, 417–443
FEDERATIONS: 11 J. A. O. LARSEN, Representative Government in Greek and Roman History, 1955 12 Id., Greek Federal States, 1968. P.J.R.

II. CHRISTIAN

Ekklesia of God was one of the terms used by early Christians to refer to themselves, i.e. the congregation of the eschaton, brought together by God through Jesus. The term originates in the language of Jewish apocalypticism and the LXX (for Hebrew *qāhāl* — 'assembly', 'cultic congregation') and became the standard term for → church, also in Latin (*ecclesia*). In the NT, the term *ekklesia* is rarely evident outside of Acts and Paul's letters (→ Paulus [2]); the only documented uses in the → gospels (Mt 16,18; 18,17) are generally disputed, as far as their attribution to the historical → Jesus is concerned.

The worldwide *ekklesia* of God is as an entity also present in each house group, local congregation, or any Christian assembly; for that reason, each of these is also in itself referred to as *ekklesia* (1 Cor 1,2; 11,18; 16,19; Apc 1,20). In → Hermas' visions (of *c.* AD 140), *ekklesia* already appears personified as both a very old woman and a virgin.

→ Church

O. LINTON, s. v. E., RAC 4, 1959, 905–921; J. ROLOFF, Die Kirche im NT, 1993; K. L. SCHMIDT, s. v. ἐκκλησία, ThWB 3, 1938, 502–539. S. GE.

Ekklesiasterion (ἐκκλησιαστήριον; *ekklēsiastḗrion*). Meeting-place of a Greek public assembly. Among the cities where the word *ekklesiasterion* is used are Olbia (SIG³ 218) and Delos during the period of the Athenian *kleroucboi* in the 2nd cent. BC (SIG³ 662). In Athens, the regular meeting-place was the Pnyx in the southwest part of the city, where three different building stages from the 5th and the 4th cent. were identified. From the late 4th cent., the theatre of Dionysus came to be used more and more as a meeting place. As opposed to the Romans, the Greeks sat during their assemblies. Thus, the use of theatres or buildings similar to theatres was common. A survey of the evidence for *ekklesiasteria* can be found in [1. 44–75].

→ Ekklesia; → Assembly buildings

1 M. H. HANSEN, T. FISCHER-HANSEN, Polis, politeuma and politeia. A note on Arist. Pol. 1278b, in: D. WHITEHEAD (ed.), From Political Architecture to Stephanus Byzantinus, 1994, 44–75. P.J.R.

Ekkobriga Central town of the north-western → Trocmi tetrarchy, a fortified settlement of the Trocmi and a joint posting station for the roads to Ancyra and Tavium (Tab. Peut. 9,5: *Eccobriga*; It. Ant. 203,6: *Ecobrogis*), modern Kalekişla east of Sulakyurt [1. 148–151; 2. 28]. E. consisted of a steeply rising castle mount and an extensive walled lower town; scattered finds indicate settlement into the Byzantine period. The name of this obviously Celtic new foundation is derived from *briga* ('fortified high place'), and can most probably be traced back to the common Gallic-Danubian stem *Ecc-/Ekk-*, presumably a reference to the 'sharpness of the sword blade' (cf. [3]).

1 K. Strobel, Galatica I: Beitr. zur histor. Geogr. Ostgalatiens, in: Orbis Terrarum 3, 1997, 131–153 2 Id., State Formation by the Galatians of Asia Minor, in: Anatolica 28, 2002, 1–46 3 Holder 1, 529, 533, 1404 f. K. ST.

Ekkyklema (ἐκκύκλημα; *ekkýklēma*). Theatre machine, through which 'interior scenes' could be made visible: a platform which 'rolled out' of the fly tower. Since the word *ekkyklema* is not documented prior to Poll. 4,128 (Aristophanes, however, uses the related verbs) and since clear archaeological indications are lacking, the existence of such a device in the theatre of the 5th cent. was called into question despite better knowledge of the texts [1; 2]. The tragedians removed bloody acts of violence from the audience's eyes, but then presented the perpetrators and the victims in tableaux that caused the audience's shuddering and lamentation. For this, it could not suffice to simply open the door of the fly tower. Instead, they moved the horrible events into broad daylight on the *ekkyklema*. The *ekkyklema* naturally belonged to tragedy, just as the *mechane* belonged to the appearance of gods. Aristophanes used the *ekkyklema* obviously for the purpose of parody (Ach. 408f.; Thesm. 95–98), Menander apparently declined its use (Dysk. 758 does not offer conclusive evidence).
→ Mechane

1 E. Bethe, E. und Thyromata, in: RhM 83, 1934, 21–38
2 A.W. Pickard-Cambridge, The Theatre of Dionysus in Athens, 1946, 100–122.

H.-D. Blume, Einf. in das ant. Theaterwesen, 31991, 66–72; N. C. Hourmouziades, Production and Imagination in Euripides, 1965, 93–108; H.-J. Newiger, E. und Mechane in der Inszenierung des griech. Dramas, in: WSA 16, 1990, 33–42. H.BL.

Eknomon (ἔκνομον; *éknomon*). Massif in southern Sicily near the mouth of the Salso above Licata. The discovery of remnants from archaic times (chthonic sanctuary, necropolis) in Mollarella and newer studies about the mountain [1], which was bordered by a subsidiary of the ancient Himeras and was located towards the sea, suggest [2] the location of E. west of Monte S. Angelo (Poliscia plateau) and not on its eastern foothills as was previously thought. References: Diod. Sic. 19,108 (fortress of Phalaris [3]); 107–110 (311 BC: defeat of Agathocles); Plut. Dion 26 (on 357 BC); Pol. 1,25 (on 256 BC: Roman base).

1 G. Bejor, s.v. Ecnomo, BTCGI 7, 101f. 2 A. De Miro, s.v. Licata, EAA, II Suppl. 1971–1994, 1995, 354
3 G. Manganaro, Instituzioni pubbliche e culti religiosi, in: L. Braccesi, E. De Miro (ed.) Agrigento e la Sicilia greca, Atti della settimana di studio Agrigento 2–8 maggio 1988, 1992, 214. GI.F.

Ekphora (ἐκφορά; *ekphorá*) From Aeschylus (Sept. 1024; clearly terminologically in Thuc. 2,34,3), *ekphora* denotes the funeral procession which takes the body from the place where it was laid out to cremation or burial. Detailed descriptions can be found first in Hom. Il. 23,131–139. As indicated by representations on late geometrical funeral receptacles [1. fig. 53–55], the *ekphora* was performed by wealthy families in the older Athens with great splendour (deathbed on a wagon, cf. clay model of the hearse from Attica [3. fig. 22]) and a large number of participants. After the prohibition of special extravagance and public mourning in the 6th cent. BC (Ps.-Demosth. 43,62 = Sol. F 109 Ruschenbusch), the *ekphora* took place quietly in the early morning of the third day after death. Restrictions in the way it was carried out and in the number of participants are also evidenced for the 5th cent. BC in Iulis on Ceos (Syll.3 1218,7–9) and Delphi (LSCG 77 C 11–28).
→ Burial

1 G. Ahlberg, Prothesis and E. in Greek Geometr. Art, 1971, 220–239 2 M. Andronikos, Totenkult, Arch Hom III W, 1968 3 D.C. Kurtz, J. Boardman, Thanatos, 1985 (Greek Burial Customs, 1971) 4 E. Stein-Hölkeskamp, Adelskultur und Polisgesellschaft, 1989, 116f. W.K.

Ekphrasis (ἔκφρασις; *ékphrasis*)
I. Literature II. Archaeology

I. Literature
A. Greek B. Latin

A. Greek
1. Definition 2. Vividness and Illusion

1. Definition
In the rhetorical terminology of the Imperial period, *ekphrasis* is a description which aims at vividness (ἐνάργεια, *enárgeia*) (thus in Rhet. Her., Theon, Hermogenes, Aphthonius, etc.), that is, a description which tries to bring its object clearly in front of the readers' eyes: persons, things, situations, cities, seasons, celebrations, etc. (cf. [8; 17]). The object was not specified until Nicolaus Rhetor (5th cent. AD) as 'primarily statues, visual works (εἰκόνες), and related things'. The *ekphrasis* pursues this goal most of all through clarity (σαφήνεια, *saphḗneia*) in the details (κατὰ μέρος). This, according to Nicolaus, distinguishes it from other, more general forms of description (καθ' ὅλου). The

handbooks of the → *progymnasmata* refer to *ekphrasis* as a rhetorical exercise and as a possibility of composition. Although *ekphrasis* does not become an independent genre until the → Second Sophistic (2nd–5th cents. AD), it can be found in Greek literature from the beginning in many primarily literary and dramatic works: In drama, we find it in narrative passages which describe events outside of the scenes (e.g. Aesch. Eum. 39–59) or which dress up the relatively sparse realism of the stage (e.g. Soph. El. 4–10; Soph. Phil. 15–21; 1081–1094; Soph. OC 668–706). *Ekphrases* of both types are very numerous in Euripides, the most detailed is *Ion* 82–183 [16].

Even if we disregard the cases in which a detailed, vivid description is not the goal but the means of literary communication (e.g. the illustration of diseases in the Hippocratic *Epidemics*, of human types in the *Charakteres* by Theophrastus, of cities in the *Perihēgḗseis*), *ekphrasis* of highly varied, even non-pictorial objects is very common in Greek literature.

2. Vividness and Illusion

The most common object of detailed *ekphrasis* can be found in works of art and pictorial representations (engraved objects, statues, paintings, etc.). This fact is based, on the one hand, on the highly influential model of Hom. Il. 18,468–608 (description of Achilles' shield) — similarly, Hephaestus is the creator of works of art in two other famous epic *ekphrases* (Apoll. Rhod. 1.721–767; Mosch. Europa 37–62), and, on the other hand, on the always relevant concept of → *mimesis* in Greek literature, which justified the details of the *ekphrasis* with the pictorial nature of the content (the *ekphrasis* thus also became the description of a description, the poet emulating the visual artist).

The goal of vividness in the *ekphrasis* of visual works of art is usually achieved in two ways: Either the author 'replaces' the artist by allowing the reader to take in the scenes depicted on an object through the narrative force of words and through the pictorial nature of the details, or he 'dramatizes' the description by including an audience of viewers in the *ekphrasis* and then describing to the readers the effect of reality experienced by the viewers (he thereby tells not so much about the object itself but about the process of its observation). Homer lends an independent verbal life to the scenes on Achilles' shield, on the one hand through his integrating narrative, which transforms the static scenes into chronological sequences (e.g. Il. 18,504–506; 513; 516; 520), and on the other hand through numerous references to the making of the shield by Hephaestus (ἐν ... ποίησε, ἐν ... ἐτίθει etc., Il. 18,483; 490; 541; 550; 561, etc.).

In (Ps.-)Hes. *Aspis*, the description is more static, but this is compensated by the emphasis on the realistic effect of the scenes on Hercules' shield on the viewers. This effect is achieved by optical (cf. 189; 194; 216–218; 241–244; in Homer, there are only two indications of this kind: Il. 18,539; 548) and acoustical illusions (cf. 164; 243; 278–280). The difference between the developing reality and the illusion of a movement, which, however, is irrefutably static (310f.) is made quite clear. Correspondingly, (Ps.-)Hes. needs fewer direct references to the activity of the shield's maker (the one in 219 is isolated). The emphasis on artistic illusions remains one of the most consistent aspects of *ekphrasis* (not even the truest readoption of the Homeric model of shield descriptions is free from it, Quint. Smyrn. 5,3–101; cf. 12f.; 24). In contrast, the *ekphrasis* of the shepherd's cup found in Theoc. 1,27–56, while analogous in form, should be regarded as an antithesis to the Homeric model in its typically bucolic topics versus Homer's epic and martial topics. In an effort to increase the *enárgeia*, Apoll. Rhod. 1,721–767 integrates anticipation of the characters' future into the *ekphrasis* (esp. 731; 736), which again points to the illusionist effect which the object would have on a potential audience of viewers (e.g. 765–7).

The practice of praising the illusion's closeness to reality develops fully in dramatic and paradramatic works, in which a real or fictitious audience of viewers is already taken for granted prior to the conventions of the respective genre — both in the classical (clearly Aeschyl. *Theoroi* fr. **78a Radt, cf. also Epicharmus *Thearoi* and Sophron *Tai thamenai*) as well as esp. in the Hellenistic period (Theoc. 15,78–86; Herodas 4; cf. also Euphron *Theoroi*, PCG 5,288). Parallel to this is the 'dramatization' of the *ekphrasis* of a festival in Callim. H. 5,1–54, 137–142, which he conducts in the role of the chorus leader. The emphasis on the effect of artistic illusion is also very common in the Hellenistic epigram (e.g. Anth. Pal. 6,354 and 9,604: Nossis; 16,182: Leonidas; 16,120: Archelaus), which furthermore foregrounds the illusion itself by imagining an audience of viewers that questions the statues about their significance — or in turn is questioned by them (e.g. Anth. Pal. 16,275: Posidippus; 16,136: Antiphilus; 9,709; 16,25: Philippus; cf. [9]).

We often encounter the exact symbolic correspondence of the images in an *ekphrasis* with their context, cf. e.g. Aesch. Sept. and on this [18]; Apoll. Rhod. 1,763f. (Phrixus / expedition of the Argonauts) and especially Mosch. Europa 37–62 (with strong symbolic valency of Io and the cow, Zeus/Europa, and Zeus and the bull; Ach. Tat. 1,1 (the leitmotif of Eros' power and the fate of the female protagonist are anticipated in the *ekphrasis* of a painting of Europa; other symbolic *ekphrases* in 3,6–8 and 5,3; cf. [1]). A special form of symbolic *ekphrasis* is the allegoric-didactic type of the *pinax* by → Cebes, whose precursors must be traced in Pl. Criti. 110d–111d and 114d–115c, but according to Cic. Fin. 2,69, primarily in the didactic practice of → Cleanthes.

The *ekphrasis* was one of the favourite topics of rhetoric from the Second Sophistic up to the Justinianic period (2nd–6th cents. AD): from → Lucianus (most of all *De domo*, *Herodotus*, *Zeuxis*, *Imagines*; but cf. *Quomodo historia conscribenda sit* 19f. and on this [12]), Philostratus, Callistratus up to Johannes of Gaza, Paulus Silentiarius, and Procopius of Gaza (cf. [7]). On the afterlife of the ancient theory and practice of *ek-*

phrasis in Byzantium, cf. [10], in Renaissance paintings, [14].

1 S. Bartsch, Decoding the Ancient Novel: The Reader and the Role of Description in Heliodorus and Achilles Tatius, 1989 2 A.S. Becker (cur.), A Rhetoric of Early Greek Ekphrasis, 1995 3 G. Downey, s.v. E., RAC 4, 921–944 4 W. Elliger, Die Darstellung der Landschaft in der griech. Dicht., 1975 5 E.C. Evans, Literary Portraiture in Ancient Epic, in: HSCPh 58–59, 1948, 189–217 6 D.P. Fowler, Narrate and Describe: the Problem of Ekphrasis, in: JRS 81, 1991, 25–35 7 P. Friedländer, Johannes v. Gaza und Paulus Silentiarius: Kunstbeschreibungen justinianischer Zeit, 1912 8 G. Geissler, Ad descriptionum historiam symbola, thesis 1916 9 S. Goldhill, The Naive and Knowing Eye: E. and the Culture of Viewing in the Hellenistic World, in: S. G.-R. Osborne (ed.), Art and Text in Ancient Greek Culture, 1994 10 H. Maguire, Truth and Convention in Byzantine Descriptions of Works of Art, in: Dumbarton Oaks Papers 28, 1974, 113–140 11 F. Manakidou, Beschreibung von Kunstwerken in der hell. Dichtung, 1993 12 F. Montanari, E. e verità storica nella critica di Luciano, in: Filologia e critica letteraria della grecità (Ricerche di filologia classica II), 1984, 113–123 13 J. Palm, Bemerkungen zur E. in der griech. Lit., in: Kungl. Human. Vetenskaps-Samf. i Uppsala, Arsb. 1965–66, 108–211 14 D. Rosand, E. and the Generation of Images, in: Arion 1, 1990, 61–105 15 G. Rudberg, Zum hellenischen Frühlings- und Sommergedicht, in: Symbolae Osloenses 10, 1932, 1–15 16 Schmid/Stählin I, 787, n. 3 17 G. Zanker, Enargeia in the Ancient Criticism of Poetry, in: RhM 124, 1981, 297–311 18 F. Zeitlin, Under the Sign of the Shield. Semiotics and Aeschylus' Seven against Thebes, 1982. M.FA.

B. Latin

1. Introduction 2. Epics 3. Lyric poetry 4. Prose

1. Introduction

Latin literature is essentially based in this respect — as usual — on the Greek models [2; 3]. The significance of particularly the first literary *ekphrases,* the Homeric description of the shield, is overwhelming for Roman tradition as well. Of similarly strong influence on Latin literature were the efforts of rhetoric theory, largely Greek in character, towards conceptual clarity (cf. on the function of description, *descriptio*, in speech, Rhet. Her. 4,51; Cic. De or. 3,96ff; Quint. Inst. 6,2,32; 8,3,66f; 9,2,40 and passim; Serv. Aen. 10,653 [4; 6]).

The question of the influence of rhetoric on the development of *ekphrasis* is contested. *Ekphrasis* cannot be a central argument in a speech aimed at the affect on the listener, but was developed in the rheotrical schools as a 'virtuoso etude' [6. 149]. The simplified view that *ekphrasis* is a point of rest in the plot, a delaying element, may be based on Quint. Inst. 4,3,12f., but is short-sighted nevertheless. From the Hellenistic period, we witness an increase in the desire to turn the *ekphrasis* into the focal point of the plot, and to employ it for greater emphasis of its statements, esp. in epic poetry [1; 5. 151; 3; 10]. We therefore cannot necessarily assume a function of symbolic heightening in *ekphrasis*, but it certainly conveys a mood and offers an interpretative reflection of the plot. At the same time, the 'demonstration of poetic virtuosity' [5] also plays an important role. In the Augustan period, the poetic description of works of art with an ideological programme leads to the result that the *ekphrasis* itself becomes politicized.

Examples of *ekphrasis* in the modern sense, which is restricted to works of art [7; 5], can be found in Latin literature in → epics, → epigrams, and → lyric poetry, in → novels and in oration (→ rhetoric). Subjects of *ekphrasis* in the narrower sense are the accessories of weapons, esp. — following Homer — shields, fabric, pieces of jewellery, receptacles, representations of figures in paintings or sculptures primarily on buildings, and, finally, invisible phenomena. The representation is presented directly or indirectly, that is, conveyed through a fictitious recipient, in realistic spacial conceptions or 'as an illusion' [6] (see above I. A. 2.). Linguistic patterns can be identified esp. in the use of introductory formulas, and in a special use of tenses and adverbs [11; 12; 6. 26ff.].

2. Epics

In Hellenistic tradition, *ekphrases* obviously appear already in → Ennius (fr. 23 V.) and → Naevius, then in → Catullus Carm. 64. → Virgil, in Ecl. 3,36–47 (a receptacle) and in Georg. 3,13–39 (Temple of Octavian), does not yet demonstrate the independence of statement which is characteristic for *ekphrasis* in the *Aeneid* (survey: [8]). The representations on the temple doors in Carthage (Aen. 1,421–493; cf. also 1,159ff.; 6,19ff.) and the shield of Aeneas (8,625–731), aside from a few shorter *ekphrases,* offer, as it were, a 'window into the future' [5. 150; 22]. In matters of form, Virgil also trod new paths in clearly bringing out the reaction of the fictitious viewer and in using it for increasing the pathos [17]. The post-Virgilian epic reveals the type of *ekphrasis* that interprets the events, in fact by clearly offering intertextual connections. In the *ekphrasis*, → Valerius Flaccus informs the viewer and the reader about the mythical prehistory (1,129ff.; 2,400ff.; 5,416ff.); Statius plays in a masterly way and almost ironically with the claim that *ekphrasis* adds vividness to what is represented (e.g. Theb. 1,540ff.; 2,215ff.; 4,168ff.). In the description of Hannibal's shield 2,406ff., Silius presents the events leading up to the present from the Punic perspective. Ovidius, above all, more and more renounces 'realistic' presentation and develops the description into the fantastic or allegorical (Ov. Met. 6,68ff.: fabric; 2,1ff.: *regia Solis* [18]). The temporal sequence and spatial arrangement becomes increasingly unclear. An illusionist technique dominates [6]; optical traits are complemented by acoustical ones. A preference for the miraculous over the plausible characterizes also the descriptions by → Claudianus [2] (rapt. Pros. 1,238ff.; cf. 2,21ff.; 41ff.).

3. Lyric poetry

In their descriptions of Augustan Rome, Prop. 2,31 and also Ov. Ars am. 1,67–74 indicate a sceptical attitude towards the political aspect of the buildings. Examples of *ekphrasis* in epigrammatic poetry can be found in Martial (6,42; 9,43; 8,51). There, the description offers both a positive and negative characterization of the subject. Statius apparently is also influenced by the epigram in the *Silvae* (1,1; 4,6). Epic descriptions of landscapes may have influenced the descriptions of villas 1,3; 2,2. The emphasis on precious details can also be found in the *ekphrases* of → Sidonius Apollinaris (Carm. 15; 22).

4. Prose

Regarding novels in the Latin realm, we can mention only → Petronius 83,2, in which the description of images motivates the viewers to think about their own worries. A direct path leads from the descriptions of villas by the younger Pliny (Epist. 2,17; 5,6) to the authors of late antiquity (→ Gregory of Nyssa, → Paulinus of Nola). Christian literature of late antiquity is extraordinarily rich in ekphrastic representations in poetry and prose [1; 2].

→ Ekphrasis

1 P. Friedländer, Johannes von Gaza, Paulus Silentiarius und Prokopios von Gaza, 1912 (repr. 1969) 2 G. Downey, s.v. E., RAC 4, 921–944 3 D. Fowler, Narrate and Describe, in: JRS 81, 1991, 25–35 4 G. Boehm, Bildbeschreibung, in: G. Boehm, H. Pfotenhauer (ed.), Beschreibungskunst — Kunstbeschreibung, 1995, 24–40 5 F. Graf, E., in: ibid., 143–155 6 G. Ravenna, L'e. poetica di opere di arte in Latino, in: QIFLPadova 3, 1974, 1–51 7 Id., s.v. E., EV 2, 183–185 8 M. Krieger, E., 1992 9 S. Goldhill, The Naive and Knowing Eye, in: S. Goldhill, R. Osborne (ed.), Art and Text in Ancient Greek Culture, 1994, 197–223 10 G. Kurman, E. in Epic Poetry, in: Comparative Literature 26, 1974, 1–13 11 A. Szantyr, Bemerkungen zum Aufbau der Vergilischen E., MH 27, 1970, 28–40 12 M. v. Albrecht, Zur Funktion der Tempora in Ovids elegischer Erzählung, in: M. v. Albrecht, E. Zinn, Ovid, 1968, 451–467 13 F. Klingner, Catulls Peleus-Epos, SBAW 1956, 6 14 R. F. Thomas, Callimachus, the Victoria Berenices, and Roman Poetry, in: CQ 33, 1983, 92–113 15 A. Laird, Sounding out E.; in: JRS 83, 1993, 18–30 16 W. Clausen, Virgil's Aeneis and the Tradition of Hellenistic Poetry, 1987 17 W. B. Boyd, Virgil's Camilla and the Traditions of Catalogue and E., in: AJPh 113, 1992, 213–234 18 H. Herter, Ovids Verhältnis zur Bildenden Kunst, in: N. I. Herescu (ed.), Ovidiana, 1958, 49–74.

CH.R.

II. Archaeology

A. Competition between the arts B. Functions and aesthetic categories C. Art and literature

A. Competition between the arts

The central element of *ekphrasis* can be found in the various interactions between art and literature: Most descriptions are based explicitly or implicitly on a competition between the arts (cf. the performance of a singer in Homer's description of shield, Il. 18,603ff.), wherein literature ultimately claims victory. Its superiority is due, among other things, to the possibilities of simultaneous interpretation, the integration into a historical-aetiological context, and the description of effects on the viewer. In contrast to a picture, which is locally fixed and even in case of duplication (copies of statues, vases) accessible only to a limited audience, a text can proclaim the fame of transitory works of art (fabric, wood) world-wide and make them eternal. The difficulties inherent in the topic (the reproduction of colour and light, the conversion of synchrony in the image to the diachrony of narration, etc.) elevate the author's achievement.

B. Functions and aesthetic categories

Hellenism is the first period in which buildings, festivals, works of art, and their literary descriptions are consistently placed in the service of courtly culture: Lavish temporary scenes, mechanical games, processions and festival productions served the increased demonstration of luxury and the legitimization of rulership of the new elite of leaders [8; 10], cf. the great procession of → Ptolemy II (Callixenus 197C–203B) [12]. Augustus' reshaping of Rome and the large-scale introduction of marble are reflected in *ekphrases* of mythical (Ov. Met. 2,1ff.: palace of Sol), historical (Verg. Aen. 1,418ff.: Carthage; 7,145ff.: palace of Latinus), contemporary (Prop. 2,31: Temple of Apollo; Ov. Tr. 3,1: house of Augustus), and astronomical themes (Ov. Met. 1,188ff.: godly residences in the Milky Way in the style of the aristocratic houses on the Palatine) and can be employed for panegyrics or criticism [14]. In the Imperial period (esp. under Nero and Domitian), buildings and *ekphrases* serve the praise of the ruler (Stat. Silv. 4,2; Calp. Ecl. 7) and the criticism of luxury (Luc. 10,104ff.; Sen. Ep. 55 and 86).

The *ekphrases* are therefore usually situated in a fixed framework of reasoning and interpretation. By means of certain descriptive categories, which become fixed in treatises on rhetorics of late antiquity (cf. Theon, Progymnasmata 11,241f. Spengel; Nicolaus 3,492,19ff. Spengel), the author directs the eye of the reader to the desired qualities: Within the general topoi — beauty, splendour, size, material value, animation — thematically conditioned values take shape. Images of gods, for example, are attributed special sacredness through enormous size and weight, exalted dignity, and old age (cf. Quint. Inst. 12,10,7–9); on satyrs and centaurs, realistic representations of the body and sensual pleasure are emphasized, etc. [3. 43ff., 78ff.; 4; 11. 49ff.].

The perspective moves from the outside to the inside, from the overall impression to the detail, from the centre to the periphery, from the ceiling to the floor. Archaeology can help clarify the preconditions and the origins of these aesthetic categories: its findings document, for instance, that the (stadium) length was an

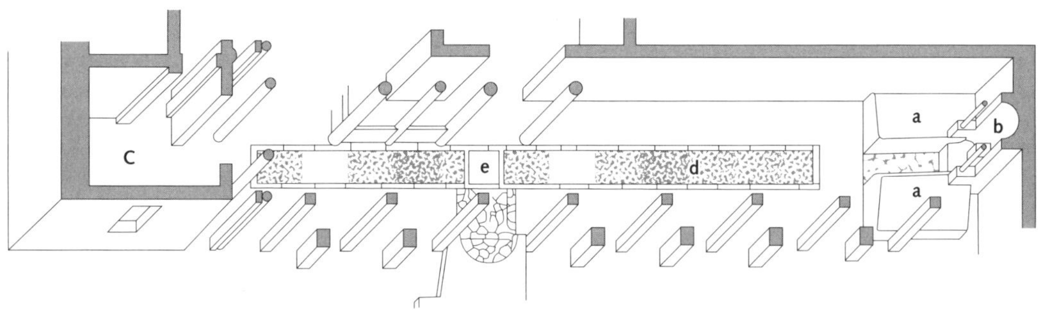

Garden architecture in the house of Loreius Tiburtinus (Pompeii):
The water-*biclinium* (a) with nymphaeum (b) and the house shrine (*sacellum*) (c) opposite it serve as visual focus for each other. The canal (d), running underneath a long and narrow pergola and with a bridge (e) at half-length, emphasizes the axial relation.
The layout of this site is closely related to the sequence of rooms in the villa described by Pliny.
There, a stibadium with water feature is situated opposite a room (*cubiculum*) with an attached cabinet (*zotheca*).
Instead of the canal with bridge, in Pliny a centrally situated fountain directs the viewer's glance.

independent value of architecture [7. 86ff.], that the perfection of perspective was the basis for greater realism, and that the emergence of mirror scenes and light and shadow effects were the root of the category of 'shine, glimmer, reflection' [1; 13. 115ff.].

C. Art and literature

Art and literature only rarely exist in a relationship of obvious interdependence. More often, we find parallel trends which originate within the cultural framework of each epoch and which influence each other. Thus, Hellenistic images increasingly appeal to the imagination of the viewer, who is supposed to fill in gaps, interpret symbols, and solve cryptograms. → Epigram and *ekphrasis* simultaneously include the reader more and more in the interpretation [2; 7; 9; 15]. The achievements of Hellenism continue to have an effect in Rome: Thus, Virgil's cycle of images on the Trojan War (Aen. 1,441ff.) takes up tragic → historiography, the early Hellenistic image of the battlefield (cf. the → Alexander Mosaic), and the Roman → triumphal painting (App. B Civ. 2,101). All three genres appeal to the viewer's emotional empathy through their pathos [11. 20ff.], as illustrated by Virgil in Aeneas' reaction.

The works of art described in *ekphrases* survived only rarely [16]. Since *ekphrasis* strives neither for completeness nor objectivity and is marked by literary stylization, reconstruction must remain hypothetical and is not the goal of *ekphrases*: Thus, Pliny's villa letters offer no ground plan that can be paced out, but rather a portrait of the owner with his preferences and desires. However, archaeological findings can illustrate the architectural forms which underlie certain *ekphrases*. For example, the end of the Tuscan hippodrome (Epist. 5,6,36ff.), a combination of water *stibadium*, fountain, and axially corresponding summer room, finds its counterpart in the garden architecture of the city villa of Loreius Tiburtinus in Pompeii. Both spatial arrangements unify the principles of axiality, a system of reciprocal views and eye-catchers, technically clever waterworks, and an artificial layout of nature [6. 83ff.] (cf. fig.). The structure of this installation is closely related to the spatial arrangement in the villa described by Pliny. There, a water *stibadium* is placed opposite of a room (*cubiculum*) complete with a side room (*zotheca)*. Instead of a bridged canal, in Pliny the view is captured by a centrally placed fountain.

→ Architecture; → Art, theory of; → Mimesis; → Villa; → Wall paintings

1 L. Balensiefen, Die Bed. des Spiegelbildes als ikonographisches Motiv in der ant. Kunst, 1990 2 P.H. van Blanckenhagen, Der ergänzende Betrachter, in: Wandlungen, FS E. Homann Wedeking 1975, 193–201 3 H. Cancik, Untersuchungen zur lyrischen Kunst des P. Papinius Statius 1965 4 Id., Größe und Kolossalität als rel. und ästhetische Kategorien, in: VisRel 7, 1990, 51–68 5 H. Drerup, Zum Ausstattungsluxus in der röm. Architektur 1957 6 R. Förtsch, Arch. Komm. zu den Villenbriefen des jüngeren Plinius, 1993 7 H. v. Hesberg, Bemerkungen zu Architekturepigrammen des 3. Jh.v.Chr., in: JDAI 96, 1981, 55–119 8 Id., Mechanische Kunstwerke und ihre Bed. für die höfische Kunst des frühen Hell., in: MarbWPr 47–72 9 Id., Bildsyntax und Erzählweise in der hell. Flächenkunst, in: JDAI 103, 1988, 309–365 10 Id., Temporäre Bilder oder die Grenzen der Kunst, in: JDAI 104, 1989, 61–82 11 T. Hölscher, Röm. Bildsprache als semantisches System, 1987 12 E.E. Rice, The Grand Procession of Ptolemy Philadelphus, 1983 13 I. Scheibler, Griech. Malerei der Ant., 1994 14 T.P. Wiseman, Conspicui postes tectaque digna deo, in: Id., Historiography and Imagination, 1994, 98–115 15 G. Zanker, Pictorial Description as a Suppl. for Narrative, in: AJPh 117, 1996, 411–423 16 G. Zimmer, Das Sacrarium des C. Heius. Kunstraub und Kunstgeschmack in der späten Republik, in: Gymnasium 96, 1989, 493–520.

UL.EG.

Ekthesis see → Rubrica

Ekthesis pisteos (ἔκθεσις πίστεως; *ékthesis písteōs*). A decree of faith issued by Emperor Heraclius in AD 638, probably written by the Patriarch Sergius, with the objective of stopping the christological controversies (regarding the nature and energy of Christ). The Ekthesis pisteos forbade further discussion of the one- or two-energy theories and instead assumed two natures and one will of Christ. However, a reconciliation was not effected. Rather, it created the monotheletic doctrine (→ Monotheletism). In 648 Emperor → Constans II revoked it and the 6th Ecumenical Council (680) condemned it as heretical.

R. Riedinger (ed.), Acta conciliorum oecumenicorum, Ser. II,1, 1984, 156–162; V. Grumel, Recherches sur l'histoire du monothélisme, in: Échos d'Orient 29, 1930, 16–28; G. Ostrogorsky, Gesch. des byz. Staates, ³1963; F. Winkelmann, Die Quellen zur Erforschung des monenergetisch-monotheletischen Streites, in: Klio 69, 1987, 515–559, 526f. (no. 50). G.MA.

El (Ugaritic *ʾil*, Hebrew *ʾēl*, Akkadian *ilu*). Common Semitic appellation for 'god' (except in Ethiopian) and also the *nomen proprium* of a deity attested in Mesopotamia since the 3rd millennium BC that apparently belonged to the original Semitic pantheon. Of several etymological hypotheses, the derivation from the root *ʾwl*, 'be in front, the first, strong,' deserves consideration.

While *il* in Old Akkadian and Amoritic, but also in the texts of → Ebla (3rd millennium) only appears in theophoric personal names, Ugaritic texts (2nd half of the 2nd millennium) reveal a much more defined profile of the god El. El was in second or third place in the lists of gods and sacrifices (after *ilib* and *il ṣpn*—two aspects of El that had become independent), but in the mythical texts of → Ugarit he was clearly at the head of the pantheon and presided as the reigning king in the assembly of gods. El was labelled the 'Creator of Creatures' (*bny bnwt*) and 'Father of Humanity' (*ab adm*), whose strength and fertility was expressed in the epithet 'Bull' (*ṯr il*). Simultaneously, he was together with his spouse Aširatu the 'Creator of the Gods' (*qny ilm*), who address him as 'My Father' (*aby*). All deities except for → Baʿal and his sister Anat were considered his sons and the 'family of El' (*bn il*; *dr il*). It even included the gods Jammu and Mot, who threatened the cosmic balance. In this manner the unavoidable negative experiences of the world were integrated as essential features into the cosmic balance. El stood above the cycle of seeding and harvest, of becoming and wasting, which were determined by Baʿal and Mot. He had no need to reconquer his kingdom over again like Baʿal but had always been king: his kingdom was of 'eternity' (*ʿlm*). As such he was known as the 'Father of Years/the Height' (?) (= World Mountain?) (*ab šnm*), whose 'wisdom' was expressed in the epithet 'the Benevolent, God of the (Understanding?) Heart' (*ltpn il dpid*). Although creation myths are not yet known from Ugarit, it is possible to deduct them for Ugarit from a contemporary Canaanitic myth in a

Hittite transmission (CTH 342 [8]), which is about *ᵈel-ku-ni-ir-sa* (i.e. *ʾl qn ʾrṣ*, 'El, Creator of the Earth', cf. Gen 14,19, the inscriptions of Karatepe [KAI No. 26 A III 18, 8th cent. BC], Leptis Magna [KAI No. 129,1: 2nd cent. AD] and four tesserae from Palmyra, where El is equated with Ποσειδῶν γαιηός in an altar inscription). El's location, which was imagined to be at the primal water ('the source of the two rivers in the depth of the two primal seas', *mbk nhrm, qrb apq thmtm*) or on the World Mountain (*ḫršn*), perhaps indicates the separation of the cosmic waters as the act of creation. Against an understanding of El as *deus otiosus*, which is derived from the Baʿal myth, speak his great significance in naming and the sacrifice lists, his role as an active god who fathered deities (in the myth of *Šaḥar* and *Šalim*), as well as his being the giver of blessings and progeny and, therefore, the preserver of the dynasty in the epic of Aqhat and Keret. The concepts of El and Baʿal differ but may only be interpreted in relation to each other: 'a superior and fundamental creator function is attributed to El but it is not sufficient for establishing a perfect cosmic order in its specific aspects (both at the divine and human level). The actual originator of this balance is Baal, who establishes it by confronting Yam and Mot' [7. 283].

The texts from Ugarit (since 1929) led to a re-evaluation of references to El in the patriarchal tradition of the OT (Gen. 14,18–20; 16,13; 21,33; 33,20; 35,7; 46,3; 49,25 etc.). The religion of the Proto-Israelites is now generally interpreted either as a religion of El, or as considering the clan gods as person-specific manifestations of El or assumed to have a transition phase in which the clan gods were identified with El before all merged in Yahwe. This reconstruction is of necessity hypothetical because El is always identical with Yahwe in the context of the evidence. Mythological substance was preserved in the patriarchal tradition (especially in Deut. 32,8–9; Ps. 19,2; 29; 82; cf. Is. 14,13; Ez 28,2) in which El plays a role (superior to Yahwe?), but throughout the OT El is used as an appellative. Numerous epithets and ideas that were originally associated with El (such as god as king, creator, judge and sacred god) were transferred in Israel to Yahwe. The identification of Yahwe with El is also demonstrated in the small number of epigraphical findings of Judea under the monarchy (Ḫirbat al-Kūm and Ḫirbat Bait Layy [2. 215, 248]). Whether El next to Baʿal in an inscription on the wall plaster of the caravanserai Kuntillat ʿAǧrūd (9th cent. BC) is a divine name or designation of Yahwe remains uncertain [2. 59].

Overall, El only played a subordinate role in the 1st millennium BC. Philo of Byblus (in Eus. Pr. Ev. 1,10,16) equated El with → Kronos and named him together with his divine siblings → Baitylus and → Atlas as being in only the third divine generation after Eliun with Berut and → Uranus with → Gaia. In inscriptions he is only encountered on statues of Panammuwas I and II (Zincirli) after → Hadad and before Rakibel, the god of the dynasty (KAI No. 214,2.11.18; No. 215, 22), and next to ʿEljan among the paired divine witnesses in the state treaty of Sfire I (KAI No. 222 A 11). The fragments of Tall Dair ʿAllā in the central Jordan valley (late 9th cent. BC), which are difficult to interpret, know of a divine assembly, over which El possibly presided, and also El in an active role (cf. Num. 23,22). Among the Phoenicians and Aramaeans Baʿalšamēn increasingly appeared in the foreground (for the first time in the inscription of Yehimilk of Byblus [KAI No. 4]) and was increasingly equipped with El's traits (e.g., in Palmyra: 'the Great and Merciful', 'Lord of Eternity') so that in him the 'El and Baal traditions converged in a Zeus-like concept' [1. 185].

1 H. Gese, Die Religionen Altsyriens, 1970 2 J. Renz, W. Röllig, Hdb. der althebrä. Epigraphik, 1995 3 J. Hoftijzer (ed.), The Balaam Text from Deir ʾAlla Reevaluated, 1991 4 M. Köckert, Vätergott und Väterverheißungen, 1988, 67–91 5 H.-P. Müller, Die aram. Inschr. von Deir ʾAlla und die älteren Bileamsprüche, in: ZATW 94, 1982, 214–243 6 M. H. Pope, The Status of El at Ugarit, in: Ugarit-Forschungen 19, 1987, 219–230 7 P. Xella, Aspekte rel. Vorstellungen in Syrien nach den Ebla- und Ugarit-Texten, in: Ugarit-Forschungen 15, 1983, 279–290 8 E. Laroche, Catalogue des textes hittites, 1971, 342. M.K.

Elaeus (Ἐλαιοῦς; *Elaioûs*).

[1] City in the south of the Thracian Chersonesus near modern Eceabat (Turkey), foundation of the Athenians in the 6th cent. BC to control the southern access to the Propontis, important port town. Used by Militiades the Younger as the base for expeditions against Lemnos and Lesbos (Hdt. 6,140). E. was used as an achorage by Xerxes (Hdt. 7,22). The sanctuary of Protesilaus was defiled by the Persians (Hdt. 7,33). Member of the Delian and of the 2nd. Athenian League. E. remained an Athenian possession when the Chersonesus became part of the Odrysae kingdom. Alexander [4] the Great used it as the base for his Asian campaign in 334 BC (Arr. Anab. 1,11,5). I.v.B.

[2] Attic *paralia* (?) deme of the Hippothontis phyle, from AD 126/7 the Hadrianis, Ἐλαία (*Elaía*) in the inscription IG I³ 472 l. 10, which attests Hercules cult for E. One *bouleutes*. [1. 138] suggests a location east of Magula near Mavraki at a site where a dedicatory inscription was found. [2. 6f.]. As for which *trittys* it belonged to, s. IG II² 1927 [1. 115].

1 J. S. Traill, Demos and Trittys, 1986
2 E. Vanderpool, Three inscriptions from Eleusis, in: AD 23, 1968, A, 1–9.

Traill, Attica 12, 52, 69, 110 No. 37 Tab. 8, 10; Whitehead, 209, 372. H.LO.

Elaeussa (Ἐλαιοῦσσα; *Elaioûssa*). This city in Cilicia Pedias, originally situated on an island 200 m from the shore, arose as → Diocaesarea [1] from a temple sanctuary belonging to Corycus, and is first attested in the early 1st cent BC. In 12 BC E. became the residence of Archelaus of Cappadocia, who had renamed E. Sebaste after his patron Augustus. In the 2nd cent. AD expansion onto the mainland, and extensive construction. In 260 conquered by the Sassanids (R. Gest. Div. Saporis 29). From the beginning of the 4th cent. it belonged to the province of Cilicia Isauria; bishopric (suffragan to Seleucia on the Calycadnus). Arch. finds: remarkable necropolis.

A. Machatschek, Die Nekropolen und Grabmäler im Gebiet von Elaiussa Sebaste und Korykos im Rauhen Kilikien, 1967; Hild/Hellenkemper, s.v. Sebaste. F.H.

Elagabalus

[1] Name of a deity, based on its earliest attestation (Palmyrene stele of Nazala, 1st cent. AD), it can be etymologically derived from *ʾlhʾbl* (Hdt. 5,3,4: Elaiagabalos). Since *ʾlhʾ* is present in the *status emphaticus*, E. must be read as the 'God Mountain' [8. 503f.]. The image on the stele also speaks for this [1. 707]. The mountain signifies the citadel mountain of → Emesa (Ḥimṣ) with the temple of E. [6. 257f.; 8. 509f.], which is indicated in ancient descriptions (Avien. Descriptio orbis 1083–1093) and an altar find with the dedication 'To the god Helios Elagabalus' [6. 257–259; 9]. Because the elite of Emesa has been Arabic since the pre-Christian period, an Arabic origin of E. has been considered. However, his name is Aramaic. The deification of mountains is documented since the 2nd millennium BC, especially in Anatolia, Syria and Palestine, so E. probably was a deity of the pre-Arabic population of Emesa. E. was worshipped as a stone (Betyl, → Baitylia), a cultic custom also practiced in Anatolia, Syria and Palestine. As *páredros* of Elegabalus, the Arabic goddess al-Lāt [5. 150–153] is encountered in the cult of Emesa.

Elegabalus achieved more than regional importance when his priest Varius Avitus became emperor under the name M. Aurelius Antoninus (→ E. [2]) in AD 218. He took the cult stone of E. from Emesa to Rome, where the god reached the pinnacle of the Roman pantheon, was provided with Juno/Pallas Athene/al-Lāt and Urania/Dea Caelestis/Tanit as *páredroi* (Hdn. 5,6,3–5) and equated with Jupiter and/or Sol (HA Heliog. 1,5; 17, 8, Carac. 11,7) or even placed above them (Cass. Dio 79,11,1; Herodian 5,5,7; HA Heliog. 7,4). He was invoked as *(Deus) Sol A/Elagabalus* (CIL III 4300; VI 708; 2269) or as *Invictus Sol Elagabalus* (CIL X 5827): the Hellenized Heliogabalus was based on the name E. (HA Opil. 9,2; Aur. Vict. Caesares 23,1; cf. Cass. Dio 79,31,1; Hdn. 5,3,4) and indicates the 'solarization' of the god, which had already begun in Emesa. A temple was built for him on the Palatine to which his cultic image was transferred. After the death of Emperor E. (AD 222), it was returned to Emesa [2. 966f.]. Worship of E. is still attested under Aurelianus because he attributed his victory over Zenobia (AD 272) to the god E. The mention of E. as the Great Sun on the incense altar of Cordoba (3rd cent. AD) is based on private piety. Its Greek inscription mentions Aphrodite/al-ʾUzza and

Athena/al-Lāt together [4]. Iconographically, E. appears — especially on altars and coins — as a mountain, an eagle or a beehive-shaped Betyl (Hdn. 5,3,5) [1. 706f, 542] and, thus, stands in the tradition of the mountain iconography of Asia Minor.

1 C. Augé, P. Linant de Bellefonds, s.v. E., LIMC III/1, 705–708, III/2, 542 2 K. Gross, s.v. E., RAC 4, 987–1000 3 G.H. Halsberghe, The Cult of Sol Invictus, 1972 4 F. Hiller von Gaertringen et al., Syr. Gottheiten auf einem Altar aus Cordova, in: ARW 22, 1923/4, 117–132 5 S. Krone, Die altarab. Gottheit al-Lāt, 1992, 150–156 6 M. Moussli, Griech. Inschr. aus Emesa, in: Philologus 127, 1983, 254–261 7 H. Seyrig, Le culte du Soleil en Syrie à l'époque romaine, in: Syria 48, 1971, 337–373 8 J. Starcky, Stèle d'Elahagabal, in: Mélanges de l'Université Saint Joseph 49, 1975/6, 503–520 9 R. Turcan, Héliogabale et le sacre du soleil, 1985.

M. Frey, Unt. zur Religion und zur Religionspolitik des Kaisers Elagabal, 1989; M. Petrzykowski, Die Religionspolitik des Kaisers E., in: ANRW II 16,3, 1806–1825 Zu Emesa: M. Moussli., Tell Ḥoms (Qalʿat Ḥoms), in: Zschr. des Deutschen Palästina-Vereins 100, 1984, 9–11. H.NI.

[2] **Elagabalus = Imperator Caesar M. Aurelius Antoninus Augustus.** Roman emperor AD 218–222. Before his elevation his name was Varius Avitus Bassianus. He was the son of Sex. Varius Marcellus of Apamea and Iulia Soaemias of Emesa, a niece of the Empress Iulia Domna (Cass. Dio 78,30,2) and was probably born in 203. He was raised in Rome by his grandmother Iulia Maesa (Hdn. 5,3,2f.). After 217 he became the priest of the god E. in Emesa (Hdn. 5,3,6), as his great-grandfather Bassianus ([Aur. Vict.] Epit. Caes. 21,1; 23,2) had been. The ambitious Maesa achieved that the Syrian *legio II Gallica* proclaimed E. emperor on 16 May 218 as the alleged bastard son of his mother's cousin Caracalla (Cass. Dio 78,30,2ff.; Hdn. 5,3,2–12). Macrinus sent his praetorian prefect Ulpius Iulianus from Antioch, but his legions changed sides to E. On 8 June Macrinus was defeated and soon afterwards killed (Cass. Dio 78,38–40; Hdn. 5,4,6ff.). E. travelled via Nicomedia, where he spent the winter, to Rome, where he arrived about August/September 219. He brought with him the sacred stone from Emesa, his aniconic god, and immediately began to establish his cult in the capital (→ E. [1]). E. married the noble Iulia Cornelia Paula in 219. His grandmother Maesa and his mother Soaemias conducted the governmental affairs especially with the help of P. Valerius Comazon, who despite his low birth became *cos. ord.* in 220 and repeatedly held the office of urban prefect. Numerous other persons from the lower classes were elevated by E. to high offices (Cass. Dio 79,16,1ff.; SHA Heliog. 6,1–4; 10,2–11,1). Late in 220 E. began a determined religious policy: his god was declared the supreme god of the empire. E. himself was officially called *sacerdos amplissimus dei invicti Solis Elagabali*; the god was solemnly married to the Carthaginian Dea Caelestis (Hdn. 5,6,3–5).

E. separated from his first wife to marry the Vestal Iulia Aquilia Severa. There were strong protests in Rome against E.'s behaviour (Cass. Dio 79,5,1ff.; Hdn. 5,6,1) and especially among the soldiers he lost all respect. Maesa was able to persuade E. late in June 221 to adopt his young cousin Alexianus (= → Severus Alexander) and proclaim him Caesar (Cass. Dio 79,17,2ff.; SHA Heliogab. 10,1), also to dissolve the marriage to the Vestal and to marry a great-granddaughter of Marcus Aurelius, Annia Faustina (Cass. Dio 79,5,4). However, in religious matters E. was not willing to make any concessions: the coinages of the years 221 and 222 emphasize the Syrian deity without interruption. Before the end of 221, he separated from his third wife and, allegedly after a short fourth and fifth marriage, brought back his second wife, the Vestal Aquilia (Cass. Dio 79,9,4). According to SHA Heliogab. 13–15, E.'s attempts to murder his Caesar, who was popular among the soldiers, were supposedly foiled by the praetorians. This detailed representation is probably based on the contemporary imperial biographer Marius Maximus (otherwise, his Vita is largely fictional). *Cos. III* in 222 with Alexander, E. again attempted to kill him (SHA Heliogab. 16,1) but soldiers killed E. and his mother on 11 March 222. His body was thrown into the Tiber (Cass. Dio 29,20,2; Hdn. 5,8,6ff.; SHA Heliogab. 16,5–17,2).

RIC 4/2 23–45; C. Chad, Les dynastes d'Emèse, 1972; M. Frey, Unt. zur Religion und zur Religionspolitik des Kaisers Elagabal, 1969; E. Kettenhofen, Die syr. Augustae in der histor. Überlieferung, 1979; Kienast, ²1996, 173. A.B.

Elam (Elamite *haltamti*; Sumerian *elam(a)*, graphically 'explained' as NIM.KI, 'Upper Land '; Akkadian *elamtu*; Hebrew *ʿēlām*). The name was adopted in the West with the Bible (Gen 14) serving as intermediary. The geographical boundaries of E. varied but the core region was the lowland of modern Ḫuzestān (Khuzistan) with → Susa (settled since about 4,000 BC), later also the Iranian highland (→ Persis) centred on Anšan (the largest known Proto-Elamite site [2. 123]; modern Tappe Malyān, 42 km west of → Persepolis). In the east it extended to Kermān and the margins of the great deserts of Dašt-e Lūt and Dašt-e Kavīr. E.'s history was reconstructed from native sources and to a fair extent from the epigraphical record in Mesopotamia. The first rulers known by name are from the period of about 2600–2100 BC (dynasty of Awan [3. 102; 7. 25f.]). Late in the 3rd millennium E. consisted of an association of states (Susa, Awan, Šimaški, Anšan, Marḫaši), with Susa being under the suzerainity of Mesopotamian rulers for a longer period. The 'period of the Sukkalmaḫ', named after a Sumerian title taken over from Mesopotamia (there meaning 'great chancellor'), lasted from about the 19th to the 15th cent. BC. Elamite rulers formed a kind of triumvirate: 1. the *sukkal.maḫ* (the supreme ruler), 2. the *sukkal* of E. and Šimaški (coregent) und 3. the *sukkal* of Susa (a younger local ruler, usually the son or nephew of the *sukkalmaḫ*). In the early 2nd millennium E. was one of the most powerful states in the Middle East. Its rulers advanced as far as the regions to the west of the upper Tigris and in the age of → Ḫammurapi of Babylon claimed suzerainity over Mesopotamia. E.'s trade relations extended to the Mediterranean (Elamite tin to Karkemiš, Aleppo and Qaṭna in central Syria).

In the Middle Elamite period (*c.* 1450–1100) there was a flowering of construction under the kings of Anzan and Susa. Untaš-Napiriša (*c.* 1274–1240) founded a sacred city of about 100 ha (Dūr-Untaš, modern Čoġā Zaṇbīl, 40 km southeast of Susa). A → ziggurat and temple with numerous inscriptions grant a good insight into the Elamite pantheon. E. expanded the furthest under Šutruk-Nahhunte (*c.* 1185–1155 BC) and his brother Šilḫak-Inšušinak (*c.* 1150–1120). Their campaigns extended to the → Euphrates and into the Assyrian heartland. Babylonian trophies were dedicated in Susa. After a historically dark age of 300–400 years, E. re-emerged in the 8th cent. BC involved in Assyrian-Babylonian struggles while in the northeast the Medes and Persians advanced against E. Assurbanipal delivered a crushing blow against the Elamite kingdom in 646 BC with the destruction of Susa. In this context a Persian ruler by the name of → Cyrus (I), whose family had already seized power in the ancient capital of Anšan, appeared for the first time. E. merged in the 6th cent. into the newly created empire of the Achaemenids (→ Achaemenidae).

→ Elamite; → Iran

1 P. Amiet, Elam, 1966 2 E. Carter, M.W. Stolper, Elam, 1984 3 W. Hinz, Das Reich Elam, 1964 4 Id., Persia *c.* 2400–1800 B.C., in: CAH I,2, 31971, 644–680, II,1, 1973, 256–288 5 W. Hinz, H. Koch, Elam. WB, 1987 6 R. Labat, Elam *c.* 1600–1200 B.C., in: CAH II,2 31975, 379–416, 482–506 7 F. Vallat, Suse et l'Élam, 1980 8 Id., s.v. E., Répertoire Géographique des Textes Cunéiformes 11, 1993.

H.KO.

Elamite An agglutinative language without relationship to any other languages; a possible relationship to Dravidian remains unproven [5]. Whether the Ḫamazi languages, which were mentioned in Sumerian texts of the late 3rd millennium BC, are part of the same language family as Elamite is uncertain. Elamite was deciphered (→ DECIPHERMENT) with the aid of Achaemenid → trilingual texts, especially the inscription of → Darius' [1] I (→ Bisutun). The grammar and meaning of many words is still obscure. Numerous administrative records — mostly from Susa but also from East Iran — contain *c.* 400–800 pictographic symbols [1]. Texts in Proto-Elamite linear script (with fewer than 100, largely deciphered symbols [3]) are known from the period about 2200 BC. Even earlier the Elamites had adopted the Sumerian-Akkadian → cuneiform script. The earliest preserved text is a treaty with → Naramsin of Akkad (23rd cent. BC). Soon a simplified writing system developed with about 150–160 graphically modified symbols. Their number remained almost the same over the centuries but the use of Sumerian logograms increased over the centuries. The linguistic development of Elamite is represented by four language phases: Old Elamite (23rd–14th cents.), Middle Elamite (13th–11th cents.), New Elamite (8th–7th cents.) and Achaemenid Elamite (from the 6th cent.). The last Elamite inscriptions are from → Persepolis (period of Artaxerxes III, 358–337 BC).

→ Achaemenid; → Elam; → Iran

1 P. Damerow, R. Englund, The Proto-Elamite Texts from Tepe Yahya, 1989 2 F. Grillot-Susini, Eléments de grammaire élamite, 1987 3 W. Hinz, Iranica Antiqua 2, 1962, 1–21 4 W. Hinz, H. Koch, Elam. WB, 1987 5 D.M. McAlpine, Proto-Elamo-Dravidian. The Evidence and its Implications, 1981 6 E. Reiner, The Elamite Language, in: HbdOr I/2, 1969, 54–118 7 M.-J. Steve, Syllabaire Elamite, 1992.

H.KO.

Elaphebolos (Ἐλαφηβόλος; *Elaphēbólos*, 'Stag Slayer'). Poetic (Anac. fr. 1 Calame; Soph. Trach. 213) and cultic epiclesis of → Artemis. Her feast of Elaphebolia (with characteristic ritual destruction in the Phocian federal sanctuary of Hyampolis, Plut. Mor. 244 BD; Paus. 10,1,6; [1; 2; 3]) and the Athenian month name → Elaphebolion derived from the festival attest to the significance of the association of the goddess with her quarry. The association has been attested in literature since Homer (Od. 6,104) as well as the myths surrounding → Iphigenia's sacrificial substitution (since Eur. IT) and in iconography since the late Archaic period through many vase images and dedicatory reliefs [4].

1 Nilsson, Feste, 221–225 2 R. Felsch, Tempel und Altäre im Heiligtum der Artemis E. von Hyampolis bei Kalapodi, in: R. Étienne, M.-Th. Le Dinahet (ed.), L'espace sacrificiel dans les civilizations méditerranéennes de l'antiquité, 1991, 85–91 3 Graf, 410–417 4 L. Kahil, s.v. Artemis, LIMC 2.2, No. 686; 1231 etc.

F.G.

Elate (Ἐλάτη; *Elátē*, 'spruce'). Sister of the → Aloads Otus and Ephialtes. She was similar in stature to them. When she mourned the demise of her brothers she was transferred into a spruce tree towering to the sky (Lib. Narrationes 37; Eust. on Hom. Od. 5,239 and on Hom. Il. 5,560; 14,287).

R.B.

Elatea (Ἐλάτεια; *Eláteia*).

[1] In antiquity together with → Delphi (Str. 9,3,2) the largest (Paus. 10,34,1–2; Str. 9,2,19; Harpocr., Suda s.v. E.) and most famous Phocian town. Located in the farthest north of the Cephissus valley near modern Elatia (Leftà), E. dominated the road that led south from Thessaly and Locris through the passes of Thermopylae and Hyampolis. This location made E. a lively centre with local links and station for all who wanted to travel from the north to the south of the country (Str. 9,3,2; cf. Dem. Or. 18,168). Etymologically the name is derived from Arcadian *Elatos* (Paus. 10,34,1f.). Significant remains of neolithic settlements [1; 2] and a protogeometric necropolis of the Mycenaean period are preserved [3; 4]. The large number of graves, the quality and origin of grave goods and variety of the typology of goods attributable to the later period permit conclusions to be drawn on the town's standard of living and connections to the rest of the Greek world in the Mycenaean period as well as on its high productivity and technological capacity between the 12th and 10th cents. while the rest of Greece regressed. This also indicates a simultaneous population growth that was very likely caused by new settlers in the context of the Post-Mycenaean migrations of Greek peoples, the favourable position of E. on the north-south axial land route, and the fertility of the surrounding Cephissus valley. The flowering of the city finally came to an end, the burial ground was abandoned in the Archaic and Classical periods and only used again in the Hellenistic-Roman period. E. does not appear in the Homeric catalogue of Phocian towns, but burning by the Persians (480 BC, Hdt. 8,33) and destruction by Philip II (346 BC, Paus. 10,33,2) are recorded.

In the Hellenistic and Roman periods E. was repeatedly the scene of military confrontations, endured sieges, occupations and also a mass flight of the population (Liv. 32,24,1; MORETTI 1, 55) [5]. Quoted in the Price Edict of Diocletian, temporarily a bishop's seat after AD 347, E. is still attested in the 4th cent. AD and the Byzantine period with the name *Elatina* (Hierocles, Synekdemos 643,8; Constantine Porphyrogennetus, De thematibus 89; Steph. Byz. s.v. E.). The remains of the monumental acropolis walls (4th cent. BC and the Hellenistic period) and the fortress dating from Justinian's reign confirm E.'s function as a military base to ward off invasions of Phocis and southern Greece. In antiquity the city was also home to the sanctuary of Athena Kranaia — of which a few remains are preserved on a hill *c.* 20 stadia from E. — the most important cult of E. (Paus. 10,34,7f.). Inscriptions: IG IX 1, 97–185; SEG 3, 416ff.; 9, 1107 (= 18, 197); 19, 327.

1 S. WEINBERG, Excavations at prehistoric E., in: Hesperia 31, 1962, 158–209 2 R. HOPE SIMPSON, O.T. P. K. DICKINSON, A Gazetteer of Aegean Civilisation in the Bronze Age 1, 1979, 259f. 3 S. DEGER-JALKOTZY, E. und die frühe Gesch. der Griechen, in: AAWW 127, 1990, 79 4 S. DEGER-JALKOTZY, P. DAKORONIA, E., in: Arch. Österreichs, 3/1, 1992, 68 5 C. HABICHT, Pausania's guide to ancient Greece, 1985, 67–69.

J. BUCKLER, Philip II. and the third Sacred War, Mnemosyne, Suppl. 1989; P. DAKORONIA, E., in: Phokika Kronika 5, 1993, 25–39; J. M. FOSSEY, The Ancient Topography of Eastern Phokis, 1986, 86–91; MÜLLER, 487; P. NTASIOS, Symbolè sten Topographian tes archaias Phokidos, 1992, 27f.; N.D. PAPACHATZIS, Παυσανίου Ἑλλάδος Περιήγησις [Pausaníon Hellâdos Periḗgēsis] 5, ²1981, 432–436; PRITCHETT, IV 1982, 170–175; F. SCHOBER, Phokis, 1924, 29f.; TIB I, 153f.; L.B. TILLARD, The Fortifications of Phokis, in: ABSA, 17, 1910/1, 54–75. G.D.R.

[2] Town in Thessaly at the western entrance of the Tempe valley. E. surrendered in 171 BC simultaneously with the town Gonnus located on the other (north) side of the Peneius (Liv. 42,54) to Perseus when he marched into Thessaly. Localization near modern E. is uncertain.

K. GALLIS, in: AD 29, 1973/4 II, 582 (reports of finds and investigations); F. STÄHLIN, Das hellen. Thessalien, 1924, 88f. HE.KR.

Elatus (Ἔλατος; *Élatos*, 'spruce man'). Name of several mythical figures.

[1] Centaur, pierced by Hercules' poisoned arrow, which simultaneously wounded → Chiron (Apollod. 2,85).

[2] Prince of the Lapiths in Larisa. He was the father of the Argonaut Polyphemus (Schol. Apoll. Rhod. 1,40–41; Apollod. 1,113) and of → Caeneus/Caenis (Hyg. Fab. 14,2.4; 173,3; 242,3; Ov. Met. 12,189; 497).

F. BÖMER, P. Ovidius Naso, Met. B. 12–13, 1982, 63.

[3] *Eponymos* of → Elatea [1] in Phocis (Paus. 8,4,2–4). Son of Arcas and of Leaneira, Meganeira, the nymph Chrysopeleia (Apollod. 3,102) or the dryad Erato (Paus. 8,4,2). He was the father of Aepytus (Pind. Ol. 6,33), Stymphalus, Pereus, Ischys (Hes. Cat. 60,4) and Cyllen. Initially in possession of the Cyllene Mountains in Arcadia, he later founded Elatea after helping the Phocians in a war against the Phlegyans. In Elatea and in Tegea Pausanias saw sculptures of E. (Paus. 10,34,6; 8,48,8).

C. LOCHIN, s.v. E., LIMC 3.1, 708–709.

[4] Trojan ally from Pedasus, who was killed by Agamemnon (Hom. Il. 6,32–35).

P. WATHELET, Dictionnaire des Troyens de l'Iliade, Bd. 1, 1988, 507–508.

[5] Suitor of Penelope who was killed by Eumaeus (Hom. Od. 22,267). R.B.

Elaver River in Aquitania, modern Allier, source at 1,430 m elevation on Mont Lozère; flows from the left side into the Liger below Noviodunum after a course of 375 km (Caes. B Gall. 7,34,2; 35,1). E.O.

Elder Two shrubs of the genus *Sambucus* in the family *Caprifoliaceae* occur in Europe, the common elder (*Sambucus nigra* L., *sa(m)bucus*, ἀκτῆ; *aktê*) and the red-berried elder (*Sambucus racemosa* L.; Verg. Ecl. 10,27: Pan was said to be red because of the berries of the *ebulum*, according to Serv. ad loc. a comparable plant). A third type is the herbaceous, black-fruited dwarf elder (*Sambucus ebulus* L., *ebulus/um*, χαμαιάκτη; *chamaiáktē* in Dioscorides 4,173,2 WELLMANN = 4,172 BERENDES; Plin. HN 24,51: *chamaeactis* or *helion acte*). A good description of the species is found in Theophr. Hist. pl. 3,13,4–6.

Their medicinal use (Dioscorides, ibid.; Plin. HN. 24,52) was extensive: the roots and bark were recommended as laxatives and emetics. The leaves, drunk in wine, supposedly helped against snakebite and, placed on inflamed wounds, were cooling. The berries were considered diuretic and were used to dye hair (black). The pith (*medulla*) of the stem was used to seal branches of precious apples (Plin. HN 15,64) and pomegranates (Columella 12,46,3; Pall. Agric. 4,10,9,) for storage. Posts of elder wood were a permanent support for vines (Plin. HN 17,151 and 174; Columella 4,26,1). The smoke of the dwarf elder drove away snakes (Plin. HN 25,119). The unidentifiable *actaea* has nothing to do with elders (Plin. HN 27,43). C.HÜ.

Elea (Ἐλέα; *Eléa*).

[1] Coastal town in Epirus at the mouth of the Acheron near modern Veliani, main settlement of the Eleatis region (wrongly Elaia/Elaiatis in Thuc. 1,46,4) in Thesprotia. Origin of the *pólis* before 350 BC, first minting between 360 and 335 BC. Of the 10-ha. town mainly the 1.5-km-long walls are preserved. Documents: Scyl. 30; Str. 7,7,5.

Archaeological Reports 41, 1994/5, 26; P. CABANES, L'Épire, 1976; S.I. DAKARIS, Thesprotia, 1972; P.R. FRANKE, Die ant. Mz. von Epirus, 1961, 300–307. D.S.

[2] in Lower Italy → Velia.

Eleatic School Conventional term for the immediate successors of Parmenides (Zenon of Elea, Melissus).

A. THE HISTORY OF ELEATICISM B. TEACHINGS

A. THE HISTORY OF ELEATICISM

Plato's suggestion (Soph. 242d) that Eleatic philosophy began with → Xenophanes and even earlier is inserted into a scheme of the development of philosophical thought that cannot be taken at face value. However, → Parmenides' thought had such an immense effect on later Greek thought that one can justifiably speak of an Eleatic School. It is uncertain to what extent there actually was an organization for the discussion and dissemination of the philosophical thought of Parmenides in Elea. → Zeno's relationship to Parmenides is apparent (both were from Elea and Zeno's work supplements Parmenides' poem) but it is unknown how → Melissus may have come by his Eleaticism.

Though this is not necessarily so, Parmenides' influence assumes a teacher/student relationship, which has been claimed for Parmenides and → Empedocles or Zeno and → Leucippus. At least, however, it assumes that Parmenides' didactic poem was available for discussion and that such discussions took place in the entire Greek world (from Plato, Parm. 127b, in which Parmenides and Zeno take the latter's book to Athens, one may conclude that Parmenides' book was easily accessible, otherwise the young Socrates would not have been able to level the accusation of plagiarism against Zeno).

B. TEACHINGS

The basic teaching of Eleaticism is the statement that Non-Being does not exist. The characteristics ('signs', σήματα) of Being necessarily arise from this first fundamental decision. Since the results of this derivation contradict intuition — Parmenides claims that Being did not originate, is imperishable, one, continuous, immobile and spherical (cf. 28 B 8 DK) —, Eleatic philosophers regularly presented arguments for the testimony of the senses contradicting itself so that the senses cannot cancel results that were achieved through intellectual examination. Zeno's work did not contain anything but a collection of such antipluralistic arguments. Therefore, one may question to what extent he followed the positive teachings of Parmenides. Melissus introduced at least one significant change to the structure of Parmenides' teaching by claiming that Being is infinite in extent.

After Melissus no Eleatic philosophers in the strict sense are known. When Plato has a stranger from Elea appear in his late dialogues, he suggests that the school continued to exist and prepared the ground for Platonic ontology. However, all this may be no more than a recognition of the inspiration that some Socratic schools and Plato received from Eleaticism.

With its rejection of ordinary experience, Eleaticism inherently criticized the → Milesian school, which attempted to present a reflected representation of this experience. The Milesians did not intend to contradict arguments regarding Non-Being; they related every phenomenon to a change in the eternal and continuous basic principle (ἀρχή, *arché*) but they allowed for changes of this *arché*. The Eleatic analysis of change (cf. 28 B 8.34–41, 30 B 8 DK) was to show that changes were not possible without the introduction of Non-Being. Post-Parmenidian philosophers accepted this link of Non-Being and change to varying degrees. Representatives of → Atomism gladly took up the concept of Non-Being and claimed that it must exist as a void beside Being, which exists in indivisible parts of matter. → Empedocles and → Anaxagoras left no room for changes in their *archaí* but they maintained their plurality; their rearrangement can change phenomena. → Diogenes of Apollonia returned to the explanatory scheme of the Milesians. Previous attempts to avoid the Eleatic conclusions perhaps convinced him that it was not necessary to privilege spatial movement at the expense of qualitative change: either the Eleatic arguments are not conclusive or both are to be excluded.

Excavations in an Asclepieion of the 1st cent. AD in Elea produced a stele of Parmenides among the steles of the school's dignitaries (cf. [1]). This only means that at the time Parmenides was considered an outstanding member or even the founder of the school but does not prove that there was a link between the work of Parmenides and his students and the medical school in Elea.

1 PH. MERLAN, Neues Licht auf Parmenides (1966), in: Id., KS, 1976, 8–17.

G. Calogero, Studien über den Eleatismus, 1970; G. E. L. Owen, Eleatic Questions (1960), in: Id., Logic, science and dialectic, 1986, 3–26. I.B.

Eleazarus (Hebrew *ʾælʿāzār*, 'God has helped'; Greek Ἐλεάζαρος; *Eleázaros*, Λάζαρος; *Lázaros*). A name that is particularly common in priestly Jewish families (cf. 2 Macc 6,18–31; 4 Macc 5,1–7,23).

[1] Son of → Aaron and father of Pinhas. In the OT genealogy the ancestor of the Sadducean high priests (Ex 6,23; 28,1; Lev 8ff; Nm 20,25–28; Dt 10,6; 1 Chr 5,29); grave in Gibea (Jos 24,33); considered an ancestor of → Ezra [1] (Ezra 7,5).

[2] Guardian of the Ark of the Covenant in Kiryat-Yearim (1 Sam 7,1).

[3] High priest who sent Ptolemy Philadephos the 72 Bible translations and supposedly received in return gifts for the Jerusalem sanctuary (→ Aristeas [2]; Jos. Ant. Iud. 1,10f.; 12,16; 40–117.)

[4] Brother of → Judas Maccabaeus (1 Macc 2,5; 6,43ff; 2 Macc 8,23; Jos. Ant. Iud. 12,266. 373f.).

[5] Pharisee who disputed the legitimacy of the High Priest John → Hyrcanus I and only wanted to concede the office of monarch to him (Jos. Ant. Iud. 13,291–294).

[6] Priest and guardian of the temple treasure in Jerusalem, was not able to prevent Crassus [2] from plundering it in 54 BC (Jos. Ant. Iud. 14,107ff.).

[7] Son of Boethus, high priest in 4 BC (?) (Jos. Ant. Iud. 17,339).

[8] Son of Dinai, zelot. His campaign of revenge against the Samaritans was put down by the *procurator* Cumanus (AD 48–52) (Jos. BI 2,234ff.; Jos. Ant. Iud. 20,121); → Felix (AD 52–60) sent him as a prisoner to Rome for sentencing (Jos. Ant. Iud. 20,161).

[9] Son of the High Priest Ananias, head of the temple. With the abolition of the daily sacrifice to the emperor he sparked the 1st Jewish War AD 66–70 (Jos. BI 2,409f.) and at the beginning of the war eliminated the Messiah claimant Menachem and the Roman garrison in Jerusalem (Jos. BI 2,441–454). Commander in Idumaea during the war (ibid., 2,566).

[10] Jew with the byname Gigas, whom → Artabanus [5] II (12 — *c.* AD 38) made a gift to Tiberius (Suet. Vit. 2) or Caligula (Suet. Cal. 14) (Jos. Ant. Iud. 18,103).

[11] Son of Simon, leader of the priestly group of zelots. Before and during Titus' siege of Jerusalem he attempted in vain to establish his claim to leadership against his rivals John of Gishala and Simon bar Giora (Jos. BI 2,564f.; 4,225; 5,5–21; 5,98–105; 5,250).

[12] Son of Jair, zelot and defender of the fortress → Masada against the Romans (AD 74). He persuaded the garrison and the civilian population that had fled there to commit collective suicide before the conquest by → Flavius Silva (Jos. BI 7,320–400).

[13] Name of several important rabbis [1]. In the NT cf. Lk 16,19–31; Jn 11,1–44.

→ Aaron; → Ezra; → Pharisees; → Zelots

1 G. Stemberger, Einleitung in Talmud und Midrasch, [8]1992, 364, Index s.v. Eleazar. A.M.S.

[14] **E. ben Qallir.** (also Qillir), probably lived late in the 6th or early in the 7th cent. AD in Palestine before the Arab conquest, his life is largely unknown. He was among the most important representatives of the classical piyyūṭ poetry, which is dedicated to religious themes and in life is embedded in worship at the synagogue. He created piyyūṭīm (< ποιητής, *poiētḗs*) for all feast days but especially for the Sabbath and fasting days. His works are characterized by numerous allusions to biblical passages and Aggadic traditions as well as neologisms and new morphological formations, so that his work is considered to be difficult to understand. As with his predecessor Yannai — but in a more complex way — rhymes and acrostichs play a significant role in his poetry.

Encyclopedia Judaica 10, 1971, s.v. Kallir, Eleazar, 713–715 (Lit.); T. Carmi (ed.), The Penguin Book of Hebrew Verse, 1981, 89, 221–251 (a selection of his poems with Engl. translations). B.E.

Elections Within the sphere of state and politics, elections serve to appoint organs (individuals or committees), who were generally entrusted for a set period of time by the majority of qualified voters with the preparation or execution of community tasks; in monarchic systems, political elections are of no importance. There is no information regarding the appointment of functionaries (for military tasks or within the jurisdiction) in early aristocracies, but it is likely that selection was based on consensus or on rotation of office (→ reciprocity) rather than on majority voting. It was only as a consequence of the expansion of military and political rights to the peasant classes (cf. → *hoplítai*) — a phenomenon observable in almost all ancient societies from the 7th cent. BC onwards, resulting in a consolidation of statehood (→ *pólis*; → *res publica*; → State) — which made it increasingly necessary to develop institutionalized election procedures in order to entrust certain tasks to functionaries (→ *archaí*; → *magistratus*) and to legitimize their actions through the will of the majority. However, as this led to the formation of 'temporary elites', procedures for the control of power developed in parallel, covering the entire range from the admission to candidature, conduct in office, to full rendition of accounts. These aims shaped election procedures in Greece (best documented for Athens) as well as in Rome, but also demonstrate at the same time how the difference in social structures resulted in very different solutions regarding the transfer, legitimization and control of power.

Both systems had in common that the right to vote was restricted to adult free men in possession of full → citizenship; in contrast with Rome, however, poor citizens were not allowed to vote in oligarchically structured Greek communities (→ *oligarchía*). As a fundamental rule, all women, but also permanently resident free men without citizenship were barred from voting. Another common feature was the principle of rotation (annuity) through annual elections (in Rome with the exception of the → *censores* and diluted through the role of the → *promagistratus*), the strict prohibition of immediate re-election (in Athens with the exception of the → *stratēgós*), and also through impediments applied to a further candidature to the same office (in Athens, a second candidature was only permitted for the → *boulḗ*, and in Rome it was compulsory from the 2nd cent. BC to leave a ten-year gap between two candidatures for → *consul*, while a repetition of other offices was in practice prevented by the compulsory → *cursus honorum*). Common to both systems was also the internal control by appointing several officials to the same office (collegiality). Furthermore, in principle, both showed a restriction of eligibility to member of the wealthy elite: even in the democratic Athens of the 5th cent. BC, the highest revenue officers (→ *hellēnotamíai*) came exclusively from the first property class (→ *pentakosiomédimnoi*), and in the 4th cent. BC, *strategoi* and archonts hailed from the wealthiest families — even though members of the second property class (→ *hippeís*) were eligible for these offices from 487 and those of the third class (→ *zeugîtai*) from 457 BC; however, these restrictions did not apply to the majority of the (allegedly) 700 Athenian officials. In Rome, a political career was only ever open to the highest census class of the → *equites*, as even the lowest office (→ *quaestor*; → *tribunus* [7] *plebis*) required several years of equestrian military service, a rule which still applied in the Imperial period (→ *tres militiae*).

However, significant differences are manifest in the differentiation of electoral bodies and the choice of meeting-places. In Greece, the electoral assembly (→ *ekklēsía*; → *apélla*) met on the → *agorá* for all municipal elections (in Athens also on the → Pnyx or inside the theatre of Dionysus). In Rome, magistrates with full military authority (→ *imperium*: → *consules*; → *praetores*) as well as *censores* were elected by the whole people (→ *populus*), who for that purpose assembled on the Campus Martius outside of the → *pomerium* in the centuriate assembly (→ *comitia centuriata*), based on the structure of military units (while the red flag of war flew on the Capitolium); the elections of other officials (→ *aediles*; → *quaestores*) took place within the walls: in this case the entire people were divided into → *tribus*. A Roman peculiarity was the election of the people's tribunes and of the plebeian aediles (on the Forum or the Capitolium) by the assembly of the → *plebs*, also subdivided into *tribus*, but only representing a part of the entire people; nonetheless, from the 3rd cent. (*lex Hortensia*, 287 BC), all laws passed by the plebeian assembly (*concilia plebis*) under the chairmanship of the tribunes applied to all Roman citizens.

The way in which votes were cast was also distinctly different. To start with, all votes in Greece were of equal importance, whereas in Rome, the principle of group voting at times negated the value of individual votes: each Roman → *centuria* (193 in total) or respectively each of the 35 → *tribus* only had one vote, irrespective of the number of voters actually present. In Rome, the weight of votes was further distorted by the unequal number of citizens in the various subdivisions of the electoral bodies, and by the cessation of voting in the *comitia centuriata*, as soon as a majority was reached (with the remaining divisions never even casting their votes). In principle, all elections in Greece were public — voting took place by show of hands (→ *cheirotonía*), in Sparta by acclamation; in Rome, secret ballots were introduced with the *leges tabellariae* of 139 BC (cf. Papirius [I 5] Carbo), using voting tablets (*tabellae*), upon which the name of the candidate was written (however, it seemed to have been customary to show the tablet in the voting process, cf. Plut. Cato min. 46; → *pons* [2]). Furthermore, election by → lot played a far greater role in Greece (at least in Athens) than in Rome: from the mid 5th cent. onwards, with the exception of the *strategoi* and the *hellēnotamíai*, all Athenian officials (including member of the → *boulḗ*) were appointed by casting lots; even though lots played a certain part in the organization of electoral procedures in Rome (order in which votes were cast or order of candidates, see → Lot, election by C.1.), they never replaced an election by the citizens.

There were also significant differences in the control of candidates and officials and also in the accountability of office holders: in Athens, it was customary for candidates to be vetted by a committee of judges and frequently also by the council (→ *dokimasía* 2.); officials could be checked upon at any time during their tenure of office and could be put under legal investigation; at the end of their period of office, they had to account to two different committees (→ *eúthynai*), whose decisions could lead to a judicial trial. In Rome, it was only the election official who checked the admissibility of any candidate or voter (he had the authority to refuse admission); during his period of office, any → *magistratus* was immune from prosecution, nor was he obliged to account for his actions afterwards, even though he could be taken to court (generally by his political opponents) for misconduct in office. The lack of institutionalized control in Rome was replaced by an even stricter social control by the peers of the → *candidatus*, who was subjected to great pressure to conform during his political career and could only ensure his success — esp. as a political novice (*homo novus*) — by appearing politically correct in the eyes of the Senate and the → *nobiles*. From the time of Caesar onwards and esp. in the Imperial period, this peer pressure was replaced by proximity to the powerful, because the only way for a candidate to ensure election was by a direct recommendation by the → emperor or through recommendation by a committee of senators and *equites*, formed on the emperor's orders (→ *commendatio*; → *destinatio*; → *Tabula Hebana*). Election by the people became a mere formality and died out in the course of the 1st cent. AD. The → *municipia* and → *coloniae* of the empire's western provinces followed Rome's example: Members of the municipal council (→ *curiales*; → *decurio* [1]) co-opted further members, these councils then elected the magistrates (→ *duoviri*; → *quattuorviri*; cf. → *lex Irnitana*; → *lex Malacitana*). In the eastern provinces, elections in the Greek poleis continued throughout the Imperial period.

The widespread use of lots in the appointment of officials in Greece (cf. → Lot, election by) meant that bribery of voters was a marginal problem; its only importance was in the election of the *strategos*, where opportunities arose to influence the outcome of the election through financial generosity (see → Cimon [2]), through the removal of the political opponent (see → *ostrakismós*), or the formation of political clubs (→ *hetairía* [2]). However, there is no knowledge of Greek laws regulating manipulative practices. In Rome, by contrast, electoral corruption (→ *ambitus*) seems to have been omnipresent; in his 'election campaign handbook' (*Commentariolum petitionis*), Q. → Tullius [I 11] Cicero lists measures against attempted bribery by political opponents as standard actions in an election campaign. This resulted in numerous — largely ineffectual — laws dealing with *ambitus*, and finally, at the end of the 2nd cent. BC, the institution of a permanent court of law for this particular offence.

C. NICOLET, The World of the Citizen in Republican Rome, 1980, 207–315; R. FREI-STOLBA, Unt. zu den W. in der röm. Kaiserzeit, 1967; R. RILINGER, Der Einfluß des Wahlleiters bei den röm. Konsulwahlen von 360–50 v. Chr., 1976; E. S. STAVELEY, Greek and Roman Voting and Elections, 1972; L. R. TAYLOR, Roman Voting Assemblies, 1966. W. ED.

Electra (Ἠλέκτρα; *Ēléktra*).

[1] The daughter of → Oceanus and → Tethys; wife of Thaumas, mother of → Iris and the → harpies Aello and Ocypete (Hes. Theog. 265ff.; 349; Hom. H. 2,418; Apollod. 1,10).

[2] The daughter of → Danaus and the Naiad Polyxo (Apollod. 2,19; Hyg. Fab. 170).

[3] The daughter of → Atlas and Pleione. One of the → Pleiades. E.'s place of birth is the Cyllene range in Arcadia (Dion. Hal. Ant. Rom. 1,61; Apollod. 3,110), but she is also associated with Samothrace (Hes. Fr. 177 MW; Conon FGrH 26F1,21; Apoll. Rhod. 1,916; Val. Fl. 2,431). By Zeus the mother of → Dardanus (Hyg. Poet Astr. 2,21), of → Iasion (or Aëtion) and → Harmonia (Hellanicus FGrH 4F23; Diod. Sic. 5,48f.), through whom she probably also entered the Theban cycle of myths (cf. Paus. 9,8,4). On Rhodes she was worshipped as Alectrona (→ Electryone [2]) and considered the daughter of Helius and Rhodus (IG XII 1, 677; Diod. Sic. 5,56).

[4] The daughter of → Agamemnon and → Clytaemnestra (Hes. Fr. 23a15f. MW), sister of → Iphigenia and → Orestes, not mentioned in the epic. Equated by Xanthus (fr. 699f. PMG) with Homer's Laodice (Il. 9,145). In the 'Orestia' of Stesichorus (fr. 210ff. PMGF) she supposedly played a significant role. The most important source for her tale is the Attic tragedies. After the murder of Agamemnon by Clytaemnestra and → Aegisthus, E. mourned her father and waited for Orestes, who had been taken to safety with Strophius in Phocis (Pind. Pyth. 11,17f.; Eur. El. 16ff.; 416; according to Soph. El. 296f.; 1348f.; Hyg. Fab. 117 with E.'s help) and from whom E. expected revenge for her father. She is kept like a prisoner by Clytaemnestra and Aegisthus (Aesch. Cho. 445ff; Soph. El. 312f.; 516ff.; 911f.; differently in Eur. El. 19ff., where she has been married off to a peasant). After the mutual recognition of E. and Orestes after the latter's return with his friend Pylades (Aesch. Cho. 212ff.; Soph. El. 1113ff.; Eur. El. 508ff.), revenge is plotted but only in Euripides is Electra involved in carrying it out (El. 1224f.). Later she cares for Orestes when he is driven to insanity by the → Erinyes, the two are sentenced by the Argives but saved by Apollo, who marries E. to Pylades (Eur. El. 1249; 1340f.; IT 695f.; Or. 1078f.; Paus. 2,16,7; according to Eur. El. 312f. she was promised to Castor). Her children are Strophius and Medon (Hellanicus FGrH 4F155). Hyg. Fab. 122, possibly according to Soph. Aletes, reports a further meeting of the siblings.

G. BERGER-DOER, s.v. E. 3), LIMC 3.1,719; E. BETHE, s.v. E. 2), RE 5, 2309–2314; P. BRUNEL, Le mythe d'Electre, 1971; S. GRUNAUER-VON HÖRSCHELMANN, s.v. Elektryone, LIMC 3.1, 719–720.; I. MCPHEE, s.v. E. 1), LIMC 3.1, 709–719. R.HA.

Electric ray Aristotle sufficiently clearly described this electric marine fish (Torpedo spec.), a representative of the flat cartilagenous fish known to him, as νάρκη/ *nárkē* with reference to eye witnesses (Aristot. Hist. an. 8(9),37,620b 19–23; cf. Plin. HN 9,143: *torpedo*; Ael. NA 9,14 and Plut. Mor. 878b-d; [1. 238 f.]). Pliny (loc.cit.) praises the tenderness of its liver.

1 LEITNER. C. HÜ.

Electryon (Ἠλεκτρύων; *Ēlektrýōn*). Tirynthian or Mycenaean hero, son of Perseus and Andromeda, husband of Anaxo, the daughter of → Alcaeus, father of → Alcmene. He lost almost all his sons fighting the Teleboans (Taphians). When the cattle stolen from E. were handed over, he was killed by his son-in-law → Amphitryon. This was the occasion for the latter and Alcmene to emigrate to Thebes (Hes. Sc. 3; 11–12; Apollod. 2,52–56; Hyg. Fab. 244,1; 4; Paus. 2,25,8). R.B.

Electryone (Ἠλεκτρυώνη; *Ēlektryṓnē*).

[1] Patronymic of Alcmene, the daughter of → Electryon (Hes. Sc. 16; 35; 86).

[2] (also Ἀλεκτρώνα; *Alektrṓna*). Heroine on Rhodes, daughter of Helios and Rhodus (Diod. Sic. 5,56; Schol. Pind. Ol. 7,24; Syll.[3] 338–340). She is depicted on coins from Rhodes.

[3] → Electra [3] R.B.

S. GRUNAUER-VON HOERSCHELMANN, s.v. E., LIMC 3.1, 719f.

Elegantia see → Art theory

Elegiae in Maecenatem In some manuscripts of the → Appendix Vergiliana there are 89 distichs under the heading 'Maecenas' that were correctly divided into two parts by J.J. SCALIGER (1572f.). The first part (v. 1–144) is a lamentation and defence of Maecenas that ends with an epitaph. The second is a speech of the dying Maecenas to Augustus. The use of myth is on occasion obscure, expression and metre are consistent with the Augustan period. The relationship to the → Consolatio ad Liviam and to → Seneca the Younger is disputed and, therefore, its dating is uncertain.

EDITIONS: W.V. CLAUSEN (et al.), Appendix Vergiliana, 1966.
COMMENTARY: H. SCHOONHOVEN, Elegiae in Maecenatem: Prolegomena, text and commentary, 1980. J.A.R.

Elegy
I. GREEK II. LATIN ELEGY

I. GREEK
A. DEFINITION B. ARCHAIC AND CLASSICAL PERIOD C. HELLENISM D. IMPERIAL PERIOD

A. DEFINITION
Poem in elegiac verse metre (alternating a dactylic catalectic hexameter and a pentameter). This important Greek literary genre is documented since *c.* 650 BC. Once the inscriptional → epigram had developed into the literary epigram and the elegiac distich had become its customary verse metre, often no difference was recognizable between the two genres. The Greek metric term for the couplet is *elegeíon* (ἐλεγεῖον; formed from *élegos*, ἔλεγος), first in Pherecrates PCG VII, fr. 162,10 (in plural) and Critias 4,3 WEST, later documented in Thuc. 1,132,2–3. In ML 95(c),5 — as often later — it means 'elegiac poem' for which the substantive *elegeía* (ἐλεγεία) was also used (first in Aristot. Ath. Pol. 5,2, later in Theophr. Hist. pl. 9,15). Poems of this type were presumably called ἔλεγοι (*élegoi*) (first attested in 586 BC, cf. → Echembrotus ap. Pausanias 10,7,4–6), which perhaps simply meant (dactylic?) songs accompanied by the *aulós*, a wind instrument (→ musical instruments) (on the link between elegy and *aulōdía*, cf. Plut. De musica 1132c on Clonas and 1134a on Sacadas). The earliest poem that reveals the ancient etymological link of *élegos* with mourning (ἒ ἒ λέγειν; Etym. m. 326,48–49 = 935 GAISFORD; Suda ii, 241 No. 774 ADLER s.v. ἔλεγος; cf. Marius Plotius Sacerdos, GL VI, 509,31) is the lament of Hippias for a boy *chorós* that had drowned several generations earlier (cf. [1. 22–27] and Paus. 5,25,2–4). This meaning is also already evident in the late work of Euripides and in Aristophanes (Eur. Tro. 119; Eur. Hel. 185; Eur. Or. 968 [conjectured]; Eur. Hypsipyle I, iii,9; Eur. IT 146; Aristoph. Av. 217). It is perhaps also related to the Armenian word *elegn*, 'flute' or 'reed'. Although scepticism is appropriate in this case [2], archaic and classical elegies normally seem to have been accompanied by the *aulós* (so in Thgn. 239–43; 533; 825; 941; 943; 1056; on the Duris cup of *c.* 480 BC a symposiast sings dactylic verse accompanied by an aulete (ουδυναμου = οὐ δύναμ' οὐ[...]?) [3]. This cup and Thgn. 239–52 (cf. 467; 503; 825; 837; 1047; 1129; Xenophanes B 1 WEST; Simonides El. 25 WEST; Dionysios Chalcus 1–5 WEST; Ion 26–7) show that elegies were typically sung at symposia. Other contexts for the presentation of short elegies are difficult to identify [1; 4].

None of the preserved fragments of archaic elegies (which are often no longer than one distich) can be proven to be a complete poem. These short poems of no more than 76 lines (Solon 13 WEST) have an exhortatory (as war and consolation poetry), reflecting, encomiastic or (quasi-) autobiographic character but are rarely erotic-narrative poems (maybe Theognidea 261–2; 263–6; 1063–4; Simonides 21.22 WEST) or personal invectives (unlike the → iambus). Some of the cited poets also composed longer elegies (up to *c.* 1,000 verses?) that dealt with current and perhaps more remote events in the history of their polis and were probably first presented at public celebrations.

B. ARCHAIC AND CLASSICAL PERIOD
The earliest poets of whom we still have fragments (→ Archilochus, → Callinus, → Mimnermus, → Tyrtaeus; nothing by Polymnastos is preserved) were active *c.* 660–640 BC. This source constellation is probably due to the spread of literacy in the 7th cent. BC. Some Ionic epic forms of the Laconian Tyrtaeus show that the genre was considered Ionic in his period (640?). The technical mastery of these earliest preserved poems suggests that the genre had been flowering for some time in Ionia though it is impossible to calculate for how long, but perhaps since the introduction of the *aulós* from the East (that elegies originated in the East is unlikely because of their metrical form and the shared vocabulary with hexametric poetry). It was already established in the 7th cent. (→ Clonas of Tegea or Thebes), and definitely after the early 6th cent. BC, in central Greece (→ Solon in Attica, → Sacadas in Argus, → Theognis in Megara). The 1,400 verses that tradition ascribes to Theognis cover a great range of (mainly incomplete) archaic sympotic elegies, some from the 5th cent. (e.g., Thgn. 757–768, and three by → Evenus). Elegies by Simonides, Panyassis, Ion of Chios, Melanthius and Sophocles prove that the genre was alive at least to the last quarter of the 5th cent. The accident of transmission (or stereotyping selection?) has mainly preserved exhortatory war poetry by Callinus and Tyrtaeus, cynical self-portrayal by Archilochus, melancholic reflection on love, the briefness of youth and the unpleasantness of old age by Mimnermus and Simonides as well as moral and political disputes and complaints by Solon and Theognis, a selection that probably does not represent an objective image of the work of these poets. Metapoetic themes (as in Thgn. 237–254 and Xenophanes B 1) play a rather more prominent role in pre-

served poems of the 5th cent. (→ Critias, → Dionysius [30] Chalcus).

Longer elegies that obviously treat events in polis history are only infrequently recorded: the *Eunomía* of Tyrtaeus (1–4 WEST), the *Smyrnēís* of Mimnermus (13a and 13 WEST?), the 'Samian Antiquities' (Ἀρχαιολογία τῶν Σαμίων) of Semonides (Suda ιω 360,12 ADLER) the 'Founding of Colophon' (Κολοφῶνος κτίσις) and 'The Migration to the Italian Colony of Elea' (ὁ εἰς Ἐλέαν τῆς Ἰταλίας ἀποικισμός) by Xenophanes (2,000 vv., Diog. Laert. 9,20), the 'Ionian History' (Ἰωνικά) of Panyassis (7,000 vv.), and perhaps the 'Founding of Chios' (Χίου κτίσις) by Ion of Chios (Schol. Aristoph. Pax 835) (cf. [1]). Only the new papyrus fragments of Simonides brought to light significant passages from the beginning of a poem that celebrates the Spartan departure for Plataea and their victory there (10–17 and 18 WEST?), as well as smaller fragments on the victories at Artemisium (2–4 WEST) and Salamis (6–7 WEST?) [5; 6]. The polished beginning of the Plataea poem (10–11 WEST, an Achilles hymn) fits well with a larger and methodically elevated composition (cf. Mimnermus 13 WEST) and supports the hypothesis of its presentation at a celebration and perhaps a competition (cf. the presumed competition between Aeschylus and Simonides over an elegy to commemorate the dead of Marathon, Vita Aeschyli 8 = TrGF III 33f). So far only the products of Xenophanes and Panyassis offer an impression of size and even Solon's 100-line *Sálamis* (1–3 WEST) is perhaps a short festive elegy rather than a long elegy for a symposium.

Sympotic elegies are, like symposia, less well represented in the 4th cent. (but s. Philiscus 1 WEST, an encomium on Lysias, which Plut. Vitae decem oratorum 836c describes as an epigram, and Aristotle's poem to Eudemus, in which he praises Plato, 673 ROSE). Later elegiac poems reveal an even greater influence of the epigram; when musical accompaniment was dropped is uncertain [7]. With the beginning of the 4th cent anthologies of shorter and longer poems were compiled in book form for a growing readership: in his *Lýdē*, Antimachus linked in two books myths of (erotic?) misfortune to a consolatory poem to himself on the occasion of his female partner's death (Plut. Consolatio ad Apollonium, 106b). He may have been the first to collect the elegies of Mimnermus under the title *Nannṓ* [8] (without it being possible to dismiss earlier collections, one even by Mimnermus himself). Presumably, in Athens a collection of poems by Theognis, perhaps also of Tyrtaeus, was circulating.

C. HELLENISM

In the 3rd cent. BC Philetas adopted the narrative form. He joined the etymology of the mourning song by speaking in his *Demeter* of mourning for Kore and the goddess' search for her; in his *Paígnia* he also used the elegiac verse measure (although these might also possibly be epigrams). His friend and student → Hermesianax, primarily an elegiac poet (cf. Paus. 8,12,1; 9,35,5), further developed the Antimachian model of combining tales and wrote an elegy in three books entitled *Leóntion*, named for the girl to whom it was addressed. He also composed an elegy on the centaur Eurytion (Paus. 7,18,1). Alexander of Pleuron also compiled in his elegy *Apollon* tales of unhappy love that the god predicts, and used another, the *Mousai*, for a history of literature. In his 'Love Stories' (Ἔρωτες ἢ καλοί) → Phanocles compiled a catalogue of the love of heroes and gods for youths. → Poseidippus, mainly known as an epigram writer, used the elegiac form for prayers to the Muses and Apollo (for recognition and an honourable old age) and, in the process, picked up several themes of the archaic elegists (SH 705). → Callimachus, as the Roman elegians later did, named Mimnermus and Philetas as the most important models (Kall. *Aítia*, Fr. 1,9–12), although in his *Aítia* (4 B.) he rather combined the tradition of Antimachus and Hermesianax with Hesiodic elements, perhaps as an answer to the cataloguing elegy [7. 263–386]. His use of the elegiac verse metre in the fifth *Hymnos* is also an innovative hybrid and perhaps was supposed to recall the position of Sacadas of Argus in the elegiac tradition (similar to the elegiac verse of Euripides in Andr. 103–116).

In the Hellenistic period, some of the poems of Nicander were elegies, the *Ophiaká* (a collection of legends about snakes) and the didactic poem *Kynēgētiká*, likewise in the 1st cent. BC some works of → Parthenius, notably three books on the death of his wife Arete. Papyrus fragments from the Hellenistic or Roman periods contain encomia with various addressees (SH 958), among them a monarch (SH 969, maybe the same poem), the reminiscence of a poet on his participation in a competition during the Museia at Thespiae (SH 959), a wedding (SH 961, an epithalamion?), erotic myths (SH 962–3; 964), reflection (SH 968) and a curse (SH 970).

D. IMPERIAL PERIOD

In the Imperial period elegies were used, though rarely, for didactic poetry, e.g., the 174 verses on cures for snake bite, which Nero's doctor → Andromachus [4] addressed to Nero (quoted by Galen 14,32 [9]). Some epigrams achieved the extent of elegies and perhaps also adopted some archaic elegiac motifs (e.g., the at least 38-line poem that welcomed back Herodes Atticus, who returned in 174/5 BC (?) from exile, IG II/III[2] 3606). However, the role of elegies in symposia was taken over by recited epigrams, Anacreontea that were perhaps sung, and the songs of professional citharodes.

1 E.L. BOWIE, Early Greek Elegy, Symposium and Public Festival, in: JHS 106, 1986, 13–35 2 D.A. CAMPBELL, Flutes and Elegiac Couplets, in: JHS 84, 1964, 63–68 3 F. LISSARRAGUE, Un flot d'images, 1987, fig. 101 (= The Aesthetics of the Greek Banquet, 1990) 4 E.L. BOWIE, Miles ludens, in: O. MURRAY (ed.), Sympotica, 1990, 221–229 5 P.J. PARSONS, Oxyrhynchus papyri 59, 1992, No. 3965 6 IEG 2[2] 7 A. CAMERON, Callimachus and his Critics, 1995 (especially 24–103 on the question of verbal

performance in the Hellenistic period) 8 M.L. West, Studies in Early Greek Elegy and Iambus, 1974, 75f. 9 E. Heitsch, Die griech. Dichterfragmente der röm. Kaiserzeit 2, 1964, No. 62.

Editions: F.R. Adrados, Líricos griegos: elegiacos y yambógrafos arcaicos (siglos vii-v a.C.), 2 vol., ²1981; Gentili/Prato, vol. 1, ²1988, vol. 2 1985; IEG1², 2²; M.L. West, Delectus ex iambis et elegis graecis, 1980.
Hellenistic period: CollAlex; SH.
Literature: D.E. Gerber, Early Greek Elegy and Iambus 1921–1989, in: Lustrum 33, 1991, 7–225; 401–9; B. van Groningen, La composition littéraire archaique grecque, 1958; A.W.H. Adkins, Poetic Craft in the Early Greek Elegists, 1985; K. Bartol, Greek Elegy and Iambus, 1993; B. Gentili, Poesia e pubblico nella Grecia antica, 1984 (= Poetry and its Public in Ancient Greece, 1988); R.L. Fowler, The Nature of Early Greek Lyric, 1987, ch. 3.

E.BO.

II. Latin elegy

A. Beginnings and genre characteristics
B. Development in the imperial period
C. Later reception

A. Beginnings and genre characteristics

In the form of a longer poem in elegiac verse meter and in character the Latin elegy attaches itself to the Greek genre: it is an 'open genre', i.e. it has (during its creation and development) both separated and enriched itself in confronting r, the Roman love elegy in the closer sense has a specific profile.

After elegiac verses by → Ennius and → Lucilius and the Hellenistic love epigrams about 100 BC (→ Porcius Licinus, → Valerius Aedituus and Q. → Lutatius Catulus), → Calvus (mourning for his wife Quintilia), → Varro Atacinus (*Leucadia*) and perhaps P. → Valerius Cato (*Lydia*; not preserved) all wrote elegies. The original text of the 'Roman love elegy' is often considered to be → Catullus' great 'Allius elegy' (Carm. 68, 41–148; all-encompassing love to Lesbia, to Clodia who was probably noble, dampened by mourning for his dead brother, interpretation in mythology). → Cornelius Gallus probably wrote the first elegiac poetry book around 40 BC (*Amores*). Though he is considered the archegete of the elegiac canon only by later generations (e.g., Ov. Ars am.3,536–538 and Quint. Inst. 10,1,93, also Prop. 2,34,85–94 and Ov. Am. 3,9,59–66), one can for the first time grasp the entire concept of 'Roman love elegy' ([17]; general [11; 6]). It is a counter-design answering to the late Republican crisis from a deliberately restricted perspective — the subjectivity of the *poeta amator*: simultaneously a literary role [18] and fulfilment of personal experience in the medium of art. Everything is governed by the love of a girl, the *puella* (motifs of loyalty and death): the man enmeshed in the madness of love (*furor*) serves his mistress (*domina*), a libertine, in *servitium amoris* [10; 13], in unrequited love. Therefore, the elegy is both paraenesis and lament. The myth functions in many ways as the level of reference. The choice in lifestyle of love and love poetry is a protest against politics, war, fame, *negotium*, wealth, the primacy of men, etc. (in Tibullus also against urban life). At the same time, the elegy defends Roman values, e.g., *fides*, with new accents [2] or inverts them metaphorically (*militia amoris* [12] etc.). Poetry is also the theme (as courting a woman [16], apology of the minor form, → *recusatio* of 'great' subject matter). Miscellaneous literary forms were adapted (→ Paraklausithyron, complaint of the locked-out lover, *exclusus amator* [19], → propemptikon, → prayer, → epikedeion etc.). The idea that it was modelled on a Greek subjective and erotic elegy (as distinct from the objective and mythological elegy) has been rejected by most scholars since [7] (but s. POxy. LIV 3725). → Epigraphy, → comedy, → novels and → rhetoric are particularly influential. The elegists envisioned themselves as being part of the Alexandrian tradition. (e.g., Prop. 3,1,1; [14]).

B. Development in the imperial period

→ Propertius sings of his love to Cynthia (published after *c.* 29/28 BC) to the point of breaking up and rejection. The 'Augustan' book 4 then crosses Roman aitia with erotic themes that are 'objectivized' by changing perspective (for example, 4,3: Arethusa letter; 4,11: the deceased Cornelia speaks to her husband), thus conceptually and formally overcoming the subjective 'Roman love elegy'. → Tibullus (published after *c.* 26/25 BC) creates — largely without mythological *exempla* — both love and an idyllic peaceful rural life but then sees his hopes fail in this conflict: in book 1 through Delia and (in a separate cycle) through the boy Marathus, in book 2 through the money-hungry Nemesis. His relationship to his benefactor → Messalla is added as a social and political theme.

Young → Ovid (*Amores* after *c.* 25 BC), to whom the *pax Augusta* already was normality and the elegy convention, played (in epigrammatic-rhetorical poetic structures) with the literary tradition, confronted it with the reality of everyday life in Rome [9], disavowed subjective rhetoric with concluding punchlines, poem pairing, etc. A new concept of an unburdened, free, changeable love took shape in the process (e.g., in the pan-erotic Ov. Am. 2,4). In the casuistry of the typical lover, the latter's unity with the poetic ego is dissolved (cf. Ov. Am. 1,1), enabling the ego to become the teacher of all lovers (Ov. Am. 2,1,5–10; [4]) and to compose erotic poetry of a very different nature and even at a high level (Ov. Am. 2,18; 3,1. 15). In fact, Ovid was developing new elegiac forms (from beginnings in Prop. 4 and Ov. Am. 3): with the mythical *Heroides* the 'elegiac → epistle' was created [15]; the *Ars amatoria* (book 3 for women) and *Remedia amoris* are erotic → didactic poems (cf. the *didaxis* in Prop. 4,5, Tib. 1,4, Ov. Am. 1,8), and the *Fasti* an aetiology of the Roman calendar. There the 'elegiac narrative' was able to unfold [5]. The exile elegies processed a personal catastrophe in elegiac complaints and topics. Even in his epic, the *Metamorphoses*, Ovid adapts and quotes elegiac elements (in eroticism, psychology; cf. already in Verg. Aen. 4).

Almost nothing by C. → Valgius Rufus, L. → Varius Rufus and → Domitius Marsus is preserved. The 3rd book of the Tibullus corpus contains the elegies of → Sulpicia (13–18 = book 4), five anonymous elegies commenting on her fate in love (8–12) and the epigonal poems of a certain → Lygdamus to his unfaithful wife Neaera (1–6). Ovid mentions contemporaries and students (Ov. Tr. 2,467f.; 4,10,55; Pont. 4,16; on → Sabinus' mythological letters Ov. Am. 2,18,27–34). Non-erotic themes were developed in → *Copa*, → *Nux*, → *Consolatio ad Liviam* and → *Elegiae in Maecenatem*. (Erotic) elegies are attested for the later emperor → Nerva, L. → Arruntius Stella, one Varro (Mart. 5,30,4), → Pliny the Younger (Plin. Ep. 7,4,7) and C. Passennus Paulus (Plin. Ep. 6,15,1. 9,22,1f.) (cf. generally Pers. 1,32–43 and Juv. 1,3f.). The elegiac tradition shapes later epigrams of → Martial and several *carmina epigraphica* (→ Funerary epigram). In late antiquity [1. 1048–1051] distich poems by → Ausonius (lament for the dead), → Claudianus, → Rutilius Namatianus (travel account) are encountered; the love elegy is continued by (the aging) → Maximianus. Christian approaches are encountered in → Sedulius, → Orientius, → Ennodius, → Arator, → Boethius, → Dracontius, → Venantius Fortunatus (e.g., Carm. 8,3,227–248: letter of a nun to Christ).

C. Later reception

In the MA Marboduus of Rennes and Baudri of Bourgueil composed erotic elegies, Hildebert of Lavardin laments for Rome and his exile. The elegiac distich enters almost all genres; the erotic 'elegiac comedies' of the 12th/13th cents. drew upon Ovid. Nine alliterative Old English laments were also called 'elegies'. In the modern period elegies were particularly important in periods of a strong reception of antiquity, but also as a genre of individual subjectivity. Both apply to humanism and the Renaissance: in the Neo-Latin elegy with ancient metre the theme of love prevails (e.g., Sannazaro's *Eclogae piscatoriae* or the *Basia* of Iohannes Secundus). The vernacular elegy was founded in Italy by Sannazaro and Ariosto, in France by Marot and Ronsard, in Spain by Garcilaso de la Vega and Lope de Vega, in England by Spenser, in the Netherlands by Heinsius, in Germany first by Opitz. In part it is characterized by theme and tone (death, melancholy, contemplation of the world; thus, especially in England after Milton), partially by its metrics (especially in Germany: since Opitz the alexandrine has been used as a substitute metre for the distich, since Klopstock the ancient metre). The 'pastoral elegy' (cf. the allegorical *egloga* of Radbertus in the 9th cent.) and the 'heroic letter' (already in the Middle Ages and, e.g., allegorically in the humanist Eobanus Hessus; [3]) were common. The 18th cent. (which appreciated Tibullus to an increased degree, while otherwise the oeuvre of Ovid dominated the elegy reception) was the climax of sensitivity ('graveyard elegy' since Gray), the classicism of Chénier and the 'classical German elegy ' (Goethe's 'Roman Elegy' [8], which was close to the Augustans but filled with *joie de vivre*, Schiller, Hölderlin's hymnal elegies). The pain of living is expressed in Lamartine, Leopardi, the English Romantics, Pushkin, etc. In the 20th cent. only Rilke (in his own peculiar rhythms, the symbolic 'Duinese Elegies'), Celan and Brecht ('Buckower Elegies'), Jiménez and García Lorca shall be named; English literature continues the tradition of the funerary poem.

→ Elegy

1 L. Alfonsi, W. Schmid, s.v. Elegie, in: RAC 4, 1026–1061 2 E. Burck, Röm. Wesenszüge der augusteischen Liebes-E., in: Hermes 80, 1952, 163–200 3 H. Dörrie, Der heroische Brief, 1968 4 B. M. Gauly, Liebeserfahrungen, 1990 5 R. Heinze, Ovids eleg. Erzählung, in: Id., Vom Geist des Römertums, ³1960, 308–403 6 N. Holzberg, Die röm. Liebes-E., 1990 7 F. Jacoby, Zur Entstehung der röm. E., in: RhM 60, 1905, 38–105 8 F. Klingner, Liebes-E., in: Id., Röm. Geisteswelt, ⁵1965, 419–439 9 M. Labate, L'arte di farsi amare, 1984 10 R. O. A. M. Lyne, Servitium amoris, in: CQ 29, 1979, 117–130 11 Id., The Latin Love Poets, 1980 12 P. Murgatroyd, Militia amoris and the Roman elegists, in: Latomus 34, 1975, 59–79 13 Id., Servitium amoris, in: Latomus 40, 1981, 589–606 14 M. Puelma, Die Aitien des Kallimachos als Vorbild der röm. Amores-E., in: MH 39, 1982, 221–246; 285–304 15 H. Rahn, Ovids eleg. Epistel, in: A&A; 7, 1958, 105–120 16 W. Stroh, Die röm. Liebes-E. als werbende Dichtung, 1971 17 Id., Die Ursprünge der röm. Liebes-E., in: Poetica 15, 1983, 205–246 18 P. Veyne, L'élégie érotique romaine, 1983 19 J. C. Yardley, The Elegiac Paraclausithyron, in: Eranos 76, 1978, 19–34.

F.SP.

Elektron

I. Middle East II. Greece and Rome

I. Middle East

Elektron as a natural alloy of gold and silver that was mostly worked as found in the Middle East and Egypt. According to analysis, objects seemingly consisting of gold usually contain a large amount of silver, which may constitute more than 40% (e.g., vessels from the royal graves of Ur, *c.* 2600 BC). Later, elektron was also artificially produced as an alloy. Elektron is harder than gold and, therefore, was preferred for jewellery, display weapons, statues, plating, inlays and units of value (e.g., as rings).

→ Gold; → Amber

J. R. Lucas, Ancient Egyptian materials and industries, ⁴1962, 234f.

R.W.

II. Greece and Rome

A name for → amber and a naturally occurring (Sardes: Soph. Ant. 1037; Spain: Plin. HN 33,22,1) or artificial alloy (Serv. Aen. 8,402; Isid. Orig. 16,24,2) of gold and silver, usually in the ratio of 3:1 with an admixture of copper [1. 201ff.]. Elektron is harder than gold and has been used for jewellery and vessels since the Mycenaean period [2. 102; 3], since the archaic period also for minting coins. Elektron coins were minted, for example, in the towns of western Asia Minor up to the 4th cent. BC, later Carthage, Syracuse and the western Celts and in late antiquity the Kušan and their successors [1. 202f.; 4. 34f.].

1 J.F. HEALY, Mining and metallurgy in the Greek and Roman world, 1978 2 G.E. MYLONAS, Mycenae and the Mycenaean Age, s.v. E., 1966 3 B. DEPPERT-LIPPITZ, Griech. Goldschmuck, s.v. E., 1985 4 GÖBL, passim.

F. BODENSTEDT, Phokäisches E.-Geld von 600–326 v.Chr. Stud. zur Bed. und zu den Wandlungen einer ant. Goldwährung, 1976; L. WEIDAUER, Probleme der frühen E.-Prägung, Typos. Monographien zur ant. Numismatik 1, 1975. A.M.

Elements, theories of the Elements (Greek στοιχεῖα; *stoicheía*, 'letters') are unalterable 'simple' natural substances, which cannot be further subdivided into any other constituents. The mixture of the elements forms the composite substances constituting the material aspect of all things natural.

According to the Hylozoists (→ Anaximander, → Anaximenes) change transformed the original substances into all naturally occurring conditions and properties. According to the ontology of the → Eleatic School, by contrast, even the material world was immutable (ungenerated and stable), whereas the unity of the Eleatic being was conceived as uniformity: both the atomists (→ Atomism) and Anaxagoras assumed an infinite variety (and infinite number of that which is, the former conceiving these as made up of 'indivisible' constituents, whereas the latter viewed these as infinitely divisible). Closer to the epic tradition (Hom. Il. 15,187–193; Hes. Theog. 736–738), → Empedocles saw four fundamentally different elements, still designated by their divine names: earth, water, air, and fire, perceived as the 'four roots of all things' (Frg. B 6: τέσσαρα πάντων ῥιζώματα), tracing all natural substances back to — in each case — specific proportions in the mixture of these root elements (particularly fr. A 34,43; B 23,96), in which 'coherence' (durability and cohesion) lies in their 'harmony' (B 96: ἁρμονίης κόλλησιν) and the pores of the elements (A 86,87).

By permitting only relatively stabile elements to shift states through external stimuli, Plato and Aristotle tried to integrate the pre-Eleatic view of the alterability of matter onto this theory of the elements. Plato's expository and epistemological level in his *Timaeus* assumes immaterial mathematics as the means of depicting ideas: following the model of the atoms, he reduces qualities to quantities (form and size), and equates four of the five regular polyhedra (whose number had only just been set at that by Theaetetus) with the four Empedoclean elements: tetrahedron/fire, octahedron/air, icosahedron/water, hexahedron/earth. The equilateral triangles of the three first-named polyhedra would in each case be formed by the six right-angled triangles along the three central verticals (cathetus ratio 1:3) as the 'protosurfaces', in such a way that in the surfaces and bodies congruent angles and sides abut, thus creating stability. By contrast, the squares of the hexahedron (cube) are formed by the four equilateral triangles built from the diagonals (and thus the fourfold character of the elements is founded in the mathematics). These prototriangles and polyhedra surfaces could be divided by external forces (e.g. 'pointed' fire) and subsequently re-formed as other polyhedra.

However, such a 'transformation' is limited to the first three of the polyhedra, as the prototriangles of equilateral triangles and squares cannot be transformed into one another, metals are thus not understood as 'earth', but rather as very dense 'meltable water'. Aristotle (esp. in Gen. corr. 2,1–5) avoids this difficulty by transposing the principles (correspondingly totalling four) into the natural bodies themselves and also by defining the material principle (ὕλη/*hýlē, causa materialis*) itself as a 'natural' feature, i.e. as a—in contrast to Empedocles and Plato—homogenous and infinitely divisible mixture of the four (earthly) simple bodies, whose formal principle is based on simple qualities of the opposites dry/moist and cold/warm: earth/dry-cold, water/moist-cold, air/wet-warm, fire/dry-warm. Individually or as groups, external forces can transform these 'intrinsic' properties into their opposites, and thus the transformation of an element also includes the commensurate new properties.

Deduced through abstraction, the 'prime matter' (πρώτη ὕλη/*prṓtē hýlē, materia prima*), the material principle which is the prerequisite of the transformability common to all elements, is necessarily devoid of both property and form. Later, alchemists sought to create this state in order to fix infinite properties into the black (proto-)matter; thus Aristotle's theory of elements retained its validity up to the onset of the modern era.

However, as a further natural property of the four elements, Aristotle (esp. in Cael. 1,3; 3,4–5 and 4) connected to each a basic movement which (in the absence of obstacles) would propel them towards, and keep them in, their 'natural places' (mixed forms would move according to their dominant tendency): earth and water 'downward' ('place': centre of the world), air and fire 'upward' ('place': periphery of the terrestrial world), producing the 'shell' structure and geocentricity of this world. This vertical and straight movement towards the 'natural places' manifests itself as 'heaviness', or respectively, 'lightness' (i.e., negative, not relative heaviness); however, in the case of 'upward' motion, it required the existence of a concentric-spherical body constituting the boundary, which Aristotle deduces to be ether, as the fifth element: this body's natural motion is the (regular) rotation around the centre. These 'bodies in circular motion' (whereby complex layering allowed some to be set inside the others, to permit a description of the movement of individual celestial bodies) are devoid of any other properties and utterly immutable, as their circular movement has no opposite. The result is a dualistic world, later modified however, by Neoplatonists and Stoics who followed Plato in identifying the goal of the upward or downward movements not as the 'natural place' itself, but rather the accumulation of similar matter there and the 'reasonable order' (τάξις/*táxis*, *ordo*) of 'nature' as a whole. Ether as a fifth element was thus rendered—at least partly—superfluous (celestial bodies again being viewed as 'fiery').

In his dispute with Anaxagoras, Aristotle (Ph. 1,4) also assumed that certain homogenous mixtures of organic substances — in contrast to the elements themselves — have a specific lower limit up to which they can be divided into equal parts. Over time, in the commentaries on Aristotle from Late Antiquity and the Middle Ages, these ἐλάχιστα (*eláchista*) of the organic domain (as a fixed term already used by Alexander [26] of Aphrodisias) become the *minima naturalia* (in the sense of stabile molecules), each with their own specific 'form', applied also to inorganic and even elementary substances.

→ Elements, theories of the

R. Hooijkaas, Het begrip element, 1934; H. Happ, Hyle. Studien zum aristotelischen Materie-Begriff, 1971; F. Krafft, Gesch. der (spekulativen) Atomistik bis John Dalton. Vorlesungen, 1992. F.KR.

Elenchos see → Refutation

Eleon (Ἐλεών, Ἑλεών; *Eleṓn, Heleṓn*). Boeotian town (Plin. HN 4,26), already mentioned in Hom. Il. 2,500, between Thebes and Tanagra near the mod. Harma (formerly: Dritsa). The town, which was fortified anew during the Middle Ages, was settled from the Early Helladic to the Roman period. Still independent in the classical period (Paus. 1,29,6), later E. together with Harma, Mycalessus, and Pharae formed a synoecism dependent on Tanagra (Str. 9,2,12; 14; 17; 9,5,18). Plut. Quaest. Graec. 41 mentions sanctuaries of the τρεῖς Παρθένοι (*treîs Parthénoi*, 'three virgins') near E.

Fossey, 89–95; Lauffer, Griechenland, 209f.; N.D. Papachatzis, Παυσανίου Ἑλλάδος Περιήγησις [Pausaníou Helládos Periḗgēsis] 5, [2]1981, 125f.; P.W. Wallace, Strabo's Description of Boiotia, 1979, 56f. P.F.

Eleos (Ἔλεος; *Éleos*). 'Compassion'. Appears personified in Timocles fr. 33 PCG. An altar dedicated to E. stood on a market square in Athens (Paus. 1,17,1; Diod. Sic. 13,22,7) [1], a well-known → asylon/asylum (Lucian Demonax 57 and schol.; Schol. Aeschin. 2,15). According to Apollod. 2,167, it was there that the Heraclides sought refuge, according to Philostr. Epistula 39, they even appear as the founders of the altar. According to Aristotle's poetic theory, through *éleos* and *phóbos* ('pity and fear'), tragedy should lead to → katharsis (Aristot. Poet. 5, 1449 b 27f.; cf. also Rh. 2,8, 1385b 13–15) [2].

1 E. Vanderpool, The 'Agora' of Paus. 1,17,1–2, in: Hesperia 43, 1974, 308–310 2 M. Fuhrmann, Einführung in die ant. Dichtungstheorie, 1973, 90–98. R.B.

Elephant

I. Early History II. Classical Antiquity

I. Early History

In the Early Holocene, the Asian elephant, *Elephas maximus*, was common from central China to the Syrian Mediterranean coast. Written sources, representations, and, in particular, bones found in the excavations of settlements, indicate that some survived along the Syrian rivers into the 7th/8th cents. BC. Today their habitat is restricted to parts of southern Asia. Because of their physical strength and intelligence, Asian elephants were trained as working animals without actually being domesticated. Seal images of the Harappan civilization provide the earliest documentary evidence. In the pre-Christian era, the African elephant, *Loxodonta africana*, was found across the variety of African landscapes, with the exception of extreme deserts. However, probably as early as the Roman period, it became extinct in North Africa. Apart from small, isolated populations in West and East Africa, only intense protection has ensured the survival of sizeable numbers in Central Africa: even in prehistoric times, the ivory tusks, which in bulls can grow to a total length of 3.5 m and weigh more than 100 kg, were a much sought after raw material for carvings.

→ Ivory

C. Becker, Elfenbein aus den syr. Steppen? Gedanken zum Vorkommen von Elefanten in Nordostsyrien im Spätholozän, in: M. Kokabi, J. Wahl (ed.), Beiträge zur Archäologie und Prähistorischen Anthropologie, Kolloquium Konstanz 1993, Forsch. und Ber. zur Vor- und Frühgesch. Baden-Württembergs 53, 1994, 169–181; F. Kurt, Das Buch der Elefanten, 1986; H.H. Scullard, The E. in the Greek and Roman World, 1974; S.K. Sikes, The Natural History of the African E., 1971. CO.BE.

II. Classical Antiquity

Prior to Alexander's expedition (→ Alexander [4]; map) Greeks knew only of → ivory through trade, which supplied the etymological root of the animal's name: ἐλέφας; *eléphas*, Lat. *elepha(n)s* or *elephantus*, but also *barrus* (Indian (?), cf. Isid. Orig. 16,5,19). Herodotus transferred the name to the animal itself (3,114; 4,191). Arrianus (Anab. 5,35) mentions elephants presented to Alexander the Great as a gift. Aristotle seems to have based his detailed description of bodily form (Hist. an. 2,1,497b 22–31), sexual organs (2,1,500b 6–14), and teeth (2,5,501b 29–502a 3) on anatomical studies. It appears that elephants kept in zoos were observed for their rutting behaviour (6,18,571b 32–572a 5), mating times, and gestation period (Arist. Hist. an. 6,27,578a 17–24), their fights within the herd (8(9),610a 15–19), their nutritional requirements and quantities consumed (6, 9,596a 3–9), their illnesses and their cures (7(8),26,605a 23–b 5), as well as their character and way of life (8(9),46,630b 18–30). According to contemporary comments, Aristotle (Hist. an. 8(9),610a 24–33) provides a better description of the capture and subsequent taming of Indian elephants than → Ctesias. An extensive discussion of the question of → domestication of both species, the African as well as the Indian elephant, is provided by ZEUNER [2. 234–253] (with many illustrations). Elephants were only occasionally bred in captivity; as a rule, wild-born animals were tamed and kept. The lost monograph by king → Juba of Mauretania in North Africa, describing the capture of elephants in pits and at watering holes, was apparently known to both Pliny (HN 8,24) and Aelianus (HN 4,24; 8,10). Elephants, who were seen as clever and docile, careful, good-natured, grateful, faithful, fair, and even pious (because of their alleged veneration of sun and moon [3. 267]) (cf. Plin. HN 8,1), appear in numerous anecdotes (int.al. in Plin. HN 8,5–15, Plut. Soll. an. 12; 14; 17–18; 20; 25 or respectively Mor. 968B-E; 970C-E; 972B-F; 974C-D; 977D-E; Ael. NA passim). According to Pliny (HN 8,3), in India elephants were used for ploughing, but also for heavy toil such as uprooting trees and road building. After the Greek Diadochian states had first encountered elephants in the battle of → Gaugamela in 331 BC, they themselves employed the animals for military use: up to 500 were used to carry warriors into battle, creating panic amongst human and equine opponents, until appropriate defensive tactics were developed.

In 282 BC, King Pyrrhus of Epirus used elephants against the Romans (Plut. Pyrrhus 16f.; Iust. 18,1; Plin. HN 8,16), initially referred to by the Romans as 'Lucanian bulls' (*boves Lucas*, cf. Varro, Ling. 7,39, and Isid. Orig. 12,2,15). Some elephants were paraded in the triumphal procession after the victory over Pyrrhus in 275 BC. In the First Punic War (252 BC), the Romans captured between 120 and 142 elephants on Sicily and shipped them to Italy on rafts. Allegedly, they were later put to death in the circus. Hannibal even crossed the Alps with elephants; the Romans themselves rarely used them (in 221 BC against the Gauls, in 46 BC at Thapsus). From 169 BC they were regularly on show in the circus (Liv. 44,18,8). Exhibition fights between animals and people were fashionable in the 1st cent. BC, but in the Imperial period, elephants were frequently found in artwork (i.a. Ael. NA 2,11; Plin. 8,5f.; Sen. Ep. 85,41). Images of African or Indian elephants are found on Etruscan, Carthaginian, Ptolemaic, and Seleucid coins, but also those of Roman emperors since Augustus, sometimes as a quadriga ([4. pl. IV,1–7] cf. also [5. 375]), but also on ancient cameos [4. pl. XIX,37–45]. Elephants are occasionally found depicted in late Roman hunt mosaics, also in book illustrations (Cod. Ven. Marc. Gr. l. 479, 10th/11th cent., fol. 36r and v [6. fig. 165,2, fig. 166,1], and Cod. Par. Gr. 2736, 1554, fol. 31r and v [6. fig. 212,2, fig. 213,1]). Elephants are also found in not very lifelike medieval miniatures of the creation and of paradise, but also in bestiaries of the same period, as well as in sculptures adorning portals and capitals of churches of the 11th–13th cent. [7]. It was predominantly through Pliny and Aristotle (in the Latin translation by Michael Scotus) that ancient knowledge of this largest of terrestrial animals was passed on to the Middle Ages, e.g. to Thomas of Cantimpré (4,33 [8. 126–131]).

1 TREU, in: Philologus 99, 1955, 151 2 F.E. ZEUNER, Gesch. der Haustiere, 1963 3 A. MOMIGLIANO, in: Athenaeum 11, 1933, 267 4 F. IMHOOF-BLUMER, O. KELLER, Tier- und Pflanzenbilder auf Münzen und Gemmen des klass. Altertums, 1889 (repr. 1972) 5 KELLER II 6 Z. KÁDÁR, Survivals of Greek zoological illustrations in Byzantine manuscripts, 1978 7 M. BOSKOVITS, s.v. E., LCI 1, 598–600 8 H. BOESE (ed.), Thomas Cantimpratensis, Liber de natura rerum, 1973. C.HÜ.

Elephantine (Egypt. *ꜣbw*, 'elephant' or 'ivory island'). Island at the northern end of the first cataract of the Nile; the settlement on its southern tip [1] dates back to late prehistoric times. During the 1st dynasty, a fortress was built in this border region between Egypt and Nubia; at the time of the Old Kingdom, it was extended into a fortified town. From then on, E. was the capital of the first Upper Egyptian nome and its southern border city, controlling both the trade route to Nubia and the quarries of the cataract region. The cults of E. gained importance because of their link with the arrival of the Nile inundation, which was thought to originate in the cataract region (Hdt. 2,28). Satet was the goddess of the city; her temple, a modest arrangement in the Archaic period and the Old Kingdom, was lavishly extended from the 11th dynasty onwards. It was probably only under → Ptolemy VIII that a new construction of the temple was begun; work continued on its entrance buildings, river terrace, and Nilometer into the Augustan period [2]. From the 12th dynasty, the island also housed a temple of Khnum (→ Chnubis), the ram-headed god, which soon outshone that of Satet in importance. A rebuilding of the temple was begun under → Nectanebus II, and continued into Augustan times with the addition of a forecourt, pylon, terrace, and also a Nilometer (mentioned in Str. 17,1,48) [2]. The Roman Khnum temple also included a cemetery with the graves of sacred rams. A temple of Amenophis III and a smaller one of Ramses II were only pulled down in the 19th cent. Several archives of Aramaic papyri confirm that during the 26th and 27th dynasties, a contingent of Jewish soldiers of the border garrison of → Syene was stationed on the island and maintained its own → Jahwe temple [3].

1 W. KAISER et al., Stadt und Tempel von E., MDAI(K) 26, 1970, 87ff. and subsequent vols. 2 H. JARITZ, Die Terrassen vor den Tempeln des Chnum und der Satet, 1980 3 B. PORTEN, Archives from E., 1968. S.S.

Elephenor (Ἐλεφήνωρ; *Elephḗnōr*). Son of Chalcodon, grandson of Abas and king of the → Abantes on Euboea. He was one of Helena's suitors (Apollod. 3,130) and the leader of the Abantes against Troy (Hom. Il. 2,540–541). He was expelled from Euboea following the accidental killing of his grandfather; for that reason, he was only able to call the Abantes to battle by shouting from a cliff top near Euboea (Lycoph. 1034 with Tzetz.). The sons of Theseus were among those who followed him to Troy (Paus. 1,17,6). E. was killed by → Agenor [5] (Hom. Il. 4,463–469).

E. VISSER, Homers Katalog der Schiffe, 1997, 415–418; W. KULLMANN, Die Quellen der Ilias, Hermes ES 14, 1960, 122–123. R.B.

Eleusinia (Ἐλευσίνια; *Eleusínia*). Festivals held in Eleusis, often confused by modern scholars with the Eleusinian mysteries (never referred to as Eleusinia in Attic sources). They were apparently celebrated as a kind of 'harvest festival' (Schol. Pind. Ol. 9,150), probably in late spring (against the modern view that they were held in the *metageitnion*, i.e. August/September); an Athenian decree [1] listing the order Eleusinia, Panathenaea (Hekatombaion), mysteries (Boedromion) seems to indicate that they took place before the Hekatombaion (June/July). These games were held every four years on a larger scale (penteric games in the third year of an Olympiad), and on a smaller scale always two years after that (trieteric celebration in the first year of an Olympiad) [2]. They included a procession and sacrifices (IG II² 930, 8; 1028, 16; the sacrificial animals listed in IG I³ 5 were part of the mysteries, and not the Eleusinia, as previously assumed [3]), and there were athletic, riding, and music competitions as well as a so-called 'Ahnenwettkampf'. The prize was a certain quantity of grain from the Rarian field (IG II² 1672, 258–262). The Eleusinia and the Panathenaea were Athens' most important agonistic festivals.

The games of the '*Eleuhýnia*' (= *Eleusýnia*) in Laconia (IG V 1, 213, etc.), which were probably held in conjunction with the Eleusinion in Therai [4], seem to date back to Eleusinian influence in the protogeometric period. The same applies to cults of Demeter Eleusinia in Arcadia and Ionia [5], many of which were exclusively for women.

1 B. HELLY, Gonnoi II, no. 109, 35–38 2 J. D. MORGAN, The Calendar and the Chronology of Athens, in: AJA 100, 1996, 395 3 K. CLINTON, IG I² 5, the Eleusinia and the Eleusinians, in: AJPh 100, 1979, 1–12 4 R. PARKER, Demeter, Dionysus and the Spartan Pantheon, in: R. HÄGG, N. MARINATOS, C. NORDQUIST (ed.), Early Greek Cult Practice, 1988, 101–103 5 GRAF, 274–277.

DEUBNER, 91–92; NILSSON, Feste, 334–336. K.C.

Eleusinian mysteries see → Mysteria

Eleusis

[1] (Ἐλευσίς; *Eleusís*, mod. Elefsina).

A. LOCATION B. HISTORY C. BUILDINGS D. POST-ANTIQUITY

A. LOCATION

Attic Paralia deme of the phyle Hippothontis with urban character, 11 (?) bouleutai, *c.* 21 km west of → Athens [1] on a low coastal hill range west of Thriasia, whose north-western summit with Hellenistic fortress and medieval tower is now completely razed. Excavations by the Greek Archaeological Society since 1882 have concentrated on uncovering the famous mystery cult sanctuary south-east of E.

B. HISTORY

Eleusis, which displayed urban characteristics even as early as the Bronze Age (Mycenaean fortifications questionable [11. 91]) presumably lost its independence when in Late Helladic IIIA Athens rose to become Attica's predominant power (Paus. 1,38,3; [13. 39]). E. developed during the Iron Age from a small late Geometric settlement [13. 64, 89, 128]. Archaeological finds beneath the Telesterion can confirm neither the presumably prehistoric origin of the mysteries [5] nor their roots in Eleusis; however, both are evident in the cultic finds, even if the *pólis* of Athens exercised control over the mysteries even prior to the appointment of the *árchōn epónymos* (683/2 BC?) through the office of the (*árchon*) *basileús* (Aristot. Ath. Pol. 57,1; [4. 112]). Neither Herodotus' observation (1,30,5) nor the mention in the Homeric Hymn to Demeter of *basileís* in E. (Hom. h. 2,473, according to [2] not an official Eleusinian hymn) are proof of E.'s independence in the 7th cent. BC [13. 66, 144]. The mystery cult and the procession from E. along the Sacred Way (Paus. 1,36,3–38,6; [11. 177–190]) were (from the time of Solon?) regulated in great detail [1]. Peisistratus' relationship with the Eleusinian mystery cult is unclear; an increase in building activities is evident at the earliest from the end of the 6th cent. BC [13 241]. According to TRAVLOS [11. 93f., fig. 136–138, 144–148], the Peisistratid fortifications were razed in the Persian Wars and later rebuilt under Cimon [11. 94, fig. 149–153]. A strongly fortified garrison town in the classical period, E. was occupied by the Thirty Tyrants in 403 BC, reunited with Athens in 402/1, in 295 BC taken by → Demetrius [2] Poliorcetes, in 286/5 liberated by → Demochares [3], and in 255 restituted to Athens by → Antigonus [2] Gonatas. In AD 170, E. was laid waste by the Costoboci [8], and again in 395 by Alaric's Goths. It is possible that Theodosius' edict of AD 381 meant the end of the mystery cult. Recovery in the early Byzantine period.

C. BUILDINGS

Many details of the architectural history of both town and sanctuary, especially for the earlier periods, remain uncertain. The Mycenaean, late Archaic, and classical periods as well as particularly the middle Imperial and early Byzantine periods were the high points. The archaeologically verifiable beginnings of the sanctuary on a spur of the hill on which the town is built (above the well of Callichorus—no. 6; Hom. h. 2,270ff.) date back into the geometric period at least ([11. 92, fig. 113–118; 119–122]: 'Sacred House'). The Telesterion (no. 16), built by Ictinus on the site of smaller Solonic (?) and Peisistratid predecessors (Str. 9,1,12;

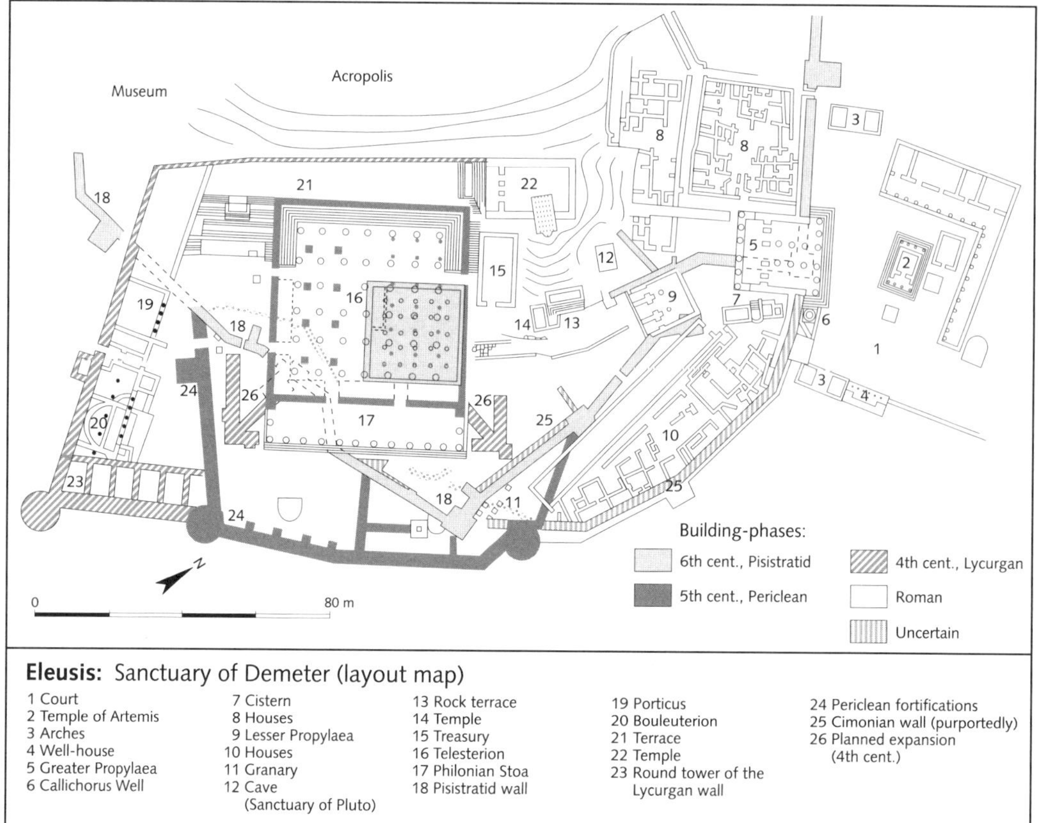

Eleusis: Sanctuary of Demeter (layout map)

1 Court
2 Temple of Artemis
3 Arches
4 Well-house
5 Greater Propylaea
6 Callichorus Well
7 Cistern
8 Houses
9 Lesser Propylaea
10 Houses
11 Granary
12 Cave (Sanctuary of Pluto)
13 Rock terrace
14 Temple
15 Treasury
16 Telesterion
17 Philonian Stoa
18 Pisistratid wall
19 Porticus
20 Bouleuterion
21 Terrace
22 Temple
23 Round tower of the Lycurgan wall
24 Periclean fortifications
25 Cimonian wall (purportedly)
26 Planned expansion (4th cent.)

Vitr. De arch. 7,16), was completely renewed after AD 170 [7; 10], as was Philo's porch (τὸ προστῷον, Vitr. De arch. 7,17, [11. 95]); the planning (352/1 BC) and construction (completed 317/08 BC) of the latter is documented in great detail (IG II² 1666, 1671, 1673, 1675, 1680). Large-scale architectural copies of imperial buildings dominate the square in front of the sanctuary [14. 179]. Work on the 'Greater Propylaea' (no. 5), modelled on the Athenian Propylaea, began under Hadrian; destroyed in AD 170, they were completed by Marcus Aurelius [3; 6; 7]. The 'Lesser Propylaea' (no. 9; 50–30 BC) led into the inner area of the sacred precinct, replacing an older building of the 4th cent. BC [11. 95]. There is also a church dating from the early Byzantine period: [11. 98, fig. 213–214].

1 K. Clinton, A law in the city Eleusinion concerning the mysteries, in: Hesperia 49, 1980, 258–288 2 Id., The author of the Homeric Hymn to Demeter, in: OpAth 16, 1986, 43–49 3 Id., Hadrian's contribution to the renaissance of E., in: S. Walker (ed.), The Greek renaissance [see n. 12], 56–68 4 Id., The sanctuary of Demeter and Kore at E., in: N. Marinatos, R. Hägg (ed.), Greek sanctuaries, 1993, 110–124 5 P. Darque, Les vestiges mycéniens découverts sous le Télestérion d'E., in: BCH 105, 1981, 593–605 6 K. Fittschen, Zur Deutung der Giebel-Clipei der großen Propyläen von E., in: S. Walker (ed.), The Greek renaissance [see n. 12], 76
7 D. Giraud, The Greater Propylaia at E., a copy of Mnesikles' propylaia, in: S. Walker (ed.), The Greek renaissance [see n. 12], 69–75 8 C.P. Jones, The Levy at Thespiae under Marc Aurelius, in: GRBS 12, 1971, 45–48
9 G.E. Mylonas, Προϊστορικὴ Ἐλευσίς [Proistorikē Eleusís], 1932 10 R.F. Townsend, The Roman rebuilding of Philon's porch and the Telesterion at E., in: Boreas 10, 1987, 97–106 11 Travlos, Attika 12 S. Walker (ed.), The Greek renaissance in the Roman empire. Papers from the Tenth British Museum Classical Colloquium London 1986, 1989 13 K.W. Welwei, Athen, 1992
14 D. Willers, Der Vorplatz des Heiligtums von E., in: M. Flashar, H.-J. Gehrke, E. Heinrich (ed.), Retrospektive. Konzepte von Vergangenheit in der griech.-röm. Ant., 1996, 179–225.

K. Clinton, Myth and cult. The iconography of the Eleusinian mysteries, 1992; H. Hörmann, Die inneren Propyläen von E., 1932; G.E. Mylonas, E. and the Eleusinian Mysteries, 1961; F. Noack, E., 1927; Traill, Attica, 21, 52, 59, 67, 110 no. 38, table 8; Travlos, Attika, 91–169 fig. 103–214; Whitehead, Index s.v. E. H.LO.

D. After antiquity

The small Arvanite village Λεψῖνα (*Lepsîna*), Alba. Lepsinë (mod. again Ελευσῖνα; *Eleusîna*) retained its name despite its insignificance since the end of antiquity. While this alone points to a continuity of settlement, it is confirmed with certainty by the frequent mention of its name in works by Byzantine and Latin authors of the time of the crusades. Nothing seems to have remained of the medieval κάστρον (*kástron*)

[1. 154], a basilica on the site of the ancient settlement has been partially excavated.

→ Mysteria; → ELEUSIS

1 J. KODER, s.v. E., TIB J.N.

[2] Early Boeotian settlement site on the south-western shore of Lake Copais; according to tradition, steeped in both Boeotian and Attic folklore, it was founded by Cecrops together with Athens [2], and quite early submerged by the waters of Lake Copais; however, it resurfaced after being drained by Crates, under Alexander the Great (Paus. 9,24,2; Str. 9,2,18). E. may be identified as either the settlements of Dekedes near the mod. Agia Paraskevi (formerly: Agoriani) [1] and Lyoma near Kalami south-east of the mod. Lafistion [3. 123ff.], both dating back to the Early Helladic period, or the farming region of Xinos, about 4 km east of the mod. Mavrogija [2].

FOSSEY, 335f. 2 J. KNAUSS, Die Melioration des Kopaisbeckens durch die Minyer im 2. Jt.v.Chr., 1987, 16–31 3 S. LAUFFER, Kopais, 1986. P.F.

Eleutherai (Ἐλευθεραί; *Eleutheraí*). A settlement of Boeotian origins on the pass-route across Mt. Cithaeron from Eleusis [1] to Thebes, near the mod. Kaza; after the cult of Dionysus Eleuthereus was relocated from E. to the southern slopes of the Acropolis in Athens [1] in the 2nd half of the 6th cent. BC, it belonged to Attica, without, however, ever forming an independent → *dḗmos*; Source references: Eur. Supp. 757ff.; Xen. Hell. 5,4,14; Str. 9,2,31; Plin. HN 4,26; Paus. 1,38,8f.; Arr. Anab. 1,7,9; Ath. 11,486D; Steph. Byz. s.v. Ἐλευθεραί; IG [3]I 892; 1162,96f.; remains of the settlement and two early Christian basilicas are to the south below the hill with the mod. name of Gyphtokastro, on which is the well preserved Attic border fortress of E., dating from the 4th cent. BC (often mistakenly equated with the Attic fortress of Panactum).

J. KODER, E., TIB 1, 154f.; M.H. MUNN, The Defense of Attica, 1993, 8f.; J. OBER, Fortress Attica, 1985, 160–163; TRAVLOS, Attika, 170–176; E. VANDERPOOL, Roads and Forts in Northwestern Attica, in: California Studies in Classical Antiquity 11, 1978, 227–245. P.F.

Eleutheria see → Freedom

Eleutherios see → Zeus

Eleutherna (Ἐλευθέρνα; *Eleuthérna*). City in central Crete on the northern slopes of the Ida range, settled from the late Minoan period. Some vestiges have survived near the mod. village of Prinès (cisterns, town walls, bridge, Byzantine tower). In around 260 BC, E. joined the *isopoliteia* of Miletus with Cnossus, Gortyn, Phaestus and their allies [2. 482]. In *c.* 225 BC, the city entered into an alliance with the Macedonian king Antigonus [2] Gonatas [1. 20; 2. 501]. In 220 BC, as a consequence of disputes among the Cretan cities, but also involving Rhodes, the Aetolians, Achaeans, and Macedonians, E. was besieged by Polyrrhenia and its allies (Pol. 4,53–55). In 183 BC, E. joined the alliance of the 31 Cretan cities with Eumenes II (Syll.[3] 627,4). In 67 BC, the city was captured by Q. Caecilius Metellus (Cass. Dio 36,18,2; Flor. Epit. 1,42,4). In late antiquity, E. was a bishop's seat (Not. Episc. 8,226; 9,135).

1 M. GUARDUCCI (ed.), Inscriptiones Creticae vol. 2, 1939 2 StV 3.

H.v. EFFENTERRE, La Crète et le monde grec de Platon à Polybe, 1948; LAUFFER, Griechenland, 213; I.F. SANDERS, Roman Crete, 1982, 162f. H.SO.

Eleutherolakones (Ἐλευθερολάκωνες; *Eleutherolákōnes*). League of Laconian coastal settlements; as former *perioikoi* settlements, they were placed under the protection of the Achaean Confederacy following the defeat of Nabis by the Romans in 195 BC. After the failure of the Achaean uprising in 146 BC, they were permitted to unite in the *koinòn tôn Lakedaimoníōn* (κοινὸν τῶν Λακεδαιμονίων) (Liv. 35,13,2; 38,31,2) [2. 51]. In 21 BC, Augustus reorganized the league [1. 60], which was thenceforth known as *koinòn tôn Eleutherolakṓnōn* (Str. 8,366; Paus. 3,21,6f.; IG V 1 1161; 1167; 1243; 1360).

1 S. GRUNAUER-V. HOERSCHELMANN, Die Münzprägung der Lakedaimonier, 1978 2 TH. SCHWERTFEGER, Der Achaiische Bund von 146 bis 27 v.Chr., 1974.

P. CARTLEDGE, A. SPAWFORTH, Hellenistic and Roman Sparta, 1989, 101; 113f.; 138f.; 149f.; 173f. K.-W.WEL.

Eleuthia see → Eileithyia

Elias

[1] (Elijah, prophet). The biblical character of E., according to the evidence of the Deuteronomic History, appears as a prophet of the northern kingdom at the time of king Ahab (871–852 BC) (cf. the E. traditions in 1 Kgs 17–19; 21; 2 Kgs 1–2); probably because of his miraculous translation to heaven (2 Kgs 2), E. comes to play a very important role in post-biblical Judaism. Thus, even in early Judaism, the notion arose of E.'s eschatological return (cf. Mal 3,23; cf. also Mt 11,14; 17,10–13). Ps.-Philo 48,1–2 identifies E. with Pinchas the Zealot, a role model of particular importance especially among the Zealots. In the Rabbinic literature, which deals comprehensively with E.'s family background, left ambiguous in the biblical tradition (cf. Ber 99,11; 71,10), the translated E. participates in divine secrets (bBM 59b; bHag 15b), while at the same time keeping a record of human deeds (WaR 34,8). This omniscience made E. a helper of people in distress or persecution, appearing either in their dreams or in a variety of different disguises; at the same time, he acted as an advisor, teacher of great scholars (i.a. bShab 109b; bAZ 18b; bBM 85b; bTaan 22a). However, there are also attempts to marginalize the peculiarities of E.'s charac-

ter by denying his ascension (bSuk 5a). In the hymnic poetry of the Ancient Church, the legend of E. is dealt with on a number of occasions: in Ephraim, in an anonymous fr. (probably 1st half of the 6th cent. AD [1]), in Romanos' E.-kontakion (Canticum 45 MAAS/TRYPANIS, in imitation of a sermon Basilius of Seleucea [2]). In medieval esoteric or Kabbalistic traditions, E.'s character played a prominent part as a revelatory intermediary. The acceptance of E. in neo-Greek popular belief is evident in the numerous chapels dedicated to E., mainly on mountain tops or at least raised terrain, frequently on the site of former Zeus or Apollo sanctuaries. However, it is questionable whether this implies a direct link with pre-Christian Greek traditions [3].

1 P. MAAS, Frühbyz. Kirchenpoesie. Anonyme Hymnen des V.-VI. Jh., 1910, 20–23, no. 3 (Kleine Texte für theol. und philol. Vorlesungen und Übungen 52/3) 2 Id., KS, 1973, 386–388 3 E. Rein, Zu der Verehrung des Propheten Elias bei den Neugriechen, in: Öfversigt af Finska Vetenskaps-Societetens Förhandlingar 47, 1904/5, 1–33.

M. W. LEVINSOHN, Der Prophet Elia nach den Talmudim und Midraschim, 1929; N. OSSWALD, s.v. Elia II. Judentum, TRE 9, 502–504 (bibliography); G.F. WILLEMS (ed.), Elie le Prophète. Bible, Tradition, Iconographie. Colloque des 10 et 11 novembre 1985 Bruxelles, Publications de l'Institutum Judaicum, 1988, 96–102 (bibliography).
B.E.

[2] The name of this Neoplatonic philosopher, known from Byzantine scholia and from authors and who lived in the 6th cent. AD, points to Christian origins. The only work preserved under his name is the introduction to a commentary of Aristotle's *Analytica Priora* [1]. It is questionable whether the ambiguous official title ἀπὸ ἐπάρχων; *apò epárchōn*, in the heading of this commentary, allows an identification with E., the *praefectus Illyrici* of AD 541 (Iustin. Nov. 153). Of the commentaries which the editor BUSSE attributes to E. — the anonymous commentary of Porphyrius' Isagoge (CAG 18,1) and the commentary of the Categories, listed in the MSS under the name of David (ibid.) —, the latter is most definitely a work of David of Armenia [2], confirmed by the Armenian translation, also bearing David's name. It is probable that E., like David (Elias, In Aristot. An. pr., Armenian trans.), studied in Alexandria as a disciple of Olympiodorus and Eutocius.
→ Alexandrian School; → David

1 E. on the Prior Analytics, ed. by L. G. WESTERINK (1961), in: L. G. WESTERINK, Texts and Studies in Neoplatonism and Byzantine Literature, 1980 2 Simplicius, Commentaire sur les Catégories, traduction commentée sous la direction d'I. Hadot, fasc. I, 1990, S. VII, fn. 2, and Appendice 2 (= J. P. MAHÉ).
I.H.

[3] of Nisibis (*Eliyā bar Šināyā*), 975–1046. Metropolite of Nisibis (Eastern Church), author writing in Syrian and Arabic. Amongst his key works are an important chronography in Syrian and Arabic, mainly in the form of tables, also a report on seven conversations (*Kitāb al-Mağālis*, 'Book of Meetings', Arab.) with vizier Abū'l-Qāsim al-Mağribī in July 1026, characterized by a remarkable openness towards Islam, as well as a collection of aphorisms (Kitāb Daf' al-Hamm, 'Expulsion of Worry') in Arabic, and a lexicographical work (*at-Tarğumān*, 'The Translator') in Arabi and Syrian. Other works deal with theology and canon law.

EDITIONS: E. W. BROOKS, J. B. CHABOT, CSCO Scr. Syri 21–24, 1909/10, (chronography, with Lat. trans.); L. DELAPORTE, Chronographie de Mar Elie bar Shinaya, 1901 (chronography, French trans.).
BIBLIOGRAPHY: D. SERRUYS, Les canons d'Eusèbe, d'Annianos et d'Andronicos d'après Élie de Nisibe, in: ByzZ 22, 1913, 1–36.
ARAB. WORKS: G. GRAF, Gesch. der christl. arab. Lit. II, 1947, 178–189; S.K. SAMIR, Foi et culture en Irak au Xième siècle: Élie de Nisibe et l'Islam, 1996 (bibliography); Dictionnaire de spiritualité 4, s.v. E., 1960, 572–574; E. DELLY, s.v. E., Dictionnaire d'histoire et de géographie ecclésiastique 15, 1963, 192–194.
S.BR.

Elicius see → Jupiter

Eliezer ben Hyrkanos Rabbi Eliezer ben Hyrkanos (*c.* end 1st/early 2nd cent.) is one of the most frequently mentioned Tannaites in the Mishnah and Talmud. Records of his life have survived in numerous legends: he only found his way to the Torah after the age of twenty and left the home of his wealthy parents to devote himself to studying the Torah as one of the disciples of Rabbi Jochanan ben Zakkais. There he was noted because of his outstanding exegetical abilities, which were so remarkable that they even convinced his father not to disinherit him (Abot de Rabbi Natan A 6, 30f. Par.; Pirqe de Rabbi Eliezer 1, 2). Later he headed a school in Lod/Lydda, a settlement on the Palestinian coastal plain. Several remarks indicate his utter disregard for non-Jews (e.g. bBB 10b; bGit 45b). He may have travelled to Rome together with Rabbi Gamaliel and Rabbi Jehošua (ySan 7, 19 (11) [25d]). In Jewish tradition, he is also thought to be the author of the *Pirqe de Rabbi E.*, a kind of Midrash; however, in reality, it is likely to have been written later, in Islamic times.

Y. D. GILAT, A Scholar Outcast, 1984; Y. D. GILAT, s.v. E. ben Hyrcanus, Encyclopedia Judaica, 6, 1971, 619–623 (bibliography).
B.E.

Elijah see → Elias [1]

Elimea (Ἐλίμεια; *Elímeia*). Region, originally belonging to Epirus (Str. 9,5,11), east of the Pindus range on the upper course of the Haliacmon south of Orestis and Eordaea; from the 5th. cent. BC, the people of the Elimiotaea in upper Macedonia took their name from E. (Thuc. 2,99). The location of the eponymous town is uncertain (Kozani, Palaiogratsiano?). Cities of the Hellenistic and Roman era are → Aeane and Caesarea (bishop's seat: Hierocles Synekdemos 642,11). Despite its dependence on the Macedonian king (Perdiccas), E. managed to maintain its own royal house, related to the → Argeadae, into the times of Alexander the Great. Under Alexander, Elimiotai fought at Arbela, and later under Perseus against the Romans. After 167 BC, the Romans assigned E. to *Macedonia IV* (Liv. 45,30,7), which was considered independent (Str. 7,7,8). Inscriptions [1. 35f.] testify to a *koinón* of the Elimiotai in the 2nd cent. AD. Following the Tetrarchy's reorganization of provinces in the 4th cent. AD, it became part of the province of *Thessalia*.

1 Th. Rizakis, G. Touratzoglou, Epigraphes ano Makedonias, 1985.

N. G. L. Hammond, A history of Macedonia 1, 1972; 2, 1979; 3, 1988; F. Papazoglou, Les villes de Macédoine a l'époque Romaine, 1988, 249–255. D.S. and MA.ER.

Elis (῏Ηλις; *Êlis*).
[1] Region of the Peloponnese
I. Definition II. Region III. History

I. Definition

Doric *Ális*, Elean *Wális*, probably 'valley', cf. Mycenaean *e-nwa-ri-jo* (= **en-walios*), ethnicon Ἠλεῖοι (Ϝαλεῖοι 'valley dwellers'), the north-western coastal region of the Peloponnese. E. is defined as the lower Peneius valley (later also Κοίλη ῏Ηλις; *Koílē Êlis*, 'Hollow Elis'), the largest (1160 km^2) and most fertile part of the region. Not least because of its advantageous climate (wet, constant), E. was a favourite for agriculture even in antiquity [1. 103–104], dominated by large estates ([2]; esp. for animal husbandry and cattle breeding). Its northern border with Achaea was the Larisus, but at times the border also moved further north to Cape Araxos (Paus. 6,26,10 [3]); in the east, E. also bordered on Achaea (Skollion mountains, mod. Santomeri) as well as Arcadia (the river Erymanthus), and in the south the border followed a line from Cape Phe(i)a (Katakolo) to the north-east. After E. had taken possession of, the formerly independent regions of Pisatis on the Alpheius river and Triphylia south of the Alpheius, these also became part of E., resulting in the Neda forming the southern border to Messenia (secured only in the course of the Roman conquest).

II. Region

On the whole, E. consists mainly of an alluvial plain bordered by a broad belt of hills, likewise formed of Neocene sand and marl, with an average height of about 200 to 400 m above sea level. The long shallow bend of the coastline, formed by a strong surf, is only broken by some isolated rocky headlands; it offers not a single good natural harbour. Along the coastline, there is a chain of shallow lagoons, separated from the sea by belts of dunes (some formed since antiquity). E.'s main river is the Peneius [4. 293–303], joined in the hill country of its central course by the Elean Ladon, from the south. Apart from the eponymous capital, other ancient settlements in E. are named: Pylos [5] northwest of Agrapidochoria at the confluence of the Ladon with the Peneius, Thalamae (Pol. 4,75,2), Myrtuntion 4 km west of Kapeleton on the eastern shore of the Kotiki lagoon (Str. 8,3,10)—possibly not to be identified with the Homeric Myrsilus [3. 19f.]—, Oenoe in the south of E. on the left bank of the Ladon (Str. 8,3,5), furthermore, along the coast, Cyllene (Glarentsa near the mod. Kyllini) [6], E.'s main port (Str. 8,3,4), and also the fortified harbour town of Phe(i)a (Thuc. 7,31,1; Xen. Hell. 3,2,30). To the east follows the Akroreia ('mountain county'), generally an Elean dependency: in the hill country between Peneius and Alpheius, partly on the 6–800 m high Pholoe conglomerate plateau lying to the east Further east towards the Arcadian border on the upper reaches of the Ladon on the Pholoe plateau was Lasion, near the mod. Kumani; it was also an Elean dependency whose territory also included the upper Peneius valley between Astras and Skiadovuni. The road running through the valley of the Ladon linked E. with Arcadia and near Lasion joined the road from Olympia to Psophis.

III. History

A. Prehistory to the Archaic Period
B. Classical and Hellenistic Periods
C. Early Christian and Byzantine Period

A. Prehistory to the Archaic Period

The formation of a kingdom in Mycenaean times is questionable (hardly any remains of Mycenaean settlements). The Eleans, who judging by their dialect [7], came from north-western Greece (→ Doric/North-west Greek), arrived on the Peloponnese towards the end of the 2nd millennium at the time of the → Doric migration, having come via Aetolia—according to a legend, upon which Pausanias (5,1–9) based a late, but complete reconstruction. Further sources: Hom. Il. 2,615–624; 11,670–761; H. Hom. Apoll., 418–429; Str. 8,3,1–33, with extensive use of Homeric geography. Traditions about the *Epeioí* (Ἐπειοί), an Aetolian tribe, whose kingdom comprised Buprasion, E., the *pétrē Ōleníē* (πέτρη Ὠλενίη), as well as Alesion (Hom. Il. 2,615–618), contain references to the revival of the north-western Peloponnese after the destruction of the last remaining Mycenaean palaces [3; 8. 158]. In *c.* 700/660 BC, the Eleans founded colonies in Epirus (Harpocr. s.v. Ἐλάτεια). From fairly early on, the ruling aristocracy tried to extend its power to the neighbouring regions, which were seized and reduced to dependent *perioikoi* regions, such as the Akroreia in the east, but mainly the smaller Pisatis districts south towards the Alpheius. This conquest was of particular importance, as the Eleans thus gained Olympia and with it the control of the Games. Olympia with its Zeus sanctuary — a focus of regional identification — as well as the settlements along the 'mountain road' to E. along the valley of the Lestenitsa became immediate Elean territory. It is generally believed that the organization of the Games initially lay with the Pisatians; in *c.* 576, it was passed to the Eleans who enjoyed Spartan support.

B. Classical and Hellenistic Periods

Despite its membership in the Peloponnesian League, E. was not involved in the main events of the Persian Wars (Hdt. 8,72; 9,77,3); however, its name nonetheless appears on the votive offering in Olympia and Delphi (Paus. 5,23,2; Syll.³ 31,27). In 472/1 BC, a democratic revolution transformed the constitution following the Attic pattern; the foundation of the capital E. dates to the same period [9. 174–199]. In the mid 5th cent. BC, Triphylia was conquered (Hdt. 4,148; Str. 8,3,30), with the exception of Lepreum, which, however, came under Elean control soon after (Thuc. 5,31,2). In the Peloponnesian War, E. initially fought alongside Sparta; however, a dispute over Lepreon led to E. breaking with Sparta and joining the → Delian League after the Peace of Nicias. In 402/400, during an armed dispute with Sparta, E. was forced to grant freedom to all of its *perioikoi* districts and to rejoin the Peloponnesian League (Thuc. 5,49f.; Xen. Hell. 3,2,21–31; Diod. Sic. 14,17,4–12; 34,1; Paus. 3,8,3–5; [9. 232–256]). Independent once more following the battle of Leuctra in 371 BC, E. regained its *perioikoi* districts north of the Alpheius and Scillus (Xen. Hell. 7,4,12–14; Paus. 5,6,6). Initially, E. sought a closer union with the Arcadian League, but later went to war against the league in 365–363 BC (battle on the Altis); for a short while, Olympia was separated and became the independent state of Pisa. Over the following decades, alliances changed several times; there were also repeated reforms to the constitution. Following its affiliation with the Aetolian Confederacy, E. succeeded in 245 BC in recapturing Triphylia and Lasion; however, in 219/8, Philippus V undertook a victorious campaign in E. and Triphylia [10. 28–30, 58–76], resulting once again in E.'s loss of Triphylia and Lasion in the peace of 217. In 191 BC, E. was forced to join the Achaean Confederacy, thus ending its independent history; however, from 146 BC Triphylia was again united with E.

→ Synoikismos

1 Gehrke 2 S. Zoumbaki, Röm. Grundbesitzer in Eleia, in: Tyche 9, 1994, 213–218 3 B. Sergent, Sur les frontières de l'Elide aux hautes époques, in: REA 80, 1978, 16–35 4 A.D. Rizakis (ed.), Achaia und E. in der Ant. (Meletemata 13), 1991 5 J. Coleman, Excavations at Pylos in E., Hesperia Suppl. 21, 1986 6 J. Servais, Recherches sur le port de Cyllène, in: BCH 85, 1961, 123–161 7 A. Thévenot-Warelle, Le dialecte grec d'Elide, 1988 8 G. Maddoli, L'Elide in età arcaica: il processo di formazione dell'unità regionale, in: F. Prontera (ed.), Geografia storica, 1991, 150–173 9 U. Bultrighini, Pausania e le tradizioni democratiche (Argo ed Elide), 1990 10 Pritchett 6, 1989, 1–78.

Y.L.

C. Early Christian and Byzantine Period

From the 4th to the 6th cent. AD, the region belonged administratively to the province of Achaea, whereas in ecclesiastical law it was directly under the jurisdiction of the pope in Rome. E. as well as Phigalia appear amongst the cities of the Peloponnese, quoted by Hierocles in his register *Synekdemos* (6th cent.); both are Corinthian suffragan episcopal seats (→ Corinth) Recent archaeological research has confirmed this information. Other early Christian settlements, mainly agricultural, are also found within the region, such as → Olympia, → Pylos, Samicon, Scillus, Lepreum, Anailion. Most of these settlements survived into the 6th/7th cents., in spite of repeated earthquakes and invasions of the 4th, 5th, and 6th cents.

In Byzantine times (9th to early 13th cent.), following the institution of the → Thema of the Peloponnese and a reform of its ecclesiastical structure, the region blossomed once again. New cities or dioceses such as Olenus and Moreas developed. We know of a number of Byzantine settlements in E.: Zourtsas (Koimesis church, end 10th cent.), Olenus (bishop's seat, Metamorphosis church, 1st half 10th cent.), Manolada (Koimesis church, end 12th cent.), Gastouni (church of St. Mary, end 12th or very early 13th cent.), Glarenza, Anailiion, Hagios Dimitrios (Church of St. Dimitrios, mid 11th cent.) and many more.

A.D. Rizakis (ed.), Achaia und E. in der Antike. Akten des 1. internat. Symposiums (Athen 1989), Meletemata 13, 1991; N. Gialoures, Ἀρχαία Ἤλιδα. Τό λίκνο τῶν Ὀλυμπιακῶν ἀγώνων, 1997; J.E. Coleman, K. Abramovitz, Excavations at Pylos in E., in: Hesperia Suppl., 21, 1986; A. Lampropoulou, Παύλιτσα Ἠλείας Ἱστορικές καί ἀρχαιολογικές μαρτυρίες, in: Symmeikta 8, 1989, 335–359; Id., Θέματα τῆς ἱστορικῆς Γεωγραφίας τοῦ νομοῦ Ἠλείας κατά τήν παλαιοχριστιανική περίοδο, Meletemata 13, 1991, 283–291; A. Moutzale, Ἡ Ὀλυμπία κατά τήν πρωτοβυζαντινή περίοδο. Προβλήματα καί προσεγγίσεις. Πρακτικά τοῦ Ἠλειακοῦ πνευματικοῦ Συμποσίου, 1994, 260–278; X. Boura, 'Zourtsa', in: Cahiers Archéologiques 21, 1971, 137–150; W.K. Pritchett, Studies in Ancient Greek Topography, Classical Studies 33, 1989, 46–78.

A.LAM.

[2] Capital city of E. [1], founded in 472/1 BC (Diod. Sic. 11,54,1; Str. 8,3,2; Paus. 5,9,5), located where the Peneius flows from the hill country into the plain, between the mod. villages of Palaiopolis, Kalyvia, and Buchiotis. To the northwest of the Acropolis (mod. Hagios Ioannis), lay the administrative districts, the agora and the theatre, on the banks of the river. E. was never permanently fortified with walls (Xen. Hell. 3,2,27; Str. 8,3,33). Archaeology: ancient remains dating from the Bronze Age to the Byzantine period. Literary evidence: Paus. 6,23–26,3.

→ Synoikismos

M. Moggi, I sinecismi interstatali greci I, 1976, 157–166; N. Yalouris, s.v. E., PE, 299–300; Id., in: Ergon 37, 1990 (1991), 36–45.

Y.L.

Elisaios Wardapet see → Elischē (Ełišē)

Elis and Eretria, School of A construct of both ancient and modern historians of philosophy, based on the following facts: Hellenistic historians of philosophy grouped together → Phaedon of Elis and his disciples and their disciples as the School of Elis (Ἠλιακὴ αἵρεσις), and Phaedon's second or third generation disciple → Menedemus of Eretria and his followers as the School of Eretria (Ἐρετρικὴ or Ἐρετριακὴ αἵρεσις) (Diog. Laert. 1,18–19 and passim). Modern historians of philosophy combined both traditions in the School of Elis and Eretria. As it is not known whether Phaedon's disciples and successors, apart from their direct or indirect descent from him, shared any philosophical views (no such similarities are found between Phaedon and Menedemus, at any rate), it is not really possible to talk of a 'school' in the traditional sense. For that reason it is not recommendable to use the term 'school' in relation to Phaedon and his successor.

EDITION: SSR III AH.

BIBLIOGRAPHY: K. DÖRING, Phaidon aus Elis und Menedemos aus Eretria, GGPh² 2.1, § 18. K.D.

Elisha ben Abuja (Eliša b. Abuja). Jewish scholar of the first half of the 2nd cent. AD, in the Rabbinic literature considered a prototypical apostate and probably therefore bearing the name Aḥer (Hebrew 'the Other'). However, Rabbinic legendary tradition attributes to him a number of very different heresies: the reference in bHag 15a, according to which he believed in the existence of two heavenly powers, seems to point to Gnostic ideas (→ Gnostics); according to yHag 2,1 (77b), he is supposed to have killed anyone who studied the Torah (cf. also throwing into doubt the idea of a just reward for obedience to the Torah, ibid.). Following his renouncement of Judaism, he supposedly led a hedonistic life (bHag 15a), but on his deathbed did penance for his life in apostasy (yHag 2,1 [77b]).

SH. SAFRAI, s.v. E. ben Avuyah, Encyclopedia Judaica 6, 668–670 (bibliography); G. STEMBERGER, Einleitung in Talmud und Midrasch, ⁸1992, 83 (bibliography). B.E.

Elishē (Ełišē). Author of a history of the Vardanids and the Armenian wars in the Armenian language, describing the uprising of the Armenian people under the leadership of Vardan Mamikonyan against the Sassanid occupation forces in AD 450/1. However, E. did not himself witness the historical events which he describes, but is likely to have lived in the 6th cent. AD. It was his aim to provide a martyrological anchor for the foundation of the Armenian church.

→ Armenia; → Armenians, Armenian literature; → Sassanids

E. TER-MINASSJAN, Vasn Vardanay ew Hayocʿ paterazmicʿ, 1957 (repr. 1993); R. W. THOMSON (ed.), Elishē. History of Vardan and the Armenian War (Harvard Armenian texts and studies, 5), 1982 (translation and commentary). K.SA.

Elision see → Punctuation; → Orthography; → Sandhi

Elk (*Alces alces*, American 'moose') A large northern species of deer, originally common across all of Central Europe [1]; its earliest ancient reference is found in Pliny (HN 8,39). He describes it similar to a mule (*iumentum*), but with a long neck and ears. He only knows of this species from hearsay, as with the related Scandinavian *achlis* with its protruding upper lip, forcing the animal to walk backwards while grazing. Its (slender) legs without knee joints supposedly forced the *achlis* to lean against trees when sleeping. To catch an *achlis* in the → Hercynia silva, one needed do no more than saw a cut into the tree it habitually leaned against. This assertion is repeated in the interpolation in Caes. B. Gall. 6,27,1–5. The assumption [2. 281ff.] that the *achlis* was identical with the giant prehistoric deer (*Cervus megaceros euryceros Aldrov.*) has found some followers [3. 6], but, to name but one, Solin. 20,6f. refers only to the elk. Thomas of Cantimpré (4,5 *aloy*; 4,7 *alches* [4. 111f.]) as well as Albertus Magnus (de animalibus 22,15 [5. 1356]) only repeat what is said in these sources.

→ Deer

1 H. PRELL, Die Verbreitung des Elches in Deutschland zu gesch. Zeit, 1941 2 W. RICHTER, Achlis. Schicksal einer tierkundlichen Notiz, in: Philologus 103, 1959 3 LEITNER 4 H. BOESE (ed.), Thomas Cantimpratensis. Liber de natura rerum, 1973 5 H. STADLER (ed.), Albertus Magnus. De animalibus, 2, 1920. C.HÜ.

El Kalb see → Eileithyiaspolis

Ellipsis (Greek ἔλλειψις; *élleipsis*: 'omission', Lat. *ellīpsis*: Quint. Inst. 8,6,21, cf. 9,3,58); in contrast with brachylogy, it refers to the actual omission of a syntactically essential constituent of a sentence, which can, however, be restored verbatim (not merely in its meaning) from context and situation (cf. Donat. 4,395,11: *e. est defectus quidam necessariae dictionis*). Some examples from everyday language: Καλλίας ὁ Ἱππονίκου (sc. υἱός), Pl. Ap. 20a; *ad Dianae* (sc. *fanum* or *aedem*), Ter. Ad. 582. As an element of rhetorical style, ellipses serve to render a text more concise and to liven up descriptions. An ellipsis of several clauses always includes the verb. Frequently, an ellipsis is applied to the predicate, e.g. a verb of speaking. In its immediate context, one finds neither an identical nor any other form of the syntactic element(s) subjected to an ellipse.

Examples: στῆσε δ' ἐν Ἀμνισῷ (sc. νῆα), Hom. Od. 19,188; μή, πρός σε γονάτων τῆς τε νεογάμου κόρης (sc. ἱκετεύω), Eur. Med. 324; *satis ferax, frugiferarum arborum impatiens, pecorum fecunda, sed plerumque improcera* (sc. *est* or respectively *sunt*), Tac. Germ. 5,1.

→ Style; → Syntax

KÜHNER/GERTH, 2,1, 265–271; 2,2, 558–560; M. LEUMANN, J. B. HOFMANN, A. SZANTYR, Lat. Gramm., vol. 2, 1965, 61, 419–425, 822–825; KNOBLOCH, vol. 1, 750–755; LAUSBERG, 346f. R.P.

Ellops see → Sturgeon

Elm (Latin *ulmus*, f.). Several species of this genus of trees in the *Ulmaceae* family grow in the Mediterranean region, notably the smooth-leaved elm (*Ulmus carpinifolia Gled.*, Greek πτελέα/*pteléa*) and the wych elm (*U. scabra Mill.*), which only grows as a shrub in Greece. It is already encountered in Homer (Il. 6,419 f.; 21,242–245 and 350). Theophrastus (Hist. pl. 3,14,1) differentiates in his excellent description a ὀρειπτελέα/*oreipteléa* (*Ulmus scabra*; *atinia* in Plin. HN 16,72; cf. Columella 5,6,2 and De arboribus 16,1) from the shrubby common elm, probably *U. nemoralis L.* or *U. carpinifolia*. Columella (loc. cit.) also appears to know the white or water elm. (U. laevis = U. effusa Willd.). The *gallica* and the *genus silvestre* (in Plin. loc. cit.) are unidentifiable. The erroneus assumption of the infertility of some elm species (Plin. loc. cit.) perhaps led to their association with death and the Underworld (Hom. Il. 6,419 f. as plantings on a cremation burial; Verg. Aen. 6,282–284 as the seat of dreams in the realm of the dead). Because of its particular suitability as a support for grapevines, elms were already raised in nurseries (*seminaria*) in antiquity. The desired growing together of elm and vine, which Columella 5,6,6–22 (cf. 4,1,6; De arboribus 16,1–4; Plin. loc. cit. and Gp. 4,1,2) describes in detail, was called *maritare* (Columella 5,6,18; Pall. Agric. 3,10,7). The young shoots growing after cutting back were fed to livestock (Columella De arboribus 16,2) and used for whipping slaves (cf. e.g., Plaut. Amph. 1029; Plaut. Rud. 636). The yellowish, heavy (cf. Plin. HN 16,228), tough and durable (ibid. 16,218) wood was used for precious doors (Theophr. Hist. pl. 3,14,1), esp. for door hinges and fillings (ibid. 5,3,5; cf. Plin. HN 16,210), but also for hammer and drill handles (ibid. 16,230) as well as ship parts (Theophr. Hist. pl. 5,7,3).

M. Schuster, s. v. U., RE 9 A, 544–554. C. HÜ.

Elocutio (λέξις; *léxis*). When first mentioned (Cic. Inv. 1,9) and discussed (Rhet. Her. 1,3; 4,10ff.) in Latin, *elocutio* was seen as the third stage of the work of the orator (→ *officia oratoris*). According to these sources, *elocutio* consists of four parts, the *aretaí tês léxeōs* (*virtutes elocutionis*): 1. ἑλληνισμός (*hellēnismós*), *latinitas*: grammatical correctness; 2. σαφήνεια (*saphéneia*), *explanatio*: clarity; 3. πρέπον (*prépon*), *decorum, aptum* (missing in Rhet. Her.; according to Cic. De or. 1,132, it is impossible to teach *decere* in an *ars*): aptness; 4. κατασκευή (*kataskeuḗ*), *dignitas, ornatus*: embellishment. *Dignitas* is mainly concerned with → figures and tropes. This subdivision into four *aretaí* is based on the influence of poetry on rhetorical theory and practice (→ prose-rhythm); Protagoras' observations on the theory of language — an approximation to a theory of the verbal moods [4. 176f.] — had some influence on Aristotle's *schḗmata tēs léxeōs* (*entolḗ, euchḗ, diḗgēsis, apeilḗ, erṓtēsis*). The earliest definite example of a complete separation of → grammar and *elocutio* is found in Rhet. Her. 4,17: In his introduction to the part dedicated to *elocutio*, the author promises to elaborate the *latinitas* in an *ars grammatica*; however, this was long preceded by the development of a Peripatetic grammar (Theophrastus), then an Alexandrian (Zenodotus, Aristophanes, Aristarchus) as well as a Stoic (Diogenes of Babylon). Prodicus' discrimination of synonyms and Protagoras' distinction of speech situations (*modi*) together with Homeric studies formed the basis for linguistic studies relevant to orators [10. 43ff; 8. 311f.]. The doctrine of *elocutio* reached its final form with Theophrastus, and was later only enriched by the Stoics. Of the four *aretaí tês léxeōs*, *hellēnismós* belongs more to grammar than rhetoric, and was primarily treated in studies of barbarisms and solecisms. Undoubtedly, Theophrastus contributed significantly to this development with a book on solecisms (Diog. Laert. 5,48); he developed the four *aretaí* and perhaps added the three *charaktḗres* (*plásmata*) *tēs léxeōs*: *charaktḗr hadrós* (*genus grande*), *ischnós* (*g. humile*), *mésos* (*g. medium*). According to Cic. Orat. 96, the Sophists already used a fourth *genus*, i.e. *florens (floridum)/anthērón* (in-depth in [6]). The Stoics added *syntomía* (conciseness) [13. 46], which had apparently already been listed by Theodectes amongst the virtues of a good storyteller (according to Quint. Inst. 4,2,32, brevity was one of Isocrates' strengths as a story teller; cf. Aristot. Rh. 1416b 30–35).

In Rome in particular, *elocutio* played a major part in the polemic debate about → Asianism vs. → Atticism. Also worthy of note is the relation between *elocutio* and → literary criticism, demonstrated by [8. 326ff.] particularly in the case of Dionysius of Halicarnassus. Other main works in this field are → Demetrius' *Perì hermēneías*, → Horatius' *Ars poetica*, and Ps.-Longinos' *Perì hýpsous*.

1 W. Ax, Quadripertita Ratio, in: Historiographia Linguistica 13, 1986, 191–214 2 M. Baratin, La naissance de la syntaxe à Rome, 1989 3 K. Barwick, Probleme der stoischen Sprachlehre und Rhet., Abh. Sächs. Akad. d. Wiss., Phil.hist. Kl. 49,3, 1957 4 G. Calboli, I Modi del Verbo Greco e Latino 1903–1966, in: Lustrum 11, 1966, 173–349 5 Id., From Aristotelian λέξις to E., in: Rhetorica 6 L. Calboli Montefusco, Consulti Fortunatiani *Ars Rhetorica*, 1979 7 Id., Exordium, Narratio, Epilogus, 1988 8 C. J. Classen, Rhet. und Literarkritik, in: Entretiens 40, 1994, 307–360 9 W. W./A. Fortenbaugh, Theophrastus of Eresus, 1992 10 R. Pfeiffer, History of Classical Scholarship, 1968 11 D. M. Schenkeveld, Figures and Tropes, in: G. Ueding (ed.), Rhet. zwischen den Wiss., 1991, 149–157 12 F. Striller, De Stoicorum studiis rhetoricis, 1886 13 J. Stroux, De Theophrasti virtutibus dicendi, 1912. G.C.

Elogium

[1] An honorary inscription placed by the Romans on the tombs of deceased men of rank, on statues and wax masks within buildings or on public places. Most of the *elogia* on public display were removed by the censors of

158 BC. Most extant material dates from the Imperial period, where it was at times employed in the exalted reconstruction of times long since past. This also applies to the most important and best known examples of *elogia*, i.e. the inscriptions on the marble statues of the Mars temple on the Forum Augustum. Augustus had them erected together with the statues as a memento of Roman history and legendary prehistory, starting with Aeneas. According to Plin. HN 22,6,13, Augustus wrote these texts himself — probably an exaggeration, but a clear demonstration of the influences exerted by the *princeps* on the design as a whole. Similar and probably at least in parts identical *elogia* are extant in Arretium (Arezzo).

[2] In Roman law, *elogium* carried a number of quite different meanings. In testaments, the term referred to those elements which did not contain any concrete regulations (naming of heirs, bequeathals), but only served to provide reasons (particularly for disinheritance, *exhereditatio*) or to set out intentions ('last wishes' as opposed to 'last will'). Their practical importance was based on the possibility that in the interpretation of a testament the *elogium* could be used to draw conclusions or to prove an irremediable error by the deceased. In late antiquity, *elogium* is used almost as a synonym for the testament as a whole. In the context of police and criminal law, an *elogium* refers predominantly to written record, e.g. of an illegal or criminal offence or a criminal procedure, including the sentence passed. For that reason, *elogium* is occasionally used as an expression for a criminal judgement itself (Amm. Marc. 14,7,2).

1 InscrIt. XIII 3 Elogie, 2 E. Meyer, Einführung in die lat. Epigraphik, ²1973, 66f. 3 A. v. Premerstein, s.v. E., RE 5, 2440–2452 4 P. Zanker, Forum Augustum, 1968, 15f. G.S.

Elpenor (Ἐλπήνωρ; *Elpḗnōr*). Evocative name, whose exact meaning is disputed ('on whom rest the hopes of men' or 'who hopes for manly vigour') [1]. He was one of Odysseus' companions, who were turned into swine by Circe; reverted to his normal shape, he fell off the roof of her house in a sleepy drunken stupor, broke his neck, and was left without burial. His shadow begged Odysseus to bury him, when the latter visited the Underworld; his wish was granted (Hom. Od. 10,551–560; 11,51–83; 12,10; Apollod. epit. 7,17; Hyg. Fab. 125,11–12; Ov. Met. 14,252; Trist. 3,4,19f.; Juv. 15,22). According to Paus. 10,29,8, E. was depicted on → Polygnotus' Nekyia. Etruscan mirrors portray him together with Odysseus, who threatens Circe [2]. His grave was on show in Circeii (Scyl.8; Theophr. Hist. pl. 5,8,3; Plin. HN 15,119).

1 Kamptz 27, 61f., 99f. 2 O. Touchefeu, s.v. E., LIMC 3.1, 721–722.

M. Lossau, E. u. Palinurus, in: WS 14, 1980, 102–124; H. Rohdich, E., in: A&A; 31, 1985, 108–115. R.B.

Elpinice (Ἐλπινίκη; *Elpiníkē*). Daughter of Miltiades and sister or stepsister of → Cimon. A number of scandalous tales grew up around her. Intimations of an incestuous relationship with Cimon are already found in Eupolis (PCG, fr. 221). Another tradition assumes a legal marriage, which would have been entirely possible between stepsiblings; however, there is no doubt that E. was married to → Callias (Nep. Cimon 1). She was supposed to have had an affair with the painter → Polygnotus (Plut. Cimon 4). When Cimon was accused of treason in 463 BC and also when his return from banishment was discussed in 457 BC, E. herself supposedly intervened with Pericles on his behalf (Plut. p. 10). Davies, 8429.

R. Just, Women in Athenian Law and Life, 1980, 109ff. E.S.-H.

Elpis (Ἐλπίς; *Elpís*, from ἔλπομαι/ἐλπίζω; *élpomai/elpízō*, 'expect, hope'). As a term and a character a *vox media*, which in its fundamentally neutral quality ('expectation') alternates between 'hope' (positive or false) and — less often — 'apprehension' (Pl. Leg. 644c; Hom. Od. 16,101; 19,84; Semonides fr. 1,6–7 IEG 2; Pind. Fr. 214).

In Hes. Op. 90–105, the personified E. remains in → Pandora's box, while the other evil spirits (κακά; *kaká*) escape (cf. Babr. 58; [1; 2; 3]). According to Thgn. 1135–1146, E. was the only benevolent power to remain on earth. To her should go the first and the last sacrifice. It was only in the Jewish-Christian context that E. was seen as entirely positive [3; 4].

→ Spes

1 J. N. O'Sullivan, s.v. E., LFE 2, 559 2 V. Leinieks, E. in Hesiod, Works and Days 96, in: Philologus 128, 1985, 1–8 3 E. F. Beall, The Contents of Hesiod's Pandora Jar: Erga 94–98, in: Hermes 117, 1989, 227–230 4 A. Dihle et al., s.v. Hoffnung, RAC 15, 1159–1250.

A. Corcella, E. Punti di vista sul valore delle aspettative humane nel V secolo, in: Annali della Facoltà di Lettere e Filosofia di Bari 27–28, 1984, 41–100; F. W. Hamdorf, s.v. E., LIMC 3.1, 722–725; O. Lachnit, E., Eine Begriffsunt., thesis 1965. R.B.

Elusa Chief place (Amm. Marc. 15,11,14) of the Celtic Elusates (Caes. B Gall. 3,27,1; Plin. HN 4,108) in Aquitania, mod. Eauze (Dép. Gers). Roman *colonia* from the early 3rd cent. AD (CIL XIII 546), in the 4th cent. *metropolis* of the *prov. Novempopulana* (Notitia Galliarum 14). E.O.

Elymaei (Ἐλυμαῖοι; *Elymaîoi*).

[1] Inhabitants of the → Elymais, described by ancient authors mainly as mountain dwellers or rather, in a military context, as mounted archers (cf. i.a. App. Syr. 32; Str. 16,1,17; Liv. 37,40,9).

[2] According to Pol. 5,44,9 neighbours to the inhabitants of → Media Atropatene in the Elburz region along the south-western corner of the Caspian Sea. Plut. Pom-

peius 36 reports of a 'king of the Elymaei and Medes' who sought diplomatic relations with the Romans. Undoubtedly, this refers to the Delymaei (as in Ptol. 6,2,2), who later appear in Byzantine sources as *Dolomítai* (Procopius), *Dilimnítai* (Agathias), *tò Dilmaínon éthnos* (Theophanes), and in Oriental ones as inhabitants of the Sassanid and post-Sassanid province of Dēlān/Dēlām/Dailamān (Gēlām).

W. Felix, s.v. Deylamites, EncIr 7, 1996, 342f. J.W.

Elymais ('Ελυμαΐς; *Elymaís*). Greek name of a region in south-west Iran (*Ḫūzestān*) within the territory of the ancient empire of → Elam. Originally probably mainly used for the mountainous *Baḫtiārī* region (in contrast with the Susiana plains), the term increasingly also included the expanding territory of the Hellenistic-Parthian 'kingdom' of E. [1. 39–45; 2. 3–8].

E./Susiana was one of the political and economic core regions of the Achaemenid and Seleucid empires; however, for the actual E., it is to be expected that some special forms of political relations developed between the central power and the mountain dwellers [8. 747–753]. Ancient authors describe the Hellenistic E. as a region characterized by large sanctuaries of local deities [3. 40–49], whose wealth tempted the Seleucid kings Antiochus III (187 BC) and IV (164 BC) into ill-fated plundering campaigns in order to satisfy their financial needs (Diod. Sic. 28,3; 29,15; Str. 16,1,18 and, respectively, 1 Macc 3,31.37; 6,1–3; 2 Macc 1,13–17; 9,1; Pol. 31,9; Diod. Sic. 31,18a).

Presumably not least for that reason, a local independent dynasty (under Kamnaskires I) was established in about the mid 2nd cent. BC for a short period, but was soon forced to acknowledge Parthian supremacy (Iust. 41,6,8; Str. 16,1,18). 'Kings' of E. continued to reign—and kept the right to mint coins [4. 119–124; 5] as well as other privileges (double diadem: Hdn. 6,2,1) — on behalf of the Arsacids, until the dynasty came to an end in the struggle with the Sassanid ruler → Ardashir [1] at the beginning of the 3rd cent. AD. Archaeological research of the last decades in Bard-e Nešānde, Marǧed-e Soleimān, Tang-e Sarvak and other places has been able to establish an important role for E. in the cultural and artistic history of Iran as a whole (esp. cult, rock carvings, and sculpture) [2; 6; 7].

1 U. Kahrstedt, Artabanos III. und seine Erben, 1950 2 L. Van den Berghe, K. Schippmann, Les reliefs rupestres d'Elymaïde, 1985 3 M. Boyce, F. Grenet, A History of Zoroastrianism 3, 1991 4 M. Alram, Die Vorbildwirkung der arsakidischen Münzprägung, in: Litterae Numismaticae Vindobonenses 3, 1987, 117–146 5 J. Hansman, Coins and Mints of Ancient Elymais, in: Iran 28, 1990, 1–11 6 T.S. Kawami, Monumental Art of the Parthian Period in Iran, 1987 7 H.E. Mathiesen, Sculpture in the Parthian Empire I-II, 1992 8 Briant.

G. Le Rider, Suse sous les Seleucides et les Parthes, 1965. J.W.

Elymi (Ἔλυμοι; *Élymoi*). Pre-Greek tribe in western Sicily, thought by Thucydides (6,2,3; cf. Str. 13,1,53) to be descendants of Trojan refugees (→ Elymus); according to Hellanicus (FGrH 4 F 79b), they were forced out of southern Italy by the Oinotroi. They were generally allied with the Phoenicians and hostile towards the Greeks. Following their Hellenization in the 5th cent. BC, they are no longer mentioned as a tribe. The names of their towns (→ Eryx, Segesta, → Entella) point to Ligurian origins. However, recent archaeological research [1; 2] has unearthed inscriptions [3; 4; 5] expanding our knowledge of the places within the territory of the E., which extended from Belice in the east to the northern line of Monte Iato, Partinico, and Monte Lepre [6]: The finds, which date from the 8th/9th cents. BC ('proto-Elymian'), prove relations of the E. to the Italic regions and seem to point to their Italic descent [7; 8].

1 Gli Elimi e l'area elima fino all'inizio della prima guerra punica. Atti del Seminario di Studi, Palermo — Contessa Entellina, 1989 (ASS IV, XIV-XV, 1988/9) 2 Giornate Internazionali di studi sull'area elima (Gibellina 1991), 1992 3 L. Agostiniani, L'elimo nel quadro linguistico della Sicilia anellenica, in: Giornate Internazionali [see n. 2], 1–11 4 L. Biondi, Nuovi graffiti elimi, in: Giornate Internazionali [see n. 2], 111–127 5 A. M. G. Calascibetta, Un graffito elimo da Monte Castelluzzo di Poggireale, in: ASNP 20,1, 1990, 19–22 6 G. Nenci, Per una definizione dell'area elima, in: ASS [see n. 1], 21–26 7 S. Tusa, Preistoria e protostoria nel territorio degli Elimi, in: Giornate Internazionali [see n. 2], 603–615 8 Id., La 'problematica elima' e testimonianze archeologiche da Marsala, Paceco, Trapani e Buseto Palazzolo, in SicA, 25, 1992, 71–102.

Nissen, 1, 469, 546; A. Schenk Graf v. Stauffenberg, Trinakria, 1963, 22f., 306, 329. GI.F.

Elymian Some sparse indication of the language of the Elymians (→ Elymi) can be gleaned from the legends of coins from Eryx and Segesta (5th cent. BC) as well as the about 300 mainly short graffiti on pottery from Segesta known only since 1960 (8th–6th cents.): it probably was an Indo-European Italic dialect, possibly similar to those of the Siculans. Older attempts to establish a similarity with the 'Ligurian' or 'Illyrian' languages or a non Indo-European origin, have been shown to be untenable.

→ Italy: Languages; → Sicel (Siculan)

Edition: L. Agostiniani, Iscrizioni anelleniche di Sicilia. Le iscrizioni elime, 1977.

Bibliography: U. Schmoll, Die vorgriech. Sprachen Siziliens, 1958; A. Zamboni, Il Siculo, in: A.L. Prosdocimi (ed.), Lingue e dialetti dell' Italia antica, 1978, 951–1012; M. Lejeune, Le problème de l'élyme, in: Gli Elimi e l'area elima, 1989, 339–343. J.U.

Elymus Trojan, eponymous forefather of the → Elymi. He came to Sicily either with Aegestus (Dion. Hal. Ant. Rom. 1,47; 52f.; Tzetz. schol. Lycoph. 965) or Aeneas (Str.13,1,53), and settled in the region around the

→ Eryx. Virgil, who refers to him as Helymus, depicts him as the winner in a competition (Verg. Aen. 5,73; 323). According to Serv. Aen. 5,73, he was the founder of the cities of Asca, Entella, and Egesta. R.B.

Elyrus (Ἔλυρος; *Élyros*). Extensive urban settlement in south-western Crete (Steph. Byz. s.v. E.) near Rodovani east of Kandans. Archaeological data: some Roman ruins (town walls, theatre, aqueduct). Syia was Elyrus' port (Steph. Byz. s.v.). It is possible that E. belonged to the *koinon* of the western Cretan Oreioi, who probably entered an alliance with Magas of Cyrene between 280 and 250 BC [1. 1; 2. 468]; from 183 BC, it was part of the alliance of thirty-one Cretan cities with Eumenes II (Syll. 3 627,7). Donation of a bronze goat in Delphi (Paus. 10,16,5). In late antiquity, E. was a bishop's seat (Not. Episc. 8,229; 9,138). The settlement was abandoned in the 9th cent.

1 M. Guarducci (ed.), Inscriptiones Creticae vol. 2, 1939 2 StV 3.

C. Bursian, Geogr. von Griechenland 2, 1872, 548f.; Lauffer, Griechenland, 216; I.F. Sanders, Roman Crete, 1982, 171. H.SO.

Elysium (Ἠλύσιον; *Ēlýsion*, *Elysium*). In the beginning of its tradition E. was a 'paradise' for heroes. It appears only once in Homer: in Od. 4,561–5 Proteus tells Menelaus that he will not die but the gods will instead send him, as Zeus' son-in-law, to a paradise with perfect climate, to the Elysian fields at the end of the earth, where Rhadamanthys resides. Belief in a paradise for an elite few is not at all a significant feature of Homeric eschatology but it becomes increasingly important after Homer. In Hes. Op. 167–173 the paradise that heroes attain, instead of dying, is named μακάρων νῆσοι (*makárōn nêsoi*), 'Islands of the Blessed', but otherwise corresponds to E. The paradisiacal concept of the Islands of the Blessed came to predominate Greek eschatologies (even → Leucae, where Achilles was taken by Thetis, bore features of such an island, Procl. EpGF p. 47), without E. ever disappearing; it continued to be mentioned for example in Ibycus fr. 10 PMG; Simonides fr. 53 PMG; Apoll. Rhod. 4,811; Paus. 8,53,5; Apollod. 3,39; Epit. 6,30 and Quint. Smyrn. 2, 650–2. Because of the extremely close connection between → Rhadamanthys and E., Pherecydes' account (FGrH 3 F 84) of Hermes' carrying off Alcmene after her death to the Islands of the Blessed, on Zeus' orders, and marrying her there to Rhadamanthys can be seen as an early identification of E. with the Islands of the Blessed or, more likely, as a merging of the two (cf. also Pind. Ol. 2,75, another connection of Rhadamanthys and the Islands of the Blessed). E. finally ends up being described as a 'field' on the Islands of the Blessed (cf. Lucian Jupiter confutatus 17; Ver hist. 2, 6–14).

Like E. the Islands of the Blessed were initially a paradise for heroes but then, as concepts of death and burial changed and gave rise to hopes for life after death, they became a paradise for the righteous, a place attainable even by ordinary souls, if they had led good and just lives, after they had been sentenced by the Judges of the Underworld, Rhadamanthys and Minos (e.g. Pind. Ol. 2,68–80; Pl. Grg. 523a-b; E. Lucian Cataplus 24; De luctu 7; Dialogi mortuorum 24,1 Macleod). A few post-classical tomb epigrams express the belief that those interred had not died but had gone to the Islands of the Blessed and were living in E. (e.g. [1]). Str. 3,2,13 refers to the Homeric E. as 'the dance-floor of the god-fearing' (εὐσεβῶν χορός, *eusebōn chorós*). In Virgil's version of Platonic eschatology E. replaced the *makárōn nêsoi*: in Pl. Grg. 524a behind the meadow where the dead come for judgement there are two roads, one of which leads to the *makárōn nêsoi*, the other to → Tartarus; in Verg. Aen. 6 540–3 the road has two branches, one leading to E., the other to Tartarus. The term *elysium* is not uncommon in Latin literature (cf. e.g. Sen. Herc.f. 744; Sen. Tro. 159; Ov. Am. 2,6,49; 3,9,60).

The view that E. is of Minoan origin is a modern misconception; even the term E. has now been established as Greek. Not long before the epics assumed their final form, the Homeric E. developed as one single construct from a combination of elements of different origin. Their integration expressed the novel idea that — in stark contrast to the prevailing Homeric view that all heroes, even Hercules, had to die — some great heroes did not die but lived on in a paradise at the end of the earth. The name E. was one of the merged elements, the connection between a Minoan ruler and life after death was another; this latter also appears in another form in Hom. Od. 11,567–71, where Rhadamanthys' brother Minos enjoys a privileged position among the dead.

1 W. Peek, Griech. Versinschr. I, 1955, no. 1830.

W. Burkert, E., in: Glotta 39, 1961, 208–213; R. Garland, The Greek way of death, 1985, 60–1, 156; M. Gelinne, Les champs Elysées et les îles des Bienheureux chez Homère, Hesiode et Pindare. Essai de mise au point, in: Les études classiques 56, 1988, 225–240; L. Malten, E. und Rhadamanthys, in: JDAI 28, 1913, 35–51; C. Sourvinou-Inwood, 'Reading' Greek death, 1995, 17–56; R. Vermeule, Aspects of death in early Greek art and poetry, 1979, 72, 76–7, 229–230 fn. 58; Waser, s.v. Elysion, RE V 2, 2470–2476; M.L. West (ed.), Hes. erg., 1978, 192–5. C.S.I.

Emanation (ἀπόρροια/*apórrhoia*, *emanatio*). The term emanation is used to describe the relationship between an origin and what was derived from it; it is based on the concept of discharge of fluidity. It was significant in Gnosticism and Neoplatonism. Gnosticism used the concept of emanation to diminish the distance between an extraterrestrial god and the world. Plotinus used the term sparingly and with qualifications and emphasized that the origin is not diminished in the process (Plot. Enneades 3,8,10; 3,4,3,26f.): The spirit emanates from the overflow of the One (Enneades 5,2,1,9), and the soul from it. Even Christianity (following Solomon, Proverbs 7,25) made use of emanation initially, to describe the son's subordination to the father, but this was condemned by Athanasius as gnostic. The concept of emanation began then to disappear in the East but survived longer in the West, even if Augustine did not admit it into the doctrine of creation or of the Trinity.

H. DÖRRIE, E. Ein unphilosophisches Wort im spätantiken Denken, in: Platonica Minora, 1976, 70–88; M. HARL, A propos d'un passage du Contre Eudome de Grégoire de Nysse ... (1967), in: Id., Le déchiffrement du sens, 1993, 281–290; K. KREMER, HWdPh 2, 1972, 445–448; J. RATZINGER, RAC 4, 1959, 1219–1228. S.M.-S.

Emancipatio Under Roman law the → *pater familias* generally held paternal authority over his children for as long as he lived. Releasing sons from the control of the *pater* was possible only by means of a formal and complicated legal process: the *emancipatio*. It was linked to formal alienation by → *mancipatio*, by which not only a *dominus* could sell his slaves but also a father his sons. By means of this 'sale' a father gave his sons into servitude with another *pater*. Even in the period of the Twelve Tablets (5th cent. BC) no suitable business practice other than the 'sale' was available for that commercial purpose. Because of that background, however, it often happened that the new holder of authority resold the son to the *pater*. Otherwise, the son came under the authority of his *pater* again, if the purchaser gave him his freedom as if he were a slave. The Twelve Tablets (4,2, and [4] as well) had the provision that: *si pater ter filium venum dederit, filius a pater liber esto* (the son is free of his *pater* 's control after the third sale). That provision formed the basis of the *emancipatio*: it could be triggered by the *pater* 's selling his son symbolically three times and then the purchaser's granting him his freedom by → *manumissio*, to which he had been fiduciarily committed from the start. By itself, though, that still did not suffice, because in the process of manumission the 'purchaser' would acquire the rights of patron (→ *patronatus*), e.g. the claim to service (→ *operae libertorum*) and a right to inheritance on the death of the freedman. Therefore, the 'purchaser' sold the son back to the father one more time and the father then gave him his freedom. The 'expedient' of the threefold sale was necessary because the *patria potestas* was so strong in law that it not only revived by the manumission on the part of the purchaser, but also remained unaffected by the manumission on the part of the *pater* himself.

As the Twelve Tablet provision specifically mentioned sons, the *emancipatio* of daughters and nieces was easier: in their case a once only *mancipatio* sufficed to put an end to paternal authority, after re-mancipation and manumission by the former parent. In the later Principate the father could be obliged under the → *cognitio extra ordinem* to perform a promised *emancipatio* (Papinian Dig. 37,12,5). The emperors of the Late Period, Constantine in particular, sought to encourage *emancipatio* by offering the *pater* inducements. The *emancipatio* itself, however, survived until the vulgarization of the law in late antiquity. In AD 531, Justinian (Cod. Iust. 8,48,6) radically simplified the *emancipatio*: from then on it sufficed for the father to make a declaration, with the child's assent, before an authorized imperial official.

The emancipated person was *sui iuris*, that is to say fully competent in terms of law, contracts and property. At the same time he was excluded from the laws of succession, as earlier constituted, so that no share of the inheritance was legally conferred upon him by his *pater*. The praetor later granted an emancipated person a 'legal' right of succession in the class *unde liberi* (on behalf of children), which, however, they had to offset with property acquired after the *emancipatio* (→ *collatio*).

1 WIEACKER, RRG, 331f. 2 H. HONSELL, TH. MAYER-MALY, W. SELB, Röm. Recht [4]1987, 418f. 3 KASER, RPR I, 68–71 4 D. FLACH, Die Gesetze der frühen röm. Republik, 1994, 130f. G.S.

Emar Central city of the kingdom of Aštata at the knee of the Euphrates, near Maskana in north-west Syria, *c.* 100 km east of → Aleppo; the Byzantine name was Barbalissos, the Islamic name Bālis. Known already from the palace archives of → Ebla and → Mari, this trading town was studied archaeologically in 1972–76 by a French team which uncovered several temples and residences from the late Bronze Age and discovered *c.* 900 clay tablets — primarily in Akkadian language [2]. Since 1996, a German-Syrian mission has been conducting excavations and has reached layers from the middle and early Bronze Age [8].

In contrast to its great geographical and commercial significance as a place of contact between Mesopotamia, Anatolia, and the Mediterranean coast, E. did not exert any political influence beyond its own region but was under the rule of larger powers such as Ebla, Jamḫad (→ Aleppo), and the Hittite kingdom (→ Ḫattusa). The cuneiform material consists primarily of legal documents, which offer information about local institutions and customs and also reveal the effects of the Hittite conquest on society and writing system. In addition, the finds include a number of rituals of local origin, lexical → lists, texts of omens and conjuration (cf. → Divination) as well as literary compositions from the Sumeric-Babylonian scribal tradition.

1 A. ARCHI, Imâr au IIIème millénnaire d'après les archives d'Ebla, in: Mari 6, 1990, 21–38 2 D. ARNAUD, Emar: Recherches au pays d'Aštata, 4 vols., 1985–1987 3 Id., Textes syriens de l'âge du bronze récent, 1991
4 D. BEYER, E. IV: Les sceaux, 2001 5 Id. (ed.), Meskéné-E.: Dix ans de travaux 1972–1982, 1982 6 M. W. CHAVALAS (ed.), E.: The History, Rel., and Culture of a Syrian Town in the Late Bronze Age, 1996 7 J.-M. DURAND, La cité-état d'Imâr à l'époque des rois de Mari, in: Mari 6, 1990, 39–92 8 U. FINKBEINER, E. & Bālis 1996–1998, in: Berytus 44, 1999–2000, 5–34. B. FA.

Emathia (Ἠμαθία; *Ēmathía*). Old name for Lower Macedonian regions (Hom. Il. 14,226; Str. 7, fr. 11), later only an imprecise poetic term for Macedonia west of the → Axius without Pieria (Ptol. 3,13,9). By E. Pol. 23,10,4 understood Paeonia, Str. l.c. (cf. Steph. Byz. s.v.) knew of a city E.

N.G. L. HAMMOND, A History of Macedonia I, 1972, 155f. MA.ER.

Embas see → Shoes

Embaterion (ἐμβατήριον/*embatḗrion*, sc. μέλος/*mélos*, ᾆσμα/*âisma*). Military march, often sung, usually played by an *auletes* (flute-player), although Phillis of Delos speaks of κινήσεις ἐμβατηρίους (*kinḗseis embateríous*) in connection with ἀρχαίους κιθαρῳδούς (*archaíous kitharōidoús*; Ath. 1,21f–22a). The proto-Corinthian Chigi vase of *c.* 630 BC (Rome, VG 22679) shows warriors marching with a flute-player (cf. Thuc. 5,70). The rhythm was undoubtedly anapaestic: Dion Chrys. 2,59 (PMG 856; cf. PMG 857) quotes one such song, supposedly by Tyrtaeus. Ath. 14,630f recounts that the *embatḗria* of the Spartans were called *enhóplia* (not to be confused with the rhythm of the same name in dances in full arms) and that the Spartans sang the poems of Tyrtaeus on the way to war. Plut. Lycurgus 5,22 mentions the Spartan *embatḗrios paián* as well as the *kastóreion* (→ Work songs). According to Heph., Alcman is said to have been keen to replace the anapaests with spondees in catalectic anapaestic verses; Marius Victorinus calls the anapaestic catalectic trimeter *embatḗrion* (TB 13 (iv),(v),(vi),(xi) PMGF). These lyrical *embatḗria* are possibly an intermediate step between war songs and the anapaestic marches of tragic *parodoi*: Polybius tells us that the youth of Arcadia practised '*embatḗria* in theatres' (ἐμβατήρια ... ἐν τοῖς θεάτροις) (4,20,12). Outside the Peloponnese we know of such songs on Crete: Hsch. s.v. ἰβυκτήρ (*ibyktḗr*; cod. ἰβηκ-; *ibēk-*) mentions this as an epithet of Ibrias (cod. *Íbrios*; cf. → Hybrias), singer of *embatḗria*. E.R.

Embateuein (ἐμβατεύειν; *embateúein*). In Athens the seizure of immovable objects (even ships, Dem. Or. 33,6) by 'stepping upon' them, due to a claim of ownership (law of succession of the son of the house, right of distraint, court judgement). In Egyptian papyri ἐμβαδεία (*embadeía*) signified official seizure as the third stage of compulsory acquisition in real estate matters.

→ Succession, law of

A. KRÄNZLEIN, Eigentum und Besitz im griech. Recht, 1963, 94ff. A. R. W. HARRISON, The Law of Athens I, 1968, 156; 272; 283 H.-A. RUPPRECHT, Einführung in die Papyruskunde, 1994, 149. G.T.

Emblemata see → Mosaic

Embossing see → Coin production

Emendation of texts An important part of textual criticism are conjectures (emendations of passages that are corrupted in the editor's opinion). There are no → autographs or authorized → copies extant of any ancient literary work. Since it is impossible to produce entirely error-free handwritten copies, texts became increasingly corrupted during → scribal reproduction (→ Text, corruption of the). Critical readers already attempted to improve corrupted texts in antiquity (→ Textual history) and during the Middle Ages. But only in the Renaissance did the number of interventions into apparent text anomalies (violation of syntactic rules or contradiction of the usual language usage of an author) increase, e.g. by means of → interpolation. → Papyri found at a later date (often at least a millenium older than previously known medieval MSS) often supported the correctness of the emendation (e.g., P Oxy 2545 confirms conjecture of BLAYDES' ἑκάστοθ' ὡς in Aristoph. Equ. 1070), though the examination of previously neglected medieval MSS has yielded few results. All modern scientific editions contain a multitude of conjectures that are supposed to reflect the presumed wording of the original. The problem with this is that the ancient languages have on occasion not been examined in sufficient detail, that ancient authors apparently give words special meanings and that the correct assessment of possible language use is no longer possible because the completeness of the original stock is lost.

The humanists of the 15th cent. had little Greek but all the better Latin linguistic knowledge, cf. the anonymous emendations (corrections) of the Lucrecius text in the Cod. Laur. 35.31. HEINSIUS was a remarkable Latin philologist who often made several suggestions at once for textual problems in Ovid [1]. R. BENTLEY'S knowledge of both ancient languages was equal but his logical approach occasionally went amiss. In the 19th cent. J. N. MADVIG for Latin and C. G. COBET for Greek applied the grammatical rules very strictly — with greater success (correct text) for prose than for poetry. There was an insistence on being able to find the inherent logical precision of the texts of ancient authors. While this method was defended in particular by A. NAUCK, it was criticized by BLAYDES (very large number of conjectures in Sophocles and Aristophanes), whose emendations did not withstand crutiny. One of the most typical examples of a conjectural critique for Greek was provided by J. JACKSON, although he never produced a complete edition [2].

→ Philology; → Scribes; → Textual history; → Text, corruption of the ; → PHILOLOGICAL METHODS

1 R. J. TARRANT, in: P. HARDIE et al. (ed.), Ovidian Transformations, 1999, 288–300 2 J. JACKSON, Marginalia scaenica, 1955.

L. HAVET, Manuel de critique verbale, 1911; P. MAAS, Textkritik, ³1957; R. G. M. NISBET, How Textual Conjectures Are Made, in: Materiali e discussioni 26, 1991, 65–

91; G. PASQUALI, Storia della tradizione e critico del testo, [2]1952; M. L. WEST, Textual Criticism and Editorial Technique, 1973, 53–59.

S. H. and N. W.

Emerald (σμάραγδος/*smáragdos*, Lat. *smaragdus* or *zmaragdus*). Greenish gemstone, variety of beryl, in the famous ring of → Polycrates [1] (in Hdt. 3,41) among others, one of the 12 stones of → Aaron (Ex 39,10). Theophr. De lapidibus 25 [1. 66] mentions the copper mines of → Cyprus and an island near Chalcedon as the main places where the stone is found. Plin. HN 37,62–75 distinguishes 12 types depending on their origin. Particularly transparent and shiny mirroring specimens were highly regarded.

1 D. E. EICHHOLZ (ed.), Theophrastus, De lapidibus, 1965.

A. SCHRAMM, s. v. Smaragd, RE Suppl. 7, 1217–1219.

C. HÜ.

Emergency, state of is the extreme form of an internal crisis, to which state authorities respond with extraordinary, i.e. unlawful measures. A similar response to internal crises by state authorities did not arise in the Greek city states. As responses to crisis-like situations there, we find trials against individual citizens, instigated by other individual citizens (see → Herms, mutilation of the); or on occasion groups sought to resolve a crisis by means of a *putsch* (see → Oligarchy), or conditions developed similar to a civil war (→ *Stasis*). In Rome the state of emergency could be declared only by the state authorities and involved the suspension of a citizen's personal rights of protection (→ *Provocatio*; *lex Sempronia de capite civis*). Declaration of a state of emergency in a concrete situation is always a question of relative strengths and so also a matter of controversy. Caesar provides the best definition of this state of affairs (B Civ. 1,7,5f.): The state of emergency has been declared to proceed against pernicious legislation, the arbitrary rule of the popular tribunes and a popular uprising, which involved the occupation of temples and commanding heights (*in perniciosis legibus, in vi tribunicia, in secessione populi templis locisque editioribus occupatis*).

During the → Struggle of the orders (until 287 BC) the dictatorship (→ *Dictator*) functioned as a patrician state of emergency-magistrature against the plebeians. From the 2nd cent. the Senate, as the designated guardian of the constitution, set up extraordinary courts in cases of widespread criminality (*quaestiones extraordinariae*; → *Quaestio*), e.g. in the Bacchanalian scandal of 186 BC (→ Bacchanalia; → *Senatus consultum de Bacchanalibus*). In 133 BC, however, there was no legal instrument available against the popular tribune Ti. → Sempronius Gracchus, who was accused of insurrection: in the absence of a decision by the Senate → Cornelius [I 84] Scipio Nasica set himself, as a private citizen, at the head of volunteers by virtue of an *evocatio/coniuratio* (levy at a time of sudden external danger). With the *senatus consultum ultimum* (*videant consules, ne quid detrimenti res publica capiat*, 'the consuls should ensure that the state suffers no damage') the Senate found — first of all in 121 BC against Gaius → Sempronius Gracchus — a mechanism against popular tribunes who were a nuisance, in that it assured the consuls of its solidarity in use of unlawful measures and urged them to mobilize the *boni* ('citizens loyal to the State '). The implicit assumption of *hostes* (→ *Hostis*) within the city was formalized in 88 BC in the *hostis*-declaration against Marius [I 1] and some of his supporters. L. Cornelius [I 90] Sulla went far beyond the state of emergency and the means to counteract when he established his dictatorship and the → Proscriptions.

Instituting a constitutional procedure (*lex Lutatia* and *lex Plautia de vi*) was to no avail, as became evident in the conspiracy of → Catilina in 63. In the riots that were mainly instigated by Clodius [I 4] and Annius [I 14] Milo in the 50s BC all mechanisms for maintaining public order failed to a large extent. The riots, however, did not affect the foundations of the Republican constitution. The dictatorship of Caesar, Cicero's extension of legitimate self-defence to the self-declared protectors of the Senate Junius [I 10] Brutus and Cassius [I 10]) (Phil. 11,26–28), and the so-called 2nd → Triumvirate of Antonius [I 9], Octavianus and Lepidus (*lex Titia* of 27 November 43 BC), with yet again the dread proscriptions, were no more than symptoms of a state of emergency in the Republic that was collapsing in civil wars.

1 L. A. BURCKHARDT, Politische Strategien der Optimaten in der späten röm. Republik, 1988 2 W. KUNKEL, Staatsordnung und Staatspraxis der röm. Republik, 1995 3 A. W. LINTOTT, Violence in Republican Rome, 1968 4 CHR. MEIER, Der Ernstfall im alten Rom, in: A. PEISL, A. MOHLER (ed.), Der Ernstfall, 1979, 40–73 5 A. DUPLÀ ANSUATEGUI, Videant consules. Las medidas de excepción en la crisis de la República Romana, 1990 6 W. NIPPEL, Public Order in Ancient Rome, 1995 7 G. PLAUMANN, Das sog. Senatusconsultum ultimum, die Quasidiktatur der späten röm. Republik, in: Klio 13, 1913, 321–386 8 J.V. UNGERN-STERNBERG, Unt. zum spätrepublikanischen Notstandsrecht, 1970.

J.v.U.-S.

Emeriti see → Veterans

Emesa (Amm. Marc. 14,8,9; Plin. HN 5,19,81 *Hemeseni*), city in Syria on the Orontes, today's Ḥimṣ (< Byzantine Χέμψ; *Chémps*). According to archaeological evidence it had been settled from the 3rd millennium BC but E. has been known to us only from Pompey's time as the seat of a clan of Arab 'kings', who were Roman vassals from the time of → Herodes Agrippa I (Jos. Ant. Iud. 18,5,4; 19,8,1; → Aristobulus [5]) and M. Iulius Agrippa II. (Jos. Ant. Iud. 20,7,1), who were related to them until the end of the Jewish War (Jos. Ant. Iud. 20,8,4; Jos. BI 2,18,9; 3,4,2; 7,7,1; Tac. Hist. 2,81; 5,1). After their regime was brought to an end by Domitian, a related clan of priests of E.s → Baal, who was called

→ Elagabal and venerated in a famous temple (Avien. 1082–1093), stepped into the political limelight. The priestly daughter Iulia Domna, who later inspired Philostratus to write his *Vita Apollonii Tyanensis*, became the wife of the later emperor Septimius Severus, on whose striving for universal dominion she conferred some legitimacy, and mother of Caracalla. In AD 218 her sister Iulia Maesa had the son of one of her daughters, Iulia Soaemias, proclaimed emperor. According to the *Historia Augusta* he received the name of his god → Elagabal [2]). She repeated that action in 222 with the son of her other daughter, Iulia Mammaea, who (according to Origen) cultivated a literary clique. Like Elagabalus, that son was a priest of the god of E. and was called as an emperor Severus Alexander. → Heliodorus, author of the *Aithiopiká*, came from E. The exegete Eusebius, who was accused of Sabellianism, worked here in E. as Bishop until 359; likewise, around 400, the Platonist Nemesius. In 636 E. came under Arab control. The Umayyad commander Ḫālid b. al-Walīd had a mosque tomb on a church square.

F. Altheim, Die Soldatenkaiser, 1938; Id., Helios und Heliodor von E., 1942; Id., Literatur und Gesellschaft 1, 1948; K. Gross, s.v. Aurelianus, RAC 1, 1004ff.,; Id., s.v. Elagabal, RAC 4, 987ff.; E. Kornemann, Große Frauen des Altertums, [3]1952; M. Moussli, Tell Homs (Qala'at Ḥoms), in: Zeitschrift des Deutschen Palästina-Vereins 100, 1984, 9–11. C.C.

Eminentissimus Rank at the Roman imperial court; originally used of officials from the equestrian class. With their growing status as representatives and direct subordinates of the emperor (→ *praefectus praetorio*), their position and form of address was brought into line with the senatorial *summae potestates* (Dig. 1,11,1) and its nomenclature (cf. Cod. Theod. 12,12,3). In the courtly order of ranking (*ordo dignitatum*) in late antiquity the title then had the same meaning as *excellentissimus*, *magnificentissimus*, *gloriosissimus*, *sublimissimus* or *illustrissimus* (even in their non-superlative forms) and was reserved for people of the first courtly and senatorial rank (ahead of the *spectabiles* and the *clarissimi*): the *praefecti praetorio*, *praefecti urbi*, the *consules*, the *magistri militum*, *magistri officiorum*, *praepositi sacri cubiculi*, the *quaestor sacri palatii*, *comes sacrarum largitionum*, *comes rerum privatarum* and the *proconsulares et legati* (Cod. Iust. 12,3–7; 1,35,2). From the rank of *eminentissimus* derives the church title 'Eminence' for cardinals, still in use today.
→ Senatus; → Spectabilis

Jones LRE 378, 525. C.G.

Emmaus
[1] (Ἐμμαοῦς; *Emmaoûs*, Arabic ʿAmwās). City situated *c.* 30 km north-west of Jerusalem. In 166/5 BC → Judas Maccabeus defeated the → Seleucids at E.. In the Jewish War → Vespasian stationed the 5th Legion there. Re-founded at the start of the 3rd cent. AD at the time of Iulius Africanus, E. was given the name Nicopolis. From the 4th cent. to the period of the Crusades E. was considered to be the place where the resurrected Jesus appeared to two disciples (Lk 24, 13).
[2] (Arabic al-Qubaiba) Its identification with the E. named by Luke, first demonstrated in the 13th cent. and especially espoused by the Franciscans, became established from the 15th cent. and relies on the fact that the 11 km distance to Jerusalem corresponds to the 60 *stadia* mentioned by Luke.
[3] (Ἀμμαοῦς; *Ammaoûs*). At E., 30 km from Jerusalem, → Vespasian settled 800 veterans (Jos. BI 7, 217), probably identical with Κολωνία (*Kolōnia*, Arabic al-Qālūniya, (*c.* 6 km north-west of Jerusalem).

L.-H. Vincent, F.-M. Abel, Emmaus: sa basilique et son histoire, 1932; B. Bagatti, Emmaus-Qubeibeh, 1993. J.P.

Emmenidae Sicilian dynasty of tyrants from Acragas, who were closely related to the → Deinomenids in Syracuse (genealogical table with the Deinomenids). W.ED.

Emmenides (Ἐμμενίδης; *Emmenídēs*). Writer of New Comedy [1] known to us only epigraphically; won a victory at the Lenaia in the 2nd cent. BC.

1 PCG V, 1986, 130. B.BÄ.

Emmer The emmer (Babylonian *kunasu*) variety of wheat was well known from 2800 BC and was the second most important form of grain in the whole of the Ancient Near East, as e.g. in Ugarit (*ksm*; Hebrew *kussemet*) [2. 114f.] and the Jewish colony in Elephantine (Aramaic *kntn*) [4. 83]. Its yield could occasionally be higher than that of barley [1. 96]. That emmer was supplanted by the more resistant barley because of increasing saltiness is now disputed; barley's higher status is thought to derive from its 'superior reliability' [5]. The oldest texts distinguish between black, white and red emmer, from which → beers were produced. Groats, → flour and → bread from emmer were appreciated; they even played a role in cult [3. 25f.]. As the corn of spelt wheats like emmer does not detach during threshing, it has to be roasted and crushed; later texts call the husked emmer 'pistachio nut', by which is meant a kind of pearls of unripe emmer. Emmer was also made into a soup. Since its rediscovery in old texts at the beginning of the 20th cent. it is being cultivated again.
→ Grain; → Barley; → Wheat

1 K. Maekawa, Acta Sumerologica 4, 1982 2 L. Milano, in: Dialoghi di archeologia, N.S. 3, 1981, 88–91 3 L. Milano, s.v. Mehl, RLA 8/1–2, 1993 4 B. Porten, Archives from Elephantine, 1968 5 M. A. Powell, in: ZA 75, 1985, 12–19.

F. Hrozny, Das Getreide im alten Babylonien, 1914; I. Löw, Die Flora der Juden I, 1928, 767–776; Bull. of Sumerian Agriculture 1, 1984, 9, 12f., 18, 24f., 33f., 51–56, 81, 90, 92, 109, 114–152.; D. Zohary, M. Hopf, Domestication of plants in the Old World, [2]1993, 39–47. MA.S.

Emodus (Ἡμωδός/*Ēmōdós*, Ἡμωδὸν ὄρος/*Ēmōdòn óros*, [*H*]*emodus*; derived through Middle Indian from the Old Indian *Haimavata*, also Imaos, Ἴμαον ὄρος; *Ímaon óros*, *Imaus*, from Old Indian *Himavān*, 'covered with snow'). Name of the eastern part of the Hindukuš-Pamir-Himalaya taken as one single mountain range. There were several views about the location of this mountain range; sometimes Imaos was named as the more easterly (Eratosth. in Str. 15,1, 11; Plin. HN 6, 64; Arr. Ind. 2, 3 et al.), sometimes Emodos. (Ptol.).

O. VON HINÜBER, in: G. WIRTH, O. VON HINÜBER (ed. and trans.), Arrian. Der Alexanderzug – Indische Gesch., 1985, 1084. K.K.

Emona now Ljubljana (Laibach). Favourably situated on the amber route and on the link between the Balkans and Italy on the banks of the navigable Ljubljanica. Intensively settled from the 12th cent. BC (Necropoleis from the Urnfield culture and the early Iron Age). Probably a military settlement under Augustus (garrison of the *legio XV Apollinaris*). City founded as *colonia Iulia Emona* (Plin. HN 3,147), systematically designed in rectangular form (522 × 432 m) around the → *cardo* and → *decumanus maximus*; city wall with four main gates and 26 towers.

In the 1st cent. AD. E. belonged to Pannonia; from the 2nd cent. to the 10th region of Italy. Indigenous cults of Aecorna and Laburus are attested. With the advance of Maximinus in AD 238, E. was burnt down (Hdn. 8,1,4; SHA Maximinus 21), reconstruction followed. Zos. 5,29 attests to the presence of West Goths under Alarich in 408. E. was seat of a bishop from the 4th cent.; Jerome (Ep. 11; 12) communicated with Christians from E. An early Christian centre (*insula XXXII*) of the 4th cent. was extended at the beginning of the 5th cent. with a cathedral and baptistery.

L. PLESNICAR-GEC, Old Christian centre in Emona, 1983; J. ŠAŠEL, s.v. E., RE Suppl. 11, 540–578; Id., Zur verwaltungstechnischen Zugehörigkeit E.s, in: Acta Antiqua Academiae Scientiarum Hungaricae 41, 1989, 169–174. H.GR.

Empedocles (Ἐμπεδοκλῆς; *Empedoklês*).

[1] from Agrigentum Pre-Socratic (*c.* 490–430 BC). His most important works: the Nature poem 'On the origins of the world' (so-called Περὶ φύσεως, *Perì phýseōs*) and the 'Purifications' (Καθαρμοί, *Katharmoí*), both in epic hexameters. The following presentation distinguishes between the two works. [1; 2] argue for unity.

A. SOURCES B. THE NATURE POEM (Περὶ φύσεως) C. THE 'PURIFICATIONS' D. THE STRASBOURG EMPEDOCLES PAPYRUS

A. SOURCES

A large part of our knowledge about E. depends on the quotations and comments in Plutarch's *Moralia*; his monograph is unfortunately lost. For the most part, however, we are indebted to Aristotle and his commentators, especially → Simplicius, who used the original text of the Nature poem and transcribed other excerpts from it. On the other hand, without the → Doxography we would often be unable to fathom the sense of individual verses quoted elsewhere; it provides us with the framework and connects the epic episodes that belong together.

B. THE NATURE POEM (Περὶ φύσεως)

The central ontological intuition is focussed on the One; it maintains the Eleatic principle of Being with its predicates but gives a radically new interpretation as a unifying force, bound more to life and bound more strongly to appearance, that dominates the whole system right to the end. Worldly objects are indeed kept apart from one another, but are even more often brought together. Philosophically the change in overall perspective, detaching itself from the strict logic of → Parmenides, ended up bringing into the foreground the becoming of Being. In the first phase of this theogony there consequently reigned an integrated, all-encompassing principle, alone and self-contained as the god Sphaerus, named after the geometrical sphere, monotheistic perfection, so to speak, from which everything else, other gods first, is derived.

The origin, holding everything together that derives from it, is God, and yet this initial state is not eternal; after its own destruction it survives, en route to its own restoration, in all worldly forms. No necessity imposed itself on the divine, timeless status of bliss. If it dissolved 'after the oracle of necessity' (B115, cf. 110 BOLLACK), that demonstrates that this law expresses a meaningfulness, standing over the gods and making them useful to the perfecting and deifying of mankind. The god becomes finality, he has no existence outside the process of becoming. His reign is overcome by an adversary who, as his restraining element, is an aspect of himself; he bears the name 'strife' or 'hate', Neikos, in the framework of an accented polyonymy. This second generation of gods involves a pair of abstract powers that incarnate themselves in the worldly process as an outer and an inner and share the realms between them. Neikos' counterpart is called Love (generally Philotes). The real creative force is reserved for a female figure who is dependent on her partner in a radical contra-legality and collaborates with him on the basis of separation. To that extent it is not a genuine dualism but a constantly reassessed attempt to master the relationship between destruction and reconstitution, to integrate Non-being and so overcome it.

The third generation of elements, similarly conceived of as proceedings and as divine forces, arise as compact masses in a transitional stage when all elementary particles that were mixed together in the sphere of Sphairos withdraw from the supremacy of separation. The number of four elements has a central place in E. In contrast to other systems the four elements are equal powers, as Aristotle was to codify them later in his own world system. Seen from the revised religious perspective, it is easy to understand why E. equated them to the Olympic gods. Thus, for example, Zeus is called fire, and Hera, air. The elements survive in combinations of, e.g. on land or in the sea. This is the explanation for the sun's corporeal disappearance. Particles of fire are mixed with air in the hemisphere of light that circles the earthly globe. This globe now has the ability to gather beams from the cosmic light source surrounding it. It thus reproduces itself in a circular, mirror image of itself on the crystal heavenly arch — a shining reflection of the earth. People think it is the sun, although it is nothing but light and fire. The astronomical construction demonstrates how strongly the components ought to relate to one another and the whole entity ought to be organically held together.

Understanding the cosmogony in its individual stages within the one, unifying principle is *sine qua non* for reconstructing the 'Nature poem' and putting the extant quotations into order. People have often assumed — not without a certain naïveté being attributed to the author — that E. had, experimentally as it were, crafted two cosmogonies, one of love and the other of hatred. That was to misunderstand the sense of reciprocal dominance. The two worlds theory (not yet in KARSTEN [3]) was postulated towards the end of the 19th cent. and has been constantly re-advocated; even today it has its supporters [4]. Actually, the 'at one time' and 'at another' that are so characteristic of E. refer to the separation, incessant even on a microscopic plane, of contrary influences and pulse beats. Hatred is merely a destructive force. Conversely, there is nothing that cannot be achieved by love. A special significance attaches to the genetic representation. In contrast to Parmenides, the Having Become is incorporated in the Being. Above all the description of demiurgical creativity has the advantage of showing the dynamic force of the aetiological principle and outlining an overall plan. Plato was inspired by it in the *Timaeus*. There is no lack of teleology in E. either.

The doxographic tradition is especially informative for an understanding of the origin of the living creatures that each presuppose various phases of cosmic upheavals. In one episode, like a demiourgos in his workshop, Aphrodite created individual limbs; these were in some way autonomous units. They existed on their own behalf until later, though at first haphazardly and uncoordinatedly, they came together; a bull's head paired up with a human neck. Here, E. referred to the monsters of mythology and gave new meaning to mankind's animal past. A harmony was reached when in the third phase figures that had their origin in the earth (σπάρτοι; *spártoi*, 'grown from seed') shot out of the pregnant earth and then, in keeping with predetermined paradigms, developed into homogeneous shapes. Even natural history is subservient to new conditions of life. Mankind and animals, too, develop into superelevated creatures, and thus poetic imagination is closely associated with the decisive battle that E. led against blood

sacrifice and with the migration of the soul (metempsychosis).

C. THE 'PURIFICATIONS'

Reconstructing the *Katharmoí* presents even greater difficulties. It has had a more meagre transmission. However, an attempt is perhaps not altogether futile. The reshaping of human coexistence is based on the same preconditions as in the other poem. Along with the structure of the cosmic cycle, the relationship between the two works is *the* great Empedoclean question. As long as scientific discovery was placed in the foreground, by virtue of the interest that extends, as in Aristotle, to all natural phenomena, it has been difficult to reconcile the mystical, religious content and the plaintive tones that rivalled tragic choral songs with the interest in biological science. Debate today is no longer limited by that deceptive aporia; nevertheless, the contrast further obstructs an understanding of the transition from one poem to the other. The book that establishes the real doctrine (Περὶ φύσεως; *Perì phýseōs*) is dedicated to a certain Pausanias, who symbolizes the transfer of knowledge, whereas in the *Katharmoí* an Ego is speaking who announces the extraordinary message of a new life, and indeed in Pythagorean tradition nothing less than the promise of peace among men and the cities in conflict. War is combated. In the poem's prologue (B115) the Ego heads off into the wide world as the emissary of the Agrigentian community. It presents itself as one of the fallen 'demons' (souls), who 'entrusted' themselves to the divine struggle (probably in order to overcome it dialectically). According to one ancient account, E. had his doctrine of salvation recited at the Olympic Games by a famous rhapsode before the assembled Greeks (Diog. Laert. 8,63). That amounted to a strategic counterblow by Italian philosophy, politically universally oriented, against the cultural pre-eminence of Athenian tragedy. The same myths, like the story of the Atrides family, with the sacrilege committed by Thyestes and the slaughter of people, were given a new interpretation. By chance the sacrificial scene has been transmitted to us (B137). The *Katharmoí* are doubly allegorical in their ethical claim to being a history of both humanity and spirituality. On the one hand the depictions of the 'Nature poem' are taken as the basis and biological anthropology is extended to communal living and cult; consequently, in the course of the transformation of tradition a connection is made, on the other hand with the mythologems on which the familiar ideas depend. A strict analogy between the realms cannot be created; the *Katharmoí* have their own logic. Thus, the Sphaerus is indeed a model of that divine community to which committed people aspire, but it is not a real equivalence.

FRAGMENTS: DIELS/KRANZ (31), vol. 1, 276–375; J. BOLLACK, Empédocle, 4 vols., 1965/69.

1 C. OSBORNE, E. recycled, in: CQ 37, 1987, 24–52 2 B. INWOOD, The Poem of E., 1992 3 S. KARSTEN, Empedocles, 1838 4 J. BARNES, The Presocratic Philosophers, 1982, 308–310.

JE.BO.

D. The Strasbourg Empedocles papyrus

The papyrus *P.Strasb. gr. 1665–1666* (end of the 1st cent. AD) are fragments of a scroll that once contained the first book of Empedocles' Nature poem (περὶ φύσεως; *perì phýseōs*). The papyrus was acquired in Achmim/Panopolis in 1904 by the Deutsche Papyruskartell but not identified until 1992. Remnants of *c.* 80 verses have been preserved; 20 of these are identical to Empedocles quotations from the indirect transmission. The papyrus offers i.a. 34 verses that are directly linked to DK 31 B 17. The start of love's expansion (cf. DK 31 B 35,3–5) is described in the papyrus as a cyclically recurring process; four verses that Aristotle cites (Metaph. 1000a 26–32) as evidence that, as well as the zoogony of love, Empedocles (for each cycle) assumed also a separate zoogony of strife, appear for the first time in their original context (not = DK 32 B 21); they confirm Aristotle's interpretation. The third zoogonic step, directly preceding our era (cf. DK 31 A 72 and DK 31 B 62) is depicted in the papyrus in terms of the narrator's (= Empedocles' demon?) own experience; in this natural-philosophical connection is also to be found the self-accusation, previously attributed to the 'Purifications' (*Katharmoí*), of a homicide committed for the sake of nourishment (DK 31 B 139). A stichometric marker identifies DK 31 B 17 (without v. 90) as vv. 233–266 of the 1st book of the *Physiká*, and this creates space for a prooemium at the beginning of the book.

→ Pre-Socratics

A. Martin, O. Primavesi, L'Empédocle de Strasbourg, 1999; O. Primavesi, Kosmos und Dämon bei E.: Der Papyrus P. Strasb. gr. Inv. 1665–1666 und die indirekte Überlieferung (Hypomnemata, H. 116, forthcoming).

O.P.

[2] According to Suda ε 1001 grandson of → Empedocles [1]; wrote 24 tragedies, otherwise unknown.

TrGF 50 and TrGF 238.

F.P.

Emperors, child The term child emperors (after Lat. *principes pueri*, SHA Tac. 6,5; Sid. Apoll. Carm. 7, 533) has been applied, since Hartke [1], to the members of the Valentinian-Theodosian dynasty (genealogical tree see → Theodosius) who ascended the throne as one- to eight-year-old boys: the sons of Valentinianus I, Gratianus [2] (born in AD 359; Augustus in 367), and Valentinianus II (born in 371; Augustus in 375); the sons of Theodosius I, Arcadius (born in 377; Augustus in 383) and Honorius (born in 384; Augustus in 393) as well as his grandsons Theodosius II (born in 401; Augustus in 402) and Valentinianus III (born in 419; Augustus in 423). As a reaction to the serious crisis of the Western Empire at the turn of the 4th to the 5th cent. AD, the authors of late antiquity draw a connection between the child emperors and the image of the emperor who is locked inside the palace (*princeps clausus*), politically powerless and estranged from his subjects, the victim of a regime of favourites, eunuchs and women (Pan. Lat. 2,21,3f.; Synesius De regno 15 [16D]; Sid. Apoll. Carm. 5,354–57; 7,532–36; Sulpicius Alexander in Greg. Tur. Franc. 2,9; projected back into the 3rd cent.: SHA Gord. 23,6–24,2; SHA Alex. Sev. 66,1–3; SHA Tac. 6,5f.).

1 W. Hartke, Röm. Kinderkaiser, 1951, esp. 207– 242
2 F. Kolb, Unters. zur Historia Augusta, 1987, 52–67.

K.-L.E.

Emphyteusis (hereditary leasehold). The technical term first appeared in an Imperial constitution of AD 386 (Gratianus/Valentinianus/Theodosius/Arcadius Cod. Iust. 11,62,7). Even earlier, the term *fundus emphyteutici iuris* (Cod. Iust. 11,62,1) crops up in a constitution of 315. Around that time *emphyteusis* appears, along with the original Roman right to *ager vectigalis,* as the Hellenistic form of hereditary leasehold. *Ager vectigalis* is communal land (→ *ager publicus*) that is made available, in exchange for rent (→ Taxes), for cultivation in perpetuity (*in perpetuum*) (Dig. 6,3,1 pr.). The leaseholder is not the property owner but, as distinct from an ordinary tenant, is protected by an *actio in rem*—even from the community (Dig. 6,3,1,1). As well, he enjoys security of property through the → *interdictum uti possidetis*. The right to leasehold is transferable and mortgageable (Dig. 20,1,31 pr.,1; 13,7,16,2). In AD 480 Emperor Zeno combined both hereditary leasehold and the right to *ager vectigalis* into one unified *ius emphyteuticarium* (Cod. Iust. 4,66,1). It appears in that form in the rubric of Dig. 6,3 (*Si ager vectigalis, id est emphyteuticarius, petatur*) and is identifiable in the parenthetical qualification in Dig. 2,8,15,1 (... *qui vectigalem* [*id est emphyteuticum*] *agrum possidet* ...). At the same time Zeno settled the old dispute as to whether the right to *ager vectigalis* was subject to the *emptio venditio* or the *locatio conductio* (Gai. Inst. 3,145), by separating it from both of them in a *ius tertium* (Inst. Iust. 3,24,3). The leaseholder could forfeit his rights to the property if he fell into arrears with his rent for three years (Cod. Iust. 4,66,2 of 529).

H. Honsell, Th. Mayer-Maly, W. Selb, Röm. Recht [4]1987, 192f.; Kaser, RPR I, 455; II, 308–312.

D.SCH.

Empires, Concept of empire

I. Ancient Orient II. Classical Antiquity

I. Ancient Orient

The idea of a → rulership that encompassed the entire known world was expressed in Mesopotamia in various royal epithets—i.a. 'Ruler of the Four Regions (of the world)' (*šar kibrāt arbaʾim/erbettim*), 'Ruler over the Totality' (*šar kiššatim*), 'Ruler of Rulers' (*šar šarrāni*). The title 'Ruler of the Four Regions (of the world)' is first documented for the Akkadian ruler → Naramsin (23rd cent. BC). However, the claim inherent in this title did not hold true according to contemporary documents, since Naramsin's sphere of control reached, at most, to the boundaries of the 'Fertile Crescent', that is, in the east to the → Zagrus, in the north to the Taurus range (→ Taurus [2]), in the west to the Mediterranean, and in the south to the → Persian Gulf, thus from the 'upper to the lower sea', although the knowledge about the existing world went far beyond it (Iranian plateau, Indus delta, Oman). The succeeding Mesopotamian dynasties from the 21st to the 18th cents. BC deserved the title even less [1. 305–308]. In the 14th cent. BC, the title 'Ruler of Four Regions' at times became part of the forms of address for the rulers of Egypt, → Ḫattusa, Assyria, and Babylonia, who, however, preferred to call themselves → Great King in their mutual correspondence; that title expressed both a regional supremacy and the mutual acceptance as a major power.

From the 11th cent. BC until the end of the Assyrian Empire (end of the 7th cent. BC), Assyrian rulers consistently designated themselves as Great Kings, which was justified since no other power in the Near East was equal to them. The claim of ruling the world was made from Assurnaṣirpal II (883–859 BC) with the inclusion of the title 'Ruler of the Four Regions' into the form of address for the Assyrian king.

Claiming world rulership and the ambition of attaining it went hand in hand with a successful military expansion far beyond the borders of Mesopotamia. The purpose of this expansion lay primarily in controlling and securing the trade routes (→ Commerce I), an essential necessity for Mesopotamia, which was lacking in raw materials and was existentially dependent on access to the sources of goods needed for strategic reasons and for prestige (e.g. metals, building lumber, aromatic substances, precious stones).

Although the rulers of Egypt and Ḫattusa at times advanced and conquered areas beyond their own, geographically recognizable borders, their titles show few signs of claiming rulership of the world that would be comparable to the Mesopotamian → rulers. The virulence of these ideas about global rulership in the Near East towards the end of the 1st millennium, is demonstrated by the episode of → Nebuchadnezzar [2]'s dream and the four empires in Dan 2, where we find the claim, particularly about the iron empire, that it will 'rule over the entire earth' (v. 39). Clearly, we can draw a parallel between this and the epithet for Achaemenid rulers (Darius [1] I, Xerxes I, Artaxerxes [2] II): 'king of the earth' (*šar qaqqari*).

→ Great King; → Ruler; → Rulership

1 J.-M. Seux, Epithètes royales akkadiennes et sumériennes, 1967, 292–320 2 J. Wiesehöfer, Das ant. Persien, ³1998.

J. RE.

II. Classical Antiquity

A. Introduction: 'Three-Empire Scheme' B. Hellenistic 'Four-Empire Scheme' C. The Roman 'Five-Empire Model' D. World Empires in Jewish Tradition E. Pagan and Jewish-Christian Translatio imperii

A. Introduction: 'Three-Empire Scheme'

The tendency of old oriental rulers to equate their empires with the boundaries of the world (see above, I.) probably lies at the root of the idea of a series of empires —an idea that was developed in the 5th cent. BC (Greek *oikouménē*; Lat. *orbis terrarum*) and quickly became an ideology. The initial introduction of this scheme of empires, which first can be grasped in Herodotus [1], (1,95; 1,130) as a sequence of three empires (Assyria–Media–Persia), is usually attributed by modern research to the → Achaemenids [2] (Cyrus [2] the Great or late Achaemenid kings, [11; 8. 197–212; 14] includes the older literature). On the basis of three reasons, however, it seems more plausible to attribute the scheme to Herodotus: firstly, the scheme is missing in the royal inscriptions (cf. → Bisutun), secondly, the historical existence of the middle element—a fully developed 'Median kingdom'—remains doubtful, and thirdly, the model corresponds to the Herodotean view of the history of the → *oikouménē* ([15]; cf. [12; 9]). For Herodotus, only the Persian empire could attain rulership over all of Asia (and, in the process, incorporate the entire territorial heritage of the previous empires) and the rise of fall of empires was linked substantially to the moral qualities of the rulers, but → Ctesias, on the other hand, who more clearly expresses the 'three-empire-scheme', also attributes the rulership over all of Asia to the Assyrians (FGrH 688 F 1 and 5).

B. Hellenistic 'Four-Empire Scheme'

After the destruction of the Achaemenid empire by the Macedon Alexander [4] the Great, a similarly optimistic 'four-empire-scheme' must have evolved (theories about its emergence quoted in [7. 16–18]). This is indicated by the four empires in the OT book of Daniel (Dan 2: Babylonia – Media – Persia – Greece/Macedon, but here combined with the wish of overcoming the present situation) and by the five-empire scheme of Roman historiography (see below II. C). Although the sequence Assyria–Media–Persia–Macedon is not documented in Hellenism, much speaks for attributing the → Seleucids with expanding the three-empire scheme (and not already Alexander [4] or even an anti-Hellenic oriental opposition) [14].

C. The Roman 'Five-Empire Model'

Beginning with the 1st cent. BC (following the reorganization of the East in 63 BC by Pompeius [I 3]; cf. Cass. Dio 37,21,2; Plut. Pomp. 45,5–7), Rome appears as the uncontested fifth member in the chain of empires (originator: Theophanes [1] of Mytilene?, Posidonius [3]?) [14], even though the Romans probably had claimed world rulership even earlier (Pol. 1,2,2–8) and Aemilius Sura [2] (in Vell. Pat. 1,6,6; Sura in the 1st, not in the 2nd cent. [3. 63 f.], differing: [2. 111]) as well as Pompeius [III 3] Trogus tried to bestow great significance for world history on the Roman victories over the Antigonids (cf. → Macedonian Wars). The oriental series of four empires, expanded to include Rome in acknowledgement of the existing situation and of the Imperium Romanum as an everlasting empire and, moreover established for the sake of this last empire, can also be found later in Tacitus (Hist. 5,8), in Appian (praef. 9), in the speech by Aelius Aristides [3] (26,91), as well as in Claudianus [2] (De consulatu Stilichonis 3,159–166) and Rutilius [II 1] Namatianus (1,81–92).

For Dionysius [18] of Halicarnassus, who probably adopted the original three-empire scheme (see above II.A.) from Herodotus and Ctesias, the Antigonids (not the Seleucids) were the Macedonians whose (fourth) empire was superseded by Rome as the last and the greatest of all the previous empires [1. 413–417]. In Pompeius [III 3] Trogus, who structures his *Historiae Philippicae* according to the sequence of the *imperia* and thus succinctly expresses the idea of a 'transfer of rulership' (*imperium transferre*; see below II. E), the eastern empires of the Assyrians, Medes, and Persians are followed by the rule of Alexander the Great, who added the *imperium Asiae* (11,14,6) to the *imperium Europae* (Iust. 12,16,5) and who was the first rightly to be called *rex terrarum omnium et mundi* ('king of all countries and the world': 12,16,9). Following the dispute of his successors about *regnum et imperia* (13,1,8) and the division of the empire as a whole (15,4,10), the Romans (Rome as *caput orbis*, 'capital of the world': 43,1,2) and the Parthians became the successors of the *imperium Macedonicum* (*divisio orbis*, 'division of the world' 20 BC: 41,1,1) [13].

D. World Empires in Jewish Tradition

The four-empire scheme of the Book of Daniel (Dan 2) is probably also based on the traditional (Herodotean) sequence of three. However, due to its Jewish tradition and history, it replaces Assyria with Babylonia. While the eschatological hope of an eternal Kingdom of God is not felt urgently in Dan 2 (the dating is therefore prior to the struggle with Antiochus [6] IV.), the vision of the animals of chaos in Dan 7 is already strongly characterized by this hope [4].

The (originally perhaps non-Jewish [4. 168]) 4th book of Sibylline oracles (→ *Sibyllini libri*; completed in *c*. AD 80 [10. 1064; 5. 454]) is based on the Hellenistic 'four-empire scheme' (with Assyria as the first empire). In the 3rd book, 158–161 (2nd or the end of the 1st cent. BC [5. 447 f.]), we find a scheme of eight and of ten empires ([Kronos–]Egyptians – Persians – Medes – Aethiopians – Assyrians – Macedonians – Egyptians – Romans–[Messianic Kingdom]).

E. Pagan and Jewish-Christian Translatio imperii

In Pompeius [III 3] Trogus, we cannot find the idea of a higher legitimacy of the *translatio* nor the idea of 'a ruling power 'divorced from historical 'reality' [13. 234]. His theory combines the idea of a sequence of empires with the model of a continuous development of rulerships and states, which is oriented towards a theory that understands the processes of emerging, becoming and passing-away as based on natural law yet still leaves open the possibility of human intervention [13]. The contradiction between the simultaneous existence of two world powers (Rome and Parthia) and the idea of the *translatio imperii* which assumes a single world empire can be resolved in Trogus when we consider that he may have understood *imperium* (with the added word *terrarum* or *orbis*) as world rulership without intending it at the same time as a world empire [13. 222]. There is no connection between the pagan scheme of four or five empires and the documents from Jewish-apocalyptic, rabbinical, and Christian literature, which are almost exclusively based on the four-empire scheme from the Book of Daniel (with a subsequent Messianic Kingdom and/or Kingdom of God) [8. 221]. Clearly separate from Trogus' idea is also the notion communicated by → Hieronymus (in his translations of the texts from the OT [such as Dan 2,21; Sir 10,8] and in his history of the world) of a *regna transferre* — with the notion of God as the creator and of sin and *virtus* as the reason for the *translatio* — as well as the later Christian *translatio* theories [6. 17–36].

→ Roma I. E.

1 J. M. Alonso Núñez, Die Abfolge der Weltreiche bei Polybios und Dionysios von Halikarnassos, in: Historia 32, 1983, 411–426 2 Id., Aemilius Sura, in: Latomus 48, 1989, 110–119 3 P. Burde, Untersuchungen zur ant. Universalgeschichtsschreibung, 1974 4 J. J. Collins, Daniel. A Commentary on the Book of Daniel, 1993 5 J.-D. Gauger, Sibyllinische Weissagungen, 1998 6 W. Goez, Translatio Imperii, 1958 7 K. Koch, Europa, Rom und der Kaiser vor dem Hintergrund von zwei Jahrtausenden Rezeption des Buches Daniel, 1997 8 R. G. Kratz, Translatio Imperii: Untersuchungen zu den aramäischen Danielerzählungen und ihrem theologiegeschichtlichen Umfeld, 1991 9 D. Mendels, The Five Empires: A Note on a Hellenistic Topos, in: AJPh 102, 1981, 330–337 10 H. Merkel, Apokalypsen, 1998 11 D. Metzler, Beobachtungen zum Geschichtsbild der frühen Achämeniden, in: Klio 57, 1975, 443–459 12 A. Momigliano, The Origins of Universal History, in: R. E. Friedman (ed.), The Poet and the Historian, 1983, 133–154 13 B. R. van Wickevoort Crommelin, Die Universalgeschichte des Pompeius Trogus, 1993 14 J. Wiesehöfer, Vom 'Oberen Asien' zur 'gesamten bewohnten Welt': Die hell.-röm. Weltreiche-Theorie, in: M. Delgado et al. (ed.), Europa: Tausendjähriges Reich und Neue Welt. Zwei Jahrtausende Gesch. und Utopie in der Rezeption des Danielbuches, 2003 15 J. Wiesehöfer, The Medes and the Idea of the Succession of Empires, in: G. Lanfranchi, R. Rollinger (ed.), Continuity of Empire: Assyria, Media, Persia, 2004.

J. W.

Empiricists
A. History B. Doctrine C. Therapy
D. Connection with Philosophy

A. History
The Empiricists are a Greek school of physicians founded in about 250 BC by Philinus of Cos, a pupil of → Herophilus (Ps.-Galen Introductio; Gal. 14,683). According to Celsus (De med. pr. 10) it was founded somewhat later by Serapion of Alexandria. According to some doxographers the founder was Acron of Acragas (about 430 BC; fr. 5–7 Deichgräber). It is mentioned in the medical doxographies as one of the leading movements in Greek medicine even in the time of Isidorus of Sevilla (d. AD 636); but its last followers known to us by name are → Sextus Empiricus and Theodosius (fr. 219) in the late 2nd cent. AD. The epithet 'Empiricus', which was given to Marcellus of Bordeaux (about AD 380), meant only that in his practice he relied upon *experta*, i.e. on medications proven to be reliable, and not that he subscribed to the teachings of the Empiricists.

The Empiricists did not form a 'school' in the narrow sense, with a fixed number of school heads, but a series of different groupings led by teachers like Glaucias, Heraclides of Tarentum, Theodas and Menodotus. The best (but not uncritical) account of their teachings is to be found in Galen's *Subfiguratio empirica* (originally written in about AD 163) as well as his early work *De experientia medica*.

B. Doctrine
The Empiricists refused to search for hidden causes of illnesses, as they regarded that as too unreliable, time-consuming and speculative. In spite of the recognition they gave to anatomy, they even disputed the possibility of gaining a better understanding of the living body's functions by conducting autopsies. Instead, they insisted that everything needed for medical studies could be obtained from books that had collected all the fruits of earlier research (fr. 68, Celsus de med., pr. 27). In order to identify the appropriate method of therapy, they preferred to employ direct examination, together with written notes on similar cases. They were not interested in diagnosis in the sense of searching for specific illnesses but tended to describe illnesses, rather than define them (fr. 12–13). At the heart of their therapeutical approach was the principle of transition from 'like to like', in which no distinction was made as to whether the 'like' was a bodily part, an illness or an item of medication (fr. 15).

C. Therapy
Careful, written notes on cases of illness, based on experience, were among the central principles of empirical therapy. The Empiricists did not only offer therapeutic guidance but aimed at achieving an understanding of 'hypomnematic signs' that were essential for comprehending the stages in a case's development (fr. 79–81). They likewise paid close attention to a diagnosis based on the pulse, even if their explanation for it was essentially different from that of Galen (fr. 71–77). To the latter's regret, they tended to think in more far-reaching categories in their treatment of a patient (fr. 114). Although they recognized bloodletting, they were disinclined to use it in practice (fr. 120–124); instead they preferred medicinal treatment, which they both researched and documented in detail (fr. 105–106). This confidence in the medicinal experience of their predecessors led some Empiricists to a deep appreciation of Hippocrates; some Empiricists, including Heraclides of Tarentum, composed commentaries on the Hippocratic works.

D. Connection with Philosophy
Attitudes of a section of Empiricists, including Menodotus of Nicomedia, Theodas of Laodicea and Sextus Empiricus, were close to scepticism. This expressed itself in their mistrust of theories that took for granted the thesis of theoretical units (e.g. atoms). They preferred to stick with what was easy to observe and they relied on judgements from everyday life (*epilogismoi*). Some Empiricists (e.g. Menodotus) probably accorded a high place for perception, others, however, had a more subtle attitude towards empiricism, as e.g. Sextus Empiricus, who, like the Methodists, did not take sides in the debate about recognition of what has been hidden (Sextus, Subfiguratio 1,236ff.).

Editions: 1 K. Deichgräber, Die griech. Empirikerschule, Sammlung der Fragmente u. Darstellung der Lehre, 21948 2 R. Walzer, Galen, On medical experience, 1944 3 M. Frede, Galen, Three Treatises on the Nature of Science, 1985 4 J. Atzpodien, Galens Subfiguratio empirica, 1986.
Bibliography: 5 Edelstein, AM, 195–204 6 R.J. Hankinson (ed.), Method, Medicine and Metaphysics, 1988 7 C. Opsomer, R. Halleux, in: P. Mudry, J. Pigeaud (ed.), Les écoles médicales a Rome, 1991, 160–178. V.N.

Emplekton see → Masonry

Emporia As Emporia in a strict sense are to be understood all the cities of the Syrtis Minor but in a broader sense the cities of the Syrtis Minor and the Byssatis or the Syrtis Minor and the Tripolitania or the Syrtis Minor, the Byssatis and the Tripolitania.

A. Bresson, P. Rouillard (ed.), L'emporion, 1993; R. Rebuffat, Où étaient les emporia?, in: Semitica 39, 1990, 111–126. W.HU.

Emporiae (Emporion). Sea-trading port, now Ampurias, on the eastern edge of the Pyrenees, in the province Gerona, on the Costa Brava. Sources: [1; 2]. Archaeological activity that was unparalleled in Spain took place here from the start of the 20th cent. and has been extensively covered in several publications [3. 334ff.;

4. 66ff.; 5. 94; 6; 7; 8. 273ff.]. The inscriptions have produced very little; two of them were Christian [9]. Coin finds have been rich and significant [7. 251ff.; 10; 11; 12].

E. grew up from four different settlements. The oldest part is Palaiopolis, probably founded by Massalia after 520 BC (Str. 3,4,8) on the island, today's peninsula, off San Martín de Ampurias, with a temple of the Ephesian → Artemis. In any event the finds go even further back in time (as far as 600 BC). To the south lay the harbour, still protected today by a Greek mole. Neapolis, which has been built up in terraces on the mainland beach, probably arose after 500. To the west lay the Iberian city Indike [13], separated from Neapolis by a wall (a description of both peoples in Str. 3,4,8; Liv. 34,9.) Neighbouring it was the Roman colony founded by Caesar in 45 BC. As well, Greek, Roman and Iberian Necropoleis [14; 15] have been uncovered. There have been numerous finds, including many pieces of classical art [16. 275f.].

E. was the starting point for Roman military operations in Spain (Scipiones, Cato [1] the Elder) and developed into a rich city. Invasion by the Franks (AD 265) seems to have been a disaster for E. but it still played a role as a bishopric in the West Gothic period [17]. That came to an end after invasion by the Arabs, although a *condado de Ampurias* survived [18].

1 A. SCHULTEN (ed.), Fontes Hispaniae Antiquae, 2, 1925 2 M. ALMAGRO, Las fuentes escritas referentes a Ampurias, 1951 3 A. SCHULTEN, Ampurias, Neue Jbb. für das klass. Altertum 10, 1907, 334ff. 4 Id., Eine unbekannte Top. von Emporion, in: Hermes 60, 1925, 66ff. 5 Id., Forsch. in Spanien, in: AA I/2, 1940 6 A. FRICKENHAUS, Zwei top. Probleme. 1. Emporion, in: BJ 118, 1909, 17–27 7 M. ALMAGRO, Ampurias, 1951 8 P. GARCÍA, La España primitiva, 1950 9 M. ALMAGRO, Las inscripciones ampuritanas griegas, ibéricas y latinas, 1952 10 H. DESSAU, s.v. Emporia, RE V 2, 2526f. 11 A. VIVES, La moneda hispánica, 1926 12 J. AMORÓS, Les monedes empuritanes anteriores a les dracmes, 1934 13 A. SCHULTEN, s.v. Indiketes, RE IX 2, 1368 14 M. ALMAGRO, Las Necrópolis de Ampurias, 2 vols., 1953/1955 (Reviews cf. Gnomon 26, 1954, 284 and Gnomon 29, 1957, 238) 15 M. ALMAGRO, P. DE PALOL, La Ampurias paleocristiana y visigoda, (Monografias Ampuritanas, 4), 1958 16 P. GARCÍA, La España primitiva, 1950, 275ff. 17 Fontes Hispaniae Antiquae 9, 1947, 447ff. 18 Enciclopedia Universal Ilustrada 5, 274.

Anuari de l'Institut d'Estudis Catalans 1907–1927 (Research reports); E. SAMARTI I GREGO et al., Emporion, in: W. TRILLMICH, P. ZANKER (ed.), Die Monumentalisierung hispanischer Städte zwischen Republik und Kaiserzeit, 1990, 117–144; E. SAMARTI I GREGO et al., La presencia comercial etrusca en la emporion arcaica, determinada a partir de las Anforas, in: J. REMESAL, O. MUSSO, La Presencia de Material Etrusco en la Península Ibérica, 1991, 83–94; R. MAR, J. RUIZ DE ARBULO, El foro de Ampurias y las transformaciones augusteas de los foros de la Tarraconense, in: W. TRILLMICH, P. ZANKER (ed.), Die Monumentalisierung hispanischer Städte zwischen Republik und Kaiserzeit, 1990, 145–164; TOVAR, 3, 1989, 427–430.

P.B.

Emporikai dikai (ἐμποϱικαὶ δίκαι; *emporikaì díkai*). Commercial suits in Athens involving maritime imports and exports. Traders and shipowners were the parties but also foreigners and → *métoikoi*. The *emporikai dikai* could be brought on only in winter months when maritime traffic was resting. First they came under the jurisdiction of the *nautodíkai*, then the → *eisagogeís* and finally (Aristot. Ath. Pol. 59,5) under that of the → *thesmothétai*. Under the jurisdiction of the *eisagogeís* they had to be completed speedily within one month. Execution of the judgement was assured by the conditions set for pledge and arrest.

E. E. COHEN, Ancient Athenian Maritime Courts, 1973.

G.T.

Emporikoi nomoi (ἐμποϱικοὶ νόμοι; *emporikoì nómoi*). The Athenian laws on maritime trade, grouped systematically on the basis of their subject matter (not, as was customary, according to the jurisdiction of individual authorities) (Dem. Or. 35,3); in particular, they probably laid down strict provisions for the protection of the city's grain supplies. They covered also speedy judicial process (→ Emporikai dikai) and the avoidance of frivolous complaints against traders and shipowners (Dem. Or. 58,10f.).

E. E. COHEN, Ancient Athenian Maritime Courts, 1973.

G.T.

Emporion Although ἐμπόϱιον (*empórion*, Lat. *emporium*) could originally be translated by 'port/trading centre', there arise a variety of problems of definition because of the changing meaning in antiquity due to regional differences and historical developments, and this caused the term to become a reflection of economic and cultural structures. Consequently, in modern research *emporion* is neither used as a topographical term, or as a distinct form of settlement, nor as a well-defined economic institution, but only to cover some fundamental, distinctive features: 1. An *emporion* is normally found on the border of a political community or between two culturally different systems. 2. It is found either outside or on the border of an indigenous population. 3. It is a place where different communities come together to exchange goods, even if the relationship between the communities can take widely differing forms. 4. The residents of an *emporion* are actively engaged in trade, whereas the neighbouring population is probably not. 5. An *emporion* offers infrastructure and institutions that preserve the rights and living standards of its inhabitants, as well as fair trade (temples, authorities for controlling the market etc.). 6. Unlike the polis, the *emporion* offers a space in which foreigners can mingle unhindered.

From a historical-archaeological point of view there were many forms of *emporia*. First of all, there were entire settlements — usually situated on the coast — with a large proportion of traders (Al-Mina, Tartessus, Emporion-Ampurias, Pithecussae). These settlements developed separately from their agrarian-oriented surroundings. The special case of Naukratis is to be distinguished from that, being declared by Amasis in the 6th cent. BC as the only trading place for Greeks in Egypt (Hdt. 2,178f.). The *emporia* that were geographically part of a city or polis and belonged to its politico-legal system form another category. Again a distinction has to be made between various topographical and institutional circumstances. Piraeus, for example, lay 7 km from Athens but within the city walls after the long walls were constructed under Pericles; on the other hand, Dikaiarchia, the *emporion* of Cumae, lay outside the polis (Str. 5,4,6); the *emporion* of Alexandria was a quarter integrated into the city. Cities that were called *emporion* only in terms of their function as ports supplying for the hinterland constitute a third category. Thus, Ephesus and Alexandria came to be called the *emporion* of Asia Minor and Egypt respectively. Even the ports of archaic Corinth, Aegina, Athens or in the Hellenistic period, Delos and Rhodes served as trade centres for the whole Mediterranean.

Earlier research focussed on the special economic and social situation and the demarcation of *emporia*. Ancient political theory and what has been transmitted of the special control measures for ports and trading supported that line of approach. Contemporary research, however, tends to look at individual variations in the kind and extent of economic and social integration.

1 A. Bresson, P. Rouillard (ed.), L'emporion, 1993 2 R. Garland, The Piraeus, 1987 2 Gehrke 3 P. Millett, Maritime Loans and the Structure of Credit in Fourth-Century Athens, in: Garnsey/Hopkins/ Whittaker, 36–52 4 C. Mossé, The World of the *Emporion* in the Private Speeches of Demosthenes, in: Garnsey/ Hopkins/ Whittaker, 53–63. S.v.R.

Emporos (ἔμπορος; *émporos*). In the Odyssey *emporos* is a passenger travelling on a foreign ship (Hom. Od. 2,319; 24,300f.). The merchant and shipowner trading in goods for profit, however, is called πρηκτήρ (*prēktḗr*) or ἀρχὸς ναυτάων (*archós nautáōn*) in Od. 8,161–164. In keeping with epic language travellers on land and sea are *emporoi* in Attic tragedies. Hesiod, however, already uses ἐμπορή (*emporḗ*; Hes. Op. 646) to describe trading by ship and Herodotus also uses the word in that sense. In the Classical period *emporos* was used in particular of a merchant trading over long distances who imported and exported his goods over the polis boundaries by foreign ships. The retail trader relying on the local market (κάπηλος, *kápēlos*; Pl. Resp. 371d) and the shipowner (ναύκληρος, *naúklēros*) were distinguished from the *emporos*. In contrast to the retail trader, who was not highly regarded, the *emporos* was thought likely to make a fortune quickly (Xen. Mem. 3,4,2) and thus enjoyed high social standing; the *emporoi* did not, however, exercise any political influence. Grain merchants were particularly important to Athens; they were subject to special regulations and ἐμπορίου ἐπιμεληταί (*emporíou epimelētaí*) monitored their compliance (Aristot. Ath. Pol. 51,4, cf. Lys. or. 22). *Emporoi* frequently took out maritime loans that did not need to be repaid in the event of wreckage; such loans were frequently the object of legal suits (Dem. Or. 32; 34; 35; 56; a contract for a maritime loan: Dem. Or. 35,10–13). In Athens loans could be granted only to merchants that brought in specific goods, grain in particular, to Attica (Dem. Or. 35,51). Special complaint procedures (ἐμπορικαὶ δίκαι, → *Emporikaí díkai*) were used in Athens to settle commercial disputes. To increase revenue for Athens Xenophon proposed various privileges for *emporoi* and *naúklēroi* (Xen. Vect. 3). In the Hellenistic period Rhodes and then Delos, which was declared a free port, were the main trading centres for *emporoi* and *naúklēroi*, who owned warehouses and depots there. Overseas traders very often formed their own religious and social associations (κοινά, *koiná*).

→ Loan; → Trade; → Kapelos; → Nauclerus

1 V. Ehrenberg, Aristophanes und das Volk von Athen, 1968 2 D. Gray, Seewesen, ArchHom G, 1974 3 M. V. Hansen, Athenian Maritime Trade in the 4th Century B.C. Operation and Finance, in: CeM 35, 1984, 71–92 4 J. Hasebroek, Staat und Handel im Alten Griechenland, 1928 5 H. Knorringa, Emporos, 1926 6 G. Kopcke, Handel, ArchHom M, 1990 7 P. Millett, Lending and Borrowing in Ancient Athens, 1991, 188–196 8 C. Mossé, The 'World of the *Emporion*', in: Garnsey/Hopkins/Whittaker, 53–63 9 C. Mossé, Homo oeconomicus, in: J.-P. Vernant (ed.), Der Mensch der griech. Antike, 1993, 31–62 10 N.K. Rauh, The Sacred Bonds of Commerce, 1993 11 W.E. Thompson, The Athenian Entrepreneur, in: AC 51, 1982, 53–85. W.S.

Emptiness see → Space

Emptio venditio The *emptio venditio* applied to the exchange of goods for money. The detailed interest taken by Roman jurists in this economically important contract has led to the development of many legal institutions that have left their fundamental stamp on the patterns and procedures of civil law to this day.

A. The precursor: Mancipatio B. The reciprocal contract C. Main obligations and guarantee D. Collateral agreements

A. The precursor: Mancipatio

In the oldest form of Roman law, purchase was a cash transaction: with the → *Mancipatio*, the conclusion of the sale, the payment of the price and the transfer of ownership of a → *Res mancipi* took place as one single legal process. From unregulated transactions between Romans for *res nec mancipi*, or between Romans and peregrines in legal proceedings, there arose till the 2nd cent. BC the *emptio venditio* that functioned as an obligatory commitment in transactions.

B. The reciprocal contract

In the Principate the *emptio venditio* was a synallagmatic (reciprocal) consensual contract, based on *bona fides* and arrived at through an informal agreement on goods and price. Acquisition of the property involved in the purchase required an additional transaction procedure (→ *Traditio* or *mancipatio* or → *In iure cessio* with *res mancipi*).

The price had to involve a specific sum of money. The parties were free to fix the amount. In late antiquity the vendor had a right to appeal if the price was less than half the value of the goods (so-called *laesio enormis*).

Both concrete objects and entitlements could be sold. Contracts involving the sale of free men or of objects that were outside the scope of civil law (→ *Commercium*), or did not exist at the time the contract was agreed, were not valid. It was, however, possible to sell prospective items (*emptio rei speratae*) or opportunities for making a profit (*emptio spei*). Roman sources were familiar with purchases of individual items or from stock (limited generic purchases). (Straightforward generic purchases were effected by means of reciprocal → Stipulations on goods and price.)

C. Main obligations and guarantee

The *actio empti* of the purchaser and the *actio venditi* of the vendor served primarily to establish the main reciprocal obligations — provision of the sale item and payment of the purchase price. In their dispute clauses they contained an instruction to the judge to decide the case *ex fide bona*. To make clear what *oportere ex fide bona* involved, Roman jurists developed regulations on secondary contractual obligations, disruptions in performance etc.

The vendor was liable for any culpable damage to, or destruction of the item purchased, as well as its theft (→ *custodia*), between the time of the contract and the item's being handed over. The purchaser, on the other hand, bore the risk of accidental deterioration or ruin after settlement and had to pay the purchase price in full. (The *emptio venditio* was settled if there was no postponement or other condition in the way and the goods were individually specified.)

The vendor was originally liable for any shortcomings in the purchase item only in cases of malice or given guarantees. With marketplace sale of slaves and draught-animals, edicts of the curulian aediles obliged the vendor to disclose specific shortcomings. For breaches of that obligation or for false claims of quality, the *actio redhibitoria* could be applied within 6 months to nullify the transaction, or the *actio quanti minoris*, within 12 months, for a reduction in the price. Later on these principles of guarantee against material defects (independent of culpability) were applied under the *actio empti* to all commercial sales.

The sale of someone else's object was valid. The vendor was not obligated to hand over the property but only to guarantee undisturbed possession. He was liable, however, if a third party successfully challenged the purchaser for the item (eviction): in a *mancipatio* purchase the purchaser could institute the *actio auctoritatis* for repayment of double the purchase price; otherwise it was open to him to bring a suit for the imposition of the penalty (*stipulatio duplae*) customary in that situation. Moreover, with the *actio empti*, the purchaser could in the case of eviction and the deliberate sale of someone else's object, suit for compensation.

D. Collateral agreements

By means of a collateral agreement (*pactum adiectum*) the vendor could be permitted to sell the item on better terms (*in diem addictio*) within a given timeframe or to cancel the contract if the agreed price was not paid on time (*lex commissoria*). The buyer could stipulate a trial period for checking the purchase item out (*pactum displicentiae*). With the sale of slaves it was customary to impose a ban on prostitution and to impose conditions on the grant of freedom (*ut/ne servus manumittatur*) or the export of the slave (*ut servus exportetur*). If the agreement was breached, the slave was returned to the vendor.

→ Auctoritas; → Consensus; → Damnum; → Pactum; → Synallagma

Kaser, RPR I, 545–562, II, 385–394; H. Honsell, Th. Mayer-Maly, W. Selb, Röm. Recht, [4]1987, 304–322; M. Talamanca, s.v. Vendita (diritto romano), Enciclopedia del diritto XLVI, 1993, 303–475; L. Vacca (ed.), Vendita e trasferimento della proprietà nella prospettiva storico-comparatistica I/II, 1991; R. Zimmermann, The Law of Obligations, 1990, 230–337.

R.GA.

Empusa (Ἔμπουσα; *Émpousa*, etymology unclear [1]). Ghostly female figure (*phásma*) who was remarkable for her ability to transform her appearance (*polýmorphos*) and belonged to the group of spectral → Demons in Greek popular belief [2; 3] (→ Lamia). She adopted various forms and in Aristoph. Ran. 285–295 appeared to Dionysus and his slave Xanthias, on their journey through the underworld [4], as a cow, a mule, a pretty woman and finally as a dog [5]. Her face was lit by fire, one leg was made of ore, the other of cow-dung (cf. Aristoph. Eccl. 1056f.). Aeschines' mother → Glaukothea is said to have been nicknamed E. because of her many wheelings and dealings (Dem. Or. 18,130; Idomeneus FGrH 338 F2; cf. also Alci. 3,26,3). E. also appeared as a ghost of the night and as an enticing and seductive vampire (Philostr. VA 2,4; 4,25). She was therefore included with the ghosts of → Hecate (Hekataia) (Schol. Apoll. Rhod. 3,861; Schol. Aristoph. Ran. 293; cf. also Aristoph. fr. 515 PCG).

1 Frisk, 1, 508 2 H. Herter, Böse Dämonen im frühgriech. Volksglauben, in: KS, 1975, 43–75 3 G. Lanata, Medicina magica e religione popolare in Grecia, 1967, 34 4 F. Graf, Eleusis und die orphische Dichtung Athens in vorhellenistische Zeit, 1974, 40–50 5 K. Dover, Aristophanes, Frogs, ed. with introduction and commentary, 1993, 229f.

E.K. BORTHWICK, Seeing Weasels: The Superstitious Background of the Empusa Scene in the Frogs, in: CQ 18, 1968, 200–206; CH.G. BROWN, Empusa, Dionysus and the Mysteries: Aristophanes, Frogs 285ff., in: CQ 41, 1991, 41–50; NILSSON, GGR 725; O. WASER, s.v. E., RE V 2, 2540–2543. R.B.

Empylus (Ἔμπυλος; *Émpylos*). Rhetor of the 1st cent. BC from Rhodes; he lived in Rome in the house of M. → Iunius Brutus and composed a small work on Caesar's assassination, taking the side of his friend Brutus. Plut. Brut. 2,4 used the work and passed a positive judgement on it. Quint. Inst. 10,6,4 mentioned E., praising his extraordinary memory.

EDITION: FGrH 2 B 191. M.W.

Empyra see → Sacrifices

Enagonius (Ἐναγώνιος; *Enagṓnios*). Epiclesis of the deities responsible for the Gymnasium, the athletic exercises and the young men engaging in them there; it was especially widespread from the Hellenistic period onwards. → Hermes in particular bears this epithet in many Greek cities but it is also found with Apollo (in various cities), Aphrodite (Athens) and even Dionysus (Magnesia on the Maeandrus). F.G.

Enallage see → Figures I

Enalus (Ἔναλος; *Énalos*). Lesbian hero from the Poseidon circle, entangled in the foundation myth of Lesbos. According to Myrsilus of Methymna (FGrH 477 F 14), the Penthilidae (→ Penthilus), because of an oracle of Amphitrite, threw the daughter of Smintheus (or Phineus) into the sea; her lover E. jumped in but was saved by a dolphin and carried to Lesbos. Plut. Mor. 20, p. 163 a-d is more detailed: E. was one of the colonists of Lesbos who had to sacrifice a maiden to Amphitrite and the Nereids and a bull to Poseidon. E.'s beloved was elected by lot. According to Anticlides (FGrH 140 F 4), both disappeared in the waves: E. tended Poseidon's mares; his beloved became a Nereid. R.B.

Enamel Coloured molten glass decoration applied to metal (mostly bronze). The Celtic → La Tène Culture (late 5th–1st cent. BC) was the heyday for enamel in Central Europe, the knowledge for it possibly originating in the Achaemenid East. The Celts used almost only red enamel ('blood-enamel'), probably because of its similarity to → Coral. → Jewellery (fibulae, necklaces, parts of belts etc.), bronze vessels, and → weapons (helmets, swords) etc. were decorated with enamel. Workshops for enamel were found in → *oppida* in particular (→ Bibracte). Enamel had little importance in Greek, Etruscan and German culture; only in the Roman provinces there were important workshops (e.g. in the Rhineland).
→ Achaemenids; → Glass; → Crafts

G. HASELOFF et al., s.v. Email, in: RGA 7, 1989, 197–228; V. CHALLET, Les Celtes et l'émail, 1992. V.P.

Enarete see → Aenarete

Encaustic (painting) From the Greek ἐγκαίειν (*enkaíein*), to burn in, heat up. A painting technique with → wax as binder for the pigments. The colour emulsion was applied cold or warm or fused with the surface by heating. The process, described incompletely by Pliny (HN 35,122f.; 149) and especially valued by Greek panel painters in the 4th cent. BC, gave the paintings a brilliant quality as well as durability but it was protracted, complicated and expensive. In spite of a great deal of research, even experimental, individual techniques and painting tools have still not been authoritatively explained and reconstructed even today, as they each varied depending on the kind of painting surface. On wood, the soft to melted hot wax paste was painted on with a spoon-shaped metallic instrument, the *cauterium*, or a hairbrush. Small-shaped ivory tablets were scratched with the *cestros*, a chisel-like caustic stylus, and the lines filled in with liquid colour. Examples of encaustic painting are Egyptian → Mummy portraits and early icons, that also promoted the of oil-painting. The process, which has been in use for painting ships since time immemorial, is also said to have been employed for → Wall paintings but no evidence of it has been found in houses of the Vesuvian cities. For encaustic colouring processes in architecture and sculpture, see → Polychromy.

Since the Renaissance, debate on encaustic painting, forgotten until then, has been revived on the basis of Pliny's text. A. Caylus experimented with it in the 18th cent. and in the 19th cent., some painters of the Munich School used the technique in wall paintings.

B. BORG, Mumienporträts, 1996, 5–18; R. BÜLL, Vom Wachs, vol. I, issue 7/1, in: Hoechster Beitr. zur Kenntnis der Wachse, 1963; R. KÖNIG, G. WINKLER (ed.), Plinius, Naturkunde. B. 35, [2]1997, 267–270; I. SCHEIBLER, Griech. Malerei der Antike, 1994, 97–100. N.H.

Enceladus (Ἐγκέλαδος; *Enkélados*, 'The Raging One', from κελαδέω; *keladéō*; EM. s.v. E. 310,35 GAISFORD; Hsch. s.v. E.). One of the → giants, son of Tartarus and Ge (Hyg. Fab. praef. 4). He fought against Zeus (Batr. 283), Dionysus (Eur. Cycl. 5–9) and—according to the most widely disseminated version—Athene, who threw the island of Sicily or Mt. Aetna on him (Callim. Fr. 1,36; Eur. HF 907–909; Apollod. 1,37; Verg. Aen. 3,578). He is commonly represented in the visual arts [1].

1 F. VIAN, s.v. E., LIMC 3.1, 742–743.

R. ROCCA, s.v. E., EV 2, 217–218; F. VIAN, La guerre des géants, 1952, 201; 221. R.B.

Enclitic see → Accent

Encomium (ἐγκώμιον/*enkṓmion*, sc. μέλος/*mélos*, ᾆσμα/*âisma*). A song of praise. Praise (ἔπαινος, *épainos*) and reproach (ψόγος, *psógos*) are two important functions in oral poetry widely used and documented in early Greece [1. 141–151]. Reproach is largely the subject of the iambographers while praise is, for example, found in the poem addressed by → Alcaeus to his brother (350 VOIGT [2]), the poems of → Sappho to her female friends, in the Partheneia of → Alcman, in the erotic poetry dedicated by → Anacreon and → Ibycus to beautiful youths, in a threnos by → Simonides for the warriors killed at Thermopylae (531 PMG [3]) and in Attic drinking songs (→ Skolion). The Alexandrine editions of → Bacchylides and → Pindar separated their encomia from the → epinikia that celebrated the victors in athletic competitions. However, in his epinician poetry Pindar used the terms ἐγκώμιος (*enkṓmios*) and ἐπικώμιος (*epikṓmios*).

The κῶμος (κômος) was the celebration by delirious enthusiasts after a victory, initially at the site of the games, then in the hometown of the victor. In the former case they were accompanied by an improvized or traditional refrain, then by a song (→ *epinikion*) written by a commissioned poet. It is not clear from the texts if the mention of the *kômos* by Bacchylides and Pindar (e.g., Bacchyl. Epinikia 11; 12; Pind. Ol. 14,16) should be understood as a note to the chorus regarding its own role [4], or as an allusion by the poet to the delirious context into which his monodic song fit [5], or, finally, if the poet used the term for his own song that was to be presented by the chorus [6].

The victory songs contain many references to *kômoi* with respect to the occasion of their presentation but none to *choroí*. However, it is certain that even at the time of composition of the first epinician poem by Pindar (Pind. Pyth. 10 in 498 BC) the adjective *enkṓmios* was entirely independent of the circumstances of presentation used in the meaning of 'praise' (53–54): there Pindar refers to various elements of his song [7. 500; 511] and the subordination of myth, gnomic sayings, religious wisdom, poetic theory and opportunistic comment under the dominating aim of praise [8. 35]. In a similar vein *kōmázein* (κωμάζειν; Pind. Isthm. 4,90b) may simply mean 'to praise' (= ἐγκωμιάζειν; *enkōmiázein*). Fragments of encomia by Pindar are preserved for many contemporary rulers — Xenophon of Corinth, Alexander of Macedonia, Hieron of Syracuse, Theron of Acragas —, also erotic praise of the son and nephew of Theron as well as Theoxenus of Tenedus (fr. 118–128 SNELL-MAEHLER), who was allegedly particularly dear to Pindar. These poems are not occasional poetry such as the victory songs. Fragments of the encomia of Bacchylides are also preserved (fr. 20a-g SNELL-MAEHLER); among them are poems addressed to the same audience. In his famous poem dedicated to Scopas, Simonides supplies a description of the type of man who is a suitable subject of the encomium [9].

1 B. GENTILI, Poesia e pubblico nella Grecia antica, 1984 2 E.-M. VOIGT, Sappho et Alcaeus, 1971 3 PMG 4 C. CAREY, The victory ode in performance: the case for the chorus, in: CPh, 86, 1991, 192–200 5 M. LEFKOWITZ, First-person fictions: Pindar's poetic 'I', 1991 6 K. A. MORGAN, Pindar the professional and the rhetoric of the ΚΩΜΟΣ, in: CPh 88, 1993, 1–15 7 H. FRÄNKEL, Dichtung und Philos. des frühen Griechentums, ²1962 8 E. BUNDY, Studia Pindarica, repr. 1986 9 G. W. MOST, Simonides' ode to Scopas in contexts, in: I. J. F. DE JONG, J. P. SULLIVAN (ed.), Modern critical theory and classical literature, 1994, 127–152.

E.R.

Encyclopaedia

I. GENERAL II. GREECE III. ROME 1. VERSE WRITINGS 2. ARTISTIC PROSE 3. PROSE

I. GENERAL

An encyclopaedia is a work containing the 'totality of knowledge' for a whole field or for individual disciplines. The word is derived from Greek → *enkýklios paideía* (ἐγκύκλιος παιδεία), whose Latin translation *orbis doctrinarum* is closer to the modern understanding of encyclopaedia. The term is first documented in a letter of AD 1490 to Poliziano [12; 13]. Encyclopaedia and 'Encyclopaedism' (cf. French *encyclopédisme*, Italian *enciclopedismo*) are modern words and concepts that may be used within certain limits for antiquity (on their origin cf. [14. 716–717]). The intentionally 'encyclopaedic' book in the proper sense only appeared in the Latin world (see III.) [25].

II. GREECE

However, the history of the encyclopaedia as a literary genre may have begun with Homeric poetry whose function was the preservation of the ethical, mythical and also technical heritage of an oral culture. Herder called it the 'encyclopaedia' of the Greeks ('Homer, a favourite of time', 1795), Burckhardt an 'encyclopaedia of legends' [2. 81] but the Iliad and Odyssey are more than that: they are a 'tribal encyclopaedia' [11] or, better yet, in an extended meaning an 'encyclopaedia of the collective knowledge' of the Greeks [19. 87–92]. According to Xenophanes 'everyone learned from Homer from the beginning' (frg. 10 DK) although Heraclitus turned against the supposed 'wisdom' of Homer and the 'teacher' (διδάσκαλος; *didáskalos*) Hesiod (frg. 56 and 57 DK). Plato's polemic (Resp. 598d-e) against the rhapsodes in his 'Ion' and against the widespread opinion that poets 'knew all arts' takes the same direction. This criticism of the knowledge of poets that was mistakenly considered universal cannot be separated from the more general polemics against 'knowing much' (πολυμαθίη; *polymathíē*) (cf. Heracl. frg. 40 and 129 DK; Democrit, frg. 64 and 65 DK; on Plato especially Alc. 2,146d–147d and the criticism of the conservative, memory-based 'encyclopaedism' of the sophist → Hippias, on the latter [3. 111–115]). Likewise, the Pseudoplatonic dialogue *Ērāstaí* contradicts the thesis that the philosopher must have an encyclopaedic knowledge (excluding, however, a knowledge of the crafts).

Nevertheless, uncritically accepted Homeric 'wisdom', disseminated by the schools, was generally the base of Greek *paideía* (education) [2. 97–102] only thrown into doubt in the Second Sophistic, and even then with difficulty (e.g., Dion Chrys. Or. 11; cf. [6]). On a specific use of Homeric poetry as a technical 'encyclopaedia' in the 2nd cent. AD, cf. Philostr. Heroikos 11,5 and 25,3.

The necessity of codifying technical knowledge in writing in a manual form emerged as early as the 5th cent. BC [10], even though the written representation of a special discipline only achieved definitive theoretical authority with Aristotle [15; 23]. Therefore, the first systematization of knowledge in the sense of book writing is due to the peripatetic school [1. 11–19]. The 'thematic' subtitles of Plato's dialogues (which may derive from the Academy [22]) also represent an attempt to systematize philosophical thinking by indicating — even though in a very simplified manner — the main subject, so that an 'encyclopaedia' of sorts resulted [5].

Although → Speusippus is often named as the precursor of encyclopaedias, the first theoretically reflective approach to combining knowledge in an encyclopaedia must be attributed to → Aristotle. In Meteor. 338a20–339a10 (praef.) Aristotle provides a clear depiction of the strands linking the individual natural sciences [4]. Towards the end of the 'Nicomachean Ethics' (1181b12–23) he describes how he wishes to carry the treatment of the 'philosophy of human affairs' (ἡ περὶ τὰ ἀνθρώπεια φιλοσοφία) to a conclusion and thereby provides a summary announcement regarding the subject of the 'Politics'. An encyclopaedia of knowledge is possible for Aristotle since all sciences share formal principles. He dedicated the *Organon* and the first four books of the *Analytica* to the methods and instruments required for the treatment of individual disciplines, while the texts that were to enter the *Metaphysics* were to supply the ontological foundation for a differentiation of categories of things that were the subject of the sciences [23].

Subsequent concepts of encyclopaedias may be understood as a continuation of the Aristotelian model or opposition to it. The large institutions of Ptolemaic Egypt (the → Museion and the → Library of Alexandria) developed in a direction that was contrary to the Aristotelian unity of science (partially based on the unifying role of the respective 'school master'): instead they pursued the route of specialization and sectorialization [9; 21].

By contrast, the Lyceum conveyed (in succession to Aristotle) to Hellenistic-Alexandrian culture a specific model of library organization as the place of collecting and systematizing all the world's books (cf. Strabo 13,608c). Thus, the idea was created of the encyclopaedia as a kind of 'library' [20]. The most famous example is the 'inventory' of available books that the patriarch → Photius attempted to realize in the 9th cent. AD in his work (known from the 16th cent. by the title *Bibliothḗkē*) but its model is much older. This type of 'encyclopaedism' must be related to those learned works of varied content compiled by the Greeks in particular (*solam copiam sectati*, as Gellius writes at the end of a long list of titles in the *praefatio* to the *Noctes Atticae*). Among these works the *Pandéktai* (books 'that include everything') already clearly show their 'encyclopaedic' character in their titles. Tiro wrote a work with a title of this type (*tamquam omne rerum atque doctrinarum genus continens*; 13,9) for the Latin area and Dorotheus for the Greek sphere (Clem. Al. Strom. I 21,133,1). This title appears as a genre label in Pliny, HN Praef. 24. 'Encyclopaedic' intentions are also evident in → Apollodoros' [7] *Bibliothḗkē* of myths that promised the reader, if the introductory epigram preserved by Photius is genuine, that one could find 'everything in the world' there.

In the discussions of the 2nd and 3rd cents. AD on the function and legitimacy of theoretical knowledge, the encyclopaedia of Aristotelian type found its most important representative in → Galen. He composed a very extensive but only partially preserved encyclopaedic work that extended from literary criticism to medical treatises. While Galen addressed all *téchnai* (De placitis Hippocratis et Platonis 8,482 De Lacy), → Sextos Empeirikos systematically opposed this in his 'anti-encyclopaedia' [24]. The Aristotelian encyclopaedia as a system reached its climax, though in a sense far removed from the empirical vision of Aristotle, in Arab culture and from there entered the Latin Middle Ages.

A special form of encyclopaedism that survived into the Middle Ages emerged in the 2nd and 3rd cents. AD from a response to the Aristotelian encyclopaedia: the collection of *mirabilia*, i.e. phenomena that cannot be explained scientifically (→ Paradoxographi). Thus, → Antigonus [7] of Carystus made it his programme to compile *xéna* (unusual things) and *parádoxa* (unexpected things) from the writings of Aristotle (Ἱστοριῶν παραδόξων συναγωγή, 60). However, collections of *mirabilia* are found even earlier in the Pseudo-Aristotelian treatise Περὶ θαυμασίων ἀκουσμάτων. The papyrus known as *Laterculi Alexandrini* [16] of the 2nd cent. AD with its list of the 'most beautiful' places and the 'most famous' men in various *téchnai* represents a remarkable example of cataloguing and canonization of *mirabilia* for educational purposes. The intentions of paradoxographers were quite scientific and may, therefore, be called 'encyclopaedic' (and, consequently, differ from the sensationalism evident in the work Περὶ θαυμασίων by → Phlegon of Tralleis).

Also considered as 'encyclopaedism' is the writing of compendia, corpora or books of diverse content that begins with the 4th cent. AD and is peculiar to Byzantine culture. On one hand they replaced traditional manuals and on the other document the contemporary tendency towards conserving knowledge [17]. The → Suda, which was compiled in the 9th cent. AD, is the best known Byzantine work of encyclopaedic character. And the → etymologika, too, are no more than large, grammatically oriented encyclopaedias proving access to the entire preceding scholarship in the field of lexicography.

1 R. Blum, Die Literturverzeichnung im Alt. und MA, 1983, 11–19 2 J. Burckhardt, Griech. Kulturgesch. III, 1900 3 G. Cambiano, Platone e le tecniche, 1971 4 W. Capelle, Das Proömium der Meteorologie, in: Hermes 47, 1912, 514–535 5 F. Della Corte, Enciclopedisti latini (1946), in: Opuscula VI, 1978, 1–99 6 P. Desideri, Tipologia e varietà di funzione comunicativa negli scritti dionei, in: ANRW II 33.5, 3916–3922 7 U. Dierse, Enzyklopädie, 1977 8 A. Dihle, Philos. — Fachwiss. — Allgemeinbildung, in: Entretiens 32, 1986, 185–231 9 P. M. Fraser, Ptolemaic Alexandria, 3 vols., 1972 10 M. Fuhrmann, Das Systematische Lehrbuch, 1960 11 E. A. Havelock, Preface to Plato, 1963, 61–144 12 J. Henningsen, Enzyklopädie, in: ABG 10, 1996, 271–357 13 J. Henningsen, Orbis doctrinae: encyclopaedia, in: ABG 11, 1967, 241–245 14 G. Hummel, s.v. E., TRE 9, 716–742 15 W. Jaeger, Studien zur Entstehungsgesch. der Metaphysik des Aristoteles, 1912 16 H. Diels, Laterculi Alexandrini aus einem Papyrus ptolemäischer Zeit, in: Abh. der Königlich Preussischen Akad. der Wiss., 1904, 3–16 17 P. Lemerle, Le premier humanisme byzantin, 1971, 100–102 and 267–300 18 G. Rechenauer, s.v. Enkyklios paideia, HWdR 2, 1160–1185 19 L. E. Rossi, I poemi omerici come testimonianza di poesia orale, in: R. Bianchi Bandinelli (ed.), Storia e civiltà dei Greci I, 1978, 87–92 20 A. Salsano, s.v. Enciclopedia, Enciclopedia Einaudi, I, 1977, 3–64 21 H. v. Staden, Herophilus, 1989 22 M. Untersteiner, Problemi di filologia filosofica, 1980, 8–10 23 M. Vegetti, Aristotele, il Liceo e l'enciclopedia del sapere, in: Cambiano, Canfora, Lanza (ed.), Lo spazio letterario della Grecia antica I/1, 1992, 587–611 24 C.A. Viano, Lo scetticismo antico e la medicina, in: G. Giannantoni (ed.), Lo scetticismo antico, 1981, II, 645–656 25 B. Zimmermann, Osservazioni sulla 'Enciclopedia' nella letteratura latina, in: M. Picone (ed.), L'enciclopedismo medievale, 1994, 41–51. S.FO.

III. Rome

In Roman literary history 'encyclopaedia' (not a book title before the 16th cent.: [1]) meant a sequence of treatises categorized according to subjects useful in the practical life of non-experts, generally intended for the self-education of young adults (often dedicated to the author's sons) outside of school. Since these writings neither developed a fixed canon of subjects nor a typical generic form (they are not text books in the strict sense), the classification of many works is often arbitrary in the grey zone between unsystematic → Buntschriftstellerei and methodical teaching books of the seven (or nine) → Artes liberales .

While the term → *enkýklios paideía*, as Greek education, had been integrated *in toto* into the curriculum of the *artes liberales* since Cicero (De or. 3,21), → Cato's *Disciplinae* already aimed at a general Roman education with an anti-Greek tendency, which can still be felt in → Pliny and partially in → Celsus, but dissolved in a general encyclopaedism because the Roman disciplines were also dependent on Greek materials (e.g., medicine). Real Greek models for didactic and practical collections of materials were lacking — the *Homoia* of the academic → Speusippus come closest [1]. In Cato (as far as can be made out in *Agr.*) teaching (imperatively *ad Marcum filium*) prevails over science (descriptive and enumerative) in the subjects of agriculture, rhetoric, healing and war. In the following period the didactic component increasingly took a back seat to the demonstrative component. The *Artes* of Celsus [7] (more than 30 books) were at a very respectable level for a layperson, if one may so conclude from the preserved *De medicina*. The *Naturalis historia* of Pliny (37 books) uses every opportunity for instructive asides in a didactically skilful manner that results in encyclopaedic breadth and scientific depth that fails to reach the standard of the specialist but also, in the interest of readability, does not aim for that. Another tendency became apparent in the mid 1st cent. BC in → Varro, whose *Antiquitates rerum humanarum et divinarum*, which touched upon all material and linguistic areas, exhibited a programmatic historical and antiquarian (→ Antiquarians) leaning, aimed at a humanistic rather than a pragmatic education (Varro's *Disciplinae* belong into the systematics of the *artes liberales*). This tendency was elaborated in → Suetonius' *Pratum*, concentrating on interesting and unusual subjects as well as cultural curiosa and exotic items, as the subtitles show (e.g., *de spectaculis, de lusibus puerorum*). Subsequently, this branch of encyclopaedias merged with the rich → Buntschriftstellerei of the 2nd cent. AD (→ Favorinus, Aelianus, Telephus, Athenaeus of Naucratis) among which the *Noctes Atticae* of → Gellius (dedicated to his sons) again strongly emphasizes the educational objective. In the end, the purely scientific-oriented anthologies structured in alphabetical order (→ Stephanus of Byzantium; the → Suda) or by subject (→ Isidore, *Origines*) constituted, as reference works and thesauri of ancient knowledge, the bridge to the modern encyclopaedia. Collections restricted to particular subjects such as the *res reconditae* of → Serenus Sammonicus, the *Saturnalia* of → Macrobius or the (poetic) *Chrestomatheiai* of → Helladios take an intermediate position.

The idea of an *encyclios disciplina,* executed by → Vitruvius (1,1,1–18) (see Plin. HN praef. 14; Quint. Inst. 1,10,1), describes, probably due to a misinterpretation of the adjective, the diversity of knowledge as a continuum linked at the disciplinary boundaries. This resulted in a stock of learning for the specialist who must also know many subjects at the margins of his field (cf. already Cic. De or.). This basic thought led to the concept of broad knowledge, understood as an end in itself as well as the archiving of all things researched or recognized that finally converged with the encyclopaedias of the collectanea and manuals.

→ Encyclopaedia

1 H. Fuchs, s.v. Enzyklopädie, RAC 5, 504–515 2 F. Kühnert, Allgemeinbildung und Fachbildung in der Ant., 1961 3 H. Koller, Enkyklios Paideia (1955), in:

H.-TH. JOHANN (ed.), Erziehung und Bildung in der heidnischen und christl. Ant., 1976, 3–21 4 TH. BALLAUFF, Pädagogik vol. 1, 1969, 172–183 5 H.J. METTE, Enkyklios Paideia (1960), in: Erziehung 1976 (No. 3), 31–41 6 R. MEISTER, Die Entstehung der Höheren Allgemeinbildung in der Ant. (1956), in: JOHANN (No. 3), 22–30 7 MARROU, 1957, 259–274; 355–372 8 K. SALLMANN, in: NHL 4, 1997, ch. 13. KL.SA.

Endeis see → Aeacus

Endeixis (ἔνδειξις; *éndeixis*). Literally 'charge': in Athens the endeixis was a special form of public intervention by a private person that resulted in the immediate arrest of the accused or an order for a material surety by the head of the court (the 'Eleven ', the *Árchōn Basileús* or the *thesmothétai*; → archontes). It was permissible against persons (state debtors, exiles and *átimoi* (→ atimia) who visited places (their home town, the public assembly, council, courts, sanctuaries, the market) that they were forbidden to visit by law or popular resolution or who exercized legally proscribed activities (Aristot. Ath. pol. 52,1; Dem. Or. 24,22). The procedure following the charge was also called the endeixis. In contrast to the → *apagogḗ*, the intervening person was not required to arrest the accused. The penalties were decided by the court, differing according to the type of the offence, and included the death penalty. → Delatio nominis; → Delator

H. M. HANSEN, Apagoge, E. and Ephegesis, 1976. G.T.

Endelechius Probably identical with the rhetor Severus Sanctus E. who taught in Rome in AD 395, was of Gallic origin and friends with → Paulinus of Nola. About 400 he composed a bucolic Christian poem (→ Bucolics) in 33 stanzas (i.e. the number of years of Christ's life), each of three asclepiads and one glyconeus: Bucolus reports to Aegon the loss of his flock due to a cattle disease while Christ points out to Tityrus that his flock was preserved by the power of the cross. Thereupon, the other two convert to Christianity.

EDITION: D. KORZENIEWSKI, Hirtengedichte aus spätröm. und karolingischer Zeit, 1976, 58–71.
BIBLIOGRAPHY: HLL § 626. J.GR.

Endesa Siculan town [1] in the territory of Himera, mentioned in a dedication to Hera Thespis (rather than to Leukaspis [2]) inscribed on both sides of a relief. It was found in the Heraion of Samos and shows on one side a round shield and on the other the bow of the ship Samaina. The dedication was probably presented by citizens of Samos when they besieged Endesa (500 BC).

1 M. MASSA, s.v. E., BTCGI 7, 1989, 181
2 G. MANGANARO, Una dedica di Samo rivolta non a Leukaspis, ma a Hera Thespis?, in: ZPE 101, 1994, 120–126. GI.F.

Endius (Ἔνδιος; *Éndios*). Spartan, son of Alcibiades. In 420 BC, E. attempted in vain as a delegate in Athens to prevent a symmachia between the Athenians and Argos, Mantineia and Elis (Thuc. 5,44–47). As ephor he voted in 413/2 on the advice of Alcibiades [3], who was banned from Athens and with whose family he was associated by *proxenia*, for a rapid shift of the war theatre to the territory of Athens' allies in Asia Minor (Thuc. 8,6; 17). After the Spartan defeat at Cyzicus (410 BC) E. attempted in vain to broker a peace in Athens (Diod. Sic. 13,52f.). M.MEI.

Endive (*Cichorium endivia L.*) was one form of the cultivated σέρις (*séris*) of Dioscorides (2,132 [2. 203f.] and 2,159 [3. 224f.]), which was considered as tolerable to the stomach, astringent and cooling in effect. A poultice of its leaves was prescribed as soothing medication for heart ailments, podagra, eye infections, scorpion stings, etc. Then as now it was popular as a salad. Pliny (HN 19,126) mentions it under the name *intubus* amongst the *lactuca* species ('lettuce'). As *sponsa solis* it is found, i.a., in the Salernitan *Circa instans* and in Thomas of Cantimpré (12,26 [1. 348]).

1 H. BOESE (ed.), Thomas Cantimpratensis, Liber de natura rerum, 1973 2 WELLMANN 1 3 BERENDES. C.HÜ.

Endoeus (Ἔνδοιος; *Éndoios*) Sculptor in Athens in the late 6th cent. BC. He made statues of goddesses in ivory and wood for Ephesus, Erythrae and Tegea, the latter were later brought to the forum of Augustus in Rome. His seated marble figure of Athena, the dedicatory gift of a certain Nicias on the Athenian Acropolis, is identified as the statue Athens, AM Inv. No. 625 (*c.* 520 BC). The suppletion of his signature on the votive relief of a potter is plausible, but the association of a signed base with the kore Athens, AM Inv. No. 602 is uncertain. The painting at the base of the funerary monument of Nelonides (530–520 BC) is not necessarily from his hand.

FUCHS/FLOREN, 297–299; OVERBECK, No. 348–353 (sources); A. E. RAUBITSCHEK, Dedications from the Athenian Akropolis, 1949, 491–495; B.S. RIDGWAY, The Archaic style in Greek sculpture, 1977, 138, 284, 288; D. VIVIERS, Recherches sur les ateliers de sculpteurs et la cité d'Athènes à l'époque archaique, 1992. R.N.

Endowments

I. DEFINITION AND HISTORICAL DEVELOPMENT
II. ENDOWERS AND THEIR MOTIVES

I. DEFINITION AND HISTORICAL DEVELOPMENT

In antiquity, endowments were private donations for specific and perpetual purposes, often repeated at set intervals: → sacrifices, banquets, games (→ *ludi*), monetary payments to a specified group of people, or commemorative rites (→ Dead, cult of the). They were based on single transfers of property; whose yields were then used to finance the purpose of the endowment (Pliny [2]: CIL V 5262 = ILS 2927), such as e.g. the transfer of a piece of land, whose lease income was to be used (Plin. Ep. 7,18), or gifts in kind, the proceeds of whose sale then constituted the financial assets of the endowment (→ Grain; Pol. 31,31(25)). It was crucial that the capital of the endowment or its main asset remained untouched to ensure that the intended recipients could receive their bestowments in perpetuity.

Endowments fall into the sphere of → euergetism and have to be differentiated from single donations and → dedications. In the Greek world, endowments only become evident in the late 5th cent. BC. Beyond purely private interests, endowments developed into an important institution for public, social, and religious concerns. Early records in particular are often associated with → sanctuaries (Xen. An. 5,3,4–13) or family cults (IG XII 3,330). Endowments reached their first peak in the 3rd and 2nd cents. BC, not least under the influence of dynastic munificence, which on a supraregional level frequently took its place alongside the commitments of the urban elites, and often benefited sanctuaries like Delphi or Delos. From the Hellenistic period onwards, western Asia Minor, in particular, occupied a special position, which continued into the 2nd and 3rd cents. AD (the period of greatest bloom for endowments).

In the Latin West, endowments are documented in the early Principate for Italy in particular (Rome and environs). Of the western provinces, only Africa and to some extent Gallia played a certain part. There are hardly any epigraphical records dating from late antiquity, which is undoubtedly linked with a decline in endowment activities, but maybe also with an abandonment of their written certification. Endowments were widespread within the Christian communities, but are not individually epigraphically documented.

II. Endowers and their Motives

Endowments were made by individuals, amongst them women, from all social ranks — from → freedpersons (CIL III 6998 = ILS 7196) to Hellenistic kings (OGIS 383) and Roman emperors (→ princeps) —, but also by families, → associations,→ *collegia*, and other groups of people. Equally wide-ranging were the motives for setting up endowments. Apart from assets gained from the spoils of war, ascent to an office is often quoted as a motive (CIL VIII 26591b). Gaining the benevolence of fellow citizens, subjects, or foreign powers (Pol. 31,31(25) with the help of an endowment was also an important political motive. An element of self-presentation and rivalry within the political elites also played its part. The numerous endowments in favour of imperial or other → ruler cults also belong into this context. However, other motives such as piety and the wish to be remembered (μνῆμα/*mnêma*; Lat. *memoria*) have to be considered as well. The commemoration of family members is often explicitly cited as a motive, but the endower might also have wanted to ensure the memory of his or her own person (CIL XIV 353 = ILS 6148; CIL XIV 367 = ILS 6164). Quite frequently, this has to be taken as the endower's real motive, especially as it was quite common to honour the institution of an endowment with the erection of a statue.

According to [7], the purpose and content of endowments fall into three, albeit quite fluid, categories: religious, agonal, and social. Apart from the construction and upkeep of sanctuaries, the category of religious endowments comprises mainly → sacrifices for deities and → heroes, often in conjunction with a festive → procession (πομπή/*pompḗ*; Lat. *pompa*) and a banquet. It also encompassed everything associated with the ruler cult (CIL XIV 2795 = ILS 272). Of particular importance were family cults or cults of the dead (CIL V 7906 = ILS 8374). Agonal endowments were concerned with the institution of musical or gymnastic agons (→ sports festivals), who could then be named after their initiator, or with the financing and equipping of existing → competitions.

Social endowments favoured certain specified groups (priests, office holders, *collegia*) as well as the general public; the oil endowment of Phaenia in Gytheium explicitly also included foreigners and slaves (IG V 1,1208). Examples of office endowments, whose means were used for the perpetual financial support of generally costly offices, are the → gymnasiarchy or the → stephanephoria in Asia Minor. The Attalids, for example, financed several school endowments (Rhodes, Eumenes [3] II. Soter: Pol. 31,31(25); Delphi, Attalus [5] II.: Syll.[3] 672). The distribution of → *sportulae* to a part of the population on certain feast or commemorative days also needs to be mentioned, as well as building endowments, which paid for the erection as well as upkeep of a building (Pliny [2] for a library: CIL V 5262 = ILS 2927).

Alongside alimentary endowments on the initiative of the *princeps* (→ *alimenta*), private endowments were also of importance, such as an endowment of Pliny the Younger [2] (CIL V 5262 = ILS 2927; Plin. Ep. 7,18): He gave a plot of land to the town of Comum, in order to lease it back for his own use. In that way, Comum had use of the rental income of 30,000 HS in order to support the freeborn boys and girls of the town.

In all, endowments contributed in a considerable way to the quality of life in ancient towns, even though they never played a decisive role in public life. Endowers and their descendants enjoyed a certain social prestige, at times expressed in public honours. The ultimate reason for the decline in the endowment culture was a continuous → devaluation of money, with the consequence that the yields of the endowment assets in the long run were insufficient to pay for its original purpose.

→ Alimenta; → Building trade; → Euergetes; → Euergetism; → Liberalitas, largitio

1 K. Bringmann, H. von Steuben (ed.), Schenkungen hell. Herrscher an griech. Städte und Heiligtümer, vol. 1, 1995 2 W. Eck, Der Euergetismus im Funktionszusammenhang der kaiserzeitl. Städte, in: Actes Xe Congr. Inter-

national d'Épigraphie grecque et latine, 1997, 306–331 3 PH. GAUTHIER, Les cités grecques et leurs bienfaiteurs (IVe-Ie s. av. J. C.), 1985 4 C. HABICHT, Gottmenschentum und griech. Städte, 21970 5 D. JOHNSON, Munificence and Municipia, JRS 75, 1985, 105–125 6 J. U. KRAUSE, Das spätant. Städtepatronat, in: Chiron 17, 1987, 1–80 7 B. LAUM, Stiftungen in der griech. und röm. Ant., 1914, repr. 1964 8 A. MANNZMANN, Griech. S.-Urkunden, 1962 9 F. QUASS, Die Honoratiorenschicht in den Städten des griech. Ostens, 1993 10 P. VEYNE, Le pain et le cirque, 1976 (English tr. by B. Pearce, Bread and Circuses, 1990) 11 G. WESCH-KLEIN, Liberalitas in rem publicam, 1990 12 M. WÖRRLE, Stadt und Fest im kaiserzeitl. Kleinasien, 1988. GA. W.

Endoxa see → Opinion

Endromis see → Shoes

Endymion (Ἐνδυμίων; *Endymíōn*). Son of Aethlius (or Zeus) and Calyce, a daughter of Aeolus (Paus. 5,8,1; Apollod. 1,56). In the Peloponnesian legend cycle the king of Elis (Ibycus Fr. 284 PMGF; Paus. 5,8,1), who led the Aetolians there from Thessaly, has his sons Paeon, Epius and Aetolus compete for their inheritance in a race. This is probably why a funerary monument of E. was shown at the stadium in Olympia (Paus. 5,1,4; 6,20,9). In Hesiod (Fr. 245 MERKELBACH-WEST) E. as a favourite of Zeus was permitted to decide on his own death. However, when he boldly desired Hera he was punished by being plunged into Hades (Hes. fr. 260 MW) or falling asleep for eternity (Epimenides FGrH 457 fr. 10). The love of the moon goddess → Selene for a beautiful hunter (Schol. Theoc. 3,49) or shepherd E. (Theoc. 20,37; Serv. Georg. 3,391; not yet in Hesiod) is always associated with Asia Minor and the Latmus mountains. When Selene, with whom he had 50 daughters (Paus. 5,1,4), obtained a wish for him from Zeus, E. choose eternal sleep in youth and immortality (Sappho Fr. 199 VOIGT; Apoll. Rhod. 4,57f.; Lucian Dial. deor. 19), or E. is finally heard by Selene because of his particularly white sheep. Hypnos, the god of sleep, also loves E. and, therefore, permits him to sleep with open eyes (Licymnius of Chios fr. 771 PMG). While rationalists made him the first astronomer (Plin. HN 2,6,43; Nonnus, Dion. 41,379) and Lucian (Ver. hist. 1,11) even calls him the king of the moon dwellers, the eternally sleeping E. was a favourite motif of Imperial age sarcophagus art. In Heraclea on the Latmus his grave or adyton was shown in a cave (Str. 14,1,8; Paus. 5,1,5).
→ Hypnos; → Calyce

E. BETHE, s.v. E., RE 5, 2557–2560; H. GABELMANN, s.v. E., LIMC 3.1, 726–742; L. ROBERT, Retour dans le Latmos à Héraclée; in: Id., A travers l'Asie Mineure, 1980, 351–353; H. SICHTERMANN, Späte E.-Sarkophage, 1966; Id., G. KOCH, Griech. Mythen auf röm. Sarkophagen, 1975; L. v. SYBEL, s.v. E., ROSCHER 1.1, 1246–48. T.S.

Enechyrasia (Ἐνεχυρασία; *Enechyrasía*). In Greek law the enforcement of a demand for money or the release of goods. It was used against movable and immovable assets (outside of Athens also against the person) of the debtor after the expiry of a term that is not precisely known. It was based on a judgement or an enforceable document and took the form of the creditor personally taking a colleratal. In Athens the *dḗmarchos* (→ Demarchoi) of the debtor's community of residence gave him access to the collateral. The creditor was free to choose the collateral objects (however, see Dem. Or. 47,58) but was liable for any excess (Dem. Or. 47,57). In Ptolemaic Egypt the *enechyrasia* was the first step of the enforcement, initiated after the creditor's request and performed by an enforcement official.

A. R. W. HARRISON, The Law of Athens II, 1971, 188ff.; H.-A. RUPPRECHT, Einführung in die Papyruskunde, 1994, 149. G.T.

Enema (*klystḗr*/*klystḗrion*, Lat. *clyster*/*clysterium*; also *klýsma*/*klysmós* and *éngklysma*, derived from *klýzein*/*engklýzein*, Lat. *inicere*: to pour, to rinse, and *enetḗr*/*énema*, from: *eniénai*: to inject) or clyster: pharmaceutical substance of, and device for, administering parenteral (in this case, often in combination with the adverb *kátō* or the verb *hypoklýzein*) or (in gynaecological treatises) vaginal injections of therapeutic solutions.

The instrument consisted of a flexible and compressible container (animal skin or bladder) with two openings at opposite ends, one for filling, the other for fastening to a tapering attachment of variable length made of natural (horn or bone) or artificial (metal) material with an opening at its tip, and perhaps more openings at the sides, the number and size of which could vary depending on the amount and the viscosity of the liquid to be injected. The injected solution consisted of any type of base, sometimes a mixture for creating an emulsion, and of a medical substance that was first boiled or soaked in the solution. The mixture was filled into the container, which had the attachment at one end, and the opening was closed. The doctor or (in gynaecology) the patient herself applied the mixture at different temperatures, depending on the desired effect, by progessive and continuous compressing of the container. An instrument of a similar kind but of smaller shape was used for injections into the ears or other anatomical openings. The therapeutic goal of the enema (in all its forms) was not only the purging of the (possibly pathogenic) content of the treated organ, but also (as far as the therapeutic effect is concerned, esp. in gynaecology) the application of medicinal substances, or of nutritional substances in the case of parenteral injection (the invention of this enema is attributed to Lycus of Naples).

The originators of the enema were considered to be the Egyptians, who copied the behaviour of the → ibis: the latter supposedly uses its long beak to inject water into its intestine. In Babylonian medicine, injections apparently were among the most important methods of administering medications [2. 78–82]. During all of antiquity, the enema was used in gynaecology, particularly in Hippocratic medicine; it was possibly the topic of a special treatise by Mantias. In later times, its use appears to have become less frequent, but it remained part of western medicine for a very long time and gave cause to an apocryphal writing distributed under Galen's name [1].

→ Galenus; → Lycus of Neapolis; → Mantias

1 L. ELAUT, Le traité galénique des clystères et de la colique, in: Janus 51, 1964, 136–151 2 D. GOLTZ, Stud. zur altoriental. und griech. Heilkunde, 1974.

E. KIND, s.v. K., RE 21, 881–890. A.TO.

Enepiskepsis (ἐνεπίσκηψις; *Enepískēpsis*). In Athens, when property was confiscated (→ *dḗmeusis*, → *dēmióprata*) a third party was able to claim that a particular part of the assets belonged to him or was mortgaged to him. If he objected, by using the form of an *enepiskepsis*, there would be a → *diadikasía* between him and the person initiating the confiscation (→ *apographḗ*) in which it was determined if the state debtor 'owed' cession of the asset parts to the third party (Dem. Or. 49,45ff.; Hesperia 10, 1941, 14).

A. R. W. HARRISON, The Law of Athens II, 1971, 216ff. G.T.

Energeia The abstract nomen ἐνέργεια (*enérgeia*) was (apparently) formed by Aristotle from the adjective ἐνεργός (*energós*: at work/acting/active) and introduced into philosophy as a technical term. He differentiates between (I) a δύναμις (*dýnamis*/potential) of being something and the ἐνέργεια (*enérgeia*/realization/actual state/activity) of being something, (II) two degrees of potential and two degrees of *enérgeia*, and (III) a narrow and a broad meaning of *enérgeia*. (Ia) To Aristotle matter is a potentiality, the form an *enérgeia*; for something is ἐνεργείᾳ (really) what it is — it is shaped as it is — because of its form (cf. An. 2,1,412a 19–21; Metaph. 8,6, 1045a 23–25). (Ib) Any change (motion) is to be understood as the *enérgeia* of a potentiality; for something is before potentially (δυνάμει) what (where) it later really (ἐνεργείᾳ) is (cf. Phys. 3,1,201a 10–b15) [1; 2]. The two degrees of potentiality and *enérgeia* (II) may be illustrated as follows: every human has a potentiality for acquiring language and the *enérgeia* of this potentiality is learning the language. Once, for example, speaking English has been learned, this is itself the (further) second potentiality for speaking English. The actual speaking of a language that one has mastered is an activity based on the acquired second potentiality and thus also a (second) *enérgeia* (III) However, in the strict sense, changes (such as learning) of first to second potentialities are → motions (κινήσεις) that (i) require time, (ii) can be described with adverbs like 'fast' or 'slow' and (iii) are not perfect in themselves but aim for completion (cf. Aristot. Eth. Nic. 10,3,1173a 29– b 4; Metaph. 9,6,1048b 18–36). (i) and (ii) are relatively clear. On (iii): Aristotle would say that someone who is learning English is not simultaneously someone who has learned English. However, if someone speaks English he is also one who has spoken English. In general (ϕ is a variable for verbs, x for possible subjects): if the following conclusion is *not* valid, then ϕ describes a *kínēsis*: if ϕx (present tense), then x has already and simultaneously ϕx-ed (perfect tense); e.g., if someone builds a house, he has *not* already and simultaneously built a house. However, if the conclusion is valid, then ϕ describes a true, i.e. a second *enérgeia*; e.g., when someone thinks, he has already thought and is simultaneously thinking. With this differentiation of realization and *enérgeiai* (in the narrow sense) Aristotle attempts to do justice to the internal structure of events. Motions *are*, but transitions from second potentialities to their respective realizations are *not*, temporal processes (Eth. Nic. 10,4,1174a13–b9). However, that does not mean that they are timeless but rather that if a second potentiality is 'activated', it is used at every point in time whithin the time period that it is used, e.g., when someone sees, his potential to see is fully activated (1174a 14–15; Metaph. 9,6,1048b 23) [3; 4; 5]. The difficult thoughts of significance to posterity that the soul is an *entelécheia* (An. 412a27), an *enérgeia* expressing the goal (*télos*) in life of a creature — in the meaning of a life appropriate to its kind —, and that God is a pure *énergeia* that is not based on a potential — that god is only active and completely active (cf. Metaph. 12,7,1072b14–21 and 12,9,1074b15–35; Eth. Nic. 10,8,1178b 7ff.) —, should be understood in this context.

1 S. WATERLOW, Nature, Change and Agency, 1982 2 R. HEINAMAN, Is Aristotle's Definition of Change Circular?, in: Apeiron 27, 1994, 25–58 3 T. PENNER, Verbs and the Identity of Actions, in: G. PITCHER, O. P. WOOD (ed.), Hyle: A Collection of Critical Essays, 1971 4 M. FREDE, Aristotle's Notion of Potentiality in Metaphysics Θ, in: T. SCALTSAS, D. CHARLES, M. L. GILL (ed.), Unity, Identity and Explanation in Aristotle's Metaphysics, 1994, 173–193 5 A. KOSMAN, The Activity of Being in Aristotle's Metaphysics, in: ibid., 195–213. WO.M.

Energy

A. MODERN CONCEPT OF ENERGY AND ANCIENT CONCEPT OF MOTION AND FORCE B. THE USE OF ENERGY IN ANTIQUITY 1. HUMAN MUSCLE POWER 2. ANIMAL TRACTION 3. WATER POWER 4. THERMAL ENERGY

A. MODERN CONCEPT OF ENERGY AND ANCIENT CONCEPT OF MOTION AND FORCE

Since the middle of the 19th cent., the term energy describes the capacity of matter to perform work in various forms. A precise definition of the terms force, work and energy became unavoidable because of technological development during the industrial revolution and the increasing cooperation of technicians and scientists. The law of the preservation of energy formulated by modern physics makes it possible to describe the transformation of one form of energy into another exactly, and to clearly record the degree of effectiveness of various energy forms. A distinction is made between kinetic and thermal energy. In ancient natural philosophy no idea comparable to the modern concept of energy was developed. Aristotle defined four relevant variables in his theory of motion — the mover, the moved, distances and time (Phys. 249b–250b) — but did not arrive at a clear concept of work as used by modern physics. In Aristotelian mechanics the effect of mechanical instruments, especially the lever, is seen in moving large weights with little force (Ps.-Aristot. Mech. 847a–850b). In the subsequent development of mechanics the focus was on using a given force as effectively as possible, e.g., by lifting heavy loads with rollers and pulleys. However, there was no means of saving energy by technical means.

B. The use of energy in Antiquity

1. Human muscle power

In the history of economy and technology energy potentials and forms of energy use are fundamental criteria for the analysis of an economy; in the ancient economy it is almost impossible to quantify energy sources but energy use may be described in outline. Essentially, one must assume that the most commonly used sources of energy in Antiquity were human and animal muscle power as well as firewood and charcoal. Thermal energy — excepting → automaton technology — was not transformed into kinetic energy and there was no propulsion using fossil fuels. Many labour processes in agriculture and the crafts were performed by people with simple tools so that no demand for energy other than human muscle power arose. In transportation the share of human muscle power should not be underestimated either: in towns, on estates and in ports loads were transported by people, in part with such simple means as a staff that rested on the shoulders of two bearers.

2. Animal traction

The option of using animals for labour opened a further energy potential — technical progress that was already reflected in Greek literature: in the tragedies Prometheus boasted of having been the first to harness the animals who saved human beings so much effort (Aesch. PV 462–466). In agriculture this initially applied to soil cultivation, especially ploughing. In the Mediterranean region oxen (→ Cattle) and less frequently cows or → donkeys were used. Oxen were also used to pull heavy loads placed on carts with two lateral disc wheels and an axle. Mules (→ Hinnies) were already important draught animals in the archaic period and normally drew light wagons with spoked wheels. However, due to a lack of good roads, transportation did not always use the cart but rather to a large extent pack animals that carried goods of all sorts (grain, firewood, metal ingots etc.) on their backs. Among pack animals donkeys and mules were the most important. In the Near East the → camel was already used at an early time for this purpose. The issue of which animals were used in the economy did not depend only on the harnessing but also the temperament of the animals, feeding costs and susceptibility to disease. Since animals were not suited for the monotonous work in agriculture and transport, far reaching intervention in their natural disposition was required to adapt them to their respective tasks. Castration modified the temperament of the bull, and mules were bred by crossing donkeys and horses to combine the good qualities of both. Since animal traction was an important energy source animal breeding must be considered to a significant degree from this perspective: cattle were especially bred to use the workforce of oxen, a perspective already found in Plato (Pl. Resp. 370e).

The development of complicated tools and instruments also created the option of using human and animal muscle power as a propulsive force. This applied to such a simple instrument as the potter's wheel, put into motion by the potter's assistants. Humans also powered the great bucket wheels that controlled the water level in Roman mines or cranes equipped with a tread wheel. Once rotating mills were available for grinding grain, animals were used: the mills of Pompeii were constructed to be turned by → horses or donkeys who walked blindfolded in a small circle.

3. Water and wind power

Water power was first used to grind grain: a vertical water wheel drove a millstone via a transmission mechanism; a system of this type was first described by Vitruvius (10,5). In the → *Edictum Diocletiani* water mills and rotation mills turned by horses or donkeys are mentioned together (15,52–54); in late antiquity several water mills are documented in literature and archaeology, among them the milling centre at the Ianiculum in Rome. Since rivers in the Mediterranean region had little water during the summer, mills such as at the Ianiculum and the similar system in southern France near Arles used water from aqueducts. In the 6th cent. AD boat mills that adapt to the water level are first mentioned on the Tiber (Procop. Goth. 1,19,19ff.). According to Ausonius (Mos. 361–364) marble saws were powered by water in the 4th cent. AD near Trier. In this case the rotational movement of the water wheel was transformed into the linear motion of the saw. The use of wind power was restricted to navigation. Military craft were usually rowed and, thus propelled, by humans, while commerce usually used sail ships that exploited the wind on their voyages in the Mediterranean, the Atlantic and to India.

4. Thermal energy

→ Wood and → charcoal were important energy sources; for the preparation of metals, firing pottery, bricks and glass production thermal energy was required on a large scale; households also required considerable amounts of fuel for preparing foods.

If one looks at energy use as a whole in antiquity, the primacy of human and animal muscle power as well as wood as a fuel is apparent. The water mill was by no means as widespread in the Imperium Romanum as in the Middle Ages, but the fundamental step in terms of a history of technology of an economically effective use of water power was performed in late antiquity.
→ Automatata; → Fuels; → Edictum Diocletiani

1 L. Casson, Energy and Technology in the Ancient World, in: Id., Ancient Trade and Society, 1984, 130–152 2 R. Halleux, Problèmes de l'énergie dans le monde ancien, in: Etudes Classiques 45, 1977, 49–61 3 J. G. Landels, Engineering in the Ancient World, 1978, 9–33 4 White, Technology, 49–57 5 Ö. Wikander, Exploitation of Water-Power or Technological Stagnation?, 1984 6 Id., The Use of Water-Power in Classical Antiquity, in: Opuscula Romana 13, 1981, 91–104. AS.S.

Engomi Fortified Bronze Age port settlement of the late Cypriote phase (LC III A) in east Cyprus with palace and sanctuaries (e.g. of the 'horned' or 'ingot god'); workshops for coppersmiths; graves in the town and necropolis; rich finds, especially of metallic material (some inscribed in the Cypriote syllabic script), several hoardfinds. Probably founded early in the 2nd millennium, flowered in the 16th/15th cents. BC because of the international copper trade. Rich burial finds of the 14th/13th cents. (including Mycenaean ware). After destruction in the 13th cent. a planned reconstruction can be demonstrated archaeologically. *C.* 1075 BC the town was completely destroyed by an earthquake and as a result → Salamis was founded. Both towns existed side by side for *c.* 25 years until Engomi was completely abandoned about 1050 BC, probably also because the port was silted up. English, French and Cypriote digs. The equation of Engomi (and also Citium) with the town (?) → Alaschia, mentioned in Hittite, Akkadian and Egyptian sources, is disputed.

J. C. Courtois et al., Enkomi et le Bronze Récent à Chypre, 1986; P. Dikaios, Enkomi I-III (1969–1971); V. Karageorghis, Cyprus from the Stone Age to the Romans, 1982; O. Masson, Les Inscriptions chypriotes syllabiques, ²1983. A.W.

Engye (ἐγγύη; *engýē*). Surety or bail, later also termed → *engýēsis*. Its oldest form, the hostage surety, can be seen in Hom. Od. 8,266–366. Therefore, the *engye* was a guarantee in case the main debtor did not fulfil his duty of repayment. The security consisted of access to the hostage, the ἔγγυος (*éngyos*), provided to the creditor. Like a pawn, he became the creditor's who proceeded on his own if the guaranteed success did not materialize, hence also the post-verbal expression *engye* from ἐγγυάω (*engyáō*) 'to hand over' as pledge [1]. In classical Greek law there was a reinterpretation into 'taking over the debtor's person'. However, there was also the legal form of the surety through *bona fide* promise. The 'payment security', ἐγγύη εἰς ἔκτισιν (*engyē eís éktistin*), also a pure issue of liability, did not develop from the hostage security but from the surety for the providing of foods. Although the exact wording was not defined, the assumption of a guarantee required explicitness, and the names of the guarantors were entered into a written contract regarding the principal debt. Unlike modern law, the *engye* was not dependent on a claim (e.g., a loan repayment) and could also be assumed for future obligations. Recovery of damages to twice the amount of the claim was possible against the principal debtor (IPArk. 17, 109–111). The *engye* is encountered in all areas of debt law, in business transactions (Dem. Or. 33,10), work contracts and leasing by the public as well as in procedural law in sureties for the providing of goods and for performance. In the Egyptian papyri a mutual obligation of two or more debtors occurs, the ἀλληλεγγύη (*allēllengýē*), which in the end only resulted in a joint liability of the debtors.

1 Frisk, s.v. E.

J. Partsch, Griech. Bürgschaftsrecht I, 1909; K. Sethe-H. Partsch, Demot. Urkunden zum Bürgschaftsrecht, 1920, 516ff.; D. M. MacDowell, The Law in Classical Athens, 1978, 76. 167; A. Biscardi, Diritto greco antico, 1982, 161ff.; G. Thür-H. Taeuber, Prozeßrechtliche Inschr. Arkadiens, 1994, 172, 179.; H.-A. Rupprecht, Einführung in die Papyruskunde, 1994, 131. G.T.

Engyesis (ἐγγύησις; *engýēsis*). In Greece a festive legal act concluded between the bridegroom and the → *kýrios* of the bride in the presence of witnesses on which the husband's rights are founded (also called ἐγγύη, *engýē*), formerly wrongly interpreted as 'engagement'. It only became fully effective with the transfer of the bride to the husband (→ *ékdosis*). In Gortyn the *engýēsis* is never mentioned but it is by Plato (Leg. 774e). In the papyri *engýēsis* is a synonym of → *engýē*.

H. J. Wolff, Beiträge zur Rechtsgesch. Altgriechenlands, 1961, 170 (from 1944); Id., Die Grundlagen des griech. Eherechts, in: TRG 20, 1952, 160ff.; A. R. W. Harrison, The Law of Athens I, 1968, 3ff. G.T.

Engyon (Ἔγγυον; *Énguon*). City in the interior of Sicily, supposedly founded by Cretans (Diod. Sic. 4,79; Plut. Marcellus 20), taken by Timoleon from the tyrant Leptines (Diod. Sic. 16,72); in the 2nd Punic War on the side of Carthage and yet treated gently by Marcellus (Plut., ibid.); according to Cic. Verr. 3,103 a *civitas decumana*, according to Plin. HN 3,91 *stipendiarii*; the sanctuary of the 'mothers' (Plut. ibid.) was famous, in Cic. Verr. 2,4,97 of the *Mater Magna*, 2,5,186 *Mater Idaea*, with relics of Meriones and Odysseus. Undoubtedly identical with Troina [1. 130[13]; 2].

1 G. Manganaro, Alla ricerca di mikrai poleis della Sicilia centro-orientale, in: Orbis Terrarum 2, 1996 2 G. Bejor, s.v. Engio, BTCGI 7, 185–188. GI.F.

Enipeus (Ἐνιπεύς; *Enipeús*).
[1] A tributary to the right of the → Alpheius [1] in Elis, also Βαρνίχιος (*Barníchios*, 'River of Lambs') [1], mod-

ern Lestenitsa west of Olympia (Str. 8,3,32; Hom. Od. 11,238ff.).

1 E. Curtius, Peloponnesos 2, 1852, 71f. C.L. and E.O.

[2] Main river of the West Thessalian plain, modern Tsanarlis. Its source is in the Othrys range near Melitaea under the name *Elipeus* (IG IX 2, 205 and add.). After running in places through gorges, to the north it enters the plain *c.* 10 km east of Pharsalus where it turns northeast. About 5 km before entering the Peneius it receives, with the → Apidanus (whose name it may have born in antiquity), the waters of the West Thessalian plain. The swamps in this area (→ Limnaeum) have largely disappeared because of drainage and dykes. The valley of the Enipeus was the scene of the battles of Cynoscephalae and Pharsalus as well as other military actions, e.g., by Persian troops in 480 BC (Hdt. 7,129ff.; [1]), Philippus V after 198, during the war against Antiochus in 192/1 and the war against Perseus in 169 BC [2].

1 J.-C. Decourt, La vallée de l'E. en Thessalie, 1990
2 F. Stählin, Das hellen. Thessalien, 1924, 83.
HE.KR. and C.L.

Enklema (ἔγκλημα; *énklēma*). In general Greek usage 'reproach', in the laws of Athens 'suit' in civil trials, in the criminal law of Egyptian papyri 'charge'. Before the law, which in Athens required written form for the court file (presumably 378/7 BC), the *enklema* was a verbal application to the head of the court (→ *dikastḗrion* 3.) to open the trial, which included the name of the parties, the suit and, if provided, (in the → *tímētos agṓn*), an estimate of the judgement sum. Written *enklḗmata* are preserved in Dem. Or. 37,22–32; 45,46, and imprecisely called → *graphḗ* or (with the response to the suit) → *antigraphḗ*. The rigid formalism of the *dikasteria* resulted in the judgement merely being able to confirm or reject the *enklema* but not to modify it. Documentation outside Athens: e.g., IPArk. 16,14,16; 17,36; 92; 131; 25,2.

G. Thür, Formen des Urteils, in: Akten des 26. Dt. Rechtshistorikertages, ed. by D. Simon, 1987, 475f. H.-A. Rupprecht, Einführung in die Papyruskunde, 1994, 152 G. Thür, H. Taeuber, Prozeßrechtliche Inschr. Arkadiens, 1994. G.T.

Enktesis (Ἔγκτησις; *Énktēsis*). In the Greek states the acquisition of property was reserved to citizens. Individual foreigners were granted the privilege of *énktesis*, the right to acquire 'land' or 'a house' (or both) by a popular resolution. In Athens some → *métoikoi* were thus provided, generally perhaps the → *isoteleís*. In the Doric area the term ἔμπασις/ἵμπασις (*émpasis/ímpasis*) was used instead of *enktesis*.

J. Pečirka, The Formula for the Grant of E. in Attic Inscriptions, 1966 A.R. W. Harrison, The Law of Athens I, 1968, 237f. A.S. Henry, Honours and Privileges in Athenian Decrees, 1983 M.H. Hansen, The Athenian Democracy in the Age of Demosthenes, 1991, 97 G. Thür, H. Taeuber, Prozeßrechtliche Inschr. Arkadiens, 1994, No. 36. G.T.

Enkyklios paideia (ἐγκύκλιος παιδεία; *enkýklios paideía*).
A. Term B. Nature C. History

A. Term

The term *enkýklios paideía* (and similar ones, e.g., *enkýklia mathḗmata/paideúmata*) is only attested since *c.* 50 BC [1. 370–375; 2. 6–18; 3. 263–293]. Diogenes Laertios (2,79; 7,32) and Stobaeus (2,206,26–28; 3,246,1–5) seemingly ascribe the expression to Hellenistic philosophers, but perhaps it was only an attempt to provide ancestry for their own terminology (contrary [2. 6f.]). That the concept of *e.p.* originally supposedly described the musical training acquired by Attic citizens united in a circle to sing and dance [4] has been accepted by some [1. 369f.] and rejected by others [2. 14–17]. In general there are two opinions: 1. 'ordinary education' [1. 371], 2. 'general, non-expert education', acquired with the help of a circle of educational objects [2. 14]. The idea of a 'circle of sciences' should, however, probably be assigned to Roman authors (Vitruvius, Quintilian); in the Greek sphere it can only be demonstrated from the 2nd half of the 3rd cent. AD (Porphyrius in Tzetz. Chiliades 11,377) [1. 372–375; 5. 113f.]. The argument that the term *paideía* already contained the notion of 'non-expert' [2. 13] is insufficient because *enkýklios* also certainly adds the aspect of 'customary': *enkýklios paideía*, therefore, would be the 'normal' or 'standard education'. This would allow a term appearing later to be plausibly associated with an activity of much older date. (The designation of the 'ordinary' [2. 13f.] musical-gymnastic education as *paideía* appears to have not been a technical term but only one of several used; Aristophanes Nub. 961 calls it *archaía paideía.*).

B. Nature

The *e.p.* represents an educational concept that was to train the intellect and form the character of a youth through a general study of grammar, rhetoric, dialectics, arithmetic, geometry, astronomy and music, thus encouraging personal development [5. 260f., 335–338]. Philosophers, rhetoric teachers and even experts considered it a propaedeutic for philosophy and rhetorical education or expert training, for example, as a philologist, geographer, architect; but others, e.g. epicureans, cynics, sceptics, some stoics, rejected it as useless [2. 47–111]. Depending on the situation, philosophy (often instead of dialectics) or rhetoric were placed in or above the system of subjects. The incompleteness of some catalogues (see the summary at the end of [2]), reflects the deficit in educational reality, to the extent that completeness was intended. However, there is no need to speak of 'extensions' by other subjects [2. 18–42; 337]: → Menecles of Barca (FGrH 3, 270,9), who listed *technítai* (persons exercizing professions) certainly was not including painting, gymnastics and medicine in the *e.p.* (see also [2. 31f.]). → Maximus of Tyrus discussed *eleuthérioi téchnai*, which can also include gymnastics [6. 79–129]. → Galen included (Protreptikos 5,14) medicine and jurisprudence among the *téchnai logikaí*, which are also not identical to the *e.p.* and therefore represent the professional pride of intellectuals [6. 120–125].

Together with the contemporary understanding of the *artes liberales*, the *e.p.* was also questioned [3. 263–293]: from Vitr. De arch. 1,1,1–3; 1,1,12; 1,1,15f.; Quint. 1,10,1; 1,10,11; 1,10,34; 1,10,37 and Plin. HN praef. 14 it was conjectured that *e.p.* meant the '*culture complète*' of a minority of the educated and the specialized *technítai*; Schol. Dion. Thrax p. 112,16–20 HILGARD demonstrates the identity of *enkýklioi téchnai* (a synonym of *e.p.*) and *logikaí téchnai*. This thesis is not tenable: a) In Quintilian the disciplines of law and philosophy, which are only discussed in book 12, are not part of the *e.p.* treated in the first book; in Pliny *e.p.* is a subcategory, not a category of the areas of knowledge listed by him. The *e. p.* is part of Strabo's Polymathia (1,1,1) [2. 90f.]. b) *Enkyklios paideia* and *logikaí téchnai* are not identical. Only the *technítai* speak of *logikaí téchnai*, but not the theoreticians of education because they wished to distinguish themselves from physical labourers [6. 74–129]. c) Testimonials such as Diod. Sic. 33,7,7 are wrongly dismissed [3. 264]: the context demonstrates that Viriathus was not lacking '*culture complète*', but quite simply general education. This was also meant in Str. 1,1,22 with *enkýklios agōgḗ* (otherwise [3. 290f.]). d) In the education of Nicolaus of Damascus (Suda 3,468,3 ADLER) we have a complete progress through the *e.p.* ([3. 36[34]] relating 'knowledge of mathematics' to dialectics; but the meaning of 'mathematical sciences' — e.g., Pl. Leg. 817e — fits without difficulties into the context of other disciplines). e) Regarding the sources as a whole, it should be considered that the authors who speak of general education are discussing something that was a matter of course to their readers (insightful S. Emp. adversus mathematicos 1,7). It is the *technítai*, who in an attempt to profit from the respectability of the *e.p.*, give explanations — mostly such that manipulate the nature of the *e.p.*

C. HISTORY

In essence, the *enkyklios paideia* was already developed by the sophists [1. 366; 2. 42–50; 7. 114–123]. An important component of their teaching was the explanation of poems which aimed at a refinement of language sensitivity and formal logic (Pl. Prt. 338e–348a; Grg. 484bc). This required linguistic and grammatical knowledge. Thus, → Protagoras, → Prodicus and → Hippias contributed to the development of grammatical knowledge [4. 45]. → Thrasymachus and → Gorgias made decisive contributions to the development of rhetorical artistic prose. Thrasymachus wrote a rhetorical *téchnē* and gave rhetoric lessons; Gorgias explicitly described rhetoric as the only subject he taught (Pl. Grg. 449a, 452de), while Protagoras taught both the technique of coherent discourse as well as rapidly held discussion (Pl. Prt. 334e f., 329ab). Hippias claimed that he could respond to any question directed at him in improvized speech (Pl. Hp. mi. 363cd). The sophists copied the formal technique of disputation — to distinguish it from philosophical dialectics, Plato called it *eristic* — from the Eleates → Zeno and → Melissus [4. 46]. In particular, Hippias — taking up the Pythagorean tradition — included arithmetic, astronomy, geometry and music into the sophist teaching programme (Pl. Prt. 318de; Hp. mi. 366c–368a; mai. 285b-d).

With Plato, in whose philosophical *paideía* the mathematical disciplines acquired special importance, and Isocrates, who gave the *e.p.* its form for the subsequent period, the history of the *e.p.* merged with that of ancient education in general and, with the acceptance of the latter by the Romans into that of the *artes liberales*.

→ Artes liberales; → ARTES LIBERALES; → Education; → Paideia; → Sophistry

1 H. FUCHS, s.v. E.P., RAC 3, 365–398 2 F. KÜHNERT, Allgemeinbildung und Fachbildung in der Ant., 1961 3 I. HADOT, Arts libéraux et philosophie dans la pensée antique, 1984 4 H. KOLLER, Ἐγκύκλιος παιδεία, in: Glotta 34, 1955, 174–189 5 H. I. MARROU, in: Gnomon 36, 1964, 113–116 6 J. CHRISTES, Bildung und Ges., 1975 7 MARROU.

J.C.

Enlil (Sumerian 'Lord Wind'). City-god of → Nippur and highest god of the Sumerian-Akkadian Pantheon in the 3rd and the 1st half of the 2nd millennium BC. His place was taken in the 1st millennium by → Marduk, the god of Babylon. His spouse was Ninlil (→ Mylissa).

→ Marduk; → Mesopotamia; → Nippur

T. JACOBSEN, Treasures of Darkness, 1976.

J.RE.

Ennia Aequa Wife of L. Vitrasius Flamininus, *cos. suff.* in 122, mother of L. Vitrasius Ennius Aequus. CIL X 4123 = CAMODECA, EOS I 531.

W.E.

Ennius

[1] **E., Q.** Latin writer of the pre-classical period.

A. LIFE B. LITERARY WORK 1. DRAMATIC POETRY 2. OPERA MINORA 3. ANNALS C. RECEPTION

E. (239–169 BC) is the most important and versatile Latin writer (Fronto p. 134,1 H.[2]) of the pre-classical period. Although 'a foreigner in Rome' [21] (sociologically a dependent poet, *poeta cliens* [33]) and representative of Hellenistic education, he contributed to shaping the Roman national consciousness through sentences such as *moribus antiquis res stat Romana virisque* (Ann. 500 V.; see Cic. Rep. 5,1).

A. Life

Most of the preserved biographical details appear to be based on statements in the works of E. [38] that were collected by → Varro [1] in *De poetis*. E. was born in 239 BC (Gell. NA 17,21,43; Cic. Brut. 72) in Rudiae (Ann. 377) in ancient Calabria (Hor. Carm. 4,8,20) and claimed descent from the tribal hero Messapus (Ann. 376; cf. Sil. Pun. 12,393–397); variants (Jer. Chron.: born 240 in Tarento) are not credible. Culturally, his home was part of *Magna Graecia* (*E. semigraecus*: Suet. Gram. 1,2; *Graecus*: Fest. 374 L/293 M), politically part of Rome's sphere of influence since 266. E. claimed to have *tria corda* because he spoke Greek, Oscan and Latin (Gell. NA 17,17,1). According to Nepos (Cato 1,4), M. Porcius → Cato [1], then the quaestor of P. Scipio (Africanus) brought E. in 204 from Sardinia to Rome. There E. appears to have lived in modest circumstances on the Aventine (Jer. Chron. a. Abr. 1777, Cic. Cato 14). According to Suet. Gram. 1,2f. he gave lessons in Greek and Latin (apparently privately as a *grammaticus*). As he celebrated Africanus maior in his *Scipio*, he probably (initially?) enjoyed the protection of the Scipiones (cf. Cic. De or. 2,276). Since at least 189 M. → Fulvius Nobilior was E.'s real patron. He accepted him as court poet (later severely reprimanded by Cato, ORF p. 59f. = fr. 109, 112 Sb.) and took him on his campaign against the Aetolians and their capital Ambracia (Cic. Arch. 27, Tusc. 1,3; Symmachus, Ep. 1,20,2; Vir. ill. 52,3); perhaps also → Caecilius [III 6] Statius (according to Jer. Chron. a. Abr. 1838 = 179 BC *contubernalis* of E.). E. fulfilled his expectations with the praetexta (?) *Ambracia* and later the *Annales*. Perhaps under E.'s influence, Fulvius founded the *aedes Herculis Musarum* ('Temple of Hercules, the Leader of Muses') in Rome in 187 or perhaps later as censor in 179. Through a member of his *gens* (Cic. Brut. 79: son Q.; differently [16. 183–185]), Fulvius obtained Roman citizenship in 184 for E. (cf. Cic. Arch. 22), who boasted of this honour (Ann. 377). E. died in 169 (despite Prop. 3,3,8 not in 167) at the age of 70 (Cic. Cato 14), according to Jer. Chron. a. Abr. 1849 (168 BC) from gout (but cf. [38. 233–236] on Sat. 64 V).

B. Literary work

E. shaped Latin epics by replacing Saturnian with hexameter verse (→ Metrics II). With innovative content and form E. took up Hellenistic themes in several smaller poems, from manneristic or even parody (*Hedyphagetica*) to philosophical, Pythagorean influenced teaching (*Epicharmus*; in *Euhemerus* for the first time in Rome in literary prose). With the *Satura* (→ Satire) he created a medium of direct personal expression. Apart from hexameter and Sotadean metre, he introduced another verse measure to Rome: he wrote → epigrams in elegiac distiches, which also replaced Saturnian verse. Since Plautus alludes to his tragedies (Poen. 1–11), E. must have emerged as a dramatist right after 204; shortly before his death he had the tragedy *Thyestes* staged (Cic. Brut. 78). Individual works cannot be dated more closely. E. was working on the *Annales* in 184 (the year in which he received citizenship) and in 172 was still occupied with book 12 (of 18) (thus Gell. NA 17,21,43; the number of books should be increased [38. 115–120, 133f.]). Because E. was credited with the introduction of consonant doubling (Fest. 374 L/293 M) and 1,100 (stenographic) abbreviations (Isid. Orig. 1,22,1), *duos libros de litteris syllabisque, item de metris* were assigned to him as *philólogos* (*dicti studiosus*, Ann. 216) by the 1st cent. BC at the latest (differently in Suet. Gram. 1,3: a *posterior Ennius* as author; Fest. 482, 19 L).

1. Dramatic poetry

Titles and fragments of at least 20 tragedies with more than 400 verses are preserved [39]. Essentially, they are all translations [31. 41–67], often with comments interspersed, or, more precisely, reworkings of Greek models (by contrast Cic. Fin. 1,4 and Ac. 1,10). Attested are (on the double counting of no. 1 and 14: [35]): 1. *Achilles* (= *Achilles Aristarchi*?), 2. *Aiax*, 3. *Alcmeo*, 4. *Alexander*, 5. *Andromacha* (*aechmalotis*), 6. *Andromeda*, 7. *Athamas* (on the remarkable metrics [32. 119–125]), 8. *Cresphontes*, 9. *Erechtheus*, 10. *Eumenides*, 11. *Hectoris lytra* (relationship to No. 1 disputed), 12. *Hecuba* (Gell. NA 11,4 compares Enn. scaen. 199–201 with Eur. Hec. 293–295), 13. *Iphigenia*, 14. *Medea* (= *Medea exul*?), 15. *Melanippa*, 16. *Nemea*, 17. *Phoenix*, 18. *Telamo*, 19. *Telephus*, 20. *Thyestes*. Furthermore, a 21st tragedy called *Alcumena* (following Euripides) is often deduced from Plaut. Rud. 86 [37. 177–181]. All titles refer to the well-known world of Greek heroes, which appealed to audiences in Rome, six of them even to heroines and almost half belong to the Trojan legend cycle (4, 19, 13, 1, 11, 2, 5, 12, 18). The works of → Euripides are generally assumed to be the models (attested for 4, 5, 12, 14, deduced for 6, 9, 13, 15, 17, 19, 20 as well as 3, 7, 8). Glossographi Latini 1,568 L suggests in some cases (not only 1) → Aristarchus [2], a contemporary of Euripides. However, a direct comparison with a preserved model is only possible in four cases (10, 12–14; on this [31]). Indications (especially for 14, 11 and 10) suggest that the 'contamination' (the amalgamation of several models), which is explicitly documented for E.' comedies in Ter. Andr. 15–21, also applies to his tragedies. With this practice E. continued an analogous development in Hellenistic theatre. The same applies to the strengthening of solo song by replacing the spoken verses of the model (→ Canticum). Stylistically, E. often attempts to elevate the pathos, for example with borrowings from religious and legal speech. Phonetic figures are sought, especially → alliteration [25. 160–222]. The metaphors are also often elaborated, which → Plautus already parodies. Nevertheless, *E. tragicus* must have remained close to everyday speech (see Cic. De or. 109. 183f.). A wealth of *sententiae* was excerpted by the rhetor schools (Rhet. Her. 4,4,7; → gnome).

Because of their titles, the following are considered to be → praetextae [39. 361]: 1. *Sabinae* (cf. H. D. Joce-

LYN [22. 82–88, 93–95]); 2. *Ambracia*, probably a celebratory play for the triumph of Fulvius in 187, the first praetexta to glorify a living person. E. was not much admired as a → palliata poet (in last place in the 'canon' of → Volcacius Sedigitus in Gell. NA 15,24). No more than fragments of 3–4 comedies are attested [39. 361f.].

2. OPERA MINORA

These share a personal and auctorial, even autobiographical element. Of the *libri saturarum* (surely not the authentic ancient name because *satira* [→ satire] of the older type is itself a synonym of *liber*) there appear to have been six (Donat. Ter. Phorm. 339) and not four 'books' (Porph. Hor. Sat. 1,10,46). The recognizable content resembles a moralizing cynic → diatribe rather than the iambics of → Callimachus. Because of Gellius' prose paraphrase (2,29), the Aesopian fable of the crested lark, which in the original was composed *in saturis versibus quadratis* (certainly over 50 trochaic septenaries), is the only piece in the entire works of E. that continued to have an effect in the Middle Ages and later, as it was included in anthologies of fables [21. No. 569].

In → *Epicharmus* [4. 276–289], composed in trochaic septenaries, E., who in a dream was placed in the Underworld as a dead person, received revelations in natural philosophy, especially with respect to the four elements and their relationship to the deities, from the title character [38. 92–94]. An even stronger demythologization of the deities is evident in *Euhemerus* (a rendition of the Greek travel novel of → Euhemerus of Messene, created after 316; [4. 133–137, 289–308; 45]; → Euhemerism) which was presumably written before the burning of the 'Pythagorean' Numa books in 181 BC. Fame is the theme in all four extant epigrams that are of significance in intellectual history: the so-called image and grave epigrams of E. (Cic. Tusc. 1,34; [38]) and the two epigrams on Scipio Africanus maior, in the second of which E. makes him claim divinity in the first person. A panegyric tendency is also evident in *Scipio* [38. 103–105, 239–248; 18. 161–167]. Only three fragments in trochaic septenares that may be attached to the tradition of triumphal poetry in *versus quadratus* are explicitly attested (the genre is disputed). No impression is to be had of the *Sota*, which was still appreciated in the 2nd cent. AD. Title and verse measure (Sotadean) point to → Sotades as the model. The content of *Protrepticus* (only one word preserved) and *Praecepta* (one fragment in trochaic septenaries) may only be attributed to philosophy because of their titles. The *Hedyphagetica* (11 ponderous hexameters preserved), in the Alexandrian tradition, constitute a translation of the parodying Greek didactic poem of → Archestratus [2] of Gela on delicacies; the reference to Ambracia demands a date after 189.

3. ANNALES

In this hexametric → Epic in 18 books (more than 600 fragments preserved; recent addition: PHerc. 21 from Ann. B. 6: [40]) E. for the first time presents all of Roman history in Latin: beginning with the departure of Aeneas (in E. the grandfather of Romulus) from Troy to his own day. E. was the first Latin literary figure to divide his work into books (though they were relatively small and cannot be reconstructed). It particularly gave weight to the Monarchy and the more recent past. A division in triads is evident: early Roman history to the end of the Monarchy (books 1–3), the Republican period to the war with Pyrrhus (280–275; book 4–6). After a leap over the First Punic War (264–241), which was omitted out of consideration of → Naevius, book 7, marked by a prooemium, treats contemporary history: the war with Hannibal (218–201; books 7–9). An invocation of the muses at the beginning of book 10 opens the description of the (2nd) Macedonian war (200–197). After that E. must have narrated in more detail or set more scenes (books 10–15 = 200–189/187). Book 12 possibly had an epilogue.

From Plin. HN 7,101 it was concluded that E. originally wanted to conclude the *Annales* with book 15, presumably with the triumph of his benefactor Fulvius over the Aetolians in 187. However, the work was restarted again with a new prooemium in Ann. 16 and extended by the barely tangible books 17–18. His structuring of Roman history is E.'s own achievement [cf. 20. 133f.]. His historical sources were Greek, but also Romans such as → Fabius Pictor, and sub-literary Latin records such as the *Annales Pontificum*. E.'s most important achievement in his presentation consisted of Roman history (and not just as in Naevius' *Bellum Poenicum* the 'Archaeology') being 'homerized': the appearance of deities, speeches, *aristeiai*, similes [35. 38–62], *ekphraseis* and the subdivision of events in single days. His self-styling in the prooemium of book 1 as *Homerus redivivus*, which E. underpinned rationally through the theory of the transmigration of souls, must, like the motif of the consecration of the poet and the memory of Callimachus cloaked in a dream (and the Hesiodeic-enlightening tendency of the poet) be understood in programmatic terms. However, the *Annales* also display un-Homeric, Hellenistic and, therefore, 'modern' traits, not only its factual aspects (such as cavalry and naval battles), but especially its pronounced autobiographical, meta-literary and panegyric elements (cf. in this respect [46]). They especially appear in the prooemia of books 1, 7 and 16 [38; 18. 143–171], but also in his consideration for contemporaries [16; 33; 23; 27] and the indirect self-portrait as the 'Good Companion' (Gell. NA 12,4; [38. 142f.]).

C. RECEPTION

E. is considered the greatest Roman poet before Varro and Cicero (material: chronologically [1. XX-CXLIV]; according to genera [6. 8–44]; on this [17. 1–223]). The *Annales* were the representative epic of Rome until displaced by the *Aeneid* of → Virgil (which borrows language from E.). → Lucilius parodied E., → Lucretius admired him. Philologists of the 2nd/1st cents. BC examined him (Q. → Vargunteius; M.

→ Pompilius Andronicus: Suet. Gram. 2,4. 8,1). Roman annalists and historians (explicitly attested for → Coelius [I 1] Antipater) to including → Livy were stylistically influenced by E.'s epic. They took over principles of evaluation and representation for 'moral' and 'dramatic' orientation.

In the 1st half of the 1st cent. BC the → Neoterics established a new 'Alexandrian' ideal of literary style so that E. increasingly was perceived as a *vetus*, the representative of an archaic, dated period. Therefore, Ovid's 'appreciation' (Trist. 2,424) *Ennius ingenio maximus, arte rudis* is actually a condemnation. In the 1st cent. AD Seneca's judgement marked a low point in the assessment of E. (in Gell. NA 12,2,3–14). However, Sil. 12,390–414 appreciated E. as a person and a poet, Quint. Inst. 10,1,88 with detached respect. In the 2nd cent., the period of → archaism, E. was again read by the educated, especially by → Gellius (Gell. NA 18,5) and even publicly recited. Afterwards, reading E. must have declined strongly. In late antiquity few philologists knew E. first hand, e.g., → Servius does, but not Macrobius. → Nonius did not own the *Annales*, but owned two tragedies by E. as well as glossaries and Gellius. The last traces of a direct knowledge of E. are probably not the interlined glosses in the text of Orosius, but (late 4th cent.) in → Ausonius [6. 18f., 25f.]. Apparently no E. ms. survived into the Middle Ages. Sporadic mentions are secondary. Petrarca made E. into an *alter Petrarca* (W. Suerbaum in [22. 293–352]).

Complete works: 1 J. Vahlen, Ennianae poesis reliquiae, ²1903 incl. Curae Ennianae ultimae, ed. by. A. Lunelli, 1989 2 A. Traglia, Poeti latini arcaici 1, 1986, 274–515 (with translation/notes; textual criticism 126–157).
Anthologies: 3 J. Heurgon, E. vol.1/2 (Annals, tragedies.), 1958 4 G. Garbarino, Roma e la filosofia greca dalle origini alla fine del II sec. a. C., vol. 1/2, 1973 5 R. Till, Res publica. Texte zur Krise der frühröm. Tradition, 1976, 147–163, 348–354.
Annals: 6 O. Skutsch, 1985, rev. 1986 (commentary) 7 M. Bandiera, 1978 (book 1).
Scaenica: 8 TRF 17–85 9 CRF 5f. 10 L. Castagna, Lexikon Q. Ennii et M. Pacuvii sermonis scaenici, 1996
Tragoediae: 11 R. Argenio, 1951 (with translation) 12 H. D. Jocelyn, 1967 (commentary).
Saturae, Fragmenta varia: 13 E. Bolisani, E. minore, 1935 14 E. Courtney, 4–43
Bibliography: 15 Albrecht, 106–119 16 E. Badian, E. and his friends, in: [22], 149–208 17 M. Barchiesi, Nevio epico, 1962 18 M. Bettini, Studi e note su E., 1979 19 N. Catone, Grammatica enniana, 1964 20 C. J. Classen, E.: ein Fremder in Rom, in: Gymnasium 99, 1992, 121–145 21 G. Dickel/K. Grubmüller (ed.), Die Fabeln des Mittelalters und der frühen Neuzeit, 1987. 22 Ennius. Entretiens 17, 1971 23 S. M. Goldberg, Epic in Republican Rome, 1995, 83–110; also 111–134 (this first in 1989) 24 A. S. Gratwick, E.' Annales. The minor works of E., in: CHCL-L 60–76, 156–160 25 A. Grilli, Studi enniani, 1965 26 Id., E., in: Dizionario degli scrittori greci e latini 1, 1988, 709–718 27 E. S. Gruen, Studies in Greek culture and Roman policy, 1990, 106–122 28 H. D. Jocelyn, The fragments of E.' scenic scripts, in: AC 38, 1969, 181–217 (report on research since the 16th cent) 29 Id., The poems of Quintus E., in: ANRW I 2, 1972, 987–1026 30 Leo 150–211 31 K. Lennartz, Non verba sed vim, 1994 32 S. Mariotti, Lezioni su E., ²1991 (= 1951, repr. 1963) 33 M. Martina, E. 'poeta cliens', in: Quaderni di Filologia Classica 2, 1979, 13–74 34 E. Norden, E. und Vergilius, 1915 (repr. 1966) 35 W. Röser, E., Euripides und Homer, 1939 36 F. Skutsch, s.v. E., RE 5,2, 2589–2628 37 O. Skutsch, Studia Enniana, 1968 38 W. Suerbaum, Unt. zur Selbstdarstellung älterer röm. Dichter, 1968 39 Id., E. als Dramatiker, in: A. Bierl (ed.), Orchestra, 1994, 346–362 40 Id., ZPE 106, 1995, 31–52 41 Id., HLL § 117 42 S. Timpanaro, Per una nuova edizione critica di E., in: SIFC 21, 1946, 41–81; 22, 1947, 33–77; 179–207; 23, 1948, 5–58 43 Id., Forschungsber. E., in: AAHG 5, 1952, 195–212 (from *c.* 1939) 44 Id., Contributi di filologia e di storia della lingua latina, 1978 (especially 623–671 on [42]) 45 M. Winniarczyk, RhM 137, 1994, 274–291 46 K. Ziegler, Das hell. Epos, ²1966, 23–37, 53–77 (Italian translation 1988 with additions by M. Fantuzzi). W.SU.

[2] **P.E. Saturninus Karus.** Senator from Bisica Lucana in Africa; his career is known to the office of aedile; descendant of a veteran of the *legio III Augusta*. AE 1979, 657.

M. Corbier, in: EOS II, 710f. W.E.

Ennodius, Magnus Felix Born in AD 473–74, probably in Arles, derived from Gaulish aristocracy. Raised in Pavia according to his rank, he entered into the service of the Church in 493 and became bishop of Pavia in 513. In 515 and 517, he was in Constantinople on behalf of Pope Hormisdas for the settlement of the Acacian schism and died in 521 (epitaph CIL VI 16464). His *c.* 500 writings, among them 297 letters in the manner of → Symmachus, were written before his tenure as bishop and were preserved in the manuscripts in approximately chronological order. Their affected and therefore often difficult to understand language is in keeping with the style cultivated by the Roman nobility under Theoderic. In addition to Christian topics (*vitae* of Antonius of Lérins, of Bishop Epiphanius of Pavia; *Eucharisticum de vita sua*, autobiography in the manner of the *Confessiones* of Augustine) there are secular topics (Panegyric on Theoderic, in 507; *Paraenesis didascalica*, a schedule for the study of rhetoric in a prosimetrical form). The speeches (*dictiones*) are either model speeches and treat the traditional topics of *controversiae* or mythological subjects, or they were earmarked for special events (e.g. birthday of a bishop, consecration of a basilica, school celebration). The occasional poems in various metres show similar style, but hardly any poetic talent. The 151 epigrams are mostly descriptions or epitaphs. Attached to the ancient culture and full of admiration for the political and literary traditions of the Romans, E. clearly sees the decline of the old world power (in the image of the aged Roma: Opuscula 1,48; 2,130) under Theoderic; however, he feels attached to Theoderic's cultural policy. He believes the → *artes liberales* to be indispensible for the education of young clerics and therefore emphasizes not only their intellectual value, but also their ethical value. Mastery of the art of rhetoric is proof for him of one's aptitude for public offices; indeed, it bestows immortal fame. His Christian conviction retreats behind this belief in education.

EDITIONS: W. HARTEL, CSEL 6, 1882; F. VOGEL, MGH AA 7, 1885.
LITERATURE: J. KÜPPERS, HLL § 785; J. GRUBER, s.v. E., LMA 3,2015f.; J. FONTAINE, s.v. E., RAC 5, 398–421. J.GR.

Ennoeus (Ἔννοιος; *Énnoios*) Author of an epitaph on a marble block that was rediscovered in Catania (Anth. Pal. append. 2,491 COUGNY = GVI 883) and is to be dated in the 3rd–4th cents. AD. The name of the poet, which stands under the three insipid as well as damaged distichs, is not otherwise documented. E.D.

Enodia see → Hecate

Enomotia (ἐνωμοτία; *enōmotía*). Literally a 'sworn band', the *enomotia* was the smallest unit in the regular Spartan army, allegedly instituted by Lycurgus (Hdt. 1,65,5) and consisting in principle of one Spartan from each of the 40 active service year-classes (aged 20–59). In practice, however, not only was the age distribution of the citizen population of military age imperfect but in response to the increasingly severe shrinkage of citizen numbers (ὀλιγανθρωπία, *oliganthrōpía*) from the mid 5th cent. BC onwards, the *enomotia* was brought up to an average strength of 32–36 (Thuc. 5,68; Xen. Hell. 6,4,12) by the inclusion of hoplites among the *perioikoi*.
→ Hoplites, Lycurgus, Perioikoi; → Sparta

1 J. F. LAZENBY, The Spartan Army, 1985. P.C.

Ensérune Fortified high-altitude settlement (*oppidum*?) between Béziers and Narbonne on a hill c. 120 m high, well protected by steep slopes to the north and to the east; it ruled a plain surrounded by ponds and crossed by an important traffic route between the Iberian and Italian peoples. Three settlement phases are documented by ceramic finds (end of 6th cent. BC—end of 1st cent. AD). The second phase (*c.* 425–220 BC) includes the building of a city wall (4th cent.), and of the necropolis with its numerous Celtic finds; there is evidence of trading relations with countries around the Mediterranean Sea. In spite of romanization, E. to a great extent preserved its original Ibero-Ligurian character.

M. SCHWALLER, Ensérune (Guides archéologiques de la France 28), 1994. Y.L.

Ensigns The ensigns of the Roman army fulfilled an important tactical function: the transfer of commands from the commander; in this case they were accompanied by the sound of the *cornu* (Veg. Mil. 2,22). Due to their importance, they achieved an almost religious validity (cf. for instance Tac. Ann. 1,39,4). According to tradition, Romulus provided the first legion with animal symbols such as the eagle, the wolf, the horse, the wild boar and the minotaur (Plin. HN 10,16).

At that time, each of the thirty maniples supposedly received a *signum* (Ov. Fast. 3,115; Plut. Romulus 8). In the republic the *hastati* were also called *antesignani* during the battle, since they fought in front of the legion's ensigns (Liv. 8,8,5; 9,39,7). In peace times the ensigns were handed to the quaestors and preserved in the → *aerarium populi Romani* (Liv. 3,69,8).

The units of the allied cities (the *socii)*, received *signa* for the infantry and *vexilla* for the cavalry. Marius presented each legion with an eagle of silver that became its symbol. This eagle (*aquila*) was the common ensign of an entire legion and was born by the first cohort (Veg. Mil. 2,6; 2,13; [6]). There is agreement that the *signum* remained the ensign of the maniple. The hypothesis that the *cohortes* of the legions also received such *signa* is not convincing because in the text in question (Caes. B Gall. 2,25,1) reference is not to this but rather to a *signifer* of the 4th cohort. In the Principate, the praetorian cohorts, and perhaps also the *centuriae,* received *signa* that were equipped with the image (*imago*) of the *princeps,* one *signum* for each maniple. The *urbaniciani* followed the model of the Praetorians, while the *vigiles* only had a *vexillum* for each cohort. The legions guarded their eagle, which in this period was made of gold,

Ensigns of the Roman army

The standards of the Roman legions during the Principate

Units	1st–2nd cents.	Gallienus (253–268)	Victorinus (269–271)	Carausius (286–293)
Leg. I Adiutrix	Ibex, Pegasus	Ibex, Pegasus		
Leg. I Italica	Boar,Bull, Bos marinus	Boar, Bull		
Leg. I Minerva	Minerva, Ram	Minerva	Ram	Ram
Leg. II Adiutrix	Boar, Pegasus	Boar, Pegasus		
Leg. II Augusta	Ibex, Pegasus, Mars			Ibex
Leg. II Italica	She-wolf, Ibex, Stork	She-wolf with twins, Ibex		
Leg. II Parthica	Centaur	Centaur		Centaur
Leg. II Traiana	Hercules			Hercules
Leg. III Augusta	Ibex, Pegasus			
Leg. III Gallica	Bull			
Leg. III Italica	Stork	Stork		
Leg. IV Flavia	Lion	Lion	Lion	Lion
Leg. IV Macedonica	Bull, Ibex			
Leg. V Macedonica	Bull, Eagle	Eagle	Bull	
Leg. VI Victrix	Bull			
Leg. VII Claudia	Bull, Lion	Bull		Bull
Leg. VIII Augusta	Bull	Bull		Bull
Leg. X Fretensis	Bull, Boar		Bull	
Leg. X Gemina	Bull	Bull		
Leg. XI Claudia	Neptune	Neptune		
Leg. XII Fulminata	Lightning			
Leg. XIII Gemina	Lion	Lion	Lion	
Leg. XIV Gemina	Ibex, Eagle	Ibex	Ibex	
Leg. XVI Flavia	Lion			
Leg. XX Valeria	Boar, Ibex		Boar	Boar
Leg. XXI Rapax	Ibex			
Leg. XXII Primigenia	Ibex, Hercules	Ibex	Ibex	Ibex
Leg. XXX Ulpia	Neptune, Ibex, Jupiter	Neptune	Ibex	Neptune

and entrusted it to an *aquilifer* (Tac. Ann. 1,39,4; Hist. 1,56,2; 2,89,1; cf. also ILS 2338–2342); this ensign of the legions had the form of an eagle that held Jupiter's lightning bolt in its talons. It was attached to the tip of a long lance. In addition, each legion owned several emblems, god, animal or zodiac sign.

A soldier, the *imaginifer*, carried the portraiture or *imago* of the *princeps*. In the legion and in other units, the *signum* remained the ensign of the maniple; it was entrusted to a *signifer*. In the Principate, the *signum* represented a more or less richly ornamented long lance: tassel and crescent moon on the lower end, discs in the middle, crown, hand and a short transverse pole with ribbons on the tip. The cohorts of the *auxilia* as well as the *numeri* of the infantry were identified by their *signum*. Each cavalry unit followed a *vexillum* that was carried by a *vexillarius* (the form *vexillifer* is wrong); this was of course the case for the *alae* and the *turmae*. The *vexillum* was a rectangle of fabric that hung down from a horizontal pole; this was again fastened to a long lance. The *signiferi turmae* and the *imaginiferi* are also documented for the *auxilia* [1]. In the course of the 2nd cent. AD, the cavalry received new ensigns resembling our windsocks, that were called *draco* (dragon). The same ranks of the *signifer* and of the *vexillarius* are found for the *equites singulares Augusti*. In peace times, all ensigns, especially the *signa* and the *aquilae*, were preserved in a small sanctuary, the *aedes signorum*, that was located behind the *principia* in the centre of the camp. The navy received ensigns as well: each trierarch was supported by two *signiferi*; each ship and each league of ships identified itself with a *vexillum* [10].

The army of late antiquity appears to have kept the old ensigns to a great extent, but only allocated them second-rank tactical tasks. The *aquilifer* (Veg. Mil. 2,7) as well as the *signifer* (CIL 5, 5823; Amm. Marc. 25,5,8), which from this time on was often described as *semaforus* (CIL 5, 8752; ILS 2802), survived. The *signifer* was now allocated to the *centuria*, while the *draconarius* carried the ensign of the cohorts (ILS 2805). The *vexillum* served the *turma* as ensign (Veg. Mil. 2,14; Amm. Marc. 27,10,9; 27,10,12). In contrast to some assertions, even the imperial *imago* survived, albeit only for a short time; it was carried by the *imaginarius* (Veg. Mil. 2,7). Added since the battle at the Milvian bridge in the year 312 was the *labarum*; in this ensign were engraved the Greek letters X and P, the monogram of Christ (Eus. Vita Const. 1, 28–31).

1 G.L. Cheesman, The Auxilia of the Roman Imperial Army, 1914, 39 2 J.C.N. Coulston, The Draco Standard, in: Journal of Roman Military Equipment Stud. 2, 1991, 101–114 3 A. von Domaszewski, Die Fahnen, in: Aufsätze 1972, 1–80 4 M. Durry, Cohortes prétoriennes, [2]1968, 104 5 R. Grosse, Röm. Militär-Gesch., 1920, 229–234 6 J. Harmand, L'armée et le soldat, 1967, 237–238 7 Le Bohec, 50–51 and 262–263 8 W. Liebenam, s.v. Feldzeichen, RE 6, 2151–2161 9 H.M.D. Parker, Legions, [2]1980, 261–263 10 M.P. Speidel, The Master of the Dragon Standards, in: Id., Roman Army Studies 2 (Mavors 8), 1992, 390–395.

Y.L.B.

Entasis A term transmitted by Vitruvius (3,3,13), a term, that however is not documented in Greek architectural inscriptions, for the swelling of the → column, which is to express the tension of this architectural part under the load of the entablature. Together with the → inclination and the → curvature, the entasis forms the most important element of the → optical refinements in Greek column construction; the entasis turns up in an extreme form in the archaic architecture of Western Greece (e.g. Paestum, 'Basilica'), is reduced in the later 6th, the 5th and 4th cents. BC to a curved contour line that is sometimes scarcely recognizable, and in Hellenism is increasingly rare in favour of evenly tapering shafts. Entasis was planned beforehand as shown by the preserved column sketches of the temple of Apollo by → Didyma (→ Building trade); it was presumably executed in connection with the fluting of the columns as a relatively late operation in the work.

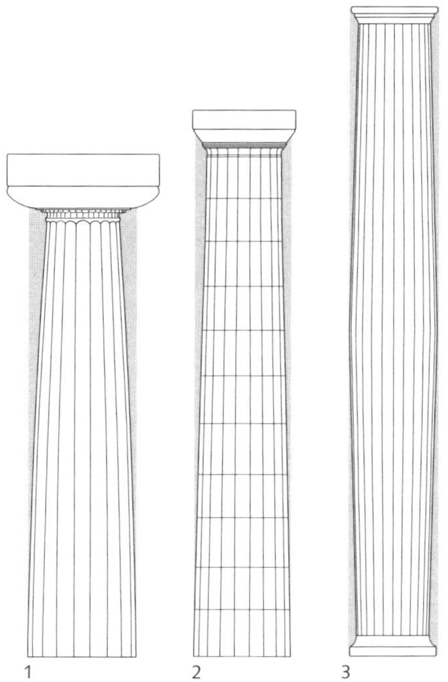

1. Paestum, Temple of Hera I (6th cent. BC)
2. Athens, Parthenon (5th cent. BC)
3. Contour of Renaissance column

Entasis was rediscovered in the Renaissance in the course of the Vitruvius reception (e.g. in Leon Battista Alberti, De re aedificatoria VI, 13 and Andrea Palladio, I quattro libri dell'architettura I, 13). The column outline common since the 16th cent., that in the area of the base again reduces the shaft that swells from the capital base down to the middle in a regressive curve, is a Renaissance construction and unknown in monuments of antiquity; here the lower column diameter always marks the maximum of the entasis.

EBERT, 24; D. MERTENS, Zur Entstehung der Entasis griech. Säulen, in: Bathron. FS für H. Drerup, 1988, 307–318; W. MÜLLER-WIENER, Griech. Bauwesen in der Antike, 1988, 91, 114. C.HÖ.

Entelechy see → Energeia

Entella (Ἔντελλα; *Éntella*), modern Rocca d'Entella west of Corleone. City of the → Elymi in the west of Sicily (Thuc. 6,2,3), often named in the wars of Dionysius I and of Timoleon with the Carthaginians (Diod. Sic. 14,9; 48; 61; 15,73; 16,67; 73), numbered by Cic. Verr. 2,3,103 among the *civitates decumanae*, by Plin. HN 3,91 to the *stipendiarii*, not destroyed until the 13th cent. by Frederick II. The investigation of the settlement and of the area belonging to it (begun in 1983) has brought finds to light from archaic times up into the Middle Ages [1; 2]. A series of written copper tablets [3; 4] (from the antiques trade) has thrown new light on historical events (expulsion of the inhabitants and ensuing *synoikismós*) and the topographical organization of the city and its international relations in the course of the 3rd cent. BC. Coins: HN 137.

1 G. NENCI (ed.), Alla Ricerca di Entella, 1993 2 A. DI STEFANO, Attività della Soprintendenza per i beni culturali e ambientali di Palermo, in: Kokalos 49/50, 1993/94, 1110–1112 3 G. NENCI, Fonti epigrafiche, in: Alla Ricerca di Entella, 1993, 35–50 4 J. B. CURBERA, Sulla cronologia relativa dei decreti di Entella, in: ASNP 24,2, 1994, 879–894. GI.F.

Entellus Imperial freedman who performed the task of *a libellis* under Domitian. He participated in the plot against Domitian. His *domus* and his gardens are mentioned by Martial 8,68. His property became part of the imperial *patrimonium*. PIR² E 66. W.E.

Entertainers

I. PRELIMINARY COMMENT II. SPECIALISTS III. THE CONTEXT OF PERFORMANCES IV. SOCIAL STATUS

I. PRELIMINARY COMMENT

Acrobats, tumblers, fools, jesters and magicians appeared as entertainers before audiences in town and country. These specialists, who earned their living with their performances, either had a fixed abode or were travellers in the Graeco-Roman world. Their presentations were geared towards audience expectations and often reflected societal conventions, their counter-images or merely wishful thinking.

II. SPECIALISTS

A. JUGGLERS B. ACROBATS C. TIGHT-ROPE PERFORMERS D. TRAPEZE ARTISTS E. JESTERS F. PERFORMERS G. MAGICIANS

A. JUGGLERS

In the Phaeacian section of the 'Odyssey' (Hom. Od. 8,370–379; → *Phaíakes*) the sons of king Alcinous [1] perform a leaping dance that involved tossing up and catching a ball. This agonistic performance conformed to the values of the Greek aristocratic elite in the 8th cent. BC. In the Classical period (5th/4th cents. BC) juggling objects was part of the repertoire of professional entertainers. [1]. In the Roman Imperial period an added difficulty was introduced into juggling by playing with glass balls that would break if they hit the ground (CIL VI 9797).

B. ACROBATS

Entertainers who had mastered hand- and headstands or somersaulted were called *kybistētêres* (κυβιστητῆρες). In the 'Odyssey' these leaping dancers are first mentioned in the context of a wedding feast (Hom. Od. 4,15–19). Artistic leapers were prized also in agonistic competitions as demonstrated by an image on a pseudo-Panathenaean amphora in Paris (about 540 BC; Bibl. Nationale 243 [6]). In the 5th cent. BC professional entertainers performed head-first leaps between swords (Xen. Symp. 2,11). Indian performers created an airborne sommersault as a dangerous attraction during the Imperial period (cf. Philostr. VA 2,28).

C. TIGHT-ROPE PERFORMERS

Dancers balancing on a thin rope were called *neurobátai* (νευροβάται). It is apparent from the prologue of → Terence [III 1] to his comedy *Hecyra* (Ter. Hec. 4 f.) that they competed with theatre performances: the spectators preferred to watch tight-rope performers.

D. TRAPEZE ARTISTS

These artists and in a wider sense tumblers in general were called *petauristêres* (πεταυριστῆρες; original form perhaps *peteuristêres*, Latin *petauristae* or *petauristarii*). The name is probably derived from the frame or board they used (*pétauron*, Latin *petaurum*). Occasionally, these performers also used a ladder and performed their tricks on its rungs (Petron. Sat. 53,11 f.).

E. JESTERS

Jesters were masters of a broad repertoire of pranks and amusing peculiarities. Jesters and fools were called γελωτοποιοί (*gelōtopoioí*), Latin *derisores*, *scurrae* or *moriones*. They performed at markets and in streets, but often in homes and temples during drinking-bouts. Some had physical defects (Lucian Symposium 18 f.). From the audience's perspective these entertainers with their unconventional appearance and improper conduct represented the opposite of the ideal for ancient society. This inversion confirmed the value perceptions of the audience because of its ridiculousness [2].

Scurrae as professional jesters are already documented in Cicero (Cic. Verr. 2,3,146). As companions and parasites they appeared at the table (cf. the struggle of two bragging *scurrae* in Hor. Sat. 1,5,52–70, which was modelled on epic combat). The wealth of a host was made apparent by their participation.

F. Performers

The Latin term *praestigiator* (just as θαυματοποιός/*thaumatopoiós*) does not describe the practitioner of a particular skill but the most diverse tumblers, conjurers and magicians. They included soothsayers, ventriloquists and hypnotists. The future emperor L. Verus brought along a troop of entertainers, which included *praestigiatores*, on his Asian campaign (SHA Lucius Verus 8,11).

A *thaumatopoiós* or *thaumaturgós* was an entertainer who presented θαύματα/*thaúmata* ('marvels'), i.e., things considered extraordinary or peculiar when heard or seen [3].

G. Magicians

The most familiar performances of magicians included making small stones or balls disappear under cups (Alci. 3,20). These performances might even take place in the *orchḗstra* of a → theatre. Thus, the people of → Histiaea on Euboea set up a bronze statue for the magician Theodorus, which depicted him with stones of this type, in the theatre (Ath. 1,19b).

III. The context of performances

Public squares which provided visibility for many spectators were particularly suitable for entertainers to present performances (Apul. Met. 1,4). During festive periods they performed in rural and urban sanctuaries (Aristot. Rh. 1401b 25) [4]. At feasts and drinking-bouts entertainers earned their livelihood in the homes of citizens and the palaces of the elite [5].

Public space has been subject to a continuous process of multiplication and differentiation since the origins of the → town. The creation of a new leisure architecture also provided entertainers with new venues for their activities. Performers and acrobats also displayed their arts in the → gymnasium, → theatre, amphitheatre (→ *amphitheatrum*) and → thermal baths.

IV. Social Status

Professional entertainers, like actors, (→ *histrio*) usually belonged to the lower stratum of ancient society. They were often travelling performers and perceived as strangers or foreigners. Slaves have also been found as acrobats, jesters, etc. Public statues for entertainers suggest that some made a career of this occupation and were even perceived as upwardly mobile.

→ Leisure; → Marginal groups; → Spectacles

1 A. Schäfer, Unterhaltung beim griech. Symposion, 1997, 70; 79, pl. 37,1 2 Id., Ein grotesker Tänzer im histor. Museum von Sibiu, in: Acta Musei Napocensis 35.1, 1998, 61–67 3 H. Blümner, Fahrendes Volk im Altertum (SBAW 6), 1918, 8–53 4 M. Maass, Das ant. Delphi, 1993, 83 5 L. Giuliani, Die seligen Krüppel, in: AA 1987, 714–716 6 CVA Paris, Bibl. Nationale, vol. 2, 1931, III He, pl. 88.

AL. SCH.

Enthousiasmos In Greek religion enthusiasm (ἐνθουσιασμός/*enthousiasmós*) refers to being taken by a higher power, usually personified by the gods (cf. θειασμός/*theiasmós*, 'inspiration'; ἔνθεος/*éntheos*, 'possessed by god'). The individual leaves an ordinary state and enters one that is determined from without and strange, to being no longer 'him- or herself' (ἔκστασις/*ékstasis*; cf. → Ecstasy). What humans achieve in this state, which is experienced as paranormal, is god-given (cf. Heraclitus [1] fr. 22 B 92; B 93 DK; → Pythia [1]). How this possession (*katokōchḗ*, Pl. Phdr. 245a) or influence happens in a specific case, whether as a breath (→ *pneûma*, Hes. Theog. 31), a blow (the action of an affect: *katáplēxis*, *ékplēxis*, cf. Aesch. PV 878 f.) or by other means (wine: Eur. fr. 265, cf. → Dionysus; → Intoxicating substances IV.; smoke: Dion. Hal. Demosthenes 22; music: Hom. Od. 12,44; dance: Str. 10,3,7), varies [5; 8].

The ecstatic effect of poetry on recipients is reflected at an early time in poetology (Gorg. fr. B 11 DK, § 9; 11; 16–17). Whether *enthousiasmos* already becomes formulaic in the early → epic is difficult to determine; in any case the divine *pneûma* does not preclude cognitive or poetic achievements in humans [4]. Democr. fr. B 18; B 21 DK (earliest reference to *enthousiasmos*) makes high poetic output dependent on an enthusiastically affected soul (*psychḗ theázousa*; because of a special material structure of the soul? cf. [2. 56, n. 4]). Plato [1] (Phdr. 244a–245a) differentiates four forms of enthusiastic μανία/*manía* ('frenzy'): mantic (→ Apollo; → *mántis*), 'telestic' (service of the gods or mysteries; cf. → Dionysus I. C.8.), poetic *manía* (→ Muses; cf. → Muses, acclamation of the), erotic *manía* (→ Eros, → Aphrodite; cf. → Eroticism). In the 'Ion' (533d–535a 2) he discusses the question of whether the → rhapsode — for lack of other ability — draws his knowledge from *enthousiasmos* (cf. also [1]); the image of a 'magnetic' chain of god — poet — performer — recipient is conjectured.

Aristotle [6] derives *enthousiasmos*, as a special gift (cf. Pl. Men. 99c-d), from → melancholia and, therefore, gives it a physiological explanation (Aristot. Pr. 30,1). On the other hand, *enthousiasmos* to him also characterizes the effect of poetry and speech (Aristot. Rh. 3,7) on listeners as an intense emotion: thus poets and orators step into the original place of the deity [6]. → Ps.-Longinus separates this pathetic *enthousiasmos* in terms of an aesthetic of effect and result by making *ékplēxis* (see above) the criterion of the sublime (*hýpsos*) that must be striven for (1,4), and recommends → *mímēsis* as the source of inspiration (13).

In the Roman cultural sphere, *enthousiasmos* was initially a Greek import (→ Divination VII), which Cicero represents with the verbs *in-/adflare*, *inspirare*

(Cic. Div. 1, 12 and 38; Cic. Nat. D. 2,167). Only the Augustan poets fit the → *vates* out with a higher social authority as an inspired visionary.

1 S. Büttner, Die Lit.-Theorie bei Platon und ihre anthropologische Begründung, 2000 2 H. Flashar, Der Dialog Ion als Zeugnis Platonischer Philos., 1958 3 A. Gellhaus, E. und Kalkül, 1995 4 P. Murray, Poetic Inspiration in Early Greece, in: JHS 101, 1981, 87–100 5 F. Pfisterer, s. v. Ekstasis, RAC 4, 1959, 944–987 6 Th. Schirren, Persuasiver E. in Rhetorik 3, 7 und bei Ps.-Longin, in: J. Knape, Th. Schirren (ed.), Aristotelische Rhet.-Trad. (in print)
7 W. H. Schröder, s. v. E., Ästhetische Grundbegriffe (ed. by K. Barck), vol. 2, 2001, 223–240 8 K. Thraede, s. v. Inspiration, RAC 18, 1998, 329–365. TH. SCH.

Entremont Celtic-Ligurian *oppidum*, main location of the Salluvii, 3 km north of Aix-en-Provence. In *c.* 2nd cent. BC two residential estates, the second of which surrounds the first without having destroyed it, proves the development of the town formation, which was stopped by the Romans between 124 and 90 BC. Ancient remains: town wall, roads, sanctuary (heroon?), sculptures, coins from Massalia, numerous crafts products.

P. Arcelin et al., Voyage en Massalie, 1990, 101–106; F. Benoît, Entremont, capitale celto-ligure des Salyens de Provence, 1969; F. Salviat, Entremont antique, 1973. Y.L.

Enūma eliš The Enūma eliš (EE) [1; 2], the so-called Babylonian creation epic, received its name in accordance with the beginning words, 'When up there [heaven not yet being named]'. The song, written down on seven tablets and probably created in the 12th cent. BC, is counted among the most important witnesses to ancient Oriental literature. Following a theogony leading up to → Marduk, it describes his battle against → Tiamat ('the Sea') who embodies the original chaos, and whom he defeats and kills. From her body, he forms heaven and earth and sets up the order of the existing world. His work of creation is crowned by the creation of mankind. As thanks for his deeds, the gods of the world raise him up as their king and build his temple → Esagil and the city → Babylon in the center of the world.

In the EE, while consciously exploiting numerous considerably older mythemes of vastly differing origins, the originally unimportant god Marduk is equated with → Enlil, the king of the Sumerian pantheon, and by further syncretisms is declared the origin of all divinity. This so-called promotion of Marduk reflects the political advancement of Babylon in the 2nd millennium BC. The EE served the Babylonian kingship as legitimation of a claim to world domination and was symbolically presented in the rituals of the Babylonian New Year's celebrations, but it was also performed. even → Berosus delivers a quite reliable summary of the EE [3].
→ Cosmology; → Cosmogony

1 B.R. Foster, Before the Muses, 1993, 351–402 2 W.G. Lambert, TUAT III/4, 1994, 565–602 3 P. Schnabel, Berossos, 1923, 254–256. S.M.

Environment, Environmental behaviour
I. Methodological Comments II. Relationship to the natural environment III. Environmental destruction caused by war IV. Environmental damage caused by civilization V. Environmental problems in large cities VI. Decline and destruction of animal populations

I. Methodological Comments

The concept of the environment *per se* is very young. The public environmental debate began in the early 1970s and with it came a previously unheard-of elevated ecological awareness. Neither the environmental ethics resulting from it nor ecological research have a long tradition. This often results in scepticism towards the soundness and the issues of environment historical research whose methodological premises are questioned as being modern awareness projected back onto earlier periods. This criticism can only apply to an evaluation of historical results. The results themselves are a product of the self-evident interdependence of nature and society, which legitimizes research in environmental history (regarding fundamental methodological reservations [1. 7 f.]).

II. Relationship to the natural environment

That which 'grows' or 'is created' without a human contribution is described as φύσις/*phýsis* or *natura*. On the one hand, humans are a part of this process, but on the other hand humans intervene with their civilization and → technology in this process and actively shape it. The trend is towards eroding or disrupting a → Golden Age of primal harmony between humans and nature as proposed in mythology — the *autómaton* motif of a Mother Earth supplying humans with all their needs (Hes. Op. 117–119; Verg. G. 1,125–146; Ov. Met. 1,101–112), which is a reflection of the concept of humans who are not yet shaping their environment. Consequently, civilizing activities such as agriculture and → mining may be considered violations of what has grown naturally (Verg. Ecl. 4,39–41; Ov. Met. 1,101 f.; 1,138; cf. Ps.-Sen. Octavia 414–419; digging in the bowels of Mother Earth as a topos in ancient criticism of mining: Plin. HN 33,1 f.; 2,158).

The cultic worship of phenomena in the natural environment was an essential trait of ancient religiosity. Independent of scientific and rational examination, nature appeared to be populated by innumerable supernatural beings that needed to be approached with respect. Closely related to this belief were the personifications of various local and regional features of the natural environment: rivers, streams, springs, caves, groves, trees, mountains, etc. were personified and worshipped as nature demons (→ Nymphs, list of cult sites [2]). Roman *religio* also extended to these locations (mocking mention of their great number in Petron. Sat. 17,5), which as holy sites were to some extent expressly protected from human intervention (sacred → groves: CIL VI 2107,15 f.; CIL X 4104; restriction in favour of economic use: Varro Ling. 5,49, speaks of *avaritia*). In Virgil's didactic poetry this idea is combined with that of a continuously required 'taming' of nature by humans (especially Verg. G. 2, cf. 2,22–176 and 458–540; [3]). This thought is also reflected in the interpretation of → natural disasters as a divine reaction to disturbances in the interaction between humans and a deified nature (Cic. Nat. D. 2,14; Plin. HN 33,1 f.).

Apart from respect and fear, the ancient 'sentiment of nature' (the term is problematic given its lack of specificity) was also characterized by joy in, and love of, nature. Scenery with flowers in bloom (Bacchyl. 13,87 f.), trees and springs (Pl. Phdr. 230b) were considered beautiful. A beautiful grove away from the city with cool water and in whose shadow shepherds rested was considered the *locus amoenus* of the Hellenistic period (Theocr. 5,31–34; 5,45–49; 7,135–145). Comparable descriptions of scenery that were inspired by Hellenistic models are found in Roman literature (Lucr. 2,30–33). The Imperial elite's sentiment of nature is reflected in building palace-like villas in an enchanting environment (Quint. Inst. 3,7,27) or a gentle rolling landscape in which a view into the distance was given great significance (Sen. Epist. 86,8; Plin. Ep. 5,6,7; Hor. Epist. 1,10,23). This ideal shows a desire for a superiority over nature, which is also reflected in the growing tendency from the 1st cent. BC to 'domesticate' nature by setting up parks with the help of garden artisans (*topiarii,* Cic. Ad Q. Fr. 3,1,5; Plin. Ep. 5,6,33–36).

Greeks and Romans found little joy in wild 'romantic' landscapes. High mountains, deep gorges and impenetrable forests, deserts and swamps as well as the raging sea as 'natural spaces hostile to life' caused fear and dislike (Aesch. Supp. 792–799; Lucr. 5,200–217 and 5,1000 f.; Liv. 21,58,3: *foeditas Alpium*, 'the hideousness of the Alps'). Humans considered themselves to be in opposition to the natural environment whose domination was praised as the progress of civilization (Anth. Gr. 7,626).

Actual conduct towards the environment cared little for religious reservations. In the conflict between preserving and exploiting the natural environment, military, economic and civilizing interests generally prevailed. The immediate problems were generally minor in comparison with the environmental damage occuring since the 19th cent., but their effects on later generations were not marginal. The lack of 'environmental awareness' occurred to some extent because it was not a pressing problem. In modern terms the 'environmental mentality' of antiquity may be sketched as follows: an economy without sustainability or analysis of consequences, short-term thinking regarding profit and success, hardly any long-term investment planning, general disinterest in extending and renewing resources.

III. Environmental destruction caused by war

War was not only directed against human opponents but also against their land. The devastation of Attica was an essential part of the Spartan strategy of attrition in the → Peloponnesian War (Thuc. 3,26,3 f.). The extensive felling of olive trees caused particularly lasting damage (Lys. 7,7). Devastation of the landscape and → agriculture was also part of Roman strategy of warfare (Tac. Agr. 30,3 f.): Declarations of war explicitly included the *agri* of the enemies (Macrob. Sat. 3,9,10). In the 2nd → Punic War a scorched-earth strategy was even practised in Roman territory (Pol. 9,4,3; Liv. 23,41,13 f.; regarding the consequences [4. 101]; cf. Caes. B Gall., also [5]).

IV. Environmental damage caused by civilization

→ Wood was one of the most important raw materials of antiquity (as an energy source; in building and → ship building, → crafts, → agriculture and → mining). With the increase in population from the Neolithic, the demand for wood and agricultural land grew. Clearing of large forest areas (including treed slopes) resulted in erosion damage in many places. The earliest description of this karstification is found in Pl. Criti. 111a-e. The consequences of complete clearing were known: for the sake of initially above-average yields, a later decline in production resulting from the humus layer being washed away were accepted (Columella 2,1,5–7). From the 5th cent. BC, the transport routes for wood resources probably lengthened for many Greek states because timber needs were initially satisfied close to the settlement and no reforestation was undertaken (although there is a hint of this notion in: POxy. 1188; CIL III 180). Athens imported large quantities of timber for ship-building in the 5th and 4th cents. BC from Thessaly and Macedonia (Thuc. 4,108,1; Xen. Hell. 6,1,11). Reliable wood supplies from forested regions were also a major factor in the politics of other naval powers such as Rhodes in the Hellenistic period and later Rome [6].

From a modern ecological perspective, this reckless deforestation must be considered pillaging. The island of Elba may be considered a model of a short-sighted exploitative mentality that was only interested in short-term demand. Smelting of the ore mined there had to be relocated to the mainland in the Augustan period because the island's wood reserves had been exhausted (Str. 5,2,6; Diod. Sic. 5,13,1). But on the whole Italy was still considered rich in woods at that time (Dion. Hal. Ant. Rom. 1,37,4) until during the Imperial period the deforestation of the Apennine slopes increased — for example, because of the enormous charcoal demand of → thermal baths (Sid. Apoll. Carm. 5,441–445). Despite firewood imports from Africa, which are attested for late antiquity (Cod. Theod. 13,5,10), there were no bottlenecks for timber as a resource. Exaggerated ideas of huge karst damage, especially in higher altitudes, during antiquity are contradicted by medieval and early modern sources. The most significant ecological interventions into the forests of the Mediterranean region only began in the much more technologically advanced 19th cent. [7. 386–403; 8. 36–38]. In antiquity irreversible damage to the environment through clear cutting was primarily caused near the coast. Erosion damage resulted in some areas from overgrazing of slopes bearing sparse Mediterranean macchia [9. 77–90; 10].

Mining entailed massive intervention into the appearance of the landscape and the ecosystem of affected regions. The thought of recultivating former mining districts was foreign to antiquity; waste and slag dumps characterized the appearance of these areas (e.g., → Laurium, where the silver veins were exhausted by the 4th cent. BC.). Roman gold mining practices included rerouting rivers to wash away the soil (Plin. HN 33,74–76; Str. 4,6,7; [11]) and making mountains collapse artificially without certainty of actual ore occurrences (Plin. HN 33,70–78; especially 76 f.; indications of the landscape-destroying consequences of these mining methods). Criticism was not so much motivated by ecological considerations as by moral and religious ones even though the relationship of cause and effect was known (Plin. HN 33,1–6). Nevertheless, the effects of ancient mining and quarrying were only local or at most regional. This applies — despite the building of high chimneys (Str. 3,2,8; the critical comments in Plin. HN 18,3 do not explicitly refer to this) — also to the contamination of air by poisonous gases that were caused by silver and lead smelting.

One of the more worrisome effects of civilization on the natural environment was the tendency to oversettle areas considered beautiful since the late Republican period. 'Landscape consumption' for luxurious elite villas (Sen. Epist. 89,21) was particularly high in the Campanian coastal region. Nature was considered a challenge by builders and → architects, who imposed the architectual concept on it even to the extent of 'levelling mountains and bridging the sea ' (Sall. Catil. 13,1; construction of a canal to supply artificial fish ponds with sea water: Varro, Rust. 3,17,9; Plin. HN 9,170). The 'wilderness' (*natura*) was there to be domesticated by human creativity (Stat. Silv. 2,2,52–62; Sen. Epist. 122,8; Hor. Carm. 3,1,33–37). This also included the widespread Imperial period fashion of 'cultivating' parks by integrating sculptures, water fountains and architectural elements [12. 65–85; 13] as well as laying out symmetrical plant arrangements and 'vegetation sculptures' (*nemora tonsilia*: Plin. HN 12,13; Plin. Ep. 5,6,16; 5,16,35).

V. Environmental problems in large cities

The only source material worth mentioning with respect to environmental restrictions on life in large ancient cities relates to Imperial Rome. As a million-strong metropolis and by far the most populous city of antiquity, Rome was a special case, but a comparable settlement structure (strong concentration of the population in the centre) suggests that the environmental problems noted there also occurred in other large cities such as Alexandria [1] and Athens [9. 156]. Often a smog-like, oppressive air hung over Rome (*gravitas urbis*: Sen. Epist. 104,6), which encumbered breathing. It consisted of the emissions of innumerable open hearths (Hor. Carm. 3,29,11 f.) and the crematoria near the centre of town (*ustrina*, e.g., on the → Campus Martius), street dust blowing in the air and the smoke of fires erupting almost daily somewhere in town (Sen. Controv. 2,1,12; Juv. 3,190–198). Air pollution (*gravius caelum*, Frontin. Aq. 2,88,3) caused many residents of the capital to have a pale complexion (Mart. 10,12,7–12). Life in the streets of the overpopulated metropolis was described as hectic and stress-inducing. Despite the basic daytime driving prohibition (CIL I² 593,56–61), traffic was often clogged by pedestrian jams (Sen. Clem. 1,6,1). The satirically exaggerated description of the risks of accident (Juv. 3,243–261; Hor. Epist. 2,2,70–75) may dramatize reality but nevertheless is based on it. The unceasing → noise (*strepitus Romae*: Hor. Carm. 3,29,12) during day and night was described as causing illness (Juv. 3,233–238; Mart. 12,57; [12. 208–227]). Only the rich were able to escape the noisy city (*clamosa urbs*: Stat. Silv. 4,4,18; on Alexandria: Call. fr. 260,63–69) by retreating to a *villa suburbana* or a country mansion (Hor. Epist. 2,2,76–78; Mart. 4,64; 12,18; 12,57) — an early form of 'environmentally triggered moves'.

Whether → rubbish constituted a serious problem in ancient metropolises cannot be answered with certainty. Considering that a rubbish removal service is attested for Rome (though its nature is not known, CIL I² 593,66 f.), it is perhaps inappropriate to speak of 'conditions that were worrisome in terms of street hygiene' in general [15. 25]. However, rubbish dumps were often located near the edge of town, sometimes even close to residential areas. Rubbish removal using rivers (Tiber: Suet. Aug. 30,1; Tac. Ann. 15,18; a river as a sewer in Amastris in Asia Minor: Plin. Ep. 10,98 f.), ports and lakes was common.

VI. Decline and destruction of animal populations

The relationship between humans and animals was characterized throughout antiquity by a combination of proximity and distance. Already in classical Greece, manifestations of a love of animals (animals as playmates, lap dogs, → domestic animals; CLE II,2 1512; 1174–1177) and close relationships especially to → dogs and → horses (Hom. Od. 17,290–323; Ath. 12,520c-f), stood in marked contrast to mercilessly staged animal fighting, especially between roosters (→ cockfighting), → dogs and → cats. Essentially, a pragmatic approach to animals prevailed, seeing them especially as economic property for the benefit of humans [16. 80 f., 140 f.]. The concepts of animal welfare and conservationism were unknown in antiquity.

The vegetarian rules of the Pythagoreans (→ Vegetarianism) did not constitute an exception because they were based on belief in the → migration of souls.

The cutting down of forests and the expansion of agricultural land restricted the habitat of some species from the Neolithic. Some animal populations were reduced and pushed into remote regions (Paus. 8,23,9). Considering the danger that wild animals constituted for humans and their livestock (Lucr. 5,990–993), it is understandable that their forced retreat was often celebrated as a victory for civilization.

Overhunting of animal stocks through 'normal' hunting did not generally lead to an ecological imbalance, even though close seasons were unknown. Only the uninhibited capture of almost all wild animal species for → *venationes* in amphitheatres (→ *amphitheatrum*) and stadiums of the Graeco-Roman world had significant and even disastrous effects on the fauna of some regions. From the late Republican period the demand in 'material' for animal-baiting rose sharply. The number of victims rose into the hundreds, even the thousands (R. Gest. Div. Aug. 22; Cass. Dio 66,25,1; 68,15; details: [17. 26–29]). The general popularity of *venationes* — even in the East of the empire — and rising demand for the quantity and exotic 'quality' demanded a logistic of continuous restocking. Many animals probably died on the long transport routes (cf. map in [17. 29], Apul. Met. 4,14,1 f.).

A certain imperialist mentality was expressed in mass killings of animals during show *venationes* and delighted in refined stagings of the suffering of creatures (Mart. Liber spectaculorum 9–14). Similarly, a systematic 'emptying' of some territories of dangerous animals was interpreted as an expression of the imperial and civilizing superiority of humans who were able to extend their settlement and economic space as a result (Claud. De consulatu Stilichonis 3,317–332; 343–369; Anth. Gr. 7,626; Str. 2,5,33). → Elephants, → rhinoceroses and zebras were largely exterminated in North Africa by the 4th cent., while → hippopotamus and → crocodile populations had been pushed far back to the south (Amm. Marc. 22,15,24).

1 O. Rackham, Ecology and Pseudo-Ecology: the Example of Ancient Greece, in: G. Shipley, J. Salmon (ed.), Human Landscapes in Classical Antiquity. Environment and Culture, 1996 2 W. Ruge, s. v. Nymphai, RE 17, 1527–1599 3 H. Heckel, Das Widerspenstige zähmen (Bochumer Alt.-wiss. Coll. 37), 1998 4 A. J. Toynbee, Hannibal's Legacy, vol. 2, 1965 5 H. Cancik, Rationalität und Militär — Caesars Kriege gegen Mensch und N., in: H. Cancik, Antik — Modern, 1998, 103–122 6 A. C. Johnson, Ancient Forests and Navies, in: TAPhA 58, 1927, 199–209 7 R. Meiggs, Trees and Timber in the Ancient Mediterranean World, 1982 8 K.-W. Weeber, Smog über Attika. U.-Verhalten im Alt., 1990 9 J. D. Hughes, Pan's Travail. Environmental Problems of the Ancient Greeks and Romans, 1994 10 C. A. Yeo, The Overgrazing of Ranch Lands in Ancient Italy, in: TAPhA 79, 1948, 275–307 11 P. Lewis, G. D. B. Jones, Roman Gold-Mining in Northwest Spain, in: JRS 60, 1970, 169–185 12 R. Pörtsch, Arch. Kommentar zu den Villenbriefen des Jüngeren Plinius, 1993 13 E. Lefèvre, Plinius-Stud. I. Röm. Baugesinnung und Landschaftsauffassung in den Villenbriefen, in: Gymnasium 84, 1977, 519–541 14 H. Dahlmann, Über den Lärm, in: Gymnasium 85, 1978, 206–227 15 G. E. Thüry, Müll und Marmorsäulen. Siedlungshygiene in der röm. Ant., 2001 16 W. Martini, M. Landfester in: P. Dinzelbacher (ed.), Mensch und Tier in der Gesch. Europas, 2000, 29–86; 87–144 17 K.-W. Weeber, Panem et circenses. Massenunterhaltung als Politik im ant. Rom, 1994.

A. Biese, Die Entwicklung des Naturgefühls bei den Griechen und Römern, 2 vols., 1882/1884; E. Bernert, I. von Lorentz, s. v. N.-Gefühl, RE 16, 1811–1885; R. Fairclough, Love of Nature among the Greeks and Romans, 1930; G. Jennison, Animals for Show and Pleasure in Ancient Rome, 1937; J. Healy, Mining and Metallurgy in the Greek and Roman World, 1978; J. V. Thirgood, Man and Mediterranean Forest, 1981; J. M. C. Toynbee, Tierwelt der Ant. Bestiarium romanum, 1983; Th. A. Wertime, The Furnace versus the Goat, in: Journal of Field Archeology 10, 1983, 445–452; J. K. Anderson, Hunting in the Ancient World, 1985; P. Fedeli, La natura violata. Ecologia nel mondo romano, 1990; T. H. van Andel et al., Land Use and Soil Erosion in Prehistoric and Historical Greece, in: Journal of Field Archeology 17, 1990, 379–396; K. Schneider, Villa und N. Eine Studie zur röm. Oberschichtkultur, 1994; E. Thüry, Die Wurzeln unserer U.-Krise und die griech.-röm. Ant., 1995; X. Dupré Raventós, J.-A. Remolà (ed.), Sordes urbis. La eliminación de residuos en la ciudad romana, 2000.

K.-W. WEE.

Envoys (Greek ἄγγελοι/*ángeloi*, πρέσβεις/*présbeis*, ἀπόστολοι/*apóstoloi*; Lat. *missi*, *nuntii*). Despite a lively inter-state exchange, antiquity had no fixed institution for maintaining contact with foreign states through envoys in the sense of constant representation. Envoys were mostly appointed for a certain period, for certain duties and with set competencies. The importance of the work is shown from the fact that they were never appointed by → lot but in Greece as a rule were selected by the public assembly and in Rome by the Senate. In the process, personal contact with citizens of the target towns or special familiarity with the region to be visited were taken into consideration; depending on the scope of their duties, envoys were provided with 'travel money' (*ephódion*, Lat. *viaticum*) but received no salary. Envoys were considered to be under special divine protection and if they were killed, it was grounds for war (*bellum iustum*; → Law of war). Regarding the Greek-Hellenistic envoy system cf. → *presbeía*; → *proxenía*; → *theōría* [1]; → Hospitality; re the Roman envoys cf. → *legatio*; → *legatus* (1.–3.); → *cliens*.

→ Diplomacy

W. ED.

Enyalius (Ἐνυάλιος; *Enyálios*, also dialect forms). Deity of close combat, called upon in historical times in the moment battle began. In antiquity it was already disputed whether E. was just an epithet of → Ares in literary texts or originally an independent deity (schol.

Hom. Il. 17,211; 22,132; schol. Soph. Aj. 179; schol. Aristoph. PAX, 457 = Alcm. fr. 104 BERGK/44 PMG). A partial answer to this question was attempted by pointing to the fact that E. appears as *E-nu-wa-ri-jo* in a list of four deities from Knosos. Independent of how the Mycenaean deity was imagined, the relation between Ares and E. in historical times is best represented 'structurally': The domain of E. is the moment of desperate conflict 'face to face' [1], while Ares was associated with destructive rage and violent death. In as far as the differentiation was felt to be significant, E. would remain an autonomous deity; otherwise he was reduced to a synonym or epithet of Ares. Reports of E.'s parentage (son of Ares and → Enyo; or of Kronos and Rhea, schol. Aristoph. PAX 457) and of his conflict with Ares in Thrace (Eust. Hom. Il. 673,45 ff) are only constructions to confer a mythical identity to E. In the Classical period (all instances are from Xen., but cf. Thuc. 4,43,3 with schol.) E. was associated with the moment immediately preceding the start of battle.

He was invoked together with Ares in a → paean, which the strategos began (Hell. 2,4,17; Cyr. 3,3,58; 7,1,26) and in which the remaining soldiers joined (Aristophan. Pax 455–57). Furthermore, he was called upon in the war cry that resounded (ἀλαλάζειν, ἐλελίζειν) as the frontlines aligned their spears for the first charge (An. 1,8,17f.; 5,2,14; 6,5,27). The connection between E. and hoplitic close combat explains the allusion to E. in the oath of the Athenian ephebes (TOD 2, no. 204. 17; Poll. 8,106), the sacrifice by the [x-ref] polemarchos (Aristot. Ath. Pol. 58,1) and the placement of the E. temple on Salamis (Plut. Solon 9,7 p. 83c). There is an archaic votive slab [4] from Argos, where → Telesilla erected an E. statue in honour of the women's defence of the city after the battle at Sepeia (Plut. Mor. 245e/f) [2. 273–5; 3]. In Sparta there was a statue of E. tied up (Paus. 3,15,7); at Therapne two Moirai of the Eirenes (ephebes) sacrificed two whelps to E. on the day before the sham battle on the Platanistas (Paus. 3,14,9) [2. 204]. On Lindos, there was a dog sacrifice; in addition, the Hoplites there had to remit $^{1}/_{60}$ of their daily salary to the god (LSCG, Suppl no. 85, around 400 BC). Otherwise, there is scarcely any proof for public worship of E. [5].

In literary texts E. was mostly just a synonym for Ares (e.g. Hom. Il. 2,651 (formula); 13,519; 20,69; Hes. Sc. 371; Archil. fr. 1; Pind. Ol. 13,106; I. 6,54; Dithyrambus 2,16; fr. 169,12 SNELL) or an epithet (e.g. Apoll. Rhod. 3, 1366) which led to the catachresis in Hom. Il. 17,210f. (cf. Eur. Phoen. 1572) and the expression ξυνὸς Ἐνυάλιος (Il. 18,309; Aristot. Rh. 2,21 1395a 16). Now and again there are also hints of an independent role on the part of E. (Hom. Il. 22,132; Pind. Nem. 9,37; Soph. Aj. 179; Eur. Andr. 1015).

→ Ares; → Enyo; → Quirinus; → Telesilla

1 R. LONIS, Guerre et religion en Grèce à l'époque classique, 1979, 121 2 P. VIDAL-NAQUET, Le Chasseur noir, 1981 3 F. GRAF, in: ZPE 55, 1984, 245f. 4 W. VOLLGRAFF, in: BCH 1934, 138–56 5 NILSSON, GGR 1, 519.

R.GOR.

Enyana (ʿenyānā). One of several Syrian expressions for a liturgical answering verse; in a special sense, a poetic text as an answer during the recitation of Psalms. The expression corresponds to the Greek στιχηρόν (*stichērón*), κανών (*kanṓn*).

O. HEIMING, Syr. ʿeniane und griech. Kanones, 1932.

S.BR.

Enyo (Ἐνυώ; *Enyṓ*). Pale feminine counterpart to Enyalius, of whose name E. is a shortened form; goddess of bloody close combat. In Homer's Iliad she appears in 5,333 with Athena and in 592 with Ares, whom she joins in encouraging the Trojans. Her identifying characteristic is Kydoimos (demon of close combat), which she swings like a weapon (Il. 5,592, cf. 18,535; schol. Hom. Il. 5,593). Genealogical constructions starting from these passages made E. the mother or daughter or wet-nurse of → Ares (schol. Hom. 5,333; Cornutus Nat. deor. 21) or of → Enyalius. There was a painting of E. in the Ares temple in Athens (Paus. 1,8,4; cf. Philostr. Imag. 2,29); together with Enyalius, Ares and Athena Areia, she appeared in the ephebic oath (Aesch. Sept. 45). In Quintus of Smyrna and Nonnus, E. became the eponym of the battle massacre.

→ Ares; → Bellona; → Demon; → Enyalius R.GOR.

Eordaea (Ἐορδαία, Ἐορδία; *Eordaía, Eordía*). Macedonian landscape east of Lyncus, west of Bermion, northeast of the watershed of the Haliacmon. Cities of E. were Arnisa, Cellis, Boceria. In 167 BC E. was annexed to *Macedonia IV* (Liv. 45,30,6). The *via Egnatia* led through E., in the Roman Imperial period apparently a *civitas*.

N.G. L. HAMMOND, A History of Macedonia I, 1972, 106–110; F. PAPAZOGLOU, Les villes de Macédoine, 1988, 159–169.

MA.ER.

Eos (Ἠώς; *Ēṓs*). Goddess of the dawn, probably of Indo-European origin, frequently equated with Hemera, the daylight. Her heavenly beauty (rosy-fingered, saffron-robed) is praised already by Homer (Il. 8,1). E. is the daughter of the Titans Hyperion and Theia, sister of → Selene and → Helios (Hes. Theog. 371ff.). Every morning she rises with her chariot and horses from Oceanus (Hom. Il. 19,1; Od. 23,244; H. Hom. Veneris 5,227). By → Astraeus she is the mother of the winds and the stars (Hes. Theog. 378; Apollod. 1,9). She snatches the beautiful → Cleitus (Hom. Od. 15,250) and kidnaps for herself the hunter → Orion, who however is torn from her by the envy of Artemis (Hom. Od. 5,121; Apollod. 1,27). Her attempt to win → Cephalus (according to some the husband of Procris) also has tragic consequences (Eur. Hipp. 454f.; Ov. Met. 7,700ff.). She abducts her beloved → Tithonus (Hom. Il. 20,237; Hom. Od. 5,1; H. Hom. Veneris 5,218ff.; Eur. Tro. 847ff.; Apollod. 3,147; Ath. 13,566d) and requests immortality for him from Zeus,

forgetting however to ask for eternal youth. E. finally transforms the aged Tithonus into a cicada (schol. Il. 11,1f.). By Tithonus she is the mother of two sons, Emathion and → Memnon (Hom. Od. 4,188; Hes. Theog. 984; Pind. Ol. 2,83; Pind. Nem. 6,5ff; Apollod. 3,147). The *Aethiopis* described their fate (PEG I p. 67): Memnon fell in single combat with Achilles, his brother Emathion was killed by Hercules (schol. Pind. Ol. 2,83). The plastic arts have frequently depicted E. as winged since the 6th cent. BC. She scarcely emerges cultically (Ov. Met. 13,588);only libations are documented in Athens (Polemon fr. 42 FHG 3 p. 127).
→ Procris

D.D. Boedeker, Aphrodite's Entry into Greek Epic, 1974; J. Escher, s.v. Eos, RE 5, 2657–2669; J. Fontenrose, Orion. The Myth of the Hunter and the Huntress, 1981, 93 and *passim*; A. Rapp, s.v. Eos, Roscher 1.1, 1252–1278; C. Weiss, s.v. Eos, LIMC 3.1, 747–789. T.S.

Epaenetus (Ἐπαίνετος; *Epaínetos*)
[1] Medicinal plant expert and author of toxicological works, who lived between the 1st cent. BC and the 3rd cent. AD. His views on the dangerous characteristics of wolfbane, hemlock, opium, mandrake, henbane, poisonous mushrooms, black chamaeleon (a plant whose leaves can change colour), of bull's blood, of litharge and of lumpsucker as well as his remedies against these poisons are reported in detail in Ps.-Aelius Promotus' *De venenis* (ed. princeps, S. Ihm, 1995).
→ Medicine; → Toxicology V.N.

[2] Greek technical author who presumably wrote in the 1st half of the 1st cent. BC. His work Ὀψαρτυτικόν (*Opsartytikón*, 'Cookbook') is mentioned numerous times in Athenaeus (e.g. 7,294de about a thorny fish; 297c reference to a type of fish treated by E. and Dorion, similarly 304cd; 312b Ray; 9,371e Leek; 14,662de detailed recipe). Alternative names for foods of all types and food ingredients appear to have been of special interest to E. Ath. 9,387de seems to imply that Athenaeus was familiar with the cookbook of E. only via the lexicon of Pamphilus and the glossographical work of Artemidorus. Schol. Nic. Ther. 585 reports that E. (probably in a separate work) wrote about vegetables and kitchen herbs; furthermore, a work about poisonous animals is documented [1].
→ Artemidorus; → Cookery books; → Pamphilius

1 E. Rhode, in: RhM 28, 1873, 264–290, especially 269–271. G.BI.

Epakria see → Diakria

Epaminondas (Ἐπαμεινώνδας; *Epameinṓndas*). Most important Theban commander of the 1st half of the 4th cent. BC. His year of birth has not been recorded. After instruction by the Pythagorean Lysis of Tarentum who lived in his father Polymis' house (Diod. Sic. 15,39,2; Plut. Mor. 583c; 585e; Paus. 9,13,1; Nep. Epaminondas 2,2), he was considered incorruptible and frugal as well as a great orator (Plut. Mor. 808e, 809a). Little is known about his political beginnings. The outline in Paus. 9,13,1–15,6 offers no replacement for Plutarch's lost biography of E. [1]. After the occupation of the *Kadmeía* by the Spartans in 382 BC, E. did not go into exile, but in 379–78 he immediately joined the liberators of Thebes after the attack of the group of exiles under Pelopidas on the pro-Spartan polemarchs (Plut. Pel. 12). He probably took part in the peace congress in Sparta in 375, however when Diod. Sic. 15,38,2 tell us that E. represented Thebes there in its claim to power in Boeotia, this is to be connected to the negotiations in 371. E. first steps into the limelight for us as Boeotarch during the congress in Sparta in 371, at which the Spartans swore an oath also in the name of their allies to a *koinḗ eirḗnē* (StV 2, 269; → Peace, concept of), while the Athenians and their *symmachoi* including the Thebans who had joined the 2nd Athenian League swore *katà póleis*. On the next day E. demanded that the name 'Thebans' be replaced in the documents by 'Boeotians' (Xen. Hell. 6,3,18–20; Diod. Sic. 15,50,4; Plut. Agesilaus 27,4–28,2; Paus. 9,13,2). Perhaps Agesilaus II of Sparta had announced a call for all Greeks (i.e. also Boeotian poleis) after the swearing of the oath to join the *koinḗ eirḗnē* and hereby provoked E.'s demand, who wanted to achieve a recognition of the hegemony of Thebes in the Boeotian League [2. 68–74; 3. 113–125]. Agesilaus rejected this and King Cleombrotus received direction from Sparta to advance from Phocis to Boeotia. A short time later at Leuctra, E. carried his battle plan in the council of the Boeotarchs and was victorious due to his new tactics of the 'oblique alignment', overrunning the Spartans with a 50–man-deep attack formation on his left wing (Xen. Hell. 6,4,3–15; Diod. Sic. 15,53–56; Plut. Pel. 23; Paus. 9,13,3–12). After his re-election as Boeotarch, in the winter of 370–69 he managed to get the Thebans to comply with a request for help from the newly constituted Arcadian League and to transfer the management of the campaign to him. Although he was unable to conquer Sparta, he did free Messenia from Spartan rulership and initiated the founding of a Messenian state, so that Sparta was decidedly weakened (Xen. Hell. 6,5,23–52; Diod. Sic. 15,62–66; Plut. Agesilaus 31–34,1; Paus. 9,14,5).

Despite unparalleled successes, he was accused of exceeding his term of office (Plut. Pel. 25,1–6; Nep. Epaminondas 7–8) [4]. After being acquitted, he again became Boeotarch and advanced into the Peloponnese again already in 369 in order to stabilize the anti-Spartan coalition of Arcadians, Argives and Eleians. He forced Sicyon and Pellene into submission, but he had no success before Corinth and was accused of collaboration with the enemy and deposed (Xen. Hell. 7,1,15–22; Diod. Sic. 15,68–72,2). After being elected Boeotarch once again, E. in 367 freed Pelopidas who had wanted to stop the Athenian exertion of influence in

Macedonia and had been taken captive by Alexander of Pherae (Plut. Pelopidas 29; Paus. 9,15,2). When Theban efforts for a *koinè eirḗnē* had failed after probes by Pelopidas in Susa in 367–66 (Xen. Hell. 7,1,33–37; Diod. Sic. 15,81,3; Plut. Pelopidas 30), E. undertook his third campaign into the Peloponnese in 366 in order to strengthen the Theban influence in Arcadia and Elis and to force the Achaeans to ally themselves to Thebes. The Thebans did not agree with his support of the oligarchs in Achaea, seeing here an imitation of Spartan practice, but they assessed the situation wrongly and provoked severe unrest in Achaea by sending their own harmosts (Xen. Hell. 7,1,41–43). It is unlikely that E. wanted to erect sea bases there, although he was preparing the construction of a Theban fleet already in 366. His maritime plans were directed at the Aegean region, where in 364 he led a fleet operation to Byzantium, Heraclea (Pontus), Chios and Rhodes in order to win these poleis for an anti-Athenian sea alliance (Diod. Sic. 15,78,4–79). But he had no long-term success with this and was forced in 362 to again intervene on the Peloponnese after, as a result of the split of the Arcadian League, anti-Theban powers in Mantinea had joined with Elis, Achaea and Sparta and had issued a request for help to Athens. In the battle of Mantinea, Boeotian hoplites again broke through the enemy's formation, but E. fell and the battle ended without a military decision (Xen. Hell. 7,5,1–27).

The *koinè eirḗnē* of 362–61 (StV 2, 292) did not bring a lasting peace. Even E., who is celebrated by an epigram on the Kadmeia (9,15,6) as the 'Liberator of Hellas', scarcely had a concept for the future that pointed to a stable balance of powers. Inner-Theban leadership structures and lacking resources on the part of his polis limited E.'s scope for action, whose policy was, initially in any case, oriented toward the traditional claim of Thebes for supremacy in Boeotia. Although he rejected the enslavement of the inhabitants of Orchomenus (Diod. Sic. 15,57.1; Paus. 9,15,3), a policy after Leuctra within the entire Hellenic context towards the connection of Theban hegemony and polis-autonomy leading beyond the older systems of Sparta and Athens [5] is not discernable.

1 C.J. Tuplin, Pausanias and Plutarch's E. (369 BC), in: CQ 78, 1984, 346–358 2 M. Jehne, Koine Eirene, 1994 3 A.G. Keen, Were the Boiotian Poleis Autonomoi?, in: M.H. Hansen, K. Raaflaub (ed.), More Studies in the Ancient Greek Polis, 1996 4 J. Buckler, Plutarch on the Trials of Pelopidas and E. (369 BC), in: CPh 73, 1978, 36–42 5 H. Beister, Hegemoniales Denken in Theben, in: Id., J. Buckler (ed.), Boiotika, 1989, 131–153.

H. Beck, Polis und Koinon, 1997; H. Beister, Unt. zu der Zeit der thebanischen Hegemonie, thesis 1970; J. Buckler, The Theban Hegemony 371–362 BC, 1980; J. Roy, Thebes in the 360s B.C., in: CAH 6^2, 1994, 187–208.

K.-W.WEL.

Epanagoge (Ἐπαναγωγή; *Epanagōgḗ*). A law book in 40 titles promulgated under the Macedonian dynasty in the year AD 886 with the goal of invalidating the so-called → Ecloge, a codification of law enacted in the year 741 under the Isaurian emperors. In addition to civil and criminal provisions, it also contains state theoretical parts probably inspired by → Photius, which assume the patriarch to be of equal rank with the emperor. The work, whose original title is 'Eisagōge' (Εἰσαγωγή, 'introduction') [1. 12–14], instituted the *Basilika*, a large-scale codification based on the *Corpus iuris Civilis* (→ Digesta, → Law, codification of), however it was soon replaced by the *Prócheiros Nómos*.

A. Schminck, Studien zu mittelbyzantinischen Rechtsbüchern, 1986.

P.E. Pieler, in: Hunger, Literatur, II, 454f.; J. Scharf, Photios und die E., in: ByzZ 49, 1956, 385–400; Id., Quellenstudien zum Prooimion der E., in: ByzZ 52, 1959, 68–81.

G.MA.

Epanalepsis see → Figures I

Epander Nicephorus (Ἔπανδρος Νικηφόρος; *Épandros Nikēphóros*) Indo-Greek king in the 1st cent. BC. He is documented only by his coins (Middle-Indian *Epadra*).

Bopearachchi 103, 305f.

K.K.

Epangelia (ἐπαγγελία; *epangelía*). In Athens the legally prescribed announcement of the submission of a → *dokimasía* against a speaker who put forward a motion in the public assembly. It could be submitted by any citizen against the applicant who had incriminated himself of an action that removed his right to speak, but who had not yet been convicted in court (Aeschin. In Tim. 28ff. 81). *Epangelia* means the announcement of a complaint against the obligor in the Egyptian papyri.

A.R. W. Harrison, The Law of Athens II, 1971, 204; M.H. Hansen, The Athenian Assembly in the Age of Demosthenes, 1987, 117; F. Preisigke, Fachwörter des öffentlichen Verwaltungsdienstes Ägyptens, 1915, s.v.

G.T.

Epaphos see → Io

Epaphroditus (Ἐπαφρόδιτος; *Epaphróditos*).

[1] Freedman of Octavian, who in the year 30 BC was supposed to keep Cleopatra from committing suicide, but was allegedly outwitted by the queen (Plut. Antonius 79,6; Cass. Dio 51,13,4f.).

K. Kraft, KS 1, 1973, 38f.

D.K.

[2] Freedman of Nero, therefore Ti. Claudius Aug(usti) lib(ertus) E. by his full name. First accepted as an imperial freedman into the city of Rome's *decuriae*, i.a. *apparitor Caesarum* and *viator tribunicius*; later *a libellis* of Nero, presumably as thanks for having contrib-

uted to the exposure of the Pisonian conspiracy in the year 65. For this he was rewarded by Nero with military honours to which only a freeborn person was entitled (ILS 9505 = [1]). He accompanied Nero in his flight in the year 68 and helped him when he committed suicide. He first lived among the Flavians without being pestered; Flavius Iosephus was friends with him and dedicated his works *Antiquitates, Vita* and the books *contra Apionem* to him. Epictetus was among his slaves (cf. [2]). Domitian had him executed, alledgedly because he had helped Nero in his suicide. His fortune was apparently confiscated, at least the *horti Epaphroditiani*, in which E. was buried. PIR² E 69; LTUR III 60.

1 W. Eck, Nero's Freigelassener Epaphroditus und die Aufdeckung der pisonischen Verschwörung, Historia 25, 1976, 381ff. 2 F. Millar, Epictetus and the Imperial Court, JRS 55, 1965, 141ff. W.E.

[3] Greek Grammarian of the 1st cent. AD.
A. Life B. Works

A. Life
Detailed biographical news in the Suda (s.v. E., ε 2004, Sources: Hermippus of Berytus, conveyed by Hesychius of Miletus). Born in AD 22–23 in Chaeronea, slave in the house of the Alexandrian grammarian → Archias [8], then acquired by *praefectus Aegypti* M. Mettius Modestus as teacher for his son Petelinus, finally set free by the same; his Lat. name was M. Mettius Epaphroditus). He lived in Rome, where he died at the age of 75 under Emperor Nerva, and came to wealth here (he owned two houses and a library of 30,000 scrolls). His statue with inscription is preserved in the villa Altieri in Rome (CIL VI 9454; identification by E. Q. Visconti, 1818; [5]).

B. Works
1. Commentaries (ὑπομνήματα; *hypomnḗmata*): a) on Homer (which likely followed in detail the order of the books of the *Iliad* and the *Odyssey*), of which fragments are preserved in the scholia, the etymologica and above all by Stephanus of Byzantium: The explanations dealt with grammatical and content issues; special notice was given to the Homeric place names and their etymology [6]. E.'s sources are: → Demetrius of Scepsis, the commentary of Apollodorus on the Homeric catalogue of ships, → Didymus of Alexandria [4. 2713]; b) on the ps.-Hesiodian *Scutum*; c) on Callimachus' *Aetia*.
2. *Léxeis* (Λέξεις: perhaps a miscellaneous work); most of the fragments contain etymologies.
3. Περὶ στοιχείων (*Perì stoicheiōn*; for the meaning of the title cf. [4. 2714]).

Edition: 1 E. Luenzer, Epaphroditi grammatici quae supersunt, 1866 (Additions to this: [4. 2713–2714]).
Literature: 2 S. F. Bonner, Education in Ancient Rome, 1977, 50, 58–59, 154, 217 3 J. Christes, Sklaven und Freigelassene als Grammatiker und Philologen im antiken Rom, 1979, 103–104 4 L. Cohn, s.v. E., RE 5, 2711–2714 5 R. A. Kaster, Sueton. De Grammaticis et Rhetoribus, 1995, 136–137 6 R. Reitzenstein, Gesch. der griech. Etym., 1897, 187. S.FO.

Eparchia (ἐπαρχία; *eparchía*). Territorial administrative unit in Hellenistic states. In the Seleucid kingdom, Antiochus [5] III especially supported the setting up of smaller provinces in order to prevent power concentrations in the areas of individual satraps, as for example → Molon (222 BC). Polybius describes their head, who evidently had military and civil power, as *éparchos* or *stratēgós* (Pol. 5,46,7; 48,14); however his terminology is misleading since from the middle of the 2nd cent. BC on, *eparchia* started taking on the meaning of Lat. *provincia* (cf. SIG³ 683,55 and 65; Arr. Parth. fr. 1,2: *éparchos* as descriptor of a Seleucid provincial governor) [1. 150ff.], such that an exact characterization of the Seleucid *eparchia* is problematic. Starting in the Imperial period *eparchia* appears officially for *provincia* (cf. SEG 16, 391; 42, 631; 43, 777; Jos. BI 1,157; Str. 12,3,37; 16,2,3; 17,1,12) and *éparchos* is used generally for *praefectus* (cf. ILS 8841; SEG 42, 676; 43, 492; Plut. Galba 2; for the *éparchos* of Egypt cf. [2]).

1 Bengtson, Vol. 2 2 G. Bastianini, ΕΠΑΡΧΟΣ ΑΙΓΥΠΤΟΥ nel formulario dei documenti, in: ANRW II 10.1, 581–597. M.MEI. and ME.STR.

Eparchos (ἔπαρχος; *éparchos*). Head of an → *eparchía*, a territorial administrative unit in Hellenistic states, especially in the → Seleucid kingdom. It is disputed whether *eparchos* ever was an official title for the holder of civil and military power in a subdivision of the satrapy (→ Satrap) because in this context it is not attested epigraphically. The first appearance of the term *eparchos* for a governor in Seleucid territory in Polybius [2] (5,46,7) suggests that *eparchos* was formed as an analogy to the term *eparchía* (the Greek term for a Roman province) and describes the function of a → *stratēgós* [1. 150–158; 275 f.; 396]. In the Roman period, *eparchos* became the Greek term for a Roman → *praefectus*, both for the → *praefectus urbi* in Rome (ἐ. τῆς πόλεως/*éparchos tês póleōs*) and the → *praefectus Aegypti* as well as other functionaries in Roman provinces (comprehensive collection in [2. 45]).

1 Bengtson, vol. 2 2 H. J. Mason, Greek Terms for Roman Institutions, 1974, 45; 138–140. W. ED.

Epasnactus (Epad[nactus]; Celt. name compilation from *epo-* 'Horse' [2. 89–90]). Pro-Roman prince of the → Arverni, who captured the rebellious Cadurcan leader Lucterius in 51 BC and turned him over to Caesar (Caes. B Gall. 8,44,3). E. is documented on several coins [1. 432–436].

1 B. Colbert de Beaulieu see Diviciacus [1] 2 Evans. W.SP.

Epeisodion (τὸ ἐπεισόδιον; *tó epeisódion*, from the adjective ἐπεισόδιος; *epeisódios*, 'inserted'). According to Aristot. Poet. 12,1452b 20f. part of a tragedy between two entire chorus parts (that is between the → parodos and the first → *stasimon* or between two *stasima*). The term *epeisodion* is found as a technical term only in the *Poetica*, other authors speak of a *méros* or *mórion*. Aristotle also uses the *terminus epeisodion* in the *Poetica* in a more general sense for 'section', 'episode' (e.g. 17,1455b 13). In the Old Comedy, the second part of the pieces can often be divided into *epeisodia*. In the New Comedy, the episodic structure develops into five acts.

→ Actus B.Z.

Epenthesis see → Phonetics

Epetium Like Tragurium a colony of Greeks from Issa on the mainland south of Salona (later province Dalmatia), in a fertile region, well protected by its position on a peninsula, today Stobreč/Croatia (cf. Pol. 32,9; Ptol. 2,16,4; Tab. Peut. 5,3: *Epetio*, *Portus Epetius*; Geogr. Rav. 4,16 or 209,5: *Epitio*). Probably founded in the 3rd cent. BC (the protected harbour was used already in the 4th cent. BC) and most assuredly some amount of time before 158 BC when Issa complained that both settlements were attacked by the → Dalmatae (Pol. 32,9); these were defeated by C. Cosconius (78–76 BC), but until their defeat E. like Salona was in their possession. E. was possibly recognized by Caesar as a possession of Issa. After the founding of the *colonia* by Caesar in Salona, E. was one of the main settlements in the area of that city. Aerial photographs show the remains of a *centuriatio*. There is no trace of an indigenous population in E.; all inhabitants were either of Italian origin or had immigrated from elsewhere. Both the Greek and the Roman E. were protected by powerful walls, erected on a narrow land bridge to Salona.

A. FABER, Bedemi Epetiona — Stobreč kod Splita (The Fortifications of Epetion [Stobreč near Split]), in: Prinosi Odjela za arheologiju 1, 1983, 17–37. M.Š.K.

Epeunaktai (Ἐπευνακταί; *Epeunaktaí*). Literally 'bedfellows'. According to Theopomp (FGrH 115 F 171 in Ath. 6,271c-d), Helots who during the 1st Messenian War were set free by the Spartans and received citizenship; they were supposed to unite with the widows of those who had fallen (cf. also Just. Epit. 3,5,6, who however dates the events in the second Messenian War). According to this, the E. would have been the fathers of the so-called → Partheniai, who appear in tradition as the founders of Tarentum (Str. 6,3,2f.) and with whom Diod. Sic. fr. 8,21 falsely identifies the E. The E. legend, which is certainly younger than the Partheniai story, probably only reflects one of the various attempts to interpret the name of the Partheniai (literally 'sons of virgins') that was already puzzling in antiquity. However, a definitive certainty regarding their true identity is not ascertainable. M.MEI.

Ephebeia (ἐφηβεία; *ephēbeía*)
I. DEFINITION II. CLASSICAL ATHENS III. HELLENISM AND PRINCIPATE

I. DEFINITION

The *ephebeia* generally described a life stage in Greece between childhood and manhood, more specifically puberty, and in the more narrow sense the phase at its conclusion. This is valid from a biological point of view and is consequently treated in medical writings. As a rule, an age between 12 and 18, sometimes 12 and 20 is used to define *ephebeia*; occasionally the previous level after the end of childhood is described with its own term (e.g. μελλεφηβία, *mellephēbía*). Specific formal and ritual aspects are characteristic of the *ephebeia* and gave the transition to adulthood a social dimension: Afterwards the young man was no longer a minor and therefore in the legal sense entitled to marriage and property. During *ephebeia*, specifically at its end, he attained the political and cultural rights and duties of a polis citizen, including compulsory military service. In this phase of their life, the juveniles formed a clearly defined group that was externally recognizable by virtue of hairstyle and clothing, and the fact that they were bound to certain rooms and modes of behaviour. They grew into the community of the polis at an accelerated tempo by getting to know its practices in the cultural, social and military-political spheres and by practising these in the execution of certain ritual actions in a manner appropriate to their age, by physical training, military education, instruction and various activities promoting community (dance and singing, common meals, training fights in groups). Their physical-social borderline situation frequently found expression in specific initiation rites and in their isolation that was also spatial (especially in the border regions of the polis territory).

In the Greek communities, such transition stages were probably widespread from the beginning onward; the considerable variation in the names that were in use for them at different locations indicates this. In the course of the formation of the polis, they were developed gradually. For the early period, those from Sparta and Crete are best known to us; here, the original initiation rites partially survived in the forms institutionalized in the archaic period (e.g., borderline situations in lingering peripheral areas and in the → *krypteía*, ritual scourgings, the temporary change in gender identity, homosexual practices). In the Spartan → *agōgḗ* [6; 3. 234–298; 1. 112–207; 12] and in the Cretan → *agélai* ('herds of youths') [7. 31–41], they were formalized due to their contribution to co-operative values.

II. CLASSICAL ATHENS

The most extensive material about the *ephebeia* comes from Athens, where the expression itself was also quite common. The institution of the *ephebeia* is documented for the first half of the 4th cent., stretching over two years and consisting of military training and service in the Attic territory (Aeschin. In Tim. 49; Leg. 167). It can be traced back to the middle of the 5th cent. due to the analogous activities of *neṓtatoi* ('youngest'; Thuc. 1,105,4; 2,13,7). The Attic *ephebeia* was probably reformed in 336–35 BC by a law from Eucrates (Lycurg. fr. 5,3), most certainly in connection with the Lycurgan restoration programme. The traditional elements were further formalized and military training was strengthened; on the whole, the reform was guided by the ideal of the citizen soldier. In the sense of observing the law of democracy, the young men were to be brought to completely identify with their polis militarily, politically and religiously. The *ephebeia* of this period is described in detail by Aristotle (Aristot. Ath. Pol. 42).

At the age of 18 the young Athenians in their respective demes were entered into the lists of citizens after checking their personal legal status, and then admitted into the *ephebeia* by phyle. A *kosmētḗs* and ten *sōphronistaí*, one per phyle who were chosen by the people, were responsible for their training. In addition, there were teachers for athletic and military training (two *paidotríbai* as well as trainers for hoplite fighting, archery, spear throwing, and handling catapults); furthermore, there were military ranks (*taxíarchoi, lochagoí*). The *sophronistai* and the ephebes received payment from the polis for their joint livelihood (1 drachma for each *sophronistes*, 4 oboli for each ephebe per day). Service began with an inspection of the sanctuaries, whereby more than likely an oath was sworn at the Aglaurus sanctuary (Tod 204; Pollux 8,105; Stob. 4,1,48; Lycurg. 76f.; Plut. Alcibiades 15,7), in which the ephebes promised military obedience, to observe the laws and religious rules of the polis, as well as to protect the constitution. They spent the first year in the fortified garrisons of the Piraeus (Munychia, Acte). At its end they demonstrated what they had learned during a public assembly in the theatre and received a shield and lance. In the second year of service the ephebes were stationed in the various fortresses and had to do patrol service in the country. During the time period mentioned they were released from remitting duties and were allowed neither to be accused nor to accuse (with the exception of cases dealing with the ownership of land, the marriage of an heiress (*epíklēros)* or an inherited priesthood). They wore special clothing, a black cape (*chlamýs*) and probably the → *pétasos* as a head covering. The ephebes participated in special ritualistic acts and ritual contests (Aristot. Ath. Pol. 53,4; Dem. Or. 19,303 with schol.; Philoch. FGrH 328 F 15f. 105).

There is clear evidence (Aristot. Ath. Pol. 42,1; Lycurg. 76), that all young Athenians were required to serve as ephebes. However, according to the ascertainable numbers of the respective age groups (around 500), participation was incomplete. This does not justify the assumption, however, that the *ephebeia* had been set up only for the citizens with hoplite census [2. 33–43].

The ephebes as well as the teachers responsible for their training were honoured from the beginning in various ways: Above all, their military discipline as well as their obedience with respect to their trainers, the laws and the political institutions of the polis were emphasized via the keywords εὐταξία (*eutaxía*), κοσμιότης (*kosmiótēs*) and φιλοτιμία (*philotimía*). Not of least importance, these awards promoted competition among the phyle groups and their inner cohesion. Even though older elements of the ritual initiation will have survived particularly in the patrolling of the frontier regions of the polis [13. 151–176], the reform indicates decidedly military-political objectives; it was oriented to the idea of an identity as citizen and soldier and was to serve the strengthening of the military capacity and traditional polis patriotism in view of the Macedonian dominance.

III. Hellenism and Principate

It is to be assumed that the pro-Macedonian oligarchies under Phocion and Demetrius of Phalerum (322–307 BC) did not undertake any special efforts with reference to the *ephebeia*. After the re-establishment of the democracy (307), the *ephebeia* was also reorganized, apparently by a law (IG II [2]556 ?), likely substantially in accordance with the old forms, however with only one year of service and only one *paidotríbēs*. During the first half of the 3rd cent. clear changes occurred that are documented in the inscriptions since the time of the Chremonidean War (268–262) (esp. instructive are IG II [2]665; 766; 900; 1006 with SEG 38,114; 1008; cf. generally [8. 159–281; 9. 289f.]): The office of the *sōphronistḗs* no longer shows up, the number of ephebes varies sharply, however it has definitely decreased (on average there were not more than 100 per age group). Apparently service was no longer obligatory, and furthermore many could no longer afford the expense since the state maintenance support had been discontinued. The leading official (*kosmētḗs*) even had to spend considerable sums from his own private fortune in order to provide the most splendid equipment possible for his *ephebeia*.

Especially striking was the change in objectives and content of the ephebate training: Although the military components as such did survive and were especially emphasized in war times, the originally military education served predominantly for the preparation and holding of athletic competitions. The unity of citizen and soldier had broken down, if for no other reason than the decreased participation. The cultic elements, especially the execution of various rites, came to the fore; in addition to *eutaxía* and *philotimía*, the εὐσέβεια (*eusébeia*, piety) appears as grounds for the prize-giving. Furthermore, physical training was increasingly accompanied by a general education of the ephebes, for example the attendance of lectures in the Attic philosopher schools. Although as always talk was of observing the law and respect for the constitution that was passed down with its institutions, when it came to patriotism, it expressed itself less in concrete imitation and more in the cultic worship of ancestors, above all the heroes of the Persian Wars. The 'benefactors' of the city, i.e. primarily the Hellenistic monarchs on whom Athens was dependent, also found particular attention. In this way the *ephebeia* became an institution for the physical and intellectual education of the elite. It was only consistent that starting towards the end of the 1st cent. BC foreigners were also accepted into the *ephēbeía*. Athens had become a seat of learning in which the *ephebeia* had a firm place, which it also retained in the Principate period with multifarious forms [9. 290f.].

Numerous inscriptions and papyri from the Hellenistic and Imperial periods document a broad distribution of the *ephebeia* in the Greek world. Although there had been varying local traditions, now the *ephebeia* offered a unified picture. The military components were still present everywhere — and in times of emergency they were also attributed increased importance — but generally the *ephebeia* became an element of athletic agones and training. The ephebes' participation in cultic activities (sacrifices, processions, religious festivals) was striking. The intellectual and cultural education was highly valued; teachers of rhetoric and philosophy participated in it. The *ephebeia* was from now on an institution of education for the elite (instructive examples IK 19,1: Sestus; SEG 27, 261: Beroea; IG XII 9, 234: Eretria; IPriene 112). Particularly due to this, it represented a fundamental factor in the self-conception and in the self-awareness of the Greek cities. However, over and beyond this it was also (in connection with its most important location, the → *gymnasium*) a specific characteristic of urban Greek life; and insofar as Hellenic culture defined itself in this period primarily via education, the *ephebeia* was a substantial element of Greek identity (2 Macc 4,7–12; Str. 5,4,7).

→ Agelai; → Agoge; → Youth

1 A. Brelich, Paides e parthenoi I, 1969,112–207 2 L. Burckhardt, Bürger und Soldaten, 1996 3 W. Den Boer, Laconian Studies, 1954, 234–298 4 H.-J. Gehrke, Gewalt und Gesetz. Die soziale und politische Ordnung Kretas in der archaischen und klassischen Zeit, in: Klio 79, 1997, 23–68 5 G. Ieranò, Osservazioni sul Teseo di Bacchilide (Dith. 18), in: Acme 40, 1987, 87–103 6 H. Jeanmaire, Couroi et courètes, 1939 7 H.Y. McCulloch, H.D. Cameron, Septem 12–13 and the Athenian ephebia, in: Illinois Classical Studies 5, 1980, 1–14 8 C. Pélékidis, Histoire de l'Éphebie attique des origines à 31 av. J.-C., 1962 9 O.W. Reinmuth, s.v. Ephebia, KlP 2,287–291 10 Id., The Ephebic Inscriptions of the Fourth Century B.C., 1971 11 P. Siewert, The Ephebic oath in fifth-century Athens, in: JHS 97, 1977, 102–111 12 C.M. Tazelaar, ΠΑΙΔΕΣ ΚΑΙ ΕΦΗΒΟΙ: Some Notes on the Spartan Stages of Youth, Mnemosyne 20, 1967, 127–153 13 P. Vidal-Naquet, Le chasseur noir, [3]1983. H.-J.G.

Ephedra (ἐφέδρα, ἐφέδρον; *ephédra, ephédron*). Type of shrub that has been identified with the almost leafless gymnospermous birch shrub *Ephedra campylopoda C.A. Mey*, which climbs up trees and cliffs in the Balkan countries. This is supported not only by the alternative name (*anábasis*, ἀνάβασις) but also by Pliny's description of the plant (HN 26,36 *scandens arborem et ex ramis propendens*). There, rubbed into dark wine, it is recommended for coughing and shortness of breath, and is supposed to help against stomach-ache when boiled as a broth and added to a bit of wine. Its straight-growing relatives *E. distachya* (or *vulgaris Rich.*, called *uva marina* or 'sea grape' in the 17th and 18th cents.) and *E. maior Host.* were confused by Pliny (HN 26,133) under terms such as ἵππουρις (*híppouris*) or *equisaetum* with the similarly appearing horsetails (→ *equisetum*) and was recommended for similar complaints due to its astringent effect (there is no confusion however in Dioscorides, 4,46 [2. 203f.] or [3. 388f.]). The agent ephedrine, extracted from the plant, used to be prescribed for asthma and poor circulation, and today has become a stimulant drug replacement.

1 H. Baumann, Die griech. Pflanzenwelt, 1982 2 Wellmann 2 3 Berendes. C.HÜ.

Ephedrismos (ἐφεδρισμός; *ephedrismós*). A game where a target (δίορος; *díoros*) on the ground is to be hit with a rock or a ball; the loser had to carry the winner, who covered the loser's eyes, on his back until he touched the target with his foot. Boys and girls participated in *ephedrismos*, which according to the evidence of monuments became popular in the 5th cent. BC and is depicted in various stages. The representations also show satyrs and Erotes playing *ephedrismos*. The piggyback motif is very widespread in the Greek and Roman art (intaglios, sculpture; group in Rome, Palazzo dei Curatori: Helbig 2, no. 1465; terracotta, vase and wall paintings); however, the *ephedrismos* game does not always have to be meant.

P. Zazoff, Ephedrismos. Ein altgriech. Spiel, in: A&A; 11, 1962, 35–42; K. Schauenburg, Erotenspiele, in: AW 7, 1976 H.3, 41–42; U. Steininger, Zwei Ephedrismos-Terrakotten im Basler Antikenmuseum, in: AK 34, 1994, 44–50. R.H.

Ephemeris (ἐφημερίς; *ephēmerís*, pl. *ephēmerídes*). A diary for personal notes, as office or accounts journal. The common term for such notes is → *hypomnēma(ta)*, Lat. → *commentarii* or → *acta*. *Ephemeris* is found as the title of literary works that have been passed down or used, i.a. for the 'war journal' of → Alexander [4] the Great used by the historian → Ptolemy I (FGrH 117) and the fictitious *Ephemerìs toû Troikoû polémou*, the Trojan War diary from the (fictitious) → Dictys Cretensis. Plutarch (Caes. 22) describes Caesar's *commentarii* as *ephemeris*; however, in the → Corpus Caesarianum only the *Bellum Africanum* and the *Bellum Hispaniense* contain diary characteristics. J.R.

Ephesia see → Artemis

Ephesia Grammata (Ἐφέσια γράμματα; *Ephésia grámmata*, 'Ephesian letters of the alphabet'). Designation for a series of words devoid of meaning — (*askion kataskion lix tetrax damnameneus aision* or *aisia*) that was used orally and in writing for apotropaic and salvation-bringing purposes. Their name comes from the fact that they were engraved on the statue of Artemis of Ephesus (Paus. ap. Eust. Od. 19,247). They were spoken in → exorcism (Plut. Mor. 706 de) for the protection of a bridal couple which was ritually encircled (Men. Fr. 313); → Croesus supposedly used them to put out the burning wood that was to burn him at the stake (Suda s.v. E. γ., E 386); written on a piece of leather and worn, the *Ephesia grammata* (EG) serve as an amulet (Anaxilas fr. 18) and bring victory in sport (Suda ibid.). The first epigraphical documentation on a small lead tablet from Halasarna in Crete (4th cent. BC; ICr 2,19,7) documents the use as amulet; a text from Selinus suggests that the series of words originally had a hexametrical form. The play with language that is incomprehensible to the user himself is something the EG have in common with a great many magical salvation aphorisms of the ancient and post-classical cultures.

K. Preisendanz, s.v. Ephesia grammata, RAC 5, 515–520; R. Kotansky, Incantations and prayers for salvation on inscribed Greek amulets, in: C. A. Farone, D. Obbink (ed.), Magika Hiera. Ancient Greek Magic and Religion, 1991, 110–112. 126f.; H. S. Versnel, Die Poetik der Zaubersprüche, in: T. Schabert, R. Brague (ed.), Die Macht des Wortes, Eranos N.F. 4, 1996, 233–297. F.G.

Ephesiaka see → Xenophon of Ephesus

Ephesis (ἔφεσις; *éphesis*). Derived from the verb ἐφίεσθαι (*ephíesthai*, to turn to someone), in Athens *ephesis* denoted a series of legal actions in which a person turned to the competent authority for a decision after a provisional decision had been reached. One certainly cannot speak of a uniform institution comparable to today's 'appeal'. Solon (around 600 BC) is said to have allowed the *ephesis* for decisions of the → archontes at the → Heliaea (Aristot. Ath. Pol. 9,1). In the classical period there was the *ephesis* to a → *dikastḗrion* against an → *epibolḗ* imposed by an archon and exceeding 10 drachmas (Aeschin. In Ctes. 27). Whoever was not satisfied with the ruling of one of the official → *diaitetaí*, turned to the *dikastḗrion* with *ephesis* (Aristot. Ath. Pol. 53,2); there he was limited to the evidence presented in the *díaita*. The *diaitétēs* who was convicted by his peers of incorrectness, also had *ephesis* at his disposal (Aristot. Ath.Pol. 53,5). There was *ephesis* also in connection with → *dokimasía* (Aristot. Ath. Pol. 45,3), → *apagogḗ* (when the accused did not confess, cf. Aristot. Ath. Pol. 52,1) and with entry into the lists of the phratry (IG II[2] 1237,96) as well as in the first Athenian League (478 BC; IG I[3] 40,71ff.). As for Ptolemaic Egypt, in spite of B I 4638,26 Preisigke, one should adhere to the view that *ephesis* does not mean 'appeal'.

H. J. Wolff, Das Justizwesen der Ptolemäer, [2]1970, 152, 159 A. R. W. Harrison, The Law of Athens II, 1971, 190f. Ch. Koch, Volksbeschlüsse in Seebundangelegenheiten, 1991, 135ff. 465. G.T.

Ephesus

I. History II. Archaeology

I. History

A. Site B. Beginning and Greek Period C. Artemisium D. Hellenistic Period E. Roman Empire F. Christianity G. Byzantine Period

A. Site

City (today Turkish county seat Selçuk) at the mouth of the Caystrus in the Aegean Sea, 80 km south of Izmir. The river sedimentation moved the coastline by about 9 km to the west since archaic times (Hdt. 2,10; Str. 14,1,24; Plin. HN 2,201; 5,115) and caused the deep bay to finally silt up by the late Middle Ages. English, Austrian and Turkish excavations convey the broad expanse of ruins of the Roman-early Byzantine city, the Artemisium and the Basilica of St. John. Important collections of artefacts are in Istanbul, AM, in the archaeological Mus. of Izmir, in London, BM, in the Mus. in Selçuk and in Vienna, Ephesus-Museum.

B. Beginning and Greek Period

The oldest settlement locations in the Ephesian bay belong to the Chalcolithic (4th–3rd millennia BC) and the early Bronze Age. The castle hill (today Ayasoluk, from *Hágios Theólogos*) was settled at the latest in the 3rd millennium BC (finds of the periods of Troy I and II). Several scholars have identified E. with the Apaša in the land Arzawa that was conquered by the Hittite king Muršilis II in the 14th cent. BC. A Mycenaean grave from the same period (level LH IIIA$_2$) and sporadic finds from the Artemis Sanctuaries document a Mycenaean outpost. According to the → *Marmor Parium*, the founding of E. occurred in 1086–85 BC. The legend influenced by Attica names the son of Codrus → Androclus as the leader of Greek colonists who found on arrival the sanctuary of → Artemis Ephesia and settlements inhabited by Carians and Lydians (Paus. 7,2,6ff.; Str. 14,1,3f.; 21). E. was a member of the Ionian League of twelve cities (Hdt. 1,142f.). The Greek city lay at a distance of seven stadia (*c.* 1200 m) from the Artemisium (Hdt. 1,26) and was called Coressus. City and sanctuary have probably withstood the attack of the Cimmerii in the middle of the 7th cent. BC, against which the poet Callinus called to battle. Starting in the 2nd half of the 7th cent. BC tyrants ruled: Pythagoras, Melas (son-in-law of the Lydian king Alyattes), and lastly his son Pindarus. In 560 BC Croesus of Lydia besieged Coressus and resettled the Greeks in the Artemisium, whereby the Greek-Lydian hybrid city of E. was formed. The Athenian Aristarchus (Suda, s.v. Ἀρίσταρχος) drew up a democratic constitution. After Croesus' defeat against

Cyrus in 541 BC the Ionian cities were conquered by the Median General Harpagus (Hdt. 1,162; 169).

The Persians in their turn supported the *tyrannis*, which the poet Hipponax avoided by moving to Clazomenae (Suda, s.v. Ἱππῶναξ). In the rebellion of the Ionian cities, E. remained pro-Persian; perhaps that is why the Greek fleet gathered in the old Coressus harbour in 498 BC (Hdt. 5,100). In 497 the Ephesians murdered the citizens of Chios who had shipwrecked on their way home after the naval battle of Lade (Hdt. 6,16). Starting in 465 BC, E. was a member of the → Delian League with a democratic constitution, against which the philosopher Heraclitus (fr. 121 DK) polemicized. E. fought in the Peloponnesian War on the side of Athens until at least 424 BC (Thuc. 4,50). In 412 at the latest E. switched to the side of the Spartans (Thuc. 8,14ff.); in 409 it was stormed to no avail by the Attic commander Thrasyllus (Xen. Hell. 1,2,6ff.), and from 407 it was the main headquarters of the Spartan Lysander (Plut. Lysander 3; Xen. Hell. 1,5,1ff.). In 401 BC E. was the starting-point of the doomed rebellion of the satrap Cyrus against his brother Artaxerxes (Xen. An. 2,2,6); from 400–399 BC it was the base of the renewed Persian war under Spartan leadership. Due to the peace of Antalcidas with Artaxerxes II, E. again came under Persian sovereignty in 387 BC (3rd *tyrannis*), from which it was not freed until 334 BC by Alexander [4] the Great.

C. Artemisium

According to legend, the cult of Artemis was either founded by Amazons, or these same fled before Hercules and Dionysus into the asylum of the already existing sanctuary (Paus. 7,2,7). Some finds go back to the Minoan-Mycenaean period. The oldest identifiable cult structure dates the 8th cent. BC: a temple courtyard with a circular hall (13.5 × 6.5 m with 8 × 4 wooden columns) around a base for the wooden cult image of Artemis Ephesia. Around 600 BC a temple that was never completed was begun (by the tyrant Pythagoras?), from *c.* 560 the giant marble temple — one of the seven ancient Wonders of the World — was erected with the help of Croesus. Its double circular hall contained 127 columns of which 36 were decorated in relief (Plin. HN 36,95–97); in the temple courtyard stood a naiskos exactly over the oldest small temple. Allegedly set on fire in 356 BC by Herostratus, the temple was newly erected by the Ephesians with their own money, having declined an offer of help from Alexander the Great (Str. 14,1,22). The sanctuary achieved international significance due to its right to grant asylum (restructured and established as extending to a *stadion* around the temple by Alexander and Augustus, Str. 14,1,23) and its bank function (minting of coins starting in archaic times; deposits documented for example at Xen. An. 4,3,4ff.).

D. Hellenistic Period

In the Diadochi wars Lysimachus won E. first in 301 and finally in 287 BC after chequered battles. In view of the increasing sedimentation, he built a new town named after his wife → Arsinoe [II 3] 2 km west of the Artemisium (Str. 14,1,21). The *c.* 8 km long city wall, partially well preserved, stretched over the ridge of Mt. Prion (today Bülbüldağ) and also surrounded Pion (today the southern part of Panayırdağ). Of the early Hellenistic structures, up to now only the commercial or Tetragonos agora has been excavated; the city centre is likely to have taken up the at that time narrow coastal strip from the theatre to the Roman harbour basin. After the death of Lysimachus in 281 BC the city became Seleucid and was again called E. From 246 until 196 BC E. belonged to the Ptolemaic empire, was then recaptured by → Antiochus [5] III and in 188 BC at the peace of Apamea was annexed to the Pergamene kingdom of → Eumenes II. After the institution of the Roman *provincia Asia,* E. became *civitas libera atque foederata* (ILS 34) from 133 BC on. In 89–8 E. changed sides to Mithridates VI and the Romans resident in the city were killed ('Ephesian Vespers'), for which Sulla imposed a judgement over the city in 84 BC (App. Mith. 61–63).

E. Roman Empire

In the winter of 30–29 BC the future Augustus, with recourse to Caesar's privileges, made E. the seat of the *proconsul* of Asia. In the saddle between Prion and Pion a new governmental quarter was built with Prytaneion, Sebasteion and Bouleuterion at the so-called State Agora whose peripteral temple was probably constructed by the *conventus civium Romanorum* for *divus Iulius* and *dea Roma* (Cass. Dio 51,20,6). The economic importance of E. as the largest harbour in Asia Minor and its rapid growth in population — Seneca (Ep. 17,2,21) described E. as the second largest city of the Orient — are particularly seen in the installation of two long distance water pipes (a further three by the middle of the 2nd cent.), the new construction of the Tetragonos Agora with a side length of 150 m and the generous residential installations at the Embolos ('terrace houses'). After a devastating earthquake in AD 23 (Tac. Ann. 4,13,1; ILS 156), Emperor Tiberius nominally acted as γραμματεὺς τοῦ δήμου ('Scribe of the public assembly') in favour of its reconstruction. In AD 88–9 at the latest, the *neokoros* temple was consecrated for the *theoí Sebastoí*, which was connected with the construction of a magnificent complex including a gymnasium, thermal baths and a sports field (*xystoí*) in the former sea area (Hellenistic harbour?). Under Trajan (before AD 114) the extension of the theatre with *c.* 25,000 seats (perhaps also the new harbour basin?) was completed. In 130–31 Hadrian, upon the occasion of his visit in E., approved the construction of a second *neokoros* temple. The unrestricted growth of the city did not run out until the middle of the 3rd cent.; E. sustained lasting damage in an earthquake in 262. A

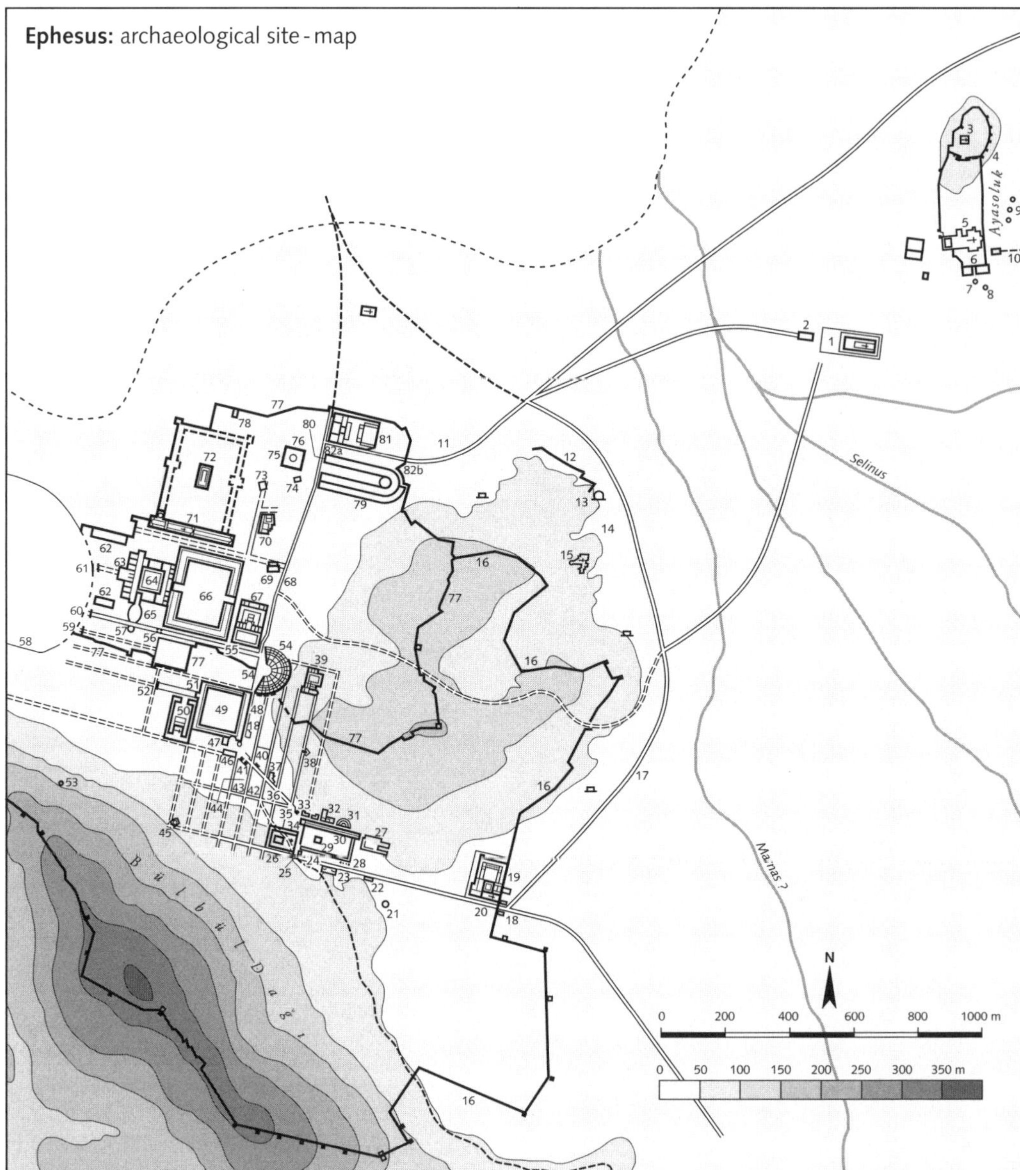

1. Artemision
2. Rostrum by the Artemision
3. Fortress (Byzantine-Turkish)
4. Early Bronze Age settlement
5. Basilica of St. John (finished AD 565)
6. 'Gate of Persecution' (Byzantine)
7. Mycenaean tomb
8. Classical tomb
9. Archaic-classical tombs
10. Byzantine aqueduct
11. Port of Coressus
12. Defence wall in Coressus
13. Rock sanctuary (of Meter or Cybele, from 5th cent. BC)
14. Byzantine aqueduct
15. Cave of the Seven Sleepers
16. Hellenistic city wall (early 3rd cent. BC)
17. Stoa of Damianus (2nd cent. BC) and colonnaded procession road
18. Magnesian Gate
19. East Gymnasium (2nd cent. AD)
20. Basilica in the East Gymnasium (5th/6th cents. AD)
21. 'Tomb of St. Luke' (1st cent. AD?)
22. Street fountain (AD 102–114)
23. Fountain (1st/2nd cents. AD)
24. South Road
25. Hydrekdochion of Laecanius Bassus (AD 78/79)
26. Temple of the Theoi Sebastoi (late 1st cent. AD)
27. Baths on the 'State Agora' (1st cent. AD)
28. Doric propylon
29. 'State Agora' with temle (Divus Iulius and Dea Roma ?)
30. Basilike Stoa (AD 13)
31. Bouleuterion (extant remains from the 2nd cent. AD)/ Odeion
32. Temenos for Augustus and Artemis Ephesia (?) and Prytaneion (early 1st cent. AD)
33. Monument of Memmius (late 1st cent. BC) and Hydreion (3rd cent. AD)
34. Fountains of Pollio and of Domitian
35. Heracles Gate (5th cent. AD)
36. Embolos ('Curetes Street')
37. Nymphaeum Traiani (AD 102–114)
38. Late Hellenistic round building (1st cent. BC)
39. Byzantine banqueting-house
40. Baths of Varius (2nd cent. AD; reconstructed in the 4th cent.: Baths of Scholasticia) with temple of Hadrian
41. Latrine and 'bordello' (2nd cent. AD)
42. Slope house 1
43. Slope house 2
44. Octagon (1st cent. BC, tomb of Arsinoe IV?) and 'Heroon' (2nd/1st cent. BC)
45. Circular tomb on the Bülbül Dağ (1st cent. BC)
46. Horologion, altar building (1st cent. AD) and Gate of Hadrian
47. Hellenistic peristyle house and 'Library of Celsus' (2nd cent. AD)
48. 'Marble Street'
49. Tetragonos Agora (archaic settlement of Smyrna) with North and South Gates and Stoa of Nero
50. Temple precinct ('Serapeion', 2nd cent. AD)
51. West Road and West Gate
52. Medusa Gate (4th cent. AD)
53. Cave of St. Paul
54. Theatre (Hellenistic, completed 2nd cent. AD; reconstruction 4th cent.) and Hellenistic well-house
55. Arcadian Way (5th cent. AD), East Gate
56. Monument with four columns (6th cent. AD)
57. Exedra fountain (4th/5th cents. AD) and 'church'
58. Quay wall, southern section of the port
59. Southern harbour gate (3rd cent. AD)
60. Central harbour gate (2nd cent. AD)
61. Northern harbour gate
62. Warehouses by the harbour (2nd cent. AD)
63. Harbour Baths (1st cent. AD?)
64. Harbour Gymnasium (1st cent. AD)
65. Atrium Thermarum (4th cent. AD)
66. Xystoi (Stoa of Verulanus, 1st/2nd cents. AD)
67. Theatre gymnasium (2nd cent. AD)
68. Plateia on the Coressus
69. Building with apses
70. Byzantine palace
71. Church of the Virgin Mary, with baptisterium and episcopium
72. Temple of Hadrian (emperor cult; Olympieion?)
73. Byzantine peristyle house
74. Byzantine well-house
75. Acropolis
76. Severian temenos ('Macellum')
77. Byzantine city wall
78. 'Crevice Temple' (4th/3rd cents. BC)
79. Stadium (1st cent. AD)
80. Church in the stadium north gate (6th cent. AD)
81. Vedius Gymnasium (2nd cent. AD)
82. 'Coressus Gate' (a: Hellenistic, b: Byzantine)

comprehensive reconstruction of the public areas was not begun until under Theodosius I (379–395).

F. Christianity

The mission of Paul (Acts 18,24–20,1) found Christian communities already existing in E. The first bishop of E., Timotheus, suffered martyrdom under Domitian (before AD 96) (Acta S. Timothei, Usener p. 11,1). Around the same time, John the Evangelist wrote the Book of Revelations (Apoc.) in E. The persecution of the Christians by Emperor Decius (249–251) led to the myth of the Seven Sleepers. Around AD 400 work was done on the church of St. Mary.

A. Bammer, U. Muss, Das Artemision von E., 1996; FiE 1–12, 1906–1996; IK 11–17, 1979–1984; S. Karwiese, Groß ist die Artemis von E., 1995 (bibl. from 1986); Id., Die Münzprägung von E. I. Die Anfänge, 1995; H. Koester (ed.), E. — Metropolis of Asia (Harvard Theological Studies 41), 1995; R.E. Oster, A Bibliography on Ancient E., 1987; P. Scherrer (ed.), E. — Der neue Führer, 1995; G. Wiplinger, G. Wlach, E. — 100 Jahre öst. Forschung, 1995; H. Friesinger, F. Krinzinger, 100 Jahre öst. Forsch. in E. (Symposium des Öst. Arch. Inst., Wien 1995), 1997; ongoing publications on archaeology, inscriptions and other aspects in: AAWW, JÖAI, ZPE.

Maps: F. Hueber, Ephesos. Gebaute Gesch., 1997.

P.SCH.

G. Byzantine Period

Despite various periods of destruction due to earthquakes (*i.a.* 262, 359–366, 467/8, 557, 614) and war (*i.a.* 263, 654–55, 781, 798, 867688, 1090–96), E. was one of the most important cities of late antiquity and the Byzantine period, which did not lose its importance until after the Turkish conquest (in 1304, Selcuk dynasty of Aydınoğlu) in the late Middle Ages. This is documented by comprehensive construction activity in the lower city area from the 4th–6th cents., which included the development on Ayasoluk hill of a second city centre around the church of St. John (domed basilica in the shape of a cross over the grave of John, erected by Justinian and Theodora until 565); this centre formed the only city centre in the Middle Ages, cf. the medieval city names. In the 7th cent. E. became the main location of the Thrakesion *thema*.

The bishops list includes, up to Stephanus who was a participant in the so-called Robber Synod in E. in 449 and dismissed at the Council of Chalcedon in 451, 27 bishops [1], of whom 18 are known by name [2. 558]. E. was the meeting-place of the Councils of 431 (3rd Ecumenical Council, declaring Mary θεοτόκος, 'bearer of God') and of 449. In the year 451 the bishop of E. loses his rank that had been confirmed in 325 in Nicaea (*canon* 6) and in 381 in Constantinople (*canon* 2) in favour of the patriarch of Constantinople. Its Pauline past as well as numerous legends, i.a. regarding the residence and death of Mary and of the evangelist John as well as the so-called Seven Sleepers, allowed E. to become a centre of Christian pilgrimage. The Isabey Mosque was built in the Selcuk period.

→ Ephesus

1 E. Schwartz (ed.), ACO II, 1, 3, 52 [411], 32f.
2 DHGE XV, 1963, 554–579.

W. Brockhoff, Studien zur Gesch. der Stadt E. vom IV. nachchristl. Jh. bis zu ihrem Untergang in der ersten Hälfte des XV. Jh., 1905 (thesis Jena); W. Elliger, E. [2]1992, 137–206; F. Hueber, E., 1997, 94–107; S. Karwiese, Groß ist die Artemis von E., 1995, 126–145, 154–161 (Sources, Bibliography); LMA III, 1986, 2048–2052; LThK[3] III, 1995, 704–707; W. Müller-Wiener, in: MDAI(Ist) 11, 1961, 85–112; RE Suppl. 12, 248–364, 1588–1704; M. Restle, RBK 2, 1971, 164–207; T. Wohlers-Scharf, Die Forschungsgesch. von E., 1995.

E.W.

II. Archaeology

The first English excavations occurred under the direction of J.T. Wood (1863–1874; carried on by D.E. Horgath 1904–05) and were concentrated on the → dipteros of Artemis made famous in the literature of antiquity as → Wonder of the World; systematic and extensive excavations occurred in campaigns extending from 1895 through the current day carried out by the Austrian Archaeological Institute, and with growing Turkish participation starting in 1954. Early finds are predominantly in London today (BM); the Austrian finds from the years 1895–1906 are kept in Vienna (KM, since 1978: E. Museum); later finds are mostly in the E. Museum of Selçuk, dedicated in 1964. As a result of the subsidence of the Asia Minor continental shelf, parts of the ancient settlement grounds, especially the area around the Artemisium, have become marshy; therefore, archaeological excavations require at times substantial technical expenditure.

The extant building substance and finds reflect in large measure the town's transition from an early Hellenistic provincial city to a Roman metropolis of late antiquity, while the appearance of the prehistoric, pregeometric-archaic and classical settlement has only recently begun to take shape thanks to targeted excavation. The ceramic finds of the Chalcolithic-Bronze Age settlement (4th–2nd millennia) resemble those of → Troy. Around 1000 BC the area is colonized; starting in *c.* 800 BC E. becomes the focus of an Ionian culture oriented on Greek patterns that for cents. presented a mixture of Greek and Oriental strands of tradition. The archaic-classical settlement places, to a great extent unknown even today, were probably grouped around the Panayır Dağ with the acropolis in the north-west. The central cult precinct of Artemis, in which a first monumental dipteros in Ionian order was built around the middle of the 6th cent. BC at the position of a predecessor reaching back into the geometric period (after the fire of 356 BC ignited by Herostratus this temple was rebuilt in the late 4th cent., i.a. from donations by Alexander the Great), lay at some distance in the north-east at the foot of the Ayasoluk and remained isolated from the city area into late antiquity.

The Hellenistic expansion of the city was erected at the beginning of the 3rd cent. under Lysimachus next to the old city between Panayır Dağ and Bülbül Dağ; it doubled the space that had been available up to then. A newly erected, massive, double wall surrounded the entire inhabited area; this city expansion is a first document for an important upturn of the town in the post-classical period. Additional city expansions from the late 1st cent. BC and the 2nd cent. AD caused E. to grow into one of the largest metropolises of the Imperium Romanum. Numerous splendidly furnished public buildings (administrative and governmental buildings, gymnasiums, thermal baths, temple, theatre, circus, library, large hall-like buildings along the larger streets and at the agora), many luxurious residences ('slope houses') and costly infrastructure (harbour constructions, wells, cisterns, water pipes, roads, latrines) underline the prosperity and importance of the city in this period; since the settlement area in the Roman period did not expand much beyond the early Hellenistic city wall, new buildings were frequently erected over older ones, resulting in a sequence of layers that has not been completely clarified in detail to this day. In the early Christian-Byzantine period the city area was once again expanded (7th cent.?); Important church complexes (church of St. Mary, Basilica of St. John's; both with baptisterium), Byzantine administrative and defence structures (fort) as well as Christian necropoleis ('Seven Sleepers Cemetery') were built in and in front of the city in several building phases.

Broad sections of the Hellenistic-Roman city were uncovered in three large excavation campaigns: In a first campaign (1895–1913, led by O. BENNDORF and R. HEBERDEY) i.a. the harbour gymnasium, the large theatre, the Celsus Library (see → Library with fig.), Hadrian's gate, the 'Marble Street', Odeum and Bouleuterion as well as the church of St. Mary; in a second campaign (1926–1935, led by J. KEIL) *i.a.* the Basilica of St. John, the 'Seven Sleepers Cemetery', the theatre gymnasium and the mausoleum of Belevi. In the third campaign, lasting from 1954 through the present day (2004) (led by F. MILTNER, F. EICHLER, H. VETTERS, G. LANGMANN, S. KARWIESE, D. KNIBBE, A. BAMMER) the area along Curetes Street, the structures at the 'State Agora' as well as the architecture and history of the building of the Artemisium were all researched. Lavish activities of historic monument preservation have made the excavation site into a first-class tourist destination, although the various anastylosis measures of the last decades have come up against a divided echo among experts and the public.

EDITION: Successive annual excavation reports in AAWW and JÖAI; Excavation publications and monographs in FiE 1ff. (since 1906).

LITERATURE: W. ALZINGER, Augusteische Architektur in E., 1974; A. BAMMER, R. FLEISCHER, D. KNIBBE, Führer durch das Arch. Mus. in Selçuk, 1974; A. BAMMER, A Peripteros of the Geometric Period in the Artemision of E., in: Anatolian Studies 90, 1990, 137–160; Id., Multikulturelle Aspekte der frühen Kunst im Artemision von E., in: JÖAI 61, 1991/2, Insert, 17–54; B. FEHR, Archäologen, Techniker, Industrielle. Beobachtungen zur Wiederaufstellung der Bibliothek des Celsus in E., in: Hephaestus 3, 1981, 107–125; F. HUEBER, E. — Gebaute Gesch., 1997; D. KNIBBE, G. LANGMANN (ed.), Via Sacra Ephesica, vol. 1, 1993, vol. 2, 1995; W. SCHABER, Die archaische Tempel von E., n.d.; T. WOHLERS-SCHARF, Die Forschungsgesch. von E., 1995 (bibliography). C.HÖ.

Ephetai (ἐφέται; *ephétai*). There were in classical Athens, besides the court of → Areopagus, three further collegiate courts for capital cases; these sat at the Palladion, at the Delphinion and in Phreatto (→ Dikasterion), and comprised 51 *ephetai* (Aristot. Ath. Pol. 57,3f.). These colleges of jurors (→ Dikastes) were small in comparison with the other *dikasteria*. It is now believed that, prior to Solon, *ephetai* also sat at the court on the Hill of Ares, but at that time not all citizens could yet be appointed.

R. W. WALLACE, The Areopagos Council to 307 BC, 1985, 22. G.T.

Ephialtes (Ἐφιάλτης; *Ephiáltēs*). Mythology → Aloads.

[1] Son of Eurydemus of Malis, he is supposed to have shown → Xerxes the path over the mountains at → Thermopylae, in the hope of a large reward. This enabled the Persians to circumvent the Greek army under Leonidas and attack it from the rear. E. himself is said to have led the elite corps of Hydarnes along this path, and so contributed to the defeat of the Spartans. Herodotus was already aware of another version, thought by him to be not credible, in which two other men were accused of the betrayal. The Delphic amphictyony later put a price on the head of E. He was killed upon returning to his homeland after a long period of flight (Hdt. 7,213–225).

→ Persian Wars

A. R. BURN, Persia and the Greeks, [2]1984, 412ff.; N. G. L. HAMMOND, CAH 4, [2]1988, 555ff. E.S.-H.

[2] Athenian politician, active during the 460s BC. Little of a personal nature is known of him. In *c.* 465 he led a naval expedition by way of Phaselis (south-western Turkey) (Plut. Cimon 13, 4). In the late 460s he became Cimon's leading opponent, and unsuccessfully opposed the dispatch of a force to aid Sparta during the 3rd Messenian War (Plut. Cimon 16,9). He appears to have been one of a group of Athenians who had a fundamental belief in the principles of democracy. Giving that he attacked individual members of the Areopagus, it is likely that while Cimon and his hoplite army were away in Messenia, he was responsible for the transfer of politically significant judicial powers (possibly those affecting the control over officials and *eisangelia* cases) from the Areopagus to the council of five hundred and the jury courts ([Aristot.] Ath. Pol. 25; Plut. Cimon 15,2). Cimon attempted to have the reforms repealed, but was ostracized. E. himself was murdered (Ath. Pol. 25,4), and there were rumours of an oligarchic conspiracy *c.* 457 at the time of the battle of Tanagra (Thuc.

1,107,4–6). But the form of democracy instituted by E. persisted, under his aid Pericles.
→ Areopagus; → Pericles

LGPN 2, Ἐφιάλτης (1); P.J. RHODES, in: CAH 5², 67–77. P.J.R.

[3] An Athenian rhetor and *strategos*, in 341/40 BC E. negotiated on behalf of the rhetors around Demosthenes for an alliance between Athens and the Persian Empire against → Philippus II, and for subsidies for Athens. E. did not achieve a formal alliance, but upon his return distributed large sums of money to leading Athenian opponents of Philip II (Plut. Mor. 847f–848a; 848e; Dem. Or. 9,71; 10,31–34; Aeschin. In Ctes. 238). E. urged Athens to join the Theban revolt against → Alexander [4] the Great in 335. For this, Alexander unsuccessfully demanded his extradition (Arr. Anab. 1,10,4; Plut. Demosthenes 23,4 and Phoc. 17,2; Suda s.v. Antipater). In 335 E. entered Persian service, and in 334 fell at the defence of Halicarnassus (Diod. Sic. 17,25,6–27,3; cf. Deinarchus 1,33; Dem. Ep. 3,31). PA 6156.
→ Thebes

A.B. BOSWORTH, A historical commentary on Arrian's History of Alexander, vol. 1, 1980, 92–96; J. ENGELS, Studien zur polit. Biographie des Hypereides, ²1993, 162–178. J.E.

Ephippion see → Riding

Ephippus (Ἔφιππος; *Éphippos*).
[1] of Olynthus, at the court of → Alexander [4] the Great during the final years; he later wrote an anecdotal work 'On the life and death of Hephaestion and Alexander'. As all extant fragments (FGrH 126) derive from → Athenaeus [3], they for the most part describe banquets. We also hear that Alexander was in the habit of putting on the insignia of various gods, and like → Gorgus sought the liberation of Samos. Identification of E. with an officer of Alexander in Egypt (cf. BERVE 2, no. 331) is erroneously based.

E. BADIAN, Studies in Greek and Roman History, 1964, 253f.; L. PEARSON, The Lost Histories of Alexander the Great, 1960, 61–67. E.B.

[2] Middle Comedy writer [1. test. 1], of whose plays twelve titles (28 fragments in total) survive. On the basis of historical references, his active period can be narrowed down to the years 375–340 BC [2. 197]; *c.* 370 victory at the Lenaea [1. test. 2]. His plays are in part mythological; but there is also a *Sapphṓ* (fr. 20) and a *Philýra* (fr. 21, probably a *hetaera* play). In his *Naúagos* ('The Castaway', fr. 14), E. satirizes Plato and his academy, in other plays the tragedies of Dionysius (fr. 16) and Chaeremon (fr. 9), in *Ártemis* (fr. 1) the tyrant Alexander of Pherae [2. 196].

1 PCG V, 1986, 131–152 2 H.-G. NESSELRATH, Die att. Mittlere Komödie, 1990, 196f., 218–221. B.BÄ.

Ephodion (ἐφόδιον; *ephódion*, 'travel money'). In Greece, *ephodion* denotes the allowance for travel expenses paid to an ambassador (e.g. in Athens: TOD 129; cf. the parody in Aristoph. Ach. 65–67; in Chios: SIG³ 402). In the Hellenistic and Roman periods a rich citizen could aid his city by declining such a payment due to him (e.g. IPriene 108). P.J.R.

Ephoroi (ἔφοροι; *éphoroi*). 'Custodians'; annual officials in Sparta and a number of Peloponnesian and Dorian *poleis* and colonies (e.g. Thera, Cyrene, Heraclea on the Siris). The most significant institution of this kind was that of the five Spartan *ephoroi*, who arrived at their decisions by majority and whose chairman (Plut. Lysander 30) gave his name to his year of office. According to ancient tradition, the Spartan ephorate was held to be an institution of Lycurgus (Hdt. 1,65), and it was later ascribed to king Theopompus during the 1st Messenian War (Aristot. Pol. 1313a27; Plut. Lycurgus 7), but both versions are as fictitious as the traditional beginning of the list of *ephoroi* in 754/53 BC. *Ephoroi* are not mentioned in the great *rhetra* (*c.* 700 or early 7th cent.?) cited by Plutarch (Lycurgus 6), or in Tyrtaeus (fr. 3 DIEHL = 14 GENTILI-PRATO). It is, however, certain that the beginnings of the ephorate go back to an early phase of the formation of institutions, as the 'election' of the *ephoroi* — like the 'election' of the *gerontes* — occurred in the popular assembly in accordance with an archaic, 'infantile' (Aristot. Pol. 1270b27f.) acclamation procedure, the volume of the acclamation being the decisive factor (Plut. Lycurgus 26).

The title of the office would seem to indicate supervisory duties: from the first, the function of the *ephoroi* was probably supervision of the established order (also helots and *perioikoi*), especially the maintenance of the *klaros* system and of helotry as the basis of the economy. An original function as 'overseer' in the five Spartan settlements is improbable, as the annual symbolic declaration of war against the helots indicates that the *ephoroi* were representatives of the *damos* as a whole. This also explains in part their political advancement alongside the dual kingship and the *gerousia*, although this is also to be seen as a general consequence of increasing institutionalization in Greek *poleis*. The Spartan custom that kings appeared before the *ephoroi* only after being summoned three times indicates conflicts during the transition of authority from the kings to the ephorate. As early as the middle of the 6th cent., however, the *ephoroi* were able, by agreement with the *gerousia*, to enforce the will of the *damos* on a king (Hdt. 5,39f.). This implies that at that time the *ephoroi* could lead the popular assembly, a function that was the prerogative of the eponymous ephors during the classical period (Thuc. 1,87). The extension of the powers of the *ephoroi* essentially reached its zenith in the early 5th cent. At the time of the Persian Wars they even supervised the manner in which a king or regent waged war (Hdt. 9,76), oversaw the execution of decisions of the popular assembly, received ambassadors or when appropriate dismissed them (Xen. Hell. 2,2,13), and possessed extensive policing powers as well as the right to inspect the function of other officials and institute proceedings even against kings (Hdt. 6,82). They themselves had to answer to their successors in office. Although the annual handover of office prevented continuity of ephorate policy, in the late 5th cent. the college became a 'command centre', where Sparta's wide-ranging military and political activities were co-ordinated. The *ephoroi* exchanged monthly oaths of office with the kings (Xen. Lac. 15,7), and every new year performed a ritual of observing the heavens that could lead to the kings' suspension (Plut. Agis 11). But they could not compete with the prestige of the kings, as the ephorate was open to all circles of the *damos*. In 227 the ephorate was abolished by Cleomenes III, to be restored after his defeat at Sellasia in 222 by Antigonus [3] Doson. After 188 it was evidently on occasion not occupied, but is attested again in the Roman period as a municipal office.

1 A.S. BRADFORD, The Synarchia of Roman Sparta, in: Chiron 10, 1980, 413–425 2 M. CLAUSS, Sparta, 1983, 132–138 3 S. LINK, Der Kosmos Sparta, 1994, 64–71 4 P.J. RHODES, The Selection of Ephors at Sparta, in: Historia 30, 1981, 498–502. K.-W.WEL.

Ephorus (Ἔφορος; *Éphoros*) from Cyme in Asia Minor; Greek universal historian, lived *c.* 400–330. On the basis of his style, in antiquity he was held to be a student of Isocrates. He was a contemporary of Theopompus (FGrH 70 T 3–5; 8; 28), and was said to have refused Alexander's invitation to accompany him on his campaign in 334 BC (T 6).

Works: *Epichṓrios lógos* ('History of our homeland'): an encomium to Cyme, which E. even made the homeland of Homer (F 1). 'On inventions': to be assigned to the realm of 'sophist polyhistory' (cf. ED. SCHWARTZ), it covered i.a. the origin of Greek letters (F 97 and 236) and types of flute (F 3). 'On style': questions of prosody and prose-rhythm. *Historíai*: a universal history in 30 bks.; avoiding the period of myth (T 8), it extended from the return of the Heraclidae (→ Doric migration) down to his own time. The final book (period 356–341/40) was by his son Demophilus (T 9).

His work is outstanding for its many innovations and distinctive features: according to Polybius (5,33,2), E. was the founder and up to that time sole exponent of universal history, and at the same time the initiator and main representative of a rhetorical strain of historiography that was marked by a particular emphasis on form and style. He was the first Greek historian to divide his own work into books, providing each book with a proem (T 10). He also gave it a structure that was based on subject areas (*katà génos*, T 11) rather than being annalistic: e.g geography of the *oikoumene* (B. 4–5), early history of the Peloponnese (6), Lydia and Persia (8 and 9), early Sicilian *tyrannis* (16), the hegemony of Sparta and Thebes (21–25). E.'s writing became more detailed as he approached the present time (cf. F 9), and was for the most part methodical and dispassionate, as long as his pro-Athenian tendency [1. 2] and his local patriotism as a Cymean did not come into play (cf. F 236). Moralizing didacticism was to the fore, encouraging the reader to imitate good actions and deterring him from evil ones. A rationalizing tone predominated, as evidenced by a critical attitude to mythology (F 31), the elimination of the divine from history and its replacement by *tyche*, in unhistorical constructions and duplication of events, which continued to be a favoured stylistic method (cf. Pol. 6,46,10). He had no political or military experience, which exposed his battle descriptions to criticism (T 20); E.'s knowledge was entirely obtained from books (Pol. 12,25f.). He was the first historian to proceed not by primary research by way of autopsy, personal experience and the interrogation of eyewitnesses, but primarily by secondary research on the basis of existing written sources and literary descriptions. To this end he used not only every earlier historian, from Hecataeus and Herodotus to Philistus, Theopompus and Callisthenes, but also orators, commentators, poets (e.g. Tyrtaeus, F 216; Aristophanes, F 196) and epigrammatists (F 122,199). He was highly regarded as the founder of the genre of universal history (cf. Pol. 5,33,2), and was quoted extensively by writers of similar works in the 1st cent. BC (Nicolaus of Damascus, Timagenes, Diodorus and Strabo); it was only in the Roman imperial period that interest in him waned.

In spite of his shortcomings, E. is of great significance for modern researchers into the ancient world. Via the mediation of Diodorus, who paraphrases E. in bks. 11–15, he provides the only continuous account of Greek history from *c.* 480–350. At the same time he is the book-learned prototype and ancestor of today's desk-bound historian, and owing to the modern call for a universal conception of history he is again of great topical interest. FGrH 70 (with comm.).

1 G.L. BARBER, The Historian Ephorus, 1935 2 W.R. CONNOR, Studies in Ephorus, 1961.

R. DREWS, Diodorus and His Sources, in: AJPh 83, 1962, 383–392; Id., Ephorus and History Written κατὰ γένος, in: AJPh 84, 1963, 244–55; O. LENDLE, Einführung in die griech. Geschichtsschreibung, 1992, 136ff.; K. MEISTER, Die griech. Geschichtsschreibung, 1990, 85ff. (lit.); C. RUBINCAM, A Note on Oxyrhynchus Papyrus 1610, in: Phoenix 1976, 357–366; K.S. SACKS, in: OCD, [3]1996, 529f.; G. SCHEPENS, Historiographical Problems in Ephorus, in: Historiographia antiqua, 1977, 95–118; ED. SCHWARTZ, s.v. E., RE 6, 1–16. K.MEI.

Ephrem Syrian poet and theologian (*c.* AD 306–373); his reputation was already known to Jerome in 392 (Vir. ill. 115). He spent the greater part of his life as a deacon in Nisibis; when in AD 363 the city was ceded to the Persians, he settled in Edessa, the modern Urfa. The 6th.-cent. *vita* is filled out with many fabulous tales. E.'s writings may be divided into three categories: verse writings, which make up the major part, artistic prose and prose.

1. VERSE WRITINGS

His verse writings in more than 50 metres, mostly in strophes (→ *madraše*, *hymni*), survive in cycles of various length. The longest are: *De fide* (87, including 5, 'The Pearl'), *Carmina Nisibena* (77), *Contra Haereses* (56), *De virginitate* (52), *De ecclesia* (52), *De nativitate* (28). Shorter cycles contain *De azymis* (21), *De paradiso* (15) and *Contra Iulianum* (4). Other works in verse are couplets (→ *memre*, *sermones*) in the 'Ephraimic metre' (7+7 syllables), among them six *memre de fide* and a number of works whose authenticity is disputed (e.g. 'Ninive', 'The sinful woman'). Many later *memre* were falsely ascribed to E.

2. ARTISTIC PROSE

The *Sermo de domino nostro* and the *Epistula ad Publium* should be mentioned under this heading.

3. PROSE

The commentaries on Genesis, Exodus and the Diatessaron probably come from his school rather than himself. The commentaries on the Acts of the Apostles and the letters of St. Paul survive only in Aramaic translation. E.'s various polemical writings in prose include five speeches 'Against false teachings', directed against Hypatius and against Bardesanes' *Domnus* (also under the title 'Against the Platonists'). E.'s opponents are → Marcion, → Bardesanes, → Mani and (in the hymns) the Arians (→ Arianism). A substantial body of work ascribed to E. has survived in Greek (and in subsequent Latin and Slav translations), but scarcely any of these works corresponds to a known work written in Syrian.

Although E. presumably had no knowledge of the Greek language, he mentions Albinus (Prose Ref. II, p. iii) and alludes at least twice to Greek mythology (Carmina Nisibena 36,5; hymnus de Paradiso 3,8).

EDITIONS: E. BECK (ed.), Corpus Scriptorum Christianorum Orientalium (CSCO), 1955–1979 (with Germ. trans., replaces older editions); R. TONNEAU (ed.), CSCO, 1955 (comm. on Gn-Ex); L. LELOIR (ed.), 1963 or 1990 (comm. on Diatesseron); C.W. MITCHELL (ed.), Prose Refutations, 1912 or 1921 (polemical writings in prose); Editions of E. Graecus: see CPG 3905–4175 (in part repr. in K. PHRANTZOLAS (ed.), I-V, 1988–1994).
BIBLIOGRAPHY: N. EL-KHOURY, Die Interpretation der Welt bei Ephraem dem Syrer, 1976; E. BECK, Ephraems Trinitätslehre, 1982; T. BOU MANSOUR, La pensée symbolique de S. Ephrem, 1988; S.P. BROCK, The Luminous Eye: the spiritual world vision of St Ephrem, 1992; Dictionnaire de spiritualité 4, 1960, 788–819; E. BECK, s.v. E., RAC 5, 520–531; R. MURRAY, s.v. E., TRE 9, 1982, 755–762 (with bibliography).
BIBLIOGRAPHY: S.P. BROCK, Syriac Studies: a classified bibliography (1960–1990), 1996, 78–94; K. DEN BIESEN (in print). S.BR.

Ephyra (Ἐφύρα; *Ephýra*).

[1] City 'in a corner of Argos' (Hom. Il. 6,152); home of Sisyphus; later equated with Corinth. Sources: Str. 8,3,5; Paus. 2,1,1; 3,10. Y.L.

[2] Str. 8,3,5 mentions an otherwise unknown town on the Elean coast, by the name of → Oinoe; Homeric commentators equate it with the Homeric E. (cf. also Steph. Byz. s.v. E.; Hsch. s.v. E).

L. DEROY, Ephyre, ville imaginaire, in: AC 18, 1949, 401–402. R.B.

[3] City in Epirote Thesprotia, later (in antiquity) called Cichyrus, situated on the Acheron, inland from the Bay of Elea. The settlement lies on the hill of Xylokastro near the modern Mesopotamon; on the plain is the Nekyomanteion, the oracle of the dead.

S.I. DAKARIS, Thesprotia, 1972; Id., The Nekyomanteion, 1993; N.G.L. HAMMOND, Epirus, 1967. D.S.

Epibatai (ἐπιβάται; *epibátai*) were initially passengers on board ship (Hdt. 8,118,3), or an armed escort of soldiers serving on warships in antiquity; in Greece the *epibatai* were normally recruited from among the hoplites. Their numbers varied: in 494 BC ships from Chios each carried 40 *epibatai* (Hdt. 6,15,1), Persian ships in 480 BC carried 30 *epibatai* (Hdt. 7,184,2); in the Athenian fleet during the Peloponnesian War, 10 *epibatai* was the normal complement (Thuc. 3,94,1 and 3,95,2; cf. IG II[2] 1951,84f.: 11 *epibatai*). More *epibatai* were necessary on the bigger Hellenistic ships. Apart from shipboard fighting, their duties included armed landings and — esp. in the Hellenistic age — the operation of catapults. In the fleet of the Roman Republic, the *epibatai* drawn from the legions (*propugnatores, milites classici*; 80 — 120 per ship) were more important, as Roman tactics in sea-fighting were based on boarding the enemy ship and doing battle with its crew (Pol. 1,22–23; Veg. Mil. 4,44). During the Principate, the often foreign crew of a ship constituted a → *centuria*; the *epibatai* as such were not strictly distinguished from the seamen.

→ Corvus LE.BU.

Epiblema (ἐπίβλημα; *epíblēma*). Greek term for → blanket, cloth, coat (Poll. 7,49f.). In modern-day archaeological terminology, *epiblema* denotes the shoulder-covering of Daedalic female statues, esp. those from Crete. As a rule the *epiblema* is fastened at the breast, but also across the neck and collarbone; the upper edge is occasionally decorated. The *epiblema* is frequently depicted on 7th-cent. BC monuments.

C. DAVARAS, Die Statue aus Astritsi, 8. Beih. AK, 1972, 26–27, 59–64. R.H.

Epibole (ἐπιβολή; *epibolḗ*) Any office-bearer in Athens (→ *Archai*, to which the → *boulḗ* also belonged) was entitled by law to impose within his sphere of responsibility an *epibole*, a small sum up to a legally determined level by way of a fine; the *epibole* was subject to → *éphesis*. The *epibole* in P.Zen. 51,15 (3rd cent. BC) is also to be understood in this sense. In papyri of the

Roman period, *epibole* (or ἐπιμερισμός, *epimerismós*) denotes the allocation of uncultivated land to individual farmers or communities for purposes of taxation.

A.R. W. Harrison, The Law of Athens II, 1971, 4ff.; H.-A. Rupprecht, Einführung in die Papyruskunde, 1994, 75. G.T.

Epic

I. Ancient Near East II. Classical Antiquity

I. Ancient Near East

The convention in ancient oriental studies is to maintain a distinction between epic and myth in so far as the protagonists of each genre are concerned, even though, in respect of genre theory and style, this remains difficult and contentious [1. 145–153; 2. 1–24]: in epic the actors are (heroicized) people, whereas myths inhabit the realm of the divine. Sumerian epic literature is woven around the legendary kings of the 1st dynasty of Uruk: Enmerkar, Lugalbanda and Gilgameš. Originating towards the end of the 3rd millennium BC, although the basic material may in part be older, and surviving primarily in copies from the Old Babylonian period (for the most part 18th cent. BC), the epics of the early kings (as mythical forebears) served to legitimize the neo-Sumerian dynasties of Ur (2111–2003 BC) [3. 133]. The epics of Enmerkar and Lugalbanda cover relations and conflicts between the southern Babylonian city of → Uruk and Aratta in Iran [4. 576–579]. The legendary king Gilgameš, who was already worshipped as a god in the 1st half of the 3rd millennium BC, is at the centre of several Sumerian epics that are regarded as the precursors of parts of the Akkadian Epic of → Gilgameš.

Regarding its form, the Sumerian epic is a narrative poem with frequent interpolation of direct speech. Frequent use is made of epic repetition. The epic also contains descriptions, song-like passages, and prayers [5. 248f.].

Alongside the most celebrated Akkadian epic, the Epic of Gilgameš, are to be set the so-called historical epics, whose subject is the deeds of Assyrian and Babylonian kings. Thus the extant fragments of the Epic of Adad-nirari describe the battles between this Assyrian king (1307–1275 BC) and Nazimaruttaš of Babylon, while the Epic of Tukulti-Ninurta describes the victory of Tukulti-Ninurta I (1244–1208 BC) over Kaštiliaš IV of Babylon. Fragments of Babylonian epics concern i.a. the deeds of Babylonian kings of the 2nd and 1st millennia BC [6. 184–187; 7. 52].

Chiasmus, rare grammatical forms and words, ambiguity, plays on words etc. are favoured stylistic devices within the individual lines of the Akkadian epic, as in Akkadian literature as a whole. Also common are i.a. similes, metaphors, repetition and the linking of lines by means of structural parallelism. An accented metre can be detected. In the more recent epics, verse may alternate with literary prose [7. 48–50].

From the literary tradition of → Ugarit (14th/13th cents. BC) we have epics with Aqhat and Keret as protagonists. The basic themes here are immortality, death and illness. The Epic of Aqhat has motifs in parallel with that of Gilgameš [8. 81–98]. The Hittites did not develop an independent epic as generally defined at the beginning of this article, but the Epic of Gilgameš was adapted in the Akkadian, Hurrite and Hittite languages [9. 75]. No epics are attested from Egypt. The extent of Greek adaptation of the ancient oriental epic is difficult to determine [10].

→ Gilgamesh Epic; → Myth

1 G. Komoróczy, Die mythol. Epik in der sumer. Lit., in: Annales Universitatis Scientiarum Budapestinensis, Sectio Classica 5/6, 1977/8 2 K. Hecker, Unt. zur akkad. Epik, 1974 3 C. Wilcke, Die Sumer. Königsliste und erzählte Vergangenheit, in: J. von Ungern-Sternberg, H. Reinau (ed.), Vergangenheit in mündlicher Überlieferung, 1988, 133–140 4 C. Wilcke, s.v. Sumer. Epen, Kindler 19 5 Id., Formale Gesichtspunkte in der sumer. Lit. in: Assyriological Stud. 20, 1975, 205–316 6 A.K. Grayson, Histories and Historians of the Ancient Near East: Assyria and Babylonia, Orientalia N.S. 49, 1980, 140–194 7 W. Röllig, s.v. Literatur, akkadische, RLA 7, 48–66 8 J.M. Sasson, Literary Criticism, Folklore Scholarship, and Ugaritic Literature, in: G.D. Young (ed.), Ugarit in Retrospect, 1981 9 E. von Schuler, s.v. Literatur bei den Hethitern, RLA 7, 66–75 10 C. Auffarth, Der drohende Untergang, 1991.

W. Röllig (ed.), Altoriental. Literaturen, 1978. H.N.

II. Classical Antiquity

A. Problems of definition, characteristics of the genre B. The body of work 1. Pre-literary phase (reconstruction) 2. Greek literature (from Homer to Nonnus) 3. Roman literature

A. Problems of definition, characteristics of the genre

(Ϝέπος: Ϝεπ- in (Ϝ)ειπεῖν as in the German *Sage* ('legend'): *sagen* ('to say'); 'that which is said; tidings'). It is evident that Ϝέπος from the earliest times meant not just 'the word', but evidently in a 'poetological' sense also 'hexametric verse', even 'hexametric lines or an individual hexametric line' (thus e.g. Hdt. 7,143; 4,29), and the epic concept in tandem with the evolving use of the hexameter post-Homer was attached to a highly varied range of poetic forms; the resulting profusion of literary forms bearing the 'epic' label makes any practical definition of the term 'epic' impossible, even within the confines of Greek and Latin literature (for attempts at definition going even beyond that sphere, [3. 1–10]). A sensible alternative is to assemble a collection of shared characteristics, starting from the premise that by the time of Hesiod and the oldest Homeric hymns two contrasting conceptions of the genre coexisted: the narrower of the two was based on the epic's (surely diachronically primary and substantive) character as a spoken narrative form (the typical mode of the epic in the Homeric age and in the Ancient Orient); the broader conception (a consequence of the disassociation of essentially non-narrative hexametric literary forms from the Homeric-type epic) being founded purely on the criterion of the hexametric form. As attempts to exclude the broader, purely formal conception (Aristot. Poet. 1447b13–20) remained ineffective, there was never in antiquity any divorce between the narrative and non-narrative forms (with a correspondingly distinct terminology); thus a broad conception of the genre became firmly established, and predominates to this day. The final cause of this development was that, with the decline of narration as the main organizing instance of the Homeric-type epic ('narration' in GENETTE [2. 15f., 199ff.]), and the concomitant decline in autonomy of the 'mimetic' elements contained within the narrative form (see the relevant catalogues in Pl. Resp. 392d–398b), the similarity between the new genres thus arising (the descriptive specialist epic; the argumentative/proselytizing, so-called philosophical epic; the cultic or religious epic [*hymnos*]; the didactic epic ['Didactic poetry'] etc.) and the mother genre, esp. as regards form (metre: hexameter; formulae; 'high' style), remained so persuasively evident as to assume the nature of an essential identity.

On practical grounds, we retain the 'broad' conception as a basis for taking account of the body of work (see B. below) and creating a fund of common characteristics. The latter is for the most part fed from the narrative epic, from time immemorial regarded as the definitive form, as reflected both in practice (Pind. Nem. 2,2; Hdt. 2,117) and in theory (cf. e.g. Pl. Resp. 392d–398b; Aristot. Poet. 1459b26: ἐποποιία = διήγησις, *dihēgēsis*, 'narrative'), and here again esp. from the Homeric epics the *Iliad* and the *Odyssey*, which served as prototypes in the context of all the post-Homeric processes of transformation and manipulation of the narrative epic:

I. formally: (1) acatalectic dactylic hexameters, in consecutive lines without strophic structure; (2) typical formal elements such as the epithet (*epitheton*), the formulaic expression, similes, catalogues, description of objects, typical scenes; and in the narrative epic (and the narrative parts of the non-narrative epic forms) direct speech (in Hom.: 67% of the *Iliad* and the *Odyssey*).

II. content and structure: — (1) insistence on the significance of the subject ('size', 'grandeur'); avoidance of the banal, the everyday, the private, and the striving for public, political meaning transcending the personal, at levels that are as 'national', even 'international' as possible: the social scenario is accordingly the upper class; in the narrative epic a preference for heroic subjects, figures, characters, motifs, virtues and attitudes (drawn from myths about heroes and gods): 'heroic poetry', 'heroic epic' [1]. — (2) Aesthetic sublimity and dignity (including an 'aesthetic of the terrible'): clarity of thought, beauty of form, cultivated language, customs, manners (sanctioning of 'heroic' ferocity, bluntness ['divine' anger], absence of restraint). — (3) Rationality: a principle of causality that embraces the depiction of humans, gods, animals, natural phenomena (including anthropomorphism), without ignoring cause and effect and factual coherence; avoidance of shamanistic elements. — (4) An aspiration to totality in depiction not only of the world, world-view, conduct, but also of objective reality and systems of thought. — (5) An aspiration to organic unity as regards narrative structure and the representation of objective reality. The drive for structural unity (μύθους συνιστάναι περὶ μίαν πρᾶξιν ὅλην καὶ τελείαν, ἔχουσαν ἀρχὴν καὶ μέσα καὶ τέλος, Aristot. Poet. 1459a18–20) declines in the narrative epic: according to Aristotle's correct observation (Poet. 1459a37–b2), this happens already directly after Homer, in the epic cycle; in the non-narrative epic, esp. the historical epic, it essentially survives, compelled by the unity of the poetic subject.

1 C.M. BOWRA, Heroic Poetry, 1952 2 G. GENETTE, Die Erzählung, 1994 3 J.B. HAINSWORTH, The Idea of the Epic, 1991. J.L.

B. THE BODY OF WORK

The production of epics in the Greek language extends from Homer (8th cent. BC) until the fall of the Byzantine Empire in 1453 (as late as 1150 Johannes → Tzetzes in his so-called *Carmina Iliaca* gives a new verse-rendering of the epic cycle). Countless epics were written during this span of some 2,150 years; the exact number even of those attested by some quotation or mention is unknown. Few epics have survived intact; we have fragments of large numbers of them (systematic collections as of now exist only for the period up to *c.* 400 BC: [1; 5]; for those of most significance in ancient and modern literary history cf. table. The history of the development of the epic turns and centres upon Homer: on the one hand, the entire body of epic production in Greek and Latin and in the early modern age arose by direct or indirect reference to Homer; on the other, Homer represents the end-point and culmination of a process of development that can be reconstructed only via him.

1. PRE-LITERARY PHASE (RECONSTRUCTION)

K. WITTE in his 1913 RE article 'Homeros' [53. 2214] summarizing German-language research since F.A. WOLF (in particular [6; 8; 14]) established that the language of Homer's works was a 'creation of the epic line'. Homer was thereby placed within a tradition of hexametric poetic composition whose main characteristic was the technique of oral improvisation [22. 25–44]. M. PARRY sought to reconstruct this technique on a systematic basis [22. 10f.; 41. XXII]. Since the eighties, after a lengthy phase of typological ('horizontal') comparative studies of *oral poetry* (cf. 2; 4; 9; 22; 35]), continuation of his investigation into the stereotyped character of the 'artificial language' [35] of the epic and the improvisatory techniques of the preliterate pre-Homeric singer- (→ Aoiden-) poets has produced increasingly concrete reconstructive results:

The ancient epic: an inventory[1]

* = completely preserved; *f* = fragments preserved; † = lost

A. The Greek epic of the archaic period

I. The narrative heroic epic
(Heroic Poetry, 8th–6th cents. BC)
1. The Trojan epic cycle
a. *Homer: *Iliad*
b. *Homer: *Odyssey*
c. [various authors]: the epic *Kyklos* (*f*)
2. The Theban epic cycle (*f*):
Epics with titles such as *Oidipodeia, Epigonoi,* etc.
3. Heracles epics (*f*)
named among others:
Pisander of Camirus;
Cinaethon; Conon; Demodocus; Diotimus;
Phaedimus; Pisinus; Minyas
4. Argonaut epics (*f*): Epimenides, etc.
5. Theseus epics (and other topics) (*f*)

II. The religious/ cultic epic of praise
1. The so-called **Homeric Hymns*
(6th/7th cents. and later)
2. Delphic oracular poetry (beginning in the 8 th cent.) (*f*)

III. The explanatory, 'technical' epic
1. Epics concerning practical life (7th/ 6th cents. BC)
a. *Hesiod: *Erga kai hemerai* ('Works and Days')
b. Phocylides: *Gnomai* (*f*)
2. Speculative epics explaining the world
a. Cosmogonic/ theogonic epics (7th/ 6th cents.)
*Hesiod: *Theogonia* ('Theogony') (*f*);
Epimenides (*f*); Abaris (*f*) etc.
b. Genealogical/ historical epics (7th/ 6th cents.) (*f*)
Pseudo-Hesiod: *Katalogoi, Phoronis*
Eumelus of Corinth: *Korinthiaka*
Hegesinus: *Atthis*
Aristeas: *Arimaspoi,* etc.
c. Philosophical epics (*c.* 500) (*f*)
Xenophanes of Colophon; Parmenides of Elea;
Empedocles of Elea (→Lucretius)

IV. The parodic epic
Margites ('The Fool') (*f*)
(hexameters and iambic trimeters; 7th/ 6th cents.)

B. The revival of the archaic epic in the classical period

I. Heroic epics
1. Panyassis of Halicarnassus: *Herakleia* (*c.* 470) (*f*)
2. Antimachus of Colophon: *Thebais* (*c.* 400) (*f*)

II. Religious/cultic epics
1. Antimachus of Colophon: *Artemis* (*c.* 400) (†)
2. Delphic oracular poetry (*f*)

III. Technical epics
1. Historical epic poetry[2]
Choerilus of Samos: *Persika* (*c.* 400) (*f*)
2. So-called didactic poetry
Archestratus of Gela: *Hedypatheia* (*c.* 350) (*f*)
(→Ennius: *Hedyphagetica*)

C. Greek epic poetry of the Hellenistic era

I. Heroic epic
*Apollonius of Rhodes: *Argonautika*
('Stories of the Argonauts') (*c.* 260 BC)

II. Religious/cultic epic
*Callimachus: 'Hymns' (*c.* 260 BC)

III. Technical epics
1. Epics on history/local history[2]
a. Euphorion of Chalcis (*c.* 250 BC):
Foundation epics
b. Rhianus of Bene (*c.* 220 BC): *Achaika, Eliaka, Thessalika, Messeniaka* (*f*)
c. Nicander of Colophon (*c.* 200 BC):
Epics on regional history (*f*)
2. So-called didactic poetry
a. *Aratus of Soli: *Phainomena*
('The heavenly phenomena') (*c.* 250 BC)
(→Cicero: *Aratea*; Germanicus; Manilius)
b. Similar topics:
Numenius: *Halieutikon* (*c.* 250 BC) (*f*)
Eratosthenes: *Hermes* (*c.* 220 BC) (*f*)
Pancrates: *Halieutika* (*f*)
Boeus: *Ornithogonia* (*f*)
Alexander Lychnus: *Phainomena* (1st cent.)
(etc.) (*f*)
c. Nicander of Colophon (*c.* 200 BC):
**Theriaka*, **Alexipharmaka, Heteroioumena* (*f*),
Georgika (*f*) (→Virgil)

IV. Mythological-idyllic epic poetry (epyllion)
(→Roman Neoterics)
1. Callimachus: *Hekale* (*c.* 260 BC) (*f*)
2. *Theocritus: *Eidyllia* (e.g. *Hylas*) (3rd cent. BC)
3. *Bion of Smyrna: *Adonis*
('Lament for Adonis') (shortly before 200 BC)
4. *Moschus of Syracuse: *Europe* (1st cent. BC)

V. Parodic epic
**Batrachomyomachia*
('The War between Frogs and Mice')

D. Latin epic poetry of the Republican period

I. The reception of Greek heroic poetry
(← Homer)
1. Livius Andronicus: *Odusia* (shortly before 200 BC) (*f*)
2. Cn. Naevius: *Bellum Punicum* (in part) (*c.* 200 BC) (*f*)

II. The reception of the Greek technical epic
1. The philosophical epic
* Lucretius: *De rerum natura* (before 55 BC) (← Empedocles)
2. Historical epics[2]
a. Naevius (*c.* 200 BC): *Bellum Punicum* (*f*)
b. Ennius (up to *c.* 170 BC): *Annales* (*f*)
3. So-called didactic poetry: Cicero: *Arata* (etc.) (1st cent. BC) (*f*)

E. Latin and Greek epic poetry of the Imperial period

I. The reception of the Greek heroic epic
*Virgil: *Aeneis* (29-19 BC)

II. The reception of the Greek technical epic
1. *Virgil: *Georgica* ('Agriculture') (37-29 BC.)
2. *Ovid: 'Metamorphoses' (before AD 8)
3. *Manilius: *Astronomica* (*c.* AD 10)

III. Reproduction of Greek heroic poetry
1. Ptolemaeus Chennus (†); Scopelianus (†); Pisander of Laranda (†); Soterichus (†)
2. *Valerius Flaccus: *Argonautica* (*c.* AD 80)
3. Papinianus Statius: **Thebais, Achilleis* (*f*) (up to AD 90)
4. *Quintus Smyrnaeus: *Posthomerica (Gk.)* (3rd cent. AD)
5. *Triphiodorus: *Iliou Halosis (Gk.)* (*'The Taking of Troy'*) (*c.* AD 300)
6. *Claudianus: *Gigantomachia (Gk.), De raptu Proserpinae* (Lat.) (*'The Rape of Proserpina'*) (*c.* AD 400)
7. *Nonnus: *Dionysiaka (Gk.)* (5th cent. AD)
8. *Pseudo-Orpheus: *Argonautika (Gk.)* (*c.* AD 500)
9. *Colluthus: *Harpage Helenes* (*f*) ('The Rape of Helen') (*c.* AD 500)

IV. Reproduction of the Hellenistic technical epic
1. Grattius: *Cynegetica* (1st cent. AD) (*f*)
2. *Dionysius Perihegetes: *Perihegesis tes Oikoumenes (Gk.)* ('Description of the Earth') (AD 124)
3. *Oppianus of Cilicia: *Halieutika (Gk.)* (*c.* AD 180)
4. *Oppianus of Apamea: *Kynegetika* (*Ixeutika*?) *(Gk.)* (*c.* AD 215)
5. Nemesianus, *Cynegetica* (shortly before AD 300) (*f*)
6. *Terentianus Maurus: *De litteris, De syllabis, De metris* (c. AD 300)
7. *Avienus: *Phainomena* (shortly before AD 400)
8. *Pseudo-Orpheus: *Lithika (Gk.)* (4th cent. AD)

V. The updating of the historical epic
1. [*Virgil: *Aeneis*]
2. *Lucanus: *Pharsalia* ('Civil War') (before AD 65)
3. *Silius Italicus: *Punica* ('The Second Punic War') (before AD 100)
4. *Claudianus: *De bello Gothico, De bello Gildonico* (*c.* AD 400)
5. *Corippus: *Iohannis* (6th cent. AD)

VI. The reception of the Hellenistic (mythological-) idyllic epic
[1. *Virgil: *Bucolica* (AD 42-39)]
2. *Appendix Vergiliana (*Culex, Ciris, Moretum, Dirae, Copa*)
3. *Ausonius: *Mosella* ('The Moselle') (*c.* AD 370)
4. *Musaeus: 'Hero und Leander' *(Gk.)* (*c.* AD 450)

VII. The reception of the religious/cultic epic
1. *Proclus: (philosophical) hymns *(Gk.)* (5th cent. AD)
2. *Christian epics
Iuvencus; Proba; Heptateuch Poet;
Nonnus: *Metabole* (= Gospel of John)*(Gk.)*;
Eudocia *(Gk.)*;
Prudentius: *Apotheosis, Hamartigenia, Psychomachia, Contra Symmachum*;
Avitus; Sedulius; Arator

1 Greek titles are transliterated and, where not obvious, marked as (Gk.)

2 The historical epic, beginning with Choerilus, is listed under the heading of the technical rather than the narrative epic, since it does not tell a story (μῦθος), but enumerates actions or chains of events, which *per se* do not result in a plot (μία πρᾶξις) directed towards a goal, (Aristot. Poet. 1451a19 and 1459a28). Thus in general it is versified historical writing (of course the genres can overlap and blend, the most famous being Virgil's *Aeneid*).

(a) The improvisational process was demonstrated hypothetically by E. VISSER [48] (the improvizing poet-singer produces the individual hexameter by an intuitive interplay of determinants, variables and free elaboration; potted account of VISSER's reconstruction: [28]). (b) Linguistic analysis of the style of the Homeric hexameter with reference to the so-called 'Mycenaean' phase of the Greek language detectable in Linear B texts, consistently developing upon the initial research described in [32, 25–34], has enabled the age of this technique to be traced back to the 16th cent. BC at least (Linear B as such had no influence on the singers and their technique; for the heroic poetry that can be surmised as an antecedent, its common Indo-European ancestry and its aristocratic ideology of renown, still recognizable in Homer, see esp. [3; 7; 46; 50. 152–156]).

These conclusions are founded on microscopically exact analyses by a great number of researchers, and have become matters of consensus since the beginning of the nineties (cf. e.g. [20]). They have been summarized and systematized, in particular in the work of M.L. WEST [50], C.J. RUIJGH [45] and G. HORROCKS [17], and rest predominantly on the following findings (the linguistic argument is for the most part supported by cultural-historical scholarship):

(a) Tmesis (ἀπὸ θυμὸν ὄλεσσεν, πρὸς μῦθον ἔειπεν) is of Indo-European origin (also attested in Vedic), but in the Linear B texts is already outdated [16; 50. 156]. (b) Reinstatement of the Indo-European short syllabic /r/ (r̥) in place of the -(δ)ρο- in our Homeric texts in word-forms such as (Ἐνυαλίωι) ἀνδρειφόντηι (ἀνδροφόντηι) or ἀνδροτῆτ(α) restores the metre to non-metrical lines or parts of lines: *anr̥g^{w}hóntāi* and *anr̥tāt'*, respectively as the syllabic /r/ in Linear B has already become ρο or ορ (e.g. *to-pe-za* τόρπεζα), lines such as (Μηριόνης ἀτάλαντος) Ἐνυαλίωι ἀνδρειφόντηι = (*Māriónās ḥatálantos) Enūwalíōi anr̥g^{w}hóntāi* and, resp., (ὃν πότμον γοόωσα,) λιποῦσ' ἀνδροτῆτα καὶ ἥβην = (*ḥwón pótmon gawáonsa,) lik^{w}óns anr̥tā́t' ide yḗg^{w}ān* stem from the pre-Mycenaean (proto-Mycenaean) phase of Greek hexametric verse ([44. 163; 50. 158]; [45. 90] significantly modified); [17. 202f.; 51. 229, 234].

(c) Reinstatement of the initial consonant /h/, still present in Linear B, in non-metrical formulae such as (Διῒ) μῆτιν ἀτάλαντος produces metrical regularity: *(Diweí) mētim hatálantos* (from *sm̥-tálantos* 'weighing as much'; with case-form attested in Mycenaean) [50. 157; 45. 77f.]).

(d) Prosodically precarious and functionally obscure Homeric titular forms such as βίη Ἡρακληείη, ἱερὴ ἶς Τηλεμάχοιο can be normalized by restitution (*F*, *h*) to *g^{w}íā Hēraklewehéjja, hierā wīs Tēlemáchojjo* etc., forms the like of which are to be assumed in the court ceremonial of Mediterranean palace cultures of the 2nd millennium BC as functional expressions of hierarchic demarcation within an aristocratic 'titular system' ([50. 158 with n. 55; 45. 82f.]: *Sa Majesté, Son Altesse Royale* etc.; cf. JANKO [20. 12]: ἱερὸν μένος Ἀλκινόοιο, approximately *His Royal Highness*). For the many other cogent arguments as regards language and content, reference must be made to the cited literature.

The pre-Mycenaean and Mycenaean phase of oral hexametric composition that can be revealed in this way was followed during the 'Dark Ages' by a phase of mixing of dialects that in some particulars is still contentious; we are able to distinguish the strains of Ionian and Aeolian tradition with particular clarity. Formulaic line-endings such as Ἴλιος ἱρή /προτὶ Ἴλιον ἱρήν (five times each in the *Iliad*) attest that 'Aeolic bards were already singing tales about a war at Troy' [20. 19] (Boeotian, Euboean and some traces of Dorian, however, appear to attest a survival of the bardic tradition that is not solely Aeolian but Panhellenic; cf. [50. 165–168; 54. 173], similarly [29; 31]). → Homer represents the only tangible conclusion to this process to have come down to us.

2. Greek literature (from Homer to Nonnus)

Vital phase. By virtue of direct relationship with the audience based on oral improvisation, each sung performance of the epic from the beginnings to Homer's time was an original, living event and artistic creation, in spite of its use of formulae and stereotypic devices (best illustration: [33]). The adoption of the alphabet in *c.* 800 (→ Alphabet II) and its extension to the practice of literature (assumed today by the majority of researchers) allows the till then fluid existence of the genre to be fixed for the first time. Use of this new technical tool, part of an all-embracing surge of innovation in the context of the general spiritual awakening of the '8th-cent. Renaissance' [11; 23. 68–73; 30. 52–56; 42. 205–256], leads to the emergence of the great Homeric epics the *Iliad* and the *Odyssey*. Their poet represents a generation in transition within the old bardic fraternity: it had grown up with the old oral technique, but, realizing the opportunities offered by written composition, had blended the two forms to create a hybrid technique; at the same time, representative of the altered *zeitgeist* set in train by a 'structural revolution' [47] in society, it replaces the old celebratory function of the aristocratic epic with a topically relevant, interpretative and expository function [26; 29]. By means of this reformation of the genre, the writer (or writers) of these two epics, evidently outstanding as to intellect and artistry, achieve(s) a height of excellence that remains singular in the history of the genre and thus ensures canonic status for his/their oeuvre [15]. A vitality of the kind that pours forth from these two narrative epics may still, on the strength of their 'existential function' ([13. 19] within an overall theory of the epic), be found in the philosophical epics of → Hesiod, the oldest → Homeric Hymns and the proselytizing philosophical epics of → Parmenides and → Empedocles, even though here it is otherwise founded, and these latter works are already determined in their technique by adoption of the written form (in Hesiod an 'oralità di reflesso' already predominates [43. 178; 26. 13]; the work of the hymnists and philosopher-poets is increasingly densely structured — i.e. lacking the skeletal tapestry indispensable for oral delivery — and artificial).

The vital phase is first succeeded by a *completion phase*, for us primarily represented by the epics of the → Epic Cycle, and in part by the pseudo-Hesiodic *Aspís* (*c.* 570: [19; 20. 14]): the 'gaps' in the cycle of myths prior to the *Iliad*, between the *Iliad* and the *Odyssey* and after the *Odyssey* are 'filled in'; non-Trojan cycles only hinted at in the *Iliad* and the *Odyssey* are 'added' (epics of Thebes, Heracles, Argonauts, Theseus i.a.). At the same time, the hexametric form and style begin to become 'multifunctional': the genre becomes a vehicle for all manner of content and purposes (see above under II. A).

The subsequent phase of *attempted revitalization* (→ Panyassis; Antimachus; Choerilus) during the Classical period of the 5th cent., which was doomed to fail in the face of competition from more vital forms such as the drama and historiography, is followed in the Hellenistic period by a *renaissance* of the form via artistic transformation in the → epyllion (Callimachus, Theocritus i.a.), the idyll (Theocritus), historiographical use (Rhianus i.a.) and → didactic poetry (Nicander i.a.); the virtuosity that results from the combination of artistic perfection and scholarship is brilliant in those cases having a poetological motivation (Callimachus, Theocritus, Apollonius of Rhodes), but enervating in those that are merely naively ambitious (esp. Nicander).

This last-mentioned negative development continues in the predominantly *reproductive* creations of the Imperial period, where, because of the change from quantitative to accented metre that was already beginning in the Hellenistic period, the loss of dichronous long syllables and of → itacism, a great deal of the genre's energy is turned to the avoidance of mistakes [18. 87–119]: the history of the living Greek epic had already come to an end with the Alexandrians.

For the direct and indirect influence of the Greek (and Latin) epic on epics and poetry in the modern age see provisionally [25] (with tabular overviews).

1 A. Bernabé (ed.), Poetae epici Graeci. Testimonia et fragmenta. Pars I, 1987. [2]1996 2 C. M. Bowra, Heroic Poetry, 1952 3 E. Campanile, Ricerche di cultura poetica indoeuropea, 1977 4 H. M. and N. K. Chadwick, The Growth of Literature, 1932–1940 5 M. Davies (ed.), Epicorum Graecorum fragmenta, 1988 6 H. Düntzer, Über den Einfluß des Metrums auf den Homer. Ausdruck, 1864, in: [22], 88–108 7 M. Durante, Sulla preistoria della tradizione poetica greca, II, 1976 8 J. E. Ellendt, Einiges über den Einfluß des Metrums auf den Gebrauch von Wortformen und Wortverbindungen im Homer, 1861, in: [22], 60–87 9 J. M. Foley, The Theory of Oral Composition. History and Methodology, 1988 10 G. Genette, Die Erzählung, 1994 11 R. Hägg (ed.), The Greek Renaissance of the Eighth Century B.C.: Tradition and Innovation, 1983 12 J. B. Hainsworth, The Idea of Epic, 1991 13 A. T. Hatto, Eine allg. Theorie der Heldenepik, 1991 14 G. Hermann, De iteratis apud Homerum, 1840 = Über die Wiederholungen bei Homer, in: [22], 47–59 15 U. Hölscher, Über die Kanonizität Homers, in: Id., Das nächste Fremde, 1994, 62–70 16 G. Horrocks, The Antiquity of the Greek Epic Tradition: Some New Evidence, in: PCPhS 26, 1980, 1–11 17 Id., Homer's Dialect, in: [38], 193–217 18 H. Hunger, Die hochsprachliche profane Lit. der Byzantiner, in: ByzHdb V 2, 1978 (= HdbA XII 5,2) 19 R. Janko, Homer, Hesiod and the Hymns, 1982 20 R. Janko, The origins and evolution of the epic diction, in: Id., The Iliad: A Commentary, Vol. IV, 1992, 8–19 21 S. Koster, Ant. Epostheorien, 1970 22 J. Latacz (ed.), Homer. Tradition und Neuerung (WdF 463), 1979 23 Id., Homer. Eine Einführung, 1985 (= Homer. Der erste Dichter des Abendlands, [3]1997) 24 Id. (ed.), Zweihundert Jahre Homer-Forschung. Rückblick und Ausblick, 1991 25 Id., Hauptfunktionen des ant. Epos in Ant. und Moderne, in: [27], 257–279 26 Id., Hauptfunktionen des ant. Epos in Ant. und Moderne (new version), in: AU 34(3), 1991, 8–17 27 Id., Erschließung der Ant., 1994 28 Id., Neuere Erkenntnisse zur ep. Versifikationstechnik, in: [27], 235–255 29 Id., Between Troy and Homer. The So-Called Dark Ages in Greece, in: Storia, Poesia e Pensiero nel Mondo Antico. Studi in onore di Marcello Gigante, 1994, 347–363 30 Id., Homer. His Art and His World, 1996 31 Id., Troia und Homer. Neue Erkenntnisse und neue Perspektiven, in: H. D. Galter (ed.), Troia (Grazer Morgenländische Studien 4), 1997, 1–42 32 A. Lesky, s.v. Homeros, RE Suppl. 11, 687–846 33 A. B. Lord, The Singer of Tales, 1960 34 A. Meillet, Les Origines indo-européennes des Mètres grecs, 1923 35 K. Meister, Die homer. Kunstsprache, 1921 36 M. N. Nagler, Spontaneity and Tradition: A Study in the Oral Art of Homer, 1974 37 G. Nagy, Comparative Studies in Greek and Indic Meter, 1974 38 A New Companion to Homer, ed. by I. Morris, B. Powell, 1997 39 Oralità. Cultura, Letteratura, Discorso, a cura di B. Gentili, G. Paioni, 1985 40 M. Parry, L' Épithète traditionnelle dans Homère, thesis 1928 41 A. Parry (ed.), The Collected Papers of Milman Parry, 1971 42 K. A. Raaflaub, Homer und die Geschichte des 8. Jh. v.Chr., in: [24], 205–256 43 L. E. Rossi, I poemi omerici come testimonianza di poesia orale, in: Storia e Civiltà dei Greci. I, 1978, 73–147 44 C. J. Ruijgh, Le mycénien et Homère, in: A. Morpurgo Davies, Y. Duhoux (ed.), Linear B: A 1984 survey, 1985, 143–190 45 Id., D'Homère aux origines proto-mycéniennes de la tradition épique, in: J. P. Crielaard (ed.), Homeric Questions, 1995, 1–96 46 R. Schmitt, Dichtung und Dichtersprache in idg. Zeit, 1967 47 A. M. Snodgrass, Archaic Greece: The Age of Experiment, 1980 48 E. Visser, Homer. Versifikationstechnik. Versuch einer Rekonstruktion, 1987 49 Id., Formulae or Single Words? Towards a new theory on Homeric verse-making, in: WJA 14, 1988, 21–37 50 M. L. West, The rise of the Greek epic, in: JHS 108, 1988, 151–172 51 Id., Homer's Meter, in: [38], 218–237 52 P. Wathelet, Les traits éoliens dans la langue de l'épopée grecque, 1970 53 K. Witte, s.v. Homeros (B. Sprache), RE 8, 2213–2247 54 W. F. Wyatt, Homer's linguistic forebears, in: JHS 112, 1992, 168–173.

J.L.

3. Roman literature

A. Republic B. Augustan Period and first century AD C. Mythological Epics under the Principate D. Historic Epics under the Principate E. Second century to Late antiquity

A. Republic

The first epic in the Latin language was the translation of the *Odyssey* in Saturnian verse by → Livius Andronicus. Here already can be observed the solemn, formal style pervaded by archaisms that became characteristic of the Roman epic [1. 603]. It was followed by the *Bellum Poenicum* of Cn. → Naevius, likewise in Saturnians. Its subject was the 1st Punic War, in which the writer himself had participated; but it also incorporated an account of the foundation of Rome from Troy, thus to some extent anticipating Virgil by linking the story of a wandering journey following the Trojan War (like the *Odyssey*) with a war epic (like the *Iliad*). Naevius probably employed traditional epic *loci* (fr. 10 Morel seems to come from a description of a shield [2]; → Ekphrasis), and was the originator of the epic as a medium for voicing a national sentiment of historic and cosmic destiny [3]. Politically fragmented Greece had only → Homer to give expression to national identity (cf. II. B.2.); As textbook authors, Ennius and later Virgil influenced their national culture in the same way that Homer had his. Most Roman epic writers (Naevius, Ennius, Virgil, Lucanus) raised matters of current importance, and adopted a more patriotic tone than did their Greek predecessors.

→ Ennius' subject in his *Annales* was Roman history from the foundation of Rome by Trojans to his own time. He gave only a brief account of the 1st Punic War, which had already been portrayed by Naevius. Ennius gave the epic a new direction, on the one hand by importing from Greece the hexameter, which became established as the standard metre for the genre, and on the other by writing the *Annales* in books structured in groups of three [4. 5]. The work appears to have been published in three parts, each part with a personalized prologue (1–6, 7–15, 16–18). In the proem to Book 1 Ennius presents himself as Homer reborn, and the openings of the first, third and fourth triads refer to the Greek Muses rather than the Italian → Camenae invoked by his predecessors (fr. 322 SK. *insece Musa* stands in direct contradistinction to Livius Andronicus fr. 1 *Camena insece*). Similarly, he refers to his work as *poema* (fr. 12 SK.), and to himself (like Homer, fr. 3 SK.) as *poeta*, both Greek terms, whereas his predecessors were *vates* (fr. 207), who wrote *carmina*. Ennius' work was rightly admired for its sublimity of language and thought, but suffered from a lack of unity and from stylistic inconsistencies. His adoption of the Homeric pantheon and his application of it to virtually contemporary events—a problem recognized by Demosthenes with regard to the historical epic (Epitaphion 9)—produces unharmonious juxtapositions: thus he has a dialogue between Jupiter and Juno during the 2nd Punic War (8,15–16); but other similar examples are missing from the fragments.

Under the influence of Ennius, Livius Andronicus' epic was rewritten in hexameters [5. 60] and divided into books (it appears that in the case of the Homeric poems this latter process was undertaken by → Aristarchus [4], after the time of Livius Andronicus). Naevius' epic too was divided into books by → Octavius Lampadio in the mid 2nd cent. BC (Suet. Gram. 2,4). The tradition of Livius Andronicus lived on, now in hexametric translations of Homer and other Greek epics: → Matius [6. 99], → Ninnius Crassus [6. 107] and perhaps also Attius Labeo in the 1st cent. AD [6. 350] translated the *Iliad* (cf. also the short summary of it in the → *Ilias Latina*, which became an important schoolbook in the Middle Ages); one Naevius [6. 108] translated the → *Cypria*, and P. Terentius → Varro the *Argonautica* of → Apollonius [2] Rhodius [6. 238].

A historical epic by the name *Bellum Histricum* (presumably about a campaign of C. → Sempronius Tuditanus 129 BC) was written by → Hostius. It probably corresponded to the type of epic current in Hellenistic poetry [7. 16] (which was perhaps more panegyric than epic [17. ch. 10]). Presumably there were personal links between Hostius and Tuditanus, likewise between M. Fulvius Nobilior and Ennius, who celebrated Fulvius' Aetolian campaign in Ann. 15. A. → Furius Antias probably wrote a similar epic about the Cimbrian campaign of Q. → Lutatius Catulus [6. 97]. P. → Varro (Atacinus) wrote a *Bellum Sequanicum* on Caesar's campaign of 58 BC [6. 238], and M. → Furius Bibaculus the *Annales Belli Gallici* [6. 195], probably likewise on Caesar's war. The character of the *Annales* of → Accius is uncertain [6. 60]. → Cicero gave the panegyric/historical epic an autobiographical turn in his *De consulatu suo* [6. 156] and his *De temporibus suis* [6. 173] on his banishment and return; the latter work, so far as is known, was never completed or published. He also wrote a *Marius* [6. 174], probably—after his return from exile?—on the banishment and return of Marius. A noteworthy aspect of these poems is that Cicero happily adapted historical facts to his literary aims [6. 157, 178], as did later authors of historical epics. The mythological apparatus here, where it is used in the service of self-glorification, is even less appropriate than in Ennius. Cicero is particularly important to the development of the hexameter [6. 150].

During the Republic epics on themes from Greek mythology, apart from translations, were written exclusively in the form of the → 'epyllion' (a modern expression), i.e. a miniature epic of some 400–500 lines. Such poems include → Catullus' Carm. 64, the *Io* of C. → Licinius Calvus, the *Zmyrna* of → Helvius Cinna and, perhaps earliest of all, Cicero's *Alcyones* [6. 152]; a late (post-Ovidian) example of this genre is the → *Ciris*. Catullus' Carm. 95 accentuates the opposition between such works and voluminous *Annales*. The *epyllion* contributed much to a more marked awareness of skill and structure and to an interest in the representation of *páthos* (emotions). It was primarily characterized by complex structure comprizing the interpolation of a secondary narrative (subtly imitated in Verg. Ecl. 6,45–60) and an interest in metamorphoses.

B. Augustan Period and first century AD

→ Ovid's 'Metamorphoses' in some respects represent a collection of such *epyllia*, and their structure must be based on → Nicander's *Heteroioumena*. They belong to a type of poetic collection that goes back in the final instance to Hesiod, comprizing a series of different individual narratives (some 250 in Ovid) under one overall theme. This type was previously represented in Rome only by the *Ornithogonia* of → Aemilius Macer. Ovid calls his 'Metamorphoses' a *perpetuum carmen* (1,4). It is held together by a predominantly chronological framework, leading from the creation of the world to the appearance of Julius → Caesar as a comet in the sky. One of the significant aspects of this work is the intention to show by means of a series of *aitia* the way things in the natural world arise through transformation. Pythagoras' speech (B.15) gives a philosophical basis to the process of eternal flux. The final books bring the narration ever nearer to Italy, and overlap the subject-material of the *Aeneid*. Continuity is also accentuated by the fluid transitions between the tales as well as between the books. The tales often have erotic or humorous overtones: the former an inheritance from the *epyllion*, the latter a personal characteristic of Ovid. The high point of the Roman epic had already been reached a generation earlier in the *Aeneid* of → Virgil, who had previously (Georg. 3,1–48) announced a panegyric epic to Augustus. Although the *Aeneid* has as its theme the flight from Troy, also recounted by Naevius and Ennius, it handles this theme in an entirely different way: (1) in presenting his readers with announcements and prophecies giving an overview and interpretation of the entire history of Rome up to the Augustan period (represented as its high point), Virgil glorifies Augustus in a much more effective way than could have been achieved in a panegyric poem. Situational parallels can for instance be determined between Augustus and Aeneas (esp. in bk. 8), but this is not a work of → allegorical poetry. Whereas Naevius and Ennius had provided their picture of Roman virtues via a series of historical personalities, Virgil concentrated his in an exemplary symbolic figure. This reflects the transition to the Principate with its emphasis on one *princeps*. Roman rulership is portrayed as being determined by *fatum*, which is identified with the pronouncements of Jupiter. (2) Many verbal and situational similarities [8] represent a kind of dialogue with the Homeric epic, whose ethos of heroic self-assurance is replaced in the *Aeneid* by the sentiment of duty to the community, and esp. by the emphasis placed on the *pietas* of Aeneas. Much of the epic technique also derives from Homer, appropriately adapted to suit the written rather than the oral form [9]. Virgil combines both Homeric epics organically in one much shorter work; he follows a story of war by one of wanderings, and begins the second half of his epic with a new appeal to the Muses (7,37). (3) Virgil gives us not only a summary of Roman history, but, by means of frequent reverentially intended imitations of Ennius and other earlier authors (cf. e.g. Macrob. Sat. 6,1–5 and [10]), to a certain extent a compendium of Roman literature. Other characteristics are his 'subjective' and 'empathic' style [7. 41] and his symbolism [11]. Despite some contemporary adverse criticism, his poetry became an accomplished model for later writers (Stat. Theb. 10,445–448; 12,816 f.).

C. Mythological Epics under the Principate

The Augustan period saw the first appearance of full-blown mythological epics on a restricted theme, e.g. the *Amazonis* of → Domitius Marsus, the *Theseis* of → Albinovanus Pedo, the *Diomedia* of Iullus Antonius, one or more epics by Pompeius Macer on the events preceding and following the *Iliad*. This tradition was continued in the early Imperial period by → Nero's *Troica* [6. 359], → Lucanus' *Iliaca* [6. 353], the *Argonautica* of → Valerius Flaccus, the *Thebais* and the *Achilleis* of → Statius.

Unlike Apollonius Rhodius, Valerius seeks to lend the voyage of the Argonauts historical significance, portraying it as first contact between Greece and Asia, as well as premonition of the dominance of Greece. He attempts to make his poem more heroic than that of Apollonius, by introducing detailed battle scenes. The *Thebais* of Statius is a complex creation, its episodes inspired not only by Homer, Virgil, Ovid, Lucan and Valerius Flaccus, but also by Greek and Senecan tragedy. He portrays a fratricidal conflict imposed by Jupiter to cleanse the godless cities of Thebes and Argos; this is finally resolved by the intervention of Athens in a just war, and the establishment of harmony and piety. Despite occasional flashes of genuine heroism, the protagonists are for the most part motivated by *furor* (which in Aen. 1,295 had been incarcerated to mark the end of the Civil War), and see cruelty, inhumanity and godlessness as vehicles for their passionate heroism. Their destructive rage is offset by their urge to self-destruction. Statius pushes Ovid's predilection for rounded personifications of abstract forces so far that they compete for significance with figures from traditional mythology. This prepares the way for the allegory of the Middle Ages (an era in which the *Thebais* was extremely popular). Statius perfects the hyperbolic, mannerist mode of expression [12; 13. 7] — it has its first roots in Ovid — and, at least to modern taste, tips it over into the bombastic. Valerius and Statius (in both his epics) follow Lucan with their panegyric proems to the emperor. In this they are doubtless influenced by the mock epic → *Culex*, which at that time was regarded as Virgilian, as well as by Verg. G. 1.

D. Historic Epics under the Principate

Alongside these works, the historical, chronicle-type epic makes another appearance, with → Cornelius Severus (*Res Romanae* and a *Bellum Siculum* about the war of 38–36 BC between Octavian and Sex. Pompeius; for uncertainties about these poems cf. [6. 320]) and presumably with → Albinovanus Pedo, by whom a long fragment on the campaign of Germanicus (AD 16) is extant. Fragments of a poem about Octavian's Egyptian campaign after Actium (→ *Carmen de bello Aegyptiaco*) have been preserved on a papyrus from Herculaneum. It appears to be part of an epic in at least 10 bks., perhaps the *Res Romanae* of Cornelius Severus [6. 334]. Some panegyric poems with historical themes (e.g. the *Panegyricus Messalae* and a work on Mark Antony by → Anser; but probably not another on Augustus by Varius; cf. [6. 275]) also have affinities with the epic. A cent. later, Statius' *De bello Germanico* [6. 360] must have been of this type. Valerius Flaccus (1,12) has Domitian writing a similar poem about the Jewish war of Vespasian and Titus.

A radical recasting of the conventions of the genre came about with Lucan's *De bello civili* (*Pharsalia*): he resolved the problem of integrating the divine apparatus into the historical context by replacing it with fate, and with gods who do not intervene personally (although at 4,110ff. he calls upon them to do so). Lucan's causes of war (*causae*, 1,67)—unlike Virgil's (Aen. 1,8)—are definitely not supernatural. This gave rise to dispute as to whether he should be regarded more as a historian than a poet (schol. Bernensia on 1,1; Serv. Aen. 1,382; Isid. 8,7,10). Despite the characteristic ambiguity of his point, → Petronius is clearly referring to Lucan when, in Sat. 118–124, the poetaster Eumolpus emphasizes the necessity of 'twists of plot, the intervention of the gods, and a plethora of fantastic ideas' (*ambages deorumque ministeria et fabulosum sententiarum tormentum*) in a work on the Civil War, and then provides an appropriate sample (295 V.) similar to Lucan's first book, but in the traditional manner. Although Lucan's epic concerns events 100 years in the past, it is imbued with the topical theme of 'monarchy versus liberty' (*libertas*, 7,695 f.).

Contrary to Virgil's *fatum* and the orthodox tenets of Stoicism, for Lucan fate is on the wrong side in this debate, and is therefore the target of many angry reproaches (going so far as to deny the existence of the gods in 7,445–447), in which the personal voice and feelings of the poet find expression over and above characters and action, in a quite non-Virgilian and basically non-epic manner (hence the remark in Quint. Inst. 10,1,90, intended as praise, that Lucan should be imitated by orators rather than by poets: *magis oratoribus quam poetis imitandus*). Lucan is modernizing the epic here. The individual acts of his characters are entirely on a human level, while Caesar's demonic *Fortuna* determines the action from behind the wings; this *Fortuna* is in practice identical to *fatum*, i.e. the outcome of the historical process, and prevails over Cato's *virtus*. On the same principle, in the traditional motif of the dinner conversation the usual mythological tale is replaced by a discussion on the flooding of the Nile (10,194–331), so that the natural takes the place of the supernatural. In the many sections on natural philosophy, Lucan is more of an orthodox Stoic than he is in his theology: for the Stoic, nature is divine (*natura parens* 10,238), and the same forces, *concordia* and *discordia* (1,98; 4,190; 9,1097 and *passim*), drive nature as drive human history.

Lucan's innovations found no disciples. → Silius Italicus in his *Punica* (17 bks., the longest extant Latin epic) returns to the traditional form, imitating episodes from Virgil and other epic writers, but is unable to give that form any topical function. He attempts to heroicize Roman generals, with episodes of single combat and *aristeíai* in the Homeric manner—hardly convincing in the context of the Roman way of waging war. Scipio's rescue (4,417–479) and the river battle (4,638–697) illustrate the old problem of combining supernatural and historical events. Equally, the highly Virgilian prologue (1,17 = Aen. 1,8.11) with its imputation of the *causae* of the war to Juno's anger goes back on Lucan. The extent to which Silius referred back to Ennius [14. 2,148] is uncertain; he has him appear as a warrior (12,387–414).

E. Second century to Late antiquity

The great revolution in taste that took place under Hadrian displaced classical forms and themes. The epic writers of the 1st cent. were unpopular, and very seldom read. The only epic known with certainty to have been written in the 2nd cent. was by one Clemens [6. 401], about Alexander the Great; the sole fragment is strongly Virgilian in style. In preference to the epic, traditionally epic themes were treated in sub-epic form, e.g. in iambic dimeters by → Alfius Avitus [6. 403] and → Marianus [6. 405]. Later on, → Avienus seems to have recast Virgil in iambs [15. 185]. The epic was not revived until → Claudianus, himself strongly influenced by Ovid and Statius. Claudianus wrote two uncompleted mythological epics, the *Gigantomachia* (evidently as a continuation of one of his own Greek poems) and *De raptu Proserpinae*, as well as, among other panegyrics, some poems on the achievements of Stilicho, on the border between → panegyric and epic. In spite of making wide use of mythic tradition, as a non-Christian at a Christian court he was unable to place Stilicho explicitly under the protection of the Graeco-Roman gods, so that for him the old problem of the mythological apparatus in historical epics was resolved of necessity.

The Christian → Dracontius lived in Vandal North Africa, where Roman settlers and Vandal invaders alike were strongly beholden to Roman tradition. His *Romulea* contain some *epyllia* displaying remarkable divergences from canonic versions of the myths [16. 207]. To him is also ascribed the *Orestis tragoedia* (hardly the original title), a recasting of a drama in hexametric

form, finding parallels in the recently discovered → *Alcestis Barcinonensis*. → Reposianus' *De concubitu Martis et Veneris* (Anth. Lat. 25, probably only an extract from a longer poem) and the → *Aegritudo Perdicae* (Anth. Lat. 808; [16. 222]) are of the same type. These works on pagan themes had their Christian counterparts in panegyric works by → Sidonius Apollinaris, → Merobaudes and → Corippus (who also wrote a full-blown epic, the *Iohannis* in 8 bks.). These late epics (the *Iohannis* too) show a new development: most of them are introduced by a short elegiac preface (*praefatio, prooemium*). — For the development of major Christian poetry in hexameters see → Biblical poetry.
→ EPIC

1 E. FRAENKEL, s.v. Livius Andronicus, RE Suppl. 5, 598–607 2 Id., The Giants in the Poem of Naevius, in: JRS 44, 1954, 14–17 (= Id., Kleine Beiträge, vol. 2, 1964, 25ff.) 3 P. HARDIE, Virgil's Aeneid, Cosmos and Imperium, 1986 4 O. SKUTSCH, The Annals of Quintus Ennius, 1985 5 F. LEO, Der saturnische Vers, AAWG 8.5, 1905 6 COURTNEY 7 B. OTIS, Virgil, 1963 8 G. N. KNAUER, Die Aeneis und Homer, [2]1979 9 R. HEINZE, Vergils ep. Technik, [3]1915 10 M. WIGODSKY, Vergil and Early Latin Poetry, 1972 11 V. PÖSCHL, Die Dichtkunst Virgils, [3]1977 12 E. BURCK, Vom röm. Manierismus, 1971 13 D. VESSEY, Statius and the Thebaid, 1973 14 R. HÄUSSLER, Das histor. Epos, 1976–1978 15 C. E. MURGIA, Avienus's supposed iambic version of Livy, in: California Studies in Classical Antiquity 3, 1970, 185–197 16 D. F. BRIGHT, The Miniature Epic in Vandal Africa, 1987 17 AL. CAMERON, Callimachus and his Critics, 1995.

W. SCHETTER, Das röm. Epos, in: M. FUHRMANN, Röm. Lit., vol. 2, 1974, 63–98; P. R. HARDIE, The Epic Successors of Vergil, 1993; D. C. FEENEY, The Gods in Epic, 1991; H. JUHNKE, Homerisches in röm. Epik flavischer Zeit, 1972; M. M. CRUMP, The Epyllion from Theocritus to Ovid, 1931; E. BURCK (ed.), Das röm. Epos, 1979; H. HOFMANN, Überlegungen zu einer Theorie der nichtchristl. Epik der lat. Spätant., in: Philologus 132, 1988, 101–159; S. M. GOLDBERG, Epic in Republican Rome, 1995. ED.C.

Epic, animal An epic narrative featuring animals instead of humans as protagonists. However, it is 'rather doubtful' that the animal epic existed as a literary genre in antiquity [1. 98]. The titles of some works ascribed to Homer [1] (*Arachnomachía*/ 'The Spider War', *Psaromachía*/'The War of the Starlings', *Geranomachía*/ 'The War of the Cranes') are preserved but nothing is certain. However, the *Geranomachía* probably refers to the battle between cranes and → pygmies in the 'Iliad' (Hom. Il. 3,3–7) [1. 99]. The only preserved ancient text that may be considered an animal epic is the late Hellenistic → *Batrachomyomachía* ('War of the Frogs and Mice'), an approx. 300-verse parody of epics, possibly reflecting the rivalry between the *Iliad* and the *Odyssey* [2. 38 f.].

Thematically, the → fable is closest to the animal epic: fables told of wars between eagles and hares, dolphins and whales (Aesop Romance 256 PERRY = 169 HAUSRATH; 62 = 73), winged snakes and ibises (Mela 3,82) etc. The *Batrachomyomachía* is related to an Aesopian fable (384 P. = 302 H.) from which it was probably elaborated [1. 91 f.]. There are also literary confrontations between humans and animals, e.g., the description of the battle between gryphons and the → Arimaspi people in the epic of → Aristeas [1], and the pseudo-Virgilian → *Culex* ('The Mosquito').

Animal epics are known from post-Antiquity: in the High Byzantine period → Theodoros [37] Prodromos (1st half of the 12th cent.) wrote a *Katomyomachía* ('The War of Cats and Mice') [3], which together with its contemporary *Ysengrimus* secured a place for the animal epic in Western literature [4. 90] (→ GERMANY I. B.1.).
→ Epic; → Fable; → Parody; → EPIC, ANIMAL

1 H. WÖLKE, Unt. zur Batrachomyomachie, 1978 2 G. W. MOST, Die Batrachomyomachia als ernste Parodie, in: W. AX, R. F. GLEI (ed.), Lit.parodie in Ant. und MA, 1993, 27–40 3 H. AHLBORN (ed.), Pseudo-Homer: Der Froschmäusekrieg, Theodoros Prodromos: Der Katzenmäusekrieg, 1968 (with German trans., reprint 1978 passim) 4 F. P. KNAPP, Das lat. Tierepos, 1979. R. DA.

Epicaste (Ἐπικάστη; *Epikástē*).
[1] Daughter of → Augeias; mother of Thestalos (Thessalus) by Hercules (Apollod. 2,166).
[2] see → Iocaste, mother and wife of → Oedipus (Hom. Od. 11,271; Apollod. 3,48). R.B.

Epic cycle (ἐπικὸς κύκλος; *epikòs kýklos*).
A. CONCEPT B. CONTENT AND AUTHORSHIP
C. INFLUENCE

A. CONCEPT

'A circle or ring of epics'. Literary historical technical term, current not 'only after Aristotle [and] before Callimachus' [1. 359], but already before Aristotle [4. 93–95], who in An. post. 77b 32f.(= T 1, p.1 BERNABÉ = T *2, p.13 DAVIES) appears to assume knowledge of it. Reference to a book-title Τραγικὸς κύκλος (*Tragikòs kýklos*; cf. Τραγῳδούμενα/*Tragōidoúmena*), by Isocrates' pupil Asclepiades of Tragilus (prose book retelling in chronological sequence the myths treated by Attic tragedy) was already accepted by WILAMOWITZ [1. 361]; *kýklos* was understood among the literati, probably as early as the 5th cent. BC, as a 'synopsis' (also in verse) of 'interrelated events over a wide range of subject-matter' [2. 43]; similarly [3. 2347]: 'accounts to some extent interrelated by content, thus so to speak forming part of a circle or ring'); additional defining attributes such as ἐπικός (*epikós*), τραγικός (*tragikós*) etc. could then easily be interpolated.

Initially, the term was probably a value-neutral collective term for all 'Homeric' (i.e. early Greek, ascribed to Homer) epics; since Aristotle (cf. [5. 98–101] restricted to a complex of early Greek hexametric epics apart from the *Iliad* and the *Odyssey*, recounting in verse and in a linear narrative style imitative of Homer all the old legends of the gods and heroes that were still known, probably with the partly unconscious, partly conscious intention of stringing together all mythological events (1) prior to the beginning of the *Iliad*, (2) between the end of the *Iliad* and the beginning of the *Odyssey* and (3) from the end of the *Odyssey* to the death of Odysseus (and thus the end of the 'heroic age') in a chronological sequence of tales (ἀκολουθία ... τῶν πραγμάτων: Phot. Bibl. 319a 30 = T 22, p.6 BERNABÉ = T *1, p.13 DAVIES), in such a way that, when the *Iliad* and the *Odyssey* were included, a narratively coherent epic was created, covering an entire branch of the mythic inheritance (individual authors seeking to dovetail with one another, in similar fashion to the historians of a later period: → Herodotus — Thucydides — Xenophon).

As the term solely referred to the aspect of continuity (not the regular recurrence of particular elements, which is also a part of the cycle concept), it being used in the same way that we speak of literary or musical 'cycles' today, and as no single edition of the epic cycle (EC) ever achieved canonic status, thereby determining which epics belonged to the EC, the number and titles of such epics varied already in antiquity: as well as (1) a very broad cycle concept, which includes epics concerning the origin of the world and the gods, there is (2) a median cycle concept, comprizing only the Theban and Trojan legends, and (3) a narrow cycle concept, concerning only the Trojan legends (also referred to as Τρωϊκὸς κύκλος, *Trōïkós kýklos*). In the following, those epics that are included more on an *occasional* basis are enclosed in square brackets; the others constitute the canon as usually conceived of: [1. *Theogonía*; see [6. 121–129], for a contrary view [7. 13]] — [2. *Titanomachía*] — 3. *Oidipódeia* — 4. *Thebaís* — 5. *Epígonoi* — [6. *Alkmaionís*] — 7. *Kýpria* — (*Iliás*) — 8. *Aithiopís* — 9. *Iliás mikrá* — 10. *Ilíou pérsis* — 11. *Nóstoi* (*Odýsseia*) — 12. *Telegón(e)ia* (for each epic mentioned see the relevant entry).

B. CONTENT AND AUTHORSHIP

All the epics belonging to the EC have been lost; only two prose synopses (by → Proclus and → Apollodorus [7]), many attestations (testimonies) and an extremely small number of short fragments (now collected in the editions of [8] and [9]) survive. Dates of origin of the individual epics were unknown even in antiquity [1. 361; 4. 99f.]: writers' names are pure speculation; the dates of origin in any case must lie *after the Iliad* and the *Odyssey* (as KULLMANN [10. 33; 11. 104f.] also now has it), most likely between 600 and 500 BC (also judging by linguistic evidence: [12], [13, more circumspect]). The *subject-matter* is older than the *Iliad* and the *Odyssey*; it is used by the EC, by the *Iliad* and the *Odyssey*: by the EC with the constant intention to *clarify* allusions to this material in the great epics already available in written form, by embedding them in their original narrative context. This consistent clarifying intention prevented any artistic autonomy, so that the epics of the EC became mere series of facts in verse ('and then — and then'), whose inferior quality the Alexandrians were already using as a foil to Homer (→ Callimachus, → Pollianus: [5. 281] for a contrary view [2. 103–110]); modern research into the epic follows them in this [14; 15. 96–99]): compared with the epics of the EC, the outstanding quality of Homer becomes apparent.

C. INFLUENCE

The EC was already cherished by Attic tragedians (esp. Sophocles: T 18 BERNABÉ = T *4 DAVIES; cf. Aristoteles' instruction in the 'Poetics': T 5 BERNABÉ p.37 = T 13 p.30 DAVIES) as a fund of material. Exploited by the mythographers (e.g. Dionysius of Samos, known as ὁ κυκλογράφος) in prose manuals, it came down in ever sparser excerpts i.a. to → Proclus, → Apollodorus, → Photius, and in the Middle Ages to the openings of several *Iliad* MSS [16. 341–346]. Via intermediaries, it also influenced the Troy novels of → Dictys and → Dares, as well as the *Posthomerica* of → Quintus of Smyrna and the *Ante-* and *Posthomerica* of → Tzetzes, from which the Middle Ages derived their knowledge of 'Homer'; via HEDERICH'S Lexicon, Goethe (*Achilleis*) and Kleist (*Penthesilea*) i.a. also depend on the EC.

1 U. v. WILAMOWITZ-MOELLENDORFF, Homer. Unt. (Der epische Cyclus), 1884, 328–380 2 F.G. WELCKER, Der epische Cyclus, [2]I, 1865 3 A. RZACH, s.v. Kyklos, in: RE 11, 2347–2435 4 M. DAVIES, Prolegomena and Paralegomena to a New Edition (with Commentary) of the Fragments of Early Greek Epic, in: AAWG 2, 1986, 91–111 5 PFEIFFER, KPI 6 M. L. WEST, The Orphic Poems, 1983 7 M. DAVIES, The Epic Cycle, 1989 8 PEG I 9 EpGF 10 W. KULLMANN, Zur Methode der Neoanalyse in der Homerforsch., in: WS 15, 1981, 5–42 (= Id., Homer. Motive, 1992, 67–99) 11 Id., Ergebnisse der motivgesch. Forsch. zu Homer (Neoanalyse), in: Id., Homer. Motive, 1992, 100–134 12 M. DAVIES, The Date of the Epic Cycle, in: Glotta 67, 1989, 89–100 13 R. SCHMITT, Zur Sprache der kyklischen 'Kypria', in: Pratum Saraviense. Festgabe für Peter Steinmetz, 1990, 11–24 14 J. GRIFFIN, The Epic Cycle and the uniqueness of Homer, in: JHS 97, 1977, 39–53 15 J. LATACZ, Homer. Der erste Dichter des Abendlands, [3]1997 16 A. SEVERYNS, Recherches sur la Chrestomathie de Proclos, III 1, 1953.

O. GRUPPE, Griech. Myth. und Religionsgesch., HdbA V 2, 1906, 380–718; A. SEVERYNS, Le Cycle épique dans l'école d'Aristarque, 1928; F. JOUAN, Le Cycle épique: état des questions, in: Association Guillaume Budé. Actes du Xe Congrès, 1980, 83–104; E. BETHE, Thebanische Heldenlieder, 1891; Id., Der Troische Epenkreis, ([2]1929 =) 1966; W. KULLMANN, Die Quellen der Ilias (Troischer Sagenkreis), 1960; A. SADURSKA, Les Tables Iliaques, 1964.

J.L.

Epicedium (ἐπικήδειον; *epikḗdeion*, sc. μέλος; *mélos*, ᾆσμα; *âisma*). Ceremonial song at mourning (κῆδος, *kḗdos*) or during burial (cf. Pind. Pyth. 4,112). The chorus in Eur. Tro. 514 sings an *epicedium* (ᾠδὰν ἐπικήδειον; *ōidàn epikḗdeion*) over the fall of Troy; similarly, Plato speaks of the women who are ἐπικήδειοι ᾠδαί (*epikḗdeioi ōidai*), professional mourners at a burial. As a substantive, however, *epicedium* is used rarely and only quite late. Ancient authors tried to distinguish it from other words for 'lament': Proclus (Phot. 321a 30–32) calls *epicedium* a song 'before the burial' (ἔτι τοῦ σώματος προκειμένου; in Eur. Alc. 828 *kēdos* means 'corpse'); the term θρῆνος (*thrênos*), on the other hand, is said to have a wider meaning. Serv. Ecl. 5,14 recounts that the *epicedium* was performed before the corpse was buried (*cadavere nondum sepulto*); he contrasts it with the 'epitaphion ... after the burial is concluded' (*epitaphion...post completam sepulturam*). The essential feature seems to be the performance at burial, although the Alexandrian publishers of the lyric poets made no distinction and collated deathbed songs and songs commemorating the dead together with the *thrênoi* of Pindar and Simonides. We know of *epikḗdeia* by Hesiod, Aratus, Euphorion and Parthenius but do not know what form of poems these were [3. 3]. Plutarch quotes an *epikedeion* by Euripides for the Athenians besieging Syracuse (Nikias 17,4); it is one of several epigrams that he refers to by the name of *epikedeion* (cf. Plut. Pel. 1,4; Mor. 1030a). Here *epikedeion* seems to be applied primarily to elegiac distichs that emphasize praise more than lament. Diomedes recounts that elegiac *epikḗdeia* actually were performed at burials [2. 20].

1 M. Alexiou, The Ritual Lament in Greek Tradition, 1974, 107f. 2 A. Hilgard, Grammatici Graeci 1,3, 1901 3 E. Reiner, Die rituelle Totenklage der Griechen, 1938, 2–4.

E.R.

Epicedium Drusi see → Consolatio ad Liviam

Epicephisia (Ἐπικηφισία; *Epikēphisía*). Attic *asty* deme of the phyle Oeneis. One (or two) *bouleut(ai)*. The approximate location of E. in the Cephissus valley at → Laciadae is evident from the name and the site where the decree on deme was found IG II^2 1205 at Dipylon, see [1. 40].

1 P. Siewert, Die Trittyen Attikas und die Heeresreform des Kleisthenes, 1982.

Traill, Attica 19, 49, 69, 110 no. 40, table 6; J. S. Traill, Demos and Trittys, 1986, 133; Whitehead, Index s.v. E.

H.LO.

Epicharmus (Ἐπίχαρμος; *Epícharmos*). Earliest and most important writer of Doric comedy.

A. Life B. Works C. Later influence

A. Life

Widely varying accounts are given for his origin: Syracuse, the Sicanian city of Crastus or Samos [1. test.1], Cos [1. test. 1. 3] or Megara Hyblaea in Sicily [1. test. 1. 2] have been mentioned; it is most probably a place in Sicily. Establishing dates for E. has to rely on the following details: he is said to have been active as a playwright 'six years before the Persian Wars', i.e. 486/5 BC [1. test. 1], or in the 73rd Olympiad, i.e. 488–485 [1. test. 9]. He has been assigned to the period of the tyrant Hieron of Syracuse (478–467) [1. test. 8], but he is also said (according to Aristotle) to have been working 'very much earlier' than the Athenian comedy writers → Chionides (attested for 486) and Magnes [1. test. 2]; finally, E.'s mockery of Aeschylus (fr. 214) does not really allow a dating before the latter's visit to Sicily in 470. If, however, Aristotle's information is correct, E. would have to have emerged as a playwright long before the 480s, and this would indeed be plausible, given his long life (90 or 97 years [1. test. 3]) and the large number of plays attributed to him.

B. Works

Altogether E. is said to have written 52 [1. test. 1] or 40 (including four that are contested [1. test. 9]) or 35 plays [1. test. 1]; [1] lists 39 play titles (including two revisions), to which another six now need to be added on the basis of two fragmentary lists preserved on papyrus [2. no. 81; 82]. With at least two plays E. apparently produced a second version ('The Marriage of Hebe'/ Ἥβας γάμος; 'The Muses'/Μοῦσαι; 'Prometheus or Pyrrha'/Προμαθεὺς ἢ Πύρρα; 'Deucalion'/ Δευκαλίων). None of his plays can be dated accurately, except for the 'Islands' (Νᾶσοι), which must have been written after 478–476 (cf. fr. 98, the only certain contemporary allusion found so far in E.'s fragments).

At least 22 titles refer to mythical subject matter (Hercules and Odysseus were favourite heroes cf. 'Bousiris' (Βούσειρις), 'The Marriage of Hebe' (Ἥβας γάμος), 'Hercules' Journey to fetch the Girdle' (Ἡρακλῆς ὁ ἐπὶ τὸν ζωστῆρα), 'Hercules with Pholus' (Ἡρακλῆς ὁ πὰρ Φόλωι); 'The Cyclops' (Κύκλωψ), 'The Sirens' (Σειρῆνες), 'Odysseus the Turncoat' (Ὀδυσσεὺς αὐτόμολος), 'Odysseus the Shipwrecked' (Ὀδυσσεὺς ναυαγός); thanks to papyrus finds we know somewhat more of two of these: in 'Odysseus the Turncoat' the hero of the play, who is unenthusiastic about a spy mission that he is about to undertake, converses with someone else [2. no. 83], in 'Prometheus or Pyrrha' Prometheus and Deucalion are talking of building the hull of the ship before the flood, when a suspicious Pyrrha turns up [2. no. 85]. However, E. also used contemporary themes (cf. the characterization of the freeloader in 'Hope or Riches' (Ἐλπὶς ἢ Πλοῦτος, fr. 34f.).

Amongst the more unusual titles are 'Earth and Sea' (Γᾶ καὶ Θάλασσα) and 'Mr. and Mrs. Word' (Λόγος καὶ Λογίνα); there may have been agons between allegorical figures (as later in Aristophanes' 'Clouds'). Not very much at all can be said about the structure of E.'s plays: they were evidently considerably shorter than Attic comedies, and choruses do not seem to have been a standard feature [3. 278–281]. Metres used were the trochaic tetrameter, the iambic trimeter and the catalectic anapaestic tetrameter (in which two plays, *Epiníkios* and *Choreutaí*, are said to have been written in their entirety), but no lyrical verse metres. Gnomic material and elements of contemporary natural philosophy (as parody?) probably featured quite strongly in E.'s plays at times and might have formed the basis for later Pseudepicharmeia (see below).

C. Later influence

Several sources place E. at the start of Greek comedy, claiming that he either virtually 'discovered' it [1. test. 1. 11] or made a substantial contribution to its development [1. test. 9]. The extent to which E. influenced the development of Attic comedy in the 5th cent. is a matter of dispute; the fact that he did influence it can hardly be denied — especially given Aristotle's testimony [1. test. 2] — [4. 39–43]. Remarkably, E. scarcely did any work at all as a comic playwright in the following period but, supposedly as a pupil of Pythagoras, composed didactic poetry with a natural philosophical, ethical, medical and even agricultural content [1. test. 3–5]: in the 4th cent. BC the tyrant Dionysius II wrote 'On the writings of Epicharmos', which was probably not restricted to the comedies [1. test. 15]; at about the same time, the Sicilian historian Alcimus (FGrHist 560 F 6) was collecting evidence to demonstrate that Plato adopted many features of his teaching from E. Towards the end of the cent. the Peripatetic Aristoxenus (fr. 45 Wehrli) was already attributing to the flute player Chrysogonus (attested to the end of the 5th cent.) a *Politeía* circulating under E.'s name; only a little later Philochorus (FGrH 328 F 79) named a Locrian or Sicyonian, Axiopistus, as author of the poems thought to be by E., Γνῶμαι and κανών (*Gnômai* and *Kanṓn*), and in the 2nd cent. BC the authenticity of the poem *Chírōn*, which apparently contained medical teachings, was also challenged by Apollodorus of Athens (FGrH 244 F 226), who compiled a complete edition of E.'s plays [1. test. 14]. Whether — and if so, when — there was a *Carmen physicum* with E.'s name is a matter of debate [3. 241–247]; likewise, the question as to which of the fragmentary verses that Alcimus (see above) quoted as models of Platonic teaching (fr. 170–173) really come from E.'s plays or from the Pseudepicharmeia [3. 247–255], upon which the *Epicharmus* of Ennius is based.

1 CGF I 1, 88–147 2 C. Austin (ed.), Comicorum Graecorum Fragmenta in Papyris Reperta, 1973, 52–83 3 A.W. Pickard-Cambridge, Dithyramb, Tragedy and Comedy, [2]1962, 230–288 4 A.C. Cassio, Two Studies on Epicharmus and His Influence, in: HSPh 89, 1985, 37–51.

H.-G.NE.

Epicheirotonia (ἐπιχειροτονία; *epicheirotonía*). *Epicheirotonia* generally means voting (literally: 'raising one's hand'). In particular *epicheirotonia* was used in the 4th cent. in Athens to mean a vote of confidence in officials that was cast in every prytany ([Aristot.] Ath. Pol. 43,5; 61,2; but *epicheirotonia* used in connection with an ostracism in 43,5 is probably an error for *diacheirotonía*) and a vote of confidence conducted annually for each of the four different subject areas of law (Dem. Or. 24,20–23).

P.J.R.

Epiclesis

A. Definition B.1 Invocation B.2 Epithet C. Later influence

A. Definition

Invocation (ἐπίκλησις < ἐπικαλέω; *epíklēsis* < *epikaleō*, cf. *advocatio*, *invocatio*), and in a narrower sense supplication, of one or more gods and demons constituted, along with the narrative section and the articulation of the wish, a standard feature of prayer [1]. In an extended sense epiclesis is the epithet (cf. Eponymia, Epitheton), by which the god was addressed in cult.

B.1 Invocation

Epiclesis originally had the function of appealing for help or inviting the deity to the sacrifice or ceremony, to the taking of an oath, to magic activities (cf. the word of summons ἐλθέ; *elthé*, *veni* — 'come!', φάνηθι; *phánēthi* – 'appear!' and the like) [2. 115–117; 3. 578–580; 4. 179–182]; the accompanying epiphany ('appearance') could be unreservedly understood as real (cf. χαῖρε; *chaîre*, *saluto te* — 'welcome!', βέβακες; *bébakes*, — 'you are here' [2. 109f.; 5. 29f.]. The most basic form of epiclesis was to invoke the gods in time of need, its weakest was the epiclesis at the start of literary works [3. 579f.]. Epiclesis in an oath, at the conclusion of a contract or at the beginning of a legal hearing ensured the presence of gods as witnesses [6. 202–205]; at sacrifices it asked the deity's epiphany to take part in the sacrificial meal and listen to the prayer of those performing the sacrifice. In the sacrifice the verbal *epiclesis* was sometimes replaced or strengthened by inarticulate cries [4. 167f.; 6. 179f.]. The literary form of epiclesis at ceremonies in which the deity was invited to the celebration or summoned to its sanctuary after some absence (Dionysus in Elis, Apollo in Delphi, Zeus Dictaeus on Crete) was the *hýmnos klētikós* (ὕμνος κλητικός [5. 29 n. 114; 7. 103, 158f., 291–293; 8. 205f.]. In the cult of the dead, the epiclesis conjured up dead heroes (ἀνακαλεῖν ψυχήν) (Maximus Tyrius, p. 88 Hobein). In magical prayer [9], which often contained an element of coercion, long *epicleses* were generally mixed with magical formulae and accompanied by magical actions. Featuring uppermost here was the care taken to name correctly the 'many-named' gods; by demonstrating his knowledge of secret epitheta, the appellant commended himself to the deity being invoked.

As a general rule epiclesis consisted of the word of summons, the god's name in the vocative form and a 'cultic relative clause' [3. 578; 4. 197–291]. a) The word of summons attracted the deity's attention to the person praying and invited the epiphany (cf. ἄκουε; *ákoue* – 'listen!', βλέψον; *blépson*, *respice* – 'see!', and the like) [1. 516f.; 2. 115–119]. b) Accurate knowledge of the deity's name, to which a special power was to some extent attached *eo ipso* [11. 205–210, 238, 281f.], facilitated contact; repetition strengthened the efficacy, especially in magic [3. 578]. If the person praying was unsure of the real name of the god he avoided mentioning that one name; even unknown gods or all gods could be invoked [2. 75–84; 5. 13f.; 6. 191; 12; 13]. c) The cultic relative clause mentioned epithets, cult centre and the deity's deeds. Their glorification sometimes took on the form of an extended aretalogy (PMG IV 2785–2879; Orph. H. QUANDT).

B.2 EPITHET

The role of epithets in the invocation was expressed in the fact that the word *epíklēsis* also means the 'epithet' by which a god was invoked at specific places or in specific situations. The epithets generally denote power, beauty (forms of πᾶν, ἄριστος, κάλλιστος) [14. 50–66] and specific qualities of a deity (Apollo Katharsios, Dionysus Lysios, Poseidon Gaiaochos, Zeus Bronton), and particularly the area where the power manifested itself, for example the protection of civic institutions (Athena Polias, Poseidon Phratrios, Zeus Agoraios), marriage (Hera Gamelios), agreements (Zeus Ephorkios), the household (Zeus Herkeios, Ktesios, Pasios), birth (Artemis Lochia), foreigners (Zeus Hikesios, Xenios), crafts (Athena Ergane), natural prosperity (Demeter Karpophoros, Dionysios Auxites) and health (Apollo Iatros, Paian). Many epithets recall genealogy (Zeus Kroneios), birthday (Apollo Eikadios), birth place (Zeus Kretagenes), cult centre (Artemis Amarysia, Poseidon Tainarios) or specific cult forms and ceremonies for a particular deity (Apollo Daphnephoros, Demeter Megalartos, Dionysus Omestes, Zeus Hekatombaios). Sometimes the epithets indicate one deity's association with another that might have related qualities or have been venerated at the same location at some earlier time (Ares Enyalios, Athena Alea, Poseidon Erechtheus) [8. 195; 15. 184].

Although most epithets initially arose from the concept of a personal god, characterized by specific qualities, functions, cult forms and legends, there are many varied associations between names of gods and epithets that cannot always be reduced to an unambiguous interpretation. Some epithets may originally have designated divine figures without individual names ('Special gods' [14. 122–247] cf. [8. 195]) e.g. Despoina, Eubuleus, Kalliste, Kourotrophos, Iatros, Meilichios, Potnia, Sosipolis, etc., which were only later transferred to individual gods (e.g. Kourotrophos to Aphrodite, Artemis, Athena, Demeter, and so on). Thus the Mycenaean Linear B texts contain numerous 'names of gods' that merely describe the deity's sphere of influence, e.g. forms from *pótnia* ('mistress, lady', *potinija asiwija, iqeja, dapu₂ritoja, sito, upoja, atanapotinija*) [15. 44; 16. 256f.]. Many names of gods could well derive from epithets (Poseidon < *Ποτει Δᾶς; *Potei Dâs*, 'master/husband of the earth', cf. Διὸς Κοῦροι; *Diòs Koûroi*, 'sons of Zeus', Dioscuri). The epithet by itself can appear as an abbreviation (e.g. Phoibos = Apollo) or as a reference to an independent quality of the god's, as distinct from the figure taken in entirety [14. 217; 17. 38f.]. From the Hellenistic period more and more epithets were used to glorify a god (Μέγας, Ὕψιστος; *Mégas*, *Hýpsistos*) and they often replaced the god's name, were transferable to other gods and expressed henotheistic tendencies [5. 12f.]. By no later than the 1st cent. BC special collections were made of the epithets of individual gods, with etymological explanations [18. 18f., 211–213]. A deity's epithets relate to the concrete form of that deity's veneration and are not interchangeable; likewise, the features of a deity invoked with different epithets are not always identical (cf. [19]). If a god happened to be invoked with the same epithet at several locations, all the myths and rituals connected with that epithet may contribute to a general understanding of the deity [17. 4]. In general a firm distinction should be drawn between cult epithets and those used by writers [6. 90f.].

C. LATER INFLUENCE

The 'invocation' that existed even in Christian prayer (usually simple in Roman liturgy but with an accumulation of attributes in Eastern liturgy) has more the character of a greeting than that of a 'summons'; its origins lie in the OT and in the early Christian church service. In the Eucharist the epiclesis asks for the dispatch of the Holy Spirit to transform the eucharistic gifts into the body and blood of Christ. On the other hand, forms of ancient epiclesis survived in Christianity in the form of appeals to the dead, in exorcism and in magic [3. 582–599].

→ Aretalogy; → Oath; → Epiphany; → Prayer; → Gods, names of; → Magic; → Theoxenia

1 C. AUSFELD, De Graecorum precationibus quaestiones, Neue Jahrbücher Suppl. 28, 1903, 502–547 2 G. APPEL, De Romanorum precationibus, 1909 3 J. LAAGER, s.v. Epiklesis, RAC 5, 1962, 577–599 4 D. AUBRIOT-SÉVIN, Prière et conceptions religieuses en Grèce ancienne jusqu' à la fin du Ve siècle av. J.-C., 1992 5 H.S. VERSNEL, Religious Mentality in Ancient Prayer, in: Id. (ed.), Faith, Hope, and Worship, 1981, 1–64 6 J. RUDHARDT, Notions fondamentales de la pensée religieuse et actes constitutifs du culte dans la Grèce classique, 1992² 7 NILSSON 8 J.M. BREMMER, Greek Hymns, in: as n. 5 9 F. GRAF, Prayer in Magic and Religious Ritual, in: C.A. FARAONE, D. OBBINK (ed.), Magika Hiera, 1991, 188–213 10 E. BRANDT, Gruß und Gebet, 1965 11 E. PETERSON, Εἷς θεός, 1926 12 E. NORDEN, Agnostos Theos, 1913 13 F. JACOBI, Pantes Theoi, 1930 14 H. USENER, Götternamen, ³1948 15 BURKERT, 126–190 16 M. GÉRARD-ROUSSEAU, Les mentions religieuses dans les tablettes mycéniennes, 1968 17 GRAF 18 A. TRESP, Die Fragmente der griech. Kultschriftsteller, 1914 19 V. PIRENNE-DELFORGE, Épithètes culturelles et interprétations philosophiques, in: AC 57, 1988, 142–157.

BRUCHMANN; NILSSON, GGR I, 385–603; M. SANTORO, Epitheta deorum in Asia Graeca cultorum ex auctoribus Graecis et Latinis, 1974; G. WENTZEL, Ἐπικλήσεις θεῶν sive de deorum cognominibus per grammaticorum Graecorum scripta dispersis, 1890.

A.C.

Epicrates (Ἐπικράτης; *Epikrátēs*).

[1] Athenian who fought with the democrats against the oligarchy in 403 BC. In 397 he and → Cephalus advocated collaboration with Persia and a clean, quick break with Sparta, even at the risk of a new war (Hell. Oxy. 10, 1–2 CHAMBERS). After Conon's victory in the Aegean in 394, he accompanied Phormisius to the Persian king as emissary of Athens. On his return he was accused of corruption but acquitted. In 392/1 he went to Sparta as an emissary for peace negotiations. The terms were rejected by the Athenian public assembly and the emissaries condemned to death *in absentia* (Dem. Or. 19,277–280; Philochorus FGrH 328 F 149a). DAVIES, 181.

P. FUNKE, Homónoia und Arché, 1980, 63f., 106, 115f. W.S.

[2] Athenian from the deme Archarnae. E. secretly sent → Themistocles' wife and children to him when Themistocles was staying with the Molossian king Admetus in Epirus. He was therefore impeached by Cimon (Plut. Themistocles 24,6).

F. J. FROST, Plutarch's Themistocles, 1980 (on the relevant passage). E.S.-H.

[3] Rhodian, son of Polystratus, admiral in the Aegean in the second Macedonian War (Syll.[3] 582) [1. 135,23] and in the War against Antiochus (Liv. 37,13,11; 14,1–4). In 190 BC he proposed to the praetor Aemilius [I 35] Regillus that a Cilician fleet be formed with the help of the Lycians (Liv. 37,15,6).

1 R. M. BERTHOLD, Rhodes in the Hellenistic Age, 1984. L.-M.G.

[4] From Ambracia, writer of Middle Comedy [1. test. 2], active around 380–350 BC [2. 197f.]; six play titles and eleven fragments are extant. Only one of the plays bears a mythical title, *Amazónes* [2. 198]; of the others, *Antilaís* mocks the aged hetaera Lais [2. 197]. Fr. 10 (untitled) is particularly noteworthy for its description of activities in the Platonic Academy (it depicts Plato discussing a gourd with two pupils [2. 277]).

1 PCG V, 1986, 153–163 2 H.-G. NESSELRATH, Die att. Mittlere Komödie, 1990. B.BÄ.

[5] Writer of New Comedy, only epigraphically attested (documenting that he won fifth place at the Dionysia in 167 BC); possibly father of the actor Elpinicus [1].

1 PCG V, 1986, 164. B.BÄ.

Epicteta (Ἐπικτήτα; *Epiktḗta*). Widow of the aristocrat Phoenix from Thera. Under the instruction of her son Andragoras, who died two years after his father, she completed the construction of a shrine to the Muses (mouseion) that Phoenix had started, as a memorial to their son Cratesilochus, but had not been able to finish. In her will (early 2nd cent. BC, preserved epigraphically: IG XII 3,330, l. 1–108), E. entrusted the *mouseion* to her 'heiress' (→ *epikleros*) daughter Epiteleia. In the will she provided for the setting up of an association of male relatives (κοινὸν τοῦ ἀνδρείου τῶν συγγενῶν), which could also co-opt women (l. 79–106), and a cult for the Muses and her family. Three days a year were dedicated to the cult activities, one for the muses, one for Phoenix and E., and one for the dead sons. The costs of maintaining the *mouseion* and the cult area were to be met from the interest on a mortgage of 3,000 drachmas secured by her landed properties. Epiteleia was responsible for administering the property and dispersing the annual interest (*c.* 7% of the mortgage). The organization of the association is clear from her instructions (IG XII 3,330, l. 109–288, νόμος): the highest priestly office fell initially to her son Epiteleias and then passed to the eldest male successor at the time; the other priestly offices (one ἐπιμήνιος for each cult day) were not hereditary. The *koinón* was administered by a senior official (ἐπίσσοφος) elected annually by the body of members (σύλλογος) and by support staff working under him. They oversaw regular conduct of the cult and had powers of sanction if members tried in any way to divert the *mouseion* and *temenos* from their intended use.

The will throws up various judicial questions, such as the opportunity for women to acquire real estate (attested in l. 32) [1. 93]. At the same time it is to be noted that E. may have composed the dispositions independently but not on her own initiative: she was acting on the instructions of her husband or her son; officially she had a spokesman in her son-in-law Hypereides (κύριος; *kurios*, l. 3).

1 R. SEALEY, Women and Law in Classical Greece, 1990.

A. WITTENBURG, Il testamento di E., 1990 (text, trans., comm. and bibliography). M.MEI. and ME.STR.

Epictetus (Ἐπίκτητος; *Epíktētos*).

[1] Early Attic red-figured vase painter (*c.* 520–490 BC); signed many of his vases as painter and collaborated with various potters (early on with Andocides, → Nicosthenes, Pamphaeus and Hischylos, later with Python and Pistoxenus). Possibly a pupil of → Psiax, E. mainly decorated bowls but also several plates, some of which rank with his best works. E. signed one of these plates as painter and potter. Amongst his early works are bilingual eyecups (→ Bilingual vases), which are red-figured on the outside and black-figured on the inside; in his middle and late periods, E. predominantly painted Type B cups, the majority of which display painting only on the inside. E. painted one eyecup in collaboration with the → Euergides painter.

E.'s fine and delicate lines and miniature style were perfectly suited to painting the edges of cups where E. was an unchallenged master. Figures have an animated effect rich in attitudes and gestures. E. favoured everyday scenes and Dionysian themes; his satyrs, comasts and erotic depictions are especially noteworthy. E. was the first painter to use a crimson colour exclusively for his inscriptions. Hipparchus was the favourite name used in → kalos-inscriptions.

→ Duris; → Oltus

Beazley, ARV², 70–81, 1623–1624, 1705; Beazley, Paralipomena, 328f.; Beazley, Addenda², 116–169; B. Cohen, Attic Bilingual Vases and their Painters, 1978, 400–438; W. Kraiker, E., in: JDAI 44, 1929, 141–197. J.O.

[2] Stoic philosopher, *c.* AD 50–125

A. Life and works B. Teachings

A. Life and works

Born in Phrygian Hierapolis, E. was a slave in the house of the imperial freedman Epaphroditus in Rome. He studied philosophy under → Musonius Rufus, whose practical approach and focus on ethics he adopted. After his manumission he taught philosophy in Rome until the general banishment of philosophers in the year 89. With his highly regarded school, attended by rich and powerful aristocrats, he then moved to Nicopolis on the other side of the Adriatic and taught there until his death. He left behind no writings but Flavius Arrianus (→ Arrianus [2]), a Greek-writing Roman, took notes of his lectures and published a collection of 'lectures' (διατριβαί, *diatribaí*), the first four books of which are extant. This collection was extremely influential, as E.'s oral teaching had been in his own lifetime. It had a lasting impact on → Marcus Aurelius and later had a major influence on Christians and non-Christians alike. A summary was also published, the 'handbook' (ἐγχειρίδιον, *encheirídion*), the influence of which extended right through late antiquity (the Neoplatonist → Simplicius wrote a commentary on it) into the modern world.

B. Teachings

Although E. also taught logic and physics, generally adopting positions of early Stoics like → Chrysippus, his public lectures on ethics were the core of his teaching. His essential contribution to ethics lay in his moulding early Stoic theories of moral responsibility into a coherent teaching of moral autonomy and the individual's inner freedom. This shaping was based on an innovative concept of moral personality, *prohaíresis* (προαίρεσις, 'resolution'), but also important was his maintenance of the Stoic distinction (ultimately derived from Socratic thought) between moral values (virtue and wickedness, good and bad) and indifferent things (like health, wealth etc.). E. specifically defined indifferent things as those that are not subject to our *prohaíresis*, i.e. are not within our power (ἐφ' ἡμῖν). He takes the view that our happiness can be attained only by limiting our own wishes and desires to what is in our power, namely to our own views, attitudes and our moral character. For although human beings live in a providentially predetermined world that was set up for the best by a rational god (Nature or the Stoic Zeus to whom E. often turns, as if to a personalized deity), they are incapable of shaping the external forces of destiny and so have to find a way of adapting their life to nature as best they can. Only then are they capable of avoiding passions, incoherence and irrationality that otherwise dominate human existence and deprive it of available repose.

The sharp dichotomy between internal and external goes even further. An essential feature of E.'s teaching is the contrast between our 'impressions' (φαντασίαι, *phantasíai*) on the one hand and the critical use (χρῆσις, *chrêsis*) that we can make of them on the other hand. Impressions can be created externally through usual perceptions of the world or summoned up by our spirit. Although E. followed the teachings of the early Stoa in most respects, he came up with the new approach that human beings possess certain innate opinions (προλήψεις, *prolḗpseis*), the elucidation of which, together with a rational analysis of the external world, could be a reliable guide to moral knowledge and moral behaviour. Impressions are to be subjected to thorough examination, without regard for their origins, before they can be accepted. This critical use of impressions, which appears to be an internalization of Socratic → refutation, is the most important of the moral exercises recommended by E.

Moral exercise (ἄσκησις, *áskēsis*) is the central principle of E.'s teaching. In fact, he did not group his teachings in the traditional categories of logic, physics and ethics, but instead proposed three *tópoi* (τόποι) or fields of exercise:

1. Mastering desires and aversions (so that we do not yearn for the unattainable or seek to escape the unavoidable); two traditional techniques are recommended for that: anticipation of possible negative events (*praemeditatio malorum*; Cic. Tusc. 3,14,29) and 'reservation' (ὑπεξαίρεσις, *hypexaíresis*), restricting one's desires with the qualification 'if it be Zeus' will'.

2. Mastering impulses and decisions, whereby we learn to do what is appropriate in various contingent situations in life.

3. Mastering one's own imaginings and consents, so that any error is avoided. That requires an extremely differentiated use of impressions. Logic, epistemology and even physics play essentially an instrumental role in helping us to free our views from incoherence and error and bring them into harmony with the rational course of the world.

→ Arrianus; → Musonius Rufus; → Epaphroditus

Editions: 1 H. Schenkl, Epicteti Dissertationes, 1894 2 W. Oldfather, Epictetus, 2 vols., 1925/1928 3 J. Souilhé, Epictète, in: Entretiens 4, 1941.
Bibliographies and overviews: 4 W. Oldfather, Contributions toward a Bibliography of Epictetus, 1927 (Supplement 1952).
Studies: 5 J. Hershbell, The Stoicism of Epictetus, in: ANRW II 36.3, 1989, 2148–2163 6 M. Billerbeck, Vom Kynismus, 1978 7 A. Bonhöffer, Epictet und die Stoa, 1890 8 Id., Die Ethik des Stoikers Epictet, 1894 9 Id., Epiktet und das Neue Testament, 1911 10 P. Brunt, From Epictetus to Arrian, in: Athenaeum 55,

1977, 19–48 11 B. HIJMANS, ΑΣΚΗΣΙΣ, 1959 12 A. A. LONG, Representation and the self in Stoicism (1991), in: Stoic Studies, 1996, 264–285 13 F. MILLAR, Epictetus and the Imperial Court, in: JHS 55, 1965, 141–148 14 M. POHLENZ, Die Stoa, [5]1978, vol. 1, 327–341 15 H. v. ARNIM, s.v. Epiktetos 3), RE 6, 126–131. B.I.

Epicurean School

A. SCHOOL OF EPICURUS B. SUCCESSORS TO EPICURUS C. THE SCHOOL IN ROME D. BETWEEN ORTHODOXY AND HETERODOXY E. PHILOSOPHICAL THOUGHT F. INTERNAL ORGANIZATION

A. SCHOOL OF EPICURUS

The school, founded in Athens in 307/6 or 305/4, survived as an institution until the 1st cent. BC. After a period of obscurity we again come across references, from the 2nd cent. AD, to some Epicurean philosophers. It was between the 4th and 1st cents. BC that the Epicurean School received its strength and vitality, extending both its range of thought and its structure. That happened under a series of school heads from Epicurus to Patron who assured its fate and ensured its continuity even in times of crisis and disruption. After his first five years as a teacher in Mytilene and Lampsacus, Epicurus (342/1–271/0) moved to Athens. There he founded the school that took its name 'garden' (Κῆπος, *Kêpos*) from its setting. Epicurus remained in Athens for the rest of his life, surrounded by numerous students who shared the commitment to a common philosophical goal (συζήτησις, *syzḗtēsis*). The first circle of friends and pupils included Metrodorus of Lampsacus, Pythocles, Polyaenus, Colotes and Idomeneus, who had met Epicurus in Lampsacus and followed him to Athens.

B. SUCCESSORS TO EPICURUS

Epicurus' first successor was Hermarchus (died *c.* 250), a pupil from Mytilene. With his death the first phase of Epicureanism, that is of pupils who had listened to the master in person, came to an end. Following Hermarchus as the school head were Polystratus (died before 220/19), Dionysius of Lamptrae (died 201/0) and Basilides of Tyrus (died *c.* 175). In the long gap between the last of these and Apollodorus Kepotyrannos we have to assume that there was at least one other head of the school (Thespis?). In the same period Philonides of Laodicea on the Pontus and Protarchus of Bargylia were also active; the influence of these significant Epicureans shows that Epicureanism was spreading even to areas far removed from Athens, to Asia Minor in particular. Even on Rhodes there existed a flourishing Epicurean circle, which appears, however, to have distanced itself from official doctrine.

The parent school in Athens experienced a heyday under → Apollodorus [10] Kepotyrannos, who was the head from *c.* 150 until *c.* 110 BC and was well-known for his extensive writing. Another famous Epicurean was Demetrius [21] Lakon (*c.* 150–75), who never became head and conducted his teaching mainly from Miletus. After the death of Apollodorus, management of the 'Garden' passed to Zeno of Sidon (*c.* 150–75). Thereafter the Athenian school survived under Phaedrus (*c.* 138–70) and Patron (still head in 51) until at least the middle of the 1st cent. BC. A pupil of Zeno's, Philodemus of Gadara (*c.* 110–40), had left Athens at the end of the 80s, however, and settled in Italy where he opened a new school at Herculaneum. It was supposed to be the ideal extension of the 'Garden' in Athens. The latter underwent a slow but steady decline until it was on the verge of ruin at the end of the 50s (Cic. Fam. 13,1,3 and Att. 5,11,6) whereas the opposite was the case in Italy.

C. THE SCHOOL IN ROME

An initial effort by Alcius and Philiscus to set up a school on the occasion of the philosophers' embassy to Rome (155 BC) was unsuccessful, as were also the clumsy propaganda activities of C. Amafinius, C. Catius and Rabirius about 100 years later. A new historical phase of Epicureanism then began in the 1st cent. BC, resulting in a large number of proselytes. Credit for this 'Roman' renaissance was attributed to the influence of the Greek-speaking Epicurean circle in Campania and to the didactic poem of → Lucretius, *De rerum natura*. The lively battle waged by Cicero against Epicureanism in those same years was symptomatic of the growing dissemination of the 'garden's' teachings in the Roman world. Epicurean philosophy spread to the West and East of the Roman Empire and left unmistakable traces behind. An example is the letter from Trajan's widow, Pompeia Plotina, to Hadrian in AD 121 (IG [2]1099): in her view the head of the Epicurean school in Athens ought to be able to nominate a successor who was not a Roman citizen and to compose his last will in Greek; the request was granted by the emperor. The letter attests to the existence of an obviously institutionalized Athenian school in the 2nd cent. AD and to the continued teaching of Epicurean philosophy (cf. also Hadrian's subsequent letters to the Epicureans in Athens: SEG 3,226; IG [2]1097). This school, however, was probably not a continuation of the institution founded by Epicurus, which had gone into decline in the middle of the 1st cent. BC. The treatise of → Diogenianus (2nd cent. AD ?) and the philosophical inscriptions of → Diogenes [18] of Oenoanda are sound evidence of the spread of Epicureanism in the Imperial period. The latter attests to the presence of Epicurean teaching in areas far removed from cultural centres, as for example in the north of Lycia. Recent efforts to assign Diogenes of Oenoanda to the 1st cent. BC/1st cent. AD instead of the 2nd/3rd cents. AD should be treated with caution but they do raise doubts as to whether the 'Garden's' philosophy lasted beyond the first centuries of the Empire.

D. Between orthodoxy and heterodoxy

Early in the history of the school there soon were schisms: even in Epicurus' lifetime Timocrates, brother of Metrodorus, left the 'Garden' and undertook a defamatory campaign against Epicurus, causing a great deal of damage. According to Philodemus, there was a whole series of Epicurean dissidents (*sophistaí*) active in the centres on Cos and Rhodes between the 2nd and 1st cents BC: there it was taught that not even sophist rhetoric could be regarded as an art (*téchnē*); Nicasicrates, possibly the head of the school on Rhodes, maintained that a wise man was not subject to the passions of flattery and anger. Timasagoras expressed similar views on anger but he was also interested in vision (ὅρασις; *órasis*). Antiphanes modified some inconsequential aspects touching on the life of gods (θεῶν διαγωγή; *theôn diagōgḗ*), while Bromius seemed to prefer political to sophist rhetoric. Although these Epicureans had probably strayed from Epicurean teaching in secondary aspects, they did not affect any of its key points.

E. Philosophical thought

The key points of philosophical thought and the basic principles described in detail by Epicurus were not set out in a canon to which adherence was expected. Epicurean teaching underwent instead an independent development, at any rate in particular secondary issues. That began in the generations succeeding Epicurus and his immediate pupils. It is only in the early stages of Epicureanism (from Epicurus to Hermarchus) that one can speak of doctrinal unity. The introduction of new features into the basic structures of the master's teaching was admittedly regarded by the Epicureans as heresy but at the same time they felt compelled by changed social and cultural conditions to reinterpret the school's dogmas. Changing the criteria seemed to them a permissible means of interpreting faithfully the word of Epicurus. In the light of those considerations it was also possible to resolve the old conflict between the 'genuine representatives' (*gnḗsioi*) and the 'Sophists' (*sophistaí*) within the Epicureans. On a theoretical level both parties were convinced that they were reading Epicurus' work in terms of the master's own principles but in practice they interpreted it at varying depths of understanding and, in both cases, to suit their own purposes at the time. Dissidence between the two groups of *gnḗsioi* and *sophistaí* played an important role. Fundamental to an understanding of this dissidence and its historical relevance is the gap between the death of Hermarchus, who was amongst Epicurus' immediate pupils, and the following generations (from Polystratus onwards). The latter engaged in interpreting those principles of his teaching that had become canonical. Common to both trends was the belief in the authenticity of their own interpretation of the school's teachings.

The concept of orthodoxy is found to the same degree amongst both the *gnḗsioi* and the *sophistaí*; but there was a fundamental difference: the former emphasized the teaching that they claimed had evolved within the school itself, whereas this codified transmission was exactly what the dissidents criticized for not reflecting the original meaning of Epicurus' teaching and that of his immediate pupils. On the basis of that interpretation it was easy to exonerate key members (Apollodorus Kepotyrannos, Demetrius Lakon, Zeno of Sidon and lastly Philodemus) from accusations of dissidence. The phenomenon of dissidence continued into the 1st cent. BC when Philodemus fought strongly against it. The reasons for its appearance are to be found in the difficult situation that arose when the pioneers (καθηγεμόνες; *kathēgemónes*) who had established the basic theories of the philosophical system — Epicurus, Metrodorus, Hermarchus and Polyaenus — had died. For free debate had then been replaced by a book culture that required interpretations, which in time altered to suit the needs of individual interpreters. The original school in Athens had always managed to maintain a strong line against dissidents. It thus prevented the survival of deviant teachings and their influence on the official direction of the 'Garden'.

F. Internal organization

More than that of any other philosophical school, the internal organization of the 'Garden' was from the beginning based on principles of emulation, memory and imitation. Epicurus had *i.a.* taught that the goal and purpose of philosophy was to imitate godliness so as to be able to live happily and undisturbed amidst the world's evil. For members of the school that meant a constant striving to imitate the pioneers who had achieved a level of the greatest perfection in their own imitation of divine bliss. From the first generation onwards, the school had been organized on the ideal model of communal partnership, in which individuals seemed to be parts of the one body. In the Epicurean community each member retained his own identity and personal individuality but was also responsible for cooperating with the others in order to achieve the common goal, bliss. In the 'Garden' there never developed an awkward hierarchical structure, with a class distinction between philosophers, philologists, teachers (καθηγηταί; *kathēgētaí*) and friends (συνήθεις; *sunḗtheis*); the ideal of free speech (παρρησία, *parrhēsía*) between teachers and pupils was more important. Communal life was characterized by the pedagogical goals of friendship (φιλία; *philía*), gratitude (χάρις; *cháris*) and goodwill (εὔνοια; *eúnoia*). It is also revealing that the school was open to female students; the sources give the names Batis, Boidion, Demetria, Hedeia, Leontion, Mammarion, Nikidion and Themista. Some of these women took an active part in philosophical discussion. Members of the school lived as a community on the grounds of the garden. The practice of celebrating commemorative days with feasts and banquets played an important part in communal life. Such occasions commemorated Epicurus, his dead brothers and friends (Metrodorus and Polyaenus). Five rituals are attested to have been held in the 'Garden': the annual cult of mourning that Epicurus instituted in honour of his parents and dead brothers; the two cults for Epicurus himself (one annually on the 20th of the month of Gamelion, his birthday, and another on the 20th of each month, honouring Metrodorus also); one day was reserved to commemorate the birthday of Epicurus' brothers in the month of Poseideon; and finally a cult for Polyaenus, in the month of Metageitnion. For the upkeep of the school Epicurus made use of the *syntáxeis* system: donations made to the 'Garden' by influential people (sometimes solicited by Epicurus).

A. ANGELI, Filodemo. Agli amici di scuola (PHerc. 1005), 1988, 82–102; C. J. CASTNER, Prosopography of Roman Epicureans, [2]1991; T. DORANDI, Ricerche sulla cronologia dei filosofi ellenistici, 1991, 45–54, 62–64; J. FERGUSON, Epicureanism under Roman Empire, ANRW II 36.4, 2257–2327; S. FOLLET, in: REG 107, 1994, 158–171.

T.D.

Epicurus (Ἐπίκουρος; *Epíkouros*).
A. LIFE B. WORKS C. TEACHING D. LATER INFLUENCE

A. LIFE

E. was born in 342/1 BC on Samos, where his father Neocles, an Athenian citizen from the deme Gargettos, had moved as a cleric in 352. His birthday was the 20th of Gamelion [1]. He had three brothers, Neocles, Chaeredemus and Aristobulus. His early interest in philosophy is attested. He associated with the Platonist Pamphilus (Diog. Laert. 10,14), and then on Teos listened to lectures given by the Democritean and acquaintance of the sceptic Pyrrhon, Nausiphanes. At the age of 18, E. went to Athens for two years to do service as an ephebe; he may have attended lectures given there by the Academic Xenocrates (Diog. Laert. 10,13). After his return he accompanied his parents who moved to Colophon (after 322), after Samos was captured by Perdiccas. We know little of the following ten years. That period was, however, of great importance for his philosophical development, which was influenced, aside from Democritus, by Platonic-Academic teaching and Aristotle's work. Around 311/0 E. began to teach philosophy and opened a school first in Mytilene and then soon afterwards in Lampsacus. In that period E. acquired loyal friends like Hermarchus (Mytilene), Metrodorus and Colotes (Lampsacus).

In 307/6 E. settled in Athens (Diog. Laert. 10,2), the centre of philosophy with the → Academy and → Peripatos as the most important schools. He acquired a house (Apollodorus in Diog. Laert. 10,11) with the famous 'garden' (κῆπος, *kē̂pos*), from which the school received its name. The community was dedicated to mutual friendship and joint enquiry (συμφιλοσοφεῖν, *symphilosopheîn*). Through visits or correspondence E. maintained close and friendly relations with like-minded groups on Greek islands and in Asia Minor (Diog. Laert. 10,10). He died in 271/0 after long and painful suffering that he bore in a manner that impressed even his opponents, as is evident from his 'Letter to Idomeneus' (Diog. Laert. 10,22 = fr. 138 USENER). Cicero translated the letter as a testimony to human courage (Fin. 2,30,96). E.' s behaviour in the face of death, as throughout his life, was an example and a moral inspiration for his students (Gnomologicum Vaticanum 36 = Hermarchus fr. 49 AURICCHIO). Emulating him would be a means of achieving a divine life on earth (Epicurus Ad Menoeceum 135). His will (Diog. Laert. 10,16–22) appointed Hermarchus of Mytilene as his successor and school head and he assigned to him the right to use the house and garden. He appointed Amynomachus and Timocrates as his heirs, who as Athenian citizens had the right to own property. As the spiritual focus of his school, E. was to receive an almost divine veneration after his death. His birthday was observed as a communal day of remembrance (εἰκάδες, *eikádes*). *I.a.*, E.'s personal qualities (Diog. Laert. 10,9–10) of understanding (εὐγνωμοσύνη; *eugnōmosýnē*) and humanity (φιλανθρωπία; *philanthrōpía*) were renowned; people saw him as the saviour who imparted truth (*rerum inventor*) and fatherly advice (*patria praecepta*) (Lucr. 3,9f.).

B. WORKS

In contrast to other Hellenistic philosophers, we have, apart from fragments by E.([2], cf. [3. 84ff.]), not only biographical and doxographical material from Diogenes Laertius, but also three significant works (letters) that have survived in their entirety (the authenticity of the Pythocles letter is admittedly disputed): a) to Herodotus (= Epist. Hdt.), offering an outline of E.'s teaching on nature (cosmos, images, senses, atoms, soul, bodies, qualities, worlds, the origin of culture and language and heavenly phenomena) together with methodological tips (Diog. Laert. 10,35–83); b) the letter to Pythocles (= Epist. Pyth.) on meteorology and astronomy (μετέωρα; *meteōra*) (Diog. Laert. 10,84–116) and c) the letter to Menoeceus (= Epist. Men.), in which E. discusses the basis of his teaching for an art of living (*ars vitae*), understood as a good life (god, death, desire), and urges continual re-examination of his teaching; a philosophical protreptic that does not demand any comprehensive education but is intended for a general readership (Diog. Laert. 10,122–135). We are also indebted to Diogenes Laertius for the so-called 'Principal Doctrines' (*Ratae sententiae*, cf. Cic. Fin. 2, 7, 20, κύριαι δόξαι (*kýriai dóxai*, = KD), 40 aphorisms in which E. collected his basic teachings as for a catechism and which were famous in antiquity. They were intended to give beginners the essential points of E.'s teaching in a short overview and, as a breviary, to facilitate the process of memorizing and meditating by more advanced students — a medicine, as it were, to keep at bay irritants that disturb one's peace of mind, as shown in the very first four aphorisms that are known in Epicureanism as 'fourfold medicine' (τετραφάρμακος; *tetrapharmakos*, cf. [4. 68ff.]). As well as the nature of the eternal, the aphorisms touch upon, *i.a.*, death, god, desire, communal life, friendship, and justice. These aphorisms were supplemented (with 13 passages overlapping) by the Gnomologium Vaticanum that was preserved in cod. Vat. Gr. 1950 and rediscovered in 1888 by C. WOTKE (now in [2]).

Of E.'s prolific written output (Diog. Laert. 10,27 offers a list of 40 titles of his best works) important remnants have survived in papyri found in the 'Villa dei Pisoni' at Herculaneum, including large segments (e.g. including copies with divergences) of his masterwork 'On Nature' (Περὶ φύσεως; *Perì phýseōs*, *De natura*, in 37 volumes, cf. [3. 94ff.]). Also extant are fragments of numerous letters that, in spite of their condition, allow some interesting insights. Quotations, excerpts, and reports are also to be found in the occasionally polemical secondary transmission, e.g. in Cicero, Seneca, Lactantius or Sextus Empiricus, and were compiled, together with the primary sources, by USENER [4] in 1887. Finally, E.'s words have been preserved on the monumental wall inscription, probably from the 2nd cent. AD, that the Epicurean → Diogenes [21] had put up in Oenoanda in Asia Minor [5]. Emulation of and remembrance of models featured as part of the life of an Epicurean, who was urged to behave always as if E. were able to observe him (Sen. Epist. 25,5 = fr. 211 USENER). Similarly, we hear of the important role that images of E. and his most important pupils played for Epicureans (Cic. Fin. 5,1,3; cf. [6. 87ff.]). Rings have been found with his image, also statues, statuettes and busts (copies of Hellenistic originals, cf. [3. 63f.]).

C. TEACHING

1. GENERAL CHARACTERISTICS 2. CANONICS 3. PHYSICS 4. COSMOLOGY 5. PSYCHOLOGY 6. THEOLOGY 7. ETHICS

1. GENERAL CHARACTERISTICS

E.'s philosophy saw itself as promoting a life-style that would create happiness (*eudaimonia*) for mankind. Elucidating Nature (physiology), epistemological reflections and ethical fundamentals were to dispel unsettling factors, while making the unknown comprehensible and showing the unattainable to be irrelevant, the unavoidable as acceptable (KD 11). In seeking a happy life, philosophy should convert help into self-help (fr. 219 USENER). 'Enlightenment' and 'soul-therapy' are two essential features of E.'s teaching known as the art of living (*ars vitae*) and therapy (*philosophia medicans*) [7]. Focussing on that objective E. disparages all forms of education in the → *enkýklios paideía* that do not appear indispensable for attaining *eudaimonia* [8. 181ff.], and as his tools uses the triad of philosophical disciplines, logic, physics and ethics, with logic and physics being subordinate to ethics. Theory thus becomes the handmaiden to practice but is accorded a higher place in the scale of values, because happiness is impossible without an explanation of Nature (KD 12). The therapeutic character of E.'s philosophy is shown in the form in which it is presented: along with detailed exposition, gnomologies, *epitomai*, manuals and letters are expected to facilitate the intended meditation on his teaching. Those texts were regarded as virtually sacrosanct and were subjected to very thorough philological interpretation, which for its part gained a form of therapeutic character [9]. The striving for orthodoxy gave the teaching a superficial appearance of being a closed unit (Numenius fr. 24 OF PLACES). Texts of later Epicureans, however, show that the impression of rigidity and lack of originality is unjustified (cf. [10] und [11]; → Epicurean School).

2. CANONICS

E.'s epistemology (Diog. Laert. 10,29f.) is closely linked to his theory of natural science (φυσιολογία, *physiología*). E. set out his epistemological teaching in a work that has not survived, entitled 'On criterion or canon'. The word 'canon' (κανών; *kanṓn*) means 'guideline'. The canonics is the teaching of the criteria (κριτήρια; *kritḗria*) of truth [12. 9ff.]. Its main proposition is that knowledge can be gained only by sense-perception. E. distinguished three criteria of truth (Diog. Laert. 10,31ff.) [13]: sense-perception (αἴσθησις, *aísthēsis*), universal or preliminary notions (προλήψεις, *prolḗpseis*) and sensations (πάθη, *páthē*). The validity of perception as a criterion derives, *i.a.*, from its non-rationality — reason (λόγος, *lógos*) is dependent on perception (Lucr. 4,724ff.) — and E.'s atomistic world vision. Sensory perception arises from the influx of clear images (Epist. Hdt. 46), in which the continuity and passivity of the recipient ensure reliability (Diog. Laert. 10,31) [14]. For that reason and because they cannot contradict each other (Lucr. 4,379–386), all perceptions are of equal value (KD 23). All perceptions have to be regarded as true (KD 24). It is not perception but erroneous inferences of reason that are responsible for irritations (Epist. Hdt. 50f.). Sensory perceptions are accompanied by pleasurable or unpleasurable sensations. These can provide a criterion for a positive or negative assessment (Diog. Laert. 10,31–34). Although judgements of proper or improper behaviour belong to the realm of ethics (cf. Epist. Men. 129), with sensations it is a matter of criteria of truth, in so far as sensations are understood as external affections (Epist. Hdt. 52f.) [15]. The criterion of 'preliminary notion' or 'anticipation' (Diog. Laert. 10,33) helps assign sense-perceptions to universal precepts. A *prólēpsis* is a general impression formed by the repeated influence of external images in sensory or non-sensory perception. The *prólēpsis* is a yardstick for measuring something particular or behavioural patterns. Whatever conforms to the *prólēpsis* of justice has to be held to be just (KD 37). Together with perceptions, language is a source of preliminary notions. Words are accompanied by an immediately apparent impression that is essentially bound up with the words' meaning (Diog. Laert. 10,33). On hearing a word, the general impression evidently takes shape, and an unchecked conventionalism should certainly be avoided so that colloquial words do not lead to false impressions (cf. Epicurus De natura 28 fr. 8 col. V 2–3 SEDLEY).

Although truth is dependent on perception, there can be understanding, according to E., even where observation is obscured or impossible. These hypothetical statements about an object await verification (Epist. Hdt. 38) through evidentiary confirmation (ἐπιμαρτύρησις, *epimartýrēsis*). Concerning things which are in principle unobservable (ἄδηλα, *ádēla*) — e.g. atoms and the void — scrutiny of truthfulness is possible indirectly through the process of counterclaim (ἀντιμαρτύρησις, *antimartýrēsis*) or non-counter-claim (οὐκ ἀντιμαρτύρησις). A thesis is thus true if its reciprocal opposite leads to evident contradictions with phenomena in the observable domain. In this way, several explanations of phenomena can validly stand alongside one another (Epist. Hdt. 80), especially in the realm of celestial phenomena, *metéōra* (Epist. Pyth. 96).

3. Physics

The teaching of natural science (φυσιολογία, *physiología*). By explaining unknown natural events E. wanted to remove mankind's fear of death, god and unnerving phenomena and thereby bring about peace of mind and happiness. The teaching of natural science uses the canonics and gives support to ethics. E.'s masterpiece *De natura*, however, also reveals a demanding treatment of physical problems just for their own sake. Principles of his natural science theory are: the Being understood as corporeal and the void (κενόν, *kenón*) as an extended space. The basic law is that nothing comes from nothing, nothing disappears to nothing (Epist. Hdt. 38,8ff.) and the universe is unchanging. E. justifies the first two statements with a reference to empirical experience. All things thus develop from appropriate causes. The proposition on the constancy of the 'universe', which cannot change because there is nothing that could ensure such a change from outside follows from the first two statements (Epist. Hdt. 39). The universe is composed of two building blocks: the physically indivisible 'bodies' or matter (ἄτομοι φύσεις; *átomoi phýseis*, *corpora individua*) and 'empty space' (Epist. Hdt. 39). Motion demonstrates the necessity of the vacuum (Epist. Hdt. 39f.).

Matter exists in the form of immutable atoms or as atomic compounds (Epist. Hdt. 40). What does not have an independent existence is to be regarded as a quality of some body: either as essential qualities (συμβεβηκότα, *symbebēkóta*) such as form, weight and size (Epist. Hdt. 54) or as casual attributes (συμπτώματα, *symptṓmata*) such as freedom or poverty (Lucr. 1,445ff.). Atoms are indivisible, imperishable and immutable. As the universe has no limits, the void and the number of atoms are infinitely large (Epist. Hdt. 41). Atoms have an unimaginable variety of forms and this explains multiplicity of differences in atomic compounds. The number of forms, on the other hand, is not unlimited (Epist. Hdt. 42), otherwise the size of atoms would be unlimited (Epist. Hdt. 55f.). The basis for this thesis is E.'s teaching on atomic parts, the *minima*, which deserves to be seen as an innovation on the work of his predecessors (Epist. Hdt. 55ff.; Lucr. 1,599–634). Atoms are not physically divisible but may be mathematically divisible — though not infinitely (Epist. Hdt. 57). Therefore there exist the smallest *minima*, even if theoretically not divisible any further.

The thesis of *minima* is also important for E.'s teaching on motion. All atoms are subject to a constant, parallel movement downwards, caused by their weight (Epist. Hdt. 61). The velocity of the atoms is unimaginably high — 'as quick as a flash' (Epist. Hdt. 61) [16]. It is the same for all atoms because in empty space there is no resistance to their movement (Epist. Hdt. 61). This gives rise to the problematic question of how atomic compounds can arise, given their parallel motion. By way of explanation E. assumes a spontaneous, not-externally caused deviation of the atoms during their descent (*clinamen*; παρέγκλισις/*parénklisis*). Admittedly this teaching is found only in → Lucretius (2,216–250) and Diogenes of Oenoanda (fr. 54 III 6 Smith) but it was attributed, probably rightly so, to E. himself. As only a minimal deviation is involved, the impression of strict regularity in the realms of sensory perceptions is maintained. This atomic deviation, however, helps avoid strict determinism and provides scope for spontaneity (Lucr. 2,244ff.), and that is why it plays a part in discussion of free will in an atomic system.

4. Cosmology

Cosmology aims to help mankind to happiness through enlightenment (KD 20). By cosmos E. understands a self-contained part of heaven encompassing the stars, the earth and all phenomena (Epist. Pyth. 88). E. proceeds on the assumption of a multiplicity of worlds (Epist. Hdt. 45). As he believes all phenomena to be caused by mechanical processes, he rejects a teleological world view (cf. Lucr. 5,419ff.); in his opinion the world is instead the result of random atomic collisions. Its creation was completed from the first clash of atoms, including living creatures, each of whose survival is important for their further development, on an atomic foundation (Lucr. 5,837ff.). Nature and reason (Epist. Hdt. 75f.), not the gods, play a role in this process. With celestial phenomena (meteorology) final verifiability is not possible, and that is why E. accepts several explanations for the same phenomenon, provided none of them contradicts the phenomenon in any way. Being aware of the existence of explanations promotes a feeling of security and contributes to a happy life.

5. Psychology

E.'s psychology aims at removing the fear of death that is, in his view, responsible for moral misconduct (KD 7; Lucr. 3,59ff.). Therefore it is important to demonstrate that death does not represent any threat to mankind (KD II), because it is a state of being without sensation and thus unimportant to mankind. 'While we are there, death is not present, and when death is present, we are no longer there' (Epist. Men. 125). The soul is born with the body and disappears with it (Lucr. 3,417–829). It is a delicately structured, bodily feature that is assigned to the body and connected to it. It is the origin of affectivity, movement and thought (Epist. Hdt. 63).

6. THEOLOGY

E.'s theology was designed to protect mankind from fear of the gods. The gods exist eternally and blissfully (Epist. Men. 123f.) in a realm that in later sources is termed 'intermediate world' (Lucr. 3,18ff.). They are inaccessible to human influence through, for example, sacrifice and prayer (KD 1); there is instead direct evidence of their existence. The existence of immortal beings is problematic in an atomic world vision. The sources do not agree in their pronouncements (schol. KD I; Cic. Nat. D. 1,49) and so far no generally accepted explanation has been found [17; 18]. The striving for divine alignment, so important for Platonism, plays a part in Epicureanism as well (Epist. Men. 135). It is the lack of any temporal limit that distinguishes gods from humans. The gods offer a model that is worth emulating, with the help of therapeutic philosophy that liberates mankind from pain and anguish of soul. For that reason the gods deserve veneration (Epist. Men. 123), although the process is more important for human well-being (cf. Gnom. Vat. 32).

7. ETHICS

E. represents a hedonistic standpoint in ethics. The goal of all activity is *eudaimonia*. In practice E. sees the greatest good in pleasure (ἡδονή, *hēdonḗ*), the greatest evil in pain. All activities should be measured in terms of pleasure. Pleasure comes as freedom from bodily pain (ἀπονία, *aponía*) and freedom from mental confusion (ἀταραξία, *ataraxía*) (Epist. Men. 128). As a happy sensation accompanies the absence of pain (Cic. Fin. 1,37), it is questionable whether it is justified to criticize a supposedly entirely negative definition of the greatest good. Because of the close connection between removal of pain and the corresponding pleasure there is no neutral position. By nature mankind strives for pleasure as something good and avoids pain as an evil. That is also supported by the so-called 'cradle-argument', reported by Cicero (Fin. 1,30), that refers to the pleasure-seeking of the young child. The proposition does not appear in E.'s extant writings but can be assigned to him [19]. Even before E. the role of pleasure in human life was discussed amongst the Sophists, by Democritus, Plato and Aristotle; E.'s position should therefore be seen against the background of long dispute. Take also → Eudoxus of Cnidus or → Aristippus and the Cyrenaics, who assign a central role to pleasure. They do not, however, see pleasure and pain as mutually exclusive but concede transitional states and an almost neutral, intermediate condition of being free of needs [20].

E. distinguishes between (Cic. Fin. 2,31–32; cf. 2,9–10) a 'pleasure in motion' (ἐν κινήσει; *en kinḗsei*) and a 'static' or 'katastematic' pleasure (καταστηματικὴ ἡδονή; *katastematikè hēdonḗ*) (Diog. Laert. 10,138), which is to be regarded as the greatest good. Katastematic pleasure means freedom from bodily pain and disquiet of the soul, a condition that cannot be heightened, only varied. Kinetic pleasure is the sensation accompanying the removal of pain and the satisfaction of a need. This definition of the greatest good earned E. criticism for being negative, but from one passage in Cicero (Fin. 1,37) it emerges that the state of pleasure being striven for was not in any way solely negative. A happy sensation is thus associated with the absence of pain [21]. The sources offer no explanation of hedonism on an atomistic basis; desire is described as an accident (Sext. Emp. Adv. math. 10,225). Although every pleasure is good in itself, one need not choose every pleasure. Sometimes a pleasure has an evil consequence, so a lesser evil should not be accepted for the sake of a greater pleasure. Thus a sober assessment (pleasure calculation) is necessary : it helps discover which wishes should be fulfilled so as to achieve the happiness being targeted. E. analyses desires (Epist. Men. 127) and shows that pain and aversion arise only if natural and necessary desires remain unsatisfied. For this, however, Nature keeps everything in readiness (Epist. Men. 130). It is therefore fitting to be grateful to Nature (fr. 469 USENER). A prerequisite for avoiding pain and aversion is the free choice of desires. By pointing to empirical method and a preliminary notion of 'free choice', Epicurus therefore puts the case for the possibility of free choice even in an atomist context. Free choices are possible through one's condition at birth, through the environment and in particular so-called 'acquired characteristics' or 'creations' (ἀπογεγεννημένα, *apogegennēména*) that are responsible for a person's mental autonomy ([22]; but cf. also [23. 123ff.]).

E.'s postulation of a rational consideration of needs and his rejection of excess lead to a modification or reassessment of conventional values such as the virtues (ἀρεταί, *aretaí*) or a change in status from purpose to means. Virtue, however, helps us on the road to happiness (Diog. Laert. 10,38). Pleasurable living cannot be separated from a morally good life (Epist. Men. 132). Above all friendship is linked to the goal of (*télos*) pleasure (KD 27). Friendship and generally virtuous living match the need for security (KD 17). Overrating of virtue is the consequence of a warping caused by cultural conventions. Crime has an unsettling effect because of the constant fear of discovery (KD 31–35).

E. offers practical guidance for a proper lifestyle. The wise man leads a godlike existence among men (Epist. Men. 135), if he is no longer dependent on external circumstances. He will no longer fall victim to chance if he acts rationally and knows how to appreciate fate and providence properly (KD 16). E. and his successors give hints on daily life in the state and the community [23]. Extant are comments on marriage and instructions on how to behave at a symposium or how to treat slaves (Diog. Laert. 10,117–120). E. urges political commitment only if necessary (Sen. De otio 3,2); this does not mean, however, a 'life in solitude'. As an appropriate surrounding is necessary for individual happiness, political commitment on the part of an Epicurean does not imply any inconsistency with his teaching [24]. Even here, then, the calculation of pleasure comes into play: occasional political activity is justified because it can assure security, and so create something good.

D. Later influence

Hints and efforts by E., and later Epicureans in particular, to give guidance, under religious, cultural or political headings, for appropriate behaviour in society and a new cultural milieu can be explained as a consequence of philosophical infighting with rival schools and also the striving for security and peace of mind. This may also be a reason for the school's having such a long tradition in antiquity ([25] and [26], overview also in [3. 188ff., 477ff.]). Epicureanism remained a presence until the time of Augustine, even if mainly as a target for predominantly Christian authors, for whom E., as herald of *homo carnalis* and especially for his rejection of providence and the immortality of the soul, was regarded as the heretic *par excellence* [27]. A dual image was registered in the Middle Ages: together with the condemnation as heretic emanating from Christian polemics, there was the accompanying attempt to credit E. historically as an ethical personality in his own right. Of significance in the modern age are the great humanists Stephanus, Scaliger, Casaubon, Lipsius, and the attempt by the Franciscan Pierre Gassendi around the middle of the 17th cent. to harmonize E.'s teaching with Christian thinking. In France in the 17th and 18th cents. Pierre Bayle's article on E. in the *Dictionnaire historique et critique* tried to gain a positive reception for Epicurean attitudes. E. encountered resistance, however, as displayed in the widely circulated and influential poem of Cardinal Polignac *Anti-Lucretius, sive de Deo et Natura* (1747). Kant found the theoretical part of E.'s teaching noteworthy but took a rather sceptical view of the practical part. Hegel criticized the apparently rigid dogmatism of the Epicurean School but after Hegel attempts were made to rehabilitate hedonism, partly with reference to E. (Fechner; Feuerbach; Marx).

→ Epicureanism

1 K. Alpers, Epikurs Geburtstag, in: MH 25, 1968, 48–51 2 Epicuro. Opere, ed. G. Arrighetti, [2]1973 3 M. Erler, Epikur — Die Schule Epikurs — Lukrez, in: GGPh[2], vol. 4, 1994, 29–490 4 H. Usener, Epicurea, 1887, repr. 1966 5 M. F. Smith (ed.), Diogenes of Oinoanda. The Epicurean Inscription, 1993 6 B. Frischer, The sculpted word. Epicureanism and philosophical recruitment in ancient Greece, 1982 7 M. Gigante, 'Philosophia medicans' in Filodemo, in: CE 5, 1975, 53–61 8 Id., Scetticismo e Epicureismo, 1981 9 M. Erler, Philologia medicans. Wie die Epikureer die Texte des Meisters lasen, in: W. Kullmann, J. Althoff (ed.), Vermittlung und Tradierung von Wissen in der griech. Kultur, 1993, 281–303 10 D. Sedley, Philosophical allegiance in the Greco-Roman World, in: J. Barnes, M. Griffin (ed.), Philosophia Togata. Essays on Philosophy and Roman Society, 1989, 97–119 11 M. Erler, Orthodoxie und Anpassung. Philodem, ein Panaitios des Kepos?, in: MH 49, 1992, 5–23 12 G. Striker, Κριτήριον τῆς ἀληθείας, in: Id., Essays on Hellenistic Epistemology and Ethics, 1996, 22–76 13 E. Asmis, Epicurus' Scientific Method, 1984 14 C. C. W. Taylor, All perceptions are true, in: M. Schofield, M. F. Burnyeat, J. Barnes (ed.), Doubt and Dogmatism. Studies in Hellenistic Epistemology, 1980, 105–124 15 A. Manuwald, Die Prolepsislehre Epikurs, 1972 16 A. Laks, Minima und noematische Geschwindigkeit, in: E. Rudolph (ed.), Zeit, Bewegung, Handlung. Studien zur Zeitabhandlung des Aristoteles, 1988, 129–143 17 D. Lemke, Die Theologie Epikurs, 1973 18 J. Mansfeld, Aspects of Epicurean theology, in: Mnemosyne 46, 1993, 172–210 19 J. Brunschwig, The Cradle Argument in Epicureanism and Stoicism, in: M. Schofield, G. Striker (ed.), The Norms of Nature, 1986, 113–144 20 K. Döring, Der Sokratesschüler Aristipp und die Kyrenaiker (AAWM 1988, 1) 21 J. S. Purinton, Epicurus on the Telos, in: Phronesis 38, 1993, 281–320 22 D. Sedley, Epicurus' Refutation of Determinism, in: Syzetesis. FS M. Gigante, vol. I, 1983, 11–51 23 J. Annas, Hellenistic Philosophy of Mind, 1992 24 A. A. Long, Pleasure and Social Utility — The Virtues of Being Epicurean, in: H. Flashar, O. Gigon (ed.), Aspects de la Philos. Hellénistique (Entretiens XXXII), 1986, 283ff. 25 H.-J. Krämer, E. und die hedonistische Tradition, in: Gymnasium 87, 1980, 294–326 26 H. Jones, The Epicurean Tradition, 1992 27 W. Schmid, s.v. E., RAC 5, 681–819 (now in: W. Schmid, Ausgewählte philologische Schriften, 1984, 151–266).

Editions: Epicuro. Opere, ed. G. Arrighetti, [2]1973; C. Bailey, Epicurus. The Extant Remains, 1926 (repr. 1975); J. Bollack, A. Laks, Epicure a Pythoclès. Sur la cosmologie et les phénoménes météorologiques, 1978; P. von der Mühll (ed.), Epistulae tres et ratae sententiae, 1922 (repr. 1966); H. Usener, Epicurea, 1887 (repr. 1966).

Bibliography: C. Bailey, The Greek Atomists and Epicurus,1928 (repr. 1964); E. Bignone, L'Aristotele perduto e la formazione filosofica di Epicuro, 1936, [2]1973; C. Diano, Scritti epicurei, 1974; W. Englert, Epicurus on the Swerve and Voluntary Action, 1987; A. J. Festugière, Epicure et ses dieux, [2]1968; D. J. Furley, Two Studies in the Greek Atomists, 1967; Id., Nothing to us?, in: M. Schofield, G. Striker (ed.), The Norms of Nature, 1986, 75–91; J. C. B. Gosling, C. C. W. Taylor, The Greeks on Pleasure, 1982; M. Hossenfelder, Epicure: hédoniste malgré lui, in: M. Schofield, G. Striker (ed.), The Norms of Nature, 1986, 245–263; Id., Epikur, 1991; F. Jürss, Die Epikureische Erkenntnistheorie, 1991; K. Kleve, Gnosis Theon. Die Lehre von der natürlichen Gotteserkenntnis in der Epikureischen Theologie (Symbolae Osloenses, Suppl. 19), 1963; H. J. Krämer, Platonismus und hell. Philos., 1971; Ph. Merlan, Studies in Epicurus and Aristotle, 1960; P. Mitsis, Epicurus' Ethical Theory. The Pleasures of Invulnerability, 1988; R. Müller, Die epikureische Ethik, 1991; D. Obbink, The Atheism of Epicurus, in: GRBS 30, 1989, 187–223; R. Philippson, Studien zu Epikur und den Epikureern, 1983; J. M. Rist, Epicurus. An introduction, 1972; J. Schmid, Götter und Menschen in der Theologie Epikurs, in: RhM 94, 1951, 97–156. M.ER.

Epicydes (Ἐπικύδης; *Epikýdēs*).

[1] Son of Euphemides of Athens. In 480 BC, he ran for the office of *strategos* but → Themistocles supposedly bribed him into withdrawing his candidacy (Plut. Themist. 6; Mor. 185A). E.S.-H.

[2] Brother of Hippocrates, grandson of Arcesilaus, a Syracusian exile in Carthage. E. grew up in Carthage as the son of a Carthaginian woman (Pol. 7,2; Liv. 24,6;

Iust. 22,8). He was a confidant of Hannibal and, in 214 BC, achieved the Carthaginian-Syracusian alliance with → Hieronymus, for whom he became advisor and general. In 213, he prevented a possible re-emergence of a pro-Roman line in Syracuse in the midst of the turmoil following the assassination of the king, and secured his position of power with the aid of Cretan mercenaries and others (Pol. 7,4–5; Liv. 24,29–33). During the Roman conquest of Syracuse, he fled to Acragas in 212, and after its fall in 211, to North Africa (Liv. 25,24; 27; 26,40) [1. 354–356, 367–370].

1 Huss. L.-M.G.

Epicydias (Ἐπικυδίδας; *Epikydídas*). Spartiate, who, in 394 BC, delivered to King Agesilaus the order of the Ephoroi to return to Sparta from Asia Minor (Xen. Hell. 4,2,2; Plut. Agesilaus 15,2). He was probably a troop commander in the battle of Aigospotamoi (405) for which he was honoured in Delphi with a memorial (Paus. 10,9,10, although the name was transmitted in a corrupt form). He fell in 378 in Boeotia under Agesilaus (Xen. Hell. 5,4,39). He is probably not identical with a troop commander of the same name mentioned in Thuc. 5,12f. M.MEI.

Epidamnos see → Dyrrhachium

Epidaurum (Plin. HN 3,143f. *Epidaurum*; Ptol. 2,16,5 *Epidaurus*). Important urban settlement with two harbours on a peninsula in the province of Dalmatia, today Cavtat in Croatia (< *civitas*; Italian Ragusa vecchia). Originally probably a Hellenistic settlement (there is no clear archaeological evidence), it was romanized in the course of the 1st cent. BC, served as *praesidium* in the conflict with Pompey Caesar, and was unsuccessfully besieged by Pompey (Bell. Alex. 44,5). Roman *colonia* (probably imperial, *tribus Tromentina*). *Epitaur(o)* is mentioned as *origo* in a military diploma (CIL XIV 14, table 2, AD 71. *Auxilia* were stationed in E.: in the 1st cent. AD, the *cohors VI* and *VIII voluntariorum c(ivium) R(omanorum)* (CIL III 1742f.; [1] 636). E. was a centre of oriental religion (two Mithraea), it also had a ruler cult. Documented as a diocese in AD 533 at the provincial synod of Salona. In *c.* AD 600, the residents of E. fled from the invading Slavs and Avars to Ragusium (= Dubrovnik: *Epitaurum id est Ragusium*, Geogr. Rav. 4,16).

1 A. Šašel, J. Šašel (ed.), Inscriptiones Latinae Jugoslaviae, 1986.

G. Novak, Quaestiones Epidauritanae, in: Rad JAZU 339, 1965, 97–140; Arheološka istraživanja u Dubrovniku i dubrovačkom području (Archeological Researches in Dubrovnik and Its Surroundings) (Izdanja Hrvatskog arheološkog društva 12), 1988. M.Š.K.

Epidaurus (Ἐπίδαυρος; *Epídauros*).
A. Location B. History C. Sanctuary of Asclepius

A. Location

City in the Argolic Acte on the southern coast of the Saronic Gulf. The city's large territory extended to the Argolic Gulf, with a good land-connection to the Argolic plain. The ancient city was located on a bay with a shallow beach and a small coastal plain, situated on a rocky hill that protruded into the bay with two peaks (Nisi) near modern Palaia-Epidavros. We have only superficial knowledge of the topography of ancient E.

B. History

E. is mentioned already in Hom. Il. 2,561. The city was a member of the Amphictyony of Calaurea (Str. 8,6,14). In the 7th/6th cents. BC it was ruled by the tyrant Procles (Hdt. 3,50–52; Paus. 2,28,8). E. participated in the fight against the Persians with its army and its fleet. In 459/8, E. suffered a defeat against Athens at Cecryphaleia (Thuc. 1,105,1; Diod. Sic. 11,78,1f.). During and after the Peloponnesian War, E. was on the side of Sparta, even after the battle at Leuctra in 371 BC. It participated in the Lamian War in 323/2 BC (Diod. Sic. 18,11,2). In 243, E. joined the Achaean Confederacy (Plut. Aratus 24,3; Paus. 2,8,5; StV 3, 489). A list of casualties for the battle on the Isthmus of 146 BC is extant (IG IV 1^2, 28). In AD 395, the Goths destroyed the sanctuary. In the mid 5th cent. AD, the old cult was given up as a result of the spread of Christianity.

C. Sanctuary of Asclepius

C. 10 KM South of E., a wide basin is home to the sanctuary of Asclepius. The cult began in the sanctuary of Maleatas — later identified with Apollo — on the slope of Mt. Cynortium in the 7th cent. BC, possibly even earlier (discovery of a cult site, Late Helladic I-II) [1; 2], and in the sanctuary itself, in the 6th cent. BC; both Apollo and Asclepius were the proprietors of the sanctuary. Esp. in the 4th cent. BC, the sanctuary was built up in a magnificent way but was then plundered by Sulla (Plut. Sulla 12,3), also by pirates (Plut. Pompey 24,5). In *c.* AD 163, E. enjoyed the rich patronage of the senator Sex. Iulius Maior Antoninus Pythorus from Nysa (Paus. 2,27,6f.) and received several new buildings. Statues of Roman emperors reach into the period of the Severi and into that of Gordianus. A Christian basilica of the 4th cent. AD is located in the northern part of the precinct. The main entry to the sanctuary from the direction of the city is in the north (Northern Propylaea). The centre of the sanctuary is the Doric peripteral temple (*c.* 380–375 BC) with the cult statue of enthroned Asclepius in gold-ivory by Thrasymedes of Paros (Paus. 2,27,2) [3], and behind it, the tholos ('thymele') by the younger Polyclitus [4], which is one of the most richly appointed cult buildings of the classical period, situated above a base made of walls arranged in concentric circles that are separated by pas-

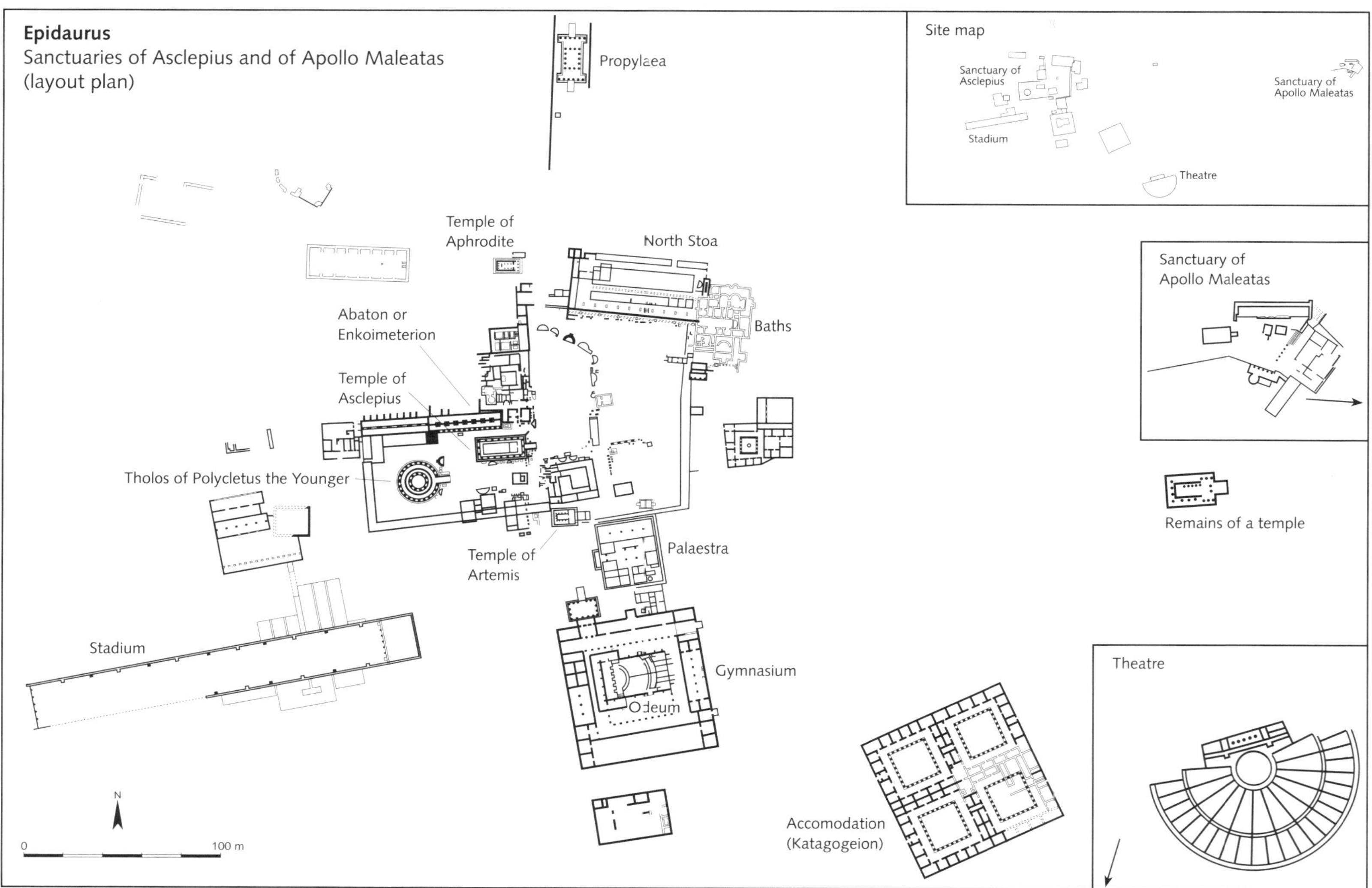
Epidaurus
Sanctuaries of Asclepius and of Apollo Maleatas
(layout plan)
Propylaea
Site map
Sanctuary of Asclepius
Stadium
Sanctuary of Apollo Maleatas
Theatre
Temple of Aphrodite
North Stoa
Baths
Abaton or Enkoimeterion
Temple of Asclepius
Tholos of Polycletus the Younger
Temple of Artemis
Palaestra
Sanctuary of Apollo Maleatas
Remains of a temple
Stadium
Gymnasium
Odeum
Theatre
Accomodation (Katagogeion)
N
0
100 m

sageways (the exact function is still in question). Several temples, esp. that of Artemis (E. of the 4th cent. BC), Themis, Aphrodite [5. 171–175], and of the 'Egyptian gods', also belong to the sanctuary complex as well as large buildings for the housing and treatment of individuals in search of cures and for other visitors. Furthermore, there were buildings for the contests of the main festival (*Asklepíeia*), whose development is linked to the spread of the cult of Asclepius [6]. There is also a gymnasium, a palaestra, a stadium [7], and an early Hellenistic theatre (2nd half of the 4th cent. BC) [8; 9], several thermal baths, auxiliary buildings, and a large number of altars and works of art. The ailing visitors searched for cures in dream-oracles which they received while sleeping in a two-part porticus (*enkoimētérion* or *ábaton*). The priests documented reports of miracle healing on large, partially preserved slabs (IG IV 1², 121–127). Some healing rites also involved the use of water [10]. Sources: Scyl. 50,54; Str. 8,6,15; Paus. 2,26–29,1 [11. 298–307]; Liv. 45,28,3. Inscriptions: IG IV 1². Coins: HN², 418; 441f.

→ Medicine; → Oracles

1 V. Lambrinoudakis, in: Praktika 140, 1984 (1988), 229–232; 142, 1987 (1991), 52–65; 143, 1988 (1991), 21–29; 144, 1989 (1992), 43–56 (excavation report) 2 V. Ch. Petrakos, in: Ergon 37, 1990 (1991), 11–21; 38, 1991 (1992), 11–23; 39, 1992 (1993), 8–20 (excavation report) 3 N. Yalouris, Die Skulpturen des Asklepiostempels von E., in: Arch. und klass. griech. Plastik. Akten des intern. Kolloquiums (22.–25.4.1985) in Athen, 1986, 175–186 4 H. Büsing, Zur Bauplanung der Tholos von E., in: MDAI(A) 102, 1987, 225–258 5 V. Pirenne-Delforge, L'Aphrodite grecque, 1994 6 M. Sève, Les concours d'E., in: REG 106, 1993, 303–328 7 R. Patrucco, Lo stadio di E., 1976 8 A. von Gerkkan, W. Müller-Wiener, Das Theater von E., 1961 9 L. Käppel, Das Theater von E., in: JDAI 104, 1989, 83–106 10 V. Lambrinoudakis, L'eau médicale à E., in: R. Ginouvès et al. (ed.), L'eau, la santé et la maladie dans le monde grec, 1994, 225–236 11 D. Musti, M. Torelli, Pausania. Guida della Grecia. II. La Corinzia e l'Argolide, 1986.

A. M. Burford, The Greek Temple Builders at E., 1969; M. Massa, s.v. E., EAA², 469–473; N. Pharaklas, Ἐπιδαυρία [Epidauría], 1972; G. Roux, L'architecture de l'Argolide aux IVᵉ et IIIᵉ siècles av. J.-C., 1961; R. Tomlinson, E., 1983; N. Yalouris, s.v. E., PE, 311–314.

Y.L.

Epideictic poetry This poetic genre corresponded to epideictic prose (→ epideixis). Above all, its aim was to praise or reprimand (thus the definitions in Aristot. Rh. 1358b12ff. and Menander Rhetor, 331f. Russel-Wilson) and it served primarily to display (ἐπιδείκνυσθαι; *epideíknysthai*) the author's δεινότης (*deinótēs*) in a public lecture (ἐπίδειξις; *epídeixis*). There is no documentation of epideictic poetry (EP) as an independent genre until the Hellenistic period. The public performance was almost always the origin of Greek lyric and classical poetry and its primary vehicle for circulation, which resulted from the fact that poetry was communicated orally: at least in the classical period, *epideíknysthai* often denotes this public performance of EP and of dramatic works (e.g. Pl. La. 183a; Leg. 658b; Aristoph. Ran. 771–776). The archaic poets show a distinct tendency to polarize their opinion into the alternative possibilities of praise (ἔπαινος; *épainos*) or reprimand (ψόγος; *psógos*), (e.g. Tyrtaeus fr. 6f. Gentil-Prado). Thus, the decision for one of the two becomes a characteristic element of lyric poetry. Already in Pindar we find a theoretical treatment of the dichotomy between praise and reprimand, esp. in P. 2,54ff.. Later, Aristotle (Poet. 1448b24–27) even made a plausible case for the idea that Attic tragedy and comedy were derived from this dichotomy (cf. [4] and [7]).

Along with the emergence of the written tradition in the 4th and 3rd cents. BC, poetry increasingly evolved into occasional literature, though it continued to aim at the short-lived purpose of *epideíxeis* for specific occasions and agonal events with their specific audience. It is often improvised and designed for a single performance in front of a crowd. The artfulness and the special qualities of the poets (child prodigies, female poets, impromptu poets), who often present their works in person, are noted much more often than content and aesthetic quality (inscription records in [6] and [9]; cf. Late Helladic 194–198 and 230). These poets, who are often professional wandering minstrels and could be regarded as descendants of the Homeric rhapsodes, practice highly diverse kinds of poetry (even theatre), but hardly find recognition in 'high' literature, which is usually geared towards written dissemination. There, the only kind of poetry that preserves the (real or fictitious) character of pointed occasional poetry is the → epigram, which came in a special, epideictic form (cf. above all the 'epideictic' epigrams in Anth. Pal. 9). As far as encomiastic occasional poetry is concerned, we must mention Theoc. 16 and 17. However, the *Argonautica* by → Apollonius [2] Rhodius supposedly underwent a public *epídeixis* as well (cf. Vitae a, b: schol. Apoll. Rhod. S. 1f. Wendel), and one can perhaps also find indications of a performance within a competition in Theoc. 24,171f.. The content of epideictic presentations in the theatre is not certain (we can at least expect adoptions from the 'classical' authors, perhaps also in the form of anthologies, cf. [2]).

The element of praise seems to have been the central interest in works of lyric and epideictic occasional poetry as early as the Hellenistic period (several of the preserved lyric texts about gods and deified political personalities can be found in CollAlex 132ff.). We must consider, however, that our principal sources (that is, essentially inscriptions which document *epideíxeis* of public importance, and historians) may only allow limited insights (cf. EpGr 618), since the speciality of ἐγκώμιον ἐπικόν (*enkṓmion epikón*) appears less often in the winner lists of poetic agons than the competition in ποίημα ἐπικόν (; *poíēma epikón*; traditional mythological epics). For the imperial period, the specialization on praise is certain: In the agons of the Muses at Thespiai, for instance, the Hellenistic competition of epic poets (ἐπῶν ποιηταί; *epôn poiētaí*) is no longer listed; instead, the two competitions appear in the groups 'poem to the Muses' (ποίημα εἰς τὰς Μούσας; *poíēma eís tàs Moúsas*) and 'poem to the emperor' (ποίημα εἰς τὸν αὐτοκράτορα; *poíēma eis tòn autokrátora*). The strong specialization on the encomium (or the invective) represents a parallel development to the epideictic prose that flourished in the Second Sophistic, as is clearly indicated by the occasional poetry of a series of wandering and court poets from the 4th and 5th cents. AD (mostly from Egypt): cf. [1; 2]; papyrus fragments in GDR I Heitsch (PBerol. 5003: Olympiodorus?; and PGr. VIN. 29788: Pamprepius ed. E. Livrea, 1978 and 1979), furthermore, PAnt. III 115 (cf. [3]).

1 G.M. Browne, Harpocration Panegyrista, in: Illinois Classical Studies 2, 1977, 184–196 2 A. Cameron, Wandering Poets: A Literary Movement in Byzantine Egypt, in: Historia 14, 1965, 470–509 3 A. Cameron, Pap. Ant. III. 115, in: CQ 20, 1970, 119–129. 4 B. Gentili, Theatrical Performances in the Ancient World, 1979 5 Id., Poesia e pubblico nella Grecia antica, [2]1989 6 M. Guarducci, Poeti vaganti e conferenzieri dell'età ellenistica, in: Memorie della Classe di Scienze morali e storiche dell' Acc. dei Lincei, S. VI, 2, 1929, 629–655 7 A. Hardie, Statius and the Silvae, 1983, 15–36, 73–102 8 G.W. Most, The Measures of Praise: Structure and Function in Pindar's Second Pythian and Seventh Nemean Odes, 1985 9 M. Pallone, L'epica agonale in età ellenistica, in: Orpheus 5, 1984, 156–166. M.FA.

Epideixis (ἐπίδειξις; *epídeixis*). One of the three → *genera causarum*. Aristotle determined the *epideixis* as the type of a speech that does not elicit the listener's judgement or decision, but simply places him into the role of spectator (*theōrós*): the speech itself is what is being tested (Rh. 1358b). It is not a necessary, but a plausible consequence that the function of directing the attention towards the speech itself is supported by certain topics, that is, topics of praise or reprimand, thus giving preference to mimetic texts over political and legal speeches. This Aristotelian limitation of a speech's function to certain subject matters was criticized in antiquity: Cicero (De or. 2,43ff.) disputes the equivalence of the third *genus* which is limited to *demonstratio* (Rhet. Her. 1,2) Quintilian (Inst. 3,4,13) foregrounds the primary function of *epideixis* in the Greek term by translating it with *ostentatio*. The alternating focus on function versus subject matter is responsible for the history of *epideixis*: as a speech for show, *epideixis* plays an important role for the development of rhetoric into a profession, in the public arena as well as in training (cf. Cic. Orat. 42; → *declamationes*). This development begins with the early sophistic rhetoric [1] and gains paramount importance in the non-decisive rhetoric of the courts during the Hellenistic and Roman imperial periods. It characterizes the discipline of rhetoric from Renaissance until the Baroque [5]. In theory and in practice, the art of *epideixis* focuses on the ornamentation of speech (→ *ornatus*) and strives for → *amplificatio* in the service of praise or reprimand [3. 208]: thus especially as rhetoric defined by *epideixis*, it becomes a theory for the production of mimetic texts and of poetry in general.

As the rhetorical 'genre' of *demonstratio*, *epideixis* leads to the formation of a 'philosophical' theory of praise [1. 84ff]: the *loci communes* of praise and reprimand allow a systematic self-assurance in evaluating the basis of fame. Correspondingly, the role of the listener for *epideixis* must be judged in a more differentiated way: in matters of content, *epideixis* especially concerns the acceptance and, if need be, the clever modification of a given consensus. The latter requires a sufficiently mobile public (→ Gorgias), the former applies primarily to wandering and court rhetors. In this context, we can find elements of *epideixis* in numerous genres (→ Ekphrasis, → Hymn, → Panegyrics, reports of all types) [4], for poetic genres → Epideictic poetry.

1 V. Buchheit, Unt. zur Theorie des Genos E. von Gorgias bis Aristoteles, 1960 2 Lausberg, 129f. 3 J. Martin, Ant. Rhet., 1974, 177–210 4 K. Berger, Hell. Gattungen im NT, in: ANRW II 25.2, 1984, 1149–1281 5 S. Matuschek, s.v. E. Beredsamkeit, HWdR 2, 1258–1267. J.R.

Epidemic diseases

I. Prehistory and early history II. Greece III. Rome IV. Byzantium V. Causes and treatment

I. Prehistory and early history

Epidemic diseases (ED), or in the broadest sense, diseases that attack a large number of living beings simultaneously have been documented archaeologically since the middle of the Bronze Age, that is, since *c.* 2800 BC. Their appearance has been linked to population growth and the resulting ease with which disease can spread from animals to humans and from person to person [9. 251]. In Egypt, smallpox appears to have been known since *c.* 1250 BC, although papyri with medicinal content do not refer to this or any other comparable epidemic. The Bible, on the other hand, often addresses the fact that large populations were attacked by a variety of scourges, be it in Egypt, Assyria, or Palestine [12. 151–157]. To identify these with diseases known to us today has proved impossible.

II. Greece

A. Archaic and Homeric period B. Classical period

A. Archaic and Homeric period

Homer's *Iliad* begins with the outbreak of plague (1,8), and Hesiod, whose world was filled with spreading diseases, draws a connection between hunger and scourges as simultaneous phenomena (Op. 102,243). It is telling that both sources locate the cause of plague in the wrath of a god, a characteristic trait which distinguishes the attitude towards ED from that towards individual sickness throughout all of antiquity (cf. Soph. OT 22–30 and Thuc. Hist. 2,47).

B. Classical period

In 430 BC a devastating pestilence broke out in Athens that reached Potidaea and other regions (Thuc. 2,47–58) and flared up anew after a break (3,87). It is claimed to have originated in Ethiopia, Northern Africa, and in Persia, and to have reached as far as Italy. Thucydides as a person affected gives a detailed description of the social causes and effects of this pandemic, the first description to be transmitted. Still, a clear identification of the disease is difficult; possibly we are dealing with smallpox or an unknown viral disease. The Thucydidic description became the model for later descriptions of ED, for instance for the epidemic that befell the Carthaginians in front of Syracuse in 397 BC (Diod. Sic. 14,70–71), and for the later description of plague in Procop. (HA 2,22–23).

III. Rome

Livy reports frequent outbreaks of ED such as lues or plague in Republican Rome, although their spread seems to have been regionally limited and did not affect the entire Mediterranean area. In other cases, entire regions seem to have been afflicted, for instance during the bubonic plague, which spread through Egypt, Libya, and Syria in the early 1st cent., according to Oribasius (CMG 9,1,345). We may assume that the growth of the city of Rome as well as the expansion of the Roman Empire into areas that were home to different diseases contributed to the rise of new diseases which authors reported in the 1st cent. AD [10. 205]. The second pandemic, probably smallpox, was brought in from Persia during AD 165/6 by the armies of Lucius Verus and quickly spread throughout the empire. Heavy population losses are confirmed by Egyptian papyri [6. 120f.] and by Galen, who also reports the outbreak of other more locally restricted diseases such as anthrax. In the mid 3rd cent. AD, another severe strain of plague raged through Northern Africa, claiming large numbers of victims.

IV. Byzantium

Locally restricted outbreaks of ED were frequent and often occurred along with famines, as was the case in Edessa in the years of 499–502 [7. 3–7]. However, they are not easily identified in most cases, (this is also true for the 'yellow pestilence', which raged in Wales in the year 547 [5. 141–155]). In 541, a new pandemic of bubonic plague spread from Egypt across Syria and Constantinople over the entire Mediterranean area [1; 11. 73–94] and claimed countless victims in the country as well as in the large cities. Furthermore, this epidemic left a reservoir of infection in its wake which resulted in ever new flare-ups of the bubonic plague over the next two hundred years at least [2. 927–932]. In Syria, plague raged repeatedly between 542 and 610 with catastrophic consequences for agriculture [3. 51–58].

V. Causes and treatment

Divine punishment was universally regarded as the main cause of an epidemic [10. 235–256]. But doctors preferred models of explanation that had to do with bad air or pollution, although there was dispute over the way they supposedly materialized — through changes in weather, poisonous vapours, or poisonous insects. The → theory of contagion was known at least since Thucydides but it was hardly ever used to explain ED in human beings or animals.

Those who believed in the divine origin of epidemic outbreaks tried to prevent them with expiatory sacrifices, which included the ritual scapegoat [10. 257–281]. Others proposed flight or recommended staying out of swampy areas that were deemed unhealthy. Doctors advised dietetic caution, reduced air intake, or even called for more appropriate city planning. A few veterinarians allowed the slaughter of infected animals. Only few cities had sufficient means to offer public assistance during an epidemic. No single city was organized tightly enough to be able to carry out strict quarantines such as those implemented in the Middle Ages and in the Renaissance throughout Europe.

→ Infection (Contagion); → Malaria; → Medicine; →

1 P. Allen, The Justinianic plague, in: Byzantion 49, 1979, 5–20 2 J. N. Biraben, Les hommes et la peste, 1975 3 L. I. Conrad, Epidemic disease in central Syria in the late sixth Century, in: Bulletin of Modern Greek Studies 18, 1994, 12–58 4 Id., Die Pest und ihr soziales Umfeld im Nahen Osten des frühen MA., in: Der Islam 73, 1996, 81–112 5 J. Cule, Wales and Medicine, 1973 6 R. P. Duncan-Jones, The Impact of the Antonine Plague, in: Journ. of Roman Archaeology 9, 1996, 108–136 7 P. Garnsey, Famine and Food Supply in the Graeco-Roman World, 1988 8 M. D. Grmek, La dénomination latine des maladies considérées comme nouvelles par les auteurs antiques, in: MPalerne 10, 1991, 195–214 9 K. F. Kiple, The Cambridge World History of Human Disease, 1993 10 R. Parker, Miasma, 1983 11 E. Patlagean, Pauvreté économique et pauvreté sociale à Byzance, 1977 12 J. Preuss, Biblical and Talmudic Medicine, 1978.

M. D. Grmek, Les maladies à l'Aube de la Civilisation occidentale, 1983; H. Haeser, Lehrbuch der Gesch. der Medicin und der epidemischen Krankheiten, 1875–1882; R. Sallares, The Ecology of the Ancient Greek World, 1991; G. Sticker, Abh. aus der Seuchengeschichte und Seuchenlehre, 1910. V.N.

Epidikasia (ἐπιδικασία; *epidikasía*). In Athens, the legitimate natural sons of the testator or those adopted during his lifetime (→ *eispoíēsis*) could claim their inheritance through the simple act of → *embateúein*, but outside heirs needed an *epidikasia* decree from the archon to do so (→ Archontes [I]). This arrangement, similar to the granting of the Roman → *bonorum possessio*, authorised the applicant to come into the inheritance, but did not exclude the possibility of a later court decision regarding the right of succession of another pretender (→ *diadikasía*). Similarly, the → *epíclērus* (heiress) was subject to the *epidikasia* as well. *Epidikasia* referred to the request of the outside heir (verb: ἐπιδικάζεσθαι, *epidikázesthai*, medium) as well as to the archon's decree (ἐπιδικάζειν, *epidikázein*). The heir of a house was able to prevent the granting of the *epidikasia* through a → *diamartyría* — a formally effective testimonial — but he was obliged to pay the → *parakatabolḗ* (deposit). The applicant for the *epidikasia*, in turn, could cancel the effect of the *diamartyría* by means of charging his opponent with bearing false witness (→ *pseudomartyriôn díkē*), although he then risked the → *epobelía* (punishment for bringing malicious action).

H. J. Wolff, Die att. Paragraphe, 1966, 122f. G.T.

Epidius, M. (?) (the praenomen appears only in the index to Suet. Gram.), rhetor and teacher of rhetoric in Rome, publicly reprimanded for calumny (*calumnia*), (Suet. Gram. 28,1). M. Antonius and Augustus attended his school, possibly Vergil as well (Verg. vit. Ber., p. 44 Diehl) [2. 301]. He is assumed to be identical with a C.E. (Plin. HN 17,243) who wrote *commentarii* to the prodigies [1; 2]. The conjecture of his name in GL 1,387,6 is improbable.

1 J. Brzoska, s.v. E. (2), RE 6, 59 2 R. A. Kaster, C. Suetonius Tranquillus, De Grammaticis et Rhetoribus, 1995. MA.D.

Epidosis (ἐπίδοσις; *epídosis*). Voluntary tax requested by Greek states during special emergencies to supplement the revenue from regular taxes and contributions furnished through public office. In Athens, *epidóseis* are documented since the 4th cent. (see for example Dem. Or. 21,161); they were probably introduced by Eubulus. P.J.R.

Epieicidae (Ἐπιεικίδαι; *Epieikídai*). Attic *asty* or *mesogeia* deme of the phyle Cecropis. One → bouleutes. In the years 303/2 and 281/0 BC, E. was without council representative. The location is unknown. Trittys-affiliation uncertain [1. 135, 135[33]].

1 J. S. Traill, Demos and Trittys, 1986.

Traill, Attica 11, 20, 51, 62, 70, 110 no. 39, table 7; Whitehead, 266, 372, 379, 428. H.LO.

Epigamia (ἐπιγαμία; *epigamía*). In the Greek world, *epigamia* refers to the right of entering into a legal marriage with a person from a different state. It also granted legitimacy and citizenship to the children of such a marriage. It was possible to be granted this right in cases when such a marriage would not have been recognized according to the prevailing laws of the respective states. Examples can be found in international treaties (for instance between Aetolia and Acarnania: SIG³ 421; Messenia and Phigalia: SIG³ 472). *Epigamia* could also be one of the special rights granted to individual non-citizens as a state honour (e.g. in Kotyrta: IG V 1, 961).

The word *epigamia* is also used as a translation for the Latin → *conubium*. P.J.R.

Epigenes (Ἐπιγένης; *Epigénēs*).

[0] E. of → Sicyon. According to the Suda s. v. → Thespis (θ 282 = TrGF I 1 T 1), the first tragedian (6th cent. BC). The audience supposedly reacted to the lack of Dionysiac content in his plays with the proverbial exclamation οὐδὲν πρὸς τὸν Διόνυσον (*oudèn pròs tòn Diónyson*, 'But this has nothing to do with → Dionysus!'; TrGF I 1 T 18,3). Perhaps E.'s activity may be related to the τραγικοὶ χοροί (*tragikoì choroí*, 'tragic choruses') attested for Sicyon in Hdt. 5,67 [2. 21–23]. → Tragedy I

1 J. Leonhardt, Phalloslied und Dithyrambos, 1991 (testimonia) 2 B. Zimmermann, Europa und die griech. Trag., 2000. B. Z.

[1] Comedy writer; although Pollux [1. test. 2] regards him as one of the 'new' comedians, he must be dated before the middle of the 4th cent. BC [1. on fr. 6,4f.]. Eight fragments and five titles of plays are extant — Ἀργυρίου ἀφανισμός (also attributed to → Antiphanes), Βακχίς (? probably a courtesan-comedy), Ἡρωίνη, Μνημάτιον, Ποντικός (about traders or philosophy students from the Black Sea area).

1 PCG V, 1986, 165–169. B.BÄ.

[2] From Teos, *strategos* of Attalus I against the Galatians and Antiochus Hierax. He donated two votive offerings for Attalus. The latter honoured E. by erecting an equestrian statue in Delos (IPergamon 30; OGIS 280; IG XI 4,1109).

[3] Commander and functionary of Seleucus III and Antiochus III. He advised the latter to march — in person — against the usurper Molon. In an intrigue in the year 221, he was accused by the chancellor Hermias of conspiring with Molon and was put to death (Pol. 5,41f.; 49f.). A.ME.

[4] Seleucid (?) or Ptolemaic city commander in the 3rd Syrian War. PP 6,15104.

F. Piejko, Episodes from the Third Syrian War in a Gurob Papyrus, 246 B.C., in: APF 36, 1990, 17 A.8. W.A.

[5] Astrologer from Byzantium who probably lived in the 2nd cent. BC, educated by Babylonians (Sen. Q Nat. 7,4,1; Plin. HN 7,193). His work was perhaps entitled Χαλδαικά (*Chaldaiká*) [2] and was probably imparted to Varro and others through Posidonius. His independent theory of comets (Sen. Q Nat. 7,4–10) is comparable to that of Apollonius of Myndus, and his assumption about a human being's maximum life span (Plin. HN 7,160; Censorinus, DN 17,4) is comparable to that of → Berosus. His calculations about the number of pregnancy months are in accordance with others (Cen-

sorinus, DN 7,5f.). It is uncertain whether he conceals himself behind the name of Perigenes in the schol. Apoll. Rhod. 3,1377.

1 A. REHM, s.v. E. 17), RE 6, 65f. 2 P. SCHNABEL, Berossos und die babylon.-hell. Lit., 1923, 109–118. W.H.

[6] see → Socratics

Epigoni (ἐπίγονοι; *epígonoi*, 'future generations', 'descendants').

[1] Second generation of successors of Alexander [4] the Great in regions of the former Alexandrian Empire. Regarding the term *Epigoni*, see → Diadochi and Epigoni. W.ED.

[2] Lost early Greek epic (only one hexameter certain to belong to it has survived, and that is the introductory verse: F 1 BERNABÉ = F 1 DAVIES, see below) which belonged to the Theban part of the → epic cycle and probably followed on directly from the (Cyclic) → *Thēbaïs* but was written by a younger poet unknown even in antiquity: [1. 2375], against [2. 109–140, 148], who regards the epic *Thēbaïs-Epígonoi* as the two-part work of a single author and dates it to the 8th cent. (later revoked: 'of a later date, perhaps the 7th or 6th cent.' [3. 67]). The attribution to an epic poet by the name of Antimachus of Teos [4. 346], and now again BERNABÉ (p. 30) is speculative (rejected already by [1. 2375]): Herodotus (4,32) as the oldest witness knew the E. as a work of 'Homer's' (although he clearly doubts it himself) and has no information regarding a different author (consequently, neither does the early sophistic study of literature: BETHE [3. 67]).

Even though the epic was new, the material must have been ancient, since the poet of the *Iliad* already puts the following words into the mouth of Sthenelus, the Epigone and son of Capaneus who attacked Thebes, in Il. 4,406: 'We have (not only besieged, as our fathers did, but) taken Thebes, the city of seven gates!' (This also gives credence to the assumption that the surviving introductory verse 'Now, in turn, let us begin with the *younger* men, Muses! ...' could have the following continuation: 'who have *taken* seven-gated Thebes!'; most recently: [5. 31]). The content of the E. can no longer be reconstructed in detail (attempts in [1. 2375–2377; 2; 6]); certain is only that the seven sons of the 'Seven against Thebes' (several lists of names in BETHE [2. 110–113], cf. [7. 150f.]) conquered Thebes, drove away the residents (some of whom returned later), and, to give thanks for the victory, sacrificed the Theban seer → Teiresias with his daughter → Manto to Apollo in Delphi (F 3 BERNABÉ = F 3 DAVIES, also containing Manto's further destiny).

1 A. RZACH, s.v. Kyklos, RE 11, 2374–2377 2 E. BETHE, Thebanische Heldenlieder, 1891 3 E. BETHE, s.v. E., RE 6, 67f. 4 U. v. WILAMOWITZ-MOELLENDORFF, Homer. Unt. (Der ep. Cyclus), 1884 5 M. DAVIES, The Epic Cycle, 1989 6 C. ROBERT, Oidipus, 1915 7 W. KULLMANN, Die Quellen der Ilias (Troischer Sagenkreis), 1960. J.L.

Epigonus (Ἐπίγονος; *Epígonos*).

[1] Sculptor in Pergamum, who participated in building the victory monuments for the Attalids according to Pliny. Signatures are preserved on the following bases for Attalus I (241–197 BC): the so-called 'Small Battle Bathron' of the *strategos* Epigenes [2]; round base of the so-called 'Great Anathema' (*c.* 228 BC; the attribution of the 'Ludovisi Gaul' remains in dispute); the so-called 'Great Bathron' (*c.* 223 BC) with the 'Dying Trumpeter', which is documented in writing and was recognized in a copy on the Capitol. His 'Dying Amazon with her Child' came perhaps from the same monument and is similar to a copy from the so called 'Small Athenian Anathema' of Attalus II in Naples.

E. KÜNZL, Die Kelten des E. von Pergamon, 1971; P. MORENO, Scultura ellenistica, 1994, 282–287; OVERBECK, no. 2095 (Sources); B. S. RIDGWAY, Hellenistic sculpture, 1, 1990, 284–296; H.-J. SCHALLES, Unt. zur Kulturpolitik der Pergamenischen Herrscher im 3. Jh.v.Chr., in: IstForsch 36, 1985, 68–104; R.R. R. SMITH, Hellenistic sculpture, 1991, 99–104 fig.; R. WENNING, Die Galateranatheme Attalos' I., 1978, 42–43. R.N.

[2] Musician from Ambracia, whose school is mentioned by Aristoxenus (3 MEIBOM) in connection with Lasus. He is attributed with the invention of the Epigoneion, a harp with 40 strings arranged in a special order (Ath. 4,183 c-d). F.Z.

[3] Epigrammatist from Thessalonica, author of a funny epideictic poem from the 'Garland' of Philippus about an old grapevine (however, the word σταφυλή (*staphylḗ*) alludes to the woman's name of Σταφύλη; *Staphŷle*), who once was rich with grapes and is now covered in wrinkles (Anth. Pal. 9,261). Even plausible identifications must be ruled out due to the commonality of the name. The proposal by Planudes to attribute E. with the poems 9,260 (Secundus) and 9,406 (Antigonus of Carystus) cannot claim much validity.

GA II,1, 244f.; 2, 277f. E.D.

Epigram

I. GREEK II. LATIN

I. GREEK

A. BEGINNINGS B. ARCHAIC PERIOD
C. CLASSICAL PERIOD D. HELLENISM
E. SCHOOLS F. IMPERIAL PERIOD AND LATE ANTIQUITY G. LATE ANTIQUITY AND MIDDLE AGES

A. BEGINNINGS

The epigram was a part of Greek literature throughout its entire history (the oldest documents coincide with the first examples of alphabetic script) and originally consisted of a short verse inscription or label on vases, cups, votive gifts, funeral steles, herms, etc. The occasion was always real and could be public or private in nature. The metre of the epigram was the epic hexameter, sporadically in combination with a dactylic pentameter, an iambic trimeter, or in rare exceptions appearing in yet other combinations (cf. [1]). The purpose of the epigram was to keep memory alive or to consecrate objects: of the *c.* 900 *carmina epigraphica Graeca* from the 8th to the 4th cent. BC that now have been published by HANSEN (CEG 1–2), more than half are funeral inscriptions, almost 400 are votive inscriptions (most of which are votive epigrams), and only 50 owe their purpose to various other occasions (the so-called Dipylon Vase = CEG 432 and the famous Nestor Cup = CEG 454, both from the second half of the 8th cent., fall into this category).

B. ARCHAIC PERIOD

Numerous inscriptions in bronze and especially on stone represent the heritage of the 7th and 6th cents.: at the beginning of the 7th cent., we have the inscription on the Boeotian statuette of Manticlus (CEG 326), at the end of the 7th cent., the inscription which adorned the Kenotaphion of Glaucus, Archilochus' friend and son of Leptines, on Thasos (GVI 51a). During the course of the 6th cent., the elegiac distich emerges, which becomes the epigram's most common metrical combination by far in only a short time (one of the earliest examples is the inscription of the Cypselides in the temple of Hera at Olympia, which must be dated earlier than 582 BC, cf. FGE 397f.). In the epigrams of this period, we often encounter the 'speaking monument', esp. in funeral epigrams. The other well-known model of composition — the deceased person who informs about himself and his death — does not emerge until the 5th cent., and finally becomes a topos in its own right in the 4th cent. Characteristic for the archaic epigram aside from its brevity (rarely more than a pair of verses; more often we find monostichic forms) are the following qualities: a sober and serious style, a restrained and strictly impersonal tone, a practical purpose (as a rule, the epitaphs list the name, city, family, and age of the deceased) as well as the author's anonymity.

C. CLASSICAL PERIOD

In the 5th cent., first the Persian Wars, then the countless interior disputes esp. in Attica and Athens resulted in a large demand for public as well as private inscriptions: thus we can explain the rampant production to which even famous authors such as Euripides contributed at times — according to Plutarch (Nicias 17,4), he was the author of the funeral inscription for the Syracusian soldiers killed in action (GVI 21, the authenticity, however, is strongly contested, cf. FGE 129 and 155f.) — and, above all, Simonides of Ceos. Literary tradition attributes the latter with *c.* 90 epigrams (FGE 186–302), although rarely with the certainty which we have in the case of the inscription to the seer Megistias (FGE 196), whose authenticity is guaranteed by Herodotus (7,228,3). The state epigrams for large communal cemeteries (*polyándria*) are highly representative. They are often brief, easily remembered, and reduced to the essential (cf. GVI 4, the famous distich on the Spartans who fell at Thermopylae). Less emotional restraint is apparent in private funeral inscriptions, some of which are exquisite and remarkably expressive (cf. e.g. CEG 161, from Thasos, early 5th cent.). Compared to the archaic epigram, the classical epigram evolves, on the one hand, into more flexible and graceful, even pompous forms at times. This development reveals a careful effort to achieve greater harmony and style. On the other hand, we find in the sepulchral genre a focus on didactical and idealizing purposes, resulting in epigrams that often present the deceased as a paradigm of virtue. The influences of elegy, of tragedy, and of rhetoric (the influence of the Sophists can at times be felt in the over-subtlety and precision of some poems) lead to an obvious pathos and to a powerful density of expression which even includes theatrical gestures and expresses itself occasionally through dialogue.

In the 4th cent., the epigram is enriched with new formal structures, such as the use of a conditional clause in the beginning (GVI 1686), the comparison of the deceased with a hero (GVI 1727 = Nicarchus Anth. Pal. 7,159), and the comparison of his present situation to that in his lifetime (GVI 1702). At the same time, the first examples of fictitious epitaphs begin to emerge (cf. Theocritus of Chios, epigr. 1 FGE): the poets step out of anonymity and begin to place their own name into the poem (e.g. Ion of Samos as one of the first to do so, cf. CEG 819). Characteristically, the poem is now sometimes called ἐλεγεῖον (*elegeîon*). Noticeable innovations can be found on the content level as well: after the political and military events of the Peloponnesian War, fame, heroism, and the desire to deify man gradually disappear to be replaced by gnomic reflection and the attempt to render gods and heroes in a way that more resembles humans. The trend was towards simple, natural, and concise expressions and away from emphatic and rhetorical grandeur. These were the tender beginnings of modest, antiheroic motifs which later received further development. We would find support for this, for instance, in the three preserved epigrams of the → Erinna, if they were only authentic (the female poet should probably be dated to the turn of the 5th to the 4th cent., cf. most recently [2]); however, they appear to be the result of later endeavours — as is doubtlessly the case for the numerous poems attributed to Plato (FGE 125–130) and to various archaic and classical poets (Archilochus, Sappho, Anacreon, Bacchylides, etc.).

D. HELLENISM

The Hellenistic poets turned the epigram into a substantially new form with an altogether different function. What originally began as an inscription now becomes essentially literary: the occasion increasingly becomes fictitious as is obvious, above all, in the epitymbia (funeral inscriptions) to personalities who had died centuries earlier. The repertoire of topics was increased and renewed to a large extent: among the most frequently used topics are wine and love, also bucolic excursions, the realistic search for the 'primitive' and 'folksy', the unexpected and surprising, as well as descriptions of works of art, anecdotes, sententia, literary polemics, funny splashes of inspiration, satire of types (such as the drunk old woman of Timon) — anything and everything could become the subject of an epigram in the end. Moreover, subjectivity and autobiography become essential but not exclusive characteristics: as an expression of feelings, the epigram at this time is the heir of sympotic song, of elegy, even of archaic choral lyric, whereby it exerted an important influence on Latin elegy. Even the requirement of brevity clearly becomes less binding, resulting sometimes in a downright dramatic presentation in dialogue form. Elegance, a high stylistic standard, and careful observation of form characterize the Hellenistic epigram in all of its phases.

E. Schools

Epigram poetry is rightfully divided into three different schools (although such delimitations are always problematic): the 'Peloponnesian', the 'Ionian-Hellenistic', and the 'Phoenician' school. The first largely refers to the poets of the mainland who had strong connections to the Peloponnese, even though they came from other regions and their influence was noticeable in all of Greece: the 'rural', 'folksy' tendency of Leonidas, Anyte, Perses, Mnasalces, Simia, and of several others. In contrast to them stands the second group of the clever, mostly erotic-sympotic 'Musa urbana' of poets such as Callimachus, Asclepiades, Posidippus, Hedylus, etc. In the last decades of the 3rd cent., several important epigones stand between the two schools (beginning with → Dioscorides up to → Alcaeus of Messene) who had aligned themselves with so-called Dorism, that is, they openly showed their political engagement in favour of Sparta and the Aetolian League, both of whom resisted the repressive imperialism of Macedonia. In the period from 150 to 50 BC, the 'Phoenician' school finally gains in influence, named after its most famous representatives who were Phoenicians, such as → Antipater [8] of Sidon, → Meleager and → Philodemus (both came from Gadara and were a little younger), probably also → Archias [7] of Antiochia. Antipater already introduced a custom which quickly spread among the Greek intellectuals: he moved to Rome. He was soon followed by Philodemus and Archias, who, together with Mucius Scaevola, Tullius Laurea, and others, belonged to the famous literary circle around Cicero.

F. Imperial period and late antiquity

Thus the preconditions were established for the rise of the so-called 'Roman epigram', whose representatives are, above all, Crinagoras of Mytilene and the Thessalonians → Philippus and → Antipater [9]. In the time of Nero, satirical *epigrams* particularly by Lucillius and Nicarchus became successful and made obligatory the characteristically short form (usually one or two distichs) complete with a punch-line at the end: several professions were taken under scrutiny (doctors, philosophers, grammarians, astrologers, athletes, artists, *et al.*) as well as certain human types (misers, sweet-toothed persons, old women with make-up, etc.), and in doing so, the mocked persons were addressed directly by name in complete accordance with the iambic-Aristophanic tradition.

Among the more eccentric examples of this period are the isopsephic poems by Leonidas of Alexandria and the anacyclic poems of Nicodemus of Heraclea. In the centuries following, we can observe a clear decline of the Greek epigram. Epigrams remained fashionable within high society, since the emperors and their entourage amused themselves with creating them (two of Germanicus' have survived, perhaps one of Trajan's, seven of Hadrian's, and two of Julian's), but real schools did not exist and outstanding personalities became rare. The few exceptions include Straton of Sardeis, Rufinus, and, in the 4th cent., Palladas of Alexandria, while the Christian epigram found a glowing admirer in Gregory of Nazianzus, whose ambitious and confusing production becomes the 8th book of the *Anthologia Palatina*.

G. Late antiquity and Middle Ages

In the period of Justinian, the epigram has a last revival with Agathias and, above all, with → Paulus Silentiarius. The traditional themes, aside from the openly rejected pederasty (jurisdiction at this time imposed severe punishments for pederasty), are varied and combined with original inspirations. Thus, an encomium of the deceased is readily included in the *epitaphios*, while the epideictic ἔκφρασις (→ *ékphrasis*) becomes increasingly panegyrical in character by replacing the praise of the work of art more and more with praise for the depicted dignitary. Clever elegance and a classical perfection of form are the trademarks of this last height of the genre, in which we find no traces of the new faith whatsoever. In the cents. to follow, the epigram still finds individual representatives, beginning with Georgius Pisides (7th cent.), then Johannes Geometres (10th cent.), Christophoros of Mitylene (11th cent.), and Johannes Mauropous (11th cent.) up to Theodoros Prodromos (12th cent.) and Manueles Philes (14th cent.).

1 P.A. Hansen, Lapidary Lyrics, in: CR 34, 1984, 286f.
2 C. Neri, Studi sulle testimonianze di Erinna, 1996.

Editions: G. Kaibel, Epigrammata Graeca ex lapidibus conlecta, 1878; E. Cougny, Epigrammatum Anthologia Palatina cum Planudeis et appendice nova, 3, 1890; GVI; J. Ebert, Griech. E. auf Sieger an gymnischen und hippischen Agonen, 1972; FGE; CEG; P.A. Hansen, Carmina Epigraphica Graeca saeculi IV a. Chr. n., 1989.
Bibliography: R. Reitzenstein, Epigramm und Skolion, 1893; A. Wifstrand, Studien zur griech. Anthologie, 1926; Div. Authors, L'epigramme Grecque, Entretiens 14, 1968.

E.D.

II. Latin

A. Term B. History C. Afterlife and history of research

A. Term

The word *epigramma* is documented in Latin since Varro and Cicero. It is not only used for 'inscriptions' (for this purpose, there is also the term *titulus*), but also for shorter poems in general, whereby we cannot count on a strict delimitation from other types of poems (cf. Plin. Ep. 4,14,2). Martial, who often uses the term, has perhaps the most clearly developed notion of this genre, but he opposes any limitation of its scope. A modern presentation should be based on other factors besides the use of the term itself, such as the literary tradition and the formation of a corpus, both of which offer insights into the ancient understanding of the genre.

B. History

Latin epigrammatic poetry in antiquity develops more or less closely in connection to the Greek. Especially at its height with → Catullus and → Martialis, it has brought forth important independent achievements. Since the 2nd half of the 3rd cent. BC, the custom of inscriptional funeral epigrams is adopted from Greece first by upper class families like the Scipio clan; the first metre to be used is the Saturnian. Ennius introduces the elegiac distich and begins the tradition of the Latin literary epigram with verses about his own poetic achievements. C. 100 BC, authors such as → Lutatius Catulus, → Valerius Aedituus, and → Porcius Licinus adopt the Hellenistic love epigram. Among the three parts of Catullus' poetry collection, the shorter poems in elegiac distichs constituting the third part are today usually called epigrams. Catullus himself never uses the term, but Quint. Inst. 1,5,20 already refers to one of these poems as *epigramma*. As models for his epigrams, Martial not only used Catullus' poems from the 3rd part, but also the shorter poems of the 1st part. In Catullus, these two groups of poems are clearly distinguished from each other, for instance in regard to diction. Catullus' work differs from Hellenistic epigram poetry, which he took up esp. in Carm. 70, in its serious presentation of love. Furthermore, a poem such as Carm. 76 goes beyond the usual scope of the epigram in its formal aspects as well.

Catullus' influence is present in the collection entitled → *Catalepton*, transmitted under Vergil's name. The papyrus finding on → Cornelius Gallus shows four-liners that are separated from each other, which perhaps refers to epigrams as poems that cannot be clearly distinguished from → elegy. As far as the epigrammatic poetry from the Augustan period is concerned, only that by → Domitius Marsus can be traced. The authenticity of the epigrams attributed to → Seneca the younger is uncertain, but at least one part, such as the epigrams on the triumph of Claudius, stem from his time. The collection of the *Carmina* → *Priapea* shows a brilliant artistry of form in the variation of a single topic, which chronologically may belong to the vicinity of Martial. Mocking verses, handed down from various epochs, that circulated orally and Pompeian graffiti show the popularity of pithy humour also in the sub-literary realm.

Martial aims at elevating the literary status of the genre by imposing high demands on quality, in contrast to the common perception that regarded the epigram as a playful side activity for amateurs. Aside from the mocking epigrams most often noticed in literary reception, most other types of epigrams (except for love epigrams) are represented as well. In his supreme utilization of the Latin and Greek traditions, Martial led epigram poetry to a high point in which keen pointedness is connected to a rich and lively description of detail.

Of the literary epigrammatic poetry from the 2nd and 3rd cents., only little is comprehensible. The 4th cent. brings a new beginning. → Publilius Optatianus Porfyrius practices the special form of → technopaignia. → Ausonius deals with a broad variety of topics, primarily following Greek tradition. A similar picture is presented by the collection of the → *Epigrammata Bobiensia* written in *c.* 400. A new development begins with Christian epigrams, which appear from the 4th cent. on. They are used on inscriptions in the martyr epigrams by Damasus (→ Epigrammata Damasiana), as building inscriptions in churches and baptisteria, and in the side captions of picture cycles, which is the form in which literary tradition has preserved them (→ Ambrosius, → Prudentius, → Rusticus Helpidius). → Prosper of Aquitaine entitles a collection of versified sententia from Augustinus *Epigrammata*; they share a didactic function with church inscriptions (cf. Aug. Serm. 319,8). Authors of late antiquity, such as → Claudianus, → Sidonius Apollinaris, → Ennodius, and → Venantius Fortunatus primarily practised the secular tradition, above all descriptive epigrams. As far as the anthology of the Codex Salmasianus is concerned, which was created in Northern Africa in 534, the epigram book by → Luxurius should be mentioned in particular. In 7th-cent. Spain, → Isidorus and → Eugenius of Toledo carry on with epigrammatic poetry.

C. Afterlife and history of research

The themes and forms we find in the epigrammatic poetry of late antiquity are taken up again in the early Middle Ages. The high Middle Ages embrace Martial as a moral-satirical author. In addition to the Greek anthology, he and Catullus represent the principal models for early modern epigrammatic poetry. In comparative evaluations, Catullus is often regarded as more closely connected to the Greeks and seen in contrast to Martial. In the 16th cent., Catullus takes precedence, but in the 17th cent. Martial becomes more important, a development which corresponds to the trend of that time towards pointed brevity. Theories of epigrams in the poetics focus primarily on *brevitas* and *argutia* as characteristic qualities of the genre. Lessing's division of the epigram into 'expectation' and 'explanation' was based on Martial and still maintains its influence on more recent epigram research. A complete account of the genre's history is still lacking. Even partial areas such as the Christian epigram above all have yet to be researched adequately.

→ Funeral epigram; → EPIGRAM

1 W. BARNER, Vergnügen, Erkenntnis, Kritik. Zum E. und seiner Tradition in der Neuzeit, in: Gymnasium 92, 1985, 350–371 2 G. BERNT, Das lat. E. im Übergang von der Spätant. zum frühen MA, 1968 3 M. CITRONI, La teoria Lessinghiana dell' E. e le interpretazioni moderne di Marziale, in: Maia 21, 1969, 215–243 4 P. HESS, E., 1989 5 N. HOLZBERG, Martial, 1988 6 R. KEYDELL, s.v. E., RAC 6, 539–577 7 P. LAURENS, L'abeille dans l'ambre. Célébration de l'E. de l'époque alexandrine à la fin de la Renaissance, 1989 8 M. LAUSBERG, Das Einzeldistichon, 1982 9 W. MAAZ, Lat. Epigrammatik im hohen MA, 1992 10 F. MUNARI, Die spätlat. Epigrammatik, in: Philologus 106, 1958, 127–139 11 G. PFOHL (ed.), Das E., 1969 12 R. REITZENSTEIN, s.v. E., RE 6, 71–111 13 E.A. SCHMIDT, Catull, 1985 14 J.P. SULLIVAN, Martial, the unexpected classic, 1991 15 H. SZELEST, Martial eigentlicher Schöpfer und hervorragendster Vertreter des röm. E., in: ANRW II 32.4, 1986, 2563–2623 16 T. VERWEYEN, G. WILLING, E., in: HWdR 2, 1273–1283 17 H. WIEGAND (ed.), Kleine Formen. Das E. (= AU 38,6), 1995.

MA.L.

Epigramma Paulini A conversation between two monks and a person who appears to be a former member of the monastery, documented in the *cod. Parisinus* 7558 in 110 hexameters (with small gaps). The point of departure is the devastating invasion of Gaul by the Vandals and Alans (AD 407–409). While its effects are being smoothed out, the moral disaster continues and is rendered in a satirical fashion (*interior pestis*, V. 15): the striving towards a knowledge denied to humankind, the vices of women, which, of course, are encouraged by men who thereby are held responsible. (On the problem of theodicy, cf. Ps.-Prosp. Carm. de prov.; Salv. Gub.) The poem is of southern Gallic origin, the author appears under the name of S. Paulinus in literary tradition but cannot be identified.

EDITION: C. SCHENKL, CSEL 16,499–510.
BIBLIOGRAPHY: 1 A. GALLICO, Note per una nuova edizione dell'E.P., in: SSR 6, 1982, 163–172 2 E. GRIFFE, L'E.P., in: Revue des études augustiniennes 2, 1956, 187–194 3 R. HERZOG, HLL § 628.3 4 K. SMOLAK, Zur Textkritik des sog. Sancti Pauli Epigramma, in: WS 102, 1989, 205–212.

W.-L.L.

Epigrammata Bobiensia The title of this poetry book which was created *c.* AD 400 and structured by a later editor refers to a codex of the monastery Bobbio (north of Genoa). The codex is no longer extant but a copy of it has been kept in the Vatican Library since the humanist period (Cod. Vat. lat. 2836 f. 268r–278v; fig.: [3] appendix; [4. 140f., 152f.]). The collection contains 71 poems of varying lengths and metre (mostly distichs, less often iambic trimeter and stichic hexameter) and is divided into two parts of almost equal length by the 70 verses of the 'Lamentation of Sulpicia about the condition of the state and the times of Domitian' (no. 37). Poems by different authors and from different time-periods are joined together (→ Naucellius, friend of Symmachus: no. 1–9; → Domitius Marsus: no. 39f.; Ps.-Sulpicia: no. 37, explicit anonyma: no. 38; 43). Independent poems are placed next to the literal or free renderings of works by Greek poets (above all Anth. Gr.) and prose writers (Epicurus, Demosthenes). This poetry book, of which certain poems were already known prior to 1955 from the appendices of the Opuscula by Ausonius, offers insights into the education, the taste, and the intellectual goals of the pagan aristocrats in the circle surrounding → Symmachus and → Ausonius. Christian material is lacking, although polemics against Christianity may lurk beneath the surface (e.g., no. 37; 42f.). This notion also finds support in the inclusion of the epigram by Domitius Marsus on Atia that alludes to conception through Apollo (no. 39). The sight of the poets and of the editor is directed backwards: onto the classical poetry of the Greeks and the Romans, the classical and post-classical fine arts of the Greeks, their history and their opinions. In addition to this there are curiosities, invectives, biographical and erotic material. The Epigrammata Bobiensia have inspired Italian humanists to create free renderings ([3. 87f.]; more still unedited).

→ Anthology; → Poetry book

1 F. MUNARI (ed.), E.B., vol. 2: Introduzione e edizione critica, 1955 2 SC. MARIOTTI, s.v. E.B., RE Suppl. 9, 37–68 3 W. SPEYER (ed.), E.B., 1962 4 M. FERRARI, Le scoperte a Bobbio nel 1493, in: IMU 13, 1970, 139–180.

WO.SP.

Epigrammata Damasiana According to [1], the Epigrammata Damasiana (ED) are the epigraphic and epigrammatic work of the Roman bishop → Damasus' I, consisting of 57 mostly metrical, primarily hexametrical inscriptions from Rome and of two poems designed for literary publication. In addition to building inscriptions, we find cemeterial inscriptions, above all on martyrs, designed to help find their graves and to emphasise their significance (Rome ideology). This purpose is served by → Filocalus' calligraphy as well as by the high literary standard (imitation of Vergil). The ED belong to the earliest non-liturgical Christian poetry in Latin (cf. Jer. Vir. ill. 103: *elegans in versibus componendis ingenium habuit.*) Sources: partially on marble plates, partially in medieval anthologies [2] which go back to copies made by pilgrims to Rome. The afterlife is quite extensive: names that were only known from the ED find entrance into martyrologies [3]. The ED had a literary influence esp. on → Prudentius, and epigraphically, we find many imitations on Christian graves. In the Middle Ages, the ED was used beyond Italy at monastery schools, thus exerting influence on Hrabanus Maurus, Alcuin, Aldhelm et al. It also influenced the design of grave inscriptions as far away as Trier.

→ Anthology; → Epigram; → Funeral inscriptions; → Martyrs; → Pilgrimage

1 A. FERRUA, E.D., 1942 2 G. WALSER, Die Einsiedler Inschr.-Slg. und der Pilgerführer durch Rom (Codex Einsidelensis 326), 1987 3 E. SCHÄFER, Die Bedeutung der Epigramme des Papstes Damasus I. für die Gesch. der Heiligenverehrung, 1932 4 J. FONTAINE, Naissance de la poésie dans l'Occident Chrétien, 1981 5 Saecularia Damasiana, Studi di Antichità Cristiana 39/1986 (conf. Rome 1984).

A.GL.

Epigrapheis (ἐπιγραφεῖς; *epigrapheîs*). In the 390s BC in Athens, the *epigrapheis* kept registers of people whom they obliged to pay a special wealth tax, the *eisphora* (Isoc. Or. 17, 41; Lys. fr. 92 SAUPPE).
→ Eisphora

R. THOMSEN, Eisphora, 1964, 187–189.

P.J.R.

Epigraphical style The term epigraphical style refers to the script of the oldest Greek literary papyri and papyrus documents (*c.* 4th–3rd cents. BC); it is a majuscule imitating the style of contemporary inscriptions. Among the extant examples are the papyrus containing the 'Persians' by → Timotheus of Miletus [3], the Derveni Papyrus [1], the so-called 'lament of Artemisia' [4] and a few other papyri from Sakkara and Hibeh [2]. The script's epigraphical character manifests itself in its bilinear, rigid, uniform and unwieldy strokes — the shapes of the E (written in four strokes), the Z (two horizontal lines connected by a vertical one), the Θ (a circle with a dot in its centre), the M (written in four separate strokes), the angular Σ, the Ξ (three parallel lines) and the Ω, in its archaic shape typical of inscriptions. In the course of the 3rd cent. BC, with writing becoming more widespread, the epigraphical template develops softer shapes, and a more rapidly written cursive begins to become distinguished from bookhands.
→ Majuscule, A. Greek script

1 S.G. KAPSOMENOS, Ὁ ὀρφικὸς πάπυρος τῆς Θεσσαλονίκης, in AD 19, 1964, 17–25. 2 E. G. TURNER, Ptolemaic Bookhands and Lille Stesichorus, in Scrittura e Civiltà 4, 1980, 26–27. 3 U. VON WILAMOWITZ-MOELLENDORF (ed.), Timotheos, die Perser, aus einem Papyrus von Abusir, 1903 (facsimile: Der Timotheos-Papyrus gefunden bei Abusir am 1. Februar 1902, 1903) 4 U. WILCKEN, Urkunden der Ptolemäerzeit I, 1927, 97–104.

E. CRISCI, Scrivere greco fuori d'Egitto (Papyrologica Florentina XXVII), 1996, 9–15.; E.G. TURNER, Ptolemaic Bookhands and Lille Stesichorus, in Scrittura e Civiltà 4, 1980, 19–40.

G.M.

Epigraphy Epigraphy, from Greek ἐπιγράφειν (*epigráphein*, 'to write on something'). The term refers to ancient texts that were documented on various, mostly permanent materials (stone, bronze, etc.), as well as to the respective sub-discipline of archaeology.
→ Inscriptions; → EPIGRAPHY

M.MEI. and ME.STR.

Epii (Ἐπειοί; *Epeipoí*). The oldest population in Elis (Pind. Ol. 9,58). → Augeias was regarded as one of their kings (Pind. Ol. 10,35; Hom. Il. 11,698). According to the Homeric catalogue of ships, the E. fall into four different groups (Hom. Il. 2,618–625). Nestor reports of conflicts between the E. and Pylians in Hom. Il. 11,670–762. According to Paus. 5,1,4; 8, they were named after Epius, but later their name was changed into Elii (cf. also Hecat. FGrH 1 F 25).

E. VISSER, Homers Katalog der Schiffe, 1997, 195; 556–557; 562–563; B. HAINSWORTH, The Iliad, B. 9–12 (comm.), 1993, 296–298.

R.B.

Epikichlides (Ἐπικιχλίδες; *Epikichlídes*) is the title of an erotic poem attributed to Homer (Ath. 14,639a). Menaechmus associates it with the word for thrush (κίχλη, *kíchlē*), which suggests a travesty or parody, set in the animal kingdom, of the Homeric epics (cf. → Batrachomyomachia). The title may perhaps refer to *kichlismoí*, which denotes exuberant laughter.

U. v. WILAMOWITZ-MOELLENDORFF, Die Ilias und Homer, 1916, 18, n. 2.

C.S.

Epikleros (ἐπίκληρος; *epíklēros*). Not quite correctly translated as 'heiress'. If an Athenian citizen or → *métoikos* was survived only by daughters, they were not entitled to the inheritance in their own right, but their legitimate sons were, and so the inheritance (→ *klḗros*) could in some circumstances benefit a different family. Because of that danger the law allowed the nearest male collateral relative of the testator (→ Anchisteia), to obtain at the same time from the archon or polemarch (→ Archontes I), by a process of → *epidikasía*, the immediate assignment of the *klḗros* and even that of a still childless daughter, as a married woman, even if she were already married elsewhere. The *epidikasía* replaced the → *engýesis*. Sons produced from the union of the collateral relative with the *epikleros* were considered sons of the testator (their grandfather). In that manner the sacred continuity of the household (οἶκος, *oíkos*) was preserved and the property remained within the family. The legal institution of the 'heiress' was also known in Doric territory (*patroioúchos* in Sparta, *patroiokos* in Gortyn).
→ Succession, law of; → Kleros

H.J. WOLFF, Die Grundlagen des griech. Eherechts, in: TRG 20, 1952, 1ff. G. THÜR, Armut. Gedanken zu Ehegüterrecht und Familienvermögen in der griech. Polis, in: D. SIMON (ed.), Eherecht und Familiengut, 1992, 121ff.

G.T.

Epikrisis (ἐπίκρισις; *epíkrisis*). The term was unknown in Athens. *Epicrisis* was used in inscriptions as a judicial control on penalties imposed by the authorities (IPArk. 3, 19,50: Tegea; Syll.[3] 1075, 6: Epidaurus) or as an objective third party's assent to a settlement reached by the contesting parties [1. 190ff.]. The verb ἐπικρίνεσθαι (*epikrínesthai*) is found in Hellenistic court language meaning 'to resolve' (SHERK 194f.), in IPArk. 31 B 22 meaning *decernere* (*decretum*) of a Roman authority. In Roman Egypt *epikrisis* was the procedure for establishing membership of a privileged taxation group [2. 155, 212].

1 A. STEINWENTER, Streitbeendigung durch Urteil, Schiedsspruch und Vergleich nach griech. Rechte, [2]1971 2 H.-A. RUPPRECHT, Einführung in die Papyruskunde, 1994 3 G. THÜR, H. TAEUBER, Prozeßrechtliche Inschr. Arkadiens, 1994. G.T.

Epilepsy From 1050 BC onwards we find careful descriptions of epilepsy and its various manifestations in Babylonian texts [1]. There, epilepsy is linked to gods, spirits, or demons. The belief in a religious cause of epilepsy and the corresponding treatment of it through religious, magical, and folk-medicinal methods can be traced throughout all of antiquity and across cultural borders. In *c.* 400 BC, the Hippocratic author of *De morbo sacro* propagated a purely somatic interpretation of epilepsy, wherein he suspected that changes in the balance of bodily fluids were to blame, thus opening the possibility of a somatic therapy, an interpretation which was adopted by most doctors [2]. However, an agreement was never reached among doctors regarding the aetiology or the therapy of epilepsy. Some took dietetic irregularities to be the cause, others looked to the moon or the climate, still others believed that the brain was affected by disorders of other parts of the body. Some advocated surgical procedures, phlebotomies, or trepanations; others preferred dietetic measures; sometimes magical remedies were rejected as 'Persian nonsense', sometimes they were adopted and made to fit with one's own cultural habits. Occasionally, blood cures were regarded as acceptable medical remedies, then were rejected, only to be included yet again into the therapeutic repertoire. A peony root worn around the neck may have had a pharmacological or else a symbolic explanation. Christianity, which designated the case described in Mt 17,11–14 as the rule, increasingly rejected patterns of explanation that were based on the moon or on an imbalance of bodily fluids, and explained epilepsy as a demonic possession (e.g. Orig., Comm. in Mt 17,14), although certain doctors continued to insist on a strictly somatic point of view.

In Babylonian, Greek, and Roman law, epileptic sickness was regarded as such a 'reduction of worth' that an owner could return a slave to the seller or claim compensation from him. Aristotle regarded epilepsy in the context of melancholy and genius as the 'Herculean disease' (Probl. 30,1), whereby he distilled a positive aspect from a socially highly disturbing condition.
→ Medicine

1 M. STOL, Epilepsy in Babylonia, 1993 2 O. TEMKIN, The falling sickness, 1971. V.N.

Epilogue (ἐπίλογος; *epílogos*, *peroratio*, *conclusio*). Conclusion of a speech. It had the double function of reminding the listener of what was discussed in the → *argumentatio* and, at the same time, of completing the → *captatio benevolentiae*, for which the orator had employed the method of moving the audience's emotions from the beginning on (Quint. Inst. 6,1,1). Of these two functions, that of recapitulation appears to have been regarded as the one particularly reserved for the epilogue in pre-Aristotelian rhetoric (Corax in Anonym., RABE, RhG XIV 26,2; Pl. Phdr. 267d). But already in Aristotle's teachings (Rh. 1419b 10ff.), we find a rudimentary differentiation into two kinds, one being πρακτικόν (*praktikón*), the other being παθητικόν (*pathētikón*; cf. e.g. in Anonym. Seguerianus, SPENGEL-HAMMER, RhG I 453ff. or in Maximus Planudes, WALZ, RhG V 285,8ff.), a differentiation which remains practically constant in the Latin as well as in the Greek rhetoric tradition. In the εἶδος πρακτικόν (*eídos praktikón*, *enumeratio*, *rerum repetitio*), the points presented in the *partitio* (*kephálaia*) had to be repeated (thus the name *anakephalaíōsis*), and that is, in the same order in which they were discussed (Rhet. Her. 2,47; Gregorius of Corinth, WALZ, RhG VII 1220,22). If, on the other hand, they were repeated in the opposite order, the recapitulation was called ἐπάνοδος (*epánodos*; Syrianus, RABE, RhG XVI 2,89,20).

Prosecutor as well as defendant employed this method, albeit in a different way. However, the diverse ways in which this part of the speech could be prepared were always treated with great care in order to avoid boredom from the side of the audience and to disguise the fact that it was a trick (Cic. Inv. 1,98; Part. 60; Quint. Inst. 6,1,2). Even in the earliest formulations of a theory of the epilogue, we can identify the goal of bringing out the audience's goodwill for the speaker and of arousing their suspicion against the opponent (Aristot. Rh. Alex. 1444b29f; Aristot. Rh. 1419b 10ff.). The *eídos pathētikós,* on the other hand, had the double function of turning the audience against the opponent (*indignatio, amplificatio*, δείνωσις, *deínōsis*) and of arousing pity for the speaker (*miseratio, conquestio*, ἔλεος, *éleos*). For both parts, a theory for special *loci communes* (cf. e.g. Rhet. Her. 2,47ff.; Cic. Inv. 1,100ff.) was developed for the use by both prosecutor and defendant depending upon the circumstances.

C.F. LAFERL, s.v. E., HWdR 2, 1286–1291; LAUSBERG; J. MARTIN, Ant. Rhet., 1974; L. CALBOLI MONTEFUSCO, Exordium, Narratio, E., 1988; R. VOLKMANN, Die Rhet. der Griechen und Römer in systematischer Übersicht, [2]1885 (repr. 1963); M. WACHTLER, Der E. in der röm. Rhet., PhD thesis, Innsbruck 1973 (type-written). L.C.M.

Epilycus (Ἐπίλυκος; *Epílykos*).
[1] Comedy writer, whose surviving work consists of the title of one play (Κωραλίσκος; *Kōralískos, The little lad from Crete*? cf. Phot. p. 198,15) and of nine fragments; fr. 3 (remnants of catalectic anapaestic tetra-

meters) and fr. 4 (catalectic anapaestic dimeter in Doric dialect) show that he belonged to the Old Comedy (late 5th, early 4th cent. BC).

1 PCG V, 1986, 170–173. H.-G.NE.

[2] The son of Teisander, nephew of Andocides [1], of the lineage of the → Philaïdae [1] (cf. [1. 296–298]), perhaps the secretary (*grammateús*) of the council in 424/3 BC. E. participated as an Athenian delegate in a treaty of unknown date and content with the Persian great king (And. Or. 3,29). It probably was the treaty with Darius [2] II, which came about shortly after his ascension to the throne (424), with Heraclides [1] ([2. 207–211]; [3. 422 n. 132]) acting as the intermediary. E. died in Sicily (And. Or. 1, 117), probably during the Athenian campaign (→ Peloponnesian War) between 415 and 413 BC [4].

1 Davies 2 H. T. Wade-Gery, Essays in Greek History, 1958 3 D. M. Lewis, The Archidamian War, in: CAH 5, ²1992 4 Traill, PAA 395845. W. ED.

Epimachia (ἐπιμαχία; *epimachía*). Thucydides (1,44,1; 5,48,2) uses the term *epimachia* for a purely defensive alliance, which obliges the participants to give assistance only in the case of an attack, as opposed to the *symmachía*, which is an offensive as well as defensive alliance to the full extent, wherein the participants have 'the same friends and enemies'. The Greeks, however, failed to always make a clear distinction between the two terms: the → Athenian League of the 4th cent. was a defensive alliance, but the treatise which promoted it consistently uses *symmáchein* and related words (Tod 125; 127).

→ Athenian League P.J.R.

Epimeletai (ἐπιμεληταί; *epiméletai*). Functionaries, who 'take care of something' (*epimeleîsthai*). The word is used as the title for several Greek officials; see also *epískopoi*, *epistátai*.

1. The author of the Aristotelian *Athenaion Politeia* mentions for Athens the *epimeletai* of wells (43,1), of the market (51,4), of the festival of Dionysia (56,4), and of the Eleusinian Mysteries (57,1). Also documented are *epimeletai* as court officials who deal with the tributes in the Delian-Athenian League (ML 68), *epimeletai* of shipyards (such as IG II² 1629, 178–179; Dem. Or. 22,63), of the *symmoria* for the equipment of triremes ([Dem.] Or. 47,21f.), of the metics' *symmoria* (i.e. taxation-group) for the *eisphora* (IG II² 244), and, in the post-classical period, an *epimeletḗs* of the harbour (IG II² 1012; 1013). Corporations within the state had *epimeletai* as well: in the phyle, they were in charge of nominating the *chorēgoí* (Dem. Or. 21,13), of heiresses (*epíklēroi*), and of the phyle's possessions (IG II² 1165). In the phratria (i.e. phyle-subdivision), *epimeletai* were involved in the purchase and the sale of property (IG II² 1597) and could be nominated *ad hoc* for special tasks.

2. *Epimeletai* can be found in numerous other cities of the Greek world. Delphi had an *epimeletḗs* who was nominated by the Aetolians (Syll.³ 534), later we find an *epimeletḗs* of the Amphictyons (Syll.³ 813 A). In the 2nd cent., the Athenians employed an *epimeletḗs* of the Klerouchoi in Delos (Syll.³ 664), and Megalopolis nominated *epimeletai* for the *kṓmē* of Lycosura (Syll.³ 800). In Rhodes, there was an *epimeletḗs* for strangers (Syll.³ 619), in Olbia, one for the walls (Syll.³ 707), in Chalcis, one for public works (Syll.³ 905), similarly, one in Oropus (IG VII 4255). In Kalauria, *epimeletai* leased sacred land (Syll.³ 993), and in Andania, an *epimeletḗs* administered the treasure of the mysteries (Syll.³ 736 § 11).

Epimelētḗs was also used as a translation of the Latin *curator* or *procurator*.

→ Episkopoi; → Epistatai P.J.R.

Epimenes (Ἐπιμένης; *Epiménēs*) from → Miletus. After the fall of the Neleids in the 7th cent. BC, he was supposedly elected by the deme as → *aisymnḗtēs* with authority over life and death (Nic. Damasc. FGrH 90 F 53). The purges attributed to him there — proscription, exile, confiscation of property — correspond to the rules of a decree from the 5th cent. (ML 43), which states that the office of the ἐπιμήνιοι (*epimḗnioi*) is to carry out such measures which are common in coups d'états. This is probably the basis for the later, possibly Peripatetic construction of the *aesymneteia* of E.

H.-J. Gehrke, Zur Gesch. Milets in der Mitte des 5. Jh., in: Historia 29, 1980, 17–31. K.-J.H.

Epimenides Cretan religious figure, of whom many legends and miracles have been reported (FGrH 457 T 1–11). He lived to be 154, 157, or 299 years old, of which he supposedly spent 40 or 50 years as a young man asleep in a grotto of the nymphs (nourished by special food which he kept in the hoof of an ox). His soul could leave the body and then return if it desired. He also claimed to have lived several lives (FGrH 457 T 1; 2; 4d). He shares several of these qualities (migration of the soul, reincarnation) with other archaic sages, e.g. → Hermotimus of Clazomenae and → Pythagoras, who are regarded as heirs to the Thracian-Scythian shamans ([1; 2]; opposing [3]). E.'s most famous deed (first directly witnessed in Aristot. Ath. Pol. 1) was the expiation of Athens from the consequences of the 'sin of Cylon' in the early 6th cent. by means of new sacrificial rites. Historians are still discussing the historical background [4]. A part of the narrative could have been created during the Peloponnesian War [5]. Plato estimates E.'s workings in Athens to be almost 100 years later than the myth of expiation would require, and that is '10 years prior to the Persian Wars' (Leg. 642d). E. was also extolled as a prophet — since the functions of 'priest of expiation' and 'seer' often were combined — and had ties to several Peloponnesian states in this position (FGrH 457 F 1; T 1,5). Sparta as well as Argus claimed that E. was buried there (FGrH 457 T 1; 5e).

Various pseudepigrapha were attributed to E. (cf. FGrH 457 and [6]); the most famous one was a theogony, which can be compared in its kind and its dating (6th/5th cents. BC) approximately to the poetry attributed to Orpheus [7].
→ Cylon; → Orphic poetry

1 E.R. Dodds, The Greeks and the Irrational, 1951, 140–147 2 C. Ginzburg, Storia notturna, 1989, XX 3 J. Bremmer, The Early Greek Concept of the Soul, 1983, 24–53 4 P.J. Rhodes, A Commentary on the Athenaion Politeia, 1981, 81–84 5 S. Hornblower, A Commentary on Thucydides, I, 1991, 518 6 Diels, Vorsokr. I, 27–37 7 M.L. West, The Orphic Poems, 1983, 45–53. R.PA.

Epimerismi ἐπιμερισμοί (*epimerismoí*) are 'subdivisions' (Apollonius Dyscolus, Syntaxis 491,13 Schneider-Uhlig; Lat. *partitiones*, → Priscianus) 'of verses or sentences into words' (this is the sense, in which Sext. Emp. Adv. Math. 1,159–168 in the 2nd cent. AD used μερισμός; *merismós*): each word was analyzed grammatically and prosodically, and sometimes also semantically. It is a teaching aid of the Byzantine School (Tzetzes on Hes. Op. 285); in the 11th–12th cents., it was referred to as *schedographia* ('writing of didactic pieces', σχέδη (*schédē*), of uncertain etymology [7. 127]). It was mainly applied to Homer's works, but also to those of Philostratus and Aelianus, the Bible and other religious texts as well as Agapetus (the tradition of writing 'Homeric glosses' dates back to at least the 5th cent. BC: Aristoph. fr. 233 PCG). → Herodianus also wrote *epimerismi*, but the transmitted version, published by J. Fr. Boissonade in 1819, is not authentic [6. 23–24]. The *epimerismi* to Homer [2; 3] list the following: the 'basic form' of a word (θέμα; *théma*, nom. sing., 1st pers. present indicative), dependent forms (παραγωγή; *paragōgḗ*) divisions into parts of speech according to the categories defined by → Dionysius [17] Thrax, and also synomyms and 'applications' (χρήσεις; *chrḗseis*) of the form. In many of these explanations, there is agreement between the Homeric *epimerismi* and Choeroboscus' anthology of *Epimerismi in Psalmos* [1] in tenet, method, and presentation; for that reason it has been assumed that the latter was the author of both anthologies. At any rate, the time of Choeroboscus (9th cent. AD) is seen as *terminus post quem* for the Homeric *epimerismi* (the oldest work, in which they are used, is the Etymologicum Gudianum, 2nd half of the 9th cent. AD; for an earlier dating into the 6th cent. AD, see [8. 206]).

Initially, the Homeric *epimerismi* followed the text ('scholiastic *epimerismi*'), later they were ordered alphabetically. The extant *epimerismi* were compiled by alphabetically lemmatizing the commentaries to the second, third, and first book of the Iliad (in that order). In the course of this, mistakes in the alphabetical order of the lemmata were corrected; they had either been caused by some disarray in the sheets of the commentaries, upon which the *epimerismi* were based, or by interpolations and additions from other excerpted sources. Herodianus is the most frequently quoted source, and it is possible that his *epimerismi* have been absorbed into the addition to the Homeric *epimerismi* in alphabetical order, to be found in Cramer's edition of MS *Oxon. bibl. Novi Colleg.* 298 [3. 37–40]; cf. [9]. Amongst other sources and [2. 27–36] are the Homeric D-scholia (esp. on the meaning of words). In the first part of the latest edition [2], 'scholiastic *epimerismi*' are restored for the first book of the *Iliad* ([3]: edition of the alphabetical *epimerismi*. The Homeric *epimerismi* constituted an important source for the *Etymologicum Parvum* [8. 200–204; 2. 38f.], then the *Etymologicum Genuinum*, the encyclopaedia αἱμωδεῖν (*haimōdeîn*) (edition: [3. 825–1016]), the compilation of so-called *Eklogaí* [4], and the *Regulae in Homericas voces* (edition [5]), were also used by Tzetzes, *Exegesis in Homeri Iliadem*, by Eustathius, Zonaras, and in the scholia on Oppianus' *Halieutiká*.

Editions: 1 Georgii Choerobosci Epimerismi in Psalmos, ed. Th. Gaisford, 1842 (repr. 1963) 2 Epimerismi Homerici, Pars Prior, ed. A.R. Dyck, 1983 (SGLG 5/1) 3 Epimerismi Homerici, Pars Altera Lex. ΑΙΜΩΔΕΙΝ, ed. A.R. Dyck, 1995 (SGLG 5/2) 4 Cramer, Anecdota Graeca Oxoniensia 2, 427–487 5 P. Matranga, Anecdota Graeca, 1850, 536–555 (repr. 1971).
Literature: 6 Hunger, Literatur, II, 22–29 7 R.H. Robins, The Byzantine Grammarians, 1993, 125–148 8 R. Reitzenstein, Gesch. der griech. Etymologika, 1897 9 A.R. Dyck, ANRW II 34.1, 1993, 792f. S.FO.

Epimetheus see → Prometheus

Epinetron (ἐπίνητρον; *epínētron*). A curved cover, wrongly referred to as *ónos* (ὄνος), for the protection of thighs and knees during the cleaning and combing of wool; according to Hesychius s.v., the *epinetron* was used to card the fibres, but more likely to prepare the rovings (see illustr.). *Epinetra* were generally made from clay or wood; some painted clay *epinetra* from the 5th cent. BC are extant.
→ Eretria Painter

A. Lezzi-Hafter, Der Eretria-Maler, 1988, 253–262; A. Pekridou-Gorecki, Mode im antiken Griechenland, 1989, 16–20. I.S.

Representations: C.H. E. Haspels, A Fragmentary Onos in the Allard Pierson Museum, in: BABesch 29, 1954, 25–30; G. Bakalakis, Zur Verwendung des Epinetrons, in: JÖAI 45, 1960, Beibl., 199–208.

Epinicus (Ἐπίνικος; *Epínikos*).
[1] Comic poet; two titles of his plays and two fragments are extant. The dating of his life (late 3rd/early 2nd cent. BC) is based on the title of his play, *Mnēsiptólemos*: it refers to the court historiographer (FGrH 164) of Antiochus III (223–187 BC), a remarkably late example for the mockery of a named character

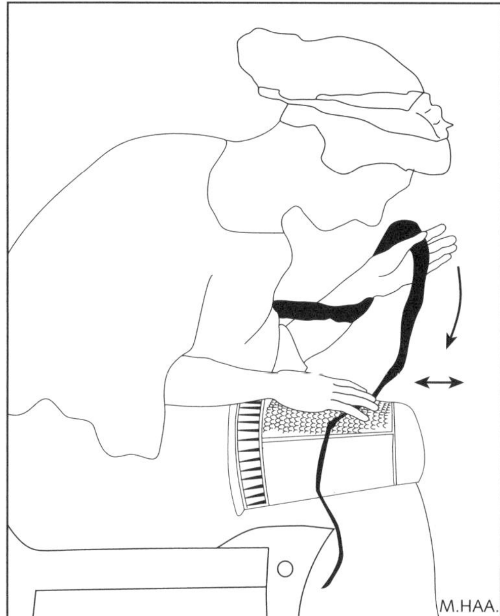

Production of the roving with the help of the *epinetron*: the raw material is held by the left hand, while the right hand stretches the fleece and rubs it up and down the *epinetron*. Its surface is roughened by scratching or scales, so as to stop the material from slipping.

(ὀνομαστὶ κωμῳδεῖν; *onomastì kōmōideîn*). Fr. 1 sees Mnesiptolemus speaking for himself, parodying the ornate, almost dithyrambic style, in which he describes the banalest of acts performed by his sovereign.

1 PCG V, 1986, 174–176. H.-G.NE.

[2] High-ranking revenue officer under Leo I († AD 474), a favourite of Leo's wife Verina. In 475, E. was made *praef. praetorio Orientis* by Verina's brother Basiliscus, the usurper against emperor Zeno. After Zeno's victory in August 476, E. was deposed, but otherwise left in peace. In 478 he was exiled to Isauria after an uprising against Zeno, but he soon returned to Constantinople following mediation by the influential Illus. In the summer of 480, he revolted again, and was subsequently executed.

PLRE 2, 397; Stein, Spätröm. R. 2, 8–17. F.T.

Epinikion (ἐπινίκιον; *epiníkion*, sc. μέλος; *mélos*, ᾆσμα; *âisma*), 'victory song'.
A. Term B. Development

A. Term

The adjective *epiníkios* is used for the closer definition of ἀοιδή (*aoidḗ*; song) in Pind. Nem. 4,78, whereas in Aesch. Ag. 174 the neutr. pl. *epiníkia* represents a shout of victory. In prose, the term, in conjunction with θύειν (*thýein*) or ἑστιᾶν (*hestiân*), generally refers to the sacrifices (sc. ἱερά; *hierá*), which followed a victory in battle (Dem. Or. 19,128) or took place as part of festival celebrations ([Dem. or.] 59,33; cf. Pl. Symp. 173a). The neutr. sing. *epiníkion* was first used by Alexandrian scholars to describe the songs about the victors in the Panhellenic Games. Poets themselves rather tend to use the terms *enkṓmios* or *epikṓmios hýmnos* (cf. Pind. Pyth. 10,53): a song on the occasion of a *kṓmos*, a procession in celebration of a victory, and thus a paean.

B. Development

Its origins are unknown. In Ol. 9,1–3 Pindar goes back to a chorus by Archilochus, which was sung in Olympia in honour of the victor, the words of which are preserved in the corresponding scholion (324 West [1]): it was an invocation of Hercules and Iolaus. Eratosthenes, who is quoted in the scholion, maintains that this song was not an *epinikion*, but Pindar seems to have seen it as an example of occasional poetry and a forerunner to his own, much more elaborate, composition which was meant to be performed upon the victor's return home. *Hýmnoi* addressed the gods directly; as this is the term most frequently used by poets of *epinikia* to describe their songs, it seems obvious to take a *hymnos* to the deified Hercules as a forerunner of an *epinikion* on mortals and the beginnings of a partial secularization of the genre. Pindar also uses the expression of a *hymnos* to Castor and Iolaus (Pind. Pyth. 2,69; Isthm. 1,16); this also suggests the view of a song in praise of superhuman competitors (*athlētaí*). The term *Kastóreion* was seen as 'synonymous with *epinikion*' [2. 494, n. 18]: in Pind. Ol. 3,34–37, it is Hercules and the Dioscuri who together organize and attend the games in Olympia. It was a common literary view that the roots of the *epinikion* lay in the tribute to characters of such distinction; this is confirmed by Pindar's statement that in the moment of victory, mortal men came the closest ever to the gods, as well as by his (and also Bacchylides') repeated reminders that men have but a limited life span.

Members of the aristocracy demanded tributes which went beyond the singing of simple choruses; and when from the 6th cent. BC the games in Olympia were joined by those in Delphi, in Nemea and those on the Isthmus, poets were commissioned to write them. The earliest known writer of epinician poetry was Simonides (506–519 PMG). In 520 BC, he wrote a poem for the wrestler Glaucus of Carystus, in which he draws an exaggerated comparison between the young athlete and Hercules and Polydeuces (509 PMG); an anecdote told by Cicero and Quintilian further emphasizes the importance of the Dioscuri (=Tyndaridae) in Simonides' poetry [510 PMG]. As a rule, the elaborate *epiníkia* of → Pindarus and → Bacchylides tell a mythical tale, most often centred around Hercules. In its most accomplished form at the peak of its development, this genre probably owed as much to tradition as to the clients' wishes [3]. The songs themselves provide no indication as to whether the lyrics of epinician poetry were monodic or choral [4].

1 IEGi 2 H. Fränkel, Dichtung und Philosphie des frühen Griechentums, [2]1962 3 W. Schadewaldt, Der Aufbau des Pindarischen Epinikions, [2]1966
4 M. Heath, M. Lefkowitz, Epinician Performance, in: CPh 86, 1991, 173–191. E.R.

Epione (Ἠπιώνη; *Ēpiṓnē*). Wife of → Asclepius, with whom she had the daughters → Hygieia, Aceso, Panacea, and Aegle, and the sons → Machaon and → Podalirius (in great detail in the epigraphical paeans of Macedonius, the so-called Erythraean paean, and of Dion, CollAlex 136–139 Powell); she was reputedly a daughter of → Heracles. In contrast with the sons who in Homer are frequently referred to solely as sons of Asclepius, i.e. only indirectly linked to her, there is a close and direct link with her daughters, whose evocative names embody aspects of expected healing in the same way as her own (< ḗpios; *ḗpios*, 'gentle'); presumably, this mythology was an Epidaurian invention. Her cult is evident in Epidaurus (inscriptions from the imperial age; two statues: Paus. 2,27,5; 2,29,1) as well as in Cos (LSCG 152; 159, 3rd cent. BC; with priestess), in both locations closely connected with Asclepius; epigraphical paeans indicate that there must have been other locations, too, where E. and her daughters were venerated jointly with Asclepius. F.G.

Epiorkia (ἐπιορκία; *epiorkía*) means 'perjury', ever since Homer and throughout (with the exception of a single incidence in Solon's Laws as 'oath', Lys. 10,17). It was common practice for every → oath to conclude with a curse for a potential perjurer. As *epiorkia* was not a secular offence, its punishment — which was not limited to the offender himself, but could extend to his entire household — was in the remit of the gods, who were witnesses and guarantors of the oath (Xen. An. 2,5,21; Dem. Or. 23,68; 19,220; Lys. 32,13).
→ Oath

K. Latte, s.v. Meineid, RE XV 1, 346ff. G.T.

Epiparodos The return of the chorus after it had left the orchestra during the performance of a play (μετάστασις χοροῦ; *metástasis choroû*, cf. Poll. 4,108), as in: Aesch. Eum. 231, 244; Soph. Aj. 814, 866; Eur. Alc. 746, 861, Hel. 385, 515, Rhes. 564, 674; Aristoph. Eccl. 310, 478.
→ Parodos

O. Taplin, The Stagecraft of Aeschylus, 1977, 377–381. B.Z.

Epiphaneia (Ἐπιφάνεια; *Epipháneia*).
[1] City in Cilicia Pedias (Ptol. 5,8,7; Steph. Byz. s.v. E., 274 Meineke), previously Oeniandus (Plin. HN 5,93), renamed E. after → Antiochus [6] IV Epiphanes. Road station (Geogr. Rav. 2,16,93; [2. 766]). In AD 260, E. was captured by Šapur I [1. 312f.]. After the restructuring of the province in AD 408, E. was seen as one of the cities of *Cilicia II* (Hierocles, 705,5). Its ruins (well preserved theatre and aqueduct) are *c.* 8 km west of Erzin in Gözene/Gözcucler Harabeleri.

1 A. Maricq, Res Gestae Divi Saporis, in: Syria 35, 1958, 312f. 2 Miller, 766.

M. Gough, s.v. E., PE, 315; Hild/Hellenkemper, s.v. E., 249f. M.H.S.

[2] (Ḫamat, mod. Ḥamāh). City in central Syria on the → Orontes.
A. Ancient Orient and Hellenism B. Roman and Byzantine Period

A. Ancient Orient and Hellenism

An important regional centre from the Bronze Age onwards. Danish excavations (1931–1938) found evidence of settlement from the 5th millennium BC. The earliest reference to the town in the Ebla Texts (→ Ebla) of the 3rd millennium BC is controversial. There is no record of the ancient name of Ḫamat in the 2nd millennium, even though archaeological remains of the middle and late Bronze Age have been found. From the 9th cent. BC, the settlement is evident in Assyrian texts (generally as 'land of Ḫamat') and in the Old Aramaic stele inscription of king Zakkūr of *c.* 800 BC. Inscriptions in Luwian hieroglyphs date from the 1st millennium BC. In 710 BC, Ḫamat was destroyed by Sargon II, but the reference 'land of Ḫamat' can still be found in Neo-Babylonian texts. There are frequent references to the city in the OT. Archaeological findings confirm a break in settlement activity during the Achaemenid period. Habitation only began again in the Hellenistic period; the city was probably renamed E. under → Antiochus [6] IV Ephiphanes. However, the old name survived as *Amathe* in Josephus as well as in the Arabic *Ḥamāh*.

J.D. Hawkins, Hamath, RLA 4, 67–70; H. Klengel, Syria 3000 to 300 B.C., 1992; A. de Maigret, La Cittadella Aramaica di Hama, 1979. G.LE.

B. Roman and Byzantine Period

In Roman times, the town expanded downwards into the valley of the Orontes, where a 3rd-cent. temple marks the development of a new centre of cult worship in the place now occupied by the Ummayad Mosque. The temple was converted to a church in the 4th/5th cents., but E. had been a bishop's seat from as early as 325. During the Muslim conquest of Syria (636/7), E. surrendered and was again renamed Ḥamāt. As a small insignificant town, it remained to the 10th cent. part of the military district of Ḥimṣ. The tell of E./Ḥamāt continued to be settled up to the Mongol invasion of 1260.

M. Buhl, s.v. Hamath, Anchor Bible Dictionary 3, 33–36; Hama, fouilles et recherches 3, 1986; 4.2, 1957; 4.3, 1969. T.L.

[3] see → Ecbatana

Epiphanes (Ἐπιφανής; *Epiphanḗs*, 'god manifest'). Epithet of Hellenistic rulers, already evident in Athens in the early Hellenistic period (307 BC) in the godlike veneration of Antigonus [1] Monophthalmos and his son Demetrius Poliorketes and the decrees issued in their honour. In this, the beneficial power (→ Epiphany) of the manifest deities was transferred to and celebrated in the physically present (*parousía*) king, who was venerated as a god (*theós*) and who, it was hoped, would act as saviour (*sotḗr*) and benefactor (*euergétēs*) (Demochares, FGrH 75 F 2; Duris, FGrH 76 F 13; Diod. Sic. 20,46,1–3; Plut. Demetr. 10–13; 23f.). It was particularly in conjunction with or rather through the concepts of *soter* and *theos* that Epiphanes became the epithet of a ruler, with Ptolemy V (OGIS 90,5: 27.3.196) the earliest example; subsequently, it was borne by Antiochus IV (174–164, popularly parodied as 'Epimanes': Pol. 26,1; 1a), of the Seleucid rulers also by Antiochus VI and Seleucus VI, and also by the rulers of Commagene, who traced their line back i.a. to the Seleucids, namely Antiochus I and IV and the latter's son as well as their more distant descendant Antiochus Philopappus.

→ Epiphany

E. Pax, s.v. Epiphanie, RAC 5, 832–909, esp. 842ff.; F. Taeger, Charisma 1, 1957, 257f., 270ff., 318ff. A.ME.

Epiphanius (Ἐπιφάνιος; *Epiphánios*).
[1] of Salamis
A. Biography B. Works

A. Biography

E. was born between 310 and 320 in the Palestinian Beṯ Guvrin/Eleutheropolis (short biography in GCS Epiphanius 1,1 Holl), more precisely in the nearby village of Besanduke/Beṯ Zedek (= Dair Saʿad?), probably as the son of Christian parents. He became an ascetic early on in his life, and in conjunction with that may have spent longer periods in Egypt (Sozom. Hist. eccl. 6,32,3); at the age of about 20, he founded a monastery in his home village. At about the same time, he was ordained to the priesthood. The extent of his fame is well illustrated by the fact that in 367 (or 366) he was elected bishop of Constantia/Salamis on Cyprus. On the other hand, for reasons no longer known, he did not succeed his local bishop Eutychius of Eleutheropolis after the latter's death after 363. In 374, he tried in vain to mediate between the parties in the Antiochene schism. In his episcopate, he was particularly concerned with safeguarding the 'orthodoxy' of the Church: in 382 he took part in a Roman synod, and together with → Hieronymus, spearheaded the opposition to the Origenist position. In 390, he engaged his fellow bishop Iohannes of Jerusalem in a kind of 'sermonical duel' (Jer. Contra Iohannes Hierosolymitanum 11), and continued his fight against him for several years, during which time he presumably stayed in Palestine. Following mediation by the Alexandrian bishop Theophilus (Socr. 6,10), the two opponents were reconciled. In the spring of 396, E. returned to Cyprus. He became briefly involved in the controversy surrounding → Iohannes Chrysostomus in Constantinople, and died on his return journey from there to Cyprus in 403 (or 402).

B. Works

Alongside several letters, which on the whole have survived only as fragments (CPG 2, 3750–3760), in 374, E. wrote a compendium of Church dogmatics under the appropriate title of Ἀγκυρωτός (*Ankyrōtós*, 'The well-Anchored', CPG 2, 3744). Originally, this work ended, as evident in the Ethiopian tradition, with the Nicene symbol (=profession of faith) of 325 [6]. His main work is considered to be the representation and refutation of 80 pagan, Jewish, and Christian 'heresies' (with extensive quotes from source texts) in the 'Medicine Chest' (πανάριον εἴτουν κιβώτιον; *panárion eítoun kibṓtion, Adversus haereses*), completed in 377. Both works were published between 1915 and 1933 by K. Holl in an edition which is quite partial to conjecture, but still as yet unsurpassed (CPG 2, 3745: GCS Epiphanius 1–3; GCS 2–3 ²1980/1985 Dummer). E. is also the author of a biblical encyclopaedia, extant in Greek and Syriac (περὶ μέτρων καὶ σταθμῶν; *perì métrōn kaì stathmôn, De mensuris et ponderibus*, 'On Weights and Measures', CPG 2, 3746), and of a treatise, which is only completely extant in Georgian, on the precious stones in the vestments of the Jewish high priest (*De XII gemmis*, CPG 2, 3748). Both his theological originality and the source value of his polemics are nowadays seen in a much more positive light.

1 F. Williams, The Panarion of Epiphanius of Salamis, 2 vols., 1987/1993 2 E. A. Clark, The Origenist Controversy, 1992, 85–104 3 K. Holl, Gesammelte Aufsätze zur Kirchengesch. II, 1964 (first in 1928), 204–224, 310–387 4 A. Pourkier, L'hérésiologie chez Épiphane de Salamine, 1992 (see also review by Uthemann, in: ByzZ 86/7, 1994, 135f.) 5 W. Schneemelcher, s.v. Epiphanius von Salamis, RAC 5, 909–927 6 B. M. Weischer, Die ursprüngliche Form des ersten Glaubenssymbols im Ankyrōtos des Epiphanios von Salamis, in: Theologie und Philosophie 53, 1978, 407–414. C.M.

[2] Bishop of Ticinum (Pavia) 466–496; through his intervention with the (Arian) Gothic kings → Odoacer and → Theoderic, he managed to ease the lot of the Roman people. A *vita* of E. was written by → Ennodius.

Edition: M. Cesa, 1988 (= Ennod. p.331–383 Hartel = CSEL 6, p. 84–109 Vogel = MGH AA 7).

[3] E. Scholasticus. Around the mid 6th cent. AD, he was commissioned by → Cassiodorus to translate Greek works into Latin [4], the most important of which is the *Historia tripartita* [1; 2; 5].

1 W. Jacob, R. Hanslik, 1952 (CSEL 71)
2 R. Hanslik, E. Scholasticus oder Cassiodor?, in: Philologus 115, 1971, 107–113 3 PLRE 3, 446 4 ThlL Index ²1990, 45–46 5 F. Weissengruber, E.S. als Übersetzer, 1972.

[4] Syrian, who according to → Eunapius [1] worked in Athens during the 1st half of the 4th cent. as a teacher of rhetoric along with Prohaeresius [2; 3]. It is uncertain whether he is identical with either E. of Petra, whose rhetorical works are listed in the Suda E 2741, or with the Sophist E., who taught in Laodicea (Sozom. Hist. eccl. 6,25,9–10) [4] (Fr.: on the doctrine of stasis [6], on Demosthenes [5]).

1 Eunapius ed. GIANGRANDE 1956, 79–80 2 PLRE 1, E. 1 3 G.A. KENNEDY, Greek Rhetoric under Christian Emperors, 1983, 137, 140 4 R.J. PENELLA, Greek Philosophers and Sophists in the 4th Cent. A.D. 1, 1990, 94–97, 101f. 5 M.R. DILTS (ed.), Scholia Demosthenica, 1983, p. 134,3; 203,20 6 WALZ, 4, 463–465.

[5] Member of the Sophist circle of Gaza at the turn of the 5th to the 6th cent. He was the recipient of letters by → Procopius and → Aeneas [3] of Gaza.

PLRE 2, E. 4/5.

[6] Lat. bishop, author of an *interpretatio evangeliorum*, discovered in 1905 by G. MORIN. The Vulgar Latin tinge of its language indicates that it cannot have been written any earlier than the 5th cent.

EDITIONS: 1 A. ERIKSON, 1939 = Migne Suppl. 3, 1963, 834–964.
LITERATURE: 2 Id., Sprachliche Bemerkungen zu E., 1939. O.HI.

Epiphany (ἐπιφάνεια; *epipháneia*, 'manifestation, appearance') refers to the manifestation of a deity in a spontaneous vision, or during an actual ritual process (→ Ecstasy), as well as in stories; such appearances are the essence of superhuman beings. Because divine existence mainly manifests itself in the active help given to human beings, deities, who had been helpfully present, were from the Hellenistic period onwards denoted with the → epiclesis 'becoming apparent' (ἐπιφανής, → *epiphanḗs*, Lat. *praesens*). Epiphany seems to have played an important role within the Minoan religion; several seal rings bear illustrations of a male or female deity appearing from above within a circle of—mostly dancing—female worshippers [1]; epiphany in the form of a bird is more problematic—according to some scholars, it is still apparent in Homer ([2. 330–340; 3], rejected by [4]). In Homer's world of heroes, the gods are mostly incognito when they appear to humans; it is only some minor details which might give the deity away after all (Aphrodite: Hom. Il. 3,396f.; Poseidon: Il. 14,385), or a god might chose to show himself to some chosen individuals (Athena and Achilles: Il. 1,188–222). For that reason, a stranger could always be a god in disguise.

The set narrative form of an epiphany is manifest ever since the Homeric hymns, when → Aphrodite reveals her divine nature to → Anchises after their night of love (H. Hom. 5,172–183), or → Demeter her true identity to the Eleusinian kings after having been disturbed by Metanira (H. Hom. 2,188–190; 275–280). It is a standard element of such epiphanies that the deity is larger than life, and surrounded by light and a divine sweet fragrance; mortals react with fear, which the deity seeks to dispel. This narrative pattern can be found throughout ancient literature (e.g. Callim. Fr. 1,21–28; Ov. Fast. 1,93–101), but also in the NT (epiphany of the angels in the Christmas story, Lc 2,13ff.). Epiphanies of deities and heroes mainly occur in crisis situations, but they can also serve to legitimize political claims, as in the case of Peisistratus and Phye (Hdt. 1,60). In war in particular, gods and heroes appear in order to provide support in battle; Archilochus emphasizes Athena's help in securing victory (IEG fr. 94), Polygnotus' picture of Marathon shows → Ajax, the helping hero (Paus. 1,15,2f.), Herodotus stresses the achievements of gods and heroes in the Persian War (8,37f.; individual hero: 6,117), and throughout antiquity numerous tales and inscriptions illustrate the living faith in such epiphanies [5; 6]. Frequently, the beginning of a cult was the result of an epiphany: The Athenian cult of → Pan was instituted as a result of his intervention at Marathon (Hdt. 6,105f.) [7]. The same pattern can still be recognized in the apotheosis of a Roman emperor (→ Deification).

Cultic epiphanies belong to the ecstatic cults, e.g. that of → Dionysus, where pictorial evidence shows the appearance of the god and his followers (Apulian calyx krater: [8. 133f.]); However, in the majority of Hellenistic and Imperial cults of individual helpers in time of need, epiphanies are replaced by dream visions (→ Asclepius, → Isis, → Incubation). Neoplatonic philosophers and theurgists sought the epiphany of a deity through private ecstatic rituals (Plot. 5,8,2), but it is also said of Iamblichus that he was able to call for local deities to appear (Eunap. VS 5,2,2–7). It was part of the magicians' stock in trade to evoke an individual epiphany of a powerful deity as well as to conjure up → demons. The shape of an epiphany is determined by culture. Whereas a heroified dead appeared in an epiphany or in a dream looking the same as he had in real life, deities generally appeared in the form familiar from their cult images [9]; in some rites, masks were used to represent the deities (Paus. 4,27,1–3; Polyaenus, Strat. 8,59; Plut. Dion 56, 982d-f). Christianity continues in the same tradition: reports of epiphanies in the NT use the familiar narrative structure (e.g. the epiphany of the angels before the shepherds, or Saul's epiphany in Acts 9,3ff. [10]). However, the divine epiphany was eclipsed by the epiphany of saints, whose support now replaced the earlier one of gods and heroes [6].

1 R. HÄGG, Die göttliche Epiphanie im minoischen Ritual, in: MDAI 101, 1986, 41–62. 2 NILSSON, MMR 3 F. MATZ, Göttererscheinung und Kultbild im minoischen Kreta, Abh. der Akad. der Wiss. Mainz, 1958, H. 7 4 H. BANNERT, Zur Vogelgestalt der Götter bei Homer, in: WS 12, 1978, 29–42 5 SEG 26, 1986, 1581 6 W. SPEYER, Die Hilfe und Epiphanie einer Gottheit, eines Heroen und eines Heiligen in der Schlacht, in: E. DASSMANN, K.S. FRANK (ed.), Pietas 1980, 55–77 7 PH. BORGEAUD, Recherches sur le dieu Pan, 1979 8 A. BOTTINI, Archeologia della salvezza, 1992 9 H. VERSNEL, What did An-

cient Man see when he saw a God? Some Reflections on Graeco-Roman Antiquity, in: J. VAN DER PLAS (ed.), Effigies Dei, 1987, 42–55 10 F. E. BRENK, Greek epiphanies and Paul on the road to Damaskos, in: U. BIANCHI (ed.), The Notion of Religion in Comparative Research, 1994, 415–424. F.G.

Epirrhematic Derived from *tó epírrhēma* (τὸ ἐπίρρημα, 'that which is said afterwards'), i.e. the speech following a lyric part. The succession of lyrical and spoken (or rather recited) parts is referred to as an epirrhematic composition. Aeschylus frequently used this form in semi-lyrical → amoibaia. In the Old Comedy, epirrhematic composition can be found in the → parabasis and in the epirrhematic agon.

TH. GELZER, Der epirrhematische Agon bei Aristophanes, 1960; B. ZIMMERMANN, Unt. zur Form und dramatischen Technik der Aristophanischen Komödien I, [2]1985, 253–261. B.Z.

Epirus (Ἤπειρος; *Épeiros*, Epirus)
I. REGION II. POPULATION III. HISTORICAL DEVELOPMENT

I. REGION
E. is located at the north-western fringe of the Greek cultural sphere, nowadays comprising northern Greece and southern Albania. From Homer (8th cent. BC) to the late 5th cent., the geographical term ἤπειρος (*ḗpeiros*) referred to the mainland north of the Gulf of Ambracia. There is a wide variation in the attribution of individual tribes to E. both in ancient and modern literature, making it impossible clearly to define E.'s geographic expansion [1]. E. was bordered in the west by the Ionian Sea, its southern border (to the → Acarnanians and → Amphilochi) was the Gulf of Ambracia, and its eastern one to the Macedonians (→ Macedonia), → Thessalians, and Athamanes (→ Athamania) the high mountains of the Pindus range, passable only in a few places; its northern border is taken to be the Aous and the Acroceraunian Mountains, but both culturally and linguistically, the boundaries to the Illyrians in the transitory area of Amantia and → Byllis are fluid. West to east communication within E. is very restricted, because the region is dissected from NNW to SSE by four mighty limestone and flysch mountain ranges, with a height of up to 2,633 m. The rivers in the mountainous regions are not navigable, even though they carry a lot of water because of the high level of precipitation; the Aous (mod. Vjosë) has its mouth in Albania, the Thyamis (Kalamas) in a sizeable delta opposite Corcyra, the Acheron south of the mod. Parga, and the Luros and Arachthus flow into the Gulf of Ambracia.

II. POPULATION
Life and economy in central E. differed markedly from that of southern Greece: it was dominated by pasture farming in woodlands and on distant pastures (transhumance) with both summer and winter pastures; any sizeable arable farming was only possible in the basin region around the mod. Ioannina (→ Dodona), the fertile hills of Cassopaea, and also the plains of the river deltas. The three main tribes of the → Chaones, Thesproti, and Molossi were themselves made up from small tribes, which in turn consisted of numerous *ethne* (list of tribes: [2. 134–141]). Ancient authors saw the inhabitants of E. as *bárbaroi* (βάρβαροι, Thuc. 1,47,3; Scymn. 444f.; Str. 7,7,1) and as related to the Macedonians (Str. 7,7,8). However, there was an early Hellenization of the elite, the inhabitants of the coastal towns (Hecat. FGrH 1 F 105 lists → Buthrotum, Argos Amphilochicum, and Orikos Poleis), and also the sanctuaries (Dodona, Nekyomanteion). The original language is unknown; rare early written evidence from Dodona shows Corinthian letters with local (?) deviations [13. 228–230, 452], the earliest (longer) inscriptions of *c.* 380 BC are written in a north-west Greek dialect.

III. HISTORICAL DEVELOPMENT
A. EARLY HISTORY AND ARCHAIC PERIOD
B. CLASSICAL PERIOD C. HELLENISTIC PERIOD
D. IMPERIAL PERIOD E. BYZANTINE PERIOD

A. EARLY HISTORY AND ARCHAIC PERIOD
In the Late Helladic period, the Mycenaean-Helladic culture can only be ascertained as a marginal influence in E. Late Helladic material (ceramics, swords) and architecture ('Cyclopean' walls, tholos graves) are found up to a line of the mod. Parga – Dodona — Ioannina [3. 31–33; 4. 195–207; 5. 233–265]; to the north of that line, tumulus graves and grave gifts indicate a link with the Macedonian-Illyrian region [6. 619–656]. Earliest written references are in Homer, to the Zeus oracle of Dodona, and also to the oracle of the dead (Nekyomanteion) of → Ephyra [3]. In the Archaic period, Greek culture advanced into E. from the Corinthian colonies of Corcyra, → Ambracia, and → Apollonia [1], as well as the Eleian ones of Buchetion, Elatria, Pandosia, Batiae in Cassopaea [7. 134], e.g. through the import of ceramics into the rural uplands [3. 53–64; 8].

B. CLASSICAL PERIOD
Till the 4th cent. BC, there is no indication of the development of 'state-like' structures. The monarchy had been abolished by the Thesproti and Chaones (two annual chief magistrates, Thuc. 2,80,5) as early as the 5th cent. BC, but survived somewhat longer in the interior of the country (Atintanes, Molossi, and with the Athamanes into the 2nd cent.). Initially, the leading role was played by the Thesproti (Str. 7,7,11; Hdt. 2,56; Hecat. FGrH 1 F 108); however, from the 6th cent., the Chaones assumed greater importance [9. 479], until finally, towards the end of the 5th cent., the Molossi expanded westward and took control of Dodona and parts of the coast opposite Corcyra and along the Gulf of Ambracia [10. 22f.]. The leading role of the Molossi

probably originated with Tharypas, who had been educated in Athens and who at the end of the 5th cent. entered into an alliance with that city (in the → Peloponnesian War, the Molossi — in line with all the other tribes — had supported Corinth [9. 506–508]). His successor Alcetas [2] I was from 375 BC a member of the Second → Athenian League. The structure of the Molossian state developed under these rulers: one king (at times two), who ruled with limited authority (military monarchy, Arist. Pol. 1313a 19–29), officials and representatives (δαμιοργοί, *damiorgoí*; συνάρχοντες, *synárchontes*) of the Molossian, Thesprotian and Chaonian (?) tribes, who formed a council as part of the Molossian confederation [9. 536–539]; onset of minting of coins [11. 85–106]. In *c.* 360, the Molossi and the Macedonians entered into an alliance, and in 357, Philip II married Olympias, a niece of the Molossian king → Arybbas. However, the latter was deposed in 343/2 and replaced by → Alexander [6], beginning a period in which E. began to open up. The capture of the Eleian colonies (Dem. Or. 7,32; Theopomp. FGrH 115 F 206; F 207) provided Molossia with access to the sea. From 334 to 331, Alexander pursued an unsuccessful military campaign in southern Italy (Aristot. fr. 614 Rose). Whereas before *c.* 360, most settlements retained a village character (Scyl. 26–33; IG IV[2] 95), this period saw towns like Cassope, Titane, Elea, Buthrotum, Antigonea, Byllis, and Amantia being founded as (or expanded to) *póleis* of Greek character.

C. Hellenistic Period

After the death of Alexander [6], the three largest tribes (later also joined by Ambracia, Amphilochia, etc. al) formed an alliance (between 331 and 325) [10. 25–31], minting coins with the legend ΑΠΕΙΡΩΤΑΝ (*APEIRŌTAN*). The Aeacids (named after → Aeacides [2], from 313 BC) on the Molossian throne acted as *hēgēmṓn* of the alliance, but never became king of all Epirotes. Pyrrhus' (297–272) accession to the throne signalled the beginning of E.'s heyday: the tribes were unified, the territory expanded though marriages as well as armed conquests, towns were founded, and the new capital of Ambracia was embellished. In *c.* 232, the last of the Aeacids were murdered, the Molossian monarchy deposed, and the Epirote League founded as a tribal state. (τὸ κοινόν; *tò koinón*, or respectively τὸ ἔθνος; *tò éthnos* [1. 198–396], differently in [3. 125–134]), within which the smaller *koiná* continued to exist as sovereign communities. But in the Social War, the newly formed league was powerless against Aetolian intrusions (219: pillage of Dodona). In both the First and the Second Macedonian War, E. fought against Rome alongside Philip V; however, after the peace of 196, it was nonetheless admitted to Rome's *amicitia*. In the Third Macedonian War, the *koinón* split: in 170/69, the Chaones and Thesproti supported App. Claudius, but Molossia went with Perseus (Liv. 43,21,4). In a dreadful act of revenge, Molossia and parts of Thesprotia were given up to pillage in 167: 70 settlement were destroyed, and 150,000 people became slaves (Str. 7,7,3; Liv. 45,34,1–6; Plut. Aem. 29). The war resulted in a reorganization of the borders (SEG 35, 665), fragmentation into regional *koiná* (Syll.[3] 653A. B; 654A) [3. 23–27, 151–158], settlement of Roman landowners, known as *synepirotae* [3. 245–254], levying of troops (SEG 36, 555), and in the 1st cent. BC the foundation of Roman colonies (Dyrrhachium, Byllis, Buthrotum).

D. Imperial period

The foundation of Nicopolis in 27 BC absorbed urban life in the south of E. [12]. The coastal towns benefited from their location along the Roman imperial roads [15. 225–261; 9. 690–705]. North of the Oricus, E. belonged to the *prov. Macedonia*, south of it to *Achaia*. At the latest under Trajan, E. became a province in its own rights [12. 201–204]; under Diocletian, the province was split into *E. Nova* (capital: Dyrrhachium) and *E. Vetus* (capital: Nicopolis). Initially, E. belonged to the diocese of *Moesia*, later (mid 4th cent) to *Macedonia*. Epigraphical evidence: [14; 2. 534–592]. Coins: [11].

1 Philippson/Kirsten 2, 1 2 P. Cabanes, L'Épire, 1976 3 Id. (ed.), L'Illyrie méridionale et l'Épire dans l'antiquité 1, 1987 4 K. Soueref, Das prähistorische Epeiros, in: P. Berktold (ed.), Akarnanien, 1996 5 ΦΗΓΟΣ [PHĒGOS]. FS S.I. Dakaris, 1994 6 CAH 3, 1, [2]1982 7 S.I. Dakaris, Cassopaia and the Eleian Colonies, 1971 8 I. Vokotopoulou, Vitsa, 1986 9 N.G. L. Hammond, E., 1967 10 P. Cabanes, Problèmes de géographie administrative et politique dans l'Épire, in: La géographie administrative et politique d'Alexandre à Mahomet, 1979, 19–38 11 P.R. Franke, Die antiken Münzen von E., 1961 12 D. Strauch, Die Umgestaltung NW-Griechenlands unter röm. Herrschaft, 1996 13 LSAG 14 P. Cabanes, F. Drini, Corpus des inscriptions grecques d'Illyrie méridionale et d'Épire 1, 1995 15 P. Cabanes, L'Illyrie méridionale et l'Épire dans l'antiquité 2, 1993.

Z. Andrea, Archaeology in Albania, in: Archaeological Reports 30, 1983/4, 102–119; 38, 1991/2, 71–88; A. Eggebrecht (ed.), Albanien, 1988; Soustal, Nikopolis, 47–54 and *passim* D.S.

E. Byzantine Period

Because of the scarcity of written sources, the history of post-Graeco-Roman E. depends largely on the consideration of archaeological and linguistic material, even though the evaluation of the great number of Slavic toponyms has only just begun.

The early Byzantine period was still characterized by the Diocletian administrative structure, i.e. the division into *Epirus nova* (→ Dyrrhachium) and *Epirus vetus* (→ Nicopolis) [1. 47ff.]. Neither the pillage by the Visigoths in 395/397, nor the piratical incursions of the Vandals from 467 (Procop. Vand. 3,5,23), which culminated in the occupation of Nicopolis, resulted in significant changes in the Late-Roman structures. Of great significance, however, was the settlement of Avars and Slavs, whose first incursion is documented for 548/9

(Procop. Vand. 7,29,1f.). For centuries, the region slipped out of Byzantine control ([3. 251]; recapture by the Byzantine empire in the 8th cent.); hardly any of the numerous fortifications reported by → Procopius (Aed. 4,1,35ff.; 4,4) have been located [2. 69ff.]. The Slavs settled mainly in the interior, in clan communities according to the evidence of place names (this aspect of toponyms is as yet insufficiently evaluated in [2]). The indigenous population fled to the islands, which remained under central (Byzantine) control (ascertainable for Euroea, whose inhabitants together with their bishop fled to → Corcyra in 591 [1. 51]). The central power had little interest in the interior of the country; only those islands of strategic importance for the sea traffic to Italy remained within the navy's sphere of control: the naval theme of Cephallenia was founded in the mid 8th cent. whereas the → theme of Nicopolis only followed towards the end of the 9th cent. As Nicopolis itself had already fallen into decline by that time, it was → Naupactus which became the seat of the *strategos*.

1 SOUSTAL/KODER TIB 3, 1981 2 E. CHRYSOS, Συμβολή στὴν ἱστορία τῆς Ἠπείρου κατὰ τὴν πρωτοβυζαντινὴ ἐποχὴ, Epeirotika Chronika 23, 1981, 9–104 3 G. SCHRAMM, Anfänge des albanischen Christentums, 1994 4 T.E. GREGORY, s.v. Epiros, ODB 1, 715f.

J.N.

Episkopos, Episkopoi

[1] The lexical meaning of *epískopos* equates to 'supervisor'. In the Greek world, *episkopos* habitually referred to an official, similar to → *epimelētaí* and → *epistátai*, but used less frequently. The Delian League sent *epískopoi*, who were Athenian officials, into allied cities, e.g. in order to set up a democratic constitution (Erythrae: ML 40; cf. Aristoph. Av. 1021–1034). Rhodian officials also included *episkopoi* (Syll.[3] 619), Massilia appointed an *episkopos* for its colony of Nicaea (ILS 6761), and Mithridates VI sent one to Ephesus (App. Mith. 187). In Egypt, an *episkopos* was answerable to a *dioikētḗs* (MITTEIS/WILCKEN 2, 2, no. 5).

P.J.R.

[2] Christian texts also used the term in its lexical meaning, e.g. for Christ (1 Petr 2,25) or God (Ignatius, Epistula ad Magn. 3,1). Initially, *episkopos* was also used as 'supervisor', in the sense of looking on benevolently from above (LXX translates פקד 'visit/haunt' as *episkopeîn*), also in respect of particular ways of supervision, such as visits to the sick (cf. Mt 25,36; 43), but equally in the sense of instruction, assignation, authorization. From the late 1st cent. BC, the Greek word is also used as a precise technical term for the (respectively initially a) leading spiritual office within the Christian congregations. It is possible that the development of an institution with that name was not only rooted in the documentary evidence from the pagan sphere, but also in the fact that the term *episkopos* was used for the office of 'supervisor' (מבקר) by the Qumran congregation: it was his task to admit new members, to teach and to preach, to call the congregation to assemble, and also to act a judge (QD 13,7; 1 QS 6,12; 14; 20). However, the earliest evidence of *episkopos* as a title of office originates from pagan-Christian congregations: as early as the mid 1st cent., in the greetings of his letter to the Philippians, Paul mentions special *epískopoi kaì diákonoi* (1,1), even though it is almost impossible to provide an exact definition of the function of these officials. By contrast, in the Milesian farewell speech, which Luke attributed to Paul, the elders of the congregation (=presbyters) were quite unspecifically referred to as *episkopoi* (Acts 20,28). However, it seems that within the small Pauline congregations of Asia Minor, as evident in the 'pastoral letters', such an office had developed as early as the 1st cent.

In this early period, the title of office is mainly used in the plural. For that reason, it is better to refer to them as *episkopoi* rather than 'bishops'; following the introduction of the Jewish presbyterian constitution to the Pauline congregations, they obviously represented a subgroup of presbyters. Similar to rabbis at their ordination (סמיכה), *episkopoi* were instituted in office through the laying-on of hands. They were required to show exemplary behaviour both in public and within their families (1 Tim 3,2–4); newly converted Christians were not admissible. The earliest precise accounts of the function of *episkopoi* is found in the first letter of Clement (→ Apostolic Fathers; end of the 1st cent.): *Episkopoi* should be 'men of trust' (1 Clem 44,2), their task seems to have been predominantly cultic, and they were not to be deposed (44,4). Only a little later, during the rule of → Traianus, the Antiochene bishop → Ignatius propagated in his letters to replace the traditional collegiate leadership structure with a 'monepiscopacy', i.e. to have only one *episkopos* at the head of a congregation, with a clearly understood difference in rank between him and the remaining presbyters: 'Wherever the *episkopos* appears, there is the congregation, the same as the *katholikḗ ekklesía* is found, wherever Jesus Christ is' (earliest documentary evidence for the linking of these terms). In the absence of an *episkopos*, neither baptisms nor eucharists were to be performed, but, whatever the *episkopos* approved, would also find favour in the eyes of God (Smyrn 8,1–2). The intensity of the arguments based on the philosophical concept of archetype and copy indicates that at the time this was a radically new and as yet unimplemented model of ecclesiastical organization; there is general consensus amongst modern scholars that the tripartite hierarchical structure (bishop, presbyter, deacon) generally only became established in the second half of the 2nd cent.

In Rome, monoepiscopacy only succeeded as a constitutional model in *c.* 189, after an initial authoritative advantage of the presbyter, who was charged with looking after outside contacts. It is possible that monoepiscopacy developed as the result of natural processes within collegially structured organs (as argued by HARNACK), but certainly also in answer to the perceived need in the 2nd cent. of having an authoritative leader figure lead the opposition against any 'heretical' movements (e.g. Gnosis). Recently, the theologumenon of the church as the 'house of God' has been cited: the *monoepiskopos* would thus equate to the 'sovereign head of the house' (DASSMANN).

From the 3rd cent., the 'monoepiscopacy' developed into the 'monarchical episcopate'; bishops demanded (at least in parts) such a level of authority above presbyters to make it impossible for the latter still to be involved in the leadership of a congregation. However, the extent of this power must not be overestimated; in the mid 3rd cent., Gregory Thaumaturgus officiated as *episkopos* for a congregation of 17 Christians (Greg. Nyss. vit. Greg. p. 16,2f HEIL). The concept of an uninterrupted chain of office holders gained in strength, tracing them back via the apostles to Christ himself (*diadochḗ/successio*); in contrast with the pagan succession of philosophers, it was also meant to imply the handing down of an unchanging tradition of faith. Lists of bishops for the most prominent of the episcopal seats were compiled retrospectively. The anonymous Church regulations, published as *Traditio Apostolica* and attributed to → Hippolytus (in its basis dating from the early 3rd cent.), complete this stage of the development. *Episkopoi* were inducted into office by laying-on of hands and prayer for the Holy Spirit. They were elected by the people as a whole (§2); some bishops of neighbouring congregations as well as the presbyterate were involved in the election. It is almost impossible to reconstruct the exact electoral procedure; however, the effect of the popular vote was limited by the fact that the election was only validated by the laying-on of hands by the neighbouring bishops. According to the regulations of the First Council of Nicaea (325; Canon 4), all bishops of a province should be involved in the laying-on of hands, but at least three bishops had to attend and lay on hands in person. Absent bishops as well as the metropolitan bishop of the province in question had to give their consent to the election and the induction into office. The precedence of the metropolitan bishops, which had developed in the course of the 3rd cent., was set as standard by the synodal canons of the 4th cent. (e.g. 9th Canon of Antioch). It was only in the 4th cent. that the political precedence of the metropolites of Rome, Alexandria, Antioch, and Constantinople as well as the honorary precedence of the metropolite of Jerusalem was codified (Council of Nicaea, canon 6/7, and of Constantinople 381, canon 3); the establishment of the primacy of Rome began at the latest under → Damasus of Rome (366–384). Leading clergy in rural areas (*chōrepískopoi*/ 'chorebishops') were stripped of their episcopal rights of precedence (Council of Serdica 342, canon 6). In the 3rd cent. it became more common that, alongside *confessores*, men of influence or high social standing were also elected bishops; on the other hand, there continued to be amongst the bishops prominent theologians, such as → Theopilus of Antioch; → Cyprianus of Carthage, or → Dionysius [52] of Alexandria).

However, alongside or even inside the majority church, there were circles who still did not accept the tripartite hierarchy of ecclesiastical office. → Epiphanus [1], for example, reports on a group which he referred to as Aerians (Haer. 75): they refuted that 'a bishop was worth more than a presbyter' (75,3,3).

In line with the increasing number of privileges the Church was granted by the state in the course of the 4th cent. BC, the office of bishop also underwent considerable changes: with the structures of the states collapsing, it gained immensely in political importance. This development, which also led to the adoption of all means employed in political dispute (such as bribery i. a.), unquestionably met with quite a critical reception within the Church. One of the causes of this change were the prerogatives, which had already been granted to the bishops by → Constantinus [1]: 313 saw the first convention of an episcopal law court, constituted by the *princeps* as an imperial law court (Optatus, Parm. 1,23,1–2); probably in June 318, the episcopal court of arbitration was recognized as the court of first instance dealing with civil cases, provided that both parties agreed to this (Cod. Theod. 1,27,1), and in 313/333, bishops were exempted from the *munera civilia* (Cod. Theod. 16,2,2) and permitted to use the → *cursus publicus* (cf. only Cod. Theod. 8,5,54). Various honorary privileges (the title of *vir clarissimus*, privileged dress etc.) demonstrate how bishops gained a more and more equal standing with officials of the state, without however ever directly becoming some themselves. Typical for the new 'political dimension' of the episcopal office from the 4th cent. are the 'court bishops' (e.g. → Eusebius of Nicomedia, but not → Eusebius of Caesarea), also 'court theologians' (cf. the work of the Homoean bishops Ursacius and Valens under Constantius II), also those bishops, who acted sovereignly within the sphere of Church politics (e.g. → Ambrosius of Milan, but also → Athanasius, → Basilius, → Cyrillus of Alexandria, or → Iohannes Chrysostomos), furthermore those bishops who acted as imperial judges or as patrons for members of the congregation (for the *intercessionis officium* cf. e.g. Aug. Epist. 151,2), and finally the *episkopos* as a municipal benefactor. It was in 5th-cent. Galllia that the foundations were laid for the 'secular rule' of bishops which was to dominate the Middle Ages. In view of the increasing importance of holy men in late antiquity, it is no surprise that it became more and more common for bishops to be recruited from monastic circles; most of the prominent late-antique theologians were bishops, even if they did not always take pleasure in carrying out their public office (e.g. → Gregorius of Nazianzus).

H.W. BEYER, H. KARPP, s.v. Bischof, RAC 2, 394–407; H. FREIHERR VON CAMPENHAUSEN, Kirchliches Amt und geistliche Vollmacht in den ersten drei Jh., 1953; E. DASSMANN, Ämter und Dienste in den frühchristlichen Gemeinden, 1994; A. HARNACK, Entstehung und Entwicklung der Kirchenverfassung und des Kirchenrechts in den ersten zwei Jh., 1910 (= 1990); H. LIETZMANN, Zur altchristlichen Verfassungsgesch., in: Id., KS, TU 67, 1958, 144–148; CH. MARKSCHIES, Zwischen den Welten wandern, 1997, 208–227; Id., Die politische Dimension des Bischofsamtes im vierten Jh., in: J. MEHLHAUSEN (ed.), Recht, Macht, Gerechtigkeit, 1997. C.M.

Epistatai (ἐπιστάται; *epistátai*, 'chairmen', 'superiors'). Title for various officials of the Greek world; see also *epimelētaí*, *epískopoi*.

1. *Epistatai* are most frequently found within the administration of both sacred treasures and public works. In Athens, committees of *epistatai* existed to oversee several of the public building projects of the Periclean era (e.g. ML 59 regarding the Parthenon), to supervise the treasure of the goddesses of Eleusis (IG I[3] 32; II[2] 1672), as well as other sacred funds. *Epistatai* of this nature were also found in other locations, such as Cyzicus (Syll.[3] 799), Ilion (330), and Rhodes (340; 931). In Miletus, *epistatai* looked after boys supported by a charitable foundation (Syll.[3] 577, 73).

2. In a more specific meaning, *epistates* referred to the chairman of a committee or an assembly. In Athens, the *prytáneis* and the *próhedroi* had one *epistates* for each day ([Aristot.] Ath. pol. 44). In many other cities, *epistateîn* described the position of chairman of the council or the citizens' assembly, amongst them Ilium (e.g. OGIS 219), Zelia (e.g. Syll.[3] 279), Magnesia on the Maeandrus (e.g. Syll.[3] 589: *epistates* of the *próhedroi*), Miletus (IMilet 1, 3 139 B), and Iasos (IK Iasos 32).

3. Hellenistic kings frequently appointed an *epistates* to act as their representative in a certain city, as e.g. the Antigonids in Thessalonica (IG X 2,1,3), a Bithynian king in Prusa at the Mysian Olympus (IK Prusa ad Olympum 1), and the Seleucids in Seleucea in Pieria (IGLS 3, 2, 1183). The *epistates* of the *koinón* of Zeus Panamaros near Stratoniceia was initially appointed by Philip V, later by Rhodes (IK Stratonikeia 4; 9); in a similar fashion, Rhodes also appointed an *epistates* for Syros (IG XII 5,1, 652).

→ Epimeletai; → Episkopoi P.J.R.

Episteme see → Epistemology

Epistemology

A. TERM B. PLATO C. ARISTOTLE D. HELLENISM AND IMPERIAL PERIOD

A. TERM

There is no single term used by ancient philosophers, which could be translated as 'epistemology'; they used various categories for the introduction of their epistemological reflections: Plato outlines them as the 'perception of perception', Aristotle deals with them under the heading of analytics, the Stoa as part of logic, and Epicurus as part of canonics.

Within ancient philosophy, epistemology as a distinct philosophical discipline or at least as a clearly definable set of philosophical theses first makes a real appearance in the works of Plato and Aristotle. However, philosophical reflection on perception is about as old as Occidental philosophy itself. First traces are found in Presocratic texts by Xenophanes and Heraclitus, both of whom — disregarding any differences in their fundamental position — were engaged in clarifying the relationship between empirical and theoretical perception. Xenophanes emphasizes the absence of reliable indicators for truth and thus the finite nature of human perception, especially in the field of theories and explanations, but at the same time, he also talks of the possibility of improving human perception (fr. 21 B34, B35, B18 DK). Heraclitus points to the importance, but also the unreliability of sensory perception (fr. 22 B46, B54–56, B101a, B107 DK); he defines true perception and reason as being in harmony with the cosmic and divine → logos, but at the same time he acknowledges even on this level the restrictedness of human insight (fr. 22 B41, B50, B112, B114; B47, B78, B86 DK). Philosophers of the Eleatic and atomistic schools became increasingly stronger in their reservations regarding sensory perception and the reliance on the possibility of non-empirical cognition (Parmenides fr. 28 B1, B2, B4, B6 V. 1–2, B6 V. 3–9, B7–8 V. 50–61 DK; Democr. fr. 68 B6–11, B117–119, B125 DK). Some of the most influential Sophists, such as Protagoras or Gorgias, even converted to a radical epistemological scepticism (Protagoras fr. 80 B1, B4, B6a DK; Gorg. fr. 82 B1, B3 DK). It was not least this development which prompted Plato and Aristotle to develop the concept of an independent epistemology (Pl. Prt. 313a–314c, 348cff.; Tht. 155e–187b).

B. PLATO

Plato discovered that for any given 'F' with observable features which are 'F', there is a difference between the various observable 'F' objects and the structure of 'F' (e.g. Pl. La. 190d–192b, Euthphr. 5d–6e). It is his fundamental epistemological assumption that perception primarily only exists in respect of structures (forms, ideas) (e.g. Pl. Phd. 65b–66a; 99d–100a; Resp. 475b–480a; 504a–517a). These structures or ideas contain a finite amount of general qualities, which are constant and which can be expressed as universal principles. The thesis that the structure F has the general quality G, can be substantiated by citing those F objects which are G, and disproved by referring to those observable F objects, which are not G (e.g. Pl. La. 192c–193d; Chrm. 159b–162b). It is essential to the perception of structures that all and only the universal qualities are stated. In his early dialogues, Plato shows a number of — mainly unsuccessful — attempts to gain perception of certain structures, which comply with this elementary standard of rationality; at the same time, he also tries to prove that these standards themselves follow on from preconditions: those involved in a conversation have to acknowledge them from the very outset of their search for a definition of the meaning of structures, and again in their final admission of the failure of their search. One of the most elementary of these preconditions is the implicit conviction that universal principles can be used sensibly and that they — provided they are true — refer to some cosmic entity, and,

Schematic representation of Stoic epistemology and theory of action

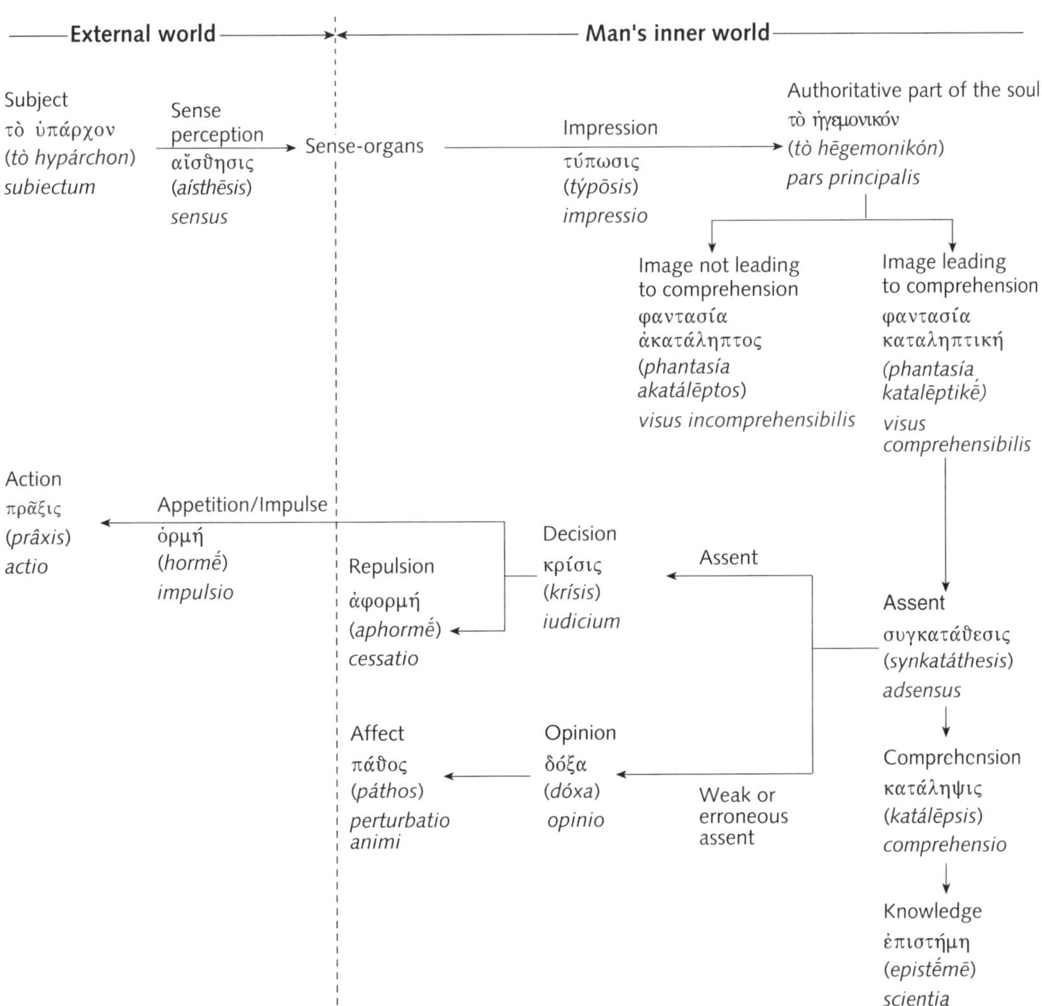

Cognition is the result of the soul's processing of sense-perception. The soul remains passive in receiving the impression; the perception is actively transformed by means of the logos (λόγος; *ratio*).

Assent can be contolled through the concepts abstracted from similar imaginings (ἔννοιαι; *notiones*). Epistemology forms a link between Stoic logic and ethics.

M. HAA.

most of all, that they can be discussed rationally. It is also assumed that each use of 'F' as a general term permits the hypothesis that 'F' refers to a structure of F and that in the course of a definition of F the meaning of all important terms under this definition have to be kept constant. In the later dialogues, these elementary assumptions were moulded into the epistemological Platonism which was then to explain how humans can relate to outstanding human qualities, geometric theorems, or cosmic regularities.

According to Plato, all human beings have an *a priori* innate epistemic ability to recognize structures within singular observable objects or facts. Sensory perception alone is not the same as perception in the primary sense, but the correct application of sensory perception is necessary in order to perceive structures (e.g. Pl. Men. 82b–85e; Phd. 75a-b; Resp. 523b-e). Once the human soul has been changed by philosophy, i.e. once it has learned to recognize the implications of ideas and their theories for rational dialogue, it is also in a position to recognize observable single objects as being representative of mathematical or other structures, and eventually to recognize as a hierarchically ordered continuum the field of structures themselves and that of all objects in existence, within which the principles of order (unity) and variety (plurality) — the highest levels of perception — appear in a variety of combinations (e.g. Pl. Resp. 509c–511e; Phlb. 57b–59b). The method of a (mostly) dichotomic terminological division, which Plato developed in his later dialogues in order to define structures, reflects the blending of unity and variety within the field of ideas, and represents the highest form of a method-based search for insight and perception, which Plato calls 'dialectics' (e.g. Pl. Soph. 218b–232a; 251a–254b; Phlb. 14c–18e). But even → dialectics continue to depend on structural, propositional perception. Even though Plato refers to philosophical perception in the primary sense as 'always true', this is no more than a terminological observation: the analytical corollary of the sentence 'P perceives that X ...' is that 'X' is true, but in Plato's view, these trivial findings do not alter his tenet that there remains an openness to objections and improvements in all philosophical assumptions regarding the fundamental definition of structures and of existence itself, as well as all in respect of all attempts at a dialectical definition of specific structures (e.g. Pl. Plt. 262cff.; 263eff.).

C. Aristotle

For Aristotle, too, perception in its highest sense pertains to eternal structures, though at the time it is based on sensory perception as the ability to differentiate, which can be found in all animals and allows them to distinguish between various qualia. In addition to that, humans have the epistemic capacity of memory and experience, enabling them to describe the qualia, which they have perceived, as singular set of circumstances, to register their similarities, and to commit them to memory. Aristotle refers to the explicit listing of a great number of similar singular sets of circumstances as 'induction' (ἐπαγωγή; *epagōgḗ*). Induction, in turn, makes it possible to formulate a philosophical hypothesis regarding the existence of a universal structure, whose unambiguity and closer definition — through universal tenets — can be checked and made more precise by means of further inductions.

This hypothesis presupposes a clear philosophical knowledge of the ontological status and the epistemological preconditions of universal structures; for suitable inductions, it leads to the cognition of general regularities e.g. of the form 'A applies to all B' ('AaB'), in which both A and B are structures (Aristot. An. post. 2,19; for 'inducting' cf. e.g. Top. 8,2,157a). However, this process does not yet lead to the highest level of perception. Inductively established tenets of the form 'AaB' have to be submitted to a logical (i.e. syllogistic) analysis, which detects all 'middle terms' (terminus medius) C_1, ..., C_N, to which the following applies: AaC_1, C_1aC_2, ..., C_NaB, and for whom no further middle terms exist (i.e. which are 'unmediated'). For each inductively established universal tenet, logical analysis is to establish the finite quantity of its unmediated syllogistic premises; it needs to be noted that each of these premises itself has to be inductively confirmed. In this way, a sequence of syllogisticly correct and inductively established deduction of the form AaC, CaB → AaB (e.g. Aristot. An. post. 1,23) is obtained. In a further step, each one of these deductions can be tested as to whether its subpremises indicate one of the Aristotelian causes for its conclusion — i.e. either the beginning or target of a motion, or material, or (definitory) form. If that is the case, Aristotle speaks of a 'demonstration' or deductive explanation (e.g. Aristot. An. post. 1,2; 2,1–2; 2,8–10). Finally, for each branch of science, it needs to be checked, whether all its demonstrations can be put into a logical and explanatory order. If that is also the case, the highest unmediated explanatory premises of a specific scientific discipline are referred to as its 'definitory principles'.

However, according to Aristotle, a closer reflection on this procedure does reveal that the establishment of definitory principles requires two further categories of fundamental assumptions, namely existential postulates in view of the fundamental entities of each specific scientific discipline ('hypothesis'), and logical theorems and other preconditions, which apply to all disciplines ('axioms'; Aristot. An. post. 1,2,72a 14–24). It is up to philosophers to establish theses and axioms (e.g. Aristot. Metaph. 4; 13). The highest form of perception of universal structures is to understand the definitory principles as well as the hypotheses and axioms of each specific science. Along with Plato, Aristotle, too, describes perception — especially in its highest scientific form — as 'always true'; however, similar to Plato, Aristotle thus only defines the ideal of perception as well as the standards of rationality, with which any epistemological postulates have to comply. According to Aristotle, it is however rarely possible to establish a final epistemological basis for actual scientific supposition within a specific research context: even though a philosopher can provide a definiton of perception, it is difficult to establish whether perception has actually occurred (Aristot. An. post. 2,19,100b; 1,9,76a 26–30). This applies even more to those weaker forms of perception: in the fields of ethics or politics, these are aimed at contingencies: because no scientific methodology exists for them, they can only resort to a procedure based on experience and → 'dialectics' in order to specify generally held convictions, to make them consistent and to provide arguments in their support (Aristot. Eth. Nic. 6,5,1140a31–1141a4; 7,1,1145b; Ph. 4,4,211a).

D. Hellenism and Imperial Period

In the views of both Plato and Aristotle, perception — as a condition as well as an objective — is of high ethical value, because it represents the good order of the soul and because it brings with it the most sublime forms of → happiness. In the most influential of the Hellenistic philosophical schools, epistemology is even more decidedly subordinate to their ethical programmes, aimed at devaluating those things which are unattainable in order to optimize the attainment of self-defined objectives — and thus happiness. Stoics and Epicureans employ an epistemological sensualism to underpin the unattainability of external objects and their future development, which reduces all perception to the receptive capacity of sensory perception (e.g. SVF II 88, 56; Epicurus fr. 35; 36; 260; 261 USENER.; Epicurus Epist. Herod. 38; 52; 82).

Furthermore, both schools work on the assumption that repeated similar sensory perceptions instinctively lead to the formation of certain 'preconceptions' (προλήψεις, *prolépseis*), based on which reason as a spontaneous epistemic ability can arrive at further insights (e.g. SVF II 83; 87; 473; 764; Epicurus fr. 255 USENER; Diog. Laert. 10,32–33). Within the framework of this sensualism, the truth criteria for sensory perception become by necessity the central epistemological problem. These criteria — for the Stoics to have reason to agree to the reality contained in sensory impressions, and for the Epicureans the conditions for the infallibility of sensory impressions — together with the application of the preconceptions are to ensure that perception is directed at the true nature of objects and thus looks beyond the mere surface of phenomena. However, neither the Stoics nor the Epicureans succeeded in formulating a satisfactory epistemological foundation to this 'dogmatic' position — a fact which played to the advantage of the arguments provided by ancient Sceptics. Ancient Scepticism never denied that all humans, including the Sceptics themselves, have to have certain opinions in order to be able to act in daily live; it only denied the sensibility of striving towards any kind of 'dogmatic' convictions, which claim to refer to the true nature of things. Sceptics do not deny that they have certain perceptions, they only deny that the perceptions of a few human beings have any bearing on the true nature of things, and for that reason they recommend to their fellow humans to refrain from any judgement, and thus ensure their own peace of mind (documentary evidence in [5]).

1 J. BARNES, The Presocratic Philosophers, 2 vols., 1987 2 TH. EBERT, Meinung und Wissen in der Philosophie Platons, 1974 3 W. DETEL, Aristoteles, Analytica Posteriora, 2 vols., 1993 4 M. HOSSENFELDER, Stoa, Epikureismus und Skepsis (Gesch. der Philosophie, ed. by W. RÖD, vol. III), 1985 5 M. FREDE, Des Skeptikers Meinungen, in: Neue Hefte für Philosophie 15/16, 1979.

W.DE.

ANCIENT SOURCES: SVF I, fr. 52–73, 205–215.
REFERENCES TO FIGURE: J.M. RIST, Stoic Philosophy, 1969 repr. 1980, 133–151 P. STEINMETZ, Die Stoa, in: GGPh[4], vol. 4, 528–533, 541–549, 593–595, 612–618.

Epistle

A. TERM, TERMINOLOGY, ORIGINS B. MATERIAL, CONVEYANCE C. FORMULAE D. PRIVATE LETTERS E. OFFICIAL LETTERS F. LETTER WRITERS AND THEORY OF LETTER WRITING G. LITERARY LETTERS H. ANTHOLOGIES OF LETTERS

A. TERM, TERMINOLOGY, ORIGINS

A letter is a written message to an absent recipient. The Greek *epistolḗ* (ἐπιστολή) is the verbal noun for ἐπιστέλλειν; *epistéllein*, 'to give a message (to a messenger)' or 'to send a written or oral message (to s.o.)'; *epistolḗ* means 'a sent message', which in earlier times could also include an oral message. Synonyms: *grámmata* (γράμματα), literally 'piece of writing', Lat. *epistula, litterae.* Wherever script was developed, writing letters was one of its first applications. For that reason, communication by writing letters is found in all scriptural cultures; the Greeks undoubtedly encountered this practice in the Orient. However, there is no example of a letter amongst the Linear B-tablets. The only letter mentioned in Homer (Il. 6,169: an 'Urias' letter') is handed to Bellerophon to take from Argos to Lycia; the entire episode is full of Oriental references.

B. MATERIAL, CONVEYANCE

Originally, letters were written on wax-covered wooden tablets (δέλτοι; *déltoi, tabellae*); a pair (δίπτυχον; *díptychon*) could be folded and sealed. Later on, → papyrus was used; the address of the recipient was written on the outside of the scroll (ἐπιγραφή; *epigraphḗ, inscriptio*). As a further variant, lead foils were used occasionally, which could also be rolled up; some very old examples are extant (*c.* 500 BC [25]; *c.* 400: Syll.[3] III 1259 and 1260). Letters were delivered by messengers or by travellers on behalf of acquaintances. Letters of recommendation (a particularly ancient and frequent use of letters) were carried by the recommendee. Wealthy people sent slaves to deliver their letters (γραμματοφόρος; *grammatophóros, tabellarius* [19]); from the Hellenistic age, official institutions had their own messenger service. There was no development of a public postal service [16; 17]. An old form of the secret letter was the → skytale.

C. FORMULAE

Conventional fomulas as set elements of letter writing only become evident after the 2nd half of the 5th cent. BC; they are independent of Oriental patterns. They are of lesser importance in letters of high stylistic qualities; such letters tend to begin and end abruptly. The evolution of conventional formulae can be traced with the help of the wealth of Greek letters on Egyptian papyri [12]. The most important elements were: (1) introductory formula (initial greeting: 'Greetings from Philippus to Theon': Φίλιππος Θέωνι χαίρειν; *Phílippos Théōni chaírein*, 'Cicero greets Atticus': *Cicero Attico salutem dat* or *dicit.* The phrase χαίρειν (*chaírein;* cf. Aristoph. Nub. 608f.) should be complimented with a phrase such as: ἐπιστέλλει (*epistéllei*) or λέγει (*légei*) [13]. (2) *formula salutis*: εἰ ἔρρωσαι (*ei érrōsai*), εὖ ἂν ἔχοι· (*eû àn échoi*) ἐρρώμεθα δὲ καὶ αὐτοί(*errṓmetha dè kaì autoí*) (and similar); *Si vales, bene est, ego valeo* (obsolete according to Sen. Ep. 15,1). (3) following the main body of the letter (corpus): care fomula (Hellenistic): ἐπιμέλου σεαυτοῦ ὅπως ὑγιαίνῃς; *epimélou seautoû hópōs hygiaínēis*, *cura ut valeas*. (4) sending of regards: ἀσπάζου τὸν δεῖνα; *aspárou tòn deîna*, ἀσπάζεταί σε καὶ ὁ δεῖνα; *aspázetaí se kaì ho deîna* (and similar). (5) final greeting: ἔρρωσο; *érrōso*, *vale*. (6) It was rare for letters to contain a date.

Three linguistic peculiarities are noteworthy: (1) the 1st pers. sg. is replaced by the 1st pers. pl. in the majority of cases, this plural was probably a *pluralis modestiae*. In the letters of the Hellenistic kings, it became the *pluralis maiestatis* [24]. (2) The 2nd pers. pl. as the *pluralis reverentiae* gradually developed under the Roman emperors. (3) Periphrastic courtesy addresses became prevalent in the 4th cent. AD, e.g. ἡ σὴ μεγαλειότης; *he sḕ megaleiótēs*, *maiestas tua* ('your greatness'); conversely ἡ ἐμὴ ὀλιγότης; *he emḕ oligótēs*, *mea parvitas* ('my humble self'). This development seems to have been Latin-led [23].

D. Private Letters

Into this group fall letters between relatives, friends, and members of private groups, but also business letters. A great number of Greek letters of this kind have survived on Egyptian papyri, some Latin ones were found in the British Vindolanda [1]. This proves that the ability to read and write was widespread; in Egypt, illiterate people are known to have employed the services of professional scribes. Letters were not only written in answer to practical needs, but also to nurture human relations (friendship, φιλία; *philía*); some letters contain hardly any practical information.

E. Official Letters

(Letters to and from officials). The Hellenistic monarchies used letters as the vehicle of state administration, a practice later adopted by the Roman emperors. Most official decrees were published in the form of letters. Again, copious material has survived on Egyptian papyri; royal letters are preserved epigraphically [7; 8]. In Rome, the correspondence between → Plinius and the emperor Trajan during the former's term as provincial governor is extant (Plin. Ep., 10th bk.). → Cassiodorus issued his official edicts in the form of letters. In international relations, diplomatic letters were exchanged. Chanceries employed professional letter writers (*epistolográphoi*, ἐπιστολογράφοι); the office of *ab* → *epistulis* was an important one at the Roman imperial court.

F. Letter Writers and Theory of Letter Writing

Instructions how to write letters [5] have been around from the Hellenistic age, initially in form of elementary introductions for general use and particularly for private correspondents; there was initially a 'gap' in respect of the writing of official letters (to be filled by Ps.-Demetrius, *Týpoi epistolikoí*/Τύποι ἐπιστολικοί). Finally, rhetoric instructions also touched upon the composition of letters. In the latter, letters were not part of the system, but were dealt with more incidentally, within the topic of → progymnasmata as an application of ethopoeia (first in Theon, vol. II p. 115 Spengel [14. 70–73]). Compilations of Imperial age model letters are extant: Pap. Bononiensis 5; Ps.-Demetrius, *Týpoi epistolikoí*; Ps.-Libanius and Ps.-Proclus, *Epistolimaîoi charaktêres*/Ἐπιστολιμαῖοι χαρακτῆρες (two recensions of the same basic compilation). 21 (Ps.-Demetrius) or respectively 41 (Ps.-Proclus) different types of letters are listed. Theoretical discussions: Demetrius, *Perí hermēneías* (Περὶ ἑρμηνείας 223–235); Philostr. *Diálexis* (Διάλεξις 1, vol. II p. 257f. Kayser), Gregory of Nazianzus Epist. 51 (ed. princeps Galley, Paris 1964, vol. I p. 126); → Iulius Victor (Lat.) in the addenda to his 'Rhetoric' (ch. 27).

The earliest verifiable theoretical statement originates from Artemon, the editor of Aristotle's letters: in a manner of speaking, a letter represented one side of a dialogue and therefore should adopt the same style (Demetrius, ibid. 223). This concept was later frequently repeated (similar in Cic. Att. 12,53 and Phil. 2,7: *amicorum conloquia absentium*). Added to this were scattered remarks on the style of letters, e.g. in Cicero, Fam. 2,4 and 4,13 [21. 27–47]. Some stylistic characteristics of letters are [20. 192–195; 15; 21]: (1) language: simplicity, closeness to colloquial language. Figures and periods are to be avoided. Discrete elegance is the aim (χαρίεν; *charíen*, Demetrius ibid. 235). (2) Content: serious arguments do not belong in a letter (Demetrius ibid. 230), in contrast with literary quotations, proverbs, and jokes. Letters can be evidence of education and culture, they can be witty and pointed; letters became the expression of the urban way of life. In this, the actual communication content can almost disappear. (3) Clarity of expression is of eminent importance; this is the main difference in style between letters and speeches (Philostratus) but also colloquial language (because the recipient cannot ask for clarification, Iulius Victor). (4) Brevity, a frequently emphasized demand; Gregory of Nazianzus warns of exaggeration (many examples of which can be found after the Greek letters of → Brutus): letters must not turn into riddles (γρῖφος; *grîphos*). (5) Ethos: Demetrius ibid. 227: σχεδὸν γὰρ εἰκόνα ἕκαστος τῆς ἑαυτοῦ ψυχῆς γράφει τὴν ἐπιστολήν (the letter as the mirror of the soul). The writer also has to adapt to the recipient (ibid. 234), also including tactful consideration. (6) Friendship: all letters are basically a sign of friendship (Demetrius ibid. 231: φιλοφρόνησις σύντομος; *philophrónēsis sýntomos*); they should not be restricted to factual information, but be used to nurture personal relations, thus leading to the development of a wealth of topics dealing with friendship [21].

EDITIONS OF COMPILATIONS: 1 A.K. BOWMAN, J.D. THOMAS, The Vindolanda Writing-Tablets (Tabulae Vindolandenses II), 1994, 183–343 2 P. CUGUSI (ed.), Epistolographi Latini Minores, 1970 3 G. DAUM (ed.), Griech. Papyrusbriefe aus einem Jahrtausend antiker Kultur, 1959 4 R. HERCHER (ed.), Epistolographi Graeci, 1873 (repr. 1965) 5 A.J. MALHERBE (ed.), Ancient Epistolary Theorists, 1988 6 S.K. STOWERS (ed.), Letter-writing in Greco-Roman Antiquity, 1986 7 WELLES 8 A. WILHELM (ed.), Griech. Königsbriefe, 1943.
LITERATURE: 9 A. DEISSMANN, Licht vom Osten, [4]1923 10 DZIATZKO, s.v. Brief, RE III 1, 836–843 11 F.X. J. EXLER, The Form of the Ancient Greek Letter, 1923 12 P.J. PARSONS, in: Genèse et développement d'un genre littéraire. La lettre antique..., Didactica Classica Gandensia 20, 1980, 3–19 13 G.A. GERHARD, Unt. zur Gesch. des griech. Briefes 1, in: Philologus 64, 1905, 27–55 14 G.A. KENNEDY, Greek Rhetoric under Christian Emperors, 1983 15 H. KOSKENNIEMI, Studien zur Idee und Phraseologie des griech. Briefes bis 400 n.Chr., 1956 16 REINCKE, s.v. Nachrichtenwesen, RE XVI 2, 1496–1541 17 W. RIEPL, Das Nachrichtenwesen des Altertums, 1913 18 J. SCHNEIDER, s.v. Brief, RAC 2, 564–585 19 SCHROFF, s.v. Tabellarius, RE IV A2, 1844–1847 20 SYKUTRIS, s.v. Epistolographie, RE Suppl. 5, 185–220 21 K. THRAEDE, Grundzüge griech.-röm. Brieftopik, Zetemata 48, 1970 22 F. ZIEMANN, De epistularum Graecarum formulis ..., 1910 23 H. ZILLIACUS, s.v. Anredeformen, JbAC 7,1964,167–182 24 H. ZILLIACUS, Selbstgefühl und Servilität, 1953 25 Proc. of the Cambridge Philological Society 199, 1973, 35f. H.GÖ.

G. LITERARY LETTERS

Epistula est, habet quippe in capite quis ad quem scribat. Augustinus' quote from the *Retractationes* to a longer treatise (2,20) demonstrates that in Roman understanding a letter was any piece of writing, which contained a salutation, naming both sender and recipient, regardless of whether it had actually been sent. A letter became literature not by its content, but through publication, regardless of whether that was due to its content or its writer, after the writer's death or even during his lifetime, by others or the writer himself. It is thus clear that the modern distinction between a 'genuine' letter and an 'artistic letter' or 'epistle' does not apply to ancient conditions [2. 550f.]. The large volume of the letter genre results from the dual task of acting as a 'substitute for conversation', i.e. both the conveyance of information and the nurturing of personal relationships. The familiar tone and the unconstrained form proved particularly suited to introducing a wide variety of topics to a large circle of readers or listeners (Varro, *Epistolicae quaestiones*; Seneca, *Epistulae morales ad Lucilium*); legal and medical specialists preferred to use letters to publish their scientific treatises (Proculus, Marcellus Empiricus). The majority of the surviving letters of Hieronymus (125) and Augustinus (308) are indeed treatises in letter form. Romans in particular were fond of letters in verse form (Lucilius; Horatius, *Epistulae*; *Ars poetica*; Ovid, *Heroides*; Ausonius; Paulinus of Nola). Exercises in ethopoeia, part of the teaching of rhetoric, were the starting point for fabricated letters — for their understanding, it is important to remember that antiquity applied different rules to the concept of originality than the modern view: it was common to include fabricated letters in historical works (*Historia Augusta*), as individual letters or whole compilations, under the name of important personalities (pseudonymous letters).

The theory, however, was different. Anyone who was educated was aware of the Greek scholarly epistolary theory (see F above), which defined the nurturing of friendship as the main purpose of a letter and postulated a length (or rather brevity) commensurate with that purpose, a choice of language and expression devoid of exaggeration and appropriate to the recipient ('conversational tone': *iocari*), a limitation to only one topic, and an avoidance of anything to do with current politics or exceedingly private matters. The recollection of the ancient tradition in the 4th cent. AD gave renewed importance to the original task of a letter, i.e. as a sign of friendship, combined with very artistic stylization: in excess, this resulted in some letters of almost no substance.

H. ANTHOLOGIES OF LETTERS

Anthologies of letters from outstanding personalities were compiled from very early on. → Cato the Elder' s letters to his son or those of → Cornelia, Mother of the Gracchi, were in circulation, and several anthologies existed of Caesar's letters. Tacitus made use of a literary correspondence on the best oratorical style by C. Licinius Calvus and M. Brutus with Cicero. An insight into ancient correspondence is provided by the surviving letters of Cicero and his friends (a total of 864, of which 774 were written by Cicero himself; about the same number is assumed lost). Amongst them are hastily scribbled messages, artistically styled letters of recommendation, congratulation or consolation, as well as treatises, personal letters (not meant for publication, such as those to his friend Atticus), and letters, which Cicero himself had made public. Alongside two special anthologies (*ad Quintum fratrem*; correspondence with Brutus), there is also extant a corpus (16 bks.) of mixed correspondence (*ad familiares*), based on individual letters ordered according to addressees, and also Cicero's letters to Atticus, published about 100 years after their author's death.

As far as we know, → Plinius the Younger was the first to publish an anthology of his own beautifully crafted letters; in accordance with epistolary theory, each one of them was geared to the personal circumstances and interests of its respective recipient. He divided them into 9 bks., taking guidance from the stylistic principle of *variatio*; the 10th book, containing his official correspondence with emperor Trajan, was probably added posthumously. The incompletely extant corpus of letters by → Fronto, tutor to Marcus Aurelius and his brother, consists of various individual compilations, ordered according to addressee or topic; these letters have frequently been criticized for their lack of content, which did, however, comply with ancient epistolary theory, less so though the rather stilted language. In full awareness of their tradition as Roman noblemen, both the rhetor → Symmachus and bishop → Ambrosius imitate great ancient models by compiling their own letters in anthologies: following Pliny's example, they collate 9 bks. of private correspondence and 1 bk. of official letters, with Symmachus copying Cicero in ordering his letters according to their addressee, and Ambrosius like Pliny employing the principle of *variatio*. Whereas the over 900 letters which Symmachus had written to his friends are frequently 'words without content', Ambrosius used the form of a letter to friends for his explanations of individual theological problems. Following that example, → Sidonius Apollinaris used the letter genre in order to convey the problems of his times to future generations without causing offence [2. 547ff.]; in order and presentation, he took his lead from Pliny's example. Much admired, these letters also influenced the subsequent epistolography (Ennodius, Ruricius of Limoges, Avitus of Vienne). → Cassiodorus compiled a voluminous anthology of his edicts, all composed in artistic style, which he called *Variae* (sc. *epistulae*) after the various styles of letters used as appropriate to the various recipients.

→ LETTER, EPISTOLARY LITERATURE

1 H. PETER, Der Brief in der röm. Lit., 1901
2 M. ZELZER, Der Brief in der Spätantike, in: WS 107/8, 1994/5, 541–551 3 Id., NHL 4, 377–402. M.ZE.

Epistolary novel The epistolary novel is a literary subgenre, almost exclusively familiar in numerous modern examples dating from the 18th and 19th cents. (RICHARDSON, ROUSSEAU, LACLOS, GOETHE etc.), yet was already known in classical antiquity. However, ancient examples of this genre have only been critically studied in terms of their authenticity and sources, but never evaluated in terms of literary aspects. At least this was true prior to the publication of the latest works in this field. The following texts could be taken as part of this genre: the fictitious letters by → Plato (1st cent. AD), → Euripides (1st cent. AD), → Hippocrates (1st cent. AD), → Aeschines (2nd cent. AD), → Chion (end of 1st cent. AD), → Themistocles (end of 1st cent. AD), as well as those by → Socrates and the Socratics (2nd cent. AD); furthermore, one should also consider the letters by Phalaris, the Seven Sages, and Xenophon, the preserved forms of which probably differ considerably from the original ones, as well as the papyrus fragments of the letters by Alexander the Great. Historical characters — generally taken from the mythical 5th cent., a period which also formed the backdrop to the historical novel by → Chariton — and their relationship with political power stand at the centre of all of these works. With the exception of the letters by Themistocles, story lines are developed chronologically, concentrating fully on their inherent dynamics, and sometimes employing comical or satirical elements (as in the Hippocrates and Aeschines novels). Like their modern counterparts, ancient epistolary novels made full use of the dramatic potential of such a 'tale without a narrator', and sometimes even aimed for multi-perspective effects. It is also noticeable that such novels are generally more subjective in character (in line with the topos of a letter as the 'mirror of the soul'), thus inviting the reader to an affective identification.

→ Chione (novel); → Epistolography; → Novel

R. HERCHER (ed.), Epistolographi Graeci, 1873 (1965); N. HOLZBERG (ed.), Der Griech. Briefroman, 1994; W. G. MÜLLER, Der Brief als Spiegel der Seele, in: A&A; 26, 1980, 138–157; P. A. ROSENMEYER, The Epistolary Novel, in: J. R. MORGAN, R. STONEMAN (ed.), Greek Fiction, 1994, 144–165. M.FU.

Epistolography

A. TERM B. PUBLICATION OF ANTHOLOGIES OF PRIVATE LETTERS C. OPEN LETTERS D. LETTERS OF DEDICATION E. DIDACTIC LETTERS F. FICTITIOUS LETTERS G. POETIC LETTERS H. INFLUENCE

A. TERM

This term is mainly applied to literary letters; however, the transition from private letters (→ Epistle) to literary ones is fluid, because even in private, correspondents aimed for a cultivated form of expression, which was also suitable for public consumption. A stylistically well-written letter was seen as a gift to its recipient (Demetrius [41], *Perí Hermēneías* 224). Such letters were shared within the recipient's circle of friends, they were shared with acquaintances, enjoyed and praised (Synes. Epist. 101; Lib. Ep. 1583 WOLF; Greg. Nyss. Epist. 14). There are several ways in which letters were made public:

B. PUBLICATION OF ANTHOLOGIES OF PRIVATE LETTERS

The earliest tangible examples are letters by Plato (already in the early edition of the corpus by Aristophanes of Byzantium *c.* 200 BC, Diog. Laert. 3,61f.) and Aristotle (by Artemon *c.* 100 BC) [14]. In Rome, → Cornelia's letters to C. Gracchus probably are the first published anthology [16]; then, of course, there is the extensive and extant corpus of → Cicero's letters which is of great importance in every way. Cicero himself prepared them for publication by Atticus (Att. 16,5,5); however, the (particularly intimate) letters to Atticus were only published long after his death (Seneca epist. 118,1–2 criticized their everyday topics; he himself may have thought along more literary lines from the start). The letters of → Pliny the Younger constitute another extant corpus; it seems that he wrote his letters primarily as works of art and published them himself; vol. 10 of his letters also includes his official letters to the emperor; likewise preserved are letters of → Fronto and → Marcus Aurelius. In the course of the 4th cent. AD, Christians, too, embraced these traditions. Some adopted the urban educated style (e.g. → Gregorius I [3] of Nazianzus, who — for the first time in the Greek cultural sphere — published his letters himself as didactic examples); others were dominated by the ponderous seriousness of their religious and official duties. Amongst the important anthologies from pagan writers are those by the emperors → Iulianus, and → Libanius (in Greek), and → Symmachus (in Latin); from Christian writers by → Athanasius, → Basilius, → Gregorius of Nazianzus, → Gregorius of Nyssa, → Johannes Chrysostomos, → Synesius, Neilus, Isidorus of Pelusium, → Procopius, and → Aeneas of Gaza (in Greek), as well as (in Latin) by → Ambrosius, → Jerome, → Augustinus, → Paulinus of Nola, → Sidonius Apollinaris, and → Ruricius.

C. Open Letters

From the 4th cent. BC, there are letters not just written to a particular recipient, but also intended for wide distribution. Into this category fall the letters of Isocrates and Demosthenes, preserved in the form of anthologies; furthermore Plato Epist. 7 and 8; Philip II's letter to the Athenians (preserved as Dem. Or. 12 [15]). In all of these cases, authenticity is a matter of controversy. Letters by Hellenistic kings were frequently made public in the form of inscriptions [20; 21]. In Rome, it became common practice in the Civil War for letters to be published [13. 213–216], extant: Sallustius, *Epistulae ad Caesarem* (authenticity disputed).

D. Letters of Dedication

Originally, these are the letters which accompanied a first edition, e.g. Archimedes' 'On the Sphere and Cylinder' (Περὶ σφαίρας καὶ κυλίνδρου) I (to Dositheus). Where the closing formula of the letter is omitted, the work appears as part of the letter, as in Archimedes ibid. II. Both of these forms became customary in specialized scientific works, esp. in → Hippiatrics and Roman jurisprudence. In the fields of magic, hermetics, alchemy, and astrology, letters were often used as a frame [17. 572]. Poetry books with prose letters of dedication: Martial, bk. 2, 8, and 12; Statius, *Silvae* i.a.

E. Didactic Letters

They share the same origin as the letters of dedication (see above), with the additional influence of the paraenetic literature (e.g. Hesiod's *Erga* and Isocrates' *Ad Nicoclem*). This was particularly suited to ethical and philosophical letters. An outstanding example of this is → Epicurus (O. Gigon [8. 117–132]). The → consolation literature in letter form (since → Crantor) falls into the same category. Q. Tullius Cicero wrote his *Commentariolum petitionis* to his brother Marcus in letter form, which elicited the reply ad Q. fr. 1 on provincial administration. This genre reached its peak with → Seneca's *Epistulae morales ad Lucilium*. The letters by early Christians constitute a separate development, initially those by → Paulus, later those by the Apostolic Fathers (Ignatius, Polycarp, Clement et.al.). Paul was familiar with the Greek culture of letter writing; Deissmann [3] wanted to restrict this to private letters only, but it is certain to have included literary letters. Nonetheless, early Christian letters display certain distinctive characteristics [17. 574–576; 1; 2. 190–198; 4], which only gradually disappeared with the increasing assimilation to the surrounding culture.

F. Fictitious Letters

A distinction must be made between letters which were forged with the intention of personal deception, and those which were fictitiously attributed to important personalities for the propagandistic support of a certain point of view, such as the correspondence between Paulus and Seneca [18. 258, 328]. When historians quote letters (or speeches, for that matter), one has to expect stylistic changes (Thuc. 7,8–15) or even pure fiction. Another category altogether are fictional letters which were frequently written as a series of letters with the sole purpose of developing characters and situations from the classic past as an art form. The primary readership was probably aware of the fiction; but later such letters were taken as authentic documents: from the Renaissance onwards, they were important tools in recreating a vivid picture of life in antiquity (the character of Democritus as the 'laughing philosopher' was thus established by the Hippocrates letters); this is the background for the reaction when philologists later proved the true origin of these letters. The decisive work was Bentley's *A dissertation upon the Epistles of Phalaris* (1699), leading to a general disregard for such 'brazen forgeries'. Attempts were made to explain them as rhetorical exercises in ethopoeia; however, there is no way of proving this. It is more likely that they were reading material that was both educational and entertaining; there are some similarities to the → novel. It is difficult to establish when they were first written. The Anacharsis letters are thought to originate from the 3rd cent. BC, and a papyrus confirms the 7th letter by Heraclitus for the 2nd cent. AD. However, most of the letters date from the Imperial period. It is possible that in some cases individual authentic letters were included (Letters of the Socratics no. 28: Speusippus to Philippus II; Plato, letter no. 7). The presence of a clearly structured plot allows the classification as an → 'epistolary novel'. According to ([9] with extensive bibliography), the following collections of letters fall into this category: Plato, Euripides, Aeschines, Hippocrates, Chion, Themistocles, Socrates, and the Socratics. It is less obvious with regards to the letters of Phalaris (not in their original order?), of the Seven Sages and Xenophon (only some quotes extant), of Alexander the Great (attempted reconstruction in [11. 230–252]). 'Mimic letters' [19. 216] are also of fictional character, but in their title bear the name of the real author. They were particularly popular in the → Second Sophistic. The main focus was on description of everyday life in ancient Attica; the characters themselves were mainly fictional. Topics were often taken from comedies. To this category belong: → Alciphron (letters by fishermen, peasants, parasites, and hetaera), → Aelianus [2] (peasants' letters), → Philostratus (love letters), → Aristaenetus (love letters), → Theophylactus Simocatta (characters, peasants, hetaera). Of particular interest for the history of religion are the 'Letters from Heaven' [17. 572f.], in literary forms in Menippus (Diog. Laert. 6,101) and Lucian, Ἐπιστολαὶ Κρονικαί (*Epistolaì Kronikaí; epistulae saturnales*).

G. Poetic Letters

Some of these are real letters, such as the unique poem by Pindar to Hieron (P. 3). The Romans developed this form into a favourite poetic genre [13. 178–179]: → Lucilius (some of his satires were written in letter form), → Horatius (Epist., bk. 2 contains didactic letters), → Ovidius (*Epistulae ex Ponto*); the tradition continues to → Ausonius and → Paulinus of Nola. In lyric poetry: → Catullus (15; 32 i.a.). Whereas in the previously listed works, the poets themselves spoke, Ovid in his *Heroides* developed a unique genre of mythical-fictional letters [5], in which the art of ethopoeia reached its peak.

H. Influence

In Byzantium, the patterns of ancient letters were intensively studied and copied [10. 199–239]. In the West, the teachings of the art of letter writing in the *Ars dictaminis* was based on the rules of speaking in a court of law rather than the ancient style of letters [7. II,54–68]. In the Renaissance, letters became once again popular for expressing the experiences and thoughts of an individual (Petrarca, Familiarum rerum libri 1,1,32: following Cicero and Seneca). The rediscovery of Cicero's letters (1345) made a deep impression and led to a revival of the ancient style of letter writing. Erasmus (*De conscribendis epistolis*) continued the tradition of rhetorization [6]. 'The letter — a mirror of the soul' [12] — remains a leitmotif. In literature, the 'heroic letter' experienced a renewed bloom [5]. The ancient style of letters influenced Thornton Wilder's *The Ides of March* (1948).

→ Letter, Epistolary Literature

Literature: cf. → Epistle. Additionally: 1 K. Berger, Hell. Gattungen im Neuen Testament, ANRW II 25.2, 1984, 1031–1432, letters: 1326–1363 2 Id., Apostelbrief und apostolische Rede. Zum Formular frühchristl. Briefe, in: ZNTW 65, 1974, 190–231 3 A. Deissmann, Licht vom Osten [4]1923 4 D. Dormeyer, Das NT im Rahmen der ant. Literaturgesch., 1993 5 H. Dörrie, Der heroische Brief, 1968 6 H. Funke, Epistolographie und Rhetorik. Beobachtungen zu Erasmus' De conscribendis epistolis, in: Res publica litterarum, Studies in the Classical Tradition 10, 1987, 93–99 7 J. de Ghellinck, L'essor de la litterature latine au XIIe siècle, 1946 8 O. Gigon, in: Genèse et developpement d'un Genre littéraire. La lettre antique ..., Didactica Classica Gandensia 20, 1980 9 N. Holzberg (ed.), Der griech. Briefroman. Gattungstypologie und Textanalyse (Classica Monacensia 8), 1994 10 H. Hunger, Die hochsprachliche profane Lit. der Byzantiner I (HdbA XII 5,1), 1978 11 R. Merkelbach, Die Quellen des griech. Alexanderromans (Zetemata 9), [2]1977 12 K.A. Neuhausen, Der Brief als 'Spiegel der Seele' bei Erasmus, in: Wolfenbütteler Renaissancemitteilungen 1986, 97–110 13 H. Peter, Der Brief in der röm. Lit., 1901 14 M. Plezia (ed.), Aristotelis privatorum scriptorum fragmenta, 1977 15 M. Pohlenz, Philipps Schreiben an Athen, in: Hermes 64, 1929, 41–62 16 P.L. Schmidt, Catos Epistula ad M. filium und die Anfänge der röm. Brieflit., in: Hermes 100, 1972, 568–576 17 J. Schneider, s.v. Brief, RAC 3, 564–585 18 W. Speyer, Die lit. Fälschung, 1971 (HAW I 2) 19 Sykutris, s.v. Epistolographie, RE Suppl. 5, 185–220 20 Welles 21 A. Wilhelm, Griech. Königsbriefe, 1943.

H.GÖ.

Epistulis, ab Correspondence constituted one of the central tasks of the administration; this had to be undertaken within the bounds of the responsibility of a particular authority in an impersonal businesslike manner and in accordance with generally applicable instructions (*officii formae*). The term *epistula* (→ Epistle), adopted into Latin administrative terminology from the original Greek, officially referred to a written communication by an authority, delivered to a real addressee. An *epistula* could result from a previous enquiry, petition, or application by a member of the public (Lat. *preces*, Greek ἐντεύξεις/*enteúxeis*), or alternatively follow from reports, initiatives, and consultations by the authorities themselves (*relationes*, *suggestiones*, *consultationes*). If the aim of an enquiry or application was to receive some legal advice from an authority without a lawsuit, it was referred to in Latin as a → *rescriptum*. During the Roman Republican era, it was the task of the magistrates to issue epistles and rescripts within their specific remit but the task of responding to enquiries was at times delegated to lawyers of great practical experience and reputation — whose main job was teaching. Imperial Rome retained the Republican traditions regarding written dealings within administration and law. However, from the reign of Augustus onwards, only specifically authorized lawyers were permitted to exercise the *ius publice respondendi* (Dig. 1,2,2,49). At this time, within the official structure of the imperial court, the specifically legal political *officium ab epistolis* developed; the preposition '*a*' indicates a subsection within the entire organization of subaltern civil servants (*officiales*) with responsibility for the imperial administration. The administrative body was subdivided into offices (*officia*, later called *scrinia*); it was initially headed by *liberti*, who from the time of Hadrian onwards were increasingly replaced by *equites*. Names, remits, and the internal structures of these offices kept changing, but there was a continuity in the main focus of activity, according to which there was one section dealing with petitions and directives (*ab epistulis*) alongside one for appointments to offices as well as other matters concerning military and administrative personnel (*a* → *memoria*), a section dealing with legal procedures, esp. with appellations (*a* → *libellis, a decretis*), as well as one or more other sections with different remits as directed by the emperor (e.g. *a dispositionibus*). In late antiquity, the *Notitia dignitatum* defines the remit of the *scrinium ab epistulis* as follows: *Magister epistolarum legationes civitatum, consultationes et preces tractat* (Not. Dign. Or. 19,8f.); however, the other *scrinia* were also charged with dealing with *preces*. The number of regular subaltern civil servants within the *scrinium ab epistulis* was 34 under emperor Leo, 62 in the *a memoria*, and again 34 in the *a libellis* (Cod. Iust. 12,19,10). The activities of the *officium/scrinium ab epistulis* are excellently documented in the Codices Theod. and Iust., particularly from the 3rd cent. AD, as the constitutional law, which has been summarized here, was as a rule based on imperial rescripts.

HIRSCHFELD, 321ff.; JONES, LRE, 504ff.; WENGER, 427ff.

C.G.

Epistylion Ancient technical term, frequently appearing In Greek architectural inscriptions as well as in Vitruvius (4,3,4 and *passim*); applicable to all ancient orders of column construction, it refers to that part of the entablature of the peristasis which rests immediately on top of the columns. Modern architectural terminology often refers to the *epistylion* as 'architrave', whereas the entablature in its entirety — i.e. architrave, → frieze, and cornice (→ geison) together — are referred to as *epistylion*.

The translation of the initially wooden *epistylion* to stone represents a critical moment in Greek stone architecture; the *epistylion* is that element in a columned building bearing the greatest load. Spanning the gaps between two columns required building elements of considerable weight (due to the strain placed on the material); this constituted a significant technical challenge in transport, emplacement, and building statics. At times, the challenge proved too much and remained unsolved, leading to the abandonment of a building project (Selinunte, Temple G), even though some effective solutions to these problems had been developed quite early on: metal reinforcements (Athens Propylaea of the Acropolis; Bassae, temple of Apollo), weight reduction through grooves (Syracuse, temple of Apollo), as well as the parallel placement of two or three clamped blocks with mitred corners (*bilithes*, *trilithes epistylion*).

The top of a Doric *epistylion* ends with an overhanging cornice (ταινία, *tainía*), connected to the → *regulae* by a row of → *guttae*, corresponding to the → *mutulus* in the → *geison* and the → triglyphs in the → frieze — a purely decorative element, a technical anachronism in reminiscence to earlier wooden building techniques, which characterize the formal appearance of the Doric order. The *tainíai* of some of the archaic buildings in western Greece were richly decorated with a variety of mouldings; decorative reliefs on the *epistylion*, as found in the Athena temple in Assos, remained an exception, as did the late-archaic Doric-Ionic hybrid form of the Demeter temple of Sangri/Naxos. Between the 6th and

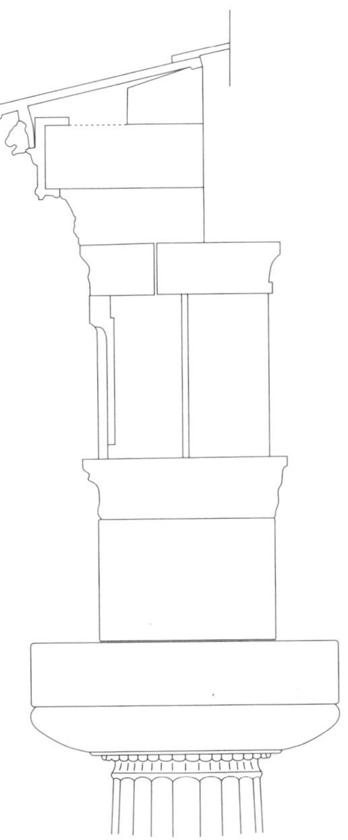

1. Paestum, Temple of Hera I (monolithic epistylion)

the late 4th cents. BC, the Doric *epistylion* loses noticeably in height in relation to the frieze, following the trend towards lighter design.

The early form of the Ionic *epistylion* is largely unknown; some of the fragments from the archaic temple of Apollo of → Didyma (→ Dipteros) show the — later customary — profiling with three horizontal fasciae (→ Ornaments) and closes with a powerful → *kymation* (→ Egg-and-dart moulding), but in some instances also figurative ornamental reliefs. The outer *epistylion* as well as the inner one with two fasciae are part of the standard Ionic order; in Asia Minor, the height of the fasciae generally tended to increase towards the top, whereas fasciae of equal height were the rule in Attic-Ionic buildings.

The Ionic *epistylion* was integrated into the pure Corinthian as well as into the composite Ionic-Corinthian order; in Roman architecture, it was increasingly combined with the Doric order (Miletus, warehouse; peristyles of dwelling houses in Delos and Pompeii). From the late Classical period, the *epistylion* was used to place ornaments — carved in relief or applied — such as shields, wreaths, and garlands, and in the Hellenistic-Roman period particularly also for architectural inscriptions.

EBERT, 29; O. BINGÖL, Überlegungen zum ion. Gebälk, in: MDAI(Ist) 40, 1990, 101–108; H.R. GOETTE, Ein dor.

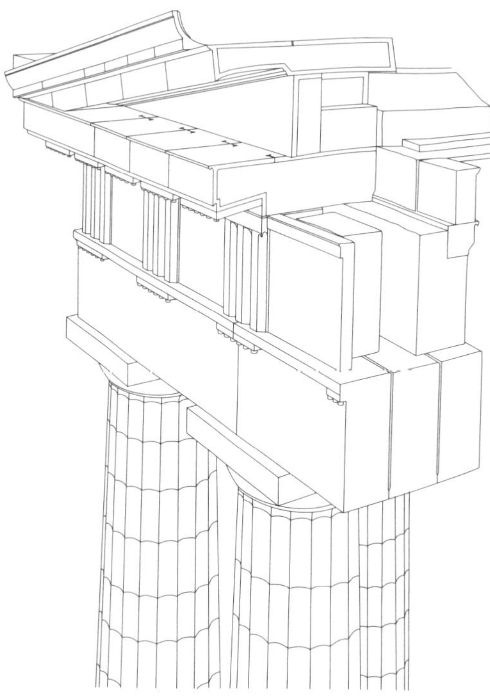

2. Athens, Parthenon (drawing depicting the structure of an epistylion in three sections)

3. Priene, Temple of Athena (view of one of the long sides)

Architrav im Kerameikos von Athen, in: MDAI(A) 104, 1989, 92–96; G. GRUBEN, Griech. Un-Ordnungen, in: DiskAB 6, 1996, 70–74; D. MERTENS, Der alte Heratempel in Paestum und die archa. Baukunst in Unteritalien, 1993, 28–29, 129–140; W. MÜLLER-WIENER, Griech. Bauwesen in der Ant., 1988, s.v. Architrav (Register); W. v. SYDOW, Die hell. Gebälke in Sizilien, in: MDAI(R) 91, 1984, 239–358.

C.HÖ.

Epitadeus (Ἐπιτάδευς; *Epitádeus*). An ephor from Sparta; according to Plutarch (Agis 5), out of anger against his son, he passed a law making it permissible to give away or pass on house and → *kleros* at will, no doubt with the aim of increasing the number of Spartiates. Plutarch dates this → rhetra vaguely to 404 BC, but cites this law as the reason for significant differences in wealth amongst the Spartiates in *c.* 250 BC. Aristotle (Pol. 1270a 15–34) seems to see the deplorable state of affairs in Sparta's cosmos in the mid-4th cent. BC as a consequence of this law, but does not mention E. by name. There are significant variations in the interpretation and dating of this law [2. 188–192], and some even assume the character to be fictitious [1. 163].

1 M. CLAUSS, Sparta, 1983 2 P. OLIVA, Sparta and her Social Problems, 1971.

J. CHRISTIEN, La loi d'É., in: Revue d'histoire du droit 52, 1974, 197–221; D. M. MACDOWELL, Spartan Law, 1986, 99–110; G. MARASCO, La retra di Epitadeo e la situazione sociale di Sparta nel IV secolo, in: AC 49, 1980, 131–145.

K.-W.WEL.

Epitalium (Ἐπιτάλιον; *Epitálion*). Town in Triphylia on the left bank of the → Alpheius [1]. References: Xen. Hell. 3,2,29; Pol. 4,80; Str. 8,3,12; 8,3,24. Archaeology: significant remains from Roman times.

Chroniques des fouilles, in: BCH 94, 1970, 996; E. MEYER, Neue peloponnesische Wanderungen, 1957, 50, 60.

Y.L.

Epitaphios (ἐπιτάφιος; *epitáphios*).

[1] → Funerary epigram

[2] (sc. ἀγών or λόγος; *agṓn* or *lógos*: funeral games or funeral oration). Funeral games are known since Hom. Il. 23; for Athens, Aristot. Ath. Pol. 58 mentions an *epitáphios agṓn* (for Sparta cf. Paus. 3,14,1). The term 'funeral oration' (ἐπιτάφιος λόγος; first in Pl. Menex. 236b) is only confirmed for Athens; it refers to the *laudatio* for a well-respected citizen in accordance with the πάτριος νόμος; *pátrios nómos*, 'the inherited order' (Thuc. 2,34). The funeral oration given by Pericles (431) is the first example preserved (although he had given an earlier one in 439; Plut. Pericles 8,6). All extant examples of this genre adhere to the same formula: introduction, praise (with reference to ancestors and descent), lament (sometimes rejected as unseemly), and consolation.

Dion. Hal. Rhet. 6,1–4 deals with this type of speech. Plato's *Menéxenos* contains an *epitaphios*, given by Socrates and allegedly written by Aspasia for Pericles. The fragment of an *epitaphios* by Gorgias is extant (82 B 6 DK). An *epitaphios*, attributed to Lysias is seen as genuine by some, whereas the one attributed to Demosthenes (Or. 60) is generally seen as fake (differently on both points in [3]). Demosthenes gave a speech (not extant) for those who lost their lives in the battle of Chaeronea in 338 BC (De corona 285). Hypereides' *epitaphios* was dedicated to the fallen of the Lamian War in 322 BC; his singling out of one warrior — Leosthenes — is unusual. Traces of this genre are also found in Lycurg. Or. in Leocratem 39–40 and Isocrates Panegyricus 74–81. *Epitáphioi* by Archinus and Dion (Pl. Menex. 234b) as well as Naucrates (Dion. Hal. Rhet. 6,1) are also mentioned. In later periods, the distinction between the *epitáphios agṓn* and the *epitáphios lógos* was absorbed within the feast of *epitaphia* [1. 64–66].

1 F. Jacoby, Patrios Nomos, in: JHS 64, 1944, 37–66 2 G. Kennedy, The Art of Persuasion in Greece, 1963, 154–166 3 M. Pohlenz, Zu den att. Reden auf die Gefallenen, in: Symbolae Osloenses 26, 1948, 46–74.

E.R.

Epithalamion see → Hymenaus

Epitherses Author of a treatise 'On comic and tragic Attic idioms' (Περὶ λέξεων Ἀττικῶν καὶ κωμικῶν καὶ τραγικῶν (Steph. Byz. s.v. Νίκαια), probably mentioned in Erotian, Vocum Hippocraticarum coll. 24,3 Nachmanson (the MS Text Θέρσις was corrected by Meineke as Ἐπιθέρσης; Nachmanson suggests the abbreviation Θέρσης). If he was indeed identical with the grammarian from Nicaea, he would be the father of the orator Aemilianus (cf. Sen. Controv. 10,5,25); because he is mentioned in Plut. De defectu oraculorum 419b-e, he can be dated to the period of emperor Tiberius, i.e. the latter half of the 1st cent. AD.

L. Cohn, s.v. E., RE 6, 221.

S.FO.

Epitome (ἐπιτομή; *epitomḗ*, Lat. *epitoma* and *epitome*) A. Definition B. Historical Epitomes C. Philosophical Epitomes D. Grammatical Epitomes E. Medical Epitomes F. Theological Epitomes G. Later Reception

A. Definition

Epitomḗ (from ἐπιτέμνειν; *epitómnein*, 'abbreviate', 'cut to size', Aristot. Soph. el. 174b 29; Theophr. Hist. pl. 6,6,6): as an ideal type, it is a form of reduced written text [10] somewhere between an excerpt and a paraphrase, generally of prose works (exception *i.a.* the lost Virgil epitomes [2]), and themselves written in prose (exception: Ausonius' *Caesares*). Extreme brevity is the declared aim of an epitome: decorative features of the original, such as speeches, or digressions, or lengthy passages of text, are omitted or ordered differently. However, the wording of the original is often kept in the retained passages (e.g. M. → Cetius Faventinus' epitome of Vitruvius' *De architectura*); however, occasionally changes were made deliberately (e.g. → Ianuarius Nepotianus 1,1 with Val. Max. 1,1). Alternative terms for epitome are: *breviarium, liber breviatus* (ThlL 2, 2169f. and 5,2,692 [11. 175]), ἐπιδρομή (*epidromḗ*), ἐκλογαί (*eklogaí*), ἐγχειρίδιον (*encheirídion*), and συναγωγαί (*synagōgaí*) [7. 946].

Epitomes are differentiated from related forms of a less stringent coherence (periocha, excerpta, → florilegium, → catene, and → hypothesis) by a specific editorial plan [7. 944], which reproduces basic outlines, as particularly obvious in the auto-epitomists (i.a. Epicurus, Galen, and Lactantius). The original editorial order is changed in favour of a new one with a lesser number of book(roll)s, while the order of the original books is retained as the internal subdivision within an epitome, i.a. in Justin and Galen [2. 21 and *passim*]). This first kind of epitome, conveying the works of one particular author (*epitome auctoris*), was joined by a second, based on a broader choice of literature and providing a condensed overview of a particular subject (*epitome rei tractatae* [7. 945], i.a. Vegetius). At times, epitomes were used as evidence of educated reading, esp. of historiographical works (SHA Triginta Tyranni 30,22), with a view to possible publication later (cf. epitome of Brutus: Cic. Att. 12,5,3; 13,8; Plut. Brutus 4,6–8).

Of the more than 120 known pagan epitomes, 38 are partially or completely extant, of the 36 Christian epitomes, 33 have survived (listed in [7. 947–957, 963–966], cf. [2; 3]). Their subject matters are accounts of historical events, philosophical and theological treatises, as well as other specialized literature.

B. Historical Epitomes

The earliest known epitome of a Greek historian is that of Theopompus of Chios (in two books from the original nine by Herodotus). The earliest completely extant one is 2 Macc in LXX; the epitomist (latest 2nd half 2nd cent. AD) describes his work (2,23 and 28) as an epitome of 5 bks. by Iason of Cyrene (2nd cent. BC), and lists among his aims the guidance of the soul (ψυχαγωγία; *psychagōgía*), facilitating memorization, and usefulness for all of his readers (ibid. 2,25); he strives for concision in his expressions (τὸ σύντομον; *tò sýntomon*, ibid. 31) — therefore, his work does not represent a mere collection of material, but a consciously rhetorically styled account [9. 1318].

In the Latin sphere, a variety of abridged versions of Livy's works are either documented or extant (such as the *Periochae*, and Iulius Obsequens' *Prodigia*); however, the Livy epitomes of the Imperial period are controversial [1; 6. XXVI-LV; 11. 190f.]: it was only later tradition which bestowed on Florus' historical work (with his own goals) the title of *Epitomai de Tito Livio* [5. 53, 138–141]; Aurelius Victor's *Historiae abbreviatae* (*c.* AD 360), Eutropius' *Breviarium ab urbe condita* (after AD 396), Festus' *Breviarium de breviario* (sc. of Eutropius) (*c.* AD 370), as well as the *Libellus breviatus* from Aurelius Victor (after AD 395) are epitomes of the second kind (see above), as they also draw from other sources apart from Livy himself; the same applies to the content of the epitomes by Iulius Paris (4th cent. AD), Ianuarius Nepotianus (end of 5th cent.), and Titius Probus (before AD 600), all contained in the nine-volume collection of exempla by Valerius Maximus [11. 193–210].

Justin's epitome of Pompeius Trogus' *Historiae Philippicae* (dating uncertain), which takes its internal structure from the 44 bks. of the original, is more than a *periocha* (outline), but he includes only those items selected 'because of the desire for knowledge' (*voluptate cognoscendi iucunda*) or 'their importance as role models' (*exemplo necessaria*) (praef. 4). Sozomenus (5th cent. AD) epitomizes in two bks. the period from Christ's ascension to the onset of his history of the Church.

C. Philosophical Epitomes

The earliest known example is Aristotle's epitome in three books of Plato's *Nómoi* (12 bks).; the earliest entirely extant epitome is → Epicurus' letter to Herodotus (Diog. Laert. 10,35–83) from his Περὶ φύσεως (*Perì phýseōs*; 37 bks.). He justifies writing this epitome, because it provides an overview for those of his readers who are not familiar with the details of his teachings, but may also help more advanced students with an overall orientation as well as more detailed problems (ibid. 10,35 and 83). → Arrianus recorded the lectures of his teacher Epictetus as verbatim as possible in 8 bks. (4 bks. extant) in the form of ὑπομνήματα (records; → *hypómnēma*), and later presented a systematic and concise summary of Epicetus' philosophy in an *encheirídion*.

D. Grammatical Epitomes

The earliest known example is Varro's epitome in 9 bks. of *De lingua Latina* (25 bks.). Hephaestion in particular provides a good example of the continuing process of abridgement: he first epitomized his 'Metrics' (48 bks.) in 11 bks., then wrote a second (lost) epitome in 3 bks., and finally produced the extant *encheirídion* (1 bk.).

E. Medical Epitomes

→ Galen epitomized the works of other authors and also produced a (largely extant) brief *sýnopsis* (9, 431–549 Kühn) of his own work on the pulse (transmitted in 16 bks.). While he only considers those epitomes useful, which an individual produces for himself from the more comprehensive original (ibid. 431), he found himself forced to epitomize his own works, because of faulty epitomizations by others.

F. Theological Epitomes

In the epitome (1 bk.) of his *Divinae institutiones* (7 bks., AD 304–311), which → Lactantius produced after the *Konstantinische Wende* (latest AD 321 [8. 16]), he states his aim (praef. 4) to make the text more concise (*substringere*) and to abridge it (*breviare*); however, at the same time he corrected his judgement of the Roman state: this epitome is equivalent to a second edition [8. 32; 4. XXII]. Two Greek epitomes are extant on the pseudo-Clementine *Homilies*, and one Arabic on the *Recognitiones* and *Homilies* [7. 963, 969–972].

Especially in late antiquity, epitomes fulfilled an important role in the transfer of knowledge. In Christian late antiquity, they seem to have been used in theological disputes to increase the circulation and persuasive power of a particular work (e.g. Fulgentius Ferrandus' *Breviatio canonum*). Within the isolated world of the monasteries, epitomes were important intellectual tools, such as the epitomes of some works by Cassianus of Marseilles by Eucherius of Lyon for the monastery of Lérin.

G. Later Reception

Both forms of epitome (see above A.) were in common use throughout the Middle Ages and modern times, especially the second, which established its prevalence as early as late antiquity, in the form of a compendium (in the more modern sense), a handbook, also a reference book [9. 1318].

1 L. Bessone, La tradizione epitomatoria liviana, in: ANRW II 30.2, 1230–1263 2 H. Bott, De epitomis antiquis, thesis 1920 3 M. Galdi, L' e. nella letteratura latina, 1922 4 E. Heck, A. Wlosok (ed.), Lactanti epitome divinarum institutionum, 1994 5 M. Hose, Erneuerung der Vergangenheit, 1994 6 P. Jal (ed.), Abrégés des livres de l' histoire romaine de Tite-Live, 1984 7 I. Opelt, s.v. E., RAC 5, 944–973 (fundamental and comprehensive) 8 M. Perrin (ed.), Lactance, Épitomé des institutions divines, 1987 9 H. Rahn, s.v. E., HWdR 2, 1316–1319 10 W. Raible, Arten des Kommentierens — Arten der Sinnbildung — Arten des Verstehens, in: A. Assmann, B. Gladigow (ed.), Text und Kommentar, 1995, 51–73 11 HLL 8,5, 101–211 12 E. Wölfflin, E., in: Archiv für lat. Lexikographie und Gramm. 12, 1902, 333–344.

H.A.G. and U.E.

Epitome de Caesaribus see → Aurelius Victor

Epitome of Livy see → Livius

Epitropos (ἐπίτροπος; *epítropos*).

[1] Alongside a great number of other titles, this was the term generally used for a steward who supervised the management of an estate on behalf of the (generally absent) owner. The duties of an *epitropos* as well as the degree of independence in decision-making varied from case to case, but, as a rule, it was his duty to supervise the workforce, to purchase supplies required for the estate, to sell surplus agricultural produce, and to be accountable to the estate owner. For that reason, he had to be able to have specialized knowledge in agriculture, be trustworthy, and be able to write and reckon. As the estates of the wealthy tended to become ever larger in the course of Greek history and were increasingly scattered, more and more *epitropoi* were employed, accompanied by a rise in their social standing. Incidental references to *epitropoi*, who worked for wealthy Athenians in the 5th cent. BC, show that the employment of estate managers was not unusual in Attica — and the same will probably apply to other developed regions of the Greek world. The earliest known prose treatise

about the running of an *oíkos* and the management of its associated estates is Xenophon's *Oikonomikós* (*c.* 370–360 BC); several of its sections are devoted to the selection and treatment of an *epitropos* (Xen. Oec. 12–15) and also that of a housekeeper (ταμία, *tamía*; Xen. Oec. 9). At that time, it was common for *epitropoi* to be slaves. Even though Xenophon mentions the option that a free man could work as a salaried estate manager (Xen. Mem. 2,8,3; here he uses the term *epistateîn*; cf. also Xen. Oec. 1,4), this was significantly hampered by the fact that working for someone else was seen as a curtailment of one's own personal freedom and honour. The *epitropoi* mentioned by Herodotus — apparently born free (Hdt. 1,108,3; 3,27,2; 3,63,2; 4,76,6; 5,30,2; 5,106,1) — were authorized agents of Persian or Scythian kings. Whereas throughout the following periods, slaves were largely appointed *epitropoi* in Greece, it was quite common to find free *epitropoi* in the Hellenistic kingdoms as well as under Roman rule; this can be traced back to differing local traditions. During these periods, a hierarchy of land agents is evident, particularly on larger estates; their different titles (amongst them *epitropos*) mostly referred to different functions and roles within this hierarchy. The best examples for this come from Egypt, and in time extend from Zeno, Apollonius' [1] estate manager in the 3rd cent. BC (even though no document actually contains a title which refers to his role) via Heroninus the *phrontistḗs* together with his colleagues and superiors (*epítropoi*, *oikonómoi*, *boēthoí*, etc.) on the estates of Aurelius Appianus in the 3rd cent. AD to the *pronoētaí* and other administrators on the estates of the Flavii Apiones from the 5th to the 7th cents. AD.

→ Heroninus Archive; → Vilicus; → Zeno-Papyrii

1 G. Audring, Über den Gutsverwalter (E.) in der att. Landwirtschaft des 5. und 4. Jh.v. u. Z., in: Klio 55, 1973, 109–116 2 S. B. Pomeroy, Xenophon Oeconomicus. A Social and Historical Commentary, 1994 3 W. Scheidel, Freeborn and Manumitted Bailiffs in the Graeco-Roman World, in: CQ 40, 1990, 591–593. D.R.

[2] In Athens, the 'guardian' for young people who had no father to care for them. An *epitropos* was generally appointed by the father in his will; it was not uncommon for a father to appoint several *epitropoi* from within his immediate family (→ *diathḗkē*) for each to keep an eye on the others. In case of intestacy, a legal guardian was appointed. In such instances, the order of succession determined which relatives were appointed guardian. The legal *epitropos* was confirmed in his position by the archon. The role of the guardian was set out in law (Dem. Or. 27,58; Lys. 32,23): the *epitropos* was responsible for the personal care and the administration of property, as well as the legal representation of the ward. After the termination of his guardianship, the *epitropos* had to transfer the assets previously under his administration to the ward, and account for his actions — this could be enforced by law with the δίκη ἐπιτροπῆς (*díkē epitropês*). Guardians were fully liable for damages (Aristot. Ath. Pol. 56,6), if they did not put their ward's property out to lease. In Diogenes Laertius' 'philosophers' wills', *epitropos* refers to the 'executor', in the Egyptian papyri (as earlier in Dem. Or. 27,19) to a representative of the proprietor or principal.

A. R. W. Harrison, The Law of Athens I, 1968, 97ff.
G. Thür, Tyche 2, 1987, 234 n. 6. G.T.

Epius (Ἐπειός; *Epeiós*).

[1] Son of Panopeus of Phocis (Eur. Tro. 9 with schol.; Paus. 2,29,4). He took part in the Trojan War, and won the boxing match at Patroclus' funeral games (Hom. Il. 23,664ff.), but was less successful in throwing Eëtion's iron discus (835ff.). E.'s subordinate social position as the 'water-carrier of the Atreids' is documented in Stesichorus (fr. 200 PMGF; cf. also Pl. Ion 533b). E. had the reputation of being a proverbial coward — in punishment for his father's perjury (Lycoph. 930ff. with schol.). In the siege of Troy, however, he excelled as the builder of the Wooden Horse and also as one of the warriors concealed in it (Hom. Od. 8,493; Verg. Aen. 2,264); sources differ on the exact number of heroes allegedly hidden inside the horse (Il. parv. fr. 8 PEG I; Tryphiodorus 152ff.). During the building of the horse, Athena took pity on him and helped him (Quint. Smyrn. 12,108ff.). Paus. 2,19,6 names E. as making statues of the gods in Argus. After the fall of Troy, he went to Italy and founded the cities of Lagaria near Thurii (Lycoph. 930ff. with Tzetz.; 946ff.; Str. 6,1,14), Metapontum (Iust. 20,2), and Pisae (Serv. Aen. 10,179). Both Lagaria and Metapontum claimed to hold in their respective Athena sanctuaries the original tools used by E. in the building of the Trojan Horse.

M. Robertson, s.v. Epeios, LIMC 3.1, 798–799; R. Wagner, s.v. Epeios, RE 5, 2717f.; Id., Conjectures in Polygnotus' Troy, in: ABSA 62, 1967, 5–12.

[2] Son of the mythical king → Endymion, winner of the running race which his father organized to decide the rule of Elis, beating his brothers → Aetolus and Paeon (Paus. 5,1,4ff.).

W. M. Stoop, Acropoli sulla Motta, in: Atti e Memorie della Società Magna Grecia 15/17, 1974/1976, 107–167, 1; R. Wagner, s.v. Epeios, RE 5, 2717–18; P. Weizsäkker, s.v. Epeios, Roscher 1.1, 1278f.; P. Zancani-Montuoro, Necropoli, in: Atti e Memorie della Società Magna Grecia 15/17, 1974/76, 9–106. T.S.

Epobelia (ἐπωβελία; *epōbelía*). Athenian law stipulated that in some private law proceedings, the losing plaintiff had to pay a fine equivalent to a sixth of the sum in dispute — i.e. an → *obolos* to the drachma (hence *epobelia*) to the defendant for wilful litigation. The same applied to litigants who were unsuccessful in a → *paragraphḗ* or who lost an appeal against a → *diamartyría*, but in this instance only if they had not even succeeded in securing the support of one fifth of the judges' votes for their case (Isoc. Or. 18,12).

A. R. W. HARRISON, The Law of Athens II, 1971, 183ff. G.T.

Epoche (ἐποχή; *epoché*). Expression used in sceptic philosophy (Sext. Emp. P.H. 1,196), meaning that the sceptic suspends judgement or refrains from a particular notion (ἐπέχειν; *epéchein*). A sceptic refrains from judgement, not only because it is not proven that a certain notion is true, but also because there is not a single reason for its acceptance, which was not opposed by a different reason. Later sceptics distinguish between various kinds of 'assent' — and thus of *epoché* —, in order to say that in some sense, sceptics always refrain from assent, but in another sense are quite able to agree with certain notions (Cic. Acad. 1,104). Thus → Carneades and → Cleitomachus allowed themselves assent as in a point of view, but not an opinion (*dógma*). This differs from the followers of → Philo of Larissa, such as Cicero, who allowed themselves opinions, but not knowledge (Cic. Acad. 1,148), and is different again from the Pyrrhonians (S. Emp. P.H. 1,19). M.FR.

Epochs and their divisions see → Era; → EPOCHS, UNDERSTANDING OF; → Periods, division into; → Chronography

Epode see → Horace; → Metrics

Epoikia (ἐποικία; *epoikía*). *Epoikia* was occasionally used instead of *apoikía* for Greek colonies, e.g. the early 5th-cent. BC Locrian colony near Naupactus (ML 20). The Athenian decree of 325/4 BC regarding the foundation of a colony on the Adriatic coast contains the reconstructed [*apoi*]*kía* as well as *épοi*[*koi*]. It has been claimed that strictly speaking *epoikia* and *époikoi* did not refer to the original settlement, but to its later reinforcement with additional settlers [1]. This special meaning may occasionally have been intended, but it is unlikely that it was taken into account every time this term was used.
→ Apoikia

1 T. J. FIGUEIRA, Athens and Aigina in the Age of Imperial Colonization, 1991, 7–39. P.J.R.

Epona Celtic goddess of horses, in Gallo-Roman times tutelary goddess of all equines (horses, mules, donkeys), stables, riders, waggoners, travellers, of trade and transport. Diverse images of E. exist, but all display at least one horse. She is frequently mentioned in ancient sources. The greatest concentration of her monuments is found in northern, eastern and central Gaul, from where her cult presumably originated. From the early 2nd cent. AD, her cult began to spread. These monuments — at a total of *c.* 300 particularly numerous — are found all across the European sector of the Roman empire, and one as far afield as Mauretania. This distribution can on the one hand be a result of the movement of Roman troops, on the other of trade and transport. Military dedications show that E. was not only a particular favourite of all mounted troops, but enjoyed the status of an official Roman military deity. Her importance for the entire network of trade and transport is evident in her veneration together with Mercurius and Hercules, in the inscriptions of certain colleges, as well as in the frequent dedications by *beneficiarii*. In both iconography and content, E. is closely related to other fertility goddesses; on this level, she is also linked with Bacchus. As horse goddess, E. is twice depicted together with the Thracian hero-horseman. Interpretations of E. as a chthonic goddess have been proven unsustainable. Attempts to establish E.'s elusive myth in the Insular Celtic literature stretch the limits of methodological permissibility.

G. BAUCHHENSS, SCHMIDT, s.v. E., RGA 7, 414ff.; BOUCHER, s.v. E., LIMC 5.1, 985ff.; M. EUSKIRCHEN, E., in: BRGK 74, 1993, 607ff. M.E.

Eponyms in chronology
I. ANCIENT ORIENT II. GREECE AND ROME

I. ANCIENT ORIENT

In the Ancient Orient, the custom of naming or numbering years after the annually changing occupants — high-ranking dignitaries of the royal administration — of an eponymous office *(līmum/limmum)* is only confirmed for Assyria from *c.* 1900 to 612 BC, i.e. to the end of the Neo-Assyrian empire. For the 1st millennium BC, the following order generally applied:' king, commander-in-chief, chief cup-bearer, palace herald, chamberlain, provincial governor'. Under Salmanassar III (858–824 BC), after 30 years in government, a new such sequence was started again with the eponymate of the king.

The origins of the Assyrian eponymous office are unknown. It is assumed that it developed from a rotational responsibility to take care of the sanctuary and cult of the god → Assur [2]. According to the list of Assyrian kings, it is likely that a king's years on the throne were counted eponymously from the reign of Erišum I (*c.*1900 BC). Documents from the Old Assyrian trading colonies in Asia Minor (19th cent. BC; → Kaniš) are dated eponymously. Under Šamši-Adad I of Assyria (1813–1781 BC), → Mari, too, adopted Assyrian eponym dating. After that, further evidence of eponymous dating only sets in again from *c.* 1400 BC. Up to the 11th cent., it is only sporadically possible to reconstruct the order of eponyms. The eponyms of the 11th and 10th cents. are largely unknown.

Eponymous dating basically presupposed the existence of lists of eponyms, and these are known from virtually the beginning of the Old Assyrian period in the 1st half of the 2nd millenium BC. A virtually complete list of eponyms is preserved from the earliest period, but the sequence is not continuous as the next specimens date to the 1st millenium BC. Several lists of eponyms, which as a rule start with the eponymate of a king, com-

mence in 910 BC with the reign of Adad-Nerari II; they compliment each other and thus ensure the sequence of eponyms up to the fall of the Assyrian empire. Only one specimen originally also covered the period up to *c.* 1200 BC. According to their layout and the detail provided, lists of eponyms are grouped into two categories: The first provides nothing but a list of the eponyms in chronological order, with the possible addition of their official functions. Texts of the second category are also referred to as eponymous chronicles, because they link an eponym with other significant political or other events (the target of a military campaign, the foundation of a temple, an epidemic, an uprising, or a solar eclipse).
→ Chronicle; → Chronography

H. Freydank, Beitr. zur mittelassyr. Chronologie, 1991; M.T. Larsen, The Old Assyrian City-State, 1976; A. Millard, The Eponyms of the Assyrian Empire 910–612 BC, 1994; A. Ungnad, s.v. Eponymen, RLA 2, 1938, 412–457; K.R. Veenhof, The Old Assyrian List of Year Eponyms from Karum Kanish 2003. H.FR.

I. Greece and Rome

A. Definition B. Greece C. Rome

A. Definition

It is defined as the designation of a year according to the name of a religious or secular magistrate. Strictly speaking, an eponym is an annually elected official or priest, whose name is used by the state to date *all* of the documents of his particular community ('true eponym') and whose accession to office coincided with the beginning of the year. However, the dating formulae on documents might also contain the name of further officials (scribe, treasurer, *agonothetes* etc.) or priests ('false eponyms'), mostly because they were involved in the specific activity concerned; thus, documents relating to sanctuaries were frequently named after the incumbent priest, who might not always have been identical with the municipal eponym [1. I 256].

The eponyms of different states assumed office at different times throughout the year: the Athenian *archon eponymos* on the 1st *hekatombaion* (July/August), the Spartan *ephoroi* probably in autumn, Roman consuls on March 15 (222–153 BC) or respectively January 1 (from 153 BC). It could also happen that the period of eponymous office did not coincide with that of other officials within the same community: the period of office of the Athenian *archon eponymos* ('calendar year') often exceeded that of the *boulē*; and Roman tribunes assumed office on December 9 [2. 34, 64f.]. The use of eponymous officials to establish dates led to some confusion in ancient historiography (Thuc. 5,20,2) and thus to the development of other dating methods (Olympiads, *ab urbe condita*). Nonetheless, eponymous dating provides the basis for ancient chronology, especially for those communities where long lists of eponymous officials have survived (Assur, Athens, Miletus, Sparta, Rome, Alexandria etc.), — always under the condition that the name of the eponym can be linked to a clearly dateable event. The list of eponyms from Miletus (see below) can be dated accurately, because Alexander the Great held the eponymous office in the year that the town was liberated (333 BC). Notes in the margins of such lists, chronicling events such as eclipses, wars, etc., also help to determine the absolute chronology; the Assur list of eponyms is thus dateable thanks to the reference to the solar eclipse of June 15, 763 BC [3. 414]. Particularly fundamental to the chronology of the ancient world are the—at times incomplete—lists of eponymous *archontes* in Athens [4; 5; 6; 7; 8; 9; 10. 198–237] and consuls in Rome [10. 256–276; 11; 12; 13; 14; 15. I 1041–1045, II 1242–1245, III 1457; 16].

B. Greece

Clear evidence of eponymous dating in Greece, where this practice was possibly adopted from the Orient, only exists from the 6th cent. BC. While Sosthenes (1st cent. BC) dates the beginning of his vita of Archilochus after an eponymous archon from Paros (FGrH 502), it is doubtful whether he actually found his name on an official list of eponyms going back as far as the 7th cent. BC. It is only from the mid-6th cent. onwards that annual lists of office holders were regularly compiled — although by no means in all of the cities. The Athenian list of eponyms, which was epigraphically recorded in *c.* 425 BC, sets in at perhaps 682/1; however, its earliest part may well have been a later reconstruction (ML 6; [10. 196; 17. 193, 207]. The lists of *theoroi* and *archontes* from Thasos, recorded in *c.* 360 BC, starts with the mid-6th cent. BC [1. II 292–294; 17. 194]; the list of Milesian *aisymnētai* (334/3) starts with 525 BC [1. I 251f., IV 229f.; 17. 196]. Sporadic examples of eponymous dating of documents exist from the 6th cent. BC. (Athens, Cyzicus; Solon fr. 49a, 70 Ruschenbusch; Syll.[3] 4) [1. III 245], they only become more frequent after the mid-5th cent. (Athens, Argos, Sparta, Delphi, Gortyn, Chios, Erythrae, Halicarnassus; ML 32, 37, 41 col. V 5–6, 42 B 43, 53; StV 134, 188; CID I 9; I Erythrae 1, 17); in Athens, the name of the eponymous *archon* only appears regularly in the introductory formula of decrees after *c.* 421 [1. I 270–272; 18]. Probably at about the same time, in any case before Thucydides, eponymous dating also became popular in historiography (cf. Thuc. 5,20,2). It is only in the Hellenistic period that attempts at keeping regular and orderly lists are documented (Syll.[3] 723, 793 [17. 210]).

A great number of eponyms existed within the various city, tribal, and confederate states, such as in Athens the *archon eponymos*, the *ephoroi* in Sparta, the *kosmoi* in the Cretan cities, the Milesian *stephanephoros* (compilation of documentary evidence in geographical order in [1. I-V]). Frequently, the eponym was either the most important official (strategos in the Acarnanian League), or an official, whose office had risen in importance after a constitutional reform (e.g.

the *archon* in Athens after the abolition of the monarchy, the Spartan *ephoroi* after Chilon, or the *patronomoi* after Cleomenes III, and the *prytanis* in Pergamum) [1. I 269, II 241f., IV 238f.]. However, it may also in some instances have merely been an office whose holder had been appointed annually from the earliest period—frequently, these were priestly offices (e.g. the priest of Athena Alea in Tegea). In Ptolemaic Egypt, the eponymous office was that of the priest to the royal cult in Alexandria, which was so important to the legitimization of the dynasty [1. IV 259–265]. Changes in the eponymous office were quite common [1. V 280–282, 288], especially with the purpose of signalling a new political beginning (e.g. Timoleon's introduction of the eponymous priestly office of Zeus Olympios in Syracusae in 345 BC; Diod. Sic. 16,70,5–6). Altogether, there is documentary evidence for the classification of around 40 religious and secular offices as eponymous ones [1. V 277–280].

As a rule, religious eponymous officials were priests (*hiereús*, *amphípolos*, *hierapólos*, *theokólos*) of the primary deity (Despoina in Lycosura, Asclepius in Epidaurus, Helios on Rhodes) or respectively a city's eponymous deity (Aphrodite in Aphrodisias, Caunus in Caunus, Dionysus in Dionysopolis). From the 2nd cent. BC, priests of Dea Roma appear as additional eponyms alongside the traditional one [1. V 281], joined in the Imperial period also by the priests of the imperial cult. Apart from priests, other religious officials also served as eponyms (*hierothýtēs* in Tymnos and Acragas, *hieromnḗmōn* in Byzantium, Perinthus, and Entella, *hieropoiós* in Erythrae, *neopoiós* in Amyzon and Halicarnassus). The term *stephanēphóros* ('wreath-wearer', e.g. in Calymna, Chios, Iasos, Magnesia on the Maeander, Miletus, Mylasa, and Priene)—frequently used to describe an eponymous officials—covers a number of religious as well as secular offices (e.g. *aisymnētai* in Miletus, *prytanis* in Chios, priests of Aphrodite in Aphrodisias) [1. II 264f., III 231, IV 230f., 242].

Secular eponymous officials represented a number of different magistracies. Sometimes, the eponym was the basileus — degraded to an annual office —, as in Argus, Aegosthena, Megara, Samothrace, Callatis, Calchedon, Chersonesus, Heraclea) [1. V 277]; very often, particularly in confederacies, the eponym was a military official (the strategos in the Acarnanian League, the tagos in Thessaly, the hipparchos in Cyzicus, Dascylium, and Prokonessos), or an important political official: the prytanis for many cities, esp. in the Aeolis and in Ionia [19. 733–749], the Cretan *kosmoi*, the monarchos on Cos, the *aisymnētai* in Naxos, Miletus, Olbia,and Sinope), the *demiurgoi* particularly on the Peloponnese, but also the Aegean islands and in Asia Minor [22], the *archon* (or *archontes*) as well as the *prostates* (Epirus, Amyzon, Paphos). Finally, there are amongst the eponymoi magistrates of the council (the *archiprobulos* in Termessos, the *boularchos* in Amphissa) as well as scribes [1. V 278]. 'False' or additional eponymoi of confederations or amphictionies were the *agonothetai*, responsible for the organization of agones (Aetolian Confederacy, west-Locrian *koinon*, Ilian amphictiony) [1. I 260, II 246, III 258].

Sometimes, the eponymous office was held by a magisterial committee, e.g. the five *ephoroi* in Sparta itself and in communities under Spartan influence (Thera, Heraclea, Taras), the seven *strategoi* of the Acarnanian League in the 5th cent. BC, the Cretan *kosmoi* [1. I 256, 260f., II 241f., 267–269; 21. 672]; it was common practice for the name of only one committee member to appear in the dating formula [e.g. 1. I 264; II 242; 19. 672]. In most of the confederacies (Achaean, Aetolian, Acarnanian, Boeotian), individual poleis dated their documents with reference to the municipal eponym as well as to the confederate one, e.g. in Epidaurus with reference to the priest of Asclepius and also the Achaean *strategos* [1 I.256–261, 279–288, V 280f.]. According to the Rhodian synoecism (408/7 BC), the participating communities (Lindus, Ialysus, Camirus) retained their respective eponymoi, but also dated documents in accordance with the eponym of the Rhodian state as a whole, i.e. the priest of Helios [1. II 279–287, V. 282]. Documents involving two states (e.g. international treaties) were generally dated with reference to the eponymoi of both communities [1 V. 280]. In the Imperial period, the emperor's name as well as references to local eras appear alongside local eponyms [1 V. 281].

As with all other official positions, eponymous offices came with considerable expenditure. From the Hellenistic period onwards, there was an increasing lack of citizens with adequate means (IEphesos 10; Syll.[3] 708 l. 26ff.); for that reason, the costs of office were often paid for from a temple fund — thus more than 120 times, Apollo took care of the office of the eponymous *prytanis* in Colophon [1 V. 283–285; 22]. The various duties of the eponym were then carried out by an 'administrator' (e.g. ἐπιμελητὴς τῆς θεοῦ Λυκούργου πατρονομίας in Sparta, IG V 1, 541). For the same reason, eponymous offices were also taken on by the emperor or members of the imperial family [1. V 285–288], by the senate in Rome (Hieromnemon in Pylae, 2nd cent. AD) [23. 79f.], as well as by wealthy women, particularly in Asia Minor (thus Attalis was for 13 years *stephanephoros* in Aphrodisias) [1 V. 290f.]. It was also quite common for wealthy citizens to donate large sums of money to ensure the future funding of the eponymous office [1. V 289f.; 24].

The compilation of lists of eponyms (πίναξ, ἀναγραφή; *pínax*, *anagraphḗ*) for individual cities was among the tasks of the ancient historians [17. 186f., 205–219]. Such 'literary' lists of eponyms are preserved for Athens (Demetrius of Phaleron, Stesiclides, Philochorus) (FGrH 228 F 1–3; 245 F 1–3; 328 T 1), Sparta (Charon of Lampsacus) (FGrH 262 T 1), Smyrna (Hermogenes) (FGrH 579), as well as Alexandria (Charon of Naucratis) (FGrH 612). The older view that Greek historiography had its origins in pre-literary lists of eponyms, which allegedly served as a kind of chronicle, can no longer claim any validity [17. 188–192]. Lists of local eponyms are preserved in inscriptions. Apart from inscriptions, which only list the names of office holders of one particular year (some of these covering a succession of years — [17. 187 n. 396f.]), there are also epigraphical lists of eponyms, which cover longer periods of time [17. 187–192]: a) lists, which gradually developed through the annual addition of the names of office holders [17. 187 n. 395; cf. 1. I 253f.]. It was the responsibility of the incumbent eponymoi to ensure that their names were added to the lists (IDidyma 218; Syll.[3] 723 [17. 187f.]), sometimes with the addition of short references to the most important events of the year [17. 188–192]. b) lists of eponymoi over a longer period of time, compiled in one go, perhaps as copies of archived annual lists of the type described above [17. 192–219]. The oldest extant example is probably the fragmentary list of Athenian *archontes* (earliest recorded year: 682/1 BC), compiled in *c.* 425 BC (see above). The list of eponymous Helios priests, which sets in with the Rhodian synoecism (408/7 BC), was made public epigraphically in 383/2 and from then on continued with annual additions into the 3rd cent. BC [17. 194 L3]. From the mid-4th cent., such lists become increasingly common (Athens, Anthedon, Thasos, Lindus, Camirus, Odessus, Miletus, Amyzon, Tauromenium [17. 194–204]; cf. [1. I 251–255]). As a rule, either kind of list begins with the year of an important historical event (constitutional change, synoecism, liberation, victory) [17. 210–212].

C. Rome

In Rome, the consuls were the eponyms [10. 249f., 253–255], allegedly ever since the institution of the office in 509 BC; however, prior to 222 BC, a consul could accede to or resign from office at any time throughout the year, so that initially there was no stringent correspondence between his period of office and the calendar year [2. 70; 25]. The *pontifices*, who were responsible for keeping the calendar, also compiled the lists of the leading magistrates, to which were added important events of the city's religious and political life. Dating according to consular office holders — alongside dating 'from the foundation of the city' (*ab urbe condita*), a literary invention — was used in both Roman and Greek historiography. Lists of consuls were publicly accessibly in epigraphical form — perhaps from as early as 304 BC (Liv. 9,56,5) —, such as the *fasti Capitolini* [26] and the *fasti Ostienses* [27], but also in the form of books (*codicilli fastorum*, Atticus' *liber annalis*) (Cic. Att. 4,8a,2; cf. FGrH 579). Dating after the *consules* was abandoned in AD 537 (611 in Egypt), when Iustinian (Nov. 47) introduced dating according to the emperor's year of reign.

→ Annales; → Archon; → Atticus; → Chronicle; → Consul; → Ephoros; → Fasti; → Pontifex; → Prytany

1 R. Sherk, The Eponymous Officials of Greek Cities I, in: ZPE 83, 1990, 249–288; II, in: ZPE 84, 1991, 231–295; III, in: ZPE 88, 1991, 225–260; IV, in: ZPE 93, 1992, 223–272; V, in: ZPE 96, 1993, 267–295 2 E.J. Bickerman, Chronology of the Ancient World, [2]1980 3 A. Ungnad, s.v. Eponymen, RLA 2, 1938, 412–457 4 W.B. Dinsmoor, The Archons of Athens in the Hellenistic Age, 1931 5 B.D. Meritt, The Athenian Year, 1961 6 Chr. Habicht, Unt. zur polit. Gesch. Athens im 3. Jh. v.Chr., 1979 7 Id., Studien zur Gesch. Athens in hell. Zeit, 1982 8 M.J. Osborne, The Chronology of Athens in the Mid Third Century B.C., in: ZPE 78, 1989, 209–242 9 S. Follet, Athènes au IIe et IIIe siècle, 1976 10 A.E. Samuel, Greek and Roman Chronology, 1972 11 T.R. S. Broughton, The Magistrates of the Roman Republic I-III, 1951–1986 12 Degrassi, FCIR 13 Alföldy, Konsulat 14 Leunissen 15 PLRE 16 Bagnall 17 A. Chaniotis, Historie und Historiker in den griech. Inschr., 1988 18 A.S. Henry, Archon-Dating in Fifth Century Attic Decrees, in: Chiron 9, 1979, 23–30 19 F. Gschnitzer, s.v. Prytanis, RE Suppl. 13, 730–816 20 Chr. Veligianni-Terzi, Damiurgen, 1977 21 F. Gschnitzer, s.v. Protokosmos, RE Suppl. 10, 670–675 22 L. Robert, Divinités éponymes, in: Hellenica 2, 1946, 51–64, 154f. 23 T. Corsten, Neue Denkmäler aus Bithynien, in: Epigr. Anat. 17, 1991, 79–99 24 L. Robert, Opera Minora Selecta II, 1969, 810–812 25 K. Hannell, Das altröm. eponyme Amt, 1946 26 Degrassi, FCap. 27 L. Vidman, Fasti Ostienses, 1982.

W. Eck, Consules ordinarii et consules suffecti als eponyme Amtsträger, in: Epigrafia. Actes du colloque A. Degrassi (Rome, 27–28 May 1988), 1991, 15–44; E. Manni, Fasti ellenistici e Romani, 1961. A.C.

Eponymus (Ἐπώνυμος; *Epṓnymos*), also eponym or eponymous hero, refers to a mythical character, whose name was given to a tribe, a town or settlement, or another group of people, or a mountain range. The Greek word *eponymos* in the sense of 'name giving' is particularly well documented in references to the heroes of the ten Attic phyles, whose images were displayed on the agora (decree in And. 1,83; Paus. 1,5,1); in the (passive) sense of 'name bearing', it is evident from Aesch. Supp. 252 for this very phenomenon (→ Pelasgus).

The phenomenon is as old as the earliest references to Greek mythology. In systematic form, they are evident in Hesiod, whose catalogues begin with Hellen, Magnes, Makedon, and Graikos, the *epṓnymoi* of the Hellenes, Magnetes, Macedonians, and Graikoi (the north-western Greek tribe, from whose name the Latin *Graeci* originated). In its (post-Hesiodic) conclusion, Hesiod's 'Theogony' also mentions Latinus, son of Circe and eponym of the Latini (Theog. 1013), and Medus, son of Medea and eponym of the Medes (Theog. 1001). As in these cases, the name of the eponym is generally traced back from the name, for which an explanation is sought. However, the reverse was also possible: the names of the ten Cleisthenic → phyles in particular were derived from heroes, who were well known even before Cleisthenes. As the mythical focus of a political identity, eponyms enjoyed regular cultic veneration by the cities and their subdivisions; as heroes, they often had graves, as the cult centre of a polis frequently located on the agora. Even in those cases where a later formation of such a cult can be clearly proven, modern feelings regarding the 'artificiality' of such religion have to be avoided: in ancient religions, myth and cult played a central role in the focussing and legitimization of identity.

U. KRON, Die zehn attischen Phylenheroen. Gesch., Mythos, Kult und Darstellung, 1976; T.S. SCHEER, Mythische Vorväter. Zur Bedeutung griech. Heroenmythen im Selbstverständnis kleinasiatischer Städte, 1993.

F.G.

Eponymy see → Eponyms in Chronology

Epopeus see → Antiope [1]

Epopteia (ἐποπτεία; *epopteía*, 'the seeing'). One of the levels of initiation into the → mysteries; whoever attained it, was *epóptēs*. In → Eleusis, whence the term originated, *epopteia* refers to the stage of initiation after the initial → myesis — *epopteia* either refers to the public 'display' during the celebration of the mysteries, in which *myesis* was the individual dedication which could take place outside of the celebrations, or rather a second facultative stage following on from the obligatory *mýēsis* [1; 2]. In any case, the term underlines the importance of vision within the Eleusinian mysteries. This aspect of the mysteries also finds regular emphasis in beatitudes, beginning with Homer's hymn to Demeter (480ff.); it is also evident in the title of the chief priest of the mysteries, the *hierophant* ('he who brings to view what is holy'). In contrast, *mýēsis* might point to the 'closing of the eyes'.

From Eleusis, the term was adopted by other mystery cults, such as in → Samothrace [3] or Andania in Messenia (LSCG 65).

1 W. BURKERT, Ant. Mysterien, 1990, 117, n. 13 2 K. DOWDEN, Grades in the Eleusinian Mysteries, in: RHR 197, 1980, 409–427 3 S. G. COLE, Theoi Megaloi. The Cult of the Great Gods at Samothrace, 1983, 30–36.

F.G.

Eporedia Mod. Ivrea, Celtic settlement at the confluence of the Dora and the Padus. the Roman citizen colony was founded in 100 BC at the order of the Sibylline oracle (Plin. HN 3,123) within the territory of the → Salassi (Ptol. 3,1,30; falsely Vell. Pat. 1,15,5 *in Bagiennis*). According to Str. 4,6,7, there was a slave market in E. for the subjugated Alpine tribes, and Plin. HN 21,43 mentions E. for its perfume production. In late antiquity, it became a bishop's seat. Archaeological monuments: town walls (rectangular enclosure), theatre, aqueduct, amphitheatre.

A. PERINETTI, Ivrea romana, 1968.

H.GR.

Eporedorix Celtic composite name: 'king of the riders?' (cf. also Plut. Mor. 259A; C (Ποϱηδόϱιξ MS].

[1] E. was the leader of the Haedui against the Sequani prior to Caesar's arrival,. In 52 BC, he fell into Roman captivity at Alesia (Caes. B Gall. 67,7).
→ Alesia; → Haedui; → Sequani

[2] Young equestrian leader of the Haedui, of noble descent. With Caesar's help, E. and Viridomarus had risen to highest office. At Gergovia in 52 BC, E. betrayed a conspiracy by Litaviccus to Caesar and thus foiled it. When after the Roman defeat at Gergovia the two leaders of the Haedui warned Caesar once more of Litaviccus' subversive activities, they were released to their tribe; in view of the general situation, they went over to Vercingetorix. They then looted the main Roman supply camp in Noviodunum, and tried to prevent Roman troops from crossing the Loire river. From then on, E. and Viridomarus were amongst Vercingetorix' most important military commanders (Caes. B Gall. 7,38,2; 39,1–3; 40,5, 54–55; 63,9; 64,5; 76). Descendant (?): CIL XIII 2728 = ILS 4659 (Bourbonne-Lancy).
→ Gergovia; → Haedui; → Litaviccus; → Noviodunum; → Vercingetorix; → Viridomarus

B. KREMER, Das Bild der Kelten bis in augusteische Zeit, 1994, 246–257.

W.SP.

Eposognatus ('Ἐποσόγνατος; *Eposógnatos*). Celtic name; pro-Roman tetrarch of the Galatian Tolistobogii [1. 155]. E. remained loyal to Eumenes II of Pergamum and did not support Antiochus [5] the Great. For that reason, C. → Manlius Vulso asked him during his campaign against the Galatians in 189 BC to talk the Tolistobogii into voluntary submission, but without success (Pol. 21,37; Liv. 38,18).
→ Tolistobogii

1 L. WEISGERBER, Galatische Sprachreste, in: Natalicium. FS J. Geffken, 1931.

W.SP.

Epostrakismos (ἐποστϱακισμός; *epostrakismós*). Boys' game, in which a shard or flat stone is skimmed on the water to make it hit the surface and skip. The winner was the one whose stone or shard made the most skips and went the furthest (Poll. 9, 119; Hes. s.v. E.; Min. Fel. 3; Eust. in Hom. Il. 18,543). R.H.

Eppia Wife of a senator, who under Domitian allegedly left her husband to follow a gladiator to Egypt (Juv. 6,82–114; cf. PIR^2 E 79, F 91). W.E.

Epponina Wife of the Lingonian Iulius Sabinus, whom, following his participation in the Gallic uprising against Rome in AD 69/70, she kept hidden in a cave for nine years, during which time she bore him two sons. Following their discovery, Vespasian had her and Sabinus executed in AD 79. PIR^2 E 81. W.E.

Eppuleius see → Tettienus

Eprius T. Clodius E. Marcellus. Descendant of a socially unimportant family from Capua (where the province of Cyprus later had a monument erected in his honour, ILS 992); *homo novus*. He probably entered the Senate under Claudius, and became praetor in AD 48. After commanding a legion, he was posted to Lycia as praetorian governor (*c.* 53–56); he was charged with extortion by the province, but acquitted. Under Nero, he became proconsul of Cyprus (SEG 18, 587 [1]), and *cos. suff.* in 62 [2]. He excelled as an orator, and under Nero publicly accused several senators, amongst them in AD 66 Paetus Thrasea, for which he received a reward of 5 million sesterces. After Nero's death, Helvidius Priscus and others tried to take action against him in the Senate, however without success. His position was too strong. Nonetheless, his three-year proconsulate in the province of Asia (70–73) can be seen as Vespasian's attempt to remove him for a period of time from the political debate within the Roman capital. In 74, he became *cos. suff. iterum*, he was a member of three priestly colleges, and had close links with Vespasian. Therefore, it is surprising that in AD 79, he was accused of being part of a conspiracy against Vespasian; brought to trial before the Senate, he evaded condemnation by committing suicide (Cass. Dio 65,16,3f.). PIR² E 84.

1 Bradley, SO 1978, 171ff. 2 V. Arangio-Ruiz, G. Pugliese Carratelli, in: PP 9, 1954, 69 W.E.

Epulo

[1] Name (probably Roman nickname 'the feaster') of the king of the Istri (*rex E.* Enn. Ann. 408 SK.; *rex Aepulo* Liv. 41,11,1, *Apulo* Flor. 1,26 [1]). In 178 he defeated consul A. → Manlius Vulso (MRR 1,395), but was ejected again from the captured Roman camp, where the victors were enjoying their supplies (*rex accubans epulari coepit*, Liv. 41,2,12; 41,4,7). In 177 he was besieged in Nesactium, and killed himself after the capture of the city (41,11,6; a different account in Flor. 1,26). E. is also the cognomen of C. Cestius [I 4]. Another E. is a fictional character in Virgil (Aen. 12,459).

1 O. Skutsch, The Annals of Q. Ennius, 1985, 574. K.-L.E.

[2] **(Jupiter)** An epithet of Jupiter, attested in two inscriptions (CIL I² 2, 988; AE 1936, 95); it refers to the *epulum Iouis*, in which the other two divinities of the Capitoline triad (Juno, Minerva) were also involved. This *epulum* (cult feast) was celebrated every year on the Capitol on the occasion of the → *Ludi Romani* (13 September) and the *Ludi Plebei* (13 November). Senators and knights participated in this public feast, along with the *tibicines*. It is one of the best-attested Roman sacrificial feasts. The priesthood of the *epulones*, created in 196 BC, supervised the *epulum* and the games that followed. Analogously in the private cult, Jupiter was called *dapalis* after the sacrificial meal shared with him (Cato Agr. 132).

Wissowa, Religion und Kultus der Römer, ²1912, 120. J.S.

Epulones see → Septemviri

Epyllion The term *epyllion*, in the sense of a 'short epic poem', evidently entered philological usage in German between 1817 and 1824 with F.A. Wolf [cf. 7], with reference to the ps.-Hesiodic *Aspís* (already in Ath. 2,65a ἐπύλλιον for the ps.-Homeric *Epikyklídes*). The word *epyllion* (ἐπύλλιον) occurs very infrequently in Ancient and Byzantine Greek, and not with this specific sense. It possibly had a negative undertone, thus Aristoph. Ach. 398, Pax 531 and Ran. 942, where *epyllion* refers to the 'bad iambs' of Euripides (schol. Aristoph. Ach. 398 and Pax 531; Hsch. ε 5575; in schol. Ran. 942 'bad speeches'); the use of *epyllion* for the individual hexameter in Clem. Alex. Strom. 3,3,24 could also be pejoratively intended. Already used in a value-neutral sense by M. Haupt for the *carmina docta* of Catullus and their Hellenistic precursors (1855), *epyllion* quickly became established [cf. 9] as a useful term for various kinds of short dactylic poems from the Hellenistic period and later (according to [5] only for poems in hexameters; according to [2] also for those in elegiac metre, as it is used for the most part today).

The following poems in Greek may be termed *epyllia*: Moiro, *Mnēmosýnē*; Philetas, *Hermḗs*, *Tḗlephos* (? cf. CollAlex adesp. 3 infra) and *Dēmḗtēr* (elegiac); Alexander Aetolus, *Halieús* and *Kírka*; Hedyle, *Skýlla* (elegiac); Simias, *Apóllōn*; Callimachus' *Hekálē* (elegiac), *Galáteia*, *Glaúkos* (? Suda, cf. Alexander Aetolus' *Halieús*); Theoc. 13; 18; 22; 24; [25]; 26; Nicaenetus, *Lýrkos*; Eratosthenes, *Hermḗs*, *Anterinýs* and *Ērigónē* (elegiac); some works by → Euphorion; Moschus' *Eurṓpē*, Parthenius' *Anthíppē* (cf. Erot. path. 32), *Heraklḗs* (fr. 17 Eratosth. Erig.?); Bion(?), 'Epithalamium of Achilles and Deidamia', PVind. Rainer 29801; Musaeus, 'Hero and Leander' (examples not fitting the pattern, at least as regards cyclic theme and deficient unity of action: Coluthus' 'Rape of Helen' and Triphiodorus, *Ilíou hálōsis*); also some *adespota epica* CollAlex 1 (on Actaeon), 2 (Diomedes and Pheidon), 3 (Telephus), 4 (monologue of a poor old woman, cf. Call. *Hekálē*), adesp. SH 901A (Hero and Leander?), 903A (Heracles and the Meropians), 939 (Arganthona and Rhesus?), 951 (Hero and Leander); cf. also 906, 922 (Eratosth. *Hermḗs*?), 955f., 962.

The Hellenistic *epyllia* show some typical characteristics of the aesthetic of the ἔπος τυτθόν, going back to Callimachus, or the characteristics typical of the narrative epic of the archaic period are lacking: although the theme is mythological, it is presented in the manner of light-hearted parody. In contrast to the themes of the earlier poems, there is a preference for marginal myths of lesser significance, and esp. for romantic/sentimental stories, for aetiology, for a humanized, domestic perspective to characters (tales of erotic relations between gods and humans are very common). Interest in a 'realistic' psychology of character, in particular developed through dialogues and monologues, comes to the fore. Length is limited (lying between the 75 lines of Theoc. 13 and the 1,000 lines at least of the *Hekálē* or the 1,500 lines of Eratosthenes' *Hermês*). Unity of action is observed, but priority is given to colour and variety rather than continuity; trivial details are emphasized, the action broken up by descriptions of the landscape (for the most part rural/bucolic); use is made of detailed description (→ Ekphrasis) and other interpolations (dreams, prophecies etc.), surprising new beginnings and endings.

Almost all of these peculiarities have their exact model in the non-monumental post-Homeric epic: aetiology in the 'Homeric' hymns to Demeter and Apollo; humanization and light-hearted parody in the hymn to Hermes; unions between gods and humans and the taste for myths of lesser significance in Hesiod's catalogue of women (where moreover at least some myths, like those of Mestra and Atalante, display the autonomous character, the length and other particular traits of the epyllion); length, aetiology and detailed description in the ps.-Hesiodic *Aspís*. The Hellenistic *epyllion* is set apart only by its stronger emphasis on these devices, and its systematic use of them, perhaps due to fortuities of taste, later to be reinforced by the influence of a few models (Philetas and Callimachus), together with an elaborate style (which is characteristic of the Hellenistic period and is not restricted solely to the literary genres particular to it): [5] esp. is inclined to assume critical awareness of the *epyllion* as a literary genre in antiquity (but see [1] and [10]); Crinagoras (Anth. Pal. 9,545,1) undoubtedly calls the *Hekálē* of Callimachus an *épos*, and it is not even certain whether and how the form of the miniature epic form was designated: *poíēma* as in Lucil. 376–385 KRENKEL (cf. [6. 124–127])? Not at first, but predominantly from the 3rd cent. BC, a combination of some of these factors can also be found in narrative poems not belonging to the miniature form. This circumstance lends relatively long narratives within large-scale epics the autonomous character of *epyllia* (e.g. Apoll. Rhod., *Argonautica*, cf. [2]; Nonn. Dionys., cf. [3]) or parts of a verse collection (e.g. Hes. Cat., Callim. Aet. fr. 75; cf. Ov. Met.).

1 W. ALLEN JR., The Epyllion, in: TAPhA 71, 1940, 1–26 (and Studies in Philology 55, 1958, 515–518) 2 M. M. CRUMP, The Epyllion from Theocritus to Ovid, 1931 3 G. D'IPPOLITO, Studi nonniani, 1964 4 K. J. GUTZWILLER, Studies in the Hellenistic Epyllion, 1981 5 J. HEUMANN, De epyllio Alexandrino, 1904 6 S. KOSTER, Ant. Epostheorien, 1970 7 G. W. MOST, Neues zur Gesch. des Terminus 'Epyllion', in: Philologus 126, 1982, 153–156 8 G. PERROTTA, Arte e tecnica nell' e. alessandrino, in: A&R; 4, 1923, 213–229 (= Poesia ellenistica, 1978, 34–53) 9 J. F. REILLY, Origins of the Word 'Epyllion', in: CJ 49, 1953/4, 111–114 10 D. VESSEY, Thoughts on the Epyllion, in: CJ 66, 1970, 38–43.

M.FA.

Addenda

Citations, law governing The law known in modern literature as the law governing citations is an order by the Roman emperor declaring which jurists from earlier centuries should be drawn on and cited in legal decisions. With the crisis of the Roman empire in the mid 3rd cent. AD even Roman jurisprudence (→ *iuris prudentia*) lost the political, social and economical conditions for productive continuation. Legal literature from the 1st cent. BC, the beginning of its 'classical' period, therefore changed from being a fund for a discourse of ideas on specific legal questions to a 'mine' of citations — some more comprehensible than others — on almost any tenable legal opinion. It therefore appeared to be a requirement for legal security to establish for the 'normal jurist' of late antiquity by force of imperial authority which legal opinions could be taken as valid. In a first step → Constantinus [1] therefore decided in AD 321 in a 'law of reversal' that the *notae* ('notes') of Iulius [IV 16] Paulus and Ulpianus on → Papinianus were not binding (Cod. Theod. 1,4,1). Not long afterwards, by a further law he declared the authority of Paulus' own works, including the (inauthentic) *Pauli sententia* as beyond doubt (Cod. Theod. 1,4,2). In AD 426 the law governing citations of the emperors → Theodosius [3] II and → Valentinianus [4] III (Cod. Theod. 1,4,3) in the manner of a 'tribunal of the dead' or 'spiritual collegium' [1. 533] declared the jurists → Papinianus, → Iulius [IV 16] Paulus, → Ulpianus, → Modestinus and → Gaius [2] to be jurists 'with legal force'. Where opinions differed, the 'majority of votes' would apply, and where votes were equal the opinion of Papinianus. Besides this, the older jurists could of course still be cited if their opinion could be proved from demonstrably authentic MSS. → Iustinianus [1] abolished the law governing citations in AD 533 (Const. Deo auctore § 6).

1 Wenger 2 F. Wieacker, Textstufen klassischer Juristen, 1960, 156–160.

G. S.

City deity

I. Ancient Orient II. Classical antiquity

I. Ancient Orient

The religion of Mesopotamia is characterized by a system of tutelary deities for the numerous city settlements that has its origin in the Sumerian religion of the 4th millennium BC. There is evidence of the existence and worship of city deities from the 3rd to the 1st millennium. Individual city deities achieved supraregional importance in the course of history (e.g. → Assur [2]; → Enlil; → Ištar, → Marduk; → Nabû).

→ Asia Minor IV.; → Pantheon; → Religion II. and III.

J. RE.

II. Classical antiquity

For Graeco-Roman antiquity the term 'city deity' describes a deity who occupies an outstanding position in the cult (→ Ritual), in theological reflection (→ Myth) and the public forms of representation of a city. This position also finds expression as a rule in the local festive calendar, the cult infrastructure or the iconographic media of the city [1]. In this way, an important, often identity-creating role is accorded for example to → Athena, the city deity of Athens, who was presumably named after the place name At(h)ana/Athens, or to → Jupiter Optimus Maximus in Rome, both in the political rituals and in the official economic and cultural activities of the city.

These cases are however the exception. From the pragmatic point of view of the cult, local history of religion examines complex local panthea of the gods, since the welfare of a city and its territory as well as the way in which the inhabitants viewed themselves in a religious sense depended on the activities of many gods. The category of 'city deities' is therefore problematical for ancient → polytheism from the point of view of methodology and the identification of a deity as 'city deity' in particular is moreover frequently difficult [2. 293–305; 3. 207–210]. Greek titles and epithets that above all since the Hellenistic period describe the special protective function and responsibility of a deity for a → *pólis* are the original local epithets πολιάς (*poliás*) or πολιεύς (*polieús*) among others, in addition the epithets naming 'leadership' πολιοῦχος (*polioûchos*), the → *archēgétēs* brought in line with the nomenclature of political offices and *prokathēgemṓn tês póleōs* or simply *ho tês póleōs theós*, 'the god of the city'. These descriptions however can also be used to describe groups of gods or the entire local Pantheon [1. 211–223; 2. 301–305]. The 'city deity' is therefore only a — politically, cultural historically, culturally motivated — option for the internal structuring of a pantheon of gods differentiated from each other according to sociomorphic models. Among the tasks of research is the investigation of this option, using concrete cases, as to in what way local group-specific power and prestige claims were to be legitimated through reference to a city deity on the level of divine hierarchies.

→ Pantheon [1] III.; → Patrii di; → Polytheism; → Theoi patrioi

1 U. Brackertz, Zum Problem der Schutzgottheiten griech. Städte, thesis Berlin 1976 2 S. G. Cole, Civic Cult and Civic Identity, in: M. H. Hansen (ed.), Sources for the Ancient Greek City-State (Historisk-filosofiske Meddelelser 72), 1995, 292–325 3 W. Burkert, Greek *Poleis* and Civic Cults, in: M. H. Hansen, K. Raaflaub (ed.), Stud. in the Ancient Greek *Polis*, 1995, 201–210.

A. BEN.

City state see → Civitas; → Polis; → State; → Town/ City

Civil War (Already in Hdt. Greek ἔμφυλος στάσις/ *émphylos stásis*; πόλεμος/*pólemos*; Latin *bellum civile*). Fight between armed citizens of the same state on its territory, which could be particularly fierce in Graeco-Roman antiquity given that 'citizens' and 'soldiers' were identical and therefore battle-experienced troops encountered each other. The causes lay in social conflicts, political differences or the power aspirations of individuals. Because the boundaries of civil wars are undefined, differentiation from 'revolts' and 'uprisings' is difficult.

I. Greece II. Rome

I. Greece

The small territory of the Greek → polis, the low yield increases of agrarian production combined with population increases and rivalries among leading families, who often gathered followings (→ *hetairíai* [2]) about themselves, made internal unrest a common phenomenon of the archaic period. The term *stásis* (literally: 'standpoint', in the meaning of 'obstinacy' directed against other communities or groups), which was used to differentiate it from *pólemos* ('interstate war'), is unclear and its meaning extends from 'dispute' and 'unrest' ([Aristot.] Ath. Pol. 5,2) to 'civil war' with the objective of the opponents' physical destruction (Thuc. 3,82,1). In the archaic period the causes were often found in social conflicts that were not seriously alleviated by → colonization (IV) and which often led to the use of arbitrators (→ *aisymnḗtēs*; → legislation) or even a → tyrannis because of the irreconcilability of the 'positions'.

With the expansion of the social groups involved in politics, in the classical period political dissent over shaping the → constitution, which was deepened by the dualism of → Sparta ('oligarchic') and Athens ('democratic'; → Athens; cf. → Peloponnesian War; → Pentekontaetia), was added to social conflicts since the conflicting parties could now expect external help. This intermingling of internal dissent with external influence continued in the Hellenistic period through support for particular persons or groups by competing Hellenistic monarchs (→ Hellenistic politics) and later also Rome (cf. → Social conflicts II).

II. Rome

Unlike Greece, Rome was spared violent internal conflict before the late 2nd cent. BC because of the strong internal coherence of its elite (→ *patricii*; → *nobiles*), strong vertical bonds between the elite and the people (→ *cliens*), and the option of quelling social conflicts through land distributions in conquered territories. Even the → struggle of the orders (5th–3rd cent. BC) was not conducted as a military conflict. The preconditions for violent conflicts only arose when the elite consensus fell apart, the burdens of the wars of expansion on the rural population increased in the 3rd and 2nd cents. BC, and the army was restructured (which resulted in a closer bond between the army and its generals). These conflicts permeated the late Republic from 133 BC (Tib. → Sempronius [I 16] Gracchus) to the conquest of Egypt by Octavian (30 BC): the 'Age of Civil Wars', so called because of the time frame in App. B Civ. = ἐμφύλια/*emphýlia* ('Wars among Kindred'). Appian did not differentiate between rioting with numerous casualties (e.g., during legislation and elections, mostly associated with petitions by the popular tribunes; → *tribunus* [7] *plebis*; → *populares*), which Latin authors called → *seditio* (e.g., Cic. Har. resp. 41; 43) and civil war (*bella civilia*) proper, which — in marked contrast to Greek civil wars — was fought by regular units of the Roman citizen army against the Roman civilian population or each other. In the term → *seditio* the military aspect is weaker; (similar to Greek *stásis*) it emphasizes the active deviation of one group (*seditiosi*) from political harmony (*concordia*).

The march of L. Cornelius [I 90] Sulla on Rome (88 BC), the subsequent fighting (87/6) between Marius and L. Cornelius [I 18] Cinna for power in Rome and the war in Italy after Sulla's return from Asia (83/2) were civil wars in a narrower sense. The uprising of Aemilius [I 11] Lepidus (77), the war against → Sertorius (76–73) and the final phase of the uprising of → Catilina (63/62) may also be considered civil wars.

The best-known civil wars are the wars between → Caesar and Pompeius [I 3] and their followers (49–46 BC) and the wars after Caesar's death (44 BC), in which troops of → Octavian, Anthony [I 9], Aemilius [I 12] Lepidus (→ *tresviri* [3]), the regular consuls and Caesar's murderers Brutus and Cassius participated. After the victory over Caesar's murderers at Philippi (42), fighting among Roman troops continued until Octavian's victory over Sextus Pompeius [I 5] in 36 BC, when the Civil War was declared to be finished (App. B Civ. 5,13, 128; 130; 132)>. However, the decisive struggle between Mark Antony and Octavian (31/30 BC) also counts as a civil war even though the war was officially waged as an external war against Cleopatra [II 12].

Whether the wars for the Imperial crown under the Principate and in late antiquity should be called civil wars is doubtful. While the civil wars of the late Republic touched upon the commitment and interests of all citizens (because the parties were at least superficially fighting about the shape of the → *res publica* and therefore were also fighting about the constitution), this aspect receded completely since the Principate. The wars after the death of Nero (AD 68/9; → Year of Four Emperors) and the death of Commodus (AD 192; → Severan dynasty, see Addenda) come closest to being civil wars because the decisive battles were mostly fought by citizen soldiers in the traditional territory of the citizenry, i.e., Italy. The many wars between emperors and usurpers in the 3rd cent. AD (→ Soldier emper-

ors) and between the armies of late antiquity, which largely no longer consisted of 'citizens', should rather be considered as 'wars of pretenders'.
→ Social conflicts

P. Tasler, P. Kehne, s. v. B., in: H. Sonnabend (ed.), Mensch und Landschaft in der Ant., 1999, 76–82 (with bibiliography). W. ED.

Claudius

[II 2a] C. Agrippinus. *procurator Asiae* under Hadrian.

J. Reynolds, New Letters of Hadrian to Aphrodisias, in: Journal of Roman Archaeology 13, 2000, 5–20.

[II 3a] Ti. C. Antoninus Son of a Tiberius, from the *tribus Sergia*. Prefect of the *cohors II Galatarum* (= *Gallorum*?), tribune of the *cohors I Hispanorum milliaria*, prefect of the *ala Tauriana*, procurator of the *vicesima hereditatium* in the Gaulish-Germanic provinces, procurator in Macedonia under Hadrian, procurator of Britain (unpublished inscriptions from Apollonia Mygdonia in Macedonia: Devijver V C 118 bis).

[II 20a] C. Cornel(ius/ianus) Latro Apellianus. Senator; *quaestor pro praetore* of the province Lycia-Pamphylia in the 3rd cent. AD

S. Şahin (ed.), Inschr. von Perge, vol. 2, 290 (in print).

[II 33a] Ti.C. Heraclas. Procurator with the rank of ducenarius; father of Ti. → C. [II 51a] Plotinus (see Addenda).

S. Şahin (ed.), Inschr. von Perge, vol. 2, 293 (in print).

[II 35a] Ti. C. Isidorus. Son of a father of the same name who was *gymnasiárchēs* and *hypomnēmatographeús* in Alexandria [1]; Roman *tribunus militum* and *epistratēgós* of Thebais [1. 125 ff.], according to [1. 125 ff.] son of the → Isidorus [3] mentioned in Phil. in Flaccum 20 ff.

1 A. Lukaszewicz, Tiberius Claudius Isidorus: Alexandrian Gymnasiarch and Epistrategus of Thebaid, in: T. Gagos (ed.), Essays and Texts in Honor of J. D. Thomas, 2001.

[II 41a] C. Lucilianus. Not *praefectus Aegypti*, as earlier assumed because of papyri Basel II, but only *praefectus montis Berenicidis et alae Herculianae* in AD 190.

H. Cuvigny, Claudius Lucilianus, Préfet d'Aile et de Bérénice, in: T. Gagos (ed.), Essays and Texts in Honor of J. D. Thomas, 2001, 171–174.

[II 50a] C. Nysius. Pretorian imperial governor of Cilicia either under Caracalla or under Elagabalus [2] (the name of the emperor is erased).

M. H. Sayar (ed.), Inschr. von Anazarbos, 2000, 11.

[II 51a] Ti. C. Plotinus. Equestrian, son of → Claudius [II 33a] Heraclas. From Caracalla he received the *militiae equestres*; *procurator* of Narbonensis and of Liguria maritima; *procurator Africae dioeceseos Lepcitanae*; *procurator* of Lycia-Pamphylia; designated *procurator* of Cilicia.

S. Şahin (ed.), Inschr. von Perge, vol. 2, 293 (in print). W. E.

Cockroach English name for the representatives of the Blattaria order of insects which can be found throughout the world in *c.* 3,000 types since the Carboniferous, one of them the German cockroach *Blatella germanica*. The Latin name is usually *blatta*; in Isid. Orig. 12,8,7, however, this name is used for a type of butterfly — actually a moth whose name was derived from its colour: when touched, its wings leave a blackish-blue spot on the hand (*blatteum colorem*, 'crimson'). In this text, the only zoological piece of information about the animal is its aversion to light in contrast to the fly's (*musca*) attraction to light (adjective: *lucipeta*). As a place of its origin, Pliny (HN. 11,99) furthermore mentions warm and humid baths (cf. Verg. G. 4,243). The unsightly animal (*animal inter pudenda*) is divided by Plin. HN 29,140 f. into three types: one of them soft, one of them residing in mills (*myloecon* = μύλοικος/*mýloikos*), and one of them foul-smelling with a pointy back part of the body (*exacuta clune*). The heads of these three types of cockroaches (Plin. HN 29,139–142, see [1. 56 f.]) or rather the whole insects were boiled in oil and placed, for example, on warts or sores that were slow to heal, also on injured ears or used as drops for treating ear infections (here, Dioscorides 2,36 Wellmann = 2,38 Berendes recommends the type of cockroach σίλφη/*sílphē* found in bakeries), or they were spread on the body to treat uterine cramps (Plin. HN 30,131).

1 Leitner C. HÜ.

Commerce see map on following page

Competitions, artistic
I. Stage competitions II. Literary competitions

I. Stage competitions

Competitions, which included the → *skēnḗ* (the stage and the podium in front of it for the actor's appearance) in Greek theatre, that is dramatic performances. Originally, the *skēnḗ* was away from the *orchḗstra* (→ Theatre I) and was used only for changing costumes and masks; it probably was not moved into the audience's view and integrated into the play until 458 BC with the 'Orestia' of → Aeschylus [1]. Nevertheless, early dramatic competitions are also thought to have been staged.

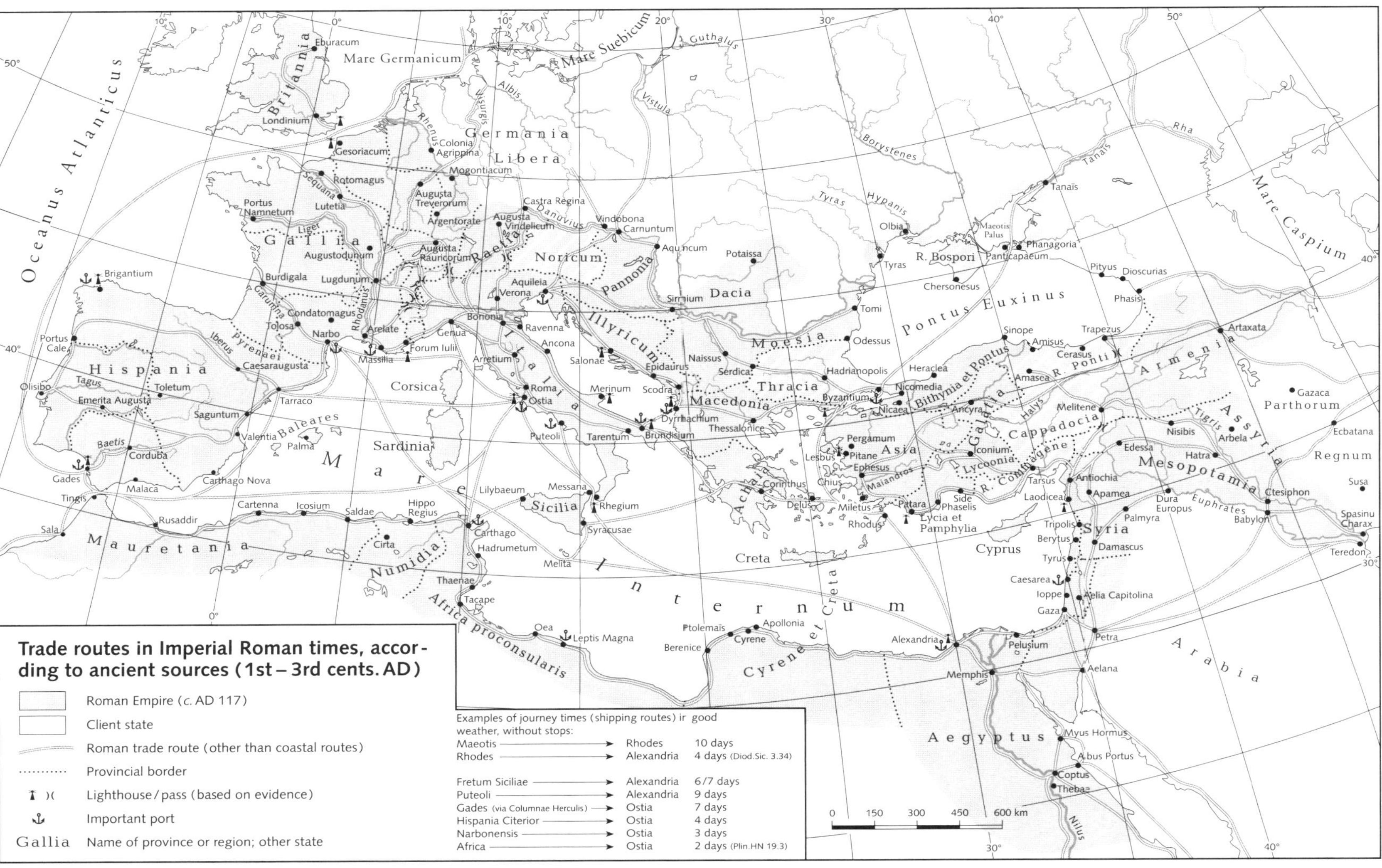
Oceanus Atlanticus
Mare Germanicum
Mare Suebicum
Mare Caspium
Pontus Euxinus
Mare Internum
Britannia
Gallia
Hispania
Germania Libera
Noricum
Pannonia
Illyricum
Dacia
Moesia
Thracia
Macedonia
Italia
Corsica
Sardinia
Sicilia
Creta
Cyprus
Asia
Cappadocia
Armenia
Mesopotamia
Assyria
Syria
Arabia
Aegyptus
Cyrene
Africa proconsularis
Numidia
Mauretania
Parthorum Regnum
0 150 300 450 600 km
Trade routes in Imperial Roman times, according to ancient sources (1st – 3rd cents. AD)
Roman Empire (c. AD 117)
Client state
Roman trade route (other than coastal routes)
Provincial border
Lighthouse / pass (based on evidence)
Important port
Gallia Name of province or region; other state
Examples of journey times (shipping routes) in good weather, without stops:
Maeotis → Rhodes 10 days
Rhodes → Alexandria 4 days (Diod. Sic. 3.34)
Fretum Siciliae → Alexandria 6/7 days
Puteoli → Alexandria 9 days
Gades (via Columnae Herculis) → Ostia 7 days
Hispania Citerior → Ostia 4 days
Narbonensis → Ostia 3 days
Africa → Ostia 2 days (Plin. HN 19.3)

A. GREECE B. ROME

A. GREECE

1. DEVELOPMENT IN ATHENS

Since the archaic period agonal thought characterized the societal and religious life in Greece [1]. Stage competitions in Athens were just as closely tied to cult as sport (→ Olympia IV; → Sport festivals IV. C.) and musical (→ Pythia [2]) ones. Naturally, when → Thespis first performed a → tragedy between 536 and 533 BC at the city → Dionysia, there was no competition, but no more than a generation later the official responsible for the celebration was able to present three tragedians annually who competed for the prize and this regulation remained in effect.

After the ten Attic → phyles contested the glory of the most beautiful cultic song (→ *dithýrambos*) on the first day, the three tragedians competed and after 486 also five comic poets as the conclusion. The prize was symbolic: a tripod (→ *trípous*) for the → *chorēgós* of the victorious phyle chorus, which was then set up as a dedication, and an ivy wreath for the best poet. The → *pólis* made the maximum effort to guarantee the same chances for all participants in the organization and execution of the competition. Thus, every tragedian had to submit a → tetralogy, each comic poet an individual piece and only a fixed number of *choreutai* (→ Chorus) and actors were available for the staging. Thereupon, the practice period was regulated, the place of performance the same, and, to avoid bribery, the judges were only selected at the last moment. The audience's reaction also influenced the victory in a stage competition [2]. Apart from the tragic interpretation of the myth or the originality of the comical subject, the acting skills of the main actor (→ *prōtagōnistḗs*) were decisive. It became independent to such a degree that after 447 a special actors' competition was introduced for the protagonists. This resulted in the poets' selection of actors no longer being by preference of but, rather, the archonts assigned them by lot (→ *árchontes*). When stardom was in its heyday in the 4th cent., the three competing tragedians received a different protagonist for each of their pieces in alternation [3]. More on the course of stage competitions: → Theatre (III. A.2.).

2. COMPETITIONS OUTSIDE OF ATHENS

Outside of Athens, drama eventually lost its exclusive association with the cult of Dionysus. Performances adorned the most varied festivals, at times without any specific cultic aspect. Often well-known pieces were replayed [4], but prolific comic poets such as → Alexis and → Antiphanes [1] also produced for external festivals. The art of acting became increasingly central, so that stage competitions were primarily fought out among the protagonists (→ Neoptolemus [6], → Lycon [3], → Satyrus [5]), e.g., in the performances held by Philip [4] II and Alexander [4] the Great (→ Plays I. A.). The situation in Athens is most clearly reflected in the documents of the Dionysia of Delos (which [5] prepared in exemplary fashion); in the Delphic → Soteria three groups competed against each other [5. 71–74].

Aeschylus' *Aitnai(ai)* of 475 BC were not performed in the context of a competition: a celebration on the occasion of the foundation of → Aetne [2] in Sicily by → Hiero [1] I; the same applies to the restaging of the 'Persians' *c.* 470 in Syracuse to celebrate the victory over the Carthaginians and Etruscans (TrGF 3, testim. 1, line 33 and 68; testim. 56). Similarly, → Euripides [1] did not present his *Archelaos* and possibly other dramas at the Macedonian court during the last decade of the 5th cent. in the context of a competition.

B. ROME

In Rome there were no stage competitions. At several festivals individual pieces were performed for the entertainment of the audience (→ *ludi* II. C.; III), which had to hold their own against all sorts of circus spectacles (→ Circus II) (→ Theatre III. B.1.). The low number of dramatists and the low social rank of actors (→ *histrio*) precluded competitions from the start.

1 B. SEIDENSTICKER, Die griech. Trag. als literarischer Wettbewerb (ADAW 2), 1996, 11 f. 2 PICKARD-CAMBRIDGE/GOULD/LEWIS, 97 f.; 274 f. 3 METTE, 91 f. 4 P. E. EASTERLING, From Repertoire to Canon, in: The Cambridge Companion to Greek Tragedy, 1997, 211–227 5 G. M. SIFAKIS, Studies in the History of Hellenistic Drama, 1967.

H.-D. B.

II. LITERARY COMPETITIONS

A. GREECE 1. MUSICAL AND RHETORICAL COMPETITIONS AT FESTIVE EVENTS 2. RHETORICAL COMPETITIONS IN VARIOUS LITERARY GENRES
B. ROME 1. HELLENISTIC AGONS IN THE ROMAN REPUBLIC 2. THE NERONIAN GAMES 3. THE DOMITIANIC GAMES 4. LATER COMPETITIONS

A. GREECE

Literary competitions included on the one hand (fictional) rhetorical *agṓnes*, which represent an element of → tragedy and → comedy (as well as other rhetorical *agṓnes* in various literary works before an audience within the work), and, on the other, the competition actually taking place in the context of a festive event at which a jury evaluated and awarded prizes.

1. MUSICAL AND RHETORICAL COMPETITIONS AT FESTIVE EVENTS 2. RHETORICAL COMPETITIONS IN VARIOUS LITERARY GENRES

1. MUSICAL AND RHETORICAL COMPETITIONS AT FESTIVE EVENTS

From the beginning agonal thought (→ *agṓn*, see Addenda) shaped all areas of life in ancient Greece. The objective of Homeric heroes 'to be the best and to excel beyond others' (Hom. Il. 6,208) may be considered a motto for competitions of all sorts. Human life as a permanent competition with others was already a theme in → Hesiod (Op. 21–26), who according to his own statement (ibid. 656 f.) won at a musical *agṓn* in Chalcis with a *hýmnos* and, therefore, is the earliest known victor in a competition. Later tradition, possibly going back to the rhetor → Alcidamas recounts a poetic agon between Homer [1] and Hesiod in three rounds, but there is no evidence of its historicity (→ Contest between Homer and Hesiod). A reflection of a poetic competition is the five-round *agṓn* conceived by Aristophanes [3] in the 'Frogs' between the tragedians Aeschylus [1] and Euripides [1] in the Underworld for the title of greatest tragic poet (Aristoph. Ran. 830–1471).

At the great → sport festivals of the Greek world, musical competitions, especially in the disciplines of solo and chorus singing as well as cithara and flute playing [1], established themselves along with the sports. Especially at the Pythian games (→ Pythia [2]) in honour of the god Apollo at Delphi musical competitions played a prominent role. A laurel wreath and high honours in society beckoned to the victor. The flutist → Sacadas, who won three known victories including at the Pythian games in 586 BC, was famous. At the → Panathenaea of 442 BC Pericles [1] organized a musical competition at which singers, citharists and flute players performed (Plut. Pericles 13,9–11).

Musical competitions also took place at smaller festivals, with rhetorical competitions having their place especially at the symposium, where participants in the feast competed with each other in improvized speeches on a predetermined topic (→ Feast; → Symposium literature).

2. RHETORICAL COMPETITIONS IN VARIOUS LITERARY GENRES

Reflections of rhetorical competitions are already found in the Homeric epics, where the skills of orators were presented under competition-like conditions to an audience that was present with the work. The most famous example is the rhetorical competition between Agamemnon and Achilles regarding ownership of the prisoner Briseis, which consisted of several exchanges, in the first book of the 'Iliad' (Hom. Il. 1,121–187; 223–244; 285–303).

The variety of topics in this competition is large: Ajax and Odysseus conduct a spoken agon for ownership of the weapons of Achilles (earliest example: Hom. Od. 11,543–564); the goddesses Hera, Athena and Aphrodite dispute who is the most beautiful before Paris as the judge (originally in the → *Cypria*; cf. Eur. Tro. 924–931), the personifications of virtue and evil each want to draw young Hercules on their side (Xen. Mem. 2,1,21–33). Topics of this nature also entered Roman literature (cf. already Enn. Sat. fr. 20 VAHLEN: competition of life and death) and were dealt with in great number for practice in Greek and Roman schools of rhetoric [2. 264–294].

In historiography rhetorical competitions have played a major role since Herodotus [1] and were often inserted by authors at decisive turning-points in history. Famous examples are the Persian constitutional debates over the advantages and disadvantages of the three forms of government (monarchy, aristocracy and democracy) in Herodotus (Hdt. 3,80–82), the debate on the punishment of renegade Athenian allies in Thucydides [2] (Thuc. 3,37–48) and the dialogue between Athens and Melos over the relationship between power and morals in politics (Thuc. 5,85–113).

In almost all preserved Attic comedies and the majority of tragedies, especially those of Euripides (cf. [3]), rhetorical competitions appear at decisive points in the action. The agon in tragedy is formally basically characterized by two lengthy disputations separated by a few commenting chorus verses, which are then often followed by the confrontation of the competitors in speech and rejoinder, often with a change in speaker after each verse (→ Stichomythia). An agreement is never achieved and the positions of the disputing parties rather harden as in the famous *agônes* between Creon and Antigone or between Creon and Haemon in the 'Antigone' of Sophocles (Soph. Ant. 450–525 and 639–765). Often the → chorus gives a judgment on whose arguments are more persuasive (→ Tragedy).

In → comedy the rhetorical *agṓn* is integrated into an even stricter scheme [4]; in contrast to the tragedy there routinely is a victor. An example is the competition of the allegorical figures of just and unjust speech in Aristophanes' 'Clouds' (Aristoph. Nub. 949–1104).

The system of speech and rejoinder, which is seen to be possible in principle for any topic, was taken to a higher level of perfection in the → rhetoric of the → sophists and entered forensic rhetoric. In his three tetralogies the orator Antiphon [4] presents sets of speeches in which plaintiff and defendant each have two turns [5].

Agonal elements are also contained in many of Plato's [1] dialogues; particularly typical are the three exchanges that Socrates [2] conducts in the 'Gorgias' with his opponents Gorgias, Polus and Callicles. With the six praise speeches on → Eros in the 'Symposium' Plato designed a broad rhetorical competition (Pl. Symp. 178a–212c), whose climax is Socrates' presentation of the speech of the priestess → Diotima on the nature of Eros (Pl. Symp. 207c–212a). In the Hellenistic period the bucolic *agṓn* between two shepherds is remarkable as a new form of the rhetorical competition. It is repeatedly used in the corpus of → Theocritus (Theoc. Eidyllia 5, 6, 8, 9) and later becomes a fixed part of the motif stock in Roman bucolics. These competitions are partly aggressive in tone (Theoc. Eidyllion 5), partly friendly [6]. In the literature of the Imperial period the satirical oratorial agons of → Lucian [1] must be noted [2. 360–381].

1 M. WEGNER, Das Musikleben der Griechen, 1949, 107–109 2 W. J. FROLEYKS, Der ΑΓΩΝ ΛΟΓΩΝ in der ant. Lit., 1973 3 M. DUBISCHAR, Die Agonszenen bei Euripides, 2001 4 TH. GELZER, Der epirrhematische Agon bei Aristophanes, 1960 5 M. FUHRMANN, Die ant. Rhetorik, 1984, 22 6 B. EFFE, G. BINDER, Ant. Hirtendichtung, [2]2000, 21 f.; 35; 63–67; 86 f.; 105 f.

TH. P.

B. Rome

1. Hellenistic agons in the Roman republic

Given the known aversion of the Romans against Greek gymnastics and their own fixed, religiously based system of *ludi publici* with (agonistic) *ludi circenses* and (non- agonistic) *ludi scaenici* (→ Circus II, → *ludi*) attempts to permanently translate Greek *agṓnes* (→ *agṓn*, s. Addenda → Sport festivals) to the Roman system [1. 169] remained without result. In information on early, only occasional appearances of Greek *artifices* ('artists') in Rome, a kind of stage competition (*theatrales artes ... id genus spectaculi*, 'acting ... this [i.e., the Greek] genre of spectacle'; Tac. Ann. 14,21,1) is only dedicated in 145 BC 'in the games' (*ludi curatius editi*) staged with great care by the conqueror of Corinth L. Mummius [I 3]; also in the triumphal games of Cornelius [I 3] Sulla in 82 a complete programme of sport and musical competition appears to have been offered (App. B Civ. 1,99), likewise by Pompeius [I 3] at the dedication of the Theatre of Pompey in 55 BC (Plut. Pompeius 52,4). Inversely, the penteteric (i.e., held on a four-year cycle) *ludi pro valetudine Augusti* ('games for the well-being of → Augustus'), which were held after 28 BC, were restricted to *circenses*, *agones gymnici* and gladiator fights [2].

2. The Neronian games

It is hardly astonishing that the theatre fanatic → Nero [1] was the first to attempt to implant the musical *agṓn* in Rome. He initially attempted to probe acceptance in his private → Iuvenalia from 59 to at least 63 (in his *theatrum peculiare*, 'private theatre': Plin. HN 37,19), but in 60 had the Neronia held (celebrated in August in the Theatre of Pompey), and then in 64 in Naples and in 64/65 [3] at the second Neronia in Rome he himself performed [4]. The Neronia supplemented the gymnastic and hippic competitions already celebrated under Augustus with a preceding *certamen musicum* ('musical competition': Suet. Nero 12,3; Tac. Ann. 14,20,1), which specifically envisioned a competition in each of rhetorical presentation, poetic recitation and cithara playing. In the first category no victor was recognized in 60 (Tac. Ann. 14,21,4); in the second the young → Lucan [1] won with a panegyric on Nero and the emperor was acclaimed in the citharode competition after all other competitors were disqualified in advance as a precautionary measure (Cass. Dio 61,21,2). In the second (Suet. Nero 21,1) Neronia of 64, which was held early, Nero took part in all three competitions (Suet. Nero 21); after he rejected the prizes that the Senate offered him in advance in rhetoric and the poetry recital, he gratefully accepted them from the other competitors (Tac. Ann. 16,4). Only in cithara playing did he not wish to be fobbed off in this manner, but appeared as a professional citharode (Suet. Nero 21,2; Tac. Ann. 16,4,3 f.), but then had the prize-awarding delayed to 65.

3. The Domitianic games

Like Nero, though not as professionally committed, Domitian [1] complemented his private *ludi Albani*, which were held annually in March in his villa at Alba and in which orators and poets competed (Suet. Dom. 4,4; Cass. Dio 67,1,2; [5. vol. 2, 232]), with the *certamen Capitolinum* (Suet. Dom. 4,4; → Capitolia), which was established in 86. In 90 both the young African (*puer*) → Florus [1] (Flor. Vergilius orator an poeta) and the established poet → Statius [II 2] performed in the category of 'recited poetry' on the same theme, the imperial triumph (in 89) over Germans and Dacians [6. 3098 f.]. It is uncertain if Florus, like Statius (Silv. 3,5,28–31; 4,2,65–67; 5,3, 225–227) received the prize, a golden olive wreath; in any case his verses remained famous in Rome according to his own claim.

Unlike the Neronia, which lapsed with the death of their founder, the Capitoline *agṓn* of Domitian (Cens. 18,15) maintained itself despite his → *damnatio memoriae* to late antiquity, i.e., until the general cancellation of festivals dedicated to pagan deities in 407 (cf. for example Auson. Commemoratio professorum Burdigalensium 5,5–8).

The Capitoline *agṓn* was set up according to the model of the Olympic games; it was dedicated to Iuppiter/Zeus and was first held in AD 86 to celebrate the restoration of the Capitoline temple (→ Capitolina), and then every four years from late April/early May to June 12. Together with the four old Greek festivals, and the Augustan → Actia (in → Nicopolis, after 27 BC) as well as the → Sebasteia (Augustalia, AD 2 in Naples), it took its place in the festival circuit (→ *períodos*), with Capitoline victories being named first in the series from the 2nd cent. As with the Greek → Pythia [2] and the Neronia, the musical competitions, for which more than 30 days were allotted, came first; 6 days sufficed for the hippic and two for the gymnastic parts [7. 171 f.].

The programme contained elements of the Neronia but was broader. It began (1) as in Olympia with a competition of trumpeters and heralds [7. 183] as a necessary precondition of the later programme. These were probably followed (in the sequence of the Neronia), by (2) Greek and Latin panegyrics, (3) Greek and Latin recited poetry and (4) singing to the cithara. However, unlike the Neronia's, the programme also included other components. These were instrumental music, i.e., (5) cithara accompanied by a chorus (*chorocitharistae*), also without reference to a text (*psilocitharistae*, 'cithara solo'), (6) solo flute and accompanying the singing of a pythic chorus; (7) stage competitions, single tragic and comic songs (*fabula cantata* [4. 154 f.]), and finally held, probably in the final years of the 2nd cent. [1. 173; 7. 182 f.], (8) also the → *pantómimos* = *fabula saltata* [1. 101 f.; 173–176]. (2) and (5) no longer appeared in the programme after the early 2nd cent. (cf. Suet. Dom. 4,4: *nunc*), but the essential continuity of (2) appears to be confirmed by the evidence of the *Hermeneumata* (CGL 3, 656 No. 6). (1)–(6) took place in an → Odeion specially built by Domitian on the Campus Martius, but (7) and (8) were held in the → theatre. The emperor functioned as agonothete (→ *agōnothétēs*) among a circle of other judges (Suet. Dom. 4,4), with his vote naturally being decisive, as in Florus' case (see below). In (2) and (3) topics from the field of the praise of Jupiter (Quint. Inst. 3,7,4) or mythology relating to Zeus were required [8. 87 f.] and after a limited period of preparation presented as an improvisation ([9. 100 f.]; but cf. [8. 88 f.]). In (3) the participation of pupils (*pueri*) was common ([5. vol. 2, 200; 9. 101]; however, cf. [8. 90[17]]). With Q. Sulpicius Maximus (see below) *inter Graecos poetas* (ILS 5177) 52 competitors had entered and each individual performance had to be appropriately short (for Sulpicius only 43 hexameters). The prize of victory was an oak wreath that may possibly have been conferred by the emperor himself.

For the initial decades of the festival names of victors are known from contemporary writers (Statius, Martialis [1], Juvenal) and inscriptions, later from inscriptions only: in 86, a Collinus, probably as Latin poet (Mart. 4,54,1–4), in 86–94 Palfurius Sura as *orator Latinus* (Suet. Dom. 13,1), in 94 Scaevus Memor in tragic song (Mart. 11,9; cf. [10. 156 f.]), in 106 the thirteen-year old L. Valerius Pudens *inter poetas Latinos* (ILS 5178). In 90, Florus was not able to prevail despite support from the audience against Domitian (as a *puer*, Flor. Vergilius orator an poeta 1; → Florus [1]). In 94, the eleven-year old Sulpicius also honourably failed in the category of Greek poetry — his text (cf. [9]; on Ovid's influence [11]) was added to the funerary monument by his proud parents during their mourning —, likewise in the same year Statius (Silv. 5,3,231 f.) in singing to the cithara (ibid. 3,5,31–39; [12. 286]). Whether the Greek poet Diodorus, coming from Alexandria, ever reached Rome (Mart. 9,40) is uncertain; on the social status of the victors, cf. [8].

4. Later competitions

Later Imperial agons in Rome or competitions imitating the Greek agons in the Roman provinces [1. 172 f.; 5. 232 f.] were probably organized in a similar way; on the Greek Asclepia and the *Pythicus agon* in Carthage, cf. [13. 794–798].

1 H. Leppin, Histrionen, 1992 2 L. Polverini, La prima manifestazione agonistica di carattere periodico a Roma, in: L. Gasperini (ed.), Scritti storico-epigrafici in memoria di M. Zambelli, 1978, 325–332 3 M. Malavolta, I Neronia e il lustrum, in: Miscellanea greca e romana 6, 1978, 395–415 4 P. L. Schmidt, Nero und das Theater, in: J. Blänsdorf (ed.), Theater und Ges. im Imperium Romanum, 1990, 149–171 5 Friedländer 2, 150 f., 231 f.; 4, 276–280 6 K. M. Coleman, The Emperor Domitian and Literature, in: ANRW II 32.5, 1986, 3097–3100 7 B. Rieger, Die Capitolia des Kaisers Domitian, in: Nikephoros 12, 1999, 171–203 8 P. White, Latin Poets and the Certamen Capitolinum, in: P. Knox (ed.), Style and Tradition. FS W. Clausen, 1998, 84–95 9 S. Döpp, Das Stegreifgedicht des Q. Sulpicius Maximus, in: ZPE 114, 1996, 99–114 10 I. Lana, I ludi Capitolini di Domiziano, in: RFIC 79, 1951, 145–160 11 H. Bernsdorff, Q. Sulpicius Maximus, Apollonios von Rhodos und Ovid, in: ZPE 118, 1997, 105–112 12 G. Wille, Musica Romana, 1967 13 Robert, OMS 5, 1989.

M. L. Caldelli, L'Agon Capitolinus, 1993; IGUR 3, 1979, 189–193. P. L. S.

Constellations

I. Ancient Orient II. Classical Antiquity

I. Ancient Orient

In Mesopotamia, the visible stars were combined into constellations; some of these notions about constellations were communicated to other cultures as early as the 2nd millennium BC and, through Greek-Roman transmission, are still common today. The constellations of the → zodiac — Taurus, Gemini, Cancer, Leo, Libra, Scorpio, Sagittarius, and Pisces — can be traced back to Babylonian models, also the Big Dipper (*Ursa Maior*), the Raven, and the Eagle, among others.

Babylonian → lists of constellations have existed since the early 2nd millennium [4]. A systematic organization of the constellations can be found in the series called ^{mul}Apin (→ Fixed stars). Most of these constellations can be identified, but it is often difficult to determine which stars belong to a particular constellation [2]. The constellations play an important role in heavenly omens, while planetary phenomena (nuances of colour, etc.) can mean different things depending on the constellation to which they belong [5]. One description of constellations (*c.* 8th cent. BC) has survived [8]. Two clay tablets from the Hellenistic period show scratched drawings of constellations [10].

→ Astrology; → Astronomy; → Fixed stars; → Zodiac

1 H. Hunger, Astrological Reports to Assyrian Kings, 1992 2 Id., D. Pingree, Astral Sciences in Mesopotamia, 1999, 271–277 (survey) 3 S. Parpola, Letters from Assyrian and Babylonian Scholars, 1993 4 E. Reiner, M. Civil, Materials for the Sumerian Lexicon 11, 1974, 30 f.; 40 f.; 107 f. 5 E. Reiner, D. Pingree, Babylonian Planetary Omens, vol. 1–3, 1975–1998 6 W. H. van Soldt, Solar Omens of Enuma Anu Enlil, 1995 7 E. von Weiher, Spätbabylon. Texte aus Uruk, 1988, no. 114 and 116 8 E. Weidner, Eine Beschreibung des Sternenhimmels aus Assur (AfO 4), 1927, 73–85 9 Id., s. v. S., RLA 3, 1959, 72–82 10 Id., Gestirn-Darstellungen auf babylonischen Tontafeln, 1967. H. HU.

II. Classical Antiquity

A. Origin B. Iconography C. Catalogues D. Alternatives E. Individual Stars F. Representation G. Function H. Afterlife

A. Origin

In antiquity, it was assumed — despite a few opposing views (e.g. Geminus 1,23) — that all Graeco-Roman fixed stars were divine and therefore spirited beings who were 'attached' to an eighth sphere, on the outer shell of the cosmos, beyond the seven → planets (→ Fixed stars). The claim of Greek 'discoverers' of constellations (Thales, Cleostratus, Euctemon) lacks credibility since many of the constellation names are

English names	Greek	Latin
1. Ram	*Kriós*	*Aries*
2. Bull	*Taúros*	*Taurus*
3. Twins	*Dídymoi*	*Gemini*
4. Crab	*Karkínos*	*Cancer*
5. Lion	*Léōn*	*Leo*
6. Virgin	*Parthénos*	*Virgo*
7. Scales	*Zygós*	*Libra*
8. Scorpion	*Skorpíos*	*Scorpius* (*-io*)
9. Archer	*Toxótēs*	*Sagittarius*
10. Goat	*Aigókerōs*	*Capricornus*
11. Water-carrier	*Hydrochóos*	*Aquarius*
12. Fishes	*Ichthýes*	*Pisces*

Table 1: Zodiac

English names	Greek	Latin
1. Little Bear	*Árktos mikrá*	*Ursa minor*
2. Great Bear	*Árktos megálē*	*Ursa maior*
3. Dragon	*Drákōn*	*Draco*
4. Cepheus	*Kēpheús*	*Cepheus*
5. Herdsman	*Boṓtēs*	*Arcturus*
6. Northern Crown	*Stéphanos* (*bóreios*)	*Corona* (*borealis*)
7. Hercules	*ho Engónasin*	(*In*)*nixus*
8. Lyre	*Lýra*	*Lyra*
9. Swan	*Órnis*	*Olor*
10. Cassiopeia	*Kassiépeia*	*Cassiepia*
11. Perseus	*Perseús*	*Perseus*
12. Charioteer	*Hēníochos*	*Auriga*
13. Serpent-bearer	*Ophioúchos*	*Ophiuchus*
14. Serpent	(*ho echómenos*) *Óphis*	*Serpens*
15. Arrow	*Oïstós*	*Sagitta*
16. Eagle	*Aetós*	*Aquila*
17. Dolphin	*Delphís*	*Delphinus*
18. Little Horse	*Híppou protomḗ*	*Equi cisio*
19. Pegasus	*Híppos*	*Pegasus*
20. Andromeda	*Androméda*	*Andromeda*
21. Triangle	*Deltōtón*	*Triangulum*

Table 2: Constellations north of the zodiac

English names	Greek	Latin
1. Whale	*Kḗtos*	*Cetus*
2. Orion	*Ōríōn*	*Orion*
3. River Eridanus	*Potamós*	*Eridanus*
4. Hare	*Lagōós*	*Lepus*
5. Great Dog	*Kýōn*	*Canis* (*maior*)
6. Little Dog	*Prokýōn*	*Procyon*
7. Argo	*Argṓ*	*Argo*
8. Water-snake	*Hýdros*	*Hydra*
9. Goblet	*Kratḗr*	*Crater*
10. Crow	*Kórax*	*Corvus*
11. Centaur	*Kéntauros*	*Centaurus*
12. Wolf	*Thēríon*	*Bestia*
13. Altar	*Thymiatḗrion*	*Turibulum*
14. Southern Crown	*Stéphanos nótios*	*Corona australis*
15. Southern Fishes	*Ichthýs nótios* (*mégas*)	*Piscis austrinus*

Table 3: Constellations south of the zodiac

already documented for the Babylonians [6] (see above I.), even if they do not always refer to the same constellations. Homer knows the → Pleiades, → Hyads, Orion, the Bear (the Dipper), and → Bootes. Of oriental origin forms such as the winged Saggitarius-Centaur, the Goat-Fish (Capricorn), or the Flying Fish. Egyptian influences played a much smaller role.

B. Iconography

In antiquity, we find only sparse theoretical reflection about the origin and the naming of constellations (schol. Arat. 27 p. 75,7–16 Martin): 1. names based on similarity (Scorpio), 2. based on affect (πάθος/*páthos*: the angry dog), 3. the origin based on myth (Callisto), 4. based on honour (Dioscuri), or 5. purely mnemotechnical names (διδασκαλία/*didaskalía*). Compared to today, stars were seen much more as beings capable of motion: barges, sheep, fishes, rivers (→ Milky Way), then again also as flowers, lamps, or souls immortalized into stars; thus, we often encounter the motif of flight and persecution in the sky: the Bears at the North Pole move only slowly in a circle, while other stars move faster the closer they approach the equator of the sky. According to an explanation by → Manilius [III 1] (2,197–202), the Argo and three signs of the zodiac — Taurus, Gemini, and Cancer — move backwards, because the sun seems to move the slowest there (apogaeum). Perseus, Hercules, and Lyra are pictured in the sky in reverse position, while Taurus, Pegasus, and Argo are only halfway immortalized into stars. Some constellations appear in double form: Gemini did so already in Babylon, later the Great and the Lesser Bear, the Great and Lesser Dog, the Northern and the Southern Crown, the Horse (Pegasus) and the Foal. This tendency of doubling is continued into early modern times.

In the course of time, individual constellations were combined into larger groups: the two Bears with the Polar Dragon that winds through them became the circumpolar triad; Hydra, Cup and Raven were combined into the Apollinic myth (Eratosth. *Katasterismoí* 41). Human-shaped figures at times hold two attributes in their hands (Orion with sword and *kerykion* (caduceus) or with club and lionskin; Hercules, whose arms reach out to the lyre — with the bright star Vega, and to the Crown — with the bright star Gemma). Often, several figures in the sky perform a 'drama', sometimes up to five of them as is the case for the Erigone group [17] or the Andromeda group [10. 197–201]. Overall, a large region of water was identified in the south, being close to the horizon and therefore to the ocean [21. 5], while the northern sky was seen to contain various creatures flying through the air [10. 221 f.].

C. Catalogues

The Babylonians, based on the → Pleiades ([mul]Apin), used identifying stars for the lunar course, while the Greeks paid particular attention to the solar course (→ Zodiac). The course of the sun divided the constellations into three groups: 1. constellations of the zodiac, 2. constellations to the north of it, and 3. constellations to the south of it (cf. tables 1–3). The oldest surviving catalogues of constellations are poetic: the work by → Aratus [4], which was based on *Eudoxus*' [1] work → Phainómena by the same title and the plentiful works following its model, the *Katasterismoí* by → Eratosthenes [2] with its influential immortalizations into stars. Prose catalogues were created by Hipparchus [6] (cf. [2]), Geminus [1] (3,7–15), and Martianus Capella (8,838 probably following Varro), among others. A classic is Ptolemy's catalogue of fixed stars (Syntaxis 7,5 and 8,1; → Ptolemaeus [65] II. A. 1.), which lists 21 northern, 12 zodiacal, and 15 southern constellations, thus altogether 48 constellations with 1,025 individual stars, each with details about their ecliptic length, breadth, and brightness. The details of the catalogues vary in their counts, since some figures (such as the Snake and the Snake Holder) were at times combined. The catalogues also vary in their distinctions between individual signs (Ptol. Syntaxis 7,4 p. 37,11 HEIBERG), and some groups of stars between the known signs remained unnamed (ἀμόρφωτοι/*amórphōtoi*, ἀνώνυμοι/*anṓnymoi*, σποράδες/*sporádes*). In interpreting ecliptic lengths, it was attempted to combine and to modify the qualities of the signs of the zodiac with those of the accompanying constellations (→ *paranatéllonta*) in a speculative way [12].

D. ALTERNATIVES

The names in tables 1–3 are more or less commonly used. However, poets as well as authors writing in the field of astrology sometimes used other names as well — or they named different figures altogether. Homer already emphasized that the Bear was also called 'Cart'. A fundamentally different approach can be found in the *Sphaera barbarica* by → Teucer, which was used by Manilius [III 1], Firmicus Maternus, Rhetorius, and following him, by Johannes Kamateros as late as the 12th cent. [3].

This catalogue can be reconstructed in part from the anonymous compilation of the 10th cent. contained in the *Liber Hermetis*, even if the signs are difficult to identify in detail [12]. It also includes the Egyptian 'Twelve-hour-circle', or *dōdekáōros*, which either replaces the twelve signs of the zodiac or forms a ring north or south of it [11]. New constellations were invented to serve panegyrical purposes: → Conon [3] invented the Lock of Berenice, others invented the *Thronos Caesaris* (Plin. HN 2,178), Antinous [2] (Hadrian's favourite who drowned in the Nile, as part of Aquarius, which was already interpreted as Ganymede) as well as Ptolemy instead of Canopus (modern Carinae) (Mart. Cap. 8,838). This practice was continued in the 17th–19th cents.

E. INDIVIDUAL STARS

A few constellations hold smaller groups within themselves: Taurus holds the Pleiades and the Hyads, Cancer holds two donkeys with a manger, Aquarius holds his stream and Pisces hold their band. The goat with the little billy-goats, which the Charioteer carries on his arm, are probably remnants of an older nomenclature.

Compared to the Arabs in later times, the Greeks did not assign many names to individual stars: in the zodiac, the main star of Taurus was called Λαμπαύρας/*Lampaúras* (something like 'the shining one') (?), and, located diametrically opposite (and also reddish), the main star of Scorpio, Ἀντάρης, 'Antares', the heads of the two Gemini Hercules and Apollo, the main star of Leo, Βασιλίσκος/*Basilískos* ('little king'; *Regulus* is a modern translation), in Virgo, Στάχυς/*Stáchys* (*Spica*) as well as Προτρυγητήρ/*Protrygētḗr* (*Vindemiatrix*), on the garment of the Aquarius Ganymede.

At times it is uncertain whether a name refers to the entire constellation or only to its main star (Arcturus/Bootes, Canicula, Procyon). Catalogues that list the yearly rising and setting of the 30 or 34 brightest individual stars are offered by → Ptolemy [65] in his *Pháseis* (with weather data), the Anonymus from the year 379 (CCAG V 1, 1904, 194–211), and Ps.-Ptolemy [4. 71–82], a catalogue of 68 bright individual stars is used in *Liber Hermetis* (ch. 3 and 25: [8. 123–159]). Classes of brightness or colour are first mentioned by Manilius [III 1] (5,710–745), Ptolemy uses six of them in his *Sýntaxis* with the addition of 'fog-like' stars. In the *Apotelesmatiká* (1,9), he classifies the constellations, parts thereof, or individual stars according to planetary qualities [4].

F. REPRESENTATION

Aside from the signs of the → zodiac, only few ancient representations of constellations are still extant on a *sphaera solida* ('massive ball'). In addition to the incomplete Farnese Atlas (from the Augustan period, see → Cartography II.), the first complete globe of the sky (2nd cent. AD) has recently been discovered [14]. The Egyptians represented the sky as the goddess Nut leaning over the Earth. Accordingly, the constellations appear on the interior walls of rooms or on the inside of the lids of sarcophagi. Plato (Phdr. 247bc) refers to the outer side of the sky as the 'back', which led to the question whether the constellations were visible from the front (below) or from behind (above). Globes of the sky usually reversed the interior earthly view and offered an outer view, one that is humanly impossible to attain (schol. Arat. 248 p. 198,11 σφαιρογραφία/*sphairographía* — οὐρανοθεσία/*ouranothesía*) and one that resulted in much confusions about left and right. Ancient planispheres have not survived. The iconography of the individual constellations has been preserved by the illuminated Germanicus-MSS of the Carolingian period (→ Germanicus [2].

G. FUNCTION

Since ancient times, the observation of constellations was used to aid navigation, to organize agriculture in the absence of generally applicable calendars, and to predict the weather (easily recognizable stars were, in particular, the Pleiades and Hyads, Arcturus, Sirius). Practical → astrology limited itself, with few exceptions, to the constellations of the → zodiac, although didactic poetry and handbooks also dealt with the *paranatellonta* [3; 12]. The aesthetic beauty of the constellations remained in constant view; educated Romans received instruction about the sky in school based on the *Phainómena* by Aratus [4] (on this topic: [22]), a fact that proves the immense effect of the latter through translations, new renderings and commentaries.

H. Afterlife

The Gnostics offered a Christian interpretation of the Aratean sky (Hippolytus, Refutatio omnium haeresium 4,46–49). The Latin-Greek names of constellations were adopted by India from the time of Alexander's campaign (327 BC), while the Chinese went their separate way towards the end of the 3rd cent. AD with their 283 constellations comprised of 1,464 stars. The canonical constellations as well as the decan zodiac (figures of the zodiacal thirds à 10°) of the Greeks, Indians, and Persians arrived in Arabia via Persia. Chapter 6,1 of the influential 'Great Introduction' by Abū Maʿšar (9th cent.) was instrumental in spreading the whole work to the West, and it stimulated the scientific and encyclopaedic interest of the 12th cent. as well as the artistic imagination. In the Renaissance period, the constellations were rediscovered in their aesthetic beauty and were displayed on wall and ceiling paintings, the artist at times working together with astronomers in order to capture a constellation at a specific point in time.

→ Astronomy; → Fixed stars; → Cartography (II.); → Hyads; → Milky Way; → Pleiades; → Stars, legends about; → Zodiac; → Natural Sciences V.

1 R. H. Allen, Star Names. Their Lore and Meaning, 1963 (¹1899) 2 F. Boll, Die Sternkataloge des Hipparch und des Ptolemaios, in: Bibliotheca Mathematica 3.2, 1901, 185–195 3 Id., Sphaera, 1903 4 Id., Ant. Beobachtungen farbiger Sterne, 1916 5 Id., W. Gundel, s. v. S., Sternglaube und Sternsymbolik, Roscher 6, 867–1071 6 F. Gössmann, Planetarium Babylonicum, 1950 7 W. Gundel, Sterne und S., 1922 8 Id., Neue astrologische Texte des Hermes Trismegistos, 1936 9 W. Hübner, Zodiacus Christianus, 1983 10 Id., Manilius als Astrologe und Dichter, in: ANRW II 32.1, 1984, 126–320 11 Id., Zur neuplatonischen Deutung und astrologischen Verwendung der Dodekaoros, in: D. Harlfinger (ed.), Philophronema, FS M. Sicherl, 1990, 73–103 12 W. Hübner, Grade und Gradbezirke der Tierkreiszeichen, 1995 13 Id., Die *Lyra cosmica* des Eratosthenes, in: MH 55, 1998, 84–111 14 E. Künzl, Der Globus im röm.-germanischen Zentralmus. in Mainz, in: Der Globusfreund 45/6, 1997/8, 7–80 15 A. Le Bœuffle, Les noms latins d'astres et de constellations, 1977 16 F. Lassere (ed.), Die Fr. des Eudoxos von Knidos, 1966 (with German translation) 17 R. Merkelbach, Die Erigone des Eratosthenes, in: Miscellanea di Studi Alessandrini in memoria di A. Rostagni, 1963, 469–526 18 O. Neugebauer, R. A. Parker, Egyptian Astronomical Texts, 1960–1969 19 A. Scherer, Gestirnnamen bei den idg. Völkern, 1953 20 A. Stückelberger, Sternglobеn und Sternkarten, in: MH 47, 1990, 70–81 21 G. Thiele, Ant. Himmelsbilder, 1898 22 H. Weinhold, Die Astronomie in der ant. Schule, 1912.

W. H.

Contagion see → Infection

Coronea

[2] see → Koroneia

Corrector (Italiae) At the beginning of the 3rd cent. AD there is evidence for the senator C. Octavius Appius → Suetrius Sabinus as *corrector Italiae* (*CI*) while *iuridici* (→ *iuridicus*) still held office simultaneously: CIL X 5178 and 5398 = ILS 1159 (under Caracalla); possibly T. Pomponius [II 5] Bassus was also *CI*: CIL VI 3836 = 31747 = 41237 (probably in 268/9). [3. 221 ff.]. So they had not replaced the *iuridici* as occurred from the late 3rd cent. These *correctores* were special authorized representatives, as the description in CIL X 5398 = ILS 1159 for Octavius Appius Suetrius Sabinus shows (but cf. in this regard [3. 223 n. 9]): *elect(us) ad corrig(endum) statum Ita[l(iae)]*, i.e. they took on similar roles to the → *correctores* in the provinces in the 2nd and 3rd cents. Whether C. Ceionius Rufius Volusianus, CIL X 1655 (under Carus) should also be considered as one of them, remains unclear. Most of the *correctores* in PLRE 1, 1092 were probably already limited to a part of Italy (most probably to a region), so would have already more or less been governors whose titles were not however meant to show the equal status of Italy and the provinces.

1 W. Eck, L'Italia nell'Impero Romano, 1999, 274 f. 2 G. A. Cecconi, Governo imperiale e élites dirigenti nell'Italia tardoantica, 1994, passim 3 M. Christol, Essai sur l'évolution des carrières sénatoriales, 1986.

W. E.

Cosconius

[II 0] **C. Celsus.** Presiding procurator in Raetia until AD 139 when he was replaced by Sempronius Liberalis [1]; his name should probably also be added to RMD II 94 = AE 1984,706.

1 K. Dietz, Ein neues Militärdiplom aus Alteglofsheim, Lkr. Regensburg, in: Beiträge zur Arch. in der Oberpfalz 3, 1999, 225–256.

W. E.

Cossonius L. C. Gallus Vecilius Crispinus Mansuanius Marcellinus Numisius Sabinus. Senator whose career is known from an inscription from Antioch [5] in Pisidia (CIL III 6813 = ILS 1038). Quaestor in the province of Pontus-Bithynia, people's tribune, praetor, *curator viarum Clodiae, Cassiae, Ciminiae, Traianae novae, praef. frumenti dandi, legatus legionum I Italicae et II Traianae, proconsul Sardiniae* (*c.* AD 111), praetorian imperial legate of Galatia, Pisidia *c.* AD 113–115; suffect consul probably in 116 [1. 9–35] or even not until

117, *VIIvir epulonum*; first known consular governor of the province of Judea in *c.* 118–120 [2].

1 H. Wolff, Neue Militärdiplome aus Künzing (Ldkr. Deggendorf) und der Stadt Straubing, Niederbayern, in: Ostbairische Grenzmarken 41, 1999, 9–35
2 H. M. Cotton, W. Eck, Governors and Their Personnel on Latin Inscriptions from Caesarea Maritima, in: The Israel Academy of Sciences and Humanities, Proc. 7.7, 2001, 215–240. W. E.

Cradle (λίκνον/*líknon*, σκάφη/*skáphē*; Lat. *cunae*, *cunabula*, n. pl.). The *líknon*, actually the 'grain rocker', was used as a cradle (H. Hom. 4,150; 254; 290; 358; [1. 298, fig. 285]; cf. Callim. H. 1,48). A container similar to a tub served as a second form of the cradle (Soph. TrGF IV, 385; Ath. 13,606f; 607a; → *scáphē*). There were often notches or small struts on the frame of the cradle for attaching cords. Safety belts could be drawn crosswise over the cradle. From time to time two children could be accommodated in them (Plut. Romulus 3,4). Depictions of infants in *skáphai* are known since the Bronze Age in terracotta and marble i.a. Remains of wooden cradles are extant from the towns at the foot of Vesuvius — from Herculaneum even a specimen with a child's skeleton [2nd fig. p. 82].
→ Child, Childhood

1 E. Simon, Die Götter der Griechen, [2]1980 2 R. Ross Holloway, The Town of Hercules, 1995.

F. von Zglinicki, Die Wiege, 1979; H. Rühfel, Ammen und Kinderfrauen im klass. Athen, in: Ant. Welt 19.4, 1988, 43–57, esp. 50 with figs. 10–12; St. T. A. M. Mols, Wooden Furniture in Herculaneum, 1999, 43 f., 123 f., 164 f., fig. 72–80. R. H.

Criminal procedure From a historical perspective it is only possible to speak of a criminal procedure (CP) in the technical sense if we can distinguish a field of criminal prosecution in the public (state) interest (→ Punishment; Criminal law) from legal prosecution in the civil interest (including any civil law penalties, Lat. → *poena*). The fact, for example, that private → revenge is channelled via the obligation to conduct a judicial procedure still does not constitute a CP: to protect public peace and state authority, only the administering of private punishment is made dependent upon a prior formal procedure (→ Procedural law). The differentiation between the CP and the civil law procedure is made additionally difficult by the fact that, in antiquity, the institution of the public prosecutor who brings the charge in the CP was unknown. Regularly a private individual also tended to be the plaintiff in the CP.

In Greece, esp. in Athens, private individuals could submit the formal (criminal) statement of claim, the → *graphḗ* [1] (see also → *eisangelía*), on which a judgement was then reached in a very large people's (jury-) court (→ *dikastḗrion*). If criminals were caught in the act and arrested, the fast-track procedure of → *apagōgḗ* was also possible, otherwise a criminal charge against them was brought before the president of the court (→ *éndeixis*). The indictment of private individuals in the CP was of course regularly associated in Athens with the risk of a procedural penalty if the prosecutor did not win over at least $^1/_5$ of the jury's votes for his petition.

The most important CP in the development of Roman law was the → *quaestio*, as it was introduced particularly by Cornelius [I 90] Sulla (around 80 BC): a jury court acting on private charges (→ *delatio nominis*; → *delator*). There was however provision for the examination of the indictment by the → praetor (similar to the procedure *in iure* in civil law trials) prior to the judicial proceeding. In the Imperial period this procedure increasingly changed to an official procedure (→ *cognitio*) conducted by the imperial official.
→ Criminal law

A. R. W. Harrison, The Law of Athens, vol. 2, 1971; B. Santalucia, Diritto e processo penale nell'antica Roma, [2]1998. G. S.

Critical signs (Greek σημεῖα/*sēmeîa*, Lat. *notae*). One of the most important technical and methodological inventions of Alexandrian → philology were the critical signs (CS) used in philological exegetic work. Their development and use cannot be followed continuously as there are gaps in the evidence. One exception, however, is the edition and exegesis technique of the Alexandrian grammarians with reference to Homer, about which we are adequately informed both through a small number of anonymous grammatical excerpts and by Homeric scholia (cf. [4; 6]) and through papyrus fragments of Homeric texts and commentaries (cf. [5; 8]); we also have some information regarding Plato.

The earliest inventor of CS was → Zenodotus of Ephesus (1st half of the 3rd cent. BC) who introduced the → *obelós*, a short horizontal line (–) with which he marked each Homeric verse that he wanted rejected (i.e. crossed out as spurious). Here it was not just a matter of a technical working instrument; rather its significance lay in the fact that the philologist expressed his own critical judgement without drastic intervention in the text that was the object of his → publication (*ékdosis*) and in this way allowed others plenty of leeway for their evaluation. Several decades later → Aristophanes [4] of Byzantium took the method further and also perfected the philological technique by using an increased number of CS: he introduced the → *asterískos* (⋇) and *sígma* (C) and *antísigma* (Ɔ) (with the two last-mentioned signs he described two verses with the same content following one another).

The system of CS was finally perfected by → Aristarchus [4] of Samothrace who again increased their number giving structure and precision to their use; the CS ensured the connection between the publication of the Homeric text in which they were noted beside the respective verse and the commentary (*hypómnēma*) that interpreted it. Apart from traditional *obelós* (for suggestions for rejections), → *diplḗ* (> to show various explanations and scholarly notes) and *diplḗ periestigménē* (⋗, i.e. 'dotted': to show differences of opinion from → Zenodotus) were characteristic of Aristarchus; with the *asterískos* he marked repeated verses (*asterískos* alone in passages where he considered them suitable, *asterískos* with *obelós* in passages where he considered them unsuitable and in this way recommended their deletion; he also used *antísigma* (verses in the reverse order), *antísigma periestigménon* (i.e. 'dotted', to show two verses with the same content), *stigmḗ* (i.e. 'dot', apparently to suggest less doubt regarding authenticity than the *obelós* indicated) and perhaps also the *keraúnion* ('sign shaped like lightning' that looked something like this: ⊤).

In the Augustan period the grammarian → Aristonicus [5] dedicated one of his works to the explanation of the CS of Aristarchus with reference to the Homeric text; his material was incorporated (together with that of Didymus [1] of Alexandria) via the → Four-Men Commentary in the Homeric scholia. The famous Cod. Venetus A of the *Iliad* in particular gives us a large number of these CS used in the margins beside the verses along with the scholia that explain them (over 2,000). In addition CS appear sporadically in papyrus fragments of Homeric texts.

For other literary genres we lack material that is equally informative, but it is certain that CS were used in philological practise. In this way, the *asterískos* of Aristophanes [4] of Byzantium, for instance, was used in his Alcaeus publication to show a change in the verse measure, and by Aristarchus, on the other hand, to show the beginning of a new poem (Hephaestion 74,5–13). The papyrus fragments provide examples of the application of CS to lyrical and dramatic literary texts (tragedy as well as comedy) as well as to prose texts [5; 8. 112–118].

A passage in Diog. Laert. (3,66) and the papyrus PSI 1488 (from the 2nd cent. AD, and thus independent of this) prove an analogous system of CS for the Plato text. It differs from that used in the Homeric text but many CS are identical and are often used in exactly the same way. Aside from the *obelós* to mark sections rejected (deletions), the *obelós periestigménos* (÷) represents arbitrary rejections; furthermore here there are — with a specific meaning in each case — *diplḗ*, *diplḗ periestigménē*, *antísigma*, *antísigma periestigménon*, *asterískos* and *keraúnion* as well as, to mark a stylistic usage common in Plato, the Greek letter χ, in the form of *chi periestigménon* (.χ.) to designate selected wording and elegant expressions (also in lyrical and dramatic texts to mark certain passages).

For further CS used sporadically and in particular instances cf. [4; 5].

→ Asteriskos; → Diple; → Correction marks; → Obelus; → Philology; → Scholia

1 H. Alline, Histoire du texte de Platon, 1915, 86ff. 2 A. Carlini, Studi sulla tradizione antica e medievale del Fedone, 1972, 18–23 3 M. Gigante, Un papiro attribuibile a Antigono di Caristo?, in: PSI 1488, in: Div. Autoren, Papiri Filosofici. Miscellanea di studi, 1998, 111–114 4 A. Gudeman, s.v. Kritische Zeichen, RE 11, 1916–1927 5 K. McNamee, Sigla and Select Marginalia in Greek Literary Papyri, 1992 6 F. Montanari, Studi di filologia omerica antica, vol. I, 1979, 43–75 7 Pfeiffer, KP I, passim (index s.v. σημεῖα) 8 E. G. Turner, Greek Papyri. An Introduction, ²1980, 100–124 9 Id., Greek Manuscripts of the Ancient World (2nd ed., ed. von P. J. Parsons), 1987, passim (index s.v. Critical signs). F.M.

Cuballum Fortress in → Galatia (C. *Gallograeciae castellum*: Liv. 38,18,5), can be identified with the spacious plateau situated near modern Ortakişla (north of Sülüklü) in a bend in the valley, with edges that fall away steeply and have to some extent obviously been consolidated for fortification purposes, and the drop of a massive cut embankment to provide a barrier against the rear elevations; otherwise no identifiable building remains [1. 31]. C. controlled the west-east link through the → Axylus from the upper → Sangarius to → Tatta Limne and to → Lycaonia. Here Cn. Manlius [I 24] Vulso was successfully attacked in 189 BC on the march east by the cavalry of the Galatians (→ Celts III. B.) and forced to withdraw behind the Sangarius (glossed over by Liv. 38,18,5–8).

1 K. Strobel, State Formation by the Galatians of Asia Minor, in: Anatolica 28, 2002, 1–46. K. ST.

Cugerni (Cuberni). Presumably a part of a tribe, certainly one of the groups succeeding the → Sugambri resettled by the Romans in 8 BC on the lefthand side of the Rhine (on the motives [1]). According to Pliny (HN 4,106: *Cuberni*) they lived between the → Ubii in the south and the → Batavi in the north and probably already created in the 1st cent. AD a → *civitas* based on peregrine law. On the basis of an extant fragmentary inscription (AE 1981, 690 = AE 1984, 650) from AD 68, Cib[ernodurum] was developed close to the later → Colonia Ulpia Traiana as a major town [2]. The C. were involved in the uprising of Julius [II 43] Civilis (Tac. Hist. 4,26,3; 5,16,1; 5,18,2). The Britannic military diploma CIL XVI 48 (AD 103) names a *cohors I Cugernorum* (cf. also [4. 1524, 2313]) that, according to CIL XVI 69 and 70 from AD 122 or 124 (cf. also AE 1974, 535 and AE 1980, 603), is called *cohors I Ulp(ia) Traiana Cuger(norum) c(ivium) R(omanorum)* (cf. in this regard [3]). A Cugerni cavalryman *domo Cugernus* (CIL III 2712, Dalmatia, from the middle of the 1st cent. AD). From the 2nd cent. AD onwards the term C. was superseded by Traianenses.

1 J. Heinrichs, Röm. Perfidie und german. Edelmut?, in: T. Grünewald (ed.), Germania inferior, 2001, 54–92 2 J. Bogaers, Zum Namen des »oppidum Cugernorum«, in: Naamkunde 16, 1984, 33–39 3 R. W. Davies, Cohors I Cugernorum, in: Chiron 7, 1977, 385–392 4 R. G. Collingwood, R. P. Wright, The Roman Inscriptions of Britain, 1965.

C. B. RÜGER, Germania inferior, 1968, 96–101; Id., Colonia Ulpia Traiana, in: H. G. HORN (ed.), Die Römer in Nordrhein-Westfalen, 1987, 626–629; G. NEUMANN, s. v. C., RGA 5, 103 f.; M. GECHTER, Small Towns of the Ubii and C./Baetasii civitates (Lower Germany), in: A. E. BROWN (ed.), Roman Small Towns in Eastern England and Beyond, 1995, 193–203; L. WIERSCHOWSKI, Cugerner, Baetasier, Traianenser im überregionalen Handel der Kaiserzeit, in: see [1], 409–430. RA. WI.

Curia

[2] C. (pl. *curiae*) was the name of the assembly place of the municipal council in Rome (→ *senatus*; Fest. p. 42) and also in many → *coloniae* and *municipia* (→ *municipium*) of Italy and the Roman provinces (cf. → *curiales*). As opposed to the *comitium* (→ *comitia*), the assembly place of the people in the open air, the *curia* is always a building on a piece of land belonging to the community or a god and mostly it is at the → *forum* of the town or close to it. Council chambers of non-Roman towns can also be called *curiae* (Liv. 24,24,5 and 9: Syracuse Ov. Met. 13,197: Troy).

In Rome the earliest *curiae* are the meeting-chambers of the → *curiae* (cf. Tac. Ann. 12,24; Fest. p. 180); the building of the first *curia* for the Senate (which as a committee was likewise called *curia*: Liv. 2,23,14; Suet. Caes. 76,3) is attributed to King Hostilius [4] (*C. Hostilia*). Basically any public building could serve as *curia* if the auspices could be consulted from there (→ *augures*), so this also applied to temples within the → *pomerium* and a mile in front of it: on the Campus Martius possibly the temples of Apollo and Bellona or a room in the theatre complex of Pompey [I 3], where → Caesar was murdered [1. 926–936].

When new towns were founded in Italy and in the provinces, a place was regularly set aside on the main forum as the location of the *curia* (cf. Vitr. De arch. 5,1–2; [2. 25–61; 77 f.]), ideally next to the office buildings of the magistrates (→ *duoviri*) and opposite the main temple of the city (cf. the plan of → Pompeii, no. 31 and 38).

→ Meeting; → Assembly buildings

1 MOMMSEN, Staatsrecht 3 2 J. E. WYMER, Marktplatz-Anlagen der Griechen und Römer, 1916 3 LTUR 1, 329–337. W. ED.

Curiatius

[1] **C. Maternus.** Roman orator and writer of tragedies who is known only from → Tacitus' *Dialogus* in which he appears as the host on the day after the recitation of his tragedy *Cato*. Furthermore the tragedies *Thyestes*, *Medea* and *Domitius* (3,4) and probably an *Agamemnon* (9,2) are attributed to him by Tacitus (Dial. 2 f.; 9–11). While Tacitus (about AD 76) personalizes the contrast of writing about great men and limited public speech in C. as a writer, Cass. Dio 67,12,5 reports on the execution of a rhetor Maternus because of his criticism of tyranny. One identification is worthy of consideration; C. may have been a close relative of M. → Cornelius [II 36] Nigrinus C. Maternus or even identical to him.

PIR [2]C 1605/[2]M 360; W. ECK, Jahres- und Provinzialfasten der senatorischen Statthalter von 69/70 bis 138/139, in: Chiron 12, 1982, 281–362, esp. 324, n. 172. J. R.

Curtain (παραπέτασμα/*parapétasma*, προκάλυμμα/*prokálymma*, αὐλαία/*aulaía*; Lat. *velum*, *aulaea*). In Greek and Roman tents (Ath. 12,538d), houses, palaces, occasionally also in temples (Lk 23,45; cf. Paus. 5,12,4), curtains were attached to doors, windows (Juv. 9,105), as wall decoration (Juv. 6,227) and to the intercolumnia of the atria and peristyles; they served to keep out the rain or sun (Ov. Met. 10,595). Depictions of such curtains are known from Greek and Roman art (e.g. the *parapétasma* representations on Roman relief sarcophagi) and are extant in original fragments from late antiquity (→ Textile art). Curtains were attached to rings (Plin. HN 13,62) and mounted on rails. The pulled-back curtains were attached by means of curtain holders to door posts or walls.

I. NIELSEN, Hellenistic Palaces, 1999, 97, 134. For further bibliography, see also → Textile art. R. H.

Curtius

[II 2a] **A. C. Crispinus.** Suffect consul in AD 159 (CIL VI 32321 = [1]). The family probably came from Aspendus in Pamphylia; his sons could be A. Curtius Crispinus Arruntianus and A. Curtius Auspicatus Titinnianus (IGR III 803; CIL XIV 2695; 3030 = ILS 7788).

1 P. WEISS, Ein Konsulnpaar vom 21. Juni 159 n. Chr., in: Chiron 29, 1999, 160–167.

[II 9a] **Cn.C. Severus.** *praefectus alae* [1]; also named in Tac. Ann. 12,55,1 f. He honoured Ummidius [2] Quadratus with a monument in an exedra in Apamea.

1 J.-CH. BALTY, in: CRAI 2000, 465 f. W. E.

Cuttlefish The class of cuttlefish called *Cephalopoda* ('Cephalopod') belongs to the μαλάκια/*malákia* that live in the sea (cf. Plin. HN 32,149), Lat. *mollia*, modern molluscs, and to the subphylum *Conchifera*. Today's system differentiates the two orders of the ten-armed cuttlefish (*Decabrachia*) and eight-armed cuttlefish (*Octobrachia*).

I. DECABRACHIA II. OCTOBRACHIA

I. DECABRACHIA

Of the *Decabrachia* that have, in addition to the eight tentacles on the head (πλεκτάναι/*plektánai*: Aristot. Hist. an. 4,1,524a 3 f.), two longer, retractable tentacles (προβοσκίδες/*proboskídes*: ibid. 523b 29–33), Aristotle describes: (1st) the common cuttlefish (*Sepia officinalis L.*), Greek σηπία/*sēpía*, Lat. *sepia* or *sepiola*.

The pigment obtained from it was used in antiquity as low-value → ink (Plin. HN 35,43; cf. Pers. 3,12 f.; Auson. epist. 4,76 and 7,54). Aristot. ibid. 524b 15–17 mentions the ink sack on the rectum (θολός/*tholós*) whose content the frightened animal (cf. Plin. HN 9,84) expels through the mouth. The ink that is distributed in the sea water makes it invisible to its enemies. The animal reproduces with the aid of a special pointed arm in the male, the hectocotylus (Aristot. ibid. 524a 5–9) that introduces the spermatophore. The characteristic chalky cuttlebone that lies under the dorsal skin (σήπιον/*sḗpion* or ξίφος/*xíphos*; 'sword') is thinner and more cartilaginous in the (2nd) slimmer cuttlefish (Aristot. ibid. 524b 22–27); there are two species of the latter, the smaller τευθίς/*teuthís* (*Loligo vulgaris*; e.g. Aristot. ibid. 5,18, 550b 12–19) and the τεῦθος/*teûthos* (squid, *loligo* = *Todarodes sagittatus*; e.g. Aristot. ibid. 4,1,524a 25–33). Like flying fish or scallops (*pectunculi*), both species of *lolligines* can, according to Plin. HN 9,84 (cf. 18,361 and 32,14 as signs of storms), shoot out over the surface of the water (*volitare*, 'flying'; cf. [1. 155 f.]).

II. Octobrachia

The *Octobrachia* include (1.) the musky octopus (*Eledone moschata*), ἑλεδώνη/*heledṓnē*, probably identical to βολίταινα/*bolítaina*, ὄζολις/*ózolis* (Aristot. ibid. 525a 16–20; Ath. 7,318e) and ὀσμύλος/*osmýlos* (Ath. loc.cit.) that is conspicuous because of its musk odour (Plin. HN 9,89: *ozaena* [1. 187]) and the single row of suckers on the tentacles; (2.) the common octopod or octopus (*Octopus vulgaris*), πολύπους/*polýpous*. Catching them with a trident, fishing rod or net for use in cooking was not easy because these animals hold fast to rocks with their tentacles (Opp. Hal. 2,232–236) and can spit out fishing hooks. After losing individual tentacles (that could be regrown later) — people interpreted this wrongly as self-mutilation for reasons of hunger (Ael. NA 1,27 and 14,26; Opp. Hal. 2,243–245; Ath. 7,316e-f), rejected by Aristot. Hist. an. 7(8),2,591a 4; Plin. HN 9,87 and Plut. De sollertia animalium 27 (= Mor. 978f) — the cuttlefish were able to continue living, and could also survive on land for short periods (Aristot. ibid. 8(9),37,622a 31–33; Plin. HN 9,71 and 9,92 on a giant specimen). The colour changes reminiscent of the → chamaeleon were interpreted in different ways (Plut. loc.cit.: for reasons of prudence; Theophr. fr. 172 and 188: for reasons of cowardice). The boneless animal (ἀνόστεος/*anósteos*) in Hes. Op. 524 probably refers to the octopus. (3.) Of the so-called paper nautilus (*Argonauta argo*), Greek ναυτίλος/*nautílos* or ποντίλος/*pontílos* (in Plin. HN 9,88 wrongly *pompilus*) only the female lives in a paper-thin shell up to 20 cm in length. Aristotle describes the species very precisely (Hist. an. 4,1,525a 20–29), but with fantastic characteristics (ibid. 8(9),37,622b 5–18 = Plin. HN 9,88).

The common octopus is found on many coins [2. pl. 8,3, 8,15–22, 13,1] from Greek cities close to the sea such as Tarentum and Syracuse and on cameos [2. pl. 24,44–46], whilst the cuttlefish is found on coins [2. pl. 8,23–25] and cameos [2. pl. 23,13, 23,37, 24,32, 24,47].

1 Leitner 2 F. Imhoof-Blumer, O. Keller, Tier- und Pflanzenbilder auf Mz. und Gemmen des klass. Alt., 1889, repr. 1972.

H. Aubert, Die Kephalopoden des Aristoteles, 1862; Keller 2, 507–518; A. Steier, s. v. T., RE 6 A, 1393–1406.

C. HÜ.

Cypress Of the conifer genus Lat. *cupressus* (since Enn. Ann. 262 (223) and 490 (511); late Lat. *cyparissus*, Isid. Orig. 17,7,34; κυπάρισσος/*kypárissos*, probably from the pre-Indogermanic, already in Hom. Od. 5,64) with 14 species, only the wild form *C. sempervirens L.* with the variant *C. horizontalis* (*C. mas* in Plin. HN 16,141) occurred in south-east Europe. However, the old culture strain [1. 34 ff.] of the variant *C. pyramidalis* (*C. femina*: Plin. HN 16,141; it was already sown by Cato: Cato Agr. 48,1; 151), widespread and well known on Cyprus and Crete (the supposed home: Theophr. Hist. pl. 3,1,6; Plin. HN 16,141), the plant that (perhaps because of its flame shape) was sacred to → Apollo, was cultivated more often, especially around sacred places such as tombs. Cut-off branches were considered to be a symbol of mourning. According to Ovid (Met. 10,106–142) the youth → Cyparissus, beloved of Apollo, was transformed into a cypress because of his mourning over the unintentional killing of a sacred deer [2. 35]. This conifer was also dedicated to → Asclepius and → Hades (Pluto), the goddesses (in their chthonic aspects) → Cybele, → Artemis, → Eurynome, → Persephone and black → Aphrodite (in Corinth), → Hera and → Athena as well as on Cyprus to the Phoenician Beroth. It was therefore considered to be a general symbol of a female deity in its dual relationship with procreation and death.

The durable and fragrant wood was worked to form images of deities, palace doors (e.g. those of Odysseus, Hom. Od. 17,340) and temple gates (as in the Artemis temple in → Ephesus, Theophr. Hist. pl. 5,4,2; Plin. HN 16,215), to build houses (Theophr. Hist. pl. 5,7,4) and among other things for little jewellery boxes (Hor. Ars P. 332), and the Phoenicians also used it for ships. The cones in particular, as well as the leaves of the cypress, were used as an astringent and cooling remedy (Dioscorides 1,74 Wellmann = 1,102 Berendes) as well as in veterinary medicine (cf. Pall. Agric. 14,4,1; 14,7,2; 14,34,3).

1 K. Koch, Die Bäume und Sträucher des alten Griechenlands, [2]1884 2 H. Baumann, Die griech. Pflanzenwelt, 1982.

C. HÜ.